Contemporary Authors

Contemporary Authors

A Bio-Bibliographical Guide to
Current Writers in Fiction, General Nonfiction,
Poetry, Journalism, Drama, Motion Pictures,
Television, and Other Fields

JANE A. BOWDEN

Editor

volumes 69-72

GALE RESEARCH COMPANY • BOOK TOWER • DETROIT, MICHIGAN 48226

CONTEMPORARY AUTHORS

Published by
Gale Research Company, Book Tower, Detroit, Michigan 48226
Each Year's Volumes Are Revised About Five Years Later

Frederick G. Ruffner, *Publisher*   James M. Ethridge, *Editorial Director*

Jane A. Bowden, *Editor*
Frances Carol Locher, *Associate Editor*
James Carlton Obrecht, Susan A. Stefani,
and Barbara A. Welch, *Assistant Editors*
Barbara Bedway, Otto Penzler,
and Carole Potter, *Contributing Editors*
Johanna P. Zecker, *Research Assistant*

Alan E. Abrams, *Consultant*
Eunice Bergin, *Copy Editor*
Conrad Corda, Andrea Geffner, Frank M. Soley,
Joseph Sullivan, Arlene True, and Benjamin True, *Sketchwriters*
Norma Sawaya and Shirley Seip, *Editorial Assistants*
Michaeline Nowinski, *Production Manager*

Copyright © 1978
GALE RESEARCH COMPANY

ISBN 0-8103-0030-3

Preface

Authors, as persons who express opinions or report facts which influence the actions of others, or who tell tales which stimulate the minds of others, have always had a special interest for everyone who has read their works.

Until recently, it was writers of books who had primary interest for readers. Now, however, the newspaper reporter famous in his own right, the television anchorperson or correspondent, the influential editor or columnist of a popular magazine, and many other persons active in communications have an equal claim on the public's interest. In fact, individuals often move rapidly from one area of communications to another, and the medium is of less significance than the communicator.

CA Has Changed Its Scope

Therefore, with Volumes 65-68 *Contemporary Authors* changed its scope to include significant personalities from all media—books, magazines, newspapers, television, radio, films, etc. The title page has a new subtitle to reflect this change:

Contemporary Authors:
A Bio-Bibliographical Guide to Current Writers in Fiction,
General Nonfiction, Poetry, Journalism, Drama, Motion Pictures,
Television, and Other Fields.

Besides authors of nontechnical books, *CA* now includes newspaper and television reporters, columnists, prominent newspaper and periodical editors, syndicated cartoonists, screenwriters, television scriptwriters, and other media people.

Among the media people now covered are Walter Cronkite, David Frost, Eric Sevareid, Edwin Newman, Bob Woodward, John Chabot Smith, Malcolm Johnson, T George Harris, and Melville Bell Grosvenor in this volume, as well as Barbara Walters, Daniel Schorr, Federico Fellini, Mike Wallace, Sally Quinn, Mel Brooks, John Scali, Max Frankel, and Marlene Sanders in Volumes 65-68. Also covered are major television, Capitol, and foreign correspondents, wire service reporters and bureau chiefs, important by-line contributors to newspapers and magazines, and other writers of interest to the public.

Further Suggestions Are Welcome

Interest in media people on the part of librarians and users of *CA* is very high, as indicated by the numerous suggestions *CA* has received in recent years concerning the need for a reliable, on-going source of information on non-book and non-print communicators. Suggestions and comments in both individual letters and responses to our surveys have been very helpful in planning the present change.

CA will, of course, continue to focus primarily on persons whose work appears in book form, but the editors believe the addition of other media people will make *CA* even more useful.

Further comments from users will be welcomed.

No Obligation for Inclusion

An unusual number of biographical publications appears to be springing up, and the question is now often asked whether a charge is made for listings in such publications. Although some publishers charge for listings or require purchase of a book by biographees, there is absolutely no charge or obligation of any kind attached to being included in *CA*. Copies of the volumes in which their sketches appear are offered at courtesy discounts to persons listed, but less than five percent of the biographees purchase copies.

Cumulative Index Should Always Be Consulted

Since *CA* is a multi-volume series which does not repeat author entries from volume to volume, the cumulative index published in alternate new volumes of *CA* should always be consulted to locate an individual author's listing. Each new volume contains authors not previously included in the series and is revised approximately five years after its original publication. The cumulative index indicates the original or revised volume in which an author appears. Authors removed from the revision cycle and placed in the *CA Permanent Series* are listed in the index as having appeared in specific original volumes of *CA* (for the benefit of those who do not hold *Permanent Series* volumes), *and* as having their finally revised sketches in a specific *Permanent Series* volume.

CONTEMPORARY AUTHORS

Indicates that a listing has been compiled from secondary sources believed to be reliable, but has not been personally verified for this edition by the author sketched.

ABERNETHY, Peter L(ink)   1935-

PERSONAL: Born July 26, 1935, in Hickory, N.C.; son of Peter L., Sr. (a civil engineer) and Jessie (White) Abernethy. *Education:* University of North Carolina, B.A., 1963, M.A., 1965, Ph.D., 1973. *Home:* 2419 22nd St., Lubbock, Tex. 79411. *Office:* Department of English, Texas Tech University, Lubbock, Tex. 79409.

CAREER: University of North Carolina, Chapel Hill, part-time instructor in English, 1964-65; University of Arizona, Tucson, instructor in English, 1965-67; University of North Carolina, part-time instructor in English, 1967-70; Texas Tech University, Lubbock, instructor, 1971-73, assistant professor of English, 1973—. *Military service:* U.S. Army, 1956-58. *Member:* Modern Language Association of America, American Association of University Professors, Rocky Mountain Modern Language Association.

WRITINGS: (Editor with J. W. Kloesel Christian and Jeffrey R. Smitten) *English Novel Explication: Supplement I,* Shoe String, 1976. Contributor to *A Biographical Guide to Southern Literature.* Contributor of articles, a poem, and reviews to journals, including *Eighteenth Century Life, Critique, American Transcendental Quarterly,* and *American Studies.*

WORK IN PROGRESS: Research on Walt Whitman and Saul Bellow.

AVOCATIONAL INTERESTS: Building and playing old musical instruments, including gamba, recorder, rebec, and harpsichord.

*   *   *

ABRAMSON, Michael   1944-

PERSONAL: Born July 5, 1944, in Plainfield, N.J.; son of Philip (a merchant) and Frieda (a merchant; maiden name, Belsky) Abramson. *Education:* Kenyon College, A.B., 1966; University of Chicago, M.A., 1968. *Home and office:* 84 University Pl., New York, N.Y. 10003.

CAREER: Photojournalist and writer, 1969—. *Awards, honors:* Photography grant from CAPS (Creative Artists in Public Service), 1975.

WRITINGS: Palante: Young Lords Party (with own photographs), McGraw, 1971.

Photographer: Robert Hamberger, *Our Portion of Hell,*
Link Books, 1973; Mario Puzo, *Mario Puzo's Vegas,* Grosset, 1977.

Anthologized in *Eyes of Conscience,* edited by Milton Metzer and Bernard Coles, Follett, 1974.

*   *   *

ABRECHT, Mary Ellen (Benson)   1945-

PERSONAL: Born December 18, 1945, in Granby, Mass.; daughter of Donald Dean (a personnel manager) and Mary Ellen (a dietician; maiden name, Ballard) Benson; married Gary Lorne Abrecht (a police lieutenant), September 7, 1968. *Education:* Mount Holyoke College, B.A., 1967; graduate study at Union Theological Seminary, New York, N.Y., 1967-68, and American University, 1969-70; Georgetown University, J.D., 1974. *Religion:* Protestant. *Residence:* Washington, D.C. *Office:* U.S. Attorney's Office, Third & Constitution Ave. N.W., Washington, D.C. 20001.

CAREER: Substitute teacher in public schools in Washington, D.C., 1968; Metropolitan Police Department, Washington, D.C., police officer, 1968-72, patrol sergeant, 1972-75; U.S. Attorney's Office, Washington, D.C., assistant prosecuting attorney, 1975—. Member of Bars of U.S. District Court, U.S. Court of Appeals and District of Columbia Court of Appeals. Lecturer and consultant on women offenders and the use of women in police work. *Member:* American Bar Association, American Civil Liberties Union, District of Columbia Bar Association.

WRITINGS: (With Barbara Lang Stern) *The Making of a Woman Cop,* Morrow, 1976. Contributor to *Social Action.*

WORK IN PROGRESS: A chapter on women in law enforcement, to be included in a book on sex discrimination counseling, edited by Virginia E. Pendergrass, publication by Kendall/Hunt expected in 1978.

*   *   *

ABT, Clark C(laus)   1929-

PERSONAL: Born August 31, 1929, in Cologne, Germany; came to the United States in 1937, naturalized citizen, 1944; married Wendy Peter (a researcher), November 3, 1971; children: Thomas Peter, Emily Peter. *Education:* Massachusetts Institute of Technology, B.S., 1951, Ph.D., 1965; Johns Hopkins University, M.A., 1952. *Home:* 19 Follen St., Cambridge, Mass. 02138. *Office:* 55 Wheeler, Cambridge, Mass. 02138.

CAREER: Johns Hopkins University, Baltimore, Md., instructor in literature, 1951-52; Raytheon Co., Bedford, Mass., manager of advanced systems department, 1957-64; Abt Associates, Inc., Cambridge, Mass., founding president and treasurer, 1965—. Visiting lecturer at Harvard University, 1968-69; visiting professor at State University of New York at Binghamton, 1975-76. *Military service:* U.S. Air Force Reserve, 1952-62, active duty as navigator and intelligence officer, 1952-57; became captain. *Member:* Operations Research Society of America. *Awards, honors:* Thoreau Grand Award for Landscape Architecture, 1975.

WRITINGS: Serious Games, Viking, 1970; (editor) *The Evaluation of Social Programs,* Sage Publications, 1977; *The Social Audit for Management,* American Management Association, 1977. Contributor of more than twenty articles to professional journals.

WORK IN PROGRESS: Policy Research Management.

* * *

ABUN-NASR, Jamil Miri 1932-

PERSONAL: Born August 8, 1932, in Bassa, Palestine; son of Miri Khalil (a landowner) and Salwa (Freiwat) Abun-Nasr; married Marlies Siegmund (a secretary), December 21, 1963; children: Sonie, Nadia. *Education:* American University of Beirut, B.A. (with distinction), 1958; St. Antony's College, Oxford, D.Phil., 1961. *Home:* Dahlemer Weg 205, 1000 Berlin 37 (West), Germany. *Office:* Institut fuer Islamwissenschaft, Freie Universitaet Berlin, Boltzmannstrasse 4, 1000 Berlin 33, Germany.

CAREER: United Nations Relief and Works Agency, Schools for Palestine Refugees, Sidon and Beirut, Lebanon, teacher, 1949-54; Harvard University, Cambridge, Mass., research fellow at Center for Middle East Studies, 1962-63; American University of Beirut, Beirut, assistant professor of history and cultural studies, 1963-68; University of Ibadan, Ibadan, Nigeria, senior lecturer, 1968-70, associate professor of history, 1970-75; Freie Universitaet Berlin, Berlin, Germany, Wissenschaftlicher Angestellter, 1976—. *Member:* Middle East Studies Association of North America, Deutsche Morgenlaendische Gesellschaft.

WRITINGS: The Tijaniyya: A Sufi Order in the Modern World, Oxford University Press, 1965; *A History of the Maghrib,* Cambridge University Press, 1971, 2nd edition, 1975.

WORK IN PROGRESS: Research on the socio-political functions of Muslim religious institutions in North Africa.

SIDELIGHTS: Abun-Nasr writes: "The greatest turning point in my career was studying with Albert Hourani, the well-known Oxford historian of the Middle East, when he was a visiting professor at the American University of Beirut. His trust in my ability made him arrange for me to carry out my graduate studies with him at Oxford. This meant, apart from an Oxford education, the friendship and support of a man of understanding and professional distinction."

* * *

ADAIR, Ian 1942-

PERSONAL: Born December 20, 1942, in Scotland; son of John (a manager) and Isabell (a tracer; maiden name, Henderson) Adair; married Susan Ann Becraft, September 17, 1975; children: Kylie, Antony. *Education:* Educated at private academy in Scotland. *Home and office:* 20 Ashley Ter., Bideford, Devonshire, England.

CAREER: Children's entertainer, 1954—; magician and writer, 1960—. Partner in Supreme Magic Company Ltd. (theatrical suppliers), Bideford, Devon, England, 1965-73. Has also worked as a shoemaker, 1957, a television presenter, 1959, and a free-lance scriptwriter, 1960. Active in Round Table movement. *Member:* International Brotherhood of Magicians, Associated Wizards of the South (England; honorary vice-president), India Ring (honorary member), Inner Magic Circle (London). *Awards, honors:* Invention awards from U.S. branch of International Brotherhood of Magicians, 1962, 1975, and 1976; gold medal from Inner Magic Circle, 1974.

WRITINGS—All published by Supreme Magic Co., except as indicated: *Adair's Ideas,* 1957, 3rd edition, 1970; *Entertaining Children,* 1960; *Magical Menu,* three volumes, 1960-63; *Encyclopaedia of Dove Magic,* four volumes, 1961-76; *Mental Magic,* 1962; *Dove Magic,* Part I, 1962, Part II, 1962; *Dove Magic Finale,* 1962; *Television Dove Magic,* 1963; *Illusions,* 1963; *My Card, Sir!,* 1963; *"Twenty-One",* 1963; *Dove Magic Encore,* 1963; *Television Dove Steals,* 1964; *Doves in Magic,* 1964; *Doves from Silks,* 1964; *New Doves from Silks Methods,* 1964; *Dove Classics,* 1964; *Further Dove Classics,* 1965; *More Modern Dove Classics,* 1965; *Stunners with Stamps,* 1965; *Television Card Manipulations,* 1966; *Classical Dove Secrets,* 1966; *Diary of a Dove Worker,* 1966; *Magic on the Wing,* 1966; *Cabaret Dove Act,* 1966; *A La Zombie Plus,* 1967; *Pot Pourri,* 1967; *Balloon-o-Dove,* 1967; *Spotlight on Doves,* 1967; *Watch the Birdie,* 1967; *Rainbow Dove Routines,* 1967; *Heads Off!,* 1967; *Tricks and Stunts with Rubber Doves,* 1967; *Magic with Doves,* 1968; *Dove Dexterity,* 1968; *Twin Dove Production,* 1968; *Magic with Latex Budgies,* 1968; *Paddle Antics,* 1969; *Television Puppet Magic,* 1969.

Conjuring As a Craft (self-illustrated), A. S. Barnes, 1970; *Party Planning and Entertainment* (self-illustrated), A. S. Barnes, 1971; *Magic Step by Step,* Arco, 1972; *Papercrafts,* Arco, 1975; *Complete Guide to Conjuring,* A. S. Barnes, 1977; (with Heather Amery) *The Knowhow Book of Jokes and Tricks* (juvenile), Urborne Publishing, 1977.

Author of "Adair's Ideas" and "The Dove Column," monthly columns in *Magigram.* Contributor of more than three thousand articles to more than thirty-five magic journals in the United States and England.

WORK IN PROGRESS: The Complete Party Planner, publication by A. S. Barnes expected in 1979; *Complete Guide to Conjuring,* publication by A. S. Barnes expected in 1980.

SIDELIGHTS: Adair writes: "At the age of ten years I received a birthday present from my grandmother which completely changed my life. It was a toy box of conjuring tricks. Within a day I had learnt and perfected all and had given my first performance the following day, receiving praise from my friends who formed the audience. 'Conjuring' and 'magic' was to be my life and not being content with the toy variety magic tricks which were available to anyone, I, now eleven years of age, invented my own. Entering a television talent show at eleven years of age, presenting a six-minute act, I won the major prize.

"Inventing of magical principles and routines occupied most of my young life and at fourteen years, my first book was published. At sixteen years of age, although still inventing and writing, I became involved in television work, both local and national. When eighteen years of age, I was given my own television show. At twenty, I joined a thriving company, specialised in supplying original material for theatricals.

"During this time, my magical and novelty subject writings flourished, with books on puppetry, origami, party planning techniques being published regularly by leading non-fiction publishers.

"Perhaps, one of my most pleasurable writing experiences has been that of compiling and writing, in collaboration with Heather Amery, *The Knowhow Book of Jokes and Tricks*. Printed in full colour with thousands of illustrations, we believe this to be the most comprehensive book, providing magic and secrets, by using the comic strip process.

"Inventing, lecturing, performing, writing, manufacturing, publishing, and promoting the craft to its fullness are my only interests. I live, eat, and sleep magic, just like the poet does with his words, the painter with his transformations to the canvas.

"I always make a point of presenting my own originations before an audience and do this by using television and stage. Making personal appearances on top BBC television shows, at leading cabaret venues, and more often before groups of children at birthday, Christmas, and annual treat parties is one way of ensuring that I learn the modern techniques which every performer can benefit from."

*   *   *

ADAMS, Elsie B(onita)   1932-

PERSONAL: Born August 11, 1932, in Atoka, Okla.; daughter of Mike (a mechanic) and Verdy (a clerical worker; maiden name, Long) McKaskle; married Dion G. Myers, January 25, 1954 (divorced, 1958); married Goerge R. Adams, October 11, 1959 (divorced, 1972); children: Jae Leslie, Geoffrey Richard. *Education:* University of Oklahoma, B.S., 1953, M.A., 1959, Ph.D., 1966. *Residence:* San Diego, Calif. *Office:* College of Arts and Letters, San Diego State University, San Diego, Calif. 92182.

CAREER: Northeastern Oklahoma Agricultural & Mechanical College, Miami, instructor in English, 1953-54; high school English teacher in Del City, Okla., 1955-56; Ginn & Co. (publishers), Boston, Mass., English editor, 1961-63; University of Wisconsin—Whitewater, assistant professor, 1966-67, associate professor of English, 1967-71; San Diego State University, San Diego, Calif., assistant professor, 1971-74, associate professor, 1974-77, professor of English, 1977—, associate dean of College of Arts and Letters, 1975—. *Member:* Modern Language Association of America.

WRITINGS: Bernard Shaw and the Aesthetes, Ohio State University Press, 1971; *Israel Zangwill,* Twayne, 1971; (with Mary Louise Briscoe) *Up Against the Wall, Mother: On Women's Liberation,* Glencoe Press, 1971. Contributor of about a dozen articles and reviews to language and literature journals.

WORK IN PROGRESS: GBS: An Annotated Bibliography of Writings About Him, with Donald H. Haberman and John P. Pfeiffer, for Northern Illinois University Press.

SIDELIGHTS: Adams writes to *CA:* "The work on Shaw focusses mostly on his place in the late nineteenth century milieu, especially his relationship to the prevailing art theories and movements of the period. Other scholarly writings deal with late nineteenth century British minor writers, in an attempt to reassess their contribution to English letters.

"The feminist anthology (*Up Against the Wall, Mother . . .*) was one of the first such readers in the contemporary women's movement. Its thesis is that Western literature had traditionally stereotyped woman: as sex object, as femme fatale, as goddess, as the Great Mother, and more recently—as the 'career girl' or the 'women's libber.' The result is that there are few portraits of women in literature that women can identify with or sympathize with."

*   *   *

ADAMS, Frank C(lyde)   1916-

PERSONAL: Born March 4, 1916, in Sparta, Ill.; son of Frank Wilson (in retail furniture) and Pearl (in retail furniture; maiden name, Schellenger) Adams; married Mary Calhoun (an editor), 1941. *Education:* Monmouth College, Monmouth, Ill., B.Ed., 1941; Southern Illinois University, M.S., 1951, Ph.D., 1962. *Religion:* Protestant. *Home and office:* 2726 West Murphysboro Rd., Route 7, Carbondale, Ill. 62901.

CAREER: U.S. Cartridge Co., St. Louis, Mo., metallurgist, 1942-44; Eastman Co., Oak Ridge, Tenn., supervisor of industry, 1944-45; high school teacher of biology in Sparta, Ill., 1947-52, counselor, 1952-54, principal, 1956-57; Southern Illinois University, Carbondale, instructor, 1957-62, assistant professor, 1962-69, associate professor, 1969-73, professor of higher education, 1973-77; American Work-Education Foundation, Carbondale, Ill., co-founder and president, 1976—. *Military service:* U.S. Army, special agent for Military Intelligence, 1945-46.

MEMBER: American Personnel and Guidance Association, National Association of Work and the College Student, Vocational Guidance Association, Cooperative Education Association, Midwest Association of Student Employment Administrators, Phi Delta Kappa.

WRITINGS: (With Clarence W. Stephens) *College and University Student Work Programs: Implications and Implementations,* Southern Illinois University Press, 1970; (with Stephens) *A Student Job Classification Plan,* Southern Illinois University Press, 1972; (editor with Roland Keene and John E. King) *Money, Marbles, or Chalk,* Southern Illinois University Press, 1975; (editor with Keene and King) *Work and the College Student,* Southern Illinois University Press, 1976; *National Journal: Work and the College Student,* National Conference of Work and the College Student, in press.

SIDELIGHTS: Adams writes: "With Dr. John E. King and Dr. Roland Keene, I have formed the National Work-Education Foundation, a not-for-profit organization, to support national work conferences, regional work education reorganization, and provide consulting services to universities and colleges. Also projected are several books and pamphlets on many aspects of student employment, both on and off campus, as well as cooperative educational areas."

*   *   *

ADAMS, Richard P(errill)   1917-1977

August 17, 1917—March 25, 1977; American professor of American literature and author of fiction and poetry and a work on William Faulkner. He died in New Orleans, La. Obituaries: *New York Times,* March 27, 1977; *AB Bookman's Weekly,* June 27, 1977. (*CAP*-2; earlier sketch in *CA*-33/36)

*   *   *

ADAMS, Robert (Franklin)   1932-
(Frank Adamson, Peter Eberhardt)

PERSONAL: Born August 31, 1932, in Danville, Va.; son of Frank Griffith (a sales manager) and Elnora (a registered nurse; maiden name, Lillard) Adams; married Joanna Jeffers, February, 1959 (divorced, March, 1964). *Politics:* Conservative. *Religion:* Unitarian-Universalist. *Residence:* Highland Springs, Va. *Agent:* Lyle Kenyon Engel, Book Creations, Inc., Canaan, N.Y. 12029.

CAREER: In sales and sales management for twenty years; now a writer. *Military service:* U.S. Army, 1951-54, 1961-62. *Member:* Science Fiction Writers of America.

WRITINGS: The Coming of the Horseclans, Pinnacle Books, 1975; *The Swords of the Horseclans,* Pinnacle Books, 1976; *The Return of the Horseclans,* Pinnacle Books, 1977; *The Queen and the Gladiator,* Pinnacle Books, 1977. Author of science fiction, sometimes under pseudonym Frank Adamson, and pornography, under pseudonym Peter Eberhardt.

WORK IN PROGRESS: Chattan House, a historical trilogy; *Castaways in Time,* the first volume of a new series; science fiction books.

SIDELIGHTS: Adams writes: "I feel that a fiction writer is an *entertainer* and I hotly disagree with those writers who consider their fiction a vehicle for their own narrow, political, sociological or religious beliefs—in essence, I write to provide escape for the reader, not to preach or lecture."

*   *   *

ADAMS, Russell B(aird), Jr. 1937-

PERSONAL: Born March 30, 1937, in Fredericksburg, Va.; son of Russell B. (an airline executive) and Frances (Nordin) Adams; married Nancy Weber (a teacher), February 20, 1960; children: Kathryn, Russell B. III. *Education:* Dickinson College, A.B., 1959. *Home:* 44 Harrison St., Brookline, Mass. 02146. *Agent:* L. David Otte, Otte Co., 9 Park St., Boston, Mass. 02108.

CAREER: Jewelers' Circular—Keystone, Philadelphia, Pa., associate editor, 1959-61; *Business Week,* assistant news bureau manager in Philadelphia, 1961-63, news bureau manager in Denver, Colo., 1963-66, and in Boston, Mass., 1967-70; Boston University, Boston, director of Office of Public Information, 1970-71; *Boston,* Boston, executive editor, 1971-73; *Purchasing,* Boston, news editor, 1974-75; freelance writer, 1975—.

WRITINGS: The Boston Money Tree (nonfiction), Crowell, 1977; *The Privy Papers* (nonfiction), Quail Street Publishing, 1977; *King Gillette* (biography), Little, Brown, in press. Contributor to *Women's Almanac.* Contributor of articles and reviews to magazines and newspapers, including *Nation* and *New Englander.*

*   *   *

ADAMSON, Joy(-Friederike Victoria) 1910-

PERSONAL: Born January 20, 1910, in Troppau, Silesia (now Opava, Czechoslovakia); daughter of Victor (an architect and urban planner) and Traute (Greipel) Gessner; married Victor von Klarwill, 1935 (divorced); married Peter Bally, 1938 (divorced); married George Adamson (a game warden), January, 1943. *Education:* Educated in Vienna, Austria, 1933-35. *Religion:* Protestant. *Home and office:* P.O. Box 254, Naivasha, Kenya.

CAREER: Illustrator of African botany texts and painter, 1938—, work has been exhibited by Kenya National Museum and Tryon Gallery in Nairobi and Fort Jesus Museum in Mombasa; ethologist, 1956—; author, 1958—. Founder and head of Elsa Wild Animal Appeal in England, 1961—,

United States, 1969—, Canada, 1971—, and Japan, 1976—. *Member:* Nanyuki Club, Nairobi Club. *Awards, honors:* Gold Grenfall medal from Royal Horticulture Society, 1947; award of merit from government of Czechoslovakia, 1970; Joseph Wood Krutch medal from U.S. Humane Society, 1971; Ehrenkreutz fuer Kunst und Wissenschaft (Austria), 1977.

WRITINGS—Adult: Born Free: A Lioness of Two Worlds, Pantheon, 1960; *Living Free,* Harcourt, 1961; *Forever Free,* Harcourt, 1962 (published in England as *Forever Free: Elsa's Pride,* Harvell, 1962); (self-illustrated) *The Peoples of Kenya,* Harcourt, 1967; *The Spotted Sphinx,* Harcourt, 1969; *Pippa's Challenge,* Harcourt, 1972; (self-illustrated) *Joy Adamson's Africa,* Harcourt, 1972.

Collections: *The Story of Elsa* (includes *Born Free, Living Free,* and *Forever Free*), Harcourt, 1966.

Children's books: *Elsa, The True Story of a Lioness,* Pantheon, 1961; *Elsa and Her Cubs,* Harcourt, 1965; *Pippa the Cheetah and Her Cubs,* Harcourt, 1970.

Illustrator: Arthur J. Jex-Blake, editor, *Gardening In East Africa,* Longmans, 2nd edition (Adamson not associated with 1st edition), 1939, 4th edition, 1957; Muriel Jex-Blake, *Some Wild Flowers of Kenya,* Longmans, 1948; *Flore des spermatophytes,* National Parc de Congo Belge, 1955; W. J. Eggeling, *Indigenous Trees of the Uganda Protectorate,* Government Printer (Entebbe, Uganda), 1957; Ivan R. Dale and Percy J. Greenway, *Kenya Trees and Shrubs,* Hatchards (London) for Buchanan's Kenya Estates (Nairobi), 1961.

Contributor of articles to magazines, including *Journal of the Royal Geographical Society, Country Life,* and *Geographical Journal.*

WORK IN PROGRESS: Research on the lion, cheetah, and leopard.

SIDELIGHTS: Joy Adamson's books are said to be the most moving animal stories yet to come out of Africa. Her books describe her and her husband's attempts to return two large African cats, a lioness and a cheetah, to life in the bush.

The lioness, Elsa, was adopted and raised by the Adamsons after George had killed the mother in self-defense. The Adamsons were outraged at the thought of turning Elsa, who lost her natural training in hunting and killing, over to a zoo—the accepted practice when such animals became full grown. Against local and scientific advice the Adamsons decided to train Elsa to live in the wild themselves. This story is told in *Born Free* and continued in *Living Free.* Elsa's death and the tale of her cubs is told in *Forever Free.* In 1964 through 1967, Mrs. Adamson repeated the experience with a cheetah named Pippa who had been raised by a British Army officer.

Four of Mrs. Adamson's successful and popular books have been made into movies. *Born Free* was adapted for the screen in 1966, *The Spotted Sphinx* was filmed in 1970, and *Living Free* and *Forever Free* were both done in 1971. All the films appeared under the original book titles.

Mrs. Adamson told *CA:* "The more I learn from wild animals, the more I am convinced that they communicate by thought communication—which we humans may also have possessed before we developed speech and mechanical means of communication. Our telepathy gradually atrophied, except in very rare cases. I had it with Elsa and Pippa, but not with humans."

As founder of the Elsa Wild Animal Appeal, an organization dedicated to the preservation of threatened wildlife species, Mrs. Adamson urged everyone to "save the wild cats of Africa and the world . . . by boycotting the trade of furs and other organic parts of the animal's body sold as jewelry or trinkets." She especially urged writers to "help the wild animals of the U.S.S.R., Poland, Hungary, Czechoslovakia, Roumania, and Bulgaria with book royalties sold in those countries."

*   *   *

ADDY, John   1915-

PERSONAL: Born June 3, 1915, in England; son of John (an engineer) and Elizabeth Addy. *Education:* Attended St. John's College of Education; University of Leeds, B.A., 1957, M.A., 1960, Ph.D., 1970. *Home:* 66 Long Lane, Clayton West, Huddersfield, England. *Office:* Department of Historical Studies, College of Ripon and York St. John, Lord Mayor's Walk, York Y03 7EX, England.

CAREER: Engineer in Huddersfield, England, 1931-47; teacher of history and divinity in secondary schools in York, Penistone and Barnsley, England, 1948-70; College of Ripon and York St. John, York, England, senior lecturer in history, 1970—, archivist, 1976—. Schoolmaster fellow at Balliol College, Oxford, 1962-63. *Member:* Royal Historical Society, Historical Association, Surtees Society, British Records Association.

WRITINGS: The Archdeacon and Ecclesiastical Administration, 1559-1714, St. Anthony's Press, 1963; *The Agrarian Revolution,* Longmans, Green, 1964; *Parliamentary Elections and Reform,* Longmans, Green, 1965; *A Coal and Iron Community in the Industrial Revolution,* Longman, 1969; *The Agrarian Revolution: Seminary Studies,* Longman, 1972; *The Textile Revolution,* Longman, 1976; *The Industrial Revolution Source Book,* Longman, 1976. Contributor to British history journals.

WORK IN PROGRESS: Research on Consistory Court files of Chester Diocese, 1600-1800, and on the church in the eighteenth century; *The Diary of Beilby Porteus: Bishop of London, 1787-1809; The Diary of Henry Prescott: Registrar of Chester, 1690-1719.*

SIDELIGHTS: Addy told *CA:* "In outlook and thinking I am very much a European rather than just an insular Englishman. Perhaps that is the result of undertaking research in European universities and libraries."

*   *   *

ADELMAN, Bob   1930-

PERSONAL: Born October 30, 1930, in New York, N.Y.; son of Samuel (a builder) and Anna (Pomerantz) Adelman; married Trudy Viner, June 21, 1964; children: Samantha. *Education:* Rutgers University, B.A., 1951; Harvard University, graduate study, 1952; Columbia University, M.A., 1955. *Politics:* Democrat. *Religion:* Jewish. *Home:* 27 West 96th St., New York, N.Y. 10025. *Office:* 119 Fifth Ave., New York, N.Y. 10003.

CAREER: Free-lance photojournalist, 1962—. Lecturer at Philadelphia College of Art, Columbia University, New School for Social Research, and at School of Visual Arts, 1968-71. Creative director of Prairie House. Group shows include exhibitions at Martha Jackson Gallery, Smithsonian Institution, and American Federation of Arts Gallery. *Military service:* U.S. Marine Corps Reserve, active duty, 1951.

MEMBER: American Society of Magazine Writers.

Awards, honors: Awards from Missouri School of Journalism, 1964, Art Directors Club of New York, 1965, 1971, and Art Directors Club of Washington, D.C., 1965; Guggenheim fellowship, 1965.

WRITINGS: Cambridge Readers, New York Times, 1968; (with Irving Weinstein) *A Proud People: Black American,* 1970; (with Susan Hall) *On and Off the Street,* Viking, 1970; *Street Smart,* McGraw, 1972; *Down Home,* McGraw, 1972; *Gentleman of Leisure,* New American Library, 1973; *Ladies of the Night,* Simon & Schuster, 1974; *Out of Left Field,* Prairie House, 1976. Author of material for National Broadcasting Co.-Television; educational writer for major publishers, including Random House, Dell, Cowles, and Holt. Contributor to *Photography Annual.* Contributor of stories, photographs, and cover photographs, to national magazines, including *Newsweek, Look, Fortune, Harper's, Saturday Review,* and *Esquire.*

SIDELIGHTS: Adelman writes briefly: "I have been a close student of social events and issues. My books have grown out of these preoccupations."

*   *   *

ADELSON, Daniel   1918-

PERSONAL: Born September 19, 1918, in New York, N.Y.; son of Louis Hirsch (a hotel and restaurant owner) and Esther Fay (Edelson) Adelson; married Suzanne B. Maricq (a psychologist and social worker), July 23, 1948; children: Isabelle Rachel, Ann Deborah, Mark David. *Education:* City College (now of the City University of New York), B.A., 1940, graduate study, 1941-42; further graduate study at University of Chicago, 1948, and University of California, Berkeley, 1949-50; New School for Social Research, M.A., 1953; Columbia University, Ph.D., 1957. *Politics:* Democrat. *Religion:* Jewish. *Home:* 299 Uplands, Berkeley, Calif. 94705. *Office:* California School of Professional Psychology, Berkeley, Calif.

CAREER: Altro Health and Rehabilitation Service, New York City, research assistant, 1953-54; Jewish Board of Guardians, New York City, social science associate on mental health of children,1954-55; Child Welfare League of America, New York City, research consultant, 1955-56; Napa State Hospital, Napa, Calif., principal investigator of ataraxic drugs, 1957-61; University of California, San Francisco, lecturer, 1960-67, associate professor of psychology, 1967-74, director of community mental health training program, School of Nursing, 1966-72, member of psychology group, 1967-74; California School of Professional Psychology, San Francisco, member of faculty, 1976—. Team officer for United Nations Relief and Rehabilitation Acministration (UNRRA) at Children's Center of U.S. Zone in Germany, 1946; volunteer agency liaison officer and deputy chief of UNRRA and International Refugee Organization, U.S. Zone, Germany, 1946-48. Research associate at Institute of Human Development, University of California, Berkeley, 1960-70; assistant director at Center for Training in Community Psychiatry and Mental Health Administration, 1961-65. *Military service:* U.S. Army, organizer of displaced persons centers, 1943-45; served in Europe; received Bronze Star with oak leaf cluster.

MEMBER: American Psychological Association (fellow), American Association for the Advancement of Science (fellow), American Association of University Professors, Society for the Psychological Study of Social Issues (fellow).

WRITINGS: (Contributor) Francis J. Rosenbaum, editor, *Work and the Heart,* Paul B. Hoeber, 1959; (contributor)

Marion E. Kalkman, editor, *Psychiatric Nursing,* 3rd edition (Adelson was not associated with earlier editions), McGraw, 1969; (editor with Betty L. Kalis, and contributor) *Community Psychology and Mental Health,* Chandler Publishing, 1970; (editor and contributor) *Man as the Measure: The Crossroads,* Behavioral Publications, 1972. General editor of the "Community Psychology" series, Division of Community Psychology, American Psychological Association. Contributor to *Handbook of Community Psychiatry* and *Handbook of Community Mental Health.* Contributor of about twenty articles and reviews to professional journals.

WORK IN PROGRESS: Community Psychology: A Base for Prevention in Community Mental Health (tentative title), for Holt; books on names and on group cohesiveness and value conflict under extreme conditions.

SIDELIGHTS: Adelson writes: "There can be joy and love with dance and song—as I felt it and experienced it in my childhood—at various moments at home—the larger ideological community being the Workmen's Circle and Central Park with free concerts of the twenties with no fear in the streets, and the hard working but fairly carefree song, dance, and laughter summer evenings of the Borscht Circuit—but also the Depression with its separation of our family—and then overriding the Nazi period—the Army and Displaced Persons and UNRRA and the International Refugee Organization—and lessons learned there about the importance of culture and community for those just freed from the camps, and social organization (the Kibbutz) for morale—and the importance for the individual of individual approaches, but their relative ineffectiveness when faced with a mass problem of millions of refugees, and so the need for a *community* approach.... The writer as writer and artist may be closer to the truth than the psychologist as scientist—because the former if true puts life down whole—capturing the emotion with the form—and the latter must put things in categories.

"I joined about 38 other psychologists in an exciting workshop which gave rise to the official birth of Community Psychology as a new sub-area of psychology. The significance of this new sub-discipline for community mental health, for community psychiatry, and for psychology and the social sciences in general has been a central concern since—either in my positions conceptualizing, writing, and teaching—or editing as general editor of the 'Community Psychology' series for the Division of Community Psychology of the American Psychological Association, the first volume of which is *Man as the Measure: The Crossroads*—in which my own introductory article points up the need for a psychology which sees man whole and in historical perspective—and emphasizing his own cultural roots, rejects the pathological stereotypes through which rational psychology appears to have viewed many minorities.... I am particularly interested now in the meaning of psychology and psychological mindedness for man's relations with his fellow man and the contribution it can make. The book on Community Psychology on which I am now doing the finishing touches has as a central idea the designation of Community Psychology as Man's Encounter with History."

* * *

ADLER, Freda 1934-

PERSONAL: Born November 21, 1934, in Philadelphia, Pa.; daughter of David R. (an industrialist) and Lucia Green (DeWolfson) Schaffer; married Herbert M. Adler (a physician), June 18, 1955 (divorced, 1975); married Gerhard O.W. Mueller (chief of United Nations Crime Section), February 29, 1976; children: (first marriage) Mark, Jill, Nancy. *Education:* University of Pennsylvania, B.A., 1956, M.A., 1968, Ph.D., 1971. *Home:* 30 Waterside Plaza, Apt. 37J, New York, N.Y. 10010. *Office:* School of Criminal Justice, Rutgers University, 53 Washington St., Newark, N.J. 07102.

CAREER: Temple University, Philadelphia, Pa., instructor in psychiatry, 1971, research coordinator at Addiction Science Center, 1971-72; Medical College of Pennsylvania, Philadelphia, assistant professor of psychiatry and research director of Section on Drug and Alcohol Abuse, 1972-74; Rutgers University, Newark, N.J., associate professor of criminal justice, 1974—. Member of faculty of National College of State Judiciary, 1973—, and of National College of Criminal Defense Lawyers and Public Defenders, 1976; visiting fellow at Yale University, 1976. Member of board of directors of Institute for the Continuous Study of Man, 1974—. Consultant to National Commission on Marijuana and Drug Abuse and the United Nations. *Member:* International Association of Penal Law, American Sociological Association, American Society of Criminology (executive counselor, 1971-72, 1974-75), University of Pennsylvania Alumnae Association (member of board of directors, 1974-77). *Awards, honors:* Herbert Bloch Award from American Society of Criminology, 1972; Ancient Order of Chamorri (Guam).

WRITINGS: (Editor with G.O.W. Mueller) *Politics, Crime and the International Scene: An Interamerican Focus,* North-South Center Press, 1972; (with Arthur D. Moffett, Federick B. Glaser, and others) *The Treatment of Drug Abuse in Pennsylvania,* Governor's Council on Drug and Alcohol Abuse, 1973; (contributor) William White, Jr. and Ronald F. Albano, editors, *North American Symposium on Drugs and Drug Abuse,* North American Publishing, 1974; (with Moffett, Glaser, and others) *A Systems Approach to Drug Treatment,* Dorrance, 1974; (with Moffett, Glaser, and Diana Horvitz) *Medical Lollipop, Junkie Insulin, Or What?: Patient and Staff Views of the Chemotherapy of Addiction,* Dorrance, 1974; *Sisters in Crime,* McGraw, 1975. Contributor to criminology, sociology, and psychiatry journals, law and medical journals, and *Washington Post.* Member of editorial board of *Criminology: An Interdisciplinary Journal,* 1971-73; consulting editor of *Journal of Research in Crime and Delinquency,* 1977.

WORK IN PROGRESS: Women in Crime and Women in Criminal Justice; a cross-cultural comparison of female criminality.

SIDELIGHTS: Freda Adler writes: "Several years ago while working for the government as an evaluator of drug and alcohol treatment centers it was part of my task to interview addicts in treatment. One of the important areas of concern was in each individual's arrest record. After studying hundreds of these profiles, I became aware that there was a change in the types of crime in which females were involved. No longer content with shoplifting and prostitution they were turning to crimes such as robbery and burglary. This realization led me to a three-year research study involving visits with inmates, administrators, police officers, judges, etc. These changing female crime patterns and their relationship to women's emancipation became the subject of *Sisters in Crime.* Since that time I have been studying female criminality and lecturing on the topic in many countries, including Mexico, Venezuela, Brazil, Canada, Switzerland, Germany, Finland, Poland, Hungary, Guam, Australia, Ivory Coast, and Saudi Arabia."

AVOCATIONAL INTERESTS: Horseback riding, skiing, sailing.

* * *

ADLER, Norman Tenner 1941-

PERSONAL: Born June 7, 1941, in Chicago, Ill.; son of Arthur (a businessperson) and Mary (Barricks) Adler; married Shelley Goodman, 1968; children: Shira Tamar, Tanya Aviv, Ari Chaim, Kiva Tal. *Education:* Harvard University, B.A. (magna cum laude), 1962, graduate study, 1962-63; University of California, Berkeley, M.A. and Ph.D., both 1967; University of California, Los Angeles, post-doctoral study, 1967-68. *Office:* Department of Psychology, University of Pennsylvania, 3815 Walnut St., Philadelphia, Pa. 19104.

CAREER: University of Pennsylvania, Philadelphia, assistant professor, 1968-71, associate professor, 1971-76, professor of psychology, 1976—, member of Graduate Group in Biology and Institute of Neurological Sciences, both 1970—. Visiting scientist at University of Edinburgh, spring, 1975; visiting professor at University of Texas, spring, 1977. Director of Philadelphia Jewish Free University, 1970-73. Ad hoc member of National Institutes of Health Committee on Reproduction, 1973, 1976; chairperson of Eastern Regional Conference on Reproduction Behavior, 1971.

MEMBER: International Society for Psychoneuroendocrinology, International Society for Developmental Psychobiology, American Psychological Association, American Society of Zoologists, American Behavior Society, Endocrine Society, Society for Neuroscience, Phi Beta Kappa, Sigma Xi. *Awards, honors:* Woodrow Wilson fellowship, 1962-63; National Institute of Mental Health grant, 1967-68; National Institutes of Health grant, 1969—; early career award from American Psychological Association, 1974; Lindbach Award for Distinguished Teaching from University of Pennsylvania, 1976, National Science Foundation grant, 1976—.

WRITINGS: (Editor) *Psychology Today: Readings in Experimental-Biological Psychology,* CRM Books, 1970; (contributor) Donald Dewsbury and D. A. Rethlingshafer, editors, *Comparative Psychology: A Modern Survey,* McGraw, 1973; (contributor) William Montagna and William Sadler, editors, *Reproductive Behavior,* Plenum, 1974; (contributor) B. L. Hart, editor, *Laboratory Manual on Experimental Psychobiology,* W. H. Freeman, 1975; (contributor) J. B. Hutchison, editor, *Biological Determinants of Sexual Behavior,* Wiley, in press. Contributor of more than twenty-five articles and reviews to scientific journals. Associate editor of *Hormones and Behavior,* 1973—; member of editorial board of *Motivation and Emotion,* 1975; member of neuroendocrine editorial board for Plenum, 1975.

WORK IN PROGRESS: A *Textbook of Biological and Physiological Psychology,* with C. R. Gallistel; editing *A Primer of Neuro-Endocrine Function for Behaviorists,* for Plenum; "Behavioral and Social Control of Reproductive Process," to be included in *Advances in the Study of Animal Behavior,* edited by Jay Rosenblatt, R. H. Hinde, and Evelyn Shaw.

* * *

ADLER, Warren 1927-

PERSONAL: Born December 16, 1927, in Brooklyn, N.Y.; son of Sol and Fritzie (Goldman) Adler; married Sonia Kline (a magazine editor); children: David Allen, Jonathan Robert, Michael Adam. *Education:* New York University, B.A., 1947; further study at New School for Social Research. *Home:* 3301 Woodbine St., Chevy Chase, Md. 20015. *Agent:* Peter Lampack, William Morris Agency, 1350 Avenue of the Americas, New York, N.Y. 10019. *Office:* 3301 New Mexico Ave. N.W., Washington, D.C. 20016.

CAREER: Has worked as a copy person for *New York Daily News;* was editor of *Queens Post,* Forest Hills, N.Y.; president of an advertising and public relations agency in Washington, D.C., 1959—. Publisher and president of apartment shoppers guide, 1961—. President of radio and television stations, 1966—. Bank director, 1974—. *Military service:* U.S. Army, Washington correspondent for Armed Forces Press Service, 1951-53. *Member:* Public Relations Society of America, Authors Guild, National Press Club.

WRITINGS—Novels: *Options,* Whitman Publishing, 1974; *Banquet Before Dawn,* Putnam, 1976; *The Henderson Equation,* Putnam, 1976; *Trans-Siberian Express,* Putnam, 1977.

Contributor to magazines and journals. Writer of newspaper column, "Pepper on the Side," for several newspapers, 1947-53. Also author of two novels and numerous short stories, as yet unpublished.

WORK IN PROGRESS: A novel set in South America.

* * *

AFRICANO, Lillian 1935-
(Lillian Atallah)

PERSONAL: Born June 7, 1935, in Paterson, N.J.; daughter of John and Nadwa (Gorab) Tabeek; married Arthur Africano (a physician), June 28, 1958 (divorced); children: David, Nina, Arthur. *Education:* Barnard College, B.A., 1957; Columbia University, graduate study, 1957-58. *Home and office:* 45 West 10th St., New York, N.Y. 10011. *Agent:* Julia Coopersmith Literary Agency, 10 West 15th St., New York, N.Y. 10011.

CAREER: Teacher in Union City, N.J., 1957-59; *Villager,* New York, N.Y., theater critic and entertainment editor, 1970-75; *Acupuncture News Digest,* New York City, editor, 1975; writer of syndicated column, "Theatre U.S.A.," 1975—. Theater critic for *Asbury Park Press,* 1973—. Conducted exclusive interview with Egypt's first lady, Madame Sadat; has also interviewed Tennessee Williams. *Member:* Outer Critics' Circle, Drama Desk (vice-president, 1974-75, secretary, 1975-77).

WRITINGS: The Businessman's Guide to the Middle East, Harper, 1977. Writer of monthly news column for *Forum;* regular contributor to syndicated column, "One Woman's Voice"; contributor of medical articles (under pseudonym Lillian Atallah) and other articles to popular magazines and newspapers, including *National Review, Penthouse, Cue, Nation, Worldview, Harper's Bazaar, Woman's Day, Viva,* and *Christian Science Monitor.*

WORK IN PROGRESS: An as yet untitled book on women and social/sexual love, publication by Wentworth expected in 1978; extensive research on recent economic developments in Arab countries; travel in the Middle East in connection with future writings. *Avocational interests:* Travel (Europe, the Caribbean, the Middle East—speaks Arabic).

* * *

AGAY, Denes 1911-

PERSONAL: Born June 10, 1911, in Hungary; came to

United States in 1939, naturalized citizen, 1943; son of Martin (a businessman) and Louise (Lustig) Agay; married Mary Roberts, November 1, 1947; children: Susan Louise (Mrs. Charles J. Rothschild III). *Education:* Liszt Academy of Music, diploma, 1933; University of Budapest, Ph.D., 1934. *Home:* 1052 Pine St., Norton, Va. 24273. *Office:* Music Sales Corp., 33 West 60th St., New York City, N.Y. 10023.

CAREER: Composer of works for piano, orchestra, band, chorus and solo voice; arranger and editor of instructional materials for piano. Consultant to music publishers, including Music Sales Corp., Yorktown Music Press, and Consolidated Music Publishers. Lecturer. *Military service:* U.S. Army, 1942-46. *Member:* American Society of Composers, Authors, and Publishers (ASCAP), Associated Music Teachers League (board member), American College of Musicians, Piano Teachers Congress of New York (board member). *Awards, honors:* Numerous awards from *Piano Quarterly;* award from National Guild of Piano Teachers.

WRITINGS: (Editor) *An Anthology of Piano Music,* four volumes, Yorktown Music Press, 1968; (arranger and editor with William Kaufman) *Children's Songs of the World,* Stackpole, 1971; *Best Loved Songs of the American People,* Doubleday, 1975. Contributor of articles to music journals.

WORK IN PROGRESS: A guide book for piano teachers.

SIDELIGHTS: Agay says that he "preaches and practices the acceptance and enjoyment of all kinds of *good* music from Baroque to jazz."

*   *   *

AGNEW, Patience McCormick-Goodhart 1913(?)-1976

1913(?)—December 25, 1976; British-born American author, needlepoint designer, and craftswoman. She died in Greenwich, Conn. Obituaries: *New York Times,* December 28, 1976; *AB Bookman's Weekly,* February 14, 1977.

*   *   *

AINSWORTH, Dorothy Sears 1894-1976

March 8, 1894—December 2, 1976; American professor and author of books on physical education. Ainsworth was a member of several committees on physical education and received awards from various nations, including the United States, France, Finland, and Sweden. She died in Moline, Ill. Obituaries: *New York Times,* December 4, 1976.

*   *   *

AJAY, Betty 1918-

PERSONAL: Born June 26, 1918, in California; daughter of Walter (a contractor) and Eva (Palmer) Raymond; married Peter Barry, August 7, 1941 (divorced, 1943); married Abe Ajay (an artist), December 16, 1947; children: Robin Dickinson. *Education:* University of California, Berkeley, B.A., 1939. *Religion:* None. *Home address:* Walnut Hill Rd., Bethel, Conn. 06801.

CAREER: Self-employed landscape designer and interior designer in Connecticut and New York, 1956—.

WRITINGS: Betty Ajay's Guide to Home Landscaping, McGraw, 1970.

WORK IN PROGRESS: Color for All Seasons, on gardening.

ALBERT, Louise 1928-

PERSONAL: Born May 20, 1928, in White Plains, N.Y.; daughter of Benjamin Leopold (an electrical engineer) and Esther (a psychotherapist and writer; maiden name, Pfeffer) Spitzer; married Floyd Albert (a manufacturer of dental education aids), April 15, 1951; children: Elizabeth, David, Alice. *Education:* Cornell University, B.A. (honors), 1949; University of Michigan, M.A., 1950. *Politics:* "Liberal/Radical—if that means anything." *Home:* 35 Park Rd., Scarsdale, N.Y. 10583. *Agent:* Richard Huttner, 330 East 33rd St., New York, N.Y. 10016.

CAREER: Elementary school teacher in Poughkeepsie, N.Y., 1950-52, and White Plains, N.Y. 1952-53; private remedial reading teacher, 1953-60; writer, 1968—. *Member:* Authors Guild of Authors League of America, Phi Beta Kappa.

WRITINGS: But I'm Ready to Go (novel), Bradbury, 1976.

WORK IN PROGRESS: Another novel.

SIDELIGHTS: Louise Albert writes: "I write out of my own experience and deep emotional needs. Although my first book is fiction with characters and events made up, and this will be true for my next book, my imagination, so far, is fueled by the deepest and most tragic parts of my life. . . . Writing helps me, and I hope others, learn to accept and understand and go beyond these things in life."

AVOCATIONAL INTERESTS: Reading (adult and juvenile fiction), music.

*   *   *

ALDEN, Douglas William 1912-

PERSONAL: Born September 11, 1912, in Washington, D.C.; son of Alanson Gilbert and Grace Anderson (Hunt) Alden; married Martha Seaver Bowditch, September 11, 1937; children: Claire Douglas (Mrs. Dennis C. Drehmel), Barbara Bowditch (Mrs. Richard C. Giangiulio). *Education:* Dartmouth College, A.B., 1933; Brown University, A.M., 1934, Ph.D., 1938; also attended University of Paris, 1931-32, 1935-36. *Home:* 1880 Westview Rd., Charlottesville, Va. 22903. *Office:* Department of French Literature and General Linguistics, University of Virginia, Charlottesville, Va. 22903.

CAREER: Texas Tech College (now University), Lubbock, instructor in French, 1938-41; Amherst College, Amherst, Mass., instructor in French, 1941-42; Texas Tech College, assistant professor of French, 1943; Princeton University, Princeton, N.J., instructor, 1945-46, assistant professor, 1947-54, associate professor of French, 1954-61; University of Maryland, College Park, professor of French and chairman of department of foreign languages, 1961-64; University of Virginia, Charlottesville, professor of French, 1964—, chairman of department of modern languages, 1964-71, chairman of department of Romance languages, 1966-71. Chairman of advisory council for Sweet Briar College junior-year-in-France program, 1950—. *Military service:* U.S. Army Air Forces, Office of Strategic Services, 1942-45; became captain; received Bronze Star and Croix de Guerre.

MEMBER: Association Internationale des Etudes Francaises, Modern Language Association of America, American Association of Teachers of French (member of executive council, 1968-71; national president, 1972-76), Alden Kindred Society, Societe des Professeurs Francais en Amerique, South Atlantic Modern Language Association (president of Association of Departments of Foreign Languages,

1969-70), South Central Modern Language Association, Alpha Sigma Phi, Appalachian Mountain Club. *Awards, honors:* Chevalier of Ordre des Palmes Academiques, then officier.

WRITINGS: Marcel Proust and His French Critics, Lymanhouse, 1940, 2nd edition, 1973; *Introduction to French Masterpieces,* Appleton, 1948; *Cortina's·French in Twenty Lessons,* Cortina, 1950; *Premier Manuel,* Appleton, 1954; *Jacques de Lacretelle: An Intellectual Itinerary,* Rutgers University Press, 1958; (with Andre Maman) *Grammaire et Style,* Appleton, 1967; *Marcel Proust's Grasset Proofs,* University of North Carolina Department of Romance Languages, 1977; (editor) *A Critical Bibliography of French Literature: The Twentieth Century,* Syracuse University Press, Volumes I-III, 1977. Editor-in-chief of *French XX Bibliography,* French Institute and Camargo Foundation, 1949—. Review editor for *French Review,* 1964-71.

WORK IN PROGRESS: Editing additional volumes of *A Critical Bibliography of French Literature: The Twentieth Century,* for Syracuse University Press.

* * *

ALDOUS, Anthony Michael 1935-
(Tony Aldous)

PERSONAL: Born December 20, 1935, in London, England; son of Leslie R. (a journalist) and Queeni (Lawrence) Aldous; married Ruth Vivian Field (a librarian), January 6, 1962; children: Simon, Katherine, Jessica. *Education:* University of Bristol, LL.B., 1959. *Politics:* "Political agnostic." *Religion:* None. *Home and office:* 12 Eliot Hill, London SE13 7EB, England.

CAREER: Staff reporter for weekly and daily provincial newspapers in England, 1960-67; *Times,* London, England, staff reporter, 1967-73, environment and architectural reporter, 1970-73; free-lance architectural, planning, and environmental journalist, 1973—. Member of conservation advisory group of Department of the Environment. *Member:* Land Use Society, Architecture Club (London).

WRITINGS: Battle for the Environment, Collins, 1972; *Goodbye, Britain?,* Sidgwick & Jackson, 1975. Contributor to magazines and newspapers, including *Building Design, Country Life, New Scientist,* and *New Society.*

SIDELIGHTS: Aldous writes: "For the past seven years I have specialized in architecture, town planning, and environmental subjects, and especially urban conservation. I have extensive contacts among British architects, town planners, and environmentalists; and some contacts in Europe—notably France, Germany, Denmark, Poland, and Italy."

* * *

ALDWINCKLE, Russell (Foster) 1911-

PERSONAL: Born November 9, 1911, in Leicester, England; son of Arthur William (an engineer) and Alice Jane (Foster) Aldwinckle; married Muriel Owen, 1942; children: David. *Education:* University of London, B.A. (honors), 1932; Oxford University, B.A., 1936, M.A., 1948; University of Strasbourg, D.Th., 1938. *Home:* 704-33 Robinson St., Hamilton, Ontario, Canada L8P 1Y8. *Office:* McMaster Divinity College, McMaster University, Hamilton, Ontario, Canada.

CAREER: Ordained Baptist minister, 1939; pastor of Baptist churches in Coventry, England, 1939-43, and North Finchley, England, 1943-47; McMaster University, Hamil-

ton, Ontario, assistant professor, 1947-55, associate professor, 1955-60, professor of systematic theology, 1960—. Member of Faith and Order Commission of World Council of Churches, 1962, and Commission on Doctrine of Baptist World Alliance. *Member:* Canadian Theological Society (president), American Academy of Religion. *Awards, honors:* Lord Nuffield travel award, Oxford University, 1955; Canada Council senior fellowship and American Association of Theological Schools fellowship, both to Oxford University and University of Basel, both 1959-60; D.D. from Acadia University, 1965.

WRITINGS: Death in the Secular City, Allen & Unwin, 1974, Eerdmans, 1975; *More Than Man: A Study in Christology,* Eerdmans, 1976.

Work anthologized in *New Theology Number Five,* Peerman Macmillan, 1968. Contributor to theology journals.

WORK IN PROGRESS: Christians Without Ecstasy; The God Beyond and the God Within: A Study in Christian Theism.

SIDELIGHTS: Aldwinckle writes: "My research at present is in the area of religious ecstasy with a view to discovering the criteria for judging the validity or otherwise of the claims made for these unusual types of experience. There are chapters on the role of emotion and feeling in religion, the biblical concept of Spirit, non-Christian ecstatic experiences, mysticism and drug-induced 'mystical' experience, Jungian integration, and the modern Christian charismatic movement.

"My second manuscript deals with the Christian Doctrine of God in the light of recent vigorous philosophical discussion about the 'proofs' and the possibility of some kind of natural theology. The basic thrust, however, is to argue that Christian theism is more than, even though it may include, a philosophical theology. A section is devoted to a critique of the currently popular process theology."

AVOCATIONAL INTERESTS: Oil painting.

* * *

ALEXANDER, Harold Lee 1934-
(Zane Alexander)

PERSONAL: Born June 20, 1934, in Dallas, Tex.; son of Theron Lee (a clergyman) and Anna Belle (Moore) Alexander; married Gloria Faye Sawyer, January 24, 1959; children: Donna Lynn, Dawn Lee. *Education:* Union University, Jackson, Tenn., B.A. (cum laude), 1955; Southeastern Theological Seminary, earned B.D., M.Div., 1958; also attended Princeton Theological Seminary, 1959-60, and University of Heidelberg, 1965-66. *Politics:* Democrat. *Home and office address:* P.O. Drawer 922, Fort Clayton, Canal Zone, A.P.O., N.Y. 09827.

CAREER: Ordained Baptist minister, 1952; pastor of First Baptist church in Benson, N.C., 1960-61; U.S. Army, chaplain, 1961-76, served in Germany, Vietnam, and Panama Canal Zone, retiring as lieutenant colonel; writer, 1976—. Licensed marriage counselor in State of California. *Member:* American Association of Marriage and Family Counselors (clinical member), Group Psychotherapy Association of Southern California.

WRITINGS: (Under pseudonym Zane Alexander) *Till Death Do Us Part or Something Else Comes Up,* Westminster, 1976.

WORK IN PROGRESS: Marriage, Among Other Things, Doesn't Work Any More: How to Make It When Your Institutions Don't, under psuedonym Zane Alexander.

SIDELIGHTS: Alexander writes: "I am a marriage counselor with over ten thousand hours of clinical experience and
out of this broad experience has grown my conviction that
marriage and other institutions in the United States have
become dysfunctional. My literary work is an attempt to
state this and to point out what can be done about it. I believe that the dyad is a product of institutional romanticism
and that it must be expanded into a larger group in order to
meet basic human needs."

*   *   *

ALEXANDER, John N. 1941-

PERSONAL: Born August 30, 1941, in Loudon, Tenn.; son
of Noel O. (a teacher) and Alma (Maples) Alexander; married Sheila Hunt, October 12, 1963; children: Cynthia
Robin, Angela Page. Education: Attended University of
Tennessee. Home: 18616 Tanterra Way, Brookeville, Md.
20729. Office: WMAL-FM Radio, 4400 Jenifer St. N.W.,
Washington, D.C. 20015.

CAREER: Director of news operations for radio stations in
Knoxville, Tenn., Albany, N.Y., Richmond, Va., and Atlanta, Ga., 1962-70; WMAL-AM Radio, Washington, D.C.,
Maryland correspondent, 1970-76; WMAL-FM Radio,
Washington, D.C., director of news and public affairs,
1976—. Member: Radio and Television Correspondents
Association. Awards, honors: Ohio State Award, 1971, for
documentary "Washington Revisited"; Freedoms Foundation Award, 1972, for documentary "As American As";
George Foster Peabody Award from University of Georgia,
1976, for documentary "Legend of the Bermuda Triangle."

WRITINGS: Ghosts!: Washington's Most Famous Ghost
Stories, Washingtonian Books, 1976. Author of radio documentaries, including "The Centennial Commemoration of
the Battle of the Little Big Horn."

*   *   *

ALEXANDER, W(illiam) M(ortimer) 1928-

PERSONAL: Born December 5, 1928, in Jacksonville, Fla.;
son of Leon Wilson (a lawyer) and Ruth Louise (Chese-
brough) Alexander; married Katherine Alice Fryer (a
teacher), June 5, 1953; children: John Edward, Susan Dorman, David Leon. Education: Davidson College, A.B.,
1950; Louisville Presbyterian Seminary, B.D., 1953; Harvard University, S.T.M., 1957; Princeton Theological Seminary, Ph.D., 1961. Religion: Presbyterian. Office: Division
of Religion and Philosophy, St. Andrews College, Laurinburg, N.C. 28352.

CAREER: St. Andrews College, Laurinburg, N.C., assistant professor, 1961-63, associate professor, 1963-67, professor of religion and philosophy, 1967—, chairman of division, 1971-73. Military service: U.S. Army, chaplain, 1953-
56; served in Korea.

MEMBER: American Philosophical Association, Metaphysical Society of America, American Academy of Religion, Society for Philosophy and Public Affairs, American
Association of University Professors. Awards, honors:
Grants from American Council of Learned Societies, summer, 1966, Piedmont University Center, 1969-71, Council
for Philosophical Studies, 1974, and National Endowment
for the Humanities, 1976.

WRITINGS: Johann Georg Hamann: Philosophy and
Faith, Nijhoff, 1966; Sex and Philosophy, Mouton & Co., in
press. Contributor to Encyclopedia of Philosophy and to
philosophy and religion journals.

ALEXIOU, Margaret 1939-

PERSONAL: Born March 25, 1939, in Birmingham, En-
gland; daughter of George Derwent (a university professor)
and Katharine (a musician; maiden name, Stewart)
Thomson; married Christos Alexiou (a lecturer), July 14,
1961 (separated, 1975); children: Dimitris George and
Pavlos Michael (twins). Education: Newnham College,
Cambridge, degree in classics (first class honors), 1961,
Ph.D., 1967. Politics: "Enlightened self-interest." Religion:
None. Home: 755 Pershore Rd., Selly Park, Birmingham
B29 7NY, England. Office: School of Hellenic and Roman
Studies, University of Birmingham, Birmingham B15 2TT,
England.

CAREER: University of Birmingham, Birmingham, En-
gland, lecturer in Byzantine and modern Greek, 1964—.
External examiner at Oxford University, 1967-69, 1976—,
Cambridge University, 1968-71, and University of London,
1977-78. Member: International Society for Byzantine
Studies (member of national committee), Society for the
Promotion of Hellenic Studies (member of council, 1973-76),
Modern Greek Studies Association (United States).

WRITINGS: The Ritual Lament in Greek Tradition, Cambridge University Press, 1974. Contributor to professional
journals. Co-editor of Mandataforos: Bulletin of Modern
Greek Studies.

WORK IN PROGRESS: Studying modern Greek folk ballads in relation to past history and contemporary culture.

SIDELIGHTS: Margaret Alexiou writes that her approach
lies in the "inter-relatedness of historical, literary, and cultural factors—the significance of contemporary cultural context as well as the origins and evolution of particular traditions." Avocational interests: Classical music, folk music
(of Greece and the Balkans), walking, wine.

*   *   *

al-FARUQI, Ismai'il Raji 1921-

PERSONAL: Born January 1, 1921, in Jaffa, Palestine;
came to the United States in 1948, naturalized citizen, 1973;
son of Ibrahim Adham (a lawyer) and Raifah (Abul-Huda)
al-Faruqi; married Lois R. Ibsen (an ethnomusicologist and
writer), September 2, 1951; children: Sakhr, Hawazin,
Anmar, Marwan, Tayma'. Education: American University
of Beirut, B.A., 1941; Indiana University, M.A., 1949,
Ph.D., 1952; Harvard University, M.A., 1951; post-doctoral study at Al-Azhar University, 1955-58, and McGill
University, 1959-61. Religion: Muslim. Home: 323 Bent
Rd., Wyncote, Pa. 19095. Office: Department of Religion,
Temple University, Philadelphia, Pa. 19122.

CAREER: McGill University, Montreal, Quebec, research
and assistant professor of Islam and Christianity, 1958-61;
Central Institute of Islamic Research, Karachi, Pakistan,
professor of Islamics, 1961-63; University of Chicago, Chicago, Ill., visiting scholar in the history of religion, 1963-64;
Syracuse University, Syracuse, N.Y., associate professor
of Islamics and history of religion, 1964-68; Temple University, Philadelphia, Pa., professor of Islamics and religion,
1968—. Decennium lecturer at Internationales Forschung-
zentrum fur Grundfragen der Wissenschaften, 1961; visiting
lecturer at University of Libya, 1971-72, and Muslim Education Board (South Africa), 1971—; Fulbright Professor at
Universiti Kebangsaan, Kuala Lumpur, 1974. District governor in Galilee district of the Mandate Government of Palestine; member of League of Arab States' Board of Arabic
Studies, and Commission on Religious Studies, both 1961-

63; chairman of board of trustees of North American Islamic Trust; consultant to Arab universities in the Philippines, Malaysia, Libya, South Africa, Egypt, and Saudi Arabia.

MEMBER: International Association for the History of Religions, American Oriental Society, Union for the Study of World Religions, American Academy of Religion (chairman of Islamic studies group), Society for Biblical Literature, American Association for Asian Studies, Association of Muslim Social Scientists (president, 1972—), North American Islamic Trust, Oriental Society of Manchester. *Awards, honors:* Rockefeller Foundation fellowship, 1959-61; Spalding Trust fellowship, 1962; fellowship from Inter-University Association for Institution Building, 1968-69.

WRITINGS: Min Huna Nabda', Khalid Muhammad Khalid, translation published as *From Here We Start,* American Council of Learned Societies, 1953; *Min Huna Na'lam,* Muhammad al Ghazzali, translation published as *Our Beginning in Wisdom,* American Council of Learned Societies, 1953; *The Policy of Tomorrow,* American Council of Learned Societies, 1953; *On Arabism: 'Urubah and Religion—An Analysis of the Dominant Ideas of Arabism and of Islam as Its Highest Moment of Consciousness,* Djambatan, 1962; *Usul al Sahyuniyyah fi al Din al Yahudi* (title means "The Basis of Zionism in Judaism"), Institute of Higher Arabic Studies, 1964; *Christian Ethics: A Systematic and Historical Analysis,* McGill University Press, 1968; *Al Milal al Mu'asirah fi al Din al Yahudi* (title means "Contemporary Sects in Judaism"), Institute of Higher Arabic Studies, 1968; (with W. T. Chan, P. T. Raju, and Joseph Kitagawa) *Islam,* Part IV: *The Great Asian Religions,* Macmillan, 1969; *The Historical Atlas of the Religions of the World,* Macmillan, 1975; *The Life of Muhammad,* American Trust Publications, 1977.

Contributor to professional journals. Chairman of board of editors of American Trust Publications; member of editorial board of *Islamic Studies, Journal of Ecumenical Studies, Islam and the Modern Age, Zygon, Journal of South Asian and Middle Eastern Studies.*

WORK IN PROGRESS: Islam and the Modern Age, for Islam and the Modern Age Society; editing "Pakistan: The Modernization of an Islamic State," a series of articles; editing and translating *Kitab al Intisar wa al Radd 'ala Ibn al Rawandi* (title means "Book of Victory and the Response to Ibn al Rawandi"), by A. H. al Khayyat.

* * *

ALGARIN, Miguel 1941-

PERSONAL: Born September 11, 1941, in Puerto Rico; came to the United States in 1950. *Education:* University of Wisconsin, Madison, B.A., 1963; Pennsylvania State University, M.A., 1965; further graduate study at Rutgers University. *Home:* 524 East Sixth St., New York, N.Y. 10009. *Office:* Livingston College, Rutgers University, New Brunswick, N.J. 08903.

CAREER: Brooklyn College of the City University of New York, Brooklyn, N.Y., lecturer in English, 1965-67; Middlesex County College, Edison, N.J., instructor in English, 1968; Rutgers University, New Brunswick, N.J., assistant professor of English, 1971—. Editor of Nuyorican Press. Director of El Puerto Rican Playwrights'/Actors' Workshop; executive director of Nuyorican Theater Festival; founder of Nuyorican Poets' Cafe. Visiting poet at Naropa Institute; has given poetry readings in the United States, the Netherlands, and France; has appeared on New York and Philadelphia television programs; consultant to German

television. Director of the film "Underground Weathermen" and a video-film on William Carlos Williams. *Awards, honors:* Grant from Samuel Rubin Foundation, 1975, for Nuyorican Theater Festival; Judy Peabody grant from Peabody Foundation; grant from New York State Council of the Arts for El Puerto Rican Playwrights'/Actors' Workshop.

WRITINGS: (Editor with Miguel Pinero, and author of introduction) *Nuyorican Poetry: An Anthology of Puerto Rican Words and Feelings,* Morrow, 1975; (translator and author of introduction) Pablo Neruda, *Song of Protest,* Morrow, 1976; *Mongo Affair,* Nuyorican Press, 1977.

Plays: "Olu Clemente, the Philosopher of Baseball," first produced in New York City at Delacorte Theater, August 31, 1973; "Apartment 6-D," first produced in New York City at Lincoln Center, August, 1974; "The Murder of Pito," first produced in New York City at Nuyorican Poets' Cafe, summer, 1976. Also author of "Blue Heaven."

Television: "Side Show, the Making of a Play," WNET-Television, October 20, 1975; "Salsa Ballet," WNET-Television, spring, 1977.

Represented in anthologies, including *The New Consciousness,* edited by Albert La Valley, Winthrop Publishing, 1972; *New Writing in the Caribbean,* edited by A. J. Seymour, 1972; and *Roof,* edited by Tom Savage, 1977. Contributor to literary journals, including *Dodeca, Salamander,* and *Box 749.* Contributing editor of *Revista Chicano-Riquena* and *Margins.*

* * *

ALLAMAND, Pascale 1942-

PERSONAL: Born September 22, 1942, in Montreux, Switzerland; daughter of Pierre (a travel agent) and Yvette (Milharoux) Allamand. *Education:* Attended schools in Montreux, Switzerland, and studied photography in Montreux and later in Lausanne, Switzerland. *Home and office:* Grand Rue 25, 1095 Lutry, Switzerland.

CAREER: Has worked as a fashion, news, and food photographer, and as an author and illustrator of children's books in Lutry, Switzerland, 1970—.

WRITINGS—All juveniles; all self-illustrated: *The Boy and His Friend the Bear,* J. Cape, 1974; *The Pop Rooster,* Scribner, 1975; *The Camel Who Left the Zoo,* Scribner, 1976; *The Little Goat in the Alps,* J. Cape, 1977. Photographer: *A la mode de chez nous* (cookbook; title means "Our Art of Cooking"), Payot, 1976.

WORK IN PROGRESS: The Bear Who Wanted to Change Colour, for J. Cape, publication expected in 1978.

SIDELIGHTS: Pascale Allamand told *CA:* "If I make books for children, it is for three reasons: I love children, I love to paint, and I love to listen to stories and to tell them. Now at my age, as much as when I was small, I still love to listen to stories being told, whether they are for adults or children. So why shouldn't I tell them myself?"

* * *

ALLAND, Guy 1944-

PERSONAL: Born September 16, 1944, in St. Augustine, Fla.; son of Clive F. (a salesman) and Antoinette (a legal secretary; maiden name, Milano) Alland. *Education:* Cooper Union for the Advancement of Science and Art, B.Arch., 1972. *Agent:* Helen Brann, Helen Brann Agency, 14 Sutton Pl. S., New York, N.Y. 10022. *Office:* Knowhow Workshop, Inc., 17 East 16th St., Seventh Floor, New York, N.Y. 10003.

CAREER: Self-employed as architect, collaborating with Stromsen & Scofidio (architects) on various Caribbean islands projects; self-employed as planner-designer, 1967—; Knowhow Workshop, Inc., New York, N.Y., president and director, 1972—.

WRITINGS: (With Tony Hiss) *Knowhow: A Fix-It Book for the Clumsy But Pure of Heart,* Little, Brown, 1975; (with Patricia Drake Hemingway) *Auto-Mechanics for Beginners,* Little, Brown, in press.

WORK IN PROGRESS: Writing about alternate energy, carpentry, and motorcycle mechanics.

SIDELIGHTS: Alland's Knowhow Workshop is designed to teach anyone home repair, carpentry, automobile mechanics, bicycle mechanics, quilt making, and "functional recycling, alternate energy."

BIOGRAPHICAL/CRITICAL SOURCES: New York Times, June 15, 1973; *New Yorker,* September 24, 1973.

* * *

ALLEN, Carl 1961-

PERSONAL: Born October 19, 1961, in Watertown, N.Y.; son of David E. (a florist) and Marjorie (a writer; maiden name, Nicholson) Allen. *Education:* Attending high school in Pittsfield, Mass. *Home:* 39 Montgomery Ave., Pittsfield, Mass. 01201.

CAREER: Writer.

WRITINGS: (With mother, Marjorie N. Allen) *Farley, Are You for Real?* (juvenile fiction), Coward, 1976; (with M. N. Allen) *The Marble Cake Cat* (juvenile fiction), Coward, 1977.

WORK IN PROGRESS: Not Again, Farley!, a juvenile fiction, to follow *Farley, Are You for Real?; The Puzzlers,* a picture book, with Arlene Mogavero.

SIDELIGHTS: Allen comments briefly that he would like to become involved in book design and illustration. *Avocational interests:* Sports, theater, art, music.

* * *

ALLEN, Charlotte Vale 1941-

PERSONAL: Born January 19, 1941, in Toronto, Ontario, Canada; came to the United States in 1966; Canadian citizen; married Walter Bateman Allen, Jr., July, 1970 (divorced, 1976); children: Kimberly Jordan Allen (daughter). *Education:* Attended drama school in Toronto, Ontario. *Politics:* No affiliation. *Religion:* No affiliation. *Home:* 262 Old Kings Highway S., Darien, Conn. 06820. *Agent:* Paul R. Reynolds, Inc., 12 East 41st St., New York, N.Y. 10017.

CAREER: Actress, model, and singer; worked in England, 1961-64; night club singer, 1961-71; writer, 1971—.

WRITINGS—Novels: *Love Life,* Delacorte, 1976; *Hidden Meanings,* Warner Books, 1976; *Sweeter Music,* Warner Books, 1976; *Gentle Stranger,* Warner Books, 1977; *Another Kind of Magic,* Warner Books, 1977; *Mixed Emotions,* Warner Books, 1977; *Running Away,* New American Library, 1977; *Becoming,* Warner Books, 1977.

WORK IN PROGRESS: Another novel for New American Library; more novels for Warner Books.

SIDELIGHTS: Allen told *CA:* "I write books about women predominantly, not *for* women—for everyone. I like to include issues of both social and emotional significance." She has studied drama, ballet, piano, art, and guitar. *Avocational interests:* Needlepoint, tennis, scuba diving and snorkeling, water color painting, collage, gardening.

ALLEN, Kenneth (William) 1941-

PERSONAL: Born October 7, 1941, in Mount Vernon, Ill.; son of Loren H. (a librarian) and Doris (Trout) Allen; married Janet R. Adams (a teacher), September 23, 1967; children: Andrew Jon. *Education:* Southern Illinois University, B.S., 1963, M.S., 1964; Northern Illinois University, Ed.D., 1970; Rosary College, M.A.L.S., 1971. *Home:* 210 Orchard, Oswego, Ill. 60543. *Office:* Waubonsee Community College, Route 47 at Harter Rd., Sugar Grove, Ill. 60554.

CAREER: Director of instruction materials at a high school in Peoria, Ill., 1965-70; Waubonsee Community College, Sugar Grove, Ill., director of learning resources, 1967-70, assistant dean of instruction, 1971—. Part-time instructor at Rosary College. Chairperson of Learning Resources Commission, 1975. *Member:* American Library Association, Association for Educational Communications and Technology, Community College Association for Instruction and Technology (Midwest vice-president, 1977), Illinois Library Association (chairman of audiovisual committee, 1976-77).

WRITINGS: Use of the Community College Libraries, Shoe String, 1971; (with father, Loren Allen) *Administration and Organization of a Community College Learning Resources Center,* Shoe String, 1973. Contributor to education, library, and audiovisual instruction journals.

WORK IN PROGRESS: Journalistic writing.

SIDELIGHTS: Allen says that the book he and his father Loren Allen wrote, *Administration and Organization of a Community College Learning Resources Center,* was completed at a time when no comprehensive book on the subject was available and community colleges were rapidly being created. Both authors, Allen writes, created or administered five such centers from 1966 to 1972.

AVOCATIONAL INTERESTS: Stained glass, fishing, golf.

* * *

ALLEN, Marjorie 1931-

PERSONAL: Born December 8, 1931, in Manchester, N.H.; daughter of Andre (a salesman) and Lauretta (an executive secretary; maiden name, Elliott) Nicholson; married David Allen (a salesman), July 6, 1957; children: John, Carl, Dena. *Education:* Currently attending University Without Walls at University of Massachusetts, 1976—. *Religion:* Methodist. *Home:* 39 Montgomery Ave., Pittsfield, Mass. 01201.

CAREER: Berkshire Medical Center, Pittsfield, Mass., personnel clerk, 1974-76, unit co-ordinator, 1976—. Continuing education instructor in writing for children, Berkshire Community College, 1976.

WRITINGS—all juvenile: (With Alice Schick) *The Remarkable Ride of Israel Bissell as Related by Molly the Crow,* Lippincott, 1976; (with Carl Allen) *Farley, Are You for Real?,* Coward, 1976; (with Carl Allen) *The Marble Cake Cat,* Coward, 1977. Contributor to *Humpty Dumpty, Happy Times, Grit, Denver Post,* and other periodicals.

WORK IN PROGRESS: The Purple Martin Pyramid; Lavender and Listerine; The Tree House Book, with David Allen; *Return of the Blue Whales; Tua's Island.*

SIDELIGHTS: Allen told *CA:* "My goal is to make every children's book I write better than the one before it; to make what I write a pleasurable experience for a child; to write about children's books in columns, book reviews and articles until I finally say something that will break through a few barriers. Children deserve the very best in books offered them. The majority of the general public, including teachers, know little or nothing about children's literature. With about 2000 new children's books being published every year, there is an enormous need for educating the public on how to be selective, how to evaluate not just children's books, but adult books for children as well and to be able to say, 'This book is worthwhile, and this book is not.' These values need to be passed down to children so that they in turn will learn to be selective. I am not necessarily talking about classical literature. I am simply talking about good books, mediocre books and bad books—and being knowledgeable enough to tell the difference.''

AVOCATIONAL INTERESTS: Reading, summer theatre, woman's barbershop chorus.

*　　*　　*

ALLEN, Merrill J(ames)   1918-

PERSONAL: Born August 2, 1918, in San Antonio, Tex.; son of Millard (an optometrist) and Mildred (a bookkeeper; maiden name, Windnagle) Allen; married M. Joan Gower, December 25, 1942; children: M. Jayne Allen Granger, Merrill James, Jr. *Education:* Ohio State University, B.Sc., 1941, M.Sc., 1942, Ph.D., 1949. *Politics:* Republican. *Religion:* Methodist. *Home:* 1311 Valley Forge Rd., Bloomington, Ind. 47401. *Office:* School of Optometry, Indiana University, Bloomington, Ind. 47401.

CAREER: Frankfort Arsenal, Philadelphia, Pa., physicist, 1943-44; Ohio State University, Columbus, assistant professor of optometry, 1949-53; Indiana University, Bloomington, associate professor, 1953-57, professor of optometry, 1957—. Member of American Optometric Foundation, 1955—. Member of advisory panel on automotive safety, of U.S. General Servies Administration, 1966-69. *Military service:* U.S. Naval Reserve, active duty, 1946-49; became lieutenant commander.

MEMBER: American Optometric Association, American Academy of Optometry, Association for Research in Vision and Ophthalmology, American Association for the Advancement of Science. *Awards, honors:* Grant from American Optometric Foundation, 1961-67; Omega Epsilon Phi Outstanding Optometrist Award, 1966; Iowa's John E. Martin Award, 1969; research medal from British Optical Society, 1970; named optometrist of the year by Indiana Optometric Association, 1973; Apollo Award from American Optometric Association, 1974.

WRITINGS: Vision and Highway Safety, Chilton, 1970. Contributor of about two hundred articles to professional publications.

WORK IN PROGRESS: Vision Therapy of Amblyopia, Strabismus and Learning Disorder; Effects of Windshields and Spectacles on Highway Seeing.

*　　*　　*

ALPER, M(ax) Victor   1944-

PERSONAL: Born March 23, 1944, in Wilkes-Barre, Pa.; son of Samuel (a newspaperman) and Hannah Robin (a department store executive) Alper. *Education:* Boston University, A.B., 1964; New York University, M.A., 1967, Ph.D., 1972; also attended Harvard University. *Home:* 145 West 79th St., #11-C, New York, N.Y. 10024. *Agent:* Betty Marks, 51 East 42nd St., Suite 1406, New York, N.Y. 10017.

CAREER: Educational Research Associates of America, New York City, assistant to the president, 1966-67; New York University, New York City, instructor in College of Arts and Sciences, 1969-73; Montclair State College, Upper Montclair, N.J., assistant professor of humanities, 1973—. Guest lecturer at University of Massachusetts and Rutgers University; visiting assistant professor at City University of New York, summer, 1976; assistant to executive vice-president, Rutgers University, 1977-78. Author and narrator of "Historic Sites of America," on WGBH-Radio, 1976—; guest on radio and television programs; consultant to *Newsweek.*

MEMBER: International Platform Association, Modern Language Association of America, American Association of UniversityProfessors, National Academy of Television Arts and Sciences (member of council, 1977), American Federation of Arts, Organization of American Historians, New York State English Council. *Awards, honors:* Fellow of American Council on Education, 1977.

WRITINGS: America's Freedom Trail, Macmillan, 1976; *America's Heritage Trail,* Macmillan, 1976. Contributor to *Encyclopedia of English Literature.* Contributor of about forty articles and reviews to magazines, including *New Republic.* Contributing editor of *Arts,* 1970-74; member of editorial board of New York State English Council monograph series.

WORK IN PROGRESS: A study of the Greek epic; research on American higher education.

SIDELIGHTS: Alper writes that his main areas of interest are: "interdisciplinary studies, especially in the culture and history of the eighteenth and nineteenth centuries, art criticism and consultation, and educational trends." *Avocational interests:* Skiing, photography (has had exhibitions in New York City), classical music.

*　　*　　*

ALPERN, Andrew   1938-

PERSONAL: Born November 1, 1938, in New York, N.Y.; son of Dwight K. (a college professor, engineer, and mineralogist) and Grace (in public relations; maiden name, Michelman) Alpern. *Education:* Columbia University, B.Arch., 1964. *Home and office:* 315 Eighth Ave., New York, N.Y. 10001.

CAREER: Haines Lungberg Waehler (architectural firm), New York City, student trainee, 1959-61, architect, 1962-67; W. T. Grant (department store chain), New York City, architect, 1967-68; Saphier Lerner Schindler Environetics (space planning and design firm), New York City, project director, 1968-72; Environmental Research & Development, Inc. (planning, design, and real estate firm), New York City, vice-president and director of architecture, 1972-75; independent consulting architect, 1975—. Certified by National Council of Architectural Registration Boards, 1967; registered in New York, Pennsylvania, California, Washington, D.C., and West Virginia; licensed real estate salesman in New York. Member of advisory board of Institute of Applied Psychotherapy, 1969-72, therapist in New York State drug abuse program, 1970-72; national arbitrator of American Arbitration Association, 1971—; lecturer. *Member:* American Institute of Architects, Society of Architectural Historians, National Fire Protection Association, Association of Collegiate Schools of Architecture, New York State Association of Architects, Metropolitan Association of Urban Designers and Environmental Planners, New York Historical Society, Long Island Historical Society, Municipal Art Society, Real Estate Board of New York. *Awards, honors:* Sc.D. from London College of Applied Science, 1971.

WRITINGS: Apartments for the Affluent: A Historical Survey of Buildings in New York, McGraw, 1975; *Garret Ellis Winants: 1818-1890,* privately printed, 1976. Editorial advisor and consultant to McGraw-Hill periodicals for architects.

WORK IN PROGRESS: The Architect's Vade Mecum, publication expected in 1978; editing the *Handbook of Specialty Elements in Architecture* for McGraw, publication expected in 1979; editing the *Handbook of Records Management* for McGraw, publication expected in 1979.

SIDELIGHTS: "I am concerned with making people more aware of the man-made environment around them," Alpern told *CA.* "Looking at architecture and enjoying it isn't only for tourists and scholars. *Apartments for the Affluent* was written with that in mind. In a similar vein, for several years I was a part-time therapist with a state-funded drug program helping young people realize that there is much beauty and interest around them that can be seen and enjoyed without the aid of drugs."

Concerning the future of his profession, Alpern said: "Architects have designed too long for themselves, rather than for their clients and for society at large. A building that looks good on paper, or in a photograph, may not meet the needs of the client for reasons of livability or of cost (and this means maintenance cost as well as initial cost). Indigenous architecture reflects the detailed needs of the specific area in which it is built; buildings for a hot climate should by their nature be different from those for colder areas. But the technology that enables us to eat strawberries out of season has lead architects to design buildings with total disregard for their natural environment; there has never been a logical rationale for identical facades on all four sides of a building. For too long we have taken for granted the natural resources with which we have worked. Perhaps the economic pressures of the oil-producing nations of the world are a good thing, since they are forcing us all, architects and laymen alike, to reevaluate our basic approach to construction. Renovation and reuse have finally become socially acceptable. Conservation of all our resources has finally become an important component in the process of preparing a program for a building project. At long last the old New England proverb is getting a fresh hearing:

> Use it up,
> Wear it out,
> Make it do,
> Or do without."

*   *   *

ALTMAN, Irwin 1930-

PERSONAL: Born July 16, 1930, in New York, N.Y.; married; children: two sons. *Education:* New York University, B.A., 1951; University of Maryland, M.A., 1954, Ph.D., 1957. *Home:* 2827 Commonwealth Ave., Salt Lake City, Utah. *Office:* Department of Psychology, University of Utah, Salt Lake City, Utah 84112.

CAREER: American University, Washington, D.C., assistant professor of psychology, 1957-58; Human Sciences Research, Inc., Arlington, Va., vice-president and research scientist, 1958-60; American University, associate professor of psychology and senior research scientist, 1960-62; Naval Medical Research Institute, Bethesda, Md., research psy-

chologist, 1962-69; University of Utah, Salt Lake City, professor of psychology, 1969—, chairman of department, 1969-76. Adjunct professor at American University, 1960-69, and University of Maryland, 1968-69. Member of research advisory panel of American Institute of Architects, 1970-72; member of National Institute of Mental Health grant review committee, 1970-73, 1974—. Consultant to Battelle Memorial Institute. *Military service:* U.S. Army, personnel psychologist, 1954-56; became lieutenant.

MEMBER: American Psychological Association (fellow; chairman of task force on environment and behavior, 1973-76), American Association for the Advancement of Science (fellow), Society for the Psychological Study of Social Issues, Society of Experimental Social Psychology (chairman; member of executive committee, 1974-76), Association for the Study of Man-Environment Relations (founder; member of board of directors, 1967-73), Environmental Design Research Association (member of board of directors, 1976-79), Interior Designer Educators Council (honorary member), Western Psychological Association, Sigma Xi.

WRITINGS: (With J. E. McGrath) *Small Group Research: Synthesis and Critique of the Field,* Holt, 1966; (with D. A. Taylor) *Social Penetration: The Development of Interpersonal Relationships,* Holt, 1973; *Environment and Social Behavior: Privacy, Personal Space, Territory, and Crowding,* Brooks/Cole, 1975; (editor with J. F. Wohlwill, and contributor) *Human Behavior and Environment: Advances in Theory and Research,* Plenum, Volume I, 1976, Volume II, 1977.

Contributor: M. Appley and R. Trumbull, editors, *Psychological Stress,* Appleton, 1967; B. Indik and I. Berrien, editors, *People, Groups, and Organizations: An Effective Integration,* Columbia University Press, 1968; H. Proshansky and W. Ittelson, editors, *Environmental Psychology,* Holt, 1970; J. E. McGrath, editor, *Social and Psychological Factors in Stress,* Holt, 1970; L. Pastalan and D. H. Carson, editors, *Spatial Behavior of Older People,* University of Michigan-Wayne State University Press, 1970; D. A. Taylor, editor, *Small Groups,* Markham, 1971; A. H. Esser, editor, *Behavior and Environment: The Use of Space by Animals and Men,* Plenum, 1971; Carson and J. F. Wohlwill, editors, *Environment and the Social Sciences: Perspectives and Applications,* American Psychological Association, 1972; J. E. Rasmussen, editor, *Human Behavior in Isolation and Confinement,* Aldine, 1973; S. Friedman and Juhasz, editors, *Environments: Notes and Selections on Objects, Spaces, and Behavior,* Brooks/Cole, 1973; S. M. Margulis, editor, *Privacy* (proceedings), Environmental Design Research Association, 1974; T. L. Huston, editor, *Perspectives on Interpersonal Attractions,* Academic Press, 1974; G. Miller, editor, *Explorations in Interpersonal Communication: Sage Annual Review of Communication,* Volume IV, Sage Publications, 1976; D. Forgays, editor, *Primary Prevention of Psychopathology,* University of Vermont Press, 1977; D. Stokols, editor, *Psychological Perspectives on Environment and Behavior: Conceptual and Empirical Trends,* Plenum, 1977; A. Baum and Y. Epstein, editors, *Human Response to Crowding,* Erlbaum, 1977.

Contributor to *International Encyclopedia of Neurology, Psychiatry, Psychoanalysis, and Psychology* and *Handbook of Cross Cultural Psychology.* Contributor of more than forty articles and reviews to professional journals. Member of editorial board of *Man-Environment Systems,* 1967-73, *Comparative Group Studies,* 1970, *Contemporary Psychology,* 1975—, *Environment and Behavior,* 1975—, *Environmental Psychology and Nonverbal Behavior,* 1976—, and

Psychology, 1976—; member of editorial board and reviewer of *Sociometry,* 1973-76, *Journal of Applied Social Psychology,* 1973, and *Journal of Personality and Social Psychology,* 1974-76; book reviewer for *Psychological Review, Journal of Experimental Social Psychology,* and *Science.*

*   *   *

ALTMANN, Berthold   1902(?)-1977

1902(?)—June 4, 1977; German-born American historian and author. Altmann specialized in medieval history. He came to the United States in 1939 and served as a colonel in the Army Reserves. He died in Alexandria, Va. Obituaries: *Washington Post,* June 7, 1977.

*   *   *

AMES, Mildred   1919-

PERSONAL: Born November 2, 1919, in Bridgeport, Conn.; daughter of Edward John and Amelia (Miller) Walsh; married William Ames (a technical writer), April 19, 1946. *Education:* Attended secondary school in Bridgeport, Conn. *Home:* 4415 Via Pinzon, Palos Verdes Estates, Calif. 90274.

CAREER: Writer, 1965—. *Member:* Society of Children's Book Writers, Surfwriters Club, Southern California Council on Literature for Children and Young People.

WRITINGS: Shadows of Summers Past (teen and adult), Bouregy, 1973; *The House of the Haunted Child* (teen and adult), Bouregy, 1974; *Is There Life on a Plastic Planet?* (juvenile), Dutton, 1975; *Without Hats, Who Can Tell the Good Guys?* (juvenile), Dutton, 1976; *The Wonderful Box* (juvenile), Dutton, 1977. Contributor to *Young Miss* and *Cricket.*

WORK IN PROGRESS: Research on the early West.

SIDELIGHTS: Mildred Ames writes: "I wrote my first story at the age of eight or nine, a tearful melodrama. When the teacher read it in class, I thought it so achingly beautiful, I wanted to cry. Instead of admiration from my classmates, one little boy shot up and said, 'Well, I just don't believe she wrote it.'

"I have worked in a magic factory and in a five and ten, and learned that while there may be magic in a five and ten, there is none in a magic factory. I have sold hats, run an elevator, worked as a telephone operator, travelled for a chain of photography studios, and, as a clerical worker, worked for two aircraft plants, an air base, and an automobile dealer.

"I write for children because I share so many of their beliefs. Like them, I believe that there *can* be happy endings, that people *can* live happily ever after, and that if you wish hard enough and work hard enough, a dream can come true."

*   *   *

AMES, (Polly) Scribner   1908-

PERSONAL: Born February 16, 1908, in Chicago, Ill.; daughter of Edward Scribner (a clergyman and professor of philosophy) and Mabel (Van Meter) Ames. *Education:* University of Chicago, Ph.B., 1928; attended Art Institute of Chicago, 1929, Chicago School of Sculpture, and Goodman Theatre; studied privately with Hans Hofmann, Jose de Creeft, and Hans Schwegerle. *Politics:* Republican. *Religion:* Christian. *Home:* 5834 South Stony Island, Chicago, Ill. 60637.

CAREER: Painter and sculptor. Art teacher in school in New York, N.Y., 1939-41; gave private classes in New York and Chicago, 1939-68. Secretary and general assistant at American British Art Center, during the 1940's; with Active Recordings for the Blind, since 1958. Paintings exhibited in France, the Hague, and Curacao; paintings and sculptures exhibited in United States. Has appeared on educational television programs. *Member:* National Trust for Historic Preservation, Smithsonian Associates, Oriental Institute, Chicago Archaeological Institute, Arts Club (Chicago; member of board of directors, 1957—), Quadrangle Club. *Awards, honors:* Purchase award from Illinois State Museum, 1962, for bronze "Young Satyr and Friend."

WRITINGS: Marsden Hartley in Maine (self-illustrated), Maine Studies, University of Maine, 1972. Author of "Creative Women," a column in *Realm.* Contributor to magazines.

WORK IN PROGRESS: Poems; short stories.

SIDELIGHTS: Ames told *CA:* "I was born and educated in Chicago, the last of four children. My father Edward Scribner Ames and brother Van Meter Ames are both published philosophers. I lived almost twenty years in New York City, not counting two years in France (where one is all of a piece as an artist), and nine months in Curacao, Netherlands West Indies. I started with clay but under the influence of Jose de Creeft, went into carving directly in wood; eventually I felt more drawn to color. I've had individual exhibitions in many cities in the United States. Abroad I showed in Paris, Aix-en-Provence, the Hague, and at the Culture Center in Curacao.

"There has been since childhood a compulsion to put my overflow into words but I never thought of myself as a writer. My little manuscript of *Marsden Hartley in Maine* sat in the Archives of American Art many years before the University of Maine, inquiring about letters to me from another artist, asked to see the Hartley manuscript. It includes sketches made when I visited the lobster fisherman and his wife who harbored Hartley in his last summers; it is really their story.

"My father gave me belief in life; Marsden Hartley told me never to be afraid of reality; Hans Hofmann gave me challenging principles of painting.

"The sale of a painting done as an impression of Geraldine Page in 'Sweet Bird of Youth' made it possible for me to go to Greece where I had the privilege of staying at the American School of Classical Studies between sessions. Intermittently when in Athens I worked on the ancient pots in the Stoa Attalos Museum in the Agora below the Acropolis. I met one of Athena's little owls above the Dionysius Theatre; encountered the famous Sisyphus beetle struggling up the path to Acrocorinth pushing a minute dung ball; at the summit I was startled by a large black snake guarding the ruins of the temple of Aphrodite. By the Dicte cave (Dionysius' birthplace) in the Lassithi mountains of Crete, twenty eagles glided low enough for me to see their feathered leggings, perhaps mistaking me for carrion as I lay resting from the hot climb. They only circled away when I rose and hurled stones at them.

"One of my high points was exhibiting in Aix-en-Provence during the International Music Festival. The conductor Hans Rosbaud let me go to rehearsals mornings; evenings I went to the performances. For once my hunger for music was satisfied. In Paris Georges Braque's protege Nicholas de Stael made possible my renting a pavillion Braque built in Parc Montsouris which gave me a place to prepare for my exhibition. It was so perfect for work, he said I must tell Braque. Walking into that great artist's studio at the appointed time, my mind went blank in all languages. He put out his hand and said, 'Nous sommes des voisins!' ('we are neighbors').

"In Curacao, I painted Frater Rudolphus, the beneficent 'Father Flannagan' of the island. A highly cultured Dutch gentleman who spoke impeccable English, he surprised me by asking if I'd like a Coca Cola! On a sandy hill at the extreme end of the same island, as I painted the cove and thatched huts below, I thought myself alone in the silence. Stepping back to study my canvas I found I was surrounded by about fourteen squatting natives who'd come to watch, proud that I painted their African village established hundreds of years earlier by their runaway slave ancestors. They smiled, leaned over the palette to all but taste the colors, then when I finished, helped me down the sandy shell-littered hill, carrying my folding easel and gently steadying me.

"In Norway I rented a goatherd's hut above Lillehammer where I could paint until late at night while defending my watercolors from a too curious goat who dragged his beard across the page in his eagerness to smell the pigment! I took photos of Sigurd Undset's sod roof house in Lillehammer. Back in New York after the invasion when she spoke for the benefit of Norwegian children, I offered her the photos which she accepted with gratitude as she'd left too hurriedly to take any mementos with her.

"Nature, music, and books are important to me. A few special moments have been a chipmunk sitting in my hand to eat; seeing an eagle at dawn on Mount Equinox in Vermont; holding a migrant bird while I released his foot caught in a nylon stocking supporting a city tomato plant; sitting on a camel in Morocco; being blasted by a young elephant who was friendly until he discovered I had no peanuts (his zoo keeper said he was spoiled by T.V. appearances); stroking the arm of a barbary ape on Gibraltor while the natives stared with apprehension.

"Like William James I have a 'rage for privacy' and at the same time a hunger for people. So it's a constant seesaw. Withdrawing to digest and incubate for work, then emerging to share life again. Like the process of living, it is the process of creating that is important to me. . . . In that which continually renews itself, lies my security."

*   *   *

AMORY, Cleveland   1917-

PERSONAL: Born September 2, 1917, in Nahant, Mass.; son of Robert and Leonore (Cobb) Amory; married Cora Fields Craddock, 1941 (divorced, 1947); married Martha Hodge, 1953; children: Gaea McCormick. *Education:* Harvard University, A.B., 1939. *Home:* 150 East 72nd St., New York, N.Y. 10021. *Office:* 140 West 57th St., New York, N.Y. 10021.

CAREER: Began as newspaper reporter in Nashua, N.H., and Tucson, Ariz.; managing editor of *Prescott Evening Courier,* Prescott, Ariz.; *Saturday Evening Post,* Philadelphia, Pa., associate editor, 1939-41, 1943; free-lance writer, lecturer, and television commentator, 1943—. Member of board of directors, Bide-a-Wee Homes, Inc. *Member:* World Federation for the Protection of Animals (member of board of directors), National Society for Animal Welfare (honorary vice-president), Fund for the Animals (president), Harvard Club, Dutch Treat Club.

WRITINGS: The Proper Bostonians, Dutton, 1947; *Home Town,* Harper, 1950; *The Last Resorts,* Harper, 1952; (ed-

itor with Frederic Bradlee) *Vanity Fair; Selections from America's Most Memorable Magazine; A Cavalcade of the 1920s and 1930s,* Viking, 1960; *Who Killed Society?,* Harper, 1960; *The Proper Bostonians Revisited,* Dutton, 1972; *Man Kind?: Our Incredible War on Wildlife,* Harper, 1974; *Cleveland Amory's Animail,* Windmill Books, 1976.

Editor of *Celebrity Register* (U.S. edition of *International Celebrity Register),* Harper, 1959—. Writer of syndicated newspaper column, "Animail"; columnist for *TV Guide.* Editor-at-large of *World,* beginning 1972, and of *Saturday Review.**

*   *   *

ANCEL, Marc   1902-

PERSONAL: Born July 14, 1902, in Paris, France; son of Leon (a director of a normal school) and Marie-Therese (Cambus) Ancel; married Yvonne Comte, August 12, 1935; children: Jacqueline, Jean-Pierre. *Education:* University of Paris, received lic. es lettres and dr. en droit. *Home:* 120 bis, boulevard du Montparnasse, Paris 14eme, France. *Office:* Cour de Cassation, Palais of Justice, Paris le, France.

CAREER: Revue de Science Criminelle et de Droit Penal Compare and *Revue Internationale de Droit Compare,* both in Paris, France, editor-in-chief, both 1949—. Counsellor for Cour de Cassation, Palace of Justice, in Paris, 1954—. Secretary-general of French Centre of Comparative Law, 1956—; president of European Committee on Crime Problems of the Council of Europe, 1957-62.

MEMBER: La Societe de Legislation Comparee (president, 1964), Louisiana Law Institute (United States; honorary member). *Awards, honors:* Officer of the Legion of Honor, Palmes Academiques, Ordre de la Couronne (Belgium), and Ordre du Merite Italien; Chevalier de la Sante publique; commander of the Equestrian Order of Saint Agatha (Republic of San Marino); honorary doctorates from University of Geneva and University of Edinburgh.

WRITINGS—In English: *La Defense sociale nouvelle: Un Mouvement de politique criminelle humaniste,* Editions Cujas, 1954, translation and revision by J. Wilson and the author published as *Social Defence: A Modern Approach to Criminal Problems,* Routledge & Kegan Paul, 1965, Schocken, 1966, 3rd French edition, Editions Cujas, 1971.

Other works: *La "Common Law" d'Angleterre* (title means "The Common Law of England"), Rousseau & Sons, 1927; (editor) *La Condition de la femme dans la societe contemporaine: Etat actuel des legislations concernant les droits politiques, l'activite professionnelle, la capacite civile, la situation de la femme dans la famille et la condition de la femme au regard du droit penal* (title means "The Condition of Women in Contemporary Society: The Present Status of Legislation Concerning Political Rights, Professional Activity, Civil Capacity, the Situation of Women in the Family, and the Condition of Women with Respect to Penal Law"), Recueil Sirey, 1938; *L'Adoption dans les legislations modernes: Essai de synthese comparative suivi du releve systematique des legislations actuelles relatives a l'adoption* (title means "Adoption in Modern Legislation: An Essay in Comparative Synthesis Followed by a Systematic Statement of Existing Legislation Relating to Adoption"), Recueil Sirey, 1943, 2nd edition, 1958; *Le Probleme de l'enfance delinquante* (title means "The Problem of Delinquent Childhood"), 1947.

Les Grands Systemes penitentiaires actuels (title means "The Great Penitential Systems of the Present Day"), 1950;

(editor with Leon F. Julliot de la Morandiere) *L'Oeuvre juridique de Levy-Ullmann: Contribution a la doctrine moderne sur la science du droit et le droit compare* (title means "The Juridicial Work of Levy-Ullmann: Contribution to the Modern Doctrine on the Science of Law and Comparative Law"), Centre francais de droit compare, 1955; (editor with Antonin Besson) *La Prevention des infractions contre la vie humaine et l'integrite de la personne* (title means "The Prevention of Infractions Against Human Life and the Integrity of the Person"), two volumes, Editions Cujas, 1956; (editor with Yvonne Marx) *Les Codes penaux europeens presentes dans leur texte actuel, avec un notice speciale sur chaque code et une introduction comparative generale* (title means "The European Penal Codes Presented in Their Existing Texts, with a Special Notice on Each Code and an Introduction"), Centre francais de droit compare, 1956; (editor with L. Radzinowicz) *Introduction au droit criminel de l'Angleterre* (title means "Introduction to British Criminal Law"), Editions de l'epargne, 1959; (editor and author of introduction) *La Reforme penale sovietique: Code penal, loi d'organisation judiciaire de la R.S.F.S.R. due 27 octobre 1960* (title means "Soviet Penal Reform: Penal Code, Code of Penal Procedure, Law of Judicial Organization for the R.S.F.S.R. of October 27, 1960"), Centre francais de droit compare, 1962; (editor with Nikola Srzentic and others) *Le Droit penal nouveau de la Yougoslavie* (title means "The New Penal Law of Yugoslavia"), Editions de l'epargne, 1962; (editor with Louis B. Schwartz) *Le Systeme penal des Etats-Unis d'Amerique* (title means "The Penal System of the United States of America"), Editions de l'epargne, 1964; *Utilite et methodes du droit compare: Elements d'introduction generale a l'etude comparative des droits* (title means "Uses and Methods of Comparative Law: Elements of General Introduction to the Comparative Study of Law"), Editions Ides et Calendes, 1971.

Contributor to scholarly journals.*

* * *

ANCHOR, Robert 1937-

PERSONAL: Born May 18, 1937, in Detroit, Mich.; son of Bernard (an engineer) and Pearl (Dashkin) Anchor. *Education:* Wayne State University, B.A., 1959; University of Rochester, Ph.D., 1965. *Residence:* North Hollywood, Calif. *Office:* Department of History, University of Southern California, Los Angeles, Calif. 90007.

CAREER: Yale University, New Haven, Conn., instructor in modern European history, 1964-66; University of Southern California, Los Angeles, assistant professor, 1966-70, associate professor of modern European history, 1970—. *Member:* American Historical Association. *Awards, honors:* Fulbright grant, Germany, 1959-60; National Endowment for the Humanities senior fellowship, 1973-74.

WRITINGS: (Contributor) Lewis W. Beck, editor and translator, *Kant on History,* Bobbs-Merrill, 1963; *The Enlightenment Tradition,* Harper, 1967; (translator) Georg Lukacs, *Goethe and His Age,* Merlin Press, 1968; *Germany Confronts Modernization,* Heath, 1972; *The Modern Western Experience,* Prentice-Hall, in press.

WORK IN PROGRESS: Research on modern European intellectual history, especially Germany.

SIDELIGHTS: Anchor writes: "I have traveled extensively in western Europe and studied two years in Germany. Both of my books and other published material have been the outgrowth of my abiding interest in the thought and culture of modern Europe, beginning with the Enlightenment."

ANDERSEN, Christopher P(eter) 1949-

PERSONAL: Born May 26, 1949, in Pensacola, Fla.; son of Edward Francis (a commander in the U.S. Navy) and Jeanette (Peterson) Andersen; married Valerie Hess (a banker), February 3, 1972. *Education:* University of California, Berkeley, B.A., 1971. *Home:* 213 East 66th St., Apt. 2C, New York, N.Y. 10021. *Office: People,* Time & Life Building, New York, N.Y. 10020.

CAREER: Time, New York City, correspondent from San Francisco, 1969-71, staff writer in New York City, 1971-72, and in Montreal, Quebec, 1972-74; *People,* New York City, assistant editor, 1974-75, associate editor, 1975—.

WRITINGS: The Name Game, Simon & Schuster, 1977.

SIDELIGHTS: Andersen writes: "As a professional journalist since the age of seventeen, I have done stories on thousands of personalities, from presidents to axe murderers to movie stars. Thus it seemed only natural to write a book about the one thing they all have in common: a name. Names, I discovered, are not mere identity tags. They carry strong psychological overtones that have a profound impact on virtually every aspect of our lives. *The Name Game* has afforded me the rare opportunity of writing something entirely new and exciting about a universal subject."

* * *

ANDERSON, Alan H., Jr. 1943-

PERSONAL: Born February 22, 1943, in New York, N.Y.; son of Alan H. (in advertising) and Nancy (Swan) Anderson; married Gloria Monteiro (in sales), December 7, 1968; children: Jennifer. *Education:* Yale University, B.A., 1964; Columbia University, received M.S. *Home address:* R.R.1, Athens, Ill. 62613. *Agent:* Wendy Weil, Julian Bach Agency, 3 East 48th St., New York, N.Y. 10017. *Office: Illinois Times,* 512 South Eighth St., Springfield, Ill. 62703.

CAREER: Smithsonian Institution, Washington, D.C., bird ecology researcher; *Time,* New York, N.Y., correspondent, 1969-72; *Saturday Review,* San Francisco, Calif., senior editor, 1972-73; *Time,* correspondent, 1973-74; *Illinois Times,* Springfield, editor, 1975—. *Member:* National Association of Science Writers.

WRITINGS: The Drifting Continent, Putnam, 1971; (with John Sanders and Robert Carola) *Physical Geology,* Harper, 1976. Contributor to *Science Digest, Saturday Review,* and *New York Times Magazine.*

WORK IN PROGRESS: Editing *The Blue Reef,* about a biologist studying a coral reef, for Knopf.

SIDELIGHTS: Anderson writes: "I began my career studying sea bird migration in the central Pacific, but decided I would rather write about science than be a scientist. I take great satisfaction in explaining complex issues or events in clear and dramatic language."

* * *

ANDERSON, Bob 1947-

PERSONAL: Born December 28, 1947, in Manhattan, Kan.; son of William Brady and Ester (Fullmer) Anderson; married Rita Weimer (an executive assistant), July 31, 1971; children: Lisa Marie, Michael Jon. *Education:* Attended Kansas State University, 1966-69. *Home:* 12000 Moody Springs Ct., Los Altos Hills, Calif. 94022. *Office:* World Publications, 1400 Stierlen Rd., Mountain View, Calif. 94042.

CAREER: World Publications, Mountain View, Calif.,

founder, president, and publisher of *Runner's World*, 1966—, *Down River*, 1974—, *Nordic World*, 1974—, and of "Runner's Book Series" and *Bike World Quarterly*, publisher and editor of *Bike World*, 1972—, and *Soccer World*, 1974—. Founder, owner, and president of Starting Line Sports (retail and mail order). President of World Sport Tours. *Member:* Magazine Publishers Association.

WRITINGS: (Editor with Joe Henderson) *Guide to Distance Running*, World Publications, 1972; (editor) *Sport Source*, World Publications, 1976.

SIDELIGHTS: Anderson told *CA:* "All the magazines that I publish are written for participants in the various sports. We are not interested in just publishing a magazine because there is a market for it. We are interested in promoting the sport. And in most cases we develop our own market.

"When I started *Runner's World* (first called *Distance Running News* until 1970) we did not publish for the obvious high school and college track people. We wrote for people outside of school. They were the ones that needed a publication. We promoted road racing, marathoning, and what we later called fun-runs.

"Today we have a circulation of 150,000 and in addition to publishing *Runner's World* we have also published 60 books on running, started a national fun-run program that now has 125 sites across the country, sponsor and put together National Running Week every other year, promote an event we call the 24-Hour Relay, and so forth.

"We'll be doing the same in the other four sports."

* * *

ANDERSON, Elbridge Gerry 1907-

PERSONAL: Born March 2, 1907, in Chicago, Ill.; son of Norman Kendall (a lawyer) and Louise (Holden) Anderson; married (Anna) Helen Nielsen (a teacher), December 17, 1958. *Education:* Attended University of Wisconsin, 1925-26; Yale University, B.A., 1930; attended Elizabeth Holloway School of Acting, 1934-37, University of Melbourne, 1942, and Maren Elwood College for Writers, 1948-51. *Politics:* "I'm for the best of both sides—a Roman rider with a hopeful foothold on each." *Religion:* "The Great Cathedral Within." *Home:* 31575 Moonglow Lane, San Juan Capistrano, Calif. 92675.

CAREER: Worked various jobs, including gas station attendant, shoveler on a track crew for a lumber camp in the Black Hills, stock boy, and slack wire performer in late 1920's; technician and writer for Metro-Goldwyn-Meyer, Hollywood, Calif., 1931-32, and for Columbia Studios, Hollywood, 1932-33; teacher of acting and ballroom dancing for U.S. Government Emergency Education Program, San Francisco, Calif., 1934-37; busboy, soda jerk, and night clerk in Hollywood, 1937-42; secretary to a psychologist in Hollywood, 1952-54, and for Los Angeles Blinded Veterans, 1954-56; church custodian, 1956-58; Butler Models (architectural models), Burbank, Calif., model builder, 1958-71; full time writer, 1971—. *Military service:* U.S. Air Force, 1942-45. *Awards, honors:* John Gassner Playwriting Award, 1976 for "Checkmates."

WRITINGS: Through The Awakening Eye (poems), Pygmalion Press, 1976; "Checkmates," one-act play; first produced in Norton, Mass., at Wheaton College, 1977. Contributor of poems to *Yale Review*, and *Marilyn*.

WORK IN PROGRESS: "The Last Enemy," a teleplay; "Tiger in a Paper Cage," a stage/film play.

SIDELIGHTS: Anderson told *CA* that his interest in playwriting began in high school when he made several films with a friend who "happily owned the first home movie camera." He recalls, "We co-produced two comedies and a full length drama, which, incidentally, turned out to be funnier than the other two put together!" His decision to write seriously, however, came years later: "It was complete misery of spirit, compounded by aloneness and the Depression in 1934, which finally forced me, at age twenty-seven, into the humiliating (and fearsome) process of recording fragments of thoughts streaming before my mind's eye. I got a little dizzy until I accepted fewer barriers and wider horizons than I had previously supposed, and from there started to build on my new-to-me concepts and expanded sympathies."

"I wrote more stream-of-consciousness pieces and my ever hopeful plays, for what turned out to be all but a lifetime, for smidgens of recognition. And now (a study in irony, or better-late-than-never), forty-two years later, all the highlights of the stream-of-consciousness pieces have been published—right out of the bottom of my trunk—as *Through the Awakening Eye.*"

Anderson added that when he goes to see his play, "Checkmates," produced at Wheaton College he will "happen to have all my play scripts under one arm as I arrive—the other arm reaching for the brass ring, with hope springing eternal. Though, if the glass slipper is discovered to fit at age seventy, it may be a little tough to dance."

Looking forward, Anderson envisions writing another play while "lying back on a world cruise—taking my wife this time, instead of her taking me. I love to travel because I'm always trying to expand my horizons." In a broader sense, he admits: "The horizon I long for most is the vast, all encompassing one—possible only within the human spirit—which could put our circles of thought and emotion into such perspective that we could see how to skip war. Don't blame me for trying!"

* * *

ANDERSON, George Christian 1907-1976

January 30, 1907—December 19, 1976; British-born American clergyman, consultant in field of mental health, and author. He died in Swarthmore, Pa. Obituaries: *New York Times*, December 21, 1976. (*CAP*-2; earlier sketch in *CA*-29/32)

* * *

ANDERSON, Irvine H(enry) 1928-

PERSONAL: Born March 29, 1928, in Natchez, Miss.; son of Irvine Henry and Elizabeth Ogden (Reed) Anderson; married, 1950 (divorced, 1974); married Donna B. Denoon (a counselor), June 14, 1975; children: Emily, Grace; (stepchildren) Craig, Eric, Mary. *Education:* Southwestern College at Memphis, B.A., 1950; University of Cincinnati, M.A., 1968, Ph.D., 1973. *Politics:* Republican. *Religion:* Presbyterian. *Home:* 2619 Ardmore Ave., Cincinnati, Ohio 45237. *Office:* Raymond Walters College, University of Cincinnati, Cincinnati, Ohio 45236.

CAREER: Memphis International Center, Memphis, Tenn., associate director in foreign trade promotion, 1950-52; General Electric Co., New York City, in employee relations (worked in Syracuse, N.Y., Pittsfield, Mass., and Cincinnati, Ohio), 1956-67; University of Cincinnati, Cincinnati, instructor, 1970-73, assistant professor, 1973-76, associate professor of history, 1976—. Moderator of numerous television programs for "World Front" series in Cincinnati, 1974-76. *Military service:* U.S. Naval Reserve, active duty in Naval Air Intelligence, 1952-56; served in Pacific theater; became lieutenant commander.

MEMBER: American Historical Association, Organization of American Historians, Society for Historians of American Foreign Relations, Midwest-China Seminar, Cincinnati Council on World Affairs. *Awards, honors:* Woodrow Wilson fellowship, summer, 1971; Louis Knott Koontz Award from *Pacific Historical Review,* 1976, for article on oil embargo to Japan; Thomas Newcomen Award from Newcomen Society and *Business History Review,* 1977, for a book on the Standard-Vacuum Oil Company.

WRITINGS: The Standard-Vacuum Oil Company and the United States East Asian Policy, 1933-1941, Princeton University Press, 1975. Contributor of articles and reviews to history journals.

WORK IN PROGRESS: A study of the Arabian American Oil Company and American Middle Eastern policy, 1941-1950.

SIDELIGHTS: Anderson writes that his "principal current interest is international affairs in general and the relationship of multinational corporations to American foreign policy in particular. My general viewpoint has been heavily influenced by the work of Pierre Teilhard de Chardin."

* * *

ANDERSON, Madelyn Klein

PERSONAL: Born in New York, N.Y.; daughter of Max W. and Fannie (Siegel) Klein; married Douglas Ray Anderson (deceased); children: Justin Lee. *Education:* Hunter College (now of the City University of New York), B.A., 1951; New York University, certificate in occupational therapy, 1958; Pratt Institute, M.L.S., 1974. *Home:* 80 North Moore St., New York, N.Y. 10013. *Agent:* Patricia Lewis, 390 Riverside Dr., New York, N.Y. 10001. *Office:* Julian Messner, Inc., 1230 Avenue of the Americas, New York, N.Y. 10020.

CAREER: Beth Israel Hospital, New York, N.Y., director of occupational therapy, 1959-63; New York Infirmary, New York City, director of occupational therapy, 1968-72; Julian Messner, Inc., New York City, editor, 1974—. *Military service:* U.S. Army, Women's Medical Specialist Corps, 1954-55; became lieutenant. *Member:* World Federation of Occupational Therapists, American Occupational Therapy Association, Beta Phi Mu.

WRITINGS: Iceberg Alley, Messner, 1976.

WORK IN PROGRESS: A book on the U.S. Coast Guard; research on the Arctic.

SIDELIGHTS: Madelyn Anderson comments that the death of her husband in Vietnam "led to a drastic career change which in turn led to a basic interest which had never been developed—writing. I have traveled extensively as a military wife, but the most exciting trip was in connection with *Iceberg Alley,* when I traveled on a Coast Guard C130 to Newfoundland and Greenland. This has led to a profound respect for the Coast Guard—and to several books on the subject—and a deep interest in the Arctic."

* * *

ANDERSON, Margaret J(ean) 1931-

PERSONAL: Born December 24, 1931, in Gorebridge, Scotland; came to the United States in 1963; daughter of John A. (a clergyman) and Margaret (Reid) Hall; married Norman H. Anderson (a professor of entomology), September 15, 1956; children: Richard, Judy, Susan, Karen. *Education:* University of Edinburgh, B.Sc. (honors), 1953. *Religion:* Presbyterian. *Home:* 1930 Northwest 29th Pl., Corvallis, Ore. 97330.

CAREER: East Malling Research Station, Kent, England, statistician, 1953-55; Canada Department of Agriculture, Summerland, British Columbia, entomologist, 1955-56; Oregon State University, Corvallis, Ore., statistician, 1956-57. Writer.

MEMBER: Society of Children's Book Writers. *Awards, honors:* Writing competition award from Canadian Entomological Society, 1973, for "Making a Case for the Caddisfly"; *Exploring the Insect World* was named an outstanding science book for children by National Science Teachers Association and Children's Book Council, 1974; *To Nowhere and Back* was named outstanding book of the year by *New York Times Book Review,* 1975.

WRITINGS: Exploring the Insect World (juvenile nonfiction), McGraw, 1974; *To Nowhere and Back* (juvenile), Knopf, 1975; *Exploring City Trees, and the Need for Urban Forests* (juvenile nonfiction), McGraw, 1976; *In the Keep of Time* (juvenile fiction), Knopf, 1977; *Clairmont House* (juvenile fiction), Knopf, in press. Contributor to magazines, including *Nature and Science, Ranger Rick's Nature Magazine, Insect-World Digest,* and *Instructor.*

WORK IN PROGRESS: In the Circle of Time, for juveniles.

SIDELIGHTS: Margaret Anderson writes: "I am interested in environmental issues, which is reflected in both my nature books and fiction. All my fiction books (so far) have been set in England, or Scotland, where I grew up."

* * *

ANDERSON, R. C. 1883(?)-1976

1883(?)—October 2, 1976; British maritime historian and author. Anderson's greatest area of expertise was in 16th and 17th century sailing ships. He died in England. Obituaries: *AB Bookman's Weekly,* November 15, 1976.

* * *

ANDERSON, Ruth Nathan 1934-

PERSONAL: Born January 28, 1934, in New York, N.Y.; daughter of Solomon (a pediatrician) and Anna (a seamstress; maiden name, Cornick) Gans; married Arthur Aksel Anderson, Jr. (a construction supervisor), September 11, 1971; children: (stepchildren) Barbara Anderson Stasioski, Terri Anderson, Jack Anderson; *Education:* Attended New York University and George Washington University. *Politics:* Independent. *Religion:* "Believer—Universal God." *Home and office:* 161 Nasa Circle, Round Lake, Ill. 60073.

CAREER/WRITINGS: Washington Post, Washington, D.C., newsletter editor, 1952-53; National Multiple Sclerosis Society, New York City, chief medical writer and press officer, 1953-55; Crusade for Freedom, New York City, feature editor, 1955-58; *TV Revue,* New York City, editor of junior television department, 1958-61; North American Newspaper Alliance/Women's News Syndicate, New York City, feature reporter, 1961-69; National Features Syndicate, Chicago, Ill., writer of "Doctor's Grapevine" column, appearing in newspapers in Texas, Florida, Pennsylvania, and New York, and special features writer, 1969-73; writer of self-syndicated column, "VIP Medical Grapevine," and free-lance writer, 1973—. Notable assignments include an interview with President Eisenhower at Gettysburg and with Mrs. Eleanor Daley. Has also taught journalism for Florida Adult Board of Education, 1968-69, and conducted faculty seminars at University of Chicago, 1971-74. News broadcaster, WNYC-Radio, 1967-69; television show panelist. Singer under contract to Nashville Artist & Repertoire, 1974—; singer for commercials. Author of a booklet for United Nations, 1959. Contributor to periodicals, including *Pageant, Parents, Mademoiselle, Reader's Digest, Saturday Evening Post,* and to *Encyclopedia Brittanica. Member:* Future Physicians of America, Chicago Press Club, Chicago Women in Broadcasting, Lake County Association of Journalists, Chicago Unlimited.

WORK IN PROGRESS: Adaptation of column for television and radio; a non-fiction book on enduring marriage.

SIDELIGHTS: Anderson told *CA:* "I consider myself a natural writer vs. someone who painfully acquires the skills; not overly aggressive, non-brash, but persistent, relying on personal persuasion rather than 'contacts' or 'influence' to obtain extremely hard-to-get interviews or stories. I started a second career as a professional singer in 1974; after an audition I won a renewable contract as a recording artist (melodic pop—no rock); have recorded four songs to date—no big name label yet."

* * *

ANDERSON, Tom 1910-

PERSONAL: Born November 7, 1910, in Nashville, Tenn.; son of William J. and Nancy Anderson; married Carolyn Jennings, 1936; children: one daughter (Mrs. Sam Porter, Jr.). *Education:* Vanderbilt University, B.A., 1934. *Politics:* American Party. *Religion:* Southern Methodist. *Office:* 100 River Rd., Pigeon Forge, Tenn. 37863.

CAREER: Southern Farm Publications (publisher of fourteen farm magazines), Nashville, Tenn., publisher, 1948-71; American Way Features, Pigeon Forge, Tenn., president, 1965—. Owner and operator of 4,300 acre cattle and timber ranch in middle Tennessee. Lecturer. American Party, national chairman, 1972—, presidential nominee, 1976. *Member:* American Agricultural Editors Association (president, 1953-54). *Awards, honors:* Honorary LL.B. from Bob Jones University.

WRITINGS: Straight Talk, Western Islands, 1967; *Silence Is Not Golden—It's Yellow,* Western Islands, 1973. Writer of "Straight Talk" column syndicated by American Way Features to over sixty newspapers, 1958—. Notable assignments include interviews with Generalissimo Franco and Rhodesian prime minister Ian Smith; travel to over thirty-seven nations.

SIDELIGHTS: Anderson told *CA* the motivation for his writing is to help restore and preserve freedom.

* * *

ANDRADE, Victor (Manuel) 1905-

PERSONAL: Born March 6, 1905, in Chulumani, Bolivia; son of Manuel (a businessman) and Maria (a concert pianist; maiden name, Usquiano) Andrade; married Blanca Salmon Tapia, October 17, 1937; children: Lupita (Mrs. Esteban Krsul), Mario Victor. *Education:* University of La Paz, Bach. Arts and Sciences, 1923; also attended University of San Andres. *Politics:* Movimiento Nacionalista Revolucionario. *Religion:* Roman Catholic. *Home and office:* Heriberto Gutierrez, La Paz, Bolivia. *Mailing address:* Casilla 451, La Paz, Bolivia.

CAREER: American Institute, La Paz, Bolivia, professor of mathematics, 1925-30; Bolivian Government, undersecretary of education, 1930-36, director of Social Security, 1936-43, minister of labor, 1943-46, minister of foreign relations, 1943-44, ambassador to the United States in Washington, D.C., 1944-46; New School for Social Research, New York, N.Y., visiting professor, 1948-50; Bolivian Government, ambassador to the United States, 1952-58, minister of foreign relations, 1958-60, ambassador to the United States, 1960-62, member of parliament, beginning 1940, served as deputy and senator; candidate for president, 1964. In mining business, 1936-37. Representative of International Basic Economy Corp. in Ecuador, 1949-52; representative of Organization of American States to Ecuador, 1970-71, and Brazil, 1971-74. Director general of Savings and Security Bank, 1937-43; member of board of trustees of American Institute (La Paz) and Inter-American Committee of Social Security. *Military service:* Bolivian Army, 1932-35; received Medalla de Guerra and Merito Militar. *Member:* Club de La Paz, Club de Golf (Mallasilla), Metropolitan Club (Washington, D.C.), Burning Tree Club (Washington, D.C.). *Awards, honors:* Has received decorations from most of the countries of Latin America, including Condor de los Andes.

WRITINGS: Elementos de las condiciones sociales de Bolivia, Seguro Obrero, 1943; *My Missions for Revolutionary Bolivia, 1944-1962,* University of Pittsburgh Press, 1976. Also author of *Aritmetica aplicada,* 1931. Contributor to *Encyclopaedia Britannica* and *Encyclopedia Americana.*

WORK IN PROGRESS: Books on the economic and social effects of the Bolivian revolution; *Derrumbe,* a novel set during Bolivia's Chaco War; research on Bolivian culture, especially Incan and pre-Incan culture.

SIDELIGHTS: Andrade was most active in Bolivian politics during the 1940's, when he participated in the military overthrow of the government in 1943. When the new government was itself overthrown in 1946, Andrade led the opposition to the new regime and spent the next few years in exile. *Avocational interests:* Music (playing the piano).

* * *

ANDRAIN, Charles F(ranklin) 1937-

PERSONAL: Born February 22, 1937, in Fortuna, Calif.; son of Milton (a dentist) and Alberta W. (Gatton) Andrain. *Education:* Whittier College, A.B., 1959; University of California, Berkeley, M.A., 1961, Ph.D., 1964. *Office:* Department of Political Science, San Diego State University, San Diego, Calif. 92182.

CAREER: San Diego State University, San Diego, Calif., assistant professor, 1964-67, associate professor, 1967-70, professor of political science, 1970—, chairman of department, 1972-74. Research associate at Institute of International Studies, University of California, Berkeley, 1975-76. Member of political science advisory panel of California Statewide Social Study Committee, 1967-68. *Member:* American Political Science Association, American Sociological Association. *Awards, honors:* Woodrow Wilson fellowship, 1959-60; Ford Foundation fellowship, 1968-69; National Institute of Mental Health fellowship, 1971-72.

WRITINGS: (Contributor) David E. Apter, editor, *Ideology and Discontent,* Free Press, 1964; (contributor) Walter A. E. Skurnik, editor, *African Political Thought,* University of Denver Social Science Foundation and Graduate School of International Studies, 1968; *Political Life and Social Change,* Wadsworth, 1970, 2nd edition, 1975; *Children and Civic Awareness,* C. E. Merrill, 1971; (editor with

Apter) *Contemporary Analytical Theory*, Prentice-Hall, 1972. Contributor to political science journals.

WORK IN PROGRESS: Research on comparative public policy in Western democracies.

* * *

ANDRE, Evelyn M(arie) 1924-

PERSONAL: Born July 13, 1924, in Pennsylvania; daughter of J. Clyde (a carpenter) and Lillian (Haley) Andre. *Education:* Adrian College, student, 1946-48; Capital University, Columbus, Ohio, B.A., 1950; Hartford Seminary Foundation, M.A., 1952. *Religion:* United Methodist. *Residence:* Nashville, Tenn. *Office:* United Methodist Publishing House, 201 Eighth Ave. S., Nashville, Tenn. 37203.

CAREER: Research assistant at Allegheny Ludlum Steel Corp., 1942-46; Court Street Methodist Church, Flint, Mich., director of Christian education, 1952-59; United Methodist Board of Discipleship, Nashville, Tenn., editor of nursery materials, 1959—.

WRITINGS: Things We Like to Do (juvenile), Abingdon, 1969; (juvenile songbook; compiler with Jeneil Menefee) *Rejoice and Sing Praise*, Abingdon, 1977; (teachers' manual; compiler with Margie McCarty) *I Can Teach Young Children*, Board of Discipleship, 1977.

* * *

ANDREW, John (Alfred III) 1943-

PERSONAL: Born January 16, 1943, in Boston, Mass.; son of John Alfred, Jr. (a salesman) and Deborah (a clerk; maiden name, Marston) Andrew; married Rosanne Gonye, September 3, 1966; children: John Francis, Lea Whitney. *Education:* University of New Hampshire, B.A., 1965, M.A., 1967; Univeristy of Texas, Ph.D., 1973. *Politics:* "Left-of-center Democrat." *Religion:* Unitarian-Universalist. *Home:* 727 College Ave., Lancaster, Pa. 17603. *Office:* Department of History, Franklin & Marshall College, Lancaster, Pa. 17604.

CAREER: High school social studies teacher and chairman of department in White Mountains, N.H., 1966-68; University of Texas, Austin, lecturer in Evening Division, 1968-73, assistant instructor in history, 1973; Franklin & Marshall College, Lancaster, Pa., assistant professor of history and chairman of American studies, 1973—. *Member:* Organization of American Historians, American Studies Association, New Hampshire Historical Society, Phi Alpha Theta, Pi Sigma Alpha, Pi Gamma Mu. *Awards, honors:* American Philosophical Society grant, 1975.

WRITINGS: Rebuilding the Christian Commonwealth: New England Congregationalists and Foreign Missions, 1800-1830, University Press of Kentucky, 1976. Contributor of articles and reviews to history journals.

WORK IN PROGRESS: A biography of Jeremiah Evarts and an interpretation of post-Revolutionary American reform; a history of American Indian policy, 1815-1840.

SIDELIGHTS: Andrew comments: "I am interested in why reform activity takes place, and why certain people support, and oppose, reform movements—and am a 'political groupie' of sorts." *Avocational interests:* Sports, "caulking windows, and swatting flies."

* * *

ANDREWS, Arthur (Douglas, Jr.) 1923-
(Ana Ort)

PERSONAL: Born March 19, 1923, in Terre Haute, Ind.; son of Arthur Douglas (a sales engineer) and Kathryn (Marlowe) Andrews; married Jean Elizabeth Williams (a bookkeeper), December 25, 1943 (divorced); married Margaret Jean Jonakin, January 14, 1963 (deceased); children: Cathy Jean Andrews Bray, Arthur Douglas III, Kathryn Jonakin. *Education:* Attended Wooster College, 1941-43, Western Reserve University (now Case Western Reserve University), 1943, and Ohio State University, 1945; Washington University, St. Louis, Mo., B.S.-M.S., 1953; San Jose State University, graduate study, 1964-70. *Religion:* Religious Society of Friends (Quakers). *Home address:* P.O. Box 5963, San Jose, Calif. 95150. *Office:* Western Lifetime Housewares, Campbell, Calif. 95008.

CAREER: Has worked in construction and as a construction superintendent in Cleveland, Ohio, 1945-50; manager of advertising, sales promotion, and marketing for industrial firms, all in St. Louis, Mo., 1956-62; high school teacher of English and science in San Jose, Calif., 1963-70; Western Lifetime Housewares, Campbell, Calif., owner, 1971—. *Military service:* U.S. Army, Medical Corps, 1943-45.

WRITINGS: A Dog-Eared Book (humorous poetry), Ashley Books, 1974. Contributor of articles and poems (sometimes under pseudonym Ana Ort) to magazines, including *Hygienic Review*.

WORK IN PROGRESS: Children's books; health books.

SIDELIGHTS: Andrews told *CA:* "In my writings and in my life I attempt to express life and living as a joy, an opportunity, a privilege and a responsibility. I am convinced one can be ecstatically happy and quite serious about life at the same time. My experiences assure me that growth comes best from hardship and tribulation, and that grief offers a special lesson and has its own beauty. The surest promise of happiness lies in work."

* * *

ANDREWS, Dorothea Harris 1916-1976

March 9, 1916—December 3, 1976; American journalist, civil servant, and author of books and articles about child welfare. Worked with the Department of Health, Education and Welfare. She died in Washington, DC. Obituaries: *Washington Post*, December 6, 1976.

* * *

ANDROS, Dee G(us) 1924-

PERSONAL: Born October 17, 1924, in Oklahoma City, Okla.; son of Gus D. (a restaurant owner) and Harriett (Roberts) Andros; married Luella Thomas, January 24, 1949; children: Jeanna. *Education:* University of Oklahoma, B.A., 1950, M.A., 1952. *Politics:* Democrat. *Religion:* Protestant. *Home:* 715 Elizabeth Dr., Corvallis, Ore. 97330. *Office:* Athletic Department, Oregon State University, Gill Coliseum 103, Corvallis, Ore. 97331.

CAREER: University of Oklahoma, Norman, assistant football coach, 1950-52; University of Kansas, Lawrence, line coach, 1953; Texas Tech University, Lubbock, line coach, 1954-55; University of Nebraska, Lincoln, line coach, 1956; University of California, Berkeley, offense/defense coordinator, 1957-60; University of Illinois, Champaign, offense/defense coordinator, 1960-61; University of Idaho, Moscow, head coach, 1962-65; Oregon State University, Corvallis, professor of education, 1965—, head coach, 1965-75, athletic director, 1975-76. *Military service:* U.S. Marine Corps, 1943-46; served in Pacific theater; became sergeant; received Bronze Star. *Member:* National

Football Association (member of board of directors, 1973-75), Chamber of Commerce, Ambassadors Club, Country Club, Masons, Shriners, Elks, Moose Club, Acacia Club.

WRITINGS: (With Roland Red Smith) *Power T Football,* Parker & Son, 1971. Contributor to sports manuals.

SIDELIGHTS: Andros was head coach of the All-American Game, 1968, and of the East-West Shrine Game, 1967 and 1968; he was assistant coach of the Sugar Bowl, 1950 and 1951, the Sun Bowl, 1956, the Rose Bowl, 1959, the East-West Shrine Game, 1967 and 1968, and of the Hula Bowl, 1968 and 1971.

* * *

ANGEL, Heather 1941-

PERSONAL: Born July 21, 1941, in Fulmer, England; daughter of Stanley Paul and Hazel Marie (Sherwood) Le Rougetel; married Martin Angel (a biological oceanographer), October 3, 1964; children: Giles Philip. *Education:* University of Bristol, B.Sc. (with honors), 1962, M.Sc., 1965. *Home and office:* Sunset Cottage, Clovelly Rd., Hindhead, Surrey GU26 6RT, England.

CAREER: National Institute of Oceanography, Godalming, Surrey, England, assistant biologist, 1966-67; self-employed wildlife and biological photographer, author, and lecturer, 1967—. *Member:* Royal Photographic Society (fellow; council member, 1976—; co-founder and chairman of nature group, 1976), Institute of Incorporated Photographers (fellow), Marine Biological Association, Scottish Marine Biological Association, Conchological Society. *Awards, honors:* Hood medal from Royal Photographic Society, 1975, for contributions to advancement of nature photography.

WRITINGS: Nature Photography: Its Art and Techniques, Fountain Press, 1972, International Publications Service, 1973; *Your Book of Fishes,* Transatlantic, 1972; *The World of an Estuary,* Faber, 1975; *All Colour Book of Ocean Life,* Octopus, 1975; *Seashore Life on Rocky Shores,* Jarrold, 1975; *Seashore Life on Sandy Beaches,* Jarrold, 1975; *The World of a Stream,* Faber, 1976; *Sea Shells of the Sea Shore,* Jarrold, 1976; *Fact Finder Seashore,* Macmillan, 1976; *Life in the Oceans,* Octopus, 1976; *Wild Animals in the Garden,* Jarrold, 1976; *Life of Our Estuaries,* Jarrold, 1977; *British Wild Orchids,* Jarrold, 1977; *Seaweeds of the Seashore,* Jarrold, 1977; *The Countryside of the New Forest,* Jarrold, 1977; *Life in Our Rivers,* Jarrold, 1977.

"Photographing Nature" series; published by Argus: *Trees,* 1975; *Insects,* 1975; *Seashore,* 1975; *Flowers,* 1975, Morgan, 1976; *Fungi,* 1975, Morgan, 1976.

Contributor to *British Journal of Photography, Practical Photography, Wildlife, Hasselblad* (magazine), and *Professional News* (of the Eastman Kodak Co.).

WORK IN PROGRESS: The Countryside of Devon; The Countryside of Cornwall; The Countryside of North Wales.

SIDELIGHTS: Heather Angel's preference to photograph plants and animals in their natural environment has taken her to many unusual places. "I have skin-dived and photographed underwater the coral reef life of Zanzibar and the Seychelles in the Indian Ocean. I have pony-trekked high up in Kashmir in search of rare alpine flowers, stalked lemurs in the tropical rain forest in Madagascar, and climbed volcanoes in Hawaii. But one of my most unforgettable experiences was seeing the large population of giant tortoises (4,000-odd) lumbering over the floor of Alcedo Crater on Isabela Island in the Galapagos. I camped with my husband for four days inside this crater. When we woke at 5:30 AM, the crater was filled with early morning mist. As the sun rose the mist cleared and the giant tortoises clambered from the temporary muddy pools in which they spend their nights.

"Most recently I spent a week on a tiny island (Stephens Island) north of the South Island of New Zealand making a comprehensive study of a living fossil reptile called the tuatara."

Her desire to accurately depict natural life goes beyond photographing the habitat. She feels that a single photograph cannot adequately illustrate the biology of a species. "Take for instance, the common limpet which to most people is simply a conical shell found clamped on to rocks on the seashore at low water. The 80-odd transparencies in my files of this snail illustrate many facets of its life: exposure at low water, browsing areas, feeding tracks, scars made in soft rock, living as a rock pool inhabitant, its huge muscular foot, shells washed up on the shore, movement underwater and specimens marked with paint for experimental work." She also has little tolerance for scientifically inaccurate pictures. "Pictures of stuffed animals and pinned insects propped up in natural surroundings, of deep sea fish with opaque eyes and of opaque plankton do, alas, manage to pass via agencies to picture researchers, designers and editors on to the printed page. An agency obviously accepts pictures in good faith, and so here the blame must lie fairly and squarely with the photographer who takes and supplies such pictures."

A photograph of a vanilla orchid Heather Angel took in the Republic of the Seychelles has been used for the design of that country's new fifty-cent piece.

* * *

ANSELL, Jack 1925-1976

November 21, 1925—September 20, 1976; American television network director and novelist. He died in New York City. Obituaries: *New York Times,* September 22, 1976. (See index for previous *CA* sketch)

* * *

ANSPACH, Donald F. 1942-

PERSONAL: Born August 10, 1942, in Hershey, Pa.; son of Donald R. (an appraiser) and Evelyn (a realtor; maiden name, Yeacley) Anspach; children: Jennifer Lynn. *Education:* Franklin & Marshall College, A.B., 1964; Case Western Reserve University, M.A., 1966, Ph.D., 1970. *Home:* 752 Ocean Ave., Portland, Maine 04103. *Office:* Department of Sociology, University of Maine, Portland, Maine 04103.

CAREER: University of Maine, Portland, associate professor of sociology, 1970—, chairperson of department. *Member:* American Sociological Association, National Council on Family Relations.

WRITINGS: (With George S. Rosenberg) *Working Class Kinship,* Lexington Books, 1973. Contributor to *Journal of Marriage and the Family.*

* * *

ANTHONY, Geraldine C(ecilia) 1919-

PERSONAL: Born October 5, 1919, in Brooklyn, N.Y.; daughter of William (a pharmacist) and Agnes (Murphy) Anthony. *Education:* Attended Boston College, 1945-47; Mount St. Vincent University, B.A., 1951; St. John's University, New York, N.Y., M.A., 1956, Ph.D., 1963; postdoctoral study at Exeter College, Oxford, University of Minnesota, and Columbia University. *Home and office:* Department of English, Mount St. Vincent University, Halifax, Nova Scotia, Canada.

CAREER: Member of Roman Catholic women's community, the Sisters of Charity, 1939—; junior high school teacher at Roman Catholic schools in Dorchester, Mass., 1942-48, Lowell, Mass., 1948-51, and Bellmore, N.Y., 1951-62; high school teacher of English in Halifax, Nova Scotia, 1963-65; Mount St. Vincent University, Halifax, Nova Scotia, associate professor of English, 1965—, director of summer school, 1966-68. *Member:* Association of Canadian University Teachers of English, Canadian Theatre History Research Association, Canadian Conference of the Arts. *Awards, honors:* Journalism fellowship from University of Minnesota, 1965; Canada Council grants, 1975, 1976, 1977.

WRITINGS: John Coulter, G. K. Hall, 1976; (editor) *Twelve Canadian Dramatists,* Doubleday, 1977; *Gwen Pharis Ringwood,* G. K. Hall, in press. General editor of *Profiles in Canadian Drama,* Gage, 1977—. Contributor to *Canadian Drama, Canadian Theatre Review, Canadian Library Journal,* and to *Cithara.* Member of editorial Board, *Canadian Drama/L'Art Dramatique Canadien.*

WORK IN PROGRESS: John Herbert, publication by Gage expected in 1979; *Two Languages, One Theme: The Canadian Theatre of Liberation,* with Renate Usmiani, completion expected in 1980.

SIDELIGHTS: Geraldine Anthony writes: "My interest in theatre stems back to my childhood in New York. Because my parents loved Broadway plays, they stimulated my interest in them. I have been in Canada since 1963 and my research interests have centered on Canadian and American drama. My publications since 1973 have been entirely within the field of Canadian drama which has suddenly become a source of major development throughout Canada."

*　　*　　*

ANTRIM, William H.   1928-

PERSONAL: Born September 29, 1928, in Johnstown, Pa.; son of G. Harold (a high school superintendent) and Florence (a teacher; maiden name, Trimble) Antrim; married Katherine M. Mathie (a teacher), December 27, 1952; children: Ann Marie, Carolyn. *Education:* Syracuse University, B.S., 1950; graduate study at University of Minnesota, 1962, and Arizona State University, 1963; University of Arizona, M.A., 1968. *Politics:* Independent. *Religion:* Christian. *Home:* 4153 Camino de la Colina, Tucson, Ariz. 85711. *Office:* College of Education, University of Arizona, P.O. Box 308, Tucson, Ariz. 85721.

CAREER: High school teacher in Tucson, Ariz., 1962-68; University of Arizona, Tucson, faculty member in education, 1968—. Member of advisory committee of Pima College, 1972—. Member of Arizona State Distributive Education Advisory Commission, 1975-77, and Arizona Advisory Committee for Economic Education, 1976-77. *Military service:* U.S. Air Force, transportation officer, 1952-54; served in Morocco; became captain.

MEMBER: Council for Distributive Teacher Education, National Association of Distributive Teachers, Distributive Education Clubs of America (honorary life member), American Vocational Association (life member), National Business Education Association, Cooperative Education Association, Arizona Association of Distributive Teachers (honorary life member), Arizona Business Education Association, Arizona State Vocational Association, Sales and Marketing Executives of Tucson (member of board of directors, 1972-77), Phi Delta Kappa. *Awards, honors:* Distinguished service award from Arizona chapter of Distributive Education Clubs of America, 1959.

WRITINGS: (Contributor) *Readings in Distributive Education,* University of Michigan, 1968; *Advertising,* Gregg, 1970, teacher's manual, 1973. Contributor to education journals.

WORK IN PROGRESS: Revising *Advertising;* research on a job-oriented curriculum for entry-level distributive education programs.

SIDELIGHTS: Antrim writes that he is "interested in curriculum development for vocational and career education, with special interest in business and office education and marketing and distributive occupations education."

*　　*　　*

APPEL, Benjamin   1907-1977

September 13, 1907—April 3, 1977; American author of works of fiction and nonfiction, best known for his book *Brain Guy.* He died in Princeton, N.J. Obituaries: *New York Times,* April 4, 1977; *AB Bookman's Weekly,* June 27, 1977. (See index for previous *CA* sketch)

*　　*　　*

APPLEBY, Joyce Oldham   1929-

PERSONAL: Born April 9, 1929, in Omaha, Neb.; daughter of Junius Graham and Edith (Cash) Oldham; married Andrew Bell Appleby, 1959; children: Ann Lansburgh, Mark Lansburgh, Frank. *Education:* Stanford University, B.A., 1950; University of California, Santa Barbara, M.A., 1959; Claremont Graduate School, Ph.D., 1966. *Home:* 3568 Front St., San Diego, Calif. 92103. *Office:* Department of History, San Diego State University, San Diego, Calif. 92182.

CAREER: San Diego State University, San Diego, Calif., assistant professor, 1967-70, associate professor, 1970-73, professor of American history, 1973—. Member of board of fellows of Claremont Graduate School and University Center. *Member:* American Historical Association, Organization of American Historians.

WRITINGS: (Editor) *Materialism and Morality in the American Past: Themes and Sources, 1600-1860,* Addison-Wesley, 1973; *The Ideology of the Market Economy,* Princeton University Press, in press. Contributor to history journals.

*　　*　　*

APPLEGARTH, Margaret Tyson   1886-1976

July 8, 1886—October 30, 1976; American author of thirty-five books and lecturer on ecumenicism and other religious subjects. She died in Manhattan. Obituaries: *New York Times,* November 2, 1976.

*　　*　　*

ARAGON, Louis   1897-
(Saint Romain Arnaud, Francois La Colere [Lacolere])

PERSONAL: Born October 3, 1897, in Paris, France; son of an innkeeper; married Elsa Triolet Kagan (a writer), February 28, 1939 (died June 16, 1970). *Education:* Studied medicine at University of Paris, 1916-17. *Politics:* Communist. *Home:* 56 rue de Varenne, Paris 7e, France.

CAREER: Poet and novelist. As a young writer, involved with avant-garde movements of dada and cubism; founder with Andre Breton and Philippe Soupault of magazine, *Litterature,* 1919, and subsequently of the surrealist movement; became a member of the Communist party in 1927; member of staff of political newspapers, *L'Humanite* and *Commune,* in early 1930's; *Ce Soir* (Communist daily newspaper), Paris, France, co-director, 1937-39; editor of clandestine French periodical, *La Drome en armes,* during World War II; Editeurs France Reunis (publishers), Paris, founder and managing director, 1944—; *Ce soir,* editor, 1947-53; *Les Lettres Francaises* (weekly literary and political review), Paris, staff member, 1949-53, director, 1953—. Member of central committee of French Communist Party, 1950-60; member of advisory board of *Europe* (monthly literary review), 1958—; member of Academie Concourt, 1967-68. *Wartime service:* Medical auxiliary with the French Army in early World War I; entered combat with 355th Infantry Regiment in 1917; awarded croix de guerre. In World War II, served as auxiliary doctor with French Army and was at Dunkirk when government fell; fought remainder of war as a member of the French resistance; received croix de guerre and medaille militarie. *Member:* International Association of Writers for the Defense of Culture (founder, 1935; now secretary of French section), Association of Combatant Writers (vice-president, 1945-60), French National Committee of Authors, American Academy of Arts and Letters (honorary member). *Awards, honors:* Prix Renaudot, 1936, for *Les Beaux Quartiers;* Lenin Peace Prize, 1957; Ph.D., University of Prague, 1963, University of Moscow, 1965.

WRITINGS—Poetry: *Feu de joie* (title means "Bonfire"), Au Sans-Pareil (Paris), 1920; *Le Mouvement perpetuel* (title means "Perpetual Motion"), Nouvelle Revue Francaise (Paris), 1925; *La Grande Gaite* (title means "High Spirits"), with drawings by Yves Tanguy, Gallimard (Paris), 1929; *Persecute persecuteur,* Editions Surrealistes (Paris), 1931; *The Red Front,* translation by E. E. Cummings of "Front rouge," Contempo Publishers, 1933; *Hourra l'Oural* (title means "Hurrah, the Urals"), Denoel & Steele (Paris), 1934; *Le Creve-Coeur* (title means "Heart-break"), Gallimard, 1941, [New York], 1942, new edition, Gallimard, 1946; *Cantique a Elsa* (title means "Canticle to Elsa"), Editions de la Revue Fontaine (Algiers), 1941; *Broceliande,* Editions de la Baconniere (Neuchatel, Switzerland), 1942; *Les Yeux d'-Elsa* (title means "Elsa's Eyes"), Cahiers du Rhone (Neuchatel), 1942, Pantheon, 1944, new edition with critical essays, P. Seghers (Paris), 1945; (under pseudonym Francois La Colere) *Le Musee Grevin* (title means "The Grevin Museum"), Editeurs Francais Reunis (Paris), 1943; *France ecoute* (title means "France Listen"), Editions de la Revue Fontaine, 1944; *En Etrange pays dans mon pays lui-meme* (includes *Broceliande* and *En Francais dans le text),* P. Seghers, 1945; (under pseudonym Francois Lacolere) *Neuf Chansons interdites, 1942-1946* (title means "Nine Banned Songs"), Bibliotheque Francaise (Paris), 1945; *La Diane francaise* (title means "The French Diana"), P. Seghers, 1945; *Le Musee Grevin, les poissons noirs, et quelques poemes inedits* (title means "The Grevin Museum, the Black Fishes, and Some Unpublished Poems"), Editions de Minuit (Paris), 1946; *Le Nouveau Creve-Coeur* (title means "The New Heartbreak"), Gallimard, 1948.

Les Yeux et la memoire (title means "Eyes and Memory"), Gallimard, 1954; *Mes Caravanes et autres poemes (1948-1954)* (title means "My Caravans and Other Poems"), P. Seghers, 1954; *Le Roman inacheve* (autobiographical poem; title means "The Unfinished Romance"), Gallimard, 1956,

revised and corrected edition, 1969; *Elsa,* Gallimard, 1959; *Poesies: Anthologie, 1917-1960,* Le Club du Meilleur Livre (Paris), 1960; *Les Poetes* (autobiographical poem; title means "The Poets"), Gallimard, 1960, revised edition, 1969; *Le Fou d'Elsa* (title means "Elsa's Madman"), Gallimard, 1963; *Il ne m'est Paris que d'Elsa* (anthology; title means "There Is Only Elsa's Paris for Me"), Laffont (Paris), 1964, new edition with photographs, 1968; *Le Voyage de Hollande,* P. Seghers, 1964, 5th edition published as *Le Voyage de Hollande et autres poemes,* 1965; *Elegie a Pablo Neruda* (title means "Elegy to Pablo Neruda"), Gallimard, 1966; *Le Mouvement Perpetuel procede de feu de joie et suivie de ecritures automatiques* (includes "Perpetual Motion," "Bonfire," and "Automatic Writings"), Gallimard, 1970.

"Le Monde reel" ("The Real World") series of novels: *Les Cloches de Bale,* Denoel & Steele (Paris), 1934, translation by Haakon M. Chevalier published as *The Bells of Basel,* Harcourt, 1936; *Les Beaux Quartiers,* Donoel & Steele, 1936, translation by Chevalier published as *Residential Quarter,* Harcourt, 1938; *Les Voyageurs de l'imperiale,* Gallimard, 1942, translation by Hanna Josephson published as *The Century Was Young,* Duell, Sloane & Pearce, 1941 (published in England as *Passengers of Destiny,* Pilot Press, 1947), definitive French edition, 1947; *Aurelien,* Gallimard, 1944, translation by Eithne Wilkins published under same title, Duell, Sloane & Pearce, 1947; *Les Communistes,* six volumes, Bibliotheque Francaise, 1949-51.

Other novels: *Anicet; ou, Le panorama roman* (title means "Anicet; or, The Panorama Novel"), Nouvelle Revue Francaise, 1921; *Les Aventures de Telemaque* (title means "The Adventures of Telemachus"), Gallimard, 1922; *Le Paysan de Paris,* Gallimard, 1926, translation by Frederick Brown published as *Nightwalker,* Prentice-Hall, 1970, translation by Simon Watson Taylor published as *Paris Peasant,* J. Cape, 1971; *La Semaine sainte,* Gallimard, 1958, translation by Haakon Chevalier published as *Holy Week,* Putnam, 1961; *La Mise a mort* (title means "The Kill"), Gallimard, 1965; *Blanche ou l'oubli* (title means "Blanche or Forgetting"), Gallimard, 1967; *Irene,* L'Or du Temps (Paris), 1968; *Henri Matisse: Roman,* Gallimard, 1971, translation by Jean Stewart published in two volumes as *Henri Matisse: A Novel,* Harcourt, 1972; *Theatre/Roman,* Gallimard, 1974.

Short stories: *Servitude et Grandeur des Francais: Scenes des annees terribles* (seven stories; title means "Servitude and Greatness of the French: Scenes from the Terrible Years"), Bibliotheque Francaise, 1945; (under pseudonym Saint Roman Arnaud) *Trois Contes* (title means "Three Tales"), Burrup, Mathieson, 1945; *Shakespeare* (original title, "Murmure"), translation by Bernard Frechtman, with illustrations by Pablo Picasso, Abrams, 1966.

Plays: "L'Armoire a glace un beau soir," published in *Le Libertinage,* Nouvelle Revue Francaise, 1924, translation published as "The Mirror-Wardrobe One Fine Evening" in *Modern French Theatre,* edited by Michael Benedikt and George E. Wellwarth, Dutton, 1964; "Au pied du mur," 1924; (with Andre Breton) "Le Tresor des Jesuites," 1929, included in *Trois Pieces surrealists,* edited by Robert G. Marshall and Frederic C. St. Aubyn, Appleton, 1969.

Collections: *Le Libertinage* (includes essays, creative work, and a play), Nouvelle Revue Francais, 1924; *Aragon, Poet of the French Resistance* (includes translations of wartime poetry and prose and critical essays on Aragon), edited by Hanna Josephson and Malcolm Cowley, Duell, Sloane & Pearce, 1945 (published in England as *Aragon: Poet of Re-*

surgent France, Pilot Press, 1946); *Aragon* (selections), edited and a critical essay by Claude Roy, P. Seghers, 1959; *L'Un ne va pas sans l'autre: Un perpetuel printemps suivi de paroles a Saint Denis* (poetry and address), privately printed, 1959; *La Diane francaise suivi de en etrange pays dans mon pay lui-meme* (contains "The French Diana" and "In a Strange Country in My Own Country"), P. Seghers, 1962; *Anicet; ou, Le panorama* [and] *Le Libertinage,* Laffont, 1964; *Oeuvres romanesques croisees d'Elsa Triolet et Aragon* (complete works of Aragon and his wife, Elsa Triolet), 38 volumes, Laffont, 1964—; *Aragon* (selected works), edited and introduction by George Sadoul, P. Seghers, 1967; *Les Yeux d'Elsa suivi de la Diane francaise* (contains "The Eyes of Elsa" and "The French Diana"), P. Seghers, 1968.

Nonfiction: *Traite du style* (literary criticism and surrealist manifesto), Nouvelle Revue Francaise, 1928; *La Peinture au defi* (essays), Editions Surrealists, 1930; *Pour un realisme socialiste* (lectures), Denoel & Steele, 1935; (with others) *Authors Take Sides on the Spanish War,* Left Review (London), 1937; *En Francais dan le texte* (essay), Ides et Calendes (Paris), 1943; *Le Crime contre l'esprit (les martyrs) par le temoin des martyrs,* Editions de Minuit, 1944; *Apologie de luxe* (art criticism), Skira (Geneva, Switzerland), 1946; *L'Enseigne de Gersaint* (essays), Ides et Calendes, 1946; *L'Homme communiste* (title means "The Communist Man"), Gallimard, Volume I, 1946, Volume II, 1953; *Chroniques du bel canto* (essays and lectures), Skira, 1947; *La Culture et les hommes* (essays), Editions Sociales (Paris), 1947; *Hugo, poete realiste* (literary criticism), Editions Sociales, 1952; *L'Example de Courbet* (art criticism), Cercle d'Art (Paris), 1952; *Le Neveu de M. Duval, suivi d'un lettre d'icelui a l'auteur de ce livre* (title means "The Nephew of M. Duval, Followed by a Letter from Him to the Author of This Book"). Editeurs Francais Reunis, 1953; *Journal d'une poesie nationale* (critical anthology), Ecrivains Reunis (Lyons), 1954; *La Lumiere de Stendhal* (essays and lectures), Denoel, 1954; *Litteratures sovietiques* (essays and lectures), Denoel, 1955; *J'Abats mon jeu* (esssys), Editeurs Francais Reunis, 1959; (with Maurice Thorez) *Il faut appeler les choses par leur nom* [and] *Problemes de notre epoque* (addresses; the former by Aragon, the latter by Thorez), Parti Communiste Francaise, 1959.

(With Andre Maurois) *Histoire parallele* (historical study of the United States and the Soviet Union; Aragon author of Volume I and Volume II and co-author of Volume IV), four volumes, Presses de la Cite, 1962, updated edition published in five volumes as *Les Deux Geants: Histoire des Etats-Unis et de l'U.R.S.S. de 1917 a nos jours,* Editions du Pont Royal (Paris), 1962-64, translation of Volume I and Volume II by Patrick O'Brian published as *A History of the U.S.S.R. from Lenin to Khrushchev,* two volumes, McKay, 1964, Volume I and Volume II also published in three volumes as *Histoire de l'U.R.S.S., 1917-1960,* Union Generale d'Editions (Paris), 1972; *Les Collages* (criticism), Hermann (Paris), 1965; (with others) *Dictionnaire abrege du Surrealisme,* new edition (Aragon not associated with earlier edition), Corti (Paris), 1969; *Je n'ai jamais appris a ecrire ou les incipit,* Skira, 1969.

Author of preface or introduction: (Under pseudonym Francois La Colere) Jean Cassou, *33 Sonnets composes au secret,* Editions de la Baconniere, 1946; Andre Fougerson, *Dessins,* Les 13 Epis (Paris), 1947; Pablo Picasso, *Sculptures et dessins* (exhibition catalogue), Maison de la Pensee Francaise (Paris), 1952; (and of reviews) IUrii IAnovs'kyi, *Les Cavaliers,* Gallimard, 1957; Fernand Leger, *Contrastes: 13 Aquarelles,* Au Vent d'Arles (Paris), 1959; *Marc Cha-*

gall: Recent Paintings, 1966-68 (exhibition catalogue), Pierre Matisse Gallery (New York), 1968.

Other: (Translator) Louis Carroll, *La Chasse au snark, une agonie en huit crises,* Hours Press, 1928; (contributor) Gabriel Peri, *Toward Singing Tomorrows,* International Publishers, 1946; (translator and author of preface) *Cinq Sonnets de Petrarque,* A la Fontaine de Vaucluse, 1947; (contributor) *Henri Matisse,* Philadelphia Museum of Art, 1948; (editor and author of commentaries) *Avez vous la Victor Hugo?,* Editeurs Francais Reunis, 1952; (editor and author of preface) *Introduction aux litteratures sovietiques: Contes et nouvelles,* Gallimard, 1956; (with Jean Cocteau) *Entretiens sur la musee de Dresde,* Cercle d'Art, 1957; (translator) Tchinghiz Aitmatov, *Djamilia,* Editeurs Francais Reunis, 1959; (editor and author of critical essay) *Elsa Triolet choisie par Aragon,* Gallimard, 1960; *Entretiens avec Francois Cremieux* (ten radio interviews), Gallimard, 1964; (contributor) Roger H. Guerrand, *L'Art nouveau en Europe,* Plon (Paris), 1965; *Aragon parle avec Dominique Arban,* P. Seghers, 1968; *Fernand Sequin recontre Louis Aragon,* Editions de l'Homme (Montreal), 1969.

SIDELIGHTS: While Aragon is above all a poet, he has also established other reputations—as a novelist, as a founder of surrealism and dadaism, as a literary spokesman for communism, and as a patriot and intellectual leader of the underground resistance to the Nazi occupation of France in World War II. His Russian-born wife, Elsa Triolet, the sister-in-law of the Russian poet Mayakovsky, and herself a writer, was a life-long source of inspiration to him, and the subject of many of his poems.

His involvement with communism, which began in 1927, resulted in his break with the surrealist movement in 1933. During World War II his poems of resistance, published by the underground, deeply stirred many French people and became symbolic of the swelling of French patiotism after the crushing defeat of 1940. He emerged from the war a national hero.

A striking aspect of his work has been its sheer volume. The *New York Times Book Review* pointed out that Aragon has "written a seemingly endless flow of words—over 60 books, including novels, his excellent lyrics, history, [and] reviews. . . ."

J. W. Kneller observed: "The case of Louis Aragon is one of the most controversial in contemporary French letters. Aside from political matters, he has been a source of disagreement among critics on purely literary grounds. Some consider him one of the most gifted writers of his generation. Others call him an elegant failure—a *precieus* who, for reasons of his own, has refused to write the poetry for which he is best suited by nature."

BIOGRAPHICAL/CRITICAL SOURCES: Yale Review, September, 1945; *Transformation,* III, 1945; Malcolm Cowley and Hannah Josephson, editors, *Aragon: Poet of the French Resistance,* Duell, Sloan & Pearce, 1945; *Yale French Studies,* fall-winter, 1948; *French Review,* December, 1952, May, 1965; Germaine Brie and Margaret O. Guitor, *An Age of Fiction: The French Novel from Gide to Camus,* Rutgers University Press, 1957; Stanley Burnsham, editor, *The Poem Itself,* Holt, 1960; Catherine Savage, *Malraux, Sartre, and Aragon as Political Novelists,* University of Florida Press, 1965; M. Adereth, *Commitment in Modern French Literature: Politics and Society in Peguy, Aragon, and Sartre,* Schocken, 1968; Lucille Becker, *Louis Aragon,* Twayne, 1971; *Contemporary Literary Criticism,* Volume 3, Gale, 1975.*

ARBUZOV, Alexei Nikolaevich 1908-

PERSONAL: Born May 26, 1908, in Moscow, U.S.S.R. *Education:* Educated in Leningrad at Theatrical School, 1922-23. *Address:* c/o Union of Soviet Writers, 52 Ulitsa Vorovskogo, Moscow, U.S.S.R.

CAREER: Actor, director, and dramatist in Moscow and Leningrad, U.S.S.R. Worked with mime group and as stage manager, 1923-30; traveled with Communist Party touring company, 1930, and became associated with Proletkult Theatre in Moscow; also worked on collective farm-theatre before becoming serious playwright, 1934—; organizer with V. N. Pluchek of Moscow Theatrical Studio, 1938. *Wartime service:* Took Moscow Theatrical Studio to front for performances during World War II. *Member:* Union of Soviet Writers. *Awards, honors:* Order of Red Banner of Labor, 1958, 1968.

WRITINGS—Plays: Shestero liubimykh (title means "Six Loved Ones"), Iskusstvo, 1936, 1958; *Evropeiskaia khronika* (title means "European Chronicle"), Iskusstvo, 1953; *Tania* (title means "Tania"), Iskusstvo, 1954, 1967; *Domik na okraine* (title means "Little House in the Outskirts"), Iskusstvo, 1956; *P'esy* (title means "Plays"), Sovietsky Pisatel, 1957; *Dal'niaia doroga* (title means "The Longest Road"), Iskusstvo, 1958.

Dvenadsatyi chas (title means "The Twelfth Hour"), Iskusstvo, 1960; *Irkutskaia istoriia,* Sovietskaia Rossiia, 1960, Vsesoiuznoe upravlenie po okhrane avtorskikh prav, 1963, annotated edition in Russian with introduction in English published as *An Irkutsk Story,* Pitman, 1963; *Teatr* (title means "Theater"), collected plays, Sovietsky Pisatel, 1961; *Moi bednyi Marat* (title means "My Poor Marat"), Vsesoiuznoe upravlenie po okhrane avtorskikh prav, 1965, translation by Ariadne Nicolaeff published as *The Promise* (first produced in London; produced on Broadway at the Henry Miller Theater, 1967), Oxford University Press, 1967; *Neozhidannaia osen'* (title means "The Unexpected Autumn"), Vsesoiuznoe upravlenie po okhrane avtorskikh prav, 1965; *Poteriannyi syn* (title means "The Lost Son"), Vsesoiuznoe upravlenie po okhrane avtorskikh prav, 1966; *Nochnaia ispoved',* Vsesoiuznoe upravlenie po okhrane avtorskikh prav, 1967, translation by Nicolaeff published as *Confession at Night* (first produced in London at Nottingham Playhouse, 1968), Davis-Poynter, 1971; *Gorod na zare* (title means "City at Sunset"), Vsesoiuznoe upravlenie po okhrane avtorskikh prav, 1969; *Dramy* (title means "Plays"), Iskusstvo, 1969.

Gody strantsvii (title means "Years of Wandering"), Vsesoiuznoe upravlenie po okhrane avtorskikh prav, 1971; *Skazki starogo Arbata* (title means "Tales of Old Arbat"; first produced at Drama Theater, Moscow, 1970), Vsesoiuznoe upravlenie po okhrane avtorskikh prav, 1971.

Other: (Edited by Vladimir Fedorovich Pimenov) *O trude dramaturga* (title means "On the Work of a Playwright"), Iskusstvo, 1957.*

* * *

ARDALAN, Nader 1939-

PERSONAL: Born March 9, 1939, in Tehran, Iran; son of Abbas (an economist) and Faranguis (Davar) Ardalan; married Laleh Mehree Bakhtiar (a writer), June 11, 1960 (divorced); children: Mani, Iran, Karim. *Education:* Carnegie Institute of Technology (now Carnegie-Mellon University), B.Arch., 1961; Harvard University, M.Arch., 1962. *Religion:* Moslem. *Home:* Saman Iran Dne, Apt. 65, Boulevard Elizabeth, Tehran, Iran. *Office:* Mandala Collaborative, Architects & Planners, 33/35 Kushk St., Tehran, Iran.

CAREER: Architect and principal of Mandala Collaborative, Architects & Planners, Tehran, Iran; associate professor of fine arts faculty at Tehran University, Tehran. Visiting critic at Yale University; lecturer at Harvard University, University of California at Los Angeles and Berkeley, Princeton University, and University of Pennsylvania. Participant in National Museum of Design (New York) opening exhibition; jury member of International Architectural Competition in Tehran. Official adviser to government of Iran, to expansion project in Mecca (Saudi Arabia), and to King Abdol Aziz University.

WRITINGS: (With wife, Laleh Mehree Bakhtiar) *The Sense of Unity,* University of Chicago Press, 1973; (with Jose Luis Sert, Moshe Safdie, and B. V. Doshi) *Habitat Bill of Rights,* Ham Dami Foundation (Tehran), 1976.

WORK IN PROGRESS: The History and Construction of the Holy Kaaba, Mecca.

SIDELIGHTS: Ardalan predicted: "After a period of forgetfulness, in emulation of a world movement (particularly sensed in western Europe and North America) already underway, the Middle East will confront the absence of spirituality in the arts and in particular, architecture. If the confrontation is genuine, an ensuing architecture of great richness and profound purpose will result."

* * *

ARMSTRONG, Arthur Hilary 1909-

PERSONAL: Born August 13, 1909, in Hove, England; son of W. A. (a clergyman) and E. C. (Cripps) Armstrong; married Deborah Wilson, 1933; children: two sons, three daughters. *Education:* Cambridge University, B.A., 1932, M.A., 1935. *Office:* Department of Classics, Dalhousie University, Halifax, Nova Scotia, Canada.

CAREER: University College, Swansea, Wales, assistant lecturer in classics, 1936-39; Royal University of Malta, Valletta, professor of classics, 1939-43; Beaumont College, Old Windsor, Berkshire, England, classical sixth form master, 1943-46; University College, Cardiff, Wales, lecturer in Latin, 1946-50; University of Liverpool, Liverpool, England, Gladstone Professor of Greek, 1950-72, professor emeritus, 1972—; Dalhousie University, Halifax, Nova Scotia, Canada, Killam Senior Fellow, 1970-71, visiting professor of classics and philosophy, 1972—. Visiting professor, Manhattanville College, 1966. *Member:* British Academy (fellow, 1970), American Catholic Philosophical Association. *Awards, honors:* Acquinas Medal, American Catholic Philosophical Association, 1973.

WRITINGS: The Architecture of the Intelligible Universe in the Philosophy of Plotinus: An Analytical and Historical Study, Cambridge University Press, 1940; (translator) *Plotinus,* Allen & Unwin, 1953, Collier, 1962; *An Introduction to Ancient Philosophy,* Methuen, 1947, 4th edition, Methuen, 1966; (with R. A. Markus) *Christian Faith and Greek Philosophy,* Darton, Longman & Todd, 1960, Sheed, 1964; (editor with E.J.B. Fry) *Re-discovering Eastern Christiandom: Essays in Commemoration of Dom Bede Winslow,* Darton, Longman & Todd, 1963; (translator) *Plotinus,* three volumes, Harvard University Press, 1966-67; *St. Augustine and Christian Platonism,* Villanova University Press, 1967; (editor) *The Cambridge History of Later Greek and Early Medieval Philosophy,* Cambridge University Press, 1967; *The Church of England, the Methodists and Society: 1700 to*

1850, Rowman & Littlefield, 1973. Contributor to professional journals, including *Classical Quarterly, Mind, Journal of Hellenic Studies, Journal of Theological Studies,* and *Downside Review.*

AVOCATIONAL INTERESTS: Travel, gardening.*

* * *

ARMSTRONG, Brian G(ary) 1936-

PERSONAL: Born August 1, 1936, in Guys Mills, Pa.; son of Ray H. (a lumberman) and Donna (Winans) Armstrong; married Carol Demarest (a professor), June 20, 1959; children: Brett Gregory, Curt Jeffrey. *Education:* Houghton College, A.B., 1958; Gordon Divinity School, B.D., 1961; Princeton Theological Seminary, Th.M., 1962, Ph.D., 1967. *Religion:* Presbyterian. *Home:* 5461 Walker Rd., Stone Mountain, Ga. 30088. *Office:* Department of History, Georgia State University, Atlanta, Ga. 30303.

CAREER: Georgia State University, Atlanta, assistant professor, 1967-70, associate professor of early modern European history, 1970—, assistant dean of College of Arts, 1974—. Member of board of directors of Historical Foundation of the Presbyterian and Reformed Churches. *Member:* American Historical Association, American Society for Reformation Research, American Society of Church History, Renaissance Society of America, Sixteenth Century Studies Conference, Societe de l'etude du dix-septieme siecle, Southern Historical Association, Friends of the French Protestant Library (Paris). *Awards, honors:* American Council of Learned Societies fellowship, Geneva, Switzerland, 1973-74.

WRITINGS: Calvinism and the Amyraut Heresy, University of Wisconsin Press, 1969. Contributor of articles and reviews to academic journals.

WORK IN PROGRESS: A book on Pierre du Moulin, 1568-1658; research on the history of thought in seventeenth-century France, relating the new science and new philosophy especially to the intellectual tradition of the French Calvinists.

SIDELIGHTS: Armstrong writes: "I am concerned particularly with the general principle that meaningful action and practice must spring from carefully-developed theoretical frameworks. Hence I find life fulfilling and meaningful at the point where it is clear that clear, identifiable reasons exist for any action, reasons which are recognized and applauded by rational men. I'm also deeply concerned to see how different cultures respond theoretically to problems. I have concentrated on the 'Great Century' in France (the seventeenth century) and have traveled extensively in France and French-speaking European countries."

AVOCATIONAL INTERESTS: All sports.

* * *

ARMSTRONG, Christopher J(ohn) R(ichard) 1935-
(Anthony C. Armstrong)

PERSONAL: Born June 16, 1935, in Cambridge, England; son of Arthur Hilary (a university professor) and Deborah Pease (Wilson) Armstrong; married Meriel P. L. Moir, September 2, 1967; children: Bridget. *Education:* Attended Pontifical University, Salamanca, Spain, 1958-59; University of Fribourg, lic. theology, 1961; Christ's College, Cambridge, M.A., 1964; attended Cambridge University and Sorbonne, University of Paris, 1965-68. *Home:* Bredenbury Rectory, Bromyard, Herefordshire HR7 4TF, England.

CAREER: Ordained priest of Church of England, 1959; University of Aberdeen, Aberdeen, Scotland, lecturer in French language and literature, 1968-74; assistant priest of Church of England in Ledbury, England, 1974-76; Bredenbury Rectory, Bromyard, England, parish priest for parishes of Bredenbury, Wacton, Thornbury, Edvyn Ralph, Collington, Pencombe, and Little Cowarne, 1976—.

WRITINGS: (Translator, under pseudonym Anthony C. Armstrong) Philippe dela Trinite, *What Is the Redemption?,* Burns & Oates, 1962; *Evelyn Underhill: An Introduction to Her Life and Writings,* Mowbray, 1975, Eerdmans, 1976; (contributor) Peter Sharratt, editor, *French Renaissance Studies, 1540-70: Humanism and the Encyclopedia,* Edinburgh University Press, 1976. Contributor to *Downside Review* and *Aberdeen University Review.*

WORK IN PROGRESS: Renaissance studies and research on Christian theology.

SIDELIGHTS: Armstrong comments: "I had no ambition to embark on biography. My encounter with Evelyn Underhill was, for me, a happy accident. I have learnt a number of things from the experience, about myself, about publishers, about mysticism. I suspect that the art of biography aspires to the art of writing novels, which in its turn, aspires to the art of writing gospels. It is the last of these arts which is supreme—and least understood."

AVOCATIONAL INTERESTS: The wilderness, music, cinema, beekeeping, making cider, "talking with bookdealers."

* * *

ARNOLD, Richard K(lein) 1923-

PERSONAL: Born August 15, 1923, in San Francisco, Calif.; son of Maxwell (a hotel owner) and Lela (Klein) Arnold; married Mary Louise Blair, June 19, 1946; children: William Maxwell. *Education:* Stanford University, A.B., 1948. *Residence:* Portola Valley, Calif. *Office:* Arnold & Palmer & Noble, Inc., 150 Post St., San Francisco, Calif. 94108.

CAREER: Consultants, Inc. (public relations firm), San Francisco, Calif., vice-president, 1951-60; Guild, Bascom & Bonfigli (advertising agency), San Francisco, Calif., copy chief, 1960-61; Public Relations Counselors, San Francisco, Calif., executive vice-president, 1961-63; Arnold & Palmer Associates, San Francisco, Calif., partner, 1963-67; Arnold & Palmer & Noble, Inc. (public relations firm), San Francisco, Calif., president and chairman of board of directors, 1967—. Guest lecturer at University of California, Berkeley, San Francisco State University, and San Jose State University. Member of Support for Promoting the Utilization of Resources (SPUR) and Committee for Green Foothills. *Military service:* U.S. Navy Reserve, active duty, 1943-46; served in Pacific theater; became lieutenant, junior grade.

MEMBER: Public Relations Society of America, Sierra Club, Navy League, California Historical Society, Sigma Nu, Bohemian Club, Hammer and Coffin.

WRITINGS: Call It Frisco (libretto for musical play), Grabhorn-Hoyem, 1972; (editor) *Adams to Jefferson and Jefferson to Adams* (history), Jericho Press, 1975.

Also writer of musical plays, "Sweet Executive," 1958; "The Khan Game," 1963; "Back at the Front," 1966; "Fifty-Fifty," 1967.

Work anthologized in *Stanford Short Stories, 1948,* edited by Wallace Stegner, Stanford University Press, 1948; *Stan-*

ford Short Stories, 1949, edited by Stegner, Stanford University Press, 1949; *Poets of the Pacific,* edited by Yvor Winters, Stanford University Press, 1949.

WORK IN PROGRESS: Research on the 1930's for a book and lyrics of a musical play.

SIDELIGHTS: Arnold writes: "My literary career—such as it is—has been achieved on time borrowed or stolen from my business and family obligations and from my leisure time. I'm more a musical comedy librettist than anything else, probably because the form combines my interest in both poetry and prose and in the American Popular Song. My librettos have also reflected my deep interest in American history (as did the Adams-Jefferson book). I write to express my own particular visions of the human comedy/tragedy—and if economics allowed, I would attempt that expression more regularly."

* * *

ARNOSKY, Jim 1946-

PERSONAL: Born September 1, 1946, in New York, N.Y.; son of Edward J. (a draftsman) and Marie (Telesco) Arnosky; married Deanna L. Eshleman, August 6, 1966; children: Michelle L., Amber L. *Education:* Attended high school in Pennsylvania. *Residence:* South Ryegate, Vermont.

CAREER: Draftsman in Philadelphia, Pa., 1964; Braceland Brothers (printers), Philadelphia, Pa., art trainee, 1965-66, creative artist, 1968-72; free-lance illustrator and writer, 1972—. *Military service:* U.S. Navy, 1966-68.

*WRITINGS—*Self-illustrated children's books: *I Was Born in a Tree and Raised by Bees,* Putnam, 1977; *Outdoors on Foot,* Coward, 1977; *Nathaniel,* Addison-Wesley, in press.

Illustrator: Melvin and Gilda Berger, *Fitting In: Animals in Their Habitats,* Coward, 1976; Miska Miles, *Swim, Little Duck,* Atlantic Monthly Press, 1976; Miles, *Chicken Forgets,* Atlantic Monthly Press, 1976; Miles, *Small Rabbit,* Atlantic Monthly Press, 1977; Marcel Sislowitz, *Look: How Your Eyes See,* Coward, 1977.

WORK IN PROGRESS: Writing and illustrating *Beartracks, Buckrubs and Beaver Patties,* for children; illustrating *Porcupine Baby,* by Berniece L. Freschet, for children; writing and illustrating *Freshwater Fishing with Jim Arnosky,* for children.

SIDELIGHTS: Arnosky writes: "I had no formal art training but learned a great deal about drawing from my dad who is a skillful patent draftsman. With this training at home I began working in the art field as a trainee.... It wasn't until I had been on my own freelancing in illustration for nearly five years that I was introduced to the writing end of books.... Like solid, well-written poetry, writing for children emphasizes structure and the need for every word to count.

"I have always had a deep connection with the natural world and find its rhythm close to my own. I think of myself as an artist/naturalist. Most of my close friends are working naturalists, teachers, writers, photographers, farmers, and woodsmen. For four and a half years my wife, my two daughters, and I lived in a tiny cabin at the base of Hawk Mountain in Pennsylvania. There I matured as a writer and illustrator of natural subjects.... We have made our home in the hills of northern Vermont because its natural pace of life fits our needs best as a family and mine as a writer and illustrator.

"My books are autobiographical. I have difficulty contriving a story that doesn't come from a personal experience. (I admire writers who can.) The character Crinkleroot is a vehicle I use to express the teacher and father in me. He is an old grandfatherly woodsman who knows endless wonders about the natural world and teaches them to his readers through activities they can join in. The character Nathaniel is a caricature of the everyday part of me. He is a countryman. A gardener and outdoorsman. His individual approaches to living in the country sometimes lead into predicaments. Most of Nathaniel's wordless adventures are based on experiences of my own. Nathaniel's stories are wordless because, like myself, Nathaniel feels no need to talk when he's off on a walk or busy building or working around the farm. He is a perfect vehicle for me to share some of my own everyday adventures with youngsters."

AVOCATIONAL INTERESTS: Leisurely walking, growing food, fishing, watching wildlife, "thinking, listening, worrying, and smiling."

* * *

ARNOW, L(eslie) Earle 1909-

PERSONAL: Born June 22, 1909, in Micanopy, Fla.; son of Joseph Leslie and Mable Annie (Thrasher) Arnow; married Jennie McLemore Martin, July 17, 1933 (died September 19, 1976); children: Peter Leslie. *Education:* University of Florida, Ph.G. and B.S., 1930; University of Minnesota, Ph.D., 1934, M.B. and M.D., 1940. *Home:* 14 Fairfield Dr., Convent Station, N.J. 07961.

CAREER: University of Minnesota, Minneapolis, instructor, 1934-40, assistant professor of physiological chemistry, 1940-42; Sharp & Dohme, Inc., West Point, Pa., director of biochemical research in Medical Research Division, 1942-44, director of research for the company, 1944-53; Merck & Co., Inc., West Point and Rahway, N.J., vice-president and director of research for Sharp & Dohme Division, 1953-56; vice-president of Merck Sharp & Dohme Research Laboratories and executive director of Merck Institute for Therapeutic Research, both 1956-58; Warner-Lambert Co., Morris Plains, N.J., vice-president, and president of Warner-Lambert Research Institute, 1958-65, president of Warner-Lambert Research Institute of Canada, 1965, senior scientific consultant, 1965-74; writer, 1974—.

MEMBER: American Association for the Advancement of Science (fellow), American Society for Clinical Pharmacology and Therapeutics, American Chemical Society, American Medical Association, American Society of Biological Chemists, Society for Experimental Biology and Medicine, Association of Research Directors, New York Academy of Sciences (fellow), Medical Society of New Jersey, Morris County Medical Society, Morris County Golf Club, Philadelphia Art Alliance, Phi Beta Kappa, Sigma Xi, Alpha Omega Alpha, Gamma Sigma Epsilon, Rho Chi, Phi Sigma, Alpha Epsilon Delta, Sigma Chi, Phi Beta Pi, Gamma Alpha. *Awards, honors:* Centennial award from University of Florida, 1953; outstanding achievement award from University of Minnesota, 1955; award from Philadelphia Science Council, 1958.

WRITINGS: Introduction to Laboratory Chemistry, Mosby, 1939, 9th edition, 1976; *Introduction to Physiological and Pathological Chemistry,* Mosby, 1939, 9th edition, 1976; (with H. C. Reitz) *Introduction to Organic and Biological Chemistry,* Mosby, 1943, 2nd edition, 1949; *Health in a Bottle: Searching for the Drugs That Help,* Lippincott, 1970; *Food Power: A Doctor's Guide to Commonsense Nutrition,* Nelson-Hall, 1972.

Also author of cassette tape recordings, published by Spenco Medical Corp., 1976, "The Story Behind All Prescription Drugs," "Lose That Ugly Fat Forever," and "Eating Our Way to Heart Attacks." Contributor of about sixty articles to technical journals.

* * *

ASHLEY, Michael (Raymond Donald) 1948-

PERSONAL: Born October 1, 1948, in Southall, Middlesex, England; son of Albert Cecil (a laboratory technician) and Ada (Locke) Ashley; married Susan Mary Ogilvie (an audio-typist), July 6, 1972. *Education:* Maidstone College of Further Education, ONC in Public Administration, 1970. *Home:* 59 Watson's Hill, Sittingbourne, Kent, England. *Agent:* Cosmos, 32 Tynedale Ave., Wallsend, Tyne and Wear, England.

CAREER: Kent County Highway Department, Kent, England, local government official, 1967—. Writer.

WRITINGS: The History of the Science Fiction Magazine, includes representative examples from other authors edited by Ashley, New English Library, Volume I: *1926-35,* 1974, Regnery, 1976, Volume II: *1936-45,* 1975, Regnery, 1976, Volume III: *1946-55,* 1976, Volume IV: *1956-65,* in press; (contributor) Brian Ash, editor, *The Visual Encyclopedia of Science Fiction,* Trewin Copplestone, 1977.

Editor, except as noted: *Weird Legacies,* Star, 1977; *Souls in Metal,* St. Martin's, 1977; *Science Fiction Choice,* Quartet, 1977; *The Best of the British,* two volumes, Dobson, 1977; (compiler) *Who's Who in Horror and Fantasy Fiction,* Elm Tree, 1977; *Splinters from the Mind,* Dobson, in press.

Contributor of articles to *Science Fiction Monthly* and to *Dark Horizons* (journal of the British Fantasy Society).

WORK IN PROGRESS: The History of the Science Fiction Magazine, Volume V: *1966 To the Present,* publication expected in 1979; research on modern horror fiction for a number of books; a science fantasy, an historical fantasy, and a comic novel; a critical index to the leading popular magazines of the turn of the century; biographies of leading science fiction writers.

SIDELIGHTS: Ashley told *CA:* "My main delight is doing research and making facts as thorough as possible. I hate gaps in knowledge. I am appalled at the slipshod 'research' evident in the science fiction/horror/fantasy fields where most people take facts for granted and constantly repeat errors. There are a great many writers in these fields who are undeservedly overlooked. I want to research their writings and resurrect their names."

* * *

ASHLEY, Rosalind Minor 1923-

PERSONAL: Born October 10, 1923, in Chicago, Ill.; daughter of Jack (a salesman) and Frances (Wasser) Minor; married Charles Ashley (a vice-president in sales), March 1, 1942; children: Stephen David, Richard Arthur. *Education:* Attended Moser Business College, University of Illinois, 1956-57, and Roosevelt University, 1957-58; Northwestern University, B.S., 1963; graduate study at Northeastern Illinois University and National College of Education. *Home:* 724 Becker Rd., Glenview, Ill. 60025.

CAREER: Secretary in Chicago, Ill., 1942-46; WEAW-Radio, Evanston, Ill., co-producer and performer, 1955-56; elementary school teacher in Evanston, 1963-68, and Wilmette, Ill., 1968-70; Scott, Foresman & Co., Glenview, Ill.,

associate editor in language arts, 1970-72; volunteer worker for National Cancer Society, 1975—. *Member:* Alpha Sigma Lambda.

WRITINGS—All published by Parker Publishing: (Editor) Marion Monroe, *Language and How to Use It: Beginning Levels,* with record, 1970; *Successful Techniques for Teaching Elementary Language Arts* (Macmillan Book Club selection), 1970; *Activities for Motivating and Teaching Bright Children* (Instructor Book Club selection), 1973; *Simplified Teaching Techniques and Materials for Flexible Group Instruction,* 1976; *Portfolio of Daily Classroom Activities, with Model Lesson Plans,* in press. Author of radio scripts. Contributor of articles and a poem to education journals and to *Feline Defenders.*

SIDELIGHTS: Rosalind Ashley writes: "I enjoy writing for teachers, and hope to improve the teaching and learning experiences for teachers and students by making lessons relevant and interesting. It is also important to me to provide materials and ideas that will teach practical skills and stimulate new ideas. I want to provide new, different, *useful* lessons.

"I plan to continue writing. I have written two novels as well as poetry and children's stories. I would like to write screen plays for educational films. Also, I hope to continue creating original games and simulation games."

AVOCATIONAL INTERESTS: Reading, tennis, belly dancing, cooking, golf, table tennis, painting, gardening, bowling, latch hooking tapestries, knitting, sewing, cats, travel (United States, England, France, Italy, Portugal, Switzerland, Greece, Spain, Hawaii, Turkey, the Caribbean, the Orient).

* * *

ASHTON-WARNER, Sylvia (Constance) 1908-
(Sylvia Henderson, Sylvia)

PERSONAL: Born December 17, 1908, in Stratford, New Zealand; married Keith Dawson Henderson (a teacher). *Education:* Attended Wairarapa College, Masterton, New Zealand, and Teachers' College, Auckland, New Zealand, 1928-29. *Home:* Whenua, 5-9 Levers Rd., Otumoetai, Tuaranga, New Zealand. *Agent:* Monica McCall, International Creative Management, 1301 Avenue of the Americas, New York, N.Y. 10019.

CAREER: Novelist. Taught at several country schools in New Zealand; former professor of education at Aspen Community School Teaching Center, Aspen, Colo.

WRITINGS—Novels: *Spinster,* Simon & Schuster, 1959; *Incense to Idols,* Simon & Schuster, 1960; *Teacher,* Simon & Schuster, 1963; *Bell Call,* Simon & Schuster, 1964; *Greenstone,* Simon & Schuster, 1967; *Three,* Knopf, 1970.

Autobiography: *Myself,* Simon & Schuster, 1967; *Spearpoint: Teacher in America,* Knopf, 1972.

Contributor of short stories, sometimes under names Sylvia and Sylvia Henderson, and of poetry to *New Zealand Listener, New Zealand Monthly Review,* and other periodicals.

SIDELIGHTS: Together with her husband, Ashton-Warner taught Maori children in country schools in New Zealand for a number of years, and much of her subject matter, fictional and otherwise, is based on her experiences at that time. She devised new teaching methods in reaction to some children's readers entitled *Janet and John* (the New Zealand equivalent to the American "Dick and Jane") that she felt were patently unsuited to Maori needs. Elizabeth

Janeway wrote that Ashton-Warner's methods, essentially based on the importance of personal communication, "seem to me a real and important contribution to the new approach to education our society so desperately needs."

"She is really a much more successful teacher than she represents herself to be," contended Sister M. Marguerite, "and [in her autobiography *Myself*] she traces her development with a humility and insight that show her to be—what most geniuses are—a simple and sincere personality," though John Holt cautioned that "Ashton-Warner is, after all, an authority with a big following, and her ideas should not be uncritically accepted. More explicitly than she has ever said before, she says [in *Myself*] that our aim in educating children must be to bring together, to integrate, their inner and outer life, so that they will be at peace with themselves and others. Feeling as I do that the violence and irrationality of our public life reflects the disorder of our inner lives, I agree. But I disagree completely with her view that this integration is to be brought about by teachers exerting a kind of magic spell over children."

A British film, "Two Loves" (1961), was based on one of her novels.

BIOGRAPHICAL/CRITICAL SOURCES: Sylvia Ashton-Warner, *Myself*, Simon & Schuster, 1967; *Best Sellers*, October 1, 1967; *New York Times Book Review*, October 8, 1967; *Life*, November 3, 1967; *Landfall*, September, 1969; *New York Times*, May 22, 1970; Ashton-Warner, *Spearpoint: Teacher in America*, Knopf, 1972.*

*　　*　　*

ASTRACHAN, Samuel 1934-

PERSONAL: Born January 4, 1934, in New York, N.Y.; son of Isaac (a physician) and Ethel (Kagan) Astrachan; married Claude Jeanneau (a sculptor), March 25, 1959; children: Isaac. *Education:* Columbia University, B.A., 1955. *Home:* 84220, Gordes, France. *Agent:* Elaine Markson, Elaine Markson Literary Agency, 44 Greenwich Ave., New York, N.Y. 10011.

CAREER: Northern Illinois University, De Kalb, writer-in-residence, 1967-68; Marquette University, Milwaukee, Wis., writer-in-residence, 1968-69; Wayne State University, Detroit, Mich., writer-in-residence, winters, 1971—. *Military service:* U.S. Army, 1957-59. *Member:* P.E.N. Club. *Awards, honors: Partisan Review* fellowship, 1957.

*WRITINGS—*All novels: *An End to Dying*, Farrar, Straus, 1956; *The Game of Dostoevsky*, Farrar, Straus, 1965; *Rejoice*, Dial, 1970; *Katz-Cohen*, Macmillan, in press.

*　　*　　*

ATHERTON, Pauline 1929-

PERSONAL: Born December 2, 1929, in Berwyn, Ill.; daughter of John and Ann (Jakovich) Blazina; divorced; children: Linda Myers. *Education:* Illinois College, A.B., 1951; Rosary College, M.A., 1954; graduate study at University of Chicago, 1955-70. *Home:* K-3, 126 Jamesville Ave., Syracuse, N.Y. 13201. *Office:* School of Information Studies, Syracuse University, 113 Euclid Ave., Syracuse, N.Y. 13210.

CAREER: Chicago Teachers College, Chicago, Ill., acting reference librarian, 1956-58, assistant professor of library science, 1958-61; Field Enterprises Educational Corp., Chicago, cross reference editor of *World Book Encyclopedia*, 1958-59; American Institute of Physics, New York, N.Y., associate director of documentation, 1961-66; Syracuse

University, Syracuse, N.Y., professor of library science, 1966—. Consulting librarian, Rodfei Zedek Congressional Library, Chicago, 1960-61; consultant, *World Book Encyclopedia*, 1960—; member of board, Salt City Playhouse, 1970-75. Consultant to UNESCO, National Library of Medicine, and others. *Member:* American Library Association, American Society for Information Science, Phi Beta Kappa.

WRITINGS: (Editor) *Classification Research*, Munksgard, 1965; *Putting Knowledge to Work*, Vikas (Delhi), 1973; *Guidelines for Education and Training Workshops in Scientific Information Work*, Unesco, 1975. Also author of pamphlets, including American Institute of Physics series, 1962-68. Contributor of articles and book reviews to journals in her field. Editor of newsletters and of two series for Syracuse University school of library science, 1972 and 1974.

WORK IN PROGRESS: A subject access project for Council on Library Resources; a book on computer-based reference service, for Knowledge Publications.

*　　*　　*

ATKESON, Ray A. 1907-

PERSONAL: Born February 13, 1907, in Grafton, Ill.; son of James M. (a farmer) and Danielle (Barber) Atkeson; married Mira E. Crane, June 14, 1930 (deceased); children: Eleanor J. Atkeson Schmeer. *Education:* Attended high school in Kansas City, Mo. *Politics:* Republican. *Religion:* Interdenominational. *Home and office:* 1675 Southwest Westwood Dr., Portland, Ore. 97201.

CAREER: Photo Art Commercial Studio, Portland, Ore., chief cameraman, 1929-46; free-lance photographer in Portland, 1946—. *Member:* Photographic Society of America, National Press Photographers Association. *Awards, honors:* Named distinguished citizen by the governor of Oregon; awarded Doctor of Fine Arts from Linfield College.

*WRITINGS—*Self-illustrated: *Ski and Snow*, U.S. Camera, 1961; *Northwest Heritage: Cascade Range*, Charles H. Belding, 1969; *Western Impressions*, Beautiful West Publishing, 1976. Contributor of photography to books by others. Contributor to photography, travel, and nature magazines.

WORK IN PROGRESS: The World of Mira Atkeson, a picture book with photographs by wife, Mira Atkeson.

AVOCATIONAL INTERESTS: Environmental issues ("involving preservation of nature wherever possible").

*　　*　　*

ATKINS, Paul Moody 1892-1977

April 3, 1892—January 31, 1977; American financial and management consultant, professor, and author. Atkins wrote books and articles on economics and business subjects. He died in Glen Ridge, N.J. Obituaries: *New York Times*, February 2, 1977.

*　　*　　*

ATKINSON, Anthony Barnes 1944-

PERSONAL: Born September 4, 1944, in Caerleon, England; son of Norman Joseph (a teacher) and Esther Muriel Atkinson; married Judith Mary Mandeville (a social worker), 1965; children: Richard, Sarah, Charles. *Education:* Churchill College, Cambridge, M.A., 1966. *Politics:* Socialist. *Residence:* Brightlingsea, Essex, England. *Agent:* Curtis Brown Ltd., Craven Hill, London, England. *Office:* Department of Political Economy, University College, University of London, London, England.

CAREER: Cambridge University, Cambridge, England, fellow of St. John's College, 1967-71; University of Essex, Colchester, England, professor of economics, 1971-76; University of London, London, England, professor of political economy, 1976—. Chairman of Colchester Poverty Action Group, 1972-73. *Member:* Econometric Society (fellow).

WRITINGS: Poverty in Britain and the Reform of Social Security, Cambridge University Press, 1969; *Unequal Shares: Wealth in Britain,* Penguin, 1972; *The Tax Credit Scheme and the Redistribution of Income,* Institute of Fiscal Studies, 1973; (editor) *Wealth, Income, and Inequality,* Penguin, 1973; *The Economics of Inequality,* Oxford University Press, 1975; (with A. J. Harrison) *The Distribution of Wealth in Britain,* Cambridge University Press, 1977. Editor of *Journal of Public Economics.*

WORK IN PROGRESS: Lectures on Public Economics, with J. E. Stiglitz, for McGraw.

SIDELIGHTS: Atkinson told *CA* his "work on income and wealth tries to apply professional skills to important economic and social problems."

* * *

ATTHILL, Robin 1912-

PERSONAL: Born March 7, 1912, in Netherhampton, Salisbury, England; son of Robert Thomas (a schoolmaster) and Olive K. (Hill) Atthill; married Elizabeth Thackeray (an artist), April 12, 1939; children: Thomas, Charles, Catherine. *Education:* Trinity College, Oxford, B.A., 1935, M.A., 1938. *Religion:* Church of England. *Home:* Stoneleigh Cottage, Oakhill, Bath, Somerset BA3 5BG, England.

CAREER: Schoolmaster, teaching English and classics, in Ampleforth, York, England, 1935-42, and Sherborne, Dorset, England, 1942-48; Downside School, Somerset, England, English master, 1948—.

WRITINGS: If Pity Departs (poems), Andrew Dakers, 1947; *The Curious Past,* Wessex Press, 1955; *Old Mendip,* David & Charles, 1964; *The Somerset and Dorset Railway,* David & Charles, 1967; *Picture History of the Somerset and Dorset Railway,* David & Charles, 1970; (editor and contributor) *Mendip,* David & Charles, 1976. Contributor to professional journals, and to *Country Life* and *West Country.*

WORK IN PROGRESS: Research on historical subjects.

SIDELIGHTS: Atthill writes: "I have lived most of my life on Mendip, and write about its historical significance and interest. Being a schoolmaster, I have had time to research and explore the environment in which I live in an attempt to understand it."

* * *

AULETTA, Ken 1942-

PERSONAL: Born April 23, 1942, in New York, N.Y. *Education:* State University of New York College, Oswego, B.S., 1963; Syracuse University, M.A., 1965. *Politics:* "Registered Independent." *Home:* 295 Central Park Ave. W., New York, N.Y. 10024. *Office: New York Daily News,* 220 East 42nd St., New York, N.Y. 10017; and *New Yorker,* 43 West 43rd St., New York, N.Y. 10017.

CAREER/WRITINGS: New York magazine, New York City, contributing editor, 1975-76; *Village Voice,* New York City, staff writer and weekly columnist, 1975-76; *New Yorker,* New York City, writer, 1976—; *New York Daily News,* New York City, political columnist, 1976—. Co-host of a weekly WNET-TV interview program, 1976—. Contrib-

utor of articles to *New York Times* and *More.* Notable assignments include coverage of the New York City fiscal crisis, the presidential campaign of Jimmy Carter, and the media. *Awards, honors:* Media award from the Bar Association, 1976; media award from the Public Relations Society of America, 1976, for an article on New York's fiscal crisis, and 1977, for an article outlining an agenda to save New York.

SIDELIGHTS: Auletta writes: "Most of my work is concerned with political and economic and governmental matters, though I do stray off and write of the media frequently. I very much enjoy having a regular magazine and newspaper outlet. Before resigning, that was the case at *New York* magazine and the *Voice;* it is again the case at the *New Yorker* and the *Daily News.* What I find is that the magazine work comes to represent those subjects that require more depth and thought and, because they afford more time, more careful writing. But magazines usually have a long leadtime and the journalistic impulse is often satisfied by newspapers. There one can break a story, experience the communal sweat and nervousness of a city room, react quickly. A newspaperman, like a firefighter, responds to alarms; a magazine writer can set off his own alarms. There are advantages to each. By having a career that combines newspaper and magazine work, I like to think I have the best of both worlds."

* * *

AUSTER, Paul 1947-

PERSONAL: Born February 3, 1947, in Newark, N.J.; married Lydia Davis (a writer); children: one. *Education:* Columbia University, B.A., 1969, M.A., 1970. *Residence:* Stanfordville, N.Y.

CAREER: Poet, 1970—. *Awards, honors:* Poetry grant from Ingram Merrill Foundation, 1975; P.E.N. Translation Center grant, 1977.

WRITINGS: Unearth: Poems, 1970-1972, Living Hand, 1974; (translator) Jacques Dupin, *Fits and Starts: Selected Poems of Jacques Dupin,* Living Hand, 1974; (translator with wife, Lydia Davis) Saul Friedlander and Mahmoud Hussein, *Arabs and Israelis: A Dialogue,* Holmes & Meier, 1975; *Wall Writing: Poems, 1971-1975,* Figures, 1976; "Eclipse" (play), first produced in New York City by Artists' Theatre, March, 1977. Also translator, with L. Davis, of *Life/Situations,* by Jean-Paul Sartre. Contributor of articles and translations of poetry to magazines, including *New York Review of Books, Commentary, Harper's, Tri-Quarterly,* and *Saturday Review.*

WORK IN PROGRESS: A new book of poems.

* * *

AUSTIN, Charles M(arshall) 1941-

PERSONAL: Born May 17, 1941, in Sioux City, Iowa; son of Wilbur T. and Anna (Swanson) Austin; married Janet Singer (a librarian), August 17, 1963; children: Adam Paul, Glenda Marie. *Education:* Midland Lutheran College, B.A., 1963; Lutheran School of Theology, Chicago, Ill., M.Div., 1967; Aquinas Institute, Dubuque, Iowa, M.Th., 1971. *Residence:* Geneva, Switzerland. *Agent:* Alexandria Hatcher, 150 West 55th St., New York, N.Y. *Office:* Lutheran World Federation, 150 Route de Ferney, 1211 Geneva, Switzerland.

CAREER: Ordained minister of Lutheran Church of America; *Proviso Herald,* Maywood, Ill., reporter, 1963-65;

pastor of Lutheran church in Dubuque, Iowa, 1967-70; Religious News Service, New York City, staff writer, 1970-71; Lutheran Council in the U.S.A. (LCUSA), New York City, staff writer, 1971-76; Lutheran World Federation, Geneva, Switzerland, director of News Bureau, 1976—. Free-lance journalist; photographer. *Member:* American Society of Journalists and Authors, Religion News Writers Association.

WRITINGS: Let the People Know, Augsburg, 1975. Contributor of several hundred articles and reviews to magazines.

WORK IN PROGRESS: Refugees: Political Prisoners.

AVOCATIONAL INTERESTS: The arts, current affairs, travel (Europe, Africa, Chile, Argentina, Brazil).

* * *

AUSUBEL, Herman 1920-1977

April 24, 1920—March 3, 1977; American history professor, authority on Victorian England, editor of Macmillan's "Historical Reconsiderations" series and Crowell's "Historical Classics" series, and author of books and contributor to journals in his field. He died in New York City. Obituaries: *New York Times,* March 4, 1977; *AB Bookman's Weekly,* June 20, 1977. (See index for previous *CA* sketch)

* * *

AVRIEL, Ehud 1917-

PERSONAL: Born October 19, 1917, in Vienna, Austria; son of Israel Uiberall (a factor) and Helena (a teacher; maiden name, Segel) Avriel; married Hannah Marie Eliasberg (a teacher), May 5, 1940; children: Dina Avriel Rosner, Dorith, Ruthi Avriel Asulin, Athalia. *Education:* Educated in secondary school in Vienna, Austria. *Politics:* Democrat. *Religion:* Jewish. *Home:* Neot Mordechai Magalil, Haelyon, Israel.

CAREER: Israel Foreign Service, Jerusalem, minister to Czechoslovakia, 1948, Hungary, 1949, and Rumania, 1950, director-general of prime minister's office in Jerusalem, 1951-57, director-general of Treasury, 1952-53, ambassador to Ghana and Liberia, 1957-61, and to the Congo, 1960-61, deputy director-general of African affairs and of Ministry of Foreign Affairs, 1961-66, ambassador to Italy and Malta, 1966-69, chairman of World Zionist Action Committee in Jerusalem, 1969-72, diplomatic adviser and ambassador extraordinary to Ministry of Foreign Affairs, 1972, consul-general to the Midwest, 1975—. Chairman of board of directors of Upper Galilee Development Corp.

WRITINGS: Open the Gates, Atheneum, 1975.

WORK IN PROGRESS: History of the Kibbutz; a book on the first thirty years of Israel's independence.

SIDELIGHTS: Avriel told *CA* he hopes "to acquaint the younger generation with the Hitler holocaust and with the struggle of the Jewish people for the right to exist in security." *Avocational interests:* Photography.

* * *

AVRUTIS, Raymond 1948-

PERSONAL: Born February 28, 1948, in Washington, D.C.; son of William J. (an attorney) and Adelaide (a bookkeeper; maiden name, Sofrance) Avrutis. *Education:* Attended Georgetown University, summer, 1965, and University of Virginia, Arlington, 1966-67; American University, B.A., 1970; New York University, M.A., 1975. *Politics:* "If

you're unemployed, run for a seat on your city or county council. You may do more good in public office than on unemployment or welfare." *Religion:* Jewish. *Home:* 9202 Piney Branch Rd., #102, Silver Spring, Md. 20903.

CAREER: Free-lance writer, 1966—; National Council on Crime and Delinquency, Washington, D.C., research writer, 1972. Guest on television and radio programs.

WRITINGS: How to Collect Unemployment Benefits: Complete Information for All Fifty States, Schocken, 1975. Contributor to *Daily Rag* (Washington, D.C., alternative newspaper).

WORK IN PROGRESS: A Creation of Growth and Meaning; Jewish Poverty in America; The Ph.D. Fact Book; research on astrology.

SIDELIGHTS: Avrutis writes that he is "one of a kind." He adds, "Although my mother loved me deeply . . . she was unable to give me proper mothering during the first year of my life. I had a strong searchlight, and held on to a portion of the 'cosmic quality' that is in our souls when we are born, but which most people lose quite early in life."

* * *

AYER, Jacqueline 1930-

PERSONAL: Born May 2, 1930, in New York, N.Y.; married Frederic Ayer; children: Margot, Elizabeth. *Education:* Attended Art Students League, New York, N.Y., Syracuse University for two years, and Ecole des Beaux Arts, Paris, France.

CAREER: Writer and illustrator. Fashion illustrator in Paris, France; International Basic Economy Corp., fabric and fashion designer, started a small division called Design Thai, 1960-66; consultant and head fashion designer in London, England, 1966—. Has exhibited work at American Institute of Graphic Arts. *Awards, honors:* Gold medal from the Society of Illustrators.

WRITINGS—All self-illustrated: *Nu Dang and His Kite,* Harcourt, 1959; *A Wish for Little Sister,* Harcourt, 1960; *The Paper-Flower Tree: A Tale from Thailand,* Harcourt, 1962; *Little Silk,* Harcourt, 1970; *Oriental Costume,* Studio Vista, 1974.

Illustrator: Petr Pavlovich Ershov, *Humpy,* translation by William C. White, Harcourt, 1966; Grimm Brothers, *Rumpelstiltskin,* Harcourt, 1967; William Somerset Maugham, *Princess September,* Harcourt, 1969.

BIOGRAPHICAL/CRITICAL SOURCES: Diana Klemin, *The Art of Art for Children's Books,* Clarkson Potter, 1966; *Illustrators of Children's Books: 1957-1966,* Horn Book, 1968; *Graphis 155,* Volume 27, Graphis Press, 1972.

* * *

AYERS, Bradley Earl 1935-

PERSONAL: Born March 7, 1935, in St. Paul, Minn.; married; children: three sons. *Education:* Attended Minnesota Metropolitan State University. *Politics:* "Pragmatic social and civil liberalism and reality democracy." *Religion:* Roman Catholic. *Residence:* Minnesota.

CAREER: U.S. Army, Infantry, 1953-64, trained as a paratrooper, specialized in unconventional warfare and ranger-commando operations, qualified as master parachutist, underwater demolitions swimmer, mountaineer, aircraft pilot, and flight instructor, attached to U.S. Central Intelligence Agency, 1963-64, leaving service as captain; organized own air charter company, 1965. Has also worked as a real estate broker and private investigator.

WRITINGS: The War That Never Was (non-fiction account of Central Intelligence Agency covert operations against Cuba), Bobbs-Merrill, 1976. Contributor to technical military publications and to popular and inspirational magazines.

WORK IN PROGRESS: Another book.

SIDELIGHTS: Ayers was among the first young career officers in the military to express opposition to the Vietnam war and to the "growing military-industrial influence in American foreign policy." His most recent writing encompasses a wide variety of subjects, including the psychic sciences, "esoteric thinking," extra-sensory perception, religious philosophy, and phenomena of an undetermined nature, including unidentified flying objects.

AVOCATIONAL INTERESTS: Running, physical fitness, ice hockey, motor-cycling, water skiing, boating, photography, painting, flying (certified as commercial pilot and flight instructor), classical music and concerts, films, "small gatherings with friends."*

* * *

AYLING, (Harold) Keith (Oliver) 1898-1976

1898—August 9, 1976; British-born American author and journalist. Served in the Royal Air Force during World War I. A writer of both fiction and non-fiction, much of his work focused on aviation and adventure. He died in Freeport, Long Island. Obituaries: *New York Times*, August 11, 1976.

* * *

AYVAZIAN, L. Fred 1919-
(Kenneth Flagg, Fred Levon)

PERSONAL: Born October 3, 1919, in Ordu, Turkey; came to United States in 1923, naturalized citizen, 1927; son of Haig A. (a physician) and Shnorhig (a teacher; maiden name, Kylyjian) Ayvazian; married Gloria Beatrice Bedikian (a teacher), June 8, 1947; children: Leslie Ann, Andrea Jo, Gina Kate. *Education:* Columbia University, B.A., 1939; New York University, M.D., 1943. *Politics:* Democrat. *Religion:* Protestant. *Home:* 201 Turrell Ave., South Orange, N.J. 07079. *Agent:* Elizabeth Otis, McIntosh & Otis, Inc., 475 Fifth Ave., New York, N.Y. 10017. *Office:* Veterans Administration Hospital, East Orange, N.J. 07019.

CAREER: Bellevue Hospital, New York City, intern and resident, 1944-47; Boston City Hospital, Boston, Mass., resident and research fellow at Thorndike Memorial Laboratory, 1947-48; National Academy of Sciences, Washington, D.C., investigator for National Research Council, 1948-51; Goldwater Memorial Hospital, Welfare Island, N.Y., worked with sterilization of blood plasma against hepatitis virus, 1953-54; Veterans Administration Hospital, New York City, assistant chief of medical service, 1954-61; Will Rogers Hospital, Saranac Lake, N.Y., medical director and chief of O'Donnell Memorial Research Laboratories, 1961-71; Veterans Administration Hospital, East Orange, N.J., chief of pulmonary section, 1971—. Diplomate of American Board of Internal Medicine, 1951. New York University Medical Center, fellow in medicine, 1944-45, associate professor of medicine, 1947-71; fellow in medicine, Harvard Medical School, 1947-48; professor of medicine, New Jersey Medical School, 1971—. Member of advisory board of New Jersey's health commissioner; consulting physician for New Jersey Medical School Affiliated Hospitals. *Military service:* U.S. Army, Medical Corps, 1951-53; served as captain.

MEMBER: Mystery Writers of America (charter member), American College of Physicians (fellow), American College of Chest Physicians, American Thoracic Society, Federation of Clinical Research, Harvey Society, American Lung Association of New Jersey (member of board of directors), Academy of Medicine of New Jersey (fellow), New Jersey Thoracic Society (president), New York Academy of Sciences (fellow), Alpha Omega Alpha. *Awards, honors:* Scroll from Mystery Writers of America, 1956, for *Much Ado About Murder*.

WRITINGS: (Under pseudonym Fred Levon) *Much Ado About Murder*, Dodd, 1955; (under pseudonym Kenneth Flagg) *Andrew* (novel), Putnam, 1959; (under pseudonym Fred Levon) *The Manx Cat* (suspense novel), World Publishing, 1967. Author of television script, "Jonathan," for Alfred Hitchcock. Contributor of articles to scientific journals and to *New York Times Book Review;* contributor of short stories to *Ellery Queen's Mystery Magazine, Alfred Hitchcock's Mystery Magazine, New Yorker, Collier's,* and *Saturday Evening Post*.

WORK IN PROGRESS: A medical novel; medical research.

SIDELIGHTS: Ayvazian wrote: "I first began writing at Bellevue Hospital to supplement my meager income as an intern, and sold my first stories without an agent. I took the first Mystery Writers of America course, then at Columbia, and lampooned the course in *Much Ado About Murder*. I also studied under Hiram Haydn and Simon Michael Bessie (at the New School for Social Research), and found this of great help in the non-mystery field."

* * *

BADDELEY, Alan D(avid) 1934-

PERSONAL: Born March 23, 1934, in Leeds, England; son of Donald (a composer) and Nellie (Hanson) Baddeley; married Hilary Ann White (a physiotherapist), February, 1964; children: Roland John, Gavin Timothy, Bartholomew Thomas Daniel. *Education:* University of London, B.A. (honors), 1956; Princeton University, M.A., 1957; Cambridge University, Ph.D., 1962. *Office:* Applied Psychology Unit, Medical Research Council, 15 Chaucer Rd., Cambridge CB2 2EF, England.

CAREER: Medical Research Council, Cambridge, England, research scientist with Applied Psychology Unit, 1958-67; University of Sussex, Brighton, England, lecturer, 1967-69, reader in psychology, 1969-72; University of Stirling, Stirling, Scotland, professor of psychology, 1972-74; Medical Research Council, director of Applied Psychology Unit, 1974—. Research associate at University of California, San Diego, 1970-71. *Member:* British Psychological Society, Experimental Psychology Society, Underwater Association.

WRITINGS: The Psychology of Memory, Basic Books, 1976. Associate editor of *Journal of Verbal Learning and Verbal Behavior*.

WORK IN PROGRESS: Research on human memory and on human performance under stress, with publication expected to result.

* * *

BADER, Julia 1944-

PERSONAL: Born August 14, 1944, in Hungary. *Education:* Goucher College, B.A., 1965; University of California, Berkeley, M.A., 1966, Ph.D., 1971. *Office:* Department of English, University of California, Berkeley, Calif. 94705.

CAREER: University of California, Berkeley, professor of English, 1970—. *Member:* Modern Language Association of America. *Awards, honors:* Woodrow Wilson fellowship, 1965; National Endowment for the Humanities fellowship, 1974.

WRITINGS: Crystal Land: Artifice in Nabokov's English Novels, University of California Press, 1973.

* * *

BAILEY, Beryl Loftman   1920(?)-1977

1920(?)—April 18, 1977; Jamacian-born educator and writer on linguistics. Bailey specialized in Black and Puerto Rican Studies and served as consultant to national organizations. She died in New York City. Obituaries: *New York Times,* April 21, 1977.

* * *

BAILEY, Robert W(ilson)   1943-

PERSONAL: Born November 30, 1943, in Lynchburg, Va.; son of David Lee (a Baptist minister) and Mildred Katheryne (a director of volunteer services; maiden name, Chocklett) Bailey; married Mary Frances Prillaman (a freelance writer), August 7, 1965; children: Robert Kevin, Mary Courtney. *Education:* Bluefield College, student, 1960-61; Carson-Newman College, B.A., 1964; Southern Baptist Theological Seminary, B.D., 1967, S.T.D., 1970. *Politics:* Democrat. *Home:* 441 Claymont St., Concord, N.C. 28025. *Office:* First Baptist Church, P.O. Box 643, Concord, N.C. 28025.

CAREER: Pastor of Baptist churches in Clinchport, Va., 1961-64, Flemingsburg, Ky., 1964-69, and Durham, N.C., 1970-75; First Baptist Church, Concord, N.C., pastor, 1975—. Retreat master. Lecturer at Rowan Technical Institute, 1975, 1976, and Mars Hill College, 1975. Leader of state-wide preaching and worship workshops and of state Family Life Conference, both 1976. Member of board of directors of Durham's Volunteer Services Bureau, 1972-75, and Family Counseling Service, 1974-75; member of Research Triangle Missions Committee, 1971-75. Assistant director and assistant producer of "Creative Arts Festival," on WTVD-Television, 1973. Consultant to Southern Baptist Convention. *Member:* Concord Ministerial Association, Cabarrus Baptist Ministers' Association, Phi Theta Kappa, Pi Kappa Delta, Phi Alpha Theta, Circle K, Blue Key.

WRITINGS: The Minister and Grief, Hawthorn, 1976; *God's Questions and Answers,* Hawthorn, 1977; (contributor) James C. Barry, editor, *Partners in Worship,* Convention Press, 1977. Contributor of several dozen articles to religious magazines.

SIDELIGHTS: Bailey told *CA:* "In my writing I seek to touch the needs and hurts of people today. The book on grief offers help to caring persons in relating to those who are dying and to those struggling with the aftermath of grief. My basic premise is that the one who would minister to others needs to face and affirm death as a part of his own life. Persons who seek to hide from or escape death can mean little or nothing to those who are dying or bereaved.

"The book, *God's Questions and Answers,* concentrates on the issues facing people twenty-four centuries ago in the days of the prophet Malachi. In a forensic, rhetorical manner, the prophet raised and answered burning questions on behalf of God. These questions are appropriate to be asked in our present day. Many of our social, economic and religious contexts are similar to the prophet's."

BAILEY, Sydney D(awson)   1916-

PERSONAL: Born September 1, 1916, in Hull, England; son of Frank Burgess (a grain broker) and Elsie (a teacher; maiden name, May) Bailey; married Jennie Elena Brenda Friedrich (a social worker), April 26, 1945; children: Martin Dawson, Marion Elizabeth Bailey Hartwell. *Education:* Attended secondary school in Worksop, Nottinghamshire, England. *Religion:* Society of Friends (Quakers). *Home and office:* 19 Deansway, London N2 0NG, England.

CAREER: National Newsletter, London, England, editor, 1946-48; Hansard Society for Parliamentary Government, London, England, secretary, 1948-54; Society of Friends, New York City, Quaker representative to the United Nations, 1954-58; Carnegie Endowment for International Peace, New York City, research fellow, 1958-60; writer, 1960—. Member of advisory committees of British Foreign Office. *Wartime service:* Society of Friends, attached to ambulance unit, 1940-46; served in China-Burma-India theater. *Member:* International Institute for Strategic Studies, Royal Institute of International Affairs, American Society for International Law.

WRITINGS: (Editor) *Aspects of American Government,* Hansard Society for Parliamentary Government, 1950; *Constitutions of British Colonies* (pamphlet), Hansard Society for Parliamentary Government, 1950; (editor) *Parliamentary Government in the Commonwealth,* Philosophical Library, 1951; *Lords and Commons* (pamphlet), H.M.S.O., 1951; *Parliamentary Government* (pamphlet), British Council, 1952, 2nd edition, 1958; *Ceylon,* Hutchinson, 1952; (editor) *The British Party System,* Praeger, 1952, 2nd edition, 1953; *Naissance du nouvelles democraties* (title means "The Birth of New Democracies"), Armand Colin, 1953; *Parliamentary Government in Southern Asia,* Institute of Pacific Relations, 1953; (editor) *Problems of Parliamentary Government in Colonies,* Hansard Society for Parliamentary Government, 1953; (editor) *The Future of the House of Lords,* Praeger, 1954; *British Parliamentary Democracy,* Houghton, 1958, 3rd edition, 1970.

The General Assembly of the United Nations, Praeger, 1960, 2nd edition, 1964; *The Secretariat of the United Nations,* Praeger, 1962, 2nd edition, 1964; *The Troika and the Future of the United Nations* (pamphlet), Carnegie Endowment for International Peace, 1962; (contributor) Saul H. Mendlovitz, editor, *Legal and Political Problems of World Order,* World Law Fund, 1962; *A Short Political Guide to the United Nations,* Praeger, 1963; (contributor) Evan Luard, editor, *The Evolution of International Organization,* Thames & Hudson, 1966; (contributor) *Peace is Still the Prize,* S.C.M. Press, 1966; (contributor) Richard A. Falk and Mendlovitz, editors, *The Strategy of World Order,* World Law Fund, 1966; (contributor) Robert W. Gregg and Michael Barkun, editors, *The United Nations System and Its Functions,* Van Nostrand, 1968; *The Veto in the Security Council* (pamphlet), Carnegie Endowment for International Peace, 1968.

Voting in the Security Council, Indiana University Press, 1970; *Chinese Representation in the Security Council and General Assembly of the United Nations,* Institute for the Study of International Organization, 1970; (contributor) George Cunningham, editor, *Britain and the World in the Seventies,* Weidenfeld & Nicolson, 1970; *The Peaceful Settlement of International Disputes,* United Nations Institute for Training Research, 1970, 3rd edition, 1971; *Prohibitions and Restraints in War,* Oxford University Press, 1972; *The Procedure of the United Nations Security Council,* Clarendon Press, 1975. Contributor of several hundred articles to periodicals, including *Economist, Spectator, Review of Politics, World Today, Survival, Theology, International Affairs,* and *American Journal of International Law.* Editor of *Parliamentary Affairs,* 1948-54.

WORK IN PROGRESS: A multi-volume study of the United Nations Security Council, regarding cease-fires, truces, and armistices.

SIDELIGHTS: Bailey told *CA* that his concerns are "world peace, human rights, and the rule of law." A disabled person, he has nonetheless traveled widely in western and eastern Europe, the Middle East, Asia, and Africa, and has lived in the United States. His books have been published in Portuguese, Japanese, Hindi, French, and Arabic.

AVOCATIONAL INTERESTS: Music, people.

* * *

BAINE, Rodney M(ontgomery) 1913-

PERSONAL: Born June 30, 1913, in Kosciusko, Miss.; married, 1940; children: three. *Education:* Southwestern at Memphis, A.B., 1935; Vanderbilt University, further study, 1935-36; Oxford University, B.A., 1938, B.Litt., 1939, M.A., 1951; Harvard University, Ph.D., 1951. *Office:* Department of English, University of Georgia, Athens, Ga. 30601.

CAREER: University of Missouri, Columbia, instructor in English, 1939-41; Massachusetts Institute of Technology, Cambridge, instructor in English, 1941-44; University of Richmond, Richmond, Va., associate professor of English, 1946-54; Delta State College, Cleveland, Miss., head of Division of Languages and Literature, 1954-57; Alabama College (now Alabama State University), Montgomery, chairman of department of English, 1957-62; University of Georgia, Athens, 1962—, began as associate professor, became professor of English. *Military service:* U.S. Army, 1944-46. *Member:* Modern Language Association of America, South Atlantic Modern Language Association. *Awards, honors:* Rhodes scholar at Oxford University, 1938-39.

WRITINGS: (Editor and author of introduction) Thomas Warton, *A History of English Poetry: An Unpublished Continuation,* William Andrews Clark Memorial Library, University of California, 1953, Kraus Reprint, 1967; *Thomas Holcroft and the Revolutionary Novel,* University of Georgia Press, 1965; *Robert Munford: America's First Comic Dramatist,* University of Georgia Press, 1967; *Daniel Defoe and the Supernatural,* University of Georgia Press, 1968; (editor) *A History of English Poetry,* Folcroft, 1973. Contributor to scholarly journals.*

* * *

BAKER, Oleda 1934-

PERSONAL: Born August 12, 1934, in Florida; daughter of Marvin and Thelma Freeman; married David Pettis, 1956 (divorced, 1962); married Steven Baker, December 9, 1967 (separated); children: David Pettis, Jr. *Education:* Attended New York University. *Office:* Oleda Unlimited, Inc., 770 Lexington Ave., New York, N.Y. 10021.

CAREER: Model in New York City, 1960-73; Oleda Unlimited, Inc. (in beauty products), New York City, president, 1976—. Artist; has had solo exhibitions of primitive art; co-producer, writer, and hostess of "Oleda's Beauty and Health Tips," television program syndicated by Dolphin Productions, 1977—. *Awards, honors:* Dame of Knights of Malta, 1977.

WRITINGS: The Models' Way to Beauty, Slenderness, and Glowing Health, Prentice-Hall, 1973; *The I Hate to Makeup Book,* Prentice-Hall, 1975; *Be a Woman,* Ballantine, 1975; *Oleda Baker's Face Savers* (booklet), Mega Woman, 1975; *Oleda Baker's Hair Savers* (booklet), Mega Woman, 1976; *Oleda Baker's Age-Less Diet,* Mega Woman, 1976; *How to Create the Illusion of a More Perfect Figure,* Prentice-Hall, 1976; *Twenty-Nine Forever,* Putnam, 1977; *The Teenage Beauty Care Book,* Putnam, in press; *How to Renovate Yourself from Head to Toe,* Doubleday, in press. Beauty editor of *Models' Circle,* 1975.

WORK IN PROGRESS: The First Aid Beauty Book, for Putnam; *The Reluctant Goddess,* a novel.

SIDELIGHTS: Baker told *CA:* "Although I enjoyed my career as a model, I enjoy far more transferring the beauty techniques that I learned as a model to other women. This transfer of created beauty and prolonged youth takes two primary forms in my work: publications and products. Both have the same goal in mind—to share my discoveries, after a lifetime of concentration in the beauty field, with women of all ages, and all heredities, who either need or desire it. In my writings, I give them what they can *do* to build this self-created desirability; with my products, I sell them the ingredients they need to build it with. I have found that these techniques and these ingredients have, for all practical purposes, helped to freeze my own external age. I have seen the tragedy of needless aging in these women—I wish therefore to prevent as much of this tragedy, in all other women, as I can."

* * *

BAKHTIAR, Laleh Mehree 1938-

PERSONAL: Born July 29, 1938, in Tehran, Iran; daughter of Abol (a physician) and Helen (a public health nurse; maiden name, Jeffreys) Bakhtiar; married Nader Ardalan (an architect), June 11, 1960 (divorced, 1976); children: Mani, Iran, Karim. *Education:* Chatham College, B.A., 1960. *Religion:* Moslem. *Home:* Maidan-i-Kakh, Kh. Tus, Kooche Tabriz #38, Tehran, Iran.

CAREER: Mandala Collaborative, Tehran, Iran, head of graphics, 1974-76; Hamdami Foundation, Tehran, managing director, 1976—.

WRITINGS: (With Nader Ardalan) *The Sense of Unity,* University of Chicago Press, 1971; *Sufi Expressions of the Mystic Quest,* Avon, 1976.

WORK IN PROGRESS: Articles; a book on the Ka'ba and surrounding Masque, with Nader Ardalan.

SIDELIGHTS: Bakhtiar found the most interesting aspect of researching *The Sense of Unity* was "the study of tradition and in particular how Iranians have expressed themselves becoming part of tradition."

* * *

BAKKER, Elna S(undquist) 1921-

PERSONAL: Surname is pronounced Bocker; born August 4, 1921, in Los Angeles, Calif.; daughter of August and Ellen Sundquist; married Gerhard Bakker, Jr. (a professor of biology), November, 1948. *Education:* University of California, Los Angeles, B.A., 1945. *Home:* 450 West Ave., #43, Los Angeles, Calif. 90065.

CAREER: Elementary school teacher in Los Angeles, Calif., 1946-65; travelogue and nature photographer and lecturer, 1965-70; free-lance writer, 1969—. Training and demonstration teacher at University of California, Los Angeles, 1948-56. Naturalist, teacher, and photographer for Oakland Museum, 1965-71; naturalist for Placerita Canyon Nature Center and tour escort for Los Angeles Geographical Society, 1965-73. Member of board of trustees of Sierra Club Foundation. *Member:* Nature Conservancy (executive secretary of southern California chapter, 1961-72). *Awards, honors:* Nonfiction award from Border Regional Library Association, 1973, for *The Great Southwest.*

WRITINGS: An Island Called California, University of California Press, 1971; (with Richard G. Lillard) *The Great Southwest,* American West, 1972; (with Raymond B. Cowles) *Desert Journal,* University of California Press, 1977; *Green Champagne: An Adventure in Ecoverse,* Feathered Serpent Press, in press.

WORK IN PROGRESS: A book about sagebrush, "the West's most famous unknown plant."

SIDELIGHTS: Elna Bakker writes: "I am a self-taught naturalist, blessed with a biologist husband. We have traveled in Africa many times, Central America twice, Mexico times without number, the Caribbean three times (I made a film on Trinidad), of course many times throughout the West, in Canada, and once to Alaska, several times in Europe, Outer Mongolia, Central Asia (the U.S.S.R.), Thailand, Australia, Hongkong, Japan, South America, and the Galapagos."

AVOCATIONAL INTERESTS: Bach, cooking (especially Chinese food), painting with watercolors, conservation work.

*   *   *

BALDWIN, Arthur W.   1904(?)-1976

1904(?)—July, 1976; British biographer. One of his most famous works was a biography of his father, former Prime Minister Stanley Baldwin. He died in England. Obituaries: *AB Bookman's Weekly,* October 4, 1976.

*   *   *

BALLER, Warren Robert   1900-

PERSONAL: Born June 19, 1900, in Trenton, Neb.; son of Albert Ernest (a farmer) and Mary Louise (Taylor) Baller; married Dorothy Gwendolyn Jensen; children: William Warren, John Timothy, Elizabeth Claire Baller Clarke. *Education:* York College (now Westmar College), A.B., 1923; University of Nebraska, M.A., 1927, Ph.D., 1935; also attended Columbia University, 1930, University of Minnesota, 1932, and University of Chicago, 1940-41. *Politics:* Democrat. *Religion:* Presbyterian. *Home:* 3275 Loma Riviera Dr., San Diego, Calif. 92110. *Office:* Graduate School of Human Behavior, U.S. International University, 8655 Pomerado Rd., San Diego, Calif. 92131.

CAREER: High school principal in Calloway, Neb., 1923-24; superintendent of schools in Cheney, Neb., 1925-28; York College (now Westmar College), Le Mars, Iowa, associate professor of psychology, 1928-34, academic dean, 1933-34; University of Nebraska, Lincoln, assistant professor, 1935-38, associate professor, 1938-43, professor of educational psychology, 1943-67, director of Student Counseling Center, 1942-48, dean of Lower Division, 1949-51, chairman of department, 1960-65; U.S. International University, San Diego, Calif., professor of psychology, 1967—. Diplomate of American Board of Examiners in Psychology, 1949. Visiting professor at University of Texas, 1949, Northwestern University George Peabody College for

Teachers, and University of Florida, all 1950, and University of California, Los Angeles, summer of 1951, and 1955-57; professor at California Western University, 1967-68. Past member of board of directors of Lincoln, Neb., Young Men's Christian Association. Chief civilian psychologist at Fort Leavenworth Induction Station, 1941.

MEMBER: American Psychological Association (fellow), American Educational Research Association, College Teachers of Education (president, 1964-65), American Academy of Political and Social Science, National Education Association, American Association of University Professors, National Society for the Study of Education, American Association for the Advancement of Science, Western Psychological Association, Midwest Psychological Association, Nebraska Psychological Association, Nebraska Schoolmasters Club, San Diego County Psychological Association, Sigma Xi, Phi Delta Kappa. *Awards, honors:* LL.D. from George Williams College, 1962; Worcester Memorial Award from University of Nebraska, 1967, centennial award, 1969.

WRITINGS: The Evaluation of Teachers' Understanding of Child Growth and Development, Commission on Teacher Education, American Council on Education, 1941; (with E. M. Troyer) *Evaluative Materials in Teacher Education,* Commission on Teacher Education, American Council on Education, 1941; (with M. E. Ahrens and Zach Henderson) *Physiological Aspects of Growth and Development,* Commission on Teacher Education, American Council on Education, 1941; *The Study of Mickey Murphy: An Instrument in Evaluation,* University of Nebraska Press, 1943, 7th edition, 1966; (contributor) C. E. Erickson, editor, *A Basic Text for Guidance Workers,* Prentice-Hall, 1948; (contributor) W. W. Cook and W. C. Trow, editors, *Educational Psychology in Teacher Education,* National Society of College Teachers of Education, 1953.

(With Don C. Charles) *Psychology of Human Growth and Development,* Holt, 1961, 2nd edition, 1968; (editor) *Psychology of Human Growth and Development: A Book of Readings,* Holt, 1962, 2nd edition, 1969; *Nocturnal Enuresis (Bedwetting): Origins and Treatment,* Pergamon, 1975. Contributor of more than fifty articles to education and psychology journals.

WORK IN PROGRESS: A book on the psychology of human development.

SIDELIGHTS: Baller comments that one of his major influences was his child and adolescent study at University of Chicago, 1940-41.

*   *   *

BANGERTER, Lowell A(llen)   1941-

PERSONAL: Born June 23, 1941, in Ogden, Utah; son of Alma H. (a civil servant) and Helen (Lone) Bangerter; married Judy Lee Pearson, September 16, 1964; children: Grant W., Stephen A., Carl W., Tamara Lynn, Janine Ann. *Education:* Stanford University, B.A., 1966, M.A., 1967; University of Illinois, Ph.D., 1970. *Religion:* Church of Jesus Christ of Latter-day Saints (Mormons). *Home:* 1114 Mitchell, Laramie, Wyo. 82070. *Office:* Department of Modern and Classical Languages, University of Wyoming, Box 3603 University Station, Laramie, Wyo. 82071.

CAREER: University of Wyoming, Laramie, assistant professor, 1970-76, associate professor of German, 1976—. *Member:* Modern Language Association of America, American Association of Teachers of German, Rocky Mountain

Modern Language Association, Verband deutschsprachiger Autoren in Amerika.

WRITINGS: Schiller and Hofmannsthal, Dos Continentes, 1974; *Hugo von Hofmannsthal,* Ungar, 1977. Contributor to *Encyclopedia of World Literature in the Twentieth Century.* Contributor of articles and poems to language journals.

WORK IN PROGRESS: A book on the East German writer, Anna Seghers; translating poetry of Johann Wolfgang von Goethe, for an anthology of Goethe's poetry in translation, edited by Frederick Ungar, publication by Ungar expected in 1978.

SIDELIGHTS: Bangerter writes that his "interest in German language and literature was first aroused during my initial stay in Germany as an American Field Service exchange student in summer, 1958, and further stimulated during thirty months spent in Germany from 1961 to 1964, when I served as a missionary for the Church of Jesus Christ of Latter-day Saints. Language studies include German, French, Old Norse-Icelandic, Modern Danish, and Russian.... Most of my own poetry has been stimulated by the experience of the vast panorama of nature in the American West."

* * *

BARAHENI, Reza 1935-

PERSONAL: Born April 7, 1935, in Tabriz, Iran; came to the United States in 1974; son of Mohammad-Taghi (a worker) and Zahrasoltan (Shokoohetaze) Baraheni; married Angela Marangozidi, 1959 (divorced June 22, 1966); married Sanaz Sihhati (a teacher), September 24, 1971; children: Aleca, Oktay-Mohammad. *Education:* University of Tabriz, B.A., 1957; University of Istanbul, Ph.D., 1960. *Religion:* "Born to a Moslem family." *Home:* 150 West 225th St., Apt. 14K, Bronx, N.Y. 10463. *Agent:* Hoffman/Sheedy Literary Agency, 145 West 86th St., New York, N.Y. 10024. *Office:* Department of English, University of Maryland, 5401 Wilkens Ave., Baltimore, Md. 21228.

CAREER: Technical Faculty of Teheran, Teheran, Iran, lecturer in English, 1961-62; Teheran University, Teheran, assistant professor, 1964-68, associate professor of English literature, 1968-74, dean of students, 1965-68, chairperson of English department for correspondence faculty, 1974; University of Iowa, Iowa City, poet-in-residence for International Writing Program, 1974; Indiana University, Bloomington, professor of creative writing, 1975; Bard College, Annandale-on-Hudson, N.Y., professor of English, 1977; University of Maryland, Baltimore, professor of English, 1977—. Distinguished visiting professor at American University in Cairo, spring, 1971; visiting associate professor at University of Texas, autumn, 1972, and University of Utah, 1973. Lecturer in Iran and the United States; has given poetry readings. Active in organizations working toward the release of political prisoners. *Military service:* Iranian Army, 1960-62.

MEMBER: International P.E.N. (U.S. branch; member of freedom to write committee), Writers Association of Iran (founding member; chairperson of committee of campaign against censorship, 1969—), Committee for Artistic and Intellectual Freedom in Iran (honorary chairperson, 1975—), Council of Latin American Human Rights, Mustafa Zjemilev Committee.

WRITINGS—In English: *Zillulah,* Abjad Publications, 1975, translation by the author published as *God's Shadow* (prison poems), Indiana University Press, 1976; *The Crowned Cannibals* (poems and prose), Vintage, 1977; *Oil and Revolution: The Case of Iran,* Random House, in press.

Other: *Ahovan-e bagh* (poems; title means "The Deer of the Garden"), Sepehr House, 1962; *Jangal-o-shahr* (poem; title means "The Jungle and the City"), Javid Publications, 1963; *Shabi az nimrooz* (poems; title means "Night—Starting from Midday"), Chehr House, 1965; *Tala dar mes* (criticism; title means "Gold in Copper"), Chehr House, 1965, 2nd edition, Zaman, 1970; *Quesseh-nevisi* (title means "The Writing of Fiction"), Ashraf Publications, 1969; *Mosibati zir-e afetab* (poems and prose), Amir Kabir Publications, 1970; *Gol bar gostare-ye mah* (poems; title means "A Flower upon Moon—Moonflower"), Zaman, 1970; *Roozegar-e doozakhi-ye agha-ye Ayyaz* (novel, the first volume of a trilogy; title means "The Infernal Times of Mr. Ayyaz"), Amirkabir Publications, 1972; *Tarikh-e mozakkar: Resale-i piramoon-e tashattot-e farhang dar Iran* (title means "Masculine History: A Manifesto on the Causes of Cultural Disintegration in Iran"), Pindar, 1973; *Jonoone neveshtan* (title means "The Insanity of Writing"), Iranmehr, 1973; *Safar-e Mesr* (title means "Journey into Egypt"), Iranmehr, 1973; *Do baradar akhar-e khat dar yek khat* (novel; title means "Two Brothers on the Same Line at the End"), Neguin, 1974; *Chah be chah* (novel; title means "From One Well to Another"), Payam Daneshjoo, 1976.

Translator into Persian: William Shakespeare, *Richard III,* Amir Kabir, 1963; Ivo Andric, *The Bridge over Drina,* Franklin Pocket Books, 1963, 3rd edition, Nil Publications, 1977; Maxim Rodinson, *Israel and the Arabs,* Kharazmi Publications, 1969, 3rd edition, 1973; David Caute, *Franz Fanon,* Kharazmi Publications, 1973.

Author of "Play No Play" (one-act play), first produced in Salt Lake City, Utah, at Salt Lake City Public Auditorium, May 1, 1973.

Represented in about a dozen anthologies in Persian and English, including *City Lights Anthology,* City Lights, 1974, and *Anthology of Middle East Literature,* edited by Leo Hamalian and John Johannan, New American Library, in press. General editor of Abjad Publications. Contributor of more than a hundred articles, poems, and translations to scholarly journals and popular magazines, including *Penthouse, Iowa Review,* and *American Poetry Review.* Editor-in-chief of *Jahane No* (title means "Modern World"), 1966. Literary editor of *Ferdowsi,* 1964-70.

WORK IN PROGRESS: A novel set in Iran, 1941-73; *An Evil under the Sun,* a translation of *Mosibati zir-e afetab;* poems.

SIDELIGHTS: The writer as witness seems to be emerging as perhaps the most characteristic artist of the twentieth century, and Reza Baraheni, a well-known writer and chronicler of tortures in Iran, is among the most important, according to E. L. Doctorow.

Many critics believe that politics makes bad art; some subscribe to the aesthetic dogma that denies the writer any other function than to place words in pleasing patterns. For the writer witnesses, such as Baraheni, Doctorow finds that the major problem is "how to communicate to those who insulate themselves in literature the terrible inadequacy of aesthetic criteria as applied to human suffering." Baraheni has apparently resolved this problem, since critics generally agree that his works are successful both aesthetically and as eloquent statements of the human condition.

Baraheni's chronicles may be of special interest to Americans, for they are involved, indirectly or directly, in the U.S.

support of the repressive Iranian government. John Leonard says of Baraheni's writing: "And if his documentation of SAVAK terror, his prison memoirs, his compendium of tortures—names, dates, devices, sound familiar, we ought to remind ourselves that the Gulag seems to be the preeminent form of modern architecture, a franchise built of human bones, and that in this case, with the Shah, we are responsible."

Baraheni told *CA:* "Since 1974, I have appealed directly to the American public and through them to the world at large. I have spoken and read my poetry and prose on more than fifty American campuses and talked to the people on almost all the major news media. My aims have been: first, to expose the Shah's dictatorial regime and the U.S. government's complicity with that regime; second, to force the Shah to open his jails and release all the political prisoners of Iran and to let the people take their own destiny in their own hands; next, to prevent the Shah, the Pentagon, and the CIA from arming our people to the teeth through the help of multinational corporations, and to allow our people to use their natural wealth the way they see fit; fourth, to force the Shah to stop harassing Iranian dissidents and students in the U.S. and to force his SAVAK (the Iranian secret police) out of this country; and finally, to stop the Shah from extending his dictatorship to American universities through his attempts to bribe the academic community here.

"Since 1953, Americans have been directly responsible for the dictatorship in Iran. The legally elected government of Dr. Mohammad Mossadeq was overthrown by the CIA in that year and the Shah who had run away earlier was brought back and reinstalled on the throne. The American-trained SAVAK came to existence in 1957. The number of Americans in Iran is estimated at 30,000, with most of them involved in the training of the army, the police and the gendarmerie, or acting as representatives and employees of American corporations.

"Americans should ask their government to open the files of the CIA, the FBI, and the State Department on Iran. They should force their government to stop selling arms to the Shah, and to stop supporting his dictatorial rule. Public opinion in the U.S. should openly voice its opposition to the President's silence on the miserable situations of human rights in Iran.

"The people of Iran have come to the realization that they, and only they, should decide what form of government they want for their future. Whatever the form of that government, it will not be genuine unless the underprivileged majority of the people have the representation they rightly deserve. I can imagine that representation being achieved before we are through with the last decade of this century."

In a discussion of his literary influences, Baraheni wrote: "If I hadn't read the works of Rumi, the great Iranian poet, I wouldn't have known the meaning of poetry. My learning from the West taught me how to rationalize about the irrational (hence, my literary criticism). I have learned from Marx, Lenin, and Trotsky, as well as many others who were not revolutionary socially: Proust, Joyce, Mann, Yeats, and Charles Olson. But at heart I am deeply rooted in the culture of the Middle East. My knowledge of Persian, Turkish, and Arabic, as well as French and English, is my window to the world."

Baraheni, who is considered to be the founder of modern literary criticism in Iran, was imprisoned and tortured by Iranian secret police for 102 days in 1973. His release was due to public pressure generated by the American branch of P.E.N., Amnesty International, and the Committee for Artistic and Intellectual Freedom in Iran. His works have been published in Arabic, Armenian, French, German, Polish, Russian, Spanish, and Turkish.

BIOGRAPHICAL/CRITICAL SOURCES: Ehsan Yar-Shater, *Iran Faces the Seventies,* Praeger, 1970; *New York Times,* December 16, 1973, June 17, 1977, June 20, 1977; *City Lights Anthology,* City Lights, 1974; *Village Voice,* March 3, 1975, February, 1976; *Index on Censorship,* spring, 1976; *Harper's,* May, 1977.

* * *

BARBER, Stephen Guy 1921-
(Guy Bernard)

PERSONAL: Born December 24, 1921, in Tanta, Egypt; son of Clement (a broker) and Margaret (a teacher; maiden name, Mole) Barber; married Deirdre Christine Knewstub (a decorator), March 21, 1953; children: Simon Guy. *Education:* Attended Bristol University, 1938. *Politics:* None. *Religion:* Protestant. *Home:* 2700 35th Pl. NW, Washington, D.C. 20007. *Office:* Daily Telegraph, 50 Rockefeller Plaza, New York, N.Y. 10020.

CAREER: Associated Press, New York City, war correspondent in Mideast, North Africa, Italy and Greece, 1942-45; *News Chronicle,* London, England, roving correspondent, 1945-56, assistant editor, 1956-61; *London Daily Telegraph,* London, correspondent in India and South Asia, 1961-62, special correspondent for *London Sunday Telegraph,* 1963-69, chief correspondent in U.S., 1969—. Notable assignments include World War II, death of Mussolini, Greek Civil War, Palestine and Mideast War, 1948, Korean War, 1950-53, war in Indochina, 1954, war in Cyprus, 1955-59, tours with Queen of England and Harold MacMillan, assassination of John Kennedy, and tours with Richard Nixon and Gerald Ford. *Military service:* British Army, 1939-45. *Member:* Institute of Journalists, Press Club, National Press Club, White House Correspondents' Association, Overseas Writers.

WRITINGS: (With R. S. and W. S. Churchill) *The Six Day War,* Houghton, 1967; (contributor) K. Halle, *The Grand Original,* Norton, 1969; *America in Retreat,* Stacey, 1970.

WORK IN PROGRESS: America Rebounds, a sequel to *America in Retreat.*

SIDELIGHTS: Barber told *CA:* "To be a foreign correspondent for a first-class newspaper is to have a free front-row seat at history in the making. It is not just a job but a whole way of life. If I were rich, I would happily pay for the privilege of doing what I do. But at the same time, I feel that we journalists should take care not to presume too much—our public is fickle."

* * *

BARBOUR, Douglas (Fleming) 1940-

PERSONAL: Born March 21, 1940, in Winnipeg, Manitoba, Canada; son of Harold Douglas (a fundraising executive) and Phyllis (Wilson) Barbour; married M. Sharon Nicoll, May 21, 1966. *Education:* Acadia University, B.A., 1962; Dalhousie University, M.A., 1964; Queen's University, Kingston, Ontario, further graduate study, 1967-68. *Politics:* "Anarchist (at heart)." *Residence:* Edmonton, Alberta, Canada. *Office:* Department of English, University of Alberta, Edmonton, Alberta, Canada T6G 2E1.

CAREER: Alderwood Collegiate Institute, Toronto, Ontario, teacher of English, 1968-69; University of Alberta,

Edmonton, assistant professor, 1969-77, associate professor of English, 1977—. *Member:* Association of Canadian University Teachers, League of Canadian Poets (co-chairman, 1972-74).

WRITINGS—Poetry: *Land Fall,* Delta Books, 1971; *A Poem As Long As the Highway,* Quarry Press, 1971; *White,* Fiddlehead Books, 1972; *Song Book,* Talon Books, 1973; *He and She and,* Golden Dog Press, 1974; *Visions of My Grandfather,* Golden Dog Press, 1977. Member of editorial board of *Quarry,* 1965-68, and *White Pelican,* 1972-76; poetry reviewer for *Dalhousie Review.*

WORK IN PROGRESS: Continuing research on his family history; a collection of shorter poems; "cooperative sound poetry."

SIDELIGHTS: Barbour writes briefly that he regards "language as experience leading to speech."

* * *

BARKER, Gerard A(rthur) 1930-

PERSONAL: Born March 4, 1930, in Essen, Germany; came to the United States in 1940; naturalized citizen, 1944; son of Arthur J. (a merchant) and Ella (Davids) Barker; married Ann Silezin, June 26, 1965; children: Madeleine, Derek. *Education:* University of California, Berkeley, B.A., 1952, M.L.S., 1953; Stanford University, Ph.D., 1961. *Residence:* Dix Hills, N.Y. *Office:* Department of English, Queens College of the City University of New York, Flushing, N.Y. 11367.

CAREER: Queens College of the City University of New York, Flushing, N.Y., instructor, 1961-67, assistant professor, 1968-74, associate professor of English, 1975—. *Military service:* U.S. Army, 1953-55. *Member:* American Society for Eighteenth-Century Studies.

WRITINGS: Henry Mackenzie, Twayne, 1975. Contributor to literature journals.

WORK IN PROGRESS: Twice-Told Tales: An Introduction to Short Fiction, an anthology of short stories, publication expected in 1979.

* * *

BARNARD, William Dean 1942-

PERSONAL: Born September 18, 1942, in Birmingham, Ala.; son of Cecil Dean (a freight line representative) and Dorothy (Bates) Barnard; married Hollinger Farmer, December 21, 1964; children: William Harrison III, Margaret Pace, Joshua Bates. *Education:* Birmingham-Southern College, B.A., 1964; University of Virginia, Ph.D., 1971. *Home:* 17 Pinemont Dr., Tuscaloosa, Ala. 35401. *Office:* Office of the Chancellor, University of Alabama, Box BT, University, Ala. 35486.

CAREER: University of South Alabama, Mobile, instructor, 1968-71, assistant professor of history, 1971-72; Alabama Commission on Higher Education, Montgomery, research associate, 1972-73, associate director of academic affairs, 1973-77; University of Alabama, Tuscaloosa, assistant to the chancellor, 1977—. Member of Alabama Committee on the Humanities and Public Policy; member of local board of directors of American Red Cross. *Member:* Organization of American Historians, Association for Institutional Research, Southern Historical Association, Alabama Historical Association, Association of Alabama Historians (member of board of directors, 1974-75; president, 1976-78). *Awards, honors:* Woodrow Wilson fellowship, 1964-65.

WRITINGS: A Guide to the Papers of Edward R. Stettinius, Sr., Library, University of Virginia, 1968; *Dixiecrats and Democrats: Alabama Politics, 1942-1950,* University of Alabama Press, 1974. Contributor to Alabama magazines.

WORK IN PROGRESS: Research on recent political history of Alabama and the South.

* * *

BARNETT, Franklin 1903-

PERSONAL: Born January 27, 1903, in Chicago, Ill.; son of John George and Jeanette A. (Schloesser) Barnett; married Joan Elizabeth Andrews, March 24, 1945. *Education:* Attended Western School of Estimating and Plan Reading and Polytechnic College of Engineering. *Politics:* Democrat. *Religion:* Roman Catholic. *Home:* 2403 Country Park Dr., Prescott, Ariz. 86301.

CAREER: U.S. Army, 1919-45, intermittently in Infantry, Cavalry, and Coast Artillery, 1919-34, in Corps of Engineers, 1934-45; technical writer, 1950-65; free-lance writer and archaeologist, 1965—. Has also worked as cartographer, commercial designer, and draftsman and designer of laboratory equipment. *Member:* Disabled American Veterans (life member). *Awards, honors:* Grand Awards from New Mexico State, 1951, 1953, 1956, and 1959, from Denver Philatelic Society, 1953, and from National Society of Philatelic Americans, 1959.

WRITINGS: Viola Jimulla: The Indian Chieftress (biography), privately printed, 1968; *Birds on Rio Grande Pottery,* Albuquerque Archaeological Society, 1968; *Tonque Pueblo* (excavation report), Albuquerque Archaeological Society, 1969; *Matli Ranch Ruin* (excavation report), Museum of Northern Arizona, 1970; *San Ysidro Pueblos,* Albuquerque Archaeological Society, 1973; *Dictionary of Prehistoric Indian Artifacts of the American Southwest,* Northland Press, 1973; *Lonesome Valley Ruin in Yavapai County, Arizona,* Museum of Northern Arizona, 1973; *Excavation of the Main Pueblo at Fitzmaurice Ruin,* Museum of Northern Arizona, 1974; *Sandstone Hill Pueblo Ruin: Cibola Culture in Catron County, New Mexico,* Albuquerque Archaeological Society, 1974; *Excavation of a Lower Room at Fitzmaurice Ruin,* Yavapai College, 1975; *Las Vegas Ranch Ruin—East and Las Vegas Ranch Ruin—West,* Museum of Northern Arizona, 1977; *Crooked Arrow* (prehistoric Indian novel), Paul Hughes & Associates, 1977. Contributor to philately journals.

WORK IN PROGRESS: Viviana, a historical novel set in revolutionary Texas; *Head of Caleb Reed,* a historical novel set in early Arizona; research for an archaeological ceramic report of prehistoric Prescott's Indian culture.

SIDELIGHTS: Barnett writes that he has been involved with southwestern archaeology since 1955, when it became a dedicated avocation. He has excavated more than five hundred prehistoric Indian rooms since then. He has also taught college-level workshops on southwestern archaeology and set up the Indian rooms for Sharlot Hall Museum in Prescott and the Western Museum in Wickenburg, Ariz.

AVOCATIONAL INTERESTS: Sports (coached basketball, football, softball, and semi-professional baseball), philately (has had exhibits all over the United States).

* * *

BARNEY, Kenneth D. 1921-

PERSONAL: Born August 28, 1921, in Thayer, Kan.; son of Joseph D. Barney (an electrician); married Rosaleigh

Montgomery, October 24, 1942; children: Kenneth D., Kristy Gail. *Education:* Central Bible Institute, Springfield, Mo., received diploma, 1948. *Politics:* Republican. *Religion:* Assemblies of God. *Home:* 215 South Schuyler, Ottumwa, Iowa 52501. *Office:* 733 Church St., Ottumwa, Iowa 52501.

CAREER: Liberty Life Insurance Co., Topeka, Kan., clerk, 1938-40; Rock Island Railroad, Topeka, secretary, 1940-41; Santa Fe Railway, Topeka, secretary, 1941-43; Assemblies of God Churches in Kansas, Missouri, New Mexico, Texas, and Iowa, pastor, 1945—. Member of board of directors, Evangel College, 1970-73. *Military service:* U.S. Army Air Corps, 1943-45; became first lieutenant; prisoner of war, 1944.

WRITINGS: Christ Speaks to the Church, Gospel Publishing House, 1970; *The Fourth Watch of the Night,* Gospel Publishing House, 1973; *Preparing for the Storm,* Gospel Publishing House, 1975. Also author of *Seven Lamps of Fire.* Contributor to periodicals.

WORK IN PROGRESS: The Communion of the Holy Spirit.

AVOCATIONAL INTERESTS: Jogging, music.

*   *   *

BARON, Salo W(ittmayer) 1895-

PERSONAL: Born May 26, 1895, in Tarnow, Austria; came to the United States in 1926; son of Elias and Minna (Wittmayer) Baron; married Jeannette G. Meisel, June 12, 1934; children: Shoshana Baron Tancer, Tobey Baron Gitelle. *Education:* University of Vienna, Ph.D., 1917, Pol.Sc.D., 1922, Jur.D., 1923; Jewish Theological Seminary, Vienna, Austria, M.H.L. (rabbi), 1920. *Home address:* Yifat Shalom, Honey Hill Rd., Canaan, Conn. 06018; and 29 Claremont Ave., New York, N.Y. *Office:* 420 West 118th St., New York, N.Y. 10027.

CAREER: Ordained rabbi, 1920; Juedisches Paedagogium, Vienna, Austria, lecturer in history, 1919-25; Jewish Institute of Religion, New York City, visiting lecturer, 1926, professor of history and acting librarian, 1927-30, director of department of advanced studies, 1928-30; Columbia University, New York City, professor of Jewish history, literature, and institutions, 1930-63, professor emeritus, 1963—, director of Center of Israel and Jewish studies, 1950-68, director emeritus, 1968—; writer, 1968—. Has served as rabbi of Jewish congregations. Rauschenbusch lecturer at Colgate-Rochester Divinity School, 1944; visiting professor at Jewish Theological Seminary, 1954-72, Hebrew University (Jerusalem), 1958, Rutgers University, 1964-69, and Brown University, 1966-68. President of Jewish Cultural Reconstruction, Inc., 1947—. Chairman of survey commission of National Jewish Welfare Board, of library information for American Jewish Committee, and of cultural advisory committee of Conference for Jewish Material Claims against Germany, 1953-55; corresponding member of UNESCO's international committee for the scientific history of mankind, 1953—. Trustee of Jewish Institute of Religion, 1937-55; president of academic council of Hebrew University, 1940-50; member of board of governors of Tel-Aviv University, 1968—, and Haifa University, 1970—.

MEMBER: American Academy for Jewish Research (fellow; president, 1940-43, 1958-63, 1965-67, 1969—), American Academy of Arts and Sciences (fellow), American Jewish Historical Society (president, 1953-55), American Historical Association, Society for Biblical Literature,

Conference for Jewish Social Studies (honorary president). *Awards, honors:* Decorated knight of the Order of Merit (Italy); honorary degrees include D.H.L. from Hewbrew Union College, 1944, LL.D. from Dropsie University, 1962, Litt.D. from Rutgers University and Columbia University, both 1963, Golden Doctorate from University of Vienna, 1969, and Ph.D. from Tel-Aviv University, 1970.

WRITINGS: Die judenfrage auf dem Wiener kongress, auf grund von zum teil ungedruckten quellen dargestellt von dr. Salo Baron, R. Loewit, 1920; *Die politische theorie Ferdinand Lassalle's,* C. L. Hirschfeld, 1923; *A Social and Religious History of the Jews,* fifteen volumes, Columbia University Press, 1937, 2nd edition, Volumes 1-2, 1952, Volumes 3-5, 1957, Volumes 6-8, 1958, Volumes 9-10, 1965, Volumes 11-12, 1967, Volumes 13-14, 1960, Volume 15, 1973.

The Jewish Community: Its History and Structure to the American Revolution, three volumes, Jewish Publication Society of America, 1942, reprinted, Greenwood Press, 1972; *Modern Nationalism and Religion,* Harper, 1947, reprinted, Books for Libraries, 1971; (editor with Ernest Nagel and Koppel S. Pinson) *Freedom and Reason: Studies in Philosophy and Jewish Culture, in Memory of Morris Raphael Cohen,* Free Press, 1951; (editor with Joseph L. Blau, and author of introduction and notes) *Judaism: Postbiblical and Talmudic Period,* Liberal Arts Press, 1954; (author of introduction) *Jerusalem: City Holy and Eternal,* Hemisphere Publications, 1954; (contributor) Leo Walder Schwarz, editor, *Great Ages and Ideas of the Jewish People,* Random House, 1956.

From a Historian's Notebook: European Jewry Before and After Hitler, Institute of Human Relations, American Jewish Committee, 1962; *World Dimensions of Jewish History,* Leo Baeck Institute, 1962; (editor with Blau) *The Jews of the United States, 1790-1840: A Documentary History,* three volumes, Columbia University Press, 1963; *The Russian Jew under Tsars and Soviets,* Macmillan, 1964, revised edition, 1976; (editor) *Essays on Maimonides: An Octocentennial Volume,* reprinted, AMS Press, 1966; *Steeled by Adversity: Essays and Addresses on American Jewish Life,* edited by his wife, Jeannette Meisel Baron, Jewish Publication Society of America, 1971; *Ancient and Medieval Jewish History: Essays,* edited by Leon A. Feldman, Rutgers University Press, 1972; (with Arcadius Kahan) *Economic History of the Jews,* edited by Nachum Gross, Schocken, 1975.

Also author of *Azariah de Rossi's Attitude to Life,* 1927, *The Israelitic Population under the Kings* (in Hebrew), 1933, *Bibliography of Jewish Social Studies, 1938-1939,* 1941, *Historiyah hevrutit vedatit shel 'am Yisrael,* 1954, and *History and Jewish Historians,* 1964; also editor of *Jewish Studies in Memory of G. A. Kohut,* 1935.

Editor-in-chief of series, "A Documentary History of American Jews," 1954—, and "World History of the Jewish People," Volumes 14-20, 1957—. Contributor to periodicals. Editor, *Jewish Social Studies,* 1939—.*

*   *   *

BARONDESS, Sue K(aufman) 1926-1977
(Sue Kaufman)

August 7, 1926—June 25, 1977; American author of novels and short stories on the stresses of modern urban life. Her novel *Diary of a Mad Housewife* was made into a successful motion picture. She died in New York City. Obituaries: *New York Times,* June 26, 1977; *Washington Post,* June 28,

1977; *Newsweek,* July 11, 1977; *Time,* July 11, 1977. (See index for previous *CA* sketch)

* * *

BARR, Donald Roy 1938-

PERSONAL: Born December 10, 1938, in Durango, Colo.; son of Russell W. (a farmer) and Elizabeth G. (a nurse) Barr; married Loudean Suttle (an artist), June 14, 1958; children: Mark Edward, Bryan Michael. *Education:* Whittier College, B.A., 1960; Colorado State University, M.S., 1962, Ph.D., 1965. *Home:* 422 Pine Ave., Pacific Grove, Calif. 93950. *Agent:* Jack Thornton, 555 Abrego, Monterey, Calif. 93940. *Office:* Department of Operations Analysis, Naval Postgraduate School, Monterey, Calif. 93940.

CAREER: Colorado State University, Fort Collins, instructor in mathematics, 1963-65; University of Wisconsin, Oshkosh, assistant professor of mathematics, 1965-66; Naval Postgraduate School, Monterey, Calif., assistant professor, 1966-70, associate professor, 1970-76, professor of operations research, 1976—. Consultant to Litton Industries. *Member:* Institute of Mathematical Statistics, Mathematical Association of America, American Statistical Association, American Mathematical Association, Operations Research Society of America, Sigma Xi, Phi Kappa Phi.

WRITINGS: College and University Mathematics, Allyn & Bacon, 1968; *Finite Statistics,* Allyn & Bacon, 1969; *Probability,* Brooks/Cole, 1971; *Analytic Geometry,* Allyn & Bacon, 1971.

WORK IN PROGRESS: Inference, a textbook.

* * *

BARR, Jeff 1941-

PERSONAL: Born December 21, 1941, in Aurora, Ill. *Education:* California State University, Long Beach, B.A., 1974. *Home address:* P.O. Box 7785, Van Nuys, Calif. 91409.

CAREER: Free-lance writer, 1963-73; *Quincy Patriot Ledger,* Quincy, Mass., jazz critic, 1973—. Member of board of directors of Foundation for Jazz Broadcasting.

WRITINGS: Nobody's Children, Brandon, 1969. Contributing editor of *Record Collector's Journal,* jazz editor, 1975; record reviewer for Sabin's Radio Free Jazz.

SIDELIGHTS: Barr comments: "My current interest is to help publicize the resurgence of good jazz music on record."

* * *

BARRETT, Dean 1942-
(Yum Char)

PERSONAL: Born October 10, 1942, in New London, Conn.; son of Jack and Jacqueline (McCarthy) Barrett; married Louella Harteam (a public relations manager for a hotel), December 3, 1971. *Education:* Mitchell College, A.A., 1962; University of Hartford, B.A., 1964; University of Hawaii, M.A., 1970. *Politics:* "Very liberal." *Home:* Baguio Villa, 550 Victoria Rd., Block 36, 18th Floor, Hong Kong. 5-518739.

CAREER: Orientations, Tokyo, Japan, assistant editor, 1970-72; *Pacific,* Tokyo, associate editor, 1973; *Hong Kong Standard,* Hong Kong, columnist under pseudonym Yum Char, 1974—; *Seasons,* Hong Kong, editor, 1976—; Thai International, Hong Kong, publisher and editor of *Sawasee,* 1976—. Lecturer at Baptist College, Hong Kong, 1975. *Military Service:* U.S. Army, Chinese linguist for Security Agency, 1964-68; served in Thailand and Taiwan.

MEMBER: Amnesty International, Society of American Travel Writers, Foreign Correspondents Club, Royal Asiatic Society, Siam Society, Hong Kong Journalist Association, Studio One Film Society (member of executive board).

WRITINGS: (Author of text) *Aberdeen: Catching the Last Rays* (photograph book on the boat people of Hong Kong), Perennial Press, 1974.

Books of satire, under pseudonym Yum Char: *Yum Char's Travels: A Voyage to Gnokgnoh,* Hong Kong Publishing Co., 1976; *Hong Kong Joshsticks,* James Dean Enterprises, 1976; *More Hong Kong Joshsticks,* James Dean Enterprises, 1977.

Writer of "Uncle Yum Char" column, under pseudonym Yum Char, *Hong Kong Standard,* 1976—.

Author of film scripts for advertising purposes. Contributor of articles and photographs to magazines in the United States and Asia.

WORK IN PROGRESS: A feature length film script; novels.

SIDELIGHTS: Barrett writes: "I have lived in Asia for ten years and in Hong Kong for over six years. I speak, read, and write Chinese Mandarin and speak Thai. My wife is Chinese. My field of expertise is writing and travel photography on Asia and satire in the vein of Jonathan Swift and Twain. I am also now becoming involved in writing film scripts for advertising and also for feature films. I specialize in the late seventeenth century history of Siam."

AVOCATIONAL INTERESTS: Travel to places not open to tourists (lower Burma, parts of Indonesia, upper Laos).

* * *

BARRETT, Laurence I(rwin) 1935-

PERSONAL: Born September 6, 1935, in New York, N.Y.; son of Harold (a postal official) and Ruth (Gaier) Barrett; married Paulette Francois Singer, April 9, 1957; children: Paul Meyer, David Allen, Adam Singer. *Education:* New York University, A.B., 1956; Columbia University, M.S., 1957. *Politics:* Independent. *Religion:* Jewish. *Home:* 28 Tenafly Rd., Tenafly, N.J. 07670. *Agent:* MacIntosh & Otis, Inc., 475 Fifth Ave., New York, N.Y. 10017. *Office:* Time & Life Bldg., Rockefeller Center, New York, N.Y. 10020.

CAREER: New York Herald Tribune, New York City, metropolitan political reporter, 1958-62, Washington correspondent, 1962-65; *Time* Magazine, New York City, national affairs writer, 1965-70, senior editor, 1970-75, New York bureau chief and senior political reporter in middle Atlantic region, 1975—.

WRITINGS: The Mayor of New York (novel), Doubleday, 1965. Writer of news stories and editorial page columns for *New York Herald Tribune* and of cover stories for *Time.* Contributor to *Nation* and *Columbia Journalism Review.*

* * *

BARRETT, Marvin 1920-

PERSONAL: Born May 6, 1920, in Des Moines, Iowa; son of Edwin Galbraith (a professor) and Esther (Kruidenier) Barrett; married Mary Ellin Berlin (a writer), October 14, 1952; children: Elizabeth, Irving, Mary Ellin, Katherine. *Education:* Harvard University, B.A., 1942; Drake University, M.A., 1976. *Politics:* Independent. *Religion:* Protestant. *Agent:* Russell & Volkening, Inc., 551 Fifth Ave., New York, N.Y. 10017.

CAREER: Time, New York, N.Y., contributing editor, 1948-52; free-lance writer, 1952-55; *Newsweek,* New York City, radio-television editor, 1955-59; *Show Business Illustrated,* New York City, executive editor, 1960; *Show,* New York City, editor, 1961-64; *Atlas,* New York City, editor, 1965-67; free-lance writer, 1967—. *Military service:* U.S. Naval Reserve, active duty, 1942-46; became lieutenant. *Awards, honors:* Distinguished service award from Sigma Delta Chi, 1975, for *Moments of Truth?.*

WRITINGS: The Jazz Age, Putnam, 1959; *The Years Between,* Little, Brown, 1961; *Meet Thomas Jefferson,* Random House, 1964; *Survey of Broadcast Journalism,* Grosset, 1969; *Year of Challenge, Year of Crisis,* Grosset, 1970; *State of Siege,* Grosset, 1971; *The Politics of Broadcasting,* Crowell, 1973; *Moments of Truth?,* Crowell, 1975; *The End of the Party,* Putnam, 1976. Contributor to magazines.

WORK IN PROGRESS: A Company of Lovers, a novel; a book on broadcast journalism; another novel.

* * *

BARRIGER, John Walker 1899-1976

December 3, 1899—December 9, 1976; American railroad executive and author of a book on the railroads. He died in St. Louis, Mo. Obituaries: *New York Times,* December 11, 1976.

* * *

BARRON, Ann Forman
(Annabel Erwin)

PERSONAL: Born in Oakdale, La.; daughter of Royal Clinton (a professor) and Anne (a pianist; maiden name, Erwin) Forman; married Del D. Barron (a realtor); children: Douglas Del, Robert Bruce (deceased). *Education:* Studied under private tutors. *Home and office:* 7212 Evergreen Rd., Fort Worth, Tex. 76118. *Agent:* John K. Payne, Lenniger Literary Agency, 437 Fifth Ave., New York, N.Y. 10016.

CAREER: Writer. *Member:* Women in Communication.

WRITINGS: Murder Is a Gentle Kiss, Bouregy, 1960; *Spin a Dark Web,* Bouregy, 1961; *Strange Legacy,* Fawcett, 1969; *Dark Vengeance,* Fawcett, 1972; *Serpent in the Shadows,* Berkeley Publishing, 1973; *Bride of Menace,* Fawcett, 1973; *Banner Bold and Beautiful,* Fawcett, 1975; (under pseudonym, Annabel Erwin) *Liliane,* Warner Books, 1976; *Firebrand,* CBS-Fawcett, 1977. Contributor of articles to periodicals, including *Redbook* and *Reader's Digest.*

WORK IN PROGRESS: Two novels, *River of Passion,* and one set in Texas.

SIDELIGHTS: Ann Barron writes: "I had my own typewriter at the age of six, writing my first short novel at that age, entitled 'Woolly, the Worm.' My shrewd and kindly father paid me by the line for all the classics I could memorize. By the time he removed this financial carrot from in front of my nose, I was full of quotes and he had achieved his purpose. I was firmly hooked on good reading.

"I have loved and studied American history—and world history—all my life. There are hundreds of great love stories that can be imagined, teeming with conflict and passion set against the tapestry of the past. *Banner Bold and Beautiful* is the accumulation of years of reading, and listening to folklore, an inescapable occupation to any resident of Texas."

BARRON, Charlie Nelms 1922-1977

January 8, 1922—January 7, 1977; American veterinary pathologist and writer of works in his field. Barron edited the journal *Pathologia Veterinaria* and belonged to several veterinary organizations. He died in Washington, D.C. Obituaries: *Washington Post,* January 14, 1977.

* * *

BARRY, Jack 1939-

PERSONAL: Born May 9, 1939, in Syracuse, N.Y.; son of Vincent J. (a laborer) and Irene (Mahoney) Barry; married Judith Ann DeBell (a nursing student), August 28, 1965; children: Brian, Denise, Jonathan. *Education:* University of Notre Dame, B.A., 1963; Syracuse University, M.A., 1965. *Home:* 509 Buckingham Ave., Syracuse, N.Y. 13210. *Office:* McKinley-Brighton School, 104 West Newell St., Syracuse, N.Y.

CAREER: Junior high school teacher in Syracuse, N.Y., 1968-76; director of Westside Educational Center in Syracuse, 1976—. McKinley-Brighton School, Syracuse, administrative assistant, spring 1972. Conductor of creative writing workshops for students, teachers, and parents at University of Vermont, summer, 1974, and Cazenovia College, 1976. *Member:* Poets and Writers, Phi Delta Kappa.

WRITINGS: Hints and Hunches (poems), The Garlic Press, 1973; (compiler and editor) *Drawing Dreams,* Syracuse School District, 1973.

Contributor of poems and articles to *America, Notre Dame Magazine, American Poetry Review,* and *Upstate New York.*

WORK IN PROGRESS: Fleadh Cheoil (title means "Feast of Music"), a book of poems tracing the author's grandparent's journey from Listowel, Ireland, to Syracuse, N.Y.

* * *

BARTHELMES, (Albert) Wes(ley, Jr.) 1922-1976
(Sisyphus)

PERSONAL: Son of Albert Wesley Barthelmes, an insurance representative; married wife, Dorothy; children: Lisa, Victoria; (stepchildren) Elizabeth Stevens, Robert Stevens. *Education:* Tufts University, B.A., 1947; Columbia University, M.A., 1949; additional study at University of Geneva. *Home:* 6006 Welborn Dr., Wood Acres, Md.

CAREER/WRITINGS: Worcester Telegram Gazette, Worcester, Mass., reporter and editor, 1950-53; *Washington Post,* Washington D.C., general assignment reporter, 1953-58, assistant city editor, 1958-62; United States Congress, Washington, D.C., administrative assistant to Oregon Congresswoman, Edith Green, 1962-65, press secretary to Massachusetts Senator Robert Kennedy, 1965-66, assistant to Oregon Congressman Robert Duncan, 1966, administrative assistant to Missouri Congressman Richard Bolling, 1967-70; special assistant to Idaho Senator Frank Church, 1970-73, administrative assistant to Delaware Senator Joseph R. Biden, Jr., 1973-76. Journalistic assignments concentrated on District of Columbia planning and development, including coverage of District transit, building, finance, tax, and budgeting problems. Writer of column "Washington Report," for *Commonweal,* under pseudonym Sisyphus. Member of Montgomery County and Maryland State Democratic Central Committees, 1970-74. *Military service:* U.S. Army, 1943-46; served as paratrooper. *Member:* Newspaper Guild (chairperson of *Washington Post* unit, 1956), Washington Newspaper Guild (president, 1958). *Awards, honors:* Guildsman of the Year award from Newspaper Guild, 1965; Journalism Award of Catholic Press Association, 1975, for "Washington Report" columns.

OBITUARIES: Washington Post, June 24, 1976.*

(Died June 22, 1976, in Wood Acres, Md.)

* * *

BARTLEY, Diana E(sther) Pelaez-Rivera 1940-

PERSONAL: Born May 18, 1940, in New York, N.Y.; daughter of Manuel (an attorney) and Lila Esther (Camacho) Pelaez-Rivera; children: R. Christian Manuel. *Education:* Rosemont College, B.A., 1961; Middlebury College, M.A. (Spanish and Italian), 1963; Stanford University, A.M. (education), 1964, Ph.D., 1970; also attended University of Fribourg, University of Madrid, and University of Florence. *Home:* 203 West Highview Dr., Mequon, Wis. 53092. *Office:* Department of Curriculum and Instruction, School of Education, University of Wisconsin, Milwaukee, Wis. 53201.

CAREER: U.S. Information Agency, Bi-National Center, Madrid, Spain, teacher of English as a foreign language, 1961-62; French and Spanish teacher in Fairfield, Conn., 1963; junior high school teacher of French and Spanish in Palo Alto, Calif., 1964-66; University of Wisconsin, Milwaukee, instructor in Spanish and Portuguese, 1969-70, assistant professor of curriculum and instruction, 1970-73, associate professor of curriculum and instruction, 1973—, also director of bilingual bicultural teacher education program. Chairman and participant in seminars, national conventions, and workshops; organized bilingual bicultural education program for WUWM-Radio, 1975-76. Guest on television and radio programs. Member of board of directors of Florentine Opera Auxiliary, 1973-76, Literary Services of Wisconsin, Laubach Literacy Center, 1975-76; member of Library League of Mequon, 1970-73; member of American Field Service, 1966—.

MEMBER: Modern Language Association of America, American Association of Teachers of French, American Association of Teachers of Spanish and Portuguese, American Council on the Teaching of Foreign Languages, National Association for Bilingual Education, American Educational Research Association, Teachers of English to Speakers of Other Languages, Adult Education Association (chairperson of Teaching of English to Speakers of Other Languages—TESOL section), American Association of University Professors (member of local executive committee, 1973-76), American Association of University Women, Research Society of Hertzen Pedagogical Institute (honorary member), Wisconsin Bilingual Association, Wisconsin Teachers of English to Speakers of Other Languages Association, Wisconsin Association for Bilingual Education, Pi Lambda Theta, Sigma Delta Pi. *Awards, honors:* Has received more than $600,000 in grants from the U.S. Office of Education and the State of Wisconsin.

WRITINGS: (With Robert L. Politzer) *Practice-Centered Teacher Training: Spanish,* Center for Research and Development in Teaching, Stanford University, 1967, revised edition, Center for Curriculum Development, 1970; *Standard English and Nonstandard Dialects: Phonology and Morphology* (monograph), Center for Research and Development in Teaching, Stanford University, 1969; *Standard English and Nonstandard Dialects: Elements of Syntax* (monograph), Center for Research and Development in Teaching, Stanford University, 1969; (with Politzer) *Standard English and Nonstandard Dialects: Suggested Teaching Behaviors and Microlessons* (monograph), Center for Research and Development in Teaching, Stanford University, 1970; *Soviet Approaches to Bilingual Education,* Center for Curriculum Development, 1971; (with Politzer) *Practice-Centered Teacher Training: Standard English for Speakers of Non-Standard Dialects,* Center for Curriculum Development, 1972; (editor) *The Latin Child Goes Forth: Bilingual Early Education Experience Based Lessons—A Guide for Teachers,* Bilingual Bicultural Early Childhood Development Center, United Migrant Opportunity Services, 1975; (editor) *ABE-TESOL: A Handbook for Educators,* Collier, 1977. Also author of about fifteen technical reports.

Video-tapes: "Methodology in the Bilingual Pre-School and Elementary Classroom," "The Bilingual Secondary Classroom," "The Adult Bilingual Classroom."

Contributor of about twenty-five articles and reviews to professional journals and to newspapers. Editorial reviewer for *Foreign Language Annals, Modern Language Journal, Foreign Language Education,* and Blaisdell.

WORK IN PROGRESS: Developing an evaluation model for bilingual bicultural teacher education.

* * *

BARTLEY, Numan V(ache) 1934-

PERSONAL: Born October 29, 1934, in Ladonia, Tex.; son of Numan V. (a farmer) and Rosa (a nurse; maiden name, Rollin) Bartley; married Morraine Matthews (in real estate), June, 1968. *Education:* East Texas State College, B.A., 1955; North Texas State University, M.A., 1961; Vanderbilt University, Ph.D., 1968. *Home:* 220 Lavender Rd., Athens, Ga. 30606. *Office:* Department of History, University of Georgia, Athens, Ga. 30601.

CAREER: Georgia Institute of Technology, Atlanta, instructor, 1964-66, assistant professor, 1966-70, associate professor of history, 1970-72; University of Georgia, Athens, associate professor, 1972-75, professor of history, 1975—. *Military service:* U.S. Navy, 1955-58, became lieutenant, junior grade. *Awards, honors:* Postdoctoral fellowships from Johns Hopkins University Institute of Southern History, 1969-70, University of Michigan Inter-University Consortium for Political Research, 1971, and Woodrow Wilson International Center for Scholars, 1972; Chastain Award for best book on the South, from Southern Political Science Association, 1976, for *Southern Politics and the Second Reconstruction.*

WRITINGS: The Rise of Massive Resistance: Race and Politics in the South During the 1950's, Louisiana State University Press, 1969; *From Thurmond to Wallace: Political Tendencies in Georgia, 1948-1968,* Johns Hopkins University Press, 1970; (with Hugh D. Graham) *Southern Politics and the Second Reconstruction,* Johns Hopkins University Press, 1976; (with Kenneth Coleman and others) *A History of Georgia,* University of Georgia Press, 1977. Contributor of articles to journals in his field.

WORK IN PROGRESS: A history of modern Georgia.

* * *

BASILE, Gloria Vitanza 1929-
(McKayla Morgan; Michaela Morgan)

PERSONAL: Born June 29, 1929, in Westfield, N.Y.; daughter of Alphonse and Guisepa (Guido) Vitanza; divorced; children: Louis, Robert, David. *Education:* Attended San Jose State University and University of California, Los Angeles. *Religion:* "Science of Mind." *Agent:* Reece Halsey Agency, 8733 Sunset Blvd., Los Angeles, Calif. 90069.

CAREER: Gloria's (women's apparel shop), San Jose, Calif., owner and designer, 1950-56; actress for television and motion pictures, in Hollywood, Calif., 1956-62; music composer, 1956—; novelist, 1969—. Owner and designer of Down the Aisle (women's apparel shop), Beverly Hills, Calif., 1967-71. Director of actor's workshop in San Jose, Calif.; literary agent for motion pictures. *Member:* American Society of Composers, Authors, and Publishers, Authors Guild of Authors League of America, Screen Actors Guild, American Federation of Television and Radio Artists.

WRITINGS—Novels: *The Godson,* Pinnacle Books, 1976; (under pseudonym Michaela Morgan) *Madelaina,* Pinnacle Books, 1977; *Appassionato,* Pinnacle Books, in press. Composer of music, under pseudonym McKayla Morgan.

WORK IN PROGRESS—Novels: *Iago,* for Pinnacle Books; *Phaedra,* a novel set in the 1850 of Napoleon III; *Aurora,* a novel dealing with American Indians, the Gold Rush, and the Civil War; *Bethaynia,* a novel set in Italy and France during the reign of Napoleon Bonaparte.

SIDELIGHTS: Gloria Basile writes: "Having been raised in a highly prejudiced area in an era when Sicilian Italians were considered the lowest on the totem, the attitudes of my contemporaries were as puzzling as they were traumatic. Inclined to withdraw and survey the situation as if it was happening to another—not me, I found myself wondering at the differences in man. What makes one man better than the next or more acceptable? As a second generation Sicilian American, I lacked true self identification until I was in my thirties. Poised between two world cultures, American and Sicilian, my childhood was one of ambivalence and moody introversion. However outgoing I was to offset these insecurities, by participating in school activities, and politics . . . I immersed myself in books, and became a voracious reader—anything I could lay my hands on.

"Over the years, after three children and two divorces, there still fermented inside me the need to know my roots—and to eliminate the childhood feelings of unworthiness cemented into my mentality by a bigoted people. I began to involve myself in extensive research to learn for myself what this stigma was concerning Italo-Sicilians. Out of this frustration and exhaustive research came *The Godson,* to be re-titled *House of Lions* for a coming motion picture, and *Appassionato,* a story of post-war Sicily.

"In the late 1950's I pursued a career in Hollywood in the motion picture industry. Unsure of which facet of the industry I'd find my niche, I began as student of drama, actress, writer, composer, director, and worked up. I authored and composed lyrics and music for *Ballad of One Eyed Jacks* for the Brando movie. Hopefully, perhaps I may be able to produce a motion picture with the necessary integrity so terribly lacking in many of the films in recent years."

AVOCATIONAL INTERESTS: Travel (Mexico, Baja California, Italy, Sicily), free-form wall macrame, weaving, oil painting, botany, music.

* * *

BASON, Lillian 1913-

PERSONAL: Born October 17, 1913, in Albany, N.Y.; daughter of Victor and Gertrude (Nilson) Peterson; married Charles R. Bason, June 2, 1939; children: Frank, Christine Bason Becker, Roger. *Education:* Attended Adelphi College; New York University, B.A., 1938. *Religion:* Presbyterian. *Home address:* R.R. 1, South Salem, N.Y. 10590.

CAREER: New York Stock Exchange, New York, N.Y., secretary, 1932-39; writer, 1964—. Has worked as substitute teacher and volunteer story teller. Town historian of Lewisboro, N.Y., 1972—. *Member:* Authors Guild of Authors League of America, Forum of Writers for Young People, Lewisboro Historical Society (president, 1973—).

WRITINGS—For children: *Isabelle and the Library Cat,* Lothrop, 1966; *Pick a Raincoat, Pick a Whistle,* Lothrop, 1966; *Eric and the Little Canal Boat,* Parents' Magazine Press, 1967; *Castles and Mirrors and Cities of Sand,* Lothrop, 1968; *Spiders,* National Geographic Society, 1974; (translator) *Those Foolish Molboes* (Danish folk tales), Coward, 1977. Writer and producer of radio scripts for Church Women United during the 1940's.

WORK IN PROGRESS: Translating more Danish folk tales; nonfiction for children, about storks and white owls.

SIDELIGHTS: Lillian Bason writes: "I like to share my sense of wonder at the world and all it contains with young children. Wherever I travel, I find inspiration in the people, places, and stories of the countries I visit. My interest is equally in stories and non-fiction subjects that fascinate me."

* * *

BASS, Howard L(arry) 1942-

PERSONAL: Born February 6, 1942, in Brooklyn, N.Y.; son of Samuel and Estelle (Gold) Bass. *Education:* Adelphi College, B.A., 1963; Brooklyn Law School, J.D., 1966. *Home and office:* 330 East 49th St., New York, N.Y. 10017.

CAREER: Erdheim & Shalleck, New York City, associate trial attorney, 1967-68; associate trial attorney in New York City, 1968-70; Blumenthal, Barandes, Bass, Matson & Arnold, New York City, law partner, 1970-72; Mitchell, Salem, Fisher & Kemper, New York City, special counsel, 1974—. Private consultant and counsel to Herbert Siegal, Buffalo, N.Y. Lecturer at New School for Social Research. Has given poetry readings and song recitals at schools, clubs, and on television and radio programs; has appeared on local television programs. *Member:* International Society on Family Law, American Bar Association, New York State Trial Lawyers Association. *Awards, honors:* Poetry awards from *Bardic Echoes,* 1975, for "The Dream," and "Backroads of My Mind," and *Amateur Writers Journal,* 1976, for "Eulogy for Paul".

WRITINGS: Divorce or Marriage: A Legal Guide, Prentice-Hall, 1976.

Work represented in anthologies, including *New Worlds Unlimited Anthology,* edited by John Buttaci and Susan Gerstle, 1974, *Bouquets of Poems,* edited by Arnando Troni, Centro Studi e Scambi Internazionali (Rome), 1975, and 1976, and *Man! The Poet,* edited by James Romnes, Northwoods Press, 1975.

Contributor of articles and poems to law journals, literary magazines, including *New York State Trial Lawyers Quarterly, American Bar Association Journal, Janus, Driftwood East Poetry Quarterly,* and *Bardic Echoes,* national magazines, including *Girl Talk, Face to Face, Town and Country, Ladies' Home Journal, Cosmopolitan,* and *Viva,* and newspapers.

WORK IN PROGRESS: For the Children of Tomorrow, with J. Louise Despert; *Hyphens: Toward the New Age Relationship,* with M. L. Rein, a sequel to *Divorce or Marriage: A Legal Guide.*

SIDELIGHTS: Bass comments that he began writing poetry as an adolescent, as an outlet for his feelings about social issues, love, and death. He adds: "Extensive travel to the Mediterranean, Greece, and Europe brought contact with collective unconscious parts of me." He came to feel "that simplicity held life's answers and affected my philosophy of life." *Avocational interests:* Reading, nature, music of all lands.

*   *   *

BASSOFF, Bruce 1941-

PERSONAL: Born January 18, 1941, in New York; son of Isidore (a lawyer) and Sylvia (a pre-medical adviser; maiden name, Flexer) Bassoff; married Evelyn Silten, June 13, 1965; children: Leah, Jonathan. *Education:* Brandeis University, B.A., 1962; Columbia University, M.A., 1963; City University of New York, Ph.D., 1970. *Home:* 3033 Jefferson St., Boulder, Colo. 80302. *Office:* Department of English, University of Colorado, Boulder, Colo. 80302.

CAREER: University of Paris, Sorbonne, Paris, France, teaching fellow, 1969-70; Brooklyn College of the City University of New York, Brooklyn, N.Y., instructor in English, 1970-72; Ohio University, Athens, assistant professor of English, 1972-75; University of Colorado, Boulder, associate professor of English, 1975—. *Member:* Modern Language Association of America.

WRITINGS: Toward Loving: The Poetics of the Novel and the Practice of Henry Green, University of South Carolina Press, 1975.

WORK IN PROGRESS: A book on contemporary American fiction.

*   *   *

BATE, Lucy 1939-

PERSONAL: Born March 19, 1939, in Washington, D.C.; daughter of Immanuel (a musician) and Ruth (Schmerler) Neumark; married Michael Bate (a computer scientist), March 15, 1965; children: Gabrielle, Rebecca. *Education:* Brandeis University, B.A., 1960. *Politics:* Liberal. *Home:* 195 Lakeview Ave., Cambridge, Mass. 02138.

CAREER: Crown Publishers, New York City, editorial assistant, 1961; American Book Co., New York City, assistant editor, 1962-63; Hart Publishing Co., New York City, writer, 1964-65; freelance writer, 1965—. *Member:* Overseas Press Club. *Awards, honors:* New plays award from Skidmore College, 1969, for "The Great Silkie of Sule Skerrie."

WRITINGS: Little Rabbit's Loose Tooth (juvenile), Crown, 1975.

Plays: "The Great Silkie of Sule Skerrie" (radio play), first produced by Liberi Artisti, 1973; "Little Red Riding Hood" (juvenile), first produced in Cambridge, Mass. by Tobin Players, 1974; "An Antigone Play" (one-act), first produced in Boston, Mass. by Octopus, 1974; "King David" (three-act), first produced in Boston by Jewish Repertory Theatre, 1975; "A Long Drive to Quincy" (one-act), first produced in Cambridge by Tobin Players, 1975; "Events in a Beerhall" (one-act), first produced in Cambridge by Tobin Players, 1975.

AVOCATIONAL INTERESTS: Jazz piano.

BATES, Robert H(inrichs) 1942-

PERSONAL: Born December 5, 1942, in Brooklyn, N.Y.; son of David H. (a physician) and Lucy (Thomas) Bates; married Margaret Rouse (a college administrator), June 6, 1964; children: Elizabeth. *Education:* Haverford College, B.A. (summa cum laude), 1964; Massachusetts Institute of Technology, Ph.D., 1969. *Office:* Division of Social Sciences, California Institute of Technology, Pasadena, Calif. 91125.

CAREER: California Institute of Technology, Pasadena, assistant professor, 1969-76, associate professor of social sciences, 1976—. *Member:* American Political Science Association, African Studies Association, Phi Beta Kappa. *Awards, honors:* Woodrow Wilson fellowship, 1964-65; fellowship from Center for International Studies at Massachusetts Institute of Technology, 1969; Social Science Research Council fellowship, 1969-70; National Institutes of Health fellowship, 1971-73.

WRITINGS: Unions, Parties, and Political Development, Yale University Press, 1971; *Patterns of Uneven Development,* University of Denver Graduate School of International Studies, 1974; *Rural Responses to Industrialization,* Yale University Press, 1976. Contributor to political science and African studies journals.

WORK IN PROGRESS: Research on peasant politics, rural development, and agricultural development.

*   *   *

BATESON, Charles (Henry) 1903-

PERSONAL: Born August 4, 1903, in Wellington, New Zealand; immigrated to Australia, 1922; married Coy C. Lynam, August 27, 1923 (died, 1962); married Ann Graham, November 28, 1964; children: (first marriage) one daughter. *Education:* Educated in private schools in New Zealand. *Home:* 10 Burra Birra Ave., Vaucluse, New South Wales 2030, Australia.

CAREER: Writer. Served as editorial manager of Mirror Newspapers in Australia, 1960-66. *Member:* City Tattersalls Club, New Zealand Club (Sydney, Australia), New South Wales Sports Club.

WRITINGS: The Convict Ships, 1787-1868, Brown, Son & Ferguson, 1959, 2nd edition, 1969; *Gold Fleet for California: Forty-Niners from Australia and New Zealand,* Ure Smith, 1963, Michigan State University Press, 1964; *Patrick Logan: Tyrant of Brisbane Town,* Ure Smith, 1966; *A Soldier,* Oxford University Press, 1968; *The War with Japan: A Concise History,* Michigan State University Press, 1968; *Australian Shipwrecks: Including Vessels Wrecked en Route to or from Australia and Some Strandings,* A. H. & A. W. Reed, Volume I, 1972; *Dire Strait: A History of Bass Strait,* A. H. & A. W. Reed, 1973. Also author of *First into Italy,* 1944, *Early Sailor,* 1968, and *Early Surveyor,* 1970; also co-author of *Spitfires over Malta,* 1943.*

*   *   *

BATIUK, Thomas M(artin) 1947-

PERSONAL: Born March 14, 1947, in Akron, Ohio; son of Martin (an engineer) and Verna (Greskovics) Batiuk; married Catherine L. Wesemeyer. *Education:* Kent State University, B.F.A., 1969. *Office:* Field Newspaper Syndicate, 401 North Wabash Ave., Chicago, Ill. 60611.

CAREER: Teacher of art at Eastern Heights junior high school in Elyria, Ohio, 1969-72; Field Newspaper Syndicate, Chicago, Ill., creator of comic strip "Funky Winkerbean," syndicated to about two hundred thirty publications, 1972—. *Member:* Newspaper Comics Council.

WRITINGS: Funky Winkerbean (cartoons), Xerox Education Publications, 1973; *Play It Again Funky* (cartoons), Tempo Books, 1975; *Funky Winkerbean, Closed Out,* Tempo Books, 1977.

BIOGRAPHICAL/CRITICAL SOURCES: Cartoonist Profiles, June, 1974.

*   *   *

BATTERBERRY, Ariane Ruskin 1935-

PERSONAL: Born September 18, 1935, in New York, N.Y.; daughter of Simon Lyon (a physician) and Frances (a lawyer; maiden name, Reder) Ruskin; married Michael C. Batterberry (an author), May 15, 1968. *Education:* Barnard College, B.A., 1955; Cambridge University, M.A., 1960. *Home:* 1100 Madison Ave., New York, N.Y. 10028.

CAREER: Writer. *Harper's Bazaar,* New York, N.Y., contributing editor, 1972-73.

WRITINGS: Pantheon Story of Art, Pantheon, 1964; *Spy for Liberty,* Pantheon, 1965; *Nineteenth Century Art,* McGraw, 1969; *17th and 18th Century Art,* McGraw, 1969; (with husband, Michael Batterberry) *Greek and Roman Art,* McGraw, 1970; *Art of the High Renaissance,* McGraw, 1970; *Prehistoric Art and Ancient Art of the Near East,* McGraw, 1971; (with M. Batterberry) *Primitive Art,* McGraw, 1972; (with M. Batterberry) *Children's Homage to Picasso,* Abrams, 1972; (with M. Batterberry) *On the Town in New York,* Scribner, 1973; *History in Art,* F. Watts, 1974; *Pantheon Story of American Art,* Pantheon, 1976; (with M. Batterberry) *Bloomingdale's Book of Entertainment,* Random House, 1976; (with M. Batterberry) *Fashion, the Mirror of History,* Holt, in press.

Contributor of articles to *New York, Harper's Bazaar, Playbill, Wine and Food, Travel and Leisure,* and other periodicals.

SIDELIGHTS: Ariane Batterberry wrote: "I feel strongly that art and social history share or even exceed the importance of political history in teaching the young about the past. Political history is largely the record of human error, while cultural history is the record of human achievement."

*   *   *

BAUER, Marion Dane 1938-

PERSONAL: Born November 20, 1938, in Oglesby, Ill.; daughter of Chester (a chemist) and Elsie (a kindergarten teacher; maiden name, Hempstead) Dane; married Ronald Bauer (an Episcopal priest), June 25, 1959; children: Peter Dane, Elizabeth Alison, Teresa Sue (foster daughter). *Education:* Student at La Salle-Peru-Oglesby Junior College, 1956-58, and University of Missouri, 1958-59; University of Oklahoma, B.A., 1962. *Politics:* Democrat. *Religion:* Episcopalian. *Home:* 13908 McGinty Rd., Minnetonka, Minn. 55343. *Agent:* Ann Elmo Agency, Inc., 52 Vanderbilt Ave., New York, N.Y. 10017.

CAREER: High school English teacher in Waukesha, Wis., 1962-64; Hennepin County Vo-Tech School, Minneapolis, Minn., instructor in creative writing for adult education program, 1975—. *Member:* Authors Guild of Authors League of America, Society of Children's Book Writers.

WRITINGS: Shelter from the Wind (juvenile novel), Seabury, 1976; *Foster Child* (juvenile novel), Seabury, 1977.

WORK IN PROGRESS: Sing, O Barren, an adult novel; a novel for young adults, set in Lake Superior's Apostle Islands.

SIDELIGHTS: Marion Bauer writes: "In 1972, when my last excuse for not writing walked out the door to go to first grade, I embarked on a five-year-plan to work consistently and professionally at my writing, agreeing to take a full-time job at the end of the five years if I couldn't achieve some small measure of 'success'. . . . This work is my joy and my truest play. How glad I am not to need a job."

*   *   *

BAUER, Robert A(lbert) 1910-

PERSONAL: Born August 29, 1910, in Vienna, Austria; came to United States, 1940; naturalized U.S. citizen, 1946; son of Robert and Rosa (Schwarz) Bauer; married Maria von Kahler (a writer and interpreter), July 14, 1940; children: Virginia Rose (Mrs. Martin A. Ceaser), Robert Felix. *Education:* School for International Studies, Geneva, Switzerland, graduated, 1931; Economic University, Vienna, Austria, M.A., 1932; University of Vienna, J.D., 1933; American University of Cairo, M.A., 1967. *Politics:* Democrat. *Religion:* Protestant. *Home and office:* 3733 Massachusetts Ave. N.W., Washington, D.C. 20016; and 24 Playhouse Lane, Woodstock, N.Y. 12498.

CAREER: Admitted to Austrian bar, 1933; practiced law in Vienna, Austria, 1933-38; reporter to *New York Times* in Prague, Czechoslovakia, 1938-39; chief of Austrian Freedom Broadcasting Station in France, 1940; division chief, policy officer, and commentator for Voice of America, 1942-58; U.S. Department of State, officer in U.S. Foreign Service, 1958-72, director of center in Tehran, Iran, 1958-60, cultural attache in Paris, France, 1960-61, deputy director of cultural presentation in Washington, D.C., 1961-63, first secretary of cultural affairs at American embassy in Cairo, Egypt, 1963-66, counsellor for public affairs in Cairo, 1966-67, director of U.S. Information Agency Foreign Press Center in Washington, D.C., 1967-71, cultural attache and international relations specialist at American embassy in New Delhi, India, 1971-72; *West-Ost Journal,* Vienna, correspondent, 1972—. Kenyon College, adjunct professor, 1972-74, director of Kenyon Public Affairs Forum, 1972—. Lecturer on international affairs in the United States and abroad, 1958—. Member of school board of American College (Cairo), 1964-67. Consultant to U.S. Information Agency. *Member:* American Foreign Service Association, American Political Science Association, American Academy of Political and Social Science, Dacor Club. *Awards, honors:* Meritorious honor award from U.S. Government, 1972; silver medal of honor from the Republic of Austria, 1977.

WRITINGS: The United States in World Affairs: Leadership, Partnership or Disengagement?, University Press of Virginia, 1975; *The Interaction of Economics and Foreign Policy,* University Press of Virginia, 1975.

WORK IN PROGRESS: Bureaucracy and the Citizen in an Open Society; a conference and book, *The Making of American Foreign Policy.*

SIDELIGHTS: Bauer told *CA:* "Continuous study of international affairs and frequent lecture tours in West and East Europe, the Middle East, and Africa have strengthened my conviction that the last quarter of this century will be a most difficult period in mankind's history. The international economic problems are of a magnitude that defies traditional theories and methods. Nuclear proliferation, the armament race, the Middle East problem, the widening gap between the rich and the poor nations, and a sharpening ideological struggle between the Western world and the communist countries foreshadow periods of intense crises and confrontation. The world begins to understand the importance and the implication of the events in sub-Sahara Africa.

"At the same time," he observed, "I notice a renewed confidence abroad in U.S. leadership and with it a decline of what is known as anti-Americanism. The question on my mind is whether the American people know this and whether they are prepared once more to rise to the demands and sacrifices of world leadership. The communication media can and should increase the flow of information and analyses which will form the basis for the peoples' judgment."

*   *   *

BAUGH, Daniel A(lbert) 1931-

PERSONAL: Born July 10, 1931, in Philadelphia, Pa.; son of Albert C. (a professor of English literature) and Nita (Scudder) Baugh; married Carol Allen, June 18, 1955; children: Nancy, Charles Scudder, John Allen. *Education:* University of Pennsylvania, B.A., 1953, M.A., 1957; Cambridge University, Ph.D., 1961. *Religion:* Episcopalian. *Home:* 536 Cayuga Heights Rd., Ithaca, N.Y. 14850. *Office:* Department of History, McGraw Hall, Cornell University, Ithaca, N.Y. 14853.

CAREER: Princeton University, Princeton, N.J., instructor, 1961-64, assistant professor of history, 1964-69; Cornell University, Ithaca, N.Y., associate professor of history, 1969—. *Military service:* U.S. Navy, 1954-57; became lieutenant.

MEMBER: American Historical Association, Economic History Society, Navy Records Society, Society for Nautical Research, Conference on British Studies, American Society for Eighteenth-Century Studies, Royal Historical Society (fellow), Economic History Association. *Awards, honors:* Social Science Research Council grant, 1966-67; National Endowment for the Humanities fellowship, 1977-78.

WRITINGS: British Naval Administration in the Age of Walpole, Princeton University Press, 1965; (editor) *Aristocratic Government and Society in Eighteenth-Century England,* F. Watts, 1975; (editor) *Naval Administration, 1715-1750,* Navy Records Society, 1977. Contributor to *Economic History Review.*

WORK IN PROGRESS: The Great Darths and the Old Poor Law in England, 1795-1801.

SIDELIGHTS: Baugh writes: "My research field is mainly England, 1660-1840. By studying administration chiefly in terms of administrative problems, I hope to improve our understanding of both the nature of society and the development of government."

*   *   *

BAUMGAERTEL, (Max) Walter 1902-

PERSONAL: Born December 22, 1902, in Delitzsch, Germany; son of Max (a master bookbinder) and Maria (Maerz) Baumgaertel. *Education:* Educated in secondary school in Germany. *Home address:* c/o Hornbacher, Kirchenweg 4, D8203 Oberaudorf, Reisach, West Germany. *Agent:* Julian Bach Literary Agency, Inc., 3 East 48th St., New York, N.Y. 10017.

CAREER: Bookseller, 1919-21, and 1928-34; actor, 1922-28; shopkeeper, 1934-39, and 1945-49; writer, 1950—; innkeeper, 1955-69. *Military service:* South African Air Force, 1939-45.

WRITINGS: Koenig in Gorillaland (title means "King in Gorillaland"), Franchkh'scge Verlagshandlung, 1960; *Up Among the Mountain Gorillas,* Hawthorn, 1976; *Unter Gorillas* (title means "Under Gorillas"), Universitas Verlag, 1977. Author of material for German radio stations.

AVOCATIONAL INTERESTS: Wildlife protection, gorillas, evolution, travel (Uganda and other parts of Africa).

*   *   *

BEACH, Mark B. 1937-

PERSONAL: Born January 24, 1937, in Westfield, N.J.; son of Emmett (a chemist) and Olive (Brocklebank) Beach; married, 1960; children: Alisa, Shana. *Education:* University of Wisconsin, Madison, B.S., 1958, Ph.D., 1965; University of Minnesota, M.A., 1961. *Office address:* P.O. Box 12305, Portland, Ore. 97212.

CAREER: State University of New York College at Plattsburgh, assistant professor of history of education, 1964-66; Cornell University, Ithaca, N.Y., assistant professor of history of education, 1966-67; Smithsonian Institution, Washington, D.C., visiting research associate in history of science, 1967-68; University of Rochester, Rochester, N.Y., assistant professor of history and associate dean of College of Arts and Science, 1968-74; writer, 1974—. Past president of local community association (Rochester). *Member:* American Historical Association, Organization of American Historians, History of Education Society.

WRITINGS: (Contributor) George Daniel, editor, *Nineteenth Century American Science,* Northwestern University Press, 1972; *Interracial Neighborhoods Bibliography,* National Neighbors, 1975; *Bibliographic Guide to the History of American Colleges and Universities,* Greenwood Press, 1975; (with Marion Walker) *Minority Student Guide to Making It in College,* Mason Charter, 1976. Contributor to education journals.

WORK IN PROGRESS: Interracial Neighborhoods in the Urban Community.

SIDELIGHTS: Beach writes: "My main intent is to write books stimulated by my personal and civic life—where I live, how I live, and the problems I share with my friends, neighbors, and family."

*   *   *

BEAL, Gwyneth 1943-
(Gwyneth Morgan)

PERSONAL: Born March 18, 1943, in Coventry, England; daughter of Thomas Edward (a school teacher) and Mary Constance (a school teacher; maiden name, Thomas) Morgan; married Petergeorge Beal (a publisher's researcher), July 24, 1974. *Education:* Bedford College, London, B.A. (honors), 1965; Cambridge University, certificate in education, 1967-68; University of Nancy, Licence-es-lettres, 1971; Leeds Polytechnic, teacher-librarian certificate, 1976. *Home:* 7 Lickless Dr., Horsforth, Leeds, West Yorkshire, England.

CAREER: Research assistant to writer, 1966; assistant housemother to children's family group in Berkshire, England, 1967; history teacher at convent school in Cambridge, England, 1968-71; writer, 1972-73; history teacher in Hertfordshire and Essex, England, 1973-74. *Member:* Historical Association, Convocation of University of London.

WRITINGS: (Under name Gwyneth Morgan) *Life in a Medieval Village* (high school text), Cambridge University Press, 1975.

WORK IN PROGRESS: A book on medieval England; local history books for use in schools.

SIDELIGHTS: Gwyneth Beal comments: "I've only written one short school history book. I wrote that because I was very hard up and thought most school history books were unsuitable for real pupils. I'd like to write more." *Avocational interests:* Travel (especially in France), exploring old places, historical novels, old films, dressmaking and handcrafts, French comic books, collecting Victorian children's books.

* * *

BEAM, George D(ahl) 1934-

PERSONAL: Born May 30, 1934, in Pittsburgh, Pa.; married, 1958; two children. *Education:* Westminster College, New Wilmington, Pa., B.A., 1956; University of Pittsburgh, M.A., 1957; University of Michigan, Ph.D., 1963. *Home:* 1001 South Grove, Oak Park, Ill. 60304. *Office:* Department of Political Science, University of Illinois, Chicago, Ill. 60680.

CAREER: Monmouth College, Monmouth, Ill., assistant professor of political science, 1963-65; University of Illinois, Chicago Circle, assistant professor, 1965-70, associate professor of political science, 1970—. *Military service:* Army National Guard, 1957-63.

WRITINGS: (Editor with John Buechner) *Readings on American Government,* Wadsworth, 1968; *Usual Politics: A Critique and Some Suggestions for an Alternative,* Holt, 1970; (with Dick Simpson) *Strategies for Change,* Swallow Press, 1976.

* * *

BEARDMORE, George 1908-
(Cedric Beardmore, Cedric Stokes, George Wolfenden)

PERSONAL: Born May 18, 1908, in England; son of Frank (a potter) and Sissie (Bennett) Beardmore; wife deceased; children: Victoria Beardmore Knowles, Tiffa Beardmore Meadows. *Education:* Educated in England and Scotland. *Politics:* "Nil on all." *Religion:* Sufi. *Home:* Trim's Cottage, West Stour, Gillingham, Dorset, England.

CAREER: Writer.

WRITINGS: (Under pseudonym Cedric Beardmore) *Dodd the Potter,* Doubleday, 1931; (under pseudonym George Wolfenden) *The House in Spitalfields,* Hurst, 1937; (under pseudonym George Wolfenden) *The Undefeated,* Hurst, 1940; (under pseudonym George Wolfenden) *The Spy Who Died in Bed,* Hurst, 1941; (under pseudonym George Wolfenden) *The Little Doves of Destruction,* Hurst, 1942; (under pseudonym Cedric Stokes) *All Space My Playground,* Macdonald & Co., 1943; *Madame Merlin,* Macdonald & Co., 1946; *A Tale of Two Thieves,* Macdonald & Co., 1947; *Far Cry,* Macdonald & Co., 1947; *The Staffordshire Assassins,* Macdonald & Co., 1950; *A Thousand Witnesses,* Macdonald & Co., 1953; *Charlie Poccok's Indian Bride,* Macdonald & Co., 1967, Viking, 1968; *Waldo Rush 48%,* Macdonald & Co., 1968; *Arnold Bennett in Love* (biography), Bruce & Watson, 1972.

Books for young adults: *Going into the Country,* Phoenix House, 1948; *The Isle of Apes,* Macdonald & Co., 1950;

North Wind, Macdonald & Co., 1952; *Belle of the Ballet's Gala Performance,* Hulton Press, 1956; *Belle of the Ballet's Country Holiday,* Hulton Press, 1957; *Jack O'Lantern and the Fighting Cock,* Hulton Press, 1958; *Lesley's Great Adventure,* Paul Hamlyn, 1967; *Islands of Strangers,* Macdonald & Co., 1968; *Expedition to Faollen,* Macdonald & Co., 1970; *The Maid of the Isles,* Macdonald & Co., 1974; *Ladies of Spain,* Macdonald & Co., 1975, published as *The Treasure of Spanish Bay,* Thomas Nelson, 1976.

Contributor of over ninety stories to *Eagle* and *Girl.*

WORK IN PROGRESS: A serious study of a child's life during World War I, "largely but not entirely autobiographical."

SIDELIGHTS: Beardmore discusses his book *Arnold Bennett in Love* for *CA:* "The biography of Arnold Bennett's marriage arose from the fact that I am Bennett's nephew and therefore had unique insight into his character. Outwardly, he gallantly endeavoured to be amiable, generous, of assistance to young writers. In this he succeeded. It would appear that I alone am left to know that *chez lui* he was arrogant and intolerant. Following the late war, I visited his French widow, Marie Marguerite, at her home near Montauban, France. Subsequently, she bequeathed to me all Arnold's letters to her (these are now in the library of Keele University, England), and I was thereby enabled to shed light on his private life and the burden he carried of a stern Victorian upbringing that he tried to amend. The book makes unpleasant reading, but was necessary in the interests of truth."

Beardmore told *CA* that he is motivated by "the necessity to write stories as an escape from an otherwise intolerable life." He says he writes, "like everyone else—alone."

AVOCATIONAL INTERESTS: Gardening, bee keeping, astronomy, and natural history.

* * *

BEATTY, Robert Owen 1924-1976

November 12, 1924—December 8, 1976; American conservationist, publisher, civil servant, and author on conservation. He belonged to several national conservation organizations, including the National Audubon Society, the Sierra Club, and The Wilderness Society. Beatty served as Assistant Health, Education and Welfare Secretary from 1971-73. He died in Boise, Idaho. Obituaries: *New York Times,* December 10, 1976.

* * *

BEBEY, Francis 1929-

PERSONAL: Born July 15, 1929, in Douala, Cameroon; son of Fritz N'Dedi (a pastor) and Maria N'Gobo Eyidi; married Jacqueline Edinguele, August 14, 1956; children: Eyidi, Christiane, Fanta, Francis, Jr., Patrick. *Education:* Attended Sorbonne, University of Paris, and New York University. *Religion:* Protestant. *Home:* 18 Rue du Champ de l'Alouette, 75013 Paris, France. *Agent:* Today's Artists, Inc., P.O. Box 465, Berkeley, Calif. 94701.

CAREER: Radiodiffusion Outre-mer, Paris, France, radio producer and journalist, 1957-61; UNESCO, Paris, France, program specialist, 1961-74; free-lance writer and guitarist, 1974—. Has worked for Radio Ghana and Radio Cameroon. *Member:* Cercle Renaissance, Association des Escrivains de Langue Francaise, Societe des Auteurs, Compositeurs et Editeurs de Musique. *Awards, honors:* Grand prix litteraire de l'Afrique noir from Association des Ecrivains de Langue

Francaise, 1968, for the novel *Le Fils d'Agatha Moudio;* prix jeune chanson from S.A.C.E.M., Paris, 1977, for recording "La Condition Masculine."

WRITINGS: La radiodiffusion en Afrique noire (title means "Broadcasting in Black Africa"), Editions Saint-Paul, 1963; *Le Fils d'Agatha Moudio* (novel), Editions CLE, 1967, 3rd edition, 1971, translation by Joyce A. Hutchinson published as *Agatha Moudio's Son,* Heinemann, 1971, Lawrence Hill, 1973; *Embarras et cie: Nouvelles et poemes* (stories and poems; title means "Embarrassment and So On"), Editions CLE, 1968; *Musique de l'Afrique,* with recording, Horizons de France, 1969, translation by Josephine Bennett published as *African Music: A People's Art,* Lawrence Hill, 1975; *Trois petits cireurs* (novel; title means "Three Little Shoeblacks"), Editions CLE, 1972; *La poupee ashanti* (novel), Editions CLE, 1973, translation by Joyce A. Hutchinson published as *The Ashanti Doll,* Lawrence Hill; *Le Roi Albert d'Effidi* (novel; title means "King Albert of Effidi"), Editions CLE, 1974; *La Musique africaine moderne* (title means "Modern African Music"), Editions Presence Africaine, 1975; *Le Petit Fumeur* (story; title means "The Little Smoker"), Editions Rencontres, 1976.

Author of script for film "Sonate en bien majeur."

WORK IN PROGRESS: Two novels; "Musique africaine," a film on African music.

SIDELIGHTS: Bebey comments: "As a performing guitarist (classical, African, and my own music), I travel very much, through which as an author I discover how wonderful the world is, and how similar human beings are wherever I meet them." His books have been published in German, Polish, and Russian.

*   *   *

BECKER, Marion Rombauer   1903-1976

January 2, 1903—December 28, 1976; American newspaper stringer and school art director during early career, author of book on wild flowers, and best known as co-author with her mother of *The Joy of Cooking.* A record among cookbooks, it has sold five million copies, distributed strictly through the book trade. She died in Cincinnati, Ohio. Obituaries: *New York Times,* December 30, 1976; *Time,* January 10, 1977; *AB Bookman's Weekly,* March 7, 1977. (See index for previous *CA* sketch)

*   *   *

BECKINSALE, Monica   1914-

PERSONAL: Born April 19, 1914, in Bath, Somerset, England; daughter of William George (in Royal Navy) and Mary (Cotterell) Crump; married Robert Percy Beckinsale (a university lecturer and writer), June 23, 1939; children: Monica, Robert Dover, Mary. *Education:* University of Reading, B.A., 1935. *Home:* 194 Iffley Rd., Oxford OX4 1SD, England.

CAREER: Teacher of geography in high schools in Plymouth and Oxford, England, 1936-70; writer, 1970—.

WRITINGS: (With husband, Robert Beckinsale) *Southern Europe,* Hodder & Stoughton, 1975. Contributor to *Encyclopaedia of Knowledge* and to *Reader's Digest.*

WORK IN PROGRESS: The English Heartland.

SIDELIGHTS: Beckinsale told *CA:* "My writing started very gradually with looking up details and checking facts for my husband, preparing his indexes, and acting as proofreader. It was only as housekeeping for a family was less time-consuming that I began to write seriously. We travelled a lot in Europe and found that so much had changed since 1940 that we wanted to record it. *The English Heartland* is an expression of my anxiety about the English landscape which is undergoing great changes with urbanization and increasing mechanization of its agriculture and changing farming patterns. I wanted to describe the aspects both physical and cultural of a particular English landscape which has been of great significance in English history before time and change had blurred them perhaps forever."

*   *   *

BECKMANN, Petr   1924-

PERSONAL: Born November 13, 1924, in Prague, Czechoslovakia; came to the United States in 1963, naturalized citizen, 1974; son of Rudolf (a lawyer) and Katerina (Fischer) Beckmann; married Irene Hairgrove, May 31, 1965. *Education:* Prague Technical University, B.Sc., 1949, Ph.D., 1955. *Office:* Department of Electrical Engineering, University of Colorado, Boulder, Colo. 80309; and Access to Energy, P.O. Box 2298, Boulder, Colo. 80306.

CAREER: Research Institute for Telecommunications, Prague, Czechoslovakia, research engineer, 1951-54; Czechoslovak Academy of Science, Prague, scientist at Geophysics Institute, 1955, and at Institute of Radio Engineering and Electronics, 1955-63, head of wave propagation department, 1955-63; University of Colorado, Boulder, visiting professor, 1963-64, professor of electrical engineering, 1965—. Registered professional engineer in Colorado. Founder of Golem Press, 1967. *Military service:* Royal Air Force, radar mechanic, 1942-45. *Member:* Institute of Electrical and Electronics Engineers (fellow), Operations Research Society of America, Society for Industrial and Applied Mathematics. *Awards, honors:* D.Sc. from Czechoslovak Academy of Sciences, 1962.

WRITINGS: Technicka anglictina pro castecne pokrocile (title means "Technical English"), two volumes, State Publishing House for Technical Literature, 1948, 2nd edition, 1959; *Die Ausbreitung der Ultrakurzwellen* (title means "Propagation of Ultra-Short Waves"), Akademische Verlagsgesellschaft Geest und Portig, 1963; (with Andre S. Spizzichino) *The Scattering of Electromagnetic Waves from Rough Surfaces,* Pergamon, 1963; *Probability in Communication Engineering,* Harcourt, 1967; *Introduction to Elementary Queuing Theory and Telephone Traffic,* Golem, 1968, 2nd edition, *Lee's ABC of the Telephone,* 1977; *Elements of Applied Probability Theory,* Harcourt, 1968; *The Depolarization of Electromagnetic Waves,* Golem, 1968; *Whispered Anecdotes: Humor from Behind the Iron Curtain,* Golem, 1969; *A History of Pi,* Golem, 1970, 3rd edition, St. Martin's, 1976; *The Structure of Language: A New Approach,* Golem, 1972; *Orthogonal Polynomials for Engineers and Physicists,* Golem, 1973; *Eco-Hysterics and the Technophobes,* Golem, 1973; *The Health Hazards of Not Going Nuclear,* Golem, 1976.

Translator from the Russian: L. A. Weinstein, *Open Resonators and Open Waveguides,* Golem, 1969; L. A. Weinstein, *The Theory of Diffraction and the Factorization Method,* Golem, 1969; L. N. Zakharyev, A. A. Lemanski and K. S. Shcheglov, *Radiation from Apertures in Convex Bodies,* Golem, 1970; V. V. Shevchenko, *Continuous Transitions in Open Waveguides,* Golem, 1971; Y. S. Shifrin, *Statistical Antenna Theory,* Golem, 1971.

Contributor of more than sixty articles to scientific journals. Founder and editor of *Access to Energy* (monthly newsletter), 1973—.

WORK IN PROGRESS: A fourth edition of *A History of Pi;* a history of energy generation and consumption in the United States.

SIDELIGHTS: Bechmann told *CA:* "In the early 70's, realizing that science and technology were under attack from a wide segment of intellectuals, I limited my research on esoteric scientific problems and devoted much of my literary activity to the defense of science and technology, especially the fields of environment and energy. In the last few years, much of my activity was taken up by pointing out the well-established, but consistently ignored fact that nuclear power, by any criterion (not excluding major disasters, waste disposal or sabotage), is incomparably safer than any of our present methods of generating electricity, and that it annually saves thousands of lives by replacing more dangerous energy sources."

AVOCATIONAL INTERESTS: History, language and linguistics, music, nature, and playing bassoon.

* * *

BEDE, Jean-Albert 1903-1977

April 2, 1903—January 19, 1977; French-born American educator and author. His specialty was nineteenth-century French literature. Bede was the editor of the *Dictionary of Modern European Literature* and the author of books in French. He was a member of several professional organizations. He died in New York City. Obituaries: *New York Times,* January 21, 1977; *AB Bookman's Weekly,* February 14, 1977.

* * *

BEEDELL, Suzanne (Mollie) 1921-

PERSONAL: Born April 14, 1921, in Sheffield, England; daughter of Reginald (a politician) and Olive (Coppen) Chambers; married Harry Beedell (a merchant navy officer), April 1, 1947; children: Jane Beedell Kippenberger, Catherine. *Education:* Attended high school in Norwich, England. *Religion:* None. *Home:* 12 Saint Georges Rd., Deal, Kent, England. *Agent:* Barbara Hargreaves, Mains of Faillie, Daviot, Inverness, Scotland.

CAREER: Writer, 1953—.

WRITINGS: Country Dishes: Traditional Farmhouse Recipes from the Counties of Great Britain, edited by Barbara Hargreaves, Countrywise Books, 1962; *The A to Z of Sailing: Maintenance, Manoeuvring, Rigging, Navigation, Mooring, Racing,* Parrish, 1962; *The Compleat Angler's Wife: A Complete Guide to Cooking the Angler's Catch,* Countrywise Books, 1964; *Cookery Plus,* Countrywise Books, 1964; (editor) *The Farmer's Bedside Book* (collected articles from *Farmers Weekly*), Countrywise Books, 1964; (editor) *The Diary of a Farmer's Wife, 1796-1797,* Countrywise Books, 1964; *Converting a Cottage,* Sphere Books, 1968; *Winemaking and Home Brewing: A Complete Guide,* Sphere Books, 1969.

Restoring Junk, McKay, 1970; *Suzanne Beedell's Menopause: Questions and Answers,* Arlington Books, 1972; *Herbs for Health and Beauty,* Sphere Books, 1972; *Pick, Cook, and Brew,* Hippocrene Books, 1973; *Delicatessen Cook Book,* Pelham, 1973; *Brasses and Brass Rubbing,* Bartholomew, 1973; *Water in the Garden,* David & Charles, 1973; *The Amateur's Guide to Leisuretime Photography,* Bartholomew, 1975; *Windmills,* Scribner, 1975; *The Wall Book,* Macdonald & Janes, 1977. Also author of *Time Photography,* Bartholomew, and *What on Earth Shall I Cook Today?,* Pelham. Contributor to *Punch* and *Small Boat.*

WORK IN PROGRESS: Country Living, a guide for the "new countryman."

SIDELIGHTS: Suzanne Beedell began as a feature writer, now concentrates on books. Her special interests include "practical and country subjects, windmills, and brasses." All the photographs in her books are her own; she lectures, using her own photographs, on the subjects that interest her most. *Avocational interests:* Sailing a racing dinghy, golf, travel (Europe and New Zealand).

* * *

BEELER, Nelson F(rederick) 1910-

PERSONAL: Born April 5, 1910, in Adams, Mass.; married wife, Marion (a nurse), 1937; children: Deborah, Richard, Charles, Linda. *Education:* University of Massachusetts, B.A., 1933; Columbia University, M.A., 1937; New York University, Ph.D., 1957. *Office:* Department of Chemistry, State University of New York College at Potsdam, Potsdam, N.Y. 13676.

CAREER: Teacher in Adams, Mass., 1933-36, and in Nyack, N.Y., 1936-46; Clarkson College of Technology, Potsdam, N.Y., assistant professor, 1946-49; State University of New York College at Potsdam, professor, 1949—. *Military service:* United States Army, civilian instructor, 1940-42. *Member:* American Chemistry Society, National Science Teacher Association, National Association of Residence Science Teaching. *Awards, honors:* Thomas Alva Edison Foundation Award, 1962, for *Experiments in Sound.*

WRITINGS—All published by Crowell: all with Franklyn M. Branley: *Experiments in Science,* 1947, revised edition, 1955; *Experiments in Electricity,* 1949; *More Experiments in Science,* 1950; *Experiments in Optical Illusion,* 1951; *Experiments in Chemistry,* 1952; *Experiments with Airplane Instruments,* 1953; *Experiments with Atomics,* 1954, revised edition, 1965; *Experiments with a Microscope,* 1957; *Experiments with Light,* 1957, revised edition, 1964; *Experiments in Sound,* 1961. Co-author of science page for *Young America.*

* * *

BEHNKE, John 1945-

PERSONAL: Born February 26, 1945, in Syracuse, N.Y.; son of Harold Frederick (a pattern maker) and Pauline (Bogensperger) Behnke. *Education:* St. Bernard's Seminary, B.A., 1966, M.Div., 1969. *Home and office:* St. Paul's Church, 415 West 59th St., New York, N.Y. 10019.

CAREER: Ordained Roman Catholic priest. Monroe County Penitentiary, Rochester, N.Y., chaplain, 1969-71; Catholic Information Center, Boston, Mass., member of staff, 1972; St. Paul's Church, New York City, priest, 1973—. Part-time chaplain for New York State Corrections Department.

WRITINGS: A Children's Lectionary, Paulist Press, 1974.

WORK IN PROGRESS: A Teacher's Aid to Children's Liturgies, three volumes; *Stories of Jesus.*

AVOCATIONAL INTERESTS: Sightseeing in large cities, visiting museums.

* * *

BELANGER, Jerome D(avid) 1938-

PERSONAL: Born April 2, 1938, in Wisconsin; son of Mose P. (a musician) and Cecilia C. Belanger; married Diane O. Landskron (a registered nurse), May 30, 1959; children:

Anne-Marie, David, Steven, John. *Education:* University of Wisconsin, Madison, B.A., 1962. *Home address:* Route 1, Waterloo, Wis. 53594.

CAREER: Wisconsin State Journal, Madison, Wis., reporter, 1961-62; General Telephone of Wisconsin, Madison, employee communications administrator, 1962-64; CUNA International, Madison, business manager of publications, 1964-69; hog farmer, 1970—. Publisher of *Telco Call,* 1960-64; Countryside Publications Ltd., editor and publisher of *Countryside,* 1969—, president of company, 1974—. President of Waterloo (Wis.) Chamber of Commerce, 1977. *Military service:* U.S. Marine Corps, 1956-58.

WRITINGS: (With John Prindle, Ed Magdol, and Paul Butler) *It's Not Just Money,* CUNA International, 1967; *Country Living,* Award Books, 1973; *Homesteader's Handbook to Raising Small Livestock,* Rodale Press, 1974; *Raising Milk Goats the Modern Way,* Garden Way, 1975; *Soil Fertility,* Countryside Books, 1977; *Raising the Homestead Hog,* Rodale Press, 1977; *Managing Your Personal Food Supply,* edited by Ray Wolfe, Rodale Press, 1977. Author of column "Beyond the Sidewalks" in *Countryside.* Contributor to farming and country living magazines.

WORK IN PROGRESS: "A book about the *real* energy crisis: food."

SIDELIGHTS: Belanger writes: "Just the other day Lewis Mumford said that the salvation of mankind will depend on backyard gardens. Since most people still get enough to eat, they don't think about food, but I've always been a few years ahead of my time. Famine is possible in America. Mumford is a city planner. I'm a farmer. I work on this single facet of Mumford's vision, *showing* people how to live from their gardens (which includes goats, pigs, chickens, and rabbits). With the depletion of fossil fuels and the problems of the cities and technology in general, including industrial agriculture, there are no alternatives but to live lightly upon Spaceship Earth. We must reassess our priorities, and increase our self-reliance. My writing provides a practical approach to this philosophy."

* * *

BELLAH, James Warner 1899-1976

September 14, 1899—September 23, 1976; American foreign correspondent for *Aero Digest,* novelist, short-story writer, and author of screenplays on the American West. He died in Los Angeles, Calif. Obituaries: *New York Times,* September 24, 1976; *Washington Post,* September 25, 1976; *AB Bookman's Weekly,* November 15, 1976. (See index for previous *CA* sketch)

* * *

BELLMAN, Richard (Ernest) 1920-

PERSONAL: Born August 26, 1920, in New York, N.Y.; married, 1963; children: two. *Education:* Brooklyn College (now of City University of New York), B.A., 1941; University of Wisconsin, Madison, M.A., 1943; Princeton University, Ph.D., 1946. *Office:* Department of Mathematics, University of Southern California, Los Angeles, Calif. 90007.

CAREER: Truax Field, Madison, Wis., instructor in electronics, 1942-43; Princeton University, Princeton, N.J., instructor in mathematics, 1943-44; U.S. Navy, Radio and Sound Laboratory, San Diego, Calif., mathematician and physicist, 1944-45; U.S. Army, Los Alamos, N.M., mathematician and physicist, 1945-46; Princeton University, in-

structor, 1946-47, assistant professor of mathematics and research associate, 1947-48; Stanford University, Stanford, Calif., associate professor of mathematics, 1948-52; RAND Corp., Santa Monica, Calif., mathematician, 1952-65; University of Southern California, Los Angeles, professor of mathematics and electrical engineering, 1965—, professor of medicine in School of Medicine, 1974—; associate fellow of Institute of Higher Studies, 1975—. Associate of Center for the Study of Democratic Institutions, 1969—.

MEMBER: American Mathematical Society, National Academy of Engineering. *Awards, honors:* First Norbert Weiner Prize in Applied Mathematics from American Mathematical Society and Society for Industrial and Applied Mathematics, 1970; first Dickson Prize from Carnegie-Mellon University, 1970; D.Sc. from University of Aberdeen, 1973; D.Laws from University of Southern California, 1974; D.Math. from University of Waterloo, 1975; American Academy of Arts and Sciences fellowship, 1975; John von Neumann Theory Award from Institute of Management Sciences and Operations Research Society of America, 1976.

WRITINGS: Stability Theory of Differential Equations, McGraw, 1953; *Dynamic Programming,* Princeton University Press, 1957; *What Is Dynamic Programming?,* RAND Corp., 1959.

Introduction to Matrix Analysis, McGraw, 1960, 2nd edition, 1970; (with Edwin F. Beckenbach) *An Introduction to Inequalities,* Random House, 1961, revised edition, Springer-Verlag, 1965; *A Brief Introduction to Theta Functions,* Holt, 1961; (editor) *A Collection of Modern Mathematical Classics: Analysis,* Dover, 1961; *Adapted Control Processes: A Guided Tour,* Princeton University Press, 1961; (with Stuart E. Dreyfus) *Applied Dynamic Programming,* Princeton University Press, 1962; (editor) *Symposium on Mathematical Optimization Techniques,* University of California Press, 1963; *A Mathematical Model of Drug Distribution in the Body,* RAND Corp., 1963; (with Robert E. Kalaba and Marcia C. Prestrud) *Invariant Imbedding and Radiative Transfer in Slabs of Finite Thickness,* American Elsevier, 1963; (with Kenneth L. Cooke) *Differential-Difference Equations,* Academic Press, 1963; (editor with Kalaba) *Selected Papers on Mathematical Trends in Control Theory,* Dover, 1964; (with Kalaba and H. H. Kagiwada) *Invariant Imbedding and Time-Dependent Transport Processes,* American Elsevier, 1964; *Perturbation Techniques in Mathematics, Physics, and Engineering,* Holt, 1964; (with Kalaba) *Quasilinearization and Nonlinear Boundary-Value Problems,* American Elsevier, 1965; (with Kalaba) *Dynamic Programming and Modern Control Theory,* Academic Press, 1965; (with Kalaba and Jo Ann Lockett) *Numerical Inversion of the Laplace Transform: Applications to Biology, Economics, Engineering, and Physics,* American Elsevier, 1966; *Introduction to the Mathematical Theory of Control Processes,* Academic Press, 1967; *Modern Elementary Differential Equations,* Addison-Wesley, 1968, 2nd edition (with Kenneth L. Cooke), 1971; *Some Vistas of Modern Mathematics: Dynamic Programming, Invariant Imbedding, and the Mathematical Biosciences,* University Press of Kentucky, 1968.

(With L. A. Zadeh) *Decision-Making in a Fuzzy Environment,* National Aeronautics and Space Administration, 1970; (with Cooke and Lockett) *Algorithms, Graphs, and Computers,* Academic Press, 1970; *Methods of Nonlinear Analysis,* Academic Press, Volume I, 1970, Volume II, 1973; (with John C. Hogan and Ernest M. Scheuer) *Programmed Statistics, with Chapters on Probability, Com-*

puter Theory, and Programmed Instruction, Holt, 1970; (with Charlene Paule Smith) *Simulation in Human Systems: Decision-Making in Psychotherapy,* Wiley, 1973; (with John Wilkinson) *The Dynamic Programming of Human Systems,* MSS Information Corp., 1973; (with G. M. Wing) *An Introduction to Invariant Imbedding,* Wiley, 1975; *Introduction to Artificial Intelligence,* Boyd & Fraser, in press.

Has written numerous other technical books and pamphlets in his field. Editor of series "Mathematics in Science and Engineering" for Academic Press, and "Modern Analytic and Computational Methods in Science and Mathematics" for American Elsevier. Contributor of more than five hundred articles to research periodicals. Editor of *Journal of Mathematical Analysis and Applications.*

WORK IN PROGRESS: Introduction to Analytic Number Theory; Mathematics in Medicine; research on energy and ecology.

*   *   *

BELTON, John Raynor 1931-

PERSONAL: Born November 30, 1931, in Milwaukee, Wis.; son of Harry F. (a musician) and Neva (McLaughlin) Belton; married Jordis Lambrecht, July 17, 1953; children: Dana, Mark, Paul, Victoria, Scott, Amy. *Education:* University of Wisconsin, Milwaukee, B.S., 1957, M.S., 1959; Marquette University, Ph.D., 1968. *Politics:* Republican. *Religion:* Protestant. *Home:* W189N4978 Crest View Ter., Menomonee Falls, Wis. 53051. *Office:* Glendale Schools, 2600 Mill Rd., Glendale, Wis. 53209.

CAREER: Elementary school teacher in Brookfield, Wis., 1957-60; school psychologist in West Allis, Wis., 1960-65; supervisor of instruction for public schools in Milwaukee, Wis., 1965-76; Glendale Schools, Glendale, Wis., superintendent of schools, 1976—. Part-time instructor at University of Wisconsin, Milwaukee, 1957-68. *Military service:* U.S. Army, Artillery, 1952-54; became second lieutenant. *Member:* American Association of School District Administrators, American Psychological Association. *Awards, honors:* George Washington Medal from Freedoms Foundation, 1967, for filmstrip series "Robert and His Family."

WRITINGS—Juveniles: (With Joella Cramblit) *Let's Play Cards,* Raintree, 1975; (with Cramblit) *Card Games,* Raintree, 1976; (with Cramblit) *Solitaire Games,* Raintree, 1976; (with Cramblit) *Dice Games,* Raintree, 1976; (with Cramblit) *Dominoe Games,* Raintree, 1976.

Co-author of filmstrip series "Robert and His Family," Society for Visual Education, 1967. Editor of "Know About" series (juvenile), for Franklin Publishers, 1976—.

WORK IN PROGRESS: Developing full-color, photo-illustrated, factual books for young children; using audio-visual media to teach reading skills to young children.

SIDELIGHTS: Belton is interested in "developing fun-type books for young children, to motivate them to read about real-life situations they see on television and in the world around them. I would like to develop books for international distribution."

*   *   *

BEN-AMOS, Dan 1934-

PERSONAL: Born September 3, 1934, in Tel-Aviv, Israel; came to the United States in 1961; son of Zalman (a construction worker) and Rivka (Feinzilber) Ben-Amos; married Paula D. Girschick (an anthropologist), 1960; children:

Ilana (daughter). *Education:* Hebrew University of Jerusalem, B.A., 1961; Indiana University, M.A., 1964, Ph.D., 1967. *Home:* 539 East Durham St., Philadelphia, Pa. 19119. *Office:* Folklore and Folklife Program, University of Pennsylvania, Philadelphia, Pa. 19174.

CAREER: University of California, Los Angeles, assistant professor of anthropology, 1966-67; University of Pennsylvania, Philadelphia, assistant professor, 1967-70, associate professor, 1970-77, professor of folklore and folklife, 1977—, acting chairman of folklore and folklife program, 1973-74. Assistant professor at Indiana University, summer, 1970. Intern of Midwest Universities Consortium for International Activities, with field research in Benin City, Nigeria, 1965-66. Member of joint committee on African studies of Social Science Research Council, 1976.

MEMBER: International African Institute, International Association for Semiotic Studies, World Union of Jewish Studies, American Folklore Society (fellow), American Anthropological Association (fellow), African Studies Association. *Awards, honors:* Annual prize from Israeli Society for Folk Narrative Research, 1958-59; honorable mention from Chicago Folklore Competition, 1967, for "Narrative Forms in the Haggadah: Structural Analysis"; grants from National Science Foundation, 1968, 1970, National Institute of Mental Health, 1968, and African Studies Association, 1971; fellowships from American Council of Learned Societies, 1972-73, and Guggenheim Foundation, 1975-76.

WRITINGS: (With Dov Noy) *Folktales of Israel,* University of Chicago Press, 1963; (editor with Jerome R. Mintz, and translator) *In Praise of the Baal Shem Tov,* Indiana University Press, 1970; (editor with Kenneth S. Goldstein) *Thrice-Told Tales: Folktales from Three Continents,* Hammermill Paper Co., 1970; (with Goldstein) *Folklore: Performance and Communication,* Mouton, 1975; (editor) *New Theories in Oral Literature: Literary Forms in Social Context,* Tel-Aviv University, 1975; *Sweet Words: Story-telling Events in Benin,* Institute for the Studies of Human Issues, 1975; (editor) *Folklore Genres,* University of Texas Press, 1976.

Contributor: Richard M. Dorson, editor, *African Folklore,* Doubleday, 1972; Americo Paredes and Richard Bauman, editors, *Toward New Perspectives in Folklore,* University of Texas Press, 1972; Linda Degh, Henry Glassie, and Felix Oinas, editors, *Folklore Today: A Festschrift for Richard M. Dorson,* Research Center for Language and Semiotic Studies, and Indiana University, 1976; (author of introduction) Bin-Gorion, editor, *Mimekor Yisrael: Classical Jewish Folktales,* Indiana University Press, 1976; Dorson, editor, *Folklore in the Modern World,* Mouton, in press.

Past associate editor of "Monographs in Folklore and Folklife," University of Pennsylvania; editor of "Translations in Folklore Studies and Texts." Institute for the Study of Human Issues; co-editor of publication series of American Folklore Society, 1973. Contributor of more than fifty articles and reviews to scholarly journals. Associate editor of *Research in African Literatures;* member of advisory board of *Genre.*

*   *   *

BENDER, Frederic L(awrence) 1943-

PERSONAL: Born April 13, 1943, in New York, N.Y.; son of Joe David (a worker) and Ethel (an executive; maiden name, Geller) Bender; married Sarah Eleanor Masland (a learning disabilities specialist), August 1, 1976. *Education:* Polytechnic Institute of Brooklyn, B.S., 1965; Northwestern

University, M.A., 1967, Ph.D., 1969. *Politics:* Socialist. *Home:* 45-126B William Henry Rd., Kaneohe, Hawaii 96744. *Office:* Department of Philosophy, University of Hawaii at Manoa, 2560 Campus Rd., Honolulu, Hawaii 96822.

CAREER: U.S. Gypsum Co., Staten Island, N.Y., chemist, 1963-65; Northwestern University, Evanston, Ill., instructor in philosophy, 1968-69; Lake Forest College, Lake Forest, Ill., instructor in philosophy, 1969; University of Hawaii at Manoa, Honolulu, assistant professor, 1969-73, associate professor of philosophy, 1973—, chairman of department, 1972-74. *Member:* American Philosophical Association.

WRITINGS: (Editor) *Karl Marx: The Essential Writings,* Harper, 1972; (editor) *The Betrayal of Marx,* Harper, 1975. Contributor of articles and reviews to scholarly journals.

WORK IN PROGRESS: A critical edition of *The Communist Manifesto,* for Norton; a multi-volume study of the development of the political thought of Karl Marx and Friedrich Engels.

* * *

BENFORD, Gregory (Albert) 1941-

PERSONAL: Born January 30, 1941, in Mobile, Ala.; son of James Alton (in the military) and Eloise (a teacher; maiden name, Nelson) Benford; married Joan Abbe (an artist), August 26, 1967; children: Alyson Rhandra, Mark Gregory. *Education:* University of Oklahoma, B.S., 1963; University of California, San Diego, M.S., 1965, Ph.D., 1967. *Agent:* Richard Curtis, 156 East 52nd St., New York N.Y. 10022. *Office:* Department of Physics, University of California, Irvine, Calif. 92717.

CAREER: Lawrence Radiation Laboratory, Livermore, Calif., fellow, 1967-69, research physicist, 1969-71; University of California, Irvine, assistant professor, 1971-73, associate professor of physics, 1973—. Visiting fellow at Cambridge University, 1976. Consultant to Physics International Co. *Member:* American Physical Society, Science Fiction Writers of America, Royal Astronomical Society. *Awards, honors:* Woodrow Wilson fellowship, 1963-64; Nebula Award from Science Fiction Writers of America, 1975, for *If the Stars Are Gods.*

WRITINGS—Science fiction novels: *Deeper Than the Darkness,* Ace Books, 1970, revised edition published as *The Shrouded Stars,* Putnam, in press; *Jupiter Project,* Thomas Nelson, 1975; (with Gordon Eklund) *If the Stars Are Gods,* Putnam, 1977; *In the Ocean of the Night,* Dial, 1977; *The Man with a Million Faces,* Doubleday, in press; *What Will You Be When You Grow Up, Mark?,* Lippincott, in press.

Represented in anthologies, including *Again, Dangerous Visions,* edited by Harlan Ellison, Doubleday, 1972; *Universe 4,* edited by Terry Carr, Random House, 1974; *New Dimensions, 5,* edited by Robert Silverberg, Harper, 1975.

Contributor of articles and stories to magazines, including *Smithsonian* and *Natural History.*

SIDELIGHTS: Benford writes: "I'm probably the only research scientist now writing science fiction. I've concerned myself with facets of the alien, of the immensity of the universe. I see science fiction as an attempt to incorporate the landscape of modern science into human scales, including the theological realm. I've written much nonfiction, but I feel the new worldview emerging demands the flights of fiction as well."

BENFORD, Timothy B(artholomew) 1941-

PERSONAL: Born May 29, 1941, in Jersey City, N.J.; son of Timothy Bartholomew (a businessman) and Margaret (Luzzu) Benford; married Marilyn Fabula, September 15, 1962; children: Susan, Timothy. *Education:* Attended Rutgers University, 1960-61. *Home:* 1464 Whippoorwill Way, Mountainside, N.J. 07092. *Office:* 605 Fifth Ave., New York, N.Y. 10017.

CAREER: Bayonne Times, Bayonne, N.J., began as printer's devil, became journeyman printer, 1959-65; Hudson County Publishing and Printing, Bayonne, owner and printer, 1965-67; *Travel Weekly,* New York City, night editor, 1967-75; Travel Trade Publications, New York City, managing editor, 1975—. Candidate for New Jersey Assembly, 1969. Appeared as expert witness on the socio-economic impact of tourism promotion before New Jersey Assembly Commission on Tourism. *Member:* North Jersey Press Association (former president, vice-president, secretary, and treasurer).

WRITINGS: Contributor of articles on travel, antique cars, politics, coins, and crime to New Jersey and national periodicals. Notable free-lance assignments include space program (Mercury thru Skylab) and the coverage of airline service worldwide.

WORK IN PROGRESS: A book dealing with documented phenomena with Elizabeth Pate, a recognized authority in the field.

AVOCATIONAL INTERESTS: "Heavy interest in history, detail, and trivia"; historical autographs, coins, antique automobiles (once owned a modest collection), politics, the space program, motor racing, and reading.

* * *

BENJAMIN, Edward Bernard 1897-

PERSONAL: Born November 18, 1897, in New Orleans, La.; son of Emanuel Victor and Rachel (Goldsmith) Benjamin; married Blanche Sternberger, October 19, 1921; children: Edward Bernard, Jr., William Mente Sternberger, Jonathan Sternberger. *Education:* Harvard University, A.B. (magna cum laude), 1918. *Home:* 383 Walnut St., New Orleans, La. 70118. *Office:* Suite 825, Whitney Building, New Orleans, La. 70130.

CAREER: E. V. Benjamin Co., Inc. (family business), New Orleans, La., vice-president, 1919-29, president, 1939-47; president of Benjamin Minerals Co., 1947—. President of Starmount Co., 1929-67, Bay Chemical Co., 1938-47, Myles Salt Co., 1940-47, and Friendly Center, Inc., 1953-67. Member of board of directors of U.S. Coast Guard Academy Foundation and Grayson Foundation; president of Benjamin Fund (donor of Benjamin Awards for Restful Music); member of board of directors of Human Betterment League. Founder and trustee of Sternberger Children's Hospital (now Guilford County Welfare Center). Member of export advisory committee of U.S. Department of Commerce, 1946; member of National Board for Morality in the Media. Director of Whitney National Bank, 1924-64. Member of New Orleans Welfare Committee, 1930-32; member of board of directors of New Orleans Opera House Association; chairman of organizing committee and first president of Cultural Attractions Fund of Greater Orleans, 1960-61; Community Concert Association, president, 1960-67, honorary president, 1967—.

MEMBER: Merchants and Manufacturers Club (Greensboro, N.C.), Round Table, Southern Yacht Club (New Orleans), Turf and Field Club (New York City), New Orleans Country Club, Starmount Forest Country Club, Greensboro Country Club, Saratoga Golf Club, Royal Thomas Yacht Club. *Awards, honors:* L.H.D. from University of Rochester, 1960.

WRITINGS: The Larger Liberalism: Outlines of a Social Philosophy for the United States of America, Cambridge University Press, 1918; *The Restful in Music,* Restful Music, 1970. Also author of *Restful and Tranquil Composition,* 1956. Contributor to trade journals and popular magazines.*

* * *

ben-JOCHANNAN, Yosef 1918-

PERSONAL: Born December 31, 1918; married Gertrude. *Education:* "Not important to my writings." *Home:* 40 West 135th St., New York, N.Y. 10037.

CAREER: Writer. Has taught at colleges in the United States, Europe, South America, and Africa. UNESCO and civilian adviser to the ambassador of Zanzibar, 1963-64. *Member:* Afro-American History Association, Society of African Historians and Anthropologists.

WRITINGS: Africa: Land, People, Culture, Sadlier, 1969; *Southern Lands,* Sadlier, 1969; *Southern Neighbors,* Sadlier, 1970; *The Black Man of the Nile and His Family,* Alkebu-Ian Books Association, 1972; *Africa: Mother of "Western Civilization,"* Alkebu-Ian Books Association, 1972.

WORK IN PROGRESS: A ten-volume work.

SIDELIGHTS: Ben-Jochannan writes because of "the fact that the major presses did not want to publish anything other than the myths about African people. Moreso, because my teacher in eighth grade said that 'Negroes have no history.'"

BIOGRAPHICAL/CRITICAL SOURCES: Harold Cruse, *Crisis of the Negro Intellectual,* Morrow, 1967; Albert Cleage, Jr., *Black Christian Nationalism: New Directions for the Black Church,* Morrow, 1972.*

* * *

BENNETT, Jay 1912-

PERSONAL: Born December 24, 1912, in New York, N.Y.; son of Pincus Shapiro (a businessman) and Estelle Bennett; married Sally Stern, February 2, 1937; children: Steven Cullen, Randy Elliott. *Education:* Attended New York University. *Home:* 402 Ocean Parkway, Brooklyn, N.Y. 11218.

CAREER: Writer. Has worked as a farmhand, factory worker, lifeguard, mailman, salesman, and senior editor of an encyclopedia. English features writer and editor, Office of War Information, 1942-45. *Member:* Mystery Writers of America, Dramatists Guild, Writers Guild of America, Authors League of America. *Awards, honors:* Edgar Allan Poe Award of Mystery Writers of America for best juvenile mystery novel, 1974, for *Long Black Coat* and 1975, for *The Dangling Witness.*

WRITINGS: Catacombs, Abelard-Schuman, 1959; *Death Is a Silent Room,* Abelard-Schuman, 1965; *Murder Money,* Fawcett, 1963; *Deathman, Do Not Follow Me* (juvenile mystery), Meredith Press, 1968; *The Deadly Gift* (juvenile mystery), Meredith Press, 1969; *The Killing Tree* (juvenile mystery), F. Watts, 1972; *Masks: A Love Story,* F. Watts, 1972; *The Long Black Coat* (juvenile mystery), Delacorte, 1973; *Shadows Offstage,* Nelson, 1974; *The Dangling Witness* (juvenile mystery), Delacorte, 1974; *Say Hello to the*

Hit Man, Delacorte, 1976; *The Birthday Murderer,* Delacorte, 1977.

Plays: "No Hiding Place" (three-act), first produced in New York at President Theatre, November 10, 1949; "Lions After Slumber" (three-act), first produced in London at Unity Theatre, June 2, 1951.

Also author, for all leading networks, of radio scripts, including "Miracle Before Christmas" and "The Wind and Stars Are Witness." Author of television scripts for "Alfred Hitchcock Presents," "Crime Syndicated," "Wide, Wide World," "Cameo Theater," and "Monodrama Theatre."

WORK IN PROGRESS: Guttering Candle, Ladder to Death, Nothing Man, all suspense novels.

SIDELIGHTS: Bennett told *CA:* "I always look for a central character and then let him find the story for me. In a way, I embark upon a voyage of discovery. I constantly find myself surprised at the revelations that come through the unconsciousness and onto the page. However, this must be kept in mind, I have spent many long years learning my craft of writing, particularly that of the suspense genre. So this knowledge always comes into play.

"As to writing for young adults, I have come to know them and they have come to know me. My work for them has been translated into French, Japanese and Swedish. I am particularly well received in Sweden. I respect my readers. I am a totally committed writer when I work for them. I know of no other way to function in the Young Adult field."

* * *

BENNETT, John W. 1918-

PERSONAL: Born July 18, 1918, in Milwaukee, Wis.; son of William H. and Elsa (Biersach) Bennett; married Kathryn Goldsmith (a social worker), December 7, 1940; children: John Michael, James Peter. *Education:* Beloit College, B.A., 1937; University of Chicago, Ph.D., 1946. *Office:* Department of Anthropology, Washington University, St. Louis, Mo. 63130.

CAREER: Japan Occupation, Tokyo, research director, 1948-51; Ohio State University, Columbus, instructor, 1946-48, assistant professor, 1952-57, associate professor of anthropology, 1958-59; Washington University, St. Louis, Mo., professor of anthropology, 1960—. Visiting professor at University of Wisconsin, Madison, University of Puerto Rico, Waseda University, University of Calgary, and University of California. Consultant to University of Wisconsin Land Tenure Center, Ford Foundation, Agency for International Development, and *Encyclopedia Americana.* *Member:* International House of Japan, American Anthropological Association, Canadian Society for Sociology and Anthropology, Asian Studies Association, Rural Sociological Society, Scientists Institute for Public Information.

WRITINGS: Archeological Explorations in Illinois, University of Chicago Press, 1947; (with Herbert Passim) *In Search of Identity: The Japanese Overseas Scholar in America and Japan,* University of Minnesota Press, 1958; (with Iwao Ishino) *Paternalism in the Japanese Economy,* University of Minnesota Press, 1963; *Hutterian Brethren: The Agricultural Economy and Social Organization of a Communal People,* Stanford University Press, 1967.

Northern Plainsmen: Adaptive Strategy and Agrarian Life, Aldine, 1970; (editor) *The New Ethnicity: Perspectives from Ethnology* (proceedings), West Publishing, 1975; *The Ecological Transition: Cultural Anthropology and Human Adaptation,* Pergamon, 1976.

Member of editorial board of *Reviews in Anthropology* and *Annual Review of Anthropology*.

WORK IN PROGRESS: A book on theory of culture in the social sciences; a book on economic behavior, based on field research in agricultural and rural development.

SIDELIGHTS: Bennett told *CA:* "I have three main specialties: the sociology and ecology of agrarian and rural development; the commune, particularly the traditional forms like Hutterites and the Kibbutz; and Japanese society and its modern development." His field research includes work in Mexico, Taiwan, India, Israel, and Thailand.

* * *

BENNETT, Rita (Marie) 1934-

PERSONAL: Born September 8, 1934, in Port Huron, Mich.; daughter of William H. (a merchant) and Loretta (Jesse) Reed; married Dennis J. Bennett (a clergyman and writer), October 15, 1966; children: (step-children) Margi (Mrs. Ted Jones), Stephen, Conrad. *Education:* Attended Tampa University, 1953-56; University of Florida, B.A.E., 1958. *Religion:* Episcopalian. *Home:* 1428 Olympic Ave., Edmonds, Wash. 98020. *Office:* Christian Renewal, P.O. Box 70563, Seattle, Wash. 98107.

CAREER: Child welfare worker for the State of Florida, 1959-61; Christian Renewal, Seattle, Wash., vice-president and treasurer, 1969—. Presented "Walk in the Spirit," a radio broadcast talk show, on KHOF-Radio, 1968-70, and "St. Luke's Broadcast" on KTW-Radio, 1968-75. *Member:* Women's Aglow Fellowship International, Alpha Chi Omega.

WRITINGS: (With husband, Dennis Bennett) *The Holy Spirit and You,* Logos International, 1971, supplement, 1973; *I'm Glad You Asked That,* Logos International, 1974. Author of "Questions and Answer Column," in *National Courier,* 1977.

WORK IN PROGRESS: The Balanced Life; The Triune Person.

SIDELIGHTS: Rita Bennett has spoken to women's groups and church congregations in England, Scotland, Germany, Norway, and Jamaica. *Avocational interests:* Singing, piano, swimming, cooking, studying nutrition, gardening.

BIOGRAPHICAL/CRITICAL SOURCES: Anchorage Daily Times, May 5, 1971; *Christianity,* May, 1971; *Christian Life,* June, 1974; *Longview Daily News,* February, 1975.

* * *

BENNIE, William A(ndrew) 1921-

PERSONAL: Born October 9, 1921, in Linton, Ind.; son of Andrew R. (a civil servant) and Sylvia (VanMeter) Bennie; married Betty Jean Burks (a teacher), January 31, 1944; children: James Andrew, Carol Ann. *Education:* Indiana State University (Terre Haute), B.S., 1943, M.S., 1949; Indiana University (Bloomington), Ed.D., 1955. *Home:* 7205 Waterline Rd., Austin, Tex. 78731. *Office:* Department of Education, University of Texas, Austin, Tex. 78712.

CAREER: Bloomfield High School, Bloomfield, Ind., teacher, 1946-48; Miami University, Oxford, Ohio, professor of education, 1949-61; University of Texas, Austin, professor of education, 1961—, chairman of department, 1973—. Teacher education consultant for several colleges. *Military service:* U.S. Army, 1943-46; became staff sergeant; received three battle stars. *Member:* National Society

for Study of Education, Association of Teacher Education (executive committee, 1967-70), Phi Delta Kappa, Phi Kappa Phi.

WRITINGS: Cooperation for Better Student Teaching, Burgess, 1966; *Supervising Clinical Experiences in the Classroom,* Harper, 1972. Contributor of articles to more than twelve professional journals.

* * *

BENSEN, Alice R. 1911-

PERSONAL: Born February 14, 1911, in Charlotte, Mich.; daughter of Harry E. (an accountant) and Ida (Rhodus) Bensen. *Education:* Washington University, St. Louis, Mo., A.B., 1932, M.A., 1933; Sorbonne, University of Paris, further graduate study, 1933-34; University of Chicago, Ph.D., 1943. *Home:* 3416 Edgewood, Ann Arbor, Mich. 48104.

CAREER: Valparaiso University, Valparaiso, Ind., instructor, 1938-40, 1942-45, assistant professor of English, 1945-47; Eastern Michigan University, Ypsilanti, associate professor, 1947-57, professor of English, 1957-76; writer, 1976—. *Member:* Modern Language Association of America, American Association of University Professors, American Association of University Women, Alliance Francaise, Phi Beta Kappa.

WRITINGS: Rose Macauley, Twayne, 1969. Contributor to literature journals.

AVOCATIONAL INTERESTS: International travel.

* * *

BENSON, A. George 1924-

PERSONAL: Born November 17, 1924, in Chicago, Ill.; son of George A. (a clergyman) and Judith (Anderson) Benson; married Anne Schultz, 1949; children: George, Anne, Rebecca Benson Schreiber. *Education:* University of Cincinnati, B.S., 1950, M.D., 1954; Chicago Institute for Psychoanalysis, certified psychoanalyst, 1966. *Religion:* Episcopal. *Home:* 4961 Pershing Pl., St. Louis, Mo. 63108. *Office:* 4524 Forest Pl., St. Louis, Mo. 63108.

CAREER: Psychoanalyst in private practice in St. Louis, Mo., 1966—. Guest on television and radio programs. Member of Medical Director Therapy Consultants. *Military service:* U.S. Army, 1942-45; became staff sergeant. *Member:* American Psychoanalytic Association, Medical Director Care and Counseling, St. Louis Psychoanalytic Society, Chicago Psychoanalytic Society.

WRITINGS: Then Joy Breaks Through, Seabury, 1972; *What to Do When You're Depressed,* Augsburg, 1975.

SIDELIGHTS: Benson comments: "In teaching clergy and talking with religious people I find it imperative to explain that psychological growth is an inherent part of the religious life. Psychological growth is an essential prerequisite to spiritual development."

* * *

BENTON, John Frederic 1931-

PERSONAL: Born July 15, 1931, in Philadelphia, Pa.; son of Frederic E. (a businessman) and Josephine (a writer; maiden name, Moffet) Benton; married Elspeth Hughes (a teacher), December 31, 1953; children: Helen Benton Anderson, Josephine, Anna, Laura. *Education:* Haverford College, A.B., 1953; Princeton University, M.A., 1955, Ph.D., 1959; also attended University of Dijon, 1956-57. *Home:* 285 South Holliston Ave., Pasadena, Calif. 91106.

Office: Department of History, California Institute of Technology, Pasadena, Calif. 91125.

CAREER: Reed College, Portland, Ore., instructor in history and humanities, 1957-59; University of Pennsylvania, Philadelphia, instructor, 1959-60, assistant professor of history, 1960-65; California Institute of Technology, Pasadena, assistant professor, 1965-66, associate professor, 1966-70, professor of history, 1970—. Fulbright Professor at University of Reims, 1972; professor at University of Southern California, 1973-74.

MEMBER: American Historical Association, Mediaeval Academy of America (member of council, 1969-72), Medieval Association of the Pacific (member of advisory board, 1971-75), Phi Beta Kappa. *Awards, honors:* Fulbright fellowship, University of Dijon, 1956-57; American Philosophical Society grants, for France and Italy, 1962, 1968, 1972; Guggenheim fellowship, France, 1963-64; American Council of Learned Societies grant, France, 1963-64.

WRITINGS: Town Origins: The Evidence from Medieval England, Heath, 1968; (contributor) Francis X. Newman, editor, *The Meaning of Courtly Love,* State University of New York Press, 1968; (editor) *Self and Society in Medieval France: The Memoirs of Abbot Guibert of Nogent,* Harper, 1970; (editor with Thomas N. Bisson) *Medieval Statecraft and the Perspectives of History: Essays by Joseph R. Strayer,* Princeton University Press, 1971; (contributor) William E. Miller and Thomas G. Waldman, editors, *Bibliographical Studies in Honor of Rudolph Hirsch,* University of Pennsylvania, 1975. Contributor of about twenty articles to scholarly journals. Contributing editor of *History of Childhood Quarterly,* 1974—; member of editorial board of *Viator,* 1976—.

WORK IN PROGRESS: Charters of the Counts of Champagne, 1152-1198; History of Abelard and Heloise; Self-Awareness in Twelfth-Century Europe; research on space technology as it applies to the reading of ancient manuscripts.

SIDELIGHTS: Benton writes: "My interest in the study of medieval history is based on the belief that history, like psychoanalysis, provides the living some chance to understand the present and shape the future." He has traveled extensively in Europe.

* * *

BENVENISTE, Asa 1925-

PERSONAL: Born August 25, 1925, in New York City; immigrated to England, 1950; naturalized British citizen, 1965; son of Samaya and Alegre (Levy) Benveniste; married Penelope Walker (an artist), December 9, 1949; children: Jasper, Paul, Mark. *Education:* New School for Social Research, B.A., 1948. *Politics:* "Anarchist, but benign." *Religion:* Jewish. *Home and office:* 22 Leverton St., London NW5, England.

CAREER: Poet. Jewish News Agency, New York, N.Y., researcher, 1947; *Zero Quarterly,* Paris, Tangier, and London, co-editor, 1948-56; *Nugget Magazine,* London, correspondent, 1957-58; Paul Hamlyn Ltd., London, senior art editor, 1959-61; Studio Vista Ltd., London, senior editor, 1961-63; Trigram Press, London, executive editor and publisher, 1965—. *Military service:* U.S. Army, 1943-46.

WRITINGS—Poems: Poems of the Mouth, Trigram Press, 1966; (with Jack Hirschman) *A Word in Your Season,* Trigram Press, 1967; *Count Three,* Maya, 1969; *The Atoz Formula,* Trigram Press, 1969; *Free Semantic No. 2.,* Wallrich Books, 1970; *Umbrella,* Wallrich Books, 1972; (with Ray Di Palma and Tom Raworth) *Time Being,* Blue Chair (London), 1972; *Blockmakers Black,* Steam Press (London), 1973; *Certainly Metaphysics,* Blue Chair, 1973; *It's the Same Old Feeling Again,* Trigram Press, 1973; *Edge,* Joe DiMaggio Press (London), 1974; (with Brian Marley) *Dense Lens,* Trigram Press, 1975.

Nonfiction: *Autotypography: A Book of Design Priorities,* Latimer New Dimensions, 1974.

Also author of radio plays "Tangier for the Traveller," 1956, and "Piano Forte," 1957.

WORK IN PROGRESS: A book on typography, poems.

SIDELIGHTS: Benveniste told *CA:* "I am trying to find and work in the obscurest language possible, in order to find the final clarity. I did not speak English, or any other language, until I was five. The first word caused the most excruciating pleasure I have ever felt."

* * *

BERCOVICI, Rion 1903(?)-1976

1903(?)—August 6, 1976; American journalist, public relations executive, and author. He worked for several newspapers in New York, including the *New York Graphic* and the *New York Post,* and he was president of a public relations firm. Bercovici also wrote a novel about public relations. He died in New York City. Obituaries: *New York Times,* August 8, 1976.

* * *

BERENDT, Joachim Ernst 1922-

PERSONAL: Born July 20, 1922, in Berlin, Germany; son of Ernst (a minister) and Maria (Hammerschmidt) Berendt; children: Christian. *Home:* Auf der Alm 11, D-7570 Baden-Baden, West Germany. *Office:* Sudwestfunk, Baden-Baden, West Germany.

CAREER: Sudwestfunk (Southwestern German Radio and Television Network), Baden-Baden, Germany, co-founder and broadcaster, 1945—; ARD (German TV), Baden-Baden, host and writer of "Jazz—Heard and Seen" program, 1954-72; producer of over 250 jazz albums, including "Jazz Meets the World" series, 1969—; lecturer. Founder, American Folk Blues Festival, 1962; founder, Berlin Jazz Days, 1964. *Awards, honors:* Preis der Deutschen Fernsehkritik, 1957, for best musical television production of the year; Deutsche Bundesfilmpreis in Gold, 1962, for best film music of the year.

WRITINGS: Der Jazz, Deutsche Verlagsanstalt (Stuttgart), 1950; *Das Jazzbuch,* S. Fischer Bucherei, 1953; *Jazz Optisch,* Nymphenburger Verlagshandlung, 1954; *Variationen uber Jazz,* Nymphenburger Verlagshandlung, 1956; *Blues,* Nymphenburger Verlagshandlung, 1957, *Prisma der Gegenwartigen Musik,* Furche, 1959; *Das Neue Jazzbuch: Entwicklung und Bedeutung der Jazzmusik,* Fischer Bucherei, 1959, translation by Dan Morganstern published as *The New Jazz Book, A History and Guide,* Hill & Wang, 1962; (with Ed van der Elsken) *Foto-Jazz,* Nymphenburger Verlagshandlung, 1959; *Jazzlife,* Burda Druck und Verlag, 1961; *Blues, English-Deutsch,* Nymphenburger Verlagshandlung, 1962; *Das Jazzbuch: Von New Orleans bis Free Jazz,* Fischer-Bucherei, 1968, translation by Dan Morganstern and Helmut and Barbara Bredigkeit published as *The Jazz Book—From New Orleans to Rock and Free Jazz,* Lawrence Hill, 1975; *Blues,* Gerig, 1970; *Das Jazzbuch: von Rag bis Rock,* Fischer-Taschenbuch Verlag, 1975; *Ein Fenster aus Jazz,* S. Fischer Buecherei, 1977.

Editor, "Calendar Jazz and Rock," 1954—.

WORK IN PROGRESS: A Foto History of Jazz.

SIDELIGHTS: CA asked Berendt what relationships he sees between European and American Jazz. He responded: "There is a strong influence of Folk Blues and archaic blues on today's scene. Contemporary jazz forms like soul and funk are unthinkable without the jazz tradition. Jazz as a whole is unthinkable without its tradition—not only in blues, but also in spirituals and gospel, and, of course, all the way back to West Africa (especially Yoruba and Dahomey cultures). The central figures of jazz are Louis Armstrong, Duke Ellington, Charlie Parker, John Coltrane, and Ornette Coleman.

"Jazz in Europe is considered much more as an art form than in America (where it is still part of the huge entertainment industry). European jazz from the twenties to the early sixties was not much more than an imitation of American jazz. But during the sixties, there was an emancipation process, and now, there are musicians in Europe who play their own kind of jazz, without looking much to America. For instance: German trombone player Albert Mangelsdorff, British saxaphonist John Surman, Polish violinist Zbiggniew Seifert, etc. These musicians are using part of their own European tradition—in a way similar to American musicians using their tradition."

* * *

BERESINER, Yasha 1940-

PERSONAL: Born June 12, 1940, in Turkey; son of Lazar David (a company chairman) and Rachel (Saltiel) Beresiner; married Zmira Goldman, January 7, 1964; children: Guy David, Dana. *Education:* Hebrew University of Jerusalem, LL.B., 1968. *Home address:* P.O. Box 97, London NW4 2LD, England. *Office:* Paramount International Coin Ltd., 238 Grand Buildings, London W.C.2, England.

CAREER: Commodities & Equipment Ltd., London, England, director, 1969-74; Paramount International Coin Ltd., London, director, 1974—. *Military service:* Israeli Armed Forces, Paratroop Regiment, 1962-65. *Member:* International Bank Note Society (member of board of directors), Royal Numismatic Society (fellow), Numismatic Literary Guild (member of board of directors), American Numismatic Society, American Numismatic Association (life member), Latin American Paper Money Society (past president). *Awards, honors:* Writing award from Numismatic Literary Guild, 1974, for "Numismatic Scrapbook."

WRITINGS: Catalogue of the Paper Money of Colombia, Stanley Gibbons, 1973; *The Story of Paper Money,* David & Charles, 1974; *A Collector's Guide to Paper Money,* Stein & Day, 1977.

Author of columns in *International Banknote Journal,* 1971-74, in *Bank Note Reporter,* 1975, and in *Coins and Medals,* 1975—. Contributor of several hundred articles to numismatic journals in England and the United States, principally to *Numismatic.* Editor for Latin American Paper Money Society; former editor for International Bank Note Society.

WORK IN PROGRESS: A History of Casino Games, publication expected in 1979.

SIDELIGHTS: Beresiner writes that his book in progress "evolved from collecting gaming tokens. It involves research into the origins of dice, playing cards, and roulette, and the development of gambling through these specific methods. Taboos, religion, and psychology are involved, and a brief background of famed gambling houses in Europe and the U.S.A.

"My writing allows for a greater appreciation of my hobby; the inclination for research has always been present. Activities in society affairs led to editorships, beginning with editorial columns later developed into specialised articles which led to books. I consider a hobby to be essential to a more balanced way of life. Hard work on a hobby is always somehow less trying than normal work!"

He adds: "My cosmopolitan background (Russian father, Greek mother, Israel nationality and Israeli wife) led to fluent knowledge of English, Italian, Spanish, French, Hebrew, and Turkish, languages I use in travel; I know Latin America and Western Europe very well."

AVOCATIONAL INTERESTS: "Main interest outside collecting (I collect books, maps, coins, playing cards, prints, etc.) is sport. In Judo I represented Israel at a students' Olympics in Tokyo in 1967; I am active still in golf and rugby football. I enjoy bridge and backgammon."

BIOGRAPHICAL/CRITICAL SOURCES: Bank Note Reporter, September, 1976.

* * *

BERG, Goesta 1903-

PERSONAL: Born July 31, 1903, in Oerebro, Sweden; daughter of Oskar (a teacher) and Stina (Johansson) Berg; married Gunnel Hazelius-Berg, May 10, 1929; children: Jonas, Ann-Sofi Topelius. *Education:* University of Uppsala, Ph. Lic., 1929; University of Stockholm, Ph.D., 1936. *Home:* Ludvigsbergsgatan 16, S-117 26 Stockholm, Sweden.

CAREER: Nordiska Museet and Skansen, Stockholm, Sweden, assistant, 1924-28, assistant director, 1929-55, director, 1956-69. President, R. Gustavus Adolphus Academy, 1968—.

WRITINGS: Artur Hazelius (biography), Bokfoerlaget Natur och Kultur, 1933; (with Sigfrid Svensson) *Svensk bondekultur,* A. Bonnier, 1934; *Sledges and Wheeled Vehicles,* Levin & Munksgaard, 1935; (editor) *Det glada Sverige,* Natur och Kultur, 1947-48; *The Origin and Development of the Skis,* Generalstabens, 1950; *Skansens oertagard,* Nordiska museet, 1971; (editor) *Circumpolar Problems,* Pergamon, 1973.

Co-editor, *Fataburen,* 1925-69; editor, *Rig,* 1947—; editor, *Ethnologa Standinavica,* 1971—.

* * *

BERG, Thomas L(eRoy) 1930-

PERSONAL: Born June 3, 1930, in Glenville, Minn.; son of Alvin Otinius and Ruut Julia (Karhoja) Berg; married Toshiko Betsumiya, March 20, 1965 (divorced, 1972). *Education:* University of Minnesota, A.L.A., 1951, B.B.A., 1952; Columbia University, M.S., 1956, Ph.D., 1960. *Politics:* Independent. *Religion:* Lutheran. *Home and office address:* R.D. Box 141D, Scannell Rd., Chatham, N.Y. 12037.

CAREER: Columbia University, New York, N.Y., instructor, 1956-60, assistant professor of marketing, 1960-64; New York University, New York, N.Y., associate professor, 1964-67, professor of marketing, 1967-74, chairman of department, 1968-74; American Maize Products Co., New York City, vice-president of corporate planning, 1974-76, assistant to chairman of the board, 1976-77. *Military service:* U.S. Naval Reserve, active duty, 1952-55; became lieutenant senior grade.

MEMBER: International Oceanographic Foundation, Academy of Management, American Academy of Political and Social Science, American Marketing Association, Wilderness Society, Beta Gamma Sigma. *Awards, honors:* Author award from New Jersey Association of Teachers of English, 1970, for *Mismarketing: Case Histories of Marketing Misfires.*

WRITINGS: (Editor with Abe Shuchman) *Product Strategy and Management,* Holt, 1963; (with Ralph S. Alexander) *Dynamic Management in Marketing,* Irwin, 1965; *Mismarketing: Case Histories of Marketing Misfires,* Doubleday, 1970. Contributor to business and management journals.

WORK IN PROGRESS: Bottomline Marketing (tentative title), a book on marketing for profit; research on human development, especially personal and institutional growth and change processes.

SIDELIGHTS: Berg mentions that he is "concerned about ecology and preservation of wildlife" and "believes personal spiritual development requires contact with—and reverence for—nature." *Avocational interests:* Fishing, beachcombing, nature walks.

* * *

BERGER, John J(oseph) 1945-

PERSONAL: Born May 8, 1945, in New York, N.Y.; son of Laszlo (a customer's broker) and Agnes (a statistician; maiden name, Hollo) Berger; married Nancy Ann Guinn (an ecologist), October 31, 1976. *Education:* Stanford University, B.A., 1966. *Agent:* Theron Raines, Raines & Raines, 475 Fifth Ave., New York, N.Y. 10017. *Office:* Friends of the Earth, 529 Commercial St., San Francisco, Calif. 94111.

CAREER: KPFA-FM Radio, Berkeley, Calif., volunteer news writer and producer, 1968-70; *News Observer,* Fremont, Calif., staff reporter and author of column "Darts 'n Dashes," 1969-70; Alternative Features Service, Berkeley, managing editor, 1970-73; Far West Laboratory for Educational Research and Development, San Francisco, Calif., editorial specialist, 1973-75; Friends of the Earth, San Francisco, energy products director, 1976—. Member of board of directors of Alternative Features Service; adviser on nuclear power plant performance study to Council on Economic Relations. *Member:* Investigative Reporters and Editors. *Awards, honors:* Fellowship from Experiment in International Living and University of Southern California for study in Tunisia, 1967.

WRITINGS: Nuclear Power, the Unviable Option: A Critical Look at Our Energy Alternatives (introduction by Linus Pauling; foreword by U.S. Senator Mike Gravel), Ramparts, 1976. Contributor to magazines, including *Nation, Progressive, Newsweek, Not Man Apart,* and *Enterprise Science News,* and to newspapers.

WORK IN PROGRESS: Energy research for Friends of the Earth; preliminary research for books on energy and the environment.

SIDELIGHTS: John Berger writes: "Despite billions of dollars in federal subsidies and decades of development, nuclear power in this country is in a real sense a failed technology. It has proven costly, unreliable, and unable to contain its radioactivity. Most importantly, nuclear power is unnecessary to our energy future. For all these reasons, the nuclear industry has many foes and is quite properly on the defense throughout the U.S. and in many parts of the world. New domestic reactor orders this year will be at or near zero.

"Ultimately, our economy must be converted to primary dependence on solar energy, with some power from clean coal and geothermal technologies. Naturally, there will be no instantaneous conversion, and so in the interim, we will need comprehensive energy conservation policies. Yet in order for adequate development of clean energy technologies to occur, we must renounce the absurdly expensive nuclear option which has starved and stunted the development of safe energy alternatives. By giving solar energy the top priority in our energy research and development budget, we will both be minimizing our dependence on imported oil and greatly reducing the environmental consequences of our energy use. In developing the renewable energies, we should devote a major portion of our efforts to commercializing cheap, decentralized, small-scale energy technologies which contribute to individual self-sufficiency and self-reliance, helping people to reduce the power of large corporations over their lives."

AVOCATIONAL INTERESTS: Jogging, hiking, folk dancing, and music.

* * *

BERGESON, John B(rian) 1935-

PERSONAL: Born January 5, 1935, in Sycamore, Ill.; son of Stanley B. (a tavern owner) and Lillian (Carlson) Bergeson; married Alice Schauer, June 17, 1961; children: John Stanley, Kristin Marie. *Education:* Knox College, B.A., 1957; Northern Illinois University, M.S., 1960, Ed.D., 1966. *Home:* 418 East Grand, Mount Pleasant, Mich. 48858. *Office:* Instructional Materials Center, Central Michigan University, Mount Pleasant, Mich. 48859.

CAREER: Teacher in public schools in Illinois, 1959-62; junior high school social studies teacher in East Aurora, Ill., 1962-65; Western Michigan University, Kalamazoo, assistant professor, 1966-68, associate professor of education, 1968-69; director of media sources for public school system in Wyoming, Mich., 1969-70; Central Michigan University, Mount Pleasant, professor of secondary education, and director of Instructional Materials Center, 1970—.

MEMBER: Association for Supervision and Curriculum Development, National Society for Programmed Instruction, Association for Educational Communications Technology, Michigan Association for Media in Education, Mid-Michigan Society for Instructional Technology, Phi Delta Kappa. *Awards, honors:* Otto Gabel Award from Phi Delta Kappa, 1962.

WRITINGS: (Contributor) Mary Caine, editor, *An Analysis of the Effects of a Training Program for Teachers of the Disadvantaged,* U.S. Department of Health, Education & Welfare, 1968; (with George Miller) *Learning Activities for Disadvantaged Children,* Macmillan, 1971. Contributor to education journals.

WORK IN PROGRESS: Research on the use of media in the public school setting in Michigan.

AVOCATIONAL INTERESTS: Restoring and flying antique aircraft, building experimental aircraft "from scratch."

* * *

BERGMAN, Hannah E(stermann) 1925-

PERSONAL: Born June 17, 1925, in Hamburg, Germany; came to the United States in 1933, naturalized citizen, 1939; daughter of Immanuel (a physicist) and Rosa (Chwolles) Estermann; married John Bergman (a lawyer), August 5, 1953; children: Michael. *Education:* Carnegie Institute of Technology (now Carnegie-Mellon University), B.S., 1946;

Smith College, M.A., 1947; University of California, Berkeley, Ph.D., 1953. *Residence:* New York, N.Y. *Office:* Department of Romance Languages, Herbert H. Lehman College of the City University of New York, Bedford Park Blvd. W., Bronx, N.Y. 10468.

CAREER: Smith College, Northampton, Mass. instructor in Spanish, 1947-48; Brandeis University, Waltham, Mass., instructor in Spanish, 1951-53; Hunter College (now of the City University of New York), New York City, instructor in Spanish, 1953-57; New York State Department of Education, New York City, reviewer of foreign films, 1958-59; Herbert H. Lehman College of the City University of New York, Bronx, N.Y., assistant professor, 1961-68, associate professor, 1968-71, professor of Romance languages, 1971—, chairperson of department, 1968-69, executive officer of Ph.D. program in Spanish, 1975-76. *Member:* Asociación Internacional de Hispanistas, Modern Language Association of America, American Association of Teachers of Spanish and Portuguese, Hispanic Society of America (corresponding member).

WRITINGS: Luis Quinones de Benavente y sus Entremeses (title means "Luis Quinones de Benavente and His Interludes"), Castalia, 1965; (editor) Luis Quinones de Benavente, *Entremeses* (title means "Interludes"), Anaya, 1968; (editor) *Ramillete de Entremeses* (title means "Anthology of Interludes"), Castalia, 1970; *Luis Quinones de Benavente,* Twayne, 1972. Contributor to professional journals.

WORK IN PROGRESS: Research on seventeenth century Spanish drama.

SIDELIGHTS: Hannah Bergman writes: "My approach to teaching and research in Spanish drama strives to consider not only the literary values of the written text but to include the circumstances of performance (acting, staging, etc.) in an attempt to recreate for the modern reader the total theatrical experience of the audience for whom the works were first written. Only contemporary television is comparable to Golden Age Spanish theatre in quantity, quality, and mass audience reached."

* * *

BERGMANN, Ernst W.   1896(?)-1977

1896(?)—May 22, 1977; American author and editor. Bergmann edited *Business Week* and *Money* magazines. He also wrote television scripts. He died in New York City. Obituaries: *New York Times,* May 23, 1977.

* * *

BERKEY, Barry Robert   1935-

PERSONAL: Born September 28, 1935, in New Kensington, Pa.; son of Saul M. (a clothier) and Esther Frances (Freedlander) Berkey; married Velma Ann Levin (a writer), June 23, 1960; children: Kent Elliot, Richard Eric, Lori Susan. *Education:* Washington and Jefferson College, A.B. (magna cum laude), 1957; University of Pittsburgh, M.D., 1961. *Office:* 8301 Arlington Blvd., Fairfax, Va., 22030.

CAREER: Licensed to practice medicine in Virginia, Wisconsin, and Pennsylvania; diplomate of National Board of Medical Examiners, 1962; diplomate in psychiatry of American Board of Psychiatry and Neurology, 1969; Harrisburg Hospital, Harrisburg, Pa., intern, 1961-62; University of Wisconsin Medical Center, Madison, resident in neurology, 1962-63, in psychiatry, 1963-65; part-time psychiatrist in private practice, Petersburg, Va., 1966-67; part-time psychia-

trist in private practice, Fairfax, Va., 1968; Georgetown University School of Medicine, Washington, D.C., instructor in psychiatry, 1968; Fairfax General Hospital, Fairfax, active member of psychiatric staff, 1968-73; psychiatrist in private practice, Fairfax, 1968—. Lecturer at hospitals and at various civic, church, and health organizations. Clinical director, Northern Virginia Mental Health Institute, 1967-68. President of Berkey, Gilmore & Co. (psychological consultation firm), 1970-72. Consultant to Virginia State Department of Vocation Rehabilitation, 1966-67, Northern Virginia Mental Health Institute, 1968-69, Group Health Association, 1968—, Human Resource Associates, 1969—, Pastoral Counseling and Consultation Centers of Greater Washington, 1970-73, Accotink Academy, 1971-72, B'nai B'rith Career and Counseling Service of Greater Washington, 1973—. *Military service:* U.S. Army, Medical Corps, 1965-67; became captain.

MEMBER: American Group Psychotherapy Association, American Orthopsychiatric Association (fellow, 1975), American Psychiatric Association (fellow, 1974), National Writers Club, Washington Psychiatric Society, Phi Beta Kappa, Phi Delta Epsilon, Phi Sigma, Delta Phi Alpha, Chi Epsilon Mu.

WRITINGS: Halfway through the Tunnel, Philosophical Library, 1972; (with wife, Velma Berkey) *The Mind Is a Funny Thing,* T. S. Denison, 1973, musical tape to accompany book (also with Jon Carow), 1975; (contributor) Jhan Robbins, *The Anatomy of a Prostitute,* New American Library, 1974; (with V. Berkey and Richard Berkey) *Chincoteague for Children,* Tidewater, 1975; *Save Your Marriage,* Nelson-Hall, 1976; *The Fat's in Your Mind,* Chateau, 1977; (with V. Berkey and R. Berkey) *The Brothers Ward: Lem and Steve,* Tidewater, 1977; (with V. Berkey) *The Guilty Book,* T. S. Denison, 1977; (with V. Berkey) *Robbers, Bones, and Mean Dogs,* Addison-Wesley, in press. Author of column, "The Inner Limits," in *Virginia Cardinal* (magazine), 1972-74. Contributor of more than fifty articles to professional journals, including *Sexual Behavior, Journal of Psychiatry,* and *Sexology,* and to consumer magazines. North Virginia Chapter of Washington Psychiatric Society newsletter, *The Group,* reporter, 1970-71, news, honors, and awards editor, 1971-73.

AVOCATIONAL INTERESTS: Photography, snorkeling and shallow diving, bird watching, wildfowl carvings.

* * *

BERKIN, Carol Ruth   1942-

PERSONAL: Born October 1, 1942, in Mobile, Ala.; daughter of Saul (a businessman) and Marian (a bookkeeper; maiden name, Goldreich) Berkin; married John Paull Harper (a dean of curriculum), June 21, 1970. *Education:* Barnard College, A.B., 1964; Columbia University, M.A., 1966, Ph.D., 1972. *Religion:* Jewish. *Home:* 118 West 79th St., Apt. 14B, New York, N.Y. 10024. *Office:* Department of History, Bernard M. Baruch College of the City University of New York, 17 Lexington Ave., New York, N.Y. 10010.

CAREER: Editorial assistant for "Papers of Alexander Hamilton," New York City, 1964; Hunter College of the City University of New York, New York City, lecturer in history, 1968; member of editorial staff for "Papers of John Jay," New York City, 1972; Bernard M. Baruch College of the City University of New York, New York City, assistant professor, 1972-75, associate professor of history, 1975—.

MEMBER: American Antiquarian Society (fellow), American Historical Association, Organization of American Historians (member of bicentennial celebration committee, 1975—), Coordinating Committee for Women in the Historical Profession, Smithsonian Institution, Essex Institute, New York Historical Society, Columbia University Seminar in Early American History and Culture. *Awards, honors:* Bancroft Award from Bancroft Foundation and Columbia University, 1974, for doctoral dissertation on Jonathan Sewall; National Endowment for the Humanities grant, 1974; American Council of Learned Societies grant, 1975.

WRITINGS: Jonathan Sewall: Odyssey of an American Loyalist, Columbia University Press, 1974; *Within the Conjurer's Circle: Women in Colonial America* (pamphlet), General Lerarning Press, 1974.

WORK IN PROGRESS: Men in Crisis: The Loyalist Experience of the American Revolution, for Columbia University Press; editing *The Women of America: Original Essays and Documents,* with Mary Beth Norton, for Houghton.

SIDELIGHTS: Carol Berkin told *CA:* "My primary focus in my work has been to examine the personalities of men or women whose life style, ideology, or career patterns have placed them on the 'losing side' or out of the mainstream. Thus, the American Loyalists, for whom, in many ways, the world was turned upside down; thus, also, the study of American women who have always been outsiders as the 'second sex' in our history. Recently it has been noted that, 'while the patriots won the revolution, the Loyalists seem to be winning the bicentennial' because of the many sympathetic studies of these men and women in the 1960's and 70's. Perhaps with the new and exciting examination of women in our past, being done by so many able scholars today, it will also be said that women lost many struggles for equality, but they are winning a sense of their past."

* * *

BERLANSTEIN, Lenard R(ussell) 1947-

PERSONAL: Born November 29, 1947, in Brooklyn, N.Y.; son of K. David and Belle (Barnett) Berlanstein. *Education:* University of Michigan, B.A., 1969; Johns Hopkins University, M.A., 1971, Ph.D., 1973. *Office:* Department of History, University of Virginia, Charlottesville, Va. 22903.

CAREER: University of Virginia, Charlottesville, lecturer, 1973-75, assistant professor of modern European history, 1975—. *Member:* American Historical Association.

WRITINGS: The Barristers of Toulouse in the Eighteenth Century, Johns Hopkins Press, 1975.

WORK IN PROGRESS: Research on juvenile delinquency in nineteenth-century France.

* * *

BERLIN, Michael J(oseph) 1938-

PERSONAL: Born December 5, 1938, in New York, N.Y.; son of Jacob M. (a salesman) and Mary (a teacher; maiden name, Jacobson) Berlin; married: Nancy Goodman (an artist), April 8, 1962; children: Meredith Joy. *Education:* Columbia College, B.A., 1959, M.S., 1960. *Office:* United Nations Bureau, *New York Post,* Room 306, United Nations Bldg., New York, N.Y. 10017.

CAREER: Philadelphia Inquirer, Philadelphia, Pa., copy editor, 1960-62; *Houston Post,* Houston, Tex., copy editor, 1962-63; *San Francisco Chronicle,* San Francisco, Calif., copy editor, 1963-65; *New York Herald Tribune,* New York City, rewrite man and copy editor, 1965-66; *New York Post,* New York City, reporter, 1966—. Notable assignments include the coverage of all United Nations events, 1967—, and Middle East peace talks in Geneva and the Middle East, 1973-74. Teaching associate in journalism, Columbia University, 1972—. *Member:* United Nations Correspondents Association (secretary, 1976 and 1977), Columbia Journalism Alumni (secretary, 1974-77).

WRITINGS: (With Ralph Blumenfeld and others) *Henry Kissinger: The Private and Public Story,* New American Library, 1974. Contributor of articles to *Columbia Journalism Review, Columbia Today* and *New York,* of scripts to Canadian Broadcasting Corp. and Australian Broadcasting Corp., and of articles to various newspapers.

* * *

BERLINER, Joseph S(cholom) 1921-

PERSONAL: Born September 4, 1921, in New York, N.Y.; son of Michael (a neckwear cutter) and Yetta (Eisenberg) Berliner; married Ann Korenbaum (a teacher), October 7, 1943; children: Paul, Carl, Nancy. *Education:* U.S. Coast Guard Academy, student, 1941-43; Harvard University, B.A., 1947, M.A., 1949, Ph.D., 1953. *Politics:* Democrat. *Religion:* Jewish. *Home:* 3 Compton Circle, Lexington, Mass. 02173. *Office:* Department of Economics, Brandeis University, Waltham, Mass. 02154.

CAREER: Harvard University, Cambridge, Mass., assistant director of Russian Research Center, 1953-54; Corporation for Economic and Industry Research, Washington, D.C., economist, 1954-56; Syracuse University, Syracuse, N.Y., assistant professor, 1956-59, associate professor, 1959-61, professor of economics, 1961-63; Brandeis University, Waltham, Mass., professor of economics, 1963—. *Wartime service:* U.S. Maritime Service, 1943-46; became first engineer.

MEMBER: American Economic Association, American Association for the Advancement of Slavic Studies (president, 1963-64), Association for Comparative Economic Studies (president, 1975-76), Association for the Study of Soviet-Type Economies (executive secretary, 1959-62). *Awards, honors:* T.S.M. Award from Association of American Publishers, 1976, for *The Innovation Decision in Soviet Industry.*

WRITINGS: Factory and Manager in the U.S.S.R., Harvard University Press, 1957; *Soviet Economic Aid,* Praeger, 1958; (contributor) Henry Rosovsky, editor, *Industrialization in Two Systems,* Wiley, 1966; *Economy, Society, and Welfare,* Praeger, 1972; *The Innovation Decision in Soviet Industry,* M.I.T. Press, 1976. Contributor to economics and anthropology journals.

WORK IN PROGRESS: The Economics of Social Institutions.

* * *

BERMEL, Albert (Cyril) 1927-

PERSONAL: Surname is accented on last syllable; born December 20, 1927, in London, England; came to United States, 1955; naturalized U.S. citizen, 1962; son of Harry (a shoe stall holder in an open-air market) and Rae (a partner in husband's business; maiden name, Sanders) Bermel; married Joyce Hartman (a magazine editor and writer), 1956; children: Neil, Derek. *Education:* London School of Economics and Political Science, London, B.Sc., 1952. *Politics:* "Nonpartisan egalitarian." *Religion:* Nonsectarian Jewish.

Residence: New Rochelle, N.Y. *Agent:* Elaine Markson, Elaine Markson Literary Agency, 44 Greenwich Ave., New York, N.Y. 10011. *Office:* Department of Speech and Theatre, Herbert H. Lehman College of the City University of New York, Bronx, N.Y. 10468.

CAREER: Advertising and publicity copywriter in London, Montreal, Toronto, and New York City, 1951-56; free-lance writer in New York City, 1956-58; magazine and book editor in New York City, 1958-60, 1961-63; free-lance writer in New York City, 1963-66; Columbia University, New York City, associate professor of theatre, 1966-72; Herbert H. Lehman College of the City University of New York, New York City, associate professor, 1972-75, professor of theatre, 1975—. Visiting professor at Rutgers University, 1966-67, and Juillard School, 1971-72. Member of board of Bronx Council on the Arts; secretary of Glenwood Lake Association, 1975-76. Adviser to several theatre companies. *Military service:* British Army, 1946-48; served in West Germany. *Member:* Authors League of America, Dramatists Guild, New Drama Forum. *Awards, honors:* Guggenheim fellow in playwriting, 1965-66; George Jean Nathan Award for best dramatic criticism published in 1973-74, for *New Leader* theatre reviews and book *Contradictory Characters.*

WRITINGS: (Editor) *The Genius of the French Theater,* New American Library, 1961; (editor and translator) *The Plays of Georges Courteline,* Theatre Arts, 1961; (translator and author of introduction) Corneille, *Horatius (Horace),* Chandler Publishing, 1962; (translator and author of introduction) *One-Act Comedies of Moliere,* World Publishing, 1964, 2nd edition, Ungar, 1975; *Contradictory Characters: An Interpretation of the Modern Theatre,* Dutton, 1973; (translator and author of notes) *Three Popular French Comedies,* Ungar, 1975; *Artaud's Theatre of Cruelty,* Taplinger, 1977.

Plays; full-length: "One Leg over the Wrong Wall" (based on *The Song of Roland*), first produced in London at Royal Court Theatre, 1960; "Herod First," produced in London at Saville Theatre, 1965; "Thrombo," produced in New York City at Columbia Summer Theatre, 1968; "Family Weather," produced under title "The Terror of Suspension" in New York City at House Theatre, 1975. Also author of "Whose Play?," as yet unproduced.

One-acts: "The Workout," first produced in London at Questors Theatre, 1963, and in New York City at New Theatre Workshop, 1967; "The Adjustment," first produced in Spoleto, Italy, at Theatre of Two Worlds, 1963; "The Recovery," first produced in Edinburgh at Traverse Theatre Club, 1965, produced in New York City at New Theatre Workshop, 1967; "The Seizure, a Web, the Imp or Imps," first produced in New York at Assembly Theatre, 1970.

Translator and adaptor of plays by others for production, including Georges Courteline's "The Commissioner," Arthur Adamov's "Professor Taranne," and Jean Cocteau's "The Infernal Machine."

WORK IN PROGRESS: The Comic Agony, "a book-length view of modern drama that conflicts with the traditional view that there are genres (tragedy, comedy, farce, melodrama, tragicomedy) and involves a close reading of about fifteen plays."

SIDELIGHTS: Bermel told *CA:* "I try to write on a fairly specialized topic, theatre, for a general audience, those hypothetical people, intelligent readers, in the belief that theatre is, by its nature, a popular art form that touches politics, economics, sociology, and other social sciences, as well as all the other arts, from painting to sculpture (and graffiti) to fiction, music, dance, mime, and conjuring.

"Of the plays I have written, I have junked at least twice as many plays as these, and hope to do so with many more. Edward Bond, who recently said that he writes plays to avoid going mad, is a respected British playwright who acted in my first play, 'One Leg over the Wrong Wall.' I believe I write plays to avoid going sane. Directors I have worked with will confirm this. Some years ago one play was done in a plushy, expensive staging which poisoned my feelings about the commercial theatre (they were none too friendly before that experience); since then I have tried to shun the horrors of bigness."

* * *

BERNHEIMER, Martin 1936-

PERSONAL: Born September 28, 1936, in Munich, Germany; came to United States in 1940, naturalized citizen, 1946; son of Paul Ernst (an art dealer) and Louise (Nassauer) Bernheimer; married Lucinda Pearson (an audiologist), September 30, 1961; children: Mark, Nora, Erika and Marina (twins). *Education:* Brown University, B.A. (with honors), 1958; Munich Conservatory, student, 1958-59; New York University, M.A., 1962. *Office: Los Angeles Times,* Times-Mirror Sq., Los Angeles, Calif. 90053.

CAREER/WRITINGS: Free-lance music critic, 1958-65; *Los Angeles Times,* Los Angeles, Calif., music editor and critic, 1965—. Contributor to more than twenty national and international periodicals, including *New York Times, Musical Quarterly, Opera News, Christian Science Monitor, Nation,* and *Commonweal.* Member of music staff, *New York Herald Tribune,* 1959-62; assistant music editor, *Saturday Review,* 1962-65; managing editor, *Philharmonic Hall Program* (magazine), 1962-65; contributing editor, *Musical Courier;* New York correspondent, *Opera* (British magazine). Member of music faculty, New York University, 1960-62, Rockefeller Program for the Training of Music Critics at University of Southern California, 1966-73, University of California at Los Angeles, 1969-75, and University of Southern California, 1971—. Author of liner annotations for RCA Victor, Columbia, and London Records. Frequent guest on radio and television programs in New York City and Los Angeles. *Awards, honors:* Deems Taylor Award, 1974, from American Society of Composers, Authors, and Publishers (ASCAP), for "outstanding service to music and journalism."

* * *

BERNSTEIN, Hillel 1892(?)-1977

1892(?)—April 5, 1977; Russian-born American journalist and author. He served in the United States Navy during World War I and wrote for the British Broadcasting Corporation during World War II. He also wrote several novels. Bernstein was writing his memoirs at the time of his death. He died in Colebrook, Conn. Obituaries: *New York Times,* April 7, 1977; *Washington Post,* April 7, 1977.

* * *

BERRY, Boyd M(cCulloch) 1939-

PERSONAL: Born May 29, 1939, in Chicago, Ill.; son of Albert McCulloch (in industry) and Carolyn (a teacher; maiden name, Fischer) Berry; married Sara Sweezy (a college teacher), December 29, 1961; children: Rachel E. A.,

Jonathan E. A. *Education:* Harvard University, B.A., 1961; University of Michigan, M.A., 1962, Ph.D., 1966. *Home:* 1114 Grove Ave., Richmond, Va. 23220. *Office:* Department of English, Virginia Commonwealth University, Richmond, Va. 23284.

CAREER: Indiana University, Bloomington, assistant professor of English, 1966-74; Virginia Commonwealth University, Richmond, associate professor of English, 1974—. *Member:* Modern Language Association of America, Milton Society of America, Southeastern Renaissance Society.

WRITINGS: Process of Speech: Puritan Religious Writing and Paradise Lost, Johns Hopkins Press, 1976. Contributor to journals.

WORK IN PROGRESS: Renaissance Attitudes toward Childhood; a book on Renaissance botanists, vegetarians, and pastoral poets.

SIDELIGHTS: Berry told *CA:* "I began writing out of an effort to see Milton's epic in terms of the religious sensibilities of the common man of his age, rather than against the 'greats' of Christian theologizing. I tread the by-ways of renaissance publication, studying human behavior rather than 'ideas' or poetic traditions. . . . In focus, in ideological outlook, and in style, I try in my writing to be popular."

*   *   *

BERRY, Charles H.   1930-

PERSONAL: Born January 6, 1930, in Ottawa, Ontario, Canada; son of F. William (a businessman) and Lucinda B. (Pratt) Berry; married Gisella Erdody; children: William, Rachael, Katherine. *Education:* McGill University, B.Sc., 1951; University of Connecticut, M.Sc., 1953; University of Chicago, Ph.D., 1956. *Home:* 47 Maclean Circle, Princeton, N.J. 08540. *Office:* 219 Woodrow Wilson School, Princeton University, Princeton, N.J. 08540.

CAREER: Yale University, New Haven, Conn., assistant professor of economics, 1957-63, director of undergraduate studies, 1959-62; Brookings Institution, Washington, D.C., senior staff member, 1963-66; Princeton University, Princeton, N.J., associate professor, 1966-71, professor of economics, 1971—, director of Sloan Foundation, 1975—, associate dean and director of graduate studies at Woodrow Wilson School, 1975—. Director of National Bureau of Economic Research, 1969—. Member of Princeton Regional Planning Board and Princeton Hospital Liaison Committee. Consultant to U.S. Department of Justice, Internal Revenue Service, Royal Commission on Health Services, and Social Science Research Council. *Member:* American Economic Association, Econometrics Society.

WRITINGS: Voluntary Medical Insurance and Prepayment, Queen's Printer, 1965; *Corporate Growth and Diversification,* Princeton University Press, 1975. Contributor to professional journals. Member of editorial board of *Explorations.*

WORK IN PROGRESS: Research on the impact of the Medicare Program.

*   *   *

BESHOAR, Barron B(enedict)   1907-

PERSONAL: Born April 26, 1907, in Trinidad, Colo.; son of Ben B. (a physician) and Fay (an artist; maiden name, Shanly) Beshoar; married Sally Throckmorton, September 7, 1929; children: Ben B., John Michael, Daniel Joseph, Barron B., Jr. *Education:* Attended University of Denver

and University of Colorado. *Politics:* Democrat. *Religion:* Roman Catholic. *Home:* 615 Maple St., Trinidad, Colo. 81082.

CAREER: Rocky Mountain News, Denver, Colo., reporter and rewrite man, 1935-37, 1937-42; *Des Moines Register,* Des Moines, Iowa, reporter, 1937; regional minority representative in eight states for Labor Division of War Production Board, 1942-43; regional chief of information in eight western states for War Manpower Commission, 1943-44; *Memphis Commercial Appeal,* Memphis, Tenn., reporter, 1944; *Rocky Mountain News,* reporter and rewrite man, 1944-46; Time, Inc., New York City, bureau chief and deputy director of news service in Denver, New York City, and Los Angeles, and staff correspondent for *Fortune, Time, Life,* and *Sports Illustrated,* 1944-67; Colorado College, Colorado Springs, director of information, 1968; writer, 1969—. Consultant for Education Commission of the States, 1969-75.

WRITINGS: Out of the Depths (story of the 1913-14 Colorado coal strike against the Rockefeller's Colorado Fuel & Iron Corp.), World Press, 1954; *Hippocrates in a Red Vest* (biography of a Confederate Army surgeon and frontier doctor), American West, 1973. Also author of *Western Trails to Calvary,* 1949, and *No Windy Promises,* 1961, and, with Clifford Dochterman, *Future Directions for School Financing* and *Directions to Excellence in Education.* Contributor to magazines, including *Newsweek, Collier's,* and *Coronet.*

WORK IN PROGRESS: Research on the Navajos.

BIOGRAPHICAL/CRITICAL SOURCES: Denver Post, March 27, 1957, July 28, 1967; *Time,* May 12, 1961, March 16, 1962, February 27, 1963.

*   *   *

BESSER, Milton   1911-1976

PERSONAL: Born January 12, 1911, in Denver, Col.; married wife, Betty, 1937; children: Mary Ruth Besser Swan, David, William, Ralph, Robert, James. *Education:* University of Colorado, B.A., 1933. *Home:* 2672 North Pershing, Wichita, Kan. 67220.

CAREER/WRITINGS: Star Herald, Scotts Bluff, Neb., city editor, 1933-37; Associated Press, New York, N.Y., state editor, 1947-44, foreign news desk editor, 1944-57, United Nations correspondent, 1951-71; Wichita State University, Wichita, Kan., associate professor of journalism, 1971-76. *Member:* Association of Education in Journalism.

OBITUARIES: New York Times, July 24, 1976.*

(Died July 23, 1976, in Wichita, Kan.)

*   *   *

BEST, Judith A.   1938-

PERSONAL: Born April 7, 1938, in Chicago, Ill.; daughter of Dominic M. and Dorothy (Ahrbeck) Vairo; children: Michael, David. *Education:* Michigan State University, B.A., 1958; University of Michigan, M.A., 1963; Cornell University, Ph.D., 1971. *Office:* Department of Political Science, State University of New York College at Cortland, Cortland, N.Y. 13045.

CAREER: Cornell University, Ithaca, N.Y., instructor in American government, 1970-71, research associate on Rann Energy Project, 1971-73; State University of New York College at Cortland, assistant professor, 1973-75, associate professor of American government and theory, 1976—.

Member: American Political Science Association, American Academy of Political Science, Caucus on Women's Rights (State University of New York).

WRITINGS: The Case Against Direct Election of the President: A Defense of the Electoral College, Cornell University Press, 1975.

* * *

BEST, Otto F(erdinand) 1929-

PERSONAL: Born July 28, 1929, in Steinheim, Main, Germany; son of Conrad and Christina (Rapp) Best; married wife Brigitte; children: Bettina, Christoph, Philipp, Daniel. *Education:* University of Munich, Ph.D., 1963. *Home:* 2100 Ardleigh Court, Bowie, Md. 20716. *Office:* Department of Germanic and Slavic Languages, University of Maryland, College Park, Md. 20742.

CAREER: College Hippolyte Fontaine, Dijon, France, assistant, 1952-53; Insel Verlag in Wiesbaden, Germany, Verlag Kiepenheuer & Witsch in Cologne, R. Piper & Co., Munich, editor, 1954-63, editor-in-chief, 1963-1968; University of Munich, Munich, Germany, lecturer in German philology, 1965-68; University of Maryland, College Park, Md., associate professor, 1969-71, professor of German and comparative literature, 1971—.

WRITINGS: Peter Weiss, Francke Verlag, 1971, translation by Ursule Molinaro under same title, Ungar, 1975; *Handbuch literarischer Fachbegriffe,* Fischer Verlag, 1972; *Mameloschen, Jiddisch,* Insel Verlag, 1973; (editor) *Moses Mendelssohn,* Wissenschaftliche Buchgegesellschaft, 1974; (editor with H. J. Schmitt) *Die deutsche Literatur,* 16 volumes, Reclam, 1974-77; *Das verbotene Gluck,* Piper, 1977.

WORK IN PROGRESS: Weisheit und Uberleben, publication by Suhrkamp expected in 1978.

* * *

BEYER, Andrew 1943-

PERSONAL: Born November 17, 1943, in Carbondale, Ill.; son of Ricahrd L. (a teacher) and Pauline (Sorgen) Beyer. *Education:* Harvard University, student, 1961-66. *Home:* 2457 Tunlaw Rd. N.W., Washington, D.C. 20007. *Office: Washington Star,* 225 Virginia, Washington, D.C.

CAREER: Washington Post, Washington, D.C., reporter, 1966-69; *Washington Daily News,* Washington, D.C., author of sports column, 1969-72; *Washington Star,* Washington, D.C., author of sports column, 1972—. *Military service:* U.S. Army, 1968-70.

WRITINGS: Picking Winners: A Horseplayer's Guide, Houghton, 1975.

WORK IN PROGRESS: A book on horse race betting, publication by Harcourt expected in 1979.

* * *

BEZIO, May Rowland ?-1977

?—April 9, 1977; American religious organization official and author of books on religion. She died in Kansas City, Mo. Obituaries: *New York Times,* April 10, 1977.

* * *

BIBLE, Charles 1937-

PERSONAL: Born April 22, 1937, in Waco, Tex.; son of Julius Vernon and Willie Mae (Chapman) Bible; married Evelyn Nebeling, July 13, 1969; children: Ava, Philip, Jennifer, Charles, Jax. *Education:* Attended San Francisco State College (now University), 1966-67; Pratt Institute, 1969-70; Queens College of the City University of New York, B.A., 1976; also studied art privately under Gerald Marks. *Home and office:* 94-11 34th Rd., Jackson Heights, N.Y. 11372.

CAREER: Good Publishing Co., Ft. Worth, Tex., boardman and cartoonist, 1952-54; Jamerson Printing Co., San Francisco, Calif., art director, 1956-63; Amistad Litho Co., San Mateo, Calif., art director, 1963-69; artist and book illustrator, 1969—. Work exhibited at museums, galleries, and universities in New York and California, including San Francisco State University, Queens College of the City University of New York, and New Muse Community Museum of Brooklyn; posters included in many permanent library collections. Summer high school teacher, New York, N.Y., 1971; instructor at Metropolitan Museum of Art, 1976—. *Military service:* U.S. Navy, 1954-56. *Member:* National Conference of Artists (acting regional director of New York/New Jersey region, 1975-76), College Art Association, American Institute for Graphic Artists, Pratt Graphics Center, Council on Interracial Books for Children, Queens College Veterans Association.

WRITINGS—Self-illustrated: *Eating at the Y* (poetry), privately printed, 1974; *Jennifer's New Chair,* Holt, in press.

Illustrator: Sharon Mathis, *Brooklyn Story,* Hill, 1970; pupils of P.S. 150, *Black Means . . . ,* Hill, 1970; Nikki Giovanni, *Spin a Soft Black Song,* Hill, 1971; *Hamdaani* (Zanzibar folk tale), Holt, 1977.

Correspondent for "Illustrators Showcase" column in Council on Interracial Books for Children bulletin, 1974—. Contributor of illustrations to *Bayviewer.*

WORK IN PROGRESS: Writing, with own illustrations, *That Little Colored Boy.*

SIDELIGHTS: Bible told *CA:* "In my attempts to make beautiful pictures for other people to see, I always use the butterfly as reference. The wonderful colors and the peaceful attitude of the butterfly encourage me to try to find as much beauty in other animals, in people, and in all the creations of the earth. Besides, I have never even heard of an *ugly* butterfly!"

* * *

BICKELHAUPT, David L(ynn) 1929-

PERSONAL: Born May 16, 1929, in Syracuse, N.Y.; son of Lynn John (an insurance agent) and Susan Helen (Metcalfe) Bickelhaupt; married Ona Lee Barron, June 8, 1952; children: Tina Gay Bickelhaupt Erwin, Janet Lynne, Paul Barron, Carol Lee. *Education:* University of Pennsylvania, B.S., 1951, Ph.D., 1959; Columbia University, M.S., 1952. *Religion:* Episcopal. *Home:* 2239 Buckley Rd., Columbus, Ohio 43220. *Office:* Ohio State University, 1775 South College Rd., Columbus, Ohio 43210.

CAREER: Van Voast & Leonard Agency, Saratoga Springs, N.Y., insurance agent, 1952-55; University of Pennsylvania, Wharton School of Finance and Commerce, Philadelphia, part-time instructor in insurance, 1957-58; Georgia State University, Atlanta, assistant professor of insurance, 1959; Ohio State University, Columbus, associate professor, 1959-65, professor of insurance and finance, 1965—. Part-time instructor at Skidmore College, 1953-55; executive director of Griffith Foundation for Insurance Education, 1959-65; member of board of trustees of Ohio State Teachers Retirement System, 1976—. Diplomate of Insurance Institute of America, 1968.

MEMBER: International Insurance Seminars, American Risk and Insurance Association (president, 1972-73), American Finance Association, American Society of Chartered Life Underwriters, American Society for Insurance Management, Society of Chartered Property Casualty Underwriters, American Association of University Professors, Sigma Phi Epsilon, Beta Gamma Sigma, Gamma Iota Sigma. *Awards, honors:* Award from *Library Journal,* 1964.

WRITINGS: The Transition to Multiple-Line Insurance Companies, Irwin, 1961; *General Insurance,* 9th edition (Bickelhaupt was not associated with earlier editions), Irwin, 1974, 10th edition, 1978. Contributor to *Property and Liability Insurance Handbook, Encyclopaedia Britannica Yearbook,* and *Lincoln Library of Essential Information.* Contributor of about thirty articles to professional journals.

WORK IN PROGRESS: Research on university retirement systems.

SIDELIGHTS: Bickelhaput's textbook on general insurance is widely used in colleges and universities, and for professional courses, including those of Insurance Institute of America.

*   *   *

BILSLAND, E(rnest) C(harles) 1931-
(Bilko Bilsland)

PERSONAL: Born March 27, 1931, in Chicago, Ill.; son of Ernest C., Sr. and Anna (Bozik) Bilsland; married Joyce Edna Holmes, October 21, 1950; children: Bonita Jean, Ernest C. III, Roxann. *Education:* Educated in Chicago, Ill.; additional study from Cartoonist Exchange, 1952. *Home:* 7832 La Castana Way, Buena Park, Calif. 90620. *Agent:* B. P. Singer Features, Anaheim, Calif.

CAREER: Has been a postal worker in Chicago, Ill., 1949-55; has worked in fire departments in Chicago, 1955-59, Buena Park, Calif., 1959-62; works for Los Angeles Fire Department, Los Angeles, Calif., 1962—, inspector, 1970-75. Cartoonist. Lecturer on cartooning.

WRITINGS: (With Jim Whitehead; under name Bilko Bilsland) *Stick Shifter's Glove Box Companion,* Sports Car Press, 1971. Columnist for Los Angeles Fire Department's magazine. Contributor to magazines.

*   *   *

BING, Elisabeth D. 1914-

PERSONAL: Born July 8, 1914, in Berlin, Germany; came to the United States in 1949; daughter of George Felix (an architect) and Kate (Born) Koenigsberger; married Fred M. Bing (in shipping), April 19, 1951; children: Peter. *Home:* 164 West 79th St., New York, N.Y. 10024.

CAREER: Mt. Sinai Hospital, New York, N.Y., in childbirth education program, 1952-60; Flower & Fifth Avenue Hospitals, New York City, instructor in childbirth education, 1960—. Assistant professor at New York Medical College, 1974—; gives private classes and public lectures on childbirth education. *Member:* American Society for Psychoprophylaxis in Obstetrics (co-founder).

WRITINGS: Six Practical Lessons for an Easier Childbirth, Grosset, 1967; (editor) *The Adventure of Birth: Experiences in the Lamaze Method of Prepared Childbirth,* Simon & Schuster, 1970; (with Gerald Barad) *A Birth in the Family,* Bantam, 1973; *Moving Through Pregnancy,* Bobbs-Merrill, 1975; (with Tarvez Tucker) *Prepared Childbirth,* Tobey Publishing, 1975; (with Libby Colman) *Making Love During Pregnancy,* Bantam, 1977.

SIDELIGHTS: Elisabeth Bing is responsible for the training record "Practice for Childbirth" and consultant for the record album "The Lamaze Experience."

*   *   *

BIRKIN, Charles (Lloyd) 1907-
(Charles Lloyd)

PERSONAL: Born September 24, 1907, in Nottinghamshire, England; son of Charles Wilfrid (a colonel) and Claire (Howe) Birkin; married Janet Johnson, June 16, 1940; children: Jennifer Claire de Clermont, Amanda Jane, John Christian. *Education:* Attended private secondary school in England. *Politics:* Conservative. *Religion:* Church of England. *Home:* West Kella, Sulby, Isle of Man.

CAREER: Fiction writer, 1934—. Worked for Philip Allan & Co. (publishers), 1933-35; advertising copywriter for Bernard & Co., 1936-38. *Military service:* British Army, Eighth Sherwood Foresters, 1940-46; became captain. *Member:* Carlton Club. *Awards, honors:* Second prize from *Argosy,* 1968, for "Fairy Dust."

WRITINGS—All collections of stories, except as indicated: *Devil's Spawn,* Philip Allan, 1934; *I'll Have My Gun* (animal story), privately printed, 1940; *The Kiss of Death* (includes stories first published singly under pseudonym Charles Lloyd), Tandem, 1964, Award Books, 1969; *The Smell of Evil,* Tandem, 1965, Award Books, 1969; (editor) *The Tandem Book of Ghost Stories,* Tandem, 1965; (editor) *The Tandem Book of Humor Stories,* Tandem, 1965; *My Name Is Death,* Panther, 1966, Award Books, 1970; *Where Terror Stalked,* Tandem, 1966; *Dark Menace,* Tandem, 1968; *So Pale, So Cold, So Fair,* Tandem, 1970; *Spawn of Satan,* Award Books, 1970. Also author of radio scripts.

Work represented in anthologies, including *Quiver of Horror,* edited by Dennis Wheatley, Arrow, 1964; and *John Creasey's Mystery Bedside Book,* edited by Herbert Harris, Hodder & Stoughton, 1971. Contributor of stories to magazines, including *Tatler, Sketch,* and *Bystander.*

WORK IN PROGRESS: Horror stories for inclusion in anthologies, to be published by Fontana and W. H. Allen.

SIDELIGHTS: Sir Charles Birkin (5th Baronet Birkin) writes: "With the post-war closedown of most magazines in England, I specialized in short stories of a *grand guignol* character."

*   *   *

BIRKS, Tony 1937-

PERSONAL: Born November 1, 1937, in Manchester, England; son of Edwyn Ainsworth (a publisher) and Nora Lilian (a writer) Birks; married Margaret Leslie Hay (an editor), July 14, 1972; children: Paul Raphael. *Education:* Slade School of Fine Art, D.F.A., 1958; St. Edmund Hall, Oxford, M.A., 1961; University of Grenoble, ler Degre, 1964. *Home and office:* Manor Farm, Caundle Marsh, Sherborne, Dorsetshire DT9 5LX, England.

CAREER: Oxford School of Art, Oxford, England, lecturer in ceramics and sculpture, 1959-63; Thames & Hudson (publisher), London, England, art editor, 1964-68; George Rainbird Ltd., London, England, sponsor editor, 1968-71; Alphabet & Image, Sherborne, England, managing director, 1972—. Member of Crafts Centre of Great Britain. *Awards, honors:* Slade sculpture prize, 1958; award from TV Westward, 1973, for ceramics.

WRITINGS: The Art of the Modern Potter, Country Life

Books, 1967, 2nd edition, Van Nostrand, 1977; *Building the New Universities*, David & Charles, 1972; *The Potter's Companion*, Dutton, 1974; *Meyer's Ornament*, Duckworth, 1974; (contributor) Emmanuel Cooper and Eileen Lewenstein, editors, *New Ceramics*, Van Nostrand, 1974; *Outline Guide to Pottery*, Blandford Press, 1975.

WORK IN PROGRESS: A biography of William Dampier, publication expected in 1980; *Crafts Guide to Pottery*, for Pan Books.

SIDELIGHTS: Birks writes briefly that he is "interested in all forms of design of all periods, especially architecture and carpets."

* * *

BISSELL, Richard (Pike) 1913-1977

June 27, 1913—May 4, 1977; American pajama-factory superintendent, riverboat pilot, novelist, and playwright. He was best known as co-author of smash Broadway musical "The Pajama Game" which he adapted from his own best-selling novel, *7½ Cents*. He died in Dubuque, Iowa. Obituaries: *New York Times*, May 5, 1977; *Newsweek*, May 16, 1977; *Time*, May 16, 1977. (See index for previous *CA* sketch)

* * *

bissett, bill 1939-

PERSONAL: Born November 23, 1939, in Halifax, Nova Scotia, Canada; son of Frederick William and Katherine Hamilton (Covert) Bissett; children: Ooljah. *Education:* Attended Dalhousie University, 1956-57, and University of British Columbia, 1963-65. *Politics:* "equality." *Religion:* "erth air fire n watr." *Home address:* Box 48870, Station Bentall, Vancouver, British Columbia, Canada. *Agent:* Arlene Lampert, League of Canadian Poets, 651 Spadina Ave., Toronto, Ontario, Canada.

CAREER: Has worked as a record store clerk, library clerk, house painter, ditch digger, gas station attendent, bean picker, disk jockey, construction worker, sign painter, English tutor, fence builder, and hauler. Associate director, Mandan Ghetto, Vancouver, British Columbia, 1967-68; editor and printer, Blewointmentpress, 1964—. *Member:* League of Canadian Poets, Association of Canadian Publishers, Literary Press Group. *Awards, honors:* Canada Council grants, 1967, 1969, 1971, 1974.

WRITINGS—Poetry: *we sleep inside each othr all*, ganglia, 1967; *th jinx ship Or fires in the tempul*, very stone house, 1967; *of th land/divine service*, weed/flower press, 1967; *what poetiks*, blewointmentpress, 1967; *where is miss florence riddle*, luv press, 1976; *(Th) Gossamer Bed Pan*, blewointment press, 1967; *lebanon voices*, weed/flower press, 1968; *sunday work (?)*, blewointment press, 1968; *liberating skies*, blewointmentpress, 1969; *lost angel mining co.*, blewointmentpress, 1969; *AWAKE IN TH RED DESERT*, Talonbooks, 1969; *Killer Whale*, Sea Hear Productions, 1969; *Th Outlaw*, blewointmentpress, 1970; *s th story i to*, blewointmentpress, 1970; *blew trewz*, blewointmentpress, 1970; *air 6*, air press, 1971; *dragonfly*, weed/flower press, 1971; *tuff shit*, bandit black moss, 1971; *drifting into war*, Talonbooks, 1971; *NOBODY OWNS TH EARTH*, House of Anansi, 1971; *IBM*, blewointmentpress, 1972; *RUSH what fukin thery*, blewointmentpress, 1972; *TH ICE BAG*, blewointmentpress, 1972; *pomes for yoshi*, blewointmentpress, 1972; *th first sufi line*, blewointmentpress, 1973; *pass th food release th spirit book*, Talonbooks, 1973; *Van-*

couver Mainland Ice & Cold Storage, Writers Forum, 1973; (with Earle Birney, Judith Copithorne, and Andy Suknaski) *FOUR PARTS SAND*, Oberon Press, 1973; *Air 10-11-12*, air press, 1973; *living with th vishyun*, New Star Books, 1974; *MEDICINE my mouths on fire*, Oberon Press, 1974; *(Th) Gossamer Bed Pan REVISD*, blewointmentpress, 1974; *what*, blewointmentpress, 1974; *drawings*, blewointmentpress, 1974; *yu can eat it at th opening*, blewointmentpress, 1974; *th fifth sun*, blewointmentpress, 1975; *image being*, blewointmentpress, 1975; *venus*, blewointmentpress, 1975; *space travl*, air press, 1975; *stardust*, blewointmentpress, 1975; *plutonium missing*, Intermedia, 1976; *an allusyun to macbeth*, black moss, 1976; *th wind up tongue*, blewointmentpress, 1976.

Illustrator, Jim Brown, *The Circus in the Boy's Eye*, very stone house, 1966.

WORK IN PROGRESS: bissett told *CA* he is "continuing to xploor vizual n sound writing as well as conversahunal vois writing with accent on/tord picture in th word sound utterance—chants—nd what speech is for—wher it comes from—often without any correct grammar spelling syntax linear meening spelling mor 'phonetik' as sound."

SIDELIGHTS: bissett said: "painter and poet, collage-maker n sound poet, th drawings n pomes feed each othr, ar sources i don't know from th same fire."

* * *

BITTER, Gary G(len) 1940-

PERSONAL: Born February 2, 1940, in Hoisington, Kan.; son of Solomon and Elvera Bitter; married Kay Burgat (a writer), August 19, 1962; children: Steve, Mike, Matthew. *Education:* Kansas State University, B.S., 1962; Kansas State Teachers College, M.A., 1965; University of Michigan, further graduate study, 1965-66; University of Denver, Ph.D., 1970. *Home:* 8531 East Osborn, Scottsdale, Ariz. 85251. *Office:* College of Education, Arizona State University, Tempe, Ariz. 85281.

CAREER: Teacher of mathematics and science at public high schools in Derby, Kan., 1962-65, and mathematics in public schools in Ann Arbor, Mich., 1965-66; Washburn University, Topeka, Kan., instructor in mathematics education, 1966-67; Colorado College, Colorado Springs, instructor in mathematics and computer education, 1968-70; Arizona State University, Tempe, assistant professor, 1970-74, associate professor of mathematics education, 1974—. Professor of mathematics education at University of Northern Colorado, summer, 1973, and at Montana State University, summer, 1975; lecturer at University of Colorado, 1968-70. Consultant to Kaman Nuclear Co. and General Cassette Corp.

MEMBER: American Association of University Professors, Association of Educational Data Processing (member of national board of directors, 1974-75), Mathematical Association of America, National Council of Teachers of Mathematics, School Science and Mathematics, Association for Computing Machinery, Arizona Association of Educational Data Systems (president, 1972-74; member of board of directors, 1974-75), Arizona Association of Elementary-Kindergarten-Nursery Education, Arizona Association of Teachers of Mathematics (member of board of directors, 1972-75), Phi Delta Kappa.

WRITINGS: (With Lyle Mauland) *Limits: Computer Extended Calculus*, University of Denver Press, 1970; (with W. Y. Gateley) *Basic for Beginners*, McGraw, 1970; (with

W. S. Dorn and D. L. Hector) *Computer Applications for Calculus,* Prindle, 1972; (with Jon Knaupp) *Mathematics Activity Manual,* Addison-Wesley, 1972; (with Gateley) *Basic Fibel,* R. V. Deckers, 1973; (with Mauland) *Functions: Computer Extended Calculus,* University of Denver Press, 1973; (contributor) N. K. Silvaroli and Lynn Searfoss, editors, *Communications, Reading, and Mathematics,* D. A. Lewis Associates, 1975; (with Charles Geer) *Materials for Metric Instruction,* ERIC, 1975; (with Jerald Mikesell) *Investigating Metric Measure,* McGraw, 1975; (with Mikesell) *Discovering Metric Measure,* McGraw, 1975; (with Tom Metos) *Exploring with Metrics,* Messner, 1975; (with Mikesell) *Multiplication and Division Games and Ideas,* McGraw, 1976; (with Mikesell) *Activities Handbook for Teaching the Metric System,* Allyn & Bacon, 1976; (with Mikesell) *Addition and Subtraction Games and Ideas,* McGraw, 1976; *Calculator Power* (six workbooks), EMC Corp., 1977; (with Metos) *Exploring with Pocket Calculators,* Messner, 1977. Contributor to mathematics and education journals. Editor of *Computer Corner;* member of editorial board of *Two Year College Mathematics Journal;* editor of metric corner of *Teacher* magazine.

WORK IN PROGRESS: A 2nd edition of *Basic for Beginners,* with W. Y. Gateley, for McGraw; *Handheld Pocket Calculator Book,* for Allyn & Bacon; *Mathematics Methods Book,* for Allyn & Bacon; pocket calculator film and filmstrips, for Centron Corp.

* * *

BITTNER, Vernon (John)   1932-

PERSONAL: Born November 26, 1932, in Lamberton, Minn.; son of John and Mildred Bittner. *Education:* St. Olaf College, B.A., 1954; graduate study at Garrett Theological Seminary and McCormick Theological Seminary; Northern Baptist Theological Seminary, M.Th., 1961; San Francisco Theological Seminary, S.T.D., 1973. *Home:* 3135 Kyle Ave. N., Minneapolis, Minn. 55422. *Office:* North Memorial Medical Center, 3220 Lowry Ave. N., Minneapolis, Minn. 55422.

CAREER: Fairview Hospital, Minneapolis, Minn., chaplain intern, 1959-60; co-pastor of Lutheran church in Minneapolis, Minn., 1960-64, senior pastor of another Lutheran church in Minneapolis, 1964-69; North Memorial Medical Center, Minneapolis, Minn., director of religion and health, and supervisor of clinical pastoral education, both 1969—. Lecturer at Luther Theological Seminary and Northwestern Lutheran Theological Seminary; adjunct professor at San Francisco Theological Seminary, autumn, 1973. Marriage and family counselor; assistant supervisor of clinical pastoral education at Fairview Hospital, summer, 1964, acting supervisor, summer, 1965; supervisor of clinical pastoral education in Rickling, Germany, summer, 1972. Founder and program coordinator for Northwest Suburban Hennepin County Emergency Chaplaincy Corps. *Member:* American Association of Pastoral Counselors, Association for Clinical Pastoral Education, American Protestant Hospital Association, American Association of Marriage and Family Counselors.

WRITINGS: Senior High Leadership Training Manual, American Lutheran Church, 1962; *Getting the Message of the Bible* (for high school students), Augsburg, 1963; *Make Your Illness Count,* Augsburg, 1976. Author of "The How of Supervision," a film for Field Education National Consultation, 1969. Contributor to *Journal of the Academy of Parish Clergy.*

WORK IN PROGRESS: Lord, I Want to Be Healed (tentative title), "to explain the self-destructive nature of refusing to accept illness, and the resulting loss of meaningfulness, as opposed to finding purpose for the time remaining in one's life."

SIDELIGHTS: Bittner writes: "I have seen many people with terminal and otherwise debilitating illness waste their lives. My aim is to see them 'turned around' by new insights." *Avocational interests:* Vocal music, German music, food, and language (has lived in Germany).

* * *

BIXLER, Paul (Howard)   1899-

PERSONAL: Born October 27, 1899, in Union City, Mich.; son of Miles and Lida (Gillett) Bixler; married Norma Hendricks (a columnist and editorial writer), October 6, 1926; children: Giles, Jon, Mark. *Education:* Hamilton College, A.B., 1922; Harvard University, M.A., 1924; Western Reserve University, B.L.S., 1933. *Politics:* Independent. *Office:* Antioch Review, Antioch College, Yellow Springs, Ohio 45387.

CAREER: Ohio Wesleyan University, Delaware, Ohio, instructor in English, 1924-26; *Cleveland Press,* Cleveland, Ohio, reporter, 1927; Western Reserve University, Cleveland, Ohio, instructor in English, 1928-33; Antioch College, Yellow Springs, Ohio, librarian, 1935-65, librarian emeritus, 1965—; *Antioch Review,* Yellow Springs, Ohio, member of editorial board, 1941-42, 1958—, managing editor, 1943-58, editor, 1974—. Member of staff, Ford Foundation Study on Policy and Program, 1949; executive secretary, Intellectual Freedom Committee, American Library Association, 1952-56; advisor, Social Science Library, University of Rangoon, 1958-60; visiting scholar, University Center, Atlanta, 1963; library consultant. *Member:* American Library Association, Association for Asian Studies, Ohio Library Association (president, 1948-49), American Civil Liberties Union (ACLU).

WRITINGS: (Contributor) Guy R. Lyle, editor, *Administration of the College Library,* H. W. Wilson, 1944; (editor) *Antioch Review Anthology,* World Publications, 1953; (editor) *Freedom of Book Selection,* American Library Association, 1954; *The Mexican Library,* Scarecrow, 1967; *Southeast Asia: Bibliographic Directions in a Complex Area,* Choice, 1974.

Editor, *Intellectual Freedom Newsletter,* 1952-56; editor, *Antioch Review,* 1974—.

WORK IN PROGRESS: People in My Life, autobiographical; a study of "American Librarians Abroad within the whole context of American foreign aid."

SIDELIGHTS: CA asked Bixler what changes he has noted in the quantity and quality of material submitted to *Antioch Review* over the last thirty-five years. He responded: "Clearly we receive more unsolicited manuscripts today than we did in the 1940's and 50's. Inaugurated as a journal of social and political comment, the *Antioch Review* in the 1940's published essays and articles which came from government personnel and labor leaders as well as from academic sources. We published our first fiction and poetry in the 1950's, and today our range is wide and fairly general. Presently, we receive more poetry than contributions in other categories; fiction is an also-ran, and nonfiction a poor third.

"The quality of the fiction and poetry we publish appears higher than in the 1950's; in both categories we are highly selective. As to nonfiction, substance and authority once seemed to take occasional precedence over style. But today even style itself is in some abeyance. Of nonfiction, otherwise acceptable, perhaps two out of three manuscripts require some revision by the authors before publication, and now and then, although an author's subject material may be significant, his style is so opaque I have to do extensive revision myself. There has been an increasing loss in the ability to communicate."

* * *

BJOERNEBOE, Jens 1920-1976

PERSONAL: Born in 1920 in Kristiansand, Norway. *Education:* Studied painting in Oslo, Norway.

CAREER: Taught at Rudolph Steiner school in Oslo, Norway, before becoming a novelist, dramatist, essayist, and poet.

WRITINGS—in English: *Jonas* (novel), Aschehoug, 1955, translation by Bernt Jebsen and Douglas K. Stafford published as *The Least of These*, Bobbs-Merrill, 1959; *Frihetens oeyeblikk* (novel), Gyldendal, 1966, translation by Esther Greenleaf published as *Moment of Freedom: The Heiligenberg Manuscript*, Norton, 1975; translation from the Norwegian by Walter Barthold published as *Without a Stitch*, Grove Press, 1969.

Other : *Dikt*, Aschehoug, 1951; *Foer Hanen galer* (novel), Aschehoug, 1952; *Ariadne* (poetry), Aschehoug, 1953; (contributor) Olaf Bull, editor, *Norske studentersamfund*, [Oslo], 1954; *Under en haardere himmel*, Cappelen, 1957; *Den store by*, Cappelen, 1958; *Vinter i Bellapalma*, Cappelen, 1958; *Blaamann*, Aschehoug, 1959, reprinted by Pax, 1974.

Den onde hyrde (novel), Aschehoug, 1960; *Droemmen og hjulet* (novel), Aschehoug, 1964; *Til lykke med dagen* (title means "Many Happy Returns"), Pax, 1965; *Fugleelskerne* (title means "The Bird Lovers"), Gyldendal, 1966; *Foer hanen galer*, Pax, 1967; *Aske, vind og jord* (title means "Ashes, Wind, and Soil"), Gyldendal, 1968; *Norge, mitt Norge* (essays), Pax, 1968; *Semmelweis: Et anti-autoritaert skuespill*, Gyldendal, 1968; *Kruttaarnet: La Poudriere*, Gyldendal, 1969.

Amputasjon, Gyldendal, 1970; *Vi som elsket Amerika* (essays), Pax, 1970; *Hertug Hans* (novel) Gyldendal, 1972; *Politi og anarki* (essays), Pax, 1972; *Samlede skuespill*, Pax, 1973; *Stillheten: En anti-roman og absolutt aller siste protokoll*, Gyldendal, 1973; *Til fellet Torgersen*, Pax, 1973; *Haiene: Historien om et mannskap og et forlis*, Gyldendal, 1974; *Dongery: En collage om forretningsstanden og om markedsfoererens liv*, Pax, 1976.

OBITUARIES: Washington Post, May 12, 1976; *New York Times*, May 15, 1976; *AB Bookman's Weekly*, June 28, 1976.*

(Died May 10, 1976, in Oslo, Norway)

* * *

BLACKBURN, Graham (John) 1940-

PERSONAL: Born February 19, 1940, in London, England; came to the United States in 1965; son of John (a builder) and Verena (Watson) Blackburn; married Janice Lucas, August 31, 1962 (divorced September 25, 1970). *Education:* Attended Juilliard School of Music, 1965-67. *Home:* 1890 La Jolla Ranch Rd., La Jolla, Calif. 92037; and Crown & Anchor, Meads Mountain Rd., Woodstock, N.Y. 12498 (summers). *Office address:* 3 Tinker St., Woodstock, N.Y. 12498.

CAREER: Writer and illustrator, 1958—. Musician (conducted tours; recorded rock and roll music), 1965-74; builder and cabinet maker, 1968-72. *Member:* American Federation of Musicians, American Philatelic Society.

WRITINGS—All self-illustrated: *Illustrated Housebuilding*, Overlook Press, 1974; *The Illustrated Encyclopedia of Woodworking Handtools, Instruments, and Devices*, Simon & Schuster, 1974; *Illustrated Basic Carpentry*, Bobbs-Merrill, 1976; *The Postage Stamp Gazetteer*, Bobbs-Merrill, 1977; *Illustrated Furniture Making*, Simon & Schuster, 1977; *Illustrated Interior Carpentry*, Bobbs-Merrill, 1977; *The Illustrated Encyclopedia of Ships and Boats*, Overlook Press, in press.

Illustrator: Bob Ross and Carol Ross, *Modern and Classic Woodburning Stoves*, Overlook Press, 1976.

Author of columns, "Music" and "Take Another Look: An Essay in Philatelic Journalism," in *Woodstock Times*, 1973-75.

SIDELIGHTS: Blackburn writes: "My main concerns at this time are sailing and playing Chopin, to which I intend devoting my future. I am concerned with the apparent demise of this 'culture' and hope, through my books, to preserve some of the better qualities of this life before mass production, pollution, and political competition destroy individualism."

* * *

BLACKBURN, Norma Davis 1914-

PERSONAL: Born October 10, 1914, in Salt Lake City, Utah; daughter of Charles B. (a railroad engineer) and Madge M. (Denkle) Davis; divorced; children: Richard Lindsay Blackburn. *Education:* University of Utah, B.S., 1934; University of Southern California, Los Angeles, M.S., 1962. *Residence:* Fresno, Calif. *Office:* Fresno City College, 1101 University Ave., Fresno, Calif. 93741.

CAREER: Federal Bureau of Investigation, Washington, D.C., secretary in Salt Lake City, Utah, 1936, secretary in Washington, D.C., 1937-42; legal secretary for two law firms in Salt Lake City, 1948-52; University of Utah, Salt Lake City, secretary, 1960-61; Fresno City College, Fresno, Calif., instructor in secretarial skills, 1961—. *Member:* California Business Education Association (past president of central section), Theta Alpha Delta (past president), Delta Kappa Gamma, Delta Pi Epsilon.

WRITINGS: Legal Secretaryship, Prentice-Hall, 1971; *Secretaryship*, Goodyear Publishing, 1974.

* * *

BLACKBURN, Thomas C(arl) 1936-

PERSONAL: Born December 4, 1936, in Pasadena, Calif.; son of Albert and Ruth (Miller) Blackburn; married Joyce Gibbs (an employment development officer), January 27, 1956; children: Lisa Marie, Robert Alan. *Education:* Attended Reed College, 1954-56; University of Hawaii, B.A., 1959; University of California, Los Angeles, Ph.D., 1974. *Politics:* Democrat. *Religion:* None. *Home:* 527 Clark Ave., Claremont, Calif. 91711. *Office:* Department of Social Sciences, California State Polytechnic University, Pomona, Calif. 91768.

CAREER: California State Polytechnic University, Pomona, assistant professor, 1965-74, associate professor of anthropology, 1974—. *Member:* Society for American Archaeology, Society for California Archaeology.

WRITINGS—Nonfiction: (Editor) *December's Child,* University of California Press, 1975; (editor with Lowell J. Bean) *Native Californians,* Ballena, 1976; (editor) *Flowers of the Wind,* Ballena, 1977; (editor with Travis Hudson, Rosario Curletti, and Janice Timbrook) *Eye of the Flute,* Santa Barbara Museum of Natural History, 1977. Co-editor of "Anthropology Papers," for Ballena. Contributor to anthropology and folklore journals.

WORK IN PROGRESS: Research on Indians of California, mythology, and symbolism.

* * *

BLACKFORD, Charles Minor III   1898-

PERSONAL: Born October 4, 1898, in Washington, D.C.; son of Charles Minor, Jr. (a physician) and Winifred Julia (Sears) Blackford; married Sara Louise Dickens (a pianist), August 20, 1930; children: two (both deceased). *Education:* Attended private and public primary and secondary schools. *Politics:* Democrat. *Religion:* Unitarian-Universalist. *Home:* 25 Flamingo Rd., Crystal River, Fla. 32629. *Agent:* Broome Agency, P.O. Box 3649, Sarasota, Fla. 33578.

CAREER: U.S. Merchant Marine, deck officer, 1919-31; free-lance writer, 1931-41, 1945—. Port director for Citrus County Port Authority. President of Citrus County Library Board; member of board of trustees of Central Florida Regional Library. President of Homosassa (Fla.) Chamber of Commerce. *Military service:* U.S. Navy, 1916-19. U.S. Coast Guard Reserve, active duty, 1941-45, 1950-51; served in the Atlantic and Pacific theaters; became lieutenant commander. *Member:* Veterans of Foreign Wars, Reserve Officers Club, Civitan Club.

WRITINGS: Letters from Lee's Army, Scribner, 1947; *Deep Treasure,* Winston's, 1954; *Torpedoboat Sailor,* U.S. Naval Institute, 1964; *The Making of a Skipper,* Seven-Seas Press, 1977. Columnist for *Crystal River Sentinel,* 1962-73. Contributor of articles and stories, mainly on marine subjects, to magazines.

WORK IN PROGRESS: That Hanna Ketch; Gunboat, fiction, based on rumors of a German Navy attempt to gain a base in the West Indies before World War I.

SIDELIGHTS: Blackford writes: "Being the fourth generation of what is known as a 'Family of Letters' it was only natural that I write, and about my chief love, the sea. Foreseeing involvement in World War I, I enlisted in the Navy at seventeen and was lucky that I was on one of the first six destroyers to go overseas, which made the material for *Torpedoboat Sailor.* On discharge I went to Navigation School and emerged with a license as Second Mate. After twelve years seafaring on the Atlantic and Pacific the Great Depression pushed me ashore in 1931 to make out as I could as a free-lance writer, getting married and living aboard a thirty-four-foot ketch in Florida. In 1941 I was commissioned in the Coast Guard Reserve and went on active duty. The first part of the war I was on convoy duty in the Atlantic, then commanded the *LST 19* in seven invasions in the Pacific. I returned to take up writing again but was recalled in 1950-51 and commanded the cutter *Ariadne* on the Key West Station. On discharge I returned to Tarpon Springs with a contract from Winston's to write *Deep Treasure,* on the Greek spongers there. Later I moved to Citrus County, living first in Homosassa and then in Crystal River."

BLACKSTONE, Bernard   1911-

PERSONAL: Born February 15, 1911, in Knaresborough, Yorkshire, England; son of Edward and Ruth (King) Blackstone. *Education:* Cambridge University, B.A., 1933, Ph.D., 1936, M.A., 1937. *Office:* Department of English, University of Aleppo, Aleppo, Syria.

CAREER: Cambridge University, Cambridge, England, supervisor of students at Trinity College, 1936-40; University of Brazil, Rio de Janeiro, visiting professor of English literature, 1941-45; University of Wales, University College of Swansea, Swansea, senior lecturer in English literature, 1946-49; University of Istanbul, Istanbul, Turkey, professor of English, 1949-52; University of Athens, Athens, Greece, Byron Professor of English Literature, 1952-61; University of Benghazi, Benghazi, Libya, professor of English, 1961-65; University of Rhodesia, Salisbury, professor of English, 1965-67; American University of Beirut, Beirut, Lebanon, professor of English, 1967-76; University of Aleppo, Aleppo, Syria, professor of English literature, 1976—. *Awards, honors:* Freedom of the City of Missolonghi, 1954, for services to Anglo-Greek understanding; Litt.D., Cambridge University, 1963.

WRITINGS: The Ferrar Papers: The Manuscripts of Little Gidding, Cambridge University Press, 1938; (editor) *Obras-Primas do Conto Inglese* (title means "Masterpieces of the English Short Story"), Carioca Press, 1946; *English Blake,* Cambridge University Press, 1948; *Virginia Woolf: A Commentary,* Harcourt, 1949, reprinted, 1972; *Advanced English for Foreign Students,* Longmans, Green, 1954; *A Modern Quintet* (study of five modern English writers), Ikaros Press, 1956; *The Consecrated Urn: A Study of Keats in Terms of Growth and Form,* Longmans, Green, 1959.

Virginia Woolf, Longmans, Green, 1960; *The Lost Travellers: Variations on a Romantic Theme,* Longmans, Green, 1962; (contributor) Paul West, editor, *Byron: Twentieth Century Views,* Prentice-Hall, 1963; *English Prosody,* Longmans, Green, 1965; (contributor) Shiv Kumar, editor, *British Romantic Poets,* New York University Press, 1966; (contributor) A. W. Thomson, editor, *Wordsworth's Mind and Art,* Oliver & Boyd, 1969; *Byron: Lyric and Romance,* Longman, 1970; *Byron: Literary Satire, Humor, and Reflection,* Longman, 1971; *Byron: Social Satire, Drama, and Epic,* Longman, 1971; *Byron: A Survey,* Longman, 1975.

Contributor to literary journals and to *Times Literary Supplement, Theology, Journal of European Studies, Ariel, Cambridge Journal,* and *Review of English Studies.*

WORK IN PROGRESS: A series of books on Byron's mind and art, including *Byron: The Classical Background* (tentative title); a further book on Virginia Woolf, discussing her use of analogy; *The Kingdoms of Silence,* a collection of quietest texts with running commentary.

SIDELIGHTS: Having lived abroad for most of his adult life, Blackstone speaks French, Portuguese, modern Greek, Italian, and some Turkish, German, Arabic, and Spanish.

The *Economist* described Blackstone as "a scholar and a critic who has preserved his independence of judgement—perhaps by keeping away, for much of his life, from English universities. . . . He insists, like a good European, that Byron's was a very great and comprehensive genius." Blackstone insists on understanding Byron within his Gestalt, which is Mediterranean and to a large degree Oriental, and on exploring the complexities of Byron's mind and not of his love affairs.

While considering himself an apolitical animal (Blackstone

reports he has never cast a vote for any party), he feels his stance is plainly traditionalist. Blackstone told *CA:* "I feel that the main current of my writing career is this mingling of an interest in religion and particularly in mysticism with a growing cosmopolitanism. It was in Rio, while giving a series of public lectures on William Blake, that I first came in contact with the Sufis, and my interest in Oriental mysticism has deepened during my long sojourn in the Maghreb and the Eastern Mediterranean. Greece remains my greatest love, however, as it was Byron's; and it is through a direct, living and continuous contact with Greece that I have sought to 'place' Byron and to penetrate his mystery. I spend my summer months on the island of Crete where a Gestalt similar to that of Attica in Byron's day still survives, and where the dryness of the air, the brilliance of the light, and the silence of shores and mountains combine to provide a 'lens' through which the Byronic texts can be adequately scrutinised. This 'Gestalt' approach, which may be detected in my other critical writings to a lesser degree, is my most original contribution to Byron scholarship.

"My Islamic studies now centre largely on the dervishes, whose practice of the Sufic silence may be expected to figure prominently in my work in progress. My latest book will thus be thematically related to my first, *The Ferrar Papers,* in which the manuscripts of Little Gidding were used to illustrate a way of life or *tarikah* which, in Nicholas Ferrar's words, 'might prove a pattern in an age that needs patterns.' I feel that in our own age, which provides no patterns but the mechanical, the possibility of learning from more traditional ways of life offers a slight hope of salvation. The emergence of the Arab nation as a political force could prove decisive, provided always that its Islamic identity is preserved."

AVOCATIONAL INTERESTS: Music (especially woodwind chamber music; plays baroque flute, recorder, and clavichord), architecture and archaeology, international travel, cats.

BIOGRAPHICAL/CRITICAL SOURCES: Economist, December 27, 1975.

* * *

BLAIR, John M. 1914(?)-1976

1914(?)—December 21, 1976; American professor, economist, civil servant and author. Blair was an economist with the Senate Anti-Trust and Monopoly Subcommittee. He published articles and books in his field. Blair died in St. Petersburg, Fla. Obituaries: *New York Times,* December 23, 1976; *Washington Post,* December 23, 1976.

* * *

BLAISDELL, Foster W(arren) 1927-

PERSONAL: Born January 3, 1927, in Omaha, Neb.; son of Foster Warren (an accountant) and Helen (Gwin) Blaisdell; married Karen E. Michelson, August 16, 1952; children: Peter, Anne, Amy. *Education:* University of California, Berkeley, B.A., 1950, M.A., 1951, Ph.D., 1956; attended University of Copenhagen, 1954-55. *Residence:* Bloomington, Ind. *Office:* Department of Germanic Languages, Indiana University, Bloomington, Ind. 47401.

CAREER: Indiana University, Bloomington, instructor, 1956-59, assistant professor, 1959-63, associate professor, 1963-67, professor of Germanic languages, 1967—, associate dean of graduate school, 1968-76. Fulbright exchange teacher in Germany, 1960-61; visiting assistant professor, University of Washington, 1962-63. *Military service:* U.S.

Army, 1945-46. *Member:* Society for the Advancement of Scandinavian Study (president, 1975-77), Modern Language Association of America, American Association for Teachers of German, Linguistic Society of America, International Arthurian Society (president, North American branch, 1975—), Phi Beta Kappa. *Awards, honors:* Johnson Memorial Fellow, 1954-55; grants from American Council of Learned Societies, summers, 1960, 1970; National Endowment for the Humanities summer fellow, 1976.

WRITINGS: Preposition-Adverbs in Old Icelandic, University of California, 1959; *Erex saga Artuskappa,* Munksgaard (Copenhagen), 1965; (contributor) Evelyn Firchow, and others, editors, *Studies for Einar Haugen,* Mouton (The Hague), 1972; (with Marianne E. Kalinke) *Erex Saga and Ivens Saga,* University of Nebraska Press, 1977. Contributor of more than seventeen articles to journals in his field, including *Scandinavian Studies.*

WORK IN PROGRESS: Editing *Ivens Saga* for Editiones Arnamagnaeanae (Copenhagen); research on style and syntax of the Old Norse riddarasogur.

* * *

BLAKE, Minden V(aughan) 1913-
(Mindy Blake)

PERSONAL: Born February 13, 1913, in New Zealand; son of Charles Minden (a schoolmaster) and Emma (Wootten) Blake; married Mary Jessie Seldon (an accountant), May 24, 1947; children: Belinda, Robyn. *Education:* New Zealand University, M.Sc. (honors), 1936. *Religion:* Church of England. *Home:* Carnanton, Woodlands Rd. E., Virginia Water, Surrey, England.

CAREER: New Zealand University, Christchurch, New Zealand, lecturer in physics, 1935-36; Royal Air Force, fighter pilot, 1936-58, retiring as wing commander; Simoniz Car Wax, West Drayton, England, factory manager, 1958-61; Penn Elastic Co., Swansea, England, managing director, 1962-65; inventor, 1965—. *Awards, honors*—Military: Distinguished Service Order and Distinguished Flying Cross. Other: New Zealand gymnastic champion and pole vault champion, both 1936.

WRITINGS: (Under name Mindy Blake) *Golf Swing of the Future,* Souvenir Press, 1972, Norton, 1973.

WORK IN PROGRESS: Another golf book.

SIDELIGHTS: Blake writes: "I have a few patents being manufactured and as an inventor I have been applying scientific and athletic principles to bringing the golf swing up to date."

* * *

BLAKEY, Walker Jameson 1940-

PERSONAL: Born July 3, 1940, in Beattyville, Ky.; son of Frank Trimble and Anne (Jameson) Blakey. *Education:* Harvard University, A.B., 1963; Ohio State University, J.D., 1967. *Politics:* Democrat. *Religion:* Episcopal. *Home:* Sharon Heights 10-G, Chapel Hill, N.C. 27514. *Office:* School of Law, University of North Carolina, Chapel Hill, N.C. 27514.

CAREER: Private practice of law in Columbus, Ohio, 1967-69; University of North Carolina, Chapel Hill, assistant professor of law, 1971—. Reporter for North Carolina Pattern Charges Committee, 1972-76. *Member:* American Bar Association, Coif.

WRITINGS: (With J. D. Howe) *Assignments in Trial Prac-*

tice, Little, Brown, 1971, 4th edition, 1975. Contributor to law journals.

WORK IN PROGRESS: Research on hearsay and on a proposed evidence code for North Carolina.

* * *

BLAKISTON, Georgiana 1903-

PERSONAL: Born January 28, 1903, in London, England; daughter of Harold (a barrister) and Victoria (Leveson-Gower) Russell; married Noel Blakiston (a writer), October 10, 1929; children: Rachel Blakiston Campbell, Caroline Blakiston Hunter. *Education:* Educated privately. *Politics:* Liberal. *Religion:* Church of England. *Home:* 6 Markham Sq., London, England.

CAREER: Writer, 1962—.

WRITINGS: Lord William Russell and His Wife, 1815-1846, J. Murray, 1972, Scholarly Resources, 1973.

WORK IN PROGRESS: Woburn and the Russells, for Constable.

* * *

BLANCHARD, Allan E(dward) 1929-

PERSONAL: Born September 4, 1929, in Detroit, Mich.; son of Frank (a clerk) and Blanche (McCartney) Blanchard; married Shirley Aman (a teacher), June 22, 1957; children: Stephen, John. *Education:* Wayne State University, B.S., 1952, B.A., 1954. *Home:* 6722 Weaver Ave., McLean, Va. 22101. *Office: Detroit News,* Washington Bureau, 511 National Press Building, Washington, D.C. 20045.

CAREER/WRITINGS: Detroit News, Detroit, Mich., reporter and correspondent, 1954-68, author of "Al Blanchard" column, 1968-70, national editor, 1970-75, Washington bureau chief, 1975—. Notable assignments include the trial of Jack Ruby, 1964, Dominican revolution, 1965, and Six-Day Mid East War, 1967. Member of New Detroit Committee, 1968. *Military service:* U.S. Army, 1947-54; became staff sergeant. *Member:* Detroit Press Club (president, 1967-68). *Awards, honors:* Detroit Press Club Foundation Award, 1967 and 1968, for reporting under pressure of deadline; Associated Press newswriting award, 1968.

SIDELIGHTS: Blanchard writes: "I firmly believe that a creditable journalist's first dedication is to his profession, that he or she should not be involved in ideologies or institutions that would influence their reporting and writing, that journalism, while a creative craft, first should be dedicated to the presentation of news fairly, and second to the personal creative expression of the journalist."

Blanchard, who has traveled in Canada, Caribbean and South America, is an amateur musician and sailing enthusiast.

* * *

BLANCHARD, Kendall A(llan) 1942-

PERSONAL: Born November 21, 1942, in Kankakee, Ill.; son of Craig Allan (a clergyman) and Lois (a professor of English; maiden name, Kendall) Blanchard; married Helen Martin, June, 1963 (divorced, 1972); married Kathy Arbeiter (a clinical psychologist), December, 1976. *Education:* Olivet Nazarene College, A.B., 1964; Vanderbilt University, M.Div., 1968; Southern Methodist University, M.A., 1970, Ph.D., 1971; Johns Hopkins University, postdoctoral study, 1976-77. *Home:* 1315 East Castle, #P-3, Murfreesboro, Tenn. 37130. *Office:* Department of Sociology and Anthro-

pology, Middle Tennessee State University, Murfreesboro, Tenn. 37132.

CAREER: High school English teacher and basketball coach in Grant Park, Ill., 1964-65; Tennessee Securities, Nashville, Tenn., account executive, 1969; Middle Tennessee State University, Murfreesboro, assistant professor, 1971-75, associate professor of anthropology, 1975—. Visiting professor at University of Tennessee, 1972, and Vanderbilt University, 1972, 1973.

MEMBER: American Anthropological Association (fellow), Association for the Anthropological Study of Play (fellow; member of executive board), Society for Applied Anthropology, Tennessee Anthropological Association (member of board of directors, 1975-77). *Awards, honors:* Fellowship from National Endowment for the Humanities, 1976-77.

WRITINGS: The Ramah Navajos: The History of a Growing Sense of Community, Navajo Tribe, 1971; *The Economics of Sainthood: Religious Change among the Rimrock Navajos,* Associated University Presses, 1977. Contributor to anthropology and education journals, and *Journal for the Scientific Study of Religion.*

WORK IN PROGRESS: Native North America: The Anthropology of Adaptation, with Steven Fox; *The History and Function of Sport among the Mississippi Choctaw.*

SIDELIGHTS: Blanchard writes briefly: "I'm committed to anthropology. In a rapidly shrinking world its message is essential. A basic anthropology course should be a required element in all liberal arts education programs." *Avocational interests:* Jogging, tennis.

* * *

BLAZIER, Kenneth D(ean) 1933-

PERSONAL: Born March 17, 1933, in Topeka, Kan.; son of Edwin B. and Hazel E. (Spencer) Blazier; married R. Elaine Kellogg (a nursery school director), August 25, 1956; children: Lynnette, Gregory, Kyle. *Education:* Ottawa University, Ottawa, Kan., B.A., 1955; American Baptist Seminary of the West, B.D., 1959. *Residence:* Norristown, Pa. *Office:* American Baptist Churches, Valley Forge, Pa. 19481.

CAREER: Pastor of Baptist churches in Hudson, N.Y., 1959-62, and Cazenovia, N.Y., 1962-66; American Baptist Churches, Valley Forge, Pa., director of department of educational planning services for Educational Ministries, 1966—. *Member:* Association of Voluntary Action Scholars.

WRITINGS: (With Joseph J. Hanson) *Launching the Church School Year,* Judson, 1972; (with Evelyn Huber) *Planning Christian Education in Your Church,* Judson, 1974; *Building an Effective Church School,* Judson, 1976. Author of "Checklist for Administrators," a monthly column in *Baptist Leader.*

WORK IN PROGRESS: Research for *The Growing Church School.*

SIDELIGHTS: Blazier writes: "My books have been part of my work as director, Department of Educational Planning Services. My department is responsible for services (training and materials) for local church planners and administrators of Christian education. I consider my active role as a volunteer leader in Calvary Baptist Church, Norristown, Pa., indispensable in my research and experimentation for my writings in the field of Christian education planning and administration. My involvement as trainer of local church educational leaders is also essential to my work."

BLEGVAD, Lenore 1926-

PERSONAL: Born May 8, 1926, in New York, N.Y.; daughter of Julius C. (a mechanical engineer) and Ruth (a teacher; maiden name, Huebschman) Hochman; married Erik Blegvad (an illustrator), September 12, 1950; children: Peter, Kristoffer. *Education:* Vassar College, B.A., 1947; studied art in New York, N.Y. and Paris, France. *Home:* 4 Crescent Mansions, 113 Fulham Rd., London S.W.3, England.

CAREER: Artist. Writer, 1965—. Exhibited abstract paper mache sculpture in London showing, 1975.

WRITINGS—Children's books; illustrated by husband, Erik Blegvad: *Mr. Jensen and the Cat,* Harcourt, 1965; *One Is for the Sun,* Harcourt, 1968; *The Great Hamster Hunt,* Harcourt, 1969; *Moon-Watch Summer,* Harcourt, 1972; *Mittens for Kittens,* Atheneum, 1974; *Hark Hark the Dogs Do Bark,* Atheneum, 1975.

WORK IN PROGRESS: This Little Pig-a-Wig, nursery rhymes illustrated by Erik Blegvad; a novel for children; translating French fables.

SIDELIGHTS: Lenore Blegvad comments: "I divide my time between writing and painting, and which one I do at any given moment is dictated by various things: mood, inspiration, location (we live half the year in London and half in the South of France). I find the creative effort for each equally exciting, arduous, and absorbing. The change from one occupation to the other brings new insights every time and somehow suits me to perfection."

Blegvad has studied under Moses Sayer, Andre Lhote, Fernand Leger, and other contemporary artists.

* * *

BLIGHT, John 1913-

PERSONAL: Born July 30, 1913, in Unley, South Australia; married; children: two daughters. *Home:* 34 Greenway St., The Grange, Queensland 4051, Australia.

CAREER: Poet; worked as a ring-barker and miner during the Depression; became an accountant in Australia during the late 1930s; Commonwealth Government costing officer, 1942-45; Commissioner for Queensland government inquiry into the timber industry, 1949-50; worked as a cost accountant and part-owner of three sawmills and as an honorary golf club committee-man during the 1950s and 1960s; named Senior Fellow by Australia Council Literature Board for full time writing, 1973—. *Member:* Australian Society of Authors, Australian Society of Accountants. *Awards, honors:* Myer Award for poetry for *A Beachcomber's Diary,* 1964; Dame Mary Gilmore Medal, 1965; National Book Council Literary Award for *Selected Poems 1939-75,* 1976; Patrick White Literary Award, 1976, for consistently high quality of poetry.

WRITINGS—Poems: *The Old Pianist,* Dymock's (Sydney), 1945; *The Two Suns Met,* Edwards & Shaw (Sydney), 1954; *A Beachcomber's Diary,* Angus & Robertson (Sydney), 1963; *My Beachcombing Days,* Angus & Robertson, 1968; *Hart,* Nelson (Australia), 1975; *Selected Poems 1939-75,* Nelson, 1976. Contributor of poems to *Melbourne Age, Sydney Morning Herald, Nation Review, The Australian, Texas Quarterly, London Magazine,* and other periodicals.

WORK IN PROGRESS: Pageantry for a Lost Empire, publication by Nelson expected in late 1977.

SIDELIGHTS: Blight told *CA* of his frequent use of the sonnet form and setting of the sea: "I had recourse to the sonnet form in my two 'sea-sonnet' books, *A Beachcomber's Diary* and *My Beachcombing Days,* because at the time of their writing I was involved in a small group of sawmills as director/secretary/accountant/log buyer etc. with a concurrent 18 years as a golf club committee-man who could find no extra time to write except in the hour or so before dawn. I needed a form which was organically complete and yet confluent. Before adopting the sonnet, I had written for years in formalist styles. I soon recognized and loved the strict discipline, yet remarkable pliability of the sonnet form and still return to the sonnet occasionally.

"The sea I knew from early childhood and later, sea-trips to the Barrier Reef, besides sojourns along the whole Eastern coast of Australia. Our Countryside has been ravaged by the 'cockies' (farmers) from the beginning in a lazy, wasteful way of scrub-clearing, use of humus of ages to grow quick profitable crops, soil exhaustion, then more scrub-falling. I saw this happening progressively as a lad when I went on numerous trips with my father who was a farm estate agent and valuator. Writing poetry, I turned towards the sea as a backdrop of virginal purity against which to portray the idiosyncrasies of human behavior. Unfortunately, our seas are rapidly being ravaged and the ocean is not the great unconquerable domain formerly idealised by me.

"However, I recognise that no ideal is eternal and, whatever is lost in an evolutionary process, is replaced by other phenomena of human interest which shouldn't err into despair and bitterness, the lozenges of mental old age and death."

When asked by *CA* of his particularly rugged use of language, Blight responded: "this derived from my impatience with the tediousness of much of our classical poetry which verges on the precious to me. Perhaps, unwittingly, I have developed on the lines of your current U.S.A. poets. Only in the last half year have I begun to read them. I think, only Emily Dickinson, Whitman, and Frost were in my reading before Longfellow and your past writers. Therefore U.S.A. influences can scarcely apply in any plagiaristic sense."

* * *

BLIVEN, Bruce 1889-1977

July 27, 1889—May 27, 1977; American lecturer in field of communications, free-lance writer, journalist, and author of an autobiography and books on American history. He served as editor of the *New Republic* magazine (1930-55), during which time he wrote the first comprehensive account of President Warren G. Harding's corrupt "Ohio Gang," helping to expose the Teapot Dome oil scandals of the 1920's. Bliven contributed articles to magazines, including *Saturday Evening Post, Harper's,* and *Redbook.* He died in Palo Alto, Calif. Obituaries: *New York Times,* May 29, 1977; *Washington Post,* May 29, 1977; *Time,* June 13, 1977; *AB Bookman's Weekly,* June 27, 1977. (See index for previous *CA* sketch)

* * *

BLOM, Karl Arne 1946-
(Bo Lagevi)

PERSONAL: Born January 22, 1946, in Naessjoe, Sweden; son of Karl Axel (a hotel owner) and Ester (Skoeld) Blom; married Karin Ann-Marie Gyllen (a nurse), June 29, 1969; children: Karl Anders Bertil, Kristina Magdalena. *Education:* University of Lund, B.A., 1972. *Politics:* "Liberal, cosmopolitan, anti-Communist." *Religion:* Agnostic. *Home and office:* Smaaskolevaegen 22, S-223 67 Lund, Sweden. *Agent:* Lennart Sane, P.O. Box 25044, S-200 47 Malmoe 25, Sweden.

CAREER: Free-lance writer, 1970-75. *Member:* Union of Swedish Authors, Swedish Academy of Detection, Society of Detective Story Writers of Skane (chairman), Mystery Writers of America, Crime Writers Association (England), Poe Club (Denmark). *Awards, honors:* Sherlock Award from *Expressen* (newspaper), 1974, for *The Moment of Truth.*

WRITINGS: Sanningens oegonblick, Almqvist & Wiksell/Gebers, 1974, English translation by Erik J. Friis published as *The Moment of Truth,* Harper, 1977.

Books not translated into English: *Naagon borde soerja* (title means "Somebody Should Mourn"), Almqvist & Wiksell/Gebers, 1971; *Naagon aer skyldig* (title means "Somebody Is Guilty"), Almqvist & Wiksell/Gebers, 1972; *Naagon slog tillbaka* (title means "Somebody Hit Back"), Almqvist & Wiksell/Gebers, 1973; *Ett gammalt mord* (title means "An Old Murder"), Gleerups, 1974; (editor) *Brottpunkter* (title means "Murderous Points"), Lindqvist, 1975; *Vaaldets triumf* (title means "Triumph of Violence"), Almqvist & Wiksell/Gebers, 1975; *Resan till ingenstans* (stories; title means "Journey into Nowhere"), Zindermans, 1975; *Lund,* Hermods, 1975; (editor) *Skaanska Brottstycken* (title means "Pieces of Crimes"), Bra Deckare, 1976; *Kortaste straaet* (title means "Second Best"), Lindqvist, 1976; *Noedhamm* (title means "Harbor of Refuge"), Lindqvist, 1976; *Lyckligt lottade* (title means "The Happy People"), Almqvist & Wiksell/Gebers, 1976; (under pseudonym Bo Lageri) *Allt vad du gjort mot naagon* (title means "All the Things You Did"), B. Wahlstroem, 1976; *Noedvaern* (novel; title means "Self-Defense"), Zinderman, 1977; *40° Kallti Solen* (stories; title means "40 Degrees Cold in the Sun"), Zindermans, 1977; *Frihetssoekarna* (title means "Searchers of Freedom"), Almqvist & Wiksell/Gebers, 1977; (under pseudonym Bo Lageri) *Utan personligt ansvar* (title means "Without Personal Responsibility"), B. Wahlstroem, 1977.

Translator into Swedish: Jack Higgins, *Bikten* (title means "A Prayer for the Dying"), Lindqvist, 1975; Emile Gaboriau, *Den lille mannen i Batignolles* (title means "The Little Man in Batignolles"), Lindqvist, 1975; A. Conan Doyle, *En studie i roett* (title means "A Study in Scarlet"), Almqvist & Wiksell/Gebers, 1977; Hanning Hjuler, *Raattorna* (title means "The Rats"), Bra Deckare, 1977; Doyle, *Minnena* (title means "The Memoirs of Sherlock Holmes"), Almqvist & Wiksell/Gebers, 1977. Author of material for television series. Contributor of articles and stories to magazines.

SIDELIGHTS: Blom writes: "So far most of what I have written is crime novels . . . because this is the kind of novel by which you can best describe and try to analyze time, society, and human beings. I try to tell about our time—people as they are now and the problems people are facing in a Swedish so-called welfare society. My other novels and most of my short stories are efforts to describe the surrealistic and absurd realities of life.

"I regard the mystery genre as not inferior to so-called real literature. In my opinion a crime novel, a mystery, or whatever it happens to be, can be as good a book as any book of fiction. . . . A good mystery or crime novel is like an iceberg. You see what's on the surface and a lot of things are hidden.

"My first three books deal with crime and murder and violence. But the first one is also a book about how lonely people can be when they are apparently among many others. The second one is about the economic problems students are facing, and the third one is about unemployment among students with degrees. From there on I have dealt with the basic elements of violence among people, with violence in our time and how violence has become almost a natural way of expressing oneself."

In addition to English, Blom's books have been translated into German, Danish, Norwegian, Dutch, and Japanese.

* * *

BLOUNT, Margaret   1924-

PERSONAL: Born May 14, 1924, in Watford, England; daughter of Ernest John (a builder) and Eve (a headmistress; maiden name, Clarke) Blount; married Bryan Ingle-Finch (a motorcycle dealer), April 15, 1950; children: Jan Robert, Dinah Margaret Hogan. *Education:* Somerville College, Oxford, M.A., 1946. *Politics:* None. *Residence:* Poole, Dorsetshire, England. *Agent:* Richard Scott Simon, College Cross, Islington, London, England.

CAREER: High school teacher of English in Worthing, England, 1947-50; writer, 1967—. *Member:* International Dolls House Society, Somerville Dramatic Society (president, 1944). *Awards, honors:* Fiction prize from *Guardian,* 1970, for *When Did You Last See Your Father.*

WRITINGS: Mirror Here, Mirror There (novel), Hutchinson, 1967; *When Did You Last See Your Father* (novel), Hutchinson, 1970; *Animal Land* (guide to humanized animals in literature), Morrow, 1974. Contributor to *Winter's Tales.*

WORK IN PROGRESS: Two novels, *A Woman of Property* and *The Queen and Mr. Punch* (tentative title).

SIDELIGHTS: Margaret Blount writes: "I write novels because life is so boring I have to do something about it. I wrote *Animal Land* because the whole of Aesop suddenly struck me as extraordinary. I think one's first seven years are quite the most interesting. After seventeen nothing interesting really happens at all which is why most of my books have children in them."

AVOCATIONAL INTERESTS: Period furniture as seen in dolls' houses, making miniature models ("in other words, playing with toys").

* * *

BLUNK, Frank M.   1897(?)-1976

1897(?)—December 15, 1976; American journalist. Blunk was a sports reporter for over fifty years with several newspapers and wire services. He was also a sports enthusiast; he was a stunt man in early air races and, along with several other people, he introduced soaring and gliding in the United States. He died in New York City. Obituaries: *New York Times,* December 16, 1976.

* * *

BOARDMAN, Francis   1915-1976

October 2, 1915—December 22, 1976; American economist, civil servant, and author of works in his field. He died in Washington, D.C. Obituaries: *Washington Post,* December 24, 1976.

* * *

BOBA, Imre   1919-

PERSONAL: Born October 23, 1919, in Gyor, Hungary; came to the United States in 1956, naturalized citizen, 1956; son of Laszlo K. and Ilona (Faludy) Boba; married Elizabeth Herndon Hudson, December 22, 1954; children: Eleanor, Leslie. *Education:* University of Budapest, doctoral candidate, 1941-46; University of Washington, Seattle, Ph.D., 1962. *Religion:* Roman Catholic. *Home:* 7336 55th Ave. N.E., Seattle, Wash. 98115. *Office:* Department of History, DP-20, University of Washington, Seattle, Wash. 98195.

CAREER: Active in Polish underground, 1946-56; Polish Research Centre, London, England, research librarian, 1956-59; free-lance journalist, 1959-62; University of Washington, Seattle, assistant professor, 1962-67, associate professor, 1967-71, professor of medieval history, 1971—. *Member:* American Historical Association, American Association for the Advancement of Slavic Studies. *Awards, honors:* Received Silver Cross of Merit for activities in Polish underground.

WRITINGS: (With Howard Kaminsky and others) *Master Nicholas of Dresden,* American Philosophical Society, 1965; *Nomads, Northmen, and Slavs: Eastern Europe in the Ninth Century,* Mouton, 1967; *Moravia's History Reconsidered: A Reinterpretation of Medieval Sources,* Nijhoff, 1971. Contributor to *Slavic Review.* Contributing editor of *Dictionary of Political Science.*

WORK IN PROGRESS: Medieval History of East Central Europe.

SIDELIGHTS: Boba told *CA:* "Having acquired training also as a philogist, I subject medieval sources to analysis in depth in respect to their exact syntactic structure and semantic peculiarities. This method allowed me to revise several widely held assumptions, such as that the name of the Russians developed from the word Rus which means retainers; that Saint Zoreardus came to Hungary in the eleventh century not from Poland but from the city of Pola in Istria; and that the medieval state of Moravia should be associated not with the region around the river Morava in present-day Czechoslovakia but with a city Morava near Belgrade in present-day Yugoslavia."

* * *

BOCOCK, Robert (James) 1940-

PERSONAL: Born September 29, 1940, in Lincoln, England; son of Frank William (a farmer) and Jessie (Drake) Bocock. *Education:* University of Leeds, B.A., 1962; University of London, diploma, 1963; Brunel University, Ph.D., 1973. *Home:* 30 Oakwood Rd., London N.W.11, England. *Office:* Department of Sociology, Brunel University, Uxbridge, Middlesex UB8 3PH, England.

CAREER: Brunel University, Uxbridge, England, lecturer in sociology, 1966—. Annual lecturer at University of Birmingham; director of B.C.W. Publications; consultant to Richmond Fellowship. *Member:* International Conference of Sociology of Religion, British Sociological Association, Association of University Teachers, Association of Pastoral Care and Counselling.

WRITINGS: Ritual in Industrial Society, Allen & Unwin, 1974; *Freud and Modern Society,* Thomas Nelson, 1976. Contributor to sociology journals.

WORK IN PROGRESS: Research on relations between psychoanalysis and sociology, on the sociology of morals, and on symbols.

SIDELIGHTS: Bocock writes: "I'm interested in the use of Freudian ideas to provide a basis for a view of man-in-society to act as a source of political legitimation in North American and West European societies, to provide an alternative to traditional Christianity (which has little appeal to bright young intellectuals in these societies), and as an alter-

native to Marxism (which is attractive to intellectuals, but lacks an awareness of human feelings). I aim to increase *tolerance of ambiguity* in individuals and organisations and between states."

* * *

BODE, Janet 1943-

PERSONAL: Surname is pronounced *Boe*-dy; born July 14, 1943, in New York; daughter of Carl J. (a writer and professor) and Margaret (Lutze) Bode. *Education:* University of Maryland, B.A., 1965; graduate study at Michigan State University and Bowie State College. *Politics:* "Varies, but I'd never vote for a Republican." *Home:* 1920 Laguna, San Francisco, Calif. 94115. *Agent:* Jean Naggar, Manuscripts Unlimited, 420 East 72nd St., New York, N.Y. 10021.

CAREER: Writer. Has worked in Germany, Mexico, and the United States as personnel specialist, program director, community organizer, public relations director, and teacher. Member of San Francisco Women's Center, special projects task force of San Francisco Commission on the Status of Women, and San Francisco Women Against Rape.

WRITINGS: Kids School Lunch Bag (on the National School Lunch Program), Children's Foundation, 1972; *View from Another Closet: Exploring Bisexuality in Women,* Hawthorne, 1976. Co-author of "Women Against Rape" (television documentary film), 1975.

SIDELIGHTS: Janet Bode writes: "Women's issues are my primary concern, but I have a strong undercurrent of interest in all people regardless of gender. Continually I find myself questioning the motivating factors and thought processes behind actions. I then take this information and translate it into the written word."

* * *

BODKIN, Cora 1944-

PERSONAL: Born December 27, 1944, in New York, N.Y.; daughter of Mac (a real estate manager) and Lillian (a secretary; maiden name, Cohen) Modell; married Jerome Bodkin (a high school teacher), June 25, 1966; children: Kenneth, Daniel. *Education:* Hunter College of the City University of New York, B.A.,1966, M.A., 1970. *Home:* 7 Bellwood Dr., New City, N.Y. 10956.

CAREER: Elementary school teacher in New York, N.Y., 1966-73; Harvest House, Spring Valley, N.Y., arts and crafts teacher, 1973—. Partner in novelty photography company, Picture Yourself, 1971—. Member of National Council of Jewish Women (Rockland section).

WRITINGS: (With Helene Leibowitz and Diana Wiener) *Crafts for Your Leisure Years,* Houghton, 1976.

WORK IN PROGRESS: The Grandparent's Babysitting Guide: How to Spoil the Grandchildren and Still Be Loved by Your Children; research on "childproofing" a home, stages of child development, how to select appropriate and welcome gifts for grandchildren, handling sick children and emergencies, and how to make extra money as a professional babysitter.

SIDELIGHTS: Cora Bodkin writes: "*Crafts for Your Leisure Years* was written as a result of several years of experience working with a senior citizen craft group." She is presently initiating a community service project, co-sponsored by Rockland Community College, offering recreational activities to homebound members of the community. She adds that her "interest in the grandparent's babysitting guide developed as a result of my occasional use of Grandma as babysitter. When my baby was three months old, Grandma wanted to know if she would need a high-chair. . . . I didn't know whether to laugh or cry—how out of touch she was with babies!. . . Grandma needed a refresher course, plus a special guide for the uncharted course of 'grandparenthood.'''

* * *

BOEGEHOLD, Betty (Doyle) 1913-
(Donovan Doyle)

PERSONAL: Surname is pronounced *Berg*-a-hold; born September 15, 1913, in New York, N.Y.; daughter of James and Myrtle Doyle; divorced; children: Karen Simon. *Education:* Wellesley College, B.A., 1935; Columbia University, M.A., 1943. *Politics:* Independent Democrat. *Religion:* Protestant. *Home:* 64 Sagamore Rd., Bronxville, N.Y. 10708. *Office:* Publications Division, Bank Street College, 610 West 112th St., New York, N.Y. 10025.

CAREER: Preschool teacher in New York City, 1936-40; elementary school teacher, librarian, assistant principal, and remedial reading specialist, in Mount Vernon, N.Y., 1946-68; Bank Street College, New York City, senior editor of publications and staff writer, instructor in graduate programs, and director of writer's workshop, 1968—. Once owned a nursery school. *Member:* Association for Childhood Education International, National Organization of Women, League of Women Voters, Common Cause, Citizens Council, Save the Children Foundation, Defenders of Wildlife, Animal Protection League, Wild Horse Organized Assistance, Fund for Animals, Friends of Animals, Phi Beta Kappa.

WRITINGS—For children: *Three to Get Ready,* Harper, 1968; *Paw Paw's Run,* Dutton, 1969; *Pippa Mouse* (Junior Literary Guild selection), Knopf, 1973; *What the Wind Told,* Parents' Magazine Press, 1974; (with Cyndy Szekeres) *Here's Pippa Again* (Junior Literary Guild selection), Knopf, 1975; *Small Deer's Magic Tricks,* Coward, 1977. Also author of *The Carmen Book, The Jack Book, The Rosa Book,* and *The Victor Book,* all published by Macmillan; also author, under pseudonym Donovan Doyle, of *Gray Gull, Bugs, The Old Woman Who Couldn't Keep a Secret, Almost There, Perseus and Andromeda: A Retelling,* and other books, all published by Houghton.

Senior associate editor of Macmillan's "Bank Street Readers" series, 1967, and Houghton's "Discovery" series, 1976.

WORK IN PROGRESS—For children: *The Chipper Stories; The Night Stories; The Grabbits; Goober's Great Day.*

SIDELIGHTS: Boegehold writes: "I'm most interested in writing for young children—in using sensory images that will reach them—hopefully, in illuminating some small bit of their world, their concerns. I believe they deserve the best possible writing and the greatest respect—for books that touch them will not be forgotten by them. They are the most receptive of audiences—and should never be addressed as less wise than adults—only as less knowledgeable."

* * *

BOER, Charles 1939-

PERSONAL: Born June 25, 1939, in Cleveland, Ohio. *Education:* Western Reserve University (now Case Western Reserve University), A.B., 1961; graduate study at University of Florence, 1961-62, and Harvard University, 1962-63; State University of New York at Buffalo, Ph.D., 1967. *Home address:* R.F.D. 1, Box 69, Pomfret Center, Conn. 06259. *Office:* Department of English, University of Connecticut, Storrs, Conn. 06268.

CAREER: University of Connecticut, Storrs, assistant professor, 1966-71, associate professor, 1971-75, professor of English, 1975—. *Member:* International P.E.N. *Awards, honors:* Fulbright fellowship, 1961; Woodrow Wilson fellowship, 1962; nominated for National Book Award, 1972, for *The Homeric Hymns.*

WRITINGS: The Odes (poems), Swallow Press, 1969; (translator) *The Homeric Hymns,* Swallow Press, 1970; *Varmint Q* (poems), Swallow Press, 1972; *Charles Olson in Connecticut* (biography), Swallow Press, 1975; (editor with George Butterick) *The Maximus Poems of Charles Olson,* Volume III, Viking, 1976.

Translation of *The Bacchae* included in *An Anthology of Greek Tragedy,* edited by Arthur Cook and Edwin Dolin, Bobbs-Merrill, 1972. Contributor to magazines in the United States and abroad, including *Spring, Journal of Archetypal Psychology, Tri-Quarterly, New Republic,* and *Chelsea Review.*

* * *

BOGARD, Travis (Miller) 1918-

PERSONAL: Born January 25, 1918, in San Francisco, Calif.; son of Verner Edward and Gertrude (Travis) Bogard; married Jane Malmgren, June, 1946; children: John George, Sara Snow. *Education:* University of California, Berkeley, A.B., 1939, M.A., 1940; Princeton University, Ph.D., 1947. *Home:* 7 West Parnassus Court, Berkeley, Calif. 94708. *Office:* Department of Dramatic Art, University of California, Berkeley, Calif. 94720.

CAREER: Yale University, New Haven, Conn., instructor in English, 1942-43; University of California, Berkeley, instructor, 1947-49, assistant professor, 1949-55, associate professor, 1955-59, professor of English, 1959-66, professor of dramatic art, 1966—, chairman of department, 1960-66. Director of artistic and educational program at Eugene O'Neill Tao House Foundation. *Military service:* U.S. Army, 1942-46. *Member:* American Theatre Association. *Awards, honors:* Guggenheim fellowship, 1958; silver medal from Commonwealth Club of California, 1973.

WRITINGS: The Tragic Satire of John Webster, University of California Press, 1957; (editor with W. I. Oliver) *Modern Drama: Essays in Criticism,* Oxford University Press, 1965; (editor) *The Later Plays of Eugene O'Neill,* Modern Library, 1967; *Contour in Time: The Plays of Eugene O'Neill,* Oxford University Press, 1972; (editor) Frederick G. Ross, *The Actor from Point Arena,* Friends of Bancroft Library, 1977; (contributor) T. W. Craik, editor, *Revels History of Drama in English,* Methuen, in press. Contributor to theater journals.

WORK IN PROGRESS: Editing correspondence between Eugene O'Neill and Kenneth Macgowan, with Jackson R. Bryer, for Yale University Press.

* * *

BOHN, Joyce Illig 1940(?)-1976

1940(?)—August 22, 1976; American journalist. She wrote a literary column for the *Washington Post.* She was previously an associate of television critic Gene Shalit in the firm of Scrooge & Marley. She died in New York City. Obituaries: *New York Times,* August 24, 1976; *Washington Post,* August 24, 1976.

* * *

BOLTHO, Andrea 1939-

PERSONAL: Surname is pronounced *Bol-*toe; born October 13, 1939, in Berlin, Germany; son of Alexander (a journalist) and Ellis (von Hedenstroem) Boltho von Hohenbach; married Maya Nandi, July 15, 1967; children: Fabrice, Alexei. *Education:* London School of Economics and Political Science, University of London, B.Sc., 1962; University of Paris, D.E.S., 1963; Nuffield College, Oxford, B.Litt., 1965. *Politics:* Progressive. *Home:* 2 Rue du Bel Air, 92 Meudon, France. *Office:* Department of Economics, Organization for Economic Co-operation and Development, 2 Rue Andre-Pascal, 75016 Paris, France.

CAREER: Organization for Economic Co-operation and Development (OECD), Paris, France, administrator, 1966-71, head of division, 1971—. *Awards, honors:* Japan Foundation fellowship, 1973-74.

WRITINGS: Foreign Trade Criteria in Socialist Economics, Cambridge University Press, 1971; *Japan: An Economic Survey,* Oxford University Press, 1975.

WORK IN PROGRESS: Research on European growth since World War Two.

SIDELIGHTS: "I was born of Russian parents," Boltho told *CA,* "brought up in Italy, speaking five languages (plus some rudimentary Japanese). I am strongly interested in comparative economic work and drawn to international institutions."

* * *

BOND, Douglas Danford 1911-1976

July 2, 1911—October 30, 1976; American physician, educator, and author of books in his field. Bond was a consultant to several organizations and was a member of many professional societies. He died in Cleveland, Ohio. Obituaries: *New York Times,* November 1, 1976.

* * *

BONE, Robert (Adamson) 1924-

PERSONAL: Born August 12, 1924, in New Haven, Conn.; son of Robert Burns (a printer) and Isabelle (Adamson) Bone; married Dorothea Darrow (a high school teacher), September 2, 1945; children: Debora, Keira Bone Burtch. *Education:* Yale University, B.A., 1945, M.A., 1948, Ph.D., 1955. *Politics:* "Democratic Socialist." *Religion:* None. *Home:* 560 Riverside Dr., New York, N.Y. 10027. *Office:* Department of Languages and Literature, Teachers College, Columbia University, New York, N.Y. 10027.

CAREER: Yale University, New Haven, Conn., instructor in English, 1954-59; University of California, Los Angeles, assistant professor of English, 1959-64; Columbia University, Teachers College, New York, N.Y., associate professor, 1965-67, professor of English, 1967—, chairman of department, 1974—. Fulbright lecturer at University of Grenoble, 1967-68; visiting fellow of Center for Twentieth Century Studies, University of Wisconsin, Milwaukee, 1973-74. *Member:* Modern Language Association of America, National Council of Teachers of English, American Studies Association, American Association of University Professors.

WRITINGS: The Negro Novel in America, Yale Univer-

sity Press, 1958, revised edition, 1965; *Richard Wright* (monograph), University of Minnesota Press, 1969; *Down Home: A History of Afro-American Short Fiction from Its Beginning to the End of the Harlem Renaissance,* Putnam, 1975. Contributor to literary journals.

WORK IN PROGRESS: The Promised Land: Afro-American Short Fiction from 1935 to the Present, completion expected in 1982.

SIDELIGHTS: Bone writes: "My major areas of vocational interest include Afro-American literature, American literature, and British literature, especially Shakespeare. A white man and critic of black literature, I try to demonstrate by the quality of my work that scholarship is not the same thing as identity." *Avocational interests:* Swimming, sailing, canoeing, skiing, spending the summers on Nantucket.

* * *

BONFANTE, Larissa

PERSONAL: Born in Naples, Italy; came to the United States in 1940, naturalized citizen, 1952; daughter of Giuliano (a professor) and Vittoria Bonfante; married Peter Beach Warren, September, 1950 (divorced, August, 1962); married Leo Raditsa (a professor and writer), May 2, 1973; children: Alexandra Bonfante Warren. *Education:* Attended Radcliffe College and University of Rome; Barnard College, B.A.; University of Cincinnati, M.A.; Columbia University, Ph.D. *Home:* 50 Morningside Dr., New York, N.Y. 10025. *Office:* Department of Classics, New York University, 25 Waverly Pl., New York, N.Y. 10003.

CAREER: New York University, New York City, instructor, 1963-64, assistant professor, 1964-68, associate professor of classics, 1968—. *Member:* Archaeological Institute of America, Istituto di Studi Etruschi (foreign member), Phi Beta Kappa (past president of Beta chapter, New York University).

WRITINGS: (Translator) E. J. Bickerman, *Chronology of the Ancient World,* Thames and Hudson, 1968; (with Rolf Winkes) *Bibliography of the Works of Margarete Bieber for her Ninetieth Birthday.* Columbia University Press, 1969; *Etruscan Dress,* Johns Hopkins Press, 1975; (editor, with Helga von Heintze) *In Memoriam Otto J. Brendel: Essays in Archaeology and the Humanities,* von Zabern (Mainz), 1976. Contributor of articles and reviews to professional journals. Contributor of translations for *Encyclopedia of World Art,* McGraw-Hill; consultant for *The Etruscans* in "The Emergence of Man," series, Time-Life, 1975.

WORK IN PROGRESS: The Etruscans, publication by Phaidon; *Ancient Greek, Etruscan, and Roman Dress,* Thames and Hudson; *The Plays of Hrotswitha of Gandersheim: A Translation; The Situla People;* research on the Etruscan influence in Europe.

* * *

BOONE, Muriel 1893-

PERSONAL: Born January 27, 1893, in Shanghai, China; daughter of Henry William (a physician) and Annie (a teacher; maiden name, Kirkby) Boone. *Education:* Hollins College, student, 1908-11; University of California, Berkeley, B.A., 1916; Yale University, graduate study, 1945. *Politics:* Republican. *Home:* 119 Camino Santiago, Santa Fe, N.M. 87501. *Agent:* Roland Tapp, 428 Tamal Plaza, Corte Madera, Calif. 94925.

CAREER: Presbyterian missionary in China, 1917-50; refugee relief worker in Hong Kong, 1953-58; writer. Employed as war relief worker, 1938-43; member of Commission on International Relations and School of American Research. *Member:* American Association of University Women, United Church Women, Historical Society of Santa Fe, Santa Fe Gem and Mineral Club.

WRITINGS: Seed of the Church in China, United Church Press, 1973; *Spring Bamboo,* Omega Books, 1976.

WORK IN PROGRESS: A book "to cover the impact of World War II and of the takeover of the country by Communism, as both occurred in China."

SIDELIGHTS: Muriel Boone writes: "Outsiders were not permitted to enter China, much less reside there, until after the Opium War and the Treaty of 1842. *Seed of the Church in China* is a historical biography covering the years 1837 to 1864. It follows the early entrance of Americans and their missionaries into China, based on letters written from there by my grandfather, the Right Reverend William J. Boone. It depicts what was taking place both in the United States and in China during that period and their interaction. *Spring Bamboo* attempts to show normal Chinese life during the period of 1917-1930 as I lived intimately with the Chinese in the far interior of that time before Communism."

*   *   *

BOOTH, Stephen 1933-

PERSONAL: Born April 20, 1933, in New York, N.Y.; son of Frank Walter and Ruth Joan (Friedman) Booth; married Susan Patek, June 20, 1959; children: Jason Michael, Mary. *Education:* Harvard University, A.B., 1955, Ph.D., 1964; Trinity College, Cambridge, B.A., 1957, M.A., 1961. *Politics:* Democrat. *Religion:* Episcopalian. *Home:* 98 The Uplands, Berkeley, Calif. 94705. *Office:* Department of English, University of California, Berkeley, Calif. 94720.

CAREER: University of California, Berkeley, assistant professor, 1962-69, associate professor, 1969-74, professor of English, 1974—, vice-chairman of department, 1974-76. *Awards, honors:* Marshall scholarship, England, 1955-57; Guggenheim fellowship, 1971.

WRITINGS: An Essay on Shakespeare's Sonnets, Yale University Press, 1969; *The Book Called Holinshed's Chronicles* (monograph), Book Club of California, 1969; (contributor) Norman Rabkin, editor, *Reinterpretations of Elizabethan Drama,* Columbia University Press, 1969; (editor and author of commentary) *Shakespeare's Sonnets,* Yale University Press, 1977.

Work represented in anthology, *Literary Criticism: Idea and Act,* edited by William Wimsatt, University of California Press, 1974.

*   *   *

BORDLEY, James III 1900-

PERSONAL: Born December 7, 1900, in Centerville, Md.; son of James, Jr. and Margaretta (Hollyday) Bordley; married Julia Ross, July 4, 1936; children: Patricia (Mrs. Roderic D. Wiltse), James, Donald R. *Education:* Yale University, Ph.B., 1923; Johns Hopkins University, M.D., 1927. *Politics:* Independent. *Religion:* Episcopal. *Home and office:* 13 Main St., Cooperstown, N.Y. 13326.

CAREER: Johns Hopkins Hospital, Baltimore, Md., intern, 1927-28; National Research Council, medical fellow in Cambridge, Mass. and Philadelphia, Pa., 1930-32; Johns Hopkins University, Baltimore, Md., resident physician at Hospital, 1932-34, instructor, 1932-33, assistant professor,

1933-37, associate professor, 1937-47, associate physician and chief of Cardiovascular Division, 1937-47; Albany Medical College, Albany, N.Y., clinical professor of medicine, 1947-77. Associate clinical professor at Columbia University, 1947, clinical professor, 1948-67; visiting professor at National Defense Medical Center (Taiwan), 1967-68. Director and chief physician at Mary Imogene Bassett Hospital, 1947-67, director emeritus, 1967—, trustee, 1947—. Trustee of Clark Foundation, 1948—, Regional Hospital Review and Planning Council of Northeastern New York, 1948-76 (president, 1962-71); director and member of executive committee of Health Systems Agency of Northeastern New York; consultant to Surgeon General of the U.S. Army, 1955-66, and Naval Medical Research Unit (Taiwan), 1967-68. *Military service:* U.S. Army, chief of medicine at 118 General Hospital and later commanding officer, 1942-46; received Bronze Star Medal.

MEMBER: Association of American Physicians, American Clinical and Climatological Association (president, 1957), American Society for Clinical Investigation, American Heart Association, American Physiological Society, Society of Medical Consultants of the Armed Forces, American Association for the Advancement of Science, New York State Historical Association (trustee, 1949—). *Awards, honors:* D.Sc. from Hartwick College, 1953, and Union University, 1964.

WRITINGS: (With A. M. Harvey) *Differential Diagnosis: The Interpretation of Clinical Evidence,* Saunders, 1955, 2nd edition, 1970, abridged edition, 1972; (with B. N. Chiang) *Hypertension: A Symposium,* privately printed, 1967; (with Harvey) *Two Centuries of American Medicine,* Saunders, 1976. Contributor to medical journals. Managing editor of *Bulletin of the Johns Hopkins Hospital,* 1936-42.

WORK IN PROGRESS: Differential Diagnosis: The Interpretation of Clinical Evidence, 3rd edition, with A. M. Harvey, for Saunders.

SIDELIGHTS: Bordley comments: "A. M. Harvey . . . has stimulated me to do things which otherwise I might never have done. The book on hypertension was written in English, with a summary of each chapter in Chinese."

*   *   *

BORETZ, Benjamin (Aaron) 1934-

PERSONAL: Born October 3, 1934, in New York, N.Y.; son of Abraham (a mathematician) and Leah (an artist; maiden name, Yollis) Boretz; married Naomi Messinger (a painter), September 1, 1954; children: Avron Albert. *Education:* Brooklyn College (now of the City University of New York), B.A., 1950; Brandeis University, M.F.A., 1957; Princeton University, M.F.A., 1960, Ph.D., 1970. *Home address:* River Rd., Barrytown, Red Hook, N.Y. 12571. *Office:* Department of Music, Bard College, Annandale-on-Hudson, N.Y. 12504.

CAREER: Perspectives of New Music, Annandale-on-Hudson, N.Y., co-founder and associate editor, 1961-62, editor, 1963—. Assistant professor at Brandeis University, 1962-63, New York University, 1964-69, and Columbia University, 1969-72; Fulbright-Hays lecturer at University of Southampton, 1971-72; lecturer at Princeton University, 1972-74; associate professor at Bard College, 1973—; visiting member of faculty at University of California, Los Angeles, University of California, Berkeley, University of Chiago, and University of Michigan. Participant in international music seminars and congresses; consultant to Fromm Music Foundation, 1959-70.

MEMBER: International Society for Contemporary Music (member of board of governors), American Society of University Composers (co-founder; executive secretary, 1966-68), American Composers' Alliance, American Musicological Society, New York Music Critics Circle. *Awards, honors:* Composition award from Fromm Foundation, 1956, for "Violin Concerto"; grant from Ingram Merrill Foundation, 1966-67; fellowship from Council of Humanities at Princeton University, 1972-73; MacDowell fellowship, 1974.

WRITINGS: (Editor with Edward T. Cone) *Perspectives on Schoenberg and Stravinsky,* Princeton University Press, 1968, revised edition, Norton, 1972; *Meta-Variations: Studies in the Foundations of Musical Thought,* Perspectives of New Music, 1969; (editor with Cone) *Perspectives on American Composers,* Norton, 1971; (editor with Cone) *Perspectives on Contemporary Music Theory,* Norton, 1972; (editor with Cone) *Perspectives on Notation and Performance,* Norton, 1976.

Composer: "Chamber Concerto," 1954; "Concerto Grosso," 1955; "Partita for Piano," 1955; "Wind Quintet," 1956; "Violin Concerto," 1956; "String Quartet," 1957; "Divertimento," 1957; "Donne Songs," 1959-60; "Ensemble Variations," 1962-64; "Brass Quintet," 1963-64; "Group Variations I" (for chamber orchestra), 1967; "Group Variations II" (for computer), 1973; "First Music" (for piano), 1977.

Contributor to philosophy and music journals, and to *Nation.* Music critic for *Nation,* 1962-69. Member of editorial board of *Dutton's Dictionary of Twentieth Century Music, Contemporary Music Newsletter,* and American Composers' Alliance, 1970-72.

WORK IN PROGRESS: Studying theory of language by way of music and modes of musical description.

*   *   *

BORUCH, Robert F(rancis)   1942-

PERSONAL: Born October 14, 1942, in Bayonne, N.J.; married Nancy Braund (a banker), September 21, 1970. *Education:* Stevens Institute of Technology, B.E., 1964; Iowa State University, Ph.D., 1968. *Office:* Department of Psychology, Northwestern University, Evanston, Ill. 60201.

CAREER: U.S. Air Force, Operations Analysis Group, Washington, D.C., research associate, 1965-66; American Council on Education, Washington, D.C., research associate, 1968-70; Northwestern University, Evanston, Ill., assistant professor, 1970-72, associate professor of psychology, 1972—. Research associate of National Academy of Sciences, 1968-70; staff associate of Social Science Research Council, 1971; president of Council for Applied Social Research; chairman of career education evaluation group, National Institutes of Education, 1972—. *Member:* American Psychological Association, American Educational Research Association, Psychometric Society, American Statistical Association, New York Academy of Sciences.

WRITINGS: (Co-author) *Science in Liberal Arts Colleges,* Columbia University Press, 1971; (with H. W. Riecken, D. T. Campbell, and others) *Social Experimentation: A Method for Planning and Evaluating Social Interaction,* Academic Press, 1974; (editor with Riecken) *Experimental Tests of Public Policy,* Westview, 1975. Contributor to psychology and sociology journals.

WORK IN PROGRESS: Methods for Assuring Privacy and Confidentiality of Social Research Data: Legal, Statis-

tical, Procedure; Methodology for Planning and Evaluating Social Programs.

SIDELIGHTS: Boruch attributes his success in his profession to "brains, sweat, intestinal fortitude."

*   *   *

BOSCO, (Fernand Marius Joseph) Henri   1888-1976

PERSONAL: Born November 16, 1888, in Avignon, France; son of Louis (an opera singer) and Louise (Falena) Bosco; married Marie-Madeleine Rhodes, July 16, 1930. *Education:* Graduate of Faculty of Arts in Grenoble and French Institute in Florence, Italy. *Residence:* Nice, France.

CAREER: Language teacher at schools in Avignon, France, 1912, in Bourg-en-Bresse, France, 1913, in Philippeville (now Skikda), Algeria, 1914, at French Institute in Naples, Italy, 1920-30, and at school in Rabat, Morocco, 1931-41; writer in Rabat, 1945-55; writer in Nice, France, 1955-76. Administrator of R. Laurent-Vibert a Lourmarin Foundation, 1941-76; member of council of University of Nice, 1966-76. *Military service:* French Army, 1914-18 and 1940-45. *Member:* Academie d'Aix-en-Provence, Academie rhodanienne.

AWARDS, HONORS: Received first literary award for poetry, 1901; prix Theophraste-Renaudot, 1945, for *Le Mas Theotime;* prix Louis Barthou from Academie francaise, 1946, for *Le Jardin d'Hyacinthe;* prix des Ambassadeurs, 1947, for *Malicroix;* grand prix national des Lettres francaises, 1953; grand prix de litterature de Academie francaise, 1968; medal from the city of Marseille, 1969; named citizen of honor by Avignon and Nice, both 1970; Croix de Guerre; medaille militaire serbe; commander of Legion d'honneur; commander of Palmes academiques; commander of Arts et des Lettres; commander of Nichan-Iftikhar; chevalier de la Couronne d'Italie.

WRITINGS—Novels in English translation: *Hyacinthe,* Gallimard, 1940, translation by Mervyn Savill published as *The Dark Bough,* Staples Press, 1955; *Le Mas Theotime,* Charlot, 1946, translation by Savill published as *The Farm Theotime,* Aldor, 1946, and as *Farm in Provence,* Doubleday, 1947; *Monsieur Carre-Benoit a la campagne,* Charlot, 1947, translation by Savill published as *Monsieur Carre-Benoit in the Country,* Staples Press, 1956; *L'Enfant et la riviere,* Gallimard, 1953, translation by Gerard Hopkins published as *The Boy and the River,* Pantheon, 1956; *Le Renard dans l'ile,* Gallimard, 1956, translation by Hopkins published as *The Fox in the Island,* Oxford University Press, 1958; *Barboche,* Gallimard, 1957, new edition published as *Le Chien Barboche,* 1966, French language edition edited by Clifford King, Harrap, 1965, translation by Hopkins published as *Barboche,* Oxford University Press, 1959.

Other work in English: *The Wonderful Life of John Bosco* (adaptation by Mary Cousins of biography, *La Vie extraordinaire de saint Jean Bosco,* written with wife Marie-Madeleine Bosco and first published in France), Chapman, 1963; *Don Bosco,* illustrated by Leonard von Matt, Spes, 1964, Universe Books, 1967.

In French: *Pierre Lampedouze* (novel), [France], 1924, Gallimard, 1931; (with N. Vesper) *Les Poetes* (poetry), [France], 1925; *Eglogues de le mer* (poetry), [France], 1928; *Irenee* (novel), Nouvelle revue francaise, 1928; *Noels et chansons de Lourmain* (poetry), [France], 1929; *Le Quartier de Sagesse* (novel), Gallimard, 1929; *Le Sanglier,* Gallimard, 1932; *Le Trestoulas* (novel), Gallimard, 1935; *Devant le mur de pierre,* [France], 1936; *L'Ane Culotte* (novel), Gallimard, 1937.

Bucoliques di Provence (poetry), Revue Fontaine, 1944; *Le Jardin d'Hyacinthe* (novel), Gallimard, 1946; *Malicroix* (novel), Grasset, 1948; *Le Roseau et la source* (poetry), Gallimard, 1949; *Sylvius* (novel), Gallimard, 1949; *Un Rameau de la nuit* (novel), Flammarion, 1950; *Des Sables a la mer: Pages marocaines* (poetry and essays), Gallimard, 1950; *Sites et mirages* (essays), Gallimard, 1951; *Antonin* (novel), Gallimard, 1952; *L'Antiquaire* (novel), Gallimard, 1954; *Les Balesta* (novel), Gallimard, 1955; *Sabinus* (novel), Gallimard, 1957; *Bargabot suivi de Pascalet* (novel), Gallimard, 1958; *Saint Jean Bosco* (biography), Gallimard, 1959.

Un Oubli moins profond (first volume of memoirs trilogy), Gallimard, 1961; *Le Chemin de Monclar* (second volume of memoirs trilogy), Gallimard, 1962; *L'Epervier* (novel), Gallimard, 1963; *Le Jardin des Trinitaires* (third volume of memoirs trilogy), Gallimard, 1966; *Mon compagnon de songes,* Gallimard, 1967; *Le Recif,* Gallimard, 1971; *Tante Martine,* Gallimard, 1972; *Trobo prouvencalo: Pieces provencales* (poetry in French and Provencal), L'Astrado, 1974.

Also author of novels first published in *Les Oeuvres libres* periodical, including *Malicroix* (also see above), 1946, "A l'enseigne des deux bossus," 1951, and "Un Secret de famille," 1954.

Author of preface: Frederic Mistral, *Mireille: Poeme provencal,* Club des libraires de France, 1959; Jean C. Godin, *Une Poetique due mystere,* [France], 1968.

WORK IN PROGRESS: L'Ombre, title means "The Shadow."

OBITUARIES: New York Times, May 6, 1976; *Washington Post,* May 8, 1976; *AB Bookman's Weekly,* May 31. 1976.*

(Died May 4, 1976, in Nice, France)

* * *

BOWEN, Ralph H(enry) 1919-

PERSONAL: Born September 21, 1919, in Bellows Falls, Vt.; son of Floyd Byron (a farmer) and Mildred Davis (Severens) Bowen; married Susan Heath Beardslee (a television producer); children: Sarah Heath, Paul Davis. *Education:* Amherst College, A.B., 1940; Columbia University, A.M., 1941, Ph.D., 1946. *Politics:* Independent. *Home:* 924 Dawn Court, DeKalb, Ill. 60115. *Agent:* Walter Pitkin, Jr., 11 Oakwood Dr., Weston, Conn. 06880. *Office:* Department of History, Northern Illinois University, DeKalb, Ill. 60115.

CAREER: U.S. Department of State, Washington, D.C., country economic specialist, 1942-45; Columbia University, New York, N.Y., instructor, 1946-48, assistant professor of history, 1948-56; Elmira College, Elmira, N.Y., associate professor of history, 1956-57; State University of New York, Long Island Center, professor of social science, 1957-60; Northern Illinois University, DeKalb, professor of history, 1960—. Fulbright lecturer at University of Nantes, 1967-69, visiting professor, 1975-76; lecturer at University of Nice, summer, 1968. President of DeKalb County Fine Arts Association, 1962—. *Member:* American Historical Association, Economic History Association, Society for French Historical Studies, Phi Beta Kappa.

WRITINGS: German Theories of the Corporate State, McGraw, 1947, reprinted, Russell, 1971; (co-translator and editor) *Rameau's Nephew and Other Works of Diderot,* Doubleday, 1954; *A Frenchman in Lincoln's America,*

Lakeside Press, Volume I, 1974, Volume II, 1975. Also co-author of *Chapters in Western Civilization.* Contributor of articles and reviews to learned journals.

WORK IN PROGRESS: The Great Words in American Life, completion expected in 1978; *Diderot and Rousseau: A Dual Biography,* 1979.

SIDELIGHTS: Bowen's special interests are history of ideas, Franco-American cultural relations, and translating.

* * *

BOWEN, Robert Sidney 1901(?)-1977

1901(?)—April 11, 1977; American journalist and author. Bowen was a reporter for several newspapers, was an editor, and wrote adventure novels. He died in Honolulu, Hawaii. Obituaries: *New York Times,* April 14, 1977.

* * *

BOWLES, Chester (Bliss) 1901-

PERSONAL: Born April 5, 1901, in Springfield, Mass.; son of Charles Allen (a paper mill supplier) and Nellie (Harris) Bowles; married Julia Mayo Fisk, 1925 (divorced, 1933); married Dorothy Stebbins, February 11, 1934; children: (first marriage) Barbara, Chester Bliss, Jr.; (second marriage) Cynthia, Sally, Samuel. *Education:* Yale University, B.S., 1924. *Religion:* Unitarian-Universalist. *Home address:* Hayden's Point, Essex, Conn. 06426.

CAREER: Springfield Republican, Springfield, Mass., reporter, 1924-25; George Batten Co. (now Batten, Barton, Durstine & Osborn), New York City, copy writer, engaged in merchandising and marketing research, 1925-29; Benton & Bowles (advertising firm), co-founder, 1929, partner, 1929-36, chairman, 1936-41; Office of Price Administration, Washington, D.C., state director for Connecticut, 1941-43, national general manager, 1943, national price administrator, 1943-46; Office of Economic Stabilization, Washington, D.C., director, 1946; United Nations, New York City, special assistant to the secretary-general, 1947-48; governor of the state of Connecticut, 1949-51; American ambassador to India and Nepal, 1951-53; Bryn Mawr College, Bryn Mawr, Pa., Shaw lecturer, 1953-54; University of California, Berkeley, Berkeley lecturer, 1956; Harvard University, Cambridge, Mass., Godkin lecturer, 1956; Yale University, New Haven, Conn., Chubb lecturer, 1957; Democratic member of U.S. Congress and foreign policy adviser to then Senator John F. Kennedy, 1959-60; became U.S. under-secretary of state, 1960-61; became president's special representative for Asian, African, and Latin American affairs, 1961; American ambassador to India, 1963-69; writer, 1969—.

Head of Connecticut state rationing board, 1941; member of War Production Board and Petroleum Council for War, 1943-46. Member of American National Commission for UNESCO, 1946-47; head of United Nations Appeal for Children, 1948. Platform chairman of Democratic National Convention, 1960. Member of board of advisers of Fletcher School of Law and Diplomacy (of Tufts University); chairman of advisory committee of Yale Center for Economic Growth. Past director of Institute for International Education, American Council of Learned Societies, Fund for the Peaceful Development of Atomic Energy, and Fund for the Republic; trustee of Franklin Delano Roosevelt Foundation, Eleanor Roosevelt Memorial Fund, and Woodrow Wilson Foundation; chairman of advisory committee of Rockefeller Foundation. Past director of Britannica Films.

MEMBER: Asia Society, Connecticut Grange, Essex Yacht Club, Cruising of America Club, Yale Club (New York City). *Awards, honors:* LL.D. from American University, 1946, Howard University, 1955, Oberlin College, 1957, Bard College, 1957, Rhode Island University, 1958, University of Michigan, 1961, Yale University, 1968, and Davidson College, 1972; Franklin D. Roosevelt Award, 1953, for fighting racial discrimination; Roosevelt College Award, 1953, for outstanding public service; D.Sc. from New School for Social Research, 1954.

WRITINGS: Tomorrow without Fear, Simon & Schuster, 1946; Ambassador's Report, *Harper, 1954;* The New Dimensions of Peace, *Harper, 1955, reprinted, Greenwood Press, 1974;* Africa's Challenge to America, *University of California Press, 1956;* American Politics in a Revolutionary World, *Harvard University Press, 1956;* Dangers in Our Foreign Policy *(pamphlet), Teamsters Joint Council, 1957;* Ideas, People, and Peace, *Harper, 1958;* The Coming Political Breakthrough, *Harper, 1959.*

Agenda 1961: New Principles for a New Age, foreword by Eleanor Roosevelt, National Committee for an Effective Congress, 1960; *The Foundations of World Partnership* (pamphlet), U.S. Department of State, 1961; *The Conscience of a Liberal: Selected Writings and Speeches,* edited by Henry Steele Commager, Harper, 1962; *The Makings of a Just Society: What the Postwar Years Have Taught Us About National Development,* University of Delhi, 1963; *The Objectives and Instruments of U.S. Policy in Asia* (pamphlet), United Board for Christian Higher Education in Asia, 1963; *Indian-American Relations: A Current View,* Harold Laski Institute of Political Science, 1966; *A View from New Delhi: Selected Speeches and Writings, 1963-1969,* Yale University Press, 1969.

Promises to Keep: My Years in Public Life, 1941-1969, Harper, 1971. Also author of *Waging the Peace,* 1955, and *Behind American Foreign Policy: The Need to Redefine Our National Purpose,* 1956, and contributor to *New Global Strategy for Trade and Tea,* edited by Anthony Hyde, 1954. Contributor to magazines, including *Common Sense.* Past director of *Encyclopaedia Britannica.*

SIDELIGHTS: Bowles's work for the Office of Price Administration began with serious efforts to control the wartime black market dealing with rationed goods. His next attempt was to lower prices, but was somewhat less successful. As governor of Connecticut, his main achievements were in the areas of child care, housing, and welfare. His diplomatic career was concerned with promoting America's image abroad and committing the United States to assist developing nations. He has traveled all over the world, and his books have been published in Spanish, Tamil, and Bengali.

BIOGRAPHICAL/CRITICAL SOURCES: Harper's, November, 1952; *Saturday Review,* January 9, 1954; Edward Roscoe Murrow, *This I Believe,* Simon & Schuster, 1954; Deane Heller and David Heller, *The Kennedy Cabinet,* Monarch, 1961; *Newsweek,* August 23, 1965; Chester Bowles, *Promises to Keep: My Years in Public Life, 1941-1969,* Harper, 1971; *New York Times,* March 27, 1973.*

*   *   *

BOWMAN, Kathleen (Gill) 1942-

PERSONAL: Born December 19, 1942, in Minneapolis, Minn.; daughter of Albert (a postman) and Inga (a nurse; maiden name, Thompson) Gill; married Daniel Clifford Bowman (an archaeologist), June 12, 1974; children: Susan,

William, Geoffrey. *Education:* Attended Lawrence University, 1960-61; University of Minnesota, B.S. (with high distinction), 1964, M.A., 1967, Ph.D., 1977. *Home:* 436 Oliver Ave. S., Minneapolis, Minn. 55405. *Office:* 400 Southwest State Office Building, St. Paul, Minn. 55155.

CAREER: Junior high school teacher of English and Spanish in Robbinsdale, Minn., 1964-66; University of Minnesota, Minneapolis, instructor in education, 1968-71; Hamline University, St. Paul, Minn., director of human relations, 1972-75; Minnesota Department of Education, St. Paul, program consultant, 1976-77; research associate of Legislative Advisory Council on the Economic Status of Women, 1977—. *Member:* American Civil Liberties Union, National Organization for Women, Women's Equity Action League, Women in State Employment, Phi Beta Kappa, Eta Sigma Epsilon.

WRITINGS—All for young people; all published by Creative Education Press: *New Women in Media,* 1976; *New Women in Entertainment,* 1976; *New Women in Social Science,* 1976; *New Women in Medicine,* 1976; *New Women in Art and Dance,* 1976; *New Women in Politics,* 1976; *Johnny Cash* (biography), in press; *Elvis Presley* (biography), in press. Also author of monographs, *Minnesota Women: State Government Employment* and *Minnesota Women: Education Training and Job Market Reentry.* Editor of "New Women" series, Creative Education Press, 1976. Contributor to *Insports.*

WORK IN PROGRESS: Research on women in Minnesota state government employment, the status of the family, and women as homemakers.

SIDELIGHTS: Bowman writes: "I have been trained as an academician, but I am most comfortable writing for young people and the general public, specifically on issues of a social or political nature. The driving force behind much of my work is the notion that equality requires not sameness, but *diversity,* along dimensions of age, sex, race, religion, and life-style."

AVOCATIONAL INTERESTS: Weaving, classical piano.

*   *   *

BOWSER, Eileen 1928-

PERSONAL: Born January 18, 1928, in Columbia Station, Ohio; daughter of Roy and Florence (Doyle) Putt; married William Patton Bowser, June 12, 1950. *Education:* Marietta College, B.A., 1950; University of North Carolina, M.A., 1953. *Office:* Department of Film, Museum of Modern Art, 11 West 53rd St., New York, N.Y. 10019.

CAREER: Museum of Modern Art, New York, N.Y., member of staff, 1953-55, secretary to curator of film department, 1955-57, research assistant, 1957-59, curatorial assistant, 1959-61, cataloger for D. W. Griffith Collection, 1961, curatorial assistant, 1961-65, assistant curator, 1965-69, associate curator, 1969-76, curator of film department, 1976—, member of archives advisory committee, 1971—, chairman of committee on film and television resources and services, 1973-74. Member of executive committee of Federation Internationale des Archives du Film, 1969—, president of Documentation Commission, 1972—, vice president, 1977—.

WRITINGS: Carl Dreyer (monograph), Museum of Modern Art, 1964; (author of revision) Iris Barry, *D. W. Griffith: American Film Master* (monograph), Museum of Modern Art, 2nd edition, 1965; (editor and contributor) *Film Notes* (revision of *The Movies,* by Richard Griffith and Arthur Mayer), Museum of Modern Art, 1969; (editor and author of introduction) *Biograph Bulletins, 1908-1912,* Farrar, Straus, 1973; (contributor) Ted Perry, editor *Performing Arts Resources,* Volume II, Drama Book Specialists, 1975. Author of film series "D. W. Griffith," 1965, and "From the D. W. Griffith Collection," 1975; also "Films from the Archive" and "Recent Acquisitions." Contributor to professional journals.

WORK IN PROGRESS: Editing a basic manual for film archives, with John Kuiper, for Federation Internationale des Archives du Film.f

*   *   *

BOY, Angelo V(ictor)   1929-

PERSONAL: Born June 3, 1929, in Malden, Mass.; son of Victor (a bookkeeper) and Philomena (Palladino) Boy; married Barbara Sarnie, April 14, 1956; children: Stephanie, Eleanor, Bernadette, Monica. *Education:* University of Notre Dame, A.B., 1953; Boston University, Ed.M., 1955, Ed.D., 1960. *Religion:* Roman Catholic. *Home:* 40 Coe Dr., Durham, N.H. 03824. *Office:* Morrill Hall, University of New Hampshire, Durham, N.H. 03824.

CAREER: Secondary school teacher in Everett, Mass., 1953-56, counselor, 1956-61; counselor in Lexington, Mass., 1961-65; University of New Hampshire, Durham, associate professor, 1965-69, professor of counselor education, 1969—. Visiting professor at University of Arizona, 1964, University of Hawaii, 1967, University of Toronto, 1968, and University of Colorado, 1969. *Member:* American Psychological Association, American Personnel and Guidance Association, New Hampshire Psychological Association, Massachusetts Psychological Association, New Hampshire Personnel and Guidance Association.

WRITINGS: (With G. J. Pine) *Client-Centered Counseling in the Secondary School,* Houghton, 1963; (with Pine) *The Counselor in the Schools: A Reconceptualization,* Houghton, 1968; (with Pine) *Expanding the Self: Personal Growth for Teachers,* W. C. Brown, 1971; (with Pine) *Learner-Centered Teaching: A Humanistic View,* Love Publishing, 1977. Contributor of about one hundred articles to professional journals and to newspapers.

WORK IN PROGRESS: Research on child-centered counseling and on psychological education, consulting, and synergistic counseling.

SIDELIGHTS: Boy told *CA:* "I have devoted my career to the preparation of therapeutic professional counselors from a client-centered and existential-humanistic viewpoint. I support the counselor functioning as a therapeutic agent rather than as an information dispenser, moralist, judge, or enforcer of institutional policy. I believe that the counseling profession should safeguard human rights and personal dignity through the counseling process."

AVOCATIONAL INTERESTS: Golf, photography, the psychology of sports.

*   *   *

BOYCE, Richard Fyfe   1896-

PERSONAL: Born March 24, 1896, in Lansing, Mich.; son of James Burton and Grace (Miles) Boyce; married Katherine Randall (an author), August 24, 1921; children: Richard Fyfe, Mary Elenore. *Education:* Harvard University, A.B., 1918, graduate study, 1920-21. *Politics:* Republican. *Religion:* None. *Home and office:* 1639 Northeast 26th St., Apt. 311, Wilton Manors, Fla, 33305.

CAREER: U.S. State Department, Foreign Service, Washington, D.C., vice-consul in Kingston, Jamaica, 1920-22, and Nassau, Bahamas, 1922-23, consul in Nassau, 1923-24, Hamilton, Ontario, 1924, Nueva Laredo, Mexico, 1928, Barcelona, Spain, 1931, Yokohama, Japan, 1933, Callao-Lima, Peru, 1941, first secretary in Lima, 1942-43, first secretary and consul general in Havana, Cuba, 1943-45, consul general in Melbourne, Australia, 1945-48; Georgetown University, Washington, D.C., lecturer, 1949-50; Philco Corp., Washington, D.C., sales representative, 1950-61; free-lance writer and researcher, 1961—. *Military service:* Canadian Engineers, 1918-19. *Member:* American Foreign Service Association, Diplomatic and Consular Officers, Retired.

WRITINGS: The Diplomat's Wife, Harper, 1956; *A History of Dacor (Diplomatic and Consular Officers, Retired),* Dacor, 1969; (with wife, Katherine Boyce) *Bibliography of American Foreign Service Officers,* Scarecrow, 1973. Contributor to *American Foreign Service Journal.*

WORK IN PROGRESS: Studies of U.S. Foreign Service.

*   *   *

BOYD, Beverly M(ary)   1925-

PERSONAL: Born March 27, 1925, in Brooklyn, N.Y.; daughter of James Gray (a salesman) and Elspeth (Mossop) Boyd. *Education:* Brooklyn College (now of the City University of New York), B.A., 1946; Columbia University, M.A., 1948, Ph.D., 1955. *Office:* Department of English, Wescoe Hall, University of Kansas, Lawrence, Kan. 66045.

CAREER: Brooklyn College (now of the City University of New York), Brooklyn, N.Y., instructor in English, summer, 1947; University of Texas, Austin, instructor in English, 1955-59; Virginia Polytechnic Institute, Radford College, Radford, professor of English, 1959-62; University of Kansas, Lawrence, assistant professor, 1962-64, associate professor, 1964-69, professor of English, 1969—. Visiting associate professor at University of Wisconsin, spring, 1966. *Member:* Modern Language Association of America, Mediaeval Academy of America, American Association of University Professors, Midwestern Medieval Institute, Kansas University Medieval Society (founding member). *Awards, honors:* Guggenheim fellowship, 1969-70.

WRITINGS: (Editor) *The Middle English Miracles of the Virgin,* Huntington Library, 1964; *Chaucer and the Liturgy,* Dorrance, 1967; *Chaucer and the Medieval Book,* Huntington Library, 1973; (contributor) Paul G. Ruggiers, editor, *The Variorum Chaucer,* University of Oklahoma Press, 1978. Contributor of articles, poems, and reviews to literary journals, including *Modern Language Quarterly,* and to literature journals.

WORK IN PROGRESS: Editing *The Caxton Chaucers.*

SIDELIGHTS: Beverly Boyd writes briefly: "I am a medievalist with a specialty in Middle English literature. I spend a lot of my time at the Huntington Library. I also visit libraries in England." *Avocational interests:* Collecting rocks, playing piano.

*   *   *

BOYD, William Harland   1912-

PERSONAL: Born January 7, 1912, in Boise, Idaho; son of Harland D. and Cordelia (Crumley) Boyd; married Mary Kathryn Drake, June 25, 1939; children: Barbara A. Boyd Voltmer, William Harland, Jr., Kathryn Louise. *Education:* Riverside Junior College, A.A., 1933; University of California, Berkeley, B.A., 1935, M.A., 1936, Ph.D., 1942; graduate student at Fresno State College, Garrett Biblical Institute, Northwestern University, and University of California, Irvine. *Politics:* Republican. *Religion:* American Baptist. *Home:* 339 Cypress St., Bakersfield, Calif. 93304.

CAREER: High school teacher of history, music, and English in McArthur, Calif., 1937-38, Watsonville, Calif., 1941-42, and San Mateo, Calif., 1942-44; Trans-World Airlines, San Francisco, Calif., agent, 1944-46; Bakersfield College, Bakersfield, Calif., instructor, 1946-63, professor of social sciences, 1964-73, professor emeritus, 1973—, chairman of department, 1967-73. Instructor at Fresno State College, summers, 1949-55, assistant professor, autumns, 1961-63, spring, 1965; adjunct lecturer at California State College, Bakersfield, 1972-73. Member of advisory committee of Kern County Museum, 1955—; chairman of Fort Tejon Restoration Committee, 1952-55.

MEMBER: American Historical Association, Western History Association, California Historical Society, California Retired Teachers Association, Kern County Historical Society (past president), Tulare County Historical Society, Friends of the Bancroft Library, Phi Alpha Theta. *Awards, honors:* Merit award from Kern County Board of Trade, 1960.

WRITINGS: Land of Havilah, 1854-1874: The Story of Keyesville, Kernville, and Havilah, in the Kern River Country, California, Kern County Historical Society, 1952; (with G. J. Rogers) *San Joaquin Vignettes: The Reminiscences of Captain John Barker,* Kern County Historical Society, 1955; (with J. D. Stockton and G. J. Rodgers) *Spanish Trailblazers in the South San Joaquin,* Kern County Historical Society, 1957; *A Centennial Biography of Kern County, California,* Kern County Historical Society, 1966; *A California Middle Border: The Kern River Country, 1772-1880,* Havilah Press, 1972; *A Climb Through History: From Caliente to Mount Whitney in 1889,* Havilah Press, 1973; *Kern County Wayfarers, 1844-1881,* Kern County Historical Society, 1977. Contributor to *Encyclopaedia Britannica* and to history journals.

WORK IN PROGRESS: Continuing research on the history of Kern County, Calif., and on the history of stagecoaching in the San Joaquin Valley.

SIDELIGHTS: Boyd writes: "My interest in California local history began while I was a graduate student and part-time employee of the Bancroft Library at the University of California, Berkeley. My research in Kern County history began when I became a member of the history faculty at Bakersfield College. This interest has continued into my retirement years."

* * *

BOYER, Richard Lewis 1943-

PERSONAL: Born October 13, 1943, in Evanston, Ill.; son of Paul Frederick (an attorney) and Betty (Hatton) Boyer; married Elaine Smudsky, June 29, 1968; children: Clayton Paul, Thomas Edwards. *Education:* Denison University, B.A., 1961-65; University of Iowa, M.F.A., 1968. *Home:* 689 Bedford St., Concord, Mass. 01742. *Agent:* L. David Otte, Otte Co., 9 Park St., Boston, Mass. 02108. *Office:* College Division, Little, Brown & Co., 34 Beacon St., Boston, Mass. 02106.

CAREER: High school English teacher in Winnetka, Ill., 1968-70; Little, Brown & Co. (publishers), Boston, Mass., textbook salesman traveling throughout the Midwest, 1971-73, editor of College Division, 1973—. *Member:* American

Political Science Association, Smithsonian Society, Boston Young Men's Christian Union Athletic Club, Art Institute of Chicago (life member), Alumni Association of University of Iowa.

WRITINGS: The Giant Rat of Sumatra (novel), Warner Communications, 1976.

WORK IN PROGRESS: The Adventure of Bell Rock Light and Other Tales (tentative title), four stories that form a sequel to *The Giant Rat of Sumatra;* a partly-fictional biography of his ancestor, Meriwether Lewis; mystery-adventure stories.

SIDELIGHTS: Boyer writes that he began *The Giant Rat of Sumatra* in 1970. "From the time of its conception, it was to be a serious attempt to continue the Sherlockian saga much as Sir Arthur Conan Doyle would have written it were he still alive."

* * *

BRACE, Geoffrey (Arthur) 1930-

PERSONAL: Born February 18, 1930, in Bristol, England; son of Arthur Henry (a clerk) and Mabel (Hobbs) Brace; married Sylvia Jean Powell (a dressmaker), September 4, 1954; children: Nicholas Powell, Cynthia Nancy, Natalie Ann Mary. *Education:* Attended Sorbonne, University of Paris, 1949; University of Bristol, B.A., 1951; Royal Academy of Music (England), L.R.A.M., 1956. *Home:* White Barn, Whimple, Exeter, Devonshire EX5 2QL, England.

CAREER: Director of music at schools in London, England, 1954-59, Cambridge, England, 1960-63, and Dorset, England, 1963-70; King's School, Ottery St. Mary, England, director of music, 1972—. Director of Mikrokosm (a youth singing group.) *Military service:* Royal Navy, Russian interpreter, 1951-53; became sub-lieutenant. *Member:* Incorporated Society of Musicians, English Folk Dance and Song Society, Sing for Pleasure.

WRITINGS: Something to Sing, four volumes, Cambridge University Press, 1963-68; *The Story of Music,* Ladybird Books, 1965; *Something to Play,* Cambridge University Press, 1965; *Something to Sing at Assembly,* Cambridge University Press, 1965; *Thirty-Five Songs from Thirty-Five Countries,* Cambridge University Press, 1970; *Music and Nature,* Cambridge University Press, 1976; *Music and You,* Cambridge University Press, 1977; *Music and Civilization,* Cambridge University Press, 1977; *Music and Musicians,* Cambridge University Press, 1978.

Musical plays: "A Young Man's Fancy," first produced in Gillingham, England, at Gillingham School, July 11, 1972; "Aucassin and Nicolette," first produced in Ottery St. Mary, England, at King's School, July 10, 1975; "Patelin," first produced in Ottery St. Mary, at King's School, April 1, 1976. Contributor to education and music journals.

WORK IN PROGRESS: A musical drama based on the life of soprano Nancy Storace; research on music education.

SIDELIGHTS: Brace writes: "I am particularly interested in promoting a non-elitist, irreverent if necessary, and socially non-divisive attitude to all aspects of the art and craft of music, musical 'ecumenicalism' and the accent on music-*making,* enjoyment of things because they are entertaining, not because they are 'clever' or 'noble,' and working like this with children so that they may be less pompous than their parents about music."

AVOCATIONAL INTERESTS: Musical holidays in Austria, directing amateur choirs and orchestras, chamber music, playing the cello, and folk dance.

* * *

BRACE, Richard Munthe 1915-1977

August 11, 1915—June 5, 1977; American professor of history and author of books on French and Algerian history. He also contributed articles to journals in his field. Brace died in Paris, France. Obituaries: *New York Times,* June 15, 1977. (See index for previous *CA* sketch)

* * *

BRADY, Leo 1917-

PERSONAL: Born January 23, 1917, in Wheeling, W. Va.; son of Joseph T. (a bookbinder) and Nannie (Beans) Brady; married Eleanor Buchroeder, April 17, 1945; children: Brigid Brady Witkowski, Peter, Monica, Ann, Martin, Elizabeth, Daniel, Stephen. *Education:* Catholic University, A.B., 1940, M.A., 1942. *Religion:* Roman Catholic. *Home:* 3605 Dunlop St., Chevy Chase, Md. 20015. *Office:* Catholic University, Washington, D.C. 20064.

CAREER: Catholic University, Washington, D.C., 1946—, became professor of drama. *Member:* Phi Beta Kappa.

WRITINGS: Brother Orchid (play), Samuel French, 1939; *The Edge of Doom,* Dutton, 1949; *Signs and Wonders,* Dutton, 1953; *The Quiet Gun,* Curtis, 1972. Also author of film and television scripts.

WORK IN PROGRESS: A novel.

* * *

BRADY, Maxine L. 1941-

PERSONAL: Born July 22, 1941, in Brooklyn, N.Y.; daughter of Norman (a businessman) and Toby (Bronzman) Kalfus; married Frank Brady (a writer and editor), March 31, 1963. *Education:* Brooklyn College of the City University of New York, B.A., 1961; City University of New York, M.A., 1963; Northwestern University, M.A., 1968. *Politics:* Democrat. *Religion:* Jewish. *Home:* 175 West 72nd St., New York, N.Y. 10023. *Office:* Media Systems, 919 Third Ave., New York, N.Y. 10022.

CAREER: Eros (magazine), New York, N.Y., correspondent, 1961-63; elementary school teacher in New York City, 1963-65; Science Research Associates, Chicago, Ill., editor, 1965-66; A.B. Dick Co., Chicago, Ill., editor, 1966-69; Multi-Media Education, Inc., New York, N.Y., editor, 1969-70; Media Systems, Inc., New York City, senior project editor, 1973—. *Member:* New York Oratorio Society.

WRITINGS: The Assessment Cycle, Words & Pictures, Inc., 1969; *The Monopoly Book,* McKay, 1974; (with Goro Hasegawa) *The Othello Book* (English version from Japanese), Harcourt, in press.

Author of "The Truth About Drugs," an audio script for Multi-Media Education, Inc., 1970, and "Study in Black and White," a radio documentary script for British Broadcasting Corp., 1972.

SIDELIGHTS: Maxine Brady writes: "The most successful writing is that which is easy to understand and comfortable and pleasant to read. Needlessly obscure language, convoluted sentence structure, and esoteric jargon interfere with communication and can make reading a tedious, unpleasant experience. Naturally, a well-varied vocabulary and syntax will enhance a piece of writing, but the writer should never . . . use words to impress or restrict his audience."

BIOGRAPHICAL/CRITICAL SOURCES: Forbes, November 1, 1974; *New York Times,* December 4, 1974; "The Today Show," December 4, 1974; *San Francisco Chronicle,* January 15, 1975.

* * *

BRANCATO, Robin F(idler) 1936-

PERSONAL: Born March 19, 1936, in Reading, Pa.; daughter of W. Robert and Margretta (Neuroth) Fidler; married John J. Brancato (a teacher), December 17, 1960; children: Christopher Jay, Gregory Robert. *Education:* University of Pennsylvania, B.A., 1958; City College of City University of New York, M.A., 1976. *Residence:* Teaneck, N.J.

CAREER: John Wiley & Sons, New York, N.Y., copy editor, 1959-61; Hackensack High School, Hackensack, N.J., teacher of English, journalism, and creative writing, 1967—.

WRITINGS: Don't Sit Under the Apple Tree, Knopf, 1975; *Something Left to Lose,* Knopf, 1976; *Winning,* Knopf, 1977.

WORK IN PROGRESS: A young adult novel, tentatively titled *Blinded by the Light.*

* * *

BRANDON, Donald (Wayne) 1926-

PERSONAL: Born May 14, 1926, in Portland, Ore.; son of Elmer Irving (an insurance salesman) and Edna Louise (a religious worker; maiden name, Plog) Brandon; married Rosemary Vollmar (a teacher of Asian art), June 9, 1948; children: Elisabeth, Margaret, Catherine, Jennifer. *Education:* Reed College, student, 1946-48; University of California, Berkeley, B.A., 1949, M.A., 1950, Ph.D., 1954. *Politics:* Moderate Independent. *Religion:* Roman Catholic. *Home:* 524 Moraga St., San Francisco, Calif. 94122. *Office:* Department of Government, University of San Francisco, San Francisco, Calif. 94117.

CAREER: Portland Oregonian, Portland, Ore., staff writer, 1946-48; University of San Francisco, San Francisco, Calif., instructor in political science, 1953-55; Central Intelligence Agency, Washington, D.C., intelligence analyst, 1955-56; U.S. Embassy, Bonn, West Germany, cultural affairs officer, 1956-58; University of San Francisco, assistant professor, 1958-62, associate professor, 1962-66, professor of government, 1966—. *Military service:* U.S. Army, 1944-46; served in European theater; received combat infantryman badge and two battle stars. *Member:* American Political Science Association, American Council on Germany, U.S. Tennis Association, World Affairs Council of Northern California.

WRITINGS: American Foreign Policy: Beyond Utopianism and Realism, Appleton, 1966; (contributor) Kevin McEvoy, editor, *Two Kennedys,* Paulist/Newman, 1969; (contributor) Robert R. Jones and Gustave L. Seligmann, Jr., editors, *The Sweep of American History: A History in Readings,* Volume II, Wiley, 1970, 2nd edition, 1974. Contributor of about fifty articles and reviews to academic journals.

WORK IN PROGRESS: Trilateralism: Carter's Foreign Policy.

SIDELIGHTS: Brandon has traveled in Europe, Asia, and Latin America.

BRANDON, Dorothy 1899(?)-1977

1899(?)—June 15, 1977; American newspaperwoman and author. She was an award-winning reporter in New York, Pittsburgh, the western United States, and Asia. Brandon also wrote a biography of Mamie Eisenhower. She died in New York City. Obituaries: *Washington Post,* June 18, 1977.

* * *

BRANDON, James Rodger 1927-

PERSONAL: Born April 10, 1927, in St. Paul, Minn.; married, 1961; children: one. *Education:* University of Wisconsin, Madison, Ph.B., 1948, M.S., 1949, Ph.D., 1955. *Office:* Department of Drama and Theatre, University of Hawaii, Honolulu, Hawaii 96822.

CAREER: University of Connecticut, Storrs, instructor in drama and speech, 1950; U.S. Information Agency, Washington, D.C., assistant cultural attache in Djakarta, 1955-56, radio officer, 1956-57, Japanese language officer in Tokyo, 1958-59, assistant cultural attache, 1959-61; Michigan State University, East Lansing, associate professor of drama, 1961-67, professor of Asian theater, 1967-68; University of Hawaii, Honolulu, professor of theater, 1968—. *Military service:* U.S. Army; became sergeant. *Member:* Asia Society, Japan Society, American Theatre Association. *Awards, honors:* Ford Foundation research grant for Southeast Asia, 1963-64; Fulbright research grant, Japan, 1966-68; National Endowment for the Humanities senior research fellowship, 1971-72.

WRITINGS: (Editor with Tamako Niwa) *Kabuki Plays,* Samuel French, 1966; *Theatre in Southeast Asia,* Harvard University Press, 1967; (editor and author of introduction) *On Thrones of Gold: Three Javanese Shadow Plays,* Harvard University Press, 1970; (editor and author of introduction) *The Performing Arts in Asia,* UNESCO, 1971; (editor and author of introduction) *Traditional Asian Plays,* Hill & Wang, 1972; (translator) *Kabuki: Five Classic Plays,* Harvard University Press, 1975; *Brandon's Guide to Theater in Asia,* University Press of Hawaii, 1976.

* * *

BRANDT, Anthony 1936-

PERSONAL: Born November 21, 1936, in Cranford, N.J.; son of Axel E. (in railroad insurance) and Grace (Scott) Brandt; married Barbara Rescorla, June 21, 1958 (divorced, 1977); children: Katherine, Evan. *Education:* Princeton University, A.B., 1958; Columbia University, M.A., 1961. *Home:* 17 Maurice Ave., Ossining, N.Y. 10562. *Agent:* Paul R. Reynolds, Inc., 12 East 41st St., New York, N.Y. 10017.

CAREER: Fairchild Camera & Instrument, New York, N.Y., personal researcher and writer for chairman of company, 1962-71; free-lance writer, 1971—.

WRITINGS: Reality Police: The Experience of Insanity in America, Morrow, 1975. Contributor of articles and poems to magazines, including *Soundings, Atlantic Monthly, Prairie Schooner,* and *New York Quarterly.*

WORK IN PROGRESS: A book about the American dream, which "will attempt to define the dream and trace its origins and development."

SIDELIGHTS: Brandt writes: "My interest is in uncovering the hidden myths, the unconscious fantasies and unquestioned assumptions, the characteristic fears, obsessions, and desires which determine our behavior, our attitudes, our systems of belief. My first book was devoted to the attitudes, and their underlying assumptions, which support the mental health system; my second will explore those peculiarly American fantasies and myths which make American culture what it is."

* * *

BRANDTS, Robert (Percival) 1930-

PERSONAL: Born September 1, 1930, in Orange City, Iowa; son of Percy K. and Kathryn (a pianist; maiden name, Brower) Brandts; married Lois Rasner (a teacher), February 6, 1954; children: Dirk Robert, Daren Anne. *Education:* California State University, Long Beach, A.B., 1957, M.A., 1963. *Politics:* "Non-voter." *Religion:* "Poetry—cello." *Home:* 43 San Marcos Trout Club, Santa Barbara, Calif. 93105. *Office:* English Department, 5892 Hollister, Goleta, Calif. 93017.

CAREER: Life guard in Long Beach, Calif., 1954-64; Ministry of Education, Nairobi, Kenya, education officer, 1964-66; University of Colorado, Boulder, instructor in English, 1966-68; University of California, Santa Barbara, lecturer in English, 1968-76; English Department (tavern), Goleta, Calif., owner and bartender, 1976—. *Military service:* U.S. Army, 1951-52.

WRITINGS: As We Drifted (poems), Christopher Books, 1972; *Dear 732:* (epistolary narrative), Christopher Books, 1976. Contributor to literary journals, including *Ohio Review* and *Spectrum.*

WORK IN PROGRESS: Back to Square One, a study in Biblical genealogies, with Pat Carlin; a novel, "a mythical summary of ten years' life guard service on the Dream Coast."

SIDELIGHTS: Brandts writes: "Like rabies, literacy is incurable; therefore, I've learned to live with my infection by occasional bleedings—a poem, a short story, an essay, every once in a while seems to do the trick. If the blood's red, I know I'm still alive.

"Writing now seems to have evolved into my taking inventory of the past, then tempering the bits and pieces into a form that provides a reader with a pretty damn good hint of what I think about things. I avoid the sleeping bag scenes probably because I don't try to make a dime from writing. A working wife plus the income from a beer and wine saloon (The English Department . . .) make me independently wealthy."

AVOCATIONAL INTERESTS: Wandering, loafing, playing basketball.

BIOGRAPHICAL/CRITICAL SOURCES: Santa Barbara News and Review, October 10, 1975.

* * *

BRANT, Irving (Newton) 1885-1976

January 17, 1885—September 18, 1976; American newspaperman turned historian and author of books in his field, best known for his six-volume biography of President James Madison. He was a frequent contributor to newspapers on constitutional law and American history. Brand died in Eugene, Ore. Obituaries: *New York Times,* September 20, 1976; *Washington Post,* September 21, 1976. (See index for previous *CA* sketch)

* * *

BRASHER, Thomas L(owber) 1912-

PERSONAL: Surname is pronounced *Bray*-zer; born December 16, 1912, in Roswell, N.M.; son of Marcellus Hampton (an educator) and Lula (Snow) Brasher; married Christine Guzzino, July 12, 1947; children: Mark. *Education:* Student at Texas A & M University, 1930-31, and University of Texas, 1932-33; Hardin-Simmons University, B.A., 1949, M.A., 1951; Louisiana State University, Ph.D., 1956. *Politics:* "Moderately Liberal." *Religion:* "Skeptic." *Home:* 1408 Highland Dr., San Marcos, Tex. 78666. *Office:* Department of English, Southwest Texas State University, San Marcos, Tex. 78666.

CAREER: Owner of a private business in Abilene, Tex., 1934-42, 1946-48; commercial credit investigator in Abilene, 1949-52; Louisiana State University, Baton Rouge, part-time instructor in English, 1952-56; Southwest Texas State University, San Marcos, assistant professor, 1956-57, associate professor, 1958-61, professor of English, 1962—. Part-time instructor at Hardin-Simmons University, 1949-52. *Military service:* U.S. Army Air Corps, Air Intelligence, 1942-46; became first lieutenant. *Member:* South Central Modern Language Association, Texas Association of College Teachers. *Awards, honors:* Named Minnie Stevens Piper Professor by Minnie Stevens Piper Foundation, 1970.

WRITINGS: (Editor) *Collected Writings of Walt Whitman: The Early Poems and the Fiction,* New York University Press, 1963; *Whitman As Editor of the Brooklyn Daily Eagle,* Wayne State University Press, 1970. Contributor of articles and reviews to literary journals. Member of editorial board of *Studies in American Humor.*

WORK IN PROGRESS: "Trying to find a suitable approach to present experiences of several months in an alcoholic treatment center; the purpose is to debunk the prevailing distorted idea held by 'straight' people about alcoholics and alcoholism and treatment centers—that alcoholics are skidrow bums deficient in all humanly sensitive virtues."

SIDELIGHTS: Brasher writes: "My writings are simply an over-flow from my teaching. I try to persuade my students to enter into divergent life-philosophies with open and sympathetic minds and with a healthy skepticism. My three favorite graduate courses are Walt Whitman (the complete optimist aware of the other side of the coin—St. Walt to some of my students), Herman Melville (the complete pessimist), and Emily Dickinson (the complete skeptic)."

AVOCATIONAL INTERESTS: Gardening, "murdering snails," "rereading *A La Recherche.*"

*   *   *

BRAUN, Arthur E. 1876-1976

November 23, 1876—December 5, 1976; American banker and publishing executive. Braun had been the publisher of two newspapers and the president of several companies. He was also noted for his philanthropic efforts; in 1950 he was given Greece's highest civilian award for his services to the Greek War Relief Society. He died in Pittsburgh, Pa. Obituaries: *New York Times,* December 6, 1976.

*   *   *

BRAVERMAN, Harry 1920-1976

December 9, 1920—August 2, 1976; American publishing director (Monthly Review Press), founder of *American Socialist* and its co-editor (1954-60), and author of works on economic issues from a Marxist perspective. For his 1974 book *Labor and Monopoly Capital* he received the C. Wright Mills award from the Society for the Study of Social Problems. Braverman's early career included work as a coppersmith and as a master mechanic. He died in Honesdale, Pa. Obituaries: *New York Times,* August 5, 1976; *Publishers Weekly,* September 6, 1976. (See index for previous *CA* sketch)

*   *   *

BRECHER, Jeremy 1946-

PERSONAL: Born March 8, 1946, in Washington, D.C.; son of Edward M. (a writer) and Ruth (a writer; maiden name, Cook) Brecher. *Education:* Attended Reed College, 1963-65; attended Institute for Policy Studies, 1965-68; Union Graduate School, Yellow Springs, Ohio, Ph.D., 1975. *Residence:* West Cornwall, Conn. *Agent:* Mary Yost Associates, 141 East 55th St., New York, N.Y. 10022.

CAREER: Staff assistant to Representative Robert Kastenmeier in Washington, D.C., 1966; Friends Committee on National Legislation, Washington, D.C., member of staff, 1966-67; Council of Churches of Greater Washington, Washington, D.C., member of urban staff, 1968; Institute for Policy Studies, Washington, D.C., associate fellow, 1969-70; Yale University, New Haven, Conn., visiting lecturer in American studies and guest fellow, 1976-77; Institute for Labor Education and Research, New York City, member of staff, 1977; writer, 1977—. *Member:* Work Relations Group.

WRITINGS: Strike!, Straight Arrow Books, 1972; (editor with Rick Burns, Elizabeth Long, Paul Mattick, Jr., and Peter Rachleff) *Root and Branch,* Fawcett, 1975; (with Tim Costello) *Common Sense for Hard Times,* Two Continents Publishing, 1976; (wiht Leon and Shirley Zussman) *A Guidebook to Sexual Enrichment,* Morrow, in press. Contributor to journals. Former editor of *Inter/Change;* associate editor of *Radical America;* advisory editor of *Talking Back.*

WORK IN PROGRESS: Common Preservation; Rank and File on Strike, with Tim Costello.

SIDELIGHTS: Common Sense for Hard Times has been well-received as an analysis of modern times, written in a popular, rather than scholarly style. It is based on hundreds of interviews with all kinds of working people.

*   *   *

BREGER, Louis 1935-

PERSONAL: Born November 20, 1935, in Los Angeles, Calif.; son of Leo I. (a social worker) and Lillian (a nursery school teacher) Breger; married Gail Heller (a teacher), January 27, 1957; children: Lisa, Samuel, Josie. *Education:* University of California, Los Angeles, B.A., 1957; Ohio State University, M.A., 1959, Ph.D., 1961. *Office:* Division of Humanities and Social Sciences, California Institute of Technology, Pasadena, Calif. 91125.

CAREER: University of Oregon, Eugene, assistant professor of psychology, 1961-66; Langley Porter Neuropsychiatric Institute, San Francisco, Calif., staff psychologist, 1966-70; California Institute of Technology, Pasadena, associate professor of psychology, 1970—. Psychoanalyst in Los Angeles, Calif. *Member:* American Psychological Association, Association for the Psychophysiological Study of Sleep, American Academy of Psychoanalysis, Southern California Psychoanalytic Institute.

WRITINGS: (Editor) *Clinical-Cognitive Psychology,* Prentice-Hall, 1969; (with Ronald W. Lane and Ian Hunter) *The Effect of Stress on Dreams,* International University

Press, 1971; *From Instinct to Identity: The Development of Personality,* Prentice-Hall, 1974. Contributor to psychology journals.

WORK IN PROGRESS: The Nature of Human Nature, completion expected in 1979.

* * *

BREHM, Shirley A(lice) 1926-

PERSONAL: Born July 30, 1926, in Flint, Mich.; daughter of Frank F. (a farmer) and Margaret (a teacher; maiden name, Schmidt) Brehm. *Education:* Michigan State University, B.A., 1948, M.A., 1955, Ph.D., 1964. *Residence:* East Lansing, Mich. *Office:* Department of Elementary and Special Education, Michigan State University, 358 Erickson Hall, East Lansing, Mich. 48824.

CAREER: Teacher in public elementary schools, Alma, Mich., 1948-49; Michigan Department of Natural Resources, East Lansing, conservation education consultant, 1950-52; Michigan Capitol Area Girl Scout Council, district advisor, 1952-53; Michigan State University, East Lansing, instructor in elementary education, 1953-56; elementary school teacher, Battle Creek, Mich., 1956-58, Ann Arbor, Mich., 1958-59; Michigan State University, East Lansing, instructor, 1959-64, assistant professor, 1964-68, associate professor, 1968-72, professor of elementary education and science, 1972—. Vice-president and member of board, Michigan Capitol Area Girl Scout Council, 1973-76. *Member:* National Science Teachers Association, Central Association of Science and Mathematics Teachers, Council of Elementary Science Instructors, Phi Kappa Phi, Phi Delta Kappa, Kappa Delta Pi.

WRITINGS: Teacher's Handbook for Study Outside the Classroom, Merrill, 1969. (Contributor) William Matthews, editor, *Helping Children Understand Earth-Space Science,* National Science Teachers Association, 1971; (contributor) Edward Victor and Marjorie J. Lerner, editors, *Readings in Science Education for the Elementary School,* Macmillan, 1971. Contributor to *Science and Children* and *School Science and Math.*

* * *

BRENNER, Erma 1911-

PERSONAL: Born November 1, 1911, in New York, N.Y.; daughter of Robert (a salesman) and Amy (Schoenbrunn) Brandt; married Charles Brenner (a psychoanalyst and writer), September, 1935; children: Elsa Brenner Cohen, Lucy Brenner Biven. *Education:* Attended Harvard University, 1930-34. *Politics:* Liberal. *Religion:* None. *Home:* 30 Rugby Lane, Scarsdale, N.Y. 10583. *Agent:* Maximilian Becker, 115 East 82nd St., New York, N.Y. 10028. *Office:* 35 East 85th St., New York, N.Y. 10028.

CAREER: Piano teacher; owner of a girls' camp in Bridgton, Maine, 1933-40; Children's Center, Roxbury, Mass., in training as child therapist, 1942-44; nursery school teacher in Crestwood, N.Y., 1948-51; White Plains Day Care, White Plains, N.Y., therapist, 1977; Einstein College of Medicine, New York, N.Y., member of department of child psychiatry, 1977—. Guest on television and radio programs. *Awards, honors:* Christopher Award from the Catholic Church, for *A New Baby!: A New Life.*

WRITINGS: A New Baby!: A New Life, McGraw, 1973. Contributor to local newspapers.

WORK IN PROGRESS: Lovers and Fathers, nonfiction; *Echoes,* a novel.

SIDELIGHTS: Erma Brenner writes: "My chief interest is children. I know them well, and have worked successfully on all levels with them. McGraw-Hill was prompted to have me write a psychological book on the first year of life for undereducated parents in a fourth grade vocabulary. It was to include the physiological aspects of the first year as well as the psychological. This has been a very successful book, unfortunately not put to its full use as it had been intended."

* * *

BRENTON, Howard 1942-

PERSONAL: Born December 13, 1942, in Portsmouth, England; son of Donald Henry and Rose Lilian (Lewis) Brenton; married Jane Margaret Fry, January 31, 1970; children: Samuel John. *Education:* St. Catherine's College, Cambridge, B.A. (honors), 1965. *Agent:* Margaret Ramsey, 14A Goodwin's Court, St. Martin's Lane, London WC2, England.

CAREER: Has worked as stage manager for various repertory companies in England. Royal Court Theatre, London, England, resident dramatist, 1972—. Performed as an actor with Brighton Combination, 1969. *Awards, honors:* Bursary awards from Arts Council of Great Britain, 1971, for "Christie in Love."

WRITINGS—Poetry: Notes from a Psychotic Journal and Other Poems, privately printed, 1969.

Plays: *Revenge* (first produced in West End at Royal Court Theatre Upstairs, 1969), Eyre Methuen, 1969; *Christie in Love and Other Plays,* includes "Christie in Love" (produced in West End at Royal Court Theatre Upstairs, March 10, 1970), "Heads," and "The Education of Skinny Spew," Methuen, 1970; *Plays for Public Places,* Eyre Methuen, 1972; *Magnificence* (first produced in West End at Royal Court Theatre, 1973), Methuen, 1973; (with David Hare) *Brassneck* (first produced in Nottingham, England at Nottingham Playhouse), Methuen, 1974; *The Churchill Play,* Methuen, 1974; *Weapons of Happiness* (first produced in London), Methuen, 1976.

Unpublished plays: "Ladder of Fools," first produced in Cambridge, England, 1965; "Winter, Daddykins," first produced in Dublin, Ireland, 1965; "It's My Criminal," first produced in London, 1966; "Gargantua," first produced in Brighton, England, 1969; "Fruit," first produced in London at Royal Court Theatre Upstairs, 1970; "A Sky-Blue Life" (adaptations of stories by Gorky), first produced in London at Open Space Theatre, 1971; "Lay By," first produced in Edinburgh, Scotland, 1971; "How Beautiful with Badges," first produced in London at Open Space Theatre, 1972; "Hitler Dances," first produced in London at Traverse Theatre Workshop, 1972; "Measure for Measure" (adaptation from Shakespeare), first produced in Exeter, England, 1972; (co-author) "England's Ireland," first produced in Amsterdam, Netherlands, 1972; (with David Edgar) "A Fart for Europe," first produced in London, 1972; "The Screens" (adaptation from Genet), first produced in Bristol, England, 1973.

Television Plays: "Lushly," 1971; "The Saliva Milkshake," 1975; "The Paradise Run," 1976. Author of screenplay "Skin Flicker," based on a book by Tony Bicat, for British Film Institute, 1973.

WORK IN PROGRESS: Another play.

BIOGRAPHICAL/CRITICAL SOURCES: Plays and Players, February, 1972.

BRESLAU, Alan Jeffry 1926-

PERSONAL: Born March 18, 1926, in New York, N.Y.; son of Louis Stanley (an attorney) and Julia (a bookkeeper; maiden name, Rosenberg) Breslau; married Grace Tauscher (a speech therapist), June 18, 1950; children: Leigh Stanton, Cory Archer, Tod David. *Education:* Attended Juilliard School, 1943-44, Amherst College, 1944, and Sampson College, 1946-47; New York University, B.Ch.E., 1950; Columbia University, M.S.Ch.E., 1954; further graduate study at Polytechnic Institute of Brooklyn (now of New York). *Home:* 11 Rust Hill Rd., Levittown, Pa. 19056. *Agent:* Julian Bach Literary Agency, Inc., 3 East 48th St., New York, N.Y. 10017. *Office:* A. J. Breslau Associates, Rust Hill Rd., Levittown, Pa. 19056.

CAREER: Essex Rubber Co. (rubber reclaimers), Trenton, N.J., plant manager, 1950-51; Thiokol Chemical Corp. (plastics machinery manufacturers), Philadelphia, Pa., technical director, 1959-61; Rico Internationale Ltd. (plastics molders), New York City, technical director in New York City and Hong Kong, 1961-63; A. J. Breslau Associates (plastics consultants), Levittown, Pa., president, 1963—. Instructor at Philadelphia College of Textiles and Science, 1959-67, at Rider College, 1965-67, and at Bucks County Technical School, 1975—. Member of board of directors and vice-president of Valley Day School for Emotionally Disturbed Children; member of board of trustees of Burlington College. President of Parent-Faculty Association of St. Mary's Hall, Doane Academy; chairman of Middletown Township Arts and Culture Commission; member of Middletown Democratic Association. *Military service:* U.S. Army, 1944-46; served in European theater. *Member:* Society of Plastics Engineers (president of Delaware Valley section, 1967—), American Chemical Society (senior member), American Society for Testing and Materials, Phi Lambda Upsilon. *Awards, honors:* First Prize for fine art from engineering art show at New York University, 1950; first prize in Paul Masson design contest, 1964; award from Society of Plastics Engineers, 1973.

WRITINGS: (Contributor) Clayton May and Yoshio Tanaka, editors, *Epoxy Resins: Chemistry and Technology,* Dekker, 1973; *The Time of My Death* (autobiographical), Dutton, 1977. Contributor to professional and technical journals. Editor of *Spectator* (of Society of Plastics Engineers), *Alembic,* and *Quadrangle.* Member of editorial advisory board of *Journal of Elastomers and Plastics.*

WORK IN PROGRESS: The Collins Avenue Gang, an ethnic mystery; a historical novel about the Mamelukes.

SIDELIGHTS: Breslau writes: "In 1963 I was the victim of a commercial plane crash that destroyed my face and hand, leaving me severely disfigured. This is the story in my recent book *The Time of My Death.* In spite of my disfigurement and disability, I am totally unhindered. I play a fair game of tennis and have not lost my touch at the piano."

AVOCATIONAL INTERESTS: Chess.

BIOGRAPHICAL/CRITICAL SOURCES: Rochester Times, March 2, 1977, April 10, 1977, April 11, 1977; *Brighton-Pittsford Post,* March 10, 1977; *Bucks County Courier Times,* March 13, 1977; *Trenton Times Advertiser,* March 13, 1977; *Irondequit Press,* March 17, 1977; *Rochester Democrat & Chronicle,* April 7, 1977, April 10, 1977.

* * *

BRETT, Simon (Anthony Lee) 1945-

PERSONAL: Born October 28, 1945, in Surrey, England; son of John (a surveyor) and Margaret (a school teacher; maiden name, Lee) Brett; married Lucy Victoria McLaren, November 27, 1971; children: Sophie Victoria Margaret McLaren. *Education:* Wadham College, Oxford, B.A. (first class honors), 1967. *Politics:* None. *Religion:* "Some." *Home:* 7 Graemesdyke Ave., London SW14 7BH, England. *Agent:* Michael Motley, 78 Gloucester Ter., London W.2, England. *Office:* British Broadcasting Corp., London W1A 1AA, England.

CAREER: British Broadcasting Corp., London, England, radio producer of light entertainment, 1968—. *Awards, honors:* Award from Writer's Guild, 1973, for best radio feature script.

WRITINGS—The Charles Paris series; suspense novels: *Cast, in Order of Disappearance,* Gollancz, 1975, Scribner, 1976; *So Much Blood,* Gollancz, 1976, Scribner, 1977; *Star Trap,* Gollancz, 1977, Scribner, in press.

WORK IN PROGRESS: Another suspense novel in the "Charles Paris" series; a stage play; "a pseudonymous romp."

SIDELIGHTS: Brett writes briefly: "I write to entertain."

* * *

BRIDGE, Raymond 1943-

PERSONAL: Born February 5, 1943, in Princeton, N.J.; son of Herbert Sage (a physicist) and Jeanne (Hall) Bridge; married Madeleyne Claire DeSimone (an office manager), March 17, 1961; children: Diane Michelle, Cynthia Jeanne. *Education:* Attended California Institute of Technology, 1959-62, and University of California, 1963-65. *Politics:* "Civil libertarian-conservationist-populist." *Home and office:* 435 South 38th St., Boulder, Colo. 80303.

CAREER: KPFA-FM RAdio, Berkeley, Calif., non-commercial radio journalist, 1964-69; writer, 1973—. Director of Boulder Mountaineering School, 1974-76; has also worked as a photographer and as a political campaign manager.

MEMBER: Authors Guild of Authors League of America, Sierra Club (member of Indian Peaks group executive committee, 1973-75), American Canoe Association, American Whitewater Affiliation, Colorado Mountain Club (member of Boulder group executive council, 1974-76), Colorado Open Space Council (member of board of directors, 1975-76), Colorado Whitewater Association.

WRITINGS: The Complete Snow Camper's Guide, Scribner, 1973; *America's Backpacking Book,* Scribner, 1973; *Freewheeling: The Bicycle Camping Book,* Stackpole, 1974; *Tourguide to the Rocky Mountain Wilderness,* Stackpole, 1975; *The Camper's Guide to Alaska, the Yukon, and Northern British Columbia,* Scribner, 1976; *Climbing: A Guide to Mountaineering,* Scribner, 1976. Contributor of stories and articles on the outdoors, conservation, and politics to magazines.

WORK IN PROGRESS: Books on kayaking, canoeing, and running; research for books on the Alaska pipeline, the history of mountaineering, and the relation of memory patterns to thought processes.

SIDELIGHTS: Bridge writes: "I am an active climber, kayaker, canoeist, and runner, and in my outdoor books I try to reflect personal experience and to communicate my strong conservationist position. I have led and participated in mountaineering expeditions, and I am particularly fond of the wilderness regions of northwestern Canada and Alaska. I believe that it is man's and woman's responsibility to husband the resources of the race and of the Earth, rather than unthinkingly exploiting them for the gain of a few, and to the detriment of the less fortunate, of future generations, and of other species of life.''

AVOCATIONAL INTERESTS: History, philosophy.

* * *

BRIGGS, Berta N. 1884(?)-1976

1884(?)—November 12, 1976; American artist and author. She began painting in 1928 and her works were shown all over the United States and in London. Briggs wrote two books. She died in New York City. Obituaries: New York Times, November 16, 1976.

* * *

BRIGGS, Walter Ladd 1919-

PERSONAL: Born May 9, 1919, in Dale, Ind.; son of Walter Merrill (a clergyman) and Anita (Ladd) Briggs; married Margaret Liang, June 6, 1948; married Antoinette Ho (a librarian), November 26, 1976; children: (first marriage) Mark Barut. Education: Attended University of Chicago, 1937-40. Politics: Independent. Home: 4546 North Teilman, Fresno, Calif. 93705. Agent: Ann Buchwald, 4327 Hawthorne St., Washington, D.C. 20016.

CAREER: United Press, correspondent from the Far East in New Delhi, India, 1940-43; Christian Science Monitor, special correspondent from the Far East in Hong Kong, 1947-49; New York Herald Tribune, New York City, foreign correspondent from the Far East, 1950-60; worked for National Broadcasting Co. (NBC), New York City, 1963-65; Arizona Republic, Phoenix, foreign correspondent, 1966-67; New Mexico, Santa Fe, editor, 1968-74; writer, 1974—. Military service: U.S. Marine Corps, 1944-45; became sergeant; received Purple Heart. Member: Regional Publishers Association.

WRITINGS: Without Noise of Arms, Northland Press, 1976.

* * *

BRIGHT, Richard (Eugene) 1931-

PERSONAL: Born July 14, 1931, in Gonzales, Tex.; son of William Joe (a surveyor) and Tillie Mae (McGill) Bright; married Flora Stryker, September 14, 1957 (died February 1, 1971); married Jean Stapleton (a professor of journalism), January 13, 1973; children: Lynn Denise, Paul Eugene. Education: University of Texas, B.A., 1953; Southern Methodist University, Th.M., 1957; Azusa Pacific College, further graduate study, 1973-74. Politics: Democrat. Home and office: 3232 Philo St., Los Angeles, Calif. 90064.

CAREER: Boys club leader in Nashville, Tenn., 1953-54; ordained United Methodist minister, 1956; associate pastor of United Methodist church in San Antonio, Tex., 1957-58; campus minister at North Texas State University, Denton, 1958-62, and University of New Mexico, Albuquerque, 1962-63; private practice as marriage, family, and child counselor in Los Angeles, Calif., 1964—. Former chairman of education department of New Mexico Interchurch Agency. Member: National Organization for Women (member of coordinating council), California Association of Marriage, Family and Child Counselors.

WRITINGS: (With wife, Jean Stapleton) Equal Marriage, Abingdon, 1976. Contributor to Eighteen Almanac and Christian Home.

SIDELIGHTS: Bright comments: ''Of special overall interest to me is the bridging of the gap between the teachings of the Judeao-Christian religious tradition and the behavioral sciences.''

* * *

BRINES, Russell (Dean) 1911-

PERSONAL: Born March 13, 1911, in Denver, Colo.; son of Curry (a sales manager) and Edna Dean (Brainard) Brines; married Barbara Borey (an artist), July 29, 1939; children: Coralie Ann (Mrs. Frederick Mayer). Education: Pomona College, B.A., 1932; graduate study at Claremont College, 1932-33. Politics: Independent. Home: 4518 North Glebe Rd., Arlington, Va. 22207. Agent: Collins-Knowlton-Wing, Inc., 575 Madison Ave., New York, N.Y. 10022.

CAREER: Reporter and correspondent for various newspapers in southern California, 1926-33; social service visitor in Pomona, Calif., 1933-34; Honolulu Star-Bulletin, Honolulu, Hawaii, reporter and columnist, 1934-35; Associated Press, correspondent in the Pacific and Japan, 1935-41, war correspondent in Pacific theatre of operations, 1941-45, chief of bureau in Japan and Korea, 1946-51, war correspondent in Korea, 1950-51, Washington correspondent, 1951-55; Copley News Service, San Diego, Calif., founder, editor, and columnist, 1955-60; International Press, Washington, D.C., editor and columnist, 1960—. Notable assignments include the search for Amelia Earhart, interviews with most of the Japanese leaders tried as war criminals, MacArthur and his dismissal during the Korean War, Nixon's near assassination in Caracas, Khrushchev's tour of the United States, the Indo-Pakistani War, and the Vietnam War, periodically, 1949-72. Lecturer, 1944—. Member: National Press Club, Overseas Writers, State Department Correspondents' Association. Awards, honors: Pulitzer Prize nomination for international reporting, 1945, for series on U.S. landing in Japan and Japanese account of war.

WRITINGS: Until They Eat Stones, Lippincott, 1944; MacArthur's Japan, Lippincott, 1948; (with William J. Sebald) With MacArthur in Japan, Norton, 1965; The Indo-Pakistani Conflict, Pall Mall, 1968.

SIDELIGHTS: Brines said: ''My work has been based on the conviction that journalism is a profession, a very demanding one, and that the reporter is obligated to acquire the maximum possible professional expertise to practice it. This means, particularly in foreign-war or Washington correspondence, that the journalist should prepare himself by study and experience to provide on his own responsibility the balanced judgment necessary to untangle most major stories. His responsibility to his readers, as I see it, is to make it possible for them to see the world more clearly and more realistically, so that the judgments they may have to make, either tacitly or directly, will be as soundly based as possible.

''The lack of expertise, for example, was an important factor behind some of the quite obvious mis-reporting from Vietnam. A great many of the most influential correspondents did not have, or did not use, enough knowledge of Asia or of communism or of military affairs to put the conflict into proper perspective for an American public that desperately wanted solid reporting.

''In short, the old bromide, that every reporter can cover any story, no longer is valid, if it ever was, in complicated stories. The need for expertise, outside of the sports press box and politics, is certain to grow. I anticipate and would welcome the time when journalists are regarded as professionals, required to perform as professionals—and paid accordingly.

"But I believe also that the tensions of the past decade require a complete review of the principles on which the news business is based. In particular, we need a formula to write 'good' and constructive news stories—and to see them printed. Reality has outmoded the validity of a news judgment based on the thesis that only conflict makes news; this is not only untrue, but it has been seriously manipulated over the years. My professional would have the authority and the competence to expose manipulation, regardless of its source. He also would be authorized to resist competitive pressures to match the opposition or the prevailing current of the news, if his background and his legwork convinced him otherwise.

"These conclusions and others like them were reached long ago in the heat of wire service competition.

"In all, I have reported from eighty countries, many of them often, and I travel regularly. I speak Japanese; speak and read French and Spanish."

During Brines' wartime reporting he was captured and held for two years, first in Manila and then in Shanghai, by the Japanese. He received three ribbons with six battle stars and was given the simulated rank of full colonel.

AVOCATIONAL INTERESTS: "World-watching is so fascinating that it dominates my time and much of my reading. But I am devoted also to good theatre, good music, mystery and adventure fiction, and all sports. I count an occasional fling into sports-writing as a recreational activity. I am an enthusiastically incompetent golfer—but I can still body surf."

* * *

BROADBENT, W. W. 1919-

PERSONAL: Born April 29, 1919, in Niagara Falls, N.Y.; son of Wilfred (a businessman) and Minerva (a seamstress; maiden name, Warren) Broadbent; married Lillian Grasso, March 10, 1946; children: Mark, Melody (Mrs. Stephen McCutcheon). *Education:* Niagara University, B.A., 1941; University of California, Long Beach, B.S., 1956; Loma Linda University, M.D., 1961. *Home:* 4517 Whitewood, Long Beach, Calif. 90808. *Agent:* Donald Shepherd, 1680 Vine St., Hollywood, Calif. 90028. *Office:* Broadbent Medical Psychiatric Clinic, 3740 Long Beach Blvd., Long Beach, Calif. 90807.

CAREER: President of Broadbent Advertising Agency, 1947-52, and Broadbent Investment Corp., 1953-57; University of Southern California, Medical Center, Los Angeles, psychiatric resident, 1961-65, assistant director of psychosomatic department and assistant clinical professor of psychiatry, 1966—, member of attending staff, training psychiatrists, 1968—. Director of Broadbent Medical Psychiatric Clinic, 1968—. Former violinist with Niagara Falls and Buffalo Symphony Orchestras. *Military service:* U.S. Army, French interpreter and instructor in French, 1942-45; became technical sergeant. *Member:* American Psychiatric Association, Southern California Psychiatric Society.

WRITINGS: How to Be Loved, Prentice-Hall, 1976.

WORK IN PROGRESS: Your Words Can Attack You; Belonging, completion expected about 1978; general research on semantics, philosophy, and psychiatry.

SIDELIGHTS: Broadbent writes: "My conviction is that belonging, the drive to be a 'part' of another, is an instinctual phenomenon activated early in life.... The intent of the book is to introduce the reader to some of his own ineffective ways of trying to belong and provide him with some solid principles and techniques whereby he can do something about it. The book is a melding of eastern thinking and western ingenuity—a 'doing something about it.' It encapsulates my interest in linguistics, specifically general semantics, religion and sociology—all courses, incidentally, which at this writing are not required curriculum for the practice of psychiatry but which, I believe, with the advances that are being made today will eventually become required."

* * *

BROCE, Thomas Edward 1935-

PERSONAL: Born October 27, 1935, in Fort Meade, Md.; son of Thomas Louis and Arlene Broce; married Barbara Lynn Barnes; children: Ashley Beth, Thomas Allan, David Edward. *Education:* Baylor University, B.A., 1957; University of North Carolina, M.A., 1965; University of Oklahoma, Ph.D., 1970. *Religion:* Christian Church (Disciples of Christ). *Office:* Phillips University, Enid, Okla. 73701.

CAREER: Waco Tribune-Herald, Waco, Tex., reporter, 1953-57; University of Arkansas, Little Rock, instructor in journalism and director of public relations and development, 1959-61; Duke University, Durham, N.C., director of development, 1961-67; Southern Methodist University, Dallas, Tex., vice-president, 1967-69; University of Oklahoma, Norman, lecturer in higher education and executive assistant to the president, 1970-73; Phillips University, Enid, Okla., president, 1973-76, chairman of board of trustees, 1976—. Lecturer for American Academy of Fund Raising Sciences (Institutes on Foundations and Capital Campaigns), 1969—. Lecturer and director of Institute for Resource Development for College and University Administrators, 1972—; chairman of board of directors of Baylor University Journalism Alumni Advisory Board, 1972-75; member of board of trustees of Foundation for Research on the Nature of Man; member of board of governors of Philanthropic Management Institute at Nova University, 1976—. Member of board of trustees of Fellowship of Christian Athletes, 1970—; member of Christian Church Foundation, 1976—. *Military service:* U.S. Air Force, 1957-59; became first lieutenant. U.S. Air Force Reserve, 1958-69 (liaison officer for U.S. Air Force Academy); became captain.

MEMBER: Council for the Advancement and Support of Education, All Sports Association, Urban Coalition (member of financial council, 1969—), Pith Helmet Society, Oklahoma Heritage Association, Oklahoma City Petroleum Club, Oklahoma City Men's Dinner Club, Rotary International, Phi Delta Kappa, Sigma Delta Chi.

WRITINGS: Directory of Oklahoma Foundations, University of Oklahoma Press, 1973; *Fund Raising,* University of Oklahoma Press, 1978. Contributor to *Handbook of College and University Administration* and to academic journals.

AVOCATIONAL INTERESTS: Golf, tennis, flying (licensed private pilot), reading.

* * *

BROER, Lawrence R(ichard) 1938-

PERSONAL: Original name, Lawrence Highsmith; name legally changed in 1945; born September 11, 1938, in Baltimore, Md.; son of Richard (an electrician) and Ruth (a federal employee; maiden name, Wolfrum) Highsmith; married Carmen Avila, December 28, 1963 (divorced, November, 1969); married Kris Shields (a poet), December 6, 1969; children: Joshua. *Education:* Florida State University, B.A., 1960, M.A., 1963; Bowling Green State University, Ph.D.,

1968. *Residence:* Odessa, Fla. *Office:* Department of English, University of South Florida, Tampa, Fla. 33620.

CAREER: Part-time basketball and football coach and instructor in archery for public recreation departments in St. Petersburg and Tallahassee, Fla., 1956-63; University of South Florida, Tampa, instructor, 1965-68, assistant professor, 1968-73, associate professor of English, 1973—. *Member:* Popular Culture Association, South Atlantic Modern Language Association.

WRITINGS: Counter Currents: An Introduction to Current Fiction, Kendall/Hunt, 1973; *Hemingway's Spanish Tragedy,* University of Alabama Press, 1973; (editor with Herb Karl and Charles Weingartner) *The First Time: Initial Sexual Experiences in Fiction,* Bobbs-Merrill, 1975.

Author of "The Father" (one-act play), first produced in Bowling Green, Ohio, at Bowling Green State University, November, 1964. Contributor to *Lost Generation Journal.* Book reviewer for *Tampa Tribune.*

WORK IN PROGRESS: Dancing Fools and Weary Blues: A Cultural Anthropology of the 1920's; Pilgrim's Progress: The Schizophrenic World of Kurt Vonnegut, Jr.

SIDELIGHTS: Broer writes: "The book on Hemingway culminated many years of interest in Hemingway, and of concentrated study of the twentieth century novel. The book on Vonnegut represents a focus in recent years upon trends in the contemporary American and English novel. In the last several years I have been teaching the contemporary novel."

AVOCATIONAL INTERESTS: Travel (England and France), outdoor sports (especially cross-country running), reading, "the sun and the wind."

*　　*　　*

BROOKINS, Dana   1931-

PERSONAL: Born February 22, 1931, in St. Louis, Mo.; daughter of William H. and Mildred (Wilson) Martin; married Elwood Brookins, January 15, 1949 (divorced); children: Victoria, Valerie Brookins Neilson, William, Danile. *Education:* California State College, San Bernardino, B.A., 1977. *Politics:* Independent. *Home:* 207 North Date, #A, Rialto, Calif. 92376. *Office:* Learning Center, Chaffey Community College, Alta Loma, Calif.

CAREER: Chaffey Community College, Alta Loma, Calif., instructional associate in English, 1975—. Former Little Theatre director. Has directed local political campaigns. *Member:* Society of Children's Book Writers.

WRITINGS: Rico's Cat (juvenile), Seabury, 1976.

WORK IN PROGRESS: The Aloners (tentative title), a juvenile book, for Seabury; *Hilding,* juvenile; research for *The People,* a fictionalized history of the Guachama clan of early California.

SIDELIGHTS: Dana Brookins writes: "I write because writing is a natural act for me. Also it helps me control a rather formidable imagination. A lot of children inside me are demanding recognition." She has taught Spanish to speakers of English, and English to speakers of Spanish.

*　　*　　*

BROOKS, Deems M(arkham)   1934-

PERSONAL: Born September 1, 1934, in Cleveland County, N.C.; son of Elijah B. and Virginia Marie Brooks; married Barbara King, August 27, 1956; children: Melissa, Mark. *Education:* David Lipscomb College, B.A., 1956;

Southern Illinois University, M.A., 1965, Ph.D., 1968. *Religion:* Church of Christ. *Home address:* Route 5, Box 156, Warrensburg, Mo. 64093. *Office:* School of Arts and Sciences, Central Missouri State University, Warrensburg, Mo. 64093.

CAREER: Florida State University, Tallahassee, assistant professor of communication and director of speech education, 1968-71; Central Missouri State University, Warrensburg, associate professor, 1971-76, professor of speech communication, 1977—, chairman of Division of Language, Literature, and Communication, 1973-74, assistant dean of School of Arts and Sciences, 1974—. *Military service:* U.S. Army, 1967-69. *Member:* Speech Communication Association of America, Central States Speech Association, Missouri Mental Health Association (member of board of directors; president, 1975-76), Phi Kappa Phi, Phi Delta Kappa.

WRITINGS: (Contributor) Lee Thayer, editor, *Communication: General Semantics Perspectives,* Spartan, 1970; *Speech Communication Instruction: A Reader,* McKay, 1972.

WORK IN PROGRESS: Don't Speech to Me!

*　　*　　*

BROUE, Pierre   1926-

PERSONAL: Born May 8, 1926, in France; son of Leon and Rene (Verrot) Broue; married Andree Jacquenet (a professor); children: Michel, Francoise, Catherine, Martine, Jean-Pierre. *Education:* University of Grenoble, diplome d'etudes superieures, 1952; University of Paris, Nanterre, doctorat es lettres (with high honors), 1972. *Politics:* "Militant Trotskyite." *Home:* 6 rue St. Ferjus, Grenoble, France 38000. *Office:* Institut d' Etudes Politiques, BP 17 Grenoble, France 38040.

CAREER: High school teacher of history in Nyons, Switzerland, and Beaune, Paris, and Moutereau-faut-Yonne, France, 1948-65; Institute d'Etudes Politiques, Grenoble, France, assistant historian, 1965-69; assistant master, 1969-72; lecturer, 1972—.

WRITINGS: (With Emile Temime) *La revolution et la guerre d'Espagne,* two volumes, Minuit, 1961, translation by Tony White published as *The Revolution and the Civil War in Spain,* M.I.T. Press, 1972; *Le parti bolchevique: Histoire du P.C. de l'U.R.S.S.,* Minuit, 1963, 2nd edition, 1972; *Revolution en Allemagne, 1917-1923,* Minuit, 1971; *La revolution espagnole, 1931-1939,* Flammarion, 1973.

Editor: Nikolai Ivanovich Bukharin, *ABC du communisme,* Maspero, 1963; *Les proces de Moscou: Comptes rendus du commissariat du peuple a la justice, dossiers de la revision depuis le XXe congres du P.C. de l'U.R.S.S.,* Julliard, 1964; (and author of preface) *Le question chinoise dans l'-internationale communiste, 1926-1927,* Etudes et Documentation Internationales, 1965; *Pologne-Hongrie, 1956; ou, "Le printemps en octobre,"* Etudes et Documentation Internationales, 1966; Leon Trotsky, *Le mouvement communiste en France, 1919-1939,* Minuit, 1967; (and author of preface) *Ecrits a Prague sous la censure,* Etudes et Documentation Internationales, 1973; (and author of preface) *La premier congres de l'internationale communiste,* Etudes et Documentation Internationals, 1974. Contributor to history and political science journals.

WORK IN PROGRESS: Editing the next two volumes in the history of Communist international movement, covering the periods between the first and second congresses and the period of the second congress.

BROWN, Barbara B(anker)   1917-

PERSONAL: Born November 16, 1917, in Columbus, Ohio. *Education:* Ohio State University, A.B., 1938; graduate study at Western Reserve University (now Case Western Reserve University), 1938-41; University of Cincinnati, Ph.D., 1950. *Home:* 9609 Oakpass Rd., Beverly Hills, Calif. 90210. *Office:* Veterans Administration Hospital, 16111 Plummer St., Sepulveda, Calif. 91343.

CAREER: Lab technician at Mead Johnson & Co., 1941-42; William S. Merrell Co., Cincinnati, Ohio, lab technician, 1943-53, head of division of pharmacology, 1953-57; Riker Laboratories, Inc., Northridge, Calif., research neuropharmacologist, 1957-63; Veterans Administration Hospital, Psychopharmacological Research Laboratories, Sepulveda, Calif., consulting neurophysiologist, 1963-65, chief experiential physiologist, beginning 1967; full-time writer. University of California, Center of Health Science, Los Angeles, associate clinical professor of pharmacology, 1957-62, lecturer in psychiatry, beginning 1972; University of California, Irvine, associate professor of pharmacology, beginning 1967. Visiting professor, University of California, Santa Barbara and San Diego; frequent lecturer at conferences and scientific meetings. Consultant to National Institutes of Health and to other organizations.

MEMBER: American Association for the Advancement of Science (fellow), American Society for Pharmacology and Experimental Therapeutics, Biofeedback Research Society (founder, 1969; president, beginning 1969), Society for Psychophysiological Research, Society of Biological Psychiatry, Society for Experimental Biology and Medicine. *Awards, honors:* Council for Tobacco Research fellowships from Veterans Administration Hospital, Sepulveda, 1963-65, 1967, 1969, and 1970; Licensed Beverage Industries fellow, 1968; National Institute of Mental Health fellow, 1969-70, 1972—; National Institutes of Health fellow, 1973.

WRITINGS: (Contributor) W. L. Dunn, editor, *Smoking Behavior,* V. H. Winston, 1973; *New Mind, New Body Biofeedback: New Directions for the Mind,* Harper, 1974; (editor with Jay Klug) *The Alpha Syllabus: A Handbook of Human EEG Alpha Activity,* C. C Thomas, 1974; (editor) *The Biofeedback Syllabus,* C. C Thomas, 1975; *Stress and the Art of Biofeedback,* Harper, 1976. Also author of *Mind and Supermind,* 1976. Contributor of articles to proceedings and to journals in her field.

WORK IN PROGRESS: Travels through the Mind of India.

SIDELIGHTS: Besides being responsible for the development of several pharmacological therapeutic agents, Brown has been involved in a wide variety of research activities in the field of neurophysiology and psychophysiology. Known as a creative researcher, she has many "firsts" to her credit, including demonstrating the coexistence of two etiologic mechanisms in auricular arrhythmias, and that visual recall is related to a specific type of brain electrical response during visual perception.

Brown is also a traveler and has circled the globe five times, concentrating most of her travel in India. She has had opportunities to study at leisure the philosophic and scientific influences of Indian life and thought in many areas of India. Her lifelong research in physiology and medicine led her to participation in the discovery of biofeedback. In the last few years she has developed new concepts of mind-consciousness and their relationship to mental and physical health which are being accepted. One of her major interests is fostering East-West understanding.

BROWN, F. Keith   1913(?)-1976

1913(?)—October 16, 1976; American attorney and writer of works in his field. He died in New York City. Obituaries: *New York Times,* October 19, 1976.

*   *   *

BROWN, Frank A(rthur), Jr.   1908-

PERSONAL: Born August 30, 1908, in Beverly, Mass.; son of Frank Arthur (an artist) and Arletta (Robinson) Brown; married Jennie Pettegrove (a teacher), June 24, 1934; children: Charlotte Brown Russell, Frank Arthur III, M. Diane Brown Maranchie. *Education:* Bowdoin College, A.B., 1929, Harvard University, M.A., Ph.D., 1934. *Politics:* Republican. *Religion:* Congregational. *Home:* 906 Greenleaf Ave., Wilmette, Ill. 60091. *Office:* Northwestern University, Department of Biological Sciences, Evanston, Ill. 60201.

CAREER: University of Illinois, Urbana, instructor in zoology, 1934-37; Northwestern University, Evanston, Ill., assistant professor, 1937-40, associate professor, 1940-46, professor of zoology, 1946-57, Morrison Professor of Zoology, 1957—, chairman of department of biological sciences, 1949-57. Instructor, Mt. Desert Biology Lab, 1941; Marine Biology Lab, Woods Hole, Mass., head invertebreate zoologist, 1945-49, trustee, 1946—, consultant, 1949—; chairman, Biology Advisory Panel, Office of Naval Research, 1953-58; trustee of John M. Shedd Aquarium, Chicago; corporate member and member chemical advisory panel for Bermuda Biology Lab and Mt. Desert Biology Lab. *Member:* International Society of Chronobiology, International Society of Biometeorology, American Society of Zoologists (vice-president, 1956), American Society of Naturalists (vice-president, 1956), American Association for the Advancement of Science (fellow), American Physiological Society, American Geophysical Union, Ecological Society of America, American Institute of Biological Science, American Society of Limnology and Oceanography, Society of General Physiologists (president, 1955), Animal Behavior Society (fellow), Society for Plant Physiology, Society for Developmental Biology, Society for Experimental Biology and Medicine, Illinois Academy of Science, Sigma Xi, Delta Upsilon. *Awards, honors:* Award of merit from Foundation for the Study of Cycles, 1966.

WRITINGS: (Contributing editor) *Selected Invertebrate Types,* Wiley, 1950; (with C. Prosser, D. Bishop, T. Jahn, and V. Wulff) *Comparative Animal Physiology,* Saunders, 1950, (with Prosser) revised ed., 1961; *Biological Clocks,* Heath, 1962; (with J. Hastings and J. Palmer) *The Biological Clock: Two Views,* Academic Press, 1970.

Contributor to encyclopedias, textbooks, and to journals and periodicals in his field. Member of editorial board of *Physiological Reviews, Biological Bulletin, International Journal of Chronobiology,* and *Journal of Interdisciplinary Cycle Research.*

WORK IN PROGRESS: Research on the nature of biological clocks, the response of organisms to atmospheric electromagnetic fields, and field interactions among organisms.

*   *   *

BROWN, Harrison Scott   1917-

PERSONAL: Born September 26, 1917, in Sheridan, Wyo.; son of Harrison Harvey and Agatha (Scott) Brown; married Rudd Owen, November 11, 1949; children: Eric Scott. *Education:* University of California, Berkeley, B.Sc., 1938;

Johns Hopkins University, Ph.D., 1941. *Home:* 623 East California St., Pasadena, Calif. 91106. *Office:* Division of Humanities and Social Sciences, California Institute of Technology, Pasadena, Calif. 91109.

CAREER: Johns Hopkins University, Baltimore, Md., instructor in chemistry, 1941-42; University of Chicago, Chicago, Ill., research associate in chemistry, 1942-43; Clinton Laboratories, Oak Ridge, Ill., assistant director of Chemical Division, 1943-46; University of Chicago, assistant professor, 1946-48, associate professor of chemistry at Institute for Nuclear Studies, 1948-51; California Institute of Technology, Pasadena, professor of geochemistry, 1951—, professor of science and government, 1969—. Civilian employee of U.S. Office of Scientific Research and Development, 1944. Trustee of Charles F. Kettering Foundation.

MEMBER: International Council of Scientific Unions (vice-president), National Academy of Sciences (foreign secretary, 1962—), American Geophysical Union, Geological Society of America, American Chemical Society, American Association for the Advancement of Science, Resources for the Future (member of board of trustees), Phi Beta Kappa, Sigma Xi. *Awards, honors:* Honorary degrees include LL.D. from University of Alberta, 1961, Johns Hopkins University, 1969, University of California, 1970, University of Wyoming, 1971; Sc.D. from Rutgers University, 1964, Amherst College, 1966, Cambridge University, 1969; awards from American Association for the Advancement of Science, 1947, American Chemical Society, 1952, and Lasker Foundation, 1958; Carnegie-Mellon Award from Mellon Institute, 1971.

WRITINGS: Thermal Diffusion of Gases: The Construction of a Mass Spectrometer, Lancaster Press, 1941; *Must Destruction Be Our Destiny?: A Scientist Speaks as a Citizen,* Simon & Schuster, 1946; (editor with Gunnar Kellerud and Walter Nichiporuk) *A Bibliography on Meteorites,* University of Chicago Press, 1953; *The Challenge of Man's Future: An Inquiry Concerning the Condition of Man during the Years That Lie Ahead,* Viking, 1954; (with James Bonner and John Weir) *The Next Hundred Years: Man's Natural and Technological Resources,* Viking, 1957; *The Age of the Solar System,* W. H. Freeman, 1957; *Problems of Survival,* University of Minnesota, 1958; *Requisites for Survival,* Institute of Government and Public Affairs, University of Illinois, 1958; (with James Real) *Community of Fear* (foreword by Reinhold Niebuhr), Center for the Study of Democratic Institutions, 1960; (with Bonner and Weir) *The Next Ninety Years: Man's Natural and Technological Resources,* California Institute of Technology, 1967; (with Chloe Zerwick) *The Cassiopeia Affair,* Doubleday, 1968; (editor) *Population: Perspective, 1971,* Freeman, Cooper, 1972; (editor) *Are Our Descendants Doomed?,* Viking, 1972. Also editor of *Proceedings of the Caltech-JPL Lunar and Planetary Conference, Pasadena, California, 1965,* published, 1966. Contributor to Smithsonian Institution annual reports. Editor-at-large for *Saturday Review.*

SIDELIGHTS: Brown made the phonotape "Help for the Have Nots," for American Chemical Society. *Avocational interests:* Music.

BIOGRAPHICAL/CRITICAL SOURCES: Chemical and Engineering News, February 2, 1948, April 21, 1952.

* * *

BROWN, Harry (Peter McNab) 1917-
(Artie Greengroin)

PERSONAL: Born April 30, 1917, in Portland, Maine; son of Harry McNab and Bessie (Hiles) Brown; divorced. *Education:* Harvard University, student, 1936-38. *Residence:* Hollywood, Calif.

CAREER: Copyboy for *Time* Magazine and sub-editor for *New Yorker* magazine, both before World War II; *Yank* magazine, writer in New York City, 1941-42, in London, England, 1942-44; Office of War Information, London, England, worked in Films Division, 1944-45; poet, novelist, playwright, and screenwriter, 1945—. *Military service:* U.S. Army, Corps of Engineers, member of Anglo-American Film Unit, 1941-45; served in England. *Awards, honors:* Co-winner of "Oscar" from Motion Picture Academy, 1952, for screenplay of "A Place in the Sun."

WRITINGS: The End of a Decade (poems), New Directions, 1940; *The Poem of Bunker Hill,* Scribner, 1941; *The Violent: New Poems,* New Directions, 1943; *A Walk in the Sun* (novel), Knopf, 1944; *Artie Greengroin, P.F.C.* (stories originally published in *Yank,* under pseudonym Artie Greengroin), Knopf, 1945, published in England as *Artie Greengroin: Some Episodes in His Life in the Army,* Secker & Warburg, 1945; *Poems, 1941-44,* Secker & Warburg, 1945; *A Sound of Hunting* (three-act play), Knopf, 1946; *The Beast in His Hunger* (poems), Knopf, 1949; *The Stars in Their Courses,* Knopf, 1960; *A Quiet Place to Work* (novel), Knopf, 1968; *The Wild Hunt* (novel), Harcourt, 1973. Also author of *The Wake of the Red Witch,* 1949, and *Thunder on the Mountain,* 1954.

Films: "El Dorado" (based on *The Stars in Their Courses*), Paramount, 1967; "A Walk in the Sun"; "A Place in the Sun."

Contributor to poetry journals and popular magazines, including *New Yorker, Atlantic Monthly, Vogue, Harper's Bazaar, Town and Country,* and *Horizon.*

AVOCATIONAL INTERESTS: Hunting, fishing, guns, "avoiding work, being dull at parties, and not answering letters."

BIOGRAPHICAL/CRITICAL SOURCES: New York Times, November 30, 1941; *New York Herald Tribune,* June 24, 1944; *Poetry,* January, 1948; *Saturday Review of Literature,* December 24, 1949, April 20, 1968; *Publishers Weekly,* February 12, 1968; *Library Journal,* March 1, 1968; *New York Times Book Review,* April 28, 1968; *Best Sellers,* May 1, 1968; *Book World,* May 19, 1968; June 16, 1968; *Hudson Review,* autumn, 1968; *Virginia Quarterly Review,* winter, 1969.*

* * *

BROWN, Janet 1947-

PERSONAL: Born March 18, 1947, in Los Angeles, Calif.; daughter of Robert H. and Mary (Maffe) Brown; children: Ona Blossom Lesser. *Home address:* P.O. Box 656, Woodacre, Calif. 94973.

CAREER: Naturalist and writer.

WRITINGS: (With Eugene Lesser, Stephanie Mills, and Ed Buryn) *Two Births,* Random House, 1972.

* * *

BROWN, Jim (M.) 1940-

PERSONAL: Born May 28, 1940, in Shreveport, La.; son of Clyde (an oil worker) and Martein (a secretary; maiden name, Atkins) Brown; married Arlene Pendas (a college teacher), August 12, 1967; children: Matthew. *Education:* Baylor University, B.A., 1962; McNeese State University,

M.Ed., 1967; North Texas State University, Ph.D., 1971. *Politics:* Democrat. *Religion:* Southern Baptist. *Home:* 916 Audubon Ln., Lake Charles, La. 70609. *Office:* McNeese State University, Department of Health and Physical Education, Lake Charles, La. 70609.

CAREER: Peace Corps volunteer teacher in Colombia, South America, 1962-64; *Lake Charles American Press,* Lake Charles, La., news writer, 1965-67; McNeese State University, Lake Charles, associate professor of health and physical education, 1967—; Lake Charles Country Club, Lake Charles, tennis pro, 1976—. *Member:* American Alliance for Health, Physical Education, and Recreation, Association for the Advancement of Health Education, United States Tennis Association, Louisiana Association for Health, Physical Education, and Recreation.

WRITINGS: Tennis: Teaching, Coaching, and Directing Programs, Prentice-Hall, 1976; *Tennis Without Lessons,* Prentice-Hall, 1977. Contributor of articles to *World Tennis, Tennis Illustrated, Tennis Trade, Health Education,* and other periodicals.

WORK IN PROGRESS: Secondary Heath Methods; Tennis Strategy.

SIDELIGHTS: "The writing I do," Brown told *CA,* "is an outgrowth of my experience as a teacher, coach, program director, consultant, and participant in various health and physical education activities. The books and articles I produce are simply a record of my work. Making that record a marketable literary item is a challenge because people in my field are expected to perform physically, not mentally or academically. Conducting tennis clinics in the South, Southwest, and Mexico gives me the opportunity to develop teaching techniques which, in turn, provide new material for writing."

*   *   *

BROWN, Letitia Woods   1915-1976

October 24, 1915—August 3, 1976; American educator and author. Her specialty was the history of the black community in Washington, D.C. She was also active in the field of historic preservation in the Washington area. In 1961, she and her husband assisted in the training of the first Peace Corps volunteers at the University of California at Berkeley. She died in Washington, D.C. Obituaries: *New York Times,* August 5, 1976; *Washington Post,* August 5, 1976.

*   *   *

BROWN, Marc Tolon   1946-

PERSONAL: Born November 25, 1946, in Erie, Pa.; son of Leroy Edward and Renita (Toulon) Brown; married Stephanie Marini (a ballet teacher), September 1, 1968; children: Tolon Adam, Tucker Eliot. *Education:* Cleveland Institute of Art, B.F.A., 1968. *Home and office:* 100 Cushing Way, Scituate, Mass. 02066.

CAREER: Writer and artist, 1969—. Art director for WICU-Television, 1968—. Guest lecturer at colleges and universities; has had exhibits of his work at Society of Illustrators.

WRITINGS—Self-illustrated children's books: *Arthur's Nose,* Little, Brown, 1976; *One, Two, Three* (Book-of-the-Month Club selection), Little, Brown, 1976; *Marc Brown's Full House,* Addison-Wesley, 1977.

Illustrator: Louise Moeri, *How the Rabbit Stole the Moon,* Houghton, 1977; Jan Willem Van de Wetering, *Little Owl Henry,* Houghton, in press.

WORK IN PROGRESS: Lenny and Lola, a self-illustrated children's book, for Dutton.

AVOCATIONAL INTERESTS: Collecting early nineteenth-century American art and antiques, gardening, small-scale farming (horses and chickens).

*   *   *

BROWN, Virginia (Suggs)   1924-

PERSONAL: Born July 14, 1924, in St. Louis, Mo.; daughter of Clarence and Viola (Hampton) Suggs; married Charles F. Brown. *Education:* Stowe Teachers College, B.A., 1947; Washington University, St. Louis, Mo., M.A., 1952, further graduate study, 1953-56. *Home:* 4106-A San Francisco Ave., St. Louis, Mo. 63115. *Office:* Webster Division, McGraw-Hill Book Co., Manchester Rd., Manchester, Mo. 63011.

CAREER: Elementary school teacher in St. Louis, Mo., 1948-65, in charge of Banneker Reading Clinic, 1956-60, supervisor of elementary education, 1960-65; Office of Economic Opportunity, Human Development Corp., St. Louis, Mo., director of Head-Start program, 1965-66; McGraw-Hill Book Co., Manchester, Mo., director of early childhood education in Webster Division, 1966—. In-service teacher at Harris Teachers College, 1961-64; member of staff of Knoxville College, summers, 1963-64; television teacher of adult reading classes for CBS-Television (St. Louis), summers, 1963-67. Active on boards of directors of children's and civic organizations.

MEMBER: International Reading Association, National Association for the Education of Young Children, Association for Childhood Education. *Awards, honors:* Hannah G. Solomon Award from National Council of Jewish Women, 1966, for outstanding service to the young children of St. Louis.

WRITINGS: (With others) *Watch Out for C-* (juvenile), McGraw, 1965; (with Billie Phillips and Elsa Jaffe) *Who Cares?* (juvenile), McGraw, 1965; (with others) *The Hidden Lookout* (juvenile), McGraw, 1965; *Out Jumped Abraham* (juvenile), McGraw, 1967. Also co-author of an art education book, 1970. Contributor to professional journals and popular magazines.

*   *   *

BROWNLEE, W(ilson) Elliot, Jr.   1941-

PERSONAL: Born May 10, 1941, in La Crosse, Wis.; son of Wilson Elliot (a chemist) and Pearl (Woodings) Brownlee; married Mary Margaret Cochran (a writer), June 25, 1966; children: Charlotte Louise, Martin Elliot. *Education:* Harvard University, B.A., 1963; University of Wisconsin, Madison, M.A., 1965, Ph.D., 1969. *Home:* 859 Cambridge Dr., Santa Barbara, Calif. 93111. *Office:* Department of History, University of California, Santa Barbara, Calif. 93106.

CAREER: University of California, Santa Barbara, assistant professor, 1967-74, associate professor of economic history, 1974—. *Member:* American Historical Association, Organization of American Historians, Economic History Association, Economic History Society. *Awards, honors:* Haynes Foundation fellowship, 1969.

WRITINGS: Dynamics of Ascent: A History of the American Economy, Knopf, 1974; *Progressivism and Economic Growth,* Kennikat, 1974; (with wife, Mary M. Brownlee) *Women in the American Economy: A Documentary History,* Yale University Press, 1976; (with R. M. Current, T. H. Williams, and Frank Freidel) *Essentials of American His-*

tory, 2nd edition, Knopf, 1976. Contributor of articles and reviews to history and economics journals.

WORK IN PROGRESS: A History of Women in the American Industrial Revolution, 1820-1930; A History of American Taxation.

* * *

BROWNSON, William C(larence), Jr. 1928-

PERSONAL: Born June 27, 1928, in Charlotte, N.C.; son of William Clarence (a corporate executive) and Juanita (Clements) Brownson; married Helen Stewart (a high school special needs coordinator), August 25, 1951; children: William Clarence IV (deceased), David Alexander, James Victor, Jonathan Clements. *Education:* Davidson College, Davidson, N.C., A.B., 1949; Columbia Theological Seminary, Decatur, Ga., B.D., 1952; Princeton Theological Seminary, Th.D., 1963. *Politics:* Independent. *Religion:* Protestant. *Home:* 1347 Heather Dr., Holland, Mich. 49423. *Office:* 700 Ball Ave., Grand Rapids, Mich. 49501.

CAREER: Pastor at churches in Lodi, N.J., 1953-59, and in Chicago, Ill., 1959-64, Western Theological Seminary, Holland, Mich., professor of preaching, 1964-74; radio and television minister appearing on "Words of Hope" program, 1974—. *Member:* Phi Beta Kappa.

WRITINGS: The Plan is God's, Half Moon Press, 1965; *Tried by Fire,* Baker Book, 1972; *Distinctive Lessons from Luke,* Baker Book, 1974; *Do You Believe?,* Zondervan, 1975. Contributor of articles to journals and magazines, including *Christianity Today, Church Herald, Banner, Eternity, Reformed Review.*

WORK IN PROGRESS: A biography of his late handicapped son; a book on learning how to pray.

SIDELIGHTS: Brownson told *CA* that his "major motivation is communicating the Christian faith." He is proficient in New Testament Greek, French, Latin, Hebrew, and German.

* * *

BRUCKER, Herbert 1898-1977

October 4, 1898—April 5, 1977; American journalist, former editor of the *Hartford Courant,* educator in the field of journalism, and author of books on First Amendment privileges and responsibilities. He died in Hartford, Conn. Obituaries: *New York Times,* April 7, 1977; *AB Bookman's Weekly,* May 9, 1977. (See index for previous *CA* sketch)

* * *

BRYSON, Phillip J(ames) 1939-

PERSONAL: Born October 11, 1939, in Salt Lake City, Utah; son of Ivan Miles (a telephone technician) and Violet (Peterson) Bryson; married Patricia Anderson, June 19, 1963; children: Miles, Amy, Emily, Jennifer, Bret. *Education:* University of Utah, B.A. (magna cum laude), 1964; Ohio State University, Ph.D., 1967. *Religion:* Church of Jesus Christ of Latter-day Saints (Mormons). *Home:* 340 West Camino Fairhaven, Tucson, Ariz. 85704. *Office:* College of Business and Public Administration, University of Arizona, Tucson, Ariz. 85721.

CAREER: University of Arizona, Tucson, assistant professor, 1967-72, associate professor, 1972-77, professor of economics, 1977—. *Member:* American Economic Association, Phi Beta Kappa, Phi Kappa Phi, Omicron Delta Epsilon. *Awards, honors:* Mershon postdoctoral fellowship from

Ohio State University, in Germany, summer, 1968; research fellowship from Alexander von Humboldt Foundation, 1973-74.

WRITINGS: Scarcity and Control in Socialism: Essays on East European Planning, Lexington Books, 1976. Contributor of about a dozen articles and reviews to academic journals.

WORK IN PROGRESS: Research on East German relations with other Council of Mutual Economic Assistance countries, and on planning and consumer theory.

SIDELIGHTS: Bryson comments: "Much of the research effort of the book *Scarcity and Control in Socialism* was done in West Berlin at the East European Institute of the Free University."

* * *

BUCK, George C(rawford) 1918-

PERSONAL: Born March 20, 1918, in Meriden, Conn.; son of Morris Hemingway and Elizabeth F. (Meiklem) Buck; married Anna Marie Reichrath, November 22, 1943; children: Keith H., Barbara Ann Dickerson, George Crawford III. *Education:* Amherst College, B.A., 1942; Yale University, M.A., 1948, Ph.D., 1954; attended Middlebury College, 1946-47. *Home:* 2206 Omani Lane, Redmond, Wash. 98052. *Office:* 340 Denny Hall: DH-30, Dept. of Germanics, University of Washington, Seattle, Wash. 98195.

CAREER: University of Washington, Seattle, instructor, 1950-54, lecturer, 1954-56, assistant professor, 1959-62, associate professor of Germanics, 1962—, associate dean, 1970-73, department chairman, 1973—. Guest professor at Columbia University, 1954. *Military service:* U.S. Navy, 1942-46. *Member:* Modern Language Association of America (member of delegate assembly), American Association of University Professors (treasurer), American Council on Teaching of Foreign Languages, Philological Association of the Pacific Coast, Pacific Northwest Conference on Foreign Languages, Washington Association of Foreign Language Teachers, American Association of Teachers of German, Western Association of German Studies, Phi Beta Kappa. *Awards, honors:* Fulbright senior research grant, 1957-58.

WRITINGS: (Translator with Frithjof A. Raven) W. von Humboldt, *Linguistic Variability and Intellectual Development,* University of Miami Press, 1971; (translator) Walter Berendsohn, *Thomas Mann: Artist and Champion in Disturbed Times,* University of Alabama Press, 1975.

WORK IN PROGRESS: Research on Goethe, Lessing, R. Borchardt, and Herder.

AVOCATIONAL INTERESTS: Golf, fishing, photography, travel.

* * *

BUCKLEY, Michael F. 1880(?)-1977

1880(?)—January 7, 1977; American editor. He was the editor of *Standard & Poor's Daily News* from 1939 until 1961. Buckley had also been an editor with The New York News Bureau Association. He died in New York City. Obituaries: *New York Times,* January 9, 1977.

* * *

BUFERD, Norma Bradley 1937-

PERSONAL: Born June 23, 1937, in Plainview, Tex.; daughter of Vernon (a rancher) and Winifred (a writer)

Bradley; married James D. Kerley, August 13, 1957 (divorced, 1964); married Richard M. Buferd, August 30, 1965 (separated, May 1977); children: Bradley M., Brenda. *Education:* Attended Southern Methodist University, Richland College, Texas Tech University, and Southwest School of Photography. *Politics:* Democrat. *Home and office:* 7326 Spring Valley Rd., Dallas, Tex. 75240.

CAREER: Stewardess for Continental Airlines, 1954-55; KCLV-Radio, Clovis, N.M., presented "Woman's Day," 1956-57; Southwest Quilt Guild, Dallas, Tex., co-founder and president, 1973—. *Member:* Authors Guild of Authors League of America, League of American Authors, Historical Preservation Society, Mes Amie, Society for Abandoned and Neglected Children.

WRITINGS: The Quilters: Women and Domestic Art, Doubleday, 1977. Contributor to women's magazines. Editorial representative for *Better Homes and Gardens* and *Woman's Day.*

WORK IN PROGRESS: Folklore of American Quilts and *Hometown, Texas,* an oral history, both with Patricia Cooper.

SIDELIGHTS: Buferd writes: "Most of my work has been with women whose families were pioneers of the harsh American Southwest. They have shared their reminiscences, and reflections, their strengths and spirit and allowed me to know them as well as giving me a personal view of my historical roots. My greatest pleasure lies in capturing history through the spoken words of those who have lived it."

* * *

BULGER, William T(homas) 1927-

PERSONAL: Born January 16, 1927, in Flint, Mich.; son of William T. (a lumber dealer) and Isabelle (Todd) Bulger; married Margery Servis (a professor), April 21, 1967; children: Ann Marie. *Education:* Kenyon College, A.B., 1949; University of Michigan, Ann Arbor, A.M., 1950, Ph.D., 1957. *Home:* 660 Aspen Ct., Mt. Pleasant, Mich. 48858. *Office:* Dept. of History, Central Michigan University, Mt. Pleasant, Mich. 48859.

CAREER: Central Michigan University, Mt. Pleasant, assistant professor, 1957-65, associate professor of history, 1965—. *Military service:* U.S. Army, 1945-46. *Member:* American Historical Association, Organization of American Historians, Michigan Historical Society.

WRITINGS: (With Frank O. Ranger) *The Great American Quiz Book,* Pagurian Press, 1977.

WORK IN PROGRESS: Research on history of sports.

* * *

BULL, John 1914-

PERSONAL: Born February 28, 1914, in New York, N.Y.; son of John Lewis and Grace (King) Bull; married Edith Hellman (a teacher and editor), September 16, 1944; children: Doris. *Education:* Attended James Clark Taxidermy Studio, 1932-33. *Home:* 1148 Virginia St., Far Rockaway, N.Y. 11691. *Office:* American Museum of Natural History, 79th St. and Central Park W., New York, N.Y. 10024.

CAREER: American Museum of Natural History, New York, N.Y., in department of entomology, 1940-42; U.S. Customs, New York City, examiner of wild bird plumage, 1942-59; National Audubon Society, Miami, Fla., special investigator of live bird imports and nature leader, 1960-61;

American Museum of Natural History, research assistant in ornithology, 1962-65, field associate, 1965—. Chief investigator of bird hazards and jets at J.F.K. International Airport, for U.S. Fish & Wildlife Service, 1965. Instructor at New School for Social Research, 1974-75; faculty member at Asa Wright Nature Centre (Trinidad), 1975-77. Consultant to Environmental Analysts, Terrestrial Environmental Specialists, and Environmental Engineers.

MEMBER: International Council for Bird Protection, American Ornithologists Union, Cooper Ornithological Society, Wilson Ornithological Society, British Ornithologists Union, Eastern Bird Banding Association (member of council, 1954-55), Northeastern Bird Banding Association, Federation of New York State Bird Clubs, Linnaean Society of New York (fellow; president, 1953-55).

WRITINGS: Birds of New York City: A Museum Guide, Natural History Press, 1958; *Birds of the New York Area,* Harper, 1964; (editor) Shelley and Mary Louise Grossman and John Hamlet, *Birds of Prey of the World,* C. N. Potter, 1964; (contributor) *Bird Watcher's America,* McGraw, 1965; (editor) Gardner Stout, *Shore Birds of North America,* Viking, 1967; (contributor) Sidney Bahrt, editor, *A Wilderness of Birds,* Doubleday, 1974; *Birds of New York State,* Doubleday, 1974; *Great White Heron,* Communication Ventures, 1975; *Pygmy Owl,* Communication Ventures, 1976; *Wood Duck,* Communication Ventures, 1976; *Barn Swallow,* Communication Ventures, 1976; (with John Farrand) *Audubon Society Field Guide to Birds of Eastern America,* Knopf, 1977. Contributor to ornithology journals and magazines, including *Audubon,* and *New York Times.*

SIDELIGHTS: A nature leader since 1967, Bull has had two round-the-world tours and trips to Trinidad and Tobago; he led a trip to Australia and New Zealand, and two Caribbean cruises.

BIOGRAPHICAL/CRITICAL SOURCES: New York Herald Tribune, June 14, 1959, April 24, 1960; *New York Mirror,* November 26, 1959; *New York Times,* November 8, 1964, April 23, 1965, April 18, 1966, June 27, 1971, December 15, 1974; *Newsday,* February 5, 1975.

* * *

BULLEN, Robert 1926(?)-1976

1926(?)—August 21, 1976; American editor, translator, and author. He died in New York City. Obituaries: *Publishers Weekly,* September 6, 1976.

* * *

BULLOUGH, Bonnie 1927-

PERSONAL: Born January 5, 1927, in Delta, Utah; daughter of Ruth Uckerman; married Vern L. Bullough (a college professor), August 2, 1947; children: James, Steven, Susan, Robert. *Education:* University of Utah, R.N., 1947; Youngstown State University, B.S., 1957; University of California, Los Angeles, M.S. (nursing), 1962, M.A. (sociology), 1965, Ph.D., 1968, postdoctoral study, 1970-74. *Home:* 10301 Orton Ave., Los Angeles, Calif. 90064. *Office:* Department of Nursing, California State University, 1250 Bellflower Rd., Long Beach, Calif. 90840.

CAREER: Santa Rosa General Hospital, Santa Rosa, Calif., nurse, 1947-48; Salt Lake General Hospital, Salt Lake City, Utah, operating room head nurse, 1948-51; University of Chicago Clinics, Chicago, Ill., operating room nurse, 1951-52; City of Chicago, field nurse for health department, 1952-54; Youngstown State University, Youngstown, Ohio, part-time instructor in nursing, 1956-59; Northridge Hospital, Northridge, Calif., part-time nurse, 1959-61; Cairo University, Higher Institute of Nursing, Cairo, United Arab Republic, Fulbright lecturer in nursing, 1966-67; San Fernando Valley State College, Northridge, part-time instructor in sociology, 1967-68; University of California, Los Angeles, assistant professor, 1968-72, associate professor of nursing, 1972-75; California State University, Long Beach, professor of nursing, 1975—, associate director of pediatric nurse practitioner program, 1971-75, chairperson of primary care section, 1972-74, coordinator of graduate nursing program.

MEMBER: American Nurses Association (member of local board of directors, 1973-74), American Public Health Association, American Sociological Association, National League for Nursing, Nursing Fund (founder; member of board of directors). *Awards, honors:* Award from Los Angeles Nursing Fund, 1976; grants from National Center for Health Services, Research, and Development, 1970-72, and W. K. Kellogg Foundation, 1975—.

WRITINGS: (With husband, Vern Bullough) *What Color Are Your Germs?* (pamphlet), Committee to End Discrimination in Chicago Medical Institutions, 1954; (with V. Bullough) *The Emergence of Modern Nursing,* Macmillan, 1964, 2nd edition, 1969; (editor with V. Bullough) *Issues in Nursing,* Springer Publishing, 1966; *Social Psychological Barriers to Housing Desegregation,* Center for Real Estate Reserach and Urban Economics, University of California, Berkeley, 1969; (editor with V. Bullough) *New Directions for Nurses,* Springer Publishing, 1971; (contributor) Saleem A. Farag, editor, *Selected Papers on Health Issues in California,* State of California, 1971; (with V. Bullough) *Poverty, Ethnic Identity, and Health Care,* Appleton, 1972; (contributor) Judith Lorber and Eliot Friedson, editors, *Medical Men and Their Work,* Aldine-Atherton, 1972; (contributor) V. Bullough, editor, *The Subordinate Sex: A History of Attitudes Toward Women,* University of Illinois Press, 1973; (editor and contributor) *The Law and the Expanding Nursing Role,* Appleton, 1975; (editor with V. Bullough, and contributor) *Expanding Horizons for Nurses,* Springer Publishing, 1976; (with V. Bullough) *Sin, Sickness, and Sanity: A History of Sexual Attitudes,* New American Library, 1977; (with V. Bullough) *Prostitution,* Crown, in press; *The Management of Common Human Miseries,* Springer Publishing, in press. Contributor of more than thirty-five articles and reviews to professional journals.

WORK IN PROGRESS: A revision of *Poverty, Ethnic Identity, and Health Care;* articles on the career ladder in nursing and on breast cancer.

SIDELIGHTS: Bullough writes: "I consider this an exciting time to be involved in nursing. The role of the nurse is in a period of rapid change as nurses take on more responsibility in acute, long term, and primary care. This means that the education of nurses must necessarily be strengthened and nurses need to expand their horizons to exploit the opportunities which are opening up. Since social change of this proportion is always somewhat painful, the profession is also beset by many problems, and problems, if they are not overwhelming, can be interesting."

*   *   *

BUNN, Thomas 1944-

PERSONAL: Born February 22, 1944, in Detroit, Mich.; son of Clark William (in insurance) and Myra (in horticulture; maiden name, Petzholdt) Bunn; married Mary M.

Kennedy (a social researcher), August 14, 1973. *Education:* University of Michigan, student, 1961-64; Michigan State University, B.A., 1971. *Agent:* Robert Lescher, 155 East 71st St., New York, N.Y. 10021.

CAREER: Writer, 1973— ("writing is a no-collar job and I like it best"). *Military service:* U.S. Navy, 1966-68. *Member:* Authors Guild of Authors League of America, Phi Beta Kappa.

WRITINGS: Closet Bones (detective novel), Putnam, 1977.

WORK IN PROGRESS: Two mainstream novels; one detective novel.

SIDELIGHTS: Bunn writes briefly: "I enjoy writing and can think of nothing else I'd rather do, except, perhaps, fish the surf."

*   *   *

BUNT, Lucas N(icolaas) H(endrik) 1905-

PERSONAL: Born June 10, 1905, in Edam, Netherlands; came to U.S. in 1968; son of Hendrik and Jannetje (Klinkert) Bunt; married Elizabeth Catharina Huisman, January 4, 1932; children: Lydia Elizabeth Maria van Welzenis, Hendrik Cornelis. *Education:* University of Amsterdam, Netherlands, doctorandus, 1929; University of Groningen, Netherlands, Ph.D., 1934. *Religion:* Protestant. *Home:* 331 East Laguna Dr., Tempe, Ariz. 85282. *Office:* Department of Mathematics, Arizona State University, Tempe, Ariz. 85281.

CAREER: High school teacher of mathematics in Netherlands, 1929-46; scientific head of mathematics at University of Utrecht and University of Groningen, both in Netherlands, 1946-68, head of department of mathematics and science at University of Utrecht, 1957-68; Arizona State University, Tempe, professor of mathematics, 1968—. Docent at University of Leyden, 1952-53. Counselor to the Minister of Education of Brazil, 1956-57. *Member:* Mathematical Center (Netherlands), Wiskundig Genootschap (Netherlands), Mathematical Association.

WRITINGS: (With Howard F. Fehr and George Grossman) *An Introduction to Sets, Probability and Hypothesis Testing,* Heath, 1964; (with Alan Barton) *Probability and Hypothesis Testing,* Harrap, 1967; (with Phillip S. Jones and J. D. Bedient) *The Historical Roots of Elementary Mathematics,* Prentice-Hall, 1976.

Author of about twenty mathematical textbooks and reports for various organizations in Dutch, Portuguese, and Baha Indonesia language editions. Contributor of articles to professional journals.

WORK IN PROGRESS: An article on pre-columbian mathematics.

*   *   *

BURBANK, Garin 1940-

PERSONAL: Born April 14, 1940, in Atchinson, Kan.; son of John M. (an accountant) and Mary A. Burbank. *Education:* University of California, Berkeley, B.A., 1962, M.A., 1965, Ph.D., 1974. *Office:* Department of History, University of Winnipeg, Winnipeg, Manitoba, Canada R3B 2E9.

CAREER: University of Saskatchewan, Regina, assistant professor of history, 1969-73; University of Winnipeg, Winnipeg, Manitoba, assistant professor of history, 1973—.

WRITINGS: When Farmers Voted Red: The Gospel of Socialism in the Oklahoma Countryside, 1910-1924, Greenwood Press, 1976. Contributor to history and American studies journals.

WORK IN PROGRESS: A History of Capitalist Development in Alberta, Canada.

SIDELIGHTS: Dr. Burbank told *CA:* "When I reached adulthood at the beginning of the 1960's, I became aware of the ferocious inequalities that had not been reduced by the New Deal and successive social legislation. The onrush of the disastrous policy of intervention in Vietnam made me despair of the possibility that America in her maturity could be anything other than an arrogant imperial power abroad and a leviathan state consuming its own children at home and abroad. I began my studies of American history wondering if it had ever been different and could possibly be different—and better—for Americans in the future.

"As a native of the Midwest, I was especially intrigued to discover in that region earlier instances of protest against social inequality, political repression, and imperial adventures. The Socialists in rural Oklahoma, like the Populists of Texas, were remarkable for their ability to affirm the best of American political culture—democratic openness, a cooperative spirit, and a preference for equal rights and roughly equal conditions. These abilities and qualities had their origins less in formalized socialist doctrine than in the collective urgency of evangelical religion. The experience of the agrarian socialists then, and maybe even the Presidency of Jimmy Carter now, are enough to give me hope for America, even though I am no longer an American citizen."

*   *   *

BURBY, Raymond J(oseph) III   1942-

PERSONAL: Born June 26, 1942, in Los Angeles, Calif.; son of Raymond Joseph (a sales manager) and Barbara (in community service; maiden name, Del Pino) Burby; married Nannie Harbour (an editorial assistant), December 27, 1965; children: Barbara Derina, Raymond Joseph IV. *Education:* University of Washington, Seattle, student, 1960-62; George Washington University, A.B., 1964; University of North Carolina, M.R.P., 1966, Ph.D., 1969. *Home:* 138 Ridge Trail, Chapel Hill, N.C. 27514. *Office:* Center for Urban and Regional Studies, University of North Carolina, 067A Hickerson House, Chapel Hill, N.C. 27514.

CAREER: University of North Carolina, Chapel Hill, assistant professor of planning, 1969-72, research associate of Center for Urban and Regional Studies, 1968-72, senior research associate, 1972-76, assistant director of research, 1976—. President of Village West Homeowners Association, 1976-77. *Member:* American Institute of Planners, American Society of Planning Officials, American Real Estate and Urban Economics Association, Regional Science Association, Southern Regional Science Association.

WRITINGS: Lake-Oriented Subdivisions in North Carolina: Decision Factors and Policy Implications for Urban Growth Patterns—Developer Decisions (monograph), Center for Urban and Regional Studies, University of North Carolina, 1967; *Planning and Politics: Toward a Model of Planning-Related Policy Outputs in American Local Government,* Center for Urban and Regional Studies, University of North Carolina, 1968; (editor with Shirley F. Weiss and Edward J. Kaiser) *New Community Development: Planning Process, Implementation, and Emerging Social Concerns,* two volumes, Center for Urban and Regional Studies, University of North Carolina, 1971; (with Weiss and Thomas G. Donnelly) *Multipurpose Reservoirs and Urban Development,* Center for Urban and Regional Stud-

ies, University of North Carolina, 1972; (with Weiss and Robert B. Zehner) *Evaluation of New Communities: Selected Preliminary Findings,* Center for Urban and Regional Studies, University of North Carolina, 1974; (contributor) Daniel H. Carson, editor, *Man-Environment Interactions: Evaluations and Applications,* Halsted, 1975; (with Weiss) *New Communities, U.S.A.,* Lexington Books, 1976; *Recreation and Leisure in New Communities,* Ballinger, 1976; (with N. H. Loewenthal) *Health Care in New Communities,* Ballinger, 1976; (with Donnelly) *Schools in New Communities,* Ballinger, 1977. Editor of "New Community Research Series," Ballinger, 1976. Contributor to professional journals. Manuscript reviewer for *Journal of Leisure Research,* 1964—.

WORK IN PROGRESS: Energy and Human Settlement; Second Home Communities and Recreational Land Development; Development and Utilization of Flood Plains.

*   *   *

BURDGE, Rabel J(ames)   1937-

PERSONAL: Born December 14, 1937, in Columbus, Ohio; son of Alonzo M. (an insurance executive) and Mariam F. Burdge; married Sharon Sue Payne, 1962 (deceased); children: Stephanie Lee, Jill Marie, Amy Louise. *Education:* Ohio State University, B.S., 1959, M.S., 1961; Pennsylvania State University, Ph.D., 1965. *Politics:* Democrat. *Religion:* Methodist. *Home:* 2110 Burlison, Urbana, Ill. 61801. *Office:* Institute for Environmental Studies, University of Illinois, 408 South Goodwin, Urbana, Ill. 61801.

CAREER: University of Kentucky, Lexington, assistant professor, 1968-71, associate professor of sociology, 1971-76; University of Illinois, Urbana, associate professor of environmental studies, 1976—. Lecturer at University of Colorado, 1966-68. Consultant to U.S. Forest Service, National Park Service, and U.S. Army Corps of Engineers. *Military service:* U.S. Army, 1965-68, technical publications writer, 1965-66, assistant professor of sociology at U.S. Air Force Academy, 1966-68; became captain.

MEMBER: American Sociological Association, Rural Sociological Society, National Recreation and Park Association, Society of Park and Recreation Educators, Southern Sociological Society, Alpha Kappa Delta, Gamma Sigma Delta.

WRITINGS: (With Everett M. Rogers) *Social Change in Rural Societies,* Prentice-Hall, 1960, 2nd edition, 1971; (with Rogers) *Rural Social Change and Speck's "A Stake in the Land",* Patterson Smith, 1971; (contributor) J. W. Coleman and others, editors, *Kentucky: A Pictorial Review,* University Press of Kentucky, 1971; (with Neil H. Cheek, Jr. and Donald R. Field) *Leisure and Recreation Places: Ann Arbor,* Ann Arbor Sciences Publisher, 1976. Editor of *Journal of Leisure Research,* 1972-75; co-editor of *Leisure Sciences: An Interdisciplinary Journal,* 1975.

WORK IN PROGRESS: Leisure in Mass Society, publication expected in 1979.

AVOCATIONAL INTERESTS: Backpacking, camping, canoeing, fishing, travel, gourmet cooking, guitar.

*   *   *

BURGER, Sarah Greene   1935-

PERSONAL: Born September 7, 1935, in Providence, R.I.; daughter of Denison W. and Louise (Hill) Greene; married Edward J. Burger (a physician), June 17, 1960; children: Heidi, Hilary. *Education:* Connecticut College, B.A., 1957; Radcliffe-Massachusetts General Hospital School of Nursing, R.N., 1959. *Home and office:* 3403 Woodley Rd. N.W., Washington, D.C. 20016.

CAREER: Brookline Health Department, Brookline, Mass., in research, 1959-61; Washington Home, Washington, D.C., nursing supervisor, 1970-75; Episcopal Home, Washington, D.C., nursing supervisor, 1976—. Consultant to Urban Institute. *Member:* American Nurses Association, District of Columbia Nurses Association, Washington Hospice Society (president, 1977).

WRITINGS: (With Martha D'Erasmo) *Living in a Nursing Home: A Complete Guide for Residents, Their Families, and Friends,* Seabury, 1976.

WORK IN PROGRESS: Articles.

SIDELIGHTS: Sarah Burger writes: "Having worked in nursing homes for a number of years, Ms. D'Erasmo and I repeatedly found both patients and families without a source of information about nursing homes. Our book fills that gap."

* * *

BURNESS, Wallace B(inny) 1933-
(Tad Burness)

PERSONAL: Born July 11, 1933, in Berkeley, Calif.; son of Thomas B. (a club manager) and Wallea Tormey (in real estate; maiden name, Draper) Burness; married Sandra Kay Chapman, July 9, 1967; children: Tammy Lynn. *Education:* Attended San Jose State University, 1951-58. *Religion:* Christian. *Residence:* San Jose, Calif. *Agent:* Toni Mendez, Inc., 140 East 56th St., New York, N.Y. 10022. *Office:* c/o United Feature Syndicate, 200 Park Ave., New York, N.Y. 10017.

CAREER: In real estate and property management in San Jose, Calif., 1956-63; civil service in California, 1960-65; United Feature Syndicate, New York, N.Y., author of syndicated weekly column "Auto Album," 1966—. Radio announcer in San Jose, Calif., 1955-61; automotive history consultant. *Member:* International Edsel Club, Antique Automobile Club of America, Society of Automotive Historians, Edsel Owners Club, Contemporary Historical Vehicle Club, Metropolitan Owners Club, WPC Club (Walter P. Chrysler/Chrysler Products Restorer's Club).

WRITINGS—Under name Tad Burness: *Cars of the Early 'Twenties',* Chilton, 1968; *Auto Album,* Scholastic Book Services, Volume I, 1969, Volume II, 1976; *Cars of the Early 'Thirties',* Chilton, 1970; *American Car Spotter's Guide, 1940-1965,* Motor Books International, 1973; *Indianapolis 500 Winners,* Scholastic Book Services, 1974; *American Car Spotter's Guide, 1920-1939,* Motor Books International, 1975; *American Truck Spotter's Guide,* Motor Books International, 1978. Contributor of articles on automobiles and mobile homes to magazines.

WORK IN PROGRESS: The Streamlined Years; Shadycreek, a novel; *Waldo* and *Michael,* cartoons.

SIDELIGHTS: Burness told *CA:* "I am interested in all phases of 20th century history and Americana, and have a large collection of old advertisements, books, magazines, phonograph records, etc. This reference collection is always undergoing changes and improvements." *Avocational interests:* History, popular twentieth-century American music, railroad history.

BIOGRAPHICAL/CRITICAL SOURCES: San Jose Mercury News, May 21, 1967; *Antique Automobile,* May, 1971.

BURNS, Norman T(homas) 1930-

PERSONAL: Born July 25, 1930, in Brooklyn, N.Y.; son of John J. (a machinist) and Elizabeth (Donaldson) Burns; married Dorothy O'Neill, August 30, 1958; children: Caroline Mary (a ward), Andrew, Hugh, Emily. *Education:* Queens College (now of the City University of New York), A.B., 1952; University of Michigan, A.M., 1953, Ph.D., 1967. *Home:* 417 West Benita Blvd., Vestal, N.Y. 13850. *Office:* Department of English, State University of New York at Binghamton, Binghamton, N.Y. 13901.

CAREER: University of Michigan, Institute of Science and Technology, Ann Arbor, assistant editor, 1958-62, head of publication service, 1962-68; State University of New York at Binghamton, assistant professor, 1968-73, associate professor of English, 1973—. *Member:* American Association of University Professors, Milton Society of America. *Awards, honors:* Research fellow at Henry E. Huntington Library and Art Gallery, summer, 1973; younger humanist fellowship from National Endowment for the Humanities, 1974-75.

WRITINGS: Christian Mortalism from Tyndale to Milton, Harvard University Press, 1972; (editor with Christopher Reagan) *Concepts of the Hero in the Middle Ages and the Renaissance,* State University of New York Press, 1975.

WORK IN PROGRESS: Research on Milton's views of church membership and inspiration.

* * *

BURNS, Richard W(ebster) 1920-

PERSONAL: Born September 12, 1920, in Waterloo, Iowa; son of James C. (a salesman) and Florence G. (Berry) Burns; married Patsy Mulhern; children: James M., Cathleen Ann Burns Perkins, Bruce C. *Education:* University of Northern Iowa, B.A., 1946; University of Iowa, M.S., 1950, Ph.D., 1952. *Religion:* Episcopalian. *Home:* 213 Maricopa, El Paso, Tex. 79912. *Office:* Department of Curriculum and Instruction, University of Texas, El Paso, Tex. 79968.

CAREER: University of Texas, El Paso, assistant professor, 1952-58, associate professor of education, 1958-61, professor of curriculum and instruction, 1963—, director of Office of Institutional Studies, 1963-67. *Military service:* U.S. Marine Reserve, active duty, 1942-46; became chief pharmacist's mate. *Awards, honors:* Bronze Medal from Freedoms Foundation, 1962.

WRITINGS: (Editor with Gary D. Brooks) *Curriculum Design in a Changing Society,* Educational Technology Piblications, 1970; *New Approaches to Behavioral Objectives,* W. C. Brown, 1971, 2nd edition, 1977; (editor with Joe Lars Klingstedt) *Competency-Based Education,* Educational Technology Publications, 1973.

Contributor: W. Robert Houston and Robert B. Howsam, editors, *Competency-Based Teacher Education: Progress, Problems, and Prospects,* Science Research Associates, 1972; Robert C. Maxon and Walter E. Sistrunck, editors, *A Systems Approach to Educational Administration,* W. C. Brown, 1973; Philip G. and Miriam B. Kapfer, editors, *Learning Packages in American Education,* Educational Technology Publications, 1973; Elliot W. Eisner and Elizabeth Vallance, editors, *Conflicting Conceptions of Curriculum,* McCutchan, 1974; Lawrence Lipsitz, editor, *The Test Score Decline,* Educational Technology Publications, 1977; Lipsitz and Jerrold Ackerman, editors, *Instructional Television,* Educational Technology Publications, 1977.

Contributor to education journals. Co-editor of *Educational*

Technology, April-May, 1970, November, 1972; contributing editor of *Educational Technology,* 1967-74, *Continuing Educational Review,* 1968, and *NSPI Journal,* 1970—.

WORK IN PROGRESS: Construction and Use of Classroom Measurement Devices, with Everett E. Davis.

SIDELIGHTS: Burns writes: "I would class myself educationally as an interactive behaviorist with a wide interest in technology. My goal is to train teachers to be effective in classrooms so my major efforts are to explain and implement theory into practice. I believe education should move more toward problem solving, integrated curricula, decision making, and process learning."

* * *

BURR, Charles 1922(?)-1976

1922(?)—October 10, 1976; American editor and writer. He died in New York City. Obituaries: *New York Times,* October 12, 1976.

* * *

BURR, Gray 1919-

PERSONAL: Born March 20, 1919, in Omaha, Neb.; son of Alfred Earnest (a lawyer) and Geraldine (Gray) Burr; married Carol T. Hayes, September 8, 1943 (divorced, 1959); married Ellen Krohn, August 6, 1960; children: Elizabeth Burr Coogan, Rebecca Burr Cassidy, Katherine, Martha. *Education:* Harvard University, A.B., 1943, M.A., 1948. *Home address:* R.D.2, Box 525, New Paltz, N.Y. 12561. *Office:* Department of English, State University of New York College at New Paltz, New Paltz, N.Y. 12561.

CAREER: Phillips Exeter Academy, Exeter, N.H., instructor in English, 1948-49; Tufts University, Medford, Mass., instructor in English, 1950-56; Wheaton College, Norton, Mass., assistant professor of English, 1956-61; State University of New York College at New Paltz, assistant professor, 1962-67, associate professor of English, 1967—. *Military service:* U.S. Navy, 1943-45; became lieutenant. *Awards, honors:* Poetry grant from Ingram-Merrill Foundation, 1970.

WRITINGS: A Choice of Attitudes (poems), Wesleyan University Press, 1969.

Poems anthologized in *A Controversy of Poets,* edited by Paris Leary and Robert Kelly, Doubleday, 1963; *The New Yorker Book of Poems,* edited by the editors of *New Yorker,* Viking, 1969; *Decade,* edited by Normon Holmes Pearson, Wesleyan University Press, 1969. Contributor of poems to literary journals, including *New Yorker* and *Poetry.*

WORK IN PROGRESS: Two books of poems.

SIDELIGHTS: Burr comments briefly: "Poetry is its own motivation, circumstances are irrelevant. I always hope to get printed, but write out of personal necessity."

* * *

BURSTEIN, John 1949-

PERSONAL: Born December 25, 1949, in Mineola, N.Y.; son of Herbert (an attorney) and Beatrice (a state Supreme Court judge; maiden name, Sobel) Burstein; married June Beznover (a teacher), June 26, 1976. *Education:* Hofstra University, B.A., 1972. *Home:* 1092 Alicia Ave., Teaneck, N.J. 07666. *Office address:* P.O. Box 773, New York, N.Y. 10013.

CAREER: One-man health education musical performer in

elementary schools in United States, under stage name Mr. Slim Goodbody, 1974—.

WRITINGS: Mr. Slim Goodbody Presents the Inside Story, McGraw, 1977. Also author of and performer on "The Inside Story" record album, Macmillan, 1975.

WORK IN PROGRESS: A book on health subjects.

SIDELIGHTS: Wearing a body suit with pictures of organs, muscles, and bones in appropriate places, Burstein performs his Mr. Goodbody's "The Inside Story" to help schoolchildren counter anxieties and confusion about the workings of their bodies. "I believe it is vitally important," he told *CA,* "that children learn to appreciate their bodies and love themselves. Our educational system has been based on learning facts about the world 'out-there' and it's time we learned to focus on each individual's creative potential and inner worth."

* * *

BURT, Frances R(iemer) 1917-

PERSONAL: Born March 23, 1917, in Brodhead, Wis.; daughter of Arthur Paul (a farmer) and Lavina (Baird) Riemer; married A. Oren Burt (a salesman), November 30, 1939; children: Meredith Edward, Orene Elizabeth Burt Dunzweiler, Michael Joseph. *Education:* Attended Green County Normal School, 1935, and Whitewater State Teachers College, 1937. *Politics:* Republican. *Religion:* Methodist. *Home:* 5720 Holstein Way, Sacramento, Calif. 95822.

CAREER: Writer and artist. Member of board of directors of Sacramento Regional Arts Council, 1967-76; president of Sacramento Ballet Guild, 1962, and Northern California Arts, 1964. *Member:* National League of American Penwomen (local vice-president, 1962-64, 1974-76; president, 1964-66; chairman of national board of directors, 1976-78). *Awards, honors:* Regional awards for poems and plays.

WRITINGS: Random Rhymes, Albany Herald, 1948. Also author of plays. Author of "Sal Sez" in *Albany Herald.* Contributor to *Together* and to newspapers. Editor of *Norcal News* and of newsletters for National League of American Penwomen.

WORK IN PROGRESS: An autobiography, dealing with Wisconsin farm life in the 1920's and 1930's "before mechanization and freezers."

SIDELIGHTS: Frances Burt writes: "I have something to share and preserve—country schools, the dignity of farm labor—honesty and integrity—a gentle way of life where SEX is *not* the most important end or means. My poetry and articles also are devoid of morbid or sordid ideas. I am a happy person. I am also an artist and illustrator—I paint the way I write."

* * *

BUSH, Barbara Holstein 1935-

PERSONAL: Born September 8, 1935, in California; daughter of Walter Edwin (an educator) and Beulah (an artist; maiden name, Williams) Holstein; married Richard Merrell Bush (a clergyman), June 16, 1956; children: Stephen, David, Gary, Patricia. *Education:* Los Angeles Harbor Junior College, A.A., 1954; California State University, Long Beach, B.A. (with great distinction), 1956. *Religion:* Protestant. *Home:* 27031 Pinjara Circle, Mission Viejo, Calif. 92675.

CAREER: Elementary school teacher in Los Angeles,

Calif., 1956-57, Ewing Township, N.J., 1957-59, Princeton Township, N.J., 1959-60, Madera, Calif., 1965-66, and Mission Viejo, Calif., 1968-70. *Member:* P.E.O. Sisterhood, Pi Lambda Theta.

WRITINGS: I Can't Stand Cindy, Lord (on her teaching experiences), Zondervan, 1976. Author of column "Still Learning," in *Saddleback Valley News* (Mission Viejo), 1969-70.

WORK IN PROGRESS: A Funny Thing Happened on the Way to the Ivory Tower, a fictional account of some of the subtle cultural pressures on the modern pastor; *Still Learning,* a book of essays.

SIDELIGHTS: Barbara Bush writes: "The area of prime importance to me in my writing is that of improved quality of life, especially in regard to human relationships. My approach will undoubtedly continue to be practical rather than theoretical, specifically trying to show how a personal relationship with Jesus Christ and an application of Biblical principles enriches daily life and mends torn interpersonal relationships.

"I sustain an enduring interest in the preservation of the family unit, public education, and church music, having served as church organist and choir director."

AVOCATIONAL INTERESTS: Travel (United States, Israel, Cyprus, Turkey, Greece), sewing and stitchery, reading.

*   *   *

BUSIA, Kofi Abrefa 1913-

PERSONAL: Born July 11, 1913, in Wenchi, Brongahafo District, Ghana; married, 1950; children: two sons, two daughters. *Education:* Earned B.A. degrees from Achimote College and University of London, and M.A. and Ph.D. degrees from Oxford University. *Home address:* Brighthampton Rd., Standlake, Oxford, England.

CAREER: Member of staff at Wesley College, Kumasi, Ghana, 1932-34, and at Achimota College, Accra, Ghana, 1936-39; district commissioner of Government of the Gold Coast, 1942-49, officer in charge of sociological surveys, 1947-49; University College of the Gold Coast (now University of Ghana), Accra, research lecturer in African studies, 1949-51, senior lecturer in sociology, 1952-54, professor, 1954-59; Institute of Social Studies, the Hague, Netherlands, professor of sociology, 1959-62; University of Leiden, Leiden, Netherlands, professor of sociology and culture of Africa, 1960-62; World Council of Churches, Birmingham, England, director of studies, 1962-64; Oxford University, St. Antony's College, Oxford, England, professor of sociology, 1964-66; National Liberation Advisory Council in Ghana, vice-chairman, 1966-67, chairman, 1967-69; founder of Progress Party in Ghana, 1969; prime minister of Ghana, 1969-72, minister of economic planning and the interior, 1971-72. Lecturer in sociology at Oxford University, 1973—. Leader of Ghana Congress Party, 1952-57, leader of parties in opposition to Nkrumah's Convention People's Party (United Party), 1957-59; chairman of Centre for Civic Education, 1967. Visiting professor at Northwestern University, 1954, Nuffield College, Oxford, 1955, Agricultural University of Wageningen, 1956, El Colegio de Mexico, 1962, and University of York.

MEMBER: International Sociological Association (executive member, 1953-60), International Social Science Council, International African Institute, Association of Social Anthropologists. *Awards, honors:* Carnegie Foundation research fellowships, 1941-42, 1945-47; D.Litt. from University of Ghana, 1970.

WRITINGS: Report on a Social Survey of Sekondi-Takoradi, Crown Agents for the Colonies on Behalf of the Government of the Gold Coast, 1950; *The Position of the Chief in the Modern Political System of Ashanti: A Study of the Influence of Contemporary Social Changes on Ashanti Political Institutions,* Oxford University Press, for International African Institute, 1951, International Scholastic Book Service, 1968; *Education for Citizenship,* Bureau of Current Affairs (London, England), 1951; *Judge for Yourself,* West African Graphic Co., 1956; *Africa in Transition: A Social and Anthropological Observation,* Division of Studies, World Council of Churches, 1957.

The Sociology and Culture of Africa, University of Leiden Press, 1960; *The Challenge of Africa,* Praeger, 1962; *Purposeful Education for Africa,* Mouton & Co., 1964, Humanities, 1969; *Urban Churches in Britain: A Question of Relevance,* Lutterworth, 1966; *Ghana Will Be Truly Free and Happy,* Ghana Students Association, 1966; *Africa in Search of Democracy,* Praeger, 1967; *The African Consciousness: Continuity and Change in Africa,* American-African Affairs Association, 1968; (contributor) Akwasi A. Afrifa, editor, *Civil Rule Returns to Ghana,* Ministry of Information (Accra-Tema, Ghana), 1969; *The Way to Industrial Peace,* Ghana Publishing Corp., 1970; *Apartheid and Its Elimination,* Ghana Public Relations Department, 1971; *Dr. Busia in Singapore* (speeches), Ministry of Information (Accra, Ghana), 1971.

Also author of *Self-Government,* 1955, and *Industrialization in West Africa,* 1955.

SIDELIGHTS: Busia is a member of the royal family of Wenchi, of the Ashanti people. In 1957, Nkrumah's government, of which Busia was opposition leader, arrested several leaders and charged them with conspiracy to assassinate Nkrumah. At the time, Busia was lecturing abroad, and chose to remain in the Netherlands in exile. When Nkrumah was overthrown by a military coup, Busia returned to Ghana to serve as prime minister. Another military coup occurred while Busia was in office, but he chanced to be abroad again, where he remains in a second period of exile.

AVOCATIONAL INTERESTS: Music, walking.

BIOGRAPHICAL/CRITICAL SOURCES: Times Literary Supplement, November 2, 1967; *Listener,* November 23, 1967; *New Statesman,* December 22, 1967; *Time,* September 12, 1969; *Ghana,* January 14, 1973.

*   *   *

BUTLER, David Jonathon 1946-

PERSONAL: Born June 8, 1946, in Berkeley, Calif.; son of Harry Nathaniel (in sales) and Gloria Eileen (Chapman) Butler; married Nancy E. Bracker, April 24, 1971 (divorced). *Education:* Attended University of Oregon. *Politics:* "Conservative radical populist isolationist." *Residence:* Eugene, Ore. *Office:* Lane Intermediate Education District, 1900 Highway 99N, Eugene, Ore. 97402.

CAREER: WYFM-Radio, Charlotte, N.C., copywriter and announcer, 1970; Lane Community College, Eugene, Ore., media relations specialist, 1972; Lane Intermediate Education District, Eugene, Ore., director of public relations, 1975—. *Military service:* U.S. Marine Corps, 1966-70; became sergeant. *Member:* National School Public Relations Association. *Awards, honors:* Sweepstakes award from American Newspaper Publishers Association, 1964, for high school feature writing; Thomas Jefferson Award from *Newsweek,* 1969, for editing.

WRITINGS: Cat's Whiskers on Sunday (juvenile), Carolrhoda, 1975; *Fourth and Madison* (history), Lane Community College Press, 1976. Contributor to magazines.

WORK IN PROGRESS: A children's book on dreams.

SIDELIGHTS: Butler writes: "We had this class in high school and out of that class of seventeen came a couple of people who are newspapering, another book writer, a big shot in poetry, and a Pulitzer Prize-winning photographer.... The motivator was a teacher named Dutton. The first day in class Dutton threw five-hundred spelling words at us. Miss one and you get an F. Ditto the next day. And the next, and the next, and the next ... F, F, F, F, F. Along the way, he had us write things, in-ver-ted pyramid style. We got the picture.

"Then he started putting signs up all over the place, notably one that read, 'When you are satisfied, you can leave by this door.' After a while, some of us learned how to write and how to spell, and it wasn't long before I thought I might want to do this for a living.

"So I got motivated. The motivation has hung in there. It's gotten me over the rough spots—I don't particularly care for writing, but I enjoy having written—and now feel I have a nice combination of fluid creativity and the discipline to keep it in line."

*   *   *

BUTLER, Lucius (Albert, Jr.) 1928-

PERSONAL: Born May 2, 1928, in St. Petersburg, Fla.; son of Lucius Albert (an engineer) and Mable Rose (Tubbs) Butler; married Dona Mae Medchill (a teacher), 1950; children: Stephen Paul, Thomas Albert, Susan Joy Butler May. *Education:* University of Puget Sound, B.A., 1952; Northern Baptist Seminary, M.R.E., 1954; Bethel Theological Seminary, B.D., 1955; University of Minnesota, M.A., 1955, Ph.D., 1968; University of Hawaii at Manoa, M.L.S., 1974. *Office:* Department of Educational Communications, University of Hawaii at Manoa, 1776 University Ave., Honolulu, Hawaii 96822.

CAREER: Baptist General Conference, Evanston, Ill., missionary at Japan Mission, 1955-66; University of Minnesota, Minneapolis, instructor in education, 1966-68; University of Hawaii at Manoa, Honolulu, assistant professor, 1968-70, associate professor of education, 1970—, chief-of-party for contract team in Laos, 1971-73. *Military service:* U.S. Army, 1946-49, 1950-52; became sergeant. *Member:* World Educational Fellowship, Association for Educational Communications and Technology, Pacific Association for Communications and Technology, Hawaii Audio-Visual Association (president, 1970-71), Phi Delta Kappa.

WRITINGS: (Editor with Neville Pearson) *Instructional Materials Centers: Selected Readings,* Burgess, 1969; (editor with Pearson) *Learning Resource Centers,* Burgess, 1973. Contributor to education journals.

*   *   *

BUTLER, Ron(ald William) 1934-

PERSONAL: Born March 8, 1934, in New York, N.Y.; son of William J. and Rose M. (Fink) Butler; married Barbara Buechner, 1960 (divorced, 1967); married Greta Grudel, 1968 (divorced, 1975); children: (second marriage) Alexandra, Adrian. *Education:* University of Arizona, B.A., 1960.

Residence: New York, N.Y. *Agent:* Bill Berger, Bill Berger Associates, Inc., 444 East 58th St., New York, N.Y. 10022.

CAREER: Esquire, New York City, staff writer, 1960-65; *True,* New York City, associate editor, 1965-70; free-lance writer, 1970—. *Military service:* U.S. Air Force, public information officer, 1952-56; served in French Morocco; became staff sergeant. *Member:* Society of American Travel Writers, New York Travel Writers.

WRITINGS: Esquire's Guide to Modern Etiquette, Lippincott, 1970; *Fodor's Guide to Trains of the World,* McKay, 1977. Author of "Passport to Everywhere," a weekly travel column syndicated by Columbia Features Syndicate, 1973—. Contributor to popular magazines, including *Penthouse, Travel and Leisure, Gallery,* and *Argosy.*

SIDELIGHTS: Butler describes himself briefly as a "born wanderer. I have visited virtually every country in the world."

*   *   *

BUTTERICK, George F. 1942-

PERSONAL: Born October 7, 1942, in Yonkers, N.Y.; son of George W. (a factory worker) and Kathleen (a clerk; maiden name, Byrnes) Butterick; married Colette Marie Hetzel (a painter), June 19, 1965; children: George Adam, Aaron. *Education:* Manhattan College, B.A. (honors), 1964; State University of New York at Buffalo, Ph.D., 1970. *Home:* 194 North St., Willimantic, Conn. 06226. *Office:* Literary Archives, University of Connecticut Library, Storrs, Conn. 06268.

CAREER: Wilson College, Chambersburg, Pa., instructor, 1968-69, assistant professor of English, 1969-70; University of Connecticut, Storrs, assistant professor, 1970-72, lecturer in English, 1972—, curator of Literary Manuscripts, 1972—.

WRITINGS: The Norse (poems), Institute of Further Studies, 1973; *Reading Genesis by the Light of a Comet* (poems), Ziesing Brothers, 1976; *A Guide to the Maximus Poems of Charles Olson,* University of California Press, in press.

Editor: (With Albert Glover) *A Bibliography of Works by Charles Olson,* Phoenix Book Shop, 1967; Charles Olson, *Poetry and Truth: The Beloit Lectures and Poems,* Four Seasons Foundation, 1970; Olson, *Additional Prose,* Four Seasons Foundation, 1974; (with Charles Boer) Olson, *The Maximus Poems, Volume Three,* Grossman, 1975; Olson, *The Post Office,* Grey Fox Press, 1975; Vincent Ferrini, *Selected Poems,* University of Connecticut Library, 1976; Olson, *The Fiery Hunt and Other Plays,* Four Seasons Foundation, in press; Olson, *Muthologos: Collected Interviews and Lectures,* Four Seasons Foundation, in press.

Co-editor of *Audit,* 1966-68; editor of *Olson: The Journal of the Charles Olson Archives,* 1974—; contributing editor of *Magazine of Further Studies,* 1968-70, and *Athanor,* 1970-75.

WORK IN PROGRESS: Poems; a biography of Charles Olson; editing more writings of Charles Olson, including his letters; editing an anthology of recent American poetry.

*   *   *

BUXTON, (Evelyn June) Bonnie 1940-

PERSONAL: Born June 25, 1940, in Radway, Alberta, Canada; daughter of Earl William (a professor) and Dorothy Lee (a teacher; maiden name, Cox) Buxton; married Brian Anthony Philcox (an information director in the Canadian Government), February 12, 1971. *Education:* University of

Alberta, B.A., 1960; Stanford University, graduate study, 1962. *Office:* Waxwing Productions, 198 Glebe Ave., Ottawa, Ontario, Canada K1S 2C7.

CAREER: Worked as advertising copywriter, 1962-66; freelance magazine writer, 1966-68; *Toronto Star Weekly,* Toronto, Ontario, travel editor and author of travel column, 1968; *Chatelaine,* Toronto, Ontario, contributing travel editor and author of monthly travel column, 1969-73; Waxwing Productions (publishers), Ottawa, Ontario, co-founder, partner, and executive editor, 1974—. *Member:* Media Club of Canada, Periodical Writers Association of Canada, Association of Canadian Publishers.

WRITINGS: (With Betty Guernsey) *Montreal Inside Out,* Waxwing Productions, 1974, revised edition, 1976; (with Guernsey) *Great Montreal Walks,* Waxwing Productions, 1976. Author of weekly column "Montreal Inside Out" in *Montreal Gazette,* 1973-75. Contributor to magazines in Canada, the United States, England, and Australia, including *Cosmopolitan* and *American Home.*

WORK IN PROGRESS: A biography of Princess Agnes zu Salm-Solm.

SIDELIGHTS: Bonnie Buxton writes: "Having spent many years as a travel writer and five years as a travel editor, I have been able to visit many parts of the world—including most Caribbean countries, Eastern Europe, and India. Over these years, I have grown to realize how fortunate we in North America are, to have such bountiful resources—and I also have become aware of how quickly, ruthlessly and stupidly we are wasting them.

"My chief concern these days deals with the over-mechanization and over-industrialization of this continent. I hope, in both my journalism and in the books published by my company, to encourage a re-examination of the North American lifestyle. How can we return to a simpler, saner way of life—without plunging our continent into recession? How can we conserve our resources for later generations—so that our grandchildren won't curse our profligacy? How can we learn to be happy with less?

"My own examination of values has led me to adopt a strong Canadian nationalist viewpoint, although our books are sold in the United States, and I write for many U.S. periodicals. U.S. conglomerates that have in various ways despoiled much of the United States currently own a great deal of Canada—close to a hundred percent in some resource industries. If we Canadians wish to preserve what is important to us and our descendants, we must somehow become the guardians of our own resources."

BIOGRAPHICAL/CRITICAL SOURCES: Ottawa Citizen, July 14, 1976; *Chatelaine,* October, 1976.

* * *

BYERS, R(ichard) McCulloch 1913-

PERSONAL: Born September 7, 1913, in St. Paul, Minn.; son of Maxwell Cunningham (a railroad executive) and Janet (a teacher; maiden name, McCulloch) Byers. *Education:* Lehigh University, B.S. (honors), 1934. *Politics:* Republican. *Religion:* Presbyterian. *Home:* 3 Fairfield Dr., Catonsville, Md. 21228.

CAREER: Baltimore Gas & Electric Co., Baltimore, Md., principal electrical engineer, 1934-74; writer, 1974—. Has appeared on television and radio programs. *Military service:* U.S. Naval Reserve, active duty in mine warfare, 1943-46; became lieutenant senior grade. *Member:* Institute of Electrical and Electronics Engineers (senior member), Power

Engineering Society, Catonsville Historical Society, Phi Beta Kappa, Eta Kappa Nu, Theta Xi. *Awards, honors:* Awards for engineering papers.

WRITINGS: The Hard Hat Girl: Power Engineer (novel), Fairfield House, 1976.

WORK IN PROGRESS: A tetralogy of novels about Andromache of Troy.

SIDELIGHTS: Byers comments: "I wrote *The Hard Hat Girl: Power Engineer* mainly to encourage young women to enter the engineering professions and to inform Americans of the IEEE-PES cures for the energy crisis today; an engineering novel seemed a novel way to get my messages across to my fellow Americans."

* * *

CABLE, John L(aurence) 1934-

PERSONAL: Born May 22, 1934, in Lancaster, N.Y.; son of Laurence N. and Edith (Wilson) Cable. *Education:* University of Buffalo, B.A., 1956, M.S., 1960. *Home:* 18701 West Oakmont Dr., Miami, Fla. 33015. *Office:* Department of Mathematics and Physics, Miami-Dade Community College, 11380 Northwest 27th Ave., Miami, Fla. 33167.

CAREER: Secondary school teacher in Wilson, N.Y., 1956-67; Miami-Dade Community College, Miami, Fla., associate professor of mathematics, 1967—. Instructor at State University of New York at Buffalo, 1961-67. *Member:* Mathematical Association of America, National Council of Teachers of Mathematics, American Mathematical Association of Two Year Colleges.

WRITINGS: (With Maurice Bosstick) *Patterns in the Sand,* Glencoe Press, 1971, 2nd edition, 1975; (with J. Louis Nanney) *Developing Skills in Algebra,* Allyn & Bacon, 1974, 2nd edition, 1976; (with Nanney and Barr) *Basic Skills in Technical Mathematics,* Allyn & Bacon, 1977; (with Nanney) *College Algebra: A Skills Approach,* Allyn & Bacon, 1977.

WORK IN PROGRESS: Trigonometry: A Skills Approach.

* * *

CAHILL, Daniel J(oseph) 1929-

PERSONAL: Born March 3, 1929, in Chicago, Ill.; son of John Joseph (a railroad employee) and Bridget (Armstrong) Cahill; married Karma Zan Johnson (a businesswoman), June, 1963; children: Kara. *Education:* Loyola University, Chicago, Ill., B.S., 1951, M.A., 1954; University of Iowa, Ph.D., 1966. *Home:* 2618 Willow Lane, Cedar Falls, Iowa 50613. *Office:* Department of English, University of Northern Iowa, Cedar Falls, Iowa 50613.

CAREER: St. Ambrose College, Davenport, Iowa, assistant professor of English, 1955-62; St. Olaf College, Northfield, Minn., assistant professor of English, 1965-68; University of Northern Iowa, Cedar Falls, associate professor, 1968-71, professor of English, 1971—, head of department, 1971-76. Vice-president of Conference on Christianity and Religion, 1969-71. *Military service:* U.S. Army, Corps of Engineers, 1953-55. *Member:* International P.E.N., Modern Language Association of America, National Council of Teachers of English, American Academy of Religion, Central Modern Language Association.

WRITINGS: Harriett Monroe, Twayne, 1973. Contributor to *Twentieth Century Literature, New Republic, North American Review,* and *Contemporary Literature.*

WORK IN PROGRESS: Editing a collection of essays on

Jerzy Kosinski; research on Katherine Mansfield, Philip Larkin, and Walter Pater.

SIDELIGHTS: Cahill writes: "One writes, I guess, to stay professionally alive in academe." *Avocational interests:* Sailing.

* * *

CAHN, William 1912-1976

May 12, 1912—October 13, 1976; American free-lance writer who began his career in journalism and in public relations and advertising, and later turned to writing profiles of labor unions and corporations. His books included pictorial histories on comedy and other aspects of the entertainment world, as well as studies of the history of labor. Cahn died in New Haven, Conn. Obituaries: *New York Times,* October 15, 1976. (See index for previous *CA* sketch)

* * *

CALABRESE, Alphonse F. X. 1923-

PERSONAL: Born April 27, 1923, in Brooklyn, N.Y.; son of Charles (a retail store owner) and Josephine (Ambrosino) Calabrese; married Florence Schumacher (a social worker), August 4, 1950; children: Charles, Therese, Eileen, Thomas, Cathy, John, Bernadette, James. *Education:* St. John's University, B.A., 1949; Catholic University of America, M.S.W., 1951; Florida State Christian College, Ph.D. in psychology, 1963; New York University, Ph.D. in religious education, 1977. *Politics:* Republican. *Religion:* Roman Catholic. *Home:* 120 Hunters Dr., Syosset, N.Y. 11791. *Office:* Christian Institute for Psychotherapeutic Studies, 183 S. Broadway, Hicksville, N.Y. 11801.

CAREER: Catholic Charities Psychiatric Clinic, New York City, psychotherapist, 1950-52; Postgraduate Institute for Mental Health, New York City, psychotherapist, 1952-53, fellow in psychoanalysis, 1953-56, fellow in analytic group therapy, 1956-58; Long Island Consolation Center, Jamaica, N.Y., faculty and training supervisor, 1958-60; Christian Institute for Psychotherapeutic Studies, Hicksville, N.Y., executive director, 1965—. *Member:* Academy of Psychotherapists, Council of Psychoanalytic Psychotherapists, American Group Therapy Association, Christian Association of Psychological Studies.

WRITINGS: (With William Proctor) *The Christian Love Treatment,* Doubleday, 1976. Contributor to *Sign, National Courier, Journal of Psychology and Theology,* and other periodicals.

WORK IN PROGRESS: Research in "inner healing."

AVOCATIONAL INTERESTS: Synthesis of Christianity and the findings of psychotherapy; research in psychotherapy with poverty groups.

* * *

CALAMANDREI, Mauro 1925-

PERSONAL: Born March 5, 1925, in Florence, Italy; son of Pietro and Italia Calamandrei; divorced; children: Camilla *Education:* University of Florence, Doctor of Letters, 1947; Univeristy of Chicago, Ph.D., 1952. *Home:* 121 West 72nd St., New York, N.Y. 10023. *Office:* 850 Seventh Ave., New York, N.Y. 10019.

CAREER: Julliard School of Music, New York, N.Y., professor of history, 1953-60; *Edizioni di Comunitá,* Milan, Italy, editorial director, 1955-57; University of Florence, Florence, Italy, professor of American history, 1955-57;

L'Espresso, Rome, Italy, chief U.S. correspondent, chief of New York and United Nations bureaus, 1958—. Visiting professor of Italian civilization, Middlebury College, 1950-51, 1953. *Military service:* Served in Italian underground, 1944. *Member:* Associazione Stampa Italiana, American Historical Association, Foreign Press Association, United Nations Correspondents Association.

WRITINGS: Pianeta: USA e Canada, two volumes, CEI (Milan), 1968-70; *Le Americhe,* three volumes, CEI, 1968-70; *Arte e vita nell 'America di oggi,* F. Fabbri (Milan), 1974; (with G. Mammarella) *Quale America,* Vallecchi (Florence), 1976; *Chi comanda in USA, Bari,* Laterza, 1976. Also editor of *Classics of American History,* twelve volumes, Il Mulino (Bologna), 1956-66.

Contributor to *Church History, Preuves, William & Mary Quarterly, La Stampa, Il Ponte,* and other periodicals.

* * *

CALDE, Mark A(ugustine) 1945-

PERSONAL: Surname is pronounced *Kall*-dee; born December 1, 1945, in Los Angeles, Calif.; son of Emil Anthony and Eleanor (Ferrera) Calde; married Shelley Cavanaugh, July 12, 1969; children: Steven Mark. *Education:* Loyola University, Los Angeles, Calif., B.A., 1967, M.A., 1969. *Residence:* Los Angeles, Calif.; *Agent:* Peggy Lanpher, 1352 Ballena Blvd., Alameda, Calif. 94501.

CAREER: Novelist and screenwriter; Mobile Draperies, Inc., Los Angeles, Calif., manager and vice president of sales, 1970-73.

WRITINGS: Shadowboxer (suspense novel), Putnam, 1976. Screenwriter for television series "Emergency," National Broadcasting Co. (NBC), 1974—.

WORK IN PROGRESS: Research for a novel; a feature-length screenplay.

SIDELIGHTS: Calde writes briefly: "Since my initial introduction to the professional ranks of writing was through films and television, I try to carry over a highly visual sense into my prose, and also a tightness of style. The screenplay is the leanest form of narrative writing, and I have a built-in prejudice against books that take 800 pages to say what could have been said in half that space.

"I enjoy the process of writing and try to convey this enjoyment to the reader. A novel should be first and foremost entertaining, no matter how 'important' the topic may be. I hope never to bore a reader with polemics, but rather strive to give him something to think about while he enjoys an entertaining story.

"I am a writer because it is the only occupation that makes sense to me."

* * *

CALDER, Robert (a pseudonym) 1941-

PERSONAL: Born 1941, in Illinois; married; children: two. *Education:* B.A. (English). *Politics:* "Humane." *Religion:* "Vague." *Agent:* Theron Raines, Raines & Raines, 475 Fifth Ave., New York, N.Y. 10017.

CAREER: Full-time writer. "Various other occupations, brief, years ago." *Military service:* "My war was with the military, our own." *Awards, honors:* "A few minor awards, some under real name, from book clubs and guilds."

WRITINGS: The Dogs, Delacorte, 1976. Writer of almost twenty other books, under real name and other pseudonyms. Contributor of numerous short pieces to magazines.

WORK IN PROGRESS: "A second Robert Calder book—again of ecological concern, some unconscious mysticism, the nature of violence."

SIDELIGHTS: "I write because I have to, emotionally. The nature of reality, and the human soul, are the only subjects of abiding interest."

* * *

CALDWELL, Kathryn (Smoot) 1942-
(Kathryn Alexander)

PERSONAL: Born March 11, 1942, in Salt Lake City, Utah; daughter of Reed (a sugar industry executive) and Stella (Madsen) Smoot; married David E. Caldwell (a television director), August 6, 1971; children: Jason, Sherilyn. *Education:* University of Utah, Salt Lake City, B.A. (honors), 1964; Northwestern University, M.S., 1965; graduate study at University of California, Los Angeles, 1965-70; University of Southern California, Ph.D., 1972. *Religion:* Church of Jesus Christ of Latter-day Saints (Mormons). *Home:* 1212 Peninsula Dr., Westwood, Calif. 96137. *Office:* Communications by Design, 1455 Airport Blvd., San Jose, Calif.

CAREER: University of Utah, Salt Lake City, science writer for College of Medicine, 1965-66; *Clinical Orthopaedics and Related Research* (journal), Los Angeles, Calif., editorial assistant, 1966-67; University of California, Los Angeles, communications coordinator for California regional medical programs, 1967-70, communications coordinator for medical media network, 1970-72; Foundation for Applied Communications Technology, Denver, Colo., director of experimental design, 1972-75; Communications by Design, San Jose, Calif., director of instructional design and vice-president, 1975—. *Member:* Society of Children's Book Writers, National Association of Science Writers. *Awards, honors:* William Randolph Hearst Award, 1963; award to support reportage of psychological effects of Alaskan earthquake from *Reader's Digest*, 1964.

WRITINGS—Under pseudonym Kathryn Alexander: *Medical Media: An Approach to Learning,* University of California Medical Media Network, 1971; (editor) *A Source Book: Social and Physical Rehabilitation of the Patient with Spinal Cord Injury,* Veterans Administration, 1971.

Also author of health education films, under pseudonym Kathryn Alexander before 1971. Contributor of articles to professional journals and childrens' magazines, under pseudonym Kathryn Alexander before 1971.

WORK IN PROGRESS: A fictional account of the termination of polygamy in Salt Lake and Provo, Utah, for young adults, entitled *My Name Used to be Karen Madsen.*

* * *

CALDWELL, Louis O(liver) 1935-

PERSONAL: Born February 6, 1935, in Edna, Tex.; son of Lewis J. and Sidney (McDonald) Caldwell; married Mamie Carrico (a receptionist), July 18, 1958; children: Terri Lynn, Louis Regan, David Andrew, Paul Bradley. *Education:* Student at Southern Bible College; University of Houston, B.S., 1958, M.Ed., 1961, Ed.D., 1970. *Religion:* Protestant. *Home:* 1111 Loire Lane, Houston, Tex. 77090. *Office:* 1000 FM 1960 W., Suite 106, Houston, Tex. 77090; and 10950 Beaumont Hwy., Caldwell Building, Houston, Tex. 77015.

CAREER: Southern Bible College, Houston, Tex., staff member in psychology, 1960-76, head of department of education, 1960-73, founder and director of Christian Coun-

seling Center, 1966—, academic dean, 1973-76. Junior high school mathematics teacher in Houston, Tex., 1958-66. *Member:* Texas Psychotherapy Association.

WRITINGS: It's Great to be YOUng, Baker Book, 1962; *His Eye on YOUth,* Baker Book, 1963; *He Speaks to YOUth,* Baker Book, 1964; *Parables of the Master: A Discussion Guide for Teens,* Baker Book, 1964; *Speaker's Source Book for Talks to Teens,* Baker Book, 1966; *Good Morning, Lord: Devotions for College Students,* Baker Book, 1967; *After the Tassel Is Moved: Guidelines for High School Graduates,* Baker Book, 1968; *The Adventure of Becoming One,* Baker Book, 1969; *Another Tassel Is Moved: Guidelines for College Graduates,* Baker Book, 1970; *Miracles of the Master: A Discussion Guide for Teen-Agers,* Baker Book, 1970; *When Partners Become Parents,* Baker Book, 1971; *Good Morning, Lord: Meditations for Modern Marrieds,* Baker Book, 1974; *Through the Years: An Anniversary Remembrance,* Abingdon, 1976; *A Birthday Remembrance,* Abingdon, 1977. Contributor to *Christianity Today.*

WORK IN PROGRESS: The Total Person for Troubled Times, an interpretation of the "beatitudes"; *The Church and the Kissing Gate,* on courtship and marriage; *The Voice on the Waters,* "a Christian psychotherapist's response to the needs of hurting and confused people"; booklets on mental health, marriage, and youth.

AVOCATIONAL INTERESTS: Fishing, hunting, flying (licensed private pilot), boating.

* * *

CALLAHAN, Raymond (Aloysius) 1938-

PERSONAL: Born November 30, 1938, in Trenton, N.J.; son of Raymond Aloysius, Sr. (a civil servant) and Esther (a civil servant; maiden name, Reynolds) Callahan; married Mary Helen McPeek (an executive secretary), September 26, 1964; children: Sarah Reynolds, Brian Patrick. *Education:* Georgetown University, A.B., 1961; Harvard University, A.M., 1962, Ph.D., 1967. *Home:* 303 Beverly Rd., Newark, Del. 19711. *Agent:* John McLaughlin, 31 Newington Green, London N16 9PU, England. *Office:* Department of History, University of Delaware, Newark, Del. 19711.

CAREER: University of Delaware, Newark, assistant professor, 1967-72, associate professor, 1972-76, professor of history, 1976—. *Member:* American Historical Association, Conference for British Studies, American Committee on the History of the Second World War. *Awards, honors:* Woodrow Wilson fellow, 1961-62; Danforth fellow, 1961-67.

WRITINGS: The East-India Company and Army Reform, 1784-1796, Harvard University Press, 1972; *The Worst Disaster: The Fall of Singapore, 1942,* University of Delaware Press, 1977; *The Burma Campaigns, 1942-1945,* Davis-Poynter Ltd., in press. Contributor to history and military journals.

WORK IN PROGRESS: Sir Ian Jacob: A Life of Service, completion expected in 1978; *Churchill and India,* 1979; continuing research on British history, especially between 1933 and 1945.

SIDELIGHTS: Callahan writes: "I think that Britain was in fact one of the principal losers in World War II, suffering its defeat largely at the hands of the United States. The nature of this final American defeat of the British Empire shaped much of the postwar world. I have spent a great deal of time in England during the last ten years and these views have been shaped as much by personal contacts and conversations as by documents.''

* * *

CALLMANN, Rudolf 1892-1976

PERSONAL: Born September 29, 1892, in Cologne, Germany; came to United States in 1936; son of Max and Clara (Meyer) Callman; married Maria Hess, April 20, 1919; children: Ellen. *Education:* University of Freiburg, L.L.D., 1919; Harvard University, L.L.B., 1939. *Home:* 117-14 Union Turnpike, Kew Gardens, Long Island, N.Y. *Office:* 10 East 40th St., New York, N.Y. 10016.

CAREER: Private law practice in Cologne, Germany, 1922-36; private practice in New York City, specializing in unfair competition, trademarks, copyrights, and antitrust law, 1943-76. Counsel to Golenbock & Barell, New York City. Honorary professor, University of Cologne, 1954. *Member:* American Bar Association, New York City Bar Association, American Association of International Law; U.S. Trademark Association, New York Patent Law Association, American Federation of Jews from Central Europe (past president; chairman of board), Conference on Jewish Material Claims Against Germany (vice-president and member of executive committee, 1955-76), Council of Jews from Germany (member of presidium), Leo Baeck Institute (executive member).

WRITINGS: Der unlautere Wettbewerb, J. Bensheimer, 1929, revised edition, 1932; *Das deutsche Kartellrecht,* Philo Verlag (Berlin), 1934; *The Law of Unfair Competition and Trademarks,* three volumes, Callaghan, 1945, second editiop, five volumes, 1950, third edition published as *The Law of Unfair Competition, Trademarks, and Monopolies,* five volumes, 1967.

OBITUARIES: New York Times, March 15, 1976.*

(Died March 12, 1976, in Kew Gardens, Long Island, N.Y.)

* * *

CALMER, Ned 1907-

PERSONAL: Born July 16, 1907, in Chicago, Ill.; son of Henry Edgar and May (Regan) Calmer; married Priscilla A. Hatch, March, 1929; married Carol Church, August, 1957; children: Alden (daughter), Regan (son). *Education:* Attended University of Virginia, 1930. *Home and office:* 125 Ocean Ave., Lawrence, N.Y. 11559.

CAREER: Chicago Tribune, Chicago, Ill., and *Herald-Tribune,* New York City, reporter and foreign correspondent, 1927-34; Agence Havas, France, foreign news editor in New York City, 1934-40; Columbia Broadcasting System (CBS), New York City, news editor and broadcaster, 1940-67; writer. War correspondent with U.S. Armed Forces in Europe, 1944-45, and Mediterranean correspondent, 1951-53. *Member:* New York County Grand Jury Association, Association of Radio News Analysts, Players Club and Fencers Club (both New York City), Rockaway Hunting Club.

WRITINGS: The Strange Land, Scribner, 1950; *All the Summer Days,* Little, Brown, 1961; *The Anchorman,* Doubleday, 1970; *The Avima Affair,* Doubleday, 1973.*

* * *

CAMERON, Elizabeth Jane 1910-1976
(Jane Duncan, Janet Sandison)

March 10, 1910—October 20, 1976; Scottish-born author of

books under her own name as well as under pseudonyms Jane Duncan and Janet Sandison. Besides the ''My Friend'' series published under the Duncan pseudonym, Cameron wrote juvenile books and her memoirs under her own name. Obituaries: *Publishers Weekly,* November 22, 1976. (See index for previous *CA* sketch)

* * *

CAMPANILE, Archille 1900(?)-1977

1900(?)—January 4, 1977; Journalist, playwright, television critic, and author. He died in Italy. Obituaries: *New York Times,* January 5, 1977; *AB Bookman's Weekly,* February 14, 1977.

* * *

CAMPBELL, Alexander 1912-1977

October 19, 1912—January 13, 1977; Scottish-born journalist, foreign correspondent (variously from South Africa, India, Korea, Japan, the Middle East, and most recently from Washington, D.C., for the London *Economist*), former managing editor of the *New Republic,* international affairs writer for *U.S. News and World Report,* and author of books on subjects he has covered as a journalist. He died in Washington, D.C. Obituaries: *New York Times,* January 14, 1977. (See index for previous *CA* sketch)

* * *

CAMPBELL, Charles S(outter) 1911-

PERSONAL: Born April 9, 1911, in Essex Falls, N.J.; son of Charles S. (a businessman) and Mary (Abbe) Campbell; married Anne Howson (an art historian), May 1, 1944; children: Patrick C. *Education:* Yale University, B.A., 1933, M.A., 1937, Ph.D., 1938. *Home:* 694 West 11th St., Claremont, Calif. 91711. *Office:* Department of History, Claremont Graduate School, Claremont, Calif. 91711.

CAREER: Yale-in-China (now Yale-China), Changsha, China, teacher of English and history, 1933-35; American University of Beirut, Beirut, Lebanon, adjunct professor of economics, 1938-40 and 1946-47; U.S. State Department, Washington, D.C., worked in commercial policy division, 1940-46; Johns Hopkins University, Baltimore, Md., assistant professor, 1947-57, associate professor of history, 1957-58; Claremont Graduate School, Claremont, Calif., associate professor, 1958-60, professor of history, 1960—. Visiting professor at University of Wisconsin, Madison, 1962; Fulbright-Hays senior lecturer at University of East Anglia, 1977-78.

WRITINGS: Special Business Interests and the Open Door Policy, Yale University Press, 1951; *Anglo-American Understanding, 1898-1903,* Johns Hopkins University Press, 1957; *From Revolution to Rapprochement: The United States and Great Britain,* Wiley, 1974; *The Transformation of American Foreign Relations, 1865-1900,* Harper, 1976.

WORK IN PROGRESS: Research on U.S. foreign relations, 1848-1905.

* * *

CAMPBELL, Donald 1940-

PERSONAL: Born February 25, 1940, in Wick, Caithness, Scotland; son of William Henry (a plumber) and Mary Elizabeth (a cook; maiden name, Mackenzie) Campbell; married Jean Elliot Fairgrieve (a teacher), October 15, 1966; children: Gavin Douglas. *Education:* Educated in Edinburgh,

Scotland. *Politics:* Socialist. *Religion:* Agnostic. *Home and office:* 53 Viewforth, Edinburgh, Scotland. *Agent:* Joanna Marston, Rosica Colin Ltd., 4 Hereford Sq., London, England.

CAREER: Writer. Writer-in-residence for Lotian Region of Scotland, 1971—; creative writing coach in Scottish schools; involved in community arts programs. Governor of Newbattle Abbey College. *Member:* Scottish Society of Playwrights, Scots Language Society. *Awards, honors:* Bursary award from Scottish Arts Council, 1973; playwright award from Arts in Fife, 1975.

WRITINGS: Poems, Akros Publications, 1971; *Rhymes 'n Reasons,* Gordon Wright, 1972; *Murals,* Lothlorien, 1975; *The Jesuit,* Paul Harris, 1976.

Author of plays "Culture Vulture," "Jean Dundee," and "Somerville the Soldier." Author of radio plays "Poet at Large," "Moods," "Living with Others," "Testament of Cresseid," and "Robert Garioch's Edinburgh."

WORK IN PROGRESS: Research on his Caithness ancestry, for a stage play.

BIOGRAPHICAL/CRITICAL SOURCES: Leonard Mason, *Two Younger Poets: Duncan Glen and Donald Campbell,* Akros Publications, 1976.

* * *

CAMPBELL, F(enton) Gregory, Jr. 1939-

PERSONAL: Born December 16, 1939, in Columbia, Tenn.; son of Fenton G. (an engineer) and Ruth (Hayes) Campbell; married Barbara Kuhn (a writer), August 29, 1970; children: Fenton, Matthew. *Education:* Baylor University, A.B., 1960; Emory University, M.A., 1962; Yale University, Ph.D., 1967; also attended University of Marburg and Charles University. *Politics:* "No party." *Religion:* Baptist. *Office:* Office of the Acting President, Yale University, New Haven, Conn. 06520.

CAREER: Yale University, New Haven, Conn., research staff historian, 1966-68; University of Wisconsin, Milwaukee, assistant professor of history, 1968-69; University of Chicago, Chicago, Ill., assistant professor of European history, 1969-76; Yale University, special assistant to the acting president of the university, 1977—. Fellow at Woodrow Wilson International Center for Scholars, 1976-77; consultant to International Research and Exchanges Board. *Member:* American Historical Association, American Association for the Advancement of Slavic Studies. *Awards, honors:* Woodrow Wilson fellowship, 1961-62; Fulbright fellowship, 1960-61 and 1973-74; grant from East European Exchange, 1965-66 and 1973-74.

WRITINGS: (Editor with International Editorial Commission) *Akten zur deutschen auswaertigen Politik,* 1918-1945 (title means "Documents on German Foreign Policy, 1918-1945"), Vandenhoech & Ruprecht, 1966; *Confrontation in Central Europe: Weimar Germany and Czechoslovakia,* University of Chicago Press, 1975.

WORK IN PROGRESS: Masaryk's Czechoslovakia in the Wilsonian Order (tentative title), a general comparative history.

SIDELIGHTS: Campbell comments: "I believe in the civilizing impact of liberal education, particularly in its espousal of creative individuality. This is the basic motive force behind my activities as an historian and a college teacher and administrator. By helping to mold rational and moral individuals, educators can do much more for society than those who would settle for collective mediocrity."

CAMPBELL, James Marshall 1895-1977

September 30, 1895—March 25, 1977; American Roman Catholic clergyman, educator, and author. His specialty was the classics. Campbell was a member of several professional organizations. He died in Washington, D.C. Obituaries: *Washington Post,* March 26, 1977.

* * *

CAMPBELL, Margaret

PERSONAL: Born in London, England; daughter of Alexander (a singer) and Mabel (an actress; maiden name, Norton) Gollan; married Richard Beare (a dealer in musical instruments), September 23, 1947; children: Steve, Sally, Bruce. *Education:* Studied music privately; presently attending Open University. *Home and office:* White House, 160 Piccotts End. Hemel Hempstead, Hertfordshire, England. *Agent:* Curtis Brown Ltd., 1 Craven Ter., London W.2, England; and John Cushman Associates, Inc., 25 West 43rd St., New York, N.Y. 10036.

CAREER: Began as commercial photographer in London, later became free-lance "society" journalist and writer of short fiction; free-lance feature writer on music and musical instruments, 1960—. *Member:* Society of Authors, National Book League, Galpin Society (member of executive committee), Oxford Foundation for Historical Musical Instruments (founder), Dolmetsch Foundation (member of board of governors). *Awards, honors:* Winston Churchill Memorial Travelling Fellowship, United States, France, and Belgium, 1971.

WRITINGS: Dolmetsch: The Man and His Work, University of Washington Press, 1975. Author of material for British Broadcasting Corp. Author of "Associates," column formerly in *Screenwriter.* Contributor to *Grove's Dictionary of Music and Musicians.* Contributor of articles, stories, and reviews to magazines and newspapers. Editor of *British Journal of Music Therapy.*

WORK IN PROGRESS: The Great Violinists, "a history of performing styles told through the lives of the famous players from Corelli to the present time."

SIDELIGHTS: Margaret Campbell writes: "My father was a singer and I was reared against a musical background. My own talents in music are limited but I studied singing and have always sung in a first class choir. I have been fortunate in that I am able to use my one talent (which is writing) to its best advantage in pursuing music subjects. Thus I get paid for doing something which is also the greatest pleasure. I live in the country and love the quiet and the clean air."

AVOCATIONAL INTERESTS: Reading, walking, yoga.

* * *

CAMPBELL, Robert B(lair) 1923-

PERSONAL: Born January 3, 1923, in Herrin, Ill.; daughter of Charles W. (a politician) and Edith L. (a piano teacher; maiden name, Blair) Campbell; married Jennie Ruth Pope (a teacher), June 13, 1949; children: Blair Bruce, Laura Beth Campbell Unland, Ross Richard, Martha Sue, Jennifer Andrea. *Education:* Southern Illinois University, B.S., 1944; Indiana State University, B.A., 1944; University of Wisconsin, Madison, M.S., 1951, Ph.D., 1956. *Office:* Department of Sociology, Southern Illinois University, Edwardsville, Ill. 62025.

CAREER: University of North Dakota, Grand Forks, 1951-62, began as instructor and became professor of sociology, chairman of department of sociology and anthropology, 1956-62; Southern Illinois University, Edwardsville, associate professor, 1962-70, professor of sociology, 1970—, chairman of department, 1963, dean of social sciences, 1967-69. Visiting professor at Michigan State University and University of Manitoba. *Military service:* U.S. Naval Reserve, active duty, 1943-46; became lieutenant junior grade. *Member:* American Sociological Association (fellow), American Academy of Political and Social Sciences, American Association of University Professors (past local president), Midwest Sociological Society.

WRITINGS: (With S. C. Kelley, Jr., Ross Talbot, and B. K. Wills) *The Williston Report: The Impact of Oil on the Williston Area of North Dakota,* University of North Dakota Press, 1956; *Geology of Glenlyon Map-Area, Yukon Territory,* privately printed, 1967; (with Gunter Remmling) *Basic Sociology: An Introduction to the Study of Society,* Littlefield, 1971. Contributor to professional journals.

WORK IN PROGRESS: International Organization.

*   *   *

CAMPEN, Richard N(ewman)   1912-

PERSONAL: Born August 1, 1912, in Cleveland, Ohio; son of Morris J. (in manufacturing) and Ottille (a teacher; maiden name, Newman) Campen; married Helen Selden, April 26, 1937; children: Richard Selden, Selden William. *Education:* Dartmouth College, A.B., 1934; graduate study at Case Western Reserve University, 1941-45, and Kent State University, 1969. *Politics:* Republican. *Religion:* "Unaffiliated Unitarian." *Home and office:* 27 West Summit St., Chagrin Falls, Ohio 44022.

CAREER: Stoner-Mudge, Inc., Pittsburgh, Pa., in technical sales, 1948-52; Celanese Corp., Pittsburgh, in technical sales, 1952-56; Air Reduction Chemical and Carbide, Pittsburgh, in product development, 1956-67; writer and photographer, 1962—. Owner of West Summit Press. Member of local Planning and Zoning Commission, 1971-75. *Member:* Society of Architectural Historians (founding member; first president of Cleveland chapter, 1964—), American Institute of Archaeology. *Awards, honors:* Western Reserve Award from Society of Architectural Historians, for *Architecture of the Western Reserve.*

WRITINGS: George Brown of Gates Mills: Stonemason, privately printed, 1969; *Architecture of the Western Reserve,* Press of Case Western Reserve University, 1971; *Ohio: An Architectural Portrait* (with own photographs), West Summit Press, 1973; *Our Valley . . . Our Villages: An Illustrated Story of the Chagrin Valley* (with own photographs), West Summit Press, 1976; *Sanibel and Captiva: Enchanting Islands* (with own photographs), West Summit Press, in press. Contributor to *Cleveland Plain Dealer.*

SIDELIGHTS: Campen writes: "Circa 1967 I made an abrupt change in the direction of my career from chemically-related pursuits to writing in the realm of architectural history. Membership in the Society of Architectural Historians has been a great stimulus to my growth. The West Summit Press is a sole proprietorship of my own. I am proud that I have successfully designed and marketed the Ohio book and *Our Valley . . . ,* etc. Every one of the numerous photos was taken and processed by me. This is the achievement of a 'renaissance man.'"

*   *   *

CAMPOLO, Anthony, Jr.   1935-

PERSONAL: Born February 25, 1935, in Philadelphia, Pa.;

son of Anthony (a radio repairman) and Mary (Piccirelli) Campolo; married Margaret Davidson (in real estate sales), June 7, 1958; children: Lisa Davidson, Bart Anthony. *Education:* Eastern Baptist College (now Eastern College), B.A., 1956; University of Pennsylvania, graduate study, 1958-59; Eastern Baptist Theological Seminary, Th.M. and B.D., both 1960; Temple University, Ph.D., 1968. *Home:* 486 Glenmary Lane, St. Davids, Pa. 19087. *Office:* Department of Sociology, Eastern College, St. Davids, Pa. 19087.

CAREER: Ordained Baptist minister, 1959; pastor of American Baptist church in King of Prussia, Pa., 1961-65; Eastern College, St. Davids, Pa., associate professor, 1965-73, professor of sociology, 1973—, chairman of department, 1966—. Visiting associate professor at University of Pennsylvania, 1966-75; visiting lecturer at Eastern Baptist Theological Seminary, 1968-73. Staff member of WCAU-Television; host of television programs; has appeared on the "Mike Douglas Show." Democratic candidate for U.S. Congress, 1976. Vice-president of American Baptist Sociological Association, Evangelical Association for the Promotion of Education (president).

WRITINGS: A Denomination Looks at Itself, Judson, 1971. Contributor to periodicals, including *Watchman-Examiner, Foundations,* and *Observer.*

WORK IN PROGRESS: A book on family life.

SIDELIGHTS: Campolo writes: "My book, *A Denomination Looks at Itself,* is an attempt to use sociological methods to analyze a major American denomination. It illustrates how the church can become captive to sociological processes which will eventually mold its nature, its message, and its lifestyle.

"Perhaps the most important aspect of my life right now is that I have been involved in developing a new university in the Dominican Republic, and I have also developed a program to create job training for Dominicans. Related to this is a program called SELF-HELP, in which we market products manufactured in the Dominican Republic here in the United States, thus creating a market for village people who can produce craft products. We feel this represents a new way of expressing missionary concern."

*   *   *

CANDELARIA, Nash   1928-

PERSONAL: Born May 7, 1928, in Los Angeles, Calif.; son of Ignacio N. (a railway mail clerk) and Flora (Rivera) Candelaria; married Doranne Godwin (a fashion designer), November 27, 1955; children: David, Alex. *Education:* University of California, Los Angeles, B.S., 1948. *Politics:* "I usually vote for the wrong person." *Religion:* "Non-church-going monotheistic and cultural Christian." *Home:* 1295 Wilson St., Palo Alto, Calif. 94301. *Office:* Varian Associates, Inc., 611 Hansen Way, Palo Alto, Calif. 94303.

CAREER: Don Baxter, Inc. (pharmaceutical firm), Glendale, Calif., chemist, 1948-52; *Atomics International,* Downey, Calif., technical editor, 1953-54; Beckman Instruments, Fullerton, Calif., promotion supervisor, 1954-59; Northro-Nortronics, Anaheim, Calif., in marketing communications, 1959-65; Hixon & Jorgensen Advertising, Los Angeles, Calif., account executive, 1965-67; Varian Associates (in scientific instruments), Palo Alto, Calif., advertising manager, 1967—. *Military service:* U.S. Air Force, 1952-53; became second lieutenant.

WRITINGS: Memories of the Alhambra (novel), Cibola Press, 1977. Contributor to *Science.* Editor of *Via.*

WORK IN PROGRESS: Rancho Grande (tentative title), a "novel about the Mexican War from the point of view of the Mexicans who afterwards became Americans by conquest."

SIDELIGHTS: Candelaria writes: *"Memories of the Alhambra* is about the Chicano heritage myth of being descendants of Conquistadors. *Rancho Grande* is a look at the war that made Americans of these people. I plan a third novel about this subject matter, but a contemporary middle-class novel with Spanish surname heroes. I am a descendant of one of the founding families of Albuquerque, New Mexico, and though born in·California I also consider myself a New Mexican."

AVOCATIONAL INTERESTS: Travel (Mexico, Europe, including Spain), the arts.

* * *

CANNON, Beth 1951-

PERSONAL: Born August 30, 1951, in Kansas; daughter of J. Thomas (a consultant) and Ann (Tuller) Cannon. *Education:* Rhode Island School of Design, B.F.A., 1972. *Home and office:* 84 Christopher St., New York, N.Y. 10014. *Agent:* John Brockman, 241 Central Park W., New York, N.Y.

CAREER: Artist, book illustrator, and writer.

WRITINGS: A Cat Had a Fish About a Dream (self-illustrated), Pantheon, 1976.

Illustrator: Shirley Ross, *Plant Consciousness, Plant Care,* Quadrangle, 1973; Ann Cameron, *The Seed,* Pantheon, 1975; Ross, *First Aid for House Plants,* McGraw, 1976.

WORK IN PROGRESS: A picture book based on the work of Proust.

SIDELIGHTS: Beth Cannon has had three shows at Gotham Bookmart Gallery in New York, N.Y. Two of them have been solo shows of her art.

* * *

CANNY, Nicholas P(atrick) 1944-

PERSONAL: Born January 4, 1944, in Ireland; son of Cecil R. (a teacher) and Helen (Joyce) Canny; married Morwena Denis (a teacher), January 5, 1974; children: Solenn (daughter). *Education:* National University of Ireland, University College at Galway, B.A., 1964, M.A., 1967; further graduate study at University of London, 1969-70; University of Pennsylvania, Ph.D., 1971. *Home:* 8 Sylvan Heights, Galway, Ireland. *Office:* Department of History, National University of Ireland, University College, Galway, Ireland.

CAREER: University of Pennsylvania, Philadelphia, fellow, 1967-71; National University of Ireland, University College, Galway, assistant lecturer, 1971-72, lecturer in history, 1972—. Visiting fellow at Harvard University, autumn, 1974, and Yale University, spring, 1975. *Member:* Irish Economic and Social History Society (committee member, 1976—), Irish Association for American Studies (committee member, 1976—), Irish Historical Society. *Awards, honors:* Fulbright-Hays senior fellowship, 1974-74.

WRITINGS: The Elizabethan Conquest of Ireland: A Pattern Established, 1565-1576, Harvester Press, 1976; (editor with K. R. Andrews and P.E.H. Hair) *The Westward Enterprise: The English in the Atlantic, Ireland, and America, 1550-1650,* Liverpool University Press, 1977.

WORK IN PROGRESS: A comparative study of English settlement in Ireland and Virginia, 1580-1650, completion expected in 1980.

SIDELIGHTS: Canny describes himself briefly as "a bilingual Irishman devoted to understanding the European colonization experience from the point of view of the colonized as well as the colonizer."

* * *

CANTOR, Leonard M(artin) 1927-

PERSONAL: Born November 25, 1927, in London, England; son of Abraham (a telephonist) and Fanny (Rosenberg) Cantor; married Betty Louise Philpott (a registered nurse), March 15, 1961; children: David John, Martin John. *Education:* University of London, B.A. (honors), 1951, certificate in education, 1952, M.A., 1960. *Home:* 14 Stoop Lane, Quorn, Leicestershire, England. *Office:* Department of Education, Loughborough University of Technology, Loughborough, Leicestershire, England.

CAREER: School teacher in Portsmouth, England, 1952-58; University of Keele, Keele, England, lecturer, 1958-67, senior lecturer in education, 1967-69; Loughborough University of Technology, Loughborough, England, Schofield Professor of Education, 1969—, dean of School of Education, 1969-73, senior pro-vice chancellor, 1976—. Also taught at Reed College, 1964-5, University of Michigan, summers of 1967 and 1969, and University of California, Long Beach, summer, 1974. *Military service:* Royal Air Force, 1946-48.

WRITINGS: Water and Man, Chatto & Windus, 1963; *A World Geography of Irrigation,* Oliver & Boyd, 1967, 2nd edition, Praeger, 1970; (with I. F. Roberts) *Further Education in England and Wales,* Routledge & Kegan Paul, 1969, 2nd edition, 1972; *Recurrent Enducation in the United Kingdom,* Organization for Economic Co-operation and Development, 1974; (contributor) A. D. M. Phillips and B. J. Turton, editors, *Environment, Man, and Economic Change,* Longman, 1975; (with G. F. Matthews) *Loughborough: From College to University,* Loughborough University of Technology, 1977; (with Roberts) *Further Education Today: A Critical Analysis,* Routledge & Kegan Paul, in press.

SIDELIGHTS: Cantor told *CA* that his writings on irrigation, notably on the California State Water Project, "are concerned with the geographical aspects of irrigated agriculture, particularly its role in transforming the landscape. Writings on further, adult, and recurrent education are concerned with the organisation and provision of post-school education, primarily in the United Kingdom. Writings on the English medieval landscape, largely in the form of articles in English historical and archaeological journals, are concerned primarily with the problems and techniques of mapping the English medieval landscape, particularly in respect of the medieval park."

AVOCATIONAL INTERESTS: Badminton, bridge, crossword puzzles, and gardening.

* * *

CARLETON, R(eginal) Milton 1899-

PERSONAL: Born July 16, 1899, in Chicago, Ill.; son of Charles August (an engineer) and Ellen (Du Aubrey) Carlton; married Frances Griffith (a musician and composer); children: Shelley Diane Carleton Seccombe, Nancy Lynne Carleton Pennington, Daniel Webster. *Education:* University of Illinois, B.S., 1918; University of Uppsala, Ph.D., 1920. *Politics:* Independent. *Religion:* "Agnostic Humanist." *Home:* (Winter) 1938 High Point Dr., Sarasota, Fla. 33577; (summer) Matinicus, Maine 04851.

CAREER: U.S. Gypsum Co., Chicago, Ill., agronomist, 1920-35; consulting agronomist, 1935-38; Vaughan's Seed Co., Chicago, Ill., research director, 1938-68; Growth Systems, Inc., Glenview, Ill., research director, 1968-76; horticultural consultant, 1976—. Founder of Chicago's Municipal Rose Garden. *Military service:* U.S. Army, Allied Expeditionary Force, 1918-20; became first lieutenant. *Member:* American Horticultural Society (founding member; past member of board of directors; past vice-president), American Society for Horticultural Science (president), American Association for the Advancement of Science (fellow), Chicago Horticultural Society (president, 1958-60). *Awards, honors:* Charles Hutchinson Medal from Chicago Horticulture Society, 1966.

WRITINGS: Hardy Bulbs, Rinehart, 1955; *A New Way to Kill Weeds in Your Lawn and Garden,* Fawcett, 1957; *Index to Common Names of Herbaceous Plants,* G. K. Hall, 1959; *Your Lawn: How to Make It and Keep It,* Van Nostrand, 1959, 2nd edition, 1971; *Your Garden Soil: How to Make the Most of It,* Van Nostrand, 1961; *Vegetables for Today's Gardens,* Van Nostrand, 1967, revised edition, 1972; *Indoor Gardening Fun: Year-Round Projects for Children,* Reilly & Lee, 1970; *The Small Garden Book,* Macmillan, 1971; *False Profits of Pollution: How Fake Ecologists Sidetrack America's Progress,* Trend Publications, 1973; *The New Vegetable and Fruit Garden Book,* Regnery, 1976. Contributor of more than a thousand articles on gardening to magazines in Canada, England, and the United States.

WORK IN PROGRESS: Tests for Cancer: Can We Trust Them?; a lawn book; a greenhouse book; a book of garden verse and miscellany.

SIDELIGHTS: Carleton writes: "As research director for Vaughan's Seed Co., I visited every major state and federal experiment station in the United States and Canada. I met four Nobel Prize winners, dozens of top scientists, and was able to study many important research projects before publication. This enabled me to participate in research on D.D.T., 2.4.D., Merion Blue Grass, horticultural vermiculite, and many other firsts."

* * *

CARLISLE, Howard M(yron) 1928-

PERSONAL: Born September 30, 1928, in Salt Lake City, Utah; son of Myron C. and Hazel (Checketts) Carlisle; married Colleen Boss (a secretary), December 18, 1956; children: Richard, Julie, Jana Lou, Michael. *Education:* Utah State University, B.S., 1950, graduate study, 1969-70; University of Wisconsin, Madison, M.S., 1952; University of California, Berkeley, further graduate study, 1952-54. *Home:* 1525 East 1220 N., Logan, Utah 84321. *Office:* Department of Business Administration, Utah State University, Logan, Utah 84322.

CAREER: U.S. Atomic Energy Commission, Oakland, Calif., budget officer, 1954-58; Thiokol Corp., Brigham City, Utah, director of budgeting and planning, 1958-64; Utah State University, Logan, assistant professor, 1964-67; associate professor, 1967-75, professor of business administration, 1975—, head of department, 1967—. Member of W. S. Sigler & Associates (consultants). *Member:* Academy of Management, Utah Teachers Association, Rotary International. *Awards, honors:* Writers award from *Aerospace Management,* 1964, for an article.

WRITINGS: Situational Management, American Management Associations, 1973; *Management: Concepts and Situations,* Science Research Associates, 1976. Contributor of about twenty-five articles on management to journals.

WORK IN PROGRESS: A book on organizational behavior, with Y. K. Shetty and Newman Perry; a book on management for use in junior colleges; research on planning and motivation.

SIDELIGHTS: Carlisle writes that his major interest in travel and research relates to industrial management in foreign countries. In 1976-77 he lived in England, teaching U.S. military officers.

* * *

CARMEL, Catherine 1939-

PERSONAL: Name legally changed in 1975; born June 6, 1939, in Oakland, Calif.; daughter of Joseph B. (a farmer) and Carmella (Lima) Canciamilla; married Herbert Wheeler, February 3, 1957 (divorced, 1964); children: Michelle Wheeler, Donna Wheeler. *Education:* Attended San Jose State University and Sophia University, Tokyo, Japan. *Home:* 320 Brook Dr., Boulder Creek, Calif. 95006. *Office:* Mercury Communications, Inc., 730 Mission, Santa Cruz, Calif. 95060.

CAREER: GTE/Novar Corp., Mountain View, Calif., consultant, 1971-72; Reizes, Wechler & Wheeler, Sunnyvale, Calif., consultant, 1972-76; Mercury Communications, Santa Cruz, Calif., director and vice-president of marketing, 1976—. *Member:* Electronic Defense Association.

WRITINGS—All published by Mercury Communications: *How to Create a Winning Proposal,* 1976; *The War On Fat,* 1976; *You Can Do It!,* 1977. Also author of data communications systems and equipment manuals. Contributor of articles to technical magazines.

* * *

CARMEN, Arlene 1936-

PERSONAL: Born April 5, 1936, in New York; daughter of Jacob and Mina (Goldberg) Carmen. *Education:* City College of the City University of New York, B.A., 1962. *Home:* 237 Thompson St., New York, N.Y. 10012. *Office:* Judson Memorial Church, 55 Washington Sq. S., New York, N.Y. 10012.

CAREER: Judson Memorial Church, New York, N.Y., administrator, 1967—.

WRITINGS: (With Howard Moody) *Abortion Counseling and Social Change,* Judson, 1973.

* * *

CARMER, Carl (Lamson) 1893-1976

October 16, 1893—September 11, 1976; American professor of English, journalist, folklorist, historian of upstate New York, and novelist. His published books include volumes of poetry, juveniles, and books on upstate New York. Carmer died in Bronxville, N.Y. Obituaries: *New York Times,* September 12, 1976. (See index for previous *CA* sketch)

* * *

CARNEVALI, Doris L(orrain)

PERSONAL: Born in Seattle, Wash.; daughter of Helmer and Hannah (Anderson) Scholin; married Armando Carnevali; children: Nick, Jeffrey. *Education:* Swedish Hospital School of Nursing, diploma, 1943; University of Washington, Seattle, B.S.N., 1947, M.N., 1961. *Home:* 3250 36th Ave. S.W., Seattle, Wash. 98126. *Office:* School of Nursing, University of Washington, Seattle, Wash. 98195.

CAREER: Swedish Hospital, Seattle, Wash., staff nurse,

1944-45; head nurse, 1945-46; clinical instructor, 1947-51; Veteran's Administration Hospital, Seattle, supervisor, 1951-53; Washington State Nurses Association, Seattle, assistant executive secretary, 1953-55; University of Washington, School of Nursing, Seattle, instructor, 1947-51, 1961-66, assistant professor, 1966-69, associate professor of nursing, 1969—. *Member:* American Nurses Association (member of Council of Nurse Researchers, 1971), National League for Nursing, Sigma Theta Tau (charter member of Psi chapter). *Awards, honors:* Honorable mention from *American Journal of Nursing,* 1968, for best feature article "Rendevous in Nursing"; Book of the Year award from American Journal of Nursing, 1969, for *Nursing Care Planning.*

WRITINGS: (With Dolores Little) *Nursing Care Planning,* Lippincott, 1969, 2nd edition, 1976; (with Maxine Patrick) *Handbook for Geriatric Nurse Clinicians,* Lippincott, in press.

Contributor: Edith M. Lewis, editor, *The Clinical Nurse Specialist,* American Journal of Nursing Co., 1970; Margaret Auld and Linda Birum, editors, *The Challenge of Nursing,* Mosby, 1973; Joan P. Riehl and Joan Wilcox McVay, editors, *The Clinical Nurse Specialist,* Appleton, 1973; Pamela Mitchell, editor, *Concepts Basic to Nursing,* McGraw, 1973, 2nd edition, 1977; Marjorie V. Batey, editor, *Communicating Nursing Research,* Volume VIII, Western Interstate Commission for Higher Education, 1975; Ann Marriner, editor, *The Nursing Process: A Scientific Approach to Nursing Care,* Nursing Publications, 1975; Judith Walter, Geraldine Pardee, and Doris M. Molbo, editors, *Dynamics of Problem Oriented Approaches,* Lippincott, 1976. Contributor of about twenty articles to nursing journals.

SIDELIGHTS: Doris Carnevali told *CA* that her writings focus on the diagnostic and management areas of nursing, and on nursing skills which help patients to effectively manage health and illness related aspects of daily living. She added that interdisciplinary health team development and the role of the nurse on such teams is an area of current activity and research for her.

* * *

CARNEY, John J(oseph), Jr. 1932-

PERSONAL: Born September 8, 1932, in Yonkers, N.Y.; son of John Joseph (a machinist) and Julia (Donegan) Carney; married Margaret Kane (a book seller), July 18, 1959; children: John Joseph III, Caralee, Julie, Christy. *Education:* State University of New York College at Geneseo, B.S., 1960; Pennsylvania State University, M.A., 1961, Ph.D., 1976. *Home:* 44 Elm St., Oneonta, N.Y. 13820. *Office:* Department of Speech and Theatre, State University of New York College at Oneonta, Oneonta, N.Y. 13820.

CAREER: Board of Cooperative Educational Services, Avon-Livonia, N.Y., speech correctionist, 1960; State University of New York College at Potsdam, assistant professor of speech, 1961-65; State University of New York College at Oneonta, associate professor, 1965-70, professor of speech, 1970—. Lecturer at Speech Communication Institute, summer, 1973; guest lecturer at colleges; public speaker. *Military service:* U.S. Air Force, 1953-57; became airman first class. *Member:* American Committee for Irish Studies, Irish American Cultural Institute, Speech Communication Association of America, Eastern States Communication Association, New York State Speech Association (president, 1970-71).

WRITINGS: (Editor and contributor) *Communication for*

Education, International Textbook Co., 1971; (editor) *Crises in Communication: Three Speeches,* New York State Speech Association, 1971. Contributor to speech and communication journals. Co-editor of *New York State Forensic League Newsletter,* 1966-70.

WORK IN PROGRESS: A book on nineteenth-century Irish attitudes toward deliberative oratory.

SIDELIGHTS: Carney writes: "I am seriously concerned with the effects of television on all aspects of the rhetorical-situation. I've had a life-long interest in my Irish heritage, especially as it provides insight into how people attempt to persuade other people politically." *Avocational interests:* Collecting books.

* * *

CARO, Francis G(eorge) 1936-

PERSONAL: Born September 28, 1936, in Milwaukee, Wis.; son of Walter (an engineer) and Elizabeth (Voss) Caro; married Carol Bauer (in public administration), December 28, 1965; children: Paul, David. *Education:* Marquette University, B.S., 1958; University of Minnesota, Ph.D., 1962. *Politics:* Democrat. *Home:* 262 Farrington Ave., North Tarrytown, N.Y. 10591. *Office:* Community Service Society, 105 East 22nd St., New York, N.Y. 10010.

CAREER: Community Studies, Inc., Kansas City, Mo., research associate, 1962-64; Community Progress, Inc., New Haven, Conn., research associate, 1964-65; Marquette University, Milwaukee, Wis., assistant professor of sociology, 1965-67; University of Colorado, Boulder, associate professor of sociology, 1967-70; Brandeis University, Waltham, Mass., associate professor of social welfare, 1970-74; Community Service Society, New York, N.Y., director of office of Program Planning and Research, 1974—. *Member:* American Sociological Association, Society for the Study of Social Problems.

WRITINGS: (Editor) *Readings in Evaluation Research,* Russell Sage, 1970, 2nd edition, 1977. Contributor to sociology journals.

* * *

CARONIA, Guiseppe 1884(?)-1977

1884(?)—January 15, 1977; Italian pediatrician and author of works in his field. He died in Rome, Italy. Obituaries: *New York Times,* January 17, 1977; *Washington Post,* January 17, 1977.

* * *

CARR, John Dickson 1906-1977
(Carr Dickson, Carter Dickson; John Rhode, a joint pseudonym)

November 30, 1906—February 27, 1977; American writer for British Broadcasting Corp. during World War II, best-selling mystery novelist, short-story writer, and author of works of nonfiction, including the official biography of Sir Arthur Conan Doyle. The famous mystery novel detectives Dr. Gideon Fell and Sir Henry Merrivale were his creation. Carr was considered master of the "locked-room" crime puzzle both under his own name and under pseudonym Carter Dickson. He received Edgar awards in 1949 and 1962, and received the *Ellery Queen* prize twice for short stories. He died in Greenville, S.C. Obituaries: *New York Times,* March 1, 1977; *Washington Post,* March 2, 1977; *Newsweek,* March 14, 1977; *Time,* March 14, 1977; *AB Bookman's Weekly,* May 9, 1977. (See index for previous *CA* sketch)

CARRIKER, Robert C(harles) 1940-

PERSONAL: Born August 18, 1940, in St. Louis, Mo.; son of Thomas B. (a postal employee) and Vivian (Spaunhorst) Carriker; married Eleanor R. Gualdoni, August 24, 1963; children: Thomas, Robert, Andrew. *Education:* St. Louis University, B.S., 1962, A.M., 1963; University of Oklahoma, Ph.D., 1967. *Politics:* Independent. *Religion:* Roman Catholic. *Home:* 3604 Northwest Blvd., Spokane, Wash. 99205. *Office:* Department of History, Gonzaga University, Spokane, Wash. 99258.

CAREER: Gonzaga University, Spokane, Wash., assistant professor, 1967-71, associate professor, 1971-76, professor of history, 1976—. Visiting lecturer at Arizona State University, 1971-72. Executive vice-president of Pacific Northwest Indian Center (museum). Staff supervisor for Ford Motor Co. exhibit at "Expo '74." *Member:* Organization of American Historians, Council on Abandoned Military Posts, Western History Association. *Awards, honors:* Henry H. Huntington Library fellowships, 1969, 1971; American Philosophical Society grant, 1971.

WRITINGS: Fort Supply, Indian Territory, University of Oklahoma Press, 1970; *The Kalispel People,* Indian Tribal Series, 1973; (editor) *Captain Robert Gray's Charts Discovered after Two Centuries,* Gonzaga University Press, 1975; (editor with wife, Eleanor R. Carriker) *Army Wife in the West,* University of Utah Press, 1975; (with C. L. Carroll and Walter Larsen) *Guide to the Microfilm Edition of the Oregon Province Archives of the Society of Jesus Indian Language Collection: The Alaska Native Languages,* Gonzaga University Press, 1976. Contributor to history and regional studies journals.

WORK IN PROGRESS: A biography of frontier military hero, Lieutenant Frank D. Baldwin; a book of early Alaska photographs; research on Indian Claims Commission documents.

*   *   *

CARROLL, Theodus 1928-

PERSONAL: Given name is pronounced The-*odd*-us; born September 26, 1928, in Pittsburgh, Pa.; daughter of Randolph and Eleanor (Scanlon) Foster; children: Michael, Randolph. *Education:* Attended Duquesne University, 1946-48, and Carnegie Institute of Technology (now Carnegie-Mellon University), summers, 1946-48. *Home:* 148 Silvermine Ave., Norwalk, Conn. 06850. *Agent:* Arthur Pine Associates, Inc., 1780 Broadway, New York, N.Y. 10019.

CAREER: Fiorelli Films, Stamford, Conn., writer, 1967; Health Care Publications, New Canaan, Conn., executive editor, 1968—.

WRITINGS: Evil Is a Quiet Word (novel), Warner Books, 1976.

WORK IN PROGRESS: A historic novel.

SIDELIGHTS: Theodus Carroll writes: "Adults need the security behind the horror story in the same way that children need the scary fairy tale—to give them a stable framework on which to hang their fears, and say—that couldn't happen to me."

*   *   *

CARSTAIRS, George Morrison 1916-

PERSONAL: Born June 18, 1916, in Mussorie, India; son of George C. (a clergyman and missionary) and Elizabeth (a missionary; maiden name, Young) Carstairs; married Vera Hunt (a sociologist), December 14, 1950; children: Susan, Mungo, Benjamin. *Education:* University of Edinburgh, M.A., 1938, M.B.Ch.B., 1941, M.D., 1958. *Office:* Vice-Chancellor's Lodge, University of York, Heslington, York Y01 5DD, England.

CAREER: Maudsley Hospital, London, England, registrar, 1953; Medical Research Council, member of scientific staff with Psychiatry Research Unit, 1954-60; University of Edinburgh, Edinburgh, Scotland, professor of psychiatry, 1961-73; University of York, York, England, vice-chancellor, 1974—. Reith Lecturer for British Broadcasting Corp., 1962. Director of research unit for Medical Research Council, 1960-71. Consultant to World Health Organization. *Military service:* Royal Air Force, medical officer, 1942-46. *Member:* World Federation for Mental Health (president, 1967-71), Royal College of Physicians (Edinburgh; fellow), Royal College of Psychiatrists (London; fellow). *Awards, honors:* Commonwealth fellowship to the United States, 1948-49; Rockefeller research fellowship, India, 1950-51; Henderson research scholar in India, 1951-52.

WRITINGS: The Twice Born, Indiana University Press, 1957; *This Island Now,* Basic Books, 1963, 3rd edition, 1964; (with R. L. Kapur) *The Great Universe of Kota,* University of California Press, 1976. Contributor to medical journals.

WORK IN PROGRESS: A thirty-year study of a village community in Rajasthan, India.

SIDELIGHTS: Carstairs is as much involved in social anthropology as in psychiatry. He has conducted extensive field studies in India, and speaks Hindi. His current interest is in psychiatric services in developing countries, especially in Southeast Asia. *Avocational interests:* Travel, theater, athletics (Scottish champion three-mile runner, 1937-39).

*   *   *

CARTER, James Earl, Jr. 1924-

PERSONAL: Born October 1, 1924, in Archery, Ga.; son of James Earl (a grocer, farm machinery salesman, and politician) and Lillian (a nurse; maiden name, Gordy) Carter; married Rosalynn Smith, July 7, 1946; children: John William, James Earl III, Donnel Jeffery, Amy Lynn. *Education:* Attended Georgia Southwestern College, 1941-42, and Georgia Institute of Technology, 1942-43; U.S. Naval Academy, B.S., 1946; Union College, Schenectady, N.Y., graduate study, 1952. *Politics:* Democrat. *Religion:* Baptist. *Home:* 1 Woodland Dr., Plains, Ga. 31780. *Office:* White House, 1600 Pennsylvania Ave. N.W., Washington, D.C. 20500.

CAREER: Thirty-ninth president of United States. Farmer, owner, and chief executive of general purpose seed and farm supply firm, 1953-62; Georgia state senator, 1962-66; unsuccessful Democratic candidate for governor of Georgia, 1966; farmer and operator of family business, 1966-70; governor of Georgia, 1970-74, served on various regional gubernatorial commissions, on Committee on Natural Resources and Environmental Management of National Governor's Conference, and as chairman of Democratic national committee for the 1974 elections; Democratic candidate for U.S. presidency, with Walter Mondale as vice-presidential running mate, 1976, elected with 297 electoral votes. President, Plains Development Corp., 1963, Sumter Redevelopment Corp., 1963; West Central Georgia Planning and Development Commission (now Middle Flint Area Planning and Development Commission), president, 1964-66, member of executive board, 1967-69. Deacon of Baptist Church. *Military service:* U.S. Navy, 1947-53; became lieutenant commander. *Member:* Georgia Planning Association (president, 1968-69), Georgia Crop Improvement Association (president, 1968-69), Lions International. *Awards, honors:* LL.D. from Morris Brown College, 1972.

WRITINGS: Why Not the Best? (autobiography), Broadman, 1975.

BIOGRAPHICAL/CRITICAL SOURCES—Books: Gary Allen, *Jimmy Carter—Jimmy Carter,* Seventy Six, 1976; Bob Slosser and Howard Norton, *The Miracle of Jimmy Carter,* Logos, 1976; Robert Turner, *I'll Never Lie to You: Jimmy Carter in His Own Words,* Ballantine, 1976; Leslie Wheeler, *Jimmy Who?,* Barron's, 1976.*

* * *

CARTER, Peter 1929-

PERSONAL: Born August 13, 1929, in England; son of Percy (a seaman) and Evelyn (a spinner; maiden name, Giles) Carter; married Gudrun Willege (a photographer), February 17, 1974. *Education:* Wadham College, Oxford, M.A., 1962. *Politics:* None. *Religion:* Anglican. *Home:* c/o Holbeinstrasse 2, D-2 Hamburg, Germany.

CAREER: Worked a wide variety of jobs ranging from construction work to road making, office work to schoolteaching. Churchwarden at St. Barnabas Church, Birmingham, 1973-76. Writer. *Awards, honors:* Guardian Award runner-up, 1974, for *Gates of Paradise.*

WRITINGS—All published by Oxford University Press: *The Black Lamp* (novel), 1973; *Madatan* (novel), 1974; *Gates of Paradise* (novel), 1974; *Mao* (biography), 1976.

WORK IN PROGRESS: The Pipers of Belfast (tentative title), a novel set in contemporary Belfast.

SIDELIGHTS: An extensive traveler, Carter has visited the United States, Canada, India, the Middle East and Europe. He told *CA:* "I write because I enjoy it." *Avocational interests:* Rock climbing, cricket, bird watching.

* * *

CARVER, (Richard) Michael (Power) 1915-

PERSONAL: Born April 24, 1915, in Blechingley, England; son of Harold Power (a merchant) and Winifred Annie Gabrielle (Wellesley) Carver; married Edith Lowry-Corry, November 22, 1947; children: Susanna, Andrew, Alice Carver Walters, John. *Education:* Attended Winchester College and Royal Military College, Sandhurst, 1933-34. *Politics:* None. *Religion:* Church of England. *Home:* Shackleford Old Rectory, Godalming, Surrey GU8 6AE, England. *Agent:* David Higham Associates Ltd., 5-8 Lower John St., London W1R 4HA, England.

CAREER: British Army, career officer, 1935-76, in Royal Tank Corps, 1935, general staff officer in Seventh Armored Division, 1942, commanding officer of First Royal Tank Regiment, 1943, commander of Fourth Armored Brigade, 1944, technical staff officer in Ministry of Supply, 1947, assistant quartermaster-general of Allied Land Forces in Central Europe, 1951, colonel with general staff of Supreme Headquarters, Allied Powers, Europe, 1952, deputy chief of staff in East Africa, 1954, chief of staff in East Africa, 1955, director of plans in War Office, 1958-59, commander of Sixth Infantry Brigade, 1960-62, general officer commanding Third Division, 1962-64, commander of Joint Truce Force in Cyprus and deputy commander of United Nations Force in Cyprus, 1964, director of army staff duties for Ministry of Defence, 1964-66, commander of Far East Land Forces, 1966-67, commander-in-chief in the Far East, 1967-69, general officer commander-in-chief of Southern Command, 1969-71, chief of general staff, 1971-73, commandant of Royal Electrical and Mechanical Engineers, 1966-76, Royal Tank Regiment, 1968-72, Royal Armoured Corps, 1974-76, aide-de-camp (general), 1969-72, chief of defense staff, 1973-76, retiring as field marshal; writer, 1976—.

MEMBER: Anglo-Belgian Club. *Awards, honors*—Military: Military Cross; companion of the Distinguished Service Order, with bar; commander of the Order of the British Empire; Companion of the Bath, Knight Commander, Knight Grand Cross.

WRITINGS: El Alamein, Batsford, 1962; *Tobruk,* Batsford, 1964; (editor) *The War Lords,* Little, Brown, 1976.

WORK IN PROGRESS: A biography of Field Marshal Lord Harding.

* * *

CASEY, John 1939-

PERSONAL: Born January 18, 1939, in Worcester, Mass.; son of Joseph Edward (a lawyer) and Constance (Dudley) Casey; married Jane Barnes (a writer), June 17, 1967; children: Maud Innis, Eleanor Dudley. *Education:* Harvard University, B.A., 1962, LL.B., 1965; University of Iowa, M.F.A., 1968. *Agent:* Brandt & Brandt, 101 Park Ave., New York, N.Y. 10017. *Office:* Department of English, Wilson Hall, University of Virginia, Charlottesville, Va. 22904.

CAREER: University of Virginia, Charlottesville, associate professor of English, 1972—. Admitted to North Carolina Bar, 1966. *Military service:* U.S. Army Reserve, active duty, 1959-60.

WRITINGS: An American Romance, Atheneum, 1977. Contributor to magazines, including *New Yorker, Sports Illustrated, Harper's,* and *Shenandoah,* and to newspapers.

WORK IN PROGRESS: A collection of stories.

* * *

CASEY, Lawrence B. 1905-1977

September 6, 1905—June 15, 1977; American Roman Catholic clergyman. He founded *The Beacon,* the diocesan newspaper for Paterson, N.J., where he served as bishop. His collected weekly columns were published in book form. Casey gained national attention when he opined in a controversial case that no extraordinary life support measures are necessary to prolong life in the terminally ill. He died in Paterson, N.J. Obituaries: *New York Times,* June 16, 1977.

* * *

CASPER, Barry M(ichael) 1939-

PERSONAL: Born January 21, 1939, in Knoxville, Tenn.; son of Barry (a government personnel specialist) and Florence (Becker) Casper; married Myra Barrett (a professor of psychology), June 24, 1961; children: Daniel, Benjamin, Michael. *Education:* Swarthmore College, B.A., 1960; Cornell University, Ph.D., 1966. *Home:* 100 Nevada St., Northfield, Minn. 55057. *Office:* Department of Physics, Carleton College, Northfield, Minn. 55057.

CAREER: Cornell University, Ithaca, N.Y., instructor in physics, 1965-66; Carleton College, Northfield, Minn., assistant professor, 1966-71, associate professor, 1971-77, professor of physics and chairman of department, 1977—. *Member:* Federation of American Scientists (member of executive committee, 1971-75), American Physical Society Forum on Physics and Society (member of executive committee, 1972-77, vice-chairman, 1973, chairman, 1974), American Association of Physics Teachers. *Awards, honors:* Rockefeller Foundation fellowship in humanities, Harvard University, 1975-76; National Science Foundation fellowship, University of Minnesota, 1976-77.

WRITINGS: (With Richard J. Noer) *Revolutions in Physics,* Norton, 1972.

WORK IN PROGRESS: Scientists and the Politics of Technology (tentative title).

* * *

CASTELLS, Matilde O(livella) 1929-

PERSONAL: Born December 20, 1929, in Santiago, Cuba; daughter of Fernando (a physician) and Maria A. (a physician; maiden name, Rivery) Olivella; married Rodolfo Castells (a manager of an airline), 1952; children: Rodolfo, Ricardo, Rafael. *Education:* Attended Mount Aloysius Junior College, 1947-48; University of Havana, Ph.D., 1956; postdoctoral study at Trenton State College, 1961-62, and New York University, 1962. *Office:* Department of Spanish, California State University, Los Angeles, Calif. 90032.

CAREER: Instituto Vedado, Havana, Cuba, instructor in Spanish, 1956-59; high school teacher of Spanish in Pennsylvania, 1961-63; Rutgers University, New Brunswick, N.J., instructor, 1963-66, assistant professor of Spanish, 1966-72; California State University, Los Angeles, associate professor of Spanish, 1972—. Member of Spanish discipline committee for College Entrance Examination Board, 1974-77. *Member:* Modern Language Association of America, American Association of Teachers of Spanish and Portuguese (vice-president of southern California chapter, 1976-78), American Council on the Teaching of Foreign Languages.

WRITINGS: (With Phyllis Boring) *Lengua y lectura: Un repaso y una continuacion,* with instructor's manual, Harcourt, 1970; (with Harold Lionetti) *La lengua espanola: Gramatica y cultura,* with exercise book and instructor's manual, Scribner, 1974. Contributor to language and Spanish studies journals.

WORK IN PROGRESS: A grammar textbook for second-year students, completion expected in 1980.

* * *

CASTLE, William 1914-1977

April 24, 1914—May 31, 1977; American producer, director, and author. Castle produced horror movies, the best known of which was "Rosemary's Baby". He also wrote his autobiography. Castle died in Los Angeles, Calif. Obituaries: *New York Times,* June 2, 1977; *Washington Post,* June 3, 1977.

* * *

CATUDAL, Honore (Marc, Jr.) 1944-

PERSONAL: Born October 17, 1944, in Washington, D.C.; son of Honore M. (a government official) and Gertrude (Hemm) Catudal; married Renate Goerz, April 1, 1967; children: Raymond, Sandra. *Education:* Free University of Berlin, Zertifikat, 1968; Syracuse University, B.A. (cum laude), 1969; American University, M.I.S., 1971, Ph.D., 1973. *Re-*

ligion: Catholic. *Home:* 537 Andrews Dr., Angus Acres, Apt. 3, St. Cloud, Minn. 56301. *Office:* Department of Politics, St. John's University, Collegeville, Minn. 56321.

CAREER: St. John's University, Collegeville, Minn., assistant professor of international relations, 1973—. *Military service:* U.S. Army, 1962-65. *Member:* Oral History Association, American Society of International Law, American Political Science Association, International Studies Association, Conference Group on German Politics, Phi Alpha Theta, Pi Sigma Alpha. *Awards, honors:* Phi Alpha Theta prize, 1969, for essay on Steinstuecken.

WRITINGS: Steinstuecken: A Study in Cold War Politics, privately printed, 1971; *The Enclave Problem of Western Europe,* University of Alabama Press, 1977. Contributor to national and international journals in the fields of geography, history, political science and international relations.

WORK IN PROGRESS: Two books, *The Future of Berlin in East-West Relations,* and *Kennedy and the Berlin Wall Crisis.*

SIDELIGHTS: Catudal's writing on Berlin and enclaves (pieces of one state situated in another) stems from his experience as an army private stationed in the divided city during the early 1960's. There he served as a security guard for Rudolph Hess.

While in college, he traveled to Washington, D.C., New York City, and Cambridge, to interview more than a dozen military and diplomatic officials, who at one time or another have been deeply involved in a Berlin crisis. Among those he talked with were Dwight Eisenhower, Lucius Clay, Maxwell Taylor, James Gavin, Dean Rusk, Robert Murphy, Foy Kohler, Eleanor Dulles, and Allen Dulles.

Catudal spent his "junior year abroad" as a student in Berlin, and took out a second residence in the small enclave community of Steinstuecken, legally part of the American sector but lying as a separate "island" inside East Germany. Encouraged by its 180 inhabitants, who made their personal archives available to him, he proceeded to write its political history. Before Catudal was suddenly barred by East German border guards in 1968, he was one of the few outsiders ever to visit the cut-off village.

When the four-power talks on Berlin got underway in 1970, Catudal proposed that the Steinstuecken enclave be joined to the mainland through an exchange of territory. This idea was soon injected into the conversations with the Russians by American diplomats. The Russians, after some preliminary discussion, accepted the idea of a swap of territory, and so when the quadripartite accord was finally signed in 1971, the inhabitants of Steinstuecken were provided with a Western controlled corridor linking their village with the rest of West Berlin.

AVOCATIONAL INTERESTS: Chess, tennis, and long-distance running.

BIOGRAPHICAL/CRITICAL SOURCES: Washington Post, January 2, 1972.

* * *

CAWLEY, Winifred 1915-

PERSONAL: Born January 24, 1915, in Felton, Northumberland, England; daughter of Percy Frazer (a butler and shopkeeper) and Lottie (a housemaid; maiden name, Dunning) Cozens; married Arthur Clare Cawley (a university professor), January 3, 1939; children: John Cozens. *Education:* University of Durham, B.A. (with honors), 1936; graduate study at University College, London, 1937-39. *Home and office:* Moor Croft, Moor Rd., Bramhope, Leeds LS16 9HH, England.

CAREER: Teacher of English at British Institutes in Romania, 1939-40, and Yugoslavia, 1940-41, and in Cairo, Egypt, 1942-45; College of Commerce and Technology, Leeds, England, part-time teacher, 1949-54; English teacher in Leeds, 1954-59 and 1966-73, and in Brisbane, Australia, 1960-64; writer, 1964—. Has given radio talks in Australia. *Awards, honors:* Guardian award for children's fiction and Carnegie Medal runner-up, both 1974, both for *Gran at Coalgate.*

WRITINGS—Children's novels: *Down the Long Stairs,* Oxford University Press, 1964, Holt, 1965; *Feast of the Serpent,* Oxford University Press, 1969, Holt, 1970; *Gran at Coalgate,* Oxford University Press, 1974, Holt, 1975; *Silver Everything and Many Mansions* (two novellas), Oxford University Press, 1976.

WORK IN PROGRESS: "I am at present writing a novel for young adults which is set in Romania in 1939-40—the years I lived there."

SIDELIGHTS: Winifred Cawley explained that her international teaching experience came about because her husband worked for the British Council overseas and accepted visiting professorships. "I like living abroad although I'm not particularly fond of travelling for holidays," she said. "My books so far have all concerned the north of England where I grew up in what I have heard described years later, to my surprise, as a slum. To me it was home and to some extent I feel myself a permanent exile from it and from the working class I grew up with."

* * *

CHACE, William M(urdough) 1938-

PERSONAL: Born September 3, 1938, in Newport News, Va.; son of William Emerson (a teacher and publicist) and Grace (Murdough) Chace; married Joan Elizabeth Johnstone (a teacher), 1964; children: William J., Katherine E. *Education:* Haverford College, B.A., 1961; University of California, Berkeley, M.A., 1963, Ph.D., 1968. *Home:* 1325 Cowper St., Palo Alto, Calif. 94301. *Office:* Department of English, Stanford University, Stanford, Calif. 94305.

CAREER: Stillman College, Tuscaloosa, Ala., instructor in English, 1963-64; Stanford University, Stanford, Calif., assistant professor of English, 1968—. *Member:* Modern Language Association of America. *Awards, honors:* Woodrow Wilson fellowship, 1961-62.

WRITINGS: (With Peter Collier) *Justice Denied: The Black Man in White America,* Harcourt, 1970; (editor with wife, Joan E. Chace) *Making It New* (anthology of poems), Canfield Press, 1973; *The Political Identities of Ezra Pound and T. S. Eliot,* Stanford University Press, 1973; (editor) *James Joyce: A Collection of Critical Essays,* Prentice-Hall, 1973. Contributor to magazines, including *Novel, Mosaic,* and *American Quarterly.*

WORK IN PROGRESS: A book on Lionel Trilling.

SIDELIGHTS: Chace writes: "I have a strong interest in the relationship between literary culture and political circumstances."

* * *

CHADWICK, Lee 1909-

PERSONAL: Born March 29, 1909, in London, England; married Paxton Chadwick (an artist; deceased, 1961); children: Peter. *Education:* University of London; B.A. *Home:* The Studio, Leiston Common, Leiston, Suffolk, England.

CAREER: Teacher at Summerhill School, Leister, England; writer. *Member:* Society of Authors, Suffolk Conservation Society, Suffolk Naturalist Society.

WRITINGS: Fish from the Sea, Cassell, 1963; *The Shell Fish We Eat,* Cassell, 1963; *Science and Fishing,* Cassell, 1963; *How the Fish Is Caught,* Cassell, 1963; *Marketing the Fish,* Cassell, 1963; *The Fishing Fleet,* Cassell, 1963; *Soil and Fruit,* Cassell, 1966; *Science and Fruit,* Cassell, 1966; *On a Fruit Farm,* Cassell, 1966; *Insects in the Orchard,* Cassell, 1966; *Harvesting the Fruit,* Cassell, 1966; *London's Fruit and Vegetable Markets,* Cassell, 1966; *Seeds of Plenty: Agriculture in a Scientific Age,* Methuen, 1968, Coward, 1969; *Lighthouses and Lightships,* Dobson Books, 1971; *A Cuban Journey,* Dobson Books, 1975, published as *Cuba Today,* Lawrence Hill, 1976. Contributor to *Times Educational Supplement, SHE, Harper's Bazaar,* and other periodicals.

WORK IN PROGRESS: Our Vanishing Heathlands (tentative title); editing a book on lighthouses for Dobson Books; articles on Portugal.

SIDELIGHTS: "How far do people themselves change with a changing pattern of society?" is the question which stimulated Lee Chadwick to travel. In recent years she has visited Italy, France, Czechoslovakia, Rumania, and Cuba. She told *CA* of her 1975 visit to Cuba: "I was particularly attracted to Cuba by reports of experiments in education with an emphasis upon creating a 'whole' people, and by the Cubans' endearing sense of humor and ability to take a critical look at themselves. Four months stay on the island as a writer with a special interest in young people enabled me to travel throughout the island when grass root organisations were debating the proposed new state institutions of 'People's Power.' In 1975, for instance, all Cuba was talking about the new Family Code which critically re-examined the question of sex equality in the home and in public life in present day Cuba. Notes taken on the spot from conversations in schools, on farms and sugar mills, in friends' houses and in casual encounters during solitary rambles round Havana, form the basis of *Cuba Today.*"

AVOCATIONAL INTERESTS: Cinema, ballet, music, agriculture, "the position of women in various societies."

* * *

CHAET, Bernard 1924-

PERSONAL: Born March 7, 1924, in Boston, Mass.; son of David and Golda (Benjamin) Chaet; married Ninon Lacey (a printmaker), 1951; children: Leah. *Education:* Boston Museum of Fine Arts School, student, 1942-46; Tufts University, B.S., 1949. *Home:* 141 Cold Spring St., New Haven, Conn. 06511.

CAREER: Yale University, New Haven, Conn., professor of painting, 1951—. Has held about twenty-five solo exhibitions of paintings; work is represented in more than fifty collections, including Brooklyn Museum, Addison Gallery, and Rhode Island School of Design. *Awards, honors:* Grant from National Foundation for Humanities and the Arts, 1966-67.

WRITINGS: Artists at Work, Webb Books, 1960; *The Art of Drawing,* Holt, 1970, revised edition, 1977; *The Artist's Notebook: Materials of Painting and Drawing,* Holt, in press. Editor of column "Studio Talk" in *Arts,* 1956-59.

CHAFETZ, Janet Saltzman 1942-

PERSONAL: Born February 14, 1942, in New Jersey; daughter of Laurence (a motion picture distributor) and Ruth (Effros) Saltzman; married Henry S. Chafetz (a professor of geology), March 18, 1969. *Education:* Cornell University, B.A., 1963; University of Connecticut, M.A., 1965, further graduate study, 1965-66; University of Texas, Ph.D., 1969. *Politics:* "Feminist." *Home:* 1924 Swift, Houston, Tex. 77030. *Office:* Department of Sociology, University of Houston, Houston, Tex. 77004.

CAREER: Wayne State University, Detroit, Mich., assistant professor of sociology, 1968-69; Trinity University, San Antonio, Tex., assistant professor of sociology, 1969-71; University of Houston, Houston, Tex., assistant professor, 1971-73, associate professor of sociology, 1973—, chairperson of department, 1973-76, administrative intern, office of academic vice-president, 1975-76. Assistant field supervisor of Tracor, Inc., summer, 1967. Public lecturer; guest on local television and radio programs. Consultant to Southwest Center for Urban Research.

MEMBER: American Sociological Association, Sociologists of Women in Society (second vice-president, 1973-74), National Organization for Women, Women's Political Caucus, Southwestern Social Science Association (chairperson of Committee on Social Problems, 1974-75, secretary and treasurer, 1976—), Southwestern Sociological Association (chairperson of subcommittee on sex roles, 1973-74), Houston Civil Liberties Union (member of board of directors), University of Houston Faculty and Professional Staff Women's Association (president, 1974-75). *Awards, honors:* Hogg Foundation grant, 1974-75.

WRITINGS: Masculine/Feminine Or Human? An Overview of the Sociology of Sex Roles, F. E. Peacock, 1974, 2nd edition, in press; (contributor) *Impact E.R.A.: Limitations and Possibilities,* Les Femmes, 1976; (with P. Beck, P. Sampson, J. West, and B. Jones) *Who's Queer: A Study of Homo and Heterosexual Women,* Omni, 1976; *A Primer on the Construction and Testing of Theories in Sociology,* F. E. Peacock, in press; (with Elizabeth Almquist, Barbara Chance, and Judy Corder-Bolz) *Sociology: Women, Men, and Society,* West Publishing, in press; (contributor) Almquist, editor, *Sex Roles: Tradition and Change,* West Publishing, in press.

Contributor of articles and reviews to sociology and social science journals. Member of editorial board of *Social Science Quarterly,* 1972—. Special reader for *Social Forces, American Sociological Review, Social Problems,* and *Youth and Society;* manuscript reviewer for publishing companies.

WORK IN PROGRESS: Research on a model of rates of labor force participation and patterns of occupational deployment by gender, race, and ethnicity; a study of the division of labor among white middle-class spouses; a study of 1960 high school graduates; research on the sociology of sex roles and theory development.

SIDELIGHTS: Janet Chafetz comments: "Most of my research interests and writings spring from two sources: my feminist commitments and my teaching. Several of my books have been prompted by my own need for appropriate reading to assign to students."

* * *

CHAMELIN, Neil Charles 1942-

PERSONAL: Born January 16, 1942, in New York, N.Y.; son of I. M. (a biochemist) and Estelle (Kaye) Chamelin;

married Vicki Peterson, June 21, 1964; children: Christopher R., Todd M. *Education:* Florida State University, student, 1959-61; Michigan State University, B.S. (high honors), 1963; Stetson University, J.D., 1968. *Home:* 3029 Corrib Dr., Tallahassee, Fla. 32302. *Office:* Standards and Training Division, Florida Department of Criminal Law Enforcement, Tallahassee, Fla. 32302.

CAREER: National Aeronautics & Space Administration, Houston, Tex., security clerk, summer, 1963; police patrolman in Sarasota, Fla., 1964; Montgomery Ward & Co., Chicago, Ill., special investigator, 1964-65; St. Petersburg Junior College, St. Petersburg, Fla., faculty member in criminal law, procedure, and police administration, 1965-71, chairman of department, 1970-71; Florida Institute for Law Enforcement, St. Petersburg, director, 1970-71; University of Georgia, Athens, administrator of Police Science Division of Institute of Government, 1971-77; Florida Department of Criminal Law Enforcement, Tallahassee, director of Florida Police Standards and Training Commission, 1977—. Adjunct member of faculty at Valdosta State College, 1972—, and Appalachian State University, 1976—; adjunct professor at Nova University, 1976—; visiting lecturer at Tallahassee Community College, University of Oklahoma, Reinhardt College, and southern police academies. Member of standards and accreditation committee of Academy of Criminal Justice Sciences.

MEMBER: International Association of Chiefs of Police (section vice-chairperson), American Bar Association, American Society for Public Administration, Southern Association of Criminal Justice Educators (first vice-president, 1977—), Florida Bar Association, Florida Criminal Justice Educators Association (charter president), Florida Police Chiefs Association, Georgia Criminal Justice Educators Association (past president), Tampa Bay Area Chiefs of Police Association, Phi Alpha Delta, Alpha Phi Sigma, Phi Kappa Phi.

WRITINGS: (With Kenneth R. Evans) *Criminal Law for Policemen,* Prentice-Hall, 1971, 2nd edition, 1975; (with Evans) *Handbook of Criminal Law,* Prentice-Hall, 1971; (with Vernon Fox and Paul Whisenand) *Introduction to Criminal Justice,* Prentice-Hall, 1975; (contributor) Vernon Rich, editor, *Law and the Administration of Justice,* Wiley, 1975; (contributor) W. Ken Katsaris, editor, *Evidence and Procedure in the Administration of Justice,* Wiley, 1975; (contributor) Donald T. Shanahan, editor, *Issues in the Administration of Criminal Justice,* Holbrook, 1977; (with C. R. Swanson and Leonard Territo) *Criminal Investigation,* Goodyear Publishing, 1977; (with Swanson and Territo) *The Police Personnel Selection Process,* Bobbs-Merrill, 1977; (contributor) *Legislative Issues in Crime Control,* Institute of Government, University of Georgia, 1977; (contributor) John T. O'Brien and Marvin Marcus, editors, *Criminal Justice Beyond 1984,* Prentice-Hall, in press. Contributor to *Police Chemical Agents Manual.* Contributor to police administration and education journals.

WORK IN PROGRESS: Revising *Introduction to Criminal Justice,* with Vernon Fox and Paul Whisenand; writing an article.

* * *

CHAMPLIN, Charles (Davenport) 1926-

PERSONAL: Born March 23, 1926, in New York; son of Francis Malburn (a wine chemist) and Katherine (a bank teller; maiden name, Masson) Champlin; married Margaret Derby (a librarian), September, 1948; children: Charles,

Katherine, John, Judith, Susan, Nancy. *Education:* Harvard University, A.B. (cum laude), 1947. *Home:* 2169 Linda Flora Dr., Los Angeles, Calif. 90024. *Agent:* Ned Brown, Inc., 403 North Maple, Beverly Hills, Calif. 90210. *Office: Los Angeles Times,* Times-Mirror Sq., Los Angeles, Calif. 90053.

CAREER: Time, Inc., New York, N.Y., writer and correspondent for *Life* in New York City, 1948-49, Chicago, Ill., 1949-52, Denver, Colo., 1952-54, assistant editor in New York City, 1954-59, writer and correspondent for *Time* in Los Angeles, Calif., 1959-62, and London, England, 1962-65; *Los Angeles Times,* Los Angeles, Calif., arts editor, 1965—, film critic, 1967—, author of column "Critic at Large," appearing in about three hundred fifty newspapers all over the world, 1965—. Adjunct lecturer at Loyola Marymount University, 1969—; lecturer at colleges and universities. Host of "Homewood" series and "Film Odyssey," both for Public Broadcasting Service, and of "Citywatchers" for KCET-Television. *Military service:* U.S. Army, Infantry, 1944-46; served in European theater; became corporal; received Purple Heart, three battle stars, and combat infantryman's badge.

MEMBER: National Society of Film Critics, National Society of Journalists, Harvard Club of Southern California (member of board of directors, 1972—).

WRITINGS: (With Charles Sava) *How to Swim Well,* Simon & Schuster, 1960; *The Flicks: Or, Whatever Became of Andy Hardy,* Ritchie, 1977.

Represented in anthologies, including *Cinema 72/73,* edited by David Denby, Bobbs-Merrill, 1973; *Cinema 73/74,* edited by Denby and Jay Cocks, Bobbs-Merrill, 1974; *Focus on Orson Welles,* edited by Ronald Gottesman, Prentice-Hall, 1976; *Movie Comedy,* edited by Stuart Byron and Elisabeth Weiss, Viking, 1977.

Contributor to magazines, including *Saturday Review, McCall's, New Society,* and *Millimeter.*

SIDELIGHTS: Champlin writes: "I can't remember a time when I seriously wanted to do anything except write for a living. My seventeen years as a writer-correspondent for Time-Life in Chicago, Denver, Los Angeles, New York and London were a post-graduate education in the world and led (it now seems inevitable) to the arts and at last to reviewing movies. The movies have been in a period of revolutionary change as an art-form since 1946 (and the arrival of television) and I am able to watch and report at close hand. My writing about movies and other arts at the *Los Angeles Times* has led to a number of related and very satisfying activities: hosting 'Film Odyssey' and other television programs, teaching at a university, and lecturing widely on the changed movie scene, and on criticism."

* * *

CHANNELS, Vera G(race) 1915-

PERSONAL: Born January 28, 1915, in Trenton, N.D.; daughter of John T. (a businessman) and Mae (Hoover) Whitted; married Lloyd Channels (a clergyman), September 4, 1938; children: Luan Channels Gardner, Noreen Channels Dulz, Paul, Janice Channels Pierce. *Education:* University of Illinois, B.A., 1935, M.A., 1939; Indiana State University, further graduate study. *Religion:* Christian Church (Disciples of Christ). *Home:* 928 Elizabeth Lane, Terre Haute, Ind. 47802. *Office:* Department of Home Economics, Indiana State University, Terre Haute, Ind. 47809.

CAREER: Peoria Mental Hygiene Society, Peoria, Ill.,

clinical psychologist, 1940-43; Center College of Kentucky, Danville, instructor in psychology and education, 1963-66; Indiana State University, Terre Haute, instructor, 1966-72, assistant professor of child development and family life, 1972—. Member of board of directors of Vigo County Coordinating Council, 1969-73, Health and Welfare Council, 1966-69, and Vigo County Council on Aging, 1974-76. *Member:* International Transactional Analysis Association, National Council of Family Relations, Indiana Council of Family Relations (vice-president; member of board of directors).

WRITINGS: (With Penelope Kupsinel) *Career Education in Home Economics,* Interstate, 1973; (with Kupsinel) *Home Economics Careers,* Interstate, 1974; *Experiences in Interpersonal Relationships,* Interstate, 1975; (contributor) Rebecca Smith, compiler, *Resources for Teaching about Family Life Education,* National Council on Family Relations, 1976; *Freedom Is an Inside Job,* John Knox, in press. Contributor to *Family Coordinator.*

WORK IN PROGRESS: My First Year Alone, with Virginia Stumbough.

SIDELIGHTS: Vera Channels writes: "A major concern of mine is working for the equality of all human beings; I thoroughly enjoy working with and teaching college-age people; they are stimulating and refreshing." *Avocational interests:* Weaving, ceramics, travel (including Mexico, Canada, Jamaica, Europe, England, Scotland, Wales).

* * *

CHAPLIN, George 1914-

PERSONAL: Born April 28, 1914, in Columbia, S.C.; son of Morris (a merchant) and Netty (Brown) Chaplin; married Esta L. Solomon, January 26, 1937; children: Stephen M., Jerri (Mrs. Naftali Liberman). *Education:* Clemson College, B.S., 1935; Harvard University, graduate study, 1940-41. *Politics:* Independent. *Religion:* Jewish. *Home:* 4437 Kolohala St., Honolulu, Hawaii 96816. *Office: Honolulu Advertiser,* P.O. Box 3110, Honolulu, Hawaii 96802.

CAREER: Greenville Piedmont, Greenville, S.C., reporter, 1935-36, city editor, 1937-42; *Camden Courier-Post,* Camden, N.J., managing editor, 1946-47; *San Diego Journal,* San Diego, Calif., managing editor, 1948; *New Orleans Item,* New Orleans, La., managing editor, 1949, editor, 1949-58; *Honolulu Advertiser,* Honolulu, Hawaii, associate editor, 1958, editor, 1958—. Chairman of Hawaii governor's Conference on the Year Two Thousand and Hawaii State Commission on the Year Two Thousand. Director of Friends of the East-West Center, Honolulu Symphony Society, Pacific and Asian Affairs Council and Hawaii Jewish Welfare Fund. *Military service:* U.S. Army, editor in charge of Pacific Stars and Stripes, 1942-46; became captain.

MEMBER: International Press Institute, American Society of Newspaper Editors (president, 1976-77), National Conference of Editorial Writers, Sigma Delta Chi. *Awards, honors:* Nieman fellow at Harvard University, 1940-41; citations from Overseas Press Club, 1962, 1972; award from National Headliners Club, 1963, for distinguished feature writing; John Hancock Award for Excellence from John Hancock Mutual Life Insurance Co., 1972, 1974, for economic reporting; Edward Willis Scripps Award, 1976, for First Amendment reporting.

WRITINGS: (Editor with Glenn D. Paige) *Hawaii 2000: A Continuing Experiment in Anticipatory Democracy,* University Press of Hawaii, 1973.

SIDELIGHTS: Chaplin has traveled in and written about the Soviet Union, eastern and western Europe, Morocco, Israel, Australia, New Zealand, Japan, Hong Kong, Thailand, Malaysia, Singapore, the People's Republic of China, Korea, New Guinea, New Hebrides, New Caladonia, Fiji, and Samoa.

* * *

CHAPMAN, Carleton B(urke) 1915-

PERSONAL: Born June 11, 1915, in Sycamore, Ala.; son of John G. (an engineer) and Mary (Anderson) Chapman; married Ruth Horine (a social worker), August 30, 1940; children: Nancy C. (Mrs. Jack A. Collins), John G., Mary A. Chapman East. *Education:* Davidson College, A.B., 1936; Oxford University, B.A., 1938, M.A., 1953; Harvard University, M.D., 1941, M.P.H., 1944. *Politics:* Democrat. *Religion:* Nonc. *Home:* 18 East 84th St., New York, N.Y. 10018. *Office:* Commonwealth Fund, 1 East 75th St., New York, N.Y. 10021.

CAREER: Boston City Hospital, Boston, Mass., intern, 1941-42, resident, 1942-44, intern at Mallory Institute of Pathology, 1946; University of Minnesota, Minneapolis, member of faculty, 1947-50, associate professor of medicine, 1950-53; University of Texas, Southwestern Medical School (now Health Science Center), Houston, professor of medicine, 1953-66; Dartmouth College, Hanover, N.H., dean of Medical School, 1966-73, vice-president, 1972-73; Commonwealth Fund, New York, N.Y., president, 1973—. Diplomate of American Board of Internal Medicine, 1948; member of staff at Parkland Hospital (Dallas). Adviser to Bishop College, 1962-63. Consultant to U.S. Army (Surgeon-General) and U.S. Veterans Administration. *Military service:* U.S. Public Health Service, 1944-46.

MEMBER: American Academy of Arts and Sciences, Association of American Physicians, American College of Physicians (fellow), American College of Cardiology (fellow), American Heart Association (president, 1964-65), American Medical Association, American Association for the Advancement of Science, Society for Experimental Biology and Medicine, American Federation for Clinical Research, American Society for Clinical Investigation, American Physiological Society, Central Society for Clinical Research, Southern Society for Clinical Research, Texas Medical Association, New York Academy of Medicine, Dallas County Medical Society, Century Club. *Awards, honors:* Rhodes scholar, Oxford University, 1939; Rockefeller Foundation fellowship, 1944-46; career professorship award from U.S. Public Health Service, 1963; Guggenheim fellowship, 1964; M.A. from Dartmouth College, 1968; LL.D. from Davidson College, 1968.

WRITINGS: Development, 1797-1968: The Next Logical Step, Dartmouth College, 1962; *Ernest Henry Starling: The Clinician's Physiologist,* American College of Physicians, 1962; (editor and author of commentary) Starling, *Starling on the Heart: Facsimile Reprints, Including the Linacre Lecture on the Law of the Heart,* Dawsons of Pall Mall, 1965; (editor with Marvin Pollard) *Treatment of Heart Failure,* Harper, 1965; (editor) *Physiology of Muscular Exercise* (proceedings), American Heart Association, 1967; *Dartmouth Medical School: The First Hundred Seventy-Five Years,* University Press of New England, 1973; (with Elinor C. Reinmiller) *The Physiology of Physical Stress: A Selective Bibliography,* Harvard University Press, 1975. Contributor of about one hundred articles to medical journals. Editor of *American Oxonian,* 1963-64; member of editorial board of *Archives of Internal Medicine,* 1963-68.

WORK IN PROGRESS: The Right to Die; Ethics and Malpractice Law.

SIDELIGHTS: Chapman writes that his main concerns are "the future of higher education, basic medical and legal ethics, and national health policy."

* * *

CHARNLEY, Mitchell V(aughn) 1898-

PERSONAL: Born April 9, 1898, in Goshen, Ind.; son of William H. (a lawyer) and Louise (Carmien) Charnley; married Margery Lindsay, September 12, 1922 (divorced, 1936); married Jean Mary Clifford (a psychotherapist), July 24, 1937; children: Donn, Blair, Deborah Fort. *Education:* Williams College, B.A., 1919; University of Washington, Seattle, M.A., 1921. *Politics:* "Loosely Democrat." *Home:* 88 Orlin Ave. S.E., Minneapolis, Minn. 55414. *Office:* College of Liberal Arts, University of Minnesota, Minneapolis, Minn. 55455.

CAREER: Reporter for newspapers in Honolulu, Hawaii, and Detroit, Mich., 1921-23; American Boy (magazine), Detroit, assistant managing editor, 1923-30; Iowa State College (now Iowa State University), Ames, 1930-34, began as assistant professor, became associate professor of journalism; University of Minnesota, Minneapolis, 1934—, began as assistant professor, professor of journalism until 1968, assistant dean of College of Liberal Arts, 1958-68 and 1970—. Fulbright lecturer in journalism, University of Florence, Italy, 1952-53. President, Minnesota Mental Health Association, 1958-60. *Military:* U.S. Army, 1918. *Member:* Association for Education in Journalism (president, 1958-59), Society of Professional Journalists, Newspaper Guild. *Awards, honors:* Knopf fellowship in biography, 1941; award from Radio-Television News Directors Association, 1963, for contributions to broadcasting; honored as journalism teacher of the year by Society of Professional Journalists, 1970.

WRITINGS: Secrets of Baseball, Appleton, 1927; *Boys Life of Wright Brothers,* Harper, 1928; *Boys Life of Herbert Hoover,* Harper, 1931; *Play the Game: The Book of Sports,* Viking, 1931; *Jean Lafitte, Gentleman Smuggler,* Viking, 1934; (with Blair Converse) *Magazine Writing and Editing,* Cordon, 1937; *News by Radio,* Macmillan, 1948; *Il Giornalismo negli Stati Uniti* (title means "Journalism in the U.S."), Fulbright Commission, 1953; *Reporting,* Holt, 1959, 3rd edition, 1975. Editorial consultant to newspapers and mental health organizations.

WORK IN PROGRESS: Fourth edition of *Reporting,* publication by Holt in 1979.

SIDELIGHTS: Charnley writes: "I travel widely (I have spent a total of at least four years abroad) in all of western Europe, North Africa, Japan, Manchuria, South America, and the Caribbean. I have a well-equipped woodworking shop in which I produce furniture and gift items."

* * *

CHARRON, Shirley 1935-

PERSONAL: Surname is pronounced like Sharon; born April 22, 1935, in Norwich, Conn.; daughter of John B. and Edwardina (Martin) Charron. *Education:* Massachusetts College of Art, B.S., 1958; Columbia University, M.A., 1963; apprentice to pewtersmith Frances Felton, 1966-73; further study at Eastern Connecticut State University, University of Bridgeport, and Southern Connecticut State College. *Residence:* Ridgefield, Conn. *Agent:* (art) Kruger-Van Eerde Gallery, 842 Madison Ave., New York, N.Y.

CAREER: Art teacher in high schools in Hartland, Mich., 1958-59, Hillsdale, N.Y., 1959-60, and Haverstraw, N.Y., 1960-63; Norwalk High School, Norwalk, Conn., crafts teacher and acting chairman of department, 1963—. Professional pewtersmith, 1966—. Participates in national and state pewter exhibitions; has had solo shows in Connecticut and Philadelphia. Member of advisory board of Connecticut Scholastic Art Awards Competitions. Member: American Craftsmens Council, Society of Connecticut Craftsmen, Philadelphia Art Alliance, Brookfield Craft Center. Awards, honors: Awards for pewter work.

WRITINGS: Modern Pewter, Van Nostrand, 1973.

WORK IN PROGRESS: Pewter Casting.

SIDELIGHTS: Charron told CA that Modern Pewter is "the first 'how to do it' book on pewtersmithing since 1935." "I am dedicated," she added, "to the revival of the ancient art of pewtersmithing as a contemporary art medium."

BIOGRAPHICAL/CRITICAL SOURCES: Bridgeport Post, October 11, 1973.

*   *   *

CHARRY, Elias 1906-

PERSONAL: Born February 4, 1906, in Brooklyn, N.Y.; son of Marim (a teacher and choir leader) and Dora (Romm) Charry; married Ruth Epstein Revsen, December 31, 1930; children: Marim, Adina Charry Ben-Chorin, Dana. Education: City College (now of the City University of New York), B.S.S., 1926; Jewish Theological Seminary of America, rabbi and M.H.L., 1930. Home: 6910 McCallum St., Philadelphia, Pa. 19119. Office: Germantown Jewish Center, 400 West Ellet St., Philadelphia, Pa. 19119.

CAREER: Rabbi of Jewish congregations in Youngstown, Ohio, 1930-32, and Indianapolis, Ind., 1933-42; Germantown Jewish Center, Philadelphia, Pa., rabbi, 1942-71, rabbi emeritus, 1971—. Member of Philadelphia Board of Rabbis; chairman of United Synagogue of America Commission on Jewish Education, 1951-53. Governor of Indiana Commission on Education, 1938. Founder of Akiba Hebrew Academy, 1947; member of board of directors of Gratz College, 1944—; member of board of overseers of Jewish Theological Seminary of America, 1948-51. Member: Rabbinical Assembly of America, Zionist Organization of America (local vice-president, 1944—). Awards, honors: Has received numerous awards for community service.

WRITINGS: (With Abraham Segal) The Eternal People: An Ideological History of the Jewish People, United Synagogue of America, 1967.

WORK IN PROGRESS: Midrash for Today.

*   *   *

CHASIN, Barbara 1940-

PERSONAL: Born June 8, 1940, in New York, N.Y.; daughter of Melvin James (a mail carrier) and Carolyn (a clerk; maiden name, Koerpel) Fischer. Education: City College of the City University of New York, B.A., 1961; University of Iowa, Ph.D., 1966. Home: 363 Washington St., Somerville, Mass. 02143. Office: Department of Population Sciences, School of Public Health, Harvard University, Boston, Mass. 02115.

CAREER: St. Mary's College, Halifax, Nova Scotia, assistant professor of sociology, 1967-68; University of Massachusetts, Boston, assistant professor of sociology, 1968-70; Montclair State College, Montclair, N.J., assistant pro-

fessor of sociology, 1970-76; Harvard University, Boston, Mass., research fellow of School of Public Health, 1976—. Awards, honors: Ford Foundation fellow, 1976-78.

WRITINGS: Power and Ideology: A Marxist Approach to Political Sociology, Schenkman, 1974. Contributor to Science for the People and Sociological Quarterly.

WORK IN PROGRESS: The West Africa Famine, 1968-1973, completion expected in 1979.

*   *   *

CHASTON, Gloria Duncan 1929-

PERSONAL: Born October 7, 1929, in Murray, Utah; daughter of Leon (a construction foreman) and Evelyn (Johnson) Duncan; married A. Norton Chaston (a professor of electrical engineering), September 12, 1949; children: Larry, Keith, John, Carolyn, Anne. Education: Brigham Young University, A.S., 1965, B.A. (magna cum laude), 1977. Religion: Church of Jesus Christ of Latter-day Saints (Mormons). Home and office: 31 East 2050 N., Provo, Utah 84601.

CAREER: Burnt Hills School District, Burnt Hills, N.Y., teacher of continuing education, 1973; Utah Valley Branch Genealogical Library, Provo, Utah, member of staff of continuing workshop program, 1976—. Guest lecturer. Co-owner of Genealogy Tree (mail-order company), 1975—. Conducted genealogical research in Scotland, Sweden, England, and the United States. Member: Utah Genealogical Association, Phi Kappa Phi.

WRITINGS: (With Laureen R. Jaussi) Fundamentals of Genealogical Research, Deseret, 1966, 3rd edition, 1977; (with Jaussi) Register of Latter-day Saints Church Records, Deseret, 1968; (with Jaussi) Genealogical Records of Utah, Deseret, 1972. Editor of newsletters of Utah Genealogical Association, 1973-75, and Utah Valley Branch Genealogical Library, 1976—.

SIDELIGHTS: Gloria Chaston writes that Fundamentals of Genealogical Research "is a basic genealogical reference which emphasizes the first four generations of ancestry and lays a foundation for extending the pedigree. It provides the beginning genealogist with instructions on how to perform his own genealogical research; provides the experienced genealogist with a convenient ready-reference, and provides the genealogical teacher with well-organized source material and corresponding lesson assignments. Genealogical Records of Utah is a follow-up book to Fundamentals for individuals who have Utah ancestry, and the Register of LDS Church Records contains over 13,000 microfilm numbers of LDS Church Records, most of which are discussed in the Utah book."

*   *   *

CHATHAM, Russell 1939-

PERSONAL: Born October 27, 1939, in San Francisco, Calif.; son of Russell Wilson (in lumber business) and Romy Charlotte (Piazzoni) Chatham; married Mary Howard Fanning (an artist; marriage ended); married Doris Clark Meyer (an artist; marriage ended); children: Georgina Romy Piazzoni Chatham, Lea Irene Piazzoni Woodville Chatham. Education: Self educated. Politics: "Smash the State." Religion: "Salmon Fishing." Residence: Livingston, Mont.

CAREER: Writer and artist.

WRITINGS: The Angler's Coast, Doubleday, 1976; Striped Bass on the Fly: A Guide to California Waters, Hearst Corp., 1976.

SIDELIGHTS: Chatham told *CA:* "I write and paint for money; fish, cook, shoot pool, and chase women for fun."

* * *

CHEIFETZ, Dan 1926-

PERSONAL: Surname is pronounced *Shay*-futz; born January 18, 1926, in Kansas City, Mo.; son of Samuel (a publicist) and Bessie (Webber) Cheifetz; children: Amy, Richard. *Education:* Attended University of California, Los Angeles, 1947-48; New School for Social Research, B.A., 1953; Columbia University, M.F.A., 1958. *Home and office:* 865 West End Ave., New York, N.Y. 10025.

CAREER: Free-lance writer. Publicist for Paramount Pictures and Universal Studios, 1948-50; Wunderman Ricotta & Kline, New York City, group head, 1960-63; "21" Brands, New York City, advertising director, 1969-71; City College of the City University of New York, New York City, instructor in education, 1974-77. Workshop leader. *Member:* Teachers and Writers Collaborative.

WRITINGS—Juvenile: Washer in the Woods (fiction), Lion Press, 1967; *Theatre in My Head* (nonfiction), Little, Brown, 1973. Contributor to *Learning* and *Teachers and Writers.*

WORK IN PROGRESS: A book for teachers and parents, to help them teach skills for effective living to children, based on classroom and workshop experience.

SIDELIGHTS: Cheifetz told *CA:* "I have always written—poems, novels, plays. But what I have *published* are my educational works—the outgrowth of my work with, and love of, children. The current focus of my writing is my teaching experiences and insights, and the drive I have to help myself and others, teachers and parents, bring out the inner powers and talents and self-respect of kids. Fiction is still a love of mine, and someday something worth saying will come out of that, maybe. But right now, the way I connect best with the world, and make my contribution, is through facilitating the inner lives of children—and helping other teachers do the same—and that's what I am motivated to write about."

* * *

CHENG, Hang-Sheng 1927-

PERSONAL: Born October 13, 1927, in Hangchow, China; came to the United States in 1950, naturalized citizen, 1967; son of Chen-Chuin and Chin-Yin (Tai) Cheng; married Angela Chen (an accountant), June 16, 1956; children: Anthony, Lawrence, Michael, David. *Education:* Tsing Hwa University, B.A., 1948; George Washington University, M.A., 1953; further graduate study, Johns Hopkins University, 1958-61; Princeton University, Ph.D., 1963. *Religion:* Roman Catholic. *Home:* 4108 Fairway Ave., Oakland, Calif. 94605. *Office:* Research Department, Federal Reserve Bank of San Francisco, 400 Sansome St., San Francisco, Calif. 94120.

CAREER: International Monetary Fund, Washington, D.C., research assistant in research department, 1951-56, economist, 1956-61; Iowa State University, Ames, assistant professor, 1963-66, associate professor of economics, 1966-73; Federal Reserve Bank of San Francisco, San Francisco, Calif., economist in research department, 1973-74, senior economist, 1975, assistant vice-president and economist in charge of International and Pacific Basin section, 1975—. Lecturer at University of California, Berkeley, 1973-74, summer, 1975, and 1977-78. Adviser to chairman and director of research for Commission on Taxation Reform in the Republic of China, 1968-69; international economist for U.S. Treasury Department, 1971-73.

WRITINGS: The International Bond Issues of the Less-Developed Countries, Iowa State University Press, 1969. Contributor of about a dozen articles and reviews to professional journals.

* * *

CHENG, Hou-Tien 1944-

PERSONAL: Born May 30, 1944, in Banfu, China; came to the United States in 1972; son of Yan-Ren (in trading business) and Kuei-Shiang Cheng; married Fu-Hua Huang, August 13, 1976. *Education:* Attended industrial high school in Taipei, Taiwan. *Home:* 125 East Broadway, Apt. 3C, New York, N.Y. 10002.

CAREER: Illustrator, demonstrator, and designer of Chinese paper cutting. Has had individual shows and exhibitions in New York City; has appeared on television programs in the United States and Japan. *Awards, honors:* Winner of paper cutting competition for Taiwan, in Japan, 1970; *The Chinese New Year* named a notable book by American Library Association, 1976.

WRITINGS: The Chinese New Year (self-illustrated), Holt, 1976.

WORK IN PROGRESS: A series of "how-to" books, illustrating the art of paper cutting with scissors.

SIDELIGHTS: Cheng Hou-tien learned the art of paper cutting from his grandmother (in the face of parental disapproval), rather than by studying with a master. His innovations in the art have been systematized into a method of instruction. He gives lectures and demonstrations, with hopes of popularizing his art in the United States, especially among school children. He has also designed industrial items, toys, furnishings, costumes, oriental lanterns, and landscapes.

* * *

CHERRY, Colin 1914-

PERSONAL: Born June 23, 1914, in St. Albans, England; son of Arthur Leonard and Margaret Ellen Cherry; married Heather White, 1956; children: Lucy Helen, Anna Frances. *Education:* University of London, B.Sc., 1936, M.Sc., 1940, D.Sc., 1958. *Politics:* Labour. *Religion:* "Not a member of any church." *Home:* Combe House, Chichester Rd., Dorking, Surrey, England. *Office:* Department of Electrical Engineering, Imperial College of Science and Technology, University of London, London SW7 2BT, England.

CAREER: General Electric Co., Research Laboratories, London, England, member of scientific staff, 1936-45; University of London, Imperial College of Science and Technology, London, England, lecturer, 1947-52, reader, 1952-58, Henry Mark Pease Professor of Telecommunication, 1958—. Member of assessment board of Open University; member of United Kingdom National Commission for UNESCO; member of St. Dunstan's Scientific Committee. *Member:* British International Studies Association, Institution of Electrical Engineers, British Experimental Psychology Society, Royal Horticultural Society, Royal Society of Arts.

WRITINGS: Pulses and Transients in Communication Circuits, Chapman & Hall, 1949; *On Human Communication,* M.I.T. Press, 1957, 3rd edition, 1977; *World Communication: Threat or Promise?,* Wiley, 1971. Contributor of about a hundred twenty articles to technical journals. Member of editorial board of *Telecommunication Policy*.

WORK IN PROGRESS: Research and experimentation on the psychology of reading.

SIDELIGHTS: Cherry comments: "I have always been highly critical of the traditional teaching of technology, especially that of communication, arguing that is meaningful if considered only as a political matter. My students are largely drawn from developing countries and this has forced me to study the nature of the human communication process socially, psychologically, and philosophically in order to understand and advise better on specification of telecommunication systems to be of real value to development. I have travelled widely and lectured in some thirty countries of Europe, North and South America, and Asia."

* * *

CHEYETTE, Irving 1904-

PERSONAL: Surname is pronounced Shay-*ette;* born August 1, 1904, in New York, N.Y.; son of Samuel (a merchant) and Fanny (Levy) Cheyette; married Ruth Netter, August 29, 1925 (died July 29, 1974); married Ruth Marcus (a psychotherapist), July 12, 1975; children: Herbert Basil, Fredric Laurance. *Education:* Columbia University, B.S., 1929, M.A., 1930, Ed.D., 1936. *Politics:* Democrat. *Religion:* Jewish. *Home:* 2560 South Ocean Blvd., Palm Beach, Fla. 33480. *Agent:* Murray Benson, Sands Point, Long Island, N.Y.

CAREER: State Teachers College (now Indiana University of Pennsylvania), Indiana, Pa., professor and director of music education, 1938-48; Syracuse University, Syracuse, N.Y., professor of music and education, 1948-54; Tokyo University of Fine Arts, Tokyo, Japan, Fulbright Professor of Music, 1954-55; State University of New York at Buffalo, professor of music and music director, 1955-72; Fordham University, New York City, adjunct professor of art, 1973—. Consultant to Creative Education Foundation and National Council for Accreditation of Teacher Education.

MEMBER: International Music Education Association (Pennsylvania president, 1943), Music Educators National Conference (life member; member of board of directors, 1948-50), American Association of University Professors, New York School Music Association, Phi Delta Kappa, Phi Mu Alpha Sinfonia. *Awards, honors:* American Music Achievement Award from American Music Foundation, 1940.

WRITINGS: Four and Twenty Folk Tunes for Beginning Orchestra, Carl Fischer, 1930; *Basic Piano for Music Educators,* Presser, 1950; *Elements of Sight Reading for Instrumentalists,* Pro Art Music, 1951; (with Joseph Paulson) *Basic Theory: Harmony for School Musicians,* Pro Art Music, 1952; (with son, Herbert Cheyette) *Teaching Music Creatively in Elementary Schools,* McGraw, 1969. Contributor of about forty articles to professional journals.

WORK IN PROGRESS: A Child's Year in Japan: A Humanities Approach for Middle Schools.

SIDELIGHTS: Cheyette writes: "I have had published about eighty-five works in all fields of music education, choral and instrumental, theory and piano. All of my materials have been based on direct classroom needs and have been tested in the classroom. I have traveled extensively in Mexico, Europe, South America, North Africa. I have taught all ages from kindergarten through octogenarians, my last post at Fordham being in the College at Sixty program

teaching a course in understanding the arts. In my younger years I was active in the theater as an actor. I performed professionally as a violinist-violist, and still play chamber music."

* * *

CHI, Madeleine 1930-

PERSONAL: Born April 16, 1930, in Shanghai, China; came to United States in 1952, naturalized citizen, 1975; daughter of Matthew (an importer) and Agnes (Jung) Chi. *Education:* Manhattanville College, B.A., 1955, M.A., 1960; Fordham University, Ph.D., 1968; Columbia University, certificate from East Asian Institute (M.A. equivalent), 1971. *Religion:* Roman Catholic. *Office:* Department of History, Manhattanville College, Purchase, N.Y. 10577.

CAREER: International School of the Sacred Heart, Tokyo, Japan, teacher, 1959-62; Sacred Heart College, Taipei, Taiwan, president, 1967-68; Manhattanville College, Purchase, N.Y., professor of history, 1969—, director of East Asian studies program, 1971—. Co-chairperson of seminar on modern China, Columbia University, 1975-76. *Member:* Association for Asian Studies. *Awards, honors:* Awards from National Humanities Faculty, 1972, 1973; grant from Social Science Research Council, 1972-73; grant from American Philosophical Society, 1975.

WRITINGS: China Diplomacy, 1914-1918, Harvard University Press, 1970. Contributor of articles to professional journals. Contributor to *Encyclopedia of Japan.*

WORK IN PROGRESS: Research on women elite in Republican China, 1912-1949.

AVOCATIONAL INTERESTS: Photography and painting.

* * *

CHILL, Dan S(amuel) 1945-

PERSONAL: Born August 17, 1945, in Miami Beach, Fla.; son of Henry (a clothing manufacturer) and Dina (Mann) Chill; married Abigail Gerstein (a teacher), June 16, 1968; children: Jordan Henry, Caleb Aaron. *Education:* New York University, B.A., 1966; Harvard University, M.P.A. and J.D., both 1970. *Politics:* None. *Religion:* Jewish. *Home and office:* 12 Lehi St., Kiryat Ono 55000, Israel.

CAREER: Law clerk to chief judge of U.S. District Court in Boston, Mass., 1970-71; Brown, Rudnick, Freed & Gesmer, Boston, associate, 1972-75; attorney with corporate law practice in Israel, 1975—. Chairman of Boston's Lawyers Committee on Soviet Jewry. Member of Bars of Israel, Massachusetts, and U.S. District Court. *Member:* Phi Beta Kappa, Pi Sigma Alpha.

WRITINGS: The Arab Boycott of Israel: Economic Aggression and World Reaction, Praeger, 1976. Contributor to *Harvard International Law Journal.*

WORK IN PROGRESS: Updating Arab boycott material.

SIDELIGHTS: Chill writes that his family has been in Israel/Palestine since 1809. He adds: "I began my research on the Arab boycott in 1964 and have been involved in this endeavor ever since. At first I was intrigued by the boycott's incompetence; later I was surprised at Israel's refusal to come to grips with the problem; and most recently, it has been of great interest to observe which of the major countries are willing to succumb to the boycott's demands. The Arabs need the world a great deal more than the world needs the Arabs, publicity is a great weapon against the boycott and yet it is used very poorly."

AVOCATIONAL INTERESTS: Photography, tennis.

*   *   *

CHILSON, Robert   1945-

PERSONAL: Born May 19, 1945, in Ringwood, Okla.; son of Morris G. (a pioneer) and Flora M. (Coones) Chilson. *Education:* Educated in high school in Appleton City, Mo. *Politics:* None. *Religion:* None. *Home address:* Route 3, Box 181, Osceola, Mo. 64776. *Agent:* Virginia Kidd, Box 278, Milford, Pa. 18337.

CAREER: Writer, 1967—. *Member:* Authors Guild of Authors League of America, Science Fiction Writers of America, Liars' Club of America (founding member; past president).

WRITINGS—Science fiction: *As the Curtain Falls,* DAW Books, 1974; *The Star-Crowned Kings,* DAW Books, 1975; *The Shores of Kansas,* Popular Library, 1976.

Work represented in anthology, *Universe Seven: Astrology and the Man,* edited by Norma L. Browning, Doubleday, 1977. Contributor of stories to science fiction magazines, including *Analog, Galileo,* and *Cosmos.*

WORK IN PROGRESS: A Flame Within, a fantasy; *The Shilmereth,* a novel; *Cluster 'Round the Sun,* a novel examining the classic Dyson sphere economically and for its psychological and political impact.

SIDELIGHTS: Chilson writes: "Despite early flirtations with policemen (for the uniform) and firemen (for the excitement), I intended to be a writer from age about six or seven on; I had never heard of time clocks, but instinctively I knew a writer does not punch one. Science fiction is my principal interest, though I have dabbled in fantasy. I will read anything, nearly; though I do not ride horses, I have a book titled *How to Shoe a Horse* waiting to be read. It's all grist for the mill, and besides, I'm interested. That sums up my whole attitude (and philosophy) toward life."

*   *   *

CHINN, Robert (Edward)   1928-

PERSONAL: Born October 25, 1928, in Newark, N.J.; son of Ernest (a musician) and Susie (a beautician; maiden name, Grier) Chinn; married Ethel Mae Hall, August 8, 1946 (separated, 1948). *Religion:* Agnostic. *Home:* c/o S. Bowman, 1905 McCarter Hwy., Newark, N.J. 07104.

CAREER: Worked as a printing pressman in Newark, N.J., 1947-50; as trombonist and musical composer and arranger in Newark, 1950-71. *Member:* New Directions Drug Program, National Association for the Advancement of Colored People (NAACP).

WRITINGS: Dig the Nigger Up—Let's Kill Him Again, Zebra/Scorpio Books, 1976. Work represented in anthologies, *Over the Wall,* edited by Frank Andrews, Pyramid Press, 1974; *Prose and Cons,* edited by Andrews, Pyramid Press, 1975.

WORK IN PROGRESS: Sha, a novel; a booklet of poems.

SIDELIGHTS: Chinn told *CA:* "I believe all New Jersey ex-cons should try in some way to change the appalling conditions that now exist in New Jersey's penal institutions."

*   *   *

CHOY, Bong-youn   1914-

PERSONAL: Born May 25, 1914, in Korea; son of Ki Ok (a farmer) and Bong-nae (Chang) Choy; married Jung-suck, January, 1941 (died August 1, 1971); married Yong-ja Kim (a teacher); children: Sae-chun, Cora Choy Snow, David, Francis, Sunnie Choy Yuk. *Education:* Aoyama College, A.A., 1938; University of California, Berkeley, B.A., 1944, M.A., 1946. *Religion:* Christian. *Home:* 101 Tamalpais Rd., Berkeley, Calif. 94708. *Office:* Asian American Studies, Contra Costa College, San Pablo, Calif. 94800.

CAREER: University of California, Berkeley, instructor in Japanese and Korean and lecturer in Korean American history, 1942-46; Seoul National University, Seoul, Korea, professor of political science and chairman of department, 1946-48; Seattle Pacific College, Seattle, Wash., visiting professor of political science and Far Eastern history, 1949-52; Contra Costa College, San Pablo, Calif., member of staff of Asian-American studies. Advisory member of Korean Multi-Service Center (San Francisco). *Member:* Pi Sigma Alpha.

WRITINGS: Korean Reader for Beginners, University of California Press, 1943; *Korea: A History,* Tuttle, 1971; *Koreans in America from 1882 to 1976,* Nelson-Hall, in press.

*   *   *

CHU, Samuel C.   1929-

PERSONAL: Born March 25, 1929, in China; came to the United States in 1941, naturalized citizen, 1960; son of Shih-Ming (an Army officer) and Grace (a cooking authority; maiden name, Zia) Chu; married Lucy Kao (a music teacher), June, 1967; children: Elaine, Laura, Jonathan. *Education:* Dartmouth College, A.B., 1951; Columbia University, M.A., 1953, Ph.D., 1958. *Politics:* Democrat. *Religion:* Protestant. *Home:* 3553 Olentangy Blvd., Columbus, Ohio 43214. *Office:* Department of History, Ohio State University, Columbus, Ohio 43210.

CAREER: Yale University, New Haven, Conn., research assistant on China for Human Relations Area Files, 1955-58; State University of New York College at New Paltz, assistant professor of history, 1958; Bucknell University, Lewisburg, Pa., assistant professor of history, 1958-60; University of Pittsburgh, Pittsburgh, Pa., associate professor of history, 1960-69; Ohio State University, Columbus, professor of history and director of East Asian program, 1969—. Visiting associate professor at University of Michigan, 1957-58.

MEMBER: American Historical Association, Association for Asian Studies (member of board of directors, 1970-71), Asia Society, National Committee on U.S.-China Relations, American Association of University Professors, Phi Beta Kappa. *Awards, honors:* Fulbright grant, 1961-62; Social Science Research Council fellowship, 1965-66; American Council of Learned Societies grant, 1974-75.

WRITINGS: (With Chang-tu Hu, Leslie Clark, Yuan-li Wu) *China: Its People, Its Society, Its Culture,* Human Relations Area File Press, 1960; *Reformer in Modern China: Chang Chien (1853-1926),* Columbia University Press, 1965; (with Daniel Chu) *Passage to the Golden Gate,* Doubleday, 1968. Co-editor of series "Inquiries into the Living Past," Macmillan, 1975—. Contributor to Asian studies journals.

WORK IN PROGRESS: A book on the Sino-Japanese War of 1895.

SIDELIGHTS: Dr. Chu told *CA* his primary interests in the 1970's and 1980's include: "Seeing that Americans have a more realistic view of China; active efforts for the Asian-Americans in this country; putting into practice a broad plan for education for the future, stressing written and verbal expressions, historical and ethical awareness, scientific 'literacy' for all, physical fitness (in the Chinese mold), and global involvement."

AVOCATIONAL INTERESTS: Piano, tennis, reading.

* * *

CHUMAN, Frank Fujio 1917-

PERSONAL: Born April 29, 1917, in Montecito, Calif.; son of Hitsuji (a businessman) and Kiyoko (Yamamoto) Chuman; married Ruby Ryoko Dewa, June 27, 1948 (divorced, August, 1968); married Teruyo Nishimura, October 22, 1970; children (first marriage) Daniel Christopher, Paul Randolph; Anthony James Akimoto (stepson). *Education:* University of California, Los Angeles, B.A., 1938; attended University of Southern California, 1940-42, and University of Toledo, 1943-44; University of Maryland, J.D., 1945. *Politics:* Democrat. *Religion:* Episcopalian. *Residence:* Studio City, Calif. *Office:* Broadway Plaza Building, 700 South Flower St., 22nd Floor, Los Angeles, Calif. 90017.

CAREER: Los Angeles County Probation Department, Los Angeles, Calif., clerk, 1939-42; Goodyear Tire & Rubber Co., Baltimore, Md., accountant, 1945; attorney in Los Angeles, 1947—. Member of Bars of Maryland, California, and U.S. Supreme Court. General partner of Japanese Village Plaza, 1976—. Legal adviser to Office of the Japanese Consulate General (Los Angeles), 1952—, and Little Tokyo Towers (housing for senior citizens), 1973—. Chairman of board of directors of Founders Savings and Loan Association, 1975—; member of advisory committee of Sumitomo Bank of California, 1952—. *Wartime service:* U.S. Public Health Service, hospital administrator at Manzanar Relocation Center, 1942-43.

MEMBER: American Bar Association, Criminal Courts Bar Association (charter member), American Trial Lawyers Association, National Association of Immigration and Nationality Lawyers (local president, 1958), Council on Foreign Relations (member of Los Angeles committee), Japanese American Citizens League (national president, 1960-62), California Trial Lawyers Association, Southern California Japanese Chamber of Commerce (member of board of directors), Los Angeles County Bar Association, Los Angeles Trial Lawyers Association, University of California, Los Angeles, Alumni Association (general counsel, 1969-71), University of California, Los Angeles, Chancellor's Associates, University of California, Los Angeles, Foundation, Blue Shield. *Awards, honors:* Received Silver Beaver Award from Boy Scouts of America; awarded community service award from University of California, Los Angeles, Alumni Association.

WRITINGS: The Bamboo People: The Law and Japanese-Americans, Publishers (Las Vegas, Nev.), 1976.

AVOCATIONAL INTERESTS: Golf, music, fishing.

* * *

CHURCHILL, Creighton 1912-

PERSONAL: Born October 1, 1912, in Cornish, N.H.; son of Winston (a writer) and Mabel Harlakenden (Hall) Churchill; children: Alexandra (Mrs. Massimo Pabis-Ticci), Daniel C., Patricia M., Mabel H. *Education:* Attended Harvard University and Mozarteum Conservatorium in Salzburg, Austria. *Politics:* Independent. *Religion:* Episcopal. *Home address:* 27 W. 44, New York, N.Y. 10036. *Agent:* Julian Bach Literary Agency, Inc., 3 East 48th St., New York, N.Y. 10017. *Office:* American Airlines, 633 Third Ave., New York, N.Y. 10017.

CAREER: Guest conductor of symphony orchestras in Buffalo, N.Y. and Hartford, Conn., 1935-37; *Cue,* New York, N.Y., associate editor, 1939-40; free-lance writer, 1960—. Lecturer and consultant on wines; consultant to American Airlines. *Military service:* U.S. Army, Military Intelligence, 1940-43; became captain. *Member:* Century Club, Harvard Club, Chevy Chase Club, Wine Writers Circle, Importers' Tuesday Club, Confrerie de Chevaliers de Tastevin (Burgundy, France; commandeur-majeur).

WRITINGS: A Notebook for the Wines of France, Knopf, 1960; *The World of Wines,* Collier, 1964, revised edition, 1974; *The Great Wine Rivers,* Macmillan, 1971. Contributor to popular magazines, including *Gourmet, Saturday Review, Harper's, Status, House Beautiful,* and *Quest;* contributing editor of *House Beautiful.*

SIDELIGHTS: When asked his opinion of "soda pop" wines Churchill told *CA:* "I do not believe that 'soda pop' wines were part of a plot—they just happened. At least they have led more people to drink wine, which is good. From 'soda pop' one progresses to something better." He added, "In my memory one of the most exciting things that happened is the progress (in quality) of California and Washington State wines over the past ten years."

* * *

CIEPLAK, Tadeusz N(owak) 1918-

PERSONAL: Born October 7, 1918, in Tarnopol, Poland; came to the United States in 1957, naturalized citizen, 1963; son of Antoni (a farmer) and Agnieszka (Pszeniczna) Cieplak; married Irena Kondraciuk (a nurse), June 19, 1948; children: Bozena M. Dobrzynska (stepdaughter). *Education:* Attended Lvov and Warsaw universities, 1936-39; Oxford University, B.C.L., 1946; McGill University, LL.M., 1955, Ph.D., 1962. *Home:* 372 Burns St., Forest Hills, N.Y. 11375. *Office:* Department of Government and Politics, St. John's University, Grand Central & Utopia Parkways, Jamaica, N.Y. 11439.

CAREER: International Peasant Union, New York, N.Y., secretary to the president, 1957-61; San Francisco State College (now University), San Francisco, Calif., assistant professor of political science, 1961-63; Pennsylvania State University, State College, assistant professor of political science, 1963-64; Alliance College, Cambridge Springs, Pa., associate professor of political science, 1964-65; St. John's University, Jamaica, N.Y., associate professor of political science, 1965—. Foreign service officer of Polish Government-in-Exile, serving in the Soviet Union, Turkey, and Portugal, 1941-45. Host of "Conference Call" on WABC-Radio, 1975—. *Member:* International Platform Association, American Political Science Association, American Association for the Advancement of Slavic Studies, Polish Institute of Arts and Sciences in America, Center for the Study of Democratic Institutions, Kosciuszko Foundation, Delta Tau Kappa (life member).

WRITINGS: (Editor and contributor) *Poland since 1956: Readings and Essays,* Twayne, 1972; *Sorel and European Radicalism* (monograph), Hippocrene, in press. Contributor to academic journals.

WORK IN PROGRESS: Postwar Changes in the Attitudes and Behavior of Polish Peasantry; The Emerging Pattern of Opposition to the Political System in Eastern Europe; The Role and Function of Non-Communist Parties in the Polish People's Republic: The Case of the Democratic Party.

SIDELIGHTS: Cieplak writes: "After the war, I felt that I

should complement my war-time experiences with graduate studies in law and politics so that I could become an effective college teacher and writer. A concerted, dynamic, and creative cooperation of the Free World, in the political, economic, and intellectual realms, should decidedly tilt the scales in favor of democracy before the end of the century."

* * *

CIVILLE, John R(aphael) 1940-

PERSONAL: Born July 8, 1940, in Athens, Ohio; son of George P. (a government employee) and Mary (a teacher; maiden name, Guerra) Civille. *Education:* Athenaeum of Ohio, A.B., 1962; Xavier University, Cincinnati, Ohio, M.Ed., 1965; Alfonsiana, S.T.D., 1972. *Politics:* Democrat. *Home and office:* 5440 Moeller, Cincinnati, Ohio 45212.

CAREER: Ordained diocesan Roman Catholic priest; associate pastor of Roman Catholic church in Cincinnati, Ohio, 1966-69; Mount St. Mary's Seminary, Cincinnati, Ohio, assistant professor of moral theology, 1972—. Assistant professor at Xavier University, 1974—. Director of World Justice and Peace Commission of the Archdiocese of Cincinnati, 1973—. Chaplain of Sisters of St. Ursula, Cincinnati, 1974-76. *Member:* American Society of Christian Ethics, Catholic Theological Association of America.

WRITINGS: Tanzania and Nyerere, Orbis, 1976.

WORK IN PROGRESS: Research on Tanzania's UJAMAA socialism.

SIDELIGHTS: Civille has studied in Rome, East Africa, and South America, and visited more than sixty countries. He told *CA:* "I have a great interest in social justice and in trying to understand what that means in practice especially concerning international questions. I feel that my experiences from living in Africa and South America have given me more sensitivity to the problems people of the Third World face, as well as a greater realization of their struggle for economic advancement. I am using these insights in my teaching of social ethics and in my World Justice and Peace Commission work to stress the interdependence of the human family."

* * *

CLABAUGH, Gary K(enneth) 1940-

PERSONAL: Born August 22, 1940, in Altoona, Pa.; son of Harry Kenneth (a barber) and Thelma (Barger) Clabaugh; married Marjorie A. Marks, May 26, 1960; children: Erik Kenneth. *Education:* Indiana University of Pennsylvania, B.S., 1962; Temple University, M.S., 1968, Ed.D., 1972. *Religion:* Unitarian-Universalist. *Home:* 1061 Cushmore Rd., Southampton, Pa. 18966. *Office:* Department of Education, LaSalle College, 20th & Olney, Philadelphia, Pa. 19141.

CAREER: Junior high school teacher of geography in Red Lion, Pa., 1964-67; LaSalle College, Philadelphia, Pa., assistant professor, 1969-74, associate professor of education, 1974—. *Military service:* U.S. Army, 1962-64; became first lieutenant. *Member:* Association of Teacher Educators, American Association of Sex Educators, Counselors, and Therapists, Pennsylvania Association of Teacher Educators (president of Eastern region), Phi Delta Kappa. *Awards, honors:* Ralph D. Owen Prize from Phi Delta Kappa, 1969.

WRITINGS: Thunder on the Right: The Protestant Fundamentalists, Nelson-Hall, 1974; *The Radical Right in Twentieth Century America,* Nelson-Hall, 1977.

WORK IN PROGRESS: "Serious fiction."

SIDELIGHTS: Clabaugh writes: "I wrote my first book as a result of being attacked by the Fundamentalists segment of the radical right. The incident involved my teaching of a unit on evolution. The more I looked into the individuals and groups responsible for the harassment, the more fascinated I became. Eventually I published the results under the first title listed above. More generally, I am profoundly interested in all expressions of Fascism as well as in the nature of the phenomenon itself. While I suspect this interest will endure, I anticipate researching and writing on other social issues."

* * *

CLAMMER, David 1943-

PERSONAL: Born August 18, 1943, in Dorchester, Dorsetshire, England; son of George (a businessman) and Doris (Board) Clammer; married Elizabeth Caroline Budd, April 12, 1966; children: James, Paul. *Education:* St. Luke's College of Education, teacher qualification, 1965. *Politics:* "I would like to see the re-establishment of the British Empire!" *Religion:* None. *Residence:* St. Ives, Huntingdon, England.

CAREER: Teacher of students with learning disabilities and behavior problems at a secondary school in Bristol, England, 1965-72, head of careers department, 1970-72; Longsands School, St. Neot's, Huntingdon, England, deputy head of remedial education department, 1972-75, head of Hardy House, 1975—, teacher of humanities, 1976—.

WRITINGS: The Zulu War, St. Martin's, 1973; *The Victorian Army in Photographs,* Hippocrene Books, 1975; *The Last Zulu Warrior,* Purnell, 1977.

WORK IN PROGRESS: Soldiers of the Queen, a study of the Victorian Army; research on the Boer War and on British campaigns in Egypt and the Sudan, in the 1880's and 1890's.

SIDELIGHTS: Clammer writes: "I'm not an historian by profession, but my hobby, military history, has by now become rather more than just a hobby—a sort of cottage industry!" His special interest, as his writings indicate, is the British Army and its activities. *Avocational interests:* Travel in western Europe, gardening, horseback riding.

* * *

CLARK, Bruce B(udge) 1918-

PERSONAL: Born April 9, 1918, in Georgetown, Idaho; son of Marvin E. (a farmer) and Alice (Budge) Clark; married Ouida Raphiel, November 7, 1946; children: Lorraine, Bradley, Robert, Jeffrey, Shawn, Sandra. *Education:* University of Utah, B.A., 1943, Ph.D., 1951; Brigham Young University, M.A., 1948. *Religion:* Church of Jesus Christ of Latter-day Saints (Mormons). *Home:* 365 East 1655 S., Orem, Utah 84057. *Office:* College of Humanities, 129 J.K.B.A., Brigham Young University, Provo, Utah 84602.

CAREER: Brigham Young University, Provo, Utah, assistant professor, 1950-56, associate professor, 1956-59, professor of English, 1959—, director of department of humanities, 1958-60, chairman of department of English, 1960-65, dean of College of Humanities, 1965—. *Military service:* U.S. Army, 1943-46.

MEMBER: Modern Language Association of America, National Council of Teachers of English, Comparative Education Society, Conference on College Composition and Communication, Browning Society, Rocky Mountain Modern Language Association, Phi Kappa Phi. *Awards, honors:* Certificate of merit for distinguished service to education from International Biographical Association, 1967; Karl G. Maeser Distinguished Teaching Award from Brigham Young University, 1972.

WRITINGS: (Editor) *Out of the Best Books: An Anthology of Literature,* five volumes, Deseret, 1964-69; *Romanticism through Modern Eyes,* Brigham Young University Press, 1970; *Oscar Wilde: A Study in Genius and Tragedy,* Press Publishing, 1970; (editor) *Richard Evans Quote Book,* Publishers Press, 1971; *Idealists in Revolt: An Introduction to Romanticism,* Brigham Young University Press, 1975. Author of booklets. Contributor to professional journals.

WORK IN PROGRESS: Great Short Stories for Discussion and Delight (tentative title); *Poetry without Pain* (tentative title); research on Robert Browning and Oscar Wilde; anthologies.

SIDELIGHTS: Clark writes: "Although administrative duties and writing take much of my time, first and last I am a teacher. My field is English literature, and my approach to teaching is to experience literature for its beauty and for its human insights and values. I love literature, I love my family, I love people generally, I love teaching, I love service, and I think of myself as a champion of traditional ideals and principles."

* * *

CLARK, Electa 1910-

PERSONAL: Born May 17, 1910, in Chicago, Ill.; daughter of Richard H. (an engineer) and Rose (Dougherty) Carter; married James E. Clark, September 4, 1932; children: James E., Jr. (deceased), Jenifer Alice (Mrs. Warren Edward Leet). *Education:* Purdue University, B.S., 1933. *Politics:* Democrat. *Religion:* Methodist. *Home address:* R.R.1, Box 63-H, Nashville, Ind. 47448.

CAREER: Writer, 1949—. Docent of Children's Museum, Indianapolis, Inc., 1957-64.

WRITINGS—For children, except as indicated: *The Pennywinks,* Bobbs-Merrill, 1949; *Pennywink Carnival,* Bobbs-Merrill, 1951; *The Seven Q's,* Bobbs-Merrill, 1953; *Robert Peary, Boy of the North Pole,* Bobbs-Merrill, 1953; *Tony for Keeps,* John C. Winston Co., 1954; *Wildcat the Seminole,* Aladdin, 1955; *The Dagger, the Fish, and Casey McKee,* McKay, 1955; *Spanish Gold and Casey McKee,* McKay, 1956; *Osceola, Young Seminole Indian,* Bobbs-Merrill, 1957; *Show Folks,* McKay, 1958; *John Ross, Cherokee Chief,* Macmillan, 1972; *Leading Ladies* (for adults), Stein & Day, 1976.

WORK IN PROGRESS: Two books for children, one fiction and one nonfiction.

* * *

CLARK, Norman H(arold) 1925-

PERSONAL: Born May 10, 1925, in Mesa, Ariz.; son of Leigh and Sadie (O'Horton) Clark; married Kathy Henningsen, 1949; children: Karen Louise, Kenneth Norman. *Education:* Southern Methodist University, B.A., 1949; University of Washington, Seattle, M.A., 1950, Ph.D., 1964. *Office:* Everett Community College, Everett, Wash. 98201.

CAREER: High school teacher of English and history in Anacortes, Wash., 1951-53, Kirkland, Wash., 1953-56, and San Jose, Calif., 1956-57; Everett Community College, Everett, Wash., teacher of English and history, 1958—, president of college, 1975—. Associate professor at University of Washington, Seattle, 1964-66, visiting lecturer, 1970-71; visiting professor at Lewis & Clark College, summers, 1966-69. Member of Washington Commission for the Humanities, 1976—. *Military service:* U.S. Marine Corps, 1943-46; served in the Far East; became second lieutenant.

MEMBER: American Historical Association, Organization of American Historians, Washington Association of Community Colleges. *Awards, honors:* Award of merit from Seattle Historical Society, 1966; research grant from American Philosophical Society, 1966; grant from National Endowment for the Humanities, 1967; award of merit from American Association for State and Local History, 1971; Washington State Governor's Award, 1971; Pacific Northwest Bookseller's Award, 1971.

WRITINGS: The Dry Years: Prohibition and Social Change in Washington, University of Washington Press, 1965; *Mill Town,* University of Washington Press, 1970; (author of introduction) James G. Swan, *The Northwest Coast,* University of Washington Press, 1972; *Deliver Us from Evil: An Interpretation of American Prohibition,* Norton, 1976; *Washington: A Bicentennial History,* Norton, 1976. Contributor to *Funk & Wagnell's Standard Reference Encyclopedia.* Contributor of articles and reviews to education and history journals, and to *Pacific Northwest Quarterly* and *Seattle.* Member of editorial board of *Pacific Northwest Quarterly,* 1969—.

AVOCATIONAL INTERESTS: Reading, classical music, swimming, boating and fishing (has worked summers as a commercial fisherman), hiking.

* * *

CLARK, Ruth C(ampbell) 1920-
(Alan Porter)

PERSONAL: Born March 22, 1920, in Boston, Mass.; daughter of Angus (a dentist) and Frances (a social worker; maiden name, Porter) Campbell; married Douglas Alan Clark (a professor), September 16, 1944; children: Jonathan Alden, Stephen Alan, Stanley Andrew. *Education:* Gordon College, B.A., 1940; Eastern Baptist Theological Seminary, M.R.E., 1944; West Texas State University, M.A., 1962. *Politics:* Independent. *Religion:* Baptist. *Home:* 4207 Blaine Rd., Shawnee, Okla. 74801. *Office:* Oklahoma Baptist University, Shawnee, Okla. 74801.

CAREER: Wayland Baptist College, Plainview, Tex., instructor in English, 1959-65; Aurora College, Aurora, Ill., assistant professor of English, 1965-66; Oklahoma Baptist University, Shawnee, assistant professor of English, 1966-71 and 1973—. Visiting lecturer, Acadia University, Wolfville, Nova Scotia, summer 1963; lecturer, Mt. Lawley Teachers College, Perth, Western Australia, 1972-73.

WRITINGS: Object Lessons for Special Occasions, Standard Publishing, 1958; *Vacation Bible School Manual,* Evangelical Teacher Training Association, 1959; *Modern Methods for Modern Man,* Conservative Baptist Foreign Mission Society, 1968; *Let's Face It,* Conservative Baptist Foreign Mission Society, 1969; *Help Wanted,* Conservative Baptist Foreign Mission Society, 1971; (under pseudonym, Alan Porter) *You've Really Got Me, God!,* Baker Book, 1977.

WORK IN PROGRESS: Three books, completion expected in 1978, *Footprints in the Sand,* about missions in Hawaii, *From Eden to Eden,* about missions in Micronesia, and *How to Do Micronesia on $?? a Day,* about travel in Micronesia.

SIDELIGHTS: Mrs. Clark has traveled to Canada, Melanesia, Polynesia, Australia, Singapore, Bali, Africa, Spain, Portugal, Caribbean islands, Micronesia, and all states but Alaska, and says that her interest is in work being done in church missions in each of these areas. *Avocational interests:* Photography and philately.

* * *

CLARKE, James F(ranklin) 1906-

PERSONAL: Born June 5, 1906, in Monastir, Turkey; son of William Paine (a missionary) and Martha (a missionary; maiden name, Gisler) Clarke; married Esther Nichols (a social worker), August 18, 1935; children: Robert William. *Education:* Amherst College, A.B., 1928; Harvard University, M.A., 1929, PH.D., 1938. *Politics:* "Usually Democrat." *Religion:* Unitarian-Universalist. *Home:* 207 Church Lane, Pittsburgh, Pa. 15238. *Office:* Department of History, University of Pittsburgh, Pittsburgh, Pa. 15260.

CAREER: Massachusetts Institute of Technology, Cambridge, instructor in history, 1938; College of Idaho, Caldwell, professor of history and government and head of department, 1939-41; Office of Strategic Services, Washington, D.C., chief of Balkan section, 1941-43; Office of War Information, Washington, D.C., chief of Balkan branch, 1943-45; Allied Mission for Observing Greek Elections, Salonika, Greece, district secretary, 1946; U.S. Political Mission to Bulgaria, Sophia, press attache, 1946; U.S. Department of State, Washington, D.C., section chief in Office of Intelligence Research, 1946-49, branch chief, 1949-50; Indiana University, Bloomington, professor of history and director of East European Institute, 1951-54; Associates for International Research, Inc., Cambridge, senior research associate, 1955-56; University of Pittsburgh, Pittsburgh, Pa., associate professor of European history, 1956-76, writer, 1976—. Member of ethnic studies planning committee of Pittsburgh Council on Higher Education. Consultant to Voice of America and U.S. Information Agency. *Wartime service:* U.S. Army, Psychological Warfare Branch, 1944; served in Mediterranean theater.

MEMBER: American Historical Association, American Association for the Advancement of Slavic Studies, American Association for Southeast European Studies (vice-president, 1976-77; president, 1977-78), Association for the Study of Nationalities, Bulgarian Studies Group, Polish Institute of Arts and Sciences of America, Romanian Academic Society (Munich), Phi Beta Kappa. *Awards, honors:* Ford Foundation fellowship, 1954-55.

WRITINGS: (Contributor) D. C. McKay, editor, *Essays in the History of Modern Europe,* Harper, 1936, reprinted, 1968; (contributor) H. S. Hughes, editor, *Teachers of History,* Cornell University Press, 1954; (contributor) Horace Lunt, editor, *Slavic Studies III,* Harvard University Press, 1957; (contributor) P. L. Horecky, editor, *Southeastern Europe: Guide to Basic Publications,* University of Chicago Press, 1969; *Bible Societies, American Missionaries, and the National Revival of Bulgaria,* Arno, 1971. Contributor to history and Slavic studies journals.

WORK IN PROGRESS: America and Bulgaria: A History, completion expected in 1979; *The Russian Bible Society in the Balkans,* 1980; *History of the Bulgarians,* 1981; *Literary History, Culture, and Nationalism in Southeastern Europe; The Macedonian Question in Historical Perspective; Dear Uncle Henry,* for children.

SIDELIGHTS: Clarke writes: "Born and brought up in what once was called 'The Whirlpool of the Balkans' or the 'Cockpit of Europe', I naturally took to history—as an alternative to four generations of clergymen, two of them missionaries. Add to this inspiring teachers of history. Personal experience directed me to Eastern and Southeastern Europe; a penchant for collecting (especially books) and showing indicated teaching (I have one of the largest private collections of Bulgarian books in this country).

"Vocational and avocational interests are somewhat merged and include an interest in languages (German, French, Russian, Bulgarian, etc.) and travel—as far east as Samarqand, and as far south as Khartoum and Accra, north to Finland and west to San Francisco (I have never visited Luxembourg). I am fascinated with Byzantine churches and taking their pictures. Thus, vocational-avocational interests resulted in talks with kings, presidents, patriarchs, and premiers, as well as lesser but often more interesting mortals. I once crossed the Atlantic on one of the last cattle boats (tending mules), another crossing on a plane next to Trygve Lie. I have been called a Communist (McCarthy era) and a fascist (today's era), a Roman Catholic, and an atheist—all of which pleases me no end. I like to climb, cultivate, and cook nature, especially Balkan.

"I believe everyone in this country should give up something—not just for Lent but for the good of the country and therefore of themselves (except those who have nothing). And what is desperately needed, I believe, are higher standards, not only in the quality of bread and TV; and greater integrity for all, but especially for elected officials. Lastly, I'm against 'growth' and believe 'small is beautiful.'"

* * *

CLARKE, Stephan P(aul) 1945-

PERSONAL: Born January 18, 1945, in Watertown, N.Y.; son of Albert J. and Marjory R. (Grieb) Clarke; married Mary E. Hawley (a high school teacher), May 23, 1970. *Education:* State University of New York College at Geneseo, B.S.Ed., 1966; Bowling Green State University, M.A., 1968. *Politics:* Republican. *Religion:* Protestant. *Home:* 110 Greenway Blvd., Churchville, N.Y. 14428. *Office:* Spencerport Central Schools, Spencerport, N.Y. 14559.

CAREER: Spencerport Central Schools, Spencerport, N.Y., high school English teacher, 1970—. *Military service:* U.S. Naval Reserve, active duty, 1968-70; became lieutenant. *Member:* Mystery Writers of America, Rochester Area English Council, National Council of Teachers of English.

WRITINGS: Crimes and Clues (textbook), Prentice-Hall, 1977.

WORK IN PROGRESS: Editing *Popular Opinions* (tentative title), an anthology of critical essays by Dorothy L. Sayers, dealing with mystery and detective fiction, completion expected in 1979.

SIDELIGHTS: Clarke writes that his book "uses mystery and detective fiction short stories, an essay, and poems as vehicles to assist in teaching basic logic and organization skills in thinking, reading, and composition." He adds: "The course from which the text is derived results from a strong personal conviction that too many students are unable to reason clearly or express their thinking effectively. Public education seems to place too little value on the ability to handle the basic tools of learning."

AVOCATIONAL INTERESTS: Collecting rare and first editions of mystery and detective fiction, model railroading, travel.

CLAYBAUGH, Amos L(incoln) 1917-

PERSONAL: Born December 11, 1917, in Waukesha, Wis.; son of Robert Parks (a salesman) and Marion (Holloway) Claybaugh; married Patricia Norman (a manager of a college bookstore), December 18, 1948; children: Donna Claybaugh Schenk, Norman R., Kristy Claybaugh Johnson. *Education:* Wisconsin State University, Whitewater, B.E., 1945; University of Wisconsin, Madison, M.S., 1950; University of Northern Colorado, Ed.D., 1960. *Religion:* Protestant. *Home:* Box 276, Allenspark, Colo. 80510. *Office:* Department of Elementary Education, University of Northern Colorado, Greeley, Colo. 80639.

CAREER: Teacher and principal in elementary school in Racine County, Wis., 1938-47, teacher in Beloit, Wis., 1947-48, principal and audio-visual coordinator in Davenport, Iowa, 1948-58; University of Northern Colorado, Greeley, instructor, 1958-61, assistant professor, 1961-62, associate professor, 1962-67, professor of elementary education, 1967—. *Member:* International Reading Association, National Education Association, Colorado Council International Reading Association (president, 1970-71), Phi Delta Kappa.

WRITINGS: (With Arnold Burron) *Concepts in Reading Instruction,* C. E. Merrill, 1972, 2nd edition, 1977; (with Burron) *Using Reading to Teach Subject Matter,* C. E. Merrill, 1974.

SIDELIGHTS: Claybaugh comments that his "writings have been an outgrowth of experience and observations in the public schools of three states. The purpose has been to contribute to the betterment of classroom teaching." *Avocational interests:* Color photography (especially in central and western Europe).

* * *

CLAYTON, Bruce 1939-

PERSONAL: Born March 14, 1939, in Wakenda, Mo.; son of Roy Roosevelt (a farmer) and Lilly Ruth (Gilbert) Clayton; married Carrah Ann Hendrix, May 2, 1959; children: Elisabeth Anne, Jennifer Hendrix, John Edward, Sarah Jane. *Education:* Kansas City Junior College, A.A., 1959; University of Missouri, Kansas City, B.A., 1961; Duke University, M.A., 1963, Ph.D., 1966. *Politics:* Liberal Democrat. *Religion:* None. *Home:* 296 Loomis, Meadville, Pa. 16335. *Office:* Department of History, Allegheny College, Box 74, Meadville, Pa. 16335.

CAREER: King College, Bristol, Tenn., assistant professor of history, 1963-65; Wake Forest University, Winston-Salem, N.C., instructor in history, 1965-66; Allegheny College, Meadville, Pa., assistant professor, 1966-70, associate professor, 1970-76, professor of history, 1976—. *Member:* Organization of American Historians, Conference on Peace Research in History, National Association for the Advancement of Colored People, Southern Historical Association. *Awards, honors:* Woodrow Wilson fellowship, 1961-62; National Endowment for the Humanities fellowships, summer, 1967, summer, 1977; American Philosophical Society grant, 1972.

WRITINGS: The Savage Ideal: Intolerance and Intellectual Leadership in the South, 1890-1914, Johns Hopkins Press, 1972. Contributor to *Encyclopedia of Southern History.* Contributor of articles and reviews to history journals.

WORK IN PROGRESS: An intellectual biography of Randolph Bourne, 1886-1918; *Radical Women in the Progressive Era.*

SIDELIGHTS: Clayton writes: "I write because I need intellectual and literary stimulation to think clearly; although teaching allows me to do a certain amount of this, I need to feel that I am speaking to an audience of peers. I enjoy the feeling I have when I communicate something to scholars and intellectuals. And I enjoy the challenge and the (small) rewards. I also enjoy the base reward of seeing my writings and my name in print. I would like also to think that my writings about the American past have helped clarify the issues, particularly in the area of race relations. I also hope to help clarify the liberal dimension of the past."

AVOCATIONAL INTERESTS: Baseball, playing the trombone (with the Cussewago Jazz Band).

* * *

CLEAVES, Peter S(hurtleff) 1943-

PERSONAL: Born December 4, 1943, in Washington, D.C.; son of Richard Delaplane (a senior government official) and Margaret (Shurtleff) Cleaves; married Dorothy Barcham, July 31, 1968; children: Geoffrey, Rachel. *Education:* Dartmouth College, A.B., 1966; Vanderbilt University, M.A., 1968; University of California, Berkeley, Ph.D., 1972. *Home:* Alejandro Dumas 42, Polanco, Mexico City 5, Mexico. *Office:* Office for Latin America and the Caribbean, Ford Foundation—Peru, 320 East 43rd St., New York, N.Y. 10017.

CAREER: Ford Foundation, Lima, Peru, adviser to advanced social science program, 1972-76; Yale University, New Haven, Conn., visiting fellow, 1976-77; Ford Foundation, Mexico City, Mexico, representative, 1978—. *Member:* American Political Science Association, American Society for Public Administration, Southern Political Science Association.

WRITINGS: Developmental Processes in Chilean Local Government, Institute of International Studies, 1969; *Bureaucratic Politics and Administration in Chile,* University of California Press, 1974.

WORK IN PROGRESS: Agriculture, Bureaucracy, and Society in Peru, with M. J. Scurrah; *In Search of the Mexican State,* completion expected in 1980.

SIDELIGHTS: Cleaves writes: "An abiding interest in international affairs since early childhood, and fascination by Latin America over the past decade, have motivated my research and writing."

* * *

CLEGG, Stewart (Roger) 1947-

PERSONAL: Born September 4, 1947, in Bradford, England; son of Willie (a sales representative) and Joyce Sylvia (Rogers) Clegg; married Caroline Lynne Bowker (a teacher), August 7, 1971. *Education:* University of Aston, B.Sc. (honors), 1971; University of Bradford, Ph.D., 1974. *Politics:* Socialist. *Religion:* None. *Agent:* A. D. Peters & Co., 10 Buckingham St., London W.C.2, England. *Office:* School of Humanities, Griffith University, Nathan, Brisbane, Queensland 4111, Australia.

CAREER: University of Bradford, Bradford, England, research fellow of European group for organization studies, 1975-77; Griffith University, Brisbane, Australia, lecturer in sociology, 1977—. *Member:* British Sociological Association.

WRITINGS: Power, Rule and Domination: A Critical and Empirical Understanding of Power in Sociological Theory and Organizational Life, Routledge & Kegan Paul, 1975; (editor with David Dunkerley) *Critical Issues in Organizations,* Routledge & Kegan Paul, 1977. Contributor to professional journals.

WORK IN PROGRESS: Research on power.

SIDELIGHTS: Clegg told *CA:* "I have chosen to write about 'power' in order to understand it, and, in that understanding, oppose the intellectual obfuscations which have so often passed as 'understanding,' but which merely lead to delusion, rather than enlightenment. If my writing aids in a more realistic grasp of practice, and the possibilities of changing that practice, then it will have been of value to more than just myself. My writing is always a political, as well as intellectual, activity. Sometimes it seems to me to be my fate, with many others, to substitute the former as no more than a manifestation of the latter."

* * *

CLEMENTS, Harold M., Sr.   1907-

PERSONAL: Born October 21, 1907, in Beaumont, Tex.; son of Francis Lemuel (a traffic manager) and Elizabeth C. (Upington) Clements; married Mary Virginia Burke, November 26, 1935; children: Cornelius F., Harold M., Jr., David J. *Education:* Georgetown University, A.B., 1930; Texas A & M University, M.S., 1936; University of Florida, Ph.D., 1966. *Home:* 3409 North St., Apt. 108, Nacogdoches, Tex. 75961. *Office:* Department of Sociology, Stephen F. Austin State University, Nacogdoches, Tex. 75962.

CAREER: Assistant gauger for a pipe line company in Corpus Christi, Tex., 1933-41; operated grocery and cleaning businesses in Marble Falls, Tex., 1941-48; inventory supervisor for supermarkets in Houston, Tex., 1948-49, store manager, 1949-54; operated filling station in Houston, 1954-62; University of Florida, Gainesville, interim instructor in sociology, 1966; Stephen F. Austin State University, Nacogdoches, Tex., assistant professor, 1967-69, associate professor, 1969-70, professor of sociology, 1970—, head of department, 1970-76. Visiting faculty member at Texas A & M University, 1971—.

MEMBER: American Sociological Association, Rural Sociological Society, Latin American Studies Association, Southern Sociological Society, Southwestern Sociological Association, Alpha Kappa Delta, Phi Kappa Phi, Lions Club.

WRITINGS: The Mechanization of Agriculture in Brazil, University of Florida Press, 1969; (contributor) T. Lynn Smith, editor, *Brazil: People and Institutions,* 4th edition, Louisiana State University Press, 1972; (contributor) Smith, editor, *Brazilian Society,* University of New Mexico Press, 1975; (contributor) Smith, editor, *The Race Between Population and Food Supply in Latin America,* University of New Mexico Press, 1977.

WORK IN PROGRESS: An Analysis of the Extent of Farm Improvement in the Agricultural Regions of Brazil; a textbook on minority relations.

SIDELIGHTS: Clements writes: "My interest in sociology and the field of teaching led to my entrance into the academic field after thirty years in non-academic occupations. I am intensely aware of the need to develop new areas of concentration for younger students in keeping with changing socioeconomic conditions, as well as continuing education for many seeking career improvement, new careers after early retirement, and/or newly-awakened interest in acquiring additional knowledge. I feel that fairly well-balanced academic and nonacademic experiences are quite valuable to anyone."

* * *

CLEMENTS, John   1916-

PERSONAL: Born July 23, 1916, in Wilkes-Barre, Pa.; son of Dillon F. (a businessman) and Lynn (Hershberger) Clements; married Gladys Johnston (a secretary); children: Lynn Clements Burleson, Daphne Clements Firestone, Allan. *Education:* Attended University of Minnesota. *Politics:* Independent. *Religion:* Methodist. *Home:* 6140 Spring Valley, Dallas, Tex. 75240. *Office:* Political Research, Inc., Fifth Floor, Continental Building, Dallas, Tex. 75201.

CAREER: Writer for McGraw-Hill Book Co. in New York City; board chairperson of McCullers Press, Inc.; board chairperson of Political Research, Inc., in Dallas, Tex.

WRITINGS: Taylors Encyclopedia of Government Officials, Political Research, Inc., 1967, 6th edition, 1977; *Clements Encyclopedia of World Governments,* Political Research, Inc., 1974, 2nd edition, 1976; *Chronology of the United States,* McGraw, 1975.

WORK IN PROGRESS: The Story of Tegoland.

SIDELIGHTS: Clements writes that he has served as special analyst to two U.S. presidents and to other federal and state officials.

* * *

CLEMENTS, Traverse   1900(?)-1977

1900(?)—May 4, 1977; American politician, editor, and author. He was secretary of the Socialist Party and editor of the party's weekly publication from 1939-1942. Clements also co-authored a book of radical political history. He died in Neuchatel, Switzerland. Obituaries: *New York Times,* May 9, 1977.

* * *

CLODFELTER, Micheal   1946-

PERSONAL: Born December 6, 1946, in Winfield, Kan.; son of Lutie D. (a truck driver) and Betty (a clerk; maiden name, Hotchkin) Clodfelter; married Rena Katherine Dyce (a keypunch operator), August 1, 1967; children: Thomas Debs. *Education:* Fort Hays Kansas State College, A.B., 1971. *Politics:* Socialist. *Religion:* None. *Home:* 1515 Maryland, Lawrence, Kan. 66044.

CAREER: Has worked as a dishwasher, farmhand, janitor, painter, and night watchman; writer, 1967—. *Military service:* U.S. Army, 1964-67; served in Vietnam; became sergeant; received Purple Heart.

WRITINGS: The Pawns of Dishonor, Branden Press, 1976. Contributor to student underground newspapers.

WORK IN PROGRESS: Casualties, an investigation into the military losses of modern warfare; writing poems.

SIDELIGHTS: Clodfelter writes: "My one published work . . . concerns my months of service in the Vietnam War. My current literary efforts continue to be focused on military history and upon the effects of war upon the human condition. I hope that my research and writing may in some small way help to illuminate the experience of war in both a personal and historical sense."

* * *

CLOKE, Richard   1916-

PERSONAL: Born January 23, 1916, in Seattle, Wash.; son

of Harold E. (an army officer) and Alice Bird (Findley) Cloke; married Shirley Jane Rodecker (a teacher); children: Kenneth, William. *Education:* Attended Unitersity of Virginia; University of California, B.A., 1940; graduate study at California State University, Northridge. *Address:* c/o Kent Publications, 18301 Halsted St., Northridge, Calif. 91324.

CAREER: Has worked variously as auto worker, pile driver operator, shipwright, carpenter, poultry rancher, electronics technician in a television factory, account executive at KDUO-FM Radio in Los Angeles, teacher, and principal; now a writer.

WRITINGS: Mister Pistol-John (Western novel), Kent Publications, 1976; *Vector Lee* (science fiction spy novel), Kent Publications, 1977. Contributor of poems to small literary magazines.

WORK IN PROGRESS: A gangster novel, *Jerry the Put;* a World War I novel, *My Pal Al;* a historical novel, *Yvar, Prince of Rus;* a historical novel based on the American Revolution, *Liberty Boys and Belles*.

* * *

CLOUGH, William 1911(?)-1976

1911(?)—November 5, 1976; American physician and author of works in his field. He died in New London, N.H. Obituaries: *New York Times,* November 8, 1976.

* * *

CLUBB, Louise George 1930-

PERSONAL: Born July 22, 1930, in New York, N.Y.; daughter of Alexander (an Army officer) and Ethel Louise (a singer; maiden name, Wright) George; married William Graham Clubb (a scholar), November 6, 1954. *Education:* Universita degli Studi di Firenze, corso per stranieri, 1951; George Washington University, A.B., 1952, M.A., 1956; University of Florence, graduate study, 1952-53; Columbia University, Ph.D., 1963. *Home:* 135 Evergreen Lane, Berkeley, Calif. 94705. *Office:* Department of Comparative Literature, University of California, Berkeley, Calif. 94720.

CAREER: English and history teacher at private school in Washington, D.C., 1955-56; University of Maryland, College Park, instructor in English, 1956-57, autumn, 1960, assistant professor of English and comparative literature, 1961-62; George Washington University, Washington, D.C., assistant professor of English and comparative literature, 1962-64; University of California, Berkeley, visiting assistant professor, 1964-65, associate professor, 1966-70, professor of Italian and comparative literature, 1970—. Member of national screening committee of Institute for International Education, 1972.

MEMBER: International Comparative Literature Association, Associazione Internazionale per gli Studi della Lingua e Letterature Italiana, Renaissance Society of America, Shakespeare Society of America, Dante Society, American Association of Teachers of Italian, American Comparative Literature Association, Philological Association of the Pacific Coast. *Awards, honors:* American Association of University Women fellowship, 1959-60; Folger Library fellowship, 1963; Guggenheim fellowship, 1965-66; American Philosophical Society grant, 1972-73; American Council of Learned Societies grant, 1976-77.

WRITINGS: Giambattista Della Porta, Dramatist, Princeton University Press, 1965; *Italian Plays (1500-1700)*

in the Folger Library, Leo S. Olschki, 1968; (contributor) J. A. Molinaro, editor, *Petrarch to Pirandello,* University of Toronto Press, 1973; (contributor) G. A. Tarugi, editor, *Interrogativi dell' Umanesimo,* Leo S. Olschki, 1976; (contributor) Dale Randall, editor, *Renaissance Background of English Literature,* Duke University Press, 1977. Contributor to academic journals.

WORK IN PROGRESS: Editing and translating Della Porta's *Gli duoi fratelli rivali,* originally published in 1601; a book on Italian comic dramatic forms in Shakespeare's time.

SIDELIGHTS: Clubb writes: "My writing, like my teaching and my views on education, is determined by concern for the continuity of humanistic values through the study of historical and linguistic traditions central to European and American civilization. I am especially interested in English, Italian, Spanish and French literature in the Renaissance and the Middle Ages. I am of Scottish ancestry, received my early schooling in Japan and have lived in Central America and West Africa as well as in Europe."

* * *

CLUM, John M(acKenzie) 1941-

PERSONAL: Born September 29, 1941, in Asbury Park, N.J.; son of Henry George (a lighting engineer) and Edythe (Black) Clum. *Education:* Princeton University, A.B., 1963, M.A., 1966, Ph.D., 1967. *Home:* 4006 Inwood Dr., Durham, N.C. 27705. *Office:* Drama Program, 6436 College Station, Durham, N.C. 27708.

CAREER: Duke University, Durham, N.C., assistant professor, 1966-76, associate professor of English, 1976—, director of drama program, 1975—, also theatrical director and managing director of summer theater. *Member:* Modern Language Association of America, American Theatre Association, American Society for Theatre Research, Southeastern Theatre Conference, North Carolina Theatre Conference.

WRITINGS: Ridgely Torrence, Twayne, 1972; *Paddy Chayefsky,* Twayne, 1976.

Co-author of "Sanctuary" (two-act play), first produced in Durham, N.C., at Duke University Chapel, February 1976. Contributor of articles and reviews to literary journals, including *South Atlantic Quarterly* and *American Literature*.

WORK IN PROGRESS: Co-author of a mystery novel, *Death's Ghoulish Dance;* a study of the plays of Simon Gray.

SIDELIGHTS: Clum writes: "I like to juggle a number of roles at once—teacher, administrator, scholar/critic with a particular interest in contemporary theater and a growing interest in film, creative participant in theater, dabbler in creative writing. To me these roles fit a larger pattern—they inform one another."

* * *

CLYNE, James F. 1898(?)-1977

1898(?)—January 22, 1977; American educator and writer of works in his field. Clyne was on the staff of New York University as a professor as well as in several administrative positions. After his retirement in 1968, he worked as a consultant. He died in New York City. Obituaries: *New York Times,* January 24, 1977.

* * *

COAKLEY, Lakme 1912-

PERSONAL: Born December 21, 1912, in New Orleans,

La.; daughter of Leonard and Lillian (McNeely) Perez; married John M. Coakley, August 29, 1941; children: Kate Coakley Collins, John, Peter, Mark. *Education:* Webster College, B.A., 1933; Wichita State University, M.E., 1965. *Politics:* Democrat. *Religion:* Roman Catholic. *Home:* 2055 Porter, Apt. 121, Wichita, Kan. 67203. *Agent:* Walter Powers, Wichita State University, 1847 North Chautauqua, Wichita, Kan. 67214. *Office:* Wichita Public Schools, 1847 North Chautauqua, Wichita, Kan. 67214.

CAREER: Wichita Public Schools, Wichita, Kan., high school reading specialist, 1965—. Lecturer at Wichita State University, 1966—. *Member:* International Reading Association (member of Wichita council, Kansas council, and national council, all 1966—; president of local chapter, 1972—), Kansas Council of Teachers of English (member of board of directors, 1968-79), Wichita Council of Teachers of English (president, 1969). *Awards, honors:* Wakan Award from National Council of Campfire Girls, 1956, Gulick Award, 1957; Benemerenti Medal from Pope Pius XII, 1957.

WRITINGS: Wichita Reading Inventory, Tarmac, 1977.

* * *

COAN, Richard Welton 1928-

PERSONAL: Born January 24, 1928, in Martinez, Calif.; son of Otis Welton (an instructor in English) and Dorothy (a secretary; maiden name, Wilson) Coan; children: Lisa Coan Cooper, Cynthia. *Education:* Los Angeles City College, A.A., 1946; University of California, Berkeley, A.B., 1948, M.A., 1950; University of Southern California, Ph.D., 1955. *Home:* 1240 East Mabel St., Tucson, Ariz. 85719. *Office:* Department of Psychology, University of Arizona, Tucson, Ariz. 85721.

CAREER: University of Illinois, Urbana, research associate in psychology, 1955-57; University of Arizona, Tucson, assistant professor, 1957-60, associate professor, 1960-64, professor of psychology, 1964—. *Member:* American Psychological Association, Association for Humanistic Psychology, Society for Multivariate Experimental Psychology.

WRITINGS: The Optimal Personality: An Empirical and Theoretical Analysis, Columbia University Press, 1974; *Hero, Artist, Sage, or Saint?: A Survey of Views on What Is Variously Called Mental Health, Normality, Maturity, Self-Actualization, and Human Fulfillment,* Columbia University Press, 1977.

Contributor: O. K. Buros, editor, *The Sixth Mental Measurements Yearbook,* Gryphon, 1972; S. V. Zagona, editor, *Studies and Issues in Smoking Behavior,* University of Arizona Press, 1967; V. S. Sexton and H. Misiak, editors, *Historical Perspectives in Psychology,* Brooks/Cole, 1971; O. K. Buros, editor, *The Seventh Mental Measurements Yearbook,* Gryphon, 1972; R. M. Dreger, editor, *Multivariate Personality Research,* Claitors, 1972. Contributor to psychology journals.

WORK IN PROGRESS: Patterns of Theoretical Orientation in Psychology: Their Nature and Personal Roots; a book on the psychology of human adjustment.

SIDELIGHTS: Coan writes: "My primary areas of research have been personality theory and patterns of theoretical orientation in psychology, but I have a general interest in the symbolic systems of mankind. I want to understand the psychological roots common to science, art, mythology, religion, and philosophy." *Avocational interests:* Musical composition, writing poetry.

COATES, Willson H(avelock) 1899-1976

August 1, 1899—September 23, 1976; Canadian-born specialist in British studies and Western European cultural history, professor of history at University of Rochester, and author of books in his field. He died in Rochester, N.Y. Obituaries: *New York Times,* September 24, 1976. (See index for previous *CA* sketch)

* * *

COBB, Robert A. 1941-

PERSONAL: Born October 19, 1941, in Augusta, Maine; son of Willis I. (a farmer) and Aldea (a secretary; maiden name, Maheuk) Cobb; married Shayne Dooling (a secretary), August 26, 1961; children: Tracy Helen, Casey Dooling. *Education:* Springfield College, B.S., 1964, M.S., 1967, D.P.E., 1969. *Politics:* Democrat. *Religion:* Roman Catholic. *Home address:* M.R.B. 446, Bangor, Maine 04401. *Office:* College of Education, University of Maine at Orono, Orono, Maine 04473.

CAREER: University of Maine, Orono, faculty member in health, physical education and recreation, 1969—, and coordinator of Division of Health, Physical Education and Recreation. Consultant to Health Education Research Center. *Member:* American Alliance of Health, Physical Education and Recreation, Maine Association for Health, Physical Education and Recreation (president).

WRITINGS: Contemporary Philosophies of Physical Education and Athletics, C. E. Merrill, 1973; *Psychomotor Competencies in Primary Grades K-3,* Maine Department of Education, 1976; *Psychomotor Competencies in Intermediate Grades 4-6,* Maine Department of Education, 1977.

WORK IN PROGRESS: Competition and the Child; The Relationship of Psychomotor and Affective Variables.

* * *

CODERE, Helen (Frances) 1917-

PERSONAL: Born September 10, 1917, in Winnipeg, Manitoba, Canada; came to the United States in 1919, naturalized citizen, 1924; daughter of Charles Francis (a businessman) and Mabelle Helen (Prosser) Codere. *Education:* University of Minnesota, B.A. (summa cum laude), 1939; Columbia University, Ph.D., 1950. *Office:* Graduate School of Arts and Sciences, Brandeis University, Waltham, Mass. 02154.

CAREER: Vassar College, Poughkeepsie, N.Y., instructor, 1946-50, assistant professor, 1951-53, associate professor, 1955-57, professor of anthropology, 1958-63; Bennington College, Bennington, Vt., professor of anthropology, 1963-64; Brandeis University, Waltham, Mass., professor of anthropology, 1964—, dean of Graduate School of Arts and Sciences, 1975—. Visiting lecturer at University of British Columbia, 1954-55, and Northwestern University, winter, 1963; has conducted field work on the Indians of British Columbia and in Rwanda, 1959-60.

MEMBER: American Anthropological Association (fellow; member of executive council, 1966-69), American Ethnological Society (president), American Association for the Advancement of Science (fellow), African Studies Association, Society for Applied Anthropology, Northeastern Anthropological Association (president, 1973), New York Academy of Sciences, Phi Beta Kappa. *Awards, honors:* Social Science Research Council fellowships, 1956, 1962-63; Guggenheim fellowship, 1959-60.

WRITINGS: Fighting with Property: A Study of Kwakiutl

Potlatching and Warfare, 1792-1930, J. J. Augustin, 1950; (editor) Franz Boas, *Kwakiutl Ethnography,* University of Chicago Press, 1966; *The Biography of an African Society: Rwanda, 1900-1960—Based on Forty-Eight Rwandan Autobiographies,* Musee royal de l'Afrique centrale, 1973. Contributor to *International Encyclopedia of the Social Sciences* and to professional journals.

WORK IN PROGRESS: Rwanda: Social and Cultural Change.

* * *

COE, Lloyd 1899(?)-1976

1899(?)—October 10, 1976; American illustrator, cartoonist, and author. Coe's cartoons appeared in *The Saturday Review* for many years. He died in Gloucester, Mass. Obituaries: *AB Bookman's Weekly,* November 15, 1976.

* * *

COHAN, Avery B(erlow) 1914-1977

July 12, 1914—February 21, 1977; American professor of finance at University of North Carolina, consultant to the United Nations and to business concerns, and author of books on financial subjects. He died in Chapel Hill, N.C. Obituaries: *New York Times,* February 23, 1977. (See index for previous *CA* sketch)

* * *

COHEN, Aharon 1910-

PERSONAL: Born June 3, 1910, in Bessarabia, Russia; son of Yosef and Rachel (Kliger) Cohen; married Rivka Ghivelder, 1931; children: Tirtza, Yossef. *Politics:* "Socialist Zionism." *Religion:* None. *Home and office:* Kibbutz Shaar Haamakim 30097, Israel. *Agent:* Virginia Barber, 44 Greenwich Ave., New York, N.Y. 10011.

CAREER: Founding member of Kibbutz Shaar Haamakim, Israel, 1935—. Member of Hashomer Hatziar Central Committee, 1935; delegate to World Zionist Congress, Lucerne, 1935; member, executive committee of Hakibbutz Haartzi Hshomer Hatzair Kibbutz Federation, 1937-54; founder and director, Arab department, Hasomer Hatzair, 1940-50; secretary, League for Arab-Jewish Rapprochement and Cooperation, 1941-48; member, Central Committee of Mapam, 1948-63.

WRITINGS: Hascala Vehinuk Ba'olam Ha'arovi (title means "Culture and Education in the Arab World"), Histadrut, 1944; *Al-kadiya Al-yahudia Wamushkilat Falastin* (title means "The Jewish Question and the Problem of Palestine"), Hasomer-Hatzair, 1945; *Tenuat Hapoalim Ha'aravit* (title means "The Arab Workers Movement"), Histadrut, 1947; *Hamizrach Ha'aravi* (title means "The Arab East"), Sifriat Poalim, 1955, 3rd edition, 1960; *Ha'olam Ha'aravi Shel Yameinu* (title means "The Contemporary Arab World"), Sifriat Poalim, 1959, 2nd edition, 1960; *Skenenu Ha'aravim* (title means "Our Arab Neighbors"), Sifriat Poalim, 1964; *Israel Veha'olam Ha'aravi,* Sifriat Poalim, 1964, translation by Aubrey Hodes, Naomi Handelman, and Miriam Shimeoni, published as *Israel and the Arab World,* Funk, 1969, abridged edition, Beacon Press, 1976; (contributor) M. H. Kerr, editor, *The Elusive Peace in the Middle East,* State University of New York Press, 1975. Contributor to *Encyclopedia of Social Science* and to scholarly journals (in Hebrew, Arabic, English, and Yiddish). Member of editorial board of *New Outlook.*

WORK IN PROGRESS: The Kurds; Soviet Orientalism; *The New Romania;* a new edition of *Israel and the Arab World.*

SIDELIGHTS: Cohen has been described as a man who has "lived a life of total commitment to an ideal and to a movement. The ideal is socialist Zionism and the movement is the socialist-Zionist enterprise in its various forms. Since the most serious problem Zionism had to face has been that of relations with the Arabs, Cohen devoted a lifetime of work toward achieving "a real, lasting, just and honorable peace between the two peoples in the Middle East." Cohen speaks Romanian, Arabic, Russian, and German.

* * *

COHEN, I. Bernard 1914-

PERSONAL: Born March 1, 1914, in Far Rockaway, N.Y.; son of Isador and Blanche (Bernstein) Cohen; married Frances Parsons Davis, June 23, 1944; children: Frances. *Education:* Harvard University, B.S. (cum laude), 1937, Ph.D., 1947. *Home:* 22 Gray Gardens E., Cambridge, Mass. 02138. *Office:* 235 Science Center, Harvard University, Cambridge, Mass. 02138.

CAREER: Carnegie Institution, Washington, D.C., fellow in the history of science, 1938-41; Harvard University, Cambridge, Mass., instructor in physics, 1942-46, instructor in physical science, 1946-47, instructor, 1947-49, assistant professor, 1949-53, associate professor, 1953-59, professor of the history of science, 1959—. Special lecturer at University of London, 1959; Lowell lecturer, 1961; Wiles lecturer at Queen's University, Belfast, 1966; visiting fellow at Clare Hall, Cambridge, 1965; visiting overseas fellow at Churchill College, Cambridge, 1968.

MEMBER: International Union for the History and Philosophy of Science (first vice-president, 1962-68; president, 1968-71), International Academy for the History of Science (chairman of membership committee, 1961-62), U.S. National Committee for the History and Philosophy of Science (chairman, 1961-62), Institute for Early American History and Culture (member of council, 1957-60), History of Science Society (member of executive council, 1945-58; president, 1961, 1962), American Association for the Advancement of Science (fellow; vice-president, 1959-60), American Association for the History of Medicine, American Antiquarian Society, American Academy of Arts and Sciences (vice-president), American Historical Association, Royal Astronomical Society (fellow), Royal Society of the Arts (fellow), Massachusetts Historical Society, Colonial Society of Massachusetts, Athenaeum Club (London), Club of Odd Volumes (member of council, 1965-69), Phi Beta Kappa, Sigma Xi. *Awards, honors:* Guggenheim fellowship, 1956; National Science Foundation postdoctoral fellowship, 1960-61; LL.D. from Polytechnic Institute of Brooklyn, 1964; George Sarton Medal of History of Science Society.

WRITINGS: Benjamin Franklin's Experiments, Harvard University Press, 1941; *Roemer and the First Determination of the Velocity of Light,* Burndy Library, 1942; *Science, Servant of Man: A Layman's Primer for the Age of Science,* Little, Brown, 1948; *Some Early Tools of American Science: An Account of the Early Scientific Instruments and Mineralogical and Biological Collections in Harvard University* (foreword by Samuel Eliot Morison), Harvard University Press, 1950, Russell, 1967; *Ethan Allen Hitchcock: Soldier, Humanitarian, Scholar, Discoverer of the "True Subject" of the Hermetic Art,* American Antiquarian Society, 1952; (editor with F. Watson) *General Education in Science,* Harvard University Press, 1952; *Benjamin*

Franklin: His Contribution to the American Tradition, Bobbs-Merrill, 1953; (editor) Benjamin Franklin, *Some Account of the Pennsylvania Hospital,* Johns Hopkins Press, 1954; *Franklin and Newton: An Inquiry into Speculative Newtonian Experimental Science and Franklin's Work in Electricity as an Example Thereof,* American Philosophical Society, 1956, revised edition, Harvard University Press, 1973; *Issac Newton's Papers on Natural Philosophy,* Harvard University Press, 1957.

The Birth of a New Physics, Doubleday, 1960; *Science and American Society in the First Century of the Republic,* Department of Physics and Astronomy and the Graduate School, Ohio State University, 1961; (editor with Howard Mumford Jones) *A Treasury of Scientific Prose: A Nineteenth Century Anthology,* Little, Brown, 1963; *Introduction to Newton's "Principia,"* Harvard University Press, 1971; (editor with A. Koyre and A. Whitman) *Issac Newton's Philosophiae Mathematica, the Third Edition (1926) with Variant Readings,* Harvard University Press, 1972; *Isaac Newton's "Theory of the Moon's Motion" (1702) with a Bibliographical and Historical Introduction,* Dawson's of Pall Mall, 1975.

Author of introductions, all published by Johnson Reprint: Jean Baptiste Joseph Delambre, *Histoire de l'astronomie moderne,* 1969, Walter William Rouse Ball, *An Essay on Newton's Principia,* 1972; Stephan Peter Rigaud, *Historical Essay on the First Publication of Sir Isaac Newton's Principia,* 1972; William Whiston, *Sir Isaac Newton's Mathematick Philosophy More Easily Demonstrated,* 1972.

Contributor of articles and reviews to professional journals. Managing editor of *Isis,* 1947-52, editor and chairman of editorial committee, 1953-58; editorial adviser to "The Papers of Benjamin Franklin."

*   *   *

COLBACH, Edward M(ichael)   1939-

PERSONAL: Born September 14, 1939, in Chicago, Ill.; son of Edward Michael, Sr. (an attorney) and Julia (a secretary; maiden name, Miller) Colbach; married Josephine Taraska (a physician), June 13, 1964; children: Christine, Michael. *Education:* Loyola University, Chicago, Ill., B.S., 1962; Northwestern University, M.D., 1964; Menninger School of Psychiatry, graduated, 1968. *Politics:* Independent. *Religion:* Roman Catholic. *Residence:* Tualatin, Ore. *Office:* 10175 Southwest Barbur Blvd., Suite 316-B, Portland, Ore. 97219.

CAREER: Pacific Medical Center, San Francisco, Calif., intern, 1964-65; Menninger School of Psychiatry, Topeka, Kan., psychiatry resident, 1965-68; psychiatrist in private practice, Portland, Ore., 1970—. University of Oregon, assistant professor, 1970-73, associate clinical professor of psychiatry, 1973—. *Military service:* U.S. Army, psychiatrist in Medical Corps, 1968-70; became major; received Bronze Star.

WRITINGS: (With Charles D. Fosterling) *Police Social Work,* C. C Thomas, 1976. Contributor of short stories to *U.S. Catholic* and *Extension.*

WORK IN PROGRESS: Novels on Vietnam and on cultism.

SIDELIGHTS: Edward Colbach writes: "In my professional work with the criminal justice system, I have become convinced that we as a society are too litigious and depend too much on attorneys. Attorneys often seem more interested in obscuring the facts and hiding them than at getting at the truth.

"I think that in dealing with criminal behavior we as a society have become far too lenient. I often see people with tremendous potential for violence turned loose with inadequate supervision on an unsuspecting society. I think the pendulum of individual rights has swung too far away from those rights which society has. Someday, I would like to expand on this in my writing."

*   *   *

COLE, Charles L(eland)   1927-

PERSONAL: Born April 20, 1927, in Long Beach, Calif.; son of Charles (a dentist) and Verda (Baugher) Cole. *Education:* University of Southern California, A.B., 1951, Ph.D., 1963; Stanford University, M.B.A., 1955; attended Worcester College, Oxford, 1975. *Religion:* Episcopalian. *Residence:* Long Beach, Calif. *Office:* Department of Economics, California State University, Long Beach, Calif. 90840.

CAREER: California State College (now University), Los Angeles, assistant professor of economics, 1962-63; Occidental College, Los Angeles, assistant professor of economics, 1963-67; California State University, Long Beach, associate professor, 1967-72, professor of economics, 1972—. *Military service:* U.S. Army, 1945-46. *Member:* American Economic Association, History of Political Science Society, Western Economic Association, Town Hall of California, Los Angeles World Affairs Council, Phi Beta Kappa, Omicron Delta Epsilon, Pi Sigma Alpha. *Awards, honors:* Grant from Haynes Foundation, 1965-66.

WRITINGS: The Economic Fabric of Society, Harcourt, 1969; *Microeconomics: A Contemporary Approach,* Harcourt, 1973.

WORK IN PROGRESS: Research for a book on economic (distributive) justice.

SIDELIGHTS: Cole told *CA* his opinion of distributive justice: "The purpose of our economic system is not to distribute goods justly but to produce those goods. But justice need not be incompatible with efficiency, and people will not support an economic system unless they perceive or believe that it is just. The more viable an economic system, then, the more likely it is regarded by its members as being just. Thus, to some extent, the justice of an economic system can be judged by its staying power and the degree of its popular (uncoerced) support."

BIOGRAPHICAL/CRITICAL SOURCES: Journal of Economic Literature, June, 1969.

*   *   *

COLE, Charles Woolsey   1906-

PERSONAL: Born February 8, 1906, in Montclair, N.J.; son of Charles Buckingham and Bertha Woolsey (Dwight) Cole; married Katharine Bush Salmon, August 29, 1928 (died, 1972); children: Elizabeth (Mrs. Hugh M. Hamill, Jr.), Katharine (Mrs. John C. Esty, Jr.). *Education:* Amherst College, A.B., 1927; Columbia University, A.M., 1928, Ph.D., 1931. *Religion:* Congregationalist. *Home address:* P.O. Box 66, Amherst, Mass. 01002.

CAREER: Columbia University, New York, N.Y., instructor in history, 1929-35; Amherst College, Amherst, Mass., associate professor, 1935-37, George C. Olds Professor of Economics, 1937-40; Columbia University, professor of history, 1940-46; Amherst College, president, 1946-60, president emeritus, 1960—; Rockefeller Foundation, vice-president, 1960-61; U.S. ambassador to Chile, 1961-64;

Federal Reserve Bank, Boston, Mass., director, 1966-68; writer, 1968—. Visiting lecturer at Yale University, 1938-39; member of teaching staff of U.S. Navy School of Military Government and Administration, and lecturer at U.S. Army School of Military Government, both 1943-44; faculty member of Manhattan School of Music, 1944-46. New York region price executive for U.S. Office of Price Administration, 1942-43; member of national selective service scientific advisory committee, 1948-51; member of Council on Foreign Relations. Trustee of Charles E. Merrill Trust and Clarke School for the Deaf.

MEMBER: American Academy of Arts and Sciences, Economic History Association, American Association of University Professors, American Historical Association (member of council, 1947-50), Phi Beta Kappa, Delta Kappa Epsilon, Delta Sigma Rho, Century Club, Anglers' Club (New York City). *Awards, honors:* Social Science Research Council traveling fellowship to Paris, 1932-33; L.H.D. from Amherst College, 1942, University of Massachusetts, 1951, and Trinity College, 1953; LL.D. from Wagner College, 1946, Wesleyan University, 1946, Williams College, 1946, American International College, 1952, Doshisha University, 1953, Columbia University, 1954, Amherst College, 1960, and Emerson College, 1964; Litt.D. from Hamilton College, 1948; Sc.D. from Clarkson College, 1948; grand cross of the Order of Merit of Chile; grand officer of the Order of Morazan of Honduras.

WRITINGS: French Mercantilist Doctrines Before Colbert, R. R. Smith, 1931, Octagon, 1969; *French Mercantilism, 1683-1700,* Columbia University Press, 1943, Octagon, 1965; (with Carlton Joseph Huntley Hayes and M. Baldwin) *History of Europe Since 1500,* Macmillan, 1949, revised edition, 1956; (with Shepard Bancroft Clough) *Economic History of Europe,* 3rd edition, Heath, 1952; *Colbert and a Century of French Mercantilism,* two volumes, revised edition, Archon Books, 1964; (with Hayes and Baldwin) *History of Western Civilization,* 2nd edition, Macmillan, 1967; (with Bragdon) *History of a Free People,* Macmillan, 1973. Also author, with Henry Wilkinson Bragdon and S. P. Mc-Cutcheon, *A Free People,* Volume I: *The United States in the Formative Years,* Volume II: *The United States in the Twentieth Century,* 1970. Editor of Macmillan's "Career Books."

AVOCATIONAL INTERESTS: Fly fishing for trout, gardening.

BIOGRAPHICAL/CRITICAL SOURCES: Time, February 4, 1946.*

* * *

COLE, Frank R(aymond) 1892-

PERSONAL: Born June 29, 1892, in Redlands, Calif.; son of Joseph Morrison (a farmer) and May E. (Cram) Cole; married Dorothy G. Stonnell, December 12, 1925; children: Richard, James, Lewis. *Education:* Pomona College, B.A., 1913; Stanford University, M.S., 1921, Ph.D., 1922. *Politics:* Republican. *Religion:* Congregationalist. *Home:* 4221 George Ave., #7, San Mateo, Calif. 94403.

CAREER: Bureau of Entomology, Washington, D.C., scientific assistant in southern California, 1914-15, junior entomologist in Washington, D.C., 1915-16, and Oregon, 1917-19; U.S. Department of Agriculture, Washington, D.C., field entomologist in Florida and California, 1924-33; consulting entomologist in San Bernardino, Calif., 1934-46; citrus grower and writer in San Bernardino, 1946-54; U.S. Naval Engineering Laboratory, Port Hueneme, Calif., sci-

entific illustrator, 1954-56; University of California, Berkeley, research fellow and writer, 1957-69; writer, 1969—.

MEMBER: Entomological Society of America, American Museum Society, Audubon Society, Wilderness Society, Wildlife Society, Pacific Coast Entomological Society, California Academy of Science, Washington Entomological Society, Sigma Xi.

WRITINGS: The Flies of Western North America, University of California Press, 1969. Author of monographs. Contributor to entomology journals.

SIDELIGHTS: Cole conducted research on cereal and forage pests during World War I in Western States and British Columbia. *Avocational interests:* Philately.

* * *

COLE, Robert E(van) 1937-

PERSONAL: Born October 14, 1937, in New York, N.Y.; son of Bernard M. (a pharmacist) and Beatrice (Goldberg) Cole; married Ingrid Emlsson (a weaver), April 17, 1961; children: Anders Johan, Rebecca Leah. *Education:* Hobart College, B.A., 1959; studied in Sweden, 1960-61; University of Illinois, M.A., 1962, Ph.D., 1967. *Home:* 369 Hilldale, Ann Arbor, Mich. 48105. *Office:* Department of Sociology, University of Michigan, Ann Arbor, Mich. 48105.

CAREER: University of Michigan, Ann Arbor, assistant professor, 1967-73, associate professor of sociology, 1973—, director of Center for Japanese Studies, 1974—. *Member:* American Sociological Association, Association for Asian Studies, Social Science Research Council, Joint Committee on Japanese Studies. *Awards, honors:* National Science Foundation grant, 1973-75; Fulbright research scholar, 1977-78.

WRITINGS: Japanese Blue-Collar: The Changing Tradition, University of California Press, 1971; *Work in Modern Japan: A Comparative Perspective,* University of California Press, 1978. Contributor to economics and labor relations journals.

WORK IN PROGRESS: A study of worker participation in management in Japan and Sweden.

* * *

COLE, Sylvan, Jr. 1918-

PERSONAL: Born January 10, 1918, in New York, N.Y.; son of Sylvan and Dorothy (Stein) Cole; married Vivian Vanderpool, May, 1944; married second wife, Lillyan Wood, August 20, 1953; children: Nancy, Robert, James. *Education:* Cornell University, B.A., 1939. *Home:* 1112 Park Ave., New York, N.Y. 10028. *Office:* 663 Fifth Ave., New York, N.Y. 10022.

CAREER: Sears, Roebuck & Co., New Brunswick, N.J., executive trainee, 1939-41; Associated American Artists, New York City, worked in direct mail order, and advertising and promotion departments, 1946-58, president and director, 1958—. Member of dealers advisory committee of Print Council of America; member of board of directors of Pratt Graphic Art Center. *Military service:* U.S. Army, 1941-46; became major. *Member:* Art Dealers Association of America (member of board of directors).

WRITINGS: (Editor) Raphael Soyer, *Raphael Soyer: Fifty Years of Printmaking, 1917-1967,* Da Capo Press, 1967; (editor) Joseph Hirsch, *The Graphic Work of Joseph Hirsch,* Associated American Artists, 1970; (editor) *Will Barnet: Etchings, Lithographs, Woodcuts, Serigraphs, 1932-*

1972—Catalogue Raisonne, Associated American Artists Gallery, 1972; (editor) Frank Kleinholz, *Kleinholz Graphics: Catalogue Raisonne, 1940-1975,* University of Miami Press, 1975; (editor) *The Lithographs of John Steuart Curry: A Catalogue Raisonne,* Associated American Artists, 1976.

WORK IN PROGRESS: Ivan LeLorraine Albright: Catalogue Raisonne; Stuart Davis: Catalogue Raisonne; Grant Wood: Catalogue Raisonne.

* * *

COLEMAN, William L(eRoy) 1938-

PERSONAL: Born September 25, 1938, in Barkhill, Md.; son of Marion Oscar and Novella (Fringer) Coleman; married Patricia Ann Marshall, August 25, 1962; children: Mary Elizabeth, James Marshall, June Christine. *Education:* Washington Bible College, B.A., 1962; Grace Theological Seminary, M.Div., 1965. *Politics:* "Mobile." *Home:* 1308 14th St., Aurora, Neb. 68818. *Office:* Professional Building, Aurora, Neb. 68818.

CAREER: Ordained Baptist minister, 1966; pastor of Baptist church in St. Clair Shores, Mich., 1965-70, Mennonite church in Sterling, Kan., 1970-73, and Evangelical Free Church in Aurora, Neb., 1973-75; Aurora Community Improvement Development, Aurora, Neb., chairman, 1975—. Chairman of Aurora police committee; vice-president of Aurora Community Theatre.

WRITINGS: Lord, Sometimes I Need Help, Hawthorn, 1976; *Counting Stars,* Bethany Fellowship, 1976; *Those Pharisees,* Hawthorn, 1977. Contributor of about ninety articles to Evangelical periodicals.

WORK IN PROGRESS: The Happy Christ: Humanity and Deity; When Sunday Was King: Billy Sunday's 1917 Campaign in New York; The Death They Whisper About: The Christian and Suicide; The Sea Is His: The Bible and the Modern Ocean.

SIDELIGHTS: Coleman comments: "I enjoy writing for two reasons, . . . for the fun of it . . . to help people by making the Christian faith easy to understand."

* * *

COLLETT, Rosemary K(ing) 1931-

PERSONAL: Born December 11, 1931, in Shanghai, China; daughter of Donald Key (a newspaperman) and Alexandra (Brannicova) King; married George Richard Collett, Jr., May 16, 1962; children: Janice Elaine. *Education:* Attended St. Petersburg Junior College. *Politics:* "Registered Democrat—vote for the best man." *Religion:* Episcopalian. *Home address:* P.O. Box 1002, Venice, Fla. 33595.

CAREER: St. Petersburg Times, St. Petersburg, Fla., newsroom receptionist, 1949-50; clerk in a jewelry store, 1950-51; secretary in an elementary school in Venice, Fla., 1953-55; cashier, 1960-62; writer, photographer, and lecturer, 1965—. Director of Felicidades Wildlife Foundation. Guest on television and radio programs. *Member:* Florida Audubon Society. *Awards, honors:* Conservation awards from Florida Audubon Society and from Sarasota County, both 1969; award from Florida Federation of Humane Societies, 1970; commendation from U.S. Department of the Interior's Fish & Wildlife Service, 1970; certificate from National Park Service, 1972; patriot's award from Sarasota County, 1976; educational award from the Women's Auxiliary of Atlanta Humane Society, 1977.

WRITINGS: Beginning with Gerbils, T.F.H. Publishing Co., 1967; *Enjoy Keeping Wild Pets,* Pet Library, 1970; *My Orphans of the Wild: Rescue and Home Care of Native Wildlife,* Lippincott, 1974; *Rescue and Home Care of Native Wildlife,* Hawthorn, 1976. Author of "Wild Orphan Notebook," column in *Animals.* Contributor of articles and photographs to magazines, including *Good Housekeeping, Florida Naturalist,* and *Florida Wildlife.*

WORK IN PROGRESS: Help! There's a Duck Up My Chimney, anecdotes from her thirteen years of experience with wildlife; research for a book on eastern brown pelicans presently disabled and nesting in her yard.

SIDELIGHTS: Rosemary Collett writes: "I live on an acre of ground . . . two blocks from the Gulf of Mexico.

"I have had two vital interests all my life, since childhood: 1) I have always loved animals and 2) I have always wanted to write. I wrote a column for a weekly newspaper . . . when I was in high school in China.

"Since 1964 I have worked with injured, ill, and orphaned wildlife here on Florida's west coast. Our acre is home to a hundred or more birds and beasts at all times. I have hand-raised thousands of orphaned birds and mammals, and ministered to thousands more who were ill or injured. My prime aim is to release my patients, returning them to their own natural environment as soon as possible.

"I am concerned with our entire earth and every living thing upon it. I am vitally concerned with the preservation and wise use of our natural resources. And I feel that Man has need of the wildlife that share the earth with him—not simply for biological survival, but for aesthetic reasons as well. I am especially concerned that seventy-five to eighty per cent of my wildlife patients come to me with injuries caused by Man. Unhappily, Man is the most destructive creature on the face of the earth.

"I feel that my educational efforts are extremely important. Education is the key to preserving our natural resources, and to protecting our wildlife—and, in the long run, Man himself.

"I enjoy travel, and would like to spend a great deal more time traveling and photographing in all parts of the world. I have traveled in much of the United States, and have been to East Africa (a most memorable experience!), Mexico, and the Caribbean. I would most like to go to the Galapagos (before they are completely destroyed) and Hawaii, also Alaska. I prefer the wild and natural areas to the cities, but one must see both to get a full understanding of each area, its people and problems.

"I'm not really keen on Florida—it's too hot and sticky. I'd rather live on a mountaintop in North Carolina!"

* * *

COLLIER, David 1942-

PERSONAL: Born February 17, 1942, in Chicago, Ill.; son of Donald (an anthropologist) and Malcolm (an anthropologist; maiden name, Carr) Collier; married Ruth Berins (a political scientist), March 10, 1968; children: Stephen, Jennifer. *Education:* Harvard University, A.B., 1965; University of Chicago, M.A., 1967, Ph.D., 1971. *Home:* 915 Eastside Dr., Bloomington, Ind. 47401. *Office:* Department of Political Science, Indiana University, Bloomington, Ind. 47401.

CAREER: Institute of Peruvian Studies, Lima, Peru, lecturer in political science, 1968-69; Indiana University, Bloomington, lecturer, 1970-71, assistant professor, 1971-75, associate professor of political science, 1975—. Visiting fellow at Princeton University and at Institute for Advanced Study, both 1975; visiting scholar at University of Chicago, 1977. *Member:* American Political Science Association, Latin American Studies Association. *Awards, honors:* Ford Foundation research grant, 1972-73; Social Science Research Council grant, 1975; National Science Foundation research grant, 1975-78.

WRITINGS: (Contributor) David Chaplin, editor, *Peruvian Nationalism: A Corporatist Revolution,* Dutton, 1973; *Squatter Settlements and Migrant Adaptation in Lima* (monograph), Center for International Studies, Massachusetts Institute of Technology, 1976; *Squatters and Oligarchs: Authoritarian Rule and Policy Change in Peru,* Johns Hopkins Press, 1976. Contributor to *Comparative Politics* and *American Political Science Review.*

* * *

COLLINS, Orvis F(loyd) 1918-

PERSONAL: Born June 3, 1918, in Montesana, Wash.; son of William Lee (a logger) and Mary Lee (Fitch) Collins; married June McCormick (a professor of anthropology), April 22, 1942; children: Anne Collins Lundquist, Mary Collins Demski, Orvis Floyd, Jr. *Education:* University of Chicago, M.A., 1962, Ph.D., 1964. *Politics:* "Befuddlement." *Religion:* Episcopal. *Home:* 146 North Brier Rd., Tonawanda, N.Y. 14150. *Office:* Department of Sociology, State University of New York College at Buffalo, 1300 Elmwood Ave., Buffalo, N.Y. 14222.

CAREER: University of Chicago, Chicago, Ill., research associate in human development, 1958-59; Michigan State University, East Lansing, assistant professor, 1960-64, associate professor of management, 1964-65; Southern Illinois University, Edwardsville, professor of behavioral sciences, 1965-68, chairman of department, 1965-68; State University of New York College at Buffalo, professor of sociology, 1968—. Executive director of Center for the Study of Human Interaction. Consultant to Social Research, Inc. and Municipal Manpower Commission. *Member:* American Sociological Association (fellow), American Anthropological Association (fellow), Semiotic Society of America.

WRITINGS: (With W. Lloyd Warner, Paul P. Van Riper, and Norman H. Martin) *The American Federal Executive,* Yale University Press, 1963; (with David C. Moore and D. B. Unwalla) *The Enterprising Man,* Michigan State University Press, 1964; (with Moore) *The Organization Makers,* Prentice-Hall, 1970; (with wife, June M. Collins) *Interaction and Social Structure,* Mouton & Co., 1973. Contributor to academic journals.

WORK IN PROGRESS: Comparative Sociology: Interaction Sequencing in Humans and Non-Humans.

SIDELIGHTS: Collins comments: "My attention has been increasingly drawn to *simple interaction* as a device for simplifying and thereby making comparative basic social processes which occur throughout animal forms."

* * *

COLLINS, Robert E(mmet) 1927-

PERSONAL: Born December 2, 1927, in Grand Rapids, Mich.; son of John A. (an executive) and Sarah G. Collins; married Beverly M. Burnett (a secretary), June 25, 1955; children: Patrick, Stephen, Therese, Sharon, Daniel. *Education:* Sacred Heart Academy, Detroit, Mich., B.A., 1950; Marquette University, M.A., 1958, Ph.D., 1960. *Home:* 204

East Seventh St., Winona, Minn. 55987. *Office:* Department of Philosophy, College of St. Teresa, Winona, Minn. 55987.

CAREER: College of St. Teresa, Winona, Minn., instructor, 1960-63, assistant professor, 1963-68, associate professor, 1968-73, professor of philosophy, 1973—. *Military service:* U.S. Army, 1953-55. *Member:* American Philosophical Association, American Catholic Philosophical Association, Society for the Advancement of American Philosophy, Minnesota Philosophical Association.

WRITINGS: Theodore Parker: American Transcendentalist, Scarecrow, 1973. Contributor to *Journal of the History of Philosophy.*

WORK IN PROGRESS: A book on Ralph Waldo Emerson; a philosophic defense of B. F. Skinner; a critique of Lawrence Kohlberg.

* * *

COLLINS, William Alexander Roy 1900-1976

May 23, 1900—September 21, 1976; British publisher. Collins was chairman of William Collins Sons & Co. Ltd., which published such authors as Agatha Christie, Ngaio Marsh, and Victoria Holt. He died in Tonbridge, England. Obituaries: *Publishers Weekly,* October 4, 1976.

* * *

COLLYNS, Robin 1940-

PERSONAL: Born July 21, 1940, in Auckland, New Zealand; son of Arthur Bridge (a broadcaster, producer, and government statistician) and Irene (a secretary; maiden name, Forde) Collyns. *Education:* Attended Auckland University, 1967-68. *Politics:* "Non-involvement in politics." *Religion:* "Non-involvement in religion." *Home:* 22 Rarangi Rd., St. Heliers, Auckland 5, New Zealand.

CAREER: Electronic faults inspector, 1956-69; writer and researcher, 1969—.

WRITINGS: Did Spacemen Colonize the Earth?, Pelham Books, 1974, Regnery, 1976; *Laser Beams from Star Cities?,* Pelham Books, 1975; *Ancient Astronauts: A Time Reversal?,* Pelham Books, 1976.

WORK IN PROGRESS: These Men Knew the Future!, "case histories of people who predicted the future"; *The DNA Code: Programmed on Planet X?,* an expansion of his own theories of genetic engineering; a book "exploring Maori legends in connection with visits to Earth by extraterrestrials"; a book examining the spiritual nature of Man and of all life forms.

SIDELIGHTS: Collyns has conducted research at museums in New Zealand and England. He has also conversed with Buddhist monks at Colombo's Kotahena shrine in Sri Lanka. He writes: "Basically, my interest in writing 'spaceman' books centres on my hypothesis that life on Earth did not 'evolve' but was brought to this planet from distant worlds. The old legends relating to the existence of the two now submerged continents of Atlantis and Mu must be accepted as true, and I have spent several years gathering evidence in this connection. For according to many old legends it was on these two continents—and particularly on Mu in the Pacific—that mankind was first resettled after being brought from outer space. The submergence of these two continents around twelve thousand years ago according to legends, also destroyed most of mankind. Cro-Magnon man who 'suddenly' appeared in Europe was apparently a surviving race from Atlantis. But the hominoids? When people have been taught to believe in the theory of evolution how would one react to the question that the 'ape men' may have been the result of deliberate sophisticated 'genetic engineering' experiments undertaken on apes by advanced civilizations on Mu, Atlantis and possibly China in antiquity, and that the Yeti, Bigfoot and similar creatures surviving today are degenerate or degenerating hominoid survivors—apes changed by intentional gene tampering?

"In *Laser Beams from Star Cities?* I investigated the possibility that the tiny unexplained 'cup marks' found indented into rock in many countries may be ancient remnant traces of a laser beam communication attempt with Earth by beings from another constellation. In *Ancient Astronauts: A Time Reversal?* the main theory relates to some new scientific evidence which suggests that it may be possible to travel faster than light, hence this could explain how beings could travel to Earth from their homes many light years away. One point which fascinated me during research were some centuries-old Maori legends (from New Zealand) about the rings of Saturn and the bands of Jupiter. The Maoris knew of these things long before Galileo and it does suggest that they are a remnant race from the lost Pacific continent of Mu. For only a telescope would reveal the rings of Saturn and the bands of Jupiter. The Maoris also have legends about a hominoid creature called the 'Taniwha', and space visitors."

AVOCATIONAL INTERESTS: Photography.

*   *   *

COLMER, Michael (J.) 1942-

PERSONAL: Born March 12, 1942, in Gillingham, England; son of Ernest and Patricia (Ladbrooke) Colmer; married Linda Gillian Scott (divorced); married Gillian Irene Froud; children: Sarah Louise, James Philip. *Education:* "Vague recollection of English public school." *Politics:* "Naive optimism." *Religion:* "Pisces with strong Mercury (and rising Scorpio!)." *Agent:* Aaron Priest, Aaron M. Priest Literary Agency, 150 East 35th St., New York, N.Y. 10016; and David Grossman, 101 Seddon House, The Barbican, London EC2, England. *Office:* 7 Bell Yard, Fleet St., London WC2, England.

CAREER: Was a senior staff journalist for *Financial Times* (daily newspaper), London, England; presently a writer. Liberal candidate for Parliament. Lecturer in visual communications to corporations, including International Telephone & Telegraph (ITT), and to art colleges and business schools. Regular judge at national and international photography competitions. Visual consultant to Barclays Bank. *Member:* American Canal Society, National Union of Journalists, Royal Photographic Society (member of photo-journalism group), Inland Waterways Association (United Kingdom; life member), Society of Authors.

WRITINGS: Industry in Focus, Cahners, 1974; *Management Information Manual,* Samsom, 1976; *Glamour Calendar Art,* Regnery, 1976 (published in England as *Calendar Girls,* Sphere Books, 1976); *Pinball,* New American Library, 1976. Contributor to photographic journals. Managing editor of *Cosmetic World News.*

WORK IN PROGRESS: History of the Slot Machine, for Regnery; *History of Swimwear/Bathing Beauties,* for Sphere Books; *Complete Video Book.*

SIDELIGHTS: Colmer writes: "Basically I am a communicator, versed in words, illustration, broadcasting, and lecturing. A strong marketing sense based on gut reaction and anticipation of the public pulse plus the challenge of exploring new horizons turns me on."

COLVER, Alice Mary (Ross) 1892-
(Mary Randall)

PERSONAL: Born August 28, 1892, in Plainsfield, N.J.; daughter of Louis Runyan (a salesman) and Sarah Greenleaf (Wyekoff) Ross; married Frederick B. Colver, September 8, 1915 (deceased); children: Frederick R. (deceased), Joan Colver Brink, John Richard. *Education:* Wellesley College, A.B., 1913. *Religion:* Presbyterian. *Residence:* Tenafly, N.J.

CAREER: Writer, 1917—.

WRITINGS: If You Should Want to Write (a handbook for beginning writers), Dodd, 1939; (with Helen Brant Birdsall) *Dream Within Her Hand* (biography of Dr. Cornelia Chase Brant), 1940; (under pseudonym Mary Randall) *Call If You Need Me,* Revell, 1977.

Children's fairy tales; all published by Henry Altemus, all 1917: *The Long Ago Years Stories; The Wish Fairy of the Sunshine and Shadow Forest; The Wish Fairy and Dewy Dear.*

Juvenile; all published by Penn Publishing: *Babs,* 1918; *Babs at Birchwood,* 1919; *Babs at College,* 1919; *Babs at home,* 1920; *Jeanne,* 1920; *Jeanne's Houseparty,* 1921; *Jeanne's Happy Year,* 1922; *Jeanne at Rainbow Lodge,* 1923.

Juvenile; all published by Dodd, except as noted: (With Charlotte Lockwood) *Adventure for a Song,* 1938; (with Jack Colver) *Adventure in the West,* 1939; *Adventure on a Hilltop,* 1941; *Joan Foster, Freshman,* 1942; *Joan Foster, Sophomore,* 1948; *Joan, Freelance Writer,* Messner, 1948; *Joan Foster, Junior,* 1949; *Joan Foster, Senior,* 1950; (with Jack Colver and Phyllis Colver) *Joan Foster in Europe,* 1951; *Joan Foster, Bride,* 1952; *Janet Moore, Physical Therapist,* 1965; *Vicky Barnes, Junior Hospital Volunteer,* 1966; *Sally, Star Patient,* 1968; *Say Yes to Life,* 1969.

Adult fiction; all published by Penn Publishing: *The Dear Pretender,* 1924; *If Dreams Come True,* 1925; *Under the Rainbow Sky,* 1926; *The Lookout Girl,* 1928; *The Dimmest Dream,* 1929.

Adult fiction; all published by Dodd: *The Redheaded Goddess,* 1929; *Hilltop House,* 1930; *Windymere,* 1931; *Modern Madonna,* 1932; *Passionate Puritan,* 1933; *Three Loves,* 1934; *Wild Song,* 1935; *I Have Been Little too Long,* 1935; *Strangers at Sea,* 1936; *Substitute Lover,* 1936; *Only Let Me Live,* 1937; *One Year of Love,* 1937; *Where the Heart Goes,* 1939; *The Measure of the Years* (historical novel), 1954; *There Is a Season* (historical novel), 1957.

Adult fiction; all published by Macrae: *When There is Love,* 1940; *Not Just to Remember,* 1941; *There's Only One,* 1941; *The Heart Does Not Forget,* 1941; *Forever Is So Long,* 1942; *The Merrivales,* 1943; *Fourways,* 1944; *Homecoming,* 1945; *Uncertain Heart,* 1946; *Three Loves Are Mine,* 1946; *Kingsridge,* 1949; *The Parson,* 1951.

WORK IN PROGRESS: An autobiography.

SIDELIGHTS: Alice Colver told *CA* that she feels writers have a responsibility for what they write. Her own writing is based on experiences and she uses authentic backgrounds. Among her concerns are "lawlessness, corruption, indifference, and the breakup of marriages and families." *Avocational interests:* Theatre, gardening, crewel embroidery, music.

*   *   *

COLWELL, Richard J(ames) 1930-

PERSONAL: Born May 27, 1930, in Sioux Falls, S.D.; son

of George L. (a furrier) and Mildren (Muchow) Colwell; married Ruth Crockett, June 4, 1960; children: Robert, Catherine, Mary. *Education:* University of South Dakota, B.F.A. and M.M., both 1953; University of Illinois, Ed.D., 1961. *Home:* 406 West Michigan, Urbana, Ill. 61801. *Office:* Music Building, University of Illinois, Urbana, Ill. 61801.

CAREER: Teacher of instructional music in public schools in Sioux Falls, S.D., 1955-57; Eastern Montana College, Billings, assistant professor, 1957-60, associate professor of music, 1960-61; University of Illinois, Urbana, assistant professor of music, 1961-64, associate professor, 1964-68, professor of music and secondary education, 1969—, chairman of department of music, 1974—. Member of Music Education Research Council, 1968-74. *Military service:* U.S. Army Reserve, 1953-55; U.S. Army National Guard, 1955; became lieutenant colonel.

MEMBER: Music Educators National Conference, Council for Research in Music Education, American Educational Research Association, National Council for Measurement in Education, National Education Association, American Federation of Teachers, Illinois Music Educators Association, Phi Delta Kappa, Phi Mu Alpha. *Awards, honors:* Guggenheim fellowship, 1975-76.

WRITINGS: The Teaching of Instrumental Music, Appleton, 1967; *Music Achievement Tests,* Numbers 1-4, Follett, 1968-70; *The Evaluation of Music Teaching and Learning,* Prentice-Hall, 1970; *Concepts for a Musical Foundation,* Prentice-Hall, 1975. Contributor to music and education journals. Editor for Illinois Music Educators Association, 1962-65; editor of bulletin of Council for Research in Music Education, 1963—; member of editorial board of *Journal of Aesthetic Education,* 1968-74; book review editor of *Journal for Research in Music Education,* 1976—.

WORK IN PROGRESS: A music appreciation text for Prentice-Hall; *Criterion-Referenced Tests for Grades 1-6,* Silver Burdett.

SIDELIGHTS: Colwell writes that his current interest is "cross cultural aspects of music perception."

* * *

COMMIRE, Anne

PERSONAL: Born in Wyandotte, Mich.; daughter of Robert (in U.S. Navy) and Shirley (Moore) Commire. *Education:* Earned B.S. from Eastern Michigan University; also attended Wayne State University, University of Birmingham, Birmingham, England, and New York University. *Home:* 81R Oswegatchie Rd., Waterford, Conn. 06385. *Agent:* Esther Sherman, William Morris Agency, 1350 Avenue of the Americas, New York, N.Y. 10019. *Office:* 1332 Third Ave., New York, N.Y. 10021.

CAREER: High school teacher in Waterford Twp., Mich., 1961-66; Gale Research Co., Detroit, Mich., editor of *Something About the Author,* 1967—, and *Yesterday's Authors of Books for Children,* 1976—. Wardrobe mistress for Meadowbrook Theatre, Rochester, Mich., 1967; stage managing and various other jobs in summer stock and off-off Broadway, 1968-72; panel member in playwriting for Creative Artists Program, 1976 and for Massachusetts Arts and Humanities Foundation, 1977. *Member:* Dramatists Guild. *Awards, honors:* O'Neill Playwright Award, 1974, for "Shay"; playwriting grant from Creative Artists Program, 1975.

WRITINGS—Plays: "Matinee Ladies" (two one-acts), first produced in New York City at Columbia University,

1973; "Shay" (three-act), first presented in Waterford, Conn., at Eugene O'Neil Memorial Theatre, 1975; first produced in Westport, Conn., at Westport Country Playhouse, 1974; "Transatlantic Bridge" (three-act), first presented in New York at Playwrights Horizon, 1976. "Betty MacDonald" (three-act), as yet neither published nor produced.

"That Lowry Kid" (teleplay), for CBS-TV. Contributor of material to "Dick Cavett Summer Show."

WORK IN PROGRESS: A full length play entitled, "Put Them All Together."

* * *

COMO, (Michael) William 1925-

PERSONAL: Born November 25, 1925, in Williamstown, Mass.; son of Michael and Janet (Caporale) Como. *Education:* American Academy of Dramatic Arts, B.A., 1947. *Home:* 360 West 55th St., New York, N.Y. 10019. *Agent:* Chris Huizenga, *After Dark,* 10 Columbus Cir., New York, N.Y. 10019. *Office:* Danad Publishing Co., 10 Columbus Cir., New York, N.Y. 10019.

CAREER: Dance Magazine, New York City, sales manager, 1954-60, advertising manager, 1961-69, editor-in-chief, 1970—. Editor-in-chief of *After Dark* (magazine), New York City, 1968—. Writer of monthly column, "Speaking Out," in *After Dark.* Editor of a series of books for Danad, containing material previously published in *Dance Magazine.* Free lance lecturer on professional journalism and on the history of dance. *Military service:* U.S. Army, 1944-46. *Member:* Association of American Dance Companies. *Awards, honors:* Received an award from Dance Teachers Club of Boston, 1974.

WORK IN PROGRESS: A biography.

* * *

CONARROE, Richard R(iley) 1928-

PERSONAL: Born February 28, 1928, in New Jersey; son of Elvin H. (a business executive) and Elizabeth (a secretary; maiden name, Lofland) Conarroe; married Doris P. Nermaier, 1949 (divorced, 1957); married Nancy S. Morse, 1969 (divorced, 1975); children: Richard R., Jr., Ronald R. *Education:* New York University, B.S.J., 1950. *Home:* 59 Bluff Ave., Rowayton, Conn. 06853. *Office:* Walden Public Relations, Inc., 246 Post Rd. E., Westport, Conn. 06880.

CAREER: Administrative Management Society, Philadelphia, Pa., editor and director of public relations, 1950-56; Scott Paper Co., Chester, Pa., in public relations, 1956-57; Business Management, Greenwich, Conn., editor and vice-president, 1957-61; Walden Public Relations, Inc., Westport, Conn., founder and chairperson, 1961—. *Military service:* U.S. Navy, 1945-47.

WRITINGS: The Decision Makers, Prentice-Hall, 1958; *Bravely, Bravely in Business,* American Management Association, 1972; *Executive Search: How Companies Recruit Outstanding Executives,* Van Nostrand, 1976; *Public Relations for Professional Organizations,* Walden Public Relations, Inc., 1977. Contributor of several dozen articles to professional magazines.

WORK IN PROGRESS: Two novels; two business books; a book on public relations; a book on health for executives.

* * *

CONE, Fairfax Mastick 1903-1977

February 21, 1903—June 20, 1977; American advertising

executive and author. He died in Carmel, Calif. Obituaries: *Newsweek,* July 4, 1977; *Time,* July 4, 1977.

* * *

CONINE, (Odie) Ernest 1925-

PERSONAL: Born December 31, 1925, in Dallas, Tex.; son of Odie Ernest and Myrtle (Elkins) Conine; married Phyllis Joan Hoyland, November 28, 1953. *Education:* Attended Central Washington College of Education (now Central Washington State College), 1944; Southern Methodist University, B.S., 1948. *Home:* 3460 West Seventh St., Los Angeles, Calif. 90005. *Office: Los Angeles Times,* Times Mirror Sq., Los Angeles, Calif. 90012.

CAREER/WRITINGS: United Press International, staff writer in Dallas, Tex., 1948-51; *Houston Chronicle,* correspondent in Washington, D.C., 1952-55; *Business Week* magazine, correspondent in Washington, D.C., 1955-59, in Moscow, U.S.S.R., 1960-61, and in Boston, Mass., 1962-63; *Los Angeles Times,* foreign correspondent in Vienna, Austria, 1963-64, member of editorial board in Los Angeles, Calif., 1964—. Author of weekly column syndicated by *Los Angeles Times-Washington Post* New Service, 1964—; contributor of articles to *Harper's, Harvard Business Review, Coronet, Catholic Digest,* and other magazines; lecturer. Notable assignments include the coverage of Khrushchev's U.S. summit tour, 1959, the trial of U-2 pilot Gary Powers in Moscow, and interviews with U.S. cabinet members, members of Congress, scientists, foreign diplomats, businessmen, and academicians. *Military service:* U.S. Army Air Corps, 1944-46. U.S. Army, 1951-52, served as staff officer at psychological warfare school; became first lieutenant. *Member:* National Press Club, Sigma Delta Chi.

* * *

CONLEY, Phillip Mallory 1887-

PERSONAL: Born November 30, 1887, in Charleston, W.Va.; son of George and Alice (Simpson) Conley; married Pearl Scott, August 15, 1914 (deceased); children: Phyllis. *Education:* West Virginia University, B.S., 1914. *Politics:* Republican. *Religion:* Methodist. *Home:* 2504 S. Kanawha Ave., Charleston, W.Va. 25304. *Office:* 810 Virginia St. West, Charleston, W.Va. 25302.

CAREER: Teacher and superintendent of public schools in coal fields area near Farmington, W.Va., 1910-1918; Consolidation Coal Co., Jenkins, Ky., director of welfare work, 1919-21; *West Virginia Review,* Charleston, W.Va., editor, 1923-46; *West Virginia Encyclopedia,* Charleston, editor-in-chief, 1929; Education Foundation, Inc., Charleston, founder and president, 1938—; Charleston Printing Co., Charleston, president, 1938—. Liaison officer for American Mission to Greece, 1947-48; *Cincinnati Enquirer,* Cincinnati, Ohio, special European correspondent, 1950; special assignment by Institute of Inter-American Affairs to Latin American countries, 1952; specialist for Department of State to Greece, 1955. Writer. *Military service:* U.S. Army, 1918-19; became second lieutenant.

MEMBER: American Legion (national vice-commander, 1937-38), West Virginia Centennial Commission, Kanawha Valley Heart Associaton (past president), Masons, Shriners, Rotary International, Emeritus Club (West Virginia University), Phi Beta Kappa. *Awards, honors:* Litt.D. from West Virginia Wesleyan College, 1936; Chevalier of the Legion of Honor, 1937; LL.D. from Concord College, 1960; Gold Cross of Royal Order of George I (Greece), 1962; named West Virginia Son of the Year by West Virginia Society of the District of Columbia, 1964.

WRITINGS: (Editor-in-chief) *The West Virginia Encyclopedia,* West Virginia Publishing Co., 1929; *West Virginia Yesterday and Today,* West Virginia Review Press, 1931, 4th edition (with Boyd Stutler) Education Foundation, 1966; *Beacon Lights of West Virginia History,* West Virginia Publishing Co., 1939; *The Mountain Murder,* West Virginia Publishing Co., 1939; *Uncle Amos, Politician,* West Virginia Publishing Co., 1940; *West Virginia: A Brief History of the Mountain State,* West Virginia Publishing Co., 1940; (with Grace Turkington) *Your Country and Mine* (textbook), Ginn, 1943; *Everyday Philosophy,* West Virginia Publishing Co., 1944; *History of the West Virginia Coal Industry,* Education Foundation, 1960; *America's Debt to Greece,* Education Foundation, 1961; *As I See It,* Education Foundation, 1965; *West Virginia Reader: Stories of Early Days,* Education Foundation, 1970. Also author of monograph, *Life in a West Virginia Coal Mine,* 1923. Contributor to *Coal Review.*

* * *

CONNOLLY, Robert D(uggan, Jr.) 1917-
(Pat Duggans)

PERSONAL: Born January 2, 1917, in Phillipsburg, N.J.; son of Robert D. and Florence (Duggan) Connolly; married Florence Sarson, May 3, 1942; children: Ann Louise Connolly Dodson, Robert D. III, Thomas M., David F., Florence Connolly Smith, Richard P. *Education:* Lafayette College, A.B., 1940; Georgetown University, certificate in international relations, 1954; Oregon State University, M.Ed., 1962. *Home and office:* 168 Del Norte Way, San Luis Obispo, Calif. 93401.

CAREER: Easton Plain Dealer, Easton, Pa., reporter, 1936-38; *Easton Free Press,* Easton, reporter and news editor, 1939-41; U.S. Army, served in infantry, 1941-45; *Easton Daily Express,* Easton, reporter, 1945-48; U.S. Army, career officer, 1948-63, retiring as lieutenant colonel; teacher in California Public Schools, 1963-73; free-lance writer, 1973—. Served as public information officer for Eighth Army in Japan and Korea, 1948-52, and at Camp San Luis Obispo, Calif., 1952-53; instructor at Army Psychological Warfare School, Fort Bragg, N.C., 1954-57; executive and commanding officer of Signal Battalion in Germany, 1957-60; associate professor in Reserve Officers Training Corps (R.O.T.C.), Oregon State University, Corvallis, 1960-63. *Awards, honors—*Military: Bronze Star Medal and oak leaf cluster.

WRITINGS: A History of Phillipsburg Elks' Lodge, privately printed, 1947; *The Story of a Basic Trainee,* Blake Printing, 1953; *The New Collector's Directory,* Padre Productions, 1976.

Author of "Collectibles," a column in *Mankind;* (under name Pat Duggans) author of column on hot jazz for English edition of *Mainichi* (Japanese newspaper.) Contributor of articles, poems, and word puzzles, sometimes under name Pat Duggins, to military magazines, puzzle magazines, and to *Jazz World, Freeman, Fanfare, Escapade, Acquire, American Collector,* and *Antique Trader.* Correspondent for *Stars and Stripes,* Far East edition, 1949-53; managing editor of *JLC Journal,* 1951-52.

WORK IN PROGRESS: Collectibles from A to Z; research on the history of woven-silk items manufactured in the United States.

AVOCATIONAL INTERESTS: Hot jazz and collecting phonograph records.

CONSIDINE, Douglas M(axwell) 1915-

PERSONAL: Born May 24, 1915, in Norwalk, Ohio; son of Benjamin Maxwell (a business executive) and May Louise Considine; married Glenna Louise Taylor (a registered nurse), August 14, 1940; children: Glenn Douglas. *Education:* Case Western Reserve University, B.S., 1937. *Home and office:* 3420 Chesley Dr., Columbus, Ga. 31904.

CAREER: Registered professional engineer in state of California. D. W. Haering & Co. (chemicals), Chicago, Ill., director of research, 1937-40; Honeywell, Inc., Philadelphia, Pa., manager of Market Extension Division, 1940-54; P. R. Mallory & Co. (electronic and metallurgical products), Indianapolis, Ind., manager of marketing, 1954-57; Hughes Aircraft Co. (weapons systems), Culver City, Calif., manager of advanced control engineering, 1957-69; writer, 1969—. Consultant to Beckman Instruments, General Signal Corp., Varian Associates, and Dun & Bradstreet. *Member:* American Association for the Advancement of Science (fellow), Instrument Society of America (fellow), American Institute of Chemical Engineers (senior member).

WRITINGS: Van Nostrand's Scientific Encyclopedia, Van Nostrand, 1938; *Industrial Weighing,* Reinhold, 1948; *Process Instruments and Controls Handbook,* McGraw, 1958, 2nd edition, 1975; *Handbook of Applied Instrumentation,* McGraw, 1964; *Encyclopedia of Instrumentation and Control,* McGraw, 1973; *Chemical and Process Technology Encyclopedia,* McGraw, 1974; *Energy Technology Handbook,* McGraw, 1977. Contributor of more than seventy articles on management sciences, instrumentation, and automation to magazines.

SIDELIGHTS: Considine told *CA* that his special areas of professional interest are instrumentation and control systems engineering, energy and environmental systems, food production and food processing analyses and systems, and chemical and photochemical process engineering. He holds U.S. patents for thermocouples, flowmeters, protecting tubes and control systems, and is co-inventor of a laser fabric cutter used in garment and textile industries. During World War II, Considine was active in the development of automatic control systems for synthetic rubber and aviation gasoline plants.

* * *

COOK, Don Lewis 1928-

PERSONAL: Born January 28, 1928, in Craig, Colo.; son of Lewis E. (a contractor) and Leora (Saylor) Cook; married Betty Mary Walker (a librarian), July 25, 1952; children: Cynthia, Julia. *Education:* University of California, Los Angeles, A.B., 1949, M.A., 1957, Ph.D., 1960. *Politics:* Democrat. *Home:* 1911 Wexley Rd., Bloomington, Ind. 47401. *Office:* Department of English, Indiana University, Bloomington, Ind. 47401.

CAREER: University of California, Los Angeles, associate instructor in English, 1955-58; Indiana University, Bloomington, instructor, 1959-62, assistant professor, 1962-66, associate professor, 1966-71, professor of English, 1971—. Fulbright lecturer in Japan, 1968-69. *Military service:* U.S. Naval Reserve, active duty, 1951-54; became commander. *Member:* Modern Language Association of America (chairman of committee on scholarly editions, 1976—), National Council of Teachers of English, American Studies Association. *Awards, honors:* American Philosophical Society fellowship, 1966.

WRITINGS: (Editor with James H. Justus and Wallace E. Williams) *The Current Voice,* Prentice-Hall, 1967, alternate edition, 1971; (editor) Royall Tyler, *The Algerine Captive,* University College Press, 1970. Also contributor to *Proof,* Volume II, University of South Carolina Press, 1972. General editor of "A Selected Edition of W. D. Howells," Indiana University Press, 1969-75.

WORK IN PROGRESS: A book on anti-idealism in American writing, painting, and philosophy, 1870-1910; studies in textual scholarship and editing.

* * *

COOK, James W(yatt) 1932-

PERSONAL: Born September 8, 1932, in Hickman, Ky.; son of William J. and Kathleen (Wyatt) Cook; married Barbara Marie Collier (an executive), July 10, 1954; children: Christopher Wyatt, Kathleen Marie, David Geoffrey, *Education:* Attended Albion College, 1950-51; Wayne State University, B.A., 1954, Ph.D., 1964; University of Michigan, M.A., 1955. *Residence:* Albion, Mich. *Office:* Department of English, Albion College, Albion, Mich. 49224.

CAREER: High school English teacher in Livonia, Mich., 1955-56, 1958-61; Albion College, Albion, Mich., instructor, 1962-64, assistant professor, 1964-67, associate professor, 1967-73, professor of English, 1973—, chairman of department, 1971—. Founder and president of Validated Instruction Associates, Inc., 1972-75, chairman of board of directors, 1975—; member of board of directors of Institute for Innovation (at William Patterson College of New Jersey) and Rayswift Foundation. Regional dean of graduate studies at Walden University, 1974-76; visiting professor at Pontifical Institute of Mediaeval Studies (at University of Toronto), 1975-76. *Military service:* U.S. Army, 1954-56.

MEMBER: Modern Language Association of America, Mediaeval Academy of America. *Awards, honors:* Distinguished service award and award of merit from Michigan Education Association, both 1960; grants from U.S. Department of Health, Education and Welfare and Great Lakes College Association, 1964, Carnegie Corp. and Great Lakes College Association, 1967, Kellogg Foundation and Association of Independent Colleges and Universities of Michigan, 1927-73, National Council for American and Indian Studies and Kansas City Regional Council on Higher Education, 1970, and Kellogg Foundation, 1976; named outstanding educator of the year by Outstanding Educators of America, 1972, 1975; Newberry Library fellow, 1977.

WRITINGS: Poetry: Method and Meaning—A Program in Poetic Analysis and Criticism, Educational Methods, 1962; *Chaucer's Canterbury Art: Echoes and Reflections,* Writer's Workshop Press (Calcutta, India), 1976; (with Kirsten Hinsdale, J. P. Zink, Lanny Morreau, and Paula Smith) *The Illinois Regional Resource Center Diagnostic Teaching Model: A Systems Approach to Assessment and Programming for children with Unexplained Handicaps,* Bureau of Education for the Handicapped, U.S. Department of Health, Education and Welfare, 1976.

Video-tapes with accompanying test; all with Paul Loukides, John Shtogren, and Zink; all for State of Michigan Department of Social Services, 1976; "Building Trust and Mutual Respect," Parts I and II; "Designing and Implementing Feedback Systems"; "Establishing Training Systems"; "Integrating the New Employee: The Supervisor's Role"; "Integrating the New Employee: The Staff's Role"; "Interactive Job Descriptions"; "Problem Solving," Parts I, II, and III; "The Care and Feedbacking of Supervisors." Author of technical reports for U.S. Navy training programs. Contributor of articles and poems to professional journals and to *Heenyana*.

WORK IN PROGRESS: Old Fool, Young Fools: Polonius and His Children; A Team Approach to Diagnosing and Prescribing for Low Incidence Learning Disabilities, with Kirsten Hinsdale and Paula Smith; a verse translation of Petrarch's *Canzoniere*, with Germaine Warkentin.

SIDELIGHTS: Cook has lived in Europe, especially Italy. In 1970, he visited India as a guest of the Indian Government, in 1972 visited Egypt, and in 1976, Spain, Iran, India, Nepal, and England. *Avocational interests:* Glass crafting; Indian literature in English, playing the viola.

* * *

COOKSON, Frank Barton 1912-1977

September 27, 1912—February 2, 1977; British-born American educator, editor, composer, and author of works in his field. Cookson was a professor of music at the University of Chicago and the University of Connecticut, where he was also dean of the School of Fine Arts. He was a former editor of *Education Music* magazine. He died in Willimantic, Conn. Obituaries: *New York Times*, February 4, 1977.

* * *

COOL, Ola C. 1890(?)-1977

1890(?)-May 3, 1977; American publishing executive, public accountant, labor relations expert, and author. He died in Bernardsville, N.J. Obituaries: *New York Times*, May 4, 1977.

* * *

COOLEY, Peter 1940-

PERSONAL: Born November 19, 1940, in Detroit, Mich.; son of Paul John (an insurance executive) and Ruth Esther Cooley; married Jacqueline Marks, June 12, 1966; children: Nicole, Alissa. *Education:* Shimer College, A.B., 1962; University of Chicago, M.A., 1964; University of Iowa, Ph.D., 1970. *Politics:* Democrat. *Religion:* Episcopalian. *Home:* 4546 South Galvez, New Orleans, La. 70125. *Office:* Department of English, Tulane University, New Orleans, La. 70118.

CAREER: University of Wisconsin, Green Bay, assistant professor, 1970-72, associate professor of English, 1972-75; Tulane University, New Orleans, La., assistant professor of English, 1975—. *Member:* International P.E.N., Modern Language Association of America, Poetry Society of America, South Central Modern Language Association.

WRITINGS: How to How (poetry chapbook), G.S.S.C. Publications, 1968; *The Company of Strangers* (poems), University of Missouri Press, 1975; *Miracle, Miracles* (poems), Juniper Press, 1977. Poetry editor of *North American Review*, 1970—.

WORK IN PROGRESS: More poems.

* * *

COON, Nelson 1895-

PERSONAL: Born March 26, 1895, in Rhinebeck, N.Y.; son of Elmer (a florist) and Mattie (Dedrick) Coon; married Vesta Van Vredenburgh, August, 1919 (died, 1976). *Education:* Attended Union College, 1917. *Politics:* Republican. *Religion:* Episcopalian. *Home and office:* Waterview Gardens, Hines Point, Vineyard Haven, Mass. 02568.

CAREER: Worked as a florist and nurseryman in Rhine-

beck, N.Y., 1919-31; Perkins School for the Blind, Watertown, Mass., superintendent of maintenance, 1931-45, head librarian, 1945-60; writer on gardening. *Military service:* U.S. Aviation Service, 1917-18; became sergeant-major. *Member:* Royal Horticultural Society, International Society for Horticultural Science, Garden Writers of America, New England Botanical Club (president, 1955), Dukes County Historical Society (president, 1968-71). *Awards, honors:* American Horticulture Society citations, 1973 and 1975.

WRITINGS: The Small Nursery, De la Mare, 1923; *Practical Violet Culture*, De la Mare, 1925; *Nursery Sales and Management*, De la Mare, 1925; *Using Wayside Plants*, [Watertown, Mass.], 1957, 4th revised edition, Hearthside, 1969; *A Brief History of Dog Guides for the Blind*, Seeing Eye, 1959; *Using Plants for Healing*, Hearthside, 1963; *Fragrance and Fragrant Plants for House and Garden*, Diversity Books, 1967; *Using Plants for Fragrance*, [Grandview, Mo.], 1967; *Wild Flowers of Martha's Vineyard*, Vineyard [Haven, Mass.], 1969; *Gardening for Fragrance*, Hearthside, 1970; *Dictionary of Useful Plants*, Rodale Press, 1974; *Complete Book of Violets*, A. S. Barnes, 1977.

Author of "The Island Gardener" column, *Vineyard Gazette*, 1974—. Contributor of articles to gardening magazines and *New York Times*.

WORK IN PROGRESS: Several ideas for future books.

SIDELIGHTS: Coon writes: "From age 1-10 I annoyed everyone and learned about violet-growing while from 10-20 was 'book-larnin'; then 20-30 the Air Force in England and marriage; 40-50 widening viewpoints in Boston; 50-60 librarianship and the beginning of Island life; 60-70 in book writing and community action and 70-80 in growth through travel."

Impressed by the work of America's "greatest horticultural writer," Liberty Hyde Bailey, Coon decided at retirement to write about horticulture until age 92—the same age at which Bailey finished his work.

"I garden constantly," Coon added, "and welcome visitors to my garden and get daily phone calls for help. Presently I am advertising nationally as having for sale the only stock in the U.S. of a special variety of fragrant double Parma violets."

* * *

COOPER, Harold H. 1911(?)-1976

1911(?)—August 2, 1976; American intelligence agent and writer. Cooper joined the Central Intelligence Agency after World War II. After leaving the CIA in 1966, he wrote articles and a novel about the agency. He died in Randolph, Va. Obituaries: *Washington Post*, September 16, 1976.

* * *

COOPER, Henry Spotswood Fenimore, Jr. 1933-

PERSONAL: Born November 24, 1933, in New York, N.Y.; son of Henry S. F. (a physician) and Katherine G. F. Cooper; married Mary Luke Langren, October 13, 1966; children: Elizabeth, Hannah, Mary. *Education:* Yale University, B.A., 1956. *Home:* 1165 Fifth Ave., New York, N.Y. 10029. *Agent:* Robert Lescher, 155 East 71st St., New York, N.Y. 10021. *Office: New Yorker*, 25 West 43rd St., New York, N.Y. 10036.

CAREER: New Yorker, New York City, staff writer, 1958—. Trustee of Wrexham Foundation, 1957— (chairperson, 1965-68, 1974-77), Yale University Art Gallery, 1970—,

New York Society Library, 1972—, Yale Library Associates, 1976—, and Glimmerglass Opera Co. Judge of National Book Awards, 1972. *Military service:* U.S. Army, 1956-58.

MEMBER: Authors Guild of Authors League of America, American Association for the Advancement of Science, Municipal Art Society (member of New York City board of directors, 1965-68), Century Association (member of board of trustees, 1973-76), Grolier Society, Coffee House. *Awards, honors:* Guggenheim fellowship, 1975; science writing award from American Association for the Advancement of Science, 1977, for an article "Life in a Space Station."

WRITINGS: Apollo on the Moon, Dial, 1969; *Moon Rocks,* Dial, 1970; *Thirteen: The Flight That Failed,* Dial, 1973; *A House in Space,* Holt, 1976.

WORK IN PROGRESS: The Viking Spacecraft and the Search for Life on Mars.

SIDELIGHTS: Cooper writes: "Having no academic background in the sciences myself, I proceed on the assumption that there is no basic division between the sciences and the humanities, and accordingly I try to treat science (in particular space science) as though it were simply another branch of human thought—like poetry or art."

* * *

COOPER, I(rving) S(pencer) 1922-

PERSONAL: Born July 15, 1922, in Atlantic City, N.J.; son of David (a salesman) and Eleanor (Cooper) Cooper; married Mary Dan Frost, December 15, 1944 (died, 1968); married Sissel Holn Svenningsen, January 31, 1970; children: Daniel Alan, Douglas Paul, Lisa Frost, David Erik Louis, Eric. *Education:* George Washington University, B.A., 1942, M.D., 1945; University of Minnesota, M.S. and Ph.D., both 1951. *Home:* 3753 Fort Charles Dr., Port Royal Club, Naples, Fla. 33940. *Agent:* Russell & Volkening, Inc., 551 Fifth Ave., New York, N.Y. 10017. *Office:* St. Barnabas Hospital of Chronic Diseases, 4422 Third Ave., New York, N.Y. 10457.

CAREER: U.S. Naval Hospital, St. Albans, N.Y., intern, 1945-46; Mayo Foundation, Rochester, Minn., resident in neurosurgery, 1948-51; New York University, New York City, assistant professor, 1951-57, professor of neurosurgery at Bellevue Medical Center, 1957-66, associate attending neurosurgeon at university hospital, 1951-66; New York Medical College, New York City, research professor of neuroanatomy, 1966—. Director of department of neurosurgery at St. Barnabas Hospital, 1953—. Diplomate of American Board of Psychiatry and Neurology, 1951, and American Board of Neurological Surgery, 1953. Eliza Savage Visiting Professor in Australia, 1962; visiting professor at Mayo Foundation and University of London, both 1974. *Military service:* U.S. Naval Reserve, active duty in Medical Corps, 1946-48; became lieutenant junior grade.

MEMBER: American College of Surgeons (fellow), American Association for Neurological Surgery, American Medical Association, Neursurgial Society of America, American Academy of Neurology, American Geriatric Society (fellow), American Federation of Clinical Research, American Congress of Physical Medicine and Rehabilitation, Pan American Society of the United States, Harvey Cushing Neurosurgical Society, Society of Cryobiology (governor), Society of Cryosurgery (president), Medical Honor Society, Luther Rice Society, Royal Academy of Medicine (Madrid; foreign academic correspondent), Scandinavian Neurosurgical Society, Czechoslovak Neurosurgical Society, Neurological Society of Czechoslovakia, Neurological and Neurosurgical Society of Argentina, Society for Neurology and Neurosurgery (Cuba), Egyptian Neurosurgical Society, New York Academy of Medicine (fellow), New York Academy of Science (fellow), Sigma Xi, Alpha Omega Alpha. *Awards, honors:* Hektoen Bronze Medal from American Medical Association, 1957, 1958, certificate of merit, 1961; Lewis Harvey Taylor Award from American Therapeutic Society, 1957; award from New York Philanthropic League, 1960; civic award in medicine from Bronx Board of Trade, 1961; award from National Cystic Fibrosis Foundation, 1962; humanitarian merit award from Chicago National Parkinson Foundation, 1962, and United Parkinson Fund, 1965; Henderson Lecture Award from American Geriatric Society, 1967; gold medal from Worshipful Society of Apothecaries (London), 1967; bronze award from American Congress of Rehabilitation Medicine, 1967; Comenius Medal from University of Bratislava, 1971; D.Sc. from Trinity University, Hartford, Conn. and Fordham University, both 1974.

WRITINGS: The Neurosurgical Alleviation of Parkinsonism, C. C Thomas, 1956; *Parkinsonism: Its Medical and Surgical Therapy,* C. C Thomas, 1961; *Involuntary Movement Disorders,* Hoeber, 1969; *The Victim Is Always the Same* (autobiographical), Harper, 1973; *It's Hard to Leave While the Music's Playing,* Norton, 1977. Contributor to medical journals.

WORK IN PROGRESS: Chronic Cerebellar Stimulation: The Brain Pacemaker, for Raven Press; *The Peacemaker.*

SIDELIGHTS: Cooper developed the first brain operation that would relieve some of the symptons of Parkinson's disease without paralyzing the patient. He also became the first surgeon to use freezing (cryosurgery) during surgery. In 1972 he began work on a stimulator or pacemaker for the brain, to aid victims of untreatable epilepsy, stroke, cerebral palsy, and other movement disorders. Other of his innovations include the technique of chemopallidectomy or chemothamectomy (which can be performed with only a local anesthetic).

Cooper uses a part of his own income to finance his ongoing research in these areas, and his lecture tours have taken him around the world at least four times.

AVOCATIONAL INTERESTS: Tennis, reading, language study (speaks six languages).

* * *

COOPER, Will 1929-

PERSONAL: Born September 23, 1929, in Possum Trot, Tenn.; son of Arthur Andrew (a miner) and Verble (Winningham) Cooper; married June Mitschrich (a personnel supervisor), January 27, 1952; children: Sara Elizabeth, Jennifer Diane. *Education:* University of Oklahoma, B.A., 1954; graduate study at Ohio State University, 1954-55, and Mexico City College, 1955-56. *Politics:* "Neanderthal." *Residence:* Dallas, Tex. *Agent:* Robert P. Mills Ltd., 156 East 52nd St., New York, N.Y. 10022. *Office:* 10875 Shady Trail, Dallas, Tex. 75220.

CAREER: Writer. *Military service:* U.S. Navy, fireman, 1946-51.

WRITINGS: Death Has a Thousand Doors (novel), Bobbs-Merrill, 1976. Author of "Space & Time," a weekly column in *Financial Trend.* Editor of *Northtown News.*

WORK IN PROGRESS: Brothers Have I None, a novel; a sequel to *Death Has a Thousand Doors,* set on a Mescalero Apache reservation in New Mexico.

SIDELIGHTS: Cooper writes: "I have held more than a hundred jobs in twenty-one professions, including farmer, seaman, cabinet maker, newspaper reporter, trapper, actor, salesman, advertising writer, building contractor, teacher." He adds: "I would like to travel the world, specifically to Southeast Asia, Australia, New Zealand, India, and Polynesia, writing as I go. I prefer to write adventure/suspense novels, which reflect current fashions in sex, religion, politics—with the accent on the more violent aspects of these mores."

AVOCATIONAL INTERESTS: Hunting, fishing, sailing.

* * *

COOPER, William F(razier) 1932-

PERSONAL: Born in 1932, in Louisville, Ky.; son of William L. (an educator) and Catherine (a music professor; maiden name, Tomlinson) Cooper; married Thelma Lou Smith (a music professor), 1959; children: Richard, Jonathan, Doris Anne. *Education:* Baylor University, B.A. (cum laude), 1954, M.A., 1959; Southern Baptist Theological Seminary, B.D., 1958; Indiana University, Ph.D., 1967. *Home:* 204 Guittard, Waco, Tex. 76706. *Office:* Department of Philosophy, Baylor University, Waco, Tex. 76703.

CAREER: Lycoming College, Williamsport, Pa., assistant professor of philosophy, 1964-65; Baylor University, Waco, Tex., assistant professor, 1965-68, associate professor, 1968-71, professor of philosophy, 1971—, chairman of Latin American Studies program, 1969—. Attended National Consortium for Latin American Studies and Southwest Alliance for Latin America. Summer camp counselor, director, and athletic supervisor in Mississippi, Alabama, Georgia, and Maryland, 1951-57.

MEMBER: American Philosophical Association, American Association of University Professors (local vice-president, 1967-68; local president, 1968-69), Latin American Studies Association, Southwest Council of Latin American Studies, Southwestern Philosophical Society. *Awards, honors:* Fulbright research grant to Argentina, 1962-63.

WRITINGS: (Translator) Francisco Romero, *Theory of Man,* University of California Press, 1964; *Francisco Romero's Theory of Value,* Baylor University Press, 1966. Contributor of articles and reviews to philosophy, history, Latin American studies, and religion journals.

* * *

COOPER, William J(ames), Jr. 1940-

PERSONAL: Born October 22, 1940, in Kingstree, S.C.; son of William James (a farmer) and Mamie (Mayes) Cooper; married Patricia Holmes, September 1, 1962; children: William James III, Michael Holmes. *Education:* Princeton University, A.B. (cum laude), 1962; Johns Hopkins University, Ph.D., 1966. *Office:* Department of History, Louisiana State University, Baton Rouge, La. 70803.

CAREER: Louisiana State University, Baton Rouge, assistant professor, 1968-70, associate professor of history, 1970—. Senior fellow of Johns Hopkins University's Institute for Southern History, 1971-72; research fellow of Harvard University's Charles Warren Center for Studies in American History, 1975-76. *Military service:* U.S. Army, 1966-68; became captain. *Member:* Organization of American Historians, Southern Historical Association.

WRITINGS: The Conservative Regime: South Carolina, 1877-1890, Johns Hopkins Press, 1968; *The Politics of Slavery: Politics and Parties in the South, 1828-1856.* Louisiana State University Press, in press. Contributor to history journals.

WORK IN PROGRESS: Editing the reprint of *Social Relations in Our Southern States,* by Daniel R. Hundley (originally published in 1860), for Louisiana State University Press.

* * *

COPPER, John Franklin 1940-

PERSONAL: Born October 30, 1940, in Omaha, Neb.; son of Russell B. (a businessman) and Ina (Townsend) Copper; married Athena Chen, December 7, 1966; children: Harrison Blair, Elizabeth Allison, Anne Devona. *Education:* University of Nebraska, B.A., 1961; University of Hawaii, M.A., 1965; University of South Carolina, Ph.D., 1975. *Home:* 3473 Cowper St., Palo Alto, Calif. 94306. *Office:* Hoover Institution on War, Revolution and Peace, Stanford University, Stanford, Calif. 94305.

CAREER: U.S. Department of Defense, San Francisco, Calif., research analyst, 1965-67; College of Notre Dame, Belmont, Calif., instructor in political science, 1967-68; Tamkang College of Arts and Sciences, Taipei, Taiwan, associate professor of political science, 1968-69, 1971; University of Maryland, Far East Division, Tokyo, Japan, lecturer in government and politics, 1971-76; Stanford University, Stanford, Calif., research fellow at Hoover Institution on War, Revolution and Peace, 1976—. *Military service:* U.S. Air Force Reserve, 1962-68.

MEMBER: International Studies Association, American Political Science Association, Association of Asian Studies, East-West Center Alumni Association. *Awards, honors:* Publication awards from University of Maryland's Far East Division, 1972-75 for articles, and 1976, for *China's Foreign Aid: An Instrument of Peking's Foreign Policy.*

WRITINGS: (Translator with Sun Li-feng) Lawrence J. Peter and Raymond Hull, *Pi-teh Yuan-li* (title means "The Peter Principle"), Prometheus Book Co., 1971; (translator with Sun Li-feng and Chen Hui-Guang) Peter, *Pi-teh Ling-fang* (title means "The Peter Prescription"), Prometheus Book Co., 1975; *China's Foreign Aid: An Instrument of Peking's Foreign Policy,* Heath, 1976. Contributor of over twenty articles to Asian studies journals, and to *Current Scene, Japan Times,* and *Bangkok Post.*

WORK IN PROGRESS: Peking's World Power Prospects: An Analysis of China's National Power Capabilities and Its Role in an Evolving International System, a monograph.

SIDELIGHTS: Copper writes: "In the future all important problems will be political problems. Hence political science is the master science. The study of international relations and Asia are the most challenging part of this field: they are the most complex and least understood, while the need for understanding is most crucial." He has lived in Taiwan, Japan, Korea, Thailand, Vietnam, and Laos.

* * *

COREN, Alan 1938-

PERSONAL: Born June 27, 1938, in London, England; son of Samuel (a builder) and Martha (Phelps-Cholmondeley) Coren; married Anne Kasriel (a doctor), October 14, 1963; children: Giles, Victoria. *Education:* Wadham College, Oxford University, B.A., 1960, M.A., 1970; attended University of Minnesota, 1961, Yale University, 1962, and University of California, Berkeley, 1962-63. *Home:* 26 Ranulf Rd., London, England. *Agent:* A. D. Peters & Co. Ltd., 10 Buckingham St., London WC2N 4DD, England. *Office:* *Punch* Magazine, 23-27 Tudor St., London EC4Y 0HR, England.

CAREER: Punch magazine, London, England, assistant editor, 1963-67, literary editor, 1967-69, deputy editor, 1969—. Television critic for *The Times* (London), 1971—; writer of columns, "Alan Coren" for *Daily Mail,* 1972-77, and "Alan Coren's Monday View" for *Evening Standard,* 1977—. Rector of St. Andrew's University, 1973-76.

WRITINGS—Adult satirical fiction: *The Dog It Was That Died,* Hutchinson, 1965; *All Except the Bastard,* Gollancz, 1969; *The Sanity Inspector,* Robson, 1974, St. Martin's, 1975; *The Collected Bulletins of Idi Amin,* Robson, 1974; *The Further Bulletins of Idi Amin,* Robson, 1975; *Golfing for Cats,* Robson, 1975, St. Martin's, 1976; *The Lady from Stalingrad Mansions,* St. Martin's, 1977; *The Peanut Papers,* St. Martin's, 1977.

Children's fiction; all published by Robson, except as noted: *Buffalo Arthur,* 1976, Little, Brown, in press; *Arthur the Kid,* 1976, Little, Brown, in press; *The Lone Arthur,* 1976, Little, Brown, in press; *Railroad Arthur,* 1977, Little, Brown, in press; *Klondike Arthur,* 1977, Little, Brown, in press; *Arthur's Last Stand,* 1977, Little, Brown, in press.

Television scripts: "That Was the Week That Was," BBC-TV, 1963-64; "Not So Much a Programme," BBC-TV, 1965-66; "At the Eleventh Hour," BBC-TV, 1967; "The Punch Review," BBC-TV, 1976-77; "Every Day in Every Way" (play), BBC-TV, 1977; "Nuts" (situation comedy), Yorkshire-TV, 1977.

Radio plays: "The Shelter," BBC-Radio, 1965; "End As a Man," BBC-Radio, 1965; "Black and White and Red All Over," BBC-Radio, 1966.

Documentaries: "The British Hero," BBC-TV, 1972; "A Place in History," Thames-TV, 1974.

Contributor to *Atlantic, Playboy, TV Guide, Harper's, Cosmopolitan,* and *Sunday Times* (London).

WORK IN PROGRESS: A feature filmscript; a television comedy series, production expected in 1978; a novel, publication expected in 1978.

SIDELIGHTS: "My greatest pleasure in recent years," began Coren, "came from being told, in a *Washington Post* review of *Golfing for Cats* that I was 'the first transAtlantic humorist since Thurber and Perelman.' That pleasure emanates from the desire throughout my working life to be able to commend myself to both cultures. Educated in both countries, steeped in the literature (particularly the humour) of both countries, and loving both countries equally, I have always wanted to have a part in what one might call the CisAtlantic Tradition. I have now taken the ultimate risk with a new book, *The Peanut Papers,* ostensibly written by Mrs. Lillian Carter, which is to be published simultaneously in England and in the States in December, 1977. I doubt that an English humorist has ever stuck his neck out quite so far!

"In spring 1978, though, the neck remains out: six of my children's books are to be published in the United States by Atlantic-Little, Brown, and since these are Westerns, my reputation with both American kids and adults goes right on the line. Still, if it all works, I can't think of a better way of welding the Anglo-American culture than by working with small children, and since I have always seen our destinies as inextricably interlinked, politically as well as culturally, I make no excuse for grinding this little axe."

When *CA* asked Coren about the large amount of work he has recently accomplished in such widely different fields, he replied: "As for the regularly reiterated press comments on my output, I make no excuses here, either: I am as happy with daily journalism as I am with fiction, drama, TV writing, reviewing, or anything else. To me, it is all writing; I see no point, for me, in exclusivity of area—there are things I wish to say which can't be said in fiction, therefore must be said in journalism, there are things which don't work as drama but will as magazine stories, there's stuff I want to say to kids that I can't say to adults. And it shouldn't be forgotten that variety, for a writer, is the best form of creative regeneration."

AVOCATIONAL INTERESTS: Riding, shooting, collecting English Delft pottery, playing bridge, and rebuilding old motorcars. He is currently doing the design and planting the flora for a small park in London.

BIOGRAPHICAL/CRITICAL SOURCES: Clive James, *The Metropolitan Critic,* Faber, 1974.

* * *

COREY, Dorothy

PERSONAL: Born in Rush Lake, Saskatchewan, Canada; married Edward Corey (an engineer); children: Richard, Jan Khouri. *Education:* Attended school in Nebraska. *Home:* 16654 Parthenia St., Sepulveda, Calif. 91343.

CAREER: Writer. Active in a cooperative nursery school, Parent/Teacher Association; leader in Girl Scouts of America. *Member:* Society of Children's Book Writers (charter member).

WRITINGS—All children's books: *You Go Away,* Albert Whitman, 1975; *No Company Was Coming to Samuel's House,* Blaine Ethridge, 1976; *It Isn't Even Christmas,* Parents' Magazine Press, in press. Contributor of short stories to *Humpty Dumpty.*

WORK IN PROGRESS: Robby and the Cavity, for Elk Grove Press; more concept stories for very young children.

SIDELIGHTS: Corey told *CA* that she wrote *No Company Was Coming to Samuel's House* because she felt there was a need for a Thanksgiving story to which Spanish-American children could relate.

* * *

CORMILLOT, Albert E. J. 1938-

PERSONAL: Born August 31, 1938, in Buenos Aires, Argentina; son of Emilio Alberto and Esther (Rehermann) Cormillot; married Monika Arbogast, December, 1961; children: Renee, Adrian. *Education:* University of Buenos Aires, physician's degree, 1961. *Religion:* Catholic. *Home:* Paraguay 3358, Buenos Aires, Argentina 1425. *Agent:* Sanford J. Greenburger Associates, 825 Third Ave., New York, N.Y. 10022. *Office:* Clinica Cormillot, Paraguay, Buenos Aires, Argentina.

CAREER: Cormillot Clinic, Buenos Aires, Argentina, director, 1961—. *Military service:* Served in the Argentine Navy. *Member:* Pan American Medical Association (Latin American chairman for alcoholism section, 1976), Latin American Association of Diabetes, Argentine Society of Obesity, Association for the Study of Obesity (London), Argentine Association of Endocrinology, Argentine Association of Psychosomatic Medicine.

WRITINGS: El arte do no estar gordo, Editorial Planeta, 1973, translation by author published as *Thin Forever,* Regnery, 1976; *Obesidad, clinica y tratamiento,* Ed Medica Panamerica, 1976. Also author *Como bien y adelgace* (title means "Eat well and reduce"), with Dona Petrona C. de Gandulfo, 1973, and of *The Art of Fasting,* 1977.

Editor, *Argentine Review of Obesity and Alcoholism,* 1975-76.

AVOCATIONAL INTERESTS: Playing tennis and chess.

BIOGRAPHICAL/CRITICAL SOURCES: Village Voice, February 7, 1972; *Town and Country,* January, 1973; *Woman's Day,* July, 1976.

* * *

CORNELL, James (Clayton, Jr.) 1938-

PERSONAL: Born September 25, 1938, in Niagara Falls, N.Y.; son of James C. (an accountant) and Mary Elizabeth (Linick) Cornell; married Carole Fusaro (a musician and teacher), September 8, 1962; children: Jennifer. *Education:* Hamilton College, B.A., 1960; Boston University, M.S., 1968. *Residence:* Boston, Mass. *Office:* Harvard-Smithsonian Center for Astrophysics, 60 Garden St., Cambridge, Mass. 02138.

CAREER: Worcester Telegram & Gazette, Worcester, Mass., promotion and feature writer, and editor of in-house publication, 1960-62; Rust Craft Publishers, Dedham, Mass., public relations and advertising copywriter, 1963; Harvard-Smithsonian Center for Astrophysics, Cambridge, Mass., public information officer for Smithsonian Astrophysical Observatory, 1963-71, manager of publications department, 1971—. Instructor at Cambridge Center for Adult Education, 1969, and Boston University, 1971; lecturer at Suffolk University, 1976—. *Military service:* Massachusetts Army National Guard, broadcast media specialist, 1964-69. *Member:* World Union of Science Writers, International Science Writers Association, National Association of Science Writers.

WRITINGS: The People Get the Credit, Spiegel, Inc., 1965; *Strange, Sudden, and Unexpected* (juvenile), Scholastic Book Services, 1972; (with John Surowiecki) *Pulse of the Planet,* Crown, 1972; *Mythical Monsters* (juvenile), Scholastic Book Services, 1973; *Fakes, Frauds, and Phonies* (juvenile), Scholastic Book Services, 1973; *It Happened Last Year,* Macmillan, 1974; *Nature at Its Strangest* (juvenile), Sterling, 1974; *Unbelievable But True!* (juvenile), Scholastic Book Services, 1974; (with E. Nelson Hayes) *Man and Cosmos,* Norton, 1975; *Catastrophe, Calamity, and Cataclysm* (juvenile), Scholastic Book Services, 1975; *Where Did They Go?* (juvenile), Scholastic Book Services, 1976; *The Great International Disaster Book,* Scribner, 1976; *The Loch Ness Monster* (juvenile), Scholastic Book Services, in press. Author of book review column for "Limelight Page" in *Quincy Patriot-Ledger,* 1970—. Contributor of science articles to *Boston Globe* and *Science World* and travel articles to newspapers. Executive editor of *Beacon Hill News,* 1965-68, contributing editor, 1968-70.

WORK IN PROGRESS: A book for young readers on the origins of prehistoric cultures; research on expatriate Americans in Mexico during the revolutionary period; research on the prospects for world catastrophes, including economic collapse, ecological disaster, and population emergency.

SIDELIGHTS: Cornell writes: "I consider myself primarily a journalist who happens to write books about natural science topics. My motivation is simply to share with others my fascination and sense of wonder about the natural world, including both its extraordinary physical phenomena and the diverse human cultures that have evolved to cope with these processes of nature."

* * *

CORNMAN, James W(elton) 1929-

PERSONAL: Born August 16, 1929, in Philadelphia, Pa.; son of Ralph Miller (a manufacturer) and Rose (Scharfe) Cornman; married Elizabeth Marie Pedrotty (a volunteer worker), February 2, 1955; children: Deborah, Julie, Diane, Elizabeth. *Education:* Dartmouth College, B.A., 1956; Brown University, M.A., 1957, Ph.D., 1960. *Politics:* Democrat. *Religion:* Atheist. *Home:* 201 Walnut Ave., Wayne, Pa. 19087. *Office:* Department of Philosophy, University of Pennsylvania, Philadelphia, Pa. 19174.

CAREER: Ohio State University, Columbus, instructor in philosophy, 1960-63; University of Rochester, Rochester, N.Y., assistant professor, 1963-65, associate professor of philosophy, 1965-67; University of Pennsylvania, Philadelphia, associate professor, 1967-69, professor of philosophy, 1969—, chairman of department, 1970-72. Member of board of directors of Radnor, Pa. Better Chance Program. *Member:* American Philosophical Association, Philosophy of Science Association. *Awards, honors:* Andrew Mellon fellowship, 1965-66; National Science Foundation grant, 1968-70; American Council of Learned Societies fellowship, 1970-71; Guggenheim fellowship, 1974-75.

WRITINGS: Metaphysics, Reference, and Language, Yale University Press, 1966; (with Keith Lehrer) *Philosophical Problems and Arguments,* Macmillan, 1968, 2nd edition, 1974; *Materialism and Sensations,* Yale University Press, 1971; *Perception, Common Sense, and Science,* Yale University Press, 1975. Contributor of about forty articles to philosophy journals, including *The Journal of Philosophy* and *Nous.*

WORK IN PROGRESS: Skepticism, Justification, and Explanation, "an attempt to refute epistemological skepticism by combining the strengths of foundational theories with those of explanatory coherence theories."

SIDELIGHTS: Cornman writes: "My primary philosophical goal has long been to complete a comprehensive philosophical theory of man, the world around him, his perception and knowledge of that world, and the place of ethics and art in the resulting metaphysical and epistemological world view. Thus far I have tried to develop and justify a metaphysical theory that is a unification of the common sense view of man and the world with the scientific view that so many thinkers (such as Galileo, Newton, Descartes, and Locke) have thought requires the rejection of our common sense view. I believe that this reconciliation of science and common sense opens the way for a fuller understanding and more judicious balancing of the scientific world view and the humanistic, artistic construals of man and his world. I am currently finishing work on an epistemological theory, and have begun to develop a theory of moral obligation. Work in aesthetics lies somewhere in the future."

* * *

CORRIGAN, (Helen) Adeline 1909-

PERSONAL: Born May 31, 1909, in Cleveland, Ohio; daughter of Patrick James (a businessman) and Norah (Walsh) Corrigan. *Education:* Notre Dame College, South Euclid, Ohio, B.A., 1930; Western Reserve University (now Case Western Reserve University), M.S.L.S., 1931. *Home:* 3716 Lytle Rd., Shaker Heights, Ohio 44122.

CAREER: Cleveland Public Library, Cleveland, Ohio, children's librarian, 1931-48, assistant supervisor of Work with Children, 1949-53, supervisor, 1954-65, assistant to director of library and head of branch libraries and Bookmobile Services, 1965-72; writer, 1972—. Lecturer at Case Western Reserve University, 1947-72. *Member:* Delta Kappa Gamma.

WRITINGS: (Editor and author of introduction) *Holiday Ring: Festival Stories and Poems,* Albert Whitman, 1975. Contributor of articles and reviews to library journals. Member of editorial advisory board of *Highlights for Children.* Consultant to H. W. Wilson Co.

WORK IN PROGRESS: Editing an anthology of prose and poetry for children.

AVOCATIONAL INTERESTS: "I enjoy music and dance, travel, nature and the outdoor world. I have had the collecting spirit, from music-boxes to Belleek porcelain and Lalique crystal, and the Cinderella legend in literature. No hobby has brought me more pleasure than bringing young readers and books together. In introducing books to children, I have used story, poetry, puppets, films, and recordings."

*　*　*

COSGROVE, Stephen E(dward) 1945-
(Edward Stevens)

PERSONAL: Born July 26, 1945, in Spokane, Wash.; son of Patrick R. and Edith M. (a secretary; maiden name, Townsend) Cosgrove; married Joanne Ferrante, January 18, 1968 (divorced, March, 1977); children: Jennifer Joanne, Julie Ann. *Education:* Attended Stephen's College for Women, 1963-64. *Politics:* "Extremely emotional." *Religion:* Roman Catholic, Methodist. *Home:* 16630 Sunset Rd., Bothell, Wash. 98011. *Office:* Serendipity Communications Ltd., P.O. Box 707, Bothell, Wash. 98011.

CAREER: C-Star Concrete, Everett, Wash., assistant manager, 1964-68; Fleet Investment, Seattle, Wash., vice-president, 1968-74; Serendipity Communications Ltd., Bothell, Wash., president, 1974—. Horse breeder and rancher.

WRITINGS—All juvenile fantasies; all published by Serendipity Press: *In Search of the Saveopotomas,* 1974; *The Gnome from Nome,* 1974; *The Muffin Muncher,* 1974; *Tail of Three Tales,* 1974; *Wheedle on the Needle,* 1974; *Serendipity,* 1975; *The Dream Tree,* 1976; *Hucklebug,* 1976; *Jake O'Shawnasey,* 1976; *Morgan and Me,* 1976; *Creole,* 1976; *Flutterby,* 1977; *Bangalee,* 1977; *Leo the Lop,* 1977; *Cap'n Smudge,* 1977.

WORK IN PROGRESS: Dominoes Fall Down and *Boyce Adaho,* adult novels; "Weather War," a television script for adults; "Wheedle on the Mountain," a television Christmas special presentation and series, for children.

SIDELIGHTS: Cosgrove writes that Serendipity Communications Ltd. was formed because he and illustrator Robin James did not agree with editorial or creative policies of the New York publisher who wanted their books. They believed it was possible to create inexpensive fantasy books for children without giving up the quality of production. Since then, their books have been distributed in Canada, Africa, Australia, and Europe, and published in Spanish. An animated television series, "Serendipity," will be presented in Japan and later in the United States.

*　*　*

COTE, Richard G(eorge) 1934-

PERSONAL: Born September 14, 1934, in Lewiston, Maine; son of Albert C. and Mae Agnes (Davis) Cote. *Education:* Oblate College, Bar Harbor, Maine, student, 1952-54; Oblate College and Seminary, Natick, Mass., B.A., 1957, M.Th., 1961; University of Angers, lic. theology, 1964; University of Strasbourg, D.D., 1966. *Politics:* "Liberation and Justice." *Home and office address:* National University of Lesotho, P.O. Roma, Lesotho.

CAREER: Roman Catholic priest of Oblates of Mary Immaculate (O.M.I.), 1960—; Pius XII University College, via Maseru, Lesotho, assistant lecturer of philosophy, 1961-63; University of Botswana, Lesotho and Swaziland, Roma, Lesotho, lecturer of theology, 1967-75, director and chief administrative officer of Division of Adult Education and Extra-Mural Services, 1973-75; National University of Lesotho, Roma, Lesotho, senior lecturer in theology, 1975—. Director of Theological Winter School, 1968-70; vice-provincial of more than two hundred Oblate missionaries in Lesotho, 1970-73; member of 1974 Synod of Bishops (Rome, Italy).

WRITINGS: Could It Be?: A Theological Reflection on America, Alba, 1976; *Universal Grace: Myth Or Realtiy?,* Orbis, 1977. Contributor to theology journals. Member of editorial board of *Concilium,* 1975—.

WORK IN PROGRESS: A Contemporary Theology of Laughter; Liberation in Southern Africa.

SIDELIGHTS: Cote writes: "The overriding motivation behind all my thoughts, endeavors, and writings at the moment can perhaps best be described in terms of that challenge of which Chesterton said: 'The Christian ideal has not been tried and found wanting. It has been found difficult and left untried.' My main interest and concern is precisely the 'untried' dimension of Christianity, its potentially 'subversive' and dangerous character, and just what might happen if the radical demands of Christ were carried to their logical and faithful conclusions. This challenge takes on a special urgency—if it isn't too late already—in the context of the present liberation struggle here in the whole of southern Africa."

*　*　*

COURT, Wesli 1940-

PERSONAL: Born April 1, 1940, in Oswego, N.Y.; son of Putnam and Suella (Larsen) Court. *Education:* Attended school in Oswego, N.Y. *Home address:* P.O. Box 362, Oswego, N.Y. 13126. *Office:* Mathom Publishing Co., 219 West First St., Oswego, N.Y. 13126.

CAREER: Longshoreman and seaman in Oswego, N.Y., 1956—. Writer, 1965—.

WRITINGS: Courses in Lambents (poems), Mathom Publishing Co., 1977; *Murgatroyd and Mabel* (juvenile), Mathom Publishing Co., 1977; *Curses and Laments* (poems), Song Magazine Press, 1977. Contributing editor for Mathom Publishing Co., 1977—.

WORK IN PROGRESS: Ancient Music, modern versions of ancient Welsh, Irish, and Anglo-Saxon poems.

SIDELIGHTS: Court writes: "I have done manual labor for many years, writing *in camera.* Suddenly, this year, I have three books coming out. I have no idea how or why."

*　*　*

COWAN, Wood (Messick) 1896-1977

PERSONAL: Born November 1, 1896, in Algona, Iowa; son of James McKelvey and Marian (Foster) Cowan; married Frances Daines Metcalf, December 15, 1928; children: Conrad Metcalf, Thaddeus McKelvey. *Education:* Attended Chicago Art Institute, 1908-12. *Politics:* Republican. *Religion:* Congregationalist. *Home:* 18 Godfrey Rd., Weston, Conn. 06880.

CAREER: Chicago Inter-Ocean, Chicago, Ill., cartoonist, 1912-13; *New Orleans Item,* New Orleans, La., cartoonist, 1913-14; *Washington Times,* Washington, D.C., cartoonist, 1914-16; author of sports columns and cartoons "Spotlight on Sports," "Them Were the Days," and "Auto Bugs and Buggies," all syndicated by George Mathew Adams Syndicate, 1917-23; *New York World,* New York City, author of comic strip "Vivian the Vamp," 1924-26; author of "Carrie and Her Car," a comic strip syndicated by *Philadelphia Ledger,* 1926-28; author of syndicated comic strips "Mom'n Pop" and "Our Boarding House," 1932-42; *Bridgeport Evening Post,* Bridgeport, Conn., cartoonist, 1948-50; *New Haven Evening Register,* New Haven, Conn., cartoonist, 1960-68; free-lance writer and cartoonist, 1968—. Founder of Artists and Writers Service, 1945. Member of Connecticut General Assembly, 1951-55; first selectman of Weston, Conn., 1955-57. Lecturer on cartooning history. *Awards, honors:* Best cartoon of the year award from National Foundation for Highway Safety, 1960.

WRITINGS: (With Tom Curry) *Famous Figures of the Old West* (self-illustrated), Monarch, 1965. Also author of *Iowa Cracker Barrel* (self-illustrated), 1972. Contributor of drawings and comic panels to magazines, including *Collier's, Argosy,* and *New Yorker.*

SIDELIGHTS: Cowan's paintings have been exhibited in Connecticut and Georgia.

(Died June 10, 1977)

[Sketch verified by son, Thaddeus M. Cowan]

* * *

COWEN, Emory L(eland) 1926-

PERSONAL: Born April 20, 1926, in New York, N.Y.; son of Philip H. and Rose D. Cowen; married Renee Senna (a teacher), January 28, 1947; children: Richard Jan, Peter Rolf, Lisa Allyson, Andrew Philip. *Education:* Brooklyn College (now of the City University of New York), A.B. (cum laude), 1944; Syracuse University, A.M., 1948, Ph.D., 1950. *Home:* 32 Aberthaw Rd., Rochester, N.Y. 14610. *Office:* Center for Community Study, University of Rochester, Rochester, N.Y. 14627.

CAREER: University of Rochester, Rochester, N.Y., assistant professor, 1950-55, associate professor, 1955-60, professor of psychology, 1960—, associate in psychiatry, 1960-67, professor of psychiatry, 1967—, professor of education, 1973—, director of Undergraduate Counseling Service, 1956-61, director of clinical psychology training program, 1956-69, director of Center for Community Study, 1969—. New York State Board of Examiners in Psychology, member, 1962-68, vice-chairman, 1963-64, chairman, 1964-66; consultant to Veterans Administration, 1955—. Member of National Science Foundation visiting scientist program; member of psychology training subcommittee for National Institute of Mental Health, 1964-68. *Military service:* U.S. Navy, 1944-46; became lieutenant junior grade.

MEMBER: American Psychological Association (fellow; member of executive committee, 1973-77), Eastern Psychological Association, New York State Psychological Association (past member of board of directors), Genessee Valley Psychological Association (past president), Sigma Xi, Psi Chi. *Awards, honors:* National Institute of Mental Health special senior research fellow at Institut de Psychologie, University of Paris, 1961-62; research award from American Personnel and Guidance Association, 1962.

WRITINGS: (Contributor) W. M. Cruickshank, editor, *A Psychology of Exceptional Children and Youth,* Prentice-Hall, 1955, 2nd edition, 1963; (with R. P. Underberg, R. T. Verrillo, and F. G. Benham) *Adjustment to Visual Disability in Adolescence,* American Foundation for the Blind, 1961; (contributor) L. H. Lofquist, editor, *Psychological Research and Rehabilitation,* American Psychological Association, 1963; (editor with E. A. Gardner and M. Zax, and contributor) *Emergent Approaches to Mental Health Problems,* Appleton, 1967; (with Zax, D. R. Beach, and others) *Follow-Up Study of Children Who Participated in a Preventive Mental Health Program* (monograph), U.S. Office of Education, 1967; (contributor) C. D. Spielberger, editor, *Progress in Clinical Psychology and Community Mental Health,* Academic Press, 1969; (contributor) J. W. Carter, editor, *Research Contributions from Psychology to Community Mental Health,* Behavioral Publications, 1969.

(Contributor) Spielberger and I. Iscoe, editors, *Community Psychology: Perspectives on Training and Research,* Appleton, 1970; (with J. Rappaport and J. M. Chinsky) *Innovations in Helping Chronic Patients: College Students in a Mental Hospital,* Academic Press, 1971; (with Zax) *Abnormal Psychology: Changing Conceptions,* Holt, 1972, 2nd edition, 1976; (contributor) H. H. Barten and L. Bellak, editors, *Progress in Community Mental Health,* Volume III, Grune, 1975; (with R. V. Isaacson, L. D. Izzo, and others) *New Ways in School Mental Health: Early Detection and Prevention of School Maladaptation,* Human Sciences, Inc., 1975; (contributor) V. L. Allen, editor, *Tutoring and Inter-Age Interaction,* Academic Press, 1976; (contributor) B. B. Wolman, J. Egan, and A. O. Ross, editors, *Handbook of Treatment of Mental Disorders in Childhood and Adolescence,* Prentice-Hall, 1976; (contributor) Iscoe, Spielberger, and B. L. Bloom, editors *Community Psychology in Transition,* Hemisphere Press, 1977.

Contributor to *International Encyclopedia of Neurology, Psychiatry, Psychoanalysis, and Psychology.* contributor of more than one hundred articles to professional journals. Advisory editor of *Journal of Consulting and Clinical Psychology,* 1967-76; associate editor of *American Journal of Community Psychology,* 1972—.

* * *

COX, Keith (Kohn) 1931-

PERSONAL: Born April 21, 1931, in Austin, Tex.; son of Lambuth and Pearl Cox; married Sue Johnson (a teacher), July 1, 1961; children Suzanne, Gregory. *Education:* University of Texas, B.B.A., 1953, M.B.A., 1959, Ph.D., 1963. *Politics:* Democrat. *Religion:* Methodist. *Home:* 7315 Carew, Houston, Tex. 77074. *Office:* Department of Marketing, University of Houston, Cullen Blvd., Houston, Tex. 77004.

CAREER: Kent State University, Kent, Ohio, assistant professor of marketing, 1963-67; University of Houston, Houston, Tex., 1967—, began as associate professor, became professor of marketing. *Member:* American Marketing Associaton (vice-president in education, 1975; vice-president in finance, 1976).

WRITINGS: (Editor) *Analytical Viewpoints in Marketing,* Prentice-Hall, 1968; *Experimentation for Marketing Decisions,* Intext Publishing, 1969; (with Ben Enis) *The Mar-*

keting Research Process, Goodyear Publishing, 1972; (editor with Enis) *Marketing Classics,* Allyn & Bacon, 1969, 3rd editon, 1977.

* * *

COX, Warren E(arle) 1895-1977

August 27, 1895—May 22, 1977; American antiques dealer, authority on porcelain and pottery specializing in Oriental antiques, and author of books in his field, including the two-volume *Book of Pottery and Porcelain,* regarded as a standard reference. He died in New York City. Obituaries: *New York Times,* May 23, 1977. (*CAP*-2; earlier sketch in *CA*-33/36)

* * *

CRABBE, Buster (Clarence Linden) 1908-

PERSONAL: Born February 7, 1908, in Oakland, Calif.; son of Edward and Agnes (McNamara) Crabbe; married Virginia Held, April 13, 1933; children: Susan Fletcher, Caren, Cullen. *Education:* University of Southern California, B.A., 1932. *Politics:* Republican. *Religion:* Episcopal. *Home:* 11216 North 74th Street, Scottsdale, Ariz. 85260. *Agent:* Ventura Associates, 40 East 49th Street, New York, N.Y. 10017.

CAREER: Signed as actor by Paramount Pictures, Hollywood, Calif., after winning 400-meter race in 1932 Olympics; appeared in motion pictures for Paramount Pictures, Universal Studios, and Producers Releasing Corporation, the most notable of which include "Tarzan the Fearless," 1933, "King of the Jungle," 1933, "Nevada," 1936, "Flash Gordon's Trip to Mars," 1938, "Mars Attacks the World," 1938, "Buck Rogers," 1939, "Queen of Broadway," 1943, "Last of the Redmen," 1947, "Caged Fury," 1948, "Gunfighters of Abilene," 1959, "Arizona Raiders," 1965, and in the "Buck Rogers," "Flash Gordon," and "Billy the Kid" serials in the 1930's and 1940's; appeared in lead role in "Captain Gallant of the French Foreign Legion" television series syndicated by National Broadcasting Company (NBC), 1955-61; The Concord, Kiamesha Lake, N.Y., director of water sports, 1951-69; Cascade Industries, Edison, N.J., vice-president, 1956—. Lecturer. *Member:* Sigma Chi. *Awards, honors:* Elected to Swimming Hall of Fame, 1965.

WRITINGS: Energistics, Playboy Press, 1976.

WORK IN PROGRESS: A book about Hollywood, *From the Outside Looking In.*

SIDELIGHTS: Crabbe writes: "I have completed some eighty-five college lectures on the movies of the 1930's, 1940's, and 1950's. In conjunction with the nostalgia lectures am now lecturing on physical fitness and weight control for convention groups, most recently the annual conventions for Holiday Inns, Mechanical Contractors Association of America, and Rockwell International."

* * *

CRAIB, Ian 1945-

PERSONAL: Born December 12, 1945, in Croydon, Surrey, England; son of Gwen (Langdon) Craib; married. *Education:* Borough Polytechnic, London, England, B.A., 1970; University of Manchester, Ph.D., 1973. *Politics:* Marxist. *Religion:* None. *Agent:* Curtis Brown (Academics) Ltd., 13 King St., Covent Garden, London W.C.2, England. *Office:* Department of Sociology, University of Essex, Wivenhoe Park, Colchester, Essex, England.

CAREER: University of Essex, Colchester, England, lecturer in social theory and philosophy, 1973—.

WRITINGS: Sociology and Existentialism: A Study of Jean-Paul Sartre, Cambridge University Press, 1976. Contributor to sociology and philosophy journals.

WORK IN PROGRESS: Theoretical study of the sociology of literature.

SIDELIGHTS: Craib comments: "My main concern is the development of a Marxist theory of consciousness and its implications for political organisation and activity. I am interested in the political nature of all forms of experience and, through that, in making some contribution to radical change in modern capitalist society."

* * *

CRANDALL, Norma 1907-
(Norma McCarty; joint pseudonym, Wilson Chamberlain)

PERSONAL: Born November 20, 1907, in Brooklyn Heights, N.Y.; daughter of Edward (in hotel and real estate business) and Marie Vanderveer (Hall) Crandall; married Wilson Chamberlain McCarty (a journalist), September 15, 1933 (deceased). *Education:* Attended Barnard College, 1926-28. *Politics:* Democrat. *Religion:* Protestant. *Home and office:* 44 East 63rd St., New York, N.Y. 10021.

CAREER: Harcourt, Brace Co., New York, N.Y., editorial adviser, 1939; free-lance writer and translator from French into English, 1939—. *Member:* Authors Guild of Authors League of America, Poetry Society of America, Academy of American Poets (patron), Bronte Society (England), Barnard College Club (New York City; librarian and member of board of directors).

WRITINGS: Emily Bronte: A Psychological Portrait, R. R. Smith, 1957, reprinted, Kraus Reprint, 1970. Contributor of articles, poems, and reviews (sometimes under name Norma McCarty) to magazines, including *Town and Country Review, New Leader, New Republic, Humanist, Chicago Review, Pageant, Collier's,* and to newspapers; contributor with husband, Wilson McCarty, under name Wilson Chamberlain, to *Reader's Digest.*

WORK IN PROGRESS: Revising *Emily Bronte: A Psychological Portrait;* continuing to present "Evening with the Brontes: A Dramatic Reading"; several literary-critical biographies; translating a new biography of Cardinal Mazarin from French to English.

SIDELIGHTS: Norma Crandall told *CA,* "although I feel an academic background is valuable to a writer, I do not believe that writing, itself, can be taught. It seems to me the chief value is in providing beginners with professional criticism from established writers, many of whom now teach in the universities."

* * *

CRAVEN, Roy C., Jr. 1924-

PERSONAL: Born July 29, 1924, in Cherokee Bluffs, Ala.; son of Roy C., Sr. and Edna (Morris) Craven; married Lorna Andreae (an artist), September 19, 1948; children: Curtis Andreae, Hillary Yvonne. *Education:* Studied at University of Tennessee, 1942; University of Chattanooga, B.A., 1949; studied at Art Students League of New York, 1949-50; University of Florida, M.F.A., 1956. *Home:* 6818 Northwest 65th Ave., Gainesville, Fla. 32601. *Office:* University Gallery, University of Florida, Gainesville, Fla. 32611.

CAREER: Tivoli Theatre, Chattanooga, Tenn., theater display artist and photographic assistant, 1938-41; *Chattanooga Times,* Chattanooga, Tenn., photographer, 1946-47; U.S. Army, Fort Oglethorpe, Ga., civilian artist and illustrator, 1947; free-lance commercial artist in New York, N.Y., 1949-50; Stratford College, Danville, Va., head of department of art, 1950-52; University of Chattanooga, Chattanooga, Tenn., instructor in art, 1952-53; University of Florida, Gainesville, instructor at Jacksonville Art Museum, 1954-55, instructor at Gainesville campus, 1955-57, assistant professor, 1957-64, associate professor, 1964-67, professor of art, 1967—, director of University Gallery, 1966—. Graphic designer for Purse Advertising Co., 1952-54; paintings have been exhibited in New York, including Metropolitan Museum of Art, and throughout the South; included in American Federation of Arts exhibits, 1957-58; one-man show in Mexico; guest curator of High Museum of Art, 1974; lecturer at museums and universities in the United States and abroad; guest on television programs. *Military service:* U.S. Army Air Forces, photographer, 1942-46; served in India.

MEMBER: Asia Society, Association for Asian Studies, American Association of Museums, Southeastern Museums Conference (past member of board of directors), Florida League of Arts (past member of board of directors), Florida Art Museum Directors Association, Phi Beta Kappa, Alpha Society, Phi Kappa Phi. *Awards, honors:* Chattanooga Art Association fellowship, Mexico, 1947; purchase award from Virginia Museum of Fine Arts, 1950, Ringling Museum of Art, 1961, and Sears, Roebuck Foundation, 1969; special award from American Institute of Graphic Design, 1950; first prize from Brooks Memorial Gallery, 1952; Fulbright senior research scholarship, India, 1962-63; National Defense Education Act grant for traveling exhibitions, 1968-73, and for South America, 1975; American Philosophical Society Travel Grant to India, 1977.

WRITINGS: Indian Sculptures in the John and Mabel Ringling Museum of Art (monograph), University of Florida Press, 1961; *Ceremonial Centers of the Maya,* University of Florida Press, 1974; *A Concise History of Indian Art,* Thames & Hudson, 1976. Author of exhibition catalogs. Contributor to art journals and other professional periodicals. Former editor of journal of the Southeastern Museums Conference.

WORK IN PROGRESS: Continual study and research on eighteenth century miniature paintings from India and the iconographic development of the *makara,* a mythical beast symbolizing fertility and waters, found in the art of Hinduism and Buddhism.

SIDELIGHTS: Craven has been commissioned to do architectural sculptures including a sixteen feet by thirty-two feet structure for Jacksonville, Florida's Civic Auditorium, 1962, a facade for the medical building of Wesley Manor Retirement Village in St. Johns County, Fla., 1963, and a facade for the music and fine arts building at Jacksonville University, 1964. He has just completed making a comprehensive collection of Andean folk art of Bolivia, Peru, Ecuador, and Columbia for University of Florida.

AVOCATIONAL INTERESTS: Travel (North America, Switzerland, Iran, Greece, France, England, South and Central America).

*   *   *

CRAWFORD, Stanley (Gottlieb)   1937-

PERSONAL: Born October 2, 1937, in San Diego, Calif.; son of A. Bergman (a teacher) and Helen (Ikinger) Craw-

ford; married Rosemary Wilton (a journalist), December 20, 1967; children: Stefan Adam, Kate. *Education:* University of Chicago, A.B., 1958; University of California, Berkeley, M.A., 1962. *Home address:* P.O. Box 56, Dixon, N.M. 87527.

CAREER: Northern Branch College, Santa Cruz, N.M., instructor in English, 1973—.

WRITINGS—All novels: *Gascoyne,* Putnam, 1966; *Travel Notes,* Simon & Schuster, 1967; *Log of the S. S. the Mrs. Unguentine,* Knopf, 1972; *Some Instructions* (satire), Knopf, 1978.

*   *   *

CREDLAND, Peter (Francis)   1946-

PERSONAL: Born September 9, 1946, in Sheffield, England; son of Stanley (an insurance manager) and Mollie (Glossop) Credland; married Jennifer Susan Brown (a secretary), September 19, 1970; children: Victoria Louise. *Education:* University of Nottingham, B.Sc. (honors), 1967, Ph.D., 1971. *Politics:* "Usually Conservative." *Home:* Tylers Green, High Wycombe, Buckinghamshire, England. *Office:* Department of Zoology, Bedford College, University of London, Regents Park, London NW1 4NS, England.

CAREER: University of London, Bedford College, London, England, lecturer in zoology, 1970—. *Member:* Royal Entomological Society (fellow), Zoological Society (fellow).

WRITINGS: (With Gillian Standring) *The Living Waters: Life in Lakes, Rivers, and Seas,* Aldus Books, 1975, Doubleday, 1976. Contributor to scientific journals.

WORK IN PROGRESS: Working on problems in insect physiology, especially with midges.

SIDELIGHTS: Credland writes: "In the job which I now occupy the writing of scientific papers in a necessity. The opportunity to write a book aimed at a wider audience provided me with a chance to explore what I regard as an important part of modern science—the communication of scientific discovery and expertise to the non-professional scientists and, hopefully, the public who may be frightened by the idea of 'science' in our time. I hope to do more in the years to come."

*   *   *

CREEKMORE, Betsey B(eeler)   1915-

PERSONAL: Born May 23, 1915, in Knoxville, Tenn.; daughter of Ulysses D. (a manufacturer) and Bessie (Hoskins) Beeler; married Frank B. Creekmore, November 10, 1938 (deceased); children: David D., Betsey B. *Education:* Vassar College, A.B., 1935; University of Tennessee, graduate study, 1935-36. *Politics:* Republican. *Religion:* Presbyterian. *Home and office:* 4734 Sylvan Lane, Knoxville, Tenn. 37919.

CAREER: Writer. Vice-president and director, Fidelity Federal Savings & Loan Association; trails adviser for Dogwood Arts Festival (first chairman, 1957-60). *Member:* Authors Guild of Authors League of America, Junior League of Knoxville (president, 1938-40), Garden Club of America, Knoxville Garden Club (president, 1954-56), Blount Mansion Association, Phi Beta Kappa. *Awards, honors:* Bicentennial citation from Greater Knoxville American Revolution Bicentennial Commission, 1976, for revised edition of *Knoxville.*

WRITINGS: Knoxville, University of Tennessee Press, 1958, 3rd edition, 1976; *Arrows to Atoms,* University of

Tennessee Press, 1959; *Dark and Bloody Ground,* Fell, 1968; *Traditional American Crafts,* Hearthside, 1969; *Making Gifts from Oddments and Outdoor Materials,* Hearthside, 1970; (with daughter, Betsey Creekmore) *Your World in Miniature,* Doubleday, 1976. Zone editor of *Garden Club of America Bulletin,* 1958-60.

SIDELIGHTS: "Since 1975," Creekmore told *CA,* "I have been representing the states of Arkansas, Louisiana, Mississippi, Tennessee, and Texas on the Conservation Committee of the Garden Club of America. Of necessity, I've learned a great deal about such national concerns as natural resources, air and water quality, public lands, highway beautification, endangered underdeveloped areas and endangered species, strip mining and reclamation, historic preservation, and urban revitalization. I've also discovered that conservationists and environmentalists do not always see eye-to-eye on controversial issues. In general, the environmentalist orders 'Touch it not,' while the conservationist urges 'Use it well!'"

*　　*　　*

CREEL, Stephen Melville 1938-
(E. B. Sachem)

PERSONAL: Born June 13, 1938, in Denver, Colo.; son of George William (a professor of English) and Josephine (a customs broker; maiden name, Shields) Creel; married Dorothy Willet, January 25, 1964 (divorced April 19, 1969); married Julie Dolan (a nurse), July 2, 1976; children: Bradley, Emory. *Education:* Sacramento State College, B.A., 1960; University of Colorado, M.D., 1964; Harvard University, postdoctoral study, 1970-71. *Politics:* Democratic Socialist. *Religion:* None. *Home:* 1049-2 Chena Rd., Fort Wainwright, Alaska 99703. *Office:* Bassell Army Hospital, Fort Wainwright, Alaska 99703.

CAREER: Hartford Hospital, Hartford, Conn., intern, 1964-65; Boston State Hospital, Boston, Mass., resident in psychiatry, 1967-69; Veterans Administration Hospital, Boston, resident in psychiatry, 1969-70; Massachusetts General Hospital, Boston, resident in psychiatry, 1969-70; private practice of medicine in Boston, 1971-76; U.S. Army, chief of psychiatry at Basset Army Hospital, Fort Wainwright, Alaska, 1976—; present rank, lieutenant colonel. Staff psychiatrist of Community Mental Health Activity, 1976—. Clinical instructor at Harvard University, 1972-75. Staff psychiatrist at Boston City Hospital, 1972-74. Smallpox researcher for World Health Organization in India, 1963. *Military service:* U.S. Army, Medical Corps, 1965-67; served in Germany; became captain.

MEMBER: Amnesty International, Common Cause, Taxation with Representation, Public Citizen, Wilderness Society, Massachusetts Medical Society, Alaskan Conservation Society, Chi Sigma Rho, Blue Key.

WRITINGS: (Under pseudonym E. B. Sachem) *Poppy Children* (novel), Myrmidon, 1975. Contributor to professional journals and to *Atlantic Monthly.*

WORK IN PROGRESS: A historical novel, set during the Taiping Rebellion, 1850-64.

SIDELIGHTS: Creel writes: "My principal theme in not only the above works but in several other unpublished novels is old and nowadays seemingly trite, yet it is unfailingly both universal and at the same time close to our daily lives and even lies within the depths of our souls. That theme is the constant, gargantuan, mortal struggle between 'good' and 'evil,' now with one the victor, and now the other.

'Evil,' when seen in the light of realism, often seems to take the honors, yet 'good' is always running just behind it, close enough to keep it in check (almost). The present novel in progress explores this question from a socio-politico-religious aspect."

AVOCATIONAL INTERESTS: Playing classical and Flamenco guitar, jogging.

*　　*　　*

CREER, Thomas L(aselle) 1934-

PERSONAL: Born November 2, 1934, in Lund, Idaho; son of Laselle L. (a pipefitter) and Naomi (Jones) Creer; married Patricia J. Plummer, July 7, 1961; children: Jennifer, Matthew. *Education:* Brigham Young University, B.S., 1956; Utah State University, M.S., 1961; University of Wisconsin, Madison, further graduate study, 1962-63; Florida State University, Ph.D., 1967. *Politics:* Democrat. *Home:* 8043 East Oberlin Pl., Denver, Colo. 80237. *Office:* National Asthma Center, 1999 Julian, Denver, Colo. 80204.

CAREER: Utah State University, Logan, counselor, 1959-61; Dayton Children's Psychiatric Hospital, Dayton, Ohio, clinical psychologist, 1961-62; Veterans Administration Hospital, Coral Gables, Fla., intern, 1966-67; National Asthma Center, Denver, Colo., research clinical psychologist, 1967-70, director of Division of Behavioral Science, 1970—. *Military service:* U.S. Army, Adjutant General's Corps, 1956-58. U.S. Army Reserve, 1958-65. *Member:* American Psychological Association, Psychonomic Society, American Association for the Advancement of Science, Association for the Advancement of Behavior Therapy. *Awards, honors:* National Institute of Mental Health grant, 1972-74.

WRITINGS: (With Walter P. Christian) *Chronically-Ill and Handicapped Children,* Research Press, 1976. Contributor to psychology journals.

WORK IN PROGRESS: When I Get Asthma, juvenile; *Childhood Asthma: A Practical Handbook,* completion expected in 1978; *Parenting Children with Chronic Afflictions,* 1978.

SIDELIGHTS: Creer told *CA:* "Most of my writings have been oriented towards describing how social learning principles can be applied to improve the health and well-being of chronically ill individuals. Behavioral and technological breakthroughs offer greater hope for this segment of our population than at any other time in our history. What I hope to achieve is to communicate to others how recent developments can assist in mainstreaming the handicapped and physically impaired into our society."

*　　*　　*

CREGIER, Don M(esick) 1930-

PERSONAL: Surname is pronounced *Cree*-ger; born March 28, 1930, in Schenectady, N.Y.; landed Canadian immigrant; son of Harry M. (a mechanical engineer) and Marion (Shovea) Cregier; married Sharon Kathleen Ellis (a journalist), June 29, 1965. *Education:* Union College, Schenectady, N.Y., B.A., 1951; University of Michigan, M.A., 1952; further graduate study at Clark University, 1952-54, and London School of Economics and Political Science, London, 1957-58, 1961-62. *Residence:* Kinloch, Prince Edward Island, Canada. *Office:* Department of History, University of Prince Edward Island, Charlottetown, Prince Edward Island, Canada C1A 4P3.

CAREER: Clark University, Worcester, Mass., assistant

instructor in government, 1952-54; Conquistador Press, Schenectady, N.Y., president and managing director, 1954-56; University of Tennessee, Knoxville, instructor in history and political science, 1956-57; Baker University, Baldwin City, Kan., instructor, 1958-59, assistant professor of history and political science, 1959-61; Keuka College, Keuka Park, N.Y., assistant professor of history and political science, 1962-64; St. John's University, Collegeville, Minn. visiting assistant professor of history, 1964-65; Mark Hopkins College, Brattleboro, Vt., senior fellow in history and political science, 1965-66; St. Dunstan's University, Charlottetown, Prince Edward Island, assistant professor, 1966-68, associate professor of history, 1968-69; University of Prince Edward Island, Charlottetown, associate professor of history, 1969—.

MEMBER: Canadian Historical Association, American Historical Association, Conference on British Studies, Oral History Association, American Political Science Association, Conference on Latin American History, Association for Contemporary History, National Writers Club (United States), Historical Association (England), National Library of Ireland Society, London Library, Phi Beta Kappa, Phi Kappa Phi, Pi Gamma Mu. *Awards, honors:* Canada Council fellowship, 1972-73.

WRITINGS: Bounder from Wales: Lloyd George's Career Before the First World War, University of Missouri Press, 1976. Contributor to professional journals. Editor of *Quest for Education,* 1966-67.

WORK IN PROGRESS: Two more biographical studies of David Lloyd George, the first covering 1914-1922, and the second concerning the remainder of his political life; a monograph on Lloyd George's Irish home rule negotiations of 1916; a historical and comparative study of university history-teaching methods.

SIDELIGHTS: Cregier told *CA:* "My wife and I shuttle between Canada and the U.S. customarily spending three or four spring and summer months in Vermont where one of our horses is domiciled. Although Canada has treated us very well, and we are landed immigrants, we see ourselves as cultural Americans with the need to touch base regularly on American soil. Rising energy costs and the need to find a permanent home for our horses and nearly ten thousand books may soon force us to end this paripatetic life-style. Plans for a rammed-earth, partially undergound, fuel-conserving house are on the drawing board. It probably will be built in rural Prince Edward Island. Both of us belong to the *Mother Earth News, Prevention,* and *Provoker* schools of health-fooders, vegetarians, ecologists, and do-it-yourselfers, insofar as time and circumstances permit. We are also contributors to and participants in organizations and movements for the protection of wild and domestic animals from human exploitation. A blue Land Rover, known as Kew/II, is a member of our family; we hope to keep her in good working order for at least fifteen years. Our two family mottos are "Illegitimati non carborundum' and 'Impermanence is the curse of eccentricity.'"

AVOCATIONAL INTERESTS: Travel, cooking organic foods, keeping horses.

* * *

CREIGHTON, Joanne V(anish) 1942-

PERSONAL: Born February 21, 1942, in Wisconsin; daughter of William J. (a forest ranger) and Bernice Vanish; married Thomas F. Creighton (an administrator), November 9, 1968; children: William Troy. *Education:* University of

Wisconsin, Madison, B.A., 1964; Harvard University, M.A., 1965; University of Michigan, Ph.D., 1969. *Home:* 18000 Muirland, Detroit, Mich. 48221. *Office:* Department of English, Wayne State University, Detroit, Mich. 48202.

CAREER: Wayne State University, Detroit, Mich., instructor, 1968, assistant professor, 1969-75, associate professor of English, 1975—. *Member:* Phi Beta Kappa, Phi Kappa Phi. *Awards, honors:* National Endowment for the Humanities grant, 1976.

WRITINGS: William Faulkner's Craft of Revision, Wayne State University Press, 1977; *Joyce Carol Oates,* Twayne, in press.

* * *

CRELLIN, John 1916-

PERSONAL: Born February 29, 1916, in Port Huron, Mich.; son of Charles (a reporter) and Kathleen (Carroll) Crellin; married: Grace Reuther, April, 1936; children: James, John, Michael, Thomas, Kathleen, Jeffrey, Christopher. *Home:* 34590 Jefferson, Mount Clemens, Mich. 48045. *Office: Detroit News,* 615 Lafayette, Detroit, Mich. 48231.

CAREER/WRITINGS: Detroit Times, Detroit, Mich., reporter, 1935-61; *Detroit News,* Detroit, 1961—, worked as rewrite person, business writer, assistant city editor, city editor, and labor reporter. Notable assignments include coverage of labor since 1942, including the election of Walter Reuther, the attempted assassinations of Walter and Victor Reuther, and presidency of Jimmy Hoffa; also directed coverage of 1967 race riot in Detroit. *Military service:* U.S. Navy, 1943-45. *Member:* Detroit Press Club. *Awards, honors:* Headliner Award, 1967, for coverage of Detroit race riot; United Press International Award, 1973, for coverage of automative investigations; also received Newspaper Guild One Award, and Detroit Press Club Foundation Award.

* * *

CROCKER, Helen Bartter 1929-

PERSONAL: Born July 30, 1929, in Columbia Station, Ohio; daughter of Milford Hale (a farmer) and Edna (a teacher; maiden name, Bracy) Bartter; married Kenneth Wayne Crocker (a veterinarian), June 16, 1951; children: Scott, Kelly, Daniel, Timothy Stephen, Benjamin. *Education:* Attended Baldwin-Wallace College, 1947-50; Ohio State University, B.A., 1951; Western Kentucky University, M.A., 1970; further graduate study, Vanderbilt University, 1972-75. *Religion:* Protestant. *Home:* 413 South College St., Franklin, Ky. 42134. *Office:* Department of History, Cherry Hall, Western Kentucky University, Bowling Green, Ky. 42101.

CAREER: Western Kentucky University, Bowling Green, assistant professor of history, 1970—.

WRITINGS: The Green River of Kentucky, University Press of Kentucky, 1976. Contributor to state history journals.

WORK IN PROGRESS: A biography of William E. Barton.

SIDELIGHTS: Crocker writes: "The Green River valley of Kentucky takes in nearly one-fourth of the Commonwealth. Born in the foothills of the Appalachian Mountains, the Green River flows past the famous Mammouth Cave in its upper reaches and through the western Kentucky coalfields in its lower reaches. Ever since its first settlement in the 1780's, valley residents have depended on the Green River for transportation, and today it carries well over a million tons of coal a year to Ohio River markets. Its waters have an unusual green tint and a high mineral content as a result of its large number of underground feeders. Though the valley's population has remained small, its proximity to urban areas is making it a favorite recreational area, and canoeists, water-skiers, fishermen, and swimmers increasingly enjoy its beauty.

"My own interest in the Green River began when I was planning to write a master's thesis in Kentucky history, and my professor dropped the suggestion that no regional study had been done on the Green River valley. This appealed to me because I had grown up along the Rocky River of Ohio, and had come to realize that rivers recalled the best of my past. What better subject could there be for the historian than something that recalled the past? My master's thesis dealt only with the steamboat era on the river (1828-1931), but the book, *The Green River of Kentucky,* deals more generally with the life along the river and its tributaries for the past two hundred years. My research included a number of oral interviews—with retired steamboat captains, lock masters, and collectors of river lore, and I have concluded that Green River residents are unusually friendly and always interesting."

*   *   *

CRONKITE, Walter (Leland, Jr.)   1916-

PERSONAL: Born November 4, 1916, in St. Joseph, Mo.; son of Walter Leland (a physician) and Helen Lena (Fritsche) Cronkite; married Mary Elizabeth Simmons Maxwell (a journalist), March 30, 1940; children: Nancy Elizabeth, Mary Kathleen, Walter Leland III. *Education:* Attended University of Texas, 1933-35. *Politics:* Independent. *Religion:* Episcopalian. *Office:* Columbia Broadcasting System, 524 West 57th St., New York, N.Y. 10019.

CAREER: Scripps-Howard Bureau, Austin, Tex., reporter on state capitol staff, 1933-35; *Houston Press,* Houston, Tex., reporter, 1935-36; KCMO-Radio, Kansas City, Mo., news and sports editor and broadcaster, 1936-37; United Press International (UPI), organized El Paso (Tex.) bureau, 1937; WKY-Radio, Oklahoma City, Okla., football announcer, 1937; worked for Braniff Airways, Kansas City, 1937; UPI, reporter, 1937-48, war correspondent from Germany, North Africa, Normandy, and Belgium, 1941-45, established bureaus in Belgium, the Netherlands, and Luxembourg, 1945, chief correspondent from the Nuremberg trials of Nazi war criminals, 1945-46, chief correspondent for the Soviet Union in Moscow, 1946-48; broadcaster, lecturer, and journalist from Washington, D.C., 1948-50; Columbia Broadcasting System (CBS)-News, New York City, Washington, D.C., news commentator and analyst, 1950—, discussion chairman of "Man of the Week," beginning 1951, moderator of "Pick the Winner," 1952, narrator of "You Are There," beginning 1953, coordinator and master of ceremonies of "Morning Show," 1955, host of "It's News to Me," beginning 1954, narrator of "Twentieth Century," managing editor and anchor of "CBS Evening News with Walter Cronkite," 1963—. Broadcaster from Washington, D.C., to Midwest radio stations, 1948-50.

MEMBER: Overseas Press Club, Overseas Writers Club, National Press Club, Academy of Television Arts and Sciences (president, 1959), Association of Radio News Analysts, Chi Phi, Players Club, New York Yacht Club, Indian Harbor Yacht Club. *Awards, honors:* George Foster Pea-

body Radio and Television Award, 1962; William Allen White Award of Journalistic Merit, 1969; Emmy Award from Academy of Television Arts and Sciences, 1970; George Polk Memorial Award from Long Island University, 1971. Honorary degrees include LL.D. from Rollins College, Bucknell University, and Syracuse University, and L.H.D. from Ohio State University and University of Missouri; has also received degrees from American International College (now University), Dartmouth College, and from Duke University.

WRITINGS: (Contributor) M. Mirkin Stanford, editor, *Conventions and Elections, 1960: A Complete Handbook,* Channel Press, 1960; *Vietnam Perspective: A CBS News Special Report,* Pocket Books, 1965; *Eye on the World,* Cowles Book Co., 1971; *The Challenge of Change,* Public Affairs Press, 1971. Contributor of articles and reviews to magazines, including *Theatre Arts,* and to newspapers.

SIDELIGHTS: Walter Cronkite's favorite critical review noted that "viewers rarely recall and relish a Cronkite statement. They believe it instead." The man who quickly became one of the most respected figures on television, and undoubtedly the most trusted anchorman, has established high standards of professional and journalistic excellence throughout the entire duration of his career. As a United Press International reporter, he shared with his fellow UPI reporters the thrill of scooping the Associated Press—often by a ten-minute margin!, and was known to be highly aggressive. David Halberstam observed that "no one, particularly anyone who had ever worked on a story against him, would ever accuse Walter Cronkite of a lack of hunger; he was, from his earliest days, wildly competitive—no one was going to beat Walter Cronkite on a story." He added, "As he grew older and more successful, the marvel of it was that he never changed, the fires still burned."

It is said that no one could cover a story and be better prepared than the young Cronkite. Every fact had to be verified and stand up under the harshest investigation. His instinct for excellence was fierce and continued burning after his years at UPI and during his period with radio, and certainly it became a shining aspect of his work on television. "Yet, fortunately for his television career," remarked Halberstam, "he did not *look* competitive. He looked comfortable, reassuring, and very much in control. It was an admirable and lucky combination. . . . In addition, he had physical strength and durability. Iron pants, as they say in the trade. He could sit there all night under great stress and constant pressure and never wear down, never blow it. And he never seemed bored by it all, even when it got boring."

In little more than a decade, Cronkite had become a comforting fixture in American life, a symbol of unity and stability, of good faith and trust; he had become senior journalist in the broadcast news medium by sheer force of his energies and his talent and his excellence. What he said during a news broadcast now was grounded in the truth, in verifiable evidence, just as it had always been, or at least so he thought. If Cronkite's own standards were impeccable, then so must the standards of his sources, but Halberstam reflected that at that time Cronkite "was inclined to take without question the word of men who had titles and positions." This became a particularly acute problem in reporting on the Vietnam situation. Cronkite found the younger correspondents brash and cynical in their attacks against the conventional and optimistic official reports, and it did not make him feel comfortable, but he was also the man who had to pass on the critical data. When he went to Vietnam in the summer of 1965, Halberstam wrote, "it was a crucial moment for him, because for the first time he saw the credibility gap, face front.

"He was shocked, not so much by the ferocity of fighting, but because to his mind the men in charge of the war were not to be trusted." When Cronkite reported that the war didn't work, and that the United States had to start thinking of getting out, it is said that President Lyndon Johnson told his press secretary, George Christian, that this was evidently a turning point, because if he had lost Walter Cronkite, then he had lost Mr. Average Citizen. As Halberstam observed, Johnson's estimation of this loss "solidified his decision not to run for re-election. He had lost his consensus."

AVOCATIONAL INTERESTS: Yachting, dancing, spectator sports, playing golf and tennis, bowling, reading history, mystery novels, and humor.

BIOGRAPHICAL/CRITICAL SOURCES: New York Times, July 20, 1952; *Newsweek,* February 9, 1953, November 12, 1973; *New York Post Magazine,* March 21, 1954; Carlyle Wood, *Television Personalities Biographical Sketch Book,* Television Personalities, 1956; *Saturday Evening Post,* March 16, 1963; *Look,* August 25, 1964, November 17, 1970, March 26, 1971; *Time,* October 14, 1966, November 21, 1969, September 10, 1973, November 11, 1973; *Reader's Digest,* December, 1969; *Publishers Weekly,* May 3, 1971; *Today's Health,* autumn, 1972; *Esquire,* April, 1973; *Broadcasting,* October 15, 1973; *Atlantic Monthly,* February, 1976.

*   *   *

CROOKENDEN, Napier 1915-

PERSONAL: Born August 31, 1915, in Chester, England; son of Arthur (a colonel in the British Army) and Dorothy (Rowlandson) Crookenden; married Patricia Nassau Kindersley, August 3, 1948; children: James Napier, Elisabeth Jane (Mrs. Samuel G. Hughes), Charles Stephen Napier, Catherine Mary. *Education:* Attended Royal Military College, 1934-35. *Religion:* Church of England. *Home:* Sissinghurst Place, Cranbrook, Kent TN17 2JP, England.

CAREER: British Army, career officer, 1935-72, commissioned to Cheshire Regiment, 1935, Sixth Airlanding Brigade, 1943-44, commanding officer of Parachute Regiment, 1944-46, general staff officer to director of operations in Malaya, 1952-54, commander of Sixteenth Parachute Brigade, 1960-61, at Imperial Defence College, 1962, director of Land/Air Warfare for Ministry of Defence, 1964-66, commandant of Royal Military College of Science in Shrivenham, 1967-69, colonel of Cheshire Regiment, 1969-71, commander-in-chief of Western Command, 1969-72, retiring as lieutenant general. Colonel commandant of Prince of Wales Division, 1971-74; lieutenant of Tower of London, 1975—. Member of board of trustees of Imperial War Museum, 1973—.

MEMBER: Soldiers', Sailors', and Airmen's Families Association (chairman, 1974—), Ski Club of Great Britain. *Awards, honors:* Distinguished Service Order, 1945; officer of Order of the British Empire, 1954; Knight Commander of the Bath, 1970.

WRITINGS: Drop Zone Normandy, Scribner, 1976.

WORK IN PROGRESS: A comparative study of American, British, and German airborne troops, for Ian Allan; a history of the Battle of the Ardennes, 1944-45, Ian Allan; *The Life of a Parachute Battalion, 1942-47,* Ian Allan.

SIDELIGHTS: Crookenden writes: "I know America well

and having fought alongside American Airborne Troops, I find my work on the history of our combined operations is stimulating. I speak French and German and find equal interest in my researches into World War Two battles."

*   *   *

CROSHER, G. R.
(G. R. Kesteven)

HOME: 99 Langley Way, Watford, Hertfordshire WD1 3ED, England.

CAREER: Writer. Has also worked as a gardener, fire fighter, teacher (sometimes of retarded teenagers), and in insurance and advertising.

WRITINGS—All for children, except as indicated—Under name G. R. Crosher: *Ken and the Kidnappers,* Cassell, 1954; *The Limping Smuggler,* Cassell, 1954; *The Strange Lodger,* Cassell, 1954; *The Robbery at Blairs,* Cassell, 1954; *Fire at Brean House,* Cassell, 1954; *Castaway on Green Rock,* Cassell, 1954; *Fireman Joe,* Methuen, 1955; *Cowboy Dave,* Methuen, 1955; *Footballer Steve,* Methuen, 1955; *Lone Eagle,* Methuen, 1955; *Island Adventure,* Methuen, 1955; *House on Fire,* Methuen, 1955; *A Convict Has Escaped,* Methuen, 1955; *Treasure in the Ruins,* Methuen, 1955; *Mail-Bag Robbery,* Cassell, 1956; *Attack on a Stranger,* Cassell, 1956; *A Spy on the Falcon,* Cassell, 1956; *Trail to Adventure,* Cassell, 1956; *Night Chase,* Cassell, 1956; *A Bomb in the Submarine,* Cassell, 1956; *Laughter from the Past* (one-act plays based on European folk tales), Methuen, 1956; *Mystery at Camp,* Methuen, 1957; *A Night in the Old House,* Methuen, 1957; *A Man Without Memory,* Methuen, 1957; *A Gun from Nowhere,* Methuen, 1957; *A Drive into Danger,* Cassell, 1959; *Mystery Cottage,* Cassell, 1959; *The Man from the Sea,* Cassell, 1959; *Blackmailer's Hide-Out,* Cassell, 1959; *Hunt the Necklace!,* Cassell, 1959; *The Drifting Yacht,* Cassell, 1959.

More Laughter from the Past (one-act plays), Methuen, 1961; *Holiday Mystery,* Methuen, 1961; *Uncle Bill Comes Home,* Methuen, 1961; *Adventure in the Snow,* Methuen, 1961; *The Strange Artist,* Methuen, 1961; *Country Stories,* Cassell, 1962; *Seaside Days,* Cassell, 1962; *At Home,* Cassell, 1962; *Round the Town,* Cassell, 1962; *Along the Chiltern Ways* (adult travel book), Cassell, 1973; *The Match on the Patch,* Cassell, 1975; *A Find on the Patch,* Cassell, 1975; *Christmas on the Patch,* Cassell, 1975; *A Pinch on the Patch,* Cassell, 1975; *Along the Cotswold Ways* (adult travel book), Cassell, 1976; *No Sun at Sunnyside,* Cassell, 1976; *Attack in Dark Lane,* Cassell, 1976; *Runaway into Danger,* Cassell, 1976; *Strangers in the Village,* Cassell, 1976.

Under pseudonym G. R. Kesteven: *The Peasants' Revolt,* Chatto & Windus, 1965; *The Reformation in England,* Chatto & Windus, 1965; *The Armada,* Chatto & Windus, 1965; *The Mayflower Pilgrims,* Chatto & Windus, 1966; *The Execution of the King,* Chatto & Windus, 1966; *The Glorious Revolution of 1688,* Chatto & Windus, 1966; *1485, from Platagenet to Tudor,* Chatto & Windus, 1967; *Peterloo, 1819,* Chatto & Windus, 1967; *The Triumph of Reform, 1832,* Chatto & Windus, 1967; *The Forty-Five Rebellion,* Chatto & Windus, 1968; *The Loss of the American Colonies,* Chatto & Windus, 1968; *1851, Britain Shows the World,* Chatto & Windus, 1968; *1870, Year of Change,* Chatto & Windus, 1970; *The Boer War,* Chatto & Windus, 1970; *1914,* Chatto & Windus, 1970; *The Why of Our Towns and Villages,* Chatto & Windus, 1972; *The Pale Invaders* (futuristic fiction), Chatto & Windus, 1974; *Where Do You Live?: The Story Behind English Place-Names,* Chatto &

Windus, 1976; *The Awakening Water* (futuristic fiction), Chatto & Windus, 1977.

Author under real name, with D. R. Crawford, of arithmetic book series, "Problem Practice," Methuen, 1959-60; and with N.W.N. Sagar, of English book series, "Pilot English," Methuen, 1965-66.

WORK IN PROGRESS: Four books in the "Onward Books" series, for Cassell.

SIDELIGHTS: Crosher writes: "I can remember at quite an early age trying verses, usually intended to be humorous.... By my teens I was trying more ambitious stories and essays; I was, I think, drawn by the challenge of giving shape to often-vague ideas, fascinated by the variety and subtlety of words, and intrigued by working out the intricacies of a plot....

"When asked to try teaching retarded youngsters, I found that almost the only simply written books then available were those for five-year-olds. My teenagers were not encouraged by such books, so I wrote ... exciting stories in a controlled vocabulary and a deliberately repetitive style.... The forty-eighth is due early in 1977, and many have been published ... in European countries where they are used in teaching English as a second language.

"The writing of those stories taught me much. Their simple language and controlled sentence construction make them, of course, of no literary value ... though some stories are more than mere adventures. But ... that these stories have enjoyed a long life, and many have been given a more up-to-date appearance and re-issued, suggests that they did their job well.

"Meanwhile, perhaps to relieve the strain of teaching retarded children, I had been asked to take Social Studies with brighter classes. As part of this work I tried to get away from the conventional and often superficial approach to History by taking a series of incidents and trying to discover what contemporaries thought about them. The results often gave very different impressions from the text-book summary ... and so I wrote my findings.

"A few years ago, on my doctor's advice, I left teaching. Since then I have written two adult travel books.... I have also written two futuristic (definitely not Science Fiction) novels for children.... To me, these last seem unexpected works, and I'm unsure of my reasons for attempting them ... perhaps partly an extension of my interest in History, partly a distrust of those futuristic works which appear to me suspect in their assumptions and improbable in their conclusions, partly a feeling which many of us must share of being subjected to forces too large for our comprehension, partly a belief that, whatever comes, we humans will retain our essential humanity."

* * *

CROSLAND, (Charles) Anthony (Raven)   1918-1977

August 29, 1918—February 19, 1977; British politician, economist, and author of works in his field. In addition to being a former member of Parliament, Crosland held several cabinet posts, the last being Foreign Secretary which he held at the time of his death. He died in Oxford, England. Obituaries: *New York Times*, February 20, 1977; *Newsweek*, February 28, 1977; *Time*, February 28, 1977; *Current Biography*, April, 1977.

* * *

CROWE, Philip Kingsland   1908-1976

January 7, 1908—October 16, 1976; American diplomat, conservationist, and author. Crowe served as American ambassador to Ceylon, South Africa, Norway, and Denmark. He was very active in the conservation movement and belonged to several national and international conservation groups. Crowe was author of six books on nature and wildlife. He died in Easton, Md. Obituaries: *New York Times*, October 18, 1976; *AB Bookman's Weekly*, November 15, 1976; *Publishers Weekly*, November 15, 1976.

* * *

CROWE, Robert L(ee)   1937-

PERSONAL: Born August 14, 1937, in Macomb, Ill.; son of Edward C. and Helen (Purdy) Crowe; married Sandra Rae Haring, August 12, 1961; children: Cassandra, Tracy, Robert, Jr., David. *Education:* Western Illinois University, B.S.E., 1959; St. Louis University, A.M., 1967; Southern Illinois University, further graduate study, 1970-71; Indiana University, Ed.D., 1972. *Home:* 4 Sunnydale, Jacksonville, Ill. 62650.

CAREER: English and speech teacher in junior high schools in Macomb, Ill., 1959-60, and Ferguson, Mo., 1960-61; speech teacher and director of speech in high school in Macomb, Ill., 1961-63; Parkway School District, Chesterfield, Mo., high school teacher of speech and head of department, 1963-68, personnel director, 1968-72, assistant to superintendent, 1972-75; superintendent of schools in Jacksonville, Ill., 1975—. Instructor at University of Missouri—St. Louis, 1967, and Northeast Missouri State University, 1975. Member of executive committee of Four Rivers Special Education District. *Member:* American Association of School Administrators, Illinois Association of School Administrators, Illinois Association of Supervision and Curriculum Development, Phi Delta Kappa, Elks, Kiwanis, Jacksonville Chamber of Commerce.

WRITINGS: (Contributor) Robert Rea and Robert Arnspiger, editors, *Professional Development Programs, Education*, Part II: *Instructional Personnel*, University of Missouri, School of Education, 1970; *The Fastest Trip in the History of Turtle* (juvenile), Creative Ideas, Inc., 1975; *Clyde Monster* (juvenile), Dutton, 1976. Contributor of about a dozen articles to education journals. Editor of *Indiana School Boards Journal*, 1971-72.

* * *

CROWLEY, John W(illiam)   1945-

PERSONAL: Born December 27, 1945, in New Haven, Conn.; son of John A. (a patent lawyer) and Mary (McKenna) Crowley; married Sheila Myers, 1967 (divorced, 1977); children: John Matthew, Anne Marie. *Education:* Yale University, B.A. (magna cum laude), 1967; Indiana University, M.A., 1969, Ph.D., 1970. *Religion:* Roman Catholic. *Office:* Department of English, Syracuse University, Syracuse, N.Y. 13210.

CAREER: Syracuse University, Syracuse, N.Y., assistant professor, 1970-74, associate professor of English, 1974—. *Member:* Modern Language Association of America, Phi Beta Kappa. *Awards, honors:* Woodrow Wilson fellowship, 1967.

WRITINGS: George Cabot Lodge, Twayne, 1976; *George Cabot Lodge: Selected Fiction and Verse*, John Colet Press, 1976; (editor) W. D. Howells, *A Foregone Conclusion*, Indiana University Press, in press. Contributor of articles and reviews to periodicals.

WORK IN PROGRESS: A book on fiction from and about New England since 1850.

SIDELIGHTS: Crowley writes: "I am interested in the applications of psychology to literary criticism."

* * *

CRUMLEY, James 1939-

PERSONAL: Born October 12, 1939, in Three Rivers, Tex.; son of Arthur Roland (an oil field supervisor) and Ruby (Criswell) Crumley; married Judith Ann Ramey (an editor), June 28, 1975; children: Mary, Elizabeth, David. *Education:* Georgia Institute of Technology, student, 1957-58; Texas A & I University, B.A., 1964; University of Iowa, M.F.A., 1966. *Home:* 423 South Lee, Mathis, Tex. 78368. *Agent:* Owen Laster, William Morris Agency, 1350 Avenue of the Americas, New York, N.Y. 10019.

CAREER: University of Montana, Missoula, instructor in English, 1966-69; University of Arkansas, Fayetteville, assistant professor of English, 1969-70; Colorado State University, Fort Collins, assistant professor of English, 1971-74; free-lance writer, 1974-76; Reed College, Portland, Ore., visiting associate professor of creative writing, 1976-77; writer. 1977—. *Military service:* U.S. Army, 1958-61. *Member:* Associated Writing Programs.

WRITINGS: One to Count Cadence (novel), Random House, 1969; *The Wrong Case* (novel), Random House, 1975; *The Last Good Kiss* (detective novel), Random House, in press. Contributor to literary magazines, including *Aspen Leaves, California Quarterly,* and *Ploughshares.*

* * *

CRUMPLER, Gus H(unt) 1911-

PERSONAL: Born March 7, 1911, in Lowry, Ark.; son of Thomas Newton (a merchant-farmer) and Phebe Sue (Dunlap) Crumpler; married Mary Afton Chappelle, February 7, 1942; children: Anna Jean Smith, Saundra Kaye Villines. *Education:* Attended University of Missouri and North Arkansas Community College; also studied at Newspaper Institute of America. *Politics:* Independent Democrat. *Home:* 413 North Center St., Harrison, Ark. 72601. *Office:* Times Publishing Co., 111 West Rush, Harrison, Ark. 72601.

CAREER: United States Post Office, Lowry, Ark., postmaster, 1933-42; owner and operator of country store in Lowry, Ark., 1934-42; Real Estate Development, Lowry, Ark., owner and operator, 1952-76; Times Publishing Co., Harrison, Ark., member of newspaper advertising staff, 1953-76. Has served as Democratic Party committee member and as secretary of local Democratic Party. *Military service:* U.S. Army, 1943-46. *Member:* Veterans of Foreign Wars, American Legion (vice-commander, 1947-49), Northwest Arkansas Archaeological Society (vice-president, 1957-76), Arkansas Archaeological Society.

WRITINGS: Under the Burmese Pagoda, School of the Ozarks Press, 1975. Contributor of articles to *Central States Archaeological Journal, The Ozarks Mountineer,* to poetry publications and to local newspaper.

WORK IN PROGRESS: Family histories; a novel about a Hindu lad and an American soldier.

SIDELIGHTS: Crumpler told *CA:* "*Under the Burmese Pagoda* is the saga of a small group of American servicemen whose plane crashes in the forbidding jungle of northern Burma during World War II." He went on to say that he has had writing as a goal since his high school days. Aside from his principal vocations, Crumpler said that he has worked as a "cedar post dealer, a fishing lure manufacturer, a salesman of sporting goods, candy and notions, a fur buyer and prospector."

AVOCATIONAL INTERESTS: Fishing, archaeology, exploring, hunting.

* * *

CUDDY, Don 1925-

PERSONAL: Born May 30, 1925, in Wilkes-Barre, Pa.; son of Alfred (a salesman) and Mabel (Gardner) Cuddy; married Joan Vaughan, August 5, 1949 (divorced, 1970); married Claudia Lambert Hughes (an insurance agent), November 14, 1970; children: Paul Brandt, Tricia (Mrs. Bruce VanderJagt), Michael Lawrence, Stephen Hughes, Michael Hughes, Brian. *Education:* Cornell University, student; University of Miami, Coral Gables, Fla., A.B., 1948; attended U.S. Navy Post-Graduate School, 1952. *Politics:* Democrat. *Religion:* Methodist. *Home:* 3349 Park Rd., Hollywood, Fla. 33021.

CAREER: Florida Sun, Miami Beach, Fla., sports editor, 1949-52; *Coral Gables Times-Guide,* Coral Gables, Fla., managing editor, 1955-58; *Miami Herald,* Miami, Fla., assistant state editor, 1958-59; Diplomat Hotel, Hollywood, Fla., public relations director, 1960-65; Don Cuddy Public Relations, Fort Lauderdale, Fla., owner, 1965-75; City of Hollywood, Fla., bicentennial coordinator, 1975-76; free-lance writer and public relations consultant, 1976—. Vice-chairperson of transportation committee for Broward County Charter Commission; chairman of transportation task force for Fort Lauderdale Area Chamber of Commerce; director of local American Red Cross. *Military service:* U.S. Naval Reserve, active duty, 1943-45, 1952-54; served in Pacific theater; became lieutenant.

MEMBER: Sigma Delta Chi (past president), Broward Gridiron Club (chairman), Tower Club. *Awards, honors:* Community service award from Florida Press Association, 1957, for articles; tourism award from State of Florida, 1964, for films.

WRITINGS: Tales of Old Hollywood, Spectator Books, 1977. Contributor to popular and local magazines, including *Collier's, Saga, Sport, Boxing, Cavalier,* and *Signature.*

WORK IN PROGRESS: Second Marriage Survival, a book of practical advice for persons planning to remarry; *The Indispensable Woman,* a novel; *Sandspur,* a historical novel.

SIDELIGHTS: Cuddy writes: "*Tales of Old Hollywood* is an anecdotal history of Hollywood, Florida, resulting in part from an oral history project involving interviews with early (1925) residents to record the personal recollections of people and events that shaped the growth of a real estate development into a city of over one hundred twenty-five thousand population in fifty years, and especially to clarify some controversial aspects of Joseph W. Young's career as founder of the city and Port Everglades."

* * *

CULBERT, Samuel Alan 1938-

PERSONAL: Born July 27, 1938, in Chicago, Ill.; son of Richard (a salesman) and Rose (Greenberg) Culbert; children: Samantha Rachel, Gar Robert. *Education:* Northwestern University, B.S., 1961; University of California, Los Angeles, Ph.D., 1966. *Home:* 2710 Nichols Cyn., Los Angeles, Calif. 90046. *Office:* Graduate School of Management, University of California, Los Angeles, Calif. 90024.

CAREER: Professor of management at University of California, Los Angeles. Licensed clinical psychologist in State of California, 1967—. *Military service:* U.S. Army. *Member:* National Institute of Applied Behavioral Science, American Psychological Association.

WRITINGS: The Organization Trap, Basic Books, 1974.

WORK IN PROGRESS: Ego Patrol.

SIDELIGHTS: Culbert writes that his "research laboratory is the organizational world" where he "uses his skills in facilitating organization effectiveness as a lever for helping people see the self-defeating assumptions made when participating in our society's work system."

* * *

CUNNINGHAM, Joseph F. X. 1925-

PERSONAL: Born March 4, 1925, in Jersey City, N.J.; son of Joseph (a traffic manager) and Mary (Snell) Cunningham; married Rita Horrigan, September 6, 1952, (died August 15, 1972); married Janette Hart (a teacher), August 9, 1975; children: Joseph, Elizabeth, Rita, Mary-Jo, Thomas. *Education:* Seton Hall University, A.B., 1946, M.A., 1950; New York University, Ed.D., 1964. *Politics:* Democrat. *Religion:* Catholic. *Home:* 118 Kenneth Ter., South Orange, N.J. 07079. *Office:* Seton Hall University, South Orange, N.J. 07079.

CAREER: Seton Hall University, South Orange, N.J., associate professor of education, 1947—, associate dean of graduate school, 1961-70. *Member:* American Association of University Professors, National Education Association, National Catholic Education Association, New Jersey Education Association.

WRITINGS: Functional English, Washington Irving, 1956; *Summit of a Century,* Washington Irving, 1957; *Behind the Bamboo Curtain,* St. Paul Press, 1961; *The Rise of a University,* New York University Press, 1964; *Research for Teachers,* University Press of Washington, in press. Writer of television series, "Channels of Learning," 1955-60.

* * *

CURNOW, (Thomas) Allen (Monro) 1911-

PERSONAL: Born June 17, 1911, in Timaru, New Zealand; son of Tremayne Monro (an Anglican clergyman) and Jessamine Towler (Gambling) Curnow; married Elizabeth Jaumaud Le Cren, 1936 (divorced, 1965); married Jenifer Mary Tole, August 31, 1965; children: Wystan Tremayne Le Cren, Belinda Elizabeth Allen Curnow Morley, Timothy Charles Monro. *Education:* Attended St. John's College, Auckland, New Zealand, 1931-33; University of New Zealand, B.A., 1933; University of Auckland, Litt.D., 1966. *Home:* 62 Tohunga Cres., Parnell, Auckland, New Zealand. *Agent:* Curtis Brown Ltd., P.O. Box 19, Paddington 2021, Australia.

CAREER: Press, Christchurch, New Zealand, reporter, 1936-40, sub-editor, 1941-48; *News Chronicle,* London, England, reporter and sub-editor, 1949; University of Auckland, Auckland, New Zealand, senior lecturer, 1951-67, associate professor of English, 1968-76. *Awards, honors:* Jessie Mackay Memorial Prize from New Zealand branch of International P.E.N. and State Literary Fund, 1957, for *Poems, 1949-1957,* and 1962, for *A Small Room with Large Windows;* New Zealand Poetry Award from P.E.N. and State Literary Fund, 1975, for *Collected Poems;* Litt.D. from University of Canterbury, 1975.

WRITINGS—Poems: *Enemies,* Caxton Press, 1937; *Not in Narrow Seas,* Caxton Press, 1939; *Island and Time,* Caxton Press, 1941; *Sailing or Drowning,* Progressive, 1943; (editor) *A Book of New Zealand Verse,* Caxton Press, 1945, revised edition, 1950; *Jack Without Magic,* Caxton Press, 1946; *At Dead Low Water,* Caxton Press, 1949; *Poems, 1949-1957,* Mermaid, 1957; (editor) *The Penguin Book of New Zealand Verse,* Penguin, 1960; *A Small Room with Large Windows,* Oxford University Press, 1962; *Trees, Effigies, Moving Objects,* Catspaw, 1972; *An Abominable Temper,* Catspaw, 1973; *Collected Poems,* A. H. & A. W. Reed, 1974.

Plays: *The Axe: A Verse Tragedy* (three-act; first produced in Christchurch, New Zealand at Little Theatre, Canterbury University College, April 24, 1948), Caxton Press, 1949; *Four Plays* (includes "The Axe," revised version, and three radio plays: "The Overseas Expert," 1962, "The Duke's Miracle," 1967, and "Resident of Nowhere," 1969), A. H. & A. W. Reed, 1972.

WORK IN PROGRESS: Satirical pieces and more poems.

BIOGRAPHICAL/CRITICAL SOURCES: Landfall, Volume XVII, number 1, 1963; *Islands,* Autumn, 1975.

SIDELIGHTS: Curnow told *CA:* "My first very youthful poems came from a personal religious crisis during studies for the Anglican ministry and the social crisis of the nineteen thirties depression. A few of the poems which followed touched on New Zealand life and history: a poet's attempt to solve questions about where he was, the language and tradition being almost everywhere, and his country rather inconveniently but ineluctably *somewhere.* There was 'The Unhistoric Story' about Cook's first southern voyage, 'The Victim' about a Dutch crewman killed in a clash with the Maori when Abel Tasman made the first European discovery of New Zealand (in 1642), and 'Landfall in Unknown Seas,' written on commission by the New Zealand government to celebrate the 300th anniversary of Tasman's voyage. There was also a sonnet, 'The Skeleton of the Great Moa,' about New Zealand's giant extinct bird. "It pleases me," Curnow continued, "that all these works have continued to be quoted, nearly forty years after their first appearance—not only in literary works, but occasionally in historical and even scientific studies. It pleased me less when one or two younger writers chose to regard me as a banner-bearer for some kind of hole-and-corner poetic nationalism. The truth was that for a few years my island nation served me the way Yeats said his 'System' served him—it 'gave me metaphors for poetry.'

"Like some other New Zealand authors," Curnow recalled, "I was to find dramatic writing (especially for the stage) a somewhat frustrating exercise in a country without dramatic tradition or well-established theatre. Since 1970 I have persisted with poems about the troublesome question of how to be in two (or more) places at once, i.e. Aukland, New Zealand and Washington, D.C. A title like 'Trees, Effigies, Moving Objects,' for instance, is an excuse for arranging in perspective a giant kauri tree, the Washington Memorial, a roadside effigy of the Virgin at Paraparaumu, and Nebuchadnezzar's golden idol. Can I perhaps unite a memory of the Duomo in Florence, by way of the assassin's dagger which killed Giuliano de'Medici in 1948, with my own rusty fishing knife and a *kahawai* landed at Kare Kare, and the chemistry of a garden poison for snails? This may sound far-fetched, but isn't one of the tasks of a poet to transform the far-fetched into the self-evident?"

CURRY, David 1942-

PERSONAL: Born January 10, 1942, in Springfield, Ill.; son of George Bruce (a municipal worker) and Jessie (a nurse; maiden name, Agnew) Curry. *Education:* Trinity College, Hartford, Conn., student, 1960-63. *Politics:* "Timid Anarchist." *Religion:* "Poet." *Home:* 1111 South Second St., Springfield, Ill. 62704.

CAREER: International Order of the Golden Rule, Springfield, Ill., advertising director, 1965-76; free-lance writer, 1976—. *Awards, honors:* National Endowment for the Arts writing fellowship, 1976-77; Yaddo Colony fellowship, 1977.

WRITINGS: Here: Poems, 1965-1969, New Rivers Press, 1970; *Theatre* (poems), Best Cellar Press, 1973; *Contending to Be the Dream* (poems), New Rivers Press, in press. Editor of *Apple,* 1967-76.

WORK IN PROGRESS: A Clash of Songs (tentative title), a novel.

SIDELIGHTS: Curry comments briefly: "As Theodore Roethke wrote in one of his notebooks, 'I have only a few ideas and some of them are almost dead from overwork.'"

* * *

CURRY, George E(dward) 1947-

PERSONAL: Born February 23, 1947, in Tuscaloosa, Ala.; son of Homer (an auto mechanic) and Martha (Harris) Curry; married Jacqueline Smith (a Social Security Administration operations analyst), May 23, 1970. *Education:* Attended Knoxville College, 1967-70. *Politics:* "Closet Independent." *Religion:* Baptist. *Home:* 36 Conway Cove, St. Louis, Mo. 63017. *Office: St. Louis Post-Dispatch,* 900 North 12th Blvd., St. Louis, Mo. 63101.

CAREER: Sports Illustrated, New York, N.Y., reporter, 1970-72; *St. Louis Post-Dispatch,* St. Louis, Mo., reporter, 1972—. *Member:* Society of Professional Journalists, National Association of Black Journalists, St. Louis Journalism Review (board member), Metropolitan St. Louis Sickle Cell Anemia Association (member of board of directors).

WRITINGS: Jake Gaither (biography), Dodd, 1977. Contributor to *National Observer, Tuesday, Sports Illustrated,* and other periodicals.

WORK IN PROGRESS: A book about Mark Essex, tentatively titled *The New Orleans Sniper.*

SIDELIGHTS: Curry told *CA* of his first encounter with the Jake Gaither legend: "In the late 1950's and early 1960's, my public housing playmates, especially the older ones, would tell me about Jake Gaither and his Florida A&M Rattlers. Having been afraid of green snakes all of my life, not to mention Rattlers, I wasn't sure I wanted to hear the full story. When I enrolled at Druid High School, then all-Black, my football coaches spoke frequently and favorably of Gaither and how he liked his players 'ag-ile, mo-bile and hos-tile,' accenting the first syllable of each word. I suspect my coach had a motive for telling me that, but it failed to change my style of play. I later attended Knoxville College, and I learned that this was Gaither's alma mater. I should have given up on avoiding the Gaither ghost at that point, but I didn't. When I became a reporter with *Sports Illustrated* in 1970, I heard still more about the man *Sports Illustrated* called 'the most famous Black coach in America.' Finally, I decided to stop trying to run away from Gaither and take a look at what made him so famous—and ever present. The book, I hope, reveals what I found."

Curry also told of his youth in Alabama, and of his desires to succeed despite the disadvantages Southern Blacks faced during the 1950's and early 1960's: "I suspect a prime source of my motivation then was a desire to leave Alabama. Some of my earliest recollections were of seeing my mother, who worked as a domestic, being driven home in the back seat of a white woman's automobile, my being told to drink from 'colored' water fountains (I always drank 'white' water, I never did like 'colored' water), and white persons who purported to be ministers appearing on television to say that had God wanted the races to mix, he would have made all of us the same color. My parents taught me at an early age to be proud of my Blackness and I can at no time recall ever feeling Blacks were inferior to Whites. Deep down, perhaps as early as age 9, I kept telling myself: *I'm going to show you.*

"Of course, no one could have survived that era alone. Fortunately, my family, my extended family of neighbors and friends, along with a dozen teachers at the elementary and secondary level, were extremely supportive. My teachers always told me to prepare myself for the day when the South would no longer be segregated. 'You should be prepared when integration comes,' they would often say. Thus, at an early age I knew who I was and I knew what it would take to get ahead. I used segregation, as cruel as it was, as a positive factor in my life. I was determined not to let any system or anyone deter me from reaching my goals. The disadvantage of such an inhumane and unjust system, however, is that for every George Curry who has 'made it,' there are thousands of others whose aspirations and dreams were crushed by this vicious system."

* * *

CURRY, Thomas A. 1901(?)-1976

1901(?)—October 7, 1976; American author of more than one hundred twenty adventure stories. Recently, he had been writing articles on nature and conservation. He died in Norwalk, Conn. Obituaries: *New York Times,* October 9, 1976; *AB Bookman's Weekly,* November 15, 1976.

* * *

CURTIS, Patricia 1924-

PERSONAL: Born July 31, 1924, in Orange, N.J.; daughter of Harry A. (a chemical engineer) and Irene (Hall) Curtis; married William Palitz, 1948 (deceased); children: Wendy, Stephen. *Education:* University of Missouri, B.A., 1945. *Agent:* McIntosh & Otis, Inc., 475 Fifth Ave., New York, N.Y. 10017. *Office: Family Circle,* 488 Madison Ave., New York, N.Y. 10022.

CAREER: Fawcett Publications, New York City, editor, 1959-61; *House and Garden,* New York City, assistant managing editor, 1961-66; Cowles Book Co., New York City, senior editor, 1967-68; *This Week* (magazine), New York City, copy editor, 1969; *Family Circle,* New York City, copy director, 1970—. *Member:* American Society of Magazine Editors.

WRITINGS: The Breakfast and Brunch Book, Winter House, 1972; *Animal Doctors,* Delacorte, 1977; (editor) Barbara and Gideon Seaman, *Women and the Crisis in Sex Hormones,* Rawson Associates, 1977. Contributor to *College Management* and to popular magazines, including *Family Circle, House and Garden, Cue,* and *Pageant.*

WORK IN PROGRESS: Another book on animals, for Delacorte.

SIDELIGHTS: Patricia Curtis writes briefly: "I have had a

rich career as an editor in magazine and book publishing, especially in the women's magazine field. My main current interests are feminism and humane treatment of animals.''

*   *   *

CUSACK, Michael J(oseph) 1928-
(Samuel F. O'Gorman)

PERSONAL: Born June 27, 1928, in Cork, Ireland; came to the United States in 1947, naturalized citizen, 1954; son of Samuel F. (in hardware business) and Ellen (O'Gorman) Cusack; married Anne E. Longstreet (a writer), September 3, 1966; children: Deborah, Deirdre, Jennifer. *Education:* Attended Columbia University, 1949-50, and Fairleigh Dickinson University, 1955-58. *Religion:* "Not sure." *Home:* 560-4 Main St., North Roosevelt Island, New York, N.Y. 10044. *Office:* Scholastic Magazines, Inc., 50 West 44th St., New York, N.Y. 10036.

CAREER: General Precision, Inc., Little Falls, N.J., editor of external house organs, 1957-67; Scholastic Magazines, Inc., New York, N.Y., associate editor of *Science World*, 1967-76, editor, 1976—. *Military service:* U.S. Air Force, 1950-54.

WRITINGS: Is There a Bermuda Triangle?, Messner, 1976; (with wife, Anne Cusack) *How Sensitive Are Plants?*, Messner, 1977. Author of filmstrip scripts for "Human Issues in Science." Contributor to *Funk & Wagnall Encyclopedia Year Book* and *Grolier Encyclopedia Year Book*. Contributor of about two hundred articles, sometimes under pseudonym Samuel F. O'Gorman, to *Science World*.

WORK IN PROGRESS: Biographies of Giordano Bruno, Samuel F. Cody, and Dame Kathleen Lonsdale; science mystery books.

SIDELIGHTS: Cusack writes that his main concern is ethical considerations of technological developments, particularly "social costs of certain developments viewed from a global perspective; considerations of the allocation of limited resources, particularly in health care; and should certain types of research, such as recombinant DNA, be restricted?"

AVOCATIONAL INTERESTS: Travel, archaeology, philately, old maps, and European history primarily of the medieval period.

*   *   *

CUSICK, Philip A. 1937-

PERSONAL: Born September 16, 1937, in Elmira, N.Y.; son of John F. (a salesman) and Agnes K. Cusick; married wife, Georganne, October, 1973; children: Greg, Jean, Philip. *Education:* John Carroll University, A.B., 1959; Elmira College, M.S., 1965; Syracuse University, Ph.D., 1970. *Politics:* Democrat. *Religion:* Roman Catholic. *Office:* 409 Erickson Hall, Michigan State University, East Lansing, Mich. 48824.

CAREER: Michigan State University, East Lansing, professor of education, 1970—.

WRITINGS: Inside High School, Holt, 1973.

*   *   *

DABNEY, Dick 1933-

PERSONAL: Born October 26, 1933, in Charlottesville, Va.; son of Wythe Overton, Jr. (a lawyer) and Reba (a government executive; maiden name, Lawson) Dabney; married Paige Pentecost, December 10, 1962 (divorced August

5, 1969); married Dana Elisabeth Trice (an artist), August 9, 1969; children: Vaden, John, Norah. *Education:* Attended University of Virginia, 1951-53, and Davidson College, 1954; American University, B.A., 1966, M.A., 1968; George Washington University, Ph.D., 1971. *Religion:* Evangelical Christian. *Home and office:* 4638 North 23rd St., Arlington, Va. 22207. *Agent:* Scott Meredith Literary Agency, Inc., 845 Third Ave., New York, N.Y. 10022.

CAREER: American University, Washington, D.C., researcher and editor for Center for Research in Social Systems, 1965-68; George Washington University, Washington, D.C., instructor in American literature, 1969-72; American University, visiting assistant professor of American civilization, 1971-73, visiting associate professor of literature, 1976-77. *Awards, honors:* Award from National Endowment for the Arts, 1974, for *The Honor System*.

WRITINGS: Someone to Talk To (short stories), Varlet Press, 1965; *Old Man Jim's Book of Knowledge* (novel), Random House, 1973; *A Good Man: The Life of Sam Ervin*, Houghton, 1976; *The Honor System* (novel), Harper, 1976. Author of monthly column "Side Streets" in *Washingtonian*, 1976-77.

WORK IN PROGRESS: American Suckers, a novel based on the Duke family, for Putnam.

SIDELIGHTS: Dabney writes: "I am first and last a Christian, although it would be hard to tell it from my books thus far, because I am writing for a secular humanist society and am not cut out to be a preacher. It's ironic, because some of my books, including both novels thus far, are said to be savage and bleak and utterly without hope. But I am not without hope."

*   *   *

DACHS, David 1922-
(Dave Stanley)

PERSONAL: Born January 23, 1922, in Brooklyn, N.Y.; son of Morris (a garment worker) and Ethel (a dress shop owner; maiden name, Krieg) Dachs; married Julie Mandel (a songwriter), June, 1951; children: Joshua. *Education:* Attended City College (now of the City University of New York), 1941. *Politics:* Independent. *Home and office:* 6923 Loubet St., Forest Hills, N.Y. 11375.

CAREER: Broadcast Music Inc. (BMI), New York City, radio scriptwriter, 1954-55; feature writer for North American Newspaper Alliance (NANA), 1957-58; Pope Publications, New York City, reporter for *Drug and Cosmetic Industry* and *Beauty Fashion* magazines, 1959-60; Caedmon Records, New York City, director of public relations, 1961-64; American Guild of Authors and Composers (AGAC), New York City, director of public relations, 1965-68; writer, 1968—. Free-lance publicist. *Member:* American Guild of Authors and Composers, National Academy of Recording Arts and Sciences.

WRITINGS: Straw Hat: Guide to Summer Theatres, Musical Tents, and Shakespeare Festivals, Frank Productions, 1957; *Anything Goes: The World of Popular Music*, Bobbs-Merrill, 1964; *Inside Pop*, Scholastic Book Services, 1968; *American Pop*, Scholastic Book Services, Book I, 1969, Book II, 1970; *Pop/Rock Question and Answer Book*, Scholastic Book Services, 1971; *Encyclopedia of Pop and Rock*, Scholastic Book Services, 1972; *TV's Top Comedians* (profiles and notes), Scholastic Book Services, 1973; *Tops in TV* (portraits of television personalities), Grosset & Dunlap, 1974; *John Denver* (biography), Pyramid Books, 1976.

Under pseudonym Dave Stanley: (With Jack Gaver) *There's Laughter in the Air* (comedy radio anthology), Greenberg, 1945; *A Treasury of Sports Humor* (short stories and essays), Lantern Press, 1946; (with George Ross) *The Golfer's Own Book* (essays and articles), Lantern Press, 1955.

Also author of books for several unproduced musicals, including "Miss Seedless Raisin" and "Expense Account." Contributor to magazines, including *Saturday Review, Redbook, Saga, High Fidelity, Down Beat, Family Weekly,* and *Variety.*

WORK IN PROGRESS: A contemporary satirical novel; the books for two musicals.

SIDELIGHTS: Dachs told *CA* he has an "ambivalent love-hate relationship with pop culture. I enjoy pop music (mostly show music and jazz), theatre, comedy (on TV, movies, theatre). I'm concerned with cultural impact of pop and how mass taste is manipulated. Having been a press agent, I know how cultural products are pushed. However, good products are also promoted by skillful PR as schlock (Bernstein records, the Met, good films) so taste and seasoning yardsticks become more crucial. My feelings find their way (sometimes) into my work, particularly in *Anything Goes: The World of Popular Music,* which I am quite proud of.

"As a publicist, reporter, scriptwriter, friend of songwriters, I've watched the pop music business closely. Since 1964, when *Anything Goes* was published, much has happened. New names are on the best-seller charts, there are softer sounds heard (John Denver, Neil Sedaka, Olivia Newton-John). There's less protest music. More foreign tours by U.S. pop people, notably in the U.S.S.R. And books and films have come out similar to 'A Star Is Born,' portraying the unlovely side of pop.

"However, new big talents are few, and the music machine goes on its way: 1) There's too much hype; 2) too many records and the over-production is glutting warehouses; 3) pop music coverage that is an extension of PR, or pretentious super-serious puffery with little critical analysis; 4) formula radio that misshapes the taste of millions by heavy airplay of junk music; 5) vast overpraising of Elton John, Bob Dylan, Paul Simon, Carole King, Neil Sedaka, Barry Manilow, who are weak musically, although lyrically some of them are superior in choice of imagery and theme; 6) concert audiences are getting more unruly and indulge in vandalism.

"About hype: PR is a neutral tool used to sell everything from politicians to pop. It can sell the Met, good films, as well as schlock. But it can be particularly powerful in pop because most of the record-buyers and those who go to pop concerts (the life-support system of the music business) are 11-18, the impressionable years.

"Call it hype, call it legitimate public relations, call it taste manipulation—today's pop is full of it—and there's more of it than ever before. With so much money to be made on records, on concerts, and from TV, the battle for mere exposure grows more fierce. Consequently more press agents are hired, more full-page ads are taken in pop-minded media (*Rolling Stone, The Village Voice,* etc.). Specialists in disc jockey promotion criss-cross the land daily seeking airplay. Payola is not unknown either, as government trials in Newark, N.J. have shown.

"While hype cannot create pop stars and groups automatically (groups promoted lavishly often fail) hype leaves an imprint. People's critical faculties are softened up. Generally speaking more dollars are spent on what is commercial than what is creative.

"One of the biggest villains in my songbook is formula radio where hits and popstars are made. In its pursuit of profit, radio stations pick an audience target, and then tailor an approach. Often this leads to musical segregation: stations playing one kind of music, hard-rock, soft rock, middle of the road, country music, classical music, or Top 40 (which is based on *Billboard* charts or *Record World* charts, plus samplings of record shop sales).

"A good station should play a little of everything—show music (Broadway and Hollywood musicals), jazz, rock and roll, country, contemporary folk, Tin Pan Alley, middle of the road. Where are the stations of this sort? Practically nonexistent. So the pop audience, mostly young people, are push-overs for the latest hype-sensation, since they have little musical knowledge of the great traditions of popular music. Their ears, minds, and tastes are programmed by the stations they listen to, to a certain sound.

"Ask the average teen record buyer if he knows the works of Gershwin ('Who's he?'), Richard Rodgers, Stephen Sondheim, Burton Lane, E. Y. Harburg, Larry Hart, Frank Loesser, Irving Berlin, Fats Waller, Duke Ellington, Harold Arlen. You'll get a glazed look. Most kids today do not know their musical 'roots.'

"Millions of poor teen-agers are being hurt by the airwaves (ostensibly owned by the people) as are the adults. Adults who enjoy jazz, swing, the big bands, and Broadway theatre music can't abide much of today's pop. There are those in the record business who recognize this.

"About cultural impact: Pop is the most pervasive cultural force among young people. It influences what music they listen to, as well as manners, fashions, speech, courtship, sexual behaviour. It is unmistakably true that certain pop figures and groups have popularized and glamourized the taking of hard and soft drugs.

"Pop is also getting increasingly sexual with blue lyrics, lp's of girls experiencing an orgasm, and songs like 'The More You Do It,' 'It's All Right To Make Love on the First Night,' and 'Shake Your Body.' Reverend Jesse Jackson traces the rise in illegitimate births and abortions to milieu fashioned by pop.

"Of course, the picture isn't all bleak. A lot of material today is less dreamy, more realistic. There are songs celebrating brotherhood, the joys of nature, the processes of growing up. Protest songs aren't banned. There's more black music on, but a lot of 'soul' is monotonous, repetitious, and sugared-up, typical of the worst of Tin Pan Alley of yesteryear. (Incidentally, a lot of black-oriented stations will not play white artists.) And on the positive side, too, there are fine songs that do come along such as 'Feelings,' and good story-songs such as Harry Chapin's portrait of a high-intensity disc jockey, called 'W O L D.'"

AVOCATIONAL INTERESTS: Pop culture, politics, travel, walking, and good talk with friends.

* * *

DAGG, Anne Innis 1933-

PERSONAL: Born January 25, 1933, in Toronto, Ontario, Canada; daughter of Harold Adams (a professor) and Mary (a writer; maiden name, Quayle) Innis; married Ian Ralph Dagg (a professor), August 22, 1957; children: Hugh Eric, Ian Innis, Mary Christine. *Education:* University of Toronto, B.A., 1955, M.A., 1956; University of Waterloo, Ph.D., 1967. *Home:* 81 Albert St., Waterloo, Ontario, Canada.

CAREER: Waterloo Lutheran University, Waterloo, Ontario, lecturer in biology, 1962-65; University of Guelph, Guelph, Ontario, assistant professor of zoology, 1967-72; free-lance biology writer and researcher, 1972—. Member: Canadian Society of Environmental Biologists (member of board of directors, 1977—), American Society of Mammalogy. Awards, honors: Named one of Canada's top female biologists, by the National Museums of Canada, 1975, for International Women's Year.

WRITINGS: (With C. A. Campbell) Mammals of Waterloo and South Wellington Counties, Otter Press, 1972; Canadian Wildlife and Man, McClelland & Stewart, 1974; Mammals of Ontario, Otter Press, 1974; (with J. B. Foster) The Giraffe: Its Biology, Behavior, and Ecology, Van Nostrand, 1976; Wildlife Management in Europe, Otter Press, 1977; Running, Walking, and Jumping: The Science of Locomotion, Taylor & Francis, 1977.

WORK IN PROGRESS: A scientific treatise on the camel in the northwest and western Sahara.

SIDELIGHTS: Anne Dagg writes: "The two driving forces in my life are to increase our knowledge of wildlife, both by doing basic research and by popularizing such work, and to help women scientists gain equality with male ones, an uphill task in Canada."

*   *   *

D'AGOSTINO, Joseph David 1929-

PERSONAL: Born May 30, 1929, in Garfield, N.J.; son of Anthony (a business owner) and Maria (Romeo) D'Agostino. Education: Attended Juilliard School. Home and office: 240 Midland Ave., Garfield, N.J. 07026.

CAREER: Musician and musical composer for the theatre. Member: American Society of Composers, Authors and Publishers (ASCAP), Dramatists Guild.

WRITINGS: Tarot: The Royal Path to Wisdom, Samuel Weiser, 1976.

Writer of musical compositions, including "Key to My Heart," "Withering Words," "Teach Me How to Dance," and "Baddest Kind of Blues."

WORK IN PROGRESS: A sequel to Tarot: The Royal Path to Wisdom, completion expected in 1978; a musical play centered around the controversial nineteenth-century mystic Madame Blavatsky.

SIDELIGHTS: D'Agostino writes: "I continue to pursue, through the study and practice of the mystical and the occult, the practical knowledge and inner enlightenment it offers to the undeviating student."

*   *   *

DAHLBERG, Edward 1900-1977

July 22, 1900—February 27, 1977; controversial American writer, poet, critic, and author of novels, beginning with Bottom Dogs (with an introduction by D. H. Lawrence), books of criticism, and autobiography. He wrote much about his start as an illegitimate son of a hairdresser and his years with American expatriate writers in Paris during the 1920's. Dahlberg died in Santa Barbara, Calif. Obituaries: New York Times, February 28, 1977; Washington Post, March 2, 1977; Time, March 14, 1977. (See index for previous CA sketch)

*   *   *

DAIN, Phyllis 1929-

PERSONAL: Born November 29, 1929, in New York, N.Y.; daughter of Jacob Louis (a wall paper hanger) and Bessie (Melofsky) Segal; married Norman Dain (a historian), March 10, 1950; children: Bruce Russell. Education: Brooklyn College (now Brooklyn College of the City University of New York), B.A., 1950; Columbia University, M.S., 1953, M.A., 1957, Doctor of Library Science, 1966. Home: 110 Crescent Ave., Leonia, N.J. 07605. Office: School of Library Service, Columbia University, New York, N.Y. 10027.

CAREER: Columbia University, New York City, university libraries, cataloger, 1953-55, senior cataloger, 1955-58, chief of medical cataloging section, 1958-60; School of Library Service, lecturer, 1960-66, assistant professor, 1966-71, associate professor, 1971-77, professor of library service, 1977—. Member of board of directors, New York City Mental Health Materials Center; member of board of trustees, Leonia Public Library.

MEMBER: American Library Association, American Historical Association, American Society for Information Science, American Civil Liberties Union, Freedom to Read Foundation, Women's National Book Association, New York Library Association, Phi Beta Kappa, Beta Phi Mu. Awards, honors: Columbia University School of Library Service Virgil Fuller Award; Council on Library Resources fellow, 1973-74; National Endowment for the Humanities research grant, 1973-74.

WRITINGS: The New York Public Library: A History of Its Founding and Early Years, New York Public Library, 1972. Contributor of articles and reviews to library science journals, including Library Quarterly, Library Journal, and College and Research Libraries. Member of editorial board for Journal of Library History.

WORK IN PROGRESS: A second volume of the history of the New York Public Library; co-editing article for Library Trends.

*   *   *

DALE, Edwin L., Jr. 1923-

PERSONAL: Born September 7, 1923, in Philadelphia, Pa.; son of Edwin L. (in the textile buisness) and Janet (Lord) Dale; married Mary Todd Hastings, March 11, 1952. Education: Yale University, B.A., 1944. Home: 4526 Lowell St. N.W., Washington, D.C. 20016. Office: New York Times, 1920 L St. N.W., Washington, D.C. 20036.

CAREER: Worcester Evening Gazette, Worcester, Mass., reporter and editorial writer, 1947-51; New York Herald Tribune, New York, N.Y., reporter at Washington bureau, 1951-55; New York Times, New York City, reporter at Washington bureau, 1955-60, European economic correspondent from Paris, 1960-63, reporter at Washington bureau, 1963—. Military service: U.S. Navy, 1944-46; became lieutenant junior grade. Member: National Press Club. Awards, honors: Loeb Award, 1963, for international economic reporting.

WRITINGS: Conservatives in Power, Doubleday, 1960; (editor) W. Howard, Contemporary Economics, Heath, 1972. Contributor to popular magazines, including New Republic, Harper's, Yale Review, Money, New York Times Magazine, and Economist.

SIDELIGHTS: Dale comments: "I have specialized in economic reporting for twenty-five years, all but three in Washington. I continue to be fascinated at the subject of government economic policy and its evolution. I enjoy daily journalism, with some opportunity for commentary in the

Times." *Avocational interests:* Golf, travel (almost entirely abroad).

* * *

DALY, Donald F(remont)

PERSONAL: Born in Montana; son of Charles F. (a contractor) and Annie L. (a teacher; maiden name, Johnson) Daly; married Clara E. Rawlins (a clerk typist), February 9, 1936. *Education:* Utilities Engineering Institute (Chicago), A.S., 1938; also pursued additional home study. *Politics:* Independent Democrat. *Religion:* Protestant. *Home:* 2113 21st St., Bakersfield, Calif. 93301.

CAREER: Worked in construction as apprentice, journeyman, supervisor, and application and test engineer; writer, 1943—. *Military service:* U.S. Navy, 1920-22. U.S. Merchant Marine, 1923-25. U.S. Coast Guard, 1931-33. *Member:* United Association of Plumbers and Steamfitters (chairman of local examining board, 1956-73).

WRITINGS: The Refrigeration Contractors Estimating Guide, Nickerson & Collins, 1948; *Know Your Union: A Guide to Jobs in the Building Trades,* Dorrance, 1964; *Aim for a Job in Air Conditioning and Refrigeration,* Richards Rosen, 1968, revised edition, 1970, paperback edition published as *Your Future in Air Conditioning and Refrigeration,* Arco, 1971, revised edition, 1974; *Aim for a Job in the Pipe Trades,* Richards Rosen, 1969, revised edition, 1971; *Aim for a Job in the Building Trades,* Richards Rosen, 1970, revised edition, 1972; *Indirections for Vocational Technical Education,* privately printed, 1973. Contributor to *Science of Mind* magazine, *Consumer Bulletin, Appliance Service News,* and other magazines.

WORK IN PROGRESS: Working toward a better understanding between labor/management sponsored apprentice training programs and equivalent programs in public and private educational agencies.

SIDELIGHTS: Daly writes: "My own early efforts to prepare for a rewarding career, plus the fact that much vocational education and trade-technical education is of little value has been my chief motivation. Both apprentice training and vocational education have improved, somewhat, but still have a long way to go if they are to serve the best interest of students who hope for a career in this area."

* * *

DALY, John Jay 1888(?)-1976

1888(?)—December 16, 1976; American journalist, poet, and author. Daly was a newspaper reporter and editor from 1911 to the mid-1940's. He wrote his most famous work, a poem called "A Toast to the Flag" in 1917. He wrote articles for many magazines; he also wrote several books. Daly died in Washington, D.C. Obituaries: *Washington Post,* December 18, 1976.

* * *

DAM, Kenneth W. 1932-

PERSONAL: Born August 10, 1932, in Marysville, Kan.; son of Oliver W. (a farmer) and Ida (Heupplesheuser) Dam; married Marcia Wachs (a college professor), June 7, 1962; children: Eliot. *Education:* University of Kansas, B.S., 1954; University of Chicago, J.D., 1957. *Home:* 5609 South Kenwood Ave., Chicago, Ill. 60637. *Office:* School of Law, University of Chicago, 1121 East 60th St., Chicago, Ill. 60637.

CAREER: U.S. Supreme Court, Washington, D.C., law clerk, 1957-58; Cravath, Swaine & Moore (law firm), New York, N.Y., associate, 1958-60; University of Chicago, Chicago, Ill., visiting assistant professor, 1960-61, associate professor, 1961-64, professor of law, 1964-71; U.S. Office of Management and the Budget, Washington, D.C., assistant director, 1971-73; U.S. Council on Economic Policy, Washington, D.C., executive director, 1973; University of Chicago, professor of law, 1974-76, Harold J. and Marion F. Green Professor of Law, 1976—. *Member:* American Law Institute.

WRITINGS: (With Lawrence Krause) *The Treatment of Foreign Income,* Brookings Institution, 1964; *The GATT: Law and International Economic Organization,* University of Chicago Press, 1970; *Oil Resources: Who Gets What How?,* University of Chicago Press, 1976; (with George P. Shultz) *Economic Policy Beyond the Headlines,* Stanford Alumni Association, 1977. Contributor to law journals.

SIDELIGHTS: Dam writes that he is "interested in the borderline between the legal system and the economic system." His area of expertise is international economy.

* * *

D'AMATO, Barbara 1938-

PERSONAL: Born April 10, 1938, in Grand Rapids, Mich.; daughter of Harold (a department store owner) and Yvonne (Watson) Steketee; married Anthony D'Amato (a law professor), September 4, 1958; children: Brian, Paul. *Education:* Cornell University, 1956-58; Northwestern University, B.A., 1972, M.A., 1973. *Home:* 716 Greenwood, Glencoe, Ill. 60022. *Agent:* Roger Parson, 800 Third Ave., New York, N.Y. 10022.

CAREER: Writer, 1973—. *Member:* Phi Beta Kappa.

WRITINGS—Plays: "The Magic Man" (two-act), first performed in Chicago, Ill., at First Chicago Center, November, 1974; "The Magic of Young Houdini" (two-act), first performed in Niles, Ill., at Mill Run Theater, December, 1975.

Contributor of articles to *Journal of Personality and Social Psychology.*

WORK IN PROGRESS: A series of detective novels.

AVOCATIONAL INTERESTS: Furniture making and wood carving.

* * *

DANCE, S(tanley) Peter 1932-

PERSONAL: Born February 3, 1932, in Maidenhead, Berkshire, England; son of Stanley and Elsie Rose (Coleman) Dance; married Una Hearne; children: Robert Alexander, Philip Russell. *Education:* Attended school in Maidenhead, England. *Politics:* "No strong political affiliations." *Religion:* Church of England. *Home and office:* Priory Hall, Priory Wood, Clifford, Hereford HR3 5HF, England.

CAREER: British Railways Stock Registration Office, London, England, clerk, 1948-50; door-to-door salesman, Waverley Book Co., 1956; British Museum (Natural History), London, zoologist, 1957-66; zoologist at Manchester Museum, 1966-68; National Museum of Wales, Cardiff, zoologist, 1968-72; Richard Booth (bookseller), Hay-on-Wye, England, bookseller, 1972-74; writer, 1974—. Co-owner of Arvona Gallery (art gallery), Hay-on-Wye. *Military service:* Royal Air Force, 1950-55. *Member:* Society for the Bibliography of Natural History, Conchological Society of Great

Britain and Ireland, British Shell Collectors Club, Woolhope Naturalists Club.

WRITINGS: Shell Collecting: An Illustrated History, Stanford University Press, 1966; *Rare Shells,* Stanford University Press, 1969; *Sea Shells,* Paul Hamlyn, 1971, Grosset, 1973; *Shells and Shell Collecting,* Paul Hamlyn, 1972, Bantam, 1974; *The Collector's Encyclopedia of Shells,* McGraw, 1974; *The World's Shells,* McGraw, 1976 (published in England as *The Shell Collector's Guide,* David & Charles, 1976): *Animal Fakes and Frauds,* Low, 1976. Contributor of about fifty articles to scientific and popular magazines.

WORK IN PROGRESS: Animal Art; a biography of W. H. Hudson; a book on seashell identification.

SIDELIGHTS: Dance writes: "My scientific background has given me an approach to writing which has made it difficult to relax into an easy-going popular style, but my books, aimed at a wide audience, have sold well. My interests are very broad and cover subjects in the natural sciences and the arts. As well as nonfiction, I have tried poetry, rather vapid nature writings (none offered or thought fit for publication), and humorous writing. I have an ambivalent attitude toward science and the fine arts. The charlatanry, selfishness, and pettiness I have observed in both spheres is only partially offset by the disinterested search for truth and personal expression I have also observed. I hope to write a book—fictional probably—on these observations."

*   *   *

DANENBERG, Leigh   1893-1976

September 23, 1893—December 3, 1976; American publisher. He died in Westport, Conn. Obituaries: *New York Times,* December 4, 1976.

*   *   *

DANIEL, James   1916-

PERSONAL: Born June 6, 1916, in Davidson County, N.C.; son of James Manly (an attorney) and Bert (Fletcher) Daniel; married Ramona Teijeiro, April 15, 1939; children: Jane (Mrs. John Nagy), Nina (Mrs. Mark Ritts). *Education:* University of North Carolina at Chapel Hill, A.B., 1937; graduate study, Harvard University, 1942-43. *Home:* 183 Good Hill Rd., Weston, Conn. 06883. *Agent:* Thomas Lowry Associates, 156 West 86th St., New York, N.Y. 10024.

CAREER: Raleigh News & Observer, Raleigh, N.C., reporter, 1937-40; *Washington Daily News,* Washington, D.C., feature writer, 1941, city editor, 1946-47; Office of War Information, Washington, D.C., staff member, 1943-45; Scripps-Howard Papers, New York, N.Y., Washington correspondent, 1948-56; *Time,* New York City, associate editor, 1957-60; *Reader's Digest,* Pleasantville, N.Y., roving editor, 1961—. First selectman, Weston, Conn., 1967-69; president, Aspetuck Land Trust, Fairfield County, Conn. *Member:* National Press Club, Harvard Club. *Awards, honors:* Nieman fellow, 1942-43.

WRITINGS: (Editor) *Private Investment: The Key to International Industrial Development,* McGraw, 1958; (with John G. Hubbell) *Strike in the West,* Holt, 1963; *Rural Violence in Columbia Since 1946,* Princeton University, 1964.

WORK IN PROGRESS: Articles for *Reader's Digest.*

SIDELIGHTS: Daniel told *CA:* "I have done a great deal of work on money, economics and business, also on educa-

tion, travel and art. I have no preference as to subject matter. I believe there are two basic problems: content and form. I distrust formulas for writing that palm off slick readable pieces without a thought in them. On the other hand, I know the public's attention span is limited. But I am not happy unless the content meets my own standard. I think commercial writing today must be understandable to the masses but have insights for experts as well."

*   *   *

DANK, Milton   1920-

PERSONAL: Born September 12, 1920, in Philadelphia, Pa.; son of Charles (a barber) and Olga (Olessker) Dank; married Naomi Rand (a hospital administrator), March 18, 1954; children: Gloria, Joan. *Education:* University of Pennsylvania, B.A., 1947, Ph.D., 1953. *Politics:* "Unenthusiastic Democrat." *Religion:* "Diabolist (lapsed)." *Home:* 1022 Serpentine Ln., Wyncote, Pa. 19095.

CAREER: Owens-Illinois Glass, Toledo, Ohio, research physicist, 1953-56; General Electric (Aerospace), King of Prussia, Pa., research manager, 1958-72; research consultant in thermonuclear fusion power, laser applications, and space vehicle vulnerability, 1972—. *Military service:* U.S. Air Force, 1940-45; became first lieutenant. *Member:* American Physical Society, National Association of World War II Glider Pilots.

WRITINGS: The French Against the French, Lippincott, 1974; *The Glider Gang,* Lippincott, 1977; *The Dangerous Game,* Lippincott, 1977.

WORK IN PROGRESS: A narrative history on the civil population of Europe during World War II.

SIDELIGHTS: Dank told *CA:* "My books are all derived from my wartime experiences. *The French Against the French* and *The Dangerous Game* were based on my study of the behavior of the French under the German occupation. As squadron translator and liaison officer, I found the French civilians most reluctant to talk of the fifty months during which the Nazis occupied France.

"The Glider Gang is a tribute to the Allied glider pilots, my comrades-in-arm. They flew in fragile canvas and wood motorless craft at low altitudes over enemy guns, and brought in jeeps, howitzers and antitank guns to the paratroopers. Their casualties were high, as much from poor planning and faulty intelligence as from enemy resistance. They wore no parachutes because their passengers wore none. I thought it was wrong that their story should go untold.

"In my fourth book, I am going back to the theme that fascinated me while researching my first book: the permissible limits of collaboration under a foreign military occupation."

*   *   *

DANKY, James Philip   1947-

PERSONAL: Born October 3, 1947, in Los Angeles, Calif.; son of Philip Harper (a probation officer) and Elizabeth (an elementary school principal; maiden name, James) Danky; married Pamela Anne Johnson, May 6, 1969 (divorced August 20, 1974). *Education:* Ripon College, A.B., 1970; University of Wisconsin, Madison, M.A.L.S., 1973. *Religion:* None. *Residence:* Fort Atkinson, Wis. *Office:* State Historical Society of Wisconsin, 816 State St., Madison, Wis. 53706.

CAREER: Department of Public Social Services of Los

Angeles County, Los Angeles, Calif., welfare clerk, 1970-71; Department of Social Services of Jefferson County, Jefferson, Wis., social worker, 1971-72; State Historical Society of Wisconsin, Madison, order librarian, 1973-76, newspapers and periodicals librarian, 1976—. *Member:* American Library Association, American Historical Association, State Historical Society of Wisconsin.

WRITINGS: Undergrounds: A Union List of Alternative Periodicals in Libraries of the United States and Canada, State Historical Society of Wisconsin, 1974; (editor with Eleanor McKay) *Women's History: Resources of the State Historical Society of Wisconsin,* State Historical Society of Wisconsin, 1975, 2nd edition, 1976; *Book Publishing in Wisconsin* (proceedings), Library School, University of Wisconsin, Madison, 1977. Author of column "Alternative Periodicals" in *Wilson Library Bulletin,* 1975—; co-editor of column "Wisconsin History Checklist" in *Wisconsin Magazine of History,* 1973-74, 1976-77. Editor of *Collectors' Network News,* 1977—.

WORK IN PROGRESS: A History of Western Publishing Company, completion expected in 1980; a group of essays "on the place/value of alternative literature in libraries."

SIDELIGHTS: Danky writes: "In writing and editing, my emphasis has been to create works that are useful in promoting an alternative or progressive view of American society. To the degree that these goals are met, the writings are successful." *Avocational interests:* Raising pigs, making cider, tending "a large garden on a small farm."

* * *

D'ARCY, Martin C(yril)   1888-1976

June 15, 1888—November 20, 1976; British Jesuit Roman Catholic priest credited to have converted well-known writers and intellectuals, including Dame Edith Sitwell and Evelyn Waugh, lecturer, and author of philosophical and religious works. He served as provincial superior of the British Jesuits (1945-50). D'Arcy died in London, England. *Obituaries: New York Times,* November 22, 1976; *Current Biography,* March, 1977. (See index for previous *CA* sketch)

* * *

DARDIG, Jill C(arolyn)   1948-

PERSONAL: Born November 13, 1948, in New York, N.Y.; daughter of Ben V. and Evelyn (Shapiro) Dardig; married William L. Heward (a college professor), August 21, 1976. *Education:* Mount Holyoke College, A.B., 1969; University of Massachusetts, M.Ed., 1971, Ed.D., 1974. *Home:* 1094 F Fountain Lane, Columbus, Ohio 43213. *Office:* Office of Habilitation Services, Room 1236, State Office Tower, 30 East Broad St., Columbus, Ohio 43215.

CAREER: Northeast Regional Media Center for the Deaf, Amherst, Mass., research assistant, 1970-74; Russell Sage College, Troy, N.Y., assistant professor of education, 1974-76; Office of Habilitation Services, Ohio Division of Mental Retardation and Developmental Disabilities, Columbus, Ohio, curriculum development specialist, 1976—. *Member:* American Association on Mental Deficiency, Council for Exceptional Children, Midwest Association of Behavior Analysis.

WRITINGS: (With husband, William L. Heward) *Sign Here: A Contracting Book for Children and Their Parents,* with leader's guide, Behaviordelia, 1976. Contributor to education journals.

WORK IN PROGRESS: Parenting the Exceptional Child

(tentative title), with husband, William L. Heward, and Allison Rossett, publication by Behaviordelia expected in 1978.

* * *

DAVAR, Ashok

PERSONAL: Born in Gwalior, India. *Education:* Graduate study at University of Pennsylvania and University of Nebraska. *Office address:* P.O. Box 2257, Philadelphia, Pa. 19103.

CAREER: Has worked as an illustrator, writer, architect, philosopher, and self-employed architectural consultant. *Awards, honors:* Rotary International fellowship, 1968.

WRITINGS: A Book of Elephants, Eriksson, 1969; *God Is,* Eriksson, 1969; *Talking Words* (juvenile), Bobbs-Merrill, 1969; *The Flower and the Bee* (juvenile), National Book Trust (India), 1974; *Homage to Philadelphia* (drawings), Goldner, 1976; *The Kiss,* Theosophical Publishing, 1976; *The Wheel of King Asoka* (juvenile), Follett, 1977; *Joy of Reincarnation,* Theosophical Publishing, 1978.

WORK IN PROGRESS: The Subway System of the Mind, for Argus; a science fiction novel; short stories.

* * *

DAVIDSON, Rosalie   1921-

PERSONAL: Born July 25, 1921, in Paoli, Ind.; daughter of Roger Carl and Annabel (McIntosh) Davidson. *Education:* University of Louisville, student, 1939-41; University of Denver, B.A., 1948, M.A., 1950; University of California, San Diego, graduate study, 1970. *Home:* 6315 Connie Dr., San Diego, Calif. 92115. *Office:* San Diego Unified Schools, Grant School, 1425 Washington Pl., San Diego, Calif. 92103.

CAREER: Seagram's Distillery, Louisville, Ky., in quality laboratory, 1941-43; public school teacher in Denver, Colo., 1948-50; Grant School, San Diego, Calif., first grade teacher, 1950—. *Military service:* U.S. Navy, Women Accepted for Volunteer Emergency Service (WAVES), chief storekeeper, 1943-46. *Member:* National Science Association, Society of Children's Book Writers, National Education Association, California Teachers Association, San Diego Teachers Association.

WRITINGS—For children: *Dinosaurs: The Terrible Lizards,* Golden Gate, 1969; *When the Dinosaurs Disappeared,* Golden Gate, 1973. Contributor to *Grade Teacher.*

WORK IN PROGRESS: Tidepool Animals; Sea Dragons of Long Ago; Warm-Blooded Dinosaurs; a book on nutrition.

SIDELIGHTS: Rosalie Davidson writes: "I wanted to be a journalist, but observed a first grade class in Denver, fell in love with the children, and went back to school to get a degree in education. I taught a third grade summer class of boys who were poor readers. I asked them what they wanted to read about. They said 'Dinosaurs!' So I read about dinosaurs—told them each day what I'd read. . . . We each wrote our own dinosaur book! I feel that many science books talk down to primary children, or try to entertain them with funny things. Children want to know the *facts,* that's entertainment enough for them. I have worked with children for twenty-nine years. I understand their reading vocabulary, their interests and the importance of helping them develop accurate concepts."

AVOCATIONAL INTERESTS: Collecting books on western Americana, natural history.

DAVIES, A(lfred) Mervyn 1899-1976

November 20, 1899—December 23, 1976; British-born freelance writer, long-time confidential secretary to Joseph Pulitzer, editor and publisher of *St. Louis Post-Dispatch*, and author of biographical works. He died at his home in Wilton, Conn. Obituaries: *New York Times*, December 25, 1976. (See index for previous *CA* sketch)

*   *   *

DAVIES, John Gordon 1919-

PERSONAL: Born April 20, 1919, in Chester, England; son of Arthur Gordon (a wine merchant) and Elsie Elizabeth Mary (a school teacher; maiden name, Speakman) Davies; married Emily Mary Tordoff (a researcher), January 27, 1945; children: Elizabeth Jane, Sally Claire Davies Skilbeck, Arthur Mark. *Education:* Christ Church, Oxford, B.A., 1942, M.A., 1945, B.D., 1946, D.D., 1956; Westcott House, Cambridge, graduate study, 1942-43; University of Birmingham, M.A., 1952. *Home:* 28 George Rd., Birmingham B15 1PJ, England. *Office:* Department of Theology, University of Birmingham, Birmingham B15 2TT, England.

CAREER: Curate of Church of England in Rotherhithe, England, 1942-48; University of Birmingham, Birmingham, England, assistant lecturer, 1948-50, lecturer, 1950-57, senior lecturer, 1957-59, reader, 1959-60, Edward Cadbury Professor of Theology and head of department, 1960—, director of Institute for the Study of Worship and Religious Architecture, 1962—, dean of faculty of arts, 1967-70. Bampton Lecturer at Oxford University, 1958. Hereditary freeman of the City of Chester.

MEMBER: Society for the Study of Theology, Ancient and Worshipful Company of Skinners and Felt Makers, Studiorum Novi Testamenti Societas, Guild for Religious Architecture (United States; honorary member). *Awards, honors:* Named honorary canon of Birmingham Cathedral, 1965; Conover Memorial Award, 1967, for *Guide for Religious Architecture;* D.D. from University of St. Andrews, 1968.

WRITINGS: The Theology of William Blake, Clarendon Press, 1948, Archon Books, 1966; *The Origin and Development of Early Christian Church Architecture,* S.C.M. Press, 1952, Philosophical Library, 1953; *Daily Life in the Early Church: Studies in the Church Social History of the First Five Centuries,* Lutterworth, 1952; *Daily Life of Early Christians,* Duell, Sloan & Pearce, 1953; *Social Life of Early Christians,* Lutterworth, 1954; *The Spirit, the Church and the Sacraments,* Faith Press, 1954; *He Ascended into Heaven: A Study in the History of Doctrine,* Lutterworth, 1958, Association Press, 1959; *Members One of Another: Aspects of Koinonia,* Mowbray, 1958; (with Gilbert Cope and Donald A. Tytler) *An Experimental Liturgy,* John Knox, 1958.

The Making of the Church, Skeffington, 1960; *Intercommunion,* British Council of Churches, 1961; *The Architectural Setting of Baptism,* Barrie & Rockliff, 1962; *God's Will and Gift,* British Council of Churches, 1962; *Holy Week: A Short History,* John Knox, 1963; *The Early Christian Church,* Holt, 1965; *A Select Liturgical Lexicon,* John Knox, 1965; *Worship and Mission,* S.C.M. Press, 1966, Association Press, 1967; *Dialogue with the World,* S.C.M. Press, 1967; *The Early Christian Church,* Doubleday, 1967; *The Secular Use of Church Buildings,* Seabury, 1968; (editor) *A Dictionary of Liturgy and Worship,* Macmillan, 1972; *Every Day God: Encountering the Holy in World and Worship,* S.C.M. Press, 1973; (editor) *Worship and Dance,* Institute for the Study of Worship and Religious Architecture, University of Birmingham, 1975; *Christians, Politics, and Violent Revolution,* Orbis, 1976; *Looking to the Future: Prospects for Worship, Religious Architecture and Socio-Religious Studies,* Institute of the Study of Worship and Religious Architecture, University of Birmingham, 1976; *Playing Before the Lord: New Perspectives on Worship,* S.C.M. Press, 1977.

Translator: Oscar Cullmann and F. J. Leenhardt, *Essays on the Lord's Supper,* John Knox, 1958; Max Thurian, *The Eucharistic Memorial,* John Knox, Volume I, 1960, Volume II, 1961; Jacques Rossel, *Mission in a Dynamic Society,* S.C.M. Press, 1968.

Contributor: Basil Minchin, editor, *Becoming a Christian,* Faith Press, 1954; G. Henton Davis and Alan Richardson, editors, *The Teachers' Commentary,* S.C.M. Press, 1955; Cope, editor, *Making the Building Serve the Liturgy,* Mowbray, 1962; William Lockett, editor, *The Modern Architectural Setting of the Liturgy,* S.P.C.K., 1964; C. P. M. Jones, editor, *A Manual for Holy Week,* S.P.C.K., 1967; Robert L. Hunt, editor, *Revolution, Place and Symbol,* First International Congress on Architecture, Religion and the Visual Arts, 1969; Cope, editor, *Cathedral and Mission,* Institute for the Study of Worship and Religious Architecture, University of Birmingham, 1969; D. R. Dudley and D. M. Lang, editors, *Penguin Companion to Literature,* Volume IV: *Classical and Byzantine, Oriental and African,* Penguin, 1969; F. G. Healey, editor, *Preface to Christian Studies,* Lutterworth, 1971. Contributor to *The Concise Encyclopaedia of Living Faiths, Encyclopaedia Britannica,* and *A Dictionary of Christian Theology.* Contributor to scholarly journals.

SIDELIGHTS: Davies explained that his works fall into four main categories: thought and history of the early Church, worship, the history of architecture and worship, and contemporary theological issues, e.g. revolution. *Avocational interests:* Cooking.

*   *   *

DAVIS, Ann E(lizabeth) 1932-

PERSONAL: Born September 17, 1932, in Cleveland, Ohio; daughter of Bill (an electrician) and Ilona (a seamstress; maiden name, Nagy) Schwarcz; married Morton S. Davis (a regional corporate manager), October 20, 1956; children: William Keith, Steven Scott. *Education:* Ohio State University, B.A., 1954, Ph.D., 1971; University of Louisville, M.S.S.W., 1960; University of California, Los Angeles, further graduate study, 1965-66. *Politics:* Independent. *Religion:* Unitarian-Universalist. *Home:* 1460 Glosser Rd., Lebanon, Ohio 45036. *Office:* Department of Sociology and Anthropology, Miami University, 213 Harrison Hall, Oxford, Ohio 45056.

CAREER: Washington National Insurance, Evanston, Ill., saleswoman, 1954-56; Kentucky Department of Mental Health, Louisville, social worker, 1958-60; Ohio Psychiatric Institute, Columbus, in social work research, 1960-62; Covina Mental Health Center, Covina, Calif., counselor, 1965-66; Miami University, Oxford, Ohio, instructor, 1969-71, assistant professor, 1971-74, associate professor of sociology, 1974—. Adjunct associate professor of sociology at Wright State Medical School. Member of board of directors of Warren County Mental Health Services, 1976-77. Vice-president of Waynesville Parents Swim Team Association, 1975.

MEMBER: National Association of Social Workers, American Sociological Association, Association for Humanist Sociology (secretary-treasurer, 1976-77), North Central Sociological Association (secretary, 1977-80), Kent School Student Association (president, 1959), Kent School Alumni Association (president, 1961).

WRITINGS: (With Simon Dinitz and Benjamin Pasamanick) *Schizophrenics in the New Custodial Community: Five Years after the Experiment,* Ohio State University Press, 1974. Contributor to sociology and psychiatry journals.

WORK IN PROGRESS: Sociology Views Medicine, an introductory textbook; research on "an optimal fit between research and practice," on problems with professional careers, and on the relationship of personal biography to social theory.

SIDELIGHTS: Ann Davis writes: "My primary interest is in specifying the interface between personality and social structure and culture; to try and develop a workable quasi-predictive social theory. My background is analytically-oriented social work and academic training in sociology has enabled me to look at personality and structure as interactive. My primary motivation is to understand and then to convey this to the public.

"Themes and problems with which I am concerned are: the future of the family, emotional disturbance, and social arrangements as they affect adjustment, energy, objectivity and science, ethics and science.

"Thinkers who have influenced my views in the past include Freud, Marx, Sorokin, and Weber; I often integrate perspectives gained from their works. Most recently I've been interested in the writings of Habermas and Horkheimer from the Frankfort School of Sociological Thought.

"My family has had a vital impact upon my work; they constitute the 'warm place' from which I gain strength. Our farm in Ohio as well as home in the Florida Keys offer beautiful settings that allow retreats from the 'overly paced' system—these sources of human and natural beauty help me think from afar.

"In the near future I shall try my hand at novels and articles for the public. In many ways the dramatic can convey more about human existence than any empirical study—at least to a public who has little access to academician's works."

*   *   *

DAVIS, Elise Miller   1915-

PERSONAL: Born October 12, 1915, in Corsicana, Tex.; daughter of M. M. and Rachelle (Daniels) Miller; married Jay A. Davis, June 27, 1937 (died June 12, 1973); married Leo M. Davis, August 23, 1974; children: Rayna Miller (Mrs. Michael E. Loeb). *Education:* Attended University of Texas, 1930-31, and University of Oklahoma, 1938-40. *Residence:* Dallas, Tex. *Agent:* Paul R Reynolds, Inc., 12 East 41st St., New York, N.Y. 10017.

CAREER: Jay Davis, Inc., Amarillo, Tex., director and buyer, 1956-73; writer. *Member:* American Society of Journalists and Authors.

WRITINGS: The Answer Is God, McGraw, 1955, Pyramid Publications, 1973. Contributor to major national magazines, including *Reader's Digest.*

WORK IN PROGRESS: Articles for *Reader's Digest.*

SIDELIGHTS: Elise Davis writes: "*The Answer Is God* is the personal story of Dale Evans and Roy Rogers and the miracle that changed their lives. It is a glowing story of triumphant faith and hope. Roy and Dale have provided through their own lives a meaning, an understanding, and a shining inspiration to countless thousands throughout the world.

"My work has always displayed my interest in character with unshakable beliefs. I abandoned fiction for non-fiction because I wanted to tell my readers, 'This *did* happen,' not 'This *could* happen.' And when I was sent by *Reader's Digest* to undertake a story about the Roy Rogers family, I soon realized theirs was one of the great stories of our time. I felt, however, that it could never be properly told in a short article, that it had to be a book. Because the enormity hit me squarely—whatever happened in the hearts of this home could echo in homes all over the world.

"So I lived with the Rogerses, went with them on tour, and became almost a member of the family in order to write, for the first time, this story of their life together."

*   *   *

DAVIS, Hope Harding   1915(?)-1976

1915(?)—August 1, 1976; American artist and writer. She wrote for several magazines as well as being a screenwriter for MGM. She died in Lincolnville, Me. Obituaries: *New York Times,* August 18, 1976.

*   *   *

DAVIS, Lloyd (Moore)   1931-

PERSONAL: Born February 23, 1931, in Charleston, W.Va.; son of Lloyd M. and Eva (Simms) Davis; married Mary McIntosh, October 1, 1955 (divorced April 15, 1974); children: David, Owen, Jessica. *Education:* West Virginia University, A.B., 1953; Vanderbilt University, M.A., 1954; New York University, graduate study, 1956-59. *Residence:* Morgantown, W.Va. *Office:* Department of English, West Virginia University, Morgantown, W.Va. 26506.

CAREER: Presbyterian College, Clinton, S.C., instructor in English, 1954-55; Hartford Accident & Indemnity, New York, N.Y., underwriter, 1955-56; Hofstra University, Hempstead, N.Y., instructor in English, 1956-59; West Virginia University, Morgantown, instructor, 1959-67, assistant professor, 1967-74, associate professor of English, 1974—.

WRITINGS: Fishing the Lower Jackson (poems), Best Cellar, 1974; *Contemporary American Poetry: A Checklist,* Scarecrow, 1975.

Work anthologized in *This Book Is a Movie,* Delta, 1971; *Art Work: No Commercial Value,* Grossman, 1972. Contributor of poems to literary magazines, including *Ohio Review, Georgia Review, Foxfire, Pebble,* and *Poetry Now.* Editor of *Appalachian Review,* 1966-69.

WORK IN PROGRESS: A book of poems, mainly autobiographical, set in West Virginia.

SIDELIGHTS: Davis writes: "Emphasizing images and sounds, I try to write out of honest emotion and avoid the trickeries of rhetoric. My concern is for the few things of beauty remaining in a world made ugly, impersonal, and inhuman by technology."

*   *   *

DAVIS, Millard C.   1930-

PERSONAL: Born August 19, 1930, in Utica, N.Y.; son of A. Graham (a pediatrician) and H. Leah (Corkran) Davis; married Virginia Bierds, June 21, 1958; children: Millard P., Virginia E., Leah E., Richard G., Lynn Inga. *Education:*

Middlebury College, A.B., 1953; Cornell University, M.S. (entomology), 1958; University of Wisconsin, Madison, M.S. (journalism), 1970. *Politics:* Republican. *Religion:* Presbyterian. *Home:* 919 Edgemoor Rd., Cherry Hill, N.J. 08034. *Agent:* Fran Collin, Marie Rodell-Frances Collin Literary Agency, 141 East 55th St., New York, N.Y. 10022. *Office:* Solid Waste Advisory Council of Camden County, 2276 North 43rd St., Pennsauken, N.J. 08110.

CAREER: Biology teacher at private school in Blairstown, N.J., 1958-63; high school biology teacher in Alexandria, Va., 1966-69; U.S. Department of Agriculture, Soil Conservation Service, Madison, Wis., information specialist, 1969-70; National Science Teachers Association, Washington, D.C., editorial associate, 1970-71; coordinator of outdoor education for public schools in Pennington, N.J., 1972-73; high school teacher of ecology and botany in Willingboro, N.J., 1973-75; Burlington County College, Pemberton, N.J., assistant professor of English, 1976; Solid Waste Advisory Council of Camden County, Pennsauken, N.J., environmental planner, 1976—. Program director of Pennington's Nature Education Center at Washington Crossing State Park, summers, 1972-73. Instructor at Brookdale Community College, summer, 1975. *Military service:* U.S. Air Force, 1953-55.

MEMBER: American Nature Study Society (president, 1978-79), Audubon Wildlife Society (New Jersey; president, 1974-75), New Jersey Audubon Society (chairman of Extension Education for Southern New Jersey, 1974-75), Philadelphia Writers Conference (member of board of directors, 1976—), Sigma Xi, Gamma Alpha. *Awards, honors:* Scholarship to Breadloaf Writers Conference, 1959, summer, 1962; National Science Foundation grants, summers, 1959, 1960, 1963.

WRITINGS: The Near Woods, Knopf, 1974. Contributor of more than twenty-five articles to professional and conservation magazines. Associate editor of *Ranger Rick's Nature Magazine,* 1971-72.

WORK IN PROGRESS: Nature Notes; Garden Insects, completion expected in 1978; *Our House by the Sea,* 1978.

AVOCATIONAL INTERESTS: Travel (to natural areas), tennis, photography.

BIOGRAPHICAL/CRITICAL SOURCES: Interpreting Environmental Issues, University of Wisconsin Press, 1973.

*   *   *

DAVIS, Myrna (Mushkin)   1936-

PERSONAL: Born April 27, 1936, in New York; daughter of Herman and Sylvia (Optican) Mushkin; married Paul Davis (an artist); children: Matthew. *Education:* Barnard College, B.A., 1956. *Home address:* Rector St., Sag Harbor, N.Y. 11963.

CAREER: Woman's Home Companion, New York City, editorial assistant, 1956; Columbia Records, New York City, editor of house organ "Insight," 1957-58; George Nelson & Co., New York City, publicity writer, 1959-60; Push Pin Studios, Inc., New York City, editor, writer, and researcher, 1960-65; free-lance writer, 1964—. Member of board of trustees of Hampton Day School; co-chairman of Sag Harbor Preservation Commission, 1973-74.

WRITINGS: The Potato Book, Morrow, 1973. Contributor to *New York* and *Arts.* Editor of *Push Pin Graphic,* 1960-65.

WORK IN PROGRESS: Free-lance writing projects, with graphic designer, Milton Glaser; research and writing about the death of a young friend from anorexia nervosa.

SIDELIGHTS: Myrna Davis writes: "*The Potato Book* was a fund-raising project for my son's school which was (and is) housed in a former potato barn and among potato fields, so the subject seemed appropriate. My husband designed the book, and a few other parents and I laid it out and pasted up the type. We produced the first edition ourselves and sold three thousand copies. Then it was published in hard-cover by Morrow (using the original plates). . . . Since then I have done various free-lance projects and now that my parental duties are lessening I want to do a lengthier and more personal work." Her book has been published in German, Dutch, Italian, and Japanese.

*   *   *

DAVIS, Norman Maurice   1936-

PERSONAL: Born in 1936, in Philadelphia, Pa.; son of Milton B. and Esther P. Davis. *Education:* American University, B.A., 1958. *Politics:* "Some." *Religion:* "Some." *Office:* NMD Features, 4915 Chevy Chase Blvd., Chevy Chase, Md. 20015.

CAREER: Employee of NMD Features, Chevy Chase, Md. *Military service:* U.S. Navy, 1958-62.

MEMBER: Authors Guild of Authors League of America, American Numismatic Association, Numismatic Literary Guild, Baker Street Irregulars, Red Circle, Six Napoleons of Baltimore, Sherlock Holmes Society of London.

WRITINGS: The Complete Book of United States Coin Collecting, Macmillan, 1971, revised edition, 1976. Contributor to coin magazines and other journals, including *McCall's, Bowling,* and *Baker Street Journal.*

WORK IN PROGRESS: Books on coin collecting and other subjects.

*   *   *

DAVISON, Verne E(lbert)   1904-

PERSONAL: Born January 10, 1904, in Ashland, Kan.; son of George Elbert and Sibyl Inez (Van Laningham) Davison; married Mildred Lashley, April 25, 1923; children: Barbara Jean (Mrs. S. M. Craft), Meredith Verne. *Education:* Educated in high school in Wichita, Kan. *Politics:* Republican. *Religion:* Presbyterian. *Home:* 245 Marla Ave., Jackson, Miss. 39204.

CAREER: State Game Department, Ellis County, Okla., ranger and manager of game refuge, 1923-35; U.S. Department of Agriculture, Soil Conservation Service, Washington, D.C., soil, water, fisheries, and wildlife regional biologist in South Dakota, North Dakota, Wyoming, and Montana, 1935-37, in Virginia, North Carolina, South Carolina, Georgia, Florida, Alabama, Mississippi, Tennessee, Kentucky, Louisiana, and Arkansas, 1937-64, and in western states, 1964-69; writer and researcher, 1969—. Cattle rancher in Ellis County, Okla., 1921-35. Conducted research and demonstrations on the lesser prairie chicken, 1931-35. Fisheries research scientist for American Embassy, Burma, 1952; aquatic biologist for U.S. Department of State, 1952; fisheries specialist in South Vietnam, 1966.

MEMBER: Wildlife Society (charter member), Soil Conservation Society, National Audubon Society, National Wildlife Federation, American Ornithologists Union. *Awards, honors:* Conservation award from Nash Motors, 1954; outstanding performance award from Soil Conservation Service, 1958; superior service award from U.S. Department of Agriculture, 1959.

WRITINGS: Bobwhites on the Rise, Scribner, 1949; *Homemade Fishing,* Stackpole, 1953; *Attracting Birds: From the Prairies to the Atlantic,* Crowell, 1967. Contributor of about two hundred articles to technical and popular magazines.

WORK IN PROGRESS: Manuscripts "about myself, parents, grandparents, and earlier ancestors—each family and the times and accomplishments of record."

SIDELIGHTS: Davison writes: "I liked to try new methods, determine failures or successes by comparison. Wildlife, fishponds, and landuse related to conservation and management were my forte, my delightful interests. I felt that whatever I learned worthy of use by others, demanded publication. Futhermore, I always found it very helpful to draft the article to see what further studies would be necessary to assure its dependability. I wrote simply."

BIOGRAPHICAL/CRITICAL SOURCES: Our Ellis County Heritage, Ellis County Historical Society, 1974.

* * *

DAWE, (Donald) Bruce 1930-

PERSONAL: Born February 15, 1930, in Geelong, Australia; son of Alfred (a laborer) and Mary Ann (Hamilton) Dawe; married Gloria Desley, January 1, 1964; children: Brian, Jamie, Katrina, Melissa. *Education:* University of Queensland, B.A., 1969, M.A., 1975; University of New England, Litt. B., 1973. *Religion:* Roman Catholic. *Home:* 30 Cummings St., Toowoomba, Queensland, Australia. 4350. *Office:* School of Arts, Institute of Advanced Education, Darling Heights, Toowoomba, Queensland, Australia. 4350.

CAREER: Has worked as a laborer, postman, gardener; Institute of Advanced Education, Toowoomba, Australia, lecturer in literature, 1971—. *Military service:* Royal Australian Air Force, 1959-68; became sergenat. *Awards, honors:* Myer Award for poetry, 1966, for *A Need of Similiar Name,* and, 1969, for *An Eye for a Tooth*; Ampol Arts Award for Creative Literature, 1967; Dame Mary Gilmore Medal, 1971, for *Condolences of the Season.*

*WRITINGS—*Poems: *No Fixed Address,* Cheshire (Melbourne), 1962; *A Need of Similiar Name,* Cheshire, 1965; *An Eye for a Tooth,* Cheshire, 1968; *Beyond the Subdivision,* Cheshire, 1969; *Heat-Wave,* Sweeny Reed (Melbourne), 1970; *Condolences of the Season,* Cheshire, 1971; *Bruce Dawe Reads from His Own Work,* University of Queensland Press, 1971.

WORK IN PROGRESS: A Ph.D. thesis on Graham Greene's collected works.

SIDELIGHTS: Dawe writes: "One of the reasons why the use of various verse forms may help me to capture something of the evanescence of the contemporary Australian idiom is that the use of various traditional rhyme-forms and some metrical regularity together with elements of the contemporary scene and idiom provide a 'mix' of past and present in an acceptable form overall."

In response to *CA*'s question as to how he chose the dramatic monologue as one of his major poetic forms, Dawe said: "I never *consciously* chose the dramatic monologue form—it just occurred as a form frequently enough to confirm its possibilities. I am sure this is the general way things happen—forms choose us."

"Regional poetry," Dawe continued, "is not (as in the United States) a very obvious and characteristic kind of po-

etry here, Australian society being culturally and linguistically far more homogeneous than American—urban and rural are the significant 'regions' rather than Southwest, West, Midwest, East, etc. This is one of our greatest losses, I feel, artistically."

BIOGRAPHICAL/CRITICAL SOURCES: Basil Shaw, editor, *Times and Seasons: An Introduction to Bruce Dawe,* Chesire, 1973.

* * *

DAWES, Frank 1933-

PERSONAL: Born August 15, 1933, in Ilford, England; son of Wilfred (à merchant) and Jennie Dawes; married Catherine Connelly (a nursing sister), May 19, 1956; children: Amanda Patricia, Timothy John, Catherine. *Education:* Attended technical secondary school in Essex, England. *Home:* Mariners, Dormans Park, East Grinstead, Sussex RH19 3NU, England. *Agent:* Lorna Vestey, 22 Holmbush Rd., London S.W.15, England. *Office:* British Broadcasting Corp., Broadcasting House, Portland Place, London WIA 1AA, England.

CAREER: Reporter for provincial evening newspapers in England, 1956-60; *Daily Herald-Sun,* London, England, defense and shipping correspondent, 1960-72; British Broadcasting Corp., London, news editor and senior producer, 1972—. *Military service:* Royal Air Force, 1951-53. *Member:* Society of Authors, National Union of Journalists.

WRITINGS: Not in Front of the Servants: Domestic Service in England, 1850-1939, Wayland, 1973, Taplinger, 1974; *A Cry from the Streets: A History of the Boys' Club Movement in England, 1850 to the Present,* Wayland, 1975. Contributor to *Daily Telegraph.*

WORK IN PROGRESS: Not Just Wives and Mothers, a history of women's employment in England from 1830 to 1977; *Dear Bella,* a biography of cookbook author Mrs. Beeton.

SIDELIGHTS: Dawes writes: "My interest in the Victorian period in England was stimulated by my first book which was published as the 'Upstairs, Downstairs' programme and reached peak popularity on television in the United Kingdom and the United States. Working as a producer in radio for the British Broadcasting Corp., I compiled and narrated a programme on servants. I also present a weekly radio programme 'Holiday Scene' on holidays and travel, visiting many places around the world."

* * *

DAWKINS, Richard 1941-

PERSONAL: Born March 26, 1941, in Kenya; son of C. John (a farmer) and Jean (Ladner) Dawkins; married Marian Stamp (a university teacher), August 19, 1967. *Education:* Balliol College, Oxford, B.A., 1962, M.A., 1966, D.Phil., 1966. *Religion:* None. *Office:* Department of Zoology, New College, Oxford University, South Parks Rd., Oxford, England.

CAREER: University of California, Berkeley, assistant professor of zoology, 1967-69; Oxford University, Oxford, England, lecturer in zoology and fellow of New College, both 1970—.

WRITINGS: The Selfish Gene, Oxford University Press, 1976. Honorary editor of *Animal Behaviour,* 1974—.

BIOGRAPHICAL/CRITICAL SOURCES: Spectator, January 15, 1977; *Science,* May 13, 1977.

DAWSON, Frank G(ates, Jr.) 1925-

PERSONAL: Born July 6, 1925, in Alliance, N.C.; son of Frank G. (a farmer) and Lola (Paul) Dawson; married Beta Holmes, October 31, 1947; children: Richard, Geraldine (Mrs. Bruce Myers), Diana. *Education:* North Carolina State University, B.E.E., 1950; graduate study, Oak Ridge School of Reactor Technology, 1955-56; University of Washington, Seattle, Ph.D., 1973. *Home:* 4586 Hayden Run Rd., Amlin, Ohio 43002. *Office:* Battelle Memorial Institute, 505 King Ave., Columbus, Ohio 43201.

CAREER: Test Engineers Program, Schenectady, N.Y., test engineer, 1950-51; General Electric Co., Aircraft Nuclear Propulsion Department, Cincinnati, Ohio, nuclear instruments engineer, 1951-53, senior engineer in critical experiments, 1953-55, principal engineer in nuclear analysis, 1956-60; General Electric Co., Hanford Laboratories, Richland, Wash., technical specialist in applied reactor physics, 1960, manager of applied physics, 1960-63, manager of reactor physics, 1963-65; Battelle Memorial Institute, manager of reactor physics at Battelle-Northwest Physics and Instruments in Richland, 1965-68, Columbus, Ohio, manager of physics and engineering, 1968-71, assistant laboratory director, 1971, director of Battelle Energy Program, 1973—, director of Battelle/Northwestern Mutual Life Insurance Co. Solar Energy Program, 1975—, director of corporate technical development, 1976—. Acting assistant professor at University of Cincinnati, 1958-60. Member of U.S. Atomic Energy Commission's advisory committee on reactor physics, 1964-70; member of European-American Committee on Reactor Physics, 1970—; U.S. delegate to United Nations Conference on Peaceful Uses of Atomic Energy, 1971; chairman of International Atomic Energy Agency panel meeting in Vienna, 1971. *Military service:* U.S. Army Air Forces, bombardier, 1943-46; became first lieutenant.

MEMBER: American Nuclear Society (member of executive committee on reactor physics, 1970—), American Association for the Advancement of Science, Tau Beta Pi.

WRITINGS: *Nuclear Power: Development and Management of a Technology,* University of Washington Press, 1976. Contributor to scientific journals. Member of editorial advisory committee of *Nuclear Science and Engineering,* 1968—; member of critical reviews committee of *Reactor Technology,* 1971—.

WORK IN PROGRESS: Energy research.

SIDELIGHTS: Dawson comments: "My long term professional interest has been energy research, over twenty years in the field of nuclear energy, more recently in coal, energy utilization, and solar energy.

"All sources of energy and conservation are necessary for the maintenance of our economic health. A vote against one form is a vote for the others. This should be recognized by all who have a voice in energy policy making and direction of our energy developments."

*   *   *

DAY, (Truman) Owen 1890-

PERSONAL: Born July 17, 1890, in Portland, Ore.; son of Franklin John (a clergyman) and Ellen (Morford) Day; married Mary Coolidge Terry, August 26, 1914 (deceased); children: Lee Franklin, Josephine (Mrs. Harold P. Ford). *Education:* Attended University of Puget Sound, 1910-13; Linfield College, A.B., 1914, D.D., 1955; Newton Theological Institution, B.D., 1917. *Politics:* Republican. *Home:* 1161 Palmetto Ave., Chico, Calif. 95926.

CAREER: Ordained Baptist minister, 1917; pastor of Baptist churches in Watertown, Mass., 1917-19, Portland, Ore., 1919-25, Spokane, Wash., 1925-32, Selma, Calif., 1932-39, and Los Angeles, Calif., 1939-45; First Baptist Church, Grand Junction, Colo., pastor, 1945-53. Worked for Young Men's Christian Association during World War I and for National Council of Churches during World War II.

WRITINGS: (With Nancy C. Thomas) *The Hallelujah Hole: The Story of a Frontier Preacher,* Judson, 1976. Also author of *Dramas: The Modern Prodigal and The Better Way,* 1923, and *Law and Sentiment,* 1932.

WORK IN PROGRESS: *Lives I Have Seen Transformed by Christ; The Mitchell Meeting; Going to Grandpa's.*

AVOCATIONAL INTERESTS: Mountain climbing, golf.

*   *   *

DAYTON, Donald W(ilber) 1942-

PERSONAL: Born July 25, 1942, in Chicago, Ill.; son of Wilber Thomas (a professor and college president) and Donna (a librarian and college teacher; maiden name, Fisher) Dayton; married Lucille Sider, June 9, 1969; children: Charles Soren. *Education:* Houghton College, B.A. (magna cum laude), 1963; Columbia University, graduate study, 1963-64; Yale University, B.D., 1969; University of Kentucky, M.S. in L.S., 1969; also attended American Institute in Jerusalem, Asbury Theological Seminary, and University of Chicago. *Politics:* Independent Democrat. *Religion:* Wesleyan Church of America. *Home:* 5104 North Christiana Ave., Chicago, Ill. 60625. *Office:* Mellander Library, North Park Theological Seminary, 5125 North Spaulding, Chicago, Ill. 60625.

CAREER: Asbury Theological Seminary, Wilmore, Ky., instructor, 1970-71, assistant professor of bibliography, 1971-72, acquisitions librarian, 1969-72; North Park Theological Seminary, Chicago, Ill., assistant professor, 1972-77, associate professor of theology, 1977—, director of Mellander Library, 1972—. Member of board of directors of Chicago Urban Life Center, 1972—.

MEMBER: World Methodist Historical Society, Karl Barth Society of North America (member of board of directors, 1972—), American Society of Church History, Wesleyan Theological Society (member of executive committee, 1974—), American Academy of Religion, Society of Biblical Literature, Conference on Faith and History, Society for Pentecostal Studies, American Theological Library Association (member-at-large of board of directors, 1976-79), Christian Holiness Association (member of board of administration, 1973—), Chicago Area Theological Library Association (chairman, 1975-76), Theta Phi. *Awards, honors:* Woodrow Wilson fellowship, 1964-65.

WRITINGS: *Theological Bibliography and Reference Resources,* Asbury Theological Seminary, 1970, revised edition, 1972; *The American Holiness Movement: A Bibliographic Introduction,* Asbury Theological Seminary, 1971, 2nd edition, in press; (with David Faupel and Susan Schultz) *Resources for Research,* Asbury Theological Seminary, 1972; (editor and author of introduction) *Five Sermons and a Tract by Luther Lee,* Holrad House, 1975; (editor) *Contemporary Perspectives on Pietism,* Covenant Press, 1976; *Discovering an Evangelical Heritage,* Harper, 1976.

Contributor: Paul Hostetler, editor, *Perfect Love and War,* Evangel Press (Nappanee, Ind.), 1974; Craig Ellison, editor, *The Urban Mission,* Eerdmans, 1974; H. Vinson Synan, editor, *Aspects of Pentecostal and Charismatic Origins,*

Logos International, 1975; Robert Welsh, editor, *Ecumenical Exercise IV*, World Council of Churches, 1976; (contributor of bibliography) Richard and Joyce Boldrey, *Chauvinist Or Feminist?: Paul's View of Women*, Baker Book, 1976.

Contributor to *Baker's Dictionary of Christian Ethics*, to *The New International Dictionary of the Christian Church*, and to theology journals. Book editor of *Sojourners*, 1975—; contributing editor of *Post-American*, 1974—; member of editorial committee of *Covenant Quarterly*, 1974—, acting editor, 1975; editorial associate of *Other Side*, 1975—; member of editorial network of ethics section of *Religious Studies Review*, 1975—.

WORK IN PROGRESS: Karl Barth in English: An Annotated Bibliography of Primary and Secondary Literature, publication by Scarecrow expected in 1978; editing *Women Called and Chosen: Historical Sources for a Distinctively Christian Feminism*, with wife, Lucille Sider Dayton and Nancy Hardesty, John Knox, 1978; editing *The Wesleyans*, with Howard Snyder, 1978; editing an anthology of essays showing the significance of Karl Barth for American life and theology, with Walt Lowe, 1978; co-author of "Women in the Holiness Movement: Feminism in the Evangelical Tradition," to be included in *Women of Spirit: Female Leadership in Religion, Past and Future*, edited by Rosemary Reuther and Eleanor McLaughlin, Simon & Schuster, 1978; research for a book on the theological roots of Pentecostalism.

SIDELIGHTS: Dayton writes: *"Discovering an Evangelical Heritage* was an effort to get my head together with regard to relating to my own roots in 'evangelicalism.' By reaching back behind recent fundamentalist experience I was able to recover a tradition of social activism rooted in evangelical religion that supported commitments I had made in the 1960's to civil rights movements and other currents for social justice. . . . One of the most formative experiences in my life was to spend most of 1967 in Israel, living through the Six-Day War in Jerusalem and then living five months on a kibbutz near Haifa."

AVOCATIONAL INTERESTS: Modern drama, book collecting.

* * *

DEACON, Joseph John 1920-

PERSONAL: Born May 24, 1920, in Camberwell, London, England; son of Joseph (a leather craftsman) and Gladys Deacon. *Education:* Entirely self-educated. *Home:* St. Lawrence Hospital, Caterham, Surrey, England. *Agent:* Victoria Shennan, National Society for Mentally Handicapped Children, Pembridge Hall, 17 Pembridge Sq., London W2 4EP, England.

CAREER: Hospital patient since age seven. *Awards, honors:* Christopher Award, adult book category, 1977, for *Joey.*

WRITINGS: (With Ernie Roberts, Michael Sangster, and Tom Blackburn) *Tongue Tied*, National Society for Mentally Handicapped Children (London), 1974, published as *Joey*, Scribner, 1976.

SIDELIGHTS: Joey Deacon was born severely handicapped—spastic in all four limbs, unable to walk, speak, or even feed himself. He entered St. Lawrence Hospital at the age of seven, first for leg operations, and later as a patient in the subnormality unit.

In 1944 Joey met two friends, Ernie Roberts and Tom. All three were handicapped in some way, but they began to function as a team. Tom, who had no physical handicap, taught Ernie his first steps. Ernie discovered that he could understand and interpret Joey's sound expressions. In 1946 the three met another friend, Michael Sangster, who was able to assist Tom in pushing the wheelchairs of Ernie and Joey.

It was not until twenty-five years later that the idea of recording Joey's thoughts and emotions was born. Victoria Shennan described the process: "Slowly, incoherently, and painfully, Joey communicated the details of his life to Ernie who translated the sounds into words and equally slowly and laboriously, Michael wrote them down. Each day's task produced 80 to 100 words." They decided that Michael's painful scribbling should be transferred to a more legible form, and got hold of a second-hand typewriter. Tom (who cannot read or write and had never typed a word in his life) mastered a code which enabled him to transfer on to the typewriter words which Michael spelled out letter by letter. In this manner, the three men were able to help Joey to relate his thoughts and, therefore, reduce his isolation.

Victoria Shennan added that, while the resulting book is no literary masterpiece, "It is the authentic first-hand account of the thoughts and feelings, pleasures and pains of one who speaks out of his own affliction, on behalf of thousands who cannot speak for themselves."

Tongue Tied has been translated into Dutch, Swedish, Italian, Japanese, German, and French. "Joey," an award-winning documentary adapted by British Broadcasting System's "Horizon" team, has been released worldwide.

* * *

DEAN, Basil 1888-

PERSONAL: Born September 27, 1888, in Croydon, England; married Esther Van Gruisen; married Victoria Hopper; children: Winton, Martin, Joseph, Tessa. *Education:* Educated in Croydon, England. *Home:* 102 Dorset House, Gloucester Pl., London N.W.1, England.

CAREER: Miss Horniman's Repertory Co., Manchester, England, actor, 1906-10; Liverpool Repertory Theatre, Liverpool, England, organizer and first director, 1911-13; Reandean Productions, London, England, managing director, 1919-26; Basil Dean Productions, London, governing director, 1926-64; writer, 1964—. Managing director of St. Martin's Theatre, 1919-25; joint managing director of Theatre Royal, 1924-25; chairman, managing director, and general European representative of Radio Keith Orpheum Corp., 1930-32. Founder, first chairman, and joint managing director of Associated Talking Pictures and its studios (now Ealing Studios), 1928-38; governing director of Basil Dean Enterprises, 1939—. Shute Lecturer at University of Liverpool, 1932-33. Director of entertainments for Navy and Army Canteen Board, 1917, and Navy, Army, and Air Force Institutes, 1939; director of National Service Entertainment, 1941-46. Organized first British Repertory Theatre Festival, 1948. *Military service:* British Army, Cheshire Infantry Regiment, 1914; became captain. *Member:* Entertainment National Service Association (founder; director general, 1939-46). *Awards, honors:* Member of the Order of the British Empire, 1918, Commander, 1947.

WRITINGS: The Repertory Theatre: Being the Substance of a Lecture Delivered on the Fifth Day of October, 1911, Philip, 1911; *The Theatre in Reconstruction*, Tonbridge, 1945; *The Theatre at War: A History of the Entertainment National Service Association*, Harrap, 1956; *Seven Ages*, Hutchinson, Volume I: *An Autobiography, 1888-1927*, 1970,

Volume II: *Mind's Eye: An Autobiography, 1927-1972,* 1973. Also author of *The Actor and His Workshop,* 1922, and *The Theatre in Emergency,* 1939.

Plays: "Marriages Are Made in Heaven" (one-act), produced in Manchester, England, 1908; "Mother to Be" (one-act), produced in Manchester, 1909; "Effie" (one-act), produced in Manchester, 1909; "The Love Cheats" (three-act), produced in London, 1910; (with Barry V. Jackson) *Fifinella: A Fairy Frolic* (children's Christmas play), Philip, 1912; (with Margaret M. Kennedy) *The Constant Nymph* (three-act; based on the novel by Margaret Kennedy), Doubleday, 1926; (with Kennedy) *Come with Me,* Heinemann, 1928; (editor of acting edition and author of introduction) James Elroy Flecker, *Hassan* (musical), Heinemann, 1951, revised edition, 1970; (arranger with Richard Blake) George Grossmith and Weedon Grossmith, *The Diary of Nobody,* Samuel French, 1955. Also author of "Murder Gang," with George Munro, 1933, and of dramatizations, "Beau Geste," with Christopher Wren, 1928, "Sleeveless Errand," with Norah James, 1933, and "The Heart of the Matter," with Graham Greene, 1949.

SIDELIGHTS: Dean is considered a pioneer of stage lighting, having imported new equipment from the United States and Germany, and devised equipment of his own.

BIOGRAPHICAL/CRITICAL SOURCES: Basil Dean, *Seven Ages,* Hutchinson, Volume I: *An Autobiography, 1888-1927,* 1970, Volume II: *Mind's Eye: An Autobiography, 1927-1972,* 1973.

* * *

DEAN, Luella Jo 1908(?)-1977

1908(?)—April 9, 1977; American artist and author. She died in Washington, D.C. Obituaries: *Washington Post,* April 12, 1977.

* * *

DEAN, Morton 1935-

PERSONAL: Born August 22, 1935, in Fall River, Mass.; married; children: Two daughters, one son. *Education:* Emerson College, B.A., 1957. *Office:* CBS News, 524 West 57th St., New York, N.Y. 10019.

CAREER/WRITINGS: Columbia Broadcasting System (CBS News), New York City, editor and writer for "Good News America" program, 1975, anchorman of "CBS Sunday Night News with Morton Dean," 1975, of "CBS Sunday Evening News with Morton Dean," 1976—, and of "Newsbreak" reports, Sunday through Friday, 1977—. Notable assignments include lunar space shots, Vietnam War, and American politics.

* * *

DEBO, Angie 1890-

PERSONAL: Born January 30, 1890, in Beattie, Kan.; daughter of Edward Peter (a farmer) and Lina Elbertha (Cooper) Debo. *Education:* University of Oklahoma, A.B., 1918, Ph.D., 1933; University of Chicago, A.M., 1924. *Politics:* Democrat. *Religion:* United Church of Christ. *Home and office address:* P.O. Box 133, Marshall, Okla. 73056.

CAREER: Rural school teacher near Marshall, Okla., 1907-09, 1913-15; principal of village school in Enid, Okla., 1918-19; high school teacher of history in Enid, 1919-23; West Texas State Teachers College (now West Texas State University), Canyon, assistant professor of history, 1924-33;

Panhandle-Plains Historical Museum, Canyon, Tex., curator, 1933-34; free-lance writer, 1934—. Member of faculty at Stephen F. Austin State Teachers College, summer, 1935; Oklahoma State University, member of history faculty, 1945, 1946, and 1957-58, curator of maps and member of library staff, 1947-55. State director of Federal Writers Program for Oklahoma, 1940-41. *Member:* Association of American Indian Affairs (member of board of directors, 1956-66), American Civil Liberties Union (Oklahoma; member of board of directors, 1973-77), Oklahoma Historical Society (honorary life member), Oklahoma Writers Federation (honorary life member), Stillwater Writers (honorary life member), Marshall Woman's Club, Rebekah Lodge. *Awards, honors:* John H. Dunning Award from American Historical Association, 1935, for *The Rise and Fall of the Choctaw Republic;* Alfred A. Knopf History Fellowship, 1942; fellow of University of Oklahoma, 1946; inducted into Oklahoma Hall of Fame, 1950; extraordinary service award from Navajo Community College, 1972; Henry G. Bennett Distinguished Service Award from Oklahoma State University, 1976.

WRITINGS: (With J. Fred Rippy) *The Historical Background of the American Policy of Isolation,* Smith College, 1924; *The Rise and Fall of the Choctaw Republic,* University of Oklahoma Press, 1934; *And Still the Waters Run: The Betrayal of the Five Civilized Tribes,* Princeton University Press, 1940; *The Road to Disappearance: A History of the Creek Indians,* University of Oklahoma Press, 1941; (editor with John M. Oskison) *Oklahoma: A Guide to the Sooner State,* University of Oklahoma Press, 1941; *Tulsa: From Creek Town to Oil Capital,* University of Oklahoma Press, 1943; *Prairie City: The Story of an American Community,* Knopf, 1944; *Oklahoma: Foot-Loose and Fancy-Free,* University of Oklahoma Press, 1949.

(Editor) *The Cowman's Southwest: Being the Reminiscences of Oliver Nelson,* Arthur H. Clark, 1953; *The Five Civilized Tribes of Oklahoma: A Report on Social and Economic Conditions,* Indian Rights Association, 1961; (editor) H. B. Cushman, *History of the Choctaw, Chickasaw, and Natchez Indians,* Redlands Press, 1962; *A History of the Indians of the United States,* University of Oklahoma Press, 1970; *Geronimo: The Man, His Time, His Place,* University of Oklahoma Press, 1976.

Columnist, "This Week in Oklahoma History" column in *Oklahoma City Times,* 1952-54. Contributor to *Encyclopedia Americana. Contributor of articles and reviews to magazines and newspapers.*

WORK IN PROGRESS: Advising Nebraska Educational Television Network on Indian-white relations in the settlement of the Northern Great Plains, as told by Indian participants.

SIDELIGHTS: Debo writes: "In 1899 my father bought a farm near Marshall, Oklahoma Territory, and brought his family there in a covered wagon. I have a distinct memory of the warm, sunny day, the lively little new town, and the greening wheat fields we passed as we lumbered slowly down the road to our new home. I attended rural one-room schools in Kansas and Oklahoma. There was no library, no magazines, and only the one book our parents managed to buy for each of us children as a Christmas present.

About her writing, she comments: "I have only one goal: to discover truth and publish it. My research is objective, but when I find all the truth on one side, as has sometimes happened in my study of Indian history, I have the same obligation to become involved as any other citizen."

De BONVILLE, Bob 1926-

PERSONAL: Born July 31, 1926, in Fitchburg, Mass.; son of A. A. and Kathleen (Connors) De Bonville; married Batty Forcier (a teacher), February 2, 1952; children: Joe, John, Tom, Patty, Dan. *Education:* University of Wisconsin, Madison, B.S., 1950. *Religion:* Roman Catholic. *Home:* 219 South Ashland, Green Bay, Wis. 54303. *Office:* WFRV-Television, 1181 East Mason, Green Bay, Wis. 54305.

CAREER: WFRV-Television, Green Bay, Wis., regional sales manager, 1962—. Member of board of directors of Old Fort Howard Project and Green Bay Area Visitor and Convention Bureau. *Military service:* U.S. Navy, 1944-46. *Member:* Green Bay Advertising Club (past president), Milwaukee Advertising Club, Madison Advertising Club, Green Bay Ambassadors, Sentry Club (charter president).

WRITINGS: Every Fourth Tuesday (nonfiction), Agape, 1976.

WORK IN PROGRESS: The Audible Father, an "impertinent look at a father's association of four boys playing football on grade school, high school, and college level."

SIDELIGHTS: De Bonville comments briefly: *"Every Fourth Tuesday* has given me a better insight into individual needs, into the futility of building walls instead of bridges. We are a society in caring attempts to solve all human problems but fail miserably in the administration of justice."

BIOGRAPHICAL/CRITICAL SOURCES: Milwaukee Sentinel, November 20, 1976; *Madison Capitol Times,* December 15, 1976.

* * *

de CAMPI, John Webb 1939-

PERSONAL: Born February 4, 1939, in Chicago, Ill.; son of J. Webb (a newspaperman) and Margaret (Horner) de Campi; married Robin L. Watson (an editor), October 3, 1964; children: Alexandra Sarah Webb. *Education:* Rochester Institute of Technology, B.F.A., 1960; Harvard University, M.B.A., 1968. *Politics:* Republican. *Religion:* Protestant. *Home:* Spruchaven Farm, Chester Heights, Pa. 19017.

CAREER: In management, 1968—; E. I. DuPont, Wilmington, Del., equipment export manager in Electronic Materials Division, 1976—. Member of Chester Heights Borough Council, 1970—, president, 1975—. *Military service:* U.S. Navy, 1962-66; became lieutenant. *Member:* Society of Automotive Historians, Rolls-Royce Owners Club (president, 1976-77).

WRITINGS: Rolls-Royce in America, Dalton-Watson, 1975. Contributor to automotive journals.

* * *

DE JONG, Arthur J(ay) 1934-

PERSONAL: Surname is pronounced De Young; born February 24, 1934, in Paterson, N.J.; son of Peter A. (a clergyman) and Anna (Vander Schaaf) De Jong; married Joyce Van Doorn (a teacher), December 21, 1957; children: Mark, Beth, Paul, Ruth, Richard. *Education:* Central College, Pella, Iowa, A.B., 1956; Western Theological Seminary, Holland, Mich., B.D., 1959; Princeton Theological Seminary, Th.M., 1962; San Francisco Theological Seminary, S.T.D., 1971. *Home address:* R.R. 3, Pella, Iowa 50219. *Office:* Office of the President, Central College, Pella, Iowa 50219.

CAREER: Ordained Reformed Church in America clergy-

man, 1959; Central College, Pella, Iowa, professor of religion, 1960—, chaplain, 1960-66, director of counseling, 1966-69, associate dean, 1969-70, acting dean, 1970-71, assistant to the president, 1971—. Adjunct professor, San Francisco Theological Seminary. Trustee of Bethesda Hospital (Denver, Colo.). *Member:* American Psychological Association.

WRITINGS: Making It to Adulthood: The Emerging Self, Westminster, 1972. Contributor to church magazines.

WORK IN PROGRESS: Marriage; Life-Planning for Adults.

* * *

DE JONG, Peter 1945-

PERSONAL: Surname is pronounced De Young; born November 18, 1945, in Grand Rapids, Mich.; son of Peter Ymen (a clergyman) and Joanne (a nurse; maiden name, Heyns) De Jong; married Charlotte Jean Bergsma (a teacher), May 6, 1967; children: Christopher James, Paul Richard. *Education:* Calvin College, A.B., 1967; Western Michigan University, M.A., 1969, Ph.D., 1972. *Religion:* Protestant. *Home:* 1636 Woodcliff S.E., Grand Rapids, Mich. 49506. *Office:* Department of Sociology, Calvin College, East Beltline, Grand Rapids, Mich. 49506.

CAREER: Calvin College, Grand Rapids, Mich., instructor, 1969-71, assistant professor, 1972-74, associate professor of sociology, 1974—. *Member:* American Sociological Association. *Awards, honors:* Research grants from Christian Reformed Church, 1971 and 1974-75, and Model Cities Program, 1973.

WRITINGS: Content Analysis of Church Publications: Their Treatment of Race, Race Commission, Christian Reformed Church, 1971; *Resource Manual for Race Relations in the Christian Schools,* Synodical Committee on Race Relations, 1975; *Patterns of Intergenerational Occupational Mobility of American Females,* R & E Research Associates, 1977. Contributor to sociology journals. Referee for *American Journal of Sociology* and National Science Foundation.

WORK IN PROGRESS: The Division of Labor Between Husbands and Wives in the Christian Family (tentative title).

SIDELIGHTS: De Jong writes: "My primary professional interests have been in poverty, race relations, and sex roles. In all of these areas I feel societal definitions have limited the development of human potentials. I have attempted to explicate this problem through marshalling the concepts and findings of social science as well as a Christian perspective. This approach is especially evident in the manuscript I have just completed."

* * *

DE LA GRANGE, Henry Louis 1924-

PERSONAL: Born May 26, 1924, in Paris, France; son of Amaury (a politician) and Emily (Sloane) De La Grange. *Education:* Attended Sorbonne, University of Paris; University of Aix en Provence, Licence en Lettres, 1944; studied music with Nadia Boulanger and Yvonne Lefebure. *Politics:* Liberal Socialist. *Home:* 23 rue du Conseil, Vevey 1800, Vaud, Switzerland.

CAREER: Music critic in Paris for *Arts* (newspaper) and *Disques,* 1955-60; free-lance critic for various French, English, American, and German publications, 1960—. Lecturer in the United States, Canada, and France; has made television appearances in France and the United States. Music festival organizer. *Military service:* French Army, 1945. *Member:* International Mahler Society, Mahler Society (Los Angeles), Alban Berg Society, Berlioz Society, Association des Amis d'Alziprato. *Awards, honors:* Deems Taylor Award from American Society of Composers, Authors, and Publishers (ASCAP), 1974, for *Mahler.*

WRITINGS: Mahler, Doubleday, Volume 1, 1973; *Mahler in Vienna,* Rizzoli, 1976. Contributor to international music journals, including *Opera News, Paris Review,* and *Music & Musicians;* contributor to dictionaries and encyclopedias. Also author of concert program notes.

WORK IN PROGRESS: Mahler, Volume II; a complete edition of the letters of Gustave Mahler.

SIDELIGHTS: Henry De La Grange writes: "Most of my interest lies in the direction of Mahler. A huge amount of time and effort, in fact most of my life—has been spent doing research and investigating every moment, every detail, every event in Mahler's life. I believe my biography to be unusual in this respect. I was utterly amazed—and I must admit, profoundly happy—to find that so many critics and readers found this tremendous amount of detail interesting and even stimulating. It has given me new strength and energy for Volume II. The work has progressed slowly, nevertheless, because I discovered so many new documents. I still sincerely hope that the new volume will be finished and published within the next two years."

AVOCATIONAL INTERESTS: Oriental music and wine making.

*   *   *

DELON, Floyd G(urney) 1929-

PERSONAL: Born August 7, 1929, in Shirley, Ind.; son of Horace L. and Reola (Phelps) Delon; married Elizabeth Taylor, May 29, 1949; children: Laura Delon Stephens. *Education:* Ball State Teachers College (now University), B.S.Ed., 1951; Butler University, M.S., 1954; University of Arizona, Ed.D., 1961. *Religion:* Methodist. *Home:* 305 Devine Court, Columbia, Mo. 65201. *Office:* College of Education, 209 Hill Hall, University of Missouri, Columbia, Mo. 65201.

CAREER: High school teacher of mathematics in Arlington, Ind., 1951-54; principal of public schools in Hillsboro, Ind., 1954-56, and Mays, Ind., 1956-60; Northwest Missouri State College, Maryville, assistant professor of education, 1961-62; University of Missouri, Columbia, associate professor of education, 1962-67; South Central Region Educational Laboratories, Little Rock, Ark., director, 1967-69; University of Missouri, professor of education and associate dean of College of Education, 1969—. Fulbright lecturer in Iran, 1975-76.

MEMBER: National Organization on the Legal Problems of Education, American Association of School Administrators (member of board of directors, 1973-75), Missouri State Teachers Association, Phi Delta Kappa, Kappa Delta Pi, Lions (member of board of directors).

WRITINGS: (Contributor) Warren E. Gauerke and Jack R. Childress, editors, *The Theory and Practice of School Finance,* Rand McNally, 1967; (with Lee O. Barber) *The Law and the Teacher in Missouri,* Interstate, 1971, 2nd edition, 1977; *Substantive Legal Aspects of Teacher Discipline,* National Organization on the Legal Problems of Education, 1972; (editor) *The Yearbook of School Law,* National Organization on the Legal Problems of Education, 1974. Con-

tributor to *Handbook of Contemporary Education,* and to education journals.

WORK IN PROGRESS: Two monographs, *Legal Controls on Teacher Conduct,* for National Organization on the Legal Problems of Education, and *School Administrators and the Courts,* for Educational Research Service.

*   *   *

DEMPSEY, Hugh Aylmer 1929-

PERSONAL: Born November 7, 1929, in Edgerton, Alberta, Canada; son of Otto L. (a civil servant) and Lily (Sharp) Dempsey; married Pauline S. Gladstone, September 30, 1953; children: L. James, Louise, John, Leah, Lois. *Education:* Educated in primary and secondary schools in Edmonton, Alberta. *Religion:* Anglican. *Home:* 95 Holmwood Ave. N.W., Calgary, Alberta, Canada T2K 2G7. *Office:* Glenbow-Alberta Institute, Calgary, Alberta, Canada.

CAREER: Edmonton Bulletin, Edmonton, Alberta, reporter and editor, 1949-51; Government of Alberta, Edmonton, publicity writer, 1951-56; Glenbow Foundation, Calgary, Alberta, archivist, 1956-67; Glenbow-Alberta Institute, Calgary, technical director, 1967-70, director of history, 1970—. Lecturer at Canadian universities. Alberta member of Historic Sites and Monuments Board of Canada; associate director of Calgary Exhibition and Stampede, 1958—; member of Alberta Records Publication Board; vice-chairman of Alberta Public Advisory Committee on Conservation of Archaeological and Historical Resources, 1971-74, chairman, 1974-76.

MEMBER: Canadian Historical Association (chairperson of archives section, 1961-62), Canadian Museums Association (executive member, 1968-70), Indian-Eskimo Association of Canada (executive member, 1960-65), Champlain Society (member of council, 1972-74), Historical Society of Alberta (executive member, 1952—; vice-president, 1955-56; president, 1956-57), Indian Association of Alberta, Fort Calgary Preservation Society (executive member), Kainai Chieftainship. *Awards, honors:* Annual award from Historical Society of Alberta, 1963; Alberta Achievement Award, 1974, 1975; D.U.C. from University of Calgary, 1974; Order of Canada, 1975; Alberta Non-Fiction Award, 1975, for *The Best of Bob Edwards.*

WRITINGS: Historic Sites of Alberta, Government of Alberta, 1952; (editor) *The Big Chief of the Prairies* (on Father Lacombe), Palm Publishers, 1953; *Blackfoot Winter Count* (monograph), Glenbow-Alberta Institute, 1965; *Jerry Potts, Plainsman* (monograph), Glenbow-Alberta Institute, 1966; *Blackfoot Ghost Dance* (monograph), Glenbow-Alberta Institute, 1968; *Indian Names for Alberta Communities* (monograph), Glenbow-Alberta Institute, 1969; *Tailfeathers, Indian Artist* (monograph), Glenbow-Alberta Institute, 1970; *Crowfoot: Chief of the Blackfeet,* University of Oklahoma Press, 1972; *William Parker, Mounted Policeman,* Hurtig, 1973; (editor) *A Winter at Fort Macleod,* McClelland & Stewart, 1974; (editor) *Men in Scarlet,* McClelland & Stewart, 1974; (editor) *The Best of Bob Edwards,* Hurtig, 1975; (editor) *The Wit and Wisdom of Bob Edwards,* Hurtig, 1976.

Former author of column "Tawasi," in the daily *Edmonton Bulletin.* Contributor to national and international journals, including *Journal of American Folklore, Plains Anthropologist,* and *Journal of the Washington Academy of Science.* Editor of *Canadian Archivist,* 1963-66; associate editor of *Alberta History,* 1953-58, editor, 1958—; Northern and Canadian editor of *Montana Magazine of History;* contributing editor of *American West;* member of editorial board of Royal Canadian Geographical Society.

WORK IN PROGRESS: Charcoal's World; The Life of Red Crow.

SIDELIGHTS: While associated with the Government of Alberta, Dempsey was responsible for historical work, including a historic highway sign program and historic sites research. His interest in history developed alongside his work with and research on Canadian Indians. His wife is a Blood Indian and in 1967 Dempsey was made an honorary Blood chief. Beginning with work for the Indian Association of Alberta, he assisted attempts to organize locals on Blackfoot and Peigan Reserves. Much of his writing concerns the Indian tribes of Alberta. He directed the documentary film "Okan, Sun Dance of the Blackfoot" and served as consultant for "West to the Mountains."

*   *   *

DENNIS, Wayne 1905-1976

September 1, 1905—July 21, 1976; American child psychologist, anthropologist, professor of psychology, and author or editor of many works in his field. He died in Richmond, Va. Obituaries: *AB Bookman's Weekly,* August 23-30, 1976. (See index for previous *CA* sketch)

*   *   *

DENNISTON, Denise 1946-

PERSONAL: Born November 11, 1946, in Albuquerque, N.M.; daughter of Douglas Gilbert (an art professor) and Patricia (Davidson) Denniston. *Education:* University of Arizona, B.A., 1969. *Home:* 1844 North Vine, Tucson, Ariz. 85719. *Office:* Three Rivers Press, 5806 Elizabeth, Allen Park, Mich. 48101.

CAREER: World Plan Executive Council (transcendental meditation program), Los Angeles, Calif., Omaha, Neb., and New York, N.Y., teacher, 1970—. Partner, Three Rivers Press, 1975—.

WRITINGS: (With Peter McWilliams and Barry Geller) *The TM Book: How to Enjoy the Rest of Your Life,* Three Rivers Press, 1975; (with Nat Goldhaber and McWilliams) *The TM Phenemenon: An Alphabetical Guide to the TM Program,* Ballantine, 1976.

WORK IN PROGRESS: Further research into the transcendental meditation program and its effects; books and articles on transcendental meditation.

*   *   *

DENTON, Jeremiah A(ndrew), Jr. 1924-

PERSONAL: Born July 15, 1924, in Mobile, Ala.; son of Jeremiah Andrew (a businessman) and Irene (Steele) Denton; married Kathryn Jane Maury, June 6, 1946; children: Jeremiah III, Donald, James, William, Madeleine, Michael, Mary Elizabeth. *Education:* Attended Spring Hill College, 1942-43; U.S. Naval Academy, B.S., 1947; George Washington University, M.A., 1964. *Religion:* Roman Catholic. *Home:* Illinois House, 478 Powhatan St., Naval Station, Norfolk, Va. 23511. *Office:* Office of the Commandant, Armed Forces Staff College, Norfolk, Va. 23511.

CAREER: U.S. Navy, career officer, 1946—, currently rear admiral. Officer on U.S.S. *Valley Forge,* 1946-47; involved in the testing, evaluation, and flying of airships, 1948-52, and airborne early warning aircraft, 1952-56; attack carrier air wing operations officer, prospective commanding officer,

and attack aircraft pilot on U.S.S. *Independence,* 1964-65; prisoner of war in North Vietnam, 1965-73; commandant of Armed Forces Staff College, 1974—. Lecturer. Member of board of regents, Spring Hill College. *Member:* Reserve Officers Association, Ends of the Earth Society, Knights of columbus, Rotary International.

AWARDS, HONORS—Military: Navy Cross, Distinguished Service Medal, three Silver Stars, Distinguished Flying Cross, five Bronze Stars, two Air Medals, two Purple Hearts.

Other: Doctor of Humane Letters from Spring Hill College, 1973; John Paul Jones Award from Navy League, 1973; Court of Honor Award from Alabama National Exchange Club, 1973; honored by a resolution of the State Legislature of Alabama, 1973; Silver Medal from Pope Paul VI in private audicnce, 1974; two awards from Valley Forge Freedoms Foundation, 1974 and 1976; Armed Forces Award from Veterans of Foreign Wars, 1974; For God and Country Award from Capitol Hill First Friday Club, 1974; Celtic Cross Award from Catholic War Veterans, 1974; Cross of Military Service from United Daughters of the Confederacy, 1975.

WRITINGS: (With Ed Brandt) *When Hell Was in Session,* Readers Digest Press, 1976. Contributor of article to *Columbia* (magazine).

WORK IN PROGRESS: A book, proposed title either *Thy Kingdom Come* or *One Nation under God.*

SIDELIGHTS: Denton writes that further books will deal with "progress of the United States toward material and social greatness," which he defines as, "free enterprise moderated by love of God and neighbor. Both progress and survival are now at risk because in having difficulty coping with an unprecedented national affluence, we are forgetting and abandoning the values by which we have survived and achieved affluence."

*   *   *

DEPAS, Spencer 1925-

PERSONAL: Born August 27, 1925, in Haiti; came to the United States in 1960; son of Gaston S. (an artist) and Sophie (Montplaisir) Depas; married Rosalind M. V. Drummond (a professor), April 23, 1965; children: Sophie M., Albert. *Education:* Studied at J. B. Damier Professional Academy, 1942-46, Centre d'Art, Haiti, 1947-49, Cranbrook Academy of Art, 1954-55, Wayne State University, 1956, and Lili Blumenau Weaving Workshop, 1960-62. *Home:* 227 Cumberland St., Brooklyn, N.Y. 11205.

CAREER: Artist; about forty group and individual exhibitions in the United States, Canada, Haiti, Brazil, and Germany. Taught painting in Haiti, 1950-54, and ceramics, 1957-59; teacher of weaving and textile design at Lili Blumenau Weaving Workshop, 1962-65; owner and teacher of weaving, macrame, and sculpture at Spencer Depas Studio, 1968—. Co-founder of Le Foyer des Arts Plastiques, secretary-manager, 1950-59; folklore consultant, choreographer, and dancer for Bacalou Dance Co., 1957-59. Member of advisory committee for Brooklyn Museum Community Gallery, 1972—. Appeared on television and radio programs in New York, Haiti, Canada, Puerto Rico, and Germany.

AWARDS, HONORS: Silver medal from Exposition Internationale Bicentenaire, 1949; honorary award from Haiti's Bureau of Tourism, 1959, for sculpture and painting; certificate of merit from New York Craftsmen, 1961; award from Fence Art Show at Brooklyn Museum, 1971.

WRITINGS: Macrame, Weaving, and Tapestry: Art in Fiber, Macmillan, 1973. Contributor to *Merit Students Encyclopedia*.

BIOGRAPHICAL/CRITICAL SOURCES: Lili Blumenau, *Creative Design in Wall Hangings*, 1967; Virginia Harvey, *Macrame: The Art of Creative Knotting*, 1967; Rose Slivka, Aileen Webb, and Margaret Patch, *The Crafts of the Modern World*, 1968.

* * *

De PIETRO, Albert 1913-

PERSONAL: Born September 11, 1913, in Brooklyn, N.Y.; son of Philip (a designer) and Elsie (Vecchione) De Pietro; married Sophia Barbiero, December 12, 1937; children: Elsie (Mrs. Robert L. Russo), Philip, Loraine (deceased). *Education:* St. John's University, Brooklyn, N.Y., B.B.A., 1935, LL.B., 1938, J.S.D., 1939. *Home:* 350 Harmon, Garden City, N.Y. 11530. *Office:* Department of Accounting and Business Administration, Nassau Community College, 230 Kilburn Rd., Garden City, N.Y. 11530.

CAREER: Admitted to the Bar of New York, 1940; F. C. Gnazzo & Co. (certified public accountants), senior staff member, 1939-45, partner, 1945-52; maintains private practice in taxation, 1952—. Brooklyn College (now of the City University of New York), Brooklyn, N.Y., lecturer in accounting, 1955-63; Nassau Community College, Garden City, N.Y., assistant professor, 1963-65, associate professor, 1966-70, professor of law, 1971—, chairman of department of accounting and business administration, 1967-70. Attorney in Mineola, N.Y., 1960-74. *Member:* International Poetry Society (fellow), Poetry Society of America, New Mexico State Poetry Society, Rhode Island State Poetry Society, New York State Bar Association (chairman of tax law committee, 1962-63). *Awards, honors:* Second prize from Rochester Festival of Religious Arts, 1965.

WRITINGS—Poetry: Moments in Passing, J.R.D. Publishing, 1967; *Sounds of Shadow*, J. & C. Transcripts, 1970; *Island City and Other Poems*, J. & C. Transcripts, 1970; *Of Hush and Whispers*, J. & C. Transcripts, 1972; *Circles of Flight*, J. & C. Transcripts, 1974. Contributor to *The Practical Lawyer's Law Office Manual* and to tax and law journals.

WORK IN PROGRESS: A sixth book of poems.

SIDELIGHTS: De Pietro comments: "I am motivated to express the life force existing in the commonplace experiences; the essence of pure and simple living realized or diluted or lost. In this search I find the challenge of poetry most enlightening, most difficult. Its brevity conforms to life; its lyric discipline to the beauty and limits of nature."

* * *

DERBY, Pat 1942-

PERSONAL: Born June 7, 1942, in Sussex, England; daughter of Thomas Boswell (a professor) and Mary (Hall) Shelley; married Ted Derby (divorced). *Education:* Columbia University. *Home:* 3651 Calzada, Los Olivos, Calif. 93441. *Agent:* McIntosh & Otis, Inc., 475 Fifth Ave., New York, N.Y. 10017. *Office:* Pat Derby Enterprises, P.O. Box 212, Los Olivos, Calif. 93441.

CAREER: Pat Derby Enterprises (wild animal trainers), Los Olivos, Calif., president, 1975—.

WRITINGS: The Lady and Her Tiger, Dutton, 1976. Author of screenplay "Lori."

WORK IN PROGRESS: A book about grizzly bears.

DERWENT, Lavinia

PERSONAL: Born in Scotland. *Religion:* Protestant. *Home:* 1 Great Western Ter., Glasgow G12 OUP, Scotland. *Agent:* Campbell, Thomson & McLaughlin, 31 Newington Green, London, England.

CAREER: Writer. Has appeared on television; storyteller in schools. *Member:* International P.E.N., Society of Authors, Writer's Guild, Soroptimists. *Awards, honors:* Member of Order of the British Empire.

WRITINGS: (Compiler with John Redgwick Crossland) *Ten Modern Mystery Stories*, Collins, 1935; (compiler) *My Own Book of Animals*, Collins, 1937; *Brer Rabbit* (adapted from *Uncle Remus* by Joel Chandler Harris), Collins, 1938; *More Brer Rabbit* (adapted from *Uncle Remus* by Harris), Collins, 1940; *The Woodland Readers*, Collins, 1940; *The Witch* (verse play), Thomas Nelson, 1941; *Brer Rabbit Again* (adapted from *Uncle Remus* by Harris), Collins, 1942; *The Book of Fables* (adapted from *Fables* by Aesop), Collins, 1945; *Clashmaclavers: A Mixty-Maxty of Prose and Verse in the Couthy Tradition*, Oliver & Boyd, 1947.

Kirk Moose, Maclellan, 1951; *Children's Picture Dictionary*, Collins, 1957; *Macpherson*, Bobbs-Merrill, 1961; *The Coat of Many Colours*, Burke Publishing, 1965; *The Story of Hiawatha* (adapted from *Hiawatha* by Henry Wadsworth Longfellow), Collins, 1965; *The Boy and the Giant*, Burke Publishing, 1967; *The Boy in the Basket*, Burke Publishing, 1968; *Macpherson's Skyscraper*, Burke Publishing, 1969; *Sula* (juvenile), Gollancz, 1969; *Fisher Boy*, Burke Publishing, 1969; *Picture Dictionary*, Burke Publishing, 1969.

Macpherson's Island, Burke Publishing, 1970; *Return to Sula* (juvenile), Gollancz, 1971; *Boy Named Samuel*, Burke Publishing, 1972; *Macpherson's Winter Sports*, Burke Publishing, 1972; *The Boy from Sula* (juvenile), Gollancz, 1973; *The Adventures of Tammy Troot*, Holmes-McDougall, 1975; *Further Adventures of Tammy Troot*, Holmes-McDougall, 1975; *A Breath of Border Air* (for adults), Hutchinson, 1975; *Song of Sula* (juvenile), Gollancz, 1976; *Another Breath of Border Air* (for adults), Hutchinson, 1977; *Joseph and the Coat of Many Colors* (juvenile), Scholastic Book Services, in press.

WORK IN PROGRESS: A juvenile and a "looking-back book for grown-ups."

SIDELIGHTS: Lavinia Derwent spent her childhood on a Scottish farm; her books deal with her experiences of farm life. *Avocational interests:* Travel.

* * *

DESCHARNES, Robert (Pierre) 1926-

PERSONAL: Born January 1, 1926, in Nevers, France; son of Guy (a businessman) and Marie (Auclair) Descharnes; married Raymonde Treiber, April 29, 1952; children: Olivier, Nicolas. *Education:* Attended Ecole des Beaux-Arts, Paris, France. *Home and office:* 12 Rue Guenegaud, Paris 75006, France.

CAREER: Free-lance artist, photographer, and filmmaker.

WRITINGS: The World of Salvador Dali, translated by Albert Field, Harper, 1962; (with Jean-Francois Chabrun) *Auguste Rodin*, translated by Haakon Chevalier, Macmillan, 1967; *La Vision artistique et religieuse de Gaudi*, Edita (Lausanne, Switzerland), 1969, translation by Frederick Hill published as *Gaudi, the Visionary*, preface by Dali, Viking, 1971; *Vilallonga*, translated and adapted by Malcolm Spicer, Juventud, 1971; *Dali*, Nouvelles Editions Francaises, 1973, translation by Eleonor R. Morse published under same title, Abrams, 1976; *Antonio Pitxot, pittore,* preface by Dali, Fondazione Dalle Molle (Venice), 1974; (with Tadao Ogura) *Salvador Dali,* Shuei-Sha (Tokyo), 1974. Also author, or co-author with Salvador Dali, Georges Mathieu, Jean Christophe Averty, and Orson Welles, of screenplays and television films.

Photographs: Roger Nimier, *Versailles que j'aime,* Editions Sun, 1958, translation published as *The Versailles I Love,* Tudor, 1959; Carlo Coccioli, *Florence que j'aime,* Editions Sun, 1959, translation by Ruth Whipple Fermaud published as *The Florence I Love,* Tudor, 1960; Pierre Devambez, *Sculptures grecques,* Editions Sun, 1960, translation by Barbara M. Bell published as *Greek Sculpture,* Tudor, 1961, revised edition, 1965; Michel Deon, *The Greece I Love,* Tudor, 1961.

Contributor to French magazines and to *Horizon, Time, Art News,* and *Life.*

WORK IN PROGRESS: Research on Dali's drawings, sculpture in India, photography in twentieth-century India, and stereoscopy.

SIDELIGHTS: Descharnes has organized and participated in major Dali exhibitions in Japan, New York City, Rotterdam, and Germany.

*   *   *

DESPERT, J(uliette) Louise 1892-

PERSONAL: Born June 9, 1892, in Versailles, France; came to U.S., 1920; became U.S. citizen, 1930; daughter of Louis (an architect) and Alice (Renon) Despert. *Education:* University of Paris, B.S., 1910; Barnard College, B.A., 1928; New York University, M.D., 1932. *Home and office:* 229 East 79th St., New York, N.Y. 10021. *Agent:* McIntosh & Otis, 475 Fifth Ave., New York, N.Y. 10017.

CAREER: High school teacher of science and hygiene in Versailles, France, 1912-15; Hospital Laennee, Paris, France, intern, 1916-17; nurse for French Army and organizer of refugees in Franco-British Sector, 1917-20; private nurse in New York, N.Y., 1921-26; Bellevue Hospital, New York City, intern, 1933-34; New York Psychiatric Institute, New York City, resident, 1934-37; researcher and child psychiatrist, 1937—. Artist and writer.

WRITINGS: Emotional Problems in Children, New York State Hospital Press, 1938; *Preliminary Reports on Children's Reactions to the War,* Josiah Macy, Jr. Foundation, 1942; (with Helen Pierce) *The Relation of Emotional Adjustment to Intellectual Function,* Journal Press, 1946; (contributor) *Modern Trends in Child Psychiatry,* International University Press, 1946; (with Gustav Bychowski) *Specialized Techniques in Psychotherapy,* Basic Books, 1952; *Children of Divorce,* Doubleday, 1953; *The Emotionally Disturbed Child, Then and Now,* Vantage, 1965, published as *The Emotionally Disturbed Child: An Inquiry into Family Patterns,* Doubleday, 1970; *Schizophrenia in Children* (collected papers), Brunner, 1968; *The Inner Voices of Children,* Brunner, 1975.

Contributor of aritcles to *American Journal of Psychiatry, Nursery Education Digest, Journal of Educational Sociology, Psychiatric Quarterly,* and other periodicals.

WORK IN PROGRESS: The Satirical Drawings of Doctor Despert, Volumes I and II.

AVOCATIONAL INTERESTS: Writings and art, especially sculpture.

DESSEN, Alan C(harles) 1935-

PERSONAL: Born November 16, 1935, in Baltimore, Md.; son of Maurice M. (a business executive) and Shirley (a retail merchant; maiden name, Kaplan) Dessen; married Cynthia Sheldon (a college professor), August 4, 1963; children: Michael, Sarah. *Education:* Harvard University, B.A. (magna cum laude), 1957; Johns Hopkins University, M.A., 1961, Ph.D., 1963. *Home:* 1100 Willow Dr., Chapel Hill, N.C. 27514. *Office:* Department of English, University of North Carolina, Chapel Hill, N.C. 27514.

CAREER: University of Wisconsin, Madison, instructor, 1963-65, assistant professor, 1965-68, associate professor of English, 1968-69; Northwestern University, Evanston, Ill., associate professor of English, 1969-73; University of North Carolina, Chapel Hill, professor of English, 1973—. Member of Institute of Renaissance Studies' Oregon Shakespeare Festival, 1974-77. *Military service:* U.S. Army Reserve, 1957-63, active duty, 1957-58.

MEMBER: Modern Language Association of America, Renaissance Society of America, Shakespeare Association of America, American Association of University Professors, South Atlantic Modern Language Association, Southeastern Renaissance Conference, Phi Beta Kappa. *Awards, honors:* National Endowment for the Humanities senior research fellowship at Folger Shakespeare Library, 1976-77.

WRITINGS: Jonson's Moral Comedy, Northwestern University Press, 1971; (editor) *Renaissance Drama: Essays on Dramatic Antecedents,* Northwestern University Press, 1975; *Elizabethan Drama and the Viewer's Eye,* University of North Carolina Press, 1977. Contributor of articles and reviews to scholarly journals. Associate editor of *Renaissance Drama,* 1973, co-editor, 1974, presently member of editorial committee; member of editorial board of *Studies in Philology* and *Shakespeare Quarterly.*

WORK IN PROGRESS: Elizabethan Dramaturgy for the Open Stage, completion expected in 1979.

SIDELIGHTS: Dessen writes: "My current goal is to unite, as much as possible, the 'academic' skills of the theatrical historian or textual scholar or literary critic with the 'theatrical' perspective of the director or actor in order to understand more fully drama in the age of Shakespeare. I also believe that we can learn much about the greatest plays by studying the techniques and assumptions found in second and third rate plays rarely acknowledged by modern scholars. My continuing contact with students and festival personnel in Ashland, Oregon has enabled me to test my ideas and findings in the context of contemporary productions of Shakespeare."

*   *   *

de SWAAN, Abram 1942-

PERSONAL: Born January 8, 1942, in Amsterdam, Netherlands; son of Meier (a tradesman) and Roos de Swaan; married Ellen Ombre (a social worker), May 27, 1972; children: Meik. *Education:* University of Amsterdam, Drs.Pol.Sci., 1966, Dr.Soc.Sci., 1973; graduate study at Yale University, 1966-67, and University of California, Berkeley, 1967-68. *Office:* Sociologisch Instituut, Universiteit van Amsterdam, 3 Korte Spinhuissteeg, Amsterdam, Netherlands.

CARÈER: Free-lance writer and filmmaker, 1968-73; University of Amsterdam, Institute of Sociology, Amsterdam, Netherlands, lector, 1973-77, professor of sociology, 1977—. Lector at University of Rotterdam, 1971-73. *Member:* Dutch Association of Psychotherapy, Dutch Association of

Psychoanalysis (candidate member). *Awards, honors:* Biennial social science award from Holland Society for Sciences, 1975.

WRITINGS: Amerika in Termijnen (title means "Reports from the U.S.A."), Polak & Van Gennep, 1968; *Een Boterham met Tevredenheid* (title means "Bread with Satisfaction?"), Van Gennep, 1971; *Coalition Theories and Cabinet Formations,* American Elsevier, 1973; *Coping with Anxiety in a Cancer Ward,* Aula, 1977. Author of television documentary programs on the United States, Peru, and Dutch factory workers. Editor of *De Gids* (cultural monthly), 1970—.

WORK IN PROGRESS: Research on the welfare state and the police state; *Professionalization and Clientele Formation in Psychotherapy,* in press.

SIDELIGHTS: de Swaan writes: "General theoretical sociology and psychotherapeutic practice provide the inspiration for investigations and reflections on the ways in which people cope together with the adversities of disease, poverty, and ignorance in small units such as the family and the neighborhood, or in larger bureaucratic entities, and within the state apparatus, as an agency of welfare and terror."

*　*　*

de TIRTOFF, Romain 1892-
(Erte)

PERSONAL: Born November 10, 1892, in St. Petersburg, Russia; son of Peter (an admiral in the Russian Navy) and Nathalie (Nikolenko) de Tirtoff. *Education:* Attended public school in St. Petersburg, Russia. *Politics:* "Antiwar." *Religion:* Russian Orthodox. *Home and office:* 21 Rue Gutenberg, 92100 Boulogne-sur-Seine, France. *Agent:* Seven Arts Ltd., 48 South Molton St., London W1Y Z5U, England.

CAREER: Artist-painter; fashion designer. *Member:* Motion Picture and Television Costume Designers' Guild (honorary). *Awards, honors:* L'ordre de Merite Culturel from the French Government, 1972; Officier de l'Ordre des Arts et des Lettres, 1976.

WRITINGS: Erte Fashions, Academy Editions, 1972; *Erte: Things I Remember* (autobiography), Quadrangle and New York Times Co., 1975.

AVOCATIONAL INTERESTS: Travel, music, visual entertainment.

BIOGRAPHICAL/CRITICAL SOURCES: Roland Barthes, *Erte,* Ricci Parma, 1970; Charles Spences, *Erte,* Studio Vista, 1970; Stella Blum, *Designs by Erte,* Dover, 1977.

*　*　*

DEVEREUX, George 1908-

PERSONAL: Born September 13, 1908, in Lugos, Hungary; son of Eugene (a lawyer) and Margaret. *Education:* University of Paris, lic. es lettres, 1931, dr. es lettres, 1971; University of California, Berkeley, Ph.D., 1935; graduate of Topeka Institute for Psychoanalysis. *Home:* 2 Square Gabriel Faure, Antony 92160, France.

CAREER: Winter Veterans Administration Hospital, Topeka, Kan., director of research, 1946-53; Devereux Foundation, Devon, Pa., director of research, 1953-55; Temple University, Philadelphia, Pa., associate professor, 1956, professor of research in ethnopsychiatry, 1956-63; Ecole des Hautes Etudes en Sciences Sociales, Paris, France, professor of ethnopsychiatry, 1963-77. Roheim Memorial Lec-

turer and visiting fellow at All Souls College, Oxford, 1972. *Military service:* U.S. Naval Reserve, active duty, 1943-44; became lieutenant junior grade. *Member:* International Psychoanalytical Association, Societe Psychoanalytique de Paris.

WRITINGS: Reality and Dream: The Psychotherapy of a Plains Indian, International Universities Press, 1951, revised edition, New York University Press, 1969; (editor and contributor) *Psychoanalysis and the Occult,* International Universities Press, 1953; *A Study of Abortion in Primitive Societies,* Julian Press, 1955, revised edition, International Universities Press, 1976; *Therapeutic Education,* Harper, 1956; (editor) Ralph Linton, *Culture and Mental Disorder,* C. C Thomas, 1956; *Mohave Ethnopsychiatry,* Bureau of American Ethnology, 1961, revised edition, 1969; *From Anxiety to Method in the Behavioral Sciences,* Mouton & Co., 1967; *Essais d'Ethnopsychiatrie Generales* (title means "Essays in General Ethnopsychiatry"), Gallimard, 1970, 3rd revised edition, 1977; *Ethnopsychoanalyse Complementariste,* Flammarion, 1972, translation published as *Ethnopsychoanalysis,* University of California Press, 1977; *Tragedie et Poesies Grecques* (title means "Greek Tragedy and Poetry"), Flammarion, 1975; *Dreams in Greek Tragedy,* University of California Press, 1976. General editor of "Bibliotheque d'Ethnopsychiatrie." Contributor of about two hundred thirty articles to scientific journals.

WORK IN PROGRESS: Femme et Mythe, essays on Greek goddesses and heroines, publication by Flammarion; translation of *Essais d'Ethnopsychiatrie Generales,* for University of Chicago Press; *Euripides: Bacchantes* and *Oidipous: Mythes et Tragedies,* both book-length ethnopsychoanalytic studies (in French); continuing research on ethnopsychiatry and ethnopsychoanalysis.

SIDELIGHTS: Devereux writes to *CA:* "My work was systematically overlooked for 30 years. Thus, *From Anxiety to Method* was published only 30 years after it was written and is now available in five languages (as are two other volumes, which are made up of essays that achieved no recognition when originally published). I was concerned with laying the theoretical and methodological foundations of ethnopsychiatry at a time when this science was just coming into being. This may be due to my antecedent training in mathematics and theoretical physics which safeguarded me from conceptual sloppiness."

*　*　*

DeVITO, Joseph A(nthony) 1938-

PERSONAL: Born August 1, 1938, in New York, N.Y.; son of James and Theresa (DeMartino) DeVito. *Education:* Hunter College (now of the City University of New York), B.A., 1960; Temple University, M.A., 1962; University of Illinois, Ph.D., 1964. *Religion:* Roman Catholic. *Home:* 133 East 35th St., New York, N.Y. 10016. *Office:* Department of Communication Arts and Sciences, Queens College of the City University of New York, Flushing, N.Y. 11367.

CAREER: Hunter College of the City University of New York, New York, N.Y., instructor in communication, 1964-66; Herbert H. Lehman College of the City University of New York, Bronx, N.Y., assistant professor, 1967-69, associate professor of speech, 1969-71; Queens College of the City University of New York, Flushing, N.Y., associate professor, 1971, professor of communication arts and sciences, 1972—. *Member:* International Society for General Semantics (member of board of directors), International Communication Association, Speech Communication Association of America.

WRITINGS: The Psychology of Speech and Language: An Introduction to Psycholinguistics, Random House, 1970; (editor) *Communication: Concepts and Processes*, Prentice-Hall, 1971, revised edition, 1976; *General Semantics: Guide and Workbook*, Everett/Edwards, 1971, revised edition, 1973; *Psycholinguistics*, Bobbs-Merrill, 1973; (editor) *Language: Concepts and Processes*, Prentice-Hall, 1973; (with Jill Giattino and T. D. Schon) *Articulation and Voice: Effective Communication*, Bobbs-Merrill, 1975; *The Interpersonal Communication Book*, Harper, 1976; *Instructional Strategies for The Interpersonal Communication Book*, Harper, 1976; *Communicology: An Introduction to the Study of Human Communication*, Harper, in press. Author of "General Semantics: Nine Cassette Lectures," Everett/Edwards, 1971. Contributor to speech and communication journals, and to *Sexology*.

WORK IN PROGRESS: Communication and Sexual Behavior; Movie Quiz.

SIDELIGHTS: DeVito writes: "From a relatively narrow interest in the psychology of language my interests expanded to encompass the entire range of human communication. Right now I am most interested in the relationship between communication and sexual behavior, the assumption being that we can learn a great deal about each from the other. A related interest is the sociological and psychological dimension of sexual 'deviation' particularly as these relate to communication."

*   *   *

DEVLIN, Patrick (Arthur) 1905-

PERSONAL: Born November 25, 1905, in Chislehurst, England; son of William John (an architect) and Frances Evelyn (Crombie) Devlin; married Madeleine Oppenheimer, February 12, 1932; children: Gilpatrick, Clare, Virginia, Dominick, Timothy, Matthew. *Education:* Christ's College, Cambridge, B.A., 1927, M.A., 1964. *Home:* West Wick House, Pewsey, Wiltshire, England.

CAREER: Barrister-at-large, Gray's Inn, 1929; appointed King's counsel, 1945; master of the bench (master of the governing body) of Gray's Inn, 1947; justice of the High Court, 1948-60; president of the Restrictive Practices Court, 1957-60; lord justice of appeal, 1960-61, lord of appeal in ordinary, 1961-63; treasurer (head) of Gray's Inn, 1963. Attorney general of Duchy of Cornwall, 1947-48. Chairman of Committee of Inquiry into Dock Labor Scheme, 1956, Commission on Nyasaland, 1959, Committee on Port Transport Industry, 1965, Joint Board for National Newspaper Industry, 1965-69, Commission on Inquiry into Industrial Representation, 1971-72, Committee on Identification in Criminal Cases, 1974-75, and on other committees. Chairman of council of Bedford College, London, 1953-59; high steward of Cambridge University, 1966—. Member of Privy Council, 1960—. *Member:* British Maritime Law Association (president, 1962-76), British Academy (fellow), Press Council (chairman, 1964-69). *Awards, honors:* Created knight, 1948, and life peer, 1961; LL.D., University of Glasgow and University of Toronto, both 1962, and Cambridge University, 1966; D.C.L., Oxford University, 1965, University of Leicester and University of Sussex, both 1966, University of Durham, 1968, and University of Liverpool, 1970.

WRITINGS: Trial by Jury, Stevens & Sons, 1956, 2nd edition, 1966; *Summing Up of the Honourable Mr. Justice Devlin*, privately printed, 1957; *The Criminal Prosecution in England*, Yale University Press, 1958; *Nyasaland Commis-*

sion of Inquiry Report, H.M.S.O., 1959; *The Enforcement of Morals*, Oxford Univeristy Press, 1959.

Samples of Lawmaking, Oxford University Press, 1962; *Committee of Inquiry into Certain Matters concerning the Port Transport Industry Report*, H.M.S.O., 1965; *Committee of Inquiry under Lord Devlin into the Wages Structure and Level of Pay for Dock Workers Report*, H.M.S.O., 1966; *The House of Lords and the Naval Prize Bill, 1911*, Cambridge University Press, 1968.

(Contributor) Michael Zander, editor, *What's Wrong with the Law?* (radio talks), British Broadcasting Corp., 1970; *Too Proud to Fight: Woodrow Wilson's Neutrality*, Oxford University Press, 1974.

WORK IN PROGRESS: Aspects of the English Judge; Mankind on the March: Woodrow Wilson at the Paris Peace Conference, 1919.

*   *   *

de VRIES, Jan 1943-

PERSONAL: Born November 14, 1943, in the Netherlands; came to the United States in 1948, naturalized citizen, 1954; son of Cornelius (a construction worker) and Elly (a sales clerk; maiden name, van Konynenburg) de Vries; married Jeannie Green, September 25, 1968; children: Nicholas, Saskia. *Education:* Columbia University, A.B., 1965; Yale University, Ph.D., 1970. *Religion:* Protestant. *Home:* 1701 La Vereda Rd., Berkeley, Calif. 94709. *Office:* Department of History, University of California, Berkeley, Calif. 94720.

CAREER: Michigan State University, East Lansing, assistant professor of history, 1970-73; University of California, Berkeley, associate professor, 1973-77, professor of history, 1977—. Visiting assistant professor at Yale University, 1972. *Member:* Economic History Association.

WRITINGS: The Dutch Rural Economy in the Golden Age, Yale University Press, 1974; *The Economy of Europe in an Age of Crisis*, Cambridge University Press, 1976.

WORK IN PROGRESS: Barges and Capitalism: Passenger Transportation in the Dutch Economy, 1632-1837, for Landbouwhogeschool (Netherlands); *The Urbanization of Europe, 1500-1800*, completion expected in 1979.

SIDELIGHTS: De Vries writes: "My chief interest is long-term economic history and the blending of the New Economic History with the 'Annales School.'"

*   *   *

DE VRIES, Walter (Dale) 1929-

PERSONAL: Born November 13, 1929, in Holland, Mich.; son of Martin and Katherine (Vander Leek) De Vries; married Lois Cook, September 6, 1950; children: Michael, Robert, Steven, Walter Dann. *Education:* Hope College, B.A. (cum laude), 1954; Michigan State University, M.A., 1955, Ph.D., 1960. *Politics:* Independent. *Religion:* Presbyterian. *Home:* 9 Bahama Dr., Wrightsville Beach, N.C. 28480. *Agent:* Sterling Lord Agency, Inc., 660 Madison Ave., New York, N.Y. 10021. *Office:* P.O. Box 501, Wrightsville Beach, N.C. 28480; and Old Chemistry Building, Room 16, Duke University, Durham, N.C. 27706.

CAREER: Calvin College, Grand Rapids, Mich., instructor in political science, 1955-56; Hope College, Holland, Mich., instructor in psychology, 1958-59; Calvin College, instructor, 1959-60, 1960-61, assistant professor of political science, 1961-62; executive assistant to Governor George Romney, in Lansing, Mich., 1962-67; Harvard University, Cambridge, Mass., fellow of J. F. Kennedy Institute of Politics, 1968-69; De Vries & Associates, Inc., Wrightsville Beach, N.C., president, 1970—. Professor at University of Michigan, 1969-72; associate professor at Duke University, 1972—. President of North Carolina Opinion Research, Inc. Assistant to speaker of Michigan House of Representatives, 1957-61; delegate to Michigan Constitutional Convention, 1961-62; member of Detroit Metropolitan Regional Planning Commission, 1963-65; senior consultant to Market Opinion Research (Detroit); member of Interstate Cooperation Commission, 1963-67; member of committee on future operations of Council of State Governments, 1965-66; member of Michigan Civil Service Commission, 1971-72; member of advisory board of U.S. Bureau of the Census, 1972-74. *Military service:* U.S. Army, 1948-51.

MEMBER: International Association of Political Consultants, American Association of Political Consultants (vice-president, 1974-77), American Association for Public Opinion Research, American Political Science Association.

WRITINGS: (With Lance Tarrance) *The Ticket-Splitter: A New Force in American Politics,* Eerdmans, 1972; (with Jack Bass) *The Transformation of Southern Politics,* Basic Books, 1976.

WORK IN PROGRESS: A revision of *The Ticket-Splitter.*

* * *

DEWDNEY, Selwyn (Hanington) 1909-

PERSONAL: Born October 22, 1909, in Prince Albert, Saskatchewan, Canada; son of Alfred Daniel Alexander (an Anglican bishop) and Alice Ashwood (Hanington) Dewdney; married Irene Maude Donner (a psychiatric art therapist), 1936; children: Donner, Keewatin, Peter, Chris. *Education:* University of Toronto, B.A., 1931, education certificate, 1932; Ontario College of Art, associateship, 1936. *Politics:* "A skeptical Socialist." *Religion:* "Humanist." *Home:* 27 Erie Ave., London, Ontario, Canada N6J 1H9.

CAREER: Collegiate-Vocational Institute, Owen Sound, Ontario, art specialist and teacher of English and geography, 1932-34; Sir Adam Beck Collegiate Institute, London, Ontario, head of art and geography departments, 1936-45; Westminster Hospital, London, part-time psychiatric art therapist, 1953-72. Executive director of Artists Workshop of London, 1960-62; president of Western Art League, 1957-60; member of board of directors of N'Amerind (Indian Friendship Centre), 1966-69, Indian Crafts of Ontario, 1970-72, and Western Ontario Therapeutic Community Hostel (founding member), 1970-72. Research associate in pictography at Royal Ontario Museum, 1966—, research assistant in archaeology, 1970-71; co-founder and senior associate of Canadian Rock Art Research Associates, 1969—; coordinator of Trent University Rock Art Research Project, 1972-74. Book illustrator, 1947-59. Conducted field research all over Canada since 1957. Reproductions of rock paintings and petroglyphs represented in collections at Royal Ontario Museum, Glenbow-Alberta Institute, and National Museum of Man. *Member:* Indian-Eskimo Association (member of Ontario board of directors, 1968-69).

WRITINGS: Wind Without Rain (novel), [Toronto], 1946, reprinted, New Canadian Library, 1974; (editor and author of introduction) Audrey Saunders, *Algonquin Story,* Ontario Department of Lands and Forests, 1946; (illustrator) Mabel Dunham, *Kristli's Trees,* McClelland & Stewart, 1960; (with Kenneth E. Kidd) *Indian Rock Paintings of the Great Lakes,* University of Toronto Press, 1962, revised edition, 1967; *The Map that Grew* (juvenile; self-illustrated), Oxford University Press, 1963; (author of introduction) Norval Morriseau, *Legends of My People: The Great Ojibway,* Ryerson Press, 1965; *They Shared to Survive: An Illustrated History of Canada's Native People,* Macmillan, 1975; *Sacred Scrolls of the Southern Ojibway,* University of Toronto Press, 1975; *Christopher Breton* (novel), McClelland & Stewart, in press.

Illustrator of numerous textbooks. Contributor of articles on pictography, ethnology and ethnohistory, education, geography, art therapy, and native artists to journals and popular periodicals.

WORK IN PROGRESS: My Love Affair with the Canoe, completion expected in 1979.

SIDELIGHTS: In 1928, Dewdney accompanied the Bishop of Keewatin on a thirty-eight-hundred-mile journey to northern Indians, traveling eight hundred miles by canoe. In 1929 and 1930 he worked as an Anglican student missionary at Lac Seul Post. In 1933 he was traverse man on a Geological Survey of Canada crew in Kapuskasing district. In 1937 he helped lead a Schools Exploration Society expedition to survey an unmapped area in the Cassiar Mountains of British Columbia. In 1940, he was a member of a timber-cruising party for a timber company northeast of Lake Superior.

Dewdney's field work in aboriginal pictography includes work for Royal Ontario Museum, Quetico Foundation, Glenbow Foundation, Canada Council, Saskatchewan Museum of Natural History, Quetico-Superior Wilderness Research Center, Manitoba Department of Mines and Natural Resources, and Ontario Ministry of Natural Resources. He has examined hide and bark pictography in British, French, and Soviet museums and in private collections in Canada and the United States.

* * *

DI CAVALCANTI, Emiliano 1898(?)-1976

1898(?)—October 26, 1976; Brazilian painter and author. He was most famous for his nudes and landscapes. He produced more than 5,000 works in his career. His book, *Lyrical Memories of a Perfect Carioca,* was a best-seller. He died in Rio de Janeiro, Brazil. Obituaries: *Washington Post,* October 28, 1976.

* * *

DICE, Lee R. 1889(?)-1976

1889(?)—December 27, 1976; American educator, geneticist, and author of works in his field. He was a member of several professional organizations. He died in Ann Arbor, Mich. Obituaries: *New York Times,* January 3, 1977.

* * *

DICKERSON, Nancy H(anschman) 1930-

PERSONAL: Born January 19, 1930, in Milwaukee, Wis.; daughter of Frederick (an architect) and Florence (Connors) Hanschman; married Claude Wyatt Dickerson, February 24, 1962; children: Elizabeth Dickerson Earls, Ann Dickerson Harrower, Jane, Michael, John. *Education:* Attended Clarke College, 1944-46; University of Wisconsin, B.A., 1948; graduate study, Harvard University, 1949. *Politics:* Independent. *Religion:* Roman Catholic. *Home and office:* Merrywood, 700 Chain Bridge Rd., McLean, Va. 22101.

CAREER: Teacher at public schools in Milwaukee, Wis.,

1948-50; Georgetown University, School of Linguistics, Washington, D.C., registrar, 1950; U.S. Senate, Washington, D.C., staff assistant to Senate Committee on Foreign Relations, 1951-53; Columbia Broadcasting System (CBS), Washington, D.C., producer of radio and television news programs, including "The Leading Question" and "Face the Nation", during 1950's, became first woman CBS news correspondent, 1960-63, covered Democratic presidential campaign, 1960; National Broadcasting Co. (NBC), Washington, D.C., news correspondent for radio and television news, 1960-70; Public Broadcasting Service (PBS), representative on all-network interview of President Nixon, 1970; Dickerson Co. (producers of syndicated television programs), president, producer, and news analyst for nationally syndicated television program, "Inside Washington", 1971-74; board member of Hospital Corporation of America, 1976—. Lecturer.

MEMBER: Woman's National Press Club, American Women in Radio and Television, Radio-Television News Analysts, Washington Press Club (vice-president), Federal City Club. *Awards, honors:* Woman of the Year Award from *Radio TV Daily,* 1964, for outstanding reporting of President Kennedy's assassination; Spirit of Achievement Award from Yeshiva University, 1966; associate fellow of Yale University, 1972; has also received H.H.D. from American International College, Collegian Award from La Salle College, Sigma Delta Chi award from Boston University, Pioneer Award from New England Women's Press Association, and an award for excellence in reporting from *Variety.*

WRITINGS: Among Those Present, Random House, 1976. Contributor to *McCalls* and other magazines.

WORK IN PROGRESS: A book about the press after Watergate.

* * *

DICKEY, Charley   1920-

PERSONAL: Born November 25, 1920, in Bulls Gap, Tenn.; son of Charles H. and Billie (Hall) Dickey; married Bunty Goddard, October 19, 1972; children: (step-children) Katie Theg, Steve Theg, Ellie Theg. *Education:* University of Tennessee, B.A., 1947. *Politics:* Independent. *Religion:* "Spiritualist." *Home and office:* 2230 Monaghan Dr., Tallahassee, Fla. 32303.

CAREER: Sporting Arms and Ammunition Manufacturers' Institute, New York, N.Y., wildlife consultant, 1954-63; National Shooting Sports Foundation, Riverside, Conn., director, 1963-71; writer and photographer, 1971—. *Military service:* U.S. Navy, torpedo bomber pilot, 1942-45, 1952-53; became lieutenant commander; received Navy Cross, Distinguished Flying Cross, and Air Medal.

MEMBER: Outdoor Writers Association of America (adviser), Southeastern Outdoor Press Association (member of board of directors), Florida Outdoor Writers Association, Tennessee Outdoor Writers Association. *Awards, honors:* Awards from Southeastern Outdoor Press Association, all 1976, for best photograph, best magazine article, and best newspaper column.

WRITINGS: Charley Dickey's Bobwhite Quail Hunting, Oxmore, 1974; *Charley Dickey's Trout Fishing,* Oxmore, 1975; *Charley Dickey's Dove Hunting,* Oxmore, 1976; *Charley Dickey's Deer Hunting,* Oxmore, 1977; *Backtrack* (short stories), National Sporting Fraternity Ltd., 1977. Author of "Woods and Water," a column in *Tallahassee Democrat.* Contributor of articles and photographs on hunt-

ing, horses, flying, farming, and travel to outdoor magazines.

WORK IN PROGRESS: Writing for magazines.

SIDELIGHTS: Dickey writes: "I am a photo-journalist specializing in general outdoor coverage. I mostly travel in the Southeast but have hunted and fished in every state of the nation except Alaska, plus many of the Canadian provinces and Yucatan, Costa Rica, Panama, Japan, Korea, and the Pacific islands."

* * *

DIEKHOFF, John S(iemon)   1905-1976

October 23, 1905—August 20, 1976; American Milton scholar, professor of English, research consultant, and author of Milton studies and books on higher education. He died in Cleveland, Ohio. Obituaries: *New York Times,* August 24, 1976. (*CAP-2;* earlier sketch in *CA-29/32*)

* * *

DIENES, C(harles) Thomas   1940-

PERSONAL: Born January 9, 1940, in Chicago, Ill.; son of Walter N. (a teacher) and Florence (Weisbaar) Dienes; married Peggy Clements (a teacher), August 14, 1965; children: Kimberly. *Education:* Loyola University, Chicago, Ill., B.S., 1961; Northwestern University, J.D. (cum laude), 1964, Ph.D., 1968. *Home:* 11806 Charen Lane, Potomac, Md. 20854. *Office:* Washington College of Law, American University, Massachusetts & Nebraska Aves. N.W., Washington, D.C. 20016.

CAREER: Admitted to Illinois Bar, 1964; University of Houston, Houston, Tex., assistant professor of law, 1967-70, and political science, 1969-70; American University, Washington, D.C., associate professor, 1970-73, professor of law and government, 1973—. Visiting assistant professor at Indiana University, summer, 1970; instructor for Bar Review, Inc., 1971—. Reviewer of proposals for National Science Foundation, 1972—.

MEMBER: Law and Society Association, American Political Science Association, American Bar Association, American Academy of Political and Social Science, Society for the Study of Social Problems, American Civil Liberties Union, Association of American Law Schools, Coif.

WRITINGS: (Editor with others) *Welfare Law Handbook,* National Institute for Education in the Law and Poverty, 1968; *Law, Politics, and Birth Control,* University of Illinois Press, 1972; (with Jerome Barron) *Constitutional Law: Principles and Policy, Cases and Materials,* Bobbs-Merrill, 1975. Contributor of articles and reviews to law journals and to *American Behavioral Scientist.* Former notes and comments editor of *Northwestern University Law Review;* member of editorial board of *Law and Society Review.*

WORK IN PROGRESS: A handbook on free speech and free press with Jerome Barron, publication by Little, Brown, expected in 1978; a book outlining the multi-state bar exam, publication expected in 1978; research on the role of the police in a therapeutic response to alcoholism, and on processes for dispute settlement.

* * *

DIETZE, Charles Edgar   1919-

PERSONAL: Born January 21, 1919, in Savannah, Ga.; son of Ernest and Mary (Fetzer) Dietze; married Mary Nettie Peavyhouse (a farm manager), December 28, 1940; children:

Mary Katherine Dietze Lamm, Charles William. *Education:* Transylvania University, B.A., 1940; Lexington Theological Seminary, B.D., 1944. *Politics:* Democrat. *Home:* 805 Trinity Dr., Wilson, N.C. 27893. *Office:* Christian Church in North Carolina, P.O. Box 521, Wilson, N.C. 27893.

CAREER: Ordained minister of Christian Church (Disciples of Christ); Christian Church in North Carolina, Wilson, currently regional minister. President of Conference of Regional Ministers of the Christian Church; chairman of Wilson County Human Relations Commission; past president of North Carolina Council of Churches. *Awards, honors:* D.D. from Atlantic Christian College, 1965.

WRITINGS: God's Trustees, to Whom Much Is Given, Bethany Press, 1976.

WORK IN PROGRESS: Whatever Happened on the Way to Happiness, completion expected in 1978; *Payoff,* a novel about a clergyman, 1979.

SIDELIGHTS: Dietze writes: "During the past five years I have become interested in experiential learning and have been engaged in a group which uses this process. It has changed my life through helping me find a new freedom as a person. *God's Trustees* and *Whatever Happened on the Way to Happiness* are outgrowths of these experiences."

*   *   *

DILKE, O(swald) A(shton) W(entworth)   1915-

PERSONAL: Born April 26, 1915, in Hove, England; son of Clement Wentworth (a company director) and Jessie (Phelps) Dilke; married Margaret Williamson (a geographer and university lecturer), August 9, 1949; children: Stephen Wentworth. *Education:* King's College, Cambridge, B.A. (first class honors), 1938, M.A., 1945; University of South Africa, D.Litt. et Phil., 1963. *Religion:* Church of England. *Home:* Moorfield, Huby, Leeds LS17 0BP, England. *Office:* Department of Latin, University of Leeds, Leeds LS2 9JT, England.

CAREER: University of Hull, Hull, England, assistant lecturer, 1946, lecturer in classics, 1946-50; University of Glasgow, Glasgow, Scotland, lecturer, 1950-64, senior lecturer in humanity, 1964-67; University of Leeds, Leeds, England, professor of Latin, 1967—. Professor of classics at Rhodes University, 1961-62; visiting professor at Ohio State University, 1969; Sir D. Owen Evans Memorial Lecturer at University College of Wales at Aberystwyth, 1975. Representative to Council for British Archaeology. *Military service:* British Army, Intelligence Corps, 1940-46; became captain.

MEMBER: Classical Association (local president, 1975-77), Hellenic Society, Roman Society, Yorkshire Archaeological Society, Glasgow Archaeological Society, Athenaeum. *Awards, honors:* Augustus Austen Leigh studentship to British School in Athens, 1938-39.

WRITINGS: (Editor) Statius, *Achilleid,* Cambridge University Press, 1954; (editor) Horace, *Epistles I,* Methuen, 1960, 3rd edition, 1966; (author of revision) J. P. Postgate, editor, Lucan, *De Bello Civili VII,* Cambridge University Press, 1961; *The Roman Land Surveyors,* David & Charles, 1971; (contributor) D. R. Dudley, editor, *Neronians and Flavians,* Routledge & Kegan Paul, 1972; *The Ancient Romans: How They Lived and Worked,* David & Charles, 1975; *Roman Books and Their Impact,* Elmete Press, 1977. Contributor to *Geographical Magazine* and *Progress in Geography.*

WORK IN PROGRESS: Studying ancient books, Roman roads, Roman sites in Great Britain, the Roman land survey-

ors, Latin poetry, and the history of cartography and ancient geography.

SIDELIGHTS: Dilke comments: "I am interested not only in Greek and Latin language and literature but in modern languages, a knowledge of which helped my wartime work." *Avocational interests:* Travel (especially Italy), writing chess problems.

*   *   *

DILLON, David   1941-

PERSONAL: Born August 24, 1941, in Fitchburg, Mass.; son of John Joseph (a teacher) and Lauretta (Morris) Dillon; married Sally Ann Hall (a sculptor), June 5, 1971. *Education:* Boston College, B.A. (magna cum laude), 1963; Harvard University, M.A., 1965, Ph.D., 1970. *Politics:* Independent. *Religion:* Roman Catholic. *Home and office:* 5119 Vanderbilt, Dallas, Tex. 75206.

CAREER: Southern Methodist University, Dallas, Tex., assistant professor of English, 1969—. *Member:* American Studies Association, Texas American Studies Association. *Awards, honors:* Texaco Foundation scholarship, 1963; Fellowship from Rotary International, at University of London, 1964-65.

WRITINGS: Writing: Experience and Expression, Heath, 1976. Contributor of articles and reviews to magazines, including *Southwest Review, D,* and *Critique.*

WORK IN PROGRESS: Another book on writing; a book of interviews with contemporary American writers; an oral history of the "out islands" of the Maine Coast, completion expected in 1978.

SIDELIGHTS: Dillon writes: "My first writing book came directly out of my work in the classroom. As the title suggests, I'm concerned with helping students generate writing from their experience; I'm workshop and process oriented, not a rules person." *Avocational interests:* Travel (especially the deserts and rivers of the American West), photography, watching hockey games.

*   *   *

DiMENTO, Joseph F(rank)   1947-

PERSONAL: Born April 14, 1947, in Syracuse, N.Y.; son of Joseph Anthony and Theresa (a saleswoman; maiden name, Riccardo) DiMento. *Education:* Harvard University, B.A. (cum laude), 1969; University of Michigan, Ph.D. and J.D., both 1974. *Home:* 10 East 38th Pl., Long Beach, Calif. 90803. *Office:* Program in Social Ecology, University of California, Irvine, Calif. 92717.

CAREER: Model Cities Program, Ann Arbor, Mich., assistant to the director, 1969-71; Washtenaw County Planned Parenthood Association, Ann Arbor, Mich., intake interviewer, 1971-74; University of California, Irvine, assistant professor of social ecology, 1974—, consultant to Public Policy Research Organization, 1975—. Member of State Bar of California. Research assistant of State of Michigan, Department of Natural Resources, 1972. Member of California Orange-San Diego Counties Environmental Task Force, 1975. *Member:* American Bar Association, Society for the Psychological Study of Social Issues, Environmental Defense Fund, California Trial Lawyers Association.

WRITINGS: (Contributor) Don M. Flourney, editor, *The New Teachers,* Jossey-Bass, 1971; *Managing Environmental Change,* Praeger, 1976. Contributor to law journals.

WORK IN PROGRESS: Citizen Environmental Legislation and Its Institutional Impact.

DINNAN, James A. 1929-

PERSONAL: Born October 7, 1929, in West Haven, Conn.; son of Raymond and Genieve (Withington) Dinnan; married Louise Heuberger, 1947; children: James, Thomas, Jane, Barbara, Joseph. Education: Hofstra University, B.A., 1954, M.S., 1956; Fordham University, Ph.D., 1959. Home: 190 Ponderosa Dr., Athens, Ga. 30605. Office: Aderhold Hall, University of Georgia, Athens, Ga. 30602.

CAREER: Elementary school teacher in public schools in Baldwin, N.Y., 1954-62; University of Scranton, Scranton, Pa., associate professor, 1962-67; University of Virginia, Fairfax, associate professor, 1967-68; University of Georgia, Athens, professor, 1968—. Military service: U.S. Marine Corps, 1944-49.

WRITINGS: Spanish Reading Laboratory, U.S. Agency for International Development, 1968; Teaching Reading to the Disadvantaged Adult, Prentice-Hall, 1971; Communication: A Meta-Theory of Language, Jaddy Enterprises, 1976.

SIDELIGHTS: Dinnan has created a series of four kits, "Key to Learning Series," 1977.

*   *   *

DINSKY, Lazar 1891(?)-1976

1891(?)—August 20, 1976; American labor organizer, poet, and author. Many of his works, published in Yiddish, were about the early labor movement. He died in New York City. Obituaries: New York Times, August 22, 1976.

*   *   *

DITCHBURN, R(obert) W(illiam) 1903-

PERSONAL: Born January 14, 1903, in Lancashire, England; son of William (a schoolmaster) and Martha Kathleen Ditchburn; married Doreen May Barrett, January 14, 1929; children: Barbara Jean, Robert Keith, Moira Jill Ditchburn Holt, Clodagh Rosalind Ditchburn Jakubovics. Education: University of Liverpool, B.Sc., 1922; Trinity College, Cambridge, B.A., 1924, M.A., 1927, Ph.D., 1928; University of Dublin, M.A., 1928. Politics: Labour. Religion: "Not associated with any church." Home: 9 Summerfield Rise, Goring, Reading, Berkshire RG8 0DS, England.

CAREER: University of Dublin, Dublin, Ireland, fellow of Trinity College, 1928-46, professor of natural and experimental philosophy, 1929-46, registrar for social studies at Trinity College, 1940-44; University of Reading, Reading, England, professor of physics, 1946-68, professor emeritus, 1968—. Visiting professor at University of Rochester. Chairman of Diamond Research Committee, 1956—. Consultant to government and industry. Wartime service: British Admiralty, civilian principal experimental officer, 1942-45.

MEMBER: Royal Society (fellow), Institute of Physics (fellow; vice-president, 1960-62), Royal Irish Academy, Optical Society of America (fellow). Awards, honors: Thomas Young Oration from Physical Society, 1959; National Science Foundation fellowship, 1964.

WRITINGS: Light, Blackie & Son, 1952, 3rd edition, Academic Press, 1975; Eye-Movements and Visual Perception, Clarendon Press, 1973.

Contributor: (With E. W. J. Mitchell and others) Defects in Crystalline Solids, Physical Society, 1954; (with U. Oepik) D. R. Bates, editor, Atomic and Molecular Processes, Academic Press, 1962; (with J. F. H. Custers) R. Berman, editor, The Physical Properties of Diamond, Clarendon Press, 1965.

Contributor to Encyclopaedia Britannica. Contributor of about a hundred articles to scientific journals.

WORK IN PROGRESS: Research on the information capacity of the visual system and on technical processes of the diamond industry.

SIDELIGHTS: Ditchburn writes that he has made many scientific visits to the United States, several countries of Europe, and South Africa. He lived in Jamaica and visited the University of the West Indies. He is a member of the Pugwash movement "which is concerned principally with nuclear disarmament. While loving my own country, I believe that rapid progress toward World Government is the only hope for the future of mankind."

AVOCATIONAL INTERESTS: Walking, music.

BIOGRAPHICAL/CRITICAL SOURCES: Stewart Duke-Elder and K. Wybar, System of Ophthalmology, Volume VI, Kimpton, 1973.

*   *   *

DIXON, S(ydney) L(awrence) 1930-

PERSONAL: Born July 9, 1930, in Liverpool, England; son of Sidney (a bus driver) and Florence (Ditchfield) Dixon; married Nancy Hancock, March 30, 1957 (divorced); married Rosaleen Dunphy (a nurse), September 7, 1968; children: Caroline, Elisabeth, Heather, Steven, Avril, Penny. Education: Attended Liverpool College of Technology, 1946-51; University of Liverpool, B.Eng. (first class honors), 1954, Ph.D., 1968. Home: 34 Westwood Rd., Noctorum, Birkenhead, Merseyside L43 9RQ, England. Office: Department of Mechanical Engineering, University of Liverpool, Liverpool L69 3BX, England.

CAREER: D. Napier & Son Ltd., Liverpool, England, student apprentice, 1946-51; Royal Aircraft Establishment, Farnborough, England, scientific officer, 1956-57; A. V. Roe & Co. Ltd., Manchester, England, 1957-59, began as aircraft intake designer, later in charge of Transonic Wind Tunnel; University of Liverpool, Liverpool, England, lecturer in mechanical engineering, 1959—. Member of Council of Engineering Institutions. Member: Institution of Mechanical Engineers, Association of University Teachers.

WRITINGS: Fluid Mechanics: Thermodynamics of Turbomachinery, Pergamon, 1966, 3rd edition, in press; (contributor) R. K. Penny, editor, The Experimental Method, Longmans, 1974; Worked Examples in Turbomachinery, Pergamon, 1975.

WORK IN PROGRESS: Secondary Flows in Turbine Blade Rows, an experimental investigation to be followed by a theoretical investigation.

SIDELIGHTS: Dixon writes: "I can only work hard when under strong pressure to complete in a given period—otherwise time is frittered away on a multitude of little jobs." Avocational interests: Mountain walking (used to rock climb and pothole), skiing (especially ski touring).

*   *   *

DJONOVICH, Dusan J. 1920-

PERSONAL: Born May 17, 1920, in Belgrade, Yugoslavia; came to the United States in 1955, naturalized citizen, 1961; son of Jovan and Angelina (Wouk) Djonovich; married Maria Romanov (a textile stylist), October 19, 1954. Education: University of Belgrade, diploma in law, 1943; Columbia University, M.L.S., 1964, further graduate study, 1964-66, received certificate of advanced librarianship. Reli-

gion: Serbian Orthodox. *Home:* 70 East 10th St., New York, N.Y. 10003. *Office:* Brooklyn Law School, 250 Joralemon St., Brooklyn, N.Y. 11201.

CAREER: Worked in American branch of Allied Military Government, Trieste Free Territory, 1949-54; United States Department of State, Washington, D.C., consul general in Genoa, Italy, 1954-55; after immigrating to United States, held a variety of jobs, mainly in banking and insurance industry, 1955-63; New York University, New York, N.Y., foreign law librarian, 1964-74; Brooklyn Law School, Brooklyn, N.Y., professor of law and librarian, 1974—. *Military service:* Royal Yugoslav Army, 1941-45; became second lieutenant. *Member:* International Law Library Association, American Association of Law Libraries, Law Library Association of Greater New York, Beta Phi Mu.

WRITINGS: (With Robert Sperry) *The Law of Notary Public,* Oceana, 1967; *Legal Education: A Selective Bibliography,* Oceana, 1970; (editor) *United Nations Resolutions,* Oceana, First Series: *General Assembly,* thirteen volumes, 1972-77, Second Series: *Security Council,* seven volumes, in press. Editor-in-chief of "Current Publications in Legal and Related Fields," a series, Oceana, 1965-66; consultant to Oceana, 1965-74.

SIDELIGHTS: Djonovich writes that his "vocational as well as avocational interest is public law, especially international public law and comparative law." He has traveled extensively through Europe. He mentions that during World War II he was an active participant in the resistance movement in Yugoslavia led by General Draza Mihailovich. *Avocational interests:* Collecting rare books on international law and Roman law.

* * *

DOBB, Maurice (Herbert) 1900-1976

July 24, 1900—August 17, 1976; British Marxist economist and theoretician, professor of economics at Cambridge University, and author of books in his field, including *Socialism, Capitalism, and Economic Growth.* He died in England. Obituaries: *AB Bookman's Weekly,* October 4, 1976. (See index for previous *CA* sketch)

* * *

DOBBINS, Dorothy Wyeth 1929-

PERSONAL: Born March 31, 1929, in East Orange, N.J.; daughter of Herbert Hummel Hock (a pharmacist) and Carol (Wyeth) Hock; married Dwight Dobbins (an art director and illustrator), August 23, 1953; children: Richard Keith, Alisa Gay (deceased), Charity Anne. *Education:* Attended Traphagen School of Art and Pratt Institute. *Politics:* Liberal. *Religion:* Christian. *Home and office:* 33 Liberty Ave., Berkeley Heights, N.J. 07922. *Agent:* Wieser & Wieser, 52 Vanderbilt Ave., New York, N.Y. 10017.

CAREER: Eleanor Pepper, New York City, interior designer; Ethan Allen Furniture Co., New York City, advertising designer; Street & Smith Publications, New York City, decorating editor of *Living for Young Homemakers;* free-lance interior designer and manufacturers' advertising designer, 1965—.

WRITINGS: What Do You with a Drawbridge? (juvenile), Addison-Wesley, 1976.

WORK IN PROGRESS: Conversations with a Carpenter; Ways with a Window; Melinda at the Met, for children.

SIDELIGHTS: Dorothy Dobbins writes: "The children's

books (done with my husband's illustrations) are for fun. I have also done considerable puppet-work with children of grammar school age."

* * *

DOBBS, Betty Jo Teeter 1930-

PERSONAL: Born October 19, 1930, in Camden, Ark.; daughter of Ransom Alexander, Sr. (a Methodist minister) and Mary Gladys (Greer) Teeter; married Dan Byron Dobbs (a professor of law and writer), May 31, 1953; children: Katherine Roan, George Byron II, Gladys Rebecca, Jean Frances. *Education:* Hendrix College, B.A., 1951; University of Arkansas, M.A., 1953; University of North Carolina, Ph.D., 1974. *Office:* Department of History, Harris Hall, Northwestern University, Evanston, Ill. 60201.

CAREER: Northwestern University, Evanston, Ill., assistant professor, 1975-76, associate professor of history, 1976—. *Member:* History of Science Society, Society for the History of Alchemy and Chemistry. *Awards, honors:* Postdoctoral fellowship from North Atlantic Treaty Organization (NATO), 1974-75.

WRITINGS: The Foundations of Newton's Alchemy: Or, the Hunting of the Greene Lyon, Cambridge University Press, 1975. Contributor of articles and reviews to history of science and philology journals.

WORK IN PROGRESS: Continuing research on seventeenth-century alchemy and chemistry, especially that of Newton and Sir Kenelm Digby.

SIDELIGHTS: B. J. Dobbs told *CA:* "As a former teacher of twentieth century chemistry, I find the period of transition in the seventeenth and eighteenth centuries, when alchemy was becoming more of a chemical discipline but yet still was the carrier of many ancient and esoteric traditions, especially fascinating. My research takes me occasionally to England, where exploration of libraries rich in seventeenth century books and manuscripts can alternate with punting on the Cam, visits to Stonehenge, etc., all which serve to make scholarly work in this area very attractive indeed."

* * *

DOIG, Desmond 1921-

PERSONAL: Born August 17, 1921, in Allahabad, India; son of Sydney Stanford (a marine engineer) and Katie (an army nurse; maiden name, Carrington-Cox) Doig. *Education:* Received equivalent of American high school diploma in Kurseong, India. *Home:* 8A Minto Park, 13 Debendralal Khan Rd., Calcutta 700 027, India. *Office: The Statesman* Ltd., 4 Chowringhee Sq., Calcutta 700 001, India.

CAREER: The Statesman (English-language daily), Calcutta, India, worked as artist, writer, assistant editor, and roving correspondent, 1948-67, editor of *JS* (fortnightly magazine for young people), 1967—. Notable assignments include the first reporting from Nepal, Bhutan, and Nagaland, the flight of the Dalai Lama into India, 1959, the Indo-Chinese War, 1962, the assassination of Bhutanese prime minister, Jigme Dorji, and execution of the assassins, 1964, and the crusade of Mother Teresa. Director of Nachiketa Publications, 1971—. *Military service:* Indian Army, Fifth Royal Gurkha Rifles, 1939-47; became captain; received Africa Star and Italy Star. *Awards, honors:* President's Award for excellence in printing and design from Indian Ministry of Information and Broadcasting, 1974, for *Once Upon A Time, Many Moons Ago.*

WRITINGS: (Self-illustrated) *Calcutta, An Artist's Impres-*

sion, The Statesman Ltd., 1970; (with Jean Perrin) *Sikkim,* Pietro Mele, 1971; (with Edmund Hillary) *High In the Thin, Cold Air,* Doubleday, 1972; (self-illustrated) *Once Upon A Time, Many Moons Ago,* Dunlop India, 1974; (illustrated with others) *Mother Teresa, Her People and Her Work,* Harper, 1976. Articles of Hillary Expeditions syndicated throughout the world by Opera Mundi, 1960-63; contributor to journals and magazines, including *National Geographic, Time, Life,* and to newspapers.

WORK IN PROGRESS: These Moving Stones, a historical self-illustrated sketch-book of the seven cities of Delhi, for Collins and Nachiketa; *My Kind of Kathmandu,* a self-illustrated sketch-book of Nepal, for Collins; *My Resistance Is Low* (tentative title), an autobiography in two parts; *Pematong,* a prose poem set in a mythical Himalayan country.

SIDELIGHTS: Doig told *CA:* "Though I was determined to become an artist, World War II made me a professional soldier, and serving with the famed Gurkhas of Nepal give me a lifelong interest in the Himalayas; I speak Nepalese and Sherpa fluently. I tried to visit Tibet, but the Chinese got there first. Another ambition was to explore the southern approach route to Mt. Everest, then in forbidden Nepal. I mounted an expedition with fellow officers of my Regiment, received written interest from the National and Royal Geographic Societies, but the plans fizzled in the chaos that followed the partition of India in 1947. I remained in India, after leaving the Army, to explore the Himalayas.

"I was selected from among several well-known international journalists to accompany Sir Edmund Hillary on his highly prestigious scientific and mountain climbing expedition (which also looked for the Yeti) in 1960-61 and again in 1963 I accompanied Sir Edmund on his first school-building expedition.

"Most of my writing is not concerned with mountaineering, but the mountains are in my blood. I have not been on top of the world myself, but following Hillary up a mountainside I have often looked at his large, size thirteen boots and marvelled and tried to share the exaltation he must have felt as he stood atop Everest for the first time. There is a grandeur, a remoteness and amazing sense of humility in being perched high above the world, the clouds and the rising and setting sun. As to why men climb mountains, I would say for the sheer ecstasy and exhilaration. To use a purely Indian comparison, it would be like achieving 'samadhi.'"

* * *

DOLS, Michael W(alters) 1942-

PERSONAL: Born July 6, 1942, in Baltimore, Md.; son of William Ludwig and Isabel Louise (Walters) Dols. *Education:* Trinity College, Hartford, Conn., B.A., 1964; graduate study, University of London, 1964-65; University of North Carolina, M.A., 1967; Princeton University, Ph.D., 1971. *Politics:* Democrat. *Religion:* Episcopalian. *Home:* 150 Henry St., San Francisco, Calif. 94114. *Office:* Department of History, California State University, Hayward, Calif. 94542.

CAREER: California State University, Hayward, assistant professor, 1971-75, associate professor of history, 1975—. Member of American Research Center in Egypt. *Member:* Mediaeval Academy of America, Middle East Studies Association of North America, American Oriental Society, American Numismatic Society. *Awards, honors:* Grant from American Council of Learned Societies and Social Science Research Council, 1974-75; fellowship from American Research Center in Egypt, 1974-75; National Endowment for the Humanities fellowship, 1976.

WRITINGS: The Black Death in the Middle East, Princeton University Press, 1977. Contributor of articles and reviews to oriental and Middle East studies journals.

WORK IN PROGRESS: Translating *Risalat fi daf' madarr al-abdan bi-ard Misr* (title means "On the Prevention of Bodily Ills in Egypt"), by Ali ibn Ridwan, completion expected in 1979; *The Madman in Medieval Muslim Society,* 1980; research on the leper and leprosy in medieval Muslim society; working on an excavation of the medieval Egyptian city of Qusayr.

SIDELIGHTS: Dols comments: "I am primarily interested in medieval Muslim social history that has been greatly neglected by historians. The investigation of such history is greatly aided by comparable studies in medieval European history. I believe that the study of Islamic history in general is of vital importance today because of the significant role of the Middle East in world affairs."

* * *

DONAHUE, Don 1942-

PERSONAL: Born May 18, 1942, in San Francisco, Calif.; son of Leo (a dock worker) and Jessie (Hamilton) Donahue. *Education:* Attended University of California at Berkeley, 1961-63. *Home:* 2750-A Adeline St., Berkeley, Calif. 94703.

CAREER: Berkeley Barb, Berkeley, Calif., production manager, 1967; Apex Novelties, San Francisco, Calif., owner, 1967—; West Coast Print Center, Berkeley, pressman, 1975—. Instructor of printing, University of California at San Francisco, 1975.

WRITINGS: (Co-editor and author of introduction) *The Apex Treasury of Underground Comix,* Links Books, 1974. Contributor of articles to *Berkeley Barb* and *Organ.*

WORK IN PROGRESS: Research in Catholicism.

AVOCATIONAL INTERESTS: Real estate, gambling, writing tunes, and drawing pictures.

* * *

DONALDSON, (Charles) Ian (Edward) 1935-

PERSONAL: Born May 6, 1935, in Melbourne, Australia; son of William Edward (a physician) and Elizabeth (Weigall) Donaldson; married Tamsin Jane Proctor (a linguist), March 6, 1962; children: Benjamin, Sadie. *Education:* University of Melbourne, B.A. (honors), 1957; Magdalen College, Oxford, B.A. (honors), 1960, M.A., 1964; attended Merton College, Oxford, 1962. *Politics:* Labour. *Religion:* None. *Home:* 22 Dugan St., Deakin, Canberra, Australian Capital Territory 2600, Australia. *Office:* Humanities Research Centre, Australian National University, Canberra, Australian Capital Territory 2600, Australia.

CAREER: University of Melbourne, Parkville, Victoria, senior tutor in English, 1958; Oxford University, Oxford, England, lecturer in English and fellow of Wadham College, 1962-69; Australian National University, Canberra, Australian Capital Territory, professor of English, 1969—, director of Humanities Research Centre, 1974—. Visiting assistant professor at University of California, Santa Barbara, 1967-68. *Member:* International Association of University Professors of English, Australasian and Pacific Society for Eighteenth-Century Studies, Australian Universities Language and Literature Association, Australia Academy of the Humanities (fellow), American Society for Eighteenth-Century Studies.

WRITINGS: The World Upside-Down: Comedy from

Jonson to Fielding, Clarendon Press, 1970; (editor) *Ben Jonson: Poems,* Oxford University Press, 1975. Co-editor of *Essays in Criticism,* 1965-69; theater reviewer for *Guardian* (London), 1961-69; member of editorial board of *Oxford Review,* 1966-69, *A.U.M.L.A.,* 1973—, and *Southern Review,* 1975-77.

WORK IN PROGRESS: A book on comedy; a study of the myth of Lucretia.

* * *

DONELSON, Kenneth L(avern)   1927-

PERSONAL: Born June 16, 1927, in Holdrege, Neb.; son of Lester Homer Irving (a meatcutter) and Minnie Irene (Lyons) Donelson; married Virginia J. Watts, May 11, 1948 (divorced October, 1969); married Annette E. Whetton (a legal secretary), June 5, 1970; children: Sheryl Lynette Donelson George, Kurt Allen. *Education:* University of Iowa, B.A., 1950, M.A., 1951, Ph.D., 1963. *Politics:* Democrat. *Home:* 5012 South Birch, Tempe, Ariz. 85282. *Office:* English Department, Arizona State University, Tempe, Ariz. 85281.

CAREER: High school English teacher in Glidden, Iowa, 1951-56, and in Cedar Rapids, Iowa, 1956-63; Kansas State University, Manhattan, assistant professor of English and education, 1963-65; Arizona State University, Tempe, assistant professor, 1965-67, associate professor, 1967-70, professor of English, 1970—. *Military service:* U.S. Navy, 1945-46. *Member:* American Civil Liberties Union, National Council of Teachers of English (executive committee member, 1974-76), Conference on English Education (executive committee member, 1974-77; national chairman, 1974-76), Freedom to Read Foundation, Popular Culture Association, Southwest Institute of Film Teachers (executive committee member, 1970-74), Arizona English Teachers Association (executive committee member, 1967-76).

WRITINGS: The Students' Right to Read, National Council of Teachers of English (Urbana, Ill.), 1972; (with Dwight Burton, Bryant Fillion, and Beverly Haley) *Teaching English Today,* Houghton, 1975; (editor) *Books for You,* National Council of Teachers of English, 1976; *Teaching Guide to E. L. Doctorow's Ragtime,* Bantam, 1976. Writer of column, "Ruminating and Rambling," in *English Journal,* 1973-74. Contributor of more than two hundred articles to journals, including *English Journal, Journal of the Producers Guild of America, Media and Methods,* and *Dime Novel Roundup.* Editor, *Arizona English Bulletin,* 1967-76.

WORK IN PROGRESS: Two books, one on history and criticism of adolescent literature, and the other on censorship in the schools; articles.

SIDELIGHTS: Donelson told *CA:* "I write for at least a couple of reasons. Sometimes I think I have something to say somebody else might like to hear. Mostly it's because I am an English teacher, the only game I've known most of my life and still the best one in town. I believe every teacher ought to write if he is to have any understanding of the difficulties his students face in finding words to match thoughts and stringing them together to make attractive sense. Teachers who don't write to prove their literacy but who ask students to write are hypocrites or intellectual frauds, nothing more.

"I write what I write because I'm committed to English teaching and English teachers, and I continue to worry about pretty much what worried me when I taught high school thir-

teen years ago. That means I write a lot about censorship (still a big worry for teachers and getting worse as teachers try to lead or push communities into the twentieth century some eighty years late), adolescent literature and film (still unexplored territories for too many teachers), and composition (more art than science but the frustrating and important work any teacher can do). I've been told I worry too much about things I can directly affect but little, and that's probably true. Occasionally, I tell my classes that when I'm buried, I'd like the headstone to read simply, 'He gave a damn.' Most students think I'm joking. I'm not.

"As for something I'm avocationally interested in, I'd say traveling, when my wife and I can afford it on a teacher's pay. Camping whenever possible. Traveling is for fun, camping is for survival. If we didn't go camping (and I mean a tent on the ground, not some van or camper) for a few weeks each summer we'd both lose our way. Our favorite place is Bandelier National Monument about forty or fifty miles north but mostly west of Santa Fe, New Mexico. It's quiet and I can think and wander and wonder and watch birds and eat oreo cookies and drink dark beer (sounds awful and it would be anyplace else but we stumbled onto the combination at Bandelier and it's great there), as close to heaven as I expect to get. Walking down Frijoles Canyon and coming alive has nothing directly to do with my writing or so it would seem, but most of the writing I've done comes in one way or another from Bandelier."

* * *

DONOHUE, Joseph (Walter, Jr.)   1935-

PERSONAL: Born September 12, 1935, in Brookline, Mass.; son of Joseph Walter and Marcella Hannah (Warren) Donohue; married Marie Therese Brady, 1959; children: Sharon Marie, Maura Cathleen, Sheila Patricia. *Education:* Johns Hopkins University, A.B., 1956; Georgetown University, M.A., 1962; Princeton University, Ph.D., 1965. *Home:* 17 Juniper Lane, Amherst, Mass. 01002. *Office:* Department of English, University of Massachusetts, Amherst, Mass. 01003.

CAREER: Mount Vernon Seminary, Washington, D.C., instructor in English, 1958-60; Dunbarton College, Washington, D.C., instructor in English, 1960-61; Princeton University, Princeton, N.J., assistant professor of English, 1966-71, John E. Annan bicentennial preceptor, 1967-70; University of Massachusetts, Amherst, associate professor, 1971-75, professor of English, 1975—. Visiting associate professor at Columbia University, 1973-74. *Military service:* U.S. Army Reserve, 1957-65, active duty, 1957, 1961-62; became first lieutenant.

MEMBER: International Federation for Theatre Research, Modern Language Association of America, American Society for Theatre Research (member of executive board, 1973-76), American Theatre Association, Society for Theatre Research (London). *Awards, honors:* Fulbright junior fellowship, University of London, 1965-66; American Council of Learned Societies grants, 1967, 1969, 1973; Folger Shakespeare Library fellowship, 1968; Huntington Library grant, 1973; Folger Library senior fellow, 1978.

WRITINGS: Dramatic Character in the English Romantic Age, Princeton University Press, 1970; (editor) *The Theatrical Manager in England and America,* Princeton University Press, 1971; *Theatre in the Age of Kean,* Basil Blackwell, 1975; (editor with James Ellis) *The British Theatre, 1800-1900: Essays on the Nineteenth Century Stage,* Theatre Survey, 1976.

WORK IN PROGRESS: The First Production of "The Importance of Being Earnest"; long-range research on the London stage between 1800 and 1900, with a calendar of performances.

SIDELIGHTS: Among Donohue's professional interests are the "history and criticism of theatrical and dramatic art, especially British, also American and European, with emphasis on study of the performed play and its relationship to audience, community, and society."

* * *

DOODY, Margaret Anne 1939-

PERSONAL: Born September 21, 1939, in St. John, New Brunswick, Canada; daughter of Hubert (an Anglican clergyman) and Anne (a social worker; maiden name, Cornwall) Doody. *Education:* Dalhousie University, B.A. (honors), 1960; Lady Margaret Hall, Oxford, B.A. (first class honors), 1962, D.Phil., 1968. *Politics:* "Much the same as Dr. Johnson's." *Religion:* Anglican. *Residence:* Berkeley, Calif. *Office:* Department of English, University of California, Berkeley, Calif. 94720.

CAREER: University of Victoria, Victoria, British Columbia, instructor, 1962-64, assistant professor of English, 1968-69; University of Wales, University College, Swansea, lecturer in English, 1969-76; University of California, Berkeley, visiting associate professor of English, 1976-77. *Member:* Societe d'Etudes Anglo-Americaines.

WRITINGS: A Natural Passion: A Study of the Novels of Samuel Richardson, Clarendon Press, 1974. Contributor of articles and a poem to literary journals.

WORK IN PROGRESS: Fanny Burney, Novelist; Bread of Independence: The Working Woman in Eighteenth Century Fiction; a biography of L. T. Meade.

SIDELIGHTS: Margaret Doody writes: "I like reading novels—and trying to write them—so I find it thoroughly congenial to write about them. My interest in Richardson developed my interest in the literature of the seventeenth and eighteenth centuries. I enjoy teaching very much, especially when the subject matter concerns the seventeenth and eighteenth centuries, or the novelists of the Victorian Age."

AVOCATIONAL INTERESTS: Children's books, books on housekeeping and cooking, detective stories, travel (Netherlands, France, Spain, Italy, Greece, Turkey).

* * *

DORFMAN, John 1947-

PERSONAL: Born April 19, 1947, in Chicago, Ill.; son of Isaiah Sol (a lawyer) and Lillian (a secretary; maiden name, Schley) Dorfman; married Deborah Levinson, June 20, 1971; children: Laura, Jessica. *Education:* Princeton University, A.B., 1969; Columbia University, M.F.A., 1972. *Home and office:* 1915 Noyes St., Evanston, Ill. 60201. *Agent:* Jane Rotrosen Agency, 212 East 48th St., New York, N.Y. 10017.

CAREER: Home News, New Brunswick, N.J., reporter, 1970-72; Associated Press, New York, N.Y., reporter, 1972-73; *Consumer Reports*, Mount Vernon, N.Y., assistant editor, 1973-74; free-lance writer, 1974—. *Member:* American Society of Journalists and Authors, U.S. Chess Federation. *Awards, honors:* Certificate of merit from American Bar Association, 1974, for *Consumer Reports* series on landlord-tenant relations.

WRITINGS: Consumer Survival Kit, Praeger, 1975; *A Consumer's Arsenal*, Praeger, 1976. Contributor to *Chicago, Money*, and *Consumer Reports.*

WORK IN PROGRESS: Well-Being, a health text book, publication by Scott, Foresman expected in 1979; *The Master Matrix*, a novel.

SIDELIGHTS: John Dorfman writes that he is interested in "the environment, fiction writing, medicine, sex, crime, business, consumerism, and the arts. My first novel, *The Brontosaurus Affair*, remains unpublished to date."

* * *

DORN, Sylvia O'Neill 1918-

PERSONAL: Born February 27, 1918, in New York, N.Y.; daughter of Albert Arpad (an inventor and manufacturer) and Leona (Newberger) Schwartz; married Dick O'Neill (died, 1954); married Samuel David Dorn, February 20, 1959 (died, 1973); children: Philip H. (stepson). *Education:* University of Cincinnati, B.A., 1938. *Politics:* "Maverick." *Religion:* "Orthodox Atheist." *Office:* 1050 Fifth Ave., New York, N.Y. 10028.

CAREER: Macy's, New York City, antiques department manager, 1940-43; Bloomingdale's, New York City, antiques buyer, 1943-48; editor of *Giftwares*, 1951-54; editor of *Home Furnishings*, 1954-60; free-lance writer, 1960—. Lecturer at New York University's School for Adult Education.

WRITINGS: The Insider's Guide to Antiques, Art, and Collectibles, Doubleday, 1974; *The How to Collect Anything Book*, Doubleday, 1976. Antiques and collecting feature writer for *Better Living*, and scriptwriter for "What's New in Collecting," both in the 1950's.

WORK IN PROGRESS: The What to Collect Book.

SIDELIGHTS: Sylvia Dorn writes that she is an advocate of "Collector Protection," and that her books and articles "aim to make the reader more of an equal and less of a victim when buying or selling their treasures. I explain the techniques and tricks of the trade of dealers, auctioneers, and appraisers and show collectors their weaknesses and strengths."

* * *

DOUGAN, Michael B(ruce) 1944-

PERSONAL: Born February 26, 1944, in Burbank, Calif.; son of Will Leigh (an aviator) and Helen (North) Dougan; married Carol Warner (a historical archaeologist), March 30, 1970. *Education:* Southwest Missouri State University, B.A. (cum laude), 1966; Emory University, M.A., 1967, Ph.D., 1970. *Politics:* Democrat. *Religion:* Unitarian-Universalist. *Home:* Bell House, 303 West Cherry, Jonesboro, Ark. 72467. *Office:* Department of History, Arkansas State University, State University, Ark. 72467.

CAREER: Arkansas State University, State University, assistant professor of history, 1970—. Member of Arkansas State Historical Records Advisory Board. *Member:* American Society for Legal History, Southern Historical Association, State Historical Society of Missouri, Arkansas Historical Association, Craighead County Historical Society (member of board of directors). *Awards, honors:* Award from Colonial Dames of the State of Georgia, 1968; Mrs. Simon Baruch University Award from United Daughters of the Confederacy, 1972, for *Confederate Arkansas.*

WRITINGS: Confederate Arkansas, University of Alabama Press, 1976. Contributor to regional history journals.

WORK IN PROGRESS: The Arkansas Stories of Octave

Thanet, completion expected in 1979; *Outlaws in Anglo-American Legal History,* 1980.

SIDELIGHTS: Dougan comments: *"Confederate Arkansas* is partly politics and partly about the plain people of the state. In addition to scholarly writings, I am interested in opera and have written the life of Mary Lewis, the Arkansas opera singer." *Avocational interests:* Canoeing, gardening, collecting records of Beniamino Gigli.

* * *

DOUGLAS, Paul Howard 1892-1976

PERSONAL: Born March 26, 1892, in Salem, Mass.; son of James Howard (a traveling salesman) and Annie (Smith) Douglas; married Dorothy S. Wolff, 1915 (divorced, 1930); married Emily Taft, 1931; children: (first marriage) Helen (Mrs. Paul Klein), John, Dorothea (Mrs. Robert John), Paul; (second marriage) Jean (Mrs. Edward Bandler). *Education:* Bowdoin College, A.B., 1913; Columbia University, M.A., 1915, Ph.D., 1921; Harvard University, graduate study, 1915-16. *Religion:* Unitarian-Universalist. *Home:* 2909 Davenport St. N.W., Washington, D.C. 20008.

CAREER: University of Illinois, Urbana, instructor in economics, 1916-17; Reed College, Portland, Ore., instructor, 1917, assistant professor of economics, 1918; Emergency Fleet Corp., Philadelphia, Pa., industrial relations employee, 1918-19; University of Washington, Seattle, associate professor of economics, 1919-20; University of Chicago, Chicago, Ill., assistant professor, 1920-23, associate professor, 1923-25, professor of industrial relations, 1925-48; U.S. Senate, Washington, D.C., Democratic Senator from Illinois, 1949-66; New School for Social Research, New York, N.Y., professor of economics, 1966-69; writer, 1969-76. Visiting professor at Amherst College, 1924-27, and Oberlin College, 1930-31. Acting director of Swarthmore unemployment study, member of Pennsylvania Commission on Unemployment, and economic adviser to New York Commission on Unemployment, all in 1930; member of Illinois Housing Commission, 1931-33; member of National Recovery Administration's consumers advisory board, 1933-35; member of advisory committee to U.S. Senate and Social Security Board on the Federal Social Security System, 1937; chairman of the President's Commission on Urban Problems, 1967-68. Delegate-at-large to Democratic national conventions, 1948, 1952, 1956, 1964, and 1968; alderman of Chicago City council, 1939-42. Chairman of board of trustees of Freedom House, 1967-69. *Military service:* U.S. Marine Corps, 1942-46; became lieutenant colonel; received Bronze Star.

MEMBER: Econometric Society (fellow), American Academy of Arts and Sciences (fellow), American Philosophical Society, American Economic Association (president, 1946-47), American Statistical Association, Royal Economic Association, Phi Beta Kappa, Delta Upsilon, Federal City Club (Washington, D.C.), Quadrangle Club, Chicago Literary Club. *Awards, honors:* Guggenheim fellowship, 1931; Sidney Hillman Award, 1957; John F. Kennedy Award from Catholic Interracial Council, 1970. Awards for books include Karelsen Prize from American Economic Association, 1921, for *What Can a Man Afford?* and first prize in Hart, Schaffner, and Marx international competition, 1927, for *The Theory of Wages.* Recipient of over twenty honorary degrees, including LL.D. from DePaul University, College of William and Mary, New School for Social Research, Bucknell University, and Brandeis University; L.H.D. from Lincoln College, Southern Il-

linois University, and University of Illinois at Chicago Circle; Litt.D. from Rollins College.

WRITINGS: American Apprenticeship and Industrial Education, Columbia University, 1921, reprinted, AMS Press, 1968; (with first wife, Dorothy Douglas, and Carl S. Joslyn) *What Can A Man Afford?* (essays), American Economic Association, 1921; (with Curtice N. Hitchcock and Willard E. Atkins) *The Worker in Modern Economic Society: Materials for the Study of Business,* University of Chicago Press, 1923, reprinted, Arno, 1969; *Wages and the Family: Materials for the Study of Business,* University of Chicago Press, 1925; (with others) *Adam Smith, 1776-1926,* University of Chicago Press, 1928.

(With Florence Tye Jennison) *The Movement of Money and Real Earnings in the United States, 1926-28: Studies in Business Administration,* University of Chicago Press, 1930; *Real Wages in the United States, 1890-1926,* Houghton, 1930, reprinted, Augusta M. Kelley, 1966; (with Aaron Director) *The Problem of Unemployment,* Macmillan, 1931; *The Coming of a New Party,* foreword by John Dewey, McGraw, 1932; *Know America: Its Ills and Cures,* Buti-Lami Press, 1933; *Standards of Unemployment Insurance,* University of Chicago Press, 1933; *The Theory of Wages,* Macmillan, 1934, published with new foreword and additional material, Kelley & Millman, 1957; *Controlling Depressions,* Norton, 1935; *Social Security in the United States: An Analysis and Appraisal of the Federal Social Security Act,* McGraw, 1936, 2nd edition, 1939, reprinted, Da Capo Press, 1971.

(With Harold Gregg Lewis) *Studies in Consumer Expenditures: 1901, 1918-1919, 1922-1924,* University of Chicago Press, 1947.

Economy in the National Government, University of Chicago Press, 1952; *Ethics in Government,* Harvard University Press, 1952, reprinted, Greenwood Press, 1972.

American in the Marketplace: Trade, Tariffs, and the Balance of Payments, Holt, 1966; (with J. Enoch Powell) *How Big Should Government Be?,* American Enterprises Institute for Public Policy Research, 1968; *In Our Time,* (collected lectures), Harcourt, 1968; (with Robert C. Weaver and William E. Zisch) *The Urban Environment: How It Can Be Improved,* New York University Press, 1969.

In the Fullness of Time: The Memoirs of Paul H. Douglas, Harcourt, 1972.

Also author of many reports, addresses, lectures, and papers on government, economics, social conditions, and international trade published by government and public organizations. Contributor to professional journals.

BIOGRAPHICAL/CRITICAL SOURCES: Edward R. Murrow, *This I Believe,* Simon & Schuster, 1954; *Look,* June 13, 1967; *Newsweek,* November 16, 1970; *In the Fullness of Time* (autobiography), Harcourt, 1972.

OBITUARIES: Washington Post, September 25, 1976; *New York Times,* September 25, 1976; *New Republic,* October 9, 1976; *Current Biography,* November, 1976.*

(Died September 24, 1976, in Washington, D.C.)

* * *

DOUGLASS, William A(nthony) 1939-

PERSONAL: Born December 4, 1939, in Reno, Nev.; son of Jack Raymond (a businessman) and Barbara Josephine (French) Douglass; married Patricia Ann Nylen, August 20, 1961; children, John, Ana, Matthew. *Education:* University of Nevada, A.B., 1961; University of Chicago, M.S., 1966, Ph.D., 1967; also attended University of Madrid, 1959-60, University of Oslo, 1960, and University of California, Berkeley, 1962-63. *Residence:* Reno, Nev. *Office:* Basque Studies Program, University of Nevada, Reno, Nev. 89507.

CAREER: University of Nevada, Reno, assistant professor, 1967-71, associate professor of anthropology, research associate in professional anthropology, and coordinator of Basque studies at Western Studies Center of Desert Research Institute, all 1971—. *Member:* American Anthropological Association, Current Anthropology, Instituto Americano de Estudios Vascos (Buenos Aires). *Awards, honors:* National Institute of Mental Health research scientist career development grants, 1971-76, 1976-81.

WRITINGS: Death in Murelaga: The Social Significance of Funerary Ritual in a Spanish Basque Village, University of Washington Press, 1969; *Achalar and Murelaga: Opportunity and Rural Depopulation in Two Spanish Basque Villages,* St. Martin's, 1975; (editor with Joseph B. Aceves) *The Changing Faces of Rural Spain,* Schenkman, 1975; (with Jon Bilbao) *Amerikanuak: Basques in the New World,* University of Nevada Press, 1975.

Also editor, with Richard Etulain, *Anglo-American Contributions to Basque Studies: Essays in Honor of Jon Bilbao,* 1977; author of *Beltran: Basque Sheepman of the American West,* in press, and *The Strategy of Emigration in a South Italian Hill Town,* in press. Contributor to anthropology, history, and Basque studies journals.

WORK IN PROGRESS: Basques in America: A Guide to Information Sources; editing *The Basque-Americans: A Bibliography,* completion expected in 1979; research for a social history of a Nevada mining town, 1979; a comparative study of Basque and Italian sugar cane cutters in northern Australia (Queensland).

SIDELIGHTS: Douglass writes: "I have been the recipient of two National Institute of Mental Health awards. These have been instrumental in allowing me to do comparative studies of how persons who are socialized into single-resource economies react when during their productive years they lose their livelihoods due to circumstances beyond their control. Vocationally, I am interested in social anthropology, social change, ethnic and immigration studies, and peasant studies (particularly European peasant society). I have language competency in Spanish, French, Italian, Latin, and Basque." *Avocational interests:* Gardening, fly fishing.

*   *   *

DRAKE, George Randolph 1938-

PERSONAL: Born March 27, 1938, in Trenton, N.J.; son of Edward H. (an administrator for New Jersey state highway department) and Catharine (Hunt) Drake; married Mary J. Margerum (a speech therapist), October 1, 1960; children: Natalie J., Jeffrey E., Paul R. *Education:* Bucknell University, student, 1956-58; Temple University, A.E.T., 1961; University of Baltimore, B.S., 1969. *Home and office:* 4209 Thorncliff Rd., Baltimore, Md. 21236.

CAREER: Martin-Marietta Corp., Baltimore, Md., technical writer and instructor for Gemini Space Program, 1961-67; AAI Corp., Cockeysville, Md., publications and training manager, 1969-74; free-lance writer, 1974—. Consultant to business, industry, and government. *Member:* American Society for Training and Development (member of board of directors, 1976-77).

WRITINGS: Everyone's Book of Hand and Small Power Tools, Reston, 1974; *The Complete Handbook of Power Tools,* Reston, 1975; *The Repair and Maintenance of Small Gasoline Engines,* Reston, 1976; *The Repair and Servicing of Small Appliances,* Reston, 1977. Author of technical manuals. Contributor to popular magazines, including *Popular Science, Woman's World,* and *Swimming World.*

WORK IN PROGRESS: A book on "home weatherization for the do-it-yourselfer," for Reston.

SIDELIGHTS: Drake describes his writing briefly: "My concerns (and hence written materials) are for the do-it-yourselfer—the detailed step by step how-to-do-it-yourself for self-satisfaction and dollar savings." *Avocational interests:* Woodworking, photography, amateur radio, sailing, swimming (Red Cross swimming instructor).

*   *   *

DRAKE, William Daniel 1941-

PERSONAL: Born October 22, 1941, in Anniston, Ala.; son of William (an Army officer) and Laura (a writer; maiden name, Garrison) Drake; married Sally Perkins (divorced, 1973); children: Zachary. *Education:* Dickinson College, B.A., 1965. *Home:* 3118 Drexel, Dallas, Tex. 75205.

CAREER: Has worked as a "singer, poet, manual laborer, activist, worldsaver, and lover."

WRITINGS: Cultivator's Handbook of Marijuana, Wingbow Press, 1970; *Connoisseurs Handbook of Marijuana,* Straight Arrow Books, 1971; *International Cultivators Handbook,* Wingbow Press, 1974.

WORK IN PROGRESS: Powerful Fathering—Handbook for Divorced Fathers; Weekend Father's Cookbook; Royal Foods; Report From the Other Side; a revision of *Cultivator's Handbook of Marijuana.*

SIDELIGHTS: CA asked Drake if he encountered any opposition to the publication of his books, and how his audience has changed since they were first published. He responded: "I do find that the audience and reaction to my books have changed. There is little of the clandestine air left to the buying, owning and display of the books. They have come out of the closet and on to the coffee table. Marijuana has now become a viable drug of choice of many millions of people, and the laws against it have become vestigial. The audience for my books is growing rapidly, and I am responding by updating and completely revising my first book, *Cultivator's Handbook.* I think it will become a widely known, generally accepted book on marijuana cultivation and lore. It's already sold several hundred thousand copies, mostly underground. Now, however, I am talking with three mass-market paperback companies who want to acquire rights, so I think that the market for marijuana books is about to come aboveground.

"I had a good deal of trouble in publishing my first book. In fact, Treasury and BNDD agents visited the first three printers I had contracts with to print the book, and I finally had to get the SDS chapter in Oregon to print the first 3000 copies. After that the government quit trying to stop publication, and has instead concentrated on watching and trying, on two occasions, to entrap me in conspiracy schemes. That hasn't worked either."

*   *   *

DRAPER, John William 1893-1976

July 23, 1893—November 30, 1976; American philologist,

professor of English, and author of books and articles on Shakespeare as well as volumes of poetry and works on other aspects of English literature. He died in Morgantown, W.Va. Obituaries: *New York Times,* December 1, 1976. (*CAP*-1; earlier sketch in *CA*-9/10)

* * *

DRAPER, Ronald Philip 1928-

PERSONAL: Born October 3, 1928, in Nottingham, England; son of Albert William and Elsie Draper; married Irene Margaret Aldridge, June 19, 1950; children: Anne, Isabel, Sophia. *Education:* University of Nottingham, B.A., 1950, Ph.D., 1953. *Home:* 50 Queen's Rd., Aberdeen, Scotland. *Office:* Department of English, University of Aberdeen, Aberdeen, Scotland.

CAREER: University of Adelaide, Adelaide, South Australia, lecturer in English, 1955-56; University of Leicester, Leicester, England, lecturer, 1957-68, senior lecturer in English, 1968-73; University of Aberdeen, Aberdeen, Scotland, professor of English, 1973—. *Military service:* Royal Air Force, flying officer, 1953-55.

WRITINGS: D. H. Lawrence, Twayne, 1964; *D. H. Lawrence,* Routledge & Kegan Paul, 1969; (editor) *D. H. Lawrence: The Critical Heritage,* Routledge & Kegan Paul, 1970; (editor) *Hardy: The Tragic Novels,* Macmillan, 1975.

Co-author of two playscripts, "The Corker and the Rose," 1964, and "An Evening with D. H. Lawrence," 1966; author of television script, "The Country of My Heart," 1977. Contributor of articles and reviews to literature journals, and to *Times Literary Supplement* and *New Literary History.*

WORK IN PROGRESS: Editing a casebook on *The Mill and the Floss* and *Silas Marner* by George Eliot.

SIDELIGHTS: Draper told *CA:* "To me, D. H. Lawrence is essentially a writer of the English midlands, though his views of his home background were radically changed by his nomadic existence after the First World War which took him wandering all over the world. He is a writer whose thought and critical attitude towards society have had a profound influence on me personally, but not always in the form of acceptance. Indeed, my strongest reaction has often been one, if not of outright rejection, at least of disagreement and a wish to correct and modify.

"One of his wisest remarks is the famous 'Never trust the artist. Trust the tale. The proper function of a critic is to save the tale from the artist who created it.' This, however, I do not interpret as meaning that one should ignore the life and opinions of the artist in favour of a 'practical criticism' approach to the text treated as an autonomous work of art. The relationship between a writer and his work is fascinating and very important. But, as Lawrence demonstrates in his own criticism, it is a relationship which needs to be approached circumspectly. The imagination has its own way of responding which is not always that of the conscious, purposive mind, and frequently tells truths that the writer might want to deny.

"A similar attitude governs my approach to the other novelists in whom I have a special interest, notably George Eliot and Thomas Hardy. With George Eliot, however, the accent for me is on her breadth of sympathy and her belief in the importance of religious forms which symbolize human rather than theological values. She is one of the first great prophets of the secular imagination, which it seems to me, is the necessary condition of artistic health in the twentieth century.

"In this she is followed closely by Thomas Hardy, though he also interests me as being, like Lawrence, a regional writer who transcends his region to become a universal figure and a novelist who yet has a primarily poetic vision.

"Needless, perhaps, to say, my interest in literature is not restricted to these three writers, but ranges over writers of all periods from the sixteenth century to the present day. And it is the *literary* quality of literature which above all interests me—not 'literary' in the effete sense, but in the sense of being a product of the imagination working through language and focusing the whole being of the writer in a work of art. The uniqueness of literature—that which makes it something other than philosophy or history or politics or social comment or psychology or any other extraneously non-literary subject—is to me the most important thing about literature. It frequently overlaps with these other interests, but it should never allow itself to be taken over by them. I believe that a vigorous imagination always, in fact, resists such takeovers; and it is a sign of imaginative health when writers and works of literature stand firmly as individualistic beings, interested in all these other activities of the human mind, but owing allegiance only to the imaginative way of exploring and representing experience."

* * *

DREISER, Vera

PERSONAL: Born in New York, N.Y.; daughter of Edward M. and Mai V. (Skelly) Dreiser; married Alfred E. Scott, July 8, 1939 (deceased); children: Sheri Dreiser Redi. *Education:* New York University, Ed.D., 1944. *Residence:* Atlanta, Ga.

CAREER: Queens College (now of the City University of New York), Flushing, N.Y., instructor in psychology, 1940-43; Manhattan State Hospital, New York City, psychological researcher, 1944-45; Brooklyn Center for Psychotherapy, Brooklyn, N.Y., senior psychologist, 1945; consulting psychologist with practice in New York City (psychological expert for television programs "The Ella Mason Show" and "Food for Thought"), 1947-61; correctional counselor and staff psychologist, California Institution for Women, 1962-66, administrator of Psychiatric Treatment Unit, 1966-72. Visiting lecturer, 1940-47. Lecturer for Los Angeles Assistance League and other organizations, and at California State Polytechnic College and Mount San Antonio College. Licensed in states of New York and California. Has appeared on television and radio programs, including some on NBC-Television and KGBS-Radio.

MEMBER: Association for the Advancement of Psychotherapy, National Association of Mental Hygiene, National League of American Pen Women, American Society of Composers, Authors and Publishers, California Probation, Parole and Correctional Association, Greater Los Angeles Press Club, New York University Alumni Association, Pi Lambda Theta.

WRITINGS: My Uncle Theodore (about Theodore Dreiser), Nash Publishing, 1976. Author of column syndicated by King Features, and "Let Dr. Dreiser Help You," a column in *Screenplay.* Contributor to magazines, including *Playgirl, Modern Maturity, Self, Real Story, Everywoman's,* and *Good Reading Rack.*

WORK IN PROGRESS: A prison expose.

AVOCATIONAL INTERESTS: Composing music.

BIOGRAPHICAL/CRITICAL SOURCES: Atlanta Journal, June 27, 1976; *Indianapolis Star,* October 3, 1976.

DRESANG, Eliza (Carolyn Timberlake) 1941-

PERSONAL: Surname is pronounced *Dree*-sang; born October 21, 1941, in Atlanta, Ga.; daughter of Gideon Baskette (a physician) and Ruth (a teacher and secretary; maiden name, Rudder) Timberlake; married Dennis Lee Dresang, August 10, 1963; children: Lee Timberlake, Steven Edward, Anna Ruth. *Education:* Emory University, B.A., 1963; University of Southern California, graduate study, 1964; University of California, Los Angeles, M.L.S., 1966; University of Wisconsin, Madison, further graduate study, 1974. *Politics:* Democrat. *Religion:* Presbyterian. *Home:* 440 Virginia Ter., Madison, Wis. 53705. *Office:* Lapham Elementary School, 1045 East Dayton St., Madison, Wis. 53705.

CAREER: High school English teacher in Atlanta, Ga., 1963; high school Spanish teacher in Lake Mills, Wis., 1963-64, high school Spanish and French teacher in Los Angeles, Calif., 1964-65; Los Angeles Public Library, Los Angeles, children's and reference librarian at Encino-Tarzana Branch, 1966-67; Atlanta Public Library, Atlanta, head of children's department at Ida Williams Branch, 1967-68; Madison Board of Education, Madison, Wis., director of Instruction Materials Center at Lapham Elementary School, 1974—. Volunteer story teller, 1967.

MEMBER: American Library Association, Association for Educational Communications and Technology, Society of Children's Book Writers, National Organization for Women, Wisconsin Library Association, Wisconsin Audio-Visual Association, Phi Beta Kappa, Phi Eta Sigma, Beta Phi Mu.

WRITINGS: African Educational Research: A Bibliography, Ford Foundation, 1974; *The Land and People of Zambia,* Lippincott, 1975. Contributor to *School Library Journal.*

WORK IN PROGRESS: Research on racism and sexism in education, specifically in printed and non-printed materials for children; research on service to the exceptional child in the school media center.

SIDELIGHTS: Eliza Dresang lived in Zambia, 1968-69, and Kenya, 1971-72; she has traveled in Ethiopia, Tanzania, Uganda, Nigeria, Malawi, and Morocco, and her adopted daughter is from Korea.

She writes: "My residence and research in Zambia and Kenya were vital to the publication of my book. My position as director of the Instructional Materials Center in a school which served over a hundred handicapped children and two hundred fifty non-handicapped children in a non-restrictive environment has given me the arena for studying my current interest in service to *all* children. The main emphasis of my work and writing is meeting individual needs without regard to sex, race, or disability and to actively pursue change in publishing for children to correct the great imbalance and inaccuracies that exist in these areas. In the summer of 1976, I attended preconference seminars on Children and Television and on Mainstreaming the Special Child at the American Library Association in Chicago."

BIOGRAPHICAL/CRITICAL SOURCES: Wisconsin Library Bulletin, November-December, 1976, March-April, 1977.

* * *

DRESSER, Davis 1905(?)-1977
(Brett Halliday, Peter Shelley, Anderson Wayne)

1905(?)—February 4, 1977; American novelist. His most famous books were the Mike Shayne series of detective stories, written under the pseudonym Brett Halliday. He wrote over fifty other books under twelve different pseudonyms. Dressor also edited anthologies of mystery stories and was a founding member of the Mystery Writers of America. He died in Montecito, Calif. Obituaries: *New York Times,* February 6, 1977; *AB Bookman's Weekly,* May 9, 1977.

* * *

DRINKWATER, Terry 1936-

PERSONAL: Born May 9, 1936, in Denver, Colo.; son of Terrell (an airline president) and Helen (an artist; maiden name, Kiddoo) Drinkwater; married Judith Wilsey, September 5, 1965; children: Croft, Angela. *Education:* Pomona College, B.A., 1958; University of California at Berkeley, M.A., 1960. *Office:* CBS News, 7800 Beverly Blvd., Los Angeles, Calif. 90036.

CAREER: KTTV New, Los Angeles, Calif., writer, 1956-60; WBAI-TV, New York, N.Y., station manager, 1961; KPFK, Los Angeles, station manager, 1961; KTLA-TV, Los Angeles, producer, 1963-64; Columbia Broadcasting System (CBS) News, Los Angeles, correspondent, 1964—. Notable assignments include the Robert Kennedy, Richard Nixon, George McGovern and Ronald Reagan presidential campaigns, the assassination of Robert Kennedy, antiwar riots on U.S. campuses, return of U.S. prisoners of war, Alaska and California earthquakes, and manned space programs. *Military service:* U.S. Army, 1959-60; became first lieutenant. *Awards, honors:* Peabody Award, 1960.

* * *

DUBERMAN, Lucile 1926-

PERSONAL: Born March 19, 1926, in New York, N.Y.; daughter of Joseph (a dress manufacturer) and Josephine (an antique dealer; maiden name, Bauml) Duberman; married Morris Beldon (a dress manufacturer), 1943 (divorced, 1956); married Irving Milberg (a physician), 1960 (divorced, 1969); married Ralph Kaminsky (an associate university dean), 1973 (divorced, 1977); children: Nanette Beldon Faughnan, Scott Beldon, Michael Beldon. *Education:* Brooklyn College of the City University of New York, B.A., 1968; New York University, graduate study, 1968-70; Case Western Reserve University, Ph.D., 1973. *Politics:* Liberal. *Religion:* None. *Home:* 3 Washington Square Village, New York, N.Y. 10012. *Office:* Department of Sociology, Rutgers University, Newark, N.J. 07102.

CAREER: Brooklyn College of the City University of New York, Brooklyn, N.Y., assistant professor of sociology, 1971-72; Rutgers University, Newark, N.J., assistant professor of sociology, 1972—.

WRITINGS: Marriage and Its Alternatives, Praeger, 1974, 2nd edition published as *Marriage and Other Alternatives,* 1977; *(with Helen Hacker) Gender and Sex in Society,* Praeger, 1975; *The Reconstituted Family,* Nelson-Hall, 1975; *Social Inequity: Class and Caste in America,* Lippincott, 1976; (with Clayton A. Hartjen) *Sociology: The Study of Human Interaction,* 3rd edition (Duberman not associated with earlier editions), Random House, 1976. Contributor to sociology journals.

SIDELIGHTS: Lucile Duberman's main interests are feminist activities, step-families, and interpersonal relationships.

* * *

DUBIE, Norman (Evans) 1945-

PERSONAL: Born April 10, 1945, in Barre, Vt.; son of

Norman E., Sr. (a clergyman) and Doris (a registered nurse) Dubie; married Francesca Stafford, December 28, 1968 (divorced); married Pamela Stewart (a poet and teacher), November 28, 1975; children: Hannah. *Education:* Goddard College, B.A., 1969; University of Iowa, M.F.A., 1971. *Politics:* None. *Religion:* None. *Home:* 2117 South Granada Dr., #14, Tempe, Ariz. 85282. *Office:* Department of English, Arizona State University, Tempe, Ariz. 85281.

CAREER: University of Iowa, Iowa City, lecturer at Writers Workshop, 1971-74; Ohio University, Athens, assistant professor of English, 1974-75; Arizona State University, Tempe, writer-in-residence, 1975-76, lecturer in English and director of graduate writing program, 1976—. Poetry director for Prison Writers and Artists Workshop, 1973-74; has given poetry readings all over the United States. *Awards, honors:* Bess Hokin Prize from *Poetry* and Modern Poetry Association, 1976, for "The Negress, Her Monologue of Dark Crepe"; Guggenheim fellowship, Mexico, 1977-78.

WRITINGS: Alehouse Sonnets, University of Pittsburgh Press, 1971; *The Prayers of the North American Martyrs* (poetry), Penumbra Press, 1975; *Popham of the New Song* (poetry), Graywolf Press, 1975; *In the Dead of the Night* (poetry), University of Pittsburgh Press, 1975; *The Illustrations* (poetry), Braziller, 1977; *A Thousand Little Things* (poetry), Cummington Press, 1977; *The City of the Olesha Fruit* (poetry), Doubleday, in press; *Odalisque in White* (poetry), Porch Publications, in press.

Poetry represented in anthologies, including *The American Poetry Anthology: Poets Under Forty,* Avon, 1975; *Poetry As Process: Fifty Contemporary American Poets,* edited by Alberta Turner, McKay, 1977; *The Face of Poetry: One Hundred Poets,* Gallimaufry, 1977. Contributor of articles and several dozen poems to literary journals, including *American Poetry Review, Iowa Review, Poetry, Field,* and to *New Yorker.* Poetry editor of *Iowa Review,* 1971-72, and *Now,* 1973-74.

WORK IN PROGRESS: "Comes Winter, the Sea Hunting," a long poem.

SIDELIGHTS: The Norman Dubie collection is housed at the University of Iowa.

* * *

DU BOIS, Shirley Graham 1907-1977

November 11, 1907—March 27, 1977; American-born Ghanian biographer, playwright, and composer. DuBois, widow of civil rights leader W.E.B. DuBois, wrote biographies of several famous black Americans for children. In 1934, she wrote the musical play "Tom-Tom"; she later turned it into an opera. She and Dr. DuBois moved to Ghana in 1961 and became citizens there. She was forced to flee in 1967 and has lived abroad since that time. She died in Peking, China. Obituaries: *New York Times,* April 5, 1977; *Washington Post,* April 5, 1977; *AB Bookman's Weekly,* June 27, 1977; *Current Biography,* June, 1977.

* * *

DUCKETT, Eleanor Shipley 1880(?)-1976

1880(?)—November 23, 1976; British-born American educator, reviewer, and author of works in her field. Duckett was a professor at Smith College from 1916 to 1949. A movie made in 1969, "Alfred the Great," was based on one of her works. Duckett wrote reviews for the "Sunday Book Review" of the *New York Times.* She died in Northampton, Mass. Obituaries: *New York Times,* November 30, 1976.

DUGGAN, William Redman 1915-

PERSONAL: Born February 11, 1915, in Durango, Colo.; son of Willian Edward (a banker) and Pansy (Redman) Duggan; married Florence Olive Jewell (a secretary), August 30, 1952; children: David William. *Education:* Western State College of Colorado, student, 1933-35; University of Notre Dame, A.B., 1938, M.A., 1939; Boston University, further graduate study, 1955-56. *Politics:* Democrat. *Religion:* Roman Catholic. *Home:* 550 Waldo Ave. S.E., Salem, Ore. 97302.

CAREER: Social Security Board, Washington, D.C., manager of field office in Ogden, Utah, and Alamosa, Colo., 1940-44; U.S. Foreign Service, Washington, D.C., vice-consul in Durban, South Africa, 1944-47, and Vancouver, British Columbia, 1948-50, second secretary at consulate in Copenhagen, Denmark, 1951-55, political liaison officer for U.S. delegation to United Nations General Assembly, 1956-57, officer in charge of West African Affairs for U.S. Department of State, 1957-58, consul general in Dar-es-Salaam, Tanzania, 1958-62, member of policy planning council of U.S. Department of State, 1962-67, consul general in Durban, 1967-71; Willamette University, Salem, Ore., professor-diplomat-on-campus of political science, 1972—. Member of Oregon Education Commission, 1975—. Member of Democratic State Central Committee, 1973—, delegate to National Convention, 1976. Consultant to Ford Foundation, 1971-72.

MEMBER: American Political Science Association, American Foreign Service Association, African Studies Association, Rotary International (member of board of directors, 1975-76), Explorers Club (New York City), Durban Club. *Awards, honors:* Meritorious service award from U.S. Department of State, 1963, distinguished service award, 1971.

WRITINGS: A Socio-Economic Profile of South Africa, Praeger, 1973; (with John Civille) *Tanzania and Nyerere,* Orbis, 1976. Contributor to professional journals. Assistant editor of *Review of Politics,* 1938-40.

WORK IN PROGRESS: Articles on Africa for newspapers.

* * *

DUKE, Charles (Richard) 1940-

PERSONAL: Born July 6, 1940, in West Stewartstown, N.H.; son of George T. and Evelyn (Murray) Duke; married Jonquelyn R. Simpson (a teacher), May 20, 1973. *Education:* Plymouth State College, B.Ed., 1962; Middlebury College, M.A., 1968; Duke University, Ph.D., 1972. *Home address:* P.O. Box 186, Plymouth, N.H. 03264. *Office:* Department of English, Reed House, Plymouth State College, Plymouth, N.H. 03264.

CAREER: High school English teacher and department chairman in Sunapee, N.H., 1962-68; Plymouth State College, Plymouth, N.H., instructor, 1968-72, assistant professor, 1972-73, associate professor of English, 1973—. *Member:* National Council of Teachers of English, American Association of University Professors, Popular Culture Association, Conference on English Education, American Film Institute, New England Association of Teachers of English (member of advisory board, 1973-74; publicity chairman, 1974-75; president-elect, 1976-77; president, 1977-78), New Hampshire Association of Teachers of English (vice-president, 1971; president, 1973-77), Kappa Delta Pi.

WRITINGS: (Editor) *Granite State Writers,* New Hampshire Association of Teachers of English, 1972; *Creative*

Dramatics and English Teaching, National Council of Teachers of English, 1974; (contributor) R. Baird Shuman, editor, *Creative Approaches to the Teaching of English: Secondary,* F. E. Peacock, 1974; *Teaching Fundamental English Today,* J. Weston Walch, 1976. Contributor of articles and reviews to English language journals.

WORK IN PROGRESS: Teaching Literature Today; editing an anthology on the use of commercial television to teach communication skills; research for a history of New England summer theater.

SIDELIGHTS: Duke writes: "I find that my writing is almost always a direct product of my teaching interests; both of the books I have done thus far have grown out of classroom experiences and needs. My writing is addressed to a definite audience—the practicing teacher—and I derive a good deal of satisfaction from being able to translate theory into practical applications which can be of use to others."

AVOCATIONAL INTERESTS: Camping, fast European cars.

* * *

DULANY, Don E., Jr. 1928-

PERSONAL: Born December 9, 1928, in Shreveport, La.; son of Don E. (a minister) and LaVera (Jackson) Dulany; married Elizabeth Gjelsness (an editor), March 19, 1955; children: Christopher. *Education:* University of Tennessee, A.B., 1948; Universty of Michigan, Ph.D., 1955. *Home:* 73 Greencroft, Champaign, Ill. 61820. *Office:* Department of Psychology, University of Illinois, Champaign, Ill. 61820.

CAREER: University of Illinois, Champaign, assistant professor, 1956-59, associate professor, 1959-64, professor of psychology, 1964—. *Military service:* U.S. Army, 1954-56.

WRITINGS: (With John Street) *A Method for Teaching English to Spanish-Speaking Military Personnel,* United States Army Information and Educational Office, 1954; (with R. W. Brown, I. M. Copi, W. K. Frankena, Paul Henle, and C. W. Stevenson) *Language, Thought, and Culture,* University of Michigan Press, 1958; (editor with David Beardslee, Russell DeValois, and Marian Winterbottom) *Contributions to Modern Psychology,* Oxford University Press, 1958, 2nd edition, 1963.

Contributor: C. W. Eriksen, editor, *Behavior and Awareness,* Duke University Press, 1962; Theodore Dixon and David Horton, editors, *Verbal Behavior and General Behavior Theory,* Prentice-Hall, 1968; Walter Weimer and David Palermo, editors, *Cognition and Symbolic Processes,* Laurence Erlbaum Associates, 1974.

Contributor of aritcles to several journals. Consulting editor, *Psychological Bulletin,* 1964-70.

WORK IN PROGRESS: Research on theory of intention and causal attribution.

* * *

DULL, Jonathan R(omer) 1942-

PERSONAL: Born August 15, 1942, in Celina, Ohio; son of Earl L. (a lawyer) and Mary (Romer) Dull; married Agnes West (a nutritionist), July 9, 1965; children: Veronica, Caroline, Robert. *Education:* University of Notre Dame, A.B., 1964; University of California, Berkeley, M.A., 1967, Ph.D., 1972. *Office:* "The Papers of Benjamin Franklin," Yale University Press, 1603A Yale Station, New Haven, Conn. 06520.

CAREER: University of California, Berkeley, acting instructor in European history, 1973-74, administrative assistant, 1974-75; University of Texas, Austin, assistant professor of European history, 1975-77; Yale University Press, New Haven, Conn., assistant editor of "The Papers of Benjamin Franklin," 1977—. *Military service:* U.S. Naval Reserve, active duty, 1964-66; became lieutenant junior grade. *Awards, honors:* Gilbert Chinard Prize from Society for French Historical Studies and Institut Francais de Washington, 1976, for *The French Navy and American Independence.*

WRITINGS: The French Navy and American Independence: A Study of Arms and Diplomacy, 1774-1787, Princeton University Press, 1975.

WORK IN PROGRESS: Research on the French Navy during the French Revolution, 1787-1799.

SIDELIGHTS: Dull writes: "My major research interest continues to be the relationship between armaments and diplomacy. As assistant editor of the 'The Papers of Benjamin Franklin' I will continue to work with the War of American Independence; my independent research will take me into the French Revolution. These interests are naturally related to my own personal experiences, particularly in the Vietnamese war and the political movements of the 1960's such as the McCarthy campaign of 1968."

* * *

DUMAS, Frederic 1913-

PERSONAL: Born January 14, 1913, in Albi, France; son of Horace (a college professor) and Jeanne (Sagnier) Dumas; married Marie Jeanne Meggle (divorced); children: Juliette (Mrs. Francois Tilquin), Helene. *Education:* Received B.A. by correspondence. *Home:* Portissol, Sanary, Var, France.

CAREER: Specialist in underwater archaeology. Marine Nationale, Toulon, France, civilian employee, 1945—; member of numerous diving expeditions, mainly with Captain Jacques Cousteau. *Military service:* French Army, 1936-37, 1939-40. *Awards, honors:* Prix de la mer, 1972, and later medal from Academie de Marine, for *Trente Siecles sous la mer.*

WRITINGS: (With Jacques-Yves Cousteau and Philippe Taillez) *Par dix-huit metres de fond: Histoire d'un film* (title means "Sixty Feet Down: The Story of a Film"), Durel, 1946; (with Jacques-Yves Cousteau) *The Silent World* (Reader's Digest Book Club selection; Book-of-the-Month Club selection), Harper, 1953; *Trente Siecles sous la mer,* France Empire, 1972, translation by Philip A. Facey published as *Thirty Centuries Under the Sea,* Crown, 1976; *La Mer sauvage* (title means "The Wild Sea"), France Empire, 1974; *Chimeres de la mer,* (title means "Chimeras of the Sea"), France Empire, 1976.

WORK IN PROGRESS: Joies et angoisses dans la mer (title means "Joy and Anguish in the Sea"), just finished; *Retour a la mer* (title means "Back to the Sea").

SIDELIGHTS: Dumas told *CA,* in his passion for the sea, he has dived in all the oceans for many various reasons. He has contributed to the development of diving with his friends Commandant Cousteau and Commandant Tailliez, and is very interested in ancient shipwrecks which he often mentions in his books.

He also said: "Generally speaking I disagree with Commandant Cousteau when he says the oceans are dying. In 30 years I have not observed any change under the oceans. As for the death of some coral reefs, it is a natural death which always existed, due to conditions of change in the water or an abnormal increase of certain kinds of animals.''

* * *

DUMOND, Dwight Lowell 1895-1976

PERSONAL: Born Aguust 27, 1895, in Kingston, Ohio; son of James Frances and Laura (Bell) Dumond; married Irene Margaret Hettel, June 6, 1921; children: Jack Wesley, Caryl-Bell. *Education:* Baldwin Wallace College, A.B., 1920; Washington University, M.A., 1928; University of Michigan, Ph.D., 1929. *Home:* 1613 Morton, Ann Arbor, Mich. 48104.

CAREER: Ohio Wesleyan University, Delaware, acting professor of history, 1929-30; University of Michigan, Ann Arbor, assistant professor, 1930-35, associate professor, 1935-39, professor of history, 1939-65, professor emeritus, 1965-76. Commonwealth Foundation lecturer, University College, London, 1938-39; distinguished visiting professor, at Northern Michigan University, summer, 1965, Howard University, 1965-66; O'Connor Professor of American institutions, Colgate University, 1968-69. *Military service:* American Expeditionary Force; served during World War I. *Member:* Society of American Historians, American Historical Association, Mississippi Valley Historical Association (member of executive committee, 1939-40; president, 1948-49), Southern Historical Association. *Awards, honors:* Distinguished Achievement Award, 1963, from University of Michigan; D.Litt., 1965, from Northern Michigan University,; Anisfield-Wolf Award, 1961, for *Antislavery: Crusade for Freedom in America.*

WRITINGS: (Editor) *Southern Editorials on Secession,* Century, 1931; *The Secession Movement, 1860-1861,* Macmillan, 1931, reprinted, Octagon, 1963; *Roosevelt to Roosevelt: The United States in the Twentieth Century,* Holt, 1937; *Antislavery Origins of the Civil War in the United States,* University of Michigan Press, 1939; *A History of the United States,* Holt, 1942; *America in Our Time, 1896-1946,* Holt, 1947; (with Edward E. Dale and Edgar B. Wesley) *History of the United States,* Heath, 1948; *Antislavery: The Crusade for Freedom in America,* University of Michigan Press, 1961; *A Bibliography of Antislavery in America,* University of Michigan Press, 1961; *America's Shame and Redemption,* Northern Michigan University Press, 1965; (with John W. Christie) *George Bourne and The Book and Slavery Irreconcilable,* Historical Society of Delaware, 1969; (editor) *Letters of Theodore Dwight Weld,* Da Capo, 1970. Also author of *The Fourteenth Amendment Trilogy in Historical Perspective,* 1957.

SIDELIGHTS: Widely known for his authoritative studies of the history of slavery, Dumond disagreed with the views held by many of his contemporaries. He maintained that Lincoln, from the beginning, was fully aware of slavery as a problem that could only be solved by war. It was Dumond's contention that Lincoln condemned slavery as morally and politically wrong.

Dumond was highly critical of static teaching methods. The *New York Times* reports that at a conference of the Mississippi Valley Historical Association in 1946, he "urged that 'dull teaching' be eliminated and that dynamic, wide-awake instructors be found for history classes".

OBITUARIES: New York Times, June 2, 1976; *A. B. Bookman's Weekly,* July 5, 1976.*

(Died May 30, 1976, in Ann Arbor, Mich.)

DUNBABIN, J(ohn) P(aul) D(elacour) 1938-

PERSONAL: Born June 26, 1938, in London, England; son of T. J. (an academic) and A. D. D. (a teacher; maiden name, de Labilliere) Dunbabin; married Jean Hymers Mackay (an academic), September, 1962; children: Bridget Jane, Penelope Ann. *Education:* Oxford University, B.A. (first class honors), 1959, M.A., 1961. *Office:* St. Edmund Hall, Oxford, England.

CAREER: Ministry of Transport, London, England, assistant principal, 1961-62; Oxford University, Oxford, England, research lecturer in modern history at Christ Church, 1962-63, fellow and tutor in politics and modern history at St. Edmund Hall, 1963—. Visiting associate professor at Fordham University, 1968-69. *Member:* Royal Historical Society (fellow).

WRITINGS: Rural Discontent in Nineteenth Century Britain, Holmes & Meier, 1974. Contributor to history journals.

WORK IN PROGRESS: Research on British social and political history since 1830; research on international relations in contemporary history and politics since 1918.

* * *

DUNCAN, Elmer H(ubert) 1933-

PERSONAL: Born May 26, 1933, in Fullerton, Ky.; son of Homer Earl (a shoe worker) and Elizabeth Augusta (O'Roark) Duncan; married Rosemary Hack (a medical technologist), June 9, 1956. *Education:* University of Cincinnati, B.A., 1958, M.A., 1960, Ph.D., 1962. *Politics:* Democrat. *Religion:* Presbyterian. *Home:* 4813 Lake Englewood, Waco, Tex. 76710. *Office:* Department of Philosophy, Baylor University, Waco, Tex. 76703.

CAREER: Baylor University, Waco, Tex., assistant professor, 1962-65, associate professor, 1965-71, professor of philosophy, 1971—. *Military service:* U.S. Army, 1953-56; became sergeant. *Member:* American Philosophical Association (Western division), American Society for Value Inquiry, American Society for Aesthetics, American Association of University Professors, Aristotelian Society, Mind Association, Southwest Philosophical Society (president, 1974). *Awards, honors:* Travel grant from American Council of Learned Societies and American Society for Aesthetics, 1976.

WRITINGS: Twenty-Year Cumulative Index to the Journal of Aesthetics and Art Criticism, Volumes I-XX: *1941-1962,* AMS Press, 1964; (with Danny Floyd Walker) *Makers of the Modern Theological Mind: Soeren Kierkegaard,* Word, Inc., 1976. Writer of "Aesthetics for the Contemporary Artist, "a column in *Leonardo.* Contributor of more than seventy articles and reviews to journals in philosophy and aesthetics. Assistant editor of bibliography for *Journal of Aesthetics and Art Criticism,* 1970-76.

WORK IN PROGRESS: Research on eighteenth-century Scottish philosophy, especially aesthetics and ethics.

SIDELIGHTS: Touching on a few areas, Duncan told *CA:* "I like to argue that the arguments used in aesthetics are *not* really quite like those used in ethics, as many philosophers (e.g., A. J. Ayer) have supposed.

"In my book on Kierkegaard I claim that the influence of Feuerbach has not been sufficiently recognized, and that Kierkegaard was *not* an 'irrationalist.'

"As I grow older, I become more interested in history, especially the history of Scottish philosophy. I am convinced that the Scottish philosophy of common sense is really quite plausible, and that its influence on American thought has been strangely neglected in recent years."

Duncan has traveled in Western Europe, especially Scotland and Germany.

* * *

DUNHAM, Robert   1931-
(Bob Dunham, Dan Yuma)

PERSONAL: Born July 6, 1931, in Portland, Me.; son of Earl T. (an automobile dealer) and Charlotte (Dean) Dunham; married third wife, Setsuko Sazawa, February 28, 1969; children: Barbara-Ann, Dan, Dee-Anne, Marcia. *Education:* Williams College, B.A., 1953; attended Tokyo Institute of Japanese, 1956-57. *Politics:* Republican. *Religion:* Protestant. *Home:* #2 Village Lane, South Wellsfleet, Mass. 02663. *Agent:* Dial-A-Writer, American Society of Journalists and Authors, 123 West 43rd St., New York, N.Y. 10025. *Office address:* Box 292, South Wellsfleet, Mass. 02663.

CAREER: Dunham Pontiac, Needham, Mass., sales manager, 1955-57; Pan Commerical Pacific, Tokyo, Japan, managing director, 1957-66; High Performance Engineering, Tokyo, owner, 1967-72; full-time writer and journalist, 1972—. Factory race and test driver, Hino Motors Ltd., Tokyo, 1964-67. President of Truro Police Association, 1977—; president of adult fellowship, Tokyo Union Church. Technical advisors, Nippon Auto Club. *Military service:* U.S. Marine Corps, 1953-56; became first lieutenant. *Member:* International Motor Press Association, Federation Internationale Association des Journalistes de l'-Automobile, American Society of Journalists and Authors, Delta Kappa Epsilon.

WRITINGS: (Under pseudonym Dan Yuma) *Tokyo Unzipped,* Yuma (Tokyo), 1961; (under name Bob Dunham) *The Art of Being Japanese,* Charles E. Tuttle (Tokyo), 1964; (under pseudonym Dan Yuma) *Alice in Blunderland,* Yuma, 1965; "The Return of Father" (play), first produced in Tokyo at Tokyo Imperial Theatre, 1975.

Author of "The Time Travelers," a science-fiction movie for television, released by National Educational Television (NET), 1965.

Writer of weekly column, "MotoReport," in *Mainichi Daily News* (Tokyo). Editor of *Motoring News International;* associate editor of *All About Japanese Automobiles* magazine; *editorial consultant to* Mainichi Daily News.

WORK IN PROGRESS: A novel about the Korean War, *Even the Blessed and the Damned Must Die;* a "how-to" book, *You, Your Money, and Your Car,* completion expected, 1977; an adventure novel, *Back of the Sun,* 1977; a romantic novel, *Suddenly It's Spring,* 1978.

* * *

DUNN, John (Montfort)   1940-

PERSONAL: Born September 9, 1940, in Fulmer, England; son of Henry G. M. (an Army officer) and Catherine M. (Kinloch) Dunn; married Susan Fyvel, 1965 (divorced, 1973); married Judy Pace (a research psychologist), 1973. *Education:* Kings College, Cambridge, B.A. (first class honors), 1962. *Politics:* "Democratic socialist." *Home:* 3 Tenison Ave., Cambridge CB1 2DX, England. *Office:* Department of History and Politics, Kings College, Cambridge University, Cambridge CB2 1ST, England.

CAREER: Cambridge University, Cambridge, England,

fellow of Jesus College, 1965-66, fellow and director of studies at Kings College, 1966—, lecturer in political science, 1972-77, reader in politics, 1977—. Visiting lecturer at University of Ghana, 1968-69; Cecil H. and Ida Green Visiting Professor at University of British Columbia, 1977. *Member:* Political Studies Association of the United Kingdom, Past and Present Society, American Society for Political and Legal Philosophy.

WRITINGS: The Political Thought of John Locke, Cambridge University Press, 1969; *Modern Revolutions: An Introduction to the Analysis of a Political Phenomenon,* Cambridge University Press, 1972; (with A. F. Robertson) *Dependence and Opportunity: Political Change in Ahafo,* Cambridge University Press, 1973.

Contributor: John Yolton, editor, *John Locke: Problems and Perspectives,* Cambridge University Press, 1969; David Martin, editor, *Anarchy and Culture: The Problem of the Contemporary University,* Columbia University Press, 1969; Eric Homberger, William Janeway, and Simon Schama, editors, *The Cambridge Mind,* J. Cape, 1970; Gordon J. Schochet, editor, *Life, Liberty, and Property: Essays on Locke's Political Ideas,* Wadsworth, 1971; Peter Laslett, W. G. Runciman, and Quentin Skinner, editors, *Philosophy, Politics and Society,* fourth series, Blackwell, 1972; Dennis Austin and Robin Luckham, editors, *Politicians and Soldiers in Ghana 1966-1972,* F. Cass, 1975; W. H. Morris-Jones, editor, *The Making of Politicians: Studies from Africa and Asia,* Athlone Press, 1976.

Contributor to journals of history, political studies, and philosophy, and to *Listener.*

WORK IN PROGRESS: Research for books on the problem of political obligation, the political theory of post-colonial states, the development of the concept of revolution, and the fundamentals of political analysis.

SIDELIGHTS: Dunn wrote: "All of my work is concerned with the effort to develop a less grossly inadequate understanding of the political realities of most of the world today than is at present provided either by American political science or sociology or by the self-conscious heirs of the social and political theories of Karl Marx."

* * *

DUNNE, Robert Williams   1895-1977

June 1, 1895—January 21, 1977; American association executive, editor, and author. With Roger Baldwin, Dunne founded the American Civil Liberties Union in 1920. He served on its executive committee from 1923 to 1940. In 1927, Dunne founded the Labor Research Association, and served as executive secretary for that organization. He edited seventeen volumes of *The Labor Fact Book,* a biennial reference book. He also wrote other books dealing with labor relations. Dunne died in New York City. Obituaries: *New York Times,* January 23, 1977; *AB Bookman's Weekly,* March 14, 1977.

* * *

DUVAL, Jean-Jacques   1930-

PERSONAL: Born February 8, 1930, in Strasbourg, France; came to the United States in 1951, naturalized citizen, 1957; son of Jule Wiell and Alice Sittler Duval; married Elga Liverman, 1955, (divorced, 1972); children: Jean-Audouin. *Education:* Attended Art Decoratif and Art Students League of New York. *Politics:* None. *Residence:* Pawling, N.Y. *Office:* Duval Studios, Scottsville, Va. 24590.

CAREER: Stained glass designer, painter, and printmaker. Owner of Duval Studios, 1959—. *Military service:* French Army, 1949-50. U.S. Army, 1955-57. *Member:* Guild for Religious Architecture, Union of American Hebrew Congregations (accredited artist), Architectural League (New York City). *Awards, honors:* Winner of international competition at New York Worlds Fair, 1964-65, for stained glass design for the Vatican pavillion.

WRITINGS: Working with Stained Glass, Crowell, 1972.

WORK IN PROGRESS: A book on vegetable gardening.

SIDELIGHTS: Duval described his work as "very abstract, in stained glass as well as in painting and printmaking." He has had several exhibitions and some of his work has been included in the permanent collections of Bezalem Museum (Jerusalem) and Springfield Museum of Art (Springfield, Mass.). *Avocational interests:* Vegetable gardening, travel, skiing, fishing.

BIOGRAPHICAL/CRITICAL SOURCES: Craft Horizon: February, 1959, July, 1959, January, 1968, August, 1971; *TWA Ambassador,* January, 1972; *Intellectual Digest,* February, 1973.

* * *

DYCK, Harvey L(eonard) 1934-

PERSONAL: Born March 16, 1934, in Winnipeg, Manitoba, Canada; son of Isaac J. (a teacher) and Anna (Warkentin) Dyck; married Anne Justine Konrad (a writer), July 5, 1957; children: Maria, Elizabeth, Alexander. *Education:* University of British Columbia, B.A., 1957, M.A., 1958; Columbia University, Ph.D., 1963; attended University of Hamburg, 1955-56. *Home:* 187 Sherwood Ave., Toronto, Ontario, Canada M4P 2A9. *Office:* Department of History, University of Toronto, Toronto, Ontario, Canada.

CAREER: Wesleyan University, Middletown, Conn., instructor in Russian history, 1962-63; Columbia University, New York, N.Y., assistant professor of Russian history, 1963-66; University of Toronto, Toronto, Ontario, assistant professor, 1966-67, associate professor of Russian history, 1967—. Associate secretary of Commission on Post-Secondary Education in Ontario, 1972-73; consultant to Time-Life Books. *Member:* University Faculty Associations (vice-chairperson of Ontario Council), American Association for the Advancement of Slavic Studies; University of Toronto Faculty Association. *Awards, honors:* Canada Council fellowship, 1968-69 and 1973-74.

WRITINGS: Weimar Germany and Soviet Russia, 1926-1933: A Study in Diplomatic Instability, Columbia University Press, 1966; (editor with H. Peter Krosby, and contributor) *Empire and Nations: Essays in Honor of F. H. Soward,* University of Toronto Press, 1969. Contributor to *Slavic Review.*

WORK IN PROGRESS: The Russian Minorities: An Anthology, completion expected in 1979; *Mastering the Russian Fact: Prince Kaunitz and the Catherinian Empire,* completion expected in 1980.

SIDELIGHTS: Dyck writes: "My research interests have broadened considerably in recent years to include the . . . minorities in eastern Europe, and Russia's unique qualities as a great power in the eighteenth century, stemming from its location on the flank of the European balance system and on the fringes of a vast settlement frontier."

DYER, Wayne W(alter) 1940-

PERSONAL: Born May 10, 1940, in Detroit, Mich.; son of Melvin Lyle and Hazel (a secretary; maiden name, Vollick) Dyer; married Susan Elizabeth Casselman (a teacher of the deaf and a counselor); children: Tracy Lynn. *Education:* Wayne State University, B.S., 1965, M.S., 1966, Ed.D. (jointly with University of Michigan), 1970. *Residence:* Fort Lauderdale, Fla. *Agent:* Arthur Pine, 1780 Broadway, New York, N.Y. 10019.

CAREER: High school teacher and counselor in Detroit, Mich., 1965-67; Mercy High School, Farmington, Mich., director of guidance and counseling, 1967-71; St. John's University, Jamaica, N.Y., assistant professor, 1971-74, associate professor of counselor education, 1974-76; on promotional tour, 1976—. Counselor and therapist in private practice, Huntington, N.Y., 1973—. Staff consultant to hospitals, school districts, and public health agencies in the United States and Germany. Wayne State University, instructor, and practicum supervisor, 1969-71, member of summer school faculty, 1970-73, professor of counselor education in overseas program in Berlin, West Germany, and Istanbul, Turkey, 1974. Has made numerous guest appearances on national radio and television programs. Lecturer. *Military service:* U.S. Navy, 1958-62.

MEMBER: American Personnel and Guidance Association, Association of Counselor Educators and Supervisors, National Vocational Guidance Association, Association for Specialists in Group Work, New York Personnel and Guidance Association, New York Association of Counselor Educators and Supervisors.

WRITINGS: (With John Vriend) *Counseling Effectively in Groups,* Educational Technology Publications, 1973; (with Vriend) *Counseling Techniques that Work: Applications to Individual and Group Counseling,* American Personnel and Guidance Association Press, 1974; (with Vriend) *Group Counseling for the School Practitioner,* American Personnel and Guidance Association Press, 1976; *Your Erroneous Zones: Bold but Simple Techniques for Eliminating Unhealthy Behavior Patterns,* Funk, 1976; *Pulling Your Own Strings,* Crowell, 1978.

Also author of professional tapes, tapes series, and testing material. Contributor to professional counseling and guidance journals. *Educational Technology,* contributing editor, 1971—, co-editor of special issues, January and February, 1973.

WORK IN PROGRESS: A television show based on his book *Your Erroneous Zones;* a guide to self-actualization for children, *Hoard Your Toys.*

SIDELIGHTS: Wayne Dyer's best-selling book, *Your Erroneous Zones,* has been described as an indictment of what he calls the "psychological establishment." Dyer told R. Allen Leider: "Psychology as practiced today is all off-center. It tells people to look for the reasons for their unhappiness, upsets, hangups, and illnesses in terms of outside places and events—how their parents treated them, how their friends reacted to them, etc. That's looking backward for answers. Those explanations are gimmicks—slick gimmicks. Mental health is not complex, expensive or involved, hard work. It's only common sense."

He told *CA:* "I feel a mission to change the mental health of our country. Far too many people are addicted to tranquilizers, anti-depressants, alcohol, etc. . . . looking for answers every place but within the self. We need to return to a no-nonsense, common-sense approach to mental health and begin to take responsibility for our own lives rather than blame others.''

Dyer explains that his philosophy is ''based on the reality that you can be whatever you want to be by going out there and making it happen.'' He defines erroneous zones as areas of self-defeating behavior which result in a person's immobilization. Immobilization, Dyer told an interviewer, ''is any state in which you are not functioning the way you would like to be.'' His solution to immobilization is to eliminate these erroneous zones by living for the moment. He says in *Celebrity* magazine: ''Anxiety is nothing more than the avoidance of 'now.' If you live each moment as it comes, you can't be anxious or neurotic.''

Dyer's own life can be seen as proof of the success of his theories. He says that until ten years ago, he was ''just as messed up as everyone else.'' According to *People* magazine, when Dyer became convinced that he had to be in control of his own life, ''he learned to stop worrying about being bald or feeling guilty about his divorce from his first wife. . . . He no longer depended upon other people's opinions of him. In sum, he began deciding for himself, minute by minute, how he would live his own life.''

Then Dyer decided to write a best-seller. The first draft of *Your Erroneous Zones* was completed in thirteen days, after two years of research, and the book has been near or at the top of most national best-seller lists for more than eleven months. He left his teaching position and lucrative private practice, bought a new car, loaded it with copies of his book, and set out on what *People* called ''a self-marketing tour-de-force.''

In four months, Dyer had visited forty-eight states promoting the book, and had done more than 600 radio and television interviews. He told a *Newsday* reporter of the tour: ''I never had a day when I didn't do an interview. Sometimes I'd do a dozen in one day. No, I didn't get tired. Each interviewer was a chance to meet someone new. I would tell the listeners that they could buy the book at such and such a bookstore. Then, in the morning, I'd go to the bookstore, and tell the manager, 'Here's 25 copies, but you better put in a big order because you're going to need them.' I went to all the bookstores. It just began to mushroom.''

Dyer's book has received criticism for trivializing substantial problems. His response to a *Newsday* reporter: ''I know it all sounds too simple to some people, but what's the other choice? To be unhappy with yourself? That's the least effective choice of all.''

BIOGRAPHICAL/CRITICAL SOURCES: Miami News, July 13, 1976; *Deseret News,* August 10, 1976; *Newsday,* November 18, 1976; *Miami Herald,* December 14, 1976; *Chicago Tribune,* December 19, 1976; *Celebrity,* December, 1976; *People,* January 10, 1977.

* * *

EAKIN, Sue 1918-

PERSONAL: Born December 7, 1918, in Loyd Bridge, La.; daughter of Samuel Pickles, Sr. (a planter) and Myrtle (Guy) Lyles; married Paul Mechlin Eakin, Sr. (a financial consultant), January 31, 1941; children: Paul Mechlin, Jr., Russell Lyles, Sara Eakin Kuhn, Samuel Fred, Frank. *Education:* Louisiana State University, B.A., 1941, M.A. (history), 1964, M.A. (journalism), 1965; University of Southwestern Louisiana, doctoral study, 1976. *Politics:* ''Just an alert, concerned citizen.'' *Religion:* Methodist. *Home:* 203 South Marshall, Bunkie, La. 71322. *Office:* Department of History, Louisiana State Unviersity, Alexandria, La. 71301.

CAREER: Worked during the 1950's as a columnist and feature writer for the *Alexandria Daily Town Talk,* Alexandria, La., as editor and co-owner of *Bunkie Record,* Bunkie, La., and as feature editor, columnist and reporter for *Opelousas Daily World,* Opelousas, La.; Louisiana State University, Alexandria, assistant professor of history, 1964—. Archivist for Louisiana State Archives and Records Service. *Member:* Louisiana Historical Association (member of board of directors, 1973-76), Historical Association of Central Louisiana (member of board of directors, 1975), Les Avoyelles Commissiones. *Awards, honors:* National Endowment for the Humanities fellow, 1974; outstanding American history professor award from Daughters of the American Revolution, 1975; Louisiana Committee of the American Revolution Bicentennial research award, 1976.

WRITINGS: (Editor with Joseph Logsdon) *Twelve Years a Slave, 1841-1853,* Louisiana State University Press, 1968; (editor and author of introduction) Manie Culbertson, *Let Me Speak,* Pelican Press, 1970; (editor) Walter Prichard, *Outline of Louisiana History,* Pelican Press, 1972; *Some History of Rapides Parish: A Sourcebook,* Louisiana Committee of the American Revolution Bicentennial, 1976; (with Norman Ferachi) *Vanishing Louisiana,* Beauregard Press, 1977.

Filmstrips: ''Louisiana's Cultural Heritage,'' ''Louisiana's Physical Features,'' ''Louisiana's Wildlife Resources,'' ''Louisiana Manufacturing,'' ''Louisiana Minerals,'' ''Louisiana Mineral Conservation,'' ''Plantation Revolution: Planters, Negroes and Machines,'' ''Acadians of Louisiana,'' and ''A Louisiana Boucherie.''

Contributor to *Louisiana Heritage.* Editor of *Back Tracking,* 1974-76.

WORK IN PROGRESS: With the Help of the Lord, a study of private black academies from about 1880 to the Depression; editing *The Way We Were: Margery Cushman, a Southern Girl's Journal of the 1850's,* with Sidney Kilpatrick; *Louisiana Socialists, 1900-1928; Ezra Bennett and the World He Lived In, 1830-1875; Bayou Boeuf Country; George Washington Bolton in the Civil War; Plantation Revolution: Planters, Negroes, and Machines in the 1950's; Vanishing Louisiana,* Volume II.

SIDELIGHTS: Sue Eakin writes: ''I was born in central Louisiana where blacks, plantation whites and blacks, and hill country people were represented in the society. This was at the end of the Bourbon period when the planter class Redeemers and Southern industrialists banded together to re-create the Southern caste system. I grew up caught in the position of empathizing with all three groups, and even as a child planned what I wanted to write, and wrote since I can remember, to show these different peoples in the affectionate light in which I saw them. To me, none of the groups seemed to accepted by the other two, and to me there was a great deal of positive good in all of them. I planned to study in a scholarly way a long list of subjects—English, sociology, journalism, history, and economics, which would help me to understand the Southern people, my people, all of them.''

* * *

EAMES, John Douglas 1915-

PERSONAL: Born October 6, 1915, in London, England; son of Edward Douglas and Winifred (Mason) Eames. *Education:* Attended London Polytechnic, 1929-30. *Politics:* Liberal. *Religion:* Episcopal. *Home:* 25 Nassau Rd., London S.W.13, England.

CAREER: Child actor (for Cosmopolitan-Goldwyn film "Under the Red Robe") in New York, N.Y., 1923; English-American Library, Cannes, France, librarian, 1930-32; Metro-Goldwyn-Mayer, London, England, publicity clerk, 1933-48, assistant director of publicity, 1948-59, director of advertising, 1959-71; writer, 1971—. *Military service:* Royal Air Force, 1940.

WRITINGS: The MGM Story: A Complete History of Fifty Roaring Years, Crown, 1975. Contributor of articles, stories, and reviews to British magazines, including *Reality* and *Passing Show.* Editor and contributor to *The Lion's Roar,* 1932-58.

WORK IN PROGRESS: History/filmography studies of Warner Brothers, Twentieth Century Fox, and Paramount.

SIDELIGHTS: Eames writes: "A product of the movie generation which devoted as much time and enthusiasm to the cinema as the TV generation now does to the smaller screen, I was further nudged toward show business by the profession of my father, an English actor on Broadway." Regarding *The MGM Story,* he comments: "I decided to make this the first book to cover the entire output of one of the major film companies; relating its history and at the same time incorporating facts, comment, and illustration for every one of its movies. The book's international approval by critics, film buffs, general readers, and (not least) reference librarians encourages me in the preparation of companion volumes."

AVOCATIONAL INTERESTS: Tennis, gardening.

*   *   *

EAST, W(illiam) Gordon   1902-

PERSONAL: Born November 10, 1902, in London, England; son of George Richard and Jemima (Nicoll) East; married Dorothea Small; children: Penelope Jane East Menuge, Jonathan Robert, Catherine East Singh, Richard Gordon. *Education:* Peterhouse, Cambridge, B.A. (honors), 1924, M.A., 1928. *Home:* Wildwood, Oxshott, Surrey KT22 OLU, England.

CAREER: University of London, London, England, lecturer at London School of Economics and Political Science, 1927-46, reader in geography, 1946-47, professor of geography at Birkbeck College, 1947-70, head of department, 1947-70; writer, 1970—. Visiting professor at University of Minnesota, 1952, University of California, Los Angeles, 1959-60, University of Michigan, 1966-67, University of Wisconsin, Milwaukee, 1969-70, and University of Saskatchewan, 1971; Myres Memorial Lecturer at Oxford University, 1971. Temporary administrative officer for Ministry of Economic Warfare and the Foreign Office, 1941-45. *Member:* Royal Geographical Society (member of council, 1956-59), Institute of British Geographers (president, 1959-60). *Awards, honors:* Thirlwall Prize from University of Cambridge, 1929; Murchison Award from Royal Geographical Society, 1972.

WRITINGS: The Union of Moldavia and Wallachia, Cambridge University Press, 1929, reprinted, 1961; *An Historical Geography of Europe,* Dutton, 1935, 4th edition, 1960; *The Geography Behind History,* Thomas Nelson, 1938, 2nd edition, 1960; *Mediterranean Problems,* Thomas Nelson, 1942; (editor with O.H.K. Spate) *The Changing Map of Asia,* Methuen, 1950, 4th edition, 1971; (with Spate and C. A. Fisher) *The Spirit and Purpose of Geography,* Hutchinson, 1951, 3rd edition (with S. W. Wooldridge), 1966; *The Soviet Union,* Van Nostrand, 1963, 2nd edition, 1976; (ed-

itor) *The Caxton Atlas,* Caxton, 1960; *Our Fragmented World,* Macmillan, 1975. Editor of "Nelson's Regions of the British Isles," for Hutchinson geographical library and Batsford's historical geography series. Contributor to professional journals.

WORK IN PROGRESS: "Historical Geography," to be included in the 4th edition of *A Geography of Europe,* edited by G. W. Hoffman, for Ronald.

SIDELIGHTS: East told *CA:* "It has been my main purpose in my books and articles to highlight the nature and importance of environmental conditions in history and international politics."

*   *   *

EASTHOPE, Gary   1945-

PERSONAL: Born May 29, 1945, in Liverpool, England; married wife, Christine (a lecturer); children: one son. *Education:* Attended University of Leeds, 1963-67, and University of Exeter, 1968-73. *Office:* School of Social Studies, University of East Anglia, Norwich, England.

CAREER: Secondary school teacher, 1967-68; Exeter Institute of Education, Exeter, England, research officer, 1968-71; New University of Ulster, Coleraine, Northern Ireland, lecturer in education, 1971-73; University of East Anglia, Norwich, England, lecturer in sociology, 1973—.

WRITINGS: A History of Social Research Methods, Longmans, 1974; *Community, Hierarchy, and Open Education,* Routledge & Kegan Paul, 1975. Contributor to technical journals.

WORK IN PROGRESS: Research on "alternative medicine" and on early English society, 1500-1750.

*   *   *

EATON, William Edward   1943-

PERSONAL: Born February 19, 1943, in Cedar Rapids, Iowa; son of Edward L. (a salesman) and Helen (a teacher; maiden name, Carlson) Eaton; married Judith Kukarola, 1964; children: Gregory M., Leslie Ann. *Education:* Eastern Illinois University, B.S., 1965; Southern Illinois University, M.S., 1968; Washington University, St. Louis, Mo., Ph.D., 1971. *Home:* 2914 Kent Dr., Carbondale, Ill. 62901. *Office:* Department of Educational Administration and Foundations, Southern Illinois University, Carbondale, Ill. 62901.

CAREER: High school social studies teacher in Granite City, Ill., 1965-68; Southern Illinois University, Carbondale, assistant professor, 1971-75, associate professor of education, 1976—. *Member:* History of Education Society, American Educational Research Association, American Educational Studies Association, Midwest History of Education Society, Jackson County Historical Society (member of board of directors), Phi Delta Kappa.

WRITINGS: The American Federation of Teachers: A History of the Movement, Southern Illinois Press, 1975.

WORK IN PROGRESS: A book about educational leader, George S. Counts; a textbook on social foundations of education, with Raymond Callahan; a monograph on nineteenth-century educator, Robert Allyn.

SIDELIGHTS: Eaton writes: "Nearly all of us who work closely with the public schools are continually besieged by the sense of overwhelming problems that face the teachers, the schools, and the students. The work that I have done and am trying to continue to do is based on the assumption that we need to achieve a better historical and philosophical perspective on problems before we can hope for truly creative solutions.''

* * *

EBB, Fred 1935-

PERSONAL: Born April 8, 1935, in New York, N.Y.; son of Harry and Anna (Gritz) Ebb. *Education:* Attended New York University and Columbia University. *Address:* c/o Morton Leavy, 437 Madison Ave., New York, N.Y. 10022. *Agent:* International Creative Management, 40 West 57th St., New York, N.Y. 10019.

CAREER: Lyricist and librettist. *Awards, honors:* Emmys from National Academy of Television Arts and Sciences, 1973, for "Liza with a Z," and 1975, for "Gypsy in My Soul"; Academy Awards (Oscars) from American Academy of Motion Picture Arts and Sciences, 1974, for "Norman Rockwell," and 1976, for "How Lucky Can You Get"; "Chicago" received Antoinette Perry (Tony) Award from League of New York Theatres and Producers for book and lyrics, Grammy Award from National Academy of Recording Arts and Sciences for the album, and Golden Globe Award from Hollywood Foreign Press Association, all 1976.

WRITINGS—Musicals; lyricist: "Flora, the Red Menace," produced on Broadway at Alvin Theatre, May, 1965; *Cabaret* (produced on Broadway at Broadhurst Theatre, November 20, 1966), Random House, 1967; "The Happy Time," produced on Broadway at Imperial Theatre, January 18, 1968; *Zorba* (produced on Broadway at Imperial Theatre, November 17, 1968), Random House, 1969; (and author of book) "70, Girls, 70," produced on Broadway at Broadhurst Theatre, April 15, 1971; (and librettist with Bob Fosse) "Chicago," produced, 1975; "In Person," produced in Chicago, July 4, 1977, produced in New York City, October, 1977.

Screenplays: (Lyricist) "Cabaret," Allied Artists, 1972; "Norman Rockwell," produced, 1974; (lyricist) "Funny Lady," Columbia, 1975; (lyricist) "Lucky Lady," Twentieth Century-Fox, 1975, (lyricist) "A Matter of Time," American International Pictures, 1976; (lyricist) "New York New York," United Artists, 1977.

Television specials: "Liza," produced June, 1970; "Liza with a Z," produced, 1972; "Ole Blue Eyes Is Back," produced, 1974; "Gypsy in My Soul," produced, 1976.

WORK IN PROGRESS: Unspecified projects.

SIDELIGHTS: "In a country where each generation measures out its milestones in the words of popular songs," writes Judy Gordon in response to a query from *CA*, "the writing of lyrics has long been an important form. Recently, it has been the fashion for critics to bemoan the drying-up of a field once made fertile by such talented poets as Lorenz Hart, Oscar Hammerstein, Cole Porter, Dorothy Field, and Howard Dietz.

"If the list is shorter today, the quality is as high as ever—as evidenced by the wit and sophistication of lyricist Fred Ebb. Early in 1977, a sampler of Fred Ebb's work with composer John Kander, a cabaret called '2 by 5' opened at New York's Village Gate Theatre. One prominent critic wrote: 'One cannot appreciate Fred Ebb's lyrics enough without writing a book length study of them. There is no better lyricist around. Ebb can be as wizardly with words as any pyrotechnician but he has long since mastered a rare simplicity. Moreover, in the midst of a mocking song such as "Class" from "Chicago" he can off-handedly introduce the touching ("Even kids will kick your shins and give you sass"). He is a

master.' Another critic wrote that 'one of Fred Ebb's great strengths is the ability to convey the emotions of lonely people who have been hurt by love or have never felt it and are willing to settle for something a good deal less than searing passion.'

"A native New Yorker with a Master's degree in English literature from Columbia University," Gordon continues, "Fred Ebb had collaborated with several composers when in 1963 a music publisher suggested that he try working with John Kander. Although their first musical was not produced, it was impressive enough to persuade George Abbott to assign them to write the score of 'Flora the Red Menace' for a seventeen-year-old named Liza Minelli, a happy and enduring association.

"Their next show, 'Cabaret,' was a smash hit, both on Broadway and in the film starring Liza Minnelli. Since 'Cabaret,' Kander and Ebb have written five shows for the Broadway theatre, five films, four television specials, and special material for Barbra Streisand, Liza Minnelli, Shirley MacLaine, Joel Grey, and Chita Rivera. 'Writing comes easily to us,' Fred Ebb explains. 'Unlike many other composing teams, we never have to worry about which comes first, the music or the lyrics. We do it all together. We compose as a whole. And we can do it in a hurry.' In writing a show tune, they begin with the episode in the story. John Kander comments, 'We set out to musicalize the moment. The boy is coming in the door, he's just lost his job and he has to tell his girlfriend. We start talking about the moment, what they are really feeling. Sometimes we even improvise the scene ourselves.'

"They reject comparison to movie hit song writers. 'We're strictly theatre guys, writing the moment, as it happens in the play,' Ebb notes. 'And the moment very often does not result in a structured song; it's not an A-A-B form, not a standard popular form. So we don't write "hits." In fact, it's not considered good form to try for one, and the writers who reach for them catch it from the critics. "And All That Jazz" from "Chicago" is not a hit; it's a successful song that's performed a lot.'

Gordon concludes, "Working with fresh ideas in an old tradition, Fred Ebb is an outstanding contributor to the enrichment of our musical theatre."

AVOCATIONAL INTERESTS: Collecting musical show albums.

* * *

EBERT, Roger (Joseph) 1942-

PERSONAL: Born June 18, 1942, in Urbana, Ill.; son of Walter H. and Annabel (Stumm) Ebert. *Education:* University of Illinois, B.S., 1964; also attended University of Cape Town, 1965, and University of Chicago, 1966-67. *Home:* 509 W. Dickens, Chicago, Ill. 60614. *Office: Chicago Sun-Times,* 401 North Wabash, Chicago, Ill. 60611.

CAREER: News Gazette, Champaign-Urbana, Ill., staff reporter, 1958-66; *Chicago Sun-Times,* Chicago, Ill., film critic, 1967—. Author of interviews and film reviews syndicated by Sun-Times wire service to about one hundred twenty newspapers, 1967—. Instructor at Chicago City College, 1967-68; lecturer at University of Chicago, 1969—; lecturer at Columbia College (Chicago), 1973-74, 1977—. Co-host, "Sneak Previews," for WTTW-TV, Chicago; contributor, "Critics at Large," for WBBM-Radio, Chicago. Member of juries at Venice, Chicago, and U.S.A. film festivals; has also covered Cannes, Teheran, Moscow, and New

York film festivals; consultant to National Endowment for the Humanities and National Endowment for the Arts.

MEMBER: American Newspaper Guild, Writers Guild of America (West), National Society of Film Critics, Arts Club of Chicago, Cliff Dwellers Club of Chicago, University of Illinois Alumni Association (member of board of directors, 1975—), Phi Delta Theta. *Awards, honors:* Overseas Press Club award, 1963; award from Chicago Headline Club, 1963; Stick o'Type Award from Chicago Newspaper Guild, 1973; Pulitzer Prize for distinguished criticism, 1975, for reviews and essays in *Chicago Sun-Times.*

WRITINGS: An Illini Century, University of Illinois Press, 1967.

Author of screenplay "Beyond the Valley of the Dolls," Twentieth Century Fox, 1970. Contributor to popular magazines and newspapers, including *Esquire, Oui, Film Comment, American Film, Critic,* and *Rolling Stone.*

WORK IN PROGRESS: A screenplay, "The Last Demo Derby," with Bob Dahlin.

*   *   *

ECKSTEIN, Alexander 1915-1976

December 9, 1915—December 4, 1976; Yugoslavian-born expert and pioneer in the field of Chinese economics, professor of economics, and author of books, including his best known work, *Communist China's Economic Growth and Foreign Trade.* Eckstein founded the National Committee on United States-China Relations, and was chairman during the visit to this country of the Chinese table-tennis team. He died at his home in Ann Arbor, Mich. Obituaries: *New York Times,* December 6, 1976. (See index for previous *CA* sketch)

*   *   *

EDBERG, Rolf 1912-

PERSONAL: Born March 14, 1912, in Lysvik, Sweden; married Astrid Persson, 1937; children: Jorgen, Ranveig Jacobsson, Birgitta. *Home:* Hagtornsgatan 3, 652 30 Karlstad, Sweden.

CAREER: Oskarshamns Nyheter, Oscarshamn, Sweden, chief editor, 1934-37; *Oestgoeten,* Linkoeping, Sweden, chief editor, 1938-44; *Ny Tid,* Gothenburg, Sweden, chief editor, 1945-56; Swedish ambassador to Norway, 1956-67; governor of Swedish province of Vaarmland, 1967-77. Member of Swedish Parliament, 1940-44 and 1948-56. Delegate to Council of Europe, 1949-52, United Nations, 1952-55, 1957, 1960-61, Northern Council, 1953-56, and Disarmament Conference, 1961-65. *Member:* Swedish Press Club (president, 1951-53), Swedish Association of Writers, Pen Club, Swedish Association of Biologists, Swedish Royal Academy of Sciences, Swedish Society for Anthropology and Geography. *Awards, honors:* Socrates Prize, 1972, from School of Adult Education; gold medal, 1974, from Royal Swedish Academy of Science; Doctor Honoris Causa, 1974, from University of Gothenburg; gold medal, 1976, from Geographical-Anthropological Society; Selma Lagerloef's Prize, 1976.

WRITINGS: Nansen, european: En studie i vilja och godvilja (title means "Nansen, the European: A Study in Will and Good Will"), Tiden, 1961; *Spillran av ett moln,* Norstedt, 1966, translation by Sven Aahman published as *On the Shred of a Cloud: Notes in a Travel Book,* University of Alabama Press, 1969, same translation published as *On the Shred of a Cloud: Reflections on Man and His Environ-*

ment, Harper, 1971; *Vid traedets fot,* Norstedt, 1971, translation by David Mel Paul and Margareta Paul published as *At the Foot of the Tree: A Wanderer's Musings Before the Fall,* University of Alabama Press, 1974; *Ett hus i kosmos* (title means "A House in the Cosmos), Esselte Studium, 1974; *Dalens Ande,* Norstedt, 1976.

Also author of *Ge dem en chans* (title means "Give Them a Chance"), 1939; *I morgon Norden* (title means "Tomorrow Nordic"), 1944; *Demokratisk linje* (title means "Democratic Line"), 1948; *Femte etappen* (title means "The Fifth Stage"), 1949; *Oeppna grindarna* (title means "Open the Gates"), 1952; *Paa jordens villkor* (title means "On Earth's Terms"), 1974.

WORK IN PROGRESS: Skuggor oever Savannen (title means "Shadows Over the Savannah").

SIDELIGHTS: Edberg writes to *CA:* "I grew up in a fresh and beautiful countryside and very early I got in contact with the science of evolution, which started a lifelong interest in natural sciences. The first book about man's condition was created in order to disentangle my own meditating threads and to put man's moment on earth in a bigger continuity. We have in our constantly greedy searching acquired an ever increasing richness in knowledge of details and have been forced into an even harder specialization. However, nature is interaction, not separation. What we have to do today is to place our varying knowledge under a unifying comprehensive view giving us a vision of our destiny. My ambition as a layman has been to arrive at such a comprehensive view.

"The scientific literature—especially in the environmental field—published in the United States has given me great inspiration in my work. Europe has a lot to learn from the American research which is the most advanced in the world. But I believe that America, highly urbanized, has some to learn from the Scandinavian people with their natural love of nature.

"And that is the way it ought to be: that we learn from each other's research, thinking, and experience."

*   *   *

EDELSTEIN, Morton A. 1925-

PERSONAL: Born July 31, 1925, in Chicago, Ill.; son of Harry (a salesman) and Charlotte (a saleswoman) Edelstein; married Sylvia Berkowitz, January 5, 1929; children: Jeffrey, Donna. *Education:* Attended Wright Junior College; Hardin-Simmons University, B.A. *Religion:* Jewish. *Residence:* Chicago, Ill. *Office: Chicago Daily News,* 401 North Wabash, Chicago, Ill. 60611.

CAREER/WRITINGS: Associated Press, New York City, newsman in Charlotte, N.C., 1950-51; *Chicago American,* Chicago, Ill., reporter, foreign correspondent and sports editor, 1951-62; Columbia Broadcasting System (CBS)-TV, New York City, city editor in Chicago, 1963-65; National Broadcasting Company (NBC)-TV, New York City, city editor in Chicago, 1965-67; American Broadcasting Company (ABC)-TV, New York City, city editor in Chicago, 1967-68; CBS-Radio, chief investigative reporter in Chicago, 1968-70; Chicago Park District, Chicago, public information director, 1971; *Chicago Daily News,* Chicago, author of "Mort's Column," 1972—. Contributor to *Coronet* and *Reader's Digest. Military service:* U.S. Marine Corps, 1943-46; received Presidential Unit Citation. *Member:* Chicago Press Club, Chicago Newspaper Reporters Association. *Awards, honors:* Prizes for investigative reporting from Associated Press; Emmy Award from National Academy of

Television Arts and Sciences, 1963; Edward R. Murrow Award for investigative reporting, 1970.

SIDELIGHTS: Edelstein writes that although he originally planned on becoming a sports writer, he decided during World War II to become a general assignment reporter. He told *CA:* "Motivation was from my innards. I wanted to be where events happened and cover them. I did. I covered sports, NFL, baseball, and college sports. I worked beats: City Hall, labor, crime, county board, state government, and had one foreign assignment, infiltrating an anti-Castro group in Chicago, then going with them to Miami, before they eventually landed in Cuba."

* * *

EDEN, (Robert) Anthony 1897-1977

June 12, 1897—January 14, 1977; British statesman and author of memoirs. After his election to the House of Commons in 1923, Eden rose rapidly in Conservative Party ranks and became foreign secretary in 1935, a post he resigned three years later to protest Chamberlain's policy of appeasement for Hitler. He was reinstated as foreign secretary by Winston Churchill in 1940 and succeeded Churchill as prime minister in 1955. Eden defied other Commonwealth countries and the United States by directing British troops to join with France in the ill-fated 1956 invasion of the Suez Canal Zone. Two months later bad health forced him to resign. He died in Wiltshire, England. Obituaries: *New York Times,* January 15, 1977; *Washington Post,* January 15, 1977; *Time,* January 24, 1977; *Newsweek,* January 24, 1977; *Current Biography,* March, 1977.

* * *

EDGAR, Frank Terrell Rhoades 1932-
(Bill Ritchie)

PERSONAL: Born May 3, 1932, in Fort Wayne, Ind.; son of Merton Wesley (an electrical engineer) and Annalydia (Hall) Edgar; married Judith Mae Benson, October 9, 1965; children: Kristine Alexandra. *Education:* University of Denver, B.A., 1954; Northern Illinois University, M.S., 1957; University of California, Berkeley, Ph.D., 1966. *Politics:* Independent. *Religion:* "Oecumenicalist. Churchmanship: Lutheran." *Home:* 907 North Seventh St., Canton, Mo. 63435. *Office:* Division of Social Science, Culver-Stockton College, Canton, Mo. 63435.

CAREER: Northern Illinois University, DeKalb, instructor in history and government, 1958-59; San Francisco State College, San Francisco, Calif., lecturer in history, 1965-66; Syracuse University, Utica College, Utica, N.Y., assistant professor of history, 1967-69; Culver-Stockton College, Canton, Mo., associate professor of history and political science, 1969—. *Military service:* U.S. Army, 1954-56. *Member:* National Historical Society, Canton Historical Society, Canton Round Table, Tory Club (co-founder).

WRITINGS: Sir Ralph Hopton, the King's Man in the West: A Study in Character and Command, Clarendon Press, 1968. Contributor of stories (under pseudonym Bill Ritchie), articles, and a play to magazines, including *Limbo.*

WORK IN PROGRESS: Cornwall for the King, a historical novel; *The Golden Chacma* or *Fellow Primates,* a short novel; *Images of Women in the West,* a long essay; a historical novel about the Greek war of independence.

SIDELIGHTS: Edgar writes: "I got my first urge to write when reading serials in *Collier's* magazine back in the early 1940's. I wrote my first short story at the age of nine. Two

formative books were a book on Greek myths which I encountered when I was five and which led me in 1959 to visit Greece and make a journey to Mount Olympus; also, V. M. Hillyer's *Child's History of the World.* I decided the two things I most wanted to do were write and travel, avocationally if not vocationally. And I wanted to write historical novels above all else. Kenneth Roberts became my model for that.

"My travels led me to Mexico; army service led me to Korea, Japan, Okinawa, and China. I have been to Europe five times: including five months in Greece and a year in England. I have studied Spanish, French, modern Greek, a very little German and Japanese.

"I find that it is very difficult to combine teaching with writing. At the small colleges the teaching load is too heavy, and at the universities scholarship is too monographic and specialized. I don't know what the answer is. If I could get out of teaching, I would like to do research and editorial work: being a county archivist is my idea of a job which might allow a little more time for writing: or possibly library work.

"I don't know if I will ever finish the projects I have started, but I will surely try."

* * *

EDGAR, Neal Lowndes 1927-

PERSONAL: Born June 21, 1927, in New York, N.Y.; son of William J. B. (a professor) and Margaret B. (an editor; maiden name, Thomas) Edgar; married Susanna Capper (a librarian), May 7, 1966. *Education:* Trinity College, Hartford, Conn., A.B., 1950; State University of New York at Albany, M.A. and M.S.L.S., both 1958; University of Michigan, A.M.L.S., 1964, Ph.D., 1965. *Home:* 1378 Athena Dr., Kent, Ohio 44240. *Office:* Library, Kent State University, Kent, Ohio 44242.

CAREER: State University of New York at Albany, acquisitions librarian, 1958-61; University of Michigan, Ann Arbor, coordinating librarian for Residence Hall Libraries, 1961-65; Library of Congress, Washington, D.C., serials cataloger in Descriptive Cataloging Division, 1965-66; Kent State University, Kent, Ohio, acquisitions librarian, 1967-68, serials librarian, 1968—, associate professor of library administration, 1969-74, professor of library science, 1972—, professor of library administration, 1974—. Has served as institutional representative to professional organizations, including Ohio College Library Center, Northeast Ohio Major Academic Libraries, and Ohio Inter-University Library Council's Technical Services Group.

MEMBER: American Library Association, American Association of University Professors, Tri-State Association of College and Research Librarians, Academic Librarians Association of Ohio, Northern Ohio Technical Services Librarians, Akron Area Librarians Association.

WRITINGS: A History and Bibliography of American Magazines, 1810-1820, Scarecrow, 1975; (contributor) Sidney L. Jackson, editor, *A Century of Service: Librarianship in the United States and Canada,* American Library Association, 1976. Contributor of about twenty-five articles to professional magazines.

WORK IN PROGRESS: Research for a comprehensive bibliography of American magazines published between 1741 and 1820; a register of editors, engravers, printers, and publishers of early American magazines and a study of some of the illustrations used therein.

SIDELIGHTS: Edgar writes that his "career in librarianship has focused on technical services, especially in serials and cataloging. The highlight has been selection as a member of the American Library Association's RTSD Catalog Code Revision Committee."

* * *

EDINGER, Edward F(erdinand) 1922-

PERSONAL: Born December 13, 1922, in Cedar Rapids, Iowa; son of Edward F. (a contractor) and Gladys M. (Rechel) Edinger; married Frances E. McCarthy (a biology researcher), August 5, 1950; children: Ronald, Bruce, Clara. *Education:* Attended Indiana University, 1940-43; Yale University, M.D., 1946. *Home:* 567 Grandview Ave., Suffern, N.Y. 10901. *Office:* 230 Central Park W., New York, N.Y. 10024.

CAREER: Yale-New Haven Hospital, New Haven, Conn., intern, 1946-47; Washington University, St. Louis, Mo., research fellow in hypertension at Barnes Hospital, 1949-50; Yale-New Haven Hospital, assistant resident, 1950-51; Rockland State Hospital, Orangeburg, N.Y., resident in psychiatry, 1951-53, supervising psychiatrist, 1953-55; practising Jungian analyst in New York, N.Y., 1955—. Chairman of C. G. Jung Training Center, 1969—. *Military service:* U.S. Army, 1947-49; became captain. *Member:* International Association for Analytical Psychology, American Psychiatric Association, New York Association for Analytical Psychology, Alpha Omega Alpha.

WRITINGS: Ego and Archetype, Putnam, 1972. Contributor to psychology and psychiatry journals.

WORK IN PROGRESS: American Nekyia, a psychological commentary on Melville's *Moby Dick; The Psychological Meaning of Alchemy; The New Myth of Meaning.*

SIDELIGHTS: Edinger writes briefly: "I am interested in promoting the realization of C. G. Jung's towering contribution to the problems of modern man."

* * *

EDLIN, Herbert 1904(?)-1976

1904(?)—December 25, 1976; British forester and author of books in his field. He died in England. Obituaries: *AB Bookman's Weekly,* February 14, 1977.

* * *

EDMONDS, R(obert) H(umphrey) G(ordon) 1920-
(Robin Edmonds)

PERSONAL: Born October 5, 1920, in London, England; son of Charles Humphrey (an aviator) and Lorna (Osborn) Edmonds; married Georgina Combe, September 20, 1951 (divorced, December, 1975); married second wife Enid Flora Albu (a psychoanalyst; widow of Dr. Michael Balint), January 26, 1976; children: Charles, Dominic, Robert, James. *Education:* Brasenose College, Oxford, M.A., 1946. *Office:* Foreign and Commonwealth Office, London SW1A 2AH, England.

CAREER: Diplomat. Entered British Foreign Service, 1946; served in Cairo, 1947-49, in Foreign Office, London, 1949-53, in Rome, 1953-57, in Warsaw, 1957-59, in Foreign Office, London, 1959-62, Counsellor in Caracas, 1962-66, head of American department of Foreign Office, London, 1966-67, head of Mediterranean department at Commonwealth Office, London, 1967-68, head of Southern European department, Foreign and Commonwealth Office, London,

1968-69, Minister in Moscow, 1969-71, High Commissioner in Nicosia, 1971-72; Glasgow University, Glasgow, Scotland, visiting fellow in politics, 1973-74; Foreign and Commonwealth Office, London, Assistant Under-Secretary of State, 1974-77; Woodrow Wilson International Center for Scholars, Washington, D.C., visiting fellow, 1977—. *Military service:* British Army, 1940-46; became major. *Member:* Royal Institute of International Affairs, International Institute of Strategic Studies, British International Studies Association, Turf Club.

WRITINGS: (Under name Robin Edmonds) *Soviet Foreign Policy, 1962-73: The Paradox of Super-Power,* Oxford University Press, 1975. Contributor of articles to *Times Literary Supplement.*

WORK IN PROGRESS: Research on the Anglo-American special relationship from 1947-57.

* * *

EDMUNDS, Stahrl W(illiam) 1917-

PERSONAL: Born May 15, 1917, in Cambridge, Minn.; son of Adoniran Walter (a salesman) and Axeline (a printer; maiden name, Holmgren) Edmunds; married Amy Margaret Klein (an artist), August, 1940; children: Dewey, Laura Edmunds Newman, Rollin. *Education:* University of Minnesota, B.B.A., 1939, M.A., 1940. *Home:* 1921 Arroyo Dr., Riverside, Calif. 92506. *Office:* Graduate School of Administration, University of California, Riverside, Calif. 92521.

CAREER: Northwestern National Life Insurance Co., Minneapolis, Minn., executive assistant to the president, 1945-53; Ford Motor Co., Dearborn, Mich., economist, 1955-58; Hughes Aircraft Co., Culver City, Calif., director of market planning, 1959-65; U.S. State Department, Agency for International Development, Washington, D.C., industrial development adviser in Washington and Ecuador, 1965-67; University of California, Riverside, vice-chancellor, 1967-70, dean of Graduate School of Administration, 1970—. Economist for National City Bank of New York, 1953-55, McGraw-Hill Book Co., 1953-55, Booz Allen & Hamilton, and Northwestern National Life Insurance Co. Member of assembly of science and technology advisory committee to the state legislature, 1972-75; member of State Economic Development Commission, 1960-64. Member of board of directors of Riverside Community Hospital, 1968-70. *Military service:* U.S. Navy, 1942-45; became lieutenant senior grade.

MEMBER: American Economic Association, American Marketing Association, American Society for Public Administration, American Institute for Decision Science, Royal Economic Society.

WRITINGS: Economics for You and Me, Macmillan, 1952; *Environmental Administration,* McGraw, 1972; *Alternative U.S. Futures,* Prentice-Hall, in press; *Basics of Private and Public Management,* Heath, in press. Contributor to business, marketing, and management journals.

WORK IN PROGRESS: Two stories; research on the impact of capital productivity on economic growth and inflation, especially with respect to small business.

SIDELIGHTS: Edmunds writes: "I have always tried my hand at story and novel writing in the hopes of becoming a fiction writer; but my professional experience and skill has made it easier for me to succeed in nonfiction. Also I am very interested in social and economic problems. . . . I tend perhaps to idealize the world, which in nonfiction tends toward romanticism or non-reality, which appears to be out of synchronization with our times."

EDWARDS, Richard Alan 1934-

PERSONAL: Born December 31, 1934, in West Mahanoy Twp., Pa.; son of Francis Reed (a clergyman) and Helen Irene (Mates) Edwards; married June Caroline Kirkhuff (a teacher), September 3, 1958; children: Jennifer, Emily, Jonathan. *Education:* Princeton University, B.A., 1956; Philadelphia Lutheran Seminary, graduate study, 1956-57; University of Chicago, M.A., 1962, Ph.D., 1968. *Home:* 1402 Locust Ave., Blacksburg, Va. 24060. *Office:* Department of Philosophy and Religion, Virginia Polytechnic Institute and State University, Blacksburg, Va. 24061.

CAREER: Bethany College, Lindsborg, Kan., instructor in religion, 1962-63; Susquehanna University, Selinsgrove, Pa., instructor in religion, 1963-66; Thiel College, Greenville, Pa., associate professor of religion, 1968-72; Virginia Polytechnic Institute and State University, Blacksburg, assistant professor, 1972-73, associate professor of religion, 1973—. *Member:* Society of Biblical Literature, Studiorum Novi Testamenti Societas. *Awards, honors:* Kinsman Trust fellowship to Kent, England, 1951-52; grants from Lutheran Church in America, 1969.

WRITINGS: The Sign of Jonah in the Theology of the Evangelist and Q, S.C.M. Press, 1971; *A Concordance to Q,* Scholars Press (Missoula, Mont.), 1975; *A Theology of Q: Eschatology, Prophecy, and Wisdom,* Fortress, 1976. Contributor of articles and reviews to religious periodicals.

WORK IN PROGRESS: The Lukan Travel Narrative, a monograph; computer studies of Luke and Acts and other Biblical materials, including the "Wisdom Material" in the Old and New Testaments.

SIDELIGHTS: Edwards writes that his "recent interests are concentrated on the early phases of Christianity in Egypt (first two centuries A.D.), and especially the social context for the development of and change in the use of wisdom traditions."

*   *   *

EFRON, Arthur 1931-

PERSONAL: Born November 2, 1931, in Chicago, Ill,; son of Miles J. (a salesman) and Esther (Kaufman) Efron (stepmother); married Esther Weisberg (a vegetarian restaurant worker), September 12, 1954 (separated); children: Sonia. *Education:* University of Washington, B.A., 1958, Ph.D., 1964; graduate study at University of California, Los Angeles, 1958-60. *Religion:* Jewish. *Home:* 123 Woodward Ave., Buffalo, N.Y. 14214. *Office:* 311 Clemens Hall, State University of New York at Buffalo, Buffalo, N.Y. 14260.

CAREER: State University of New York at Buffalo, Buffalo, instructor, 1963-64, assistant professor, 1964-68, associate professor, 1968-76, professor of English, 1976—. Cervantes lecturer at Fordham University, 1973. Chairman of executive committee of Independent School of Buffalo, 1967-68. *Military service:* U.S. Army, 1952-54; served in Japan and Korea; became sergeant; received Bronze Star. *Member:* International Psychohistorical Association, Modern Language Association of America, American Society for Aesthetics, Committee of Small Magazine Editors and Publishers (COSMEP), Coordinating Council of Literary Magazines, Virginia Woolf Society, Northeast Modern Language Association, Phi Beta Kappa. *Awards, honors:* State University of New York faculty research awards, summers, 1965, 1968, and 1971.

WRITINGS: Don Quixote and the Dulcineated World, University of Texas Press, 1971. Contributor to journals, including *International Review of Psychoanalysis, Minnesota Review, Dissent, Energy and Character,* and *Catalyst.* Founder and editor of *Paunch,* 1963—.

WORK IN PROGRESS: A study of Virginia Woolf, *Parenthetical Fire: Radical Vision in "To the Lighthouse"; The Mind-Body Problem in Lawrence, Reich, and Stephen C. Pepper;* a projected work, *The Body in the Novel: A Study in the Nature of Fiction,* completion expected, 1979; a self-analytic study of Hardy's *Tess of the d'Urbervilles;* further research on Cervantes, the body in literature, the philosophy of Stephen C. Pepper, and Wilhelm Reich and literature.

SIDELIGHTS: Efron told *CA:* "The body in literature has been my one continuous interest, going back as far as a sophomore paper I wrote for Wayne Burns, 'The Chemistry of Legs in *Great Expectations.*' The body is somehow the source and location of freedom, going beyond cultural conditioning of any kind; that is an extremely frightening thing. Some of that fear as well as the joy is visible in the only fiction so far published by *Paunch,* Lyle Glazier's novel 'Stills from a Moving Picture,' a bisexual autobiographical narrative. I have built up *Paunch* as a place where I can publish precisely the kind of academic and creative work that I want to see in print, much of it undoubtedly of a kind that would not be permitted in the university presses or the standard scholarly journals. I believe in a community of study, so that *Paunch* contributors quite often are undergraduates telling about their reading, and some of them are not academics at all: Donna Pinder, writing on Brecht, Shakespeare, and Lawrence is a dancer. *Paunch* has received a few infusions of subvention support—not that I wouldn't like more—and is NOT backed by any stock or personal fortunes. I am proud to have kept it going as a deliberately small-circulation non-profit endeavor, scrounging for support, and bucking the academic tide."

*   *   *

EHRESMANN, Donald L(ouis) 1937-

PERSONAL: Born October 11, 1937, in Newark, N.J.; son of Louis (a chemical engineer) and Anna (Strebinger) Ehresmann; married Julia M. Moore (a college teacher and librarian), September 19, 1964; children: Anna Sibylle. *Education:* Rutgers University, B.A., 1959; New York University, M.A., 1964, Ph.D., 1966. *Religion:* Lutheran. *Home:* 217 North Third St., Geneva, Ill. 60134. *Office:* Department of History of Architecture and Art, University of Illinois at Chicago Circle, Box 4348, Chicago, Ill. 60680.

CAREER: Bloomfield College, Bloomfield, N.J., assistant professor of art history and chairman of department, 1964-68; State University of New York College at Brockport, assistant professor, 1968-69, associate professor of art history, 1969-71, art history coordinator, 1969-71; University of Illinois at Chicago Circle, Chicago, associate professor of art history, 1971—, acting chairman of department, 1973-75, chairman, 1975—. Participated in colloquia and congresses in the United States and abroad. *Member:* College Art Association of America, Mid-West Art History Society. *Awards, honors:* Alexander von Humboldt-Stiftung fellow, 1967-68.

WRITINGS: Fine Arts: A Bibliographic Guide to Basic Reference Works, Histories, and Handbooks, Libraries Unlimited, 1975; *Applied and Decorative Arts: A Bibliographic Guide to Basic Reference Works, Histories, and Handbooks,* Libraries Unlimited, 1977. Also translator of *The German National Museum, Germanisches Nationalmuseum,* 1971. Contributor to *McGraw-Hill Encyclopedia of World Art* and *Dictionary of Art.* Contributor of articles and reviews to art journals. English-language coordinator for *Schrifttum zur deutschen Kunstgeschichte,* 1969—.

WORK IN PROGRESS: The Oberwesel Altarpiece and the Early Winged Altarpiece; compiling three bibliographic guides on painting, sculpture, and architecture for Libraries Unlimited.

* * *

EHRMAN, Lee 1935-

PERSONAL: Born May 25, 1935, in New York, N.Y.; daughter of Sidney M. and Lillian (Adler) Rothschild; married Richard Guy Ehrman, January 29, 1955; children: Esther Pearl, Judith Louise. *Education:* Queens College (now of the City University of New York), B.S., 1956; Columbia University, M.A., 1957, Ph.D., 1959. *Home:* 2 Jennifer Lane, Rye, N.Y. 10573. *Office:* Division of Natural Sciences, State University of New York College at Purchase, Purchase, N.Y. 10577.

CAREER: Barnard College, New York City, lecturer in zoology, 1956-58; Rockefeller University, New York City, research fellow, 1962, research associate, 1963-64, assistant professor, 1964-71, associate professor of natural science, 1971-74; State University of New York College at Purchase, professor of natural science, 1974—. Lecturer at New School for Social Research, 1969-70, and at State University of New York College at Purchase, 1970-71; Rockefeller University, adjunct associate professor, 1971-74, adjunct professor, 1974-75. Research associate in animal behavior at American Museum of Natural History, 1973—. *Member:* American Association for the Advancement of Science (fellow), Society for the Study of Evolution, Genetics Society of America, American Association of University Women (life member), American Society of Naturalists, Mensa, Eugenics Society of America, Animal Behavior Society, New York Academy of Sciences, New York Zoological Society, Phi Beta Kappa, Sigma Xi. *Awards, honors:* U.S. Public Health Service fellowships, 1959-62; Shirley Farr postdoctoral fellowship from American Association of University Women, 1962-63; Sigma Xi grants, 1963 and 1971; career development awards from National Institute of Child Health and Human Development, of U.S. Public Health Service, 1964-74; named Faculty Exchange Scholar of State University of New York College at Purchase, 1976.

WRITINGS: (Editor with Gilbert S. Omenn and Ernst Caspari) *Genetics, Environment, and Behavior: Implications for Educational Policy,* Academic Press, 1972; (with Peter A. Parsons) *The Genetics of Behavior,* Sinauer, 1976.

Contributor: E. O. Price, editor, *Animal Behavior in Laboratory and Field,* 2nd edition, W. H. Freeman, 1975; T. Wright and M. Ashburner, editors, *The Genetics and Biology of Drosophila,* Volume II, Academic Press, 1976; S. Hass, editor, *Encyclopedia of Bioethics,* Macmillan, 1977. Contributor of nearly two hundred articles to professional journals.

Past associate editor of *Evolution* and *Midland Naturalist;* associate editor of *American Naturalist,* 1976—; member of editorial board of *Behavioral Science; Behavior Genetics,* former member of editorial board, presently co-editor.

* * *

EINSTOSS, Ron 1930(?)-1977

1930(?)—June 26, 1977; American journalist. While with the *Los Angeles Times,* he was co-winner of two Pulitzer Prizes, one for a series of articles covering the Watts riots, and one for a series of articles on corruption in the Los Angeles city government. He died in Reno, Nev. Obituaries: *New York Times,* June 28, 1977.

* * *

EISINGER, Peter K(endall) 1942-

PERSONAL: Born July 9, 1942, in Ann Arbor, Mich.; son of Chester E. (a professor of English) and Marjorie (a weaver; maiden name, Kendall) Eisinger; married Erica Mendelson (a professor of French), September 6, 1967; children: Jesse, Sarah. *Education:* University of Michigan, B.A., 1964, M.A., 1965; Yale University, Ph.D., 1969. *Office:* Department of Political Science, University of Wisconsin, Madison, Wis. 53706.

CAREER: University of Wisconsin, Madison, assistant professor, 1969-74, associate professor of political science, 1974—, associate chairman, 1976—, senior member of research staff at Institute for Research on Poverty, 1970—. Visiting lecturer at University of Essex, 1972-73. *Awards, honors:* Social Science Research Council grant, 1970.

WRITINGS: The Patterns of Interracial Politics, Academic Press, 1976.

Contributor: J. P. Crecine, editor, *Financing the Metropolis,* Sage Publications, 1970; Harlan Hahn, editor, *People and Politics in Urban Society,* Sage Publications, 1972; Susan Glass and Jeffrey Obler, editors, *Ethnic Conflict in Urban Areas,* Institute for Research in Social Science, University of North Carolina, in press. Contributor of articles and reviews to journals in the political and behavioral sciences. Member of editorial board of *Policy and Politics.*

WORK IN PROGRESS: A textbook on American politics, with Booth Fowler, Joel Grossman, Richard Merelman, Dennis Dresang, and Burdette Loomis, for Little, Brown; a "study of the modes of adjustment by formerly dominant racial and ethnic elites recently displaced from formal political power by newly emerged groups," comparing recent field research in Detroit and Atlanta with Yankee response to Irish succession in Boston at the turn of the last century.

* * *

ELBIN, Paul Nowell 1905-

PERSONAL: Born April 21, 1905, in Cameron, W. Va.; son of Harry (a banker) and Nellie (Nowell) Elbin; married Helen Elizabeth Pierce (a teacher of vocal music), September 3, 1929. *Education:* Fairmont State College, student, 1923-25; Ohio State University, A.B., 1926; Columbia University, A.M., 1928, Ph.D., 1932. *Religion:* Presbyterian. *Home address:* Colonial Heights, West Liberty, W. Va. 26074.

CAREER: High school teacher of English in Cameron, W. Va., 1926-27; West Liberty State College, West Liberty, W. Va., professor of speech, 1928-35, 1970-71, president of college, 1935-70, head of department and chaplain, 1928-35, dean of interfaith chapel, 1970-72; writer, 1971—. Executive director of Oglebay Institute, 1944-46. Visiting professor at Ohio University, Belmont Branch, 1971-73. President of Wheeling Symphony Orchestra, 1973-75. *Member:* American Guild of Organists (past dean of Wheeling chapter). *Awards, honors:* D.D. from Davis & Elkins College, 1960; Litt.D. from West Virginia University, 1965.

WRITINGS: The Improvement of College Worship, Columbia University Press, 1932; *The Bible Question Bee,* Association Press, 1943; *Brotherhood Through Religion,*

Dorrance, 1944; *The Enrichment of Life,* Association Press, 1945; *Fifty Devotional Services,* Revell, 1950; *Worship for the Young in Spirit,* Bethany Press, 1957; *The Paradox of Happiness,* Hawthorn, 1975. Contributor to magazines and newspapers, including *Parade, Christian Century,* and *National Observer.* Music editor of *Wheeling News-Register,* 1947-61; record editor and staff writer for *Etude,* 1953-56.

AVOCATIONAL INTERESTS: European travel, public speaking, playing the pipe organ.

* * *

ELDRED, Vince 1924-

PERSONAL: Born August 15, 1924, in Newburgh, N.Y.; son of Vincent (a golf professional) and Alice (O'Brien) Eldred; married Ann Talmadge. *Education:* Providence College, B.A., 1943; University of Bridgeport, B.S., 1950; University of Massachusetts, M.S., 1964. *Religion:* Roman Catholic. *Residence:* West Palm Beach, Fla. *Office:* Cardinal Newman High School, 512 Spencer Dr., West Palm Beach, Fla. 33409.

CAREER: Teacher of English, history, and social studies at public and private schools; University of Massachusetts, Amherst, assistant basketball coach, 1963-64; Massachusetts Institute of Technology, Cambridge, instructor in physical education, 1964-69; Pennsylvania State University, State College, assistant professor of physical education, 1969-71; professional tennis instructor, 1971-76; Cardinal Newman High School, West Palm Beach, Fla., teacher of English and basketball coach, both 1976—. Professional tennis teacher. *Military service:* U.S. Navy, 1943-46. *Member:* U.S. Professional Tennis Association.

WRITINGS: Tennis Without Mistakes, Putnam, 1975. Contributor of more than fifty articles to sports and sports education journals.

WORK IN PROGRESS: A basketball textbook.

SIDELIGHTS: Vince Eldred writes: "After being heavily involved in college athletics for several years, in my opinion, I'm in a good position to know something about deviancy in athletics as well as drug abuse in athletics. The basketball text I'm working on deals only with the complexities of coaching phases of the game, but I am working on a lengthy article dealing with drug abuse in athletics and another article pertinent to deviancy in athletics." He is also interested in violence in athletics.

* * *

ELDRIDGE, Frank R. 1889(?)-1976

1889(?)—November 28, 1976; American economist, educator, historian, and author. His area of expertise was the Far East. He was the author of several books on the Far East as well as a history of the Coast Guard during World War II. He died in Washington, D.C. Obituaries: *Washington Post,* December 2, 1976.

* * *

ELEK, Paul 1906(?)-1976

1906(?)—October 18, 1976; Hungarian-born British head of publishing firm bearing his name. He was author of and collector of works on art and architecture. Elek died in London, England. Obituaries: *AB Bookman's Weekly,* December 20-27, 1976.

ELIAS, John L(awrence) 1933-

PERSONAL: Born December 23, 1933, in Asheville, N.C.; son of F. George (a pharmacist) and Josephine (a dressmaker; maiden name, Anastasi) Elias; married Eleanor J. Flanigan (a teacher), March 16, 1972; children: Rebecca, Rachel. *Education:* St. Charles College, B.A., 1955; St. Charles Seminary, M.Div., 1959; Temple University, Ed.D., 1974. *Politics:* "Democrat-Socialist." *Religion:* Roman Catholic. *Home:* 1131 Colonial Way, Bridgewater, N.J. 08807. *Office:* Department of Educational Foundation, Trenton State College, Trenton, N.J. 08625.

CAREER: High school teacher in Easton, Pa., 1959-64, and in Bethlehem, Pa., 1964-66; Trenton State College, Trenton, N.J., assistant professor of education, 1972—. Fordham University, New York City, associate professor of religion and religious education, 1977—. Visiting lecturer at La Salle College, 1968—. *Member:* Society for Educational Reconstruction (member of executive board, 1976—), Religious Education Association, American Educational Studies Association.

WRITINGS: Psychology and Religious Education, Catechetical Communications, 1975; *Conscientization and Deschooling: Freire's and Illich's Proposals for Reshaping Society,* Westminster, 1976. Contributor to education journals and inspirational magazines.

WORK IN PROGRESS: Approaches to Moral Education; Education and Liberation, completion expected in 1978.

* * *

ELIAV, Arie L(ova) 1921-
(Ben Ami)

PERSONAL: Born November 21, 1921, in Moscow, U.S.S.R.; came to Israel in 1924; son of Joseph and Matilda Eliav; married Tanya Zvi, October 12, 1947; children: Zvi, Ofra, Eyal. *Education:* Attended University of Reading and Cambridge University, both 1953; Hebrew University of Jerusalem, diploma (cum laude), 1958. *Home:* 3 Karl Netter St., Tel Aviv, Israel. *Office:* Labor Party, Hayarkon St., Tel Aviv, Israel.

CAREER: Israeli government official in Settlement Department, Ministry of Agriculture, and Ministry of Finance, 1949-53; instructor in immigrants' village of Moshav Nevatim, 1954; first director of Lachish regional project, 1955-57, Arad and Chazvin projects, 1960-63; Israeli Embassy, Moscow, U.S.S.R., first secretary, 1958-60; head of Israeli aid and rehabilitation team to earthquake stricken Ghazvin region of Iran, 1962-64; Mapai Organization Department, head and member of the Knesset (Israeli Parliament), 1965; deputy minister of Commerce and Industry, 1966-67, Immigration and Absorption, 1969; Labor Party, Tel Aviv, Israel, secretary general, 1969—. Head of Israeli aid mission to earthquake stricken Managua, Nicaragua, 1973. Member of mission on behalf of Beit Hillel to the United States, 1964. *Military service:* Served in Hagana (Jewish underground defense organization), 1936-40. British Army, served in artillery and engineering units during World War II. Served in illegal immigration operations, 1945-47. Israel Defence Forces, 1948-49; became lieutenant colonel. Commanded during Sinai campaign, 1956.

WRITINGS: Some Observations on Regional Planning Practice, Tahal, 1964; (under pseudonym Ben Ami) *Ben hapatish veha-magel,* Am Oved Publishers, 1965, translation published as *Between Hammer and Sickle,* Jewish Publication Society of America, 1965; *Ha-Sefinah Ulu'ah: Seporo shel Artor,* Am Oved Publishers, 1967, translation by Israel I. Taslitt published as *The Voyage of the Ulun,* Funk, 1969; *Ye'adim hadashim le-Yisrael,* Levin Epstein, 1970, translation published as *New Targets for Israel,* Jerusalem Post Publications, 1969, 3rd Hebrew edition, Levin Epstein, 1971; *Kefitsat ha-derekh,* Am Oved Publishers, 1970, translation by Dov Chaikin published as *No Time for History: A Pioneer Story,* Sabra Books, 1970; *Eretz ha-tsvi,* Am Oved Publishers, 1972, translation by Judith Yalon published as *Land of the Hart: Israelis, Arabs, the Territories, and a Vision of the Future,* Jewish Publication Society of America, 1974.

Other works: *Sipurah shel sefinat ma'pilim* (reader; title means "The Story of an Illegal Immigrants' Ship"), World Zionist Organization, 1965; *The Wind Shall Not Carry Them Away* (in Hebrew language), Am Oved Publishers, 1974; *Shalom* (in Hebrew language), Massada, 1975; *Israel's Ladder: A Dream and Its Meaning* (in Hebrew language), Zemora Bitan Modan, 1976. Also author of *Ba-yam, be-derekh mahteret,* 1964.

Contributor to periodicals in Israel and abroad.

SIDELIGHTS: Eliav served as commander of the rescue ship "Ulun" which carried two thousand Jewish refugees from Europe to Palestine. He participated in the Sinai Campaign, and in the rescue evacuation of Jews from Port Said. After bringing thousands of refugees into Israel, he continued thereafter to help them adjust to their new homes. His books, which have also been translated into French and Spanish, reflect his ongoing concern for the Jewish immigrants and for the country which they have helped to shape.

BIOGRAPHICAL/CRITICAL SOURCES: Washington Post, May 31, 1969; *Christian Science Monitor,* August 19, 1969; *Time,* January 26, 1970.

*   *   *

ELKOURI, Frank 1921-

PERSONAL: Born September 3, 1921, in Byron, Okla.; son of David and Adel (Elkouri) Elkouri; married Edna A. Asper (an attorney and writer), August 26, 1956. *Education:* University of Oklahoma, B.A., 1943, LL.B., 1947; University of Michigan, LL.M., 1948, S.J.D., 1951. *Home:* 1001 Whispering Pines, Norman, Okla. 73069. *Office:* College of Law, University of Oklahoma, 300 Timberdale Rd., Norman, Okla. 73019.

CAREER: Quinlan & Elkouri, Oklahoma City, Okla., attorney, 1948-49, 1950-51; National Wage Stabilization Board, Washington, D.C., attorney in the District of Columbia and in Dallas, Tex., 1951-52; University of Oklahoma, Norman, associate professor, 1952-55, professor of law, 1955—. Arbitrator of labor-management disputes, 1948—; special justice of Oklahoma Supreme Court, 1967. Member of executive reserve of U.S. Department of Labor, 1963—; member of Oklahoma governor's special advisory committee on workmen's compensation, 1975. *Military service:* U.S. Army, Field Artillery, 1943-44; became second lieutenant.

MEMBER: Industrial Relations Research Association, National Academy of Arbitrators, American Arbitration Association, Oklahoma Bar Association, Phi Beta Kappa, Coif.

WRITINGS: Trade Regulation: Cases and Materials, Little, Brown, 1957; *How Arbitration Works,* Bureau of National Affairs, 1952, 3rd edition, 1973. Author of teaching handbooks. Contributor to law journals.

WORK IN PROGRESS: A 4th edition of *How Arbitration Works.*

ELLIOT, Ian 1925-
(Colin Davies)

PERSONAL: Born November 17, 1925, in New York, N.Y.; son of Walter (a United Nations employee) and Marjorie (a social worker; maiden name, Powell) Elliot; married Ann Murray, February, 1951 (divorced, 1964); married Judith Jackson, August, 1966; children: (second marriage) Kristin, Colin. *Education:* Cornell University, A.B., 1950, graduate study, 1951-53. *Home:* Indian Hill, Norwalk, Conn. 06850. *Agent:* Manuscripts Unlimited, 420 East 72nd St., New York, N.Y. 10021. *Office:* Early Years, Darien, Conn.

CAREER: Syracuse Herald Journal, Syracuse, N.Y., reporter, 1961-64; *New York Purchasing Review,* New York City, editor, 1964-67; *School Management,* Greenwich, Conn., associate editor, 1967-69; *Grade Teacher,* Greenwich, Conn., senior editor, 1969-72; *Early Years,* Darien, Conn., senior editor, 1972—. *Military service:* U.S. Army, 1944-47; became sergeant. *Awards, honors:* Jesse H. Neal Award from American Business Press, 1967, for business writing; awards from Educational Press Association of America, 1970-75, for writing on education.

WRITINGS: (Editor) *How to Study in College,* Houghton, 1962, 2nd edition, 1974; *James Monroe, 1758-1831,* Oceana, 1969; *James Madison, 1751-1836,* Oceana, 1969; *Abraham Lincoln, 1809-1865,* Oceana, 1970.

Author of "Second Degree" (one-act play), first produced in Ithaca, N.Y., at Cornell University Theatre, February 19, 1963. Contributor to magazines, sometimes under pseudonym Colin Davies.

WORK IN PROGRESS: Children's Dreams, a study of how, what, and why children dream the way they do.

SIDELIGHTS: Elliot writes: "I have been a professional writer for more than twenty years and I am still not sure what writing is. Certainly, it is a craft: a good writer should be able to write almost anything, just as a good carpenter should be able to build anything made of wood. And yet writing is different from other crafts. First, writers must think constantly, not only about what they are trying to say but also about how they are saying it. Second, writers—unlike carpenters—are rarely sure they have done a competent job. Finally, writers seldom master their craft, perhaps because writers' standards are constantly growing more demanding. I believe it was Kenneth Roberts who said that writing is one of the few things that keeps getting harder, the more one knows about it. He was right."

*   *   *

ELLIOTT, Donald 1928-

PERSONAL: Born October 26, 1928, in Baltimore, Md.; son of John Planner (a professor) and Irene (Semadeni) Elliott; married Cielito Obina (a pianist and teacher), October 31, 1958; children: Estella, Julia, Fermin, Bruce, J. Gary. *Education:* St. John's College, Annapolis, Md., B.A., 1948. *Politics:* "John Stuart Millianism." *Religion:* Episcopal. *Home and office address:* Garrison Forest School, Garrison, Md. 21055. *Agent:* Johnson & Thompson, 2805 O St. N.W., Washington, D.C. 20007.

CAREER: Baltimore Life Insurance Co., Baltimore, Md., manager of actuarial department, 1957-66; Garrison Forest School, Garrison, Md., teacher of English and the humanities, 1966—. President of Romblon Associates (a company importing products from the Philippines). *Military service:* U.S. Army, Infantry, 1951-54; became first lieutenant.

Member: Life Office Management Association (fellow), Cum Laude Society (charter member).

WRITINGS: Alligators and Music, Gambit, 1976. Contributor to *Baltimore Sun.*

SIDELIGHTS: Elliott writes: "I lead a generally dull life, illuminated from time to time by association with flexible minds and receptive souls—almost invariably those of young people, perhaps primarily because of the sort of human contacts I have—and by occasional and momentary flashes of insight usually resulting from the experience of literature or music.

"I have great aspirations, a high sense of idealistic purpose, and practically no ability to make any of it work. Life and experience bring to me a constantly renewed awareness of the multitude of paradoxes and enigmas in which I flounder: of American democracy as the noblest political effort of humanity and probably one of its most unworkable; of Socrates and Christ as rare purveyors of truth who are seldom really believed; of the innocence, paralysis, and limited vision of humanity and of its viciousness and cruelty; of the unbelievably vast potential of man and of his essential and ultimate failure; of understanding and insight and of stupidity and incapacity. I see the universe, and I cannot often see myself; I see myself, and I cannot with any consistency see beyond myself, and I vacillate between the eternal beauties and truths of Michelangelo, Shakespeare, and Beethoven, and the shattering realities of relativity and the 'now.'

"But I keep my eyes open, for now and then something of value comes flitting by, and I want, if possible, not to be blinking at those rare moments."

BIOGRAPHICAL/CRITICAL SOURCES: Baltimore Sun, November 17, 1976.

*   *   *

ELLIOTT, Emory   1942-

PERSONAL: Born October 30, 1942, in Baltimore, Md.; son of Emory Bernard and Virginia Louise (Ulbrick) Elliott; married Georgia A. Carroll (an English instructor), May 14, 1966; children: Scott, Mark, Matthew, Laura, Constance. *Education:* Loyola College, Baltimore, Md., A.B., 1964; Bowling Green State University, M.A., 1966; University of Illinois, Ph.D., 1972. *Home:* 7 College Rd., Princeton, N.J. 08540. *Office:* Department of English, Princeton University, 22 McCosh, Princeton, N.J. 08540.

CAREER: Cameron State College, Lawton, Okla., part-time instructor in English, 1967; U.S. Military Academy, West Point, N.Y., instructor in English, 1968-69; Princeton University, Princeton, N.J., assistant professor, 1972-77, associate professor of English, 1977—, Richard Stockton Bicentennial Preceptor, 1975-78, director of undergraduate studies in English, and director of American Studies Program, 1977—. *Military service:* U.S. Army, 1966-69; became captain. *Member:* Modern Language Association of America, American Studies Association, American Society for Eighteenth-Century Studies. *Awards, honors:* Woodrow Wilson fellowship, 1971-72; American Council of Learned Societies fellowship, summer, 1973; Guggenheim fellowship, 1976-77.

WRITINGS: Power and the Pulpit in Puritan New England, Princeton University Press, 1975; (contributor) Earl Miner, editor, *Figuralism in Literature,* Princeton University Press, 1976; (contributor) John Karl Franson, editor, *Milton Reconsidered,* [Salzburg, Austria], 1976; (contributor) Anthony James and Lawrence Leder, editors, *Eco-*

nomics and Empire in the Eighteenth Century: Third Lawrence Henry Gipson Symposium, [Bethlehem, Pa.], 1977; (contributor) Alexander Leitch, editor, *A Princeton Companion,* Princeton University Press, in press; (editor and contributor) *Puritanism and American Literature: Representative Writers,* University of Illinois Press, in press. Contributor of articles and reviews to scholarly journals. Member of editorial board of *American Quarterly.* Reader for Cambridge University Press, Oxford University Press, Princeton University Press, and University of Virginia Press.

WORK IN PROGRESS: The Literary Calling in Early America; a long essay on Charles Brockden Brown for *American Writers Series.*

SIDELIGHTS: Elliott told *CA:* "I have a strong interest in improving technical writing."

*   *   *

ELLIOTT, Errol T(homas)   1894-

PERSONAL: Born November 10, 1894, in Carthage, Mo.; son of Elisha M. and Alice (Elleman) Elliott; married Ruby Kelly, 1916 (died, 1973); married Evelyn R. Clark, 1975; children: (first marriage) Errol, Jr., Harriet Combs, Paul, Robert. *Education:* Friends University, A.B., 1927; attended Iliff School of Theology, 1929; University of Colorado, M.A., 1930. *Home:* 1617 May, Apt. 9, Wichita, Kan. 67213.

CAREER: Five Years Meeting of Friends, Richmond, Ind., spiritual life secretary, 1930-36; pastor of Friends (Quaker) meeting in Indianapolis, Ind., 1936-42; William Penn College, Oskaloosa, Iowa, president, 1942-44; Five Years Meeting of Friends, general secretary and editor of *American Friend,* 1944-57; pastor of Friends meeting in Indianapolis, Ind., 1957-65; writer and researcher, 1965—. Chairman of Friends World Committee, 1952-58. First chairman of board of advisers of Earlham School of Religion, 1960-63, later research associate. President of Richmond Community Welfare Council, 1954; chairman of Richmond Civic Forum and actor with Richmond Civic Theater, 1950-53. *Awards, honors:* Litt.D. from Friends University, 1952; L.H.D. from Earlham College, 1965.

WRITINGS: Quakers on the American Frontier, Friends United Press, 1969; *Quaker Profiles from the American West,* Friends United Press, 1972; *Life Unfolding* (autobiography), Friends United Press, 1975; *Sing the Faith* (poems), Friends United Press, 1976; *R. Ernest Lamb: Irish American Quaker,* Friends United Press, 1977.

SIDELIGHTS: In 1898, Elliott moved by covered wagon from Missouri to Kansas. Since then, his work with the Religious Society of Friends has taken him all over the world, including Europe, Kenya, England, Cuba, Jamaica, Korea, Japan, Hong Kong, Bangkok, and India.

*   *   *

ELLIOTT, Osborn   1924-

PERSONAL: Born October 25, 1924, in New York, N.Y.; son of John and Audrey (Osborn) Elliott; married Deirdre Spencer, May 8, 1948 (divorced December 28, 1972); married Inger Abrahamsen McCabe (a designer and photographer), October 20, 1973; children: Diana, Dorinda, Cynthia. *Education:* Harvard University, A.B., 1946. *Home:* 10 Gracie Sq., New York, N.Y. 10028. *Office: Newsweek,* 444 Madison Ave., New York, N.Y. 10022.

CAREER: New York Journal of Commerce, New York

City, reporter, 1946-49; *Time,* New York City, contributing editor, 1949-52; *Newsweek,* New York City, associate editor, 1952-55, senior business editor, 1955-59, managing editor, 1959-61, editor, 1961-69, editor-in-chief, 1969-72, president and chief executive officer, 1971-72, editor, 1972-75, chairman of board, 1972—, editor-in-chief, 1975—. Member of board of overseers of Harvard College, 1965-71. Trustee of American Museum of Natural History, Asia Society, New York Public Library, 1968-72, St. Paul's School, 1969-73, and Winston Churchill Foundation, 1970-73. Chairman of Citizens Committee for New York City, 1975—. *Military service:* U.S. Naval Reserve, 1944-46.

MEMBER: Council on Foreign Relations, American Academy of Arts and Sciences (fellow). *Awards, honors:* D.H.L. from Michigan State University, 1972.

WRITINGS: Men at the Top, Harper, 1959. Also editor of *The Negro Revolution in America,* 1964.

* * *

ELLIOTT, Russell Richard 1912-

PERSONAL: Born June 2, 1912, in McGill, Nev.; son of James Thomas (a bricklayer) and Mary Jane (Hodges) Elliott; married Annie Johnson, February 11, 1944; children: Patricia Ann Elliott Eastman, Anne Marie. *Education:* University of Nevada, B.A., 1934; University of Washington, Seattle, M.A., 1938; University of California, Berkeley, Ph.D., 1946. *Politics:* Democrat. *Religion:* Protestant. *Home:* 2190 Royal Dr., Reno, Nev. 89503. *Office:* Department of History, University of Nevada, Reno, Nev. 89507.

CAREER: High school teacher of history in Ely, Nev., 1934-38; Southern Oregon College of Education (now Southern Oregon State College), Ashland, assistant professor of history, 1946-49; University of Nevada, Reno, assistant professor, 1949-54, associate professor, 1954-59, professor of history, 1959-76, professor emeritus, 1976—, chairman of department, 1957-65. *Military service:* U.S. Army Air Forces, 1942-46; became first lieutenant.

MEMBER: American Historical Association (Pacific Coast branch), Organization of American Historians, American Association for State and Local History, Western History Association (member of council, 1976-79), California Historical Society, Nevada Historical Society (chairman of board of trustees, 1968-77), Nevada Corral of Westerners International, Phi Kappa Phi. *Awards, honors:* Manuscript award from Pacific Coast branch of American Historical Association, 1949; award of merit from American Association for State and Local History, for *History of Nevada* and other contributions.

WRITINGS: (With Jay A. Carpenter and Byrd Sawyer) *The History of Fifty Years of Mining at Tonopah, 1900-1950,* Nevada Bureau of Mines, 1953; *Radical Labor in the Nevada Mining Booms, 1900-1920,* University of Nevada Press, 1961; (with Helen J. Poulton) *Writings on Nevada: A Selected Bibliography,* University of Nevada Press, 1963; *Nevada's Twentieth Century Mining Boom,* University of Nevada Press, 1966; *History of Nevada,* University of Nebraska Press, 1973. Contributor of articles and reviews to national and regional history journals.

WORK IN PROGRESS: A biography of U.S. Senator William Morris Stewart, Nevada's first U.S. Senator.

SIDELIGHTS: Elliott writes: "My professional career has been devoted to the study, teaching and writing of Nevada history and the encouragement of others to do the same."

ELLIS, M(adeleine) B(lanche) 1915-

PERSONAL: Born March 10, 1915, in Vancouver, British Columbia, Canada; daughter of George Porter (a master mariner) and Lilian (Fitzmaurice) Ellis. *Education:* University of British Columbia, B.A., 1936, M.A., 1937; further graduate study at Bryn Mawr College, 1937-38; University of Toronto, Ph.D., 1944. *Religion:* Roman Catholic. *Home:* 2045 Closse St., Apt. A8, Montreal, Quebec, Canada H3H 1Z7. *Office:* Department of Modern Languages, Marianopolis College, 3880 Cote-des-Neiges, Montreal, Quebec, Canada.

CAREER: Royal Canadian Mounted Police, Toronto, Ontario, member of Intelligence Branch, 1940-44; University of Toronto, Toronto, lecturer in French and humanities, 1944-46; Marianopolis College, Montreal, Quebec, professor of French and humanities, 1946—, chairman of department of modern languages, 1964-72. Summer lecturer at University of Toronto, 1944; charge de cours at Laval Universite, summer, 1949.

MEMBER: Societe canadienne d'etude du XVIIIe siecle, Societe Jean-Jacques Rousseau (life member), American Society for Eighteenth Century Studies, Societe francaise d'etude du XVIIIe siecle, Comite du Montlouis (France). *Awards, honors:* Carnegie Foundation scholarship, Bryn Mawr College, 1937-38.

WRITINGS: Robert Charbonneau et la creation romanesque: Une etude de textes (title means "Robert Charbonneau and Fictional Creation"), Levrier, 1948; *St-Denys-Garneau: Art et realisme* (title means "St-Denys-Garneau: Art and Realism"), Chantecler, 1949; *Julie or La Nouvelle Heloise: A Synthesis of Rousseau's Thought, 1749-1759,* University of Toronto Press, 1949; *Rousseau's Venetian Story: An Essay upon Art and Truth in "Les Confessions",* Johns Hopkins Press, 1966; *Rousseau's Socratic Aemilian Myths: A Literary Collection of "Emile" and the "Social Contract",* Ohio State University Press, 1977.

Also author of *Dictionnaire international des termes litteraires* (title means "International Dictionary of Literary Terms"), published by Association Internationale de Litterature Comparee. Contributor to language and literature journals.

WORK IN PROGRESS: Art and Truth in Rousseau's "Confessions".

SIDELIGHTS: Madeleine Ellis writes: "I am mainly a scholar and a literary critic whose work is motivated by a great love of literature and the fine arts, especially French and Italian, but also those of classical antiquity. In general I prefer the literature of thought wherein important concepts are expressed in a perfectly artistic form, and beauty and truth are combined. To me, beauty is as vital to life as truth.

"My first two books, written in French, deal with French-Canadian writers, and the others, which reflect more truly my main interests, deal with the French eighteenth century and more particularly Jean-Jacques Rousseau. I have chosen the former because at the period in question European culture in general was largely French. And I have chosen Rousseau both because he is undeniably a great writer and because he is just as undeniably a major figure in shaping the course of occidental civilization and one whose influence extends into every sphere of our culture.... The study of such a writer ... enlarges the mind and expands the vision at the same time as it develops the taste.

"I find room for self-expression and the revelation of my own inner life and character not merely in literary judgments but also in the style of my work which I carefully adapt to the theme treated. Both judgments and style also reveal my love of other French writers, mediaeval, classical, and modern, as well as English and Italian writers and those of classical antiquity. They also reveal my considerable experience of life abroad, mainly in Paris, Geneva, Florence, and Greece, particularly Athens.''

*   *   *

ELLSBERG, Daniel 1931-

PERSONAL: Born April 7, 1931, in Chicago, Ill.; son of Harry Ellsberg (a structural engineer); married Carol Cummings, 1952 (divorced); married Patricia Marx, August 8, 1970; children: (first marriage) Robert, Mary. *Education:* Harvard University, B.A. (summa cum laude), 1952, M.A., 1953, Ph.D., 1959; Kings College, Cambridge, graduate study, 1952. *Home:* 10 Hilliard St., Cambridge, Mass. 02138. *Office:* Center for International Studies, Massachusetts Institute of Technology, Cambridge, Mass. 02139.

CAREER: RAND Corp., Santa Monica, Calif., analyst, 1959-64; U.S. Defense Department, Washington, D.C., staff member of Assistant Secretary of Defense for International Security Affairs, 1964-65; U.S. Department of State, adviser in South Vietnam, 1965-67, assistant to U.S. ambassador to South Vietnam, Saigon, 1967; RAND Corp., analyst, 1968-69; Massachusetts Institute of Technology, Center for International Studies, Cambridge, senior research associate, 1969—. Consultant to the U.S. Government on Vietnam policy, 1967-69. *Military service:* U.S. Marine Corps, 1954-57. *Awards, honors:* Woodrow Wilson fellow, 1952.

WRITINGS: Papers on the War, Simon & Schuster, 1972. Author of numerous pamphlets published by the RAND Corp.

SIDELIGHTS: In 1971 Ellsberg provided the "Pentagon Papers" to the *New York Times* for publication. He subsequently faced criminal charges of conspiracy, theft, and violation of the Espionage Act. The case, however, was dismissed in 1973. *Avocational interests:* Swimming, skiing.

BIOGRAPHICAL/CRITICAL SOURCES: Christian Science Monitor, June 25, 1971; *New York Times,* June 27, 1971; *Life,* July 2, 1971; *Time,* July 5, 1971, July 26, 1971; *Newsweek,* July 12, 1971, July 26, 1971, August 30, 1971, December 6, 1971, June 26, 1972, May 21, 1973; *U.S. News and World Report,* July 12, 1971; *Look,* October 5, 1971; *New York Times Magazine,* December 2, 1971; *Harper's Bazaar,* February, 1972, October, 1973; *Playboy,* October, 1972.*

*   *   *

ELMS, Alan C(linton) 1938-

PERSONAL: Born December 15, 1938, in Gorman, Tex.; son of Vernon C. (an electrician) and Letona (Mitchell) Elms; married Roslyn Ruggiero (a nurse and teacher), June 1, 1962; children: Heather, Laurel. *Education:* Pennsylvania State University, B.A., 1960; Yale University, Ph.D., 1965. *Residence:* Davis, Calif. *Office:* Department of Psychology, University of California, Davis, Calif. 95616.

CAREER: Southern Methodist University, Dallas, Tex., assistant professor of psychology, 1964-67; University of California, Davis, assistant professor, 1967-72, associate professor, 1972-77, professor of psychology, 1977—. Visiting lecturer at Trinity College, Dublin, 1972. *Member:* American Psychological Association (fellow), Society for

the Psychological Study of Social Issues (fellow), American Association for the Advancement of Science, American Association of University Professors, Western Psychological Association, Phi Beta Kappa, Phi Kappa Phi. *Awards, honors:* Woodrow Wilson fellowship, 1960-61; National Institute for Mental Health grant, 1969-71.

WRITINGS: (Editor) *Role Playing, Reward, and Attitude Change,* Van Nostrand, 1969; (contributor) Robert A. Schoenberger, editor, *The American Right Wing,* Holt, 1969; *Social Psychology and Social Relevance,* Little, Brown, 1972; *Personality in Politics,* Harcourt, 1976; *Attitudes,* Open University Press, 1976. Contributor to psychology journals and to *Journal of American Folklore.*

WORK IN PROGRESS: A book of poems; a novel; psychobiographical studies of politicians, creative writers, and personality theorists.

SIDELIGHTS: Elms comments: "My professional work is largely in personality, social psychology, and the overlapping areas of these two sub-fields of psychology. Psychobiographical research (e.g., on Sigmund Freud, Jimmy Carter, Vladimir Nabokov) enables me to indulge my personal interests in intellectual history, politics, literature, while continuing to produce professional work.''

AVOCATIONAL INTERESTS: Creative writing, letterpress printing, photography, folk music.

*   *   *

ELOVITZ, Mark H(arvey) 1938-

PERSONAL: Born May 20, 1938, in Pittsburgh, Pa.; son of Meyer David (a restaurant proprietor) and Lillian (a civil servant; maiden name, Werner) Elovitz; married Helen Arna Altheim (a teacher and counselor), October 13, 1963; children: Rachel Aliza, Michal Aviva, Reuben Jeremiah. *Education:* New York University, B.A., 1960, Ph.D., 1973; Jewish Theological Seminary of America, M.H.L., 1962, rabbi, 1964; Cumberland School of Law, J.D., 1977; also attended Hebrew University of Jerusalem, 1962-63. *Politics:* Independent Democrat. *Home:* 3712 Northcote Dr., Birmingham, Ala. 35223. *Office:* Denaburg, Schoel, Meyerson & Ogle, Brown-Mark Building, 20th St. & First Ave., Birmingham, Ala. 35205.

CAREER: Associate rabbi of Jewish congregation in Cedarhurst, N.Y., 1967-69, rabbi in Birmingham, Ala., 1970-77; Denaburg, Schoel, Meyerson & Ogle, Birmingham, Ala., attorney, 1977—. Hubert H. Humphrey Distinguished Professor of International and Cross-Cultural Affairs at Macalester College, 1977-78; visiting professor at University of Alabama at Birmingham (also special lecturer). Law clerk for U.S. Attorney's Office, Northern District, Alabama, summer, 1976. Member of Alabama Committee for the Humanities and Public Policy; member of board of directors of Birmingham Jewish Community Center; panel member of National Endowment for the Humanities Division of Public Programs. *Military service:* U.S. Air Force, chaplain, 1964-67; served in Germany, Italy, the Netherlands, Great Britain, Spain, and Libya; became captain.

MEMBER: Rabbinical Assembly of America, Association of Jewish Chaplains, Institute of Religion and Mental Health (associate), New York Board of Rabbis, Birmingham Jewish Federation (member of board of directors), Phi Beta Kappa.

WRITINGS: Like It Is (pamphlet; sermons), privately printed, 1970; *A Century of Jewish Life in Dixie: The Birmingham Experience,* University of Alabama Press, 1974; (with John Durant and John Kirklin) *The Right to Die: Med-*

ical Ethics, Law and Human Values, Alabama Committee for Humanities and Public Policy, 1976. Contributor of more than seventy-five articles and reviews to professional journals. Associate editor of *Cumberland Law Review,* 1975-77; book editor of *Reconstructionist,* 1975-76.

WORK IN PROGRESS: Whose Side Are You on Boy?, an inspection of civil rights events in May, 1963, completion expected in 1979; *Judaism at the Secular Bar,* an inspection of Judaism, Jewish life and custom as they appear in court decisions; *The Living Will: A Provocative Inspection of the Right to Live or Die,* a monograph.

SIDELIGHTS: Elovitz writes that he feels the "most critical aspect of society currently undergoing attack, revision, and readjustment [is] 'the family structure', the major impediment to political success in foreign relations is tunnel vision and expediency." He dislikes "dealing with those who serve at the level of their incompetency. *The Peter Principle* is astutely accurate and therefore increasingly irritating."

AVOCATIONAL INTERESTS: Tennis, vegetable gardening.

* * *

El SAFFAR, Ruth (Ann) 1941-

PERSONAL: Born June 12, 1941, in New York, N.Y.; daughter of John Tabb (in the military) and Ruth (a nurse; maiden name, Wheelwright) Snodgrass; married Zuhair M. El Saffar (a professor of physics), April 11, 1966; children: Ali, Dena. *Education:* Colorado College, B.A., 1962; Johns Hopkins University, Ph.D. (with distinction), 1966. *Religion:* "Faith and love." *Home:* 613 Park Ave., River Forest, Ill. 60305. *Office:* Department of Spanish, Italian, and Portuguese, University of Illinois at Chicago Circle, Box 4348, Chicago, Ill. 60680.

CAREER: University of Maryland, Baltimore, assistant professor of Spanish, 1967-68; University of Illinois at Chicago Circle, Chicago, assistant professor, 1968-73, associate professor of Spanish, 1973—. Consultant for National Endowment for the Humanities. *Member:* Modern Language Association of America (member of executive council, 1974-78), Midwest Modern Language Association. *Awards, honors:* Woodrow Wilson fellowship, 1962; National Endowment for the Humanities fellowship, 1970-71; Danforth associate, 1973-79; Guggenheim fellowship, 1975-76.

WRITINGS: Novel to Romance: A Study of Cervantes' "Novelas ejemplares", Johns Hopkins Press, 1974; *Distance and Control in "Don Quixote",* University of North Carolina Studies in Romance Languages and Literature, 1975; *Cervantes: "El casamiento enganoso" and "El coloquio de los perros",* Grant & Cutler, 1976.

Anthologized in *Kettlestrings,* 1976. Contributor to language journals.

WORK IN PROGRESS: A study of the feminine archetype in the work of Cervantes, especially in *Don Quixote;* preparing her poems for publication.

SIDELIGHTS: Ruth El Saffar writes: "We have the responsibility, both collectively and individually, to bring into better relation with ourselves that neglected and therefore dangerous part of our being which is inaccessible to reason and rational control. I am most interested, as a critic, in those writers who have worked beyond a personalistic, individualistic view of the world to one which senses our participation with the entire universe. I am thinking not only of Cervantes, whose work I have studied so long, but of Walt Whitman, the later Heidegger, Theodore Roethke, Juan Ramon Jimenez, and Doris Lessing, to offer a collection of writers that comes immediately to mind.

"I see my writing and my teaching and my contact with every living being as a challenge to draw forth and give out some measure of Truth. The trick becomes one of loosening ego bonds so as to be able to listen, to attend to everything we come across and to find in each its highest meaning and value. I write because that is the way through which my perceptions become available to me, and because it is a method of bringing myself into an attentive state with regard to the worlds around me and within me."

* * *

ELSASSER, Albert B(ertrand) 1918-

PERSONAL: Born June 7, 1918, in San Francisco, Calif.; son of William August (a master mariner) and Barbara (Campbell) Elsasser; married Winifred Hawxhurst, 1950; children: Albert H. *Education:* Attended Trinity College of Music, London, England, 1945; University of California, Berkeley, B.A., 1950, M.A., 1960, Ph.D., 1965. *Politics:* Democrat. *Religion:* "Irish Catholic." *Home:* 824 Park Way, El Cerrito, Calif. 94530. *Office:* Robert H. Lowie Museum of Anthropology, University of California, Berkeley, Calif. 94720.

CAREER: University of California, Robert H. Lowie Museum of Anthropology, Berkeley, research archaeologist, 1952-65, assistant research anthropologist, 1965-71, associate research anthropologist, 1971—. *Military service:* U.S. Army Air Forces, 1940-45; became staff sergeant. *Member:* American Anthropological Association (fellow), Current Anthropology (associate), American Association for the Advancement of Science, Society for American Archaeology, Phi Beta Kappa, Sigma Xi.

WRITINGS: The Archaeology of the Sierra Nevada in California and Nevada, Archaeological Survey Publications, University of California, 1960; (with Michael J. Harner) *Art of the Northwest Coast,* Robert H. Lowie Museum of Anthropology, University of California, Berkeley, 1965; (with Vera Mae Fredrickson) *Ancient Egypt,* Robert H. Lowie Museum of Anthropology, University of California, Berkeley, 1966; (with Robert F. Heizer) *The Archaeology of Two Sites in Northwestern California,* Archaeological Survey Publications, University of California, 1966; *Treasures of the Lowie Museum,* Robert H. Lowie Museum of Anthropology, University of California, Berkeley, 1968; (with Heizer and Theodora Kroeber) *Drawn from Life: The California Indians in Pen and Brush,* Ballena, 1977; (with Heizer) *An Annotated Bibliography of the Indians of California,* Garland Publishing, 1977; *The Indians of California,* University of California Press, in press.

Contributor of articles to *American Antiquity* and *Pacific Discovery,* and of reviews to *Journal of California Anthropology* and *California Historical Quarterly.* Book Review editor of *Journal of California Anthropology,* 1974.

SIDELIGHTS: Elsasser writes that he has done "much archaeological excavation or survey in all parts of California (from sea shore to high mountains and deserts). I have worked on the ancient pyramids of Cuicuilco in Mexico (1957) under auspices of the National Geographic Society. Archaeological excavation in South West Africa (1962) included surveys of rock drawings in the ancestral land of the Bushmen—in conjunction with State Museum, Windhock (the capital of what is now Namibia)."

AVOCATIONAL INTERESTS: Music, drama, art films, ocean liners, shipwrecks, and naval history.

EMERY, Alan E(glin) H(eathcote) 1928-

PERSONAL: Born August 21, 1928, in Manchester, England; son of Harold H. Emery (a printer); married wife Rosalind (a physician). *Education:* University of Manchester, B.Sc. (first class honors), 1952, M.Sc., 1953, M.B. and Ch.B. (honors), both 1960, M.D., 1966, D.Sc., 1970; Johns Hopkins University, Ph.D., 1964. *Home:* 1 Eton Ter., Edinburgh, Scotland. *Office:* University Department of Human Genetics, Western General Hospital, Edinburgh, Scotland.

CAREER: Senior biology master at private school in Exeter, England, 1953-55; Manchester Royal Infirmary, Manchester, England, house physician and house surgeon, 1960-61; Johns Hopkins University, Baltimore, Md., instructor in biostatistics, 1961-64; University of Manchester, Manchester, England, lecturer in medicine, 1964-66, reader in medical genetics and director of department, 1966-68; University of Edinburgh, Edinburgh, Scotland, professor of human genetics and director of department, 1968—. Harveian Lecturer for Harveian Society of London, 1970; Woodhull Lecturer at Royal Institution, 1972; Hoyman-Gillespie Lecturer at University of Edinburgh, 1972; visiting professor at University of Cape Town, 1970, 1974, University of Rangoon, 1971, University of Heidelberg, 1972, Osmania University, 1975, and University of Baghdad, 1977. Member of advisory panel of Guild of Service (Adoption); committee member of Medical Research Council. *Military service:* British Army, King's Hussars, 1945-47.

MEMBER: International Society of Internal Medicine, European Society of Human Genetics, European Teratology Society, Society for the Study of Human Biology, Scottish Society of Physicians, Royal College of Physicians (Edinburgh; fellow), Royal Society (Edinburgh; fellow), Royal Society of Medicine (fellow), Royal Institute of Public Health and Hygiene (fellow), Faculty of Community Medicine, Association for the Study of Medical Education, Genetical Society of Great Britain, Clinical Genetics Society, Association of Physicians of Great Britain and Ireland, Brittle Bone Society (medical adviser), National Association for the Relief of Paget's Disease (member of scientific advisory committee), Muscular Dystrophy Group of Great Britain (honorary president of Edinburgh branch), American Society of Human Genetics. *Awards, honors:* Ella Pringle Bequest Prize from Royal College of Physicians (Edinburgh), 1969; British Council traveling fellowships, 1971, 1973, 1975.

WRITINGS: Elements of Medical Genetics, Churchill-Livingstone, 1968, 4th edition, 1975, also published as *Heredity, Disease, and Man,* University of California Press, 1968; (editor and contributor) *Modern Trends in Human Genetics,* Butterworth, Volume I, 1970, Volume II, 1975; (editor and contributor) *Antenatal Diagnosis of Genetic Disease,* Churchill-Livingstone, 1973; (editor and contributor) *Medical Genetics,* Osmania University, 1975; (editor with J. R. Miller, and contributor) *Registers for the Detection and Prevention of Genetic Disease,* Stratton Intercontinental, 1976; *Methodology in Medical Genetics: An Introduction to Statistical Methods,* Churchill-Livingstone, 1976. Editor-in-chief of "Genetics in Medicine and Surgery," a monograph series for Churchill-Livingstone. Contributor of more than one hundred fifty articles to scientific journals. Member of international editorial board of *Excerpta Medica;* member of editorial committee of *Journal of Medical Genetics, Annals of Human Biology, Acta Anthropogenetica, Muscle and Nerve,* and *Journal Genetique Humaine;* former member of editorial board of *Journal of Biosocial Science.*

WORK IN PROGRESS: Research on medical genetics and medical education.

SIDELIGHTS: Emery told *CA* he is "particularly interested in the medical applications of advances in genetics, especially as they relate to the prevention of genetic disease." *Avocational interests:* Poetry, oil painting, marine biology.

* * *

EMERY, Edwin 1914-

PERSONAL: Born May 14, 1914, in California; son of William E. (a rancher) and Laura A. (Miller) Emery; married Mary M. McNevin, December 28, 1935; children: Michael, Laurel, Alison. *Education:* University of California, Berkeley, B.A., 1935, Ph.D., 1943. *Politics:* Democrat. *Home:* 2524 Seabury Ave., Minneapolis, Minn. 55406. *Office:* School of Journalism, University of Minnesota, Minneapolis, Minn. 55455.

CAREER: San Francisco Examiner, San Francisco, Calif., reporter, 1935; *California Monthly,* Berkeley, managing editor, 1936-43; United Press, San Francisco, Calif., correspondent and bureau chief, 1943-45, on war desk, 1944-45; University of Minnesota, Minneapolis, member of faculty, 1945-54, professor of journalism, 1954—. Taught and lectured in Taiwan and Spain, 1972-73.

MEMBER: International Press Institute, International Association for Mass Communication Research, Association for Education in Journalism (president, 1974-75), National Conference of Editorial Writers, Public Relations Society of America (president of Minnesota chapter), Phi Beta Kappa, Sigma Delta Chi. *Awards, honors:* National research awards from Sigma Delta Chi, 1950, 1954; Guggenheim fellowship, 1959-60; Social Science Research Council grant, 1960.

WRITINGS: History of the American Newspaper Publishers Association, University of Minnesota Press, 1950; (with E. H. Ford) *Highlights in the History of the American Press,* University of Minnesota Press, 1954; *The Press in America,* Prentice-Hall, 1954, 3rd edition, 1972; (with W. K. Agee and P. H. Ault) *Introduction to Mass Communications,* Harper, 1960, 5th edition, 1976; *The Story of America as Reported by Its Newspapers, 1690-1970,* Simon & Schuster, 1965; (with son, Michael Emery, and R. S. Schuneman) *America's Front Page News, 1690-1970,* Doubleday, 1971. Editorial writer for *St. Paul Pioneer Press,* summers, 1946-53; editor of *Journalism Quarterly,* 1964-73.

* * *

EMORY, Alan (Steuer) 1922-

PERSONAL: Name legally changed in 1951; born May 7, 1922, in New York, N.Y.; son of Henry (a state Supreme Court justice) and Ethel (a labor arbitrator; maiden name, Steuer) Epstein; married Nancy Goodman (a musician and teacher), October 15, 1950; children: Marc D., John A., Katharine B. *Education:* Harvard University, A.B., 1943; Columbia University, M.S., 1947. *Religion:* Unitarian. *Home:* 6302 Crosswoods Cir., Falls Church, Va. 22044. *Office:* 1273 National Press Bldg., Washington, D.C. 20045.

CAREER: Watertown Daily Times, Watertown, N.Y., city reporter, 1947-48, state editor, 1948-49, legislative correspondent, 1949-51, Washington correspondent, 1951—. United Features-North American Newspaper Alliance, Washington, D.C., contributing writer, 1954—; Washington correspondent for *Schenectady Gazette,* 1954—, *Middle-*

town Record, 1956-62, and *Binghamton Sun Bulletin,* 1962-64; Radio Press International, New York, N.Y., special correspondent, 1959-60. Notable assignments include coverage of all national conventions since 1952, a series on Alaska, 1958, Richard Nixon's trips to the Soviet Union, 1959 and 1972, President Eisenhower's South African trip, 1960, a series on Venezuela, 1966, a series on Russia, 1972, and a series on tax policy. Lecturer; occasional panelist on NBC's "Meet the Press." Director and vice-president of Lake Barcroft (Va.) Community Association, and Watertown (N.Y.) and Massena (N.Y.) Little Theatres. *Military service:* U.S. Army, European theater of operations, 1943-46; became staff sergeant.

MEMBER: National Press Club (member of speakers' committee), White House Correspondents' Association, Washington Press Club, Sigma Delta Chi (Washington professional chapter; treasurer, 1972-73; vice-president, 1973-74; president, 1974-75; director, 1975—), Gridiron Club of Washington, D.C. (member of producers' committee). *Awards, honors:* Thomas L. Stokes award from the Washington Journalism Center, 1968, for a series of articles concerning the future of atomic power in New York state.

WRITINGS: Writer of editorial page column, "From Washington," in *Watertown Daily Times,* and of syndicated column for United Features—North American Newspaper Alliances, appearing in 200 newspapers. Contributor of articles to magazines and newspapers, including *Business Week, Reporter, Nation, Electrical World, Washington Post, Washington Star, Editor and Publisher,* and *Quill* (journalism monthly). Also author of booklets on Alaska, 1958, Soviet Union, 1972, and Washington, D.C.

SIDELIGHTS: A series of articles written by Emory, was helpful in affecting a reversal of the Nixon administration's policy concerning the use of individual income tax records by federal agencies.

* * *

ENGH, M(ary) J(ane) 1933-

PERSONAL: Born January 26, 1933, in McLeansboro, Ill.; daughter of Arthur (a hatcheryman) and Bess (a secretary; maiden name, Coker) Gholson; married David W. Ferguson, May 1, 1954 (divorced April 4, 1960); married Richard Engh, October 4, 1963 (divorced September 23, 1969); children: (first marriage) Justin James, Robert Christian. *Education:* University of Chicago, B.A., 1951; University of Illinois, B.A., 1953; University of Oklahoma, M.L.S., 1973. *Home:* 2310 North Park Dr., Stillwater, Okla. 74074. *Agent:* Virginia Kidd, Box 278, Milford, Pa. 18337. *Office:* Library, Oklahoma State University, Stillwater, Okla. 74074.

CAREER: University of Chicago, Ill., library assistant, 1954-55; *American People's Encyclopedia,* Chicago, Ill., assistant vertical files librarian, 1955-56; U.S. Navy, Chicago, Ill., writer for correspondence course research project, 1957-58; Scott, Foresman & Co. (publishers), Chicago, Ill., editorial assistant, 1959-61, assistant editor, 1961-63; teacher in public schools in McLeansboro, Ill., 1964-65; C. E. Tuttle Co., Inc. (publishers), Tokyo, Japan, editor, 1968-69; Oklahoma State University, Stillwater, library clerk, 1971-72, assistant biological sciences librarian, 1973—. *Member:* Oklahoma Library Association, Higher Education Alumni Council of Oklahoma.

WRITINGS: Arslan (science fiction novel), Warner Paperback, 1976. Contributor of stories and poems to magazines.

WORK IN PROGRESS—Novels: *Tell Brave Deeds; The Oracle; The Shaft of the Dead Man; Catullus in Bithynia.*

SIDELIGHTS: Mary Jane Engh writes: "It's by no means an accident that my first novel was published as science fiction, but I am not primarily a science fiction writer. Fiction is my method of addressing problems too complex or too deep to be solved out of hand—a means of attaining knowledge, like Einstein's 'thought experiment.' Science fiction, of course, is a lovely field for this kind of exploration; but so is history. History, anthropology, ethology, and evolutionary biology are my idea of serious sciences; everything else is just playing with toys."

* * *

ENGH, Rohn 1938-
(H. T. White)

PERSONAL: Surname rhymes with "sang"; born October 13, 1938, in Ocean City, Md.; son of Lynn A. (in insurance) and Rose Alma (Harrigan) Engh; married Geralee Sullivan (a writer), January 23, 1960; children: Linn Daniel, Jim Sydney. *Education:* Attended private schools. *Home and office:* Pine Lake Farm, Star Prairie, Wis. 54026. *Agent:* Oliver Swan, Collier & Associates, Room 903, 18 East 48th St., New York, N.Y. 10017.

CAREER: Free-lance photographer and writer, 1959-66; Sunrise Photofeatures, Osceola, Wis., director, 1966—. Editor of *Expectations,* 1969-71; publisher of *Apple River Journal,* 1975-76, and *Photoletter,* 1975—. Director of Photosearch International, 1976—. Conducts yearly photojournalism workshop for World Press Institute, St. Paul; taught workshops at Wisconsin Indianhead Technical Institute. Appears on weekly segment on home gardening of "Today Show," KSTP-TV (NBC), Minneapolis; has made talk show appearances on "Today Show" and "Tonight Show." *Military service:* U.S. Army, Counter Intelligence Corps, 1956-58. *Member:* Society of American Travel Writers, Association for Retarded Children (local president), Action for Brain-Handicapped Children (president of board of directors), Lions (member of board of directors). *Awards, honors:* Freedoms Foundation Award, 1961, for a film on international students; Wisconsin Press Association Award, 1972, for a series on snowmobiles.

WRITINGS: A Very Simple Garden Book, Paul Ericksson, 1977. Author of "A View from Horse Creek," a column in *St. Paul Pioneer Press.* Contributor of articles and photographs, sometimes under pseudonym H. T. White, to *Saturday Evening Post, Argosy, Reader's Digest,* and *Rotarian.* Also contributor of photographs to *The Family of Children,* Ridge Press, 1977.

WORK IN PROGRESS: My Brother Jim, a photoessay; *Freelance Photo Marketing.*

BIOGRAPHICAL/CRITICAL SOURCES: Saturday Evening Post, December 28, 1958; *Writer's Digest,* April, 1967; *Popular Photography,* September, 1969; *St. Paul Pioneer Press,* December 15, 1974; *Minneapolis Tribune,* March 26, 1975.

* * *

ENGLISH, David 1931-

PERSONAL: Born May 26, 1931; married Irene Mainwood, 1954; children: one son, two daughters. *Education:* Attended schools in Bournemouth, England. *Office: Daily Mail,* London E.C.4, England.

CAREER: Daily Mirror, London, England, reporter, 1951-53; *Daily Sketch,* London, feature editor, 1956; *Sunday Dispatch,* London, foreign correspondent, 1959; *Daily Express,*

London, foreign correspondent, 1960, Washington correspondent, 1961-63, chief American correspondent, 1963-65, foreign editor, 1965-67, associate editor, 1967-69; *Daily Sketch*, editor, 1969-71; *Daily Mail*, London, editor, 1971—. *Member:* Press Club, Royal Temple Yacht Club.

WRITINGS: (With the staff of the London Daily Express) *Divided They Stand* (a British view of the 1968 U.S. presidential election), Prentice-Hall, 1969.

* * *

ENGLISH, John W(esley) 1940-

PERSONAL: Born October 5, 1940, in Junction City, Kan.; son of Raymond W. (a railroad worker) and June M. English. *Education:* University of Tulsa, B.A., 1962; University of Hawaii, Peace Corps training, 1962; attended Georgetown University, 1965; Columbia University, M.S., 1966; graduate study, New School for Social Research, 1967 and 1974, University of Wisconsin, 1968 and 1969; Antioch College, Ph.D., 1977. *Home:* 188 Northview Dr., Athens, Ga. 30601. *Office:* School of Journalism, University of Georgia, Athens, Ga. 30602.

CAREER: Peace Corps teacher of English in Sabah, Malaysia, 1962-64, *Peace Corps Volunteer* (magazine), Washington, D.C., assistant editor, 1964-65 and 1966; University of Tulsa, Tulsa, Okla., instructor in journalism, 1966-68; University of Wisconsin, Madison, teaching assistant, 1968-69; Hong Kong Baptist College, Hong Kong, visiting lecturer, 1969-70; University of Georgia, Athens, assistant professor, 1970—. Participant and lecturer at International Communications Seminar in Sali, Yugoslavia, 1971; consultant to University Without Walls of New York University, 1974; tutor at International University of Communications, 1974-76. *Tulsa Southside Times*, suburban weekly news editor, 1959-62; *Associated Press-Dow Jones Economic Report*, international financial wire copy editor, 1967; WIBA-Radio, Madison, Wis., reporter and air man, 1968-69; *Popular Culture Airwaves Bulletin*, member of editorial advisory board, 1973; consultant to *Media and Consumer, Seven Days*, and Houghton-Mifflin Publishers. Co-producer of films, "Mellow Yellow," 1967, and "Imago," 1970. Founding member of Hong Kong Ballet for All, 1970. *Member:* Association for Education in Journalism (member of magazine division executive board, 1975-76), Association of Authors and Journalists, Popular Culture Association (newsletter editor and executive board member of southern branch, 1974-76), American Civil Liberties Union, Friends of the Georgia Museum of Art (treasurer, 1976), Sigma Delta Chi, Omicron Delta Kappa. *Awards, honors:* Moss Faculty fellowship, 1973-74; National Critics Institute fellowship, 1974; National Endowment for the Arts grant, 1977.

WRITINGS: (Contributor) David LeRoy and Christopher Sterling, editors, *Mass News: Practices, Controversies, and Alternatives*, Prentice-Hall, 1973; (with others) *New Journalism*, Popular Culture Press, 1975. Writer of biographical film story about Nikola Tesla, produced in Yugoslavia, 1976. *Tulsa World*, special assignments correspondent, 1958-75; *Wisconsin State Journal*, arts critic, 1968-69; *Media and Consumer*, contributing editor, 1972-75. Contributor of numerous articles to magazines and journals, including *Far Eastern Economic Review, Women and Film, American Film, After Dark*, and *National Observer*, and to newspapers, including *New York Times, Village Voice, Baltimore Sun*, and *Atlanta Journal-Constitution*.

WORK IN PROGRESS: A book, *Criticizing the Critics*; a documentary film, "It's A Mean Old World"; a television show, "Open to New Ideas: New Art for Jimmy Carter"; numerous magazine articles.

SIDELIGHTS: English writes to *CA:* "The tie-in between my interest in popular culture subjects and magazine journalism is one of the joys of my life. I've written about post card images, mobile homes as business, football fan kitsch, the art of cartooning, and scads of other contemporary phenomena. Traveling and researching topics such as these give purpose and fun to one's career."

English is a performing artist in kinetic light and a collector of modern art. He is a donor of works of art to major collections in Oklahoma, Texas, and Wisconsin.

* * *

ENZLER, Clarence J. 1910(?)-1976

1910(?)—November 2, 1976; American civil servant, educator, and Roman Catholic churchman serving as deacon in Washington, D.C. Enzler was the author of books and articles on religious topics. He died in Washington, D.C. Obituaries: *Washington Post*, November 4, 1976.

* * *

EPPS, Garrett 1950-

PERSONAL: Born April 6, 1950, in Richmond, Va.; son of A. C. (a lawyer) and Rozanne (an educator; maiden name, Garrett) Epps. *Education:* Harvard University, B.A., 1972; Hollins College, M.A., 1975. *Politics:* Socialist. *Religion:* Episcopalian. *Home:* 6323 Ridgeway Rd., Richmond, Va. 23226. *Agent:* Wendy Weil, Julian Bach Literary Agency, Inc., 3 East 48th St., New York, N.Y. 10017.

CAREER: Richmond Mercury, Richmond, Va., reporter, 1972-73; *Richmond Afro-American*, Richmond, reporter, 1974-76; *Virginia Churchman*, Richmond, reporter, 1976—.

WRITINGS: The Shad Treatment (novel), Putnam, 1977. Contributor to magazines, including *New Republic, TV Guide, Boston After Dark, Real Paper*, and *Hollins Critic*, and to newspapers.

WORK IN PROGRESS: Another novel.

* * *

EPSTEIN, Anne Merrick 1931-

PERSONAL: Born October 3, 1931, in Alplaus, N.Y.; daughter of Albert William (a metallurgist) and Ketherine (Walker) Merrick; married David Epstein (a musician, conductor, and composer), June 21, 1953; children: Eve, Beth. *Education:* Antioch College, A.B., 1953; graduate study at Columbia University and Art Students League of New York, 1954-56, and Wilberforce University, 1957. *Residence:* Lexington, Mass. *Agent:* Marilyn Marlow, Curtis Brown Ltd., 575 Madison Ave., New York, N.Y. 10022.

CAREER: Look, New York City, assistant in circulation promotion department, 1956-57; teacher of art and music in Enon, Ohio, 1957-61; writer. *Member:* American Society of Composers, Authors and Publishers (Writer Division). *Awards, honors:* Ford Foundation recording grant, 1976, for "Night Voices."

WRITINGS: Stone Man, Stone House, Doubleday, 1972; *Good Stones*, Houghton, 1977. Author of poetic narration for "Night Voices" (for narrator, orchestra, and children's chorus), Carl Fischer, Inc., 1977.

WORK IN PROGRESS: Disappeared People, "a light-hearted novel for young readers"; research for a novel based on a sixteenth-century survival story; lyrics for choral works.

SIDELIGHTS: Anne Epstein writes: "A lonely childhood until I was six years old, telling stories to imaginary 'friends' whose names I still remember, was followed by the years of World War II. Stories of survival became harshly real. Instinct tells me that the ability to be alone and discover inner resources is important.

To amuse myself during those early years I also made up songs, so it is probably not unpredictable that I married a musician and that we wrote 'Night Voices' together. Much of my family's life revolves around the world of music, both in our enjoyment in making music at home and in traveling in Europe, where my husband conducts."

"Night Voices" was recorded by Vox/Turnabout Records in 1977.

* * *

EPSTEIN, David G(eorge) 1943-

PERSONAL: Born April 29, 1943, in New York, N.Y.; son of Lee (a lawyer) and Beatrice (an artist; maiden name, Greenberg) Epstein; divorced; children: Daniela. *Education:* Columbia University, B.A. (summa cum laude), 1963, Ph.D. (summa cum laude), 1969. *Residence:* Santa Monica, Calif.

CAREER: University of California, Los Angeles, assistant professor of anthropology, 1968-76; Levy, Koszdin, Goldschmid & Sroloff, Los Angeles, Calif., legal worker, 1976—. Visiting assistant professor at Queens College of the City University of New York, 1972-73. *Member:* American Anthropological Association.

WRITINGS: Brasilia: Plan and Reality, University of California Press, 1973.

* * *

EPSTEIN, Eugene 1944-

PERSONAL: Born November 19, 1944, in New York, N.Y.; son of Louis (a financial consultant) and Rose (a nurse; maiden name, Feuer) Epstein; married Linda Harriet Silverberg (an editor), April 2, 1967; children: Kate Elizabeth, James Eugene. *Education:* Brandeis University, B.A., 1966; New School for Social Research, M.A., 1969. *Politics:* "Lean toward anarcho-capitalism." *Religion:* None. *Home:* 240 West 98th St., New York, N.Y. 10025. *Agent:* Charles Neighbors, 240 Waverly Pl., New York, N.Y. 10014.

CAREER: St. John's University, New York City, lecturer in economics, 1969-71; Human Resources Administration of the City of New York, New York City, economic analyst for department of social services, 1972; Reynolds Securities, Inc., New York City, national director of commodity research, 1972-74; free-lance writer and consultant on economics and business, 1974—. Lecturer at Richmond College of the City University of New York, 1970-71; writing assistant to economist and writer Robert Heilbroner, 1971.

WRITINGS: Making Money in Commodities, Praeger, 1977; *Electric Power from the Wind,* Business Communications Co., Inc., 1977. Contributor to business and economic magazines and trade journals, and to *Sky, Flight-Time,* and *New Engineer.*

WORK IN PROGRESS: In Defense of Capitalism.

SIDELIGHTS: Epstein told *CA:* "*Electric Power from the Wind* is about the economics of wind energy machines. I conclude that for the most part they're toys for rich people. But there's one stunning exception: The 'tornado machine' now being developed by Dr. James Yen at Grumman Aerospace. The tornado machine has a real chance of ushering in a permanent era of cheap energy.

"*In Defense of Capitalism* argues that if people are going to get better control over their lives, achieve noncoercive communities, and overcome a sense of alienation in the workplace, then capitalism is part of the solution, not part of the problem. In other words, capitalism is the economic system that best realizes the values of the New Left movement of the 1960's. Also, the social problems that are often blamed on capitalism—for instance, racism, imperialism, and unemployment—are not capitalism's fault. By a former socialist."

* * *

EPSTEIN, Fritz T(heodor) 1898-

PERSONAL: Born August 20, 1898, in Saargemuend, Germany; son of Paul (a professor of mathematics) and Alice (Wiesengrund) Epstein; married Herta Bertelsmann, 1924 (died, 1974); married Erna Kresina, June 3, 1975; children: Rose, Klaus (deceased). *Education:* University of Berlin, Ph.D., 1924. *Home:* Erwin Vollmer-Haus, 3144 Rehlingen ueber Lueneburg, West Germany.

CAREER: University of Hamburg, Hamburg, Germany, assistant, 1927-32; Academic Assistance Council, London, England, grant recipient, 1934-36; Harvard University, Cambridge, Mass., research assistant, 1937-43; Office of Strategic Service and U.S. Department of State, Washington, D.C., research analyst, 1944-46; Inter-allied German War Documents Project, Berlin, Germany, historian, 1946-48; Stanford University, Stanford, Calif., curator of Central European and Slavic collections, 1948-51; Library of Congress, Washington, D.C., specialist in Russian and Central European area, 1951-60; Indiana University, Bloomington, Ind., professor of history and curator of Slavic collection, 1962-69, emeritus professor, 1969—. Exchange professor, Free University of Berlin, 1950; director of research, War Documentation Project, Alexandria, Va., 1951-54; lecturer, American University, Washington, D.C., 1951-59; Fulbright visiting professor, University of Bonn, 1954; visiting professor, University of Hamburg, 1966-68. *Member:* American Historical Association. *Awards, honors:* Honorary doctorate, University of Hamburg, 1968; honorary professor at University of Bonn, 1961, and University of Freiburg, 1974.

WRITINGS: Aufzeichnungen uber den Moskauer Staat, Cram, 1964; *Germany and the East: Selected Essays,* Indiana University Press, 1973. Also editor of works in German. Editor, *Dokumente zur deutschen auswaertigen Politik 1918-45,* 1960-62.

WORK IN PROGRESS: Research on Germany and Russia in the nineteenth century.

* * *

EPSTEIN, Judith Sue 1947-
(Judy Sue)

PERSONAL: Born May 11, 1947, in Brooklyn, N.Y.; daughter of Perry and Ruth (Goldman) Epstein. *Education:* Cornell University, B.S., 1969, M.A.T., 1975; University of Iowa, M.F.A., 1973. *Home:* 457 Brooktondale Rd., Brooktondale, N.Y. 14817.

CAREER: Poet and writer. Teacher in Lansing, N.Y., 1975-76; local supervisor for Literary Volunteers of America. *Member:* National Association of Teachers of English, Ithaca Community Arts.

WRITINGS: Keeping Score, Ithaca House, 1975. Author of country western songs, sometimes under name Judy Sue. Contributor of poems to literary magazines, including *Grapevine, Epoch, Lamp in the Spine,* and *Hanging Loose.*

* * *

EPSTEIN, William 1912-

PERSONAL: Born July 10, 1912, in Calgary, Alberta, Canada; came to the United States in 1946; son of Harry Louis (a merchant) and Masha Bella (Geffen) Epstein; married Edna Frances Hyman, September 22, 1946; children: Mark Gil. *Education:* University of Alberta, B.A. (first class honors), 1933, LL.B. (first class honors), 1935; London School of Economics and Political Science, graduate study, 1937-38. *Home:* 400 East 58th St., New York, N.Y. 10022. *Office:* United Nations Institute for Training and Research, 801 United Nations Plaza, New York, N.Y. 10017.

CAREER: Called to the Bar of Alberta, 1936; private practice of law in Calgary, Alberta, 1935-42; United Nations Secretariat, New York, N.Y., acting head of Middle East section, 1946-50, senior political officer in Palestine, 1948, director of Disarmament Division, 1950-73, secretary of Disarmament Commission, 1952-73, special consultant to the Secretary-General, 1973—. Special fellow of United Nations Institute for Training and Research, 1973—; visiting professor at University of Victoria, 1974—; Cecil H. and Ida Green Visiting Professor at University of British Columbia, 1975. Member of International Institute for Strategic Studies, Canadian Institute of International Affairs, Pugwash Conferences on Science and World Affairs, and North American Council of the International Peace Academy. Secretary of Canadian Claims Commission (London), 1944-46. *Military service:* Canadian Army, 1942-45; became captain.

MEMBER: Arms Control Association, American Society for International Law, Canadian Bar Association, Alberta Law Society, Calgary Bar Association. *Awards, honors:* Overseas scholarship from Imperial Order of the Daughters of the Empire (I.O.D.E.), 1937-38; LL.D. from University of Calgary, 1971; Rockefeller Foundation fellowship, 1973-75; Order of the Aztec Eagle (Mexico), 1976.

WRITINGS: (Editor) *The United Nations and Disarmament, 1945-1970,* United Nations, 1971; *Disarmament: Twenty-Five Years of Effort,* Canadian Institute of International Affairs, 1971; *The Last Chance: Nuclear Proliferation and Arms Control,* Free Press, 1976; (editor with Toshiyuki Toyoda) *A New Design for Nuclear Disarmament,* Pugwash Conferences on Science and World Affairs, 1977.

Contributor: Carlo Schaerf and Frank Barnaby, editors, *Disarmament and Arms Control,* Gordon & Breach, 1972; A.M.J. Hyatt, editor, *Dreadnought to Polaris,* Copp Clark, 1973; David Carlton and Schaerf, editors, *The Dynamics of the Arms Race,* Croom Held, 1975; Anne Marks, editor, *NPT: Paradoxes and Problems,* Arms Control Association, Carnegie Endowment for International Peace, 1975; Robert F. Scagel, editor, *Mankind's Future in the Pacific: Special Lectures of the Thirteenth Pacific Science Congress,* University of British Columbia Press, 1976; A. M. Chayes and W. Bennett Lewis, editors, *International Arrangements for Nuclear Fuel Cycle Facilities,* Ballinger, 1977; Joseph I. Coffey, editor, *Nuclear Proliferation: Prospects, Problems and Proposals,* American Academy of Political and Social Science, 1977. Contributor to international journals, popular magazines, including *Scientific American, Survival, Saturday Review, Bulletin of Atomic Scientists* and *World Today,* and to newspapers.

WORK IN PROGRESS: Canada and the Problem of Nuclear Proliferation, completion expected in 1978; *New Approaches to Comprehensive Disarmament,* 1979.

SIDELIGHTS: During Epstein's career with the United Nations, he represented the Secretary-General at official conferences in Geneva on the nuclear test ban, on nuclear non-proliferation, and on various aspects of arms control and disarmament. He was technical consultant to the Preparatory Commission for the Denuclearization of Latin America, and in 1969 was chairman of the international group of experts which prepared the report on chemical and biological weapons for the Secretary-General at the request of the General Assembly.

AVOCATIONAL INTERESTS: Walking, reading, sculpting, art.

BIOGRAPHCAL/CRITICAL SOURCES: Week End, August 9, 1975; *Monday,* October 11, 1976.

* * *

ERICKSON, Carolly 1943-

PERSONAL: Born April 12, 1943, in Los Angeles, Calif.; daughter of Roland L. and Louise (Kiger) Bliss; children: Hal. *Education:* University of Washington, Seattle, double B.A., 1963; Columbia University, M.A., 1964, Ph.D., 1969. *Residence:* Berkeley, Calif. *Agent:* Robert Briggs, R. Briggs Associates, 2154 Filbert St., San Francisco, Calif. 94123; and Peter Matson, Harold Matson Co., Inc., 22 East 40th St., New York, N.Y. 10016.

CAREER: Barnard College, New York, N.Y., lecturer in history, 1964-66; San Fernando Valley State College (now California State University, Northridge), Northridge, Calif., instructor in history, 1966-67; Mills College, Oakland, Calif., assistant professor of medieval history, 1967-70; Berkeley Writers Service, Berkeley, Calif., director, 1970-74; free-lance writer, 1974—. Lecturer at Brooklyn College of the City University of New York, 1965-66. *Member:* Mediaeval Academy of America, American Historical Association, Medieval Association of the Pacific, West Coast Association of Women Historians, Phi Beta Kappa.

WRITINGS: The Records of Medieval Europe, Doubleday, 1971; *The Medieval Vision* (History Book Club selection), Oxford University Press, 1976; *Bloody Mary,* Doubleday, 1977; *Civilization and Society in the West,* Scott, Foresman, 1977. Contributor of articles and reviews to medieval studies journals.

WORK IN PROGRESS: Great Harry, a biography of Henry VIII; *Civilization Past and Present,* with T. Walter Wallbank and Alastair Taylor, publication expected in 1979; historical fiction.

SIDELIGHTS: Carolly Erickson writes: "I have found the past compelling since the age of fourteen or so, and even before I went to college I had a feeling I might some day write history for the general reader . . . I try to immerse myself in the sources and then attempt to bring a personality, an era, a past world to life.

"In addition to working on textbooks and trade nonfiction, I plan to make time to complete several historical novels after the fall of 1978."

* * *

ERICSON, Edward E(inar) 1939-

PERSONAL: Born October 19, 1939, in Chicago, Ill.; son of Edward Einar (a railroad worker) and Ethel Marie (Hall)

Ericson; married Janice Marie Kemp (an office manager), August 27, 1960; children: Edward Einar III, William R. *Education:* Attended Grace Bible College, Grand Rapids, Mich., 1956-59; Hope College, A.B., 1961; University of Arkansas, M.A., 1963, Ph.D., 1967. *Office:* Department of English, Calvin College, Grand Rapids, Mich. 49506.

CAREER: Hope College, Holland, Mich., instructor in English, 1963-65; Westmont College, Santa Barbara, Calif., assistant professor, 1965-69, associate professor, 1969-72, professor of English, 1972, chairman of department of English and modern languages, 1970-72; Stanford University, Stanford, Calif., national fellow at Hoover Institution on War, Revolution & Peace, 1972-73; Northwestern College, Orange City, Iowa, professor of English and dean of academic affairs, 1973-77; Calvin College, Grand Rapids, Mich., professor of English, 1977—. *Member:* Modern Language Association of America, National Council of Teachers of English, Conference on Christianity and Literature (associate bibliographer, 1966—), Milton Society of America, Philadelphia Society, Phi Beta Kappa.

WRITINGS: (With Ronald M. Enroth and C. Breckinridge Peters) *The Jesus People: Old-Time Religion in the Age of Aquarius,* Eerdmans, 1972 (published in England as *The Story of the Jesus People,* Paternoster Press, 1972); (editor with G. B. Tennyson) *Religion and Modern Literature: Essays in Theory and Criticism,* Eerdmans, 1975; *Radicals in the University,* Hoover Institution, 1975. Contributor of articles and reviews to a variety of academic and religious journals. Book review editor of *Christian Scholar's Review,* 1970-74; contributing editor of *Reformed Journal.*

WORK IN PROGRESS: A critical study of Aleksandr Solzhenitsyn; research for a critical study of Mikhail Bulgakov.

AVOCATIONAL INTERESTS: Softball.

* * *

ERSKINE, Laurie York 1894(?)-1976

1894(?)—November 30, 1976; British-born American author of the "Renfrew of the Royal Mounted" series and other books. Some of his "Renfrew" adventures were adapted for films, television and radio broadcast. He served in both world wars and was co-founder of a prep school in New Hope, Pa. Erskine died in New Hope. Obituaries: *New York Times,* December 3, 1976.

* * *

ERSKINE-LINDOP, Audrey Beatrice Noel 1921-

PERSONAL: Born December 26, 1921, in London, England; daughter of A. H. (a lieutenant colonel in the military) and Ivy (Monck-Mason) Erskine-Lindop; married Dudley Gordon Leslie (a playwright and scriptwriter), 1945. *Education:* Educated in private schools in England. *Home:* Gray Tiles, Niton Undercliff, Isle of Wight PO38 2NA; and Kestor Way, Chagford, South Devon, England.

CAREER: Member of Worthington Repertory Co.; scriptwriter in England and Hollywood, Calif.; writer. Freeman of the City of London, 1954. *Member:* International P.E.N., Ghost Club. *Awards, honors:* Prix Roman Policier, 1968, for *I Start Counting.*

WRITINGS: Fortune My Foe (novel), Harper, 1947, published in England as *In Me My Enemy,* Harrap, 1948; *Soldiers' Daughters Never Cry* (novel), Simon & Schuster, 1948; *The Tall Headlines,* Macmillan, 1950; *Out of the Whirlwind,* Heinemann, 1951, Appleton, 1952; *The Singer Not the Song* (Literary Guild selection), Appleton, 1953;

The Outer Ring, Appleton, 1955, published in England as *Details of Jeremy Stratton,* Heinemann, 1955; *The Judas Figures,* Appleton, 1956; *Mist Over Talla,* Doubleday, 1957; *I Thank a Fool,* Collins, 1958; *Nicola,* Doubleday, 1959.

The Way to the Lantern (Doubleday Book Club selection), Doubleday, 1961; *The Adventures of the Wuffle* (juvenile), Methuen, 1966, McGraw, 1968; *I Start Counting,* Doubleday, 1966; *Sight Unseen,* Doubleday, 1969; *Journey Into Stone,* Doubleday, 1972; *The Self Appointed Saint,* Doubleday, 1975; *The Clip,* in press.

Plays: "Let's Talk Turkey," first produced in 1955; (with husband, Dudley Leslie) "Beware of Angels," first produced in London's West End, at Westminster Theatre in 1959.

SIDELIGHTS: The Singer Not the Song was made into a film in 1961. *Avocational interests:* Reading history, "collecting relics of favourite historical characters," the countryside and wildlife, Oriental cats, parrots.

* * *

ESTABROOK, Robert Harley 1918-

PERSONAL: Born October 16, 1918, in Dayton, Ohio; son of Charles Beason (a sales manager) and Christianne M. (Harley) Estabrook; married Mary Lou Stewart (an associate publisher), December 22, 1942; children: John Stewart, Margaret Harley, James Ross, David Morse. *Education:* Northwestern University, B.A. (highest distinction), 1939; also attended Columbia University, 1947. *Religion:* Unitarian-Universalist. *Home address:* Reservoir Rd., Lakeville, Conn. 06039. *Office: Lakeville Journal,* Pocket-Knife Sq., Lakeville, Conn. 06039.

CAREER: Emmet County Graphic, Harbor Springs, Mich., city editor, 1936; Northwestern University, Evanston, Ill., editor of *Daily Northwestern,* 1938-39; *Cedar Rapids Gazette,* Cedar Rapids, Iowa, reporter, 1939-40, editorial writer, 1940-42; *Washington Post,* Washington, D.C., editorial writer, 1946-53, editor of editorial page, 1953-61, London correspondent, 1961-62, chief foreign correspondent from London, 1962-65, associate editor, 1965-66, United Nations and Canadian correspondent, 1966-71, foreign affairs columnist, 1961-65; *Lakeville Journal,* Lakeville, Conn., editor and publisher, and author of column "Perambulating," 1971—. Lecturer at University of Maryland, 1948-49, and University of Hartford, 1972-75. Director of Connecticut Council on Freedom of Information. *Military service:* U.S. Army, in charge of newspaper and radio station in Brazil, 1942-46; became captain.

MEMBER: International Society of Weekly Newspaper Editors (director, 1977—), National Conference of Editorial Writers (founder; life member; president, 1951-52), National Press Club, Overseas Writers Association, Council on Foreign Relations, New England Press Association (director, 1977), Connecticut Editorial Association (president, 1975-76), Phi Beta Kappa, Sigma Delta Chi, Delta Tau Delta. *Awards, honors:* Award from Sigma Delta Chi, 1954, for best editorial; award from Deadline Club, 1969, for best United Nations correspondence; D.H.L. from Colby College, 1972; Golden Quill Award from International Conference of Weekly Newspaper Editors, 1973; Sigma Delta Chi award, 1976, for best editorial in Connecticut.

WRITINGS: A Manual for Correspondents, Washington Post, 1966. Contributor to magazines, including *Atlantic, Nation, Reporter, American Mercury, Masthead,* and *Grassroots Editor.*

SIDELIGHTS: Estabrook has reported the news from more than seventy countries. He interviewed heads of state and government in Asia, 1957, and in Europe and the Middle East, 1961-65. He was a member of the first delegation of the American Society of Newspaper Editors to the Soviet Union in 1962; he also covered President Kennedy's visit to Europe in 1963 and Khrushchev's visit to Scandinavia in 1964.

* * *

ESTENSSORO, Hugo 1946-
(Emilio Chartier)

PERSONAL: Born January 31, 1946, in La Paz, Bolivia; came to the United States in 1968; son of Alfredo (a professor) and Blanca (Baldomar) Estenssoro; married Nicole Cohen, December 19, 1971. *Education:* Attended high school in Bolivia, Brazil, and Venezuela. *Politics:* None. *Religion:* None. *Home and office:* 117 Macdougal St., Apt. 4, New York, N.Y. 10012.

CAREER: Bolivian Embassy, Mexico City, Mexico, cultural attache, 1966-67; *Excelsior,* Mexico City, Mexico, author of international affairs column "Comentario Internacional" under pseudonym Emilio Chartier, 1967-68; *Manchete* (magazine), Rio de Janeiro, Brazil, New York correspondent, 1969-73; *Veja* (magazine), Sao Paulo, Brazil, New York correspondent, 1973-76; *Isto E* (magazine), Sao Paulo, Brazil, New York correspondent and author of column "Carta de Nova York," 1976—. Contributing editor to Brazilian magazines, *Vogue, Status,* and *Lui,* 1977—. Covered U.S. elections, 1968-76, and the United Nations since 1969; has held interviews with Latin American heads of state and with political and literary figures in the United States.

MEMBER: American Society of Magazine Photographers. *Awards, honors:* Fellow of World Press Institute, 1968-69; second prize for sequences from World Press Photo Contest in Amsterdam, 1975; invited artist (for photography) at Sao Paulo Bienal, 1976.

WRITINGS: (Editor) *Antologia de Poesia Brasilena* (title means "An Anthology of Brazilian Poetry"), Ministerio de Educacion Publica (Mexico), 1967. Contributor to *Grolier Encyclopedia.* Contributor of articles and photographs to popular magazines, including *Commonweal, Progressive, Newsweek, Stern,* and *Photo,* and to newspapers, including *New York Times* and *Christian Science Monitor.* Literary and art critic for *O Estada de Sao Paulo* and *Excelsior.*

WORK IN PROGRESS: Still Mirror, essays on photographers.

SIDELIGHTS: Estenssoro writes that he "started in life as an artist, now am a photographer as well as a writer. I am deeply interested in economics, international affairs, literature and art." He has traveled widely in Latin America and North Africa.

* * *

EVANS, Herndon J. 1895-1976

PERSONAL: Born December 22, 1895, in Morehead, Ky.; son of John Grey and Roberta (Ham) Evans; married Mary Elizabeth Downing, March 3, 1923; children: Mary Wallis (Mrs. Baylor Landrum). *Education:* University of Kentucky, A.B., 1921. *Politics:* Democrat. *Religion:* Methodist. *Residence:* Lexington, Ky.

CAREER: Louisville Courier-Journal, Louisville, Ky., state editor, 1922; Associated Press, Frankfort, Ky., cov-

ered state capital news, 1923; *Pineville Sun,* Pineville, Ky., owner, editor, and publisher, 1923-56; *Lexington Herald,* Lexington, Ky., editor, 1956-68; writer, 1968-76. *Military service:* U.S. Army, 1917-19; served in France and Germany; became second lieutenant. *Awards, honors:* The lodge at Kentucky Mountain State Park was named in his honor.

WRITINGS: The Newspaper Press in Kentucky, University Press of Kentucky, in press.

SIDELIGHTS: After serving in the army in France and Germany, Evans stayed on during the period of occupation to serve as mayor of a small town in Germany. At home in Kentucky, he was an active conservationist, particularly interested in the Cumberland Falls area.

(Died February 24, 1976)

[Sketch verified by wife, Mary Elizabeth Evans]

* * *

EVANS, Lloyd (Lloyd Thomas) 1927-

PERSONAL: Born August 6, 1927, in New Zealand; son of Claude and Gwendolyn (Fraser) Evans; married Margaret Newell (a student counselor), August 21, 1954; children: Nicholas, John, Catherine. *Education:* University of New Zealand, B.Agr.Sc., 1948, B.Sc., 1949, M.Agr.Sc., 1950, D.Sc., 1973; Oxford University, D.Phil., 1954. *Home:* 3 Elliott St., Canberra, Australian Capital Territory 2601, Australia.

CAREER: Commonwealth Scientific and Industrial Research Organisation, Canberra, Australia, research scientist, 1956—. *Member:* Australian Academy of Science (fellow; vice-president), Australian and New Zealand Association for the Advancement of Science (president), Royal Society (London; fellow). *Awards, honors:* Rhodes scholarship, 1950; Harkness fellowship, California Institute of Technology, 1954-56; National Academy of Sciences fellowship, 1963-64.

WRITINGS: (Editor) *Environmental Control of Plant Growth,* Academic Press, 1963; (editor) *The Induction of Flowering,* Macmillan, 1969; (editor) *Crop Physiology,* Cambridge University Press, 1975; *Daylength and the Flowering of Plants,* Benjamin, 1975. Contributor of more than a hundred articles to scientific journals.

WORK IN PROGRESS: Crop Evolution and Yield.

SIDELIGHTS: Evans told *CA:* "As an experimental scientist, I am only secondarily an author to the extent that the editing and writing of books allows me to develop a broader context for my research than is possible in scientific papers. One of the many delights of being a scientist is that it gives me an unassailable excuse for trying to be an author."

* * *

EVERETT, Glenn D. 1921-

PERSONAL: Born May 6, 1921, in Sandusky, Ohio; son of David F. and Lillian (Gangloff) Everett; married June Finten, July 31, 1948; children: Paul, Dale, Karen. *Education:* Heidelberg College, B.A., 1942; University of Iowa, M.A., 1943; American University, further graduate study. *Home:* 11110 South Glen Rd., Potomac, Md. 20854. *Office:* 926 National Press Building, Washington, D.C. 20045.

CAREER: Correspondent from Washington, D.C., 1947—. *Awards, honors:* National Faith and Freedom Award from Religious Heritage Foundation of America, 1957.

WRITINGS: Religious Shrines in the Nation's Capital, St.

Martin's, 1956, 2nd edition, 1963; (with John Noble) *I Found God in Soviet Russia,* Zondervan, 1971.

* * *

EVERETT, Peter 1931-

PERSONAL: Born June 1, 1931, in Hull, Yorkshire, England. *Home:* 9 Laitwood Rd., London S.W. 12, England.

CAREER: Has been employed as gardener, foundry man, and furniture salesman; writer, 1962—. *Awards, honors:* Independent Television award for drama, 1962; Maugham award, 1965; Arts Council of Great Britain grant, 1970.

WRITINGS—Novels: A Day of Dwarfs, Neville Spearman, 1962; *The Instrument,* Hutchinson, 1962; *Negatives,* J. Cape, 1964, Simon & Schuster, 1965; *The Fetch,* J. Cape, 1966, Simon & Schuster, 1967.

Screenplays: (With Roger Lowry) "Negatives" (based on own novel), Continental, 1968; "The Last of the Long-Haired Boys," 1971. Also author of plays for radio and television. Contributor of poems to *Botteghe Oscure.*

AVOCATIONAL INTERESTS: Jigsaw puzzles, games of all sorts.

* * *

EVETTS, Julia 1944-

PERSONAL: Born August 27, 1944, in Burton-on-Trent, Staffordshire, England; son of Bernard (a railway guard) and Amy (a canteen assistant; maiden name, Inwood) Ward; married David Evetts (a metallurgist for Rolls Royce), August 19, 1967; children: Victoria, Paul. *Education:* University of Sheffield, B.A. (honors), 1966. *Politics:* "Floating voter." *Religion:* Agnostic. *Home:* 26 Katherine Dr., Toton, Nottingham, England. *Office:* Department of Sociology, University of Nottingham, University Park, Nottingham, England.

CAREER: Derby College of Technology, Derby, England, lecturer in sociology and general studies, 1967-68; University of Nottingham, Nottingham, England, lecturer in sociology and sociology of education, 1968—.

WRITINGS: The Sociology of Educational Ideas, Routledge & Kegan Paul, 1973. Contributor to sociology journals.

WORK IN PROGRESS: Research on curriculum differences in the teaching of sociology among different educational institutions.

SIDELIGHTS: Julia Evetts writes: "Being responsible for babies and young children has considerably affected my current involvement in research and writing. I am resigned to this and am prepared to wait rather than fight against my emotions."

* * *

EWEN, Stuart 1945-

PERSONAL: Born June 13, 1945, in New York, N.Y.; son of Sol Joshua (a dentist) and Sylvia (a librarian; maiden name, Scott) Ewen; married Elizabeth Wunderlich (a college teacher), October 5, 1966; children: Paul Scott, Sam Travis. *Education:* University of Wisconsin, Madison, B.A., 1968; University of Rochester, M.A., 1969; State University of New York at Albany, Ph.D., 1974. *Politics:* "Shares Jose Yglesias' wish to overthrow capitalism." *Residence:* New York, N.Y.

CAREER: Student Non-Violent Coordinating Committee (SNCC), Atlanta, Ga., field secretary in Mississippi, 1964-65; *Connections* (underground newspaper), Madison, Wis., editor, 1967-68; writer, 1968-71; State University of New York Empire State College, Albany, assistant professor of history, 1971—. Seminar associate at Columbia University, 1976-77. *Member:* American Historical Association, Authors League of America, Authors Guild, Ad-Hoc Committee for Thinking. *Awards, honors:* Woodrow Wilson fellowship, 1969; award from American Library Association, 1976, for *Captains of Consciousness.*

WRITINGS: (Editor with Elizabeth Ewen, John Kaufman, and Michael Cherniavsky) *Social Textures of Western Civilization,* Wiley, 1972; *Captains of Consciousness: Advertising and the Social Roots of the Consumer Culture,* McGraw, 1976. Contributor to journals, including *Liberation, Radical America, Sevendays, Telos,* and *Cultural Studies.*

WORK IN PROGRESS: In the Shadow of the Image, a social history of American mass culture.

SIDELIGHTS: Ewen writes: "My work focuses on the development of mass culture as a significant aspect of industrial capitalist society. Rather than writing internal and anecdotal history of the mass media industries, I have attempted to locate these industries within the broad social history of monopoly capitalism. While much of my writing has been scholarly, I see my work as essentially political. The power of mass produced images in our lives requires a historical understanding, a political analysis, and a radical response."

* * *

FABIO, Sarah Webster 1928-

PERSONAL: Born January 20, 1928, in Nashville, Tenn.; children: Cheryl, Ronnie, Renee Angela, Leslie, Thomas. *Education:* Fisk University, B.A., 1946; San Francisco State College (now University), M.A. *Home address:* c/o 2536 Baylor E., Palo Alto, Calif.

CAREER: Member of faculty at Merritt Junior College, Oakland, Calif., and currently at University of California, Berkeley. Participated in First World Festival of Negro Art (Dakar, Senegal), 1966.

WRITINGS: A Mirror [and] *A Soul* (two-part volume of poems), Julian Richardson, 1969; *Black Talk: Soul, Shield, and Sword,* Doubleday, 1973. Also author of *Race Results: U.S.A.,* 1966, and *Black Is a Panther Caged.* Contributor to magazines. Editor of *Journal of Black Arts Renaissance.*

SIDELIGHTS: Sarah Fabio has made a sound recording of her poems, "Soul Ain't, Soul Is," for Folkway Records, 1973.*

* * *

FAHLSTROM, Oyvind (Axel Christian) 1928-1976

1928—November 8, 1976; Brazilian-born Swedish artist, journalist, playwright, and inventor of games. His work in all areas was noted for its satirical content and social statement. Two of his plays were produced in New York and Stockholm. His art work is exhibited in museums in the U.S. and Europe. Fahlstrom died in Stockholm, Sweden. Obituaries: *New York Times,* November 12, 1976.

* * *

FAHY, Christopher 1937-

PERSONAL: Surname is pronounced Fay; born November 15, 1937, in Philadelphia, Pa.; son of William J. (a teacher) and Dorothy (a teacher; maiden name, Kitsch) Fahy; married Davene Sernoff (a school administrator), January 25, 1960; children: Gregory, Benjamin. *Education:* Temple University, B.A., 1959, M.A., 1962. *Politics:* "Declining." *Religion:* "Stable." *Residence:* Tenants Harbor, Maine 04860.

CAREER: Speech therapist in public schools in New Jersey, 1961-62; Bancroft School, Haddonfield, N.J., speech therapist, 1962-65, director of speech clinic and coordinator of clinical services, 1967-72; free-lance writer, 1972—. Vice-president of Friends of Jackson Library, 1975—. *Member:* International Society for General Semantics, American Speech and Hearing Association.

WRITINGS: The Compost Heap (novel), Outerbridge & Dienstfrey, 1970; *Home Remedies* (on home repair), Scribner, 1975.

Work anthologized in *Traveling America with Today's Poets,* edited by David Kherdian, Macmillan, 1977. Contributor of stories and poems to literary journals, including *Beloit Poetry Journal* and *Transatlantic Review.*

WORK IN PROGRESS: Dark Harvest, a fantasy suspense novel; *A Noise in Dreams,* a novel.

SIDELIGHTS: Fahy comments: "The earth and the brain are equal magic. Words are the plants of the mind. We have to tend our gardens lovingly but leave some stones. Nothing but bones remain when we're done, but hell, have fun." *Avocational interests:* Fixing old houses, gardening.

*   *   *

FAIR, Ronald L.   1932-

PERSONAL: Born October 27, 1932, in Chicago, Ill.; son of Herbert and Beulah (Hunt) Fair; married Lucy Margaret Jones, November 10, 1952 (divorced); married Neva June Keres, June 19, 1968; children: Rodney D., Glen A. *Education:* Attended Stenotype School of Chicago, 1953-55. *Home:* 201 West 92nd St., Chicago, Ill. 60620.

CAREER: City of Chicago, Ill., court reporter, 1955-67; writer, 1967—. Teacher of literature, Columbia College, Chicago; teacher of literature and fiction, Northwestern University, fall, 1968; Wesleyan University, Middletown, Conn., visiting fellow at Center for Advanced Studies, 1969. *Military service:* U.S. Naval Reserve, 1950-53. *Awards, honors:* Arts and Letters award of National Institute of Arts and Letters, 1970, for *World of Nothing.*

WRITINGS—Novels: Many Thousand Gone: An American Fable, Harcourt, 1965; *Hog Butcher,* Harcourt, 1966; *World of Nothing: Two Novellas* (contains "World of Nothing" and "Jerome"), Harper, 1970; *Exerpts,* Paul Breman, 1971; *We Can't Breathe,* Harper, 1972. Contributor to periodicals, including *Chicago Daily Defender* and *Chat Noir Review.*

AVOCATIONAL INTERESTS: Football, reading, sports cars.

*   *   *

FAIR, Sylvia   1933-

PERSONAL: Born January 26, 1933, in Wales; daughter of Thomas Charles (a chemist) and Elizabeth Mary (Andrews) Price; married Keith Fair (a lecturer in art), December 29, 1953; children: Alun (son), Andrea, Hywel (son), Gwilym (son), Iola (daughter). *Education:* Attended Bath Academy of Art, 1951-53. *Religion:* Society of Friends (Quakers). *Home:* Old Rectory, Tothill, Alford, Lincolnshire LN13 0NJ, England.

CAREER: Art teacher in Marlborough, England, 1953-55, and in Matlock, England, 1967-69; peripatetic home tutor in Derbyshire, England, 1969-74.

WRITINGS—Juvenile: The Ivory Anvil, Gollancz, 1974; *The Penny Tin Whistle,* Gollancz, 1976.

WORK IN PROGRESS: A third juvenile novel; *The Bedspread,* a self-illustrated picture book.

SIDELIGHTS: Sylvia Fair writes: "I grew up in the main street of a small Welsh town where we knew every inhabitant. On all sides of me life abounded and I watched, I listened, I absorbed, and still I can recall with alarming clarity odd snippets of conversations and facial expressions from those early years. A second luxury I grew up with was an attic room crammed from floor to ceiling with writing paper. So from a very early age my private world was divided between observing the lives of other people, with all their endearing, human peculiarities; and shutting myself in the attic, painstakingly mastering that stiff old typewriter so that I could write stories.... I frequently made the complete book—jacket, title page, elaborately illuminated capitals, and illustrations....

"It was not until the time came for me to leave school that ... I chose art, perhaps because I had always kept my writing activities a secret (I would never allow anybody to read those books I took so long to make!).... When I did at last collect my courage and decide to write seriously, and to let other people read my stories, I found my background of art a boon. It had sharpened my perception, and made me discover the need to express myself as sincerely and personally as I knew how.

"My books so far have been a mixture of various ingredients: my own childhood memories, the world seen afresh through the 'borrowed' eyes of my children, the relationship of people to place, and an exploration of the imaginative world. The result is an interweaving of fantasy and reality."

*   *   *

FAIRBANKS, Carol   1935-
(C. F. Myers, Carol Fairbanks Myers)

PERSONAL: Born August 19, 1935, in Fairport, N.Y.; daughter of Arthur Loren (a farmer) and Clara Louise (a teacher; maiden name, Hunt) Fairbanks; married Paul Edward Myers, July 2, 1955 (divorced December 17, 1976); children: Ted Fairbanks, Lee Arthur, Timothy Edward. *Education:* Student at Cornell University, 1953-55, and Syracuse University, 1956-57; University of Michigan, Flint, A.B. (with distinction), 1968; University of Wisconsin, Eau Claire, M.A., 1971; University of Minnesota, further study, 1972, 1976. *Politics:* Democrat. *Home:* 1719 Donald Ave., Eau Claire, Wis. 54701. *Office:* Department of English, University of Wisconsin, 359 Hibbard Hall, Eau Claire, Wis. 54701.

CAREER: University of Wisconsin, Eau Claire, instructor in English, 1971—, coordinator of women's studies, 1977—. *Member:* Common Cause, Another Mother for Peace, Great Lakes Women's Studies Organization, Wisconsin Women in Higher Education, Eau Claire Women's Center, Phi Kappa Phi.

WRITINGS: (Under name Carol Fairbanks Myers; with Theressa Rush and Esther Arata) *Black American Writers Past and Present: A Bio-Bibliographical Dictionary,* Scarecrow, 1975; (under name C. F. Myers) *Women in Literature: Criticism of the Seventies,* Scarecrow, 1976, supplement (under name Carol Fairbanks), in press; (with Eugene Engeldinger) *Black American Fiction: A Bibliography*, Scarecrow, in press. Contributor to *CLA Journal* and *Bulletin of Bibliography*. Adviser for *NOTA* (university literary magazine).

WORK IN PROGRESS: Evolutions: Stories about Women, under name Carol Fairbanks, with Edna Hood.

SIDELIGHTS: Carol Fairbanks comments: "My commitment to civil rights and research in Black American literature began while working with Marguerite Randall, Mott Adult Education Program, Flint, Michigan, 1959-1968. As was typical of many white, middle-class women in the early seventies, my focus shifted to the problems of women (and men) in American society. The university classroom provides an opportunity for me to explore with students of all ages the possibilities for more centered lives which are freed, at least to some degree, from sex-role and racial stereotypes."

* * *

FALLWELL, Marshall Leigh, Jr. 1943-

PERSONAL: Born September 8, 1943, in Raleigh, N.C.; son of Marshall Leigh (in U.S. Army) and Frances (Baker) Fallwell; married Margaret Lair (a teacher), September 14, 1964. *Education:* Florence State College, B.A., 1965; Vanderbilt University, M.A., 1967, Ph.D., 1973. *Politics:* Independent. *Home:* 1496 Woodmont Blvd., Nashville, Tenn. 37215.

CAREER: Photographer, musician, actor, and writer; currently working in press relations for country musicians, including Charley Pride. *Member:* American Federation of Television and Radio Artists, American Federation of Musicians.

WRITINGS: Allen Tate: A Bibliography, David Lewis, 1968; *Country Music Encyclopedia*, Crowell, 1974; (with Robert Cornfield) *Just Country*, McGraw, 1976. Author of scripts for public service television. Writer of column "Nashville Beat" in *Photoplay*, 1976-77. Contributor of music articles to magazines.

WORK IN PROGRESS: Editing Vegetius' *De Re Militari*, for Oxford University Press; writing songs.

SIDELIGHTS: Fallwell comments briefly: "Among my professional activities, only the academic ones were planned. Everything else just happened. Country music was here so I got involved." *Avocational interests:* Civil war, archaeology of mid-Tennessee ("I have an extensive collection of Indian artifacts").

* * *

FANCHER, Raymond E(lwood), Jr. 1940-

PERSONAL: Born April 9, 1940, in Waterbury, Conn.; son of Raymond Elwood (a salesman) and Doris (a teacher; maiden name, Crose) Fancher; married Lynn Cogburn (a teacher), February 7, 1964; children: Joelle Elise, Seth Wesley. *Education:* Wesleyan University, B.A., 1962; Harvard University, A.M., 1964, Ph.D., 1967. *Office:* Department of Psychology, York University, 4700 Keele St., Downsview, Ontario, Canada.

CAREER: University of Rochester, Rochester, N.Y., assistant professor of psychology, 1966-70; York University, Downsview, Ontario, assistant professor, 1970-72, associate professor of psychology, 1972—. *Member:* American Psychological Association.

WRITINGS: Psychoanalytic Psychology: The Develop-

ment of Freud's Thought, Norton, 1973; *Pioneers of Psychology: The Lives and Works of Great Early Psychologists*, Norton, in press. Contributor of articles and reviews to psychology and history journals.

WORK IN PROGRESS: Studying papers of Francis Galton, 1822-1911, for a psychobiographical study of his life and work; research on the history of psychology and psychoanalysis, sleep and dreams, empirical studies of psychoanalytic propositions, and "person perception."

SIDELIGHTS: Fancher writes: "Since childhood, I have been fascinated by the biographies of great scientists. Thus in my research on the early psychologists I try to get into their skins to see what motivated them and to view the problems they studied from their own points of view. I try to convey something of this in my books and teaching."

* * *

FANDEL, John 1925-

PERSONAL: Born September 10, 1925, in Yonkers, N.Y.; son of John Peter and Ivy (Ekblom) Fandel. *Education:* Trinity College, Hartford, Conn., A.B., 1948; graduate study at Yale University, 1948-49, and Fordham University, 1951-52; Middlebury College, A.M., 1952. *Religion:* Roman Catholic. *Office:* Department of English, Manhattan College, Bronx, N.Y. 10471.

CAREER: University of Notre Dame, Notre Dame, Ind., instructor in English, 1949-51; Lawrence College (now University), Appleton, Wis., visiting lecturer in English, 1952-53; Manhattan College, Bronx, N.Y., 1958—, began as lecturer, became professor of English. *Military service:* U.S. Naval Reserve, active duty, 1943-46. *Member:* International P.E.N., Poetry Society of America, Phi Beta Kappa.

WRITINGS: The World I Wake, Nordic Press, 1958; *Testament* (poems), Sheed, 1959; *Body of Earth*, Roth, 1972; *The Deserted Greenhouse*, Roth, 1974. Contributor to magazines. Poetry editor of *Commonweal*.

WORK OF PROGRESS: Bach and a Catbird.

* * *

FANG, Josephine (Maria) Riss 1922-

PERSONAL: Born April 3, 1922, in Saalfelden, Austria; came to the United States in 1950, naturalized citizen, 1957; daughter of Hugo M. (a judge) and Josefa (a teacher; maiden name, Knettner) Riss; married Pao-Hsien Fang (a research professor of physics), March 31, 1951; children: Paula, David, Maria, Anna, Peter, John, Joseph, Francis, Christopher, Teresa. *Education:* University of Vienna, absolutorium, 1947; University of Graz, Ph.D., 1948; Catholic University of America, M.S.L.S., 1954; University of Grenoble, certificate, 1961. *Home:* 156 Common St., Belmont, Mass. 02178. *Office:* School of Library Science, Simmons College, 300 Fenway, Boston, Mass. 02115.

CAREER: Catholic University of America, Library, Washington, D.C., special cataloger, 1954-60; Catholic Library Association, Washington, D.C., associate editor of *Guide to Catholic Literature*, 1961-63; *The New Catholic Encyclopedia*, Washington, D.C., research editor, 1963-66; Corpus Instrumentorum, Inc. (publisher), Washington, D.C., editor, 1967-68; Boston College, Chestnut Hill, Mass., head of library's acquisitions department, 1968-69; Simmons College, Boston, Mass., associate professor, 1969-73, professor of library science, 1974—. Adjunct lecturer at University of Maryland, 1966-68; associate professor at Catholic University of America, summers, 1963-68. Participant in international conferences; consultant to Bowker.

MEMBER: American Library Association (and its International Relations Round Table), Association of College and Research Libraries, Association of American Library Schools, Catholic Library Association (member of New England executive board, 1975—), American Association of University Professors (member of local executive board, 1972—; local vice-president and president-elect, 1974-75, president, 1975-76), American Association of University Women, Special Libraries Association, New England Library Association, New England Technical Services Librarians, New England Archivists, Massachusetts Library Association, Beta Phi Mu. *Awards, honors:* Fellowship from Institute of International Education, 1950-51; Marion and Jasper Whiting Foundation award, 1974, for research at libraries in the People's Republic of China; fellowship from Council on Library Resources, 1977-78.

WRITINGS: (Editor with Joseph Placek) *Guide to Catholic Literature: 1961,* Catholic Library Association, 1962; (editor with Placek) *Guide to Catholic Literature: 1962,* Catholic Library Association, 1963; (with Alice H. Songe) *Handbook of National and International Library Associations,* American Library Association, 1973, revised edition published as *International Guide to Library, Archival and Information Science Associations,* Bowker, 1976. Contributor to *Encyclopedia of Library and Information Sciences, New Catholic Encyclopedia, International Encyclopedia of Higher Education,* and *Corpus Dictionary of Western Churches.* Contributor of articles and reviews to library journals. Editor of *CULS* (newsletter of Catholic Library Association), 1966-68; member of editorial board of Association of College and Research Libraries, 1972-76.

WORK IN PROGRESS: Revising *International Guide to Library, Archival and Information Science Associations,* for Bowker; research on education and libraries in the People's Republic of China, with publication expected to result.

SIDELIGHTS: Josephine Fang writes: "Advances in technology and the information explosion have grown to such an extent that the need for international communication and cooperation becomes a matter of mandatory priority. Library cooperation today is not only feasible and desirable, but necessary. National and international projects of common interests are increasing and library associations play an important role in meeting the demands for national planning and international communication. In order to cooperate, we have first to know with whom we should communicate, both in our own countries, and in other parts of the world.

"Through my work, travels, lectures, and publications I hope to promote better understanding and mutual assistance of all those involved in library and information service worldwide."

BIOGRAPHICAL/CRITICAL SOURCES: Simmons Review, spring, 1974; *Janus,* October 11, 1974.

* * *

FANNIN, Allen 1939-

PERSONAL: Born November 1, 1939, in Brooklyn, N.Y.; married Dorothy Meyer (a weaver), December 12, 1964. *Education:* Attended high school in Brooklyn, N.Y. *Home and office address:* P.O. Box 62, Westdale, N.Y. 13483.

CAREER: Weaver, spinner, and producer of handloom woven textile specialties, 1965—; writer, 1967—. Sample weaver for Sutton Mills, 1965-68, and Bridgewater Woolen, 1967-72. Instructor at Haystack Mountain School of Crafts,

1968, 1974, and Brookfield Craft Center, 1972, 1973. Technical consultant for State of Vermont Arts and Crafts Service, and Shelburne Spinners, 1972-76. Has also worked as photographer and church organist. Work is represented in museums and private collections. *Member:* Handweavers Guild of America, New York State Craftsmen, New York Guild of Handweavers (past president).

WRITINGS: Handspinning: Art and Technique, Van Nostrand, 1971; (author of introduction) Godfrey Bowen, *Wool Away: The Art and Technique of Sheering,* Van Nostrand, 1974; *Handloom Weaving Technology,* Van Nostrand, in press. Also author of column, "Looming Thoughts." Contributor to magazines, including *Craft Horizons, Handweaver and Craftsman, Spin-Off Anual,* and *Craft Midwest.*

WORK IN PROGRESS: Research on the application of modern technology to the handcraft process, to make craft work more economically viable.

SIDELIGHTS: Fannin writes: "I have always, at least for as long as I can remember, been a maker of things, particularly where great detail and demanding skill is required. This carries over into writing in that I tend to write long, technical material with considerable detail. Unlike some craft writers, I do not simply treat the matter as a leisure time activity for those whose income is sufficiently superfluous to permit costly leisure work. I believe that with so much of the world's people still lacking basic things, we cannot really afford to approach craft work without fully integrating it into the mainstream of economically productive human endeavors. The majority of modern day craftsmen and craftswomen come to the field from an economically advantaged background. This has fostered the widespread craft-as-art approach so much in evidence. For myself, growing up in circumstances where I had to make rather than buy what I wanted and where I had to earn a living at an early age, it means that I approach the work in much the same way as did craftsmen of earlier times: producing what a customer wants in the best way possible. My own self-expression is generally not manifest as a primary design element."

BIOGRAPHICAL/CRITICAL SOURCES: Lee Nordness, *Objects: USA,* Viking, 1970; Carolyn Meyer, *People Who Make Things,* Antheneum, 1975; Samella Lewis, *Art: African American,* Harcourt, in press; *New Rochelle Standard Star,* September 30, 1966; *Seattle Post-Intelligencer,* May 5, 1968; *Durham Sun,* February 5, 1969; *New York Times,* April 1, 1969; *Baltimore Afro-American,* December 7, 1974; *Baltimore Sun,* December 15, 1974.

* * *

FANNING, Buckner 1926-

PERSONAL: Born March 13, 1926, in Houston, Tex.; son of Charles A. and Beryl (Buckner) Fanning; married Martha Ann Howell, June 5, 1949; children: Michael, Stephen, Lisa. *Education:* Baylor University, B.A., 1949; New Orleans Baptist Theological Seminary, graduate study; Southwestern Seminary, B.D., 1953. *Politics:* Democrat. *Home:* 2327 Blanton, San Antonio, Tex. 78209. *Office:* Trinity Baptist Church, 319 East Mulberry, San Antonio, Tex. 78212.

CAREER: Ordained Southern Baptist minister; evangelist (conducting revival crusades and evangelistic campaigns all over the United States), 1949-59; Trinity Baptist Church, San Antonio, Tex., pastor, 1959—. Member of board of trustees of Baylor University; member of advisory board of Hawaii Baptist Academy; president of Buckner Fanning Evangelistic Foundation. Member of board of directors, Planned Parenthood of Bexar County, HemisFair '68;

member of Urban Coalition of San Antonio and local Human Resources Council; chairman of Billy Graham Evangelistic Crusade of San Antonio. Former member of board of trustees, University of Corpus Christi, Howard Payne College, and Baptist Hospital of San Antonio; former vice-president of Baptist General Convention of Texas and member of its executive board; former member of Foreign Mission Board of Southern Baptist Convention. Speaker at the Pentagon, 1971; has appeared on television programs. *Military service:* U.S. Marine Corps, 1943-46; served in the Pacific and Japan. *Member:* Sigma Tau Delta. *Awards, honors:* D.D. from Howard Payne College, 1962.

WRITINGS: Christ in Your Shoes, Broadman, 1970; *Throw Away the Garbage,* Word Books, 1976. Author of television film, "Nagasaki: One Man's Return," 1976.

SIDELIGHTS: Fanning's church, under his leadership, has sponsored churches in Jamaica, a rehabilitation home for women alcoholics, and two homes for dependent and neglected young people. Fanning has led groups of people to countries behind the Iron Curtain for evangelistic purposes, and has himself traveled and preached in twenty-nine countries. His 1975 trip to Japan was televised nationally in the United States and led to an interview on the "Today Show."

* * *

FANNING, Louis A(lbert) 1927-

PERSONAL: Born January 31, 1927, in Berwyn, Ill.; son of Louis A. (an accountant) and Alice (Moysey) Fanning; married Helen Hoffsommer (a receptionist), July 14, 1952; children: Jeanne, Kurt. *Education:* University of Illinois, B.A., 1951; C. W. Post College of Long Island University, M.A., 1966; St. John's University, Jamaica, N.Y., Ph.D., 1975. *Politics:* "Conservative-Libertarian." *Religion:* "Deist." *Home:* 76 Birch Ave., Farmingdale, N.Y. 11735. *Office:* Department of History, State University of New York College at Farmingdale, Farmingdale, N.Y. 11735.

CAREER: State University of New York College at Farmingdale, instructor, 1963-66, assistant professor, 1966-68, associate professor, 1968-75, professor of history, 1975—. *Military service:* U.S. Army Reserve, intelligence officer, active duty, 1952-53; served in Japan; became major. *Member:* Irish-American Society (member of board of directors), Gilgo Yacht Club.

WRITINGS: Betrayal in Vietnam, Arlington House, 1975. Contributor to *Exchange* and *University Bookman.*

WORK IN PROGRESS: Research on the work of American revisionist historians, with particular interest in James J. Martin, Charles Tansill, and Charles A. Beard.

SIDELIGHTS: Fanning writes: "I am convinced that the American people have been, and are being, subjected to the greatest propaganda campaign in the history of any society by the government, the media, and other manipulative groups. It is my hope that I can make a contribution to our times by presenting documentary evidence of events as they actually happened, not as some power bloc wants them portrayed."

* * *

FANTE, John (Thomas) 1911-

PERSONAL: Born April 8, 1911, in Denver, Colo.; son of Nicholas Peter and Mary (Capolungo) Fante; married Joyce Smart (a poet), 1937; children: one son. *Education:* Attended University of Colorado and Long Beach Junior College. *Residence:* Roseville, Calif.

CAREER: Writer. Writes for motion picture industry. Has worked in a cannery, as a hotel clerk, stevedore, and grocery clerk; during World War II worked for Office of War Information.

WRITINGS: Wait Until Spring, Bandini (novel), Stackpole, 1938; *Ask the Dust* (novel), Stackpole, 1939; *Dago Red* (short stories), Viking, 1940; *Full of Life,* Little, Brown, 1952; *Bravo, Burro!* (juvenile), Hawthorn, 1970. Contributor to *American Mercury, Woman's Home Companion, Story, Atlantic Monthly.*

WORK IN PROGRESS: A book, tentatively entitled *Mater Dolorosa.*

BIOGRAPHICAL/CRITICAL SOURCES: Time, October 7, 1940; *San Francisco Chronicle,* March 9, 1941; Olga Peragollo, *Italian-American Authors and Their Contribution to American Literature,* S. F. Vanni, 1949.*

* * *

FARKAS, Emil 1946-

PERSONAL: Born April 20, 1946, in Hungary; came to the United States in 1965, naturalized citizen, 1975; son of Albert and Antonia Farkas; married Marika Komlos. *Education:* San Fernando Valley State College, B.A., 1970. *Religion:* Jewish. *Home:* 1127 North Laurel Ave., Los Angeles, Calif. 90069. *Agent:* Aaron M. Priest Literary Agency, 150 East 35th St., New York, N.Y. 10016. *Office:* Creative Action, Inc., 9085 Santa Monica Blvd., Los Angeles, Calif. 90069.

CAREER: Free-lance writer, 1970—. Chief instructor at Beverly Hills Karate Academy, 1970—. President and partner of Creative Action, Inc., 1974—; president of National Self-Defense Institute, 1976—. Part-time high school teacher of self-defense; part-time instructor at University of California, Los Angeles. Co-chairman of Maccabee Games for Israel (Karate Division). Technical adviser and fight coordinator for films and television, including "Mannix," "S.W.A.T.," "Killer Elite," "Easy Rider," "That Man Bolt," "Ginger," and "Mod Squad." *Member:* Screen Actors Guild. *Awards, honors:* Won black belt competitions in Judo and Karate in the United States and Europe.

WRITINGS: The Martial Arts Catalogue, Simon & Schuster, 1977; *Fight Back: A Woman's Guide to Self-Defense,* Holt, 1977.

Author of film scripts, "Anatomy of Revenge" and "Project: Silent Night." Writer of column "Western Wrap Up" in *Official Karate.*

WORK IN PROGRESS: Martial Arts Encyclopedia; Self-Defense for Senior Citizens.

SIDELIGHTS: Farkas told *CA:* "The need for self-defense training in today's society is as vital as knowing how to drive a car safely. The skills we possess may not guarantee against accidents, but they can greatly reduce the chance of suffering personal injury or property damage.

"I advocate that every woman learn practical self defense skills that are easily applied." Farkas continued. "The key, I feel, is anticipation and prevention. A person can learn to become aware, to watch for warning signals that violent behavior is imminent. Being aware enables one to avoid situations which could result in confrontation; for example, when boarding a bus one assumes a greater risk if she or he takes a window seat in the rear instead of sitting near the operator and close to other passengers. In short, I feel the best defense is to learn how to avoid danger, but to have the tools to fight back with if it becomes necessary."

BIOGRAPHICAL/CRITICAL SOURCES: *Karate Illustrated,* November, 1973; *Fighting Stars,* December, 1973; *Inside Kung-Fu,* January, 1975; *Official Karate,* autumn, 1976; *Black Belt,* December, 1976.

* * *

FARNHAM, Emily 1912-

PERSONAL: Born May 27, 1912, in Kent, Ohio; daughter of Burt Leonard and Metta (Lake) Farnum. *Education:* Kent State University, B.Sc.Ed. (honors), 1933; Ohio State University, M.A., 1934, Ph.D., 1959; also attended Cleveland School of Art, California College of Arts and Crafts, University of Southern California, Art Students League of New York, and Hans Hofmann School of Fine Arts. *Politics:* Republican. *Religion:* Presbyterian. *Home:* 1108 South Overlook Dr., Greenville, N.C. 27834.

CAREER: Ohio State University, Columbus, instructor in design, 1934-37; Michigan State University, East Lansing, instructor in painting, drawing, and design, 1937; Utah State University, Logan, instructor in painting and design, 1938-41; Stout State College (now University), Menomonie, Wis., assistant professor of painting, drawing, and design, and head of related art department, 1942-45; commercial artist in Los Angeles, Calif., 1945-47; Southern Illinois University, Carbondale, assistant professor of painting and drawing, 1947-53; Ohio State University, assistant professor of watercolor painting and costume design, 1954-55; Mary Baldwin College, Staunton, Va., associate professor of art history and painting, 1956-62; East Carolina University, Greenville, N.C., professor of art history, painting, and drawing, 1962-77, chairman of department of art history, 1966-71. Faculty member at University of Virginia, winter, 1958. Solo and group exhibitions in the United States and Germany; member of North Carolina Art Commission, 1973-80. Consultant on American artist Charles Demuth.

MEMBER: International P.E.N., College Art Association of America, American Association of University Women, Daughters of the American Revolution, North Carolina Art Society, East Carolina Art Society, Southeast College Art Conference. *Awards, honors:* National Book Award nomination, 1972, for *Charles Demuth: Behind a Laughing Mask.*

WRITINGS: Charles Demuth: Behind a Laughing Mask, University of Oklahoma Press, 1971. Contributor to art journals.

WORK IN PROGRESS: The Geometric Basis of Great Painting; Basic Lessons in Dynamic Form: A First Book on Design; Memoirs of a Professor.

* * *

FARQUHAR, Margaret C(utting) 1905-

PERSONAL: Born October 6, 1905, in Worcester, Mass.; daughter of Frank Whitney (a banker) and Amy (a music supervisor; maiden name, Peavey) Cutting; married David Farquhar (divorced). *Education:* Attended Olivet College, 1924-26; University of Michigan, A.B., 1928; Columbia University, M.A., 1935. *Religion:* Congregationalist. *Home and office:* 417 Greenfield Hill Rd., Fairfield, Conn. 06430. *Agent:* McIntosh & Otis, 475 Fifth Ave., New York, N.Y. 10017.

CAREER: Elementary school teacher in Madison, N.J., 1932-36, and Great Neck, N.Y., 1936-43; Cleveland Public Library, Cleveland, Ohio, children's librarian, 1949-51; Willimantic State Teachers College, Willimantic, Conn., assistant professor of children's literature, 1951-52; Pequot Library, Southport, Conn., head librarian, 1952-59; librarian in public schools of Fairfield, Conn., 1959-73; writer, 1973—. Assistant professor at Connecticut State Teachers College, New Haven, 1953-54. Member of Connecticut Governor's Commission on Libraries, 1962-63; member of Newbery-Caldecott Award Committee, 1966, 1968. Consultant to Grosset, 1951-58. *Member:* Authors Guild of Authors League of America, American Association of University Women, American Library Association, American School Library Association (regional director, 1969-71), Connecticut School Library Association (member of board of directors, 1959-73; president, 1970-71). *Awards, honors:* Rheta A. Clark Award from Connecticut School Library Association, 1973.

WRITINGS—For children: (Editor) *Favorite Read Aloud Stories,* Grosset, 1958; *Lights: A Book to Begin On,* Holt, 1960; *Colonial Life in America,* Holt, 1962; *Indian Children of America,* Holt, 1964; *Indians of Mexico,* Holt, 1967.

Work represented in anthology, *Read Me More Stories,* edited by Child Study Association of America, Crowell, 1951. Contributor to education and library journals and to children's magazines.

WORK IN PROGRESS: Research on Indian lore and medicine, the Pequot Indians, and lost Indian tribes.

SIDELIGHTS: Margaret Farquhar writes: "Love of reading as a child motivated my interest as a teacher and librarian in producing stories of my own. An expressed need for the non-fiction subject areas for first readers motivated the four books in the 'Books to Begin On' series."

* * *

FARRAR-HOCKLEY, Anthony Heritage 1924-

PERSONAL: Born April 8, 1924, in Coventry, Warwickshire, England; son of Arthur Farrar-Hockley; married Margaret Bernadette Wells, 1945; children: three sons (one deceased). *Education:* Attended Exeter School. *Office:* Headquarters, Fourth Division, British Forces Post Office 15, England.

CAREER: British Army, career officer, 1939—. Member of Gloucestershire Regiment, 1939-42; 1st Airborne Division, served in Greece, Italy, and southern France, 1942-45, in Palestine, 1945-46, Korea, 1950-53, Cyprus and Port Said, 1956, and Jordan, 1958; college chief instructor at Royal Military Academy, Sandhurst, England, 1959-61; commander of parachute battalion in the Persian Gulf, 1962-65; principal staff officer to director of Borneo Operations, 1965-66; commander of 16th Parachute Brigade, 1966-68; defense fellow at Exeter College, Oxford, 1968-70; director of public relations for the army, 1970; commander of land forces in Northern Ireland, 1970-71; commanding officer of 4th Division, 1971-73; commandant of Prince of Wales Division and director of army combat development in the Ministry of Defense, 1974—; present rank, major general.

MEMBER: Strategic Studies, Military Commentators' Circle, Savage Club (London). *Awards, honors*—Military: Military Cross, 1944; companion of Distinguished Service Order, 1953, with bar, 1964; Order of the British Empire, 1957; mentioned in dispatches.

WRITINGS: The Edge of the Sword, Muller, 1954; (editor) Ian Standish Hamilton, *The Commander,* Hollis & Carter, 1957; *True Book About the Second World War,* Muller, 1959; *The Somme,* Dufour, 1964; *Death of an Army,* Arthur Barker, 1967, Morrow, 1968; *The War in the Desert,* Faber,

1969; *Airborne Carpet: Operation Market Garden,* Ballantine, 1969; *Student,* Ballantine, 1973; *Goughie: The Life of General Sir Hubert Gough,* Hart-Davis, 1975; (with Elizabeth Monroe) *The Arab-Israel War, October, 1973: Background and Events,* International Institute for Strategic Studies, 1975. Contributor to *History of the Second World War* and *History of the Great War.*

AVOCATIONAL INTERESTS: Cricket, badminton, walking.*

* * *

FARRELL, Michael 1944-

PERSONAL: Born May 15, 1944, in County Derry, Northern Ireland; son of Thomas and Helena (O'Reilly) Farrell; married Orla O'Hare, 1964; children: Sean. *Education:* Queen's University, Belfast, Northern Ireland, B.A., 1967; University of Strathclyde, graduate study, 1967-68. *Politics:* "Marxist (Trotskyist)." *Religion:* None. *Home:* 20 Trench Ave., Belfast II, Northern Ireland. *Office:* Connolly Bookshop, Avoca Park, Anderstown, Belfast, Northern Ireland.

CAREER: Belfast College of Technology, Belfast, Northern Ireland, teacher of history and general studies, 1968—. Founding member and member of central committee of Peoples Democracy ("a Marxist group dedicated to achieving a united Socialist Ireland").

WRITINGS: Northern Ireland, the Orange State (political history from a socialist viewpoint), Urizen, 1976; *Northern Ireland: An Anti-Imperialist Struggle* (monograph), Merlin Press, in press. Author of political pamphlets. Contributor to magazines. Editor of *Unfree Citizen,* 1976—.

WORK IN PROGRESS: Research on the links between British forces and paramilitary armed gangs during the establishment of Northern Ireland, 1920-25.

SIDELIGHTS: Farrell writes that he was raised in a Roman Catholic family in rural Northern Ireland and studied briefly for the priesthood. He was prominent in the leadership of the civil rights struggle in Northern Ireland between 1968 and 1970. He stood for Parliament against Ian Paisley. He was jailed without benefit of trial in 1971 and again in 1973, but was released after a thirty-five-day hunger strike. He writes: "I have become steadily more committed to Marxism as I have seen the naked violence used by the world's oldest democracy (Britain) in Northern Ireland. My main interest is the struggle of mankind to be free."

* * *

FARWELL, George Michell 1911-1976

October 3, 1911—August, 1976; British-born Australian free-lance writer, literary critic, and author of popular books, including *Ned Kelly: The Life and Adventures of Australia's Notorious Bushranger.* He died in Adelaide, Australia. Obituaries: *AB Bookman's Weekly,* October 4, 1976. (See index for previous *CA* sketch)

* * *

FAXON, Alicia Craig 1931-

PERSONAL: Born July 27, 1931, in New York, N.Y.; daughter of William Donald (a military captain) and Alicia H. Craig; married Richard Bremer Faxon (a clergyman), February 21, 1953; children: Richard Paul, Thomas H. *Education:* Vassar College, B.A. (magna cum laude), 1952; Radcliffe College, M.A., 1953; Boston University, M.A.,

1971, doctoral candidate, 1975—. *Religion:* Episcopal. *Home:* 451 Concord Rd., Sudbury, Mass. 01776. *Office:* New England School of Art, 28 Newbury St., Boston, Mass.

CAREER: High school teacher of English in Washington, D.C., 1955-56; American Historical Association, Washington, D.C., research assistant, 1958; University of Maryland, College Park, instructor in American history, 1961-63; DeCordova Museum School, teacher of art history, 1972, 1973; New England School of Art, Boston, Mass., instructor in art history, 1974—. Visiting lecturer at Tufts University, 1973; instructor at Massachusetts College of Art, 1975; member of DeCordova Museum Print Council; member of board of trustees of Danforth Museum, 1974—, chairman of exhibition committee and guest curator, autumn, 1975. *Member:* National League of American Penwomen, Boston Authors Club, Vassar Club (Boston; chairman of Lockwood Seminars), Phi Beta Kappa.

WRITINGS: Collecting Art on a Shoestring, Barre, 1969; *Women and Jesus,* United Church Press, 1973. Contributor to local magazines and newspapers. Art critic for *Minute-Man,* 1971-73, and *Real Paper,* 1975, 1976.

WORK IN PROGRESS: Research on French artist Jean-Louis Forain, 1852-1931.

SIDELIGHTS: Alicia Faxon writes: "My interest at present in art history seems to be taking top priority over all forms of writing, and I hope eventually to put my findings on Forain into book form."

* * *

FECK, Luke 1935-

PERSONAL: Born August 15, 1935, in Cincinnati, Ohio; son of J. Franz and Mercedes R. Feck; married wife, Gail, August 12, 1962; children: Lisa, Mara, Paul. *Education:* University of Cincinnati, B.A., 1957. *Religion:* Roman Catholic. *Home:* 1340 Observatory Dr., Cincinnati, Ohio 45208. *Office: Cincinnati Enquirer,* 617 Vine St., Cincinnati, Ohio 45201.

CAREER: Ackerman & Feck Press, Cincinnati, Ohio, president, 1963-69; *Cincinnati Enquirer,* Cincinnati, Ohio, executive editor, 1975—, also television editor and author of column. Member of board of directors of Cincinnati Convention and Visitors Bureau. *Military service:* U.S. Army, 1957-59; became first lieutenant.

MEMBER: American Society of Newspaper Editors, Associated Press Managing Editors Association, Associated Press Society of Ohio, Cincinnati Historical Society, Sigma Delta Chi (vice-president of local chapter, 1975-76; president, 1976-77), Cincinnatus.

WRITINGS: Yesterday's Cincinnati, E. A. Seeman, 1975.

* * *

FEERICK, John D(avid) 1936-

PERSONAL: Born July 12, 1936, in New York; son of John (a bus driver) and Mary (Boyle) Feerick; married Emalie Platt, August 25, 1962; children: Maureen, Margaret, Jean, Rosemary, John D., Jr., William. *Education:* Fordham University, B.S., 1958, LL.B., 1961. *Religion:* Roman Catholic. *Home:* 41 Highridge Rd., Mount Kisco, N.Y. 10549. *Office:* Skadden, Arps, Slate, Meagher & Flom, 919 Third Ave., New York, N.Y. 10022.

CAREER: Skadden, Arps, Slate, Meagher & Flom (law firm), New York City, partner, 1961—. Chairman of board of trustees of Center for Information on America. Associate adjunct professor at Fordham University. *Member:* American Bar Association (chairman of committee on election reform), American Judicature Society (member of board of directors), New York State Bar Association (member of civil rights committee, 1972-73), Association of the Bar of the City of New York (chairperson of committee on federal legislation), Fordham University Law Review Alumni Association (president, 1971-73), Fordham University Law Alumni Association (president, 1974-78). *Awards, honors:* Special award from American Bar Association, 1966, for work on the twenty-fifth amendment to the U.S. Constitution; Eugene J. Keefe Award from Fordham University, 1975, Fordham Law Review Association Award, 1977.

WRITINGS: From Failing Hands: The Story of Presidential Succession, Fordham University Press, 1965; (with wife, Emalie P. Feerick) *The Vice Presidents of the United States,* F. Watts, 1967; *The Twenty-Fifth Amendment,* Fordham University Press, 1976. Contributor of about thirty-five articles to law journals and to newspapers. Editor-in-chief of *Fordham University Law Review,* 1960-61.

*   *   *

FEILD, Reshad   1934-

PERSONAL: Legal name Richard Timothy Field; born April 15, 1934, in England; came to the United States in 1974, became resident, 1976; son of John and Esme (Hawkesworth) Feild; married Rachael Tower, January 12, 1964 (divorced, 1971); married Denise Ann Hamilton, December 19, 1975; children: (first marriage) Robin; (second marriage) Oran (son). *Education:* Educated in private schools in England. *Office:* Mevlana Foundation, 1931 Mapleton St., Boulder, Col. 80302.

CAREER: Has worked as stockbroker, advertising agent, waterskiing instructor, antique and art dealer, and interior decorator; now spiritual adviser to Mevlana Foundation, Boulder, Colo., and to Vancouver Turning Society. *Military service:* British Navy, navigating officer, 1952-54; became sub-lieutenant.

WRITINGS: Cooperation in the Three Worlds, privately printed, 1975; *The Last Barrier: A Journey Through the World of Sufi Teaching,* Harper, 1976. Contributor to magazines, including *East-West Journal* and *New Age Journal.*

WORK IN PROGRESS: To Know We're Loved; Turning, "a book of words, photographs, and graphics"; two shorter books compiled from talks and lectures.

SIDELIGHTS: Feild comes from a family whose documented history has been traced as far back as the tenth century. He was educated in private schools, but found that the kind of life he was leading did not appeal to him. At the age of twenty-five, he traveled around the United States as a folk singer, and eventually went to Japan, where he lived in a Zen Buddhist monastery for awhile before moving on to Thailand and India. It was in the Himalayas in northern Pakistan that he encountered Sufism. From that time, he spent most of his time studying spiritual healing. *The Last Barrier* is the first book of a trilogy relating his experiences in Turkey.

He writes: "*The Last Barrier* and the sequel, and indeed nearly all of my writing comes from twenty-five years of study of the inner meaning of life in many countries in the world, particularly the study of Sufism in the Middle East and the Druids in England. I have been a professional dowser for many years and a part-time healer and counsellor. I am interested in the setting-up of communities based

on spiritual principles, which I am now doing." He has made about eighty-five tape recordings of lectures and talks which are available to the public.

AVOCATIONAL INTERESTS: Gardening, birds, animals, fishing, antiques.

*   *   *

FEIN, Irving A(shley)   1911-

PERSONAL: Born June 21, 1911, in Brooklyn, N.Y.; son of Harry (a builder) and Fannie (Milstein) Fein; married Florence Kohn, December 21, 1941 (died May 8, 1968); married Marion Shepard Schechter, June 21, 1969; children: (first marriage) Michael Anthony, Patricia Ann. *Education:* Attended University of Baltimore, 1928, and University of Wisconsin Experimental College, 1930-32; St. Lawrence University, LL.B., 1936. *Home:* 1100 North Alta Loma Rd., Los Angeles, Calif. 90069. *Agent:* Arthur Pine Associates, Inc., 1780 Broadway, New York, N.Y. 10019.

CAREER: Warner Brothers, New York City and Hollywood, Calif., publicist, 1933-41; Samuel Goldwyn Productions, Hollywood, assistant publicity director, 1941-42; Columbia Pictures, Hollywood, director of exploitation, 1942-44; Warner Brothers, director of exploitation, 1944-46; Columbia Pictures, director of exploitation, 1946-47; Amusement Enterprises, Hollywood, in public relations, 1947-51; Columbia Broadcasting System (CBS)-Radio, Hollywood, in public exploitation, 1951-53, and public relations, 1953-55, vice-president in New York City, 1955-56; J & M Productions, Inc., Beverly Hills, Calif., president, 1956-65; JB Productions, executive vice-president, 1965-74. Executive vice-president for J.A.C. Productions, 1965-75. Executive producer of Jack Benny television programs, 1958-74, and George Burns special programs, 1974—; manager for Jack Benny, 1965-74, and George Burns, 1974—. *Awards, honors:* Emmy Award from Academy of Television Arts and Sciences, 1961, for "Jack Benny Show."

WRITINGS: Jack Benny: An Intimate Biography, Putnam, 1976. Author of material for television and radio. Contributor to magazines and newspapers.

WORK IN PROGRESS: A novel; a motion picture script.

*   *   *

FEINSTEIN, Elaine   1930-

PERSONAL: Born October 24, 1930, in Bootle, England; daughter of Isidore and Fay (Compton) Cooklin; married Arnold Feinstein (an immunologist), July 22, 1957; children: Adam, Martin, Joel. *Education:* Cambridge University, B.A., 1952, M.A., 1955. *Agent:* Olwyn Hughes, 100 Chetwynd Road, London NW5, England.

CAREER: Cambridge University Press, London, England, editorial staff member, 1960-62; Bishop's Stortford Training College, Hertfordshire, England, lecturer in English, 1963-66; University of Essex, Wivenhoe, England, assistant lecturer in literature, 1967-70; has also worked as a journalist. *Member:* Poetry Society, Eastern Arts Association. *Awards, honors:* Arts Council grants, 1970, 1977; Daisy Miller Award, 1971, for fiction.

WRITING—Poems: In a Green Eye, Goliard Press, 1966; *The Magic Apple Tree,* Hutchinson, 1971; *At the Edge,* Sceptre Press, 1972; *The Celebrants and Other Poems,* Hutchinson, 1973; *Some Unease and Angels,* Green River Press, 1977.

Novels: *The Circle,* Hutchinson, 1970; *The Amerstone Exit,*

Hutchinson, 1972; *The Glass Alembic,* Hutchinson, 1973, published as *The Crystal Garden,* Dutton, 1974; *The Children of the Rose,* Hutchinson, 1974; *The Ecstasy of Dr. Miriam Garner,* Hutchinson, 1976.

Other: (Editor) *Selected Poems of John Clare,* University Tutorial Press, 1968; (translator) *The Selected Poems of Marina Tsvetayeva,* Oxford University Press, 1971; *Matters of Chance* (short stories), Covent Garden Press, 1972.

Also author of British Broadcasting Corp. (BBC) teleplay, "Breath," 1975.

WORK IN PROGRESS: A biography of Marina Tsvetayeva for Oxford University Press, publication expected in 1978; a novel; a new collection of poems.

SIDELIGHTS: Feinstein told *CA:* "I began to write poetry in the '60's very *consciously* influenced by American poets; at a time when the use of line, and spacing, to indicate the movement of poetry, was much less fashionable than it is now among young British poets. It was my translations from the Russian of Marina Tsvetayeva, however, that gave me my true voice, or at least made me attend to a strength and forward push, *against* and *within* a formal structure, that I could have only learnt from Tsvetayevea herself."

* * *

FELDERMAN, Eric 1944-

PERSONAL: Born October 14, 1944, in New York, N.Y.; son of Leon and Beatrice (Jacobson) Felderman. *Education:* Columbia University, A.B. (magna cum laude), 1965; Cornell University, M.A., 1966; State University of New York at Buffalo, Ph.D., 1969. *Religion:* Jewish. *Home:* 20 Metropolitan Oval, Apt. 11-B, New York, N.Y. 10462.

CAREER: Yale University, New Haven, Conn., instructor, 1969-70, assistant professor of English, 1970-74; Cooper Union, New York, N.Y., assistant professor of humanities, 1975; writer, 1975—. Also illustrates and draws, composes songs, and directs videotape films. *Member:* Phi Beta Kappa.

WRITINGS: The Dummy's Soliloquy (poems), Columbia Review Press, 1965; *Love Poem* (poems), Zahir, 1974; *The Book of Lies* (fiction and poetry), Cat's Pajamas Press, 1975; *Garden Street* (novel), Holmgangers Press, 1976; *Animal Book* (fiction and poetry), Holmgangers Press, 1977.

Poetry anthologized in *Academy of American Poets Award Anthology,* edited by William Meredith, Academy of American Poets, 1966; *The Young American Writers,* edited by Richard Kostelanetz, Funk, 1967. Contributor of poems to magazines and newspapers, including *Amazing Grace, Aspect, Assembling, Beyond Baroque, Columbia Review, Twigs, Wind,* and *Wisconsin Review.*

WORK IN PROGRESS: Editing a collection of his stories and poems; a screenplay; three other books.

SIDELIGHTS: Felderman writes to *CA:* "Much of my writing reflects the perennial tension between strong religious intimations and consciousness of meaningless suffering."

* * *

FELDMAN, Annette Gerber 1913-

PERSONAL: Born April 17, 1913, in Asbury Park, N.J.; daughter of Emanuel (a pharmacist) and Gertrude (Fisher) Gerber; married Irving Feldman (a merchant), July 9, 1939; children: Elaine Feldman Marks, Millicent Feldman Feiner, Jessica Feldman Danzig. *Education:* New York University,

B.S., 1935; Traphagen School of Design, graduate study, 1951. *Religion:* Jewish. *Home and office:* 1725 York Ave., New York, N.Y. 10028. *Agent:* Bertha Klausner, International Literary Agency, Inc., 71 Park Ave., New York, N.Y. 10016.

CAREER: Annette Feldman Designs, New York, N.Y., interior designer, 1951—. Writer. *Member:* National Home Fashions League, American Society of Interior Designers, Fashion Group of New York.

WRITINGS: Knit, Purl, and Design!, Harper, 1972; *Crochet and Creative Design,* Harper, 1973; *Beginner's Needlecraft,* Harper, 1974; *Handmade Lace and Patterns,* Harper, 1975; *The Needlework Boutique,* Rutledge Books, 1977. Author of column "Your Decorating Clinic" in *Woman's Homecraft,* 1970-72. Contributor to design magazines. Associate editor of *Digest and Review,* 1935. Consultant to Time-Life Books.

WORK IN PROGRESS: A Book About Hats (tentative title), publication by Van Nostrand expected in 1978; *Needlework for Home Decor* (tentative title), Rutledge Books, 1978.

SIDELIGHTS: Annette Feldman writes: "Born with talent, it is my strong motivating desire to share my gift of a sense of good design with all who want to know and enjoy the rewards of being aware of the basic principles of line, color, and perspective in relationship to a well-coordinated total whole in their home and living surroundings; and beyond this, to be able to impart a knowledge of all craft skills with which others can explore their own innate talents and learn to create beautiful designs of their own, both for home and personal dress."

* * *

FELDMAN, Leonard 1927-
(Daniel Elliot)

PERSONAL: Born February 21, 1927, in Chicago, Ill.; son of David (a realtor) and Nettie (Applebaum) Feldman; married Rayma J. Mandelbaum (a librarian), June 19, 1949; children: Dianne E. Feldman Cohen, Daniel E. *Education:* City College (now of the City University of New York), B.E.E., 1950. *Politics:* Republican. *Religion:* Jewish. *Home and office:* 97 Oxford Blvd., Great Neck, N.Y. 11023.

CAREER: Fisher Radio Corp., Long Island City, N.Y., project engineer, 1951-56; Madison-Fielding Corp., Brooklyn, N.Y., president, 1956-60; Crosby Electronics, Syosset, N.Y., director of engineering, 1961-63; Vanity Fair Electronics, Syosset, chief engineer, 1963-70; free-lance writer and consultant, 1970—. Technical director of Institute of High Fidelity. *Military service:* U.S. Navy, 1945-46. *Member:* Institute of Electronic and Electrical Engineers, Audio Engineering Society, Eta Kappa Nu, Tau Beta Pi.

WRITINGS: FM Multiplexing for Stereo, Sams, 1962, 3rd edition, 1973; *Hi-Fi Projects for the Hobbyist,* Sams, 1963, 2nd edition, 1973; *FM from Antenna to Audio,* Sams, 1969; *Four Channel Sound,* Sams, 1973; *The Rolling Stone Guide to High Fidelity,* Straight Arrow Books, 1974; *Official Guide to High Fidelity,* revised edition (Feldman not associated with first edition), Sams for Institute of High Fidelity, 1977.

Author of columns, "The Feldman Report," in *Consumer Electronics Monthly,* "Soundings," in *Genesis,* "Acoustics" (under name Len Feldman) in *Rolling Stone,* and in *Cue* (under pseudonym Daniel Elliot). Contributor to magazines, including *Esquire, Apartment Life,* and *Modern Hi-Fi and Music.* Technical editor of *FM Guide* and *Tape Deck Quarterly;* audio editor of *Modern Recording;* contributing editor of *Radio-Electronics* and *Audio.*

SIDELIGHTS: Feldman writes: "My interest in electronics dates back to childhood. A love of music motivated my specialization as an audio engineer. Even when employed, I began writing on high fidelity subjects as a 'moonlighting' activity. Consultation, and the acceptance of my writings, led to abandonment of 'regular employment' in favor of full-time consultant work and writing, which, coupled with my own laboratory, has expanded into a full-time activity."

*   *   *

FENDELMAN, Helaine Woll   1942-

PERSONAL: Born January 25, 1942, in Chicago, Ill.; daughter of Albert A. and Pearl (Loeb) Woll; married Burton M. Fendelman (a lawyer), July 4, 1965; children: Barton Douglas, Jonathan Woll. *Education:* Attended Evansville College, summers, 1960-61, and University of Illinois, 1960-62; Washington University, St. Louis, Mo., B.A., 1964; Long Island University, graduate study, 1967-70. *Home:* 1248 Post Rd., Scarsdale, N.Y. 10583.

CAREER: High School English teacher in Ladue, Mo., 1964-65; junior high school English teacher in Great Neck, N.Y., 1965-68; Simon & Schuster, Inc., New York, N.Y., proofreader, 1968; antique dealer, 1968-76; M. Schorsch, Inc., Greenwich, Conn., assistant to the president, 1976—. Antique lecturer and appraiser, 1975—. Guest curator of Museum of American Folk Art, 1975, and organizer and chairperson of its Friends Committee, 1976—, organizer of "Tramp Art Traveling Exhibition," 1976-77. Member of Alumni Council executive board of Washington University, St. Louis, Mo., 1968-75. *Member:* Fresh Air Fund (co-chairperson, 1970-75), Scarsdale Historical Society (member of board of advisers, 1975—).

WRITINGS: Tramp Art, Dutton, 1975. Contributor to *Americana* and *Fine Woodworking.*

WORK IN PROGRESS: Research on sculptured and incised stoneware pottery of the eighteenth and nineteenth centuries; research on books about antiques that were published in the 1920's.

SIDELIGHTS: Fendelman told *CA:* "Basically, Tramp Art is chip, notch or edge carved pieces of cigar box wood layered one piece on top of another to form boxes, frames and even full-sized pieces of furniture. This work was done by skilled intinerant crafts people, brick layers, stone masons, carpenters, forming a part of American cultural history spanning the sixty years around the turn of the twentieth century, 1860-1930. Until recently, the phenomena of Tramp Art had been overlooked. Sometimes the carving of cigar boxes into utilitarian and whimsical objects was a leisure time activity. Sometimes the finished objects were used as a means of barter for food or lodging."

*   *   *

FENWICK, Sheridan   1942-

PERSONAL: Born October 10, 1942, in Pittsburgh, Pa.; daughter of Robert T. (a film producer and writer) and Janet (a teacher; maiden name, Jones) Fenwick; married Murray P. Naditch (a psychologist), July 5, 1964. *Education:* Goucher College, B.A., 1963; Yale University, graduate study, 1963-64; Cornell University, Ph.D., 1975. *Agent:* Mel Sokolow, 5 West 86th St., New York, N.Y. 10024. *Office:* 249 Highland St., West Newton, Mass. 02165.

CAREER: Chicago Department of Development and Planning, Chicago, Ill., director of social policy planning, 1965-70; Montefiore Hospital, Bronx, N.Y., assistant attending psychologist, 1973-75; Columbia University, New York, N.Y., assistant professor of psychology, 1975—.

WRITINGS: Getting It: The Psychology of EST, Lippincott, 1976. Contributor of scientific articles to professional journals.

WORK IN PROGRESS: Research on the psychopathology of work.

*   *   *

FEOLA, Jose (Maria)   1926-

PERSONAL: Born May 30, 1926, in Buenos Aires, Argentina; came to United States in 1959, naturalized citizen, 1974; son of Jose Juan (a businessman) and Valentina (a pianist; maiden name, DeSantis) Feola; married Olga Figini, May 23, 1950 (divorced, 1967); married Adriana Quintanilla (a writer), August 11, 1968; children: Miguel Angel, Nicolas Jose, Natacha Adriana. *Education:* University of La Plata, Licenciate, 1963; University of Rochester, M.S., 1961; University of Minnesota, Ph.D., 1974. *Home:* 479 Lake Tower Dr. #209, Lexington, Ky. 40502. *Office:* University of Kentucky, Department of Radiation Medicine, Lexington, Ky. 40506.

CAREER: Argentine Atomic Energy Commission, Buenos Aires, radiobiological researcher, 1956-64; University of California, Berkeley, radiobiological researcher at Donner Laboratory, 1965-69; University of Minnesota, Minneapolis, instructor in radiobiology, 1970-73; University of Minnesota extension division, Minneapolis, instructor in parapsychology, 1972-75; University of Kentucky, Lexington, assistant professor of clinical medicine, 1975—. Director, Argentine Institute for Parapsychology, 1957-64. *Military service:* Argentine Army Reserve, 1949; became lieutenant. *Member:* Radiation Research Society, American Society for Psychical Research, Parapsychological Association, California Society for Psychical Study (president, 1968-70), Minnesota Society for Parapsychological Research (president, 1971-73). *Awards, honors:* Fellowship from National Academy of Sciences and International Atomic Energy Agency, 1959-61.

WRITINGS: PK, Mind over Matter, Dillon, 1975. Author of column, "Parapsychology Today," in *Gnostica,* 1974—. Contributor of articles to scientific journals and to *Psychic* magazine.

WORK IN PROGRESS: A book, *Scientist and Psychic;* a play, "The Factory;" a novel with wife, Adriana Quintanilla, about the lives of Kentucky farmers.

SIDELIGHTS: Feola, who studied English for three years before coming to the United States, said that two weeks after his arrival, "I was dreaming in English, and that was the beginning of a strong feeling for the beauties one can find in some good writers' works. I still find myself limited in my attempts to fully express myself in English. However, some excellent writers I know have told me they have the same problem. I guess it is a problem of time and I work at it, but what discourages me is that I could do it in Spanish ten times faster. But I do want to write in English, and that is why I have started with non-fiction."

Feola is more critical of American society. He told *CA:* "God is Money, and Money is God for a majority of Americans, and I truly hate this. I have no doubts that a spiritual revolution is needed, but have become skeptical as to whether or not I am going to see it. The industrial 'revolution' has worked against the creative force of the individual, and this is something that should be changed. Machines should work for us, and not the other way around as it is now. This is part of what I deal with in 'The Factory'."

AVOCATIONAL INTERESTS: Playing the violin, painting, art history, and travel.

* * *

FERGUSON, Charles Albert 1921-

PERSONAL: Born July 6, 1921, in Philadelphia, Pa.; son of Albert T. and Mary (Kohler) Ferguson; married Joanne J. Eichmuller, September 16, 1944 (divorced, 1962); children: Lisa Joanna, Christina Mary. *Education:* University of Pennsylvania, A.B., 1942, M.A., 1943, Ph.D., 1945; graduate studies at Dropsie College and Columbia University. *Home:* 680 Loma Verde, Palo Alto, Calif. 94306. *Office:* Committee on Linguistics, Stanford University, Stanford, Calif. 94305.

CAREER: University of Pennsylvania, Philadelphia, instructor in languages, 1943-46; U.S. Department of State, Foreign Service Institute, Washington, D.C., linguist, 1946-52, director of Area and Language School, Beirut, Lebanon, 1953-55; Georgetown University, Washington, D.C., lecturer in Arabic, 1951-53; Harvard University, Center for Middle Eastern Studies, Cambridge, Mass., lecturer in Arabic, 1955-59; Center for Applied Linguistics, Washington, D.C., director, 1959-66; Stanford University, Stanford, Calif., professor of linguistics and chairman of Committee on Linguistics, 1967—. Visiting professor, Georgetown University, 1955, Daccan College, 1956, University of Michigan, 1960, University of Washington, 1962, 1963, and 1964-65, and Indiana University, 1964.

MEMBER: Linguistics Society of America (member of executive committee, 1957-58; president, 1970), American Anthropological Association, American Oriental Society, Association of Asian Studies (chairman of committee on South Asian languages), Linguistic Society of India, American Folklore Association, Linguistic Circle of New York.

WRITINGS: (With Moukhtar Ani) *Lessons in Contemporary Arabic,* Center for Applied Linguistics, 1960—, revised edition, 1964—; (editor with John J. Gumperz and author of introduction) *Linguistic Diversity in South Asia: Studies in Regional, Social, and Functional Variation,* Indiana University Research Center in Anthropology, Folklore & Linguistics, 1960; *Spoken Eastern Arabic,* Foreign Service Institute, c. 1961; (with Ani and others) *Damascus Arabic,* Center for Applied Linguistics, 1961; *Glossary of Terms Relating to Languages of the Middle East,* Center for Applied Linguistics, 1962; (editor with William A. Stewart) *Linguistic Reading Lists for Teachers of Modern Languages: French, German, Italian, Russian, Spanish,* Center for Applied Linguistics, 1963; (editor) *Contributions to Arabic Linguistics,* Harvard University Press, 1964; (associate editor) *Theoretical Foundations,* Mouton, 1966; (editor with Joshua A. Fishman and Jyotirindra Das Gupta) *Language Problems of Developing Nations,* Wiley, 1968.

Language Structure and Language Use (essays), Stanford University Press, 1971; (editor with Dan Isaac Slobin) *Studies of Child Language Development,* Holt, 1973. General editor of "Contrastive Structure" book series, 1962. Member of board of editors, *Middle East Journal,* 1955—.*

FERGUSON, Franklin C(ole) 1934-

PERSONAL: Born January 12, 1934, in Nashville, Tenn.; son of John Lambuth and Christine (Franklin) Ferguson; married Elizabeth Adams, August 29, 1959; children: Luke Franklin, Benjamin Adams, Ruth Ephrave. *Education:* Vanderbilt University, B.A., 1956; Harvard University, S.T.B., 1959; University of the South, S.T.M., 1962. *Home:* 275 Ashton Dr., Athens, Ga. 30601. *Office:* Emmanuel Church, 498 Prince Ave., Athens, Ga. 30601.

CAREER: Pastor of Methodist church in Bell Buckle, Tenn., 1959-61, and Episcopal church in Paris, Tenn., 1962-66; rector of Episcopal church in Murfreesboro, Tenn., 1966-74; Emmanuel Church, Athens, Ga., Episcopal rector, 1974—. Teacher in Bell Buckle, Tenn., 1959-61; member of board of directors of Rutherford County Guidance Center, 1972-74. Member of board of examining chaplains of Diocese of Tennessee; member of executive board of Diocese of Atlanta (also member of Commission on Ministry); clergy director of DuBose Development Fund; chairman of Task Force for the Continuing Education of the Clergy. *Member:* American Society of Composers, Authors and Publishers.

WRITINGS: A Pilgrimage in Faith, Morehouse, 1975. Contributor to *Living Church* and *St. Luke's Journal.*

WORK IN PROGRESS: A book on the Christian year; a six-part educational television series on contemporary theology.

SIDELIGHTS: Ferguson writes: "My purpose in writing is to present teachings on Christian faith to laity—to interpret the meaning of theology to those in the parishes." He recorded "Lift Up Your Hearts," a record album, at Music City Workshop, Nashville, Tenn., 1972. *Avocational interests:* Folk music, composing church music.

* * *

FERGUSON, Robert Bruce 1927-
(Bob Ferguson)

PERSONAL: Born December 30, 1927, in Willow Springs, Mo.; son of John Carl (a postmaster and writer) and Mary Willie (Boles) Ferguson; married Martha Jean Lewis, May 18, 1968; children: Tivvi Anna, Tulli Allen, Robert Bruce, Jr., John Marshall, Mary Lorena, Missouri Ann. *Education:* Washington State University, B.A., 1954; Vanderbilt University, graduate study, 1966-72. *Home address:* P.O. Box 12392, Nashville, Tenn. 37212. *Office:* Radio Corporation of America—Records, 30 Music Sq. W., Nashville, Tenn. 37203.

CAREER: Personal manager for country music recording artist Ferlin Husky, 1954-56; Tennessee Game and Fish Commission, Nashville, film writer and producer, 1956-61; self-employed music publisher, 1961-63; Record Corporation of America (RCA) Records, Nashville, Tenn., record producer, 1963-65, senior record producer, 1965—. Founding director of Southeastern Institute of Anthropological Studies, 1965-74; chairman of board of trustees of Southeastern Indian Antiquities Survey, 1969; member of Tennessee Archaeology Advisory Council, 1970—. *Military service:* U.S. Army, Field Artillery, 1946-47; served in Alaska. U.S. Marine Corps, 1949-53.

MEMBER: National Academy of Recording Arts and Sciences (Nashville chapter), Country Music Association, American Philosophical Society, Society for American Archaeology, Mensa, American Anthropological Association, Society for Applied Anthropology, Choctaw Boys Club (honorary member of board of directors). *Awards, honors:*

Award from American Association for Conservation Information, 1958, for the film "The World Outdoors"; award from Broadcast Music, Inc., 1960, for the song "Wings of A Dove"; awards from Country Music Association and Broadcast Music, Inc., 1969, for the song "Carroll County Accident"; award from Association for State and Local History, 1974, for *Indians of the Southeast;* also several record production awards from American Society of Composers, Authors and Publishers, Broadcast Music, Inc., and National Academy or Recording Arts and Sciences, 1963-70.

WRITINGS: A Choctaw Chronology (pamphlet), Tennessee Archaeological Society, 1962; (with Jesse Burt) *So You Want to Be in Music!,* Abingdon, 1970; (editor and contributor) *The Middle Cumberland Culture* (self-illustrated), Department of Anthropology, Vanderbilt University, 1972; (with Burt) *Indians of the Southeast: Then and Now,* Abingdon, 1973; (contributor) *Indians of the Lower South,* Florida, 1975.

Films: "The World Outdoors," "The Big E."

Songs: "Wings of a Dove," "Carroll County Accident."

Contributor to regional magazines. Editor of *Choctaw Times,* 1968-72, and *SIAS Journal.*

WORK IN PROGRESS: A book on Choctaw leadership, 1800-1830; a report on the "First American archaeological site" in Nashville, Tenn.

SIDELIGHTS: Ferguson writes: "I wrote early—first published item was in a youth newspaper of the Methodist Church. . . . Began as a printer's devil at age thirteen and printed off and on until 1949. . . . Began on radio and worked at that during college years. . . . Also had a country band then. I have a special interest in explaining anthropological and ecological concepts so that people can relate to the abstract or difficult—or, as in the title of one of my articles, show that 'Conservation Is a Personal Matter.'"

Ferguson became interested in the American Indian after World War II, and has since become an authority on the Choctaws. (His wife is a Choctaw.) In 1961, he was one of a few non-Indians invited to attend the Chicago American Indian Conference. He is also interested in archaeology. For several years he has led a drive to develop a "see and touch" museum at Mound Bottom west of Nashville, and has involved himself with the building site in Nashville where bones from a saber-toothed tiger and other extinct fauna were found. He is presently writing a report on the results of that discovery.

*   *   *

FERICANO, Paul F(rancis) 1951-

PERSONAL: Born January 16, 1951, in San Francisco, Calif.; son of Frank Paul (a truck driver) and Josephine (Anello) Fericano; married Katherine Judeen Daly (an insurance coordinator), October 14, 1972. *Education:* Attended various universities in California, 1969-75, including University of California, Berkeley, San Francisco State University, California State University, Hayward, and St. Anthony's Theological Seminary. *Politics:* "Stoogism." *Religion:* Catholic. *Home:* 1050 Magnolia #2, Millbrae, Calif. 94030. *Agent:* Elizabeth Turpin, 141 East 55th St., New York, N.Y. 10022.

CAREER: Has worked as dishwasher, waiter, washing machine repairman, gardener, carpenter, clown, playground supervisor, truck driver, warehouseman, disc-jockey, house painter, and as a Santa Claus, 1970; editor, *The West Conscious Review* and *Crow's Nest Magazine;* has worked for

California Poetry-In-the-Schools program; writer and poet. *Member:* Committee of Small Magazine Editors and Publishers (C.O.S.M.E.P.), California Writers Club. *Awards, honors:* American Association of University Women fiction award, 1969; Creative Artists Award for poetry, 1976.

WRITINGS: Beneath the Smoke Rings (poems), Dithyramb Poetry Series, 1976; *The Cancer Quiz* (poems), Scarecrow Books, 1977; *Loading the Revolver with Real Bullets* (poems), Second Coming Press, 1977. Contributor to *Wormwood Review, Gallimaufry, Sole Proprietor,* and other magazines.

WORK IN PROGRESS: A book on poems, *Old Tennis Shoe Dreams,* dealing with early childhood; *The Gospel of a Child,* an allegorical novel.

SIDELIGHTS: Fericano wrote: "For the longest time I grew up believing that the Three Stooges were the only ones who really knew what was happening in our world—still do sometimes. If its absurd, I will believe it because insanity seems to be an obsession with just about everyone these days. I believe poets sometimes tend to get a little too serious for their own good. In at least half of all the poetry I write, I try to communicate not only a sense of wonder, but a sense of humor as well. The need for strong, valid humor is just as important to the growth of contemporary poetry, as some "restricted professionals" will have you believe it is not. Of course, I'm not suggesting every poet should be a comedian. I'm merely saying that as human beings tuned into life, we should not be afraid to communicate this feeling, because after all, poetry *is* feeling: the ability to communicate our love, hate, anger, sorrow—and laughter."

BIOGRAPHICAL/CRITICAL SOURCES: CODA: Poets and Writers, July, 1976.

*   *   *

FERRIS, Timothy 1944-

PERSONAL: Born August 29, 1944, in Miami, Fla.; son of Thomas A. (a publicist) and Jean (a literary critic; maiden name, Baird) Ferris. *Education:* Northwestern University, B.S., 1966, graduate study, 1966-67. *Home:* 127 West 86th St., New York, N.Y. 10024. *Agent:* Erica Spellman, International Creative Management, 40 West 57th St., New York, N.Y. 10019. *Office:* Department of English, Brooklyn College of the City University of New York, Brooklyn, N.Y. 11210.

CAREER: United Press International, New York, N.Y., reporter, 1967-69; *New York Post,* New York City, reporter, 1969-71; *Rolling Stone,* New York City, associate editor, 1971-73, contributing editor, 1973—. Assistant professor at Brooklyn College of the City University of New York, 1974—. Among his journalistic assignments were the Democratic and Republican national conventions in 1972, and the Viking landing on Mars in 1976.

WRITINGS: The Red Limit: The Search for the Edge of the Universe, Morrow, 1977. Contributor to national magazines, including *Harper's, Playboy, Esquire,* and *New Times.*

WORK IN PROGRESS: Coming of Age in the Milky Way, on human evolution and extraterrestrial communication.

*   *   *

FETSCHER, Iring 1922-

PERSONAL: Born March 4, 1922, in Marbach, Germany; son of Rainer (a university professor) and Clara (Mueller)

Fetscher; married Elisabeth Goette (a translator), June 7, 1957; children: Caroline, Sebastian, Justus, Christine. *Education:* University of Tuebingen, Ph.D., 1950, habilitation, 1959. *Politics:* Social Democratic Party. *Home:* Ganghoferstrasse 20, Frankfurt am Main, West Germany. *Agent:* Joan Daves, 515 Madison Ave., New York, N.Y. 10022. *Office:* University of Frankfurt, Mertonstrasse 17, Frankfort am Main 6, West Germany.

CAREER: University of Tuebingen, Tuebingen, West Germany, assistant, 1950-55, lecturer in philosophy, 1959-63; University of Frankfurt, Frankfort/Main, West Germany, professor of political philosophy, 1963—; New School for Social Research, New York, N.Y., Theodor Heuss professor of political philosophy, 1968-69. Researcher, German Research Association, 1955-59. *Military service:* German Army, 1940-45; received Iron Cross, first class. *Member:* PEN, International Institute for Political Philosophy (member of board, 1969—), International Commission of Law.

WRITINGS: Von Marx zur Sowjetideologie, Diesterweg, 1957, 4th edition, 1972; *Die Freiheit im Lichte des Marxismus-Leninismus,* Bundeszentrale fur Heimatdienst, 1959; *Rousseaus politische Philosophie,* Luchterhand, 1960, 3rd edition, Surkamp, 1975; *Rechtsradikalismus,* Europaeische Verlags-Anstalt, 1967; *Modelle internationaler Ordnung,* Internationaler Arbeitskreis Sonnenberg, 1967; *Karl Marx und der Marxismus,* Piper, 1967, published as *Marx and Marxism,* Herder and Herder, 1971; *Grossbritannien,* Fischer, 1968; *Politkwissenschaft,* Fischer-Bucherei, 1968; *Die Demokratie,* Kohlhammer, 1970; *Hegels Lehre vom Menschen,* Frommann, 1970; *Hegel, Groesse und Grenzen,* Kohlhammer, 1971; *Wer hat Dornroeschen wachgekuesst?,* Claassen, 1972; *Modelle der Freidenssicherung,* Piper, 1972; *Hegel in der Sicht der neueren Forschung,* Wissenschaftliche Buchgesellschaft, 1973; *Demokratie zwischen Sozialdemokratie und Sozialismus,* Kohlhammer, 1973; *Marxistische Portraets,* Frommann-Holzboog, 1975.

Editor: Iosif Stalin, *Uber dialektischen und historischen Materialismus,* Diesterweg, 1956; *Der Marxismus,* three volumes, Piper, 1962-65; Karl Marx and Friedrich Engels, *Studienausgabe,* four volumes, Fischer, 1966; *Der Sozialismus: vom Klassenkampf zum Wohlfahrtsstaat,* Desch, 1968; *Der Kommunismus,* Desch, 1969; Karl Marx, *Pressefreiheit und Zensur,* Europaeische Verlags-Anstalt, 1969.

General editor, *Marxismusstudien,* four volumes, Mohr, 1957-68. Editor, *Politische Texte,* 1964—.

WORK IN PROGRESS: Princes-Collective Ltd. and other Satires, political satire; *The Concept of Liberty.*

SIDELIGHTS: Fetscher told *CA:* "Fascism and War were the first important experiences of my life, I turned to philosophy and history in order to find out about it and to help build up a better free society. Next came the disillusion with socialism as practiced in East Germany and the Soviet Union, and finally the insight developed by the 'Club of Rome' study on the 'Limits of Growth'."

CA asked Fetscher what he felt was the future of political philosophy in Germany. He responded: "Conservative theories will very probably center around the concept of the late professor Arnold Gehlen (institutions as relief conferring) and less around nationalism as in the past. Technocratic conservatism argues that the 'man in the street' is generally incapable of judging adequately the more and more complex problems of contemporary government, so that the democratic consent has to be manipulated for the sake of effective and competent management by elites.

"Progressive thought will turn away from any form of dogmatic Marxism which seems to be discredited not only by the Soviet Union but as well by the very conservative and bureaucratic East German regime which is a combination of Prussianism and Soviet imports. A combination of decentralisation (wherever it can be afforded), of changes in styles of life (of individual and social 'aims') and of more equality will be justified as the only possible alternative for a centralized anonymous dictatorship in the service of technological growth and/or of the necessary adaptation of the individuals to the requirements of a less quickly growing economy (and therefore less and less acceptable inequality). The theoretical basis of such an image will be a combination of critical evaluations of the economic system, of a genetical approach to civilization (Norbert Elias, etc.) and of anthropology (genetic psychology). The elaboration of a kind of political ethic will be necessary, which would allow a critique of—for instance—happiness as pleasure, needs as demands for consumer goods, and freedom as free enterprise for the few."

CA asked Fetscher if he could forsee a political joining of East and West Germany in the future, and if it is possible, what first steps are needed. He said: "I do not think that in a forseeable future there is any chance of reuniting East and West Germany. The actual governing elite of East Germany has no interest whatsoever in such a move, neither would they accept an abdication of their rulership, which would be the inevitable outcome of a common parliament (where the majority would be anti-Communist), nor have they any realistic hope of winning Communist majorities in West Germany. The only chance for such an evolution would be (1) a change in the Soviet Union towards democracy and a real lessening of tensions, (2) a change within East Germany (or West Germany) which would bring the two different societies nearer to each other. Maybe in the long run Eurocommunism, if it should be successful in Italy, Spain, France, and also if a complete split with the Eastern Communist countries could be avoided, could have such an influence . . . but I think such an evolution very unlikely.

"The only realistic basis for a reunification is the fact that until now still a rather great part (certainly a majority) of the East German population would prefer to become members of the West German State. The constant contact via radio, television, letters and smuggled-in books and/or newspapers has until now prevented a complete separation. Nevertheless the fact that the East German population has now 44 years of dictatorship behind it and the West German population at least 28 years of experience in parliamentary liberal democracy accounts for deepgoing differences, which become bigger every day."

* * *

FEUCHTWANGER, E(dgar) J(oseph)   1924-

PERSONAL: Born September 28, 1924, in Munich, Germany; son of Ludwig (a publisher) and Erna (Rheinstrom) Feuchtwanger; married Primrose Essame, June 2, 1962; children: Antonia, Adrian, Judith. *Education:* Magdalene College, Cambridge, B.A., 1947, M.A., 1950; University of Southampton, Ph.D., 1958. *Home:* Highfield House, Dean, Sparsholt, Winchester SO21 2LP, England. *Office:* Department of Extra-Mural Studies, University of Southampton, Southampton SO9 5NH, England.

CAREER: University of Southampton, Southampton, England, lecturer in extra-mural studies, 1949-63, senior lecturer, 1966-73, reader in history, 1973—, deputy director of extra-mural studies, 1963—. *Member:* International Institute for Strategic Studies, Royal Historical Society (fellow).

WRITINGS: Disraeli, Democracy, and the Tory Party, Clarendon Press, 1968; *Prussia: Myth and Reality,* Regnery, 1970; (editor) *Upheaval and Continuity: A Century of German History,* University of Pittsburgh Press, 1973; *Gladstone,* St. Martin's, 1975; (editor with John Erickson) *Soviet Military Power and Performance: A Symposium,* Macmillan, 1977.

WORK IN PROGRESS: Research for a biography of Gustave Stresemann.

SIDELIGHTS: Feuchtwanger comments briefly that his main interests are English and German political history of the nineteenth and twentieth centuries, and that subsidiary interests include contemporary international relations and strategic studies. Some of his books have been published in German.

* * *

ffRENCH BLAKE, Neil (St. John) 1940-

PERSONAL: Born November 4, 1940, in London, England; son of Robert Lifford Valentine and Grania Bryde (Curran) ffrench Blake; married Lady Caroline Anne De Vere Beauclerk, July 19, 1969; children: Clare Eleanor De Vere. *Education:* Educated in private school in Windsor, England. *Politics:* None. *Religion:* None. *Home:* Barn House, Midgham, Berkshire, England. *Office:* Radio 210 Thames Valley, P.O. Box 210, Reading, Berkshire, England.

CAREER: Journalist for *The Journal,* Newcastle, England, 1958-59, *Sydney Daily Telegraph,* Sydney, Australia, 1959-60, and *South Pacific Post,* 1961-62. British Broadcasting Corp. (BBC), London, England, radio and television producer, 1963-70; Radio 210 Thames Valley, Reading, England, program controller and executive director, 1975—. Director of Network Broadcasting Ltd. (in television distribution and establishment of commercial radio), 1970-74, and of Television International Enterprises Ltd., 1974-75. Member of board of directors of various companies in England and Ireland.

WRITINGS: A Handbook for Adventure, Museum Press, 1962; *The World of Show Jumping,* Pelham Books, 1965, Doubleday, 1966; *The World of Dressage,* Pelham Books, 1966, Doubleday, 1967; *The Pony Club World,* Pelham Books, 1967, Doubleday, 1968. Writer for several thousand television and radio broadcasts.

WORK IN PROGRESS: The history of the start of commercial broadcasting in the United Kingdom; writing on the "analysis of innocence"; biographical essays.

SIDELIGHTS: ffrench Blake writes: "I regard myself as a communicator—rather than an 'author.' I have therefore acquired skill in such areas as photography or, say, editing videotape so that I have as wide a range of professional expertise in communications media as possible. I have travelled all over the world (including much time in the U.S.A.) so that I may be able to take on any assignment anywhere for any media at any time, and deliver at least a competent technically-correct end product. In a creative sense my motivation is dictated by two somewhat divergent obsessions—fear and innocence. The study of both and the search for their fulfillment is something that I shall plainly never achieve. But such work as I produce in the future may expect to reflect the thrill of the chase in the former and the inevitable melancholy associated with the destruction of the latter."

AVOCATIONAL INTERESTS: Skiing, cricket, tennis.

FIAROTTA, Noel 1944-

PERSONAL: Born March 13, 1944, in Meriden, Conn.; son of Anthony (an engineer) and Santa (a secretary; maiden name, Lentini) Ficarotta; married Beatriz Esteban (a teacher). *Education:* Jersey City State College, B.A., 1966; Fairleigh Dickinson University, M.A., 1973. *Politics:* "Depends on who and what." *Religion:* "I believe in God." *Home and office address:* Brook Way, Llewellyn Park, West Orange, N.J. 07052.

CAREER: Language arts teacher in elementary school in East Orange, N.J., 1967-74; King Features Syndicate, New York, N.Y., editor of column "Leisure Craftsman," 1972—. Professional singer, 1962-68; director of A. Harry Moore Camp, 1972-74.

WRITINGS—All with sister, Phyllis Fiarotta; all published by Workman Publishing: *A Hundred One Gifts You Can Make at Home,* 1968; *A Hundred One Children's Gifts You Can Make at Home,* 1970; *Sticks and Stones and Ice Cream Cones: The Craft Book for Children,* 1973; *Snips and Snails and Walnut Whales: Nature Crafts for Children,* 1975; *Pin It, Tack It, Hang It: The Big Book of Kids' Bulletin Boards,* 1975; *The You and Me Heritage Tree: Children's Crafts from Twenty-One American Traditions,* 1976; *Banker, Baker, Jewelry Maker,* 1977.

Editor, with Phyllis Fiarotta, and contributor; all published by Workman Publishing: *Sewing Without a Pattern,* 1969; *Children's Parties,* 1971; *Making It with Leather and Beads,* 1971; *Sewing Tricks,* 1971; *How to Make Stuffed Animals,* 1973; *The Complete Treasury of the Decorative Craft,* 1973; *Phyllis Fiarotta's Nostalgia Crafts Book,* 1974.

WORK IN PROGRESS: A pilot television program for children, dealing with crafts and entertainment, with sister, Phyllis Fiarotta.

SIDELIGHTS: "Living is that once in a lifetime opportunity to do everything you really want to do, and so be it with my life. I started writing at the ripe old age of ten, nothing too fancy, just childhood thoughts set to adult situations. Adolescence got the better of this shortlived literary career and the corner candy store replaced the bedroom desk, a pretzel stick took the place of my pencil.

"Caught up in the times, of rock and roll, bebop, customized cars, high school dances, and hanging out, music became my main interest. Everyone wanted to become a rock and roll star, and I was there waiting in line. I headed several rock and roll and folk groups, through my high school and college years, with many minor successes: several TV appearances, the college circuit, the Bitter End, and a couple of not-so-unsuccessful records. I even tried producing records, owned a record company called Felicia Records. The music field was getting too crowded and I was looking forward to a new career, as an English teacher.

"I taught English in an experimental school in East Orange, N.J. My main concern was teaching the writing skills to grades five through eight, in a little red school house atmosphere. Students were encouraged to undertake a yearly project: to write a novel, collection of poems, essays, etc. and through their writings they would learn what language arts is all about. The experiment lasted six years, and was replaced by traditional teaching. During the summers I worked at a camp for the physically handicapped and the mentally retarded, and eventually directed the camp for two years. The A. Harry Moore Camp really pointed out the beauty of life. My teaching experiences gave me a good foundation for preparing children's craft books.

"My future plans may possibly include a TV show for children (craft oriented): writing, directing, performing, and producing. I guess I will continue to try to keep quite active and doing it all before my name is added to the dead file with the epitaph, 'He did all he possibly could!' "

* * *

FIAROTTA, Phyllis 1942-

PERSONAL: Born August 21, 1942, in Meriden, Conn.; daughter of Anthony (an engineer) and Santa (a secretary; maiden name, Lentini) Ficarotta. *Education:* Attended Newark School of Fine and Industrial Arts, 1960-63. *Politics:* Democrat. *Religion:* Roman Catholic. *Home and office address:* Brook Way, Llewellyn Park, West Orange, N.J. 07052.

CAREER: Good Housekeeping, New York, N.Y., associate art director, 1965-71; King Features Syndicate, New York, N.Y., author and illustrator of column "The Leisure Craftsman," 1972—. Assistant art director for Pharmaceutical Advertising, 1963-65. Assistant stage manager for International Ladies' Garment Workers' Union Theatre. Guest and demonstrator on more than a hundred television and radio programs.

WRITINGS—All self-illustrated; all published by Workman Publishing: *A Hundred One Gifts You Can Make at Home,* 1968; *Sewing Without a Pattern,* 1969; *Children's Parties,* 1971; *Making It with Leather and Beads,* 1971; *Sewing Tricks,* 1971; *How to Make Stuffed Animals,* 1973; *The Complete Treasury of the Decorative Craft,* 1973; *Phyllis Fiarotta's Nostalgia Crafts Book,* 1974.

Self-illustrated books, with brother, Noel Fiarotta; all published by Workman Publishing: *A Hundred One Children's Gifts You Can Make at Home,* 1970; *Sticks and Stones and Ice Cream Cones: The Craft Book for Children,* 1973; *Snips and Snails and Walnut Whales: Nature Crafts for Children,* 1975; *Pin It, Tack It, Hang It: The Big Book of Kids' Bulletin Boards,* 1975; *The You and Me Heritage Tree: Children's Crafts from Twenty-One American Traditions,* 1976; *Banker, Baker, Jewelry Maker,* 1977. Contributor to popular magazines, including *Woman's Day, Family Circle,* and *Essence.* Art editor of *Good Housekeeping Family Christmas Book,* 1963-65. Illustrator of children's stories for Western Publishing.

WORK IN PROGRESS: Preparing scripts, sets, and puppets for a pilot television program for children, dealing with crafts and entertainment, with brother, Noel Fiarotta.

SIDELIGHTS: "Although I was born in Connecticut and presently live in New Jersey, I will be eternally a New Yorker. I have an intense love affair with this, the greatest city in the world.

"I have a passion for everything that is connected with my precious life, and I reject very little.

"My philosophy of life was summed up by Fred Flintstone of cartoon fame, saying, as he emptied a quart of milk on the floor, 'I laugh at spilt milk.'

"My extreme loves, my mother, father, brother, tacos, Mexican trees of life, opera, my house, landscaping, colors, and *The Grinch That Stole Christmas* keep me busy. My extreme dislike, DYING."

* * *

FIELD, Frances Fox 1913(?)-1977
(Frances Margaret Fox)

1913(?)—January 4, 1977; American dancer, artist and author. She was author of children's books under name Frances Margaret Fox during 1930's. Field died in New York City. Obituaries: *New York Times,* January 6, 1977; *AB Bookman's Weekly,* February 14, 1977.

* * *

FIELD, Henry 1902-

PERSONAL: Born December 15, 1902, in Chicago, Ill.; married second wife, Julia Rand Allen, February 6, 1953; children: (first marriage) Mariana; (second marriage) Juliana Lathrop. *Education:* New College, Oxford, B.A., 1925, diploma in anthropology, 1926, M.A., 1929, D.Sc., 1937; also attended University of Heidelberg, 1926, and Harvard University, 1936-37. *Home:* 3551 Main Highway, Coconut Grove, Miami, Fla. 33133. *Office:* Peabody Museum of American Archaeology and Ethnology, Harvard University, Cambridge, Mass. 02138.

CAREER: Field Museum of Natural History, Chicago, Ill., anthropologist, 1926-41, assistant curator in physical anthropology, 1926-36, curator, 1937-41; Library of Congress, Washington, D.C., conducted research for Presidents Franklin D. Roosevelt and Harry S Truman, 1941-45; Harvard University, Peabody Museum of American Archaeology and Ethnology, Cambridge, Mass., research fellow in physical anthropology, 1950-69, honorary associate, 1969—. Adjunct professor at University of Miami, Coral Gables, Fla., 1966—; Forbes Hawkes Lecturer at University of Miami and Lowell Institute, 1952. U.S. delegate to international congresses and conferences; member of U.S. mission to the Soviet Union, 1945; member of archaeological expeditions in Europe, Africa, Mongolia, and southwestern Asia; leader of Marshall Field expeditions to Europe, the northern Arabian Desert, and Iraq. Trustee of American School for Prehistoric Research.

MEMBER: American Association for the Advancement of Science (fellow), American Academy of Arts and Sciences (president, 1964—), Prehistoric Society (fellow), Zoological Society (fellow), Royal Anthropological Institute (fellow), Royal Geographical Society (fellow), Royal Central Asian Society (fellow), Asiatic Society of Bengal (fellow), Glasgow Archaeological Society (honorary member), Explorers Club. *Awards, honors:* Gold medal from Royal Anthropological Institute.

WRITINGS: The Early History of Man, with Special Reference to the Cap-Blanc Skeleton, Field Museum of Natural History, 1927; *The Field Museum-Oxford University Expedition to Kish, Mesopotamia, 1923-1929,* Field Museum of Natural History, 1929.

Arabs of Central Iraq: Their History, Ethnology, and Physical Characters, Field Museum of Natural History, 1935; (with David Hooper) *Useful Plants and Drugs of Iran and Iraq,* Field Museum of Natural History, 1937; *Contributions to the Anthropology of Iran,* two volumes, Field Museum of Natural History, 1939, Kraus Reprint, 1968.

The Anthropology of Iraq, four volumes, Field Museum of Natural History, 1940-52, Kraus Reprint, 1968; (with J. B. Glubb) *The Yezidis, Sulubba, and Other Tribes of Iraq and Adjacent Regions,* G. Banta, 1943; (editor) *Contributions to the Anthropology of the Soviet Union,* Smithsonian Institution, 1948.

Bibliography, 1926-1951, privately printed, 4th edition published as *Bibliography, 1926-1961,* privately printed, 1961; *Anthropogeographical Bibliography of the Persian Gulf Area,* privately printed, 1952; *Camel Brands and Graffiti from Iraq, Syria, Jordan, Iran, and Arabia,* American Oriental Society, 1952; *Contributions to the Anthropology of the Faiyum, Sinai, Sudan, and Kenya,* University of California Press, 1952; *Bibliography on Southwestern Asia,* University of Miami Press, 1953, supplement, Field Research Projects, 1968; *Contributions to the Anthropology of the Caucasus,* Peabody Museum of American Archaeology and Ethnology, Harvard University, 1953; *The Track of Man: Adventures of an Anthropologist,* Doubleday, 1953, revised edition, Dell, 1967; *Los indios de Tepoztlan (Mexico),* University of Miami Press, 1954; *Caves and Rockshelters in Northern Iraq,* privately printed, 1955; *Ancient and Modern Man in Southwestern Asia,* two volumes, University of Miami Press, 1956-61; *An Anthropological Reconnaisance in the Near East, 1950,* Peabody Museum of American Archaeology and Ethnology, Harvard University, 1956; *List of Archaeological Sites in Arabian Peninsula and Adjoining Areas,* University of Miami Press, 1956; *Peabody Museum-Harvard Expedition to West Pakistan, 1955,* two volumes, privately printed, 1956; *Body-Marking in Southwestern Asia,* Peabody Museum of American Archaeology and Ethnology, Harvard University, 1958; *An Anthropological Reconnaisance in West Pakistan, 1955,* Peabody Museum of American Archaeology and Ethnology, Harvard University, 1959.

(Editor) *North Arabian Desert Archaeological Survey, 1925-50,* Peabody Museum of American Archaeology and Ethnology, Harvard University, 1960; (editor) *Contributions to the Anthropology of the U.S.S.R.,* privately printed, 1961; (editor) *"M" Project for F.D.R.: Studies on Migration and Settlement,* privately printed, 1962; *Bibliography: 1926-1964,* Edwards Brothers, 1964, 2nd edition published as *Bibliography: 1926-1966,* 1966; (editor) *Scientific Use of Natural Areas* (symposium), Field Research Projects, 1965; (editor with wife, Julia Field) *Game and Wild Life Preserves in the U.S.S.R.,* privately printed, 1965; (with Edith M. Laird) *Conservation and Wildlife: A Bibliography,* Field Research Projects, 1967; *Bibliography of Soviet Archaeology and Physical Anthropology, 1936-1967,* privately printed, 1967; (with Laird) *Bibliography of the Physical Anthropology of the Peoples of India,* two volumes, Field Research Projects, 1968-70; (editor) *Contributions to the Archaeology of Armenia,* Peabody Museum of American Archaeology and Ethnology, Harvard University, 1968; (editor) Albert R. al-Haik, *Key Lists of Archaeological Excavations in Iraq,* Field Research Projects, 1968; (editor) Donald Jay, *Annotated Bibliography on Locusts in Southwestern Asia,* Field Research Projects, 1968.

(Editor) Bhuban M. Das, *Anthropometry of the Tribal Groups of Assam, India,* Field Research Projects, 1970; (editor) N. R. Gurov, *Review of Finnish Decipherment of Proto-Dravidian Inscriptions,* Field Research Projects, 1970; (editor) Moosa Hekmat, *Geographical Distribution Guide,* Field Research Projects, 1970; (editor) S.M.A. Kazmi, *Bibliography on the Botany of West Pakistan and Kashmir and Adjacent Regions,* Field Research Projects, 1970; (editor) O. Namnandorj, *Conservation and Wild Life in Mongolia,* Field Research Projects, 1970; (editor) Thomas Nelson Page, *On the Nile in 1901,* Field Research Projects, 1970; (editor) *Rock-Drawings from Saudi Arabia,* Field Research Projects, 1970; *Contributions to the Physical Anthropology of the Peoples of India,* Field Research Projects, 1970, supplement, 1971; *Tombs at Gujo in Sind, West Pakistan,* Field Research Projects, 1971; (editor) Priya Bala Das, *Growth Studies of the Kalita Children,* Field Research Projects, 1971; (editor) R. K. Gulatti, *Inter-Group Differ-*

ences in an Artisan Caste of Maharashtra, Field Research Projects, 1971; (editor) G. D. Kumar, *Anthropometric Data from Kerala, South India,* Field Research Projects, 1971; (editor) Kumar, *Ethnogenesis of Indus Valley Population,* Field Research Projects, 1971; *Bibliography: 1966-1971,* Field Research Projects, 1971; *Contributions to the Anthropology of Saudi Arabia,* Field Research Projects, 1971; (editor) McGuire Gibson, *The City and Area of Kish,* Field Research Projects, 1972; *Bibliography of Soviet Archaeology and Physical Anthropology, 1936-1972,* Field Research Projects, 1972.

Editor of "Russian Translation Series," for Peabody Museum of American Archaeology and Ethnology, Harvard University, 1960-70.

WORK IN PROGRESS: Arabian Desert Tales; Mongolian Diary; a contribution to *Pre-history of Arabia,* by Augustus Sordinas.

*   *   *

FIELDS, Rona M(arcia) 1934-

PERSONAL: Born October 27, 1934, in Chicago, Ill.; daughter of William and Kate (Goldman) Katz; married Armond Fields, June 9, 1953 (divorced, 1967); children: Louis Marc, Sean Steven, Miriam Star. *Education:* Lake Forest College (now University), B.A., 1953; Loyola University, Chicago, Ill., M.A., 1964; University of Southern California, Ph.D., 1970. *Home and office:* 2719 Sycamore St., Alexandria, Va. 22305.

CAREER: Teacher in public schools in Park Forest, Ill., 1956-57, substitute teacher in Winnetka, Ill., 1959-62; Booth Memorial Hospital, Chicago, Ill., psychometric consultant, 1962-63; National Institute of Mental Health, Chicago, project psychologist for Division of Mental Health, 1963-64; Monrovia Guidance Center, Monrovia, Calif., program psychologist, 1964-67; California State College, Los Angeles, part-time lecturer, 1966-72, assistant professor of psychology, 1967-72; Clark University, Worcester, Mass., associate professor of sociology, 1972-76; Temple University, Philadelphia, Pa., associate director of National Center for the Study of Corporal Punishment and Its Alternatives in the Schools, 1976-77; Transnational Family Research Institute, Bethesda, Md., associate, 1977—. Instructor at Pasadena City College, 1967-69; assistant professor at San Fernando Valley State College, 1968-69, visiting professor, 1971-72; professor at Pacific Oaks College, 1968-70; guest lecturer at University of Lisbon, University of Oslo, Stonehill College, University College, Dublin, University of London, University of Santa Clara, Long Beach State University, and University of California, Los Angeles. Director of East Los Angeles Free Clinic, 1968-69; associate of Betsy Hogan Associates (consultants), 1973—; director of Sozialwissenschaftliches Institut fuer Katastrophen, 1977—; coordinator of International Commission of Health Professionals and of professional workshops. Broadcaster for KPEK-Radio, Los Angeles, WAAB-Radio, Worcester, Mass., WGCY-Radio, New Bedford, Mass., and RTE-Radio, Dublin, Ireland. Research fellow at International Institute for Peace Research in Oslo, Norway, summer, 1975. Consultant to Government of Northern Ireland.

MEMBER: American Psychological Association, Psychologists for Social Action (national coordinator, 1969-72), American Sociological Association, Society for the Psychological Study of Social Issues, Royal Society for Health, Massachusetts Psychological Association, California State Psychological Association.

WRITINGS: A Society on the Run: A Psychology of Northern Ireland, Penguin, 1973; (contributor) P. Chris Garcia, editor, Chicano Politics: Readings, MSS Information Corp., 1973; (contributor) Florence Denmark, editor, Who Discriminates Against Women, Sage Publications, 1974; The Armed Forces Movement and the Portuguese Revolution, Praeger, 1976; Society Under Siege, Temple University Press, 1976; (contributor) Lawrence Graham and Harry Meckler, editors, The Portuguese Revolution, University of Texas Press, 1977; (contributor) John Nietzing, editor, Violence in Industrialized Societies, Swets (Brussels), 1977. Contributor of about thirty articles and a poem to professional journals, popular magazines, including Science for People and New Humanist, and newspapers.

WORK IN PROGRESS: Research for books on psychological torture and its effects, Irish Republicanism and Jewish Zionism, and pregnancy and decision-making.

SIDELIGHTS: "My research interests," Fields told CA, "have been focused on social prejudice and violence although my personal and academic involvement with the rights of minorities and women's status have frequently led to research and writing in those areas. I have enjoyed teaching (from my earliest teaching experiences at the elementary school level to my most recent experience in teaching graduate school). I also find that, as a psychologist, I require regular and continuing experience doing counseling and psychotherapy. Although I have seldom held any position in the field of animal or experimental psychology, my favorite pastimes and hobbies have had to do with animal breeding and training. One of my favorite consultantships was with the Los Angeles City Zoo in developing environments for young primates. In the course of this work, I studied and interacted with orangutans and chimpanzees as well as with macaques and other smaller primates."

* * *

FIENE, Donald M(ark) 1930-

PERSONAL: Surname is pronounced Fee-ny; born February 24, 1930, in Schenectady, N.Y.; son of Marcus Ernest (an electrical engineer) and Clara (Engelking) Fiene; married Judith Ivy (a social worker), November 3, 1956; children: Karen Fiene Heinz, Bruce. Education: Cornell University, student, 1947-51; University of Louisville, B.A. (high honors), 1959, M.A. (English), 1961; Indiana University, M.A. (Russian), 1967, Ph.D., 1974. Politics: "Far left." Religion: "Raised . . . Lutheran; now an admirer of Taoism and Bokononism." Home: 2215 Clinch Ave., Knoxville, Tenn. 37916. Office: Department of Germanic and Slavic Languages, University of Tennessee, Knoxville, Tenn. 37916.

CAREER: American Air Filter Co., Louisville, Ky., technical writer, 1957-59; high school teacher of English and chemistry in Louisville, Ky., 1959-60; University of Louisville, Louisville, Ky., lecturer in English, 1960-62, instructor in humanities, 1962-65, 1969-72; Indiana University and Purdue University, Columbus, part-time instructor in philosophy, 1973-74; University of Tennessee, Knoxville, assistant professor of Russian studies, 1974—, conducted tour of the Soviet Union, 1975. Military service: U.S. Air Force, navigator-bombardier, 1951-55; served in Korea; became captain.

MEMBER: American Association of Teachers of Slavic and East European Languages, American Association for the Advancement of Slavic Studies, Modern Language Association of America, American Association of University Professors, American Civil Liberties Union, Southern

Comparative Literature Association (member of board of directors), Delta Phi Alpha, Phi Kappa Phi, Dobro Slovo, National Insulator Association.

WRITINGS: (Compiler with Nicolai Barmache and Tatiana Ossorguine and author of introduction) Bibliographie des oeuvres de Michel Ossorguine (title means "Bibliography of the Works of Michel Ossorguine"), Institut de Etudes Slaves, 1973; (compiler) Alexander Solzhenitsyn: An International Bibliography of Writings By and About Him, 1962-1973, Ardis, 1973; (editor and contributor of translations and criticism) Vasily Shukshin, Snowball Berry Red and Other Stories, Ardis, 1977; (editor, translator, and author of notes) M. A. Osorgin, a Reintroduction: Selected Stories, Reminiscences, and Essays, Ardis, in press.

Work represented in anthologies, including short story in New Campus Writing Number Two, edited by Nolan Miller, Putnam, 1957; critical essays in Salinger's "Catcher in the Rye", edited by Harold Simonson and Philip E. Hager, Heath, 1963; A Symposium on "Bartleby the Scrivener," edited by Howard Vincent, Kent State University, 1966; Vonnegut in America, edited by Jerome Klinkowitz and Donald Lawler, Delacorte, 1977. Contributor to 2nd edition of Columbia Dictionary of Modern European Literature. Contributor of more than fifty articles and translations to magazines, including Liberation, New World Review, Explicator, Realist, Russian Literature Triquarterly, Chicago Review, and New York Times Book Review.

WORK IN PROGRESS: Translating stories by Vladimir Voinovich; translating the biography of Boris Vilde by Raisa Rait-Kovalaeva; long-range research on the popularity and critical acceptance of Kurt Vonnegut in the Soviet Union, and his affinities with Russian literature.

SIDELIGHTS: Fiene said he "started writing fiction after getting out of the Air Force in the 1950's; could hardly make a living at it, drifted into teaching; finally studied Russian out of love for Dostoevsky, Tolstoy, Gogol, Babel. . . . I take trips to the U.S.S.R. now and then; I persuaded Mme. Raisa Rait-Kovaleva (Rita Riat) of Moscow to translate Vonnegut into Russian; I arranged for Vonnegut to meet her in Paris in 1972. . . . I enjoy acting as an agent for the reconciliation of East and West. I intend to return to writing fiction—novels, etc., while continuing to pursue my career as Slavist, literary critic, and translator."

AVOCATIONAL INTERESTS: "I am a zealous collector of glass telephone and power insulators; I steal any I see that aren't wired down; I climb high to get them; I've got two thousand of these beautiful things in my living room, including many from Poland, the U.S.S.R., France, and other countries."

* * *

FIGGINS, Ross 1936-

PERSONAL: Born March 10, 1936, in Plainfield, N.J.; son of Albert F. (in advertising) and Frances (MacAlvanah) Figgins; married Jacque Weiss (a professor), August 1, 1974. Education: Valley College, A.A., 1958; California State University, Northridge, B.A., 1960, M.A., 1962; University of Illinois, M.A., 1965; University of Southern California, Ph.D., 1972. Home: 567 South Albertson, Covina, Calif. 91723. Office: Communications Art Department, California State Polytechnic University, Pomona, Calif. 91768.

CAREER: California State Polytechnic University, Pomona, 1965—, now member of faculty of communication arts department. Adjunct professor at University of

Southern California, 1976—. Director of Pomona Valley Writers' Workshop, 1966-69; assistant director of Institute of Multidisciplinary Studies, 1973, and of Institute of Advanced System Studies, 1974. *Military service:* U.S. Army Reserve, 1958-65. *Member:* American Business Communication Association, American Haiku Society. *Awards, honors:* Arizona State Poetry Society National Haiku Contest awards, 1974, for "Gnarled Oak," and 1976, for "Dark Bamboo"; Japan and California Yukuharu Haiku Society award, 1976, for "Walking with the Wind"; award for best feature story and general excellence from Union Teacher Press Association, 1976, for editing *Union Professors of California Advocate;* received first place awards and recognitions in contests sponsored by *Modern Haiku, Haiku Highlights, Dragonfly, Bonsai,* and *Haiku West.*

WRITINGS: Techniques of Job Search, Canfield, 1976; *Untitled Haiku Anthology,* Raindrop Press, 1977.

Work represented in anthologies, *I Am Talking about Revolution,* Harper Square (Chicago), 1973; *Haiku,* Washington Poets Association, 1974; *Haiku,* Paco Press (Lynwood, Wash.), 1975; *Anthology of the Western World Haiku Society,* J & C Transcripts, 1976. Contributor of nearly five hundred haiku to magazines. Editor of *United Professors of California Advocate.*

WORK IN PROGRESS: Career Search, for Harper; *Shadows of a Hand,* an unpublished collection of original haiku; *An Annotated Haiku Bibliography in English,* completion expected in 1980; *Tales from a Bolsa,* an unpublished collection of Mexican folk tales.

*   *   *

FINLEY, Joseph E(dwin)   1919-

PERSONAL: Born August 7, 1919, in Portageville, Mo.; son of William V. (a railroad engineer) and Nell (Whitten) Finley; married Joanne E. Otte (a physician), July 10, 1950; children: Scott M., Ethan C., Lucinda M., Willian N. *Education:* University of Missouri, B.J., 1942; Yale University, LL.B., 1951. *Politics:* Democrat. *Home and office:* 57 Brookstone Dr., Princeton, N.J. 08540. *Agent:* Susan Ann Protter, 156 East 52nd St., New York, N.Y. 10022.

CAREER: Admitted to District of Columbia Bar, 1951, and Ohio Bar, 1957; Woll, Glenn & Thatcher, Washington, D.C., attorney, 1951-54; attorney in private practice in Washington, D.C., 1954-61; Metzenbaum, Gaines, Finley & Stern, Cleveland, Ohio, partner, 1961-71; private practice of law in Philadelphia, Pa., 1971—. Has served as general counsel to American Federation of Labor, Office and Professional Employees International Union, and International Brotherhood of Pottery and Allied Workers. President of Ludlow Community Association, 1961. *Military service:* U.S. Army, 1942-46; became captain.

MEMBER: American Bar Association. *Awards, honors:* Distinguished recognition award from Friends of American Writers, 1976, for *Missouri Blue.*

WRITINGS: The Corrupt Kingdom (non-fiction), Simon & Schuster, 1973; *White Collar Union* (non-fiction), Octagon, 1975; *Missouri Blue* (novel), Putnam, 1976. Contributor of articles and stories to magazines.

WORK IN PROGRESS: A novel dealing with the U.S. Supreme Court.

SIDELIGHTS: Finley writes that he earned his way through college writing stories, radio scripts, and sports publicity. After becoming a lawyer, he sold twenty stories and articles in the first year, then gradually stopped writing. "In

later years, with a strong desire to return, and with a stable law practice, I resumed writing again, with books published as above. I hope to do several more books."

*   *   *

FISH, Peter Graham   1937-

PERSONAL: Born October 2, 1937, in Tuxedo, N.Y.; son of Laurens Hull (a businessman) and Marion (Monks) Fish; married Barbara Maly (a school librarian), November 11, 1967; children: Maria Maly, Jonathan Hull. *Education:* Princeton University, B.A., 1960; Johns Hopkins University, M.A., 1965, Ph.D., 1968. *Politics:* Republican. *Religion:* Presbyterian. *Home:* 1006 Urban Ave., Durham, N.C. 27701. *Office:* Department of Political Science, Duke University, Durham, N.C. 27706.

CAREER: Oberlin College, Oberlin, Ohio, visiting instructor in political science, 1965-66; Princeton University, Princeton, N.J., instructor, 1966-68, lecturer in political science, 1968-69; Duke University, Durham, N.C., assistant professor, 1969-71, associate professor of political science, 1971—. Member of Durham Center City Church Council, 1972-73. Member of panel for the Fourth Circuit, U.S. Circuit Judge Nominating Commission, 1977. *Member:* National Conference on State Courts (member of task force on internal procedures of the courts, 1977-78), American Political Science Association, American Association of University Professors (local president, 1974-75), Southern Political Science Association. *Awards, honors:* American Council of Learned Societies grant, 1975.

WRITINGS: The Politics of Federal Judicial Administration, Princeton University Press, 1973. Contributor to law and politics journals.

WORK IN PROGRESS: Defeat: Judge Parker and the Supreme Court, completion expected in 1979; *John J. Parker: Chief Judge.*

SIDELIGHTS: Graham told *CA:* "Federal judicial administration usually raises the time-worn topics of delayed justice, congested dockets, and economy and efficiency in court management. Yet as I make clear in *The Politics of Federal Judicial Administration,* little known institutions, personalities, and low visibility politics have played and continue to play a vital role in the manner in which the courts of the United States are administered. The focus is on the administration, as distinguished from substantive judicial decision-making, of the congressionally-created inferior federal courts from their modest beginnings in the Eighteenth Century, their proliferation and augmentation of judicial power in the Nineteenth, to the hesitant but ongoing increases in their centralized administration during the Twentieth Century".

*   *   *

FISHBEIN, Morris   1889-1976

July 22, 1889—September 27, 1976; American physician, twenty-five year editor of *Journal of the American Medical Association* and writer of its "Dr. Pepy's Diary" column, extensive lecturer, syndicated columnist, and author of books for professionals and laymen, including the best selling *Modern Home Medical Adviser.* He died in Chicago, Ill. Obituaries: *New York Times,* September 28, 1976; *Washington Post,* September 29, 1976; *AB Bookman's Weekly,* November 15, 1976. (See index for previous *CA* sketch)

FISHEL, Wesley L.   1919-1977

September 8, 1919—April 14, 1977; American educator, political scientist, and expert on Southeast Asia. Author of books on the Vietnamese War, Fishel was a close friend and advisor to Ngo Dinh Diem during the 1950's. He became the center of great controversy when his advocacy of the Vietnamese War became widely known. He died in Lansing, Mich. Obituaries: *New York Times,* April 15, 1977.

* * *

FISHER, Harvey Irvin   1916-

PERSONAL: Born June 15, 1916, in Edgar, Neb.; son of Fred Herman and Mary Blanche (Baker) Fisher; married Mildred Leone Hoch, July 11, 1937; children: Fred Harvey, George Karl, James Rilan. *Education:* Kansas State University, B.S., 1937; University of California, Berkeley, Ph.D., 1942. *Home:* High Meadows, R.R.2, Carbondale, Ill. 62901. *Office:* Department of Zoology, Southern Illinois University, Carbondale, Ill. 62901.

CAREER: University of California, Berkeley, technical curator of Museum of Vertebrate Zoology, 1942-45; University of Hawaii, Honolulu, assistant professor of zoology, 1945-48; University of Illinois, Champaign-Urbana, associate professor of zoology, 1948-55; Southern Illinois University, Carbondale, professor of zoology, 1955—, chairman of department, 1955-71, assistant dean of School of Medicine, 1971—. Exchange professor at University of Nevada, 1947-48.

MEMBER: International Academy of Zoology, American Association for the Advancement of Science (fellow), American Ornithological Union, Society for the Study of Evolution, American Institute of Biological Sciences, American Association of University Professors, Cooper Ornithological Society, Wilson Ornithological Society, Illinois Academy of Science, Sigma Xi, Phi Delta Kappa, Phi Kappa Phi, Rotary International, Exchange Club (Urbana, Ill.).

WRITINGS: (With Donald C. Goodman) *The Myology of the Whooping Crane, Grus Americana,* University of Illinois Press, 1955; (with James B. Kitzmiller) *Laboratory Exercises in General Zoology,* Saunders, 1958; (with Goodman) *Fundamental Anatomy of the Feeding Apparatus in Waterfowl (Aves: Anatidae),* Southern Illinois University Press, 1962; (with wife, Mildred L. Fisher) *Wonders of the World of the Albatross* (illustrated with own photographs), Dodd, 1974. Assistant editor of *Condor,* 1942-45; editor of *Pacific Science,* 1947-48,*Auk,* 1948-52, *Illinois Biological Monographs,* 1952-55, and *Transactions of the Illinois Academy of Science,* 1955-59.*

* * *

FISHER, Peter Jack   1930-

PERSONAL: Born November 4, 1930, in Australia; married, 1956; children: two. *Education:* University of Western Australia, B.Sc., 1951; Ph.D., 1956. *Home:* 25 Drum Rd., Cookstown, Northern Ireland. *Office:* Department of Physics, Purdue University, Lafayette, Ind. 47907

CAREER: Purdue University, Lafayette, Ind., assistant professor, 1956-63, associate professor, 1963-68, professor of physics, 1968—.

WRITINGS: Jewels, Batsford, 1965; *The Science of Gems,* Scribner, 1966; *The Polio Story,* Heinemann, 1967; *The Universe, Life, and Man,* Heinemann, 1970.

WORK IN PROGRESS: Research on soft X-ray spectroscopy of the solid state and on the infrared properties of semiconductors.*

* * *

FITCH, Geraldine T(ownsend)   1892(?)-1976

1892(?)—September 23, 1976; American writer, public relations worker for Nationalist Chinese interests and consultant to Chinese publications. Fitch died in Pomona, Calif. Obituaries: *New York Times,* September 25, 1976.

* * *

FITZGERALD, James V.   1889(?)-1976

1889(?)—August 23, 1976; American newspaperman in New York and Washington, D.C. and civil servant specializing in information services. Fitzgerald was involved with motion picture newsreels, radio broadcasts, and was author of books on biographical, sports, and business subjects. He died in Bethesda, Md. Obituaries: *Washington Post,* August 26, 1976.

* * *

FLANDERS, James P(rescott)   1942-

PERSONAL: Born November 12, 1942, in Cornwall, N.Y.; son of Dwight P. (a professor) and Mildred (Hutchison) Flanders; married Juanita Hilderbrand (a librarian), December 29, 1966; children: Carl, Leah. *Education:* University of Illinois, B.S. (honors), 1964; Vanderbilt University, M.A., 1966, Ph.D., 1968. *Office:* Department of Psychology, Florida International University, Miami, Fla. 33199.

CAREER: Bowling Green State University, Bowling Green, Ky., assistant professor of psychology, 1970-72; Florida International University, Miami, assistant professor, 1972-73, associate professor of psychology, 1973—. *Military service:* U.S. Army, research psychologist in Medical Service Corps, 1968-70; became captain. *Member:* American Psychological Association, American Assocation of University Professors, Southeastern Psychological Assocation, Sigma Xi, Psi Chi.

WRITINGS: (Contributor) P. B. Smith, editor, *Group Processes,* Penguin, 1970; *Practical Psychology,* Harper, 1976; (contributor) E. P. Hollander, editor, *Principles and Methods of Social Psychology,* Oxford University Press, in press. Contributor to psychology and education journals.

WORK IN PROGRESS: A book on children and television; a book on unified social systems theory applied to population problems, with father, Dwight P. Flanders; a theoretical analysis of social skills for academic scholarly use; a scholarly analysis of resource allocation as a basis for clinical and social psychology.

* * *

FLEISHER, Belton Mendel   1935-

PERSONAL: Born May 16, 1935, in Hayward, Calif.; son of Belton and Charlotte (Mendel) Fleisher; married Elizabeth Wells, 1964. *Education:* Stanford University, A.B. (with honors), 1957, M.A., 1959, Ph.D., 1961. *Home:* 75 East Dodridge St., Columbus, Ohio 43202. *Office:* 1775 College Rd., Columbus, Ohio 43210.

CAREER: Stanford University, Stanford, Calif., acting assistant instructor in economics, 1958-59, 1960-61; University of Chicago, Chicago, Ill., assistant professor of economics, 1961-65; Ohio State University, Columbus, assistant professor, 1965-66, associate professor, 1966-69, professor of economics, 1969—, research associate of Center for Human Resource Research, 1965—. Consultant to Institute for Defense Analysis, Battelle Memorial Institute, and National Commission on Marijuana and Drug Abuse.

MEMBER: American Economic Association, Phi Beta Kappa. *Awards, honors:* U.S. Department of Health, Education & Welfare grant, 1962-64; National Science Foundation fellowship for London School of Economics and Political Science, University of London, 1963-64; grants from U.S. Department of Labor & Manpower Administration, 1971-72, 1973-74, National Institute on Child Health & Human Development, 1973-76, and U.S. Department of Labor's Bureau of International Affairs, 1975-76.

WRITINGS: (Contributor) Mark Perlman, editor, *Human Resources in the Urban Economy,* Johns Hopkins Press, 1963; *The Economics of Delinquency,* Quadrangle, 1966; *Labor Economics: Theory and Evidence,* Prentice-Hall, 1970; (contributor) H. S. Parnes, editor, *The Pre-Retirement Years,* Volume I, U.S. Department of Labor & Manpower Administration, 1970; (contributor) M. Borus, editor, *Evaluating the Impact of Manpower Programs,* Lexington Books, 1972; (contributor) Glen G. Cain and Harold Watts, editors, *Income Maintenance and Labor Supply: Econometric Studies,* Rand McNally, 1973; (with K. J. Kopecky and D. T. Paul) *A Primer in Economics,* Glencoe Press, 1976. Contributor of articles and reviews to professional journals.

WORK IN PROGRESS: A second edition of *Labor Economics: Theory, Policy, and Evidence,* with Thomas J. Kniesner.

* * *

FLORY, Harry R. 1899-1976

June 11, 1899—November 9, 1976; American journalist and consultant to government agencies. He served as wire service newsman in Paris, London, and New York. Flory died in Bridgeport, Conn. Obituaries: *New York Times,* November 10, 1976.

* * *

FLOYD, Harriet 1925-

PERSONAL: Born August 28, 1925, in New Jersey; daughter of George Rudolph and May (a writer; maiden name, Robilliard) Bredder; married William H. Floyd (a physician), December 20, 1947; children: Robert Vincent. *Education:* New York University, B.A., graduate study. *Politics:* Republican. *Religion:* Protestant. *Home and office:* 245 Brookmere Court, Ridgewood, N.J. 07450.

CAREER: Adventures in Science, Inc. (summer science program for children), Ridgewood, N.J., founder and executive director, 1959-61; Ridgewood Board of Education, Ridgewood, member and vice president, 1965-71.

WRITINGS: Plant It Now, Dry It Later, McGraw, 1973. Contributor to magazines and newspapers.

WORK IN PROGRESS: Religion, Medicine, and Politics; The Fashion of Flowers in Antique Glass Paperweights; an elementary physics book for young children.

SIDELIGHTS: Harriet Floyd writes that her current interests include solar energy and American foreign policy. She has traveled throughout Europe, the Middle East, South Africa, Taiwan, Japan, Mexico, the Caribbean, and the United States.

FLYTHE, Starkey S(harp), Jr. 1935-

PERSONAL: Born February 15, 1935, in Augusta, Ga.; son of Starkey Sharp (a lawyer) and Mary Bradley (Bacheller) Flythe. *Education:* University of the South, B.A., 1959; University of Georgia, M.A., 1962. *Home:* 1210 Pickwick Pl., Indianapolis, Ind. 46208. *Office:* Curtis Publishing Co., 1100 Waterway Blvd., Indianapolis, Ind. 46202.

CAREER: Free-lance writer, 1962-73; *Holiday,* Indianapolis, Ind., managing editor, 1973-74; *Saturday Evening Post,* Indianapolis, Ind., executive editor, 1974-76; *Country Gentleman,* Indianapolis, Ind., managing editor, 1976—. *Military service:* U.S. Army, Security Agency, 1958-60; served in Ethiopia. *Member:* Indianapolis Athletic Club, Augusta Country Club, Water Company Club. *Awards, honors:* J.D. from Augusta Law School.

WRITINGS: (Editor) *The Saturday Evening Post Christmas Book,* Curtis Publishing, 1976; (editor) *The Holiday Restaurant Awards Cookbook,* Curtis Publishing, 1976. Also editor of *The American Story.* Contributor to magazines, including *Holiday.*

* * *

FODOR, M. W. 1890(?)-1977

1890(?)—June 25, 1977; Hungarian-born American journalist and editor. A well known foreign correspondent, Fodor was an authority on Europe and Central Europe. His most notable assignments included the rise of Hitler, Mussolini, and coverage of World War II. Fodor died in Trostberg, West Germany. Obituaries: *New York Times,* July 2, 1977.

* * *

FOELL, Earl W(illiam) 1929-

PERSONAL: Born September 21, 1929, in Houston, Tex.; son of Ernest (a sales executive) and Margaret (Kane) Foell; married Cordelia Treanor, September 22, 1962; children: David, Jonathon, Hayden. *Education:* Principia College, B.A., 1949. *Office: Christian Science Monitor,* 1 Norway St., Boston, Mass. 02115.

CAREER/WRITINGS: Christian Science Monitor, Boston, Mass., reporter, editorial writer, and foreign correspondent, 1953-63, United Nations correspondents, 1963-70; *Los Angeles Times,* Los Angeles, Calif., foreign correspondent, 1968-70; *Christian Science Monitor,* managing editor, 1970—. *Member:* Associated Press Managing Editors Association, American Society of Newspaper Editors, United Nations Press Corps (president, 1968), International Press Institute. *Awards, honors:* Rudolph Elie Award, 1957, for series on problems of American cities; Sigma Delta Chi Award, 1964, for best United Nations coverage.

* * *

FOGELQUIST, Donald Frederick 1906-

PERSONAL: Born August 23, 1906, in Sioux City, Iowa; son of Frederick C. (a teacher) and Anna (Lundgren) Fogelquist; married Helen Rasmussen (a college teacher), July 1, 1939; children: Alan Frederick, Mark Stephen, James Donald. *Education:* Washington State University, B.A. (cum laude), 1930, M.A., 1933; University of Wisconsin, Madison, Ph.D., 1941; also attended University of Washington, Seattle, and University of New Mexico. *Home:* 326 Mount Holyoke Ave., Pacific Palisades, Calif. 90272. *Office:* Department of Spanish and Portuguese, University of California, Los Angeles, Calif. 90024.

CAREER: Washington State University, Pullman, instructor in German, 1937-38; University of Florida, Gainesville, instructor in Spanish 1939-40; University of Miami, Coral Gables, Fla., assistant professor of Spanish, 1941-42. Paraguayan-U.S. Cultural Center, Asuncion, Paraguay, director, 1946-47; Washington State University, assistant professor of Spanish, 1947-48; University of California, Los Angeles, assistant professor, 1948-56, associate professor, 1956-62, professor of Hispanic literature, 1962-74. Lecturer for U.S. State Department, 1959. *Military service:* U.S. Naval Reserve, active duty, 1942-45; became lieutenant commander.

MEMBER: Instituto Internacional de Literatura Iberoamericana, American Association of Teachers of Spanish and Portuguese. *Awards, honors:* Fulbright fellowship in Spain, 1962-63.

WRITINGS: *Juan Ramon Jimenez: Vida y Obra,* Hispanic Institute in the United States, 1958; *Espanoles de America y Americanos de Espana* (title means "Spaniards of America and Americans of Spain"), Editorial Gredos, 1968; *Juan Ramon Jiminez,* Twayne, 1976. Contributor to English- and Spanish-language literary journals.

WORK IN PROGRESS: A book on humanitarians and humanitarianism in colonial Spanish America, completion expected in 1979.

AVOCATIONAL INTERESTS: Travel in Europe and Latin America.

BIOGRAPHICAL/CRITICAL SOURCES: *Cuadernos americanos,* May-June, 1969.

* * *

FOLCH-RIBAS, Jacques 1928-

PERSONAL: Born November 11, 1928, in Barcelona, Spain; married Camille Du Cap (a biologist), November, 1953. *Education:* Earned degree from architectural school in Paris, France. *Home:* 649 Milton St., Montreal, Quebec, Canada H2X 1W6. *Office:* 3634 Aylmer St., Montreal, Quebec, Canada H2X 2C2.

CAREER: Architect and town planner in Montreal, Quebec, 1954—. Writer and art critic. *Member:* International Art Critics Association, Order of Art Critics of Quebec. *Awards, honors:* Prix France-Canada, 1974, for *Northlight, Lovelight.*

WRITINGS—Novels: *Jordi Bonet: Le signe et la terre* (title means "Jordi Bonet: The Sign and the Earth"), Editions du Centre de psychologie et de pedagogie, 1964; *Le Demolisseur* (title means "The Demolisher"), R. Laffont, 1970; *Le Greffon* (title means "The Graft"), R. Laffont, 1971; *Jacques de Tonnancour: Le signe et le temps* (title means "Jacques de Tonnancour: The Sign and the Times"), Presses de l'Universite du Quebec, 1971; *Une Aurore Boreale,* R. Laffont, 1974, translation by Jeffrey Leggatt published as *Northlight, Lovelight,* Reader's Digest Press, 1976.

Contributor of television and radio scripts to Canadian Broadcasting Company. Contributor of columns and reviews to *Vie Des Arts* (Montreal), and to *Liberte* (Montreal).

* * *

FOLEY, Gerald (Patrick) 1936-

PERSONAL: Born March 1, 1936, in Derry, Northern Ireland; son of Edward Daniel (an auditor) and Kathleen (McIvor) Foley; married Lanna McCarthy (a teacher), October 3, 1961; children: Kathleen Jane, Conor Gerald. *Education:* University College, Cork, Ireland, Bachelor of Engineering, 1957; University of Leeds, diploma in concrete technology, 1959. *Home:* 12 Whitehall Gardens, London W4 3LT, England. *Office:* Architectural Association, 34-36 Bedford Sq., London WC1, England.

CAREER: Electricity Supply Board, Dublin, Ireland, engineer, 1957-58; Harris & Sutherland (consulting engineers), London, England, design engineer, 1959-62; J. Jarvis & Sons (building contractors), London, site engineer, 1962-64; Harris & Sutherland, section leader, 1964-66; Indulex Engineering, London, technical services manager, 1966-67; Building Design Partnership, London, senior design engineer and associate, 1967-71; Architectural Association School of Architecture, London, 1971—, undergraduate tutor and lecturer in energy and alternative technology, coordinator of rational technology unit, now director of postgraduate energy program. *Member:* Institution of Civil Engineers.

WRITINGS: *The Energy Question,* Penguin, 1976.

Contributor to periodicals and design journals, including *Washington Post, Ecologist, Built Environment, Building Design, New Civil Engineer,* and *Architectural Design.*

WORK IN PROGRESS: Research on energy strategies for educational buildings, effects of energy constraints on future traffic levels, and social and political implication of future energy policies.

SIDELIGHTS: Gerald Foley says that since abandoning professional engineering, he has become increasingly convinced that "industrial society is entering a period of great change during which its ability to sustain and extend its liberal institutions will be tested to the limit. Many of its problems will arise from the changing patterns of energy supply and availability. If we are to avoid a future which is poor, brutish, and oppressed, we must work to devise strategies for the preservation and enhancement of what is good in the society we have created. I am a pessimist about what can be done, but prepared to be cheerful about it.

"My engineering training impels me to use simple numbers to describe some of the economic and energy variables with which we are dealing; but I believe strongly that our problems and their potential answers are social and political rather than technological. My writing is not directed towards producing deterministic models of what must be, but towards an illumination of the range of choice which exists within the boundaries of what can be."

* * *

FOLLIARD, Edward T(homas) 1899-1976

May 14, 1899—November 25, 1976; American Pulitzer prize-winning journalist who revealed a facist-type organization based in Atlanta, Ga. He also served as a war correspondent. Folliard died in Washington, D.C. Obituaries: *Washington Post,* November 26, 1976; *Current Biography,* February, 1977.

* * *

FOOTE-SMITH, Elizabeth 1913-

PERSONAL: Born October 4, 1913, in Red Wing, Minn.; daughter of Fred Warner and Emily (Batleau) Foote; married Harry Carroll Smith (an executive), August 22, 1938; children: Elizabeth Carol Smith Harvey, Timothy J., Christy Ann Smith Murphy. *Education:* Northwestern University, B.A., 1964; University of Chicago, M.A., 1966.

Home: 338 East Center Ave., Lake Bluff, Ill. 60044. *Agent:* H. N. Swanson, 8523 Sunset Blvd., Los Angeles, Calif. 90069.

CAREER: High school English teacher in Rockford, Ill., 1964-65, and Hoffman Estates, Ill., 1965-66; University of Wisconsin, Whitewater, instructor in English, 1967-69; freelance writer, 1969—. *Member:* Mystery Writers of America.

WRITINGS: Gentle Albatross (mystery), Putnam, 1976; *Never Say Die* (mystery), Putnam, 1977. Also author of a novel, "When Shall We Love," printed in *Redbook* magazine, May, 1969. Contributor of fiction and poetry to magazines, including *Playgirl, Partisan Review,* and *Michigan Quarterly Review.*

WORK IN PROGRESS: Rattus Erectus, a "historical romance-cautionary fable"; *McFeary's Depression,* a suspense novel.

SIDELIGHTS: Foote-Smith writes: "I am motivated to write for the pleasure of it and in the belief that art does change society, not by mirroring it, but by broadening, deepening, and sensitizing the collective human experience—and by prophesy."

* * *

FORBES, Bryan 1926-

PERSONAL: Born July 22, 1926, in London, England; son of William Theobald Clarke Forbes and Judith Kate Helen Seaton; married Constance Smith, February 10, 1951 (divorced, 1955); married Nanette Newman, August 27, 1955; children: Sarah Kate Amanda, Emma Katey. *Education:* Attended Royal Academy of Dramatic Art, 1941-42. *Office:* Beaver Films Ltd., Beaver Lodge, The Green, Surrey, England; and Bookshop, Virginia Water, Surrey, England.

CAREER: Actor on stage in England, beginning 1942; film actor in London, England, beginning 1948, and in Hollywood, Calif., until 1959; Beaver Films, Surrey, England, cofounder, producer, and director, 1959; Associated British Productions Ltd. (now EMI Film & Theatre Corp.), London, head of production and managing director, 1969-71, managing director and chief executive of EMI-MGM Elstree Studios, Boreham Woods, England, 1970-71, executive producer of "The Go-Between," "The Railway Children," and "Tales of Beatrix Potter," all released by EMI, all 1971; director of Capital Radio, 1973—. Director of films by others, including "The Wrong Box," Columbia, 1965, and "The Stepford Wives," 1974. Owner and operator of Bookshop, Surrey, British Broadcasting Corp. (BBC), member of general advisory council, 1965-69, member of schools council, 1971-73. *Military service:* British Army, Intelligence Corps, 1943-48. *Member:* British Film Academy (member of experimental film board), British Screenwriters Guild (member of council; council treasurer, 1960-63), British Actors' Equity Association, Writers Guild of Great Britain (trustee), Screen Actors Guild, Writers Guild of America, Directors Guild of America, Association of Cinema Technicians. *Awards, honors:* British Academy awards, 1959, for "The Angry Silence," 1962, for "Only Two Can Play," and 1964, for "Seance on a Wet Afternoon"; award from Writers Guild of Great Britain, 1962, for "Only Two Can Play"; United Nations award, 1962, for "The L-Shaped Room"; Edgar Award from Mystery Writers of America, and best screenplay award from San Sebastian Film Festival, both 1964, both for "Seance on a Wet Afternoon."

WRITINGS: Truth Lies Sleeping and Other Stories, Me-

thuen, 1951; *The Distant Laughter* (novel), Harper, 1972; *Notes for a Life* (autobiography), Collins, 1974; *The Slipper and the Rose* (novel), Quartet Books, 1976; *Ned's Gire* (biography of Dame Edith Evans), Little, Brown, 1977.

Screenplays: (And co-producer) "The Angry Silence," British Lion, 1960; (and director) "The L-Shaped Room," Columbia, 1962; (and director) "Seance on a Wet Afternoon," allied Film Makers, 1963; "King Rat," Columbia, 1964; (and director and producer) "The Whisperers," Lopert, 1966; (and director) "Deadfall," Twentieth Century-Fox, 1967; (and co-producer and director) "The Madwoman of Chaillot," 1968; (and director) "The Raging Moon," EMI, 1970, released in United States as "Long Ago Tomorrow," 1970; (co-author and director) "The Slipper and the Rose," 1975.

Author of filmed biography of Dame Edith Evans, released by Yorkshire Television, 1973, and a filmed biography of Elton John, Associated Television, 1974.

Fiction critic for *Spectator,* 1951-52. Contributor to popular British journals.

AVOCATIONAL INTERESTS: Reading, landscape gardening, photography, collecting books, collecting Napoleonic relics, "avoiding bores."

BIOGRAPHICAL/CRITICAL SOURCES: Bryan Forbes, *Notes for a Life,* Collins, 1974.

* * *

FORBES, Cabot L(owell) 1943-
(Christopher Martin Smith)

PERSONAL: Born June 1, 1943, in Andover, Mass.; son of Lowell A. (a banker) and Andrea (an investor; maiden name, Phelps) Forbes; married Josephine Oldham, August 6, 1962 (divorced, 1963); married Jane Goold (an artist), January 3, 1964. *Education:* University of Montrose, diplome d'excellence, 1962. *Politics:* "Monarchist." *Religion:* Roman Catholic. *Home:* 16 Rue Fauquier, Paris VIIIieme 07500, France.

CAREER: University of Montrose, Geneva, Switzerland, lecturer in law, 1964; investor, 1964—. Director of Zoophone Press. *Member:* Club de Sportifs, Action d'Hiver.

WRITINGS—Novels: *Fourteen Washington Place,* Pinnacle Books, 1976; *Two West Fifty-Seventh Street,* Pinnacle Books, 1977; *Seven-Fifty Park Avenue,* Pinnacle Books, 1977.

WORK IN PROGRESS: A major novel based on the life of Marcel Proust; work under pseudonym.

SIDELIGHTS: Forbes comments: "I always wanted to be famous, rich is not enough."

* * *

FORBES, Malcolm S(tevenson) 1919-

PERSONAL: Born August 19, 1919, in Brooklyn, N.Y.; son of Bertie Charles (an editor and publisher) and Adelaide (Stevenson) Forbes; married Roberta Remsen Laidlaw, September 21, 1946; children: Malcolm S. Jr., Robert Laidlaw, Christopher Charles, Timothy Carter, Moira Hamilton. *Education:* Woodrow Wilson School of Public and International Affairs, A.B., 1941. *Politics:* Republican. *Religion:* Episcopalian. *Home:* Timberfield, Old Dutch Rd., Far Hills, N.J. 07931. *Office:* Forbes Bldg., 60 Fifth Ave., New York, N.Y. 10011.

CAREER: Fairfield Times (weekly newspaper), Lancaster,

Ohio, owner and publisher, 1941-42; *Lancaster Tribune* (weekly newspaper), Lancaster, owner and publisher, 1942; Forbes Inc., New York City, vice-president, 1947-64, president, 1964—, *Forbes* magazine, associate publisher, 1946-54, publisher, 1954—, editor, 1954-57, editor-in-chief, 1957—; founder of *Nation's Heritage* (bimonthly historical magazine), 1948. President, Forbes International Inc., Investors Advisory Institute, Slegers-Forbes Inc. (motorcycle dealership), Forbes Trinchera Inc.; board chairman or member, 60 Fifth Avenue Corp., Fiji Forbes, Sangre de Cristo Ranches Inc. Bernardsville Borough councilman, 1949-51; New Jersey state senator, 1951-58; unsuccessful Republican candidate for governor of New Jersey, 1957; delegate-at-large to Republican National Convention, 1960. Member of board of advisors, Naval War College, 1975—; trustee, St. Mark's School, 1976—; director, Coast Guard Academy Foundation, 1976—. *Military service:* U.S. Army, 1942-45; received Bronze Star.

MEMBER: International Balloonists Association, International Society of Balloonpost Specialists, National Aeronautic Association (member of board of directors, 1975—), Balloon Federation of America (member of board of directors, 1974—), Aircraft Owners and Pilots Association, Lighter Than Air Society, British Balloon and Airship Club, Confrerie des Chevaliers du Tastevin, New Jersey Historical Society, Association of the United States Army, Navy League, St. Andrew's Society, Coral Beach Club, Essex Fox Hounds, New York Racquet and Tennis Club, Links Club, New York Yacht Club, Explorers Club, Pilgrims of the United States. *Awards, honors:* Freedom Foundation Medal, 1949; Harmon Trophy, 1975. Honorary degrees from Nasson College, 1966, Oklahoma Christian College, 1973, Millikin University, 1974, Franklin Pierce College, 1975, Bryant College, 1976.

WRITINGS: Fact and Comment, Knopf, 1974. Writer of "Fact and Comment" column in *Forbes,* 1950—.

SIDELIGHTS: Forbes was the first balloonist to fly coast-to-coast in a single hot air balloon. While performing the feat in 1973 he set six world records. The world's first balloon museum was founded by him in Normandy, France, also in 1973. *Avocational interests:* Art collecting, motorcycling, ballooning.

* * *

FORD, Richard 1944-

PERSONAL: Born February 16, 1944, in Jackson, Miss.; son of Parker Carrol (a salesman) and Edna (Akin) Ford; married Kristina Hensley (a research professor), 1968. *Agent:* Gerard McCauley, P.O. Box 456, Cranbury, N.J. 08512.

CAREER: Writer, 1976—. *Member:* Writers Guild (East). *Awards, honors:* University of Michigan Society of Fellows, 1971-74; Guggenheim fellow, 1977-78.

WRITINGS: A Piece of My Heart (novel), Harper, 1976. Also author of a screenplay. Contributor of stories, articles, and reviews to magazines.

WORK IN PROGRESS: A novel set in Mexico.

SIDELIGHTS: Ford writes: "The only other thing I ever really wanted to do was be a lawyer. I went to law school a while, quit too soon, felt desperate and decided to write fictions. So: chief motivation is desperation—probably false. I might've been an average lawyer."

FOREMAN, Clark H(owell) 1902-1977

February 19, 1902—June 15, 1977; American civil libertarian, government consultant and employee. He was involved with the Supreme Court's decision to void legislation requiring registration of Communist Party members. Foreman was author of books on political and consumer issues. He died in Adjuntas, P.R. Obituaries: *New York Times,* June 19, 1977; *Current Biography,* August, 1977.

* * *

FORNARI, Harry D(avid) 1919-

PERSONAL: Born May 21, 1919, in Rome, Italy; came to the United States in 1939, naturalized citizen, 1943; son of Arthur F. (a businessman) and Valentina (Piperno) Fornari; married Maria Luisa Della Seta, 1945; children: James, Daniel. *Education:* Attended University of Rome, 1937-39; Columbia University, B.S., 1941, A.M., 1952; University of Bologna, Dr.Lettere (cum laude), 1946; City University of New York, Ph.D., 1969. *Home:* 2 Rivers Dr., Great Neck, N.Y. 11020. *Office:* Bunge Corp., 1 Chase Manhattan Plaza, New York, N.Y. 10005.

CAREER: Fortex Mills, Inc., New York City, sales manager, 1939-41; U.S. Office of War Information, New York City, news editor, 1941-42; U.S. Information Service, Rome, Italy, chief of exhibits section, 1945-47; Pavia & Co., Inc. (export-import business), New York City, vice-president, 1947-52; Bunge Corp. (exporters of agricultural commodities), New York City, vice-president, 1952—. *Military service:* U.S. Army, Psychological Warfare Branch, 1942-45; served in North Africa and Italy. *Member:* Agricultural History Society, American Fats and Oils Association (past president; member of board of directors), American Historical Association, American Management Association, Risk and Insurance Management Society, Alumni Association of the School of General Studies (Columbia University), Graduate Faculties Alumni of Columbia University (past president; member of board of directors), Lawyers' Club.

WRITINGS: La Dottrina di Monroe (title means "The Monroe Doctrine"), Zanichelli, 1947; *Mussolini's Gadfly,* Vanderbilt University Press, 1971; *Bread upon the Waters,* Aurora, 1973; *A Story of Peace and Other War Stories,* Aurora, 1977.

WORK IN PROGRESS: Papers on agricultural history; articles on modern European history; a biographical contribution to a book on Fascist chieftains, publication by Bulzoni expected in 1978.

AVOCATIONAL INTERESTS: Historiography, woodworking, mountain climbing.

* * *

FORREST, Wilbur S. 1887-1977

February 13, 1887—March 23, 1977; American journalist working as newspaper reporter, editor and wire service correspondent in the U.S. and Europe. He was assigned as a war correspondent in Europe and later reported from Asia. Forrest was noted as the first reporter to give an account of Charles Lindburgh's landing in Paris in 1927. He was author of a book on journalism. Forrest died in Newton, Pa. Obituaries: *New York Times,* March 26, 1977; *Current Biography,* May, 1977.

* * *

FOSBURGH, Hugh (Whitney) 1916-1976

February 3, 1916—November 6, 1976; American writer of

novels and outdoor books. An avid naturalist and conservationist, Fosburgh co-developed a wildlife haven in the Adirondack Mountains. He also served as a bomber pilot in World War II and was a magazine reporter. Fosburgh died in Minerva, N.Y. Obituaries: *New York Times,* November 8, 1976.

* * *

FOSHEE, John (Hugh)   1931-

PERSONAL: Born November 19, 1931, in Birmingham, Ala.; son of John H. and Grace (Thomson) Foshee; married wife, Reba, June 15, 1956 (divorced, 1966); married third wife, Marta (a teacher), July 8, 1967; children: John Greig. *Education:* Attended University of Alabama. *Politics:* None. *Religion:* Presbyterian. *Home and office:* 4820 Court V, Birmingham, Ala. 35208.

CAREER: Writer. Has worked as grocery clerk, tile setter, carpenter's apprentice, aircraft mechanic, and most recently, as electrical draftsman and designer. *Member:* Birmingham Canoe Club (founder and past president).

WRITINGS—With own photographs: *Little River Canyon: Grand Canyon of the South,* privately printed, 1971; *Alabama Canoe Rides and Float Trips,* Strode, 1975, 2nd edition, 1976; *You, Too, Can Canoe,* Strode, 1977; *Pine Tree Trails: Hiking the Forests of Alabama,* Strode, in press. Privately printed cartographer. Contributor of about fifty articles on technical subjects and the out-of-doors to magazines.

WORK IN PROGRESS: Research on old railroad stations of Alabama.

SIDELIGHTS: Foshee writes: "My writing first began with poetry. Unfortunately poetry was something I couldn't sell . . . [but] I still harbor thoughts of coming out with a book of it.

"I turned to articles next and achieved a measure of success. . . . I had interests of hiking, backpacking and canoeing . . . so many of my articles were on these subjects. My next undertaking was the surveying, drawing, and printing of a map of an area in Alabama that was a unique wilderness and a gorge. . . .

"I write about things that interest me. My problem is that too many things interest me. I do all of my own photography. . . . I love backpacking and wilderness camping as well as canoe camping. I've spent a good bit of time walking the Appalachian Trail and continue to do so. I was briefly into the kayak business—building molded fiberglass slalom boats and number kayaking among my interests. . . .

"I currently have several other writing projects in progress but am . . . vacationing just now. I find writing a hard job and a lonely job and like to relax from it at the end of a project.

"I am not a world traveler. I prefer the companionship of a few selected people off in the woods, or on a river somewhere. I dislike crowds, and need, but don't particularly like, people."

* * *

FOSTER, Genevieve W(akeman)   1902-

PERSONAL: Born February 20, 1902, in New Haven, Conn.; daughter of Charles J. (a physician) and Genevieve (a teacher of classics; maiden name, Kinne) Bartlett; married A. Maurice Wakeman, June 28, 1926 (died March 2, 1929); married Roger Sherman Foster (an attorney), July 5, 1934; children: Charles B. Wakeman, Roger Sherman Foster, Jr.,

Jane Foster Buckwalter. *Education:* Vassar College, B.A., 1922; Yale University, graduate study, 1923-25, 1932-34; University of Pittsburgh, M.S., 1956. *Politics:* Democrat. *Religion:* Unitarian-Universalist. *Home:* 6622 Broad St., Brookmont, Md. 20016.

CAREER: Yale Review, New Haven, Conn., editorial assistant, 1925-27; Vassar College, Poughkeepsie, N.Y., instructor in English, 1929-30; Bryn Mawr College, Bryn Mawr, Pa., instructor in English, 1930-32; English teacher in private school in Greenway, Md., 1940-42; Bryn Mawr College, instructor in English, 1942-46; St. Christopher's Hospital, Philadelpha, Pa., child therapist, 1946-47; Children's House (school for emotionally disturbed children), Washington, D.C., child therapist, 1948-50, director, 1950-54; University of Pittsburgh, Pittsburgh, Pa., instructor, 1956-58, assistant professor of child development and care, 1958-65; University of Maryland, College Park, lecturer in psychiatry and education, 1967-71; writer, 1971—. Child therapist at District of Columbia Mental Hygiene Clinic, 1948-49; program director at Western Psychiatric Institute's Children's Residential Treatment Service, 1956-59, assistant chief of service, 1959-60; founder and director of Technoma Workshop for Disturbed Adolescents, 1961-65.

MEMBER: Child Welfare Association of America, American Child Day Care Association, Menninger Foundation, Maryland Child Day Care Association, Analytical Psychology Club of New York (charter member), Montgomery County (Md.) Child Day Care Association, Washington Speech and Hearing Association (member of board of directors, 1969-76). *Awards, honors:* Annual award from United Mental Health Services of Allegheny County, Pa., 1963, for founding Technoma Workshop for Disturbed Adolescents.

WRITINGS: (With Karen Dahlberg VanderVen, Eleanore R. Kroner, and others) *Child Care Work with Emotionally Disturbed Children,* University of Pittsburgh Press, 1972. Contributing editor of *Child Care Quarterly,* 1972-73, member of editorial board, 1973—.

SIDELIGHTS: Genevieve Foster writes: "My interest shifted in mid-career from the study of poetry to the study of people; this necessitated a new educational effort, and meant starting afresh in a new career. I am now retired, still interested but only marginally involved."

* * *

FOSTER, Lee   1923(?)-1977

1923(?)—April 11, 1977; American newsman, writer and lecturer. Foster served as a foreign correspondent and as a member of the editorial staff of the book page, travel, and editorial page and of the *Times Encyclopedic Almanac.* He was also contributor to popular magazines. Foster died in New York City. Obituaries: *New York Times,* April 12, 1977.

* * *

FOSTER, Philip (John)   1927-

PERSONAL: Born January 22, 1927, in London, England; came to the United States in 1958; son of Philip Sydney (a bus driver) and Maud (Gibbs) Foster; married Paula Hirsch, 1956; children: Michael Paul, Graham Philip. *Education:* London School of Economics and Political Science, B.Sc., 1948; Northwestern University, graduate study, 1948-49; London Institute of Education, University of London, cert. educ., 1955; University of Chicago, Ph.D., 1962. *Home:* 5749 Dorchester, Chicago, Ill. 60637. *Office:* Comparative

Education Center, University of Chicago, 5835 South Kimbark Ave., Chicago, Ill. 60637.

CAREER: Government of Uganda, Gulu, education officer, 1955-58; University of Chicago, Chicago, Ill., instructor, 1959-61, assistant professor, 1961-64, associate professor, 1964-68, professor of comparative education, 1968—, assistant director of Comparative Education Center, 1962-72, director, 1972—. Visiting professor at University of Ibadan, 1966-67, and University of London, 1971-72. *Military service:* Royal Air Force, 1950-53; became flight lieutenant. *Member:* Comparative and International Education Society (president, 1970-71), American Sociological Association, American Educational Research Association. *Awards, honors:* Carnegie Foundation grant, Ivory Coast, 1962-65; Laing Prize from University of Chicago, 1968, for *Education and Social Change in Ghana;* National Institute of Mental Health grant, Cameroon Republic, 1968-72.

WRITINGS: Education and Social Change in Ghana, University of Chicago Press, 1966; (with Remi Clignet) *The Fortunate Few,* Northwestern University Press, 1966; *Africa South of the Sahara,* Macmillan, 1968; (editor with A. R. Zolberg, and contributor) *Ghana and the Ivory Coast: Perspectives on Modernization,* University of Chicago Press, 1971; (editor with J. R. Sheffield, and contributor) *Education and Rural Development,* Evans Brothers, 1974. Also contributor to *Problems of Education in Developing Areas,* 1969, and *Current Trends in Linguistics,* Volume VII, Mouton & Co., 1971. Contributor to scholarly journals.

WORK IN PROGRESS: Studying career patterns of graduates of the University of the West Indies, 1952-75; writing on problems of education, social stratification, and economic development.

AVOCATIONAL INTERESTS: Music, reading, cricket.

* * *

FOUHY, Ed(ward Michael) 1934-

PERSONAL: Born November 30, 1934, in Boston, Mass.; son of Joseph (a salesman) and Mary (Herlihy) Fouhy; married Barbara Mahoney (a travel agent), April 15, 1961; children: Beth, Mark. *Education:* University of Massachusetts, B.A., 1956; graduate study at Boston University, 1959-60. *Home:* 49 Eaton Rd., Larchmont, N.Y. 10538. *Office:* NBC News, 30 Rockefeller Plaza, New York, N.Y. 10020.

CAREER/WRITINGS: Columbia Broadcasting System (CBS) News, New York City, associate producer, 1966-67, bureau manager in Saigon, Viet Nam, 1967-68, bureau manager in Los Angeles, Calif., 1968-69, producer in Washington, D.C., 1969-74; National Broadcasting Company (NBC), New York City, senior producer of NBC Nightly News, 1974—. Notable assignments include the first satellite broadcast from Hawaii, coverage of the Democratic convention in Chicago in 1968, the Viet Nam war, and President Nixon's trip to China in 1972. *Military service:* U.S. Marine Corps, 1956-59; became lieutenant. *Member:* University of Massachusetts Alumni Club (president of Washington, D.C., chapter), Sigma Delta Chi. *Awards, honors:* Drew Pearson Award for investigative reporting, 1973; awards from National Academy of Television Arts and Sciences (Emmy) for Watergate stories, 1974.

* * *

FOWLES, Jib 1940-

PERSONAL: Born August 14, 1940, in Hartford, Conn.; son of Lloyd W. (a historian) and Jane (Briggs) Fowles; mar-

ried Joy Castronovo (a teacher), September 20, 1975. *Education:* Wesleyan University, B.A., 1963; Columbia University, M.A., 1967; New York University, Ph.D., 1974. *Office:* Studies of the Future, University of Houston at Clear Lake City, Houston, Tex. 77058.

CAREER: New York University, New York, N.Y., instructor in English as a second language, 1967-72; University of Houston at Clear Lake City, Houston, Tex., assistant professor, 1974-75, associate professor of studies of the future and chairman of the program, 1975—. *Military service:* U.S. Army, 1964-66. *Member:* American Sociological Association, Society for the History of Technology, World Future Society (local president). *Awards, honors:* Fulbright scholar in India, 1963-64.

WRITINGS: Mass Advertising as Social Forecast, Greenwood Press, 1976; (editor) *Handbook of Futures Research,* Greenwood Press, in press.

WORK IN PROGRESS: Pro-Industrialism, on the significance of industrial culture.

SIDELIGHTS: Fowles remarks: "My chief preoccupation is with an appreciative analysis of industrial culture—its past, present, and future."

* * *

FOX, Gilbert T(heodore) 1915-
(Gill Fox; Ted Fox)

PERSONAL: Born November 29, 1915, in Brooklyn, N.Y.; son of Theodore John (an accountant) and Florence (Gatto) Fox; married Helen Fittipaldi, June 1, 1940; children: Susan McKeeman, Donna Woodward. *Education:* Studied drawing at Grand Chaumier Art School, Paris, and by correspondence. *Politics:* Independent. *Religion:* Lutheran. *Home and office address:* P.O. Box 166, Redding Ridge, Conn. 06876.

CAREER: Fliescher Studios, (animation), New York, N.Y., inker, 1934-36; worked in Harry A. Chesler Shop of Comic Book Art, 1936-37; sports cartoonist for *Long Island Press,* 1938-39; Quality Comics, Stamford, Conn., editor and artist, 1938-52; New York Herald Tribune Syndicate, New York, N.Y., artist, 1951-53; *New York Sunday News,* New York City, creator of "Bumper to Bumper," 1953-63; Newspaper Enterprise Association, Cleveland, Ohio, artist and writer for "Side Glances," a daily comic panel syndicated to about five hundred fifty newspapers, 1962—. Freelance comic advertising illustrator; produced "light illustration" for *American Weekly. Military service:* U.S. Army, cartoonist and artist for European edition of *Stars and Stripes,* 1944-46.

MEMBER: National Cartoonists Society (member of board of governors, 1961-63), Comics Council. *Awards, honors:* "Side Glances" was nominated for Rueben Award of National Cartoonists Society in 1968 and 1969.

WRITINGS—Under name Gill Fox: *Wilbert* (collected syndicate cartoons), Pocket Books, 1956; *My Son, the Doctor* (collected medical cartoons), Gold Medal, 1963. Contributor of political cartoons to *Paris Post* under pseudonym Ted Fox, 1945-46.

WORK IN PROGRESS: Sunday feature preparation of "Side Glances."

SIDELIGHTS: Fox's cartoon "Side Glances," syndicated since 1929, is the oldest syndicate gag panel feature in the United States. His sister, Lorraine Fox, was the leading woman illustrator in America. He comments: "I feel strongly that topical humor is the wave of the future for entertainment cartoon features. It is already being used in 'Side Glances,' 'Berrys World' and "Doonesbury.' In the case of 'Doonesbury,' it resulted in the feature winning the Pulitzer Award, a breakthrough. I believe that from this point, entertainment features should be considered on the same level as 'political cartoons' by the Pulitzer committee for the award.''

BIOGRAPHICAL/CRITICAL SOURCES: Cartoonist Profiles, May 6, 1970; James Steranko, *The Steranko History of Comics, Number Two*, Supergraphics Publication, 1972.

* * *

FOX-MARTIN, Milton 1914(?)-1977

1914(?)—June 21, 1977; Internationally known business executive and author of works on sales subjects. Fox-Martin died in Amsterdam, Netherlands. Obituaries: *New York Times*, June 23, 1977.

* * *

FRACKMAN, Nathaline 1903(?)-1977
(Nata Lee)

1903(?)—January 27, 1977; American socialite and author of books on entertaining under pseudonym Nata Lee. She died in New York City. Obituaries: *New York Times*, January 28, 1977; *AB Bookman's Weekly*, February 14, 1977.

* * *

FRADIN, Dennis Brindell 1945-

PERSONAL: Born December 20, 1945, in Chicago, Ill.; son of Myron (an accountant) and Selma (Brindell) Fradin; married Judith Bloom (a high school English teacher), March 19, 1967; children: Anthony, Diana. *Education:* Northwestern University, B.A., 1967; University of Illinois, graduate study, 1968. *Religion:* Jewish. *Home:* 2121 Dobson, Evanston, Ill. 60202. *Agent:* McIntosh & Otis, Inc., 475 Fifth Ave., New York, N.Y. 10017.

CAREER: Faraday Elementary School, Chicago, Ill., teacher, 1968—.

WRITINGS—For children; all published by Children's Press: *Illinois in Words and Pictures*, 1976; *Virginia in Words and Pictures*, 1976; *California in Words and Pictures*, 1977; *Ohio in Words and Pictures*, 1977; *Cara* (fiction), 1977; *Alaska in Words and Pictures*, 1977; *Wisconsin in Words and Pictures*, 1977; *Bad Luck Tony*, 1977; *South Carolina in Words and Pictures*, in press. Contributor to magazines, including *Scholastic, Saturday Evening Post, National Humane Review, Teacher Paper, Oui*, and *Midwest*.

WORK IN PROGRESS: A series of six juvenile mystery stories, for Children's Press.

SIDELIGHTS: Fradin writes: "My star has made a sudden rise in the children's book field. Originally, I wrote adult short stories for a variety of publications. But, since I was teaching small children, I found my interest turning in the direction of children's books. One day I will resume writing adult fiction, I have no doubt." *Avocational interests:* Astronomy, playing baseball, watching baseball, "all kinds of games."

* * *

FRANDSEN, Julius 1907-1976

July 12, 1907—November 14, 1976; American newsman serving as a wire service reporter in New York and Washington, D.C. Frandsen was involved with the coverage of such notable events as the dirigible Hindenburg disaster, the attack on Pearl Harbor, and the death of Franklin D. Roosevelt at Warm Springs, Ga. Frandsen died in Washington, D.C. Obituaries: *New York Times*, November 15, 1977; *Washington Post*, November 15, 1977.

* * *

FRANKEL, Hermann F. 1899(?)-1977

1899(?)—April 18, 1977; American educator and expert on ancient Greek cultural subjects. He was the author of scholarly works in his field. Frankel died in Santa Cruz, Calif. Obituaries: *New York Times*, April 13, 1977; *AB Bookman's Weekly*, June 7, 1977.

* * *

FRANKLAND, Mark 1934-

PERSONAL: Born April 19, 1934, in London, England; son of Roger and Elizabeth (Sanday) Frankland. *Education:* Cambridge University, B.A., 1957. *Office: Observer*, 8 St. Andrew's Hill, London E.C.4, England.

CAREER: Observer, London, England, foreign correspondent, 1961—. Foreign correspondent for *Economist*, London, 1967-75. Has reported from Moscow, Saigon, Tokyo, and Washington, D.C.

WRITINGS: Khrushchev: A Political Biography, Stein & Day, 1967.

* * *

FRANKLIN, Adele 1887(?)-1977

1887(?)—February 28, 1977; American educator and founder of innovative programs for primary school children. Franklin was author of books and articles on child guidance and educational subjects. She served as a consultant to government and private agencies. Franklin died in South Bend, Ind. Obituaries: *New York Times*, March 2, 1977.

* * *

FRASER, B. Kay 1941-

PERSONAL: Born October 15, 1941, in Portland, Ore.; daughter of Albert (a marine engineer) and Mary E. (a bookkeeper; maiden name, McKay) Fraser; married Jim Wamsley, April, 1963 (divorced, 1968); married Roy F. McCurdy (a real estate broker), December 30, 1970 (died May 9, 1977); children: Derek. *Education:* University of Oregon, B.A., 1963. *Politics:* Independent. *Home and office address:* P.O. Box 398, Florence, Ore. 97439.

CAREER: University of Oregon, Eugene, editor for Bureau of Business Research, 1962-63; *Siuslaw News*, Florence, Ore., news editor, 1964; Showalker Lynch Advertising, Portland, Ore., copy writer, 1965; Department of Motor Vehicles, Salem, Ore., informational representative, 1966-68; writer, 1968—. *Member:* Outdoor Writers Association of America, Northwest Outdoor Writers Association.

WRITINGS: Tole Painting, Sterling, 1971; *Decorative Tole Painting*, Crown, 1972; *Creative Bottle Cutting*, Crown, 1973; *Decorative Plastercraft*, Crown, 1974; *Modern Stitchery*, Crown, 1976. Contributor to outdoor and craft magazines, including *Field and Stream, Hunting and Fishing Guide, Creative Crafts*, and *Women's Homecraft*.

WORK IN PROGRESS: The Peddlers, a novel.

FREDE, Richard 1934-

PERSONAL: Born March 20, 1934, in Albany, N.Y.; son of Henry (a manufacturer) and Helene (an advertising writer; maiden name, Spooner) Frede; married Judy Zwerdling, April, 1964 (divorced, 1966); married Barbara Trautenberg (a special education teacher), April 16, 1967; children: Michael Ari, Benjamin Dov. Education: Yale University, B.A., 1955. Home and office: Old Street Road, Peterborough, N.H. 03458. Agent: Monica McCall, International Creative Management, 40 West 57th St., New York, N.Y. 10019.

CAREER: Writer, photographer, sculptor. Writer for Sports Illustrated, New York, N.Y., 1955-56; director of Monadnock Indoor Tennis Club, Monadnock, N.H., 1971-75. Member: American P.E.N., Authors Guild, Dramatists Guild. Awards, honors: Awarded six MacDowell Colony fellowships, 1956-61.

WRITINGS—All novels; all published by Random House: Entry E, 1958; The Interns, 1960; The Secret Circus, 1967; Coming-Out Party, 1969; The Pilots, 1977. Also author, under pseudonym, of three novels in the mystery/suspense genre. Contributor of poetry and short stories to Harper's, Short Story International, Fantasy and Science Fiction, and American Scholar.

SIDELIGHTS: Frede's novel The Interns was made into two movies, "The Interns," 1962, and "The New Interns," 1964. Avocational interests: Politics, tennis, skiing, flying, painting, music, and cooking.

* * *

FREEDMAN, Benedict 1919-

PERSONAL: Born December 19, 1919, in New York, N.Y.; son of David (a Broadway playwright and radio writer) and Beatrice (a violinist; maiden name, Goodman) Freedman; married Nancy Mars (an author), June 29, 1941; children: Johanna, Michael, Deborah. Education: University of California at Los Angeles, Ph.D., 1970. Politics: "I vote on issues. Not locked into a given party." Religion: "Ethics." Home: 4859 Stratford Rd., Los Angeles, Calif. 90042. Agent: Scott Meredith, 845 Third Ave., New York, N.Y. 10022. Office: Department of Mathematics, Occidental College, Los Angeles, Calif. 90041.

CAREER: Began as writer for Al Jolson radio program and Metro-Goldwyn-Mayer studios, 1939; Curtiss-Wright Technical Institute, Glendale, Calif., instructor in analysis and design, 1942-43; Kaiser-Hughes Aircraft Co., Los Angeles, Calif., stress analyst, 1943-46; Occidental College, Los Angeles, lecturer in mathematics, 1970—, director of general studies, 1972-75, chairman of mathematics, 1974—. Novelist. Host of Columbia Broadcasting System (CBS) educational television series, "Ethical Alternatives," 1976. Member: Authors League, Writers Guild, Mathematic Association of America, Association for Symbolic Logic, American Mathematics Society.

WRITINGS—All novels, all with Nancy Freedman: Back to the Sea, Viking, Blue Book, 1942; Mrs. Mike, Coward, 1947; This and No More, Harper, 1950; The Spark & The Exodus, Crown, 1954; Lootville, Holt, 1957; Tresa, Holt, 1959; The Apprentice Bastard, Simon & Schuster, 1966; Cyclone of Silence, Simon & Schuster, 1969.

WORK IN PROGRESS: Ethical Alternatives.

SIDELIGHTS: "My work as a novelist, a logician and a teacher," Freedman told CA, "come together in this investigation of ethics. Ethical Alternatives is a work addressed to Everyman, a 'do it yourself ethics' in which I demonstrate the need to know just what it is a person lives by. It is a book that examines and offers choices. In a section I intend to be skipped by some readers I subject my reasoning to rigorous logical analysis."

The Freedmans' Mrs. Mike was the subject of a 1947 motion picture.

* * *

FREELAND, Stephen L. 1911(?)-1977

1911(?)—March 10, 1977; American news magazine editor, author and health specialist. He served as staff member of and consultant to government and private institutions. Freeland served during World War II as an officer in the Navy and was awarded the Silver Star. He was co-author of a volume on naval history. Freeland died in Washington, D.C. Obituaries: Washington Post, March 12, 1977.

* * *

FREEMAN, Lea David 1887(?)-1976

1887(?)—August 22, 1976; American playwright, film writer and lawyer. Freeman died in New Orleans, La. Obituaries: New York Times, August 27, 1976.

* * *

FREEMAN, Linton C(larke) 1927-

PERSONAL: Born July 4, 1927, in Chicago, Ill.; son of Willis (a bank auditor) and Kathryn Clarke (Kieffer) Freeman; married Sue Feinberg (an artist), August 2, 1957; children: Stacey, Michael. Education: University of Chicago, student, 1943-44; Roosevelt University, B.A., 1952; University of Hawaii, M.A., 1953; Northwestern University, Ph.D., 1956. Politics: Democrat. Office: Department of Social Relations, Lehigh University, Bethlehem, Pa. 18015.

CAREER: Northwestern University, Evanston, Ill., lecturer in sociology, 1954; University of Illinois, Chicago, lecturer, 1955, instructor in sociology, 1955-56; Syracuse University, Syracuse, N.Y., assistant professor, 1956-61, associate professor of sociology, 1961-67; University of Pittsburgh, Pittsburgh, Pa., professor of sociology and computer science, 1967-69; University of Hawaii, Honolulu, professor of sociology, 1969-72, professor of information science, 1970-72, associate director of Social Science Research Institute, 1967; Dalhousie University, Halifax, Nova Scotia, visiting professor and Killam Senior Lecturer in sociology, 1972-73; Lehigh University, Bethlehem, Pa., Lucy G. Moses Distinguished Professor of Sociology, 1973—. Visiting assistant professor at Northwestern University, 1958-59; professor at Williams College, summer, 1968; professor at University of Michigan, summers, 1974-76. Vice-president and director of research for Social Research Institute, 1958-59; chairman of National Academy of Science subcommittee on information storage and retrieval, 1965-67; member of International Committee on Social Sciences Documentation, 1965-69; member of fellowship review panel of National Institute of Mental Health, 1968-71; chairman of International Social Science Council task force for data inventory and retrieval, 1969-70. Member of Onondaga County, N.Y. Board of Supervisors, 1966-68. Military service: U.S. Navy, 1944-46.

MEMBER: American Association for the Advancement of Science, American Sociological Association, American Statistical Association, Alpha Kappa Delta (member of executive committee, 1965-67).

WRITINGS: (With R. W. Mack and Seymour Yellin) *Thirty Years of Research and Theory in Social Mobility,* Syracuse University Press, 1957; *Elementary Applied Statistics,* Wiley, 1965; (with P. E. Convense, W. D. Garvey, and others) *Communication Systems and Resources in the Behavioral Sciences,* National Academy of Sciences, 1967; *Patterns of Local Community Leadership,* Bobbs-Merrill, 1968; (with M. H. Sunshine) *Residential Segregation Patterns,* Schenkman, 1970; *Bibliography on Social Networks,* Council of Planning Libraries, Exchange Bibliographies, 1976.

Contributor: Robert F. Winch, editor, *Mate Selection,* Harper, 1957; Howard Becker and Alvin Boskoff, editors, *Modern Sociological Theory in Continuity and Change,* Dryden, 1957; Kimball Young, editor, *Social Psychology,* Appleton, 3rd edition, 1957 (Freeman was not associated with earlier editions); R. W. O'Brien, C. C. Schrag, and W. T. Martin, editors, *Readings in General Sociology,* Houghton, 1964; E. Wandt, editor, *A Cross Section of Educational Research,* McKay, 1966; D. P. McAllester, editor, *Readings in Anthropology,* Johnson Reprint, 1967; P. E. Mott and M. T. Aiken, editors, *The Structure of Community Power,* Random House, 1967; Irwin Deutscher and Elizabeth Thompson, editors, *Studies of the Urban Poor,* Basic Books, 1967; R. A. Manners and D. Kaplan, editors, *Theory in Anthropology,* Aldine, 1968. Contributor of about twenty-five articles and reviews to academic journals. Member of editorial committee of *Sociological Inquiry,* 1958-65; associate editor of *Sociometry,* 1965-71.

WORK IN PROGRESS: On Centrality in Social Networks; Segregation in a Social Network.

SIDELIGHTS: Freeman writes: "My major current endeavor involves teaching and research with the aim of producing a creative synthesis of materials in the foundations of social structure.

"This is an attempt at building theory in the strict sense of that word. It mobilizes the tools provided by recent discoveries in mathematics to integrate the speculations, empirical generalizations, and procedures of analysis of many scholars from many fields into a single coherent conceptual framework. It is both interdisciplinary and international. It draws together the work of sociologists, social psychologists, anthropologists, social geographers, and political scientists. Current contributions—both theoretical and empirical—come from England, France, Scandinavia, the U.S.A., and Canada. Through tying these many contributions together, into a single body of explicit theory, it is hoped that a foundation for cumulative work in social structure can be provided."

*   *   *

FREEMAN, Roger L(ouis)   1928-

PERSONAL: Born July 27, 1928, in New York, N.Y.; son of Andrew A. (a writer) and Mary Alice (a chemist; maiden name, Newton) Freeman; married Francesca Paquita (a registered nurse), June 25, 1966; children: Robert Carlos, Cristina, Rosalind. *Education:* Attended Middlebury College, 1948-51; New York University, B.A., 1966, M.A., 1973. *Religion:* Congregationalist. *Home:* Capitan Haya 22, Madrid 20, Spain. *Office:* International Telephone and Telegraph Laboratories, Avenida America KM7.2, Madrid 27, Spain.

CAREER: Military Sea Transportation Service, Brooklyn, N.Y., radio officer, 1952-59; Bendix Radio, Towson, Md., senior engineer in Spain, 1959-62; International Telephone

and Telegraph Communications Systems, Paramus, N.J., member of technical staff, 1962-66; Page Communication Engineers, Washington, D.C., staff engineer, 1966-70; International Telephone and Telegraph Laboratories, Spain, Madrid, assistant technical director, 1970—. *Military service:* U.S. Naval Reserve, 1946-70, active duty, 1946-48; became lieutenant senior grade.

MEMBER: Institute of Electrical and Electronics Engineers (senior member; secretary of Spain section), Armed Forces Communications and Electronics Association. *Awards, honors:* Civil service award from U.S. Navy, 1958, for outstanding service in high latitude operations; commendation from Bogota, Colombia Ministry of Telecommunication, 1968.

WRITINGS: A Visitor's Guide to Madrid, Editorial Everest, 1971; *English-Spanish-Spanish-English Dictionary of Telecommunications Terms,* Cambridge University Press, 1972; *Telecommunication Transmission Handbook,* Wiley, 1975. Contributor to telecommunications journals.

WORK IN PROGRESS: Telecommunication System Engineering, publication by Wiley expected in 1979; *Telecommunication Transmission Handbook,* 2nd edition, Wiley, 1981; *The Joys of Spanish,* a dictionary of colloquial and vulgar Castilian.

SIDELIGHTS: Freeman writes briefly: "I try to alternate technical and cultural works: technical in telecommunications, cultural—Hispanic studies."

*   *   *

FREGOSI, Claudia (Anne Marie)   1946-

PERSONAL: Born December 30, 1946, in Middlebury, Vt.; daughter of Claude Louis (a professor of French culture) and Almira Darrow (a high school teacher of French; maiden name, Coulter) Bourcier; married William A. Fregosi (a theatrical designer and teacher), June 13, 1970; children: Stephania Palmyra Anna, Sophia Andrea Marie. *Education:* Colby College, B.A., 1968. *Politics:* Independent. *Residence:* Roslindale, Mass. *Agent:* Danielle Deverin, 226 East 53rd St., New York, N.Y. 10026.

CAREER: Art teacher to normal and retarded children in Rutland, Vt., 1969-70; free-lance writer and artist, 1970—. Art work involves printmaking, poster design, costume and set design, and construction and painting for theatre companies and for television; member of South Shore Service League. *Member:* Open Door Society.

WRITINGS—Self-illustrated children's books: *Sun Grumble,* Macmillan, 1974; *The Mammoth, the Owl and the Crab,* Macmillan, 1975; *Almira's Violets,* Greenwillow-Morrow, 1976; *A Gift,* Prentice-Hall, 1976; *The Pumpkin Sparrow,* Greenwillow-Morrow, 1977; *Are There Spooks in the Dark?,* Scholastic Book Services, 1977; *The Happy Horse,* Greenwillow-Morrow, 1977.

WORK IN PROGRESS: Illustrating *Sound Comics,* by Pegge Dillingham, for Prentice-Hall; stories and fairy tales.

SIDELIGHTS: Fregosi writes: "My husband and I had discussed adoption as a means to build a family in an overpopulated world, even before we were married. We felt there were too many children in the world without families, there was nò need to create more. We currently have two daughters from Korea. I am active in organizations which raise funds for orphans the world over and which educate people in the need and joy of interracial adoption."

On her writing, she comments: "A current project is an allegorical fairy tale, dealing with coming of age and positive identity awareness. It makes the point that you are what you make of yourself and the world is what you make of it. The message is well put in R. W. Emerson's poem:

> Though we travel the world over
> To find the beautiful,
> We must carry it with us
> Or we will find it not.''

AVOCATIONAL INTERESTS: Cats, knitting, crocheting, sewing, embroidery, gardening, cooking, bread making, art, folk art, music, dance, skating, cross country skiing, biking, swimming, riding, reading myth, science fiction, murder mysteries, fantasy, P. G. Wodehouse, picture books.

* * *

FREIVALDS, John 1944-

PERSONAL: Born March 12, 1944, in Latvia; son of Evalds (an editor) and Margarita (Dzenis) Freivalds; married Susan Alexander (an economist); children: Jill, Karla. *Education:* Georgetown University, B.S.F.S., 1966; George Washington University, M.A., 1967. *Home:* 4344 Browndale, Minneapolis, Minn. 55424.

CAREER: U.S. Peace Corps, Washington, D.C., volunteer in Panama and Columbia, 1967-70; Development and Resources Corp., Sacramento, Calif., economist, 1970-73; I. S. Joseph Co., Minneapolis, Minn., vice-president, 1973-76; Experience, Inc., Minneapolis, Minn., project manager, 1976—. Member of board of directors of American Pollution Prevention Co.; member of Davis, Calif. Planning Commission, 1972; consultant to Vita.

WRITINGS: Grain Trade, Stein & Day, 1976. Author of column "Money" in *Minneapolis.* Editor of *Agribusiness.*

WORK IN PROGRESS: Famine Formula, a novel; *The Submerged Nations;* articles.

SIDELIGHTS: Freivalds writes that his present concerns are the need for smaller governmental units and the protection and promulgation of the rights of minorities and nationalities. *Avocational interests:* Basketball, camping, model railroading.

* * *

FRENCH, Marilyn 1929-
(Mara Solwoska)

PERSONAL: Born November 21, 1929, in New York, N.Y.; daughter of E. Charles and Isabel (Hazz) Edwards; married Robert M. French, Jr. (a lawyer), June 4, 1950 (divorced, 1967); children: Jamie, Robert M. III. *Education:* Hofstra College (now University), B.A., 1951, M.A., 1964; Harvard University, Ph.D., 1972. *Residence:* Somerville, Mass. *Agent:* Hoffman-Sheedy Literary Agency, 145 East 86th St., New York, N.Y. 10024.

CAREER: Hofstra University, Hempstead, N.Y., instructor in English, 1964-68; College of the Holy Cross, Worcester, Mass., assistant professor of English, 1972-76; Harvard University, Cambridge, Mass., Mellon fellow in English, 1976—. Artist-in-residence at Aspen Institute for Humanistic Study, 1972. *Member:* Modern Language Association of America, Society for Values in Higher Education, Virginia Woolf Society, James Joyce Society, Phi Beta Kappa.

WRITINGS: The Book As World: James Joyce's "Ulysses", Harvard University Press, 1975; *The Women's Room* (fiction), Simon & Schuster, 1976. Contributor of articles and stories, sometimes under pseudonym Mara Solwoska, to journals, including *Soundings* and *Ohio Review.*

WORK IN PROGRESS: Divisions of Experience, tracing divisions in Western thought from Shakespeare to the twentieth century.

SIDELIGHTS: Marilyn French writes: "I write fiction and literary criticism, but both come out of the same set of concerns and the same values. I believe we do not, as a culture, see the values of the past clearly. It is my intention to illuminate them, in the hope that a better set can be developed; I also hope, in some way, to suggest or sketch a more humane set of values. But I believe things are most persuasive when they are embodied in the concrete. Therefore, I prefer literary criticism or fiction writing to abstract theorizing. In fact, although I like theory, I do not believe it; theories when put into action lead too often into nightmare. I think theories must be imaginatively embodied in people and events if they are to be perceived as true, indeed, if they are to be tested at all. I find my own theories, when so realized, insufficient to 'save' humanity, although sufficient to help humans clean their moral house—which may be enough.

"The most important influences on my way of thinking and feeling have been my reading of English and foreign literatures, philosophy, psychology, art history, sociology, and anthropology, and my experience as a wife and mother. My life, when married and divorced, and the lives of my friends, the lives of my children, all seem to me rich with implication.''

AVOCATIONAL INTERESTS: Amateur musician; parties, cooking, travel.

* * *

FRENCH, Richard (De Land) 1947-

PERSONAL: Born February 25, 1947, in Montreal, Quebec, Canada; son of John Kenneth (an engineer) and Clare Erina (a teacher; maiden name, Richardson) French; married Diane Louise Boivin (a public servant); children: Elizabeth Menard (stepdaughter). *Education:* Dartmouth College, student, 1964-65; University of British Columbia, B.Sc., 1968; Oxford University, D.Phil., 1973. *Office:* Faculty of Management, Samuel Bronfman Building, McGill University, 1001 Sherbrooke St. W., Montreal, Quebec, Canada H3A 1G5.

CAREER: Princeton University, Princeton, N.J., visiting research fellow in history and philosophy of science, 1970-71, lecturer and assistant professor of history, 1971-72; Ministry of State for Science and Technology, Ottawa, Ontario, assistant science adviser, 1972-73; Science Council of Canada, Ottawa, science adviser, 1973-74; Government of Canada, Privy Council Office, Ottawa, assistant director of machinery of government, 1974-77; McGill University, Montreal, Quebec, associate professor of management, 1977—. *Awards, honors:* Woodrow Wilson fellowship, 1968; Rhodes scholarship, 1968.

WRITINGS: (With Peter Aucoin) *Knowledge, Power, and Public Policy,* Science Council of Canada, 1974; *Antivivisection and Medical Science in Victorian Society,* Princeton University Press, 1975. Contributor to history of science and public administration journals.

SIDELIGHTS: French lists his interests as: "The social and political problems raised by science and medicine; public decision-making on technically complex issues; planning in government; policy analysis in government; management of information and knowledge in the public sector; and political sociology of public service.''

FRENCH, William (Harold) 1926-

PERSONAL: Born March 21, 1926, in London, Ontario, Canada; son of Harold Edward (an engineer) and Isabel Nimmo (Brash) French; married Margaret Jean Rollo (a public health nurse), June 23, 1951; children: Jane, Mark, Paul, Susan. *Education:* University of Western Ontario, B.A., 1948; Harvard University, graduate study, 1954-55. *Home:* 78 North Hills Ter., Don Mills, Ontario, Canada M3C 1M6. *Office: Toronto Globe & Mail,* 444 Front St. W., Toronto, Ontario, Canada M5V 2S9.

CAREER: Toronto Globe & Mail, Toronto, Ontario, reporter, 1948-54, member of editorial board, 1955-60, staff writer for *Globe* (magazine), 1957-59, literary editor and author of column "Books and Bookmen," 1960—. Instructor at Ryerson Polytechnical Institute, 1955—; associate fellow at Your University, 1969—. Broadcast radio documentary programs over Canadian Broadcasting Corp., 1964—. Consultant to Canada Council. *Awards, honors:* President's Medal from University of Western Ontario, 1965, for a story on young revolutionary writers of French Canada.

WRITINGS: A Most Unlikely Village: A History of Forest Hill, Municipality of Forest Hill Village, 1960; (contributor) Ellen Stafford, editor, *The Flamboyant Canadians,* Baxter, 1964.

SIDELIGHTS: French comments: "As a literary critic my main interest is assessing the increasingly rapid development of Canadian literature while drawing the attention of my readers to the significant books by authors in other countries."

* * *

FREUDENHEIM, Leslie Ann Mandelson 1941-

PERSONAL: Born April 30; 1941; daughter of Leon Z. (a retailer) and Elinor (a retailer; maiden name, Sachs) Mandelson; married Tom L. Freudenheim (a museum director), November 14, 1964; children: Sascha, Adam. *Education:* Smith College, B.A. (cum laude), 1963; New York University, M.A., 1966; University of California, Berkeley, doctoral candidate, 1966-68; also attended University of Geneva, 1961-62. *Home:* 218 Wendover Rd., Baltimore, Md. 21218. *Office: Baltimore Morning Sun,* Baltimore, Md.

CAREER: Jewish Museum, New York, N.Y., assistant curator, 1963-65; University of California, Museum, Berkeley, prepared exhibition on California domestic architecture, 1970-71; *Baltimore Sun,* Baltimore, Md., architecture and urban affairs critic, 1973-76, author of weekly column, 1976—. Lecturer at Goucher College, spring, 1973; guest curator at Baltimore Museum of Art, 1976. Architecture and urban affairs critic for "Critic's Place," Maryland Center for Public Broadcasting, 1976. Has given public lectures in the United States and in Bucharest. *Member:* Society of Architectural Historians, National Trust for Historic Preservation.

WRITINGS: (With Elisabeth Sussman) *Building with Nature: Roots of the San Francisco Bay Region Tradition,* Peregrine Smith, 1974. Contributor to *Saturday Review* and *Architecture Plus.*

SIDELIGHTS: Leslie Freudenheim writes: "My writing reflects my involvement with and commitment to urban centers. I see my responsibility as informing people who may have lost touch or forgotten how important, stimulating, and delightful city living can be. Also, to inform people what is happening to their cities, and how they can help or hinder such changes."

FRIEDMAN, Ralph 1916-

PERSONAL: Born June 2, 1916, in Chicago, Ill.; married Phoebe Lopatin (a writer, photographer, and teacher), January 11, 1949; children: Amy. *Home:* 2845 N.E. 56th Ave., Portland, Ore. 97213.

CAREER: Friedman has worked as a newsboy, fruit tramp, cannery worker, janitor, playground instructor, warehouseman, railroad worker, book store manager, dishwasher, youth project director, and forest fire fighter. Free-lance writer. Columnist. Correspondent for North American Newspaper Alliance, Central Press Association, *Labor's Daily, Drug Topics,* and other publications. Portland bureau chief of Fairchild Publications, 1959-69. Teacher at Portland State University, Clackamas Community College; teacher of writing, travel, and folklore, Portland Community College, 1970—. Lecturer. *Military service:* U.S. Army. *Member:* Society of American Travel Writers.

WRITINGS: Oregon for the Curious, Pars, 1965; (contributor) Barnett Laschever, editor, *Shell Travel Guides,* Fodor's, 1966, 3rd revised edition, 1973; *Tales out of Oregon,* Pars, 1967; *Northwest Passages,* Pars, 1968; *A Touch of Oregon,* Pars, 1970; *See Surprising Oregon,* Northwest Bell, 1971; *Tracking Down Oregon,* Caxton, 1977; (contributor) Robert C. Fisher, editor, *Fodor's Modern Guides,* Fodor's, 1977.

Community Press, Portland, columnist, 1970—, book review editor, 1976—. Work represented in anthologies, including *This Land around Us,* edited by Ellis Lucia, Doubleday, 1969, and *Around the World with the Experts,* edited by Richard Joseph, Doubleday, 1970. Also author of short stories and poetry.

WORK IN PROGRESS: The fourth completely revised edition of *Oregon for the Curious.*

SIDELIGHTS: Friedman says that he has written on subjects including politics, ecology, sports, agriculture, technology, finance, war, revolution, guerilla movements, medicine, plastics, ceramics, dancing, theatre, and movies.

He told *CA:* "I believe the job of a journalist is to go above and beyond the perceivable data. The journalist should explain, interpret, always within the range of the objective considerations, and should seek to add a dimension to the information the reader already has, providing the reader has any at all. I do not play the tantalizing game of debating the morality or efficacy of advocacy journalism because I think that all journalism is, in one sense or another, advocacy, and that all expression is one form or another of propaganda, simply because each writer comes to the story in a unique way. I tell my students there are two aspects to every story, the subject and the writer. It is what the writer brings to the subject that makes the story good, bad, imaginative or lifeless. Obviously, the more sensitive a writer, the more in tune with life the writer is, the more sophisticated and experienced a writer is, the more imaginative and sincere a writer is, the better the story. (Of course, journalists work within the limitations of editorial policy.)"

Friedman continued: "A journalist ought to be full of questions and ought to keep his head about him or her when all others are losing theirs. (Thank you, Kipling). Think of all the stout-hearted journalists who panicked during the McCarthy period. Think of all the journalists who were ready to throw Alger Hiss to the wolves and the Rosenbergs to the electric chair. All the information that would cast serious doubt on the guilt of the Rosenbergs was there all along, but it is to the shame of American journalism that no name journalist sought to uncover the facts. Think of all the journalists who worshipped J. Edgar Hoover or who were intimidated by him. Having been an investigative reporter I know how shallow most journalists are, and how flippant the majority are, and how the largest number look for quickie sensationalist stories rather than the deeper stories which require a lot of hard work and an abundance of research skills.

"A journalist, I think, should recognize that he or she is a worker, the same as a coal miner, longshoreman, waitress, bartender, hodcarrier—and ought not to feel more important than other workers.

"What concerns me as a journalist is what concerns me as a human being," Friedman said. "And as a human being I have been involved in many things: protest marches against the war in Vietnam; leadership activity in a committee to prevent nerve gas from being shipped into Oregon; financial and physical support for environmental, civil liberties, civil rights, amnesty and help-people organizations (such as the Salvation Army). I am distressed at widespread hunger, the sickening amorality of so much crime, the factors which create so much drug usage, the factors which lead to so much schizophrenia, the penal conditions, the treatment of the mentally ill, the old, the runaway kids, the decay of the cities, the abuse of the land. I am concerned with war, and I strive for peace. I believe in human dignity, and anything which diminishes it torments and concerns me. I have never become accustomed to horror—and I have seen so much of it. At the same time, I think that in order to survive you have to have an almost innate sense of the absurd. If you cannot laugh at the madness around you, and at yourself, you are in deep trouble."

* * *

FRIEDRICH, Carl Joachim 1901-

PERSONAL: Born June 5, 1901, in Leipzig, Germany; came to the United States in 1922, naturalized citizen, 1938; son of Paul Leopold and Charlotte (Baroness von Buelow) Friedrich; married Lenore Pelham, October 6, 1924; children: Paul William, Otto Alva, Elizabeth Charlotte (deceased), Matilda Cornwall, Dorothea Amanda. *Education:* Attended University of Marburg, University of Frankfurt, and University of Vienna; University of Heidelberg, Ph.D., 1925. *Religion:* Episcopalian. *Home:* 14 Hawthorn St., Cambridge, Mass. 02138. *Office:* Study 93, Widener Library, Harvard University, Cambridge, Mass. 02138.

CAREER: Harvard University, Cambridge, Mass., lecturer, 1926-27, assistant professor, 1927-31, associate professor, 1931-37, Eaton Professor of Science of Government, 1955-71, professor emeritus, 1971—, director of School of Overseas Administration, 1943-46; writer, 1971—. Professor at University of Heidelberg, 1956-66, professor emeritus, 1966—; visiting professor at Sorbonne, University of Paris, winter, 1955, spring, 1971; Culver Lecturer at Brown University; Avalon Lecturer at Colby College. Governmental affairs adviser to the Military Governor in Germany, 1946-49.

MEMBER: International Political Science Association (president, 1967-70), International Institute of Political Philosophy (president, 1969), American Political Science Association (president, 1962), American Historical Association, American Academy of Arts and Sciences, American Society of Political and Legal Philosophy (president, 1958), Phi Beta Kappa, Athenaeum Club, Harvard Club (New York, N.Y.). *Awards, honors:* Guggenheim fellowship; first prize in Greater Boston Contest; knight commander's cross with

star, German Order of Merit, 1967; officier de l'Ordre de Leopold (Belgium), 1970; A. V. Humboldt Gold Medal. Honorary degrees include U.J.D. from University of Heidelberg, 1951, A.M. from Harvard University, 1941, LL.D. from Grinnell College, 1952, Duke University, 1963, and Washington University, St. Louis, Mo., 1968, L.H.D. from Columbia University, 1954, and Colby College, 1963, and Dr.rer.pol. from University of Cologne, 1954, and University of Padua, 1964.

WRITINGS: (With Taylor Cole) *Responsible Bureaucracy: A Study of the Swiss Civil Service, Studies in Systematic Political Science and Comparative Government,* Harvard University Press, 1932, reprinted Russell & Russell, 1967; *Constitutional Government and Politics: Nature and Development,* Harper, 1937, revised edition published as *Constitutional Government and Democracy: Theory and Practice in Europe and America,* Little, Brown, 1941, 4th edition, Blaisdell, 1968; *Foreign Policy in the Making: The Search for a New Balance of Power,* Norton, 1938.

Controlling Broadcasting in Wartime: A Tentative Public Policy, Littauer Center, Harvard University, 1940; (with Jeanette Sayre) *The Development of the Control of Advertising on the Air,* Littauer Center, Harvard University, 1940; *The Poison in Our System,* Council for Democracy, 1941; *The New Belief in the Common Man,* Little, Brown, 1942, revised edition published as *The New Image of the Common Man,* Beacon Press, 1950; (with Jeanette Sayre Smith) *Radiobroadcasting and Higher Education,* Littauer Center, Harvard University, 1942; *War: The Causes, Effects, and Control of International Violence,* National Council for the Social Studies and National Association of Secondary-School Principals, 1943; (with Evelyn Sternberg) *Congress and the Control of Radiobroadcasting,* Littauer Center, Harvard University, 1944; *American Policy Toward Palestine,* Public Affairs Press, 1944, reprinted, Greenwood Press, 1971; *Inevitable Peace,* Harvard University Press, 1948, reprinted Greenwood Press, 1969; (editor) *The Philosophy of Kant,* Modern Library, 1949.

The Age of the Baroque, 1610-1660, Harper, 1952; (editor) *The Philosophy of Hegel,* Modern Library, 1953; (editor with Robert Richardson Bowie) *Studies in Federalism,* Little, Brown, 1954; (with Bowie) *Probleme einer europaeischen Staatengemein schaft,* Institut fuer Europaeische Politik und Wirtschaft, 1954; (editor) *Totalitarianism,* Harvard University Press, 1954, Grosset, 1964; (editor with Robert G. McCloskey) *From the Declaration of Independence to the Constitution: The Roots of American Constitutionalism,* Liberal Arts Press, 1954; *Die Philosophie des Rechts in historischer Perspektive,* Springer-Verlag, 1955, translation published as *The Philosophy of Law in Historical Perspective,* University of Chicago Press, 1958, 2nd edition, 1963; (editor) *The Soviet Zone of Germany,* Human Relations Area File Press, 1956; (with Zbigniew K. Brzezinski) *Totalitarian Dictatorship and Autocracy,* Harvard University Press, 1956, 3rd edition, 1967; *Cours d'histoire des idees politiques: Evolution de la liberte constitutionnelle en Angleterre a travers les deux revolutions,* Cours de droit, 1956; *Constitutional Reason of State: The Survival of the Constitutional Order,* Brown University Press, 1957; (with Charles Blitzer) *The Age of Power* (juvenile), Cornell University Press, 1957; (editor) *Authority,* Harvard University Press, 1958; (editor with Seymour E. Harris) *Problems of Defense,* Graduate School of Public Administration, Harvard University, 1958; *Puerto Rico: Middle Road to Freedom,* Holt, 1959; *Demokratie als Herrschafts-und Lebensform* (originally appeared as part of *The New Belief in the Common*

Man), Quelle & Meyer, 1959; (editor) *Community*, Liberal Arts Press, 1959.

(Editor) *Responsibility*, Liberal Arts Press, 1960; *Die politische Wissenschaft*, K. Alber, 1961; (editor) *The Public Interest*, Atherton Press, 1962; (editor) *Liberty*, Atherton Press, 1962; (editor) *Justice*, Atherton Press, 1963; (with Geleitwort von Dolf Sternberger) *Zur theorie und Politik der Verfassungsordnung: Augewaehlte Aufsaetze*, Quelle & Meyer, 1963; *Man and His Government: An Empirical Theory of Politics*, McGraw, 1963; (editor) *Rational Decision*, Atherton Press, 1964; *Report of the Commission on Presidential Campaign Debates*, American Political Science Association, 1964; *Transcendent Justice: The Religious Dimension of Constitutionalism*, Duke University Press, 1964; (editor) *Revolution: Yearbook*, Atherton Press, 1966; *An Introduction to Political Theory: Twelve Lectures at Harvard*, Harper, 1967; *The Impact of American Constitutionalism Abroad*, Boston University Press, 1967; *Prolegomena der Politik: Politische Erfahrung und ihre theorie*, (originally appeared in *Man and His Government*), Duncker & Humblot, 1967; *Trends of Federalism in Theory and Practice*, Praeger, 1968; *Europe: An Emergent Nation?*, Harper, 1969.

The Pathology of Politics: Violence, Betrayal, Corruption, Secrecy, and Propaganda, Harper, 1972; *Tradition and Authority*, Praeger, 1972; *Ich zeichne Menschen*, Starczewski, 1973; *Limited Government: A Comparison*, Prentice-Hall, 1974.

Also editor of *American Experiences in Military Government in World War II*, 1947; author of *Philosophy of History*, published by Peter Smith; editor and translator of Alfred Weber's *Theory of the Location of Industries*, 1929, reprinted, Russell & Russell, 1971. Contributor to magazines, including *Atlantic Monthly*. Editor of *Public Policy* 1940-53, and *Nomus Yearbook* of the American Society of Political and Legal Philosophy, 1958-66.*

* * *

FRIIS, Erik J(ohan) 1913-

PERSONAL: Born April 5, 1913, in Oslo, Norway; came to the United States in 1929, naturalized citizen, 1937; son of Ingvard E. and Sigrid (Erichsen) Friis; married Sylvia Schouw, May 6, 1955; children: Erik Schouw, Elin Sylvia. *Education:* St. John's University, Jamaica, N.Y., B.S., 1938; Columbia University, M.A., 1946. *Politics:* Democrat. *Religion:* Lutheran. *Home:* 19 Shadow Lane, Montvale, N.J. 07645. *Office:* American-Scandinavian Foundation, 127 East 73rd St., New York, N.Y. 10021.

CAREER: American Scandinavian Foundation, New York, N.Y., editor and director of publications, 1946-75, editor emeritus, 1976—. Vice-chairman of Norwegian Immigration Sesquicentennial Commission; secretary-treasurer of National Committee for Norwegian Immigration Sesquicentennial.

MEMBER: Explorers Club (fellow), Norwegian Club (first vice-president, 1961—), Scandinavian-American Business Association (first vice-president, 1976—), Scandinavian Collectors Club, Societas Heraldica Scandinavica, P.E.N., Norway Ski Club of New York, Sporting Club Gjoa. *Awards, honors:* U.S. Medal for Antarctica Service, 1965; Knight first class of Norwegian Order of St. Olav, 1967, and Finnish Order of the Lion, 1976; knight of Icelandic Order of the Falcon, 1968, Swedish Order of the North Star, 1972, and Danish Order of Dannebrog, 1973; arts and letters award from Finlandia Foundation, 1974; author award from

Newark College of Engineering, 1975, for translation of *The Lost Musicians*.

WRITINGS: The American-Scandinavian Foundation, 1910-1960, American-Scandinavian Foundation, 1961; (editor with Carl F. Bayerschmidt) *Scandinavian Studies*, University of Washington Press, 1965; (editor) *The Scandinavian Presence in North America*, Harper's Magazine Press, 1976. Also editor of *The Norwegian Club, Inc., 1904-1964*, 1964, *Society of Norwegian American Engineers 1925-75*, 1975, and *They Came from Norway*, 1975.

Translator: Olaf Rynning-Tonnesen, *The Secret Transmitter*, Bobbs-Merrill, 1965; Hans Granqvist, *The Red Guard*, Praeger, 1967; (with Karen Rush) R. Broby-Johansen, *Body and Clothes*, Reinhold, 1968; Helge Ingstad, *Westward to Vinland*, St. Martin's, 1969; William Heinesen, *The Lost Musicians*, Twayne, 1971; Alfred Hauge, *Cleng Peerson I-II*, Twayne, 1975; K. Arne Blom, *The Moment of Truth*, Harper, 1977; (with the author and Gerry Bothmer) Liv Ullmann, *Changing*, Knopf, 1977.

General editor of "Library of Scandinavian Literature" and "Library of Scandinavian Studies" for Twayne; general editor of reprint series, "The Scandinavian Scene." Editor and publisher of *Scandinavian-American Bulletin*. Member of editorial board of *Explorers Journal* and Norwegian-American Historical Association.

WORK IN PROGRESS: Translating *Dreams of Roses and Fire*, by Eyvind Johnson.

SIDELIGHTS: Friis has traveled around the world, and has visited Greenland and Antarctica (including the South Pole).

* * *

FRITH, Nigel (Andrew Silver) 1941-

PERSONAL: Born November 30, 1941, in Kettering, England; son of Derrick Silver (an Army officer and sculptor) and Jessica (Willis) Frith. *Education:* St. Catherine's College, Oxford, B.A., 1963, B.Litt., 1972. *Politics:* "Tory." *Religion:* Church of England. *Home:* 21 St. Andrew's Lane, Old Headington, Oxford, England. *Agent:* Carolyn Whitaker, London Independent Books, 1A Montagu Mews N., London W1H 1AJ, England.

CAREER: Tutor in North Wales, 1965-68, and Oxford, England, 1969-72; Oxford University, Oxford, England, tutor in English literature, 1973—. Professional actor with Peter Dews Shakespeare Company, 1964. Librarian in history faculty library, Oxford, 1964. Has broadcast on British Broadcasting Corp.—Radio. *Member:* Chelsea Arts Club.

WRITINGS: The Lover's Annual: A Story in Verse, Dent, 1965; *The Legend of Krishna* (prose epic), Sheldon Press, 1975, Schocken, 1976; *The Spear of Mistletoe* (prose epic), Routledge & Kegan Paul, 1977.

WORK IN PROGRESS: Osiris, a "brief epic in English classical hexameters"; *Rome*, a historical epic in prose.

SIDELIGHTS: Frith writes: "My work is mainly written in the heroic and romantic styles of the past. In *The Lover's Annual* there are many examples of traditional English verse forms used again for the spontaneous expression of emotion. In *The Legend of Krishna*, the structural technique of the Homeric epic has been used for the narration of an adventurous and exotic tale, and in *The Spear of Mistletoe* the narrative style of Homer is also used for a subject taken from Teutonic myth."

FRITSCH, Bruno 1926-

PERSONAL: Born July 24, 1926, in Prague, Czechoslovakia; son of Josef (a civil servant) and Rosa Fritsch; married Jadwiga Przybyl, October 23, 1953; children: Martin, Caroline. *Education:* Attended University of Prague, 1964; University of Basel, Dr.rer.pol., 1952, habilitation, 1958; also attended Harvard University. *Home:* Aussichtsstrasse 13, Herrliberg 8704, Switzerland. *Office:* Eidgenoessiche Technische Hochschule-Institut fuer Wirtschaftsforschung, Zurich 8092, Switzerland.

CAREER: Basel Center for Economic and Financial Research, Basel, Switzerland, director, 1958; University of Karlsruhe, Karlsruhe, Germany, professor of economics, 1959-63; University of Heidelberg, South Asia Institute, Heidelberg, Germany, professor of economics, 1963-65; Swiss Federal Institute of Technology, Zurich, professor of economics, 1965—. Visiting instructor, Harvard University, summers, 1963-74, College of Europe, 1960-69, and Australian National University, 1971. Advisor to various governments, missions in Asia, and Latin America. *Member:* World Future Studies Federation, Swiss Future Studies Association (president), Swiss Economic Association, Swiss Association for Environmental Protection, American Economic Association, German Economic Association.

WRITINGS: World Trade Flows (translation of German edition), Polygraphischer Verlag, 1971; *Wachstumsbegrenzung als Machtinstrument,* Deutsche Verlag (Stuttgart), 1974, English translation by Claire E. Reade published as *Growth Limitation and Political Power,* Ballinger, 1976.

Books not published in English: *Die Geld-und Kredittheorie von Karl Marx: Eine Darstellung und kritische Wuerdigung* (title means "Karl Marx's Theory of Money and Loanable Funds"), Polygraphischer Verlag, 1954; (translator into German) K. William Kapp, *Volkswirtschaftliche Kosten der Privatwirtschaft* (title means "The Social Costs of Private Enterprise"), Polygraphischer Verlag, 1958; *Geschichte und Theorie ser amerikanischen Stabilisierungspolitik, 1933-1939/1946-1953* (title means "History and Theory of American Stabilization Policy, 1933-1939/1946-1953"), Polygraphischer Verlag, 1959; (editor) *Entwicklungslaender* (title means "Developing Countries"), Kiepenheuer & Witsch, 1968; (contributor) Gerhard Kocher, editor, *Zukunftsforschung in der Schweiz* (title means "Further Research in Switzerland"), Paul Haupt, 1970; *Die Vierte Welt: Modell einer neuen Wirklichkeit* (title means "The Fourth World: The Model of a New Reality"), Deutsche Verlag, 1970; *Bildung, Luxus oder Ueberlebenschance?* (title means "General Education: Luxury or Chance for Survival?"), Artemis, 1973.

WORK IN PROGRESS: Research on global modeling, the future of the world system, global energy models, the relationship between industrial and less-developed countries, and the future of the international system.

* * *

FROSCH, Thomas Richard 1943-

PERSONAL: Born March 19, 1943, in New York, N.Y.; son of John (a physician) and Annette (Godsick) Frosch; married Mary Alfred (a teacher), January 25, 1976. *Education:* Wesleyan University, B.A., 1964; Yale University, M.A., 1966, Ph.D., 1968. *Residence:* New York, N.Y. *Office:* Department of English, Queens College of the City University of New York, Flushing, N.Y. 11367.

CAREER: New York University, New York, N.Y., assistant professor of English, 1968-71; Queens College of the City University of New York, Flushing, N.Y., associate professor of English, 1971—. *Member:* Modern Language Association of America. *Awards, honors:* Woodrow Wilson fellowship, 1964.

WRITINGS: The Awakening of Albion: The Renovation of the Body in the Poetry of William Blake, Cornell University Press, 1974. Contributor of poems to magazines.

* * *

FROST, Carol 1948-

PERSONAL: Born February 28, 1948, in Massachusetts; daughter of William Arthur and Renee (Fellner) Perrins; married Richard Frost (a poet and college professor), August 21, 1969; children: Daniel Adam, Joel Richard. *Education:* Student at Sorbonne, University of Paris, 1967; State University of New York College at Oneonta, B.A., 1970; Syracuse University, M.A., 1978. *Home address:* R.D.2, Box 73, Otego, N.Y. 13825.

CAREER: Poet. Founder and administrator of Oneonta Children's School (an "alternative-to-public-school"), 1971-74. *Awards, honors:* Bread Loaf scholarship, summer, 1976; Borestone Mountain Poetry Award, 1976, for "A Woman with Her Plants Talking".

WRITINGS: The Salt Lesson (poetry chapbook), Graywolf Press, 1976.

Represented in anthologies, including *Borestone Mountain Poetry Awards: Best Poems of 1976,* 1976; *The Ardis Anthology of New American Poetry,* 1977; *Syracuse Poems,* 1976, 1977. Contributor of about forty poems to literary journals, including *Antioch Review, Shenandoah, Beloit Poetry Journal,* and *Poetry Miscellany.*

WORK IN PROGRESS: Liar's Dice or *Common Places,* poetry.

SIDELIGHTS: Carol Frost writes: "After starting college I tried to find what would satisfy and provoke me. To that end I studied French literature and art at the Sorbonne, trained with the Pan American flat-water kayak team, learned photography well enough to place some of my photographs in art shows in New York, married and had two children, and traveled for three years, learning German and some Greek, in Austria, Italy, East and West Germany, England, Yugoslavia, Hungary, Lebanon, Greece, the Bahamas, France, Mexico, and from Texas to Maine.

"Satisfied as I have been in my travels, no territory or endeavor seems more provocative than sitting in a room with the scrappy beginnings of a poem, not knowing if the fragments will ever be wholly a poem; not knowing, yet still willing to empty myself of a pleasing, conscious order or emotion, a set morality or voice. Then, in the chamber that is the unfixed imagination or at sea with the imagination, off charts, to discover what will suffice, what will shine in the eye and resolve for the ear. Not to be comforted by the usual or the unusual until it is right, right for the poem, and then to savor it and take it.

"My particular concern in writing the poems collected in my book and in a new manuscript has been to try to find the difficult balance between ambiguity and clarity; not averaging, but finding the place where matters are at once more than clear and mysterious."

* * *

FROST, David (Paradine) 1939-

PERSONAL: Born April 7, 1939, in Tenterden, Kent, England; son of Wilfrid John Paradine (a Methodist minister) and Mona Eveline (Aldrich) Frost. *Education:* Gonville and Caius College, Cambridge, B.A. and M.A. *Home:* 46 Egerton Crescent, London S.W. 3, England.

CAREER: Worked as a performer in night clubs and as a trainee with Rediffusion Ltd. (a commercial television contracting firm), London, England; performer and writer of television humorous variety shows, "That Was the Week That Was," for British Broadcasting Corp., 1962-63, for National Broadcasting Co. in America, 1963-64, "Not So Much a Programme, More a Way of Life," BBC-TV, 1964-65, and "Frost Report," BBC-TV, 1965-67; host of television interview show, "Frost Programme," for ITV and concurrently a disc jockey on BBC-Radio, 1966-68; host of three television shows for Rediffusion Ltd., "Frost on Friday" (discussion), "Frost on Saturday" (interview), and "Frost on Sunday" (variety), 1968-69; host of "David Frost Show," for Westinghouse Broadcasting Co. in America, 1969-72. Founder and chief executive of David Paradine Productions, London, and founding partner of London Television Consortium, 1967—. Performer of one-man stage act, "An Evening with David Frost," at Edinburgh Festival, 1966; producer of movie, "The Rise and Fall of Michael Rimmer," 1970.

AWARDS, HONORS: Golden rose award at the International Television Festival, Montreux, 1967, for "Frost Over England," television program; Richard Dimbleby award, 1967; Royal Television Society's Silver Medal, 1967; Television Personality of the Year Award from the Guild of Television Producers and Directors, 1967; Emmy Awards of National Academy of Television Arts and Sciences, 1970 and 1971; Order of the British Empire, 1970; Religious Heritage of America Award, 1970; Albert Einstein Award in communication arts, 1971; LL.D. from Emerson College.

WRITINGS: (Editor with Ned Sherrin) *That Was the Week That Was,* W. H. Allen, 1963; (with Christopher Booker and others) *How to Live Under Labour; or, At Least, Have as Much Chance as Anybody Else,* Heinemann, 1964; (with Anthony Jay) *To England with Love,* Hodder and Stoughton, 1967, revision published as *The English,* Stein & Day, 1968; *The Presidential Debate, 1968; David Frost Talks with Vice-President Hubert H. Humphrey and Others,* Stein & Day, 1968; *The Americans,* Stein & Day, 1970; *Billy Graham Talks with David Frost,* A. J. Holman, 1971.

Author of introduction; all published by Crown: *Bluff Your Way in Opera,* 1971; . . . *in Music,* 1971; . . . *in Cinema,* 1971; . . . *in Wine,* 1971; . . . *in Art,* 1971; . . . *in Literature,* 1971; . . . *in Antiques,* 1972; . . . *in Football,* 1972; . . . *in Interior Decorating,* 1972; . . . *in Gourmet Food,* 1972; . . . *in Theatre,* 1972; . . . *in Travel,* 1972.

Former columnist for *London Observer;* contributor of dramatic criticism to *Spectator* and of humorous articles to *Punch.*

SIDELIGHTS: David Frost turned down an offer to play professional soccer when he went to college and, according to *Time* magazine, he "emerged on a dead run." He works a twenty-hour day and regularly commutes across the Atlantic traveling up to 200,000 miles a year. Part of Frost's television appeal stems from his willingness to tackle controversial subjects, which often lands him in trouble with network executives and audiences. The BBC cancelled "That Was the Week That Was" in order to avoid charges of political partisanship in the elections of 1964 and "Not So Much a Programme, More a Way of Life" was terminated by the BBC in its second year for airing a biting sketch of the Duke

of Windsor the night his sister died. Frost is probably not convinced these cancellations are failures. He has said: "The great danger in television is not programs that arouse people to fury or offense, but those that do *not* arouse people to fury or offense. My philosophy has always been simply to oppose anything that makes life less than what it can be for people. The aim of every TV program I do is to leave the audience a little more alert, a little more aware, a little more alive."

If one part of Frost's success truly lies in his choice of controversial material, the greater part must lie in his abilities as an interviewer. "I'm more interested in talk than interrogation," he asserted. "Interviewing somebody can be so boring. I've been interviewed myself by people who have this rigid little set of questions that they are doggedly ticking off one by one. I feel like saying, 'Oh by the way, I've slept with the Pope's wife.' Because I am sure they would go right on to the next question, 'What about the shrinking gold reserves?' And I hear so many interviewers throwing out these mock tough questions which are the easiest of all to duck. If you thunder at a government leader, 'Isn't is true that your party has spent two years on self-serving policies?' then you're going to get a lousy answer. But if you ask casually, 'What is the major mistake your party has made since it has been in office?' you challenge the man, and he'll respond with something interesting."

His greatest success and exposure as an interviewer occurred in May, 1977, when four interviews with Richard Nixon appeared on television. For eleven weeks, through 1976 and the early part of 1977, Frost taped twenty-nine hours of interviews in thirty-three sessions with the former president. From these tapes, the four ninety-minute programs were edited. The segments dealt with Watergate, Nixon's foreign policy, the Vietnam War abroad and at home, and the final days. Special programs were also prepared for Britain, France, Italy, and Australia. While some critics scoffed the result as a "pseudo-event," most agreed with *Newsweek* magazine's assessment of it as "a rare combination of journalism, history and live teledrama."

Frost's writing at first was an expression of the humor that characterized his early television shows. His book with Antony Jay is a satirical look at English society. Critics agreed on the book's excellent humor but some were disappointed, oddly enough, in view of his later work, by what they considered a lack of serious purpose. Anthony Hartley said: "Culpable as the English may have been, perhaps they do not really deserve or need this kind of political prefrontal lobotomy. Fortunately, it also seems doubtful that they will get it. But Frost and Jay's book will be read, not for its solutions, but as an enjoyable bash at 'figures of authority': the judiciary, the church, Parliament—all those institutions and individuals who, naturally, make us hoot with laughter these days." Charles Poore said of the book: "The prevailing mood is blithe and spirited. At heart, of course, it poses Big Moral Questions. Our enjoyment lies in eluding preachiness and finding wit. Jousting under those ground rules, Mr. Frost and Mr. Jay give us a fair view of England today and a fine lot of savage entertainment. . . . [But] the English, like ourselves, can't seem to get the hang of tuning that airborne foolishness out and turning a good book on. I can't think why. But there it is. And on the present occasion, the references to television cockeyedness come so thick and fast that you lose track of whether you're reading example or satire. A natural confusion, come to think of it."

Frost's other books are products of his talent as an interviewer. J. M. Hamernick called *The Americans,* "an excellent opportunity for the American people to savor a close-up of a perfectionist at work.'' Suzanne Lennon commended *The Presidential Debate* for doing an almost impossible job. Frost's interviews cut through the election rhetoric to ''elicit the basic personal and political philosophy of each presidential aspirant.''

BIOGRAPHICAL/CRITICAL SOURCES: Wallace Rayburn, *Frost: Anatomy of a Success,* Macdonald, 1968; *Life,* March 22, 1968; Willi Frischauer, *Will You Welcome Now. . . David Frost,* Hawthorn, 1971; *Time,* May 9, 1977; *Newsweek,* May 9, 1977.*

*   *   *

FROST, Lawrence A(ugust)   1907-

PERSONAL: Born May 1, 1907, in Ann Arbor, Mich.; son of Elvin R. (a podiatrist) and Selema (a musician; maiden name, Teufel) Frost; married Ethel Duby, September 1, 1933; children: Jill (Mrs. William Merke). *Education:* Student at University of Toledo; Ohio College of Podiatric Medicine, D.P.M., 1929. *Religion:* Presbyterian. *Home:* 211 Cranbrook Blvd., Monroe, Mich. 48161. *Office:* 11 Scott St., Monroe, Mich. 48161.

CAREER: Podiatrist in Monroe, Mich., 1929—. Mayor of Monroe, 1960-64; member of Monroe County Planning Commission, 1964-75 (chairman, 1972-75), and Monroe County Historic Commission (chairman, 1967-69). Custer curator of Monroe County Historical Museum, 1950-70.

MEMBER: American College of Foot Surgeons (fellow; past president), Company of Military Historians (fellow), Council on Abandoned Military Posts (member of board of directors, 1974-77), First Cavalry Division Association (life member), Little Big Horn Associates (member of board of directors, 1967—), Michigan State Podiatry Association (president, 1935-37), Michigan State Historical Society (member of board of trustees, 1950-52), Monroe County Historical Society (president, 1948-50, 1966, 1973). *Awards, honors:* D.Litt. from Ohio College of Podiatric Medicine, 1968; Ohioana Book Award from Ohioana Library Association, 1970, for *The Thomas A. Edison Album.*

WRITINGS: The Custer Album, Superior, 1964; *The U.S. Grant Album,* Superior, 1966; *The Phil Sheridan Album,* Superior, 1968; *The Court-Martial of General G. A. Custer,* University of Oklahoma Press, 1968; *The Thomas A. Edison Album,* Superior, 1969; *General Custer's Libbie,* Superior, 1976; (editor with John M. Carroll) *Private Theodore Ewert's Diary of the Black Hills Expedition of 1874,* CRI Books, 1976.

WORK IN PROGRESS: Custer Had Two Lives, a novel; *Custer Legends; Their Feet Come First,* a guide for parents.

SIDELIGHTS: Frost writes: ''Living, as I have for over forty-five years, in the home town of the Custers, and knowing many of the Custer family intimately, my interest in the General and his wife Libbie grew with exposure. So many myths came to light that needed an explanation I just had to dig. I uncovered a fine man and a lovely woman. The true story about them had to be told. My last book—*General Custer's Libbie*—was a big step in that direction.''

*   *   *

FRY, Michael G(raham)   1934-

PERSONAL: Born November 5, 1934, in Brierley, England; son of Cyril Victor (a surveyor) and Margaret (Copley) Fry; married Anna Maria Fulgoni, May, 1957; children: Michael, Gabriella, Margaret. *Education:* University of London, B.Sc., 1956, Ph.D., 1963. *Religion:* Roman Catholic. *Home:* 31 Torrington Pl., Ottawa, Ontario, Canada. *Office:* School of International Affairs, Carleton University, Ottawa, Ontario, Canada.

CAREER: University of Toronto, Toronto, Ontario, lecturer in history, 1961-62; University of Saskatchewan, Saskatoon, lecturer, 1962-63, assistant professor of history, 1963-65; Carleton University, Ottawa, Ontario, assistant professor, 1965-66, associate professor, 1966-72, professor of history, 1972—, associate director of School of International Affairs, 1973-76, director, 1976—. *Military service:* British Army, 1956-58. *Member:* International Studies Association (vice-president), American Historical Association, Society for Historians of American Foreign Relations, Royal Historical Society. *Awards, honors:* North Atlantic Treaty Organization research fellowship, 1969-70; Canada Council fellowships, 1966, 1967, 1968, 1973, 1976.

WRITINGS: Illusions of Security: North Atlantic Diplomacy, 1918-1922, University of Toronto Press, 1972; *Freedom and Change,* McClelland & Stewart, 1975; *The Education of a Statesman: Lloyd George and Foreign Policy,* Volume I: *1890-1916,* McGill-Queen's University Press, 1977. Contributor to history journals.

WORK IN PROGRESS: The Education of a Statesman: Lloyd George and Foreign Policy, Volume II: *1917-1945,* for McGill-Queen's University Press.

SIDELIGHTS: Fry told *CA:* ''I am concerned with the development of the ideas of elites and anti-elites (dissenters) toward foreign and defense policy problems in Western states in the twentieth century.''

*   *   *

FRYER, Judith   1939-

PERSONAL: Born August 5, 1939, in Minneapolis, Minn.; daughter of Merrill Edwin and Josephine (Margulies) Edelston; married Joel Fryer (divorced); children: Lynn, Deborah. *Education:* University of Minnesota, B.A. (magna cum laude), 1961, M.A., 1967, Ph.D., 1973; also attended Shakespeare Institute, summer, 1959. *Home:* 110 Springwood Ave., Oxford, Ohio 45056. *Office:* American Studies Program, Miami University, 7 Old Manse, Oxford, Ohio 45056.

CAREER: University of Minnesota, Minneapolis, instructor in English, American studies, and women's studies, 1967-74; Miami University, Oxford, Ohio, assistant professor of English, 1974—, director of American studies program, 1974—. Instructor at Macalester College, 1972; Fulbright Professor at University of Tuebingen, 1976—. Director of public relations for Minneapolis Symphony Orchestra, 1961-62, 1966. *Member:* Modern Language Association of America, American Studies Association. *Awards, honors:* National Endowment for the Humanities fellowship, Yale University, summer, 1976.

WRITINGS: How We Hear: The Story of Hearing (juvenile), Lerner, 1961; (editor with Eric Watkins and Donald Vanouse), *Toward Composition,* Kendall-Hunt, 1970; (contributor) Ivan Doig, editor, *Utopian America,* Hayden, 1976; *The Faces of Eve: Women in the Nineteenth-Century American Novel,* Oxford University Press, 1976. Contributor to *American Quarterly.*

WORK IN PROGRESS: A critical book on American women novelists of the early twentieth century, including Edith Wharton, Ellen Glasgow, and Willa Cather.

SIDELIGHTS: Fryer has traveled extensively in western

Europe. *Avocational interests:* Playing the harpsichord, skiing, hiking, sailing, playing tennis, swimming.

*   *   *

FUCHS, Jerome H(erbert) 1922-

PERSONAL: Born January 7, 1922, in New York, N.Y.; son of Berthold (a chemist) and Fannie (Neushotz) Fuchs; married Eleanor May DeRoo, May 26, 1945; children: Jerome S. Taylor, Susan (Mrs. John Decker), Sandra (Mrs. Thomas Lombino.) *Education:* Syracuse University, B.S. (cum laude), 1950, M.B.A., 1951. *Home:* 30 Cabot Rd. W., Massapequa, N.Y. 11758.

CAREER: Syracuse University, Syracuse, N.Y., lecturer in industrial management, 1950-52; Johns Hopkins University, Baltimore, Md., lecturer in human relations and supervisory development, 1953-54; Drexel Institute of Technology, Philadelphia, Pa., lecturer in economics and business management, 1955-59; executive assistant to president of Rockbestos Wire and Cable, 1959; Fuchs Associates (management consultants), Massapequa, N.Y., president, 1960—, consultant for more than eighty industrial and commercial firms, government agencies, and private institutions. Lecturer at Queens College of the City University of New York, 1963-65. Vice-president of manufacturing at United Aircraft Products, 1970-71; executive vice-president of Business Supplies Corporation of America, 1972. *Military service:* U.S. Air Force, navigator, 1944-46; became second lieutenant. *Member:* Society of Professional Management Consultants (charter member; president, 1977—), Institute of Management Consultants (founding member).

WRITINGS: Making the Most of Management Consulting Services, American Management Association, 1975; *Management Consultants in Action,* Hawthorn Books, 1975; *Computerized Cost Control Systems,* Prentice-Hall, 1976; *Computerized Inventory Control Systems,* Prentice-Hall, 1977.

WORK IN PROGRESS: Two books for Prentice-Hall, *Administering the Quality Control Function,* a book covering all the primary quality control areas of activity in an industrial environment, and *Quantum Growth Management,* a book on corporate "turnarounds" that interconnects the managements' personality and business philosophy with the corporate structure as a viable entity.

SIDELIGHTS: Fuchs writes: "Management is an art, not a science. There are many subtle nuances involved in the decision-making process. My primary motivation is to develop a framework that bridges the gap between the technician in a particular functional area and the business manager so that maximum economic gain can be achieved. As managing an enterprise has grown in complexity, with heavy demands on an executive to become ever more proficient, the writer attempts to provide in a business book readily understood methods of handling various situations that impact upon a company's growth and profitability."

*   *   *

FUENTES, Carlos 1928-

PERSONAL: Born November 11, 1928, in Mexico City, Mexico; son of Rafael Fuentes Boettiger (a career diplomat) and Berta (Macias Rivas) Fuentes; married Rita Macedo (a movie actress), 1959 (divorced, 1969); children: Cecilia. *Education:* Colegio Frances Morelos, LL.B., 1948; graduate study at the National University of Mexico and the Institut des Hautes Etudes Internationales in Geneva. *Poli-*

tics: Independent leftist. *Home:* 2a Cerrada de Frontera, 14 San Angel, Mexico, D.F., Mexico. *Office:* c/o Editorial Joaquin Moritz, Tabasco 106, Mexico 7, D.F., Mexico.

CAREER: International Labor Organization, Geneva, Switzerland, member, then secretary of the Mexican delegation, 1950-52; Ministry of Foreign Affairs, Mexico City, Mexico, assistant chief of press section, 1954; National University of Mexico, Mexico City, secretary and assistant director, cultural department, 1955-56; Ministry of Foreign Affairs, Mexico City, head of department of cultural relations, 1957-59; novelist. International Law Commission of the United Nations, Geneva, secretary of the Mexican delegation, 1950-52; Mexican Embassy, Geneva, cultural attache, 1950-52; United Nations Information Center, Mexico City, press secretary, 1954. Member of jury, Locarno Film Festival, 1961, and Venice Film Festival, 1967. Lecturer at University of Mexico, University of California at San Diego, University of Concepcion in Chile, the Sorbonne, University of Paris, and in several Italian cities. *Awards, honors:* Centro Mexicano de Escritores, fellowship, 1956-57; Premio Biblioteca Breve, Seix Barral publishing house (Barcelona), 1967, for *Cambio de piel.*

WRITINGS: Los dias enmascarados (short stories), Los Presentes, 1954; *La region mas transparente* (novel), Fondo de Cultura Economica, 1958, translation by Sam Hileman published as *Where the Air is Clear,* Ivan Obolensky, 1960; *Las buenas conciencias* (novel), Fondo de Cultura Economica, 1959, translation published as *The Good Conscience,* Ivan Obolensky, 1961.

La muerte de Artemio Cruz (novel), Fondo de Cultura Economica, 1962, translation by Hileman published as *The Death of Artemio Cruz,* Farrar, Strauss, 1964; *Aura* (novel), Ediciones Era, 1962, translation by Lysander Kemp published with same title, Farrar, Strauss, 1965; *Cantar de ciegos* (short stories), J. Mortiz, 1964; *Zona sagrada* (novel), Siglo Veintiuno Editores, 1967, translation published as "Holy Place" in *Triple Cross,* Dutton, 1972; *Cambio de piel* (novel), J. Mortiz, 1967, translation by Hileman published as *A Change of Skin,* Farrar, Strauss, 1968; *Dos cuentos mexicanos* (two short stories previously published in *Cantar de ciegos),* Instituto de Cultura Hispanica de Sao Paulo, Universidade de Sao Paulo, 1969; *Cumpleanos* (short novel), J. Mortiz, 1969.

Poemas de amor: Cuentos del alma, Imp. E. Cruces (Madrid), 1971; *Chac Mool y otros cuentos* (short stories), Salvat, 1973.

Nonfiction: *The Argument of Latin America: Words for North Americans,* Radical Education Project, 1963; (contributor) *Wither Latin America?* (political articles), Monthly Review Press, 1963; *Paris: La revolucion de Mayo,* Ediciones Era, 1968; *La nueva novela hispanoamericana* (essays), J. Mortiz, 1969; (author of text) *El mundo de Jose Luis Cuevas,* Tudor, 1969; *Casa con dos puertas* (essays), J. Mortiz, 1970; *Tiempo mexicano* (essays), J. Mortiz, 1971; *Los reinos originarios: Teatro hispano-mexicano,* Barral Editores (Barcelona), 1971.

Plays: *Todos los gatos son pardos,* Siglo Veintiuno Editores, 1970; *El tuerto es rey,* J. Mortiz, 1970. Writer or collaborator on several film scripts, including *Pedro Paramo,* 1966, *Tiempo de morir,* 1966, and *Los caifanes,* 1967. Contributor of hundreds of articles on cultural and political subjects to publications in Latin America, Europe, and the United States. Editor, *Revista Mexicana de Literatura,* 1954-58, *El Espectador,* 1959-61, *Siempre,* 1960, *Politica,* 1960.

SIDELIGHTS: "Carlos Fuentes is one of Mexico's most distinguished writers, possessor of an enviable international reputation, and unquestionably an artist of the most serious intent," wrote Frank Conroy. According to Webster Schott, writing in 1967: ". . . a small group of other Americans has moved in on the American fiction establishment. They come from south of the Rio Grande. . . . Activists in a kind of intellectual Alliance for Progress in reverse, they're bringing to American fiction a quality of imagination now missing from the closed U.S. circle of writers preoccupied with black humor, gray sex, white guilt. They want to know everything—the causes of man's tragic reach beyond his grasp, the mysteries of time, space and consciousness, the alchemy of their art itself. Youngest of the group, flashing brilliance and in hot pursuit of greatness, is 39-year-old Carlos Fuentes."

A writer for the Times Literary Supplement says: "Carlos Fuentes is the chameleon among Latin American writers. Essayist, dramatist, novelist, author of a political pamphlet on the events of May, 1968, he is always provocative, although his ecclecticism sometimes obscures the fact that there is a lasting central preoccupation in his writing—that of identity."

Fuentes has traveled extensively. Because of his father's various diplomatic posts, Fuentes' early years were spent in such capital cities as Washington, D.C., Rio de Janeiro, Santiago de Chile, Buenos Aires, Montevideo, and Quito. Besides the years he spent studying and working in Geneva, Fuentes has seen much of Europe, living there for four years before returning to Mexico in 1969. He has an international circle of friends and acquaintances. His plays have been staged in Barcelona, Vienna, Paris, Avignon, and Brussels.

Fuentes' political positions have been the source of considerable controversy. At home, according to David Gallagher, "he has been particularly energetic in his denunciation of what seems to him the inauthenticity of Mexico's 'institutional' revolution. One oligarchy was exchanged for another." In Spain, his novel A Change of Skin was banned for being "Communistic, pro-Jewish and anti-German." He has been denied a United States visa on several occasions, and in 1969 he was denied entrance at San Juan, Puerto Rico, by U.S. customs and immigration officials as an "undesirable alien." This action was editorially condemned by Publishers Weekly and was strongly protested by Senator J. William Fulbright, Chairman of the Senate Foreign Relations Committee, the American P.E.N., and the Authors League.

AVOCATIONAL INTERESTS: Reading, traveling, swimming, visiting art galleries, listening to classical and rock music, attending motion pictures and the theater.

BIOGRAPHICAL/CRITICAL SOURCES: Commentary, February 7, 1965; Luis Harss and Barbara Dohmann, Into the Mainstream, Harper, 1966; Britannica Book of the Year, 1969; Walter M. Langford, The Mexican Novel Comes of Age, University of Notre Dame Press, 1971; Kessel Schwartz, A New History of Spanish American Fiction, University of Miami Press, 1971; Contemporary Literary Criticism, Volume III, Gale, 1975.*

*   *   *

FULDAUER, Ivan   1927-

PERSONAL: Born April 5, 1927, in Cleveland, Ohio; son of Richard E. and Esther (Weisman) Fuldauer; married Joyce Lee Goldberg (an interior designer), September 23, 1962. Education: Miami University, Oxford, Ohio, student, 1946-48; Case Western Reserve University, B.B.A., 1950. Politics: "Not affiliated—vote for best candidate."

CAREER/WRITINGS: Metro-Goldwyn-Mayer, Inc., Chicago, Ill., Midwest marketing director, 1949-58; The Public Relations Board, Inc., Chicago, senior vice-president, 1958-70; free-lance journalist in Geneva, Switzerland, 1970—. Author of "Bonne Cuisine," a restaurant column appearing monthly in seventeen newspapers in the United States and Canada. Contributor of articles to over twenty-five periodicals in the United States, Canada, and England, including Washington Post, Chicago Tribune, Los Angeles Times, Toronto Star, and Wine World. Swiss correspondent for Overseas American. Lecturer in public relations. Member of board of directors, Chicago Council on Foreign Relations; vice-president, International Visitors Center of Chicago. Military service: U.S. Navy, 1945-46. Member: Public Relations Society of America, International Public Relations Association, Urban Gateways. Awards, honors: Seven awards, 1964-69, from Publicity Club of Chicago; international journalistic award, 1973, from Spanish National Tourist Office.

SIDELIGHTS: Fuldauer writes principally in the fields of travel, wine and food, and international education. He has traveled extensively in the United States, South America, Asia, Europe, and Africa.

*   *   *

FULLER, Beverley   1927-

PERSONAL: Stage name, Beverley Bozeman; born July 20, 1927, in Fresno, Calif.; daughter of Edward E. (founder of a motorcycle company) and Lee (an executive secretary; maiden name, Bills) Bozeman; married Dean Fuller (a writer and composer), January 3, 1955; children: Liza, John. Education: Educated in Portland, Ore. Politics: Democrat/Liberal. Religion: None. Home: 10 Old Depot Rd., Chester, Conn. 06412. Agent: Julie Fallowfield, McIntosh & Otis, 475 Fifth Ave. New York, N.Y. 10017. Office: 136 West 16th St., New York, N.Y. 10011.

CAREER: Actress, producer, and choreographer for theatre. Made stage debut, at age four, as a member of a touring Shakespearean company; was accepted as the youngest member of San Francisco Ballet, 1942; principal dancer in American version of Folies Bergere, 1944-45; contract player and assistant to dance director at Warner Brothers studio, 1945-46; lead comedienne in touring company of "The Desert Song," 1946; made Broadway debut in "Inside U.S.A.," 1948; performed in two Valerie Bettis dance dramas, 1948 and 1949; choreographed ballet, "Capriccio for Three" (with music by Igor Stravinsky), 1949; choreographed the first stock productions of "On the Town," 1950; performed female lead in "Where's Charlie," 1949-50; acted and danced in Lee Strasberg's production of "Peer Gynt," 1951; co-produced, choreographed, and designed costumes for touring company of "Connecticut Yankee," 1951; was featured in "Panama Hattie," 1952; performed with Broadway and National touring companies of "Pal Joey," 1953; starred in "The Golden Apple," and the Chicago production of "Guys and Dolls," 1955; was featured in "The Littlest Review," by Ogden Nash and Duke Vernon, 1956; assisted Valerie Bettis in the revival of her ballet, "Virginia Sampler," for North Carolina Theatre Ballet, 1975; associate artistic director for Valerie Bettis Theatre Dance Foundation, 1977—. Member: Dramatists Guild.

WRITINGS: Cooking on Your Knees, McKay, 1973, published as Cooking Afloat, 1976.

WORK IN PROGRESS: The Flops and Grumps Books,

for children; an untitled ballet ballad; a "fireplace cookbook."

SIDELIGHTS: Beverley Fuller told *CA:* "In the last twenty years, the adventurousness of Off Broadway and the rise of skilled regional theatres has injected new ideas and new playwrights into the Broadway theatre scene and proved that audiences will respond to something other than safe classics and formula comedies.

"The dance world has exploded in popularity, not just in New York but all over the country. The American dancer's technique has improved phenomenally in recent years. They can literally do anything and the interaction, so taboo in the past, between ballet and modern techniques has enriched the repertoire of both. The impact of the dazzling power, style, and intelligence of the Russian defectors—Nureyev, Barishnikov, and Markova will be felt for years.

"Twenty years ago a season that included performances by The American Ballet Theatre, The New York City Ballet, The Stuttgart, The Graham, Joffery, and Ailey, Twyla Tharp, and Paul Taylor companies, the recreation of the dances of Denis-Shawn and Isadora Duncan, the importation of regional, foreign, and ethnic companies as well as solo and group dance concerts in halls, movie houses, churches, and even the streets—would have been unimaginable. The huge success of the dance-oriented musical 'A Chorus Line,' and the extraordinary presentation of the 19th century ballet, 'Giselle'—live from the Met *and* commercially sponsored—surely point to a response to dance unprecedented in the history of the world!"

Recalling experiences from her own career in the theatre, Fuller stated: "Two productions that I appeared in on Broadway gave me enormous pleasure and satisfaction for totally different reasons. The first was creating the role of Dewey Dell in Valerie Bettis' dance drama of Faulkner's 'As I Lay Dying'. The challenge of finding a way to act the complexities of the text while moving to Miss Bettis' highly personalized dance vocabulary was difficult and very exciting. The role of dancer/actor is now expected, but then it was a rarity and the work was a milestone in this direction. It won Miss Bettis the Choreographer of the Year award from *Dance Magazine,* 1949.

"The other role was Gladys Bumps in the 50's revival of the classic musical, 'Pal Joey.' The John O'Hara 'booh' had unusual and rather unsavory characters for a musical and was blessed with a distinctive Rodgers and Hart score. The Gladys Bumps part was hilarious but physically demanding —requiring the ability to belt out a song while arms and legs were frantically flailing in all directions. One number required point work (toe shoes). The great ballerina, Alicia Markova was reported in tears of laughter during that one."

Fuller added that while theatre is her main influence, "I am interested in all forms of expression."

AVOCATIONAL INTERESTS: Cooking, drawing and painting, and sailing.

*　　*　　*

FURRER, Juerg 1939-

PERSONAL: Born August 23, 1939, in Sisikon, Uri, Switzerland; son of Ernst and Lydia (Hilfiker) Furrer; married Elsi Zimmermann, November 12, 1965; children: Samuel Christoph, Eva Katharina. *Education:* Educated in Switzerland. *Home:* Stolten 33, Ch 5701 SEON, Switzerland. 5703. *Agent:* A.F.A. Inc., 261 Madison Ave., Room 1102, New York, N.Y. 10016.

CAREER: Worked as a window dresser in Solothurn, Switzerland, 1955-56; Swiss Railroad employee, 1956-70; freelance cartoonist and illustrator, 1970—. *Military service:* Swiss Army, 1959. *Member:* German Society for Herpetology. *Awards, honors:* Golden Pen Beograd (Yugoslavia), 1974; also received Golden Diana Novi Sad (Yugoslavia), Silver Medal Skopje (Yugoslavia), and Dattero d'oro Bordighera (Italy).

WRITINGS: (Illustrator) Jan Koopman, *Bitterballen,* Blitz, 1965; *Happy End,* Magica, 1967; *Und beim fuenften hoert der Hahn auf,* Magica, 1967; *Tortoise Island* (juvenile), translated by Bettina Huerlimann, Atlantis, 1973, Addison-Wesley, 1976; (illustrator) Adolf Steiner, *Arche zum Mond,* Eichlitten, 1974; (illustrator) James McCrea and Ruth McCrea, *The Birds,* Houghton, 1977; (illustrator), *The Big Race* (traditional tale), Harcourt, 1977. Contributor of short stories and cartoons to *Nebelspalter, Pardon, Playboy,* and other periodicals.

WORK IN PROGRESS: More juvenile books.

SIDELIGHTS: Furrer told *CA* that he has acquired a great interest in turtles because "they are 180 years old and still on this earth. I think they must have something that we do not have and I am trying to find it out." He has forty-eight turtles as pets, as well as numerous lizards, cats, ducks, birds, and chipmunks, two horses, and one Alaskan Malamute.

*　　*　　*

FURST, Alan 1941-

PERSONAL: Born February 20, 1941, in New York, N.Y. *Education:* Oberlin College, A.B., 1962; Pennsylvania State University, M.A., 1967. *Agent:* Elaine Markson, 44 Greenwich Ave., New York, N.Y. 10011.

CAREER: Writer. *Awards, honors:* Fulbright fellowship, 1969-70.

WRITINGS: Your Day in the Barrel (novel), Atheneum, 1976.

WORK IN PROGRESS: Isn't Life a Fountain?; Where's My Chocolate Chip Cookie?.

AVOCATIONAL INTERESTS: French language, literature, and culture, raising pigs, raising roses, his Irish wolfhound.

*　　*　　*

GAGE, Nathaniel Lees 1917-

PERSONAL: Born August 1, 1917, in Union City, N.J.; son of Hyman and Rose (Lees) Gage; married Margaret Elizabeth Burrows, June 27, 1942; children: Elizabeth (Mrs. Andrew K. Strawn), Thomas Burrows, Sarah, Anne. *Education:* University of Minnesota, A.B. (magna cum laude), 1938; Purdue University, Ph.D., 1947. *Home:* 845 Cedro Way, Stanford, Calif. 94305. *Office:* Center for Research and Development in Teaching, Stanford University, Stanford, Calif. 94305.

CAREER: Purdue University, West Lafayette, Ind., assistant professor of education and assistant director of Division of Educational Reference, 1947-48; University of Illinois, Champaign-Urbana, assistant professor, 1948-51, associate professor, 1951-56, professor of education, 1956-62, professor of psychology, 1961-62; Stanford University, Stanford, Calif., professor of education, 1962—, and psychology, 1963—, co-director of Center for Research and Development in Teaching, 1965-68, chairman of its executive board, 1968—, acting director, 1970-71, 1975. Distinguished lecturer at New York University, 1966; distinguished alumni lecturer at Purdue University, 1968; professor at Stanford in Germany, 1971. Fellow of Center for Advanced Study in the Behavioral Sciences (Stanford, Calif.), 1965-66; visiting scholar at National Institute of Education, 1974. Member of research advisory committee of American Council on Education, 1966-73 (chairman, 1972-73); member of executive committee of Council for Educational Development and Research, 1970-71; consultant for American Heritage Dictionary of the English Language. *Military service:* U.S. Army Air Forces, 1943-45.

MEMBER: American Psychological Association (fellow; division president, 1961-62), Society for the Psychological Study of Social Issues (fellow), American Educational Research Association (president, 1963-64), National Society for the Study of Education (member of board of directors, 1969-75; chairman, 1971), American Association for the Advancement of Science, Phi Beta Kappa, Sigma Xi, Phi Delta Kappa, Stanford Faculty Club. *Awards, honors:* National Institute of Mental Health grant, 1953-57; U.S. Public Health Service special fellowship, 1965-66; Guggenheim fellowship, 1976-77.

WRITINGS: (Editor with H. H. Remmers) *Two Thousand Test Items in American History,* State High School Testing Service for Indiana, Purdue University, 1941; (with Remmers) *Educational Measurement and Evaluation,* Harper, 1943, revised edition, 1955; (with Remmers) *Student Exercises in Measurement and Evaluation for Education and Guidance,* Harper, 1947; (with Remmers) *Student Personnel Studies in the Pharmaceutical Survey* (monograph), American Council on Education, 1949; (with Remmers and J. F. Rummel) *A Practical Intoduction to Measurement and Evaluation,* Harper 1960, 2nd edition, 1965; (with C. Hagan, N. Garvey, and R. Payette) *Principles of Democracy: A Test of Knowledge and Understanding,* Science Research Associates, 1960; (editor and contributor) *Handbook of Research on Teaching,* Rand McNally, 1963; (editor with W. W. Charters, Jr., and contributor) *Readings in the Social Psychology of Education,* Allyn & Bacon, 1963; *Teacher Effectiveness and Teacher Education: The Search for a Scientific Basis,* Pacific Books Publishers, 1972; (editor and contributor) *Mandated Evaluation of Educators: A Conference on California's Stull Act,* Capitol Publications, 1973; (with David C. Berliner) *Educational Psychology,* Rand McNally, 1975; (editor and contributor) *The Psychology of Teaching Methods* (yearbook), University of Chicago Press, 1976.

Contributor: B. N. Phillips and other editors, *Psychology at Work in the Elementary School Classroom,* Harper, 1960; *New Directions in Educational Research* (proceedings), New York State Education Department, 1963; B. J. Chandler and other editors, *Research Seminar on Teacher Education,* Cooperative Research Program, U.S. Office of Education, 1963; *Freedom with Responsibility in Teacher Education* (proceedings), American Association of Colleges for Teacher Education, 1964; R. H. Beck, editor, *Society and the Schools: Communication Challenge to Education and Social Work* (proceedings), National Association of Social Workers, 1965; M. Usdan and F. Bertolaet, editors, *Teachers for the Disadvantaged,* Follett, 1966; *The Way Teaching Is: A Report of the Seminar on Teaching,* Association for Supervision and Curriculum Development, 1966; R. C. Anderson and other editors, *Current Research on Instruction,* Prentice-Hall, 1969; H. F. Clarizio, R. C. Craig, and W. A. Mehrens, editors, *Contemporary Issues in Educational Psychology,* Allyn & Bacon, 1970; M. C. Wittrock

and D. Wiley, editors, *The Evaluation of Instruction,* Holt, 1970; R. D. Strom, editor, *Teachers and the Learning Process,* Prentice-Hall, 1971; I. Westbury and A. A. Bellack, editors, *Research into Classroom Processes,* Teachers College Press, 1971; *How Teachers Make a Difference,* Bureau of Educational Personnel Development, U.S. Office of Education, 1971; *Competency Assessment, Research, and Evaluation: A Report of a National Conference,* American Association of Colleges for Teacher Education, 1974; Kevin Ryan, editor, *Teacher Education* (yearbook), Part II, University of Chicago Press, 1975; *Toward Continuous Professional Development: Designs and Directions,* College of Education, University of Maryland, 1976.

Contributor to *Encyclopedia of Educational Research.* Contributor of about a hundred articles and reviews to academic journals. Associate editor of *Sociometry,* 1958-60 (consulting editor, 1956-58); member of board of editors of *Encyclopedia of Educational Research,* 1965-69; member of editorial advisory board of *Current Contents: Behavioral, Social, and Education Sciences,* 1969—; advisory editor of *Instructional Science,* 1971—; consulting editor of *Journal of Abnormal and Social Psychology,* 1956-64, *American Educational Research Journal,* 1964-70, *Journal of Educational Psychology,* 1963-75, *Contemporary Psychology,* 1967-73, *Educational Studies: A Journal of Book Reviews in the Foundations of Education,* 1970—, and *Educational Research Quarterly,* 1976—; referee for *Journal for Research in Mathematics Education,* 1969—.

* * *

GAIL, Marzieh

PERSONAL: Born in Boston, Mass.; daughter of Ali-Kuli (a diplomat, Baha'i scholar, and art collector) and Florence (Breed) Khan; married Howard L. Carpenter, July 29, 1929 (died November 24, 1935); married Harold E. Gail (a researcher), October 3, 1939. *Education:* Attended Vassar College, 1926, and Mills College, 1927; Stanford University, B.A. (summa cum laude), 1930; University of California, Berkeley, M.A., 1932. *Religion:* Baha'i. *Home:* 63 Beaver St., Keene, N.H. 03431.

CAREER: Writer. Chairperson of Baha'i Unity of East and West Committee, Teheran, Iran, 1934, Baha'i Assembly, Nice, France, 1955-56, Baha'i Assembly, Salzburg, Austria, 1957-63, and Austrian National Baha'i Assembly, Vienna, 1963. *Member:* Phi Beta Kappa.

WRITINGS: (Translator from the Persian) Baha'u'llah, *The Seven Valleys and the Four Valleys,* Baha'i Publishing Trust, 1945; *Persia and the Victorians,* Allen & Unwin, 1951; *Six Lessons on Islam,* Baha'i Publishing Trust, 1953; *Baha'i Glossary,* Baha'i Publishing Trust, 1955; (translator from the Persian) 'Abdu'l-Baha, *The Secret of Divine Civilization,* Baha'i Publishing Trust, 1957; *The Sheltering Branch,* Ronald, 1959; *Avignon in Flower,* Houghton, 1965; *The Three Popes,* Simon & Schuster, 1969; *Life in the Renaissance,* Random House, 1969; (translator from the Persian) 'Abdu'l-Baha, *Memorials of the Faithful,* Baha'i Publishing Trust, 1971; *Dawn Over Mount Hira,* Ronald, 1976.

WORK IN PROGRESS: A book about the troubadours in the twelfth century; translating the Tablets of 'Abdu'l-Baha from Persian and Arabic; gathering material for a biography of her father, Ali-Kuli Khan.

SIDELIGHTS: Marzieh Gail, whose father was chief diplomatic representative to the United States from Persia during the Roosevelt, Taft, and Wilson administrations, writes that as a child, she accompanied him to diplomatic posts around the world. She has made three pilgrimages to the Baha'i World Centre in Haifa, Israel, during the lifetime of the Guardian, Shoghi Effendi. Ms. Gail is fluent in French, German, and Persian.

* * *

GAINSBRUGH, Martin R(euben) 1907-1977

January 29, 1907—April 25, 1977; American educator, economist, and consultant to various government and private agencies. Gainsbrugh was an executive and chief economist for a non-profit business research organization. He was author of books in his field. Gainsbrugh died in Freeport, The Bahamas. Obituaries: *New York Times,* April 26, 1977; *AB Bookman's Weekly,* June 22, 1977.

* * *

GALBRAITH, Vivian Hunter 1891(?)-1976

British historian and educator in England and Scotland. He was an authority on the *Domesday Book* and was author of books and articles in his field. Galbraith died in England. Obituaries: *AB Bookman's Weekly,* January 3, 1977.

* * *

GALLANT, Mavis 1922-

PERSONAL: Born August 11, 1922, in Montreal, Quebec, Canada; *Home:* 14 rue Jean Ferrandi, 75006 Paris, France. *Agent:* Georges Borchardt, 145 East 52nd St., New York, N.Y. 10022.

CAREER: Writer; *The Standard,* Montreal, Quebec, reporter, 1944-50. *Member:* P.E.N., Authors Guild.

WRITINGS: The Other Paris (short stories), Houghton, 1956; *Green Water, Green Sky* (novel), Houghton, 1959; *My Heart Is Broken* (novella and short stories), Random House, 1964 (published in England as *An Unmarried Man's Summer,* Heinemann, 1965); *A Fairly Good Time* (novel), Random House, 1970; (author of introductory essay) Gabrielle Russier, *The Affair of Gabrielle Russier,* Knopf, 1971; *The Pegnitz Junction* (novella and short stories), Random House, 1973; *The End of the World* (short stories) New Canadian Library, 1974.

WORK IN PROGRESS: A book on the Dreyfus case, publication by Random House expected in 1978.

* * *

GALLERY, Daniel V. 1901-1977
(Dan Gallery)

July 10, 1901—January 16, 1977; American retired Navy rear admiral, commander of the carrier *Guadalcanal* that captured German submarine *U-505* during World War II, and author of books on naval life, including his books about the capture, *Clear the Decks!* and *Twenty Million Tons Under the Sea.* He died in Bethesda, Md. Obituaries: *Washington Post,* January 19, 1977; *New York Times,* January 20, 1977; *Time,* January 31, 1977; *AB Bookman's Weekly,* March 14, 1977; *Current Biography,* March, 1977. (See index for previous *CA* sketch)

* * *

GALLICO, Paul (William) 1897-1976

July 26, 1897—July 15, 1976; American sports columnist and editor, movie critic, free-lance fiction writer, and writer of children's literature, fables, ghost stories, screenplays, and more than forty books, including the humorous "Mrs.

'Arris" series and best-sellers *The Snow Goose* and *The Poseidon Adventure.* He died in Monte Carlo, Monaco. Obituaries: *New York Times,* July 17, 1976; *AB Bookman's Weekly,* October 4, 1976. (See index for previous *CA* sketch)

* * *

GAMBLE, Andrew (Michael) 1947-

PERSONAL: Born August 15, 1947, in London, England; son of Marcus Elkington (a company director) and Joan (Westall) Gamble; married Christine Jennifer Rodway (a social worker), June 15, 1974; children: Tom. *Education:* Cambridge University, B.A., 1968, Ph.D., 1975; University of Durham, M.A., 1969. *Home:* 4 College St., Sheffield S10 2PH, England. *Office:* Department of Political Theory and Institutions, University of Sheffield, Sheffield S10 2TN, England.

CAREER: University of Sheffield, Sheffield, England, lecturer in political economy and political theory, 1973—. *Member:* Political Studies Association. *Awards, honors:* Isaac Deutscher Memorial Prize, 1972, for *From Alienation to Surplus Value.*

WRITINGS: (With Paul Walton) *From Alienation to Surplus Value,* Sheed, 1972; *The Conservative Nation,* Routledge & Kegan Paul, 1974; (with Walton) *Capitalism in Crisis,* Macmillan, 1976.

WORK IN PROGRESS: The Politics of Decline, on the political economy of the United Kingdom; research on political ecology.

SIDELIGHTS: Gamble writes: "After two books on Marxism and one on Conservatism my interests are currently moving towards political ecology and international political economy, though I retain a strong desire to write a history of the British state and its ruling class, in their heyday and in their decline. Writing well and making things comprehensible to greater numbers of people are what matter most to me in my work. My outlook on most things was permanently transformed by being at university during the extraordinary years of the late 1960's."

AVOCATIONAL INTERESTS: "The fortunes of Sheffield United Football Club," the music of Bob Dylan.

* * *

GAMM, David B(ernard) 1948-

PERSONAL: Born November 4, 1948, in Covington, Ky.; son of Bernard C. (a salesman) and Shirley (Koelker) Gamm. *Education:* Seminary of St. Pius X, B.A., 1968; Athanaeum of Ohio, M.Div., 1972. *Home:* 3349 Bluejay Ct., Edgewood, Ky. 41017. *Office:* Church of the Blessed Sacrament, 2415 Dixie Highway, Fort Mitchell, Ky. 41017.

CAREER: Ordained Roman Catholic priest; associate pastor of Roman Catholic churches in Covington, Ky., 1972-74, and Ludlow, Ky., 1974-76; Church of the Blessed Sacrament, Fort Mitchell, Ky., associate pastor, 1976—. *Member:* Knights of Columbus (chaplain of Kehoe Council, 1974-77).

WRITINGS: On Cloud Nine (collection of liturgies for children), Ave Maria Press, 1976; *Service,* Paulist/Newman, 1976; *Change My Heart* (parish Lenten program), Paulist/Newman, 1977.

WORK IN PROGRESS: Acting out Bible passages with elementary school children.

SIDELIGHTS: Fr. Gamm writes: "I've worked with children's liturgy since 1971 when I was a deacon. The motivation was that I saw children not experiencing God or understanding what they were doing at liturgy. Catholic Mass is adult-oriented and I wanted to child-orient it to help them see the richness of worship and to derive all the benefits therefrom, spiritual as well as human."

* * *

GANDLEY, Kenneth Royce 1920-
(Oliver Jacks)

PERSONAL: Born December 11, 1920, in Croyden, England; married Stella Amy Parker (an editor), March 27, 1946. *Education:* Self-educated. *Religion:* Church of England. *Residence:* County Cork, Ireland. *Agent:* David Higham Associates, 5-8 Lower John St., Golden Sq., London W1R 11HA, England.

CAREER: Business and Holiday Travel, London, England, managing director, 1948-72, member of board of directors, 1948—; full time writer, 1972—. *Military service:* British Army, Infantry, 1939-46; served in Africa; became captain. *Member:* Crime Writers Association, Writers Action Group.

WRITINGS—Mystery novels: (Under pseudonym, Oliver Jacks) *Man on a Short Leash,* Stein & Day, 1974; *Assassination Day,* Hodder & Stoughton, 1976; *Autumn Heroes,* Hodder & Stoughton, 1977.

WORK IN PROGRESS: The Satan Touch, a novel about a multi-millionaire in Corfu.

Avocational interests: Travel, sports, jazz, antiques.

* * *

GARDEN, Robert Hal 1937-

PERSONAL: Born October 27, 1937, in Charleston, W.Va.; son of Prince Hal (an executive) and Rosamond (a nurse; maiden name, Stewart) Garden; married Sally Wright, June 10, 1958 (deceased); children: Tammy (deceased), Salena (deceased), Stephen, Patricia. *Education:* Maryville College, B.A., 1956; Ringling School of Art, B.F.A., 1958. *Home:* 7212 Skillman #2149, Dallas, Tex. 75231. *Agent:* Jane Cuthbert, 2935 Forest Hills, Richardson, Tex. 75080. *Office:* 810 Lookout Dr., Richardson, Tex. 75080.

CAREER: Robert Garden Art Enterprises, Inc., Richardson, Tex., president, 1974—; artist, lecturer, instructor. President, Panama City Art Association, 1959; president, Art Association of Corpus Christi, 1962-63. *Member:* Copinni Academy of Fine Art, South Texas Watercolor Society.

WRITINGS: Anyone Can Paint—I Promise, McKay, 1976.

WORK IN PROGRESS: Paint-a-long with Robert Garden; Anyone Can Cook—I Promise.

SIDELIGHTS: Garden writes: "I feel the most rewarding aspect of my work is pleasing other people, helping them to paint easier, helping the handicapped, emotionally disturbed, and mentally retarded."

* * *

GARDNER, (Alice) Lucille 1913-

PERSONAL: Born September 20, 1913, in Olathe, Kan.; daughter of Otho (a bank cashier) and Anna (Bruce) Vardeman; married Charles Gardner (an insurance agent), March 19, 1936; children: Stella Ann, Charles, Sharon. *Education:* Attended Bryant-Stratton Business College, 1930-31. *Politics:* "Registered Democrat but vote for candi-

date, not party." *Religion:* Baptist. *Home:* 1075 Chapman St., San Jose, Calif. 95126.

CAREER: Axton-Fisher Tobacco Co., Louisville, Ky., stenographer and secretary, 1932-36; Richmond-Chase Canning Co., San Jose, Calif., secretary, 1940-42; Joshua Hendy Iron Works, Sunnyvale, Calif., secretary and stenographer, 1942-45; International Business Machines (IBM), San Jose, assistant to research librarian and secretary, 1952-59. *Member:* California Association of Neurological Handicapped, Interfaith Religious Art Committee, Santa Clara Valley Christian Writers; California Federation of Chaparral Poets (Robert Frost chapter, president, 1965-66, director, 1969-73); Kentucky State Poetry Society. *Awards, honors:* Mt. Hermon Christian Writers award for essay, 1970, and article, 1972.

WRITINGS: There IS Hope, David Cook, 1976. Contributor of poems to anthologies and to magazines, including *Purpose, Christian Reader, Grit, For Real.* Contributor of articles to *Home Life* and *Catholic Digest.*

WORK IN PROGRESS: Dear God: A Spiritual Journal, with Ethel Herr; *Only Through Suffering,* "based on the premise that many of life's greatest blessings come by way of suffering"; poetry.

SIDELIGHTS: Lucille Gardner, whose daughter Sharon suffered brain damage as a result of a car accident, told *CA:* "I felt a driving compulsion to write *There IS Hope* in order to bring whatever help and encouragement I could to other brain-damaged persons and their families. Yet I instinctively recoiled from the thought of reliving the traumatic experiences.

"I feel society could learn much from research on the relatively few brain damaged and/or retarded persons who are able to live independently as adults. The parents and loved ones of these persons have usually struggled long years, and often have made discoveries that would be helpful to others if there was some way of correlating the information and making it available. From our experience with Sharon, I know that art is wonderful therapy, and I feel that it should be used more than it is for the handicapped.

"My elementary and high school English courses," Ms. Gardner added, "required the study and memorization of much poetry of the 'Masters' (Shelley, Keats, Browning, Tennyson, Longfellow, Kipling . . .). The rhythm, beauty and meaning of their words became part of me, and their inspiring thoughts and phrases returned to my mind again and again when the need arose. Kipling's 'If' has given me courage to fight through many a difficult situation, as have numerous other poems memorized in childhood. So I feel deeply grieved to witness the present-day degradation of poetry—to see this highest of all means of written expression become synonymous with obscenity, obscure phrases, incomplete thoughts, and bitter ramblings. If this trend continues, the present and future generations will have lost one of the world's most precious treasures—one that can provide an invisible means of support. I realize I lack the ability to become a 'great' poet, but my goal is to write at least a few verses that people will read over and over again, will clip out and copy for friends or paste in a scrapbook; ones that may bring comfort, challenge, inspiration, or joy and happiness to many—thus providing beauty for the inward soul."

* * *

GARDNER, Paul

PERSONAL: Born in Hollywood, Calif. *Education:* College of William and Mary, B.A.; also studied at University of California, Berkeley. *Home:* Eight West Ninth St., New York, N.Y. 10011. *Office: New York* Magazine, 755 Second Ave., New York, N.Y. 10017.

CAREER/WRITINGS: New York Times, New York City, staff writer and assistant editor of Sunday Arts & Leisure section. Contributor to *A Faulkner Perspective,* Franklin Library. Author of the screenplay *La Decade Prodigieuse,* with Claude Chabrol. Notable assignments include an exclusive interview with Leni Riefenstahl, the German film director. Contributor to periodicals, including *New York, New Times, Transatlantic Review, Plays & Players, Art News,* and *London Sunday Observer.*

SIDELIGHTS: Gardner writes: "Extended travel is absolutely essential to growth and maturity for the journalist-writer. Unfortunately, many print organizations do not give 'leaves-of-absence' for travel. It is considered less than serious. My advice: 'Go anyway.'"

* * *

GARDNER, Richard Kent 1928-

PERSONAL: Born December 7, 1928, in New Bedford, Mass.; son of Francis and Millicent Annetta (Kent) Gardner. *Education:* Middlebury College, Middlebury, Vermont, A.B. (cum laude), 1950; University of Paris, diploma in literature, 1954; Western Reserve University (now Case Western Reserve University), M.S.L.S., 1955, Ph.D., 1968. *Religion:* Episcopalian. *Office:* Powell Library Building 120, University of California, 405 Hilgard Ave., Los Angeles, Calif. 90024.

CAREER: Case Institute of Technology (now Case Western Reserve University), Cleveland, Ohio, assistant librarian, 1955-57; Michigan State University, East Lansing, library adviser for Vietnam project, 1957-58; Marietta College, Marietta, Ohio, librarian and assistant professor, 1959-63; *Choice* Magazine, Middletown, Conn., founding editor, 1963-66; Case Western Reserve University, School of Library Science, associate professor, 1966-69; University of Montreal, Montreal, Quebec, associate professor, 1969-70, professor of library science and director of Graduate School of Library Science, 1970-72; *Choice* Magazine, editor, 1972-77; University of California, Graduate School of Library and Information Science, Los Angeles, professor of library and information science, 1977—. Consultant to college and university libraries, 1966—. Trustee, Lake Placid Club Educational Foundation, 1972—, Russell Library, 1975-77. *Military service:* U.S. Army, 1951-53.

MEMBER: American Library Association, Canadian Library Association, Association of College and Research Libraries, Music Library Association, Association Canadienne de Bibliothecaires de Langue Francaise, Association des Bibliothecaires Francaises (France), Corporation des Bibliothecaires Professionels du Quebec (member of administrative council, 1970-72), Ohio Library Association (member of executive board, 1962-63), Ohio College Association (library section; vice-president, 1962-63; president, 1963), Tudor Singers (Montreal; vice-president, 1970-72), Beta Phi Mu, Phi Beta Kappa.

WRITINGS: (With Nguyen Xuan Dao) *Bibliography of Periodicals Published in Viet Nam,* Michigan State University, 1958; (editor) Nguygen thi Cut, translator, *The Cataloging and Classification of Books,* Asia Foundation (Saigon), 1959, revised edition, 1966; (with Dorothy Sinclair, Mary Ann Hanna, and John Rowell) *Cooperative Services for "Big Country" Libraries: Report of a Survey with Rec-*

ommendations for Cooperation among Libraries of All Types in Thirty-Six Counties of West Central Texas, [Cleveland], 1969; (editor with others) *Opening Day Collection, Choice* Magazine, 1965, 3rd edition, 1974.

* * *

GARLAND, Charles T(albot) 1910(?)-1976

1910(?)—September 11, 1976; American publisher, writer, film producer, and government consultant. During World War II he produced films for the Army Signal Corps. Garland died in Alexandria, Va. Obituaries: *Washington Post,* October 10, 1976.

* * *

GARLAND, Phyl(lis T.) 1935-

PERSONAL: Born October 27, 1935, in McKeesport, Pa. *Education:* Northwestern University, B.S.J. *Office: Ebony* Magazine, 1270 Avenue of the Americas, New York, N.Y. 10020.

CAREER: Pittsburgh Courier, Pittsburgh, Pa., junior editor, 1955-57, feature editor, columnist, reporter, and feature writer, 1958-65; *Ebony* (magazine), Chicago, Ill., assistant editor, 1965-67, associate editor, 1967-69, New York editor, 1969—; State University of New York College, New Paltz, currently associate professor of black studies and chairman of department. *Member:* Media Women, Theta Sigma Phi, Delta Sigma Theta. *Awards, honors:* Golden Quill award, 1962, for outstanding feature writing on western Pennsylvania; Headliners Award, 1971.

WRITINGS: The Sound of Soul: The Story of Black Music, Regnery, 1969.

WORK IN PROGRESS: Two books.*

* * *

GARNER, Hugh 1913-
(Jarvis Warwick)

PERSONAL: Born February 22, 1913, in Batley, Yorkshire, England; moved to Canada in 1919; son of Matthew and Annie (Fozard) Garner; married Marie Alice Gallant, July 5, 1941; children: Barbara Ann, Hugh, Jr. *Education:* Attended technical high school in Toronto, Ontario. *Home:* 33 Erskine Ave., Toronto, Ontario, Canada.

CAREER: Writer. Public relations director for J. K. Cooke Enterprises, 1951. *Military service:* Machine gunner in International Brigade, 1937; served in Spain. Canadian Army, 1939-40. Royal Canadian Navy, 1940-45; served in Africa and Atlantic theater. *Member:* Association of Canadian Television and Radio Artists, Saint George Society. *Awards, honors:* Canadian Governor General's Award for English Fiction, 1963, for *Best Stories;* receipient of three Canada Council senior arts fellowships.

WRITINGS: The Yellow Sweater and Other Stories, Collins, 1952; *The Silence on the Shore* (novel), McClelland & Stewart, 1962, Ryerson, 1968; *Best Stories,* Ryerson, 1963; *Author, Author!* (humor), Ryerson, 1964; *Men and Women* (stories), Ryerson, 1966; *Storm Below* (novel), Ryerson, 1968; *Cabbagetown* (novel), Ryerson, 1968; *A Nice Place to Visit,* Ryerson, 1970; *The Sin Sniper* (novel), Simon & Schuster, 1970; *Violation of the Virgins and Other Stories,* McGraw, 1971; *One Damn Thing After Another,* McGraw, 1973; *Three Women* (three one-act plays), Simon & Pierre, 1973.

Also author of *Present Reckoning,* 1951, and (under pseudonym Jarvis Warwick) *Waste No Tears*, 1950. Work has been represented in more than seventy anthologies. Author of television dramas aired in Canada, England, and Australia. Writer of column in *Toronto Telegram*, 1966. Contributor of about five hundred articles and stories to magazines. Associate editor of *Saturday Night*, 1952-54; editor of *Liberty*, 1963.

BIOGRAPHICAL/CRITICAL SOURCES: Saturday Night, November, 1968.*

* * *

GARRIGUE, Sheila 1931-

PERSONAL: Surname rhymes with "intrigue"; born December 30, 1931, in England; came to the United States in 1956; daughter of Edward Donaldson (a salesman) and Kathleen Norah (Hayes) Hogg; married Paul Garrigue (an insurance broker), March 14, 1959; children: Matthew, Andrew, Elizabeth. *Education:* Educated in Canada and England. *Politics:* "Citizen of the United Kingdom (with Democratic leanings)." *Religion:* Presbyterian. *Home:* 17 Ludlow Dr., Chappaqua, N.Y. 10514.

CAREER: Lange Maxwell & Springer Ltd. (publishers of foreign scientific books), London, England, secretary, 1949-53; S. H. Benson Ltd. (advertising agency), London, England, secretary, 1953-56; KCBS-Radio, San Francisco, Calif., secretary to program director, 1957-58; Columbia Broadcasting System, New York, N.Y., administrative assistant, 1958-60; writer, 1973—. Vice-president of executive board of Chappaqua Drama Group, 1977. *Member:* Authors Guild of Authors League of America.

WRITINGS: All the Children Were Sent Away (children's novel), Bradbury, 1976.

WORK IN PROGRESS: A children's novel dealing with mental retardation.

SIDELIGHTS: Sheila Garrigue writes: "Although I have no training as a writer, I have written all my life. Looking back I realize all my jobs had to do with words and their effects. I believe they are more powerful than anything else, their influence more lasting." *Avocational interests:* Travel, embroidery, reading, acting.

* * *

GARRITY, Joan Terry 1940-
("J"; Terry Garrity)

PERSONAL: Born January 15, 1940, in Minneapolis, Minn.; daughter of John B. and Grace Helen Garrity; married. *Education:* Attended University of Missouri at Kansas City and Palm Beach Junior College. *Politics:* Independent. *Home address:* P.O. Box 2922, Palm Beach, Fla. 33480. *Agent:* Don Engel, Engel & Kodys, 1 Dag Hammarskjold Plaza, New York, N.Y. 10017.

CAREER: Lyle Stuart, Inc., Secaucus, N.J., member of staff; has worked as book publicist and as free-lance writer.

WRITINGS: (Under name Terry Garrity, with Ashbel Green) *Get the Most for Your Money in New York*, Grosset, 1970; (under pseudonym "J") *The Sensuous Woman*, Lyle Stuart, 1970; (under name J. T. Garrity) *The Golfer's Guide to Florida Courses*, Cornerstone Library, 1973; (author of introduction) N. Friday, *My Secret Border*, Trident, in press; (under pseudonym "J") *Total Loving*, Simon & Schuster, in press.

WORK IN PROGRESS: Two books on sex, under pseudonym "J", with co-author using pseudonym "H"; *The Golfer's Guide to Southeastern States' Courses.*

SIDELIGHTS: The notoriety surrounding the publication of *The Sensuous Woman*, and the untimely and unexpected release of her real name in the media, has driven Joan Garrity into seclusion, but it hasn't stopped her writing, about sex, about golf, or about anything else she finds interesting. She emphasizes that her writing and her interests are not at all limited to sex. Her most recent book concerns successful marriages of several years' duration, and while there are chapters dealing with sex, the book itself is much broader than that.

BIOGRAPHICAL/CRITICAL SOURCES: Miami Herald, June 14, 1974; *Fort Lauderdale News*, June 17, 1974.

* * *

GASKIN, David Edward 1939-

PERSONAL: Born June 21, 1939, in Croydon, England; married, 1962; children: two. *Education:* University of Bristol, B.Sc., 1961; Massey University, Ph.D., 1968. *Office:* Department of Zoology, University of Guelph, Guelph, Ontario, Canada.

CAREER: British Ministry of Agriculture, Fisheries, and Food and National Institute of Oceanography, Wormley, England, whaling inspector and biologist, 1961-62; British Ministry of Agriculture, Fisheries, and Food, Lowestoft, England, assistant experimental officer in fisheries research, 1962; Fisheries Research Division, Wellington, New Zealand, whale fisheries biologist, 1962-65; Massey University, Palmerston North, New Zealand, lecturer in zoology, 1965-68; University of Guelph, Guelph, Ontario, associate professor of marine biology, 1968—. Consultant to New Zealand Department of Agriculture, 1963-64; New Zealand's scientific representative to International Whaling Commission, 1963-68. *Member:* British Institute of Biology, Royal Entomological Society (fellow), New Zealand Entomological Society (fellow). *Awards, honors:* Research grant from National Research Council of Canada, 1969—.

WRITINGS: Butterflies and Common Moths of New Zealand, Verry, 1967; *The Whaling Potential of the New Zealand Sub-Region*, New Zealand Marine Department, 1967; *The New Zealand Cetacea*, Wellington Fisheries Research Division, New Zealand Marine Department, 1968; *Whales, Dolphins, and Seals, with Special Reference to the New Zealand Region*, St. Martin's, 1972.*

* * *

GAULT, Frank 1926-

PERSONAL: Born August 14, 1926, in Cameroun, West Africa; son of Frank M. (a clergyman) and Josephine (a teacher; maiden name, Maxwell) Gault; married Clare Solberg (a teacher), August 12, 1950; children: Marsha, Bryan, Davison. *Education:* Northwestern University, B.S., 1949. *Religion:* Protestant. *Home:* 148 High Tor Dr., Watchung, N.J. 07060.

CAREER: Buick Motor Division, Chicago, Ill., assistant distributor, 1949-51; Waller Buick, Chicago, Ill., salesman, 1951-54; Handy & Harman (in precious metals), New York, N.Y., advertising manager, 1955-64; free-lance promotion writer in New York, N.Y., 1965-76; free-lance writer, 1976—. Democratic committeeman in Watchung, N.J.; member of Watchung Volunteer Fire Co. *Military service:* U.S. Army, 1945-46. *Member:* Authors Guild.

WRITINGS—For children; all with wife, Clare Gault: Norman Plays Second Base, Scholastic Book Services, 1973; *How to Be a Good Baseball Player*, Scholastic Book

Services, 1973; *Four Stars from the World of Sports,* Scholastic Book Services, 1974; *How to Be a Good Football Player,* Scholastic Book Services, 1974; *Norman Joins the Football Team,* Scholastic Book Services, 1976; *Norman Plays Ice Hockey,* Scholastic Book Services, 1976; *Pele, the King of Soccer,* Walker & Co., 1976; *Stories from the Olympics,* Walker & Co., 1976; *The Cartoon Book of Sports,* Scholastic Book Services, 1977; *How to Be a Good Basketball Player,* Scholastic Book Services, 1977; *Norman Plays Basketball,* Scholastic Book Services, 1977; *A Super Fullback for the Superbowl,* Scholastic Book Services, 1977.

SIDELIGHTS: Gault writes: "Our books encourage youngsters to read. Strong interests in the subjects plus easy-to-read texts help get kids into the habit at an early age that reaps educational rewards for life."

*   *   *

GAYLORD, William 1945-
(Billy Gaylord)

PERSONAL: Born August 5, 1945, in Mesquite, Tex.; son of Charles Cyrus (a businessman) and Nellie (Berryman) Gaylord. *Education:* Attended North Texas State University. *Religion:* Baptist. *Home and office:* 1210 Lombard St., San Francisco, Calif. 94109.

CAREER: Gump's, San Francisco, Calif., interior designer, 1970-71; William Gaylord Co., San Francisco, Calif., president, 1971—. Lecturer and consultant. Has appeared on national television talk shows. *Member:* American Society of Interior Designers, Olympic Club, San Francisco Jaycees (founding member). *Awards, honors:* Named young designer of the year by Burlington Industries, 1972, and best designer, 1975; S. M. Hexter Award, 1975, for a one-room New York City apartment created on a fifteen-hundred-dollar budget.

WRITINGS: Old Rooms, New Ideas (collection of previously-published newspaper columns), Chronicles Features Syndicate, 1976. Author of "The Gaylord Touch," a column distributed by Chronicles Features Syndicate to seventy-seven newspapers, 1974—. Contributor to over one hundred design magazines.

SIDELIGHTS: In 1972, the "Billy Gaylord Signature Collection" was introduced. He has designed a fabric and wallpaper collection based on Russian themes; he also designs stationery for major department stores as well as sheet and towel collections. He designs interiors all over the United States, and his clients include all social and economic levels. Assignments have included work for the Shah of Iran, a New York penthouse, a Hawaiian summer home. He has designed one-room apartments on low budgets, a model apartment for the U.S. Department of Health, Education & Welfare in a low-income housing development, and dormitories at an alcoholic rehabilitation center. In 1973, the B. F. Goodrich Co. commissioned Gaylord to design a room entirely of rubber, and in 1974, he was asked by the San Francisco Museum of Art for a "room of tomorrow."

*   *   *

GEDDIE, John 1937-
(M. Shannon)

PERSONAL: Born January 11, 1937, in Gilmer, Tex.; son of R. S. (in heavy construction) and Alice (Childress) Geddie; married Shannon Harris (a free-lance reporter and photographer), March 24, 1962; children: John Loughery. *Education:* East Texas State University, B.S., 1959. *Reli-*

gion: "Reared as Cumberland Presbyterian." *Home:* 1303 East Holly, Sterling, Va. 22170. *Office:* Washington Bureau, *Dallas Morning News,* 637 National Press Building, Washington, D.C. 20045.

CAREER/WRITINGS: San Angelo Standard-Times, San Angelo, Tex., reporter, 1960-61; *Dallas Morning News,* Dallas, Tex., reporter, 1962-72, chief of Washington Bureau, 1972—. Contributor to magazines, sometimes under pseudonym M. Shannon. *Military service:* U.S. Army, 1961-62. *Member:* National Press Club, White House Correspondents Association. *Awards, honors:* Texas Wire Service awards during the 1960's; first place in political writing from Texas Headliners, 1971; Charles E. Green Award from Headliners Club of Austin, 1971.

WORK IN PROGRESS: Research for a book on Robert Waters Loughery, Civil War editor of *Texas Republican.*

SIDELIGHTS: Geddie covered Hurricane Celia, President Kennedy's assassination and the Jack Ruby appeals, the 1972 and 1976 presidential campaigns, the Watergate hearings, and President Nixon's resignation. He began his career hauling pulp wood in East Texas. In the 1960's he led a trip to Yucatan. Now his major interest is Civil War history.

He writes: "I am generally opposed to 'advocacy journalism' and wary of attempting 'straight' reporting while engaged in writing columns. I have been called a leftwinger in a John Birch Society pamphlet in 1970 and a rightwinger by various liberals. . . ."

*   *   *

GEEMIS, Joseph (Stephen) 1935-

PERSONAL: Born September 28, 1935, in New York, N.Y.; son of Steve Andrew (a merchant seaman chief engineer) and Euthalia (De Pietro) Gelmis; married Ruth Rosen, December 17, 1955 (divorced, 1970); married Deborah Lynn Dobski (a professor and filmmaker), November 21, 1973; children: Steven Keith, Susan Valerie. *Education:* Brooklyn College (now of the City University of New York), B.A., 1956; Columbia University, M.S., 1960. *Office: Newsday,* New York Bureau, 1500 Broadway, New York, N.Y. 10036.

CAREER: Newsday (daily newspaper), Garden City, N.Y., general assistant reporter, 1960-64, movie critic and columnist, 1964—. Producer and host of "The Movies" radio program on WBAI-FM, New York City, 1970-71; host of six "Camera Three" shows on CBS-TV. Adjunct associate professor of theater arts, State University of New York at Stony Brook, 1974. *Military service:* U.S. Air Force, instructor navigator, Air Defense Command, 1956-59; became captain. *Member:* National Society of Film Critics, New York Film Critics (chairman, 1969, 1972). *Awards, honors:* Polk Award for investigative reporting, 1961.

WRITINGS: The Film Director as Superstar, Doubleday, 1970. Work has been represented in several anthologies. Author of monthly column in *Connecticut* Magazine; contributor of articles to magazines, including *New York, True,* and *Show.*

SIDELIGHTS: Gelmis, who said he has interviewed nearly all the notable filmmakers and producers of his time, has loved movies for as long as he can remember. He recalls his high school days, in Brooklyn, when he would often cut classes to see films at the Museum of Modern Art, and his early days as a reporter when he would finish an assignment early and sneak off to a movie before reporting back to work. Gelmis adds, "I regret only that in the past dozen years I've had to watch the decline of Hollywood, which now makes fewer, more expensive movies and is headed for self destruction.''

* * *

GEER, Stephen (DuBois) 1930-

PERSONAL: Born August 20, 1930, in Mount Kisco, N.Y.; son of Solon and Eve (DuBois) Geer; married Elizabeth White, January 2, 1953 (separated); children: William Joseph, Catherine Anne, Stephen Michael, Thomas White, Nancy Ellen. *Education:* Columbia University, B.A., 1951. *Office:* ABC Network News, 4151 Prospect Ave., Hollywood, Calif. 90027.

CAREER/WRITINGS: Reporter at stations in Connecticut and Virginia, 1952-55; WHEN-TV News, Syracuse, N.Y., correspondent, 1955-59; WBEN-TV News, Buffalo, N.Y., correspondent, 1959-63; WTOP-TV News, Washington, D.C., correspondent, 1963-69; American Broadcasting Co. (ABC) News, New York, N.Y., Washington bureau correspondent, 1969-74, Los Angeles bureau correspondent, 1974—. Notable assignments include Chappaquiddick, the Harrisburg 7 trial, the Nicaragua earthquake, 1972 national conventions, Watergate investigation and impeachment hearing, Patricia Hearst trial, the Ronald Reagan campaign, and 1976 Republican Convention. *Awards, honors:* Emmy Awards, 1966 for WTOP-Reports documentary.

* * *

GELLER, Uri 1946-

PERSONAL: Born December 20, 1946, in Tel Aviv, Israel; son of Itzhak and Margaret (Freud) Geller. *Education:* Terra Santa College, general certificate of education, 1964. *Agent:* Lawrence Lighter, 1350 Avenue of Americas, New York, N.Y. 10019. *Office:* Kadima Productions, Inc., P.O. Box 5175, F.D.R. Station, New York, N.Y. 10022.

CAREER: Performer of psychokinetic effects, lecturer, author. *Military service:* Israeli Paratroopers, 1965-68.

WRITINGS: Uri Geller: My Story, Praeger, 1975. Writer of syndicated weekly column for domestic and international newspapers, 1975—; published songwriter.

WORK IN PROGRESS: The Geller Papers; Pampini, a novel.

SIDELIGHTS: CA asked Geller if he has used his powers for the advancement of mankind. ''I have used my powers to help mankind,'' he responded, ''by working with scientists in leading laboratories, universities, and research institutes throughout the world, such as Stanford Research Institute, Kent State University, University of London Birkbeck and King's College, Lawrence Livermore Radiation Laboratory, Naval Surface Weapons Center, and many more too numerous to mention. As a result of bringing out the awareness of these powers, many children are now showing some psychic abilities. Not only have I triggered this ability, I am using it for the development of underprivileged people. Presently I am employing my powers in an attempt to locate reservoirs of water and other natural resources beneath the surface of the earth. I have participated in research expeditions trying to unveil what lies beyond such phenomenal wonders as the Bermuda Triangle, the Bimini Wall and the great pyramids of Mexico.''

Geller is scheduled to appear in the title role of ''Geller Effect,'' a motion picture by the Robert Stigwood Organisation. He has appeared on numerous radio and television programs.

BIOGRAPHICAL/CRITICAL SOURCES: Andrija Puharich, *Uri,* Bantam, 1974; *Nature,* (magazine) October 18, 1974; Thelma Moss, *The Probability of the Impossible,* J. P. Tarcher, 1975; Adam Smith, *Powers of the Mind,* Random House, 1975; John Taylor, *Superminds,* Warner Books, 1975; Martin Ebon, editor, *Amazing Uri Geller,* New American Library, 1976; Charles Panati, editor, *The Geller Papers,* HM, 1976; *Esquire,* March, 1976.

* * *

GEMMILL, Paul F. 1890(?)-1976

1890(?)—December 30, 1976; American professor of economics and performing magician. He was author of scholarly texts on economics. Gemmill died in Broomall, Pa. Obituaries: *New York Times,* January 5, 1977.

* * *

GENOVESE, Eugene Dominick 1930-

PERSONAL: Born May 19, 1930, in Brooklyn, N.Y.; son of Dominick F. and Lena (Chimenti) Genovese. *Education:* Brooklyn College (now of the City University of New York), B.A., 1953; Columbia University, M.A., 1955, Ph.D., 1959. *Office:* Department of History, University of Rochester, Rochester, N.Y. 14627.

CAREER: Polytechnic Institute of Brooklyn, Brooklyn, N.Y., 1958-63, began as instructor, became assistant professor of history and economics; Rutgers University, New Brunswick, N.J., 1963-67, began as assistant professor, became associate professor of history; Sir George Williams University, Montreal, Quebec, professor of history, 1967-69; University of Rochester, Rochester, N.Y., professor of history, 1969—, also chairman of department. Visiting professor at Columbia University, 1967, and Yale University, 1969. Fellow of Center for Advanced Study in the Behavioral Sciences (Stanford, Calif.), 1972-73. *Military service:* U.S. Army, 1953-54. *Member:* American Academy of Arts and Sciences (fellow), Agricultural History Association, Southern Historical Association. *Awards, honors:* Social Science Research Council fellowship, 1968-69.

WRITINGS: The Political Economy of Slavery: Studies in the Economy and Society of the Slave South, Pantheon, 1965; *The Legacy of Slavery and the Roots of Black Nationalism,* New England Free Press, 1966; (editor) Ulrich Bonnell Phillips, *The Slave Economy of the Old South,* Louisiana State University Press, 1968; (editor with Laura Foner) *Slavery in the New World: A Reader in Comparative History,* Prentice-Hall, 1969; *The World the Slaveholders Made: Two Essays in Interpretation,* Pantheon, 1969.

In Red and Black: Marxian Explorations in Southern and Afro-American History, Pantheon, 1971; (editor) *The Slave Economies,* Volume I: *Historical and Theoretical Perspectives,* Volume II: *Slavery in the International Economy,* Wiley, 1973; (editor with Elinor Miller) *Plantation, Town, and County: Essays on the Local History of American Slave Society,* University of Illinois Press, 1974; *Roll, Jordan, Roll: The World the Slaves Made,* Pantheon, 1974.

Contributor of articles and reviews to history journals. Member of editorial board of *Journal of Social History.*

* * *

GENSER, Cynthia 1950-
(Chinas Comidas)

PERSONAL: Born June 3, 1950, in New York, N.Y.; daughter of Eli and Esther (Weinstock) Kraman. *Education:*

University of Massachusetts, B.A., 1972; Columbia University, graduate study, 1974-75. *Residence:* Seattle, Wash.

CAREER: Has worked various part time jobs, including salesperson and file clerk in New York City, 1974, fabric painter in New York City, 1975, waitress in San Francisco, 1975, telephone representative and library page in Seattle, Wash., 1976, waitress in Seattle, 1977—. Freelance writer.

WRITINGS: Taking on the Local Color (poetry), Wesleyan University Press, 1977.

Anthologized in *Renegade,* Cross Cut Saw Unlimited, 1977. Contributor to *Paris Review* and *Antaeus,* and to *Berkeley Barb* (under pseudonym Chinas Comidas).

WORK IN PROGRESS: Club 82: Lisa, prose poems and dramatic monologues; two film scripts, one a thriller.

SIDELIGHTS: Cynthia Genser writes: "I'm attempting to position myself in the universe so as to read the books, which, as William Burroughs says, are out there. I like to hang out in bars and groceries and listen. There are people speaking the words in those places. I'm trying to be a writer a woman a human being in a world where those are all considered criminal activities."

*   *   *

GEORGE, W(illiam) R(ichard) P(hilip)   1912-

PERSONAL: Born October 20, 1912, in Criccieth, Wales; son of William (a solicitor) and Anita (a nurse; maiden name, Williams) George; married Margarete Bogner, December 19, 1953; children: Philip, Anita, Elizabeth, Louise-Gwen. *Education:* Attended private school in Wellington, Shropshire, England. *Religion:* Baptist. *Home address:* Garthcelyn, Criccieth, North Wales. *Office:* 103 High St., Porthmadog, North Wales.

CAREER: Lawyer in Wales, 1934—. County councillor in Caernarfon, 1967; deputy circuit judge, 1975. *Member:* Law Society, Royal National Eisteddfod of Wales (member of council), Court of the University of Wales. *Awards, honors:* Poetry crown from Royal National Eisteddfod of Wales, 1974.

WRITINGS: Dwyfor a cherddi eraill, 1943-1947 (title means "Dwyfor River and Other Poems"), J. D. Lewis a'i Feibion Cyf, 1948; *Cerddi 'r Neraig: Cyfrol o farddoniaeth* (title means "The Shore: A Volume of Verse"), Llyfrau'r Dryw, 1968; (editor) Eluned Morgan, *Gyfaill Hoff* (letters; title means "Dear Friend"), Gwasg Gomer, 1973; *Grawn Medi* (poems; title means "September Grain"), Gwasg Gomer, 1974; *The Making of Lloyd George,* Faber, 1976.

WORK IN PROGRESS: Continuing research on the papers of his uncle, David Lloyd George, with a book, covering the years 1890 to 1910, expected to result.

SIDELIGHTS: George writes: "As a Welshman, living in a thoroughly Welsh-speaking area of Wales, I am completely bilingual; and it is as natural for me to write or converse in Welsh as in English. I find however that the poetry I write demands Welsh as the language I write in. Both as a youth, and now in maturer years, I have found that people are often more interested in me because of my famous uncle, than on my own account. This consideration has been responsible for my putting as much as possible of my own thoughts on paper; in short, to be a poet and author."

*   *   *

GEPHART, William J(ay)   1928-

PERSONAL: Born December 26, 1928, in Uniontown, Pa.;

son of Everett W. (a foundry worker) and Ruth J. (Gladden) Gephart; married Mary J. Curry (a saleswoman), June 9, 1951; children: Jeffrey Lee, Brian William. *Education:* Adrian College, student, 1949-51; Wayne State University, B.S.Ed., 1953, M.Ed., 1958; Ohio State University, Ph.D., 1965. *Home:* 3500 Morningside Dr., Bloomington, Ind. 47401. *Office:* Phi Delta Kappa, P.O. Box 789, Bloomington, Ind. 47401.

CAREER: Teacher of science, mathematics, and speech at high school in Harper Woods, Mich., 1953-58; high school guidance director in Cleveland, Ohio, 1958-61; Ohio State University, Columbus, instructor in education, 1961-63; University of Wisconsin, Milwaukee, assistant professor of education and director of education research, 1963-66; Phi Delta Kappa, Bloomington, Ind., director of Center on Evaluation, Development, and Research, 1966—. Lecturer at Indiana University, 1966—; adjunct professor at Ohio State University, 1971-73. Member of Bloomington Human Rights Commission. *Military service:* U.S. Air Force, 1947-49; became sergeant. *Member:* American Educational Research Association, Indiana Artists and Craftsmen, Hoosier Hills Art Guild, Phi Delta Kappa.

WRITINGS: (Editor with Walter Hack, James Heck, and John Ramseyer) *Educational Administration: Selected Readings,* Allyn & Bacon, 1965; (with Robert Gagne) *Learning Research and School Subjects,* F. E. Peacock, 1968; (editor with Robert Ingle) *Educational Research: Selected Readings,* C. E. Merrill, 1969; (with Daniel Stufflebeam and others) *Educational Evaluation and Decision Making,* F. E. Peacock, 1971; (editor with L. Cunningham) *Leadership: The Science and the Art Today,* F. E. Peacock, 1973; (editor with Ingle and James Potter) *The Evaluation of Administrative Performance,* Phi Delta Kappa, 1977. Contributor to professional journals. Editor of *CEDR Quarterly* (of Phi Delta Kappa).

WORK IN PROGRESS: Editing *Measurement in Education for the 1980's,* with Jack Merwin; *Synthesizing Evaluation Models.*

SIDELIGHTS: Gephart writes: "For the past twenty-five years I have painted. During the last five years I've had numerous one-man shows, group shows, and had my watercolors on exhibit in galleries in Florida, Kentucky, Indiana, and Michigan. My work is in collections all over this country, in South Africa, Germany, Norway. My favorite subject matter is the Northwest Florida coast."

*   *   *

GERASIMOV, Gennadi (Ivanovitch)   1930-

PERSONAL: Born March 3, 1930, in Kazan, Soviet Union; came to the United States in 1972; son of Ivan (a physician) and Nina (Chernov) Gerasimov; married Margarita Ponomareva (an editor), November 26, 1953. *Education:* Attended Institute of Foreign Relations, Moscow, Soviet Union, 1948-53; graduate study at Moscow University. *Home and office:* 11 Riverside Dr., New York, N.Y. 10023.

CAREER: New Times, Moscow, Soviet Union, editor, 1955-61; *World Marxist Review,* Prague, Czechoslovakia, editor, 1962-67; Novosti Press Agency, Moscow, Soviet Union, diplomatic correspondent, 1967—. Has covered political affairs in the United States and the Soviet Union, as well as the war in Nigeria. *Member:* Union of Soviet Journalists.

WRITINGS: Stanet li tesno na zemmom share?: Problema narodonaselenia, Izd-vo Znanie, 1967, translation published as *Standing Room Only?: When?;* (with Georgi Kuznetsov and Vladimir Morev) *Nabat v nochi,* Novosti Press Agency Publishing House, 1968, English translation published as *Fire Bell in the Night,* Novosti Press Agency Publishing House, 1968; *Kljuch k miru vo Vietname,* Novosti Press Agency Publishing House, translation published as *The Key to Peace in Vietnam,* 1968. Also contributor to *Problems of War and Peace,* Progress Publishing House (Moscow), 1971.

WORK IN PROGRESS: A book on the United States.

SIDELIGHTS: Gerasimov comments briefly that his interests lie in global issues: population, survival in the nuclear age, energy resources, and ecological balance.

*   *   *

GERAUD, (Charles Joseph) Andre   1882-1974 (Pertinax)

PERSONAL: Born October 18, 1882, in Saint-Louis-de-Montferrand, France; son of Oscar (a vineyard owner and exporter) and Marthe (Faux) Geraud; married Louise Banniard, January 28, 1914. *Education:* University of Bordeaux, licencie es lettres, 1905. *Address:* 91, rue de l'Universite, Paris 7e, France; Segur-le-Chateau, Correze, France; and 58 West 10th St., New York, N.Y.

CAREER: L'Echo de Paris (daily newspaper), Paris, France, joined London bureau, 1905-08, became chief British correspondent, 1908-14, foreign editor and columnist under pseudonym Pertinax, 1917-38; *L'Europe Nouvelle* (foreign policy review), Paris, managing editor, 1938-40; left Paris at signing of Armistice of Compiegne to reside in United States, 1940-45; *France-Soir,* Paris, foreign affairs commentator, beginning 1945; retired, until 1974. Diplomatic correspondent to major French and English newspapers. Named a member of United Nations group on freedom of the press, 1947. *Military service:* French Army, 1914-17; served as interpreter. *Awards, honors:* Officier de la Legion d'honneur of France, 1936.

WRITINGS: Practique du droit de la nationalite, Editions de Presse Specialilee, 1966.

Under pseudonym Pertinax: *Le Partage de Rome* (on the reconciliation of Italy and the Vatican), Grasset, 1929; *Les Fossoyeurs: Defait militaire de la France, armistice, contre-revolution,* Volume I: *Gamelin, Deladier, Reynaud,* Volume II: *Petain,* Editions de la Maison Francaise, 1943, translation published as *The Gravediggers of France: Gamelin, Deladier, Reynaud, Petain, and Laval; Military Defeat, Armistice, Counter-Revolution,* Doubleday, Doran, 1944, new French edition published as *Les Fossoyeurs: La Bataille de France, l'armistice, la contre-revolution,* Sagittaire, 1946, reprinted English-language edition, Fertig, 1968.

Columnist on international affairs, under pseudonym Pertinax, for *Pall Mall Gazette* (London), beginning 1910, and for *London Daily Telegraph,* beginning 1912. Contributor to major Parisian and British newspapers, and to American publications, including *New York Herald Tribune, Baltimore Sun, New York Times,* and *Foreign Affairs.*

OBITUARIES: New York Times, December 12, 1974; *Newsweek,* December 23, 1974; *Time,* December 23, 1974; *AB Bookman's Weekly,* January 27, 1975; *Current Biography,* January, 1975.*

(Died December 11, 1974, in Segur-le-Chateau, France)

GETTY, J(ean) Paul   1892-1976

PERSONAL: Born December 15, 1892, in Minneapolis, Minn.; son of George Franklin (a lawyer and wildcat oilman) and Sarah McPherson (Risher) Getty; married Jeannette Dumont, 1923 (divorced); married Allene Ashby, 1926 (divorced); married Fini Helmle, 1928 (divorced); married Ann Rourk, 1932 (divorced); married Louise Lynch, 1939 (divorced); children: George Franklin II (deceased), Jean Ronald, Jean Paul, Gordon Peter, Timothy Christopher (deceased). *Education:* Attended University of Southern California and University of California, Berkeley, 1909-11; Oxford University, diploma in politics and economics, 1914. *Home:* 17985 Pacific Coast Highway, Malibu, Calif. 90265. *Office:* 3810 Wilshire Blvd., Los Angeles, Calif. 90010.

CAREER: Independent oil producer, 1914-76. Began buying and selling oil leases in Tulsa, Okla., September, 1914, and became millionaire by June 1916; continued to invest in oil stock during the Depression; became president and general manager of George F. Getty, Inc., 1930; purchased control of Pacific Western Oil Co., 1932, and became director of Petroleum Corp. and Tide Water Associated Oil Co. the same year; began to acquire control of Mission Corp., which held large shares in Tide Water and Skelly Oil, 1937; became president and principal owner of Spartan Aircraft Corp. (later named Minnehoma Financial Corp.), 1942; president, Mission Development Corp., 1948; in largest business coup of career, acquired half interest rights to Saudia Arabia's Neutral Zone, 1949, and hit oil, 1953, turning an investment of thirty million dollars into over sixteen million barrels of oil a year; won numerical control of renamed Tidewater Oil Co., 1951, and obtained control of Mission Development Corp. and its holdings in Tidewater Oil Co. and Skelly Oil, 1953; made Pacific Western into Getty Oil Co., the master link in the Getty holdings and world's largest personally controlled oil company, 1956; merged Tidewater Oil Co. and Mission Development Corp. into Getty Oil, 1967. Owner of substantial interest in over two hundred other concerns. Founder and trustee, Jean Paul Getty Museum, 1953—. Owner of Pierre Hotel, New York City.

MEMBER: New York and California chambers of commerce, Nouveau Cercle, Explorers Club, Beach Club, Los Angeles Athletic Club.

WRITINGS: The History of the Oil Business of George Franklin and J. Paul Getty from 1903 to 1939, privately printed, 1941; *Europe in the Eighteenth Century,* privately printed, 1949; (with Ethel Le Vane) *Collector's Choice,* W. Allen, 1955; *My Life and Fortunes,* Duell, 1963; *The Joys of Collecting,* Hawthorn, 1965; *How to Be Rich,* Playboy Press, 1965; *The Golden Age,* Trident, 1968; *How to Be a Successful Executive,* Playboy Press, 1971; *As I See It: The Autobiography of J. Paul Getty,* Prentice-Hall, 1976. Contributor of articles to journals in his field.

SIDELIGHTS: The son of a prosperous Minneapolis lawyer who began to wildcat for oil in the Indian Territory (now Oklahoma) in 1903, Getty began speculating with a stake from his father. His first year he made $40,000 and he realized $1 million by the time he was twenty-three. After earning his first million, young Getty retired to Los Angeles where he lived a "gaudy, girl-filled life" for two years. In 1919 he returned to Oklahoma and began his lifelong uninterrupted accumulation of wealth.

In 1923, at the age of thirty, Getty married the first of five wives, all of whom were eighteen or younger at the time of marriage. Looking back, Getty regretted that all of his marriages ended in divorce, because, he said, "I don't like anything to be unsuccessful."

In the 1920's Getty accumulated about $3 million. His Christian Scientist father, though pleased with Jean Paul's business acumen, was shocked by his marriages. When he died in 1930 he left his son only $500,000 of a $10 million estate.

During the Depression Getty went against the currents of conventional wisdom and began buying stock, particularly in Tide Water Associated Oil Co., one of the nation's major oil companies. Tide Water was later to become the foundation of his vast enterprises. "It was unquestionably a gamble," Getty recalled, "and by my standards it was an enormous one. My stock purchases were financed by every dollar I possessed and every cent of credit I could obtain." If he had lost, he added, "I would have been personally penniless and very much in debt." By 1937 Getty was well on his way to winning control of Mission Corp., a holding company with substantial shares in Tide Water and Skelly Oil.

On the day that the United States entered World War II, Getty sent a telegram to Under Secretary of the Navy James V. Forrestal: "I am 49 but in good health. Have owned three yachts and am experienced in their care and maintenance. If Navy can use me in any capacity, please advise." Though rejected for sea duty, Getty was asked by Secretary Frank Knox to work with the Tulsa-based Spartan Aircraft Co., a Skelly subsidiary. Getty personally directed the company, manufacturing trainer planes and parts. After the war the company was profitably converted to the production of mobile homes.

In 1949, in what was to become the most daring business coup of his life, Getty obtained a sixty-year concession for the Neutral Zone area belonging to Saudia Arabia. He paid King Saud $9.5 million cash and agreed to pay $1 million a year for the duration of the concession, even though no oil had been discovered in the area. After investing a total of $30 million, the gamble paid off when, in 1953, drillers hit enormous quantities of oil. The discovery of oil in the Neutral Zone rose Getty's financial status from multimillionaire to billionaire.

In 1956 Pacific Western became the Getty Oil Co. and master link in the Getty holdings. Subsequent mergers, reorganizations, and investments bolstered Getty's fortunes throughout the rest of his life.

Relatively unknown to the public before, Getty quickly became a celebrity when a 1957 issue of *Forbes* declared him to be "the richest man in America." When asked the inevitable question, how much cash would he have if he sold all his interests, Getty would respond: "I would hope to realize several billions, but remember, a billion dollars isn't what it used to be." Most people, Getty said after the *Forbes* article, were "so economically illiterate that they assume most of my fortune is in cash." In reality Getty never had more that a million dollars cash, and seldom carried over $25 on his person. Still he was plagued by over 3000 letters a month from individuals asking for money. In a magazine article entitled "It's Tough to Be a Billionaire," Getty said: "I never give money to individuals because it's unrewarding and wrong. If I were certain that by giving away my fortune I could make a real contribution toward solving the problems of world poverty, I'd give away 99.5% of all I have immediately. But a hard-eyed appraisal of the situation convinces me this is not the case. However admirable the work of the best charitable foundation, it would accustom people to the passive acceptance of money."

In his early career Getty usually worked out of hotel suites, frequently carrying his important papers in boxes tied with string. In 1959 he purchased Sutton Place, a seventy-two room mansion where Henry VIII is said to have met Ann Boleyn, from the Duke of Sutherland. Getty made worldwide headlines when he had a pay phone installed for his guests at Sutton Place. "My friends will understand, and, as for spongers, well, I just don't care," he explained.

Getty was unique among oilmen, and other industry heads, for that matter, in that he kept personal control of his financial empire. He often worked sixteen to eighteen hours a day. "I can't remember a single day of vacation in the last 45 years," he said in 1965, "that was not somehow interrupted by a cable, telegram or telephone call that made me tend to business for at least a few hours. Such work schedules and the need for devoting the majority of my time to business have taken a heavy toll of my personal life."

Toward the end of his life Getty lamented the fact that none of his sons would follow him: "None of my sons is in the business. I suppose I would have liked to keep the Getty name, but the name isn't enough. You have to be qualified too. There is nobody to step into my shoes."

When his grandson, J. Paul Getty III, was kidnapped in Italy in 1973, Getty refused to pay a $16 million ransom on the grounds that "I have 14 other grandchildren, and if I pay one penny now, then I'll have 14 kidnapped grandchildren." Eventually the boy was released when the family paid $2.8 million.

In 1974 *Forbes* asked Getty, after his sixty years in the oil industry, if the current high oil prices would remain. He responded: "I've seen worldwide shortages before. It eventually leads to overdrilling. Oil people are great ones for killing the goose that lays the golden eggs. I think the shortage will be over in two to three years perhaps, and prices will come tumbling down. By then there could be a surplus, even from conventional sources of energy."

At the time of his death in June, 1976, Getty's fortune was estimated to be worth from $2 to $4 billion, including a majority interest in the Getty Oil Co. and nearly 200 other concerns. His art collection, valued in the several hundred million dollar area, is now gathered in his Malibu museum.

One of the last of a breed of businessmen that includes the Rockefellers, Mellons, and very few others, Getty explained: "In building a large fortune, it pays to be born at the right time. I was born at a very favorable time. If I had been born earlier or later, I would have missed the great business opportunities that existed in World War I and later.

"I suppose it takes a long time and it takes extraordinary circumstances to be born at the right time, be there at the right time and have cash money available at the right time. I was fortunate due to my father's foresight and my good luck. In the Depression I did what the experts said one should not do. I was a very big buyer of oil company stocks."

Getty addressed himself to the final question: was being so rich worth all the trouble? "Though our rewards may be small," he said of himself and others like him, "we are, if our society is to remain in its present form, essential to the nation's prosperity. We provide others with incentives which would not exist if we were to disappear."

BIOGRAPHICAL/CRITICAL SOURCES: Ralph Hewins, *The Richest American,* Dutton, 1960; *Town & Country,* January, 1974; *Forbes,* March 1, 1974; *Washington Star,* September 14, 1975. *Obituaries: Washington Post,* June 7, 1976; *New York Times,* June 7, 1976; *Time,* June 14, 1976; *Newsweek,* June 14, 1976.*

(Died June 6, 1976, in Sutton Place, England)

GHELARDI, Robert (Anthony) 1939-

PERSONAL: Born November 29, 1939, in New York; son of Robert Anthony (a chemical engineer) and Elizabeth (Cassidy) Ghelardi. *Education:* University of Notre Dame, B.A., 1960; University of Chicago, M.A., 1961. *Politics:* Independent. *Religion:* Roman Catholic. *Home:* 435 Market St., Bloomsburg, Pa. 17815. *Agent:* John Brockman Associates, Inc., 241 Central Park W., New York, N.Y. 10024.

CAREER: Chase Manhattan Bank, New York, N.Y., writer, 1967-69; Ernst & Ernst, New York City, writer, 1969-71; free-lance writer, 1971-74; Consolidated Edison, New York City, writer, 1974-76; Smart Communications, New York City, writer, 1976—. *Military service:* U.S. Army Reserve, active duty, 1962-63. *Awards, honors:* Woodrow Wilson fellowship, 1960-61.

WRITINGS: Economics, Society, and Culture, Delacorte, 1976.

WORK IN PROGRESS: Economics for a New Age, revisions of macro-economic theory; *Religion and Modernity.*

SIDELIGHTS: Ghelardi remarks that he "became interested in economics as a system of social integration. I would prefer to be a full-time free-lance writer, but do not find it feasible. My main writing interest is cultural theory—I am mostly interested in economics from this angle." *Avocational interests:* Occasional travel, sports.

* * *

GIBBON, (William) Monk 1896-

PERSONAL: Born December 15, 1896, in Dublin, Ireland; son of William (a canon) and Isabella (Meredith) Gibbon; married Mabel Winifred Dingwall (a teacher), August 30, 1928; children: John, Gillian, Penelope, William, Nicole, Philippa. *Education:* Dublin University, Ph.D., 1947. *Religion:* Church of Ireland. *Home:* 24 Sandycove Rd., Sandycove, County Dublin, Ireland.

CAREER: Teacher of English at Chateau d'Oex, Switzerland, 1925-27; Oldfeld School, Swanage, England, master, 1929-40; has also taught at Clive House, Prestatyn, Wales, Aravon School, Bray, Ireland, and Brook House, Monkstown, Ireland. Tredegar lecturer, Royal Society of Literature, 1952; Tagore Centenary Lecturer, Abbey Theatre, Dublin, 1961. *Military service:* Royal Army Service Corps, 1916-18. *Member:* Royal Society of Literature (fellow), Irish Academy of Letters (vice president, 1967). *Awards, honors:* Tailteann Games Silver Medal, 1928.

WRITINGS—Poetry: *The Tremulous String,* Grayhound Press, 1926; *Wise Small Birds,* Cuala Press, 1926; *The Branch of Hawthorn Tree,* Grayhound Press, 1927; *Within a Little Field,* Cuala Press, 1927; *For Daws to Peck At,* Dodd, 1929; *A Ballad,* Grayhound Press, 1930; *Now We'll Forget the Windy Hill,* Cuala Press, 1931; *Seventeen Sonnets,* Joiner and Steele, 1932; *This Insubstantial Pageant: Collected Poems in Verse and Prose,* Devin-Adair, 1951; *The Velvet Bow and Other Poems,* Hutchinson, 1972.

Travel—*Swiss Enchantment,* Evans, 1950; *Austria,* Batsford, 1953; *In Search of Winter Sport,* Evans, 1953; *Western Germany,* Batsford, 1955; *The Rhine and Its Castles,* Putnam, 1957.

Other—*The Seals* (autobiography), Cape, 1935; *The Stapleton Children in Jersey,* privately printed, 1938; *Mount Ida* (autobiography), Cape, 1948; *The Red Shoes Ballet: A Critical Study,* Saturn Press, 1948; *The Tales of Hoffman: A Study of the Film,* Saturn Press, 1951; *An Intruder at the Ballet,* Phoenix House, 1952; *The Masterpiece and the Man: Yeats As I Knew Him,* Hart Davis, 1959; *Netta* (biography of Henrietta Franklin), Routledge, 1960; *The Climate of Love* (novel), Gollancz, 1961; *Inglorious Soldier* (autobiography), Hutchinson, 1968; *The Brahms Waltz* (autobiography), Hutchinson, 1970.

Editor—*The Living Torch: An Anthology of Prose by AE,* Macmillan, 1937; Douglas Hyde, *Poems from the Irish,* Allen Figgis, 1963; *The Poems of Katherine Tynan,* Allen Figgis, 1963; Michael Farrell, *Thy Tears Might Cease,* Knopf, 1964.

WORK IN PROGRESS: The Pigeon; An Approach to Plotinus; The Noble Art of Self Defense, a defense of poetry.

SIDELIGHTS: Dr. Gibbon told *CA:* "In the catalogue to the exhibition in the National Gallery of Ireland, 'The Irish 1870-1970', my head in bronze by Margery Fitzgibbon is captioned: 'He is best known for his poetry, but his novels *Mount Ida* (1948) and *The Climate of Love* (1961) shed more light on his personality, being mainly autobiographical.' This needs footnoting. It is true that *Mount Ida* is 100% and my so-called novel *The Climate of Love* 95% direct autobiography. But I have enjoyed writing about countries and about ballet and the cinema; and these are kind of side interests a poet is entitled to have. Similarly teaching has offered a welcome escape into other lives, although my basic interest has always been the literary one. Praise from critics like Yeats, AE [George William Russell], Rebecca West, Lord Reith of the B.B.C., Richard Church and others never made my poetry fashionable, since it ran counter to the whole trend of the Eliot Age in which so much of it was written. The earlier poems, many of them bucolic, cast back to Greek lyricism; the sonnets and later poems were cerebral. But even then they did nothing to woo contemporary taste.

"America has been generous to my work; but I did not make myself popular there by my book on Yeats, which makes it quite plain that though I regard him as the supreme poet of the age, I alienated him by my transparent admiration for AE. In his last letter to his son, AE asked that I should posthumously edit his journalism, which I have done in *The Living Torch.*

"My autobiographical work treats in detail certain epochs of my life and dilates on the two great themes, love and war, sticking closely to the factual but placing the stresses and inflexions where unquestionably they belonged. George Moore inscribed a first edition of *Hail and Farewell* to me 'To Monk Gibbon with best wishes for his success in literature.' That success, with the general public, has been a modest one; but in all my autobiographical writing I think I have been true to Moore's dictum: 'To be ashamed of nothing but to be ashamed,' and have tried to recreate the living moment in all its intensity.

"I cherish memories of a number of great writers, the lovable poet Walter de la Mare amongst them. My single most vivid memory of Yeats is of an evening when after dining with him at his home in Merrion Square he led us up to the drawing room and laying his hand on the bulky manuscript of 'The Vision' remarked, 'Seven years of labour completed this morning.' On the same occasion he detained me at the door for a moment to counsel me not to fulfill my intention of visiting the institute at Fontainbleau—where Katherine Mansfield died. 'Take the advice of an old man,' Yeats said, 'I have had a lot of experience of that sort of thing and it ends in priestcraft.'"

GIBBONS, Gail 1944-

PERSONAL: Born August 1, 1944, in Oak Park, Ill.; daughter of Harry George (a tool and die designer) and Grace (Johnson) Ortmann; married Glenn Gibbons, June 25, 1966 (died May 20, 1972); married Kent Ancliffe (a builder), March 23, 1976; children: (stepchildren) Rebecca, Eric. Education: University of Illinois, B.F.A., 1967. Home address: Coriath, Vt. 05039. Agent: Florence Alexander, 50 East 42nd St., New York, N.Y. 10017. Office: 114 West 16th St., #4E, New York, N.Y. 10011.

CAREER: WCIA-Television, Champaign, Ill., artist, 1967-69; Bob Howe Agency, Chicago, Ill., staff artist, 1969-70; WNBC-Television, House of Animation, New York, N.Y., staff artist, 1970-76; free-lance writer, 1976—. Makes graphic slides, distributed by United Press International, for use on television news programs.

WRITINGS—Self-illustrated children's books: Willy and His Wheel Wagon (Junior Literary Guild selection), Prentice-Hall, 1975; Salvador and Mister Sam, Prentice-Hall, 1976; Things to Make and Do for Halloween, F. Watts, 1976; Things to Make and Do for Columbus Day, F. Watt, 1977; Things to Make and Do for Your Birthday, F. Watts, in press.

Illustrator: Jane Yolen, Rounds About Rounds, F. Watts, 1977.

WORK IN PROGRESS: The Tail of Morris Mouse, for children.

SIDELIGHTS: Gail Gibbons comments: "I became interested in writing children's books when in college—one of my instructors was involved in illustrating children's books. I did a children's show, "Take a Giant Step," for National Broadcasting Corp. for two years, doing all the artwork; this made me more interested in writing and drawing for children."

*   *   *

GIBBS, C. Earl 1935-

PERSONAL: Born April 1, 1935, in Dallas, Ore.; son of Clyde and Addie (Martin) Gibbs; married Laurice Dashiell (a secretary), December 17, 1957; children: Douglas, Barbara, Robert. Education: Northwest Christian College, B.Th., 1957; Phillips University, M.Div., 1960; University of Oregon, M.S., 1968; San Francisco Theological Seminary, D.Min., 1974. Home: 4508 Surita St., Sacramento, Calif. 95825. Office: Arden Christian Church, 4300 Las Cruces Way, Sacramento, Calif. 95825.

CAREER: Minister of Christian Church (Disciples of Christ); pastor of Christian churches in Perry, Okla., 1959-64, and Springfield, Ore., 1964-74; Arden Christian Church, Sacramento, Calif., minister, 1974—. Seminar leader at Jesuit School of Theology, Berkeley Institute for Continuing Education. Member of Springfield City Council, 1967-70; member of board of directors of Springfield Area Chamber of Commerce, 1972-74. Member: Congress of Disciple Clergy, Academy of Parish Clergy, Greater North Area Ministerial Association (president, 1977), Rotary International (local president, 1971-72). Awards, honors: Named first citizen of Springfield, 1970.

WRITINGS: Caring for the Grieving, Omega Books, 1976. Contributor to Rotarian and Disciple.

WORK IN PROGRESS: A sequel to Caring for the Grieving, for clergymen.

SIDELIGHTS: Gibbs comments: "My major purpose in writing Caring for the Grieving was to share insights which I have found helpful with other persons in helping professions. The primary research for this was done in preparation for my doctoral dissertation."

*   *   *

GIBBS, James A(twood) 1922-
(Jim Gibbs)

PERSONAL: Born January 17, 1922, in Seattle, Wash.; son of A. James (in investments) and Vera (Smith) Gibbs; married Cherie Lola Norman, May 26, 1950; children: Debbie Ann Gibbs Pedrick. Education: Attended University of Washington, Seattle. Politics: Independent. Religion: Baptist. Residence: Yachats, Ore. 97498.

CAREER: Marine Digest, Seattle, Wash., assistant editor, 1948-55, editor, 1959-72; G.E.B. Properties, Seattle, Wash., partner, 1964—. Military service: U.S. Coast Guard, 1942-46. Member: Puget Sound Maritime Historical Society (co-founder; charter member). Awards, honors: Twelve Anchor Award from the Port of Seattle, 1954-72; award of merit from Seattle Historical Society, 1955, for Sentinels of the North Pacific.

WRITINGS—All under name Jim Gibbs: Pacific Graveyard: A Narrative of the Ships Lost Where the Columbia River Meets the Pacific Ocean, Binfords & Mort, 1950, 3rd edition, 1964; Tillamook Light, Binfords & Mort, 1953; Sentinels of the North Pacific: The Story of Pacific Coast Lighthouses and Lightships, Binfords & Mort, 1955; Shipwrecks of the Pacific Coast, Binfords & Mort, 1957; West Coast Windjammers in Story and Pictures, Superior, 1968; Shipwrecks off Juan de Fuca, Binfords & Mort, 1968; Pacific Square-Riggers: Pictorial History of the Great Windships of Yesteryear, Superior, 1969; The Unusual Side of the Sea: A Slop Chest of Sea Lore, Windward Publishing Co., 1971; Disaster Log of Ships, Superior, 1971; West Coast Lighthouses: A Pictorial History of the Guiding Lights of the Sea, Superior, 1974; Shipwrecks in Paradise, Superior, 1977; Maritime Memories of Puget Sound, Superior, 1977.

WORK IN PROGRESS: The Salty Oregon Coast; Is Your Middle Name Jonah?.

SIDELIGHTS: Gibbs told CA: "One should write about the things he enjoys most, then, even if nobody else likes his work, he feels satisfied. If people enjoy his work, he's doubly satisfied. Everything comes from the good Lord and to him all basic credit must go for any works. Without him, I could do nothing."

*   *   *

GIBNEY, Frank (Bray) 1924-

PERSONAL: Born September 21, 1924, in Scranton, Pa.; son of Joseph James (a restauranteur) and Edna (Wetter) Gibney; married Harriet Cochran Suydam, November, 1957 (divorced, 1972); married Hiroko Doi, October 5, 1972; children: Alex, Margot, Frank, Jr., James, Thomas, Elise, Josephine. Education: Yale University, B.A., 1945. Politics: Democrat. Religion: Roman Catholic. Home: 1901 East Las Tunas Rd., Santa Barbara, Calif. 93103. Office: Encyclopaedia Britannica, 425 North Michigan Ave., Chicago, Ill. 60611.

CAREER: Time, New York City, foreign correspondent, 1947-54; Newsweek, New York City, senior features editor, 1954-57; Life, New York City, editorial writer and staff writer, 1957-61; Show, New York City, publisher, 1961-64; Encyclopaedia Britannica, Chicago, Ill., president in Japan,

1966-69, vice-president in Asia-Pacific region, 1969-71, president of TBS Britannica, 1969-75, vice-president in planning and development (in Chicago), 1976—, member of board of editors, 1973—. Associate of the Center for the Study of Democratic Institutions. Member and Presidential speech writer for Democratic National Committee, 1964. *Military service:* U.S. Naval Reserve, active duty, 1942-46; became lieutenant.

MEMBER: Council on Foreign Relations, Japan Society, America-Japan Society, Overseas Press Club (vice-president, 1958-61), Century Association, Foreign Correspondents Club (Tokyo; vice-president, 1970-71), Chicago Council on Foreign Relations, Arts Club (Chicago), Tavern Club (Chicago), Tokyo Club, Yale Club. *Awards, honors:* Order of the Rising Sun, third class (Japan), 1976; Christopher Award from the Christopher Society, 1976, for *Japan: The Fragile Superpower.*

WRITINGS: Five Gentlemen of Japan, Farrar, Straus, 1953; *The Frozen Revolution,* Farrar, Straus, 1959; (with Peter Deriabin) *The Secret World,* Doubleday, 1960; *The Operators,* Harper, 1960; *The Khrushchev Pattern,* Duell, Sloan & Pierce, 1962; *The Reluctant Space-Farers,* New American Library, 1965; (editor) *The Penkovskiy Papers,* Doubleday, 1966; *Japan: The Fragil Superpower,* Norton, 1976. Contributor to popular magazines, including *Harper's, Foreign Affairs,* and *Atlantic Monthly.*

* * *

GIBRAN, Jean 1933-

PERSONAL: Born October 31, 1933, in Lynn, Mass.; daughter of Charles Thomas and Elizabeth (Forman) English; married Kahlil Gibran (a sculptor), July 1, 1957; children: Nicole. *Education:* Tufts University, B.A., 1954; Boston State College, M.Ed., 1971. *Home:* 160 West Canton St., Boston, Mass. 02118. *Agent:* International Literary Management, 167 Fifth Ave., Suite 601, New York, N.Y., 10022.

CAREER: Teacher of English in junior high schools in Lynn, Mass., 1954-58; Origins, Boston, Mass., co-owner, 1960-65; teacher of primary education in Boston, Mass., 1968—.

WRITINGS: (Co-author of foreword) Kahlil Gibran, *Lazarus and Beloved,* New York Graphic Society, 1973; (with husband, Kahlil Gibran) *Kahlil Gibran: His Life and World,* New York Graphic Society, 1974.

WORK IN PROGRESS: Short stories.

SIDELIGHTS: Jean Gibran told *CA:* "My marriage to the Godson and namesake of the poet Kahlil Gibran and my commitment to early childhood education in the South End of Boston impelled my investigation of the ever popular but oft misunderstood author of *The Prophet.* This project—a five year collaboration with my sculptor-husband—led to unexpected sources relating to Gibran's turn of the century immigrant experiences. Our finds included unpublished passages about the young Gibran in the diaries of the Cambridge poet Josephine Preston Peabody as well as several important photographs of the Gibran family taken by the colorful photographer Fred Holland Day. Our portrait analyses Gibran's two worlds—his Lebanese Maronite heritage and the Boston Brahmin Culture into which he was plunged as a precocious adolescent. Perhaps our most satisfying achievement was to demythify Kahlil Gibran, whose origins had always been cloaked in a mist, by identifying the causative factors which made him a twentieth century literary phenomenon."

GIBSON, Charline 1937-

PERSONAL: Born April 22, 1937, in Omaha, Neb.; married husband, Robert; children: Anita Renee, Annette Suzanne. *Education:* Attended University of Nebraska, Omaha. *Home:* 3624 South 94th St., Omaha, Neb. 68124.

CAREER: Has worked for the Bureau of Internal Revenue. Member of board of directors of local Planned Parenthood; member of Omaha Human Relations Board and Panel of American Women. *Member:* Black Women Unlimited.

WRITINGS: (With Michael Rich) *A Wife's Guide to Baseball,* Viking, 1970.

* * *

GILBERT, Edwin 1907(?)-1976

1907(?)—August 24, 1976; German-born American novelist, playwright and film script writer. Some of Gilbert's plays were produced in New York on Broadway. He served during World War II as a documentary film writer with the U.S. Army. One of Gilbert's most notable novels was *Native Stone* (1956). He died in Cannes, France. Obituaries: *New York Times,* August 29, 1976; *AB Bookman's Weekly,* October 4, 1976.

* * *

GILBERT, George 1922-
(Gil Jordan; Pam Stevens)

PERSONAL: Surname legally changed, 1947; born October 13, 1922, in New York, N.Y.; son of Max and Sarah (Chanin) Gelberg; married Ruth Schneck (a mental health therapist), March 26, 1943; children: Stephen, Pamela. *Education:* Attended Brooklyn College (now of the City University of New York) and University of Utah. *Religion:* Jewish. *Home:* 5550 Fieldston Rd., Riverdale, N.Y. 10471. *Agent:* Weiser & Weiser, Inc., 52 Vanderbilt Ave., New York, N.Y. 10017. *Office:* George Gilbert & Associates, 104 East 40th St., New York, N.Y. 10016.

CAREER: Sears, Roebuck & Co., New York City, advertising manager, 1951-55; Solow-Wexton, Inc., New York City, vice-president, 1955-60, senior vice-president in marketing, 1961-66; Kameny Associates, Inc., New York City, senior vice-president in marketing, 1966-72; George Gilbert & Associates (public relations and marketing counselors), New York City, president, 1972—. *Military service:* U.S. Army Air Forces, 1942-46. *Member:* American Israel Numismatic Association (member of board of directors, 1972—), Photographic Historical Society of New York (member of board of directors; president, 1970-71).

WRITINGS: Child Photography Made Easy, Amphoto, 1957; *Mother-Daughter Cookbook,* Simon & Schuster, 1967; *Photographic Advertising from A to Z,* Yesterday's Cameras, 1972; *More Photographic Advertising from A to Z,* Yesterday's Cameras, 1974; *Still More Photographic Advertising from A to Z,* Yesterday's Cameras, 1976; *Collecting Photographica,* Hawthorn, 1976. Ghost author of *Guide to Available Light Photography,* Greenberg, 1957. Author of "Photography," column in *Cue,* 1976—. Contributor to *Mechanix Illustrated, Printer's Ink, My Baby,* and photography magazines, sometimes under pseudonyms Gil Jordan and Pam Stevens. Editor of *Shekel* (numismatic magazine), 1969—, and *Photographica,* 1975—.

WORK IN PROGRESS: The Amazing American Tintype, an in-depth study; *A History of the Nineteenth Century's Photography,* a review of basic photographic processes; *Weird, Wild, and Wacky Inventions of the Nineteenth Century from the Pages of Scientific American.*

SIDELIGHTS: Gilbert writes that he has been involved in photography for most of his life. Even his career in marketing emphasizes assistance to companies seeking to sell photographic and electronic products to middle-income America. *Avocational interests:* Collecting antique photographic equipment and memorabilia.

* * *

GILBERT, Gustave M.   1911-1977

September 30, 1911—February 6, 1977; American psychologist and educator. Gilbert served as prison psychologist during the Nazi war crimes tribunal at Nuremberg, Germany. His work there led to his book, *The Nuremberg Diary.* He was also the author of other works on psychology. Gilbert died in New York. Obituaries: *New York Times,* February 7, 1977.

* * *

GILBORN, Alice   1936-

PERSONAL: Born March 12, 1936, in Denver, Colo.; daughter of Paul Wakefield (a county treasurer) and Cynthia (a horse breeder and trader; maiden name, Foster) Wolf; married Craig A. Gilborn (a museum director), August 30, 1958; children: Alexis P. (son). *Education:* Wellesley College, B.A., 1958; Bread Loaf School of English, graduate study, summer, 1961; University of Delaware, M.A., 1968. *Politics:* "Independent but sometimes Democrat." *Religion:* "Lapsed Episcopalian." *Agent:* Knox Burger Associates Ltd., 39½ Washington Sq. S., New York, N.Y. 10012. *Office:* Adirondack Museum, Blue Mountain Lake, N.Y. 12812.

CAREER: Alma Moore College, Wilmington, Del., instructor in English, 1968-70; Adirondack Museum, Blue Mountain Lake, N.Y., part-time associate editor, 1972—. Member of board of directors of county Planned Parenthood. *Member:* Authors Guild of Authors League of America. *Awards, honors:* First prize for poetry from Virginia American Association of University Women, 1964, for "Alien Woods."

WRITINGS: (Editor) *The Naphtha Launch* (monograph), Adirondack Museum, 1976; (editor) *Theodore Roosevelt's Night Ride to the Presidency* (monograph), Adirondack Museum, 1976; *What Do You Do with a Kinkajou?* (non-fiction), Lippincott, 1976; (editor) *Man and the Adirondack Environment: A Primer* (monograph), Adirondack Museum, 1977. Contributor to *Adirondack Life.*

WORK IN PROGRESS: Stories and poems; research on women in the Adirondacks.

SIDELIGHTS: Alice Gilborn writes: "I grew up with the material for my book—a mother addicted to animals—a born horse trader who collected more creatures than she had space to put them. I've been writing as long as I can remember, but it took me years to realize I had the perfect subject for a book in my own family." *Avocational interests:* "I could hardly escape inheriting a love of horses and riding; a love of skiing I've cultivated with less grace then determination simply to survive the long Adirondack winters."

* * *

GILLUM, Helen L(ouise)   1909-

PERSONAL: Born June 18, 1909, in Rainier, Ore.; daughter of Frank (a lumberman) and Clara Bertha (Pieper) McCorkle; married Herbert C. Batterson, October 28, 1928 (divorced, August, 1939); married Earl H. Gillum (a mainte-

nance engineer), August 14, 1939; children: Vernon Jay, Marlis D. *Education:* Attended Long Beach City College. *Politics:* Democrat. *Religion:* Protestant. *Home:* 317 East Smith St., Long Beach, Calif. 90805. *Agent:* Evelyn Singer, P.O. Box 163, Briarcliff Manor, N.Y. 10510.

CAREER: Writer. *Member:* Smithsonian Associates (national charter member), Long Beach Historical Society, Long Beach Writers Club.

WRITINGS: Patrick Henry (juvenile), Beckley-Cardy, 1949; *Bernardo O'Higgins* (juvenile), Beckley-Cardy, 1951; *Looking Forward to a Career: Veterinary Medicine,* Dillon, 1976. Author of scripts for Walt Disney Productions and National Park Service. Author of column "Antiques" in *Sunday Southland* and *Long Beach Independent Press-Telegram,* 1960-70. Contributor to national magazines, including *Highlights for Children, Young World, Popular Gardening, American Home, Westways,* and *Mature Years.*

WORK IN PROGRESS: Research for *Other Heroes of American History,* juvenile, and *The Other Side of the Lake,* an autobiography, for children.

SIDELIGHTS: Helen Gillum writes about her book *Heroes:* There are many men and women of importance in American history who have never received full credit for their deeds. Furthermore, many of these same people were not 'Americans' as we think of Americans today, but instead came from different lands and walks of life and were of differing races, colors, and creeds. It is the contributions of many individuals from all walks of life that make America the great land it is. I wish to give ten or twelve of the lesser-known ones due credit."

AVOCATIONAL INTERESTS: Gardening, animals, history, antiques, ecology, travel, "armchair archaeology."

* * *

GILMOUR, Robert S(cott)   1940-

PERSONAL: Born May 16, 1940, in Philadelphia, Pa.; son of Albert A. O. and Irene (Owens) Gilmour; married Nanette Farmer (a librarian), March 4, 1960; children: Robert Scott, Jr., James Owen, Kara Lynne. *Education:* University of Florida, B.A. (high honors), 1962, M.A., 1963; Columbia University, Ph.D., 1968. *Residence:* Middletown Springs, Vt. *Office:* Public Affairs Program, University of Connecticut, Storrs, Conn. 06268.

CAREER: Columbia University, New York, N.Y., assistant professor of political science, 1968-74, deputy chairman of department, 1969-70; Vermont Opinion Research Center, Rutland, director, 1974-76; University of Connecticut, Storrs, associate professor of political science, 1976—. Administrative assistant to the governor of Florida, 1962-63. *Member:* American Society for Public Administration, American Political Science Association, Academy of Political Science. *Awards, honors:* Social Science Research Council fellowship, 1967-68; Fulbright-Hays senior fellowship, the Netherlands, 1971-72.

WRITINGS: (Editor with Robert Connery) *The National Energy Problem,* Heath, 1974; (with Robert Lamb) *Political Alienation in Contemporary America,* St. Martin's, 1975; (with John Donovan and others) *Democracy at the Crossroads;* Praeger, 1977. Contributor to political science and public administration journals.

WORK IN PROGRESS: Research for a book on the professional staffs of Congress and the executive branch of the U.S. Government.

GIMPEL, Jean 1918-

PERSONAL: Born October 10, 1918, in Paris, France; son of Rene and Florence (Duveen) Gimpel; married Catherine Corre (employed in an art gallery), January 15, 1946; children: Remy, Olivier, Claire (Mrs. Jean Baptiste Touchard). *Education:* Educated in France, Switzerland, and England. *Home:* 58 Drayton Gardens, London S.W.10, England. *Agent:* Wallace, Aitken & Sheill, 118 East 61st St., New York, N.Y.

CAREER: Writer, medievalist, and social historian. Lecturer in United States, Great Britain, and France, 1950-75. Conference organizer for Annenberg Foundation symposium, 1977. Technical adviser to British Broadcasting Corp. (BBC)-TV on a ten-part history of technology, and to ORTF French television technology programming.

WRITINGS: Les Batisseurs de Cathedrales, Editions du Seuil, 1958, translation published as *The Cathedral Builders,* Grove, 1961; (editor) *Journal d'un Collectionneur,* Calmann Levy, 1963, translation published as *The Diary of an Art Dealer,* Farrar, Straus, 1965; *Contre l'art et les artistes ou la naissance d'une religion,* Editions du Seuil, 1968, revised edition, translation by Christopher Ligota published as *Cult of Art: Against Art and Artists,* Stein & Day, 1969; *The Mediaeval Machine: The Industrial Revolution of the Middle Ages,* Holt, 1976. Also author of television film, "Don't Take It for Granted," 1971.

WORK IN PROGRESS: Writing ten-part series on the parallels between the Middle Ages and contemporary Britain and United States, for British Broadcasting Corp. (BBC).

SIDELIGHTS: Gimpel's father, who founded art galleries in Paris, London, and New York, was a friend of Monet, Renoir, and Proust. Gimpel himself began with an interest in art, but soon expanded into other areas. By 1939 he had exclusive French rights to several British and American patents, and had hopes of owning his own private television network. During World War II, he worked with the French Resistance, and after the war began an attempt to build a private laboratory for the scientific study of Old Masters. It was around 1946 that he became interested in medieval technology. Presently he is concerned with industrial archaeology, "the protection and conservation of the industrial part of human history," especially in France.

He writes that he holds two salons a year, always on Sunday afternoons, and "since I am against nature, I seek to discourage Londoners from going to the country. Guests at these salons are not introduced by name, but by occupation or personal interest. One rule is firmly laid down: men are not allowed to talk to men or women to women unless a woman or man is present in the group." His books have been published in Japanese, Italian, Dutch, Spanish, Polish, Portuguese, German, and Rumanian.

AVOCATIONAL INTERESTS: Sports (especially table tennis), crowds, sunbathing, women, conversation, cats and dogs, politics, television, history, artists and intellectuals ("study artists and intellectuals as other sociologists study miners or bus conductors"), technology.

*　　*　　*

GINGRICH, Arnold 1903-1976

December 5, 1903—July 9, 1976; American publisher and editor of *Esquire* (association with this magazine beginning in 1933), editor of *Coronet* (1936-49), and author of autobiographical and nonfiction books, including *Toys of a Lifetime* and *Nothing but People: The Early Days at Esquire.* He

died in Ridgewood, N.J. Obituaries: *New York Times,* July 10, 1976. (See index for previous *CA* sketch)

*　　*　　*

GINNS, Patsy (Lee) M(oore) 1937-

PERSONAL: Born April 27, 1937, in King, N.C.; daughter of Hermie D. (a farmer) and Ethel (a teacher; maiden name, Spencer) Moore; married H. Lloyd Ginns (a social work administrator), August 13, 1960; children: Marc Lloyd, Monica Lynette. *Education:* High Point College, B.A., 1959; graduate study at University of North Carolina and Wake Forest University. *Religion:* Methodist. *Home address:* Route 1, Box 413, King, N.C. 27021.

CAREER: Elementary school teacher in Winston-Salem, N.C., 1959-60; high school English teacher in Columbia, S.C., 1960-62, Anchorage, Alaska, 1962-63, King, N.C., 1963-64, and Walnut Grove, N.C., 1966-69; Chestnut Grove Junior High School, King, N.C., teacher of language arts, 1975—. Member of board of directors of King Public Library, 1966— (chairman of board, 1967-70), and Forsyth-Stokes Area Mental Health Board, 1974-76. Organizer and charter member of Stokes County Mental Health Association, 1971— (also first chairman of board of directors).

MEMBER: North Carolina Library Association (member of board of directors, 1973-75), North Carolina Library Trustees Association (vice-chairman of board of directors, 1971-73; chairman of board, 1973-75), North Carolina Poetry Society, North Carolina Association of Educators. *Awards, honors:* Caldwell W. Nixon, Jr. Cup from North Carolina Poetry Society, 1974, for children's poetry "Squeezing Squish"; first prize from Tar Heel Writer's Roundtable, 1973, for story "Chicken, Chicken!"

WRITINGS: Rough Weather Makes Good Timber, University of North Carolina Press, 1977. Contributor of articles and poems to magazines and newspapers, including *Alive Now!, Cold Mountain Review, Raleigh News and Observer, State* magazine (N.C.), and of curriculum materials to Methodist Publishing House.

WORK IN PROGRESS: A second volume of collected folk narratives of life in the coastal area of North Carolina, with J. L. Osborne, Jr.

SIDELIGHTS: Patsy Ginns writes that her book is "a collection of folk narratives from elderly North Carolinians centering around rural life in the state from about 1885 to 1940. Some accounts are presented in prose, while others are in 'found poetry.' They are accompanied by pen and ink drawings of rural North Carolina scenes by J. L. Osborne, Jr.

"I first recorded accounts from my own grandmother, ninety-five at the time, and found my way to others like her all over the state. In this way I hope to preserve, in verbatim accounts, much of the folk customs and cultural heritage of this period and locale."

*　　*　　*

GINZBERG, Yevgeniya 1906(?)-1977

1906(?)—May 25, 1977; Soviet writer of autobiographical account of life in the Stalinist labor camps where she spent eighteen years. Her book was published in the West but never appeared in the Soviet Union. She died in Moscow, U.S.S.R. Obituaries: *New York Times,* May 26, 1977.

GIRARD, James P(reston) 1944-

PERSONAL: Born July 6, 1944, in Tillamook, Ore.; son of Preston Leroy (a teacher) and Inez May (a bookkeeper) Girard; married Barbara Joyce Scott (a teacher), June 1, 1966; children: Virginia Amanda, Preston John Amos. *Education:* University of Kansas, B.A., 1966, graduate study, 1968-69; Johns Hopkins University, M.A., 1967. *Politics:* "Burkean conservative." *Religion:* "Basketball." *Home:* 255 North Michigan, #114, Lawrence, Kan. 66044. *Office:* 1069 Wescoe Hall, University of Kansas, Lawrence, Kan. 66045.

CAREER: Wichita Beacon, Wichita, Kan., reporter, summer, 1967; College of Emporia, Emporia, Kan., instructor in English, 1967-68; *Topeka Daily Capital,* Topeka, Kan., reporter, 1969-73; University of Kansas, Lawrence, editor for habilitation personnel training project, 1973-76, instructor in English, 1976—. Has worked as political scriptwriter and public relations officer. *Member:* Science Fiction Writers of America, League of Yggdrasil (past president), Associated Writing Programs.

WRITINGS: Changing All Those Changes (novella), Yardbird Wing Editions, 1976.

Work anthologized in *New Dimensions Six,* edited by Robert Silverberg, Harper, 1976. Contributor of stories to *Kansas Quarterly, Cottonwood Review,* and *Fantasy and Science Fiction.*

WORK IN PROGRESS—Fiction: *The Late Man* or *Some Survive; Grand Tour* (tentative title); continuing research on the rock and roll generation.

SIDELIGHTS: Girard writes: "I identify with the generation born in the 1940's, and with the Midwest about which East Coast publishers are singularly ignorant. My characters never represent any group, however. My writing is strongly autobiographical, in the sense that I would rather make the reader feel an experience as I did than make up something that never happened. On the other hand, my fiction is not about *me.* . . . I am a natural novella-ist, which means I don't get published much."

AVOCATIONAL INTERESTS: Recorded popular music, "gym-rat basketball."

*   *   *

GLADSTONE, Meredith 1939-

PERSONAL: Born August 8, 1939, in Providence, R.I.; daughter of James K. (an engineer) and Clara Townsend; married Gary Gladstone (a photographer), July 7, 1967; children: Gregory T. *Education:* Rhode Island School of Design, B.F.A., 1961. *Agent:* McIntosh & Otis, Inc., 475 Fifth Ave., New York, N.Y. 10017. *Office:* Gladstone Studio Ltd., 237 East 20th St., New York, N.Y. 10003.

CAREER: Fashion designer, 1962-72; free-lance designer and writer, 1972—.

WRITINGS: (With husband, Gary Gladstone) *The Needlepoint Alphabet Book,* Morrow, 1973; (with G. Gladstone) *Kids' Clothes by Meredith Gladstone,* Morrow, 1976.

WORK IN PROGRESS: Another needlepoint book.

*   *   *

GLASGOW, Eric 1924-

PERSONAL: Born June 10, 1924, in Leeds, England; son of William Ewalt (a tax inspector) and Sybil (Harper) Glasgow. *Education:* St. John's College, Cambridge, M.A., 1948; University of Manchester, Ph.D., 1951. *Politics:* Liberal/Conservative. *Religion:* Agnostic. *Home:* 45 York Rd., Birkdale, Southport, Merseyside PR8 2AY, England.

CAREER: Open University, Buckinghamshire, England, tutor in modern history in northwest region, 1975—. Honorary member, South Vietnamese Council of Foreign Relations, 1970-74; Lundie reader at St. Deiniol's Library, 1970 and 1973-75. *Awards, honors:* Melville Cup from National Philatelic Society (England), 1951.

WRITINGS: (With Donald Read) *Feargus O'Connor, Irishman and Chartist,* Edward Arnold, 1961; (editor) *The Story of Yardley Hastings,* Belmont Press, 1973; (editor) *The Legend of Kwame Nkrumah,* Abicom Ltd. (Accra, Ghana), 1973; *Shelley's Debt to Greece,* University of Salzburg, 1973; *Matthew Arnold and Greece,* University of Salzburg, 1973; *Walter Pater and Greece,* University of Salzburg, 1975; *Some British Travellers in Greece,* University of Salzburg, 1975.

Staff writer for *Greek Gazette* (London), 1969—; contributor to Crowell's *Reader's Encyclopaedia of English Literature.*

SIDELIGHTS: Glasgow told *CA* he is dedicated to the historical study in depth of current local, national, and international issues. He also is "concerned with all aspects of the nineteenth century, especially American history and American literature." *Avocational interests:* Collecting old gardening books.

*   *   *

GLASSMAN, Jon David 1944-

PERSONAL: Born January 8, 1944, in New York; son of Jack (a businessman) and Dorothy (Witkin) Glassman; married Deborah Weiss (a librarian), June 8, 1968; children: Amanda. *Education:* University of Southern California, B.F.S., 1965; Columbia University, M.A., 1968, certificate in Russian, 1968, Ph.D., 1976. *Home:* 2900 Meadow View Rd., Falls Church, Va. 22042. *Office:* Office of Soviet Union Affairs, U.S. Department of State, Washington, D.C. 20520.

CAREER: American Embassy, Madrid, Spain, political officer, 1968-70; American Embassy, Moscow, Soviet Union, consul, 1971-73; Arms Control and Disarmament Agency, Washington, D.C., political officer, 1974-75; U.S. Department of State, Washington, D.C., political officer for Office of Soviet Union Affairs, 1975—. *Member:* Phi Beta Kappa. *Awards, honors:* International affairs fellow of Council on Foreign Relations, 1973-74.

WRITINGS: Arms for the Arabs: The Soviet Union and War in the Middle East, Johns Hopkins Press, 1976.

WORK IN PROGRESS: Research on Soviet foreign policy and security affairs.

*   *   *

GODEFROY, Vincent 1912-

PERSONAL: Born April 14, 1912, in Southampton, England; son of John and Gwendolyn (Laborde) Godefroy; married Anna Mary Hurt, December 21, 1937. *Education:* Sidney Sussex College, Cambridge, M.A., 1934. *Home:* Dolphin House, Sandbanks, Dorsetshire, England.

CAREER: Westbury School, near Winchester, England, assistant master, 1935-49; Lysses School, Fareham and Rhinefield, England, headmaster, 1949-66. *Member:* Royal Numismatic Society.

WRITINGS: The Dramatic Genius of Verdi, Volume I, Gollancz, 1957, St. Martin's, 1976, Volume II, St. Martin's, 1977.

One-act plays: "The Widow of Ephesus," first produced in London at Ambassadors Theatre, 1935; "Blessed Above Women," first produced in Bristol at Clifton Arts Club, 1936; "Y Ser Yn Eu Graddau," first produced in Cardigan, Wales, at National Eisteddfod of Wales, 1942; "The Wall," first produced at Erith Technical College, 1942; "Deluge," first produced in Nottingham at Philodramatic Theatre, 1942; "Full Circle," first produced in Colchester, Essex, 1945; "Wild Wales," first produced in Pentre by Mid-Rhondda Players, 1946; "Intermezzo," first produced at Highbury Little Theatre, 1946; "Captain Oliphant," first produced in Cleadon, 1946; "Fleuriault Mill," first produced in Douglas, Isle of Manx, at Manx Drama Festival, 1947; "Morning Break," first produced at Welwyn Festival, 1947; "The Cat," first produced in Aldershot, 1947; "The Passing of Julian Mickelthwaite," first produced in Worthing, 1948; "Poet and Parrot," first produced by BBC Repertory Players, 1948; "Fairies and Rewards," first produced by BBC Repertory Players, 1948; "1 Ae Otho," first produced by BBC Repertory Players, 1949; "The Night of Friday," first produced at Blackpool Festival, 1949; "The Green Man," first produced in Fareham, 1955.

One-act plays represented in anthologies, including *Three Prize Plays and Two Others,* edited by E. Everard, Allen & Unwin, 1936; *Best One-Act Plays of 1937-1941,* five volumes, edited by W. J. Marriott, Harrap, 1942; *Ten One-Act Plays for Women,* edited by E. Everard, Harrap, 1944. Contributor to music magazines.

WORK IN PROGRESS: Research on post-Antonine Rome, Anglo-Saxon history, and contemporary opera.

SIDELIGHTS: Godefroy told *CA:* "My intention was to divide my career between teaching and writing, with drama, poetry, topography and fiction as objectives. This was working out until I ventured into Headmastership, after which until my retirement I found no time for anything else. Since giving up education I am able to return to writing more or less without interruption.

"I do not think my views on anything can be of interest. My chief perplexity is to find the most balanced approach to modern creative art, bearing in mind how many past critics have made fools of themselves by failing to recognize the value of works that are now masterpieces. It seems that today painting, sculpture, poetry, music and drama have all entered a period of worthless anarchy. I cannot make up my mind whether I am purblind in the glare of genius which I cannot appreciate, or whether I am correct in believing that an enormous rot has set into the creative faculty of Mankind. Though I try to keep abreast, I fear I shall not float much further."

*   *   *

GODFREY, (William) Dave 1938-

PERSONAL: Born August 9, 1938, in Winnipeg, Manitoba, Canada; son of Richmond (a lawyer) and Marguerite (a teacher; maiden name, Hutcheson) Godfrey; married Ellen Swartz, 1963; children: Jonathan, Rebecca, Samuel. *Education:* Attended Harvard University, 1957, and University of Toronto, 1957-58; University of Iowa, B.A., 1960, M.F.A., 1963, Ph.D., 1966; Stanford University, M.A., 1963; attended University of Chicago, 1965. *Home:* Maple Lane Farm, R.R.1, Erin, Ontario, Canada N0B 1T0. *Office:* Press Porcepic Ltd., 70 Main St., Erin, Ontario, Canada N0B 1T0.

CAREER: Frontier College, Canada, instructor in English as a second language, summers, 1958, 1961; Adisadel College, Cape Coast, Ghana, lecturer in African literature and English and acting head of department, 1963-65; University of Toronto, Trinity College, Toronto, Ontario, assistant professor of English, 1966-68, 1969-74, writer-in-residence at Erindale College, 1973-74; York University, Downsview, Ontario, visiting professor of English, 1974-75: University of Toronto, Trinity College, visiting professor of English, 1975-76, coordinator of Canadian literature minor program; York University, associate professor of humanities, 1976-77; University of Victoria, Victoria, British Columbia, head of creative writing department, 1977—. Press Porcepic Ltd., Erin, Ontario, editor, 1972—. Co-founder, editor, and president of House of Anansi, 1966-70; senior editor of New Press, 1969-73. Member of board of trustees of Books Canada, Inc., 1973—; coordinator of Literary Presses Group, 1975—. Member of advisory panel for the arts of Canada Council, 1971-74.

MEMBER: Independent Publishers Association (president, 1972-73), Association for the Export of Canadian Books (founding director, 1972—). *Awards, honors:* President's medals from University of Western Ontario, 1964, for story "Gossip: The Birds That Flew, the Birds That Fell," and 1966, for article "Letter from Africa to an American Negro" and story "The Hard-Headed Collector"; Canada Council grants, 1965 and, for France, 1968-69; governor-general's award, 1970, for *The New Ancestors.*

WRITINGS: Death Goes Better with Coca-Cola (stories), House of Anansi Press, 1967, 3rd edition, 1976; (editor with Bill McWhinney) *Man Deserves Man: CUSO in Developing Countries,* Ryerson, 1967; *The New Ancestors* (novel), New Press, 1970; (editor with Mel Watkins) *Gordon to Watkins to You—A Documentary: The Battle for Control of Our Economy,* New Press, 1970; (with Robert Fulford and Abe Rotstein) *Read Canadian: A Book About Canadian Books,* James Lewis & Samuel, 1972; *I Ching Kanada,* Press Porcepic, 1976.

Represented in anthologies, including *Great Canadian Short Stories,* edited by Alec Lucas, Dell, 1971; *Power Corrupted,* edited by A. Rotstein, New Press, 1971; *Canadian Anthology,* edited by Carl F. Klink and Reginald Watters, Gage, 1976. Contributor of twenty short stories and of articles and reviews to periodicals, including *Tamarack Review, Canadian Literature, Saturday Night, Impulse,* and *Canadian Forum.* General editor of "Canadian Writers," New Canadian Library, 1968-72. Editor of *Porcepic,* 1972—, and *Canadian Poetry Annual,* 1976—; fiction editor of *Canadian Forum,* 1971-72.

WORK IN PROGRESS: Two novels; another collection of stories.

SIDELIGHTS: Godfrey told *CA:* "I am most interested in that portion of literature where myth meets social realities; literary dogma concerning the purity of fantasy or of realism does not interest me. The Canadian environment has influenced me greatly although I write mainly about people from cultures other than my own. A good part of my twenties was spent traveling about the U.S. and Africa. I strive for great complexity in my writing because that is how I find life; I do not believe the writer has the duty to simplify or interpret life for his readers; his major tasks are to be as intelligent as possible and to take flights of imagination into bodies, minds and situations other than his own."

BIOGRAPHICAL/CRITICAL SOURCES: Ellipse, autumn, 1970; *Mysterious East,* December, 1970; *Oxford*

Companion to Canadian Literature, Oxford University Press, 1971; *Canadian Forum,* April, 1971.

* * *

GODFREY, Eleanor S(mith) 1914-

PERSONAL: Born October 10, 1914, in Shelton, Neb.; daughter of George W. (a pharmacist) and Blanche (Lee) Smith; married James Logan Godfrey (a professor of history), June 17, 1937; children: Jean (Mrs. Curt Wittig), Anne (Mrs. N. K. Dickerson III). *Education:* Smith College, B.A. (high honors), 1935; University of Chicago, M.A., 1936, Ph.D., 1957; University of North Carolina, B.L.S., 1939. *Politics:* Democrat. *Religion:* Episcopalian. *Home:* 231 Hillcrest Circle, Chapel Hill, N.C. 27514.

CAREER: University of North Carolina, Chapel Hill, librarian, 1939-43, lecturer in naval history, 1943-44, lecturer in history for evening college, 1964-76; writer and lecturer on glass and glassmaking, 1976—. *Member:* Association Internationale pour l'Histoire du Verre, Phi Beta Kappa. *Awards, honors:* Mayflower Cup from Mayflower Society, 1976, for *The Development of English Glassmaking.*

WRITINGS: (Contributor) B. E. Schnitt, editor, *Some Historians of Modern Europe,* University of Chicago Press, 1942; *The Development of English Glassmaking, 1560-1640,* University of North Carolina Press, 1976.

WORK IN PROGRESS: Research on glassmaking in Jamestown, Va., 1608-24, and on English glassmaking in the seventeenth century.

SIDELIGHTS: Eleanor Godfrey writes: "Though the nucleus of the book was my Ph.D. dissertation, it was expanded by many years of study in England, the European continent and this country, in many other periods and aspects of glassmaking, such as technical details of manufacture, artistic merits, influence of glassmaking on architecture, links with scientists and scientific equipment, archaeological excavations, etc."

* * *

GODWIN, Joscelyn (Roland Jasper Chloestro) 1945-

PERSONAL: Born January 16, 1945, in Kelmscott, Oxford, England; came to the United States in 1966; son of Edward (an artist and writer) and Stephanie (an artist and writer; maiden name, Allfree) Godwin; married Sharyn Louise Cook (a musician), July 31, 1971. *Education:* Magdalene College, Cambridge, B.A., 1965, Mus.B., 1966, M.A., 1970; Cornell University, Ph.D., 1969. *Home address:* Dragon Acres, Earlville, N.Y. 13332. *Office:* Department of Music, Colgate University, Hamilton, N.Y. 13346.

CAREER: Cleveland State University, Cleveland, Ohio, instructor in music, 1969-71; Colgate University, Hamilton, N.Y., assistant professor, 1971-76, associate professor of music, 1976—. Church organist, 1969-75. *Member:* Royal College of Organists (fellow), American Musicological Society. *Awards, honors:* Abingdon Prize from Cambridge University, 1966, for "String Trio"; Harding Prize from Royal College of Organists, 1966.

WRITINGS: (Editor) Henry Cowell, *New Musical Resources,* Knopf, 1931, new edition, Something Else, 1969; (composer) *Epistle to Harmodius,* Novello, 1966; (composer) *A Few Thoughts for Treble Recorder,* Modern Music for Recorders, 1966; (translator) Werner Walcker-Meyer, *The Roman Organ of Acquinum,* Musikwissenschaftliche Verlagsgesellschaft, 1973; (editor) *Schirmer Scores: A Repertory of Western Music,* Schirmer Books, 1975; (editor)

Marco Attilio Regolo, Harvard University Press, 1975. Contributor to *Dictionary of Twentieth Century Music* and to music and religious journals.

WORK IN PROGRESS: A music history appreciation text; continuing research on Robert Fludd and on the philosophical and occult aspects of music.

SIDELIGHTS: Godwin writes: "My major interest is in occult philosophy and comparative religion. My musicological work proceeds from a desire to understand history through music and the other arts, and to pass on this understanding to my students. More specifically, my interest is in playing music before 1750 on the instruments for which it was composed, especially recorders, viols, harpsichord."

AVOCATIONAL INTERESTS: Travel (Europe and the Middle East), bee-keeping, bio-dynamic gardening.

* * *

GOEBEL, Dorothy (Burne) 1898-1976

PERSONAL: Born August 24, 1898, in Huntington, N.Y.; married Julius Goebel, Jr. (a legal historian). *Education:* Columbia University, A.B., 1920, A.M., 1922, Ph.D., 1926. *Home:* 21 East 90th St., New York, N.Y. 10028.

CAREER: Barnard College, New York City, staff member, 1920-26; Hunter College (now of the City University of New York), New York City, instructor, 1926-29, assistant professor, 1929-42, associate professor, 1942-48, professor, 1948-63, emeritus professor of history, 1963-76, department chairperson, 1942-48 and 1961-62. *Member:* American Historical Association (chairperson of Albert J. Beveridge Awards committee). *Awards, honors:* Guggenheim fellowship, 1947-48.

WRITINGS: William Henry Harrison: A Political Biography, Historical Bureau of the Indiana Library and Historical Department, 1926, reprinted by Porcupine Press, 1974; (with husband, Julius Goebel, Jr.) *Generals in the White House,* Doubleday, 1945, reprinted by Books for Libraries Press, 1971; (editor) *American Foreign Policy: A Documentary Survey, 1776-1960,* Holt, 1961. Contributor to professional journals. Associate editor of *The Legal Papers of Alexander Hamilton,* 1963-76.

OBITUARIES: New York Times, March 14, 1976; *AB Bookman's Weekly,* April 5, 1976.*

(Died March 12, 1976, in Huntington, N.Y.)

* * *

GOERTZEL, Ted George 1942-

PERSONAL: Born November 20, 1942, in Visalia, Calif.; son of Victor (a psychologist) and Mildred (a writer; maiden name, George) Goertzel; married Carol Zwell (a social worker), November, 1962; children: Benjamin Nathaniel, Rebecca Jo. *Education:* Antioch College, B.A., 1964; Washington University, St. Louis, Mo., M.A., 1966, Ph.D., 1970. *Politics:* Democratic socialist. *Religion:* None. *Office:* Department of Sociology, Rutgers University, Camden, N.J. 08102.

CAREER: University of Sao Paulo, Sao Paulo, Barzil, visiting instructor in sociology, 1967-68; University of Oregon, Eugene, assistant professor of sociology, 1968-73; Rutgers University, Camden, N.J., associate professor of sociology, 1973—, chairman of department, 1977—. *Member:* American Sociological Association (chairman of Marxist sociology section), Society for the Study of Social Problems, Eastern Sociological Association, East Coast Conference of Socialist Sociologists.

WRITINGS: *Political Society*, Rand McNally, 1976. Contributor to sociology journals. Associate editor of *Insurgent Sociologist*.

WORK IN PROGRESS: *An Introduction to Radical Sociology*, with Albert J. Szymanski.

SIDELIGHTS: Goertzel writes: "My work is part of the radical movement in sociology which grew up as an outgrowth of the student radical movement in the 1960's."

* * *

GOKAK, Vinayak Krishna 1909-

PERSONAL: Born August 10, 1909, in Savanur, India; son of Krishna Vinayak and Sundra (Joshi) Gokak; married Sharada Betadur, May 30, 1930; children: Yeshoda (Mrs. Narayan P. Bhat), Anil, Sarala (Mrs. Srinath B. Magal). *Education:* Attended Karnatak College (now University), 1925-31; University of Bombay, M.A., 1931; Jesus College, Oxford, M.A., 1938. *Home:* Meera Cottage, 525 Rajmahal Extension, Brindavan, Whitefield, Bangalore 6, India.

CAREER: English professor and college principal in Poona, Sangli, Osmania, Kolhapur, Visnagar, and Dharwar, India, 1931-58; director of Central Institute of English, 1959-66; Bangalore University, Bangalore, India, vice-chancellor, 1966-69; Indian Institute of Advanced Study, Simla, director, 1970-71; Sri Satya Sai All-India Organizations, Bangalore, chairman, 1971—. Professor of English at Karnatak University, 1952-58. Member of Indian Commission of UNESCO, 1967-73; member of Indian University Grants Commission, 1968-69. *Member:* World Association of World Federalists (vice-president, 1970), Indian Universities Adult Education Association (president, 1969), Indian P.E.N. *Awards, honors:* Award from Indian Literary Academy, 1961; D.Litt. from Karnataka University, 1967, University of the Pacific, 1970.

WRITING: *The Poetic Approach to Language, with Special Reference to the History of English*, Oxford University Press, 1952, Folcroft, 1969; (editor) *Literatures in Modern Indian Languages: A Series of Broadcasts from All India Radio*, Publications Division, Indian Ministry of Information and Broadcasting, 1957; *English in India: Its Present and Future*, Asia Publishing House, 1964; *In Life's Temple*, Blackie & Son, 1965; (editor) *The Flame of Truth*, Institute of Human Study (Hyderabad, India), 1968; (editor) *The Golden Treasury of Indo-Anglican Poetry, 1828-1965*, Sahitya Akademi, 1970; *Bendre, Poet and Seer*, Somaiya Publications, 1970; *Indian Response to Poetry in English*, Macmillan, 1970; *Narahari, Prophet of New India*, Somaiya Publications, 1972; *India and World Cultures*, International Scholastic Book Service, 1972; *Sri Aurobindo, Seer and Poet*, Verry, 1973; *Coleridge's Aesthetics*, Humanities, 1975; *An Integral View of Poetry*, Abhinav Prakashan, 1975; *Bhagavan Sathya Sai Baba: An Interpretation*, Abhinav Prakashan, 1975.

Works in Kannada: *Navyate hagu kavyajivana*, 1959; *Pornanabha*, 1961; *Kasmira* (under a pseudonym), 1962; *Cintana* (under a pseudonym; poems), 1964; *Indilla naje*, 1965; *Trisankuvina prajnaprabhata* (poems), 1965; *Samarasave jivana* (novel), 1967; *Samudragitagalu* (novel), 1967; *Bhavaraga* (poems), 1969; (editor) *Navyadhvani* (poems), 1969; *Koneya dina*, 1970; *Gokakara natakagalu*, 1971. Also author of *Pavana* (poems) and *Sahityadalli Pragati* (criticism).

WORK IN PROGRESS: An epic in Kannada in twelve books, *Veda Purusha*, completion expected in 1980.

GOLD, William E(mil) 1912-

PERSONAL: Born August 9, 1912, in Brooklyn, N.Y.; son of Mayer (a dental supplier) and Miriam (Feldman) Gold; married Bernice Ellman, 1934; children: Walter. *Education:* Ohio State University, B.S., 1933. *Office: Washington Post*, Washington, D.C. 20071.

CAREER/WRITINGS: *Washington Post*, Washington, D.C., author of "The District Line" column, 1947—. *Member:* White House Correspondents Association, National Press Club, Sigma Delta Chi.

SIDELIGHTS: CA asked Gold what changes in the accessibility of the President to the press have occurred in recent years. He responded: "The change is hardly visible to the naked eye. They all come into office accessible. They all go into hiding to get their work done. They all become accessible again when they get into trouble and want to go over the heads of opposition Congressmen."

* * *

GOLDBERG, E(lliott) Marshall 1930-

PERSONAL: Born December 19, 1930, in North Adams, Mass.; son of Jack and Ida (Lenhoff) Goldberg; married Darlis Ray, 1966; children: five. *Education:* University of Rochester, A.B. (high honors), 1952; Tufts University, M.D., 1956. *Agent:* Warren Bayless, WB Agency, 156 East 52nd St., New York, N.Y. 10022. *Office:* Hurley Medical Center, Flint, Mich. 48502.

CAREER: District of Columbia Hospital, Washington, intern, 1956-57; Memorial Hospital, Worcester, Mass., resident, 1960-61; University Hospitals, Madison, Wis., resident, 1962-63; Wayne State University, Detroit, Mich., assistant professor of medicine, 1964-65; Michigan State University, East Lansing, assistant professor, 1966-68, associate professor, 1968, professor of medicine, 1973—. Chief of medicine at Hurley Hospital, 1970—. Diplomate of American Board of Internal Medicine; licensed in Massachusetts, Wisconsin, and Michigan; research associate in endocrinology at St. Vincent's Hospital (Worcester, Mass.), 1960; endocrine fellow at University of Wisconsin, 1961-62; health expert for "Canada A.M." on Canadian Television (CTV). Member of board of directors of Medgar Evers Foundation. *Military service:* U.S. Army, Medical Corps, 1957-59; served in France; became captain.

MEMBER: American College of Physicians (fellow), Endocrine Society, American Federation of Clinical Research, American Diabetes Association, Royal College of Physicians (associate), Massachusetts Medical Society, Michigan Medical Society, Michigan Association for Medical Education (president, 1972-75), Genesee County Medical Society. *Awards, honors:* National Institutes of Health research grant, 1963-64; Humanitarian Award from National Association for the Advancement of Colored People, 1974.

WRITINGS—Novels: *The Karamanov Equations*, World Publishing, 1972; *The Anatomy Lesson*, Putnam, 1974; *Critical List*, Harcourt, 1977. Contributor of about twenty-five articles to medical journals and popular magazines, including *Detroit* and *Medical World News*. Book editor for Physicians' Radio Network.

WORK IN PROGRESS: *The Humanist*, a novel.

* * *

GOLDBERG, George 1935-

PERSONAL: Born January 26, 1935, in New York, N.Y.;

son of Melvin C. (a physician) and Mabel (a lawyer; maiden name, Klein) Goldberg; married Mina Shayne Goldman (former U.S. vice-consul in Europe), December 19, 1960; children: Amelia, Jeremy. *Education:* Yale University, student, 1952-54; Syracuse University, B.A., 1956; Harvard University, LL.B., 1959. *Politics:* Independent ("*very* conservative"). *Religion:* Jewish. *Office:* Kreindler, Relkin & Goldberg, 500 Fifth Ave., New York, N.Y. 10036.

CAREER: Trial lawyer, 1959—. Partner of Kreindler, Relkin & Goldberg, 1970—. Visiting lecturer at University of Vermont, 1968-69. Legal adviser to U.S. Copyright Office, 1961-63.

WRITINGS: The Peace to End Peace, Harcourt, 1969; *East Meets West,* Harcourt, 1970; *The Supreme Court in American Life,* Heath, 1970; *A Lawyer's Guide to Commercial Arbitration,* American Law Institute, 1977. Contributor to law journals.

WORK IN PROGRESS: A biography of James Kent, chancellor of New York.

AVOCATIONAL INTERESTS: Music (keyboard instruments, choral singing, lieder).

*   *   *

GOLDE, Roger A(lan)   1934-

PERSONAL: Born December 27, 1934, in Chicago, Ill.; son of Joseph A. and Marthe (Bloch) Golde. *Education:* Student at University of Chicago; Harvard University, B.A. (magna cum laude), 1956, M.B.A. (with distinction), 1959; also attended University of Strasbourg and University of Paris. *Office:* Golde Management and Education Services, 183 Larch Rd., Cambridge, Mass. 02138.

CAREER: General Foods, White Plains, N.Y., in commercial evaluation, 1959-60; Atlantic Research Corp., Alexandria, Va., director of corporate acquisitions, head of overhead control, vice-president and director of Northeast engineering, 1960-63; Golde Management and Education Services, Cambridge, Mass., president, 1963—. Senior staff associate and project director for President's Advisory Council on Executive Organization, 1969-70. Lecturer in business at Northeastern University, 1963-66, and Babson Institute, 1967.

Consultant to U.S. Air Force, Peace Corps, and U.S. Postal Service. *Member:* New England Society of Management Consultants, Phi Beta Kappa. *Awards, honors:* Fulbright grant, 1956-57.

WRITINGS: Thinking with Figures in Business, Addison-Wesley, 1966; *Can You Be Sure of Your Experts: A Complete Manual on How to Choose and Use Doctors, Lawyers, Brokers—And All the Other Experts in Your Life,* Macmillan, 1970; *Muddling Through: The Art of Properly Unbusinesslike Management,* AMACOM, 1976.

Creator and executive producer of "Turning Management On" (series of ten video-cassette workshops), distributed by Columbia, 1971-73. Contributor to business, trade, and education journals, *Pageant,* and various international periodicals.

WORK IN PROGRESS: What You Say is What You Get.

SIDELIGHTS: Golde told *CA:* "I enjoy working with new areas that require relating several different types of knowledge and skills. I am particularly interested in techniques for creative problem solving. Areas of technology transfer and parapsychology intrigue me." *Avocational interests:* Magic, choral conducting.

GOLDEMBERG, Isaac   1945-

PERSONAL: Born November 15, 1945, in Chepen, Peru; came to the United States in 1964; son of Isaac (a merchant) and Bertila (a merchant; maiden name, Bay) Goldemberg; married Mona Stern, December 19, 1963 (separated); children: David, Dina. *Education:* City College of the City University of New York, B.A. (magna cum laude), 1968; New York University, graduate study, 1968—. *Home:* 515 West 110th St., New York, N.Y. 10025.

CAREER: Worked in a kibbutz in Israel, 1962-63; insurance salesman in Barcelona, Spain, 1963; New York Public Library, New York City, clerk in Jewish Division, 1965-66; Grolier, Inc., New York City, Spanish editor, 1968-69; American Book Co., New York City, Spanish editor, 1969; New York University, New York City, lecturer in Spanish, 1970-75; writer, 1975—. *Member:* Phi Beta Kappa.

WRITINGS: Tiempo de silencio (poems; title means "Time for Silence"), Coleccion de Poesia Hispanoamericana, 1969; (with Jose Kozer) *De Chepen a La Habana* (poems; title means "From Chepen to Havana"), Editorial Bayu-Menorah, 1973; *The Fragmented Life of Don Jacobo Lerner* (novel), Persea Books, 1976. Contributor to Spanish- and English-language journals, including *Present Tense, Nimrod,* and *Mundo Nuevo.*

WORK IN PROGRESS: The Conversion of Marcos Drasinover, a novel, for Persea Books; an oral history of Peruvian Jews; a book of poems.

SIDELIGHTS: Goldemberg writes: "I am a Peruvian of Jewish, Russian, English, Italian, Spanish, and Indian descent. I traveled to Israel in 1962. Then I moved to Barcelona, where I spent a year in medical school. I decided (age eighteen) I wanted to be a writer and quit medical school. I settled in New York. Prior to my return to Peru (for the first time in fifteen years) in 1976, I wrote *The Fragmented Life of Don Jacobo Lerner,* an attempt at reconstructing my own past and that of the Peruvian Jewish community at large.

"Even though my work deals mainly with the Jewish experience in Peru, the burdens of exile and spiritual rootlessness, I am also concerned with Peruvian life as a whole, particularly that of provincial Peru, marked by narrowness and claustrophobia. This is the world depicted in my first novel, where I attempted to draw the life of the Jewish immigrant as a tragic and heroic parody of the legend of the Wandering Jew."

AVOCATIONAL INTERESTS: Chinese cooking, watching television, playing soccer.

*   *   *

GOLDENBERG, Edie N.   1945-

PERSONAL: Born June 6, 1945, in St. Louis, Mo.; daughter of Joseph William (a consulting engineer) and Katie (Needle) Goldenberg. *Education:* Massachusetts Institute of Technology, S.B., 1967; Stanford University, M.A., 1968, Ph.D., 1974. *Office:* Department of Political Science, University of Michigan, Ann Arbor, Mich. 48104.

CAREER: University of Michigan, Ann Arbor, assistant professor of political science, 1974—, research associate, Institute of Public Policy Studies, 1974—, faculty associate, Institute for Social Research, 1975—. *Member:* American Political Science Association, American Association for the Advancement of Science. *Awards, honors:* Danforth Foundation fellow, 1967; Woodrow Wilson fellow, 1967; National Institute for Mental Health fellow, 1969.

WRITINGS: Making the Papers: The Access of Resource-Poor Groups to the Metropolitan Press, Lexington Books, 1975.

WORK IN PROGRESS: Contributing to two books; research on mass media and politics.

* * *

GOLDMAN, Jacquelin (Roberta) 1934-

PERSONAL: Born April 26, 1934, in Ocala, Fla.; daughter of Leon and Mildred B. Goldman. *Education:* University of Florida, B.A. (with honors), 1956; University of Illinois, M.A., 1959, Ph.D., 1962. *Office:* Department of Clinical Psychology, Miller Health Center, University of Florida, Gainesville, Fla. 32610.

CAREER: University of Florida, Gainesville, assistant professor, 1961-69, associate professor, 1969-76, professor of clinical psychology, 1976—. Certified by American Board of Professional Psychology (Clinical). President of Florida Board of Examiners of Psychology, 1977; member of psychology advisory board of Florida Office of Vocational Rehabilitation. Member of Alacaua Conservation Council. *Member:* American Psychological Association, Society for Research in Child Development, American Academy of Psychotherapists, Southeastern Psychological Association, Florida Psychological Association, Phi Beta Kappa, Sigma Xi. *Awards, honors:* U.S. Public Health Service grant, 1956.

WRITINGS: Becoming a Psychotherapist, C. C Thomas, 1976. Contributor to psychology journals.

WORK IN PROGRESS: Psychotherapy research.

SIDELIGHTS: Goldman told *CA:* "I have always found people and their lives a source of interest and wonder. Two of my major interests have been writing and being with people. I am intrigued by how people develop meaning in their lives, the spirit and the mechanics by which this is done. I spend a good bit of my life trying to gratify this curiosity in both general and specific cases."

* * *

GOLDMAN, Martin (Raymond Rubin) 1920-

PERSONAL: Born October 3, 1920, in New York, N.Y.; son of David (a merchant) and Rose (Arkin) Rubin; married Marian Beatrice Gordon (an editor and writer), March 30, 1947; children: Susanna Linda. *Education:* New York University, B.A. (summa cum laude), 1942; Harvard University, M.A., 1947; graduate study at St. Antony's College, Oxford, 1954-56. *Politics:* Democratic. *Religion:* Jewish. *Home:* 144 East 84th St., New York, N.Y. 10028. *Office: Time* Magazine, Rockefeller Center, New York, N.Y. 10020.

CAREER: Air University, Research Studies Institute, Montgomery, Ala., research historian, 1949-57; New York University, New York City, lecturer in history, 1960-61; *Encyclopedia International,* New York City, associate editor, 1961-62; *Look* magazine, New York City, assistant managing editor, 1967-68, managing editor, 1968-71; *Intellectual Digest,* New York City, editor, 1971-74; *Time* magazine, New York City, senior editor, 1974—. Consultant, Modern Language Association of America, 1975, National Endowment for the Humanities, 1976—. *Military service:* U.S. Army Air Forces, 1942-45. *Member:* American Historical Association, American Society of Magazine Editors, Phi Beta Kappa. *Awards, honors:* Social Science Research Council grant, 1958-60.

WRITINGS: (With others) *Army Air Forces in World War II,* University of Chicago Press, seven volumes, 1948-58.

* * *

GOLDSTEIN, Leon J. 1927-

PERSONAL: Born February 6, 1927, in Brooklyn, N.Y.; son of Irving and Ida (Blechman) Goldstein; married Claire R. Kelman, October 24, 1964; children: Adina T., Daniel I. *Education:* Brooklyn College (now of the City University of New York), B.A., 1949; Yale University, M.A., 1950, Ph.D., 1954. *Home:* 11 Oak St., Binghamton, N.Y. 13905. *Office:* Department of Philosophy, State University of New York at Binghamton, Binghamton, N.Y. 13901.

CAREER: Brandeis University, Waltham, Mass., instructor in philosophy, 1955-57; University of Maryland, College Park, lecturer in philosophy, 1958; City College of the City University of New York, New York, N.Y., lecturer in philosophy, 1959-63; State University of New York at Binghamton, associate professor, 1963-66, professor of philosophy, 1966—. Researcher for American Jewish Committee, 1958-63. Educational vice-president at Hillel Academy of Broome County, 1975 (chairman of board of directors, 1970—). *Member:* American Philosophical Association, American Anthropological Association.

WRITINGS: (With Lucy S. Dawidowicz) *Politics in a Pluralist Democracy,* Institute of Human Relations Press, 1963; *Historical Knowing,* University of Texas Press, 1976. Contributor of about thirty-five articles to professional journals. Member of editorial board and chairman of executive committee for the Americas of *International Studies in Philosophy.*

WORK IN PROGRESS: Research on "the logic of concepts having inexpungible tensions, and on the prospects of an hermeneutical theory of perception."

* * *

GOLDSTEIN, Ruth Tessler 1924-

PERSONAL: Born October 12, 1924, in Philadelphia, Pa.; daughter of Abraham and Mary (Kramen) Tessler; married Abraham S. Goldstein (a professor of law), August 31, 1947; children: William, Marianne. *Education:* Student at Hunter College (now of the City University of New York), 1942-43, and New School for Social Research, 1944-45; Southern Connecticut State College, B.S., 1961. *Politics:* Democrat. *Religion:* Jewish. *Home:* 545 Ellsworth Ave., New Haven, Conn. 06511. *Agent:* Georges Borchardt, 145 East 52nd St., New York, N.Y. 10022.

CAREER: Park East (magazine), New York, N.Y., editor, 1946-47; Economic Cooperation Administration, Washington, D.C., administrative assistant in technical assistance program, 1950-51; high school teacher of English and history in New Haven, Conn., 1969-75; writer, 1975—. Student teaching supervisor at Yale University, 1973, 1974. Member of board of directors of local Travelers Aid Society and Family Service Agency. *Member:* Authors Guild of Authors League of America.

WRITINGS: The Heart Is Half a Prophet (novel), Macmillan, 1976.

WORK IN PROGRESS: Another novel.

SIDELIGHTS: Ruth Goldstein told *CA:* "While my writing explores a number of themes—conflict between the higher and lower self, faith as opposed to skepticism, spiritualism and rationalism, my ultimate concern has been to foster understanding of the pathos of human imperfection and to help us feel compassion for each other.'' She has traveled in all of western Europe and in Latin America and has lived in England and Israel.

AVOCATIONAL INTERESTS: Painting in oils.

* * *

GOLSON, G. Barry 1944-

PERSONAL: Born December 12, 1944, in Lynn, Mass.; son of George A. (an engineer) and Beverly (Barry) Golson; married Cynthia MacKenzie (a hospital employee), August 24, 1968. *Education:* Yale University, B.A., 1967; Stanford University, graduate study, 1967-68. *Home:* 2650 Lakeview, Chicago, Ill. 60657. *Office: Playboy,* 919 North Michigan Ave., Chicago, Ill. 60611.

CAREER: Atlas, New York, N.Y., managing editor and columnist, 1969-71; free-lance writer in Connecticut, 1971-72; *Playboy,* Chicago, Ill., assistant managing editor and editor of "Playboy Interview," 1972—. *Awards, honors:* First prize for satire in *Playboy* writers' awards, 1972.

WRITINGS: (Contributor) *Is Nothing Sacred?,* Playboy Press, 1973.

SIDELIGHTS: Golson's interview subjects have included John Dean, Mel Brooks, Erica Jong, Jimmy Hoffa, Jerry Brown, and Jimmy Carter.

* * *

GOMPERTZ, Rolf 1927-

PERSONAL: Born December 29, 1927, in Krefeld, Germany; son of Oscar (a business executive) and Selma (Selle) Herrmann; married Carol Brown (a teaching assistant), April 28, 1957; children: Ron, Nancy, Philip. *Education:* University of California at Los Angeles, B.A., 1951, M.A., 1953. *Politics:* Democrat. *Religion:* Jewish. *Home:* 6516 Ben Avenue, North Hollywood, Calif. 91606. *Office:* NBC, 3000 W. Alameda Ave., Burbank, Calif. 91523.

CAREER: Torrance Press, Torrance, Calif., editor, 1953-57; National Broadcasting Co. (NBC), Burbank, Calif., publicist, 1957—; University of California at Los Angeles, instructor in media, 1974—. *Military service:* U.S. Army, Quartermaster Intelligence, 1946-48. *Member:* Writers Guild of America, Publicists Guild of America, Public Relations Society of America, International Association of Business Communicators, Southern California Business Communicators, Phi Beta Kappa.

WRITINGS: (Contributor) A. H. Hoffnung, editor, *For Love of Torah,* Jonathan David, 1970; *My Jewish Brother Jesus,* WorDoctor Publications (N. Hollywood, Calif.), 1977; *Publicity Handbook for Radio and Television,* Tab Books, 1977. Author with Mel Epstein of documentary film "The Spark"; author of forty-eight radio dramas for "Heartbeat Theater." Contributor to *Jewish Spectator* and other periodicals.

WORK IN PROGRESS: Sparks of Spirit, a "spiritual first-aid kit for modern man"; *If the Messiah Came,* five short stories; *Moments of Truth,* a collection of daily reflections; and a motion picture script, tentatively titled "Messiah," from *My Jewish Brother Jesus.*

SIDELIGHTS: "I consider myself a writer," Gompertz told *CA,* "and, as such, believe in being able to handle various forms and various subjects, including commercial needs, journalistic assignments, public relations writing, and literary work. My love, obviously, is 'soul' writing. In this respect, I have been intrigued with the messianic theme since college days. Virtually all my serious writing deals with this.''

* * *

GONZALEZ-GERTH, Miguel 1926-

PERSONAL: Born August 15, 1926, in Mexico; son of Miguel S. (an Army officer) and Claire Esther (Gerth) Gonzlez; married Betty Jo Brumbalow, September 1, 1956. *Education:* University of Texas, B.A., 1950, M.A., 1955; Princeton University, M.A., 1960, Ph.D., 1973. *Religion:* Christian. *Home:* 4109 Avenue G, Austin, Tex. 78751. *Office:* Department of Spanish, University of Texas, Austin, Tex. 78712.

CAREER: Spanish and French teacher in Lawrenceville, N.J., 1956-58; Bryn Mawr College, Bryn Mawr, Pa., instructor in Spanish, 1959-64; Swarthmore College, Swarthmore, Pa., lecturer in Spanish, 1964-65; University of Texas, Austin, assistant professor, 1965-72, associate professor of Spanish, 1972—. Member of board of trustees of Central Texas Area Museum; member of board of directors of Austin Symphony Orchestra Society; member of International Institute in Spain. *Member:* Modern Language Association of America, American Association of Teachers of Spanish and Portuguese, Austin Poetry Society, Hyde Park Neighborhood Association (founding member).

WRITINGS: Desert Sequence and Other Poems, Nonpareil Press, 1956; *The Infinite Absence* (poems), Stonewall Press, 1964, bilingual edition, University of Texas, 1976; *En Visperas de Olvido,* Editorial Cultura, 1967; *The Musicians and Other Poems,* University of Texas, in press.

Anthologized in *Poetry at the University of Texas, Yearbook of Modern Poetry, The Face of Poetry: A Hundred One Contemporary American Poets,* and *Travois.* General editor of "Iberian Series," University of Texas Press. Contributor of articles, photographs, and reviews to literature and Hispanic studies journals. Editor of *Texas Quarterly,* 1972—.

WORK IN PROGRESS: Fluessferd: A Cosmic Poem, Dandelion, and *Western Haiku,* all books of poems; a study of Spanish writer Ramon Gomez de la Serna as a precursor of Hispanic contemporary literature; a study of narrative techniques in the short stories of Argentine writer Julio Cortazar.

SIDELIGHTS: Gonzalez-Gerth writes: "My profession is that of a teacher, which I think is based on sharing what one has learned for himself. My other work ... as free-lance writer and researcher, and as self-employed farmer, merely serves to spare me from boring idleness and a conventional social life.... I know that I am not a significant poet primarily because my 'tongue' is cracked, as a bell is cracked, by the ambivalence of two clashing languages. But it is curious as well as decisive for my work as a writer that though Spanish is my native language and my ear is better attuned to it, I first discovered literature in the English language. I suspect that, if anything, my principal contribution lies in my translations from Spanish and Spanish-American writers ... and yet there is no substitute for the satisfaction derived from the achievement of a totally and originally personal creation, such as a poem or a short story or an imaginative piece of criticism, regardless of how modest it might be.... My vocation as a naturalist has lead me to become an amateur agriculturist and ecologist. With my wife I own and supervise a six-hundred-acre working spread which includes pecan orchards, experimental pastures, and wildlife preserve. Nature has always had a decisive influence in my own writing, but perhaps even more now."

* * *

GOODRICH, Lloyd 1897-

PERSONAL: Born July 10, 1897, in Nutley, N.J.; son of Henry Wickes and Madeleine (Lloyd) Goodrich; married Edith Havens, January 12, 1924; children: David Lloyd, Madeleine Lloyd (Mrs. John J. Noble). *Education:* Attended Art Students League and National Academy of Design. *Office:* Whitney Museum of American Art, 945 Madison Ave., New York, N.Y. 10021.

CAREER: Employed by Macmillan Publishing Co., Inc., New York, N.Y., 1923-25; *Arts* (magazine), associate editor, 1925-27, European editor, 1927-28, associate editor, 1928-29, contributing editor, 1929-31; Whitney Museum of American Art, New York, N.Y., research curator, 1935-47, associate curator, 1947-48, associate director, 1948-58, director, 1958-68, advertising director, 1968—, also member of board of trustees. Member of advisory board of Carnegie Study of American Art; member of Smithsonian Art Commission; co-chairman of Joint Artists-Museums Committee; member of advisory committee for Art for the White House, 1960-63; member of New York regional committee for Public Works Art Project, 1933-34; member of New York regional board of Archives of American Art, and chairman of committee on government and art, 1948—; member of Sara Roby Foundation, 1956—; member of council of Cornell University's College of Architecture.

MEMBER: International Art Critics Association, American Academy of Arts and Sciences (fellow), Association of Art Museum Directors, Drawing Society, American Institute of Interior Designers (honorary member), American Federation of Arts (director; trustee; honorary vice-president), National Council on Arts and Government (vice-chairman, 1962—), American Art Research Council (founder; member of board of directors, 1942—), American Friends of Tate Gallery, Edward MacDowell Association (member of board of directors). *Awards, honors:* Awards from *Art in America*, 1959, and National Art Materials Trade Association, 1964; D.F.A. from Cornell College, Mount Vernon, Iowa, 1963, and Colby College, 1964; award of merit from Philadelphia Museum College of Art, 1964.

WRITINGS: Kenneth Hays Miller, Arts Publishing Corp., 1930; *H. E. Schnakenberg*, Whitney Museum of American Art, 1931; *Thomas Eakins: His Life and Work*, Whitney Museum of American Art, 1933, published as *Thomas Eakins*, AMS Press, 1970; *Winslow Homer*, Macmillan, 1944, reprinted, Whitney Museum of American Art, 1973; *American Watercolor and Winslow Homer* (monograph), Walker Art Center, 1945; *Albert P. Ryder Centenary Exhibition*, Whitney Museum of American Art, 1947; *Yasuo Kuniyoshi: Retrospective Exhibition*, Whitney Museum of American Art, 1948; *Max Weber: Retrospective Exhibition*, Macmillan, 1949; *Edward Hopper: Retrospective Exhibition*, Whitney Museum of American Art, 1950; *John Sloan*, Macmillan, 1952; (with Atsuo Imaizumi) *Kuniyoshi: Catalogue of Kuniyoshi's Posthumous Exhibition*, Bajutou Shuppan-sha, 1954; (editor) *The Museum and the Artist*, American Federation of Arts, 1958; (with John I. H. Baur) *Four American Expressionists: Doris Caesar, Chaim Gross, Karl Knaths, Abraham Rattner*, Praeger, 1959; *Albert P. Ryder*, Braziller, 1959.

Young America, 1960, Praeger, 1960; *American Art of Our Century*, Praeger, 1961 (published in England as *American Art of the Twentieth Century*, Thames & Hudson, 1962); (with Edward Bryant) *Forty Artists Under Forty from the Collection of the Whitney Museum of American Art*, Praeger, 1962; *The Drawings of Edwin Dickinson*, Yale University Press, 1963; (author of preface) Andrew Wyeth, *The Four Seasons: Paintings and Drawings*, Art in America, 1963; *Pioneers of Modern Art in America: The Decade of the Armory Show, 1910-1920*, Praeger, 1963; *Edward Hopper: Exhibition and Catalogue*, Whitney Museum of American Art, 1964; (author of foreword) John I. H. Baur, editor, *Between the Fairs: Twenty-Five Years of American Art, 1939-1964*, Praeger, 1964; *Edwin Dickinson*, Whitney Museum of American Art, 1965; *Art of the United States, 1670-1966*, Whitney Museum of American Art, 1966; *Three Centuries of American Art*, Praeger, 1966; *Raphael Soyer*, Praeger, 1967; *Sao Paulo Nine: United States of America*, Smithsonian Institution Press, 1967; *The Graphic Art of Winslow Homer*, New York Museum of Graphic Art, 1968; (with Patricia FitzGerald Mandel) *John Heliker*, Praeger, 1968; *Winslow Homer's America*, Tudor, 1969; *Five Paintings from Thomas Nast's Grand Caricature*, Swann Collection of Caricature and Cartoon, 1970; *Georgia O'Keeffe*, Praeger, 1970; *Edward Hopper*, Abrams, 1971; (editor) *Realism and Surrealism in American Art: From the Sara Roby Foundation Collection*, American Federation of Arts, 1971; *Americans: Individualists at Work*, American Federation of Arts, 1972; *Reginald Marsh*, Abrams, 1972; *The White House Gardens*, Great American Editions, 1973.

Also author of *Fifty Years of Painting by Max Weber*, 1969, and *Harold Sterner*, 197fl fifififififi fifi *Research in American Art*, 1945; contributor to *New Art in America*, 1957. Assistant art critic for *New York Times*, 1929. Chairman of editorial board of *Magazine of Art*, 1942-50; member of editorial board of *Art Bulletin*, 1946—, and *Art in America*, 1946—; member of international scientific council of *Enciclopedia dell'Arte*.*

* * *

GOODSELL, Fred Field 1880-1976

September 21, 1880—August 13, 1976; American agency executive director of foreign missions, educator, and author of books on religious subjects and missionary experiences. He died in Auburndale, Mass. Obituaries: *New York Times*, August 14, 1976. (See index for previous *CA* sketch)

* * *

GORDON, I(an) R(obert) F(raser) 1939-

PERSONAL: Born July 28, 1939, in Surrey, England; son of R. F. (a scientist) and H. M. Gordon; married Felicia Morris (a lecturer), January 30, 1965; children: Alexander Fraser, Clare Lockwood. *Education:* Queen's College, Cambridge, B.A., 1962, M.A., 1964; University of California, Los Angeles, M.A., 1964, Ph.D., 1970. *Politics:* "Democratic Socialist." *Home:* 36 Boxworth End, Swanvesey, Cambridge CB4 5RA, England.

CAREER: Cambridge College of Arts and Technology, Cambridge, England, lecturer in English literature, 1966-69; University of Western Ontario, London, assistant professor of English literature, 1969-71; Cambridge College of Arts and Technology, senior lecturer in English literature, 1971—. *Awards, honors:* Fulbright scholarship, 1962.

WRITINGS: (Editor and author of introduction) *Are These Things So? and the Great Main Answer*, Augustan Reprint Society, 1972: *A Preface to Pope*, Longman, 1976.

WORK IN PROGRESS: Research on eighteenth-century English literature—especially poetry.

AVOCATIONAL INTERESTS: Eighteenth-century landscape painting and gardening.

* * *

GORDON, Ira J(ay) 1923-

PERSONAL: Born January 15, 1923, in New York, N.Y.; son of Herman Paul and Esther (Feltenstein) Gordon; married Esther Goldberg, August 4, 1949; children: Gary David, Bonnie Debra. *Education:* City College (now of the City University of New York), B.B.A., 1943; Columbia University, M.A., 1947, Ed.D., 1950. *Religion:* Jewish. *Home:* 1600 Halifax Rd., Chapel Hill, N.C. 27514. *Office:* School of Education, University of North Carolina, Chapel Hill, N.C. 27514.

CAREER: City College (now of the City University of New York), New York City, director of Lamport House, 1946-48; Kansas State College (now University), Manhattan, assistant professor of psychology, 1948-49, associate professor of psychology and counseling, 1949-51; University of Maryland, College Park, assistant professor at Institute for Child Study, 1951-54, associate professor of psychology, 1954-56; University of Florida, Gainesville, associate professor, 1956-60, professor, 1960-71, graduate research professor of education, 1971-77, chairman of department of foundations of education, 1964-67, director of Institute for Development of Human Resources, 1966-77; University of North Carolina, Chapel Hill, Kenan Professor of Education and dean of School of Education, both 1977—. Director of University of Maryland Child Study Summer Workshop, 1956; visiting professor at University of Illinois, 1960, Rutgers University, 1962, and University of New Hampshire, 1969, 1970; visiting scholar at University of London Institute of Education, 1973-74. Member of Gainesville City Planning Board, 1972-73, 1975-77, chairman, 1976-77. Consultant to U.S. Air Force Human Resources Research Laboratories, 1952-54. *Military service:* U.S. Army, 1943-46; became second lieutenant. U.S. Army Reserve, 1946-51.

MEMBER: Association for Childhood Education International, American Psychological Association (fellow), Association for Supervision and Curriculum Development, National Association for Young Children, National Society for the Study of Education, American Educational Research Association, American Personnel and Guidance Association, Beta Gamma Sigma, Phi Delta Kappa, Kappa Delta Pi, Alpha Phi Omega.

WRITINGS: How to Be a Good Discusser (pamphlet), B'nai B'rith Youth Organization, 1951, revised edition, 1952; *The Teacher As a Guidance Worker,* Harper, 1956; *Children's Views of Themselves* (pamphlet), Association for Childhood Education International, 1959, revised edition, 1972; *Human Development: A Transactional Approach,* Harper, 1962, 3rd edition, 1975; *Changing Views of Childhood* (pamphlet), Florida Association for Supervision and Curriculum Development, 1964; (editor) *Human Development: Readings in Research,* Scott, Foresman, 1965; *Studying the Child in School,* Wiley, 1966; (with J. R. Lally) *Intellectual Stimulation for Infants and Toddlers,* Institute for the Development of Human Resources, University of Florida, 1967; (editor) *Criteria for Theories of Instruction* (pamphlet), Association for Supervision and Curriculum Development, 1968; *A Test Manual for the How I See Myself Scale* (monograph), Educational Research and Development Council, University of Florida, 1968; *Reaching the*

Child Through Parent Education: The Florida Approach (monograph), Institute for the Development of Human Resources, University of Florida, 1969.

Baby Learning Through Baby Play: A Parent's Guide for the First Two Years, St. Martin's 1970; *Parent Involvement in Compensatory Education,* University of Illinois Press, 1970; (editor) *Reading in Research in Developmental Psychology,* Scott, Foresman, 1971; *On Early Learning: The Modifiability of Human Potential* (monograph), Association for Supervision and Curriculum Development, 1971; (with B. J. Guinagh and R. E. Jester) *Child Learning Through Child Play: Learning Activities for Two- and Three-Year Olds,* St. Martin's, 1972; (editor and contributor) *Early Childhood Education: 1972 National Society for the Study of Education Yearbook,* University of Chicago Press, 1972; *The Infant Experience,* C. E. Merrill, 1975; (editor with W. F. Breivogel, and contributor) *Building Effective Home/ School Relationships,* Allyn & Bacon, 1976; (editor with Breivogel and M. L. Hanes, and contributor) *Update: The First Ten Years of Life,* Division of Continuing Education, University of Florida, 1977; *Baby to Parent, Parent to Baby: A Guide to Loving and Learning in the Child's First Year,* St. Martin's, 1978.

Contributor: *Portfolio of College Teaching Techniques,* A. C. Croft, 1951; *Changes in Teacher Education: An Appraisal,* National Commission on Teacher Education and Professional Standards, National Education Association, 1964; P. F. Regan and E. G. Pattishall, editors, *Behavioral Science Contributions to Psychiatry,* Little, Brown, 1965; W. B. Waetjen, editor, *Learning and Mental Health in the School,* Association for Supervision and Curriculum Development, 1966; M. R. Smith, editor, *Guidance-Personnel Work: Future Tense,* Bureau of Publications, Teachers College, Columbia University, 1966; Ralph Ojemann and Karen Pritchett, editors, *Giving Emphasis to Guided Learning,* Education Research Council of Greater Cleveland, 1966; J. L. Frost, editor, *Early Childhood Education Rediscovered,* Holt, 1968; *Education and the City Child: Some New Approaches,* Day Care Council of New York, 1969; E. Grotberg, editor, *Critical Issues in Research Related to Disadvantaged Children,* Educational Testing Service, 1969; N. J. Vigilante, editor, *Mathematics in Elementary Education: Selected Readings,* Macmillan, 1969; W. R. Baller, editor, *Readings in the Psychology of Human Growth and Development,* 2nd edition, Holt, 1969 (Gordon was not associated with 1st edition); I. D. Welch, F. Richards, and A. C. Richards, editors, *Education Accountability: A Humanistic Perspective,* Shield Publishing Co., 1973; E. G. Boyer, A. Simon, and G. Karafin, editors, *Measures of Maturation: An Anthology of Early Childhood Observation Instruments,* Volume II, Research for Better Schools, 1974; Frost, editor, *Understanding and Nurturing Infant Development,* Association for Childhood Education International, 1976; M. C. Day and R. K. Parker, editors, *The Preschool in Action: Exploring Early Childhood Programs,* Allyn & Bacon, 1977.

Contributor to *Encyclopedia of Education Research* and *Handbook of Research on Teaching.* Contributor of nearly a hundred articles and reviews to scholarly journals. National adviser to *Children's.*

* * *

GORDON, Lou 1917(?)-1977

1917(?)—May 24, 1977; American television commentator and newspaper columnist. Gordon was a controversial interviewer and heated arguments occasionally erupted. It was during a Gordon interview that George Romney made his politically disasterous remark about having been "brainwashed" during a visit to Vietnam. Gordon died in Bloomfield Hills, Mich. Obituaries: *New York Times*, May 25, 1977; *Time*, June 6, 1977.

* * *

GOREN, Charles H(enry) 1901-

PERSONAL: Born March 4, 1901, in Philadelphia, Pa.; son of Jacob and Rebecca Goren. *Education:* McGill University, LL.B., 1922, LL.M., 1923. *Home:* 5767 Alton Rd., Miami Beach. Fla. 33140.

CAREER: Admitted to Pennsylvania Bar, 1923; attorney in private practice in Philadelphia, Pa., beginning in 1923. Master of ceremonies and commentator on television program "Championship Bridge," 1965.

WRITINGS: Winning Bridge Made Easy: A Simplified Self-Teaching Method of Contract Bridge Combining All the Principles of the New Culbertson System with the Principal Features of the Four Aces, Telegraph Books, 1936, new edition published as *Contract Bridge Made Easy: A Self-Teacher*, Doubleday, 1948, revised edition, 1953; *Better Bridge for Better Players: The Play of the Cards*, with introduction by Ely Culbertson and foreword by George S. Kaufman, Doubleday, 1942; *The Standard Book of Bidding*, with introduction by W. Somerset Maugham, Doubleday, 1944, revised edition, 1947; *Contract Bridge in a Nutshell*, Doubleday, 1946; *Point Count Bidding in Contract Bridge*, Simon & Schuster, 1949, revised edition, 1958; (with Ralph Michaels) *The Complete Canasta*, Pellegrini & Cudahy, 1949; *Bridge Quiz Book*, Permabooks, 1949.

Canasta Up-to-Date, Permabooks, 1950; *The Fundamentals of Contract Bridge*, Permabooks, 1950; *The New Canasta and Samba: Including the New Official International Code of Laws*, Simon & Schuster, 1951; *Contract Bridge Complete* (includes *Better Bridge for Better Players* and *The Standard Book of Bidding*), Doubleday, 1951, 2nd edition published as *The New Contract Bridge Complete*, 1957, 3rd edition published as *Goren's Bridge Complete: A Major Revision of the Standard Work for All Bridge Players*, 1963, 4th edition published as *Goren's Bridge Complete*, 1971, new edition, 1973; *Contract Bridge for Beginners: A Simple, Concise Guide for the Novice, Including Point Count Bidding*, Simon & Schuster, 1953; *New Contract Bridge Complete*, Doubleday, 1957; *New Way to Better Bridge*, Simon & Schuster, 1958; *Goren Presents the Italian Bridge System*, Doubleday, 1958; *An Evening of Bridge with Charles H. Goren*, Simon & Schuster, 1959; *Charles Goren's New Contract Bridge in a Nutshell*, Doubleday, 1959, revised edition, 1972.

The Elements of Bridge, Doubleday, 1960; *Goren's Point Count System Made Easy*, Doubleday, 1960; *The Sports Illustrated Book of Bridge*, Time, Inc., 1961; *Goren's Winning Partnership Bridge*, Random House, 1961; *Goren's Hoyle Encyclopedia of Games: With Official Rules and Pointers on Play, Including the Latest Laws of Contract Bridge*, Greystone Press, 1961; *Advanced Bidding*, Doubleday, 1963; *Goren's Easy Steps to Winning Bridge*, F. Watts, 1963; *Championship Bridge*, Doubleday, 1964; (with Jack Olson) *Bridge Is My Game: Lessons of a Lifetime*, Doubleday, 1965; *Goren's Bridge Quizzes*, Doubleday, 1966; *Bridge Players Write the Funniest Letters to Charles H. Goren*, edited by Bill Adler, Doubleday, 1968; *Go with the Odds: A Guide to Successful Gambling*, Macmillan, 1969.

Charles H. Goren Presents the Precision System of Contract Bridge Bidding: Instructions for the Precision System, Bridge Hands, and Quizzers, edited by Robert B. Ewen, Doubleday, 1971; *Play Winning Bridge with Any Partner, Even a Stranger*, Cornerstone Library, 1972; *Goren on Play and Defense: All of Play—The Technique, the Logic, and the Challenge of Master Bridge*, Doubleday, 1974; *Goren Settles the Bridge Arguments*, Hart Publishing, 1974; *Goren's Modern Backgammon Complete*, Doubleday, 1974. Also author with Effie L. Long of *Your First Introduction to Bridge: Student Text for Goren Manual* published by Barclay Bridge.

Writer of "Goren on Bridge," a daily column for Chicago Tribune Syndicate and of weekly column in *Sports Illustrated*, 1944—.*

* * *

GORER, Geoffrey (Edgar) 1905-

PERSONAL: Born March 26, 1905, in London, England. *Education:* Jesus College, Cambridge, B.A. and M.A.; also studied at the Sorbonne, Paris, University of Berlin, and University of Florence. *Home:* Sunte House, Haywards Heath, Sussex RH16 1RZ, England.

CAREER: Participated in anthropological field studies in French West Africa, Dutch East Indies, and French Indo-China, 1934-36, and Sikkim, 1937; member of faculty at Yale University, New Haven, Conn., and at Institute of Human Relations; worked at British Embassy in Washington, D.C., and at British Control Commission in Germany; Columbia University, New York, N.Y., researcher in contemporary cultures, 1948-49; writer, 1950—. Conducted research on Soviet culture at Museum of Natural History, 1948-49. *Awards, honors:* Rockefeller Foundation grant.

WRITINGS: The Marquis de Sade: A Short Account of His Life and Work, Liveright, 1934 (published in England as *The Revolutionary Ideas of the Marquis de Sade*, Wishart, 1934), revised edition published as *The Life and Ideas of the Marquis de Sade*, P. Owen, 1953, Norton, 1963; *Africa Dances: A Book About West African Negroes*, Knopf, 1935, reprinted, Norton, 1962; *Nobody Talks Politics* (satire), M. Joseph, 1936; *Bali and Angkor: Or, Looking at Life and Death*, Little, Brown, 1936; *Hot Strip Tease, and Other Notes on American Culture*, Cresset, 1937; *Himalayan Village: An Account of the Lepchas of Sikkim*, M. Joseph, 1938, 2nd edition, Basic Books, 1967.

The American People: A Study in National Character, Norton, 1948, revised edition, 1964 (published in England as *The Americans: A Study in National Character*, Cresset, 1948); (with John Rickman) *The People of Great Russia: A Psychological Study*, Cresset, 1949, Chanticleer, 1950; (with Ronald Searle) *Modern Types*, Cresset, 1955; *Exploring English Character*, Criterion Books, 1955.

Death, Grief, and Mourning, Doubleday, 1965 (published in England as *Death, Grief, and Mourning in Contemporary Britain*, Cresset, 1965); *The Danger of Equality and Other Essays*, Cresset, 1966; (contributor) Charles Rycroft, editor, *Psychoanalysis Observed*, Constable, 1966, Coward, 1967; *Sex and Marriage in England Today: A Study of the Views and Experiences of the Under-Forty-Fives*, Humanities, 1971.

Also author of plays and contributor to magazines.

SIDELIGHTS: Gorer spent some of his time in the United States studying under noted anthropologists Margaret Mead and Ruth Benedict. *Avocational interests:* Farming, gardening.*

GORMLEY, Mike 1945-

PERSONAL: Born August 3, 1945, in Ottawa, Ontario, Canada; son of Paul (an author) and Caroline (Smith) Gormley; married Cathy Reid, September 21, 1969; children: Brendan Reid. *Education:* Attended Algonquin College and Northwestern University. *Office:* Phonogram, Inc., One IBM Plaza, Chicago, Ill. 60611.

CAREER/WRITINGS: Ottawa Journal, Ottawa, Ontario, reporter, 1967-68; *Detroit Free Press,* Detroit, Mich., columnist and feature writer, 1968-70; Phonogram, Inc., Chicago, Ill., director of public relations, 1970—. Contributor of music reviews to *Playboy;* has written stories syndicated by Chicago Sun-Times Syndicate. Lecturer at University of California at Los Angeles. *Member:* National Association of Recording Arts & Sciences (member of board of directors of midwest chapter), Country Music Association.

SIDELIGHTS: Gormley writes: "My main motivation is that few writers and editors have any creative initiative to find stories or recognize good stories." He travels throughout the United States, especially in New York and Los Angeles.

*   *   *

GORODETSKY, Gabriel 1945-

PERSONAL: Born May 13, 1945, in Israel; son of Leonid and Jenny (Silverman) Gorodetsky; married Susan Mary Flood (an archaeologist), February 22, 1974. *Education:* Hebrew University of Jerusalem, B.A, 1968; St. Antony's College, Oxford, Ph.D., 1974. *Home:* 51/3 Emek Refaim, Jerusalem, Israel. *Office:* Department of History, Tel-Aviv University, Tel-Aviv, Israel.

CAREER: Tel-Aviv University, Tel-Aviv, Israel, lecturer in Russian history and research fellow at Russian and East European Centre, 1974—.

WRITINGS: The Precarious Truce: Anglo-Soviet Relations, 1924-27, Cambridge University Press, 1977. Editor of "Slavic and Soviet Series," Russian and East European Centre, Tel-Aviv University. Contributor to professional journals.

WORK IN PROGRESS: Sir Stafford Cripps's Mission to Moscow, 1940-41.

*   *   *

GOTTMAN, John M(ordechai) 1942-

PERSONAL: Born April 26, 1942, in the Dominican Republic; married wife, Heidi. *Education:* Fairleigh Dickinson University, B.S. (magna cum laude), 1962; Massachusetts Institute of Technology, M.S., 1964; University of Wisconsin, Madison, M.A., 1967, Ph.D., 1971; University of Colorado, postdoctoral study, 1971-72. *Home:* 708 West John St., Champaign, Ill. 61820. *Office:* Department of Psychology, University of Illinois, 51 East Gerty Dr., Champaign, Ill. 61820.

CAREER: Fairleigh Dickinson University, Rutherford, N.J., instructor in mathematics, 1959-60; University of California, Berkeley, instructor in mathematics, 1964; Lawrence Radiation Laboratory, Berkeley, Calif., computer programmer, 1964-65; University of Wisconsin, Extension, Madison, school psychologist at Center of Community Leadership Development, 1967-68; Central University High School, investigator, 1968-69, director of high school equivalency program and counselor in vocational placement, 1969; researcher for public schools of Madison, Wis., and asso-

ciate director of Instructional Research Laboratory, 1969-71; Indiana University, Bloomington, assistant professor, 1972-74, associate professor of psychology, 1974-76; University of Illinois, Champaign, professor of psychology, 1976—. *Awards, honors:* Woodrow Wilson fellowship, 1962-63; U.S. Public Health Service grant, 1973-76.

WRITINGS (With R. Clasen) *Evaluation in Education: A Practitioner's Guide,* F. E. Peacock, 1972; (with S. R. Leiblum) *How to Do Psychotherapy and How to Evaluate It: A Manuel for Beginners,* Holt, 1974; (with G. V. Glass and V. Willson) *Design and Analysis of Time Series Experiments,* Colorado University Associated Press, 1975; (with J. Gonso, C. Notarius, and H. Markman) *A Couple's Guide to Communication,* Research Press, 1976; (contributor) A. E. Bergin and S. L. Garfield, editors, *Handbook of Psychotherapy and Behavior Change,* Wiley, 2nd edition (Gottman was not associated with first edition), in press; (contributor) T. Kratochwill, editor, *Strategies to Evaluate Change in Single Subject Research,* Academic Press, in press.

Films: Co-editor of "Otto: A Case Study in Abnormal Behavior," 1974, "Otto: From a Behavioral Perspective," 1975, "Otto: From a Psychoanalytic Perspective," 1975, "Otto: From a Social Perspective," 1975, and "Otto: From a Phenomenological Perspective," 1975. Co-author of "Marital Conflict," 1975, "Will You Be My Friend?," 1975, "Three Styles of Marital Conflict," 1976, and "Behavioral Interviewing with Couples," 1976. Contributor of articles and reviews to psychology and education journals.

*   *   *

GOUDEKET, Maurice 1889-1977

August 3, 1889—January, 1977; French man of letters and author of biography of his wife, the celebrated author, Colette. He was also author of other works. Goudeket died in Neuilly, France. Obituaries: *AB Bookman's Weekly,* May 9, 1977.

*   *   *

GOWAN, Donald E(lmer) 1929-

PERSONAL: Born January 31, 1929, in Cleghorn, Iowa; son of Elmer G. (a farm equipment dealer) and Lucile O. Gowan; married Darlene Rogers (an owner of a yarn shop), December 28, 1958; children: Douglas, Pamela. *Education:* University of South Dakota, B.A., 1951; Dubuque Theological Seminary, B.D., 1957; University of Chicago, Ph.D., 1964; Mansfield College, Oxford, postdoctoral study, 1971-72. *Home:* 4184 Timberlane Dr., Allison Park, Pa. 15101. *Office:* Department of Old Testament Studies, Pittsburgh Theological Seminary, 616 North Highland Ave., Pittsburgh, Pa. 15206.

CAREER: General Electric Co., Richland, Wash., computer programmer, 1951-54; ordained Presbyterian minister, 1957; pastor of Presbyterian church in Princeton, Iowa, 1955-59, assistant pastor in Chicago, Ill., 1959-60; North Texas State University, Denton, United Bible chairman and head of Bible department, 1962-65; Pittsburgh Theological Seminary, Pittsburgh, Pa., assistant professor, 1965-69, associate professor of Old Testament, 1969—. *Member:* Society of Biblical Literature, American Association of University Professors, American Schools of Oriental Research, Phi Beta Kappa.

WRITINGS: When Man Becomes God: Humanism and Hybris in the Old Testament (monograph), Pickwick Press, 1975; *The Triumph of Faith in Habakkuk,* John Knox, 1976;

Bridge Between the Testaments: A Reappraisal of Judaism from the Exile to the Birth of the Church (monograph), Pickwick Press, 1976. Contributor of articles and reviews to American and German theology journals.

WORK IN PROGRESS: Research for a book on the theological significance of the Babylonian exile for the Jewish people; continuing research on apocalyptic literature and the "wisdom literature" of the Old Testament.

SIDELIGHTS: Gowan comments briefly that his "major aim in writing is to make results of biblical research available to the Church in understandable and usable form." *Avocational interests:* Archaeology (participated in archaeological excavation at Ashdod, Israel, 1965, 1968).

* * *

GRAGLIA, Lino A(nthony) 1930-

PERSONAL: Born January 22, 1930, in Brooklyn, N.Y.; son of Pasquale (an insurance agent) and Antoinette (Romeo) Graglia; married F. Carolyn Pennington, July 17, 1954; children: Donna, Carol, Laura. *Education:* City College (now of the City University of New York), B.A., 1952; Columbia University, LL.B., 1954. *Residence:* Austin, Tex. *Office:* School of Law, University of Texas, Austin, Tex. 78705.

CAREER: U.S. Department of Justice, Washington, D.C., attorney, 1954-57; private law practice in Washington, D.C. and New York, N.Y., 1957-66; University of Texas, Austin, associate professor, 1966-68, professor of law, 1968-70, Rex G. Baker and Edna Heflin Baker Professor of Constitutional Law, 1970—.

WRITINGS: Disaster by Decree: The Supreme Court Decisions on Race and the Schools, Cornell University Press, 1976. Contributor to *University of Pennsylvania Law Review.*

WORK IN PROGRESS: A book on constitutional law.

SIDELIGHTS: Graglia writes: "My major scholarly interests are to de-mystify constitutional law and de-mythologize the courts, with the hope of increasing faith in and reliance on self-government and democratic decision-making." *Avocational interests:* Reading nonfiction, tennis, skiing, visiting national parks and national monuments.

* * *

GRAHAM, David (Duane) 1927-

PERSONAL: Born March 16, 1927, in Richmond, Ind.; son of Robert William (a salesman) and Helen (Snodgrass) Graham; married Lois Anne King, December 8, 1945 (divorced, March, 1955); married Alene Fields, June 29, 1955; children: James Clark, Linda Carol Graham Barnard. *Education:* Attended Coe College. *Politics:* "Non-partisan." *Religion:* Christian. *Home:* 405 Fifth Ave., Decorah, Iowa 52101. *Agent:* Ruth Hagy Brod Literary Agency, 15 Park Ave., New York, N.Y. 10016; and Jay Garon-Brooke Associates, Inc., 415 Central Park W., #17D, New York, N.Y. 10025. *Office:* 104 Washington St., Decorah, Iowa 52101.

CAREER: In radio and television broadcasting as newsman, salesman, and disc jockey, 1943-61; Pioneer Litho Co., Cedar Rapids, Iowa, salesman in office equipment, 1961-67; KHAK-Radio, Cedar Rapids, Iowa, news director and sales manager, 1967-72; Other Dimensions, Inc., Decorah, Iowa, vice-president in business, 1972-76; David Graham Associates, Decorah, Iowa, owner, 1976—. Host of "Country Music Scene" on KHAK-Radio, 1975—. *Military service:*

U.S. Army Reserve, 1953-56; became staff sergeant. *Member:* Country Music Association, Decorah Chamber of Commerce.

WRITINGS: Eternal Journey (on reincarnation), privately printed, 1964; (with Glenn McWane) *The New UFO Sightings,* Warner Paperback, 1974; *Dream Your Way to Happiness and Awareness,* Warner Paperback, 1975; *The Practical Side of Reincarnation,* Prentice-Hall, 1976; *He Walks with Me* (religious experiences of country music stars), Simon & Schuster, 1977. Author of "Country Music Scene," a column syndicated by David Graham Associates, 1975—. Contributor to magazines. Publisher of *Infinity Newsletter,* 1965-75.

WORK IN PROGRESS: Writing on country music, parapsychology and religion.

SIDELIGHTS: Graham writes that he began his metaphysical studies about thirty years ago, and they have resulted in books on reincarnation, dream interpretation, and unidentified flying objects. He is also interested in world religions, both contemporary and ancient, and in American Indians (he is an adopted member of New York's Seneca Tribe), but his overall interest is people and their motivations. He comments, however, that he is a "journalist, not a theorist."

* * *

GRAM, Moltke (Stefanus) 1938-

PERSONAL: Born April 23, 1938, in Waterloo, Iowa; son of Moltke Stefanus (a journalist) and Dorothy (a businesswoman; maiden name, Foremann) Gram. *Education:* University of Kiel, student, 1958-59; Indiana University, B.A. (summa cum laude), 1960, Ph.D., 1965; University of Heidelberg, graduate study, 1963-64. *Home:* 712 East Market St., Iowa City, Iowa 52240. *Office:* Department of Philosophy, University of Iowa, Iowa City, Iowa 52240.

CAREER: Indiana University, Bloomington, lecturer in philosophy, 1964-65; Northwestern University, Evanston, Ill., assistant professor of philosophy, 1965-69; University of Iowa, Iowa City, associate professor, 1969-76, professor of philosophy, 1976—. *Member:* American Philosophical Association. *Awards, honors:* Woodrow Wilson fellowship, 1960-61; Fulbright fellowship, 1963-64; Guggenheim fellowship, 1970-71.

WRITINGS: (Editor and contributor) *Kant: Disputed Questions,* Quadrangle, 1967; *Kant: Ontology and the A Priori,* Northwestern University Press, 1968; (contributor) Elmer Klemke, editor, *Essays on Frege,* University of Illinois Press, 1968; (contributor) Klemke, editor, *Essays on the Philosophy of G. E. Moore,* Quadrangle, 1969; (with Henry Veatch) *Philosophy and Ethics,* Encyclopaedia Britannica, 1970; (contributor) Klemke, editor, *Essays on Bertrand Russell,* University of Illinois Press, 1970; (contributor) Klemke, editor, *Essays on Wittgenstein,* University of Illinois Press, 1971; (with Klemke) *The Ontological Turn: Essays in the Philosophy of Gustav Bergmann,* University of Iowa Press, 1974; (contributor) W. H. Werkmeister, editor, *Reflections on Kant's Philosophy,* University Presses of Florida, 1975. Founder and executive editor of "Northwestern Publications in Analytic Philosophy," Northwestern University Press. Contributor of about thirty articles to scholarly journals.

WORK IN PROGRESS: Direct Realism; German Idealism; Philosophical Hermeneutics; Things in Themselves and Double Affection, a collection of essays.

SIDELIGHTS: Gram writes: "My philosophical activity

began with the study of the theory of categories as developed in part by C. I. Lewis. This led, however, to what I later considered to be an unavoidable concern with Kant's theory of categories and its classical background. And all of this finally issued in my concern with the nature and possibility of transcendental arguments in philosophy.

"But, at the same time, my work in the history of philosophy and metaphysics gave rise to a parallel concern with philosophical hermeneutics—an interest which originated some time ago when I studied with Hans-Georg Gadamer in Heidelberg. My work with philosophical texts thus led to the epistemological assumptions of our ability to interpret any historical document, the nature and validity of the kinds of evidence which can be adduced to support the adequacy of an interpretation, and whether these assumptions can be philosophically defended. This and an accompanying interest in the philosophy of perception have constituted my central research interests in the recent past."

*   *   *

GRANT, Bruce   1893-1977

April 17, 1893—April 9, 1977; American newspaperman and author of juveniles, novels, nonfiction, and historical books. He died in Winnetka, Ill. Obituaries: *New York Times,* April 10, 1977; *AB Bookman's Weekly,* May 9, 1977. (See index for previous *CA* sketch)

*   *   *

GRAUER, Ben(jamin Franklin)   1908-1977

June 2, 1908—May 31, 1977; American newsman who was for many years associated with broadcast journalism on both radio and television. He worked with such diverse radio programs as NBC "Symphony Broadcasts," "Information Please," and with Eleanor Roosevelt and Walter Winchell. He was a pioneer in television news, covering early televised Presidential elections with John Cameron Swayze. As a child, Grauer appeared as an actor in movies, vaudeville, and on Broadway. He was the author of books and was an avid rare book and stamp collector. Grauer died in New York City. Obituaries: *New York Times,* June 1, 1977; *Washington Post,* June 1, 1977; *Time,* June 13, 1977; *AB Bookman's Weekly,* June 20, 1977.

*   *   *

GRAY, Dorothy (Kamer)   1936-

PERSONAL: Born June 3, 1936, in Chicago, Ill.; daughter of Milton R. and Grace (Daley) Kamer; divorced; children: Michele, Danny, Jeremy, Timothy, Matthew, Teddy. *Education:* University of California, Berkeley, B.A., 1957; Loyola University, Los Angeles, Calif., graduate study, 1962-65; University of Santa Clara, further graduate study. *Politics:* Democrat. *Religion:* Roman Catholic. *Home:* 762 Edgewood Lane, Los Altos, Calif. 94022.

CAREER: Involved in federal, state, and local political activities, 1971-73; State of California, legislative analyst, 1975—. Vice-chairman of Santa Clara County Historic Heritage Commission. Delegate to California State Democratic Central Committee, 1968, 1970. Editorial consultant to Westinghouse Learning Press, 1971-73. *Member:* Sierra Club, Commonwealth Club of San Francisco.

WRITINGS: (Contributor) *Environmental Grassroots Campaigning,* Sierra Club Books, 1975; (with Phyllis Butler) *Everywoman's Guide to Political Awareness,* Les Femmes, 1976; *Women of the West,* Les Femmes, 1976.

Author of television scripts. Guest editor of *Mademoiselle,* 1957.

WORK IN PROGRESS: How to Protect Historic Sites (tentative title), for State of California; *Yesterday's Kitchen* (tentative title), Celestial Arts.

SIDELIGHTS: Dorothy Gray comments: "History, politics, writing and law have fascinated me ever since childhood probably because my parents were interested in these things. . . . My children share in much of my work and have done a great deal in motivating me to try new fields."

BIOGRAPHICAL/CRITICAL SOURCES: California Historical Quarterly, spring, 1977.

*   *   *

GRAY, Wood   1905(?)-1977

1905(?)—June 27, 1977; American professor of history and author of *Historian's Handbook* used in more than 500 colleges and universities. He served as a major in the Air Force during World War II and was active in campus and other organizations. He was also author of other works on historical subjects. Gray died in Washington, D.C. Obituaries: *Washington Post,* June 29, 1977.

*   *   *

GRAYSON, Marion F.   1906-1976

September 1, 1906—August 28, 1976; American nursery school teacher and children's book author. She died in Washington, D.C. Obituaries: *Washington Post,* September 1, 1976. (See index for previous *CA* sketch)

*   *   *

GREEN, Lawrence W(inter)   1940-

PERSONAL: Born September 16, 1940, in Bell, Calif.; son of Clifton Lawrence and Ora Elizabeth (Winter) Green; married Patricia Fahey (in adult education), June 10, 1962; children: Beth, Jennifer. *Education:* University of California, Berkeley, B.S., 1962, M.P.H., 1966, D.P.H., 1968. *Home:* 2400 Everton Rd., Baltimore, Md. 21209. *Office:* School of Hygiene and Public Health, Johns Hopkins University, 615 North Wolfe St., Baltimore, Md. 21205.

CAREER: Ford Foundation, Dacca, Bangladesh, training associate, 1963-65; University of California, Berkeley, lecturer in health education, 1968-70; Johns Hopkins University, Baltimore, Md., assistant professor, 1970-72, associate professor, 1972-77, professor of health education, 1977—, head of Health Education Division, 1972—, assistant dean of School of Hygiene and Public Health, 1975-76. Founding member of Pregnancy Testing and Counseling Center and Family Planning Training Institute of Planned Parenthood Association of Maryland, 1972-74; member of expert panel on consumer health education of National Institutes of Health, 1975-76; member of advisory committee on planning of National Center for Health Education, 1975; consultant to World Health Organization, National Center for Health Services Research, National Heart, Lung, and Blood Institute, and Arthur D. Little Co. *Military service:* U.S. Public Health Service, 1962.

MEMBER: International Union for Health Education, American Public Health Association (member of governing council, 1974-76), Society for Public Health Education (chairman of research and studies committee and monograph committee), American Sociological Association, Population Association of America. *Awards, honors:* Beryl J. Roberts

Award for research in health education from Society for Public Health Education, 1972, for monograph *The Dacca Family Planning Experiment.*

WRITINGS: (With Karol Jozef Krotki) *Seven Years of Clinic Experience under the "Traditional Planned Parenthood Approach" in Karachi: A Baseline for Evaluating the Next Phase of Family Planning in Pakistan,* Pakistan Institute of Development Economics, 1965; (with Krotki) *Demographic Implications of the First Six Years of Family Planning in Karachi, 1958-1964,* Pakistan Institute of Development Economics, 1966; *Status Identity and Preventive Health Behavior,* School of Public Health, University of California, Berkeley, 1970; (with Harold C. Gustafson, William Griffiths, and David Yaukey) *The Dacca Family Planning Experiment: A Comparative Evaluation of Programs Directed at Males and at Females* (monograph), School of Public Health, University of California, Berkeley, 1972; (with Carl Anderson) *Community Health,* Mosby, 1972, 3rd edition, 1977; (with Virginia Wang) *Not Forgotten But Still Poor,* University of Maryland Cooperative Extension, 1974.

Contributor to public health and other professional journals. Editor of *Health Education Monographs.* Member of editorial board of *International Journal of Health Education* and International Union for Health Education.

WORK IN PROGRESS: The Professional and Scientific Literature of Patient Education: A Guide to Information Sources, with Connie C. Kansler, publication by Gale expected in 1979; *The Professional and Scientific Literature of Community Health Education: A Guide to Information Sources,* with Kansler, Gale, 1980; research on patient education in hypertension and other chronic diseases, with a book expected to result.

SIDELIGHTS: Green writes: "The field of health education has been given considerable attention and priority in recent health policy decisions and legislative actions of the federal government. The relative paucity of scientific literature on the effectiveness of health education in relation to life-style changes such as diet, exercise, accident prevention, and smoking has made my work on evaluation of health education valuable or at least of interest to government planners, legislative analysts, hospital and health administrators, and others."

*   *   *

GREEN, Paul E(dgar)   1927-

PERSONAL: Born April 4, 1927, in Glenolden, Pa.; son of Joseph (a law book dealer) and Lucy Mae (Gordy) Green; married Elizabeth Ann Weamer; children: three. *Education:* University of Pennsylvania, A.B., 1950, A.M., 1953, Ph.D., 1961. *Office:* Department of Marketing, Wharton School, University of Pennsylvania, Philadelphia, Pa. 19104.

CAREER: Sun Oil Co., Philadelphia, Pa., statistician, 1950-53; Lukens Steel Co., Coatesville, Pa., commercial research analyst, 1953-54; University of Pennsylvania, Wharton School, Philadelphia, instructor in statistics, 1954-55; Lukens Steel Co., supervisor of operations research group and senior market analyst, 1955-58; E. I. duPont deNemours & Co., Wilmington, Del., market planning consultant, 1958-62; University of Pennsylvania, Wharton School, associate professor, 1962-65, professor, 1965-71, S. S. Kresge Professor of Marketing, 1971—. Guest lecturer at more than forty colleges and universities in the United States and abroad, including University of Delaware, Massachusetts Institute of Technology, Stanford University, University of Tel Aviv,

University of London, University of Leiden, University of Grenoble, and University of Paris. Chairman of Institute of Management Sciences' College on Marketing, 1970-71.

MEMBER: American Marketing Association (member of local executive council, 1965-67, 1968-69, and local board of directors, 1976-77), Operations Research Society of America, Institute of Management Sciences, American Statistical Association, Psychometric Society, Association of Consumer Behavior (member of advisory council, 1970-74). *Awards, honors:* Award from Alpha Kappa Psi, 1963, for "Bayesian Decision Theory in Pricing Strategy"; silver medal from J. Walter Thompson Agency, 1970, for "Advertisement Perception and Evaluation: An Application of Multidimensional Scaling"; first prize in research design competition sponsored by American Psychological Association, 1972; Parlin Award from American Marketing Association, 1977.

WRITINGS: (With Wroe Alderson) *Planning and Problem Solving in Marketing,* Irwin, 1964; (with D. S. Tull) *Research for Marketing Decisions,* Prentice-Hall, 1966, 4th edition, in press; (with P. T. FitzRoy and P. J. Robinson) *Experiments on the Value of Information in Simulated Marketing Environments* (monograph), Allyn & Bacon, 1967; (with R. E. Frank) *A Manager's Guide to Marketing Research: Survey of Recent Developments,* Wiley, 1967; (with Frank) *Quantitative Methods in Marketing Analysis,* Prentice-Hall, 1967; (with F. J. Carmone) *Multidimensional Scaling and Related Techniques in Marketing Analysis,* Allyn & Bacon, 1970; (with V. R. Rao) *Applied Multidimensional Scaling,* Holt, 1972; (with Yoram Wind) *Multi-Attribute Decisions in Marketing,* Holt, 1973; *Mathematical Tools for Applied Multivariate Analysis,* Academic Press, 1976; *Analyzing Multivariate Data,* Dryden, 1978.

Contributor: Wroe Alderson and Stanley Shapiro, editors, *Marketing and the Computer,* Prentice-Hall, 1963; Alderson, Shapiro, and Cox, editors, *Theory in Marketing,* Irwin, 1964; Peter Langhoff, editor, *Models, Measurement, and Marketing,* Prentice-Hall, 1964; Michael Halbert, editor, *The Nature and Sources of Marketing Theory,* McGraw, 1965; Patrick Robinson, editor, *Promotional Decision-Making: Practice and Theory,* McGraw, 1965; J. W. Newman, editor, *On Knowing the Consumer,* Wiley, 1966; George Fisk, editor, *The Psychology of Management Decision,* C.W.K. Gleerup, 1967; Frank Bass, Charles King, and Edgar Pessemier, editors, *Applications of the Sciences in Marketing,* Wiley, 1967; P. J. Robinson and C. L. Hinkle, editors, *Sales Promotion Analysis: Some Applications of Quantitative Techniques,* Allyn & Bacon, 1967; Almarin Phillips, editor, *Pricing Theories, and Policies,* University of Pennsylvania Press, 1968; Montrose Sommers and Jerome Kernan, editors, *Explorations in Consumer Behavior,* University of Texas Press, 1968; Irving Crespi, editor, *Attitude Research on the Rocks,* American Marketing Association, 1968; Fisk, editor, *Essays in Marketing Theory,* Allyn & Bacon, 1971; King, editor, *Attitude Research Reaches New Heights,* American Marketing Association, 1971; R. N. Shepard, A. Romney and Sara Nerlove, editors, *Multidimensional Scaling,* Academic Press, 1972; W. D. Wells, editor, *Life Styles and Psychoanalysis,* American Marketing Association, 1973; *Studies in Multiple Criterion Decision Making,* University of South Carolina Press, 1973; J. N Sheth, editor, *Multivariate Procedures in Marketing,* American Marketing Association, 1975; Sheth, editor, *Research for Marketing,* J.A.I. Press, 1977; Yoram Wind and Marshall Greenberg, editors, *Moving Ahead with Attitude Research,* American Marketing Association, 1977.

Co-editor of a marketing series, Holt, 1967—. Contributor to *Handbook of Marketing Management, Handbook of Marketing Research,* and *Marketing Handbook.* Contributor of more than a hundred articles to technical journals. Member of editorial board of *Journal of Marketing Research,* 1965—, *Journal of Consumer Research,* 1973—, and *Journal of Business Research,* 1973—; referee for *Psychometrika, Journal of the Operations Research Society* and *Management Science,* 1967-69, 1970-71, 1973-74.

WORK IN PROGRESS: Research on multiattribute choice theory in marketing.

* * *

GREENBERG, Bernard 1922-

PERSONAL: Born April 24, 1922, in New York, N.Y.; son of Isidore (a laundryman) and Rose (Gordon) Greenberg; married Barbara M. Dickler (a family therapist), September 1, 1949; children: Gary, Linda, Deborah, Daniel. *Education:* Brooklyn College (now of the City University of New York), B.A., 1944; University of Kansas, M.A., 1951, Ph.D., 1954. *Home:* 1463 East 55th Pl., Chicago, Ill. 60637. *Office:* Department of Biological Sciences, University of Illinois at Chicago Circle, Chicago, Ill. 60680.

CAREER: University of Illinois, Medical Center, Chicago, assistant professor, 1954-60, associate professor, 1960-66, professor of biological sciences, 1966—; University of Illinois at Chicago Circle, Chicago, professor of biological sciences, 1966—. Visiting scientist at Istituto Superiore di Sanita (Rome), 1960-61, 1967-68, and Instituto de Salubridad y Enfermedades Tropicales (Mexico City), 1962, 1963; lecturer in the United States, Rome, Madrid, Ankara, Moscow, and London; consultant to business and government. *Military service:* U.S. Army Air Forces, radio operator, 1944-46; served in Pacific theater.

MEMBER: International Bee Association, American Association for the Advancement of Science (fellow), American Association of University Professors (local president, 1965-66), Entomological Society of America, American Institute for Biological Sciences, Scientists' Institute for Public Information, Sigma Xi (local president, 1966-67). *Awards, honors:* National Science Foundation grants, 1959, 1960; U.S. Public Health Service grants, 1960-63, 1963-67; grants from U.S. Army Medical Research and Development Command, 1966-68, 1969-72; Fulbright-Hays research fellowship for study in Rome, Italy, 1967-68.

WRITINGS: Flies and Disease, Princeton University Press, Volume I: *Classification and Biotic Associations,* 1971, Volume II: *Biology and Disease Transmission,* 1973. Contributor of about sixty-five articles to scientific journals and popular magazines, including *Scientific American.*

WORK IN PROGRESS: Research on environmental entomology, especially the possible biological hazards of extremely high voltage transmission lines and other aspects of extremely low frequency fields.

SIDELIGHTS: Greenberg writes: "I do not know the origin of my interest in natural history. It was already there at age eight, growing up in a part of Brooklyn that was essentially a cement desert. But the empty lots had white butterflies and grasshoppers and that was enough for me. Doing battle with midges for harassed Chicagoans taught me quickly the illusory victory of chemicals and led me to make recommendations for the use of biological control—in this case, the introduction of a red, white and blue carp to coincide with the Bicentennial. In addition to environmental is-

sues is my continuing interest in insects as spreaders of disease. This is not too relevant in this country with its excellent sanitation and food processing. It's quite another story in the Third World, which is the main reason I spent two years in Italy and several summers in Mexico doing field and laboratory studies. These sojourns, shared by my family, were a source of great cultural enrichment for each of us. They also provided me with a rare opportunity to cultivate an interest in antiquities and folk art, while polishing up Italian, Spanish, or French. The results of our many forays into little frequented regions adorn the walls and every nook and cranny of our home. We are now incurable collectors of pre-Columbian, Etruscan, New Guinea, and other artifacts."

* * *

GREENBERG, Eliezer 1897(?)-1977

1897(?)—June 2, 1977; Russian-born poet, essayist. He was translator and editor of Yiddish literature and was dedicated to bringing Yiddish literature to English readers. He died in New York City. Obituaries: *New York Times,* June 6, 1977.

* * *

GREENBERG, Paul 1937-

PERSONAL: Born January 21, 1937, in Shreveport, La.; son of Ben and Sara (Ackerman) Greenberg; married Carolyn Levy, December 6, 1964; children: Daniel, Ruth Elizabeth. *Education:* University of Missouri, B.A., 1958, M.A., 1959; Columbia University, graduate study, 1960-62. *Politics:* Republican. *Religion:* Jewish. *Home:* 2406 West 39th St., Pine Bluff, Ark. 71601. *Office:* 300 Beech St., Pine Bluff, Ark. 71601.

CAREER/WRITINGS: Hunter College of the City University of New York, New York City, lecturer in American history, 1962; *Pine Bluff Commercial,* Pine Bluff, Ark., editorial page editor, 1962-66; *Chicago Daily News,* Chicago, Ill., editorial writer, 1966-67; *Pine Bluff Commercial,* editorial page editor, 1967—. Columnist, 1970—. *Military service:* U.S. Army; became captain. *Awards, honors:* Grenville Clark award for best editorial, 1964; National Newspaper Association award, 1968; Pulitzer Prize for editorial writing, 1969.

* * *

GREENEBAUM, Louise G(uggenheim) 1919-

PERSONAL: Born March 25, 1919, in Chicago, Ill.; daughter of Milton S. (a business executive) and Sylvia (Bender) Guggenheim; married John N. Greenebaum (an insurance executive), September 7, 1944; children: John Richard, Jill S. *Education:* Wellesley College, B.A., 1941. *Politics:* "Independent leaning Republican." *Religion:* Jewish. *Home:* 1410 Glencoe Ave., Highland Park, Ill. 60035.

CAREER: Velsicol Corp., Chicago, Ill., secretary and purchasing agent, 1941-47; writer, 1968—. Member of Highland Park Plan Commission, 1968-71, on City Council, 1971—. *Member:* League of Women Voters (Highland Park; member of board of directors and vice-president, 1960-66).

WRITINGS: Looking Forward to a Career: Electronics (juvenile), Dillon, 1975. Contributor to engineering journals, women's magazines, trade journals, *National Informer,* and local newspapers.

WORK IN PROGRESS: Contributions of Women in Politics, for children, including biographies of Jeannette Rankin, Margaret Chase Smith, Clare Booth Luce, Martha Griffiths,

Ella Grasso, and Barbara Jordan, for Dillon; a similar book on women lawyers.

SIDELIGHTS: Louise Greenebaum writes: "Ten years ago, I found myself answering an ad from a free-lance writer who needed a helper. Soon I found myself doing research, outlining, and pre-writing for a top writer of articles and fiction. I learned by doing with the help of his valuable advice, until I felt qualified to try on my own. Though I did attend a writer's workshop one season, I think learning by working for a professional writer and constant reading were my most valuable activities. . . . I hope when I leave [public] office to devote more time to pursuing a writing career—maybe combining my interest in politics and writing in a fiction or non-fiction book for adults."

AVOCATIONAL INTERESTS: Social activities, bridge, tennis, golf, exercise, bicycling, the outdoors.

*   *   *

GREENLAW, Jean-Pierre 1910-

PERSONAL: Born October 24, 1910, in Paris, France; son of Joseph John (a necktie designer and manufacturer) and Leonie (a mystic; maiden name, Michon) Greenlaw; married Dorothy Vernon Pym (a nurse), August 18, 1959; children: Marcus Joseph. *Education:* Attended Imperial Service College (England); attended Dominican Theological College, Paris and Toulouse, France, 1951-54; also studied in Florence, Italy, and in the Sudan. *Politics:* "Undecided—see both sides—just to left of centre; vote Conservative." *Religion:* Roman Catholic. *Home:* White Cottage, 37 Manor Rd., Henley-on-Thames, England. *Office:* Oratory School, Woodcote, Reading, England.

CAREER: In banking and commerce in London, England, 1927-36; Sudan Government, Institute of Education, Bakht er Ruda, El Dueim, handcraft officer-inspector, 1936-51; Gordon Memorial College, Khartoum, Sudan, founder and principal of School of Design, 1946-57; Higher Teacher-Training College, Bauchi, Northern Nigeria, education officer in art, 1956-64; teacher of art and art history in British schools, 1964-67; now employed by Oratory School, Reading, England, 1967—. Involved in Baudii training for Nigerian Government, 1956-61. Consultant to UNESCO. *Military service:* Sudan Government Volunteers, 1940-43. *Member:* International Society for Education through Art, Independent Schools Art and Design Association, Newman Association.

WRITINGS: Drawing Handwork and Design: A Scheme of Work for Training Hand and Eye in Constructive and Expressive Activities for Primary Schools in Developing Countries, Thomas Nelson, 1965; *The Coral Buildings of Suakin* (self-illustrated), Oriel Press, 1976. Also author of textbooks in Arabic. Author of scripts for art broadcasts in Nigeria and Sudan. Contributor to *Liturgical Arts.*

WORK IN PROGRESS: Creative Symbolism, on "comparative religious symbolism with a view to practical teaching"; two more books on Suakin and scale models of buildings; writing and lecturing on art, philosophy, theology, and comparative mysticism; forming a school for creative symbolism under the aegis of the Oratory School.

SIDELIGHTS: Greenlaw writes that he is "aware of a decline in spiritual values, loss of insight into the meaning of things in the West as distinct from Islam and pagan Africa. I am seeking to revive an authoritative symposium to create a respect for the sacredness of nature and art through symbolic thinking which I teach in part in school, but specifically to adults in summer courses at the Oratory. I believe this to be impossible outside orthodox Christianity which is about to see a great renewal on a world scale."

*   *   *

GREENLEE, James W(allace) 1933-

PERSONAL: Born November 25, 1933, in Chicago, Ill.; son of Robert P. (an electrician) and Eleanor (Burbank) Greenlee; married Nancy Pool (a teacher), June 8, 1955; children: Edward, Andrew, Kenneth, Aaron. *Education:* University of Illinois, B.A., 1956, M.A., 1962, Ph.D., 1967. *Politics:* Democrat. *Home:* 302 West Alden Pl., DeKalb, Ill. 60115. *Office:* Department of Foreign Languages and Literatures, Northern Illinois University, DeKalb, Ill. 60115.

CAREER: High school teacher of French in Miranda, Calif., 1959-60; University of Illinois, Urbana, instructor in French, 1965-66; California Institute of Technology, Pasadena, instructor, 1966, assistant professor of French, 1966-73; Northern Illinois University, DeKalb, associate professor of French, 1973—. Member of DeKalb County Democratic Party's central committee and precinct committeeman. *Military service:* U.S. Army, counter-intelligence agent, 1956-59; served in France.

MEMBER: Modern Language Association of America, American Association of Teachers of French. *Awards, honors:* Fulbright grant for research at Institut de Professeurs de Francais a l'Etranger, 1962-63; Mellon Fund grant, 1968; Old Dominion Fund grant, summer, 1968; National Endowment for the Humanities grant, 1970-71.

WRITINGS: Malraux's Heroes and History, Northern Illinois University Press, 1975. Contributor to language and literature journals.

WORK IN PROGRESS: Research for *Prisoners of History,* "a study of the relation between narrative and an author's philosophy of history," completion expected in 1979.

SIDELIGHTS: Greenlee writes: "I am particularly interested in investigating the individual's role in history. My first book treated Malraux's attempts to make history a surrogate religion. My next book will treat the philosophies of history that underlie French novels about World War II. I am an acknowledged Francophile, spend as much time as possible in Paris."

*   *   *

GREENLEE, Sam 1930-

PERSONAL: Born July 13, 1930, in Chicago, Ill.; married, wife's name Nienke. *Education:* University of Wisconsin, B.S., 1952; graduate study at University of Chicago, 1954-57, and University of Salonica, 1963-64. *Home:* 6240 South Champlain Ave., Chicago, Ill. 60637.

CAREER: U.S. Information Agency, Washington, D.C., foreign service officer in Iraq, Pakistan, Indonesia, and Greece, 1957-65; L.M.O.C., deputy director, 1965-69. *Military service:* U.S. Army, Infantry, 1952-54; became first lieutenant. *Awards, honors:* Meritorious service award from U.S. Information Agency; *The Spook Who Sat by the Door* was co-winner of *London Sunday Times* book of the year award, 1969.

WRITINGS: The Spook Who Sat by the Door (novel), Baron, 1969; *Blues for an African Princess* (poems), Third World Press, 1971. Also author of *Baghdad Blues* (novel), published by Bantam. Contributor of articles and stories to magazines and newspapers.

SIDELIGHTS: The Spook Who Sat by the Door has been made into a stage play.*

*   *   *

GREGORY, Bettina 1946-

PERSONAL: Born June 4, 1946, in New York, N.Y.; daughter of George A. (a doctor) and V. Elizabeth (Elson) Friedman; divorced, April, 1972. *Education:* Attended Smith College, 1964-65; Webber-Douglas Academy of Dramatic Art, professional acting diploma, 1968; International House School of Languages, diploma for teaching English as second language, 1969; Pierce College, Athens, Greece, B.A., 1972; attended New York University, 1973. Studied music and foreign languages privately. *Residence:* Arlington, Va. *Office:* ABC News, 1124 Connecticut Ave. N.W., Washington, D.C. 20036.

CAREER/WRITINGS: Actress in repertory companies in Swansea, Wales, 1968, in Bath and Wolverhampton, England, 1969; Texaco Oil Co., Athens, Greece, English teacher, 1970-72; WVBR-Radio, Ithaca, N.Y., reporter, film critic, and co-anchor on news show, 1973; WGBB-Radio, Freeport, Long Island, newscaster, reporter, and producer of news specials, 1973; *New York Times,* New York City, free-lance reporter for Long Island, 1973-74; Associated Press, New York City, writer on national wire, 1973-74; WCBS-Radio, New York City, free-lance reporter and anchorwoman, 1973-74; NBC-Radio, New York City, free-lance newscaster, 1974; American Broadcasting Corp., New York City, radio news correspondent, 1974-76, television news correspondent, 1976-77, military affairs correspondent, 1977—. Has appeared on public affairs programs and on ABC's "Issues and Answers" as guest reporter. Notable assignments include first network television report on incest, Patty Hearst trial, Democratic and Republican national conventions, 1976, and coverage of vice-presidential candidates during 1976 campaign. *Awards, honors:* Front Page Award by Newswomen Club of New York, 1976, for outstanding reporting.

AVOCATIONAL INTERESTS: Skiing, yoga, aviation.

*   *   *

GREGORY, Freida 1938-

PERSONAL: Born April 8, 1938, in Chattanooga, Tenn.; daughter of Duard B. and Bonnie D. Gregory; married Paul Malone, September 5, 1956 (divorced March 3, 1969); children: Renee Malone Hawxhurst, Greg. *Education:* University of Tennessee, Chattanooga, B.S., 1961; University of Tennessee, Knoxville, M.S., 1967. *Home:* 64 Versailles Apartments, 3000 Hillsboro Rd., Nashville, Tenn. 37215.

CAREER: Part-time teacher of home economics and human relations to adults and public school children in Chattanooga, Tenn., 1961-67; Chattanooga-Hamilton County Community Action Agency, Chattanooga, Tenn., child development coordinator, 1967-68; Sanderson Child Development Center, Chattanooga, Tenn., principal, 1968-72; Appalachia Educational Laboratory, Charleston, W.Va., associated educational development specialist, 1972-74; Tennessee Department of Education, Nashville, director of compensatory education program for preschool-age children, 1974-75, field supervisor of compensatory education, 1975-76; Webster's International Tutoring System, Nashville, Tenn., consultant in parent education, 1976—. Instructor at University of Tennessee, Chattanooga, 1970-72. Participant in national conferences. *Member:* Tennessee Child Development Association (president, 1972), Chatta-

nooga Area Home Economics Association (president, 1964-65).

WRITINGS: TV: The Family's School, Avatar Press, 1976. Contributor to *TV Guide.*

*   *   *

GREGORY, H(ollingsworth) F(ranklin) 1906-

PERSONAL: Born January 13, 1906, in Rockwall, Tex.; son of Louis Franklin (a clergyman) and Glennie (Hollingsworth) Gregory; married Sarah Elizabeth Kohr, June 24, 1944; children: Glennie Elizabeth, Hollingsworth Franklin, Jr. *Education:* Mississippi College, B.A., 1926; attended U.S. Air Corps Primary and Advanced Flying Schools, Air Corps Technical School, Armed Forces Staff College, Industrial College of the Armed Forces, and Strategic Intelligence School. *Religion:* Baptist. *Home:* 3108 East 58th Pl., Tulsa, Okla. 74105.

CAREER: U.S. Air Force, career officer, 1928-58, retiring as brigadier general. President and chairman of board of directors of World Resources Corp.; chairman of board of directors of Selindex, Inc.; owner and operator of How Fox George Enterprises; owner of Gregory Rice Farms and Hollingsworth Gregory Landing Strip; past assistant to chairman of board of directors of Telex Corp.; past vice-president and member of board of directors of Midwestern Instruments of Tulsa; past president of Mid-Continent Post. Past member of board of directors of Lee National Life Insurance Co.; past chairman of board of directors of Guaranty National Bank; past member of board of directors of City National Bank of Tulsa. Past member of honorary advisory council of Air Force Museum Foundation, honorary board of directors of Freedom Documents Foundations, and board of directors of Braille Technical Press; past director of Tulsa chapter of Americans for Constitutional Action; past vice-president and member of executive board of Indian Nations Council of Boy Scouts of America; member of advisory board of local Salvation Army.

MEMBER: American Defense Preparedness Association (life member), National Small Business Association (member of board of trustees; past vice-president), American Helicopter Society (honorary fellow), American Institute of Aeronautics and Astronautics (past associate fellow), Air Force Association, Air Force Academy Athletic Association, National Aeronautic Association, American Radio Relay League, Quarter Century Wireless Association, Ox5 Club of America, Automobile Club of France, Aero Club of France, Tulsa Chamber of Commerce, Tulsa Amateur Radio Club, Sons of the American Revolution (past president of local chapter), Rotary International, Masons, Shriners, Order of Daedalians, Old Old Timers Club. *Awards, honors*—Military: Legion of Merit with palm; Air Medal; Bronze Star; officer of French Legion of Honor. Other: French Medal of Aeronautics; Thurman H. Bane Award from Institute of Aeronautical Sciences, for contributions to military and commercial development of the helicopter.

WRITINGS: Anything a Horse Can Do: The Story of the Development of the Helicopter, Reynal, 1944; *The Helicopter: A Pictorial History,* A. S. Barnes, 1976. Contributor to technical and popular magazines. Editor of *Vistas in Astronautics.* Member of editorial board of American Division of Commonwealth and International Library of Science, Technology, Engineering, and Liberal Studies.

SIDELIGHTS: During his military career, Gregory conducted the evaluation tests on the Autogiro. He organized and operated the first Army Air Corps Rotary Wing School.

During World War II, some of the positions he held were assistant chief of staff for intelligence, assistant chief of staff of material, and assistant chief of staff of operations of the Seventh Air Force in the Pacific Ocean Area (Saipan, Okinawa, and Hawaii). He is former chief of reconnaissance, requirements directorate, deputy chief of staff of operations, headquarters, U.S. Air Force, and Air Force secretary of the committee for aeronautics of the research and development board, U.S. Department of Defense. He is a former air attache to France, and commanded the Air Force Office of Scientific Research.

Gregory is also the military man directly responsible for the successful development of the helicopter, and was the first man to land a helicopter on small platforms on merchant ships in harbor, sheltered waters, and open seas. With Courtland Perkins, he developed and towed the first pilotless glider stable.

AVOCATIONAL INTERESTS: Amateur radio.

* * *

GREGORY, Vahan 1927-

PERSONAL: Born September 18, 1927, in Pomton Lake, N.J.; son of Vincent and Haigouhi (Yosefian) Gregory; married Irene Rogers (a theatrical agent), January 1, 1972; children: Dorian. *Education:* Los Angeles State College, B.A., 1955. *Office:* 3017 Canfield Ave., Los Angeles, Calif. 90034.

CAREER: Sculptor and writer.

WRITINGS: Oh Boy, Here Comes Walt (novel), Ashley Books, 1975.

Plays: "An I For An I" (three-act), first produced in Los Angeles, Calif., Santa Monica Playhouse, November 6, 1970; "One Teaspoon Salt" (three-act), first produced in Los Angeles at Horseshoe Theatre, 1971; "Oh Boy, Here Comes Walt" (three-act), first produced in Los Angeles at Horseshoe Theatre, 1971.

WORK IN PROGRESS: Chords of Rain, a novel dealing with the trauma of first love; a novel about the Turkish massacre of Armenians in the early 1900's.

* * *

GRIERSON, John 1909-1977

January 2, 1909—May 20, 1977; British aviation pioneer, lecturer, and author of books on air travel, including *Challenge to the Poles* with an introduction by his close friend Charles Lindbergh. Grierson was the second pilot to fly solo from Europe to America in a flight that took more than a year to complete. He died in Washington, D.C. Obituaries: *New York Times,* May 23, 1977. (*CAP-2;* earlier sketch in *CA-19/20*)

* * *

GRIES, Tom 1923(?)-1977

1923(?)—January 3, 1977; American film writer, filmmaker and director of television specials. He received two "Emmy" awards for his television work. Gries died in Santa Monica, Calif. Obituaries: *New York Times,* January 5, 1977.

* * *

GRIFFITH, Kenneth 1921-

PERSONAL: Born October 12, 1921, in Tenby, Wales; children: David, Eva, Jonathan, Polly, Huw. *Education:* At-tended school in Wales. *Politics:* "Humanist (I suppose)." *Religion:* "Humanist (I suppose)." *Home:* 69A Portobello Rd., London W.11, England. *Office:* Tempest Films, 1-6 Falconberg Court, London W1V 5FG, England.

CAREER: Actor since 1937 (has appeared in more than a hundred films, and on television and radio programs) and documentary film maker; currently associated with Tempest Films, London, England. *Military service:* Royal Air Force; served in Canada.

WRITINGS: Thank God We Kept the Flag Flying, Viking, 1974.

Films: "The Shop at Sly Corner," 1945; "Bond Street," 1948; "High Treason," 1950; "Forbidden," 1950; "Waterfront," 1951; "Lucky Jim," 1957; "Brothers in Law," 1957; "I'm All Right Jack," 1959; "Only Two Can Play," 1961; "The Whisperers," 1961.

WORK IN PROGRESS: "The Individualists," a series of films for British Broadcasting Corp. and WGBH-Television, Boston, Mass.

SIDELIGHTS: Griffith's first documentary film, made late in the 1960's, was on the life of Cecil Rhodes. Films since then have focused on historical subjects, ranging from Napoleon to Irish patriot Michael Collins (this film is still banned from public viewing), from the American Revolution to a short film on the Black rubbish collectors of Pretoria. His particular interest is South African history, and that interest is reflected in his films. He writes that he is "particularly interested in the lessons historical events have to instruct us about present and incipient problems. I use history as a provocative warning."

AVOCATIONAL INTERESTS: British military history (owns a very large collection of material on this theme).

* * *

GRIGGS, Lee 1928-

PERSONAL: Born May 4, 1928, in Boston, Mass.; son of Northam Lee (a diplomat) and Ellen (Halliday) Griggs; married Susan Hunter, August 5, 1959 (divorced, 1963); married Jean Alice Paxson, December 9, 1967. *Education:* Yale University, B.A. (honors), 1951. *Residence:* Nairobi, Kenya. *Office:* Time-Life News Service, P.O. Box 30421, Nairobi, Kenya.

CAREER/WRITINGS: Buffalo Courier-Express, Buffalo, N.Y., reporter, 1951-53, financial editor, 1953-54; Time Inc., New York City, staff writer for *Sports Illustrated,* 1954-55, Atlanta correspondent for *Time,* 1955-58, sports editor for *Time,* 1958-59, African bureau chief for *Time,* 1959-62, North Asia bureau chief for *Time,* 1962-64, Middle East bureau chief for *Time,* 1964-68, Southeast Asia bureau chief for *Time,* 1968-70, associate editor of *Time,* 1970-72, Africa bureau chief for *Time,* 1972—. Notable assignments include coverage of the Congo Revolution, 1960, Viet Nam War, 1963-64, Middle East War, 1967, and interviews with dozens of heads of state in Asia, Africa, and the Middle East. *Member:* Overseas Press Club of America.

* * *

GROSSMAN, Gary H(oward) 1948-

PERSONAL: Born August 22, 1948, in Hudson, N.Y.; son of Stanley H. (a state civil service investigator) and Evelyn (an executive secretary; maiden name, Kusinitz) Grossman. *Education:* Emerson College, B.S., 1970; Boston University, M.S., 1975. *Agent:* (for writing) Otte Co., 9 Park St.,

Boston, Mass. 02108; (for lectures) American Program Bureau, 850 Boylston St., Chestnut Hill, Mass. 02167.

CAREER: WHUC-Radio, Hudson, N.Y., announcer, writer, and news broadcaster, 1962-67; WBZ-Television, Boston, Mass., technician, 1968-72, associate producer, film editor, and cinematographer for news program "First Person," 1972; Mass Media Sound (radio syndication company), Boston, president, 1973; writer and consultant, 1973—. Instructor at Emerson College, 1970-76. Producer-director of weekly program for Malden Cablevision, 1970-71, and of three documentary films, "There Ain't No Place to Go" (television film), 1969, "You Don't Chew Pot" (television film), 1970, and "I Hear You," 1971. Director of Massachusetts Media Films, 1970-72. *Member:* Alpha Epsilon Rho (president, 1969).

WRITINGS: Superman: Serial to Cereal (early television history), Popular Library, 1976. Author of "The Tested Tube," a weekly television column in *Real Paper,* 1976—. News stringer for United Press International and for radio stations in northeastern New York. Contributor to *Boston, Television International,* and to newspapers. Television editor for *Real Paper,* 1976—.

WORK IN PROGRESS: "The Rubicon Interval," a television science fiction series; "One Hundred Twenty Days of the Bomb," a historical teleplay on President Harry Truman's decision to use the atomic bomb.

*   *   *

GROSSMAN, Lee   1931-

PERSONAL: Born September 6, 1931, in Chicago, Ill.; son of Max and Rose (Levenson) Grossman; married Sandee Tatelbame (a teacher), December 21, 1958; children: Edward, Robert. *Education:* University of Illinois, B.S.M.E., 1953; University of Chicago, M.B.A., 1959. *Home:* 240 Sunset Dr., Wilmette, Ill. 60091.

CAREER: Ford Motor Co., Chicago, Ill., in systems and procedures, 1953-57; Associated Business Consultants, Chicago, management engineer, 1958-61; Lee Grossman Associates, Wilmette, Ill., director, 1961—. Registered professional engineer in California. Conducts seminars. *Military service:* U.S. Army, 1953-55. *Member:* American Society for Personnel Administrators, American Institute of Industrial Engineers, Chicago Organization Development Association (CODA).

WRITINGS: How to Organize a Company-Wide Cost Reduction Program, Dartnell, 1968; *The Change Agent,* American Management Associations, 1974; *Insurance Agency Work Distribution Manual,* Lee Grossman Associates, 1975; *Fat Paper: Diets for Trimming Paperwork,* McGraw, 1976. Contributor of more than a hundred business articles to magazines and professional journals.

WORK IN PROGRESS: Research on business management.

AVOCATIONAL INTERESTS: Ceramics, skiing.

*   *   *

GROSVENOR, Kali Diana   1960-

PERSONAL: Born November 27, 1960, in New York, N.Y.; daughter of Robert Strawbridge and Verta Mae (a writer; maiden name, Smart) Grosvenor. *Education:* Educated in New York, N.Y. *Home:* 311 West 97th St., New York, N.Y. 10025.

CAREER: WPBS-TV, New York City, project advisory member for "Watch Your Mouth" program, 1977—.

WRITINGS: Poems by Kali, Doubleday, 1970.

SIDELIGHTS: The poems in Kali Grosvenor's book were written when she was seven years old. One reviewer made these comments: "Kali has more to offer than exotic spelling and sad anti-white propaganda. She can write 'love is my color'—which is pure poetry; and she possesses a child's (or a poet's) freshness of vision and precision of statement."

BIOGRAPHICAL/CRITICAL SOURCES: Christian Science Monitor, November 12, 1970.

*   *   *

GROSVENOR, Melville Bell   1901-

PERSONAL: Born November 26, 1901, in Washington, D.C.; son of Gilbert Hovey (editor of *National Geographic Magazine*) and Elsie May (Bell) Grosvenor; married Helen North Rowland, January 24, 1924 (marriage ended); married Anne Elizabeth Revis, August 12, 1950; children (first marriage) Helen Rowland (Mrs. Richard D. Lemmerman), Alexander Graham Bell, Gilbert Melville; (second marriage) Edwin Stuart, Sara Anne. *Education:* U.S. Naval Academy, B.S., 1923. *Home:* 5510 Grosvenor Ln., Bethesda, Md. 20014. *Office:* National Geographic Society, 17th and M Streets N.W., Washington, D.C. 20036.

CAREER: National Geographic Magazine, Washington, D.C., assistant chief of illustrations division, 1924-35, assistant editor, 1935-51, senior assistant editor, 1951-54, associate editor, 1954-57, editor, 1957-67, editor-in-chief, 1967—, National Geographic Society, vice-president, 1954-57, president, 1957-67, chairman of board of trustees, 1967-76, chairman emeritus, 1976—. Member of Advisory Council of National Parks, Historic Sites, Buildings, and Monuments; advisory director of Riggs National Bank. Trustee, George Washington University and University of Miami. *Military service:* U.S. Navy, 1923-24; became ensign. *Member:* Association of American Geographers, American Geographical Society, National Audubon Society, American Museum of Natural History, Cruising Club of America, Telephone Pioneers of America (honorary member of Alexander Graham Bell chapter), National Press Club, Overseas Press Club, British Royal Geographic Society (fellow), New York Zoological Society, Cosmos Club, Chevy Chase Club, Metropolitan Club, Gibson Island Club, Bath Club (Miami). *Awards, honors:* Sc.D., University of Miami, 1954, University of New Brunswick, 1975; LL.D., George Washington University, 1959; Litt.D., Boston University, 1970.

WRITINGS—All published by National Geographic Society: (Editor) *Australia and New Zealand: A Selection of Descriptive Articles Which Have Appeared in Recent Years in the Pages of the National Geographic Magazine,* 1943; (author of foreword) *The National Geographic Book of Dogs,* 1958, revised edition published as *Man's Best Friend: National Geographic Book of Dogs,* 1971; (editor and author of foreword) *National Geographic Index, 1947-1963 Inclusive,* 1964; (contributor) *John Fitzgerald Kennedy: The Last Full Measure,* 1964; (author of foreword) *America's Historylands: Touring Our Landmarks of Liberty,* 1967.

Editor-in-chief: Rhys Carpenter and others, *Everyday Life in Ancient Times: Highlights of the Beginnings of Western Civilization in Mesopotamia, Egypt, and Rome,* 1961; James M. Darley, chief cartographer, *National Geographic Atlas of the World,* 1963, 3rd edition, revised, 1970; *Wondrous World of Fishes,* 1965; Merle Severy, editor, *Wild Animals of North America,* revised edition, 1967. Also associated with editorial staff of more than fifteen books published by National Geographic Society.

Contributor of numerous articles and photographs to *National Geographic Magazine*. Founding editor, *Wild Acres Weekly*.

SIDELIGHTS: Grosvenor, a descendant of two victims of the Salem witchcraft trials of 1692, and the grandson of inventor Alexander Graham Bell, was five months old when he performed his first official task for the National Geographic Society. With the guiding hand of his grandfather, Grosvenor helped set the cornerstone in Hubbard Hall of National Geographic's original headquarters. His first by-line article for the magazine resulted from his assignment to take photographs from a blimp over New York City and Washington, D.C. These were the first successfully published negative-color aerial photographs.

Later, as editor of the coffee-table classic, Grosvenor sharply increased research and exploration grants, education subsidies, and public service activities, expanded book publication of the Society, and produced the monumental *Atlas of the World*. He also made a number of printing and publication changes that improved the already high standards of the magazine's physical appearance, including the introduction of color photographs on the cover in place of the familiar gold-bordered cover. Grosvenor was the motivating force behind many of the Society's projects and expeditions, including those that planted the first U.S. flag on Mt. Everest and climbed the highest peak in Antarctica, uncovered the two-million-year-old fossil bones of manlike creatures in East Africa, reconstructed ancient civilizations in Mexico and the Near East, and pioneered underwater research in the Red Sea and the Mediterranean.

Grosvenor is a racing skipper in his own right, and has explored in the waters around Nova Scotia, from Bermuda to the Bras d'Or Lakes, and in the Gulf of St. Lawrence, as well as following in the wake of such explorers as Henry Hudson, Samuel Champlain, and Jacques Cartier.

* * *

GROSVENOR, Verta Mae 1938-

PERSONAL: Born April 4, 1938, in Fairfax, S.C.; married; children: Kali, Chandra. *Education:* Received high school education in Philadelphia, Pa. *Home:* 311 West 97th St., #2W, New York, N.Y. 10025. *Agent:* Ron Hobbs, 211 West 58th St., New York, N.Y. 10017.

CAREER: Writer. *Member:* People United to Save Humanity (PUSH).

WRITINGS: Vibration Cooking; or, The Traveling Notes of a Geechee Girl (autobiography), Doubleday, 1970; *Thursdays and Every Other Sunday Off: A Domestic Rap,* Doubleday, 1972; *Plain Brown Rapper* (poems), Doubleday, 1975.

Work is represented in several anthologies. Author of food column in *Amsterdam News* and of column in *Chicago Courier*. Contributor of articles and stories to magazines and newspapers.*

* * *

GROUT, Jack 1910-

PERSONAL: Born March 24, 1910, in Oklahoma City, Okla.; son of Herbert and Eleanor (Hickey) Grout; married wife Bonnie Ann, July 11, 1942; children: John, Veronica, Richard, Deborah, Thomas. *Home:* 5517 Ashford Rd., Dublin, Ohio 43017.

CAREER: Professional golf player and teacher; Muirfield Golf Club. Dublin, Ohio, golf teacher, 1974—. *Member:* Professional Golf Association of America (on tour 1932-47).

WRITINGS: Let Me Teach You Basic Golf, Atheneum, 1975.

* * *

GUGGENHEIMER, Richard 1906-1977

April 2, 1906—March 11, 1977; American artist, educator, and author of books on art. He held more than twenty one-man exhibitions in Paris and New York. Guggenheimer died in New York City. Obituaries: *New York Times,* March 13, 1977; *AB Bookman's Weekly,* May 9, 1977. (See index for previous *CA* sketch)

* * *

GUINTHER, John 1927-

PERSONAL: Born April 3, 1927, in Reading, Pa.; son of Earl (a bookkeeper) and Mary Guinther; married Elaine McCabe, September 3, 1954 (deceased); children: Carol. *Education:* Kutztown State College, B.S., 1948. *Home:* 2528 Lombard, Philadelphia, Pa. 19146. *Office:* 1420 Walnut St., Suite 1420, Philadelphia, Pa. 19102.

CAREER: Held various jobs ranging from raising show dogs to selling advertising; active in early civil rights movement in Washington, D.C., in late 1940's and early 1950's; active in political reform movements in Philadelphia, Pa., 1950's until 1971; full-time writer, 1971—. Co-founder of New Democratic Coalition, Philadelphia, 1968-69. Instructor in investigative journalism, Charles Morris Price School, Philadelphia, 1977—. Visiting professor at Temple University, 1974, 1976, 1977. *Awards, honors:* Robert F. Kennedy Memorial Award from Robert F. Kennedy Foundation, 1973, for best magazine article of the year on the problems of the disadvantaged American, "The Only Good Indian"; Silver Gavel Award from American Bar Association, 1974, for "Last Whole Justice Catalog," and 1976, for "How to Hide a Crime Wave"; best magazine article award from Sigma Delta Chi, 1975, for two-part study on investigative grand juries; Gerald Loeb award for distinguished writing on business and finance from Loeb Memorial Foundation, 1976, for article, "Don't Worry, It's Only Money."

WRITINGS: Moralists and Managers: Public Interest Movements in America, Doubleday, 1976. Author of documentary scripts for WCAU/CBS-Television. Contributor of more than sixty articles to magazines. Contributing editor of *Philadelphia.*

WORK IN PROGRESS: A book on the medical malpractice problem in America, publication by Doubleday expected in 1978; a television documentary script.

SIDELIGHTS: Guinther told *CA:* "I am principally an investigative reporter, specializing in politics and urban affairs and the operation of the criminal justice system."

* * *

GULLACE, Gino 1925-

PERSONAL: Born August 18, 1925, in Ferruzzano, Italy; son of Giovanni and Nicoletta (Audino) Gullace; married: Estelle Scala, September, 1950; *Education:* Messina University, Dottore in Lettere, 1946; Rochester University, M.A., 1952; Syracuse University, Ph.D., 1964. *Home:* 38 Van Ness Ct., Maplewood, N.J. 07040. *Agent:* Rizzoli Press Service, Via Civitavecchia 102, Milano, Italy. *Office:* 712 Fifth Ave., New York, N.Y. 10019.

CAREER: Foreign correspondent for Italian magazines, *Oggi, Annabella,* and *Novella 2000,* 1951—. Notable assignments include the coverage of the American space program, first heart transplant and other medical events. Teacher at Rochester University. *Member:* Overseas Press Club, Foreign Correspondents Association.

WRITINGS: I Grandi Nomi del Ventesimo Secolo (title means *The Big Names of the Twentieth Century*), De Agostini (Italy), 1973.

* * *

GUMPERTZ, Robert 1925-

PERSONAL: Born August 17, 1925, in California; son of William Herman and Blanche (Haet) Gumpertz. *Education:* California College of Arts and Crafts, B.A., 1950. *Home and office:* 214 Bulkley Ave., Sausalito, Calif. 94965.

CAREER: Writer, graphic designer, and cartoonist, 1951—. Co-founder of Opah Books (publishers), Mill Valley, Calif.

WRITINGS—All self-illustrated: *The International Dog* (cartoons), Golden Press, 1968; *Professor Twill's Travels* (children), Houghton, 1968; *Dream Notebook,* San Francisco Book Co., 1976; (with Patricia Waters) *The Sensuous Coloring Book,* Opah Books, 1977.

Author of "Seashell," a short theatrical film.

WORK IN PROGRESS: Another children's book.

* * *

HABER, Jack 1939-

PERSONAL: Born February 26, 1939, in New York, N.Y.; son of Michael H. (an accountant) and Ada (Weiss) Haber. *Education:* Attended Brooklyn College (now of the City University of New York), 1956-58. *Office:* Esquire Inc., 488 Madison Ave., New York, N.Y. 10022.

CAREER/WRITINGS: Men's Wear, New York City, associate editor, 1962-65; *Scene,* New York City, editor, 1965-68; *Clothes,* New York City, senior editor, 1968-69; *Gentlemen's Quarterly,* New York City, editor, 1969—. Instructor in men's wear store management, New York University, 1970-74. *Military service:* U.S. Army, 1958-60. *Member:* American Society of Magazine Editors. *Awards, honors:* Lulu award for excellence in men's fashion reporting, 1971 and 1972, from Men's Fashion Association/Menswear Retailers of America.

WORK IN PROGRESS: Editor of *The Gentlemen's Quarterly Handbook* (tentative title), publication by Crown expected in fall, 1977.

* * *

HACKING, Ian 1936-

PERSONAL: Born February 18, 1936, in Vancouver, British Columbia, Canada; son of H. E. and Margaret (MacDougall) Hacking; married Nancy Cartwright (a professor); children: Jane Frances, Daniel, Rachel. *Education:* University of British Columbia, B.A., 1956; Cambridge University, B.A., 1958, M.A., Ph.D., 1962. *Office:* Department of Philosophy, Stanford University, Stanford, Calif. 94305.

CAREER: Peterhouse College, Cambridge University, Cambridge, England, fellow, 1962-64; University of British Columbia, Vancouver, associate professor of philosophy, 1964-69; Cambridge University, university lecturer in philosophy and fellow of Peterhouse, both 1969-75; Stanford University, Stanford, Calif., fellow at Center for Advanced

Study in the Behavioral Sciences, 1975-76, professor of philosophy, 1976—.

WRITINGS: The Logic of Statistical Inference, Cambridge University Press, 1965; *A Concise Introduction to Logic,* Random House, 1971; *Emergence of Probability,* Cambridge University Press, 1975; *Why Does Language Matter to Philosophy?,* Cambridge University Press, 1975.

* * *

HADDAD, Robert M(itchell) 1930-

PERSONAL: Born October 1, 1930, in Brooklyn, N.Y.; son of Nadra Abdo (a poet) and Hadbo (Trabulsi) Haddad; married Helen Rogerson (an artist and writer of children's stories), March 6, 1964; children: Emily, Leila, Josette, George. *Education:* University of Pittsburgh, B.S., 1952; University of Michigan, M.A., 1954; Harvard University, Ph.D., 1965. *Religion:* Eastern Orthodox Christian. *Home:* 65 Kensington Ave., Northampton, Mass. 01060. *Office:* Department of History, Smith College, Northampton, Mass. 01063.

CAREER: Visiting lecturer in non-Western studies at Smith College, Amherst College, Mount Holyoke College, and University of Massachusetts, Boston, 1960-63; Smith College, lecturer, 1963-65, assistant professor, 1965-68, associate professor, 1968-73, professor of history and religion, 1973—.

MEMBER: Middle Eastern Studies Association of North America, American Historical Association, American Association of University Professors, Orthodox Theological Society (president, 1974-76). *Awards, honors:* Fulbright fellowship for Egypt, 1954-55; Ford Foundation fellowship for the Middle East and Europe, 1958-60; Social Science Research Council grant for the Middle East and Europe, 1966-67.

WRITINGS: Syrian Christians in Muslim Society: An Interpretation, Princeton University Press, 1970; (co-editor and contributor) *Aftermath of Empire,* Smith College, 1975.

WORK IN PROGRESS: The Melkite Schism, completion expected in 1979.

SIDELIGHTS: Haddad told *CA:* "*Syrian Christians in Muslim Society* seeks to clarify the role of the marginal Syrian Christian community in the formation, modification and destruction of the salient institutions of the politically dominant Muslim community. An analogy is drawn between Christians in Islam, and Jews in Christendom." *Avocational interests:* Carpentry.

* * *

HADDIX-KONTOS, Cecille P. 1937-
(Cecille Haddix, Cecille Kontos)

PERSONAL: Born August 25, 1937, in Hazard, Ky.; daughter of Homer A. and Una (Haddix) Pittenger; married Peter Kontos (a writer), March 9, 1957; children: David, Philip. *Education:* Ohio University, B.S.Ed., 1959. *Religion:* Methodist. *Home and office:* Rt. 9, Box 328, Old Flowery Branch Rd., Cumming, Ga. 30130.

CAREER: Teacher of English and speech in public schools in Cleveland, Ohio, 1958-61; EDR Corp. (educational research and development), editorial director and head writer of Institute for Contemporary Curriculum Development, 1967-74, vice-president, 1967—.

WRITINGS—Under name Cecille Haddix: *Who Speaks for Appalachia?,* Pocket Books, 1975.

Textbooks—all under name Cecille Kontos; all with others; all published by Cambridge Book Co.: *Patterns of Civilization: America*, 1972; *Patterns of Civilization: Europe*, 1973; *Patterns of Civilization: Asia*, 1974; *Patterns of Civilization: Africa*, 1975; *The United States: Past and Present*, 1975; *The City: Promise and Problem*, 1975.

Also author of film strips, "The Right to Joy" and "Music Everyone."

WORK IN PROGRESS: An American history text for high school; a reading program for high school; a study of Appalachia, using interviews and crafts as sources of history; *On a Galloping Horse*, a novel "on the back burner."

SIDELIGHTS: Cecille Haddix-Kontos told *CA:* "An Appalachian heritage emphasized my need to communicate and to relate the continuity of Appalachia's heritage to the present. I've always felt the need to express myself—as a writer, a dancer, an actress, and a talker! I've always liked people . . . to watch them, talk with them, and be with them. That's why it's extraordinarily difficult (though at the same time, necessary to me) to be a writer. In order to write, one must be alone. But to have anything to write about, one must seek the company of others. There's a moral here, but I haven't grasped it yet.

"I've always believed that a writer must approach any bit of writing as a work of art. Whether writing a textbook for children or a poem, a writer must pursue the highest standard of literary excellence. I like to write in those areas in which people have too often neglected this standard. A textbook should contain the same quality of writing as a first-rate novel."

AVOCATIONAL INTERESTS: Acting, sailing, and needlework.

* * *

HAGUE, Douglas Chalmers 1926-

PERSONAL: Born October 20, 1926, in Leeds, England; son of Laurence and Marion Hague; married Brenda Elizabeth Fereday, 1947; children: two daughters. *Education:* University of Birmingham. *Home:* 8 Knutsford Rd., Wilmslow, Cheshire, England.

CAREER: University of London, London, England, assistant lecturer, 1947-50, lecturer, 1950-57, reader in political economy, 1957; University of Sheffield, Sheffield, England, Newton Chambers Professor of Economics, 1957-63, head of department of business studies, 1962-63; University of Manchester, Manchester, England, professor of applied economics, 1963-65, professor of managerial economics, 1965—. Visiting professor at Duke University, 1960-61. Director of Manchester School of Management and Administration, 1964-65, and Centre for Business Research, 1964-66. Member of council of Manchester Business School, 1964—. Director of Economic Models Ltd., 1970—. Member of working party of National Advisory Council on Education for Industry and Commerce, 1962-63; member of Treasury Working Party on Management Training in the Civil Service, 1965-67; member of Northwestern Gas Board, 1966-72; British chairman of Carnegie Project on Accountability, 1968-72; member of working party of Local Government Training Board, 1969-70; joint chairman of Conference of University Management Schools, 1971-73; member of Price Commission, 1973—. *Member:* Northwest Operational Research Group (president, 1967-69), Manchester Industrial Relations Society (chairman, 1964-66).

WRITINGS: (With Peter Kenneth Newman) *Costs in Al-*

ternative Locations: The Clothing Industry, Cambridge University Press, 1952; (with Alfred William Stonier) *A Textbook of Economic Theory*, Longmans, 1953, 4th edition, 1972, 2nd edition, Wiley, 1961, 4th edition, 1973; (with Stonier) *The Essentials of Economics: An Introduction and Outline for Students and for the General Reader*, Longmans, Green, 1955; *The Economics of Manmade Fibres*, Duckworth, 1957; *The Economic Outlook: Retrospect and Prospect*, University of Sheffield, 1959.

(Editor) *Conference on Inflation, Helsingoer, Denmark, 1959*, St. Martin's, 1962; (editor with Roy Forbes Harrod) *International Trade Theory in a Developing World*, St. Martin's, 1963; (editor) *Price Formation in Various Economies*, St. Martin's, 1967; *Managerial Economics: Analysis for Business Decisions*, Wiley, 1969, revised edition, Longmans, 1971.

Pricing in Business, Allen & Unwin, 1971, Beekman, 1973; (editor with Bruce L. R. Smith) *The Dilemma of Accountability in Modern Government: Independence Versus Control*, St. Martin's, 1971; *Devaluation and Pricing Decisions*, Beekman, 1974; (editor with M. E. Beesley) *Britain in the Common Market: A New Business Opportunity*, Longman, 1974; *Public Policy and Private Interests*, Holmes & Meier, 1975. Also editor of *Stability and Progress in the World Economy*, 1958, *The Theory of Capitol*, 1961, and *Inflation*, 1962. Contributor to economics and finance journals.

AVOCATIONAL INTERESTS: Church organs, watching cricket and football.*

* * *

HAHN, Robert O(scar) 1916-

PERSONAL: Born October 1, 1916, in Utica, N.Y.; son of Oscar Paul (a metal worker) and Louise (Knaus) Hahn; married Genevieve Warren Smith (a sculptor), December 24, 1949; children: Christopher, Peter. *Education:* Hamilton College, B.S., 1934; Syracuse University, M.A., 1947; University of Southern California, Ed.D., 1957; also attended Claremont Graduate School, New School for Social Research, and Fordham University. *Religion:* Society of Friends (Quakers). *Home:* 3000 Santa Rosa, Altadena, Calif. 91001. *Office:* Department of Secondary Education, California State University, Los Angeles, Calif. 90032.

CAREER: Middlebury College, Middlebury, Vt., instructor in speech, 1940; junior high school teacher in Newburgh, N.Y., 1940-43, senior high school teacher of speech and drama, 1944-48; Antelope Valley Junior College, Lancaster, Calif., instructor in speech, drama, and psychology, 1948-54; California State University, Los Angeles, assistant professor, 1956-61, associate professor of secondary education, 1961-65, professor of community college education, 1955—, visiting lecturer in American studies, 1974—. Instructor at Los Angeles City College, 1956-74; Fulbright lecturer at University of Trujillo, 1965-66; visiting professor at Temple University, summer, 1969, and University of New Brunswick, summer, 1971. President of Theater Americana, a local community theater; has made television appearances in San Francisco and Los Angeles. *Member:* California Teachers Association, California State Employees Association, United Professors of California, Phi Delta Kappa.

WRITINGS: (With David Bidna) *Secondary Education: Origins and Directions*, Macmillan, 1965, revised edition, 1970; *Creative Teachers: Who Wants Them?*, Wiley, 1973: *Collectibles: A Versing* (poems), Pygmalion Press, 1976.

Films: "In the Marketplace," "Team-Teaching in Shakespeare," "The Mutual Assistance Program," and "The WHERACK Program in Operation at Pasadena." Contributor to education and theater journals.

WORK IN PROGRESS: Chain Around the Stone, a novel comparing Depression-era college students with Oneida Indians.

SIDELIGHTS: Some of Hahn's experiments in education include the School Without Walls program and in-residence program for disadvantaged youth, both in Pasadena, and use of the team-teaching concept at the college level. *Avocational interests:* Collecting Upton Sinclair first editions.

* * *

HAIG-BROWN, Roderick (Langmere) 1908-1976

February 21, 1908—October 9, 1976; British-born Canadian environmentalist and naturalist author of more than twenty works of fiction and nonfiction, including several on fishing. His early career included work as a logger, guide, trapper, fisherman, and farmer. Haig-Brown died in Campbell Iver, British Columbia, Canada. Obituaries: *New York Times,* October 11, 1976; *AB Bookman's Weekly,* November 15, 1976. (See index for previous *CA* sketch)

* * *

HAIR, Donald S(herman) 1937-

PERSONAL: Born November 24, 1937, in Strathroy, Ontario, Canada; married, 1966. *Education:* University of Western Ontario, B.A., 1960; University of Toronto, M.A., 1961, Ph.D., 1964. *Office:* Department of English, University of Western Ontario, London, Ontario, Canada N6A 3K7.

CAREER: University of Western Ontario, London, lecturer, 1964-65, assistant professor, 1965-69, associate professor, 1969-73, professor of English, 1973—. *Member:* Association of Canadian University Teachers of English, Humanities Association. *Awards, honors:* Canada Council fellowship, 1973-74.

WRITINGS: Browning's Experiments with Genre, University of Toronto Press, 1972.

* * *

HALBERSTAM, David 1934-

PERSONAL: Born April 10, 1934, in New York, N.Y.; son of Charles A. (a surgeon) and Blanche (a teacher; maiden name Levy) Halberstam; married Elzbieta Tchizevska (an actress), June 13, 1965. *Education:* Harvard University, A.B., 1955. *Office:* 2 Park Ave., New York, N.Y. 10016.

CAREER: West Point Daily Times Leader, West Point, Miss., reporter, 1955-56; *Nashville Tennessean,* Nashville, Tenn., reporter, 1956-60; *New York Times,* New York, N.Y., staff writer, 1960-67, foreign correspondent in Vietnam, 1962-63, and in Warsaw, Poland, 1965-66; *Harper's* magazine, New York, N.Y., contributing editor, 1967-71; author, 1971—. Fellow of Adali Stevenson Institute of International Affairs. *Awards, honors:* Page One Award from the Newspaper Guild of New York, 1962; George Polk Memorial Award, 1964; Louis M. Lyons Award, 1964; Pulitzer Prize for international reporting, 1964, for Vietnam reporting; Overseas Press Club award, 1973.

WRITINGS: The Noblest Roman (novel), Houghton, 1961; *The Making of a Quagmire,* Random House, 1965; (editor) Stephen Crane, *Great Stories of Heroism and Adventure,* Platt, 1967; *One Very Hot Day* (novel), Houghton, 1968;

The Unfinished Odyssey of Robert Kennedy, Random House, 1969; *Ho,* Random House, 1971; *The Best and the Brightest* (Book-of-the-Month Club alternate selection), Random House, 1972. Contributor of articles to magazines, including *Esquire, Atlantic Monthly, McCall's,* and *Harper's Bazaar.*

WORK IN PROGRESS: CBS: The Network and the News.

SIDELIGHTS: Halberstam's book, *The Making of a Quagmire,* was described by George Eagle as "a memorial to a small group of reporters stationed in Vietnam who bucked pressures from the White House on down to report, at a time of official optimism, that South Vietnam and the United States were losing the war."

While on assignment in Warsaw, Halberstam's forthright reporting incurred the official disapproval of the Polish Foreign Ministry, resulting in his expulsion from Poland in 1966.

AVOCATIONAL INTERESTS: Reading detective and suspense novels, watching late movies on television, fishing.

BIOGRAPHICAL/CRITICAL SOURCES: David Halberstam, *The Making of a Quagmire,* Random House, 1965; Gay Talese, *The Kingdom and the Power,* World Publishing, 1969; *Saturday Review,* April 10, 1971.*

* * *

HALDANE, R(obert) A(ylmer) 1907-

PERSONAL: Born April 6, 1907, in Camberley, England; son of M. M. (a lieutenant colonel and assistant director of British Intelligence M.I.5) and Mable Constance (Seymour) Haldane; married Eugenie Ivanoff, July 11, 1942; children: Tatiana Haldane Colgan, John Duncan. *Education:* Attended University of London, 1924-27. *Home:* 24 Jordan Lane, Edinburgh EH10 4Q2, Scotland.

CAREER: Royal Commission on the Press, London, England, second secretary, 1947-49; Nature Conservancy in Scotland, Edinburgh, administrative head, 1949-67; Secretary of State for Scotland, Edinburgh, director of public inquiries, 1967—. *Military service:* New Zealand Army, Auckland Mounted Rifles, 1931-33. British Army, intelligence officer, 1940-47, officer of the watch in Home Security War Room during World War II.

WRITINGS: Giants of the Ring: Story of the Heavyweights for Two Hundred Years, War Facts Press, 1948; *The Investors Vade Mecum,* W. Blackwood, 1962; *The Protection Afforded to Wild Life in Scotland: A Short Review,* Nature Conservancy, 1966; *Champions and Challenges: One Hundred Years of Queensberry Boxing,* S. Paul, 1967; *With Intent to Deceive: Frauds Famous and Infamous,* W. Blackwood, 1970; *Investment Trusts and Unit Trusts,* W. Blackwood, 1972; *The Hidden World: The Story of Ciphers,* R. Hale, 1976.

SIDELIGHTS: Haldane writes: "In 1929 I was given a steerage ticket to New Zealand and a one-pound note and told to be off and make my fortune, a function I have not yet fulfilled. There I did various jobs during the depression—worked as a milk hand on two farms, a bush-whacker (cutting down trees in the forest), in a gang laying a road surface, and so on.

"In a boxing contest with a professional . . . I was severely defeated and my sight, never good, was injured. . . . I obtained a job as a boxing instructor at a school, returned to Britain in 1934, found no work, went out to Australia where I also obtained a post at a school. I returned to Britain shortly before the war."

HALE, Clarence B(enjamin) 1905-

PERSONAL: Born December 25, 1905, in Lincoln, Vt.; son of Morton Wilbur (a clergyman) and Anna Mabel (Purinton) Hale; married Florence Suzanne Vouga, August 30, 1932; children: Everett Austin, Clarence Benjamin, Jr. *Education:* Wheaton College, Wheaton, Ill., B.A., 1928; University of Illinois, M.A., 1929, Ph.D., 1942; also attended University of Chicago, 1931-33. *Home:* 515 Scott St., Wheaton, Ill. 60187.

CAREER: Wheaton College, Wheaton, Ill., assistant professor, 1929-35, associate professor, 1935-46, professor of Greek and French, 1946-74, professor emeritus of Greek, 1974—, chairman of department of foreign languages, 1946-69. Teacher of Greek, Summer Institute of Linguistics of University of Texas at Arlington, 1974-77. *Member:* American Philological Association (life member), Society of Biblical Literature.

WRITINGS: *Let's Study Greek,* Wheaton College, 1957, revised edition, Moody, 1959; *Let's Read Greek,* Moody, 1968.

SIDELIGHTS: Hale's first book has been translated into Spanish. He writes that both books were designed to provide a steady flow of ideas, rather than to present isolated out-of-context Greek sentences.

* * *

HALE, Judson (Drake) 1933-

PERSONAL: Born March 16, 1933, in Boston, Mass.; son of Roger (a conservationist) and Marian (a singer; maiden name, Sagendorph) Hale; married Sally Huberlie, September 6, 1958; children: Judson, Jr., Daniel, Christopher. *Education:* Dartmouth College, A.B., 1955. *Home address:* P.O. Box 251, Dublin, N.H. 03444. *Office:* Yankee, Inc., Main St., Dublin, N.H. 03444.

CAREER: *Yankee,* Dublin, N.H., assistant editor, 1958-61, associate editor, 1961-63, managing editor, 1963-69, editor and vice president, 1969—; *Old Farmer's Almanac,* Dublin, editor and vice president, 1968—. Trustee, Monadnock Hospital; director, New Hope Center; member of corporation, MacDonell Colony; member, Corp. of the New Hampshire Network. *Military service:* U.S. Army, 1955-57; became tank commander. *Member:* Regional Publishers Association, Dublin Lake Club, Phi Kappa Psi.

WRITINGS: (Editor, with Robb Sagendorph) *That New England,* Yankee, 1967.

SIDELIGHTS: Hale told *CA:* "Insofar as *Yankee's* present success is concerned I might say that *Yankee* magazine is the expression and perhaps indirectly the preservation of that great culture in which every real Yank was born and by which every real Yank must live. In addition, it is a way Americans in every state of the Union can keep up with the status of the six state region from which they all (assuming there are no Virginians in the house) originated."

* * *

HALL, Ariel Perry 1906-

PERSONAL: Born December 31, 1906, in Attleboro, Mass.; daughter of Everett I. and Clara (Brigham) Perry; married Frederick Garrison Hall, January 2, 1942. *Education:* Smith College, A.B., 1928; Sorbonne, University of Paris, student, 1927; Curtis Institute of Music, student, 1932-35. *Home:* 50 Westwood Park Cir., Attleboro, Mass. 02703.

CAREER: Professional harpist in New York City, Boston, Mass., and San Antonio, Tex. Writer. Lecturer. *Member:* Daughters of the American Revolution (D.A.R.; regent, 1976—).

WRITINGS: *Pills to Purge the Paines of Love,* Branden Press, 1976.

WORK IN PROGRESS: Research on the social aspects of eighteenth century England.

AVOCATIONAL INTERESTS: Playing the harpsichord on a "magnificent instrument which is frequently exhibited."

* * *

HALL, Douglas John 1928-

PERSONAL: Born March 23, 1928, in Ingersoll, Ontario, Canada; son of John D. (a railway worker) and L. Irene (Sandick) Hall; married Rhoda Catherine Palfrey, May 28, 1960; children: Mary Kate, Christopher, Sara, Lucia. *Education:* University of Western Ontario, B.A., 1953; Union Theological Seminary, M.Div., 1956, S.T.M., 1957, Th.D., 1963. *Home:* 5562 Avenue Notre-Dame-de-Grace, Montreal, Quebec, Canada. *Office:* Faculty of Religious Studies, McGill University, 3520 University St., Montreal, Quebec, Canada.

CAREER: Ordained United Church of Canada minister, 1956; pastor of St. Andrew's United Church in Blind River, Ontario, 1960-62; University of Waterloo, Waterloo, Ontario, principal of St. Paul's United College, 1962-65; St. Andrew's College, Saskatoon, Saskatchewan, McDougald Professor of Systematic Theology, 1965-75; McGill University, Montreal, Quebec, associate professor of Christian theology, 1975—. Member of theological committee of North American Alliance of Reformed Churches. *Member:* Canadian Theological Society.

WRITINGS: (Editor with Samuel Terrien and others) Paul Scherer, *Love Is a Spendthrift,* Harper, 1960; *Hope Against Hope,* World Student Christian Federation, 1971; *The Reality of the Gospel and the Unreality of the Churches,* Westminster, 1975; *Lighten Our Darkness: Toward an Indigenous Theology of the Cross,* Westminster, 1976.

WORK IN PROGRESS: *Rethinking Christ: A Theology for the Post-Christian Era.*

SIDELIGHTS: Hall writes: "My primary concern is that of a Christian theologian who tries to understand the human situation in the light of the 'Gospel of the Cross.' I attempt to work out a theological posture indigenous to the North American experience."

* * *

HALL, Wilson (Dudley) 1922-

PERSONAL: Born November 5, 1922, in Champaign, Ill.; son of Clarence G. (a minister) and Marion (Hall) Hall; married Laurier K. Hall, March 17, 1969; children: Kimberley Marion, Kevan, Mercier (son). *Education:* University of Illinois, B.A., 1940; Yale University, M.F.A., 1951; post graduate study, New York University, 1951-52. *Home:* 2018 Dayton St., Silver Spring, Maryland 20902. *Office:* NBC News, National Broadcasting Co., 4001 Nebraska Ave., N.W., Washington, D.C.

CAREER: Instructor in speech at University of Illinois, Urbana, 1946-47, and at Connecticut State College (now University of Connecticut), Storrs, 1949-50; National Broadcasting Co. (NBC) News, New York, N.Y. correspondent in Korea, 1953, Middle East bureau chief, Cairo, Egypt, 1953-57, correspondent in New York City, 1957-60, Latin America bureau chief, 1960-64, correspondent in New York City, 1964-67, correspondent in Vietnam, 1967-68, Middle East bureau chief, Beirut, Lebanon, 1968-71, correspondent in New York City, 1971-74, correspondent in Washington, D.C., 1974—. *Military service:* U.S. Army, 1943-46, 1951-53; served in Korea; became first lieutenant; received Air Medal and Bronze Star. *Member:* Overseas Press Club, Sigma Delta Chi. *Awards, honors:* Overseas Press Club Award, 1967, for series on Vietnam.

WRITINGS: (Contributor) *Memo to JKF from NBC News,* Putnam, 1962. Contributor of articles to magazines, including *TV Guide, Quill,* and others.

WORK IN PROGRESS: A novel.

SIDELIGHTS: Hall told *CA:* "A foreign correspondent's life can be exciting, challenging, and even trench-coaty. Too often it is physically hazardous. Fortunately, the bad times are easier to forget than the good times.

"After reporting from forty nation's capitals, it's refreshing to be reporting from my own country's capital. After having been a participant in two wars, and having covered the wars in Korea and Vietnam, countless coups, counter coups, and under-the-counter coups, it's nice to be a peace correspondent for a change."

*   *   *

HALLETT, Garth L(ie)   1927-

PERSONAL: Born August 15, 1927, in Chester, Pa.; son of George H., Jr. (a political scientist) and Mary (a painter; maiden name, Lie) Hallett. *Education:* Spring Hill College, B.A., 1953; Facultes St. Albert, S.T.L., 1960; Gregorian University, Ph.D., 1964. *Politics:* Democrat. *Home:* Via del Seminario 120, Rome, Italy. *Office:* Department of Philosophy, Gregorian University, Rome, Italy.

CAREER: Entered Society of Jesus (Jesuits), 1946, ordained Roman Catholic priest, 1959; Loyola University, New Orleans, La., instructor in philosophy, 1961-62; Jesuit House of Studies, Mobile, Ala., instructor in philosophy and dean, 1964-69; Spring Hill College, Mobile, Ala., associate professor of philosophy, 1964-70, and chairman of department of philosophy, 1967-70; Gregorian University, Rome, Italy, associate professor of philosophy, 1970—. *Military service:* U.S. Navy, 1945-46.

WRITINGS: Wittgenstein's Definition of Meaning as Use, Fordham University Press, 1967; *Darkness and Light: The Analysis of Doctrinal Statements,* Paulist/Newman, 1975; *A Companion to Wittgenstein's "Philosophical Investigations",* Cornell University Press, 1977. Book review editor of *Gregorianum.*

WORK IN PROGRESS: Christian Moral Reasoning; Logic for the Labyrinth.

SIDELIGHTS: Fr. Hallett writes that areas he would like to study include: "The cognitive analysis of language; transcendent meaning of truth; the pathology of the healthy mind (as an extension of Wittgenstein's interests and views)."

*   *   *

HALLIDAY, Jerry   1949-

PERSONAL: Born February 4, 1949, in Virginia; son of Hugh C. (an engineer) and Dorothy (Lee) Halliday. *Education:* Attended Hampton Institute. *Politics:* "Leftist activist." *Religion:* Episcopalian. *Office:* WHRO-TV, 5200 Hampton Blvd., Norfolk, Va.

CAREER: Hampton Association for the Arts and Humanities, Hampton, Va., director of children's theatre, 1967-69; Troubadour Marionettes, Norfolk, Va., director and master puppeteer, 1970-72; WHRO-TV (public television), Norfolk, writer, puppeteer, and host of "Tom Foolery," a children's program, 1972—. Actor and director, Virginia Center for the Performing Arts at Wedgewood Theatre, 1971.

WRITINGS: Spaced Out and Gathered In: A Sort of an Autobiography of a Jesus Freak, Revell, 1972.

Author of plays: "Will You Please Sit Down and Finish Your Oatmeal?," "Madame Mutant's Warbox," "Apostles" (drama), "In a Tin Can" (farce), and "Pompinpuff" (musical fantasy). Also author of "Electric Love Banana Flip-Out," a multi-media presentation; adaptor of *The Wizard of Oz,* and *Beauty and the Beast* for marionette teleplays.

WORK IN PROGRESS: A novel about a rock star's rise to fame; writing rock music.

SIDELIGHTS: Halliday writes: "I was an S.D.S. freak and an L.S.D. fiend until I became a Christian. . . . Jesus is where it's at now as far as I'm concerned. I create ideas to make people happy . . . dig?" Halliday makes the puppets for his children's shows himself.

*   *   *

HALLINAN, P(atrick) K(enneth)   1944-

PERSONAL: Born November 1, 1944, in Los Angeles, Calif.; son of Kenneth Frank (a salesman) and Marguerite (Rommel) Hallinan; married Julie Spencer, September 6, 1975; children: Kenneth P., Michael T. *Education:* Attended University of California, Berkeley, 1962, Foothill College, 1963-65, and California State University, Northridge, 1969. *Politics:* "None whatsoever." *Religion:* "Makeshift all the way." *Home:* 645 Law St., San Diego, Calif. 92109.

CAREER: J. C. Penney & Co., Saratoga, Calif., sporting goods manager, 1967-69; Lockheed Aircraft Corp., Burbank, Calif., project scheduler, 1969-72; Attal, Champion & Associates Advertising, San Diego, Calif., copy writer, 1973-74; Rohr Industries (in aerospace manufacturing), Chula Vista, Calif., expediter, 1974-76; writer, 1976—.

WRITINGS—All self-illustrated children's books: *How Really Great to Walk This Way,* Children's Press, 1972; *The Looking Book,* Children's Press, 1973; *We're Very Good Friends, My Brother and I,* Children's Press, 1973; *Just Being Alone,* Children's Press, 1976; *That's What a Friend Is,* Children's Press, 1977; *I'm Glad to Be Me,* Children's Press, 1977.

WORK IN PROGRESS: Where's Michael?, a self-illustrated children's book, publication by Children's Press expected in 1978; *The Man Who Spoke in Colors,* a self-illustrated children's book.

SIDELIGHTS: Hallinan writes: "From the very first time I ever attempted to write and illustrate for children, I was fascinated with their incredible animation. I also felt strongly that a children's book should be completely honest; that the value presented not be masked behind impossible, imaginary creatures! For this reason, I never write about talking animals or dancing refrigerators. I state the truth as well as I can and then try to capture the spirit of it with my cartoons. And then, if my kids laugh at my manuscript, I figure I'm doing okay."

HAMBERGER, John 1934-

PERSONAL: Born August 17, 1934, in Jamaica, N.Y.; son of Michael and Pearl (Wandolowski) Hamberger; married Rita Backer (an agent), November 29, 1975; children: Christopher, Matthew. *Education:* Attended School of Visual Arts. *Home and office:* 120 East 34th St., New York, N.Y. 10016.

CAREER: Writer and illustrator. *Military service:* U.S. Army, 1952-56. *Member:* Society of Animal Artists (member of jury of admissions), Society of Illustrators. *Awards, honors:* Christopher Award, 1973, for illustrating *Vanishing Wings;* National Science Teachers award, 1976, for *Animals of the Sea.*

WRITINGS—Self-illustrated juvenile: *The Day the Sun Disappeared,* Norton, 1964; *The Wish,* Norton, 1967; *The Peacock Who Lost His Tail,* Norton, 1967; *Hazel Was an Only Pet,* Norton, 1968; *The Call of a Loon: Story and Pictures,* Four Winds Press, 1969; *This Is the Day,* Grosset, 1971; *The Lazy Dog,* Four Winds Press, 1971; *A Sleepless Day,* Four Winds Press, 1973; *Birth of a Pond* (juvenile), Coward, 1975.

Illustrator: Kay Hill, *Badger: The Mischief Maker,* Dodd, 1965; Elizabeth Jane Coatsworth, *The Fox Friend,* Macmillan, 1966; Charles House, *The Biggest Mouse in the World,* Norton, 1968; Millen Brand, *This Little Pig Named Curly,* Crown, 1968; Helen Ross Russell, *Clarion the Killdeer,* Hawthorn, 1970; Bernice Kohn, *Chipmunks,* Prentice-Hall, 1970; Hill, *More Glooscap Stories,* Dodd, 1970; Daniel Cohen, *Watchers in the Wild,* Little, Brown, 1971; Patricia Miles Martin, *Navajo Pet,* Putnam, 1971; Griffing Bancroft, *Vanishing Wings: A Tale of Three Birds of Prey,* F. Watts, 1972; Jane Annixter, *Sea Otter,* Holiday House, 1972; Julian May, *Wild Turkeys,* Holiday House, 1973; Irmengarde Eberle, *Prairie Dogs in Prairie Dog Town,* Crowell, 1974; Wilda S. Ross, *Can You Find the Animal?,* Coward, 1974; Ralph Louis Woods, editor, *Wit and Wonder of the Animal World,* C. R. Gibson, 1974; Joan Joseph, *Pet Birds,* F. Watts, 1975; Cohen, *Animal Territories,* Hastings House, 1975; Millicent Selsam, *Animals of the Sea,* Scholastic Book Services, 1975; Dorothy Edwards Shuttlesworth, *The Hidden Magic of Seeds,* Rodale Press, 1976; Selsam, *Sea Monsters of Long Ago,* Scholastic Book Services, 1977.

WORK IN PROGRESS: A children's dictionary, for Macmillan.

*   *   *

HAMBLETT, Theora 1895(?)-1977

1895(?)—March 6, 1977; American rural school teacher in early years who became a successful artist. She began her painting while in her mid-fifties and adopted a primitive style. Her work is represented in museums and private collections. Hamblett died in Oxford, Miss. Obituaries: *New York Times,* March 7, 1977; *Washington Post,* March 8, 1977; *AB Bookman's Weekly,* May 9, 1977.

*   *   *

HAMERSTROM, Frances 1907-
(Claire Windsor)

PERSONAL: Born December 17, 1907, in Needham, Mass.; daughter of Laurence Bertram (a criminologist) and Helen (Chase) Flint; married Frederick Nathan Hamerstrom, Jr. (a wildlife biologist), June 10, 1931; children: Alan, Elva (Mrs. Dale Paulson). *Education:* Smith College, student, 1926-28; Iowa State College (now University), B.S., 1935; University of Wisconsin, Madison, M.S., 1940. *Residence:* Plainfield, Wis. *Office:* College of Natural Resources, University of Wisconsin, Stevens Point, Wis. 54481.

CAREER: Fashion model, 1929-30; worked at Edwin S. George Reserve, Pinckney, Mich., 1940-43, 1946-49; Wisconsin Department of Natural Resources, Madison, biologist, 1949-72; University of Wisconsin, Stevens Point, research associate, 1972—. Central director of Raptor Research Foundation, 1976—.

MEMBER: American Society of Mammalogists (emeritus member), Society of Children's Book Writers, National League of American Pen Women, Citizens Natural Resources Association, Raptor Research Foundation, Wilson Ornithological Society (chairman of committee for relief to European ornithologists, 1947-48), Cooper Ornithological Society, British Ornithologists Union, British Falconry Club, Deutsche Falkenorden, Deutsche Ornithologen Gesellschaft (corresponding member), North American Falconers Association (chairman of legislative committee, 1963-70), Wisconsin Society for Ornithology (president, 1960-61), Wisconsin Academy of Science, Arts and Letters. *Awards, honors:* Awards from Wildlife Society, 1940, for *The Great Horned Owl and Its Prey in the North-Central States,* and 1957, for *A Guide to Prairie Chicken Management;* Josselyn Van Tyne Award from American Ornithologists Union, 1960; D.Sc. from Carroll College, 1961; Chapman Award from American Museum of Natural History, 1964; Silver Passenger Pigeon Award from Wisconsin Society for Ornithology, 1966, Golden Passenger Pigeon Award, 1973; distinguished service award from National Wildlife Federation, 1970; Silver Acorn Award from Citizens Natural Resources Association, 1972; research award from State of Wisconsin, Department of Natural Resources, 1973.

WRITINGS: (With P. L. Errington and husband, Frederick N. Hamerstrom, Jr.) *The Great Horned Owl and Its Prey in the North-Central States,* Iowa Agriculture Experimental Station, 1940; (with Oswald E. Mattson and F. N. Hamerstrom, Jr.) *Sharptails into the Shadows?* (bulletin), Wisconsin Department of Natural Resources, 1952; (with Mattson and F. N. Hamerstrom, Jr.) *A Guide to Prairie Chicken Management,* Wisconsin Conservation Dept., 1957; *An Eagle to the Sky,* Iowa State University Press, 1970; *Birds of Prey of Wisconsin,* Wisconsin Society for Ornithology, 1972; *Walk When the Moon Is Full* (juvenile), Crossing Press, 1975; *The Adventure of the Stone Man* (juvenile), Crossing Press, 1977. Contributor of more than a hundred articles and poems to technical journals and magazines, including *Natural History, Audubon, Parchment,* and *Beloit Poetry Journal.*

WORK IN PROGRESS: A naturalist's guide to wild foods; a read-aloud children's book about walking in the dawn; stories of a Seri Indian girl and a Polish immigrant boy; research on marsh hawks, kestrels, ospreys, Harris' Hawks, and owls.

SIDELIGHTS: Frances Hamerstrom writes: "The spate of flaccid nature writing in the last few decades is leading to enormous confusion in man's attitude toward the other animals. I try to present animals—and I include birds—as they really are. I have studied and lived with wild animals all my life. I know what it is to hear a fox scratch on a screen door to get into the house; to see a golden eagle, hardly more than a speck in the sky, circle down to play with my shoelace; to have a flying squirrel scurry inside my shirt for safety.

"I write in English and in German and for adults and for

children. May my writing have integrity to help close the gap between man and nature.'' She has been a consultant or on expeditions in Scandinavia, Lapland, Germany, Switzerland, Austria, Canada, Australia, and Mexico.

BIOGRAPHICAL/CRITICAL SOURCES: Let's See, September, 1962; *Sports Illustrated,* May 29, 1967; *National Wildlife,* April-May, 1974.

* * *

HAMILTON, Carlos D. 1908-

PERSONAL: Born October 20, 1908, in Santiago, Chile; naturalized U.S. citizen in 1955; son of Charles McDonough and Rosa (a professor; maiden name, Depassier) Hamilton; married Sara Aeraya Proromant (a social worker), 1949; children: Sara Maria, Charles Francis. *Education:* University of Chile, baschiller, 1923; Gregorian University of Rome, J.C.D., 1931. *Home:* 11 Morris Dr., Syosset, Long Island, N.Y. 11791. *Office:* Department of Spanish, Brooklyn College of the City University of New York, 4157 Boylan Hall, Brooklyn, N.Y.

CAREER: University of Chile, Santiago, professor of legal history and philosophy, 1941-51; visiting professor at Columbia University, New York, N.Y., 1952-54, and Fordham University, Bronx, N.Y., 1954-55; Vassar College, Poughkeepsie, N.Y., associate professor of Spanish, 1956-61; Brooklyn College of the City University of New York, Brooklyn, professor of Spanish, 1961—. Visiting professor, New York University, 1956-62; Fulbright lecturer in Bogota, 1963-64. Member of national Fulbright Commission, 1965—. *Member:* Instituto Cultura Hispanica, Instituto Caro y Cuervo, Facultad de Ciencias Juridicas y Sociales, Instituto de estudios legislativos, Congreso latinoamericano de Criminologia, Academia de Filosofia, American Association of Teachers of Spanish and Portuguese, Latin American Studies Association, American Association of University Professors. *Awards, honors:* Best Book by Faculty Award from University of Chile, 1951.

WRITINGS: Nuevo lenguaje poetico: de J. A. Silva a P. Neruda, Instituto Caro y Cuervo, 1955; *Historia de la literatura hispanoamericana,* 2nd edition, EPESA, 1956; *Lirica Hispanica,* McGraw, 1971; *Manual de Historica del Derecho,* 3rd edition, Editions Juridica de Chile, 1972; *El ensayo hispanoamericano,* EISA, 1972; *Pablo Neruda: poeta chileno universal,* Editions Lord Cochrane, 1973; *Ensayos iberoamericanos,* A. Bello, 1975; (author of introduction) *Obras completas de Vicente Huidobro,* A. Bello, 1975. Contributor to *Cuadernos, Rhesaurus,* and *Cuadernos Hispanoamericanos.*

WORK IN PROGRESS: Second edition of *Nuevo lenguaje poetico;* third edition of *Historia de la literatura hispanoamericana; Ensayos de laguerra defensiva; Ruben Dario y Antonia Machado; Del simbolismo frances al modernismo hispanico.*

* * *

HAMILTON, William 1939-

PERSONAL: Born June 2, 1939, in Palo Alto, Calif.; son of Alexander and Ellen (Ballentine) Hamilton; married Candida Vargas, May 9, 1969; children: Alexandra. *Education:* Yale University, B.A., 1962. *Politics:* "Confused." *Religion:* Episcopalian. *Home and office:* 1855 Broadway, San Francisco, Calif. 94109. *Agent:* Lois Wallace, Wallace, Aitken & Sheil, Inc., 118 East 61st St., New York, N.Y. 10021.

CAREER: New Yorker, New York, N.Y., cartoonist, 1964—. Author of "Now Society," a cartoon syndicated by Chronicle Features to about thirty newspapers, 1973—. *Military service:* U.S. Army, 1963-64. *Member:* American Automobile Association.

WRITINGS: The Antisocial Register, Chronicle Books, 1974; *Terribly Nice People,* Putnam, 1975; *Husbands, Wives, and Live-Togethers,* Putnam, 1976.

AVOCATIONAL INTERESTS: Art, horseracing, wine, "de luxe hotels."

* * *

HAMLIN, Charles Hughes 1907-

PERSONAL: Born August 25, 1907, in Barbourville, Ky.; son of Charles Hughes, Sr. (a tobacconist) and Sallie Bell (Hacker) Hamlin; married Hallie Inez Williams, 1932 (divorced); children: Vicki (Mrs. F. R. Warner). *Education:* Educated in private school in Asheville, N.C. *Politics:* Independent. *Religion:* Protestant. *Home and office address:* The Hawk's Nest, Route 2, Box C-44, Powhatan, Va. 23139.

CAREER: Worked as a tobacconist for R. J. Reynolds and Swain-Noel Tobacco Co., 1927-31; co-owner and manager of Ford Motor Co. dealerships in Fairmont, N.C., 1933-35, and Bennettsville, S.C., 1936-41; Veterans Administration, Danville, Va., contact representative, district and branch manager, 1946-48; Packard Auto Sales, Cincinnati, Ohio, sales manager, 1948-59; genealogist and writer, 1959—. *Military service:* U.S. Navy, 1943-45; became petty officer first class; received ten battle stars.

MEMBER: Society of Colonial Wars, Sons of the American Revolution (first vice-president in Cincinnati, 1958-59), Jamestowne Society, Founders and Patriots of America, Augustan Society, Huguenot Society, American Legion, Veterans of Foreign Wars, National Genealogical Society, Virginia Genealogical Society, Kentucky Genealogical Society.

WRITINGS: Lineage Book, Cincinnati Chapter, Ohio Society, Sons of the American Revolution, 1958; *They Went Thataway,* privately printed, Volume I, 1964, Volume II, 1965, Volume III, 1967, 2nd edition, Genealogical Publishing, 1974; *Virginia Ancestors and Adventurers,* privately printed, Volume I, 1970, Volume II, 1971, Volume III, 1973, 2nd edition, Genealogical Publishing, 1976. Contributor to genealogy magazines and regional periodicals.

WORK IN PROGRESS: Genealogical research for Virginia families, to be included in *Florida Pioneers,* edited by David A. Avant; research for a genealogical book on migrations into and out of Virginia.

SIDELIGHTS: Hamlin writes: "Genealogy and family history have been of primary interest and an avocation since 1955. Actually it was of sufficient interest that I retired from business early at the age of fifty-two. All of my books have been written and published since my semi-retirement and since I attained the status of a 'senior citizen.'''

* * *

HAMMAN, Ray T(racy) 1945-

PERSONAL: Born July 5, 1945, in Pennsylvania; son of Raymond A. (a college professor) and Irene (Beasley) Hamman; married Joan Essinger (a nurse), April 24, 1971; children: Gregory, Joshua. *Education:* Ohio University, B.S., 1968; Bowling Green State University, graduate study, 1972-73. *Home and office:* 13335 Township Rd. 108, Findlay, Ohio 45840.

CAREER: International Business Machines (IBM), Lima, Ohio, systems engineer, 1968-71; Findlay College, Findlay, Ohio, director of computer center, 1971-74; PI Associates, Inc. (computer consultants), Findlay, partner, 1974—. *Member:* Association for Computing Machines, Tau Beta Pi, Eta Kappa Nu.

WRITINGS: (With Shiv K. Gupta) *Starting a Small Business: A Simulation Game,* Prentice-Hall, 1974.

WORK IN PROGRESS: Small Business Computers and Management.

SIDELIGHTS: Hamman told *CA:* "I started the company PI Associates because of the need for technical and managerial expertise in small companies installing their first computer system. The book that I hope to complete within the next year is a non-technical guide for the manager in such a small company."

* * *

HAMMOND, Dorothy 1924-

PERSONAL: Born September 24, 1924, in Maryville, Mo.; daughter of Lee O. (a farmer), and Ella (Brunk) Martin; married Robert B. Hammond (in banking), September 1, 1944; children: Robert Kurby, Kristy Renee, Byron Kiper. *Education:* Attended Maryville State Teachers College. *Religion:* Methodist. *Home:* 6622 Abardeen, Wichita, Kan. 67206.

CAREER: Columbia Features, Inc., New York, N.Y. author of column "Antique Wise," syndicated to a hundred sixty-five newspapers; writer.

WRITINGS: The Dodge City Story, Bobbs-Merrill, 1965; *Confusing Collectibles,* Wallace-Homestead, 1969; *Advertising Collectibles,* Wallace-Homestead, 1972; *Supplement to Confusing Collectibles,* privately printed, 1972; *Mustache Cups,* Wallace-Homestead, 1973; *Price Guide to American Antiques and American Primitives,* Funk, 1975; *Pictorial Guide to American Antiques,* Dutton, 1977.

* * *

HAMMOND, Peter B(oyd) 1928-

PERSONAL: Born August 7, 1928, in Glendale, Calif.; married, 1960; children: one. *Education:* Attended University of Puerto Rico; University of the Americas, B.A., 1951; University of Paris, graduate study, 1952-53; Northwestern University, Ph.D., 1962. *Home:* 409 N St. S.W., Washington, D.C. 20024.

CAREER: University of Pittsburgh, Pittsburgh, Pa., assistant professor of anthropology, 1957-62; Indiana University, Bloomington, associate professor of anthropology and director of Human Relations Area Files, 1962-65; National Academy of Sciences/National Research Council, Washington, D.C., executive secretary of Division of Behavioral Sciences, 1965-66; researcher and writer, 1966-67; Children's Hospital, Washington, D.C., lecturer in psychiatry, 1968-72; independent researcher and writer, 1973—. Has conducted field research in Upper Volta and Mali, 1954-56, and among Indians of the southeastern United States.

MEMBER: American Anthropological Association, Society for American Archaeology. *Awards, honors:* African studies fellowship from the French Foreign Ministry, 1952-53; Africa travel and study grant from the High Commissioner for French West Africa, 1953; Ford Foundation fellowship, 1954-56, for research and training in Africa; African studies fellowship from Northwestern University, 1956-57; Ford Foundation faculty grant, 1962, at Indiana University; Wenner-Gren Foundation travel grant, 1964, in the Soviet Union; National Science Foundation senior research grant, 1968-72, at Johns Hopkins University.

WRITINGS: (Author of foreword) P. Modupe, *I Was a Savage,* Harcourt, 1958; (editor with J. D. Thompson and others, and contributor) *Comparative Studies in Administration,* University of Pittsburgh Press, 1959; (editor) *Physical Anthropology and Archaeology: Selected Readings,* Macmillan, 1964; *Yatenga: Technology in the Culture of a West African Kingdom,* Free Press, 1966; *An Introduction to Cultural and Social Anthropology,* with instructor's manual, Macmillan, 1971; (editor) *Cultural and Social Anthropology: Introductory Readings in Ethnology,* Macmillan, 1964, 2nd edition, in press.

Contributor: W. R. Bascom and M. J. Herskovits, editors, *Continuity and Change in African Cultures,* University of Chicago Press, 1957; W. Moore and A. Feldman, editors, *Labor Commitment and Social Change in Developing Areas,* Social Science Research Council, 1960; W. Lewis, editor, *Emerging Africa,* Public Affairs Press, 1964; G. Carter and A. Paden, editors, *Expanding Horizons in African Studies,* Northwestern University Press, 1969; N. Paden and E. Soja, editors, *The African Experience,* Northwestern University Press, 1970.

Author of four units of audio-visual project "Emerging Africa in the Light of Its Past," History Research, Inc., 1964-67. Contributor to *Traveler's Guide to Africa, Americana Annual, Grolier's Encyclopedia Year Book, Collier's Encyclopedia,* and *Handbook of North American Indians.* Contributor to professional journals. Editor of *Ethnology,* 1957-62.

WORK IN PROGRESS: Revising *An Introduction to Cultural and Social Anthropology,* publication by Macmillan expected in 1978; *Social Race in a Southern State;* research on Mossi ethics and Mossi technology and time allocation.

* * *

HANNAVY, John Michael 1946-

PERSONAL: Born April 30, 1946, in Edinburgh, Scotland; married. *Education:* Attended University of Manchester Institute of Science and Technology, 1963-66. *Office:* Wigan College of Technology, Wigan, England.

CAREER: Wigan College of Technology, Wigan, England, photographic historian and lecturer in photography, 1969—. *Member:* Royal Photographic Society (fellow), Institute of Incorporated Photographers (fellow).

WRITINGS: Prospect of Scotland, Bartholomew, 1974; *Roger Fenton* (biography), Godine, 1976; *Masters of Victorian Photography,* Holmes & Meier, 1976. Contributor to *Photographer.* Contributing editor of *Photo Technique.*

WORK IN PROGRESS: Research for a biography of amateur photographer Thomas Keith of Edinburgh, 1827-95.

SIDELIGHTS: Hannavy presently has a photographic exhibition touring Great Britain.

* * *

HANSEN, Harry 1884-1977

December 26, 1884—January 2, 1977; American publishing executive, literary critic, novelist, and author of works in several other fields. Hansen was editor of *The World Al-*

manac and also edited the *O Henry Prize Stories* collections for a time. He died in New York City. *Obituaries: New York Times,* January 3, 1977; *AB Bookman's Weekly,* March 20, 1977.

* * *

HARMAN, Jeanne Perkins 1919-

PERSONAL: Born July 27, 1919, in Baxter Springs, Kan.; daughter of Enoch (a mining engineer) and Maude (Himes) Perkins; married Harry E. Harman III (a writer), March 27, 1949; children: Jeanne Anne. *Education:* Smith College, B.A. (magna cum laude), 1939. *Politics:* Independent. *Religion:* Episcopalian. *Home and office address:* Route 1, Box 40, Valdosta, Ga. 31601.

CAREER: New York Herald Tribune, New York City, reporter, 1940-41; *Hearst* (magazine), New York City, editor, 1941-42; *Life,* New York City, editor and writer, 1942-49; Time, Inc., New York City, correspondent, 1951-68; full-time writer, 1968—. Instructor at University of Miami, Coral Gables, Fla., 1953-54; correspondent for McGraw-Hill News Service and for *New York Times,* both 1955-1968. Assignments include interviews with Nelson Rockefeller, Franklin D. Roosevelt, and Mary Martin. *Member:* International Platform Association, Society of American Travel Writers, Overseas Press Club, Phi Beta Kappa.

WRITINGS: The Love Junk (travel book; Book of the Month Travel Book Club selection), Appleton, 1951; *Such Is Life* (Literary Guild outstanding selection), Crowell, 1956; *The Virgins: Magic Islands,* Appleton, 1961; *Fielding's Guide to the Caribbean, Plus the Bahamas,* nine volumes, Fielding, 1969-77 (Volumes I and II with husband, Harry E. Harman III); (with H. E. Harman III) *Harman's Official Guide to Cruise Ships,* Simon & Schuster, 1972. Contributor to *Encyclopedia Americana* and to popular magazines, including *Gourmet, Sports Illustrated, Life,* and *Business Week.* Founder, editor, and publisher of *Here's How: Your Guide to St. Thomas,* 1957-68.

WORK IN PROGRESS: A guide to eating out in America; a travel guide to the Southeast.

BIOGRAPHICAL/CRITICAL SOURCES: Newsweek, February 17, 1975; *Miami Herald,* May 18, 1975; *Philadelphia Enquirer,* July 13, 1975; *Florida Times Union,* October 19, 1975.

* * *

HARMON, Margaret 1906-

PERSONAL: Born January 4, 1906, in Philadelphia, Pa.; daughter of Arthur C. and Laura (Blake) Morgan; married Arthur R. Harmon (a mechanical engineer). *Education:* Bryn Mawr College, A.B., 1928. *Home:* 6348 Sixth Ave. North, St. Petersburg, Fla. 33710.

CAREER: Has worked as an editor for a publisher and for scholarly journals, and as a technical writer for industry.

WRITINGS: Stretching Man's Mind: A History of Data Processing, Mason/Charter, 1975; *The Engineering Medicine Man: The New Pioneer* (on careers in bioengineering), Westminster, 1975; *Working with Words: Careers for Writers,* Westminster, *My Family Is Different,* Westminster, 1978. Contributor of articles and stories to adult and children's magazines.

SIDELIGHTS: Margaret Harmon comments that her "humble goal is to write about more or less technical subjects in plain English."

HARRINGTON, Denis J(ames) 1932-

PERSONAL: Born June 12, 1932, in Oak Park, Ill.; son of John D. (a certified public accountant) and Mary (Hoover) Harrington; married Mary Ann Deiter, May 2, 1964; children: Michael, Patricia, John, Sean. *Education:* Butler University, B.S., 1960; Washington University, St. Louis, Mo., M.A., 1962; University of Illinois, M.S., 1966. *Politics:* Independent. *Religion:* Christian. *Home and office:* 1487 Boulevard, West Hartford, Conn. 06119.

CAREER: WILL-FM and AM Radio and Television, Champaign-Urbana, Ill., broadcaster, 1965-66; U.S. Golf Association, Far Hills, N.J., administrative assistant, 1966-67; U.S. Department of Commerce, Washington, D.C., editor and writer for *International Commerce,* 1967; Hunter College of the City University of New York, New York, N.Y., assistant director of public relations and college relations, 1967-68; University of New Haven, West Haven, Conn., associate director of public relations, publications, and sports information, 1968-69; Greater Hartford Community College, Hartford, Conn., director of public relations, publications, and sports information, 1969-74; free-lance writer and illustrator, 1974—. Instructor at Washington University, St. Louis, Mo., 1961-62, and University of Minnesota, 1962-63; high school teacher of physical education and health in Chatard, Ind., 1963-64, and New York City, 1964-65; instructor at Greater Hartford Community College, 1970-74, and Tunxis Community College, 1975. Author of cartoon features "Turnstile Testers" and "Sportin' Life," syndicated by Trans-World News Service, 1977—. *Military service:* U.S. Army, 1955-57.

WRITINGS: The Silent Pursuit (novel), Major Books, 1976; *The Long Green* (novel), Major Books, 1977. Sports correspondent for United Press International. Author of sports columns, including "Through the Green," *Sacramento Bee,* 1970; "Sportin' Life," *Los Angeles Herald-Dispatch,* 1975. Also author of columns in *Beverly Times* (Massachussets), *Maui News* (Hawaii), *Chicago Metro News, The Facts* (Seattle, Washington) and *Nite Life.* Editorial cartoonist for *Torrington Register,* 1975. Contributor to golf magazines in the United States, Italy, England, Scotland, and New Zealand, and to *Sports Digest.*

WORK IN PROGRESS: The Adjutant, fiction; *It Happens Mostly on Sunday,* children's fiction.

SIDELIGHTS: Harrington comments that his writing on golf grew out of his extensive experience in the game as a competitor on local, state, and national levels, and from his subsequent teaching experience.

* * *

HARRIS, David (Victor) 1946-

PERSONAL: Born February 28, 1946, in Fresno, Calif.; son of Clifton G. (an attorney) and Elaine (an attorney; maiden name, Jensen) Harris; married Joan Baez (a folk singer), March 26, 1968 (divorced March 26, 1973); children: Gabriel. *Education:* Attended Stanford University, 1963-67. *Politics:* Democrat. *Religion:* None. *Home:* 880 Berkeley Ave., Menlo Park, Calif. 94025. *Agent:* Helen Brann, 14 Sutton Pl., S., New York, N.Y.

CAREER: Civil rights worker in Quitman County, Miss., 1964; organizer for United Farmworkers Union, 1965; antiwar organizer, 1966-73; *Rolling Stone* (magazine), San Francisco, Calif., contributing editor, 1973—. Democratic candidate for congress from 12th California district, 1976. Member of California Democratic State Central Committee and California Tax Reform Association. *Member:* Palo Alto Cooperative, Briarpath Auto Cooperative. *Awards, honors:* Stanford Poetry Prize; Communication Arts Award of Excellence for editorial design.

WRITINGS: Goliath, R. W. Baron, 1969; (with Joan Baez) *Coming Out,* Simon & Schuster, 1971; *I Shoulda Been Home Yesterday,* Delacorte, 1976. Contributor of articles and poetry to periodicals, including *New York Times, Playboy,* and *Penthouse.*

SIDELIGHTS: Harris, who served twenty months in prison (1969-71) for draft resistance, recalls these experiences in *I Shoulda Been Home Yesterday.* Reviewer Malcolm Braly made these comments about the book: "As an activist, a social critic, and a candidate for political office we might have expected more from him. But having said this, it must also be said that Harris can write with power and economy; his incidents emerge as small gems, and many will read this book with pleasure. Beneath all the tough talk one senses a nice man who has bitten off more than he really wants to chew, whose optimism and world view has been damaged by his walk through the dark side of our Republic."

BIOGRAPHICAL/CRITICAL SOURCES: New York Times Book Review, August 22, 1976.

* * *

HARRIS, T George 1924-

PERSONAL: Born October 4, 1924, in Simpson County, Ky.; son of Garland (a farmer) and Luna (Byrum) Harris; married Sheila Hawkins, October 31, 1953 (died January 27, 1977); children: Amos, Anne, Crane, Gardiner. *Education:* Attended University of Kentucky, 1946; Yale University, B.A., 1949. *Politics:* Democrat. *Religion:* Episcopalian. *Home:* 62 Hodge Rd., Princeton, N.J. 08540. *Office: New York* Magazine, 755 Second Ave., New York, N.Y.

CAREER/WRITINGS: Clarksville Leaf-Chronicle, Clarksville, Tenn., reporter, 1942-43; *Time* magazine, New York City, correspondent in Chicago, New York, Atlanta, 1949-55; *Time, Life, Fortune* bureau chief in the Midwest, 1955-58; *Time,* contributing editor, 1958-60, Pacific Northwest bureau chief, 1960-62; *Look* magazine, New York City, senior editor, 1962-68; *psychology today* magazine, Del Mar, Calif., now New York City, editor, 1969-76; *New York* magazine, New York City, consulting editor, 1976-77. Notable assignments include coverage of civil rights movement. Contributor of articles and interviews to *psychology today, Ms., Industry Week, Fortune,* and other magazines. *Military service:* U.S. Army, served during World War II; became first lieutenant, receiving commission on battlefield of Bastonge; received Bronze Star and Air Medal with cluster.

MEMBER: Church Society for College Work (director), Phi Beta Kappa, Yale Club (New York City), Chicago Club (Chicago). *Awards, honors:* First award for excellence in economic reporting from University of Missouri, 1965; School Bell Award, 1963, for *Look* articles on segregation struggles in schools; award from National Conference of Christians and Jews, 1964, for coverage of riots; National Magazine Award for excellence in specialized journalism, 1973, for *psychology today.*

SIDELIGHTS: Known for turning the ailing *psychology today* magazine into "a *Popular Mechanics* of human behavior—eminently readable, visually stimulating and worth more than $2 million a year in net profit," according to a *Time* magazine report, Harris installed a Ping-Pong table at the editorial offices of *pt* and is known to have said "we have

created the ultimate sweatshop, one where we have eliminated the difference between work and play."

BIOGRAPHICAL/CRITICAL SOURCES: Trenton Times, February 8, 1976; *Washington Post,* May 15, 1976; *Time,* May 17, 1976.

* * *

HARRISON, Max

PERSONAL: Born in London, England. *Home:* 8 Chatham Close, Hampstead Garden Suburb, London N.W.11, England. *Agent:* David Higham Associates, 5-8 Lower John St., Golden Square, London W.1, England.

CAREER: Editor, arranger, and orchestrator for several music publishers in London, England.

WRITINGS: Charlie Parker, A. S. Barnes, 1960; *Unpleasant for the Peasants,* Melos, 1966; *The Lieder of Brahms,* Praeger, 1972; *Modern Jazz: The Essential Records,* Hanover Books, 1975; *A Jazz Retrospect,* Crescendo, 1976; *Rachmaninoff: Life, Works, and Recordings,* Barrie & Jenkins, in press.

Work represented in anthologies, including *The Art of Jazz,* edited by Martin Williams, Oxford University Press, 1959; *Jazz,* edited by Nat Hentoff, Holt, 1960; and *Jazz on Record,* edited by Albert McCarthy, Hanover Books, 1968. Contributor to *Grove's Dictionary of Music and Musicians* and *Sohlmans Musiklexikon.* Contributor to music journals, to popular magazines, and newspapers. Critic for *Times, Gramophone, Cassettes and Cartridges,* and *Composer.*

* * *

HARRISON, Randall P(aul) 1929-

PERSONAL: Born February 3, 1929, in Eau Claire, Wis.; son of Randall Joseph and Catherine (an educator; maiden name, Paul) Harrison; married Elizabeth Halsted (a journalist), October 1, 1955 (divorced May 19, 1972). *Education:* University of Wisconsin, Madison, B.S., 1950; Michigan State University, Ph.D., 1964. *Home:* 8 Locksley Ave., Apt. 1B, San Francisco, Calif. 94122. *Agent:* Michael Larsen/Elizabeth Pomada, 1029 Jones St., San Francisco, Calif. 94109. *Office address:* P.O. Box 22541, San Francisco, Calif. 94122.

CAREER: United Press, reporter in Pierre, S.D. and Chicago, Ill., 1950-51; WKOW-Television, Madison, Wis., news editor and art director, 1953-54; McGraw-Hill Book Co., New York, N.Y., magazine editor, 1954-56; Jam Handy Organization, Detroit, Mich., motion picture writer, 1956-59; Michigan State University, East Lansing, instructor, 1963-64, assistant professor, 1964-68, associate professor, 1968-73, professor of communication, 1973-77; freelance writer, 1977—. Visiting professor at University of California, San Francisco, 1970-71, research psychologist and adjunct professor, 1974—. Writer for Motion, Inc., 1953-54; director of Communication Press. *Military service:* U.S. Air Force, 1951-53; became captain.

MEMBER: International Communication Association (past vice-president), American Psychological Association, Authors Guild, Association for Education in Journalism.

WRITINGS: (Contributor) R. Budd and B. Ruben, editors, *Approaches to Human Communication,* Spartan Press, 1972; *Beyond Words: An Introduction to Nonverbal Communication,* Prentice-Hall, 1974; *How to Cut Your Water Use in Half and Still Stay Sane and Sanitary,* Communication Press, 1977.

Contributor to *Handbook of Communication* and *Joy of Knowledge Encyclopedia.* Member of editorial board of *Journal of Communication, Communication Yearbook, Annual Review of Communication Research,* and *Visible Language.*

WORK IN PROGRESS: How to Lie with Statistics (tentative title), a collection of cartoons; research on American autobiography and on international nonverbal communication.

SIDELIGHTS: Harrison comments: "A central concern is human communication. My research has focused on nonverbal communication, ranging from facial expressions, gestures, and cartoons to the international effects of television. At least some of my current work could be described as: 'helpful, humorous, how-to—on a human scale.' Each is an experiment in communication, an exercise in making potentially complicated ideas available, enjoyable, and useful. There are other things going on in my work, but perhaps it's best to let the works speak for themselves."

* * *

HARSCH, Ernest 1951-

PERSONAL: Born February 18, 1951, in Detroit, Mich.; son of Willi (a factory worker) and Katharina (a cook; maiden name, Baumhoff) Harsch. *Education:* Attended Wayne State University. *Politics:* Socialist Workers Party. *Residence:* Brooklyn, N.Y. *Office:* 410 West St., New York, N.Y. 10014.

CAREER: Intercontinental Press (socialist weekly magazine), New York, N.Y., staff writer, 1973—.

WRITINGS: (With Stephanie Coontz, Walter Lippmann, Cliff Conner, and others) *Life in Capitalist America,* Pathfinder Press (N.Y.), 1975; (with Tony Thomas) *Angola: The Hidden History of Washington's War,* Pathfinder Press, 1976; (with Malik Miah, Pankaj Roy, and Mary Tyler) *Dictatorship in India* (pamphlet), Pathfinder Press, 1976. Contributor to *Militant* and *International Socialist Review.*

WORK IN PROGRESS: Research for a book on apartheid in South Africa.

SIDELIGHTS: Harsch writes: "The major motivation behind my becoming a writer was political. Through participation in the anti-Vietnam War movement in the late 1960's, I came to the conclusion that war was inherent in the present economic system based on 'free enterprise,' in which profits are placed above human needs and the rulers of the United States seek to maintain their domination over much of the rest of the world. I felt that the only effective way to change such an exploitative system was through a social revolution carried out by the majority of the population—those who work for a living. The construction of a more humane, socialist society could then begin. In order to give expression to these ideas, and to help win others to a socialist perspective, I turned to writing.

"Since I believe that socialism can only be achieved on a world scale, international events have received much of my attention. The continent of Africa, which is destined to play an increasingly important role in world affairs, has been a particular focus of my interest."

He has been published in Australia, Argentina, Bangladesh, Brazil, Canada, Greece, Mexico, Pakistan, and Panama.

* * *

HARTJEN, Clayton A(lfred) 1943-

PERSONAL: Born April 10, 1943, in Idaho; son of Alfred C. (a carpenter) and Ruth (a cook; maiden name, Apelgreen) Hartjen; married Sandra Stults, August 24, 1964 (divorced, January, 1976); married S. Priyadarsini (a sociologist), February 20, 1976. *Education:* University of Illinois, student, 1961-64; San Francisco State College (now University), B.A., 1966, M.A., 1968; New York University, Ph.D., 1972. *Home:* 4 Washington Square Village, #2A, New York, N.Y. 10012. *Office:* Department of Sociology, Rutgers University, Newark, N.J. 07102.

CAREER: Rutgers University, Newark, N.J., assistant professor, 1972-77, associate professor of sociology, 1977—. *Member:* American Sociological Association, Society for the Study of Social Problems, Law and Society Association, American Association of Criminology, American Association of University Professors, Eastern Sociological Association. *Awards, honors:* Grant from Indo-American Fellowship Foundation for study in India, 1978.

WRITINGS: Crime and Criminalization, Praeger, 1974, 2nd edition, in press; *Possible Trouble: An Analysis of Social Problems,* Praeger, 1977. Contributor to sociology and criminology journals.

WORK IN PROGRESS: An introductory sociology text, with Lucile Duberman, publication by General Learning Press expected in 1979; research on the dynamics of treatment in therapeutic communities.

SIDELIGHTS: Hartjen remarks: "We are the authors of our own realities."

* * *

HARTLEY, Robert F(rank) 1927-

PERSONAL: Born December 15, 1927, in Beaver Falls, Pa.; son of Frank H. (a merchant) and Eleanor (Theis) Hartley; married Dorothy Mayou, June 30, 1962; children: Constance, Matthew. *Education:* Drake University, B.B.A., 1949; University of Minnesota, M.B.A., 1962, Ph.D., 1967. *Home:* 2749 Coventry Rd., Shaker Heights, Ohio 44120. *Office:* Department of Marketing, Cleveland State University, Cleveland, Ohio 44115.

CAREER: Management employee for national department store chains, 1949-59; Dayton's Corp., Minneapolis, Minn., in merchandise management, 1959-63; University of Minnesota, Minneapolis, instructor in marketing, 1963-65; George Washington University, Washington, D.C., assistant professor, 1965-69, associate professor of marketing, 1969-72; Cleveland State University, Cleveland, Ohio, professor of marketing, 1972—. *Member:* American Marketing Association, Southern Marketing Association, Southern Casewriters Research Association, Midwest Business Administration Association.

WRITINGS: Marketing Management and Social Change, International Textbook Co., 1972; *Retailing: Challenge and Opportunity,* Houghton, 1975; *Marketing Fundamentals for Responsive Management,* Dun-Donnelley, 1976; *Marketing Mistakes,* Grid Publishing, 1976. Contributor to business and marketing journals.

WORK IN PROGRESS: A book on sales management, for Houghton.

SIDELIGHTS: Hartley writes: "I have attempted in my writings, aimed primarily at the college market, to blend the practical with the conceptual. An underlying theme in all my books has been the desirability of business to be responsive to the needs and dictums of society and the environment, rather than strictly corporate short-term self-interest."

HARTMAN, William E(llis) 1919-

PERSONAL: Born February 17, 1919, in Meadville, Pa.; son of Hartley J. and Janet A. (Ellis) Hartman; married Iva R. Decker, June 30, 1944; children: Carol, William Ellis, Donald, Paul, Beverly, Stephen, Lawrence. Education: Attended New York University, 1937-41, and Centenary College, 1943; University of Southern California, A.B., 1947, M.A., 1948, Ph.D., 1950. Home: 5199 East Pacific Coast Highway, Long Beach, Calif. 90804. Office: Department of Sociology, California State University, Long Beach, Calif. 90804.

CAREER: El Camino College, Torrance, Calif., instructor in sociology and psychology, 1950-51; California State University, Long Beach, began as assistant professor, 1951—, professor of sociology, 1967—, chairman of department, 1960-63. In private practice as marriage counselor, 1959—; director of Center for Marital and Sexual Studies, 1968—. Military service: U.S. Army Air Forces, 1940-45; became second lieutenant. Member: American Sociological Association, National Council on Family Relations, American Association of Marriage and Family Counselors, Southern California Association of Marriage Counselors.

WRITINGS: (With Marilyn A. Fithian and Donald Johnson) Nudist Society: An Authoritative, Complete Study of Nudism in America, Crown, 1970; (with Fithian) Treatment of Sexual Dysfunction: A Bio-Psycho-Social Approach, privately printed, 1972.*

* * *

HARTMANN, William K(enneth) 1939-

PERSONAL: Born June 6, 1939, in New Kensington, Pa.; son of Ernest C. (an engineer) and Erdys C. (Carmichael) Hartmann; married Gayle G. Harrison (an editor), March 22, 1970; children: Amy. Education: Pennsylvania State University, B.S., 1961; University of Arizona, M.S., 1965, Ph.D., 1966. Home: 2224 East Fourth St., Tucson, Ariz. 85719. Office: Planetary Science Institute, Science Applications, Inc., 2030 East Speedway, Tucson, Ariz. 85719.

CAREER: University of Arizona, Tucson, assistant professor of astronomy, 1966-70; IIT Research Institute, Tucson, Ariz., research scientist, 1969-71, senior scientist, 1971-72; Science Applications, Inc., Tucson, Ariz., senior scientist at Planetary Science Institute, 1972—. Visiting associate professor at University of Hawaii, 1975. Member of Tucson Advisory Committee on Air Pollution, 1970-71, and Pima County Air Pollution Advisory Committee, 1975—. Consultant to National Aeronautics & Space Administration and Smithsonian Air and Space Museum.

MEMBER: American Astronomical Society, Society of Southwestern Authors. Awards, honors: Nininger Meteorite Award from Arizona State University, 1965, for research on meteorites and the early history of the solar system.

WRITINGS: Moon and Planets, Wadsworth, 1972; (with Odell Raper) The New Mars, U.S. Government Printing Office, 1974; Astronomy: The Cosmic Journey, Wadsworth, 1977. Contributor to astronomy journals and to Scientific American and Natural History. Associate editor of Journal of Geophysical Research, 1974-77.

WORK IN PROGRESS: Forgotten Volcanoes, Devils Highway, a color photo-essay on southwestern Arizona, with the cooperation of Friends of the Earth.

SIDELIGHTS: Hartmann writes:: "By background I am an astronomer with research interests in the origin and early evolution of the planets, and the possibility of planets and life elsewhere in the universe. In my writing, I have tried to communicate some of the excitement of current space exploration to the public. This is important because many scientists are not motivated to do it at all, and because we live in an age that threatens to exchange exploration and discovery for mysticism and magic. My writings stress the reflection of space discovery back onto a new perception of earth's environment."

* * *

HARVARD, Andrew Carson 1949-

PERSONAL: Born July 29, 1949, in New Orleans, La. Education: Dartmouth College, A.B., 1971; Boston University, graduate study in law, 1975—. Home: 105 Spring Glen Ter., Hamden, Conn. 06517.

CAREER: Writer, 1973—. Has worked as mountain guide, river guide, and timber management contractor (for Green Mountain National Forest, 1971-74). Member: American Alpine Club, Himalayan Institute.

WRITINGS: (With Todd Thompson) Mountain of Storms, New York University Press, 1974. Contributor of articles, stories, and reviews to magazines.

* * *

HASPEL, Eleanor C. 1944-

PERSONAL: Born December 11, 1944, in New York; daughter of Charles and Gertrude (Takce) Cohen; married Lawrence Haspel, August 15, 1965 (divorced, 1973); children: Charles, Dyan. Education: Brooklyn College of the City University of New York, B.A., 1965; University of Chicago, M.A., 1967, Ph.D., 1971. Office: 180 North Michigan Ave., Suite 1705, Chicago, Ill. 60601.

CAREER: Clinical psychologist in private practice, 1973—. Member: American Psychological Association.

WRITINGS: Marriage in Trouble: A Time of Decision, Nelson-Hall, 1976.

WORK IN PROGRESS: A book on psychotherapy in the Age of Enlightenment.

SIDELIGHTS: Eleanor Haspel writes: "I am working in the area of transformational therapy. I use traditional analytic techniques along with natural altered states of consciousness and work with body energy fields to bring individuals into transformational energies. The basis of fulfillment and change is the level of consciousness and sharing of one's presence from an unconditionally loving place. Such sharing is the work of healing and therapy, especially when grounded in a solid theoretical base."

* * *

HAUSER, Charles McCorkle 1929-

PERSONAL: Born February 3, 1929, in Newton, N.C.; son of John N. (a U.S. Army officer) and Charlotte (McCorkle) Hauser; married Jane Edwards, December 29, 1956; children: David, Susan. Education: University of North Carolina, A.B., 1954; graduate study at Harvard University, 1968. Home: 100 Ferry Lane, Barrington, R.I. 02806. Office: Providence Journal-Bulletin, Providence, R.I. 02902.

CAREER/WRITINGS: United Press International, New York, N.Y., correspondent from Paris and London, 1958-60; Charlotte Observer, Charlotte, N.C., state editor and Washington correspondent, 1961-64; Daily News & Record, Greensboro, N.C., executive editor, 1965-68; Virginian-Pilot, Ledger-Star, Norfolk, Va., vice president and general manager, 1969-73; *Providence Journal-Bulletin,* Providence, R.I., vice president and executive editor, 1974—. Notable assignments include the 1960 summit conference in Paris. Lecturer, American Press Institute, Reston, Va., 1969-73. *Military service:* U.S. Army Reserve; active duty in Korea, 1952-53; present rank, colonel; received Bronze Star and Purple Heart. *Member:* National Press Club.

* * *

HAUSER, Hillary 1944-

PERSONAL: Born September 4, 1944, in California; daughter of Carl Richard (a restaurateur) and Mabel (Hensel) Hauser. *Education:* University of Washington, Seattle, B.A., 1966. *Home and office:* 1655 Fernald Point Lane, Santa Barbara, Calif. 93108.

CAREER: TV Guide, Los Angeles, Calif., local editor, 1966-67, national programmer, 1967-68; *Skin Diver,* Los Angeles, Calif., assistant editor, 1968-71; *Ocean Science News,* Washington, D.C., West Coast editor, 1971-75; freelance writer, 1971—. Member of Harbor Commission of Avalon, Catalina Island, 1971-72. Technical consultant for television films "Shark Kill," and "Trapped Beneath the Sea."

WRITINGS: (Associate editor) *Ski World,* Peterson, 1973; (associate editor), Corky Fowler, *Skiing Techniques,* Peterson, 1973; *Women in Sports: Scuba Diving,* Harvey House, 1976; Author of monthly features "Fish of the Month" and "News Briefs" in *Skin Diver,* 1968—. Contributor to diving magazines, *Westways, Caballero, Western's World, Women Sports, Sea Technology,* and *Exxon U.S.A.* West Coast editor of *Coastal Zone Management,* 1971-75.

WORK IN PROGRESS: Book of Fishes, collected from "Fish of the Month" feature in *Skin Diver; California Channel Islands,* natural history; *The Rock,* on marine life.

SIDELIGHTS: Hillary Hauser writes: "Dr. Carleton Ray . . . said some time ago that the marine revolution was on the way—to take place alongside the agricultural and industrial revolutions. As people turn their heads, minds, hearts to the sea—I hope to help them enlarge their concept of the ocean, by writing about the animals, the life, the underwater activities, about being in the sea. . . . In 1972 I took part in a diving expedition to the Bahamas, led by Seafinders president Willard Bascom. . . . The expedition searched for the wreck of the 'Maravilla,' a Spanish galleon sunk in 1656 on the Little Bahama Bank; I left the expedition two weeks before they found it—and two million dollars. While they handled gold, I was home writing about the porpoises which we had swum with daily."

* * *

HAUSER, William B(arry) 1939-

PERSONAL: Born May 2, 1939, in Washington, D.C.; son of Philip M. (a professor) and Zelda (a secretary; maiden name, Abrams) Hauser; married Susan Lester (an attorney), May 19, 1973. *Education:* University of Chicago, S.B., 1960; Yale University, M.A., 1962, Ph.D., 1969. *Politics:* Democrat. *Home:* 486 Rugby Ave., Rochester, N.Y. 14619. *Office:* Department of History, University of Rochester, Rochester, N.Y. 14627.

CAREER: University of Michigan, Ann Arbor, lecturer, 1967-69, assistant professor of history, 1970-74; University of Rochester, Rochester, N.Y., assistant professor, 1974-77, associate professor of history, 1977—. *Member:* Association for Asian Studies. *Awards, honors:* Fulbright fellow-

ship, Osaka University, 1964-66; National Endowment for the Humanities younger humanist fellowship, 1971-72; Japan Foundation fellowship, 1976; Social Science Research Council grant, 1976; Mellon fellowship, 1977.

WRITINGS: Economic Institutional Change in Togugawa Japan: Osaka and the Kinai Cotton Trade, Cambridge University Press, 1974. Contributor of articles and reviews to Oriental studies journals.

WORK IN PROGRESS: A history of Osaka, 1600-1900, as a city in transition, focusing on the development of the city as a commercial and administrative center, its regional role, cultural life, and the nature of urban society.

SIDELIGHTS: Hauser writes: "I am particularly concerned with social change in Japan between 1600 and 1900. I feel that too much attention has been paid to political elites and that the history of the common people, the merchants, artisans, farmers, and so forth requires additional attention. I feel this is important both for the historical profession and to make the teaching of history more attractive to contemporary students. My work on Japanese history takes me to Japan periodically and enables me to introduce Americans to Japan."

* * *

HAVENS, Daniel F(rederick) 1931-

PERSONAL: Born January 23, 1931, in Shanghai, China; son of Philip Bauer and Minerva Agnes (Sullivan) Havens; married Eleanor Jean Kirsten, August 31, 1957; children: Douglas, Leslie, Charles. *Education:* Ohio Wesleyan University, student, 1948-50; University of Michigan, B.A., 1956, M.A., 1957, Ph.D., 1965. *Home:* 436 Legion Dr., Edwardsville, Ill. 62025. *Office address:* Department of English Language and Literature, Southern Illinois University, Box 43, Edwardsville, Ill. 62026.

CAREER: University of Cincinnati, Cincinnati, Ohio, instructor in English, 1961-65; Southern Illinois University, Edwardsville, assistant professor, 1965-69, associate professor, 1969-75, professor of English, 1975—, chairman of department, 1974—, also member of board of directors of National Archive of Ragtime and Jazz. *Military service:* U.S. Navy, 1951-54. *Member:* Modern Language Association of America, American Association of University Professors, American Federation of Musicians, Midwest Modern Language Association.

WRITINGS: (Editor) *Four Early Plays,* Somerset, 1970; *The Columbian Muse of Comedy: The Development of a Native Tradition in Early American Social Comedy, 1787-1845,* Southern Illinois University Press, 1972. Editor of *Sou'wester,* 1965-69.

WORK IN PROGRESS: Editing a scholarly collection of early American Yankee plays.

SIDELIGHTS: Havens writes that he has been a professional jazz musician (cornet) since 1946; he organized and led the Boll Weevil Jass Band, 1957-65 (made nine record albums); he has also been featured with such traditional jazz bands as Gene Mayl's Dixieland Rhythm Kings, Carl Halen's Gin Bottle Seven, Chicago Salty Dogs, and George Brunies' Chicago Jazz Band. At present he leads the Mississippi Mudcats, a dixieland band in the St. Louis area (they are about to release two record albums) and the Old Guys Jazz Band, composed of faculty members at Southern Illinois University.

HAWES, Grace M. 1926-

PERSONAL: Born February 4, 1926, in Cumberland, Wis.; daughter of Clarence David and Mabel (Erickson) Maxcy; married John C. Hawes (an aerospace engineer), August 8, 1948; children: Elizabeth, John D., Mark, Amy. *Education:* San Jose State University, B.A., 1963, M.A., 1971. *Home:* 12771 Glen Arbor Court, Saratoga, Calif. 95070.

CAREER: Employed at Hoover Institution Archives, Stanford, Calif., 1976—.

WRITINGS: The Marshall Plan for China: Economic Cooperation Administration, 1948-1949, Schenkman, 1977.

WORK IN PROGRESS: Research on Sino-American relations, especially in the post-World War II period.

AVOCATIONAL INTERESTS: Reading, travel, gardening.

*   *   *

HAWES, Hampton 1929(?)-1977

American jazz pianist and composer of jazz music. He played with some of the leading jazz musicians of his time. Hawes was author of his autobiography. He died in Los Angeles, Calif. Obituaries: *Time,* June 6, 1977.

*   *   *

HAWKES, (Jessie) Jacquetta (Hopkins) 1910-

PERSONAL: Born August 5, 1910, in Cambridge, England; daughter of Sir Frederick Gowland (a biochemist) and Jessie Anne (Stevens) Hopkins; married Christopher Hawkes (an archaeologist and writer), October, 1933 (divorced, 1953); married John Boynton Priestly (a writer), July 23, 1953; children: Nicolas. *Education:* Newnham College, Cambridge, B.A. (first class honors), M.A., 1935. *Home:* Kissing Tree House, Alveston, Stratford-on-Avon, Warwickshire, England.

CAREER: Conducted archaeological research and excavation in England, Ireland, France, and Palestine, 1931-40; assistant principal of Post-War Reconstruction Secretariat, 1941-43; principal, founder, and secretary of United Kingdom Commission for UNESCO, 1943-48; writer. Archaeology adviser for Festival of Britain, 1949-51; vice president of Council of British Archaeology, 1949-52; governor of British Film Institute, 1950-55; member of culture advisory committee for UNESCO, 1966—; John Danz visiting professor, University of Washington, 1971. *Awards, honors:* Kemsley Award, 1951, for *A Land;* Order of British Empire, 1952.

WRITINGS: The Archaeology of Jersey, privately printed, 1939; (with Christopher Hawkes) *Prehistoric Britain,* Penguin, 1943, revised edition, Chatto & Windus, 1947, Harvard University Press, 1953; *Early Britain,* Collins, 1945; *Symbols and Speculations* (poems), Cresset, 1949; *A Guide to the Prehistoric and Roman Monuments in England and Wales,* Chatto & Windus, 1951, revised edition, Sphere Books, 1973, published in the United States as *History in Earth and Stone: Prehistoric and Roman Monuments in England and Wales,* Harvard University Press, 1952; *A Land* (with drawings by Henry Moore), Cresset, 1951, Random House, 1952; (with husband, J. B. Priestley) *Dragon's Mouth: A Dramatic Quartet in Two Parts,* Harper, 1952; *A Woman as Great as the World, and Other Fables,* Random House, 1953, published in England as *Fables,* Cresset, 1953; *Man on Earth,* Cresset, 1954, Random House, 1955; (with Priestley) *Journey Down a Rainbow,* Harper, 1955; *Providence Island: An Archaeological Tale,* Random House, 1959.

Man and the Sun, Random House, 1962; (editor with Frankfort and Woolley) *A History of Man,* Harper, 1963; (editor and author of introduction) *The World of the Past,* two volumes, Knopf, 1963; *King of the Two Lands: The Pharoah, Akhenaten,* Chatto & Windus, 1966, Random House, 1967; *Dawn of the Gods,* Random House, 1968; *Nothing But or Something More* (collected essays and lectures), University of Washington Press, 1972; *The First Great Civilizations: Life in Mesopotamia, the Indus Valley, and Egypt,* Knopf, 1973; *Atlas of Ancient Archaeology,* Heinemann, 1975; *The Atlas of Early Man,* St. Martin's, 1976.

Work has been anthologized in *Famous Plays of Today.*

General editor of "The Past and the Present," Thames & Hudson, 1952. Former archaeological correspondent for *Observer* and *Sunday Times.* Contributor to *Spectator,* learned journals, and to newspapers.

AVOCATIONAL INTERESTS: Gardening, antiques, natural history, walking, films.

*   *   *

HAYDEN, Martin S(choll) 1912-

PERSONAL: Born May 21, 1912, in Detroit, Mich.; son of Jay G. and Marguerite (Scholl) Hayden; married Elizabeth Dodds, July 26, 1938; children: Jay G., John D., Martin S., Jr. *Education:* University of Michigan, A.B., 1934. *Politics:* Independent. *Religion:* Episcopalian. *Home:* 218 Merriweather Rd., Grosse Pointe Farms, Mich. 48236. *Office: Detroit News,* Detroit, Mich. 48231.

CAREER/WRITINGS: Kansas City Star, Kansas City, Mo., reporter, 1929; *Detroit News,* Detroit, Mich., correspondent in Ann Arbor, Mich., 1930-34, reporter, 1934-37, city and state political writer, 1938-47, Washington correspondent, 1948-58, associate editor, 1958, editor-in-chief, 1959—. Notable assignments include coverage of Berlin foreign ministers meeting, 1954, Geneva Conference, 1955, Hungarian Revolution, 1956, and events in China, Japan, and Philippines, 1936. Associated Press, director, 1968-75, vice-chairman, 1974-75. President of Leader Dogs for the Blind; trustee of Harper Hospital. *Military service:* U.S. Army, 1941-45; became lieutenant colonel; received four combat stars. *Member:* National Press Club, Detroit Press Club, Gridiron Club, Sigma Delta Chi. *Awards, honors:* L.H.D., Detroit College of Law, 1967.

*   *   *

HAYDEN, Robert C(arter), Jr. 1937-

PERSONAL: Born August 21, 1937, in New Bedford, Mass.; son of Robert C. and Josephine (Hughes) Hayden; married Charlene Roberts (a mathematician and engineer), June 13, 1959; children: Robert III, Deborah, Kevin, Karen. *Education:* Boston University, B.A., 1959, Ed.M., 1961, doctoral candidate, 1973—; Harvard University, certificate, 1966. *Home:* 77 Beaumont Ave., Newton, Mass. 02160.

CAREER: Junior high school teacher of science in Newton, Mass., 1961-65; American Education Publications, Xerox Education Division, Middletown, Conn., editor and writer, 1966-68; Ginn & Co., Xerox Education Division, Boston, Mass., editor, 1968-69; Metropolitan Council for Educational Opportunity, Boston, Mass., executive director, 1970-73; Education Development Center, Newton, Mass., director of ethnic studies for Career Opportunities Program, 1973-74, managing director of Project Torque, 1974—. Instructor at State University of New York at Buffalo, summers, 1964, 1966, and Boston College, 1974-75; guest lecturer at Boston University, Harvard University, Boston State College, Tufts University, Simmons College, and University of Suffolk. Community fellow at Massachusetts Institute of Technology, 1976—. Member of corporation of Museum of Afro-American History; member of board of directors of Roxbury Federation of Neighborhood Centers; member of advisory board of Child's World Day Care Centers, Inc.

MEMBER: Association for the Study of Afro-American Life and History, National Association of Science Writers, National Association for the Advancement of Colored People, Kappa Alpha Psi. *Awards, honors:* All-American Award from Educational Press Association of America, 1968; local National Association for the Advancement of Colored People award, 1972; outstanding book award from National Science Teachers Association and Children's Book Council, 1976, for *Nine Black American Doctors.*

WRITINGS: Why You Are You: The Science of Heredity, Sex, and Development, American Education Publications, 1968; *Black in America: Episodes in U.S. History,* Xerox Education Publications, 1969; *Seven Black American Scientists,* Addison-Wesley, 1970; *Eight Black American Inventors,* Addison-Wesley, 1972; (with Jacqueline Harris) *Nine Black American Doctors,* Addison-Wesley, 1976. Author of "Boston's Black History," a weekly column in *Bay State Banner.* Book review editor of *Science Activities,* 1969-73; regional editor, *Western Journal of Black Studies,* 1976—.

WORK IN PROGRESS: Black Educators; Boston's Black History.

SIDELIGHTS: Hayden told *CA* he "writes to provide youth of all ethnic and racial groups with accurate, useful information on the work of black Americans in science, invention, and medicine." In his work Hayden makes extensive use of oral history.

BIOGRAPHICAL/CRITICAL SOURCES: New York Amsterdam News, April 9, 1977.

* * *

HAYDEN, Robert E(arl) 1913-

PERSONAL: Born August 4, 1913, in Detroit, Mich. *Education:* Wayne State University, B.A.; University of Michigan, M.A. *Home:* 1201 Gardner Ave., Ann Arbor, Mich. 48104. *Office:* Department of English, University of Michigan, Ann Arbor, Mich. 48104.

CAREER: Fisk University, Nashville, Tenn., 1946-69, began as assistant professor, became professor of English; University of Michigan, Ann Arbor, professor of English, 1969—. *Awards, honors:* Jules and Avery Hopwood Poetry Awards from University of Michigan, 1938 and 1942; Julius Rosenwald fellowship in creative writing, 1947; Ford Foundation fellowship in Mexico, 1954-55; grand prize from World Festival of Negro Arts, 1966, for *A Ballad of Remembrance.*

WRITINGS: Heart-Shape in the Dust (poems), Falcon Press, 1940; *Figure of Time* (poems), Hemphill Press, 1955; *A Ballad of Remembrance* (poems), P. Bremen, 1962; *Selected Poems,* October House, 1966; (editor and author of introduction) *Kaleidoscope: Poems by American Negro Poets* (juvenile), Harcourt, 1967; (contributor) Alain LeRoy Locke, editor, *The New Negro,* Atheneum, 1968; *Words in the Mourning Time* (poems), October House, 1970; (with David J. Burrows and Frederick R. Lapides) *Afro-American*

Literature: An Introduction, Harcourt, 1971; *Night-Blooming Cereus* (reissue of book originally published as *Poems*), Broadside Press, 1972; (editor with James Edwin Miller) *The United States in Literature,* Scott, Foresman, 1973; *Angle of Ascent: New and Selected Poems,* Liveright, 1975. Also author with Myron O'Higgins of *The Lion and the Archer,* 1948.

Work represented in anthologies. Contributor to literary magazines.*

* * *

HAYES, Harold T(homas) P(ace) 1926-

PERSONAL: Born April 18, 1926, in Elkin, N.C.; son of James M. (a Baptist minister) and Alice (Pace) Hayes; married Suzette Meredith, April 7, 1955; children: Thomas Pace, Carrie Meredith. *Education:* Wake Forest College, B.S., 1949; Harvard University, graduate study, 1957-58. *Home and office:* 405 East 54th St., #3N, New York, N.Y. 10022. *Agent:* Candida Donadio & Associates, Inc., 111 West 57th St., New York, N.Y. 10019.

CAREER: Southern Bell Telephone Co., Atlanta, Ga., on public relations staff, 1948-49; United Press International (UPI), Atlanta, Ga., reporter, 1949-50; *Pageant,* New York, N.Y., assistant editor, 1952, associate editor, 1953; *Tempo,* New York City, associate editor, 1953; *Picture Week,* New York City, editor, 1954; *Esquire,* New York, N.Y., assistant to publisher, 1955-59, articles editor, 1959-62, managing editor, 1962-63, editor, 1963-73, senior vice-president, 1970-73; WNET-TV, New York City, television host of "Roundtable," 1974-75; writer and magazine consultant, 1975—. Instructor at New School for Social Research, 1961-63. Member of board of visitors at Wake Forest University, 1972—, chairman of board, 1974—. Member of board of directors of *Saturday Review,* 1976. *Military service:* U.S. Naval Reserve, active duty, 1943-45. U.S. Marine Corps Reserve, active duty, 1950-52; became first lieutenant.

WRITINGS: (Editor) *Smiling Through the Apocalypse* (collection of essays), McCall's Press, 1970; *The Last Place on Earth* (nonfiction), Stein & Day, 1977. Contributor to magazines and newspapers, including *New Yorker, New York Times, New Republic,* and *New Statesman.*

WORK IN PROGRESS: A television series on biological conservation, for the Public Broadcast System, with a book expected to result.

* * *

HAYES, John Haralson 1934-

PERSONAL: Born February 6, 1934, in Camp Hill, Ala.; son of Willie Nonus and Mattie (Clardy) Hayes; married Sarah Emma Hall, September 6, 1958; children: Heather Ruth, John Alexander, Megan Elizabeth. *Education:* Samford University, B.A., 1956; Princeton Theological Seminary, B.D., 1960, Ph.D. (magna cum laude), 1964. *Politics:* Democrat. *Religion:* Southern Baptist. *Home:* 976 Swathmore Dr. N.W., Atlanta, Ga. 30327. *Office:* Candler School of Theology, Emory University, Atlanta, Ga. 30322.

CAREER: Trinity University, San Antonio, Tex., assistant professor, 1964-68, associate professor of religion, 1968-72; Emory University, Atlanta, Ga., visiting professor, 1972-76, associate professor of Old Testament, 1976—, member of Interdenominational Theological Center, 1974-76. Participated in American Archaeological Expedition to Petra in 1962, assistant to director of expedition to Hebron, 1964.

MEMBER: Archaeological Institute of America, Society of Biblical Literature (regional vice-president, 1968-69, 1976-77; president, 1969-70, 1977-78), American Academy of Religion, American Schools of Oriental Research, Catholic Biblical Association. *Awards, honors:* Fulbright scholarship, University of Edinburgh, 1956-57.

WRITINGS: Biblical Hebrew Vocabulary, Independent Publishing, 1962; (with William O. Walker, Jr.) *The Biblical Heritage,* Trinity University Printers, 1966; (with Lonnie D. Kliever) *Radical Christianity: The New Theologies in Perspective,* Grosset, 1968; *Introduction to the Bible,* Westminster, 1971; (editor) *Old Testament Form Criticism,* Trinity University Press, 1974; *Understanding the Psalms,* Judson, 1976; *Son of God to Superstar: Twentieth Century Interpretations of Jesus,* Abingdon, 1976; (editor and contributor) *Israelite and Judaean History,* Westminster, 1977. Editor of Trinity University monograph series in religion, 1971—. Contributor of about twenty articles and reviews to theology journals. Associate editor of *Quote,* 1972—; editor of *Journal of Biblical Literature,* 1977—.

WORK IN PROGRESS: Introduction to Old Testament Study, for Abingdon.

* * *

HAYS, Terence E(ugene) 1942-

PERSONAL: Born September 30, 1942, in Shenandoah, Iowa; son of George Philip (an accountant) and Ardythe (Radliff) Hays; married Patricia Hurley (a college teacher), September 2, 1968; children: Nathan Christopher. *Education:* Iowa State University, student, 1960-61; University of Omaha, B.A., 1966; University of Colorado, M.A., 1968; University of Washington, Seattle, Ph.D., 1974. *Home:* 72 Radcliffe Ave., Providence, R.I. 02908. *Office:* Department of Anthropology and Geography, Rhode Island College, Providence, R.I. 02908.

CAREER: Rhode Island College, Providence, assistant professor of anthropology, 1973—. Consultant to ABT Associates, Inc. *Member:* American Anthropological Association, Association for Social Anthropology in Oceania, Royal Anthropological Institute of Great Britain, Northeastern Anthropological Association.

WRITINGS: Anthropology in the New Guinea Highlands, Garland Publishing, 1976. Contributor to anthropology journals.

WORK IN PROGRESS: Continuing anthropological and botanical research.

SIDELIGHTS: Hays writes: "My sole book so far published (an annotated bibliography) symbolizes the broad interest I have in the anthropology and natural history of the island of New Guinea. My wife and I conducted research there for fifteen months in 1971-72 and hope to return several more times to do additional research and traveling. Anthropology allows me to vocationally pursue most of my major interests, including reading and photography."

* * *

HAYWOOD, Richard Mansfield 1905-1977

June 12, 1905—March 31, 1977; American educator in the field of classics and author of books on the ancient world, including *The Myth of Rome's Fall* and *Roman Africa.* He died in Charlottesville, Va. Obituaries: *New York Times,* April 18, 1977; *AB Bookman's Weekly,* June 27, 1977. (*CAP-*2; earlier sketch in *CA*-33/36)

HEALY, George W(illiam), Jr. 1905-

PERSONAL: Born September 22, 1905, in Natchez, Miss.; son of George William (a druggist) and Rosa (Longmire) Healy; married Margaret Alford, September 22, 1927; children: George William III. *Education:* University of Mississippi, A.B., 1926. *Politics:* Independent Democrat. *Religion:* Methodist. *Home:* 2110 State St., New Orleans, La. 70118.

CAREER: New Orleans Times-Picayune, New Orleans, La., reporter, 1926-31, city editor, 1931-36, managing editor, 1936-52, editor, 1952-72, director of Times-Picayune Publishing Co., 1939-72; writer, 1972—. Director of Advertising Council, Inc., 1954-60, and Associated Press, 1957-66. Director of domestic branch of U.S. Office of War Information, 1944. Vice-president and director of New Orleans International House; life director of local American Red Cross.

MEMBER: Inter-American Press Association (member of board of directors, 1950-57), American Society of Newspaper Editors (president, 1958-59), National Press Club, Associated Press Managing Editors' Association (president, 1943-46), Foreign Relations Association (New Orleans; member of board of directors), Sigma Delta Chi (president, 1947-48). *Awards, honors:* Order of Christopher Columbus, from the Dominican Republic, 1946; Order of Leopold II, from Belgium, 1956; Star of Solidarity, from Italy, 1958; medal of international merit, from the city of New Orleans, 1959; international reporting award, from Press Club of New Orleans, 1959.

WRITINGS: (Contributor) Francis T. Hunter, editor, *The Iron Gate,* Kriendler Memorial Foundation, 1950; (contributor) Henry Gemmill and Bernard Kilgore, editors, *Do You Belong in Journalism?,* Appleton, 1959; (contributor) James W. Webb and A. Wigfall Green, editors, *William Faulkner of Oxford,* Louisiana State University Press, 1965; *A Lifetime on Deadline* (autobiography), Pelican, 1976. Editor of *Scream,* 1925-26; contributing editor of *Collier's,* 1936-41.

WORK IN PROGRESS: Research on inequities in the distribution of revenues received from minerals developments from public lands, both offshore and inshore.

SIDELIGHTS: Healy writes: "*A Lifetime on Deadline* was written to preserve for posterity history of significant events from the point of view of an observer of and participant in those events—as well as to inform active journalists regarding practices and opinions of an editor who achieved considerable success with a prestigious newspaper."

* * *

HEATH, Charles C(hastain) 1921-

PERSONAL: Born September 7, 1921, in Sapulpa, Okla.; son of Connie C. and Keren (Boyd) Heath; married Betty Rose Abernathy, July 5, 1947; children: Janice Moon, Brian Neal, Eric Scott. *Education:* Attended University of North Carolina. *Politics:* Republican. *Religion:* Baptist. *Home:* 1205 Wesson Rd., Shelby, N.C. 28150. *Office:* Heath & Associates, 7 North LaFayette St., Shelby, N.C. 28150.

CAREER: Shelby Gas, Inc., Shelbyville, Ill., manager, 1946-49; Illinois Power Co., Decatur, superintendent of gas service, 1950-54; City of Shelby, N.C., manager of gas company, 1954-59; Heath & Associates, Shelby, N.C., president, 1959—. Member of state Emergency Gas Planning Board; charter member of North Carolina Industrial Development Foundation; member of board of directors of North Carolina Railroad Co. *Military service:* U.S. Marine Corps, 1942-46.

MEMBER: American Gas Association, Southeast Gas Association, North Carolina Congressional Club, Conservative Caucus, Shelby Junior Chamber of Commerce (past president). *Awards, honors:* George Washington Medal of Honor from Freedoms Foundation, 1962; national award from Freedoms Foundation, 1964, for an essay, award for public address, 1971; editorial award from *Gas,* 1966; award from American Security Council, 1967.

WRITINGS: You Can Save America, Pageant-Poseidon, 1972; *The Golden Egg, the Goose, and Us,* Production House, 1976. Contributor to gas industry magazines.

SIDELIGHTS: Heath writes that he began writing and speaking on national politics because of his concern about the direction in which the United States is going. He believes that the individual performs best morally, socially, and economically where there is a minimum of imposed interference from the government. Since he sees more government interference every day, he feels more need to speak out. He does, however, believe that "Americans can and will get this great republic back on track, that they will return to common sense government and that citizens will become more politically active and express themselves at the polls and to their elected representatives."

* * *

HEBBLETHWAITE, Peter   1930-
(Robert Myddleton)

PERSONAL: Born September 30, 1930, in Ashton-under-Lyne, England; son of Charles and Elsie Hebblethwaite; married Margaret Speaight, July 21, 1974; children: Dominic. *Education:* Les Fontaines, lic. philosophy, 1953; Oxford University, first class honors in medieval and modern languages, 1958; Heythrop College, lic. theology, 1964. *Religion:* Roman Catholic. *Home:* 10 Earl St., Oxford, England. *Agent:* Sheila Watson, 8/12 Old Queen St., Storey's Gate, London S.W.1, England. *Office:* Department of French, Wadham College, Oxford University, Oxford, England.

CAREER: Month, London, England, literary editor, 1965-68, editor, 1968-73; Oxford University, Oxford, England, lecturer in French, 1976—. *Member:* Secretariat for Non-Believers, Council for Science and Society.

WRITINGS: Georges Bernanos, Bowes & Bowes, 1965; *The Council Fathers and Atheism,* Paulist/Newman, 1966; *Inside the Synod,* Paulist/Newman, 1968 (published in England as *Understanding the Synod,* Michael Gill, 1968); *Theology of the Church,* Mercier Press, 1969; (translator) Ladislaus Boros, *Breakthrough to God,* Darton, Longman & Todd, 1974; *The Runaway Church,* Seabury, 1975; *Christian-Marxist Dialogue and Beyond,* Paulist/Newman, 1977; (translator) Milan Machovec, *A Marxist Looks at Jesus,* Darton, Longman & Todd, 1977. Television critic for *Tablet* (under pseudonym Robert Myddleton) and contributor to *Times Literary Supplement.*

WORK IN PROGRESS: The Gods of the French (tentative title), exploring French literature; *The Next Pope.*

SIDELIGHTS: Hebblethwaite writes that his most important book so far has been "*The Runaway Church*—an attempt to get beyond the slogans toward what had really been happening—on an international level—to the Roman Catholic Church in the years after Vatican II." *Christian-Marxist Dialogue and Beyond* is "an attempt at contemporary history—same period covered, same aims of clarification, but with a more limited field." His books have been translated into Spanish, French, Dutch, and Italian.

HEBERT, Tom   1938-

PERSONAL: Born August 9, 1938, in Wenatchee, Wash.; son of Leon and Elene C. Hebert. *Education:* Linfield College, B.A., 1960; Baylor University, graduate study, 1960-62; also attended University of Washington, Seattle, and University of Guanajuato. *Home and office:* 1801 16th N.W., Washington, D.C. 20009. *Agent:* Gerard McCauley Agency, Inc., 551 Fifth Ave., New York, N.Y. 10017.

CAREER: U.S. Peace Corps, Washington, D.C., assistant lecturer in drama at University of Ibadan, 1962-64; Texas A & M University, Prairie View, assistant professor of English, 1964-65; established and directed new United Service Organizations clubs in South Vietnam, 1966-67, became executive director of Saigon operation, 1967-68; refugee relief officer in Seattle, Wash. to help Nigerian and Biafran refugees (at times associated with United Nations Children's Fund—UNICEF and with church groups), 1968-69; Trans-Century Corp., Washington, D.C., chief personnel consultant, 1969; college management consultant, 1970-71; writer and educational consultant, 1971—. Founder of Center for the Study of Consumer Financed Education; president of Worldwide Technical Training Association, Inc.

WRITINGS: (With John Coyne) *This Way Out: A Guide to Alternatives to College,* Dutton, 1972; (with Coyne) *By Hand: A Guide to Schools and a Career in Crafts,* Dutton, 1974; (with Coyne) *Getting Skilled: A Guide to Private Trade and Technical Schools,* Dutton, 1976.

* * *

HECHTER, Michael   1943-

PERSONAL: Born November 15, 1943, in Los Angeles, Calif.; son of Oscar (a biological scientist) and Gertrude (a painter; maiden name, Horowitz) Hechter; married, 1965 (terminated); children: Joshua, Rachel. *Education:* Columbia University, A.B., 1965, Ph.D., 1972. *Home:* 618 36th Ave., Seattle, Wash. 98122. *Office:* Department of Sociology, University of Washington, Seattle, Wash. 98195.

CAREER: University of Washington, Seattle, acting assistant professor, 1970-71, assistant professor, 1971-73, associate professor of sociology, 1973—, director of Center for Studies in Macrosociology, 1974—. *Member:* International Sociological Association, International Studies Association, American Sociological Association, Economic History Association, Social Science History Association, Economic History Society (England). *Awards, honors:* Woodrow Wilson fellowship, 1965; Council for European Studies fellowship, at Universite des Sciences Sociales de Grenoble, 1975.

WRITINGS: (Contributor) N. Baster, editor, *Measuring Development,* Frank Cass, 1972; (contributor) *Society Today,* CRM Books, 2nd edition (Hechter was not included in 1st edition), 1973; *Internal Colonialism: The Celtic Fringe in British National Development, 1536-1966,* University of California Press, 1975; (contributor) T. K. Hopkins and I. Wallerstein, editors, *National Politics and the World Economy: Essays in Historical Social Change,* Routledge & Kegan Paul, in press. Contributor of about twenty articles and reviews to journals in the social sciences. Member of editorial board of *Language Problems and Language Planning* and *Theory and Society;* referee for National Science Foundation and National Endowment for the Humanities.

WORK IN PROGRESS: Status Group and Class in Industrial Society, for St. Martin's; editing *Ethnicity and the*

Cultural Division of Labor, for University of Washington Press.

* * *

HECK, Frank H(opkins)   1904-

PERSONAL: Born October 18, 1904, in Racine, Wis.; son of Victor and Ruth Alice (Perham) Heck; married Edna Drill (a teacher), October 3, 1945; children: Edward V. *Education:* Lawrence University, A.B., 1925; University of Minnesota, M.A., 1929, Ph.D., 1938. *Politics:* Democrat. *Religion:* Episcopalian. *Home:* 614 East Main St., Danville, Ky. 40422.

CAREER: High school history teacher in Rice Lake, Wis., 1926-27, and Faribault, Minn., 1928-29; Nebraska State Teachers College, Peru, assistant professor, 1929-33, associate professor of history, 1933-38; Miami University, Oxford, Ohio, assistant professor, 1938-46, associate professor of history and chairman of integrated studies, 1946-48; Centre College, Danville, Ky., professor of history, 1948-74, dean, 1955-65; writer, 1974—. *Military service:* U.S. Army Air Forces, 1942-46; became captain.

MEMBER: American Historical Association, Organization of American Historians, Southern Historical Association, Kentucky Historical Society, Minnesota Historical Society, Filson Club, Phi Beta Kappa, Beta Theta Pi.

WRITINGS: The Civil War Veteran in Minnesota Life and Politics, Mississippi Valley Press, 1941; (contributor) W. F. Craven and J. L. Cate, editors, *The Army Air Forces in World War Two,* Volume VII, University of Chicago Press, 1958; *Proud Kentuckian: John C. Breckinridge, 1821-1875,* University Press of Kentucky, 1976. Contributor to history journals.

* * *

HEDRICK, Travis K.   1904(?)-1977

1904(?)—May 30, 1977; American newsman and labor union public relations official. Hedrick worked for the Soviet News Agency Tass and for a labor news service. For refusing to acknowledge himself a Communist, Hedrick was "blacklisted" as a result of the Senate Internal Security Subcommittee hearings in the early 1950's. He died in Arlington, Va. Obituaries: *New York Times,* May 31, 1977; *Washington Post,* May 31, 1977.

* * *

HEEZEN, Bruce C(harles)   1924-1977

April 11, 1924—June 21, 1977; American geologist, oceanographer, pioneer in mapping the ocean floors, and author. Heezen helped discover and map the forty-seven thousand mile globe-encompassing system of rifts and ridges. He co-authored a multi-volume work, *The Floors of the Oceans,* and a book on undersea photography, *The Face of the Deep.* He died in a submarine off the southwest coast of Iceland. Obituaries: *New York Times,* June 23, 1977; *Time,* July 4, 1977. (See index for previous *CA* sketch)

* * *

HEFFNER, Richard D(ouglas)   1925-

PERSONAL: Born August 5, 1925, in New York, N.Y.; son of Albert Simon (a transportation executive) and Cely (Bender) Heffner; married Anne de la Vergne, December 14, 1946 (marriage annulled, 1949); married Elaine Segal (a social worker), July 30, 1950; children: Daniel Jason,

Charles Andrew. *Education:* Columbia University, A.B., 1946, M.A., 1947; University of California, further graduate study. *Home:* 90 Riverside Dr., New York, N.Y. 10024. *Office:* Rutgers University, 207 Murray Hall, New Brunswick, N.J., 08903.

CAREER: Rutgers University, New Brunswick, N.J., instructor in history, 1948-50; Columbia University, New York City, lecturer in history, 1950-52; Sarah Lawrence College, Bronxville, N.Y., professor of history, 1952-53; free-lance writer, producer, and broadcaster, 1953-55; WNBC-TV, New York City, director of public affairs programs, 1955-57, producer and moderator of "The Open Mind," 1956-59; Metropolitan Educational Television Association, New York City, director of programs, 1957-59; CBS Television Network, New York City, director of special projects, 1959-61; Educational Broadcasting Corp., Channel 13, New York City, vice-president and general manager, 1961-63; Rutgers University, university professor of communications and public policy, 1964—. Director of programs, Metropolitan Educational Television, New York City, 1957-59. Moderator and producer of "The Open Mind," for WPIX-TV, and Public Broadcasting System, 1974—. Lecturer in history and political science, New School for Social Research, 1952-62. Chairman, Code and Rating Administration of Motion Picture Association of America, Inc., 1974. Editorial consultant to CBS, Inc. Director of Twentieth Century Fund's commission on campaign costs in the electronic era, 1968-69, and Ford Foundation's study of American television's environmental value-messages, 1970-72. President, Richard Heffner Associates, Inc. (communication consultants), 1964—. *Member:* American Academy of Arts and Sciences, National Association of Educational Broadcasters, Phi Beta Kappa.

WRITINGS: A Documentary History of the United States, Mentor Books, 1952; (editor) Alexis de Tocqueville, *Democracy in America,* Mentor Books, 1954. Contributor of reviews and articles to periodicals, including *New York Times* and *Saturday Review.*

WORK IN PROGRESS: Successive volumes on the mass media in America.

* * *

HEIDEMAN, Eugene P.   1929-

PERSONAL: Born June 30, 1929, in Plymouth, Wis.; son of George Ira (a farmer) and Priscilla (Hesselink) Heideman; married Mary Jane Menninga, July 23, 1952; children: Beth, Paul, Ruth, Carl. *Education:* Central College, Pella, Iowa, B.A., 1951; Western Theological Seminary, Holland, Mich., B.D., 1954; National University of Utrecht, Th.D., 1959. *Politics:* Independent. *Home:* 547 Maple Ave., Holland, Mich. 49423. *Office:* Western Theological Seminary, Holland, Mich. 49423.

CAREER: Pastor of Reformed church in Edmonton, Alberta, 1957-60, missionary in India, 1960-70; Central College, Pella, Iowa, professor of religion and chaplain, 1970-76; Western Theological Seminary, Holland, Mich., director of professional growth, 1976—, academic dean, 1977—.

WRITINGS: The Relation of Revelation and Reason in H. Bavinck and E. Brunner, Van Gorcum, 1959; *The Reluctant Worker Priest,* Eerdmans, 1967; *Reformed Bishops and Catholic Elders,* Eerdmans, 1970; *Our Song of Hope,* Eerdmans, 1974.

WORK IN PROGRESS: A book on the relation of church and state, with particular reference to the role of the Bible in public life.

SIDELIGHTS: Heideman's main interest is in world affairs, especially in India. He speaks Dutch, German, and Tamil.

* * *

HEIDI, Gloria

PERSONAL: Born in Los Angeles, Calif.; daughter of Alonzo Cannon (a colonel in U.S. Army) and Dominica (Bianco) Hyde; married James Gail Earp (a research writer). *Education:* Attended University of California, Los Angeles. *Residence:* Sacramento, Calif.

CAREER: Television and radio performer, and free-lance lecturer in the field of self-improvement, 1955-65; KXTV, Sacramento, Calif., television women's editor, newscaster and weatherperson, and variety show hostess, 1966-70; Bauder Fashion College, Sacramento, public relations director, 1970-72; Gloria Heidi & Associates (public relations firm), Sacramento, founding president, 1972—. Free-lance fashion model and fashion coordinator, 1955-70; University of California, Los Angeles, lecturer at extension centers, 1957-60; co-hostess of radio program "A Blind Man Looks At You," for KIEV, 1955-57; hostess for a series of interviews entitled "Adoption: The Story of People Who Need People," for KXTV, 1969; private consultant and lecturer for State of California Personnel Board. *Member:* California Writers' Club, Northern California Writers Guild, Alpha Phi.

WRITINGS: Winning the Age Game, Doubleday, 1976.

WORK IN PROGRESS: Research for a book on new techniques in plastic surgery.

AVOCATIONAL INTERESTS: Travel, hiking, backpacking, bicycling, and wildlife photography.

* * *

HEILMAN, Samuel C(hiel) 1946-

PERSONAL: Born May 26, 1946, in Karlsruhe, Germany; came to the United States in 1950, naturalized citizen, 1955; son of Henry (a business executive) and Lucia (a manager of a thrift shop; maiden name, Kirschenbaum) Heilman; married Ellin M. Kaufman (a counselor), June 15, 1969; children: Adam Zachary, Uriel David. *Education:* Brandeis University, B.A., 1968; New School for Social Research, M.A., 1970; University of Pennsylvania, Ph.D., 1973. *Politics:* "Pragmatism." *Religion:* Jewish. *Residence:* New Rochelle, N.Y. *Office:* Department of Sociology, Queens College of the City University of New York, Flushing, N.Y. 11367.

CAREER: Maiden Mills, Lawrence, Mass., personnel consultant, 1969, 1971; St. Joseph's College, Philadelphia, Pa., lecturer in sociology, 1972-73; Queens College of the City University of New York, Flushing, N.Y., assistant professor of sociology, 1973—. Visiting professor at Max Weinrich Center for Advanced Jewish Studies, at YIVO Institute, 1976—. *Member:* American Sociological Association, Eastern Sociological Association.

WRITINGS: (Contributor) Peter Rose, editor, *The Study of Society,* Random House, 1967, 4th edition, 1977; *Synagogue Life: A Study in Symbolic Interaction,* University of Chicago Press, 1976. Contributor of about a dozen articles and reviews to scholarly journals.

WORK IN PROGRESS: Cosmopolitan Parochials (tentative title), discussing the antinomian character of modern Orthodoxy; *Memoirs of a Survivor's Child,* "my response to my parents' survival of the Nazi terror."

SIDELIGHTS: Heilman writes: "A year after my parents were liberated from the German death camps, I was born. My family was then living in Germany. They had come out of their experience in terror, renewed in their faith in God but in doubt about their faith in men. That astounding faith became the single organizing feature of my family and consequently of me. Surviving our voyage to America as displaced persons, we began to set down roots in Boston and in New England. There, I attended both public schools and for a short time Orthodox Jewish day schools. These two strains—the cosmopolitan and the parochial—merged in the character of my writing and my interest. I have tried to reveal some of them in the blend of sociology and Jewish ethnography in my first book, and the same themes must necessarily appear in my next work.

"Being entrepreneurial in some part of my character, I have also become a part-time diamond dealer and importer, a vocation that is really more of an avocation.

"I have travelled extensively through Europe and Israel. I speak Hebrew, French, German, Polish, and Yiddish."

* * *

HEIMDAHL, Ralph 1909-

PERSONAL: Born March 22, 1909, in Willmar, Minn.; son of Peter (a store manager) and Clara (Thorson) Heimdahl; married Esther Belfi, May, 1938; children: Laverne Dupas, Linda Day, Martha Slavin. *Education:* St. Cloud State Teachers College (now St. Cloud State University), teacher's certificate. *Politics:* Republican. *Religion:* Lutheran. *Home and office:* 218 Longley Way, Arcadia, Calif. 91006.

CAREER/WRITINGS: State School for the Deaf, Faribault, Minn., art teacher, 1931-36; Disney Studios, Burbank, Calif., artist, 1937-41; Western Publishing Co., Hollywood, Calif., cartoon strip artist and writer, 1946-75. Artist of "Bugs Bunny," a syndicated daily cartoon strip appearing in about five hundred newspapers, 1948—; producer of "Minnie Soo and Little Haha," cartoon strip, 1946. Lecturer. *Member:* Newspaper Comic Council (New York), Northern California Cartoon and Humor Society. *Awards, honors:* Silver medal from Bolex International Film Festival, 1962, for "Autumn Madness"; first prize from Cincinatti Film Festival, 1963, for "Pond Life."

SIDELIGHTS: Heimdahl writes that "Bugs, today, is a bit slimmer than the original." "Bugs Bunny" comic strips are in collection at St. Cloud State University, Kansas State University, Albright College, and at other colleges and universities.

* * *

HEINS, Marjorie 1946-

PERSONAL: Born October 9, 1946, in New York, N.Y.; daughter of Solomon (a teacher) and Jeanne (Abelson) Holt; married Greg Heins (a photographer), May 19, 1967; children: Matthew, Catherine. *Education:* Cornell University, B.A., 1967; Harvard University, graduate study, 1976—. *Politics:* "Democrat socialist." *Home:* 32 Knowles St., Newton Center, Mass. 02157.

CAREER: Department of Social Services, New York, N.Y., caseworker, 1967-68; *San Francisco Express Times,* San Francisco, Calif., writer and office manager, 1968-69; Modern Times Bookstore, San Francisco, Calif., co-manager, 1972-73; Palmer & Dodge (law firm), Boston, Mass., law associate, 1977—.

WRITINGS: Strictly Ghetto Property, Ramparts, 1972;

(with Bill Coughlin, Howie Tumlin, and David Yohalem) *The Food Co-op Handbook,* Houghton, 1975. Contributor to periodicals, including *Boston Phoenix, Real Paper,* and *Progressive.*

SIDELIGHTS: Marjorie Heins writes: "Political journalism led me to law school where I am now a third-year student. My major interests are civil rights/civil liberties law and consumer law. I hope to find time to continue writing, especially about civil rights. The law should not be so mysterious, nor the constitutional roots of justice so inaccessible, as they sometimes are."

*　　*　　*

HEINS, Paul 1909-

PERSONAL: Born February 15, 1909, in Boston, Mass.; son of Samuel and Rose L. (Golbert) Heins; married Ethel L. Yaskin (editor of *Horn Book*), June 27, 1943; children: Peter Samuel, Margery Elizabeth. *Education:* Harvard University, B.A. (magna cum laude), 1931; Boston State College, M.Ed., 1932. *Politics:* Democrat. *Religion:* Episcopalian. *Home and office:* 29 Hope St., Auburndale, Mass. 02166.

CAREER: High school English teacher in Boston, Mass., 1934-67; *Horn Book,* Boston, Mass., editor, 1967-74; Framingham State College, Framingham, Mass., instructor in children's literature, 1975; Simmons College, Boston, Mass., instructor in children's literature, 1975—. Member of Newbery-Caldecott awards committee, 1969, and Caroline Hewins scholarship committee, 1975-76; Hans Christian Andersen awards nominating committee, chairman, 1976, member. *Military service:* U.S. Army, 1944-46. *Member:* American Library Association (Children's Services Division), English Teachers Lunch Club. *Awards, honors:* Ford Foundation fellowship, 1954-55.

WRITINGS: Out on a Limb with the Critics, Horn Book, Inc., 1970; *Coming to Terms with Criticism,* Horn Book, Inc., 1970; (translator) Jacob and Wilhelm Grimm, *Snow White* (juvenile), Little, Brown, 1974; (author of introduction) Mollie Hunter, *Talent Is Not Enough,* Harper, 1976. Contributor of articles and reviews to *Cricket* and *Horn Book.* Member of editorial board of *Cricket,* 1973—.

WORK IN PROGRESS: A book of critical essays collected from *Horn Book,* 1967-77.

AVOCATIONAL INTERESTS: Travel (especially England).

*　　*　　*

HEINTZ, Bonnie L(ee) 1924-

PERSONAL: Born June 28, 1924, in Junction City, Kan.; daughter of Ralph and Dorritt (Wilgocki) Heintz. *Education:* Student at Midland College, 1941, and Pacific Lutheran University, 1943; University of Puget Sound, B.A., 1949; University of Washington, Seattle, M.A., 1961, Ph.D., 1970. *Politics:* Independent. *Religion:* Methodist. *Residence:* Winslow, Wash. *Office:* Department of Humanities, Seattle Pacific University, Seattle, Wash. 98119.

CAREER: Seattle Pacific University, Seattle, Wash., instructor, 1960-64, associate professor, 1964-77, professor of English, 1977—. Past president of Seattle Cooperative; member of board of directors of Science Fiction Hall of Fame. Member of Washington governor's Committee for the Year Two Thousand; member of executive committee of "Seattle 2000."

MEMBER: International Underwater Archaeological Association, World Wildlife Society, Society for the History of Archaeology, American Camping Association, National Council of Teachers of English, Mediaeval Academy of America, Dorothy Sayers Society, Charles Williams Society, Royal Irish Academy, Pondicherrry Lodge (bibliographer), Lambda Iota Tau. *Awards, honors:* Research fellowship from U.S. Department of Health, Education and Welfare, 1971.

WRITINGS: (Editor) *Tomorrow and Tomorrow and Tomorrow* (science fiction), Holt, 1973; *The Stones of the Field* (archaeology), U.S. Government, in press; *From Under the Horns of the Unicorn* (biography), U.S. Government, in press. Contributor to magazines. Associate editor of *Lambda Iota Tau Quarterly.*

WORK IN PROGRESS: Spriggins Holiday (tentative title), a novel; a critical biography of Dorothy Sayers; a biography of Chief Sealth; research for a biography of Charles Williams; research on Ogham.

SIDELIGHTS: Bonnie Heintz comments: "As a college professor, I see that the children of the sixties have been replaced by a group of 1970's students who are potentially ultraconservative. Public education is not doing the job of providing the students with basic education. I teach varied subjects from science fiction to Anglo-Saxon, and specialize in mythology, detective fiction, and Tolkien and Lewis. Traveling in England (with or without students) has been and continues to be most rewarding."

*　　*　　*

HELLER, H(einz) Robert 1940-

PERSONAL: Born January 8, 1940, in Cologne, Germany; came to the United States in 1960, naturalized citizen, 1970; son of H.K.W. and Karin (Hermann) Heller; married Emily E. Mitchell, December 5, 1970; children: Kimberly Karin. *Education:* Parsons College, B.A., 1961; University of Minnesota, M.A., 1962; University of California, Berkeley, Ph.D., 1965. *Office:* International Monetary Fund, Washington, D.C. 20431.

CAREER: University of California, Berkeley, acting instructor in economics, 1965; University of California, Los Angeles, assistant professor, 1965-68, associate professor of economics, 1968-71; University of Hawaii, Honolulu, professor of economics and chairman of department, 1971-74; International Monetary Fund, Washington, D.C., chief of financial studies, 1974—. Visiting professor at Universitaet des Saarlandes and Universitaet Goettingen, both 1970; exchange visitor of Nagoya University, 1970.

MEMBER: American Economic Association, Royal Economic Society, Western Economic Association, Omicron Delta Epsilon. *Awards, honors:* Ford Foundation fellowship, 1965-68; Governmental Research Association grant, Universitaet Goettingen, 1970; National Science Foundation grant, 1971-72; North Atlantic Treaty Organization fellowship, 1973-74.

WRITINGS: International Trade: Theory and Empirical Evidence, Prentice-Hall, 1968, revised edition, 1973; *The Economic System,* Macmillan, 1972; *Japanese Investment in the United States,* Praeger, 1974; *International Monetary Economics,* Prentice-Hall, 1974. Contributor to business and economics journals. Associate editor of *Journal of Money, Credit, and Banking.*

WORK IN PROGRESS: Research on international liquidity and on international monetary economics.

HELLINGER, Douglas A(lan) 1948-

PERSONAL: Born March 11, 1948, in New York, N.Y.; son of James L. (a lawyer and business executive) and Eleanor (De Young) Hellinger. *Education:* Queens College of the City University of New York, B.A., 1969; Columbia University, M.B.A., 1973. *Office:* Development Group for Alternative Policies, Inc., 2200 19th St. N.W., Suite 206, Washington, D.C. 20009.

CAREER: U.S. Peace Corps, Washington, D.C., volunteer worker in northeast Brazil, 1970-72; Inter-American Foundation, Washington, D.C., consultant, 1973-74; Developing World Industry and Technology, Inc., Washington, D.C., associate, 1975-76; Development Group for Alternative Policies, Inc., Washington, D.C., co-director, 1976. Member of project selection committee of Private Agencies Collaborating Together (PACT), Inc.; consultant to World Bank.

WRITINGS: (With brother, Stephen H. Hellinger) *Unemployment and the Multinationals: A Strategy for Technological Change in Latin America,* Kennikat, 1976. Contributor to *World Development.*

SIDELIGHTS: Development Group for Alternative Policies was formed by Hellinger and his brother for the purpose of broadening the public debate within the United States on international development issues. Hellinger writes, "It is our aim to reach out to the American public and into established development institutions so as to widen perspectives, reveal development myths, and establish as a credible goal the control of projects by poor communities. Our work plan for 1977 includes the publication of a bi-monthly newsletter and participation in the establishment of a new international social development foundation." Hellinger has traveled and worked in Latin America and Europe.

*   *   *

HELLINGER, Stephen H(enry) 1948-

PERSONAL: Born March 11, 1948, in New York, N.Y.; son of James L. (a lawyer and business executive) and Eleanor (De Young) Hellinger. *Education:* Queens College of the City University of New York, B.A., 1969; Columbia University, M.B.A., 1973. *Office:* Development Group for Alternative Policies, Inc., 2200 19th St. N.W., Suite 206, Washington, D.C. 20009.

CAREER: U.S. Peace Corps, Washington, D.C., volunteer worker in Nicaragua and Venezuela, 1970-72; Inter-American Foundation, Washington, D.C., consultant, 1973; Overseas Development Council, Washington, D.C., associate fellow, 1975-76; Developing World Industry and Technology, Inc., Washington, D.C., consultant, 1976; Development Group for Alternative Policies, Inc., Washington, D.C., co-director, 1976—. Consultant to UNESCO and World Bank.

WRITINGS: (With brother, Douglas A. Hellinger) *Unemployment and the Multinationals: A Strategy for Technological Change in Latin America,* Kennikat, 1976. Contributor to *World Development.*

SIDELIGHTS: Hellinger and his twin brother write that their Development Group for Alternative Policies was formed for the purpose of broadening the public debate within the United States on international development issues.

Hellinger told *CA:* "It is our belief that American developmental programs and policies generally have not been responsive to the expressed needs of poor people overseas. Furthermore, we believe that the narrowness of the current international development debate has kept the U.S. public virtually uninformed about alternative views on these issues. As a consequence, we are left with a limited range of approaches, none of which focuses upon the active participation of the poor in their own project identification, design, and implementation."

*   *   *

HELLMAN, Arthur D(avid) 1942-

PERSONAL: Born December 9, 1942, in New York, N.Y.; son of Charles (a teacher) and Florence (a chemist; maiden name, Cohen) Hellman. *Education:* Harvard University, B.A. (magna cum laude), 1963; Yale University, LL.B., 1966. *Home:* 6313 Fifth Ave., Apt. 304, Pittsburgh, Pa. 15206. *Office:* School of Law, University of Pittsburgh, Pittsburgh, Pa. 15260.

CAREER: Law clerk to Minnesota associate justice James C. Otis, 1966-67; William Mitchell College of Law, St. Paul, Minn., assistant professor of law, 1967-70; University of Connecticut, West Hartford, assistant professor of law, 1970-72; University of Illinois, Champaign, visiting assistant professor of law, 1972-73; Commission on Revision of the Federal Court Appellate System, Washington, D.C., deputy executive director, 1973-75; University of Pittsburgh, Pittsburgh, Pa., associate professor of law, 1975—, associate dean of faculty, 1977—. *Member:* American Law Institute, American Judicature Society; Supreme Court Historical Society.

WRITINGS: Laws Against Marijuana: The Price We Pay, University of Illinois Press, 1975. Contributor to law journals, popular magazines, and newspapers.

WORK IN PROGRESS: A major study of the work of the U.S. Supreme Court.

AVOCATIONAL INTERESTS: Travel, music.

*   *   *

HELLMAN, Geoffrey T(heodore) 1907-

PERSONAL: Born February 13, 1907, in New York, N.Y.; son of George S. and Hilda Emily (Josephthal) Hellman; married Katherine Henry, August 18, 1960; children: Daisy, Katherine. *Education:* Yale University, A.B., 1928. *Office: New Yorker,* 25 West 43rd St., New York, N.Y. 10036.

CAREER: New Yorker, New York City, reporter and associate editor, 1929-31; *Fortune,* New York City, associate editor, 1931-32; *New Yorker,* staff writer, 1932-36; *Life,* New York City, associate editor, 1936-38; *New Yorker,* staff writer, 1938—. Staff writer for Office of the Coordinator of Inter-American Affairs, 1942-44. *Wartime service:* Consultant to U.S. Army Air Forces headquarters, 1944; member of history section of Office of Strategic Services, 1944-45. *Member:* Chi Delta Theta, Grolier Club, Coffee House Club, Century Club, Dutch Treat Club, Graduates Club, Cosmos Club.

WRITINGS: Inquirendo Concerning a Peculiar Aberration or Detracking of the Collecting Impulse, Hawthorn House, 1933; *Motor-Car Touring Society of the City of New York, 1907-1919,* privately printed, 1941; *How to Disappear for an Hour,* Dodd, 1947, Books for Libraries, 1971; *Mrs. De-Peyster's Parties and Other Lively Studies from the New Yorker,* Macmillan, 1963; *Profile of a Museum,* Art in America, 1965; *The Smithsonian Octopus on the Mall,* Lippincott, 1967; *Bankers, Bones, and Beetles: The First Century of the American Museum of Natural History,* Natural History Press, 1968. Also author of *Onward and Upward with the Sciences: The Tail of Taxonomy,* 1964.

Work represented in anthologies. Contributor of profiles and satire to popular magazines, including *New Yorker*.*

* * *

HELLYER, Paul (Theodore) 1923-

PERSONAL: Born August 6, 1923, in Waterford, Ontario, Canada; son of Audrey Samuel (a farmer) and Lulla Maude (Anderson) Hellyer; married: Ellen Jean Ralph, June 1, 1945; children: Mary Elizabeth, Peter Lawrence, David Ralph. *Education:* Curtiss-Wright Technical Institute of Aerodynamics, diploma in aeronautical engineering, 1941; University of Toronto, B.A., 1949. *Religion:* United Church. *Home:* 1982 Rideau River Dr., Ottawa, Ontario, Canada.

CAREER: Fleet Aircraft Manufacturing Co. Ltd., Fort Erie, Ontario, began as junior draftsman, became group leader in engineering department, 1942-44; House of Commons, Ottawa, Ontario, representative from Davenport riding, 1949-57, and Trinity riding, 1958-74; *Toronto Sun,* Toronto, Ontario, author of syndicated column "Comment—Paul Hellyer," 1974—. Proprietor of Mari-Jane Fashions (Toronto), 1945-56; president of Curran-Hall Ltd., 1951-62, Trepil Realty Ltd., 1951-62, and Hendon Estates Ltd., 1959-62; member of Toronto Board of Trade. Distinguished visitor at York University, 1969-70. Member of Canadian Privy Council and Associate Minister of National Defence, 1957-69, Minister of National Defence, 1963-67, Minister of Transport, 1967-69, Minister responsible for housing and urban affairs, 1968-69, acting Prime Minister, 1968-69; founding chairman of Action Canada (populist movement), 1971—; committee chairman and opposition spokesman on industry, trade, and commerce for Progressive Conservative Caucus, 1973. *Military service:* Royal Canadian Air Force, 1944; Canadian Army, Royal Canadian Artillery, 1945-46.

MEMBER: Royal Society for the Encouragement of Arts, Manufactures and Commerce (fellow), Canadian Association for Adult Education, Canadian Authors Association, Commonwealth Parliamentary Association, North Atlantic Treaty Organization (NATO) Parliamentary Association, Ontario Club.

WRITINGS: Agenda: A Plan for Action, Prentice-Hall, 1971. Contributor to *Queen's Quarterly.*

WORK IN PROGRESS: Stagflation; research on five years as Minister of National Defense.

SIDELIGHTS: Hellyer told *CA:* "My central thesis has been that the division between Left and Right in politics between East and West in the world is based on a false premise, i.e., that it is not possible to operate a decentralized private capital system with full employment and stable prices. If the premise is wrong, as I believe, then the whole superstructure of bandaid programs designed to alleviate the symptoms has to be re-examined. While, theoretically, politics is the vehicle for the re-examination, the rigidity of bureaucracies and the reluctance to innovate makes the introduction of new ideas difficult."

AVOCATIONAL INTERESTS: Swimming, waterskiing, skin and scuba diving, stamp collecting.

* * *

HELMLINGER, (Benita) Trudy 1943-

PERSONAL: Born January 2, 1943, in Seattle, Wash.; daughter of Benjamin V. (in the military) and Birdie (Pettigrove) Helmlinger. *Education:* California State University, Sacramento, B.A., 1967, M.S.W., 1969. *Residence:* Carmichael, Calif. *Office:* Eskaton Mental Health Clinic, 6127 Fair Oaks Blvd., Carmichael, Calif. 95608.

CAREER: Children's Protective Services, Sacramento, Calif., psychiatric social worker, 1969-70; Children's Protective Services, Placerville, Calif., psychiatric social worker, 1970-71; Eskaton Mental Health Clinic, Carmichael, Calif., psychotherapist, 1971—. Private practice in psychotherapy in Carmichael, Calif., 1971—. *Member:* National Association of Social Workers, Sacramento Area Mental Health Association.

WRITINGS: After You've Said Good-Bye (non-fiction), Schenkman, 1977.

WORK IN PROGRESS: Diary of a Female Therapist (tentative title), completion expected in 1978.

SIDELIGHTS: Trudy Helmlinger writes: "I am *not* a writer. I'm a therapist who sometimes writes. Helping people who are hurting has always been a major theme in my life. *After You've Said Good-Bye* came from my belief and experiences that we can grow through the crises in our lives if we know how. *Good-Bye* is my way of sharing how. I hope it will be helpful to those who read it."

* * *

HELPERN, Milton 1902-1977

April 17, 1902—April 22, 1977; American forensic pathologist and author. Helpern was medical examiner in New York City from 1931 to 1954, and chief medical examiner from 1954 until his retirement in 1973. One of his books, co-authored with three other physicians, was used not only by pathologists but also by mystery writers looking for novel, but possible means of murder. Helpern had received numerous awards and honorary degrees. He died in San Diego, Calif. Obituaries: *New York Times,* April 23, 1977; *Newsweek,* May 2, 1977; *Current Biography,* June, 1977.

* * *

HEMINGWAY, Patricia Drake 1926-

PERSONAL: Born November 29, 1926, in Berwick, Pa.; daughter of H. Gladstone (a businessman) and Lela (a pianist; maiden name, Drake) Hemingway. *Education:* Attended Bloomsburg State College, 1944, and Morris Harvey College, 1945. *Politics:* Independent Democrat. *Religion:* Presbyterian. *Agent:* Helen Brann Agency, 14 Sutton Place S., New York, N.Y. 10022.

CAREER: Bull's Head Inn, Bridgehampton, N.Y., manager, 1963-68; Late Edition, Delmonico Hotel, New York, N.Y., owner and manager, 1965; Hemingway's, New York City, owner and manager, 1969-70; Witches Brew, Mojacar, Spain, owner and manager, 1971-72.

WRITINGS: The Transcendental Meditation Primer, McKay, 1975; *The Auto Repair Primer,* Little, Brown, 1977; *Clothes for Careers,* McKay, 1977.

WORK IN PROGRESS: A book on "aging, causes and cures and approaches."

SIDELIGHTS: Patricia Hemingway told *CA:* "Before I learned to read and write, the publishing/printing industry became part of me because I fell in love with a publisher and he fell in love with me. I was three. I spent every day, all day, at the newspaper office and plant. The cacaphony of the linotypes was a part of me.

"I am an avid traveller. I have been around the world by freighter once and around another time by various means of conveyances. I now travel extensively by camper both in Europe and America and Mexico. Asia and South America next.''

AVOCATIONAL INTERESTS: Photography, Eastern philosophy and religion, yoga, transcendental meditation.

*   *   *

HENDERSON, George L(eslie)   1925-

PERSONAL: Born April 7, 1925, in Brainerd, Minn.; son of David and Bernice (Froebel) Henderson; married Miriam Louise Potter, September 1, 1946; children: Larry Wayne, Lee Alan, James Leslie. *Education:* University of Minnesota, student, 1943-44; University of Illinois, B.S., 1948, M.Ed., 1954; Indiana University, M.A., 1966; also attended University of Chicago and Reed College. *Home:* 5017 Marathon Dr., Madison, Wis. 53705. *Office:* Department of Mathematics, University of Wisconsin, Eau Claire, Wis.

CAREER: Champaign-Urbana Courier, Champaign-Urbana, Ill., reporter, 1951-52; teacher of mathematics in high schools in Mansfield, Ill., 1948-51, Toluca, Ill., 1952-55, and Dixon, Ill., 1955-59; mathematics teacher and head of department at high school in Moline, Ill., 1960-64; Department of Public Instruction, Springfield, Ill., mathematics consultant, 1964-66; Department of Public Instruction, Madison, Wis., supervisor of mathematics, 1966-75; free-lance writer and consultant, 1974-76; University of Wisconsin, Eau Claire, assistant professor of mathematics, 1976—. *Military service:* U.S. Naval Reserve, active duty, 1943-46. *Member:* National Council of Teachers of Mathematics, Mathematics Education Specialists of America (executive vice-president, 1976—), Wisconsin Mathematics Council, Association of State Supervisors of Mathematics (vice-president, 1974).

WRITINGS: Let's Play Games in Mathematics, National Textbook Co., Volume K (with Adeline Walter), 1970, Volume I (with Lynn Oberlin), 1970, Volume II (with Oberlin), 1970, Volume III (with Lowell D. Glunn), 1970, Volume IV (with Glunn), 1971, Volume V (with Glunn), 1971, Volume VI (with Glunn), 1971, Volume VII (with William F. Miller), 1972; *Mathematics Supervisor's Handbook,* C. E. Merrill, 1971; (with Charles H. Johnson) *The Four Roles of Mathematics: A Liberal Arts Approach,* Prindle, 1972; *Math Games for Greater Achievement* (for underachievers), National Textbook Co., 1972; (with Glunn) *Let's Play Games in General Mathematics,* National Textbook Co., 1972; (with Glunn) *Let's Play Games in Metrics,* National Textbook Co., 1974; (with Mary I. Van Beck and Walter W. Leffin) *Introduction to Algebra: A Personalized Approach,* Prindle, 1975; (with Joan A. Martin) *Strikesville,* National Textbook Co., 1975; (with Van Beck and Leffin) *Algebra: A Personalized Approach,* Prindle, 1976; (with Sue Hildebrand, Jane Toftey, and Thomas G. Toftey) *Multidisciplinary Games and Activities,* National Textbook Co., Volume I: *K-3,* 1976, Volume II: *3-6,* 1976; (with Adeline Walter) *Motor Skills Games and Activities* (for kindergarten), National Textbook Co., 1976; (author of teacher's manual) *Measure Metric,* Agency for Instructional Television, 1977; (with Van Beck, Leffin, and Fred Janusek) *Introduction to Technical Mathematics,* Prindle, in press. Contributor of more than two hundred articles to professional and religious journals.

WORK IN PROGRESS: Several books; developing mathematical games for use in schools.

SIDELIGHTS: Henderson told *CA* he believes ''that the role of games in the mathematics classroom is to provide needed review and reinforcement of important math skills,

that games should only be used when appropriate math skills are involved.''

When not writing or teaching, Henderson conducts mathematics education workshops for teachers, including ''sessions on the metric system and the use of electronic calculators in the classroom.''

AVOCATIONAL INTERESTS: Travel, tennis, and bridge.

*   *   *

HENDERSON, Richard I(van)   1926-

PERSONAL: Born January 4, 1926, in Altoona, Pa.; son of Edgar M. and Augusta (Pasekoff) Henderson; married Jean Simonton, August 10, 1970. *Education:* U.S. Naval Academy, B.S., 1948; University of Miami, Coral Gables, Fla., M.B.A., 1967; Georgia State University, Ph.D., 1970. *Residence:* Stone Mountain, Ga. *Office:* Department of Management, Georgia State University, University Plaza, Atlanta, Ga. 30303.

CAREER: Saf-T-Bak, Inc., Altoona, Pa., plant manager, 1949-50, 1953-55; Needle Trade Industry, plant manager in Hawaii, Japan, Hong Kong, and the Philippines, 1955-58; Bertrand Frank Associates, New York, N.Y., management consultant, 1958; Saf-T-Bak, Inc., sales manager and senior salesman for southern states, 1959-67; University of Miami, Coral Gables, Fla., lecturer in management, 1967-68; Middle Tennessee State University, Murfreesboro, assistant professor of management, 1970-71; Georgia State University, Atlanta, assistant professor, 1971-75, associate professor of management, 1975—. Director of middle-management courses at University of Miami, Coral Gables, 1967—; management and planning consultant, 1967—. *Military service:* U.S. Navy, 1943-49, 1950-53; became lieutenant senior grade. *Member:* Academy of Management, American Compensation Association, Southern Management Association.

WRITINGS: Toward a Faculty Self-Appraisal System (monograph), Bureau of Business and Economic Research, Georgia State University, 1969; (with Joseph L. Reina) *Inservice Training Aid* (monograph), Tennessee Nursing Association, 1972; (with Waino W. Suojanen) *The Operating Manager: An Integrative Approach,* with workbook (with W. Michael Field and Gary L. Swallow), Prentice-Hall, 1974; *Job Descriptions: Critical Documents, Versatile Tools* (monograph), AMACOM, 1976; *Compensation Management: Rewarding Performance in the Modern Organization,* Reston, 1976; (with Stephen C. Carlson and Robert O. Wilson) *COMP-$-MAN* (workbook), Reston, 1976. Contributor of articles and reviews to management and economics journals, and to *Modern Nursing Home.*

WORK IN PROGRESS: Research on compensation practices in American organizations, executive compensation, the productivity of American organizations, and quality of work life.

*   *   *

HENDRICKS, Faye N(eidhold)   1913-

PERSONAL: Born January 12, 1913, in Wisconsin; daughter of Alvin A. (a molder and farmer) and Minnie (Schoenick) Neidhold; married George F. Guth, January 2, 1934 (divorced, February, 1957); married Russel A. Hendricks, February 15, 1968; children: Gail Marie (Mrs. Roger Meiklejohn), George Earl, Gene Arne. *Education:* Attended Marathon County Normal School. *Politics:* Republican. *Religion:* Protestant. *Home address:* P.O. Box 14, King, Wis. 54946.

CAREER: Country school teacher in Marathon County, Wis., 1931-30, and Waupaca County, Wis., in the 1950's; writer, 1974—.

WRITINGS: The Travels of Hardrock Hendricks, Ram Publishing, 1976. Contributor to *True West* and *Treasure.*

WORK IN PROGRESS: Collecting stories and photographs of people who spend most of their time on the open road, especially stories about travel adventures and hobbies.

SIDELIGHTS: Faye Hendricks writes: "My husband is a treasure hunter and his activities are most enticing. My book contains several treasure stories right from the horse's mouth." *Avocational interests:* Trailering, painting in several mediums.

* * *

HENDRY, Thomas 1929-
(Tom Hendry)

PERSONAL: Born June 7, 1929, in Winnipeg, Manitoba, Canada; son of Donald (a railway superindendent) and Martha (Best) Hendry; married Irene Chick, December 28, 1958 (divorced, 1963); married Judith Carr (general manager of a theatre), November 22, 1963; children: Thomas, Christopher, Ashleigh. *Education:* Attended University of Manitoba, 1947; Institute of Chartered Accountants of Manitoba, C.A., 1955. *Politics:* "Small 1 liberal." *Religion:* Christian ("not practiced"). *Home and office:* 34 Elgin Ave., Toronto, Ontario, Canada M5R 1G6. *Agent:* Earl Graham, 245 West 47th St., New York, N.Y. 10016.

CAREER: Hendry & Co. (accountant firm), Winnipeg, Manitoba, partner, 1955-58; Hendry & Evans, Winnipeg, partner, 1958-61. Theatre 77, Winnipeg, founder and partner, 1957-58; Manitoba Theatre Centre, Winnipeg, founder, partner, and manager, 1958-63; Canadian Theatre Centre, Toronto, Ontario, secretary general, 1964-69; Stratford Festival, Stratford, Ontario, literary manager, 1969-70; Toronto Free Theatre, Toronto, founder and president, 1971—. Writer on weekly television situation comedy, "King of Kensington." Founder and chairman of Playwrights Co-op, Toronto, 1971, and Playwrights Colony, Banff, Alberta, 1974-76. Consultant to Canada Council and Ontario Arts Council. *Member:* Association of Canadian Television and Radio Artists, Canadian Artists Representation, Canadian Institute of Chartered Accountants, Actors Equity, Arts and Letters Club (Toronto). *Awards, honors:* Centennial Medal, 1967, for services to Canada; Ontario Lieutenant Governor's Medal, 1970, for "15 Miles of Broken Glass."

WRITINGS—Under name Tom Hendry: *The Canadians* (on English-Canadian theatre), Macmillan, 1967.

Plays: "Do You Remember?" (one-act), televised by Canadian Broadcasting Corp. (CBC)-TV, 1954, produced in Winnipeg at Rainbow Stage Theatre, 1956; "Trapped" (two-act; for children), produced in Winnipeg, 1961; "Do Not Pick the Flowers" (one-act; mime play), produced in Winnipeg, 1962; (with Len Peterson) "All about Us" (two-act), produced in Winnipeg and on tour, 1964-65; *15 Miles of Broken Glass* (two-act; televised by CBC-TV, 1966), Thomas Nelson, 1968, revised edition (produced in Toronto, 1969), Playwrights Co-op (Toronto), 1972; "Satyricon" (two-act; adaptation of work by Petronius), with music by Stanley Silverman, produced in Stratford, Ontario, 1969.

The Walking Wounded (three-act; produced in Lansing, Mich., 1970; produced as "How Are Things with the Walking Wounded?" in Toronto, 1972), Playwrights Co-op, 1972; *You Smell Good to Me* (one-act), Playwrights Co-op, 1972; *That Boy—Call Him Back* (one-act; produced in Lansing, 1970), Playwrights Co-op, 1972; *The Missionary Position* (one-act), Playwrights Co-op, 1972; *The Harbour at Porto de Oro* (one-act), Playwrights Co-op, 1972; *Moving On* (one-act), Playwrights Co-op, 1972, *Naked at the Opera* (two-act; produced in Banff, 1974), Playwrights Co-op, 1972; *Costume Party* (one-act), Playwrights Co-op, 1972; *Gravediggers of 1942* (one-act; produced in Toronto, June, 1973), Playwrights Co-op, 1973; "Aces Wild" (two-act), produced in Hamilton, Ontario, 1974; "A Memory of Eden" (three-act), produced in Banff, 1975; "Byron" (two-act), produced in Toronto, 1976; "Confidence" (two-act), produced in Banff, 1976.

Television plays: "Do You Remember," CBC-TV, 1954; "The Anniversary," CBC-TV, 1955; "Box Car Ballet,, (documentary), CBC-TV, 1955; "A City in White" (documentary), CBC-TV, 1956; "A House Divided" (documentary), CBC-TV, 1957; "I Was Never in Kharkov," CBC-TV, 1972. Also author of scripts for weekly television situation comedy, "King of Kensington," and of unproduced scripts, "The Day the Freaks Took Over," a fantasy about paraplegics, and with Ron Kelly, of "Private Places."

Long-play (LP) record albums: (With Richard Foreman) "Dr. Selavy's Magic Theatre" (lyrics only; music by Stanley Silverman; produced in Lenox, Mass., and in New York City, 1972), United Artists, 1974.

Contributor to magazines. Member of editorial board of *Canadian Forum* magazine.

WORK IN PROGRESS: A play, "Labrador"; a two-act comedy, "Your Place or Mine"; a musical with Steven Jack, "Toronto the Good"; an opera, "Naked at the Opera," based on own play of the same title; plays for television, one based on own stage play, "Confidence"; a collection of short stories.

SIDELIGHTS: Hendry told *CA:* "I found that to stay alive and sane I had to make my living as a writer. Two people—John Hirsch and Ron Kelly—have been influential in encouraging me, and my wife Judith and my children have been particularly supportive and very patient.

"For me the writing of a play allows me to put down a set of questions and answers about something and out of them to make some sort of pattern. I find that life is chaotic and that unless I have the time to regularly discuss and record patterns, everything seems jumbled and meaningless.

"The people in my plays are all modelled on people I know, but the situations are necessarily pressed, exaggerated, pared down or whatever so that the particular something somebody 'wants' emerges clearly.

"Drama is edited life. That's for me!

"What I really want to do is write a novel because there it's between you and the typesetter. No directors, designers, actors. Not as a refuge from the theatre—The Big Family In The Sky—but as an alternative, somewhere to go and be by yourself with one other person—the reader. Two's company—Three's a production.

"Now I have to go to the theatre and talk to a director about 'Toronto the Good.'

"I think what I try to do is to put across a vision of that perfect world where there are discernible causes and discernible effects, not the capricious lottery we must all deal with."

HENKLE, Henrietta 1909-
(Henrietta Buckmaster)

PERSONAL: Born in 1909, in Cleveland, Ohio; daughter of Rae D. (a newspaper publisher) and Pearl (Wintermute) Henkle; married Peter J. Stephens. *Education:* Educated privately in New York, N.Y.

CAREER: Worked as book reviewer for magazines and newspapers, including *Saturday Review of Literature, Christian Science Monitor,* and *New York Sun;* editor at McFadden Publications; editor of *Harper's Bazaar;* editor of *Reader's Digest;* and writer. *Awards, honors:* Ohioana Medal, 1944, for *Deep River;* Guggenheim fellowship, 1944.

WRITINGS—All under pseudonym Henrietta Buckmaster: *Tommorrow Is Another Day* (novel), R. D. Henkle, 1934; *His End Was His Beginning* (historical novel), Henkle-Yewdale House, 1936; *Let My People Go: The Story of the Underground Railroad and the Growth of the Abolition Movement,* Harper, 1941 (published in England as *Out of the House of Bondage: The Story of the Famous Underground Railroad of the American Negro Slaves,* Gollancz, 1943); *Deep River* (historical novel), Harcourt, 1944; *Fire in the Heart* (historical novel), Harcourt, 1948; *Bread from Heaven,* Random House, 1952; *And Walk in Love: A Novel Based on the Life of the Apostle Paul,* Random House, 1956; *Lucy and Loki,* Scribner, 1958; *Flight to Freedom: The Story of the Underground Railroad,* Crowell, 1958.

All the Living: A Novel of One Year in the Life of William Shakespeare, Random House, 1962; *Walter Raleigh: Man of Two Worlds* (juvenile), Random House, 1964; *Paul: A Man Who Changed the World,* McGraw, 1965; *Freedom Bound,* Macmillan, 1965; *The Seminole Wars,* Collier Books, 1966; *Women Who Shaped History* (juvenile), Collier Books, 1966; *The Fighting Congressman: Biographies of Black and White Congressmen in the Post-Civil War Period* (juvenile), Scholastic Book Service, 1974; *Wait Until Evening,* Harcourt, 1974. Contributor to magazines and newspapers.

AVOCATIONAL INTERESTS: Theater.*

* * *

HERBERG, Will 1909-1977

August 4, 1909—March 27, 1977; American philosopher, educator, and writer. In his youth he was a Marxist radical but, after leaving the Communist Party in 1929, he became an outspoken conservative. He became a Judaic scholar, a subject he taught from 1955 until his retirement in 1976. Herberg was a prolific writer, often on religious themes. He died in Chatham, N.J. Obituaries: *New York Times,* March 28, 1977; *Washington Post,* March 29, 1977; *Time,* April 11, 1977.

* * *

HERBERT, Marie 1941-

PERSONAL: Born May 25, 1941, in Dublin, Ireland; daughter of Charles Angus (a professor) and Marie Benedicta (Byrne) McGaughey; married Wally Herbert (a polar explorer and author), December 24, 1969; children: Kari Elizabeth. *Education:* Central School of Speech & Drama, London, England, teaching certificate, 1962; University of London, diploma in dramatic art, 1962; St. Godric's Secretarial College, diploma, 1965. *Home and office:* Huntall Lane, Welford on Avon, Warwickshire CV 8HF, England. *Agent:* George Greenfield, John Farquharson Ltd., Bell House, 8 Bell Yard, London WC2A 2JR, England.

CAREER: Teacher of speech and drama at school in Battersea, England, 1963, and in London, England, 1963-64; worked as English correspondent at Lockey, Norman, Craig & Kummel A/S (advertising agency) in Denmark, 1966; director of Wally Herbert Ltd., 1970—. *Member:* Royal Geographic Society (fellow).

WRITINGS: The Snow People (Literary Guild selection), Putnam, 1973; *Great Polar Adventures,* Piccolo, 1975; *The Reindeer People,* Hodder & Stoughton, 1976. Contributor to *Expedition* (magazine).

WORK IN PROGRESS: A novel, *Sealer Horn,* about a young man marooned in the Antarctic in 1819.

SIDELIGHTS: Marie Herbert writes: "After the extraordinary success of *The Snow People,* which recounts the story of the two years I spent with my family among the Polar Eskimos of northwest Greenland, I decided I would like to get to know more about the Arctic and its peoples, hence our trip to Lapland in 1975. We spent five months travelling through Swedish and Norwegian Lapland and I made a migration with four Lapp herdsmen and their six hundred reindeer from the mountains in Karasjok to the spring pastures on the northern coast of Norway."

Marie Herbert was brought up in Ceylon and has also lived in India and Denmark. She has traveled in Europe and western Australia.

* * *

HERBERT, Walter William 1934-
(Wally Herbert)

PERSONAL: Born October 24, 1934, in York, England; son of Walter William (in armed services) and Helen (Manton) Herbert; married Marie Rita McGaughey (a writer), December 24, 1969; children: Kari Elizabeth. *Education:* Educated in Lichfield, Staffordshire, England. *Home and office:* Huntall Lane, Welford-on-Avon, Warwickshire CV37 8HF, England. *Agent:* Julian Bach Literary Agency Inc., 3 East 48th St., New York, N.Y. 10017; and George Greenfield, John Farquharson Ltd., Bell House, Bell Yard, London WC2A 2JR, England.

CAREER: Polar explorer and writer. Falkland Islands Dependencies Survey, Hope Bay Antarctica, surveyor, 1955-58; member of expedition to Lapland and Spitzbergen, 1960; surveyor with New Zealand Antarctic Expedition, 1960-62; planned and prepared for trans-Arctic expedition, 1964-66; led expedition to northwest Greenland, testing equipment and techniques for the trans-Arctic expedition, 1966-67; led British trans-Arctic expedition which made the 3,800 mile first surface crossing of the Arctic Ocean from Alaska, via the North Pole, to Spitzbergen, 1968-69; led expedition to northwest Greenland to make film about Polar Eskimos, 1971-73; led expedition to Lapland, 1975; planned and prepared for expedition to Greenland, 1976-77; led expedition making first circumnavigation of Greenland by dog sledge and skin boat, 1977-79. *Military service:* British Army, Royal Engineers, 1952-55. *Member:* World Expeditionary Association (honorary joint president), Royal Geographical Society (fellow), British Schools Exploring Society (honorary member), Lansdowne Club. *Awards, honors:* Polar Medal from Queen Elizabeth, 1962, for explorations in Antarctica; Livingstone Gold Medal of Scottish Geographical Society, 1969, for polar explorations; bar to Polar Medal, 1969, for first surface crossing of Arctic Ocean; Founder's Gold Medal of Royal Geographical Society, 1970, for outstanding contributions to Arctic and Antarctic exploration and survey.

WRITINGS: *A World of Man,* Eyre & Spottiswoode, 1968, Putnam, 1969; *Across the Top of the World,* Longmans, 1969; (contributor) *World Atlas of Mountaineering,* W. Noyce and I. McMorren, editors, Nelson, 1969; *The Last Great Journey on Earth,* Putnam, 1971; *Polar Deserts,* F. Watts, 1971; *Eskimos,* F. Watts, 1976; (contributor) *Expeditions the Experts Way,* A. Ballantine and J. Blashford-Snell, editors, Faber, 1977.

Contributor of articles to *Geographical Magazine* and *Geographical Journal.*

WORK IN PROGRESS: *The First Circumnavigation of Greenland,* for Doubleday, publication expected, 1979; a novel, *King Dog,* for Collins, publication expected, 1980.

SIDELIGHTS: Herbert told *CA* that he feels he was born sixty or seventy years too late to make his fortune as a polar writer. In *A World of Men* Herbert said that he writes, not with the purpose of answering questions, but "because the feeling needs expression and adventure needs its advocate."

British Prime Minister Harold Wilson called Herbert's North Pole journey "a feat of endurance and courage which ranks with any in polar history." Herbert's patron, Prince Philip, described the journey as ranking "among the greatest triumphs of human skill and endurance." And yet, Herbert notes that while the National Geographic Society has recognized his Arctic crossing as a truly "epic" trek, none of his polar journeys have been featured or even referred to in the text of their magazine on the grounds that his journeys are "too long." In his words: "Since each of my journeys is longer than the last it would seem that I have made my choice between instant fame and a place in history as a pioneer, and have settled for the latter."

BIOGRAPHICAL/CRITICAL SOURCES: *Times Literary Supplement,* January 8, 1970.

* * *

HERBERT, (Alfred Francis) Xavier   1901-

PERSONAL: Born May 15, 1901, in Geraldton, Western Australia; son of Benjamin (a locomotive engineer) and Amy (Scammel) Herbert; married Sadie Norden, 1953. *Education:* Perth Technical College, Diploma of Pharmaceutical Chemistry, 1922. *Home:* Redlynch, Queensland 4872, Australia.

CAREER: Writer; began career as a hospital pharmacist; has also worked as an aviator, deep-sea diver, sailor, miner, and stock rider. Superintendent of Aborigines, Darwin, 1935-36. *Military service:* Australian Imperial Force, 1942-44; became sergeant. *Awards, honors:* Commonwealth Sesqui-Centenary Literary Prize, 1938; Australian Literary Society's Gold Medal, 1940; Doctor of Letters from University of Newcastle, 1975, and University of Queensland, 1976; Miles Franklin Literature Award, 1976.

WRITINGS: *Capricornia* (novel), Rich and Cowan, 1939, Appleton Century, 1943; *Seven Emus* (novel), Angus & Robertson, 1959; *Soldiers' Women* (novel), Angus & Robertson, 1961; *Larger Than Life* (short stories), Angus & Robertson, 1963; *Disturbing Element* (autobiography), Cheshire, 1963; *Poor Fellow My Country* (novel), Collins, 1975.

* * *

HERMAN, George E(dward)   1920-

PERSONAL: Born January 14, 1920, in New York, N.Y.; son of Sydney (a banker and lawyer) and Tessie (Dryfoos) Herman; married Patricia Kerwin (a decorator), February 19, 1955; children: Charles, Scott, Richard. *Education:* Dartmouth College, B.A. (cum laude), 1941; Columbia University, M.S., 1942. *Office:* 2020 M St. N.W., Washington, D.C. 20036.

CAREER/WRITINGS: WQXR, New York, N.Y., night editor, 1942-44; Columbia Broadcasting System (CBS) News, night writer and editor, special features writer and foreign correspondent, 1949-50, staff foreign and war correspondent, 1950-54, Washington correspondent, 1954—. White House correspondent, 1954-55, 1960-63, acting Washington bureau chief, 1967. Moderator, "Face the Nation" television series, 1969—. Lecturer. Contributor to *New Leader.*

SIDELIGHTS: Herman told *CA:* "It is more important for reporters to report about the news than about themselves and each other."

* * *

HERSCHENSOHN, Bruce   1932-

PERSONAL: Born September 10, 1932, in Milwaukee, Wis.; son of Herbert Lawrene and Ida Esther (Erlichman) Herschensohn; married Bunny Domenic, March 8, 1963. *Education:* Attended high school in Los Angeles, Calif. *Home:* 2475 Virginia Ave. N.W., Washington, D.C. 20037.

CAREER: RKO Pictures, Los Angeles, Calif., studio messenger, 1950-51, in art department, 1953-55; General Dynamics Corp., Convair Division, San Diego, Calif., filmmaker and director, 1955-56; self-employed film director, producer, and writer in Los Angeles, Calif., 1956-68; U.S. Information Agency, Washington, D.C., director of Motion Picture and Television Service, 1968-72; White House, Washington, D.C., staff assistant to president, 1972-73, deputy special assistant, 1973-74; self-employed film director, producer, and writer, 1975-76; free-lance writer, 1976—. Teacher in "U.S. Image Abroad" program of University of Maryland, 1972; lecturer at universities and institutes of learning. Member of board of trustees of American Film Institute, 1967—; chairman of U.S. delegation to International Film Festival, in Czechoslovakia, 1968, member of delegation in U.S.S.R., 1969. Member of board of governors of Charles Edison Memorial Youth Foundation; consultant to Republican National Convention, 1972. *Military service:* U.S. Air Force, 1951-52.

AWARDS, HONORS: Arthur S. Flemming Award, 1969; Academy Award from Academy of Motion Picture Arts and Sciences, 1970, for short documentary film "Czechoslovakia: 1968", nominations, 1969 and 1972; distinguished service award from U.S. Information Agency, 1972; award from Council Against Communist Aggression, 1972.

WRITINGS: *The Gods of Antenna,* Arlington House, 1976.

Author of films: "Tall Man Five-Five," Strategic Air Command; "Karma," International Communications Foundation; "The President," U.S. Information Agency; "Bridges of the Barrios," U.S. Information Agency; "The Five Cities of June," U.S. Information Agency; "John F. Kennedy: Years of Lightning, Days of Drums," U.S. Information Agency; "Eulogy to 5:02," U.S. Information Agency.

Contributor of stories to *Conservative Digest* and articles to popular magazines, including *Newsday, Newsweek, Human Events, Saturday Evening Post,* and to newspapers.

HERSHEY, Robert Delp 1909-

PERSONAL: Born July 3, 1909, in Reading, Pa.; son of Harry C. and Ida May (Delp) Hershey; married Mary Billman, June 16, 1937; children: Robert Delp, Georgina Stuart. *Education:* Gettysburg College, A.B., 1931; Lutheran Seminary, Gettysburg, Pa., B.D., 1934, S.T.M., 1935; University of Pennsylvania, further graduate study, 1935-36; Temple University, S.T.D., 1938; University of Berlin, S.T.D., 1939; post-doctoral study at University of Madrid, University of Florence, Alliance Francaise, Dante Alighieri School, Knubley School, Centre for Economical and Political Studies, London, England, Hebrew University of Jerusalem, and Mansfield College, Oxford. *Home:* 340 Johnson Ave., Teaneck, N.J. 07666. *Office:* 3 West 65th St., New York, N.Y. 10023.

CAREER: Gettysburg College, Gettysburg, Pa., instructor, 1932-35; ordained Lutheran minister, 1934; pastor of Lutheran churches in Phoenixville, Pa., 1935-38, Berlin, Germany, 1938-39, Ambler, Pa., 1940-42, Glenside, Pa., 1942-45, and Philadelphia, Pa., 1946-53; Holy Trinity Lutheran Church, New York, N.Y., pastor, 1953—. Radio and television broadcaster. President of Philadelphia Council of Churches, 1952-53, and of Manhattan Division of New York City Council of Churches, 1960-62; member of U.S. committee of British-American Preachers Exchange; member of board of directors of Lincoln Square Community Council. *Member:* Foundation for Arts, Religion, and Culture, Society of Biblical Literature, Phi Beta Kappa, Alpha Kappa Alpha, Eta Sigma Phi, Phi Kappa Alpha, Lambda Chi Alpha. *Awards, honors:* D.D. from Muhlenberg College, 1949; L.H.D. from Wagner College, 1968.

WRITINGS: The Secret of God, Muhlenberg Press, 1951; *Think About These Things* (sermons), Muhlenberg Press, 1958; *Advent Landmarks: From a Preacher's Notebook,* Fortress, 1975. Also editor of *Letter to Lutherans,* 1954. Contributor to theological journals.*

*   *   *

HERTZ, Jackoline G. 1920-
(Jacky Hertz)

PERSONAL: Born July 10, 1920, in Wenatchee, Wash.; daughter of Merle Harvey (an instrument maker) and Florence Valentine (Richardson) Gooden; married William Hertz, March 11, 1939; children: Thomas, Janice, Bonnie, Lawrence, Brian, Margaret, Barbara, Darryl, Loretta, Mark, Victoria, Ted, Robin. *Education:* Attended Columbia Basin College, 1959-60; Fort Wright College, B.A. (honors), 1974; pursued additional home study through Famous Artists School and Famous Writers School. *Religion:* Roman Catholic. *Residence:* Spokane, Wash.

CAREER: Apartment house owner and manager, 1944-49; motel owner and manager in Richland, Wash., 1949-67; Spokane Falls Community College, Spokane, Wash., teacher of creative writing, 1969-73; Holy Family Hospital, Spokane, public relations secretary, became acting public relations director, 1973; Westat, Inc., Rockville, Md., survey interviewer, 1976; full-time writer, 1976—.

Director of grass roots project for Community Action Council, 1966. Member of executive board, Family Life Office of Spokane Diocese, 1975—. Volunteer for organizations, including Community Action Council, Committee for Migrants, and Mass Media Action Group. *Member:* Spokane Writers, Kappa Gamma Pi. *Awards, honors:* First place in juvenile book division from Pacific Northwest Writers Conference, 1972, for juvenile manuscript, "York" (since retitled *The Black Hunter with Lewis and Clark).*

WRITINGS—All under name Jacky Hertz: *The Christian Mother: A Mary-Martha Balance,* Hawthorn, 1976. Contributor of articles to national magazines, including *The Sign, Marriage and Family Living, Family Digest, St. Joseph,* and *National PTA.*

WORK IN PROGRESS: A historical novel of the Northwest, *Yellow Fire,* completion expected in 1977; a novel on changes within the Catholic Church from the priest's viewpoint, *Adam's Mark,* completion expected in 1977; a novel on black history and the Lewis and Clark Expedition, *The Black Hunter with Lewis and Clark,* completion expected in 1977; three books about the modern woman's place in Christian churches, *A Mother's Prayers,* completion expected in 1977, *What Wives and Mothers Wish Pastors Knew About Women,* and *Mother, Apostle for Christ,* completion expected in 1978; two humorous books, *Trial by Tenant* and *Motel, Moppets and Me,* completion expected in 1978; a juvenile novel, *Mystery of Aruba Island,* completion expected in 1979; a book about politics within community service organizations, *Always with Us,* completion expected in 1982.

SIDELIGHTS: Although Jacky Hertz' sixth grade composition "How to Make Love" was returned to her with an A-plus and the comment "Did you ever think of becoming a writer?," she didn't take writing seriously until she was married, had eight children, and was managing a 26-unit motel. One day, Mrs. Hertz relates, "a tenant left owing me $25 and offered me his beat up old Remington in payment. I took it, taught myself how to type, and one day in frustration at an early morning hassle, I wrote my feelings out. I mailed the manuscript to *Family Digest.* They named it 'Riot for Breakfast' and even reprinted it a year later in their tenth anniversary issue." She said she hasn't stopped writing since.

Mrs. Hertz told *CA:* "I am obsessed with need to know 'why' about things and I feel intensely that too many areas in life are vital for a writer to concentrate on only one. To write of religion is one of my needs. Others are a love of fiction and of humor and, of course, concern for social evils that batter modern marriage and today's woman. I write more and better by switching subjects, sometimes right in midstream, but not in the same manuscript."

While seven children were still home, her husband was injured and totally disabled, but Mrs. Hertz says, "ours has been a life of adjusting and readjusting, and I wrote harder than ever after we left the motel. Our family is united in believing that no member, including the mother, should be sacrificed on the altar of other members' preferences; but all should be aware of and generous to help with others' needs. Being mother of such a large family while simultaneously managing, first an apartment house, then a motel, is like tight-rope walking with no net. But I've had God and his providence for a balance and he's given me a sense of humor that allows me to enjoy life intensely."

Jacky Hertz and her identical twin sister are married to brothers. Her sister, whose name is Geraldine Hertz, is also a writer, which she says has "confused some editors, more readers."

BIOGRAPHICAL/CRITICAL SOURCES: Library Journal, January 15, 1977.

HESSELGESSER, Debra 1939-

PERSONAL: Born May 4, 1939, in Pasadena, Calif.; daughter of Hammond G. (a businessman) and Edithe (a painter; maiden name, Thompson) Nash; married Don Dietiker (divorced); married Guy Hesselgesser (divorced); married Brian Beckwith (an attorney), December 31, 1975; children: (first marriage) Eric, Petra Marie; (second marriage) Mercedes. Education: Oberlin College, student, 1957-59; University of Wisconsin, Madison, B.A., 1963; San Jose State University, graduate study, 1963-65. Home: 666 Greenwich St., San Francisco, Calif. 94133. Agent: Charles Webb, P.O. Box 182, Hastings-on-Hudson, N.Y. 10706.

CAREER: Oberlin Review, Oberlin, Ohio, reporter, 1957-59; Wisconsin State Historical Society, Madison, researcher, 1962-63; Bowl and Board (wholesale and retail business), San Francisco, Calif., owner, 1964-69; Coffee Gallery, San Francisco, bartender, 1969-72; Bancroft-Whitney Co. (publishers), San Francisco, Calif., copy editor, 1972—. Delegate to San Francisco Labor Council.

WRITINGS: A Small Quirk in the Fuselage (poetry), Smoking Mirror Press, 1974. Former editor of Journal Thirty-One.

WORK IN PROGRESS: Mom I Had a Nightmare Last Night, poems; a book on the development of a nuclear family, with photographs.

SIDELIGHTS: Debra Hesselgesser writes: "I have been writing all my life as a form of self-expression and release without much thought given to publication." Avocational interests: Law, labor unions, mental health, travel (South and Central America, Europe).

*   *   *

HEUER, John (Michael) 1941-

PERSONAL: Surname is pronounced like Hoy-er; original name Jay Michael Kaudy, name legally changed in 1942; born January 21, 1941, in LaCrosse, Wis.; son of Carl Edward (a police chief) and Gertrude (a clerical worker; maiden name, Meitner) Heuer; married Patricia Weinrich, December 5, 1965 (divorced October 2, 1975). Education: Attended St. Norbert College, 1959-61, and New York University, 1961-62. Politics: Liberal. Religion: Vedanta-Agni Yoga. Home: 315 West 84th St., New York, N.Y. 10024.

CAREER: Bon Marche, Inc., New York, N.Y., in sales and customer service, 1966-71; National Starch & Chemical Corp., New York City, in traffic and distribution, 1971-74; H. M. Keiser, Inc., New York City, supply supervisor, 1974-75; writer, 1975—. Circle Repertory Co., company member, 1972—, resident playwright, 1975—; associated with Circle in the Square Theatre Workshop, Writer's Stage Company Workshop, Mark Epstein Mime Co., and Four Winds Theatre Workshop. Has performed in film and stage productions since 1959, including the original Circle Repertory production of "The Hot 1 Baltimore." Awards, honors: Younger audiences program grant from New York State Council on the Arts, 1975.

WRITINGS: Cavern of the Jewels (two-act juvenile play; first produced in New York, N.Y., at Circle Repertory Co., April 2, 1976), Dramatists Play Service, 1976.

Unpublished plays: "The Good Shepherd" (one-act), first produced in New York City at Four Winds Studio-in-a-Garden, March 7, 1966; "This Unsettled Earth" (one-act), first produced in New York City, at Playwrights' Workshop Club, March 15, 1967; "When Day Becomes Night" (three-act), first produced in New York City at Bastiano's Cellar Studio, October 15, 1967; "Mrs. Tidings' Mason-Dixon Medicine Man" (two-act), first produced in New York City at Circle Repertory Co., June 11, 1973; "Innocent Thoughts and Harmless Intentions" (three-act), first produced in New York at Circle Repertory Co., December 4, 1974.

WORK IN PROGRESS: "Magnificent Ebonyfyre's Midnight Circus," a two-act play for children and adults.

SIDELIGHTS: Heuer writes: "As a playwright I am particularly interested in working toward the development of a kind of theatre which concerns itself with the human condition in such a manner as to make the casting of performers able to transcend racial, color or ethnic considerations, an expression of theatre that will have itself focus more directly on an actor or actress' ability rather than the surface. I have begun this experiment in 'Cavern' and am continuing it in my current work."

*   *   *

HEWITT, Arthur Wentworth 1883-

PERSONAL: Born June 22, 1883, in West Berlin, Vt.; son of Arthur Lee and Florence Elnora (Eddy) Hewitt; married Nina A. Battles, September 18, 1907; children: Hilda (deceased). Education: Montpelier Seminary, 1904. Politics: Democrat. Home: Highland Manse, Riverton, Vt. 05668.

CAREER: Ordained Methodist Episcopal minister, 1904; pastor of Methodist Episcopal churches in Glover, Vt., 1904-08, Plainfield, Vt., 1908-33, Moretown and South Duxbury, Vt., both 1933-35, and Northfield, Vt., 1939-56; Riverton Church, Riverton, Vt., pastor, 1956—. Superintendent of schools in Glover, Vt., 1905-06, and Plainfield, Vt., 1910-11. Slover lecturer at Southwestern University, 1952; headmaster of Montpelier Seminary and president of Vermont Junior College, 1935-38; clergyman at Middlebury College, 1927-37. Member of general conference of the Methodist Episcopal Church, 1920, 1928, 1932, and 1936; member of Federal Council of Churches, 1932-39; president of Vermont Council of Religious Education, 1933-36; former chaplain for Vermont State Grange. Member of Vermont House of Representatives, 1912-17. Vermont representative to National Conference on Vocational Education, 1917, and National Conference on Rural Education, 1918; member of Vermont State Board of Education, 1915-35, chairman, 1923-35. President of board of trustees of Montpelier Seminary, 1921-36.

MEMBER: Vermont State Teachers Association, Poetry Society of Vermont (president, 1959-67), Masons. Awards, honors: D.D. from Middlebury College, 1923; Litt.D. from Norwich University, 1956; L.H.D. from University of Vermont, 1968; quadrennial award of honor from National Methodist Town and Country Conference, 1959.

WRITINGS: Harp of the North, C. H. Simonds, 1916; Bubbles, Tuttle, 1920; Songs of the Sea, Tuttle, 1923; Steeples Among the Hills (autobiography), Abingdon, 1926; The City of Joy, Tuttle, 1926; Highland Shepherds: A Book of the Rural Pastorate, Willett, Clark & Co., 1939; God's Back Pasture: A Book of the Rural Parish, Willett, Clark & Co., 1941; The Shepherdess, Willett, Clark & Co., 1943; Jerusalem the Golden, Abingdon-Cokesbury, 1944; The Bridge, Abingdon-Cokesbury, 1948; The Mountain Troubador (poems), Golden Quill Press, 1962; The Old Brick Manse (autobiography), Harper, 1966. Contributor to theology journals.*

HEYWOOD, Philip 1938-

PERSONAL: Born March 26, 1938, in Maidstone, Kent, England; son of Oliver Bertram (a dentist) and Eileen (an actress; maiden name, Hartog) Heywood; married Sheila Mayall, June 10, 1966; children: Eileen Lara, Lucy Barbara. *Education:* Oxford University, B.A. (honors), 1961; Manchester University, diploma in town planning, 1968. *Politics:* "Social Democrat/Liberal socialist." *Religion:* "Pantheist." *Home:* White Lodge, 330 Prestbury Rd., Cheltenham, Gloucestershire GL52 3DP, England. *Office:* Department of Town & Country Planning, Gloucestershire College of Art and Design, Albert Rd., Pittville, Cheltenham, Gloucestershire GL52 3JG, England.

CAREER: Senior geography master at elementary school in Onitsha, East Nigeria, 1962-64; Ministry of Housing and Local Government, Manchester, England, research officer, 1965-69; Liverpool Polytechnic, Liverpool, England, senior lecturer in regional planning, 1969-72; Gloucestershire College of Art and Design, Cheltenham, England, principal lecturer and head of planning studies, 1972—. Founding member of Help, a Liverpool claimants' union, 1970. *Military service:* British Army, Queens Own Nigeria Regiment, 1956-58; became second lieutenant. *Member:* Royal Town Planning Institute, Town and Country Planning Association.

WRITINGS: Planning and Human Need, David & Charles, 1974. Contributor to planning journals and to *Isis.*

WORK IN PROGRESS: Research for *The Social Philosophy of Physical Planning,* completion expected in 1979.

SIDELIGHTS: Heywood writes: "My concern is with the improvement of specific human conditions in ways which people report as being what they want. I dislike concentrations of power, assumptions of superior wisdom and theories of 'false consciousness.' I think it is the role of the intellectual to invent and test publicly better futures, as well as to identify current errors and injustices. I support John Rawls' assumption that sane people are capable of recognizing the most just distributions of costs and benefits, even if they are not the ones which are most advantageous to themselves. I am currently interested in the application of Karl Popper's views of man as an innate problem solver, continuously evolving toward more significant capacities and achievements, to the theory and practice of physical planning."

*   *   *

HIGGS, E(ric) S(idney) 1908-1976

November 26, 1908—September 23, 1976; British archaeologist, expert on the early history of European agriculture, and author or editor of works on prehistory. He died in England. Obituaries: *AB Bookman's Weekly,* November 15, 1976. (See index for previous *CA* sketch)

*   *   *

HILL, Harold E(verett) 1905-

PERSONAL: Born December 10, 1905, in Manchester, N.H.; son of Arthur and Luella (Manley) Hill; married Ruth Gaertner, August 8, 1928; children: Linda Anne. *Education:* Pratt Institute, E.E., 1926. *Politics:* "Kingdom of God." *Religion:* King's Kid. *Residence:* Severna Park, Md. *Office:* c/o Logos International, 185 North Ave., Plainfield, N.J. 07060.

CAREER: R. A. Lister Co., Dursley, England, chief engineer and vice president of U.S. operations, 1927-46; Curtis Engine and Equipment Co., Baltimore, Md., vice-president, 1946-51, president, 1951-73, advisor, 1973—. *Member:* International Christian Leadership, Full Gospel Business Men's Fellowship International, Christian Business Men's Committees, Propeller Club of the U.S.

WRITINGS—All published by Logos International: *How to Live Like a King's Kid,* 1975; (with Irene Harrell) *How Did It All Begin? From Goo to You by Way of the Zoo,* 1976; *How to Be a Winner,* 1976.

WORK IN PROGRESS: Three books on successful and healthy living.

SIDELIGHTS: Hill told *CA:* "After having spent a half century seeking REALITY to life in such things as religion, philosophy, monetary successes, scientific achievement, active hobbies and worldly pleasures, I finally found the answer through a personal, first-hand hookup with the Head Man of the Universe, whose name is Jesus Christ and who IS total and complete satisfaction. My books are factual reports on how my life under God's management has worked out these past twenty-three years since meeting Jesus as my personal Counsellor, Guide, Consultant and Friend. All Boredom, Depression, Anxiety and GUILT are GONE!"

Hill also told *CA* that he "invented the Ground Energizer used for starting airplane engines on the ground," which was "an important contribution to winning World War II."

*   *   *

HILL, John Wiley 1890-1977

November 26, 1890—March 17, 1977; American public relations executive and author of works in his field. Hill was a journalist from 1909 to 1927. At that time, he quit to found the public relations firm of Hill and Knowlton, Inc., which was one of the first of its kind. The firm has since become the largest of its kind in the world. Hill died in New York City. Obituaries: *New York Times,* March 18, 1977; *Washington Post,* March 18, 1977.

*   *   *

HILL, Pati

PERSONAL: Born in Kentucky; daughter of John Robert (a real estate dealer) and Patricia (Guion) Hill; married Paul Bianchini (an art dealer); children: Paola Bianchini. *Education:* Educated in private boarding schools in the South. *Home and office:* 51 Rue de Varenne, Paris, 7e. France; and 20 Grand St., Stonington, Conn. 06378.

CAREER: Fashion model, writer, artist. Has exhibited her "Photocopied Objects" and "Photocopied Garments" at Kornblee Gallery, New York City; has participated in a UNESCO group showing, 1976, and has exhibited in Flaine, France. *Member:* P.E.N. *Awards, honors:* Grant from National Endowment for the Arts, 1976.

WRITINGS: The Pit and the Century Plant (journal), Harper, 1955; *The Nine Mile Circle* (novel), Houghton, 1957; *Prosper* (novel), Houghton, 1962; *One Thing I Know,* Houghton, 1962; *The Snow Rabbit* (poems), Houghton, 1962; (translator from the English) Diane Arbus, *Diane Arbus,* Editions Chene, 1975; *Impossible Dreams* (novel), Alice James Books, 1976; *Slave Days* (poems), Kornblee Gallery, 1976; *Dreams Objects Moments,* Kornblee Gallery, 1977.

Contributor of articles, short stories, and poems to magazines and journals, including *Paris Review, New Letters, Carolina Quarterly, Harper's, Atlantic Monthly, Evergreen Review, Mademoiselle,* and *Harper's Bazaar.*

WORK IN PROGRESS: A book of fiction; a book of photocopied garments; a book of photocopied objects.

* * *

HILTON, Della (Marion) 1934-

PERSONAL: Born October 2, 1934, in Melbourne, Australia; daughter of Albert Paul (an executive) and Gladys (an office worker; maiden name, Duncan) Hilton. *Education:* University of Melbourne, B.A., 1952. *Politics:* "English Liberal." *Religion:* Presbyterian. *Home:* 88 Roxborough Rd., Harrow, Middlesex, England; and c/o 7 Sebastopol St., Caulfield, Victoria 3161, Australia. *Office:* 121 Fleet St., London E.C.4, England.

CAREER: Australian Broadcasting Commission, Melbourne, on staff of publicity department and record library, 1953-56; management secretary in Melbourne, 1953-59 and 1962-63, in London, England, 1960-61; British Broadcasting Corp. (BBC), London, member of publicity staff, 1965-69; Wilcox Advertising, London, accounts manager, 1970-71; Beaverbrook Foundation, London, co-worker with A.J.P. Taylor, 1972—. Press officer for Ruislip Northwood Liberals. Honorary director of annual London Folk Festival.

WRITINGS: Who Was Kit Marlowe?, Taplinger, 1977. Contributor of folk music articles to magazines.

WORK IN PROGRESS: A biography of Geoffrey Chaucer; a family novel set in Australia.

SIDELIGHTS: Hilton told *CA:* "I have travelled a great deal, having visited America twice to date, and many other European and Eastern countries (some rather briefly)." *Avocational interests:* Reading, music, watching sport, theater, films.

* * *

HILTON, Peter 1913-

PERSONAL: Born March 22, 1913, in New York, N.Y.; son of Augustine J. and Dorothy (Connolly) Hilton; married Rita Williamson, February 22, 1936; children: Nancy, Pamela. *Education:* Columbia University, student, 1931-32. *Home:* Hudson House, Ardsley-on-Hudson, N.Y. 10503. *Office:* 405 Lexington Ave., New York, N.Y. 10017.

CAREER: Employed at Lord & Thomas, 1930-34; National Hotel Management Co., advertising manager, 1934-38; Maxon, Inc., vice-president, 1938-47; Peter Hilton, Inc., president, 1947-50; Hilton & Riggio, Inc., New York, N.Y., president, 1950-58; Kastor, Hilton, Chesley, Clifford & Atherton, Inc., president, 1958-66; Corporate Diversification, Inc., president, 1966—. Chairman and director of Kastor, Hilton, Chesley, Clifford & Atherton Ltd., 1957-66; founder and president of New Products Institute. Member of board of regents of St. Peter's College, Jersey City, N.J.; trustee of Midwest Research Institute. Consultant to Small Business Administration.

MEMBER: Association for Corporate Growth (founder and president), Young President's Organization, Chief Executives Forum (president), Metropolitan Club (New York, N.Y.; president), Dorset Field Club, Ekwanok Golf Club. *Awards, honors:* Decorated Knight of Malta.

WRITINGS: Planning Corporate Growth and Diversification, McGraw, 1970. Also author of *New Product Guide Book*, 1947; *Handbook for New Product Development*, 1961; *Keeping Old Products New*, 1967. Contributor to magazines.*

HINKEMEYER, Michael T(homas) 1940-

PERSONAL: Born October 18, 1940, in St. Cloud, Minn.; son of Ralph Stephen and Melania (Kuhn) Hinkemeyer; married Arlene Dingilian, August 5, 1967; children: Ellen Lara, Jonathan Edward. *Education:* St. John's University, Collegeville, Minn., A.B., 1962; Northwestern University, M.A.T., 1966, Ph.D., 1971. *Politics:* Democrat. *Religion:* "No preference." *Home:* 35 Cove Dr., Manhasset, N.Y. 11030. *Agent:* Writer's House, Inc., 132 West 31st St., New York, N.Y. 10001.

CAREER: Montgomery Ward, St. Paul, Minn., in management, 1964-65; high school teacher in Chicago, Ill., 1965-67; Northwestern University, Evanston, Ill., instructor in education, 1967-69; St. Mary's College, Notre Dame, Ind., assistant professor of education, 1969-71; Queens College of the City University of New York, Flushing, N.Y., associate professor of education, 1971-76; writer, 1976—. *Military service:* U.S. Army, 1962-64; served in Europe; became first lieutenant. *Member:* National Education Association, American Civil Liberties Union, Phi Delta Kappa.

WRITINGS: The Dark Below (suspense novel), Fawcett, 1974; *Summer Solstice* (suspense novel), Putnam, 1976; *Dark Angel Pass By* (suspense novel), Warner Paperback, in press; *The Fields of Eden* (mystery novel), Putnam, in press; *The Mistress of Coldstream* (historical romance), Dell, in press; *The Creator,* Pinnacle, in press. Author of political campaign material. Contributor of about two dozen articles to professional journals. Editor of *Clearing House.*

WORK IN PROGRESS: The Vision, a novel about life in America; *Lilac Night,* a suspense novel.

SIDELIGHTS: Hinkemeyer writes: "I am interested in the state of American life, the values of Americans, and the myths that make us unique as a people. The Great American novel has not yet been written because the American writers who were good enough to do justice to the theme did not have the necessary academic background to evaluate the value substructure of the society. I have traveled in Germany, France, Italy, Hungary, Poland, Czechoslovakia, and the U.S.S.R."

AVOCATIONAL INTERESTS: Politics, literature, tennis, skiing.

* * *

HINKLE, Douglas P(addock) 1923-

PERSONAL: Born June 9, 1923, in Stamford, Conn.; son of Frank Leslie and Kathryn (Paddock) Hinkle; married Rose-Marie Hecker (an artist), April 14, 1966; children: Anthony Barton, Monica Kathryn. *Education:* University of Virginia, B.A., 1952, M.A., 1954. *Politics:* Independent. *Religion:* Anglican Catholic. *Home:* 60 Morris Ave., Athens, Ohio 45701. *Office:* Department of Modern Languages, Ohio University, Athens, Ohio 45701.

CAREER: Teacher in public schools in Virginia, 1948-49; University of Virginia, Charlottesville, instructor in Spanish, 1953-55; American Binational Center, La Paz, Bolivia, director, 1955-57; Sweet Briar College, Sweet Briar, Va., assistant professor of Spanish and French, 1957-62; Southwestern at Memphis, Memphis, Tenn., assistant professor of Spanish, 1962-63; D. C. Heath & Co., Boston, Mass., college editor, 1963-65; Eastern Kentucky University, Richmond, associate professor of modern languages, 1965-67; Ohio University, Athens, senior lecturer in modern languages, 1967—, director of Junior Year in Spain Program, 1970-71. Member of Amesville Town Council, 1971-73.

Artist; has had individual and group shows of his paintings in New York, Ohio, Tennessee, and New England, 1970—. *Military service:* U.S. Army, 1943-46; served in European theater.

MEMBER: Modern Language Association of America, American Watercolor Society, Audubon Society, American Name Society, American Dialect Society, American Society of Sephardic Studies (co-founder), Phi Beta Kappa. *Awards, honors:* Citations from Teachers of English in Bolivia, 1955, and Newspapermen of La Paz, 1957; caballero of Order of the Condor of the Andes, 1957.

WRITINGS: (Contributor) Elsdon Smith, editor, *American Surnames,* Chilton, 1969; *Poetry Is You* (poems), St. Luke's Press (Memphis, Tenn.), 1977. Contributor of articles and reviews to academic journals. Member of editorial board of *Names,* 1969-74.

WORK IN PROGRESS: Two novels, *Doctor Tortwiler* and *The Sorrow of Frenchy Dulac.*

AVOCATIONAL INTERESTS: Woodscraft, survival, hunting, bow-hunting, fishing, and hiking.

* * *

HINKSON, James 1943-

PERSONAL: Born March 9, 1943, in Oshawa, Ontario, Canada; son of James E. (a farmer) and Alita (a teacher; maiden name, Warne) Hinkson; married Cynndy Dilling (a nurse), September 28, 1973. *Education:* Waterloo Lutheran University, B.A., 1968; University of Western Ontario, B. of Ed., 1971. *Religion:* Protestant. *Home:* 700 Dunlop St. W., #312, Whitby, Ontario, Canada L1N1V5.

CAREER: High school teacher of physical education in Ajax, Ontario, 1971-75; Philadelphia Wings (lacrosse team), Bala-Cynwyd, Pa., coach, 1975—.

WRITINGS: Box Lacrosse: The Fastest Game on Two Feet, J. M. Dent, 1974.

WORK IN PROGRESS: A revision of *Box Lacrosse.*

* * *

HIRSCHHORN, Richard Clark 1933-

PERSONAL: Born January 10, 1933, in Brooklyn, N.Y.; son of Alexander (an industrialist) and Jeannette (a lawyer; maiden name, Teicher) Hirschhorn; married Ann Michelson (a physician), February 5, 1961; children: Abigail, Elizabeth. *Education:* Harvard University, A.B., 1954, M.D., 1958. *Home:* 1067 Northampton St., Holyoke, Mass. 01040. *Agent:* Walter Pitkin, 11 Oakwood Dr., Weston, Conn. 06880. *Office:* 10 Hospital Dr., Holyoke, Mass. 01040.

CAREER: Western Reserve Medical School—University Hospitals, Cleveland, Ohio, surgical intern, 1958-59, surgical resident, 1959-60; Veteran's Administration Hospital, Boston, Mass., surgical resident, 1960-61; Massachusetts General Hospital, Boston, resident in urology, 1961-64; Hahnemann Medical School and Hospital, Philadelphia, Pa., member of urology faculty, 1964-67; urologist in private practice, Holyoke, Mass., 1967—. Member of medical staff of Holyoke Hospital, Providence Hospital, Wing Hospital, and Ludlow Hospital; president of Mt. Tom Medical Group, Masada Realty Trust, Union Plaza Realty Trust, and Pumpkin, Inc.; member of Hancock (Maine) Village Improvement Society. *Member:* American Urologic Association. *Awards, honors:* Research award from American Urologic Association, 1963.

WRITINGS: A Pride of Healers (novel), Morrow, 1977;

Target Mayflower (novel), Harcourt, 1977. Also author of *Handbook of Practical Urology,* Lea & Febiger.

WORK IN PROGRESS: Three books for Morrow, the first a medical historical novel.

* * *

HIVELY, Pete (Chester) 1934-

PERSONAL: Born July 17, 1934, in La Junta, Colo.; son of Claud N. M. and Helen M. (Love) Hively; married Barbara M. Kellogg, April 5, 1960; children: Deborah. *Education:* University of Colorado, B.A., 1956, graduate study, 1958. *Office:* ABC News, 190 North State St., Chicago, Ill. 60601.

CAREER/WRITINGS: KOA Radio and Television, Denver, Colo., editor, 1958-60; WCCO Television, Minneapolis, Minn., editor, 1960-63; American Broadcasting Co. (ABC), New York City, editor of evening news, 1963-71, television news director in Washington, D.C., 1971-73, Far East bureau chief in Hong Kong, 1973-75, Midwest bureau chief in Chicago, Ill., 1975—. Pool producer for Senate Watergate Hearings; Capitol producer for Nixon inauguration, 1972; anchor producer for several political conventions. Guest lecturer at Northwestern University. Member of American Chamber of Commerce, Hong Kong; member of vestry, St. John's Cathedral, Hong Kong. *Member:* International Press Institute, Chicago Press Club, Foreign Correspondent's Club of Hong Kong, Theta Xi, Sigma Delta Chi.

SIDELIGHTS: Hively's assignments have taken him to Moscow with Nixon, to New Delhi for talks with Indira Ghandi, to Japan with Ford, and to Saigon, Cairo, Baghdad, Teheran, and Athens.

* * *

HOBAN, Lillian 1925-

PERSONAL: Born May 18, 1925, in Philadelphia, Penn.; married Russell Hoban (an author and artist), January 31, 1944; children: Phoebe, Abrom, Esme, Julia. *Education:* Attended Philadelphia Museum School of Art, 1942-44, and the Hanya Holm School of Dance. *Residence:* Wilton, Conn.

CAREER: Illustrator of books for children. Has also worked in a slenderizing salon, and as a modern dance instructor in New York and Connecticut. *Awards, honors:* Christopher Award, Children's Book Category, 1971, for *Emmett Otter's Jug-Band Christmas* (written by Russell Hoban).

WRITINGS: (With husband, Russell Hoban) *London Men and English Men,* Harper, 1962; (with R. Hoban) *Some Snow Said Hello,* Harper, 1963; (with R. Hoban) *Save My Place,* Norton, 1967; *Arthur's Christmas Cookies* (self-illustrated), Harper, 1972; *The Sugar Snow Spring* (self-illustrated), Harper, 1973; *Arthur's Honey Bear* (self-illustrated), Harper, 1974; *Arthur's Pen Pal* (self-illustrated), Harper, 1976; *Stick-in-the-Mud Turtle,* Greenwillow Books, 1977.

Illustrator: Russell Hoban, *Herman the Loser,* Harper, 1961; R. Hoban, *The Sorely Trying Day,* Harper, 1964; R. Hoban, *Nothing to Do,* Harper, 1964; R. Hoban, *Bread and Jam for Frances,* Harper, 1964; R. Hoban, *Baby Sister for Frances,* Harper, 1964, reissued, 1976; Robert P. Smith, *When I Am Big,* Harper, 1965; R. Hoban, *What Happened When Jack and Daisy Tried to Fool with the Tooth Fairies,* Four Winds, 1965; R. Hoban, *The Story of Hester Mouse Who Became a Writer,* Norton, 1965; R. Hoban, *Tom and the Two Handles,* Harper, 1965; Felice Holman, *Victoria's*

Castle, Norton, 1966; Carl Memling, *A Gift-Bear for the King,* Dutton, 1966; Mitchell F. Jayne, *The Forest in the Wind,* Bobbs-Merrill, 1966; R. Hoban, *The Little Brute Family,* Macmillan, 1966; R. Hoban, *Charlie the Tramp,* Four Winds, 1966; R. Hoban, *Goodnight,* Norton, 1966; R. Hoban, *Henry and the Monstrous Din,* Harper, 1966; Miriam Cohen, *Will I Have a Friend?,* Macmillan, 1967; R. Hoban, *Mouse and His Child,* Harper, 1967; R. Hoban, *The Stone Doll of Sister Brute,* Macmillan, 1968; R. Hoban, *A Birthday for Frances,* Harper, 1968; R. Hoban, *Ugly Bird,* Macmillan, 1969; Jan Wahl, *A Wolf of My Own,* Macmillan, 1969; R. Hoban, *Harvey's Hideout,* Parents Magazine Press, 1969; R. Hoban, *The Mole Family's Christmas,* Parents Magazine Press, 1969; R. Hoban, *Best Friends for Frances,* Harper, 1969; Aileen T. Fisher, *In One Door and Out the Other: A Book of Poems,* Crowell, 1969.

R. Hoban, *A Bargain for Frances,* Harper, 1970; Alma M. Whitney, *Just Awful,* Addison-Wesley, 1971; Ellen Parsons, *Rainy Day Together,* Harper, 1971; Meindert De Jong, *Easter Cat,* Macmillan, 1971; R. Hoban, *Emmett Otter's Jug-Band Christmas,* Parents Magazine Press, 1971; M. Cohen, *Best Friends,* Macmillan, 1971; R. Hoban, *Egg Thoughts, and Other Frances Songs,* Harper, 1972; M. Cohen, *The New Teacher,* Macmillan, 1972; Marjorie W. Sharmat, *Sophie and Gussie,* Macmillan, 1973; M. Cohen, *Tough Jim,* Macmillan, 1974; William Cole, *What's Good for a Three-Year-Old?,* Holt, 1974; Crescent Dragonwagon, *Strawberry Dress Escape,* Scribner, 1975; Janet Schulman, *The Big Hello,* Greenwillow Books, 1976; Diane Wolkstein, *Squirrel's Song,* Knopf, 1976.

SIDELIGHTS: Hoban always wanted to be an illustrator, but gave it up for a while after her marriage in order to study dance professionally. After the birth of her third child, she began illustrating her husband's books for children, as well as the writings of other authors, and eventually wrote and illustrated her own books. Hoban finds drawing completely satisfying and cozy. She usually works in black and white or in two colors. The illustrations for *Bread and Jam for Frances* and several others have been done in pencil. She also uses a pen and ink wash.

BIOGRAPHICAL/CRITICAL SOURCES: New York Times Book Review, April 15, 1973; *Times Literary Supplement,* September 20, 1974.

*   *   *

HOCHMAN, Shel 1944-

PERSONAL: Born March 27, 1944, in New York, N.Y.; son of Abraham and Celia (Sumner) Hochman; living with Robin Abrett. *Education:* City College of the City University of New York, B.A., 1965; graduate study at City College, Hunter College, Lehman College, all of the City University of New York, 1965-67, and New York University, 1969. *Residence:* New York City.

CAREER: DeWitt Clinton High School, Bronx, N.Y., teacher of English, 1965—. Director of summer cross country tours, 1968-69. *Member:* United Federation of Teachers, United States Figure Skating Association, Sierra Club.

WRITINGS: How to Save Money on Car Repairs, Dodd, 1976.

WORK IN PROGRESS: A Time for Us, a collection of poems, photographs, and short stories; *Timmy, the Allergic Tomcat* and *The Eagle and the Siamese Cat,* a book for children.

SIDELIGHTS: Hochman writes: "In my philosophy, living has three main components: the physical, the emotional, and the intellectual. Getting involved in developing each major aspect of living adds 'fullness' to life, and is likely to produce an integrated personality—a 'together person'—and a together person is usually a happy person.

"*How to Save Money on Car Repairs* may not sound very philosophical. Actually, solving a mechanical problem involves intellect, emotion, and physical skills. (I'd like to refer anyone who's skeptical to Robert Pirsig's *Zen and the Art of Motorcycle Maintenance*.)"

AVOCATIONAL INTERESTS: Physical culture, ice dancing, photography, riding a motorcycle, thinking and traveling throughout the United States and in Canada, Europe, Greece, and Israel.

*   *   *

HODGES, Herbert Arthur 1905-1976

January 4, 1905—July, 1976; British philosopher, educator, and author of works in his field. He died in England. Obituaries: *AB Bookman's Weekly,* October 4, 1976.

*   *   *

HOEST, William 1926-
(Bill Hoest)

PERSONAL: Born February 7, 1926, in Newark, N.J.; son of Earl Sevem and Dorothea (an artist; maiden name, Gamble) Hoest Whittinghill; married Madeline Mezz Jungreis, November 4, 1973; children: Elizabeth, Suzanne, John, Charles, Sharon, Molly, Patricia, William, Julie. *Education:* Graduated from Cooper Union, 1949. *Residence:* Huntington, N.Y. *Office:* c/o King Features Syndicate, 235 East 45th St., New York, N.Y. 10017.

CAREER: Norcross, New York City, artist, 1948-51; freelance cartoonist, 1955—. Creator of comic panel, "The Lockhorns," 1968, and "Agatha Crumm," 1977. *Military service:* U.S. Navy, 1944-47. *Member:* National Cartoonists Society, Cartoonists Guild, Comics Council. *Awards, honors:* Reuben Award for best syndicated panel cartoonist of the year from National Cartoonists Society, 1976, for "The Lockhorns."

WRITINGS: A Taste of Carrot, Atheneum, 1967; (under name Bill Hoest) *What's the Garbage Doing on the Stove?: The Lockhorns,* New American Library, 1975; (under name Bill Hoest) *The Lockhorns, No. 2: Loretta, the Meatloaf Is Moving!,* New American Library, 1976; (under name Bill Hoest) *Bumper Snickers,* New American Library, 1976; (under name Bill Hoest) *Who Made the Caesar Salad . . . Brutus?,* New American Library, 1977.

Creator of comic panel, "The Lockhorns," a Sunday and daily feature syndicated by King Features with more than two hundred outlets in newspapers worldwide. Contributor of gag panels to *Cosmopolitan, Good Housekeeping, Family Circle, Ladies Home Journal, Playboy,* and other popular magazines.

WORK IN PROGRESS: A new comic strip, "Agatha Crumm," for King Features; *Hoest Toasties,* for Grosset and Dunlap.

SIDELIGHTS: Hoest, whose middle aged, big nosed and foreshortened Lockhorns squabble daily to the delight of newspaper readers worldwide, remarked in a recent interview in *Cartoonist Profiles:* "I was able to gradually, throughout the years, work up a style of drawing that I was comfortable with. I tried my hardest to be loose and free like some of the cartoonists I admired; Saxon, Dedini, Lorenz; but to no avail. My work came out messy. Apparently I am compelled to make lines meet, tidy up the ends, use backgrounds to a minimum and objects only when absolutely necessary. In short, my artwork satisfies me when it is neat, clean, simple, and uncluttered. Perhaps what I am trying to do is somehow, some way, make order out of a harried and complicated life."

Prolific in his cartooning, Hoest described his work habits: "My working day varies with the weather. If the sun is out, I play tennis first and hit the drawing board second. I have no regular working schedule, but I am not lazy. I love my work and have a real need to get to the drawing board. I also have a deep sense of responsibility and always get my work out on time, if not sooner. Each week I do twelve daily Lockhorns or two Sundays consisting of four or five panels each (and some weeks both, if I want to get ahead). I also do six roughs for 'BumperSnickers,' my weekly feature in *The National Enquirer,* twelve new cartoons for the general markets, and every month about twelve or more cartoons for *Playboy.* This does not include time on new paperback books (I have four out now) or what I call 'Research and Development' for new features in magazines or for syndication. I don't keep a rigid schedule, but obviously I spend a lot of time at the drawing board, sometimes all night long, to get the work out."

Hoest told *CA:* "At this time I'm absorbed in doing what I love the most—working on my new strip, 'Agatha Crumm.' The exhiliration of creating the character, Agatha Crumm, and watching her come alive is enormous. Interspersed with the creative pleasure was the fun of a tennis tournament that my wife, Bunny, and I won last week, and the excitement of a motorcycle trip we're planning from New Hampshire to Colorado.

"Life has been good to me and I'm very grateful."

AVOCATIONAL INTERESTS: Theatre, opera, woodworking, gardening, tennis, travel.

BIOGRAPHICAL/CRITICAL SOURCES: Cartoonist Profiles, December, 1976.

*   *   *

HOFFMAN, Anita 1942-
(Ann Fettamen)

PERSONAL: Born March 16, 1942, in Baltimore, Md.; daughter of Elias Allan (a businessman) and Leah Bina (a travel agent; maiden name, Zank) Kushner; married Abbie Hoffman (a fugitive and writer); children: america. *Education:* Goucher College, B.A. (cum laude), 1962; Yeshiva University, M.S., 1965. *Politics:* "communist." *Religion:* "Jewish by birth, pantheist by choice." *Agent:* Elaine Markson, 44 Greenwich St., New York, N.Y. 10011.

CAREER: Has worked as a New York City tour guide, secretary, waitress, bookkeeper, psychotherapist and psychological tester, and as an assistant at the New York American Civil Liberties Union, 1962-71. Founder of Downtown Welfare Advocate Center in New York City, 1975-76.

WRITINGS: (Under pseudonym Ann Fettamen) *Trashing* (novel), Straight Arrow Books, 1970; (with Abbie Hoffman) *To America With Love* (letters), Stonehill Publishing, 1976. Contributor of articles to *Village Voice* and *Oui.*

WORK IN PROGRESS: A novel.

SIDELIGHTS: "Although I have strong views on a variety of subjects (ranging from capitalism to the position of women)," Ms. Hoffman told *CA,* "I think I continue to write because writing is a cheap medium; all you need is a pencil, paper, and imagination. I hope my imagination is equal to the task I have set for myself, which is to tell stories that are entertaining and illuminating."

*   *   *

HOFFMAN, Bengt R(uno) 1913-

PERSONAL: Born April 15, 1913, in Kinna, Sweden; came to the United States in 1966; son of Carl Runo (a salesman) and Hedvig Augusta (a nurse; maiden name, Ljungberg) Hoffman; married Pearl Viola Willemssen (a librarian), October 31, 1947; children: Karin Elisabeth, Kerstin Elaine Qually. *Education:* University of Gothenburg, B.A., 1934; University of Uppsala, B.D., 1938; Yale University, M.A., 1962, Ph.D., 1964. *Home:* 607 Fairview Ave., Gettysburg, Pa. 17325. *Office:* Division of Historical and Theological Studies, Lutheran Theological Seminary, Gettysburg, Pa. 17325.

CAREER: Ordained Lutheran clergyman, 1938; pastor of Church of Sweden in Hjaelstad, 1938-39; chaplain to the student movement of Sweden, 1939-42; Prisoners Aid of the Young Men's Christian Association, secretary and camp visitor in Great Britain, 1942-43; pastor of Church of Sweden in Boraas, and chaplain to interned U.S. fliers, 1944-45; Prisoners Aid of the Young Men's Christian Association, secretary and camp visitor in United States and Canada, 1945-56; World Student Christian Federation, Geneva, Switzerland, missionary in Shanghai, China, 1946-49; World Council of Churches, Geneva, section chief during reconstruction in Germany and Austria, 1949-53; pastor of Church of Sweden in Trollhaetten, 1953-56; Lutheran World Federation, Geneva, director of department of world service, 1956-61; senior pastor of Church of Sweden in Fristad by Boraas, 1963-66; Concordia College, Moorhead, Minn., associate professor of ethics and ecumenics, 1966-67; Lutheran Theological Seminary, Gettysburg, Pa., professor of ethics and ecumenics, 1967—. *Military service:* Swedish Army, conscription service and chaplaincy to interned U.S. fliers, 1939-44; became captain.

MEMBER: North American Academy of Ecumenists, American Association of University Professors, American Society of Christian Ethics, Nathan Soederblom Society, Pro Fide et Christianismo. *Awards, honors:* D.D. from Wartburg Theological Seminary, 1959.

WRITINGS: Det fasta ordet (title means "The Solid Word"), Kyrkans Ungdom, 1942; *Varfoer jag blev praest* (title means "Why I Became a Minister"), J. A. Lindblad (Uppsala, Sweden), 1955; *Teknik och maenniskovaerde* (title means "Technique and Human Dignity"; edited by Anne-Marie Thunberg and John Eriksson), Natur och Kultur (Stockholm), 1958; *Atta vara praest* (title means "To Be a Minister"; edited by Anders Frostensson), Natur och Kultur, 1965; *Svenska Kyrkan Ekumeniken* (title means "The Church of Sweden and Ecumenicity"), Diakonistyrelsen (Stockholm), 1966; *Christian Social Thought in India, 1947-62: An Evaluation,* Christian Institute for the Study of Religion and Society (Bangalore, India), 1967; *Luther and the Mystics: A Re-Examination of Luther's Spiritual Experience and His Relationship to the Mystics,* Augsburg, 1976. Writer of cultural and socio-political columns in *Boraas Tidning,* 1966—. Contributor to theology journals.

WORK IN PROGRESS: The Moral and the Mystical; Christian Ethics: Basic Motifs and Contemporary Prob-

lems; Luther and the Invisible, translation and commentary on Luther's mystical writings; translation and commentary on *Theologia Germanica.*

SIDELIGHTS: Hoffman writes: "International service has helped increase my knowledge of Norwegian and Danish, English, German, and French. My relationship to Chinese resembles my relationship to my wife: I love her but have no command of her. After many years of pastoral and ecumenical work I became an academician again and rediscovered the usefulness of Latin and medieval German, as well as the place of mystical experience in religion."

AVOCATIONAL INTERESTS: Soccer (B-team in Swedish League I-club), tennis, pingpong (recent school championships).

* * *

HOFFMAN, Harry G.   1911(?)-1977

1911(?)—January 4, 1977; American newsman working as reporter from 1929 until 1956. He was editor of the *Charleston Gazette* and was a writer of political columns. Hoffman died in Charleston, W.Va. Obituaries: *New York Times,* January 6, 1977.

* * *

HOFMANN, Melita C(ecelia)   ?-1976

?—August 12, 1976; American association curator (Oysterponds Historical Society), artist, lecturer, and author of books on nature and history. She died in Greenport, N.Y. Obituaries: *New York Times,* August 19, 1976. (See index for previous *CA* sketch)

* * *

HOGG, Helen (Battles) Sawyer   1905-

PERSONAL: Born August 1, 1905, in Lowell, Mass.; daughter of Edward Everett (a banker) and Carrie Myra (a teacher; maiden name, Sprague) Sawyer; married Frank Scott Hogg (an astronomer), September 6, 1930 (died January 1, 1951); children: Sarah Longley, David Edward, James Scott. *Education:* Mt. Holyoke College, A.B. (magna cum laude), 1926; Radcliffe College, A.M., 1928, Ph.D., 1931. *Religion:* United Church. *Home:* 98 Richmond St., Richmond Hill, Ontario, Canada L4C 3Y4. *Office:* David Dunlap Observatory, University of Toronto, Richmond Hill, Ontario, Canada.

CAREER: Smith College, Northampton, Mass., lecturer in astronomy, 1927; Mt. Holyoke College, South Hadley, Mass., lecturer in astronomy, 1930-31; Dominion Astrophysical Observatory, Victoria, British Columbia, research assistant, 1931-35; University of Toronto, Toronto, Ontario, research assistant, 1936-38, research associate, 1938-41, lecturer, 1941-50, assistant professor, 1951-55, associate professor, 1955-56, professor of astronomy, 1957-76, professor emeritus, 1976—, research associate at David Dunlap Observatory, 1936—. Researcher at Steward Observatory (at University of Arizona), 1939; assistant professor and acting chairman of department at Mt. Holyoke College, 1940-41; visiting professor at Harvard University, summer, 1952. Program director in astronomy for National Science Foundation, 1955-56. Member of board of directors of Bell Canada, 1968—.

MEMBER: International Astronomical Union (president of Subcommission, 1955-64), Royal Society of Canada (fellow), Royal Astronomical Society of Canada (president, 1957-59), Canadian Astronomical Society (first president, 1971-72),

Royal Canadian Institute (honorary member; president, 1964-65), Canadian Women's Press Club, Canadian Science Writers, American Association of Variable Star Observers (president, 1939-41), American Astronomical Society (member of council, 1956-68), Federation of Ontario Naturalists (honorary member), Toronto Women's Press Club, Richmond Hill Naturalists, University Women's Club (Toronto), Faculty Club (University of Toronto), Phi Beta Kappa, Sigma Xi. *Awards, honors:* Honorary degrees include D.Sc. from Mt. Holyoke College, 1958, University of Waterloo, 1962, McMaster University, 1976, and University of Toronto, 1977; Annie J. Cannon Prize from American Astronomical Society, 1950; Rittenhouse Silver Medal from Rittenhouse Astronomical Society, 1967; service medal from Royal Astronomical Society of Canada, 1967; Canada centennial medal, 1967; medal of service of Order of Canada, 1968, named companion of Order of Canada, 1976.

WRITINGS: The Stars Belong to Everyone, Doubleday, 1976. Author of column "The Stars" in *Toronto Daily Star,* 1951—. Contributor to *McGraw Hill Encyclopedia of Science and Technology,* 1960, *Harper Encyclopedia of Science,* 1963, and *Encyclopaedia Britannica,* 1974.

Contributor of more than a hundred articles to scientific journals.

WORK IN PROGRESS: Continuing astronomical research.

SIDELIGHTS: Ms. Hogg told *CA* she has "devotion to astronomy in all its facets—from technical research to popularization in lectures and writing." *Avocational interests:* Stamps, knitting, gardening, photography, grandchildren.

* * *

HOGUE, C(harles) B(illy)   1928-

PERSONAL: Born January 13, 1928, in Stanton, Tex.; son of George Lee and Virgie (Milstead) Hogue; married Betty Jane Howard, 1949; children: Robert, Randy, Rodney, Ronald, Jana Li (adopted daughter). *Education:* Howard Payne College, B.A., 1949; Southwestern Baptist Theological Seminary, B.D., 1952; also attended Southern Seminary and West Texas State College. *Office:* Section on Evangelism, Southern Baptist Home Mission Board, Atlanta, Ga.

CAREER: Ordained Baptist minister, 1946; pastor of Baptist churches in Star, Tex., 1946-49, Ranger, Tex., 1950-52, Happy, Tex., 1952-57, Post, Tex., 1957-63, Odessa, Tex., 1964-69, and Ada, Okla., 1969-71; Baptist General Convention, Oklahoma City, Okla., secretary of evangelism, 1971-73; Southern Baptist Home Mission Board, Atlanta, Ga., director of evangelism section, 1973—. Host of "The Bible and Today's World" on KOSA-Television, 1964-69, "Confrontation" on KRIG-Radio, 1964-69, and "Exposure" on Television, 1969-71. Past chairman of Ector County Children's Services Board; member of board of trustees of Howard Payne College. Has preached and lectured all over the United States and in Puerto Rico. *Awards, honors:* D.D. from Howard Payne College, 1971.

WRITINGS: Love Leaves No Choice: Lifestyle Evangelism, Word Books, 1976; *I Want My Church to Grow,* Broadman, 1977.

WORK IN PROGRESS: The Doctrine of Salvation, for Convention Press.

SIDELIGHTS: Hogue has visited mission areas in Mexico, Macau, and Korea; he also preached in the New Life Movement in Japan and Hong Kong.

HOLLANDER, Herbert S.   1904(?)-1976

1904(?)—November 24, 1976; American journalist, editor, and author of books on the federal civil service. He was managing editor of the Ulman Feature Service from 1926 to 1950. He also edited *The Federal Employee,* the publication of the union from 1926 until 1972. Hollander died in Washington, D.C. Obituaries: *Washington Post,* December 1, 1976.

* * *

HOLLAWAY, Otto   1903-

PERSONAL: Born February 19, 1903, in Danville, Ala.; son of William H. (a farmer) and Ola (Higgins) Hollaway; married Myrtis C. Ford, May 28, 1922 (marriage ended, 1957); married Jewel F. Ford, August 29, 1959; children: (first marriage) Norm E., Orus L. *Education:* Alabama Polytechnic Institute (now Auburn University), B.S., 1931, M.S., 1935; Columbia University, Ed.D., 1950. *Politics:* "Vote for man not party." *Religion:* Methodist. *Home:* 1845 Oak Hill Dr. N.W., Cullman, Ala. 35055.

CAREER: School teacher and principal in Eva, Ala., 1924-27, principal in Alabama public schools, 1927-44, including positions in Owens Cross Roads, Belgreen, Waterloo, and Scottsboro; principal and assistant superintendent in Tuskegee, Ala., 1944-46; Alabama State Department of Education, Division of Administration and Finance, Montgomery, associate director, 1946-47; Alabama Polytechnic Institute (now Auburn University), Auburn, associate professor, 1947-50, professor of education, 1950-72, professor emeritus, 1972—; writer, 1972—. Chairman of Alabama Commission on the Professionalization of Supervisors and Curriculum Workers, 1968-72; member of National Commission on Core Training, 1952-60.

MEMBER: National Association for Supervision and Curriculum Development (president of Alabama chapter, 1953-57; member of national board of directors, 1953-57, 1966-70), National Education Association, Alabama Education Association, International Relations Club (Auburn University; charter president), Phi Kappa Mu, Phi Delta Kappa, Rotary International.

WRITINGS: Problem Solving: Toward a More Humanizing Curriculum, Franklin Publishing, 1975. Also author of *Let's Save Oil with Sam and Sue, Better Land for Better Living, Pioneers of a New South,* all published by Birmingham Publishing. Contributor to education journals.

SIDELIGHTS: Hollaway's book on problem solving stems from his conclusion that "education, educators, classrooms, and curriculums must not only face up to change, but decide how. The idea of underlining—and undermining—our present educational system is that a student must fit into a standardized curriculum which does not prepare him for life, job opportunities, or the reality of an increasingly complex and segmented society." Hollaway has become convinced that "problem solving—team teaching does prepare the student for a productive role inside and outside the classroom."

AVOCATIONAL INTERESTS: Building, landscaping, gardening, travel.

* * *

HOLLINGSWORTH, Mary H(ead)   1910-

PERSONAL: Born December 18, 1910, in Dahlonega, Ga.; daughter of Clemeth Clifton (a farmer) and Beulah (Phillips) Head; divorced; children: Jerry E. Markham, Doris J. (Mrs. Luke Kelly), Sara Jo (Mrs. Jimmy Spinks). *Education:* At-

tended Burlington Business College, University of North Carolina, Greensboro Evening College, Allied Arts School, and Albuquerque Technical Vocational Institute. *Politics:* Democrat. *Religion:* Baptist. *Home and office:* 509 South Third St., Mebane, N.C. 27302. *Agent:* Oliver G. Swan, Collier Associates, 280 Madison Ave., New York, N.Y. 10016.

CAREER: Durham Morning Herald, Durham, N.C., Carrboro reporter, 1930-40; *Carrboro Courier,* Carrboro, N.C., owner and editor, 1934; *Chapel Hill Weekly,* Chapel Hill, N.C., Carrboro reporter, 1960-70.

WRITINGS: How Long the Heart Remembers (novel), Houghton, 1977.

WORK IN PROGRESS: Each to His Own Journey, a historical novel, completion expected in 1979; *The Earth and the Eye* and *First the Blade,* novels; *A Marvelous Time,* nonfiction.

AVOCATIONAL INTERESTS: Flower and vegetable gardening, trees, rocks, birds.

* * *

HOLLIS, (Maurice) Christopher   1902-1977

March 29, 1902—May 6, 1977; British historian, economist, educator, politician, and author. He wrote thirty books on varying topics and contributed to periodicals. He was a history professor for ten years and, after World War II, became a member of Parliament. He died in Somerset, England. Obituaries: *New York Times,* May 9, 1977; *Washington Post,* May 9, 1977; *AB Bookman's Weekly,* September 5, 1977.

* * *

HOLMES, Nancy   1921-

PERSONAL: Born February 20, 1921, in Washington, D.C.; daughter of William Kenneth and Marion (Smith) Hartung; divorced; children: Peter Alden Thompson, Brooke (Mrs. Richard Negley). *Education:* Attended high school in Honolulu, Hawaii. *Politics:* Democrat. *Religion:* Episcopal. *Home:* 1178 Casa Verde Way, Palm Springs, Calif. 92262. *Office: Town and Country,* 717 Fifth Ave., New York, N.Y. 10022.

CAREER: New York Journal American, New York, N.Y., editor, 1950-52; *Look,* New York City, photography editor, 1952-54; Columbia Pictures, London, England, photographer, 1968-72; *Town and Country,* New York City, currently member of staff. *Member:* Eagle Club, Gstaad Suisse, Racquet Club (Palm Springs).

WRITINGS: The Dream Boats, Prentice-Hall, 1976. Writer and photographer for *Venture* and *Daily Mail.*

WORK IN PROGRESS: Rich, a historical novel about Texas during the Civil War.

SIDELIGHTS: Nancy Holmes writes: "Traveling is my life—I have lived in America, Switzerland, England, and Spain—everything and every place feeds my urge to write and it eventually comes out."

* * *

HOLT, John (Caldwell)   1923-

PERSONAL: Born April 14, 1923, in New York, N.Y.; son of Henry (an insurance broker) and Elizabeth (Crocker) Holt. *Education:* "I have come to believe that a person's schooling is as much a part of his private business as his politics or religion, and that no one should be required to answer questions about it. May I say instead that most of what I know I did not learn in school, or even in what most people would call 'learning situations.'" *Agent:* Robert E. Lescher, 155 East 71st St., New York, N.Y. 10021. *Office:* Holt Associates, Inc., 308 Boylston St., Boston, Mass. 02116.

CAREER: American Movement for World Government, New York, N.Y., worked in various posts, 1946-52; traveled in Europe, 1952-53; teacher of high school English, French, and mathematics in Carbondale, Colo., 1953-57; elementary school teacher in Cambridge, Mass., 1957-63; secondary school English teacher in Boston, Mass., 1965-67; Harvard University, Cambridge, visiting lecturer in education, fall, 1968; University of California, Berkeley, visiting lecturer in education, winter, 1969; "since 1969, writing, reading, lecturing, playing the cello, working on large issues confronting society." President, Holt Associates, Inc., Boston, 1969—. Has appeared frequently on television programs nationally; has lectured nationally and in Canada, France, Great Britain, Denmark, Sweden, and Mexico. Executive director of New York State branch of United World Federalists (now World Federalists U.S.A.), 1951-52. Trustee, Apple Hill Farm, Nelson, N.H., 1976-77. *Military service:* U.S. Navy, 1943-46; received submarine combat insignia and Pacific theater ribbon. *Member:* Center for Chamber Music. Also member of a number of other organizations.

WRITINGS: How Children Fail (Book-of-the-Month Club selection), Pitman, 1964; *How Children Learn* (Book-of-the-Month Club selection), Pitman, 1967; *The Underachieving School,* Pitman, 1969; *What Do I Do Monday?* (Book-of-the-Month Club selection), Dutton, 1970; *Freedom and Beyond,* Dutton, 1972; *Escape from Childhood,* Dutton, 1974; *Instead of Education,* Dutton, 1976. Contributor to periodicals, including *Life, Atlantic Monthly, Redbook, Saturday Evening Post, Parents' Magazine, Harper's, Ms.,* and *Psychology Today.*

WORK IN PROGRESS: A musical autobiography, *Caught by Music;* a book on space research, *The Great Space Colony Rip-Off;* a book for parents, *Growing Up Smart: Without School;* a book for children and parents, *Book of "A" and Other Letters;* a book for children, parents, and teachers, *Numbers, the Sensible Way;* research on learning disabilities for a book, *Nobody Sees Backward: Myths and Realities in Perceptual Handicaps.*

SIDELIGHTS: Detailed note-taking and observation of fourteen year's duration of teaching above-average students in selected schools revealed shocking conclusions about the American educational system as far as John Holt was concerned. He found it a degrading experience for both teachers and students.

He argued that each child, before beginning school, has a love affair with life, and that the child's attitude toward everything is to taste it, touch it, heft it, bend it, break it—and he is not afraid of making mistakes. Later in school, suddenly the child is directed by fear. He must come up with the correct answer or meet with the teacher's displeasure. Holt felt that this fear discouraged experimentation and led to the search only for the correct answer.

"Holt's basic complaint ever since has been that schools test, drill and grade children so often that they lose interest in the meaning of what is being taught, and schooling becomes a charade in which the students' real aim is to escape embarrassment and pain."

Instead, Holt contended that "the true test of intelligence is not how much we know how to do, but how we behave when we don't know what to do," and certainly schools do not attempt to foster that kind of intelligence. "We have made them intellectually weak and stunted, and worse," he wrote, "dishonest." Teachers coach and care more about the appearance of knowledge rather than a real understanding. Case in point, Holt asked, "What would happen at Harvard or Yale if a prof gave a surprise test in March on work covered in October? Everyone knows what would happen; that's why they don't do it."

Testing should be dropped and students should learn only what really interests them since "the things we most need to learn are the things we most want to learn." As *Time* noted, "Holt's system would be to avoid any system at all. A teacher's role, he contends, is to 'give children as much help and guidance as they need and ask for, listen respectfully when they feel like talking, and then get out of the way.'"

Nat Hentoff decided that in *How Children Fail,* "Holt has written an important dissection of a fundamental failure of this society, and he evidently has the imagination and intellectual tenacity to now go beyond the attack to hard thinking about how to restructure the educational system. I expect that if he does, he will discover that his smorgasbord curriculum will become more and more complicated to create. A radical redefinition of education is not that easily designed, let alone implemented." Hentoff wrote, "In any case, *How Children Fail* may at last create justified anxiety in a number of parents who deplore from a distance the ghetto schooling of the 'culturally deprived' without having realized that their own children are imprisoned in the larger educational ghetto which produces smooth, interchangeable parts to be fed into the ultimate assembly line for the dehumanized technological society—the multiversity."

Holt was not the only critic taking a hard look at the educational system. "In the free-for-all of educational commentary," observed Peter Schrag, "where the half life of ideas is pitifully short, the ashes of fallen gods often materialize in the bodies of new critics.... What makes this criticism significant, however, is not its debt to the master, but its irreverent freshness, and, more often than not, its radical refusal to accept the terms of the increasingly sterile debates of the past twenty years."

Of the new critics—Edgar Z. Friedenberg, Paul Goodman, Jules Henry, and John Holt, among others, Schrag said they "are far too independent and cantankerous to develop a consistent voice or anything that could be considered a program, but their common defense of children and adolescents and their fundamental attacks on established practices have given them a place apart from the conventional critics. They have been attacked as anti-intellectuals and hailed as saviors. But for the most part the established leadership of American education has simply ignored them."

Herbert Kohl remarked that "for all the openness and naturalness of the diaries in *How Children Learn* one senses in Holt's remarks a romanticism which places the highest trust and hope in the possibilities of the uncorrupted child. It is, however, a romanticism made bitter by Holt's view of experience." Actually, Schrag noted of Holt and critics like him that "their tone is often that of the radical left, but the values are conservative, upholding the virtues of honest, meaningful work, of community and family, and of civil human relationships."

Holt observed children carefully and found them naturally curious, learning things for their own pure satisfaction, even when no adult was looking. Kohl allowed that "*How Children Learn* is an important book. Not the least of the reasons for this is that it shows children learning without teachers."

By his fifth book, Holt declared, "For all the talk, experiments, federal fundings, special programs, revolutions in education, and so forth of the past years, most of our schools have changed very little." The answer he believed was a deschooled society, one in which "nobody would be compelled to go to school, [either] by law [or] by the threat of joblessness, poverty, discrimination, and exclusion from society—all of which are in force today. . . . It would be a society in which there were many paths to learning and advancement, instead of one school path as we have now—a path far too narrow for everyone, and one too easily and too often blocked off from the poor."

Hentoff called this "a marvelously inviting vision, but perhaps we ought not to expect those who see further than we do to also show us how we get there. It is exactly in this respect—the politics of deschooling—that John Holt is, so far, of very little use." Qualifying his statement, Hentoff added, "I am hard on Holt because I expect much of him. An extraordinarily involved citizen trying to redress all manner of injustices, not merely in schools, Holt really does know how children fail and how they learn. By using common sense—paradoxically a rarity among 'educators'—to describe the actual needs and the natural learning potential of all children, Holt has earned his present influence."

Having effectively deschooled himself by severing his direct connection with schools, Holt found himself reluctant to do much further writing or speaking about schools or what happens in schools of the reform of schools, except to say that "as long as schools remain compulsory and competitive they cannot be reformed. Two things are wrong with the very notion of education: First, it is seen as a process separate from all the rest of life; secondly, it is a process whereby one group of people do things to other groups of people, supposedly for their own good, and without getting their consent. Large-scale reform of such a system depends very much on changes in the society outside the schools." More and more Holt believes that it is only within the context of politics, of legislation, of people actually running for office, that large numbers of Americans can best become more informed, intelligent, competent, and wise.

As for himself, Holt took up French and Italian at 30, skiing at 31, cello for the first time at 40, water skiing at 47, and serious horseback riding at 48. "The results show that an old dog *can* learn new tricks," Holt said.

It is Shana Alexander's observation that "it seems to me that Holt is writing neither to children nor entirely about them. He is mostly writing about us. He is using his familiarity and empathy with children to tell us some things we badly need to know about ourselves.

"He is reminding us," she explained, "to accept children as people, just as we accept the child in ourselves, and that seems to me neither a dangerous romanticization of childhood nor a foolish siren song. Rather it is an abstraction, an ideal, a tune played on an invisible cello, difficult, but pleasant and very important to hear."

Holt's books have also been published in Great Britain, Belgium, Holland, Denmark, Norway, Sweden, Argentina, Germany, Italy, France, Japan, and Greece.

AVOCATIONAL INTERESTS: The "counter economy" movement (solar power, wind power, small scale and intensive agriculture, food raising in cities, the composting and recycling of wastes, the use of worms in recycling), music and music instruction.

BIOGRAPHICAL/CRITICAL SOURCES: Commonweal,

June 11, 1965; *Commentary,* July, 1965; *Saturday Review,* February 18, 1967, July 8, 1972; *Time,* September 1, 1967; *New York Review of Books,* January 18, 1968; *Nation,* March 11, 1968; *Grade Teacher,* September, 1969; *Newsweek,* May 24, 1971.

*   *   *

HOLT, William 1897-1977

September 1, 1897—April, 1977; British traveler, social activist, and author. His early career included work as a seaman, teacher, lumberjack, war correspondent, artist, and radio commentator. Holt bought a horse in 1964, named him Trigger, and rode him across Europe. He authored travel books, including *Trigger in Europe* and *I Haven't Unpacked,* and also novels. Holt died in Todmorden, Yorkshire, England. Obituaries: *AB Bookman's Weekly,* July 25, 1977. (*CAP*-1; earlier sketch in *CA*-17/18)

*   *   *

HOLTON, Felicia Antonelli 1921-

PERSONAL: Born November 28, 1921, in Flushing, N.Y.; daughter of Victor (a master mechanic) and Lucy (Sarle) Antonelli; married James T. Holton (an attorney), August 8, 1959; children: Lisa Maria. *Education:* University of Chicago, A.B., 1950. *Home and office:* 215 Lake St., Evanston, Ill. 60201.

CAREER: Wall Street Journal, Chicago, Ill., staff reporter, 1951-54; *University of Chicago Magazine,* Chicago, Ill., editor, 1954-57; *San Francisco News,* San Francisco, Calif., staff reporter, 1957-59; *Midway* (magazine), Chicago, Ill., founding editor, 1959-61; *Blue Cross Reports,* Chicago, Ill., contributing editor, 1966-69; free-lance writer, 1969—. Special editor of books for *Chicago Tribune,* 1966. *Military service:* Women's Army Corps, 1944-46. *Member:* American Society of Journalists and Authors. *Awards, honors:* Award from American Furniture Mart, 1952, for business reporting; Robert Sibley Award from American Alumni Council, 1957, for alumni magazine "University of Chicago Magazine."

WRITINGS: (With Stuart Struever) *Koster: Americans in Search of Their Prehistoric Past,* Doubleday, 1978. Contributor to magazines and newspapers, including *Family Circle, Today's Health, McCall's, Prism, Impact,* and *Discovery.*

WORK IN PROGRESS: A study of self-help groups, with Leonard Borman.

SIDELIGHTS: Felicia Holton writes: "I am interested in writing on a number of subjects, including alcoholism, archeology, child advocacy, the family and the law, health, the socio-economics of health, hospitals, medicine, social sciences, science, and travel. I am especially interested in taking academic subjects, and interpreting these for the lay reader. My next large writing project will be historical fiction."

*   *   *

HOOBLER, Dorothy

PERSONAL: Born in Philadelphia, Pa.; daughter of Frederick and Eleanor (Bystrom) Law; married Thomas Hoobler (a writer and editor), December 18, 1971; children: Ellen Marie. *Education:* Wells College, A.B., 1963; New York University, M.A., 1971. *Residence:* New York, N.Y. *Agent:* Phyllis Jackson, International Creative Management, 40 West 57th St., New York, N.Y. 10019.

CAREER: Has worked as an editor and genealogist; free-lance writer, 1973—.

WRITINGS—All with husband, Thomas Hoobler: *Frontier Diary*, Macmillan, 1974; *Margaret Mead: A Life in Science*, Macmillan, 1974; *House Plants*, Grosset, 1975; *Vegetable Gardening and Cooking*, Grosset, 1975; *Pruning*, Grosset, 1975; *An Album of World War One*, F. Watts, 1976; *The Year in Bloom*, Bantam, 1977; *Photographing History: The Career of Mathew Brady*, Putnam, in press; *An Album of World War Two*, F. Watts, in press; *Growing House Plants in Any Light*, Tempo, in press.

WORK IN PROGRESS: A book about trench warfare in World War One, with husband, Thomas Hoobler; a collection of biographies of Chinese people throughout history, with Thomas Hoobler; research on nineteenth-century photographers.

AVOCATIONAL INTERESTS: Oriental, American, and European medieval history, music, photography, gardening, travel.

*   *   *

HOOBLER, Thomas

PERSONAL: Born in Cincinnati, Ohio; son of John T. (a printer) and Jane Frances (Pachoud) Hoobler; married Dorothy Law (a writer), December 18, 1971; children: Ellen Marie. *Education:* University of Notre Dame, A.B., 1964; attended University of Iowa, Writer's Workshop, 1965. *Residence:* New York, N.Y. *Agent:* Phyllis Jackson, International Creative Management, 40 West 57th St., New York, N.Y. 10019.

CAREER: Worked in various positions at private schools in Cincinnati, Ohio including, teacher of English and photography, audio-visual coordinator, and basketball coach, 1965-70; trade magazine editor, 1971—.

WRITINGS—All with wife, Dorothy Hoobler: *Frontier Diary*, Macmillan, 1974; *Margaret Mead: A Life in Science*, Macmillan, 1974; *House Plants*, Grosset, 1975; *Vegetable Gardening and Cooking*, Grosset, 1975; *Pruning*, Grosset, 1975; *An Album of World War One*, F. Watts, 1976; *The Year in Bloom*, Bantam, 1977; *Photographing History: The Career of Mathew Brady*, Putnam, in press; *An Album of World War Two*, F. Watts, in press; *Growing House Plants in Any Light*, Tempo, in press.

WORK IN PROGRESS: One Day As a Lion, an adult novel; *The Hunters*, a science fiction book for young adults, with Burton Wetanson; a book about trench warfare in World War One, with wife, Dorothy Hoobler; a collection of biographies of Chinese people throughout history, with Dorothy Hoobler; research on nineteenth-century photographers.

AVOCATIONAL INTERESTS: Oriental, American, and European medieval history, music, photography, gardening, travel.

*   *   *

HOOKER, Ruth   1920-

PERSONAL: Born April 30, 1920, in Rockville Center, N.Y.; daughter of John Wilhelm (an engineer) and Ruth (Garges) Hieronymus; married Harris Hooker (an electrical engineer), August 1, 1941; children: Charlotte (Mrs. Robert Kreamer), George, Jane (Mrs. Robert Hansen), Barbara (Mrs. William Shaw). *Education:* Attended Northern Illinois University, 1938-40; attended Moser Business College, 1940-41. *Home:* 1049 Sylvan Circle, Naperville, Ill. 60540.

CAREER: Children's librarian in Naperville, Ill., 1962-64;

writer, 1964—. Trustee of Nichols Library (Naperville). *Member:* Society of Children's Book Writers, Children's Reading Round Table, Off-Campus Writers Workshop. *Awards, honors:* Award from Friends of American Writers, 1971, for *Gertrude Kloppenberg (Private)*.

WRITINGS—All juveniles: *Gertrude Kloppenberg (Private)* (novel), Abingdon, 1970; *Gertrude Kloppenberg II* (novel), Abingdon, 1974; *Kennaquhair* (science fiction novel), Abingdon, 1976; (with Carole Smith) *Pelican Mystery*, Albert Whitman, 1977. Contributor of stories to *Child Life, Boys and Girls, Red Cross Youth News, Trails, Twelve/Fifteen, Adventure*, and *Christian Science Monitor*.

WORK IN PROGRESS: Two mystery novels, with Carole Smith, for Albert Whitman; science fiction; a nonfiction book about water towers.

SIDELIGHTS: Ruth Hooker writes: "I write for children because I like them, and as I write I try to keep in mind that children are new to this world; problems that seem small to an adult are great to them; they are smart, sensitive and suggestible; and I must carefully consider all these aspects." *Avocational interests:* Sailing, reading.

*   *   *

HOPKINS, Fred W(right), Jr.   1935-

PERSONAL: Born November 19, 1935, in Staten Island, N.Y.; son of Fred W. (an office manager) and Margaret (Ullman) Hopkins; married Margaret Leverage, March, 1961; children: Michael, Timothy. *Education:* Gettysburg College, B.A., 1956; University of Maryland, M.Ed., 1963, Ph.D., 1968. *Politics:* Democrat. *Religion:* Lutheran. *Home:* 518 Springer Court, Linthicum, Md. 21090. *Office:* Graduate School, University of Baltimore, 1420 North Charles St., Baltimore, Md. 21201.

CAREER: Teacher and athletic coach in public schools in Anne Arundel County, Md., 1959-70; University of Baltimore, Baltimore, Md., associate professor of education and history, 1970-71, dean of admissions, 1971-75, dean of graduate school, 1975—. *Military service:* U.S. Army, Chinese translator for Security Agency, 1956-59. *Member:* Maryland Historical Society, Phi Beta Kappa, Alpha Kappa Alpha, Eta Sigma Phi.

WRITINGS: Thomas Boyle, Master Privateer, Tidewater, 1976. Contributor to *Chesapeake Bay*.

WORK IN PROGRESS: Research on all Navy vessels named *Baltimore;* research on Baltimore clipper *Chasseur*.

*   *   *

HORN, Pamela (Lucy Ray)   1936-

PERSONAL: Born May 2, 1936, in Derby, England; daughter of Gilbert Lawrence (a bank official) and Marjorie (Orton) Jones; married Clifford Alfred Horn (head of department of management and social studies at Oxford Polytechnic), March 30, 1963. *Education:* Attended Portsmouth Polytechnic, 1963-64; University of London, B.Sc., 1964; University of Leicester, Ph.D., 1968. *Religion:* Roman Catholic. *Home:* 11 Harwell Rd., Sutton Courtenay, Abingdon, Oxford, England. *Office:* Department of Management & Social Studies, Oxford Polytechnic, Headington, Oxford, England.

CAREER: Lecturer in shorthand and typewriting at Derby and District College of Technology, 1959-63; Oxford Polytechnic, Oxford, England, lecturer in economic and social history, 1967—. *Member:* Royal Society of Arts, Agricultural History Society.

WRITINGS: Joseph Arch: A Biography, Roundwood Press, 1971; *The Victorian Country Child,* Roundwood Press, 1974; *The Rise and Fall of the Victorian Servant,* St. Martin's, 1975; *Labouring Life in the Victorian Countryside,* Hunter Press, 1976; *Country Schools and Teachers,* Gill & Macmillan, in press. Contributor to British journals, including *Countryman.*

SIDELIGHTS: Pamela Horn writes: "I am particularly concerned with nineteenth century rural life in Britain." *Avocational interests:* Travel in Germany.

* * *

HORNE, Peter 1947-

PERSONAL: Born May 15, 1947, in New York, N.Y.; son of Herman Bernard (a laundryman) and Katherine (a teacher; maiden name, Scheiner) Horne; married Anne Silberman (an elementary school teacher), June 18, 1970; children: Stacy Lynn. *Education:* Queens College of the City University of New York, B.A., 1969; California State University, Los Angeles, M.S., 1972. *Religion:* Jewish. *Home:* 1025 Windemere, St. Louis, Mo. 63131. *Office:* Department of Criminal Justice, St. Louis Community College at Meramec, 11333 Big Bend Blvd., St. Louis, Mo. 63122.

CAREER: Police officer in Compton, Calif., 1971-72; St. Louis Community College at Meramec, St. Louis, Mo., assistant professor of criminal justice, 1972—. Reserve police officer in Ballwin, Mo., 1973-76; certified emergency medical technician. Consultant to U.S. Department of Justice. *Military service:* U.S. Army Reserve, 1969-74. *Member:* International Association of Chiefs of Police, American Academy of Professional Law Enforcement, Academy of Criminal Justice Sciences, American Civil Liberties Union, Missouri Association of Criminal Justice Educators.

WRITINGS: Women in Law Enforcement, C. C Thomas, 1975. Contributor to law enforcement journals.

WORK IN PROGRESS: Women in Law Enforcement, 2nd edition, for C. C Thomas; *Police Reserves in the United States.*

SIDELIGHTS: Horne writes: "I was aware of women's restricted and limited roles in the criminal justice system and in law enforcement particularly. As a police officer I examined the role of women in law enforcement and found there was little contemporary writing or research concerning them. This, coupled with an awareness of women's restricted role in all of our society, prompted my book. I feel that individual women can effectively perform the role of general patrol officer in the United States."

AVOCATIONAL INTERESTS: Sailing, tennis, racquetball, softball, reading.

* * *

HOROBIN, Ian M. 1899-1976

1899—June, 1976; British poet and onetime member of Parliament. He died in Tangier, Morocco. Obituaries: *AB Bookman's Weekly,* October 4, 1976.

* * *

HOROWITZ, David 1903-

PERSONAL: Born April 9, 1903, in Malmo, Sweden; emigrated to United States, 1914; naturalized citizen in 1919; son of Aaron (a Cantor and composer) and Bertha (Chazen) Horowitz; married Nan Reilly, October, 1951. *Politics:* Independent. *Religion:* Jewish. *Home:* 231 East 76th Street,

New York, N.Y. 10021. *Office:* UN Bureau, Room 373, Press Section, United Nations, New York, N.Y. 10017.

CAREER: United Nations, New York City, correspondent, 1946—; United Israel Bulletin, New York City, editor, 1944—; World Union Press Syndicate, New York City, editor and author of column, 1950—. Notable assignments include covering the United Nations from its inception, the prosecution of the Kurds, and the South Moluccan Republic within the Indonesian archipelago. Lecturer. *Member:* United Israel World Union (founder and president, 1944—), Foreign Press Association (president, 1966), United Nations Correspondents Association (secretary, 1971-72). *Awards, honors:* International House award for "outstanding contribution to international understanding," 1975; Medaliha Pro Mundi Beneficio, from Academy Brasileira de Ciencias Humanas, 1975.

WRITINGS: (Translator) Moses Guibbory, *The Bible in the Hands of Its Creators,* Society of the Bible, 1943; *Thirty-Three Candles,* World Union Press, 1949. Also author of "Behind the Scenes at the United Nations" column syndicated by World Union Press, 1952—. Contributor to *Mademoiselle, General Motors World,* and other periodicals. Editor of *American Examiner,* 1968-72.

WORK IN PROGRESS: A book, tentatively titled, *The Jews Are Not Alone: Dilemma—Who Is a Jew.*

SIDELIGHTS: In his article, "'International Reformatory'—The UN," Horowitz wrote: "That there is a need of a world body such as the UN formulated on the noble Charter principles goes without saying—especially in this uncertain atomic age in which the threat of the hydrogen bomb hangs heavily over mankind.

"With all its shortcomings—and they are multiple—one must bear in mind that this world organization, born out of the holocaust of World War II, is in its infancy. What really is thirty years when viewed in the long bloody history of millennia of conflicts among the nations? We have here, in effect, a 'baby still in its diapers.' " . . . The UN 'baby' must be given a chance to grow into a healthy body."

BIOGRAPHICAL/CRITICAL SOURCES: Intermountain Jewish News, April 25, 1975; *The Churchman,* January, 1977.

* * *

HOTCHNER, A(aron) E(dward) 1920-

PERSONAL: Born June 28, 1920, in St. Louis, Mo.; son of Samuel (a jeweler) and Sally (a Sunday school administrator; maiden name, Rossman) Hotchner; married Geraldine Mavor, May 15, 1949 (died January, 1969); married Ursula Robbins (a magazine researcher), April 18, 1970; children: Tracy, Holly, Timothy Aaron. *Education:* Washington University, St. Louis, Mo., A.B., LL.B., 1941. *Politics:* Democrat. *Home and office:* 14 Hillandale Rd., Westport, Conn. 06880. *Agent:* Phyllis Jackson, International Creative Management, 40 West 57th St., New York, N.Y. 10019.

CAREER: Admitted to Missouri State Bar, 1941; practiced law in St. Louis, Mo., 1941-42; *Cosmopolitan* (magazine), New York City, articles editor, 1948-50; free-lance writer, 1950—. *Military service:* U.S. Army Air Forces, 1942-46; became major. *Member:* Authors League of America, Dramatists Guild, Overseas Press Club, Writer's Guild of America, P.E.N., Missouri Bar Association.

WRITINGS: The Dangerous American (novel), Random House, 1958; *Papa Hemingway: A Personal Memoir,* Random House, 1966; *Treasure* (novel), Random House,

1970; *King of the Hill* (memoir), Harper, 1973; *Looking for Miracles,* Harper, 1975; *Doris Day: Her Own Story,* Morrow, 1976.

Plays: "The Capital of the World" (ballet), first produced in New York City at Metropolitan Opera House, October, 1954; "A Short Happy Life" (two-act), first produced in Los Angeles at Huntington Hartford Theatre, November, 1961; *The White House* (two-act; first produced in New York at Henry Miller's Theatre, May 19, 1964), Samuel French, 1965; "The Hemingway Hero" (two-act), first produced in New Haven, Conn. at Schubert Theatre, September, 1967; "Do You Take This Man?" (two-act), first produced in New York at Experimental Theatre, April, 1970.

Author of screenplay, "Adventures of a Young Man," released by 20th Century Fox; of teleplays for "Playhouse 90," 1958-60, including "Last Clear Chance," and "The Killers of Mussolini," and teleplays adapted from major works of Ernest Hemingway, including "For Whom the Bell Tolls," 1958, and "The Killers," 1959.

Contributor of more than 300 articles and short stories to magazines, including *Esquire* and *Saturday Evening Post.*

WORK IN PROGRESS: A factual novel, *The Man Who Lived at the Ritz;* a biography of Sophia Loren, for Morrow.

SIDELIGHTS: In a review of Hotchner's *Papa Hemingway,* Vance Bourjaily commented: "Part Boswell, part Euripides, Hotchner has written a greatly detailed and very loving book of memoirs. If it seems at first self-conscious, then a bit proprietary, it recovers quickly enough, settles into high biographical stride, and then moves, steadily and affectingly, to the inevitable and thus genuinely tragic end."

Recalling his own experiences Hotchner told *CA:* "My long association with Hemingway was the overriding influence on me as a writer and as a person. His sense of values was extraordinary and infectious."

BIOGRAPHICAL/CRITICAL SOURCES: New York Times Book Review, April 3, 1966; *Newsweek,* April 11, 1966; *New Republic,* April 23, 1966; *Harper,* June, 1966; *National Review,* June 28, 1966; *Atlantic,* August, 1966; *New Statesman,* September 23, 1966; *Kirkus Reviews,* November 1, 1973; *Publisher's Weekly,* February 2, 1976, May 10, 1976, August 16, 1976.

* * *

HOUGH, Graham Goulder 1908-

PERSONAL: Born February 14, 1908; son of Joseph and Clara Hough; married Rosamund Oswell, 1942; married Ingeborg Neumann, 1952; children: (first marriage) one son, one daughter. *Education:* Attended University of Liverpool and Queen's College, Cambridge. *Home:* White Cottage, Grantchester, Cambridge, England.

CAREER: Raffles College, Singapore, lecturer in English, 1930; University of Malaya, Kuala Lumpur, professor of English, 1946; Cambridge University, Cambridge, England, tutor in English at Christ's College, 1955-60, praelector and fellow of Darwin College, 1964-75, university reader, 1965-66, professor of English, 1966-75. Visiting lecturer at Johns Hopkins University, 1950; visiting professor at Cornell University, 1958. *Military service:* Singapore Royal Artillery (Volunteers), 1942-45. *Member:* United Oxford and Cambridge University Club. *Awards, honors:* Fellow of Christ's College, Cambridge, 1950; D.Litt. from University of Malaya, 1955; Litt.D. from Cambridge University, 1961.

WRITINGS: The Last Romantics, Duckworth, 1949,

Barnes & Noble, 1961; *The Romantic Poets,* Hutchinson, 1953, 3rd edition, 1967, Norton, 1964; *The Dark Sun: A Study of D. H. Lawrence,* Duckworth, 1956, Macmillan, 1957; *Two Exiles: Lord Byron and D. H. Lawrence,* University of Nottingham, 1956, reprinted, Folcroft, 1970; *Free Verse,* Oxford University Press, 1957.

Image and Experience: Studies in a Literary Revolution, Duckworth, 1960, University of Nebraska Press, 1964; *Reflections on a Literary Revolution,* Catholic University of America Press, 1960; (editor) *Oscar Wilde,* Dell, 1960; *Legends and Pastorals: Poems,* Duckworth, 1961; *A Preface to the Faerie Queene,* Duckworth, 1962, Norton, 1963; (editor) Lodovico Ariosto, *Sir John Harington's Translation of Orlando Furioso,* Southern Illinois University Press, 1962; *The Dream and the Task: Literature and Morals in the Culture of Today,* Duckworth, 1963, Norton, 1964; (editor) *Poems of Samuel Taylor Coleridge,* Folio Society, 1963; *The First Commentary of the Faerie Queene: Being an Analysis of the Annotations in Lord Bessborough's Copy of the First Edition of the Faerie Queene,* Folcroft, 1964; *An Essay on Criticism,* Norton, 1966, Duckworth, 1974; *Style and Stylistics,* Humanities, 1969.

Also editor of books by Michael Wood and Jean R. Brooks.

AVOCATIONAL INTERESTS: Travel.*

* * *

HOWARD, Constance 1910-

PERSONAL: Born December 8, 1910, in Northampton, England; daughter of Arthur (a teacher) and Mildred (Abbott) Howard; married Harold Wilson Parker, December 15, 1945; children: Charlotte (Mrs. Peter Busby). *Education:* Royal College of Art, A.R.C.A., 1934. *Home:* 43 Cambridge Rd., S., Chiswick, London W4 3DA, England.

CAREER: Professional embroiderer, 1947—. Lecturer at Goldsmiths School of Art, Goldsmiths College, University of London, lecturer, 1947-59, senior lecturer, 1959-73, principle lecturer, 1973-75. Member of British Craft Centre. *Member:* Art Workers Guild, Society of Designer Craftsmen (fellow; member of council), Embroiderers Guild (member of council). *Awards, honors:* Member of Order of the British Empire; honorary fellow of College of Crafts.

WRITINGS—All published by Batsford: *Design for Embroidery from Traditional English Sources,* 1956; *Inspiration for Embroidery,* 1966; *Embroidery and Colour,* 1976; *The History of Embroidery in the Twentieth Century,* Reinhold, 1977. Contributor to magazines.

SIDELIGHTS: Constance Howard was trained as a wood engraver and book illustrator until 1947. Now her embroidery is often commissioned and she lectures on the subject in England, the United States, and Canada.

BIOGRAPHICAL/CRITICAL SOURCES: Embroidery, summer, 1973.

* * *

HOWE, George Locke 1898(?)-1977

1898(?)—June 19, 1977; American architect and award-winning author. His novel, *Call It Treason,* won the Christopher Award in 1949 and was later made into a movie called "Decision Before Dawn". He wrote several other novels as well as short stories and poems. He died in Salem, Va. Obituaries: *Washington Post,* June 21, 1977.

HOWE, James Robinson 1935-

PERSONAL: Born May 11, 1935, in White Plains, N.Y.; son of James R. (a real estate manager) and Miriam Howe; married Carole Murphy (a marriage counselor), June 30, 1957; children: Laura, James, Sally, Christopher. *Education:* Dartmouth College, B.A., 1957; New York University, M.A., 1960, Ph.D., 1968. *Politics:* "Unimportant." *Home address:* Morse Dr., Shelburne, Vt. 05482. *Office:* Department of English, University of Vermont, Old Mill, Burlington, Vt. 05401.

CAREER: High school English teacher in Roselle Park, N.J., 1958-60; University of Alabama, University, instructor in English, 1960-63; University of Vermont, Burlington, associate professor of English, 1964—.

WRITINGS: The Making of Style, Chilton, 1972; *Marlowe, Tamburlaine, and Magic,* Ohio University Press, 1976. Contributor of about twenty-five poems, articles, and reviews to academic journals.

WORK IN PROGRESS: Research on Renaissance aesthetics, with special reference to English literature and the continuities in aesthetic assumptions between 1530 and 1674. Based on an amalgam of intellectual traditions including Italian art and architecture theory, on the geometric and art imagery of Nicholas of Cusa, and on the philosophical sections of Ovid, plus Renaissance neo-Platonism and Hermeticism.

*   *   *

HOWE, Quincy 1900-1977

August 17, 1900—February 17, 1977; American pioneer in radio and television news commentary, lifelong defender of civil liberties, educator, editor, and author of autobiographical and nonfiction works on foreign affairs. He was one of the first radio reporters to analyze news. Howe died in New York City. Obituaries: *New York Times,* February 18, 1977; *Newsweek,* February 28, 1977; *Time,* February 28, 1977; *Current Biography,* April, 1977. (See index for previous *CA* sketch)

*   *   *

HOWLETT, John 1940-

PERSONAL: Born April 4, 1940, in Leeds, England; son of Reginald (a civil servant) and Leila (Cagna) Howlett; married Ada Angela Finocchiaro, June 10, 1967; children: Isabel, Suzanne. *Education:* Attended Jesus College, Oxford, B.A. (with honors), 1962. *Agent:* Van Loewen, Shaftsbury Ave., London, England.

CAREER: Full time writer, 1966—.

WRITINGS: James Dean: A Biography, Simon & Schuster, 1975; *The Christmas Spy,* Hutchinson, 1975, Harcourt, 1976; *Tango November,* Hutchinson, 1976.

Screenplays: (With David Sherwin) "If . . .," released by Paramount, 1969.

WORK IN PROGRESS: Frank Sinatra, a biography; "Dean," a stage musical; a film script of *Tango November.*

*   *   *

HOYT, Clark 1942-

PERSONAL: Born November 20, 1942, in Providence, R.I.; son of Charles F. (a U.S. Navy captain) and Maude Leslie (King) Hoyt; married Jane Hauser (separated). *Education:* Columbia University, B.A., 1964. *Home:* 1615 Que

St., N.W., Apt. 102, Washington, D.C. 20009. *Office:* Knight-Ridder Newspapers, 1195 National Press Bldg., Washington, D.C. 20045.

CAREER/WRITINGS: U.S. Senate, Washington D.C., research assistant to Senator George Smathers of Florida, 1964-66; *Lakeland Ledger,* Lakeland, Fla., reporter, 1966-68; *Detroit Free Press,* Detroit, Mich., politics writer, 1969-70; *Miami Herald,* Miami, Fla., Washington correspondent, 1970-73, national correspondent (Washington Bureau), 1973-75, Washington news editor, 1975—. Notable assignments include coverage of the medical history of vice-presidential nominee Thomas Eagleton. *Member:* National Press Club (financial secretary, 1975). *Awards, honors:* Pulitzer Prize, 1973, for coverage of Eagleton's medical history.

*   *   *

HSU, Benedict (Pei-Hsiung) 1933-
(Chu Chung-yu)

PERSONAL: Born May 1, 1933, in Nanking, China; came to the United States in 1967, naturalized citizen, 1974; son of Long and Yuan-Cheng (Chao) Hsu; married Lena Chen (a computer operator), June 18, 1961; children: Johnny Yen Chung, Peter Yen Chung. *Education:* Chung-Hsin University, B.A., 1958; Georgetown University, M.S., 1971. *Home and office:* 11205 Schuylkill Rd., Rockville, Md. 20852.

CAREER: Hsin-Shen Daily News, Taipei, Taiwan, reporter, 1954-57; *China Daily News,* Taipei, reporter, 1957-60; *China Times,* Taipei, reporter, 1960-67; *Taiwan Hsin Wen Pao,* Kao-Hsiung, Taiwan, correspondent, 1967-75; *China Times,* columnist, 1975—. Teacher of Chinese language at Cromwell Collier Institute, 1968-71, and Georgetown University and Johns Hopkins University, both 1971-72. Traveled around the world, 1964-65, to meet world leaders; attended Asian and Olympic Games. *Military service:* Chinese Army, 1953-54. U.S. Air Force, interpreter in Taipei, 1955-56; became first lieutenant. *Awards, honors:* Awards from World-Wide Overseas Chinese Association, 1972, for best reporting.

WRITINGS: Little League Baseball in China, East-West Publishing, 1969; *Chi-Cheng, the Fastest Woman in the World,* East-West Publishing, 1970; *The Fight for China's Representation,* Newsdom Weekly, 1971; *The World As I See It,* Newsdom Weekly, 1975. Author of column, under pseudonym Chu Chung-yu, "Along the Potomac River," in *Newsdom Weekly,* 1973—.

SIDELIGHTS: Hsu writes: "To be a first witness of the changing of the world has been an important motivation to my career as a journalist. I have travelled to more than thirty countries around North and South America, Europe, Africa, and Asia during the last twenty-two years to express my own viewpoints on whatever I saw, heard, or was concerned about, also to expose others' opinions on the subjects about which other people are concerned."

BIOGRAPHICAL/CRITICAL SOURCES: Journalism Quarterly, December, 1972.

*   *   *

HUCKER, Charles O(scar) 1919-

PERSONAL: Born June 21, 1919, in St. Louis, Mo.; son of Edward Christian (a salesman) and Katie Vivian (Bond) Hucker; married Myrl C. Henderson, February 12, 1943. *Education:* University of Texas, B.A. (high honors), 1941; University of Chicago, Ph.D. (honors), 1950. *Home:* 1132

Clair Circle, Ann Arbor, Mich. 48103. *Office:* Department of Far Eastern Languages and Literatures, 3096 Frieze Building, University of Michigan, Ann Arbor, Mich. 48109.

CAREER: University of Chicago, Chicago, Ill., instructor, 1950-54, assistant professor of Chinese, 1954-56; University of Arizona, Tucson, associate professor, 1956-58, professor of Oriental studies, 1958-61; Oakland University, Rochester, Mich., professor of history and Asian studies, 1961-65; University of Michigan, Ann Arbor, professor of Chinese and history, 1965—, chairman of department of Far Eastern languages and literatures, 1965-71. Visiting lecturer at colleges and universities; participant in international congresses. *Military service:* U.S. Army Air Forces, 1942-46; served in Pacific theater; became major; received Bronze Star.

MEMBER: American Historical Association, Association for Asian Studies (member of board of directors, 1961-64), American Oriental Society, Chinese Language Teachers Association, Phi Beta Kappa, Phi Alpha Theta. *Awards, honors:* Rockefeller Foundation fellowships to Taipei, Taiwan, 1952-53, and Kyoto, Japan, 1953-54; National Endowment for the Humanities senior fellowship, 1968-69; H.H.D. from Oakland University, 1974.

WRITINGS: Chinese History: A Bibliographic Review, American Historical Association, 1958; *The Traditional Chinese State in Ming Times,* University of Arizona Press, 1961; *China: A Critical Bibliography,* University of Arizona Press, 1962; *The Censorial System of Ming China,* Stanford University Press, 1966; (editor) *Government in Ming China: Seven Studies,* Columbia University Press, 1969; *Two Studies on Ming History,* Center for Chinese Studies, University of Michigan, 1971; *Some Approaches to China's Past,* American Historical Association, 1973; *The Association for Asian Studies: An Interpretive History,* University of Washington Press, 1973; *China's Imperial Past: An Introduction to Chinese History and Culture,* Stanford University Press, 1975; *China to 1850: A Short History,* Stanford University Press, 1977.

Contributor: John K. Fairbank, editor, *Chinese Thought and Institutions,* University of Chicago Press, 1957; David S. Nivison and Arthur F. Wright, editors, *Confucianism in Action,* Stanford University Press, 1959; Wright, editor, *Confucianism and Chinese Civilization,* Atheneum, 1964; John L. Bishop, editor, *Studies of Governmental Institutions in Chinese History,* Harvard University Press, 1968; John Meskill, editor, *An Introduction to Chinese Civilization,* Columbia University Press, 1973; Frank A. Kierman and Fairbank, editors, *Chinese Ways in Warfare,* Harvard University Press, 1974; L. Carrington Goodrich, editor, *Dictionary of Ming Biography,* Columbia University Press, 1976.

Contributor to *Encyclopaedia Britannica, Encyclopedia Americana,* and to professional journals.

WORK IN PROGRESS: A Historical Dictionary of Chinese Official Titles, publication expected in 1979; research on premodern Chinese political institutions.

*   *   *

HUFFMAN, Carolyn   1928-

PERSONAL: Born April 1, 1928, in Austin, Tex.; daughter of Carl Anthony (a certified public accountant) and Jeanette (Parker) Barlow; married Charles H. Huffman (an Episcopal priest), March 10, 1951; children: Carl B. (deceased), Beth Ann, Heather J., Laura L. *Education:* University of Texas,

B.S., 1950. *Religion:* Episcopalian. *Home:* 6306 Highland Hills Dr., Austin, Tex. 78731.

CAREER: Elementary school teacher in San Antonio, Tex., 1950-51, and Corpus Christi, Tex., 1951-52; writer and speaker, 1971—.

WRITINGS: Bloom Where You Are, Vision House, 1976.

WORK IN PROGRESS: A sequel to *Bloom Where You Are.*

SIDELIGHTS: Carolyn Huffman told *CA:* "I really feel as if God touched me on the shoulder and helped me to write *Bloom Where You Are.* I had prayed that [it] would some way reach out and touch the brokenness of His people. I am amazed that this is exactly what seems to have happened."

*   *   *

HUGHES, Emmet John   1920-

PERSONAL: Born December 26, 1920, in Newark, N.J.; son of John L. (a judge) and Grace (Freeman) Hughes; married second wife, Eileen Lanouette (divorced); married third wife, Katherine Nouri; children: (first marriage) John; (second marriage) Mary Larkin, Kathleen Freeman; (third marriage) Caitlin, Johanna. *Education:* Princeton University, A.B. (summa cum laude), 1941; Columbia University, graduate study, 1941-42. *Religion:* Roman Catholic. *Home:* 90 Olden Lane, Princeton, N.J. 08540. *Office:* Department of Politics, Rutgers University, New Brunswick, N.J. 08903.

CAREER: American Embassy, Madrid, Spain, press attache, 1942-46; Time-Life, Inc., New York, N.Y., chief of bureau in Rome, 1947-48, and in Berlin, 1948-49; articles editor for *Life,* 1949-53; administrative assistant to President Eisenhower, 1953; Time-Life International, special European correspondent, 1953-56; editor of *Fortune,* 1956-57; Time-Life International, chief foreign correspondent, 1957-60; senior adviser on public affairs to the Rockefeller family, 1960-63; *Newsweek,* New York City, columnist, 1963-68; special assistant to New York Governor Nelson Rockefeller, 1968-70; Rutgers University, New Brunswick, N.J., professor of politics at Eagleton Institute, 1970—. Campaign speech writer for Dwight D. Eisenhower, 1956, and Nelson Rockefeller, 1960-62. Member of board of directors of Lambert International Corp., 1962. *Military service:* U.S. Army, during World War II; served with Office of Strategic Services and Office of War Information in Spain and North Africa. *Member:* Phi Beta Kappa.

WRITINGS: The Church and the Liberal Society (Catholic Book Club selection), Princeton University Press, 1944; *Report from Spain,* Holt, 1947, Kennikat, 1971; *America the Vincible: A Brief Inquiry, Written with Much Anxiety and Some Anger, Dealing with Matters of Foreign Policy, Seeking Probable Sources of Our Peril and Causes of Our Fear, as Well as the Suggestion of Possible Ways by Which We Might, While Enduring the Stern Trial, Hold Hope, Tempered by Reason, to Live in Freedom More Profound and Peace Less Precarious,* Doubleday, 1959; (editor) *Education in World Perspective,* Harper, 1962; *The Ordeal of Power: A Political Memoir of the Eisenhower Years,* Atheneum, 1963; *The Living Presidency: The Resources and Dilemmas of the American Presidential Office,* Coward, 1973. Author of television film script "War in Spain" for Columbia Broadcasting System, 1958. Contributor to magazines, including *Look.* Editorial consultant to Washington Post Co., 1963-68.

BIOGRAPHICAL/CRITICAL SOURCES: Saturday Review, March 16, 1963.*

HUGHES, Judy 1943-

PERSONAL: Born November 6, 1943, in Long Beach, Calif.; daughter of Dennis H. and Doris (Ritchie) Alex; married Larry E. Hughes (a financial analyst), May 29, 1965; children: Stephanie. *Education:* Attended public schools in California. *Home address:* Route 1, Box 32A, Bagley, Minn. 56621.

CAREER: Business and Public Relations Service, Santa Barbara, Calif., owner, 1966-68; Gemini Inc., Corvallis, Ore., property manager, 1969-71; self employed insurance agent in Corvallis, Ore., 1971-76; free-lance writer, 1975—. Federally licensed to care for injured and orphaned wildlife since 1969. Executive officer of Benton County Oregon Democrats, 1976. *Member:* Wilderness Society, Defenders of Wildlife, Sierra Club, Fund for Animals.

WRITINGS: A Bird in the Hand and a Bear in the Bush: A Halfway House for Wildlife, Chronicle Books, 1976; *Superior National Forest and the Boundary Waters Canoe Area: How Environmental Action Saved It,* Dillon, in press. Contributor to magazines, including *Pacific Search, Lady's Circle, Mother Earth News, Consumer's Digest, Oregon Territory,* and *Northwest News.*

WORK IN PROGRESS: Children's Wildlife.

SIDELIGHTS: Judy Hughes writes: "I have a deep concern and commitment to educate people about wildlife and wilderness—I feel my close relationship rehabilitating wild animals and birds—fawns, foxes, bears, skunks, raccoons, hawks, owls and many others—provides me with a unique learning experience. I feel a responsibility to arouse the public's awareness and consciousness as wildlife struggles to coexist with man. I keep up-to-date politically on wildlife issues and have done extensive research on environmental issues."

AVOCATIONAL INTERESTS: Observing nature quietly, cross-country skiing, ice skating, hiking, horseback riding, photography.

*   *   *

HUGHES, Kathleen W. 1927(?)-1977

1927(?)—April 20, 1977; British historian, specializing in the early history and culture of Britain, and author of works in her field. She died in England. Obituaries: *AB Bookman's Weekly,* July 25, 1977.

*   *   *

HUMPHREY, Hubert Horatio 1911-

PERSONAL: Born May 27, 1911, in Wallace, S.D.; son of Hubert (a pharmacist) and Christine (Sannes) Humphrey; married Muriel Fay Buck, September 3, 1936; children: Nancy, Hubert, Robert, Douglas. *Education:* Denver College of Pharmacy, received degree, 1933; University of Minnesota, B.A. (magna cum laude), 1939; Louisiana State University, M.A., 1940. *Residence:* Waverly, Minn. *Office:* Senate Office Building, Washington, D.C. 20510.

CAREER: University of Minnesota, Minneapolis, instructor in political science, 1940-41; War Production Administration, head of Minnesota branch and state director of training re-employment division, 1941-42; War Manpower Progress Commission, assistant regional director, 1943; Macalester College, St. Paul, Minn., professor for Army Air Force Training Program, 1943-44; Franklin D. Roosevelt for President campaign, Minneapolis manager, 1944; Mayor of Minneapolis, 1945-48; member of U.S. Senate from Minne-

sota, 1948-64; U.S. Delegate to the United Nations, 1956-57; 38th Vice-President of the United States, 1964-68; Democratic candidate for President of United States, 1968; University of Minnesota, Minneapolis, professor of social science, 1969-70; member of U.S. Senate, 1970—; Deputy President pro tem of the Senate, 1977—.

Co-founder of Americans for Democratic Action, 1947; U.S. Delegate to UNESCO Conference in Paris and the Nuclear Test Suspension Conference in Geneva, 1958; contended for U.S. Presidential nomination, Democratic Party, 1960; Assistant Majority Leader (Whip), U.S. Senate, 1961-64; floor manager of Civil Rights Act of 1964; chairman, Board of Consultants, Encyclopaedia Britannica Education Corporation, and member of board, Encyclopaedia Britannica, Inc., 1969-70; contended for Democratic Presidential nomination, 1972; chairman of Board of Trustees, Woodrow Wilson International Center for Scholars, 1970-72; chairman, Vice-Presidential Selection Commission, Democratic Party, 1972-74. Has served as chairman of the Congressional Joint Economic Committee; chairman of the Senate Agriculture and Forestry Committee; member of Senate Foreign Relations Committee; Select Committee on Nutrition and Human Needs; Technology Assessment Board; and National Ocean Policy Study Group. Member of twelve Senate subcommittees.

WRITINGS: The Cause Is Mankind: A Liberal Program for Modern America, Praeger, 1964; *War on Poverty,* McGraw, 1964; (editor) *Integration Versus Segregation,* Crowell, 1964; (co-author) *Moral Crisis: The Case for Civil Rights,* Gilbert Publishing, 1964; *Beyond Civil Rights: A New Day of Equality,* Random House, 1964; *The Political Philosophy of the New Deal,* Louisiana State University Press, 1970; *The Education of a Public Man: My Life and Politics,* Doubleday, 1976. Also author of a regular newspaper column distributed by the Register and Tribune Syndicate, 1969-70.

SIDELIGHTS: While serving as Vice-President of the United States, Humphrey acted as a member of the Cabinet and National Security Council and chairman of several councils, including the National Aeronautics and Space Council, Peace Corps Advisory Council, National Advisory Council to the Office of Economic Opportunity, the President's Council on Youth Opportunity, National Council on Indian Opportunities, and others. At the request of President Lyndon Johnson he undertook numerous overseas assignments, most notable of which were the Nuclear Proliferation Treaty, the Kennedy Round of Trade Negotiations and the North Atlantic Treaty Organization.

Senator Humphrey's distinguished record of accomplishment in Congress include work on such projects as Medicare, Project Headstart, Peace Corps, Department of Housing and Urban Development, the U.S. Arms Control and Disarmament Agency, the 1964 Civil Rights Act, Vista, the Nuclear Test Ban Treaty of 1963, the Federal Scholarship Program, the Council of Youth Opportunity, and Job Corps. "In my years of public life," he wrote, "I have tried to serve as a voice and worker for the cause of equal justice and equal opportunity, for the general welfare, and for the common defense of our country."

Humphrey's current legislative interests are the world food shortage, energy resources (including solar research and development), modernization of Congress, arms control and national security, child and mental health care, care for the elderly, and education of the handicapped. On January 5, 1977, Humphrey was unanimously elected Deputy President pro tem of the Senate by Democratic members of the Senate.

* * *

HUNTER, Marjorie 1922-

PERSONAL: Born June 2, 1922, in Bethany, W.Va.; daughter of Joshua Allen (a professor) and Minnie (a teacher; maiden name, Gilliland) Hunter. Education: Elon College, A.B., 1942. Religion: Episcopalian. Home: 3517 R St. N.W., Washington, D.C. 20007. Office: 1920 L St. Washington, D.C. 20036.

CAREER/WRITINGS: Raleigh News and Observer, Raleigh, N.C., reporter, 1942-49; Houston Press, Houston, Tex., reporter, 1949-50; Winston-Salem Journal, Winston-Salem, N.C., reporter, 1950-61; New York Times, reporter and editor in Washington bureau, 1961—. Notable assignments include Congress and the White House. Contributor to New York Times Magazine. Member: White House Correspondents Association, Washington Press Club (president, 1969-70), Standing Committee of Correspondents in Congress, Sigma Delta Chi (vice-president of Washington chapter, 1975-76).

* * *

HURST, Virginia Radcliffe 1914(?)-1976
(Virginia Radcliffe)

1914(?)—September 24, 1976; American writer under the name Virginia Radcliffe; public relations firm staff writer and author of articles on Fire Island and of a book on the islands of the Caribbean. Previously she wrote for the radio show "Cavalcade of America." She died in Fire Island, N.Y. Obituaries: New York Times, September 28, 1976.

* * *

HUTCHINS, Robert Maynard 1899-1977

PERSONAL: Born January 17, 1899, in Brooklyn, N.Y.; son of William James (a Presbyterian minister and college president) and Anna Laura (Murch) Hutchins; married Maude Phelps McVeigh (a sculptress), 1921 (divorced, 1948); married Vesta Sutton Orlick, May 10, 1949; children: (first marriage) Frances Ratcliffe, Joanna Blessing, Clarissa Phelps. Education: Attended Oberlin College, 1915-17; Yale University, A.B. (honors), 1921. Office: P.O. Box 4068, Santa Barbara, Calif. 93103.

CAREER: English and history teacher in private school in Lake Placid, N.Y., 1921-23; Yale University, New Haven, Conn., lecturer, 1925-27, professor of law, 1927-29, acting dean of Law School, 1927-28, dean, 1928-29; University of Chicago, Chicago, Ill., president of university, 1929-45, chancellor, 1945-51; associate director of Ford Foundation, 1951-54; chief executive officer of Fund for the Republic, beginning 1954. Writer. Founding member and president of Committee to Frame a World Constitution, beginning 1945; chief executive officer of Center for the Study of Democratic Institutions; member of board of directors of Encyclopaedia Britannica, Inc. and Encyclopaedia Britannica Films, Inc. Regional chairman of the first National Labor Board, 1933; chairman of Commission on International Economic Relations, 1933-36, and Goethe Bicentennial Foundation, 1949; member of Commission on the Freedom of the Press, 1947. Member of board of directors of St. John's College, Annapolis, Md. Military service: U.S. Army, Ambulance Service, 1917-19; served in Italy; received Croce di Guerra. Member: Chicago Bar Association (honorary member), Phi

Beta Kappa, Coif, University Club (Chicago), Tavern Club, Yale Club (New York), Metropolitan Club (New York), Century Club (New York), Authors Club (London), Chicago Club, Commercial Club (Chicago), Union League Club.

AWARDS, HONORS: M.A., 1922, and LL.B., 1925, both from Yale University; LL.D. from West Virginia University, Lafayette College, and Oberlin College, 1929, Williams College, 1930, Berea College, 1931, Harvard University, 1936, Tulane University, 1938, University of Copenhagen, 1946, University of Illinois, 1947; University of Frankfurt, 1948, University of Stockholm, 1949, Rollins College, 1950, University of Chicago, 1951, Colby College, 1956, University of Rochester, 1958, and Lewis & Clark College, 1967; D.Litt. from Georgetown University and Hebrew Union College, 1964; named officer of the French Legion of Honor; Goethe Medal from the City of Frankfurt, Germany, 1948; Aspen Founders Award, 1960.

WRITINGS: No Friendly Voice, University of Chicago Press, 1936, reprinted, Greenwood Press, 1968; The Library, American Library Association, 1936; The Higher Learning in America, Yale University Press, 1936, revised edition, 1962; Education and the Social Order, Modern Forum, 1936.

Education for Freedom, Louisiana State University Press, 1943; The Atomic Bomb versus Civilization, Human Events, Inc., 1945; The Atom Bomb and Education, National Peace Council (London), 1947; The Constitutional Foundations for World Order, Social Science Foundation, University of Denver, 1947; Saint Thomas and the World State, Marquette University Press, 1949; Morals, Religion, and Higher Education, University of Chicago Press, for Kenyon College, 1950; (contributor) America and the Atomic Age, University of Chicago, 1951; The Great Conversation: The Substance of a Liberal Education, Encyclopaedia Britannica, 1952, published as Great Books: The Foundation of a Liberal Education, Simon & Schuster, 1954; The Democratic Dilemma, Almqvist & Wiksells, 1952; The Conflict in Education in a Democratic Society, Harper, 1953; The University of Utopia, University of Chicago Press, 1953, 2nd edition, 1964; (with others) Five Tributes to Ralph A. Beals, 1899-1954, [New York], 1955; Some Observations on American Education, Cambridge University Press, 1956; Freedom, Education, and the Fund: Essays and Addresses, 1946-1956, Meridian, 1956; The Bill of Rights, Yesterday, Today, Tomorrow, Fund for the Republic, 1956.

(With Harvey Einbinder) The Britannica: An Exchange of Letters, privately printed, 1960; (co-author) What's a College For?, Public Affairs Press, 1960; (editor with Mortimer Adler) The Great Ideas Today, Encyclopaedia Britannica, 1961; The Nurture of Human Life, Center for the Study of Democratic Institutions, 1961; Two Faces of Federalism: An Outline of an Argument about Pluralism, Unity, and Law, Center for the Study of Democratic Institutions, 1961; (with Joseph P. Lyford) The Political Animal: A Conversation, Center for the Study of Democratic Institutions, 1962; (editor with Adler) Gateway to the Great Books, ten volumes, Encyclopaedia Britannica, beginning 1963; (with Arthur S. Flemming) Addresses on the Role of Government in Education, William Marsh Rice University, 1963; A Conversation on Education: Robert M. Hutchins Answers Questions from the Floor, Center for the Study of Democratic Institutions, 1963; (co-author) Science, Scientists, and Politics, Center for the Study of Democratic Institutions, 1963; (with others) Dialogues in Americanism, Regnery, 1964; Dr. Zuckerkandl! (from the film), Grove, 1968; The Learning

Society, Praeger, 1968; *The Future of International Education,* United Nations Institute for Training and Research, 1970. Also author of *Speaking of Education,* 1940, and *Some Questions about Education in North America,* 1951.

Author of scripts for about fifteen phonorecords for Center for the Study of Democratic Institutions. Co-editor of "Great Books of the Western World," fifty-four volumes, *Encyclopaedia Britannica,* beginning 1952. Contributor to magazines. Editor of *Measure: A Critical Journal,* 1950-51.*

(Died May 14, 1977, in Santa Barbara, Calif.)

*   *   *

HUTCHISON, John Alexander   1912-

PERSONAL: Born March 2, 1912, in Cedar Grove, N.J.; son of Seeley and Fannie (Elwell) Hutchison; married Julia Kley, November 28, 1936; children: John Stuart, Ralph, William, Helen, Ruth. *Education:* Lafayette College, B.S., 1932; Union Theological Seminary, New York, N.Y., B.S., 1935; Columbia University, Ph.D., 1941; post-doctoral study at University of Edinburgh, 1947-48, and University of Basel, 1948. *Home:* 473 Blaisdell Dr., Claremont, Calif. 91711. *Office:* Department of Philosophy, Claremont Graduate School and University Center, Claremont, Calif. 91711.

CAREER: Ordained Presbyterian minister, 1935; assistant pastor of Presbyterian church in Baltimore, Md., 1935-37; pastor in Bayonne, N.J., 1937-40; College of Wooster, Wooster, Ohio, instructor in philosophy, 1941-43, professor of religion, 1943-47; Williams College, Williamstown, Mass., professor of religion, 1947-55; Columbia University, New York, N.Y., professor of religion, 1955-60; Claremont Graduate School, Claremont, Calif., Danforth Professor of the Philosophy of Religion, 1960—. *Member:* Society for Religion in Higher Education, American Philosophical Association, American Academy of Religion, Phi Beta Kappa. *Awards, honors:* Fund for the Advancement of Education fellowship, 1952-53.

WRITINGS: We Are Not Divided: A Critical and Historical Study of the Federal Council of the Churches of Christ in America, Round Table Press, 1941; (with James Alfred Martin, Jr.) *Ways of Faith: An Introduction to Religion,* Ronald, 1953, 2nd edition (editor and contributor) *Christian Faith and Social Action: A Symposium,* Scribner, 1953; *Faith, Reason, and Existence: An Introduction to Contemporary Philosophy of Religion,* Oxford University Press, 1956; *The Two Cities: A Study of God and Human Politics,* Doubleday, 1957; *Language and Faith: Studies in Sign, Symbol, and Meaning,* Westminster, 1963; *Myth, Religion, and Politics,* General Board of Education, Division of Higher Education, Methodist Church of the United States, 1965; *Paths of Faith,* McGraw, 1969, 2nd edition, 1975. Also author of *Religious and Theological Statements,* 1963.*

*   *   *

HUYLER, Jean Wiley   1935-

PERSONAL: Born March 30, 1935, in Seattle, Wash.; daughter of Othello Phillip (a patternmaker) and Agnes Olive (Snarr) Dickert; married Richard K. Wiley (divorced); married Garey H. Huyler (divorced); children: Richard K. Wiley, Jr., Cynthia Jean Wiley. *Education:* Attended University of Washington, 1953-55. *Politics:* Nonpartisan. *Religion:* Christian. *Home:* 7727 Southeast Atchinson Dr., Olympia, Wash. 98503. *Office:* Washington State School Directors Association, 200 East Union, Olympia, Wash. 98501.

CAREER/WRITINGS: Lynnwood Enterprise, Lynnwood, Wash., reporter and bureau manager, 1961-63; *Everett Herald,* Western Sun edition, Lynnwood, reporter, photographer, and city editor, 1963-71; *Seattle Post-Intelligencer,* Seattle, Wash., special sections editor, 1971, general assignment reporter, 1976; Rainier Bancorporation, Seattle, senior economic editor, 1972; Fournier Newspapers, Kent, Wash., women's editor and associate editor, 1973-75; Jean Wiley Huyler (communications), Kent and Portland, Ore., communications consultant, 1975—. U.S. Department of Interior, Bonneville Power Administration, writer and editior, 1976-77. Lecturer. Notable assignments include coverage of events in Southeast Asia in 1967, and in the Caribbean and Mexico. Contributor of articles and photographs to magazines, including *Editor & Publisher, American Banker, Burroughs Clearinghouse,* and *Cat Fancy.* Publisher and writer for *National Press Woman* (magazine); contributing editorial writer for national Publisher's Auxiliary.

MEMBER: National Federation of Press Women (president of Washington affiliate, 1970-73, national vice-president, 1973-75, president, 1975-77, public affairs director, 1977-79), Women in Communications, National School Public Relations Association, Pacific Northwest Business Communicators (treasurer, 1973). *Awards, honors:* Has received more than one hundred national and state awards in editing, writing, photography, management, design, community service, and public relations.

WORK IN PROGRESS: A journalism text; an educational communications manual.

SIDELIGHTS: Jean Wiley Huyler told *CA:* "Communications technology is advancing faster than any other area of society. This challenges communicators to develop greater judgmental competence and update skills, including basics, to go online to computers or typesetters; expand knowledge to encompass a burgeoning number of topics; sharpen human sensitivity and audience orientation to produce material suited to more specialized, sophisticated, visually oriented audiences. Instead of regurgitating news from 'last night's city council meeting,' communicators need to act as interpreters, report trends, 'futurize.' They should urge clarification of language in documents and instruments, such as ballots and contracts, that citizens must understand to cope effectively in American society. They should apply their skills to eliminate all types of discrimination. They must diligently guard freedom of the press as a right of free people, remembering that a press that is free also must be responsible. To quote the American Society of Newspaper Editors: 'A newspaper should not invade private rights or feelings without sure warrant of public right as distinguished from public curiosity.'"

*   *   *

IBRAHIM, Abdel-Sattar   1939-

PERSONAL: Born November 6, 1939, in Luxor, Egypt; came to the United States, 1974; son of Mohamed Elzambily (a village mayor) and El-bollock (Nafeesa) Ibrahim; married Reda Mohamed Ali Elsayed (a psychologist), November 27, 1973; children: Lobna, Chadi. *Education:* Ain Shams University, B.A. (honors), 1962; University of Cairo, M.A., 1969, Ph.D. (first class honors), 1973. *Home:* 41001 Seven Mile Rd., Northville, Mich. 48167. *Office:* Northville State Hospital, Northville, Mich. 48167.

CAREER: Armed Forces Hospital, Abbaseya, Egypt, junior clinical psychologist, 1963-64; Al-hazar University, Eldarrasa, Egypt, faculty assistant, 1964-66; University of

Assuit, Menya, Egypt, visiting lecturer in philosophy and psychology, 1972-73; University of Cairo, Giza, Egypt, assistant professor of psychology, 1973-74, on leave, 1974—; Northville State Hospital, Northville, Mich., chief psychologist and director of psychological research, 1974—. Visiting scholar at University of Michigan, 1974-75, 1976-77; lecturer at Eastern Michigan University, 1977. Research assistant at Egyptian National Center for Research in Social and Criminological Studies, 1965. Consultant psychologist at Behman Mental Hospital, 1973-74. *Member:* International Association for Applied Psychology, Middle East Studies Association of North America (fellow), American Psychological Association, Association for Humanistic Psychology, Society for the Psychological Study of Social Issues, Egyptian Psychological Association (fellow), Egyptian Mental Health Association, Mid-Western Psychological Association.

WRITINGS: (Contributor) L. K. Meleika, editor, *Readings in Social Psychology in Arabic Countries,* Arabic Writer House, 1970; *Personal Attitudes Inventory,* Ghareeb Press, 1973; *Personality Response Styles Test,* Ghareeb Press, 1973; (with Salwa Elmoulla and M. F. Farrag) *Human Behavior: Scientific Outlook,* University Book House (Cairo), 1973; (translator into Arabic) Mischel Argyle, *Elm-Elnafs Wa Moshkeelat Almojtamaa* (title means "Psychology and Social Problems"), University Book House (Cairo), 1973. Contributor of more than twenty articles and reviews to professional journals, including *Journal of Psychological Health, National Review of Social Sciences,* and *Journal of Psychology.*

WORK IN PROGRESS: Frames of the Rigid Mind; Creativity, Creative People and Society; Political Behavior and Psychopathology; a book with Robert Frumkin, *Abnormal Psychology: Selected Readings on Sources;* research on containment theory, creativity, differences between black and white schizophrenics in terms of personality and socio-cultural processes, and on personality within socio-cultural perspective.

SIDELIGHTS: Ibrahim writes: "My professional life started with the choice of psychology and the social sciences as a career and a professional style of life. My current interests in this profession are spread, as they will hopefully continue to be, all too widely. These interests reflect major themes which are actually part of my general philosophy in the profession. I am respectful and devoted to observation, experimentation and a scientific outlook. I think that these aspects are essential if we expect to rebuild our knowledge and image of man on a realistic, non-mystical, non-fictional basis. However, I think that science contains nothing like the absolute truth or the right direction for human will. I believe that we have to maximize our efforts to establish a science which might help people to live a happier, more meaningful, self-actualizing and creative existence. I profoundly believe that ignoring such values among scientists can be delusional, dogmatic, rigid, or destructing. I have and shall continue to hold the belief in the balance between the 'shoulds' of science and the humanistic and social values that ought to give science a meaningful connotation and purpose.

"As a university teacher, I see myself as having responsibility to stimulate creative and constructive changes in both society and individuals. I consider myself a change agent, and I want to see myself and other social scientists capable of guiding social change on more positive, creative, effective and scientific principles.

"My future, as I can see it, is that of integrating my three professional interests; i.e., research and writing, teaching, and practice, into one fruitful life style, to combine the ideals with the present needs, to integrate theory with practice, and to be more aware, in terms of writing and living, of the fact that a real growth and maturity is a matter of change and awareness of choices and decisions. Professionally, I still believe that my best ideas are still to come."

* * *

IMFELD, Al 1935-

PERSONAL: Born January 14, 1935, in Galgenen, Switzerland; son of Alois (a farmer) and Franziska (Hunkeler) Imfeld. *Education:* Attended Seminary Schoeneck, 1954-60, and Gregoriana University, 1961-62; Fordham University, M.A., 1964; Northwestern University, M.S.J., 1966. *Politics:* "Social democrat; leftist." *Home:* Bethlehem Fathers, 6405 Immensee, Switzerland. *Office:* Africa/Asia/Switzerland, Konradstrasse 23, 8005 Zurich, Switzerland.

CAREER: Ordained Roman Catholic priest of Missionary Society of Bethlehem Fathers, 1960; journalist in Asia, 1966; conducted research in Rhodesia on the Shona people, 1967-68; taught courses in the sociology of development and rural journalism in Malawi, Tanzania, and Kenya, 1969-71; i3w (Information Third World), Berne, Switzerland, founder and team member, 1971-76; development consultant in Tanzania, 1976—. Development consultant at Africa/Asia/Switzerland, 1977—. Taught sociology of art in Lucerne, Switzerland, 1971-72.

WRITINGS: China als Entwick lungsmodell, Laetare Verlag, 1974, English translation by Matthew J. O'Connell published as *China as a Model of Development,* Orbis, 1976.

In German: *Die Dritte Welt im Jahr 2000* (title means "Third World in the Year 2000: Prophecies"), Benziger (Zurich), 1973; *Suedafrika: Ende des Dialogs?* (title means "South Africa: End of Dialogue"), CETIM (Geneva, Switzerland), 1974; *Deutsche China literatur der letzten Zahre* (title means "Annotated Bibliography of German Language Books on China"), Asian-Forum (Munich), 1975; *Politik des Hungers* (title means "Politics of Hunger"), Laetare Verlag, 1977. Contributor to Swiss and German newspapers and magazines.

WORK IN PROGRESS: Agrobusiness: It Integrates the Third World into Capitalism; Politics in African Literature of Today: World Criticism and Self-Criticism; Or, Politics of Hunger; Self-Reliance: A New Way of Life.

SIDELIGHTS: Imfeld writes: "After I learned de-mythologizing in scripture theology I started to apply the very same methods also to economics and politics and our way of life."

* * *

INGWERSEN, Faith 1934-

PERSONAL: Born January 27, 1934, in California; daughter of Urmson (a physician) and Anna (a rancher; maiden name, Boswell) Sloniger; married Niels Ingwersen (a professor and writer), June 3, 1961. *Education:* University of Wyoming, B.A., 1954, M.A., 1957; further graduate study at University of Oslo, 1958-59, and University of Copenhagen, 1959-61, 1962-65; University of Chicago, Ph.D., 1974. *Home:* 3601 Nakoma Rd., Madison, Wis. 53711.

CAREER: Writer, 1964—. Guest lecturer at University of Wisconsin Extension, Madison, 1975-76.

WRITINGS: (Contributor) F. J. Billeskov Jansch and

P. M. Mitchell, editors, *Anthology of Danish Literature: Bilingual Edition,* Southern Illinois University Press, 1971; (with husband, Niels Ingwersen) *Martin A. Hansen,* Twayne, 1976. Contributor of translations and reviews to magazines, including *New Mexico Quarterly, Literary Review, Choice,* and *Books Abroad.*

WORK IN PROGRESS: A book on Danish writer Martin Anderson Nexoe, with husband, Niels Ingwersen; *Gothicism and Fantasy.*

* * *

INGWERSEN, Niels 1935-

PERSONAL: Born May 18, 1935, in Horsens, Denmark; came to the United States in 1965; son of Hans Henrik and Karen (Bach) Ingwersen; married Faith Sloniger (a writer), June 3, 1961. *Education:* Attended University of Stockholm, 1957, University of Oslo, 1958-59, and University of Chicago, 1961-62; University of Copenhagen, Cand.Mag., 1963. *Home:* 3601 Nakoma Rd., Madison, Wis. 53711. *Office:* Department of Scandinavian Studies, University of Wisconsin, 1302 Van Hise Hall, Madison, Wis. 53706.

CAREER: Hellerup Seminarium, Copenhagen, Denmark, adjunct in Danish literature and language, 1964-65; University of Wisconsin, Madison, assistant professor, 1965-70, associate professor, 1970-73, professor of Scandinavian studies, 1973—. Research associate at Odense Universitet, 1971-72. *Military service:* Danish Army, Signal Corps, 1963-64. *Member:* Modern Language Association of America, Society for the Advancement of Scandinavian Study (president, 1969-71), American-Scandinavian Foundation, Dansk Magisterforening, Dansklaererforeningen, Midwest Institute for Scandinavian Culture.

WRITINGS: (With wife, Faith Ingwersen) *Martin A. Hansen,* Twayne, 1976. Contributor to Scandinavian studies journals.

WORK IN PROGRESS: A book on the Danish novelist, Martin Andersen Nexoe, with wife, Faith Ingwersen; editing an anthology of Hans Christian Andersen's tales; studying Danish prose of the 1890's.

* * *

IRBY, Kenneth (Lee) 1936-

PERSONAL: Born November 18, 1936, in Bowie, Tex.; son of Addison Craft (a physician) and Dora Elizabeth (a nurse; maiden name, East) Irby. *Education:* University of Kansas, B.A., 1958; Harvard University, M.A., 1960, additional study, 1962-63; University of California, Berkeley, M.L.S., 1968. *Home address:* c/o John Friedman, 1327 Carrison, Berkeley, Calif. 94702.

CAREER: Sandia Corporation, Albuquerque, N.M., staff administrator, 1963-64; Duncan MacAndrew (merchant tailors), San Francisco, Calif., manager, 1965; University of California, Berkeley, Institute of Traffic and Transportation Engineering, duplicating machine operator, 1968-71; Tufts University, Medford, Mass., lecturer, 1971-73, assistant professor of English, 1974-75. Visiting professor, Copenhagen University, 1973-74. *Military service:* U.S. Army, 1960-62. *Member:* Phi Beta Kappa. *Awards, honors:* Fulbright travel grant, 1974-75.

WRITINGS—Poetry: The Roadrunner, Duende Press, 1964; *Kansas-New Mexico,* Dialogue Press, 1965; *Movements/Sequences,* Duende Press, 1965; *The Flower of Having Passed Through Paradise in a Dream: Poems,* Matter Books, 1969; *Relation: Poems, 1965-66,* Black

Sparrow Press, 1970; *To Max Douglas,* Tansy Press, 1971; *The Snow Queen,* Turtle Island Foundation, 1973.

Poetry represented in anthologies, including *Poems Now,* edited by Hettie Jones, Kulchur Press, 1966; *Caterpillar Anthology,* edited by Clayton Eshleman, Doubleday, 1971; *America a Prophecy,* edited by George Quasha and Jerome Rothenburg, Random House, 1973; *Catalpa: Poems, 1968-73,* Tansy Press, 1976; *Archipelago,* Tuumba Press, 1976; *In Excelsis Borealis* (long poem), White Creek Press, 1976.

Contributor to periodicals, including *Paris Review, Poetry, New Mexico Quarterly, Caterpillar, Poetry Review* (London), and *Chicago Review.*

WORK IN PROGRESS: Editing and preparing an index for Carl O. Sauer's *Seventeenth Century North America,* publication by Turtle Island Foundation expected in 1977.

SIDELIGHTS: Irby told *CA* that his main concerns include "the imagination of land and place, the local; pastoral (that which feeds us—pasture) poetry." He added, "The work of history is how any of us orders his life."

* * *

ISH-KISHOR, Sulamith 1897(?)-1977

1897(?)—June 23, 1977; British-born American author of children's books. Several of her books have a religious theme and are based on biblical figures. She died in New York City. Obituaries: *New York Times,* June 25, 1977; *AB Bookman's Weekly,* September 5, 1977.

* * *

ISLAM, Kazi Nazrul 1899(?)-1976

1899(?)—August 29, 1976; Bangladesh poet popularly known as the "rebel poet." Author of over three thousand poems, mostly of a revolutionary nature, he was said to have inspired millions of Moslems to rise against the British on the subcontinent before their 1947 independence. He once went on a forty-two day hunger strike in jail to protest mass killings of Indians by the British. Islam died in Dacca, Bangladesh. Obituaries: *New York Times,* August 30, 1976; *Washington Post,* September 1, 1976; *AB Bookman's Weekly,* October 4, 1976.

* * *

JACKSON, Anthony 1926-

PERSONAL: Born September 4, 1926, in London, England; son of Jack Zelechin and Ester (Plotkin) Jackson; married Sarah Sherman (an artist), August 28, 1949; children: Timothy, Melanie. *Education:* London Polytechnic, diploma in architecture, 1950. *Politics:* Social Democrat. *Religion:* Jewish. *Home:* 1411 Edward St., Halifax, Nova Scotia, Canada B3H 3H5. *Office:* School of Architecture, Nova Scotia Technical College, Halifax, Nova Scotia, Canada B3J 2X4.

CAREER: Design Research Unit, London, England, designer, 1950-51; School of Architecture, Southend-on-Sea, England, assistant lecturer in architecture, 1951-56; Canadian Government Exhibition Commission, Ottawa, Ontario, designer,.1957-59; *Canadian Architect,* Toronto, Ontario, technical editor, 1959-61, managing editor, 1961-62; Nova Scotia Technical College, Halifax, associate professor, 1963-73, professor of architecture, 1973—. *Military service:* British Army, 1945-48; served in India. *Member:* Royal Institute of British Architects, Royal Architectural Institute of Canada.

WRITINGS: The Politics of Architecture: A History of Modern Architecture in Britain, Architectural Press, 1970; A Place Called Home: A History of Low-Cost Housing in Manhattan, M.I.T. Press, 1976. Contributor to architectural journals.

WORK IN PROGRESS: Research on contemporary Canadian architecture, and on an existential dialectical theory of meaning in architecture.

SIDELIGHTS: Jackson writes: "Architects are given the right to practice as a profession by society through its laws. In return for this trust, our final responsibility is to the people who live in the environment that we design, not necessarily to those who pay for it. Architects are not technicians giving their clients anything they want to buy but human beings looking for a better way of life. As such they deal with values rather than facts. These are what I write about—to insist upon their importance, clarify their role, and to advocate those in which I believe."

*   *   *

JACOB, Helen Pierce   1927-

PERSONAL: Born November 9, 1927, in Lakewood, Ohio; daughter of Clyde Cowan (a teacher) and Lena (a teacher; maiden name, Grafton) Pierce; married Louis Albert Jacob (a librarian), August 15, 1953. Education: Mount Union College, B.A., 1949; Case Western Reserve University, M.S.L.S., 1953. Politics: Liberal. Religion: Methodist. Residence: Kensington, Md.

CAREER: High school teacher and librarian in Hudson, Ohio, 1949-51; assistant librarian in junior high school in Shaker Heights, Ohio, 1952-54; American University, Washington, D.C., associate librarian, 1954-55; University of California, Berkeley, reference and circulation librarian in education library, 1955-60; Parnassus Press, Berkeley, Calif., member of staff, 1960-61; junior high school librarian in Oakland, Calif., 1962-65, high school librarian, 1965-68; librarian in private school in Bryn Mawr, Pa., 1969-72; writer, 1972—. Member: Children's Book Guild (Washington, D.C.).

WRITINGS—For children: A Garland for Gandhi (picture book), Parnassus Press, 1968; The Imperfect Princess, Children's Book Trust, 1975; The Secret of the Strawbridge Place, Atheneum, 1976. Contributor of articles, stories, and reviews to Cricket, Harper's Weekly, and School Library Journal.

WORK IN PROGRESS: The Diary of the Strawbridge Place, a sequel to The Secret of the Strawbridge Place, juvenile, for Atheneum.

SIDELIGHTS: Helen Jacob writes: "As a child I was read to constantly by my parents, and on long, slow Sunday afternoon drives in an ancient Hupmobile, my father told us such stories as the myths of the Greeks and Romans and the Norse gods, Ivanhoe and David Copperfield, and he quoted reams of poetry, some of which he had written himself. So words and stories were part of my life from the very beginning.

"I hope that my words in one of my books or stories will bring to some child the drama, the peace, the knowledge, the fantasy that I got from the books that I read as a youngster. And I hope that my readers will want to become adults who need books about them to survive, and who have bookcases about their homes filled with their favorites.

"I write about what I know and have observed. My first book grew out of admiration for Gandhi. When in India, my husband and I traced the last twenty miles of Gandhi's famous two hundred mile Salt March, and we met people at the seashore in Dandi who had been there on that fateful day in April, 1930, when Gandhi broke the British laws on salt possession.

"The Imperfect Princess was written and published in India when I was there on a second trip with my husband. It is a picture book fantasy that just wrote itself.

"The Secret of the Strawbridge Place has much of my young life in it. If you are one of those who has always said: 'Writing for kiddies must be a breeze; anyone can do it,' then I just ask you to sit down and try it. Writing for young people is no different from—nor one whit easier—than writing for adults. You merely choose themes, plots, and characters appropriate to their experience. A good children's book is like any other good book—it will stand the test of time just as any classic will."

*   *   *

JACOBSEN, Lydik S.   1897(?)-1976

1897(?)—December 21, 1976; Danish-born American professor, researcher, and consultant on construction of buildings to lessen earthquake damage. He headed the mechanical engineering department at Stanford University for nineteen years, and directed its Earthquake Research Laboratory from 1930 to 1962. During World War II he was a commander in the Naval Reserves. He died in Newport Beach, Calif. Obituaries: New York Times, December 25, 1976.

*   *   *

JAHN, Ernst A(dalbert)   1929-

PERSONAL: Born April 25, 1929, in Stettin, Germany; came to the United States in 1956; son of Curt (a general) and Carola (Vahlbruch) Jahn; married Edith Hoff, December 8, 1962; married second wife, Isabel Brito (an editor and travel writer), November 28, 1974. Education: Engineering College, Helmstedt, Germany, B.S., 1950. Religion: Evangelical. Home: 18 Blackrock Ter., Ringwood, N.J. 07456. Office: Compsco Publishing Co., 663 Fifth Ave., New York, N.Y. 10022.

CAREER: McGraw-Hill Publishing Co., New York, N.Y., representative in Germany, 1952-55; worked as publisher's representative in Brazil, 1955-57; Compsco Publishing Co., New York City, travel writer and editor, 1957—. Travel lecturer; consultant to American Automobile Association, Organization of American States, National Geographic Society, and Rand McNally Map Co. Member: International Explorers Society, Explorers Club (fellow), Society of American Travel Writers, South American Travel Organization, Globetrotters Club.

WRITINGS: (Editor, with Isabel Jahn) Latin American Travel Guide & Pan American Highway Guide, Compsco, 1966, 6th edition, 1977. Author of column "Roaming the Globe" in Travel, 1975—. Contributor of articles and photographs to Encyclopedia Americana, Encyclopaedia Britannica, Crowell-Collier Educational Encyclopedia, and D.C. Heath Encyclopedia. Contributor of more than two hundred articles and photographs to newspapers and to popular magazines, including National Geographic, Argosy, Small World, Popular Imported Cars, International Railway Journal, Americas, and Foreign Car Guide. Travel editor of New Jersey Life, 1971-74; editor of Latin American Travel Newsletter.

WORK IN PROGRESS: Revision of *Latin America Travel Guide & Pan America Highway Guide.*

SIDELIGHTS: Jahn, as a guest of the Government of Brazil, was the first American motorist to drive the entire length of the Trans-Amazon Highway on its opening day. He travels about a hundred thousand miles annually. Other assignments include the NAZCA lines of Peru, the North Slope and Brooks Range of Alaska, fauna of the Galapagos Islands, the Andes of Tierra del Fuego, flora and natives of Juan Fernandez Island, Chile, archaeological sites on Easter Island, Cuna Indians of the San Blas Islands of Panama, French Polynesian atolls, and South Africa Zulu tribe reserves. He writes: "My interest is mainly in . . . explorations of unknown areas, communications with people around the world for promotion of peace and mutual understanding."

BIOGRAPHICAL/CRITICAL SOURCES: New Jersey Life, May, 1973.

* * *

JENNINGS, Michael 1931-
(Waco Brazos; Wyatt E. Kinkaid)

PERSONAL: Born April 17, 1931, in Buena Vista, Va.; son of Glen Edward (a compositor and printer) and Vaughnye (Bays) Jennings; married Patricia Motter, August 22, 1953 (divorced, August, 1975); married Susan Berger (a marketing director of children's books), October 25, 1975; children: Marc Emery, Jason Glenn, Dana Michael. *Education:* Attended high school in Little Falls, N.J. *Politics:* "Anti-Bella Abzug and ilk." *Religion:* "Unaffiliated Christian." *Residence:* Rockland County, N.Y. *Agent:* Susan Berger, 121 Sneden Pl. W., Spring Valley, N.Y. 10977.

CAREER: Hicks & Greist, Inc. (advertising agency), New York, N.Y., began as mailboy, became copywriter, 1948-51; *Louisville Courier Journal,* Louisville, Ky., writer, 1955-56; Home Life Insurance Co., New York City, assistant advertising manager, 1956-58; Burke, Charles & Guignon (advertising agency), Long Island, N.Y., vice-president and creative director, 1958-61; Michael Jennings & Colleagues (advertising agency), Long Island, N.Y., president, 1961-65; Aeolian Piano Corp., advertising manager, 1966-68; G. P. Putnam's Sons/Coward McCann (publishers), New York City, promotion director, 1968-69; free-lance writer, 1969—. Disc jockey for WKLO-Radio, 1955-56; host of talk show for WLIR, 1965-66. Advertising and publicity chairman for Antrim Players, Inc. (community theater group), 1977; liaison representative to Rockland County Council on the Arts. *Military service:* U.S. Air Force, newspaper reporter and editor, and writer-announcer for radio programs, 1951-55. *Member:* Authors Guild of Authors League of America.

WRITINGS: (Under pseudonym Waco Brazos) *There Was a Young Lady from Windmere* (erotic fiction), Venice Publishing, 1972; *Mattie Fritts and the Flying Mushroom* (juvenile), Windmill Books, 1973; *Mattie Fritts and the Cuckoo Caper* (self-illustrated juvenile), Bobbs-Merrill, 1976; *The Bears Who Came to Breakfix* (self-illustrated juvenile picture book), Children's Press, 1977. Contributor to horror comic magazines, *Metropolitan Review,* and *National Star-Chronicle;* contributor of erotic fiction to magazines, under pseudonyms Waco Brazos and Wyatt E. Kinkaid.

WORK IN PROGRESS: Tapdancing on Quicksand; How to Be Your Own Favorite Disc Jockey, for McKay; *Be-Bop, the Musical Cat,* juvenile; *The Strange Case of Robin Goodfellow and the Bogeyman,* juvenile; *Cold Wind from Nowhere,* a novel for young adults; *The Thirty-Ninth Consecutive Season,* a novel about a community theater group.

SIDELIGHTS: When asked how he switched from writing erotic fiction to writing for children, Jennings responded: "There has been none; I'm still doing both. That I am doing either is due to the way fate has cut the cards.

"In 1965, before I ever contemplated becoming a full-time writer, I wrote a porno-comedic novel, pretty much as a lark. It amused an influential friend and, to my astonishment, was accepted by an orthodox publisher. Alas, due to a merger, that house eventually defaulted on the contract. Nobody else was interested.

"By 1972 things had changed. For one thing, the porno boom was upon us. For another, I was broke, jobless, and forced to attempt to write for a living. The dusty manuscript was retrieved from a bottom drawer, 'dirtied-up' some more, and sent on the rounds of the paperback specialty houses. By then—among other forms—I was flailing away at a children's novel inspired by fanciful correspondence with my young sons, who no longer lived with me. Coincidentally, both works—seven years apart in the writing, several million lightyears apart in content—were published within months of each other.

"Continuing endeavors along both lines have followed as logically as if I had first achieved some success with, say, a cookbook and a travel guide, and thereafter produced successive volumes of recipes and itineraries. One produces what one can sell, in order to support efforts that are perchance loftier or more ambitious, and are surely chancier.

"If at first you don't succeed, you probably never will."

AVOCATIONAL INTERESTS: Performing with Antrim Players.

* * *

JENSEN, Irene K(hin Khin Myint) 1925-

PERSONAL: Born October 31, 1925, in Rangoon, Burma; emigrated to United States; naturalized U.S. citizen, 1959; daughter of U Po (an oil representative) and Daw Ngwe (Hlaing) Thein; married J. Vernon Jensen (a university professor), June 12, 1954; children: Donald, Maythee. *Education:* Rangoon University, B.A. (first class honors), 1949; Bucknell University, M.A., 1951; University of Wisconsin, Ph.D., 1956. *Politics:* Democrat. *Religion:* Methodist. *Home:* 2432 32nd Avenue South, Minneapolis, Minn. 55406. *Office:* Department of History, Augsburg College, Minneapolis, Minn. 55454.

CAREER: Rangoon University, Rangoon, Burma, tutor in ancient history, 1949-50; Augsburg College, Minneapolis, Minn., instructor in history, 1955-56; Bethel College, St. Paul, Minn., instructor in history, 1958; Augsburg College, assistant professor, 1959-61, associate professor, 1962-67, professor of history, 1967—. Lecturer. *Member:* American Association of University Professors, American Association of University Women, Association for Asian Studies, American Historical Society, Historical Association, Upper Midwest History Association, Upper Midwest Ethnic Studies Association (charter member), Midwest China Study Resource Center (member board of directors, treasurer), Women Historians of Minnesota, Minnesota Historical Society. *Awards, honors:* Fulbright Scholarship, 1950; Shalom Research Grant from American Lutheran Church, 1976-77.

WRITINGS: The Chinese in the Philippines during the American Regime: 1898-1946, R. & E. Research Associates, 1975. Contributor to *Asian Studies* and other periodicals.

WORK IN PROGRESS: An anthology, co-edited with J.

Jensen, tentatively titled *The Religious Quest: East and West; Eighteenth Century Burma's Encounter with the West; Japanese Post-World War II Experience; Chinese-American Experiences in America.*

SIDELIGHTS: Jensen has travelled extensively, including around the world journeys in 1961 and 1976; she also toured China in 1975 and Europe in 1970. *Avocational interests:* Reading, sports, music.

* * *

JENYNS, Roger Soame   ?-1976

?—October 14, 1976; British author and authority on Far Eastern decorative arts. He was former deputy keeper of Oriental antiquities of the British Museum and author of numerous works in his area. His *A Background to Chinese Painting* is considered to be the best introduction to the subject. He died in England. Obituaries: *AB Bookman's Weekly,* December 20, 1976.

* * *

JOHNSON, Evelyne   1932-

PERSONAL: Born January 20, 1932, in New York, N.Y.; daughter of David (a mathematician, inventor, and professor) and Rose (a musician; maiden name, Geiger) Levow; married Frank A. Johnson, Jr. (an artist's representative), October 10, 1950; children: Barry. *Education:* Attended New York University, National Academy of Design, and New School for Social Research. *Politics:* Liberal Democrat. *Religion:* Jewish. *Residence:* New York, N.Y.

CAREER: Free-lance artist and copy writer. Evelyne Johnson Associates, New York City, proprietor, 1965—. *Member:* Society of Illustrators, Society of Photographers and Artists Representatives.

WRITINGS: The Elephant's Ball (juvenile), McGraw, 1977.

WORK IN PROGRESS: Children's books.

SIDELIGHTS: Evelyne Johnson writes: "I want to write books, in a humorous way, to show how people, no matter how different, can enjoy life together and share each other's customs." *Avocational interests:* Travel, art, music, animals, "the environment and caring."

* * *

JOHNSON, Eyvind   1900-1976

1900—August 25, 1976; Swedish novelist and co-winner of 1974 Nobel Prize. His best-known work is the "Olof" series, a quartet of autobiographical books. He died in Stockholm, Sweden. Obituaries: *New York Times,* August 26, 1976; *Washington Post,* August 27, 1976.

* * *

JOHNSON, Ferd   1905-

PERSONAL: Born December 18, 1905, in Spring Creek, Pa.; son of John (a railroad station agent) and Bessie (Edgett) Johnson; married Doris Lee White, February 24, 1930; children: Thomas. *Education:* Attended Chicago Academy of Fine Arts, 1923, and Otis Art Institute, 1957. *Office:* 3500 E. Coast Highway, Corona Del Mar, Calif. 92625.

CAREER/WRITINGS: Chicago Tribune-New York News Syndicate, New York, N.Y., assistant to Frank Willard, originator of "Moon Mullins" comic strip series, 1923-58, author of "Texas Slim" comic strip series, 1925-27 and 1940-58, author of "Lovey Dovey" Sunday comic strip series,

1940-42, author of "Moon Mullins" comic strip series, 1958—. Sunday sports illustrator for Westbrook Pegler, *Chicago Tribune,* 1927-30. Artist, freelance advertiser. *Member:* Cartoonists Society, Comics Council.

SIDELIGHTS: CA asked Johnson what he feels constitutes a good comic strip. He replied: "Humor. Interesting. Characters with personality of their own, not merely sticks to pin a gag on. Politics is o.k.—if funny and no sides of arguments are taken. I think moral principles should be upheld and strived for . . . some sort of punishment provided if the line is stepped over." Johnson added: "I became interested in oil painting under Norman Rockwell's suggestion. Followed through and now have paintings in several galleries."

An extensive traveller, Johnson has visited Europe and the Orient.

* * *

JOHNSON, Harry G(ordon)   1923-1977

May 26, 1923—May 8, 1977; Canadian educator and author or editor of books on economic theory and international finance. He died in Geneva, Switzerland. Obituaries: *New York Times,* May 10, 1977; *Time,* May 23, 1977; *Washington Post,* May 27, 1977; *AB Bookman's Weekly,* September 5, 1977. (See index for previous *CA* sketch)

* * *

JOHNSON, Karen   1939-

PERSONAL: Born July 18, 1939, in Kane, Pa.; daughter of Albert W. (a lawyer and politician) and Virginia (Balsley) Johnson. *Education:* Mount Holyoke College, B.A., 1961; graduate study at New School for Social Research, 1971-72. *Politics:* Independent. *Religion:* Episcopalian. *Home:* 321 West 55th St., New York, N.Y. 10019. *Office:* New York Foundation for the Arts, 60 East 42nd St., New York, N.Y. 10017.

CAREER: The Playwright's Place, New York City, co-founder, 1966-67; Manhattan Theatre Club, New York City, production coordinator and fund raiser, 1971; International Film Exchange, New York City, film sales director and office manager, 1973-75; New York State Council on the Arts, New York City, Comprehensive Employment and Training Act (CETA) arts director, 1975-76; New York Foundation for the Arts, New York City, federal funds consultant, 1977—; actress, playwright, and producer. Visiting lecturer in dramatics, Lindenwood College, 1966. *Member:* Actors Equity Association, Screen Actors Guild, American Federation of Television and Radio Artists, Dramatists Guild. *Awards, honors:* Phi Beta Kappa Award for creative achievement, 1961, for "The Dove Descending"; Clio Award, 1968, for television commercial.

WRITINGS—Plays: "The Dove Descending" (one-act), first produced in New Haven, Conn., at Yale Drama Festival, April, 1961; "The Indiscretion of the Meatpacker's Daughter" (one-act), first produced in New York City at Playwright's Place, October, 1966; "Parfumerie" (two-act), first produced in New York City at Van Dam Theatre, October, 1971; (with Joyce Stoner) *I'll Die If I Can't Live Forever* (two-act; first produced in New York City at The Improvisation, October 7, 1974), Samuel French, 1975.

WORK IN PROGRESS: "Uncle Sam the Bootlegger's Dockside Palace," a two-act play; "The Cloudberry Field," a two-act play; "Hot Pepper Jelly," a screenplay; "Alicia Kent, Lady Lawyer," a ninety second soap opera.

SIDELIGHTS: "The artist," Johnson told *CA,* "is the creative force of our society. Evolution starts with new concepts or thought patterns which must be communicated by word. Women in particular have not been heard. A woman's viewpoint in a play is vital. There are no acknowledged major American *women* playwrights currently being produced. We need more.

"A great many women are writing for the theatre, but the theatre is dominated by male producers and directors who do not give women the same chance they give their own sex. Only six percent of the plays produced currently in non-profit theatres across the country are by women. Lillian Hellman and Jean Kerr take most of that percentage. The theatres with women producers do support women's work. We need the same kind of consistent support Joe Papp gives his 'sons'—male playwrights. Thus, we must encourage and assist women producers and take political action to see that equal opportunity guidelines are followed in the hiring procedure of government funded theatres. I do not believe that women do not write plays as well as men or that their concerns are too narrow. They are actually the concerns of fifty-one percent of the population."

* * *

JOHNSON, Kendall 1928-

PERSONAL: Born April 28, 1928; son of Lyle and Edna (Curkendall) Johnson; married first wife, Mary, September 1, 1953 (divorced); married Natalie Freedman, December 21, 1974; children: Cheryl, Kimberlee. *Education:* Michigan State University, B.A., 1953; University of Miami, J.D., 1958. *Home:* 10470 Eastborne Ave., Los Angeles, Calif. 90024.

CAREER: Insurance Company of North America, Los Angeles, Calif., manager of branch claim offices, claims supervisor, and adjuster, 1960-71; Employers Insurance of Wausau, Los Angeles, agent, 1971-72; University of California at Los Angeles Neuropsychiatric Institute, Los Angeles, research associate, 1971—; Brown Brothers Adjusters, Los Angeles, independent insurance adjuster, 1974—. Research colleague of School of Social Science, University of California at Irvine, 1973-74; honorary director of faculty of medicine, Policlinica Escuela, University of Guadalajara, 1976—. Inventor, lecturer, and designer. Consultant on radiation field photography and acupuncture to the Central Intelligence Agency (CIA), National Aeronautics and Space Administration, Advanced Research Projects Agency, RAND Corp., and others. *Military service:* U.S. Army, 1950-52; served in medical corps.

WRITINGS: (Contributor) Stanley Krippner, editor, *Galaxies of Life*, Harcourt, 1973; *The Living Aura*, Hawthorn, 1976; *Photographing the Non-Material World*, Hawthorn, 1977. Contributor to *Britannica Yearbook of Science*, and of articles to *Harper's, Osteopathic Physician, Psychic*, and other periodicals.

WORK IN PROGRESS: The Navigator; Creatures of the Edge, an autobiography.

SIDELIGHTS: Johnson has been the subject of numerous television and radio programs concerned with his work in acupuncture and radiation field photography.

* * *

JOHNSON, Malcolm (Malone) 1904-1976

PERSONAL: Born September 27, 1904, in Claremont, Ga.; son of William M. (an attorney) and Willie Estelle (a teacher; maiden name, Bolding) Johnson; married Ludie Adams, December 4, 1928 (died, 1972); children: Haynes Bonner, Sarah Montie, Michael Bolding, Paul Adams. *Education:* Attended Mercer University, 1922-24. *Residence:* Killingworth, Conn.

CAREER: Macon Telegraph, Macon, Ga., reporter, 1924-28; *New York Sun*, New York City, investigative reporter, columnist, critic, war correspondent, editor, and special writer, 1928-50; International News Service, New York City, correspondent, 1950-54; Hill Knowlton, Inc., New York City, vice-president, 1954-73. Notable assignments include exposes of Ku Klux Klan in Toombs County, Ga., 1920's; failure of Bank of America; burning of steamship *Morro Castle;* invasions of Okinawa and Iwo Jima; first task force raids on Japanese mainland and Japanese surrender aboard U.S.S. *Missouri;* bombing of Hiroshima; atomic tests on atoll of Bikini; expose of crime on New York City water front, 1948; January 3, 1950, obituary of *New York Sun;* racial conditions in South Africa and Mau Mau terrorism in Kenya, 1950's. *Member:* Newspaper Guild (co-founder), Pi Kappa Phi. *Awards, honors:* Pulitzer Prize, 1948, for "Crime on the Water Front" series; Polk Award, 1949; Woman's Press Club of New York award, 1949, for "outstanding example of journalism."

WRITINGS: Crime on the Labor Front, McGraw, 1950; (co-editor) *Current Thoughts on Public Relations*, Lads, 1968. Also author of *Shoeleather and Printers' Ink*, 1974.

SIDELIGHTS: Johnson's Pulitzer Prize winning series, "Crime on the Water Front," began with an investigation of the April, 1948, slaying of a New York docks "hiring boss." Through an inside informant and months of legwork, Johnson's investigation had become by November what his paper described "a startling expose of systematic thievery, 'shake-downs,' 'kickbacks,' shylocking, and murder which is costing the Port of New York millions of dollars in lost shipping trade." Johnson recalled a year later: "The story, in all truth, snowballed. One lead led to another; various sources and contacts were developed, but only after months of hard digging.

"Several times I was almost ready to give up, convinced that the real story would never be uncovered. Then I had some lucky breaks. One was meeting and gaining the confidence of an informant, an ex-convict, who had worked with the racketeers. His story set the pattern and he steered me to other sources."

The front-page articles, published in the *New York Sun* from November 8 to December 10, 1948, prompted several threats against Johnson's life and led to three official investigations of water front crime. The 1955 eight Academy Awards winning movie, "On the Waterfront," is based on Johnson's material.

In 1950, Johnson wrote his last assignment for the *New York Sun*, "the hardest of my career," he later said. It was the January 3 obituary of the 117-year-old newspaper. "I wish I had been able to tell how newspaper people feel," he wrote in 1974, "that a good newspaper has a heart and a soul and that the death of a newspaper is as grievous and personal as a death in the family. But I didn't and I couldn't." The story is regarded as among the most poignant Johnson ever wrote.

With the 1966 awarding of the Pulitzer Prize to his son Haynes for coverage of the Selma civil rights activities for the *Washington Evening Star*, Johnson became part of the only father and son ever to win the Pulitzer Prize.

OBITUARIES: Washington Post, June 18, 1976; *New York Times*, June 19, 1976.*

(Died June 18, 1976, in Middletown, Conn.)

JOHNSON, Malcolm L. 1937-

PERSONAL: Born November 25, 1937, in Hartford, Conn.; son of Ernest H. (a contractor) and Marjorie (a social scientist; maiden name, Leishman) Johnson; married Betty Carper (a lecturer). Education: Attended Yale University, 1955-59, and Wesleyan University, 1965-67. Home: 35 Prospect St., South Coventry, Conn. 06238. Office: Hartford Courant, Broad St., Hartford. Conn. 06238.

CAREER: Hartford Courant, Hartford, Conn., reporter, 1965-67, editor, 1967-75, theater and film critic, 1975—. Military service: U.S. Reserve, 1959-60.

WRITINGS: Yesterday's Connecticut, E. A. Seeman, 1976.

WORK IN PROGRESS: A mystery novel.

*   *   *

JOHNSON, Nunnally 1897-1977

December 5, 1897—March 25, 1977; American screenwriter and motion picture producer. He wrote over one hundred screenplays, including "The Grapes of Wrath," "The Desert Fox," "The Three Faces of Eve," and "The Dirty Dozen." He wrote for newspapers in Georgia and New York before going to Hollywood in 1932. He died in Los Angeles, Calif. Obituaries: Time, April 4, 1977; Newsweek, April 4, 1977; AB Bookman's Weekly, July 25, 1977.

*   *   *

JOHNSTON, Albert H. 1914-

PERSONAL: Born January 16, 1914, in Philadelphia, Pa.; son of Albert Lyle (a toolmaker) and Elsie Louise (Hanstein) Johnston; married May Chiger, 1941 (deceased); married Lillian D. Dollar; children: Rosalind Rae, Roy Louis. Education: Attended University of Pennsylvania. Home: 145-19 20th Ave., Whitestone, New York, N.Y. 11357. Office: Publishers Weekly, 1180 Avenue of the Americas, New York, N.Y. 10036.

CAREER: Story analyst for Radio-Keith-Orpheum, Twentieth Century Fox, and Columbia Pictures, all in New York City, 1944-47; Avon Books, New York City, editor, 1948-49; Columbia Pictures, story editor, 1949-60; story editor for Walt Disney productions, New York City, 1963-67; Publishers Weekly, New York City, nonfiction review editor, 1968—. Member: National Critics Circle. Awards, honors: Playwriting award from National Theater Conference, 1948.

WRITINGS: Pablo's Mountain (novel), Crown, 1952; An Age of Wolves (novel), New American Library, 1964. Also author of plays, "Offer," "Pizzazz," and "God's Tomb as Grand Central Station."

SIDELIGHTS: Johnston began studying art in the 1920's, later began writing poetry, stories, and plays. He feels his own writing career was hampered by his several years of writing for film companies, but has, since 1975, returned to playwriting, which he considers his "original love." His interviews for Publishers Weekly include talks with Walter Cronkite and Kurt Vonnegut.

*   *   *

JOHNSTON, Basil H. 1929-

PERSONAL: Born July 13, 1929, in Parry Island, Ontario, Canada; son of Rufus Francis and Mary (Lafreniere) Johnston; married Lucie Bella Desroches, July 29, 1959; children: Miriam Gladys, Elizabeth Louise, Geoffery Lawrence. Education: Graduated from Loyola College, Montreal, Quebec (cum laude), 1954; Ontario College of Education, secondary school teaching certificate, 1962. Politics: "Apolitical." Home: 253 Ashlar Rd., Richmond Hill, Ontario, Canada. Office: Royal Ontario Museum, 100 Queens Park, Toronto, Ontario, Canada.

CAREER: History teacher in secondary school, Toronto, Ontario, 1962-69; Royal Ontario Museum, Toronto, lecturer in North, Central, and South American history, 1969-72, member of ethnology department, 1972—. Night school teacher of English, 1965-70; lecturer in Indian culture. Vice-president of Canadian Indian Centre of Toronto, 1963-69; secretary of Indian consultations with Canadian Government, 1968; committee member of Indian Hall of Fame, 1968-70. Member: Indian Eskimo Association, Toronto Indian Club (president, 1957). Awards, honors: Samuel J. Fels literary award from Coordinating Council of Literary Magazines, 1976.

WRITINGS: Ojibway Heritage, Columbia University Press, 1976. Contributor to Dictionary of Canadian Biography and of stories, essays, articles, and poems to educational readers, literary magazines, and newspapers. Translator of brochures and travel guides into Ojibway. Guest editor of Tawow, publication of Indian Affairs Branch of Canadian government.

WORK IN PROGRESS: Moose Meat Point Indians; Indian Religious Ceremonies, nonfiction; Ojibway language lexicon and course outline.

*   *   *

JOHNSTON, Hugh Buckner 1913-

PERSONAL: Born April 11, 1913, in Wilson County, N.C.; son of Hugh Bolden and Ruth (Thomas) Johnston; married Elizabeth Aldrich Briggs, November 8, 1941 (divorced, 1953); married Edna Elizabeth Long, October 23, 1953; children: (first marriage) Hugh Bolden III, Thomas Owen Drakeford; (second marriage) Hugh Bolden IV. Education: Davidson College, A.B., 1933; graduate study at University of North Carolina, 1933-34, 1934-35; George Washington University, A.M., 1946. Politics: Conservative. Religion: Presbyterian. Home: Thomas Farms, Route 4, Box 160, Wilson, N.C. 27893. Office: Department of Foreign Languages, Atlantic Christian College, Wilson, N.C. 27893.

CAREER: Teacher of French in high school in North Carolina, 1935-37; clerk at Watson Warehouse Co., 1937-40; American Red Cross, Washington, D.C., administrative assistant, 1941-46; Instituto Chileno-Norteamericano de Cultura, Santiago, Chile, instructor in English, 1947-50; clerk at Watson Warehouse Co., 1950-52; teacher of English in North Carolina public schools, 1953-55; Atlantic Christian College, Wilson, N.C., assistant professor of languages and history, 1955—. Official historian of Wilson County, N.C., 1938—.

MEMBER: Modern Language Association of America, American Association of Teachers of Spanish and Portuguese, American Association of University Professors, National Genealogical Society, Sons of the American Revolution (Virginia society), Sons of Confederate Veterans, Order of the Stars and Bars, Society of the Descendants of the Colonial Clergy, General Society of the War of 1812 (genealogist for North Carolina society), Society of Genealogists (England), Society of Colonial Wars, North Carolina Society for the Preservation of Antiquities, North Carolina Genealogical Society (president), North Carolina Society of County and Local Historians (past president), North Carolina State Literary and Historical Association (past vice-president), Carolina Charter Corp., Order of the First Families of Virginia, Jamestowne Society, Sigma Phi Epsilon. *Awards, honors:* Poetry awards from Poetry Council of North Carolina, 1953, 1954, 1972, 1973, and North Carolina Poetry Society, 1970, 1971, 1975.

WRITINGS: (Contributor) Ernestine Dew White, editor, *Genealogy of Some of the Descendants of Thomas Dew,* privately printed, 1937; (contributor) Eurie P. W. Neel, editor, *The Wilford-Williford Family Treks into America,* privately printed, 1959; (with Ruth S. Williams and Margaret G. Griffin) *Tombstone and Census Records of Early Edgecombe,* Dixie Letter Service, 1959; (with Coy K. Johnston) *William Johnston of Isle of Wight County, Virginia, and His Descendants, 1648-1964: A Genealogical Study of One Branch of the Family in the South,* privately printed, 1965; *Compiling a Genealogical History* (pamphlet), North Carolina Office of Archives and History, 1972; *The First Federal Census of Wilson County: 1860,* privately printed, 1976; *Histories of Three Old Baptist Churches,* privately printed, 1976.

Represented in anthologies, including *The Poetry Digest Annual Anthology of Verse,* [New York], 1939; *Outstanding Contemporary Poets,* [New York], 1939; and *Poets of the Southern States,* [New York], 1949. Contributor to history journals. Feature writer for *Wilson Daily Times,* 1950, and *Rocky Mount Evening Telegram,* during the 1960's.

WORK IN PROGRESS: The Bridger(s) Family, 1293-1977; The Wilson Collection; The Wilson County Collection; with Eddis Johnson, *The Johnsons of Currowaugh Swamp, Isle of Wight County, Virginia, 1669-1977.*

SIDELIGHTS: Johnston writes: "My lifelong interest in research and writing can be traced to my thirteenth year, when I began to collect local Indian artifacts and also to spend much time with my unusual maternal grandfather on the farm where I was born and that had been in his family since 1747. Old weapons, domestic items, and books soon appeared among other early acquisitions; and before I was twenty-one I had begun the local historical and genealogical compilations that currently exceed five thousand typed pages."

* * *

JOHNSTON, Velma B. 1912(?)-1977
(Wild Horse Annie)

1912(?)—June 27, 1977; American author and leader of campaign to preserve wild-horse herds in the West. She was leader of the lobbying campaign which led to the 1959 "Wild Horse Annie Law," a federal statute protecting wild horses, and the 1971 "Wild Free Roaming Horse and Burro Act" which gave the animals further protection. She died in Reno, Nev. Obituaries: *New York Times,* June 28, 1977; *Time,* July 11, 1977.

* * *

JOHNSTONE, Parker Lochiel 1903-

PERSONAL: Born June 15, 1903, in Chicago, Ill.; son of Frank Chiel (a physician) and Grace (an artist; maiden name, Parker) Johnstone; married Marguerite Sprague (a registered nurse), August 8, 1929; children: Parker Lochiel, Jr., Roger-Leigh, Penelope. *Education:* Iowa State University, B.S., 1925, M.S., 1926. *Religion:* Christian. *Home:* 193 Los Robles Dr., Burlingame, Calif. 94010.

CAREER: Associated Press, New York, N.Y., foreign correspondent, 1926-29; Continental Laboratories, Los Ange-

les, Calif., science researcher, 1930-42; conducted medical research in the area of brain surgery in Los Angeles, Calif., 1946-49; Continental Laboratories, science researcher, 1950-68, general manager, 1952-68; writer and researcher, 1968—. *Military service:* U.S. Army, in chemical warfare, 1942-45; served in the South Pacific; became major. *Member:* Burlingame Hills Association (president, 1976-78).

WRITINGS: Mission-Presidio Diary, Mission Publishers, 1968; *The Turtle Speaks!,* Mission Publishers, 1970; *San Francisco Begins, 1776,* Mission Publishers, 1974; *If You Believe in God . . .,* Theoscience Publishers, 1975; *Life, Death, and Hereafter,* Theoscience Publishers, 1976. Author of "The Turtle Speaks!," a column in *Boutique News,* 1970-72.

WORK IN PROGRESS: Life Is Forever, "how all things came to be and why we are in this existence"; *Dreamology and Dictionary,* on the science of the subconscious mind.

SIDELIGHTS: Johnstone writes: "My science research development and application work has taken me three times around the world, from the Arctic Circle to Australia, New Zealand, Tasmania, and through the entire length of Africa. One single fact stands out in all my work: Many aspects of ontology and metaphysics can now be proven scientifically as, in fact, I have reported in many of my writings and lectures. The crystallization of these facts took place while I was working with my father and his associates in brain surgery when we first discovered that the tangible brain and the intangible mind were combinations of positive-negative energy forces forming two separate entities with different functions and registering distinguishable differences in their electric impulses. This laid the foundation for further proofs that everything in the universe is similarly constructed. It is on this subject in recent years that I have based many lectures at colleges, churches of all denominations and religions, hospitals, youth groups, lodges, etc. I find that people, especially young adult students, usually resent being told what to believe, but rather, they want to learn about proven facts, and then to make their own decisions. Here, then, they find the scientific answers, repeated in many forms of human behavior, concerning *how* all things came to be, *who* we are, *why* we are in this existence, *where* and *how* we are going from here."

* * *

JONAS, Carl 1913-1976

May 22, 1913—October 1, 1976; American novelist and educator. His early career included work as a journalist and writer for radio stations. His novels include *Jefferson Selleck, Beachhead on the Wind,* and *The Sputnik Rapist.* He died in Omaha, Neb. Obituaries: *New York Times,* October 2, 1976. (See index for previous *CA* sketch)

* * *

JONES, Elwyn 1923-

PERSONAL: Born May 4, 1923, in Aberdare, Wales; son of Evan (a coal miner) and Letitia (Davies) Jones; married Angela Joan Bentley, 1951 (died, 1971); married Jennifer Moore (an actress), March, 1975; children: Malorie. *Education:* Attended London School of Economics and Political Science, 1940-42. *Religion:* Welsh Methodist. *Home:* Blaeneinon, Pont Shan, Llandyssul Dyfed, Wales. *Agent:* John Farquharson, 15 Red Lion Sq., London WC1R 4QW, England.

CAREER: News Review, London, England, reporter and

critic, 1944-51; *Radio Times,* London, television editor and editorial assistant, 1951-58; British Broadcasting Corp. (BBC), London, head of drama series and drama organiser, 1958-63; writer. *Member:* Writers Guild of Great Britain, Society of Authors, Paternosters, Savage Club. *Awards, honors:* Edgar Allen Poe Award of Mystery Writers of America for best crime-fact novels, 1965, for *The Last Two to Hang;* Writers Guild Award for teleplay, 1969, for "Softly, Softly."

WRITINGS: The Last Two to Hang, Macmillan, 1966; *Barlow in Charge,* Barker, 1973; *Barlow Comes to Judgement,* St. Martin's, 1974; *The Ripper File,* Barker, 1975; *The Barlow Casebook,* Barker, 1975; *Barlow Exposed,* St. Martin's, 1976; *Dick Barton-Special Agent,* Barker, 1976. Also author of BBC teleplays, including "Z Cars," "Softly, Softly," "Dr. Finlay's Casebook," "Doomwatch," "Barlow," and others.

WORK IN PROGRESS: A study of famous trials.

SIDELIGHTS: Jones told *CA:* "I happen to think that 'popular' television series are important. They deserve more 'serious' writing than they get. I do my best."

* * *

JONES, James 1921-1977

November 6, 1921—May 9, 1977; American writer. His first book, *From Here to Eternity,* based on his own army experiences, was a best-seller and a National Book Award winner, Jones's other works include *Some Came Running, The Pistol, A Touch of Danger, World War II,* and *Whistle.* He died in Southampton, N.Y. Obituaries: *New York Times,* May 10, 1977, May 16, 1977; *Newsweek,* May 23, 1977; *Time,* May 23, 1977. (See index for previous *CA* sketch)

* * *

JONES, James C(linton) 1922-

PERSONAL: Born December 17, 1922, in Paul, Idaho; son of James (a railroad mail clerk) and Lucile (Houghtaling) Jones; married Barbara Nancarrow, June 10, 1950; children: James, Michael, Cynthia. *Education:* University of Missouri, B.A., 1949. *Politics:* Independent. *Religion:* Protestant. *Home:* 4053 Charing Cross Rd., Bloomfield Hills, Mich. 48013. *Office: Newsweek,* 100 Renaissance Center, Suite 1984, Detroit, Mich. 48243.

CAREER/WRITINGS: Business Week, Detroit, Mich., correspondent, 1949-53; McGraw-Hill Publishing Co., Detroit, bureau chief, 1953-55, *Newsweek,* New York, N.Y., Detroit bureau chief, 1955—. Notable assignments include seven national political campaigns, eight urban riots, Attica Prison riot, Kent State student killings, and the Jimmy Hoffa disappearance. Lecturer. Contributor to *Newsweek, Saturday Evening Post, Reader's Digest,* and other periodicals. *Military service:* U.S. Marine Corps, 1942-45, 1950-51; became master sergeant. *Member:* Detroit Press Club (president, 1965-66), Detroit Athletic Club, Detroit Press Club Foundation (president, 1976-77). *Awards, honors:* Seven Detroit Press Club Foundation awards; Ohio Industrial Editors Association award, 1970.

SIDELIGHTS: Jones told *CA:* "My motivation has always been the excitement related to stories a *Newsweek* bureau chief encounters, and the effort to determine the truth. Travels have included visits to all but one of the states, widely throughout Canada and the Caribbean, the Arctic, Mexico, the Solomon Islands, New Caledonia, Japan, South Korea and North Korea."

JONES, John Paul, Jr. 1912-

PERSONAL: Born March 3, 1912, in Micanopy, Fla.; son of John Paul and Lorna Doone (McCredie) Jones; married Marion Antoinette Pecot, January 29, 1938; children: John Paul III, Judy (Mrs. Thomas Joel Glenn), Letty Kay (Mrs. Oscar Rayneri). *Education:* University of Florida, B.A.J., 1937; University of Wisconsin, Madison, M.A.J., 1939. *Politics:* Democrat. *Religion:* Methodist. *Home:* 6000 Northwest 17th Pl., Gainesville, Fla. 32605. *Office:* College of Journalism and Communications, University of Florida, Gainesville, Fla. 32611.

CAREER: University of Florida, Gainesville, instructor in journalism, 1937-38; University of Illinois, Champaign-Urbana, instructor, 1939-43, assistant professor of journalism, 1946-48; University of Florida, associate professor, 1948-51, professor of journalism, 1951—, dean of College of Journalism and Communications, 1968-76, dean emeritus, 1976—. *Military service:* U.S. Navy, 1943-46; became lieutenant.

MEMBER: American Association of Schools and Departments of Journalism (vice-president, 1975-76), Newspaper Association Managers (past president; past vice-president; past member of board of directors), National Newspaper Association (past member of board of directors), Florida Press Association (secretary-manager, 1952-68), Kappa Tau Alpha (president, 1967-69), Kiwanis International (past lieutenant governor of Florida district; past president of local chapter).

WRITINGS: (With L. R. Campbell) *Effective News Reporting,* Macmillan, 1942; (with Campbell) *News Beat,* Macmillan, 1949; *The Modern Reporter's Handbook,* Rinehart, 1949; (with Donald Brown) *Radio and Television News,* Rinehart, 1954; *News Gathering and Writing,* Nelson-Hall, 1976. Editor of *Florida Press,* 1957-68.

WORK IN PROGRESS: William McKinley and the Press; Ancient City and Other Poems; History of the Florida Press Association, completion expected in 1979; *Gold Braid,* on his experiences in World War II; *The Florida Boys on the Suwannee River,* the first book in a series of stories for young people, pointing out geographical points of interest in Florida; *Magazine and Feature Writing.*

SIDELIGHTS: Jones writes: "My entire career has been in the teaching of journalism with intense interest in the teaching of journalistic writing. I have always had a strong motivation toward helping young people develop concepts of professionalism and responsibility.

"Now, I hope to spend as much time as possible in more creative writing of my own, such as poetry, novels, fact articles, landscape photography, and research into the history of Florida, with emphasis on specific areas."

* * *

JONES, Kenley 1935-

PERSONAL: Born February 24, 1935, in Greenville, S.C.; son of J. Clyde (a merchant) and Mildred (Smith) Jones; married Margaret McPherson, December 11, 1965; children: Stephanie, Jason, Eleanor. *Education:* Northwestern University, B.S., 1957, M.S., 1963; graduate study at Columbia University, 1964-65. *Office:* NBC News, 2965 Flowers Rd. S., Atlanta, Ga. 30341.

CAREER/WRITINGS: KRNT-TV, Des Moines, Iowa, reporter and cameraman, 1963-64; WSB-TV, Atlanta, Ga., reporter and cameraman, 1965-69; National Broadcasting Co. (NBC) News, New York, N.Y., correspondent from

Saigon and Singapore, 1969-72, and Atlanta, Ga., 1972—. Notable assignments include the Vietnam and Indochina War, 1969-71, the Indo-Pakistan War, 1971, and 1976 Presidential primaries and general election campaigns. *Military service:* U.S. Navy, 1958-61; became lieutenant. *Awards, honors:* Overseas Press Club Award, 1970, for best television reporting from abroad; South Carolina Broadcasters Association Distinguished Broadcaster Award, 1973.

SIDELIGHTS: Jones told *CA:* "The most challenging aspect of my job is to present accurate, clear, concise reports—within the time limits imposed by broadcast news—to make news events more meaningful to viewers."

*   *   *

JONES, Robert R(ussell) 1927-

PERSONAL: Born October 19, 1927, in Topeka, Kan.; son of Russell A. (a cabinetmaker) and Marie (Carter) Jones; married Dorothy Vincent (a historian), September 3, 1947; children: Daniel, Mark. *Education:* Washburn University, A.B., 1949; Kansas State University, M.S., 1959. *Politics:* Democrat. *Religion:* Baptist. *Home:* 1213 Main St., Evanston, Ill. 60202. *Office:* Dun-Donnelley, 222 South Riverside Plaza, Chicago, Ill. 60606.

CAREER: Lebanon Times, Lebanon, Kan., editor and publisher, 1952-55; *Pittsburg Daily Headlight,* Pittsburg, Kan., news editor, 1955-57; Kansas State University, Manhattan, station editor, 1957-60; Agricultural Publishers, Inc., Milwaukee, Wis., assistant editor, 1960-67; University of Missouri, Columbia, science editor, 1967-72; *Industrial Research,* Chicago, Ill., associate editor, 1972-74, editor, 1974—. *Awards, honors:* Jesse H. Neal Award for Outstanding Journalism from American Business Press, 1975, for a series of editorials.

WRITINGS: (Editor) *The Unsettled Earth,* Ann Arbor Science Publishers, 1975.

*   *   *

JOSEPH, Richard 1910-1976

April 24, 1910—September 30, 1976; American authority on world cruises, tropical islands, restaurants, and hotels, travel editor of *Esquire* magazine, columnist, and author of travel books, including *Esquire's Europe in Style.* He averaged one hundred thousand miles of travel each year. Joseph died in a plane returning from the Virgin Islands. Obituaries: *New York Times,* October 2, 1976; *Washington Post,* October 3, 1976. (See index for previous *CA* sketch)

*   *   *

JOSEPHSON, Halsey D. 1906(?)-1977

1906(?)—October 20, 1977; American life-insurance agent and author of seven books in his field. He died in New York City. Obituaries: *New York Times,* October 21, 1976.

*   *   *

JOSEPHSON, Hannah 1900-1976

June 6, 1900—October 29, 1976; American writer, editor, journalist, translator, and author or co-author of biographies, including *The Golden Threads* and *Al Smith: Hero of the Cities.* She died in New Milford, Conn. Obituaries: *New York Times,* October 31, 1976. (*CAP*-2; earlier sketch in *CA*-29/32)

JUDD, H(oward) Stanley 1936-

PERSONAL: Born August 11, 1936, in Bronxville, N.Y.; son of Howard Stanley and Gladys (Johnson) Judd; married Ingrid E. Mueller (a teacher), June 23, 1962; children: Jennifer Lee. *Education:* Yale University, B.A. (honors), 1959. *Politics:* Independent. *Religion:* Independent. *Home:* 2570 Ramona St., Palo Atlo, Calif. 94306. *Agent:* Edward J. Acton, 288 West 12th St., New York, N.Y. 10014. *Office:* 1230 University Dr., Menlo Park, Calif. 94025.

CAREER: Bank of America, San Francisco, Calif., in international banking, 1963-65; H. Stanley Judd & Associates, Palo Alto, Calif., consultant, 1965-74; HSJ Publishers, Palo Alto, Calif., publisher, 1974—. Director of Manhattan Playhouse. *Military service:* U.S. Navy, gunnery officer, 1959-63; became lieutenant junior grade. *Member:* San Francisco Press Club.

WRITINGS: (With James M. Terrill and Evelyn Langenwalter) *California Weight Loss Program,* Simon & Schuster, 1977. Author of films for Bellevue Hospital, Time-Life Corp., and Children's Television Workshop.

WORK IN PROGRESS: A money-management book, discussing the psychological and technical realities of money.

SIDELIGHTS: Judd writes: "Since 1965, I have been actively involved in creating effective, low cost communications materials designed to improve personal, problem-solving skills.

"This experience has convinced me that though we have made enormous technological progress, the state of our ability to communicate effectively, to each other and to ourselves, lags far behind.

"As a generalist, and a communications consultant, I have explored a varied and wide area of subjects and worked with people who have difficult communications problems to solve.

"In 1969, I pioneered a new television concept which dramatically reduced per-hour production cost and resulted in an exciting new 'magazine' concept for television. . . .

"In 1972, I pioneered the production of new, low-cost, silent films that placed a training film in the hands of a student for under ten dollars. Subsequently, programs have been developed for the National Association for the Deaf, Bellevue Hospital, Pacific Telephone Company and other clients.

"I remain convinced that the future offers an excellent potential to deliver valid, low-cost information to literate people motivated to improve their personal skills. This challenge is an exciting and rewarding one."

*   *   *

KALT, Jeannette Chappell 1898(?)-1976
(Jeannette Chappell)

1898(?)—September 25, 1976; American poet and tennis player. She died in Glen Cove, N.Y. Obituaries: *New York Times,* September 26, 1976.

*   *   *

KAMATH, Madhav Vithal 1921-

PERSONAL: Born September 7, 1921, in Udupi, India; son of Vithal (a lawyer) and Girija (Pai) Kamath. *Education:* St. Xavier's College, Bombay, B.S., 1941. *Politics:* Independent. *Religion:* Agnostic (Hindu). *Home and office:* 4200 Cathedral Ave. N.W., Washington, D.C. 20016.

CAREER: Turkey Red Dye Works, Bombay, India, chemist, 1941-42; Kemp & Co., Bombay, analytical chemist, 1942-44; Oriental Pharmaceutical Works, Bombay, assistant manager, 1944-46; *Free Press Journal*, Bombay, reporter, 1946-49; *Free Press Bulletin*, Bombay, editor, 1949-55; *Press Trust of India*, New York, N.Y., United Nations correspondent, 1955-58; *Times of India*, European correspondent, 1959-66, Washington, D.C. bureau chief, 1969—. Notable assignments include all major international United Nations conferences in Europe, North Africa, and Latin America, 1959—. President of Bombay Union of Journalists, 1954; dean of Rajendra Prasad School of Journalism, Bombay, 1967-68.

WRITINGS: Parties and Politics in India, Dadar-Matunga Youth Association, 1946; (co-editor with Sharada Prasad) *Karnataka Darshana*, [India], 1953; *To the Captain*, Shipping Corp. of India, 1968; *Kissinger, The Incomplete Diplomat*, Jaico Publications, 1975; *The United States and India, 1776-1976*, Embassy of India, Washington, 1976. Contributing editor, *United Asia*, 1950-60. Contributor to *Current History, Le Monde Diplomatique, Illustrated Weekly of India, India Quarterly*, and to several Indian journals.

WORK IN PROGRESS: Notes on the Understanding and Meaning of Death, in three parts; a children's book on stamps; *Ma Paleshu*, a novel.

* * *

KAMISAR, Yale 1929-

PERSONAL: Born August 29, 1929, in New York, N.Y.; son of Samuel and Mollie (Levine) Kamisar; married Esther Englander, September 7, 1953 (died in October, 1973); married Christine Keller; children: David Graham, Gordon, Jonathan. *Education:* New York University, A.B., 1947; Columbia University, LL.B., 1954. *Home:* 2 Londonderry Circle, Ann Arbor, Mich. 48104. *Office:* 333 Hutchins Hall, School of Law, University of Michigan, Ann Arbor, Mich. 48109.

CAREER: American Law Institute, New York, N.Y., research associate, 1953; admitted to District of Columbia bar, 1955; Covington & Burling, Washington, D.C., associate, 1955-57; University of Minnesota, Minneapolis, 1957-65, began as associate professor, became professor of law; University of Michigan, Ann Arbor, professor of law, 1965—. Visiting professor at Harvard University, 1964-65. Co-reporter and draftsman for Uniform Rules of Criminal Procedure of National Conference of Commissioners on Uniform State Laws, 1971-73. *Military service:* U.S. Army, Infantry, 1951-52; served in Korea; became first lieutenant; received Purple Heart.

MEMBER: American Bar Association, American Judicature Society, American Law Institute, Society for the Psychological Study of Social Issues, Phi Beta Kappa.

WRITINGS: (With W. B. Lockhart and J. H. Choper) *Constitutional Law: Cases, Comments, and Questions*, published with *The American Constitution*, West Publishing, 1964, 4th edition, 1975; (with W. La Fave and J. Israel) *Modern Criminal Procedure: Cases and Commentaries*, West Publishing, 1965, 4th edition, 1974; (with F. Inbau and T. Arnold) *Criminal Justice in Our Time: Magna Carta Essays*, University Press of Virginia, 1965.

Contributor: A. B. Downing, editor, *Euthanasia and the Right to Death*, Peter Owen, 1969; Arthur Niederhoffer and A. S. Blumberg, editors, *The Ambivalent Force: Perspective on the Police*, Ginn, 1970; A. Paul, editor, *Black Americans and the Supreme Court Since Emancipation: Betrayal*

or Protection?, Holt, 1972. Contributor to law journals and newspapers. Member of board of editors of *Columbia Law Review;* member of editorial advisory board of *Criminal Law Bulletin*, 1971—; member of law school and college department educational and advisory board of West Publishing, 1968—.

* * *

KAMM, Herbert 1917-

PERSONAL: Born April 1, 1917, in Long Branch, N.J.; son of Louis (a cab driver) and Rose (Cohen) Kamm; married Phyllis I. Silberblatt (a free-lance writer), December 6, 1936; children: Laurence R., Lewis R., Robert H. *Education:* Attended Monmouth Junior College, 1934-35. *Religion:* Jewish. *Home:* 13800 Shaker Blvd., Cleveland, Ohio 44120. *Office: Cleveland Press*, 901 Lakeside Ave., Cleveland, Ohio 44114.

CAREER: Asbury Park Press, Asbury Park, N.J., began as sports writer, became reporter, sports editor, and author of column "Sports Angles," 1935-42; Associated Press, Newark, N.J., news editor, 1942-43; *New York World-Telegram & Sun*, New York, N.Y., began as rewrite man, became feature writer, picture editor, assistant city editor, feature editor, magazine editor, and assistant managing editor, 1943-63, managing editor, 1963-66; *New York World Journal Tribune*, New York City, Sunday editor, 1966, executive editor, 1966-67; Scripps-Howard Newspapers, New York City, editorial consultant, 1967-69; *Cleveland Press*, Cleveland, Ohio, associate editor and editor of editorial page, 1969—. Covered the funeral of Franklin D. Roosevelt; also conducted personal interviews with Lyndon B. Johnson and Golda Meir. Lecturer at New School for Social Research, 1963; instructor at Case Western Reserve University, 1972-75; public lecturer since 1943. Sports broadcaster for WCAP-Radio, 1939-42; presented weekly news analysis for Cleveland radio stations, 1970-73; co-anchorman for WDOK-FM Radio news, 1973-75; producer and host of "Kamm's Corner" an interview program on WVIZ-TV, 1974—. Member of board of overseers of Case Western Reserve University; member of board of directors of University for Young Americans; member of board of trustees of Cleveland Scholarship Program and Cleveland International Program.

MEMBER: National Press Club, American Society of Newspaper Editors, American Federation of Television and Radio Artists, National Academy of Television Arts and Sciences, American Cancer Society (member of local board of trustees), Jewish Community Federation (member of Cleveland board of trustees), Cleveland Advertising Club, Greater Cleveland Growth Association, City Club of Cleveland, Sigma Delta Chi, Society of Silurians. *Awards, honors:* Award from Greater Cleveland Radio-Television Council, 1975, for outstanding free-lance radio and television broadcasts.

WRITINGS: Junior Illustrated Encyclopedia of Sports, Bobbs-Merrill, 1960, 5th edition, 1975. Contributor to national magazines.

* * *

KAMSTRA, Leslie D. 1920-

PERSONAL: Born February 4, 1920, in Brookings, S.D.; son of Martin Sigruid (a farmer) and Annie (Starkenburg) Kamstra; married Marion Leach (a professor of textiles and clothing), June 20, 1948; children: Lynne Kamstra Ipina, Mark, Lance, Kim, Leigh, Lex. *Education:* Washington

Junior College, A.A., 1940; South Dakota State University, B.S., 1947, B.S., 1948, M.S., 1951; Ohio State University, Ph.D., 1955. *Politics:* Republican. *Religion:* Presbyterian. *Home:* 908 Third St., Brookings, S.D. 57006. *Office:* Department of Animal Science, South Dakota State University, Brookings, S.D. 57006.

CAREER: Farm worker in Minnesota, 1934-38; high school science teacher in Howard, S.D., 1948-50; South Dakota State University, Brookings, professor of biochemistry, 1956—. Visiting professor at University of Hawaii, 1964. *Military service:* U.S. Coast Guard, Medical Corps, 1941-45. *Member:* American Society of Animal Science, American Society of Range Management, South Dakota Academy of Science, Sigma Xi, Gamma Sigma Delta.

WRITINGS: Laboratory Manual, privately printed, 1965; *Nutrition of Farm Animals,* Kendall-Hunt, 1975; *For the Love of Life,* privately printed, 1977. Contributor of more than one hundred fifty articles to scientific journals.

WORK IN PROGRESS: Revising *Nutrition of Farm Animals,* publication by Kendall-Hunt expected in 1982.

SIDELIGHTS: Kamstra writes: "I consider myself to be a biochemical nutritionist and wish to consider subjects which solve knotty farm problems long overdue. I am a product of the Depression and therefore know about waste of natural resources. I still work and write about better utilization of natural resources.

"My other interests include a love for young people and their problems. I serve as a student counselor for about thirty students per semester."

*   *   *

KANE, Basil G(odfrey) 1931-

PERSONAL: Born December 12, 1931, in London, England; came to the United States in 1949, naturalized citizen, 1951; son of Harry (a cabinet maker) and Raychel (Spector) Kane; married Nancy Kunst, October 6, 1961; children: Jeffrey, Elisabeth, Brian. *Education:* University of Illinois, B.S., 1958; John Marshall Law School, graduate study. *Residence:* Evanston, Ill. *Agent:* John Boswell, International Literary Management, Inc., 767 Fifth Ave., Suite 601, New York, N.Y. 10022. *Office:* Menomonee Club for Boys and Girls, 244 West Willow, Chicago, Ill. 60614.

CAREER: Department of Public Aid, Chicago, Ill., social worker, 1959-64; Menomonee Club for Boys and Girls, Chicago, director, 1964—. Founding member of North Shore Soccer League and Young Sportsmen's Soccer League. *Military service:* U.S. Air Force, 1952-55; became staff sergeant.

WRITINGS: Soccer for American Spectators, A. S. Barnes, 1970; *How to Play Soccer* (juvenile), Grosset, 1973; *How to Play Soccer* (for adults), Grosset, 1975. Contributor to soccer magazines.

WORK IN PROGRESS: Two novels, *Irving and the Sheik* and *The Beercan Murders.*

SIDELIGHTS: Kane writes briefly: "Writing is a great source of enjoyment for me and has been so since I was twelve years old. It is only in the last ten years that I have realized others might want to read that which I have written, thus enabling me to derive financial benefits as well as joy from what I had always considered merely a hobby."

*   *   *

KAPLAN, Edward 1946-

PERSONAL: Born March 1, 1946, in New Jersey; son of

Philip (a salesman) and Leah (a jewelry manager; maiden name, Melnick) Kaplan; married Marcia Berman, May 11, 1969 (divorced, 1977). *Education:* Temple University, B.A., 1969, M.A., 1972; Gratz College, teaching certificate, 1973. *Religion:* Jewish. *Home and office:* 56 Main St., Millburn, N.J. 07041. *Agent:* Bonnie Gordon, 126 MacDougal St., New York, N.Y. 10012.

CAREER: Association for Jewish Children, Philadelphia, Pa., director of residences, 1971-73; Jewish Memorial Center, Altoona, Pa., executive director, 1973-75; B'nai B'rith, Millburn, N.J., regional director for northern New Jersey, 1975—. Instructor at Temple University. Has given poetry readings in New York and Pennsylvania. Member of board of directors of Blair County Day Care, 1973-75, Union County Council on Alcoholism, 1976, and Ad Hoc Committee of the National Conference on Mixed Marriage. Attended special mission to Israel, 1973.

MEMBER: National Conference of Jewish Communal Service, Artists and Writers for Peace in the Middle East, Poets of New Jersey, B'nai B'rith Century Club. *Awards, honors:* Award of merit from United Jewish Appeal, 1974; citation from northern New Jersey Council of B'nai B'rith, 1976.

WRITINGS: Alvin (poem), Triton Press, 1976; *Hard Acts* (poems), Triton/Hankshaw Press, 1977; *Book of Ghosts* (poems), Hankshaw Press, 1977; *Landing Blue* (poems), Small Press Collective, 1977. Contributor of poems to literary journals, including *Stone Country, Assembling, Human Voice Quarterly, Poet,* and *Sun Lotus Haiku.* Former poetry editor of *Rising Sun Arts Review.*

WORK IN PROGRESS: "Reflexive poetry, deep imaged"; poetry readings in the New York area.

SIDELIGHTS: Kaplan writes: "In 1971, I pioneered an experimental drug prevention workshop in the Philadelphia School System using poetry as a technique of self-awareness. In cooperation with the Philadelphia Board of Education, the program predated poetry-in-the-schools by five years. Currently, my interests are in exploring poetry as a way to live, as a way of being in the world. Poetry readings help achieve this want."

AVOCATIONAL INTERESTS: "Out of body experiences," rare books, fast cars, "anything cashmere."

BIOGRAPHICAL/CRITICAL SOURCES: New Jersey, August-September, 1977.

*   *   *

KAPLAN, Howard 1950-

PERSONAL: Born July 6, 1950, in Los Angeles, Calif.; son of Albert (a painting contractor) and Clara Kaplan. *Education:* University of California, Berkeley, B.A., 1972; University of California, Los Angeles, M.A., 1974; also studied at Hebrew University of Jerusalem, 1970-71. *Religion:* Jewish. *Home:* 2862 Anchor Ave., Los Angeles, Calif. 90064. *Agent:* Scott Meredith Literary Agency, Inc., 845 Third Ave., New York, N.Y. 10022.

CAREER: Jewish Agency, Jerusalem, Israel, lecturer, 1972-73; Los Angeles Hebrew High School, Los Angeles, Calif., teacher of Jewish history, 1973-74; writer, 1974—.

WRITINGS: The Damascus Cover (novel), Dutton, 1977.

WORK IN PROGRESS: Moscow Descent, a novel, for Dutton.

SIDELIGHTS: Kaplan writes: "At the age of twenty-two while involved in smuggling textbooks into the Soviet Union and microfilm out I was arrested by the KGB and interrogated for four days. This experience coupled with extensive travel through the Middle East combined to set the background for my first two novels.''

* * *

KAPLAN, Leonard 1918(?)-1977

1918(?)—April 26, 1977; American expert and writer on foreign torpedoes, mines and guns, and U.S. Navy's primary manager for analysis of foreign conventional naval weapons systems. He died in Baltimore, Md. Obituaries: *Washington Post,* May 6, 1977.

* * *

KARPAT, Kemal H(asim) 1925-

PERSONAL: Born February 15, 1925, in Tulca, Rumania; came to the United States in 1951; son of Hashim H. and Zubeyda (Cavush) Omer; divorced. *Education:* Attended Teacher's College, Medigidia, Rumania, 1942; University of Istanbul, LL.B., 1948; University of Washington, Seattle, M.A., 1950; New York University, Ph.D., 1957. *Office:* Department of History, University of Wisconsin, Madison, Wis. 53706.

CAREER: Attorney in Istanbul, Turkey, 1948; United Nations, New York, N.Y., staff member of Secretariat's social research department, 1952-53; Montana State University, Missoula, assistant professor, 1957-58, associate professor of history, 1959-62; New York University, New York, N.Y., assistant professor, 1962-64, associate professor of history, 1964-67; University of Wisconsin, Madison, professor of history and chairman of Middle East program, 1967—. Chairman of public administration for Middle East Technical University, 1958-59, visiting professor, 1968-72; visiting associate professor at Robert College and School of Political Science (Ankara, Turkey), 1962; visiting lecturer at Johns Hopkins School of Advanced International Studies, 1967. Fellow at Harvard University, 1960-61; research associate at Princeton University's Center of International Studies, 1972. Trustee of Institute of Mediterranean Affairs, 1967-71. Organizer and director of Social Science Research Council conference in Turkey, 1965; area director of Peace Corps training program at New York University, 1966. *Military service:* Turkish Armed Forces, 1953-55; became second lieutenant.

MEMBER: International Political Science Association, Middle East Studies Association of North America (founding member; fellow; member of board of directors, 1970-72), American Historical Association, American Political Science Association, American Oriental Society, Turkish Studies Association (president, 1971-74), American-Turkish Society (vice-president, 1967-71), Middle East Institute (fellow), Royal Asiatic Society. *Awards, honors:* Rockefeller Foundation grant, 1960; Social Science Research Council grant, 1961; postdoctoral study grants from the State of Wisconsin, 1968, 1975.

WRITINGS: Turkey's Politics: The Transition to a Multi-Party System, Princeton University Press, 1959; (editor and contributor) *Political Modernization in Japan and Turkey,* Princeton University Press, 1964; (contributor) Benjamin Rivlin and Joseph Szylowicz, editors, *The Contemporary Middle East: Tradition and Innovation,* Random House, 1966; *Turk demokrasi tarihi* (title means "History of Turkish Democracy''), [Istanbul], 1967; *Political and Social Thought in the Contemporary Middle East,* Praeger, 1968; (contributor) William Polk and Richard Chambers, editors, *The Beginnings of Modernization in the Middle East,* University of Chicago Press, 1968; *The Middle East and North Africa,* Harcourt, 1969; *Turk edebiyatinda sesyal konular* (title means "Social Topics in Turkish Literature''), 2nd edition, Varlik, 1971.

(Contributor) P. M. Hoet, Ann K. Lambton, Bernard Lewis, editors, *The Cambridge History of Islam,* Cambridge University Press, 1970; *Social Change and Politics in Turkey,* E. J. Brill, 1973; *An Inquiry into the Social Foundations of Nationalism in the Ottoman State,* Princeton University Center for International Studies, 1973; *Gecekondu uzerine* (title means "On the Squatter Settlements''), Middle East Technical University, 1973; (editor and contributor) *The Ottoman State and Its Place in World History,* E. J. Brill, 1974; (contributor) Ibrahim Abu-Lughod and Baha-Abu Laban, editors, *Settler Regimes in Africa and the Arab World,* Madina, 1974; *Turkey's Foreign Policy in Transition,* E. J. Brill, 1975; (contributor) E. D. Akarli and Gabriel Ben-Dor, editors, *Political Participation in Turkey,* Bogazici Universitesi (Bebek, Istanbul), 1975; *The Gecekondu: Rural Migration and Urbanization,* Cambridge University Press, 1976. Contributor of more than thirty-five articles and reviews to political science and international studies journals.

WORK IN PROGRESS: A study of internal and international migration and settlement, population growth, and urbanization, entitled *Population Movements in the Middle East and the Balkans, 1850-1920;* a history of modern Turkey; a book on literature and social change.

SIDELIGHTS: Karpat told *CA:* "My interest in literature and in writing has been nourished basically by my direct contact, in my childhood days, with Turkish and Romanian folklore and the literature written in these languages. However, from the very start I developed a critical attitude toward literature. The society in which I was growing up regarded literature as a means of self-expression and amusement, whereas I was trained by my Muslim culture to regard society as a whole with all its parts and activities well integrated and functioning around certain societal goals. In other words, I found the segmented and almost contradictory relationship between society and literature, advocated by some writers, unacceptable.

"The search for understanding society led me to the study of politics and social science, with history acquiring increasing importance as the record of total human experience. However, my studies led me to a very painful and personal experience. I discovered that the West had placed me in a special category on the basis of my ethnic origin, religion, and background. In the eyes of the Western people, I belonged to a different world which had been condemned in advance as uncreative and even inferior. I discovered to my great chagrin that my beloved writers—with whom I became emotionally identified and to whom I owed much for my development as a sensitive, socially and politically alert human being—were used as symbols of Western superiority rather than the common heritage of all mankind. Thus, Dickens appeared as an Englishman who could see the social evils in his society as no others, especially non-Westerners, could. Balzac and Hugo became the symbols of French uniqueness, while Tolstoy was the symbol of Russian genius and messianism. In these circumstances I, the Turk, appeared as the *bete noire* of history, on whom all the 'civilized' nations discharged their prejudice. My Muslim culture was depicted as stemming from a non-revealed religion (Islam), while the West drew the essence of its culture from a revealed, and by implication divine and superior source.

"Events in the non-Western societies, including the one to which I was identified by origin and background, were described to occur under the whimsical impulse of oppressive and corrupt tyrants. In the West, decisions were supposedly made rationally by humanitarian, civic minded, well educated leaders.

"I read all this, first with interest and amusement and then with growing indignation. The memories of beautiful folktales of humanity, tenderness, and compassion I had read in my childhood and which lay dormant in my subconscious began to awaken and arise to a new level. I began thinking that the literary masterpieces of the West which helped to mature my intellect defended the idea that all people were born equal—that differences in education, living standards, etc., resulted from objective conditions rather than inherent superior or inferior human characteristics. In this light I began to look into the history and culture of the Middle East people. There I discovered literary figures, thinkers, and artists whose depth of feeling, and sharpness of intellect were equal, if not superior, to the West's.

"I have devoted considerable time and energy to the history and cultures of the Middle East in order to bring forth the value of their contribution to the civilization of all mankind. Although the forms of Western and non-Western culture and history differ, their human essence is the same. I believe that the Western idea of inherent superiority was artificially contrived in order to justify colonialism and imperialism and that this ugly period in history is rapidly approaching its end. The message of my work is to point out the originality and importance of the periphery so that we can build, in common, a strong center belonging to all of us regardless of our ethnic, linguistic, racial, and religious differences."

* * *

KATONA, Edita 1913-

PERSONAL: Born August 10, 1913, in Vienna, Austria; daughter of Hugo and Anna (Pernitzova) Zuckermann; married Victor Katona (a film producer), 1959 (died 1968). *Education:* Educated in Austria and Switzerland. *Home:* 23 Beaumont Mews, London W1, England.

CAREER: Secret agent for the Deuxieme Bureau, 1938-44; has worked as a beautician and teacher; writer. *Awards, honors:* Croix de Guerre with Palm, and Croix de Combattant, 1944.

WRITINGS: (With Patrick Macnaghten) *Code-Name Marianne* (autobiography), Collins, 1976, McKay, 1977.

SIDELIGHTS: A Czech refugee living in France, Edita Katona began working for French Naval Intelligence in 1938. She adopted the code-name Marianne Chabot and for four years executed intelligence missions in enemy territory. Most notable among her intelligence accomplishments were photographing the Sicilian military zone, obtaining a map of the minefields in the Messina Straight, and persuading the Head of Italian Secret Police to begin defection negotiations by offering the Italian Naval Code in exchange for 3 million francs. In 1942 she escaped from the OVRA police and later survived a Gestapo interrogation.

* * *

KATTAN, Naim 1928-

PERSONAL: Born August 26, 1928, in Bagdad, Iraq; emigrated to Canada, 1954; naturalized citizen, 1959; son of Nessim and Hela (Saleh) Kattan; married Gaetane Laniel (an actress), July 12, 1961; children: Emmanuel. *Education:*

Attended University of Bagdad, 1944-47, and Sorbonne, University of Paris, 1947-52. *Religion:* Jewish. *Home:* 4803 Mira Rd., Montreal, Quebec, Canada. *Office:* 255 Albert, Ottawa, Ontario, Canada.

CAREER: Nouveau Journal, Montreal, Quebec, commentator on international affairs, 1961-62; Laval University, Quebec, Quebec, instructor in Middle Eastern affairs, 1962; Cercle Juif, Montreal, Quebec, director and editor of *Le Bulletin du Cercle Juif,* 1954-67; Commission on Bilingualism, Ottawa, Ontario, writer, 1964-67; Canada Council, Ottawa, head of writing and publication section, 1967—. Columnist, *Le Devoir,* 1962—; member of board, Place des Arts, 1964—. *Member:* Royal Society of Canada. *Awards, honors:* France Canada Award, 1971, for *Le reel et le theatral;* I. J. Segal literary award, 1976.

WRITINGS: Le reel et le theatral, Editions HMH (Montreal), 1970, translation by Alan Brown published as *Reality and Theatre,* Anansi, 1972; *Ecrivains des Ameriques,* Editions HMH, Tome I: *Les Etats Unis,* 1972, Tome II: *English Canada,* 1976; *La discretion,* l'Avant-Scene (Paris), 1973; *Dans le Desert,* Lemeac (Montreal), 1974; *La discretion, La neige, Le trajet, Les Protagonistes,* Lemeac, 1974; *Farewell Babylon,* Editions La Presse, 1976, *La Traversee,* HMH, 1976.

Author of "Litterature Etrangere" column, *Le Devoir,* 1962—.

Contributor to *Les lettres nouvelles, La Quinzaine litteraire, Tamarack Review,* and *Canadian Literature.*

WORK IN PROGRESS: Les Fruits arraches, La fiancee promise, L' echangeur, novels; *La Memoire et la Promesse,* an essay.

* * *

KAUFMAN, H(arold) G(erson) 1939-

PERSONAL: Born April 23, 1939, in Bronx, N.Y.; son of Albert (a business owner) and Norma (Olshansky) Kaufman; married wife Sybil, June 13, 1962 (divorced, August, 1969). *Education:* Cooper Union, B.M.E., 1962; New York University, M.I.E., 1964, Ph.D., 1970. *Home:* 25 Jones St., New York, N.Y. 10014. *Office:* Polytechnic Institute, 333 Jay St., Brooklyn, N.Y. 11201.

CAREER: Academy of Aeronautics, Flushing, N.Y., training researcher, 1962-63; New York University, New York City, human factors research assistant, 1963-65; International Business Machines (IBM), Armonk, N.Y., personnel researcher, 1965-66; Polytechnic Institute of New York, Brooklyn, N.Y., assistant professor, 1970-72, associate professor of management, 1972—, director of organizational behavior graduate program, 1974—. Research consultant for manpower and human resources programs and agencies. *Member:* American Psychological Association, Eastern Psychological Association, International Association for Applied Psychology, Academy of Management, American Society for Engineering Education, New York Metropolitan Association for Applied Psychology. *Awards, honors:* Fellowship from National Institute of Mental Health; Lady Davis Foundation post-doctoral fellow at Hebrew University, Jerusalem.

WRITINGS: Obsolescence and Professional Career Development, American Management Association, 1974; (editor) *Career Management: A Guide to Combating Obsolescence,* Wiley-Interscience for Institute of Electrical and Electronics Engineers, 1975; *The Unemployed Professionals,* Wiley-Interscience, 1978. Contributor to professional journals in his field. Manpower editor, *Engineering Management Review* and columnist and associate editor, Engineering Management Society newsletter (both publications of Institute of Electrical and Electronics Engineers).

WORK IN PROGRESS: A self-development approach to dealing with problems of professional obsolescence using tape cassettes; a report commissioned by the National Science Foundation dealing with continuing education; a report for the Alfred P. Sloan Foundation dealing with blacks in engineering; a report for the Ford Foundation on women and part-time work.

* * *

KEENAN, Deborah (Anne) 1950-

PERSONAL: Born December 5, 1950, in Minneapolis, Minn.; daughter of Clifford A. (a chemical engineer) and Virginia (an English teacher; maiden name, Wells) Bowman; married J. Michael Keenan (a professor of English), September 19, 1970; children: Brendan, Molly. *Education:* Macalester College, B.A., 1973. *Home:* 1463 Ashland Ave., St. Paul, Minn. 55104.

CAREER: Poet-in-residence at a private school in St. Paul, Minn., 1975—. Teacher of children's literature at South-East Alternative Education Community College, 1976-77.

WRITINGS: On Stage: The Beatles, Creative Education Press, 1976; *On Stage: Barbra Streisand,* Creative Education Press, 1976. Contributor of poems to literary magazines.

WORK IN PROGRESS: A mystery novel, with Wendy Parrish; a children's book, with Parrish.

SIDELIGHTS: Deborah Keenan writes briefly: "I write because it is difficult, necessary, and because the process keeps me sane." *Avocational interests:* Travel (Scotland, Greece).

* * *

KELLEHER, Stephen J(oseph) 1915-

PERSONAL: Born August 31, 1915, in New York, N.Y.; son of Stephen J. (a corrections officer) and Margaret (Morrissey) Kelleher. *Education:* St. Joseph College, Yonkers, N.Y., B.A., 1936; Gregorian University, S.T.B., 1938; Catholic University of America, D.C.L., 1943. *Home and office:* 457 West 51st St., New York, N.Y. 10019.

CAREER: Ordained Roman Catholic priest, 1940; named monsignor, 1959; Roman Catholic Archdiocese of New York, New York City, member of Marriage Tribunal, 1943-59; Pontifical Mission for Palestine, Beirut, Lebanon, field director, 1960-62; Roman Catholic Archdiocese of New York, presiding judge of Marriage Tribunal, 1962-68; pastor of Roman Catholic church in Scarsdale, N.Y., 1968-72; writer and lecturer, 1972-73; program specialist for New York City Department of Corrections, 1973-75; writer and lecturer, 1976; lecturer at Mercy College, Dobbs Ferry, N.Y., Marymount Manhattan College, New York City, and Iona College, New Rochelle, N.Y., 1977—. Adviser to U.S. Bishops' Committee on Canon Law; member of board of governors of Scarsdale Family Counseling Service.

MEMBER: Canon Law Society of America, American Guild of Catholic Psychiatrists (associate member), Canadian Canon Law Society, Canon Law Society of Great Britain and Ireland.

WRITINGS: Divorce and Remarriage for Catholics?, Doubleday, 1973. Contributor of about twenty articles to *America, Commonweal, Jurist,* and *National Catholic Reporter.*

WORK IN PROGRESS: A survey of two to three hundred divorced catholics groups in the United States and Canada.

SIDELIGHTS: Monsignor Kelleher writes: "The principal thrust of my life is to seek substantial change in the teaching of the Catholic Church concerning divorce and remarriage. I am seeking recognition by the Church of divorce." Kelleher has traveled extensively in the Middle East and Europe.

BIOGRAPHICAL/CRITICAL SOURCES: Time, September, 1968.

* * *

KELLER, Fred S(immons) 1899-

PERSONAL: Born January 2, 1899, in Rural Grove, N.Y.; son of Vrooman Barney (a salesman) and Minnie (Simmons) Keller; married Frances Scholl, 1936; children: Anne Simmons (Mrs. Thomas C. Cline), John Vanderveer. *Education:* Tufts College (now University), B.S., 1926; Harvard University, M.A., 1928, Ph.D., 1931. *Home:* 860 Oleander Dr. S.E., Aiken, S.C. 29801.

CAREER: Tufts College (now University), Medford, Mass., instructor in psychology, 1926-28; Colgate University, Hamilton, N.Y., instructor in psychology, 1931-38; Columbia University, New York, N.Y., instructor, 1938-41, assistant professor, 1941-46, associate professor, 1946-50, professor of psychology, 1950-64, professor emeritus, 1964—; Arizona State University, Tempe, professor of psychology, 1964-67; Institute for Behavioral Research, Silver Spring, Md., visiting scientist, 1967-68; Western Michigan University, Kalamazoo, visiting professor, 1968-70, adjunct professor, 1970-73, distinguished adjunct professor of psychology, 1973-74; Georgetown University, Washington, D.C., distinguished visiting scholar, 1974, distinguished visiting psychologist, 1974-76; writer, 1976—. Fulbright-Hayes Professor at University of Sao Paulo, 1961; professor at University of Brasilia, 1964; Cecil H. and Ida Green Honors Professor at Texas Christian University, autumn, 1973; summer professor at University of California, Los Angeles, 1948. Chairman of board of directors of Independent Learning Systems, 1970-71; member of board of directors of Individual Learning Systems, 1971-72. Participated in the film "Skinner and Behavior Change," Research Press, 1972. *Military service:* U.S. Army, American Expeditionary Forces, 1918-19; became sergeant.

MEMBER: American Psychological Association (fellow), American Association for the Advancement of Science (fellow), Eastern Psychological Association (fellow; president, 1956-57). *Awards, honors:* Certificate of merit from President Harry Truman, 1948; awards from American Psychological Association, 1974, for teaching, and 1976, for contributions to psychology; award from Society of Experimental Psychologists, 1947; Sc.D. from C. W. Post College of Long Island University, 1972, and Colgate University, 1976; D.H.L. from Institute for Behavioral Research, 1976.

WRITINGS: The Definition of Psychology, Appleton, 1937, revised edition, 1973; (with W. N. Schoenfeld) *Principles of Psychology,* Appleton, 1950; *Learning: Reinforcement Theory,* Random House, 1954, revised edition, 1969; (with J. G. Sherman) *The Keller Plan Handbook,* W. A. Benjamin, 1974; (editor with Emilio Ribes-Inesto) *Behavior Modification: Applications to Education,* Academic Press, 1974; (editor) *History of Psychology: A PSI Companion* (readings), Scholars' Press, 1975.

Co-author of films "Together," Appleton, 1972; "Keller on PSI," School of Communications, University of Texas, 1975. Contributor of about sixty articles to professional journals.

WORK IN PROGRESS: Studying the history of behavior analysis, educational technology, and the meaning of awards.

SIDELIGHTS: Keller writes: "The book that was most important to my career was B. F. Skinner's *Behavior of Organisms* (1938). This is reflected in my own writings and is responsible for what success I may have had as a teacher and an educational reformer. My major interest has been in animal learning, human training, and teaching."

BIOGRAPHICAL/CRITICAL SOURCES: American *Psychologist,* January, 1977.

* * *

KELLER, James Gregory 1900-1977

June 27, 1900—February 7, 1977; American Maryknoll priest, founder and director of the Christophers, and author of over twenty-five books. The Christophers, founded in 1945 under Roman Catholic auspices, adapted the motto "It is better to light one candle than to curse the darkness." He died in New York City. Obituaries: *New York Times,* February 9, 1977; *Time,* February 21, 1977; *Current Biography,* April, 1977.

* * *

KELLY, Martha Rose 1914-
(Marty Kelly)

PERSONAL: Born November 14, 1914, in Fort Benton, Mont.; daughter of Charles (a retail merchandiser) and Grace (Carroll) Houck; married Mike Cinker, 1936 (deceased); married Earle Reynolds, 1943 (deceased); married Robert Kelly, 1953 (deceased); children: Grace, Margaret. *Home:* 1714 Fourth Avenue, Great Falls, Mont. 59401.

CAREER: Writer. Has worked as a store detective, firefighter, electrician, waitress, and practical nurse. *Member:* American Heritage Society, Ancient Order of Hibernians, Montana Institute of Arts, Humane Society of Great Falls.

WRITINGS—All children's books: *Green-Up, The Story of a Buffalo,* American Heritage Press, 1971; *The House on Deer Track Trail,* McGraw, 1976. Contributor of short stories to *Ladies Home Journal, Majestic Montana, Playgrounds of the Rockies, True West,* and other periodicals.

WORK IN PROGRESS: The Poet in the Country House, a book of poems; *Mouse Tracks,* a children's book; and "Crickets Under the Walk," a children's story.

SIDELIGHTS: Marty Kelly told *CA* of her early career as a writer: "I didn't know how to type, but I made a deal with a merchant for a second-hand Corona, and my career began, one peck at a time. I hadn't found my style yet. There were miles of love stories which didn't sell, sheets of poetry, adventure, fantasy, mystery—you name it, I wrote them all. And then one day *True West Magazine* bought 'The Door Stop Skull.' I didn't realize that this publication was factual. My story was a combination of two different tales, dovetailed together into a hell-roaring saga of the old West."

"I belive I have been writing for a thousand years," Kelly continued, "when I wasn't putting it down on paper, I was writing it in the air. It do a great deal of reading and I still love children's books."

KEMP, Gene 1926-

PERSONAL: Born December 27, 1926, in Wigginton, England; daughter of Albert (an electric meter reader) and Alice (Sutton) Rushton; married Norman Charles Pattison, August 20, 1949 (divorced, May, 1958); married Allan William George Kemp (a bus driver and union official), August 23, 1958; children: (first marriage) Judith Eve; (second marriage) Chantal Alice, Richard William. *Education:* University of Exeter, degree in English, with honors, 1945. *Politics:* Labour. *Religion:* Church of England. *Home:* 16 Waverley Ave., Exeter, Devonshire EX4 4NL, England. *Agent:* Gerald Pollinger, 18 Maddox St., Mayfair, London W1R 0EU, England. *Office:* Saint Sidwell's School, York Rd., Exeter, Devonshire, England.

CAREER: Teacher in private schools and in public secondary schools; Saint Sidwell's School, Exeter, England, teacher, 1963-77. Manager of Central School in Exeter; lecturer at Rolle College, 1974-75. Member of Council for the Advancement of State Education and of general management committee of Exeter Labour Party. *Member:* National Union of Teachers, National Association for the Teaching of English.

WRITINGS—For children: *Prime of Tamworth Pig,* Faber, 1972; *Tamworth Pig Saves the Trees,* Faber, 1973; *Tamworth Pig and the Litter,* Faber, 1975; *The Turbulent Term of Tyke Tiler,* Faber, 1977; *The Christmas of Tamworth Pig,* Faber, 1977.

Work anthologized in *Children's Literature in Education,* edited by Terry Jones and Geoff Fox. Contributor of poems to *Welsh Press.*

WORK IN PROGRESS: Research for a juvenile book on Saint Sidwell's School; a humorous book for adults; a book entitled *The Well.*

SIDELIGHTS: Gene Kemp writes: "*Tyke Tiler* is my most interesting book—I'd done a lot of research on language for it and used Peter and Ioana Opie's *Language and Love of Schoolchildren. . . .*" *Avocational interests:* Politics, reading folklore, myths, and adult literature ("I like Saul Bellow a lot").

* * *

KENDALL, T(homas) Robert 1935-

PERSONAL: Born September 12, 1935, in Berkeley, Calif.; son of Thomas William (a mechanical engineer) and Miriam (Adams) Kendall; married Ingeborg Van de Venter (a geographer), September 16, 1965; children: Thomas Edward, Kristina Marie. *Education:* Attended Massachusetts Institute of Technology, 1954-55; Pomona College, B.A. (physics), 1959; University of Washington, B.A. (oceanography), 1964; University of Hawaii, M.S., 1966; Nova University, Ph.D., 1970. *Office:* International Center for Environmental Research, 141 Emerald Bay, Laguna Beach, Calif. 92651.

CAREER: Columbia Pictures, Hollywood, Calif., special effects cinematographer in Rhodes, Greece, for the screenplay "The Guns of Navaronne," and in Hawaii, for the screenplay "The Devil at Four O'Clock," 1960; Douglas Aircraft Co., Santa Monica, Calif., aerospace engineer, 1960-62; free-lance underwater photographer, 1962-63; International Underwater Enterprises, Honolulu, Hawaii, commercial diver, 1964-66; commercial flying boat pilot for Catalina Ltd., 1966-67; International Center for Environmental Research, Laguna Beach, Calif., oceanographer, 1970—. Holds licenses as Los Angeles (Calif.) County underwater instructor and as multiengine land and sea commercial pilot. *Member:* American Geophsical Union, Los Angeles Underwater Instructor Association. *Awards, honors:* Awarded more than twenty prizes since 1961 for underwater photography, including honors from Underwater Film Festival of Santa Monica (Calif.), International and Grand International Underwater Photographic Exhibitions of Underwater Photographic Society, International Film Festival of Academy of Underwater Photographers, and most recently, the Man in the Sea Award for Photography at Inner Space Pacifica in Honolulu (Hawaii), 1973.

WRITINGS: Pacific Equatorial Countercurrent, International Center for Environmental Research, 1970; *Photographs Underwater,* International Center for Environmental Research, 1976. Contributor to *Marine Technology Society Journal, Skin Diver* magazine, and *Underwater Photographer.*

WORK IN PROGRESS: A shark manual; research for a book on U.S. Navy Catalina patrol bombers, flying boats of World War II.

SIDELIGHTS: Kendall told *CA:* "A career in oceanography combines a variety of my intense interests in engineering, undersea exploration, photography, electronics, flying, science. Basically, I live for adventure."

BIOGRAPHICAL/CRITICAL SOURCES: Life, May 30, 1960; Jim Thorne, *Adventures under the Sea,* Walker & Co., 1965.

* * *

KENDRICK, Baynard H(ardwick)   1894-1977
(Richard Hayward)

April 8, 1894—March 22, 1977; American mystery writer, creator of the blind sleuth Captain Duncan Maclain introduced in *The Last Express* in 1937. He helped organize Mystery Writers of America, was holder of membership card No. 1, and was recipient of its Edgar award. He died in Ocala, Fla. Obituaries: *New York Times,* March 23, 1977; *Washington Post,* March 25, 1977; *Current Biography,* May, 1977. (See index for previous *CA* sketch)

* * *

KENOFER, C(harles) Louis   1923-

PERSONAL: Born July 26, 1923, in Cincinnati, Ohio; son of Charles L. Klingelhoffer (a machinist); married Doris Dillon (an artist), August 25, 1951; children: Wendy, Bruce. *Education:* University of Colorado, B.A. *Home:* 5020 Juniper St., Littleton, Colo. 80123. *Office:* Rockmont Envelope Co., Denver, Colo.

CAREER: Rockmont Envelope Co., Denver, Colo., sales manager; writer. *Military service:* U.S. Naval Reserve, active duty, 1943-46, 1951-53; became lieutenant commander. *Member:* Graphology Association, Scritology Association, Sierra Club, Colorado Mountain Club.

WRITINGS: Rocky Mountain Trails, Pruett, 1970; *Trails of the Front Range,* Pruett, 1972.

WORK IN PROGRESS: Estes Park Then (1915) and Now (1977); Gove Range—Eagles Nest Trail Guide.

SIDELIGHTS: Kenofer writes: "I am studying all the major courses of handwriting—doing work with University of Colorado Medical Center on biofeedback—working with some other friends on hypnotic regression and meditation, and I am taking pictures of the back country with a large format camera, so I can publish large photos (wall type)."

KEPES, Juliet A(ppleby)   1919-

PERSONAL: Surname is pronounced *Kay-*pash; born June 29, 1919, in London, England; came to the United States in 1937, naturalized citizen, 1957; daughter of Percy (a ship chandler) and Beatrice Maud (Smith) Appleby; married Gyorgy Kepes (a painter, professor, and writer), November 3, 1937; children: Juliet (Mrs. Henry Sawyer Stone, Jr.), Imre Peter. *Education:* Attended Askes Hatcham School and Brighton School of Art, 1933-37, and Chicago School of Design, 1937-42. *Home and office:* 90 Larchwood Dr., Cambridge, Mass. 02138.

CAREER: Artist, illustrator of children's books, and writer. Taught at School of Design and Jane Addams School in Chicago, 1938-39. Has designed rooms and rugs for children, textiles, architectural enamel murals for schools and libraries, stage sets and costumes for dance groups; has designed for playgrounds, hospitals, and schools; has had one-woman exhibitions of drawings and paintings and participated in group shows. Member of Radcliffe Institute Museum of Fine Arts. *Member:* Cambridge Art Association. *Awards, honors:* Awards from Museum of Modern Art for textiles, pictures for children, and arts and therapy; certificate of excellence from American Institute of Graphic Arts, 1958, for *Give a Guess;* citation of merit from Society of Illustrators, 1962, for *Frogs Merry;* award for best illustrated book of the year from *New York Times,* 1969, for *Birds.*

WRITINGS—Self-illustrated children's books: *Five Little Monkeys,* Houghton, 1952; *Beasts from a Brush,* Pantheon, 1955; *Two Little Birds and Three,* Houghton, 1960; *Frogs Merry,* Pantheon, 1961; *Lady Bird, Quickly,* Little, Brown, 1964; *The Seed That Peacock Planted,* Little, Brown, 1967; *Birds,* Walker & Co., 1968; *Five Little Monkeys Business,* Houghton, 1970; *Run, Little Monkeys! Run, Run, Run!,* Pantheon, 1974.

Illustrator: William J. Smith, *Laughing Time,* Little, Brown, 1953; Emilie McLeod, *The Seven Remarkable Bears,* Houghton, 1954; Herbert Reed, editor, *This Way Delight: A Book of Poetry for the Young,* Pantheon, 1956; Mary Britton Miller, *Give a Guess,* Pantheon, 1957; William Jay Smith, *Puptents and Pebbles,* Little, Brown, 1959. Contributor to magazines, including *Audience, Life, Interiors,* and *Encounter,* and newspapers.

WORK IN PROGRESS: A juvenile book; an art show, "Environment for Children," in Houston, Tex.

SIDELIGHTS: Juliet Kepes writes: "In my books I try to give children pleasure and some information about the creatures around us, at the same time trying to make books that are as attractive as possible in writing, illustration, and layout. I cannot say much more, as I am so involved in the making of a book, that I am not particularly conscious of the whys. Good children's books are for everybody, so I hope parents enjoy reading books to children as much as the children love to look and listen."

BIOGRAPHICAL/CRITICAL SOURCES: Donnarae MacCann and Olga Richard, *The Child's First Books,* H. W. Wilson, 1973.

* * *

KERN, Stephen   1943-

PERSONAL: Born January 28, 1943, in Los Angeles, Calif.; son of Seymour (a writer) and Jessie (Kraus) Kern. *Education:* University of California, Berkeley, B.A. (honors), 1964; Columbia University, M.A., 1965, Ph.D., 1970. *Agent:* Shirley Burke, 370 East 76th St., New York, N.Y.

10021. *Office:* Department of History, Northern Illinois University, Dekalb, Ill. 60115.

CAREER: Cornell Medical College, New York, N.Y., research fellow in psychiatry, 1966-70; Northern Illinois University, Dekalb, assistant professor of history, 1970—. *Awards, honors:* National Institute of Health research fellowship, 1966-70.

WRITINGS: Anatomy and Destiny: A Cultural History of the Human Body, Bobbs-Merrill, 1975.

* * *

KERR, Robert (a pseudonym) 1899-

PERSONAL: Born August 2, 1899, in Scotland. *Education:* Attended University of Edinburgh. *Address:* c/o Barrie & Jenkins, 24 Highbury Cres., London N5 1RS, England.

CAREER: Writer.

WRITINGS: The Stuart Legacy, Stein & Day, 1973; *Black Pearls,* Stein & Day, 1975; *Dark Lady,* Stein & Day, 1976.

* * *

KERR, Stanley E. 1894(?)-1976

1894(?)—December 14, 1976; American professor of biochemistry and author. His four year involvement with relief operations in Turkey and Lebanon in the early 1920's formed the basis of his book, *The Lions of Marash.* He was associated with the American University at Beirut, Lebanon, from 1925 to 1964. He died in Princeton, N.J. Obituaries: *New York Times,* December 15, 1976.

* * *

KESSLER, Ronald 1943-

PERSONAL: Born December 31, 1943, in New York, N.Y.; son of Myer (a physicist) and Minuetta (a pianist; maiden name, Shumiatcher) Kessler; married Frances Jankowski (a legal assistant), 1965; children: Gregory, Rachel. *Education:* Attended Clark University, 1962-64. *Home:* 6512 Elgin Ln., Bethesda, Md. 20034. *Office: Washington Post,* 1150 15th St. N.W., Washington, D.C. 20071.

CAREER/WRITINGS: Worcester Telegram, Worcester, Mass., reporter, 1964; *Boston Herald,* Boston, Mass., editorial writer and reporter, 1964-67; *Wall Street Journal,* New York, N.Y., reporter, 1967-70; *Washington Post,* Washington, D.C., investigative reporter, 1970—. Notable assignments include Nixon finances and F.B.I. wiretapping investigations. *Awards, honors:* United Press International first prize award in newswriting, 1965; Associated Press Sevellon Brown Award, 1965; Freedoms Foundation Award, 1966; American Political Science Association public affairs award, 1967; American Dental Society science award, 1968; *Washingtonian* Magazine Washingtonian of the Year award, 1972; Baltimore-Washington Newspaper Guild Front Page Award, 1972; George Polk Memorial award for community service, 1972; American Association of University Women public affairs award, 1973.

SIDELIGHTS: Kessler contends an investigative journalist's role is "to find the truth as nearly as it can be determined."

* * *

KESSNER, Thomas 1946-

PERSONAL: Born December 20, 1946, in Germany; came to the United States in 1950, naturalized citizen, 1958; son of Eugene (a laborer) and Livia (Farkas) Kessner; married

Rachel Roth, December 17, 1967; children: Joseph, Hadassah, Sara, Aryeh, Meir. *Education:* Brooklyn College of the City University of New York, B.A., 1967; Columbia University, M.A., 1968, Ph.D., 1975. *Residence:* Brooklyn, N.Y. *Office:* Department of History, Kingsborough Community College, Manhattan Beach, Brooklyn, N.Y. 11235.

CAREER: Brooklyn College of the City University of New York, Brooklyn, N.Y., adjunct lecturer of world history, 1969; Kingsborough Community College, Brooklyn, N.Y., assistant professor of history, 1971—. Member of faculty at New School for Social Research, 1976. Associate of the University Seminar on the City, at Columbia University. *Member:* Organization of American Historians, Social Science History Association, Phi Beta Kappa, Alpha Sigma Lambda.

WRITINGS: The Golden Door: Italian and Jewish Immigrant Mobility in New York City, 1880-1915, Oxford University Press, 1977. Contributor to history and ethnic studies journals.

WORK IN PROGRESS: Research on immigrant life in New York City during the Depression and on post-World War II immigration.

SIDELIGHTS: Kessner writes: "I consider the study of history to be far more valuable when it focuses on all the people rather than the leaders. This means that historians must find ways of learning more about the lives of the common people, their concerns, hopes, aspirations, family life and interests. This has motivated me to use a variety of quantitative techniques to study New York's immigrants."

* * *

KEVLES, Bettyann 1938-

PERSONAL: Born August 20, 1938, in New York, N.Y.; daughter of David Marshal (a lawyer) and Sondra (a theatrical producer; maiden name, Alosoroff) Holtzmann; married Daniel Jerome Kevles (a historian), May 18, 1961; children: Beth, Jonathan. *Education:* Vassar College, B.A., 1959; Columbia University, M.A., 1961. *Home:* 575 La Loma Rd., Pasadena, Calif. 91105. *Agent:* Larry Sternig Literary Agency, 742 Robertson St., Milwaukee, Wis. 53213.

CAREER: Sunbeam, Northridge, Calif., editor and writer, 1967-69; Westridge School, Pasadena, Calif., instructor in history, 1970-76. *Awards, honors:* Best older juvenile award from New York Academy of Science, 1977, for *Watching the Wild Apes.*

WRITINGS: Watching the Wild Apes, Dutton, 1976. Science fiction and spy stories represented in anthologies, including *Cassandra Rises: Science Fiction by Women,* edited by A. Lawrance, Lantern Press, in press.

WORK IN PROGRESS: Gorillas, the study of the ape in captivity, the zoo, and the laboratory, for Dutton; historical research on a nineteenth-century kidnapping.

SIDELIGHTS: Bettyann Kevles writes: "Until completing the *Wild Apes,* most of my writing has been fictional, and a lot of it was science fiction, mostly short stories. My research has proven to me that finding out what is really happening is as exciting as fantasy, and has fed my imagination so that I have more fiction planned.

"My other project at the moment is largely detective work in which I am trying to reconstruct the events of a fascinating abduction and trial in Cardiff, Wales, that happened a hundred and ten years ago. The chase is almost as thrilling as the writing, and makes life varied as well as fulfilling."

KEYSER, William R(ussell) 1916-

PERSONAL: Surname is pronounced *Ky*-ser; born April 15, 1916, in Ohio; son of Charles E. (a federal employee) and Eulalia (Trigg) Keyser; married Sarah Bradfield (a piano teacher), July 4, 1941; children: Kit K. Harper (deceased), C. Keith, Kent T. *Education:* Marietta College, A.B., 1938. *Religion:* None. *Home and office address:* Millis Rd., Stanfordville, N.Y. 12581.

CAREER: U.S. Army Air Forces, navigator, 1941-47; served in European and Pacific theaters. U.S. Air Force, 1947-56, assistant air attache in Tehran, 1951-54, leaving service as major; English teacher in Key West, Fla., 1955-56; publisher's representative for New York State, 1957—. Director of Book Club and Chautauqua Literary and Scientific Circle, Chautauqua Institution, 1962-66. Publisher of art prints, 1976-77. *Awards, honors*—Military: Air Medal with cluster.

WRITINGS: A Short History and Book List, Chautauqua Literary and Scientific Circle, Chautauqua Institution, 1964; *Days of the Week,* Harvey House, 1976; *The Creation: Wood Engravings by Howard Simon,* Endymion Press, 1976.

WORK IN PROGRESS: Jason and the Argonauts; Science Fiction Monster Book; research on Babylonian, Greek, and Norse mythology.

SIDELIGHTS: Keyser comments: "I am striving to bring the myths to a younger audience and to awaken a new interest in mythology and the classics. My motivation has been travel throughout the Middle East and Asia as well as a life-long interest in etymology and mythology."

* * *

KHALATBARI, Adel-Sultan 1901(?)-1977

1901(?)—March 25, 1977; Iranian scholar, journalist and poet. He began publishing a daily paper, *Ayandeh Iran* ("The Future of Iran"), during the 1930's, and later the *Iranian Ladies Journal.* He died in Teheran, Iran. Obituaries: *Washington Post,* April 2, 1977.

* * *

KIDO, Koichi 1890(?)-1977

1890(?)—April 6, 1977; Japanese diarist and one of Emperor Hirohito's closest advisers during World War II. He was arrested as a suspected war criminal by Allied forces and sentenced to life imprisonment in 1948. His exhaustive diary, which spanned from 1930 to 1945, was used as evidence by both the prosecution and defense in postwar trials of Japanese leaders. He was released from prison in 1955. He died in Tokyo, Japan. Obituaries: *Washington Post,* April 7, 1977.

* * *

KIEFER, Irene 1926-

PERSONAL: Born November 1, 1926, in Red Lodge, Mont.; daughter of John (a grocer) and Madalene (Giachino) Giovanini; married David Kiefer (a scientific journalist), April 9, 1955; children: Timothy, Katherine. *Education:* Montana State University, B.S. (honors), 1948. *Home:* 6917 Ayr Lane, Bethesda, Md. 20034.

CAREER: DuPont Co., chemist in Waynesboro, Va., 1948-50, and Wilmington, Del., 1950-51; *Chemical Engineering News,* Washington, D.C., assistant editor, 1952-57; free-lance writer, 1964—. Editorial consultant to National Science Foundation and Energy Research and Development Administration.

WRITINGS: Underground Furnaces (juvenile), Morrow, 1976. Author of public information booklets for U.S. Environmental Protection Agency. Contributor to magazines, including *Smithsonian, Washingtonian, Maryland, Travel, Mosaic,* and to local newspapers.

WORK IN PROGRESS: Research on plate tectonics, nuclear safety, and energy sources of the future.

SIDELIGHTS: Irene Kiefer writes: "Modern society is becoming increasingly specialized, making it imperative that specialists know how to communicate outside their own narrow fields. This is especially true in science, where public funds are frequently involved. If science is to continue to receive public support, it must be presented in a form the layman can understand. This is the reason behind my writing efforts."

* * *

KILPATRICK, Carroll 1913-

PERSONAL: Born September 2, 1913, in Montgomery, Ala.; son of Andrew Carroll (a dentist) and Mary (Anderson) Kilpatrick; married Frances Talbot Williams, March 6, 1941; children: Andrew Carroll, Frank Williams. *Education:* University of Alabama, A.B., 1935; Harvard University, graduate study, 1939-40. *Home address:* R.D.1, Warfordsburg, Pa. 17267.

CAREER: Birmingham News & Age-Herald, Birmingham, Ala., reporter and editorial writer, 1935-37, on assignment in Europe, 1937; *Montgomery Advertiser,* Montgomery, Ala., associate editor, 1937-39; *Birmingham News & Age-Herald,* Washington correspondent, 1939-43; *Chicago Sun,* Chicago, Ill., Washington correspondent, 1943-46; *San Francisco Chronicle,* San Francisco, Calif., Washington correspondent, 1946-51; *Washington Post,* Washington, D.C., staff writer, 1952-75, White House correspondent, 1961-75; free-lance writer, 1975—. National affairs writer for *Newsweek,* 1940; Washington correspondent for *Raleigh News & Observer* and *Yorkshire Post,* 1940-43; assistant chief of U.S. State Department press section, 1951-52.

MEMBER: State Department Correspondents Association (past president), White House Correspondents Association (president, 1968-69), Overseas Writers Association (president, 1967), Phi Delta Theta, Omicron Delta Kappa, Cosmos Club, Gridiron Club, Federal City Club. *Awards, honors:* Merriman Smith Award from White House Correspondents' Association, 1971, for best White House correspondence; Woodrow Wilson national fellow, 1974.

WRITINGS: (Editor) *Roosevelt and Daniels: A Friendship in Politics,* University of North Carolina Press, 1952; (editor with L. Tanzer) *The Kennedy Circle,* Luce, 1961. Contributor to popular magazines, including *Harper's, New Republic, Atlantic Monthly, Nation's Business,* and *Virginia Quarterly Review.*

SIDELIGHTS: Kilpatrick comments that he covered "most of the overseas trips of Presidents Kennedy, Johnson, Nixon, and Ford, to September, 1975. I have traveled widely overseas and at home on assignment for the *Washington Post.* I continue to write occasional articles for *Washington Post* and other publications."

* * *

KIMBALL, Dean 1912-

PERSONAL: Born April 26, 1912, in Smith Center, Kan.;

son of Edgar L. (a farmer) and Cassie R. (Hicks) Kimball; married Frances L. Michael (a writer), December 23, 1932; children: William, Charles, Jean, Bonnie (Mrs. Robert Johnson). *Education:* York College (now Westmar College), A.B., 1935; attended University of Cincinnati and Ohio State University. *Politics:* Independent ("usually vote Democratic"). *Home and office:* 2420 State Route 343, Yellow Springs, Ohio 45387.

CAREER: Electrical and mechanical designer for Lear, Inc., 1941-45, and F. J. Hooven, 1945-49; sales engineer for Stotts-Friedman Co., 1949-51; registered professional engineer in Ohio, 1950—; self-employed consulting engineer, 1951-53; Antioch College, Yellow Springs, Ohio, assistant professor, 1953-59, associate professor, 1959-63, professor of electrical engineering, 1963-73, professor emeritus, 1973—; self-employed consulting engineer in Ohio, 1973—. National Science Foundation summer instructor at University of Illinois, 1966-72. Field service engineer on leave from Antioch College for General Electric Co. in Germany, 1962-64. *Member:* Institute of Electrical and Electronic Engineers (senior member), American Radio Relay League, Dayton Engineers' Club.

WRITINGS: Constructing the Mountain Dulcimer (self-illustrated), McKay, 1975.

SIDELIGHTS: Kimball writes: "I have long been interested in crafts and music. After studying violin making with the famous researcher, Carleen Hutchins, I introduced a class in stringed instrument construction at Antioch College, with chief emphasis on mountain dulcimer construction. This led to a book on that subject."

AVOCATIONAL INTERESTS: Music, photography, amateur radio, all kinds of crafts, travel (Europe, Great Britain, Mexico).

*   *   *

KIMMICH, Christoph M(artin)   1939-

PERSONAL: Born January 16, 1939, in Germany; came to the United States in 1951, naturalized citizen, 1958; son of Emil (a teacher) and Dora (a teacher; maiden name, Dreher) Kimmich; married Flora Graham Horne (a professor of German), July, 1965. *Education:* Haverford College, B.A., 1961; Oxford University, D.Phil., 1964. *Office:* Department of History, Brooklyn College of the City University of New York, Brooklyn, N.Y. 11210.

CAREER: Earlham College, Richmond, Ind., assistant professor of history, 1964-65; Columbia University, New York, N.Y., assistant professor, 1965-69, associate professor of history, 1969-73; Brooklyn College of the City University of New York, Brooklyn, N.Y., associate professor of history, 1973—. *Member:* American Historical Association. *Awards, honors:* Woodrow Wilson fellowship, 1961-62; Fulbright scholarship, 1961-63; international affairs fellowship from Council on Foreign Relations, 1974-75.

WRITINGS: (Co-editor) *Akten zur deutschen auswaertigen politik* (title means "Documents on German Foreign Policy"), Series B, Vandenhoeck & Ruprecht, Volume I, 1966, Volume II, 1967; *The Free City: Danzig and German Foreign Policy, 1919-1934,* Yale University Press, 1968; (contributor) *Foreign Affairs Fifty-Year Bibliography,* Bowker, 1972; *Germany and the League of Nations,* University of Chicago Press, 1976. Contributor to professional journals.

WORK IN PROGRESS: A study of the conception, formulation, and execution of West Germany's new Ostpolitik.

KING, C(lyde) Richard   1924-

PERSONAL: Born January 14, 1924, in Gorman, Tex.; son of Clyde Stewart and Alice (Neill) King. *Education:* John Tarleton College, A.S., 1941; University of Oklahoma, B.A., 1948, M.A., 1949; Baylor University, Ph.D., 1962. *Religion:* Methodist. *Home:* 830 Alexander Rd., Stephenville, Tex. 76401. *Office:* Department of Journalism, University of Texas, Austin, Tex. 78712.

CAREER: Mary Hardin-Baylor College, Belton, Tex., instructor in journalism and director of news service, 1949; John Tarleton College, Stephenville, Tex., instructor in English, 1950; East Texas State University, Commerce, instructor in journalism and director of news service, 1950-55; University of Texas, Austin, assistant professor, 1956-63, associate professor, 1963-70, professor of journalism, 1970—. News and feature editor for *Stephenville Empire-Tribune;* former business manager of "Journalism Monographs," for Association for Education in Journalism. President of board of directors of Stephenville Historical House Museum. *Military service:* U.S. Army, 1943-46; served in European theater; received four Bronze Stars. *Member:* International Association of Business Communicators, Texas State Historical Association, West Texas Historical Association, Sigma Delta Chi.

WRITINGS: Ghost Towns of Texas, Naylor, 1953; *Manana with Memories,* Von Boeckman-Jones, 1964; *Wagons East,* Department of Journalism, University of Texas, 1965; *Watchmen on the Walls,* Department of Journalism, University of Texas, 1967; *Letters from Fort Sill, 1886-1887,* Encino Press, 1971; *Victorian Lady on the Texas Frontier,* University of Oklahoma Press, 1972; *Susanna Dickinson: Messenger of the Alamo,* Shoal Creek Publications, 1976. Author of "Northside Kitchen," a column in *Northside News,* 1966—. Contributor to magazines and newspapers.

WORK IN PROGRESS: A biography of Angelina Peyton; a history of the theater in Texas; a biography of James Clinton Neill of the Alamo; a revision of *Ghost Towns of Texas.*

SIDELIGHTS: King writes: "My interest in Texas also takes the form of collecting Texana: books, papers, artifacts. I'm also interested in the genealogy of the Neill, Honea, Stewart, Bailey, and King families."

*   *   *

KING, Stella

PERSONAL: Born in Birmingham, England; married Robert Glenton (a writer). *Education:* Attended Southern College of Art, Bournemouth, England, received Industrial Design Certificate. *Home:* Morar Cottage, Ridge Lane, Watford, Hertfordshire, England.

CAREER: Biographer. Former columnist and feature writer for *Evening Standard* and *Sunday Express,* both London. Free-lance illustrator. *Member:* Society of Authors (Britain), Gray's Inn.

WRITINGS: (With husband, Robert Glenton) *Once Upon a Time* (biography of Antony Armstrong-Jones) Blond, 1960; *Princess Marina: Her Life and Times,* Cassell (London), 1969, London House & Maxwell (New York), 1970. Contributor to *Reader's Digest, London Times, New York Times,* and other international magazines.

WORK IN PROGRESS: A biography of Yvonne Rudellat, secret agent, completion expected, 1978.

SIDELIGHTS: Stella King told *CA* that she is motivated by curiosity and is particularly interested in writing about subjects of recent history "when both archives and survivors can be consulted." *Avocational interests:* Travel (Europe and the Middle East), heraldry, law, and fly-fishing.

* * *

KINGSLAND, Leslie William 1912-

PERSONAL: Born January 21, 1912, in London, England; son of William Browning (a railway clerk) and Elizabeth (Regester) Kingsland; married Millie Weller (a teacher), April 14, 1934; children: Peter William. *Education:* University College, London, B.A. (first class honors), 1933. *Politics:* "I find none to admire." *Home:* 91 Abbey Rd., Grimsby, South Humberside, England.

CAREER: Head of English department in grammar schools in England, 1933-53; headmaster of school in Grimsby, England, 1953-73. Translator, 1950—. Examiner for the Civil Service Commission. *Military service:* Royal Air Force, became flight lieutenant.

WRITINGS—Translator: (From the Danish) Hans Christian Andersen, *Hans Andersen's Fairy Tales*, Oxford University Press, 1959; (from the Danish) Hans Christian Andersen, *Hans Andersen's Fairy Tales* (different collection of stories from above), Oxford University Press, 1961; (from the Danish) Poul E. Knudsen, *The Challenge*, Methuen, 1962, Macmillan, 1963; (from the Danish) Anne Holm, *North to Freedom*, Harcourt, 1965 (published in England as *I Am David*, Methuen, 1965); (from the Norwegian) Reidar Brodtkorb, *The Gold Coin*, Harcourt, 1966; (from the Danish) Anne Holm, *Peter*, Harcourt, 1968; (from the Swedish) Harry Kullman, *Under Secret Orders*, Harcourt, 1968.

WORK IN PROGRESS: Translations of the Lord's Prayer into Germanic languages.

SIDELIGHTS: Kingsland told *CA* that his career as a translator began indirectly in 1950, when he spent a year teaching English in Denmark. "At the end of that time I could speak Danish well enough to get about, and when, some years later after I had returned home, I complained that many of the current translations of Hans Andersen were rather poorly done, I accepted the challenge to have a go myself. Thereafter I was for some years in demand as a reader of children's books in the Scandinavian languages, and whenever I was asked to translate a book, I did so, on the principle that since good dictionaries are available, it is much more important to be able to write, clearly and correctly, one's own language than to have complete mastery of the original. It was my endeavour to make every sentence I wrote easy to read aloud, so that it would come trippingly off the tongue, and as for the matter, if I liked it, I would translate it. Had it not been fit for a child to read, I should not have liked it."

Kingsland added: "I've no tear-stained childhood or pious platitudes to offer. I've done a little painting and a bit of acting and won one or two trophies as an amateur producer. I grow all my own vegetables, make my own wine and can turn my hand to a bit of carpentry, brick-laying, plastering, painting (decorating this time), and papering. I read and speak French and Danish fairly fluently, have rather more trouble reading Norwegian, Swedish, Old English, Latin and Gothic, have some knowledge of Icelandic and a smattering of Greek, Russian, Serbo-Croat, and Sanskrit, besides half a dozen words in German, Italian, and Spanish. Or, if you like, I find comparative philology quite fascinating and can contemplate with great satisfaction a Greek or Sanskrit verb in all its majesty of tense and mood."

KINGSTON, Maxine Hong 1940-

PERSONAL: Born October 27, 1940, in Stockton, Calif.; daughter of Tom (a laundryman) and Ying Lan (a laundress and midwife; maiden name, Chew) Hong; married Earll Kingston (an actor), November 23, 1962; children: Joseph Lawrence Chung Mei. *Education:* University of California, Berkeley, A.B., 1962, graduate study, 1964-65. *Residence:* Honolulu, Hawaii. *Agent:* John Schaffner Literary Agency, 425 East 51st St., New York, N.Y. 10022.

CAREER: High school teacher of English and mathematics in Hayward, Calif., 1965-67, and of English in Kahuku, Hawaii, 1967; Kahaluu Drop-In School, Kahaluu, Hawaii, teacher, 1968; Honolulu Business College, Honolulu, Hawaii, teacher of English as a second language, 1969; high school teacher of language arts in Kailua, Hawaii, 1969; Mid-Pacific Institute, Honolulu, teacher of language arts, 1970-77; University of Hawaii, Honolulu, visiting associate professor of English, 1977—. *Awards, honors:* General nonfiction award from National Book Critics Circle, 1976, for *The Woman Warrior.*

WRITINGS: (Contributor) Jerry Walker, editor, *Your Reading*, National Council of English Teachers, 1975; *The Woman Warrior: Memoirs of a Girlhood among Ghosts*, Knopf, 1976. Contributor of stories and articles to magazines, including *American Girl, English Journal, Viva, New West, New Dawn, American Heritage,* and *Washington Post.*

WORK IN PROGRESS: A companion book to the stories in *The Woman Warrior;* a new novel on Chinese-American heroes.

SIDELIGHTS: Maxine Kingston writes briefly: "I have no idea how people who don't write endure their lives."

* * *

KINNEAVY, James Louis 1920-

PERSONAL: Born June 26, 1920, in Denver, Colo.; son of James (a florist) and Teresa (Peila) Kinneavy; married Floria Mitchell, February 17, 1961; children: Janice Lynn, Kathleen Diane. *Education:* College of Santa Fe, B.A., 1942; Catholic University of America, M.A., 1951, Ph.D., 1956. *Home:* 6929 Scenic Brook Dr., Austin, Tex. 78736. *Office:* Department of English, University of Texas, Austin, Tex. 78712.

CAREER: High school English teacher in New Orleans, La., 1953-55; College of Santa Fe, Santa Fe, N.M., teacher of English, chairman of department and dean of students, 1955-57; Western State College of Colorado, Gunnison, assistant professor of English, 1957-63; University of Texas, Austin, associate professor, 1963-71, professor of English, 1971—, director of English Education Center, 1963—.

MEMBER: Modern Language Association of America, Conference on College Composition and Communication, National Council of Teachers of English, Rhetoric Society of America, South Central Modern Language Association, Rocky Mountain Modern Language Association.

WRITINGS: A Study of Three Contemporary Theories of Lyric Poetry, Catholic University of America Press, 1956; (contributor) Thomas D. Horn, editor, *Foreign Language Teaching: An Anthology*, Macmillan, 1967; *A Theory of Discourse*, Prentice-Hall, 1971; (with J. Q. Cope and J. W. Campbell) *Aims and Audiences in Writing*, Kendall-Hunt, 1976; (with Cope and Campbell) *Writing: Basic Modes of Organization*, Kendall-Hunt, 1976.

WORK IN PROGRESS: A book on the modes of discourse; research toward applying notions of hermeneutic literature interpretation to the writing process.

SIDELIGHTS: Kinneavy writes: "In my academic career I have always systematically attempted to break down the barriers between artificial components of knowledge.... I have attempted to bring together in my own work interests in English, philosophy, education, and politics." *Avocational interests:* Snowskiing, boating, gardening.

BIOGRAPHICAL/CRITICAL SOURCES: Ohio English Bulletin, May, 1972; *Louisiana English Journal,* February, 1972; *Arizona English Bulletin,* April, 1973.

* * *

KINSEL, Paschal 1895(?)-1976

1895(?)—November 1, 1976; American Franciscan priest, editor, and author. He was director of the Franciscan Monastery in Washington, D.C., from 1950 until 1962. He died in Washington, D.C. Obituaries: *Washington Post,* November 4, 1976.

* * *

KIRK, Clara M(arburg) 1898-1976

May 10, 1898—October 2, 1976; American educator, authority on American novelist William Dean Howells, and author of books on Howells and on other aspects of her field. She died in Austin, Tex. Obituaries: *New York Times,* October 3, 1976. (*CAP*-1; eariler sketch in *CA*-17/18)

* * *

KISH, Kathleen Vera 1942-

PERSONAL: Born June 21, 1942, in Trenton, N.J.; daughter of Stephen E. (an engineer) and Veronica J. (Lupsa) Kish. *Education:* University of California, Berkeley, B.A., 1964; University of Wisconsin, Madison, M.A., 1965, Ph.D., 1971. *Home:* 606-H South Chapman St., Greensboro, N.C. 27403. *Office:* Department of Romance Languages, University of North Carolina, Greensboro, N.C. 27412.

CAREER: University of North Carolina, Greensboro, lecturer, 1969-71, assistant professor, 1971-76, associate professor of Spanish, 1976—. *Member:* Member of American Hungarian Foundation, International Courtly Literature Society, Modern Language Association of America, Hispanic Society of America (corresponding member), Asociacion Internacional de Hispanistas, American Society for Eighteenth Century Studies, American Hungarian Educators Association, South Atlantic Modern Language Association (chairman of Spanish section, 1976), University of California Alumni Association, Phi Beta Kappa, Alpha Mu Gamma, Sigma Delta Pi. *Awards, honors:* Fulbright fellowship, Madrid, 1966-67.

WRITINGS: An Edition of the First Italian Translation of the "Celestina", University of North Carolina Press, 1973. Contributor to language, literature, and Spanish studies journals. Editorial assistant for *Romance Philology,* 1964.

WORK IN PROGRESS: Studying translations and stage adaptations of *La Celestina;* research on the Spanish ballad tradition, parallelism in medieval verse, and eighteenth-century Spanish poetry.

SIDELIGHTS: Kathleen Kish writes: "Currently, my motivation springs from within, although my students provide important positive reinforcement. Fellowships and research grants are equally significant; without them day-to-day duties can stifle research and writing." She has studied Spanish, French, Italian, German, Latin, Russian, Arabic, and Portuguese, and has traveled in Spain, the rest of Europe, Tunisia, Venezuela, and South Africa.

* * *

KLAUCK, Daniel L. 1947-

PERSONAL: Born October 16, 1947; son of John (a superintendent of public works) and Patricia (Kelly) Klauck; married JoAnne Rosenfeld, March 7, 1968 (divorced); children: James (deceased). *Education:* Community College of Allegheny County, A.S., 1975; University of Pittsburgh, student, 1975—. *Politics:* "Outlaw, degenerate, and undesirable." *Religion:* "Heathen." *Home:* Western Penitentiary, P.O. Box 9901, Pittsburgh, Pa. 15223. *Agent:* Donna Tabor, 120 Persian Drive, Oakdale, Pa. 15701. *Office:* King Publications, P.O. Box 19332, Washington, D.C. 20036.

CAREER: Worked as a draftsman, dishwasher, aluminum sider, salesman, bookie, burglar, drug pusher and conspirator; currently serving an 11 to 22 year sentence at Western Penitentiary, Pittsburgh, Pa., 1969—. *Military service:* U.S. Marine Corps; received bad conduct discharge, 1969. *Member:* Academy of Prison Arts (president, 1975-76).

WRITINGS: (Co-editor) *Captive Voices* (anthology), Quixote, 1974; *Everything Else* (poems), King Publications, 1976. Editor of *Vibrations* (a prison newspaper). Contributor of poems to *Stonecloud, Quixote, Manroot, Nausea, Happiness Holding Tank, The New Infinity Review, Wisconsin Review,* and other periodicals.

WORK IN PROGRESS: A book of long poems, *Midnight Station,* scheduled for publication by Quixote in 1977.

SIDELIGHTS: "My personal interests," Klauck told *CA,* "are women, dope, tequila. Nothing much special about my life. Been in jail the last 7 years with 4 to go. Avocation: hating police, judges, district attorneys, informers, and feminists."

* * *

KLEIN, Edward 1936-

PERSONAL: Born October 19, 1936, in Yonkers, N.Y.; son of Meyer (a merchant) and Gertrude (a merchant; maiden name, Axelrod) Klein; married Emiko Oshikiri, June 25, 1963 (divorced, May, 1975); children: Karen, Alec. *Education:* Columbia University, B.S., 1960, M.S., 1961. *Office: New York Times Magazine,* 229 W. 43rd St., New York, N.Y. 10036.

CAREER: New York News, New York City, copyperson, 1957-60; *New York World-Telegram & Sun,* New York City, reporter, 1960; *Japan Times,* Tokyo, reporter and editor, 1961-62; United Press International (UPI), Tokyo, correspondent, 1962; *Tokyo Shipping & Trade News,* Tokyo, author of column, "Green Eyed in Ginza," 1963-64; *Newsweek,* New York City, associate editor, 1965-69, senior editor for international department, 1969-75; assistant managing editor, 1975-77; *New York Times Magazine,* New York City, editor, 1977—. Notable assignments include coverage of President Sadat of Egypt, Golda Meir and Yitzhak Rabin in Israel, Indira Gandhi, Chou En-lai, and other political leaders in Europe, the Soviet Union, and Japan. *Member:* Council on Foreign Relations. *Awards, honors:* Columbia University traveling fellowship to Japan, 1961.

WRITINGS: (With Robert Littell and Richard Chesnoff) *If Israel Lost the War* (novel), Coward, 1969.

WORK IN PROGRESS: The Parachutists, a novel.

* * *

KLEIN, Walter J(ulian) 1923-

PERSONAL: Born October 25, 1923, in Newark, N.J.; son of Jacob (a butcher) and Pauline (a teacher; maiden name, Stein) Klein; married Elizabeth Goodman, June 17, 1945; children: Richard, Robert, Kathy, Betsy. *Education:* Attended University of North Carolina. *Politics:* "Active Democrat." *Religion:* Reform Jewish. *Home:* 201 Lancelot Dr., Matthews, N.C. 28105. *Office:* Walter J. Klein Co., 6301 Carmel Rd., Charlotte, N.C. 28211.

CAREER: Walter J. Klein Co.; Charlotte, N.C., president, 1948—. President, Temple Beth El, 1960-61; president, Charlotte Biblical Garden, 1966-67, founder and president, International Quorum of Motion Picture Producers, 1966-68; president, Congregation Beth Shalom, 1970-72; vice president, Union of American Hebrew Congregations Mid-Atlantic Union, 1974-77; president, Charlotte Lodge B'nai B'rith, 1975. *Military service:* U.S. Air Force, 1942-46; became staff sergeant. *Member:* National Conference of Christians and Jews (member of boards of trustees and board of governors), Society of Motion Picture and Television Engineers, Information Film Producers of America, American Film Institute, International Quorum of Motion Picture Producers.

WRITINGS: The Sponsored Film, Hastings House, 1976. Also author of 100 sponsored motion picture scripts. Contributor to *American Cinematographer, New Age, Redbook, Saturday Review,* and other periodicals.

WORK IN PROGRESS: Trade articles.

SIDELIGHTS: Klein told *CA:* "It's delightful agony, this business of creating films that are selfishly sponsored by industry or government or organizations but that contain powerful educational and motivational values for the public good. Writing them and writing about them make for lively guilt-pride conflict."

AVOCATIONAL INTERESTS: Chess, Bible, plants, architecture, music, fishing, automobile competition.

* * *

KNIGHT, Stephen 1951-

PERSONAL: Born September 26, 1951, in Hainault, Essex, England; son of Victor Wilfred (a leather case maker) and Elsie (Hall) Knight; married Margot Kenrick (an actress), September 29, 1973; children: Natasha Estelle Argy and Nicole Felicia Argy (stepdaughters), Nanouska Maria. *Education:* Attended high school in Chigwell, England. *Politics:* "My own peculiar brand of love-based socialism." *Religion:* "A reluctant agnostic, but open. I am unconvinced by all established religions." *Home:* 10 Queenborough Gardens, Gants Hill, Ilford, Essex, England. *Agent:* Andrew Hewson, John Johnson Associates, 51-54 Goschen Buildings, 12-13 Henrietta St., London WC2E 8LF, England.

CAREER: London Electricity Board, Ilford, England, showroom salesman, 1968-69; *Ilford Pictorial* (newspaper), Ilford, junior reporter, 1969-70; *Ilford Recorder* (newspaper), Ilford, junior reporter, 1970; *Hornchurch Echo,* Hornchurch, junior reporter, 1970-72, chief reporter and drama critic, 1972-73; *East London Advertiser,* London, England, reporter, 1973; *Ilford Recorder,* reporter, 1973-74, chief reporter, 1974, feature writer, 1974-75, deputy news editor, 1975; *Travel Trade Gazette,* London, England, feature writer, 1975-76; full-time writer, 1976—. *Member:* National Union of Journalists, Society of Authors, Shakespeare-Oxford Society.

WRITINGS: Jack the Ripper: The Final Solution, McKay, 1976. Drama critic, *Plays and Players,* 1973—.

WORK IN PROGRESS: A novel, *The Grand Inquisitor;* "researching first fully factual book in seventy years on the murder of Sir Edmund Berry Godfrey in London in 1678, due to be published by Harrap on the 300th anniversary of the murder, and researching the first-ever book on the unsolved Luard murder case (1908, Kent)."

SIDELIGHTS: Knight told *CA:* "I find many of the basic values of our society quite alien. My most passionate belief, I suppose, is that people are not property. I have no wish to *own* anyone—not my wife, not my children. For me to love them I must want what is essential for their own ideal existence. By staking a claim on any aspect of my wife's being I am diminishing her, and hence my love for her is diminished. I believe no one in the world has any rights over any other person. A man does not have the 'right' to sleep with his wife just because he is married to her, whatever the law of state or church says.

"So long as there is enough to pay the bills money does not concern me. I am appalled by the self destruction I see every day perpetrated in a seemingly indiscriminate chase after wealth.

"I believe love is the most important thing in the world, and that in general the churches of the world have too little of it.

"I hate the exploitation of animals. I believe every living creature—insects and fish just as much as cattle and sheep—have a right to a place on this earth. I kill nothing. I do not eat meat.

"I am opposed to the monstrously unfair distribution of the world's natural resources.

"I am in favour of each of us being exactly what she or he wants providing it harms or interferes with no one else. I am a strong supporter of Women's Lib, the Campaign for Homosexual Equality etc. etc. and a hater of moral judgments.

"This is a quick and random rundown of my thoughts at this time. It is in no particular order and impossibly condensed."

AVOCATIONAL INTERESTS: Theatre ("I am passionately interested in the theatre and have acted in London's fringe theatres along with my wife, whom I met nine years ago in the theatre").

* * *

KNOTTS, Howard (Clayton, Jr.) 1922-

PERSONAL: Born October 13, 1922, in Springfield, Ill.; son of Howard Clayton (a lawyer) and Charlotte (Sterling) Knotts; married Ilse-Margret Vogel (a writer and artist), June 1, 1959. *Education:* Knox College, student, 1940-43; Art Institute of Chicago, B.F.A. (honors), 1949. *Home and office address:* Duell Rd., Bangall, N.Y. 12506.

CAREER: Artist and writer. Paintings exhibited in major museums across the United States, and are in collections at Phillips Gallery and Joseph Hirshhorn Museum (both Washington, D.C.) and University Museum (Berkeley, Calif.). *Military service:* U.S. Army Air Forces, 1946-49. *Awards, honors: The Winter Cat* was named best juvenile book of the year by Friends of American Writers, 1972.

WRITINGS—Self-illustrated juveniles: *The Winter Cat,* Harper, 1972; *Follow the Brook,* Harper, 1975; *The Lost Christmas,* Harcourt, in press.

Illustrator: Willis Barnstone, *A Day in the Country,* Harper, 1971; May Sarton, *Punch's Secret,* Harper, 1974; Charlotte Zolotow, *When the Wind Stops,* Harper, 1975; Eve Bunting, *Winter's Coming,* Harcourt, 1977.

WORK IN PROGRESS: Writing and illustrating *Great-Grandfather, the Baby, and Me,* publication by Harcourt expected in 1978; illustrating *Wings,* by wife, Ilse-Margret Vogel, Harper, 1978.

SIDELIGHTS: Knotts comments briefly: "I am an artist (painter) who gradually became an author-illustrator of children's books because of my wife's activity in this field and because of an apparently natural enthusiasm and affinity for the genre."

*   *   *

KOBAYASHI, Tetsuya   1926-

PERSONAL: Born December 22, 1926, in Matsumoto, Japan; son of Takehiko (a physician) and Chiyoko (Akahori) Kobayashi; married Itsuko Nagaoka (a professor of music education), April 29, 1955; children: Chiaki. *Education:* University of Tokyo, B.A., 1953; University of Reading, M.A., 1957; University of Michigan, Ph.D., 1965. *Home:* Famille Fushimi, #A302, Dewayashiki-cho, Fushimi-ku, Kyoto, Japan 612. *Office:* Faculty of Education, Kyoto University, Yoshida-honcho, Sakyo-ku, Kyoto, Japan 606.

CAREER: Elementary school teacher, 1945; member of research staff at Noma Institute for Educational Research, 1953-55; International Christian University, Tokyo, Japan, assistant, 1958-59, instructor, 1959-61, assistant professor, 1961-65, associate professor, 1965-68; UNESCO Institute of Education, Hamburg, Germany, director, 1968-72; Kyoto University, Kyoto, Japan, associate professor, 1972-74, professor of comparative education, 1974—. *Member:* Japanese Society for the Study of Education, Japanese Comparative Education Society, Comparative and International Education Society.

WRITINGS: General Education for Scientists and Engineers in the United States of America and Japan, University of Michigan, 1965; *Society, Schools and Progress in Japan,* Pergamon, 1976.

WORK IN PROGRESS: Overseas Japanese and Education of Their Children.

*   *   *

KOCH, Eric   1919-

PERSONAL: Born August 31, 1919, in Frankfurt, Germany; son of Otto (a jeweller) and Ida (Kahn) Koch; married Sonia Mecklenburg, May 11, 1948; children: Tony, Monica, Madeline. *Education:* Cambridge University, B.A., 1940; University of Toronto, LL.B., 1943. *Home:* 74 Highbourne Rd., Toronto, Ontario, Canada. *Office:* Canadian Broadcasting Corp., 354 Jarvis St., Toronto, Ontario, Canada.

CAREER: Appleby College, Oakville, Ontario, teacher, 1943-44; Canadian Broadcasting Corporation (CBC), Montreal, Quebec, head of German section, 1944-53, program organizer for public affairs, 1953-60, television producer and executive producer, 1960-68, head of television arts and science programs, 1968-71, regional director for Quebec, 1971-77, associate general supervisor of policy, 1977—.

WRITINGS: The French Kiss (novel), McClelland & Stewart, 1969; *The Leisure Riots* (novel), Tundra Books, 1973; *The Last Thing You'd Want to Know* (novel), Tundra Books, 1975.

WORK IN PROGRESS: A thriller.

KOCH, Joanne   1940-

PERSONAL: Born March 28, 1940, in Chicago, Ill.; daughter of Isadore (a pediatrician) and Ceil (Eidelsheim) Schapiro; married Lewis Koch (a writer), May 30, 1964; children: Lisa, Rachel, Joshua. *Education:* Cornell University, B.A. (with honors), 1961; Columbia University, M.A., 1962. *Religion:* Jewish. *Home:* 343 Dodge, Evanston, Ill. 60202. *Agent:* Timothy Seldes, Russell & Volkening, 551 Fifth Ave., New York, N.Y. 10017.

CAREER: Roosevelt University, Chicago, Ill., director of educational information, 1964-65; Educational Methods, Inc., Chicago, director of advertising, 1966-69; Newspaper Enterprise Association, New York, N.Y., columnist, 1972-76. *Member:* Society of Midland Authors, American Society of Journalists and Authors, Phi Beta Kappa, Phi Kappa Phi. *Awards, honors:* Barnes Shakespeare Prize, 1961; Forbes-Heerman Playwriting award, 1961; Family Service Association Media award, 1973, for "Family Lib."

WRITINGS: (With Lewis Koch) *The Marriage Savers,* Coward, 1976. Co-writer of "Family Lib" column, 1972-74, and "Coping" column, 1974-76. Contributing editor, *Chicago,* 1974—. Contributor of articles to *Psychology Today.*

WORK IN PROGRESS: A Consumers Guide to Sex Therapy, with Lewis Koch; "Teeth," a comedy in two acts.

SIDELIGHTS: Koch told *CA:* "Lewis and I find that married couples and families in this country feel beleaguered and isolated. We hope to provide them with information which will help them find the type of support and guidance they are seeking. Although we are not opposed to divorce, we tend to focus on alternatives to self-actualization which strengthen marriages and families. We believe a consumerist attitude towards married counseling and sex therapy will yield more satisfied customers and fewer heartaches."

*   *   *

KOCH, Lew(is) Z.   1935-

PERSONAL: Born August 11, 1935, in Chicago, Ill.; son of Sidney (a real estate agent) and Blanche (Landis) Koch; married Joanne Schapiro (a writer), May 30, 1964; children: Lisa, Rachel, Joshua. *Education:* Attended Drake University, 1957-59. *Religion:* Jewish. *Home:* 343 Dodge, Evanston, Ill. 60202. *Agent:* Timothy Seldes, Russel & Volkening, 551 Fifth Ave., New York, N.Y. 10017.

CAREER: City News Bureau, Chicago, Ill., reporter, 1960-61; Columbia Broadcasting System (CBS), Chicago, writer and producer, 1961-66; National Broadcasting Co. (NBC), Chicago, writer and producer, 1967-73; Newspaper Enterprise Association, New York, N.Y., columnist, 1972—. Coordinator, Urban Journalism Fellowship Program, University of Chicago, 1971-73. *Member:* Society of Midland Authors, American Society of Journalists and Authors. *Awards, honors:* Jacob Scher-Theta Sigma Phi Award, 1968 and 1969, for investigative reporting and community service.

WRITINGS: (With Joanne Koch) *The Marriage Savers,* Coward, 1976. Co-writer of "Family Lib" column, 1972-73, and "Coping" column, 1973—. Also author of documentary films, including "Forget Me . . . Forget Me Not," for Parent's Magazine Films. Contributor to *Chicago, Chicago Tribune, Chicago Daily News, Law and Disorder, Chicago Journalism Review,* and other periodicals.

WORK IN PROGRESS: A Consumer's Guide to Sex Therapy, with Joanne Koch.

KOCH, Thomas J(ohn) 1947-

PERSONAL: Born March 19, 1947, in Grand Forks, N.D.; son of Roland O. (a Lutheran minister) and Jean (Kroschel) Koch; married Laura Coffin, August 10, 1974. *Education:* Gustavus Adolphus College, B.A., 1969. *Religion:* Lutheran. *Home:* 6212 Golden Valley Rd., Minneapolis, Minn. 55422. *Agent:* Heide Lange, Sanford J. Greenburger Asso., 757 Third Ave., New York, N.Y. 10017.

CAREER: U.S. Peace Corps volunteer in Kalibo and Aklan, the Philippines, 1970-72; writer.

WRITINGS: The Year of the Polar Bear (juvenile), Bobbs-Merrill, 1975.

* * *

KOHLER, Julilly H(ouse) 1915-1976

1915—December 24, 1976; American author of children's books, including *The Boy Who Stole the Elephant.* She died in Sheboygan, Wis. Obituaries: *New York Times,* December 28, 1976; *AB Bookman's Weekly,* February 14, 1977.

* * *

KOHLER, Saul 1928-

PERSONAL: Born October 4, 1928, in New York, N.Y.; son of Abraham (a tailor) and Nettie (Diamond) Kohler; married Virginia Baum, January 10, 1956; children: Alan, Barbara. *Education:* Brooklyn College, A.B., 1948. *Politics:* Independent. *Religion:* Jewish. *Home:* 10907 Lombardy Rd., Silver Spring, Md. 20901. *Office:* Newhouse Newspapers, Suite 1320, 1750 Pennsylvania Ave. N.W., Washington, D.C. 20006.

CAREER/WRITINGS: Philadelphia Inquirer, Philadelphia, Pa., general assignments, 1956-62, chief of Harrisburg bureau, 1962-68, chief of Washington bureau, 1968-69; press secretary for Senator Hugh Scott, United States Senate Minority Leader, 1970; Newhouse Newspapers, Washington, D.C., White House correspondent and author of "The Presidency" (weekly column), 1971—. Notable assignments include all national political conventions and presidential campaigns, 1964—, world tour with President Nixon, 1969, and overseas tour with President Ford, 1975, interviews with President Ford and members of the Cabinet. *Member:* White House Correspondents' Association (member of board of directors, 1976—), Sigma Delta Chi. *Awards, honors:* Philadelphia Press Association Best Reporting Award, 1966, for coverage of airplane crash which killed Pennsylvania Attorney General Walter E. Alessandroni.

SIDELIGHTS: Kohler told *CA:* "I love what I do to earn a living and cannot imagine any job I would rather have. I was fortunate to decide early in life what my vocation would be, even more fortunate that it turned out that way." *Avocational interests:* Politics, reading.

* * *

KOHLSTEDT, Sally Gregory 1943-

PERSONAL: Born January 30, 1943, in Ypsilanti, Mich.; daughter of Frederick W. (a sales manager) and Tula (Bitzer) Gregory; married David Lee Kohlstedt (a professor), December 27, 1966; children: Kristian Gregory. *Education:* Valparaiso University, B.A., 1965; Michigan State University, M.A., 1966; University of Illinois, Ph.D., 1972. *Home address:* R.D. 1, Cortland, N.Y. 13045. *Office:* Department of History, Syracuse University, Syracuse, N.Y. 13010.

CAREER: Simmons College, Boston, Mass., instructor, 1971-72, assistant professor of history, 1972-75; Syracuse University, Syracuse, N.Y., assistant professor, 1975-77, associate professor of history, 1977—. *Member:* American Historical Association, Organization of American Historians, History of Science Society, Society for the History of Technology, Mortar Board.

WRITINGS: The Formation of a National Scientific Community: The American Association for the Advancement of Science, 1848-1860, University of Illinois Press, 1976.

Contributor: Alexandra Oleson and Sanborn Brown, editors, *The Pursuit of Knowledge in the Early American Republic: American Scientific and Learned Societies from Colonial Times to the Civil War,* Johns Hopkins Press, 1975; Gerald Holton and William Blanpied, editors, *Science and Its Public: The Changing Relationship,* Reidel, 1976. Contributor to *Isis* and other history journals.

WORK IN PROGRESS: Research on the role of women in nineteenth-century American science and on the natural history museum movement, 1860-1920.

SIDELIGHTS: Kohlstedt told *CA:* "The history of science should be seen in the context of society and culture as well as part of the history of ideas. Social patterns, economic opportunities and institutional structures shape the nature of research endeavor and the extent to which science becomes popularly recognized. My research has to date investigated science in American culture, with attention to the positive institution building which created an outstanding scientific establishment; in addition, I am considering the results of professionalization on minorities, especially women, and on the general public involvement with scientific ideas and enterprise."

* * *

KOHN, Eugene 1887-1977

1887—April 1, 1977; American rabbi, editor, and a founder of Jewish Reconstruction Movement. Obituaries: *New York Times,* April 2, 1977.

* * *

KOJIMA Shozo 1928-
(Kijima Hajime)

PERSONAL: Born February 4, 1928, in Kyoto, Japan; son of Kojima Kanichi (a silk merchant) and Mori Owa; married Kaneko Mitsuko; children: Kiri, Eri (daughters). *Education:* University of Tokyo, B.A., 1951. *Home:* 3-8-12 Mibaradai, Nerimaku, Tokyo, Japan.

CAREER: Writer. Senshu University, Tokyo, Japan, lecturer in English, 1954; Hosei University, Tokyo, Japan, professor of English, 1963—. Member of jury of Bratislava International Biennale, 1973. *Awards, honors:* Japan Nursery Rhyme Prize, 1972, for "Mogura no Uta" (title means "Male's Song").

WRITINGS: Little White Hen: A Folk Tale (juvenile), Harcourt, 1967; (editor) *The Poetry of Post-War Japan,* University of Iowa Press, 1975; (contributor) *Writing from the World,* University of Iowa Press, 1976. Author of four picture books, five books of poems, five books of stories, four books of literary essays, an opera libretto, all in Japanese. Has also translated works of Langston Hughes, Nat Hentoff and Ezra Jack Keats into Japanese.

WORK IN PROGRESS: Hanashi ga futte kita (title means "Tales Have Fallen to Us"), a collection of twenty-seven short stories.

SIDELIGHTS: Kijima's writings have been translated into Korean, Russian, Czech, Hungarian, and Romanian.

*   *   *

KOLEVZON, Edward R.   1913(?)-1976

1913(?)—August 7, 1976; American educator and author of textbooks. He spent thirty-nine years in the New York City school system. He died in New Rochelle, N.Y. Obituaries: *New York Times,* August 9, 1976.

*   *   *

KOLTUN, Frances Lang

PERSONAL: Born in New York City; daughter of Samuel and Rebecca (Lang) Koltun. *Education:* Brooklyn College (now of the City University of New York), B.A., 1942; Columbia University, M.A., 1945. *Home and office:* 45 East 66th St., New York, N.Y. 10021.

CAREER: Worked at Abraham & Strauss, New York City, 1939-45; worked for U.S. Government in New York City, 1945-46; fashion merchandizing editor for *American Girl* magazine, 1946-50; travel and vacation editor for *Charm* magazine, 1950-59; *Mademoiselle,* New York City, travel editor, 1959-72; Air Transport Association of America, commentator on daily radio show heard on 500 stations, 1975-76; National Broadcasting Co. (NBC), New York City, travel commentator on "Today," 1977—. Appeared as week-end leisure and recreation commentator on "Monitor," 1970-74, and for WNBC-TV, 1973, both for NBC. Lecturer at New York University, 1955. Guest speaker. Member of Travel Advisory Committee of U.S. Department of Commerce: member of board of directors of Discover America Travel Organization. *Member:* International Union of Travel Organizations, Phi Beta Kappa.

WRITINGS: Frances Koltun's Complete Book for the Intelligent Woman Traveler, Simon & Schuster, 1967. Author of syndicated column, "The Woman Traveler," appearing in national newspapers, including *Christian Science Monitor, Chicago Tribune,* and *Herald Tribune,* 1961-72. Contributor to periodicals, including *Atlantic, New York, Reader's Digest, Ladies Home Journal,* and *Holiday.* Member of editorial board of East/West Network; contributing editor of *L'Officiel/ USA.*

WORK IN PROGRESS: Magazine articles; television scripts for the "Today" show.

SIDELIGHTS: Koltun has worked closely with the White House, has been the White House representative on a multi-industry committee to solve balance of payment problems, and has been a consultant on tourism matters.

*   *   *

KOLYER, John (McNaughton)   1933-

PERSONAL: Born June 30, 1933, in East Williston, N.Y.; son of John (a salesman) and Mildred (a teacher; maiden name, McNaughton) Kolyer; married in 1970, 1972, 1974 (unmarried at present); children: Scott M., Paul F., Craig D., Jeffrey J. *Education:* Hofstra College (now University), B.A., 1955; University of Pennsylvania, Ph.D., 1960. *Home:* Apt. 311, 885 Sea Gull Lane, Newport Beach, Calif. 92663.

CAREER: Olin Mathieson Chemical Corp., Port Jefferson, N.Y., technician working on pesticides, 1955-56; FMC Corp., Princeton, N.J., research chemist, 1960-62; Thompson Chemical Co., Hebronville, Mass., research

chemist, 1962-63; Allied Chemical Corp., Morristown, N.J., senior research chemist in plastics division, 1964-65, group leader, 1965-67, technical supervisor, 1962-72; Rockwell International Corp., Anaheim, Calif., member of technical staff in solar energy research, 1973—. Member of Lepidoptera Foundation, 1965—. *Member:* Poetry Society of America, American Chemical Society, Lepidoptera Society. *Awards, honors:* Poetry prizes from regional organizations.

WRITINGS—Poems; all published by Branden Press: *My Last Mistress,* 1972; *Ares and the Dove,* 1973; *Sonnets from Hell,* 1973; *Blasphemies with Paradise Judged,* 1974; *Dragon's Kisses,* 1975; *Neptune Taming a Seahorse,* 1975; *A Ballet of Brokers,* 1976; *The Garden of Mars,* 1976; *The Birds of Buna,* 1976; *The Black Calla,* 1977. Contributor to literary magazines.

WORK IN PROGRESS: Drawings and Sculpture, his own drawings, for Branden Press; *Odin's Other Eye,* a long poem, Branden Press; two more books of drawings; three more books of poems.

SIDELIGHTS: Kolyer comments: "I try to be a realist, a surgeon of the psyche, and a sometime student of hate—but the more sentimental verses appeal to my readers, both of whom live in Miami, Florida."

*   *   *

KONDRASHOV, Stanislav (Nikolaevich)   1928-

PERSONAL: Born December 25, 1928, in the Soviet Union; son of Nikolai Petrovich (an engineer) and Taisia (Mikhailovna) Kondrashov; married wife Klara, February 9, 1950; children: Natalia, Tatiana, Nikolai. *Education:* Attended Moscow's Institute of International Relations, 1946-51. *Home:* Begovaya Ulica 13, Moscow, Soviet Union. *Office: Izvestia,* Pushkinskaya Sq. 5, Moscow, Soviet Union.

CAREER: Izvestia, Moscow, Soviet Union, in foreign department, 1951-57, correspondent from Cairo, 1957-61, and New York City, 1961-68, foreign commentator, 1968-71, correspondent from Washington, D.C., 1971—. *Member:* Union of Journalists, Union of Writers. *Awards, honors:* Vorovskii Prize from Union of Journalists, 1968, for international reporting (from the United States).

WRITINGS: Na Beregakh Nila (title means "On the Banks of the Nile"), Izvestia Publishing House, 1958; *Perekresti Ameriki* (title means "American Crossroads"), Politizdat, 1969; *Zhiznj i Smertj Martina Lutera Kinga* (title means "The Life and Death of Martin Luther King"), Molodaya Gvardia, 1970; *Amerikancy v Amerike* (title means "Americans in America"), Izvestia Publishing House, 1970; *Svidanie s Kaliforniei* (title means "Rendezvous with California"), Publishing House (Moscow, Soviet Union), 1975. Contributor of articles and stories on the United States and on the Middle East to Soviet magazines, including *Novyi Mir, Inostrannaya Literatura,* and *Znamya,* and to *New Times.*

BIOGRAPHICAL/CRITICAL SOURCES: Zhurnalist, December, 1971; *Kommunist,* March, 1972.

*   *   *

KONECKY, Edith   1922-

PERSONAL: Born August 1, 1922, in New York, N.Y.; daughter of Harry (a businessman) and Elizabeth (Smith) Rubin; married Murray L. Konecky, May 21, 1944 (divorced, 1965); children: Michael, Joshua. *Education:* Attended New York University, 1939-41, and Columbia University, 1959, 1960. *Home:* 511 East 20th St., New York,

N.Y. 10010. *Agent:* McIntosh & Otis, Inc., 475 Fifth Ave., New York, N.Y. 10017.

CAREER: Writer. *Member:* International P.E.N., Authors Guild of Authors League of America, Poets and Writers, MacDowell Colony Fellows. *Awards, honors:* Five fellowships to attend Yaddo Colony, 1962-69; six fellowships to attend MacDowell Colony, 1969-77; Wurlitzer Foundation fellowship, 1974.

WRITINGS: Allegra Maud Goldman (novel), Harper, 1976.

Represented in anthologies, including *Best College Writing,* 1961; *Best American Short Stories,* edited by Martha Foley, 1964; *On the Job,* 1977. Contributor of poems and stories to magazines, including *Saturday Evening Post, Esquire, Open Places, Mademoiselle, Kenyon Review, Cosmopolitan,* and *Virginia Quarterly.* Editor of *Aphra,* 1976.

WORK IN PROGRESS: View to the North (tentative title), a novel.

* * *

KOPPER, Edward A(nthony), Jr.   1937-

PERSONAL: Born May 8, 1937, in Philadelphia, Pa.; son of Edward Anthony (a teacher and politician) and Margaret Mary (a family counselor; maiden name, McBride) Kopper; married Margaret Mary Gorman (a nursing co-ordinator), June 18, 1966; children: Edward, Kevin. *Education:* St. Joseph's College, Philadelphia, Pa., B.S., 1958; Temple University, M.A., 1961, Ph.D., 1963. *Politics:* Democrat. *Religion:* Roman Catholic. *Home:* 108 Farmington Dr., Butler, Pa. 16001. *Office:* Department of English, Slippery Rock State College, Slippery Rock, Pa. 16057.

CAREER: High school English teacher in Philadelphia, Pa., 1959-61; Temple University, Philadelphia, Pa., instructor in English, 1961-63; Villanova University, Villanova, Pa., assistant professor, 1963-66, associate professor of English, 1966-67; Indiana University, South Bend, assistant professor, 1967-68, associate professor of English, 1968-69; Slippery Rock State College, Slippery Rock, Pa., professor of English, 1969—, head of department, 1970-71, director of graduate studies in English, 1976—. Appeared on local television programs.

MEMBER: Modern Language Association of America, College English Association, Association of Pennsylvania State College and University Faculty, James Joyce Foundation, Virginia Woolf Society, Northeast Modern Language Association (chairman of Early Twentieth Century British and American Literature Section, 1972; chairman of James Joyce Section, 1973; chairman of Modern and Contemporary Poetry Section, 1975). *Awards, honors:* Named distinguished professor by State of Pennsylvania, 1975.

WRITINGS: (Contributor) Michael H. Begnal and Fritz Senn, editors, *A Conceptual Guide to Finnegan's Wake,* Pennsylvania State University Press, 1974; *Lady Isabella Persse Gregory,* Twayne, 1976; *James Joyce's A Portrait of the Artist as a Young Man: A Critical Analysis,* Simon & Schuster, 1976. Contributor of articles and reviews to literature journals. Editor and publisher of *Modern British Literature,* 1976—.

WORK IN PROGRESS: A bibliography of annotated criticism on John M. Synge, for G. K. Hall; a book on Arnold Bennett.

SIDELIGHTS: Kopper comments: "I am a conservative liberal in politics, a humanist and Good Samaritan in teaching, and somewhat of an elitist in research and writing. I am iconoclastic in my belief that people are more important than the roles they play or have played upon them: I believe in human liberation through culture."

* * *

KOPPERMAN, Paul Edward   1945-

PERSONAL: Born August 29, 1945, in Barranquilla, Colombia; came to the United States in 1953, U.S. citizen; son of Abraham (a factory manager) and Elsie (a bookkeeper; maiden name, Lehman) Kopperman. *Education:* Queens College of the City University of New York, B.A., 1966, M.A., 1969; University of Illinois, Ph.D., 1972. *Politics:* "Active Republican." *Religion:* Jewish. *Home:* 67-30 Clyde St., Forest Hills, N.Y. 11375.

CAREER: Macquarie University, Sydney, Australia, lecturer in British history, 1972-74; engaged in research and writing, 1974-76; Lighthouse Industries, Long Island City, N.Y., stock-worker, 1976—. *Member:* Phi Alpha Theta, Phi Kappa Phi.

WRITINGS: Braddock at the Monongahela, University of Pittsburgh Press, 1976.

WORK IN PROGRESS: Sir Robert Heath (1575-1649): Conscience and Corruption, a biography of an early-seventeenth-century British judge; fiction and other nonfiction.

SIDELIGHTS: Kopperman writes: "My historical works are highly evidence-oriented. They are primarily intended to inform, rather than to persuade, and those who dislike being confused by the facts will probably dislike them. I write as I do out of the conviction that if a subject deserves to be dealt with at all, it deserves to be dealt with accurately. In recent years, the reading public has been deluged with works that, for the sake of promoting a particular concept of society, present or future, bring in a slanted image of the past. Historians are constantly debating the uses of their vocation. At this point in time, perhaps their main service to society lies in protecting the past from those who abuse it."

* * *

KORN, Henry James   1945-

PERSONAL: Born September 19, 1945, in New York, N.Y.; son of Samuel Henry and Ruth (Beck) Korn; married Joan Willner (an educator), December 22, 1968; children: C.M. *Education:* Johns Hopkins University, A.B., 1968. *Politics:* Democrat. *Religion:* Jewish. *Home:* 109 Willow St., Brooklyn, N.Y. 11201. *Agent:* Elizabeth Trupin, P.O. Box 276, Hastings-on-Hudson, N.Y. 10706. *Office:* Jewish Museum, 1109 Fifth Ave., New York, N.Y. 10028.

CAREER: Brooklyn Museum, Brooklyn, N.Y., assistant administrator and project writer, 1969-71; Staten Island Institute, Staten Island, N.Y., administrative coordinator, 1971-74; Jewish Museum, New York, N.Y., administrator, 1975—. Member of artists council of Participation Project Foundation. Member of advisory board of Franklin Furnace Archive. *Member:* American Association of Museums, Cosmos, Flavor, and Rhythm. *Awards, honors:* Best small press titles award from *Library Journal,* 1974, for *Exact Change;* Kola Pinto Award from International Society of Structuralist Critics, 1976, for inventing new forms of fiction.

WRITINGS: Exact Change (short fiction), Assembling Press, 1974; *Pontoon Manifesto* (novel), Assembling Press, 1975; *Proceedings of the National Academy of the Avant*

Garde (fiction), Assembling Press, 1975; *Muhammad Ali Retrospective* (collection of stories, essays, and articles), Assembling Press, 1976; *A Difficult Act to Follow* (short fiction), Assembling Press, 1977.

Editor, all published by Assembling Press: (with Richard Kostelanetz) *Assembling*, 1970; (with Kostelanetz and Mike Metz) *Second Assembling*, 1971; (with Kostelanetz and Metz) *Third Assembling*, 1972; (with Kostelanetz and Metz) *Fourth Assembling*, 1973; (with Kostelanetz and Metz) *Fifth Assembling*, 1974; (with Kostelanetz and Metz) *Sixth Assembling*, 1975.

WORK IN PROGRESS: Operation Booth (tentative title), a novel, completion expected in 1978.

BIOGRAPHICAL/CRITICAL SOURCES: Richard Kostelanetz, *The End of Intelligent Writing*, Sheed, 1973; Thomas Montag, *Learning to Read Again*, Cats Pajamas Press, 1976; *Margins*, summer, 1975.

* * *

KORNBLUM, Allan 1949-

PERSONAL: Born February 16, 1949, in New York, N.Y.; son of Seymour (a social worker) and Anne (an elementary school teacher; maiden name, Epstein) Kornblum; married Cinda Wormley (a poet and secretary), August 19, 1972. *Education:* Attended New York University, 1967-68, and University of Iowa, 1970-72. *Home and office:* 626 East Main, West Branch, Iowa 52358. *Mailing address:* P.O. Box 546, West Branch, Iowa 52358.

CAREER: Toothpaste Press, West Branch, Iowa, publisher and printer, 1970—. Instructor at Scattergood School, 1974—. *Member:* Committee of Small Magazine Editors and Publishers. *Awards, honors:* Small press grants from National Education Association, 1975-76, 1976-77.

WRITINGS—Poetry: *Famous Americans*, privately printed, 1970; *Tight Pants*, privately printed, 1971; (with Darrell Gray) *Good Morning: Fourteen Sonnets*, "J" Stone Press Weekly Special, 1975; *The Salad Bushes*, Seamark Press, 1975; *Threshold*, Toothpaste Press, 1976; (editor and contributor) *1977 Pushcart Prize: Best of Small Presses*, Pushcart Press Books, 1976. Editor of *Toothpaste*, 1970-72, and *Dental Floss*.

WORK IN PROGRESS: Poems.

SIDELIGHTS: Kornblum writes: "The essence of life is the same everywhere for everyone. Therefore it is the surface which interests me. My poems are full of coffee, the refrigerator, and the towns where I have lived. Although my private studies of history would teach me otherwise, I refuse to view the world through eyes of despair. My poetry and life are open to both quiet and wild joys, open to my mother's cancer and death, open to a beer at The Peppermint Stable in West Branch. Sometimes I can't read enough, sometimes grade B movies are all I crave. If you're on Interstate 80 and pass through Iowa, give me a call."

BIOGRAPHICAL/CRITICAL SOURCES: Michael Tarachow, editor, *Toward a Further Definition*, Pentagram Press, 1977.

* * *

KORNBLUM, Cinda 1950-
(Cinda Wormley)

PERSONAL: Born March 8, 1950, in Newton, Iowa; daughter of John H. (a farmer) and Vernabelle (an office manager; maiden name, Vanness) Wormley; married Allan

M. Kornblum (a poet and publisher), September 18, 1972. *Education:* University of Northern Iowa, student, 1968-69; University of Iowa, B.S., 1972. *Home address:* P.O. Box 546, West Branch, Iowa 52358.

CAREER: University of Iowa, Iowa City, account clerk, 1972—. *Awards, honors:* Pushcart Prize from Pushcart Press, 1976, for poem "In Iowa."

WRITINGS: Bandwagon (poems), Toothpaste Press, 1976. Contributor to literary journals (sometimes under name Cinda Wormley), including *Dental Floss, Spirit That Moves Us, Me Too, Gum*, and *J Stone Press*. Editor of *Actual Now and Then*.

SIDELIGHTS: Cinda Kornblum writes that she is associated with the Iowa City "actualist" movement.

* * *

KOUTOUKAS, H. M. 1947-

PERSONAL: Born June 4, 1947, in Endicott, N.Y.; son of Harilabie and Agnes (Dewitt) Koutoukas. *Education:* Attended New School for Social Research, 1962-65, and Middleton College, 1964-65. *Religion:* Greek Orthodox. *Agent:* Madame Nino Karlweis, 250 E. 65th St., New York, N.Y. 10021.

CAREER: Dramatist and director. Pioneer in off-off Broadway movement; chairman of drive to build Caffe Cino; founder of Chamber Theatre and Supper Theatre concepts. Associated with The Electric Circus and other theatre groups. *Member:* New York Playwrights Strategy. *Awards, honors:* National Arts Club Award, 1962; Obie Award, 1965; Professional Theatre Wing Award.

WRITINGS—All plays; all first produced in New York: "The Last Triangle," 1965; "Tidy Passions; or, Kill, Kaleidoscope, Kill," 1965; "All Day for a Dollar," 1966; "Medea," 1966; "Only a Countess May Dance When She's Crazy," 1966; "A Letter from Colette," 1966; "Pomegranada," 1966; "With Creatures Make My Way," 1967; "When Clowns Play Hamlet," 1967; "View from Sorrento," 1967; "Howard Kline Trilogy," 1968; "Christopher at Sheridan Squared," at Performance Garage, 1971; "Grandmother Is in the Strawberry Patch," at La Ma Ma Experimental Theatre, 1974; "One Man's Religion," at La Ma Ma Experimental Theatre, 1975; "The Pinotti Papers," at La Ma Ma Experimental Theatre, 1975; "Starfollowers in an Ancient Land," at La Ma Ma Experimental Theatre, December 25, 1975.

Work represented in anthologies, including *The Off-off Broadway Playbook*, Bobbs-Merrill, 1972, and *More Plays from Off-off Broadway*, edited by Michael Smith, Bobbs-Merrill, 1972.

WORK IN PROGRESS: "A musical for future anthropologists."

SIDELIGHTS: Koutoukas told *CA* he is "interested only in transmutation of life throughout to beauty. Have learned from strangers and wish to wander and report on the darker side of life's areas."

* * *

KOVACH, Bill 1932-

PERSONAL: Born September 16, 1932, in Tenn.; son of John and Olga (Sicos) Kovach; married Lynne Marie Stamm, January 15, 1956; children: Theresa, David, Charles, John. *Education:* Attended University of Miami, 1957-58; East Tennessee State University, B.S., 1959. *Reli-*

gion: Episcopalian. *Home:* 2336 Highland Ave., Falls Church, Va. 22046. *Office:* 1920 L St. N.W., Washington, D.C. 20036.

CAREER/WRITINGS: Johnson City Press-Chronicle, Johnson City, Tenn., reporter, 1959-61; *Nashville Tennessean,* Nashville, reporter, 1961-68; *New York Times,* New York, N.Y., reporter, 1968-69, Albany bureau chief, 1969-71, Boston bureau chief, 1971-73, Washington news editor, 1973—. Notable assignments include coverage of the civil rights movement in the South, the anti-war movement, occupation of Wounded Knee, presidential campaigns of 1964, 1968, and 1972, and President Ford's trip to China, 1975. Contributor of articles to *New York Times, Reporter, New Republic,* and *Field and Stream. Military service:* U.S. Navy, 1951-52. *Awards, honors:* New York State Bar award, Stanford professional journalism fellow, and National Science Foundation fellow.

AVOCATIONAL/INTERESTS: Woodworking, travel, photography, painting in water colors.

* * *

KRAMER, Gene 1927-

PERSONAL: Legal given name, Eugene; born December 4, 1927, in Lincoln, Neb.; son of Joseph (a professor) and Celia Kramer. *Education:* University of California at Berkeley, A.B., 1950. *Home:* 19 Navendra Place, Parliament St., New Delhi, India. 110001. *Office:* 50 Rockefeller Plaza, New York, N.Y. 10020.

CAREER/WRITINGS: Associated Press, New York, N.Y., editor and reporter in California, 1950-54, correspondent from Tokyo, Japan, and Seoul, Korea, 1954-61, Warsaw, 1962-67, Bonn and Berlin, Germany, 1967-68, Prague, 1968-71, United Nations correspondent, 1972-75, chief of bureau in New Delhi, India, 1977—. Radio news broadcaster, Associated Press Radio, 1967—. *Military service:* U.S. Army, 1945-57. *Member:* United Nations Correspondents Association (secretary, 1975).

SIDELIGHTS: Kramer travels yearly to Europe and Asia. *Avocational interests:* Diplomacy, quality of life, consumerism, transportation, winter sports.

* * *

KRAMER, Rita 1929-

PERSONAL: Born April 30, 1929, in Detroit, Mich.; daughter of William R. and Sophie (Joffe) Blumenthal; married Yale Kramer (a physician), March 18, 1951; children: Deborah, Miriam. *Eeucation:* University of Chicago, B.A., 1948. *Religion:* Jewish. *Agent:* Carl Brandt, Brandt & Brandt, 101 Park Ave., New York, N.Y. 10017.

CAREER: Free-lance writer, editor, and researcher, 1960—.

WRITINGS: (With Lee Salk) *How to Raise a Human Being,* Random House, 1969; *Maria Montessori: A Biography,* Putnam, 1976. Contributor to magazines, including *New York Times Magazine.*

WORK IN PROGRESS: A book on childbirth in America today, publication expected in 1978.

SIDELIGHTS: Kramer told *CA:* "My current project concerns the controversy between the obstetrical profession and those who support alternatives to the traditional management of childbirth such as midwifery, out-of-hospital and home birth. It examines such issues as the place of medical and surgical techniques and procedures in normal childbirth, the question of risk and the options open to birthing women, the role of the father in labor and delivery, and the significance of the recent research on the effects of early separation on mother-infant attachment.

* * *

KRAUSS, Rosalind E(pstein) 1940-

PERSONAL: Born November 30, 1940, in Washington, D.C.; daughter of Matthew M. (a lawyer) and Bertha (Luber) Epstein; married Richard I. Krauss, September 17, 1962 (divorced, 1971). *Education:* Wellesley College, A.B., 1962; Harvard University, M.A., 1963, Ph.D., 1969. *Home:* 12 Greene St., New York, N.Y. 10013. *Agent:* Maxine Grofsky, 1 Fifth Ave., New York, N.Y. 10011. *Office:* Department of Art, Hunter College, City University of New York, 695 Park Ave., New York, N.Y. 10021.

CAREER: Princeton University, Princeton, N.J., lecturer and director of visual arts program, 1972-74; City University of New York, Hunter College, New York, N.Y., associate professor of art, 1974—. Guest curator for exhibitions at Guggenheim and Whitney Museums. *Awards, honors:* Mather Award for Criticism from College Art Association, 1972.

WRITINGS: Terminal Iron Works: The Sculpture of David Smith, M.I.T. Press, 1971; *Joan Miro: Magnetic Fields,* Guggenheim Museum, 1972; *Line as Language,* Princeton University Museum, 1974; *Passages in Modern Sculpture,* Viking, in press. Contributor to *Artforum, Art in America, October,* and *Partisan Review.* Associate editor of *Artforum,* 1972-75; editor of *October,* 1976—.

* * *

KRAYBILL, Donald B(rubaker) 1945-

PERSONAL: Born September 24, 1945, in Mount Joy, Pa.; son of Wilmer G. and Helen (Brubaker) Kraybill; married Frances Mellinger (a registered nurse), September 1, 1966; children: Sheila, Joy. *Education:* Attended Millersville State College, 1963-65; Eastern Mennonite College, B.A., 1967; Temple University, M.A., 1971, Ph.D., 1976. *Religion:* Mennonite. *Home address:* R.D. 1, Elizabethtown, Pa. 17022. *Office:* Department of Sociology, Elizabethtown College, Elizabethtown, Pa. 17022.

CAREER: Mennonite Voluntary Service, Salunga, Pa., associate director, 1967-69; Mennonite Youth Services, Salunga, director, 1969-70; Elizabethtown College, Elizabethtown, Pa., instructor, 1971-74, assistant professor of sociology, 1974—. Lay pastor of Mennonite church in Willow Street, Pa., 1968-72. *Member:* American Sociological Association, Council on Anthropology and Education, Society for the Scientific Study of Religion.

WRITINGS: Our Star Spangled Faith, Herald Press, 1976; *Ethnic Education: The Impact of Mennonite Schooling,* R & E Research Associates, 1977; *Mennonite Education: Issues, Facts, and Changes,* Herald Press, 1977; *The Upside Down Kingdom,* Herald Press, in press. Author of column "Nuts and Bolts" in *Christian Living.*

* * *

KREMER, William F. 1919-

PERSONAL: Born June 1, 1919, in Holland; son of William (a physician) and Bernarda (Niemeyer) Kremer; married Laura E. Hill (a physician), September 27, 1947; children: Corrine V., Valerie H. *Education:* University of Amsterdam, M.D., 1943. *Home address:* Box 42A, Route 1, Dickerson, Md. 20753.

CAREER: Diplomate of the National Board of Medical Examiners, 1949; diplomate of the American Board of Internal Medicine, 1957. In private practice of medicine. University of Pittsburgh, Pittsburgh, Pa., instructor in medicine, 1952-57; pharmaceutical research consultant in Hartsdale, N.Y., 1957-71, and in Dickerson, Md., 1971—. *Military service:* Royal Netherlands Army, 1944-45; became lieutenant; received Distinguished Service Cross.

WRITINGS: The Doctor's Metabolic Diet, Crown, 1975.

* * *

KRISS, Ronald P(aul) 1934-

PERSONAL: Born April 4, 1934, in Brooklyn, N.Y.; son of Harry Judah (a salesman) and Milly (Sigall) Kriss; married Lorna Sue Smith (a television news assistant), November 16, 1954; children: Evan Jane, Erik Jon. *Education:* Harvard University, A.B., 1954; Columbia University, S.M., 1957. *Home:* 35 East 85th St., New York, N.Y. 10028. *Office: Time* Magazine, Rockefeller Center, New York, N.Y. 10020.

CAREER: United Press International, New York City; foreign correspondent, 1958-60; *New York News,* New York City, desk man, 1961; *Time* magazine, New York City, writer and senior editor, 1961-67, senior political writer, 1968, foreign editor, 1969-71; *Saturday Review,* New York City, executive editor, 1971-73; *Time* magazine, senior editor, 1973—. *Military service:* U.S. Army, 1954-56.

WRITINGS: (Contributor) *The Global Village,* University of Maryland Press, 1976. Principle journalistic work includes forty cover stories for *Time* and editorials for *Saturday Review;* speechwriter for Pennsylvania Governor William Scranton during 1964 presidential campaign; contributor to *Columbia Journalism Review* and *Reader's Digest.* Editor of special issue, *Time,* July 15, 1974.

* * *

KROCHMAL, Arnold 1919-

PERSONAL: Born January 30, 1919, in New York; son of Morris (an embroiderer) and Leah (Weissman) Krochmal; married Connie Brite (a writer), November 30, 1970; children: Stephen Glen, Maurice Manfred, Walter Lyle. *Education:* Attended New York University, 1937; North Carolina State College, B.S., 1942; Cornell University, M.S., Ph.D. *Religion:* Jewish. *Residence:* Asheville, N.C. *Office:* Forest Service, U.S. Department of Agriculture, 13 Veterans Dr., Asheville, N.C. 28806.

CAREER: Fulbright professor in Greece, 1952-53; chief research advisor of Wyoming Team, in Kabul, Afghanistan, 1957-59; Panamerican Agricultural School, El Zamorano, Honduras, head of department of horticulture, 1960-61; U.S. Department of Agriculture, Virgin Islands, assistant officer in charge and research botanist, 1961-66; U.S. Department of Agriculture, Forest Service, Asheville, N.C., principal economic botanist, 1966—. College of the Virgin Islands, economic geographer, 1964-66; summer visiting professor at Wisconsin State University, 1966; fall visiting professor at Berea College, 1967; adjunct professor at North Carolina State University and University of North Carolina, Asheville; senior research fellow at Agricultural University of Wageningen, Holland, 1976-77. Consultant to Agency for International Development, Volunteers for International Technical Assistance, and the governments of Surinam, Jamaica, Montserrat, Thailand, Dominican Republic, and British Virgin Islands. *Military service:* U.S. Army, 1942-46.

WRITINGS: Horticultura Practica, Panamerican Agricultural School, 1960; (with Russ Walters and Richard Doughty) *Guide to Medicinal Plants of Appalachia,* Forest Service, U.S. Department of Agriculture, 1971; (with wife, Connie Krochmal) *Guide to Medicinal Plants of the United States,* Quadrangle, 1973; (with C. Krochmal) *The Complete Illustrated Book of Dyes from Natural Sources,* Doubleday, 1974; (with C. Krochmal) *Indoor Gardening: Green Thumb Guide,* Drake, 1974; (with C. Krochmal) *Making It: The Encyclopedia of How to Do It for Less,* Drake, 1975; (with C. Krochmal) *Caribbean Cooking,* Quadrangle, 1975; (with C. Krochmal) *A Naturalist's Gude to Cooking with Wild Plants,* Quadrangle, 1975. Also author, with C. Krochmal, of *Gardening in the Carolinas,* Doubleday. Editor, *Caribbean Agriculture and Science* and *Ceiba.*

WORK IN PROGRESS: Tropical Horticulture; Tito, A Biography, publication by Nelson-Hall; *Indigenous Nuts of the United States,* publication by Forest Service, U.S. Department of Agriculture.

* * *

KRUCHKOW, Diane 1947-

PERSONAL: Born June 10, 1947, in Stamford, Conn.; daughter of Norman and Shirley (Shulman) Kruchkow. *Education:* University of New Hampshire, B.A., 1969, graduate study, 1969-70. *Home:* 42 Bromfield St., Newburyport, Mass. 01950. *Office: Zahir,* Box 715, Newburyport, Mass. 01950.

CAREER: Has worked as a bookstore manager, secretary, typist, bookkeeper, and waitress; University of New Hampshire, Durham, N.H., teaching fellow, 1969-71; *Zahir* (literary magazine), Newburyport, Mass., editor and publisher, 1970—; New England Small Press Association (NESPA), Amherst, Mass., co-founder and co-ordinator, 1970—, director, 1974—, vice-president, 1975—. Member of board of directors, Committee of Small Magazine/Press Editors and Publishers (COSMEP), 1973-75.

WRITINGS—All poetry: *Odd Jobs,* Ghost Dance Press, 1974; (contributor) Michael McMahon, editor, *Flowering After Frost,* Branden Press, 1975; (editor and contributor) *Changes of the Day,* Rat & Mole Press, 1975; (contributor) *Contemporary Literary Scene, 1973,* Salem Press, 1975. Writer of column "News Notes" for *Margins,* 1972—. Contributor to *New York Quarterly, Harpoon, Margins, Shore Review, The Smith, Ghost Dance,* and other periodicals. Editor, *Zahir,* 1970—, and *Stony Hills: The New England Alternative Press Review,* 1977—.

WORK IN PROGRESS: Poetry.

AVOCATIONAL INTERESTS: Gardening, conjuring up recipes, old movies.

* * *

KRUGER, Mollee 1929-

PERSONAL: Born March 28, 1929, in Bel Air, Md.; daughter of Benjamin (a merchant) and Mary (Hoffman) Coppel; married Jerome Kruger (a scientist), February 20, 1955; children: Lennard, Joseph. *Education:* University of Maryland, B.A., 1950; Catholic University of America, graduate study, 1966. *Politics:* Democrat. *Religion:* Jewish. *Home:* 619 Warfield Dr., Rockville, Md. 20850. *Agent:* Curtis Brown Ltd., 60 East 56th St., New York, N.Y. 10022.

CAREER: Joseph Katz Agency, Baltimore, Md., advertising copywriter, 1951-55; *Jewish Week,* Washington, D.C., columnist, 1967—, feature writer, 1968-72. Teacher at Jewish Community Center (Washington, D.C.), 1975—. *Member:* International Platform Association, Hadassah, Women's League for Conservative Judaism, National League of American Pen Women. *Awards, honors:* College Board Award from *Mademoiselle,* 1948; Family Tree Award from Women's League for Conservative Judaism, 1976.

WRITINGS: Unholy Writ (light verse), Maryben Books, 1970; *More Unholy Writ,* Maryben Books, 1973; *Yankee Shoes* (light verse), Maryben Books, 1975. Author of television scripts for local organizations. Author of "Unholy Writ," a column syndicated by Maryben Books, 1969—. Contributor to *Washington Post.*

WORK IN PROGRESS: The God Bubble, a novel; *Unholier Than Thou,* a collection of light verse.

SIDELIGHTS: Mollee Kruger mentions that she has "been writing since the age of ten, first published at thirteen . . ., am interested in politics, literature, and theater—have directed and been in amateur theatricals—I am primarily a person, not a writer, and live my life accordingly."

* * *

KRYMOW, Virginia P(auline) 1930-

PERSONAL: Born January 25, 1930, in Detroit, Mich.; daughter of Frank and Antonia (Arlotta) La Falce; married George J. Krymow (an engineer), October 7, 1972. *Education:* Wayne State University, B.A., 1952, graduate study, 1959, 1969; Loyola University, Chicago, Ill., M.S.W., 1956; further graduate study at University of Michigan, 1964, Smith College, 1966, University of Detroit, 1971, Case Western Reserve University, 1974, and Ohio State University, 1975. *Home:* 6340 Millbank Dr., Centerville, Ohio 45459.

CAREER: Department of Public Welfare, Detroit, Mich., welfare investigator, 1952-54; Wayne County Catholic Social Services, Detroit, counselor, supervisor of intake services, and coordinator of protective services, 1956-72; Montgomery County Children's Services Board, Dayton, Ohio, director of professional services, 1973-76; Montgomery County Juvenile Court, Dayton, administrative assistant, 1976—. Field work instructor at Wayne State University, University of Michigan, St. Patrick's College (Ottawa, Ontario), University of Detroit, and Mercy College of Detroit, 1960-72. Private practice in family and personal counseling, 1964-67. Member of board of directors of Dayton's Youth Services Bureau, 1974—; member of Centerville, Ohio, City Beautiful Commission, 1976—. *Member:* National Association of Social Workers, Social Workers Guild.

WRITINGS: (Contributor) Charles T. O'Reilly and Margaret M. Pembroke, editors, *Older People in a Chicago Community,* Loyola University (Chicago, Ill.), 1966; *Remember Anything You Want,* Arlotta Press, 1977.

WORK IN PROGRESS: A series of self-help books, based on her counseling experiences, dealing with raising children, managing money and time, and enjoying retirement; a book for parents on avoiding pitfalls and raising successful children.

SIDELIGHTS: Krymow writes: "As a social worker I counseled children and adults, in families and groups as well as individually. I found that most persons are interested in improving the quality of their lives. What they need are encouragement, guidelines, specific skills, and an approach to

problem-solving and to life that will help them achieve the desired results. In my books, the same guidance and principles which I used in counseling are presented for the reading audience. In this way, I hope to make available to larger numbers of persons the same guidance which helped the many persons who came to me for counseling."

* * *

KUNHAPPA, Murkot 1905-

PERSONAL: Born May 14, 1905, in Tellicherry, Kerala, India; son of Murkot Kumaran (a writer and teacher) and Yeshoda (Amma) Kunhappa; married wife Sitha; children: Edavalath. *Education:* Madras University, B.A. *Politics:* Democratic Socialist. *Religion:* Hindu. *Home:* "Gokula," Murkot Kumaran Rd., Tellicherry P.O., Kerala, India. *Office: Malayala/Manorama,* P.I.N. 673001, Calicut, Kerala, India.

CAREER: Eastern Railway, Calcutta, India, personnel officer, 1927-57; Railway Board, New Delhi, India, director, 1957-60; Hindustan Steel, Ltd., Ranchi, India, personnel adviser, 1960-66; *Malayala/Manorama,* Calicut, India, associate editor, 1966—. Member of executive committee, Malayalam Encyclopedia. *Member:* Lions Club (Calicut director), Folklore Society. *Awards, honors:* Akadami Prize for children's stories.

WRITINGS—in English: *Three Bags of Gold* (Indian folk tales), Asia Publishing House, 1963.

Other works; juveniles: *Vijnana Shakalangal* (title means "Short Studies"), 1950; *Oru Kuppivala Janikkunnu* (title means "A Bangale Is Born"); *Kadalassum Pencilum* (title means "Pencil and Paper"); *Thonnutty Ompathu* (title means "Ninety-nine"); *Nanella* (title means "No, Not I"); *Balakatha Tharangini* (title means "A Stream of Stories for Children"); *Urulakku Upperi* (title means "Tit for Tat"); *Rajni Kodutha Maina* (title means "Queen's Gift: A Bird"); *Kadalassinte Katha* (title means "The Story of Paper").

Essays: *Sallapa Sahityam* (title means "Slippered Ease"), 1968; *Enthayalentha* (title means "The Subject Does Not Matter"); *Oru Vakka Poya Pokku* (title means "Words and Their Ways"); *Nirupana Nirupanam* (title means "Critical Essays on Criticism").

Biography and history: *Lolakshikal* (title means "Beautiful Women"), 1950; *Cinema,* 1951; *Gandhiji,* 1955; *Gautama the Budha; Markot Kumaran; Samskara Tharangini.*

WORK IN PROGRESS: Ballads of Kerala, a collection of folk tales.

* * *

KURZMAN, Dan 1927-

PERSONAL: Born March 27, 1927, in San Francisco, Calif.; son of Joseph (a businessman) and Lillian (a writer; maiden name, Halperin) Kurzman; married Florence Knopf (an editor), February 27, 1977. *Education:* University of California at Berkeley, B.A., 1944; Sorbonne, University of Paris, certificate, 1946. *Agent:* Ruth Aley, 145 East 35th St., New York, N.Y. 10016.

CAREER: International News Service, Paris, France, correspondent, 1946-48; Marshall Plan Information Division, Paris, feature writer, 1949; National Broadcasting Co. (NBC), New York, N.Y., Middle East correspondent, 1950-53; McGraw-Hill World News Service, New York City, Tokyo bureau chief, 1954-60; *Washington Post,* Washington, D.C., correspondent, 1962-68; *Washington Star,*

Washington, D.C., contributor from Spain, 1968—. Writer. *Member:* Overseas Press Club, Pen Club, National Press Club, Tokyo Foreign Correspondents Club, Overseas Writers Club, State Department Correspondents Club, Authors League. *Awards, honors:* Overseas Press Club Best Book on Foreign Affairs award, 1963, for *Subversion of the Innocents;* Front Page Award, 1964; George Polk Award for international reporting, 1965, from Long Island University.

WRITINGS: Kishi and Japan: The Search for the Sun, Obolensky, 1960; *Subversion of the Innocents,* Random House, 1963; *Santa Domingo: Revolt of the Damned,* Putnam, 1965; *Genesis 1948: The First Arab-Israeli War,* World Publications, 1970; *The Race for Rome,* Doubleday, 1975; *The Bravest Battle,* Putnam, 1976. Contributor to *Washington Post, Washington Star,* and other periodicals.

WORK IN PROGRESS: A book on the siege of Madrid in the Spanish Civil War.

*   *   *

KYSAR, Robert (Dean) 1934-

PERSONAL: Born July 6, 1934, in Lincoln, Neb.; son of Calvin Orvis (an electrician) and Iva Pearl (Anderson) Kysar; married Myrna Christopherson (a clergywoman), May 20, 1973; children: Kathryn Adele, Karen Mara. *Education:* College of Idaho, B.A., 1956; Garrett Evangelical Theological Seminary, B.D., 1959; Northwestern University, Ph.D., 1967. *Politics:* Democrat. *Office:* Department of Religion, Hamline University, St. Paul, Minn. 55104.

CAREER: Southwestern College, Winfield, Kan., assistant professor, 1959-61, associate professor of religion, 1963-65, chaplain, 1959-61; Central Methodist College, Fayette, Mo., associate professor of religion, 1966-67; Hamline University, St. Paul, Minn., assistant professor, 1967-69, associate professor, 1969-76, professor of religion, 1976—. Visiting instructor at St. Paul School of Theology (Kansas City, Mo.), 1965-66. Pastor of Methodist church in New Haven, Conn., 1976-77. *Member:* Society of Biblical Literature, American Academy of Religion, American Association of University Professors.

WRITINGS: The Fourth Evangelist and His Gospel, Augsburg, 1975; *John, the Maverick Gospel,* John Knox, 1976; (with wife, Myrna C. Kysar) *The Asundered: Biblical Teachings on Divorce and Remarriage,* John Knox, in press. Contributor to magazines.

WORK IN PROGRESS: A survey of contemporary scholarship on the Gospel of John.

SIDELIGHTS: Kysar told *CA:* "My primary scholarly and teaching interests are in the history of Christian origins and particularly in the Gospel of John. Interest in the Gospel of John originated during research for my doctoral dissertation.

"Personal experience led my wife and me to a study and interpretation of the biblical teachings on divorce and remarriage, for we feel that an injustice by well meaning churches and Christians is often done to those who are divorced and may be remarried."

AVOCATIONAL INTERESTS: Music, tennis, and old automobiles.

*   *   *

LACERDA, Carlos 1914-1977

April 30, 1914—May 21, 1977; Brazilian politician, writer and publisher. Considered to be one of Brazil's most influen-

tial politicians between 1954 and 1968, his strong vocal opposition helped force three presidents out of office. He founded the *Tribuna da Imprensa* newspaper in 1949, and turned to financial investments after he was barred from politics by the military regime in 1968. He died in Rio de Janeiro, Brazil. Obituaries: *New York Times,* May 22, 1977.

*   *   *

LACKS, Cecilia 1945-
(Cissy Lacks)

PERSONAL: Born July 21, 1945, in St. Louis, Mo.; daughter of Louis M. (a salesman) and Lenore (Gimpelson) Lacks. *Education:* Washington University, St. Louis, Mo., B.A., 1967; Boston University, M.S., 1971. *Home:* 12311 Rossridge Court, St. Louis, Mo. 63141.

CAREER: Teacher, 1967-69; high school teacher, 1971—. Free-lance writer, photographer, and media consultant. President of local Sponsors of School Publications. Member of St. Louis board of directors of Experiment in International Living; member of Commission on Community Involvement and Taft Institute on Practical Politics.

WRITINGS: (Under name Cissy Lacks) *Downtown Lady* (juvenile; with own photographs), Beanie Books, 1976. Writer, director, and photographer of slide and sound productions, "Who's to Say What's Best?," "The Home and More: Early Childhood Education," and "Fairness in Financing: Tax Assessment in Missouri." Special correspondent for *St. Louis Dispatch.* Contributor of articles and photographs to public relations publications. Editor of *SSP Messenger, Eads Bridge Brochure,* and *Louis Latzer Homestead Brochure;* coordinator of Conference on Education newsletter.

SIDELIGHTS: Lacks told *CA:* "It's important that children at an early age come in contact with writers and all sorts of people who are spending their lives creating. The exposure opens up the way for students to be expressive and creative, to see that it's valuable and worthwhile to express themselves in an effective and original way. Excellent teachers fulfill the same function (if not even more successfully) as visiting artists. But it is good for students to be exposed to as many producing artists as possible."

*   *   *

LAI, T'ien-Ch'ang 1921-

PERSONAL: Born in 1921, in Hong Kong; son of Chi-Hsi (a professor) and Cheong (Fung-Ying) Lai; married Flora Wan-Fong (a teacher); children: Ross, Miranda. *Education:* University of Hong Kong, B.A., 1942, M.A., 1956; University of Manchester, dip. ad. ed., 1962. *Home:* Residence #1, #5B, Chinese University, Shatin, Hong Kong. *Office:* Extra-Mural Department, Chinese University, 67 Chatham Rd., Kowloon, Hong Kong.

CAREER: Secretary of Chinese Embassy, London, England, 1946-50; Chung On Trading, Hong Kong, director, 1950-54; Hong Kong University, tutor in English, 1955-56, lecturer in extra-mural department, 1957-65; Chinese University, Hong Kong, director of extra-mural studies, 1965—. Member of International Congress of University Adult Education. *Member:* Rotary International.

WRITINGS: (Editor and translator) *Selected Chinese Sayings,* University Book Store, University of Hong Kong, 1960, 3rd edition, 1966; (with Jen Tai) *Love Poetry from the Chinese,* Swindon Book Co., 1968; (editor and translator) *Chinese Couplets,* Swindon Book Co., 1969.

(With Y. T. Kwong) *Chinese Proverbs,* Kelly & Walsh, 1970; *A Scholar in Imperial China,* Kelly & Walsh, 1970; *T'ang Yin, Poet/Painter, 1470-1524,* Kelly & Walsh, 1971; (editor) Husein Rofe, *Things Chinese,* Swindon Book Co., 1971; (translator, with Kwong) *Chinese Poetry,* Swindon Book Co., 1972; *The Eight Immortals,* Swindon Book Co., 1972; (translator) *More Chinese Sayings* (bilingual text), Swindon Book Co., 1972; *Ch'i Pai Shih* (abridged autobiography of Ch'i Pai-Shih), University of Washington Press, 1973; *A Chinese Book of Freindship,* Swindon Book Co., 1973; *Chinese Calligraphy: Its Mystic Beauty,* Swindon Book Co., 1973, published in the United States as *Chinese Calligraphy: An Introduction,* University of Washington Press, 1975; *Chinese Painting: Its Mystic Essence,* Swindon Book Co., 1974; *Pa ta shan jen: Chinese Monk-Painter,* Swindon Book Co., 1974; *Three Contemporary Chinese Painters: Chang Da-chien, Ting Yin-yung, Ch'eng Shih-fa,* University of Washington Press, 1975; *Kweilin: China's Most Scenic Spot,* Kelly and Walsh, 1976; *Chinese Seals,* University of Washington Press, 1976; *Treasures of a Chinese Studio,* Swindon Book Co., 1976. Contributor to *Reader's Digest, Orientations,* and *Seasons.*

WORK IN PROGRESS: Love of Flowers and Trees (tentative title); *A Gallery of Chinese Women; Chinese Letter-Paper Designs; Mountain Love Songs; Chinese Symbols and Modern Art.*

SIDELIGHTS: Lai writes: "I believe that introduction of Chinese culture (and therefore *values*) is vital to the world's welfare, particularly at a time of rampant materialism."

* * *

LAIRD, J(ohn) T(udor) 1921-

PERSONAL: Born August 19, 1921, in Sydney, Australia; son of Walter Wilfrid (a painter) and Venetia (a nurse; maiden name, Harford) Laird; married Mary Patricia Walkom, July 3, 1946; children: Margaret (Mrs. Rainer Frisch), Patricia, Ian. *Education:* University of Sydney, B.A. (honors), 1942, M.A. (honors), 1959; University of London, further graduate study, 1962-63. *Home:* 25 Rawson St., Deakin, Canberra, Australian Capital Territory 2600, Australia. *Office:* Faculty of Military Studies, University of New South Wales, Duntroon, Australian Capital Territory 2600, Australia.

CAREER: Royal Military College of Australia, Duntroon, lecturer, 1946-59, senior lecturer in English, 1959-68; University of New South Wales, Duntroon, Australia, senior lecturer, 1968-72, associate professor of English, 1973—. *Military service:* Australian Army, 1941-46; became lieutenant. *Member:* Australasian Victorian Studies Association, Australasian Universities Language and Literature Association, Australian and New Zealand American Studies Association, Australasian and Pacific Society for Eighteenth Century Studies, Thomas Hardy Society of Great Britain.

WRITINGS: (Editor and author of notes and bibliography) *Other Banners: An Anthology of Australian Literature of the First World War,* Australian War Memorial, 1971; *The Shaping of "Tess of the D'Urbervilles,"* Clarendon Press, 1975. Contributor of articles and reviews to magazines and newspapers.

WORK IN PROGRESS: The Fiction of Henry James, especially the Italian novels and stories; research on the Australian serial version of *Tess of the D'Urbervilles.*

LAMAR, Nedra Newkirk

PERSONAL: Born in Fort Worth, Tex.; daughter of George Harmon (a sales representative) and Kathryn (an organist; maiden name, Walker) Newkirk; married Henry R. Lamar (an editor), September 10, 1933; children: Juliet (Mrs. John Macedo), Austin Newkirk. *Education:* University of Texas, B.A.; also attended Theodora Irvine School for the Theatre. *Home:* 1024 Hudnall Dr., Tyler, Tex. 75701; and Winslow Dr., West Townsend, Vt. 05359.

CAREER: Teacher of analytical reading at American Academy of Dramatic Arts, New York, N.Y., Daycroft School, Greenwich, Conn., 1956 and 1972-75, and at Principia College, Elash, Ill., 1959 and 1973-75. Lecturer at Foundation for Biblical Research and Longyear Historical Society. *Member:* Phi Beta Kappa, Pi Lambda Theta, Alpha Phi, Mortar Board.

WRITINGS: How to Speak the Written Word, Revell, 1949, revised edition, Revell, 1967. Contributor to magazines and to *Christian Science Monitor.*

WORK IN PROGRESS: Giving the Sense (tentative title), another book on analytical reading.

SIDELIGHTS: Nedra Lamar told *CA:* "Analytical reading is not just a different way of reading or a new method of teaching reading; it is a whole new subject. The main focus is on helping the reader see through the words to the ideas, thus arriving at the writer's meaning. This technique is based on *principles,* deriving from pure logic and also grammar, but it does not require of the student an extensive knowledge of grammar. It also includes conversational patterns, which enable reader, actor, minister to read as if he were just talking."

AVOCATIONAL INTERESTS: Classical culture, opera, English literature (especially Carroll, Dickens, Saki, Kenneth Grahame).

* * *

LAMB, Eleanor 1917-

PERSONAL: Born February 27, 1917, in Provo, Utah; daughter of William (a teacher and rancher) and Josephine (Bean) Schofield; married Floyd R. Lamb, November 25, 1937 (divorced, 1967); children: Laurelie (Mrs. Luther Turley), Marsha (Mrs. Clark Bingham), Monte C. *Education:* Attended Woodbury Business College. *Religion:* Church of Jesus Christ of Latter-day Saints (Mormons). *Home:* 7075 Craig Rd., Las Vegas, Nev. 89108.

CAREER: Rancher in Pahranagat Valley, Nev.; owner and manager, Cowboy Supply (western store), Las Vegas, Nevada; writer.

WRITINGS: Against a Crooked Sky (novel), Bantam, 1976.

Screenplays, all with Douglas C. Stewart: "Where the Red Fern Grows" (based on story by Wilson Rawls), 1976; "Seven Alone," 1976; "Against a Crooked Sky" (based on own novel), 1976.

WORK IN PROGRESS: Two novels, *Jamie and Little Joe* and *Johnny Appleseed;* two screenplays with Mel Marshall and Verna Holt.

SIDELIGHTS: Eleanor Lamb told *CA:* "Because of a lifetime of ranching, I write about the West. I enjoy writing about children, especially young boys."

BIOGRAPHICAL/CRITICAL SOURCES: Nevadan, September 22, 1974.

LAMBERT, Herbert H. 1929-

PERSONAL: Born March 3, 1929, in Moundsville, W.Va.; son of Leonard Napoleon (a law officer) and Juanita (Hylton) Lambert; married Esther Esaias (a psychiatric social worker), June 22, 1950; children: Timothy Jay, Geoffrey Esaias. *Education:* Bethany College, Bethany, W.Va., A.B., 1950; Union Theological Seminary, New York, N.Y., M.Div., 1953. *Home:* 3510 Manola, St. Louis, Mo. 63121. *Office:* P.O. Box 179, St. Louis, Mo. 63166.

CAREER: Ordained minister of Disciples of Christ, 1950; pastor of churches in St. Albans, W.Va., 1954-58, Wilkinsburg, Pa., 1958-65, and Rantoul, Ill., 1965-71; Christian Board of Publication, St. Louis, Mo., editor, 1971—. *Member:* Association of Christian Church Educators.

WRITINGS: Into a World on Edge, Christian Board of Publication, 1969; *For Such a Time As This,* Christian Board of Publication, 1974; *Getting Inside the Bible,* Bethany Press, 1976. Contributor of more than eighty articles to church publications.

WORK IN PROGRESS: Research and field tests on a method of teaching the Bible to adults.

SIDELIGHTS: Lambert writes: "The writers by whom I have been most influenced are Reinhold Niebuhr and Karl Barth. I would consider my theology to be neo-orthodoxy somewhat tempered by experience and thought. My approach to the Bible is historical and critical, with an emphasis on positive values. My first book dealt with current social issues. I continue to be interested in these, especially in civil rights and the concerns of minority groups."

AVOCATIONAL INTERESTS: Photography, printing, archaeology.

*   *   *

LAME DEER 1895(?)-1976

1895(?)—December 14, 1976; Sioux chief and medicine man, and author of *Lame Deer, Seeker of Visions.* His book was translated into ten languages and he was recognized as a spiritual leader among American Indians. Obituaries: *New York Times,* December 16, 1976.

*   *   *

LANDMAN, David 1917-

PERSONAL: Born October 24, 1917, in Philadelphia, Pa.; son of Isaac (a rabbi) and Beatrice (a social worker; maiden name, Eschner) Landman; married Joan Klein, September 1, 1946 (deceased); married Hedy Backlin (a museum director), December 30, 1964; children: Alicia, Michael Isaac. *Education:* Brown University, A.B. (magna cum laude), 1939; Yale University, graduate study, summer, 1954; Columbia University, M.A., 1963. *Religion:* Jewish. *Home:* 40 East Cedar St., Chicago, Ill. 60611. *Office:* 2722 University Hall, University of Illinois, Chicago, Ill. 60680.

CAREER: Union, Springfield, Mass., reporter, 1939; *Universal Jewish Encyclopedia,* New York, N.Y., associate editor, 1939-41; *Look at America,* New York City, writer, 1945-46; free-lance writer, 1946-59; Cooper Union, New York City, assistant to the president, 1959-63; Princeton University, Princeton, N.J., associate director of development, 1963-69; Harvard University, Cambridge, Mass., director of public information, 1969-73; Pathfinder Fund, Boston, Mass., director of public affairs, 1973-77; University of Illinois, Urbana, director of public information, 1977—. Lecturer at Boston University, 1973-76. Member of

board of directors of Hamilton-Madison House (settlement house), 1949-69, vice-president of board of directors, 1960-64. *Military service:* U.S. Army, Infantry, 1941-45; became major; received Bronze Star Medal.

MEMBER: American Society of Journalists and Authors, Council for the Support and Advancement of Education, Asia Society, Phi Beta Kappa, Harvard Club (Boston). *Awards, honors:* Ford Foundation fellowship, Indonesia, 1955-56.

WRITINGS: (With Joan Landman) *Where to Ski,* Houghton, 1949; (contributor) Terry Morris, editor, *Prose by Professionals,* Doubleday, 1961; (editor with Johnson E. Fairchild) *America Faces the Nuclear Age,* Sheridan House, 1961.

Contributor to professional journals and popular magazines, including *Redbook, True, Cosmopolitan, Collier's, New Republic, Coronet, Pageant,* and *Nation's Business.*

SIDELIGHTS: Landman writes: "I consider myself to be a professional writer and communicator who for almost two decades has dedicated himself to communicating for non-profit institutions, usually colleges and universities. Whether these institutions flourish or flounder depends in large part on whether their story is heard, understood, and believed—by their several publics, and, as Edward L. Bernays has repeatedly pointed out, on whether the institutions adjust to what is in fact perceived and believed."

*   *   *

LANDRY, Robert John 1903-
    (Land)

PERSONAL: Born June 14, 1903, in East Haddam, Conn.; son of Daniel F. and Pauline (an actress; maiden name, Saxon) Landry; married Marcia Smith, March 5, 1931; married second wife, Annett MacQuarrie, April 30, 1948; married third wife, Paula Bronstein (an economist), March 23, 1955. *Education:* Attended high school in Toledo, Ohio. *Religion:* Protestant. *Office:* 154 West 46th St., New York, N.Y. 10036.

CAREER: Variety, New York, N.Y., radio editor, 1932-42, managing editor, 1953—, also founder of show management awards. Publisher of *Space and Time,* 1949-52. Director of Division of Program Writing for Columbia Broadcasting System, 1942-48, and producer for Columbia Workshop. Director of New York University's summer radio and television workshops; lecturer at Columbia University, University of Pennsylvania, Harvard University, and Dartmouth College, Member of Writers War Board, 1942-45. *Member:* Authors Guild of Authors League of America, Overseas Press Club. *Awards, honors:* George Foster Peabody Award from University of Georgia, 1946, for Columbia Workshop production of "Richard III."

WRITINGS: Who, What, Why Is Radio?, George W. Stewart, 1942; *How Writers Perpetuate Racial Stereotypes,* Writers War Board, 1945; *This Fascinating Radio Business,* Bobbs-Merrill, 1948. Also author of *The Performing Arts: Encyclopedia of Careers,* 1967. Contributor to *Variety,* sometimes under pseudonym Land.

SIDELIGHTS: Landry describes himself briefly as a show business critic, dealing with film, radio, opera, and ballet.

*   *   *

LANG, Fritz 1890-1976

December 5, 1890—August 2, 1976; Austrian-born film

director and writer. First recognized as one of the leaders in the 1920's "golden age" of German films, Lang achieved worldwide recognition with his 1931 film, "M." He fled Nazi Germany in 1933, and made several successful films in Hollywood, including "Fury," "You Only Live Once," "Scarlet Street," and "Clash by Night." Critics acclaimed him as a pioneer of the dramatic use of sound. He served in the Austrian Army in World War I. Lang died in Los Angeles, Calif. Obituaries: *New York Times,* August 3, 1976; *Washington Post,* August 4, 1976.

* * *

LANGE, Gerald 1946-

PERSONAL: Born June 30, 1946, in Green Bay, Wis.; son of Carl F. and Harriet (Miller) Lange. *Education:* University of Wisconsin, Green Bay, B.A., 1970; University of Wisconsin, Madison, M.A., 1975, further graduate study, 1975—. *Home:* 124 North Page St., Stoughton, Wis. 53589.

CAREER: Bieler Press, Stoughton, Wis., printer and publisher, 1975—. Information specialist at Instructional Materials Center of University of Wisconsin, Madison, 1977. *Member:* American Printing History Association, Committee of Small Magazine Editors and Publishers, Wisconsin Library Association.

WRITINGS: Starless and Bible Black (prose poems), Bieler Press, 1975; *The New World* (broadside), Bieler Press, 1976; *Flown* (poems), Hosanna Press, 1977; *The Invisible Journey* (poem), Bieler Press, 1977.

SIDELIGHTS: Lange writes: "Since October, 1975, I have been publishing as The Bieler Press, issuing several chapbooks and broadsides of poetry and fiction by authors whose work is not widely distributed. All production work is in the tradition of fine printing and bookmaking. I've studied typography, book design, and hand paper making in the art department of the University of Wisconsin—Madison for over two-and-a-half years." Lange has had exhibits of his work at universities in Nevada and Wisconsin.

* * *

LaPENTA, Anthony V(incent), Jr. 1943-

PERSONAL: Born June 8, 1943, in Hartford, Conn.; son of Anthony Vincent (a postal supervisor) and Natalie (a saleswoman; maiden name, Carpentieri) LaPenta; married Catherine LeGrande (a statistical analyst), December 13, 1969; children: Anthony Vincent III, Joanna Kathleen. *Education:* University of Hartford, student, 1961-65; Central Connecticut State College, B.A., 1970. *Home and office:* 7 Tiffany Lane, Bloomfield, Conn. 06002.

CAREER: Aetna Life & Casualty (insurance), Hartford, Conn., group underwriter, 1966-68, administrative assistant and system analyst, 1970-71; writer, 1974—. Has worked as radio copy writer. Volunteer para-medic. Career counselor and recruiter for Army National Guard. Member of Bloomfield Transportation Advisory Board. *Military service:* Army National Guard, 1965-71. *Member:* Authors Guild of Authors League of America, Connecticut Writers League.

WRITINGS: The Sniper (novel), Ashley Books, 1976. Reporter for *Bloomfield Zip.*

WORK IN PROGRESS: Two science fiction novels in the "Wilder" series, *Beyond the Sun* and *Matabasset Project.*

SIDELIGHTS: LaPenta writes: "My writing will have some social commentary and as I grow in style, more depth in character. The books for now will be hard hitting, fairly emotional." *Avocational interests:* Writing poetry, travel.

LAPIERRE, Dominique 1931-

PERSONAL: Born July 30, 1931, in Chatelaillon, France; son of Jean (a diplomat) and Luce (Andreotti) Lapierre; married Aliette Spitzer, August 4, 1952; children: Alexandra. *Education:* Institut des Sciences Politique, Paris, 1951; Lafayette College, Easton, Pa., B.A., 1952. *Religion:* Catholic. *Home and office:* 26 Avenue Kleber, Paris 75116, France. *Agent:* Irving Lazar, 211 South Beverly Dr., Beverly Hills, Calif.

CAREER: Paris Match (magazine), Paris, France, war correspondent in Korea, 1953, editor, 1954-67; author, 1967—. *Awards, honors:* Grand prize from Foundation des bourses de Zellidja, 1949, for a study on Mexico and the United States.

WRITINGS: Un dollar les mille kilometres (title means "A Dollar for One Thousand Kilometers"), Grasset (Paris), 1949; *Lune de miel autour de la terre,* preface by Andre Maurois, Grasset, 1954, translation by Helen Beauclerk published as *Honeymoon Around the World,* Secker & Warburg, 1957; *En Liberte sur les routes d'U.R.S.S.* (title means "Freely on Soviet Highways"), Grasset, 1957; *Russie portes ouvertes* (title means "Open Doors to Soviet Russia"), Editions Vie (Lausanne, Switzerland), 1957; *Les Caids de New York* (title means "The New York Bosses"), Julliard (Paris), 1958; *Chessman m'a dit* (title means "Chessman Told Me"), Del Duca (Paris), 1960; (with Larry Collins) *Paris brule-t-il?,* Laffont (Paris), 1964, published as *Is Paris Burning?,* Simon & Schuster, 1965; (with Larry Collins) *Ou tu porteras mon deuil,* Laffont, 1967, published as *Or I'll Dress You in Mourning,* Simon & Schuster, 1968; (with Stephane Groueff) *Les Ministres du crime* (title means "The Ministers of Crime"), Julliard, 1969; (with Larry Collins) *O Jerusalem,* Laffont, 1971, published under same title, Simon & Schuster, 1972; (with Larry Collins) *Cette nuit la liberte,* Laffont, 1975, published as *Freedom at Midnight,* Simon & Schuster, 1975. Also author of filmscript adaptation of *O Jerusalem.*

WORK IN PROGRESS: A new book, "top secret for the time being."

SIDELIGHTS: Lapierre told *CA:* "My main professional interest is to bring back to life great moments of our contemporary history. I am interested in the great modern epics of humanity. History has the reputation to be dull: It's not dull if only you devote enough time and sweat to bring it back to life. I consider myself a historian using the modern technique of investigative journalism. Our books are as thoroughly and seriously researched as the most serious history books, and in this sense can be of use to professional, or rather, to 'scholarly' historians. But because of the dramatic nature of their subjects and their kaleidoscopic treatment, they are also very popular with the general public."

AVOCATIONAL INTERESTS: Tennis, horseback riding.

* * *

LAPP, Eleanor J. 1936-

PERSONAL: Born January 7, 1936, in Wausau, Wis.; daughter of Gustav (a mechanic) and Bertha (a teacher; maiden name, Luetschwager) Schram; married Richard Lapp (a logger), June 11, 1955; children: Rick. *Education:* University of Wisconsin, Stevens Point, B.S. *Home address:* Star Route, Phelps, Wis. 54554.

CAREER: Elementary school teacher, 1955—. Resort owner and operator, 1955-76. Writer. *Member:* Society of Children's Book Writers, Council for Wisconsin Writers, Wisconsin Regional Writers Association.

WRITINGS—Juvenile: *Hey, Elephant!*, Steck, 1970; *Duane the Collector*, Addison-Wesley, 1976; *The Mice Came in Early This Year*, Albert Whitman, 1976. Contributor to children's magazines.

* * *

LARSEN, Stephen 1941-

PERSONAL: Born February 17, 1941, in Flushing, N.Y.; son of Harold B. (a minister) and Mabel (Martin) Larsen; married Robin Searson (an artist), October 19, 1964; children: Merlin. *Education:* Columbia University, B.A., 1964, M.A., 1968; Union Graduate School, Yellow Springs, Ohio, Ph.D., 1974. *Religion:* "Shamanistic-vedic pantheistic Christian Buddhist." *Home:* Stone Mountain Farm, R.D. 2, Box 200D, New Paltz, N.Y. 12561. *Agent:* Timothy Seldes, Russell & Volkening, 551 Fifth Ave., New York, N.Y. 10017.

CAREER: Ulster County Community College, Stone Ridge, N.Y., assistant professor of psychology, 1968—; private practice in counseling and psychotherapy, 1971—. *Member:* American Psychological Association, Canadian Psychological Association, Association for Humanistic Psychology, C. G. Jung Foundation, Mid-Hudson Association for Humanistic Psychology (chairperson, 1972-74).

WRITINGS: The Shaman's Doorway: Opening the Mystic Imagination to Contemporary Consciousness, Harper, 1976.

WORK IN PROGRESS: A book on myth and ritual, *The Living Landscape*, with wife, Robin Larsen.

SIDELIGHTS: Larsen told *CA:* "I am an ex-mountain climber, and presently a hiker, a cross country skier, a student of karate and of Zen Buddhism, and a practitioner and teacher of yoga. I lead workshops and groups on dreams, body awareness, and have developed a psychodramatic technique which uses masks. Recently, my wife and son and I traveled through India, Ceylon, Nepal, Afghanistan, and Greece for eight months, returning in August, 1976."

BIOGRAPHICAL/CRITICAL SOURCES: Parabola, summer, 1976.

* * *

LASKY, Kathryn 1944-

PERSONAL: Born June 24, 1944, in Indianapolis, Ind.; daughter of Marven (a wine bottler) and Hortense (a social worker) Lasky; married Christopher Knight (a photographer and filmmaker), May 30, 1971. *Education:* University of Michigan, B.A., 1966; graduate study at Wheelock College. *Home:* 183 Webster St., East Boston, Mass. 02128. *Agent:* Mary Jane Higgins, 15½ Appleton St., Boston, Mass. 02116.

CAREER: Teacher.

WRITINGS—Juvenile: *Agatha's Alphabet*, Rand McNally, 1975; *I Have Four Names for My Grandfather*, Little, Brown, 1976; *Tugboats Never Sleep*, Little, Brown, in press. Contributor to *Sail*.

WORK IN PROGRESS: A book on the tall ships, for Scribner.

SIDELIGHTS: Kathryn Lasky told *CA:* "I write from my own experiences. The tugs of the tugboat book chug about right outside the window of our house which overlooks Boston harbor. When I was growing up I was always thinking up stories—whether I wrote them down or not didn't seem to matter. I was a compulsive story maker. I

was fiercely private about these early stories—never really sharing them with anybody. I always wanted to be a writer, but on the other hand it seemed to lack a certain legitimacy as a profession. It was enjoyable, not reliable, and you were your own boss. This all seemed funny. It was only when I began to share my writing with my parents (and much later my husband) and sensed their responsiveness that I began to think that it was o.k. to want to be a writer. One of the greatest things about my experiences in writing recently is that my husband has illustrated both the Grandfather and the Tugboat books with his photographs."

* * *

LASS, Betty (Lipschitz) 1908(?)-1976

1908(?)—November 20, 1976; American author. She assisted her husband, Abraham Lass, with several educational books and was co-author of *Dictionary Pronunciation*. For many years she was Philip Van Doren Stern's assistant. Lass died in Brooklyn, N.Y. Obituaries: *New York Times*, November 22, 1976.

* * *

LAURENCE, John 1939-

PERSONAL: Born October 5, 1939. *Education:* Attended Rensselaer Polytechnic Institute and University of Pennsylvania. *Office:* CBS News, 524 West 57th St., New York, N.Y. 10021.

CAREER/WRITINGS: WICC News, Bridgeport, Conn., writer and reporter, 1960-61; WWDC News, Washington, D.C., writer and reporter, 1961-62; WNEW News, New York, N.Y., writer and reporter, 1962-65; Columbia Broadcasting System (CBS) News, correspondent, 1965—. Notable assignments include coverage of the Dominican Republic Revolution, the Vietnam War, U.S. urban riots, 1966-68, the 1968 Democratic Convention in Chicago, Northern Ireland conflict, 1971-76, the 1971 India-Pakistan War, Middle East "October" War, and the Angola Civil War, 1975. *Awards, honors:* Emmy Awards, 1967-70; George Polk Memorial Award from Overseas Press Club, 1970; DuPont-Columbia Award, 1970; Sigma Delta Chi Award.

* * *

LAURENCE, William Leonard 1888-1977

March 7, 1888—March 19, 1977; American journalist and winner of two Pulitzer Prizes; best known as the only journalist to witness the nuclear blast at Alamogordo, N.M., and the only newspaperman permitted to fly on the atomic bomb mission over Nagasaki, Japan. He was with the *New York Times* from 1930 to 1964, first as a science reporter and later as science editor. Laurence died in Majorca, Spain. Obituaries: *New York Times*, March 20, 1977; *Newsweek*, March 28, 1977; *Current Biography*, May, 1977.

* * *

LAURENT, Lawrence (Bell) 1925-

PERSONAL: Born March 9, 1925, in Monroe, La.; son of Lewis Emeal (a lumber company superintendent) and John Ethel (a journalist; maiden name, Dawkins) Laurent; married Margaret Funsten Goodwille (a businesswoman), November 1, 1949; children: Richard S., Arthur H., Margaret F., Elizabeth M. *Education:* University of Virginia, B.A., 1949; American University, M.A., 1961. *Religion:* Episcopalian. *Home:* 215 Jefferson St., Alexandria, Va. 22314. *Agent:* Simon Michael Bessie, 115 East 36th St., New York,

N.Y. *Office: Washington Post,* 1150 15th St. N.W., Washington, D.C. 20071.

CAREER: Washington Post, Washington, D.C., editor of "TV Channels," 1951—. Adjunct professor at American University, 1964—. Member of executive committee of Human Family Institute (Pacific Palisades, Calif.). *Military service:* U.S. Navy, radioman for Fifth Amphibious Force, 1943-46; served in Pacific theater. *Member:* National Academy of Television Arts and Sciences (life member), National Press Club, White House Correspondents Association, Smithsonian Institution Associates, Sigma Delta Chi, Pi Delta Epsilon, Theta Chi. *Awards, honors:* Front Page Award from American Newspaper Guild, 1963.

WRITINGS: Television's Impact on American Culture, Michigan State University Press, 1956; *The Eighth Art,* Holt, 1962; *Equal Time: The Private Broadcaster and the Public Interest,* Atheneum, 1964; *Political Image Makers,* Public Affairs Press, 1972. Author of a column syndicated by Los Angeles Times-Washington Post News Service, 1961—. Chairman of editorial board of *TV Quarterly,* 1964-74.

WORK IN PROGRESS: A textbook on television programming; a study of presidential uses of television.

* * *

LAURIE, James 1947-

PERSONAL: Born June 16, 1947, in Eustis, Fla.; son of Andrew (a physician) and Geneva (a nurse; maiden name, Pryor) Laurie. *Education:* American University, B.A., 1969; graduate study at George Washington University and Georgetown University, 1974. *Office:* NBC News Worldwide, Sanko Daiichi Bldg., #6 Nishikubo Sakuragawa-Cho Shiba, Minato-Ku, Tokyo, Japan.

CAREER/WRITINGS: Metromedia Radio News, Washington, D.C., reporter and Saigon correspondent, 1969-71; National Broadcasting Co. (NBC), New York, N.Y., reporter and correspondent, 1971-72; *Far Eastern Economic Review,* Hong Kong, contributor, 1973-75; NBC, New York City, reporter and correspondent, 1975—. Notable assignments include the Vietnam moratorium, 1969; Cambodian coup d'etat and Cambodian invasion, 1970; North Vietnam offensive, 1972; fall of Cambodia, 1975; and fall of Vietnam, 1975; India's emergency, 1975; and the Lebanon War, 1975. *Awards, honors:* George Foster Peabody Award for broadcasting, 1976, for "outstanding reports from Vietnam following the fall of Saigon, 1975."

SIDELIGHTS: Laurie was the only American TV network correspondent to remain in Vietnam after the Communist take-over of the country, April 30, 1975. He told *CA:* "After all NBC News personnel were advised to leave Saigon with the American Embassy evacuation, cameraman Neil Davis and I volunteered to stay behind. I felt it was a great shame that after such intensive coverage during the previous ten years of the war that so few seemed willing to accept the risk of staying on to cover the end. Davis and I had worked in Cambodia together and hardened by the experience of some of the last few tragic days in Cambodia were ready for anything. As it turned out, working under 'Socialist' Vietnam was easier than expected. During those few weeks we travelled outside of Saigon, interviewed numerous cadre and attended state receptions for the new government. I departed Saigon by a North Vietnamese piloted Soviet Illyushin on May 26, 1975, in order to bring out a month's worth of film which was edited and shown in an NBC documentary 'NBC News Special Report: Communist Saigon,' aired on May 26th, via satellite from Hong Kong."

"As a communicator," Laurie added, "I see my place in the international arena providing a bridge, no matter how imperfect, between peoples of different nations. My specialisation to date has been Asian affairs. I believe too little emphasis has been put in American journalism on well-backgrounded, experienced communicators reporting outside the United States."

* * *

LAZARSFELD, Paul Felix 1901-1976

February 13, 1901—August 30, 1976; Austrian-born sociologist and authority on American voting patterns and popular culture; his most notable books include *The People's Choice* and *Voting.* He taught at Columbia University for over thirty years. Lazarsfeld died in New York City. Obituaries: *New York Times,* September 1, 1976; *Current Biography,* November, 1976.

* * *

LAZREG, Marnia 1941-

PERSONAL: Born January 10, 1941, in Mostaganem, Algeria; came to the United States in 1967; daughter of Aoued (a businessman) and Fatma (Belghrib) Lazreg. *Education:* University of Algiers, baccalaureate, 1960, lic.-es-lettres, 1965; New York University, M.A., 1970, Ph.D., 1975. *Home:* 295 Central Park W., New York, N.Y. 10024. *Office:* Department of Sociology, New School for Social Research, 65 Fifth Ave., New York, N.Y. 10003.

CAREER: Brooklyn College of the City University of New York, Brooklyn, N.Y., instructor in sociology, 1970-73; Hunter College of the City University of New York, New York, N.Y., fellow, 1973-75; New School for Social Research, New York City, assistant professor of sociology, 1975—. Interpreter at international conferences, 1965-68. *Member:* International Sociological Association, American Sociological Association, African Studies Association, Association of Third World Economists, Eastern Sociological Society.

WRITINGS: The Emergence of Classes in Algeria: A Study of Colonialism and Socio-Political Change, Westview Press, 1976. Contributor to anthropology and Black studies journals.

WORK IN PROGRESS: Forms of Colonial Alienation; editing *State and Social Class in Third World Social Formations;* editing a book on contemporary French sociological theory.

SIDELIGHTS: Marnia Lazreg writes: "My interest in forms of social change arises out of my early experiences in a cross-cultural setting marked by historical events, namely colonialism and decolonization. I am also extremely sensitive to shifts in political consciousness and self-awareness. My work reflects my horror of dogma, be it theoretical, methodological, or political."

* * *

LEACH, Maria 1892-1977

April 30, 1892—May 22, 1977; American editor of two-volume dictionary on folklore and author of other works on the subject. She died in Barrington, Nova Scotia. Obituaries: *New York Times,* May 24, 1977. (See index for previous *CA* sketch)

LEAF, Munro 1905-1976

December 4, 1905—December 21, 1976; American illustrator, lecturer, and author of children's books; best known for *The Story of Ferdinand*, which appeared in 1936 and has since been translated into fifty foreign editions in sixteen languages. His other popular books include the "Can Be Fun" series and *The Story of Ann*. He was an English teacher before he began writing. Obituaries: *New York Times*, December 22, 1976; *Washington Post*, December 23, 1976; *Time*, January 3, 1977; *AB Bookman's Weekly*, March 7, 1977.

* * *

LeClaire, Gordon 1905-

PERSONAL: Born January 15, 1905, in Ormstown, Quebec, Canada; son of Napoleon (a miller) and Catherine Ann (Sproule) LeClaire; married Zita Nuttall (a teacher and poet), March 28, 1942. *Education:* McGill University, B.A., 1933. *Home:* 2957 Henrietta Ave., La Cresenta, Calif. 91214.

CAREER: English language specialist in high schools in Montreal, Quebec, 1923-59; Montreal Repertory Theatre, Montreal, actor, 1930-42; Drama Group, Montreal, founder and director, 1937-43; language specialist in high schools in San Gabriel, Calif., 1959-71; lecturer and poet. Director, McGill University Workshop Players, 1931-32. *Member:* Poetry Society of America, Academy of American Poets, Royal Society of Arts (fellow), Chaparrel Poets. *Awards, honors:* Prince of Wales Gold Medal Award for "outstanding excellence in mental and moral philosophy," 1933.

WRITINGS: Intimate Moments, M. Andre, 1934; *Sonnets to the Stars*, Dorrance, 1936; *Star-Haunted*, Harrison Co., 1938; *Though Quick Souls Bleed* (poetry), Banner Press, 1939; *More Life in Living*, Mind Digest, 1947; *Carpenter's Apprentice and Other Poems*, Ryerson Press, 1957; *Poems–New and Selected 1935-1975*, Golden Quill, 1975. Contributor of poems to *Saturday Review, New York Times, New York Herald Tribune*, and other periodicals.

WORK IN PROGRESS: A book of poems, all previously published.

SIDELIGHTS: "I attempt in all my creative poetry writings," LeClaire told *CA*, "to project a definite poetic mood, utilizing techniques and forms which best adapt to the idea or emotion involved. A strict disciplinarian in all my work, I strive to emulate the highest ideals of the greatest poets both contemporary and of the past."

"Much superb poetry is being written today," LeClaire continued, "in a great variety of forms. Personally, I prefer poems to be inspiring and elevating, in which form and substance combine to effect a positive mental and emotional response. However, I do deplore a prevalent tendency of many contemporary poets to write exclusively in formless 'freak verse' which features gutter language. 'Grow towards God or go to dust.'"

* * *

LEE, Eddie H. 1917-

PERSONAL: Born March 19, 1917, in Magee, Miss.; son of Eddie H. (an engineer) and Leona Lee; married wife Geraldine, June 2, 1938 (divorced, June, 1945); married wife Myrtis (a hostess), October 18, 1968; children: Sandra Kay (Mrs. A. W. Shuttleworth). *Education:* Attended high school in Mize, Miss. *Home:* 345 Daniel Lake Blvd., Jackson, Miss. 39212. *Office:* Dacus Casket Co., West Memphis, Ark.

CAREER: U.S. Air Force, pilot in European theater; retired as captain; Dacus Casket Co., West Memphis, Ark., sales representative, 1964—. *Awards, honors*—Military: Distinguished Flying Cross, Air Medal.

WRITINGS: Journey Into Nowhere, Branden Press, 1973.

WORK IN PROGRESS: A book.

* * *

LEE, Ginffa 1900(?)-1976

1900(?)—December 25, 1976; Chinese-born poet, sculptor and diplomat. He was a founder of the symbolism school of Chinese poetry. He died in Long Island City, N.Y. Obituaries: *New York Times*, December 31, 1976.

* * *

LEEKLEY, Richard N. 1912-1976

September 5, 1912—October 26, 1976; American author, journalist, poet, and publisher. Well known for his extensive collection of scarce, scholarly and rare books, he operated an antiquarian book business in the 1960's. He died in Winthrop Harbor, Ill. Obituaries: *AB Bookman's Weekly*, December 20, 1976.

* * *

LEFFERTS, George 1921-

PERSONAL: Born June 18, 1921, in Paterson, N.J.; son of Morris (an entrepreneur) and Elinor (Jacobs) Lefferts; married Elizabeth Ruth Schaul, December 29, 1942; children: Lauren Ruth, Barbara Ellen. *Education:* Drew University, B.A. (engineering), 1940; University of Michigan, B.A. (English), 1942. *Home:* Glen Goin, Alpine, N.J. 07620; and, Robbins Rest, Fire Island, N.Y. 11782. *Agent:* William Morris Agency, 1350 Avenue of the Americas, New York, N.Y. 10019.

CAREER: National Broadcasting Co. (NBC), New York, N.Y., executive producer, director, and writer, 1947-57; U.S. Department of State, Washington, D.C., producer and writer of films, 1958-61; Bing Crosby Productions, Los Angeles, Calif., executive producer and writer of "Breaking Point" television series, 1962-64; American Broadcasting Co. (ABC), executive producer, 1966-67; "Hallmark Hall of Fame" television series, executive producer, 1969-70; George Lefferts Associates, Inc., president, 1968—. Producer of specials for NBC, 1971-72; producer and writer of full-length films and of films for the American Cancer Society and American Heart Association. Sculpture exhibited at Sculpture Gallery, New York, N.Y., 1960. *Military service:* U.S. Army, 1942-45. *Member:* National Academy of Television Arts and Sciences, Academy of Motion Picture Arts and Sciences, Dramatists Guild, Authors League of America, Writers Guild of America, Christopher Morley Knothole Association, South Bay Cruising Club, Glen Goin Club. *Awards, honors:* Award from Ohio State University, 1955, for "NBC Theatre"; George Foster Peabody Award, 1956, for "Biographies in Sound"; National Media Award, 1961; Golden Globe award, 1961, and Emmy Award, 1962, both for NBC "Specials for Women"; Fame award, 1962; Plaudit Award from Producers Guild, 1963, for "Breaking Point" series, Foreign Press Award, 1963; Emmy Award, 1970, for production of "Teacher, Teacher."

WRITINGS: Special for Women (eight plays originally broadcast on television), introduction by Margaret Mead, Avon, 1962.

Unpublished plays: "Nantucket Legend," "The Boat," and "Hey Everybody," first produced in 1970.

Writer of television scripts for NBC programs, including "Kraft Theatre," "Studio One," "Armstrong Circle Theatre," "NBC Theatre," "Alcoa Theatre," and "Chrysler Theatre"; writer of two television special reports, "Pain," 1971, and "What Price Health?," 1972. Author and producer of filmscripts, "The Living End," 1959, "The Stake," 1960, "The Teenager," 1965, and "The Harness," 1972. Contributor to *Esquire* and other magazines. Author of syndicated columns.

*   *   *

le FORT, Gertrud (Petrea) von   1897-1971

PERSONAL: Full name Gertrud Auguste Lina Elsbeth Mathilde Petrea, *Freiin* von le Fort; born October 11, 1876, in Minden, Germany; daughter of Lothar (an army officer and baron) and Elsbeth (von Wedel-Parlow) von le Fort; *Education:* Attended University of Heidelberg, 1908, 1910-13, and 1914, University of Marburg, 1913-14, and University of Berlin, 1916. *Religion:* Roman Catholic. *Residence:* Oberstdorf, Germany.

CAREER: Writer. *Wartime service:* Served the Red Cross. *Member:* Bayrische Akademie der Schoenen Kuenste, Akademie der Kuenste Berlin, Deutsche Akademie fuer Sprache und Dichtung, Academy of the Gallery of Living Catholic Authors (Webster Groves, Mo.). *Awards, honors:* Muenchner Literaturpreis, 1947; Badischer Staatspreis (Droste-Preis), 1948; Gottfried-Keller-Preis, 1952; Grosse Verdienstkreuz der Bundesrepublik Deutschland, 1953; Grosser Preis des Landes Nordrhein-Westfalen fuer Literatur, 1955; Dr. Theol. from University of Munich, 1956; Bayrischer Verdienstorden, 1959; Stern zum grossen Verdienstkreuz der Bundesrepublik Deutschland, 1966; Kultureller Ehrenpreis der Stadt Muenchen, 1969.

WRITINGS—In English translation: *Hymnen an die Kirche*, Theatiner (Munich), 1924, 7th edition, Beckstein (Munich), 1946, translation by Margaret Chanler published as *Hymns to the Church*, Sheed & Ward, 1938; *Das Schweisstuch der Veronika*, Koesel & Pustet (Munich), 1928, 15th edition published as *Das Schweisstuch der Veronika*, Book I: *Der Roemische Brunnen*, 1967, translation by Conrad M. R. Bonacina published as *The Veil of Veronica*, Sheed & Ward, 1932, reprinted, AMS Press, 1970; *Der Papst aus dem Ghetto: Die Legende des Geschlechtes Pier Leone*, Transmare (Berlin), 1930, 7th edition, Ehrenwirth (Munich), 1959, translation by Bonacina published as *The Pope From the Ghetto: The Legend of the Family of Pier Leone*, Sheed & Ward, 1934; *Die Letzte am Schafott*, Koesel & Pustet, 1931, reprinted Ehrenwirth, 1959, translation by Olga Marx published as *The Song At the Scaffold*, Holt, 1933, reprinted, Image Books, 1961, revised translation edited by Martin McMurtrey and Robert Knopp, published under same title, Catholic Authors, 1954; *Die ewige Frau, Die Frau in der Zeit*, [and] *Die zeitlose Frau*, Koesel & Pustet, 1934, revised edition, 1960, 20th edition, 1962, translation by Marie C. Buehrle published as *The Eternal Woman, The Woman in Time*, [and] *Timeless Woman*, Bruce Publishing, 1954, translation of revised edition by Placid Jordan published under same title, 1962; *Madonnen, eine Bilderfolge* (in German, English, and French), Arche (Zurich), 1948, new edition, 1962; *Die Frau des Pilatus*, Insel (Leipzig), 1955, translation by Marie C. Buehrle published as *The Wife of Pilate*, Bruce Publishing, 1957; (author of introduction) Leonard von Matt, *Rom: Das Antlitz der*

ewigen Stadt, Neptun (Kreuzlingen), 1955, translation by Wolf Friederich published as *Rome: The Eternal City*, Andermann (Munich), 1955.

Collections in English translation: *Die Tochter Farinatas* (four novellas, includes *Die Tochter Farinatas, Die Consolata, Das Gericht des Meeres*, and *Plus ultra*), Insel, 1950, translation by Isabel and Florence McHugh published as *The Judgement of the Sea (The Gate of Heaven, The Tower of the Constant, The Judgement of the Sea*, and *Plus Ultra*), Regnery, 1962.

In German: *Hymnen an Deutschland*, Koesel & Pustet, 1932; *Das Reich des Kindes: Legende der letzten Karolinger*, Langen-Mueller (Munich), 1934; *Die Magdeburgische Hochzeit*, Insel, 1938, reprinted, 1958; *Die Opferflamme: Erzaehlung*, Insel, 1938, new edition, Arche, 1962.

Die Abberufung der Jungfrau von Barby: Erzaehlung, Beckstein, 1940, reprinted, Ehrenwirth, 1960; *Das Gericht des Meeres*, Insel (Leipzig), 1943, reprinted, Insel (Frankfurt), 1975, German language edition edited by Robert O. Roeseler and published under same title, Appleton, 1959; *Der Kranz der Engel*, Beckstein, 1946, 8th edition published as *Das Schweisstuch der Veronika*, Volume II: *Der Kranz der Engel*, 1962; *Die Consolata*, Insel, 1947; *Gedichte*, Insel, 1949, reprinted, Ehrenwirth, 1970; *Unser Weg durch die Nacht, eine Rede fuer meine Schweizer Freunde*, Insel, 1949, published as *Unser Weg durch die Nacht: Rorte an meine Schweizer Freunde*, Ehrenwirth, 1962.

Die Tochter Farinatas: Erzaehlung, Insel, 1950; *Am Tor des Himmels*, Insel, 1954, German language edition edited, with introduction, notes, and vocabulary, by J. R. Foster and published under same title, Harrap, 1966; *Das kleine Weihnachtsbuch*, Arche, 1954; *Die Brautgabe* [*Gedichte und Prosa*], Arche, 1955, new edition, Sanssouci (Zurich), 1967; *Weihnachten, das Fest der goettlichen Liebe*, Evangelisch Verlagsanstalt (Stuttgart), 1956; *Der Turm der Bestaendigkeit*, Insel, 1957; *Plus ultra: Erzaehlung*, Insel, 1957; *Die letzte Begegnung*, Insel, 1959; *Die Frau und die Technik*, Arche, 1959.

Das fremde Kind: Erzaehlung, Insel (Frankfort), 1961; *Aphorismen*, Ehrenwirth, 1962; *Die Tochter Jephthas: Eine Legende*, Insel, 1964; *Haelfte des Lebens: Erinnerungen*, Ehrenwirth, 1965; *Das Schweigen, eine Legende*, Arche, 1967; *Die Verfemte: Mit einer autobiographischen Erinnerung "Heidelberg,"* Reclam (Stuttgart), 1967; *Der Dom: Erzaehlung*, Ehrenwirth, 1968; *Unsere liebe Frau vom Carneval*, Arche, 1975.

Collections in German: *Aufzeichnungen und Erinnerungen*, Benziger (Einsiedeln), 1951, 4th edition, 1958; *Die Krone der Frau*, Arche, 1952; *Geloeschte Kerzen: Zwei Eraehlungen* (two novellas, *Die Unschuldigen, ein Erinnerungsblatt* and *Die Verfemte: Dem Andenken der toten Kinder des Weltkrieges*), Ehrenwirth, 1953, 8th edition, 1963; *Das Reich des Kindes* [and] *Die Voeglein von Theres: Zwei Legenden*, Insel, 1958; *Erzaehlende Schriffen* (collected work), three volumes, Ehrenwirth and Insel, 1966; *Die Erzaehlungen* (fourteen novellas), Ehrenwirth and Insel, 1966; *Die Tochter Jephthas und andere Erzaehlungen* (seven novellas, *Die Tochter Farinatas, Die Consolata, Plus ultra, Am Tor des Himmels, Die Frau des Pilatus, Der Turm der Bestaendigkeit, Die Tochter Jephthas*), Suhrkamp (Frankfurt), 1976.

Story translation published in *The Griffin*, May, 1951; poetry anthologized in *Lieblingsgedichte*, edited by Georg Gerster, Arche, 1964. Co-editor of "Das Literarische Deutschland," 1950-52.

SIDELIGHTS: Eleonore von La Chevallerie, Miss le Fort's former secretary, told *CA* that the most important influences on Baroness le Fort's life and work were her visit to Rome in 1907, her studies in Heidelberg, 1912-13, and her conversion to Roman Catholicism in 1926. Although prevalent in all her fiction, Miss La Chevallerie believes *The Veil of Veronica* and *The Wrath of the Angels* best display these influences.

Miss le Fort frequently chose historical subjects for her novellas and legends for their deliberate parallels to the problems of the present. On several occasions she wrote and told Miss La Chevallerie: "I never felt like flying from the present back to historical times but I considered the historical setting as the distance from which you can see contemporary problems more clearly, in the same way you see a mountain better if you are not quite as close to it."

BIOGRAPHICAL/CRITICAL SOURCES: Gisbert Kranz, editor, *Gertrud von le Fort, Leben und Werk in Daten, Bildern, und Zeugnissen*, Insel, 1976; Hedwig Bach, editor, *Dichtung ist eine Form der Leibe, Begegnung mit Gertrud von le Fort und ihrem Werk*, Ehrenwirth, 1976.

(Died November 1, 1971, in Obersdorf, Germany)

[Sketch verified by Eleonore von La Chevallerie]

* * *

LEHMANN, Lotte   1888-1976

February 27, 1888—August 26, 1976; Prussian-born American soprano, lieder singer, and author. During her career from 1910 to 1945, she performed in every major opera house, under every major conductor, in Europe and the United States. A diva in the grand tradition, she was well loved by audiences. Among her best known roles were Leonore in Beethoven's "Fidelio," Sieglinde in Wagner's "Die Walkeure," and her incomparable Marschallin in Strauss's "Der Rosenkavalier." She was the author of a novel, two books of memoirs, and a book on Richard Strauss. She died in Santa Barbara, Calif. Obituaries: *New York Times*, August 27, 1976; *Washington Post*, August 27, 1976.

* * *

LEIPOLD, L. Edmond   1902-

PERSONAL: Born August 2, 1902, in Minnesota; son of George August (a businessman) and Emma (Thieling) Leipold; married Gladys Huffman, July 27, 1923; children: Jean (Mrs. Dwayne Mahlberg), L. Edmond, Jr., Darel, Lance. *Education:* Attended St. Cloud State College, 1923-24; University of Minnesota, Ph.D., 1942; post doctoral study at Harvard University, 1943. *Home:* 777 Excelsior Blvd., Excelsior, Minn. 55331.

CAREER: Superintendent of schools in Montgomery, Minn., 1928-36; principal of junior high and high schools in Minneapolis, Minn., 1936-63; writer, 1963—. Professor at University of Colorado, Greely, summers, 1947-59, and at Mexico State University, summers, 1961-65. *Member:* Minnesota Association of Secondary Principals (executive secretary, 1965-66), Minneapolis Retired Teachers Association (president, 1976-77), Excelsior Senior Citizens (president, 1976-77), Scholia Fraternity, Minnetonka Country Club.

WRITINGS: Handbook of School Law, Bureau of Educational Research, Mexico State University, 1964.

All published by Denison; "Famous American Heroes and Leaders" series: *Famous American Explorers of Our Land*, 1967; . . . *Citizens Born Abroad*, 1967; . . . *Women*, 1967; . . .

Negroes, 1967; . . . *Indians*, 1967; . . . *Scientists and Astronauts*, 1967; . . . *Founders of Fortune*, 1967; . . . *Crusaders for a Cause*, 1967; . . . *Founders of Our Cities*, 1967; . . . *Doctors*, 1969; . . . *Athletes*, 1969; . . . *Poets*, 1969; . . . *Artists*, 1969; . . . *Heroes in Time of War*, 1970; . . . *Labor Leaders*, 1972; . . . *Architects*, 1972; . . . *Musicians*, 1972; . . . *Teachers*, 1972; . . . *Engineers*, 1972; . . . *Fiction Writers*, 1972. Also author of *Famous American Founders of Fortune*, book II.

"Men of Achievement" series: *William Powell Lear: Designer and Inventor*, 1967; *Gordon A. Yock: Merchandising Expert*, 1967; *Lawrence M. Weitzel: Mechanical Specialist*, 1968; *Ronald Reagan: Governor and Statesman*, 1968; *Jeno F. Paulucci: Merchant Philanthropist*, 1968; *Win Stephens: Business and Civic Leader*, 1969; *Richard M. Nixon: President*, 1969; *Cecil E. Newman: Newspaper Publisher*, 1969; *Harold W. Greenwood: Financier*, 1970; *Dr. Christiaan N. Barnard: The Man with the Golden Hands*, 1971; *Eddie Shipstad: Ice Follies Star*, 1971; *Charles Lindberg: Aviation Pioneer*, 1972; *Alton S. Newell: Recycling Expert*, 1973.

"Folk Tales" series: *Folk Tales of Germany*, 1969; . . . *Greece*, 1970; . . . *France*, 1971; . . . *England*, 1973; . . . *Russia*, 1973; . . . *Italy*, 1973; . . . *Arabia*, 1973.

"Come Along" series: *Come Along to East Germany*, 1969; *Come Along to Luxembourg*, 1973; *Come Along to Saudi Arabia*, 1974.

"Lives of Great Americans" series: *When Our Country Was Very Young*, 1972; *Our Country Grows Up*, 1972; *America Becomes Free*, 1972; *Makers of a Better America*, 1972; *They Gave Their Lives*, 1972; *Heroes of Today—The Astronauts*, 1973; *Heroes of a Different Kind*, 1973; *Americans Born Abroad*, 1973; *Great American Artists*, 1973; *Great American Poets*, 1973.

Also author of *A Pictorial Biography of the Harold Greenwoods*, published by Denison. Contributor of about eighty-five articles to education journals.

WORK IN PROGRESS: Biographies of Charles Ritz of Multi-Foods Corp., and of Walter Ringer of Foley Co.

* * *

LEITER, Robert D(avid)   1922-1976

June 2, 1922—August 19, 1976; American educator and author of books on economics and labor, including *The Foreman in Industrial Relations* and *The Teamsters Union: A Study of Its Economic Impact*. He died in New York City. Obituaries: *New York Times*, August 20, 1976. (See index for previous *CA* sketch)

* * *

LeMAHIEU, D(an) L(loyd)   1945-

PERSONAL: Born May 9, 1945, in Wisconsin; son of Lloyd Frederick and Ruth J. LeMahieu. *Education:* Lawrence University, B.A. (summa cum laude), 1967; Harvard University, M.A., 1968, Ph.D., 1973. *Home:* 21 College Campus S., Lake Forest, Ill. 60045. *Office:* Department of History, Lake Forest College, Lake Forest, Ill. 60045.

CAREER: University of Nebraska, Lincoln, visiting assistant professor of history, 1973-74; Lake Forest College, Lake Forest, Ill., assistant professor of history, 1974—. *Member:* American Historical Association, American Society for Eighteenth-Century Studies, Common Cause, Phi Beta Kappa (president of Theta chapter, 1976-77).

WRITINGS: The Mind of William Paley: A Philosopher and His Age, University of Nebraska Press, 1976.

WORK IN PROGRESS: British Reactions to Cultural Democracy, 1919-39.

* * *

LEONARD, Phyllis G(rubbs) 1924-

PERSONAL: Born October 4, 1924, in Westerville, Ohio, daughter of Maynard Lee (a paper hanger) and Lura McEwen (Steele) Grubbs; married Walter Magruder Leonard (a writer and photographer), January 31, 1948. *Education:* Attended Cleveland College (now Case Western Reserve University), 1942-44; Universidad de San Carlos, certificate, 1948; American Graduate School of International Management, certificate, 1949. *Politics:* "Conservative and proud to be an American." *Religion:* Protestant, "not much of a church-goer but try to practice everyday Christianity." *Home and office:* P.O. Box 8009, Phoenix, Ariz. 85066. *Agent:* Phyllis Westberg, Harold Ober Associates, 40 East 49th St., New York, N.Y. 10017.

CAREER: Leonard Insurance Agency, Phoenix, Ariz., partner with husband, 1952-63, president, 1963-71; Leonard Corp. (family firm), Phoenix, president, 1971—. President of Insurance Women of Phoenix, Inc., 1956; free-lance writer, 1971—. *Member:* Authors Guild, Arizona Press Women, National Federation of Press Women, Society of Southwestern Authors, Phoenix Friends of the Library (founding member). *Awards, honors:* First prize for fiction in Arizona Press Women's annual communications contest and second prize for adult fiction in National Federation of Press Women's annual communications contest, both 1974, both for *Prey of the Eagle;* first prize for fiction from Society of Southwestern Authors, 1976, for *Phantom of the Sacred Well.*

WRITINGS: Prey of the Eagle, McKay, 1974; *Phantom of the Sacred Well,* McKay, 1976; *Warrior's Woman,* Coward, 1977; *The Street of the Madwoman,* Coward, in press. Contributor of articles to magazines, including *Christian Science Monitor, Mankind, American Horseman, National Parks and Conservation, American Girl, Child Life, Iron Worker, True Frontier,* and *Pacific Discovery.*

WORK IN PROGRESS: An untitled historical romance similar to *Warrior's Woman; Sacrifice to the Sun,* a novel with nineteenth-century Peruvian background; other novels.

SIDELIGHTS: Phyllis Leonard wrote *CA:* "I dreamed of being a novelist since I was small. I like archaeological and historical material best, including little-known trivia. (E.g., I used the fact that the Mayas worshiped Cortes' horse as a god in *Phantom of Sacred Well.*) I feel my 'mission' is to be top-notch tale-spinner, combining entertainment with education through my careful research. If I can inspire readers to broaden intellectual horizons through curiosity about authentic data I've used, as well as enjoy the books as escape literature, I will feel I have given them a 'baker's dozen.' I hope to continue specializing in Latin American cultures and Amerindian civilizations, but as a lifelong history buff will write novels with other backgrounds, too. Philosophically, although I realize good guys may not always win, at 52 I remain optimistic about life, tend to be a romantic pragmatist. My books have had happy endings and generally will."

When asked where she finds her authentic data and little-known trivia, Phyllis Leonard replied: "How do I research a book? Taking *Warrior's Woman* as an example—by choosing several excellent references by authorities such as Prescott, Soustelle, Peterson, Von Hagen, Parry, and others, I immerse myself in them, then get relevant books mentioned in their bibliographies and study those. (E.g., hero-

ine's adventures in *Warrior's Woman* were involved with Cortes' conquest of Mexico; I studied him so narrative would be accurate in every detail from the scar on his lip to the banner's motto.) I also read good fiction: Marshall, Shedd, Shellabarger, Madariaga for different viewpoints. Translations from Spanish and Nahuatl records are invaluable for on-the-spot flavor. The subjects for *Warrior's Woman* ranged from armor and Aztecs to wolfhounds and witchcraft. Research is a joy to me and I feel a great obligation to readers to be as accurate as humanly possible. If sources don't agree or if they admit some lack of information, I use common sense, qualifying the statement in some way so the reader can make up his own mind.

"As to where I find little-known trivia such as Cortes' horse's name or how Toledo blades were made—sometimes it's sheer luck—other times it's the result of hours of assiduous digging, reading, and detective work. The latter is great fun and usually uncovers other research gems. This so-called trivia brings the past to vivid life and makes readers feel they are right there. Libraries, after all, are the treasure-houses of the world.

"I have specialized in Latin American and Amerindian backgrounds in all four novels because of a deep fascination for these areas which began at American Graduate School of International Management. There my husband and I (as newlyweds) studied Spanish and Central and South American countries' commerce, customs, etc. in preparation for a foreign trade career (that we did not follow). These studies, plus the summer in Guatemala in 1948, plus southern European travel later, came to fruition first in articles and then novels. *However,* and I emphasize this, if publishers ask for novels placed in other areas, I'll be able to do those, too, applying my research techniques."

CA asked what her working habits were like. "Nothing unusual, I'm afraid. I write my novels in the front room at the dining room table and have a desk in my office for clerical and general work. Hours are 10 AM to 6 PM, generally, with snack and chat breaks with my husband. I do the first draft of the novel in longhand—*just* the right word is a passion—then type the second draft which is polished numerous times before a typed manuscript is ready for the publisher. I keep the drapes closed so I won't daydream over desert skies, quail and rabbits in front of the window, or wind in the trees! The house also has to be neat while I'm working or I'm up straightening things! Although difficult at times creatively and financially, writing is a joy and I hope I'll be fortunate enough to emulate authors I admire in versatility and output."

AVOCATIONAL INTERESTS: Bird-watching, camping, trailering to beauty spots of the Southwest, Phoenix Zoo volunteer work.

BIOGRAPHICAL/CRITICAL SOURCES: Arizona Republic, February 14, 1974; *Phoenix,* September, 1974.

* * *

LEPLEY, Jean Elizabeth 1934-
(Jean Darcy)

PERSONAL: Born February 25, 1934, in England; daughter of Clarence M. (a physicist) and Ruby L. (a teacher; maiden name, Cross) Zener; married Arthur R. Lepley (a chemist), November 29, 1957; children: Margaret, Elizabeth Jo, Jennifer, Richard. *Education:* University of Chicago, A.B., 1954, A.B. (French), 1958; attended Marshall University, 1972-74; University of Utah, M.A., 1973. *Home:* 327 11th Ave., Huntington, W.Va. 25701. *Agent:* Bertha Klausner International Literary Agency, 71 Park Ave., New York, N.Y. 10016.

CAREER: Former French teacher; Huntington Galleries, Huntington, W.Va., teacher of ballads, 1977—.

WRITINGS: (Under pseudonym Jean Darcy) *Raggle Taggle Gypsy* (autobiographical travel memoir), Hopkinson & Blake, 1977.

WORK IN PROGRESS: Research on Appalachian ballads and their Scottish-English roots.

SIDELIGHTS: Jean Lepley writes: "As an over-educated, under-employed housewife with unused language fluency, untapped energies, and a craving for adventure that found only occasional outlet in backpacking expeditions or folk festivals, I felt trapped at forty. Driven to undertake a solo vagabondage through France and to write about it. Incidentally, while my book will probably be considered 'women's lib,' I find their solutions—the solutions put forth by any political group to complex problems—entirely too pat, too dogmatic. How easy to say that everything is some man's fault!"

* * *

LEVENTHAL, Herbert 1941-

PERSONAL: Born October 9, 1941, in Brooklyn, N.Y.; son of Leo (a clerk) and Lillian (a bookkeeper; maiden name, Greenberg) Leventhal. *Education:* Brooklyn College of the City University of New York, B.A., 1962; City University of New York, Ph.D., 1973. *Politics:* Liberal Democrat. *Religion:* Jewish. *Home:* 1316 East 84th St., Brooklyn, N.Y. 11236.

CAREER: U.S. Army, Brooklyn, N.Y., management analyst, 1962-63, 1965-66; Kingsborough Community College, Brooklyn, N.Y., lecturer in American civilization, summer, 1969; Brooklyn College of the City University of New York, Brooklyn, N.Y., part-time instructor, 1970-74, visiting assistant professor of history, 1974-75; *Papers of Robert Morris*, Queens, N.Y., assistant editor, 1974—. Research associate, Program for Loyalist Studies and Publications, 1971-74. Member of Tom Paine Independent Democrats; member of executive board of Kings County Democratic Coalition, 1976—. *Military service:* U.S. Army, 1963-65. *Member:* American Historical Association, Organization of American Historians, American Association for Eighteenth Century Studies (charter member), American Studies Association, Historians Film Committee.

WRITINGS: In the Shadow of the Enlightenment: Occultism and Renaissance Science in Eighteenth-Century America, New York University Press, 1976. Contributor to proceedings of the American Antiquarian Society.

WORK IN PROGRESS: Research on occultism and on eighteenth century American culture.

SIDELIGHTS: Leventhal writes: "*In the Shadow* is a slightly revised version of my doctoral dissertation. I had planned to do a dissertation on conservative political thought with a chapter or two on aspects of old-fashioned thought in other areas; however, I found relics of occultism and Renaissance science more interesting than the political thought and at the same time doubted that there was much which was especially archaic in political thought. The result is a book whose original topic is now buried in a few passages of chapter eight.

"I hope to do other studies of eighteenth-century American culture, and in particular to find out what was read and what

was influential other than the traditional classics of the eighteenth century."

AVOCATIONAL INTERESTS: Reading science fiction, listening to music.

* * *

LEVINE, Ellen

PERSONAL: Born in New York, N.Y.; daughter of Nathan (a lawyer) and Ide (an executive assistant for an advertising agency; maiden name, Gruber) Levine. *Education:* Brandeis University, B.A. (magna cum laude), 1960; University of Chicago, M.A., 1961; further graduate study at University of California, Berkeley, Columbia University, and New York University. *Home:* 210 West 101st St., New York, N.Y. 10025.

CAREER: Free-lance photographer and writer. Has prepared video and audio portions of documentary films for Columbia Broadcasting System News, 1964-73, for National Educational Television, Amram Nowak Associates, Avco Corp., and Telpac, Inc., as well as photographic work for Ford Foundation, Pepsi-Cola, Inc., Media Medica, and magazines and publishers. Teacher for Chinatown Planning Council. Producer of television special "Conversations with History," and associate producer of "Golden Mountain on Mott Street."

WRITINGS: (With Judith Hale) *The Rebirth of Feminism,* Quadrangle, 1971; (editor with Koedt and Rapone) *Radical Feminism,* Quadrangle, 1973; *All She Needs,* Quadrangle, 1973.

Illustrator: *Manners for Minors,* Association Press, 1964. Contributor to magazines, including *Ms., Books, Donne e Bello,* and *Up from Under.* Associate editor and research director of *Diplomat.*

* * *

LEVY, David M. 1892-1977

April 27, 1892—March 1, 1977; American psychiatrist and author. A recognized pioneer in child psychology, Levy introduced the Rorschach test in America, and coined such terms as "sibling rivalry." He died in New York City. Obituaries: *New York Times,* March 4, 1977.

* * *

LEWALLEN, John 1942-

PERSONAL: Born November 14, 1942, in New Mexico; son of Walter Depew (an accountant) and Grace (Hansen) Lewallen; married wife Eleanor Sara (an editor and publisher), April 4, 1971; children: Rebecca Grace. *Education:* Whitman College, B.A., 1964. *Home and office:* 5871 Chabot Rd., Oakland, Calif. 94618.

CAREER: International Voluntary Services, Vietnam, community development volunteer worker, 1967-69; *Clear Creek* (magazine), San Francisco, Calif., features editor, 1971; *North Country Star,* Oakland, Calif., co-editor and co-publisher, 1976—. *Awards, honors:* Fulbright scholarship, University of Rajasthan, 1964-65.

WRITINGS: (Contributor) Nina Adams and Alfred McCoy, editors, *Laos: War and Revolution,* Harper, 1970; *Ecology of Devastation,* Penguin, 1971; (editor with James Robertson) *The Grass Roots Primer,* Sierra Club Books, 1975. Contributor of articles and reviews to West Coast ecology journals.

WORK IN PROGRESS: The Gentle Revolution in

Northern California, an account of the environmentally harmonious community evolving in northern California, based on material from *North Country Star.*

SIDELIGHTS: Lewallen told *CA:* "It seems perfectly obvious to me that high-energy, environmentally exploitative society is giving way to lower energy using, environmentally harmonious social forms. I work to make this transformation as gentle as possible."

* * *

LEWIN, Ted 1935-

PERSONAL: Born May 6, 1935, in Buffalo, N.Y.; son of Sidney (a retail jeweler) and Bernece (Klhen) Lewin; married Betsy Reilly (an artist). *Education:* Pratt Institute of Art, B.F.A., 1956. *Home and office:* 152 Willoughby Ave., Brooklyn, N.Y. 11205.

CAREER: Professional wrestler, 1952-65; artist and freelance illustrator, 1956—. *Military service:* U.S. Army, 1958.

WRITINGS—Self illustrated: *World Within a World: Everglades,* Dodd, 1976; *World Within a World: Baja,* Dodd, in press.

WORK IN PROGRESS: Illustrating books.

SIDELIGHTS: Lewin writes: "I am primarily an artist-illustrator, and my writing has grown out of an interest in the natural world which, until my first book, I confined to graphic form only. I am a deeply concerned environmentalist and conservationist, and travel to wilderness areas around the world for both graphic and literary material."

* * *

LEWIS, David 1942-
(David Hodgson)

PERSONAL: Born April 6, 1942, in London, England. *Education:* Educated in France, Germany, and the United Kingdom. *Agent:* Joan Daves, 515 Madison Ave., New York, N.Y. 10022.

CAREER: Journalist. As free-lance photographer, contributed to *Paris Match, Stern,* and *Life.*

WRITINGS: (With Peter Hughman) *Most Unnatural: An Inquiry into the Stafford Case,* Penguin, 1971; (with Hughman) *Just How Just?,* Secker & Warburg, 1975; *Sexpionage: The Exploitation of Sex by Soviet Intelligence,* Harcourt, 1976; (with Robert Sharpe) *The Success Factor: How to Be Who You Want to Be,* Crown, 1976; *Hitler: The Secret Life of Adolf Hitler,* Heinrich Hanau, 1977; (with Sharpe) *Thrive on Stress,* Souvenir Press, 1977, Warners, 1978; (with Sharpe) *The Anxiety Antidote,* Souvenir Press, 1978; (with Sharpe) *Fight Your Phobia and Win,* Behavioural Press, in press.

Under pseudonym David Hodgson: *All About Photographing Animals and Birds,* Transatlantic, 1975; *All About Action Photography,* Transatlantic, 1976; *Dive, Dive, Dive: A Guide to Sport Diving,* Transatlantic, 1976.

SIDELIGHTS: Lewis told *CA:* "At one time I became involved in a campaign to free from prison two men serving life sentences for murder. The result of my investigations was the book *Most Unnatural.* This resulted in the Home Secretary having the case referred back to the Court of Appeal. It was the first time in British legal history that this had happened. Sadly, there was a negative response despite massive evidence in support of our case. The men are still behind bars. My disgust at the way the system had treated these men, and thousands like them, resulted in the book *Just How Just?"*

LEWIS, David L(anier) 1927-

PERSONAL: Born April 5, 1927, in Bethalto, Ill.; son of Donald F. and Edith (Jinkinson) Lewis; married Florence Yuri Tanaka, April 5, 1953; children: Kim, Leilani, Sumiko, Lance. *Education:* University of Illinois, B.S., 1948; Boston University, M.S., 1955; University of Michigan, M.A., 1956, Ph.D., 1959. *Home:* 2588 Hawthorn, Ann Arbor, Mich. 48104. *Office:* Graduate School of Business Administration, University of Michigan, Ann Arbor, Mich. 48109.

CAREER: Edwardsville Intelligencer, Edwardsville, Ill., reporter, 1948; *Alton* Telegraph, Alton, Ill., bureau chief and state editor, 1948-50; Lincoln-Mercury Automobile Co., St. Louis, Mo., editor of employee publications, 1950-51; Ford Motor Co., Dearborn, Mich., press representative and later supervisor of industrial arts awards, 1952-55; General Motors Corp., Detroit, Mich., public relations staff member, 1959-65; University of Michigan, Ann Arbor, associate professor, 1966-68, professor of business history, 1968—. Consultant to history division of Michigan Department of State; moderator on University of Michigan's television documentary, "The Four Wheels that Changed America," 1966; judge for quality dealer awards, *Time* magazine, 1970—.

MEMBER: Public Relations Society of America, Society of Automotive Historians (director), National Automotive History Collection (trustee), Model T Ford Club of America (director), American Historical Association, Economic History Association, Historical Society of Michigan, Illinois State Historical Society. *Awards, honors:* Fulbright scholar, London School of Economics and Political Science, 1956-57; Pulitzer Prize nomination, 1977, for *The Public Image of Henry Ford;* awards for editorial contributions from Antique Automobile Club of America, Model T Ford Club, Model A Restorers Club, and American Risk and Insurance Association.

WRITINGS: (Contributor) Howard Stephenson, editor, *Handbook of Public Relations,* McGraw, 1960; *The Public Image of Henry Ford: An American Hero and His Company,* Wayne State University Press, 1976. Contributor of over 280 articles dealing with Henry Ford and Ford Motor Co. to historical and industry magazines and journals; contributor to *Collier's Encyclopedia.*

Contributing editor, *Old Car Illustrated, Horseless Carriage Gazette, Model T Times, V-8 Times;* associate editor, *Model "A" News;* feature editor, *Bulb Horn;* Ford editor, *Car & Parts.*

SIDELIGHTS: In 1961, David Lewis began to refine his doctoral thesis into a business biography of Henry Ford. The book, when finished, represented over nineteen years of research and writing. Allan Nevins said: "This is a model book of its kind. It is the best study in industrial public relations I have ever read. Not only is it thoroughly scholarly, and marked by incisive judgment throughout; it is so well-written and so colorful that it will hold the attention of the general reader while it satisfies the special student of business history and public opinion."

* * *

LEWIS, E. M.
(Mary Melwood)

PERSONAL: Born in Carlton in Lindrick, Nottinghamshire, England; daughter of John Burtwistle (a landowner) and Mary Agres (a town registrar; maiden name, Justice) Hall; married Morris Lewis; children: Robert Hall, Roderick Alan. *Education:* Attended schools in England. *Politics:* "Nil." *Religion:* "Nil." *Home:* 5 Hove Lodge Mansions, Hove St., Hove, Sussex, England.

CAREER: Has been an elementary school teacher; playwright and author. *Awards, honors:* Arts Council awards, 1964, for "Tuesday Bird," and 1965, for "Five Minutes to Morning."

WRITINGS: (Under pseudonym Mary Melwood) *Nettlewood* (novel), Deutsch, 1974, Seabury, 1975.

Plays: "Tuesday Bird," first produced, 1964; "Five Minutes to Morning," first produced, 1966; "Masquerade," first produced in Nottingham, England, at Nottingham Playhouse, 1974; "The Small Blue Hopping Stone," first produced in Detroit, Mich., at Southfield Repertory Theatre, 1976. Plays are also represented in anthologies, including *All the World's a Stage,* Delacorte.

WORK IN PROGRESS: Another play.

SIDELIGHTS: E. M. Lewis told *CA* she wrote and produced her first full-length play while she was twelve or thirteen. Interested in drama since her early childhood, she was involved in town musicals and helped establish a small company in 1936.

* * *

LEWIS, Freeman 1908-1976

January 6, 1908—August 15, 1976; American publishing executive. He worked for several publishers, including Blue Ribbon Books, and Doubleday (where he started the "New Home Library" series). Lewis retired in 1969 as executive vice-president of Pocket Books. He died in Roslyn, N.Y. Obituaries: *New York Times,* August 17, 1976.

* * *

LEWIS, Lawrence E(dwin) 1928-

PERSONAL: Born January 14, 1928, in Toledo, Ohio; son of Harold (an author and artist) and Violet (McGowan) Lewis; married Donna Davis (a college instructor), June 6, 1953; children: Linda, Laura, Martin. *Education:* Olivet College, B.A., 1953. *Politics:* Independent. *Religion:* Lutheran. *Home:* 111 South Thompson, Jackson, Mich. 49203.

CAREER/WRITINGS: Consumers Power Co., Jackson, Mich., artist and writer, 1953-69; Newspaper Enterprise Association, Cleveland, Ohio, author of "Campus Clatter" comic strip, syndicated to over two hundred fifty papers, 1970—. Instructor in cartooning, Jackson Community College, 1975—. *Military service:* U.S. Army, 1946-47. *Member:* National Cartoonist Society.

SIDELIGHTS: Lewis told *CA:* "I have always had a strong desire to express myself in writing and drawing. My primary aim in my cartoons is to entertain and amuse." *Avocational interests:* Tennis.

* * *

LIDMAN, David 1905-

PERSONAL: Born July 11, 1905, in Norfolk, Va.; son of Moses (a salesman) and Rose (Horwitz) Lidman; married Karen Ebba Proschowski, July 11, 1940; children: Karen Ebba. *Education:* Attended high school in Norfolk, Va. *Home:* 163-B Heritage Village, Southbury, Conn. 06488.

CAREER: Norfolk Post, Norfolk, Va., general assignment reporter and sports editor, 1920-23; *Suffolk News,* Suffolk, Va., managing editor, 1923; *Baltimore Post,* Baltimore, Md., general assignment reporter, 1923-26; *Philadelphia*

Sun, Philadelphia, Pa., at copy desk, 1926; *Richmond Times-Dispatch,* Richmond, Va., copy desk slot man, 1926-29; *Petersburg Progress-Index,* Petersburg, Va., member of staff, 1930-31; *Richmond Times-Dispatch,* sportswriter, 1931-34; *Washington Post,* Washington, D.C., news make-up editor, 1934; *Philadelphia Record,* Philadelphia, at copy desk, 1934; *New York Herald Tribune,* New York City, member of staff, 1934-41; *Chicago Sun,* Chicago, Ill., founding news editor, 1941-46; make-up editor and city editor, 1944-46; *Philately,* St. Louis, Mo., founding editor, 1946-47; John F. Rider (publisher), New York City, in public relations, 1947; *New York Times,* New York City, news editor, 1948-73, on national news desk, 1948-50, foreign news desk, 1950-51, editor of "International Air Edition," 1951-54, author of column "Stamps," 1961-73. Wire editor and correspondent for Associated Press in Richmond, Va., 1924-30. Former chairperson of Postmaster General's Citizens' Stamp Advisory Committee.

MEMBER; American Philatelic Congress (past president), American Philatelic Society (member of board of directors; member of board of vice-presidents, 1977), Society of Philatelic Americans (member of board of directors), Royal Philatelic Society (London; fellow), Essay-Proof Society (member of board of governors), Philatelic Literature Association (president, 1965), American Philatelic Research Library (founder and trustee), American Air Mail Society, Austria Philatelic Society, American First Day Cover Society, Roosevelt Philatelic Society (Chicago). *Awards, honors:* Luff Award, 1946, from American Philatelic Society; scroll of honor from American Philatelic Congress, 1946; Saul Newberry Award, 1946, from Chicago Philatelic Society; national award from Southeast Pennsylvania and Delaware Philatelic Federation, 1961; gold medal from American Philatelic Society, 1971.

WRITINGS: The New York Times Guide to Collecting Stamps, Golden Press, 1970; *Treasury of Stamps,* Abrams, 1976, revised edition, 1977. Author of columns "Stamps," in *New York Herald Tribune,* 1939-40, and "Stamps," in *Chicago Sun,* 1941-46. Editor of *American Philatelist, Essay-Proof Journal,* and *Congress Book* (of American Philatelic Congress).

WORK IN PROGRESS: Great Stamps, publication by Ridge Press.

SIDELIGHTS: Lidman writes to *CA:* "Comments on 52 years in newspapering: It had been a grand game, as it was called once upon a time. I don't believe that I lost it as a 'game' even on the day of my retirement for, excepting some dull days or nights, it was exhilarating just about all the time. There was something new each day. That may sound corny as hell, but not so. I found it fun. The new cold-type operations make our old one appear to be a turtle racing a rabbit who didn't stop to eat. While it has revamped the manner (especially for copy-editors), it isn't going to be what it was—but that's a part of what it's all about isn't it—onward and upward!"

* * *

LIEB, Fred(erick George) 1888-

PERSONAL: Born March 5, 1888, in Philadelphia, Pa.; son of George August and Theresa (Zigler) Lieb; married Mary Ann Peck; children: Marie Theresa (Mrs. R. Leslie Pearsall). *Education:* Attended high school in Philadelphia, Pa. *Politics:* Republican. *Religion:* "Unity." *Home and office:* Oak Lodge, 235 Third Ave. N., St. Petersburg, Fla. 33701. *Agent:* David Scott, Route 2, Box 37, Katoneh, N.Y. 10536.

CAREER: Norfolk & Western Railway, Philadelphia, Pa., clerk, 1904-10; New York Press, New York City, baseball writer, 1911-16; New York Morning Sun, New York City, baseball writer, 1916-20; New York Evening Telegram, New York City, baseball writer, 1920-27; New York Post, New York City, baseball writer, 1927-33; Sporting News, St. Louis, Mo., baseball writer, 1935-67; writer, 1967—. Official scorer for World Series, 1922-24, 1945; has covered sixty World Series. Member: Masons. Awards, honors: J. G. Taylor Spink Award from Baseball Hall of Fame, 1972; award from St. Petersburg Times, 1975.

WRITINGS: Sight Unseen: A Journalist Visits the Occult, Harper, 1939; Healing Mind, Body, and Purse, privately printed, c. 1940; The St. Louis Cardinals: The Story of a Great Baseball Club, Putnam, 1944; Connie Mack: Grand Old Man of Baseball, Putnam, 1945; The Detroit Tigers, Putnam, 1946; The Boston Red Sox, Putnam, 1947; The Pittsburgh Pirates, Putnam, 1948; The Story of the World Series: An Informal History, Putnam, 1949, revised edition, 1965; The Baseball Story, Putnam, 1950; (with Stan Baumgartner) The Philadelphia Phillies, Putnam, 1953; The Baltimore Orioles: The History of a Colorful Team in Baltimore and St. Louis, Putnam, 1955; Comedians and Pranksters of Baseball, C. C. Spink, 1958.

Author of columns "Hits Are My Bread and Butter," in Saturday Evening Post, and "Strictly Screw Ball," in Collier's. Also author of columns "Hot Stove League" and "Cutting the Plate." Contributor to Encyclopedia Americana. Contributor of stories to Baseball and Railroad Man.

* * *

LILJE, Hanns 1899-1977

1899—January 6, 1977; German theologian, author, and former president of the Lutheran Church's world movement. Jailed by the Nazis in 1944 for preaching "inner resistance" to Hitlerism, he was freed by Allied forces before his execution could be carried out. East German Communists later branded him the "NATO bishop" for supporting those Lutherans who favored West German rearmament. He died in Hanover, West Germany. Obituaries: New York Times, January 7, 1977; Washington Post, January 8, 1977.

* * *

LILLY, Eli 1885-1977

April 1, 1885—January 24, 1977; American author, philanthropist, and former president and chairman of the board of Eli Lilly & Co. Lilly played a major role in the development of insulin, barbituates, early production of penicillins and antibiotics, the Salk polio vaccine, and other drugs; he wrote on Americana and history. He died in Indianapolis, Ind. Obituaries: New York Times, January 25, 1977; Newsweek, February 7, 1977.

* * *

LIMA, Jose Lezama 1911(?)-1976
(Jose Lezama)

1911(?)—August 9, 1976; Cuban poet, novelist, lawyer and editor. He is best known for Paradiso and is considered by some critics to be Cuba's most important poet. He was editor of Origenes, a literary magazine, from 1944 to 1956, and was appointed head of the literary department of Cuban Council for Culture following the 1959 revolution. He died in Havana, Cuba. Obituaries: New York Times, August 10, 1976; Publishers Weekly, August 23, 1976.

LINDBERG, David C. 1935-

PERSONAL: Born November 15, 1935, in Minneapolis, Minn.; son of Milton B. (a clergyman) and Elizabeth (a writer; maiden name, MacKinney) Lindberg; married E. Greta Johnson (a secretary), June 20, 1959; children: Christin Lisa, Erik David. Education: Wheaton College, Wheaton, Ill., B.S. (magna cum laude), 1957; Northwestern University, M.S., 1959; Indiana University, Ph.D., 1965. Home: 5038 Marathon Dr., Madison, Wis. 53705. Office: South Hall, University of Wisconsin, Madison, Wis. 53706.

CAREER: University of Michigan, Ann Arbor, assistant professor of history, 1965-67; University of Wisconsin, Madison, assistant professor, 1967-69, associate professor, 1969-72, professor of history of science, 1972—. Member of Institute for Advanced Study, 1970-71; member of Institute for Research in the Humanities, University of Wisconsin, 1975. Member: History of Science Society, Mediaeval Academy of America, Renaissance Society of America. Awards, honors: Guggenheim fellowship, 1977-78.

WRITINGS: John Pecham and the Science of Optics, University of Wisconsin Press, 1970; A Catalogue of Medieval and Renaissance Optical Manuscripts, Pontifical Institute of Mediaeval Studies, 1975; Theories of Vision from al-Kindi to Kepler, University of Chicago Press, 1976.

WORK IN PROGRESS: A study of Roger Bacon's philosophy of nature.

* * *

LINDQUIST, Jennie Dorothea 1899-1977

1899—February 8, 1977; American author of children's books and former editor of Horn Book Magazine. Among her numerous children's books were Little Silver House and Crystal Tree. She died in Manchester, N.H. Obituaries: AB Bookman's Weekly, March 14, 1977.

* * *

LINKLETTER, John A(ustin) 1923-

PERSONAL: Born February 11, 1923, in Winnipeg, Manitoba, Canada; son of Isaac (a minister) and Edna (Stamy) Linkletter; married Joan Otterman (a nurse), August 18, 1950; children: Gayle, Scott, John. Education: University of Iowa, B.A., 1947, M.A., 1948. Home: 18 Park Ave., Old Greenwich, Conn. 06870. Office: Popular Mechanics, 224 West 57th St., New York, N.Y. 10019.

CAREER/WRITINGS: Popular Mechanics, New York, N.Y., managing editor, 1962-74, editor, 1974—. Military service: U.S. Navy, 1943-45.

SIDELIGHTS: As editor of Popular Mechanics, Linkletter points out that writers for his magazine must "popularize" technical subjects so that they can be understood by anyone: "Solar energy. Conservation of resources. Nuclear fusion. Exhaust emissions. Heat loss. These are just a few of the increasingly complicated and bewildering subjects that concern every one of us. We cannot be experts in all of them, so we must be kept aware by writers who understand the subjects and present them in layman's language.

"A good writer will cover the subject in a well-organized and logical sequence. He will explain difficult concepts in non-technical language, make use of anecdotes and do all he can to make the article bright and readable."

* * *

LIPMAN, Marilyn 1938-

PERSONAL: Born July 22, 1938, in St. Louis, Mo.;

daughter of Gustav A. (a contractor) and Gertrude (Berman) Vittert; married David Lipman (a journalist), December 10, 1961; children: Gay Ilene, Benjamin Alan. *Education:* Smith College, student, 1956-57; Washington University, St. Louis, Mo., B.A., 1959. *Politics:* Democrat. *Religion:* Jewish. *Agent:* McIntosh & Otis, Inc., 18 East 41st St., New York, N.Y. 10017.

CAREER: Des Peres School, St. Louis, Mo., elementary school teacher, 1959-63; writer.

WRITINGS: (With husband, David Lipman) *Jim Hart: Underrated Quarterback,* Putnam, 1977.

*   *   *

LIPPINCOTT, Joseph W(harton)   1887-1976

February 28, 1887—October 22, 1976; American publisher and author of children's books best known for *Wilderness Champion* and *The Wahoo Bobcat.* He began with his family's company in 1908 and retired in 1958 as chairman of the board. He died in Huntington Valley, Pa. Obituaries: *New York Times,* October 23, 1976; *AB Bookman's Weekly,* November 1, 1976.

*   *   *

LIROFF, Richard A(lan)   1948-

PERSONAL: Born June 21, 1948, in Brooklyn, N.Y.; son of Jacob S. (an attorney) and Ruth (an attorney; maiden name, Turetzky) Liroff. *Education:* Brandeis University, B.A. (cum laude), 1969; Northwestern University, M.A., 1970, Ph.D., 1976. *Office:* Environmental Law Institute, 1346 Connecticut Ave. N.W., Washington, D.C. 20036.

CAREER: Environmental Law Institute, Washington, D.C., project associate, 1973—. Member of policy board of environmental impact assessment project, Institute of Ecology, 1974. Guest scholar at Brookings Institution, 1971, research fellow, 1972. *Member:* Washington Area Bicyclist Association (co-founder and member of board of directors), Brandeis University Alumni Association (member of national executive board, 1973—). *Awards, honors:* Woodrow Wilson fellowship, 1971.

WRITINGS: (Contributor) Leslie L. Roos, editor, *The Politics of Ecosuicide,* Holt, 1971; (contributor) Stuart Nagel, editor, *Environmental Politics,* Praeger, 1974; (contributor) Khristine Hall and other editors, *Enforcement of Federal and State Water Pollution Controls,* Environmental Law Institute, 1975; *A National Policy for the Environment: NEPA and Its Aftermath,* Indiana University Press, 1976. Contributor to *Natural Resources Journal, Environmental Law Reporter,* and to scholarly journals.

*   *   *

LISAGOR, Peter   1915-1976

August 5, 1915—December 10, 1976; American journalist. He began with the *Chicago Daily News* in 1939 and became its Washington bureau chief in 1959. Courted by four presidents, Lisagor also had great popular appeal and frequently appeared on the television programs "Washington Week in Review" and "Meet the Press." During World War II he was London editor of *Stars and Stripes.* Lisagor died in Washington, D.C. Obituaries: *Washington Post,* December 11, 1976; *New York Times,* December 11, 1976, December 16, 1976; *Newsweek,* December 20, 1976.

LITTO, Gertrude   1929-

PERSONAL: Born November 24, 1929, in Mt. Vernon, N.Y.; daughter of Reubin (a businessman) and Henrietta (a businesswoman; maiden name, Wilner) Fine; married Frank Litto (a sculptor and painter), January 23, 1950; children: Claude, Leo, Corbin. *Education:* Syracuse University, B.F.A., 1951; State University of New York College at New Paltz, M.A., 1967. *Residence:* New Baltimore, N.Y. 12124. *Office:* Ravena Coeymans Selkirk Central School, Selkirk, N.Y.

CAREER: Ravena Coeymans Selkirk Central School, Selkirk, N.Y., elementary school art teacher, 1953—. Adjunct faculty member at Russell Sage College, 1975—. *Member:* New York State Art Teachers.

WRITINGS: The Visual Impact of Writing, New York State Department of Education, 1969; *South American Folk Pottery,* Watson-Guptill, 1976.

SIDELIGHTS: Gertrude Litto writes: "Throughout my education and teaching career, I have nourished a growing interest in both ancient and contemporary pottery. The continuity of traditional techniques and styles in Japan up to the present day, has especially interested me. Looking at what I consider to be the next greatest pottery heritage, that of the Pre-Columbian cultures such as the well-known Inca, Mohica, and Nazca, I found meager recorded evidence that the clay working tradition was continuing. My curiosity increased as I discovered how little investigation had been done into contemporary folk pottery on the South American continent. A sabbatical leave from my teaching postion brought the chance to explore the subject first hand. I found that the art of making good utilitarian pottery still exists in many areas.

"In other communities where ceramic traditions have flourished for hundreds of years, I was fortunate to be able to document the last generation of potters. One year was not time enough to investigate all of the pottery communities which are ever fewer in number. I am planning to return to South America soon, to continue recording the work before it vanishes completely."

*   *   *

LITVINOV, Ivy   1890(?)-1977
(Ivy Low)

1890(?)—April 29, 1977; English-born novelist and wife of Maxim Litvinov, Soviet commisar for foreign affairs under Stalin. She is best known for novels written under name Ivy Low, including *The Questing Beast* and *Growing Pains.* She was a friend to D. H. Lawrence and H. G. Wells. Litvinov died in Hove, England, where she returned after the death of her husband in 1952. Obituaries: *New York Times,* May 1, 1977; *Washington Post,* May 4, 1977; *AB Bookman's Weekly,* July 25, 1977.

*   *   *

LOCKE, Charles O.   1896(?)-1977

1896(?)—May 1, 1977; American journalist, lyricist, script writer, and novelist. He worked as a reporter in Toledo, Ohio, and New York City during the 1920's, and as a lyricist and radio script writer in the 1930's. In the 1950's he wrote several adventure novels, the most successful of which was *The Hell Bent Kid.* Locke died in Burbank, Calif. Obituaries: *New York Times,* May 2, 1977.

LOEBL, Suzanne

PERSONAL: Born in Hannover, Germany; came to the United States in 1946, naturalized citizen, 1951; daughter of Hugo and Margaret (Schwarzhaupt) Bamberger; married Ernest M. Loebl (a university professor), March 15, 1950; children: Judith Hannah, David Albert. *Education:* Attended Institut Meurice Chimie, 1944-46, and Columbia University, 1946-48, 1969. *Religion:* Jewish. *Home:* 788 Riverside Dr., New York, N.Y. 10032. *Agent:* Albert Zimmerman, McIntosh & Otis, Inc., 18 East 41st St., New York, N.Y. 10017.

CAREER: Sloan Kettering Institute for Cancer Research, New York, N.Y., research assistant, 1946-52; New York University, New York City, research assistant for department of pharmacology, 1952-54; free-lance technical writer and translator, 1958—. *Member:* National Association of Science Writers, American Society of Journalists and Authors, American Medical Writers Association, American Society of Magazine Writers. *Awards, honors:* Matrix Award from New York Women in Communications, 1974.

WRITINGS: Fighting the Unseen: The Story of Viruses, Abelard, 1967; *Exploring the Mind: Man's Search for Mental Health,* Abelard, 1968; *Conception, Contraception: A New Look,* Suzanne McGraw, 1974; (with E. Heckheimer, G. Spratto, and A. Wit) *The Nurse's Drug Handbook,* Wiley, 1977. Science editor for New York Heart Association, 1969-71, and Arthritis Foundation, 1971—.

WORK IN PROGRESS: Passport to Parenthood, for Dial.

SIDELIGHTS: Suzanne Loebl told *CA:* "Even though I never set out to become a writer—I was a chemistry major—I am delighted with my profession. I am curious by nature, and this need is satisfied by having to constantly learn about new things. I enjoy taking a difficult scientific subject, understanding it, and then explaining it to a general audience.

"In my development as a writer I seem to be gradually moving away from solid science. I am very interested in the economics of medicine, medical care delivery and the psychological aspects of disease.

"I am an art addict and a devotee of the outdoors. When I can, I take my typewriter to Maine, where we own a 'camp' on a lake near the ocean."

* * *

LOOMES, Brian 1938-

PERSONAL: Born in 1938, in Leeds, England. *Education:* University of Leeds, B.A., 1962. *Residence:* Nidderdale, Yorkshire, England. *Office:* Dusty Miller Gallery, Low Laithe, via Harrogate, Yorkshire, England.

CAREER: Dusty Miller Gallery, Low Laithe, England, antiques dealer, specializing in country clocks, 1966—. *Member:* Society of Genealogists (fellow).

WRITINGS: Yorkshire Clockmakers, Dalesman Publishing, 1972; *The White Dial Clock,* David & Charles, 1974; *Westmorland Clocks and Clockmakers,* David & Charles, 1975; *Lancashire Clocks and Clockmakers,* David & Charles, 1976; *Country Clocks and Their London Origins,* David & Charles, 1976; *Watch and Clock Makers of the World,* Volume II, NAG Press, 1976.

WORK IN PROGRESS: London Clockmakers of the Seventeenth Century, completion expected in 1978; other books on British clocks and clock making.

AVOCATIONAL INTERESTS: "Self-sufficiency, cultivation, gardening, and returning to the land."

LOVE, Sandra (Weller) 1940-

PERSONAL: Born March 28, 1940, in Louisville, Ky.; daughter of Carroll Dane (a businessman) and Alma (a teacher; maiden name, Hoffmann) Weller; married Joseph Daniel Love, August 19, 1961 (divorced, 1972); married Samuel W. Young (a personnel director), June 3, 1975; children: (first marriage) Lisa Carroll, Linda Elizabeth; (second marriage—stepchildren) Michael Lloyd, Ellen Campbell. *Education:* Purdue University, B.S., 1961; University of Louisville, M.A., 1964. *Home:* 135 North Walnut St., Yellow Springs, Ohio 45387. *Agent:* Marilyn Marlow, Curtis Brown Ltd., 575 Madison Ave., New York, N.Y. 10022.

CAREER: Teacher of English in public schools in Louisville, Ky. (also chairman of department and supervisor of student teachers), 1961-66; University of Georgia, Extension, Warner Robins, instructor in English, 1967-68; *Dayton Journal Herald,* Dayton, Ohio, reporter, 1971-72; Wright State University, Dayton, Ohio, instructor in English, 1972-75; writer, 1975—. *Member:* Martha Kinney Cooper Ohioana Library Association, Yellow Springs Library Association, Yellow Springs Writers Group. *Awards, honors:* Elizabeth Enright Award from Indiana Writers Conference, 1972, for story "Sunday Morning, Winter Morning."

WRITINGS: But What About Me? (juvenile), Harcourt, 1976; *Melissa's Medley* (juvenile), Harcourt, 1977; *The Manufacturing Cluster* (educational booklet), State of Ohio, 1977. Assistant editor of *Jefferson Reporter,* 1967-68; past editor of newsletter of Ohio Association for Retardation.

WORK IN PROGRESS: The Coffee Kitchen, for children.

SIDELIGHTS: Sandra Love writes: "I write to capture the special moments in life, the times that change one's viewpoint permanently. I write for children because they like the simplicity of language and immediacy of plot that help me explore life.

"In my stories I focus on a central problem that I know and care about. In *But What About Me?* Lucy is frightened by her mother's going to work—she feels it is desertion. When Lucy faces the problems and solves them, she becomes a different, stronger person. In my second book, Melissa has to come to terms with priorities—for her, it is complicated by the fact that she is a competitive swimmer. *The Coffee Kitchen* explores the problems created for the oldest girl, Roslyn, when her father dies and her mother decides to move the coffee business to their kitchen at home.

"I usually ignore sociological problems to concentrate on psychological ones, creating a somewhat idealistic world; it is always a world where problems can be solved, unlike real life. But if a way through a problem is found once, by someone in a specific situation, everyone benefits.

"All women, old and young, are changing, and as they do they change the world around them. I want to show this growing consciousness."

AVOCATIONAL INTERESTS: Gardening, photography, swimming (also teaches swimming).

* * *

LOVINS, Amory B(loch) 1947-

PERSONAL: Born November 13, 1947, in Washington, D.C.; son of Gerald Hershel (an engineer) and Miriam (a social worker; maiden name, Bloch) Lovins. *Education:* Attended Harvard University, 1964-67 and Magdalen College, Oxford, 1967-69; Merton College, Oxford, M.A., 1971. *Politics:* Jeffersonian. *Religion:* "Thoreauvian." *Agent:*

Bruce Colman, FOE Inc., 124 Spear St., San Francisco, Calif. 94105. *Office:* c/o FOE Ltd., 9 Poland St., London W1V 3DG, England.

CAREER: Has worked internationally as a consultant physicist, 1965—; and as a mountain guide in New Hampshire, summers, 1969—. Regents' Lecturer, University of California, Berkeley, 1978. Director, New Directions.

WRITINGS: Eryri, the Mountains of Longing, Friends of the Earth, 1971; *The Stockholm Conference: Only One Earth,* Earth Island, 1972; *Openpit Mining,* Earth Island, 1973; *World Energy Strategies: Facts, Issues, and Options,* Friends of the Earth/Ballinger, 1975; (with John Price) *Non-Nuclear Futures: The Case for an Ethical Energy Strategy,* Friends of the Earth/Ballinger, 1975; *Soft Energy Paths: Toward a Durable Peace,* Friends of the Earth/Ballinger, 1977; (editor) *Energy in Context,* Friends of the Earth/Ballinger, in press. Also author of numerous monographs, technical papers and articles in his field.

WORK IN PROGRESS: Co-photographer for Friends of the Earth/Appalachian Mountain Club/New York Graphic Society book on the White Moutains of New Hampshire.

SIDELIGHTS: "My main professional role," Lovins told *CA,* "is as a synthesist and as a translator between technical specialties: I circulate on the international energy grapevine, cross-pollinating and moving ideas and papers around faster than they might otherwise go. Though my formal education added to its main strand (physics and related sciences) parallel strands in math, classics, music, linguistics, some law, a little medicine, and mountain photography, I wish it had been broader still.

"My main avocations are music (piano and composition), mountaineering (about 100 days a year), landscape photography, writing, a few sports, and, most of all, people. I regard writing not as my profession, but rather as one of the crafts essential to my main function as an energy and resource strategist. Wordsmithing is also, however, a worthy and exacting discipline."

* * *

LOWMAN, Charles LeRoy 1880(?)-1977

1880(?)—April 18, 1977; American orthopedic surgeon and author of textbooks. Lowman came to Los Angeles in 1900 and was the only orthopedic surgeon in the Southwest for many years. He operated an outpatient clinic for children from 1909 until 1972 and founded the Orthopaedic Hospital in Los Angeles in 1909. He was awarded the Medal of Freedom in 1974. Lowman died in Los Angeles, Calif. Obituaries: *New York Times,* April 19, 1977.

* * *

LOWRY, Lois 1937-

PERSONAL: Born March 20, 1937, in Honolulu, Hawaii; daughter of Robert E. (a dentist) and Katharine (Landis) Hammersberg; married Donald Grey Lowry (an attorney), June 11, 1956; children: Alix, Grey, Kristin, Benjamin. *Education:* Attended Brown University, 1954-56; University of Maine, B.A., 1972, also graduate study. *Religion:* Episcopalian. *Home:* 8 Allen Ave. Extension, Falmouth, Maine 04105.

CAREER: Free-lance writer and photographer, 1972—.

WRITINGS: Black American Literature (textbook), J. Weston Walsh, 1973; *Literature of the American Revolution* (textbook), J. Weston Walsh, 1974; *A Summer to Die* (juve-

nile), Houghton, 1977. Contributor of stories, articles, and photographs to magazines, including *Redbook, Yankee,* and *Downeast,* and to newspapers.

WORK IN PROGRESS: A book of photographs, with text, for Durrell; *Looking for Natalie* (tentative title), a juvenile novel.

SIDELIGHTS: Lois Lowry writes: "My interests are peripatetic; that is, obvious, I think, from my published work, which ranges from the scholarly to the thoroughly lighthearted. As a photographer, I have specialized in children's portraiture, and my enjoyment of kids has been fulfilled as well in writing for them. I've quit apologizing for writing 'kids' books. My first juvenile novel deals with death; my second, in progress, with a search for heritage on the part of an adopted adolescent. These are valid themes, I think, for young people; if I can, through fiction, help adolescents answer their own questions about life, identity, and human relationships, then I feel success as a writer."

* * *

LUCAS, Joseph 1928-

PERSONAL: Born December 13, 1928, in Surrey, England; son of Joseph (an estate owner) and Dorothy Mary (Collier) Lucas; married Esther Elfreda Baker (secretary to the Lieutenant-governor of Ontario), August 11, 1950; children: Caroline Mary, Esther Jane Lucas Phillips, Joseph, Jr. *Education:* University of London, B.Sc. (honors), 1953. *Home:* 422 Finch Ave., Pickering, Ontario, Canada L1V 1H8.

CAREER: Commercial fisherman in the North Sea, 1951, and Bear Island and Barents Sea, 1952; East Africa High Commission, Lake Victoria Fisheries Service, Mwanza, Tanganyika, fisheries officer, research collaborator with East Africa Medical Research Institute, and honorary game ranger of Serengeti National Park, 1953-56; elementary and secondary school science teacher in Matlock, Derbyshire, England, 1957-58; Children's Hospital, Sheffield, England, assistant pathologist, 1958-59; Butterworth & Co. (publishers), London, England, scientific editor, 1960-62, medical editor, 1962-63; *Science Journal,* London, England, life sciences editor, 1963-67; *International Zoo Yearbook* (of Zoological Society), London, England, editor, 1967-71; International Union for Conservation of Nature and Natural Resources, Morges, Switzerland, scientific editor, 1971-73; free-lance writer, 1973-74; Metropolitan Toronto Zoo, West Hill, Ontario, superintendent of education and research, 1974—. Member of Survival Service Commission of the International Union for Conservation of Nature and Natural Resources, 1966—, also secretary and treasurer of its Canadian Committee, 1976—; chairman of International Zoo Liaison Group, 1972-75; member of Conservation Council of Ontario, 1976—. Made radio and television broadcasts for British Broadcasting Corp., 1963-71. *Military service:* British Army, pathology laboratory assistant in Medical Corps, 1947-49; served in Gibraltar.

MEMBER: Royal Geographical Society (fellow), Institute of Biology, British Ornithologists Union, Association of British Science Writers, Zoological Society (London; fellow), Federation of Ontario Naturalists.

WRITINGS: A Source Book of Animals, Ward, Lock, 1971; *Encyclopedia of the Animal World,* twenty-one volumes, Elsevier International, 1972; *A Book of Animals,* Pan Books, 1973; (with Pamela Jane Critch) *Life in the Oceans,* Thames & Hudson, 1974; (with Susan Jane Hayes) *Polar Life,* Danbury Press, 1976; (with Hayes) *Biological Aspects of Conservation,* Carolina Biological Supply Co., 1977. Science correspondent for *Daily Telegraph,* 1967-68. Contributor of articles and reviews to magazines, including *Science Journal* and *New Scientist,* and to newspapers.

WORK IN PROGRESS: Another more detailed book on the biological aspects of conservation, with Susan Jane Hayes; a book on endangered mammals, with Hayes, for Van Nostrand.

SIDELIGHTS: In 1967-68, Lucas accompanied the British Antarctic Survey, as a guest, to the Falkland Islands, South Georgia, the Weddell Sea, the South Orkneys, South Sandwiches, South Shetland, and the west coast of the Antarctic peninsula, gathering data on Crabeater and Weddell seals, Chinstrap and Adelie penguins, and various petrels, with incidental work on Southern elephant seals. He visited all British, Argentine, Chilean, Soviet, and U.S. bases in West Antarctica, returning from his trip via Chile, Argentina, Uruguay, Paraguay and Brazil. In 1969, he was a guest of Parks Canada and the Canadian Wildlife Service on a survey of the denning area of polar bears in western Hudson's Bay.

He writes: "As a widely travelled (fortunately) biologist and ecologist, I am concerned that mankind must work as rapidly as possible toward zero population growth, and the rational use of natural resources, bearing in mind that they are finite if non-renewable and non-living, and subject to catastrophic over-exploitation and ultimate extinction if living. As a professional conservationist, I am attempting to encourage the governmental and non-governmental conservationists across Canada to synthesize their viewpoints, and speak with a single voice. As an individual, I am a part-time organic farmer combining crops and livestock."

* * *

LUCENTINI, Mauro 1924-

PERSONAL: Born October 23, 1924, in Rome, Italy; son of Venanzio (a merchant) and Emma (Marzi) Lucentini; married Paolo Ajo (a photographer), January 1, 1967; children: Eric, Jack. *Education:* Rome University, law degree, 1946. *Home and office:* 156 East 79th St., New York, N.Y. 10021.

CAREER: Il Risorgimento Liberale, Rome, Italy, sub-editor, 1945-46; Ansa Italian News Agency, Rome, correspondent from London, 1955-59, and New York City, 1960-69; *Il Mondo,* Milan, Italy, New York correspondent, 1969-74; *Il Giornale Nuovo,* Milan, U.S. correspondent and author of column, 1974—. Notable assignments include all major international conferences since 1957, and interviews with political figures, including Konrad Adenauer, Charles De Gaulle, Harold MacMillan, Gamal Nasser, and Lyndon Johnson.

WRITINGS: America Che Cambia (title means "Changing America"), Rizzoli, 1967; *America Al Di La' Del Mito* (title means "America Beyond the Myths"), S.E.I., 1969.

SIDELIGHTS: Lucentini told *CA* the most difficult aspect of interviewing a major political figure is "making him understand the exact use that one is going to make of his words." Lucentini's most enjoyable interview was with "Italian Premier Alcide DeGasperi (during the postwar rehabilitation period), for his candor combined with clarity of expression and insight."

* * *

LUCHINS, Abraham S(amuel) 1914-

PERSONAL: Born March 8, 1914, in Brooklyn, N.Y.; son of Moriss A. (a carpenter) and Anne E. (Yampolsky) Luchins; married Edith Hirsch (a professor of mathematics),

November 10, 1941; children: David, Daniel, Jeremy, Ann, Joseph. *Education:* Brooklyn College (now of the City University of New York), B.A. (cum laude), 1935; Columbia University, M.A., 1936; graduate study at New School for Social Research, 1937-42; New York University, Ph.D., 1939. *Politics:* None. *Religion:* Jewish. *Office:* Department of Psychology, State University of New York at Albany, Albany, N.Y. 12203.

CAREER: Yeshiva College (now University), New York, N.Y., instructor, 1940-42, assistant professor of psychology, 1942-49, chairman of department, 1946-49, director of guidance, 1949; McGill University, Montreal, Quebec, associate professor of psychology in charge of social clinical program, 1949-55; University of Oregon, Eugene, associate professor of psychology, 1955-58; University of Miami, Coral Gables, Fla., professor of psychology, 1958-62; State University of New York at Albany, professor of psychology, 1962—. Diplomate of American Board of Professional Psychology. Clinical psychologist and director of clinical psychology training at Veterans Administration Regional Office in New York City, 1947-49. *Military service:* U.S. Army, 1943-46; became first lieutenant in field. *Member:* American Psychological Association (fellow), Psychonomic Society, Educational Research Association.

WRITINGS: Mechanization in Problem Solving: The Effect of Einstellung, American Psychological Association, 1942; *The Study of a Mental Hospital: A Functional Approach to the Training of the Psychologist,* Oregon State Hospital, 1956; (with wife, Edith Hirsch Luchins) *Rigidity of Behavior: A Variational Approach to the Effect of Einstellung,* University of Oregon Books, 1959; *A Functional Approach to Training in Clinical Psychology via Study of a Mental Hospital,* C. C Thomas, 1959.

(With Lewis Aumack and Harold R. Dickman) *Manual of Group Therapy,* Psychology Service, Veterans Administration Hospital (Roseburg, Ore.), 1960; *Group Therapy: A Guide,* Random House, 1964; (with E. H. Luchins) *Logical Foundations of Mathematics for Behavioral Scientists,* Holt, 1965; (contributor) Samual M. Seltzer, editor, *Einstellung Tests of Rigidity,* Craig Colony School and Hospital, 1966; (with E. H. Luchins) *The Search for Factors That Extremize the Autokinetic Effect,* Faculty-Student Association, State University of New York at Albany, 1969; (with E. H. Luchins) *Wertheimer's Seminars Revisited: Problem Solving and Thinking,* three volumes, Faculty-Student Association, State University of New York at Albany, 1970; *Wertheimer's Seminars in Perception,* six volumes, Bucknell University Press, 1970-75; *Wertheimer's Seminars on Character and Personality,* four volumes, Bucknell University Press, 1975-77; (with E. H. Luchins) *Revisiting Wertheimer's Seminars,* Volume I: *Value, Social Influence, and Power,* Volume II: *Problems in Social Psychology,* Bucknell University Press, 1976.

Contributor of more than one hundred twenty-five articles to journals in his field.

WORK IN PROGRESS: A biography of Max Wertheimer; editing Wertheimer's letters to Albert Einstein; continuing research on topics related to Wertheimer's seminars, especially the experimental outgrowths in the published monographs.

* * *

LUKONIN, Mikhail K. 1920(?)-1977

1920(?)—August 5, 1977; Russian poet and government official. He received a Stalin Prize and State Prize for his poetry, most notable of which were *The Working Days* and *Necessity*. He was elected first secretary of the Union of Writers Moscow branch shortly before his death. Lukonin died in Moscow, U.S.S.R. Obituaries: *New York Times,* August 6, 1976.

* * *

LUMPKIN, Grace

PERSONAL: Born in Milledgeville, Ga.; *Education:* Attended Columbia University.

CAREER: Teacher in public schools in South Carolina; worked as a county home demonstration agent in North Carolina; worked as industrial secretary for Young Women's Christian Association (YMCA) in South Carolina; worked at various office jobs and as a chamber maid in New York City. Writer. *Awards, honors:* Maxim Gorky prize for best labor novel, 1932, for *To Make My Bread.*

*WRITINGS—*All novels: *To Make My Bread,* Macaulay, 1932; *A Sign for Cain,* Lee Furman, 1935; *The Wedding,* Lee Furman, 1939, reprinted, Southern Illinois University Press, 1976; *Full Circle,* Western Islands, 1962.

Contributor of short stories to magazines and journals, including *North American Review, Virginia Quarterly Review,* and *New Masses.*

SIDELIGHTS: Grace Lumpkin, who was identified with leftist causes during the 1930's, has been superficially labeled as a writer of leftist propaganda, according to Lillian Barnard Gilkes in an afterword to Ms. Lumpkin's novel, *The Wedding.* She says, "There is a social consciousness, a great deal of it in its portrayal of the lost fortunes and psychological peculiarities of a Southern middle-class family, its emphasis on outmoded values in the changing world of the early twentieth century . . ." But Gilkes finds that "any period 'message' from the Depression years" is far outweighed by the superb artistry of Ms. Lumpkin's storytelling.

To Make My Bread was adapted for the stage by Albert Bein and opened at the Broadhurst Theatre in New York City, November 6, 1935, as *Let Freedom Ring.*

The Grace Lumpkin Collection is housed at the University of South Carolina.

BIOGRAPHICAL/CRITICAL SOURCES: Lillian Barnard Gilkes, afterword to *The Wedding,* Southern Illinois University Press, 1976.

* * *

LUSTIG, Arnost 1926-

PERSONAL: Born December 21, 1926, in Prague, Czechoslovakia; came to the United States in 1970; son of Emil and Therese (Lowy) Lustig; married Vera Weislitz, July 24, 1949; children: Josef, Eva. *Education:* College of Political and Social Sciences, Prague, Czechoslovakia, M.A., 1951, Ing. degree, 1954. *Home:* 4000 Tunlaw Rd. N.W., Washington, D.C. 20007. *Office:* Department of English, American University, Washington, D.C. 20016.

CAREER: Radio Prague, Prague, Czechoslovakia, Arab-Israeli war correspondent, 1948-49; Czechoslovak Radio Corp., correspondent in Europe, Asia, and North America, 1950-68; Barrandov Film Studios, Prague, screenwriter, 1960-68; writer in Israel, 1968-69; Jadran Film Studio, Zagreb, Yugoslavia, screenwriter, 1969-70; University of Iowa, Iowa City, member of International Writers Program, 1970-71, visiting lecturer in English, 1971-72; Drake University, Des Moines, Iowa, visiting professor of English, 1972-

73; American University, Washington, D.C., professor of literature, 1973—. Head of the Czechoslovak film delegation to the San Sebastian Film Festival, 1968; member of the jury, Karlovy Vary International Film Festival, 1968. Lecturer in film and literature at universities in Czechoslovakia, Israel, Japan, Canada, and the United States.

MEMBER: Authors Guild, Authors League of America, P.E.N., Film Club (Prague). *Awards, honors:* Klement Gottwald State Prize, 1967, nomination for National Book Award, 1974, and B'nai B'rith Award, 1974, all for *A Prayer for Katerina Horovitzova;* television film of "A Prayer for Katerina Horovitzova" received nine international prizes, including first prize at Monte Carlo Film Festival, 1966; first prize of Mlada fronta publishing house, 1962, for *Diamonds of the Night;* "Lemon" chosen as best short story, 1962, by University of Melbourne (Australia); first prize of Czechoslovak Radio Corp., 1966, for radio play, "Prague Crossroads"; first prize of Czechoslovak Radio Corp., 1967, for radio play, "A Man the Size of a Postage Stamp": second prize of San Sebastian Film Festival, 1968, for the film, "Dita Saxova."

*WRITINGS—*In English: *Noc a nodeje* (short stories), Nase vojsko, 1958, translation by George Theiner published as *Night and Hope,* Dutton, 1962 (also see below); *Demanty noci* (short stories) Mlada fronta, 1958, translation by Iris Urwin published as *Diamonds of the Night,* Artia, 1962 (also see below); *Dita Saxova* (novel), Ceskoslovensky spisovatel, 1962, translation by Theiner published as *Dita Sax,* Hutchinson, 1966; *Modlitba pro Katerinu Horovitzovou* (novel), Ceskoslovensky spisovatel, 1964, translation by Jeanne Nemcova published as *A Prayer for Katerina Horovitzova,* Harper, 1973.

Collected works; "Children of the Holocaust" series: *Darkness Cast No Shadow,* translation by Jeanne Nemcova, Inscape, 1977; *Night and Hope,* Inscape, 1977; *Diamonds of the Night,* in a new translation by Nemcova, Inscape, 1977.

Other: *Ulice ztracenych* (title means "The Street of Lost Brothers"), Mlada fronta, 1949; *Muj znamy Vili Feld* (novel; title means "My Acquaintance Willi Feld"), Mlada fronta, 1949; *Nikoho neponizis* (title means "Nobody Will Be Humiliated"), Nase vojsko, 1963; *Bile brizy na podzim* (title means "The White Birches in September"), Ceskoslovensky spisovatel, 1966; *Horka vune mandli* (title means "The Bitter Smell of Almonds"), Mlada fronta, 1968; *Milacek* (title means "Darling"), Ceskoslovensky spisovatel, 1969.

Screenplays, all released by Studio Barrandov, Prague: "Transport from Paradise," adapted from *Night and Hope,* 1963; "Diamonds of the Night," adapted from *Darkness Cast No Shadow,* 1964; "Dita Saxova," 1968.

Television scripts: "The Blue Day," for T.V. Prague, 1960; "A Prayer for Katerina Horovitzova," for T.V. Prague, 1965; (with Ernest Pendrell) "Terezin," for ABC-TV, 1965; "Stolen Childhood," for TV-Rome, 1966.

Radio scripts for Radio Prague: "Prague Crossroads," 1966, and "A Man the Size of a Postage Stamp," 1967.

Also author of text for Otmar Macha's symphonic poem, "Night and Hope." Also author of unproduced screenplays, "The Excursion" with Jan Kadar, "The Street of Lost Brothers" with Jan Nemec, "The White Birches in the Fall" with Jaromil Jires, and a screenplay about the International Writers Program at University of Iowa. Author of a short filmscript, "Bit to Eat," 1962. Correspondent for literary magazines in Czechoslovakia, 1950-58; editor, *Mlady svet* (magazine; title means "Young World"), 1958-60.

WORK IN PROGRESS: Four more volumes of "Children of the Holocaust," publication by Inscape expected in 1978; a book based on the diary of a seventeen year old girl in a concentration camp.

SIDELIGHTS: Arnost Lustig, who left his native Czechoslovakia after the Soviet invasion of 1968, says, "I was in love with my country, to tell the truth. It's a beautiful country, a very romantic country. Prague is a mystical and romantic city. Just to walk through the streets makes you feel something special. And I felt it. If somebody had told me in the first half of 1968 that I would leave, I would have laughed at him. The idea of leaving my country was not in the least milli-millimeter of my mind.

"People in Czechoslovakia love to read, and if you are a writer, they like you. This is the only country where a poet can make a living, because people stand in line for books of poetry. This was a good country for writers. For instance, I didn't write on very popular themes. I wrote on suffering in camps, about the war, but they published over a half million copies in ten years. And this is a small nation of nine million people. Hemingway is published in Prague—150,000 copies: Fitzgerald—200,000 copies. Everybody knows who Faulkner is, sometimes more than they do here. Steinbeck, whom I met once in Prague, is a favorite of Czech readers, because they know his best books.

"So to live in such a country, you don't have to be a hero; it is enough to be a writer. You feel that your life has meaning; you are working as well as you can, and people are reading your work. You don't need more. You can make a living. For a writer, it is not good to be very poor, but neither is it good for him to be very rich. Somewhere midway. This was my situation in Prague when we left."

When the Soviet regime took power in 1968, Lustig reports, "almost no books were published except by mistake." For instance, 22,000 copies of a collection of three of Lustig's novels were published in 1970, and were banned almost immediately, even though one of the novels had been reprinted seven times since 1964. Lustig explains, "Suddenly the regime thought that my descriptions of Nazi concentration camps might be an allegory for life under the present regime in Czechoslovakia. For what can you publish in these countries, if you try to be as honest as possible, yet want to avoid a situation comparable to jumping on the tail of a snake so that he can still whirl around to bite you with his teeth? The only way is to write about the past, as I did with *A Prayer for Katerina Horovitzova*. I was writing about a brave girl in a concentration camp fighting against tyrants in 1944. But people perhaps understood this book also as a book about the present.

"Once everything was lost, when the country was invaded, I was declared by the last congress of the Communist party an 'enemy of the state,' an 'imperialist agent,' a 'Zionist.' They said all my books and films were paid for by some world conspiracy."

In his twenties, Lustig was active in the earlier revolution in Prague. "That revolution in Prague, connected with the Socialist revolution later," he writes, "involved so many hopes, beautiful ideas, and we didn't know in those times that ideas are not realities. We really thought that everything for which we hoped must come because we hoped so honestly. Revolutions are romantic times, and there is something honest about them. But the bigger the hope, the bigger the disappointment. This disappointment brought the events of 1968, this disappointment created Solzhenitsyn and thousands of other writers. If you are hoping for something honestly, and if you have clean hands, and if later your hands are dirty with blood for which you are not guilty (because revolution also involves killing), and even if you are not killing people, you are guilty too. So the disappointment with the realities is extremely intensive. You try to pay for it ... to tell the truth about your time, your experience."

However, Lustig found that writing the truth in his native country was not possible. When conditions in Czechoslovakia became intolerable, Lustig and his family moved to the United States. "Under those circumstances," he explains, "it is better to be in a strange country, to start again, and to prove to yourself that you are a real writer. To be a writer under the best circumstances is not so difficult. To remain a writer under worse circumstances is, I think, a good test for a writer." Still, he thinks it is better "to be outside and keep writing, and to be free, and to keep some hope.

"Every writer has a duty to be as good as he can as a writer, to tell stories he likes in the best way he can. What he likes—this is his personal approach to life. I like stories about brave people, about how they survived under the worst circumstances. I like people who are fighting for their fate, and who are better in the end, richer, in a sense, than they were in the beginning. I think that each writer has a certain duty—to imagine himself in theory as perhaps the last human being alive under certain circumstances and that perhaps his testimony will be the last one. He is obliged to deliver that testimony."

In a recent interview, John F. Baker asked Lustig if American support for the human rights of Czechs living in Czechoslovakia is meaningful to them. He responded: "Imagine you are a man on a desert island. Wouldn't it be important to you that ships are passing by? It's very important to have hope, not to have to feel you are alone. Even in the camps in the war, it helped us to know that Britain and America were fighting, to know that hope had not vanished from the world. You want to hear someone making moral sounds, even if it is only sounds. Symbolic gestures, after all, have great power, as in all ancient religions. Man can survive a hydrogen bomb, if he must, but he can never survive a lack of moral sense."

Lustig's books and stories have been translated into more than twenty languages, including German, Spanish, Japanese, Polish, Hebrew, Hindi, Esperanto, French, Estonian, Italian, and Yiddish.

BIOGRAPHICAL/CRITICAL SOURCES: Booklist, November 1, 1973; *Best Sellers,* October 15, 1973; *Kirkus Reviews,* August 1, 1973; *New York Times Book Review,* October 21, 1973; *Proteus,* spring, 1974; *Choice,* fall, 1974; *Southwest Review,* winter, 1974; *Publishers Weekly,* February 21, 1977; *Washingtonian,* May 1977.

* * *

LUTHER, James W(allace) 1940-
(Jim Luther)

PERSONAL: Born January 23, 1940, in Butler, Tenn.; son of V. R. (a textile worker) and Trilla (Osborne) Luther; married Martha Mayo (a sales representative), June 24, 1960; children: James W. Jr., Jennifer Anne. *Education:* East Tennessee State University, B.S., 1961, graduate study, 1962. *Religion:* Baptist. *Home:* 8603 Arley Dr., Springfield, Va. 22152. *Office:* Associated Press, 2021 K St. N.W., Washington, D.C.

CAREER/WRITINGS: Elizabethton Star, Elizabethton, Tenn., sports editor, 1957-58; *Johnson City Press-Chroni-*

cle, Johnson City, Tenn., general assignment reporter, 1959-65; Associated Press, Nashville, Tenn., state legislative reporter, 1965-70, Washington, D.C., editor, 1970-73, Senate reporter with emphasis on taxation and budgetary matters, 1973—.

* * *

LYMAN, Susan Elizabeth 1906-1976

1906—September 13, 1976; American author best known for works on New York City history. She was associated with the Museum of the City of New York from 1930 to 1950. She died in Rhode Island. Obituaries: *New York Times,* September 15, 1976.

* * *

LYNCH, Etta Lee 1924-

PERSONAL: Born September 19, 1924, in Abilene, Tex.; daughter of Arthur Lewis (a carpenter) and Elsie P. (Smith) Jones; married James B. Haynes, June 17, 1941 (divorced); married Jimmy Bernard Lynch (an engineer), August 30, 1955; children: Joy Elsie Hester, Jim Tom. *Education:* University of Oklahoma, student, 1967-69. *Politics:* Democrat. *Home and office:* 5101 41st St., Lubbock, Tex. 79414.

CAREER: Hairstylist, 1947-66; writer, 1966—. *Member:* National League of American Pen Women, Authors Guild of Authors League of America, South Plains Writers Association (president). *Awards, honors:* Shamrock Fiction Award from Eastern New Mexico University, 1966, for story "Fat of the Land"; prize from annual competition at University of Oklahoma, 1967, for story "Seed of Conviction."

WRITINGS—Nonfiction: *The Power Behind the Comb,* Moore Publishing, 1970; *Help Is Only a Prayer Away,* Revell, 1971; *Tender Tyrant: The Legend of Pete Cawthon,* Staked Plains Press, 1976; *The Tactless Texan* (biography of Gene Howe), Staked Plains Press, 1977.

Author of educational film "A Different Drum," 1975. Contributor of more than one hundred-fifty stories and articles to magazines. Fiction editor of *Teenage Christian* and *Christian Woman,* 1968-69.

WORK IN PROGRESS: A history of West Texas "wildcatters" (independent oil field drillers), publication by Staked Plains Press expected in 1978.

SIDELIGHTS: Etta Lynch writes: "As a writer, I feel the responsiblitiy of raising the level of our literature and refuse to do 'negative' works. Actually, I lean toward self-help and inspirational writings but find myself accepting assignments in other fields and enjoying them." *Avocational interests:* Travel.

* * *

LYONS, Leonard 1906-1976

September 10, 1906—October 7, 1976; American journalist who wrote "The Lyons Den" Broadway column from 1934 to 1974. Originally written for the *New York Post,* his column was eventually syndicated to over one-hundred papers worldwide. He died in New York City. Obituaries: *New York Times,* October 8, 1976; *Washington Post,* October 9, 1976.

* * *

LYONS, Richard D(aniel) 1928-

PERSONAL: Born May 31, 1928, in New York, N.Y.; son

of John M. (a lawyer) and Mary (a translator; maiden name, Francis) Lyons; married Margaret McKenna, 1961 (divorced, 1969); children: David McKenna, Abigail Francis. *Education:* Brown University, A.B., 1950; Columbia University, M.S., 1955. *Home:* South Shores Dr., Port Republic, Md. 20676. *Office:* 1920 L St. N.W., Washington, D.C. 20036.

CAREER/WRITINGS: Plainfield Courier-News, Plainfield, N.J., reporter, 1953-54; *Memphis Commercial Appeal,* Memphis, Tenn., reporter, 1955-57; Reuters News Agency. London, England, subeditor, 1957-58; *New York Daily News,* New York City, science editor, 1958-67; *New York Times,* Washington, D.C., bureau, correspondent, 1967—. Has done newspaper reporting, including series on the shortage of doctors in the United States, the American arms industry, and the personal wealth of Congressmen. Notable assignments include coverage of the Thalidomide scandal, Gemini and Apollo space programs, and the Nixon impeachment hearings and resignation. Contributor of articles to *Medical World News, Family Health,* and *Medical Opinion.* Lecturer. *Military service:* U.S. Air Force, 1951-53. *Member:* National Association of Science Writers. *Awards, honors:* Empire State medical writing award, 1964; American Orthpsychiatric Association award, 1970.

* * *

LYSENKO, T(rofim) D(enisovich) 1898-1976

September 29, 1898—November 20, 1976; Soviet agricultural biologist and author most noted for *Heredity and Its Variability.* He was the leading scientist and administrator of agriculture under Stalin. He died in the U.S.S.R. Obituaries: *Current Biography,* February, 1977.

* * *

MAAS, Selve

PERSONAL: Born in Estonia; came to the United States in 1940; married Leopold Maas (deceased). *Education:* Educated in Estonia, Germany, and Washington, D.C. *Politics:* "Always for the best man." *Religion:* Lutheran. *Residence:* Washington, D.C. *Office:* Library of Congress, Washington, D.C. 20540.

CAREER: Library of Congress, Washington, D.C., librarian, 1957—. Between 1940 and 1957, worked as housekeeper, nurse's aide, bookkeeper, cashier, and language teacher. *Member:* American-Scandinavian Association, Finlandia Foundation, Washington Opera Society.

WRITINGS: (Translator) *The Moon Painters and Other Estonian Folk Tales,* Viking, 1971; (translator with Peggy Hoffmann) *The Sea Wedding and Other Stories from Estonia,* Dillon, 1977.

Author of "Stories from the Moon Painters," first broadcast on WNYC-Radio in 1972. Contributor to Estonian-language magazines.

WORK IN PROGRESS: Translating stories from German and Estonian into English.

SIDELIGHTS: "I like to observe the curious behavior of human beings. Ambitions: Few. Hopes: Fewer. Expectations: None. Principal pleasure: Living." *Avocational interests:* Travel (Europe, Bahamas, Puerto Rico), needlepoint, weekends at her cabin in the Blue Ridge Mountains of Virginia.

BIOGRAPHICAL/CRITICAL SOURCES: Horn Book, October, 1971.

MacINNES, Colin 1914-1976

PERSONAL: Born 1914, in London, England; son of J. Campbell MacInnes and Angela Thirkell (a novelist). *Education:* Educated in Australia. *Office:* c/o Hart-Davis, MacGibbon Ltd., Frogmore, St. Albans, Hertfordshire AL2 2NF, England.

CAREER: Novelist and journalist. *Military service:* British Army Intelligence Corps, 1939-45; became sergeant.

WRITINGS—Novels; all published by MacGibbon & Kee, except as indicated: *To the Victor the Spoils,* 1950; *June in Her Spring,* 1952; *City of Spades* (Part I of trilogy; see below), 1957, Macmillan, 1958; *Absolute Beginners* (Part II of trilogy), 1959, Macmillan, 1960; *Mr. Love and Justice* (Part III of trilogy; see below), 1960, Dutton, 1961; *All Day Saturday,* 1966; *Visions of London* (trilogy; including *City of Spades, Absolute Beginners,* and *Mr. Love and Justice*), 1969, published as *The London Novels,* Farrar, Straus, 1969; *Westward to Laughter,* 1969, Farrar, Straus, 1970; *Three Years to Play,* Farrar, Straus, 1970; *Out of the Garden,* Hart-Davis, MacGibbon, 1974.

Other: *England, Half English* (essays), MacGibbon & Kee, 1961, Random House, 1962; (with Kenneth Clark and Bryan Robertson) *Sidney Nolan,* Thames & Hudson, 1961; *London: City of Any Dream,* Thames & Hudson, 1962; (with editors of *Life*) *Australia and New Zealand,* Time-Life, 1964; *Sweet Saturday Night,* MacGibbon & Kee, 1967; *Loving Them Both: A Study of Bisexuality and Bisexuals,* Martin Brian & O'Keeffe, 1974; *"No Novel Reader"* (on Rudyard Kipling), Martin Brian & O'Keeffe, 1975.

Contributor of articles to *New York Times, London Times, New Society,* and of scripts to the British Broadcasting Corp. (BBC).

SIDELIGHTS: MacInnes is considered to be one of the first novelists to write about Britain's black community.

OBITUARIES: New York Times, April 24, 1976; *Washington Post,* April 25, 1976.*

(Died April 22, 1976, in London England)

* * *

MACKENZIE, Locke L. 1900(?)-1977

1900(?)—May 10, 1977; American gynecologist and obstetrician and author; helped develop the Pap test for discovering cervical cancer. An amateur ornithologist, he is the author of a book on the subject. Obituaries: *New York Times,* May 11, 1977.

* * *

MACLEAN, Una 1925-

PERSONAL: Born July 3, 1925, in Applecross, Scotland; daughter of Malcolm (a clergyman) and Winifred (Marsden) Maclean; married W. Peter Cockshott, June 23, 1951 (divorced); married John P. Mackintosh (a member of Parliament), July 13, 1963; children: (first marriage) Paul, Aysha, Tunde; (second marriage) Stuart, Deirdre. *Education:* University of Edinburgh, M.B.Ch.B. (with distinction), 1949, diploma in public health, 1964, M.D., 1965, Ph.D., 1967, postdoctoral study, 1974. *Religion:* "Humanist." *Agent:* Michael Sissons, A. D. Peters, 10 Buckingham St., Adelphi, London W.C.2, England. *Office:* Department of Community Medicine, University of Edinburgh, Warrender Park Rd., Edinburgh 9, Scotland.

CAREER: Worked in Nigeria in cancer epidemiology, 1960-63, and in medical anthropology, 1963-65; conducted research in social psychiatry, 1964-67; University of Edinburgh, Edinburgh, Scotland, senior lecturer in community medicine, 1967—. *Member:* Society for Social Medicine, British Sociological Association, American Association of Medical Anthropology.

WRITINGS: Magical Medicine: A Nigerian Case Study, Penguin, 1970; *Social and Community Medicine for Students,* Heinemann, 1971; *Nursing in Contemporary Society,* Routledge & Kegan Paul, 1974.

Editor of "Medicine in Society," medical sociology series. Contributor of articles and reviews to medical journals.

WORK IN PROGRESS: Research on lay reactions to possible heart attack, and on homosexuality; studying psychiatric illness among women of Scotland's Outer Hebrides.

SIDELIGHTS: Una Maclean writes that her current interest is the women's movement, especially as it relates to the limitations on women seeking medical careers.

* * *

MACMILLAN, Norman 1892-1976

August 9, 1892—August 5, 1976; Scottish Royal Air Force wing commander, test pilot, aviation historian, and author of books on aviation, including *The Art of Flying* and *Wings of Fate: Strange True Tales of Vintage Flying Days.* He died in England. Obituaries: *AB Bookman's Weekly,* October 4, 1976. (*CAP*-1; earlier sketch in *CA*-11/12)

* * *

MAGNUSON, Paul 1939-

PERSONAL: Born April 10, 1939, in Newton, Mass.; son of Harold Einer (an editor) and Fannie (Campbell) Magnuson; married Elizabeth Hatt Campbell, September 4, 1965; children: Elise, Katherine. *Education:* Brown University, B.A., 1961; University of Minnesota, Ph.D., 1969. *Home:* 19 Franklin Pl., Maplewood, N.J. 07040. *Office:* Department of English, New York University, 19 University Pl., New York, N.Y. 10003.

CAREER: University of Pennsylvania, Philadelphia, assistant professor of English, 1969-74; New York University, New York, N.Y., associate professor of English, 1974—, also director of graduate studies. *Military service:* U.S. Navy, 1961-63. *Member:* Modern Language Association of America.

WRITINGS: Coleridge's Nightmare Poetry, University Press of Virginia, 1974. Review editor of Wordsworth Circle.

* * *

MAGUIRE, Francis T(homas) 1911-1976

1911—August 21, 1976; American poet, lyricist, and off-Broadway actor. During World War II he was a captain in the U.S. Army and a member of military intelligence. Obituaries: *New York Times,* August 24, 1976.

* * *

MAHY, Margaret 1936-

PERSONAL: Born March 21, 1936, in Whakatane, New Zealand; daughter of Francis George (a builder) and May (a teacher; maiden name, Penlington) Mahy; children: Penelope Helen, Bridget Frances. *Education:* University of New Zealand, B.A., 1958. *Politics:* "Anarchist." *Religion:* "Humanist." *Home address:* R.D.1, Lyttelton, New Zealand. *Agent:* Mrs. H. H. Watts, 10 Waterside Plaza, Apt. 37F, New York, N.Y. 10010.

CAREER: Petone Public Library, Petone, New Zealand, assistant librarian, 1958-59; School Library Service, Christchurch, New Zealand, librarian in charge, 1967-76; Canterbury Public Library, Christchurch, New Zealand, children's librarian, 1976—. *Member:* New Zealand Library Association. *Awards, honors:* Esther Glenn Medal from New Zealand Library Association, 1969, for *A Lion in the Meadow,* and 1973, for *The First Margaret Mahy Story Book.*

WRITINGS—For children: *A Lion in the Meadow,* F. Watts, 1969; *A Dragon of an Ordinary Family,* F. Watts, 1969; *Pillycock's Shop,* F. Watts, 1969; *The Procession,* F. Watts, 1969; *Mrs. Discombobulos,* F. Watts, 1969; *The Princess and the Clown,* F. Watts, 1971; *The Railway Engine and the Hairy Brigands,* Dent, 1972; *The First Margaret Mahy Story Book,* Dent, 1972; *The Man Whose Mother Was a Pirate,* Atheneum, 1972; *The Boy with Two Shadows,* F. Watts, 1972; *The Second Margaret Mahy Story Book,* Dent, 1973; *Rooms to Let,* F. Watts, 1974; *The Witch in the Cherry Tree,* Parents' Magazine Press, 1974; *Clancy's Cabin,* Dent, 1974; *The Bus under the Leaves,* Dent, 1974; *The Rare Spotted Birthday Party,* F. Watts, 1974; *Stepmother,* F. Watts, 1974; *The Third Margaret Mahy Story Book,* Dent, 1975; *Ultra-Violet Catastrophe,* Parents' Magazine Press, 1975; *New Zealand: Yesterday and Today,* F. Watts, 1975; *David's Witch Doctor,* F. Watts, 1975; *Leaf Magic,* Parents' Magazine Press, 1976; *The Boy Who Was Followed Home,* F. Watts, 1976; *The Wind between the Stars,* Dent, 1976; *The Pirate Uncle,* Dent, 1977; *The Nonstop Nonsense Book,* Dent, 1977. Author of scripts for "A Land Called Happy," a series on TV II-New Zealand.

SIDELIGHTS: Margaret Mahy comments: "I have been interested in writing children's stories for many years. There are certain sorts of story and certain uses of language which seem most appropriate in stories intended for children. It is almost as if there are certain images left over, insufficiently assimilated during one's own childhood. All stories, even the simplest ones, seem to be little pieces of biography even if what one is recounting is only one's childhood games and dreams."

* * *

MAIER, Charles S(teven) 1939-

PERSONAL: Born February 23, 1939, in New York, N.Y.; son of Louis (a businessman and attorney) and Muriel (Krailsheimer) Maier; married Pauline Rubbelke (a professor), June 17, 1961; children: Andrea, Nicholas, Jessica. *Education:* Harvard University, A.B., 1960, Ph.D., 1967; St. Antony's College, Oxford, graduate study, 1960-61. *Home:* 60 Larchwood Dr., Cambridge, Mass. 02138. *Office:* Department of History, Duke University, Durham, N.C. 27706.

CAREER: Harvard University, Cambridge, Mass., instructor, 1967-69, assistant professor of history, 1969-74; Duke University, Durham, N.C., associate professor of history, 1976—. Guest professor, University of Bielefeld, Germany, spring, 1976. Member of steering committee of Council for European Studies, 1976—; member of Social Science Research Council Committee on Western Europe; staff associate of Brookings Institution, 1977—. *Member:* American Historical Association. *Awards, honors:* National Book Award nomination and George Louis Beer Prize from American Historical Association, both 1976, for *Recasting Bourgeois Europe.*

WRITINGS: (Editor with Dan S. White) *The Thirteenth of*

May: *The Advent of De Gaulle's Republic,* Oxford University Press, 1968; *Recasting Bourgeois Europe: Stabilization in France, Germany, and Italy in the Decade After World War I,* Princeton University Press, 1975; (with Elie Abel and Averell Harriman) *Special Envoy to Churchill and Stalin,* Random House, 1975; (author of introduction) George Kistiakowsky, *A Scientist at the White House,* Harvard University Press, 1976. Contributor to history journals.

WORK IN PROGRESS: *The United States and European Reconstruction after World War II,* completion expected in 1982.

SIDELIGHTS: Maier writes that his major interest is "political, economic, and international history—with an emphasis on Europe in the twentieth century. In connection with the Brookings Institution I am currently co-directing a research group concerned with the politics and sociology of global inflation. This combines both my historical interests and contemporary concerns—one of the rewards of doing recent history."

* * *

MAIS, S(tuart) P(etre) B(rodie) 1885-1975

PERSONAL: Born July 4, 1885, in Matlock, England; son of Brodie (a clergyman) Mais; married wife Gillian; children: four daughters. *Education:* Christ Church, Oxford, B.A. (with honors), 1909, M.A., 1913. *Home:* Flat 20, Bliss House, Finches Gardens, Lindfield, Haywards Heath, Sussex, England.

CAREER: Author. Schoolmaster at schools in Lancaster, Sherborne, and Towbridge, all in England; *London Evening News,* London, England, literary critic, 1918; *London Daily Express,* London, literary critic, 1921-23; *London Daily Graphic,* London, literary editor, 1923-26; *London Daily Telegraph,* London, writer and book reviewer, 1926-31; Radley College, Abington, England, schoolmaster, 1941-45. Broadcaster on British Broadcasting Corp.; lecturer. *Member:* Achilles Club, Sette of Old Volumes Club, Vincent's Club.

WRITINGS: (Editor) *Bell's Shakespeare for Schools,* fourteen volumes, G. Bell & Sons, 1914-16; *April's Lonely Soldier,* Chapman & Hall, 1915; *An English Course for Army Candidates,* Sidgwick & Jackson, 1915; *A Public School in War Time,* John Murray, 1916; *Rebellion* (novel), Grant Richards, 1917; *Interlude* (novel), Chapman & Hall, 1917; *From Shakespeare to O. Henry: Studies in Literature,* Grant Richards, 1917, Dodd, 1918, revised edition, Grant Richards, 1923, reprinted, Books for Libraries, 1968; (editor) *A Schoolmaster's Diary: Being Extracts from the Journal of Patrick Traherne, M.D., Sometime Assistant Master at Radchester and Marlton,* Grant Richards, 1918; *The Cornish Riviera,* Great Western Railway, 1918; *Lovers of Silver,* Grant Richards, 1918; *The Education of a Philanderer,* Grant Richards, 1919; *An English Course for Schools,* Grant Richards, 1919.

Books and Their Writers, Grant Richards, 1920, reprinted, Books for Libraries, 1968; *Color-Blind* (novel), Grant Richards, 1920; *Uncle Lionel,* Grant Richards, 1920; *Breaking Covert: A Romance of the Hunting Field,* Grant Richards, 1921; *An English Course for Everybody,* Grant Richards, 1921, 5th edition, revised and edited by Jack Cox, Frewin, 1969; *Why We Should Read* (critical essays), Dodd, 1921, reprinted, Books for Libraries, 1967; *Caged Birds,* Grant Richards, 1922; *Quest Sinister,* Grant Richards, 1922; *Oh! To Be in England: A Book of the Open Air,* Grant Richards, 1922, 2nd edition, Richards Press, 1933; *Prunello,* Grant

Richards, 1923; *Some Modern Authors*, Dodd, 1923, reprinted, Books for Libraries, 1970; *Perissa*, Grant Richards, 1924; *Eclipse*, Brentano's, 1925; *Orange Street*, Grant Richards, 1926; *See England First*, Richards Press, 1927; (compiler) *Do You Know?: The Question Book*, Brentano's, 1927; *Do You Know North Cornwall?: My Finest Holiday*, Southern Railway, 1927, published as *My Finest Holiday*, Southern Railway of England, 1928; *Royal Scot and Her Forty-Nine Sister Engines*, London Midland and Scottish Railway, 1928; *Shakespeare*, Richards Press, 1928; *The Dawn of British Literature*, Richards Press, 1928; (editor) *The Modern Pictorial Library*, Richards Press, 1928; *Glorious Devon*, Great Western Railway, 1928, 3rd edition, 1934; *The Cornish Riviera*, Great Western Railway, 1928; *First Quarter*, Cassell, 1929.

It Isn't Far from London, Richards Press, 1930; *Official Handbook of the Corporation of Brighton*, Brighton Corp., 1930; *Southern Schools: An Illustrated Publication of the Schools on the Southern Railway*, Southern Railway, 1930; *Sussex*, Richards Press, 1930; *Frolio Lady*, Cassell, 1930; *West Country Holidays*, Southern Railway, 1930; *Southern Rambles for Londoners*, Southern Railway, 1931, revised edition, 1933, 4th edition, 1936; *Delight in Books*, A. Wheaton, 1931, reprinted, Richard West, 1973; *England of the Windmills*, J. M. Dent & Sons, 1931; *The High Lands of Britain*, Richards Press, 1932; *This Unknown Land*, Putnam, 1932, new edition, Falcon Press, 1946; *Some Books I Like*, Richards Press, 1932, reprinted, Richard West, 1973; *Week-ends in England*, Richards Press, 1933; *The Unknown Island*, Putnam, 1933; *These I Have Loved* (novel), Putnam, 1933; *S.O.S. Talks on Unemployment*, Putnam, 1933; *Live in Brighton or Hove*, Brighton & Hove Chamber of Commerce, 1933; *More Books I Like* (companion volume to *Some Books I Like*), Richards Press, 1934; *Isles of the Island*, Putnam, 1934; *A Modern Columbus*, Lippincott, 1934; *The Writing of English*, Chapman & Hall, 1935, reprinted, Richard West, 1973; *Round about England* (topographical essays), Richards Press, 1935; *England's Pleasurance*, Hutchinson, 1935, new edition with new plates, 1948; (editor with Tom Stephenson) *Lovely Britain*, Odhams Press, 1935; *Pictorial Britain: The Roads of Great Britain and Ireland, Shewing the Principal Places of Interest*, H. K. McCann for Anglo-American Oil, 1936; *A Chronicle of English Literature*, William Heinemann, 1936, reprinted, Richard West, 1973; *Walking at Week-ends*, Southern Railway, 1936; *The Fun of Writing*, G. Routledge & Sons, 1937; *England's Character*, Hutchinson, 1937; *All the Days of My Life* (autobiography), Hutchinson, 1937; *A.C.E.* (Atlantic Coast Express), McCorquodale, 1937; *The Three-Coloured Pencil* (novel), Eyre & Spottiswoode, 1937; (with others) *A Historical Review of McNamara's*, McNamara, 1937; *Let's Get Out of Here: Being an Account of Twenty-Six Walks from Points on the Route of the Atlantic Coast Express*, Southern Railway, 1937; *Walking in Somerset*, W. & R. Chambers, 1938; *Britain Calling*, Hutchinson, 1938; *Light Over Lundy* (juvenile), Eyre & Spottiswoode, 1938; *Old King Coal* (novel), Cassell, 1938; *Highways and Byways in the Welsh Marches*, Macmillan, 1939; *Fifty Years of the L.C.C.*, Cambridge University Press, 1939; *Raven among the Rooks*, Eyre & Spottiswoode, 1939; *Hills of the South*, Southern Railway, 1939; *Listen to the Country*, Hutchinson, 1939.

Diary of a Public Schoolmaster, Lutterworth Press, 1940; *"There'll Always Be an England,"* Hutchinson, 1940; *Men in Blue Glasses*, Hutchinson, 1940; *Calling Again: My Kitchen Front Talks with Some Results on the Listener*,

John Crowther, 1941; (editor) *A Cluster of Grapes: My Anthology*, William Heinemann, 1941; *Black Spider*, Hutchinson, 1941; *The Home Counties: Middlesex, Surrey, Kent, Hertfordshire, and Essex*, B. T. Batsford, 1943; *A Book of Food: How It Grows and What It Does for You*, Transatlantic Arts, 1944; *Youth after the War*, Macdonald & Co., 1944; *I Return to Scotland*, Christopher Johnson, 1947; *Walks in North Devon: Being an Account of Ten Walks in the North Devon District Served by the Atlantic Coast Express*, Southern Railway, 1947; (editor) *Brighton and Hove Sports Handbook*, Brighton and Hove Sports Publicity Committee, 1947; *I Return to Switzerland*, Christopher Johnson, 1948; *I Return to Ireland*, Christopher Johnson, 1948; *The English Scene Today*, Rockliff, 1948; *Around Brighton*, Saint Catherine Press, 1948; *Caper Sauce*, Hutchinson, 1948; *The Land of the Cinque Ports*, Christopher Johnson, 1949; *I Return to Wales*, Christopher Johnson, 1949; *The Best in Their Kind*, Richards Press, 1949, reprinted, Richard West, 1973; *Little England beyond Wales*, Christopher Johnson, 1949; *Who Dies?*, Hutchinson, 1949; *A History of N. Greening & Sons, Ltd., Warrington England, from 1799 to 1949*, Mackie, 1949.

Southern Rambles, British Railways, 1950; *We Wander in the West*, Ward, Lock, 1950; *The Riviera: New and Old*, Christopher Johnson, 1950; *I Loved You Once* (novel), Hutchinson, 1950; *Montacute House, Near Yeovil, Somerset* (guidebook), Cook, Hammond & Kell, 1950; *Norwegian Odyssey*, Christopher Johnson, 1951; *Brittannia 1651-1951*, Staples Press, 1951; *Arden and Avon*, Christopher Johnson, 1951; (with wife, Gillian Mais) *Winter Sports Holiday*, Alvin Redman, 1951, Taplinger, 1960; (with G. Mais) *Madeira Holiday*, Alvin Redman, 1951; *The Story of Oxford*, Staples Press, 1951; *Come Love, Come Death*, Hutchinson, 1951; (with G. Mais) *Austrian Holiday*, Alvin Redman, 1952; *Buffets and Rewards: An Autobiographical Record, 1937-1951*, Hutchinson, 1952; *The Channel Islands*, Christopher Johnson, 1953; *The Happiest Days of My Life* (autobiography), Parrish, 1953; *The Isle of Man*, Christopher Johnson, 1954; (with G. Mais) *Italian Holiday*, Alvin Redman, 1954; (with G. Mais) *Spanish Holiday*, Alvin Redman, 1955; *Our Village Today*, Werner Laurie, 1956; (with G. Mais) *Majorcan Holiday*, Alvin Redman, 1956; (with G. Mais) *Roman Holiday*, Alvin Redman, 1957; (with G. Mais) *Mediterranean Cruise Holiday*, Alvin Redman, 1958, Taplinger, 1961; (with G. Mais) *South American Cruise Holiday*, Alvin Redman, 1959.

(With G. Mais) *Continental Coach Tour Holiday*, Taplinger, 1960; (with G. Mais) *Round Africa Cruise Holiday*, Alvin Redman, 1961; (with G. Mais) *Dutch Holiday*, Alvin Redman, 1961; (with G. Mais) *Greek Holiday*, Alvin Redman, 1962; *Clovelly . . . Gem of North Devon*, J. Salmon, 1962; (with G. Mais) *Caribbean Cruise Holiday*, Alvin Redman, 1963; (with G. Mais) *Round Britain Coach Tour Holiday*, Alvin Redman, 1964; (with G. Mais) *Round the World Cruise Holiday*, Alvin Redman, 1965; *This Delicious Madness*, Frewin, 1968, A. S. Barnes, 1969.

BIOGRAPHICAL/CRITICAL SOURCES: S.P.B. Mais, *All the Days of My Life*, Hutchinson, 1937; Mais, *Buffets and Rewards: An Autobiographical Record, 1937-1951*, Hutchinson, 1952; Mais, *The Happiest Days of My Life*, Parrish, 1953.*

(Died April 21, 1975)

*　　　*　　　*

MAITLAND, Sara (Louise) 1950-

PERSONAL: Born February 27, 1950, in London, England;

daughter of Adam (a farmer) and Hope (Fraser-Campbell) Maitland; married Donald Hugh Thomson Lee (a priest), June 24, 1972; children: Mildred McNab Lee. *Education:* Oxford University, B.A. (honors), 1971; currently attending University of London for B.D. *Politics:* Feminist/Socialist. *Religion:* Christian. *Home:* 119 Faringdon Rd., Swindon, Wiltshire, England. *Agent:* John Johnson, 12/15 Henrietta St., London W2, England.

CAREER: Free-lance academic researcher in Oxford, England, 1972-73; free-lance journalist in Wiltshire, England, 1973—. *Member:* National Union of Journalists.

WRITINGS—Stories represented in anthologies: *Happy Unicorns,* edited by S. Purcell and L. Purves, Sidgewick & Jackson, 1970; *Introduction No. 5,* Faber & Faber, 1973. Contributor of articles, Short stories, and poems to journals, including *Listener, New Society, Time Out, Spare Rib, Hecate,* and *Bananas.*

WORK IN PROGRESS: Tales I Told My Mother, a feminist collective book; *Kids' London,* a guide to London for children under five; a novel on the suffragette movement; research on childbirth and infertility for a novel.

SIDELIGHTS: Sara Maitland writes to *CA:* "I am an activist feminist, a socialist, a catholic Christian, a wife, and a mother. This is motivation, vocational and avocational involvement, and full-time commitment. Also, it is complicated. Non-professional activities range from working at a battered wives' refuge to studying for a divinity degree. If it can be simplified, I'd say that the underlying conviction of my work is that people, through grace and love, can learn from the past and transform the future of this or any society."

*   *   *

MAKTOS, John 1902-1977

November 21, 1902—February 26, 1977; Greek-born American lawyer, author, and member of U.S. State Department from 1929 until 1962. He assisted in the preparation of the United Nations Charter and participated in the 1945 conference that created the United Nations. He died in Washington, D.C. Obituaries: *Washington Post,* March 1, 1977.

*   *   *

MALLOWAN, Max (Edgar Lucien) 1904-

PERSONAL: Born May 6, 1904, in London, England; son of Frederick and (Duvivier) Mallowan; married Agatha Christie (a writer), September 11, 1930 (died January 12, 1976). *Education:* New College, Oxford University, M.A., 1925. *Home:* Winterbrook House, Wallingford, Oxford OX10 9DX, England.

CAREER: Archaeologist. Participant in University of Pennsylvania excavation at Ur of the Chaldees, 1925-30, British Museum excavation at Nineveh, 1931-32, British Museum and British School of Archaeology in Iraq excavations at Arpachiyah, 1933, at Chagar Bazar and Brak, 1934-38; University of London, London, England, professor of Western Asiatic archaeology, 1947-62, professor emeritus, 1962—; Oxford University, Oxford, England, All Souls College, fellow, 1962-71, fellow emeritus, 1971—, New College, honorary fellow, 1973—. Excavated at Nimrud, 1949-58. British School of Archaeology in Iraq, director, 1947-61, chairman, 1966-70, president, 1970—; British Academy, Schweich lecturer, 1955, Albert Reckitt archaeological lecturer, 1969; honorary fellow of Metropolitan Museum of Art, 1958—; president of British Institute of Persian Studies,

1961—; member of governing board of School of Oriental and African Studies, 1967-75; trustee of British Museum. *Military service:* Royal Air Force Volunteer Reserve, 1939-45; became wing commander; served as advisor in Arab affairs.

MEMBER: British Academy (fellow; vice-president, 1961-62), Society of Antiquaries (fellow), Egypt Exploration Society (vice-president, 1968—), Arab Academy (Baghdad), German Archaeological Institute, Academie des Inscriptions et Belles Lettres, Royal Danish Academy of Letters and Sciences. *Awards, honors:* Commander of the British Empire, 1960, knighted, 1968. Lucy Wharton Drexel gold medal from Museum of University of Pennsylvania, 1957; Lawrence of Arabia memorial medal from Royal Society for Asian Affairs, 1969.

WRITINGS: (With J. Cruikshank Rose) *Prehistoric Assyria: The Excavations at Tall Arpachiyah 1933,* Oxford University Press, 1935; *Twenty-Five Years of Mesopotamian Discovery, 1932-56,* British School of Archaeology in Iraq, 1956; (with D. J. Wiseman) *Ur in Retrospect: In Memory of Sir C. Leonard Woolley,* British School of Archaeology in Iraq, 1960; *Early Mesopotamia and Iran,* McGraw, 1965; *Nimrud and Its Remains,* Dodd, 1966; (with L. G. Davies) *Ivories in Assyrian Style,* British School of Archaeology in Iraq, 1970; (with G. Herrman) *Furniture From S.W.7,* British School of Archaeology in Iraq, 1974; *Mallowan Memoirs,* Collins, 1977.

Contributor of chapter eight, "The Development of Cities: From Al-Ubaid to the End of Uruk 5," and chapter sixteen, "The Early Dynastic Period in Mesopotamia," to *Cambridge Ancient History.* Editor of Near Eastern and Western Asiatic book series for Penguin, 1948-65. Editor of *Iraq* (journal), 1948-71.

SIDELIGHTS: Mallowan told *CA:* "I suppose it is of some value to become aware from a study of the past that man has repeated his follies over and over again and is not much inclined to benefit from preceding errors.

"I do not think that I have observed any unexpected parallels in ancient civilisation, the lessons are obvious. Slack and indifferently performed work will not endure. First class craftsmanship is a joy forever.

"One of the joys of digging up artifacts is their entertainment value and the speculation to which they give rise; function and utility as well as the aesthetic considerations, and obviously from time to time the final product is suggestive of some improvement which may be carried out in the future.

"One problem which I have always wished to solve was the purpose for the thousands of alabaster Eye Idols which I discovered at Tell Brak. They were votive dedications to some god, and perhaps one day an early text may throw some light on this intriguing subject."

AVOCATIONAL INTERESTS: Trees and travel.

*   *   *

MALLOY, Ruth Lor 1932-

PERSONAL: Born August 4, 1932, in Canada; daughter of Leip (a restaurant owner) and Agnes (a restaurant owner; maiden name, Young) Lor; married Michael T. Malloy (managing editor of *National Observer*), June 5, 1965; children: Linda, Martin, Terry. *Education:* University of Toronto, B.A., 1954, B.S.W., 1960. *Religion:* Religious Society of Friends (Quakers). *Residence:* Asia. *Office address:* c/o Asia Mail, P.O. Box 1044, Alexandria, Va. 22313.

CAREER: Asia Mail, Alexandria, Va., author of column "Think Asia," 1976—. Has worked as social worker and human rights researcher in Toronto, Ontario, and social worker in Sudbury, Ontario; free-lance writer and photographer in Asia, 1960-66; organized Quaker Conferences in Southern Asia, 1962-63; information officer for Overseas Institute of Canada, 1964; has conducted workcamp activities in Mexico, Brazil, and the Canadian Arctic. Member of board of directors of American Friends Service Committee.

WRITINGS: Travel Guide to the People's Republic of China, Morrow, 1975. Author of material for CFTO-Television. Contributor to magazines and newspapers, including *Weekend* and *National Observer*.

WORK IN PROGRESS: A novel set in the People's Republic of China between 1966 and 1973.

SIDELIGHTS: Ruth Malloy comments: "My father was born in China but emigrated as a boy; my mother was born in Canada but also of Chinese ancestry. I was brought up in Canada caught between two cultures, a conflict which was not really resolved until after my first trip to Asia in 1960 when I fell profoundly in love with the place. I hope I can help other people understand, enjoy, and learn from Asia."

AVOCATIONAL INTERESTS: Skiing, scuba diving, swimming, travel, "meeting people."

* * *

MALLOY, Terry 1950-

PERSONAL: Born July 27, 1950, in Darjeeling, India; daughter of Patrick Andrew (a physician) and Lucille (a nurse; maiden name, Brady) Malloy; married Richard Matthews (a naturalist), June 12, 1973; children: Anthony. *Education:* Dodge City Junior College, A.A., 1969; Eastern Mennonite College, B.A., 1971; Eastern School for Dental Hygienists, certificate, 1972; Ithaca Montessori Teacher Training, certificate, 1973. *Politics:* Conservative. *Religion:* Sufi. *Home:* c/o 1 Bentley Rd., Great Neck, N.Y. 11023.

CAREER: Valley Montessori Preschool, Sacramento, Calif., directress, 1973-74; Our Lady Montessori School, Darjeeling, India, directress, 1974-76; writer, 1976—. *Member:* American Montessori Society, National Committee to Legalize Laetrile.

WRITINGS: Montessori and Your Child: A Primer for Parents, Schocken, 1973; *Arf!: Cooking for Dogs*, Ambrose, 1974; *Perfect Health*, Ambrose, 1976.

WORK IN PROGRESS: A biography of Dmitri Mitrinovic.

SIDELIGHTS: Terry Malloy writes: "My youth was spent in several foreign countries including India, Yugoslavia, Finland, and Brazil. The need to communicate with those around me and my love for people and textures led, I am sure, to writing." She adds that a vital subject for her is "moving others toward life; the topic is irrelevant." *Avocational interests:* Long-distance running, rock and roll of the 1950's, Russian amber.

* * *

MALRAUX, (Georges-) Andre 1901-1976
(Colonel Berger)

November 3, 1901—November 23, 1976; French writer, archaeologist, government official, resistance hero, and author of novels, art criticism, autobiography, and other nonfiction works. For his novel, *Man's Fate* (1934), he was awarded the Prix Goncourt. The money he received from that prize he devoted to a search for the lost city of the Queen of Sheba. Malraux organized the resistance in southwest France, heading the Alsace-Lorraine brigade under the pseudonym Colonel Berger. He served as minister of culture in de Gaulle's cabinet. Malraux died in Paris, France. Obituaries: *New York Times*, November 25, 1976; *Current Biography*, February, 1977. (*CAP*-2; earlier sketch in *CA*-21/22)

* * *

MALUF, Chafic 1905(?)-1976

1905(?)—December 27, 1976; Arabic poet and philosopher. He moved to Brazil in 1926, where he did most of his writings. Critics have acclaimed him as being one of the greatest contemporary poets in the Arabic language, and his work has been translated into more than ten languages. He died in Sao Paulo, Brazil. Obituaries: *New York Times*, December 29, 1976; *AB Bookman's Weekly*, February 14, 1977.

* * *

MANFRED, Freya 1944-

PERSONAL: Born November 28, 1944, in Minneapolis, Minn.; daughter of Frederick Feikema (a novelist) and Maryanna (a critic; maiden name, Shorba) Manfred; married Thomas Whiting Popp (a screenwriter), October 2, 1976. *Education:* Macalester College, B.A. (summa cum laude), 1966; Stanford University, M.A., 1968. *Address:* R.R. 3, Luverne, Minn. 56156.

CAREER: Control Data Corp., Palo Alto, Calif., applications analyst, 1967-68; University of South Dakota, Vermillion, instructor in creative writing, English, and humanities, 1968-72; poet and writer, 1972—. Instructor and counselor for South Dakota Upward Bound program, summer, 1969; instructor for South Dakota career opportunities program, 1971. *Awards, honors:* Minnesota Poetry Prize from Minnesota State Arts Board, 1974; writing fellowships at Wurlitzer Foundation, Yaddo Foundation, and MacDowell Colony.

WRITINGS: A Goldenrod Will Grow (poems), James D. Thueson, 1971, 2nd edition, 1975; *Yellow Squash Woman* (poems), Thorp Springs Press, 1976.

Work anthologized in *Sticks and Stones: 1972 Minnesota Poetry Anthology*, edited by Mary Rudbeck, Laurence Wieland, and Donna Matson, *Sticks and Stones* Magazine, 1972; *Stoney Lonesome: Indiana University Anthology*, edited by Richard Pflum, 1973; *Women of the Future*, edited by Ellen Rosser, *Hard Pressed* Magazine, 1976; *Literature of South Dakota*, edited by John Milton, Dakota Press, 1976; *Since Feeling Is First: An Anthology of New America*, edited by David Ray and Gary Gildner, University of Missouri, Kansas City, 1976; *Traveling America*, edited by David Kherdian, Macmillan, 1977.

Contributor of more than forty articles, poems, and reviews to literary journals, including *Poetry Now, Stonecloud, Hyperion, Carleton Miscellany, American Poetry Review, North Country Anvil, Cosmopolitan*, and *Christian Science Monitor*.

WORK IN PROGRESS: American Roads, a book of poems; a novel.

SIDELIGHTS: Freya Manfred writes: "*American Roads* contains a long poem which reflects the continual travel I've been doing around—across—America, working in so many different states for Poetry-in-the-Schools, sponsored by the National Endowment for the Arts. I'm looking forward to settling in more—working only in one state perhaps, and writing longer poems, and beginning work on a novel."

MANGOLD, Tom 1934-

PERSONAL: Born August 20, 1934, in Germany; son of Fritz (a lawyer) and Dorothea (an actress; maiden name, Rares) Mangold; married wife Valerie, August, 1972; children: Sarah, Abigail. Education: Attended secondary school in Dorking, England. Agent: Deborah Rogers, 29 Goodge St., London W.1, England. Office: British Broadcasting Corp.—Television, Lime Grove, London W.12, England.

CAREER: Reporter, Croydon Advertiser, 1954-1958; reporter, Sunday Mirror, 1958-62; reporter, Daily Express, 1962-64; British Broadcasting Corp. (BBC), London, England, television news reporter, 1964-70, television reporter for public affairs program, "Panorama," 1970—. Military service: British Army, 1952-54. Awards, honors: Nominated for TV reporter of the year by London Daily Express, 1975.

WRITINGS: (With Anthony Summers) The File on the Tsar: The Fate of the Romanovs . . . Dramatic New Evidence, Harper, 1976.

AVOCATIONAL INTERESTS: Talking shop, trampolining, and trying to give up smoking.

* * *

MANIFOLD, John S(treeter) 1915-

PERSONAL: Born April 21, 1915, in Melbourne, Victoria, Australia; son of John (a grazier) and Barbara Grey (Smith) Manifold; married Katharine Hopwood (a teacher and linguist), March 9, 1940 (deceased); children: Miranda (Mrs. Philip Howard Barton Macqueen), Nicholas. Education: Jesus College, Cambridge, B.A. (honors). Home: 361 Wynnum North Rd., Brisbane, Queensland, Australia. Agent: David Higham Associates, 76 Dean St., London W.1, England.

CAREER: Free-lance writer, 1946—. Has delivered Commonwealth Literary Fund lectures at Australian universities. Military service: British Army, Intelligence Corps, 1940-46; served in West Africa and Europe; became captain. Member: National Council of Realist Writers' Groups (vice-president), Fellowship of Australian Writers (president of Queensland branch, 1959), Brisbane Realist Writers' Group (past president).

WRITINGS: Death of Ned Kelly and Other Ballads (poems), Favil Press, 1941; Selected Verse, John Day, 1947; The Amorous Flute: An Unprofessional Handbook for Recorder Players, Workers Music Association, 1948; The Music in English Drama from Shakespeare to Purcell, Barrie & Rockliff, 1956, reprinted by Scholarly Press; The Violin, the Banjo and the Bones, Rams Skull Press, 1957; Nightmares and Sunhorses (poems), Edwards & Shaw, 1961; (editor) Penguin Australian Song Book, Penguin, 1964; Who Wrote the Ballads? (nonfiction), Australasian Book Society, 1964; Op. 8 (poems), University of Queensland Press, 1971.

Also author (with H. Nicholson and D. Martin) of Trident (poems), 1944, and editor of Queensland Pocket Songbook, 1959. Work appears in anthologies, including Poems from the Forces, edited by Keidrych Rhys, Routledge & Kegan Paul, 1942; More Poems from the Forces, Routledge & Kegan Paul, 1943; War Poets, John Day, 1945; A Little Treasury of Modern Poetry, Scribner, 1952; A Book of Australian Verse, Oxford University Press, 1956; Penguin Book of Australian Verse, Penguin, 1958; Penguin Book of Australian Ballads, Penguin, 1965. Contributor to music journals and other magazines, including Eastern Horizon, Realist, and Australian. Poetry editor of Realist.

WORK IN PROGRESS: History of the Flute.

SIDELIGHTS: Manifold has been performing Australian folk music for many years; he plays recorder, guitar, and bassoon, and other regional folk instruments, but is interested as well in chamber music, organizing an amateur group and writing music for it. In connection with his writing, he has traveled in the Soviet Union and in China. Some of his work has been translated into French and Polish. Avocational interests: Cats.

* * *

MANN, Michael 1919-1977

April 21, 1919—January 1, 1977; German musicologist, educator, and author. He was the son of novelist Thomas Mann and author of his father's biography, as well as author of studies in the field of German literature and music. He died in Orinda, Calif. Obituaries: New York Times, January 4, 1977; AB Bookman's Weekly, March 14, 1977. (See index for previous CA sketch)

* * *

MANNING, Jack 1920-

PERSONAL: Born November 21, 1920, in New York, N.Y.; son of Mathew (in the millinery business) and Sally (a seamstress; maiden name, Markowitz) Mendelsohn; married Marie Louise Koch, October 9, 1970; children: Sarah-Jeanne. Education: Attended City College (now of the City University of New York), 1939-40. Home: 75 Pearce Parkway, Pearl River, N.Y. 10965. Agent: Georges Borchardt, Inc., 145 East 52nd St., New York, N.Y. 10022. Office: New York Times, 229 West 43rd St., New York, N.Y. 10036.

CAREER: Free-lance photographer in New York City, Europe, and South America, 1941-64; New York Times, New York, N.Y., staff photographer, 1964—. Photographs are represented in permanent collections at Museum of Modern Art, Metropolitan Museum of Art, and International Museum at George Eastman House. Member: National Press Photographers Association, New York Press Photographers Association.

WRITINGS: Young Puerto Rico, Dodd, 1962; Young Spain, Dodd, 1963; Young Ireland, Dodd, 1965; Young Brazil, Dodd, 1970; (with Ted Szulc) Portrait of Spain, American Heritage Press, 1972; 35mm Portraiture: A New Look at an Old Art, Amphoto, in press. Author of columns in New York Times. Contributor to technical publications.

SIDELIGHTS: Manning comments briefly: "Having traveled widely, and lived in Europe for close to twelve years, books involving other peoples and cultures do interest me. My current goal is a series of photographic books, each one aiming at being the definitive work in its area."

* * *

MANNING, Robert (Joseph) 1919-

PERSONAL: Born December 25, 1919, in Binghamton, N.Y.; son of Joseph James and Agnes P. (Brown) Manning; married Margaret Marinda Raymond (an editor), December 28, 1944; children: Richard Raymond, Brian Gould, Robert Brown. Residence: Boston, Mass. Office: 8 Arlington St., Boston, Mass. 02116.

CAREER: Binghamton Press, Binghamton, N.Y., reporter, 1936-41; Associated Press, New York City, reporter, 1941; United Press International, State Department and White House correspondent in Washington, D.C., 1944-46; United Nations bureau chief, 1946-49; Time (magazine), New York

City, writer, 1949-55, senior editor, 1955-58, London bureau chief for Time, Inc., 1958-61; *New York Herald Tribune,* New York City, Sunday editor, 1961; U.S. Department of State, Washington, D.C., assistant secretary of state for public affairs, 1962-64; Atlantic Monthly Co., Boston, Mass., executive editor of *Atlantic Monthly* (magazine), 1964-66, editor-in-chief, and vice-president of company, 1966—. Member of advisory council of Edward R. Murrow Center of Public Diplomacy, Tufts University, 1965; member of visiting committee of School of International Studies, Stanford University, 1968. *Military service:* U.S. Army, 1942-43. *Member:* Council on Foreign Relations, American Academy of Arts and Sciences (fellow), Century Association, Harvard Club, Tavern Club, Buck's Garrick. *Awards, honors:* Nieman fellowship, 1945-46; Doctor of Letters, from Tufts University, 1966; Doctor of Humane Letters, from St. Lawrence University, 1971.

WRITINGS: (Editor with Michael Janeway) *Who We Are,* Atlantic, 1969.

* * *

MANOCCHIA, Benito 1934-

PERSONAL: Born May 10, 1934, in Giulianova, Italy; son of Francesco (a lawyer) and Filomena (a teacher; maiden name, Spadacci) Manocchia. *Education:* University of Urbino, degree in journalism, 1955. *Religion:* Roman Catholic. *Home:* 730 East 236th St., Bronx, N.Y. 10466.

CAREER: Free lance writer, 1950-72; Rusconi Publishers, Milano, Italy, foreign correspondent, 1972—. Notable assignments include interviews with Robert Kennedy, Hubert Humphrey, President Jimmy Carter, and other political figures, and also interviews with Hollywood actors and actresses. *Military service:* Italian Air Force, 1953; became lieutenant. *Member:* Smithsonian Institute. *Awards, honors:* Award for best foreign correspondent, 1973, from Italian Professional Journalists.

WRITINGS: Indagine Su Dieci Squillo di Lusso, MEB (Torino), 1971; *Il Prete di Cosa Nostra,* MEB, 1971; *Amore Voodu,* IPC (Rome), 1973; *Vivremo Duecento Anni,* Campironi (Milan), 1974. Contributor to *Gioia, Eva Express, Gente, Settimanale, Qui Notizie, Gente Motori,* and other periodicals.

WORK IN PROGRESS: Hollywood Today.

SIDELIGHTS: Manocchia told *CA:* "I come from a family of journalists. Two brothers work in the same field, one in the U.S. and one in Italy. I wanted to become a reporter ever since I was fifteen. One subject valid to me, as a foreign correspondent, is life in the U.S., but sometimes I must write what editors (and readers) want. The life of a foreign correspondent is tiring. I wish someday to go back and work in editorial offices in Italy, but it won't be for a long time. I find the U.S. extremely cooperative in fields of politics, sciences, movies, sports—to me there is no other country in the world where a foreign correspondent has as easy a duty as in this country."

* * *

MAO Tse-tung 1893-1976

December 26, 1893—September 9, 1976; Chinese political leader, author, poet, and most influential revolutionary of his generation. As chairman of the central committee of the Chinese Communist Party (which he helped establish in 1921) and leader of People's Republic of China since 1949, Mao was the first leader in two centuries to unify China under a central administration. In his lifetime, Mao saw China emerge from what critics termed a "Confucian slumber" into a major force embodying what Mao called "concrete Marxism," that is, Marxism "adapted to the concrete realities of China." His *Little Red Book,* carried by virtually every Chinese, is printed in more than one billion copies. Mao died in Peking, China. Obituaries: *New York Times,* September 10, 1976; *Washington Post,* September 10, 1976; *Time,* September 20, 1976; *Newsweek,* September 20, 1976.

* * *

MARCH, Joseph 1899(?)-1977

1899(?)—February 14, 1977; American poet, screenwriter best known for screenplays of the 1930's and 1940's, including "Hell's Angeles," "Wagons Westward," and "Three Faces West." Two of his narrative poems, "The Set-Up" and "The Wild Party" were made into movies. He was a former editor of *New Yorker.* During World War I he fought in France with the U.S. Army. March died in Los Angeles, Calif. Obituaries: *New York Times,* February 16, 1977.

* * *

MARCHANT, William 1923-

PERSONAL: Born May 1, 1923, in Allentown, Pa.; son of Frederick and Elizabeth Rebecca Davis (Cassel) Marchant. *Education:* Attended Temple University, 1939-40, and Yale University, 1939-42. *Politics:* "Leftish." *Religion:* None. *Residence:* New York, N.Y.

CAREER: Playwright, journalist, and author. *Military service:* U.S. Army Air Forces, 1942-45. *Member:* Authors League of America, Screen Writers Guild West. *Awards, honors:* National Theatre Conference Award for Best First Play, 1952, for "Within a Glass Bell."

WRITINGS: Gondolier (novel), Random House, 1961; *The Privilege of His Company: Noel Coward Remembered,* Bobbs-Merrill, 1975.

Plays: "Within a Glass Bell", first produced in Westport, Conn., at Westport Country Playhouse, July 23, 1950; *To Be Continued* (first produced in New York City at Booth Theatre, April 23, 1952), Dramatists Play Service, 1952; *The Desk Set* (first produced in New York City at Broadhurst Theatre, October 24, 1955), Samuel French, 1956.

Adaptor for screen: "Dark at the Top of the Stairs" (based on the play by William Inge), 1960; "Fanny" (based on play by S. N. Behrman and Joshua Logan), 1961; and "Faster! Faster!," all for Warner Brothers. Also author of screenplays produced in France and Britain, and of teleplays broadcast in Britain.

Contributor of articles to *Holiday, Theatre Arts, Saturday Review, Horizon,* and other magazines.

WORK IN PROGRESS: A novel, *Heir Apparent;* a play, "Ding-Dong Bell."

SIDELIGHTS: Marchant writes, "Having spent eleven years of my adult life abroad (England, chiefly, but also France, Italy, Switzerland, and Greece) I tend to think and behave as a European in reacting to the changing American scene and what I regard as the total collapse of the kind of civilization into which I was born. This attitude cannot help but influence my work which, in a kind of elitist way, celebrates the standards of an educated class, politically committed yet with its own gentle refinements. I am waiting for the pendulum to swing back, yet I have my doubts that it will."

AVOCATIONAL INTERESTS: Swimming, cooking, eavesdropping.

* * *

MARDER, Herbert 1934-

PERSONAL: Born April 9, 1934, in Vienna, Austria; son of Moses and Pepi (Wagschall) Marder; married Norma Rajeck (a singer), October 6, 1956; children: Michael, Yuri. *Education:* City College (now of the City University of New York), B.A., 1955; Brandeis University, M.A., 1957; Columbia University, Ph.D., 1964. *Office:* 100 English Building, University of Illinois, Urbana, Ill. 61801.

CAREER: City College of the City University of New York, New York, N.Y., lecturer in English, 1960-63; Paterson College, Paterson, N.J., assistant professor of English, 1963-65; University of Illinois, Urbana, assistant professor, 1965-68, associate professor of English, 1968—. Founder of New Verbal Workshop.

WRITINGS: Feminism and Art: A Study of Virginia Woolf, University of Chicago Press, 1968. Also contributor to *Novel: A Forum on Fiction,* 1973. Contributor to journals, including *Bucknell Review, Prairie Schooner,* and *Quartet,* and newspapers.

WORK IN PROGRESS: A critical study of the novels of Doris Lessing.

* * *

MARGOLIN, Edythe

PERSONAL: Born in South River, N.J.; daughter of Hyman (a dress manufacturer) and Rebecca (a dressmaker; maiden name, Trachtenberg) Beckerman; married Gerald J. Margolin (a campus postmaster), November 23, 1939; children: Diane, Don. *Education:* University of California, Los Angeles, B.A., 1957, M.A., 1959, Ed.D., 1963. *Home:* 13781 Southwest 84th St., Unit G, Miami, Fla. 33183. *Office:* School of Education, Florida International University, Tamiami Trail, Miami, Fla. 33199.

CAREER: University of California, Santa Barbara, assistant professor of social studies and the education of young children, 1963-64; University of California, Los Angeles, assistant professor of social studies and the socialization of the young, 1964-69; University of Miami, Coral Gables, Fla., visiting associate professor of social studies and early childhood education, 1969-70; California State University at Northridge, San Fernando Valley, lecturer in social studies, 1970-71; University of Miami, visiting associate professor of social studies and early childhood education, 1971-72; Florida International University, Miami, associate professor of early childhood education and sociocultural elements, 1972—.

MEMBER: American Academy of Political and Social Science. *Awards, honors:* Grant from University of California, Los Angeles, for Germany, England, France, and Italy, 1967; National Institutes of Health special research fellowship, 1967-68; visiting echolar at Stanford University, 1977.

WRITINGS: Sociocultural Elements in Early Childhood Education, Macmillan, 1974; *Young Children: Their Curriculum and Learning Processes,* Macmillan, 1976. Contributor to education journals.

WORK IN PROGRESS: Research on role learning and its relationship to teachers and young children.

SIDELIGHTS: Edythe Margolin comments that she became "motivated to study young children and ways of helping them develop favorable (healthy) self-concepts after noting that adults took advantage of children's vulnerability and difficulties in expressing themselves; I felt that children needed to learn ways of helping themselves to deal effectively with the environment."

* * *

MARGOLIS, Jack S 1934-

PERSONAL: Born December 11, 1934, in Holyoke, Mass.; son of Morris and Rose (Graufman) Margolis. *Education:* Los Angeles State College, B.A., 1960; University of California, Los Angeles, graduate study. *Politics:* Pragmatism. *Religion:* None. *Home address:* P.O. Box 69685, Los Angeles, Calif. 90069.

CAREER: Cliff House Books, Los Angeles, Calif., owner, 1972—; in real estate investment, 1975—. Chairman of board of directors of Cheapskates, Inc., 1977. *Military service:* U.S. Army, 1955-56. *Member:* American Federation of Television and Radio Artists, National Association of Television and Radio Artists, Writers Guild of America.

WRITINGS: A Child's Garden of Grass, Simon & Schuster, 1970; *Cooking for Orgies and Other Large Parties,* Cliff House Books, 1974; *Linda Lovelace for President,* Playboy Press, 1975; *The Ins and Outs of Orgies,* Cliff House Books, 1975; *The Poetry of Richard Milhous Nixon,* Cliff House Books, 1975; *Impotence Is Always Having to Say You're Sorry,* Cliff House Books, 1976; *Recreational Drugs,* Cliff House Books, in press.

Author of "Linda Lovelace for President" screenplay, 1975. Author of column "The Burning Bush" in *Los Angeles Free Press,* 1973-76.

SIDELIGHTS: Margolis told *CA:* "I've made more money in six months of real estate than in a whole life of writing."

* * *

MARIANO, Frank 1931(?)-1976

1931(?)—August 9, 1976; American war correspondent best known for his coverage of the Vietnam War for American Broadcasting Co. (ABC) News. He covered the war from 1969 until the Phnom Penh evacuation in April, 1975. He served in the U.S. Army for thirteen years. He died in Washington, D.C. Obituaries: *New York Times,* August 10, 1976; *Washington Post,* August 10, 1976.

* * *

MARINE, David 1880(?)-1976

1880(?)—November 26, 1976; American pathologist who discovered cure for goiters. During World War I he headed Army hospital units in France and Germany, and later directed the laboratories at Montefiore Hospital in New York City. He died in Lewes, Del. Obituaries: *New York Times,* November 28, 1976.

* * *

MARK, Theonie Diakidis 1938-

PERSONAL: Born July 20, 1938, in Rhodes, Greece; daughter of Nicolas (a businessman) and Maria (Vasiliou) Diakidis; married Robert Burton Mark (an engineer), August 24, 1955; children: Morgan W., Theodore J., Burton N. *Education:* Archaeological Institute, diploma, 1955; Odeon of Music and Dance, diploma, 1955; attended New England Conservatory, 1956-57. *Home and office:* 328 Concord St., Carlisle, Mass. 01741.

CAREER: WGBH-Television, Boston, Mass., television performer, 1972—. Instructor at Boston City Hall Office of Cultural Affairs, 1975-76; chairman of Greek events at Decordova Museum, 1976 (now honorary member); director and performer with Helios Greek Folk Dance Group, 1976—.

WRITINGS: Greek Islands Cooking, Little, Brown, 1974. Contributor to *National Observer.*

WORK IN PROGRESS: Research on Greek folk art, multi-ethnic cooking of Rhodes, foods of ancient Greece and Rome, and Sephardic cooking.

SIDELIGHTS: Theonie Mark writes: "I am motivated by a deep interest in my own culture and its origins. I am fluent in English, Greek, and Italian, and competent in Turkish and Ladino (old Spanish spoken by Sephardic people)."

* * *

MARKFIELD, Wallace 1926-

PERSONAL: Born August 12, 1926, in Brooklyn, N.Y.; son of Max (a clothing cutter) and Sophie (Monete) Markfield; married Anna May Goodman; children: Andrea Kate. *Education:* Brooklyn College (now of the City University of New York), B.A., 1947; New York University, graduate study, 1947-49. *Politics:* Democrat. *Religion:* Jewish. *Home and office:* 15 Vista Way, Port Washington, N.Y. 11050. *Agent:* Candida Donadio, 111 West 57th St., New York, N.Y. 10019.

CAREER: Writer. Anti-Defamation League, New York, N.Y., writer, 1955-65; San Francisco State College (now University), San Francisco, Calif., assistant professor, 1966-68; Kirkland College, Clinton, N.Y., writer-in-residence, 1968-69; Queens College of the City University of New York, Flushing, N.Y., assistant professor, 1971-73. *Awards, honors:* Guggenheim fellowship; National Institute of Arts and Letters grant.

WRITINGS: To an Early Grave (novel), Simon & Schuster, 1964; *Teitlebaum's Window* (novel), Knopf, 1970; *You Could Live If They Let You,* Knopf, 1974.

Stories and articles represented in anthologies. Contributor of about forty stories and articles to magazines, including *Partisan Review, Commentary, Midstream, New York, Esquire, Cavalier, Saturday Evening Post,* and *New Leader.* Film critic for *New Leader,* 1955.

WORK IN PROGRESS: A novel about the movies, completion expected in 1979; *The Passionate Movie-Goers* (tentative title), an anthology.

SIDELIGHTS: Markfield writes: "Like it or not, I've been categorized as a black humorist, as part of the American-Jewish renaissance. As of this writing, I suppose I'd call myself a tone-poet of aggravation."

* * *

MARKHAM, Clarence M(atthew), Jr. 1911-

PERSONAL: Born June 20, 1911, in San Antonio, Tex.; son of Clarence Matthew and Lena (Dillwood) Markham; married Olga Frances Hughes, July 21, 1935; children: Clarence Matthew III, Melvin, Mrs. Olga Pierre, Leslie. *Education:* Attended Wittenberg College, 1933-35. *Politics:* Democrat. *Religion:* Roman Catholic. *Home:* 1121 West 111th Pl., Chicago, Ill.; and, 7831 E. Pima, Tucson, Ariz. *Office:* 11717 South Vincennes, Chicago, Ill. 60643.

CAREER/WRITINGS: Railroad superintendent of porter car service, 1935-39; Ann Arbor Railroad Co., superintendent of dining car service, 1938-41; *Negro Traveler* (magazine), founder, publisher, and editor, 1942—. Precinct captain in Chicago, 1938-41. *Member:* American Society of Travel Writers, Bellman Porters Association of Ohio (president).

SIDELIGHTS: Clarence Markham writes "The *Negro Traveler* started as an annual directory to help black people find a place to eat and sleep when segregation was rampant in the United States. It later branched out to travel in general."

* * *

MARKISH, David 1938-
(David Maguen)

PERSONAL: Born September 24, 1938, in Moscow, Soviet Union; son of Peretz (a poet and writer) and Esther (a translator; maiden name, Lazebnikova) Markish; married Irina Berzhanskaya (a choreographer), May, 1971; children: Peretz (son). *Education:* Institute of Literature, Moscow, M.A., 1962. *Religion:* Jewish. *Home:* 28 Tamar St., Neve Monosson, Israel. *Agent:* Ewan MacNaughton, *Daily Telegraph,* 135 Fleet St., London, England.

CAREER: Writer, 1956—. *Military service:* Israel Defence Force, 1973—. *Member:* International P.E.N., Israel Writers and Poets Association. *Awards, honors:* Prize from Israel Writers and Journalists Association, 1973, for work published in *Maariv;* literary prize in Memory of Pinchas Sapir (Israel), 1976, for *A New World for Simon Ashkenazi.*

WRITINGS: Piatero u samogo neba: Dokumental 'nya novest' (title means "Five Climbing to Skies"), Gidrometeo-izdat, 1966; *A New World for Simon Ashkenazi* (first volume of proposed trilogy), translation by Michael Glenny, Dutton, 1976 (published in England as *The Beginning: A Novel,* Hodder & Stoughton, 1976).

Translator from French into Russian: Haussu Diavara, *Chyornye Zvezdy* (title means "Black Stars"), Dyetskaya Literatura, 1967. Has written film scripts, sometimes under pseudonym David Maguen in the Soviet Union, and in Israel. Contributor to literary journals.

WORK IN PROGRESS: The second and third volumes of trilogy.

SIDELIGHTS: Markish said his leading interest and his leading theme is larger than just the *condition juive* in the Soviet Union, or even abroad. "It is *deracinement* in a way: Psychological and other implications and consequences of modern mass migrations, the loss of Fatherland, of homeland, the loneliness of *deracines* of all kinds (not only emigrants) combined with the desperate insolence."

AVOCATIONAL INTERESTS: Exploring, mountain climbing, hunting, ethnography.

* * *

MARKLE, Joyce B(onners) 1942-

PERSONAL: Born November 3, 1942, in Chicago, Ill.; daughter of Harry (a businessman) and Stella (a commercial artist; maiden name, Zmudka) Bonners; married Theodore Markle (a teacher), 1961 (deceased); children: Lawren, Todd. *Education:* Marquette University, A.B., 1964, M.A. (honors), 1966; University of Wisconsin, Madison, Ph.D., 1971. *Home:* 425 Florence Ave., Evanston, Ill. 60202.

CAREER: Marquette University, Milwaukee, Wis., instructor in English, 1965-66; Edgewood College, Madison, Wis., instructor in English, 1969-70; Loyola University,

Chicago, Ill., assistant professor of English, 1970-75; free-lance writer, speaker, and researcher, 1975— . *Member:* Popular Culture Association, Modern Language Association of America, John Updike Society (president, 1974-76), Midwest Modern Language Association, Rocky Mountain Modern Language Association (president of Women's Caucus, 1975).

WRITINGS: Fighters and Lovers: Theme in the Novels of John Updike, New York University Press, 1973; (contributor) Robert Scotto, editor, *Contemporary American Fiction,* Everett/Edwards, 1976. Contributor of articles to reviews to magazines, including *Modern Fiction Studies,* and newspapers.

WORK IN PROGRESS: Updike: A Contemporary Critical Response; What Do I Feed It?, on the care and feeding of native American animals.

* * *

MARKMAN, Howard (Joel) 1950-

PERSONAL: Born October 27, 1950, in New York, N.Y.; son of Arnold J. (a certified public accountant) and Claire (Rosenkranz) Markman. *Education:* Rutgers University, B.A. (cum laude), 1972; Indiana University, M.A., 1976, Ph.D., 1977. *Religion:* Jewish. *Home:* 1035 Colorado Blvd., Apt. 208, Denver, Colo. 80206. *Office:* Medical Center, University of Colorado, Denver, Colo. 80220.

CAREER: Indiana University, Bloomington, associate instructor in psychology, 1973-75, trainer at Laboratory of Human Social Interaction, 1975-76; University of Colorado, Denver, clinical-community psychology intern at Medical Center, 1976-77. Psychologist for Monroe County Community Mental Health Center, 1973-75. *Member:* American Psychological Association, Phi Beta Kappa.

WRITINGS: (With J. G. Gottman, C. I. Notarius, and Joni Gonso) *A Couples' Guide to Communication,* Research Press, 1976; (contributor) Sol Garfield and Allen Bergin, editors, *Handbook of Psychotherapy and Behavior Change,* Wiley, 2nd edition (Markman was not included in 1st edition), 1977. Contributor to psychology and counseling journals.

WORK IN PROGRESS: An evaluation of a community consultation program; research on couples' communication in a laboratory setting; comparing couples' and observers' ratings of couples' interaction; a model of secondary prevention applied to the longitudinal study of couples planning to marry.

SIDELIGHTS: Markman writes that his professional interests center around "longitudinal and cross-sectional study of couples' interaction; relationship formation processes; development of an empirically based, preventively oriented, pre-marital intervention program; community psychology with special interests in mental health consultation to schools and community organizations, primary and secondary prevention with particular research interest in early identification of emotional problems in pre-school children; human sexuality; treatment of sexual dysfunction; pediatric psychology."

* * *

MARKS, Stuart A. 1939-

PERSONAL: Born April 28, 1939, in Wilmington, N.C.; son of Sandy Cole (a dental professor and missionary) and Katherine (a nurse; maiden name, Woods) Marks; married Martha Singletary (a writer and educator), June 20, 1964; children: Stephan Singletary, Jon Stuart. *Education:* North Carolina State University, B.Sc. (with honors), 1961; Michigan State University, M.S., 1964, Ph.D., 1968; University of London, research certificate, 1966. *Home:* 603 Turnpike Rd., Laurinburg, N.C. 28352. *Office:* St. Andrews Presbyterian College, Laurinburg, N.C. 28352.

CAREER: Alaska Department of Fish and Game, Juneau, game biologist, 1962; Michigan State University, East Lansing, instructor, 1964-65; Oklahoma State University, Stillwater, assistant professor of zoology, 1968-70; St. Andrews Presbyterian College, Laurinburg, N.C., associate professor of anthropology and environmental studies, 1970—. Research associate and visiting scholar, University of California, Berkeley, 1976. Consultant on wildlife uses in East Africa; tour guide; vertebrate collector and curator; writer's assistant. *Member:* American Association for Advancement of Science, American Anthropological Association, Royal Anthropological Institute (fellow), Ecological Society of America, African Studies Association, East African Wildlife Society, Southern Anthropological Society, Phi Kappa Phi, Sigma Xi, Gamma Sigma Delta, Alpha Zeta. *Awards, honors:* Foreign area fellowship from Social Science Research Council, 1965-68; Piedmont Universities research award, 1973; joint African studies committee of American Council of Learned Societies and Social Studies Research Council research award, 1973; outstanding teacher's award from St. Andrews College, 1974; National Endowment for the Humanities stipend, 1976.

WRITINGS: Large Mammals and a Brave People: Subsistence Hunters in Zambia, University of Washington Press, 1976. Contributor to journals in his field.

WORK IN PROGRESS: Animal symbolisms in Central African rituals; wild animals and their uses in Africa; *Hunting Traditions and Animal Symbolism in a Changing Landscape.*

SIDELIGHTS: Marks told *CA:* "My main interests are with wild animals and with people and their dependencies and relationships through time and in space. This has led me at different times to assume the roles of anthropologist (social scientist) and of zoologist. My main motivations come from the experiences and circumstances I have experienced here and abroad and through wide reading in both biological and social sciences. I am intuitive and determined." Marks has knowledge of French, Luba, Bisa, and Spanish.

AVOCATIONAL INTERESTS: Jogging, bike riding, romping with his sons, photography, reading, collecting stamps, and stimulating conversations.

* * *

MARNEY, John 1933-

PERSONAL: Born May 7, 1933, in London, England; son of George William (a printer) and Winifred (Bird) Marney; married Meilan Chan (a nurse), 1958; children: P'ei Yu, Hsiung-meng, P'ei-heng. *Education:* School of Oriental and African Studies, London, B.A. (honors), 1962; Oxford University, diploma in education, 1963; University of Wisconsin, Madison, Ph.D., 1969. *Office:* Department of Chinese, Oakland University, Rochester, Mich. 48063.

CAREER: Professional orchestral violinist. Oakland University, Rochester, Mich., associate professor of Chinese, 1969—. *Military service:* British Army, Royal Artillery, 1951-54.

MEMBER: American Oriental Society, American Association of University Professors, Modern Language Association of America, American Council of Teachers of Foreign Languages, Association for Asian Studies, Chinese Language Teachers Association, Society for Pre-Han Studies, Michigan Academy.

WRITINGS: Liang Chien-wen Ti, A.D. 503-551, Twayne, 1976; *Handbook of Modern Chinese Grammar,* Chinese Materials Center (San Francisco), 1977; *Chiang Yen, A.D. 444-505,* Twayne, in press. Contributor to professional journals. Editor of *Six Dynasties Newsletter.*

WORK IN PROGRESS: Editing *Beyond the Mulberries,* two hundred fifty translations of poems by Chien-wen Ti.

SIDELIGHTS: Marney comments that his career in Oriental studies began with tours of the Far East as a violinist. He now speaks classical and modern Chinese and Japanese, and has resided in the Far East.

*   *   *

MARSH, Mary Val 1925-

PERSONAL: Born April 28, 1925, in Uniontown, Pa.; daughter of Roy William (an osteopathic physician) and Mary (a teacher; maiden name, Hickman) Marsh: married Dwight Ellsworth Twist (a school superintendent), August 4, 1962; children: (stepchildren) Barbara (Mrs. Roger A. Williams), Charles Russell. *Education:* University of California, Los Angeles, B.A., 1946; Claremont Graduate School, M.A., 1953. *Politics:* Republican. *Religion:* Presbyterian. *Home:* 879 Rosecrans St., San Diego, Calif. 92106.

CAREER: Elementary school teacher in Redlands, Calif., 1946-48; curriculum consultant for San Bernadino County Department of Education, Calif., 1948-52, music coordinator, 1952-59; music supervisor for public schools in Beverly Hills, Calif., 1959-62; San Diego State University, San Diego, Calif., part-time lecturer in music education, 1963-73; free-lance writer, music arranger, and consultant in music education, 1973—. Faculty member at University of Redlands, Claremont Graduate School and University Center, and Idyllwild School of Music and the Arts; director of music education workshops in the United States and Canada. Member of Music Educators National Conference-Ford Foundation "Contemporary Music Project" Committee, in San Diego, 1963-65; supervisor of local "Opera Participation Project for Youth," 1971-75; member of board of directors of Civic Youth Orchestra, 1976—.

MEMBER: International Society for Music Education, Music Educators National Conference (life member), California Music Educators Association (life member), Sigma Alpha Iota, Delta Kappa Gamma, Pi Lambda Theta.

WRITINGS: Choruses and Carols (for unchanged voices), Summy-Birchard, 1964; *Here a Song, There a Song* (for elementary and junior high school choruses), Shawnee Press, 1969; *Explore and Discover Music: Creative Approaches to Music Education in Elementary, Middle, and Junior High Schools,* Macmillan, 1970; (with Carroll Rinehart and Edith Savage) *The Spectrum of Music* (textbook series for elementary grades), Macmillan, 1974-75. Contributor to *Music Educators Journal.*

WORK IN PROGRESS: Choral arranging and composing.

SIDELIGHTS: Mary Val Marsh writes: "I am committed to the belief that arts education is essential to improving the quality of life for all, and that without a commitment to the arts, a culture will gradually deteriorate. Only as children and youth encounter the arts in meaningful situations will they develop aesthetic sensitivity. As a specialist in music education, I believe that *creating music* is one of the most effective means of learning about music and of developing a continuing interest in it. This belief led me a number of years ago to organize an experimental creative music class, which subsequently led to my writing of *Explore and Discover Music.*"

*   *   *

MARTIN, Ann Bodenhamer 1927-

PERSONAL: Born October 24, 1927, in El Dorado, Ark.; daughter of R. C. (in insurance and real estate) and Jewel (Little) Bodenhamer; married Ken D. Elliott, July 25, 1953 (died, 1969); married James E. Martin (divorced); children: (first marriage) Richard Clinton, Mark Andrew. *Education:* Attended Lindenwood College and University of Arkansas. *Home and office:* 34511-B Via Verde, Capistrano Beach, Calif. 92624. *Agent:* Jet Associates, P.O. Box 276, Hastings-on-Hudson, N.Y. 10706.

CAREER: KELD-Radio, El Dorado, Ark., disc jockey, 1948-50; KSJB-Radio, Minot, N.D., disc jockey, 1950-52; WWEZ-Radio, New Orleans, La., disc jockey, also in public relations, programming, production, and promotion, 1952-56; WJMR-Television, New Orleans, in special programming, 1956-60; WWL-Television, New Orleans, presented "Hospitality House" and "Ann Elliott Show," also in special programming, public relations, and promotion, 1960-64; WNOE-Radio, New Orleans, free-lance disc jockey, also in special programming public relations, and promotion, 1964-67; KTVE-TV, El Dorado, presented "Today in the Ark-La-Miss," 1967-68; WILZ-Radio, St. Petersburg, Fla., in special programming, public relations, and promotion, 1968-72; writer, 1972—. Conducted "A Man and a Woman" and "The Ann Martin Show," on WILZ-Radio; worked for various radio and television stations in North Dakota, 1950-52, and Louisanna, 1952-60. Fashion model, 1950-70; fashion show narrator and coordinator, 1956—; teacher of modeling, 1970—. Docent at Broward Community College, 1974-77.

MEMBER: New Thoughts Alliance, World Fellowship of Religions (India). *Awards, honors:* "Ann Elliott Show" was named outstanding local television show by *Broadcasting,* 1962;" and named most promising new television show by *TV Guide,* 1962.

WRITINGS: Calico Families (poems), Pelican, 1976. Author of scripts and commercials for television and radio, including "Some Gold of Your Own" and "The Motorcycle Madonna," both on WILZ-Radio. Contributor to magazines, including *Science of Mind, Modern Maturity, Floridian,* and *Spiritual India.*

WORK IN PROGRESS: The Radioman, a science fiction novel; *No Place for A Baptist,* memories of New Orleans during the 1950's; *Alpha Omega Metaphysics,* a handbook, for Parker Publishing; *Metaphysical Whispers from Universal Mind,* poems; *Cry of the Sandpiper,* a novel; *The Ministers,* a novel; *Honeysucklers,* memories of her brother; *A Study in Angels; Be Beautiful Now; Gentlemen, You're Next,* a metaphysical view of the universe.

SIDELIGHTS: Ann Martin writes: "I am among a growing number of women who no longer fit a pattern—neither fish nor fowl—not content to be wife *or* mistress—unable to battle a man in the marketplace *or* in bed—(and not wanting to, really) and uncertain of the validity of past values and expectations in all our relationships. For a long, long time I felt apart and different—the product of some unholy combination of circumstances which kept me searching, often falling in the dark, taking doubted, unguided steps I often lived to regret. I am not 'liberated,' but have always been free—free-spirited and avant garde but not quite strong enough to fly alone. Suddenly I have awakened from a dream of prolonged puberty, a sort of extended dormancy—not truly a 'born again' sensation, but oh, my God, just *born!* Newly born! Brave and sure of Self and Source. Perhaps everything I write (or try to) is some willful truancy—a tardy flinging of rocks at the traditional limitations of my sex, my heritage, my race, my dogmas, and my age. What age? Long ago I read, or was told, that some anthropomorphic being had promised that I was eternal. I thought I believed it. But, it seems I've just gotten the word directly and Honey, it's true!''

* * *

MARTIN, Arlan Stone 1932-

PERSONAL: Born April 27, 1932, in Everett, Wash.; daughter of Harlan R. (a clergyman) and Retta (a department manager in a department store; maiden name, Fancher) Stone; married Vernon E. Martin (a music and art director of a public library), June 30, 1956; children: Vernon, Jeffrey. *Education:* University of Southern California, B.Mus., 1955; University of Oklahoma, M.Mus., 1956; Juilliard School of Music, further graduate study, 1957; Texas Woman's University, M.A., 1970; Computer Processing Institute, Hartford, Conn., diploma, 1977. *Home address:* c/o Florence Illich, 115 Stennis, Ocean Springs, Miss. 39564.

CAREER: Teacher of piano and violin, 1956-76; performed as a violinist in professional symphonies in Texas, including Fort Worth Symphony, San Angelo Symphony, and Wichita Falls Symphony, 1966-70, in the Midwest, including Sioux Falls Symphony, Sioux City Symphony, and Omaha Symphony, 1970-74, and in New England, including Hartford Symphony and Springfield Symphony, 1975-76; solo recitals on piano and violin in the Midwest, 1970-74; solo and chamber music recitals in Hartford, 1976—. *Member:* American Federation of Musicians, Pi Kappa Lambda, Mu Phi Epsilon Alumnae.

WRITINGS: The Vivaldi Violin Concertos: A Handbook, Scarecrow, 1972.

WORK IN PROGRESS: Arranging selected concertos for violin and piano, for performance and possibly for publication.

SIDELIGHTS: Arlan Martin told *CA:* "My interest in editing and arranging the Vivaldi concertos for performance was constantly hampered by the lack of any standardized numbering system for the concertos. It was difficult to know which individual concerto had been published or recorded. To solve this problem I devised a cataloguing system for cross referencing the various numbering systems already in use, thus making it possible to give an accurate account of which of the 238 violin concertos had already been published or recorded. This cataloguing system for the concertos is what was published in my handbook. I feel the Vivaldi violin concertos have been unjustly neglected and hopefully they will be more frequently performed now that the public can locate the scores to them, and hopefully more musicians will become interested in editing and arranging them for teaching and performance.''

* * *

MARTIN, John Stuart 1900-1977

November 9, 1900—June 25, 1977; American magazine editor (*Time,* 1929-38), free-lance writer, and author of works of general nonfiction and pictorial histories. Obituaries: *New York Times,* June 26, 1977; *Time,* July 4, 1977. (See index for previous *CA* sketch)

* * *

MARTIN, Margaret Joan 1928-

PERSONAL: Born March 23, 1928, in London, England; daughter of William John (a statistician) and Margaret (Lillycrop) Martin. *Education:* University of London, B.Sc., 1951, M.Sc., 1958. *Religion:* Church of England. *Home:* 5 Brinkburn Gardens, Edgware, Middlesex, England. *Office:* British Gas, Michael Rd., Fulham, London S.W.6, England.

CAREER: Chartered chemist. British Gas, London Research Laboratories, London, England, chemist, 1952—, senior scientist, 1975—. Lecturer on cacti and succulents. *Member:* Royal Institute of Chemistry, National Cactus and Succulent Society, Cactus and Succulent Society of Great Britain.

WRITINGS: (With P. R. Chapman) *Cacti and Their Cultivation,* Faber, 1971; (with Chapman and H. A. Auger) *The Other Succulents,* Faber, 1977. Contributor of articles and photographs to gardening magazines.

SIDELIGHTS: "I own about three hundred fifty cacti," Martin told *CA,* "mainly from America. These flower when small and do well in Northern Europe. I also have a collection of South African desert plants ('the other succulents'), particularly 'mimicry plants.' Despite our climate, these flower as well as if they were in the Karroo desert! I grow them in a greenhouse in which I keep a minimum winter temperature of 40 F. I have been growing these plants for about 25 years. I started by buying a packet of mixed seed at Woolworth's. Originally the young plants lived on a window-ledge. One plant led to another and eventually to a greenhouse.''

AVOCATIONAL INTERESTS: Photography, music, attending concerts, European travel.

* * *

MARTIN, Marie-Louise 1912-

PERSONAL: Born February 2, 1912, in Lucerne, Switzerland; daughter of Fritz (a businessman) and Bertha (Syfrig) Martin. *Education:* Attended University of Berne, 1932-34, and University of Edinburgh, 1934-35; University of Basel, B.D., 1937; University of South Africa, D.D., 1963. *Politics:* None. *Religion:* Kimbanguiste and Swiss Reformed. *Home address:* B.P. 4485, Kinshasa II, Ngaliema, Zaire. *Office:* Campus de Lutendale, B.P. 4485, Kinshasa II, Ngaliema, Zaire.

CAREER: Ordained clergywoman of Swiss Reformed Church, 1938. Pastor of reformed Africa parishes of Lugauo, 1938-42, and Locaruo, 1942-44; Basel Missionary College for Women, Basel, Switzerland, part-time teacher, 1944-46; Theological Seminary, Morija, Lesotho, professor, 1957-65; Lemana Training Institution, North Transvaal, South Africa, chaplain, 1965-69; University of Botswana, Lesotho & Swaziland, Roma, Lesotho, assistant professor, 1965-69; Theological College of the Kimbanguist Church, Kinshasa, Zaire, principal and professor, 1969-77. *Member:* International Association for Missiology, Deutsche Gesellschaft fuer Missionswissenschaft.

WRITINGS: The Biblical Concept of Messiamism and Messianism in Southern Africa, [Morija, Lesotho], 1964;

(contributor) D. Barrett, editor, *African Initiative in Religion*, East African Publishing House, 1971; *Kirche ohne Weisse: Kimbangu und seine Millionenkirche im Kongo*, Friedrich Reinhardt, 1972, translation by D. M. Moore published as *Simon Kimbangu: An African Prophet and His Church*, Eerdmans, 1975.

WORK IN PROGRESS: A study on the Eucharist in the Kimbanguist Church.

SIDELIGHTS: Marie-Louise Martin writes: "My missionary activity in Southern Africa brought me in contact with African independent churches which had broken away from their missionary churches. I wanted to know the reasons and the new structures and teachings of these churches which represent an African form of the Christian message."

* * *

MARTIN, Noah S(ensenig)   1940-

PERSONAL: Born January 27, 1940, in Ephrata, Pa., son of Noah Zimmerman (a clerk) and Susanna (Sensenig) Martin; married Sandra Kay Beverlin (a teacher), June 9, 1963; children: Steven, Christopher, Kathy, Cheryl. *Education:* Eastern Mennonite College, B.A., 1963; Eastern Baptist Seminary, B.D. (magna cum laude), 1966; Princeton Theological Seminary, M.Th., 1967. *Home:* 614 Freedom Ave., Johnstown, Pa. 15904. *Office:* 536 Grove Ave., Johnstown, Pa. 15902.

CAREER: Student pastor at Mennonite church in Philadelphia, Pa., 1964-66; director of youth at United Methodist church in Drexel Hill, Pa., 1965-66; ordained minister of Church of the Brethren, 1967; Moxham Church of the Brethren, Johnstown, Pa., pastor, 1967—. Vice-president of Cambria County Association for Retarded Citizens, 1968-69, and Greater Johnstown Council of Churches, 1975-76; member of board of directors, Pennsylvania Church of the Brethren's western district, 1974-77.

WRITINGS: Beyond Renewal, Herald Press, 1976. Contributor to *Messenger*.

SIDELIGHTS: Martin writes: "There has been a renewal of religious interest in recent years. My concern is that this renewal will lead to concrete expressions of love for the brotherhood of man."

* * *

MARTON, Beryl M(itchell)   1922-

PERSONAL: Born July 27, 1922, in Montreal, Quebec, Canada; came to the United States in 1953, naturalized citizen, 1957; daughter of Charles S. (a salesman) and Marie Blanche (Kilpin) Mitchell; married Mort N. Marton (an innkeeper), March 29, 1953; children: Bruce Eric, Stewart David. *Education:* Attended secondary school in Montreal, Quebec, Canada. *Politics:* Democrat. *Home:* Fundador Lodge, P.O. South Londonderry, Vt. 05155.

CAREER: Yorktown Gourmet Cooking School, Yorktown Heights, N.Y., director and instructor, 1963-70; Fundador Lodge, South Londonderry, Vt., co-owner and chef, 1971—, instructor in gourmet cooking, summers, 1971—. Guest on television and radio programs, often for R. T. French Co. *Awards, honors:* National Tastemaker Award from R. T. French Co., 1974, for *Diet for One, Dinner for All.*

WRITINGS: The Complete Book of Salads (Cooking and Crafts Club selection), Random House, 1968; *Diet for One, Dinner for All* (Literary Guild selection), Western Publish-

ing, 1974; *Out of the Garden, Into the Kitchen*, McKay, 1977. Author of "Diary of a Cook," a monthly column in *Yorktowner*, 1967-70, *Stratton Mountain News*, 1974—, and *Window of Vermont*, 1975—. Food editor of *Window of Vermont*.

WORK IN PROGRESS: A budget-oriented beginner's cook book.

AVOCATIONAL INTERESTS: Making quilted wall-hangings of New England scenes, batik, needlepoint, ceramics, leather tooling, sewing.

BIOGRAPHICAL/CRITICAL SOURCES: New York Times, March 9, 1972.

* * *

MARTZ, Lawrence J.   1933-

PERSONAL: Born April 2, 1933, in New York, N.Y.; son of Lawrence (an executive) and Jean (Bailey) Martz; married Anne-Sophie Uldall, May 28, 1955; children: Geoffrey, Jenny. *Education:* Dartmouth College, A.B., 1954; graduate study at University of Edinburgh, 1954-55. *Office: Newsweek*, 444 Madison Ave., New York, N.Y. 10022.

CAREER/WRITINGS: Pontiac Press, Pontiac, Mich., general assignment reporter, 1955-56; *Detroit News*, Detroit, Mich., general assignment reporter, 1957-59; *Wall Street Journal*, New York, N.Y., copy editor, 1960-61; *Newsweek*, New York City, associate editor, 1961-69, senior editor of business and finance section, 1969-72, senior editor of national affairs section, 1972-75, assistant managing editor, 1975—. As national affairs editor of *Newsweek* throughout the Watergate scandal, Martz edited and directed over 40 cover stories. *Member:* Phi Beta Kappa. *Awards, honors:* National Magazine Award, 1968, for article, "The Negro in America"; University of Missouri—J.C. Penney Award, 1969, for article, "The Beauty Business."

* * *

MARX, Kenneth S(amuel)   1939-

PERSONAL: Born January 21, 1939, in Los Angeles, Calif.; son of Samuel (a film producer and writer) and Marie (Simard) Marx; married Pamela R. Pfau (a computer scientist), March 21, 1970. *Education:* Attended public schools in Beverly Hills and Los Angeles, Calif. *Home:* 10347 Monte Mar Dr., Los Angeles, Calif. 90064. *Agent:* Harvey Shotz, 666 North Robertson Blvd., Los Angeles, Calif. 90069.

CAREER: Reporter for *Newport Harbor News-Press*, 1959; *Los Angeles Herald-Examiner*, Los Angeles, Calif., reporter, 1960; *Beverly Hills Times*, Beverly Hills, Calif., editor, 1963-65; *Beverly Hills Courier*, Beverly Hills, editor, 1970-72; *Quote*, Anderson, S.C., art director, 1975; writer, 1975—. Researcher, film editor, or actor for motion pictures in Europe and the United States, including "Waterloo," "Anzio," "Damon & Pythias," and "Nefertiti." 1964-70. Chairperson of "BookWest 76," Los Angeles Book Fair. *Military service:* U.S. Coast Guard Reserve, 1955-64.

WRITINGS: (Editor with wife, Pamela Pfau) Marion Davies, *The Times We Had* (autobiography), Bobbs-Merrill, 1975; *Hollywood Genesis*, Berkely Books, 1977.

WORK IN PROGRESS: A novel, "a study of persons in frantic motion, searching for a sensible place to live and for valid things to do."

SIDELIGHTS: Marx wrote: "I consider myself a dealer in words for a lack of other penetrating arrows in my personal quiver. My experiences along the way to authorship have been of some engagement but do not bear repeating either in words here or in reality there. I still look forward to the times to come." Marx described his latest book, *Hollywood Genesis* as "a who's whose of the film world."

* * *

MASSAQUOI, Hans J(urgen) 1926-

PERSONAL: Born January 19, 1926, in Hamburg, Germany; son Al-Haj (a businessman) and Bertha (a nurse; maiden name, Baetz) Massaquoi; married Joan DeBerry, October 20, 1956 (divorced, 1971); children: Steve, Hans. *Education:* University of Illinois, B.S., 1957; graduate study at Northwestern University, 1957-58. *Office: Ebony* Magazine, 820 South Michigan Ave., Chicago, Ill. 60605.

CAREER/WRITINGS: British Military Government, Hamburg, Germany, interpreter, 1945-48; National Association of Educational Broadcasters, Urbana, Ill., editor, 1956-57; *Jet* magazine, Chicago, Ill., associate editor, 1957-58; *Ebony* magazine, Chicago, associate editor, 1958-64, assistant managing editor, 1964-67, managing editor, 1967—. Notable assignments include interviews with Dr. Martin Luther King, Jr., Muhammid Ali, Ambassador Shirley Temple Black, Elijah Muhammad, Harry Belafonte, and William Tolbert. Has also covered assignments in Africa, Europe, and Asia. *Military service:* U.S. Army, 82nd Airborne Division, 1951-53; served as paratrooper. *Member:* Sigma Delta Xi. *Awards, honors:* Overseas Press Club of America citation, 1975, for coverage of Heads of Government Conference in Kingston, Jamaica.

* * *

MASSERMAN, Jules H(oman) 1905-

PERSONAL: Born March 10, 1905, in Chudnov, Poland; came to the United States in 1908, naturalized citizen, 1917; son of Abraham (a teacher) and Czerna (Baker) Masserman; married Christine McGuire (a professor of education), February 20, 1943. *Education:* Wayne State University, M.B., 1930, M.D., 1931; Chicago Psychoanalytic Institute, certificate, 1940. *Politics:* Liberal. *Home:* 2231 East 67th St., Chicago, Ill. 60649. *Office:* Eight South Michigan Ave., Chicago, Ill. 60603.

CAREER: Stanford University, Stanford, Calif., resident in neurology, 1931-32; Johns Hopkins University, Baltimore, Md., assistant psychiatrist, 1932-35; University of Chicago, Chicago, Ill., resident in psychiatry, 1935-36, instructor, 1937-39, assistant professor of psychiatry, 1939-46; Northwestern University Medical School, Chicago, associate professor, 1946-52, professor of neurology and psychiatry, 1952-74, professor emeritus, 1974—, co-chairman of department, 1964-69. Diplomate of American Board of Psychiatry and Neurology; fellow of Center for the Advancement of the Behavioral Sciences, 1968-69. Roche Visiting Professor in Australia and New Zealand, 1968; visiting professor at universities, including University of Chicago Medical School, Miami University, University of Louisville, and University of Zagreb. Science director for National Foundation for Psychiatric Research; director of education at Illinois Psychiatric Institute, 1958-62; chairman of Illinois Research and Training Authority, 1965-68, and Chicago Psychiatry Council, 1967-69; chairman of council of Stone-Brandell Foundation, 1966-69. Consultant to World Health Organization, U.S. Navy, U.S. Air Force, and Veterans Administration.

MEMBER: International Association for Social Psychiatry (honorary life president, 1969—), American Medical Association, American Psychiatric Association (fellow; member

of council, 1965-68; vice-president, 1974-75; secretary, 1975-77; president, 1977—), American Academy of Psychoanalysis (fellow; president, 1956, 1957-58), American Society for Biological Psychiatry (president, 1955, 1957-58), American Society for Group Therapy (president, 1957), American Association for Social Psychiatry (president-elect, 1972), American Academy for Stress Disorders (executive vice-president, 1971—), Academy for Air Traffic Medicine (executive vice-president, 1972—), American College of Psychiatry, American Psychoanalytic Association. *Awards, honors:* National award in pathology from Phi Lambda Kappa, 1929; Presidential Award from Selective Service, 1942; international award from American Public Health Association, 1947; Lasker Award from Albert Lasker and National Committee for Mental Hygiene, 1946, for research in mental hygiene; Taylor Manor Award in Psychiatry from Taylor Manor Foundation, 1974; Sigmund Freud Award from American Society of Psychoanalytic Physicians, 1976.

WRITINGS: Behavior and Neuroses: An Experimental Psychoanalytic Approach to Psychobiologic Principles, University of Chicago Press, 1943, reprinted, Hafner, 1965; *Principles of Dynamic Psychiatry: Including an Integrative Approach to Abnormal and Clinical Psychology,* Saunders, 1946; *Practice of Dynamic Psychiatry,* Saunders, 1955; (editor with J. L. Moreno) *Progress in Psychotherapy,* Volumes II-V, Grune, 1957-60; *Tommy the Tipsy Tabby,* Alcoholism Research Foundation, 1957; (editor) *Biological Psychiatry,* Volume I, Grune, 1959; *Principles of Dynamic Psychiatry,* 2nd edition (Masserman was not associated with earlier editions), Saunders, 1961; (editor and contributor) *Anxiety and the Art of Healing,* Grune, 1961; (with Leo Salzman) *Modern Concepts in Psychoanalysis,* Philosophical Library, 1962; *Residency Training in Psychiatry,* Northwestern University Press, 1965; (editor and contributor) *Anxiety: The Protean Source of Communication,* Grune, 1965; *Modern Therapy of Personality Disorders,* Brown, 1966; (contributor) J. Vernon, editor, *Self-Selection Textbook of Psychology,* Brown, 1966; (editor and contributor) *The Timeless Therapeutic Trinity,* Grune, 1967; *A Psychiatric Odyssey: Memoirs of a Maverick Psychiatrist,* Jason Aronson, 1971; *Theory and Therapy in Dynamic Psychiatry,* Jason Aronson, 1973; *Psychiatric Syndromes and Modes of Therapy,* Jason Aronson, 1974.

Editor of "Science and Psychoanalysis" series, Volumes I-XII, Grune, 1958-72, and "Current Psychiatric Therapies" series, Volumes I-XVI, Grune, 1961-77. Also author of *Code of Procedures and Grants Manual of the Illinois Psychiatric Training and Research Authority,* 1966. Contributor of more than three hundred fifty articles on psychiatry, psychoanalysis, neurology, philosophy, history, and music to magazines.

WORK IN PROGRESS: Research on comparative animal and human conduct, both normal and deviant.

SIDELIGHTS: Masserman comments that he is currently contemplating "the satisfactions of world travels among many friends, and a social, esthetic (mainly musical), scientific, and creative life. Objectives: to integrate and clarify the sciences and arts of human behavior."

* * *

MAST, Gerald 1940-

PERSONAL: Born May 13, 1940, in Los Angeles, Calif.; son of George A. (a pharmacist) and Bess (Gorelnik) Mast. *Education:* University of Chicago, B.A., 1961, M.A., 1962, Ph.D., 1967. *Residence:* New York, N.Y. *Agent:* Rick

Balkin, 403 West 15th St., New York, N.Y., 10025. *Office:* College of Staten Island, 120 Stuyvesant Pl., Staten Island, N.Y. 10301.

CAREER: Oberlin College, Oberlin, Ohio, instructor in English, 1965-67; College of Staten Island of the City University of New York, Staten Island, N.Y., associate professor of performing and creative arts, 1967—. Visiting professor of English and humanities, University of Chicago, 1977—. Director of professional and university plays in Chicago, New York City, and Provincetown, Mass., 1961—; actor and extra in Hollywood movies, 1948-63. *Member:* Modern Language Association of America, Writer's Guild, Actor's Equity Association, Society for Cinema Studies.

WRITINGS: A Short History of the Movies, Bobbs-Merrill, 1971, revised edition, 1976; *The Comic Mind: Comedy and the Movies,* Bobbs-Merrill, 1973; *Filmguide to Rules of the Game,* University of Indiana Press, 1973; (with Marshall Cohen) *Film Theory and Criticism: Introductory Readings,* Oxford University Press, 1974; *Film/Cinema/Movie: A Theory of Experience,* Harper, 1977.

Contributor of articles to periodicals and film journals, including *New Republic, Cinema Journal,* and *Critical Inquiry.*

WORK IN PROGRESS: The Movies in Our Midst: Readings in the Cultural History of Film in America, publication by Oxford University Press expected in 1978.

* * *

MASTERMAN, John Cecil   1891-1977

January 21, 1891—June 6, 1977; British author and director of counterintelligence during World War II best known for *The Double-Cross System.* By giving captured German spies misleading information, Masterman succeeded in leading the Germans to believe the invasion of France would take place in Calais rather than Normandy. He was associated with Oxford University from 1913 until 1961. Obituaries: *New York Times,* June 7, 1977; *Newsweek,* June 20, 1977; *Time,* June 20, 1977. (See index for previous *CA* sketch)

* * *

MASTERSON, James F(rancis)   1925-

PERSONAL: Born March 25, 1925, in Philadelphia, Pa.; son of James Francis and Evangeline (O'Boyle) Masterson; married Patricia Cooke, January 28, 1950; children: James Francis, Richard, Nancy. *Education:* Notre Dame University, student, 1943-44, 1946-47; Jefferson Medical College, M.D., 1951. *Home:* 921 Grant Ave., Pelham Manor, N.Y. 10803. *Office:* 60 Sutton Pl. S., New York, N.Y. 10022.

CAREER: Philadelphia General Hospital, Philadelphia, Pa., intern, 1951-52; New York Hospital, New York, N.Y., resident at Payne Whitney Clinic, 1952-55, director of adolescent out-patient clinic, 1956-66, head of adolescent program, 1968-75, assistant attending physician, 1956-60, associate attending physician, 1960-70, attending psychiatrist, 1970—. Assistant professor at Cornell University, 1956-65, associate professor, 1965-70, clinical professor, 1970—. Diplomate of American Board of Psychiatry and Neurology; private practice in psychiatry, 1956—. Director of Masterson Group for the Study and Treatment of the Character Disorders (for adolescents and adults), 1977—. *Military service:* U.S. Army, Medical Corps, 1944-46; became sergeant.

MEMBER: American Psychiatric Association (fellow), American Medical Association, American College of Psychoanalysts, New York County Medical Society, New York Society of Adolescent Psychiatry (founding member; past president), New York Society for Clinical Psychiatry.

WRITINGS: (Contributor) J. M. Murphy and A. H. Leighton, editors, *Approaches to Cross Cultural Psychiatry,* Cornell University Press, 1965; *The Psychiatric Dilemma of Adolescence,* Little, Brown, 1967; (contributor) Freedman and Kaplan, editors, *Comprehensive Psychiatry,* Williams & Wilkins, 1967; *A Point of View on Diagnosis and Treatment of Adolescents: Seminars in Psychiatry,* Grune & Stratton, 1969; (contributor) S. Chess and A. Thomas, editors, *The Psychiatric Significance of Adolescent Turmoil: The Annual Progress in Child Psychiatry and Child Development,* Brunner, 1969.

(Contributor) Freedman and Zubin, editors, *Psychopathology of Adolescence,* Grune, 1970; (editor with Daniel Offer, and contributor) *Teaching and Learning Adolescent Psychiatry,* C. C Thomas, 1971; *Treatment of the Borderline Adolescent: A Developmental Approach,* Wiley, 1972; (contributor) S. Lesse, editor, *Masked Depression,* Science House, 1974; (contributor) Aaron H. Esman, editor, *The Psychology of Adolescence,* International Universities Press, 1975; *To Love and Work: Psychotherapy of the Borderline Adult—A Developmental Approach,* Burnner, 1976. Contributor to *American Handbook of Psychiatry.* Contributor of about fifty articles to professional journals.

WORK IN PROGRESS: New Perspectives: Psychotherapy of the Borderline Adult.

* * *

MASTRO, Susan (Duff)   1945-

PERSONAL: Born October 4, 1945, in Newton, Mass.; daughter of Alan Dallas, Jr. (an engineer) and Vera (a writer; maiden name, Mahon) Duff; married John Mastro (a graduate student), August 15, 1973. *Education:* Sarah Lawrence College, B.A., 1967. *Home and office:* 200 West 15th St., New York, N.Y. 10011. *Agent:* Jim Seligmann, 280 Madison Ave., New York, N.Y. 10017.

CAREER: Writer. Free-lance journalist, 1971—.

WRITINGS: The Modern Woman's Zodiac Guide to Love and Fulfillment, Pilot Books, 1973. Author of three syndicated columns, "Calorie Countdown," "The Happy Gardener," and "Who Was That Lady?" appearing in 300 weekly newspapers, in suburbs of Brooklyn, Staten Island, St. Louis, San Francisco, Miami, and others.

SIDELIGHTS: Susan Mastro has written on a variety of subjects, including diet and health, gardening, the occult, women in American history, and male/female relationships. She has lived in Argentina, southern Spain, and Italy.

* * *

MATNEY, William C., Jr.   1924-
(Bill Matney)

PERSONAL: Born September 2, 1924, in Bluefield, Va.; son of William C. (an economist) and Jane (Adams) Matney; wife deceased; children: Alma Elizabeth, Angelique Electra, William C. III. *Education:* Wayne State University, student, 1940-42; University of Michigan, B.A., 1946, graduate study, 1946. *Politics:* Independent. *Religion:* Roman Catholic. *Home:* 11220 Cherry Hill Rd., Beltsville, Md. *Office:* American Broadcasting Co.—News, 1124 Connecticut Ave. N.W., Washington, D.C. 20036.

CAREER: Michigan Chronicle (weekly), Detroit, 1946-61,

began as reporter, became city editor, then managing editor; *Detroit News,* Detroit, reporter, rewrite man, and desk assistant, 1961-63; WMAQ-Radio and Television, Chicago, Ill., reporter, 1963-65; National Broadcasting Co.—News, Chicago, Ill., Midwest network news correspondent, 1965-72; American Broadcasting Co.—News, Washington, D.C., national news correspondent, 1972—. Executive secretary of Michigan State Athletic Commission, 1959-61. Adviser to Detroit's mayor and city council. *Military service:* U.S. Army Air Forces.

MEMBER: National Academy of Television Arts and Sciences, Radio and Television Correspondents Association, National Association for the Advancement of Colored People, Urban League. *Awards, honors:* D.J. from Benedict College, 1973; national journalism awards from Lincoln University, Jefferson City, Mo., Capital City Press Club, National Academy of Television Arts and Sciences, and Southern Regional Press Institute.

WRITINGS: (Editor) *Who's Who Among Black Americans, 1976-1977,* Educational Communications, 1977.

WORK IN PROGRESS: Editing further volumes of *Who's Who Among Black Americans,* publication by Educational Communications expected every two years.

SIDELIGHTS: Matney's journalism series include "The Negro in Detroit" and "The Cities." As the first black White House correspondent on permanent assignment, he has reported on Presidential conferences from Europe and Iron Curtain countries.

* * *

MATSUTANI, Miyoko 1925-

PERSONAL: Born February 15, 1925, in Tokyo, Japan; daughter of Yojiro and Midori (Kawamura) Matsutani; married Takuo Segawa, November, 1955 (divorced March, 1967); children: Takumi Matsutani, Akemi Matsutani (daughters). *Education:* Attended high school in Japan. *Home and office:* 257-42, Higashi-oizumi, Nerima-ku, Tokyo, 177, Japan.

CAREER: Author of children's books.

Member: Children's Literature Association of Japan (member of board of directors). *Awards, honors:* Juvenile Literature Association outstanding newcomer's award, and Sankei Press Juvenile Publications cultural award, both 1961.

WRITINGS:—Children's books: *Tatsunoko Taro,* Kodansha, 1960, translation by Donald C. Boone published as *Taro, the Dragon-boy,* Kodansha, 1967; *The Fox Wedding,* translation by Masako Matsumo, Encyclopaedia Britannica Press, 1963; *Chisai Momo-chan* (title means "Little Momo-chan"), Kodansha, 1964; *Futari-no-Iida* (title means "Two Iidas"), Kodansha, 1969; *How the Withered Trees Bloomed,* Lippincott, 1971; *The Complete Works of Miyoko Matsutani,* fifteen volumes, Kodansha, 1971; *Momochan to Akanechan* (title means "Momo-chan and Akane-chan"), Kodansha, 1974.

Translations into English by Alvin Tresselt; all published by Parents' Magazine Press: *The Crane Maiden,* 1968; *The Fisherman under the Sea,* 1969; *The Witch's Magic Cloth,* 1969; *Gengoroh and the Thunder God,* 1970.

Also author of numerous children's books in Japanese, including a twelve volume collection of Japanese folk tales.

MATTHEWS, Patricia 1927-
(Pat A. Brisco; Patty Brisco)

PERSONAL: Born July 1, 1927, in San Fernando, Calif.; daughter of Roy Oliver and Gladys (Gable) Ernst; married Marvin Brisco, December, 1946 (divorced, 1959); married Clayton Hartley Matthews (a writer), November 3, 1972; children: (first marriage) Michael A., David R. *Education:* Attended California State University, Los Angeles, 1968. *Home and office:* 3783 Latrobe St., Los Angeles, Calif. 90031. *Agent:* Jay Garon, Jay Garon-Brooke Associates, Inc., 415 Central Park W., Suite 17D, New York, N.Y. 10025.

CAREER: California State University, Los Angeles, secretary and office manager, 1959—. *Member:* Mystery Writers of America.

WRITINGS—Under name Patty Brisco; with husband, Clayton Matthews: *Merry's Treasure* (juvenile) Avalon Books, 1969; *Horror at Gull House,* Belmont-Tower, 1972; *House of Candles,* Manor, 1973; *The Crystal Window,* Avon, 1973; *Mist of Evil,* Manor, 1976.

Under name Pat A. Brisco: *The Other People* (science fiction), Powell Publications, 1970; *The Carnival Mystery* (juvenile), Scholastic Book Services, 1974; *The Campus Mystery* (juvenile), Scholastic Book Services, 1977.

Historical romances; under name Patricia Matthews: *Love's Avenging Heart,* Pinnacle Books, 1977; *Love's Wildest Promise,* Pinnacle Books, 1977. Contributor of stories and poems to mystery magazines and to *Oregonian, American Bard,* and *Ladies Home Journal.*

WORK IN PROGRESS: A historical romance, under name Patricia Matthews, for Pinnacle Books.

SIDELIGHTS: Patricia Matthews told *CA* "I am interested in other creative arts, but none brings me the satisfaction of writing. In other media you can create a small piece of something. In writing you can create a whole world—one that you hope will bring enjoyment to the reader." *Avocational interests:* The occult, music (especially piano and voice), painting, writing music, growing plants, studying witchcraft.

* * *

MAVES, Carl (Edwin) 1940-
(Karl Maves)

PERSONAL: Born December 31, 1940, in Milwaukee, Wis.; son of Wilbur Wesley (an electrical engineer) and Grace (an elementary school teacher; maiden name, Tetzlaff) Maves. *Education:* Dartmouth College, B.A. (summa cum laude), 1963; New College, Oxford, graduate study, 1963-64; Stanford University, Ph.D., 1969. *Politics:* "Liberal humanist." *Religion:* "Militant atheist." *Home:* 460 Channing, Palo Alto, Calif. 94301.

CAREER: Dartmouth College, Hanover, N.H., assistant professor of English, 1969-70; Southern Methodist University, Dallas, Tex., assistant professor of English, 1970-73; writer, 1973—; Foothill College, Los Altos Hills, Calif., part-time instructor in drama, 1975—. *Member:* Phi Beta Kappa.

WRITINGS: Sensuous Pessimism: Italy in the Work of Henry James, Indiana University Press, 1973. Contributor of articles and reviews to journals and newspapers, including *Palo Alto Times, American West,* and (under name Karl Maves) *Advocate.*

WORK IN PROGRESS: An experimental fiction project.

SIDELIGHTS: Maves writes: "In 1973 I quit academe to

become a novelist; since then, I have been supporting that ambition with journalism and part-time teaching. Last year, I completed a long novel titled *Communing,* and am now in search of someone intelligent enough to want to publish it. It's the story of ten oddly and vitally assorted adults who decide to live together, and is in the great Victorian tradition plus lots of sex and contemporary humor. In short, a potential sensation. . . .''

* * *

MAXON, John 1916-1977

1916—May 24, 1977; American author and official of Chicago Art Institute. He died in Chicago, Ill. Obituaries: *New York Times,* May 26, 1977.

* * *

MAXTONE GRAHAM, James Anstruther 1924-
(James Anstruther)

PERSONAL: Born May 10, 1924, in London, England; son of Anthony James Oliphant (an insurance broker) and Joyce (a writer; maiden name, Anstruther) Maxtone Graham; married Diana Evelyn Macgregor, September 4, 1952 (divorced); married Diana Irene Pilcher, June 24, 1972 (divorced); children: Mary Alma, Robert Oliphant, Anthony James. *Education:* Attended Edinburgh College of Agriculture, 1949-50. *Politics:* "All politicians should be shot." *Religion:* "Trout fishing." *Home and office:* 80 High St., Peebles, Tweddale EH45 8SW, Scotland.

CAREER: Farmer in Perthshire, Scotland, 1950-62; freelance writer, 1962—. *Military service:* British Army, Scots Guards, 1942-47; became lieutenant. *Member:* Society of Authors, National Book League, American Society of Journalists and Authors. *Awards, honors:* Nuffield Farming Scholarship to the United States and Canada, 1960.

WRITINGS: Eccentric Gamblers, Mowbray, 1975; (editor) Carol Kennedy, *Eccentric Soldiers,* Mowbray, 1975; (editor) Alan Wykes, *Eccentric Doctors,* Mowbray, 1975. Contributor of several hundred articles and poems (under name James Anstruther) to over sixty American and British magazines, including *Atlantic, Esquire, Gourmet, Harper's,* and *Reader's Digest.*

SIDELIGHTS: Maxtone Graham comments: "I am principally a writer on travel and field sports—best of all, fishing combined with travel. Great British institutions—e.g., Lloyd's, Eton, London taxis, the Bagpipe—are also favorite subjects."

* * *

MAXTONE-GRAHAM, John 1929-

PERSONAL: Born August 2, 1929, in New Jersey; son of Patrick (a banker) and Ann Maxtone-Graham; married Katrina Kanzler (a writer), June 4, 1955; children: Sarah, Ian, Emily, Guy. *Education:* Brown University, B.A., 1951. *Politics:* "Mugwump." *Religion:* Protestant. *Home:* 126 East 78th St., New York, N.Y. 10021. *Agent:* Phyllis Seidel, 164 East 93rd St., New York, N.Y. 10028.

CAREER: Stage manager for Broadway productions in New York City, 1954-66; Vineyard Films, New York City, partner, 1966-68; writer, 1968—. Member of board of trustees of Fleming School and Gateway School. *Military service:* U.S. Marine Corps Reserve, 1951-54; became captain. *Member:* Century Club.

WRITINGS: The Only Way to Cross (nonfiction), Macmil-

lan, 1972; *Dark Brown Is the River* (novel), Macmillan, 1976.

WORK IN PROGRESS: Polar Book (tentative title), an informal history, publication by Viking expected in 1979; research for a book on the "heroic age" of polar exploration.

SIDELIGHTS: Maxtone-Graham writes: "I have a 'haute curiosite' about almost everything, particularly Edwardian or late Victorian mechanical achievements. Films interest me very much and I have a passable knowledge of the French tongue. I was raised on both sides of the Atlantic, born of a Scots father and an American mother."

AVOCATIONAL INTERESTS: "I enjoy a variety of travel, preferably by sea; ships, liners, ferry boats, vessels of any kind fascinate me although I am a terrible sailor. I am almost totally anti-sport."

* * *

MAXWELL-HUDSON, (Rachel) Clare 1946-

PERSONAL: Born July 30, 1946, in Surrey, England; daughter of Thomas (an air squadron-leader, author, and educator) and Rachel (Pearson) Maxwell-Hudson. *Education:* Attended beauty school and took courses in beauty therapy and cosmetic chemistry in London and Paris. *Office:* Institute of Beauty, 25 Princedale Rd., London W11 4NW, England.

CAREER: In private practice as beauty therapist, 1967—. Adviser to various companies, including Medical and Biological Instrumentation Ltd.; Chairman, Institute of Beauty, London, England; Beauty adviser to British Broadcasting Corp. Radio; frequently appears on television and radio programs; lecturer. *Member:* Association of Beauty Therapists, Comite Internationale d'Esthetique et de Cosmetologie, Royal Commonwealth Society.

WRITINGS: Kaleidoscope of Beauty, Octagon Press, 1968; *The Natural Beatuy Book,* Macdonald, 1976, Dial, 1977.

WORK IN PROGRESS: Research and fieldwork on traditional beauty procedures in the East; a book on women's culture; articles.

SIDELIGHTS: Clare Maxwell-Hudson said: "Dealing with an international clientele of women has led me more and more into the study of the female dimension in world culture. In this study I am now engaged in extensive travels and plan much further lecturing and publications on this theme." She has worked in Paris, and has collected "traditional beauty lore" in the Near East. She manufactures her own beauty products for private customers and salons.

AVOCATIONAL INTERESTS: Antique clothing.

* * *

MAY, Robert M(cCredie) 1936-

PERSONAL: Born August 1, 1936, in Sydney, Australia; son of Henry W. (a lawyer) and Kathleen (McCredie) May; married Judith Feiner (an editor), March 8, 1962; children: Naomi Felicity. *Education:* University of Sydney, B.Sc., 1956, Ph.D., 1959. *Office:* Department of Biology, Princeton University, Princeton, N.J. 08540.

CAREER: Harvard University, Cambridge, Mass., Gordon Mackay Lecturer in Applied Mathematics, 1960-61; University of Sydney, Sydney, Australia, senior lecturer, 1962-65; reader, 1966-70, professor of theoretical physics, 1970-72; Princeton University, Princeton, N.J., professor of zoology, 1973—. Visting professor at California Institute of Technology, 1967; visiting professor at Oxford University, 1971; honorary professor at Imperial College.

MEMBER: American Academy of Arts and Sciences, American Association for the Advancement of Science, British Ecological Society, Athenaeum. *Awards, honors:* Pawsey Award from Australian Academy of Science, 1967; Edgeworth David Medal from Royal Society of New South Wales, 1968.

WRITINGS: Stability and Complexity in Model Ecosystems, Princeton University Press, 1973, 2nd edition, 1975; *Theoretical Ecology: Principles and Applications,* Saunders, 1976. Editor of "Princeton Monographs on Population Biology." Member of editorial board of *Mathematical Biosciences, Journal of Theoretical Biology, Journal of Nonlinear Analysis, Theoretical Population Biology, Springer Lecture Notes in Biomathematics, Applied Ecology Abstracts, SIAM Journal of Applied Mathematics, Evolutionary Theory.*

WORK IN PROGRESS: Research on theoretical aspects of population biology and animal ecology, with "interest in practical applications to such areas as the dynamics of human diseases, the harvesting of natural animal populations, and strategies for control of insect pests."

SIDELIGHTS: May told *CA* he "plays chess, bridge, backgammon and table tennis competently; tennis incompetently."

* * *

MAYFIELD, James Bruce 1934-

PERSONAL: Born December 14, 1934, in San Francisco, Calif.; son of Orson Smith (a salesman) and Isobel (a registered nurse; maiden name, Merkley) Mayfield; married Merlene Jeppsen, July 23, 1959; children: James Bruce, Jr., Robert, Deborah, Stephen. *Education:* University of Utah, B.S., 1958, M.A., 1959; University of Texas, Ph.D., 1967. *Home:* 2332 Oakhill Dr., Salt Lake City, Utah 84121. *Office:* Department of Political Science, University of Utah, Salt Lake City, Utah 84112.

CAREER: University of Utah, Salt Lake City, associate professor of political science, 1967—. Public management consultant. *Military service:* U.S. Army, 1959-64; became captain. *Member:* American Society of Public Administration (president of Utah chapter), American Political Science Association, Middle East Studies Association, Rotary International. *Awards, honors:* Research fellowship from University of Michigan, summer, 1970.

WRITINGS: Rural Politics of Nasser's Egypt, University of Texas Press, 1971; *Local Institutions and Egyptian Rural Development,* Cornell University Press, 1974.

WORK IN PROGRESS: Organizational Development and Your Local Government: The First Eighty Years, a history of Utah voting behavior; *Local Government in Egypt: Change Strategies and Training Opportunities.*

* * *

MAZER, Norma Fox 1931-

PERSONAL: Born May 15, 1931, in New York, N.Y.; daughter of Michael and Jean (Garlen) Fox; married Harry Mazer (a novelist), February 12, 1950; children: Anne, Joseph, Susan, Gina. *Education:* Attended Antioch College and Syracuse University. *Politics:* "I believe in people—despise institutions while accepting their necessity." *Religion:* "Jewish by birth, pantheistic by nature." *Home and office:* 307 Hillsboro Parkway, Syracuse, N.Y. 13214.

CAREER: Writer, 1964—. *Awards, honors: A Figure of Speech* was nominated for National Book Award, 1973; Lewis Carroll Shelf Award from University of Wisconsin, 1975, for *Saturday the Twelfth of October;* awards for *Dear Bill, Remember Me?* include Christopher Award, outstanding book of the year award from *New York Times,* best book of the year award from *School Library Journal,* and best book for young adults from American Library Association, all 1976.

WRITINGS: I, Trissy (for children), Delacorte, 1971; *A Figure of Speech* (young adults), Delacorte, 1973; *Saturday, the Twelfth of October* (young adults), Delacorte, 1975; *Dear Bill, Remember Me?* (young adults), Delacorte, 1976; (with husband, Harry Mazer) *The Solid Gold Kid* (young adults), Delacorte, 1977. Contributor of stories and articles to magazines, including *Jack and Jill, Ingenue, Calling All Girls, Child Life, Children's Activities, Boys and Girls, Top O'News,* and *Redbook.*

WORK IN PROGRESS: A novel.

SIDELIGHTS: Norma Mazer writes: "Although *Saturday the Twelfth of October* has a fantasy element of moving through time, in the main I seem to deal in the ordinary, the everyday, the real. I should like in my writing to give meaning and emotion to ordinary moments. In my books and stories, I want people to eat chocolate pudding, break a dish, yawn, look in a store window, wear socks with holes in them...."

AVOCATIONAL INTERESTS: Reading, racketball in winter, "living in summer on our land in Canada with sun, rain, wind, and water, and without electricity, telephone, newspaper, radio, indoor plumbing, stove, refrigerator, lights, etc., etc., etc."

* * *

MAZO, Joseph H(enry) 1938-

PERSONAL: Born August 16, 1938, in Bronx, N.Y.; son of Louis I. (a lawyer and tax collector) and Anne (a teacher; maiden name, Simerman) Mazo. *Education:* New York University, B.Sc., 1961; University of Washington, Seattle, M.A., 1963; additional study at American Academy of Dramatic Art, HB Studios, and the New School for Social Research. *Residence:* New York, N.Y. *Agent:* John Cushman, John Cushman Associates, 25 West 43rd St., New York, N.Y. 10036.

CAREER: Has worked variously as actor, director, shoe salesman, toy salesman, media researcher, journalist, teacher, and editor; *Women's Wear Daily,* New York City, reporter, 1967-73, dance and theatre critic, 1971—, copy editor, 1973—. Dance and theatre critic for WNYC-FM Radio, New York City, 1972-74. *Member:* Actors Equity Association, New York Press Club. *Awards, honors: Dance Is a Contact Sport* named one of 100 Best Books of 1974 by *Philadelphia Inquirer,* 1974.

WRITINGS: Dance Is a Contact Sport, Saturday Review Press, 1974; *Prime Movers,* Morrow, 1977. Contributor to *Cosmopolitan, Town & Country, Dans* (Swedish magazine), and to *New York Times.*

WORK IN PROGRESS: "Working on several ideas stemming from a study of the American quest for salvation (and the American definition thereof)"; collecting material for two biographies, one political and one artistic.

SIDELIGHTS: "I became a writer by mistake—I thought I was becoming a theatrical director," Mazo told *CA.* "Like many members of that profession, I had a slight problem with earning a living. I worked at several jobs, all of which irritated me, until I was hired by a newspaper and decided that I liked the work. With the assistance of a few good editors, I taught myself to report and to write. I became the paper's second-string theatre critic and first-string dance critic, and discovered that being a first-line critic for a New York newspaper is excellent training for a writer: One must learn to see and hear, to write accurately, gracefully, cleverly and quickly, and one is facing some of the best competition in the journalistic profession. I started to learn my job. I'm still learning.

"It seemed about time for me to write a book, so I did. What reputation I had as a writer derived from my reviews of theatre and dance, so it seemed advisable to choose my subject from those fields. The idea for *Dance Is a Contact Sport* grew out of interviews I did with four young soloists of The New York City Ballet. Their lives were, of course, quite different from those the public imagines for dancers. *Contact Sport* was written to celebrate the dedication of dancers, to describe the cloistered, limiting, dangerous world they inhabit, and to provide an antidote for the many sentimental books that have been written about ballet.

"The book is a piece of journalism: I lived for a full season with The New York City Ballet, during which time I was permitted access to class, rehearsal, performance, and every other activity of the company. I followed the dancers every place but onto the stage. Then I came home to write. A chronological approach would have lacked interest for the average reader, and I did not want to write a book for balletomanes only, so, with the help of an excellent editor, I started to teach myself to write books. Fortuanately, this first book was about people about whom I cared: The opening line of the prologue is 'I have a habit of falling in love with women I've never met, especially ballerinas.'

"*Contact Sport* is, in effect, a work of anthropology, a study of a remarkable tribe of human begins; it is not 'a dance book.' It has been widely reviewed and well received; the *Philadelphia Inquirer* chose it as one of the 100 best books of 1974, and other journals were equally flattering.

"*Prime Movers,* my second book, is also about dance, but uses a historical, rather than a journalistic method. It deals with the development of American modern dance, and is a celebration and study of genius. I tried to show how a series of geniuses echoed in their art the intellectual and emotional preoccupations of their times, and how the art of modern dance changed from generation to generation. The great modern choreographers have been an eccentric lot, and it has been a delight to study them.

"I am happily possessed of what I call 'the garbage-can mind'—there are very few subjects that don't interest me at one time or another. I read extensively and omnivorously. I've traveled in Europe, the United States, and Mexico; I spent part of last summer on a horse in a wilderness area of Montana, which was highly interesting because that was the first time I'd ridden a horse. I play classical guitar and have studied voice. I've had tries at karate, Tai Chi, snorkeling, sailing, and soccer—all of which I do very badly. I fence—foil—a bit less badly. I'm a reasonably good photographer, and some of my own pictures were used among the illustrations for *Contact Sport.* I can't spell; my first book editor called my spelling 'One of the high-water marks of written American humor.'

"I find that my writing technique is very much like acting technique—I use emotion memory, sense memory, objectives and other heritages from my theatrical days. I find that I am interested in presenting people in the context of their surroundings, and ideas in the context of their times. I care about the emotions of my subjects, as well as about their actions. At the same time, I am a great respecter of facts. I am fascinated by genius, by closed societies, by the relationship between form and content in art, by the antagonisms between needs and wants in society and in individuals. I am also of the opinion that truly serious matters deserve the honor of being treated with levity now and again."

* * *

McALISTER, W(alter) Robert 1930-

PERSONAL: Born August 13, 1930, in London, Ontario, Canada; naturalized U.S. citizen, 1974; son of Walter E. (a clergyman) and Ruth Lillian (Manley) McAlister; married Gloria Garr, June, 1955; children: Walter Robert, Jr., Heather Ann. *Education:* Received degree from British Columbia Bible College, 1951. *Home:* Avenida Rui Barbosa, Quinhentos, Apt. Mil Trezentos e Dois, Rio de Janeiro, Brazil.

CAREER: Ordained minister of Pentecostal Assemblies of Canada, 1954; missionary evangelist in Japan, Formosa, Hong Kong, the Philippines, and India; New Life Pentecostal Church, Rio de Janeiro, Brazil, founder, president of church corporation, and pastor, 1960—, consecrated bishop, 1976. Producer and participant in radio programs. Pastoral counselor and lecturer on pastoral counseling. Bishop of Chiesa Evangelica Internazionale (Rome). *Member:* International Evangelical Church and Missionary Association (executive vice-president), Civitan Club (Charlotte, N.C.; chaplain).

WRITINGS: The Dilemma: Deliverance or Discipline?, Logos International, 1976. Also author of *The Foundations of Our Faith, The Kingdom of God,* and several works in Portuguese.

Author of several series of booklets on the Bible. Contributor of several hundred articles to *A Voz.* Chief editor of *A Voz,* 1967—.

* * *

McBRIDE, Mary Margaret 1899-1976

PERSONAL: Born November 16, 1899, in Paris, Mo.; daughter of Thomas Walker (a farmer) and Elizabeth (Craig) McBride. *Education:* University of Missouri, B.J., 1919. *Religion:* Southern Baptist. *Residence:* West Shokean, N.Y.

CAREER: Cleveland Press, Cleveland, Ohio, reporter, 1919; Interchurch World Movement, New York City, assistant to publicity director, 1920; *New York Evening Mail,* New York City, feature writer, 1920-24; free-lance writer, 1924-34; WOR-Radio, New York City, hosted a program under the pseudonym Martha Deane, 1934-42; Columbia Broadcasting System (CBS), New York City, radio show host, 1937-41; National Broadcasting Co. (NBC), New York City, radio show host, 1941-50; American Broadcasting Co. (ABC), New York City, radio show host, 1950-54; WGHG-Radio, Kingston, N.Y., part-time broadcaster, 1954-1976. Also appeared on NBC television. *Member:* Author's League, Women's City Club, New York Newspaper Woman's Club, Query, Heterodoxy, Kappa Alpha Theta, Theta Sigma Phi. *Awards, honors:* Has received Haiti's National Order of Honor and Merit; special medal of honor from the City of Vienna; special recognition from the Virgin Islands; One World Award, 1950.

WRITINGS: (With Paul Whiteman) *Jazz,* J. H. Sears, 1926; (with Alexander Williams) *Charm: A Book about It and Those Who Have It, for Those Who Want It,* Rae D. Henkle, 1927; *The Story of Dwight D. Morrow,* Farrar & Rinehart, 1930; *The Life Story of Clark Gable: The Child, the Trooper, the Screen Sensation,* Star Library Publications, 1932; *The Life Story of Constance Bennett,* Star Library Publications, 1932; *The Life Story of Greta Garbo,* Star Library Publications, 1932; *Here's Martha Deane,* Garden City Publishing, 1936; *How Dear to My Heart,* Macmillan, 1940; *America for Me,* Macmillan, 1941; *Tune in for Elizabeth: Career Story of an Interviewer,* Dodd, 1945; (editor) *How to Be a Successful Advertising Woman: A Career Guide for Women in Advertising, Public Relations, and Related Fields,* Whittlesey House, 1948; *Harvest of American Cooking,* Putnam, 1957; *Encyclopedia of Cooking: America's Most Complete Cook Book,* Homemakers Research Institute, 1958; *A Long Way from Missouri,* Putnam, 1959; *Out of the Air,* Doubleday, 1960; *The Growing up of Mary Elizabeth,* Dodd, 1966.

Author of daily newspaper column "Mary Margaret McBride Says," for Associated Press. Contributor of articles to magazines, including *Pictorial Review, Cosmopolitan,* and *Good Housekeeping.* Editor of woman's page of Newspaper Enterprise Association of New York City.

SIDELIGHTS: Mary Margaret McBride, "The First Lady of Radio," attracted a large following over the more than two decades her programs were aired on national radio. Readings of McBride's favorite recipes made her show as popular with housewives as did her interviews with such notables as Eleanor Roosevelt, President Harry S Truman, and Queen Elizabeth II. Food sponsors begged her to accept their products for advertisements, for her lyric descriptions of meals eaten on the air (to bring realism to the program, she said), made listeners salivate. Advertisers were careful not to offend this super saleswoman: the few who did, found themselves inundated with irate letters and phone calls from McBride's fans.

By 1948, almost six million housewives were tuning in to McBride's show. On the occasion of her fifteenth anniversary on the air, 40,000 people packed Yankee Stadium to pay tribute to her.

AVOCATIONAL INTERESTS: Books, the theatre, gardens, and flying.

OBITUARIES: New York Times, April 8, 1976; *Washington Post,* April 8, 1976; *Newsweek,* April 19, 1976; *Time,* April 19, 1976; *Current Biography,* June 1976.*

(Died April 7, 1976, in West Shokean, N.Y.)

*　　*　　*

McCANLES, Michael (Frederick) 1936-

PERSONAL: Born March 8, 1936, in Kansas City, Mo.; son of Martin and Dorothy (Kaysing) McCanles; married Penelope A. Mitchell, 1967; children: Christopher, Stephanie, Jocelyn. *Education:* Rockhurst College, B.S., 1957; University of Kansas, M.A., 1959, Ph.D., 1964. *Home:* 2640 North 89th St., Wauwatosa, Wis. 53226. *Office:* Department of English, Marquette University, Milwaukee, Wis. 53233.

CAREER: University of Cincinnati, Cincinnati, Ohio, instructor in English, 1962-64; Marquette University, Milwaukee, Wis., assistant professor, 1964-68, associate professor, 1968-76, professor of English, 1976—. *Member:* Modern Language Association of America, Malone Society, Renaissance Society of America.

WRITINGS: (Contributor) Eric Rothstein, editor, *Literary Monographs,* Volume IV, University of Wisconsin Press, 1971; (contributor) Thomas O. Sloan and Raymond Waddington, editors, *The Rhetoric of Renaissance Poetry,* University of California Press, 1974; *Dialectical Criticism and Renaissance Literature,* University of California Press, 1975. Contributor to Renaissance studies and literature journals.

WORK IN PROGRESS: Machiavelli, Sidney, and the Chain of Discourse (tentative title), a development of the theory of dialectical literary structure already discussed in *Dialectical Criticism and Renaissance Literature.*

SIDELIGHTS: McCanles comments: "I am interested in structures, whether verbal or musical, that exhibit harmonies that result from various local disharmonies; hence, my interest in dialectic. I like to play at the boundaries that separate the rational and the discursive from the intuitive and the mystical."

*　　*　　*

McCARTHY, Gary 1943-

PERSONAL: Born January 23, 1943, in South Gate, Calif.; son of Garold (in communications) and Edna (Huthman) McCarthy; married Virginia Kurzweil (an artist), June 14, 1969; children: Mary Melody, Glendon David. *Education:* University of California, Pomona, B.S., 1968; University of Nevada, M.S., 1970. *Religion:* Roman Catholic. *Home:* 1008 East Robinson St., Carson City, Nev. 89701.

CAREER: State of Nevada, Carson City, occupational specialist, 1970-76, rehabilitation program evaluator, 1977—. *Military service:* U.S. Navy, hospital corpsman, 1960-64. *Member:* Western Writers of America (associate member).

WRITINGS: The Derby Man (western novel), Doubleday, 1976.

WORK IN PROGRESS: The Pipeline Percentage, a novel about the Alaska Pipeline; *Color the Children Brown,* a futuristic novel; more western novels.

SIDELIGHTS: McCarthy writes: "I am most interested in writing fiction that elevates the reader rather than depresses him. I like happy endings and believe that humor will return and is needed in fiction. Who knows? Perhaps it might even rival the great spewings of gratuitous sex and violence we demand in today's fiction.

"My major interest is people. I find appealing anything that gives me insight into their dreams and motivations." *Avocational interests:* Astrology, graphoanalysis, "late-night rap sessions."

*　　*　　*

McCLURE, James (Howe) 1939-

PERSONAL: Born October 9, 1939, in Johannesburg, South Africa; son of James Howe (an Army officer) and Isabella (Cochrane) McClure; married Lorellee Ellis, January 6, 1962; children: James Howe, Alistair Francis, Kirsten Anne. *Home and office:* Sabensa Gakulu Ltd., 14 York Rd., Headington, Oxford OX3 8NW, England. *Agent:* A. D. Peters & Co., 10 Buckingham St., London WC2N 6BU, England.

CAREER: Commercial photographer in South Africa, 1958-59; teacher of English and art at boys' preparatory school in Pietermaritzburg, South Africa, 1959-63; *Natal Witness,* Natal, South Africa, reporter, 1963-64; *Natal Mercury,* Natal, South Africa, reporter, 1964-65; *Natal Daily News,*

Natal, South Africa, reporter, 1965; *Daily Mail*, Edinburgh, Scotland, sub-editor, 1965-66; *Mail and Times*, Oxford, England, sub-editor, 1966-69; Oxford Times Group, Oxford, England, deputy editor, 1969-74; writer, 1974—. Managing editor of Sabensa Gakulu Ltd., 1976—.

MEMBER: Detection Club, Crime Writers Association, Mystery Writers of America. *Awards, honors:* Gold Dagger Award from Crime Writers Association, 1971, for *The Steam Pig*, Silver Dagger Award, 1976, for *Rogue Eagle*.

WRITINGS—All crime novels, except as indicated: *The Steam Pig*, Gollancz, 1971, Harper, 1972; *The Caterpillar Cop*, Gollancz, 1972, Harper, 1973; *Four and Twenty Virgins*, Gollancz, 1973; *The Gooseberry Fool*, Harper, 1974; *Snake*, Gollancz, 1975, Harper, 1976; *Rogue Eagle*, Harper, 1976; *Killers* (nonfiction), Fontana Paperbacks, 1976; *The Sunday Hangman*, Harper, 1977.

WORK IN PROGRESS: Mr. Bones of Dulcet, a novel, for Macmillan; a book on police procedures; a self-illustrated juvenile picture book.

SIDELIGHTS: McClure writes: "I hope to achieve several things with my writing; primarily, however, I feel an obligation to entertain. As for my subject matter, it must both move and engross me." *Avocational interests:* Walking in the countryside, billiards, drawing, reading, watching BBC television.

* * *

McCLURE, Larry 1941-

PERSONAL: Born March 18, 1941, in Union City, Tenn.; son of Joe David (an educator) and Ernestine (an educator; maiden name, Diggs) McClure; married Eleanor Carlson, December 29, 1967; children: Douglas, Jennifer, Andrew. *Education:* University of Washington, Seattle, B.A., 1963; Oregon State University, Ed.M., 1966; University of Oregon, Ph.D., 1971. *Politics:* Democrat. *Religion:* United Methodist. *Home:* 17760 Cheyenne Way, Tualatin, Ore. 97062. *Office:* Northwest Regional Educational Laboratory, 710 Southwest Second, Portland, Ore. 97204.

CAREER: Teacher in public schools in Portland, Ore., 1963-67; Oregon State Department of Education, Salem, administrative assistant, 1967-69; Northwest Regional Educational Laboratory, Portland, Ore., senior associate, 1971—. Chairperson of local community planning advisory committee. *Member:* National Association for Career Education (member of board of directors), Phi Delta Kappa, Lions Club.

WRITINGS: (Editor with Carolyn Buan) *Essays on Career Education*, Northwest Regional Educational Laboratory, 1973; *Career Education Survival Manual*, Olympus, 1975; *Experience-Based Learning: How to Make the Community Your Classroom*, Northwest Regional Educational Laboratory, 1977; *The Regional Laboratory Connection: Improving Educational Practices Through Systematic Research and Development*, Northwest Regional Educational Laboratory, 1977. Contributor to education journals.

SIDELIGHTS: McClure writes that he is concerned about the "lack of an experiential base in schools today and how we can help learners rediscover the world as their classroom. Organizations like Northwest Regional Educational Laboratory are helping foster changes in education that are every bit as far reaching as medical and space research and development. I enjoy being at the 'cutting edge.' I also enjoy writing about what others are doing."

McCREARY, Alf(red) 1940-

PERSONAL: Born September 26, 1940, in Bessbrook, Northern Ireland; married wife, Hilary-Anne (a physiotherapist); children: Emma Jane, Mark. *Education:* Earned B.A. (with honors) from Queens University of Belfast. *Religion:* Christian. *Residence:* Belfast, Northern Ireland. *Office:* *Belfast Telegraph*, Royal Ave., Belfast, Northern Ireland.

CAREER: Journalist, 1964—. Has worked as reporter, feature writer, critic, and columnist. *Member:* British National Union of Journalists. *Awards, honors:* Named British Provincial Journalist, 1971, and British News Reporter of the Year, 1975.

WRITINGS: Corrymeela: The Search for Peace, Christian Journal Ltd., 1975; *October 1976: Survivors* (nonfiction), Century Books, 1976; *Corrymeela: Hill of Harmony in Northern Ireland*, Hawthorn, 1976. Contributor to magazines, including *Time, Worldview*, and *Good Housekeeping*, and to newspapers in Ireland, Scotland, England, and the United States.

WORK IN PROGRESS: Traveling in Africa and Asia to conduct research for a book on the Third World.

SIDELIGHTS: McCreary writes that his work is "characterised by a human interest approach to complex subjects from peace to war and from problems of affluence to problems of starvation. I believe that people read books about people more readily than about abstract theories."

* * *

McCURDY, Jack 1933-

PERSONAL: Born January 27, 1933, in Tucson, Ariz.; son of Valdie (a grocer) and Berta (Carpenter) McCurdy; married Patricia Felix, December 16, 1956; children: Kevin, Keith. *Education:* Los Angeles Valley College, A.A., 1953; University of Southern California, B.A., 1960; California State University, Northridge, M.A., 1976. *Politics:* Democrat. *Religion:* None. *Home:* 6902 Columbus Ave., Van Nuys, Calif. 91405. *Office: Los Angeles Times*, Times Mirror Sq., Los Angeles, Calif. 90053.

CAREER/WRITINGS: Van Nuys News and Greensheet, Van Nuys, Calif., sports editor, 1954; *Glendale News—Press*, Glendale, Calif., reporter, 1957-59; *Los Angeles Times*, Los Angeles, Calif., reporter, 1959-64; California State Colleges, Los Angeles, public information officer, 1964-65; *Los Angeles Times*, reporter, 1965-67, education writer, 1967—. Writer of column syndicated by Times-Post to newspapers. *Military service:* U.S. Army, 1955-57. *Awards, honors:* Sweepstakes awards from Los Angeles Press Club, 1965 and 1973; Alfred North Whitehead fellowship from Harvard University, 1970-71.

SIDELIGHTS: McCurdy's main area of interest is 19th century American history and educational history. In 1974, he interviewed a group of America's leading historians about their views on Richard Nixon's place in history.

* * *

McCURDY, Michael 1942-

PERSONAL: Born February 17, 1942, in New York, N.Y.; son of Charles E. (an artist) and Beatrice (Beatson) McCurdy; married Deborah Lamb (a social worker), September 7, 1968; children: Heather, Mark. *Education:* Boston School of the Museum of Fine Arts, student, 1960-66; Tufts University, B.F.A., 1964, M.F.A., 1971. *Politics:* Democrat. *Religion:* Protestant. *Home and office address:* Old Sudbury Rd., Lincoln, Mass. 01773.

CAREER: Illustrator, 1965—. Director of Penmaen Press. Member: Society of Printers.

WRITINGS—Self-illustrated: The Brick Moon, Imprint Society, 1971; Amauskeeg Falls, Barre, 1971; This Quiet Place, Little, Brown, 1971; Narrative of Alvar Nunez Cabeza de Vaca, Imprint Society, 1972; Madam Knight, David R. Godine, 1972; Please Explain (juvenile), Houghton, 1974; The Founding Mothers: Women in America in the Revolutionary Era (juvenile), Houghton, 1975.

WORK IN PROGRESS: Illustrating and printing Icelandic stories.

SIDELIGHTS: McCurdy told CA he considers himself an illustrator, not an author.

*   *   *

McCUTCHEON, John Tinney, Jr.   1917-

PERSONAL: Born November 8, 1917, in Chicago, Ill.; son of John (a cartoonist) and Evelyn (Shaw) McCutcheon; married Susan Dart (a columnist), February 1, 1943; children: Anne, Mary, John III. Education: Harvard University, B.B., 1939. Home: 281 W. Laurel Ave., Lake Forest, Ill. 60045. Office: Chicago Tribune, 435 N. Michigan Ave., Chicago, Ill. 60611.

CAREER/WRITINGS: City News Bureau of Chicago, Chicago, Ill., reporter, 1939-40; Chicago Tribune, reporter, 1940-41, 1946-51, author of "A Line o' Type or Two" column, 1951-57, editorial writer, 1957—, editor of editorial page, 1971—. President of Lake Forest Library, 1972. Military service: U.S. Navy, 1941-46; became commander. Member: American Society of Newspaper Editors, National Conference of Editorial Writers, International Press Institute, Geographic Society of Chicago (president, 1955-57), Sigma Delta Chi.

*   *   *

McDEARMON, Kay

PERSONAL: Born in San Francisco, Calif.; daughter of John (an engineer) and Mary (Gavin) Healy; married James R. McDearmon (a college professor), July 26, 1954. Education: University of California, Berkeley, B.A. Home: 2160 Julie, Turlock, Calif. 95380.

CAREER: High school teacher in Oakland, Calif., 1948-51; high school teacher of business education in Lafayette, Calif., 1951-54; writer, 1955—. Member: Soroptimists International. Awards, honors: Polar Bear was named outstanding science book for children by National Science Teachers Association, 1976.

WRITINGS—All for children: A Day in the Life of a Sea Otter (Junior Literary Guild selection), Dodd, 1973; The Walrus: Giant of the Arctic Ice, Dodd, 1974; Mahalia: Gospel Singer, Dodd, 1976; Polar Bear, Dodd, 1976; Cougar, Dodd, 1977. Contributor of about twenty-five articles to magazines.

WORK IN PROGRESS: Biographies; animal books.

SIDELIGHTS: Kay McDearmon told CA: "I have always liked to write; in fact, in high school I often wrote two themes when only one was required. In college I worked on the university daily. I am interested primarily in people; did a bit of 'Roots' study on a three-week trip to Ireland." Avocational interests: Travel.

*   *   *

McDERMOTT, John R(alph)   1921-1977

1921—April 20, 1977; American cartoonist and author of six novels best known for Brooks Wilson, Ltd. He was a combat artist with the Third Amphibious Marine Corps in World War II. Before the war he worked for Walt Disney. McDermott died in Westport, Conn. Obituaries: New York Times, April 21, 1977; AB Bookman's Weekly, July 25, 1977.

*   *   *

McDOWELL, Dimmes   1925(?)-1976

1925(?)—September 28, 1976; American editor. She served as editor of Cornell University Press, Dryden Books, Harvard University Press, and others. She edited eight dictionaries, including American College Dictionary. She died in Canada. Obituaries: Publishers Weekly, October 11, 1976.

*   *   *

McDOWELL, Margaret B(laine)   1923-

PERSONAL: Born August 8, 1923, in Cedar Rapids, Iowa; daughter of John H. and Etta (Regnet) Blaine; married Frederick P. W. McDowell (a professor of English), May 29, 1953; children: Steven, Gloria, Lawrence, Katherine, Elizabeth. Education: Coe College, B.A., 1944; University of Iowa, M.A., 1946, Ph.D., 1954. Politics: Democrat. Religion: Presbyterian. Home: 1118 East Court St., Iowa City, Iowa 52240. Office: 305 English-Philosophy Building, University of Iowa, Iowa City, Iowa 52242.

CAREER: MacMurray College, Jacksonville, Ill., assistant professor of English, 1947-49; Kansas State College, Pittsburg, assistant professor of English, 1949-53; University of Iowa, Iowa City, assistant professor, 1953-55, 1967-71, associate professor of women's studies and rhetoric, 1971—, chairperson of women's studies, 1974—. Member: Modern Language Association of America, National Council of Teachers of English, Popular Culture Association, Women's Caucus for Modern Languages (member of executive committee), Midwest Modern Language Association (member of executive committee), Iowa Council of Teachers of English.

WRITINGS: Edith Wharton, Twayne, 1976; Carson McCullers, Twayne, in press. Contributor to language and literature journals, and to women's studies journals.

WORK IN PROGRESS: Southern Women Writers.

*   *   *

McGHAN, Barry (Robert)   1939-

PERSONAL: Born November 30, 1939, in Flint, Mich.; son of Lawrence O. (a teacher) and Lois (Resseguie) McGhan; married Barbara Durell, June 23, 1962; children: Meredith Ellen, Pegeen Alissa. Education: Flint Community Junior College, A.A. (honors), 1959; Michigan State University, B.A., 1961, Ph.D., 1977; Syracuse University, M.S., 1964; also attended University of Michigan. Politics: Democratic Socialist. Home: 3404 Sherwood Dr., Flint, Mich. 48503. Office: Flint Public Schools, Flint, Mich. 48502.

CAREER: Flint Public Schools, Flint, Mich., teacher of mathematics, 1961—. Part-time instructor at Flint Community Junior College, 1974-75. Member of local human relations committee. Member: American Sociological Association, National Education Association, American Federation of Teachers, Science FictionResearch Association, Phi Delta Kappa.

WRITINGS: (With Elizabeth Calkins) Teaching Tomorrow, Pflaum, 1972; Science Fiction and Fantasy Pseud-

onyms, privately printed, 1973, 3rd edition, 1976; (with David Labick, Edward Soloko, and others) *An Index of Science Fiction Book Reviews in Astounding/Analog, Fantasy and Science Fiction, Galaxy,* Science Fiction Research Association, 1973; (contributor) T. W. Hipple, editor, *Crucial Issues in Contemporary Education,* Goodyear, 1973. Contributor to education magazines and to *Riverside Quarterly.*

WORK IN PROGRESS: A chapter on teaching science fiction, to be included in an anthology, *Science Fiction: Education for Tomorrow,* edited by Jack Williamson, for Mirage Press; research on science fiction students, alternative education, and John Locke.

SIDELIGHTS: McGhan writes: "Most of my articles and other publications were motivated by specific experiences encountered in teaching, in studying, or in pursuing my hobby interest of reading science fiction. No particular concepts are common to them. Rather, each writing effort arose as the result of some event which generated the main idea."

AVOCATIONAL INTERESTS: Collecting science fiction (has a library of more than 1500 volumes), photography, carpentry and mechanical work (is presently building a cabin in Michigan's Upper Peninsula).

*　　*　　*

McGOWAN, Jack 1896(?)-1977

1896(?)—May 28, 1977; American screenplay writer, playwright, and actor best known for his "Panama Hattie," "Born to Dance," and "Lady Be Good" screenplays. He also wrote "Tenth Avenue," "Excess Baggage," and "Flying High," all for Broadway. He died in New York City. Obituaries: *New York Times,* June 2, 1977.

*　　*　　*

McGOWAN, Margaret M(ary)

PERSONAL: Married Anglo Sydney (a university teacher), December, 1964. *Education:* University of Reading, B.A., Ph.D., 1959. *Office:* School of European Studies, University of Sussex, Falmer, Brighton, Sussex BN1 9QX, England.

CAREER: University of Sussex, Brighton, England, professor of French, 1974—. *Member:* Association Internationale des Etudes Francaises, Modern Language Association, Renaissance Society, Association of University Teachers.

WRITINGS: L'art du ballet de cour en France, 1581-1643, Editions du Centre national de la recherche scientifique, 1963; *Philippe d'Aglie,* [Paris], 1968; (editor and author of introduction) Jean Racine, *Bajazet,* University of London Press, 1968; *Montaigne's Deceits: The Art of Persuasion in the Essays,* Temple University Press, 1974; (editor of first four volumes) *Renaissance Triumphs and Magnificences,* Orbis, 1974.

WORK IN PROGRESS: Poetry and Art in the Sixteenth Century; a book on Ronsard's poetry of praise.

AVOCATIONAL INTERESTS: Travel, music, art collecting, book collecting.

*　　*　　*

McGOWEN, Charles H(ammond) 1936-

PERSONAL: Born May 28, 1936, in Youngstown, Ohio; son of Keith Wellington (a steelworker) and Frances (a teacher; maiden name, Owen) McGowen; married Kay Umbel, December 8, 1956; children: Wendy Kay, Charles Keith, Brenda Sue. *Education:* Hiram College, B.A., 1957; Ohio State University, M.D., 1961. *Religion:* Evangelical Friends. *Home:* 16 Centennial Dr., Poland, Ohio 44514. *Office:* 1039 Boardman-Canfield Rd., Youngstown, Ohio 44512.

CAREER: Youngstown Hospital Association, Youngstown, Ohio, intern, 1961-62, resident in internal medicine, 1964-67; physician, practicing internal medicine and endocrinology, in Youngstown, Ohio, 1967—. Diplomate of American Board of Internal Medicine. *Military service:* U.S. Air Force Reserve, 1962-69, active duty as flight surgeon, 1962-64; became major. *Member:* American College of Physicians, Creation Research Society, American Diabetes Association, Ohio State Medical Association, Mahoning County Medical Society, Christian Businessman's Committee.

WRITINGS: In Six Days, Bible Voice, Inc., 1976. Contributor to *Journal of the American Medical Association.*

WORK IN PROGRESS: Where There's Smoke ...!, a treatise in lay terms on the harmful effect of tobacco; *The Little Colt Donkey,* a children's Christmas and Easter story; *Five Who Came Alive,* nonfiction, completion expected in 1979.

SIDELIGHTS: McGowen writes: "*In Six Days* came out of a desire to convince people that the question of origins is not answerable by the evolutionary doctrine alone and that equal time for the other popular view is needed."

*　　*　　*

McGRAIL, Joie 1922(?)-1977

1922(?)—April 27, 1977; Austrian-born American fashion editor, consultant, and author best known for *Fighting Back.* She was marketing editor of *Harper's Bazaar* in the 1950's. She died in New York City. Obituaries: *New York Times,* April 28, 1977.

*　　*　　*

McGREEVEY, William Paul 1938-

PERSONAL: Born April 14, 1938, in Greenville, Ohio; son of Paul H. (an engineer) and Aletha M. (a teacher; maiden name, Myers) McGreevey; children: Sean Robb, Alicia Ireys. *Education:* Ohio State University, B.A. (with high distinction), 1960; Massachusetts Institute of Technology, Ph.D., 1964. *Home:* 1115 24th St. N.W., Washington, D.C. 20037. *Office:* Battelle Memorial Institute, 2030 M St. N.W., Washington, D.C. 20036.

CAREER: University of Oregon, Eugene, assistant professor of economics, 1964-65; University of California, Berkeley, assistant professor of history, also research associate and acting chairman of Center for Latin American Studies, 1965-71, chairman of center, 1966-69; Organization of American States, Washington, D.C., senior economist in department of economic affairs, 1971-72; Smithsonian Institution, Washington, D.C., staff social scientist with interdisciplinary communications program, 1972-76; consulting economist and writer, 1976-77; Battelle Memorial Institute, Washington, D.C., program director, 1977—. Economist with Alliance for Progress, 1962; director of migration research group in Colombia, 1965; member of panel on Latin America for World Press, 1967-71; co-director of Social Science Research Council-American Council of Learned Societies Latin American studies project, 1967-69. Member of board of directors of International Center for Research on Women. Consultant to Agency for International Development.

MEMBER: American Economic Association, Conference of Latin American Historians, Latin American Studies Association, American Historical Association, Econometric Society.

WRITINGS: An Economic History of Colombia, 1845-1930, Cambridge University Press, 1971; (contributor) Richard M. Morse, editor, *The Urban Development of Latin America,* Stanford University Press, 1971; (contributor) Jacob Price and Val Lorin, editors, *The Dimensions of the Past,* Yale University Press, 1972; (with Nancy Birdsall) *The Policy Relevance of Recent Social Research on Fertility* (monograph), Smithsonian Institution, 1974. Contributor to academic journals.

WORK IN PROGRESS: Population Growth and Development Policy.

* * *

McHUGH, Edna

PERSONAL: Born in New York, N.Y.; married James McHugh, Jr. (divorced); children: Judith. *Education:* Attended University of Southern California. *Residence:* Malibu, Calif. *Agent:* Arthur Pine, 1780 Broadway, New York, N.Y. 10019; Merrily Kane, 9171 Wilshire, Beverly Hills, Calif. 90210.

CAREER: Writer.

WRITINGS: Happy Endings, Collier Books, 1962; *Chocolate Kicks and Other Recipes for the Chocolate Addict,* Price, Stern, 1970; *The Coffee Cookbook,* Price, Stern, 1972.

WORK IN PROGRESS: A television series; a novel; and three new cookbooks.

AVOCATIONAL INTERESTS: Gardening, painting, word games, study of words.

* * *

McHUGH, Heather 1948-

PERSONAL: Born August 20, 1948, in California; daughter of John Laurence (a marine biologist) and Eileen Francesca (Smallwood) McHugh; married Michael Lelyveld, May 12, 1968 (divorced). *Education:* Radcliffe College, B.A., 1970; University of Denver, M.A., 1972. *Politics:* Independent. *Religion:* Pantheism. *Office:* Department of English, State University of New York at Binghamton, Binghamton, N.Y. 13901.

CAREER: Antioch College, Yellow Springs, Ohio, visiting lecturer in English, 1971-72; Stephens College, Columbia, Mo., instructor in English and poet-in-residence, 1974-76; State University of New York at Binghamton, assistant professor of English, 1976—. *Awards, honors:* Fellow of Cummington Community for the Arts, 1970, and Provincetown Fine Arts Work Center, 1972; prize from Academy of American Poets, 1972, for "In the Third Person"; Macdowell Colony fellowships, 1973, 1974, 1976; National Endowment for the Arts grant, 1974; winner of New Poetry Series Competition, 1976, for *Dangers.*

WRITINGS: Dangers (poems), Houghton, 1977.

Anthologized in *American Poetry Anthology,* edited by Daniel Halpern, Avon, 1976; and *Ardis Anthology of New American Poetry,* edited by David Rigsbee, Ardis, 1977. Contributor of poems to magazines, including *New Yorker, Harper's, Atlantic, Antaeus,* and *Antioch Review.*

WORK IN PROGRESS: More poems.

SIDELIGHTS: McHugh writes: "I do not choose to write. Since I was six I *had* to, hook, line, and sink. I teach to support my habit. I do not read fiction, feel as remote from it as a writer as if it were not made of the same stuff as poems (and it isn't: sentence and paragraph, instead of words). I love to learn nonfiction, physical anthropology, evolution, cross-sections of fruits and vegetables, carnal orders, all six senses, men and women. I am a student of the grammars of the physical world. Can't sit still, have lived every American-where, plus Canada, France, Italy, Peru for times. Stick things out, neck and tongue."

AVOCATIONAL INTERESTS: Rhythm and blues, shooting pool, making bread.

* * *

McINTOSH, Donal W. 1919-

PERSONAL: Born September 26, 1919, in Saskatchewan, Canada; son of Herbert (a farmer) and Gladys (Grant) McIntosh; married Kathreen Genge; children: Donal Gordon, Patricia (Mrs. Jack Price), Jock Grant, Susan Richfield. *Education:* University of Oregon, B.S., 1947, M.B.A.; University of Washington, Seattle, Ph.D. *Home:* 7148 Southwest Laview Dr., Portland, Ore. 97219. *Office:* Portland State University, P.O. Box 751, Portland, Ore. 97207.

CAREER: Worked as personnel director, editor, training director, and advertising manager with trucking and automobile finance companies; former publicist with National Safety Council in Portland, Ore., and Atlanta, Ga.; currently teaching at Portland State University, Portland, Ore. *Military service:* Royal Canadian Air Force, served as flying instructor and instrument test pilot; became officer. *Member:* American Business Communication Association, Oregon Association of Communicators, Association for Loss Prevention and Security (Portland; president), Sigma Delta Chi, Beta Gamma Sigma.

WRITINGS: Techniques of Business Communication, Holbrook, 1972, 2nd edition, 1977; *A Guide to Writing Reports,* Lake Oswego Communication Processing, 1974; (with F. L. Newton) *How to Write Your Resume,* Lake Oswego Communication Processing, 1975; *The Dynamic Supervisor,* Goodyear Publishing, in press; (with Dave Whitney) *A Procedural Manual for Retail Loss Prevention,* Association for Loss Prevention and Security, in press.

* * *

McIVER, Stuart B(etts) 1921-

PERSONAL: Surname is pronounced Mc-*Kee*-ver; born December 25, 1921, in Sanford, N.C.; son of Lynn (a physician) and Maude (Betts) McIver; married Joan Hinebaugh (a newspaperwoman), June 14, 1949; children: Stuart B., Jr., Jan, Barbara, Laurel, Margery. *Education:* University of North Carolina, A.B., 1942; Johns Hopkins University, graduate study, 1958-60. *Politics:* Democrat. *Home:* 2201 Northeast 32nd Court, Lighthouse Point, Fla. 33064.

CAREER: Baltimore Sun, Baltimore, Md., reporter, 1945-54; Martin Co., Baltimore, Md., film writer and producer, 1955-59, manager of information services for Research Institute for Advanced Study, 1960-62; Goodway, Inc., North Palm Beach and Fort Lauderdale, Fla., manager of film division, 1962-71; Stimson Associates, Fort Lauderdale, Fla., account executive, 1971-75; free-lance writer and public relations consultant, 1975—. Member of publications advisory board of Broward County Historical Commission.

MEMBER: Historical Association of Southern Florida,

Historical Society of Palm Beach County, Fort Lauderdale Historical Society, Sigma Delta Chi. *Awards, honors:* Golden Eagle from Council on International Nontheatrical Events, 1966, for "Marisa the Mermaid," and 1968, for "Alligator"; Chris Award from Columbus Film Festival, 1968, and silver medal from Venice Film Festival, 1969, both for "Alligator."

WRITINGS: Yesterday's Palm Beach, E. A. Seeman, 1976.

Author of eighty-two documentary film scripts, including "Vanguard—A Rocket for Science," 1958, "Marisa and the Mermaid," 1965, "Million Acre Playground," 1966, "Eagle in the Everglades," 1966, "Alligator," 1967, and "Gettysburg—3 Days in July," 1974.

Contributor of more than fifty articles and stories to national and regional magazines. Contributing editor of *Miami;* member of editorial board of *Broward Legacy.*

WORK IN PROGRESS: A biography of Guy Bradley, the first Audubon warden killed in the line of duty.

SIDELIGHTS: McIver comments that an "interest in the subject of extinction led to research on warden Guy Bradley, killed in the line of duty in 1905 while trying to protect endangered plume birds. Since Bradley lived in the Palm Beach area as a boy, research turned up information on early Palm Beach, which led to turn to the book. The Everglades has been a major interest, as the setting for six of my films. Much of the Bradley story also takes place in the Everglades."

BIOGRAPHICAL/CRITICAL SOURCES: Fort Lauderdale Tribune, October 2, 1969; *Palm Beach Daily News,* January 17, 1977.

* * *

McKELWAY, Benjamin M. 1895-1976

October 2, 1895—August 29, 1976; American editor and former president of Associated Press. McKelway started at the *Washington Star* as a copy editor in 1920 and retired as editorial chairman in 1976. A lifelong advocate of freedom of the press and civil rights, he was director of Associated Press from 1949 to 1957 and president from 1958 to 1963. He died in Washington, D.C. Obituaries: *Washington Post,* August 31, 1976; *New York Times,* September 1, 1976; *Newsweek,* September 13, 1976; *Current Biography,* October, 1976.

* * *

McKENNEY, Kenneth 1929-

PERSONAL: Born April 4, 1929, in Suva, Fiji; son of James Francis and Naomi McKenney; married Pamela Webster, 1952 (divorced); married Virginia Susan Whalley, October 20, 1972; children: Sarah Anne. *Education:* University of Auckland, B.Sc., 1952. *Home:* 137-5 Rio Balsas, Mexico City 5, D. F. Mexico. *Agent:* International Creative Management, 40 West 57th St., New York, N.Y. 10019.

CAREER: Geologist in northwest Queensland, Australia, 1954-55, and gold mines in Fiji, 1955-56; advertising copywriter in Auckland, New Zealand, 1957-58; Ponsonby Post (newspaper), Auckland, founder, editor, copywriter, 1960; writer and producer of television commercials in Australia, 1962-65; Young & Rubicam, London, England, television producer in Europe, Mexico, and Japan, 1967-77; director of television commercials in Mexico, 1977—. *Awards, honors:* British Drama Society Award for New Zealand, 1965, for one-act play "The Escape of Henry Springs."

WRITINGS—Novels: *The Hide-Away Man,* Barrie & Rockliffe, 1965; *The Orderly,* Deutsch, 1968; *The Terminator,* Talmy-Franklin, 1970; *The Plants* (science fiction), Putnam, 1976; *The Moonchild* (gothic horror), Simon & Schuster, in press.

Plays: "The Escape of Harry Springs" (one-act) first produced, 1964.

Contributor of stories and poems to publications in Australia, New Zealand, and England.

WORK IN PROGRESS: A long novel set in present-day Mexico.

SIDELIGHTS: McKenney writes: "I am interested in people, travel, and writing. I hope that my experiences or observations might be interesting enough to entertain or perhaps inform others. I began writing in order to present attractive ladies with small and flattering pieces which they sometimes fell for."

* * *

McKENZIE, George W(ashington) 1939-

PERSONAL: Born July 30, 1939, in Brooklyn, N.Y.; son of George (a safety engineer) and Virginia (Raeburn) McKenzie; married Sandra Short (a systems architect), 1962. *Education:* Wesleyan University, B.A. (with distinction), 1961; Fletcher School of Law and Diplomacy, Tufts University, M.A., 1963; University of California, Berkeley, Ph.D., 1967. *Home:* 59 Porchester Rd., Fareham, Hampshire, England. *Office:* Department of Economics, University of Southampton, Highfield, Southampton SO9 5NH, England.

CAREER: Record Journal, Meriden, Conn., reporter, 1961; Washington University, St. Louis, Mo., assistant professor of economics, 1966-71, director of Economics Internship Program, 1969-70; University of Southampton, Southampton, England, lecturer, 1970-77, senior lecturer in economics, 1977—, research associate for Southampton Econometric Model, 1976—. Tutor for United Kingdom Civil Service College, 1971, 1973.

WRITINGS: The Monetary Theory of International Trade, Macmillan, 1973; *The Economics of the Euro-Currency System,* Wiley, 1976. Editor of "Studies in Economic Integration," for Wiley. Contributor to economics and international studies journals.

WORK IN PROGRESS: Operational Procedures for Evaluating Economic Policies; Tariffs and Income Distribution: The Case of the United Kingdom; The Stability of the International Banking System.

* * *

McKINLEY, James (Courtright) 1935-

PERSONAL: Born December 8, 1935, in Omaha, Neb.; son of Harold Courtright (a lawyer) and Kathryn (Anderson) McKinley; married Mary Ann Underwood (a writer), April 4, 1959; children: James, Jr., Mary Kathryn, Jesse. *Education:* Washington University, St. Louis, Mo., student, 1954-57; University of Missouri, B.A. and B.J., 1959, M.A., 1968, Ph.D., 1970. *Politics:* Independent. *Religion:* Episcopal. *Home:* 7309 Northwest Maple Lane, Kansas City, Mo. 64151. *Agent:* Robert Lescher, 155 East 71st St., New York, N.Y. 10022. *Office:* Department of English, University of Missouri at Kansas City, 5315 Holmes Ave., Kansas City, Mo. 64110.

CAREER: Procter & Gamble, Inc., Cincinnati, Ohio, copy supervisor, 1960-64; Young & Rubicam Advertising, Inc.,

New York, N.Y., account executive, 1965-66; University of Missouri at Kansas City, assistant professor, 1970-76, associate professor of English, 1977—. *Military service:* U.S. Army Reserve, 1960-68, active duty, 1960-61; became first lieutenant. *Awards, honors:* National Endowment for the Humanities fellowship, 1972-73.

WRITINGS: Assassination in America, Harper, 1977. Contributor of articles, stories, poems, and reviews to magazines and newspapers, including *Playboy* and *Esquire.* Fiction editor of *New Letters,* 1974-76.

WORK IN PROGRESS: The Biography of Robert Graves, for Harper.

SIDELIGHTS: McKinley writes: "The book *Assassination in America* arose from the profound shock of John F. Kennedy's death, and a corresponding desire to know what sort of people can so injure a nation's political and psychic health. My biography of Robert Graves comes from a personal fascination with the man, and an equally strong interest in his beliefs about the proper relationship of man and woman—and how that relationship can function in a technocratic world. All my writing is intended to explain both its subject to the reader and the author to himself."

* * *

McLACHLAN, Ian   1938-

PERSONAL: Born October 20, 1938, in London, England; son of William Nicol (an engineer) and Oonagh (McMartin) McLachlan; married Dominique Isabelle (a teacher), September 20, 1960; children: Stephane, Jerome, Gavin. *Education:* St. Edmund Hall, Oxford, B.A., 1960, M.A., 1964. *Politics:* "Marx-Trotsky-Mao." *Religion:* "Polytheist." *Home address:* R.R.1; Ennismore, Ontario, Canada K0L 1T0. *Office:* Peter Robinson College, Trent University, Peterborough, Ontario, Canada.

CAREER: Longmans, Green (publisher), London, England, trainee, 1956-57; University of Hong Kong, Hong Kong, lecturer, 1960-68, senior lecturer in comparative literature and chairman of department, 1968-70; Trent University, Peterborough, Ontario, associate professor, 1970-76, professor of comparative literature, 1976—, master of Peter Robinson College, 1977—. Host of "Youth Wants to Know," on TVB (Hong Kong), 1968-69. *Awards, honors:* Books Canada Award for best first Canadian novel, 1976, for *The Seventh Hexagram.*

WRITINGS: (Contributor) C. D. Narasimhaiah, editor, *The Asian Response to American Literature,* USEFI (U.S. Educational Foundation in India), 1971; *The Seventh Hexagram* (novel), Dial, 1976; (with B. N. Weber, H. Heinen, and others) *Bertolt Brecht: Political Theory and Literary Practice,* University of Texas Press, 1977.

Author of "The Investigation of Bertolt Brecht" (two-act play), first produced in Peterborough, Ontario, at Champlain Theatre, November 14, 1975. Contributor to magazines, including *Gemini, Oxford Opinion, Paris, Eastern Horizon, Enquiry,* and *Global Digest, Casa de las Americas, Malahat Review, Saturday Night, Far Eastern Economic Review,* and to newspapers.

WORK IN PROGRESS: Ho Chi Minh in Prison; an oral history of Shanghai, completion expected in 1978; *Helen,* a novel, 1980; stories and poems; research on Bertolt Brecht, Paul Eluard, and Chinese opera.

SIDELIGHTS: McLachlan writes: "My aim is to depict the moral and political collapse of a western bourgeoisie of which I am myself a part." He adds that, as a compulsive

traveler, he has visited Europe, Soviet Central Asia and Siberia, Japan, China, Southeast Asia, Australia, and North and South America.

* * *

McLEOD, Emilie Warren   1926-

PERSONAL: Born December 2, 1926, in Boston, Mass.; daughter of Shiedls (a physician) and Alice (Springfield) Warren; children: Sara K., Susan M., Stuart C. *Education:* Mount Holyoke College, B.A., 1948. *Home:* 60 Carlton Rd., Waban, Mass. 02168. *Office:* Atlantic Monthly Press, 8 Arlington St., Boston, Mass. 02116.

CAREER: Houghton Mifflin Co., Boston, Mass., assistant editor of children's books, 1950-52; Atlantic Monthly Press, Boston, Mass., children's book editor, 1956—, associate director, 1976—. Director of Shared Educational Experiences. *Member:* American Library Association, Mount Holyoke Alumnae Association, Mount Holyoke Club (Boston president, 1970-72).

WRITINGS—For children: *The Seven Remarkable Bears,* Houghton, 1954; *Clancy's Witch,* Little, Brown, 1959; *One Snail and Me,* Little, Brown, 1962; *The Bear's Bicycle,* Little, Brown, 1975.

* * *

McLEOD, John F(reeland)   1917-
(Jay Freeland, Jeff Mackle)

PERSONAL: Born November 7, 1917, in Indiana; son of Donald G. (a builder) and Ruth (a singer; maiden name, Freeland) McLeod; married Martha Klein (a librarian), September 25, 1948; children: Mary Caroline McLeod Cigolle, Elizabeth Ruth. *Education:* Indiana University, A.B., 1939. *Politics:* Independent. *Religion:* Independent. *Home:* 2703 Weisman Rd., Wheaton, Md. 20902. *Office:* Amtrak, 955 L'Enfant Pl. S.W., Washington, D.C. 20024.

CAREER/WRITINGS: Knoxville Journal, Knoxville, Tenn., reporter, 1939-40; *Belvidere Republican,* Belvidere, Ill., reporter, 1940-41; Chicago City News Bureau, Chicago, Ill., reporter, 1941; *Yank* (U.S. Army weekly), correspondent from Sydney and Manila, 1943-45; *Washington Daily News,* Washington, D.C., picture and travel editor, 1945-72; *Amtrak,* Washington, D.C., travel editor, 1972—. Notable assignments include coverage of the first transatlantic jet flight and later Pacific flights, World's Fair opening in Brussels, New York City, Montreal, and Osaka, bootlegging trials in Tennessee, Dairy Herd Improvement Association meetings in northern Illinois, gang murders in Chicago, the retaking of Corregidor Island, and twenty-four hours with a reconnaissance troop on Mindanao (during World War II). Work represented in anthologies, including *Around the World with the Experts,* published by Doubleday. Contributor to *Fodor's U.S.A.* and to magazines, including *Family Weekly, Mademoiselle,* and travel magazines. Lecturer in Communications at American University, 1952-54. *Military service:* U.S. Army, 41st Infantry, 1942-43; journalist, 1943-45; served in Australia and the Far East; became sergeant.

MEMBER: National Press Club, Society of American Travel Writers (president, 1959; chairman of board of directors, 1960, 1964), Discover America Travel Organizations (press chairman), American Society of Travel Agents, Washington Newspaper Guild (president, 1947). *Awards, honors:* Lafayette Medal from French Government Tourist Office, 1958.

SIDELIGHTS: McLeod told *CA* that his most interesting

trips to date have been to Bali and Kenya before both places were open to mass tourism, and to Cuba just before it closed to mass tourism. He added that he enjoys traveling "anywhere at all on a good train with good company".

* * *

McMAHON, Michael 1943-

PERSONAL: Born March 10, 1943, in Palmerton, Pa.; son of Edward T. and Romaine (Peters) McMahon; married Patricia M. Dishman (area director of a community action program), April 26, 1963; children: Michael, Erin, Sean Patrick. Education: Colby College, A.B., 1965; University of Scranton, M.A., 1968. Politics: Socialist. Religion: None. Home address: Box 95, North Sutton, N.H. 03260. Office: Department of English, Colby-Sawyer College, New London, N.H. 03257.

CAREER: Colby-Sawyer College, New London, N.H., assistant professor of English, 1968—; writer. Has worked as a farm laborer. Member of board of directors, New England Small Press Association; associated with New Hampshire Poetry in the Schools. Member: College English Association. Awards, honors: Nebula Award, 1975, for poem "On Turning Down a Clear $75 a Week"; Pushcart Poetry Award, Dark Horse Poetry Award, and Aspen Literary Award, all 1976.

WRITINGS: (Editor) Flowering after Frost: An Anthology of Contemporary New England Poetry, Branden Press, 1975; A Day's Work (poems), Puckerbrush Press, 1976; The George Washington Semen on Our Teeth, Contraband Press, 1976; Ripening for Heaven, Nada Press, 1977; Northern Vices (prose poems), Thunder City Press, 1977. Work has been represented in Flowering after Frost: An Anthology of Contemporary New England, Branden Press, 1975. Contributor of many poems to small magazines.

WORK IN PROGRESS: The Effects of Christ's Work on Earth, prose poems; The Dawn Mountain Poems.

SIDELIGHTS: McMahon commented: "I write poems about living in a small rented place, ruined farm country, a land where winter lasts for six months, a north country that has nothing to do with the compass direction. I have worked as a tennis pro, a farm hand, a bartender, a jazz and rock organist, a butcher, an advertising copywriter, an assistant innkeeper, a house painter, a grocery clerk, and a caterer in the last eight years. Somehow, in retrospect, it does not seem worth it."

AVOCATIONAL INTERESTS: Playing tennis, golf, basketball, touch football, and softball.

* * *

McMANIS, Douglas R.

PERSONAL: Born in Akron, Ohio. Education: Kent State University, B.S., 1954, M.A., 1955; University of Chicago, Ph.D., 1964. Office: Department of Social Studies, Teachers College, Columbia University, New York, N.Y. 10027.

CAREER: Butler University, Indianapolis, Ind., instructor in geography, 1960-64; Eastern Michigan University, Ypsilanti, assistant professor of geography, 1964-66; Columbia University, Teachers College, New York City, associate professor of geography, 1966—. Consultant to publishers and educational firms. Member: Association of American Geographers, American Geographical Society, National Council for the Social Studies, National Council for Geographical Education, Friends of the American Ballet Theatre, Metropolitan Opera Guild.

WRITINGS: Initial Evaluation and Utilization of the Illinois Prairies, 1815-1840, University of Chicago, Department of Geography, 1964; Historical Geography of the United States: A Bibliography, Eastern Michigan University, 1965; The Traditions of Vinland, Association of American Geographers, 1969; European Impressions of the New England Coast, 1497-1620, University of Chicago, Department of Geography, 1972; Colonial New England: A Historical Geography, Oxford University Press, 1975. Editor of travel and exploration series for Greenwood Press.

WORK IN PROGRESS: Evolution of American Landscapes; research on children's perceptions of foreign landscapes.

* * *

McMICHAEL, James 1939-

PERSONAL: Born July 19, 1939, in Pasadena, Calif.; son of James M. (a realtor) and Elva (a teacher; maiden name, Lee) McMichael; married Barbara Cress, June 11, 1961 (divorced, 1969); married Phylinda Wallace (a translator), June 14, 1970; children: Robert Kenneth, Geoffrey Aaron. Education: University of California, Santa Barbara, A.B., 1961; Stanford University, Ph.D., 1965. Office: Department of English, University of California, Irvine, Calif. 92717.

CAREER: University of California, Irvine, assistant professor, 1965-71, associate professor, 1971-76, professor of English, 1976—. Awards, honors: Eunice Tietjens Memorial Award from Poetry, 1975; Guggenheim fellowship, 1977.

WRITINGS: The Style of the Short Poem, Wadsworth, 1967; Against the Falling Evil, Swallow Press, 1971; The Lover's Familiar, David R. Godine, 1977.

* * *

McMURRY, James Burton 1941-

PERSONAL: Born January 5, 1941, in Butler, Pa.; son of Lloyd Thomas (employed by a railroad) and Gertrude (a hairdresser; maiden name, Dugan) McMurry; married Erica Ann Funari (a potter), July 8, 1968; children: Caine Thomas. Education: Attended St. Fidelis Seminary. Politics: "Anarchical ('Blissy chaos at peace with itself')." Religion: "Exploratory (Astrological at present)." Home address: Whit's Lane, General Delivery, Wellfleet, Mass. 02667.

CAREER: Writer and musician. Has worked as a proofreader and copy editor for New Directions and Simon & Schuster. Member of Wellfleet Cantores, an a cappella choir.

WRITINGS: The Catskill Witch and Other Tales of the Hudson Valley, Syracuse University Press, 1974.

WORK IN PROGRESS: Going to Fairyland, poems; Diary of a Mindless Wonder, poems; Richard Brecknell's Hudson River Puppet Show; The Secret of the Rose, a gothic romance; The Autobiography of Ludwig von Beethoven, "a psychic autobiography."

SIDELIGHTS: McMurry comments that his first five or six books are motivated by love of literature and literary ambition "(also, though not essentially, for money). The Secret of the Rose and Beethoven are motivated by dreams and the spiritual necessity to explore reality. . . ."

* * *

McMURTREY, Martin A(loysias) 1921-

PERSONAL: Born April 16, 1921, in East St. Louis, Ill.; son of Martin William (a clerk) and Alice (Coever) Mc-

Murtrey. *Education:* University of Dayton, B.A., 1942; St. Louis University, M.Ed., 1949. *Religion:* Roman Catholic. *Home:* 808 Camden, San Antonio, Tex. 78215. *Office:* Central Catholic High School, 1403 North St. Marys, San Antonio, Tex. 78215.

CAREER: Entered Brothers of Mary, 1939; teacher in St. Louis, Chicago, and Belleville, Ill., 1939-50; Central Catholic High School, San Antonio, Tex., teacher of English, creative writing, and drafting, and football coach, 1950—.

WRITINGS: Loose to the Wilds (novel for young people), Harper, 1976.

WORK IN PROGRESS: Us, a novel for young people.

SIDELIGHTS: McMurtrey comments that *"Loose to the Wilds* is set in Monroe County in Southern Illinois. I spent much time in this area as a boy."

* * *

McNAMARA, John S.   1908(?)-1977

1908(?)—May 17, 1977; American reporter. He worked for the *New York Herald Tribune* from the 1930's until 1966. He later was an account executive for an advertising agency. Obituaries: *New York Times,* May 19, 1977.

* * *

McNEISH, James   1931-

PERSONAL: Born October 23, 1931, in Auckland, New Zealand; son of Arthur William (an army officer) and Geraldine (a violinist; maiden name, Bosworth) McNeish; married Felicity Wily, July 16, 1960 (divorced, August 31, 1964); married Helen Schnitzer (a photographer and author), December 27, 1968; children: (first marriage) Kathryn Ann. *Education:* University of Auckland, B.A., 1952. *Residence:* New Zealand. *Agent:* George Greenfield, John Farquharson Ltd., 15 Red Lion Sq., London WC1R 4QW, England.

CAREER: New Zealand Herald, Auckland, New Zealand, journalist and arts editor, 1950-58; teacher in London, England, 1960-62; free-lance radio broadcaster and radio documentary producer, 1962—; author, 1964—. Founder and director, with wife Helen, of Bridge in New Zealand (private educational travel trust), 1974—. *Military service:* Territorial Service Army of New Zealand. *Member:* P.E.N. International. *Awards, honors:* Katherine Mansfield fellowship, 1973.

WRITINGS: Fire Under the Ashes (biography of Danilo Dolci), Hodder & Stoughton, 1965, Beacon Press, 1966; *Mackenzie* (novel), Hodder & Stoughton, 1970; *The Mackenzie Affair* (novel), Hodder & Stoughton, 1972; (with Marti Friedlander) *Larks In a Paradise,* Collins, 1974; *The Glass Zoo* (novel), St. Martin's, 1976; *As For the Codwits* (autobiographical diary), Hodder & Stoughton, 1977.

Plays: "The Rocking Cave," first produced in New Zealand at Auckland Dramatic Festival, 1973; "The Mouse Man," first produced in Auckland at Mercury Theatre, 1975.

Author of penal report to New Zealand Minister of Justice, 1974.

WORK IN PROGRESS: A novel; a sociological/autobiographical text with working title, *Between Two Worlds: The Surviving Pacific.*

SIDELIGHTS: "My interest in people extends to penal reform, social issues, and primitive societies. The Bridge in New Zealand trust is an extension of an interest in educational matters. Each year the trust sends some twenty New Zealanders, 19-26, to Israel and Europe to stretch their hori-

zons. It's a twelve-month long non-academic non-Jewish scheme.

"Most of my broadcasting, as with writing, covers these interests. They grew out of a three year stint in West Sicily (between 1960-64) when I worked with the social reformer Danilo Dolci, subject of the *Fire Under the Ashes* biography."

* * *

McPHERSON, William (Alexander)   1933-

PERSONAL: Born March 16, 1933, in Sault Ste. Marie, Mich.; son of Harold Agnew and Ruth (Brubaker) McPherson; married Elizabeth Mosher (a writer), July 7, 1959; children: Jane Elizabeth. *Education:* Attended University of Michigan, 1951-55, Michigan State University, 1956-58, and George Washington University, 1960-62. *Home:* 2955 Newark St. NW, Washington, D.C. 20008. *Office: Book World, Washington Post,* 1150 15th St. NW, Washington, D.C. 20071.

CAREER/WRITINGS: Washington Post, Washington, D.C., copyperson, 1958, staff writer and editor, 1959-66; William Morrow & Co., New York, N.Y., senior editor, 1966-69; *Washington Post,* daily book editor, 1969-72, editor of *Book World,* 1972—. American University, lecturer, 1971, adjunct professor, 1975. Contributor of book reviews and articles to periodicals, including *New Republic,* and *Life.* Member of New York County Democratic Committee, 1969. *Member:* National Book Critics Circle (member of board of directors, 1975—), P.E.N. *Awards, honors:* Pulitzer Prize for Distinguished Criticism, 1977.

BIOGRAPHICAL/CRITICAL SOURCES: Washingtonian, December, 1976.

* * *

McSHAN, James   1937-

PERSONAL: Born August 5, 1937, in Mississippi; son of Howard Cleveland (a businessman) and Mandine (Wilson) McShan; married Mena Cruthirds (a writer and editor), August 27, 1973; children: Deborah, Elizabeth. *Education:* Attended University of Western Kentucky, 1956-58; Delta State University, B.A., 1960; graduate study at Instituto Allende, 1971-72, and University of the Americas, 1972-73, both in Mexico. *Address:* Box 30, Long Beach, Miss. 39560. *Office address:* Box 95, Schlater, Miss. 38952.

CAREER: Teacher in New Orleans, La., 1960; McShan Seed Co., Schlater, Miss., manager, 1960-70; Universities International Press, New York City, assistant editor, 1970; University of the Americas, Puebla, Mexico, writer at university press, 1972; sailor and writer, 1972—.

WRITINGS: (Contributor) James Bixler, editor, *San Miguel Writer,* Mexico City Publishing, 1971; (contributor) David Lawerence, editor, *Xalli,* University of the Americas, University Press, 1972; (contributor) Robert Olmstead, editor, *Rendezvous with the Sea,* Northwoods Press (Meadows of Dan, Va.), 1975; (contributor) Lincoln B. Young, editor, *Yearbook of Modern Poetry,* Young Publications, 1976; *Stepping Stones* (poems), Northwoods Press, 1976.

WORK IN PROGRESS: A book of poetry with wife, Mena; a novel set in Mississippi, completion expected in 1978.

SIDELIGHTS: McShan writes: "Latin America and the Caribbean have been my traveling grounds since 1971. My thirty-six foot sailboat has been the mode."

McSHANE, Philip 1932-

PERSONAL: Born February 18, 1932, in Cavan, Ireland; son of Philip (a policeman) and Agnes (Timoney) McShane; married Fiona Donovan, March 10, 1972. *Education:* National University of Ireland, B.Sc. (first class honors), 1955, M.Sc. (first class honors), 1956; St. Stanislaus College, lic.phil., 1959; Heythrop College, Oxford, S.T.L., 1964, D.Phil., 1968; graduate study in Paray-le-Monial, France, 1964-65. *Home:* 1397 Le Marchant St., Halifax, Nova Scotia, Canada. *Office:* Division of History, Philosophy, Political Studies, and Religious Studies, Mount St. Vincent University, Halifax, Nova Scotia, Canada.

CAREER: National University of Ireland, Dublin, lecturer in mathematical science, 1959-60; Milltown Institute of Philosophy and Theology, Dublin, professor of philosophy, 1967-72; Lonergan Centre, Toronto, Ontario, researcher, editor, and writer, 1972-74; Mount St. Vincent University, Halifax, Nova Scotia, associate professor, 1974-76, professor of philosophy, 1976—, chairman of Division of History, Philosophy, Political Studies, and Religious Studies, 1975—. Lecturer at York University, 1973-74.

WRITINGS: (With Garrett Borden) *Towards Self-Meaning*, Gill Macmillan, 1969; *Music That Is Soundless*, Milltown Institute, 1970, 2nd edition, University Press of America, 1977; *Randomness, Statistics, and Emergence*, Gill Macmillan, 1971; *Plants and Pianos*, Milltown Institute, 1971; (editor) *International Lonergan Congress, 1970*, Gill Macmillan, Volume I: *Foundations of Theology*, 1971, Volume II: *Language, Truth, and Meaning*, 1972; (contributor) Bernard Lonergan, *Method in Theology*, Darton, Longman & Todd, 1972; (contributor) Lonergan, *A Second Collection*, Darton, Longman & Todd, 1974; (author of introduction) Lonergan, *Introducing Bernard Lonergan*, Darton, Longman & Todd, 1974; (editor) Bernard Tyrrell, editor, *Bernard Lonergan's Philosophy of God*, Gill Macmillan, 1974; *Wealth of Self and Wealth of Nations: Self-Axis of the Great Ascent*, Exposition Press, 1975; *The Shaping of the Foundations: Being at Home in Transcendental Method*, University Press of America, 1977. Contributor to Philosophy and theology journals.

WORK IN PROGRESS: A study of "business cycle theory (especially Lonergan's unpublished contribution)"; a critique of Smith-Walras-Keynesian economics.

* * *

MEADOR, Roy 1929-

PERSONAL: Born April 23, 1929, in Cordell, Okla.; son of Walter Raymond (a carpenter) and Gladys (in politics; maiden name, Reed) Meador. *Education:* University of Southern California, A.B., 1951; Columbia University, M.A., 1972. *Politics:* "Reduce Human Suffering." *Religion:* "Questioning?" *Address:* P.O. Box 2045, Ann Arbor, Mich. 48106. *Office:* Gelman Instrument Co., 600 South Wagner Rd., Ann Arbor, Mich. 48106.

CAREER: Pfizer, Inc., New York City, advertising and technical writer, 1960-72; Gelman Instrument Co., Ann Arbor, Mich., advertising and technical writer, 1972—. *Military service:* U.S. Navy, 1951-54; served in Korea; became lieutenant. *Member:* National Guild of Bookworkers, Ann Arbor Bookbinders Guild.

WRITINGS: Future Energies, Ann Arbor Science Publishers, 1974; *Franklin: Revolutionary Scientist*, Ann Arbor Science Publishers, 1975; (editor with Howard Gordon) *Perspectives on the Energy Crisis*, Ann Arbor Science Pub-

lishers, Part I, 1977, Part II, in press; (with Bruce Watkins) *Technology and Human Values*, Ann Arbor Science Publishers, 1977. Contributor to *Newsday, Christian Science Monitor*, and *New York Times*. Member of editorial advisory board of Ann Arbor Science Publishers.

WORK IN PROGRESS: A Personal History of the Antarctic; Manual on Technical Writing; Energy Frontiers; a critical biography of H. M. Tomlinson.

SIDELIGHTS: Meador writes: "Having a book published and then another, confirmed what I saw hazily at fifteen, that for me no other activity will do except writing. In my future writing I want to understand and help others understand the challenge, the perils, and the beauty of our strange world and stranger lives. I want to write about what is going on in science to threaten us and enrich us. If my mind hides in caves for false safety, I want to leave the caves and help others leave. I hope through writing to contribute what I can in preserving a world worth living in and maybe even a human race to live here beyond the twentieth century. If I find anything true to say, I want to say it. If I find anything both true and funny to say, I want to shout it. We need a good laugh."

He explains his vocational interests thus: "Personalizing, explaining, defanging, and demystifying technology; doing what I can to keep reading alive in the age of picture boxes; learning and writing about energy for greater public awareness; exploring neglected corridors of history, science, literature, and writing about them."

AVOCATIONAL INTERESTS: Reading, the Arizona desert, book collecting, walking in New York City, bookbinding, music.

* * *

MEAGHER, Paul Kevin 1907-1976

1907—December 31, 1976; American Dominican priest, theologian, writer and editor best known for his co-editing the sixty volume English edition of the works of St. Thomas Aquinas. He was founder and rector of St. Albert's College in Oakland, Calif. He died in Washington, D.C. Obituaries: *Washington Post*, January 3, 1977.

* * *

MEAKIN, David 1943-

PERSONAL: Born August 3, 1943, in Hyde, England; son of Charles Edward (a personnel officer) and Elsie (Ratcliffe) Meakin; married Andree Laboube (a teacher), June 24, 1965; children: Philip Pierre. *Education:* Brasenose College, Oxford, B.A. (honors), 1965, B.Phil., 1967. *Politics:* Labour. *Religion:* None. *Home:* 44 Radnor Rd., Bristol 7, England. *Office:* Department of French, University of Bristol, Queens Rd., Bristol 8, England.

CAREER: University of Bristol, Bristol, England, lecturer in French, 1967—. *Member:* Association of University Teachers.

WRITINGS: Man and Work: Literature and Culture in Industrial Society, Holmes & Meier, 1976. Contributor to language and European studies journals.

WORK IN PROGRESS: Research on the French "new novel" and on the concept of "play" in modern philosophy and literary practice.

SIDELIGHTS: Meakin writes that he is preoccupied with "the social problems of work and leisure, and the reflection of these problems in literature. After looking at the *explicit* treatment of these themes in literature in my first book, I am now more concerned with the *implicit* commitment expressed in literary forms and modes of writing, and particularly with the ramifications of the play-principle as a means of liberation."

* * *

MECHANIC, Sylvia (Gertrude) 1920-

PERSONAL: Born August 4, 1920, in New York; daughter of Samuel (a realtor) and Fannie (Davidson) Mechanic. *Education:* Hofstra College (now University), B.A., 1942; Columbia University, B.S.L.S., 1943. *Office:* Brooklyn Public Library—Business Library, 280 Cadman Plaza W., Brooklyn, N.Y. 11201.

CAREER: Brooklyn Public Library, Brooklyn, N.Y., library assistant in History Division, 1943-45, chief of Social Science Division, 1946-53, chief of Science and Industry Division, 1953-61, in charge of Business Library, 1962—. Instructor at Columbia University, 1967-76; associate professor at Pratt University, 1977—. *Member:* American Library Association, Special Libraries Association (chairperson of business and finance group, 1967-68), New York Library Association, New York Library Club, Columbia University School of Library Science Alumni Association (member of board of directors, 1966-69).

WRITINGS: Annotated List of Selected Government Publications Available to Depository Libraries, H. W. Wilson, 1971. Contributor to *Financial Analyst's Handbook.* Contributor of articles and reviews to library journals.

SIDELIGHTS: Sylvia Mechanic writes: "I enjoy traveling and because I am especially interested in knitting and other handicrafts have found it a source of great pleasure to learn about the particular handicrafts and specialties in various areas. I was most pleased to be asked to take part in a film which was made by the U.S. Information Agency in Washington for the East African Library Association in Dar el Salaam."

BIOGRAPHICAL/CRITICAL SOURCES: Investment Dealers' Digest, April 15, 1975; *New York Times,* May 4, 1975.

* * *

MEDEARIS, Mary 1915-

PERSONAL: Born May 31, 1915, in North Little Rock, Ark.; daughter of Robert Summerfield (a physician) and Myrtle (a piano teacher; maiden name, Hendricks) Medearis; married Richard Franklin Reeves (divorced, 1968); children: Richard, Phoebe (Mrs. Donald Wood), Robert, Jennifer (Mrs. Mark Allen), Patrick (adopted son), Suzanne Reeves Koval (adopted daughter). *Education:* Juilliard School, student, 1941; also attended University of Arkansas. *Religion:* Society of Friends (Quakers). *Home address:* P.O. Box 134, Washington, Ark. 71862.

CAREER: Piano teacher and writer. Taught at private schools in Gwynedd Valley, Pa., 1956-59, and in Philadelphia, Pa., 1960-63.

WRITINGS: Big Doc's Girl (juvenile), Lippincott, 1942; *Washington, Arkansas: History on the Southwest Trail,* Etter Printing, 1976.

Work anthologized in *Neighborhoods* (textbooks), edited by Laurence Senesh.

WORK IN PROGRESS: Research on Hempstead County, Ark., on the early settling of the state in the area of the Red River Valley, and on cotton culture and plantation areas of Arkansas as contrasted to the Ozark region.

SIDELIGHTS: Mary Medearis writes: "My motivation in writing *Big Doc's Girl* [which has been made into a television drama] was almost one of anger; Arkansas was chiefly known as a place of hillbillies and barefooted fiddlers sitting on a barrel in front of a run-down cabin—and I knew that there was beauty and dignity in those people and that state. Therefore, I wrote of my childhood among the 'have not' people and tried to show the unique simplicity and character of my people.

"I'm still trying to do that in my new project; Arkansas was also a plantation and cotton-culture state . . . down near the Texas and Louisiana lowlands, and that part of the history has never been told. When one speaks of Arkansas, the first thought in the mind is 'Ozarks'. . . .

"My dream is to have a Southwest Arkansas Research Library established here in the old courthouse so that another side of Arkansas can become known."

* * *

MEDINA, Jeremy T(yler) 1942-

PERSONAL: Born August 1, 1942, in Orange, N.J.; son of Standish F. and Hope T. (Kiesewetter) Medina; married Jacquelyn N. Savoie, July 2, 1966; children: Carolyn Tracy, Kristin Hollyer. *Education:* Princeton University, A.B., 1964; Middlebury College, M.A., 1966; University of Pennsylvania, Ph.D., 1970. *Home:* 13 Stryker Lane, Clinton, N.Y. 13323. *Office:* Department of Romance Languages, Hamilton College, Clinton, N.Y. 13323.

CAREER: Teacher of Spanish at a private school in Andover, Mass., 1964-65; University of Pennsylvania, Philadelphia, instructor in Spanish, 1967; Hamilton College, Clinton, N.Y., instructor, 1968-70, assistant professor, 1970-75, associate professor of Spanish, 1975—, founder and general director of year-in-Spain program. *Member:* Modern Language Association of America, American Association of Teachers of Spanish and Portuguese, American Association of University Professors.

WRITINGS: Introduction to Spanish Literature: An Analytical Approach, Harper, 1974. Contributor to Romance language and Spanish studies journals, including *Hispania* and *Romance Notes.*

WORK IN PROGRESS: Spanish Realism: The Theory and Practice of a Concept in the Nineteenth Century; research on Blasco Ibanez' *Flor de mayo,* and on methods of introducing literature in a foreign language.

* * *

MEDVEDEV, Zhores A(leksandrovich) 1925-

PERSONAL: Born November 14, 1925, in Tbilisis, U.S.S.R.; forced to stay as exile in England, 1973; son of Alexandr Romanovich (a philosopher) and Yulia (a musician; maiden name, Reimann) Medvedev; married Margarita Nikolaevna Busina (a research assistant), October 25, 1951; children: Alexander, Dmitri. *Education:* Moscow Agricultural Academy, B.Sc., 1950; Institute of Physiology of Plants, Ph.D., 1951. *Office:* National Institute for Medical Research, Mill Hill, London NW7 1AA, England.

CAREER: Moscow Agricultural Academy, Moscow, U.S.S.R., senior research scientist, 1951-62; Institute of Medical Radiology, Obninsk, U.S.S.R., head of laboratory of molecular radiobiology, 1963-69; Institute of Biochemistry and Physiology of Farm Animals, Borovsk, U.S.S.R., senior research scientist, 1970-72; National Institute for Medical Research, London, England, senior research scientist, 1973—. *Military service:* Soviet Army, 1943. *Member:* American Gerontological Society, American Society for Cell Biology. *Awards, honors:* Special prize from Moscow Naturalist Society, 1965; Mendel Medal from Moravian Mendel Museum, 1969.

WRITINGS: Biosintez belkov i problemy ontogeneza, Izd "Medicina" (Moscow), 1963, translation by Ann Synge published as *Protein Biosynthesis and Problems of Heredity, Development, and Ageing,* Plenum, 1966, abridged translation by U.S. Joint Publications service published as *Protein Biosynthesis and the Problems of Ontogenesis,* CCM Information Corp., 1970; *Molekuliarno-geneticheskie mekhanizmy razvitiia,* Izd "Medicina" (Moscow), 1968, translation by Basil Haigh published as *Molecular-Genetic Mechanisms of Development,* Plenum, 1970; *The Rise and Fall of T. D. Lysenko,* translated from the manuscript by I. Michael Lerner with Lucy G. Lawrence, Columbia University Press, 1969; *The Medvedev Papers: Fruitful Meetings Between Scientists of the World* [and] *Secrecy of Correspondence Is Guaranteed by Law,* translated by Vera Rich, Macmillan, 1971, published in the original Russian as *Mezhdunarodnoe sotrudnichestvo uchenykh i natsional'nye granitsy: Taina perepiski ochranjaltsa zakonom,* Macmillan, 1972; (with brother, Roy A. Medvedev) *Kto Sumasshedshil?,* Macmillan, 1971, translation by Ellen de Kadt published as *A Question of Madness,* Knopf, 1971; *Desiat' let posie "Odnogo dnia Ivana Denisovicha,"* Macmillan, 1973, translation by Hilary Sternberg published as *Ten Years After Ivan Denisovich,* Knopf, 1973; (with R. A. Medvedev) *Khrushchev: Gody u vlasti,* Xerox University Microfilms, 1975, translation by Andrew R. Durkin published as *Khruschev: The Years in Power,* Columbia University Press, 1976.

WORK IN PROGRESS: Soviet Science, a political history, completion expected in 1977; *Molecular and Genetic Aspects of Aging,* a monograph, completion expected in 1978.

SIDELIGHTS: Medvedev told *CA* he did not emigrate to Britain. "I was officially permitted to accept a one-year invitation from the National Institute for Medical Research here in England as an attached scientist (this is an unpaid position). I arrived here and after six months I was deprived of my Soviet citizenship and had my passport confiscated. I certainly intended to return at the end of my one-year term. When I lost my citizenship the British Home Office provided me with a travel certificate of identity because I am now a stateless person. I do not plan to apply for British citizenship. My wife and son still have Soviet passports.

"Originally I felt very sad about the loss of my citizenship. I wasn't employed in Britain, and I did not feel that I had the moral right to ask for employment because I could see many British Ph.D. research workers had difficulties finding jobs. I decided to continue research work, however I did not make an application for a working permit because I hoped to support myself from fees and royalties. My colleagues at the institute decided to solve the problem and I was made a member of the senior staff. Now that I am used to life in Britain and engaged in research, I feel better. Scientific research is the same in all countries."

Medvedev continues to communicate with his colleagues and friends in the U.S.S.R. and has started a small press to publish collections of essays by some Soviet dissident writers in Russian.

When asked about his feelings toward the increased emigration of scientific and literary figures from Russia, Medvedev replied: "I admit that this is a sad development, however, better than imprisonment in labor camps or mental institutions. Few literary figures have been expelled or have emigrated, the majority continue to live and work inside the U.S.S.R. I do not think that the emigration trend will be long-term; life abroad happens not to be as easy as some emigrants expect."

Medvedev's loss of Soviet citizenship undoubtedly occurred because of the controversial nature of his books on social problems in the U.S.S.R. *CA* asked Medvedev if it wasn't unusual for a scientist to be writing about social problems. "I do not feel that my vocational and avocational writing is a strange mixture, because I write social works mostly about scientific problems; about the position of science and scientists in society, using some of my own experiences as a scientist for background in the initial analysis.

"As a scientist and geneticist I started to feel that science would probably soon reach the point where its interference into the life processes would be counterproductive if a properly designed governing policy was not implemented. A heavily overcrowded planet, ninety-five percent urbanized with nuclear energy as the main source of energy and with all aspects of life highly computerized, is not too pleasant a place for human life. The life of any individual soon will be predictable from birth to death. Medicine, able to cure almost everything, will make the load of accumulated defects too heavy in the next two or three centuries. The artificial prolongation of life, which looked like a very bright idea when I started research in aging about twenty-five years ago, has now lost its attractiveness for me. This is because I now know that the aging process is so multiform and complex that the real technology and chemistry of its prevention by artificial interference must be too complex and expensive. It would be the privilege of a few, not the method for the majority. I also was deeply concerned about the fact that most research is now either directly or indirectly related to military projects and objectives for power."

* * *

MEERLOO, Joost A(braham) M(aurits) 1903-1976

March 14, 1903—November 17, 1976; Dutch-born psychiatrist, author, and expert on "brainwashing" best known for *The Rape of the Mind.* After escaping the Nazis in 1942, Meerloo became chief of the psychological department for the Netherlands army-in-exile, and worked with Nazi torture victims. He later taught at Columbia University and New School for Social Research. Obituaries: *New York Times,* November 26, 1976; *Current Biography,* February, 1977. (See index for previous *CA* sketch)

* * *

MEGLIN, Nick 1935-

PERSONAL: Born July 30, 1935, in Brooklyn, N.Y.; married Lucille Guerriero (a medical secretary), December 28, 1956; children: Diane Elizabeth, Christopher Allard. *Education:* Brooklyn/Queens College (now of the City University of New York), A.A., 1956; School of Visual Arts, B.F.A., 1976. *Politics:* "Worked with Kennedys, Lindsay, Lowenstein." *Home:* 155 Pebble Lane, Hewlett, N.Y. 11557. *Agent:* Paul Heller, William Morris Agency, 1350 Avenue of the Americas, New York, N.Y. 10019. *Office: Mad,* 485 Madison Ave., New York, N.Y. 10022.

CAREER: Mad (magazine), New York, N.Y., editor,

1956—. Free-lance writer, 1954—; free-lance illustrator, 1956—. Instructor at School of Visual Arts, 1972—. *Military service:* U.S. Army, illustrator, 1958-60. *Member:* American Society of Composers, Authors and Publishers, Society of Illustrators, National Eagle Scout Association.

WRITINGS: On-the-Spot Drawing, Watson-Guptill, 1972; *Fountain Pen Drawing,* Grosset, 1973; *Superfan,* New American Library, 1973; *Superfan . . . Again!,* New American Library, 1974; *The Art of Humorous Illustration,* Watson-Guptill, 1975; *Honor the Godfather,* New American Library, 1976; *Mad Stew,* Warner Paperback, 1977; *The Pen,* Nostalgia Press, in press; *Rotten Rhymes,* New American Library, in press. Author of animated films and recorded songs. Contributor to magazines.

SIDELIGHTS: Meglin comments: "I have always worked in areas and on subjects I have first hand experience in—illustration, sports, humor, opera, and theater. I consider myself a writer who draws rather than an illustrator who writes, since my drawing is of a serious approach and much of my writing is in a lighter vein. I have written for performers but have never had the desire to perform myself, although someday I'd like to appear as an 'extra' on the Met Opera stage. I follow the work of Fellini, Stephen Sondheim, the composer Nino Rota, Robert Klein, Woody Allen and the field of illustration in general. I learned a lot about my life from *est* and Tim Gallwey's *Inner Game of Tennis.* I will never get on the court with Connors or Ashe!"

AVOCATIONAL INTERESTS: Tennis, camping, theater.

*   *   *

MEIJER, M(arinus) J(ohan)   1912-

PERSONAL: Born September 28, 1912, in Alphen, Netherlands; son of Marinus (a merchant) and Dirkje (Spijkcr) Meijer; married Dinah Catharine Elisabeth Bolkestein, September 1, 1947; children: Martje, Roland. *Education:* University of Leiden, LL.M., 1935, B.A., 1938; University of Indonesia, Ph.D., 1950. *Home:* Nico Bovenweg 4, Oosterbeek, Netherlands.

CAREER: University of Indonesia, Djakarta, reader in Chinese history, 1947-54; Netherlands Diplomatic Service, first secretary in Peking, 1955-58, and Tokyo, 1958-62; University of Washington, Seattle, research professor, 1962-64; Netherlands Diplomatic Service, secretary in Hong Kong, 1964-68, consul, 1968-70, counsellor, 1970-72, minister in Seoul, South Korea, 1972-73; writer, 1973—. *Member:* Netherlands-Korean Society, Association for the Study of European Criminal Law in Its Historical Development.

WRITINGS: The Introduction of Modern Criminal Law in China, Kon. Drukkerij de Unie, 1949; *Marriage Law and Policy in the Chinese People's Republic,* Hong Kong University Press, 1970; (contributor) Jerome Allen Cohen, editor, *Contemporary Chinese Law,* Harvard University Press, 1970; *Slavery in China During the Ch'ing Dynasty,* Harvard University Press, in press.

WORK IN PROGRESS: "Crimes Against Human Life," in *Traditional Chinese Criminal Law.*

SIDELIGHTS: Meijer writes: "Finally I have the opportunity to devote all my time to the study of Chinese traditional law and its theoretical foundations and to try to compare its evolution with that of the criminal law in Europe."

BIOGRAPHICAL/CRITICAL SOURCES: Hong Kong Law Journal, Volume II, number 2, 1972; *China Quarterly,* autumn, 1973.

MEILEN, Bill   1932-

PERSONAL: Born September 16, 1932, in Wales; son of William Thomas (a Merchant Navy officer) and Lilian Nancy Georgina (Poole) Mudd; married Rhuanedd Gwladys James (a music teacher), March 12, 1959 (divorced); children: Lisa Angharad, Lara Myfanwy. *Education:* Attended Heswell Naval Training School, 1948-50, and Cardiff College of Music and Drama, 1955-57; licentiate of Trinity College of Music (London). *Politics:* Welsh Nationalist ("Plaid Cymru"). *Home:* 608 College Plaza II, 8210 111th St., Edmonton, Alberta, Canada. *Agent:* Jonathan Clowes, 22 New Cavendish St., London W.1, England. *Office:* Department of Drama, University of Alberta, Edmonton, Alberta, Canada.

CAREER: Professional actor in London, England, 1954-69; University of Alberta, Edmonton, associate professor of drama and dialects, 1969—. Free-lance television playwright, 1964—, novelist, 1965—; theater producer and director and radio broadcaster. Director of KANTA 4 (film company) and of Alberta Contemporary Dance Theatre; former member of court of governors of Welsh National Theatre; founder and administrative director of Welsh Artists Workshop; administrator of Artists' Aid for Aberfan. *Military service:* French Foreign Legion, 1950-51; served in Algeria and Indo-China. British Army, 1951-54; served in Korea. *Member:* Association of Canadian Television and Radio Artists (past president), Actors' Equity Association (Canada), Canadian Association of University Teachers, British Actors' Equity (founder and chairman of Welsh Committee), Writer's Guild of Great Britain (founder and chairman of Wales and West of England Committee), Welsh Academy. *Awards, honors:* Nominated for Academy Award for his role in "Six-Sided Triangle."

WRITINGS: The Division, Panther Books, 1967; *Moving On,* Sphere Books, 1968; *The Bullpen,* Sphere Books, 1968; *Eye of Grass,* Sphere Books, 1969; *Delta Two,* Sphere Books, 1970. Also author of *Dialects and Accents for the Performer: A Handbook for the Actor,* 1975; *Doctor Hit* (novel), 1975; *Postdawn* (novel), 1975; *Walk on a Stony Road* (poems), 1975.

Films: "Chango Jade," 1975; "Whiteout," 1975.

Television plays: "Moving On," for British Broadcasting Corp.; "The Division," Granada Television; "Sayonara Harada Hideko," BBC-TV; "Practise to Deceive," BBC-TV; "The Beyond" series (in which he played the lead role), Canadian Broadcasting Corp.; "The Beachcomber" (several episodes of the series), CBC-TV.

Short stories and poems represented in anthologies; author of audio programs on poetry, theater, and human interest for CKUA-Radio; cultural critic and reviewer for Canadian Broadcasting Corp. Radio, 1969-73; personal columnist for *Thomson Press;* contributor of stories, poems, and articles to magazines. Editor of *Alta 74* (poetry journal).

SIDELIGHTS: Meilen writes: "I see myself as a chronologer of the time through which I am passing, with a strong tendency to favour the underdog. My feeling is that I have a duty to bring to light the flaws in society that have most strongly affected me, and write from experience for the most part. The catalyst that first caused me to write was anger against militarism, and for the rights of lesser folk. I am deeply concerned with the survival of ethnic culture. My current poetry deals mainly with the North American Indian."

MELEZH, Ivan 1921(?)-1976

1921(?)—August, 1976; Russian novelist considered by critics to be one of the best writers in the Byelorussian language. He won the Lenin Prize for *People in the Swamp* and *The Breathing of the Storm*. He died in Minsk, Russia. Obituaries: *New York Times*, August 13, 1976; *Washington Post*, August 14, 1976; *AB Bookman's Weekly*, October 4, 1976.

* * *

MELLON, James R(oss) 1942-

PERSONAL: Born June 25, 1942, in Philadelphia, Pa.; son of Matthew and Gertrud (Altegoer) Mellon. *Education:* Yale University, B.A., 1964. *Politics:* "Free thinker." *Religion:* Non-denominational. *Home:* 1035 Fifth Ave., New York, N.Y. 10028.

CAREER: Writer. *Member:* Kenya Wildlife Society, East African Professional Hunters' Association, Friends of the Serengeti National Park, Rolling Rock Club. *Awards, honors:* Weatherby Award, 1972, for big game hunting.

WRITINGS: African Hunter, Harcourt, 1975.

WORK IN PROGRESS: A book of photographs of Abraham Lincoln, publication by Viking expected in 1978.

SIDELIGHTS: Mellon told *CA:* "My interest in zoology, in Africa generally, and in hunting in particular, provided the motivation for my first book. However, the period of my life when I was concerned with these preoccupations has ended." *CA* asked Mellon if he felt new gun laws, such as the 1977 laws in Kenya forbidding the use of firearms for hunting, would help preserve African wildlife. "As to developments in Kenya," he answered, "I will only say that to preserve wildlife there on a scale comparable to the past would require reversing the principal trends of the 20th century: namely the trends towards ever greater human numbers with the resulting ecological disruptions, also the trend toward ever greater exploitation of natural resources, the conversion of wildlife habitat to agricultural land, and of course increasing pollution of the environment and many kinds of environmental rape, all related directly or indirectly to increasing human numbers. Against this background, the regulations which the government just made will have as little effect in the long run as those they made in the past or will make in the future."

"My forthcoming book," Mellon added, "arises from a different set of interests: antique photography, history, and a fascination with the face of Lincoln. I became interested in Lincoln photographs first because of the extraordinary face that Lincoln had, secondly because of the astounding quality of many of the photographs, and finally, in the way of background, because I have always been interested in antique photography anyway. I must mention also that the deterioration and destruction, not to mention theft, of many of the best portrait photos necessitates that they be quickly and exquisitely preserved in book form."

* * *

MELNICK, Donald 1926-1977

1926—May 19, 1977; American consultant, physicist, and author. He died in Silver Spring, Md. Obituaries: *Washington Post*, June 8, 1977.

* * *

MELTON, David 1934-

PERSONAL: Born April 10, 1934, in Springfield, Mo.; son of Denny (a recreational director) and Marguerite (Pearson) Melton; married Nancy Thatch (a secretary and editor), October 15, 1954; children: Todd David, Teresa Marguerite. *Education:* Southwest Missouri State University, B.S., 1956. *Home:* 7422 Rosewood Circle, Prairie Village, Kan. 66208. *Agent:* Mrs. Carlton Cole, Waldorf Towers, Park Ave., New York, N.Y.

CAREER: Elementary school teacher in Burnt Hills, N.Y., 1956-57; Burger-Baird Engraving Co., Kansas City, Mo., sales representative, 1957; Glenn Printing Co., Kansas City, salesman, 1958-62, art director, production coordinator, and graphics designer, 1962-67, vice-president, 1967-69; writer and illustrator, 1969—. Has appeared on local and national television and radio programs.

WRITINGS: Todd, Prentice-Hall, 1968; *I'll Show You the Morning Sun* (poems; self-illustrated), Stanyan, 1971; *Judy: A Remembrance* (biography of Judy Garland; self-illustrated), Stanyan, 1971; *When Children Need Help,* Crowell, 1972; *This Man, Jesus* (self-illustrated juvenile), McGraw, 1972; *Burn the Schools, Save the Children,* Crowell, 1975; (with Raymundo Veras) *Children of Dreams, Children of Hope,* Regnery, 1975; (editor) *Happy Birthday, America!* (art work and writing by elementary school children), Independence Press (Independence, Mo.), 1976; *A Boy Called Hopeless* (juvenile novel), Herald House, 1976; *How to Help Your Preschooler Learn More ... Faster ... and Better* (self-illustrated), McKay, 1976; *And God Created* (self-illustrated), Herald House, 1976.

Illustrator: Sybil Leek, *How to Be Your Own Astrologer,* Cowles Book Co., 1970; Glenn J. Doman, *What to Do About Your Brain-Injured Child,* Doubleday, 1974. Contributor of articles, illustrations, and stories to adult and juvenile magazines, including *On Film, Unity, Wee Wisdom,* and *Coronet.* Graphics designer for *Ruberoid News,* 1959-64.

SIDELIGHTS: Melton's first book is an account of the problems and the triumphs he and his wife experienced in seeking educational and medical help for their brain-injured son. Several of his other books concern brain-injured and mongoloid children and parent-child relationships.

Melton is also an artist. He has created book jackets, visual aids for educational purposes, and produced thirteen paintings of the astrological sun signs with Sybil Leek. In 1962, he designed "Spacerelator," a mobile of the solar system, and the visual aids to accompany it. It has been widely used in the United States and was displayed in Prague in 1963. His books have been published in Germany, Italy, and Brazil.

* * *

MENARD, Jean 1930(?)-1977

1930(?)—May 27, 1977; Canadian poet, author of French-language books, and professor. He was a professor at University of Ottawa since 1955. He died in Ottawa, Ontario. Obituaries: *New York Times*, May 27, 1977.

* * *

MENG, Heinz (Karl) 1924-

PERSONAL: Born February 25, 1924, in Baden, Germany; came to the United States in 1929, naturalized citizen, 1953; son of Richard (a chauffeur) and Elsie (a cook; maiden name, Merkel) Meng; married Elizabeth A. Metz (a professor), June 20, 1953; children: Robin Elizabeth, Peter-Paul. *Education:* Cornell University, B.S., 1947, Ph.D., 1951. *Home:* 10 Joalyn Rd., New Paltz, N.Y. 12561. *Office:* Department of Biology, State University of New York College at New Paltz, New Paltz, N.Y. 12561.

CAREER: State University of New York College at New Paltz, assistant professor, 1951-56, associate professor, 1956-61, professor of biology, 1961—. *Member:* North American Falconers Association, American Ornithologists Union (associate member), Wildlife Society (associate member), Wilson Ornithological Society (associate member), Cooper Ornithological Society (associate member).

WRITINGS: (With John Kaufman) *Falcons Return: Restoring an Endangered Species,* Morrow, 1975. Contributor of photographs to bird books.

WORK IN PROGRESS: Two motion pictures, one on birds of prey and one on releasing captive peregrine falcons to the wild; articles on falconry and its importance in preserving the endangered peregrine falcon.

AVOCATIONAL INTERESTS: Falconry, archery, fly-fishing.

* * *

MENZEL, Donald H(oward) 1901-1976

April 11, 1901—December 14, 1976; American astronomer specializing in the sun and its corona, educator, and author of technical books as well as popular works in his field. He led expeditions worldwide to view total solar eclipses. In recognition of Menzel's contributions in his field, the International Astronomical Union's Minor Planet Center recently named an asteroid for him. He died in Boston, Mass. Obituaries: *New York Times,* December 16, 1976; *Time,* December 27, 1976; *Current Biography,* March, 1977. (*CAP*-2; earlier sketch in *CA*-21/22)

* * *

MEREWITZ, Leonard (Alan) 1943-

PERSONAL: Born May 19, 1943, in New York, N.Y.; son of Max H. (a caterer) and Harriet (a caterer; maiden name, Nitowsky) Merewitz. *Education:* Harvard University, B.A. (magna cum laude), 1964; University of California, Berkeley, Ph.D., 1969. *Home:* 2529 North 23rd Rd., Arlington, Va. 22207. *Office:* 12 Willowdale Ave., Port Washington, N.Y. 11050.

CAREER: University of California, Berkeley, assistant professor of business administration, 1968-75; Motor Vehicles Manufacturers Association, Detroit, Mich., senior economist, 1975-76; J. W. Wilson and Associates, Inc., Washington, D.C., director of transportation studies, 1976—. Economist for U.S. Postal Rate Commission, 1973; consultant to RAND Corp. and Institute for Defense Analyses.

MEMBER: American Statistical Association, American Economic Association, National Tax Association, Transportation Research Forum, Phi Beta Kappa. *Awards, honors:* Woodrow Wilson fellowships, 1965, 1969; National Science Foundation fellowships, 1966, 1967; Sears, Roebuck faculty fellowship, 1973.

WRITINGS: (With Stephen H. Sosnick) *The Budget's New Clothes,* Rand McNally, 1971; (with Theodore E. Keeler) *The Full Costs of Urban Transport,* Institute for Urban Regional Development, 1975. Also author, with Richard Parker, of *The Economics of Environmental Restrictions on the Use of Urban Land,* 1973. Contributor to statistics and economics journals.

* * *

MERKIN, Donald H. 1945-

PERSONAL: Born November 12, 1945, in Bronx, N.Y.; son of Eugene (an aerospace engineer) and Hortense Ruth (Erdrich) Merkin; married Carol Ann Williams (an embroiderer and seamstress), July 22, 1967; children: Daniel Hansen. *Education:* Pennsylvania State University, student, 1963-65; Parsons College, B.A., 1968; Colorado State University, M.S., 1972; Cornell University, Ph.D., 1974; Universidad Autonoma de Ciudad Juarez, medical student, 1976—. *Home address:* c/o P.O. Box 113, Bellvue, Colo. 80521. *Office:* Bridgeport Hospital, House Staff Mail, 267 Grant St., Bridgeport, Conn. 06602.

CAREER: Boulder County Juvenile Court, Boulder, Colo., research assistant, 1967; Pennsylvania State Office of Family Services, Philadelphia, child welfare worker, 1968; Cornell University, Ithaca, N.Y., staff member of Demographic Institute and Workshop, for International Population Program, 1972; University of Southern Colorado, Pueblo, assistant professor of sociology-anthropology, 1973-74; Southern Illinois University, Springfield, assistant professor of epidemiology at School of Medicine, 1974-76; Group Health of El Paso, Inc., El Paso, Tex., assistant administrator, 1977—. Assistant professor at University of Colorado and Beth-El School of Nursing, both 1973-74. Member of Illinois Family Planning Council, 1975, vice-chairman, 1976; member of epidemiology and statistics panel of Illinois Cancer Council, 1975-76; member of board of directors of Springfield area Planned Parenthood, 1975-76. *Military service:* U.S. Marine Corps, 1969.

MEMBER: Population Association of America, American Public Health Association, Institute for Society, Ethics and the Life Sciences (Hastings Center), American Medical Students Association. *Awards, honors:* Exchange student to Brazil, 1962; Fulbright fellowship, India, summer, 1974.

WRITINGS: *Needs Assessment for the Colorado Elderly: Chaffee, Custer, Fremont and Lake Counties, Colorado,* Southern Colorado State College, 1974; *Pregnancy as a Disease: The Pill in Society,* Kennikat, 1976.

WORK IN PROGRESS: An analysis of multi-disciplinary data on iatrogenic effects of diethystilbestrol (DES), especially in relation to transplacental induction of clear-cell adenocarcinoma of the vagina in girls and young women.

SIDELIGHTS: Merkin writes: "Due to many experiences while studying and traveling in Central and South America and in India, and my life-long interest in cross-cultural systems of health and medical care, I took the opportunity to enroll as a medical student in an accelerated bi-lingual program for Ph.D.'s in Mexico. I have long been intrigued by the choices, values, and practices whereby societies intervene to provide preventive and allopathic medical care to their populations. Having taught and conducted research at universities, a nursing school, and a medical school, and seen epidemiological problems from the classroom, I elected to become a physician myself, and to use some of my ideas regarding quality medical care, accessibility, and professionalism. My special concerns include maternal and child health services, and concern with iatrogenic effects of short-sighted biomedical interventions which treat symptoms to the exclusion of many other considerations. It was precisely these issues which motivated my first book on the birth control pill.... And when I am able, my second book on the 'morning-after pill.' I take very seriously the admonition taught physicians, 'First, do no harm.' Furthermore, I believe that these issues are not solely the domain of the academician or the medical scientist, but that they must be written about and discussed at a level which permits the literate citizen to inform himself and to thereby make better choices regarding his or her own well-being, exactly in those areas of life and death, and where some control is possible.

"My interest is in primary care, the doctor-patient relationship, education for the patient and the citizenry, and the delegation of tasks, responsibility, and accountability. I write, not as an alarmist, but as a commentator on what appear to be recurring dilemmas brought about by improper premises. My contention is that with proper education and the use of currently existing technology, the population and its physicians can forestall many nagging problems; lack of childhood immunizations, dietary modification, alcohol and cigarette consumption, diabetes mellitus, blindness, hypertension, and occupational hazards are prime examples of what I mean.

"My education has included work in sociology, psychology, international nutrition and socio-economic development, demography, and medicine. I believe that a well-rounded, flexible, and humble approach to both social and medical problems offers the physician and his or her patients a more effective health and medical care system—one which is less exploitive, more personal, and better fitted to the great diversity of problems and people that fall within its boundaries."

AVOCATIONAL INTERESTS: Photography, travel, skin diving, hunting and fishing.

* * *

MERNIT, Susan 1953-

PERSONAL: Surname is accented on second syllable,; born January 23, 1953, in New York; daughter of Arthur Harold and Marilyn (Riback) Mernit; married Spencer Jarrett, June, 1977. *Education:* Bard College, B.A., 1974. *Politics:* Liberal. *Religion:* Jewish (Conservative). *Residence:* Delaware, Ohio.

CAREER: Academy of American Poets, New York, N.Y., program associate, 1974-76; poet in residence and member of artists in the schools programs in Columbus, Ohio, 1976—. Has worked as street musician; has given readings at elementary and secondary schools in New York and New England, at colleges, and at fine arts galleries. *Member:* Academy of American Poets, Poets and Writers.

WRITINGS: The Angelic Alphabet (poetry), Tree Books, 1976.

Poems anthologized in *It Is the Poem Singing into Your Eyes,* edited by Arnold Adoff, Harper, 1972; *Twentieth Century Jewish Poetry,* edited by Howard Schwartz and Anthony Rudolph, Avon, 1977; *The Big Jewish Book,* edited by Jerome Rothenberg, Doubleday, 1977; *Women Poets,* edited by Adoff, Macmillan, 1977. Contributor of poems and reviews to more than thirty magazines, including *Response, Isthmus, Truck, Hanging Loose, Long House,* and *Bard Review,* and to newspapers. Editor of *Hand Book,* 1976—.

WORK IN PROGRESS: A novel; a collection of essays; a cycle of poems about the early Christian martyrs; "Snake Corn," a poem cycle "that brings together the Serpent Mound, midwestern corn, native American Indians, and our western snake-mythology via America."

SIDELIGHTS: Susan Mernit writes: "America punishes the artist, especially the woman artist, by asking her to trade creativity for mental health, as though the two were incompatible. Sylvia Plath was made an example of—the woman artist who went too far, was too successful and therefore lost her wholeness. This is rubbish. The most important part of my growth as an artist has been in accepting my right to a regular life as well as a creative one. My writing comes out of a central stable core of me.... The mystical systems of the Kabbala and various spiritual concepts have spurred my writing. Magic is a way of perception and seeing beyond the merely physical to the forms beyond. We lose too much of that seeing in our desire for 'facts'. Poetry is shorthand for a form of intimate emotional expression that uses language as art.

"I've begun to travel, after living most of my life around New York. I am currently teaching poetry in Ohio and this seems to be the first leg of a long vagabond through America, year by year. Rootless, it is easy to go back to the cultural roots of the family and the American roots of the ground. We are too homogenized these days—don't see the great land mass of corn and stone cities as having the effect it does."

AVOCATIONAL INTERESTS: Forestry, silversmithing, pottery, winter hiking, her Jewish heritage, reading anthropology, ethnology, and history of religion.

* * *

MERRILL, Boynton, Jr. 1925-

PERSONAL: Born October 21, 1925, in Boston, Mass.; son of Boynton (a clergyman) and Virginia (Worsham) Merrill; married Marian Royster, November 12, 1952; children: Clark Addison, Frances Boynton. *Education:* Dartmouth College, B.A., 1950. *Religion:* Protestant. *Home address:* Route 4, Box 52A, Henderson, Ky. 42420.

CAREER: Farm manager in Henderson, Ky., 1950-65; self-employed, in agriculture and property development, in Henderson, 1960—; writer, 1970—. *Military service:* U.S. Navy, electronic technician, in aviation, 1944-46. *Member:* Kentucky Historical Society, Filson Club.

WRITINGS: A Bestiary (poems), University Press of Kentucky, 1976; *Jefferson's Nephews: A Frontier Tragedy,* Princeton University Press, 1976.

WORK IN PROGRESS: Fiction; a biography; poems and essays.

SIDELIGHTS: Boynton told *CA* that he is concerned about how Americans use their land and resources and how these resources have influenced American character. *Avocational interests:* Horticulture, outdoor sports, handcrafts, reading ("from comics to classics").

* * *

MERRITT, Muriel 1905-

PERSONAL: Born August 23, 1905, in Ulysses, Pa.; daughter of Harry E. (a Young Men's Christian Association secretary) and Alice Edna (a teacher; maiden name, Hosley) Merritt; married Robert A. Soule, February 13, 1932 (divorced). *Education:* State University of New York College at Geneseo, student, 1923-25; Albany State Teachers College, B.S.Ed., 1936; Buffalo State Teachers College, M.S., 1957. *Religion:* Episcopal. *Home:* 1566 Wehrle Dr., Williamsville, N.Y. 14221.

CAREER: Elementary school teacher in Ivondequoit, N.Y., 1925-28, Maplewood, N.J., 1929-31, Pelham Manor, N.Y., 1932, Kenmore, N.Y., and Buffalo, N.Y., 1943-46, and in Williamsville, N.Y., 1947-72; writer, 1972—. *Member:* American Association of University Women.

WRITINGS: Turn But a Stone (adult), Henry Stewart, 1970; *Give Them Wings: Poems for Children* (self-illustrated), Henry Stewart, 1973. Contributor to education and religious magazines.

WORK IN PROGRESS: The Light and the Shadow, poems.

SIDELIGHTS: Muriel Merritt writes: "Dr. Albert Schweitzer has influenced me with his philosophy of 'Reverence for Life.' I write about the wonders of nature, and my thoughts on the philosophy of life." Avocational interests: Caribbean and European travel.

* * *

METZNER, Ralph 1936-

PERSONAL: Born May 18, 1936, in Berlin, Germany; came to the United States in 1958, naturalized citizen, 1968; son of Wolfgang (a publisher) and Jill (Laurie) Metzner. Education: Oxford University, B.A. (first class honors), 1958; Harvard University, Ph.D., 1962, postdoctoral study, 1962-63; attended School of Actualism, 1968. Politics: "How to Make the World Work." Religion: "Cosmic consciousness." Agent: John Brockman Associates, Inc., 241 Central Park W., New York, N.Y. 10024. Office: 312 Gold Mine Dr., San Francisco, Calif. 94131.

CAREER: Concord State Prison, Concord, Mass., psychology intern, 1961-63; Castalia Foundation, Millbrook, N.Y., director of research, 1963-65; Psychedelic Review, New York City, editor and publisher, 1965-67; Mendocino State Hospital, Ukiah, Calif., staff psychologist, 1967-68; Kaiser Permanente Medical Group, Hayward, Calif., staff psychologist, 1968-69; Fairview State Hospital, Costa Mesa, Calif., staff psychologist, 1970-72; Star Mountain School (high school for emotionally disturbed adolescents), Mountain Center, Calif., founder and director, 1972-73; School of Actualism, Los Angeles, Calif., staff teacher in Los Angeles and San Francisco, 1973—. Co-director of Institute of Group and Family Studies, 1968-69; private practice in psychotherapy and consultant in Palo Alto, Calif., 1968-69. Psychologist and instructor at Stanford University, 1968-69; associate professor at California Institute of Asian Studies, 1975—. Lecturer and consultant on meditation, consciousness, transpersonal psychology, and parapsychology, 1971-75. Member: Association for Transpersonal Psychology, Association for Humanistic Psychology, National Council for Geocosmic Research, California State Psychological Association.

WRITINGS: (With Timothy Leary and Richard Alpert) The Psychedelic Experience, University Books, 1964; (editor with Leary and Gunther Weil) The Psychedelic Reader, University Books, 1966; (editor) The Ecstatic Adventure, Macmillan, 1968; (contributor) Bernard Aaronson and Humphrey Osmond, editors, Psychedelics: Uses and Implications of Hallucinogenic Drugs, Anchor Books, 1970; Maps of Consciousness, Collier-Macmillan, 1971; Know Your Type, Anchor Books, in press. Contributor to professional journals.

WORK IN PROGRESS: A novel; a book on astrology; a book on mythology.

SIDELIGHTS: Metzner writes: "Starting in 1961 I spent six years researching psychedelic drugs as tools for consciousness expansion and personal growth. Since that time I've pursued many other paths to greater awareness. The one that has engaged me most is Actualism, a teaching developed by Russell Schofield, which I have been teaching for four years now. I am also deeply interested in mythology, astrology, and any work of vision that illuminates man's evolutionary path."

AVOCATIONAL INTERESTS: "Music, mountains, movement, and magic."

* * *

MEYER, Charles R(obert) 1926- (Donald Jay)

PERSONAL: Born April 10, 1926, in New York, N.Y.; son of Nathan Philip (a garage owner) and Ella (a secretary; maiden name, Hamburger) Meyer; married Bambi Windmuller (a model and secretary), March 30, 1961; children: Charles R., Jr., Philip George, Kimberly Ann. Education: Cornell University, B.A., 1948. Politics: "Extraordinarily independent." Religion: Unitarian-Universalist. Home and office: 114 Cedar Point Dr. W., Southold, N.Y. 11971.

CAREER: Writer, photographer, and public relations consultant, 1948—. Member of Southold Town Conservation Council. Has broadcast on radio and television in the New York area. Military service: U.S. Merchant Marine, radio officer, 1943-45. U.S. Army, 1950. U.S. Coast Guard, deck officer, 1950-52. Awards, honors: Prizes for excellence in writing and photography on subjects including conservation, fishing, and recreational vehicle travel.

WRITINGS: (With Edward A. Hamilton and Charles Preston) Fishing America, Doubleday, 1958; Whaling and the Art of Scrimshaw, McKay, 1976; How to Be a Clown, McKay, 1977; How to Be a Juggler, McKay, 1977; How to Be an Acrobat, McKay, 1978; How to Be a Magician, McKay, 1978.

Contributor: Successful Ocean Fishing, Frank T. Moss, editor, International Marine Publishing Co., 1971; Consumer Guide Fishing Equipment, Consumer Guide, 1973; Successful Striped Bass Fishing, Frank T. Moss, editor, International Marine Publishing Co., 1974.

Author of documentary film script, "The Menhaden Story!" produced by Seacoast Products, 1974.

Contributor to reference books, including McClare's International Fishing Encyclopedia and The Lore of Fishing. Contributor of nearly a thousand articles (often under pseudonym, Donald Jay; some with own photographs) to magazines, including Sports Illustrated, True, Argosy, Yachting, and Outdoor Life, and to newspapers. Field editor for magazines, including Argosy, Sportfishing, and Four Seasons Trails.

WORK IN PROGRESS: A series of Ringling Brothers and Barnum & Bailey circus books for children, publication by McKay.

SIDELIGHTS: Meyer writes: "I consider myself to be a hack photo-journalist and only occasionally a writer of anything more transient than a magazine story—but writing and photography have been good to me in that I've never been forced into punching a time clock or obeying the orders of a boss. So, I suppose I'm a rugged individualist who has enjoyed the work he's done, a rarity in modern times. The philosophy of middle age, plus the changing scene in periodical writing resulting from TV inroads, leads me more and more toward hard cover books—with considerable satisfaction resulting." Meyer's writing assignments have included travel to Australia and New Zealand, the Arctic, and South and Central America.

AVOCATIONAL INTERESTS: Boating, camping, fishing.

* * *

MEYER, Elizabeth C(ooper) 1958-

PERSONAL: Born October 25, 1958, in New Haven,

Conn.; daughter of Paul W. (a professor) and Mary Louise (a librarian; maiden name, Yonker) Meyer. *Education:* Willaims College, student, 1976—. *Religion:* Presbyterian. *Residence:* Nashville, Tenn.

CAREER: Writer, 1974—. *Awards, honors:* Gold award from Art Directors of Nashville, 1974, for *The Blue China Pitcher;* Harvard Book HX ZE, 1975.

WRITINGS: The Blue China Pitcher (illustrated children's fiction), Abingdon, 1974.

AVOCATIONAL INTERESTS: Ice skating, music, nature study.

* * *

MEYERS, Carole Terwilliger 1945-

PERSONAL: Born June 30, 1945, in San Francisco, Calif.; daughter of Earl Walter (a civil servant) and Esther (Furst) Terwilliger; married Gene Howard Meyers (a computer programmer), May 2, 1971; children: David Charles. *Education:* University of California, Los Angeles, student, 1962-64; San Francisco State College, B.A., 1967; graduate study at Fresno State College, 1968-69, and University of California, Berkeley, 1969—. *Residence:* Berkeley, Calif. *Office:* Carousel Press, P.O. Box 6061, Albany, Calif. 94706.

CAREER: Secretary, 1962-68; elementary school teacher in Fresno, Calif., 1968-69, East Palo Alto, Calif., 1969-70, and Oakland, Calif., 1970-72; American Society for Psychoprophylaxis in Obstetrics, San Francisco, Calif., editor of newsletter, 1973—; Carousel Press, Albany, Calif., editor-in-chief, 1976—. *Member:* Committee of Small Magazine Editors and Publishers, California Teachers Association.

WRITINGS: (With Gail Kramer) *Eating Out with the Kids in the East Bay,* Hunger Pang Press, 1974; *How to Organize a Babysitting Cooperative,* Carousel Press, 1976; *Eating Out with the Kids in San Francisco and the Bay Area,* Carousel Press, 1976; *Weekend Adventures for City-Weary Families,* Carousel Press, 1977. Contributor to *Self-Publishing Writer* and *Mothering.*

WORK IN PROGRESS: Research on Caesarean section childbirth.

SIDELIGHTS: Carole Meyers writes: "My writing is motivated by an interest in passing information I've collected on to other people. I write in an effort to help parents cope with child-rearing and to promote healthy, happy family life." She has traveled throughout the United States and Canada, in Mexico, Europe, and the Middle East.

BIOGRAPHICAL/CRITICAL SOURCES: Oakland Tribune, December 23, 1974; *Berkeley Gazette,* December 18, 1976; *San Francisco Examiner,* January 5, 1977.

* * *

MICHAELIS, John U(dell) 1912-

PERSONAL: Surname is pronounced Mike-*ah*-lis; born August 19, 1912, in Colorado; son of Richard W. (a grocery store owner) and Mary Kate (Ford) Michaelis; married Elizabeth Ann Rank, October 5, 1935; children: Susan Ann Michaelis Hruthy. *Education:* University of Northern Colorado, B.A., 1936; University of Denver, M.A., 1940; University of Maryland, Ph.D., 1943. *Politics:* Independent. *Religion:* Presbyterian. *Home:* 331 Tampico, Walnut Creek, Calif. 94598. *Office:* Department of Education, University of California, Berkeley, Calif. 94720.

CAREER: Teacher at elementary school in Englewood, Calif., 1936-38, principal, 1939-41; Fresno State College,

Fresno, Calif., associate professor and director of teacher education, 1942-45; University of California, Berkeley, associate professor, 1945-52, professor of education, 1952—; director of teacher education, 1948-52. Consultant to *World Book Encyclopedia* and to schools in Burma, the Philippines, Lebanon, and Ecuador. *Member:* National Council for the Social Studies (past member of board of directors), Association for Supervision and Curriculum Development (past member of board of directors), American Educational Research Association, National Education Association, National Council of Teachers of English, National Council for Geographic Education.

WRITINGS: Social Studies for Children in a Democracy, Prentice-Hall, 1950, 6th edition, 1976; (with Paul Grim) *The Student Teacher in Elementary School,* Prentice-Hall, 1952, 2nd edition, 1960; (with Grim) *The Student Teacher in Secondary School,* McGraw, 1953; (with Ruth Grossman and Lloyd Scott) *New Designs for Elementary Curriculum and Instruction,* McGraw, 1968, 2nd edition, 1975; (with Robin McKeown) *Twentieth Century Asia,* McGraw, 1969; (with McKeown) *Asian Studies Inquiry Program,* Addison-Wesley, 1970; (editor with Everett T. Keach) *Readings in Elementary Social Studies,* Peacock Press (Oakland, Calif.), 1972; (with Larry Hannah) *A Comprehensive Framework for Instructional Objectives,* Addison-Wesley, 1977. Co-director of social studies series for Addison-Wesley, 1976.

WORK IN PROGRESS: Books on secondary school social studies.

AVOCATIONAL INTERESTS: Travel (Europe, the Middle East, North Africa, India, Burma, Thailand, Japan, South America, and Mexico), golf, photography, woodworking.

* * *

MICHELMAN, Irving S(imon) 1917-

PERSONAL: Born November 1, 1917, in Pittsfield, Mass.; son of Abraham M. and Rae (Goldstein) Michelman; married Shirley Stoloff (a supervisor at a university medical center), September 8, 1940; children: Nancy A. Michelman Goodfriend, John D. *Education:* Harvard University, B.S., 1939. *Home:* 10375 Wilshire Blvd., Los Angeles, Calif. 90024. *Office:* 8383 Wilshire Blvd., Beverly Hills, Calif. 90211.

CAREER: Signature Loan Co., New York City, executive vice-president, 1939-58; Budget Industries, Los Angeles, Calif., executive vice-president, 1958-72; financial business consultant in Beverly Hills, Calif., 1972—. *Military service:* U.S. Naval Reserve, active duty, 1943-46. *Awards, honors:* Silver medal from Commonwealth Club, 1969, for *Business at Bay.*

WRITINGS: Consumer Finance: A Case History in American Business, Augustus M. Kelley, 1961; *Business at Bay: Critics and Heretics of American Business,* Augustus M. Kelley, 1966; *The Crisis Meeters: Corporate Response to Social Crises,* Augustus M. Kelley, 1973. Contributor to history journals.

WORK IN PROGRESS: A social-economic history of capitalism.

* * *

MILES, (Mary) Patricia 1930-

PERSONAL: Born September 8, 1930, in Lancashire, England; daughter of Robert (a businessman) and Bridget (a teacher and writer; maiden name, Clancy) Storey; married

Francis George Miles (a company executive), October 17, 1953; children: Patrick, Siobhan, Hugh. *Education:* Somerville College, Oxford, B.A. (honors), 1953, M.A., 1956. *Politics:* "No real insight: constantly fluctuating." *Home:* Windrush, Rabley Heath, Welwyn, Hertfordshire AL6 9UF, England. *Agent:* David Higham Associates Ltd., 5-7 Lower John St., Golden Sq., London, England; and Harold Ober Associates, 40 East 49th St., New York, N.Y. 10017.

CAREER: Oxford University Press, London, England, reader of Latin and Greek books, 1953-54; Latin teacher in girls' schools in Kent, England, 1958-60, and 1963-65; Nobel Comprehensive School, Stevenage, England, teacher of French, English, and Latin, 1967-76; writer, 1976—.

WRITINGS: Nobody's Child (for children and adults), Dutton, 1975; *If I Survive* (for children and adults), Hamish Hamilton, 1976; *Don't Look Down* (juvenile humor/fantasy), Hamish Hamilton, in press. Has written for British Broadcasting Corp. Contributor of articles and stories to magazines and newspapers.

WORK IN PROGRESS: A Disturbing Influence, for adolescents, publication by Hamish Hamilton expected in 1978; *Rooms in a Great House* (historical), publication expected in 1980.

SIDELIGHTS: Patricia Miles writes: "My background is half English, half Irish, and wholly ambitious. My grandfather leapt fully grown from the murk of Manchester with a copy of *Self-Help* in his hand and founded a food business to which he fettered all his family. My father worked all his life in it, doggedly, though with distaste. My mother came from a small farm in Tipperary.... I myself was the archetypal provincial scholarship girl, cramming a four-year Greek course into six months in the effort to get into Oxford, which I did.

"How to reconcile all this determined striving with the free-wheeling inventiveness which is a good part of writing! The truth is, I'm a dreamer; I always was. The practicality and endeavour have been superimposed, for which I'm profoundly grateful—to realise any dream you've got to wake up.

"My dream is to provide satisfying entertainment. More precisely: to make the past come alive for children, with humor if possible, and to use language with vigor.

"I don't have a defined philosophy, though I do feel strongly that the ordinary business of living makes demands which many people meet gallantly: life is full of unsung heroes. My own life is easy enough at present; I teach occasionally and sometimes work as a guide in a stately home—we live twenty-odd miles from London in an ancient stretch of countryside."

AVOCATIONAL INTERESTS: Travel in France and Italy, gardening.

*   *   *

MILLAR, Jeff(ery Lynn) 1942-

PERSONAL: Born July 10, 1942, in Pasadena, Tex.; son of Daniel Lynn Millar and Betty (Shove) Millar Coons; married Lynne McDonald (a journalist), December 21, 1963. *Education:* University of Texas, B.A., 1964. *Politics:* "Vague." *Home:* 1642 Colquitt, Houston, Tex. 77006. *Office: Houston Chronicle,* 801 Texas Ave., Houston, Tex. 77002.

CAREER: Houston Chronicle, Houston, Tex., film critic, 1965—, author of column, 1972—; author of the comic strip "Tank McNamara," syndicated by Universal Press Syndicate to about a hundred fifty newspapers, 1974—.

WRITINGS—Cartoon books, all with Bill Hinds: *Tank McNamara,* Grossett, 1975; *And I'm Tank McNamara with the Norts Spews,* Sheed, 1975; *Shoot, Tank, Shoot!,* Sheed, 1976; *If I Quit Baseball, Will You Still Love Me?: A Cartoon Story for New Children—A Tank McNamara Book,* Sheed, 1976; *All Blond Boys Should Be Quarterbacks,* Sheed, 1977. Also author of "Mighty Moose and the Quarterback Kid," a television play for ABC-TV.

SIDELIGHTS: Millar writes: "The biographee leads a bland, colorless, middle-class life."

BIOGRAPHICAL/CRITICAL SOURCES: Cartoonists Profile, June, 1975; *U.S. News and World Report,* June 9, 1975; *Kansas City Star,* January 16, 1976; *Washington Post,* January 25, 1976.

*   *   *

MILLER, Arthur S(elwyn) 1917-

PERSONAL: Born March 4, 1917, in Oregon; son of Dallas D. and Irene Miller; married Dagmar Meister (an executive secretary), October 29, 1948. *Education:* Willamette University, A.B., 1938; Stanford University, LL.B., 1949; Yale University, J.S.D., 1959. *Home:* 3202 Reservoir Rd. N.W., Washington, D.C. 20007. *Office:* School of Law, George Washington University, Washington, D.C. 20052.

CAREER: George Washington University, Washington, D.C., assistant professor of law, 1950-53; Emory University, Atlanta, Ga., assistant professor, 1953-55, associate professor, 1955-57, professor of law, 1957-61; George Washington University, professor of law, 1961—. Lecturer at Brookings Institution, 1962—; associate fellow of Institute for Policy Studies, 1963. Chief consultant to U.S. Senate Select Committee on Presidential Campaign Activities, 1973-74. *Military service:* U.S. Army, 1941-46. U.S. Air Force, 1950-53. U.S. Air Force Reserve, 1953-77; became colonel.

MEMBER: American Society for International Law, American Association for the Advancement of Science, Association of Evolutionary Economics, Federation of American Scientists, American Society of Political and Legal Philosophy, Society of American Law Teachers, Federal City Club. *Awards, honors:* Guggenheim fellowship, 1957-58; Ford Foundation fellowship, 1960-61; grant from Columbia University, 1967-68.

WRITINGS: Racial Discrimination and Private Education, University of North Carolina Press, 1957; *The Supreme Court and American Capitalism,* Free Press, 1968; *The Supreme Court and the Living Constitution,* Lerner Law Book, 1969; *The Modern Corporate State,* Greenwood Press, 1976; *Presidential Power,* West Publishing, 1977; *The Supreme Court: Myth and Reality,* Greenwood Press, in press. Contributor of more than eighty articles to law journals, popular magazines, including *Progressive* and *Nation,* and newspapers.

WORK IN PROGRESS: A book on the emergency powers of the U.S. Government.

SIDELIGHTS: Miller writes: "I write because I think. I think because I have to and it is something to do. I write on such topics as interest me, principally on public law and politics. The urge to write can be (and is) a terrible curse. One should hesitate these days to perpetrate another book. But one does it because one must...."

MILLER, Casey (Geddes) 1919-

PERSONAL: Born February 26, 1919, in Toledo, Ohio; daughter of Walter Siegrist (in printing) and Laura Casey (Geddes) Miller. *Education:* Smith College, A.B., 1940; Yale University, graduate study, 1953-54. *Politics:* Democrat. *Home and office address:* P.O. Box 94, East Haddam, Conn. 06423. *Agent:* Virginia Barber, 44 Greenwich Ave., New York, N.Y. 10011.

CAREER: D. Appleton-Century Co., Inc. (publishers), New York City, editorial assistant, 1941-43, 1946-47; Colonial Williamsburg, Inc., Williamsburg, Va., 1947-53, began as assistant, became acting director of publications; Seabury Press, Inc., Greenwich, Conn., curriculum editor in Greenwich and in New York City, 1954-64; free-lance writer and editor, 1964—. Member of East Haddam Democratic Town Committee. *Military service:* U.S. Naval Reserve, active duty, 1943-46; became lieutenant junior grade. *Member:* Authors Guild of Authors League of America, Women's Institute for Freedom of the Press.

WRITINGS: (With Kate Swift) *Words and Women,* Doubleday, 1976. Contributor to magazines, including *New York, Ms.,* and *New York Times Magazine.*

SIDELIGHTS: Casey Miller and Kate Swift write: "We have an editorial partnership known as Miller/Swift, and it was out of our work as freelance editors that we became interested in the effect of language on women. After writing two articles on the subject ('Desexing the English Language' and 'One Small Step for Genkind') we found we had barely scratched the surface of this topic, which until recently was ignored. *Words and Women* is an expansion of the evidence presented in the articles and is primarily drawn from contemporary sources with historical material as backup. We document many changes occurring in English today as a result of women's changing perceptions of themselves."

* * *

MILLER, Charles D(avid) 1942-

PERSONAL: Born December 25, 1942, in Monroe, La.; son of Estelle (a clerk) Clegg; married Mary Sullivan (a pharmacist), December 19, 1971. *Education:* Fresno State College, B.A., 1964, M.A., 1965. *Residence:* Sacramento, Calif. *Office:* Department of Mathematics, American River College, Sacramento, Calif. 95841.

CAREER: American River College, Sacramento, Calif., professor of mathematics, 1966—. *Member:* Mathematical Association of America, American Mathematical Association of Two Year Colleges, National Council of Teachers of Mathematics. *Awards, honors:* First annual president's award from American Mathematical Association of Two Year Colleges, 1976.

WRITINGS—All published by Scott, Foresman: (With Vern Heeren) *Mathematical Ideas,* 1969, 3rd edition, 1978; (with Margaret Lial) *Beginning Algebra,* 1971, 2nd edition, 1976; (with Lial) *Intermediate Algebra,* 1972, 2nd edition, 1976; *College Algebra,* 1973, 2nd edition, 1977; (with Stanley Salzman) *Business Mathematics,* 1973; *Mathematics with Applications,* 1974; *Essential Calculus,* 1975; *Algebra and Trigonometry,* 1975; (with Heeren) *Mathematics: An Everyday Experience,* 1976; *Trigonometry,* 1976; (with Salzman) *Mathematics for Business,* 1977; *Finite Mathematics,* 1977.

WORK IN PROGRESS: Revisions of *Mathematics with Applications, Essential Calculus* (with Margaret Lial), and *Business Mathematics* (with Stanley Salzman).

MILLER, Florence B. 1895(?)-1976

1895(?)—October 30, 1976; American editor, writer, researcher and world traveler. Miller died in Washington, D.C. Obituaries: *Washington Post,* November 2, 1976.

* * *

MILLER, Francis Pickens 1895-

PERSONAL: Born June 5, 1895, in Middlesboro, Ky.; son of Henry (a Presbyterian minister) and Flora Boyce (McElwee) Miller; married Helen Day Hill (a writer), August 25, 1927; children: Andrew Pickens, Robert Day. *Education:* Washington & Lee University, B.A., 1914; Oxford University, B.A., 1921, M.A., 1923, and diploma in theology; Graduate Institute for International Studies, Geneva, Switzerland, further graduate study, 1927-28. *Politics:* Democrat. *Religion:* Presbyterian. *Home address:* Tamassee, Kitty Hawk, N.C. 27949.

CAREER: Young Men's Christian Association (YMCA), secretary for preparatory schools, 1914-16, assistant national secretary for colleges, 1923-26; World Student Christian Federation, Geneva, Switzerland, secretary, 1927-28, chairman, 1928-38; Council on Foreign Relations, New York City, organization director of committees on foreign relations, 1938-41; Fight for Freedom Committee, New York City, national vice-chairman, 1941; Foreign Information Service, Washington, D.C., chairman of planning board, 1942; National Committee for an Effective Congress, New York City, and Washington, D.C., member of committee, 1966—. Field secretary for Foreign Policy Association, 1934-35; co-organizer and secretary of National Policy Committee, 1935-38, vice-chairman, 1938-42; secretary of Southern Policy Committee, 1935-40; member of Public Affairs Committee, 1936, executive secretary, 1936-37. Member of Virginia House of Delegates, 1938-41; candidate for governor of Virginia, 1949, and U.S. Senate, 1952; member of board of directors of Southern Regional Council, 1959—; special assistant on educational and cultural affairs for U.S. Department of State, 1962-65; member of American Revolution Bicentennial Commission, 1967-69. Member of central committee of World Council of Churches, 1954-61; president of Virginia Council of Churches, 1957-59; coordinator of Virginia Committee on Religious Freedom, 1960; member of Friends of Presbyterian Union. Member of board of directors of Freedom House, 1958—; member of board of directors of Davidson College and board of visitors of Mary Baldwin College; chairman of board of visitors of Florida Presbyterian College, 1968-71. *Military service:* American Expeditionary Forces, 1917-19. U.S. Army, 1943-46, staff member of Office of Strategic Services, 1942-43, Supreme Headquarters, Allied Expeditionary Force in Europe, 1944-45, and Office of the Director of Intelligence in the Office of the Military Government of Germany, 1945-46; became colonel; received Legion of Merit with cluster, Order of the British Empire, Legion of Honor, French Croix de Guerre with palms, Order of Leopold I with palm, and Belgian Croix de Guerre with palm.

MEMBER: Council on Foreign Relations, Society of Cincinnati, Phi Gamma Delta, Omicron Delta Kappa, Century Club, Yale Club (New York), Cosmos Club, City Tavern Club (District of Columbia), Oxford Society. *Awards, honors:* Rhodes scholar at Oxford University, 1919-23; LL.D. from Centre College, 1954, and Davis & Elkins College, 1964; D.Litt. from Washington & Jefferson College, 1959.

WRITINGS: (With wife, Helen Hill) *The Giant of the*

Western World, Morrow, 1930; (with H. R. Niebuhr and Wilhelm Pauck) *The Church Against the World,* Willett, Clark, 1935; *The Blessings of Liberty,* University of North Carolina Press, 1936; (contributor) Dewitt C. Reddick, editor, *Church and Campus,* John Knox Press, 1956; (contributor) Malcom P. Calhoun, editor, *Christians Are Citizens,* John Knox Press, 1957; (contributor) Wayne H. Cowan, editor, *What the Christian Hopes for in Society,* Association Press, 1957; *Man from the Valley,* University of North Carolina Press, 1971. Also contributor to *We Dissent,* 1962.

SIDELIGHTS: Miller writes that, as chairman of the World Student Christian Federation, he visited the Far East and South Africa and crossed Russia, 1932-33. He has become familiar with western Europe.

BIOGRAPHICAL/CRITICAL SOURCES: Walter Johnson, *The Battle Against Isolation,* 1944; V. O. Key, Jr., *Southern Politics,* 1949; Mark Lincoln Chadwin, *The Warhawks of World War II,* 1968; Neal R. Peirce, *The Border South States,* 1975; Weldon Cooper and Thomas R. Morris, *Virginia Government and Politics,* 1976.

*　　*　　*

MILLER, John P(earse, Jr.) 1943-

PERSONAL: Born July 27, 1943, in Kansas City, Mo.; son of John Pearse (a businessman) and Joy (Vencill) Miller; married Jean Foley, December 30, 1967; children: Patrick, Nancy. *Education:* Attended University of Vienna, 1963-64; University of Missouri, B.A. (honors), 1965; Harvard University, M.A.T., 1967; University of Toronto, Ph.D., 1971. *Home:* 234 Cedar Ave., Thunder Bay, Ontario, Canada P7B 4V3. *Office:* Ontario Institute for Studies in Education, 10 Algoma St. S., Thunder Bay, Ontario, Canada.

CAREER: High school teacher of history in Scarsdale, N.Y., 1965-66; University of Missouri, Kansas City, instructor in education, 1968-69; Ontario Institute for Studies in Education, Thunder Bay, assistant professor of curriculum, 1972—. Has conducted workshops, seminars, and evaluation projects. *Member:* Association of Humanistic Psychology, Association of Transpersonal Psychology, Ontario History and Social Science Teachers Association, Phi Beta Kappa.

WRITINGS: Humanizing the Classroom: Models of Teaching in Affective Education, Praeger, 1976; (with Richard Hersh) *Values Education: Alternative Models,* McKay, 1978. Contributor of articles and reviews to American and Canadian journals.

WORK IN PROGRESS: A book on transpersonal education; a book on psychological orientation to curriculum.

SIDELIGHTS: Miller writes: "My writing in education is influenced by recent developments in humanistic psychology and transpersonal psychology. I am particularly interested in research on meditation, states of consciousness, and the brain, and its implications for education."

*　　*　　*

MILLER, Judith von Daler 1940-

PERSONAL: Born May 8, 1940, in Venezuela; daughter of F. H. and Lura Frances von Daler; married Norman Nees Miller (American Universities Field Staff associate for East Africa), March 1, 1972. *Education:* Grinnell College, B.A., 1962; attended French Institute and Goethe House, 1968-71. *Home address:* New Boston Rd., Norwich, Vt. 05055. *Office:* American Universities Field Staff, P.O. Box 150, Hanover, N.H. 03755.

CAREER: High school teacher of English and American literature in Connecticut, 1962-66; Museum of Modern Art, New York, N.Y., writer and editor, 1966-69; Contemporary Central African Stone Sculpture, New York City, gallery director, 1968-71; American Universities Field Staff, Hanover, N.H., film editor, research assistant, and archivist, 1972—. Conducted field research in eastern Africa, 1969-72. *Member:* African Studies Association.

WRITINGS: (Editor) Norman N. Miller, *Witchcraft and Sorcery in Tanzania,* Parts I-III, American Universities Field Staff, 1969-70; (editor) N. M. Miller, *Research in Rural Africa,* African Studies Center, Michigan State University, 1969; *Art in East Africa,* Muller, 1975. Contributor to arts, African studies, and civic periodicals.

WORK IN PROGRESS: The Mythology and Reality of Baobabs in Eastern Africa; research on the imagery of witchcraft in eastern Africa.

SIDELIGHTS: Judith Miller writes: "I have done extensive field research in the Far East (the Soko Islands, Hong Kong, Taiwan, Samoa, the Cook Islands, Japan, Hawaii), Eastern Africa and the Indian Ocean (Kenya, Tanzania, Uganda, Zambia, Malawi, Ethiopia, the Comoro Islands) and expect ultimately to return for further work with my husband in East Africa. We are involved in research, writing and making documentary films."

*　　*　　*

MILLER, Julian M. 1922-1976

August 5, 1922—December 14, 1976; American nuclear chemist, professor, and author best known for *Nuclear and Radio Chemistry.* He was on the faculty of Columbia University since 1949. Miller died in Berkeley, Calif. Obituaries: *New York Times,* December 16, 1976.

*　　*　　*

MILLER, Peter M(ichael) 1942-

PERSONAL: Born October 5, 1942, in Buffalo, N.Y.; son of Purdy and Alice (McCue) Miller; married Gabrielle Little, July 7, 1965; children: Michael, Melanie. *Education:* University of Maryland, B.A., 1964; University of South Carolina, M.A., 1966, Ph.D., 1968. *Office:* Hilton Head Hospital, P.O. Box 1117, Hilton Head Island, S.C. 29928.

CAREER: Licensed psychologist in South Carolina and Mississippi; South Carolina State Hospital, Columbia, staff psychologist, 1966-67, co-director of vocational rehabilitation psychology section, 1967; University of Alabama, Birmingham, instructor in psychology, 1967-68; Medical University of South Carolina, Charleston, clinical instructor in psychology, 1968-69; University of Mississippi, Medical Center, Jackson, clinical assistant professor, 1969-71, assistant professor, 1971-74, associate professor of psychiatry and human behavior, 1974-76, chief psychologist, 1975-76; Hilton Head Hospital, Hilton Head Island, S.C., director of Weight Control Center, 1976—. Diplomate in clinical psychology, American Board of Professional Psychology. Director of community consultation for Charleston Area Mental Health Center, 1968-69; staff psychologist at Pascal Clinic, 1969-71, and Veterans Administration Center (Jackson, Miss.), 1971-72, director of alcoholism unit, 1972-75. Member of state and local alcoholism committees. Consultant to National Institute on Alcohol Abuse and Alcoholism.

MEMBER: American Psychological Association, Association for the Advancement of Behavior Therapy, Behavior Therapy and Research Society, Southeastern Psychological

Association, Southeastern Association for Behavior Therapy, Mississippi Psychological Association. *Awards, honors:* Grants from Veterans Administration, 1971-75, and Mississippi State Department of Mental Health, 1973-74, 1974-75.

WRITINGS: (Editor with Michael Hersen and R. M. Eisler, and contributor) *Progress in Behavior Modification,* Academic Press, Volume I, 1975, Volume II, 1976; (contributor) W. E. Craighead, A. E. Kazdin, and M. J. Mahoney, editors, *Behavior Modification Principles, Issues, and Application,* Houghton, 1976; (contributor) R. E. Tarter and A. A. Sugerman, editors, *Alcoholism: Interdisciplinary Approaches to an Enduring Problem,* Addison-Wesley, 1976; *Behavioral Treatment of Alcoholism,* Pergamon, 1976; *Behavioral Approaches to Alcoholism,* Pergamon Press, 1976; (with Marie A. Mastria) *Alternatives to Alcohol Abuse,* Research Press, 1977; (contributor) A. R. Ciminaro, K. S. Calhoun, and H. E. Adams, editors, *Handbook for Behavioral Assessment,* Wiley, in press; (contributor) G. A. Marlatt and P. E. Nathan, editors, *Behavioral Approaches to the Assessment and Treatment of Alcoholism,* Center of Alcohol Studies, Rutgers University, in press. Contributor of about forty articles to professional journals. Editor-in-chief of *Addictive Behavior,* 1974—; member of editorial board of *Behavior Therapy* and *Behavior Modification,* both 1976—.

WORK IN PROGRESS: A book on the self-treatment of obesity, problem drinking, and smoking; research on experimental analysis of psychopathology, measurement and modification of alcoholism, obesity and smoking, prevention of substance abuse, and experimental analysis of interpersonal behavior.

SIDELIGHTS: In 1974, Miller made "Analysis and Treatment of Alcoholism by Behavior Modification," a series of tape recordings. He comments: "I believe that all addictive disorders (drinking, eating, or smoking too much) are learned patterns of behavior and, as such, can be unlearned. Also, they all can be explained and treated in a similar manner using a functional behavioral approach."

* * *

MILLER, Stanley 1916(?)-1977

1916(?)—May 3, 1977; American aide for Voice of America in Washington, D.C.; involved in program, editorial, and executive work, most recently as special assistant to the director. Previously, he was a free-lance writer and composer in New York City. He died in Washington, D.C. Obituaries: *New York Times,* May 4, 1977.

* * *

MILLINGTON, Frances Ryan 1899-1977

November 17, 1899—January 6, 1977; American novelist and film producer; worked during the 1930's and 1940's in Hollywood as a script reader and adviser to producer Stanley Kramer; later formed industrial and corporate film production company in Washington. She and her husband were identified with Paris cafe society in the 1920's. She died in Washington, D.C. Obituaries: *Washington Post,* January 10, 1977.

* * *

MILLS, J(anet) M(elanie) A(ilsa) 1894-
(H. K. Challoner)

PERSONAL: Born April 1, 1894, in London, England; daughter of Harry and Janet (Lee) Mills. *Education:* Educated in Switzerland. *Home:* Westlands, Beckley Rye, Sussex, England.

CAREER: Writer; War Office, London, England, office worker, 1914-17; has worked in an antique shop.

WRITINGS: The Way Triumphant (novel), Hutchinson, 1927; *Marsh Fires,* John Lane, 1928; *The Tomb of the Dark Ones,* Rider, 1937; *Lords of the Earth,* Andrew Dakers, 1940; *There Will Your Heart Be,* Andrew Dakers, 1945.

All under pseudonym H. K. Challoner: *Watchers of the Seven Spheres,* G. Routledge, 1933; *The Wheel of Rebirth,* Rider, 1935; *The Path of Healing,* Rider, 1938; *The Sword and the Spirit,* Rider, 1943; *Invocation and Other Poems,* Beckley, 1949; (with Roland Northover) *Antidote to Fear,* R. Hale, 1962; *Regents of the Seven Spheres,* Theosophical Publishing, 1966; (with Northover) *Out of Chaos,* Theosophical Publishing, 1967; *What of Tomorrow?,* Theosophical Publishing, 1977.

WORK IN PROGRESS: Revised version of *The Sword and the Spirit,* tentatively titled *Towards the Heights; Trumpets at Dawn.*

SIDELIGHTS: Mills told *CA:* "Motivation in all the "Challoner" books is to spread occult and spiritual ideas specially related to the chaotic condition in the world today."

When asked of the use of Tarot cards and other occult implements, Mills responded: "Very few people are capable of really interpreting the *true* Tarot cards though numbers claim that they can. As for 'occult implements,' if by these one means those used in Magic which I understand are actually advertised for sale, such implements have no use *at all* in the real sense. Occultly any instrument used in a ceremony *must* have been made throughout by the person who intends to use it. Unless his vibration has entered into the whole process it is occultly useless. In any case, the practice of magic in any form can be of extreme danger, even if it is 'worked' for allegedly 'white' magic by the ignorant and untrained. Magic in any form is best—and safest—left severely alone."

AVOCATIONAL INTERESTS: Painting pictures of mountains, gardening.

* * *

MILLS, John W(illiam) 1933-

PERSONAL: Born April 3, 1933, in London, England; son of William and Lily (Wilkinson) Mills; married Josephine Demarne (a teacher); children: Dylan Thomas, Andrea. *Education:* Hammersmith School of Art, intermediate certificate and diploma; Royal College of Art, A.R.C.A., 1960. *Home and office address:* Hinxworth Pl., Hinxworth, near Baldock, Hertfordshire, England.

CAREER: Hertfordshire College of Art and Design, Hertfordshire, England, part-time lecturer, 1960-62, lecturer, 1962-67, senior lecturer, 1967-75, principal lecturer in three-dimensional studies, 1975—. Visiting professor at Eastern Michigan University, 1970-71. Has had group and individual exhibitions in England, Scotland, France, Canada, and the United States; work has been commissioned in England; other work represented in private collections in England, the United States, Canada, Sweden, Japan, France, Germany, Belgium, and Australia. *Military service:* British Army, physical training instructor, 1954-56. *Awards, honors:* Won design competitions for Topham Trophy, 1961-62.

WRITINGS: Sculpture in Ciment Fondu, Contractors Record, 1959; *The Technique of Sculpture*, Batsford, 1964, revised edition, 1976; *The Technique of Casting for Sculpture*, Batsford, 1966; *Sculpture in Concrete*, McClaren, 1967; (with Michael Gillespie) *Studio Bronze Casting*, McClaren, 1969; *Modeling the Figure and Head*, Batsford, 1977.

WORK IN PROGRESS: Sculpture and printmaking.

SIDELIGHTS: Mills comments: "Sculpture is my main occupation, and writing is to do with it. Some of my themes are to do with the sport of springboard diving, at which I used to compete. I maintain a house in France, and so travel widely in Europe."

*   *   *

MINER, Mary Green   1928-

PERSONAL: Born October 11, 1928, in Syracuse, N.Y.; daughter of Alfred Morgan (a journalist) and Elsie (a bookkeeper; maiden name, Mcyers) Green; married Donald L. Thompson, January 22, 1956 (divorced, 1966); married John B. Miner (a professor and writer), January 11, 1967; children: Jillian Ellen, David Green; stepchildren: Barbara, John, Cynthia, Frances. *Education:* Cornell University, B.A., 1950. *Home:* 651 Peachtree Battle Ave., N.W., Atlanta, Ga. 30327. *Office:* Bureau of National Affairs, Inc., 1231 25th St. N.W., Washington, D.C. 20037.

CAREER: Bureau of National Affairs, Inc., Washington, D.C., staff editor, 1950-56; Pacific Telephone & Telegraph Co., San Francisco, Calif., employee information editor, 1956-58; Bureau of National Affairs, Inc., staff editor, 1968-71, consulting editor and director of surveys, 1971—. *Member:* Academy of Management (member of executive ·committee, 1976—), Industrial Relations Research Association.

WRITINGS: (With husband, John B. Miner) *Personnel and Industrial Relations: A Managerial Approach*, Macmillan, 2nd edition, 1973 (author not associated with first edition), 3rd edition, 1977; (with J. B. Miner) *A Guide to Personnel Management*, Bureau of National Affairs, 1973; (with J. B. Miner) *Employee Selection Within the Law*, Bureau of National Affairs, 1977; (with J. B. Miner) *Policy Issues in Contemporary Personnel and Industrial Relations*, Macmillan, 1977. Contributor to *Encyclopedia of Professional Management* and to professional journals.

WORK IN PROGRESS: Research on employee absenteeism and turnover, and on personnel department functions, budgets, and staff.

*   *   *

MINOW, Newton N(orman)   1926-

PERSONAL: Born January 17, 1926, in Milwaukee, Wis.; son of Jay A. and Doris (Stein) Minow; married Josephine Baskin, May 29, 1949; children: Nell, Martha, Mary. *Education:* Northwestern University, B.S., 1949, J.D., 1950. *Politics:* Democrat. *Religion:* Jewish. *Home:* 375 Palos Rd., Glencoe, Ill. 60022. *Office:* 1 First National Plaza, Suite 4800, Chicago, Ill. 60603.

CAREER: Mayer, Brown & Platt, Chicago, Ill., associate, 1950-51, 1953-55; U.S. Supreme Court, Washington, D.C., law clerk to Chief Justice Fred M. Vinson, 1952-53; State of Illinois, administrative assistant to Governor Adlai E. Stevenson, 1953-55; Stevenson, Rifkind & Wirtz, Chicago, partner, 1955-61; Federal Communications Commission, Washington, D.C., chairman, 1961-63; Encyclopaedia Bri-

tannica, Inc., Chicago, executive vice-president and general council, 1963-65; Sidley & Austin (law firm), Chicago, Ill., attorney, 1965—. Professorial lecturer at Medill School of Journalism, Northwestern University. Director and past chairman of Chicago Educational Television Association; governor of Public Broadcasting Service. Trustee of RAND Corp., 1965-75, 1976— (chairman of board of trustees, 1970-72), and Mayo Foundation; director of Academy for Educational Development, Adler Planetarium, and Chicago Orchestral Association; trustee of Northwestern University and University of Notre Dame; chairman of board of overseers of Jewish Theological Seminary of America. Member of International Broadcast Institute. *Military service:* U.S. Army, 1944-46; served in China-Burma-India theater; became sergeant.

MEMBER: American Bar Association, American Bar Foundation (fellow), American Judicature Society, American Society for International Law, Council on Foreign Relations (member of Chicago committee), National Academy of Television Arts and Sciences, Illinois Bar Association, Wisconsin Bar Association, Chicago Bar Association, Economic Club (Chicago; director), Law Club (Chicago), Legal Club (Chicago), Carlton Club, Century Club (New York City), Commercial Club, Federal City Club (Washington, D.C.), Mid-America Club, Mid-Day Club, Northmoor Country Club, Standard Club. *Awards, honors:* Named one of America's ten outstanding young men by Junior Chamber of Commerce, 1961; George Foster Peabody Broadcasting Award from University of Georgia, 1961; Dr. Lee de Forest Award from National Association for Better Radio and Television, 1962; LL.D. from Brandeis University, 1963, University of Wisconsin, 1963, Northwestern University, 1965, and Columbia University, 1972; distinguished service award from Phi Beta Kappa, 1965.

WRITINGS: Equal Time: The Private Broadcaster and the Public Interest, Atheneum, 1964; (contributor) *As We Knew Adlai*, Harper, 1966; (with John B. Martin and Lee M. Mitchell) *Presidential Television*, Basic Books, 1973.

BIOGRAPHICAL/CRITICAL SOURCES: TV Guide, October 16, 1976.

*   *   *

MJELDE, Michael Jay   1938-

PERSONAL: Surname is pronounced *Mel*-dee; born December 1, 1938, in Bremerton, Wash.; son of Joseph Nordahl (a musician) and Bertha (a piano teacher; maiden name, Croes) Mjelde; married Wylla R. Siegert (a secretary), September 22, 1962; children: Michael J., Arina L., Deborah R., Heather. *Education:* Attended Bremerton Business College. *Home:* 1216 Broadway, Bremerton, Wash. 98310. *Office:* Land Title Insurance Co., P.O. Box 313, Bremerton, Wash. 98310.

CAREER: Mjelde Piano School, Bremerton, Wash., piano teacher, 1957-62; San Francisco State Historical Monument, Oakland, Calif., park aide on ships, 1963; Land Title Insurance Co., Bremerton, Wash., title engineer in Seattle, 1964-71, and Bremerton, 1972—. Officer and part-time teacher at Mjelde Piano School. *Member:* National Guild of Piano Teachers, Music Teachers National Association, Nautical Research Guild, Society of Nautical Research, Land Surveyor's Association of Washington, Washington State Music Teachers Association, Mystic Seaport. *Awards, honors:* Writers day award from the governor of Washington, 1971, for *Glory of the Seas*.

WRITINGS: Glory of the Seas, Wesleyan University Press, 1970. Contributor to *Sea Chest* and *Log*.

WORK IN PROGRESS: A book on the final voyage under sail of *Glory of the Seas* in 1910; research on Donald McKay and his ships and on West Coast clipper ships.

SIDELIGHTS: Mjelde writes: "I started gathering material on the ship *Glory of the Seas* in 1957. In 1962, my wife and I moved to California where I went to work on the restoration of the historic ships which are now on display at the foot of Hyde Street in San Francisco. This inspired me to finish the book; however, I did not know that it would be 1970 before it would be published. On vacations throughout the twelve-odd years of writing, we went up and down the West Coast interviewing people and visiting places *Glory* had gone."

BIOGRAPHICAL/CRITICAL SOURCES: Seattle Times, May 10, 1970; Glen Carter, *My Waterfront,* Seagull Books, 1977.

* * *

MOCKLER, Anthony 1937-

PERSONAL: Born February 18, 1937, in London, England; son of Eamon Joseph (a surgeon in the Royal Navy) and Marjorie Mary (Barrett) Mockler. *Education:* Jesus College, Cambridge, double first class honors in the Classical Tripos, 1957; Universita di Perugia, diploma, 1960. *Politics:* "Feudal regionalist." *Religion:* Catholic. *Agent:* Hope, Leresche & Sayle, 11 Jubilee Pl., London S.W.3, England.

CAREER: Called to the Bar, Inner Temple, London, England, 1960; special correspondent in the Congo, Rhodesia, Santo Domingo, Spain, Vietnam, Angola, and other countries to *Guardian* and to other periodicals, including *Times Educational Supplement, Economist,* and *New Statesman,* 1962—. Reader in British civilization at Sorbonne, University of Paris, 1969-71. *Military service:* British Army, Queen's Dragoon Guards, 1957-59; became second lieutenant. *Member:* Society of Authors, Save London Action Group (founder member), Travellers' Club.

WRITINGS: The Mercenaries, Macmillan, 1970; *Our Enemies, the French: Being an Account of the War Fought between the British and the French, Syria, 1941,* Leo Cooper, 1976; *Francis of Assisi: The Wandering Years,* Dutton, 1976; *La Guerra del Negus* (title means "The War of the Emperor"), Rizzoli Editore (Milan), 1977.

WORK IN PROGRESS: A biography of Lobengula provisionally entitled *He Who Drives the Wind;* a three-volume novel set in the near future, *Emperor of Africa;* a study of film stars in the post-Marilyn Monroe generation, *The Amazon Decade.*

SIDELIGHTS: "I came to military history more by accident than design," writes Mockler. "I find it fascinating, for it is the study of men at the moment of probably the greatest stress in their lives. Furthermore, to approach other subjects (such as the study of St. Francis) from the standpoint of a military historian is, despite appearances, an advantage: it offers a new view from a different angle. It led me to the conclusion that the most important event in Francis's life was his going on Crusade.

"I make it a rule always to visit the countries and where possible the exact locations of which I write. This has involved travel and expeditions in many parts, notably in the remoter areas of (still Imperial) Ethiopia."

Mockler speaks French, Spanish, and Italian, and has "a smattering of many other languages, including Amharic and Arabic."

AVOCATIONAL INTERESTS: Horseback riding, architecture, bridge.

MODLEY, Rudolph 1906-1976

November 3, 1906—September 28, 1976; Austrian-born management consultant, conservationist, and author of books on pictorial symbols; also founded the monthly *Report on Credit Unions.* He was co-chairperson with Margaret Mead of Glyphs, Inc., an organization concerned with universal graphic symbols. He died in Chicago, Ill. Obituaries: *New York Times,* September 30, 1976.

* * *

MOE, Barbara 1937-

PERSONAL: Born October 10, 1937, in Cincinnati, Ohio; daughter of Gerrit W. (a physician) and Martha (a nurse; maiden name, Radtke) Raidt; married Paul G. Moe (a physician), April 10, 1959; children: Steve, Susan, Danny, David, Amy. *Education:* University of Cincinnati, B.S., 1959; Ohio State University, M.S., 1961. *Politics:* Democrat. *Religion:* Protestant. *Home:* 1770 Hudson, Denver, Colo. 80220. *Agent:* Ruth Cantor, 156 Fifth Ave., New York, N.Y. 10010.

CAREER: Peace Corps volunteer in Shiraz, Iran, 1965-67; *Denver Post,* Denver, Colo., zone writer, 1976—. *Member:* Society of Children's Book Writers, Colorado Authors League. *Awards, honors:* Top Hand Award from Colorado Authors League, 1976, for *Pickles and Prunes.*

WRITINGS: The Ghost Wore Knickers (juvenile), Thomas Nelson, 1975; *Pickles and Prunes* (juvenile), McGraw, 1976.

WORK IN PROGRESS: The Gift of the Vampire, juvenile.

* * *

MOFFAT, Alexander W(hite) 1891-

PERSONAL: Born June 26, 1891, in Brooklyn, N.Y.; son of George Barclay (a banker) and Frances Hilliard (White) Moffat; married Sally DeCamp, February 13, 1913 (deceased); children: Marian W. Moffat Welch, Frances W. Moffat Sargent, Faith Moffat Parsons, Alexander W., Jr., Lydia Moffat Mulligan. *Education:* Harvard University, A.B., 1913. *Religion:* Episcopal. *Home and office:* 4 Spy Rock Hill Rd., Manchester, Mass. 01944. *Agent:* Thomas J. O'Connor, 1 Concord Lane, Westport, Conn. 06880.

CAREER: Transport Tractor Co., Long Island City, N.Y., vice-president, 1915-17; Lord Drydock Co., West New York, N.Y., assistant superintendent, 1919-21; Conant Brothers Co., Somerville, Mass., superintendent, 1922-23; Walter Baker & Co., Milton, Mass., vice-president and general manager, 1923-33; Moffat, Inc., South Boston, Mass., president, 1933-36; Moffat & Steinert, Boston, Mass., senior partner, 1936-38; Lord Electric Co., New York, N.Y., member of board of directors, 1948-55, chairman of board of directors, 1955-65. Member of national executive board of Boy Scouts of America, 1958-65. *Military service:* U.S. Naval Reserve, active duty, 1917-19, 1939-45; became captain; received Navy Cross with Sub Chaser Bar.

MEMBER: Cruising Club of America (past national commodore), Tavern Club (Boston). *Awards, honors:* Service awards from Boy Scouts of America include Silver Beaver, Silver Antelope, and Silver Buffalo.

WRITINGS: The Galley Guide (marine cookbook), Class Journal Publishing Co., 1923, revised edition, Dodd, 1977; *Maverick Navy,* Wesleyan University Press, 1976. Contributor to *Atlantic Monthly, Yachting,* and naval journals.

WORK IN PROGRESS: A book for Wesleyan University Press.

SIDELIGHTS: Moffat comments briefly: "At age eighty-five the days are simply not long enough!"

* * *

MOFFETT, Judith 1942-

PERSONAL: Born August 30, 1942, in Louisville, Ky.; daughter of James S. (a commercial artist) and Margaret (a secretary; maiden name, Cowherd) Moffett. *Education:* Hanover College, A.B. (cum laude), 1964; Colorado State University, M.A., 1966; University of Wisconsin, Madison, further graduate study, 1966-67; University of Pennsylvania, M.A., 1970, Ph.D., 1971. *Office:* Writing Program, University of Iowa, Iowa City, Iowa 52240.

CAREER: University of Lund, Lund, Sweden, Fulbright lecturer in American studies, 1967-68; Pennsylvania State University, Behrend College, Erie, assistant professor of English, 1971-75; writer, 1975—. Teacher of writing at University of Iowa, 1977-78. *Awards, honors:* Eunice Tietjens Memorial Prize from *Poetry*, 1973, for two poems; grants from Pennsylvania State Institute for the Arts and Humanistic Studies, 1973, American Philosophical Association, 1973, Nathhorsts Foundation, 1973, and Swedish Institute, 1973, 1976; Fulbright travel grant, 1973-74; Borestone Mountain Poetry Award, 1975, for "Cecropia Terzine," Levinson Prize, 1976, from *Poetry*.

WRITINGS: Keeping Time (poems), Louisiana State University Press, 1976. Contributor of poems, translations, articles, and reviews to journals, including *New Yorker, Carolina Quarterly, Translation,* and *Minnesota Review.*

WORK IN PROGRESS: Now You've Seen Through Me, Sang the Cataract, a critical study of James Merrill's work; translating from the Swedish of Hjalmar Gullberg; new poems.

SIDELIGHTS: Judith Moffett writes: "I don't find it hard at all to be both an academic intellectual and a poet, professionally rational/analytical and emotional/creative, disciplined and free at the same time and often in the same gestures. Discipline—of form, of work schedule—is how I get poems made. And I *enjoy* putting new wine in old skins, feeling that how good the resultant poem is has little to do with the age of the skin but a lot to do with how the new wine fills it out and shapes it from within. I like making new skins too, though.

"I've never settled anywhere for long. My poems have often come in response to the physical features of where I happened to be living (Lake Erie, Colorado, Stockholm, the English countryside) but lately I sense that they want to be rooted in a *place,* not only a language and a literary tradition. My interests change, of course, but some persistent ones have been ethics, wilderness, and people I think remarkable. Politically and generally I'm concerned about liberty but still more concerned about responsibility. I'm always working on ways to make weighty subject matter into palatable and accessible poetry: get people to take in ideas and hardly notice because the active ingredient was pleasure."

AVOCATIONAL INTERESTS: Backpacking, singing (sacred music, folk, catches), "promoting various kinds of Lib."

* * *

MOGAL, Doris P(ick) 1918-

PERSONAL: Born February 25, 1918, in New York, N.Y.; daughter of Max and Ruth Pick; married Alexander Rubin, January 22, 1941 (died, 1954); married Solomon Mogal (an importer), January 13, 1959; children: (first marriage) Sara Jane (Mrs. Daniel Wigeltow), David M.; (second marriage) Joshua. *Education:* Vassar College, A.B., 1939; New York University, M.A., 1940.

CAREER: Mental Health Association, West White Plains, N.Y., in public relations; Department of Corrections, New York, N.Y., assistant to commissioner, 1954-59, member of pilot teaching project at House of Detention for Women, 1959-60; free-lance editor and writer, 1960—.

WRITINGS: Character in the Making, Parents' Magazine Press, 1972.

* * *

MOLINARO, Ursule

Residence: New York City. *Agent:* Georges Borchardt, 145 East 52nd St., New York, N.Y. 10022.

CAREER: United Nations, New York, N.Y., multi-lingual proofreader, 1946-51; writer, 1950—. Teacher of creative and literary translation at Ecole libre des Hautes Etudes, New York, 1971-72. *Member:* Coordinating Council of Literary Magazines. *Awards, honors:* Creative Artists Public Service grant, 1972-73.

WRITINGS: Rimes et raisons (poetry), Regain (Monte Carlo), 1954; *Mirrors for Small Beasts* (poetry), Noonday, 1960; *L'Un pour l'autre,* translation from the English manuscript by Edith Fournier, Julliard (Paris), 1964, manuscript published as *The Borrower: An Alchemical Novel,* Harper, 1970; *Green Lights Are Blue: A Pornosophic Novel,* New American Library, 1967; *The Zodiac Lovers* (nonfiction), Avon, 1969; *Sounds of a Drunken Summer* (novel), Harper, 1969; *Life By the Numbers: A Basic Guide To Learning Your Life Through Numerology,* Morrow, 1971. Also author of as yet unpublished novels, "The Autobiography of Cassandra, Princess and Prophetess of Troy," "Encores for a Dilettante," and "That Which Is Bright Rises Twice."

One-act plays: "The Engagement," "After the Wash," "The Sundial," "The Abstract Wife," "Breakfast Past Noon." Also author of "The Mine" and "Antiques," both as yet unpublished and unproduced.

Full-length plays; unpublished and unproduced: "The Great Emancipation" and "The Happy Hexagon."

Translator from German, Italian, Spanish, and Portuguese into French and English of work by Claude Ollier, Nathalie Sarraute, Hermann Hesse, Uwe Johnson, Jean Vauthier, Dino Buzzati, Ugo Carrega, Reinhard Lettau, Michael Horbach, and many others. Also of film subtitles from and into French and from the Italian into English.

Work represented in anthologies, including Jonathan Baumbach, compiler, *Statements 1,* Braziller, 1975, *Statements 2,* 1977; Joe David Bellamy, editor, *Superfiction,* Vintage, 1975. Contributor of short stories and articles to journals, including *Epoch, Evergreen, NAR, Iowa Review, Panache, TriQuarterly, Lettres nouvelles, Fiera letteraria,* and *Village Voice.*

WORK IN PROGRESS: A novel, tentatively titled *The House,* "each chapter concentrates on one floor of a New York brownstone and is in itself an independent short story."

SIDELIGHTS: Molinaro told *CA* her basic interest is "the position of the individual, regardless of ethnic background, sex or age." *Avocational interests:* Painting (neo-Haitian primitive; oil on wood) and philosophy (any system of self-knowledge).

MOLLOY, Robert (William) 1906-1977

January 9, 1906—January 27, 1977; American translator, newspaperman, and novelist. He translated works from the German, French, and Spanish, wrote reference articles for encyclopedias, and novels, including *Pride's Way* and *The Other Side of the Hill.* Molloy died in Paramus, N.J. Obituaries: *New York Times,* January 28, 1977; *AB Bookman's Weekly,* March 14, 1977; *Current Biography,* March, 1977. (*CAP*-2; earlier sketch in *CA*-29/32)

*　　*　　*

MOMMSEN, Katharina 1925-

PERSONAL: Born September 18, 1925, in Berlin, Germany; daughter of Hermann (a lawyer) and Anna (a teacher; maiden name, Johannsen) Zimmer; married Momme Mommsen (a conductor and professor), December 23, 1948. *Education:* University of Tuebingen, Ph.D., 1956; Free University of Berlin, Dr. habil. (German philology), 1962. *Home:* 980 Palo Alto Ave., Palo Alto, Calif. 94301. *Office:* Department of German, Stanford University, Stanford, Calif. 94305.

CAREER: German Academy of Science, Berlin, Germany, researcher in German literature, 1949-62; Free University of Berlin, Germany, privatdocent, 1962-67, associate professor of German, 1967-70; Carleton University, Ottawa, Ontario, professor of German, 1970-74; Stanford University, Stanford, Calif., professor of German literature, 1974—. Visiting professor of German at University of Giessen, 1965-66, State University of New York at Buffalo, 1966, Technical University of Berlin, 1966-67, and University of California at San Diego, 1973. *Member:* International Association for Germanic Language and Literature (vice president, 1975—), Modern Language Association (member of executive committee), Modern Humanities Research Association, American Society of Eighteenth Century Studies, American Association of University Professors, Goethe Society, Schiller Society, Hofmannsthal Society, Kleist Society. *Awards, honors:* German Research Association fellow, 1962-63; Boehringer Foundation for the Arts Award, 1964; Guggenheim fellowship, 1976-77.

WRITINGS: Die Entstehung von Goethes Worken in Dokumenten, two volumes, Akademie Verlag, 1958; *Goethe und 1001 Nacht,* Akademie Verlag, 1960; *Goethe und die Moallakat,* Akademie Verlag, 1960; *Goethe und Diez,* Akademie Verlag, 1961; *Goethe, Novellen,* DTV, 1962; *Goethe und der Islam,* Goethe Gesellschaft, 1964; *Natur und Fabelreich in Faust II,* De Gruyter, 1968; (editor) Georg Herwegh, *Literatur und Politik,* Insel Verlag, 1969; *Gesellschafskritik bei Fontane und Thomas Mann,* Stiehm, 1973; (editor) *Schiller, Anthologie auf das Jahr 1782,* Metzler, 1973; *Kleists Kampf mit Goethe,* Stiehm, 1974; (editor) *J. G. Herder: Journal meiner Reise im Jahr 1769,* Reclam, 1976; *Hofmannsthal und Fontane,* Lang, 1977.

WORK IN PROGRESS: Die Entstehung von Goethes Worken in Dokumenten, volumes three and four; *Von Herder bis Hofmannsthal; Dokumentation zu Goethes West-oestlichem Divan;* editing *Hugo von Hofmannsthal, Die Hochzeit der Sobeide.*

SIDELIGHTS: Mommsen states briefly: "My main interest is in oriental influences on European literatures, especially on Goethe."

*　　*　　*

MONACO, James 1942-

PERSONAL: Born November 15, 1942, in New York, N.Y.; son of George C. (in the food industry) and Susanne (a social worker; maiden name, Hirschland) Monaco; married Susan Schenker (a writer and story analyst), October 24, 1976. *Education:* Muhlenberg College, B.A., 1963; Columbia University, M.A., 1964. *Residence:* New York, N.Y. *Agent:* Virginia Barber, Literary Agent, 44 Greenwich Ave., New York, N.Y. 10011.

CAREER: City University of New York, New York City, lecturer in literature, film, drama, and media at various colleges of university, 1964-70, chairman of University Center Search for Education, Elevation, and Knowledge (SEEK) Program, 1969—; New School for Social Research, New York City, member of faculty, 1967—. Participated in the making of several short films and videotapes; has appeared on various radio and television programs on National Broadcasting Co. (NBC)-Radio, NBC-TV, Columbia Broadcasting System (CBS)-FM Radio, CBS-TV, and other networks. Vice-president of Village Green Recycling Team; member of New York City Solid Waste Task Force Advisory Committee.

WRITINGS: A Standard Glossary for Film Criticism, American Film Institute, 1970, 3rd edition, New York Zoetrope, 1975; *Books About Film: A Bibliographical Checklist,* American Film Institute, 1970, 3rd edition, New York Zoetrope, 1976; (contributor) Stanley Hochman, editor, *American Film Directors: A Library of Film Criticism,* Ungar, 1974; *Film: How and Where to Find Out What You Want to Know,* Unicorn (Montreal), 1975; *The New Wave: Truffaut, Godard, Chabrol, Rohmer, Rivette,* Oxford University Press, 1976; *How to Read a Film,* Oxford University Press, 1977; (editor) *Mediagraphy,* Delta, 1977; (editor) *Celebrity,* Delta, 1977; *Alain Resnais, Alain Resnais,* Secker & Warburg, 1978.

Also author of monographs, including studies of Fellini, Bergman, American Realism, Kubrick, Lester, Godard, Truffaut, the new wave, and recent British films, all published by New York Zoetrope, all in the early 1970's.

Contributor of articles to a variety of publications, including *New York Times, Village Voice, Changes, More: The Media Magazine, Liberation, Cambridge Review, Take One, Sight and Sound, American Film, Film* (London), and *Film Comment.* Associate editor, *Take One;* contributing editor, *More: The Media Magazine* and *Cineaste.*

WORK IN PROGRESS: A novel, *In the Middle of Things;* editing a series of anthologies in media for Delta; a study of contemporary American directors.

AVOCATIONAL INTERESTS: Vegetable gardening, ecology.

*　　*　　*

MONFOLO, Rodolpho 1899(?)-1976

Italian-born philosopher and author of books on classicism; was a professor of philosophy at University of Bologna until 1939, when he fled anti-Semitic persecution in Italy. He died in Buenos Aires, Argentina. Obituaries: *AB Bookman's Weekly,* January 3, 1977.

*　　*　　*

MONOD, Jacques 1910-1976

PERSONAL: Born February 9, 1910, in Paris, France; son of Lucien (a painter) and Charlotte Todd (MacGregor) Monod; married Odette Bruhl (an archaeologist and museum curator), 1938 (died, 1972); children: two sons. *Education:* University of Paris, licencie es sciences, 1931, docteur es sciences, 1941. *Home:* 16 rue Thbaud, Paris 14, France. *Office:* Institut Pasteur, 25 ruc du Docteur Roux, Paris 15, France.

CAREER: University of Paris, Faculte des Sciences, Paris, France, assistant, 1934-44; Pasteur Institute, Paris, head of microbic physiology laboratory, 1945-54, head of cellular biochemistry department, 1954-71, director, 1971-76. Fellow, California Institute of Technology, 1936-37; professor of science, University of Paris, 1959-67; professor of molecular biology, College de France, 1967-72; fellow, Salk Institute, 1968-76. *Military service:* Officer in the French Resistance and later in the French Army during World War II; received Croix de Guerre, Legion of Honor, and Bronze Star. *Member:* American Academy of Arts and Sciences, Washington Academy of Science, Royal Society of London, Czechoslovak Academy of Science, National Academy of Sciences. *Awards, honors:* Co-winner of Nobel Prize in medicine and physiology, 1965; other awards include a Rockefeller Foundation fellowship, 1936-37, Leopold Mayer Prize of the French Academy of Sciences, 1962, and several honorary degrees.

WRITINGS: Recherches sur la croissance des cultures bacteriennes, Hermann, 1941; *Le Hasard et la necessite: Essai sur la philosophie naturelle de la biologie moderne,* Editions du Seuil, 1970, translation by Austryn Wainhouse published as *Chance and Necessity: An Essay on the Natural Philosophy of Modern Biology,* Knopf, 1971; (editor) *Of Microbes and Life,* Columbia University Press, 1971; (with Maurice Caveing, Francis Halbwachs, and Jacques Roger) *Epistemologie et marxisme,* Union Generale d'Editions, 1972.

SIDELIGHTS: Monod and his co-workers Andre Lwoff and Francois Jacob are credited with the discovery of the process by which the genetic code is translated into thc production of enzymes and protein within the cell. Although deoxyribonucleic acid (DNA), the basic molecule of life, and its complement ribonucleic acid (RNA) had been discovered in the 1950's, their precise relationship was unknown until Monod and his team concluded that it is RNA which carries the information encoded in the DNA and enables the cell to produce the vital proteins and enzymes.

Monod and his team also pioneered the concept of the operon—the gene cluster which regulates protein synthesis within the cell. Without this regulator, which the team likened to a thermostat, protein synthesis would be a chaotic process.

Chance and Necessity, Monod's best selling book influenced by the existentialist ethics of his friend Albert Camus, calls for a distinction to be made between objective knowledge and the realm of values. It was Monod's belief that all existence is a product of chance and that the consequences of mankind's refusal to acknowledge this would lead to tragedy.

While some reviewers thought Monod's attempt to synthesize philosophical analysis and natural science into a natural philosophy was unsuccessful, (notably Stephen Toulmin, who found the book arrogant), most found it more rewarding. Theodore Roszak wrote of the book: "As a piece of popular science dealing with this hottest of all intellectual frontiers, it is an accomplished if rather demanding effort. . . . Whenever Nobel Prize scientists like Monod wade into the cultural mainstream to give advice and counsel, it is a noteworthy event." And George Steiner comments: "What the layman will be drawn to and what Jacques Monod himself clearly regards as paramount, is the philo-

sophic, social manifesto which is derived from the technical, biological base."

AVOCATIONAL INTERESTS: Sailing, mountain climbing, playing the cello.

BIOGRAPHICAL/CRITICAL SOURCES: Book World, October 24, 1971; *New York Times Book Review,* November 21, 1971; *Nation,* November 29, 1971; *New York Review of Books,* December 16, 1971.

OBITUARIES: New York Times, June 1, 1976; *Washington Post,* June 1, 1976; *Current Biography,* July, 1976.*

(Died May 31, 1976, in Cannes, France)

*   *   *

MONTES, Antonio Llano   1924-

PERSONAL: Born January 17, 1924, in La Habana, Cuba; came to U.S. in 1962; son of Manuel (a businessman) and Blandina Montes; married Silvia Casado, August 10, 1957 (divorced); married Anita Llano, July 15, 1966; children: John, Danny, Arlene. *Education:* Habana University, B.A., 1948, J.D., 1952. *Religion:* Roman Catholic. *Home:* 1285 Southwest 16th St., Miami, Fla. 33145. *Agent:* Cadena Capriles, Plaza Panteon, Caracas, Venezuela. *Office:* Torre de la Prensa, Caracas, Venezuela.

CAREER: Carteles, La Habana, Cuba, columnist, 1950-58; *Diario de la Marina,* La Habana, travel editor, 1956-58; *Diari El Nacional,* La Habana, columnist, 1956-58; Channel 4 Television, La Habana, reporter and commentator, 1957-60; *Ultimas Noticias,* Caracas, Venezuela, journalist, 1960-63; *Elite,* Caracas, travel editor, 1960-65; *Carteles,* Santa Domingo, Dominican Republic, editor and publisher, 1963-65; *Yates y Pesca,* Miami, Fla., editor and publisher, 1965-68; *Directorio Industrial U.S.A.,* Miami, editor and publisher, 1973-75. Notable assignments include the Costa Rican War, 1950, and the Santa Domingo Revolution, 1965.

WRITINGS: (Editor) *Libro Blanco Fuerzas Armadas Dominicanas,* C.A. (Santa Domingo), 1964; *Santa Domingo: Barricadas de Odios,* Editores Mexicanos Unidos, 1966; *Manson, Dios o Diablo?,* Lithoformas Editores, 1973. Also author of "Tras la Noticia" column, *Carteles,* 1950-58, and "Observando" column, *Diaria El Nacional,* 1956-58.

SIDELIGHTS: Montes was a reporter in Cuba during the Costa Rican War. He told *CA:* "In this war the revolutionary forces took me prisoner, and General Anastasio Somoza Sr. liberated me. In the revolution in Santa Domingo (1965) I was principle adviser of General Elias Wessin. I have been personal friends with the following presidents in America: Romulo Betancourt of Venezuela, Dumarsse Estime of Haiti, Jose Figueres of Costa Rica, Carlos Andres Perez of Venezuela, Miguel Idigoras of Guatemala, etc."

"One of my special interests," Montes added, "was to study the Maya civilization, therefore I have made trips to Yucatan, Campeche, Tabasco, Quintana Roo and Honduras throughout the years 1953-56. I have also done many trips to Europe, North Africa, South America, Central America, the Caribbean, and Middle East."

*   *   *

MONTGOMERY, Bernard Law   1887-1976

PERSONAL: Listed in some sources as Montgomery of Alamein; born November 17, 1887, in London, England; son of H. H. (an Anglican bishop); married Elizabeth Carver, 1927 (died, 1937); children: David. *Education:* Attended

Sandhurst Military Academy, 1907-08. *Home:* Isington Mill, Alton, Hampshire, England.

CAREER: British Army, 1908-58; became field marshall. Entered army, 1908; was among first to land in France, 1914; was wounded twice and mentioned in dispatches six times during World War I, becoming lieutenant-colonel and battalion commander by the armistice; commanded first battalion, Royal Warwickshire Regiment, 1931-34; commander, 9th Infantry Brigade, Portsmouth, 1937-38; became major general, 1938; commander, 8th Division in Palestine and Trans-Jordan, 1938-39, again mentioned in dispatches; commanded 3rd Division of 2nd Corps, 1939-40, successfully withdrawing his men from Dunkirk, 1940; commander, 5th Corps in Britain, 1940; general officer commanding-in-chief, Southeastern Army Command, 1941; commander, British 8th Army in Egypt, 1942-44, defeated Field Marshal Irwin Rommel's Afrika Korps at El Alamein, October-November, 1942, and pursued Germans to surrender at Tunis, then invaded Sicily and Italy, 1943; promoted to field marshal, 1944; under supreme command of General Dwight D. Eisenhower, became commander-in-chief, British Group of Armies, and Allies, which invaded Northern France (Normandy), 1944; commanded 21st Army Group through Northern France and across Rhine to receive German surrender at Luenburg, 1945; commander, British Forces of Occupation in Germany, 1945-46; created 1st Viscount Montgomery of Alamein, 1946; chief of Imperial General Staff, 1946-48; chairman, Western Alliance Commanders-in-Chief Committee, 1948-51; deputy supreme Allied commander in Europe of North Atlantic Treaty Organization (NATO), 1951-58. Writer.

AWARDS, HONORS—Military: Received numerous awards, including Distinguished Service Order and Croix de Guerre, both 1914; Order of Suvorov and Virtuti Militari, 1944; Order of King George of the Hellenes, 1944; Grand Cross of the Legion of Honor (France), Distinguished Service Medal (U.S.A.), and Grand Cordon Order of Leopold, all 1945; Medaille Militaire, 1958; Knight of Garter, Knight of Grand Cross of Bath. Other: Received numerous honorary degrees from universities, including Queen's University, Glasglow University, University of Toronto, McGill University, Liege University, St. Andrews College, and Belfast College.

WRITINGS: Forward to Victory, Hutchinson, 1946; *Ten Chapters,* Hutchinson, 1946; *Normandy to the Baltic,* Hutchinson, 1947; *El Alamein to the River Sangro,* Hutchinson, 1948; *Forward from Victory,* Hutchinson, 1948; *Memoirs,* World Publishing, 1958; *An Approach to Sanity: A Study of East-West Relations,* World Publishing, 1959; *The Path to Leadership,* Putnam, 1961; *Three Continents,* Collins, 1962; *A History of Warfare,* World Publishing, 1968; *Montgomery of Alamein,* Corgi, 1974.

SIDELIGHTS: Field Marshal Montgomery, relatively unknown before El Alamein, catapulted to the rank of national hero when he led the battered "Desert Rats," the British 8th Army, against the seemingly invincible "Desert Fox" and his Afrika Korps. With meticulous planning and superior numbers (on October 23, 1942, Montgomery had 230,000 men and 1,100 tanks in his command to Rommel's 80,000 men and 260 tanks), Montgomery succeeded in driving the Afrika Korps across the desert towards Tunisia and advancing American troops. Though the victory was hailed by Prime Minister Winston Churchill when he said, "Before Alamein, we never had a victory. After Alamein, we never had a defeat," the price was still high: the British losses were triple those of the enemy.

It was largely Montgomery's plan of concentrated landings that dictated the July 10, 1943, Allied invasion of Sicily. As General George Patton's U.S. 7th Army landed on the southern coast, Montgomery landed in the east. The 8th Army's attempt to drive up the coast to Messina was halted at Catania, and Patton reached Messina first. On September 3, 1943, Montgomery crossed the Strait of Messina and began his slice across the Italian mainland, capturing the Foggia airfields by October 1.

On June 6, 1944, Montgomery directed the British 2nd Army and the U.S. 1st Army across the English Channel to Normandy. During the first two months of the invasion Montgomery came under severe criticism for his alleged caution and slowness. His capture of Caen, which was to have been completed the first day of the invasion, was completed on the forty-second. In August he virtually destroyed two German field armies in the Argetan-Falaise pocket.

Frequently at odds with his U.S. allies, in the late summer of 1944 Montgomery fought to employ his tactics of a careful buildup of troop and material superiority followed by a massive frontal attack with secondary flanking drives (these tactics had been successful at Alamein, Mareth, the Sangro River in Italy, and Caen), to deal a death blow to the Germans. His plan was to push into the Ruhr Valley in Germany, using Belgium and Holland as springboards. The resulting broad-front attack, known as "Operation Market-Garden," collapsed when ground forces failed to take the most crucial crossing—the Arnhem Bridge. The resulting Allied casualties numbered 17,000. Later Montgomery admitted he made "a bad mistake at Arnhem," though at the time he charged Eisenhower with failing to provide enough material. Montgomery later said that "Ike had simply no experience for the job. As a field commander he was very bad."

On December 16, 1944, winter fighting came to a climax when the Germans created the Battle of the Bulge with their Ardennes counter-offensive. Montgomery commanded troops on the northern shoulder. In March, 1945, Montgomery and his forces crossed the Rhine and helped take Ruhr and then swept across Germany to the Else River. At the end of the war he commanded the British occupation forces of the Army of the Rhine.

A ruthless disciplinarian, complete tee-totaler and non-smoker, Montgomery once said, "There is only one standard of physical fitness—the standard of total war." Indeed his emphasis on endurance became legendary. As early as 1941 he demanded that all officers beneath the rank of brigadier in his command run seven miles once a week, though with the later advancement of German forces he reduced the distance to six miles. Montgomery subjected all officers and soldiers outside of the field to a rigorous series of early morning exercises, which he participated in himself. He insisted: "Every man in the Army must have the light of battle in his eyes."

As controversial in his remarks as in his strategy, and undeniably arrogant, Montgomery was once asked to name the three greatest generals in history. "The other two," he smiled, "were Alexander the Great and Napoleon." Historians, too, have contributed to the controversies inescapable in any study of Montgomery. British historian A.J.P. Taylor called him "the best British field commander since Wellington"; American history scholar Martin Blumenson has called Montgomery "the most overrated general of World War II." Field Marshal Claude Auchinleck said Montgomery was "a great soldier with great determination," and added that Monty "never had a sense of humor." Lord Chafont, who wrote a biography of Montgomery, said his subject was "vain, unimaginative and brutal." Whatever the final verdict, few generals emerged from World War II with more fame and adulation than Montgomery.

On the occasion of the death of Field Marshal Montgomery, Queen Elizabeth II sent David Montgomery a message which said, "He will be remembered as a great soldier who did so much to bring about Allied victory in World War II." And indeed, in the final analysis, Montgomery did just what generals are supposed to do: he won battles.

BIOGRAPHICAL/CRITICAL SOURCES: New York Times, November 11, 1942, November 15, 1942.

OBITUARIES: Washington Post, March 25, 1976; *Newsweek,* April 5, 1976; *Time,* April 5, 1976.*

(Died March 24, 1976, in Isington, England)

*   *   *

MOONEY, Booth   1912-1977

July 3, 1912—March 22, 1977; American writer, newspaperman, executive assistant and biographer of Senator Lyndon Johnson (*The Lyndon Johnson Story),* and author of other works of biography, political nonfiction, and novels. He died in Sumner, Md. Obituaries: *Washington Post,* March 24, 1977. (See index for previous *CA* sketch)

*   *   *

MOORE, Acel   1940-

PERSONAL: Born October 5, 1940, in Philadelphia, Pa.; son of Jerry Acel (an electrician) and Hura Mae (Harrington) Moore; married Carolyn Weaver, June, 1964 (divorced, 1972); married Cheryl Rice, October, 1975; children: Acel, Jr. *Education:* Attended Charles Morris Price School of Journalism, 1966-67. *Office: Philadelphia Inquirer,* 400 N. Broad St., Philadelphia, Pa. 19101.

CAREER/WRITINGS: Philadelphia Inquirer, Philadelphia, Pa., reporter, 1968—. Co-producer of nationally syndicated television program, "Black Perspective on the News." Lecturer. *Military service:* U.S. Army, 1959-61. *Member:* National Association of Black Journalists, Association of Black Journalists of Philadelphia (president, 1977—), Pen and Pencil Club of Philadelphia. *Awards, honors:* Pennsylvania Bar Association Scales of Justice Award, 1970, for series on juvenile court system; Sigma Delta Chi public service awards, 1972, 1976, for investigative reporting; Pennsylvania Associated Press Managing Editors Association Awards, 1975, 1976, for series on gang warfare; Pulitzer Prize, Haywood Broun Award, National Headliners Award, and Robert F. Kennedy Journalism Award, 1976, all for series on Fairview State Hospital; Philadelphia Party Journalism Award, 1976; Annual Paul Robeson Award from Afro-American History Museum, 1976; Swarthmore College Annual Upward Bound Yvonne Motley McCabe Award, 1977. Other awards include Pennsylvania Prison Society Award, House of Omoja Humanitarian Award, Youth Development Center Community Service Award, Philadelphia Bar Association Award, Woman in Communications National Clarion Award, National Business League of Philadelphia Award, North Philadelphia Mothers Concern Award, and White Rock Baptist Church Achievement Award.

SIDELIGHTS: Moore told *CA* that his series on Fairview State Hospital for Criminally Insane in Philadelphia "led to a state investigation into conditions, a significant lowering of the inmate population, and the indictment of guards for murder of inmates."

When asked if he feels that black journalists have particular responsibilities, Moore responded, "Our responsibility is to report from a black perspective when necessary, also to attempt to bring to the public issues of particular concern and interest to the black reader. Like all other journalists, black journalists have a responsibility to report fairly and accurately, using balance in stories."

*   *   *

MOORE, Arthur   1906(?)-1977

1906(?)—January 9, 1977; American editor and author of books on agriculture. He was editor of newspapers in California and Illinois before joining McGraw-Hill World News, where he served as a correspondent and later became director. He died in Charlottesville, Va. Obituaries: *Washington Post,* January 19, 1977.

*   *   *

MOORE, Bernard   1904-

PERSONAL: Born June 3, 1904, in England; son of Douglas (a solicitor) and Daisy (Draper) Moore; married Enid Guinevere Evans (a picture researcher), December 5, 1927; children: Humphrey, Jane (O'Neill), Jonathon. *Education:* Educated in London, England. *Religion:* Christian. *Home:* Cleves, Peasmarsh, Rye, Sussexshire, England.

CAREER: Bank accountant and manager in India, 1927-31; *London Daily Herald,* London, England, foreign correspondent in Geneva, Switzerland, 1932-34, accredited correspondent to League of Nations, 1934-37; night foreign editor and diplomatic correspondent in London, 1937-40; British Broadcasting Corp. (BBC), editor of overseas news broadcasts from London, 1940-47, United Nations correspondent in New York, 1947-54, in London, head of African, Caribbean, and colonial services, 1954-58, editor of external service news, 1958-65. Notable assignments include Berchtesgaden and Godesburg talks in Germany, 1938; entry of German troops into the Sudetenland and Czechoslovakia, 1938; closing of the League of Nations, 1946; opening of the United Nations, 1946. Consulting editor to encyclopedias; lecturer; picture researcher. Member of elections committee of Royal Institute for International Affairs, 1958-65; member of Sussex rent assessment committee and rent tribunal, 1965—. *Member:* United Nations Correspondents Association (vice-president, 1948-51), International Association of Journalists (former secretary-general), Royal Society of Arts (fellow), Royal African Society (vice-president, 1963-76).

WRITINGS: The First Assembly, New York: An ABC of International Organizations, United Nations Association, 1946; *The Second Assembly, New York,* United Nations Association, 1947; *Second Lesson: Seven Years at the United Nations,* St. Martin's, 1957; (compiler and contributor) *Mothers,* Paddington Press, 1976. Contributor of daily and weekly broadcast features to BBC; contributor to many magazines, including the *New York Times Magazine.* Cofounder and assistant editor of *Journal of the Indian Institute of Banking.*

*   *   *

MOORE, Keith L(eon)   1925-

PERSONAL: Born October 5, 1925, in Brantford, Ontario, Canada; son of James Henry and Gertrude M. (McCombe) Moore; married Marion Edith McDermid, August 20, 1949;

children: Warren, Pamela, Karen, Laurel, Joyce. *Education:* University of Western Ontario, B.A., 1949, M.Sc., 1951, Ph.D., 1954. *Religion:* United Church of Canada. *Home:* 1540 Elite Rd., Mississauga, Ontario, Canada L5J 3B4. *Office:* Department of Anatomy, Faculty of Medicine, University of Toronto, Toronto, Ontario, Canada M5S 1A8.

CAREER: University of Western Ontario, London, lecturer in anatomy, 1954-56; University of Manitoba, Winnipeg, assistant professor, 1956-59, associate professor, 1959-65, professor of anatomy, 1965-76, head of department, 1976—; University of Toronto, Toronto, Ontario, professor of anatomy and chairman of department, 1976—. President, TDH Enterprises (a publishing and investment company). Member of Canadian Cytology Council; chairman of board of Canadian Federation of Biological Societies, 1969-70. *Military service:* Royal Canadian Navy, sick berth attendant, 1944-46.

MEMBER: International Academy of Cytology (fellow), Royal Society of Medicine (fellow), Canadian Association of Anatomists (president, 1968-70), American Association of Anatomists, Teratology Society, American Medical Writers Association, Anatomy Society of Great Britain and Ireland. *Awards, honors:* Award from American Medical Writers Association, 1974, for excellence in medical publications.

WRITINGS: (Editor) *The Sex Chromatin,* Saunders, 1965; *The Developing Human: Clinically-Oriented Embryology,* Saunders, 1973, 2nd edition, 1977; *Before We Are Born: Basic Embryology and Birth Defects,* Saunders, 1974; *Study Guide and Review Manual of Human Embryology,* Saunders, 1975; *Study Guide and Review Manual of Human Anatomy,* Saunders, 1976; *Study Guide and Review Manual of the Human Nervous System,* Saunders, in press. Member of editorial advisory board of *Acta Cytologica,* 1962—.

SIDELIGHTS: Moore writes: "My aim has been to write books in anatomy for the medical profession, especially first-year health science students, that are easy to understand and show the clinical relevance of the material. Because it is not necessary for professionals to know the huge mass of anatomical knowledge, emphasis has been placed on essential material that has value in the practice of medicine." His books have been published in Spanish, Portuguese, French, German, Greek, Italian, and Japanese.

*   *   *

MOORE, Nicholas 1918-
(Guy Kelly)

PERSONAL: Born November 16, 1918, in Cambridge, England; son of George Edward (a Cambridge philosopher) and Dorothy (Ely) Moore; married Priscilla Craig in the 1940's (divorced, early 1950's); married Shirley Putnam, July 25, 1953; children: Juliet, Peregrine, Delphine (deceased). *Education:* Cambridge University, B.A., 1940. *Politics:* "Socialism with a human face." *Religion:* None. *Home:* 89 Oakdene Rd., St. Mary Cray, Kent BR5 2AL, England.

CAREER: Writer. Worked as editorial assistant for Editions Poetry London, London, England, and as editor of *New Poetry,* London, in the 1940's; has also worked as a horticulturist. *Member:* British Iris Society, American Iris Society, Sempervivum Society, Cambridge Union Society. *Awards, honors:* Patrons Prize from *Contemporary Poetry,* 1945; Harriet Monroe Memorial Prize from *Poetry,* 1947.

WRITINGS—Poems: A Wish in Season, Fortune Press, 1941; *The Island and the Cattle,* Fortune Press, 1941; *A Book for Priscilla,* Epsilon Pamphlets (Cambridge), 1941;

Buzzing Around with a Bee and Other Poems, Editions Poetry, London, 1942; *The Cabaret, The Dancer, The Gentleman,* Fortune Press, 1942; *The Glass Tower: Poems, 1936-43,* Editions Poetry, London, 1944; (with Fred Marnau and Wrey Gardiner) *Three Poems,* Grey Walls Press, 1944; *Thirty-Five Anonymous Odes,* Fortune Press, 1944; (under pseudonym Guy Kelly) *The War of the Little Jersey Cows,* Fortune Press, 1945; *Recollections of the Gala: Selected Poems, 1943-48,* Editions Poetry, London, 1950; *Identity,* Cadenza Press, 1969; *Resolution and Identity,* Covent Garden Press, 1970; *Spleen* (thirty-one versions of Baudelaire's poem), Menard Press (London), 1973.

Other: (Editor with John Bayliss and Douglas Newton) *The Fortune Anthology,* Fortune Press, 1942; *Henry Miller,* Opus Press, 1943, Folcroft, 1969; (editor) *The P L Book of Modern American Short Stories,* Editions Poetry, London, 1945; (editor with Newton) *Atlantic Anthology,* Fortune Press, 1945; *The Tall Bearded Iris,* Transatlantic Arts, 1956.

Contributor of poems and short stories, sometimes under a variety of pseudonyms, to *Sewanee Review, Furioso, View,* and other periodicals. Founder and editor of *Seven* (literary magazine), 1938-40.

WORK IN PROGRESS: A collection of poems; a new volume of poems, tentatively titled *Longings of the Acrobats.*

SIDELIGHTS: "I've been influenced by surrealism (mainly the paintings)," Moore told *CA,* "but perhaps my main influence has been the Southern group in America, John Crowe Ransom, John Peale Bishop, Robert Penn Warren, Allen Tate. However, I don't believe in any type of poetry exclusively. The first poet I became really enthusiastic about, as a young boy, was Conrad Aiken! How much my enthusiasms show in my work, I don't know. Of my own generation I liked best Weldon Kees, Howard Nemerov, William J. Smith, and Dustan Thompson, and most of his Vice Versa people."

Moore developed a practice in some of his poetry of using "speakers" and "authors" to achieve negative capability: "My poems are all 'me' and characteristic to me, to those who read them all, but they may seem very disparate in style—different from each other—to those who haven't read them all. But this arises deliberately from my inclusive view of poetry. I don't like being cabined and confined. I like my poems to reflect on the whole gamut of my feelings, thoughts, intuition, enthusiasms, dislikes, etc., either separately or mixed in various proportions. Because this idea still is apparently not easily digested, I found people attributed single opinions or comments or characterisations in my poems to me personally—the personal heresy. I therefore took to naming 'speakers' in some of my poems. A further more recent step was to make these 'speakers' the authors of these poems. So that the 'author' as well as the title of the poem became part of the poem. So 'Freako Charlotti by Lulupicciano Grossi' by Rosine Macoolh is actually a poem written by Nicholas Moore. In this case the author is an anagram of my own name, but I do use other names, Henry Birdsong, April Winterbottom, Harrison Blamesworthy, for instance, as well as other anagrams, for various purposes of satire or of "depersonalizing" the theme. For I don't believe poems 'make statements' or 'communicate' in the popular or journalistic sense of the words, though people may make statements in them. In some ways I regard many poems as entertainment—like Graham Greene's less serious novels—but, as with his, entertainment of a very high order.

The best are something rather more. This is independent of their particular genre—high seriousness, low comedy, or bitter satire. Or for that matter ballads or nature poetry. Shakespeare understood this, and so did the Metaphysicals and Elizabethans in general.''

"I've also been interested in gardening and plant breeding," Moore continued, "particularly alpines, irises, and sempervivums. Another of my enthusiasms is jazz, of which I have also written. Henry 'Red' Allen, and the old Luis Russell Band, Edmund Hall, the Claude Hopkins Band, Chu, Buddy Tate, Cootie Williams, Lester Young, Billie Holliday are among my greatest heroes—mostly now dead, but alive on records. Analogous, perhaps, to the writing of poetry, I like my jazz to 'swing'—to have a really fine rhythm section.

"Apart from that I'm interested in the usual run of things most people are interested in—even politics. But I even like Conservatives to have a human face—though preferably not the kind of humanity displayed by the Nixons and Stonehouses of the world. I don't believe in original sin. It seems to me either a wicked theory or weak excuse!''

*   *   *

MOORES, Richard   1909-
(Dick Moores)

PERSONAL: Born December 12, 1909, in Lincoln, Neb.; son of Charles (an executive) and Valla (a pianist; maiden name, Bowdrie) Moores; married Gretchen Stahl (a sculptor), May 1, 1937; children: William, Sara, Richard. *Education:* Attended Chicago Academy of Fine Arts, 1930. *Home address:* Box 129, Fairview, N.C. 28730. *Office:* Chicago Tribune-New York Syndicate, 220 E. 42nd St., New York, N.Y. 10017.

CAREER: Began as assistant to Chester Gould, creator of "Dick Tracy" comic strip, Chicago, Ill., 1931-36; United Features Syndicate, New York, N.Y., creator, writer and artist of "Jim Handy—Man Against the World" and "Windy and Paddles" comic strips, 1936-42; Walt Disney Studios, Burbank, Calif., artist of newspaper comics, 1942-56, and co-developer of syndicated comic strip, "Scamp," 1955; Chicago Tribune-New York News Syndicate, New York City, assistant to Frank King, creator of "Gasoline Alley" comic strip, 1956-60, artist and writer of "Gasoline Alley," daily comic strip, 1960—, and Sunday comic strip, 1975—. *Member:* National Cartoonists Society, Newspaper Comics Council. *Awards, honors:* National Cartoonists Society Reuben Award, 1974, for best story strip, and 1975, for year's outstanding cartoonist.

WRITINGS: The Smoke From Gasoline Alley, Sheed, 1976; *Gasoline Alley,* Avon, 1976; *Jim Handy,* Hyperion, 1977.

SIDELIGHTS: CA asked Moores how closely "Gasoline Alley" activity parallels activity in his own life, and to what extent characters are drawn from people he knows. "I draw on my own experiences," he responded, "both past and present, and on the experiences of my family and friends—especially in the stories which relate the adventures of the Wallet family.

"The rooming house where Clovia, Slim and Chipper live is the one I lived in while attending art school in Chicago in the early thirties. The address was 218 E. Huron. My roommates and I lived in a small basement room in the front on the north side. One of our two windows looked out into the Allerton tennis courts. Our ceiling was decorated with gray pipes. The bath was around the furnace to the left.

"Though I use some of my son Richard's traits for 'Slim', my daughter Sara's for Clovia and son Bill's (a surgeon) for Chipper, I don't think of them as being these characters. I honestly think of all my characters as being real people. It seems to me they make up their own minds about what they want to do. I just follow them around and record it. I've known them so long I can see inside their little comic strip. The Wallets do the ordinary day-to-day things. Rufus and his group do crazy, outlandish things and you can count on it. I own a goat and some of the goat's expressions, or nonexpressions, turn up on Becky, Joel's donkey. Also the trick bear was inspired by my daughter's Doberman which at a tender age used to put his arms around my neck. The Great Dane is patterned after many Danes we have owned over the years.''

*   *   *

MOORSOM, Sasha   1931-

PERSONAL: Born January 25, 1931, in Hampshire, England; daughter of Raisley and Ann (Thomson) Moorsom; married Michael Young (a sociologist and writer), 1961; children: Sophie, Toby. *Education:* Girton College, Cambridge, B.A. (first class honors), 1953. *Politics:* Labour. *Religion:* "Free-thinker." *Home:* Keeper's Cottage, Dartington Hall, Totnes, Devon, England.

CAREER: British Broadcasting Corp., London, England, features producer, 1953-61; *Where* (education journal), Cambridge, England, editor, 1962-64; free-lance journalist, 1964-68; Inner London Education Authority, London, teacher, 1968-71; writer, 1971—. *Awards, honors:* Prizes from Author's Club and *Yorkshire Post,* both 1977, for *Lavender Burning.*

WRITINGS: (Translator) *Perrault's Fairy Tales,* Doubleday, 1972; *Lavender Burning* (novel), Coward, 1976 (published in England as *A Lavender Trip,* Bodley Head, 1976).

Anthologized in *Dartington Anthology.* Author of column "Information" in *Listener,* 1965-68. Contributor of poems to magazines, including *New Statesman* and *Observer.*

WORK IN PROGRESS: A second novel, set in Africa.

*   *   *

MORAIN, Lloyd L.   1917-

PERSONAL: Born April 2, 1917, in Pomona, Calif.; son of Jesse L. and Adel (Gutheil) Morain; married Mary Dewing (a volunteer worker), July 6, 1946. *Education:* University of California, Los Angeles, A.B., 1940. *Religion:* "Humanist." *Home address:* P.O. Box 7190, Carmel, Calif. 93921. *Agent:* Betty Marks, 51 East 42nd St., New York, N.Y. 10017.

CAREER: Business executive for various water, gas, and industrial corporations, 1940-65; Edward Durant Investment Co., Cambridge, Mass., vice-president, 1965—. President of Illinois Gas Co. and Eastern Illinois Gas & Securities Co., both 1970—. Past member of board of directors of Planned Parenthood Federation of America. *Member:* International Society for General Semantics (president, 1956-67), American Humanist Association (president, 1950-55, 1968-72).

WRITINGS: Humanism As the Next Step, Beacon Press, 1954; *The Human Cougar: Our Endangered Human Species,* Prometheus Books, 1976. Editor of *Free Mind,* 1968-69.

MORAIS, Vamberto 1921-

PERSONAL: Born September 1, 1921, in Recife, Brazil; son of Napoleao (in commerce) and M. (Lopes) Morais; married M. Lourdes Goncalves (a teacher), December 23, 1958; children: Ariadne. Education: University of Recife, M.D., 1944; University of London, B.A. (honors), 1955. Home: 40 Southfields, London NW4 4NB, England. Office: External Services, British Broadcasting Corp., Bush House, London W.C.2, England.

CAREER: Physician in Brazil, 1944-46; British Broadcasting Corp. (BBC), London, England, freelance writer, 1947-50; University of Recife, Recife, Brazil, lecturer, 1956; BBC, staff member, 1957-60; University of Recife, lecturer, 1961-64; BBC, broadcaster, 1964—. Awards, honors: Nonfiction prize from Brazilian Academy of Letters, 1972, for A Short History of Anti-Semitism.

WRITINGS: A emancipacao da mulher: As raizes do preconceito anti-feminino e seu declino (title means "The Emancipation of Women"), Ed. Porto Alegre Cital, 1968; Pequena historia do anti-semitismo, Difusao Europeia do Livro, 1972, revised English translation published as A Short History of Anti-Semitism, Norton, 1976.

WORK IN PROGRESS: A book on Christ.

SIDELIGHTS: "I am fascinated by the history of ideas and myths, and by the whole phenomenon of human prejudices, particularly as they are reflected in language. Comparative religion is also one of my main interests. On studying Jewish history and anti-Semitism I was struck by the way the fate of the Jews was shaped by the image they had of themselves and the hostility and prejudice they have encountered."

* * *

MORAND, Paul 1888-1976

March 13, 1888—July 23, 1976; French diplomat and author of several novels, books of short stories, and travel pieces; especially known in the United States for his best-selling book New York, written about his favorite city. He died in Paris, France. Obituaries: AB Bookman's Weekly, August 23-30, 1976.

* * *

MORENO, Pedro R. 1947-

PERSONAL: Born December 30, 1947, in Corpus Christi, Tex.; son of Manuel (a shoeman) and Wenceslada (Rangel) Moreno; married: Lydia E. (a ward clerk), November 25, 1972; children: Christina Jean, Danielia. Education: Attended art school. Religion: "Meta-physical student." Home: 4814 Archer St., Corpus Christi, Tex. 78415. Office: P.O. Box 7081, Corpus Christi, Tex. 78415.

CAREER: Cartoonist; creator of comic strips "Brother Simon and Lucus," and "Chris," both syndicated by Trans-World News Service. President and instructor at Moreno School of Cartooning. Member and docent of Art Museum of South Texas. Investigating officer for International Unidentified Flying Object Bureau. Military service: Texas National Guard.

WRITINGS: Lucus! For Heaven Sake! (cartoons), Flaming Arrow Press, 1976. Cartoonist for the newspaper Voice.

BIOGRAPHICAL/CRITICAL SOURCES: Texas Catholic—Gulf Coast, February, 1976.

* * *

MORGAN, Brian S. 1924(?)-1976

1924(?)—July, 1976; British railroad authority and novelist; wrote several novels before turning exclusively to trains and wrote more than six classics on the subject. He died in England. Obituaries: AB Bookman's Weekly, October 4, 1976.

* * *

MORGAN, David T(aft, Jr.) 1937-

PERSONAL: Born January 5, 1937, in Fayetteville, N.C.; son of David Taft and Bessie (a sales clerk; maiden name, Herring) Morgan; married Judith McIntosh, December 28, 1958; children: Cynthia (Mrs. Edward Hinkle), Brian. Education: Baylor University, B.A., 1958; University of North Carolina, M.A., 1963, Ph.D., 1968. Politics: Democrat. Religion: Southern Baptist. Home: 9 Brookhill Lane, Montevallo, Ala. 35115. Office: Department of Social Sciences, University of Montevallo, Montevallo, Ala. 35115.

CAREER: University of Virginia, Patrick Henry College, Martinsville, instructor, 1964-66, assistant professor of history, 1966-68; Texas A & M University, College Station, assistant professor of history, 1968-73; University of Montevallo, Montevallo, Ala., professor of history and chairman of department of social sciences, 1973—. Visiting associate professor at Rhode Island College, 1970-71; reader for Educational Testing Service, 1975. Member: Organization of American Historians, Southern Historical Association, Alabama Association of Historians, Georgia Historical Society, North Carolina History and Literary Society, Lions Club.

WRITINGS: (With William J. Schmidt) North Carolinians in the Continental Congress, Blair, 1976. Contributor to history journals.

WORK IN PROGRESS: Editing John Gray Blount's papers for North Carolina archives.

SIDELIGHTS: Morgan comments briefly: "I limit my research and writing to topics in which I am interested—even if there is likely to be no outlet for publication. I do not write for a living. I write for enjoyment. I think of subjects as interesting and enlightening—never as vital."

* * *

MORGAN, Robin 1941-

PERSONAL: Born January 29, 1941, in Lake Worth, Fla.; daughter of Faith Berkley Morgan; married Kenneth Pitchford (a poet, novelist, and playwright), September 19, 1962; children: Blake Ariel Morgan. Education: Student at Columbia University. Politics: "Radical feminist." Religion: "Wiccean Atheist." Residence: New York, N.Y. Agent: Georges Borchardt, Inc., 145 East 52nd St., New York, N.Y. 10022.

CAREER: Curtis Brown Ltd., New York, N.Y., associate literary agent, 1960-62; free-lance editor, 1964-70; writer, 1970—. National and international lecturer on feminism, 1970-76; guest professor at New College (Sarasota, Fla.), 1972; has given poetry readings all over the United States. Member: Authors Guild of Authors League of America, Women's Anti-Defamation League, Susan B. Anthony National Memorial Association.

WRITINGS: (Editor with Charlotte Bunch and Joanne Cooke) The New Women, Bobbs-Merrill, 1970; (editor) Sisterhood Is Powerful, Random House, 1970; Monster: Poems, Random House, 1972; Lady of the Beasts: Poems, Random House, 1976; Going Too Far: The Personal Chronicle of a Feminist, Random House, 1977.

Represented in anthologies, including No More Masks!, edited by Howe and Bass, for Doubleday; *The Young American Writers*, edited by Kostelanetz, Funk; *Campfires of the Resistance*, edited by Gitlin, Bobbs-Merrill. Contributing editor, *Ms.*, 1977. Contributor of articles and poems to about a hundred literary and political journals, including *Atlantic, New York Times, Hudson Review*, and *Feminist Art Journal*.

WORK IN PROGRESS: Tales of the Witches, historical fiction; a third book of poems; a cycle of verse plays.

SIDELIGHTS: Robin Morgan writes: "I am an artist and a political being as well. My aim has been to forge these two concerns into an integrity which affirms language, art, craft, form, beauty, tragedy, and audacity with the needs and visions of women, as part of an emerging new culture which could enrich us all."

* * *

MORGAN, Stanley 1929-

PERSONAL: Born November 10, 1929, in Liverpool, England; moved to Ireland, 1947; son of Thomas (a transport firm manager) and Annie (Pearson) Morgan; married Josephine Peggy, February 8, 1958 (divorced, September 13, 1972); married Linda Williams, December 24, 1973; children: Jo (daughter), Robert; (stepchildren) Simon, Sarah. *Education:* Attended public schools in England. *Politics:* "Disillusioned Conservative." *Religion:* "Lapsed Church of England." *Home and office:* 15 Beech Court, Ballinclea Rd., Killiney, County Dublin, Eire. *Agent:* Eric L'Epine Smith, 10 Wyndham Pl., London W1H LAS, England.

CAREER: National Provincial Bank, Liverpool, England, clerk, 1946-51; Bank of Nova Scotia, Toronto, Ontario, teller, 1951-53; worked a variety of jobs, including sewing-machine salesman, bookkeeper on tobacco farm, menswear salesman, while pursuing acting career both in Canada and Rhodesia, 1953-58; commercial actor in London, England, 1958-73; author, 1973—. *Military service:* British Army, 1947-49. *Awards, honors:* Named actor of the year at Southern Rhodesian Drama Festival, 1958.

WRITINGS—Russ Tobin series; all fiction, except as noted; published by Mayflower, except as noted: *The Sewing Machine Man*, 1969; *The Debt Collector*, 1970; *The Courier*, 1971; *Come Again Courier*, 1972; *Tobin Takes Off*, 1973; *Tobin on Safari*, 1973; *Tobin in Paradise*, 1974; *Tobin in Trouble*, 1974; *Tobin for Hire*, 1975; *Tobin in Las Vegas*, 1975; *Tobin in Tahiti*, Futura, 1976; *Tobin Down Under*, Futura, 1976; *Tobin Bedside Guide to Smoother Seduction* (sexual advice), Star Books, 1976; *Here Comes Tobin*, Futura, 1977; *Tobin Up Tight*, Star Books, 1977; *Tobin Hard Up*, Star Books, 1977.

Fly Boys series: *The Fly Boys*, Mayflower, 1974; *The Fly Boys in London*, Mayflower, 1975; *The Fly Boys Skyjacked*, W. H. Allen, 1976.

Other series: *The Rise of Randy Comfort*, Futura, 1976; *A Blow for Gabriel Horn*, W. H. Allen, 1977; *Inside Albert Shifty*, Star Books, 1977.

Adventure books: *Octopus Hill*, Mayflower, 1970; *Mission to Katuma*, Mayflower, 1973.

WORK IN PROGRESS: The Further Doings of Randy Comfort, a novel.

SIDELIGHTS: Stanley Morgan wrote his first two novels between calls from his television agent. As an actor he was unable to leave his home because, as he explained: "I once went to the corner shop and lost a lucrative Esso commercial." So one day while sitting near a silent phone he began writing.

His first two books drew heavily on his varied occupational experiences in Canada and Rhodesia. *The Sewing Machine Man* was only published after a chance meeting with a would-be paperback publisher in a pub. But first Morgan had to buy back the manuscript from a hardback publisher, who had been stalling on publishing it for over a year, and he had to invest some of his own money in the new paperback concern. In the end, any difficulties were by far outweighed by the rewards. The Russ Tobin series has sold over four million books and has elevated its author among the ranks of the most successful paperback writers in the world.

Morgan told *CA:* "The sole motivation important to my career is that my readers should pronounce my most recent book as enjoyable, as entertaining, as my last. I possess no fervent 'literary' pretensions, merely a driving desire to entertain, and am deeply touched to receive a fan letter expressing pleasure and satisfaction. Though serious-minded about many issues—social and racial injustice, political ineptitude, the break down of law and order—I also believe strongly in the necessity of humour and thus have taken that path in my writing. Having known the agony of poverty and job-frustration in my early life, I tend to concentrate on these themes in my books, endowing my 'heroes'—Russ Tobin, Randy Comfort, Gabriel Horn, and Albert Shifty—with similar frustrations, with which my many readers undoubtedly identify.

"I consider myself most fortunate to have at last found my metier and to be able to share a life of travel and professional interest with a beautiful wife and companion, Linda. Beyond my writing day and the joy of my home life with my wife, mother, and four lovely children, my interests are few. I am neither overly-gregarious nor excessively reclusive, but find no need whatever to join clubs, fraternities, or societies. A perfect day for me is six hours of satisfactory writing, a hot shower, two large vodka-tonics, dinner with my wife, then conversation as bottomless as the coffee-pot.

"My ambition? To continue doing what I'm doing for a very long time."

Morgan's wife, Linda, helps with each book. She edits them, makes critical suggestions, and just "generally knocks them into shape." He explained: "She reads what I've written every night. If she's not laughing pretty soon, then something is very wrong. We put in a full day, and rarely take a holiday. I write a first draft with corrections, then I hand it over to Linda, who has an office downstairs. She produces the second draft." Morgan believes this husband-and-wife-team effort helps to keep the escapades fresh and exciting, and in addition, it provides the important feminine point of view. "Fifty per cent of my letters come from women," Morgan insists.

In 1974 Morgan and his family left England to live in Southern Ireland. The prohibitive taxation in England forced the emigration. "Any tax exile exiles himself with the greatest difficulty," lamented the author. "One does not uproot one's family, leave one's friends in a light way just to be richer. We miss the English parks and playing fields. But when I was living in Surrey with my family, I was writing four books for the government and one book for me. I have no securities, no private income, no pension. So I want to keep my money for my wife's and my old age. Isn't it sensible?"

For the future, Morgan plans to develop his three new character series of Randy Comfort, Gabriel Horn, and Albert

443

Shifty and to continue to expand his recent Fly Boys series; all in addition to his contract for twelve new books in the Russ Tobin series.

BIOGRAPHICAL/CRITICAL SOURCES: Sunday Independent (Ireland), November 2, 1975; *Sunday Times* (London), August 1, 1976; *Daily Express,* September 20, 1976.

* * *

MORNINGSTAR, Connie 1927-

PERSONAL: Born February 9, 1927, in Toledo, Ohio; daughter of Buhl (a contractor) and Marjorie (a bank officer; maiden name, Nichols) VanOrden; married Gale E. Morningstar (a dental ceramist), May 10, 1952; children: Warren, Alan. *Education:* Attended University of Alabama, 1945, and University of Toledo, 1945-46; University of Miami, Coral Gables, Fla., B.A. (cum laude), 1950. *Religion:* United Church of Christ. *Residence:* Murray, Utah.

CAREER: Travel agent in Miami, Fla., 1950-51, and Toledo, Ohio, 1951-52; writer, 1968—. Member of Utah Heritage Foundation. *Member:* Utah State Historical Society. *Awards, honors:* First place award from Utah State Institute of Fine Arts, 1971, for story "The Piquancy of Kumquats."

WRITINGS: Flapper Furniture and Interiors of the 1920's, Wallace-Homestead, 1971; *American Furniture Classics,* Wallace-Homestead, 1976; *Early Utah Furniture,* Utah State University Press, 1976. Author of columns "Ask Connie" in *Antique Trader Weekly,* and "Ask Us" in *Antiques Journal,* both 1972—. Contributing editor of *Antiques Journal.*

WORK IN PROGRESS: American Furniture 1876-1930 and Directory of Manufacturers; Early Utah Pottery.

* * *

MORRIS, (Murrell) Edward 1935-

PERSONAL: Born September 21, 1935, in Elkview, W.Va.; son of Charles Sennet (a laborer) and Mary Elizabeth (a laborer; maiden name, Pauley) Morris; married Norma Chapman (a photographer), February 6, 1960; children: Erin, Christopher (deceased), Jason, Rachel. *Education:* Morris Harvey College, B.A., 1958; Ohio University, M.S., 1959. *Politics:* Socialist. *Religion:* None. *Home:* 249 Crim St., Bowling Green, Ohio 43402. *Office: Writer's Digest,* 9933 Alliance Rd., Cincinnati, Ohio 45242.

CAREER: Findlay College, Findlay, Ohio, instructor in English, 1960-63; Alice Lloyd College, Pippa Passes, Ky., assistant professor of English, 1965-66; Edinboro State College, Edinboro, Pa., assistant professor of English, 1967-70; Brookside Children's Home, Charleston, W.Va., childcare worker, 1971-72; Appalachia Educational Laboratory, Charleston, W.Va., staff writer and editor, 1972-74; freelance writer, 1974-76; *Writer's Digest,* Cincinnati, Ohio, assistant editor, 1976—.

WRITINGS: (With Freida Gregory) *TV: The Family School,* Avatar Press, 1976.

Poems anthologized in *Poems from Bowling Green,* edited by Frederick Eckman, Winesburg Editions, 1967; *Poems from the Hills, 1970,* edited by William Plumley, Morris Harvey College Press, 1970. Contributor to *Writer's Yearbook.* Contributor to professional journals, and to *TV Guide, Billboard,* and *Bluegrass Unlimited.* Editor of *Findlay College Alumnus* and *Crippled Minstrel.*

WORK IN PROGRESS: Studying country and bluegrass music.

SIDELIGHTS: Morris writes: "Writing is appealing to me because it allows me to earn a living without going out-of-doors. As much as I enjoy good writing (doing it or reading it) I have almost no faith in its ability to change people's lives. And I have identical qualms about teaching. Had I been a religious man, I would have tried to sell my soul to write like Peter DeVries or S. J. Perelman."

* * *

MORRIS, Mel (Merrill) 1930-

PERSONAL: Born May 29, 1930, in Hammond, Ontario, Canada; son of Norman (a farmer) and Violet Morris; married Shirley Dworkin (a writer and editor), November 8, 1952; children: Kelly, Kathleen, Jennifer. *Education:* Carleton University, B.J. *Politics:* New Democratic Party. *Home:* 22 Rathnelly Ave., Toronto, Ontario, Canada M4V 2M3. *Office: Maclean's* Magazine, 481 University Ave., Toronto, Ontario, Canada M5W 1A7.

CAREER/WRITINGS: Reuters News Agency, London, England, North American editor, 1957-62; *Toronto Star,* Toronto, Ontario, foreign and senior editor, 1962-69; *Toronto Telegram,* Toronto, city editor, 1969-71; *Toronto Star,* national editor, 1971-73; *Maclean's* magazine, Toronto, managing editor, 1973—. *Member:* Toronto Press Club.

* * *

MORSE, Harold Marston 1892-1977

March 24, 1892—June 22, 1977; American mathematician, educator, and author of articles in his field; credited with originating the mathematical theory of analysis in the large. He taught at Harvard, Cornell, and Brown universities before joining the faculty of Institute for Advanced Study at Princeton, N.J., in 1935. There he was a close associate of Albert Einstein. He was the recipient of numerous awards, including twenty honorary degrees, and a National Medal of Science in 1965. He died in Princeton, N.J. Obituaries: *New York Times,* June 26, 1977; *Washington Post,* June 26, 1977; *Current Biography,* August, 1977.

* * *

MORTIMER, John L(ynn) 1908-

PERSONAL: Born November 3, 1908, in Smithville, Tex.; son of Charles and Minnie (Parker) Mortimer; married Fae Grimsley, October 10, 1937; children: Martha Anne, John. *Education:* University of Missouri, B.J., 1958; South Texas College of Law, J.D., 1968. *Home:* 918 Chimney Rock, Houston, Tex. 77056. *Office:* 632 West Bough, Houston, Tex. 77024.

CAREER: Worked as a reporter in Central and South America, 1928-31; worked as a newspaperman in Houston and San Antonio, Tex., Chicago, Ill., and San Francisco, Calif., writing for *New York Times, Houston Press, Houston Post, San Antonio Light,* and other papers, 1932-42; U.S. Steel Corp., Public Relations, Houston, Tex., district director, 1943-52, regional director, 1952-53, district, 1953-67; attorney in Houston, 1969—; West Bough Art Gallery, Houston, owner, 1975—. Artist. Chairman, public relations committee of State Bar of Texas, 1969-70; special counsel in law firm of Johnson, Cox & Miller, 1970-71. *Military service:* U.S. Army, 1938-43; served in military intelligence; became lieutenant. *Member:* Public Relations Society of America (co-founder), American Arbitration Association, Houston Bar Association, Houston Press Club, Houston Club.

WRITINGS: Song of the Paternales, Madrona, 1977. Contributor to *New York Times, Houston Press, Houston Post, San Antonio Light,* and other periodicals.

WORK IN PROGRESS: Last Stage for San Francisco, a novel on the old Butterfield Stage Road.

SIDELIGHTS: Mortimer told *CA*: "Historians will tell you that in ancient China the development of art preceded the evolvement of the written word, or literature; but more especially that the one grew out of the other or developed along with it. Chinese writing, so they say, is a form of painting in itself—some 5,000 characters in scope—designed to accommodate the beauty of thought visually into the beauty of language.

"It has always been a disappointment to me that when fine novelists undertake to spin a yarn in a romantic setting the beauty of the setting, countryside or city, is almost always sacrificed to action and history.

"I have always thought the locale could be brought into a good historical novel much more effectively, if the writer had a better grasp of art itself in his concept of the setting in which his story is laid.

"It was out of that kind of an approach that *Song of the Paternales* was born, and attention thereto was intended to use up a third of the length of the story, the other two thirds being devoted to the people and their life styles (i.e. colonies of Europeans, pioneer ranching families, etc.), and to the action of the period—politics, Indian wars, rigors of the post-Civil War decade."

*   *   *

MORTON, Louis 1913-1976

PERSONAL: Born December 30, 1913, in New York, N.Y.; son of Nathan and Cecelia (Edelstein) Morton; married Ruth Goldstein, December 28, 1941; children: David K., Rachel Morton Franznan, Nathaniel B. *Education:* New York University, B.S., 1935, M.A., 1936; Duke University, Ph.D., 1938. *Home:* 2 Webster Terr., Hanover, N.H. 03755.

CAREER: City College (now of the City University of New York), New York City, instructor in history, 1939-41; Colonial Williamsburg, Williamsburg, Va., research associate, 1941-42; U.S. Army, Office of Military History, Washington, D.C., chief of Pacific section, 1946-60, chief historian, 1954-60; Dartmouth College, Hanover, N.H., professor of history, 1960-68, Daniel Webster Professor of History, 1968-76, chairperson of history department, 1969-72, provost, 1971-72. Harmon Memorial Lecturer at U.S. Air Force Academy, 1961; lecturer at Rice University, 1962-64, and University of California, San Diego, 1965; research associate at Harvard University, 1967-68. Board chairperson of Historical Evaluation and Research Organization, 1962-66; member of board of directors of Social Science Research Council, 1963-66; member of National Council for Accreditation of Teachers, 1967-70, and U.S. Air Force Historical Advisory Group, 1968-71; chairperson of the advisory committee of National Aeronautics & Space Administration Historical Office, 1968-76; chairperson of Pulitzer Prize history and biography jury. Consultant to U.S. Department of Health, Education & Welfare, 1966-68. *Military service:* U.S. Army, 1942-46; became captain; received Bronze Star.

MEMBER: International Studies Association, Society of American Historians (fellow), American Historical Association, Council on Foreign Relations, Organization of American Historians, Institute for Strategic Studies, Amer-

ican Association of University Professors, New England Historical Association (president, 1968-69), Phi Beta Kappa. *Awards, honors:* Superior Performance and Outstanding Employee Awards, 1957-58, from U.S. Civil Service; Rockefeller Public Service Award, 1959; recipient of several grants, including research grant from Carnegie Corp., 1960-63; M.A. from Dartmouth College, 1962.

WRITINGS: Robert Carter of Nomini Hall, a Virginia Tobacco Planter of the Eighteenth Century, Colonial Williamsburg, 1941; *The Fall of the Philippines,* Office of the Chief of Military History, Department of the Army, 1953; *Strategy and Command: The First Two Years,* Office of the Chief of Military History, Department of the Army, 1962; (with Gene Martin) *Schools for Strategy,* Praeger, 1965; *Writings on World War II,* Service Center for Teachers of History, 1967. Also contributor to *The Historian and the Diplomat.*

General editor, "War in the Pacific: United States Army in World War II" series, eleven volumes, Office of the Chief of Military History, Department of the Army, 1949-63; general editor, "Wars and Military Institutions of the United States," series, twenty-one volumes, Macmillan, 1963-76. Contributor to *New York Times Book Review,* and to professional journals. Member of board of editors of *Military Affairs* and *Journal of Modern History.*

OBITUARIES: New York Times, February 14, 1976; *Washington Post,* February 15, 1976; *AB Bookman's Weekly,* April 12, 1976.*

(Died February 12, 1976, in Burlington, Vt.)

*   *   *

MORTON, Robert 1934-

PERSONAL: Born May 20, 1934, in Jersey City, N.J.; son of Lewis Robert and Blanche (a jeweler; maiden name, Kimmel) Morton; married Marjorie Moore (a writer), February 17, 1971; children: Alexander Robert, Andrew Max Lionel. *Education:* Dartmouth College, B.A., 1955. *Home address:* Valley Rd., Redding, Conn. 06896. *Office:* Harry N. Abrams, Inc., 110 East 59th St., New York, N.Y. 10020.

CAREER: Time-Life Books, New York City, series editor, 1962-70; New York Graphic Society, Greenwich, Conn., editor-in-chief, 1970-73; Time-Life Books, series editor, 1974-75; Harry N. Abrams, Inc., New York City, vice-president and editor-in-chief, 1976—.

WRITINGS: Southern Antiques and Folk Art, Oxmore, 1976.

WORK IN PROGRESS: Research on American decorative arts.

*   *   *

MOSLEY, Nicholas 1923-

PERSONAL: Born June 25, 1923, in London, England; son of Oswald (a politician) and Cynthia (Curzon) Mosley; married Rosemary Salmond, November 14, 1967 (divorced 1974); married Verity Raymond, July 17, 1974; children: Shaun, Iva, Robert, Clare, Marius. *Education:* Attended Balliol College, Oxford, 1946-47. *Politics:* Liberal. *Religion:* Church of England. *Home:* Church Row Studios, 21a Heath St., London NW3, England. *Agent:* A. D. Peters, 10 Buckingham St., London WC2, England.

CAREER: Writer; became third Baron Ravensdale, 1966. *Military service:* British Army, 1942-46; became captain.

WRITINGS—Novels: Spaces of the Dark, Hart Davis,

1951; *The Rainbearers,* Weidenfeld & Nicolson, 1955; *Corruption,* Weidenfeld & Nicolson, 1957, Little, Brown, 1958; *Meeting Place,* Weidenfeld & Nicolson, 1962; *Accident,* Hodder & Stoughton, 1965, Coward, 1966; *Assassins,* Hodder & Stoughton, 1966, Coward, 1967; *Impossible Object,* Hodder & Stoughton, 1968, Coward, 1969; *Natalie, Natalia,* Coward, 1971.

Nonfiction: *African Switchback* (travel), Weidenfeld & Nicolson, 1958; *The Life of Raymond Raynes,* Faith Press, 1961; *Experience and Religion: A Lay Essay in Theology,* Hodder & Stoughton, 1965, United Church Press, 1967; *The Assassination of Trotsky,* M. Joseph, 1972; *Julian Grenfell,* Holt, 1976.

* * *

MOWRER, Edgar Ansel 1892-1977

March 8, 1892—March 2, 1977; American journalist, foreign correspondent, syndicated columnist, and author of books on political affairs, including Pulitzer prize winner, *Germany Puts the Clock Back,* the book that led to his expulsion from Hitler's Germany, and his autobiography, *Triumph and Turmoil.* His intolerance of totalitarianism also led to expulsion from Mussolini's Italy and Stalin's U.S.S.R. Mowrer died on the island of Madeira. Obituaries: *New York Times,* March 4, 1977; *Washington Post,* March 4, 1977; *AB Bookman's Weekly,* May 9, 1977; *Current Biography,* May, 1977. (*CAP*-1; earlier sketch in *CA*-15/16)

* * *

MUEHLEN, Norbert 1909-

PERSONAL: Born September 20, 1909, in Fuerth, Bavaria; son of Oskar and Else Baer-Muehlen; married Ruth Berenson (an art critic), 1962. *Education:* University of Munich, Ph.D., 1932. *Home and office:* 315 West 106th St., New York, N.Y. 10025.

CAREER: Deutsche Zeitung, Bonn, West Germany, and *Deutsche Welle,* Cologne, West Germany, foreign correspondent for Switzerland, 1933, for Saarbruecken, 1934, for Paris, 1935, chief foreign correspondent for the United States and the United Nations, 1945—. Writer. *Awards, honors:* Officer's cross of order of merit from Federal Republic of Germany, 1959; medal of honor from Assembly of Captive Nations, 1962; medal of honor from American Security Council, 1967.

WRITINGS: Der Zauberer: Leben und Anleihen des Dr. Hjalmar Horace Greeley Schacht, Europa (Zurich), 1938, translation by E. W. Dickes published as *Hitler's Magician, Schacht: The Life and Loans of Dr. Hjalmar Schacht,* Routledge, 1938, published as *Schacht, Hitler's Magician: The Life and Loans of Dr. Hjalmar Schacht,* Alliance Book, 1939; *The Return of Germany, a Tale of Two Countries,* Regnery, 1953; *A Report on Germany Before the Elections,* American Council on Germany (New York), 1957; *The Incredible Krupps: The Rise, Fall, and Comeback of Germany's Industrial Family,* Holt, 1959; *Germany in American Eyes: A Study of Public Opinion,* Atlantik-Bruecke (Hamburg), 1959; (with Christopher Emmet) *The Vanishing Swastika: Facts and Figures on Nazism in West Germany,* Regnery, 1961; (with wife, Ruth Berenson) *George Grosz,* Arts (New York), 1961; *The Survivors: A Report on the Jews in Germany Today,* Crowell, 1962; *Die Schwarzen Amerikaner: Anatomie einer Revolution,* Kohlhammer (Stuttgart), 1964; *Die Amerikaner,* Scheffler (Frankfurt), 1968; *Amerika, im Gegenteil: Antiamerikanische und andere Ansichten,* Seewald (Stuttgart), 1972.

Contributor to *Readers Digest, Saturday Evening Post, This Week, National Review, Commentary, America,* and other U.S. magazines.

SIDELIGHTS: Muhlen wrote: "Writing on America for German readers, and on Germany for American readers, I've tried to build bridges of understanding between my old and my new country."

* * *

MUELLER, Erwin W. 1911-1977

June 13, 1911—May 17, 1977; German-born physicist, educator, and author of articles in his field. He was the inventor of the field ion microscope, the world's most powerful microscope which enabled him to see an atom, and the atom probe, which can identify the atomic weight of a single atom. He was professor emeritus of physics at Pennsylvania State University. He died in Washington, D.C. Obituaries: *Washington Post,* May 19, 1977.

* * *

MULLAN, Fitzhugh 1942-

PERSONAL: Born July 22, 1942, in Tampa, Fla.; son of Hugh (a physician) and Mariquita (MacManus) Mullan; married Judith Wentworth (a social worker), June 9, 1968; children: Meghan Elizabeth, Caitlin Patricia. *Education:* Harvard University, B.A., 1964; University of Chicago, M.D., 1968. *Home:* 10812 Clermont Ave., Garrett Park, Md. 20766. *Agent:* Philip G. Spitzer Literary Agency, 111-25 76th St., Forest Hills, N.Y. 11375.

CAREER: Jacobi Hospital, Bronx, N.Y., intern and resident, 1968-70; Lincoln Hospital, Bronx, resident and attending physician, 1970-72; U.S. Public Health Service, Rockville, Md., physician, 1972—. *Member:* American Academy of Pediatrics, Ambulatory Pediatric Association, Medical Committee for Human Rights.

WRITINGS: White Coat, Clenched Fist: The Political Education of an American Physician, Macmillan, 1976. Author of "Mullings," a column in *Hospital Physician.* Contributing editor, *Hospital Physician.* Book reviewer for *Washington Post.*

SIDELIGHTS: Mullan writes: "My work as a doctor and as a writer has the common intent of democratizing and equalizing the health care provided in America. I am concerned about both the inequality in the distribution of medical services in this country and their increasingly technological and (often) dehumanizing direction. I would like to see national health insurance established and, after that, a national health service. I feel that, ultimately, the government is the only vehicle large enough and representative enough to arbitrate health care. At the same I feel we must examine and re-examine the machinery and procedures we call medicine lest the entire undertaking become one glossy, costly, and injurious heart transplant or Swine Flu program."

* * *

MULLEN, Harris H. 1924-

PERSONAL: Born February 27, 1924, in Tampa, Fla.; son of Charles Gordon (a publisher) and Virginia Louise (Hopkins) Mullen; married Katharine Hoag, June 7, 1949; children: Julia Katharine (Mrs. Michael Shea), Caroline Saunders (Mrs. N. De Li), Nancy Hoag, Harris H., Jr. *Education:* University of Florida, student, 1943; Duke University, B.S., 1946. *Politics:* Republican. *Religion:* Episcopalian. *Home:* 3412 Almeria, Tampa, Fla. 33609. *Office:*

Trend Publications, Inc., P.O. Box 2350, Tampa, Fla. 33601.

CAREER: *Tampa Tribune,* Tampa, Fla., reporter, 1946-48; Florida Grower Press, Tampa, vice-president and publisher of *Florida Grower* and *Ranch,* 1949-64; Trend Publications, Inc., Tampa, president and publisher of *Florida Trend,* 1958—, and *South,* 1974—, author of "Florida Close-Ups," a monthly column in *Florida Trend.* Chairman of board of trustees of University of Tampa, 1974-76. Governor of Urban Renewal Board, 1966-68, and Tampa Hillsborough County Preservation Board, 1976-79. *Military service:* U.S. Navy, 1943-46, 1951-53; became lieutenant senior grade.

MEMBER: American Business Press Club, Council on Economic Development (governor, 1976), Florida Magazine Association (past president), Tampa Advertising Federation, Alpha Tau Omega, Tampa Yacht and Country Club, Ye Mystic Krewe of Gasparilla. *Awards, honors:* Award from Florida Industrial Development Council, 1973, for contribution to economic development of Florida; silver medal from American Advertising Federation, 1973.

WRITINGS: *The Cash-Shannon Duel,* Trend Publications, 1963; *Florida Close-Up,* Trend Publications, 1972.

SIDELIGHTS: Mullen writes: "My central objective in the past two decades has been to establish two magazines, *Florida Trend,* 1958, and the *South,* 1974. *Florida Trend* was probably the first state magazine (independent) to exceed one million dollars in sales. *South* will probably overcome *Florida Trend* in 1978 or 1979. My motivation is the end product, selecting the type of people that can do the job and helping to steer them."

AVOCATIONAL INTERESTS: Restoring old buildings (presently restoring an old cigar factory in Tampa).

BIOGRAPHICAL/CRITICAL SOURCES: *St. Petersburg Times,* May 23, 1976.

* * *

MULVANITY, George 1903(?)-1976

1903(?)—October 14, 1976; American federal government agent and author of his memoirs. The last of Eliot Ness's "Untouchables," he worked as a federal investigator in Cleveland and helped smash the notorious "Purple Gang" in Detroit. He died in Mentor, Ohio. Obituaries; *Washington Post,* October 17, 1976.

* * *

MUNDIS, Hester 1938-

PERSONAL: Born December 22, 1938, in Brooklyn, N.Y.; daughter of Max (an attorney) and Fredi (an actress and model; maiden name, Levine) Nachamie; married Daniel I. Siegel, December 1, 1957 (divorced, May, 1963); married Jerrold J. Mundis (a writer), March 5, 1966; children: (first marriage) Shepard; (second marriage) Jesse Max. *Education:* Attended Hunter College of the City University of New York and Brooklyn College of the City University of New York. *Agent:* Claire Smith, Harold Ober Associates, Inc., 40 East 49th St., New York, N.Y. 10017.

CAREER: Fawcett Publications, New York City, editorial assistant, 1957-62; MacFadden Bartell Corp., New York City, associate editor, 1962-63; Dell Publishing Co., Inc., New York City, associate editor, 1963-65, copy chief, 1965-67; Popular Library, Inc., New York City, executive editor, 1967-70; Avon Books, New York City, senior editor, 1970-71; free-lance writer, 1971—. Free-lance copywriter for William H. Schneider Agency.

WRITINGS: *Mercy at the Manor Manor* (gothic spoof), Pocket Books, 1966; *Jessica's Wife* (novel), Coward, 1975; *No He's Not a Monkey, He's an Ape and He's My Son* (nonfiction), Crown, 1976; *Separate Ways,* Coward, in press.

WORK IN PROGRESS: A historical novel, set in the Hudson Valley.

SIDELIGHTS: Hester Mundis writes: "I've always enjoyed writing, and after many years of editing decided the time had come to switch to the other side of the desk. I see life as a great comedy (albeit often a black-humored one) and write about it that way. Love, marriage, sexual roles, mores, and identities are my favorite literary targets." *Avocational interests:* Animals.

* * *

MUNDIS, Jerrold 1941-

PERSONAL: Born March 3, 1941, in Chicago, Ill.; son of James M. (a business executive) and Dolores M. (an art teacher; maiden name, Hank) Mundis; married second wife, Hester Siegel (a novelist), March, 1966; children: Shepard Siegel, Jesse Max. *Education:* Attended Beloit College, 1959-61; New York University, B.A., 1963. *Politics:* "Troubled." *Religion:* "Non-specific." *Agent:* Theron Raines, Raines & Raines, 475 Fifth Ave., New York, N.Y. 10017.

CAREER: "Various brief odd jobs following college, including a year's stint as a literary agent"; full-time writer, 1966—.

WRITINGS: (With Robert Leonard) *King of the Ice Cream Mountain* (juvenile one-act play; first produced by Wisconsin Bureau of Arts and Lectures, 1961), Dramatic Publishing, 1968; *The Guard Dog* (nonfiction), McKay, 1970; *Gerhardt's Children* (novel; Book of the Month Club selection), Atheneum, 1976.

Also author of several hardcover and softcover books of fiction and nonfiction, under confidential pseudonyms. Contributor of short stories and articles to magazines, including *American Heritage, Harper's Weekly, New York,* and *New Worlds.*

WORK IN PROGRESS: "There is always a novel in progress."

* * *

MUNRO, John M(urchinson) 1932-

PERSONAL: Born August 29, 1932, in Wallasey, England; son of Duncan M. (an engineer) and Edith Mary Doris (Smith) Munro; married H. Ingrid B. Lipp, August 10, 1956; children: Karen Christine, Peter Duncan, Stephen Hans, Kirsten Caroline. *Education:* University of Durham, B.A., 1955; Washington University, St. Louis, Mo., Ph.D., 1960. *Politics:* "Uncommitted." *Religion:* None. *Home:* AUB Avenue de Francais, Apt. 804, Beirut, Lebanon. *Office:* Department of English, American University of Beirut, Beirut, Lebanon.

CAREER: Washington University, St. Louis, Mo., part-time instructor in English, 1956-60; University of North Carolina, Chapel Hill, instructor in English, 1960-63; University of Toronto, Toronto, Ontario, assistant professor of English, 1963-65; American University of Beirut, Beirut, Lebanon, associate professor, 1965-68, professor of English, 1968—, associate dean, 1970-73. Professor at Lebanese University, 1967—. English-language announcer for Radio Kuwait, Radio Libya, Radio Tunis, and Radio Qatar.

Awards, honors: United Nations Day Award from Government of the Philippines, 1967, for organizing Kahlil Gibran International Festival; Lebanese World Union Award, 1967, for service to Lebanese culture.

WRITINGS: (With Charles Edge and T. Y. Greet) *Worlds of Fiction,* Houghton, 1964; *English Poetry in Transition,* Pegasus, 1968; *Arthur Symons,* Twayne, 1969; *Decadent Poetry of the 1890's,* American University of Beirut, 1970; *Royal Aquarium: Failure of a Victorian Compromise,* American University of Beirut, 1971; *Selected Poems of Theo Marzials,* American University of Beirut, 1974; *James Elroy Flecker,* Twayne, 1976; *A Mutual Concern,* Caravan Books, 1977. Contributor to English literature education journals and *Aramco World.* Associate editor of *Arab Economist.*

WORK IN PROGRESS: Picture books on Arabian "dhow" and on Jerusalem.

SIDELIGHTS: Munro writes: "I was jogging along quite happily in my career until I decided to go to Lebanon as a visiting professor for a couple of years. Once in Lebanon I stayed. This was partly because Lebanon is a splendid place to live, partly because I found the Middle East fascinating and began to study its culture. The latter I turned to productive account, writing articles and broadcasts about the Middle East generally, and about Arabian culture in particular. I also became interested in Armenian life and culture, publishing fairly extensively in this area as well."

* * *

MURPHY, Thomas Basil, Jr. 1935-
(Tom Murphy)

PERSONAL: Born October 12, 1935, in Wallingford, Conn.; son of Thomas Basil (a physician) and Margaret Louise (a registered nurse; maiden name, Fitzgerald) Murphy. *Education:* Harvard University, A.B., 1957. *Agent:* Writer's House, 132 West 31st St., New York, N.Y. 10001. *Office:* Bozell & Jacobs, Inc., One Dag Hammarskjold Plaza, New York, N.Y. 10017.

CAREER: Vice-president and creative supervisor at J. Walter Thompson, Co., 1961-72; vice-president and creative supervisor at de Gaunio, Inc., 1972-73; associate creative supervisor at William Esty, Co., 1973-74; Bozell & Jacobs, Inc., New York City, vice-president and associate creative supervisor, 1974—. Registered dealer in Oriental and Western art and antiquities. *Military service:* U.S. Army, intelligence analyst, 1957-60; served in Berlin.

WRITINGS—Under name Tom Murphy: *Sky High* (novel), Putnam, 1977; *Ballet!* (novel), New American Library, 1977; *Aspen Incident* (novel), New American Library, 1978.

WORK IN PROGRESS: A historical novel set largely in post gold rush California.

SIDELIGHTS: Murphy explains concisely: "I write for fun, in the hopes of entertaining people. My books contain no planned political, religious, or other moral or aesthetic message, nor do I aspire to re-create written English."

* * *

MURRAY, John F(rancis) 1923-1977
(Daisy Backgammon, Nick Carryaway)

June 25, 1923—1977; American writer, advertising copywriter, and author of short stories and a novel, *The Devil Walks on Water.* Obituaries: *New York Times,* April 30, 1977. (*CAP*-2; earlier sketch in *CA*-29/32)

MURRAY, Merrill G. 1900(?)-1976

1900(?)—November 7, 1976; American economist specializing in labor and insurance and author of a book and several articles on unemployment compensation. He died in Leesburg, Fla. Obituaries: *Washington Post,* November 11, 1976.

* * *

MUSCHENHEIM, Carl 1905-1977

February 4, 1905—April 27, 1977; American physician, educator, and author of books and articles in his field. As a specialist in diseases of the lungs, he developed a drug treatment for tuberculosis. He was a professor of clinical medicine at Cornell University College of Medicine and an editor of *Yearbook of Medicine.* Obituaries: *New York Time,* April 28, 1977.

* * *

MUSE, Patricia (Alice) 1923-
(Nell Walters)

PERSONAL: Born November 27, 1923, in South Bend, Ind.; daughter of Walter L. (an engineer) and Enid (an artist; maiden name, Cockerham) Ashdown; married Kenneth F. Muse (a civil servant), December 2, 1950; children: Patience E., Walter Scott. *Education:* Principia College, B.A., 1947; also attended Columbia University, 1946, and Seminole Community College, 1977. *Residence:* Casselberry, Fla. *Agent:* Bill Berger Associates, Inc., 444 East 58th St., New York, N.Y. 10022.

CAREER: Artist and writer. Substitute teacher in public schools in Key West, Fla. and Brunswick, Ga., during the 1960's; part-time instructor in creative writing at Valencia Community College, 1974-75. Community volunteer worker. *Member:* Mystery Writers of America, National League of American Pen Women, Southeastern Writers Association, Dixie Council of Authors and Journalists.

WRITINGS—Gothic novels: *Sound of Rain,* Bouregy, 1971; *The Belle Claudine,* Bouregy, 1971; *Eight Candles Glowing,* Ballantine, 1976. Contributor to newspapers, sometimes under pseudonym, Nell Walters.

WORK IN PROGRESS: Research on earth science and ecology.

SIDELIGHTS: Patricia Muse writes: "It hadn't occurred to me to become a writer until my childhood 'nearly-sister,' a first cousin, also an only child as I am, passed away very suddenly and unexpectedly. I wrote my first book after that. *The Belle Claudine* was the kind of book she might have liked, a Gothic set on an island in the North Woods. The setting I used was her summer home, altered slightly.

"Once this book was finished I had become fascinated with writing. My former creative outlet, which had been painting, was neglected, and so it remains.

"I have a conviction that people are dependent on the continuation of wilderness on earth in more than an ecological sense, perhaps in a subtle 'spiritual' sense, and more so than they realize. Ecology and the beauty of nature are the hidden themes in my genre writing.

"It seems to me, also, that the unusual settings of Gothics, so different from the uniformity of suburbia, are a relief for the many who read them. During two long southern summers I had read many of these books with enjoyment, nourished by the vicarious dwelling apart from a technological and automated society, and by the vicarious dwelling in rich and mysterious settings. Another thing that appealed to me in Gothics was the more complex language often used by those authors, and their detailed descriptions. Growing up with Sir Walter Scott, Robert Louis Stevenson, Charlotte Bronte and Tolstoy had made many 'modern' writings sound flat and unappealing to me. However my present inclination (writing) is away from Gothics and toward more modern mysteries—and poetry! But I suspect a touch of the Gothic sound will come out in whatever I write."

BIOGRAPHICAL/CRITICAL SOURCES: *Orlando Sentinel-Star*, June 20, 1971; *Orlando Evening Star*, November 1, 1972; *La Femme*, July 8, 1976; *Winter Park Sun Herald*, July 29, 1976.

* * *

MUSGRAVE, Susan 1951-

PERSONAL: Born March 12, 1951, in Santa Cruz, Calif.; daughter of Edward and Judith (Stevens) Musgrave. *Education:* Educated in British Columbia, Canada. *Home:* 2931 Seaview Rd., Victoria, British Columbia, Canada.

CAREER: Poet. *Member:* League of Canadian Poets, National Poetry Secretariat. *Awards, honors:* Canada Council Travel Grant, 1969-70; Arts Bursary, 1972-73; Arts Grant, 1974-75 and 1976-77.

WRITINGS: *Songs of the Sea-Witch*, Sono Nis Press, 1970; *Entrance of the Celebrant*, Macmillan, 1972; *Grave-Dirt and Selected Strawberries*, Macmillan, 1973; *Gullband* (poems for children), J. J. Douglas, 1974; *The Impstone*, McClelland & Stewart, 1976; (with Sean Virgo) *Kiskatinaw Songs*, Pharos Press, in press; *Selected Strawberries: Poems, 1969-1973*, Sono Nis Press, in press; *Becky Swan's Book*, The Porcupine's Quill, in press. Also author of pamphlets published by Sceptre Press. Contributor of poems to *Canadian Forum*, *Ellipse*, *Saturday Night*, *Toronto Globe and Mail*, *Poetry Review*, *New York Times*, *West Coast Poetry Review*, and other periodicals.

WORK IN PROGRESS: A novel, *The Charcoal Burner's Camp*.

SIDELIGHTS: Susan Musgrave told a reporter from the *Toronto Star*: "My great-grandfather was a lieutenant-governor of British Columbia, Sir Anthony Musgrave. My father inherited some money, lived on a forty-foot sailboat called Froggy, and didn't marry till he was forty-five. I left home at fourteen and went to California. Later, I became a non-ward of the B.C. court. That meant the government gave me money to live on, but didn't have much say in what I did—in other words, it was perfect."

Some critics have suggested that Musgrave will be the next major poet of English Canada. Critic Doug Fetherling concurs and says that Musgrave "displays a peculiar talent for expressing an inner drama, a tension completely self-contained and born of nothing from outside except whatever it is that sets her mind to working up these moods."

Reviewer Rosemary Sullivan says that what convinces her about the excellence of Musgrave's best poems "apart from the technical mastery—is the unity of tone and vision which underlies them: a poignant bloodlonging for warmth and relationship which is continually frustrated." Sullivan adds that although "Musgrave has honed her language to essentials and made it evocative in combination so that her words have an oracular intensity," she sometimes "asks diction to carry too much, depending heavily on the associative quality of certain favorite words that are rehearsed like ritual. The images are meant to conjure up a nightmare intensity, yet felt

meaning sometimes escapes as the words have no sensuous definition. But there are too many successes for this to be more than an incidental criticism."

Images of death dominate her work, a *Toronto Star* reviewer has noticed. Musgrave explains: "Death is really a metaphor for separation, fear of not being loved. I'm forever separating from people because I need to change my life to find a new mythology for my poems. It's awful to think that has to happen, but apparently it does."

BIOGRAPHICAL/CRITICAL SOURCES: *Saturday Night*, January, 1974; *Contemporary Verse II*, fall, 1975; *Toronto Star*, February 3, 1976.

* * *

MUSIAL, Joe 1905(?)-1977

1905(?)—June 6, 1977; American cartoonist who started drawing the "Katzenjammer Kids," the oldest continuing American comic strip, in 1952; also a pioneer in the use of comic books as educational aids. He died in Manhasset, N.Y. *Obituaries:* *New York Times*, June 8, 1977; *Washington Post*, June 9, 1977; *Time*, June 20, 1977.

* * *

MYERS, M(arvin) Scott 1922-

PERSONAL: Born January 13, 1922, in Doebay, Wash.; son of Alvin Jefferson and Virginia Stella (Boone) Myers; married Susan Pryor Sloat (a psychologist), July 15, 1944; children: James D., Suzanne Myers Amimoto, Gary S., David D. *Education:* Purdue University, B.S., 1948, M.S., 1949, Ph.D., 1951. *Home:* 181 East Sunrise Ave., Coral Gables, Fla. 33133.

CAREER: Hughes Aircraft Co., Culver City, Calif., supervisor of personnel planning, 1951-54; University of Tehran, Tehran, Iran, associate professor of public administration and director of Personnel Management and Research Center, 1954-57; Governmental Affairs Institute, Washington, D.C., training adviser in Tehran, 1957-59; Texas Instruments, Dallas, organizational psychologist and management research consultant, 1959-72; Center for Applied Management, Coral Gables, Fla., director and management consultant, 1972—. Visiting professor at Massachusetts Institute of Technology, 1969-71. *Member:* American Psychological Association.

WRITINGS: *Every Employee a Manager*, McGraw, 1970; *Managing Without Unions*, Addison-Wesley, 1976; *Managing with Unions*, Addison-Wesley, in press.

Author of "Making Human Resources Productive," a film for BNA (Bureau of National Affairs), 1970. Contributor to business and management journals.

SIDELIGHTS: Myers writes that his "particular interest is in the development of industrial democracy; e.g. union-management cooperation, motivation in the non-union organization, joint financial stake in organizational success." He has worked as a barber, union president, taxi driver, and commercial fisherman.

* * *

MYRDAL, Alva Reimer 1902-

PERSONAL: Born January 31, 1902, in Uppsala, Sweden; daughter of Albert (a building contractor) and Lova (Larsson) Reimer; married Karl Gunnar Myrdal (an economist and writer), October 8, 1924; children: Jan, Sissela, Kaj. *Education:* University of Stockholm, B.A., 1924; University of Geneva, graduate study, 1930-31; University of Uppsala, M.A., 1934. *Politics:* Social Democrat. *Religion:* Lutheran ("not practicing"). *Home:* Vaesterlaanggatan 31, 11129 Stockholm, Sweden.

CAREER: Workers Education Association, Stockholm, Sweden, teacher, 1924-32; Central Prison, Stockholm, psychological assistant, 1932-34; Training College for Preschool Teachers, Stockholm, founder and director, 1935-48; United Nations, New York City, principal director of department of social affairs, 1949-50, director of UNESCO department of social sciences, 1951-55; Government of Sweden, ambassador to India and minister to Ceylon, 1955-61, minister to Burma, 1955-58, ambassador to Nepal, 1960-61, ambassador-at-large, 1961-66, member of Swedish Parliament (Senate), 1962-70, cabinet minister for disarmament, 1966-73, and for church affairs, 1969-73; Center for the Study of Democratic Institutions, Santa Barbara, Calif., visiting fellow, 1973-74; Massachusetts Institute of Technology, Cambridge, visiting professor of sociology, 1974-75; Wellesley College, Wellesley, Mass., Visiting Distinguished Slater Professor of Sociology, 1976; Institute for Research on Poverty, Madison, Wis., research fellow, 1977. Service to United Nations includes member of Swedish delegation to General Assembly, 1962-73, chief of Swedish delegation to disarmament conference in Geneva, 1962-73, chairperson of expert group on South Africa, 1964, deputy leader, 1967-73, and chairperson of Committee on Disarmament and Development, 1972. Chairperson of Swedish Civic Organization for Cultural Relief in Europe, 1943-48, government committee on organization of social information services, 1946, International Peace Research Institute, 1965-66, Commission on Disestablishment of the Swedish State Church, 1968-72, Commission on Studies of the Future, 1971-72, and delegation for expanding international laws against brutality in war, 1972-73; member of board of directors of Stockholm School for Social Work, 1946-48.

MEMBER: International Federation of Business and Professional Women (vice-chairperson, 1938-47), Swedish Federation of Business and Professional Women (chairperson, 1935-38 and 1940-42), World Council on Preschool Education (chairperson, 1941-49), World Federation of United Nations Associations (executive member, 1948-50). *Awards, honors:* Rockefeller Foundation fellowship, 1929-30, for travel in the United States; LL.D. from Mount Holyoke College, 1950, and University of Edinburgh, 1964; Ph.D. from University of Leeds, 1962; D.H.L. from Columbia University, 1965, and Temple University, 1968; D.D. from Gustavus Adolphus University, 1971; other honorary degrees from Brandeis University, 1974, University of Gothenburg, 1975, and University of East Anglia, 1976; West German Peace Prize, 1970; Wateler Prize from Hague Academy of International Peace, 1973; prize from Royal Swedish Institute of Technology, 1975; Monismanien Prize, 1976, for protection of civil liberties; gold medal from Royal Swedish Academy of Science, 1977.

WRITINGS: (With husband, Gunnar Myrdal) *Kris i befolkningsfraegan* (title means "Crisis in the Population Question"), A. Bonnier, 1934; *Nation and Family: The Swedish Experiment in Democratic Family and Population Policy,* Harper, 1941, 2nd edition, M.I.T. Press, 1965; (with Gunnar Myrdal) *Kontakt med America* (title means "Contact with America"), A. Bonnier, 1941; *Women in the Community,* TARP (Copenhagen, Denmark), 1943; *Kommentarer* (title means "Comments on World Affairs"), A. Bonnier, 1944; *Efterkrigsplanering* (title means "Postwar Planning"), In-formationsbyraan Mellanfolkligt samarbete foer fred Svenska Kommitten, 1944.

(With Paul Vincent) *Are We Too Many?,* Bureau of Current Affairs, UNESCO (London, England), 1950; (with Arthur J. Altmeyer and Dean Rusk) *America's Role in International Social Welfare,* Columbia University Press, 1955; (with Viola Klein) *Women's Two Roles: Home and Work,* Routledge & Kegan Paul, 1956, 2nd edition, 1968; *Vaart ansvar foer de fattiga folken: Utvecklingsproblem i social naerbild* (title means "Our Responsibility for the Poor Peoples: Development Problems at Close View"), Raben & Sjoegren, 1961; (contributor) Andrew W. Cordier and Wilder Foote, editors, *The Quest for Peace,* Columbia University, 1962; *Disarmament and the United Nations,* Columbia University Press, 1965; (with Solly Zuckerman and Lester B. Pearson) *The Control of Proliferation: Three Views,* Institute for Strategic Studies (London, England), 1966; *Oekad jaemlikhet,* Prisma, 1969, abridged edition translated by Roger Lind published as *Towards Equality,* Prisma, 1971.

A Non-Aligned Look at the Future of Disarmament, Banco d'Italio (Rome, Italy), 1970; *Stickprovt paa Storbrittanien* (title means "Cross Section of Great Britain"), A. Bonnier, 1972; *The Game of Disarmament,* Pantheon, 1977; *Wars, Weapons, and Everyday Violence,* University of New Hampshire, 1977; *Solidaritaet im Zwischenstaatlichen und welweiten Bersich* (title means, "Solidarity in the International and Worldwide Field"), Evangelischer Kirchenbag (Berlin, Germany), 1977.

Also author of *City Children,* 1935, and *Disarmament: Reality or Illusion?,* 1965.

Contributor to magazines, including *Parents' Magazine, Independent Woman, Scientific American, Foreign Policy,* and *Bulletin of Atomic Scientists.* Co-editor of *Morgonbris,* 1936-38; editor of *Via Suecia,* 1945-46, and *Round Table on Social Problems,* 1946-48.

WORK IN PROGRESS: A book on quality of life with more equality for women and children.

SIDELIGHTS: Alva Myrdal, the author of pioneering works in women's rights, population control, and social philosophy, has recently written a book on possibly the most critical subject of the decade—nuclear disarmament. Critics have praised *The Game of Disarmament* as "eloquent," "magnificent," and "a disenthralling masterpiece."

Herbert Mitgang writes in the *New York Times:* "With disarmament talks coming up again, this could be one of the turning-point studies on the international agenda. I cannot imagine a more significant book, whose theme is nothing less than life or death, coming out this year."

Mitgang says that *The Game of Disarmament* is "both a primer and a sophisticated work." Not only does Myrdal cut through the technical, obtuse language of the military experts to expose meanings to the people who would be, as Mitgang writes, "on the receiving end of the newly programmed final solution," but she is commended for offering possible solutions for scaling down the arms race.

Although, according to Emma Rothschild, Myrdal admits to "a gradually increasing feeling of near despair," Rothschild finds that "her values belie this sense. Her words—and her experience as Sweden's minister of disarmament, acting with moral courage in the real world of disarmament negotiations—break the set of preconceptions that surround U.S. arms policy. I expect that most of Carter's defense advisers will read her book. I hope they see how different her way would be."

Charles L. Mee, Jr., has unqualified praise for Myrdal. He writes that she has "labored like Sisyphus on behalf of disarmament," and that her life has been "a dignified and eloquent performance in the theatre of the absurd." He concludes: "Alva Myrdal unquestionably deserves the Nobel Prize—no matter what. And I put my trust in her, and luck, and existentialism."

Myrdal told *CA:* "The prophecies I had to make in my book, *The Game of Disarmament,* were somber, to say the least. They had to be to be true to reality. But my pessimism has rather become reinforced by experiences in 1977. SALT negotiations have proceeded so haltingly. And even if a SALT II agreement is reached, it will not stifle but may actually promote the most dangerous phase of the arms race: the qualitative, technological competition for ever more sophisticated, expressive and brutal weapons, called more 'efficient,' that is: efficient for killing fellow men.

"This arms race is conducted at accelerated speed by both superpowers. Simultaneously an enormous spread of weapons to many more countries is taking place. The trade in arms is a breathtaking multi-billion dollar business where the newly rich oil countries are leading the way, but others, however poor, are not hesitant to follow. SIPRI in my home country, Sweden, as well as the UN Secretariat here, are providing the horrible documentation. The mighty ones do not listen to the warnings about the mad course of events.

"The political leaders either have no will or no capacity to hold back this evil development. To me it seems as if a kind of *collective insanity* has gripped the world. What we are living through is an era of militarization of practically all societies. In domestic affairs it makes them prone to dictatorship and repression of freedom movements. In international affairs the military build-up prepares the path for new wars. Whether they be local and small-scale, or mount to a holocaust by contending superpowers, two things are certain: (1) that they are inhuman, and (2) that they are unnecessary as they certainly will not help to solve any problems. The main result of the arms race, so visibly real already now, is that it consumes giant resources that would be needed for development."

Myrdal writes that she keeps up extensive reading, "not only in international affairs, but also novels and poetry in Swedish, English, French, German, and some Spanish." Her books have been published in German, French, Italian, Japanese, Spanish, and Scandinavian languages.

AVOCATIONAL INTERESTS: Reading, cooking, foreign travel, theater, and walking, cycling, or motor tours.

BIOGRAPHICAL/CRITICAL SOURCES: New York Review of Books, January 20, 1977; *New York Times,* February 19, 1977; *Horizon,* March, 1977; *New York Times Book Review,* March 6, 1977.

* * *

NABOKOV, Vladimir (Vladimirovich)   1899-1977
(V. Sirin [until 1940])

April 23, 1899—July 2, 1977; Russian-born American novelist, poet, playwright, critic, and entomologist best known for *The Gift, Lolita,* and *Pale Fire* and his exquisite sense of irony and remarkable verbal facility. He later remarked on his move to the United States in 1939 and its influence on his work: "It had taken me some forty years to invent Russia and West Europe, and now I was faced with the task of inventing America." An expert on butterflies, Nabokov spent six years as a fellow of the Museum of Comparative Zoology

at Harvard; two species of butterflies and one species of moths bear his name. He taught Slavic languages at Wellesley College and became a professor of European literature at Cornell University. His *Speak, Memory* is considered to be one of the finest autobiographies in the English language. Nabokov died in Montreux, Switzerland. Obituaries: *New York Times,* July 5, 1977; *Detroit Free Press,* July 5, 1977; *Washington Post,* July 5, 1977; *Time,* July 18, 1977; *Newsweek,* July 18, 1977; *Current Biography,* August, 1977; *AB Bookman's Weekly,* September 5, 1977. (See index for previous *CA* sketch)

* * *

NADEL, Frances   1905(?)-1977

1905(?)—May 6, 1977; Russian-born American contributor of short stories to magazines. She died in Arlington, Va. Obituaries: *Washington Post,* May 18, 1977.

* * *

NAHAS, Rebecca   1946-

PERSONAL: Born April 21, 1946, in Des Moines, Iowa; daughter of George Joseph (a businessman) and Mary (Nussrallah) Nahas. *Education:* Manhattanville College, B.A., 1968; Columbia University, M.F.A., 1971. *Residence:* New York, N.Y.

CAREER: Writer and actress. Has appeared on stage in the Broadway production of "No Place to Be Somebody," and other plays in New York City, Philadelphia, Pa., Stockbridge, Mass., and Buffalo, N.Y. Has also appeared on television programs, including "The Edge of Night," "The Doctors," "Search for Tomorrow," and "As the World Turns." *Member:* American Federation of Television and Radio Artists, Actors Equity.

WRITINGS: Your Acting Career: How to Break into and Survive in the Theatre, Crown, 1976.

* * *

NAISMITH, Helen   1929-
(Eppie)

PERSONAL: Born September 9, 1929, in Attleboro, Mass.; daughter of Alexander (a mechanic) and Nellie (Feather) Naismith; married Cline D. Futch, Jr., November, 1961 (divorced December 31, 1976); children: Kathryn Anne. *Education:* Attended West Palm Beach Junior College. *Politics:* Independent ("mostly Republican"). *Religion:* Presbyterian. *Home:* 2555 Rolling View Dr., Smyrna, Ga. 30080. *Office:* Trans World News Service, P.O. Box 2801, Washington, D.C. 20013.

CAREER: Epicurean, Atlanta, Ga., editor and publisher, 1974; Trans World News Service, Washington, D.C., author of syndicated columns "Celebrity Dining" and "Eppie, Your Hostess Helper," both 1976—. Lecturer on the culinary heritage of America. *Member:* Atlanta Press Club, Atlanta Writers Club, Atlanta Tip Off Club.

WRITINGS: Famous Festival Foods, Contemporary Publishing (Atlanta, Ga.), 1977; *Recipes of the Stars,* H. Jackson Brown, 1977. Feature writer for *People on Parade,* 1976. Contributor to magazines, including *Fun, Taste,* and *Sausagian.*

WORK IN PROGRESS: An "in-depth personality study" or biography of her relative, James Naismith, who created the game of basketball.

SIDELIGHTS: Helen Naismith writes: "My initial interest

was in the area of culinary arts; however, I have since ventured forth into the area of personalities. I like to write about people, but not in a controversial way. I like to spotlight what the common folks in America are doing, as well as relate interesting little-known facts about celebrity-types.''

BIOGRAPHICAL/CRITICAL SOURCES: Southern Living, October, 1974; *Tennessean,* June 23, 1976; *Atlanta,* July, 1976.

* * *

NAMIOKA, Lensey 1929-

PERSONAL: Born June 14, 1929, in Peking, China; daughter of Yuen Ren (a linguist) and Buwei (a physician and writer; maiden name, Yang) Chao; married Isaac Namioka (a mathematician), September 9, 1957; children: Aki, Michi (daughters). *Education:* Radcliffe College, student, 1947-49; University of California, Berkeley, B.A., 1951, M.A., 1952. *Home:* 2047 23rd Ave. E., Seattle, Wash. 98112. *Agent:* Patricia Lewis, 450 Seventh Ave., Room 602, New York, N.Y. 10001.

CAREER: Wells College, Aurora, N.Y., instructor in mathematics, 1957-58; Cornell University, Ithaca, N.Y., instructor in mathematics, 1958-61; broadcasting monitor for Japan Broadcasting Corp., 1969—. Translator for American Mathematical Society, 1958-66. *Member:* Seattle Free Lances.

WRITINGS: (Translator) Buwei Y. Chao, *How to Order and Eat in Chinese,* Vintage, 1974; *The Samurai and the Long-Nosed Devils,* McKay, 1976; *White Serpent Castle,* McKay, 1976. Contributor of travel and humor articles to magazines and newspapers.

WORK IN PROGRESS: Village of the Vampire Cat, a novel for children; translating *The Place of Women in China.*

SIDELIGHTS: Namioka writes: ''For my writings I draw heavily on my Chinese cultural heritage and on my husband's Japanese cultural heritage. My involvement with Japan started before my marriage, since my mother spent many years in Japan. My long years of training in mathematics had little influence on my writing, except for an urge to economy.'' *Avocational interests:* Music (''prefer to make it myself badly than to hear it performed superbly'').

* * *

NAREMORE, James 1941-

PERSONAL: Born April 7, 1941, in Shreveport, La.; son of James Lawrence and Grace (Killian) Naremore; married Rita Chandler (a professor), May 19, 1963; children: James Lawrence. *Education:* Louisiana State University, B.A., 1963, M.A., 1965; University of Wisconsin, Ph.D., 1970. *Home:* 811 South Woodlawn, Bloomington, Ind. 47401. *Office:* Department of English, Indiana University, Bloomington, Ind. 47401.

CAREER: Indiana University, Bloomington, assistant professor, 1970-74, associate professor of English, 1974—. *Member:* Modern Language Association of America, American Film Institute.

WRITINGS: The World without a Self: Virginia Woolf and the Novel, Yale University Press, 1973; *Filmguide to Psycho,* Indiana University Press, 1973. Contributor of articles to professional journals. Work represented in anthologies, including *Twentieth Century Interpretations of Portraits of the Artist,* edited by William Schutte, Prentice-Hall, 1970;

Focus on Orson Welles, edited by Ronald Gottesman, Prentice-Hall, 1976; and *Approaches to Portraits of the Artist,* edited by Bernard Benstock, University of Pittsburg Press, 1977.

WORK IN PROGRESS: The World of Orson Welles, Oxford University Press, publication expected in 1978.

* * *

NASH, J(essie) Madeleine 1943-

PERSONAL: Born September 11, 1943, in North Carolina; daughter of John Vize and Jessie (Douglas) Berry; married E. Thomas Nash (a physicist). *Education:* Bryn Mawr College, B.A. (magna cum laude), 1965. *Office:* 303 East Ohio, Chicago, Ill. 60611.

CAREER: Time, New York, N.Y., researcher, 1966-70; free-lance writer, 1971-74; *Time,* correspondent from Chicago, 1974—.

WRITINGS: Schools Where Parents Make a Difference (edited by Don Davies), Institute for Responsive Education, 1976.

* * *

NEAL, Julia 1905-

PERSONAL: Born August 15, 1905, in Auburn, Ky.; daughter of Presley Taylor (a merchant) and Nellie Lou (Pace) Neal. *Education:* Bethel Woman's College, student, 1923-25; Western Kentucky University, B.S., 1931, M.A., 1932; University of Michigan, further graduate study, 1943-45. *Politics:* Democrat. *Religion:* Southern Baptist. *Home:* 1633 Chestnut, Bowling Green, Ky. 42101.

CAREER: Elementary school teacher in Auburn, Ky., 1926-30; Western Kentucky State College (now University), Bowling Green, instructor in English, 1934-41; Kingswood-Cranbrook School for Girls, Bloomfield Hills, Mich., dean of residence, 1944-46; Florence State College (now University), Florence, Ala., assistant professor, 1946-56, associate professor of English, 1956-64; Western Kentucky University, director of Kentucky Library and Museum, 1964-72; writer, 1972—. Volunteer co-director of South Union Shaker Museum.

MEMBER: International Manuscript Society, National Historical Society, American Association for State and Local History, National Trust for Historic Preservation, American Studies Association, Pace Society, Filson Club, Kentucky Historical Society, Southern Baptist Historical Society. *Awards, honors:* Avery Hopwood Award from University of Michigan, 1945, for an essay; Southern Fellowship Fund grant, 1960.

WRITINGS: By Their Fruits: History of the South Union Shaker Society, University of North Carolina Press, 1947, reprinted, Porcupine Press, 1974; (editor) *The Journal of Eldress Nancy,* Parthenon Press, 1963; (with E. Ray Pearson and Walter M. Whitehill) *The Shaker Image,* New York Graphic Society, 1974; *The Kentucky Shakers,* University Press of Kentucky, 1977. Contributor to magazines, including *Shaker Quarterly, Filson Club Quarterly,* and *Antiques.*

SIDELIGHTS: Julia Neal writes: ''I grew up near the South Union Shaker Colony and knew the last members of the society; I have visited the major Shaker collections in the U.S.; know all of today's Shakers, have been a participant in the 1969 Hancock, Mass., Shaker Conference, and the Shaker Bicentennial in Cleveland, 1974. I have had access to all the South Union manuscript records.''

NEILAN, Sarah

PERSONAL: Born in England; married; children: four. *Education:* Oxford University, M.A.

CAREER: Book editor and writer in London, England, 1974—.

WRITINGS: The Braganza Pursuit (historical suspense novel), Dutton, 1976; *An Air of Glory* (historical suspense novel), Morrow, 1977; *Charlotte Bronte's "Shirley": A Critical Essay,* British Council, 1977. Editor of "Peter and Ann" series, juvenile travel books, for Muller. Contributor of articles, stories, and reviews to magazines.

WORK IN PROGRESS: A suspense novel set in the early nineteenth century.

SIDELIGHTS: Sarah Neilan writes: "I love reading fast-moving suspense novels, and that's what I try to write. I set them in my favourite period—the first quarter of the nineteenth century—partly because I enjoy historical research and take a pride in the authenticity of my backgrounds, and partly because the past often has something to show us which adds an extra dimension to a story.

"I have travelled widely, and on my first visit to Nova Scotia I met a descendant of a Scottish emigrant who survived a journey that none of the voyagers ever forgot. *An Air of Glory* is based on that journey."

* * *

NEIMAN, David 1921-

PERSONAL: Born September 10, 1921, in Novgorod-Seversk, Russia; son of Israel B. (a builder) and Celia (Handlin) Neiman; married Shulamith Dubno (a musician), April 21, 1955; children: Rachel, Rina, Rebecca. *Education:* City College of New York (now City College of the City University of New York), B.A., 1942; University of Chicago, M.A., 1947; Dropsie University, Ph.D., 1955. *Politics:* Social Democrat. *Religion:* Jewish. *Home:* 65 Cotton St., Newton, Mass. 02158. *Office:* Department of Theology, Boston College, Chestnut Hill, Mass. 02167.

CAREER: New School for Social Research, New York, N.Y., lecturer in history and religion, 1956-63; Brandeis University, Waltham, Mass., associate professor of Biblical studies, 1963-66; Boston College, Chestnut Hill, Mass., associate professor of theology, 1966—. Instructor at New York University, 1957-60. *Member:* American Oriental Society, Society for Biblical Literature.

WRITINGS: (Contributor) Alexander Altmann, editor, *Biblical Motifs,* Harvard University Press, 1966; *The Book of Job,* Massada, 1972; *Man Against God,* Sophia & Oratia, 1973. Contributor of articles to periodicals, including *Journal of Biblical Literature.*

WORK IN PROGRESS: A book, *Israel and World Jewry.*

* * *

NELSON, Charles Lamar 1917-

PERSONAL: Born June 9, 1917, in Lafayette County, Miss.; son of Charles Robert (a professor) and Willie Aline (Welch) Nelson; married Lena Reaves (a salesperson), 1940; children: Timothy Lamar. *Education:* University of Mississippi, B.A., 1946, M.A., 1947; further study at Auburn University, 1957, and Shorter College, 1967. *Religion:* Church of Christ. *Office:* Caledonia High School, P.O. Box 57, Caledonia, Miss. 39740.

CAREER: High school teacher in Blue Springs, Miss.,

1940-41; upper elementary school teacher in Taylor, Miss., 1941-42; high school principal in Batesville, Miss., 1948-49; high school teacher and principal in Tyrenza, Ark., 1949-50; superintendent of high school in Ripley, Miss., 1950-51; high school principal in Middleton, Tenn., 1951-52; high school teacher in Pearson, Ga., 1952-53; high school guidance counselor and teacher in Hazlehurst, Ga., 1953-54, Douglas, Ga., 1954-55, and Washington, Miss., 1955-58; welfare agent, Natchez, Miss., 1958-59; elementary school principal in Bell City, Mo., 1960-62; high school principal in Bloomfield, Mo., 1962-63; high school guidance counselor in Jackson, Miss., 1963-65, Orange Park, Fla., 1965-66, and Adairsville, Ga., 1966-67; junior high school teacher in Rome, Ga., 1967-72; Caledonia High School, Caledonia, Miss., guidance counselor, 1972—. *Military service:* U.S. Navy, 1942-45; became pharmacist's mate; served in South Pacific. *Member:* International Platform Association (chairman of press releases), National Education Association, Personnel and Guidance Association (Mississippi), Mississippi Poetry Society, Lowndes County Association of Teachers, Natchez Poetry Society (co-founder and first president). *Awards, honors:* Certificate of appreciation from President Gerald Ford, 1976.

WRITINGS: The Marble Urn (poems), Paebar Co., 1941; *William Faulkner: The Anchorite of Rowan Oak* (poems), privately printed, 1973; (contributor) Joseph Blotner, editor, *Faulkner: A Biography,* Random House, 1974; *A Chain That Breaks a Man* (poems), Triton Press, 1975; (with David Goforth) *Our Neighbor, William Faulkner,* Adams Press (Chicago, Ill.), 1977.

Represented in *National Poetry Anthology.* Contributor of articles and poems to magazines, including *Poetry Digest* and *Mid-Century Prose and Verse,* and newspapers.

WORK IN PROGRESS: Edge of the Precipice, poems.

SIDELIGHTS: Nelson writes: "I have been writing poetry since the age of eight. My first effort was romantic verse, titled 'To Mary.' I write in free verse—dislike mechanical forms. Once I feel inspired to write a poem, the words seem to overflow.

"I am a native of Oxford, Mississippi, the home of William Faulkner, and have always been an admirer and friend of Faulkner, even before the general public recognized his talent."

AVOCATIONAL INTERESTS: Collecting first editions and other rare books.

* * *

NELSON, Esther L. 1928-

PERSONAL: Born September 9, 1928, in New York, N.Y.; daughter of Rubin (a fabric cutter) and Freda (a nurse; maiden name, Seligman) Nelson; married Leon Sokolsky (an art teacher), November 18, 1949; children: Mara, Risa. *Education:* Brooklyn College (now of the City University of New York), B.A., 1949; New York University, M.A., 1951; also attended New School for Social Research and Bank Street College of Education. *Home:* 3605 Sedgwick Ave., Bronx, N.Y. 10463. *Agent:* Marcia Amsterdam, 41 West 82nd St., New York, N.Y. *Office address:* Dimension Five, P.O. Box 185, Kingsbridge Station, Bronx, N.Y. 10463.

CAREER: Knollwood School, Elmsford, N.Y., dance teacher, 1953-56; Scarsdale Dance Inc., Scarsdale, N.Y., dance teacher, 1953-70; Fieldston School, Riverdale, N.Y., dance teacher, 1958-63; Dimension Five (record company), Bronx, N.Y., partner, 1963—. Lecturer at Brooklyn College of the City University of New York. Has conducted dance and music workshops for teachers. Has performed on records for children. Member of Dance Library (Israel). *Member:* American Dance Guild, American Alliance for Health, Physical Education and Recreation (Dance Division).

WRITINGS: Dancing Games for Children of All Ages (Instructor Book Club selection), Sterling, 1973; *Movement Games for Children of All Ages* (Instructor Book Club selection), Sterling, 1975; *Musical Games for Children of All Ages* (Instructor Book Club selection), Sterling, 1976.

Co-author of material for children's records: "Dance Sing and Listen," "Dance Sing and Listen Again," "Dance Sing and Listen Again and Again," "The Way Out Record for Children," "The Electronic Record for Children," "Together," "Dance to the Music," "Funky Doodle," and "Ebenezer Electric."

Contributor to *Dance* (magazine).

WORK IN PROGRESS: A book on music and dance activities for the preschool; records to accompany books already published.

SIDELIGHTS: Esther Nelson writes: "Since a young child, I have always loved and been involved with music and dance, and so it was natural for me to continue into adulthood and to get a masters degree in dance education. My branching into the fields of recording and book writing came both times from parents of children in my dance classes. One mother said that her child loved class so much, and she couldn't wait to come back from week to week, so wasn't there anything we could do that she could take into her home. That was how our record company started. Bruce Haack and I made our first record with borrowed money and a nine-dollar mike. That was all the equipment we had at the time. Now we have a totally equipped sound studio where we record, and have to date sold more than forty-five thousand of our children's music and dance participation records to schools and libraries all over the country, and in foreign countries as well."

AVOCATIONAL INTERESTS: Yoga ("the Alexander Technique, different body and mind investigations"), international travel.

BIOGRAPHICAL/CRITICAL SOURCES: White Plains Reporter Dispatch, February 9, 1974; *Patent Trader,* September 11, 1976.

*   *   *

NELSON, R. Faraday   1931-
(R. N. Elson and Ray Nelson)

PERSONAL: Born October 3, 1931, in Schenectady, N.Y.; son of Walter Hughes (a scientist) and Marie (Reed) Nelson; married Kirsten Enge, October 4, 1957; children: Walter Trygvi. *Education:* University of Chicago, B.A., 1960; Automation Institute, Oakland, Calif., programmer's certificate, 1961. *Religion:* Unitarian. *Home:* 333 Ramona Ave., El Cerrito, Calif. 94530. *Agent:* Scott Meredith, 845 Third Ave., New York, N.Y.

CAREER: Northside Poster Co., Chicago, Ill., printer, 1954; Artcraft Poster Co., Oakland, Calif., printer and art director, 1955; Jean Linard, Vesoul, France, translator, 1959; University of California Press, Berkeley, Calif., computer programmer and accounting assistant, 1961-62; writer, 1962—. Gag writer for cartoonist Grant Canfield. *Member:* Science Fiction Writers of America, Mystery Writers of America, California Writers Club (vice-president, Berkeley

branch, 1975—), The Network, Elves, Gnomes & Little Men's Chowder and Science Fiction Society. *Awards, honors:* Hugo award nomination, 1964, for *Turn off the Sky;* Nebula award nomination, 1976, for *Blake's Progress.*

WRITINGS: (With Philip K. Dick; under pseudonym, Ray Nelson) *The Ganymede Takeover,* Ace Books, 1967; *Blake's Progress,* Laser Books, 1975; *Then Beggars Could Ride,* Laser Books, 1976; *The Ecolog,* Laser Books, 1977; *Revolt of the Unemployables,* Anthelion Press, 1977; *Dimension of Horror,* Pinnacle Books, 1978; *Arthur the Celt,* Corgi, 1978; *Arthur the Roman,* Corgi, 1978.

Also author, under pseudonyms Ray Nelson and R. N. Elson, of books for Greenleaf Classics, including *The Agony of Love,* 1969, and *The D.A.'s Wife,* 1970. Work represented in anthologies, including *Year's Best Science Fiction,* edited by Judith Merril, Dial, 1965, and *The Best from Fantasy and Science Fiction: No. 13,* edited by Avram Davidson, Doubleday, 1965. Contributor of short stories to magazines.

WORK IN PROGRESS: In the Footsteps of Jack London, a guidebook.

SIDELIGHTS: Nelson, who says that his brand of science fiction "dispenses with a lot of the furniture of science fiction, and instead concentrates on ideas," told *CA:* "I work in the tradition of Jack London, combining adventure fiction with political and philosophical speculation. I see Jack London as the founder of American science fiction, predating Hugo Gernsback and providing a literary example I do not need to feel ashamed of; for me London's role is more important than that of H. G. Wells, Jules Verne, John Campbell or the modern Harlan Ellison. With time, I may become London's equal. This is my ambition."

AVOCATIONAL INTERESTS: Walking, gardening, guitar playing, and collecting cats.

BIOGRAPHICAL/CRITICAL SOURCES: Berkeley Gazette, December 29, 1975; *Northern Michigan Life,* September 3, 1976; *San Francisco Chronicle,* February 13, 1977.

*   *   *

NEWCOMBE, John (David)   1944-

PERSONAL: Born May 23, 1944, in Sydney, Australia; son of George Ernest and Lillian Newcombe; married Angelika Pfannenberg (a writer), February 21, 1966; children: Clint, Tanya, Gigi. *Education:* Attended high school in Sydney, Australia. *Office:* Program Tennis Services, P.O. Box 469, New Braunfels, Tex. 78130.

CAREER: Professional tennis player. Director and chairman of Program Tennis Services; director of Newk Plus Four (Hong Kong) and Lotto U.S.A. *Member:* Association of Tennis Professionals (president), City Tattersalls (Sydney), North Sydney Leagues Club, White City Club (Sydney).

WRITINGS: (With wife, Angie Newcombe, and Clarence Mabry) *The Family Tennis Book,* Tennis, 1975.

SIDELIGHTS: As an amateur tennis player, Newcombe was named champion of South Australia, 1963, 1964, 1966, 1967, New South Wales, 1965, and Tasmania, 1966. He won the Australian doubles competition, 1965, 1967, French doubles, 1967, Wimbledon doubles, 1965-66, U.S. doubles, 1967, Wimbledon and U.S. singles competitions, both 1967, and West German singles, 1968. He was named top world amateur in 1967 and became a professional tennis player in 1968, was ranked number one player in the world in 1970, and won the Australian doubles in 1971. He comments: "I wanted to write a book about tennis that would emphasize the family aspects of tennis. I feel strongly that family activities are needed in today's world."

* * *

NEWMAN, Edwin (Harold) 1919-

PERSONAL: Born January 25, 1919, in New York City; son of Myron (a credit manager) and Rose (Parker) Newman; married Rigel Grell, August 14, 1944; children: Nancy Livia (Mrs. Henry M. Drucker). Education: University of Wisconsin, B.A., 1940; Louisiana State University, graduate study, 1940-41. Residence: New York City. Office: NBC News, 30 Rockefeller Pl., New York, N.Y. 10020.

CAREER: International News Service, Washington, D.C., dictation writer, 1941; United Press, Washington, D.C., reporter, 1941 and 1945-46; PM, New York City, Washington bureau reporter, 1946; Tufty News Bureau, Washington, D.C., reporter, 1946-47; Columbia Broadcasting System (CBS) News, Washington, D.C., writer for evening news with Eric Sevaried, 1947-49; free-lance journalist in London, England, 1949-52; National Broadcasting Co. (NBC) News, reporter in London, 1952-56, bureau chief in London, 1956-57, in Rome, 1957-58, and in Paris, 1958-61, television commentator in New York, 1961—, critic-at-large, 1967—. Appeared on NBC television programs, "Edwin Newman Reporting," 1960, "The Nation's Future," 1961, "JFK Reports," 1962, "Speaking Freely," 1967-76; newsman on "This Is NBC News," 1961, and "Today," 1961—; narrator for numerous radio and television documentary specials, 1961—; drama critic for WNBC-TV, 1965-71. Chairman of New York State Commission on Libraries, 1978—. Military service: U.S. Navy, 1942-45; became lieutenant.

MEMBER: Association of Radio and Television News Analysts (president, 1966), American Federation of Television and Radio Artists. Awards, honors: Overseas Press Club award for foreign news, 1961; Peabody award, 1966; Boston Press Club award, 1966; award from University of Wisconsin, School of Journalism, 1967; Emmy awards for dramatic criticism and reporting, 1966, 1968, 1970, and 1972; award from San Franciso State University, 1970; chevalier, Legion of Honor (France), 1972; award from University of Missouri, 1975; also recipient of Headliners Award.

WRITINGS: Strictly Speaking: Will America Be the Death of English?, Bobbs-Merrill, 1974; A Civil Tongue, Bobbs-Merrill, 1976. Contributor of articles to British and American periodicals, including Harper's, Atlantic Monthly, Esquire, Punch, Progressive, and The Listener.

SIDELIGHTS: When asked about the effects of his books, Newman told CA: "I believe that my books have contributed to a changing attitude to the language. This is clear from the many newspaper and magazine articles that now appear and poke fun at the bloated language of government and the academic world. It is clear from the evidence of the number of school boards making changes in their teaching and their requirements, not only for students but for teachers. We now have a President who says that he wants government regulations written in plain English. There are banks and insurance companies that advertise that their policies can be read and understood. I believe that I have had a part in all of this.

"How long did it take me to compile the material in the books? Not long. I had not made a collection over the years, except in my head. I found that once I began looking, the

material flooded in. I must add that some of the material for the second book was supplied by readers of the first.

"More material is being sent to me now, but I do not have a third book in mind."

AVOCATIONAL INTERESTS: Tennis, classical music.

* * *

NIN, Anais 1903-1977

February 21, 1903—January 14, 1977; French-born American author whose works reflect the influences of surrealism and psychoanalytic theory; best known for The Diary of Anais Nin, in six volumes. The diaries, which span sixty years of her life, recall experiences in America and bohemian Paris and contain vivid portraits of her contemporaries, including Lawrence Durrell, Henry Miller, and William Carlos Williams. Finding herself increasingly in demand among students and feminists, she commented in 1971, "Sometimes I feel like I have about ten million daughters." She died in Los Angeles, Calif. Obituaries: New York Times, January 16, 1977; Washington Post, January 16, 1977; Time, January 24, 1977; Newsweek, January 24, 1977; Current Biography, March, 1977. (See index for previous CA sketch)

* * *

NIRENBERG, Jesse S(tanley) 1921-

PERSONAL: Born May 19, 1921, in New York, N.Y.; son of Abraham H. (a fur merchant) and May (Lapin) Nirenberg; married Edna Fontek, November 21, 1954; children: Liz, Sheila, Nina. Education: New York University, B.A., 1941, Ph.D., 1952; Brooklyn Polytechnic Institute, B.Ch.E., 1943. Politics: Democrat. Religion: Jewish. Home: 107 Edgemont Rd., Scarsdale, N.Y. 10583. Office: Nirenberg Communications, 30 East 42nd St., New York, N.Y. 10017.

CAREER: New York University, New York, N.Y., instructor of psychology, 1949-52; TradeWays, Inc., New York City, industrial consulting psychologist, 1952-62; Nirenberg Communications, New York City, industrial consulting psychologist, 1962—. Military service: U.S. Army Air Forces, 1943-46; became second lieutenant. Member: International Communications Association, American Psychological Association, Authors Guild of Authors League of America.

WRITINGS: Getting Through to People, Prentice-Hall, 1963; Breaking Through to Each Other: Creative Persuasion on the Job and in the Home, Harper, 1976. Contributor to management and marketing journals.

WORK IN PROGRESS: A book on credibility, "the factors influencing it, how it's lost, and how to build it."

SIDELIGHTS: Nirenberg writes: "Communication as an interpersonal process has always interested me, particularly developing methods of getting people to listen to each other, to think and reason together, and to build parallel thought structures by keeping in touch with each other's thinking in conversation, remark by remark."

* * *

NISHIHARA, Masashi 1937-

PERSONAL: Surname is accented on second syllable; born August 4, 1937, in Osaka, Japan; son of Chikao and Yoneko Nishihara; married Susuko Osawa (a linguist), December, 1968; children: Aya, Mitsu (daughters). Education: University of North Carolina, student, 1959-60; Kyoto University, B.A., 1962; University of Michigan, M.A., 1968, Ph.D., 1972. *Home:* 21-3, 2-chome, Hashirimizu, Yokosuka-shi, Kanagawa-ken 239, Japan. *Office:* Defense Academy, 1-chome, Hashirimizu, Yokosuka-shi, Kanagawa-ken 239, Japan.

CAREER: Center for Japanese Social and Political Studies, Tokyo, Japan, research assistant, 1962-64; Kyoto University, Center for Southeast Asian Studies, Kyoto, Japan, head of Jakarta Liaison Office, 1970-72; Kyoto Sangyo University, Kyoto, Japan, associate professor, 1973-75, professor of Southeast Asian politics, 1975—. *Member:* Japan Society of International Relations, Association of Asian Political and Economic Studies, International Studies Association.

WRITINGS: Golkar and the Indonesian Elections of 1971, Modern Indonesia Project, Cornell University, 1972; (with Robert E. Ward, Frank J. Shulman and Mary Espey) *The Allied Occupation of Japan, 1945-1952: An Annotated Bibliography of Western Languages Materials,* American Library Association, 1975; *The Japanese and Sukarno's Indonesia,* University Press of Hawaii, 1976; *Tonan Ajia no seijiteki fuhai* (title means "Political Corruption in Southeast Asia"), Sobunsha, 1976. Contributor to economics and Asian studies journals.

WORK IN PROGRESS: Research on Japan's role in Asia and on Indonesia's political and military elite.

SIDELIGHTS: Nishihara writes: "I have been concerned about the lack of academic interest in the role of human personal contacts between the Japanese and other Asian countries. Pre-war and wartime contacts between the Japanese and Indonesians had lots to do with postwar binational relations. I wanted to uncover this in my book from Hawaii Press. I wish to do similar things, in the future, about other countries. It is important to me to know what Japan has done to our neighbors, for I am concerned about the future of Asia as a whole."

BIOGRAPHICAL/CRITICAL SOURCES: Wakai Chikara (title means "Young Power"), February, 1977.

* * *

NOEL, Ruth (Swycaffer) 1947-

PERSONAL: Born May 1, 1947, in San Diego, Calif.; daughter of Lloyd Jefferson (a cowboy and postmaster) and Ruth (Abbott) Swycaffer. *Education:* San Diego State University, B.A., 1971, graduate study, 1971—. *Home:* 5660 Montezuma Rd., San Diego, Calif. 92115.

CAREER: Reading Progress Center, San Diego, Calif., reading teacher, 1975-77; reading teacher-aide in public schools of San Diego, Calif., 1977—. *Member:* Delta Omicron Epsilon (life member).

WRITINGS: The Languages of Middle-Earth, Mirage Press, 1974; *The Mythology of Middle-Earth,* Houghton, 1977.

WORK IN PROGRESS: Punkinhead, a phonetic introduction to reading, revised from a manuscript by her grandmother, Claudine Swycaffer.

SIDELIGHTS: Ruth Noel writes that she is motivated by a "desire to track down many of the allusions in Tolkien's works. They are multitudinous and deserve recognition." She adds that her interest in remedial reading was inspired by the work of her grandmother, Claudine Swycaffer, with Indians. One of her research interests involves travel to the British Isles, especially Fife, Scotland, to study family history, and to Scandinavia and Russia "with one remarkable day in Gotland, which I have wanted to visit since childhood and which inspired the cover of the book *Mythology.*"

* * *

NOHRNBERG, James (Carson) 1941-

PERSONAL: Born March 19, 1941, in Berkeley, Calif.; son of Carson (a self-employed businessman) and Geneva Gertrude (a teacher; maiden name, Gibbs) Nohrnberg; married Stephanie Payson Lamport, June 14, 1964; children: Gabrielle Lamport Nohrnberg, Peter Carson Lamport Nohrnberg. *Education:* Attended Kenyon College, 1958-60; Harvard University, B.A. (magna cum laude), 1962; University of Toronto, Ph.D., 1970. *Politics:* Independent. *Religion:* Presbyterian. *Home:* 1874 Wayside Pl., Charlottesville, Va. 22903. *Office:* Department of English, University of Virginia, Wilson Hall, Charlottesville, Va. 22901.

CAREER: Yale University, New Haven, Conn., acting instructor, 1968-69, lecturer, 1969-70, assistant professor of English, 1970-75; University of Virginia, Charlottesville, professor of English, 1975—, member of Center for Advanced Studies, 1975-78. *Member:* Modern Language Association of America, Spenser Society of America, Phi Beta Kappa.

WRITINGS: The Analogy of The Faerie Queene, Princeton University Press, 1976; (contributor) Michael Seidel and Edward Mendelson, editors, *Homer to Brecht,* Yale University Press, 1977. Contributor of articles and poems to literary magazines, including *Harvard Advocate, Centrum, Varsity* (Toronto), *Jargon,* and *Hika.*

WORK IN PROGRESS: Research on the literary form and use of the Bible, allegory, Renaissance literature, Spenser, and literary theory.

SIDELIGHTS: Nohrnberg writes to *CA:* "A portrait, Pascal says, conveys both presence and absence. I am interested in pursuing this theme through studies of compound expression in literature: compound structure, and compound verbal expression—language that divides 'meaning' from 'significance,' tenor from vehicle, 'said' from 'unsaid' but implied or understood—language that seems to have it both ways. My work on the Bible, on the other hand, will tend to abridge this division."

AVOCATIONAL INTERESTS: Painting, music, collecting lamps and Oriental rugs, and building furniture.

* * *

NORTH, Joseph 1904-1976

May 25, 1904—December 20, 1976; Russian-born newspaper editor and author of an autobiography, *No Men Are Strangers,* and of other nonfiction works. He died in San Juan, Puerto Rico. Obituaries: *New York Times,* December 22, 1976; *AB Bookman's Weekly,* March 7, 1977. (See index for previous *CA* sketch)

* * *

NORTHART, Leo J(oseph) 1929-

PERSONAL: Born August 23, 1929, in Pittsburgh, Pa.; son of Lee J. (a businessman) and Mozelt (a practical nurse; maiden name, Ellington) Northart; married Thelma I. Harvey (a secretary), December 20, 1948; children: Leo J. III, Pamela Leigh. *Education:* University of North Carolina, A.B., 1952, M.A., 1953. *Politics:* Republican. *Reli-*

gion: Presbyterian. *Home:* 25 Meadow Pl., Freehold, N.J. 07728. *Office: Public Relations Journal,* Public Relations Society of America, 845 Third Ave., New York, N.Y. 10022.

CAREER: General Electric Co., Schenectady, N.Y., advertising and sales copywriter, 1953-56; *Chemistry Week,* New York City, department editor, 1956-60; American Management Association, New York City, international division manager, 1960-63; *Business Abroad,* New York City, editor, 1962-66; Gallatin Service of International Intelligence, New York City, editorial director, 1966-68; Johnston International Publishing Corp., New York City, editor, 1968-74; *Public Relations Journal,* New York City, editor, 1974—. Member of New York mayor's businessmen's committee for trade in the Port of New York. Teacher of international marketing. *Military service:* U.S. Marine Corps, 1946-48. *Member:* World Trade Writers (president, 1966), American Society of Magazine Editors, New York Business Press Editors, Lions International, Jaycees.

WRITINGS: Buy, Sell, Merge: How to Do It, Prentice-Hall, 1971.

SIDELIGHTS: Northart writes: "I have been a journalist all of my working life, except for a two-year stint as manager of the International Management Division, American Management Association. My specialization has been international business. My academic background prepared me for this concentration and I have pursued it doggedly until my present assignment, which is to upgrade the Public Relations Society of America magazine. The magazine is a professional journal, not a house organ for the society."

*   *   *

NOVITZ, Charles R.   1934-

PERSONAL: Born October 25, 1934, in Chicago, Ill.; son of Meyer and Dina (Weisman) Novitz. *Education:* University of Illinois, B.S., 1956; Columbia University, M.S., 1960; New York University, M.P.A., 1971. *Home:* 160 West End Ave., New York, N.Y. 10023. *Office:* 7 West 66th St., New York, N.Y. 10023.

CAREER/WRITINGS: City News Bureau, Chicago, Ill., news writer, 1956-57; United Press International, New York City, news writer in Chicago, 1957-59; National Broadcasting Co. (NBC), New York City, news writer in Chicago and New York City, 1959-60; American Broadcasting Co. (ABC), New York City, news writer, 1960-73, manager of television network news syndication, 1973—. Contributor of articles to professional journals, including *Quill* and *Journalism Educator,* and to other publications, including *McCall's.* Executive producer of "The Journalists," a film for Sigma Delta Chi. Adjunct professor, City University of New York, 1972-75; lecturer at New York University, Long Island University, Lehman College, and other colleges and universities. *Military service:* Served in U.S. Army and U.S. Army Reserve. *Member:* Association for Education in Journalism, Radio-Television News Directors Association, New York Deadline Club (president, 1969), Society of Professional Journalists, Sigma Delta Chi (director of northeast division). *Awards, honors:* Awards from New York Deadline Club, and Society of Professional Journalists, Sigma Delta Chi.

*   *   *

NOVOMESKY, Ladislav   1904-1976

December 27, 1904—September 4, 1976; Czechoslovakian poet and writer. With President Gustav Husak, he was involved with the movement for Slovak home rule. Between World Wars I and II, he belonged to "Dav," an influential literary group. He died in Prague, Czechoslovakia. Obituaries: *Washington Post,* September 8, 1976.

*   *   *

NUNEZ, Ana Rosa   1926-

PERSONAL: Born July 11, 1926, in Havana, Cuba; came to the United States in 1965, naturalized citizen, 1971; daughter of Jorge Manuel (an architect and professor) and Carmen G. (Burgos) Nunez. *Education:* Academia Baldor, Bach. Letras, 1945; Instituto de Ensenanza Secundaria, Bach. Letras, 1945; University of Michigan, student, 1953; University of Havana, Dra. en Filosofia y Letras and Bibliotecaria, both 1954. *Religion:* Roman Catholic. *Home:* 2130 Southwest 14th Ter., Apt. 2, Miami, Fla. 33145. *Office:* Otto G. Richter Library, University of Miami, Coral Gables, Fla. 33124.

CAREER: Colegio Cima, Havana, Cuba, professor of English as a second language, 1947-49; College of Wooster, Wooster, Ohio, staff member of foreign language department, 1949-50; Tribunal de Cuentas de la Republica de Cuba, Havana, head librarian, 1950-61; University of Miami, Coral Gables, Fla., worked at Otto G. Richter Library, 1966-69, assistant professor and assistant reference librarian, 1969-72, associate professor and reference librarian, 1972—. Elementary school teacher in Havana, Cuba, 1950-52; instructor at University of Havana, 1951; librarian for Academia de Ciencias Genealogicas, 1956-59; lecturer for Cruzada Educativa Cubana, 1973. Reader with Laramore Rader Poetry Group, 1973-76. Cultural consultant to Patronato Teatro Las Mascaras. Counselor of Federation of Cuban Students at University of Miami.

MEMBER: Asociacion Bibliografica Jose Toribio Medina (Colombia), Artistic and Cultural Society of the Americas (president, 1974-76), Instituto de Cultura Hispanica (honorary librarian; member of executive council, 1973—), Colegio Nacional de Doctores en Ciencias y Filosofia y Letras, Colegio Nacional de Bibliotecarios (founder; vice-president of executive committee, 1957-59), Seminar of Latin American Acquisition Materials, Florida Library Association, Dade County Library Association, Sociedad de Escritores, Pintores, y Artistas (Miami; honorary member), Cuban Women's Club (Miami), Sigma Delta Pi (honorary member), Phi Alpha Theta. *Awards, honors:* Scholarship from New York Institute of International Education, 1949; Henri Dunant Gold Medal from International Red Cross (Spain), 1958; diploma of honor from International Young Men's Christian Association (YMCA), 1969; Juan J. Remos Prize from Cruzada Educativa Cubana, 1971; Lincoln-Marti Prize from U.S. Department of Health, Education and Welfare, 1972; first prize in poetry from Circulo de Escritores y Artistas Iberoamericanos de New York, 1972, for unpublished book of poems "Sol de un Solo dia"; Gran Orden del Merito Ciudadano en reconocimiento de destacada labor a la Comunidad from Liceo Cubano, 1973; Order of St. Helene (Greece).

WRITINGS: La vida bibliografica de don Antonio Bachiller y Morales (title means "Bibliographic Life of don Antonio Bachiller y Morales"), Libraria Marti, 1955; *Un dia en el verso 59* (poems; title means "One Day in Verse 59"), Atabex, 1959; *Gabriela Mistral: Amor que hirio* (poems; title means "Gabriela Mistral: Love that Hurt"), Atabex, 1961; *Las siete lunas de enero* (poems; title means "The

Seven Moons of January"), Cuadernos del hombre libre, 1967; *La Florida en Juan Ramon Jiminez* (title means "Florida in Juan Ramon Jimenez"), Ediciones Universal, 1968; *Loores a la palma real* (title means "Praises to the Royal Palm"), Ediciones Universal, 1968, 2nd edtion, 1976; *Bando* (poems; title means "Edict"), Armando Cordova, 1969.

(Editor and contributor) *Poesia en exodo: El exilio cubano en su poesia, 1959-1969* (anthology; title means "Poetry in Exodus: The Cuban Exile in Poetry"), Ediciones Universal, 1970; *Requiem para una isla* (poems; title means "Requiem for an Island"), Ediciones Universal, 1970; *Nuestro Gustavo Adolfo Becquer, 1870-1970* (title means "Our Gustavo Adolpho Becquer"), Ediciones Universal, 1970; *Viaje al cazabe* (title means "Journey to Cazabe"), Ediciones Universal, 1970; *Del paredon al siglo* (poems; title means "From the Shooting Wall to the Century"), Ediciones Universal, 1971; *Escamas del Caribe: Haikus de Cuba* (title means "Scales from the Caribbean: Haikus of Cuba"), Ediciones Universal, 1971; *Ya no habra mas domingos* (title means "No More Sundays Left"), edited by Humberto J. Pena, Ediciones Universal, 1971; *Cuentos a luna llena* (title means "Short Stories at Full Moon"; edited by Jose Sanchez Boudy), Ediciones Universal, 1971; *Los oficialeros* (title means "Humble Workers"), Ediciones Universal, 1973; *Algunas fuentes de referencia en materia legal cubana* (title means "Some Reference Sources on Cuban Legal Material"), Ediciones Universal, 1973; *La Marquesina* (title means "Marquee"), Diario Las Americas, 1974; (with Florinda Alzaga) *Diccionario del pensamiento vivo de La Avellaneda* (title means "Dictionary of the Living Thought of La Avellaneda"), Ediciones Universal, 1975; (editor with Alzaga) *Antologia de la poesia religiosa de La Avellaneda* (title means "Anthology of the Religious Poetry of La Avellaneda"), Ediciones Universal, 1975. Also author of *Aspectos de una vida entre libros* (title means "Aspects of a Life among Books"), 1955. Co-translator of *Synthesis of His Life as an Artist* by Fernando Boada.

Work represented in anthologies, including *Antologia de poesia espanola, 1965-1966* (title means "Anthology of Spanish Poetry"), edited by L. Jiminez Martos, Aguilar, 1967; *Un catauro de folklore cubano* (title means "A Basket of Cuban Folklore"), edited by Antonio Carbajo, Language Research Press, 1968; *Poesia en mesa redonda: Antologia latinoamericana, 1948-1968* (title means "Poetry in Round Table: Anthology of Latin American Poetry, 1948-1968"), edited by Antonio de Undurraga, Ediciones de la Revista Caballo de Guego, 1969; *Cinco poetisas cubanas, 1935-1969: Mercedes Garcia Tuduri, Pura del Prado, Teresa Maria Rojas, Rita Geada, Ana Rosa Nunez* (title means "Five Cuban Poetesses, 1935-1969: Mercedes Gardia Tuduri, Pura del Prado, Teresa Maria Rojas, Rita Geada, Ana Rosa Nunez"), Ediciones Universal, 1970; *Poesia negra del Caribe y otras areas: Black Poetry of the Americas—A Bilingual Anthology,* edited by Hortensia Ruiz del Vizo, Ediciones Universal, 1972. Contributor of about eighty-five articles and poems to Spanish and American literary journals. Co-editor of "Las Horas Blancas" in *El Habenero,* 1974—.

WORK IN PROGRESS: Editing with Jose E. Fernandez, *Antologia de literature infantil* (title means "Anthology of Children's Literature"); editing with Fernandez, *Jorge Manach y la pintura cubana* (title means "Jorge Manach and the Cuban Paintings"); an anthology of author's poems, 1957-76, *Sin sol pero con sal* (title means "Without Sun, Yet with Salt"); *Andres y otros cuentos* (title means "Andrew

and Other Stories"); a book of poems, *Mis dos voces* (title means "My Two Voices").

SIDELIGHTS: Ana Rosa Nunez writes: "I know that I am alone with my poetry, and I also know that I have broken the original silence with my poems. But as long as each one of them can have a life of its own I am rewarded, deep in my silent world. In a poem I have put a great effort in letting silence win. Poetry does not begin with the poet who writes the poem. It really begins with the person who reads it. I believe in the order of the chaos established in the soul when the abyss is not yet forgotten. I believe in Bruegel as the master of surrealism, as the man who gave the inner man his place in a world built to fit hope and tomorrows. I do not trust fame, best-sellers, or book jackets. I believe and trust in the isolation of a sincere creator who wishes to give an order to the resemblance of the light that inherits everyday's light. I believe in Liberty and I stand for everything that could restore Human Dignity."

* * *

NURENBERG, Thelma 1903-

PERSONAL: Born December 25, 1903, in Warsaw, Poland; married Charles Greenbaus; children: Carla Lord. *Education:* Attended Columbia University, 1923-26, and Jewish Theological Seminary, 1925-27. *Religion:* Jewish. *Home:* 382 Central Park W., New York, N.Y.

CAREER: Worked as reporter for *Brooklyn Daily Eagle,* Brooklyn, N.Y., and *New York Evening Graphic,* New York City. *Member:* Authors Guild of Authors League of America.

WRITINGS: The New Red Freedom, Wadsworth, 1932; *My Cousin, the Arab,* Abelard, 1965; *New York Colony* (history), Crowell, 1969; *The Time of Anger* (novel), Abelard, 1975. Author of "The Refugee Story" (television play), 1958. Editor of *Woman Today,* 1936-38.

WORK IN PROGRESS: A historical novel dealing with Russia and Israel.

AVOCATIONAL INTERESTS: International travel (England, Europe, Soviet Union, Israel).*

* * *

OATES, John (Frederick) 1944-

PERSONAL: Born December 12, 1944, in North Wales; son of Arthur (a civil servant) and Kathleen (a college teacher; maiden name, Shead) Oates. *Education:* University College, London, B.Sc. (honors), 1966; University of London, Ph.D., 1974. *Home:* 14 Bigwood Rd., London NW11 7BD, England. *Office:* Field Research Center, Rockefeller University, Tyrrel Rd., Millbrook, N.Y. 12545.

CAREER: University of Nigeria, Nsukka, research assistant, 1967-68; biology teacher at Woodhouse School in North London, England, 1968-69; Reader's Digest Association Ltd., London, England, editorial adviser, 1969-70; New York Zoological Society, Bronx, N.Y., research assistant, 1970-72; Mitchell Beazley Multimedia Ltd., London, England, editorial head of biology group, 1973; Rockefeller University, Field Research Center, Millbrook, N.Y., research associate, 1975—.

MEMBER: Association for Tropical Biology, British Ecological Society, Mammal Society of the British Isles, Primate Society of Great Britain, Association for the Study of Animal Behaviour, Fauna Preservation Society, Bombay Natural History Society, Zoological Society (London), Sigma Xi.

WRITINGS: Web of Life (introduction to ecology for the layman), Danbury Press, 1975.

Contributor: The Living World of Animals, Reader's Digest Press, 1970; Book of the British Countryside, Drive, 1973; T. H. Clutton-Brock, editor, Primate Ecology, Academic Press, 1977; Prince Rainier of Monaco and G. H. Bourne, editors, Primate Conservation, Academic Press, 1977. Contributor to Time-Life Atlas of World Wildlife. Contributor to magazines, including Wildlife and Geographical Magazine.

WORK IN PROGRESS: Books on the domestication of plants and animals; research on the ecology of Indian rain-forest monkeys; work on conservation problems in southern India.

SIDELIGHTS: Oates writes: "I have had a long-standing interest in the natural history of tropical rain forests, an interest stimulated by two expeditions to Spanish Equatorial Africa when I was an undergraduate at University College London. I have subsequently spent several years in the tropics, undertaking ecological research in the forests of Nigeria, Uganda, and India. The emotional appeal of these wild places is quite as important to me as their scientific interest and I am stimulated by travel in new places, amongst new people. I am keen to continue writing about man's involvement with the natural world."

*   *   *

ODESCALCHI, Esther Kando 1938-

PERSONAL: Born September 30, 1938, in Budapest, Hungary; came to the United States, 1957, naturalized citizen, 1962; daughter of Francis (a lawyer) and Maria (Vesenyi) Kando; married Edmond Odescalchi (a communications manager), September 30, 1961; children: Daniel, Dominic. Education: Manhattanville College, B.A., 1960; Columbia University, M.S., 1961. Religion: Roman Catholic. Home: 6 Freedom Rd., Pleasant Valley, N.Y. 12569. Office: Adriance Memorial Library, 93 Market St., Poughkeepsie, N.Y. 12601.

CAREER: International Business Machines (IBM) Laboratory, Poughkeepsie, N.Y., cataloger, 1961-62; Adriance Memorial Library, Poughkeepsie, head of extension service, 1962—. Conducts local senior citizens' activities. Member: American-Hungarian Library Association, Dutchess County Library Association (past president). Awards, Honors: Meritorious civic service award from Dutchess County Rehabilitation Programs, 1965; New York State Office for the Aging grant, 1967-69; distinguished service award from Adriance Memorial Library, 1973; Dutchess County Office for the Aging award, 1976; Community Development Funds grant, 1976—.

WRITINGS: The Little Shoe That Ran Away (juvenile), Cyclopedia Publishing Co., 1976.

Work represented in anthologies, Dance of the Muse, edited by Jeanne Hollyfield, Young Publishing Co., 1970; Yearbook of Modern Poetry, edited by Hollyfield, Young Publishing Co., 1972; and Outstanding Contemporary Poetry, edited by Dale R. Moore, Pied-Piper Press, 1972. Author "More Wisdom from Our Senior Citizens," a column in Dutchess County Senior Citizens Action News.

WORK IN PROGRESS: Another juvenile book; an essay collection.

AVOCATIONAL INTERESTS: Playing the accordion and piano.

O'GARA, James Vincent, Jr. 1918-

PERSONAL: Born March 26, 1918, in Brooklyn, N.Y.; son of James and Sarah (McEntee) O'Gara; married Marguerite Rohmer, May 9, 1943; children: Maureen, James III, Erin. Education: New York University, B.S., 1942. Religion: Roman Catholic. Home: 75 Bedell Ave., Hempstead, N.Y. 11550. Office: 708 3rd Ave., New York, N.Y. 10017.

CAREER/WRITINGS: Religious News Service, New York, N.Y., news editor, 1946-50; free lance magazine writer, 1947—; Advertising Age, New York City, writer, 1950-57, senior editor in charge of New York office, 1958-61, executive editor, 1961-68, editor, 1969-72, editor at large, 1972—. Adjunct assistant professor of communication arts, Fordham University, 1960-66; vice president, Crain Communications, 1963—, Military service: U.S. Air Force, 1942-46; became first lieutenant. Awards, honors: Award of merit for outstanding journalism, 1954, from Association of Business Publications.

*   *   *

OHL, (Mary) Suzanne Sickler 1923-

PERSONAL: Born September 11, 1923, in Tyrone, Pa.; daughter of Harry K. (a salesman) and Isabel (McNelis) Sickler; married Paul W. Ohl; children: (stepchildren) James, Lee, Robert, David, Jeanne Glenn Young, Kathryn Glenn Pfalzgraf, Kenneth. Education: Pennsylvania State University, B.S., 1944; Columbia University, M.A., 1948; also studied at Rutgers University, 1950-52. Religion: Roman Catholic. Residence: West Orange, N.J. Office: West Orange Board of Education, West Orange, N.J. 07052.

CAREER: West Orange Board of Education, West Orange, N.J., director of home economics, 1949—. Has served as chair of committees. Member: National Education Association, American Home Economics Association, Association for Supervision and Curriculum Development, American Association of University Women, Society for Nutrition Education, Home Economics Education Association, New Jersey Home Economics Association.

WRITINGS: Homemaking in the Elementary Schools, New Jersey Department of Education, 1964; (with others) Guide to Modern Meals, 2nd edition, McGraw, 1970; (with others) Focus on Food, McGraw, 1974. Contributor of articles to education journals.

*   *   *

OHLIG, Karl-Heinz 1938-

PERSONAL: Born September 15, 1938, in Koblenz, Germany; son of Josef (a bank employee) and Gertrud (Hammes) Ohlig; married Brigitte Blasius (a teacher), July 3, 1973; children: Nadja. Education: University of Trier, B.A., 1963; University of Muenster, Ph.D., 1969. Religion: Roman Catholic. Home: Gruelingsstrasse 20, Saarbruecken, Germany D 6600.

CAREER: University of Saarbruecken, Saarbruecken, Germany, assistant in humanities, 1966-70; Paedagoge Hochschule Saarbruecken, Saarbruecken, professor of Catholic theology, 1970—.

WRITINGS: Woher nimmt die Bibel ihre Autoritaet?, Patmos-Verlag (Duesseldorf), 1970; (with Heinz Schuster) Blockiert das katholische Dogma die Einheit der Kirchen?, Patmos-Verlag, 1971; Gott, eine Hoffnung, Patmos-Verlag, 1972; Die theologische Begruendung der neutestamentlichen Kanons in der alten Kirche, Patmos-Verlag, 1972; Braucht die Kirche einen Papst?, Patmos-Verlag, 1973, translation by Robert C. Ware published as *Why We Need the Pope: The Necessity and Limits of Papal Primacy,* Abbey Press, 1975; (with Brigitte Blasius) *Jesuskurs,* Koesel-Verlag, 1973; *Jesus, Entwurf zum Menschsein,* KBW-Verlag (Stuttgart), 1974.

WORK IN PROGRESS: A study of Christology.

* * *

OLSEN, Larry Dean 1939-

PERSONAL: Born January 23, 1939, in Wendell, Idaho; son of Dean and Lola (Tilby) Olsen; married Sherrel Eslinger, June 16, 1959; children: Farah Lee, Jane, Lorinda, Paul, Reuben, Nathan, Enoch, Joshua. *Education:* Ricks College, A.A., 1960; Brigham Young University, B.A., 1972. *Religion:* Mormon. *Home:* Rt. 1 Box 59, Stevensville, Mont. 59870.

CAREER: Grade school principal and teacher in Grandview, Id., 1965-68; Brigham Young University, Provo, Utah, founder and instructor of Youth Survival Program, 1969—. *Awards, honors:* National University Extension Association award for creativity in designing "Youth Rehabilitation through Outdoor Survival" class, 1969.

WRITINGS: Outdoor Survival Skills, Brigham Young University Press, 1969; *Survival Merit Badge Book,* Boy Scouts of America, 1974.

Publisher of *New Homesteader* journal, 1977—. Columnist for *Mariah Magazine,* 1976—.

WORK IN PROGRESS: Two books on survival and homesteading self-sufficiency.

SIDELIGHTS: Olsen served as technical advisor to Robert Redford in the production of the 1972 movie, "Jeremiah Johnson."

* * *

O'NEILL, Gerard (Michael) 1942-

PERSONAL: Born September 1, 1942, in Boston, Mass.; son of Richard T. (a post office official) and Mary (a nurse; maiden name, Sweeney) O'Neill; married Janet Reardon, July 6, 1968; children: Brian, Shane. *Education:* Stonehill College, B.A. (cum laude), 1964; Boston University, M.S., 1970. *Home:* 38 Bay Rd., North Easton, Mass. 02356. *Office:* Boston Globe, Morrissey Blvd., Boston, Mass. 02107.

CAREER: Boston Globe, Boston, Mass., copy boy, 1965, intern, 1966, suburban reporter, 1967-69, state house and city hall reporter, 1968-70, member of investigative spotlight team, 1970—. *Awards, honors:* United Press International civic service award, 1970; Sigma Delta Chi public service award, 1971; Pulitzer Prize, 1972; National Press Club consumer reporting award, 1975; Scripp Howard citation, 1976, for public service.

SIDELIGHTS: O'Neill told *CA* he "likes to catch crooks." *Avocational interests:* Tennis, jogging, photography, reading.

* * *

OPPENHEIM, Paul 1885(?)-1977

1885(?)—June 22, 1977; German-born philosopher of science and author of two books and numerous articles in philosophy, methodology, and science. He died in Princeton, N.J. Obituaries: *New York Times,* June 24, 1977.

ORLOFF, Ed (Sam) 1923-

PERSONAL: Born June 17, 1923, in Detroit, Mich.; son of Zalmon R. and Ruth (Oberstein) Orloff; married Kathleen F. Ward (a ceramicist), March 17, 1950; children: Ann, Robert, Russell. *Education:* University of Illinois, B.S., 1947. *Politics:* Independent. *Religion:* None. *Residence:* Berkeley, Calif. *Office: San Francisco Examiner,* 110 Fifth St., San Francisco, Calif. 94103.

CAREER/WRITINGS: Journalist for *Milwaukee Sentinel,* 1946, *Great Falls Tribune* (Great Falls, Mont.), 1947, *Chicago Herald-American,* 1948, *Chicago Sun-Times,* 1949-50, *San Francisco Examiner,* 1950-54, and for *San Francisco News* and *San Francisco News-Call-Bulletin,* 1954-60; U.S. Industries, director of educational sciences division, 1961-64, director of Buyers Laboratory, 1964-73; *San Francisco Examiner,* assistant managing editor, 1973—. Writer of columns, "Medical Digest," a weekly appearing in newspapers in the United States, and "What's Next?," a weekly on new technologies. *Military service:* U.S. Army, 1942-45; became sergeant in Signal Corps. *Member:* Associated Press Managing Editors Association.

* * *

ORLOFSKY, Myron 1928(?)-1976

1928(?)—August 24, 1976; American lawyer, art collector, and author of a book on quilts with his wife. He died in Deposit, N.Y. Obituaries: *New York Times,* August 26, 1976.

* * *

O'ROURKE, Lawrence Michael 1938-

PERSONAL: Born March 12, 1938, in Philadelphia, Pa.; son of Lawrence M. (an accountant) and Margaret (a salesperson; maiden name, Higgins) O'Rourke; married Patricia Coe, Aguust 29, 1967; children: Christopher, Katherine, Jennifer, Timothy. *Education:* Villanova University, A.B., 1959; Georgetown University, J.D., 1970. *Religion:* Catholic. *Home:* 5616 Nevada Ave. N.W., Washington, D.C., 20015. *Office: Philadelphia Bulletin,* 1296 National Press Bldg., Washington, D.C.

CAREER/WRITINGS: Philadelphia Bulletin, Philadelphia, Pa., columnist, 1964—, White House correspondent, 1969—, chief of Washington bureau, 1970—. In private practice of law, 1970—. Lecturer. *Military service:* U.S. Army, 1960-62. *Member:* White House Correspondents Association (president, 1976), National Press Club, Overseas Writers, American Bar Association, Washington, D.C., Bar Association, Superior Court Trial Lawyers Association, Gridiron Club (Washington, D.C.) Sigma Delta Chi. *Awards, honors:* National Headliners award, 1959; award from Pennsylvania Newspaper Publishers Association, 1962; award from North City Congress, 1962; award from Philadelphia Veterans, 1973.

SIDELIGHTS: O'Rourke writes that his notable assignments include coverage of Watergate, Nixon's trip to China, conventions and campaigns since 1964, as well as Internal Revenue Service abuses, and legal issues, including abortion and criminal justice.

O'Rourke told *CA:* "I believe that this civilization can exist only as long as its people, fully informed and acting responsibly upon that information, work at its preservation. I fear the test is not being met. As the American people read less, reject their community for individual gain, choose superficiality over substance, the quality of life declines and the future deteriorates."

AVOCATIONAL INTERESTS: Travel, swimming, jogging, playing the guitar, and working with young people in the juvenile justice system.

* * *

OSBORN, James M(arshall) 1906-1976

April 22, 1906—October 17, 1976; American literary historian, curator of collection of seventeenth- and eighteenth-century literature, and author of books in his field, including *The Beginnings of Autobiography in England*. He died in New Haven, Conn. Obituaries: *New York Times*, October 19, 1976. (*CAP-2*; earlier sketch in *CA-25/28*)

* * *

OWENS, Thelma 1905-
(Ann Grafton)

PERSONAL: Born April 24, 1905, in Portsmouth, Ohio; daughter of Orrin King (a physician) and Bertha May Phlegar; married Grafton Ray Owens (a chemist); children: Donald, Douglas. *Education:* University of Richmond, B.A., 1926; Ohio State University, M.A., 1930. *Politics:* Independent. *Religion:* Presbyterian. *Home:* 3560 Idlewild Ave., Napa, Calif. 94558. *Agent:* Ruth Cantor, 156 Fifth Ave., New York, N.Y. 10010; (juveniles) Dorothy Markinko, 475 Fifth Ave., New York, N.Y. 10017.

CAREER: Writer, 1926—; Ohio State University, Columbus, assistant professor of English, 1930-38. *Member:* American Association of University Women, Daughters of the American Revolution (vice-regent in Napa), Eastern Star.

WRITINGS: Daddy Was a Doctor (humor), Dutton, 1951; *I, Roger Ellis, Know-It-All* (juvenile), Funk, 1969; (under pseudonym Ann Grafton) *Ring and Walk In* (juvenile), Little, Brown, 1969; *Love, Honor, and Hang On* (humorous essays on retirement), Ritchie, 1976. Contributor of poems and articles to literary magazines, including *Poetry, Sewanee Review,* and *Southern Review.*

WORK IN PROGRESS: A volume of humorous essays, similar to *Love, Honor, and Hang On.*

SIDELIGHTS: Thelma Owens writes: "I have written since I was eight (improving slightly with age). Poetry was my first love, but since the advent of free verse I am concentrating on prose instead. Writing is therapy—for depression, for age itself—and it is also an intensely pleasurable activity. I enjoy writing for children, but hope soon to have an adult novel published."

* * *

PACE, J. Blair 1916-

PERSONAL: Born March 20, 1916, in Thatcher, Ariz.; son of J. Verne and Janie (Blair) Pace; married Evelyn Blue, August 27, 1942; children: Glenn Ellen Pace Brun, Donna Blue, Jonathan Blair, Wilson Douglas. *Education:* Gila Junior College, A.A., 1934; attended University of Utah, 1934-35; University of Texas, 1937-38; and McGill University, 1938-40; University of Chicago, M.D., 1942. *Religion:* Church of Jesus Christ of Latter-day Saints (Mormons). *Home:* 1258 Citrus Dr., LaHabra, Calif. 90631. *Office:* 101 City Dr. S., Orange, Calif. 92668.

CAREER: Presbyterian Hospital, Chicago, Ill., intern for Anesthesia Service, Kellogg-Speed Surgical Service, and Intern Pediatric Service, all 1940; University of Chicago, Chicago, Ill., staff anethesiologist at Chicago Lying-In Hospital, 1941-42; physician in family practice, 1947-71. Li-

censed to practice medicine in California, 1946; certified by American Board of Family Practice, 1970. On staff at Mercy Hospital (San Diego), 1948-66, Palomar Memorial Hospital, 1956-68, Tri-City Hospital (Oceanside), 1961-70 (chief of staff, 1961, 1962), San Diego County Hospital, 1956-70, Rancho Los Amigos Hospital (chairman of Family Practice Service), 1968-77, San Diego County University Hospital, 1970, Hoag Memorial Hospital—Presbyterian, 1971-73, and Orange County Medical Center, 1971-76. Clinical instructor at University of California, San Diego, 1970; associate clinical professor at University of California, Irvine, 1973—. Assistant director of Hoag Memorial Hospital family practice residency, 1972-74; academic head of residency at Memorial Hospital of Long Beach; sponsor and founder of Carlsbad chapter of American Field Service, 1959. *Military service:* U.S. Navy, 1942-47, intern and resident at U.S. Naval Hospital, San Diego, chief of Orthopedic Service at U.S. Naval Hospital, Santa Margarita; served on destroyer in South Pacific; received twelve combat stars.

MEMBER: American Academy of Family Physicians (charter fellow), American Academy of General Practice (local president, 1955-56; state president, 1965-66), American Medical Association, Society of Teachers of Family Medicine (charter member), American Association of Physicians Assistants (member of advisory board), California Medical Association, Orange County Medical Association, San Diego County Medical Society. *Awards, honors:* Physicians' recognition award from American Medical Association, 1971, for work in continuing medical education.

WRITINGS: (Contributor) Howard Conn, Robert Rakel, and Thomas Johnson, editors, *Textbook of Family Medicine,* Saunders, 1973; *Pain: A Personal Experience,* Nelson-Hall, 1976. Contributor of about twenty articles to medical journals. Member of editorial board of *Journal of Family Practice.*

WORK IN PROGRESS: "Autobiographical framework for a series of essays on life problems from Family Doctor's viewpoint."

SIDELIGHTS: Pace told *CA:* "Since becoming involved in research on chronic pain, it has been my good fortune to be invited to speak at many medical meetings."

* * *

PACKARD, Karl 1911(?)-1977

1911(?)—March 20, 1977; American physician and co-author of a book on medical group practice. In 1946, he co-founded the Health Insurance Plan of Greater New York. He died in New York City. Obituaries: *New York Times*, March 22, 1977.

* * *

PACKARD, Reynolds 1904(?)-1976

1904(?)—October 15, 1976; American foreign correspondent and author of several non-fiction books and novels. Known for his first-person, flamboyant accounts (which other newsmen sometimes considered less than accurate), he covered war stories throughout the world from the 1930's to 1972, first for United Press, and then for *New York Daily News*. He died in Rome, Italy. Obituaries: *New York Times*, October 16, 1976; *Washington Post*, October 17, 1976.

* * *

PAGE, Marian

PERSONAL: Born in South Orange, N.J.; daughter of F.

Maxwell and Dorothy (Mattson) Page. *Education:* Attended private school in Orange, N.J.; also studied at Newark School of Fine and Industrial Arts and National Trust summer school (England). *Home:* 321 East 54th St., New York, N.Y. 10022.

CAREER: Mademoiselle, New York, N.Y., assistant special projects editor, 1942-48; Cowles Magazines, Inc., New York, N.Y., assistant editor in special editorial departments of *Look*, 1948-51, assistant editor of News in Living Section of *Quick*, 1951-53, chief copy writer in special editorial departments of *Look*, 1953-55; *Interiors*, New York, N.Y., associate editor, 1956-74, senior editor, 1974-75; free-lance writer, 1975—. *Member:* Society of Architectural Historians, Victorian Society, National Trust for Historic Preservation.

WRITINGS: Historic Houses Restored and Preserved, Whitney Library of Design, 1976. Also ghost writer of book on hotel design. Contributor to *Interiors* and *Look*.

WORK IN PROGRESS: Editing a book on an architect's work; ghost writing a design book.

SIDELIGHTS: Marian Page wrote: "My interest in architectural history and the preservation of historic houses is the direct result of my interest in looking at architecture—architecture that enhances a cityscape or landscape for the passerby as well as for those who work or live in it. Since I believe the variety and beauty of good historic architecture not only does this but also adds dimension to present-day life by suggesting other lives and other times, I am naturally in favor of its preservation. The critieria, of course, are that it *does* enhance the cityscape or landscape and that it can pay its way in the present, preferably as the frame for a current activity whether it be the frame for a place of work or a house. I am particularly interested in the preservation of important historic houses because the connection with the past is more immediate, more intimate.

"All this, however, does not preclude knowledge of and interest in contemporary interior design and architecture as well as in other fields of design."

Marian Page has a good reading knowledge of French.

AVOCATIONAL INTERESTS: Reading, travel (England, Scotland, Wales, Ireland), sailing, gardening.

*   *   *

PALEY, Alan L(ouis) 1943-

PERSONAL: Born February 8, 1943, in New York, N.Y.; son of George (a civil engineer) and Augusta (a teacher; maiden name, Goldstein) Paley. *Education:* City College of the City University of New York, B.A., 1964; City University of New York, M.A., 1967. *Home:* 105-34 65th Ave., Forest Hills, N.Y. 11375.

CAREER: Writer, 1967—.

WRITINGS—All juveniles; all edited by D. Steve Rahmas and published by SamHar Press: *Stalin, the Iron Fisted Dictator of Russia*, 1972; *Andrew Johnson, the President Impeached*, 1972; *Soren Kierkegaard, Modern Philosopher and Existentialist*, 1972; *H. G. Wells, Author of Famous Science Fiction Stories*, 1972; *Confucius, Ancient Chinese Philosopher*, 1973; *Theodore Dreiser, American Editor and Novelist*, 1973; *Munich and the Sudeten Crisis*, 1973; *Russo-Finnish War*, 1973; *George Orwell, Writer and Critic of Modern Society*, 1974; *Sinclair Lewis, Twentieth Century American Author and Nobel Prize Winner*, 1974; *Sigmund Freud, Father of Psychoanalysis*, 1974; *The Establishment*

of Communism in China, 1974; *Edgar Allan Poe, American Poet and Mystery Writer*, 1975; *Benito Mussolini, Fascist Dictator of Italy*, 1975; *Karl Marx, Communist Philosopher*, 1975. Writer of column "Movie and TV Nostalgia" in *Newest, Most Different Magazine*, 1976—.

WORK IN PROGRESS: "A nonfiction work of approximately 25,000 words on the history of the American movie industry. If accepted by Newbury House, it will be rewritten by an editor for adults studying English as a second language."

SIDELIGHTS: Paley told *CA:* "I have never held any job except writing. I have never had any success in submitting unsolicited manuscripts to publishers. After failing to find a publisher for a nonfiction work about the Nazi Occupation of Denmark and two novels on the same subject I made my first sale in 1969, after answering a newspaper ad for writers of sex novels. I made no more attempts to write sex novels after 1971, because I disliked some of the people I had to deal with and because I found that type of writing distasteful.

"I began writing for Story House in 1971, in response to an ad in the *New York Times Book Review*. The first topic—Stalin—was chosen by me from a list prepared by the publisher; all other topics were suggested by me. I have not been successful in other attempts to write for juveniles, because these books were written for bright high school students or students entering college, while I find that other publishers are interested in exceptionally slow readers and that here some specialized background in education is desirable.

"In general, my own experience has been that it is virtually impossible to sell a novel or a nonfiction work 'over the transom' or to interest a publisher in a work on the basis of an outline. I have found that unless a publisher is seriously interested in a particular subject, nothing which you say about a manuscript or in the manuscript itself is going to get him interested.

"I would say that the time is past when a writer like Proust or Thomas Wolfe could create a 'unified' body of work based upon vivid and immediate personal experience. It has been my experience that unless you have climbed Mount Everest or lived among the Jivaros of Ecuador no publisher is going to be interested in what you write about yourself. Unless I am writing something obviously fantastical, such as science fiction, I try to confine myself to writing about places I have personally known. But I have never been successful in writing fiction based upon immediate personal experience. In general, it is my feeling that things have never been as bad for writers as they are today. As the situation is now, you have a very small number of writers who write best sellers which are aggressively promoted, a somewhat larger number of writers who support themselves by turning out science fiction, gothics, westerns and the like for paperback houses, and a gigantic number of writers who are either starving or working at menial jobs that have absolutely nothing to do with writing. As someone who writes for a living, I feel it important not to allow myself to be influenced by published works. I think that some writers starve because they regard themselves as working in splendid isolation, producing finished works of art which are then sent out to be judged by publishers. My own feeling is that literature is becoming more like movies used to be—that is, the final form of the work, including such matters as length, will be determined by a particular publisher who has expressed interest in the work.

"I believe that the purpose of writing manuscripts is not to provide diversion for an editor but to convince him that you have an interesting approach to an interesting subject. I have the feeling that too many writers waste their time on attempting manuscripts of a type which could be written only after receiving detailed suggestions and criticism from a person seriously interested in buying it. . . .''

*   *   *

PALMEDO, Roland 1895-1977

April 5, 1895—March 15, 1977; American banker, airline executive, promoter of recreational skiing, and author of books about skiing, including *Ski New Horizons* and *Skiing: The International Sport*. He died in Williamstown, Mass. Obituaries: *New York Times,* March 17, 1977. (See index for previous *CA* sketch)

*   *   *

PALMER, (Thomas) Cruise 1917-

PERSONAL: Born April 9, 1917, in Kansas City, Kan.; son of Thomas (a lawyer) and Margaret (McFadden) Palmer; married Dorraine Humphreys, September 7, 1946; children: Thomas Jr., Martha. *Education:* Kansas State University, B.S., 1938. *Religion:* Episcopal. *Home:* 4900 W. 64th Terrace, Prairie Village, Kan. 66208. *Office:* Kansas City Star, 1729 Grand Ave., Kansas City, Mo. 64108.

CAREER/WRITINGS: Kansas City Star and Times, Kansas City, Mo., assistant city editor, 1952-58, city editor, 1958-62, news editor, 1963-64, managing editor, 1965-66, executive editor and director, 1967—. *Military service:* U.S. Navy, 1943-46; became lieutenant j.g. *Member:* American Council for Education in Journalism, Missouri Press-Bar Commission, Kansas City Press Club (president, 1953 and 1964), American Society of Newspaper Editors, Kansas City Club, Kansas State University Endowment Trustee, Sigma Delta Chi. *Awards, honors:* Kansas State University distinguished service citation, 1967; Pro-Amateur Southgate Open Golf Tournament first place award, 1973; Pro-Amateur Hawaii Open second place award, 1973.

SIDELIGHTS: An active amateur golfer, Palmer also played in the 1975 Bing Crosby National Tournament and the 1977 Bob Hope Desert Classic.

*   *   *

PAPERNY, Myra (Green) 1932-

PERSONAL: Born September 19, 1932, in Edmonton, Alberta, Canada; daughter of Michael (a businessman) and Jessie (Cohen) Green; married Maurice Paperny (a businessman), July 5, 1954; children: Marina, David, Cathy, Lorne. *Education:* University of British Columbia, B.A., 1953; Columbia University, M.Sc., 1954. *Religion:* Jewish. *Home and office:* 1224 Riverdale Ave. S.W., Calgary, Alberta, Canada T2S 0Y8.

CAREER: Vancouver Province, Vancouver, British Columbia, reporter, 1952; *Vancouver News Herald,* Vancouver, British Columbia, reporter, 1953; Mount Royal College, Calgary, Alberta, instructor of creative writing, 1965-66; University of Calgary, Calgary, Alberta, lecturer in creative writing, 1966-75. Has worked in public relations. Member of board of Calgary Region Arts Foundation, 1977—. National vice-president of National Council of Jewish Women, 1971-73. *Member:* Alberta Authors Association. *Awards, honors:* Canadian Children's Book Award, 1974-75, for *The Wooden People;* achievement award from Province of Alberta, 1975, for *The Wooden People;* Canada Council Award for children's literature, 1976.

WRITINGS: The Wooden People (juvenile), Little, Brown, 1976. Editor of *Councilwoman,* 1970-73.

WORK IN PROGRESS: Take One Giant Step, a juvenile novel; *Second Go-Around,* an adult novel; stories.

SIDELIGHTS: Myra Paperny comments briefly that she believes ''children are the most sensitive and critical of readers,'' and adds that she tries ''to communicate with them honestly and in depth.''

BIOGRAPHICAL/CRITICAL SOURCES: Quill and Quire, January, 1977.

*   *   *

PAPICH, Stephen 1925-

PERSONAL: Born May 22, 1925, in St. David, Ill.; son of Frank (a coal miner) and Frances (Tomich) Papich. *Education:* Attended Katherine Dunham's School of Dance and Cultural Arts. *Residence:* Hollywood, Calif. and Palm Springs, Calif. *Agent:* Gordon Molson, Molson-Stanton Agency, 10889 Wilshire Blvd., Los Angeles, Calif. 90024.

CAREER: Twentieth Century Fox, Hollywood, Calif., staff choreographer (including work on the films ''The Robe,'' ''The Egyptian,'' and ''Seven-Year Itch''), 1952-59; Hollywood Bowl, Hollywood, Calif., producer and director, 1955-65; producer for ''Katherine Dunham with Her Singers, Dancers, and Musicians,'' 1962—; producer and director of Josephine Baker's U.S. appearances, 1962-74; writer, 1976—. *Military service:* U.S. Coast Guard, 1942-46; received presidential unit citation.

WRITINGS: Remembering Josephine (biography of Josephine Baker), Bobbs-Merrill, 1976; *Silver Heels and Flying Arrows,* Bobbs-Merrill, in press.

WORK IN PROGRESS: A biography of Katherine Dunham; a collection of eight short stories on theatrical experiences; *Hetty,* on life and times of Hetty Green; a screenplay.

*   *   *

PARKER, Lois M(ary) 1912-

PERSONAL: Born April 18, 1912, in Nebraska; daughter of William A. (a field man for a beet sugar company) and Mamie (a teacher; maiden name, Durnin) Nelson; married William Allen Parker (a rancher), December 25, 1935 (deceased); children: Joan Parker Yeatts, George, Ellen Parker Dietel, William Allen, Jr. *Education:* Attended Scottsbluff Junior College, 1929-30, and Hastings College, 1930-31; St. Luke's Hospital School of Nursing, R.N., 1934; graduate study at Oregon Medical School, 1954, and Walla Walla College, 1965-67. *Religion:* Seventh-day Adventist. *Home address:* R.R. 1, Box 510, Bonners Ferry, Idaho 83805.

CAREER: St. Luke's Hospital, Denver, Colo., night ward supervisor, 1935; St. Valentine's Hospital, Wendell, Idaho, night nurse, 1941; Lake City General Hospital, Coeur d'-Alene, Idaho, night nurse, 1950-53; public health nurse in Coeur d'Alene, Idaho, 1953-55; Community Hospital, Bonners Ferry, Idaho, night nurse, 1956-64; Tri-Cities Junior Academy, Pasco, Wash., teacher of English, 1966-68; freelance writer, 1968—.

WRITINGS: Brave Heart (teen), Review & Herald, 1958; *Yellow Cat of Cottonwood Creek* (teen), Review & Herald, 1959; *Quack-Quack and Duck-Duck* (juvenile), Review & Herald, 1961; (with Gerald R. Nash) *Investment, the Miracle Offering,* Pacific Press Publishing Association, 1965; *A New Friend for Kelly* (juvenile), Review & Herald, 1966;

Once Upon a Summer (juvenile), Review & Herald, 1970; *Thee, Patience* (teen; on the first Quakers in Rhode Island), Review & Herald, 1974; *Princess of the Two Lands* (teen; on the Exodus from the Egyptian point of view), Southern Publishing, 1975; *Duncan, Son of Malcolm* (juvenile), Southern Publishing, in press. Contributor of more than one hundred poems and articles to adult and juvenile church publications, and to *Life and Health.*

WORK IN PROGRESS: Research on early Pennsylvania history, for a story for teenagers.

SIDELIGHTS: Lois Parker writes: "I started writing for my own entertainment, and for my children, who loved 'ancestor stories,' ranch and animal adventures, and nursing experiences, which last two provided most of the material for the shorter published material. I have written mostly family history, or fictionalized history for children and young adults. Have always enjoyed history so much it seems a shame that many young people think it dull. Hence I try to show that it is made of real people, exciting, and very much related to us."

AVOCATIONAL INTERESTS: Travel (including England), birdwatching, living in her small cabin in the woods.

* * *

PARKS, Edmund 1911-

PERSONAL: Born February 26, 1911, in London, England; son of Edmund George and Elizabeth (Wheeler) Parks; married Marguerite LaRose; children: Pierre John, Anne. *Education:* Educated in England. *Politics:* "Independent of any party." *Religion:* Church of England. *Home:* 1425 Kingsley Ave., Villa 128, Dorval, Quebec, Canada H9S 1G2. *Office:* c/o *Montreal Star,* 245 St. James St. W., Montreal, Quebec, Canada.

CAREER: Has worked variously as a general reporter, sports columnist, political columnist, and news editor for publications, including *Daily Mirror, News Chronicle, Evening News, Evening Standard,* all in London, England, and for *Quebec News Chronicle,* as managing editor, and for *Montreal Star,* Montreal, Quebec, as travel editor; presently a free-lance writer. Lecturer and public speaker. Travel editorial adviser to Air Canada. While a prisoner of war, edited a magazine for fellow prisoners; after World War II, interviewed Sir Winston Churchill. *Military service:* British Expeditionary Forces, 1939-45.

MEMBER: Federation Internationale des Journalistes et Ecrivains du Tourisme, Society of American Travel Writers, Montreal Press Club, Skal. *Awards, honors:* Canadian Wine Association trophy.

WRITINGS: Contributor to *En Route* and *Financial Post.*

SIDELIGHTS: Parks writes: "Since travel is now my main concern I have come to consider it vital. I could use cliches to describe it and they would be apt. I have discovered, however, that while it should 'broaden the mind' of those who travel, more often than not it shrinks them and strengthens prejudices. I have discovered, too, that there is a vast difference between the tourist and the traveller. They could be variously described as students and graduates. And I honestly believe that the Society of American Travel Writers is doing a good in-training job although the public might feel they are 'freeloaders,' which is quite untrue of the majority."

* * *

PARLIN, Bradley W(illiam) 1938-

PERSONAL: Born in 1938, in San Francisco, Calif.; son of

Emery J. and Stella (Crow) Ingram; married Susan Harris (a potter), November 27, 1966; children: Daniel Zacharry, Rebecca Mariah. *Education:* Indiana University, B.A., 1965; University of Illinois, M.A., 1967, Ph.D., 1972. *Home:* 1501 Highland Dr., North Logan, Utah 84322. *Office:* Department of Sociology, Utah State University, Logan, Utah 84321.

CAREER: General Tire & Rubber Co., Akron, Ohio, manager of college relations, 1968-69; Indiana University, Fort Wayne, assistant professor of sociology, 1971-73; Utah State University, Logan, assistant professor, 1973-76, associate professor of sociology, 1976—. *Military service:* U.S. Army, 1957-61. *Member:* American Sociological Association, Labor and Industrial Relations Research Association, Pacific Sociological Association, Western Social Science Association.

WRITINGS: (Contributor) Arnold Olson and Sushil Usman, editors, *Focus on Sociology,* 2nd edition, Kendall/Hunt, 1972 (author not associated with previous edition); (editor with Kooros Mahmoudi) *Sociological Inquiry: A Humanistic Perspective,* Kendall/Hunt, 1973, 2nd edition, 1975; *Immigrant Professionals in the United States: Discrimination in the Scientific Labor Makret,* Praeger, 1976; (contributor) George Bugliorello, editor, *Engineering Colleges: Their Regional Role,* Pergamon, 1977. Contributor of articles and reviews to academic journals. Editor of *Western Sociological Review,* summers, 1974-76.

WORK IN PROGRESS: American Social Problems: Popular Wisdom and Scientific Knowledge, with Marty E. Zusman.

SIDELIGHTS: Parlin writes: "My research and writings are firmly grounded in the humanistic tradition. I feel, as Raymond Cuzzort suggests, that 'Sociology can be used as an academic justification for existing inhumanities or it can be an approach to a morally critical understanding of man's injuries to man.' I also share with Robert Lynd the conviction that a responsible sociologist should 'be troublesome, to disconcert the habitual arrangements by which we manage to live along, and to demonstrate the possibility of change in more adequate directions.'"

* * *

PASCOE, Elizabeth Jean

PERSONAL: Born in Cloquet, Minn.; daughter of Truman A. (a chemist) and Floride M. (a librarian; maiden name, Vos) Pascoe. *Education:* University of Wisconsin, B.S. *Home:* 1211 Vine St., Denver, Colo., 80206. *Agent:* Shirley Fisher, McIntosh & Otis, 18 East 41st St., New York, N.Y., 10017. *Office:* Suite 239, 770 Grant St., Denver, Colo. 80203.

CAREER/WRITINGS: Time (magazine), New York City, researcher, 1962-66; *Medical Economics,* Oradell, N.J., senior associate editor, 1966-67; *Woman's Day,* New York City, editor and writer, 1967-70; *McCall's,* New York City, editor of "Right Now" department, 1973-76. Notable assignments include coverage of money management, family relations, women's news, and western Americana (1840-65). Contributor of articles to *Family Circle, Reader's Digest,* and *New York Times.*

WORK IN PROGRESS: A family medical guide.

* * *

PASSERIN D'ENTREVES, Alessandro 1902-

PERSONAL: Born April 26, 1902, in Turin, Italy; married

Nina Ferrari d'Orsara, 1931; children: one son, one daughter. *Education:* University of Turin, Dr.Jur., 1922; Balliol College, Oxford, D.Phil., 1932. *Home:* Strada ai Ronchi 48, Cavoretto, Turin, Italy; and Castello di Entreves, Courmayeur, Val d'Aosta, Italy.

CAREER: University of Messina, Messina, Italy, professor, 1934-35; University of Pavia, Pavia, Italy, professor of philosophy, law, and politics, 1935-38; University of Turin, Turin, Italy, professor of law, 1938-46; Oxford University, Oxford, England, Serena Professor of Italian studies, 1946-57; University of Turin, Turin, Italy, professor of political theory, 1948-72; retired. Fellow, Magdalen College, Oxford, 1946-57; visiting professor at University of Chicago, 1948, Harvard University, 1957, and Yale University, 1960-64. Prefect of Aosta, April-May, 1945; member of council of Val d'Aosta, December, 1945.

MEMBER: American Academy of Arts and Sciences (fellow), American Society for Political and Legal Philosophy, Royal Historical Society, Societe Academique St. Anselme (Aosta), Accademia delle Scienze (Turin), Accademia dei Lincei (Rome), Academie de Savoie (Chambery). *Awards, honors:* Laurr Spelman Rockefeller traveling fellowship, 1926-29; M.A., Yale University, 1961.

WRITINGS: La Teoria del Diritto e della Politica in Inghilterra all' Inizio dell' eta Moderna, Istituto Giuridico della R. Universita di Torino, 1929; *Riccardo Hooker: Contributo alla Teoria e alla Storia del Diritto Naturale,* Istituto Giuridico della R. Universita di Torino, 1932; *Appunti di Storia delle Dottrine Politiche: La Filosofia Politica Medioevale,* G. Giappichelli (Torino), 1934; *Il Negozio Giuridico: Saggio di Filosofia del Diritto,* Tip. R. Gayet (Torino), 1934; *The Medieval Contribution to Political Thought: Thomas Aquinas, Marsilius of Padua, Richard Hooker,* Oxford University Press, 1939, Humanities Press, 1959; (editor and author of introduction) Saint Thomas Aquinas, *Selected Political Writings,* Basil Blackwell, 1948; Barnes & Noble, 1959; *Natural Law: An Introduction to Legal Philosophy,* Hutchinson University Library, 1951, revised edition, 1964, published as *Natural Law: An Historical Survey,* Harper, 1965; *Dante as a Political Thinker,* Clarendon Press, 1952; *La Dottrina dello Stato: Elementi di Analisi e di Interpretazione,* G. Giappichelli, 1962, 2nd edition, 1967; (contributor) John Freccero, editor, *Dante: A Collection of Critical Essays,* Prentice-Hall, 1965; *The Notion of the State: An Introduction to Political Theory,* Oxford University Press, 1967; *Obbedienza e Resistenza in Una Societa Democratica e Altri Saggi* (collection of previously published articles), Edizioni di Comunita (Milan), 1970; *Per la Storia del Pensiero Politico Medioevale,* G. Giappichelli, 1970. Author of a published lecture.

AVOCATIONAL INTERESTS: Rambling in the Alps.*

*   *   *

PATOSKI, Margaret (Nancy Pearson)   1930-

PERSONAL: Born in 1930, in Midlothian, Tex.; daughter of Bob M. (a farmer) and Clara (Graham) Pearson; married Victor A. Patoski (an aerospace design engineer), 1960; children: Christina, Joe Nick. *Education:* Texas Christian University, B.A. (magna cum laude), 1968, M.A., 1970, Ph.D., 1973. *Politics:* Democrat. *Religion:* Episcopalian. *Home:* 4325 Lovell Ave., Fort Worth, Tex. 76107. *Office:* Department of Social Science, Texas Wesleyan College, Fort Worth, Tex. 76105.

CAREER: Texas Christian University, Fort Worth, fellow, 1971-73; East Texas State University, Commerce, assistant

professor of history, 1973-77; Texas Wesleyan University, Fort Worth, assistant professor of history, 1977—. *Member:* American Historical Association, American Association for the Advancement of Slavic Studies, American Association for Asian Studies, Western Social Science Association (member of executive council, 1977-80), Southwestern Association for Slavic Studies (vice-president, 1977-78), Rocky Mountain Association for Slavic Studies, Phi Alpha Theta, *Awards, honors:* Dillon Anderson Award from Texas Christian University, 1968, for "Emigre Sketches"; Pate Lincoln Essay Award, 1972, for "The Emancipators: Alexander II and Abraham Lincoln."

WRITINGS: (Translator and author of notes) Maria von Bock, *Reminiscences of My Father, Peter A. Stolypin,* Scarecrow, 1970; (translator and author of notes) Anton I. Denikin, *The Career of a Tsarist Officer: Memoirs, 1872-1916,* University of Minnesota Press, 1975. Associate editor of *Red River Valley Journal of World History;* book reviewer for *History: Reviews of New Books* and *Reprint Bulletin: Book Reviews.*

WORK IN PROGRESS: Translating and writing notes for *Iz vospominaniia* (title means "From My Memoirs"), by V. A. Maklakov, and *Perezhitoe* (title means "Living Memories"), by V. M. Zenzinov, completion expected in 1980; research on the Russian Pacific Fleet during the American Civil War, on the Soviet historian, M. N. Pokrovsky, eighteenth-century Polish gentry, and the Baltic Republics between the world wars.

SIDELIGHTS: Margaret Patoski writes: "My undergraduate majors were history and English and my minors were the Russian language and education. These interests have only intensified and become specialized. All of them betray my fascination with people and the ways in which they express themselves. As a working historian, I am particularly interested in making people of the past—their thoughts and actions—relevant and comprehensible to today's generation."

*   *   *

PATTERSON, Richard   1908(?)-1976

1908(?)—October 13, 1976; American State Department official, editor, and author of books on U.S. history. He died in Shickskinny, Pa. Obituaries: *Washington Post,* October 17, 1976.

*   *   *

PATTERSON, W. M(acLean)   1912(?)-1976

1912(?)—August 20, 1976; American editor, book collector, and authority on H. L. Mencken; began as a reporter for *Baltimore Sun,* later became managing editor; editor of *Menckeniana.* He died in Baltimore, Md. Obituaries: *Washington Post,* August 29, 1976.

*   *   *

PATTI, Ercole   1904(?)-1976

1904(?)—November 15, 1976; Italian journalist, novelist, and screenwriter. He died in Rome, Italy. Obituaries: *New York Times,* November 16, 1976.

*   *   *

PAULUS, John Douglas   1917-

PERSONAL: Born July 6, 1917, in Canton, Ohio; son of James J. (a businessman) and Helen (a couturier; maiden name, Pateas) Paulus; married Mildred Hankey (an editor), December 4, 1937. *Education:* University of Pittsburgh, B.A., 1937; Georgetown University, M.A., 1939; Ph.D., 1941. *Politics:* Independent. *Religion:* Episcopalian. *Home:* 826 North Meadowcroft Ave., Mt. Lebanon, Pittsburgh, Pa. 15216. *Office:* 2319 Oliver Bldg., Pittsburgh, Pa. 15222.

CAREER: Washington Post, Washington, D.C., sports editor, 1936-41; *Pittsburgh Press,* Pittsburgh, Pa., promotion and news editor, 1941-45; *Brooklyn Eagle,* Brooklyn, N.Y., associate publisher, 1945-51; Mid Continent Feature Syndicate, Pittsburgh, editor-in-chief, 1951—. Instructor in journalism and public relations, University of Pittsburgh, 1941-57; member of Second Hoover Commission on the Reorganization of the Executive Branch, 1954; trustee of Duquesne University, Seton Hill College, Point Park College, Pittsburgh Ballet Company, and Mercy Hospital. *Military service:* U.S. Army, served in counter-intelligence, 1943-44; became colonel. *Member:* Sigma Delta Chi, Omicron Delta Kappa. *Awards, honors:* Putman award for industrial advertising, 1955; Golden Quill award for business writing, 1956.

WRITINGS: Writer of thrice-weekly column, "Everybody's Business," syndicated by Mid Continent to 181 newspapers. Contributor of literary criticism to *New York Times, Philadelphia Inquirer, Saturday Review, Book-of-the-Month Club News,* 1940-70. Book editor of *Pittsburgh Press,* 1940-57.

* * *

PAYACK, Paul J. J. 1950-

PERSONAL: Born January 3, 1950, in Morristown, N.J.; son of Peter Paul (a trucking company owner) and Florence (a teacher; maiden name, Marcello) Payack; married Millie Lorenzo (a registered nurse and student), April 19, 1974. *Education:* Attended Bucknell University, 1968-71; Harvard University, A.B., 1974, graduate student, 1976—. *Home:* 39 Hawthorne Village, Concord, Mass. 01742. *Office:* Newbury College, 921 Boylston St., Boston, Mass. 02115.

CAREER: Newbury College, Boston, Mass., admissions officer, 1975—. Writer. *Member:* Science Fiction Writers of America, Committee of Small Magazine Editors and Publishers.

WRITINGS: A Ripple in Entropy, Chthon Press, 1973; *Legend of the Shaman,* Free Books, 1974; *Solstice; or, Star-Tales,* Samisdat Press, 1975; *The Unexpected Twist Series,* Chthon Press, 1976; *Solstice II,* Samisdat Press, 1976; *Mythomania,* New York Culture Review Press, 1977; *Solstice III,* Samisdat Press, 1977; *The Black Lists,* Chthon Press, 1977; *Microtales,* Quark Press, 1977. Contributor of fiction, essays, and poetry to *Paris Review, New Letters, Creative Computing.*

WORK IN PROGRESS: The Land of Orth, Solstice IV and V, The Book of Hours, The Dream-Cycle, Lives of the Saint, Mortality Tales.

SIDELIGHTS: In response to a query about the type of writing he does, Payack told *CA:* "I consider all my work metafiction."

Sylvia Berkman called him "a writer of great originality, seriousness, and imaginative zest, to the highest degree intellectually curious. At the age of twenty-seven he has already produced a substantial body of prose fictions (to define his work loosely and approximately), beginning with his first collection, *A Ripple in Entropy* of 1973. . . .

"What distinguishes this work and continues to distinguish

even more forcibly Paul Payack's later work, is the nature of the creative intelligence from which it stems. This is an intelligence cool yet engaged, composed, witty, immensely concerned with the broad pivotal elements of human experience ('life, death, etc.' in Virginia Woolf's words), as well as the minute arcane details of human behavior through uncounted centuries: a short note on the historical position of the onion in varied cultures, for example, or the fateful propensity for disaster darkening the Fridays of the world."

* * *

PEACOCK, Mary (Willa) 1942-

PERSONAL: Born October 23, 1942, in Evanston, Ill.; daughter of William G. and Mary W. (Young) Peacock. *Education:* Vassar College, B.A., 1964. *Home:* 46 Grand St., New York, N.Y. 10013.

CAREER/WRITINGS: Harper's Bazaar, New York City, associate literary editor, 1964-68; *Innovation,* New York City, staff editor, 1968-69; *Rags,* New York City, and San Francisco, Calif., co-founder and editor, 1970-71; *Ms.* magazine, New York City, co-founder and feature editor, 1972-77; *Rags,* co-publisher and co-editor, 1977—. Occasional panelist at writers' conferences. Contributor of articles to magazines.

* * *

PEARCE, Mary E(mily) 1932-

PERSONAL: Born December 7, 1932, in London, England; daughter of Francis James (a works manager) and Catherine (Lewis) Pearce. *Education:* Attended elementary schools in London, England. *Politics:* "Uncertain." *Religion:* Agnostic. *Home:* Old Cottage, Brookend Lane, Kempsey, Worcestershire, England.

CAREER: Writer, 1960—.

WRITINGS: Apple Tree Lean Down, Macdonald & Jane's, 1973; *Jack Mercybright,* Macdonald & Jane's, 1975; *The Sorrowing Wind,* Macdonald & Jane's, 1975; *Apple Tree Lean Down* (trilogy; including the three books above), St. Martin's, 1976. Contributor of stories to publications in England, the Netherlands, Sweden, and Denmark.

WORK IN PROGRESS: A novel.

SIDELIGHTS: Mary Pearce writes: "I am fascinated by the past; by the working and domestic lives of country people in particular. I live in a rural area rich in old houses, cottages, barns. My own house is over three hundred years old. I like to find out as much as I can about the people who lived in such places in the past, and who worked the land round about; I like to imagine their lives and loves, etc.; I like to weave stories around them."

* * *

PECK, Ralph H(arold-Henry)

PERSONAL: Born in the United States. *Politics:* Independent. *Religion:* Presbyterian. *Home and office:* 51 Harvard Pl., Orchard Park, N.Y. 14127.

CAREER: Pan American World Airways, New York City, public relations representative and editor of *Clipper,* 1953-57; Cunningham & Walsh (advertising), New York City, copywriter and account executive, 1957-62; staff editor of *Travel Agent* and *Interline Reporter,* 1962-66; Spanish Ministry of Information and Tourism, New York City, public relations director, 1966-69. Free-lance writer. Lecturer in public relations at New York University. Radio and television talk show guest. *Member:* Society of American Travel Writers, Cornell Alumni Association, Zeta Psi Fraternity Alumni Association.

WRITINGS: Budget Guide to Hong Kong, Frommer-Pasmantier, 1970; (with John Wilcock) *Budget Guide to Las Vegas,* Frommer-Pasmantier, 1970; *Getaway Guide to Las Vegas,* Frommer-Pasmantier, 1971, revised edition published as *TWA Getaway Guide to Las Vegas,* 1976; *Getaway Guide to Hong Kong,* Frommer-Pasmantier, 1971, revised edition published as *TWA Getaway Guide to Hong Kong,* 1976; *Getaway Guide to Washington,* Frommer-Pasmantier, 1971, revised edition published as *TWA Getaway Guide to Washington,* 1976; *Young City Paris,* Pinder Lane Press, 1972; *Young City Lisbon,* Pinder Lane Press, 1972; *Young City Madrid,* Pinder Lane Press, 1972; *Travel Careers,* Watts, 1976; *Hotel and Motel Careers,* Watts, 1977.

Contributor: Stanley Haggart, *Spain on $5 a Day,* Arthur Frommer, 1969; Arthur Frommer, *Europe on $5 a Day,* Arthur Frommer, 1970; Pat Dickerman, *Adventure Trip Guide,* Adventure Guides, 1974; Pat Dickerman, *Farm, Ranch & Countryside Guide,* Farm & Ranch Vacations, 1974; Pat Dickerman, *Adventure Travel U.S.A.,* Adventure Guides, 1976; Bob Christopher and Ellen Christopher, *America's Favorite Inns and Restaurants,* Travel Discoveries, 1977.

Editor: Beth Bryant, *Washington, D.C. on $10 a Day,* Arthur Frommer, 1972; Stanley Haggart, *Dollar Wise Guide to Portugal,* Arthur Frommer, 1972.

Author of column "RFD World," appearing in over sixty newspapers, 1962-69, and columns in *RFD New York* and *Bouillabaisse.* Also author of television scripts, "The World from the Air" and "The Other Hong Kong."

Contributor of articles to *New York Times, Travel Agent, Washington Post, Boston Globe, Los Angeles Times,* and other periodicals. International editor, *Bravo,* 1968-69; travel editor, *National Star,* 1973-74, *Cleveland,* 1975—.

WORK IN PROGRESS: Two children's books for Troll Associates; a travel book on U.S.A. destinations; completing research for a tongue-in-cheek book of opinions.

SIDELIGHTS: Ralph Peck told *CA:* "Advertising copywriting improved my writing style, taught me the importance of action verbs and the sparse use of 'sparkle.' My 'RFD World' column, low-key humor in a 600-word format, taught me more about quick narrative techniques, how to cope with limited space. I believe that work on trade journals is valuable to young writers, who can become quickly established within an industry as they become more deft in writing news and feature articles.

According to Peck, "American writers have a difficult time with editors insensitive to style, low-key humor, and correct English; to combat this, writers should demand the final say about editorial changes in their material." He believes Truman Capote, Tom Wolfe, and Kurt Vonnegut are the best current American authors.

Peck has interviewed such notables as Pope Paul VI, Prince Philip, Ben-Gurion, Walter Cronkite, John Glenn, Joan Crawford, and Prime Minister Harold Wilson.

AVOCATIONAL INTERESTS: Horticulture, skiing, sailing, traveling, art, architecture, and garden design "an a historical element reflecting national sensitivities."

PEET, Creighton B.   1899(?)-1977

1899(?)—May 16, 1977; American author of fifteen books for young people, contributor to magazines, and drama reviewer for a West Coast newspaper. He died in New York City. Obituaries: *New York Times,* May 17, 1977.

*   *   *

PEKIC, Borislav   1930-

PERSONAL: Surname pronounced "pekitch"; born February 4, 1930, in Podgorica (now Titograd, Yugoslavia); son of Vojislav Dusan (a lawyer) and Ljubica (an economist; maiden name, Petrovic) Pekic; married Liliana Glisic (an architect), May 11, 1958; children: Alexsandra. *Education:* Attended University of Belgrade, 1954-58. *Politics:* "Do not belong to any political party; by conviction social democrat." *Religion:* Serbian Orthodox. *Home:* 14 St. Andrews Ave., Wembley, Middlesex, England. *Agent:* Prince & Prince, Postbus 5400, Amsterdam, Holland.

CAREER: Lovcen Film, Titograd, Yugoslavia, dramaturge, 1959-64; free-lance writer in Yugoslavia, currently in England, 1964—. Editorial board member of journal *Knjizevne Novine,* 1968-69. *Member:* PEN, Association of Yugoslav Writers, Association of Film Artists of Yugoslavia. *Awards, honors:* First prize in film competition, 1958, for two filmscripts; *Hodocasce Arsenija Njegovana: Portret,* named best Yugoslav novel, 1970; "The Generals" named best Yugoslav comedy, 1972.

WRITINGS—Books: *Vreme cuda,* Prosveta (Belgrade), 1965, 2nd edition, Luca (Titograd), 1961, translation by Lovett Edwards published as *Time of Miracles,* Harcourt, 1976; *Hodocasce Arsenija Njegovana: Portret,* Prosveta, 1970, 2nd edition, 1971, translation by Bernard Johnson published as *Arsenie Negovan's Pilgrimage,* Harcourt, 1977; *Uspon i pad Ikara Gubelkijana* (title means "The Rise and Fall of Icarus Gubelkiyan"), Slovo Ljubve (Belgrade), 1975; *Odbrana i poslednji dani* (title means "The Defense and Last Days"), Slovo Ljubve, 1977; *Zlatno runo* (title means "The Golden Fleece"; parts one and two of tetralogy), Prosveta, 1977.

Plays: "Generali ili Bratsvo po oruzju" (title means "The Generals; or, a Kinship in Arms"), first produced in Belgrade at Atelje 212 Theatre, 1971; "Kako zabaviti gospodina Martina?" (title means "How Can Mr. Martin Be Amused?"), first produced in Belgrade at Serbian National Theatre, 1970; "U Edenu na Istoku" (title means "Eastwards, in Eden"), first produced in Belgrade at Atelje 212 Theatre, 1971; "Kako upokojiti vampira" (title means "How To Get Rid of a Vampire"), first produced in Belgrade at Students Theatre, 1977; "Kategoricki zahtev" (title means "Categorical Demand"), first produced in Titograd at Montenegrian National Theatre, 1977.

Radio Plays; all first broadcast in Germany: "The Generals," 1969; "Goodby, Comrade, Goodby," 1970; "How Can Mr. Martin Be Amused?," 1971; "Theseus, Did You Kill the Minotaur?," 1972; "Eastwards, in Eden," 1973; "The Destruction of Speech," 1973; "Who Killed Lilly Schwarzkopf?," 1973; "The Case of One Commercial Traveller," 1974; "Categorical Demand," 1974; "How To Get Rid of a Vampire," 1974; "Who Killed My Immortal Soul?," 1974; "The Bad Day on the Stock Exchange," 1974; "Judah Triptych" (includes "The Miracle in Jerusalem," "The Miracle in Ghadara," and "The Miracle in Jabnel"), 1975.

Television Play: "The Generals," first broadcast by TV-Belgrade, 1973.

Filmscripts: "The Fourteenth Day," Lovcen Film, 1961; "Don't Touch Into the Luck," Lovcen Film, 1963; "The Man," Lovcen Film, 1965. Also adaptator of numerous works into filmscripts.

Contributor to Yugoslav periodicals, including *Knjizevne Novine, Scena, Borba, Vidici,* and *Knjizevnost.*

WORK IN PROGRESS: Third and fourth parts of "Golden Fleece" tetralogy; another tetralogy—a continuation of "The Golden Fleece"—to be called *The Red and White* and to be about the German occupation of Yugoslavia and the Revolution through the eyes of a fallen upper middle-class family; *The Silver Hand,* a philosophical and historical novel about the lives of two famous Byzantium icon painters during the hundred years Civil War between the iconoclasts and the iconophils in the eighth century—"My intention is to show the tragic position of artists in the conditions of the spiritual totalitarianism of the 20th century"; a dramatic work about the treatment of liberal artists in mental hospitals to be called either "The Starry Heavens" or "The Moral Law"; a fimscript, "The Dreaming Cock," with V. Gilic, the film director.

SIDELIGHTS: Pekic told *CA:* "My main interest is to study the relationship between man and various forms of power, from ownership to political power; the main aims being to reveal all aspects of possession from which spiritual and moral deterioration derives and to denounce all forms of totalitarianism."

When *CA* asked if he would amplify this, he replied: "History speaks for itself. The possession of property and power over people, namely all aspects of power over someone or something, in the end, result in oneself being possessed and overcome by one's own property, and the power which one enforces. I believe this to be the direct consequence of a wrongly orientated civilization, where the occasional regulators such as religion, morality and humanitarianism are helpless. Under these circumstances no revolutions except revolutions of an objective make any valid sense. The only hope lies in the realization of the vital necessity to utterly change one's angle on the view of life. Unfortunately such a conduct would seem as hopeless as a desperate attempt of a man to draw himself out of the mud, by pulling his own hair."

Pekic is an official resident of Great Britian, but he maintains his Yugoslav passport and doesn't consider himself an emigrant. "Being temporarily away from my country, will enable me to view the present situation there from an objective distance, and therefore obtain a clearer picture of socialism. Socialism is directly or indirectly linked with the theme of my writing, and it is necessary to prevent the manifestation of any one opinion."

In his first letter, the author stated: "My six years of imprisonment as well as the lack of freedom to which I have been exposed to for the best part of my life have influenced my work a great deal."

Pekic was imprisoned for six years of a fifteen-year sentence at hard labor. He had been accused of organizing a Yugoslav social democratic student conspiracy against the state in 1948 while a student at the University of Belgrade.

Regarding the lack of literary freedom, he said; "If any work is declared as unsuitable for publication for either ideological or political reasons, in the majority of the cases the work contains an undesirable truth. In that context the prohibition takes the form of a paradoxical compliment to the work. Thinking rationally, I accept it in this way. Emotionally however, it deeply disturbs me, as it is depriving me of an audience in my own country and therefore the freedom to express my opinion. This incapacity is in most cases only momentary. Literary work is virtually impossible to destroy and the temporarily buried works eventually come to life again. Almost like vampires, dating back to the folktales, the works seek revenge.

"Censorship is undoubtedly one of the most repulsive aspects of enforcing power in the intellectual sphere. Although in the long run it does not achieve the desired effect nor prevent the further development and exchange of ideas, it is unfortunately able to, in the short run, slow down the mentioned progress. The effect is multilateral. The cases where the censorship reaches the threat of the author's banishment, it becomes, through the achieved fear and insecurity of the victims, a weapon of prevention as it forces the author into author-censorship and compromise. On the other hand it provides the people in power with the comfortable and peaceful feeling of everyone being in complete agreement."

*   *   *

PELLETIER, Kenneth R.   1946-

PERSONAL: Born April 27, 1946, in New Hampshire; son of Roger N. (a designer) and Lucy B. Pelletier. *Education:* University of California, Berkeley, A.B., 1969, Ph.D., 1974; graduate study at University of Pennsylvania, 1969, and C. G. Jung Institute, Zurich, Switzerland, 1969. *Residence:* Montclair, Calif. *Agent:* Robert Briggs Associates, 2154 Filbert St., San Francisco, Calif. 94123. *Office:* Gladman Memorial Hospital, Psychosomatic Medicine Clinic, 2510 Webster St., Berkeley, Calif. 94705.

CAREER: University of California, Berkeley, clinic intern in psychology, 1971-74; University of California, San Francisco, assistant clinical professor of psychiatry, 1974—. Clinical psychologist and director of Psychosomatic Medicine Clinic at Gladman Memorial Hospital, 1975—. Licensed clinical psychologist in California, 1976—; certified biofeedback practitioner, 1977—. Instructor at University of California Extension Division, 1971—; program coordinator at Esalen Institute (Big Sur), 1971—; intern at San Francisco Veterans Administration Hospital, 1973-74; director of Institute for the Study of Consciousness (Berkeley), 1974-76. Member of board of directors of University of California, Los Angeles, Center for Integral Medicine, 1974—, and Golden Gate National Recreation Area, 1975—; member of professional advisory board of National Health Services, Inc., 1976—; member of advisory board of East-West Academy of Healing Arts, 1976—.

MEMBER: American Association for the Advancement of Science, American Psychological Association, Academy of Psychosomatic Medicine, Society for Psychophysiological Research, Biofeedback Society of America, Association for Transpersonal Psychology, Association for Humanistic Psychology, Western Psychological Association, Biofeedback Society of California (member of board of directors, 1974-76), Phi Beta Kappa. *Awards, honors:* Woodrow Wilson fellowship, 1969; research fellowships from John E. Fetzer Foundation and Aletheia Foundation, both 1974-75.

WRITINGS: (With Charles Garfield) *Consciousness: East and West,* Harper, 1976; *Mind As Healer, Mind As Slayer: A Holistic Approach to Preventing Stress Disorders,* Delacorte, 1977.

Contributor: Demetri Kanellakos and Jerome Lukas, editors, *The Psychobiology of Transcendental Meditation,* W. A. Benjamin, 1974; P. G. Zimbardo and F. L. Ruch, editors, *Psychology and Life,* Scott, Foresman, 1975; L. Domash, J. Farrow, and David Orme-Johnson, editors, *Scientific Research on Transcendental Meditation: Collected Papers,* Maharishi International University Press, 1976; Gay Hendricks and James Fadiman, editors, *Transpersonal Education,* Prentice-Hall, 1976; Kenneth Blum, editor, *Social Psychology,* Basic Books, 1977; Dolores Krieger, editor, *The Persistent Reality,* Quest Books, 1977; D. E. Bresler and R. L. Katz, editors, *Acupuncture, Hypnosis, and Pain Management,* Simon & Schuster, in press.

Media presentations: "The Nature of Things," Canadian Broadcasting Co., 1975; "The New Medicine," National Broadcasting Co., 1976; "The Search for Something Special," National Broadcasting Co.-Television, 1976; "I Move," American Broadcasting Co.-Television, 1976; "The Long Search," British Broadcasting Corp., 1976; "Mental Stress and Physical Illness" (tape cassette), Ziff-Davis, 1977; "Two Techniques for Treating Stress Disorders" (tape cassette), Ziff-Davis, 1977. Contributor of over thirty articles to professional journals.

WORK IN PROGRESS: Toward a Science of Consciousness, "suggests links between the findings of quantum physics and current neurophysiology in determining the interaction between mind and matter."

AVOCATIONAL INTERESTS: Sailing, tennis, horseback riding, foreign travel (Europe, North Africa, Mexico, and Canada).

*   *   *

PELLICER, Carlos   1900(?)-1977

1900(?)—February 17, 1977; Mexican poet, critic, and governor of the state of Tabasco. He was a close friend of muralist Diego Rivera. He died in Mexico City. Obituaries: *New York Times,* February 18, 1977.

*   *   *

PENNIMAN, Thomas Kenneth   1896(?)-1977

1896(?)—January 16, 1977; British anthropologist, museum curator, and author of several books in his field. Obituaries: *AB Bookman's Weekly,* February 14, 1977.

*   *   *

PENNINGTON, Lee   1939-

PERSONAL: Born May 1, 1939, in White Oak, Ky.; son of Andrew Virgil (a farmer) and Mary Ellen (Lawson) Pennington; married Joy Stout (a teacher), January 28, 1962. *Education:* Baldwin Wallace College, student, 1958; San Diego State University, student, 1961; Berea College, B.A., 1962; University of Iowa, M.A., 1965; University of Kentucky, graduate study, 1966. *Home:* 11905 Lilac Way, Middletown, Ky. 40243. *Office:* Jefferson Community College, First & Broadway, Louisville, Ky. 40202.

CAREER: Newburgh Free Academy, Newburgh, N.Y., instructor in English, 1962-64; Southeast Community College, Cumberland, Ky., chairperson of English department, 1965-67; Jefferson Community College, Louisville, Ky., associate professor of English, 1967—. Poetry instructor, Murray State University, summers, 1969-72 and 1975-77, Morehead State University, summers, 1975-76, Ball State University, summers, 1976-77; instructor in Upward Bound program, 1966. Manager of Bingham Trio (musical group), 1963. *Member:* World Poetry Society Intercontinental, National Association for the Preservation and Perpetuation of Storytelling (member of executive board, 1975-77), Appalachian Consortium (member of advisory board), Kentucky

State Poetry Society, Kentucky Council of Teachers of English. *Awards, honors:* Has received eighteen awards for poetry, including four awards from Kentucky Poetry Society.

WRITINGS: The Dark Hills of Jesse Stuart (criticism), Harvest Press, 1967; *Creative Composition* (textbook), Jefferson Community College, 1976.

Poetry: *Scenes from a Southern Road,* Judson R. Dicks Publishing, 1969; *Wildflower . . . Poems for Joy,* Poetry Prevue, 1970; *April Poems,* Poetry Prevue, 1971; *Songs of Bloody Harlan,* Westburg Associates, 1975; *Spring of Violets,* Love Street Books, 1976; *I Knew a Woman,* Love Street Books, 1977.

Plays: *Appalachia, My Sorrow* (for voices; first produced in New York City at Riverside Theatre, October, 1969), Love Street Books, 1971; *The Porch* (one-act; first produced in Berea, Ky., at Berea College, March, 1962), Love Street Books, 1976; *The Spirit of Poor Folk* (one-act; first produced in Cumberland, Ky. at Southeast Community College, October, 1966), Love Street Books, 1976; *Coalmine* (for voices; first produced in Louisville, Ky., at Jefferson Community College, April, 1976), Love Street Books, 1976.

Author of screenplay, "The Moonshine War," released by Metro-Goldwyn-Mayer, 1970.

Books as yet unpublished: (With wife, Joy Pennington) *Bloody Bones and Bloody Harlan* (folktales); *Hornet Wings* (poetry); *Wind and Foxes* (short stories); *Manchild* (novel); *Letters to April* (essays).

Contributor of over 1,000 poems, short stories, and articles to more than 200 magazines, including *Southern Poetry Review, North American Mentor, Appalachian Review, American Bard,* and *Poet.* Author of column, "Have Yarn, Will Ravel," for *Greenup News,* 1970-72.

Editor, Green Bow Press, 1970, Whippoorwill Press, 1971-75; poetry editor, *Playgirl* (magazine), 1973.

WORK IN PROGRESS: A book of poetry, *Appalachian Newground;* a novel, *Run on Seven Gravels;* a drama, *Scotian Women;* a poetry writing textbook, *Feeling Trees.*

SIDELIGHTS: Lee Pennington, who grew up in Appalachia and teaches there currently, says that the major handicaps of the area have been the inhabitants' loss of pride, loss of individuality, and lack of feeling for the aesthetic. He believes the feeling for the unique beauty of the region—the crafts, traditions, and legends—must be cultivated. And, according to Pennington, this new spirit is emerging. He predicts, "There's going to be a revolution in the mountains led by creative young people."

The writing of poetry, Pennington believes, should not be limited to a few gifted writers. The most important prerequisite for writing poetry is "total involvement through total awareness." Pennington tells his students, "The action is where you are—under your feet—if You're always looking for it somewhere else, you'll miss it."

One year, students in Pennington's classes published four books of poetry and had over 1,000 pieces of creative writing published in more than 30 magazines and anthologies. He says, "If Appalachian students are backward in relation to the rest of the country, these certainly didn't show it."

Pennington told *CA:* "Students everywhere, young and old, need to be given the freedom to write, to create—the same right we afford our great writers. Every person is a unique entity in the universe and thus capable of creating something no one else can. I sincerely believe if we permit students to dream, if we encourage their dreaming and if we give them total freedom to create, they will loose on the world a love and lasting art never witnessed before by any age."

BIOGRAPHICAL/CRITICAL SOURCES: Herald-Advertiser, August 6, 1967; *Louisville Times,* November 2, 1968; *Voice-Jeffersonian,* November 2, 1972; *Courier Journal,* October 1, 1975; *Amarillo Globe-Times,* April 29, 1976.

* * *

PERKES, Dan 1931-

PERSONAL: Born February 17, 1931, in New York, N.Y.; son of Abraham (an engraver) and Edith (Sherman) Perkes; married Norma Jean O'Mary (an insurance and real estate agent), December 6, 1952; children: Kimberly, Dan. *Education:* Texas Technical University, B.A., 1957. *Home:* 17 Springvale Rd., Croton-On-Hudson, N.Y. 10520. *Agent:* George Wieser, 52 Vanderbilt Ave., New York, N.Y. 10017. *Office:* Associated Press, 50 Rockefeller Plaza, New York, N.Y. 10020.

CAREER: International News Service, New York, N.Y., copy boy, 1948-50; *Morning Avalanche,* Lubbock Tex., reporter, 1954-57; Associated Press, New York City, general executive, 1957—. *Military service:* U.S. Air Force, 1950-54; became airman first class. *Member:* Masons, New York Athletic Club, Sigma Delta Chi.

WRITINGS: (Editor) *Footprints on the Moon,* Associated Press, 1969; (project director) *AP News Annual,* Associated Press, 1969-76; (editor) *Century of Sports,* Hammond and Associated Press, 1971; (project director) *AP Sports Almanac,* Associated Press, 1975-77; *Eyewitness to Disaster,* Hammond, 1976.

WORK IN PROGRESS: Preliminary research on novel based on exploits of mariner Joshua Slocum.

SIDELIGHTS: CA asked Perkes how the recent influx of journalism students affects Associated Press. Perkes responded: "The number of journalism students never seemed to affect our employment needs since we draw the great bulk of AP staffers from among experienced newsmen in broadcasting and newspapers, mostly newspapers."

* * *

PERSINGER, Michael A. 1945-

PERSONAL: Born June 26, 1945, in Jacksonville, Fla.; son of Milo Alfred (an engineer) and Violet (Knight) Persinger. *Education:* University of Wisconsin, B.A. and B.S., both 1967; University of Tennessee, M.A., 1969; University of Manitoba, Ph.D., 1971. *Politics:* None. *Religion:* None. *Home and office:* Environmental Psychophysiology Laboratory, Laurentian University, Sudbury, Ontario, Canada P3E 2C6.

CAREER: Laurentian University, Sudbury, Ontario, assistant professor, 1971-75, associate professor of psychology and head of environmental psychophysiology laboratory, 1975—. *Member:* International Society of Biometeorology, International Society of Neurochemistry, American Association for the Advancement of Science, Parapsychology Association, Canadian Psychology Association, Society for the Investigation of the Unexplained, Canadian Meteorological Society.

WRITINGS: (Editor) *ELF and VLF Electromagnetic Field Effects,* Plenum, 1974; *The Paranormal: The Patterns,* M.S.S. Information, 1974; *The Paranormal: Mechanisms and Models,* M.S.S. Information, 1974; (with Gyslaine Laf-reniere) *Spacetime Transients and Unusual Events* (for laymen), Nelson-Hall, 1977. Contributor to journals in his fields.

WORK IN PROGRESS: A textbook, *An Introduction to Behavioral Biometeorology;* research on the effects of environmental and biogenic electromagnetic fields, the role of brain chemical pools in "unconscious" human behavior, the influence of geophysical and meteorological stimuli on human behavior, and experimental control of ostensible parapsychological experiences.

SIDELIGHTS: Persinger writes: "In a period of human history where complex and innumerable scientific disciplines and problems have dominated, there must emerge an integrater scientist who has the capacity to consolidate our present knowledge. Such a scientist would entertain problems that cross-cut the accepted but artificial territorialization of the sciences, in order to objectively determine solutions to global problems."

AVOCATIONAL INTERESTS: "Major enjoyment is derived from reading new research results in all the sciences and from the insights created when the data are combined."

* * *

PETERSON, Charles 1900(?)-1976

1900(?)—August 4, 1976; American jazz musician, photographer, and author of a book on his jazz days. He began his career as a jazz banjo and guitar player, but switched to photography on the advice of the photographer Edward Steichen. Thousands of his photographs of jazz musicians appeared in national magazines. He died in Washington, D.C. Obituaries: *Washington Post,* August 6, 1976.

* * *

PEYTON, Kathleen Wendy 1929-
(Kathleen Herald; K. M. Peyton)

PERSONAL: Born in 1929, in Birmingham, England; married Michael Peyton (a commercial artist and cartoonist), 1950; children: Hilary, Veronica. *Education:* Attended Kingston School of Art; Manchester Art School, received A.T.D. *Home:* Rookery Cottage, North Fambridge, Essex, England.

CAREER: Art teacher at high school in Northampton, England, 1952-56; writer, 1956—. *Member:* Society of Authors. *Awards, honors: New York Herald Tribune* award, 1965, for *The Maplin Bird;* Carnegie Medal, 1969; *Guardian* award, 1970, for *Flambards* and for *Flambards in Summer.*

WRITINGS—Children's books under name Kathleen Herald: *Sabre: The Horse from the Sea,* A. & C. Black, 1947, Macmillan, 1963; *The Mandrake,* A. & C. Black, 1949; *Crab the Roan,* A. & C. Black, 1953.

Children's books under name K. M. Peyton: *North to Adventure,* Collins, 1959, Platt, 1965; *Stormcock Meets Trouble,* Collins, 1961; *The Hard Way Home,* Collins, 1962; *Sea Fever,* World Publishing, 1963 (published in England as *Windfall,* Oxford University Press, 1963); *Brownsea Silver,* Collins, 1964; *The Maplin Bird,* Oxford University Press, 1964, World Publishing, 1965; *The Plan for Birdsmarsh,* Oxford University Press, 1965, World Publishing, 1966; *Thunder in the Sky,* Oxford University Press, 1966, World Publishing, 1967; *Flambards* (trilogy), Oxford University Press, 1967, World Publishing, 1968; *Fly-by-Night,* Oxford University Press, 1968, World Publishing, 1969; *The Edge of the Cloud,* World Publishing, 1969; *Flambards in Summer,* Oxford University Press, 1969, World Publishing,

1970; *Pennington's Seventeenth Summer,* Oxford University Press, 1970, published as *Pennington's Last Term,* Crowell, 1971; *The Beethoven Medal,* Oxford University Press, 1971, Crowell, 1972; *The Pattern of Roses,* Oxford University Press, 1972, Crowell, 1973; *Pennington's Heir,* Oxford University Press, 1973, Crowell, 1974; *The Team,* Oxford University Press, 1975; *The Right-Hand Man,* Oxford University Press, in press.

AVOCATIONAL INTERESTS: Riding, walking in mountains, sailing, music.

BIOGRAPHICAL/CRITICAL SOURCES: John Rowe Townsend, *A Sense of Story,* Longmans, 1971; Edward Blishen, *The Thorny Paradise,* Kestrel Books, 1975.

* * *

PHILLIPS, Bob 1940-

PERSONAL: Born December 25, 1940, in Denver, Colo.; son of Richard Ross and Evelyn (East) Phillips; married Pamela Joy MacDonald, November 28, 1964; children: Lisa Joy, Christine Lynne. *Education:* Biola College, B.A., 1964; California State University, Fresno, M.A., 1977. *Home:* 6514 North Fifth, Fresno, Calif. 93710. *Office:* Northwest Church, West & Barstow, Fresno, Calif.

CAREER: Hume Lake Christian Camps, Hume Lake, Calif., assistant director, 1964-74; Northwest Church, Fresno, Calif., associate pastor of counseling ministries, 1974—. Vice-president of board of directors of Accent Crusades, Inc. *Member:* Christian Association for Psychological Studies.

WRITINGS: The Great Future Escape, Vision House, 1973; *The World's Greatest Collection of Clean Jokes,* Vision House, 1974; *More Good Clean Jokes,* Harvest Publications, 1974; *The Last of the Good Clean Joke Books,* Harvest Publications, 1974; *Redi-Reference,* Harvest House, 1975; *Praise Is a Three-Lettered Word,* Regal Books (Glendale, Calif.), 1975; *The All American Joke Book,* Harvest Publications, 1976; *Lots O'Laughs,* Spire Books, 1976; *A Time to Laugh,* Harvest House, 1977; *The Pre-marital Workbook,* Harvest House, 1977.

Editor: (With Tim LaHaye) *The Act of Marriage,* Zondervan, 1976; (with Judy Messer) *To Know Him Is to Love Him,* Beta Books, 1976.

WORK IN PROGRESS: A pre-marriage counseling manual; a book on the attributes of God; a book on communication in marriage; a book of illustrations.

SIDELIGHTS: Phillips writes: "I am what is called a 'born again Christian.' I feel that as a Christian I have a responsibility to be an influence in my society with regard to the teachings of Jesus Christ. My writing is varied, from clean joke books to religious and family topics, and in all of these I have endeavored to carry forth my moral convictions. Martin Luther said, 'If you want to influence the world—pick up your pen.' I hope that in some small way my writings will influence my world for good."

* * *

PHILLIPS, David Atlee 1922-
(George Spelvin)

PERSONAL: Born October 31, 1922, in Fort Worth, Tex.; son of Edwin (a lawyer) and Mary (an executive; maiden name, Young) Phillips; married Helen Haasch, June 5, 1948 (divorced, 1967); married Virginia Simmons (an educator), March 28, 1968; children: David Jr., Maria, Christopher,

Deborah, Bryan, Wynne, Todd. *Education:* Attended College of William and Mary, 1940-41, Texas Christian University, 1941-42, University of Chile, 1948-49. *Politics:* Democrat. *Religion:* Protestant. *Home:* 8224 Stone Trail Dr., Bethesda, Md. 20034. *Agent:* Julian Bach Agency, 3 East 48th St., New York, N.Y. 10017.

CAREER: Worked as writer and actor in New York, N.Y., 1940-48; *South Pacific Mail,* Santiago, Chile, publisher, 1948-54; Central Intelligence Agency (CIA), Washington, D.C., intelligence officer, 1950-75, chief of Western hemisphere division, 1973-75; professional lecturer. *Military service:* U.S. Air Force, 1944-45; became staff sergeant; received Air Medal with cluster and Purple Heart. *Member:* Association of Former Intelligence Officers (founder and president, 1975—). *Awards, honors:* Intelligence Medal of Merit, 1955; Distinguished Intelligence Medal, 1975.

WRITINGS: The Night Watch, Atheneum, 1977. Editor, *South Pacific Mail,* 1948-54. Editor, under pseudonym George Spelvin, *Periscope* (a quarterly for intelligence professionals), 1975—.

WORK IN PROGRESS: The Eye of Violence, a spy novel; *Preparing for a Career in Intelligence.*

SIDELIGHTS: Phillips told *CA:* "I retired from the CIA in May 1975 to participate in the current controversy concerning intelligence in America." When asked by *CA* what the stand of the Association of Former Intelligence Officers was concerning the image of intelligence, Phillips added: "Originally the Association of Retired Intelligence Officers, our name was changed to Association of Former Intelligence Officers in December, 1976—this because our members didn't like the geriatric ring of the 'retired' as many of us are active in second careers.

"Our organizational stand on intelligence is that we believe in Congressional oversight and legislation for intelligence operations—but that an adequate intelligence capability is essential. We have *some* success in explaining the role of intelligence and improving the tarnished image of intelligence men and women. I, for instance, have appeared on all the major TV shows in this country ("60 Minutes," "Today," etc.) and have lectured all over the country. We have a speakers' bureau for civic groups and schools; a clearinghouse for the media to assist when intelligence stories are covered. At our third annual convention we expect several hundred delegates from our 1700 members around the country.

"Perhaps our most successful venture has been in assisting Congress (not lobbying). I, for instance, appeared before the Church committee to discuss the role of covert action; the others on the panel were Clark Clifford, Cyrus Vance and Morton Halperin. I have testified on AFIO's behalf before Senator Ribicoff's Government Operations Committee, and will testify to the Select Committee on Intelligence in the Senate."

* * *

PHILP, Richard Nilson 1943-

PERSONAL: Born July 7, 1943, in Plainfield, N.J.; son of Lester Perry (an industrialist and landscape painter) and Gladys Emma Linea (an artist; maiden name, Nilson) Philp. *Education:* University of North Carolina, Chapel Hill, B.A. (cum laude), 1965; Yale University, M.F.A., 1968. *Politics:* Registered Democrat. *Religion:* Episcopalian. *Home:* R.D. 3, Box 46, Route 385, Catskill, N.Y. 12414; and 551 Pacific St., Brooklyn, N.Y. 11217. *Office: Dance* Magazine, Suite 1455, 10 Columbus Cir., New York, N.Y. 10019.

CAREER: Critics Choice, New York City, associate editor 1968-70; Dance Magazine, New York City, managing editor, 1970—. Associate editor of After Dark, 1970-74. Columnist. Lecturer. Member: Dance Critics Association, Drama Desk, Hudson Valley Dairy Goat Association, American Rose Society. Awards, honors: Award from Society of Publication Designers, 1974, in recognition of work at Dance Magazine.

WRITINGS: Move to Learn, Temple University Press, 1977; Danseur: The Male in Ballet, McGraw, 1977.

Plays: "Sydney," first produced in Chapel Hill, N.C., 1964; "The Anniversary," first produced in Chapel Hill, 1965; "The Birdcage," first produced in Durham, N.C., 1965; "Dabney," first produced in Chapel Hill, 1965; "Priscilla," first produced in New Haven, Conn., 1965; "The Camel Question," first produced in New Haven, 1966; "Thrush," first produced in New Haven, 1966; "Winter Fire," first produced in New Haven, 1967; "Guests," first produced in New Haven, 1968, revised for Louisiana Arts Council, 1971; (translator and adapter) Eugene Labiche, Gladiator's Thirty Millions, first produced in New York City at Institute for Advanced Studies in Theatre Arts, 1970.

Author of columns, "The Broadway Scene," in After Dark, 1970-74, and a column about dance in the theater, in Dance Magazine, 1974—. Contributor to New York Times.

SIDELIGHTS: Philps writes that he moved from "an academic theater background to professional journalism in dance and theater." He said, "I've researched and edited a number of special issues of Dance Magazine, mostly of historical nature on subjects including Vaslav Nijinsky, Martha Graham, Anna Pavlova, Isadora Duncan and the history of dance in America, as well as influences of European styles on American dance. Other professional-related interests include photography and architecture."

* * *

PIASECKI, Bruce 1955-

PERSONAL: Born February 1, 1955, in West Islip, N.Y.; son of Walter John Piasecki and Lillian Kureczko. Education: Cornell University, B.A (summa cum laude), 1976; currently studying for Ph.D. Politics: "More critical than political." Religion: "Presently searching." Home: 358 Oakwood Ave., West Islip, N.Y. 11795. Office: 207 Linden Ave., Ithaca, N.Y. 14850.

CAREER: Cornell University, Ithaca, N.Y., assistant teacher of writing, 1976-77. Awards, honors: Long Island award from C. W. Post Center, 1974; New York Poetry Forum's Narrative Award, 1976; awards from Cornell Council on the Arts, 1976, Carnegie Fund for Authors, 1977, and P.E.N. American Center, 1977.

WRITINGS: (Editor) The First Anthology, Society of Humanities, 1974; Stray Prayers (poems), Ithaca House, 1976. Contributor to Epoch, Encore, Gryphon, Images, and other periodicals. Editor, Praxis, 1977-78.

WORK IN PROGRESS: Turbulence Today, "poetry plus two essays and three sketches"; Features of Utopia, "poetic character studies on six men and six women with coincident photography by Marc Weiner of New York City's Visual Arts"; and Take Off: An Ocean Poem, a collection of poems.

SIDELIGHTS: Piasecki told CA: "I have conceived of my first three collections as a trilogy, and would be happy to set up an exchange and correspondence with anyone interested in longer poetic sequences and the place of thought in art."

PIATIGORSKY, Gregor 1903-1976

April 17, 1903—August 6, 1976; Russian-born American virtuoso cellist and author of his autobiography. Known as a master in the nineteenth century Romantic tradition, he became principal cellist of the Bolshoi Orchestra while still in his early teens. In 1921, he escaped Russia by swimming to Poland with his cello held over his head. He was principal cellist with the Berlin Philharmonic before coming to the United States in 1942. For the next two decades he played with nearly every major conductor and orchestra in the United States and Europe. He died in Los Angeles, Calif. Obituaries: New York Times, August 7, 1976; Washington Post, August 7, 1976.

* * *

PICANO, Felice 1944-

PERSONAL: Born February 22, 1944, in New York, N.Y.; son of Phillip (a grocer) and Ann (Del Santo) Picano. Education: Queens College of the City University of New York, B.A., 1964. Residence: New York, N.Y. Agent: Jane Rotrosen Agency, 212 East 48th St., New York, N.Y. 10017.

CAREER: New York City Department of Welfare, New York, N.Y., social worker, 1964-66; Art Direction, New York City, assistant editor, 1966-68; Doubleday Bookstore, New York City, assistant manager, 1969-70; free-lance writer, 1970-72; Rizzoli's Bookstore, New York City, assistant manager and buyer, 1972-74; free-lance writer, 1974—.

WRITINGS: Smart As the Devil (novel), Arbor House, 1975; Eyes (novel), Arbor House, 1976; The Mesmerist (novel), Delacorte, in press. Contributor of articles and poems to magazines, including Out, Mouth of the Dragon, Gay Sunshine, New Dawn, and Islander.

WORK IN PROGRESS: Next to the Last (tentative title), a novel, completion expected in 1978; Chinese Boxes, stories, 1978; Gay Tragic Romances, poems; "The Lure," a screenplay.

SIDELIGHTS: Picano writes: "In my poetry I am keeping a sort of notebook of fragmentary experiences and understandings. In the past, this meant a polarization of subject matter: poems dealing either with perceptions gathered from the world of nature as revealed in Big Sur or Fire Island; or poems dealing with contemporary aspects of urban life and characters: portraits of epileptics, deformity lovers, obscene phone callers, etc. Of late, however, my poetry has become more autobiographical—though not at all confessional, integrating interior and exterior worlds. And forms have changed from lyric and monologic to more experimental structures such as self-interviews, imaginary dialogues, and letters to unknown persons.

"In fiction I write about the possible rather than the actual, and so I suppose, 'Romances' in Hawthorne's sense of the word, even with 'realistic' settings, characters, and actions. My novels, novellas, and short stories deal with ordinary individuals who are suddenly thrust into extraordinary situations and relationships which test their very existence. Unusual perceptions and abilities, extrasensory powers, and psychological abberations become tools and weapons in conflicts of mental and emotional control. Previous behavioral patterns are inadequate for such situations and must be changed to enable evolved awareness and survival, or they destroy their possessor. Thus, perspective is of the utmost importance in my fiction, both for structure and meaning. I am dedicated to experimenting with new and old points of view, which seem to have progressed little since the pioneering work of Henry James and James Joyce."

PIERCE, Paul 1910-

PERSONAL: Born July 9, 1910, in Columbia, Mo.; son of Harry (an architect) and Helen Pierce; married Mary Lea Gregory, August 17, 1933; children: Mary Stegeman, Paul, Lea. *Education:* Attended Los Angeles City College. *Politics:* "Republican or Independent." *Religion:* Episcopal. *Home address:* Box 911, Malibu, Calif. 90265. *Agent:* Mike Hamilburg, 292 S. La Cienega, Suite 212, Beverly Hills, Calif. 90211. *Office:* KMPC Radio, 5858 Sunset Blvd., Hollywood, Calif. 90265.

CAREER: Reporter and poet. *Military service:* California National Guard, 1928-30; U.S. Army, 1942-45. *Member:* Writer's Guild of America West, American Federation of Television and Radio Artists. *Awards, honors:* Los Angeles Press Club Award; California Teachers Award; Radio and Television News Directors Association National Award.

WRITINGS: Take an Alternate Route, Sherbourne, 1968; *Pennies and Tears* (poetry), Brook House, 1976.

Also author of radio scripts for "CBS Special Events" series. Contributor to *Westways, Argosy, Reader's Digest, Off Road,* and to newspapers.

WORK IN PROGRESS: A book "based on my experiences as a reporter in Southern California"; a follow up volume of poetry to *Pennies and Tears,* publication expected late 1978.

SIDELIGHTS: Pierce told *CA:* "I am basically a reporter specializing in politics, aerospace, travel, and the day to day news of crime, fires, and the doings of a very large city. By contrast, I have a flair for both romantic and humorous poetry and a very personal style of sophisticated comedy. I do not write straight joke material, and I am not much good at plotting fiction. Most of my writing is directly from personal experience, some of it quite hazardous, some of it very personal and moving. We travel in Mexico often and love the people and their language."

*   *   *

PIETSCHMANN, Richard John III 1940-
(Richard Miller; Townsend Parish)

PERSONAL: Born November 5, 1940, in New York; son of Richard John, Jr. (in films and television) and Ramona (Miller) Pietschmann; married Patricia Ann Covello (a writer), March 19, 1964. *Education:* Bucknell University, A.B., 1962. *Religion:* Protestant. *Home:* 2777 La Castana Dr., Los Angeles, Calif. 90046. *Agent:* Gary Cosay, Cosay/Werner, 9744 Wilshire Blvd., Beverly Hills, Calif. 90212.

CAREER: Fox Movietonews, New York, N.Y., assistant, 1962-63; *Contractors and Engineers,* New York City, assistant editor, 1964-66; *Discount Store News,* New York City, associate editor, 1966-68; Burson-Marsteller (public relations firm), New York City, account executive in New York, 1968-70, and Los Angeles, Calif., 1970-71; writer, 1971—. Has interviewed nationally known people in business, music, and show business; covered the 1971 earthquake in California. *Military service:* U.S. Army, 1963-64.

WRITINGS: (Contributor) *The Great Escape,* Bantam, 1974; (contributor) Min S. Yee and Donald K. Wright, editors, *The Sports Book,* Holt, 1975; *The Wild Gourmet,* Lyman, 1975; (contributor) Eugene Fodor, Stephen Birnbaum and Robert Fisher, editors, *Fodor's Far West,* McKay, 1977. Author of column "Sound & Music" in *Los Angeles.* Contributor to about twenty-five national and regional magazines and newspapers. Contributing editor of *Los Angeles* and *East/West Network.*

WORK IN PROGRESS: Cure and *East Side Story,* both novels.

*   *   *

PIKE, Dag 1933-

PERSONAL: Born January 28, 1933, in Surrey, England; son of Douglas William (a bank manager) and Racheal (McDonald) Pike; children: Kevin, Cathy. *Education:* Educated in England. *Home and office:* 25 North Rd., Bristol BS6 5AD, England.

CAREER: Worked as an officer in merchant navy, 1950-55; Lighthouse Authority, England, chief officer of Trinity House, 1955-64; Royal National Lifeboat Institute, England, inspector of lifeboats, 1964-74; Cormorant Fisheries Ltd., Wales, director, 1974-75; full-time author and journalist, 1975—. Marine surveyor and consultant. *Member:* Royal Institute of Navigation, Association of Royal Institute of Naval Architects, Institute of Journalists, Bristol Channel Powerboat Association.

WRITINGS: Power Boats in Rough Seas, Adlard Coles, 1974, International Marine Publishing Co., 1975; *Motor Sailers,* Stamford Maritime, 1976; *The History of Motor Boats,* P. Davies, 1977; *Electronic Navigation for Small Craft,* Adlard Coles, 1977; *Fishing Boats and Their Equipment, Fishing News* Books, 1977. Columnist for *Fishing News.* Contributor of articles to about twenty-five boating journals in United States, Britain, Sweden, and Italy.

WORK IN PROGRESS: A fiction book about the sea.

SIDELIGHTS: Dag Pike has navigated for the world champion in offshore powerboat racing. He told *CA:* "I have a passionate interest in the sea, ships, and boats stemming from going to sea at 16 years. When working with lifeboats, I had to test a new design which led to my first book. . . . I travel widely in Europe and U.S.A., and go to sea in boats of all types when the opportunity occurs. . . . [I] have an ambition to live in France."

AVOCATIONAL INTERESTS: Offshore powerboat racing, marine photography, sailing.

*   *   *

PILKINGTON, Betty
(Betty Alsterlund)

PERSONAL: Born in Illinois; daughter of William A. (an architect and builder) and Louise (Jamieson) Alsterlund; married Walter Pilkington, September 9, 1939 (divorced, 1959); children: Maud Jamieson (Mrs. David Easter). *Education:* Smith College, A.B., 1934; University of Michigan, graduate study, 1957. *Home:* 321 East 45th St., New York, N.Y. 10017. *Office:* Press Section, United Nations, New York, N.Y. 10017.

CAREER: American Notes & Queries, New York, N.Y., co-founder, publisher, and editor in New York City and Bennington, Vt., 1941-50; freelance writer, 1950-60; Pacifica Radio and Gemini News Service, London, England, United Nations correspondent, 1961—, covered Paris peace talks and the first United Nations conferences on trade and development and on atomic energy. Managing editor of Ballantine Books, Inc., 1960. English teacher for Chinese university students in Taiwan, 1957-58. *Member:* United Nations Correspondents Association, Foreign Press Association.

WRITINGS—Under name Betty Alsterlund: (Contributor) Stanley Kunitz and Howard Haycraft, editors, *American Authors, 1600-1900,* Wilson, 1938; (contributor) Kunitz and

Haycraft, editors, *Twentieth Century Authors*, Wilson, 1942. Author of bi-weekly column syndicated by Gemini News Service to nearly two hundred newspapers all over the world, 1969—. Contributor to magazines in the United States and England, including *Nation, New Republic,* and *Christian Century.*

WORK IN PROGRESS: Political writing.

SIDELIGHTS: Betty Pilkington writes: "Of necessity, I am an advocacy journalist. The modern media are so prolific that it's not enough just to throw certain facts into the public's face—the anti-establishment side has to emerge, along with even a little interpretation. My major concerns are political and socio-economic. I believe most radio and television coverage is too thin, and too anxious to be diverting. Hence I've stuck by a non-commercial listener-sponsored broadcasting outfit (Pacifica), independent enough to carry a solid open-ended news program. My column for Gemini enjoys the same freedom."

After mentioning her coverage of the Paris peace talks, she adds: "I believe arms are the source of most of the world's troubles.... We must also feed the hungry anywhere and restore a normal environment on land and sea." She has traveled all over the world.

* * *

PINCHIN, Jane Lagoudis 1942-

PERSONAL: Born August 21, 1942, in New York, N.Y.; daughter of Emanuel and Sarah (Magan) Lagoudis; married Hugh M. Pinchin (an economist), August 2, 1969; children: Sarah Eleni. *Education:* Harpur College of State University of New York at Binghamton, B.A., 1964; Columbia University, M.A., 1965, Ph.D., 1973. *Home address:* Quarterline Rd., Hubbardsville, N.Y. 13355. *Office:* Department of English, Colgate University, Hamilton, N.Y. 13346.

CAREER: Colgate University, Hamilton, N.Y., instructor in English, 1965-66; Brooklyn College of the City University of New York, Brooklyn, N.Y., lecturer in English, 1966-67; Neighborhood Youth Corps, New York, N.Y., part-time reading teacher for high school dropouts, 1967-69; Colgate University, assistant professor of English, 1969—. *Member:* American Association of University Professors (local vice-president). *Awards, honors:* Woodrow Wilson fellowship, 1964.

WRITINGS: Alexandria Still: Forster, Durrell, and Cavafy, Princeton University Press, 1977.

WORK IN PROGRESS: Research on E. M. Forster, Virginia Woolf, and images of mothers in literature.

* * *

PINE, Tillie S(chloss) 1896-

PERSONAL: Born March 4, 1896, in Poland; came to the United States in 1905, naturalized citizen, 1913; daughter of Louis and Rachel Schloss; married Nathan S. Pine (a co-owner of a book shop), July 17, 1924; children: Mona Pine Monroe. *Education:* Attended New York Training School for Teachers. *Home:* 400 Central Park W., New York, N.Y.; and Weston, Conn.

CAREER: Elementary school teacher in New York, N.Y., 1917-28 and 1937-61. Director of experimental Stonybrook Summer Day Camp, Weston, Conn., 1939-54; Bank Street College Workshop, member, 1946-61, part-time consultant, 1961-67. *Member:* Authors Guild of Authors League of America.

WRITINGS—All juvenile; all published by McGraw: *The Indians Knew,* 1957.

With Joseph Levine: *The Pilgrims Knew,* 1957; *Magnets and How to Use Them,* 1958; *The Chinese Knew,* 1958; *Sounds All Around,* 1958; *Water All Around,* 1959; *Air All Around,* 1960; *Friction All Around,* 1960; *Light All Around,* 1961; *Electricity and How We Use It,* 1962; *The Eskimos Knew,* 1962; *Heat All Around,* 1963; *Gravity All Around,* 1963; *The Egyptians Knew,* 1964; *Simple Machines and How We Use Them,* 1965; *Weather All Around,* 1966; *The Africans Knew,* 1967; *The Incas Knew,* 1968; *Trees and How We Use Them,* 1969; *Rocks and How We Use Them,* 1969; *The Maya Knew,* 1971; *Measurements and How We Use Them,* 1974, revised edition, 1977; *The Polynesians Knew,* 1974; *Energy All Around,* 1975; *The Arabs Knew,* 1976. Contributor to professional magazines.

WORK IN PROGRESS: Children's books, *The Scientists Knew* and *The Aztecs Knew,* both for McGraw.

AVOCATIONAL INTERESTS: Reading, cultural activities.

BIOGRAPHICAL/CRITICAL SOURCES: Lee B. Hopkins, *Books Are by People,* Citation Press, 1969.

* * *

PINKERTON, Todd 1917-

PERSONAL: Born February 11, 1917, in Antigo, Wis.; daughter of George J. (a contractor) and Mae (Petrofsky) Schoblaska; married John M. Stuber, April 15, 1939 (divorced November 20, 1948); married Hulbert B. Pinkerton (a lawyer and apartment owner), May 4, 1951; children: (first marriage) Brenda Stuber Harbaugh; (second marriage) Milo. *Education:* University of Wisconsin, Madison, B.S., 1950. *Politics:* Republican. *Religion:* Congregationalist. *Home:* 5526 Ethelwyn Rd., Madison, Wis. 53713.

CAREER: American Society of Clinical Pathologists, Madison, Wis., medical technologist, 1951-53; writer, 1965—. *Member:* Wisconsin Regional Writers Association.

WRITINGS: Breaking Communication Barriers with Roleplay, John Knox, 1976.

Plays: "Dawn of the Age of Pisces" (Christmas play), first produced in Madison, Wis., at First Congregational Church, December 17, 1972; "Communication with Youth" (one-act church play), first produced in Madison, Wis., at First Congregational Church, April 17, 1974.

WORK IN PROGRESS: Dialoguettes: A New Tool for Dialogue, short dramas made for discussion, for John Knox; *The Strange Obsession,* a novel; *The Look of "Her",* a novel; research on the Essenes, druids, Scotland, and psychics.

SIDELIGHTS: Todd Pinkerton writes: "Because I feel strongly about America and her unique possibilities for growing, I am unhappy about some of the trends in America today that appear (to me) unhealthy. Although a believer in equal opportunity and equal access to the productive facilities of the world, I believe in free enterprise and deplore a socialistic baby-sitting state with cushioned security that does *not* call forth the creative best in individuals." *Avocational interests:* Dream interpretation, interior decorating, historical costuming.

* * *

PIRTLE, Caleb (Jackson) III 1941-

PERSONAL: Born December 30, 1941, in Kilgore, Tex.;

son of Caleb Jackson, Jr. (an oil field worker) and Mary Eunice (Price) Pirtle; married Linda Sue Greer (a legal secretary), August 31, 1963; children: Joshua Jackson. *Education:* Kilgore College, A.A., 1961; University of Texas, B.J., 1963. *Home:* 129 Chieftan, Waxahachie, Tex. 75165. *Office:* Crawford, Pirtle & Lynn, Waxahachie, Tex. 75165.

CAREER: Plainfield Daily Herald, Plainview, Tex., reporter, 1963; *Fort Worth Star-Telegram,* Forth Worth, Tex., feature writer, 1963-65; Texas Tourist Development Agency, Austin, press chief, 1965-68; *Southern Living,* Birmingham, Ala., travel editor, 1968—; Crawford, Pirtle & Lynn, Waxahachie, Tex., partner, 1977—. *Member:* Society of American Travel Writers (past vice-president of Central States chapter), Discover America Travel Organizations. *Awards, honors:* Award from Southwest Journalism Forum, 1963, for feature writing; William Randolph Hearst Award, 1963; feature writing award from Texas Associated Press, 1964, and from Texas Headliners, 1964; awards from Discover America Travel Organizations, 1969, 1971, 1973, for magazine coverage of travel; named headliner of the year from local chapter of Texas Women's Press Association, 1975; award from Southeastern Library Association, 1973, for *Callaway Gardens: The Unending Season,* and 1975, for *XIT: The American Cowboy.*

WRITINGS: (With Gerald Crawford) *Callaway Gardens:. The Unending Season,* Oxmore, 1973; *XIT: The American Cowboy,* Oxmore, 1975. Contributor to magazines, including *Travel and Leisure, Travel, Sky, Holiday Inn Companion,* and *Rotarian.*

WORK IN PROGRESS: "Backroads," a syndicated television series on rural America.

SIDELIGHTS: Pirtle writes that some of his writing assignments have included interviews with former President Lyndon Johnson, former vice-president John Nance Garner, governor John Connally, and with the world's strongest man, country-western performers Tom T. Hall, Minnie Pearl, Porter Waggoner, Dolly Parton, Jimmy Driftwood, Dottie West, and Jerry Clower, with the world champion tobacco spitter, the world champion muleshoe pitcher, champion cowboys, professional golfers and tennis players. He comments: "I believe in people. And I'm convinced that what happens is not nearly as important as the people who make it happen. And that has been my approach to travel writing. Most simply tell you where to go, how to get there, and how much it's going to cost. I like to add a new dimension. I like to tell you the kind of people you're going to meet when you get there. And these include tobacco spitters, muleshoe pitchers, story tellers, chili cookers, domino players, and guitar pickers. I've been fortunate enough to travel throughout the United States, Mexico, Europe and Russia. And when I get home I find I remember the people I've talked with long after I've forgotten the sights I've seen. I write for one reason. I'm curious and like to find out what's going on . . . then I can't wait to tell someone."

*　　　*　　　*

PISTON, Walter   1894-1976

January 20, 1894—November 12, 1976; American composer, teacher of music, and author of textbooks considered classics in the field. Although he mainly composed works for orchestra and chamber ensemble, he was perhaps best known for "The Incredible Flutist," composed for a ballet. He won the Pulitzer Prize for Music in 1948 and 1961 for his Third and Seventh Symphonies. He was professor emeritus of music at Harvard University from 1926 until 1960. He

died in Belmont, Mass. Obituaries: *New York Times,* November 13, 1976.

*　　　*　　　*

PITTS, Robert F.   1908-1977

October 24, 1908—June 6, 1977; American physiologist, educator, author of a textbook and editor of professional journals; internationally known for his studies of the renal and nervous systems. He was chairman of the physiology department at Cornell University Medical College for twenty-five years. He died in Live Oak, Fla. Obituaries: *New York Times,* June 9, 1977.

*　　　*　　　*

PITZ, Henry C(larence)   1895-1976

June 16, 1895—November 26, 1976; American painter, book and magazine illustrator, educator, and author of books dealing with various aspects of art. He died in Philadelphia, Pa. Obituaries: *New York Times,* December 1, 1976. (See index for previous *CA* sketch)

*　　　*　　　*

PLATE, Thomas   1944-

PERSONAL: Born May 17, 1944, in New York, N.Y. *Education:* Amherst College, A.B., 1966; Princeton University, M.P.A., 1968. *Home and office:* 242 East 71st St., New York, N.Y. 10021. *Agent:* Theron Raines, Raines & Raines, 475 Fifth Ave., New York, N.Y. 10017.

CAREER: Newsweek, New York, N.Y., writer, 1968-70; *Newsday,* Garden City, N.Y., "Viewpoints" editor, 1970-72; *New York,* New York City, senior editor, 1972-74; freelance writer, 1974—. Member of Amherst College Alumni Committee on Publications. *Member:* Princeton Club (New York City), Phi Beta Kappa.

WRITINGS: Understanding Doomsday (nonfiction), Simon & Schuster, 1971; *Crime Pays!* (nonfiction), Simon & Schuster, 1975; (with Patrick V. Murphy) *Commissioner* (nonfiction), Simon & Schuster, 1977. *Penthouse* Magazine, author of column "Crime," and contributing editor, 1977—.

WORK IN PROGRESS: Drifting Man, a novel, for Dell.

SIDELIGHTS: Plate writes: "I am a writer because I think it is perhaps the most important continuing professional activity one can be involved in. Being a writer in America is often quite difficult, but . . . it is never just an ordinary existence."

*　　　*　　　*

PLEKKER, Robert J(ohn)   1929-

PERSONAL: Born August 23, 1929, in Grand Rapids, Mich.; son of John M. and Selma M. (Groeneveld) Plekker; married M. Jane Kooistra, November 3, 1951; children: Debra Lynn Plekker Windemuller, Susan Jayne, Tamara Helen. *Education:* Calvin College, student, 1948-49 and 1954-56; University of Michigan, D.D.S., 1960; U.S. Dental Institute, postdoctoral study, 1975—. *Religion:* Christian Reformed. *Residence:* Hudsonville, Mich. *Agent:* Duncan Boss, 55 Chapel Hill Rd., Lincoln Park, N.J. 07035. *Office:* 3427 Kelly St., Hudsonville, Mich. 49426.

CAREER: WHTC-Radio, Holland, Mich., announcer, 1948-50; dentist in Hudsonville, Mich., 1960—. Established Nigerian Dental Clinic in Takum, Nigeria, 1962. Vice-president of board of directors of Evangelistic Literature League, 1967-72; national president of Christian Reformed Layman's

League, 1967-71; partner in B.E. Productions (producers of religious films), 1971-74; member of board of directors of Calvary Rehabilitation Center, 1975—. *Military service:* U.S. Coast Guard, 1950-53; served in the South Pacific and Japan.

MEMBER: American Dental Association, Academy of General Dentistry, National Analgesia Society, Luke Society, Royal Society of Health, Western Michigan Dental Society, Kent County Dental Society, Phi Alpha Kappa. *Awards, honors:* Freedoms Foundation Award, 1969; named dentist of the year by Michigan State Dental Association, 1970.

WRITINGS: Redeemed? Say So!, Harper, 1977.

WORK IN PROGRESS: Christian Divorce? Why Not!, completion expected in 1978.

AVOCATIONAL INTERESTS: Ham radio operator, licensed private pilot, international travel, tennis, paddleball.

* * *

PLOPPER, Julie Jynelle 1916-

PERSONAL: Born May 2, 1916, in Illinois; married David Pactor, January 3, 1938 (divorced, 1945); married Curtis C. Plopper (a retired attorney), December 23, 1963; children: (first marriage) David Edward, Howard Sidney. *Education:* Attended University of Southern Illinois, 1933-34. *Religion:* Jewish. *Home:* 577-578 Heritage Lake, R.R. 2, Coatesville, Ind. 46121. *Office:* Curtis Publishing Co., 1100 Waterway Blvd., Indianapolis, Ind. 46206.

CAREER: Commercial Barge Lines, Evansville, Ind., payroll supervisor, 1950-61; Inland Container Co., Indianapolis, Ind., cost analyst, 1962-63; Curtis Publishing Co., Indianapolis, fulfillment and list rent manager, 1963-76, editor of *Young World* magazine, 1976—.

WRITINGS: (Contributor) Morrie Turner and Letha Turner, *Famous Black Americans,* Judson, 1976. Also contributor to *Jewish Customs, Stories, and Activities,* 1977. Contributor to *Child Life* magazine.

* * *

PLOTNIK, Arthur 1937-

PERSONAL: Born October 1, 1937, in White Plains, N.Y.; son of Michael (a trucker) and Annabelle (a stenographer; maiden name, Taub) Plotnik; married Veta Von Borstel (an educator), September, 1960 (separated October, 1972); children: Julia Nicole, Katya Michele. *Education:* Attended State University of New York at Albany; State University of New York at Binghamton, B.A., 1960; University of Iowa, M.A., 1961; Columbia University, M.L.S., 1966. *Home:* 2014 North Kenmore, Chicago, Ill. 60614. *Office: American Libraries,* 50 East Huron St., Chicago, Ill. 60611.

CAREER: Albany Times-Union, Albany, N.Y., reporter and reviewer, 1963-64; Scott Meredith Literary Agency, Inc., New York, N.Y., paperback author, 1964-66; Library of Congress, Washington, D.C., editorial specialist, 1966-69; *Wilson Library Bulletin,* New York City, associate editor and art director, 1969-75; *American Libraries,* Chicago, Ill., editor and art director, 1975—. Headed a team of writers for major reporting on "Washington Library Power," 1975. *Military service:* U.S. Army Reserve, 1962-67; became sergeant. *Member:* American Library Association, Freedom to Read Foundation. *Awards, honors:* Certificate of distinction from International Reading Association, 1970, for editing an issue of *Wilson Library Bulletin;* two awards for excellence

in educational journalism from Educational Press Association of America, both 1973, both for article series "Library Life in America"; Jones-World Book-American Library Association goals award, 1976, to conduct *American Libraries* prize article competition.

WRITINGS: Wizards and Cabalists and Mystics and Magicians (incantations and poems), Associated American Artists, 1966; *Library Life, American Style: A Journalist's Field Report,* Scarecrow, 1975. Also author of twenty-one popular novels under various pseudonyms, including A. P. Williams, John Dexter, William Jeffries, and Don Holliday; author of nonfiction book, *Fetishism in Modern Man,* under pseudonym Dr. Murray Stevenson.

Work anthologized in *Library Literature Three: The Best of 1972,* edited by Bill Katz, Scarecrow, 1973. Writer (later contributor and editor) of column "Booktrucking About Town" in *Wilson Library Bulletin,* 1973-74. Contributor to *Encyclopedia of Library and Information Science, Dictionary of American Library Biography,* and to encyclopedia and library association yearbooks; contributor of articles or photographs to *Parent's Magazine, Schist,* and *Story* and to library journals and newspapers.

WORK IN PROGRESS: Thirty-Five: A True and Open Journal of the Halfway Point in a Modern Life; A Handbook for All Assistant Editors; Ten Who Loved: Letters from Loving Women; Bigger and Bigger Presents, a children's book.

SIDELIGHTS: Plotnik wrote: "When I'm not worrying about deadlines—which I've been doing since writing clever-kid pieces thirty years ago for the Saturday junior page of the *White Plains Reporter-Dispatch*—I worry about the power of the printed word to screw people up and bring down institutions, about journalists including myself who in an irresponsible moment can cause irreparable damage to the innocent. Investigative reporting has become so facile and reckless that it's meaningless, except to those slandered in its path. Even in trade journalism, cheap shots and truculent prose are festering where imagination, wit, and style, accuracy and responsibility, are beyond the editors' grasp. The pleasure of writing and editing for me has always been to find the brave and the extraordinary where it was little expected; to seize excellence wherever it is found and to hold it up for emulation or to be enjoyed for its own sake. Freedom of the press means trust but it must work both ways: the people must trust the press to be truthful, and the press must trust the people to be decent and innocent until proved otherwise. And where should innocence or guilt be tried? Certainly not in the headlines, whatever the faults of our systems of justice. I write on all subjects, fiction and nonfiction, with equal agony/ecstasy, and as an editor, I edit for readers, not other editors."

When Plotnik told *CA* he also "hacked out twenty-one racy paperbacks and one pseudo-scientific work, all under various pseudonyms," in a "potboiler stable," he was naturally queried for more information. "Perhaps," he began in response, "the most that can be said to the credit of a sixties 'potboiler' writer is that the books probably harmed no one but the author.

"The potboilers of that time were generally innocuous modern adventure stories, usually with a strong male hero—a superstud. Although a sex scene was required in every chapter, obscenity was forbidden—yes forbidden!—by the major publisher in the field. Sexual descriptions tended to be metaphorical: 'His steaming desire sought her warm passion'—and worse. Some of the writers would strain like metaphysical poets to come up with new-world metaphors, so that classical images of fire, oceans, and volcanoes would give way by the third chapter to more elaborate matings of steam engines, oil wells, wrecking balls, and Bessemer furnaces.

"In writing more than twenty titles, I developed a handy chart of erotic imagery from which I could randomly select new combinations. Pick one: 'He seized her (rosy, ripe, mellow, round, rotund, smooth, taut, soft, tender, supple, pliant, firm, globular) (moons, planets, melons, orbs, loaves, rump, volleyballs)'—whatever turns one on.

"In the fifties and early sixties, the king of the potboiler publishers was William Hamling, who later went to jail in a court decision as disgusting as the book that got him there: a graphic version of the President's Commission on Obscenity and Pornography Report. In potboilers, Hamling had enough business for a whole stable of writers, who for a few years received their assignments and checks through the Scott Meredith Literary Agency. (Meredith got out of the 'skin-book' business when it no longer needed the $25,000 or so it earned each year in commissions.)

"Hamling's titles were published as 'Nightstand,' 'Leisure,' 'Bedside Reader,' or 'Midwood' books, and were said to sell about 80,000 each at prices ranging from $.75 to $3.00, whatever the traffic would bear. Their trademarks were the yellow or pink spine, a poorly airbrushed cover illustration (the amateurishness of the art gave the books a clandestine look), and what was called 'flip appeal.' The prospective buyer flipping through was sure to find some key word—such as 'naked'—on almost every page. A writer could sneak in the 'flip' words in any context, so that sentences such as 'She opened the naked window' were not uncommon.

"On the average, writers were paid $900 a book after the agency took its $100 commission. It was good money then for about three weeks' work, and many now-respectable writers chose to earn a living by it rather than take such equally destructive and less lucrative 'writing' jobs as hacking out propaganda for a government bureau. The old pros could write a book in a week, then do something clean and well lighted for the rest of the month—the only way to survive psychologically.

"Because Hamling feared convictions, there were constant directives for toning down the prose: no obscenity, no bestiality, and so on. Once I received an urgent mandate to desist from all imagery of heat and food—no more warm melons. At one point, we all had to write brief introductions to our books in order to make explicit their 'social value.' We were told to quote at least one respected authority in the social sciences to underscore the point. It was madness, as was most of the business of throwing away one's best characters and plots at the relentless rate of some twenty pages a day.

"I got into it after graduate school, when I was waiting for the Army to call and couldn't find any sort of teaching or writing job in Albany, N.Y., where I was living. A college friend, writing 'Nightstands' for a man who is now a celebrated mystery writer, heard of another Hamling regular who needed a ghost. The pay was $600 a book, and after a little tryout I became the surrogate 'Don Holliday.' (The fellow I was writing for wrote a successful novel in the meantime and is today a top screenwriter.) After the Army and a stint as a reporter for $100 a week, I was offered my own Hamling slot at full pay—some $300 a week—and I couldn't turn it down.

"No form of authorship could be more anonymous. Stable members never met one another except by accident. Meredith considered us necessary evils. We never knew what our books would be titled, and many of the authors' pseudonyms would be rotated from one writer to another. To find one's books, one had to go to the stores that carried them and flip through the new titles until recognizing some familiar characters—by which time the proprietor would be screaming, 'Pick 'em out and get moving!'

"My titles, like other Hamlings, were short and to the point. Among them were *Sin Charlatan, Sin Man, Sally's Sinners* (who said the Puritan consciousness was dead?), *Lust Lure, Lust Sisters, Lust Run, Flesh Huntress,* and, my favorite, *The Reluctant Stud.* Sometimes I was A. P. Williams, other times John Dexter, William Jeffries, or Don Holliday. A schizy business.

"I wrote one nonfiction as Dr. Murray Stevenson (Ph.D.): a study called *Fetishism in Modern Man.* I did weeks of research in medical libraries and tried to write an honest text to surround the absurd 'case histories' I was told to invent. 'Shouldn't I cite case histories from classic works?' I asked my agent. He pondered the matter and replied, 'Nah, we don't wanna step on anybody's toes.' The book was sold to Monarch Publishers for $1,500 as one of the 'Monarch Human Behaviour Series,' but I was never able to find the title on the racks. Author copies and other literary amenities were obviously not a part of the potboiler game. But at least the checks came fast, and for those writing from homes in other countries it was a goldmine. One colleague, who has done very well as a 'serious' writer, still farms out his sex-novel assignments to any literate character he meets in the London pubs. His system has worked for years.

"I bolted from the business after about two years, and just in time—in a more liberal atmosphere the potboilers became drearily pornographic, dehumanized, as pathetic to write as to read. Once out, I couldn't have written another for $9,000. But the experience was an invaluable lesson in the discipline of deadline writing—in getting those big blank pages filled. And in the alienated life of any writer, being paid, published, and read by thousands even for trash can be just the boost one needs to believe in one's self and move along to better things."

AVOCATIONAL INTERESTS: "I dabble in most of the arts, especially photography, in the sports, in Spanish and French," and travel (Scandinavia, Europe, including a solo bicycle trip through Normandy and Brittany, Greece, and the West Indies).

BIOGRAPHICAL/CRITICAL SOURCES: American Libraries, November, 1974.

*   *   *

PODHAJSKY, Alois 1898-1973

PERSONAL: Born February 24, 1898, in Mostar, Austria (now Yugoslavia); son of Alois (a cavalry officer) and Wilhelmine (Peter) Podhajsky; married Verena Dvorak, August 30, 1938 (died January 23, 1963); married Eva Kuretschka (translator of husband's books), March 2, 1964. *Politics:* "Conservative outlook on life." *Religion:* Roman Catholic. *Home:* Hofburg, Feststiege 4, 1010 Vienna, Austria.

CAREER: Austrian Army, 1916-18, began as cadet, became lieutenant in 4th Dragoons regiment; Army of the First Federal Republic of Austria, 1918-38, began as lieutenant, became major; German Army (after annexation of Austria), 1938-45, began as major, became colonel; civil servant of

Second Republic of Austria, 1945-64; full time writer, 1964-73. Director of Spanish Riding School, Vienna, Austria, 1939-64. *Awards, honors:* Received numerous decorations as director of Spanish Riding School, including Cross of Malta, Order of the Hous of Oranje, and awards from the countries of Germany, Spain, Denmark, Thailand, and Iran; bronze medal in the Grand Prix de Dressage, 1936 Olympic Games in Berlin.

WRITINGS—All original German editions published by Nymphenburger Verlag, except as noted: *Die Spanische Hofreitschule wien*, Hammer, 1948; *Lipizzaner*, Schwarz Verlag, 1959; *Ein Leben fur die Lipizzaner*, 1960, 3rd edition, 1973, translation of first edition by Frances Hogarth-Gaute published as *My Dancing White Horses*, Holt, 1965; *Triumph der Lipizzaner*, 1962, translation by Hogarth-Gaute published as *The White Stallions of Vienna*, Dutton, 1963; *Die Klassische Reitkunst*, 1965, translation by Eva Podhajsky and V.D.S. Williams published as *The Complete Training of Horse and Rider*, Doubleday, 1967; *Meine Lehrmeister die Pferde*, 1967, translation by Eva Podhajsky published as *My Horses My Teachers*, Doubleday, 1968; *Die Lipizzaner im Bild*, 1968, translation by Eva Podhajsky published as *The Lipizzaners*, Doubleday, 1969; *Die Kleine Reitlehre*, 1968; (contributor) Peter Roberts, editor, *Riding the International Way*, Kaye & Ward, 1969.

Reiten lehren and lernen, 1971, translation by Eva Podhajsky published as *The Riding Teacher: A Basic Guide to Correct Methods of Classical Instruction*, Doubleday, 1973; *Ein Besuch in der Spanishen Hofreitschule: A Visit to the Spanish Riding School* (text in German and English), 1972; *Reiten und Richten*, 1973, translation by Eva Podhajsky published as *The Art of Dressage: Basic Principles of Riding and Judging*, Doubleday, 1976.

Writer of brochures on the Spanish Riding School, in German, French, and English. Contributor to *Encyclopedia of the Horse*, published by Pelham, and to *Encyclopaedia Britannica*. Contributed numerous articles to periodicals and newspapers published in Germany, Austria, France, England, Canada, and United States.

SIDELIGHTS: Podhajsky's wife, Eva, wrote this summary for *CA:* "A son of a cavalry officer, Podhajsky always wanted to be a rider. His education and career were governed by tradition, self discipline, and idealism. These qualities made him an exemplary teacher in equestrian sports, who not only theorized but demonstrated his principles in the saddle. It was one of his rules that theory and practical experience must complement each other and that only a teacher who excelled in both could convince his pupils.

"To him, straightness of character and loyalty were the most important qualities in man. He had deep understanding and respect for the individual, be it human or animal, but was premptory in his demands. His authority, however, was generally accepted without questioning. This standpoint is expressed in his equestrian manuals in which he laid down the experiences of his lifetime as a rider and a teacher.

"Outstanding talent and perseverance enabled him to rise above the crowd of cavalry officers to become one of 'the greatest horsemen of our century,' raising equitation from the level of sport to that of art. Because of his successes as a rider and instructor he was entrusted with the directorship of the Spanish Riding School—the oldest of its kind and the last abode of classical equitation. The well-known story of how he developed it to highest standards and, with the help of the American Army under General Patton, saved it from destruction at the end of World War II, is told in his autobiog-

raphy, *My Dancing White Horses*. Walt Disney's movie, "The Miracle of the White Stallions," is based on two of its chapters.

"Early in life Podhajsky had started to lecture and write, but after his retirement in 1964 he began his true second career as an author. Seven of his ten books in German, plus their translations, were published in the years following his retirement. In this period fell extensive travels to various European countries, Mexico, Venezuela, Canada, and the United States, always with the object of teaching and lecturing."

OBITUARIES: New York Times, May 24, 1973.

(Died May 23, 1973, in Vienna, Austria)

[Sketch verified by wife, Eva Podhajsky]

* * *

POLK, James R. 1937-

PERSONAL: Born September 12, 1937, in Oaktown, Ind.; son of Raymond S. (a Navy officer) and Oeta (an educator; maiden name, Fleener) Polk; married Bonnie Becker (an education administrator), November 4, 1962; children: Geoffrey, Amy. *Education:* Indiana University, A.B., 1964. *Politics:* Independent. *Religion:* Independent. *Home:* 6621 Tucker Ave., McLean, Va. 22101. *Office:* NBC News, 4001 Nebraska Ave. N.W., Washington, D.C. 20016.

CAREER/WRITINGS: Associated Press, Washington, D.C., reporter, 1961-71; *Washington Star*, Washington, D.C., reporter, 1972-74; National Broadcasting Co. (NBC) News, Washington, D.C., correspondent, 1975—. Notable assignments include the exposure of illegal campaign contributions to 1972 Republican presidential campaign, Watergate, and similar stories. Member of board of directors, WETA-TV, Washington, D.C., 1973—, and of advisory board of Fund for Investigative Journalism, 1973—. *Member:* Investigative Reporters and Editors (member, board of directors and vice-president, 1976—). *Awards, honors:* American Political Science Association award, 1961; Raymond Clapper Award for Washington investigative reporting, 1972, 1974; Pulitzer Prize for national reporting, 1974; Sigma Delta Chi prize for general reporting, 1974.

* * *

POLLACK, Herman 1907-

PERSONAL: Born August 25, 1907, in St. Louis, Mo.; son of Jacob (a painter and paperhanger) and Tillie (Padratzik) Pollack; married Sophie Schneiderman, March 14, 1937 (died, 1976); children: Rosalind. *Education:* Hebrew Union College, B.H.L., 1928, rabbi, 1932; University of Cincinnati, B.A., 1929; Columbia University, Ph.D., 1958. *Politics:* "Democrat, interested in social and economic progress." *Religion:* Jewish. *Home:* 7 Columbia Terrace, Brookline, Mass. 02146.

CAREER: Ordained rabbi, 1932; Temple Israel, Blytheville, Ark., rabbi, 1937-41; B'nai B'rith Hillel Foundation, Indiana Univeristy, Bloomington, Ind., rabbi and adviser, 1941-44; Brooklyn College Hillel, Brooklyn, N.Y., rabbi, 1944-52; Massachussetts Institute of Technology Hillel, Cambridge, Mass., rabbi, 1952-72. Lecturer in Jewish history and culture, Brooklyn College adult education program, 1947-52; Boston University, lecturer, 1968—, adjunct associate professor of ancient history, 1975. *Member:* American Historical Association, American Oriental Society, Society of Biblical Literature and Exegesis, Society for the Scientific Study of Religion, Central Conference of American Rabbis (member of executive committee, 1958-60), National Association of Hillel Directors (president, 1959-61), American Jewish Historical Society Alpha Kappa Delta. *Awards, honors:* D.D., Hebrew Union College, 1958; Merril Trust Academic Enrichment Program grant, 1968; National Foundation for Jewish Culture grants, 1972 and 1974; George Brussel Social Action Memorial Award, 1973, from Stephen Wise Free Synagogue.

WRITINGS: Jewish Folkways in Germanic Lands (1648—1806), M.I.T. Press, 1971; (contributor) S. Feingold and William Silverman, editors, *Kivie Kaplan: A Legend in His Own Time,* Union of American Hebrew Congregations, 1977. Contributor to *American Educator Encyclopedia,* 1945. Contributor of articles to *Jewish Advocate, American Academy for Jewish Research, Boston Sunday Herald,* and other periodicals.

WORK IN PROGRESS: The History and Development of the Minhag; The Scope of History: A Survey of Human Experience; researching "the Problem of Objectivity in History" and "the Purim Mask: A Cross-Cultural Study."

SIDELIGHTS: Pollack told *CA:* "My boyhood background among East European immigrants influenced me to be interested in study, in social and ethical issues. Early in my life I learned first-hand what the struggle for existence may mean. My teachers in public school, high school, university and rabbinical school had a great influence on me. They taught me to appreciate both the written and spoken word. They made me aware that the record of simple folk deserves to be studied and recorded as a crucial part of history. I was prompted to regard history as a basic discipline since it does embrace all aspects of human experience."

CA asked Pollack his opinion on the influx and efflux of anti-Semitism in the United States. "Since colonial times," he responded, "the history of the United States has consisted of democratic and anti-democratic trends. In times of economic and political stress, religious and racial bigotry have been on the upgrade, but were held at bay by humanitarian values and sentiments. The instability since the 1960's has contributed to the increase of prejudice in general and anti-Semitism in particular. If some of the current social concerns can be resolved, anti-Semitism will no doubt recede, although it should be recognized that from ancient times on bias has persisted. Inasmuch as anti-Semitism is reenforced by myth and folklore, irrationality does have a special appeal when conditions are unstable, as was the case during the period of Nazi Germany. The recent terroristic attack on the B'nai B'rith building in Washington, D.C., is a warning that an American brand of a pogrom may be developing. The outlawing of anti-Semitism is not proposed as a solution because a conflict with the First Amendment could ensue. A wholesome, stable society based on ethical principles will be effective in coping with and checking anti-Semitism."

*   *   *

POLLARD, (Henry) Graham   1903-1976

1903—November 15, 1976; British bibliographer, antiquarian book dealer, and author of works on bibliography, book production, and history of the Oxford libraries. One of his best-known works, *Enquiring into the Nature of Certain Nineteenth Century Pamphlets,* exposed the "first edition" forgeries of T. J. Wise and caused a scandal. He died in Oxford, England. Obituaries: *AB Bookman's Weekly,* December 20-27, 1976.

PONDER, James A(lton)   1933-

PERSONAL: Born January 20, 1933, in Fort Worth, Tex.; son of Leo Alton and Mae Blair (Steerfield) Ponder; married Joyce Hutchison (a writer), September 1, 1953; children: Keli Marie, James Kenyon. *Education:* Baylor University, student, 1954; Southwestern Baptist Theological Seminary, B.D., 1955, M.R.E., 1965. *Office:* Florida Baptist Convention, 1230 Hendricks Ave., Jacksonville, Fla. 32207.

CAREER: Ordained Southern Baptist clergyman, 1953; pastor of Baptist churches in Corsicana, Tex., 1953-57, Highlands, Tex., 1957-62, Fort Worth, Tex., 1963-66, and Carmi, Ill., 1966-67; Illinois Baptist State Association, Carbondale, Ill., director of evangelism, 1968-70; Florida Baptist Convention, Jacksonville, Fla., director of evangelism, 1970—. Evangelist, 1951-53, 1967; president of pastors' conferences in Texas and Illinois; member of Baptist executive boards in Texas and Illinois; conducted more than fifty youth revivals in the early 1950's; evangelist in Panama, Korea, Brazil, Vietnam, Indonesia; preacher in Central America, Hong Kong, Israel, Japan, Jordan, Lebanon, Malaysia, Mexico, Taiwan, and Thailand. Radio sports announcer in Waco and Baytown, Tex. *Member:* International Platform Association, Fellowship of Christian Athletes.

WRITINGS: The Devotional Life, Baptist Sunday School Board, 1970; *New Church Member Training Workbook for Adults,* Baptist Sunday School Board, 1973; *Evangelism Men: Motivating Laymen to Witness,* Broadman, 1975; *Evangelism Men: Proclaiming the Doctrines of Salvation,* Broadman, 1976. Author of church school material. Contributor to *Encyclopedia of Southern Baptists.* Contributor to *Skill* and *Church Training.*

WORK IN PROGRESS—All tentative titles: *Motivating the Church to Grow; Essential Priorities for Evangelism; The Holy of Holies,* on John 13:17; *Discovering Your Spiritual Gifts,* on First Corinthians 12:14.

SIDELIGHTS: At the invitation of the Foreign Mission Board of Southern Baptist Convention and missionaries of the field, Ponder has preached crusades, spoken in evangelistic conferences, and directed evangelism training and strategy clinics in fifteen overseas countries. Over the past few years he has served as guest teacher on the faculty of the Billy Graham Schools of Evangelism.

*   *   *

PONTES, Paulo   1941(?)-1976

1941(?)—December 28, 1976; Brazilian playwright, producer, and translator; co-author with Chico Buarque de Hollanda of the prize-winning play "Gota d'Agua," and one of the founders of the Opinao Theater Workshop. He died in Rio de Janeiro, Brazil. Obituaries: *New York Times,* December 29, 1976.

*   *   *

POPE, Maurice (Wildon Montague)   1926-

PERSONAL: Born February 17, 1926, in London, England; son of Philip and Violet (Carr) Pope; married Johanna May Garle, July 1, 1958; children: Hugh, Thomas, Patrick, Helen, Francis, Quentin. *Education:* Magdalene College, Cambridge, M.A., 1948. *Residence:* Oxford, England. *Agent:* Curtis Brown Academic, 1 Craven Hill, London W2 3EW, England.

CAREER: University of Cape Town, Cape Town, South Africa, lecturer, 1949-57, professor of classics, 1957-69, dean of faculty of arts, 1965-67; University of Victoria, Victoria, British Columbia, visiting professor, 1975-76. *Military service:* Royal Naval Volunteer Reserve, 1945-46; became sub-lieutenant. *Member:* Society of Antiquaries of London. *Awards, honors:* Carnegie Traveling fellowship, 1964.

WRITINGS: (With G. P. Goold) *Preliminary Investigations into the Linear A Script,* Institute of Classical Studies, 1955; (with W. H. Hewitt) *The Angry Old Man,* Balkema (Cape Town), 1960; (with John Boardman) *Greek Vases in Cape Town,* South Africa Museum, 1961; (with B. E. Newton) *Saecula Latina,* University of Cape Town Press, 1962; *Aegean Writing and Linear A,* Paul Astrom, 1964; (with Jacques Raison) *Index du Lineaire A,* Incunabula Graeca (Rome), 1971; *The Story of Decipherment,* Thames & Hudson, 1975, published as *The Story of Archaeological Decipherment,* Scribner, 1975; *The Ancient Greeks,* David & Charles, 1976. Contributor of articles to *American Journal of Philology, Journal of Hellenic Studies, Annual of the British School of Athens,* and other periodicals.

WORK IN PROGRESS: A translation and commentary on Galen's minor physiological treatises, and a biography of Galen, both with Hymie Gordon.

SIDELIGHTS: Pope told *CA:* "Having been brought up by a father who was a farmer turned stockbroker and who then wrote novels and translations of Greek poetry, and by a mother who questioned everything, I have always found it difficult to limit myself to one narrow field as a good scholar should. If I had to name a special interest I should say Geistgeschichte or the history of ideas."

*   *   *

POPE, Phyllis Ackerman   1894(?)-1977

1894(?)—January 25, 1977; American expert on Asian art and author of books on that subject; known as an authority on prehistoric symbols and myths of Iranian culture. She and her husband, Arthur Upham Pope, were co-directors of the Asia Institute in New York City. She died in Shiraz, Iran, where she had lived for several years. Obituaries: *New York Times,* February 1, 1977.

*   *   *

POPE, Whitney   1935-

PERSONAL: Born May 3, 1935, in Summit, N.J.; son of Clifford H. (a herpetologist and writer) and Sarah (Davis) Pope; married Christine Anne Farnham (a historian), July 15, 1961; children: Dulany Lucetta, Delanie Penrose, Whitney Bancroft, Norwood Braxton. *Education:* University of Chicago, B.A., 1958, M.A., 1962; University of California, Berkeley, Ph.D., 1970. *Home:* 2994 Bankers Dr., Bloomington, Ind. 47401. *Office:* Department of Sociology, Indiana University, Ballantine Hall, Bloomington, Ind. 47401.

CAREER: University of California, Berkeley, acting instructor in sociology, 1967-68; Indiana University, Bloomington, lecturer, 1969-70, assistant professor, 1970-75, associate professor of sociology, 1975—. *Military service:* U.S. Army, 1955-57. *Member:* American Sociological Association.

WRITINGS: Durkheim's "Suicide": A Classic Analyzed, University of Chicago Press, 1976. Contributor to sociology journals. Associate editor of *American Sociological Review,* 1976-78.

WORK IN PROGRESS: Durkheim on Social Integration: A Study in Theory, a monograph; research on Durkheim, Weber, Tocqueville, and on the empirical validity of Dur-

kheim's theory of suicide; research on domination, integration, and lynchings in the South.

*   *   *

PORT, M(ichael) H.   1930-

PERSONAL: Born 1930, in England; married, 1962; children: two daughters. *Education:* Hertford College, Oxford, B.A., 1954, B.Litt., 1956, M.A., 1957. *Office:* Queen Mary College, University of London, Mile End Rd., London E1 4NS, England.

CAREER: University of London, Queen Mary College, London, England, 1961—, served as assistant lecturer and lecturer, currently senior lecturer in history. Visiting professor at Columbia University, 1968-69.

WRITINGS: Six Hundred New Churches, S.P.C.K., 1961; (with others) *The History of the King's Works,* Volume VI: *1782-1851,* H.M.S.O., 1973; (editor) *The Houses of Parliament,* Yale University Press, 1976. Contributor to history journals. Editor of *East London Papers,* 1965-70.

WORK IN PROGRESS: Building in Victorian London.

*   *   *

PORTER, Darwin (Fred)   1937-

PERSONAL: Born September 13, 1937, in Greensboro, N.C.; son of Numie Rowan (a builder) and Hazel (an artist; maiden name, Phillips) Porter; *Education:* University of Miami, Coral Gables, Fla., B.A., 1959. *Politics:* Democrat. *Home:* 75 St. Marks Pl., Staten Island, N.Y. 10301.

CAREER: Miami Herald, Miami, Fla., bureau chief, 1959-60; Frommer-Pasmantier Publishing Corp., New York, N.Y., editor, 1961—. *Member:* Sigma Delta Chi.

WRITINGS: Butterflies in Heat (novel), Manor Books, 1976.

All travel guides, all published by Frommer-Pasmantier: *England on $15 a Day,* 1964; *Spain and Morocco on $10 & $15 a Day,* 1966; *Scandinavia on $20 a Day,* 1967; *Dollar-Wise Guide to Portugal,* 1968; *Dollar-Wise Guide to Italy,* 1969; *Dollar-Wise Guide to England,* 1969; *Getaway Guide to Los Angeles,* 1969; *Getaway Guide to London,* 1970; *Dollar-Wise Guide to Germany,* 1970; *Dollar-Wise Guide to France,* 1970; *Getaway Guide to Lisbon/Madrid/Costa del Sol,* 1972; *Getaway Guide to Paris,* 1972; *Getaway Guide to Rome,* 1974; *Frommer's Guide to London,* 1977; *Frommer's Guide to Paris,* 1977; *Frommer's Guide to Lisbon/Madrid,* 1977; *Frommer's Guide to Rome,* 1977.

Contributor of articles to *Fun in Florida, After Dark, Travel, Latin Times, Ultra* and *Holiday.*

WORK IN PROGRESS: A novel, *Moonlight and Chaos,* the saga of a literary goddess.

SIDELIGHTS: Darwin Porter's assignments have included coverage of Cuban guerilla training camps in 1960, and interviews with such subjects as Eleanor Roosevelt, Robert Frost, Tennessee Williams, Harry S Truman, Richard Nixon, Sophie Tucker, Adlai Stevenson, and Lucille Ball. "I was an early Rex Reed," Porter says. "But when I wrote that a star conducted an interview in the nude, my copy was cleaned up. That was considered racy back then."

He lives in a "historic 18-room gabled and shingled house with verandas," on a street where Theodore Dreiser once lived and Henry James used to vacation.

PORTER, McKenzie 1911-

PERSONAL: Born October 21, 1911, in England; son of John McKenzie and Amy (Smith) Porter; married Kathleen Gathercole, September 5, 1936; children: Timothy McKenzie, Gathercole. *Education:* Educated in England. *Home address:* R.R. 1, Sharon, Ontario, Canada. *Agent:* Canadian Speakers and Writers Service, 44 Douglas Cres., Toronto, Ontario, Canada. *Office: Toronto Sun,* 333 King St. E., Toronto, Ontario, Canada.

CAREER: Reporter for British newspapers, including *Evening Chronicle, Daily Express, Daily Mirror, Evening Standard,* and Kemsley Newspapers Ltd., 1929-39; Kemsley Newspapers Ltd., London, Paris correspondent, 1946-48; *Macleans,* Toronto, Ontario, staff writer, 1950-61; *Toronto Telegram,* Toronto, Ontario, author of daily column, 1961-71; *Toronto Sun,* Toronto, Ontario, author of weekly theater column, 1971—, column also syndicated by Toronto Sun Services. Covered Saar Plebiscite, 1934, Olympic games in Berlin, 1936, the coronation of King George VI, 1937, the Spanish Civil War, 1939, and the wedding of Queen Elizabeth II, 1947. Has made television and radio commentaries. Trustee of East Gwillimbury Library Board. *Military service:* British Army, Cameronians, 1939-45; became lieutenant; served in Sicily; received Military Cross.

MEMBER: Royal Society of Arts (fellow), Toronto Drama Bench. *Awards, honors:* Gold Medal from City of Rome, Italy, for best article about Rome by a foreigner; president's medal from University of Western Ontario, for best article in Canada.

WRITINGS: Overture to Victoria, Longman's Canada, 1961. Contributor of more than two hundred articles to *Macleans.*

SIDELIGHTS: Porter has traveled in India, South Africa, Japan, Hong Kong, Australia, New Zealand, the Middle East, and all of western Europe but Scandinavia. He is especially interested in military affairs, theater, and Regency history. *Avocational interests:* Growing trees and raising pheasants on his small country estate.

BIOGRAPHICAL/CRITICAL SOURCES: Oxford Companion to Canadian History and Literature, Oxford University Press, 1967; *Treasury of Canadian Humor,* McClelland & Stewart, 1967.

* * *

PORTER, Philip W(iley) 1900-

PERSONAL: Born August 7, 1900, in Portsmouth, Va.; son of Albert S. and Lena May (Edmonds) Porter; married Annanette Blue Riggs, September 19, 1922 (divorced December 12, 1941); married Dorothy Rutka (an artist), April 5, 1960; children: Ann Porter Sommers, Susan Porter Wood, Mary Helen Porter Schaeffer. *Education:* Ohio State University, B.Sc., 1922. *Home and office:* 2830 Lee Rd., Shaker Heights, Ohio 44120.

CAREER: Cleveland Plain Dealer, Cleveland, Ohio, reporter, 1918-23, copy editor, 1923-24, political writer and legislative correspondent, 1924-29, day city editor, 1929-37, news editor, 1937-42, assistant Sunday editor, 1946-53, Sunday and feature editor, 1953-62, managing editor, 1962-63, executive editor, 1963-66, author of column "Inside the News," 1934-66; writer, 1966-70; Sunpapers, Cleveland, Ohio, author of column "Sun-day With Porter," 1970—. Member of Ohio Water Development Authority, 1968-74; foreman of Cuyahoga County Grand Jury, 1973. Covered Bikini atomic bomb tests in 1946, and accompanied Berlin airlift, 1949. *Military service:* U.S. Army Air Forces, 1942-45, briefing officer at British Ministry of Information, 1944-45; served in North Africa, Italy, and England; became lieutenant colonel; received Bronze Star Medal. U.S. Air Force Reserve, 1946-52.

MEMBER: American Association of Sunday and Feature Editors (president, 1961-62), Comics Council (chairman, 1962-64), City Club of Cleveland (president, 1939-40; founder of Forum Foundation and member of its board of trustees, 1940—; president of Foundation, 1968-76), Cleveland Advertising Club (president, 1957-58), Ohio State Alumni Association (member of board of directors, 1965-70), Sigma Delta Chi (Cleveland president, 1950-52), Pi Delta Epsilon, Sigma Phi Epsilon, Sphinx, Bucket and Dipper, Sons of the American Revolution, American Legion, Masons. *Awards, honors:* Wolfe Medal in Journalism from Robert F. Wolfe Foundation, 1922, for excellence in college journalism; governor's award from Ohio Newspaper Association, 1966; distinguished service citation from Sigma Phi Epsilon, 1968; distinguished achievement award from Ohio State University, 1970; distinguished service award from Sigma Delta Chi, 1974.

WRITINGS: (With Norval Neil Luxon) *The Reporter and the News* (college text), D. Appleton-Century, 1935; *Cleveland: Confused City on a Seesaw,* Ohio State University Press, 1976. Editor, *Ohio State Lantern;* former associate editor of *Sundial* and *Makio.*

WORK IN PROGRESS: An autobiography.

* * *

PORTER, William E. 1918-

PERSONAL; Born October 12, 1918, in Chetopa, Kan.; married Lois Tallman; children: James Stuart, Elizabeth Susan. *Education:* University of Kansas, B.A., 1939; University of Alabama, M.A., 1940. *Politics:* Democrat. *Religion:* "Non-believer." *Office:* Department of Journalism, University of Michigan, Ann Arbor, Mich. 48104.

CAREER: Washington State College, Pullman, instructor in speech and dramatic art, 1942-43; State University of Iowa, Iowa City, lecturer, 1944-49, instructor, 1950-51, assistant professor, 1951-55, associate professor, 1955-60, professor of magazine writing, 1960-62; University of Michigan, Ann Arbor, professor of journalism, 1962—, chairman of department, 1966-73. Lecturer at New York University, 1950; Fulbright lecturer at University of Rome, 1952-53; visiting professor at Stanford University, spring, 1972. Member of executive committee of Center for the Study of Conflict Resolution. Intern for Time, Inc., 1949, special assignment writer, 1951. Project director of Educational Policies Commission, 1956-58; assistant director of National Citizens Commission for the Public Schools, 1950; member of advisory committee of Academy for Educational Development. *Member:* Association for Education in Journalism (president, 1964).

WRITINGS: The Lawbringers (novel), Appleton, 1954; *Mass Communication and Education,* Educational Policies Commission, 1957; (editor with John D. Stevens) *The Rest of the Elephant: Perspectives on the Mass Media,* Prentice-Hall, 1973; *Assault on the Media: The Nixon Years,* University of Michigan Press, 1976. Contributor to *Encyclopedia of the Social Sciences.* Contributor of more than fifty articles and stories to *Anesthesiology* and to popular magazines in the United States and abroad, including *Saturday Evening Post, Collier's,* and *Cosmopolitan.* Chairman of editorial board of *Journal of Conflict Resolution.*

WORK IN PROGRESS: The Italian Journalist.

SIDELIGHTS: Porter comments that he began his writing career in 1936 with the pulp fiction magazines. He adds that he has developed a "continuing interest in the role of the media in society, particularly the national government-media relationship. Although recent work has been scholarly, I retain an interest in writing novels." *Avocational interests:* Travel in Italy, Italian politics.

* * *

POWELL, Evan Arnold 1937-

PERSONAL: Born September 5, 1937, in Asheville, N.C.; son of Arnold Elmore (an electrical engineer) and Mary (Reighard) Powell; married Ann Shaver, September 4, 1956 (divorced, August, 1968); married Cema Chapman (a teacher), December 20, 1969; children: Angie, Trip, Scott. *Education:* North Carolina State University, student, 1954-55; Furman University, B.A., 1958. *Religion:* Presbyterian. *Home:* 108 Morningdale Dr., Greenville, S.C. 29609. *Office:* Morningdale Studios, 108 Morningdale Dr., Greenville, S.C. 29609.

CAREER: Sears, Roebuck & Co., Greenville, S.C., technical service director, 1959-73; *How-to-Homeowner's Handbook,* New York, N.Y., contributing editor, 1973—. Feature writer for Times Mirror Magazines (*Popular Science*), 1968-73, Southeast editor, 1973—. Producer and commentator for television features, including "Update," "Bill Wheless Show," and "Scrunch Workshop." Instructor at Greenville Technical College, 1967-70. *Member:* American Society of Journalists and Authors. *Awards, honors:* Awards from Association of Home Appliance Manufacturers, 1972, 1973, and 1975, for excellence in consumer education; award from Major Appliance Consumer's Action Panel, 1975.

WRITINGS: Complete Guide to Home Appliance Repair, Harper, 1974. Author of columns "Housepower" in *Popular Science* and "Checkpoint" in *How-to-Homeowner's Handbook.* Contributing editor, *Popular Science Motorcamping Handbook,* 1976—. Contributor to *Popular Science Homeowner's Encyclopedia* and *The How-to Homeowner's Treasury.* Contributor to popular magazines, including *Sandlapper, Carolina Outdoors, Off Duty, Consumer's Guide,* and *Spotlight.*

SIDELIGHTS: Powell writes: "My motivation for writing is that I find it to be a way of sharing. Everywhere I look, I see two types of people—those who are in need of information and those who have information that needs to reach other people. Through my career, I can communicate that which I have learned (often the hard way), sometimes enabling others to accomplish things or aspire to goals that they could not have attained previously. At other times, it is a way of assisting someone else to reach out with their message or knowledge. The true reward is when you hear from those who have, through their own efforts, attained a fuller lifestyle or sometimes even raised their standard of living when armed with proper information."

* * *

POWELL, William S(tevens) 1919-

PERSONAL: Born April 28, 1919, in Johnston County, N.C.; son of Isaac Millard and Ada (Perry) Powell; married Virginia Penn Waldrop, June 14, 1952; children: John Waldrop, Charles Stevens IV, Ellen Ashley. *Education:* University of North Carolina, A.B., 1940, M.A. and B.S. in L.S., both 1947. *Politics:* Democrat. *Religion:* Episcopalian. *Home:* 307 Plum Lane, Chapel Hill, N.C. 27514. *Office:* Department of History, University of North Carolina, Chapel Hill, N.C. 27514.

CAREER: Statesville Daily, Statesville, N.C., reporter, 1941, 1945; State Department of Archives and History, Raleigh, N.C., researcher, 1949-51; University of North Carolina, Chapel Hill, librarian for North Carolina collection, 1951-58, curator of collection, 1958-73, lecturer, 1964-73, professor of history, 1973—. Member of North Carolina Highway Historical Marker Advisory Committee, 1951—. Member of board of governors of University of North Carolina Press, 1960—. *Military service:* U.S. Army, 1941-45; became master sergeant.

MEMBER: Southern Historical Association, Historical Society of North Carolina (president), North Carolina Literary and Historical Association (president), Roanoke Island Historical Association (historian). *Awards, honors:* Guggenheim fellowship, 1956; Cannon Cup from North Carolina Historic Preservation Society, 1957; Crittenden Cup from North Carolina Literary and Historical Association, 1972; award of merit from American Association for State and Local History, 1973, for *The First State University.*

WRITINGS: (Editor) *North Carolina Fiction, 1734-1957: An Annotated Bibliography,* Library, University of North Carolina, 1958; *Ye Countie of Albemarle in Carolina: A Collection of Documents, 1665-1675,* North Carolina State Department of Archives and History, 1958; *Annals of Progress: The Story of Lenoir County and Kingston, North Carolina,* North Carolina State Department of Archives and History, 1963; *Paradise Preserved,* University of North Carolina Press, 1965; *North Carolina* (juvenile), F. Watts, 1966; *The North Carolina Gazetteer,* University of North Carolina Press, 1968, revised edition, 1976; *The North Carolina Colony,* Crowell-Collier, 1969; (with James K. Huhta and Thomas J. Farnham) *The Regulators in North Carolina: A Documentary History, 1759-1776,* North Carolina State Department of Archives and History, 1971; *The First State University; A Pictorial History of the University of North Carolina,* University of North Carolina Press, 1972; (with Hugh T. Lefler) *Colonial North Carolina, a History,* Scribner, 1973; *John Pory, 1572-1636: The Life and Letters of a Man of Many Parts,* University of North Carolina Press, 1977; *When the Past Refused to Die: A History of Caswell County, North Carolina, 1777-1977,* Moore Publishing, 1977; (editor) *Dictionary of North Carolina Biography,* Volume I: *A-C,* University of North Carolina Press, 1977; *North Carolina: A Bicentennial History,* Norton, in press; *The Papers of Governor William Tryon,* two volumes, North Carolina Division of Archives and History, in press.

Author or editor of about twenty pamphlets on North Carolina history. Author of column "News of History" in *American Heritage,* 1950-55. Contributor to *Encyclopedia Americana Yearbook, Encyclopaedia Britannica,* and *Dictionary of American History.* Contributor of about forty articles to history journals, church magazines, and *American Heritage.* Editor of *History News,* 1949-57.

WORK IN PROGRESS: Editing *Dictionary of North Carolina Biography,* Volumes II-VIII, for University of North Carolina Press.

POWERS, John J(ames) 1945-
(John R. Powers)

PERSONAL: Born November 30, 1945, in Chicago, Ill.; son of John Francis (an automobile salesman) and June (a real estate broker; maiden name, Tampier) Powers. *Education:* Loyola University, B.S., 1967; Northwestern University, M.A., 1969, Ph.D., 1975. *Residence:* Downers Grove, Ill. *Office:* Northeastern Illinois University, 5500 North St. Louis Ave., Chicago, Ill. 60625.

CAREER: Elementary and junior high school teacher in Chicago, Ill., 1967-68; Northeastern Illinois University, Chicago, assistant professor of speech, 1972—. Writer. *Awards, honors: Do Black Patent Leather Shoes Really Reflect Up?* was selected for inclusion on American Library Association's list of Best Books for Young Adults, 1975, and for inclusion on University of Iowa's "Books for Young Adults" poll, 1976.

WRITINGS—Novels; under name John R. Powers: *The Last Catholic in America*, Saturday Review Press, 1973; *Do Black Patent Leather Shoes Really Reflect Up?*, Regnery, 1975; *The Original Sinver and the Ice Cream God*, Regnery, in press. Weekly columnist for *Chicago Daily News*, 1977—. Contributor of articles and short stories to magazines, including *Chicago, Travel and Leisure, Scouting,* and *Chicago Tribune Magazine.*

SIDELIGHTS: Powers, who described himself as "a product of sixteen years of Catholic education," graduated in the bottom twentieth of his high school class and was the only student in the school's history to flunk music appreciation. His two books, *The Last Catholic in America* and *Do Black Patent Leather Shoes Really Reflect Up?* are, as he called them, fictionalized memoirs recalling elementary and high school days respectively. Martin Levin praised *The Last Catholic in America* as "a well balanced mixture of pleasure and pain." He also commented: "Out of the questionable experience of elementary school, John R. Powers has salvaged a delightful reminiscence. This puts the author one up on the run of survivors of childhood, who—as a rule—have nothing to show for their misery but undeserved nostalgia."

BIOGRAPHICAL/CRITICAL SOURCES: New York Times Book Review, April 22, 1973; *Kirkus Reviews,* August 25, 1975.

* * *

PRANCE, June E(lizebeth) 1929-
(Elizabeth Shaw)

PERSONAL: Born June 29, 1929, in England; came to U.S. in 1956; daughter of George Herbert and Beatrice (Hill) Shaw; married Dewey W. Prance (newspaperman); children: Brian, Marilyn Prance Hernandez, David, John, Michael, Nancy, Dewey, Jr., Cathryn. *Education:* Hudderfield Polytechnic, England, non-degree graduate, 1944; attended Victoria College, Toronto, Canada, 1947-48; Florida State University, B.A., 1972; University of South Florida, graduate study, 1972—. *Politics:* "Non-voter, English citizen. Am ultra-conservative." *Religion:* "Christian—Baptist Church." *Home:* 1221 East Hamilton Ave., Tampa, Fla. 33604. *Office:* Tampa Bay Vocational-Technical High School, Tampa, Fla. 33610.

CAREER: Sarasota News, Sarasota, Fla., promotional artist and columnist, 1957-61; Tampa Tribune Co., Tampa, Fla., promotional artist and news writer, 1961-66; Tampa Bay Vocational-Technical High School, Tampa, instructor

in commercial art, 1966—. Free-lance writer. Illustrator. Lecturer at schools and colleges in United States and England. Judge at professional art shows. Consultant for graphic design projects for Florida Department of Education; graphic designer for local Alcoholic Abuse Center.

MEMBER: Women in Communications, Society of Children's Book Writers, National Association for Art Education Classroom Teachers Association, Travel Writers International, Florida Vocational Association, National Writer's Club, British Amateur Press Association, American Amateur Press Association. *Awards, honors:* Numerous awards for graphic design, art, and store decoration.

WRITINGS: (Self-illustrated) *Traditional British Recipes for the American Cook,* Union Jack Publishing, 1971; (contributor) *The Gift,* Northwoods Press (Minnesota), 1973; (contributor) *Northwoods Journal,* Northwoods Press, 1973-76; (contributor) *The Butterflies,* Northwoods Press, 1974; (editor) *Odyssey 1974,* Northwoods Press, 1974. Also illustrator of books by others.

Author of "Sarasota Sound Box," a column in *Sarasota News,* 1957-61. Contributor of articles to periodicals, sometimes under the pseudonym Elizabeth Shaw, including *Washington Post, Toronto Daily Star,* and *Women's Wear Daily.* Editor of *Florida Business Opportunities* (monthly), 1976—.

WORK IN PROGRESS: A quarterly magazine aimed at British citizens living in the United States and Canada; a vocational education magazine for the state of Florida.

SIDELIGHTS: Mrs. Prance told *CA:* "If you've read this far, you'll have concluded that I'm vitally interested in graphic art, education, travel and writing—not to mention children. Having eight of my own leads me to feel that I understand kids pretty well. I also *like* young people—otherwise, why teach? I'm lucky to be able to combine all of my interests and get paid a half-decent salary while doing it. I teach all forms of the creative graphic arts and this lets me demonstrate my own ideas and talents while communicating my knowledge and experience to my students. My hours are flexible enough so that I have time to devote to my writing career and since I don't work during the summer months, it allows me time to travel anywhere I please. Naturally, part, if not all, of my travel expenses are met by selling travel articles to newspapers all over the world."

* * *

PRATT, Charles 1926(?)-1976

PERSONAL: Married Julie Folansbee; children: Michael. *Education:* Yale University, received degree, 1948. *Residence:* New York, N.Y.

CAREER: Photographer, writer. Worked as stage manager of several Broadway productions, including "The Consul," "The Boyfriend," and "Take a Giant Step"; photographs have been exhibited in shows at Cobert Gallery, Metropolitan Museum of Art, the Neikring, Expo '67, and Floating Foundation of Photography; co-founder of Image Gallery. *Wartime service:* American field volunteer with the British Army; served in Italy during World War II.

WRITINGS: (With own photographs) *Here On the Island: Being an Account of a Way of Life Several Miles Off the Maine Coast,* Harper, 1974. Contributor of photographs to Rachel Louise Carson, *The Sense of Wonder,* 1965, Phillip Ressner, *At Night,* Dutton, 1967, and Carson, *The Rocky Coast,* McCall, 1971. Contributor of photographs to periodicals, including *Life, Fortune, 35mm,* and *Audubon.*

OBITUARIES: New York Times, May 26, 1976; A.B. Bookman's, July 5, 1976.*

(Died May 5, 1976, in New York, N.Y.)

* * *

PREISS, Byron (Cary)

PERSONAL: Born in New York, N.Y.; son of Edmund (an attorney) and Pearl (a corporate officer) Preiss. Education: University of Pennsylvania, B.A. (honors), 1973; Stanford University, M.A., 1974. Religion: Jewish. Home and office: 680 Fifth Ave., New York, N.Y. 10019. Agent: Sterling Lord, Sterling Lord Agency, Inc., 660 Madison Ave., New York, N.Y. 10021.

CAREER: National Periodical Publications, Inc., New York City, director of EDUgraphics program, 1970; Children's Television Workshop, New York City, editor and writer for "Electric Company," 1972-73; elementary school teacher in Philadelphia, Pa., 1973; American Broadcasting Co. (ABC-Television), San Francisco, Calif., head writer, 1974; writer and director of own films, 1974-76; Harcourt, Brace, Jovanovich, Inc., New York, N.Y., editor, 1976—. Guest speaker, 1977—. Member: Mystery Writer's Guild of America, Academy of Comic Book Arts, Sigma Alpha Mu, Friar's Club.

WRITINGS: The Electric Company Joke Book (juvenile), Western Publishing, 1973; The Silent "E's" from Outer Space (juvenile), Western Publishing, 1973; (editor and contributor) Weird Heroes, Pyramid Publications, Volume I, 1974, Volume II, 1975, Volume III (with Ron Goulart): Quest of the Gypsy, 1976, Volume IV: Nightshade, 1976, Volume V: Phoenix, 1977, Volume VI, 1977; (editor) Schlomo Raven (adult), Pyramid Publications, 1976; (with Ralph Reese) The One Year Affair (adult), Workman Publishing, 1976; Fiction Illustrated (adult), four volumes, Pyramid Publications, 1976; Starfawn (science fiction), Pyramid Publications, 1976; Son of Sherlock Holmes (mystery), Pyramid Publications, 1977. Author of screenplays, "Five on the Feiffer Side" and "Hunger."

WORK IN PROGRESS: Dragonworld, a fantasy novel for adults, for Harcourt; editing a book on growing up in America, for Harcourt.

SIDELIGHTS: Preiss writes that he has "spent much time working with children in a school room environment, developing solutions to learning problems using visual materials; this resulted in more sophisticated and extensive work with the Children's Television Workshop and National Periodicals and the emergence of a new reading technology involving the use of the comic book medium to support traditional learning activities."

BIOGRAPHICAL/CRITICAL SOURCES: New York Times Book Review, March, 1974; Mediascene, summer, 1976; Tales of Texas, winter, 1976; Los Angeles Times, January 2, 1977; Ellery Queen Mystery Magazine, February, 1977.

* * *

PREISS, David (Lee) 1935-

PERSONAL: Surname is pronounced "price"; born June 22, 1935, in Milwaukee, Wis.; son of Elmer Charles (an engineer) and Delores (Creuz) Preiss; married Eleanor Osborne (a secretary), February 15, 1958 (separated); children: Nora Susan, Jennifer Emily. Education: University of Wisconsin, student, 1953-57; New School for Social Research, student, 1969-71. Politics: Pacifist—Anarchist. Religion: Agnostic.

Home: 4 Jones St., New York, N.Y. 10014. Office: American Artist, 1515 Broadway, New York, N.Y. 10036.

CAREER/WRITINGS: Playboy (magazine), Chicago, Ill, college bureau manager, 1957-60; Collage (magazine), Chicago, editor and publisher, 1960-61; Grune & Stratton, New York City, editor, 1961-63; Motor Boating (magazine), New York City, production editor, 1963-66; American Artist (magazine), New York City, production editor, 1966-68, managing editor, 1969—. Author of "Art Books" column in American Artist. Contributor of articles to American Artist and American Way. Editor and board member, Media Mobilization, 1969-70. President, Boerum Hill Association, 1967; recording secretary, Brooklyn Heights Youth Center, 1969. Member: Society of Publication Designers.

SIDELIGHTS: Preiss covered the Mayday demonstrations in 1971. He lists his professional interests as: "pacifism, linear art, graphics, grass roots government, ecology, alternatives to censorship, nuclear energy, and war." He says that he is most motiviated by Thomas Paine, William Morris, and James M. Whistler. Avocational interests: Political pamphleteering and keeping a personal library of illustrated books and magazines.

* * *

PRENTISS, Augustin M. 1890-1977

1890—April 13, 1977; American patent lawyer, U.S. Army general, and author of a book on chemical warfare. He died in Hartford, Conn. Obituaries: Washington Post, April 16, 1977.

* * *

PREVERT, Jacques 1900-1977

February 4, 1900—April 11, 1977; French poet, screen writer, and author of children's books; collaborated with Marcel Carne on eight films; his books of poetry were bestsellers in France. He died in Omonville-La-Petite, France. Obituaries: New York Times, April 12, 1977; AB Bookman's Weekly, June 20, 1977.

* * *

PRICE, V(incent) B(arrett) 1940-

PERSONAL: Born August 30, 1940, in Los Angeles, Calif.; son of Vincent (an actor and lecturer) and Edith (Barrett) Price; married Nancy Rini (an artist), 1969; children: Jody, Keir. Education: University of New Mexico, B.A., 1962, graduate study, 1962-70; National University of Mexico, graduate study, summer, 1960. Home: 2026 Candelaria Rd. N.W., Albuquerque, N.M. 87107.

CAREER: Human Resources Institue, Albuquerque, N.M., director of education and instructor in English and philosophy, 1962-66; Albuquerque Tribune, Albuquerque, N.M., acting assistant city editor, reporter, and reviewer, 1966-67; Westinghouse Learning Corp., Albuquerque, N.M., technical editor, 1967-69; Albuquerque Model Cities Program, Albuquerque, N.M., director of arts and cultural program, 1969-70; New Mexico Independent, Albuquerque, N.M., author of column "City Review" and reviewer, 1971—. High school lecturer, 1974; lecturer at University of New Mexico, 1975-76. Member of board of trustees of Museum of Albuquerque. Member: Poetry Society of America. Awards, honors: Award from New Mexico Press Association, 1967, for straight news reporting; award of honor from New Mexico Society of Architects, 1974, and from the Governor's Cultural Properties Review Committee, 1975.

WRITINGS: The Cyclops' Garden (poems), San Marcos Press, 1969; (editor and contributor) *The Vincent Price Treasury of American Art*, Country Beautiful Press, 1972; *Semblances* (poems), Sunstone Press, 1976. Contributor of poems and translations (into Brazilian Portuguese) to several dozen literary journals and newspapers, including *New Mexico Quarterly, Calcutta Review, Fiddlehead, Discourse, Southwest Review*, and *Wild Dog*.

WORK IN PROGRESS: Several nonfiction works; a mystery novel.

* * *

PRINDL, A(ndreas) R(obert) 1939-

PERSONAL: Born November 25, 1939, in Decatur, Ill.; son of Frank Joseph (a professor) and Vivian (a teacher; maiden name, Mitchell) Prindl; married Veronica Maria Koerber (a weaver), September 12, 1963; children: Karin Anne, Christopher Andreas. *Education:* Attended University of Bonn, 1958-59; Princeton University, B.A. (magna cum laude), 1961; London School of Economics and Political Science, University of London, graduate study, 1963-64; University of Kentucky, M.A., 1963, Ph.D., 1964. *Religion:* Church of England. *Home:* 3-20 Minami Azabu 5-chome, Tokyo 106, Japan. *Office:* Morgan Guaranty Trust Co., 12-1, Yurakucho 1-chome, Chiyoda-ku, Tokyo 100, Japan.

CAREER: Morgan Guaranty Trust Co., New York, N.Y., worked in international banking division, 1964-66, assistant treasurer in Frankfurt, Germany, 1966-70, assistant vice-president in London, England, 1970-72, vice-president, 1972-76, head of International Money Management Group, 1972-76, general manager of Tokyo office, 1976—. Instructor at Pace College, 1964-66; lecturer at University of Maryland (overseas), 1969-70. *Member:* Yomiuri International Economic Society, American Economic Association, Japan-America Society, Tokyo Lawn Tennis Club, American Chamber of Commerce in Japan.

WRITINGS: (With M. J. Wasserman and C. C. Townsend, Jr.) *International Money Management*, American Management Association, 1972; *Foreign Exchange Risk*, Wiley, 1976. Contributor to business and accounting journals.

* * *

PRINGLE, Peter 1940-

PERSONAL: Born June 28, 1940, in England; son of Herbert John (an air force officer) and Leslie (White) Pringle. *Education:* Oxford University, B.A. (honors), 1962. *Home:* 84 Riverside Dr., New York, N.Y. 10024. *Office: London Sunday Times*, 201 East 42nd St., New York, N.Y. 10017.

CAREER: London Sunday Times, London, England, reporter, 1968-75, New York City bureau chief, 1975—.

WRITINGS: (With others) *Insight on Middle East War*, Viking, 1974; (with others) *Insight on Portugal*, Deutsch, 1974; (with Peter Cole) *Can You Positively Identify This Man?: George Ince and the Barn Murder*, Deutsch, 1975.

AVOCATIONAL INTERESTS: Cooking, walking, sailing, flying, collecting fossils.

* * *

PRUSINA, Katica 1935-

PERSONAL: Born November 20, 1935, in Velika Ilova, Yugoslavia; daughter of Stojan (a carpenter) and Ivka Prusina. *Education:* Educated in Rijeka, Yugoslavia. *Politics:* "Not involved." *Religion:* "Not involved." *Home:* 64 Eade

Road, London N.4, England. *Office:* American Express, Oxford St., London W.1, England.

CAREER: Has worked as a representative for an English company in Russia, and as travel agent for American Express, London, England.

WRITINGS: (Co-author with Peggy Mann) *A Present for Yanya* (children's book), Random House, 1975.

WORK IN PROGRESS: Short stories.

* * *

PUTNAM, Roy Clayton 1928-

PERSONAL: Born February 12, 1928, in Greensboro, N.C.; son of James Clyde (a mill worker) and Nellic (Edmondson) Putnam; married Elflada Bunting, June 11, 1949; children: Rendal Clayton, Marcus Bryan. *Education:* High Point College, A.B., 1949, Duke University, M.Div., 1952. *Home:* 2614 Deer Pl., Greensboro, N.C. 27407. *Office:* 2227 Pinecroft Rd., Greensboro, N.C. 27407.

CAREER: Pastor of Trinity United Methodist church in Greensboro, N.C., 1949—. Writer.

WRITINGS: In It to Win, Christian Literature Crusade, 1973; *Getting It All Together*, Abingdon, 1976; *Life Is a Celebration*, Impact, 1976.

WORK IN PROGRESS: Those He Came To Save, for Abingdon, publication expected in 1978.

* * *

QUENEAU, Raymond 1903-1976

February 21, 1903—October 25, 1976; French editor and author of novels, poetry, plays, songs, screenplays, and essays. Once associated with the Surrealist movement, he introduced colloquial language into his literary works—and sometimes spelled words the way they are pronounced. He became the top editor of one of France's leading publishing houses, Librarie Gallimard and was one of the most influential literary figures in France. Among his most popular works are *Zazie dan le metro* and *Exercises de style*. He died in Paris, France. Obituaries: *New York Times*, October 26, 1976; *AB Bookman's Weekly*, January 3, 1977.

* * *

QUIGLEY, Carroll 1910-1977

November 9, 1910—January 3, 1977; American educator and author of books in the field of history. He died in Washington, D.C. Obituaries: *Washington Post*, January 6, 1977. (See index for previous *CA* sketch)

* * *

QUINT, Bert 1930-

PERSONAL: Born September 22, 1930, in New York, N.Y.; son of George (a journalist) and Sadye (Slonim) Quint; married Janet Elias, June, 1952 (divorced); Consuelo Giner de los Rios, May 14, 1958 (divorced); Diane Schwab, April 10, 1975; children: Lara, Amy. *Education:* New York University, B.S., 1952. *Politics:* None. *Religion:* None. *Office:* CBS News, Via Condotti 61/A, Rome, Italy.

CAREER: Worcester Telegram, Worcester, Mass., reporter, 1952-53; Associated Press, Columbus, Ohio, editor, 1953-54; *New York Herald Tribune*, New York, N.Y., reporter, 1956-58; free lance reporter in Latin America, 1958-65; Columbia Broadcasting System (CBS) News, New York City, roving correspondent based in Mexico City, 1965-70,

Rome, 1970—. Notable assignments include Dominican Republic Civil War, 1965, India-Pakistan Wars, 1965 and 1971, Indo China, 1967-71, and Mid-East War, 1973.

SIDELIGHTS: CA asked Quint if he knew of any instances where his reporting changed the outcome of the event he was covering. One instance he mentioned was the coverage of American intervention in Santo Domingo, 1965, where Quint was "one of a half dozen correspondents credited (or blamed?) with forcing Washington to withdraw overt aid to rightist forces there." Quint also "was one of first American reporters to call Viet Nam War a stalemate, 1967, and other reports added to the bulk of pressure for American withdrawal."

"I must say here," Quint continued, "that I do not believe that it is the reporter's mission to influence outcomes of events, but that it is his job to present facts, pros and cons, helping public and/or governments to assess situations."

* * *

RABEN, Joseph 1924-

PERSONAL: Born September 3, 1924, in New York, N.Y.; son of Abraham (a pharmacist) and Frances (a teacher; maiden name, Goldner) Raben; married Marguerite Bloch (an editor), June 8, 1952; children: Jeremy, Elizabeth. *Education:* University of Wisconsin, B.A., 1944; Indiana University, M.A., 1949, Ph.D., 1954. *Home:* 46 Baker Hill Rd., Great Neck, N.Y. 11023. *Office:* Department of English, Queens College of the City University of New York, Flushing, N.Y. 11367.

CAREER: Princeton University, Princeton, N.J., instructor in English, 1952-54; Queens College of the City University of New York, Flushing, N.Y., instructor, 1954-61, assistant professor, 1962-67, associate professor, 1967-70, professor of English, 1970—. Philips lecturer, Haverford College, 1968; visiting lecturer, University of Pisa, 1970, 1972. Chairman of working group on humanities of International Federation of Information Processing, 1971—; member of advisory committee to Associated Universities on national institute for information systems, 1968. Consultant to International Business Machines Corp., 1964, and to RAND Corp., 1969. *Military service:* U.S. Army, 1945-46; editor of translations in Tokyo, 1946. *Member:* Modern Language Association of America, American Society for Information Science, Association for Computational Linguistics, Association for Literary and Linguistic Computing (member of advisory board). *Awards, honors:* American Council of Learned Societies fellow for computer-oriented research in humanities, 1964.

WRITINGS: (Contributor) George Gerbner and others, editors, *The Analysis of Communication Content,* Wiley, 1969; (contributor) Carlos A. Cuadra, editor, *Annual Review of Information Science and Technology,* Encyclopaedia Britannica for American Society for Information Science, 1971; (editor) *Computer-Oriented Humanistic Research, 1966-1972,* Pergamon, 1976. Founder and editor of *Computers and the Humanities* journal, 1966—.

SIDELIGHTS: Raben writes: "The motivation to establish a journal to further the interaction of computers and humanistic research was a recognition that each field would ultimately appreciate its need for the other. Complex machinery requires imaginative, inquiring minds to exploit its potential; the humanities require all the aid that technology can supply for the routine functions that support the high-level activity: indexes, concordances, bibliographies, text collations, photocomposition. In my editorial and authorial activities, I have sought to explain the benefits of this interaction to appropriate audiences around the world."

* * *

RADL, Shirley L(ouise) 1935-

PERSONAL: Born August 24, 1935, in Calif.; daughter of Robert C. (a contractor) and Henrietta Joyce (Kenna) Rogers; married Calvin A. Radl (an engineer), October 20, 1956; children: Lisa, Adam. *Politics:* Democrat. *Home:* 220 Miramonte Ave., Palo Alto, Calif. 94306. *Agent:* Rhoda Weyr, William Morris Agency, 1350 Avenue of the Americas, New York, N.Y. 10019.

CAREER: Executive secretary, Sylvania Electronics, 1959-65; Zero Population Growth, Inc., Los Altos, Calif., national executive director, 1969-71; National Organization for NONparents, Palo Alto, Calif., national executive director, 1972-73. Lecturer. *Member:* Authors Guild.

WRITINGS: Mother's Day Is Over, Charterhouse, 1973; (with Carol A. Chetkovich) *And the Pursuit of Happiness,* Book People, 1976. Contributor of articles to periodicals, including *Glamour* and *Cosmopolitan.*

SIDELIGHTS: Shirley Radl told *CA:* "I do not consider myself a writer, but instead one who is moved to write by specific circumstances or because of an avid interest in a subject. I am passionately interested in the prevention of child abuse and to that end, have done several articles for major publications and organized a crisis intervention hotline in my own community. If another major work is forthcoming, it will probably deal with something within the culture that affects us all, such as social pressure to conform, coercion, etc."

* * *

RADLAUER, Edward 1921-

PERSONAL: Born March 3, 1921, in Kentucky; son of Kurt and Hulda Radlauer; married Ruth Shaw (a writer and editor), 1947; children: David, Robin, Daniel. *Education:* University of California, Los Angeles, B.A., 1947, graduate study, 1949-50; Whittier College, M.A., 1956. *Home:* 620 West Rd., La Habra, Calif. 90631.

CAREER: Employed by California Department of Employment, 1948-49; teacher, reading specialist, and principal, 1950-68; writer, 1968—.

WRITINGS—For children: Drag Racing: Quarter Mile Thunder, Abelard, 1966; *Drag Racing* (with own photographs), Bowmar, 1967; *Karting: Fun on Wheels* (with own photographs), Bowmar, 1967; *The Mighty Midget* (with own photographs), Bowmar, 1967; *Slot Car Racing,* Bowmar, 1967; *Surfing* (with own photographs), Bowmar, 1968, revised edition, 1975; *Custom Cars* (with own photographs), Bowmar, 1968, revised edition, 1974; *Drag Racing Funny Cars* (with own photographs), Bowmar, 1968; *Dune Buggy Racing* (with own photographs), Bowmar, 1968; *Dune Buggies* (with own photographs), Bowmar, 1968; *Motorcycles: Whirling Wire Wheels,* Abelard, 1969, revised edition, Bowmar, 1975; *Drag Strip Challenge* (fiction; with own photographs), Elk Grove Press, 1969; *Karting Challenge* (fiction; with own photographs), Elk Grove Press, 1969.

Minibike Challenge (fiction), Elk Grove Press, 1970; *Drag Racing Pix Dix: A Picture Dictionary* (with own photographs), Bowmar, 1970; *Motorcycle Racing* (with own photographs), Bowmar, 1970, revised edition, 1975; *VW Bugs,* Bowmar, 1970; *Snowmobiles,* Bowmar, 1970; *Motorcycle Challenge* (fiction), Elk Grove Press, 1972; *Fast, Faster,*

Fastest, Childrens Press, 1973; *Motorcycle Mania,* Childrens Press, 1973; *Motorcyclopedia* (with own photographs), Bowmar, 1973; *Soap Box Racing,* Childrens Press, 1973; *Ready, Get Set, Whoa!,* Childrens Press, 1974; *Wild Wheels,* Childrens Press, 1974; *Flying Mania,* Childrens Press, 1974; *Minibikes* (with own photographs), Bowmar, 1975; *Race Car Drivers School,* F. Watts, 1975; *Pursuit School,* F. Watts, 1975; *Motorcycle Moto Cross School,* F. Watts, 1976; *Rodeo School* (with own photographs), F. Watts, 1976; (with son, David Radlauer) *Model Airplanes,* Childrens Press, 1976; *Racing Numbers,* Childrens Press, 1976; *Cats!,* Bowmar, 1976; *Wheels!,* Bowmar, 1976; *Racing!,* Bowmar, 1976, *Kickoff!,* Bowmar, 1976; *Shark Mania,* Childrens Press, 1977; *Boats,* Childrens Press, 1977; *Model Cars,* Childrens Press, 1977.

With wife, Ruth Shaw Radlauer: *About Missiles and Men,* Melmont, 1959; *About Atomic Power for People,* Melmont, 1960; *Atoms Afloat: The Nuclear Ship Savannah,* Abelard, 1963; *Father Is Big,* Bowmar, 1967; *What Is a Community?,* Elk Grove Press, 1967; *Water for Your Community,* Elk Grove Press, 1968; *Horses* (with own photographs), Bowmar, 1968, revised edition, 1975; *Evening,* Bowmar, 1968; *Colors,* Bowmar, 1968; *Whose Tools Are These?,* Elk Grove Press, 1968; *Quarter Midget Challenge* (fiction), Elk Grove Press, 1969.

We Go on Wheels, Elk Grove Press, 1970; *Horses Pix Dix: A Picture Dictionary* (with own photographs), Bowmar, 1970; *Buggy-Go-Round* (with own photographs), F. Watts, 1971; *On the Drag Strip* (with own photographs), F. Watts, 1971; *Scramble Cycle* (with own photographs), F. Watts, 1971; *On the Sand* (with own photographs), F. Watts, 1972; *Horsing Around* (with own photographs), F. Watts, 1972; *Chopper Cycle* (fiction; with own photographs), F. Watts, 1972; *Bonneville Cars* (with own photographs), F. Watts, 1973; *Horse Show Challenge* (fiction; with own photographs), Children's Press, 1973; *Motorcycle Mutt* (with own photographs), F. Watts, 1973; *On the Water* (with own photographs), F. Watts, 1973; *Salt Cycle* (with own photographs), F. Watts, 1973; *Foolish Filly* (with own photographs), F. Watts, 1974; *Racing on the Wind* (with own photographs), F. Watts, 1974; *Gymnastics School* (with own photographs), F. Watts, 1976.

Also author of six reading board games for Bowmar.

WORK IN PROGRESS: Three titles in the "Ready, Get Set, Go" series and four titles for a reading series, all for Childrens Press; "Starting Line II," the second in a series of reading programs, for Bowmar; editing and taking photographs, with wife R. S. Radlauer, for three books in the "National Parks" series, entitled *Mammoth Cave, Bryce Canyon,* and *Acadia National Park;* four filmstrips for Pied Piper Productions.

SIDELIGHTS: Radlauer writes: "Many authors write 'high quality' literature that is incomprehensible to the less academic student, the poor reader, the slow reader, the disappointed student. I try to write for all those who feel left out of the usual college oriented curriculum. One of my great pleasures is to get scathing reviews in snobbish journals since these reviewers demonstrate their utter contempt for the youngster who is not attuned to the mainstream of educational junk."

*   *   *

RAJAN, Balachandra 1920-

PERSONAL: Born March 24, 1920, in Toungoo, Burma; son of Arunachala (a civil servant) and Visalam (Tyagu-rajan) Rajan; married Chandra Sarma, August 29, 1946; children: Tilottoma (daughter). *Education:* Trinity College, Cambridge, B.A. (first class honors), 1941, M.A., 1944, Ph.D., 1946. *Home:* 478 Regent, London, Ontario, Canada N5Y 4H2. *Office:* Department of English, University of Western Ontario, Richmond, London, Ontario, Canada N6A 3K7.

CAREER: Cambridge University, Trinity College, Cambridge, England, director of studies in English, 1945-48, lecturer in English, 1947; officer in Indian Foreign Service, 1948-61; University of Delhi, Delhi, India, professor of English and head of department, 1961-64, dean of Faculty of Arts, 1964; visiting professor of English at Institute for Research in the Humanities, University of Wisconsin, 1964-65; University of Windsor, Windsor, Ontario, professor of English, 1965-66; University of Western Ontario, London, senior professor of English, 1966—. Chairman of administrative and legal committee of second general conference of International Atomic Energy Agency, 1959. Chairman of executive board of United Nations Children's Fund, 1955-57. *Member:* Modern Language Association of America, Renaissance Society of America, Milton Society of America (president, 1972).

WRITINGS: Paradise Lost and the Seventeenth Century Reader, Chatto & Windus, 1947, Oxford University Press, 1948; (editor) *T. S. Eliot: A Study of His Writings by Several Hands,* Funk, 1948; (editor) *Modern American Poetry,* Roy, 1952; *The Dark Dancer* (novel; British Book Society selection), Simon & Schuster, 1958.

Too Long in the West (novel), Heinemann, 1961, Atheneum, 1962; (editor) John Milton, *Paradise Lost,* Books I and II, Asia Publishing House, 1965; (editor with A. G. George) *Makers of Literary Criticism,* Asia Publishing House, 1965; *W. B. Yeats: A Critical Introduction,* Hutchinson University Library, 1965, 2nd edition, 1969; (editor) *Paradise Lost: A Tercentenary Tribute,* University of Toronto Press, 1969; (editor) Sophocles, *King Oedipus,* Macmillan (Canada), 1969, Collier Books, 1970; (editor) *The Novelist as Thinker,* reprinted, Folcroft, 1970; *The Lofty Rhyme: A Study of Milton's Major Poetry,* University of Miami Press, 1970; (editor) *The Prison and the Pinnacle: Papers,* Routledge & Kegan Paul, 1973; *The Overwhelming Question: A Study of the Poetry of T. S. Eliot,* University of Toronto Press, 1976.

Contributor to literary magazines in the United States and abroad, including *Sewanee Review* and *Toronto Quarterly.* Founder and editor of *Focus.*

*   *   *

RAMSEY, Paul W. 1905-1976

February 16, 1905—September 15, 1976; American associate editor of the U.S. State Department's monthly newsletter; previously worked as a reporter and an editor for newspapers in Pennsylvania, Illinois, and Florida. He died in Washington, D.C. Obituaries: *Washington Post,* September 16, 1976.

*   *   *

RANDALL, Mercedes M. 1895-1977

September 11, 1895—March 9, 1977; American pacifist, educator, Women's International League for Peace and Freedom executive, and author of books on issues of feminism and politics and of biographical works. She died in New York City. Obituaries: *New York Times,* March 10, 1977. (See index for previous *CA* sketch)

RANDALL, Willard Sterne 1942-

PERSONAL: Born March 13, 1942, in Philadelphia, Pa.; son of Leslie Fairbanks (an executive) and Joan (a businesswoman; maiden name, Shepherd) Randall; married Mary Anne Hogan (a photographer), January 23, 1965; children: Christopher, Mary Anne, Alice Amanda. *Education:* Attended St. Joseph's Evening College, Philadelphia, Pa., 1960-69. *Politics:* Democrat. *Residence:* Ocean City, N.J. *Agent:* Ray Lincoln, 4 Surrey Rd., Melrose Park, Pa. 19126.

CAREER: Pottstown Mercury, Pottstown, Pa., reporter, 1960-61; United States Corporation Co., Philadelphia, Pa., legal writer and assistant manager, 1961-65; *Mainland Journal,* Pleasantville, N.J., reporter, 1965-66; *Philadelphia Bulletin,* Philadelphia, Pa., reporter, editor, and feature writer, 1966-71; *Philadelphia* (magazine), Philadelphia, Pa., editorial director, 1971-72; Time-Life News Service, New York, N.Y., Philadelphia correspondent, 1972-73; freelance writer, 1973—. Founder and president of Ocean City Writers Workshop; vice-president of Ocean City Cultural Arts Center.

AWARDS, HONORS: Best feature of the year award from Sigma Delta Chi, 1970; National Magazine Award from Columbia Graduate School of Journalism, 1972; grants from American Philosophical Society, 1972, and New Jersey Historical Society, 1974-75; Sidney Hillman Award from Amalgamated Clothing Workers, John Hancock Award from John Hancock Co., Gerald Loeb Award from University of California at Los Angeles Graduate School of Management, and best story of the year award from Standard Gravure Association, all 1976, all for "54 Who Died."

WRITINGS: The Proprietary House in Amboy, privately printed, 1975; (contributor) Robert A. East and Jerome Judd, editors, *The Loyalist Americans,* Sleepy Hollow Restorations, 1975; *Journalist,* M.I.T. Press, 1975; (contributor) Carroll C. Calkins, editor, *The Story of America,* Reader's Digest Press, 1975; *Thaddeus Kosciuszko* (bookscript), Public Broadcasting Service, 1976; (editor with David R. Boldt, and contributor) *The Founding City,* Chilton, 1976; (with Stephen D. Solomon) *Building 6* (nonfiction), Little, Brown, 1977. Contributor to *Nation* and *Time.*

WORK IN PROGRESS: A chronicle of the family of Benjamin Franklin for Little, Brown; research and writing on Loyalists of the American Revolution; handbooks on investigative reporting; other nonfiction.

* * *

RANSLEY, Peter 1931-

PERSONAL: Born October 12, 1931, in Leeds, England; son of Arthur (a manager) and Hilda (Taylor) Ransley; married Hazel Rew, June, 1955 (divorced, 1970); married Cynthia Harris (a social worker), December 14, 1974. *Education:* Attended University of London, 1950-52. *Home:* 33 Dordrecht Rd., London W3, England. *Agent:* Spokesmen, 1 Craven Hill, London W2 3EW, England.

CAREER: Worked as an editor of business publications and as development manager of a publishing company, 1959-70; writer and playwright, 1971—. Chairman, Blenheim Project, 1974—. *Member:* Theatre Writers Group.

WRITINGS—All plays: "Disabled," first produced in London at Hampstead Theatre Club, 1971; "Ellen," first produced in London at Hampstead Theatre Club, 1971; "The Thompson Report," first produced in London, 1972; "Runaway," first produced in London at Royal Court Theatre, 1974.

Author of teleplays, including "Dear Mr. Welfare," 1970, "Black Olives," 1971, "Night Duty," 1972, "Blinkers," 1973, and "A Fair Day's Work," 1973. Contributor of play scripts to *Plays and Players,* and articles to *Listener.*

WORK IN PROGRESS: A trilogy of stage plays; scripts for Thames television series "Hazell."

SIDELIGHTS: Ransley told *CA* his work "up to now has been fuelled by concern grown out of various social work conditions. Now I think a lot of social work is junk. My current trilogy shows this progress (if that's progress!)."

* * *

RASCOVICH, Mark 1918(?)-1976

1918(?)—December 11, 1976; American author of novels and non-fiction; best known for his Cold War novel *The Bedford Incident,* which was later made into a motion picture. He died in West Palm Beach, Fla. Obituaries: *New York Times,* December 12, 1976; *Washington Post,* December 13, 1976.

* * *

RATTNER, David S(amuel) 1916-

PERSONAL: Born April 24, 1916, in New York, N.Y.; son of Benjamin (a businessman) and Katherine (Schiffenhaus) Rattner; married Henriette Elisabeth Judels (a teacher of French and art), July 1, 1941; children: Nina Marguerite (Mrs. William Michael Gelbart). *Education:* Attended Juilliard School of Music, 1932-34; Columbia University, B.S., 1936, M.A., 1938; New York University, graduate study, 1946-47 and 1970-71. *Home and office:* 50 East 10th St., New York, N.Y. 10003.

CAREER: High school music teacher in New York, N.Y., 1936-61, chairman of department, 1949-61; Abraham Lincoln High School, New York, N.Y., assistant principal, 1961-73; writer, 1973—. Conductor of New York All-City High School Orchestra, 1939-49, and New York City Teachers Orchestra. *Member:* Retired School Supervisors and Administrators, Music Chairman's Association of New York City Schools (past president), Bohemians, Sinfonia, Phi Delta Kappa, Kappa Delta Pi. *Awards, honors:* Ford Foundation fellowship, 1954-55, for travel and study in Europe.

WRITINGS: Enjoying the Arts: Music, Richards Rosen, 1976. Contributor of articles and reviews to music and education journals.

WORK IN PROGRESS: Enjoying the Arts: History of the Arts.

SIDELIGHTS: Rattner's current activities include teaching at the Educational Center for Retired Adults of the Emanuel Midtown Young Women's and Young Men's Hebrew Association, and at the Active Retirement Center of Pace University.

* * *

RAY, Man 1890-1976

August 27, 1890—November 18, 1976; American painter and photographer who helped launch the Dadaist and Surrealist movements and author of his autobiography; creator of several important techniques in painting and photography. He was best known for his photographs of artists, writers, and women of fashion living in Paris between the world wars. He also made several avant-garde films. He died in Paris, France. Obituaries: *New York Times,* November 19, 1976.

RAYNER, Mary 1933-

PERSONAL: Born December 30, 1933, in Mandalay, Burma; daughter of A. H. and Yoma Grigson; married E. H. Rayner, 1960; children: Sarah, William, Benjamin. *Education:* University of St. Andrews, M.A. (second class honors), 1954. *Residence:* Richmond, Surrey, England. *Address:* c/o Macmillan London Ltd., 4 Little Essex St., London W.C.2, England.

CAREER: Former editorial and production assistant at Hammond, Hammond Ltd. (publisher), London, England; Longmans, Green & Co. Ltd. (publisher), London, England, copywriter, 1959-62; free-lance book illustrator, 1962—. *Member:* Association of Illustrators.

WRITINGS—Self-illustrated: *The Witchfinder* (juvenile), Morrow, 1976; *Mr. and Mrs. Pig's Evening Out* (juvenile), Atheneum, 1976.

Work represented in anthologies, *Allsorts Six,* edited by Ann Thwaite, Methuen, 1974; *Allsorts Seven,* edited by Ann Thwaite, Methuen, 1975; *Young Winters' Tales Seven,* edited by M. R. Hodgkin, Macmillan, 1976.

WORK IN PROGRESS: Garth Pig and the Ice Cream Lady, a sequel to *Mr. and Mrs. Pig's Evening Out.*

*   *   *

REAVEY, George 1907-1976

1907—August 12, 1976; Irish poet, publisher, and translator of Russian and French literature. He became familiar with the Russian literary scene during three visits there, and subsequently translated the works of Gogol, Turgenev, Pasternak, and Yevtushenko, among others. He founded Europa Press in the 1930's. He died in New York City. Obituaries: *New York Times,* August 13, 1976.

*   *   *

REDFIELD, Margaret Park 1899(?)-1977

1899(?)—February 6, 1977; American anthropologist and author of works in her field. An authority on Yucatan folklore, she was also known for a study on the American family. She was closely associated with the work of her late husband, the anthropologist Robert Redfield. She died in Chicago, Ill. Obituaries: *New York Times,* February 8, 1977.

*   *   *

REDFIELD, William 1927-1976

January 26, 1927—August 17, 1976; American actor and author of books on acting. In his forty-year career, he made over two thousand performances on stage, film, television, and radio, most recently as Harding in the film "One Flew Over the Cuckoo's Nest." He was a founding member of the Actor's Guild, and contributed a monthly column to a craft magazine. He died in New York City. Obituaries: *New York Times,* August 18, 1976; *Washington Post,* August 19, 1976.

*   *   *

REEVES, Richard 1936-

PERSONAL: Born November 28, 1936, in New York, N.Y.; son of Furman W. (a judge) and Dorothy (Forshay) Reeves; married Carol A. Wiegand, June 1, 1959 (divorced, 1971); children: Cynthia Ann, Jeffrey Richard. *Education:* Stevens Institute of Technology, M.E., 1960. *Agent:* Lynn Nesbit, International Creative Management, 40 West 57th

St., New York, N.Y. 10019. *Office:* 3410 Reservoir Rd. N.W., Washington, D.C. 20007.

CAREER: Ingersoll-Rand Co., Phillipsburg, N.J., engineer, 1960-61; *Phillipsburg Free Press,* Phillipsburg, editor, 1961-63; *Newark News,* Newark, N.J., reporter, 1963-65; *New York Herald Tribune,* New York, N.Y., reporter, 1965-66; *New York Times,* New York, N.Y., chief political correspondent, 1966-71; *New York* Magazine, New York, N.Y., editor, 1971-77. Lecturer, Hunter College of the City University of New York, 1969-70, Columbia University, 1971-72; consultant to Ford Foundation, 1972—; host of NBC television show "Sunday," 1973-75.

WRITINGS—Political analysis: *A Ford, Not a Lincoln,* Harcourt, 1975; *Old Faces of 1976,* Harper, 1976; *Convention,* Harcourt, 1977. Columnist for *Harper's,* 1971-72. Contributor of articles to many popular magazines, including *New York Times Magazine, Harper's, Readers Digest, New York, Playboy, Saturday Review,* and *New Leader.*

SIDELIGHTS: Books by Richard Reeves on the American political scene are often criticized for their negativism. In fact, Reeves admits: "I do have a bias in writing about politicians. I don't feel any great obligation to recount their many and varied personal and professional virtues. That is what they, or the taxpayers, are paying for in salaries and fees of press secretaries, media advisers, and advertising agencies. Believe me, there is nothing good about Jerry Ford, Nelson Rockefeller or any of the Kennedys that the American people have not been told." *Time* magazine believes, "he picked up his fond contempt for politicos from the fetid municipal air of Jersey City, where he grew up as the son of a county judge." Peter Jenkins has implied Reeves may be influenced by the same general cynicism and distrust Jenkins finds in much of the press since Watergate and the Vietnam War.

However critics view Reeves' conclusions, few have argued with the work they are drawn from. For his book about the first 100 days of the Ford administration, *A Ford, Not a Lincoln,* he interviewed 150 persons and read numerous documents and reports. Interestingly, he didn't formally interview President Ford. "His reactions to questions in other interviews seemed pat. I didn't think he would be of any value to me," Reeves explained. Brad Knickerbocker said the book "is well written, apparently well-researched, and its biases are up front (where they belong). It will make readers think about their government, and that is its greatest value."

The continuing debate on Reeves' political biases and his views on politicians may be a measure of the success of his candor and style. William F. Buckley, Jr. classed him "among the two or three sprightliest political writers in America, and," he continued, "it is difficult for him to fail to be interesting."

BIOGRAPHICAL/CRITICAL SOURCES: New York Times Book Review, October 26, 1975; *Time,* November 10, 1975; *Christian Science Monitor,* November 11, 1975; *New Statesman,* March 5, 1976.

*   *   *

REICH, Kenneth 1938-

PERSONAL: Born March 7, 1938, in Los Angeles, Calif.; son of Herman (a rear admiral) and Ruth (Nussbaum) Reich; married Amelia Sherman, November 14, 1970; children: Kathleen, David. *Education:* Dartmouth College, B.A., 1960; University of California at Berkeley, M.A., 1962.

Home: 13720 Cumpston St., Van Nuys, Calif. 91401. *Office:* Times-Mirror Square, Los Angeles, Calif. 90053.

CAREER/WRITINGS: United Press International, Sacramento, Calif., reporter, 1962-63; *Life,* New York, N.Y., reporter, 1963-65; *Los Angeles Times,* Los Angeles, political writer, 1965—. Notable assignments include the McCarthy and Wallace campaigns, 1968, the Carter campaign, 1976, and California and national politics, 1968—. Lecturer. *Military service:* U.S. Army Reserve, 1956-65.

SIDELIGHTS: Reich contends the most demanding aspect of covering a political campaign is "sizing up the situation accurately in diverse primary states."

* * *

REIMANN, Viktor 1915-

PERSONAL: Born January 25, 1915, in Vienna, Austria; son of Josef (a manager) and Ottilie (Klinger) Reimann; married Alice Pfeiffer, March 30, 1946. *Education:* University of Vienna, received D.Phil. *Religion:* Roman Catholic. *Home:* Schwenkgasse 12, Vienna 1120, Austria. *Office:* Kronen-Zeitung, Muthgasse 2, Vienna 1190, Austria.

CAREER: Salzburger Nachrichten, Salzburg, Austria, vice-chief editor, 1945-49; member of Houses of Parliament, Vienna, Austria, 1949-56; Vienna State Theatres, Vienna, Austria, press officer, 1956-60; *Die Welt,* Hamburg, Germany, correspondent, 1960-61; *Kronen-Zeitung,* Vienna, Austria, editor, 1971—, and author of column. *Military service:* Served in army, 1940-45.

WRITINGS: Joseph Goebbels, Molden, 1970, English translation published as *Goebbels,* Doubleday, 1976.

Untranslated works in German: *Wenn die Nacht weicht,* Styria, 1946; *Diringenten, Stars und Buerokraten,* Deutsch, 1962; *Der Ifland-Ring,* Deutsch, 1963; *Die Adelsrepublik der Kuenstler,* Econ, 1964; *Innitzer: Kardinal zwischen Hitler und Rom,* Molden, 1966; *Zu grob fuer Oesterreich: Seipl und Bauer im Kampf um die Republik,* Molden, 1968.

SIDELIGHTS: The book on Goebbels has been translated into French, Spanish, Dutch, Slovenic, Swedish, and Italian.

* * *

REISTER, Floyd Nester 1919-

PERSONAL: Born July 19, 1919, in Tiffin, Ohio; son of Everett Henry (a truck driver) and Jennie (Cooper) Reister; married Augusta Karp, 1938 (marriage terminated, 1948); married Lois Jackson Metler, 1963 (marriage terminated, 1968); married Alice M. Hendershot Shody, September 26, 1970; children: Sheila (Mrs. Ronald L. Haudenshild), Gary Everett, Patrick Erin. *Education:* Ohio State University, B.Sc.Ed., 1944, M.A., 1950; Wayne State University, Ed.D., 1957. *Politics:* Democrat. *Home address:* R.D. 2, Box 213, Loganton, Pa. 17747.

CAREER: Teacher, athletic director, and coach in public schools in Ohio, 1944-50; Department of Public Recreation, Columbus, Ohio, director of Glenwood Recreation Center, 1950-53; superintendent of schools in Glenford, Ohio, 1953-54; high school principal in New Lebanon, Ohio, 1954-55; Eastern Michigan University, Ypsilanti, assistant professor of education, 1957-62; American Newspaper Publishers Association, New York, N.Y., training administrator, 1962-64; Montclair State College, Upper Montclair, N.J., associate professor of education, 1964-66; State Department of Education, Office of Teacher Education and Certification,

Trenton, N.J., director of programs for supervised teaching, 1966-68; Montclair State College, professor of education and coordinator of vocational teacher education, 1968-69; Planners Associates, Inc., Newark, N.J., director of educational services, 1968-70; Slippery Rock State College, Slippery Rock, Pa., associate professor of education, 1970-71; Pennsylvania Department of Labor and Industry, Williamsport district office, consultant to Bureau of Employment Security, 1971-72; Keystone Central School District, Lock Haven, Pa., adjunct instructor, 1972—. Assistant director, Youth Conservation Corps project, summer of 1971. Secretary of New Jersey Intercollegiate Council for Teacher Education, 1966-68; secretary of New Jersey Council for Vocational-Technical Teacher Education, 1968-69. Ohio representative to American Athletic Union, 1950-53; vice-president of Hilltop Community Council, 1952-53; member of Student Center advisory board, Wayne State University, 1956-57.

WRITINGS: (With Francesco Cordasco) *The American High School: Challenge and Reform,* Random House, 1966. Author of curriculum guides and administrative manuals. Contributor to education journals. Associate editor of *Action,* 1955-57; editor of *Teaching Core,* 1956.

WORK IN PROGRESS: Private Aviation: A Guide to Information Sources, publication expected in 1979.

SIDELIGHTS: Reister writes: "It is difficult for me to ascertain any given influence on my concepts and philosophy—one might credit it to a youth in semi-rural Ohio—to my mother's pressures to read, to believe in and have faith in people, to seek counsel of those more knowledgeable and to use that counsel, to dedication to egalitarianism, to the Dewey philosophy as interpreted by Boyd Bode—to a fusion of experiences into an amalgamation. . . . My experiences have influenced my education perceptions—philosophy—and emphasis. I feel that the major goal of education should/must be the development of learners who have the ability to adopt—to adjust—to utilize the knowledges they have—to know where and how to seek knowledges applicable to any problem—and the ability to use that knowledge in the solution of that problem. AND 'education' should not permit an individual to be thrust upon the labor market without a salable skill. Given the first premise and a salable skill an individual would be equipped to enter, to cope with, and to survive in our industrial-technological society and in an agrarian—even a primitive—society."

AVOCATIONAL INTERESTS: Flying (has taught at a private pilot ground school, has flown charter flights), fly fishing, selling home grown flowers and vegetables, gardening.

* * *

REMI, Georges 1907-
(Herge)

PERSONAL: Surname listed in some sources as Remy; born May 5, 1907, in Brussels, Belgium; son of Alexis Remy; married. *Office:* Studios Herge, Avenue Louise 162/Bte 7, 1050 Brussels, Belgium.

CAREER: Author and illustrator of children's books, 1929—.

WRITINGS—All under pseudonym Herge; all first published by Casterman; English translations all by Leslie Lonsdale-Cooper and Michael Turner: *Tintin au Pays des Soviets,* 1930; *Tintin au Congo,* 1931; *Tintin en Amerique,* 1932; *Les Cigares du Pharaon,* 1934, published as *The Ci-*

gars of the Pharaoh, Atlantic, 1975; Le Lotus Bleu, 1936; L'Oreille Cassee, 1937, published as Tintin and the Broken Ear, Methuen, 1975; L'Ile Noire, 1938, published as The Black Island, Methuen, 1966, Atlantic, 1975; Le Sceptre d'Ottokar, 1939, published as King Ottokar's Sceptre, Methuen, 1958; Le Crabe aux Pinces d'Or, 1941, published as The Crab with the Golden Claws, Methuen, 1958, Atlantic, 1974; L'Etoile Mysterieuse, 1942, published as The Shooting Star, Methuen, 1961; Le Secret de la Licorne, 1943, published as The Secret of the Unicorn, Methuen, 1959; Le Tresor de Rackham le Rouge, 1945, published as Red Rackham's Treasure, Methuen, 1959; Les Sept Boules de Cristal, 1948, published as The Seven Crystal Balls, Methuen, 1963, Atlantic, 1975; Le Temple du Soleil, 1949, published as Prisoners of the Sun, Methuen, 1962, Atlantic, 1975.

Tintin au pays de l'Or Noir, 1951, published as The Land of Black Gold, Methuen, 1972, Atlantic, 1975; Objectif Lune, 1953, published as Destination Moon, Methuen, 1959; On a Marche sur la Lune, 1954, published as Explorers on the Moon, Methuen, 1959, Atlantic, 1976; L'Affaire Tournesol, 1956, published as The Calculus Affair, Methuen, 1960, Atlantic, 1976; Les Exploits de Quick et Flupke, 1956; Coke en Stock, 1958, published as The Red Sea Sharks, Methuen, 1960.

Tintin au Tibet, 1960, published as Tintin in Tibet, Methuen, 1962, Atlantic, 1975; Les Bijoux de la Castafiore, 1963, published as The Castafiore Emerald, Methuen, 1963, Atlantic, 1975; Tintin and the Golden Fleece, Methuen, 1965; Vol 714 pour Sydney, 1968, published as Flight 714, Methuen, 1968, Atlantic, 1975; Popol Out West, Methuen, 1969; Tintin et le Lac aux Requins, 1973, published as Tintin and the Lake of Sharks, Methuen, 1973; Tintin et les Picaros, 1976, published as Tintin and the Picaros, Methuen, 1976.

SIDELIGHTS: Tintin and his trusty dog Milou made their first appearance in the January 10, 1929, edition of Le Petit Vingtieme. Since then these two characters have appeared in 23 books, which have a combined world sales of over 25 million copies. Originally written in French, the adventures of Tintin have been translated into English, German, Spanish, Japanese, and several other languages. Tintin strip cartoons appear regularly in newspapers in Thailand, Egypt, Turkey, Australia, New Zealand, South Africa, and Ireland.

Herge relates that the conception and production of a new Tintin book is a long process: months are spent studying the background, and the staff at Studios Herge closely research details of the trains, ships, uniforms, plants, animals and other objects that will appear in the book. This close attention to detail once led Herge to embark on a North Sea voyage in a cargo boat so that he could assure the authenticity of his drawings.

*   *   *

REMINGTON, Ella-Carrie 1914-
(Carella Alden)

PERSONAL: Born November 21, 1914, in Evanston, Ill.; daughter of Thomas Augustus (a singer) and Louise (a writer; maiden name, Peirce) Remington. Education: Attended Fashion Art School, San Francisco, Calif. Residence: New York, N.Y. Office: Metropolitan Museum of Art, Fifth Ave. & 82nd St., New York, N.Y. 10028.

CAREER: Has worked as a professional dancer, 1932-37; was actress and stage manager for professional theatres in Pasadena, Calif., Abingdon, Va., and New York City, 1940-43; toured Europe with U.S.O. productions of "Junior

Miss" and "O Mistress Mine," 1944-45; staged plays and musicals for the Soldier Show program at Ernie Pyle Theatre (now Takarazuka), Tokyo, Japan, 1946-47; directed "Our Town," Sidney, Australia, 1947; directed "Candida," Equity Library Theatre, New York City, 1948; worked as television actress, 1949; employed in the television department of Anderson & Cairns Advertising Agency, 1950-51; wrote and performed one-woman shows on tour, 1952-62; Metropolitan Museum of Art, New York City, writer and director of multi-media productions for young people, 1963—.

WRITINGS—Juveniles; under pseudonym Carella Alden: Sunrise Island, Parents' Magazine Press, 1971; From Early American Paintbrushes, Parents' Magazine Press, 1971; Royal Persia, Parents' Magazine Press, 1972.

WORK IN PROGRESS: Two books for juveniles, The Teeny Tiny Paper People, and Hurricane.

SIDELIGHTS: Ms. Remington wrote: "one of the greatest errors made in planning children's theatre is the lack of consideration given to the range of the hoped-for audience. For ages two through six, a good puppet show can't fail and a well produced fairy tale will enchant three to seven-year-olds, but by the time a child reaches eight he, or she, is no longer spellbound by the story of Sleeping Beauty unless the production gives something more than just a storyline, i.e. a ballet.

"Make no mistake, I am not for eliminating the fairy tale or ancient folklore and legends; they, perhaps more than anything else, are the first things to stimulate the imagination. I use them in some of my productions, but only as a thread of fantasy on which to hang reality.

"Children like to be treated as adults, so in 'Art Entertainments for Young People' I make them reach. Adults attend the theatre to be entertained, but when children attend I think they should also learn. I do not write for laughs or mere amusement. Using multiple slide projection (most slides are of works of art), narration, professional actors, dancers and variety artists, correct costuming and music of the period, I strive to stir the child's imagination and interest on a particular period in history and the art which that period produced. After each entertainment I never fail to have at least one performer comment, 'I've never played to such an attentive children's audience.' I answer, 'when you respect a child's intelligence he'll repay you with his attention.'"

*   *   *

REMSBERG, Bonnie K(ohn) 1937-

PERSONAL: Born April 1, 1937, in Cleveland, Ohio; daughter of Henry (a printer) and Lottie (Schindler) Kohn; married Charles Andruss Remsberg (a writer), September 14, 1958; children: Jennifer, Richard. Education: Northwestern University, B.S., 1959. Home and office: 1521 Kirk St., Evanston, Ill. 60202. Agent: Robert Lescher, 141 East 55th St., New York, N.Y. 10022.

CAREER: WMAQ-Television, Chicago, Ill., hostess of "Some of My Best Friends," 1965—. Instructor at Columbia College (Chicago), 1968-69, University of Chicago, 1970-73, and Northwestern University, 1976-77; lecturer at Indiana University, Chicago City College, and New York University. Member of board of governors of Action for Brain-Handicapped Children.

MEMBER: American Society of Journalists and Authors, National Academy of Television Arts and Sciences, American Federation of Television and Radio Artists, Society of

Magazine Writers. *Awards, honors:* Sidney Hillman Foundation Award, 1968, for "America's Hungry Families"; Penney-Missouri Award from J. C. Penney Foundation and University of Missouri, 1974, for "Catastrophic Illnesses"; four journalism awards from Illinois State Medical Society and seven local Emmy awards from the Chicago chapter of the National Academy of Television Arts and Sciences, all for television documentary programs.

WRITINGS: (With Raymond Mack, husband Charles Remsberg, and others) *Our Children's Burden,* Random House, 1968; *Smiling Through the Apocalypse,* McCall, 1970; *Radio and Television Spot Announcements for Family Planning,* Community and Family Study Center, University of Chicago, 1975.

Author of more than fifty documentary films and television scripts, including "A Matter of Life and Death" and "Discovery Is Our Business," for WMAQ-TV, Chicago, Ill., 1962-74, and "Karen Anne" for KDKA-TV, Pittsburgh, Pa., 1976.

Contributor to *World Book Encyclopedia* and to popular magazines, including *Good Housekeeping, Seventeen, Redbook, Women's Day, Esquire, Saturday Review,* and *Family Weekly.*

WORK IN PROGRESS: Trial dramas; film and television scripts.

AVOCATIONAL INTERESTS: Travel, children.

*   *   *

RENE, Natalia   1908(?)-1977
(Natalia Roslavleva)

1908(?)—January 3, 1977; Russian dance historian, critic, and author. Her book *Era of the Russian Ballet,* written under the pseudonym Natalia Roslavleva, is considered to be the most popular history of the Russian ballet written in English; also author of a column in a British dance magazine. She died in Moscow, U.S.S.R. Obituaries: *New York Times,* January 8, 1977; *AB Bookman's Weekly,* March 7, 1977.

*   *   *

REYNOLDS, Ruth Sutton   1890(?)-1977

1890(?)—May 6, 1977; American author. She was a member of the family that developed the Sutton Place area in New York City and wrote a book about her home, Sutton Manor, as well as two books on the Bible. She died in Ossining, N.Y. Obituaries: *New York Times,* May 7, 1977.

*   *   *

RHODES, Robert I.   1942-

PERSONAL: Born February 10, 1942; son of Irwin A. (a businessman) and Mildred (Goldberg) Rhodes; married Karen Farless (a psychologist); children: Eve Jennifer, Rebecca. *Education:* University of Michigan, B.A., 1963; Columbia University, M.A., 1966; Princeton University, Ph.D., 1972. *Home and office:* 4 Timber Trail, Suffern, N.Y. 10901.

CAREER: Allegheny College, Meadville, Pa., instructor, 1965-67; Newark College of Engineering, Newark, N.J., instructor, 1967-68; State University of New York at Binghamton, assistant professor of sociology, 1970-74; Lakehead University, Thunder Bay, Ontario, associate professor of sociology, 1974-75; Underdevelopment Studies Center, Suffern, N.Y., director, 1975—.

WRITINGS: (Editor) *Imperialism and Underdevelopment,* Monthly Review Press, 1970; (editor) *Agrarian Underdevelopment and Revolution,* Monthly Review Press, in press. Contributor to journals in the United States, Canada, England, Sweden, and India.

WORK IN PROGRESS: A book on Turkish development, with Dogu Ergil; research on world capitalism.

*   *   *

RICH, Daniel Cotton   1904-1976

April 16, 1904—October 15, 1976; American art museum curator and author of books and articles in his field. Formerly he was director of the Art Institute of Chicago and the Worchester Art Museum (Worchester, Mass.); most recently served as a trustee of the Soloman R. Guggenheim Foundation; known as an exponent of modern art. He died in New York City. Obituaries: *New York Times,* October 18, 1976; *AB Bookman's Weekly,* November 15, 1976.

*   *   *

RICHARDS, Blair P(atton)   1940-

PERSONAL: Born July 18, 1940, in Scranton, Pa.; son of William A. (a plant supervisor) and Dorothy (a secretary; maiden name, Kellow) Richards; divorced; children: Troy Albert. *Education:* Union College, Barbourville, Ky., B.A., 1963; Emory University, M. Christian Education, 1965; also attended University of North Carolina and Columbus College. *Politics:* Independent. *Religion:* United Methodist. *Home:* 3514 Edgewood Rd., Columbus, Ga. 31907. *Office:* St. Luke United Methodist Church, 1104 Second Ave., Columbus, Ga. 31901.

CAREER: Director of Christian education for Methodist churches in Atlanta, Ga., 1965, Scottsdale, Ariz., 1966-68, Mesa, Ariz., 1968-69, and San Pedro, Calif., 1969-70; Quincy United Methodist Church, Quincy, Pa., supervisor, 1970-71; St. Luke United Methodist Church, Columbus, Ga., director of Christian education, 1971—. Summer counselor at a camp for the blind, 1962, 1963; director of migrant and Indian ministry camp, summers, 1966-67; president of national youth group of Council of the Southern Mountains, 1962-63; member of El Redentor Day Care Center, 1968-69. Member of board of managers of Columbus-Phenix City Christian Enrichment School, 1971—. *Military service:* U.S. Naval Reserve, 1957-63.

MEMBER: Christian Educators Fellowship of the United Methodist Church (charter member), North Georgia Christian Educators Fellowship of the United Methodist Church, Alumni Association of Union College (member of board of directors, 1975—). *Awards, honors:* Newspaper National Snapshot Award from *Scranton Times,* 1965.

WRITINGS: (With Janice Sigmund) *Come, Let Us Celebrate,* Hawthorn, 1976. Contributor to church school magazines.

WORK IN PROGRESS: A book "that will result in a practical resource for local church members as they live out the Christian faith daily."

SIDELIGHTS: Richards writes: "I have spent most of my life involved with youth. I have led groups on a variety of trips, including two backpacking trips into Havasu Canyon at the western end of the Grand Canyon. I directed a trip for thirty-six youths from Columbus, Georgia to Arizona and California and back through Oklahoma where we spent time working at an Indian Mission. In 1974 I led a group of families on a ten-day canoe trip in northern Minnesota and

Canada. Then in 1976, I led an intergenerational group of thirty-seven from Columbus to Switzerland, Italy, France, England, and Holland.

"This was my second trip to Europe. Travel has enriched both my life and my work. I will be taking a group from my church, mostly senior citizens, on a trip to Europe that will include Austria, Belgium, Germany, Liechtenstein, Monaco."

AVOCATIONAL INTERESTS: Camping, swimming, horseback riding, hiking, arts and crafts, photography.

*   *   *

RICHARDSON, Cyril Charles   1909-1976

June 13, 1909-November 16, 1976; British-born American Episcopal priest, church historian specializing in literature of the early Christian church, educator, and author of books on church history, including the controversial *Doctrine of the Trinity.* His study of church documents led him to make conclusions occasionally opposed to strict tradition, such as his advocating the ordination of women. He died in New York City. Obituaries: *New York Times,* November 17, 1976. (See index for previous *CA* sketch)

*   *   *

RICHARDSON, Harry V(an Buren)   1901-

PERSONAL: Born June 7, 1901, in Jacksonville, Fla.; son of Martin V. (an engineer) and Bertha (a school teacher; maiden name, Witsell) Richardson; married Selma Theodocia White (a teacher), June 22, 1927. *Education:* Western Reserve University (now Case Western Reserve University), A.B., 1925; Harvard University, S.T.B., 1932; Drew University, Ph.D., 1945. *Politics:* Democrat. *Home:* 3127 Mangum Lane S.W., Atlanta, Ga. 30311. *Office address:* P.O. Box 42156, Atlanta, Ga. 30311.

CAREER: Ordained Methodist minister, 1928; Tuskegee Institute, Tuskegee Institute, Ala., chaplain, 1932-48; Gammon Theological Seminary, Atlanta, Ga., president, 1948-49; Interdenominational Theological Center, Atlanta, Ga., founder and president, 1959-68, president emeritus, 1968—; writer, 1968—. Executive director of United Negro College Fund, 1969-71; chairman of board of directors of Atlanta's Citizens Trust Bank, 1972-74. Member of general board of National Council of Churches of Christ in the United States; member of Council of Evangelism of the Methodist Church; life member of Methodist Rural Life Fellowship; president of Georgia Council of Churches, 1964-66. Member of board of directors of Georgia Council of Alcohol Problems, Atlanta Urban League, and local Travelers Aid Society; member-at-large of Greater Atlanta Council of Churches; member of citizens' advisory committee for the urban renewal of Atlanta; member of mayor's committee of Atlanta Coordinating Council, 1963-68.

MEMBER: American Academy of Political and Social Science, Association of Methodist Theological Schools (president, 1955), Georgia Association for Pastoral Care (member of board of directors). *Awards, honors:* D.D. from Wilberforce University, 1938; award from Association of Private Colleges and Universities in Georgia, 1976.

WRITINGS: Dark Glory: A Study of the Rural Church, Friendship Press, 1947; *Dark Salvation,* Doubleday, 1976.

Contributor: G. Paul Butler, editor, *Best Sermons,* Macmillan, 1952; Stuart Nelson, editor, *The Christian Way in Race Relations,* Friendship Press, 1953; *The Black American Reference Book,* Prentice-Hall, 1976. Contributor to *The American Negro Reference Book* and *Encyclopedia Americana,* and to religious and educational magazines.

WORK IN PROGRESS: A History of the Interdenominational Theological Center; Where Am I (tentative title), a study of religious beliefs in the light of modern scientific developments and knowledge, completion expected in 1978.

SIDELIGHTS: Richardson writes: "It is clear now that unless mankind can find a way soon to make the goodness in itself dominant and the evil in itself recessive, there is little hope for human survival on earth. Therefore, religion as man's conscious effort to make the good dominant is the most essential enterprise to which the human mind can address itself. Convinced of this, I have devoted my life to religious work as a minister, teacher, writer, and school administrator."

*   *   *

RICHEY, Russell Earle   1941-

PERSONAL: Born October 19, 1941, in Asheville, N.C.; son of McMurry (a professor) and Erika (a teacher; maiden name, Marx) Richey; married Merle Umstead, August 28, 1965; children: William, Elizabeth. *Education:* Wesleyan University, B.A., 1963; Union Theological Seminary, B.D., 1966; Princeton University, M.A., 1968, Ph.D., 1970. *Office:* Department of Church History, Drew University, Madison, N.J. 07940.

CAREER: Drew University, Madison, N.J., assistant professor of church history, 1969—; ordained United Methodist minister, 1971. *Member:* American Society of Church History (member of council), American Academy of Religion, American Association of University Professors, American Studies Association, Phi Beta Kappa.

WRITINGS: (Editor with Donald Jones) *American Civil Religion,* Harper, 1974; (editor) *Denominationalism,* Abingdon, 1977. Contributor of articles to *Church History, Journal of the American Academy of Religion, Foundations, Eighteenth-Century Studies* , and other periodicals.

WORK IN PROGRESS: Further work on American denominationalism.

SIDELIGHTS: Richey told *CA:* "Denominations need to be better understood by those within them. Otherwise bureaucracy, inertias, subservience to authority, apotheosis of the institution immobilize members, stifle the creative religious spirit, inhibit the evolution of new structures to fit new circumstances. With such understanding, members should be freed to make denominations what they once were, means to higher ends. Without such understanding they will remain ends in themselves."

*   *   *

RICHMAN, Milton   1922-

PERSONAL: Born January 29, 1922, in New York, N.Y.; son of Samuel A. (a post office employee) Clara (Ganberg) Richman. *Education:* Attended high school in New York City. *Politics:* None. *Religion:* Hebrew. *Home:* 175 West 13th St., New York, N.Y. 10011. *Office:* United Press International, 220 East 42nd St., New York, N.Y. 10017.

CAREER: Minor league baseball player in Beaver Falls, Pa.,·Williamston, N.C., and Hazleton, Pa., 1939-41; United Press (now United Press International), New York City, sports writer, 1944—, sports editor, 1973—. Notable assignments in sport include Don Larsen's perfect game, death of Babe Ruth, Roger Maris' 61st home run, and Hank Aaron's

715th home run; in general news, the sinking of the Andria Doria, the Woodridge, N.J. train disaster, and the original West Point cribbing scandal. Lecturer. *Military service:* U.S. Army, Medical Corps, 1942-44. *Member:* Association of Professional Baseball Players of America, Baseball Writers' Association, Professional Football Writers of America. *Awards, honors:* National Headliners Award for consistently outstanding sports writing, 1957; Pulitzer Prize nomination for general sports writing, 1957.

WRITINGS: Daily column, "Today's Sport Parade," syndicated by UPI, 1964—; contributor of articles on sports to *Saturday Evening Post, Collier's, This Week,* and *Sport.*

SIDELIGHTS: Richman told *CA:* "I feel that my experience in professional baseball, limited as it was, has helped me tremendously in my understanding of and relationship with all athletes. I used to think playing baseball gave me the greatest satisfaction and enjoyment in the world. I've changed my mind about that and now feel writing brings me the most satisfaction."

Richman has been around the world several times covering stories. "The high point of my travels was my visit to Peking, Shanghai, and Canton in the Peoples' Republic of China in 1975."

*   *   *

RIDENOUR, Ron 1939-

PERSONAL: Born October 1, 1939, in Mt. Vernon, Ohio; children: Malcolm Karl, Eugene Douglass. *Education:* California State University at Los Angeles, B.A., 1968. *Home:* 1642 North Coronado St., Los Angeles, Calif. 90026.

CAREER: Marketing Strategies, Inglewood, Calif., publicity director, 1968-69; *Hanford Sentinel,* Hanford, Calif., sports editor and reporter, 1969-70; *Riverside Press-Enterprise,* Riverside, Calif., makeup editor, 1970; *Citizen News,* Hollywood, Calif., reporter, 1971; *Los Angeles News-Advocate,* Los Angeles, Calif., reporter, 1971-72; *Los Angeles Free Press,* Los Angeles, reporter, 1972-73; American Civil Liberties Union, Los Angeles, editor and public relations director, 1973-75; *Los Angeles Vanguard,* Los Angeles, news editor and reporter; freelance magazine writer. Notable assignments include World Peace Assembly, 1972, and Wounded Knee, 1973. *Member:* Newspaper Guild. *Awards, honors:* Houghton & Mifflin Distinctive Short Story Award, 1970, for "Affluency's Answer."

WRITINGS: (Co-author) *Glass House Tapes,* Avon, 1973; (contributor) Donald Freed, editor, *Readings in American Government 76/77,* Dushkin, 1977. Contributing editor, *Skeptic,* 1975—. Contributor of articles to over twenty-five periodicals, including *Playboy, Washington Post, Tennis Illustrated, Sevendays, Juris Doctor, Nation, Review of Southern California Journalism, Coast,* and *Chic.*

WORK IN PROGRESS: A series of articles on Interpol; a book on "a provocative provocateur."

SIDELIGHTS: Ridenour told *CA:* "I think as an active citizen of the world, hoping to help change what is cruel and exploitative. Writing is a tool to help raise issues and understanding in order to improve the lot of humanity. Writing is an important means of communication which every craftsperson must take seriously: we are public servants. I am most interested in investigative, muckraking journalism. For relief I travel, and write an occasional piece on relaxing reprieves. I love Latin America and speak Spanish well. I have travelled and lived in Brazil, Mexico and Costa Rica. I have also written stories regarding Mexico. When not

working or politicing, I enjoy handball, tennis, hiking, cooking, swimming and being with my twin boys."

*   *   *

RIDER, Alice Damon 1895-

PERSONAL: Born July 18, 1895, in Livonia, N.Y.; daughter of Daniel and Jennie (Disbrow) Damon; married Kenneth H. Rider, 1935 (deceased); children: Christopher Damon. *Education:* Attended New York State Normal School, Geneseo, 1915-17; University of Michigan, B.S., 1934, M.A.L.S., 1938. *Religion:* Episcopalian. *Home:* 8 Seminole, Geneseo, N.Y. 14454.

CAREER: Librarian, 1921-65; State University of New York College at Geneseo, director of library education, 1950-67. *Member:* Phi Beta Kappa. *Awards, honors:* Named woman of the year by American Association of University Women, 1960.

WRITINGS: A Story of Books and Librarians, Scarecrow, 1976.

*   *   *

RIEGERT, Eduard Richard 1932-

PERSONAL: Surname is pronounced *Ree*-gert; born September 28, 1932, in Laird, Saskatchewan, Canada; son of Theodor and Anna (Rosenfeldt) Riegert; married Ladona Marilyn Carlson (a bookkeeper), August 24, 1956; children: James Eduard, Ann Ladona. *Education:* University of Saskatchewan, B.A., 1955; Lutheran College and Seminary, B.D., 1958; Union Theological Seminary, graduate study, summer, 1959; Lutheran Theological Seminary, Philadelphia, Pa., S.T.M., 1960; Princeton Theological Seminary, Ph.D., 1967. *Religion:* Lutheran. *Home:* 128 Greenbriar Dr., Waterloo, Ontario, Canada N2L 4B5. *Office:* Department of Functional Theology, Waterloo Lutheran Seminary, Waterloo, Ontario, Canada N2L 3C5.

CAREER: Ordained Lutheran minister, 1962; pastor of Lutheran church in Philipsburg, Ontario, 1962-65; Waterloo Lutheran Seminary, Waterloo, Ontario, lecturer, 1965-67, assistant professor, 1967-72, associate professor, 1972—; Wilfrid Laurier University, Waterloo, Ontario, associate professor, 1973—. Member of Joint Committee for Inter-Lutheran Relations, 1970-74. *Member:* Canadian Society of Biblical Studies, Canadian Archaeological Association, American Academy of Religion, American Academy of Homiletics.

WRITINGS: (With N. E. Wagner and L. E. Toombs) *The Moyer Site: A Prehistoric Village in Waterloo County, Ontario,* Wilfrid Laurier University Press, 1973; (with R. H. Hiers) *Proclamation: Pentecost 2, Series B,* Fortress, 1975; (contributor) Erich R. W. Schultz, editor, *Vita Laudanda,* Wilfrid Laurier University Press, 1976. Contributor to religious journals.

WORK IN PROGRESS: The Perry Site: A Prehistoric Village in Ontario, with N. E. Wagner; *Sermonizing with an Eye to Pastoral Care,* with D. J. Glebe.

SIDELIGHTS: Riegert told *CA:* "Archaeology has been an excellent way for me to establish some contact with and feeling for the native peoples of North America. My contact with their earth, i.e. the earth of their prehistoric villages where they worked and played and died, has helped me appreciate their continuing reverence for the earth and the environment. I have in this way renewed my own sense of the sacredness of the earth and the sky. Also, it has extended my own history in this land. I am a child of immigrants to

Canada—my relationship to this land is scarcely two generations long; yet now my history in this land has become immeasureably longer—and I thank the native peoples for allowing me to make some of their history also mine."

*   *   *

RINCHEN, Byambyn   1905(?)-1977

1905(?)—March 6, 1977; Mongolian novelist. His outspoken espousal of Mongolia's cultural heritage caused him to be jailed by Communists in the 1930's, but in the next decade he was awarded a major prize for a film. He died in Ulan Bator, Mongolia. Obituaries: *New York Times*, March 15, 1977.

*   *   *

RINDER, Walter Murray   1934-

PERSONAL: Born June 3, 1934, in Chicago, Ill.; son of Samuel Murray (a salesman and businessman, and Geneta (Tamblyn) Rinder. *Education:* Attended North San Antonio Junior College, 1952-54. *Home address:* Box 96, Brightwood, Ore., 97011.

CAREER: Writer and photographer. Has designed and produced posters, parchments, greeting cards, and a record album. *Military service:* U.S. Army, 1954-56.

WRITINGS—All published by Celestial Arts: *Love is an Attitude*, 1970; *This Time Called Life*, 1971; *Spectrum of Love*, 1973; *Follow Your Heart*, 1973; *The Humanness of You*, Volume I, 1973, Volume II, 1974; *Love is My Reason*, 1975; *Will You Share With Me*, 1975; *Where Will I Be Tomorrow?*, 1976.

WORK IN PROGRESS: The Courage to Love (novel); *Our Renaissance* (collection of black and white and color photographs); a photographic calendar; a series of children's stories for adults.

SIDELIGHTS: Rinder told *CA* that he is involved in social change and is looking forward to a broadening of attitudes in "total loving of all kinds." He is also planning on creating a youth ranch, "within a community of people where loving is the way of life and far more important than making money. This may be the beginning of a parallel society," he writes.

*   *   *

RIORDAN, James   1936-

PERSONAL: Born October 10, 1936, in Portsmouth, England; son of William (an engineer) and Kathleen (a cleaner; maiden name, Smith) Brown; married Annick Vercaigne, July 4, 1959 (divorced, 1964); married Rashida Davletshina (a teacher), July 1, 1965; children: Tania, Nadine, Sean, Nathalie, Catherine. *Education:* University of Birmingham, B.S., 1959, Ph.D., 1975; University of London, certificate in education, 1960; University of Moscow, diploma in political science, 1962. *Politics:* Marxist. *Religion:* Atheist. *Home:* 15 Bankfield Dr., Shipley, West Yorkshire, England. *Office:* Modern Languages Centre, University of Bradford, Bradford, West Yorkshire, England.

CAREER: British Railways, Portsmouth, England, clerk, 1956-57; translator in Moscow, Soviet Union, 1963-65; Portsmouth Polytechnic, Portsmouth, England, lecturer in Russian, 1965-69; University of Bradford, Bradford, England, lecturer in Russian studies, 1971—. *Military service:* Royal Air Force, 1954-56; served in Berlin.

WRITINGS: The Mistress of the Copper Mountain, Muller, 1974; (with Eileen Colwell) *Little Grey Neck*, Addison-Wesley, 1975; *Central Russian Tales*, Kestrel,

1976; *Tartar Tales*, Kestrel, 1977; *Sport in Soviet Society*, Cambridge University Press, 1977.

WORK IN PROGRESS: Siberian Folk Tales, completion expected in 1978; research on folklore of the people of Siberia and the Soviet Far North.

SIDELIGHTS: Riordan writes: "My writing on folk tales is based on a personal acquaintance with the people and the land. For example, with the Russian tales I lived, worked, and journeyed in Russia for five years, visiting thirteen of the fifteen republics, gathering folktale material. For my Tartar tales, I spent several months in Soviet Tartary in the homes of friends and relations of my Tartar wife Rashida. And for my Siberian tales I spent two months during 1977 travelling in Siberia. My writing on Soviet sport is based on membership in the Moscow Spartak Sports Club for five years, 1961-65."

*   *   *

RITNER, Peter V.   1927(?)-1976

1927(?)—October 28, 1976; American writer and publishing executive; associated with *Saturday Review of Literature* and Macmillan; negotiated the purchase of Albert Speer's memoirs; also author of novels and non-fiction works. He died in New York City. Obituaries: *New York Times*, October 28, 1976.

*   *   *

ROBERTS, Cecil (Edric Mornington)   1892-1976

May 18, 1892—December 23, 1976; British journalist, literary editor, poet, traveler, and author of novels, works of nonfiction, and historic-travel books. He died in Rome, Italy. Obituaries: *New York Times*, December 24, 1976. (*CAP*-2; earlier sketch in *CA*-29/32)

*   *   *

ROBERTS, Michael   1945-

PERSONAL: Born September 9, 1945, in Providence, R.I.; son of Harold S. (a merchant) and Frimette (Silverman) Roberts; married Deborah Salmanson, January 2, 1972. *Education:* American University, B.A., 1967. *Office:* Time-Life Books, 777 Duke, Alexandria, Va.

CAREER: Daily Racing Form, New York, N.Y., trackman and calltaker, 1970-72; *Washington Daily News*, Washington, D.C., author of horse racing column, 1972; *Washington Star*, Washington, D.C., author of sports column, 1972-75; Time-Life Books, Alexandria, Va., staff writer, 1975—. *Member:* American Newspaper Guild, National Turf Writers Association, Washington Independent Writers. *Awards, honors:* Front Page Award from Washington-Baltimore Newspaper Guild, 1974, for two series on the medical treatment of athletes.

WRITINGS: Fans!: How We Go Crazy Over Sports, New Republic, 1976. Author of "Robertson Racing" column in *Washington Daily News*, 1972, and "Mike Roberts" column in *Washington Star*, 1972-75. Contributor to *New Republic*.

WORK IN PROGRESS: Research for several books.

SIDELIGHTS: Roberts writes: "As a sports columnist for the *Washington Star* I discovered how many people were living life vicariously through athletes and judging their own worth on the outcome of games played by others. This led me to examine, in *Fans!*, the extent to which lives are affected and the ways in which society's institutions are distorted by the passion for spectator sports and the worship of jocks.''

*   *   *

ROBERTS, Robert C(ampbell)   1942-

PERSONAL: Born January 28, 1942, in Wichita, Kan.; son of Arthur Verne (a lawyer) and Elisabeth (Euwer) Roberts; married Elizabeth Vanderkooy (a teacher), December 18, 1976. *Education:* Wichita State University, B.A., 1965, M.A., 1970; Yale University, B.D., 1970, Ph.D., 1973; studied at Oxford University, 1970-71. *Religion:* Christian. *Home:* 925 Park St., Bowling Green, Ky. 42101. *Office:* Department of Philosophy, Western Kentucky University, Bowling Green, Ky. 42101.

CAREER: Western Kentucky University, Bowling Green, assistant professor of philosophy, 1973—.

WRITINGS: Rudolf Bultmann's Theology, Eerdmans, 1976. Contributor to theology journals.

WORK IN PROGRESS: A book on Kierkegaard; a philosophical account of moral psychology.

SIDELIGHTS: Roberts writes: "My intellectual interests are in modern British philosophy and modern Christian theology. My philosophical interests run primarily to ethics and philosophy of mind. My writings in theology have been almost wholly destructive, but I am turning now to a more positive analysis, which I hope to present in the form of a book on Kierkegaard." *Avocational interests:* Playing classical guitar, travel in Europe, studying languages and music.

*   *   *

ROBINET, Harriette Gillem   1931-

PERSONAL: Surname is pronounced Ro-bi-*nay;* born July 14, 1931, in Washington, D.C.; daughter of Richard Avitus (a teacher) and Martha (a teacher; maiden name, Gray) Gillem; married McLouis Joseph Robinet (a health physicist), August 6, 1960; children: Stephen, Philip, Rita, Jonathan, Marsha, Linda. *Education:* College of New Rochelle, B.S., 1953; Catholic University of America, M.S., 1957, Ph.D., 1963. *Politics:* Democrat. *Religion:* Roman Catholic. *Home and office:* 214 South Elmwood, Oak Park, Ill. 60302.

CAREER: Walter Reed Army Medical Center, Washington, D.C., medical bacteriologist, 1954-57; Xavier University, New Orleans, La., instructor in biology, 1957-58; U.S. Army, Quartermaster Corps, civilian food bacteriologist, 1960-61. *Member:* American Orchid Society.

WRITINGS: Jay and the Marigold (juvenile), Children's Press, 1976. Contributor to magazines.

WORK IN PROGRESS: A novel set in Louisiana swamplands and the Mississippi subdelta.

SIDELIGHTS: Harriette Robinet's seven-year-old son has cerebral palsy. Because of him, she has met many handicapped children and adults, who "have shared some of their anger, dreams, and victories." Her book is "a story book about a handicapped child who learns from a friend and a marigold how to be a winner." *Avocational interests:* Pets, bird watching, growing plants (especially orchids), knitting, crocheting, sketching.

*   *   *

ROBINSON, L(eonard) W(allace)   1912-

PERSONAL: Born November 9, 1912, in Malden, Mass.; son of Henry M. (a florist) and Ellen (Flynn) Robinson; married Patricia Goedicke (a poet); children: Roderick Wallace. *Education:* Attended Columbia University, 1931-35, New School for Social Research, 1944-47, and University of Guanajuato at San Miguel Allende, 1972-76. *Home:* Apdo. 462, San Miguel Allende, Guanajuato, Mexico. *Agent:* Sterling Lord Agency, Inc., 660 Madison Ave., New York, N.Y. 10021.

CAREER: Has worked as reporter and writer for *New Yorker* (magazine), associate editor of *Life,* executive editor of *Parade,* managing editor of *Esquire,* and editor-in-chief of *Collier's,* 1956-57; Henry Holt & Co. (now Holt, Rinehart & Winston, Inc.), New York City, executive editor, 1957—.

WRITINGS—Novels: *The Assassin,* World Publishing, 1968; *With Time Running Out,* New American Library, 1971; *The Man Who Loved Beauty,* Harper, 1976. Contributor of articles and stories to national magazines, including *Harper's.*

WORK IN PROGRESS: Easy Acres, a novel; *The Burnt Offering,* a novel.

*   *   *

ROBSJOHN-GIBBINGS, Terence Harold   1905-1976

1905—October 20, 1976; British-born American furniture designer, interior decorator, and author of several books on design; his furniture was noted for its simple lines derived from classic architecture. Since 1964 he lived in Athens, Greece, where he died. Obituaries: *New York Times,* October 29, 1976.

*   *   *

ROCHE, John P(earson)   1923-

PERSONAL: Born May 7, 1923, in Brooklyn, N.Y.; son of Walther John (a salesman) and Ruth (Pearson) Roche; married Constance Ratcliff Ludwig (an artist), June 21, 1947; children: Joanna Ratcliff. *Education:* Hofstra College (now University), A.B., 1943; Cornell University, A.M., 1947, Ph.D., 1949. *Politics:* Social Democrat. *Religion:* Society of Friends (Quakers). *Home:* 15 Bay State Rd., Weston, Mass. 02193. *Office:* Fletcher School of Law and Diplomacy, Tufts University, Medford, Mass. 02155.

CAREER: Haverford College, Haverford, Pa., instructor, 1949-50, assistant professor, 1951-53, associate professor of political science, 1953-56; Brandeis University, Waltham, Mass., Christian Herter Professor of Politics and History, 1956-73, chairman of department of politics, 1958-60, dean of faculty of arts and sciences, 1958-61; Tufts University, Fletcher School of Law and Diplomacy, Medford, Mass., Henry R. Luce Professor of Civilization and Foreign Affairs, 1973—, academic dean, 1977—. Fulbright lecturer at University of Aix-en-Provence; visiting professor at Swarthmore College, Cornell University, Columbia University, Massachusetts Institute of Technology, and University of Chicago. Member, Presidential Commission on International Radio Broadcasting, 1972-74. Member of U.S. Board for International Broadcasting. Member of U.S. Postmaster General's stamp advisory committee, 1967-69. Fellow of Hudson Institute; member of National Council on the Humanities, 1968-70; member of board of trustees of Smithsonian Institution's Woodrow Wilson International Center for Scholars, 1967-75; member of board of trustees of Dubinsky Foundation; member of board of directors of A. Philip Randolph Institute. Consultant to U.S. Department of State; special consultant to the U.S. President, 1972-74. *Military service:* U.S. Army Air Forces, 1943-46; became staff sergeant.

MEMBER: Council on Foreign Relations, Americans for Democratic Action (national chairman, 1962-65), Phi Beta Kappa, Phi Alpha Theta. *Awards, honors:* Moses Coit Tylet Prize from Cornell University, 1949, for *The Early Development of the United States Citizenship;* fellow of Fund for the Advancement of Education, 1954-55, and Rockefeller Foundation, 1961-62, 1965-66; D.Litt. from Ripon College, 1975.

WRITINGS: The Early Development of the United States Citizenship, Cornell University Press, 1949; (with Murray S. Stedman, Jr.) *The Dynamics of Democratic Government,* McGraw, 1954; *Courts and Rights,* Random House, 1961, 2nd edition, 1966; (editor with Leonard W. Levy) *Readings in American Government,* four volumes, Harcourt, 1962-63; (with Levy) *The American Image: The Political Process,* Braziller, 1963; *The Quest for the Dream: The Development of Civil Liberties and Human Relations in Modern America,* Macmillan, 1963; *Shadow and Substance: Essays on the Theory and Structure of Politics,* Macmillan, 1964; (with Stedman and Eugene Meehan) *The Dynamics of Modern Government,* McGraw, 1966; (editor) *The Origins of American Political Thought,* Harper, 1966; (editor) *American Political Thought: From Jefferson to Progressivism,* Harper, 1967; (editor) *John Marshall: Major Opinions and Other Writings,* Bobbs-Merrill, 1967; *The Vietnam Negotiations: A Case-Study in Communist Political Warfare,* American Enterprise Institute, 1973; *Sentenced to Life: Essays on Law, Politics, and Education,* Macmillan, 1974.

Contributor: Milton Knovitz and Clinton Rossiter, editors, *Aspects of Liberty,* Cornell University Press, 1958; (author of introduction) Victor Serge, *The Case of Comrade Tulayev,* Anchor Books, 1963; Alison Durham and Philip Kurland, editors, *Mr. Justice,* University of Chicago Press, 2nd edition (Roche was not included in 1st edition), 1964; (author of introduction) Lynne Rianniello, editor, *Milestones Along the March,* Praeger, 1965; Hans Morgenthau, editor, *The Crossroad Papers,* Norton, 1965; Daniel Boorstin, editor, *An American Primer,* Volume II, University of Chicago Press, 1966; Anthony Lake, editor, *The Legacy of Vietnam,* Council on Foreign Relations, 1976.

Anthologized in *The Antioch Review Anthology,* 1953. Author of "A Word Edgewise," a weekly column syndicated by King Features to about a hundred fifty newspapers, 1968—; and monthly column "News Watch," in *TV Guide.* Contributor to *International Encyclopedia of Social Science.* Contributor of dozens of articles and reviews to scholarly and popular journals.

WORK IN PROGRESS: A study of "American Immigration and Nationality: 1607-1977" for *Harvard Encyclopedia of American Ethnicity.*

SIDELIGHTS: Roche writes: "Essentially my careers in the academy, politics, and writing all mesh very well, that is, writing for me is simply an extrapolation of my main work as a teacher of American foreign policy, constitutional law, and civilization. Because of my non-intellectual background (neither of my parents graduated from high school), I think I have considerable insight into the reactions of those most uncommon men and women, the average American citizens. Also roughly thirty years of professional work as a historian and political scientist has provided me with substantial information in depth about contemporary problems. Finally, I am a one-man band with no staff—any mistakes I make are my own."

*   *   *

RODIMSTEV, Aleksandr 1905(?)-1977

1905(?)—April 16, 1977; Russian military officer and author

of several books; fought in the Spanish Civil War and at the defense of Stalingrad in World War II. Obituaries: *New York Times,* April 17, 1977.

*   *   *

RODOWSKY, Colby 1932-

PERSONAL: Born February 26, 1932, in Baltimore, Md.; daughter of Frank M. Fossett and Mary C. Fitz-Townsend; married Lawrence Rodowsky (a lawyer), August 7, 1954; children: Laurie, Alice, Emily, Sarah, Gregory, Katherine. *Education:* College of Notre Dame of Maryland, B.A., 1953. *Religion:* Roman Catholic. *Home:* 4306 Norwood Rd., Baltimore, Md. 21218. *Agent:* Theron Raines, Raines & Raines, 475 Fifth Ave., New York, N.Y. 10017.

CAREER: Teacher in public schools in Baltimore, Md., 1953-55, and in a school for special education, 1955-56; Notre Dame Preparatory School, Baltimore, assistant librarian, 1974—.

WRITINGS—For children: *What About Me?,* F. Watts, 1976; *P.S. Write Soon,* F. Watts, in press.

WORK IN PROGRESS: A novel for young people; short stories.

SIDELIGHTS: Colby Rodowsky writes: "I find writing for young people a rewarding and challenging experience—but find that I draw on my own reactions—my own memory—and am always delighted when young people say—'But how do you know how it is?'"

*   *   *

RODZINSKI, Halina 1904-

PERSONAL: Born November 18, 1904, in Warsaw, Poland; came to the United States in 1934, naturalized citizen, 1940; daughter of Franciszek (an architect) and Halina (Wieniawski) Lilpop; married Artur Rodzinski (an orchestra conductor), July 19, 1934 (died November 27, 1958); children: Richard. *Education:* Attended University of Warsaw, 1923-25. *Religion:* Roman Catholic. *Home:* 200 East End Ave., New York, N.Y. 10028.

CAREER: Committee for the Blind of Poland, New York City, president, 1959—. Member of board of directors of Polish Assistance, Inc.; member of Kosciuszko Foundation. *Member:* Polish Institute of Arts and Sciences, Pilsudski Institute. *Awards, honors:* Named honorary chairman of Harlem School of the Arts.

WRITINGS: Our Two Lives (memoirs), Scribner, 1976.

SIDELIGHTS: Halina Rodzinski writes: "I wrote that book because I felt that my life was so rich and taught me so much that I wanted to share my various experiences with the world; and also I wanted to tell the truth about my husband whose image is badly distorted by his enemies—he was a great man and I wanted him to be remembered for all he did for music in the U.S.A. and abroad."

*   *   *

ROGERS, Gayle 1923-

PERSONAL: Born May 17, 1923, in Watsonville, Calif.; daughter of Manley Duane (an auto dealer) and Gladyce (an artist; maiden name, Horton) Rogers; married Keith Charles Brown (a contractor), November 26, 1944 (divorced, 1962); children: Kendall Keith, Kevin Doran. *Education:* University of California at Los Angeles, B.A., 1948; California Lutheran College, M.A., 1974; also attended Northridge University. *Politics:* "Generally Democrat." *Religion:* "All religions." *Home:* 207 Dickenson Ave., Newbury Park, Calif. 91320. *Agent:* Scott Meredith, 845 Third Ave., New York, N.Y. 10022.

CAREER: Worked as a high school teacher in Los Angeles, Calif., 1949-55; Thousand Oaks High School, Thousand Oaks, Calif., teacher of U.S. history and minority studies, 1963—. *Member:* American Federation of Teachers.

WRITINGS: The Second Kiss, McKay, 1972, published as *Nakoa's Woman,* Dell, 1975.

WORK IN PROGRESS: Love's Sake Only, a sequel to *Nakoa's Woman;* a movie script of *Nakoa's Woman.*

SIDELIGHTS: Rogers told *CA:* "Since I was pronounced 'dead' at seven years of age I have had many, many psychic experiences, including remembering parts of so-called past lives. *Naoka's Woman* is a true story witnessed by me as an Indian woman, and I hope to write about what I witnessed in Elizabethan Cornwall, colonial Williamsburg, pre-revolutionary war Massachusetts, etc., involving the hero and heroine of *Nakoa's Woman.* I would also like time to write a book of my spiritual experiences."

*   *   *

ROGERS, Sarah F.   1923(?)-1976

1923(?)—November 18, 1976; American educator and author of a book on education; supervisor of an experimental preschool program and diagnostic tester for schools and a private referral center. She died in Harrisburg, Pa. Obituaries: *Washington Post,* November 23, 1976.

*   *   *

ROGERS, (George) Truett   1931-

PERSONAL: Born April 7, 1931, in Joliet, Ill.; son of Herschel E. (a printer) and Mary (a teacher; maiden name, O'Bryan) Rogers; married, 1952 (divorced, 1976); children: Paula (Mrs. Albert Vogelsberg), Gary B., Greg D. *Education:* Attended Baylor University, 1949-51, and Odessa College, 1951; Hardin-Simmons University, B.A., 1953; Southwestern Baptist Theological Seminary, M.Div., 1959; University of Colorado, M.A., 1973, Ph.D., 1976. *Politics:* Independent. *Home:* 354 Castlewood Dr., Devon, Pa. 19333.

CAREER: Ordained Baptist minister, 1958; pastor of Baptist churches in Colorado Springs, Colo., 1959-62, and Boulder, Colo., 1962-73; substitute teacher in Huntington, N.Y., 1974; University of Colorado, Boulder, instructor in American history, 1975-76; Central Baptist Church, Wayne, Pa., interim minister, 1976-77; Alderson-Broaddus College, Phillipi, W.V., assistant professor of history, 1977—. Member of Australia-New Zealand public speaking tour, 1964; member of board of trustees of Southern Baptist Theological Seminary, 1967-73. *Military service:* U.S. Army, 1954-56; became first lieutenant.

WRITINGS: Bibles and Battle Drums, Judson, 1976. Contributor to religious magazines.

WORK IN PROGRESS: A biography of Obadiah Holmes of colonial Rhode Island.

SIDELIGHTS: Rogers told *CA:* "The motivation to be a historian has sprung out of my background as a minister. All research in historical fields has been in the areas of church history, European and American."

*   *   *

ROHATYN, Dennis   1949-

PERSONAL: Born April 21, 1949, in New York, N.Y.; son of Frederick S. (an engineer) and Lotte (a physician) Rohatyn; married Tonya (an attorney), January 18, 1974. *Education:* Queens College of the City University of New York, B.A. (magna cum laude), 1968; City College of the City University of New York, M.A., 1969; Fordham University, Ph.D., 1972. *Office:* Department of Philosophy, University of San Diego, Alcala Park, San Diego, Calif. 92110.

CAREER: Roosevelt University, Chicago, Ill., assistant professor of philosophy, 1972-77; University of San Diego, San Diego, Calif., associate professor of philosophy, 1977—. *Member:* American Philosophical Association, American Catholic Philosophical Association, Illinois Philosophical Association, Phi Beta Kappa.

WRITINGS: Naturalism and Deontology: An Essay on the Problems of Ethics, Mouton & Co., 1975; *Two Dogmas of Philosophy and Other Essays in the Philosophy of Philosophy,* Associated University Presses, 1976.

WORK IN PROGRESS: Work on papers and books in all areas of the history of philosophy, and ethics and value theory.

SIDELIGHTS: Rohatyn writes: "My wife's influence on me is more profound than that of any books or philosophers. It has helped to make me a better person as well as, for the first time, a thinker."

*   *   *

ROLFE, Sidney   1921-1976

PERSONAL: Born June 20, 1921, in Gary, Ind.; married wife, Maria, 1960. *Education:* University of Chicago, B.A., 1943, Ph.D., 1952; attended London School of Economics and Political Science, 1949-50. *Address:* 860 United Nations Plaza, New York, N.Y.

CAREER: Princeton University, Princeton, N.J., instructor in economics, 1948-51; with Economic Stabilization Administration, 1951-52; Columbia University, New York City, research associate, 1952-53, lecturer, 1954-59; president of Charles Development Corp., 1960-76; Long Island University, Greenvale, N.Y., professor of finance, 1966-76. Consultant, U.S. Department of Labor and Economic Stabilization Administration, 1951. Economist, CIT Financial Corp., 1953-60. President and chairperson, Agora Development Corp., 1959-66. Research associate, Stanford University, 1960, Massachusetts Institute of Technology, Center for International Studies, 1970-76; Dean of business affairs, City University of New York, 1961-63. Visiting professor, New School for Social Research, 1967. *Military service:* U.S. Army, 1942-46, became 1st lieutenant. *Awards, honors:* Social Science Research Council fellow, 1949-50. *Member:* American Council of Learned Societies (fellow), American Economic Association, National Association of Business Economists (treasurer, 1962).

WRITINGS: (With Robert G. Hawkins) *A Critical Survey of Plans for International Monetary Reform,* New York University, 1965; (with Hawkins) *Gold and World Power: The Dollar, the Pound, and the Plan for Reform,* Harper, 1966; *Capital Markets in the Atlantic Economic Relationships,* Atlantic Institute (Boulogne-sur-Seine, France), 1967; *The International Corporation, with an Epilogue on Rights and Responsibilities,* International Chamber of Commerce, 1969; *The Multinational Corporation,* Foreign Policy Association, 1970; (editor) *The Multinational Corporation in the World Economy,* Praeger, 1970; (editor) *Managing the Environment: International Economic Cooperation for Pollution Control,* Praeger, 1971; (with James Burtle) *The Great*

Wheel—The World Monetary System: A Reinterpretation, Quadrangle, 1973.

SIDELIGHTS: With his book, *Gold and World Power: The Dollar, the Pound, and the Plans to Reform,* Rolfe became one of the first economists to advocate the floating foreign exchange rates later adopted by the world monetary powers. In 1967, he organized the Atlantic Council meeting in Cannes, France, where the economic chiefs of Europe and the Far East gathered to discuss Atlantic economic relationships as well as the impact of multinational concerns on the world economy.

OBITUARIES: New York Times, March 11, 1976; *Time,* March 22, 1976.

(Died March 10, 1976, in East Hampton, N.Y.)

* * *

ROMERO, Orlando 1945-

PERSONAL: Born September 24, 1945, in Santa Fe, N.M.; son of Jose (a machinist) and Ruby Anne (Romero) Romero; married Rebecca Lopez (a journalist), February 10, 1968; children: Carlota, Orlando. *Education:* College of Santa Fe, B.A., 1974; University of Arizona, M.L.S., 1976. *Politics:* "A determination to save blue corn, blue sky, and New Mexico's earth." *Religion:* "Humanity revealed through the contemplative mysteries of God and Nature." *Home address:* Rt. 1, Box 103, Santa Fe, N.M. 87501. *Office:* New Mexico State Library, P.O. Box 1629, Santa Fe, N.M. 87501.

CAREER: Office of the New Mexico Secretary of State, Santa Fe, aide, 1964-67; New Mexico State Library, Santa Fe, library assistant, 1967-69; New Mexico State Supreme Court Law Library, Santa Fe, library assistant, 1969-74; New Mexico State Library, librarian for Southwest and special collections, 1977—. *Member:* Affirmative Action Committee of New Mexico State Library, Reforma, Rio Grande Writers' Association, New Mexico Library Association, New Mexico Book League.

WRITINGS: Nambe—Year One (novel), Tonatiuh International, 1976.

WORK IN PROGRESS: The Day of the Wind, short stories; *Abuelitas: New Mexico's Grandmothers and Great-Grandmothers; Turkos: New Mexico's Gypsies;* a book on New Mexico's architecture.

SIDELIGHTS: Romero told *CA:* "What motivates my writing? Primarily, *Nambe—Year One* was the beginning of self-realization, more precisely, an autobiographical way to state the Hispano's relationship to the earth. Ritual motivates me. Ritual as in the seasons, the menstrual cycles of streams and all the life therein. Wild dogs howling at the moon and barren wombs whispering the decay of autumn. Which in essence means redefining ritual.

"What motivates my writing? Hope for mankind and the eternal dream that we can live in peace with ourselves and the earth that sustains us. It is not concrete, that inspires it, or cities like Albuquerque or Phoenix or Los Angeles, but ancient people against the background of eternally blue skies and their determination to remain self sufficient despite the cost.

"My work is regional only in the sense that spawning salmon return to their place of birth, only in the sense that all of us are part of dark, brown earth and only in the sense that I am nourished by blue corn meal and blue skies."

AVOCATIONAL INTERESTS: "I am a voracious reader.

I sculpt in wood. I tie flies and I can squander my life away in the midst of a trout stream or in a field of ripening blue corn. I also like to build with adobe bricks. And conversation, be it with a philosophical hobo or a great man of letters."

* * *

ROOK, Tony 1932-

PERSONAL: Born July 12, 1932, in Kent, England; son of Reginald James (a manager) and Cecilie (Bloomfield) Rook; married Helen Merle Travis (a teacher), March 3, 1959; children: Katherine Lucy, Sylvia Jane. *Education:* University of Leicester, B.Sc., 1957; University of London, M.Phil., 1975. *Politics:* Liberal. *Religion:* None. *Home:* 23 Mill Lane, Welwyn, Hertfordshire AL6 9EU, England.

CAREER: George Wimpey & Co., Ltd., London, England, deputy head of department of building and civil engineering research and development, 1957-60; Chalk Line & Allied Industries Research Association, Welwyn, England, deputy head of department of building and civil engineering research and development, 1960-63; science teacher and head of department at independent secondary school in Welwyn, England, 1963-73; writer and archaeologist, 1973—. *Military service:* Royal Air Force, airborne radar fitter, 1951-54; served in Germany. *Member:* Crime Writers Association, St. Albans and Hertfordshire Architectural and Archaeological Society (member of council), Welwyn Archaeological Society (member of board of directors), District Council Museums Committee, Council for British Archaeology and Hertfordshire Archaeological Council (member of executive board), Lockleys Archaeological Trust.

WRITINGS: Strange Mansion (mystery novel), Milton House, 1974. Author of a local history and archaeology column in *Review.* Contributor to archaeology and history magazines and guides. Editor of *Hertfordshire Archaeological Review.* Also creator of "Rookbooks."

WORK IN PROGRESS: Murder in the Concrete; The Labrador Trust; Foul Play at Felhurst; Dragonshyde, a novel; *Practical Archaeology;* a monograph on Roman baths.

SIDELIGHTS: Rook comments: "I have been an amateur archaeologist since school. I 'dropped out' from teaching to do research in archaeology, now am a freelance archaeologist, coupled with writing and lecturing (the latter offers some financial reward)."

* * *

ROOSEVELT, Edith Kermit 1926-

PERSONAL: Born December 19, 1926, in New York City; daughter of Archibald Bulloch (a bond salesman) and Grace Stackpole (Lockwood) Roosevelt; married Alexander G. Barmine, September 8, 1948 (divorced, 1952); children: Margot Hornblower. *Education:* Barnard College, B.A., 1948. *Home and office:* Apt. 500, 1661 Crescent Pl. N.W., Washington, D.C. 20009.

CAREER: United Press, reporter in San Francisco and Los Angeles, Calif., 1950-53, in Washington, D.C., 1953-55; Spadea Syndicate, New York City, feature writer, 1956-63, associate editor, 1957-59; Washington correspondent for *New Hampshire Sunday News,* 1959—, *Vermont Sunday News,* 1963—, *Connecticut Sunday Herald, Manchester Union Leader,* and *St. Albans Messenger,* 1967—; syndicated columnist, 1963—. Lecturer. *Awards, honors:* Award from American Academy of Public Affairs of Los Angeles for column.

WRITINGS: Writer of weekly newspaper column, "Between the Lines." Contributor of articles to *Navy, Barron's, America, National Review, American Legion, Lifetime Living, Your Health, Black Belt, Catholic Digest, Popular Medicine, Karate International,* and to newspaper Sunday supplements.

SIDELIGHTS: Ms. Roosevelt wrote: "I contribute to periodicals for widely diverse interests because I have many different types of interests and have been raised in the UPI tradition of being able to handle any type of story. I don't think it is difficult to write for any type of publication if you have had a rounded type of education and experience. . . . I suppose more than most anything else I have been interested and concerned with the impact of science and technology on political and economic problems."

AVOCATIONAL INTERESTS: "Health, preventive medicine, and fitness; in reading about it, doing it, and practicing it."

* * *

ROOSEVELT, James 1907-

PERSONAL: Born December 23, 1907, in Hyde Park, N.Y.; son of Franklin Delano (president of the United States) and Anna Eleanor (a writer and lecturer; maiden name Roosevelt) Roosevelt; married Betsey Cushing (divorced, 1940); married Romelle Schneider (divorced, 1956); married Irene Kitchenmaster (divorced, 1969); married Mary Winskill (a teacher), October 3, 1969. *Education:* Harvard University, graduate, 1930; Boston University, graduate study, 1931. *Religion:* Episcopal. *Office:* James Roosevelt & Co., 100 Newport Center Dr., Suite 200, Newport Beach, Calif. 92660.

CAREER: Roosevelt & Sargent, Inc. (insurance), Boston, Mass., organizer and president, 1931-37; in motion picture industry, 1938-40; Roosevelt & Sargent, Inc., executive vice-president of west coast office, 1946; U.S. House of Representatives, congressman from 26th California district, 1955-66, serving on committee on education and labor and select small business committee; United Nations, New York City, U.S. ambassador to Economic & Social Council, 1966-68; I.O.S. Development Co. (mutual funds), Geneva, Switzerland, vice-president, 1968-71; James Roosevelt & Co., Newport Beach, Calif., president, 1971—. Lecturer in social ecology at University of California at Irvine, 1973—. Trustee of National Foundation-March of Dimes; trustee of estate of Franklin D. Roosevelt; trustee of Chapman College; member of board of South Coast Repertory. *Military service:* U.S. Marine Corps Reserve, 1940-45; became brigadier general; received Navy Cross and Silver Star Medal. *Member:* Metropolitan Club, Harvard Club.

WRITINGS: (Editor) *The Liberal Papers,* Anchor Books, 1962; (with Sidney Shalett) *Affectionately, F.D.R.: A Son's Story of a Lonely Man,* Harcourt, 1959; (with Bill Libby) *My Parents: A Differing View,* Playboy Press, 1976.

WORK IN PROGRESS: A biography, *Evans F. Carlson: Man Extraordinare.*

* * *

ROOT, Lin (Segal)

PERSONAL: Born in Boston, Mass.; daughter of Samuel and Jennie (Kader) Segal; married Wells Root; children: Jonathan S. *Education:* Columbia University, B.A. and M.A. *Home:* 44 West 44th St., New York, N.Y. 10036.

CAREER: Science and medicine editor for *Time* Magazine;

free-lance writer and foreign correspondent. Has been a visiting professor of English at Pennsylvania State University, University Park. Has been employed as a research biochemist for Psychiatric Institute of the Manhattan State Hospitals; associate in special problems, Arcturus Oceanographic Expedition to the Galapagos and the Sargasso Sea; assistant bacteriologist, Louisiana Sugar Experiment Station. *Member:* Society of Magazine Writers (president), Overseas Press Club (governor, vice-president, and secretary), Nuclear Energy Writers, National Associaton of Scientific Writers, Council for the Advancement of Science Writing, Association for the Advancement of Science.

WRITINGS: "One Good Year" (two-act comedy), first produced in New York City at Lyceum Theatre. Author of screenplays, including "Beating Back" and "Her Wedding Night," for Paramount and Universal. Also author of serialized adaption of the Spanish novel, *Pancho Villa.* Contributor of articles to national magazines, including *Fortune, Collier's, Reader's Digest,* and *Cosmopolitan.* Author of scientific monographs.

WORK IN PROGRESS: A book about the development of nuclear energy through weapons.

SIDELIGHTS: Lin Root writes: "When I was a Distinguished Visiting Professor at the Pennsylvania State University in the English Department, I impressed upon my graduate seminar, which consisted of 20 doctoral candidates in 18 disciplines distributed almost equally between the Liberal Arts and the Natural Sciences, that writing required the same skills, fidelity to fact, and integrity, regardless of subject. Of course, the fact that I started out as a research biochemist, moved into science writing and then into the humanities gave me a special advantage. However, I think one could move in either direction as long as one's interests are sufficiently stimulated."

* * *

ROSE, Hannah T. 1909(?)-1976

1909(?)—December 14, 1976; American museum curator and author of books on museums and other subjects; programs she established while curator of education at the Brooklyn Museum influenced museums around the world. She died in Rhosneigr, Wales. Obituaries: *AB Bookman's Weekly,* February 14, 1977.

* * *

ROSEBURY, Theodor 1904-1976

August 10, 1904—November 25, 1976; British-born American bacteriologist, specialist in venereal disease, educator, and author of books on venereal disease and on bacteria and their effects on man. His work *Life on Man* won special commendation in the science category of the 1971 National Book Awards. He died in Conway, Mass. Obituaries: *New York Times,* November 28, 1976. (*CAP*-2; earlier sketch in *CA*-25/28)

* * *

ROSEN, Marvin J(erold) 1929-

PERSONAL: Born September 11, 1929, in Los Angeles, Calif.; son of Joseph (a garment pattern-maker) and Gertrude (a bookkeeper; maiden name, Rhodeside) Rosen; married Ruth Seagal (a bank representative), April 14, 1955; children: Stephen Dennis, Jennifer Lynn, Joseph Alan. *Education:* University of Chicago, student, 1946-47; University of Minnesota, B.S., 1951; University of California,

Los Angeles, M.A., 1957, Ed.D., 1968. *Home:* 2010 Linnington Ave., Los Angeles, Calif. 90025. *Office:* Department of Communications, California State University, Fullerton, Calif. 92634.

CAREER: Minneapolis Star & Tribune, Minneapolis, Minn., editorial and public relations assistant, 1947-51; elementary school teacher in Omaha, Neb., 1952-53; Town 'n Country Playhouse, Buffalo, N.Y. and Bismarck, N.D., director and stage manager, 1955-56; Kansas City Resident Theater, Kansas City, Mo., managing director, 1956-58; U.S. Civil Service, Washington, D.C., director of cultural programs in Europe, 1958-61; Circle Arts Theatre, San Diego, Calif., artistic director, 1961-62; California Western Univeristy, San Diego, theatre arts and technical director-designer, 1961-62; El Camino College, Los Angeles, Calif., technical director and instructor in theater arts, 1962; Jewish Community Center, San Diego, director of cultural arts, 1962-63; University of California, Santa Cruz, acting assistant professor of education, 1965-68; University of California, Los Angeles, lecturer in education and associate director of Research and Development Center, 1968-70; California State University, Fullerton, associate professor, 1970-73, professor of communications, 1973—. Visiting professor at Towson State University, autumn, 1976. Consultant to American Institutes for Research in the Behavioral Sciences, National Laboratory for Higher Education, and other public educational agencies. *Military service:* Minnesota Army National Guard, 1948-51. U.S. Air Force, 1951-52.

MEMBER: International Communication Association, Association for Educational Communications and Technology, Association for Education in Journalism, Phi Delta Kappa. *Awards, honors:* Teaching award from Communications Students Advisory Council, 1972.

WRITINGS: Preparing Educational Specifications for College Learning Spaces, Office of Instructional Services, University of California, Santa Cruz, 1967; *Instructional Improvement Training Series,* National Laboratory for Higher Education, 1972; (contributor) James J. Lynn and E. David Graf, editors, *Preparing for Public Service Occupations: Common Core,* California State Department of Education, 1973; *Introduction to Photography: A Self-Directing Approach,* Houghton, 1976. Contributor to education, communication, and public relations journals.

WORK IN PROGRESS: Research for *Pictorial Journalism in America,* completion expected in 1979.

SIDELIGHTS: Rosen writes: "Before I was ten years old I built my own photographic enlargers and opaque projectors, hired out as a magician, and published my own neighborhood newspapers, signaling what has since become a lifelong infatuation with the visual, performing, and communication arts.

"After that I worked as a cub reporter and photographer, produced jazz-graphic concerts, directed, designed, and performed in plays and musicals, toured Europe for nearly three years as a theatrician, and studied and taught the theory and practice of education, theater, and mass communication.

"I try to sensitize my students to their world, particularly that which is close at hand, and to motivate their use of modern communication media not only as means for artistic self-expression, but also as tools for heightening public awareness of physical, social, and psychological realities which affect the quality of life for themselves and future generations."

ROSENBLATT, Suzanne Maris 1937-

PERSONAL: Born July 2, 1937, in Hackensack, N.J.; daughter of David (an engineer) and Rose (a nursery school owner and teacher; maiden name, Richman) Freedman; married Adolph Rosenblatt (an artist), March 26, 1961; children: Sarah, Eli, Joshua. *Education:* Attended Central School of Arts and Crafts, London, England, and London School of Economics and Political Science, London, both 1957-58; Oberlin College, B.A., 1959; also attended Cooper Union, 1960, and Art Students League of New York, 1961-63. *Politics:* Democrat. *Home:* 4211 North Maryland, Milwaukee, Wis. 53211.

CAREER: Artist; has had solo and group shows in Wisconsin, Illinois, Indiana, New York (including Roko Gallery, Weyhe Gallery, and City Center Art Gallery), Tennessee, and Pennsylvania (Philadelphia Art Alliance); has made courtroom drawings for local television stations. Producer, director, and editor of "Dancers," a film of her paintings and drawings, 1975; work is included in collections at New York Library and Museum of the Performing Arts. *Awards, honors:* First prize in creative expression from Shasta Film Festival, 1976, for film "Dancers."

WRITINGS: Everyone Is Going Somewhere (self-illustrated juvenile), Macmillan, 1975; *Dancers* (drawings), privately printed, 1977. Contributor of paintings and drawings to *Insight, Chicago Tribune,* and *Milwaukee Sentinel.*

WORK IN PROGRESS: Children's books; a series of paintings and drawings; writing about soap operas.

SIDELIGHTS: Suzanne Rosenblatt writes: "I take very seriously (but with humor) the things most important to me. This is not as tautological as it sounds. As a mother and wife I'm deeply involved in the health of both the mind and the body of those who depend on me; I attempt (not always successfully) to find the best, rather than the easiest, ways to solve the problems of parenthood and personhood. As an artist, I'm most stimulated by new challenges. And as a human being I'm constantly trying to figure out what life (and death) are all about and why I and everyone else do what we do; I'm always trying to determine priorities and, concomitantly, morality. One question relating to this last problem is: Does an artist have a moral right to spend his life developing his own creativity while the world around him is deteriorating into chaos? I've concluded that the answer is 'yes' (extremely convenient for an artist). Why? Because art is what sets us above all other animals; art offers us new ways to see the world; art can be the balm for a depressed or exhausted soul; art (in one form or another) is what survives and is remembered of a civilization. There's also the converse to this question: Does an individual have a moral obligation to care for and develop the special abilities he was lucky enough to be born with?"

*   *   *

ROSENFELD, Harry M(orris) 1929-

PERSONAL: Born August 12, 1929, in Berlin, Germany; came to United States, 1939, naturalized citizen, 1945; son of Sam (a furrier) and Esther (Sherman) Rosenfeld; married Anne Hahn, February 28, 1953; children: Susan, Amy, Stefanie. *Education:* Syracuse University, A.B., 1952; graduate study at Columbia University, 1956. *Home:* 9619 Glencrest Lane, Kensington, Md. 20795. *Office: Washington Post,* 1150 15th St. N.W., Washington, D.C. 20071.

CAREER/WRITINGS: New York Herald Tribune, New York City, managing editor of news service, 1960-62, foreign editor, 1962-66; *Washington Post,* Washington, D.C., foreign editor, 1968-70, metropolitan editor, 1970-74, assistant managing editor of national news, 1974-76, assistant managing editor of *Book World* and "Outlook" sections, 1976—. Associate producer, Columbia Broadcasting System, 1962. Lecturer; contributor to *World Book Encyclopedia.* Notable assignments, as reporter include foreign correspondence from Vietnam, and as editor, directed coverage of My Lai massacre, Six Day War in Middle East, Soviet invasion of Czechoslovakia, May Day mobilization, and investigative reporting on hospitals, banks, mortgages, wiretapping, and the Watergate scandal. *Member:* Federal City Club. *Awards, honors:* Associated Press Freedom of Information Award citation, 1973; Black United Front award for community service, 1974; certificate of appreciation from Syracuse University, 1975; B'nai B'rith Anti-Defamation League First Amendment Award, 1976.

BIOGRAPHICAL/CRITICAL SOURCES: Bob Woodward and Carl Bernstein, *All the President's Men,* Simon & Schuster, 1974; Barry Sussman, *The Great Cover-Up: Nixon and the Scandal of Watergate,* New American Library, 1974; Leonard Downie, Jr., *The New Muckrackers,* New Republic, 1976; Lawrence Leamer, *Playing for Keeps in Washington,* Dial, 1977; Lou Cannon, *Reporting: An Inside View,* California Journal Press, 1977.

* * *

ROSENTHAL, Joseph J. 1911-
(Joe Rosenthal)

PERSONAL: Born October 9, 1911, in Washington, D.C.; son of David (a merchant and clothier) and Lena (Hoffman) Rosenthal; married Dorothy Lee Walch, October 5, 1946 (divorced, 1960); children: Joseph J. Jr., Anne Lee. *Education:* Attended University of San Francisco (now San Francisco State University), 1930. *Religion:* Roman Catholic ("convert from Judaism, 1939"). *Residence:* San Francisco, Calif. *Office: San Francisco Chronicle,* 905 Mission St., San Francisco, Calif. 94119.

CAREER: Newspaper Enterprise Association, San Francisco, Calif., officeboy and photographer, 1930-32; *San Francisco News,* San Francisco, photographer and reporter, 1932-35; Newspaper Enterprise Association and Acme News Pictures, both San Francisco, photographer, 1935-36; *New York Times*-Wideworld Photos, San Francisco, photographer and bureau manager, 1936-41; Associated Press, San Francisco, war photographer, 1941-46; *San Francisco Chronicle,* San Francisco, photographer, 1946—. Instructor in photojournalism, City College of San Francisco, 1949, 1950, and 1951. *Military service:* U.S. Maritime Service, 1943, served as warrant officer photographer in Atlantic theatre of operations, Great Britain, and North Africa.

MEMBER: Overseas Press Club, National Press Photographers Association, California Press Photographers Association, San Francisco Press Club (president, 1961), San Francisco Bay Area Press Photographers Association (past president), Kappa Alpha Mu. *Awards, honors: Editor and Publisher's* award for best news photograph, 1936; Pulitzer Prize for news photography, New York Photographers Association award, Catholic Institute of the Press award, *U.S. Camera* medallion, Graflex Diamond award, International News Service Medal of Valor, U.S. Treasury Department Medal of Merit, all 1945, all for photograph of flag raising on Iwo Jima; New York Press Photographers Association award, 1947; San Francisco Press Club award, 1958; honorary degree from Brooks Institute of Photographic Art and Science, 1976.

WRITINGS—Photographic illustration: James Lee, *Operation Lifeline: History and Development of the Naval Air Transport Service,* Ziff-Davis, 1946. Contributor of photographs to journals, magazines, and newspapers.

* * *

ROSETT, Arthur (Irwin) 1934-

PERSONAL: Born July 5, 1934, in New York, N.Y.; son of Milton and Bertha (Werner) Rosett; married Susan Hadas Gurfein (a teacher), June 5, 1956; children: David, Martha, Daniel. *Education:* Columbia University, B.A., 1955, LL.B., 1959. *Office:* School of Law, University of California, Los Angeles, Calif. 90024.

CAREER: U.S. Supreme Court, Washington, D.C., law clerk, 1959-60; U.S. Department of Justice, assistant U.S. attorney for southern district, 1960-63; Patterson, Belknap & Webb, New York, N.Y., attorney, 1963-65; National Crime Commission, Washington, D.C., assistant director of the President's Commission on Law Enforcement, 1965-67; University of California, Los Angeles, acting professor, 1967-70, professor of law, 1970—. *Military service:* U.S. Naval Reserve, 1956-64, active duty, 1956-58; became lieutenant junior grade. *Member:* American Law Institute.

WRITINGS: (Contributor) *ASCAP Copyright Symposium,* Columbia University Press, 1958; *Taskforce Report: The Courts,* U.S. Government Printing Office, 1967; *Materials on Litigation and Negotiation Skills,* privately printed, 1969; (contributor) Werner Z. Hirsch and others, editors, *Fiscal Pressures on the Central City,* Praeger, 1971; (with Addison Mueller) *Contract Law and Its Application,* Foundation Press, 1971; (with Donald R. Cressey) *Justice by Consent: Plea Bargains in the American Courthouse,* Lippincott, 1976. Also author, with Elliot Dorff, of *Materials on the Jewish Legal Tradition with Comparative Notes,* privately printed. Contributor to law journals. Member of editorial advisory board of *Law and Psychiatry Review.*

WORK IN PROGRESS: A book on the careers of trial judges for Twentieth Century Fund; publication expected, 1978; revised edition of *Contract Law and Its Application.*

* * *

ROSS, Betty

PERSONAL: Born in Hartford, Conn.; daughter of Harry H. (an architect) and Frances (Horowitz) Beckanstin; married Richard S. Ross (a journalist and attorney), December 2, 1950 (divorced, 1958); children: Elisabeth Hewitt. *Education:* Smith College, A.B. (cum laude), 1946. *Religion:* Jewish. *Home and office:* 3516 Albemarle St. N.W., Washington, D.C. 20008. *Agent:* Anita Diamant, Writer's Workshop, Inc., 51 East 42nd St., New York, N.Y. 10017.

CAREER: WTOP-Radio, Washington, D.C., assistant to program manager, 1948-50; Mutual Broadcasting System, Washington, D.C., assistant to commentator, 1950-51; free-lance writer and public relations representative in Washington, D.C., 1951-62; Shoreham Hotel, Washington, D.C., public relations director, 1962-71; free-lance writer and consultant, 1971—. District of Columbia delegate to Democratic National Convention, 1964.

MEMBER: Society of American Travel Writers (member of board of directors, 1975—; chairman of Middle Atlantic chapter, 1974-75), National Association of Travel Journalists, Woman's National Democratic Club (member of board of governors, 1963-69), Pacific Area Travel Association, Washington Independent Writers, Washington Print Club.

Awards, honors: Award from Metropolitan Washington Board of Trade, 1976, for excellence of writing.

WRITINGS: How to Beat the High Cost of Travel, U.S. News and World Report Books, 1975. Washington correspondent for *Group Travel,* 1971-74. Contributor to magazines, including *Family Circle, U.S. News and World Report, Better Homes and Gardens, Travel Weekly* and *Dynamic Maturity,* and to newspapers.

* * *

ROSS, Marvin C(hauncey) 1904-1977

November 21, 1904—April 24, 1977; American museum curator, authority on Byzantine art, educator, and author or editor of catalogs of various collections of Byzantine art and contributor of articles to art periodicals. He died in Washington, D.C. Obituaries: *Washington Post,* April 28, 1977. (*CAP*-2; earlier sketch in *CA*-19/20)

* * *

ROSS, Philip 1939-

PERSONAL: Born June 29, 1939, in New York; son of David Robert (a businessman) and Rose (a teacher; maiden name, Rogovin) Ross; married wife Tana, September 11, 1965 (separated, July, 1974); children: Joana Aviva, Dahlia Rebecca. *Education:* Princeton University, B.A., 1961; Columbia University, M.S., 1962. *Religion:* Jewish. *Home and office:* 17 West 94th St., New York, N.Y. 10025. *Agent:* Roberta Pryor, International Creative Management, 40 West 57th St., New York, N.Y. 10019.

CAREER: Record, Hackensack, N.J., reporter, 1962-63; *Newsday,* Garden City, N.Y., reporter, 1963-65; American Museum of Natural History, New York City, writer, 1965-69; free-lance writer, 1969-72; Children's Television Workshop, New York City, in public relations, 1972-73; free-lance writer, 1973—. Member of board of trustees of Walden School. *Military service:* New Jersey National Guard, 1962-66. *Member:* Group Therapy Associates (New York City; president).

WRITINGS: The Bribe, Harper, 1976.

Also author of unproduced screenplay, "The Middle Aged Champion of the World." Contributor to *New York, Reader's Digest, New Times,* and *New York Times.*

WORK IN PROGRESS: A screenplay; television scripts.

SIDELIGHTS: Ross comments: "I write because it's what I seem to do best. It's a tough way to make a living. *The Bribe* is about my younger brother, Burt, who in 1974, while mayor of Fort Lee, N.J., was offered a five hundred thousand dollar bribe to get a zoning variance passed for a shopping center. His undercover work with the Federal Bureau of Investigation led to convictions of seven businessmen and individuals with ties to organized crime."

* * *

ROSSELLINI, Roberto 1906-1977

May 8, 1906—June 3, 1977; Italian filmmaker. His semi-documentary film "Open City," made after the Allied liberation of Rome, established neorealism as one of the most important movements of post-war cinema. His other well-known films include "Paisan" and "Generale Della Rovere." In later years, his work was almost exclusively making documentary films for public television. He died in Rome, Italy. Obituaries: *New York Times,* June 4, 1977; *Washington Post,* June 4, 1977.

ROSSMAN, (George) Parker 1919-

PERSONAL: Born May 20, 1919, in Enid, Okla.; son of George Parker (a poet and clergyman) and Vera E. (a teacher; maiden name, Jacobs) Rossman; married Jean Fleming (a reading consultant), June 6, 1951; children: George III, Kristen (Mrs. J. Kevin MacMahon), Mary-Michelle. *Education:* University of Oklahoma, B.A., 1941; University of Chicago, B.D., 1944; Yale University, Ph.D., 1953. *Politics:* Democrat. *Religion:* Disciples of Christ. *Home and office:* 33 South Washington Ave., Niantic, Conn. 06357. *Agent:* Elizabeth Trupin, Jet Associates, P.O. Box 276, Hastings-on-Hudson, N.Y. 10760.

CAREER: World Student Christian Federation, Geneva, Switzerland, staff member, 1955-56; Board of Higher Education, Indianapolis, Ind., executive of joint commission, 1956-58; Yale University, New Haven, Conn., associate professor of religion in higher education, 1958-65; Balamand School, Tripoli, Lebanon, staff member, 1965-66; Yale University, dean of Ecumenical Continuing Education Center, 1966-72, part-time chaplain and lecturer, 1972—. Lecturer at Cambridge University, 1956; fraternal visitor at Warsaw Seminary, 1960; William Henry Hoover lecturer at University of Chicago, 1961; lecturer at Indian Institute of World Culture, 1962. Chairman of Study Commission on Revolutionary Youth in Latin America; chairman of Central Study Commission of World Council of Churches of Christ.

WRITINGS: Faiths Next Door, Bethany Press, 1970; *Sexual Experience Between Men and Boys,* Association Press, 1976; *Pirate Slave* (novel), Thomas Nelson, 1976; *Hospice,* Association Press, in press; *Damned Kids: Preventing Serious Juvenile Crime,* Association Press, in press.

Author of musical play, "When Shakespeare Dances." Author of radio scripts. Contributor to professional journals.

WORK IN PROGRESS: Can You Kidnap Yourself?, Hungry Spy, Murder Is Being Done, and *Blond Indian,* a series of youth novels, each dealing with a social issue; two non-fiction books, *Creativity: A 40-Day Check-up* and *Travel to Learn;* a trilogy of novels about modern Indians in southeastern Oklahoma.

SIDELIGHTS: Rossman told *CA* that he has completed the drafts of his trilogy of novels set in the southeastern Oklahoma Indian country where he grew up, dealing with modern, well-educated, professional Indians. He says, "Not only am I dealing with the interplay of two cultures in America, I am also attempting to draw on extensive travel and living overseas to bring certain serious sexual problems of young adolescents into focus. These novels are parallel to serious nonfiction research books on the same themes. In this way, as my skill increases, I would like to write nonfiction books which are interestingly written, using some of the craft of novel writing, as well as documenting research which underlines the novels; and I want to write novels which are 'documentary,' not only because of true incidents which lie at their roots, but also because controversial matters in them can be footnoted."

Rossman has visited most Asian and European universities, and has traveled as well in Africa, Australia, and Latin America.

* * *

ROWAN, Ford 1943-

PERSONAL: Born May 31, 1943, in Houston, Tex. *Education:* Tulane University, B.A., 1968; American University, M.A., 1972; Georgetown University, J.D., 1976. *Office:* NBC, 4001 Nebraska Ave. N.W., Washington, D.C. 20016.

CAREER/WRITINGS: WDSU News, New Orleans, La., reporter, 1964-69; WTOP News, Washington, D.C., reporter, 1969-72; WRC News, Washington, D.C., reporter, 1972-73; Television News, Inc., Washington, D.C., reporter, 1973-74; National Broadcasting Co. (NBC), Washington, D.C., reporter, 1974—. Notable assignments include the Nixon administration, the Watergate investigation, and investigations into the C.I.A. and F.B.I. Journalism fellow, University of Chicago Center for Policy Studies, 1972.

*   *   *

ROWE, H. Edward 1927-

PERSONAL: Born March 14, 1927, in Maine; son of Earl Scott (a farmer) and Mable (Perreault) Rowe; married Lois Mae Farr (a real estate agent), June 9, 1946; children: David, Rebecca Kim, Ruth Burris, Deborah Pruitt. *Education:* Gordon College, B.A.; Dallas Theological Seminary, Th.M. *Politics:* Conservative Republican. *Home and office:* 4105 West Ave., Fullerton, Calif. 92633.

CAREER: Ordained minister of Conservative Baptist Church; pastor of church in Dallas, Tex., 1955-56; executive secretary of Jewish Evangelical Witness, 1957-58; pastor of church in Los Angeles, Calif., 1959-64; Christian Freedom Foundation, assistant to president, 1964-66, executive vice-president, 1967-70, president, 1971-75; executive director of Mission to America, 1975—. President of Christians Concerned for More Responsible Citizenship, Fullerton, Calif., 1976—; chairman of Citizens for Good Government; director of Conservative Caucus in California's 39th Congressional District.

WRITINGS: Save America!: The Power of the Christian Citizen, Revell, 1976. Also author of a seminar manual on Christian citizenship, 1976. Editor, *Christian Economics,* 1965-71, and *Applied Christianity,* 1971-74.

WORK IN PROGRESS: Research "to discover the applicability of the guiding principles of the Bible to community and national issues and economic political, civic, and governmental responsibility."

SIDELIGHTS: Rowe writes: "Genuine Biblical faith has contributed significantly to the development of economic, political, and social freedom. It is urgent that those who share such faith practice it intelligently and vigorously within the leadership-selection process at the precinct level as well as at higher levels of the American political system. Otherwise, our freedoms and our entire way of life might be lost."

*   *   *

ROWE, James L(ester), Jr. 1948-

PERSONAL: Born April 2, 1948, in Chicago, Ill.; son of James L. and Marie (Carey) Rowe; married Luara Kiernan (a journalist), March 17, 1973. *Education:* Catholic University of America, A.B., 1969; University of Wisconsin, Madison, graduate study, 1969-70. *Politics:* None. *Religion:* None. *Office: Washington Post,* 1150 15th St. N.W., Washington, D.C. 20071.

CAREER: Washington Post, Washington, D.C., financial writer, 1971—. Faculty advisor, student newspaper at Catholic University of America, 1975—. Has written series on housing finance, the steel industry, and the role and purpose of economic statistics; also covers economic affairs. *Member:* American Economic Association, Society of American Business and Economic Writers, Pi Delta Epsilon.

WRITINGS: (Contributor) *Bad Times and Beyond,* Dell, 1974.

SIDELIGHTS: Rowe comments that his "principal interest as an economist is comparative systems, especially that of the U.S.S.R., but the primary journalistic interest is domestic."

*   *   *

RUANE, Gerald P(atrick) 1934-

PERSONAL: Born January 6, 1934, in Scranton, Pa.; son of Gerald Jerome (a salesman) and Winifred Cecilia Ruane. *Education:* Seton Hall University, B.A., 1956; Manhattan College, M.A., 1970; New York University, Ph.D., 1973; Immaculate Conception Seminary, M.Div., 1976; also studied at University of Louvain, and Oxford University. *Home:* Rectory, Mt. St. Dominic/Caldwell College, Caldwell, N.J. 07006. *Office:* Department of Religious Studies, Caldwell College, Caldwell, N.J. 07006.

CAREER: Ordained Roman Catholic priest of Archdiocese of Newark, N.J., 1960; associate pastor of Roman Catholic church in West Orange, N.J., 1960-67; in charge of youth work at Roman Catholic church in West Orange, N.J., 1960-67; Essex County Catholic Youth Organization Teenage Council, Montclair, N.J., moderator, 1965-66; Caldwell College, Caldwell, N.J., instructor, 1967-70, assistant professor, 1970-73, associate professor, 1973-76, professor of religious studies, 1976—, chaplain, 1967—. Chaplain of Mount St. Dominic Motherhouse and Academy, 1967-76.

MEMBER: College Theology Society (chairman of metropolitan region, 1975), Association of Christian Therapists. *Awards, honors:* Citation from New Jersey Writers Conference, 1977, for *Birth to Birth.*

WRITINGS: (Contributor) Joseph F. X. Cevetello, editor, *All Things to All Men,* Volume II, Joseph Wagner, 1967; *Daily Homilies for the Year,* Joseph Wagner, 1968; *Birth to Birth: The Life-Death Mystery,* Alba, 1976. Contributor to religious periodicals.

WORK IN PROGRESS: Conducting two lecture series on charismatic renewal and on death and dying; a book of reflections.

SIDELIGHTS: Fr. Ruane writes: "I am interested in the Charismatic Prayer Movement and leader of a group here at Caldwell and am in the healing ministry." *Avocational interests:* Tennis, swimming, travel, skiing, and writing.

BIOGRAPHICAL/CRITICAL SOURCES: Florida Catholic, January 28, 1977.

*   *   *

RUBENSTONE, Jessie 1912-

PERSONAL: Born October 14, 1912, in Elkton, Md.; daughter of Jacob (a furniture dealer) and Annie (Levin) Rubenstone; children: Joan (Mrs. E. David Abrams). *Education:* University of Pennsylvania, B.S.Ed., 1934; Drexel University, M.L.S., 1969. *Politics:* Liberal. *Religion:* Jewish. *Home:* 3900 Ford Rd., Apt. 5F, Philadelphia, Pa. 19131. *Agent:* Dorothy Markinko, McIntosh & Otis, Inc., 475 Fifth Ave., New York, N.Y. 10017.

CAREER: Home economics teacher in schools in Philadelphia, Pa., 1936-62; Joseph Leidy Elementary School, Philadelphia, Pa., librarian, 1967—. *Member:* American Library Association, Pennsylvania School Librarians Association, Philadelphia Guild of Hand Weavers, Association of Philadelphia School Librarians, Philadelphia Museum of Art, Philadelphia Children's Reading Round Table, Booksellers Association of Philadelphia, Friends of the Free Library of Philadelphia.

WRITINGS: *Knitting for Beginners,* Lippincott, 1973; *Crochet for Beginners,* Lippincott, 1974; *Weaving for Beginners,* Lippincott, 1975.

WORK IN PROGRESS: *Patchwork and Quilting.*

SIDELIGHTS: Jessie Rubenstone writes: "I have always loved the arts and crafts and have dabbled in them for many years. As a librarian in an elementary school I saw the need for a book of knitting for beginners and this launched my career as a writer. My research has taken me on many delightful trips into the Pennsylvania countryside to visit with weavers and quilters. I find that librarians and craft people are among the warmest and kindest human beings that I have met and I consider myself very lucky to be able to work in both of these areas."

* * *

RUBIN, Arnold P(erry) 1946-

PERSONAL: Born November 21, 1946, in Richmond, Va.; son of David (a transit worker) and Lillian (a saleswoman; maiden name, Rogolsky) Rubin. *Education:* Hunter College, B.A., 1969; Northwestern University, M.S.J., 1971. *Politics:* Moderate Democrat. "I believe in life, liberty, and the pursuit of happiness." *Religion:* Jewish. *Residence:* Forest Hills, N.Y. *Agent:* Curtis Brown, Ltd., 575 Madison Ave., New York, N.Y. 10022.

CAREER: New York City public schools, substitute teacher, 1969-70, teacher of the emotionally disturbed, 1970; Medill News Service, Washington D.C., Washington correspondent, 1970-71; Scholastic Magazines, Inc., New York City, assistant editor, 1971-76, coordinator of National Institute of Student Opinion, 1976—. Desk assistant, CBS-Radio; production assistant, WHN-Radio; copy editor and writer, *Long Island Press,* 1974-76. Lecturer. *Member:* Deadline Club of New York, Sigma Delta Chi, Pi Sigma Alpha. *Awards, honors:* Award from Educational Press Association of America, 1974, for news writing.

WRITINGS: *The Youngest Outlaws: Runaways in America,* Messner, 1976; *The Evil that Men Do: The Story of the Nazis,* Messner, 1977. Author of syndicated column, "Scholastic Poll," appearing in about eighty periodicals, including *Boston Herald American, Denver Post,* and *San Francisco Examiner.* Contributor of articles to periodicals, including *News Citizen, Long Island Press,* and *Commercial & Financial Chronicle.*

WORK IN PROGRESS: A novel.

SIDELIGHTS: Rubin writes that he is especially interested in how society treats minorities, and adds that his interest is not limited to ethnic groups. He says, "I have never failed to be impressed by, and admire, individuals who have overcome handicaps to fill their lives with the riches of creativity, labor, friendship, and love. It is harder for them because they operate under two handicaps: their own disabilities and an environment neither sympathetic nor empathetic to their needs. Society, I am convinced, pays a high price for its apathy and even hostility towards such individuals. In short, I guess you could say I have a great deal of compassion for the striving underdog, who may well include most of us—to one degree or another."

Rubin is particularly involved in the study of the Jewish and non-Jewish relationship because of its depth, scope, and significance to Western culture. He says, "The 'Final Solution' was directed against the Jewish people by a modern, Western state within the lifetimes of most people today. To think that anti-Semitism in particular, and genocide in gen-

eral, are relics of the past is to be dangerously naive. None of us will be truly free and fulfilled until institutionalized anti-Semitism is eradicated, or at least ameliorated."

AVOCATIONAL INTERESTS: Long walks, good music, fine food, books, films, and the company of friends and relations.

* * *

RUBIN, Jerry 1938-

PERSONAL: Born July 14, 1938, in Cincinnati, Ohio; son of Robert (a union organizer) and Esther (Katz) Rubin. *Education:* University of Cincinnati, B.A., 1961; graduate studies at Hebrew University, 1962, and University of California, Berkeley. *Office:* Royce Carlton Lecture Agency, Room 4030, 866 United Nations Plaza, New York, N.Y. 10017.

CAREER: *Cincinnati Post and Times-Star,* Cincinnati, Ohio, reporter, city desk writer, and editor of youth pages, 1956-61; Vietnam Day Committee, Berkeley, Calif., co-chairman and anti-war organizer, 1965-67; Youth International Party (Yippie), Berkeley, Calif., co-founder and activist, 1967-72; lecturer and writer, 1968—. Candidate for mayor of Berkeley, Calif., 1966; U.S. vice-presidential candidate on Peace and Freedom Party ticket, 1968; defendant in Chicago 7 trial, 1969; group leader, Esalen workshops, 1973-74; therapist in Fischer-Hoffman Psychic Therapy Process, 1974; has appeared on numerous television and radio shows.

WRITINGS: *Do It!,* Simon & Shuster, 1969; *We Are Everywhere,* Harper, 1970; (with Abbie Hoffman and Ed Sanders) *Vote,* Warner Paperback, 1972; *Growing (Up) at 37,* Evans, 1976.

WORK IN PROGRESS: A history of the 1960's; a study of male sexuality; a movie of *Growing (Up) at 37.*

* * *

RUBIN, Vitalii 1923-

PERSONAL: Born September 14, 1923, in Moscow, U.S.S.R.; immigrated to Israel, June, 1976; son of Aaron (a philosopher) and Sophia (Bakhmutskaya) Rubin; married Inessa Axelrod (a German teacher), October 7, 1956. *Education:* University of Moscow, graduate, 1951, Ph.D., 1960. *Politics:* "For the strong Jewish state; against modern Nazi-like communism." *Religion:* Judaism. *Home:* Kiryat A. Bronfman 39/15, Jerusalem, Israel. *Office:* Hebrew University, Jerusalem, Israel.

CAREER: Academy of Sciences of U.S.S.R., Moscow, senior bibliographer in social sciences library, 1953-68, senior researcher in Institute of Oriental Studies, 1969-71; Hebrew University, Jerusalem, Israel, associate professor, 1976—. Head of seminar for the study of Jewish history in Moscow, 1973-76; member of organizing committee of International Seminar for the Study of Collective Phenomena, 1974; member of leadership of movement for Aliya of Soviet Jews. *Military service:* Russian Army, 1941-44; received several medals. *Member:* Israeli Association of Asian Studies.

WRITINGS: *Individual and State in Ancient China,* translation from the Russian published with new preface, Columbia University Press, 1976. Contributor of articles about Chinese history and philosophy to scholarly journals.

WORK IN PROGRESS: *Traditional Chinese Philosophy of History,* completion expected in 1980.

SIDELIGHTS: Rubin told *CA* that during World War II he was captured by the German Army near Moscow and that he escaped after three days to rejoin the Russians. Taken from the front a year later, he said he was sent to a special Soviet investigation concentration camp for former P.O.W.s. "I was forced to do hard work in the coal mines, and in the beginning of 1944 became ill with spine tuberculosis. After my release I spent 4 years in bed."

Ruben resigned his position at the Institute of Oriental Studies in January of 1972. In July of that same year his application for immigration to Israel was refused on the grounds that he was "an important specialist." He reported: "At the same time, all my scholarly work was withdrawn from publication and citations from my previous work were prohibited. I was invited to lecture at Columbia University in New York, but my application for a visa to the U.S.A. also was refused." After four years of united effort, by Israeli and Western orientalists appealing to Soviet authorities and not cooperating with Soviet specialists, Rubin received permission to leave Russia in 1976.

Rubin wrote: "I am happy to take an active part in one of the most meaningful developments of the modern world—the Exodus of Soviet Jews from a new totalitarian slavery. The totalitarian state is the most important historical experience of the twentieth century, which makes the nineteenth century communist or socialist utopianism obsolete."

*   *   *

RUKEYSER, William Simon   1939-

PERSONAL: Born June 8, 1939, in New York, N.Y.; son of Merryle Stanley and Berenice (Simon) Rukeyser; married Elisabeth Mary Garnett, November 21, 1963; children: Lisa Ellen, James William. *Education:* Princeton University, A.B., 1961; graduate study at Christ's College, Cambridge, 1962-63. *Home:* 1160 Terrill Rd., Scoth Plains, N.J. 07076. *Office: Money* Magazine, Time and Life Bldg., Rockefeller Center, New York, N.Y. 10020.

CAREER/WRITINGS: Wall Street Journal, New York City, copyreader, 1961-62, staff reporter in Europe, 1963-67; *Fortune* magazine, New York City, associate editor, 1967-71, member of board of editors, 1971-72; *Money* magazine, New York City, managing editor, 1972—.

*   *   *

RUNYAN, Thora J.   1931-

PERSONAL: Born September 11, 1931, in Lemont Furnace, Pa.; married William S. Runyan (a professor), November 7, 1954; children: Laura, Grant. *Education:* University of Idaho, B.S., 1961; Harvard University, D.Sc., 1968. *Office:* Department of Food and Nutrition, Iowa State University, Ames, Iowa 50011.

CAREER: Worked in factories in Los Angeles, Calif., 1948-53; Mendocino State Hospital, Mendocino, Calif., psychiatric technician, 1954-57; Harvard University, Boston, Mass., research associate, 1962-63; Iowa State University, Ames, Iowa, assistant professor, 1968-75, associate professor of nutrition, 1975—. *Military service:* U.S. Army, Women's Army Corps (WAC), 1953-54. *Member:* Nutrition Today Society, American Heart Association, National Organization for Women (NOW), Zero Population Growth (ZPG), Phi Beta Kappa, Phi Kappa Phi, Alpha Lambda Delta.

WRITINGS: (Contributor) Richard A. Goldsby, editor, *Biology,* Harper, 1975; *Nutrition for Today,* Harper, 1976.

Contributor of articles to *Journal of Biological Chemistry, Journal of Nutrition,* and to *Proceedings* of Society for Experimental Biology and Medicine.

WORK IN PROGRESS: An advanced undergraduate text on nutrition; an article on relationships between estrogens and amino acid metabolism; a shortened version of *Nutrition for Today* (with Allen Schwartz) publication by Canfield Press.

*   *   *

RUSKAY, Sophie   1887-

PERSONAL: Born January 29, 1887, in New York, N.Y.; daughter of Simon (a manufacturer) and Fannie (a charity worker; maiden name, Centaberg); married Cecil Ruskay (deceased); children: three daughters, two sons. *Education:* Attended Hunter College (now of the City University of New York) and Barnard College. *Politics:* Liberal Democrat. *Religion:* Jewish. *Address:* c/o A. S. Barnes.

CAREER: Writer and lecturer.

WRITINGS: Horsecars and Cobblestones, A. S. Barnes, 1973. Also author of *The Jelly Woman* (short stories) and *Discovery at Aspen.* Contributor to *New York Times.*

SIDELIGHTS: Sophie Ruskay writes: "I wrote *Horsecars and Cobblestones* to acquaint my three daughters and two sons of the struggle to exist, of the simpler fun of those who lived on East Broadway, the Fifth Avenue of the Lower East Side in a lovely brownstone mansion."

*   *   *

RUTBERG, Sidney   1924-

PERSONAL: Born February 9, 1924, in Brooklyn, N.Y.; son of Jacob (a mechanic) and Lizzie (Burd) Rutberg; married Adele Kahn (a secretary), June 20, 1948; children: Allen Theodore. *Education:* Brooklyn College (now of the City University of New York), B.A., 1949; also attended Bernard M. Baruch College (now of the City University of New York), 1950. *Politics:* Democrat. *Religion:* Jewish. *Home:* 67-18D 195th Lane, Fresh Meadows, N.Y. 11365. *Agent:* Arthur Pine Associates, Inc., 1780 Broadway, New York, N.Y. 10019. *Office:* Fairchild Publications, 7 East 12th St., New York, N.Y. 10003.

CAREER: Fairchild Publications, New York, N.Y., buyers arrival reporter, 1949-51, reporter for *Credit News,* 1951-65, editor, 1965-67, financial editor of Fairchild Publications and Fairchild News Service, 1967—, associated with Fairchild Broadcast News, 1968-71; author of weekly columns "The Street," 1968—, and "Money Matters," 1976—. Member of faculty of New York Institute of Credit. Guest on television and radio talk shows. *Member:* Authors Guild of Authors League of America, New York Financial Writers Association (president, 1975; member of board of governors).

WRITINGS: Ten Cents on the Dollar (on bankruptcy), Simon & Schuster, 1973; *The Money Balloon* (on inflation and investment; Investors Book Club selection), Simon & Schuster, 1975. Contributor to magazines, including *Pension, Harper's Weekly,* and *Finance.*

SIDELIGHTS: Rutberg comments that he has developed strong contacts among investment and commercial bankers, securities analysts, and accountants.

*   *   *

RUTH, Claire (Merritt)   1900-1976

September 11, 1900—October 25, 1976; American author

and widow of Babe Ruth, best known for *The Babe and I*. She was a dancer and model in the 1920's, and was a co-founder of Babe Ruth Baseball International. Mrs. Ruth died in New York City. Obituaries: *New York Times*, October 26, 1976.

* * *

RYAN, Cornelius John 1920-1974

PERSONAL: Born June 5, 1920, in Dublin, Ireland; came to United States, 1948, naturalized citizen, 1950; son of John Joseph and Amelia (Clohisey) Ryan; married Kathryn Ann Morgan (an author), May 27, 1950; children: Geoffrey John, Victoria Ann. *Education:* Studied violin at Irish Academy of Music. *Home:* Old Branchville Rd., Ridgefield, Conn. 06877.

CAREER: Author. Junior secretary to Garfield Weston, Member of Parliament, in London, England, 1940-41; Reuter's News Agency, London, reporter, 1941-42; *Daily Telegraph,* London, war correspondent, 1943-45, reporter in Tokyo bureau, 1945-46, Middle East bureau chief in Jerusalem, 1946-47; *Time* magazine, New York City, contributing editor, 1947-49; "Newsweek" television show, New York City, member of special projects department, 1949-50; *Collier's* magazine, New York City, associate editor, 1956; *Reader's Digest* magazine, Pleasantville, New York, staff reporter, 1962-65, roving editor, 1965-74. Stringer for *Time* and *St. Louis Post Despatch* in Jerusalem, 1946-47. Member of board of directors, Ryan Holdings Co., Connecticut State Bank, and Boys Clubs of America; consultant to Pan American Airways; trustee of Correspondents Fund. Honorary research fellow at University of Manchester, 1964. Notable assignments as reporter include coverage of D-Day landings, General Patton's Third Army in Europe, the opening of *London Daily Telegraph*'s Tokyo bureau in 1945, postwar atomic bomb tests in the Pacific, and the 1948 Arab-Israeli war.

MEMBER: National Press Club (trustee), Author's League of America, Writers Guild, Union Interalliee Club (Paris), Mid-Ocean Club (Bermuda), Dutch Treat Club, Players Club, Silver Spring Country Club (Connecticut). *Awards, honors:* Award for distinguished magazine writing from University of Illinois, 1956; Benjamin Franklin award, Overseas Press Club award, and Christopher literature award for best book on foreign affairs, all 1959; Bancarella prize for literature (Italy), 1962; gold medal for literature from Eire Society of Boston, 1966; Medaille de la France Liberee, Legion of Honor; Litt.D. from Ohio University, 1974.

WRITINGS: (With Frank Kelly) *Star-Spangled Mikado,* McBride, 1948; (with Frank Kelly) *MacArthur: Man of Action,* Doubleday, 1950; (editor) Joseph Kaplan and others, *Across the Space Frontier,* Viking, 1952; (editor) Wernher Von Braun, *Conquest of the Moon,* Viking, 1953 (published in England as *Man On the Moon,* Sidgwick & Jackson, 1953); *One Minute To Ditch!* (short stories), Ballantine, 1957; *The Longest Day: June 6, 1944,* Simon & Schuster, 1959; *The Last Battle,* Simon & Schuster, 1966; *A Bridge Too Far* (Book of the Month Club selection), Simon & Schuster, 1974. Author of screenplay adaptations of *The Longest Day* and *The Last Battle,* and of radio scripts and plays in Ireland before 1948.

SIDELIGHTS: Because of the popularity of his World War II histories, Cornelius Ryan was said to be a new breed of historian; one who wrote history with as much emphasis on interest and suspense as he placed on accuracy. Ryan always disagreed with that description of himself. "There is nothing new in what I am doing," he said. "It's only old-fashioned reporting. Regardless of all the talk about this being a new style, it is not. It's being rarefied, redefined—but we're doing no more today than fine historians and crime reporters have done, beginning with Thucydides in his history of the Peloponnesian Wars. Take Stendhal's magnificient description of the Battle of Waterloo—when asked why he did it that way he said, 'I simply want to know what happened.'"

While refusing the label of new historian, Ryan admitted his approach was different from that of his academic contemporaries. One of the reasons he gave for writing *The Longest Day* was that he disagreed with the large view of war in terms only of the outcome of battles and the movement of huge masses of men. "What was missing was the story of wartime events told in terms of the human spirit. I wanted to write about the ordinary people who were caught up in a conflict so vast they could perceive an infinitely small segment. What I write about is not war, but the courage of man and the fact that man will prevail. I just use war as the framework to show people at every level in society in all their bravery and compassion."

Paul Montgomery said: "Mr. Ryan's method was based on an assiduous accumulation of detail, drawing on the experiences in battle of everyone from enlisted man to general. For the D-Day book, for example, he advertised in American, English, Canadian and German newspapers seeking interviews with participants. From 6,300 replies, he culled more than 1,000 interviews; parts of 400 of them appeared in the book, woven together in the writer's suspenseful narrative."

Ryan was well known for his tireless research. For *The Longest Day,* he worked out a complete chronology of D-Day on five to fifteen minute intervals, and he used no detail or anecdote that was not confirmed "by at least four people who were eyewitnesses or who had diary entries to substantiate their statements." While working on *The Last Battle,* Ryan was the first American in over forty years to consult Russian documents and the first person to interview Otto Gunshe, the man who last saw Hitler alive.

"To write each one of these books means contacting from 3,000 to 6,000 people," Ryan admitted. "*The Longest Day* dealt with the landing in Normandy, so there were thousands of English, French and so on, and equally thousands of Germans looking down from the defensive positions. Imagine the problems of finding all these people. Then when they're found, through advertisements or whatever, about 30 per cent turn out to be useless—after all, every man fighting in World War II had his own D-Day, wherever it was and I need several people to describe each incident. *The Longest Day* took ten years of work, and *The Last Battle,* although it's a longer book because the fall of Berlin is the biggest subject, took six. For *The Longest Day* I have 48 drawers of files, and for *The Last Battle,* about 64." In spite of his illness, Ryan took seven years to complete his last book, *A Bridge Too Far.* The book was published only a few weeks before his death.

Ryan's painstaking research was expensive as well as time consuming. He fell $20,000 into debt while working on *The Longest Day* and spent over $60,000 on *The Last Battle*.

While sometimes criticized for going too far into the minutia of events surrounding his subject, Ryan consistently received critical acclaim for his "brilliant reporting within the well-told story." This praise must have pleased him because he often proclaimed: "I'm a reporter. If I am some help to more serious historians, I'll be satisfied. I'm not a great writer, but I know how to combine a vast amount of material into a dramatic context. There is no reason for history to be dull."

AVOCATIONAL INTERESTS: Golf, fishing, shooting.

BIOGRAPHICAL/CRITICAL SOURCES: New York Herald Tribune, March 16, 1966; *Book World,* March 2, 1969; *Washington Post,* November 25, 1974; *New York Times,* November 25, 1974.*

(Died November 23, 1974, in New York City)

*   *   *

RYAN, John J.   1922(?)-1977

1922(?)—May 16, 1977; American publisher and writer; was head of Executive Business Media, Inc., which publishes military and civilian trade journals, as well as books. He wrote two books on military sales, television scripts, short stories, and contributed more than four hundred articles to national periodicals. He died in Baldwin, N.Y. Obituaries: *New York Times,* May 19, 1977.

*   *   *

RYAN, Joseph J.   1910(?)-1976

1910(?)—December 25, 1976; American public relations executive and writer on shipping. He died in New Brunswick, N.J. Obituaries: *New York Times,* December 27, 1976.

*   *   *

RYDBERG, Lou(isa Hampton)   1908-

PERSONAL: Born August 24, 1908, in Long Beach, Calif.; daughter of Wade Baker (a merchant) and Mabel (Hailey) Hampton; married Ernie Rydberg (a writer), June 23, 1933; children: Sonya Rydberg Cuclis. *Education:* University of California, Los Angeles, B.E., 1930. *Politics:* Democrat. *Religion:* Presbyterian. *Home:* 3742 Tennyson, San Diego, Calif. 92107.

CAREER: Taught kindergarten in Santa Ana, Calif., 1931-33; Rest Haven Preventorium (charitable health foundation for children), executive secretary, 1943-71. Red Cross volunteer; member of council, Girl Scouts of America. *Member:* National League of American Pen Women (Ocean Beach/Point Loma branch president, 1953-56, treasurer, 1956-72, secretary, 1974-76), Society of Children's Book Writers, Zeta Tau Alpha.

WRITINGS—Juvenile; sometimes under name Louisa Hampton Rydberg: *Marni,* Longmans, 1958; (with husband, Ernie Rydberg) *The Shadow Army,* Thomas Nelson, 1976. Contributor of verse and short stories to magazines including, *Seventeen, Jack and Jill, American Girl, Ladies Home Journal, Better Homes and Gardens,* and *Humpty Dumpty.*

WORK IN PROGRESS: An adult murder mystery, *Hang Together.*

*   *   *

RYKWERT, Joseph   1926-

PERSONAL: Born April 5, 1926, in Warsaw, Poland; son of Szymon Mieczyslaw (an engineer) and Elizabeth (Melup) Rykwert; married Jane Morton, 1960 (divorced, 1967); married Anne-Marie Sandersley (a lawyer), February 14, 1972; children: Simon Sebastian, Marina Joanna Engel (stepdaughter). *Education:* Attended Bartlett School of Architecture, University of London, 1942-44, and Architectural As-

sociation School of Architecture, 1944-47. *Home:* 26A Wedderburn Rd., London N.W.3, England. *Office:* Department of Art, University of Essex, Wivenhoe Park, Colchester CO4 3SQ, England.

CAREER: Architect, E. Maxwell Fry & Jane Drew, 1947; architect, Richard Sheppard & Partners, 1947-48; member of editorial staff, *Chambers Encyclopaedia,* 1948-49; studio master and lecturer in the history of architecture, Hammersmith School of Arts and Crafts, 1952-53; Royal College of Art, London, England, librarian and tutor in the history of architecture, 1961-67; University of Essex, Essex, England, professor of art, 1967—, chairman of department, 1967-70. Lecturer at Delft Polytechnic, University of Louvain, York University, Columbia University, Carnegie-Mellon University, University of Pennsylvania, Cooper Union, Harvard University, Massachusetts Institute of Technology, Cambridge University, University of Naples, and University of Palermo; visiting professor at University of Paris, 1974-76. Has broadcast on French, German, and British programs.

AWARDS, HONORS: Graham Foundation fellowship at Institute for Architecture and Urban Studies, New York, 1969-71; award from Royal College of Art, 1970; senior fellow of Princeton University's Council of the Humanities, 1971.

WRITINGS: The Golden House (poem), Anthony Froshaug, 1951; (editor) Leone Battista Alberti, *Ten Books on Architecture,* Alec Tiranti, 1955; *Church Building,* Hawthorn, 1966; *On the Early Pictures of Giorgio de Chirico: A Poem,* VERB Editions, 1969; *On Adam's House in Paradise: The Idea of the Primitive Hut in Architectural History,* Musuem of Modern Art, 1972; (editor) A. Loos, *Parole nel Vuoto,* Adelphi, 1972; *The Idea of a Town: The Anthropology of Urban Form in Rome, Italy, and the Ancient World,* Princeton University Press, 1976; *What Is the Use of Architecture?,* Praeger, in press.

Contributor: John Heath Stubbs, editor, *Image of Tomorrow,* S.C.M. Press, 1953. Also contributor to *Ideas,* Grosvenor Press, 1954, and *Art, Artists, and Thinkers,* Longman, 1956. Contributor to *Garzanti Enzyclopaedia.* Contributor of more than sixty poems, articles, and reviews to art and architecture journals, literary magazines, including *Time and Tide, Points,* and *Times Literary Supplement,* and to newspapers. Contributing editor of *Studio International* and *Lotus.*

WORK IN PROGRESS: Research on the eighteenth century in western Europe and modern architecture polemics.

*   *   *

RYLE, Gilbert   1900-1976

August 19,1900—October 6, 1976; British philosopher, educator, editor, and author of books and articles; served as editor of the leading philosophical journal *Mind.* His book *The Concept of Mind* was the basic statement of his philosophy. He died in Yorkshire, England. Obituaries: *AB Bookman's Weekly,* November 15, 1976.

*   *   *

SABIN, Francene

PERSONAL: Married Louis (a writer) Sabin; children: Keith. *Home and office:* 103 Connolly Dr., Milltown, N.J. 08850. *Agent:* James O. Brown, 22 East 60th St., New York, N.Y. 10022.

CAREER: Writer. *Member:* American Society of Journalists and Authors.

WRITINGS: (With husband, Louis Sabin) *Dogs of America*, Putnam, 1967; *Women Who Win*, Random House, 1975; (with Louis Sabin) *The One, the Only, the Original Jigsaw Puzzle Book*, Regnery, 1977. Contributor of articles to magazines, including *Exploring, Family Circle, Seventeen, Scouting, American Education, Family Health, Diversion,* and *Parade.*

WORK IN PROGRESS: Three books to be published by Putnam in 1977, *Chris Evert, Jimmy Connors,* and with Louis Sabin, a book on small and unusual pets.

SIDELIGHTS: Francene Sabin told *CA:* "I write because I love to and because it's what I do best. Almost everything interests me, whether or not I have the opportunity to use it professionally. Beyond that, I am a very private person."

*   *   *

SABIN, Louis   1930-

PERSONAL: Born June 25, 1930, in Salt Lake City, Utah; son of Philip and Betty Sabin; married Francene (a writer); children: Keith. *Education:* Brooklyn College (now of the City University of New York), B.A., 1955; New York University, M.A., 1957. *Home and office:* 103 Connolly Dr., Milltown, N.J. 08850. *Agent:* James O. Brown, 22 East 60th St., New York, N.Y. 10022.

CAREER: Editor of various magazines, including *True Detective, Saga,* and *Boys' Life,* 1953-73; full-time freelance writer, 1973—. Teacher of English at Middlesex County College, 1974. *Military service:* U.S. Air Force, 1947-49. *Member:* American Society of Journalists and Authors.

WRITINGS: (With wife, Francene Sabin) *Dogs of America*, Putnam, 1967; *Stars of Pro Basketball*, Random House, 1971; *Great Teams of Pro Basketball*, Random House, 1971; *Pete Maravich*, Scholastic, 1972; *Record Breakers of the Major Leagues*, Random House, 1974; *Hot Shots of Pro Basketball*, Random House, 1974; *Walt Frazier*, Putnam, 1976; *Pro Basketball's Greatest*, Putnam, 1976; *Pele*, Putnam, 1977; *Julius Erving*, Putnam, 1977; *Johnny Bench*, Putnam, 1977; *Pete Rose*, Putnam, 1977; (with Francene Sabin) *The One, the Only, the Original Jigsaw Puzzle Book*, Regnery, 1977; *Great Moments in Sports*, Putnam, 1978. Contributor of more than 300 articles to magazines, including *Today's Health, Family Weekly, Guideposts, Parade, Seventeen, Sport,* and *Ladies' Home Journal.*

WORK IN PROGRESS: A book on small and unusual pets, with Francene Sabin, publication by Putnam expected, 1977.

*   *   *

SACKSON, Sid   1920-

PERSONAL: Born February 4, 1920, in Chicago, Ill.; son of Aaron J. (an engineer) and Esther (Rosen) Sackson; married Bernice P. Berdick, September 7, 1941; children: Dana R., Dale E. *Education:* City College (now of the City University of New York), B.S., 1943. *Religion:* "No organized religion." *Home and office:* 1287 Arnow Ave., Bronx, N.Y. 10469.

CAREER: Licensed civil engineer. U.S. Department of the Navy, Brooklyn, N.Y., civilian chief engineering draftsman, 1940-46; Corbett-Tinghir Co., New York City, engineering designer, 1946-48; City of New York, Traffic Department, traffic engineer, 1948-51; Dorr Co., Stanford, Conn., engineering designer, 1951-55; Shapiro Associates, New York City, engineer and programmer, 1955-70; writer and inventor

of games, 1970—. *Member:* New York Game Associates (president).

WRITINGS: A Gamut of Games (adult), Random House, 1969; *Beyond Tic Tac Toe: Challenging and Exciting New Games to Be Played with Colored Pens or Pencils* (juvenile), Pantheon, 1975; *Beyond Solitaire: Challenging New Games for One to Play with Colored Pens or Pencils* (juvenile), Pantheon, 1976; *Beyond Words* (juvenile), Pantheon, 1976. Author of game review column, "Sackson on Games," now called "Briefings," in *Strategy and Tactics,* 1969—. Contributor to *Washington Post.*

WORK IN PROGRESS: Another book for Pantheon's "Beyond" series; new games; research on old and new games.

SIDELIGHTS: Sackson writes: "When I was in first grade, the high point of the day would occur when the teacher distributed pages from a magazine and instructed us to circle the words we knew. The positioning of the circles and their relationship to each other interested me much more than the words themselves. I evolved rules for joining the circles, set objectives for the growing chains, and thereby created my first game. Now, many years after my initial discovery of games in the first grade, I am just as intrigued by what makes a game tick as I was then. I have created several hundred games of my own, but I am just as fascinated by one created by a friend, one I buy in a store, or one I rediscover in a library or museum. With this as a spur—and helped by travels through the United States, Canada, and Europe—my collection of games and books on games (in eight languages) has grown to be what is, to the best of my knowledge, the largest privately owned collection."

Some of the games Sackson invented include "Acquire," "Sleuth," "Bazaar," "Executive Decision," "Venture," "Monad," "Focus," "Major Battles and Campaigns of General George S. Patton," "Major Campaigns of General Douglas MacArthur," "Totally," and "The Winning Ticket."

*   *   *

SAFDIE, Moshe   1938-

PERSONAL: Born July 14, 1938, in Haifa, Israel; immigrated to Canada in 1954; son of Leon (a merchant) and Rachel (Esses) Safdie; married Nina Nusynowicz, September 6, 1959; children: Taal, Oren. *Education:* McGill University, B.Arch., 1961. *Home:* Habitat '67, Apt. 1011, Cite du Havre, Montreal, Quebec, Canada. *Office:* 1315 Boulevard de Maisonneuve W., Montreal, Quebec, Canada.

CAREER: H.P.D. van Ginkel Associates, Montreal, Quebec, architect, 1961-62; worked with architect Louis I. Kahn in Philadelphia, Pa., 1962; Canadian Corp., Montreal, section head of planning group for 1967 World Exposition (Expo '67), 1963; co-director of "Habitat '67" apartment complex, Montreal, 1964; architect in Montreal, 1964—. Has lectured in India, China, and other Asian countries, and North and South America. *Member:* Royal Architectural Institute of Canada, Order of Architects of Quebec. *Awards, honors:* Gold medal from Lieutenant Governor of Canada, 1961; Massey Medal in architecture, 1969.

WRITINGS: Habitat: Moshe Safdie Interviewed by John Gray, Tundra Books, 1967; *Beyond Habitat* (edited by John Kettle), M.I.T. Press, 1970; *For Everyone a Garden,* M.I.T. Press, 1973. Contributor to professional journals.

WORK IN PROGRESS: Several architectural projects, including Coldspring New Town in Baltimore, Md., New

City of Keur Farah Pahlavi in Senegal, Western Wall Precinct and the Mamilah New Centre in Jerusalem, and the Desert Research Institute at Sde Boqer, Israel.

SIDELIGHTS: Safdie told *CA* of the Habitat '67 project: "Habitat '67 attempted to demonstrate that a humane environment with a high level of amenities could be achieved in a high density, multi-level urban context. Habitat '67 also attempted to demonstrate that industrialized, repetitive mass production methods could be used to make housing construction more efficient without the associated stereotyped, monotonous and scale-less environment. Habitat '67 demonstrated that a rich and varied environment is possible within the disciplined industrialized system.

"The improvement of the manmade environment in the future," Safdie continued, "will be possible only if we clearly define environmental objectives and if we then structure our bureaucracy and economics to meet these objectives. The Habitat Bill of Rights written by an international committee of architects in 1976 was submitted to the United Nations Habitat Conference in Vancouver in 1976. This document attempts to define such objectives in a manner understandable by the public at large.

"Industrialization of the building process must be treated strictly as a means to an end. New methods and building technologies should, of course, be further developed, but this should be done in the context of the stated environmental goals."

*   *   *

SAFER, Daniel J. 1934-

PERSONAL: Born June 29, 1934, in Milwaukee, Wis.; son of Mendel (a food store manager) and Belle (a social worker; maiden name, Rottman) Safer; married Elaine Berkman (a professor), June 5, 1960; children: Debra L., Alan M., Judith A. *Education:* University of Wisconsin, B.S., 1956, M.D., 1959. *Home:* 301 Radcliffe Dr., Newark, Del. 19711. *Office:* 9100 Franklin Square Dr., Rosedale, Md. 21237.

CAREER: Certified by American Board of Psychiatry and Neurology, 1973; District of Columbia General Hospital, Washington, D.C., intern, 1959-60; Cleveland Psychiatric Institute, Cleveland, Ohio, psychiatric resident, 1960-63; Institute for Juvenile Research, Chicago, Ill., fellow in child psychiatry, 1963-64; Johns Hopkins Institute, Baltimore, Md., fellow in child psychiatry, 1968-69; Baltimore County Department of Health, Towson, Md., co-director of School Child Mental Health Service, 1969-72, regional director of Child Psychiatry Service, 1972—. Instructor in psychiatry, Northwestern University School of Medicine, 1964-66, and Johns Hopkins Hospital, 1969; assistant professor of psychiatry, Johns Hopkins University School of Medicine, 1970—. Assistant attending psychiatrist, Children's Memorial Hospital, Chicago, Ill., 1964-66. Psychiatric consultant to Baltimore City Hospitals, 1966-68, and Franklin Square Hospital, Rosedale, Md., 1970-73. *Military service:* U.S. Army, 1966-68; became captain. *Member:* American Psychiatric Association (fellow, 1974—), Maryland Psychiatric Association, Baltimore County Medical Society.

WRITINGS: (With Richard P. Allen) *Hyperactive Children: Diagnosis and Management,* University Park Press, 1976.

Contributor: Rachel Gittelman-Klein, editor, *Recent Advances in Childhood Psychopharmacology,* Behavioral Publications, 1976; L. L. Iversen, S. D. Iversen, and S. H. Snyder, editors, *Handbook of Psychopharmacology,* Plenum,

1977; L. E. Arnold, editor, *Parent Guidance,* Brunner, 1977.

Also author of tape "Hyperactive Children: Treatment Considerations," for Behavior Science Tape Library, 1974. Contributor of articles to professional journals, including *New England Journal of Medicine, Pediatrics,* and *Journal of American Academy of Child Psychiatry.*

WORK IN PROGRESS: Co-editing *Disruptive Youth in Secondary Schools: Program Alternatives,* publication expected in 1978.

*   *   *

ST. GEORGE, Judith 1931-

PERSONAL: Born February 26, 1931, in Westfield, N.J.; daughter of John H. (a lawyer) and Edna P. Alexander; married David St. George (an Episcopal minister), June 5, 1954; children: Peter, James, Philip, Sarah. *Education:* Smith College, B.A., 1952. *Religion:* Episcopalian. *Home:* 290 Roseland Ave., Essex Falls, N.J. 07021.

CAREER: Suburban Frontiers (re-locating service), Basking Ridge, N.J., president, 1968-71; writer, 1970—. *Member:* Authors Guild of Authors League of America, Jean Fritz Workshop. *Awards, honors: By George, Bloomers!* was named among the best books for spring, 1976, by *Saturday Review.*

WRITINGS—For young people: *Turncoat Winter, Rebel Spring,* Chilton, 1970; *The Girl with Spunk,* Putnam, 1975; *By George, Bloomers!,* Coward, 1976; *The Chinese Puzzle of Shag Island,* Putnam, 1976; *The Shad Are Running,* Putnam, in press; *Shadow of the Shaman,* Putnam, in press; *The Halloween Pumpkin Smasher,* Putnam, in press.

SIDELIGHTS: Judith St. George writes: "As a child I loved reading above all else and remember receiving twenty-two books one Christmas. In grammar school, I used to write crazy classroom plays which I'm sure drove my teachers crazy, too. In college I took every creative writing course that was available to me.... Historical fiction and mysteries are my two loves. I guess mysteries have to come first, since I find it hard to write a book without having a mystery of some sort woven into the plot. But historical fiction gives me the opportunity to do research which I find as irresistible as eating peanuts. It also gives me a reason to visit all the interesting places I like to write about."

*   *   *

SALISBURY, Dorothy (Kendall Cleveland) 1891(?)-1976

1891(?)—October 31, 1976; American librarian and freelance writer; author of a book on plants and contributor of articles to periodicals. She died in Takoma Park, Md. Obituaries: *Washington Post,* November 4, 1976.

*   *   *

SALMON, Annie Elizabeth 1899-
(Elizabeth Ashley, Nancy Martin)

PERSONAL: Born September 26, 1899, in Croydon, England; daughter of Arthur and Annie (Griggs) Martin; married Leslie Bernard Salmon (a telecommunications engineer), September 10, 1932 (died, 1966); children: Joan Frances (Mrs. Leslie George Oppitz), Brenda Elizabeth (Mrs. Graham Whitworth Salmon). *Education:* Attended elementary school in Croydon and Norwood, England. *Politics:* Conservative. *Home:* Garden House, Church Lane, Fittleworth, Pulborough, Sussex RH10 1JG, England.

CAREER: Canadian Customs Department, London, England, secretary to investigator of values, 1922-32; Canadian customs consultant in England, 1932-33; writer, 1938—. *Member:* Society of Authors, Society of Women Writers and Journalists, Women's Press Club of London (chairman, 1961), Croydon Writers' Circle (honorary life member; president). *Awards, honors:* Berwick Sayers Memorial Prize from Croydon Writers' Circle, 1966-67.

WRITINGS—All juveniles, except as indicated; under pseudonym Nancy Martin: *Bumps,* University of London Press, 1942; *Stories for Judy and Elizabeth and Jane* (Bible stories), Victory Press, 1943; *The Holy Land,* Edinburgh House Press, 1944; *The Shepherds' Message* (nativity play), Religious Education Press, 1944; *Abwa and Her Picture,* Edinburgh House Press, 1946, 2nd edition, 1950; *Jolly Jinks,* Victory Press, 1946; *No Music for Diana,* GB Publications Ltd., 1948; *Belindamay and Her Sixpence,* Victory Press, 1949; *Belindamay and Her White Mice,* Victory Press, 1949; *Africa,* Edinburgh House Press, 1950; *Young Farmers at Gaythorne,* Macmillan, 1953; *Call the Vet,* Macmillan, 1953; *Young Farmers in Denmark,* Macmillan, 1954; *Purley Congregational Church* (adult), privately printed, 1954; *Adventure on the Alm* (geography), Macmillan, 1955; *Young Farmers in Scotland,* Macmillan, 1956; *Fifty Years of Progress* (adult), privately printed, 1957; *Vet in the Making,* Macmillan, 1957; *Occupation for Kay,* Macmillan, 1958; *Ann and Peter in Denmark,* Muller, 1959.

Jean Behind the Counter, Macmillan, 1960; *Finn the Fisherboy* (geography), Macmillan, 1961; *Probation Officer,* Macmillan, 1962; *Jean, Teenage Fashion Buyer,* Macmillan, 1964; *Three Horses,* Macmillan, 1964; *Three Dogs,* Macmillan, 1965; *Call the Nurse,* Macmillan, 1966; *Chi-Chi the Giant Panda* (nonfiction), Arlington Books, 1966; *Call the Courier,* Macmillan, 1967; *Three at the Zoo,* Macmillan, 1968; *Teresa Joins the Red Cross,* Macmillan, 1968; *The Post Office: From Carrier Pigeon to Confravision* (nonfiction), Dent, 1969; *Red Cross Challenge,* Macmillan, 1970; *Four Girls in a Store,* Macmillan, 1971; *The Fire Service Today* (nonfiction), Dent, 1972; *William Carey: The Man Who Never Gave Up* (biography), Hodder & Stoughton, 1974; *Search and Rescue: The Story of the Coastguard,* David & Charles, 1974; *Prayers for Children and Young People,* Hodder & Stoughton, 1975, Westminster, 1976; *Pilots of Sea and River Craft,* Terence Dalton Ltd., 1977.

Children's books, under pseudonym Elizabeth Ashley: *The Wonderful Holiday,* Ward Lock, 1957; *Happy Venture,* Evangelical Publishers, 1959; *The Caravan Family,* Evangelical Publishers, 1961; *A Garden for Trudy,* Evangelical Publishers, 1962; *Seven Tiny Stories About Jesus,* Dean & Son, 1963; *Day by Day Stories About Jesus,* Dean & Son, 1964; *Ten Stories About Jesus,* Dean & Son, 1965; *Alison's Choice,* Evangelical Publishers, 1965; *Wonderful Stories Jesus Told,* Dean & Son, 1967; *The Story of Jesus,* Dean & Son, 1967; *The Christmas Story,* Dean & Son, 1969; *Della's Discovery,* Evangelical Publishers, 1970; *Another Book About Jesus,* Dean & Son, 1972. Author of scripts for British Broadcasting Corp.

WORK IN PROGRESS: A biography, for Wheaton & Co.

SIDELIGHTS: Annie Salmon writes that she began by writing stories and books for very young children, and as her own children grew older, began writing for older children. She has conducted research for her writing in coal mines, hospitals, coastguard stations, naval air stations, and helicopter ports. Her books have been published in German, Norwegian, Swedish, Dutch, and Finnish.

SAMSELL, R(ay) L(ane) 1925-

PERSONAL: Born January 12, 1925, in Los Angeles, Calif.; son of Raymond Lane (in investments) and Dorothy (Thompson) Samsell; married Barbara Jean Colaianni, August 9, 1946; children: Eric C., Ellen C., Christopher L. *Education:* Manhattan College, student, 1943-44; University of California at Los Angeles, B.A. (summa cum laude), 1948; Yale University, J.D., 1952. *Home:* 10201 Valley Spring Lane, North Hollywood, Calif. 91602.

CAREER: Admitted to California Bar, 1958; lawyer in private practice, Burbank, Calif., 1959—. Member of advisory board, University of West Los Angeles Law School. *Military service:* U.S. Army, 1945; received Silver Star, Bronze Star, Purple Heart, and Presidential Unit Citation. *Member:* Lemuel Pitkin Literary Society (president), California State Bar Association, Yale Club of Southern California, Phi Beta Kappa, Pi Gimma Mu, Pi Sigma Alpha, Chi Delta Pi.

WRITINGS: (Contributor) *Pages,* Gale, 1976; *Mr. Fisher* (story), Calliope Press, 1976. Contributor to *Fitzgerald/Hemingway Annual.*

WORK IN PROGRESS: A novel set in Southern California; a book of short stories.

SIDELIGHTS: Samsell told *CA:* "My material explores the burlesque and buffoonery of American institutions, the demoralizing effects of those institutions on individuals who would search for their own workable ethic in an unfeeling society." His novel in progress "peeps beyond the judicial system's facade to its essential sleasiness." Samsell is well-known as a collector of modern American first editions.

*   *   *

SANCHA, Sheila 1924-

PERSONAL: Born November 27, 1924, in Grimsby, England; daughter of Neal (a businessman) and Phylis (Middleton) Green; married Carlos Luis Sancha (a portrait painter), August 14, 1948; children: Anita Luisa (Mrs. Douglas Lear), Jeremy Christian, Nicholas Simon. *Education:* Attended Byam Shaw School of Drawing and Painting. *Politics:* None. *Religion:* "None (nothing orthodox)." *Home:* 8 Melbury Rd., Flat 5, London W14 8LR, England.

CAREER: Shell-B.P. News, London, England, illustrator, 1957-67; writer and illustrator, 1970—. *Military service:* Women's Royal Naval Service, transport driver, 1943-46. *Member:* Royal Archaeological Institute, Society of Authors.

WRITINGS: Knight After Knight (self-illustrated juvenile), Collins, 1974.

Illustrator: Barbara Kerr Wilson, *A Story to Tell,* Garnet Miller, 1964. Contributor of drawings to magazines, including *Past and Future* and *Puffin Post.*

WORK IN PROGRESS: The Castle Story, juvenile nonfiction, self-illustrated, for Puffins and Collins.

SIDELIGHTS: Sheila Sancha writes: "When my contributions to the *Shell B. P. News* ended in 1967, I felt I needed a change of direction. I had been drawing the adventures of a knight called 'Sir Bastion' for the historical magazine *Past and Future* and I decided to enlarge on this and write a book about knights. I soon realized that I was ignorant of the architecture and conditions under which these knights lived and, before I knew what had happened, I was up to my neck in history and archaeology.... Both *Knight After Knight* and *The Castle Story* are firmly based on research. The illustrations nearly always start with a good look at mediaeval manuscript drawings, sculptures or brasses: it is great fun to put an effigy back on its feet and ask it to walk about a castle that one knows well.

"My life is busy at present.... My husband is always painting interesting people: Mr. Heath when he was Prime Minister; H.R.H. The Duke of Kent last summer, and there is to be a portrait of H.R.H. Prince Charles next year. Immersed in mediaeval history as I am, I enjoy putting down my pen and serving cups of coffee and occasional lunches to such eminent men. It emphasises the fact that history is a continuing process."

* * *

SANDUSKY, Annie Lee 1900(?)-1976

1900(?)—August 10, 1976; American social worker specializing in child welfare and author of books in her field. She died in Washington, D.C. Obituaries: *Washington Post,* August 13, 1976.

* * *

SAPIR, Richard 1936-

PERSONAL: Surname is pronounced Say-purr; born July 27, 1936, in New York, N.Y.; son of Joseph (a dentist) and Martha (Feinstein) Sapir. *Education:* Columbia University, B.S., 1960. *Home address:* East Hampstead, N.H. 03826. *Agent:* International Creative Management, 40 West 57th St., New York, N.Y. 10019.

CAREER: Has worked as newspaper reporter and editor, and in public relations; now a full-time writer.

WRITINGS: Bressio, Random House, 1975.

"Destroyer" series; all with Warren B. Murphy; all published by Pinnacle: *The Destroyer, No. 1: Created, the Destroyer,* 1971; ... *No. 2: Death Check,* 1972; ... *No. 3: The Chinese Puzzle,* 1972; ... *No. 4: Mafia Fix,* 1972; ... *No. 5: Dr. Quake, 1972;* ... *No. 6: Death Therapy,* 1972; ... *No. 7: Union Bust,* 1973; ... *No. 8: Summit Chase,* 1973; ... *No. 9: Murder's Shield,* 1973; ... *No. 10: Terror Squad,* 1973; ... *No. 11: Kill or Cure,* 1973; ... *No. 12: Slave Safari,* 1973; ... *No. 13: Acid Rock,* 1973; ... *No. 14: Judgment Day,* 1974; ... *No. 15: Murder Ward,* 1974; ... *No. 16: Oil Slick,* 1974; ... *No. 17: Last War Dance,* 1974; ... *No. 18: Funny Money,* 1975; ... *No. 19: Holy Terror,* 1975; ... *No. 20: Assassin's Play-Off,* 1975; ... *No. 21: Deadly Seeds,* 1975; ... *No. 22: Brain Drain,* 1976; ... *No. 23: Child's Play,* 1976; ... *No. 24: King's Curse,* 1976; ... *No. 25: Sweet Dreams,* 1976; ... *No. 26: In Enemy Hands,* 1977; ... *No. 27: The Last Temple,* 1977; ... *No. 28: Ship of Death,* 1977; ... *No. 29: Final Death,* 1977; ... *No. 30: Mugger Blood,* 1977; ... *No. 31: The Head Men,* in press.

Contributor to magazines.

WORK IN PROGRESS: More books in the "Destroyer" series; other novels.

* * *

SARA, Dorothy 1897(?)-1976

1897(?)—November 16, 1976; American graphologist, editor, educator, and author of several books; was associated with Cadillac Publishing Company and Ziff-Davis Publishing Company, and was a faculty member at Henry George School of Social Science. She died in New York City. Obituaries: *New York Times,* November 18, 1976.

SAUNDERS, Allen 1899-

PERSONAL: Born March 24, 1899, in Lebanon, Ind.; son of Fred Clark and Nancy Ellen (Jackson) Saunders; married Lois Long, March 27, 1923; children: John, David, Penelope, Lois Ann. *Education:* Wabash College, B.A., 1920, M.A., 1922; attended Chicago Academy of Fine Arts, 1920, Institute de Tours, France, 1921 and 1923, and University of Chicago, 1922 and 1924. *Home:* 4108 River Rd., Toledo, Ohio. *Office:* 717 Security Bldg., Toledo, Ohio.

CAREER: Wabash College, Crawfordsville, Ind., associate professor of romance languages, 1920-27; *Toledo News-Bee,* Toledo, Ohio, dramatic editor, 1927-38; cartoonist, 1938—. Creator with Elmer Woggon of comic strip "Steve Roper," with Ken Ernst of "Mary Worth," 1942, and with Nicholas Dallis of "Rex Morgan, M.D.," 1950. Lecturer on comic strips and humor. Member of board of trustees, Wabash College, 1954-74; president, Ohio State Automobile Association, 1968; vice-president, American Automobile Association, 1966-69. *Member:* National Cartoonists Society, Newspaper Comics Council (past president), The Players, Phi Beta Kappa, Phi Gamma Delta, Sigma Delta Chi. *Awards, honors:* D.H.L. from Wabash College, 1963.

WRITINGS—Plays: *Three Taps at Twelve* (three-act mystery; first produced in Maumee, Ohio, at Valley Playshop Theatre, 1932), Samuel French, 1933; *Standard Equipment,* Samuel French, 1935; *The Big Cough* (one-act melodrama), Samuel French, 1939; *A Crown on the Hall Tree* (three-act comedy; first produced in Toledo, Ohio, at Repertoire Theatre, October 12, 1937), Samuel French, 1940. Author of newspaper comic strips syndicated by Field Newspaper Syndicate (formerly Publishers-Hall), 1937—.

SIDELIGHTS: Saunders explained how he and Ken Ernst took over the work on a comic strip called "Apple Mary" and how they developed this strip into one of "psychological drama, closer to real life" called "Mary Worth." "To be strictly accurate," Saunders continued, "ours has not been the realism of a Zola, a Sinclair Lewis, or even a Norman Rockwell. We have sought, generally speaking, to show the emotional and romantic problems of women in the more or less glamorous professions—artists, actors, models, musicians, advertising writers, business executives. But in weighing every proposed new episode, as we do in several days of personal conferences, Ken and I always insist that the plot contain what we call the 'John and Mary' ingredient. Which is merely to say that, regardless of glamorous professional background, the leading characters must be involved in a problem with which the reader is familiar and with which she or he can readily identify.

"The formula is simple, deceptively so, perhaps. Mrs. Worth, a refined, well-educated widow with a generous endowment of plain common sense, has seen her late husband's once worthless securities regain sufficient value to afford her a modest income. This she augments occasionally by taking a job. While working, she usually meets some attractive younger people who have a problem. We try to avoid making her a meddlesome busybody; Mary sincerely likes people and wants to help them. Sometimes she enters actively into the solution of the problem, but equally often she is an interested and quietly concerned observer as the principals themselves work it out.

"Dealing as we do with characters who invariably become very real to us, in circumstances equally real, it is natural that the story elements and the art work should, as the years roll past, mirror the fads and foibles, the social attitudes, the mores and events of the decades in which we are living and working."

"We do not think of 'Mary Worth' as being melodramatic, but rather as concerning itself with the drama of everyday life."

AVOCATIONAL INTERESTS: Golf.

* * *

SAVAGE, Joseph P. 1895(?)-1977

1895(?)—February 4, 1977; American attorney and author best known for his participation in the prosecution of Nathan Leopold, Jr. and Richard Loeb in 1924. Savage wrote an autobiography in 1975. He died in Palm Beach, Fla. Obituaries: *New York Times,* February 6, 1977.

* * *

SAVAGE, W(illiam) Sherman 1890-

PERSONAL: Born March 7, 1890, in Wattsville, Va.; son of Adam (a farm worker) and Annie (Godwin) Savage; married Roena Eloise Muckelroy (a music instructor), August 25, 1930; children: Eloise Sherda Savage Logan, Inez Marian Savage Allen. *Education:* Howard University, A.B., 1917; University of Oregon, A.M., 1925; Ohio State University, Ph.D., 1934; also attended University of Kansas. *Politics:* Independent. *Home:* 5063 Onaknoll Ave., Los Angeles, Calif. 90043.

CAREER: Okalona Industrial School, Okalona, Miss., teacher, 1917-18; A. & T. State College (now University of North Carolina A. & T. State University), Greensboro, N.C., faculty member in English and biology, 1919-20; high school teacher of biology and French in Muskogee, Okla., 1920-21; Lincoln University, Jefferson City, Mo., professor of history, 1921-60, professor emeritus, 1960—, chairman of department of history and government; Jarvis Christian College, Hawkins, Tex., professor of history and chairman of department of history and social science, 1960-66; California State University, Los Angeles, professor of history, 1966-70; writer, 1970—. Summer professor at Whittier College, Lincoln University, Alabama State College, Wisconsin State College (now University of Wisconsin, Stevens Point), and Tuskegee Institute. *Military service:* U.S. Army, 1917-18.

MEMBER: American Historical Association, Organization of American Historians, American Association of University Professors, Association for the Study of Afro-American Life and History (member of board of awards), Association of Teachers of Social Sciences in Black Colleges (past president), Western Historical Society, Southern Historical Society, Missouri Historical Society. *Awards, honors:* Social Science Research Council grant, 1938; American Philosophical Society grant, 1942.

WRITINGS: The History of Lincoln University, privately printed, 1938; *The Controversy over the Distribution of Abolition Literature,* Association for the Study of Negro Life and History, 1939; *A Suggested Outline for the Study of Negro History,* Missouri State Department of Education, 1941; (co-author) *A History of Phi Beta Sigma Fraternity,* privately printed, 1957; *Blacks in the West,* Greenwood Press, 1976. Author of "Know Your History," a column formerly in *Kansas City Call.* Contributor to professional journals.

WORK IN PROGRESS: The Career of William Alexanser Leidesdorff; Blacks in California.

SIDELIGHTS: Savage writes: "Huntington Library is a great inspiration and resource. The subject I am most interested in is the contribution of Blacks to Western history."

SAZER, Nina 1949-

PERSONAL: Born March 2, 1949, in Houston, Tex.; daughter of Victor (a cellist) and Betty (a social worker; maiden name, Rosenthal) Sazer. *Education:* Attended University of Southern California until 1970; Antioch College, M.Ed., 1971. *Home address:* R.F.D.2, Windsor, Vt. 05089. *Agent:* Jane Wilson, John Cushman Associates, 25 West 43rd St., New York, N.Y. 10036. *Office:* New Hampshire Children '76, 7 Trinity St., Claremont, N.H. 03743.

CAREER: Elementary school teacher in Orfordville, N.H., 1970; Day Care Center, Inc., Norwich, Vt., founder, director, and teacher, 1970-74; New Hampshire Children '76, Claremont, state director, 1974—. Professor at New Hampshire Vocational College, winter, 1976. Recreation leader for Los Angeles County Special Project for Mental Health. Member of state Task Force on Early Childhood Education, Action for Foster Care Program, New Hampshire Task Force on Child Abuse, Board of Programs for the Developmentally Disabled, planning committee of New Hampshire Social Welfare Council, and steering committee of New Hampshire Early Recognition and Intervention Network. President of board of directors of Sullivan County Day Care Center. Has taught cello and folk dancing to children.

MEMBER: New Hampshire Head Start Directors Association, New Hampshire Day Care Directors Association, New Hampshire Association for the Education of Young Children. *Awards, honors:* In 1972, the Nina Sazer Fund was established in her honor at Norwich Day Care Center.

WRITINGS: What Do You Think I Saw?: A Nonsense Number Book (juvenile), Pantheon, 1976. Contributor to education journals.

* * *

SCAMEHORN, H(oward) Lee 1926-

PERSONAL: Born February 27, 1926, in Kalamazoo, Mich.; son of Elmer C. and Mary Ellen Scamehorn; married Marilou Colclasure (an accountant), 1952; children: Brenda Kay (Mrs. Francis Salazar). *Education:* Western Michigan University, A.B., 1949; University of Illinois, A.M., 1952, Ph.D., 1956. *Home:* 220 Lipan Way, Boulder, Colo. 80303. *Office:* Department of History, University of Colorado, Boulder, Colo. 80303.

CAREER: University of Colorado, Boulder, instructor, 1956-58, assistant professor, 1958-62, associate professor, 1962-66, professor of history, 1966—. Director of Western Business History Research Center, 1967—. Member of Colorado Consulting Committee for Historic Preservation and Historical Records Advisory Board of Colorado.

WRITINGS: Balloons to Jets: A Century of Aeronautics in Illinois, Regnery, 1957; *The Buckeye Rovers in the Gold Rush: An Edition of Two Diaries,* Ohio University Press, 1965; (with Leslie Fishman, Conrad McBride, and Homer Rainey) *Contemporary Colorado,* University of Colorado, 1968; *Pioneer Steelmaker in the West: The Colorado Fuel and Iron Company, 1872-1903,* Pruett, 1976; (with F. A. Allen, Ernest Andrade, M. S. Foster, and P. I. Mitterling) *The University of Colorado, 1876-1976,* Harcourt, 1976. Contributor to history journals.

WORK IN PROGRESS: A history of energy resources development and utilization in the American West in the twentieth century; a history of CF & I Co. during the Rockefeller era, 1903-1944.

SCHAFFER, Ulrich 1942-

PERSONAL: Born December 17, 1942, in Germany; son of Otto and Agathe (Beyer) Schaffer; married Waltraud Gursche, September 6, 1965; children: Kira, Silya. Education: University of British Columbia, B.A., 1965, M.A., 1970; University of Hamburg, graduate study, 1965-66. Home: 7320 Ridge Dr., Burnaby, British Columbia, Canada V5A 1B5.

CAREER: Douglas College, New Westminster, British Columbia, instructor in European literature, 1970—.

WRITINGS—In English: Love Reaches Out (meditations), Harper, 1976; A Growing Love (meditations, with author's photography and calligraphy), Harper, 1977.

Other works, all published by Oncken/Brockhaus: Trotz meiner Schuld (title means "In Spite of My Guilt"), 1971; Kreise Schlagen (title means "Making Rings"), 1973; Ich will dich Lieben (title means "Love Reaches Out"), 1974; Umkehrungen (title means "Reversals"), 1975; Gott, was willst du? (title means "What Do You Want, God?"), 1976; Jesus, Ich bin traurig froh (title means "Jesus, I Am Happy, Sad"), 1976.

WORK IN PROGRESS: A book of meditations, tentatively titled In the Updrift, with his own photographs, for Harper.

SIDELIGHTS: Schaffer writes: "Most of my writing is concerned with relating the life of faith as a Christian to the everyday questions of living. I am trying to express the relevancy of faith."

*   *   *

SCHANBERG, Sydney H(illel) 1934-

PERSONAL: Born January 17, 1934, in Clinton, Mass.; son of Louis and Freda (Feinberg) Schanberg; married Janice Leah Sakofsky, October 22, 1967; children: Jessica, Rebecca. Education: Harvard University, B.A., 1955. Office: New York Times, 229 West 43rd St., New York, N.Y. 10036.

CAREER/WRITINGS: New York Times, New York, N.Y., staff member, 1959, reporter, 1960—, bureau chief in Albany, N.Y., 1967-69, and New Delhi, India, 1969-73, Southeast Asia correspondent in Singapore, 1973-75. Notable assignments include coverage of the fall of Phnom Penh. Military service: U.S. Army, 1956-58. Member: Overseas Press Club. Awards, honors: Page One Award for foreign reporting, 1972; George Polk Memorial Award for foreign reporting, 1972, and special award, 1975, for coverage of fall of Phnom Penh; Overseas Press Club award for foreign reporting, 1972, and for foreign photography, 1974.

*   *   *

SCHANDLER, Herbert Y(ale) 1928-

PERSONAL: Born January 2, 1928, in Asheville, N.C.; son of David Sigmond (a merchant) and Sarah (Salem) Schandler. Education: U.S. Military Academy, B.S., 1952; Harvard University, M.P.A., 1956, Ph.D., 1974; also attended U.S. Army Command and General Staff College and Air War College. Home: 1400 South Joyce St., Apt. B1614, Arlington, Va. 22202. Office: Congressional Research Service, Library of Congress, Washington, D.C. 20540.

CAREER: U.S. Army, career officer, 1952-75, retiring as colonel; company commander in Korea, 1953; U.S. Military Academy, instructor, 1957-58, assistant professor of social sciences, 1958-60; commander of special forces detachments in Germany, 1961-62; plans officer in Europe, 1962-63, and of Military Assistance Command in Vietnam, 1965-66; member of policy planning staff of the assistant secretary of defense in international security affairs, 1968-69; battalion commander in Vietnam, 1969-70; director of national security policy studies at National War College, 1972-73. Library of Congress, Congressional Research Service, Washington, D.C., specialist in national defense, 1975—. Guest lecturer at Foreign Service Institute and National War College; U.S. Information Agency lecturer in Indonesia and Singapore, 1973. White House social aide, 1967-68. Member of U.S. delegation to Southeast Asia Treaty Organization (SEATO) conference in Thailand, 1969. Member: East-West Philosophers Conference (fellow). Awards, honors—Military: Four Legions of Merit, three Bronze Star Medals, thirteen Air Medals, three Vietnamese Crosses of Gallantry, presidential unit citation, two combat infantryman badges.

WRITINGS: (Contributor) William W. Whitson, editor, Foreign Policy and National Security, Praeger, 1976; The Unmaking of a President: Lyndon Johnson and Vietnam, Princeton University Press, 1977. Also author of portions dealing with the Tet offensive of the Pentagon Papers, by Neil Sheehan and E. W. Kenworthy, Quadrangle, 1971. Contributor to U.S. Department of Defense, U.S. House of Representatives, U.S. Senate, and Library of Congress publications, and to Strategic Review.

WORK IN PROGRESS: Articles on United States arms sales policies, and on the relationship between United States foreign policy and the structure of our defense forces.

*   *   *

SCHARA, Ron 1942-

PERSONAL: Born April 23, 1942, in Postville, Iowa; son of Harlan C. (a contractor) and Evelyn L. (Dickens) Schara; married Denise L. Fledderman (an entertainer), June 28, 1969; children: Simone, Laura. Education: Iowa State University, B.S., 1966. Politics: None. Religion: Lutheran. Office: 425 Portland, Minneapolis, Minn. 55488.

CAREER: South Dakota Department of Game, Fish and Parks, Pierre, editor, 1966-67; Minneapolis Tribune, Minneapolis, Minn., outdoor editor, 1968—. Member: Outdoor Writers Association of America (past member of board of directors), Ducks Unlimited.

WRITINGS: Muskie Mania, Regnery, 1977; Minnesota Fishing Guide, Waldman, 1978. Contributor of feature stories to Outdoor Life and Sports Afield.

SIDELIGHTS: Schara writes that his goal is "bringing readers the conservation message." He adds that he has traveled and fished from South America to the Arctic Circle.

*   *   *

SCHATT, Stanley 1943-

PERSONAL: Born September 14, 1943, in New York, N.Y.; son of Maurice (a businessman) and Lilyan (Goldman) Schatt; married Jane Abrams (a reading specialist), April 7, 1966; children: Daniel Brian. Education: Arizona State University, B.A., 1964, M.A., 1966; University of Southern California, Ph.D., 1970; American Graduate School of International Management, M.I.M., 1976. Home: 4815 West Gardenia, Glendale, Ariz. 85301. Office: Honeywell Process Control Division, MS 144, 2222 West Peoria, Phoenix, Ariz. 85029.

CAREER: University of Southern California, Los Angeles, instructor in English, 1969-70; University of Houston,

Houston, Tex., assistant professor of English, 1970-74; Fulbright professor of American literature in Japan at universities in Tokyo, Keio, and Hiroshima, 1974-75; administrative assistant for the city of Phoenix, Ariz., 1976; Honeywell Process Control Division, Phoenix, software instructor, 1977—. Professor of management at Institute for Professional Development, 1977—. *Member:* Modern Language Association of America, American Chemical Society, Philology Association of the Pacific Coast.

WRITINGS: (Editor) *Bartleby the Scrivener: A Casebook for Research,* W. C. Brown, 1971; (with Peter Mandelik) *A Concordance to the Poems of Langston Hughes,* Gale, 1975; *Kurt Vonnegut, Jr.,* G. K. Hall, 1976; *Understanding Modern American Literature: Cultural and Historical Perspectives,* Bunkahvoron, 1977. Contributor to literature journals and to *Southwest Review.*

WORK IN PROGRESS: A textbook on law enforcement writing; a study of polygraphy; a novel about an adolescent boy; *Software Applications to Reading,* completion expected in 1978; science fiction stories.

SIDELIGHTS: Schatt writes: "Two men who influenced me significantly are Gene Montague and Max Schulz. With a background in literature, chemistry, and computer science, I am very much interested in the relationship between science and the humanities. I have also become interested in the psychological dimension of effective management. I remain fascinated by ethnic differences and languages—particularly Spanish and Japanese. I would like to travel in the future and do some cross-cultural studies involving both management technique and popular culture."

* * *

SCHENCK, Janet Daniels 1883(?)-1976

1883(?)—October 12, 1976; American music educator and author of books in her field. She founded the Manhattan School of Music in 1917 and headed it until 1956. She died in New York City. Obituaries: *New York Times,* October 14, 1976.

* * *

SCHERER, Frances Schlosser 1912-

PERSONAL: Born April 9, 1912, in Shanghai, China; daughter of George Donald (a missionary) and Mary (a missionary; maiden name, Ogren) Schlosser; married James Arnold Scherer (a missionary, professor of church history, and writer), March 28, 1948; children: James David, Susan Marie. *Education:* Yenching University, B.A., 1937; Johns Hopkins Hospital School of Nursing, R.N., 1944. *Religion:* Lutheran. *Home:* 111 Dartmouth Rd., Flossmoor, Ill. 60422. *Office:* Lutheran School of Theology, 1100 East 55th St., Chicago, Ill. 60615.

CAREER: Part-time school nurse at Lutheran School of Theology, Chicago, Ill. Writer. *Member:* Illinois Nurses' Association.

WRITINGS: (With husband, George Scherer) *Ambassadors for Christ in China,* Light & Life Press, 1976.

WORK IN PROGRESS: A sequel to *Ambassadors for Christ in China;* a book of daily devotions; a story; a hymn.

SIDELIGHTS: Frances Scherer writes that she has lived in China and Japan, and speaks both languages. She adds that "the two most important influences were the Christian faith of my parents, and life in China. In later years I became very involved in health care and am presently involved in Orville

Kelly's 'Make Today Count' movement." *Avocational interests:* Religion, art (painter), literature, writing poems.

* * *

SCHERER, Jack F(ranklin) 1939-

PERSONAL: Born November 14, 1939, in New Jersey. *Education:* Middlebury College, B.A., 1960; New York University, LL.B., 1963, LL.M., 1972. *Home:* 1 Christopher St., New York, N.Y. 10014. *Office:* 150 East 58th St., New York, N.Y. 10022.

CAREER: Attorney in New York, N.Y., 1964—.

WRITINGS: Dealing with Divorce, Little, Brown, 1976.

AVOCATIONAL INTERESTS: Chess, squash.

* * *

SCHIEFFER, Bob 1937-

PERSONAL: Born February 25, 1937, in Austin, Tex.; son of John (a building contractor) and Gladys (Payne) Schieffer; married Patricia Penrose (a toy store owner), April 15, 1967; children: Susan, Sharon. *Education:* Texas Christian University, B.A., 1959. *Religion:* Protestant. *Office:* CBS News, 2020 M St., Washington, D.C. 20005.

CAREER/WRITINGS: KXOL Radio, Fort Worth, Tex., news reporter, 1957-59; *Fort Worth Star-Telegram,* Fort Worth, reporter, 1962-66; WBAP-TV, Fort Worth, news anchorman, 1966-68; Columbia Broadcasting System (CBS) News, Washington, D.C., correspondent, 1969—. Notable assignments include the 1962 enrollment of James Meredith at University of Mississippi, the John F. Kennedy assassination, Vietnam War, the Pentagon and White House. *Military service:* U.S. Air Force, 1959-62; became captain. *Member:* Sigma Delta Chi. *Awards, honors:* Emmy Awards, 1972 and 1974; Overseas Press Club Award, for best interpretation of foreign affairs.

* * *

SCHLESINGER, Elizabeth Bancroft 1886-1977

July 3, 1886—June 1, 1977; American feminist and author of articles on women's history. The widow and mother of well-known historians, she was among a small group of scholars who pioneered the study of women's history. Her activism spanned decades: in her twenties she marched with the suffragettes; in her eighties she marched with her granddaughters in Vietnam war protests. She died in Williamsburg, Va. Obituaries: *New York Times,* June 2, 1977; *Washington Post,* June 2, 1977.

* * *

SCHMANDT-BESSERAT, Denise 1933-

PERSONAL: Born August 10, 1933, in Ay, France; daughter of Victor (a champagne producer) and Jeanne (Crabit) Besserat; married Jurgen Schmandt (a professor), December 27, 1956; children: Alexander, Christopher, Phillip. *Education:* Ecole du Louvre, diploma, 1965. *Home:* 11 Hull Cir., Austin, Tex. 78746. *Office:* Department of Art, University of Texas, Austin, Tex. 78712.

CAREER: Harvard University, Peabody Museum, Cambridge, Mass., research fellow, 1965-71; University of Texas, Austin, member of faculty and assistant director of Center of Middle Eastern Studies, 1971—. Fellow at Radcliffe Institute, 1969-71; guest curator at University Art Museum of the University of Texas, 1975. Lecturer and symposium co-ordinator. *Member:* Archaeological Institute of America (president of Austin society, 1974-76), American Anthropological Association (fellow), Middle Eastern Studies Association. *Awards, honors:* National Endowment for the Arts grants.

WRITINGS—Juveniles: *Archaeology,* Steck, 1974; (with S. Mayer) *The Story of Sumer: The First Civilization* (exhibit catalog), University of Texas Press, 1975; (with M. Timko) *Egypt in the Days of the Pharaohs* (exhibit catalog), University of Texas Press, 1975; (with S. Otto-Diniz) *Open Sesame: The Story of Persian Locks* (exhibit catalog), University of Texas Press, 1976.

For adults: *The Legacy of Sumer: The First Civilization* (exhibit catalog), University of Texas Press, 1975; (editor) *The Legacy of Sumer,* Undena, 1976; (contributor) Theodore Wertime and J. Muhly, editors, *The Coming of the Age of Iron,* Yale University Press, 1977; (editor and contributor) *Images for Eternity,* Udena, 1977. Contributor of articles to professional journals.

WORK IN PROGRESS: "A study of an ancient system of recording consisting of small clay objects in geometric and odd shapes which preceded and announced writing by five thousand years."

SIDELIGHTS: Denise Schmandt-Besserat told *CA:* "When my children were three to twelve years old, reading together was part of our everyday lives, and it may not be exaggerated to say that often it was the best part of the day. We would read after dinner when the five of us, already tired from our busy days spent in our different ways, would at last be together in the living room. The feeling was always warm and peaceful, and I looked forward to reading time as much as the children. I realized the true importance of this sharing when Phillip was asked in class to define the word 'security.' The answer he wrote was 'security is when I am reading with my mother.' All of which leads me to say that I wrote my first book, *Archaeology,* for my children.

"I am an archaeologist and on several occasions had to leave for a whole summer to join excavations in the Middle East, especially in Iran. My children did not really know what I was doing over there, so I looked for books on archaeology which we could read together and which would help explain my work. As I could not find any which fulfilled this purpose, I decided to write one myself.

"Through my work at the University of Texas, I have been able to bring to Austin a series of exhibits on the ancient Middle East. Remembering the joy and interest my children have had in learning, I have been concerned that the children visitors appreciate and enjoy these exhibits. Thus, I have initiated a series of children's catalogues which make the information attractive and understandable to elementary school children. Many teachers have indicated to me that the books are effective teaching aids, and I have seen proof of this when one day I saw a group of third graders enter the gallery of the Egyptian exhibit proudly wearing the large paper Egyptian necklace which they had made following the catalogue instruction. They were so anxious to see the real Egyptian necklaces.

"I enjoy my work as an archaeologist immensely. My main contribution may be to have detected an early recording system consisting of small clay objects in geometric and odd shapes which preceded and anticipated writing by five thousand years. I came across these little objects, as it so often happens, totally by chance, when studying man's earliest uses of clay in the Middle East. The publication of my findings should lead to a whole new area of research and to a better understanding of the organization of primitive societies."

SCHMIDT, Jerry A(rthur) 1945-

PERSONAL: Born May 9, 1945, in Jamestown, N.D.;son of Arthur (a vocational evaluator) and Marvel (Hust) Schmidt; married Karen Lambert (an elementary school teacher), May 31, 1967; children: Cory, Ryan. *Education:* Westmar College, B.A., 1967; Iliff School of Theology, M.Div., 1970; University of Nebraska, Ph.D., 1972. *Residence:* Lakewood, Colo. *Office:* Family Enrichment Foundation, Denver, Colo. 80203.

CAREER: University of Denver, Denver, Colo., assistant professor of counselor education, 1972—. Psychologist for Family Enrichment Foundation, 1975—. *Member:* American Psychological Association, Association for the Advancement of Behavior Therapy.

WRITINGS: Help Yourself: A Guide to Self-Change, Research Press, 1976. Contributor to guidance journals.

WORK IN PROGRESS: Survival Skills for Secondary School Counselors; A Behavioral Counseling Workshop.

SIDELIGHTS: Schmidt comments: "My primary interest is preventive work in mental health. More specifically, giving laypersons practical interpersonal and intrapsychic skills, so that these life skills may be used throughout the life cycle. Anxiety management, rational self-talk, assertiveness, human potential and marriage and family life are my basic interests."

* * *

SCHNEIDER, Carl D(avid) 1942-

PERSONAL: Born November 12, 1942, in Philadelphia, Pa.; son of Carl M. (a minister) and Elsie (Gilbert) Schneider; married Carol Geary (an academic administrator), June 28, 1969; children: David Matthew. *Education:* Albright College, B.A. (summa cum laude), 1963; Union Theological Seminary, New York, N.Y., B.D. (magna cum laude), 1967; Harvard University, Ph.D., 1973. *Home:* 5524 South Cornell Ave., #3W, Chicago, Ill. 60637. *Office:* Meadville/Lombard Theological School, 5701 South Woodlawn Ave., Chicago, Ill. 60637.

CAREER: Ordained United Methodist clergyman, 1971; Meadville/Lombard Theological School, Chicago, Ill., assistant professor of religion and personality, 1973—. Lecturer at Schiller College, 1973, Antioch College, summer, 1974 and 1975, Northeastern Illinois University, spring, 1975 and 1976, University of Chicago, 1976, and University of Illinois, 1976. Staff member of Illinois Central Community Hospital, 1975-76. Member of board of directors of Guidance Institute (Berks County, Pa.), 1965-66, and Jamaica Plain Area Planning Action Council (Boston), 1969-70. Consultant to Twentieth Century Foundation (Boston), 1969, and Haslemere Pastoral Centre (Surrey, England), 1972-73. *Member:* American Academy of Religion, American Association of University Professors, Association for Clinical Pastoral Education, Society for the Scientific Study of Religion, Society for Values in Higher Education. *Awards, honors:* Danforth fellow, 1963-73; Columbia University international fellow, 1964-65.

WRITINGS: (Contributor of translations) Oscar Cullmann, *Vatican Council II: The New Direction,* edited by James D. Hester, Harper, 1968; *Shame, Exposure, and Privacy,* Beacon Press, 1977. Contributor to proceedings of the General Society for Systems Research, and to *Omega, United Methodists Today, Union Seminary Quarterly Review, Pennsylvania Psychiatric Quarterly,* and *Philosophy Today.*

SCHNEIDER, Stephen H(enry) 1945-

PERSONAL: Born February 11, 1945, in New York, N.Y.; son of Samuel (an educator) and Doris (an educator; maiden name, Swarte) Schneider. Education: Columbia University, B.S., 1966, M.S., 1967, Ph.D., 1971. Politics: "Support for candidates with long-term perspective." Office: National Center for Atmospheric Research, P.O. Box 3000, Boulder, Colo. 80303.

CAREER: Goddard Institute for Space Studies, New York, N.Y., postdoctoral research associate, 1971-72; National Center for Atmospheric Research, Boulder, Colo., fellow, 1972-73, deputy head of climate project, 1973—. Lecturer and writer. Member: American Meteorological Society, American Geophysical Union, American Association for the Advancement of Science, Federation of American Scientists, Sigma Xi.

WRITINGS: (With Lynne Mesirow) The Genesis Strategy: Climate and Global Survival, Plenum, 1976. Editor, Climatic Change, 1975—. Contributor to Science, National Observer, New Engineer, Journal of Atmospherical Science, and other periodicals.

WORK IN PROGRESS: A conceptual framework for Predicting the Unpredictable, on the environmental and institutional limits to global population and economic growth.

SIDELIGHTS: Schneider writes: "I am a research scientist concerned with both the effects of climate on society and the converse. From considerable experience in Washington I became convinced that many of the warnings from scientists and others about potential climate-related crises were being ignored by governmental politicians who were preoccupied with events whose relative time span is, at most, as far away as the next election. The need to 'go public' was apparent and led to my writing The Genesis Theory for a popular audience. The book and attendant media, government, and lecture appearances have helped to put certain issues before the public. Despite some academic resistance to public airing of uncertain scientific issues, I intend to continue to study, write and speak on the urgent need for society to anticipate potential long-term consequences of its short term policies with emphasis on issues with a technological component."

*   *   *

SCHNIREL, James R. 1931-

PERSONAL: Born October 26, 1931, in Geneva, N.Y.; son of Edwin R. (a contractor) and Charlotte (Beyer) Schnirel; married Shirley Birdwell (a teacher), June 22, 1957; children: Ben, Erica, John. Education: Delhi Agricultural and Technical Institute, certified in building construction, 1950; University of Oklahoma, B.S., 1959; Utah State University, M.S., 1975. Home address: Star Route, Box 155, Park City, Utah 84060. Office: Utah Technical College at Salt Lake, 4600 South Redwood Rd., Salt Lake City, Utah 84107.

CAREER: Utah Technical College at Salt Lake, Salt Lake City, dean of technical occupations and general education. Chairman of Park City Fire Protection District. Military service: U.S. Navy, builder, 1952-54. Member: American Vocational Association, American Technical Education Association, Utah Vocational Association, Summit Park Homeowners Association (past president), Utah Technical College Classroom Teachers Association (past president), Kiwanis.

WRITINGS: (With Ron H. Jenkins) Exploring Occupations in Communication and Graphic Arts (for young people), McGraw, 1975.

SIDELIGHTS: Schnirel writes: "Information relative to various careers has always been of interest to me and the aspect of the 'Careers in Focus' program that I was involved in was especially interesting since it not only involved reading and studying a career but also involved an activity with each career exploration. This is important since those young people trying to gain an understanding of a career need to become more directly involved in what the career is all about. I feel that career education is a necessity and is something that should be taught in one form or another from basic grades on up through the end of a high school career and further into adult life. I feel that more work should be done in the adult career exploration area. Perhaps, this will be something I can look forward to working on in the near future."

*   *   *

SCHOEN, Juliet P. 1923-

PERSONAL: Born December 25, 1923, in New York; daughter of Max (a manufacturer) and Bella (a beauty salon owner; maiden name, Brawer) Pfeffer; married Stanley R. Schoen (a lawyer), June 24, 1951; children: Mitchell David, Russell Bruce. Education: Brooklyn College (now of the City University of New York), student, 1938, 1939; University of California, Los Angeles, B.A. (magna cum laude), 1971. Home: 950 Las Lomas Ave., Pacific Palisades, Calif. 90272. Agent: Toni Milford, 50 East 86th St., New York, N.Y. 10028. Office: Palisadian Post, 839 Via de la Paz, Pacific Palisades, Calif. 90272.

CAREER: Fairchild Publications, New York, N.Y., editor, 1944-56; Palisades Publishers, Englewood, N.J., editor, 1956-63; Reisman & Kessler, Los Angeles, Calif., copy editor, 1975-76; Palisadian Post, Pacific Palisades, Calif., editor, 1976—.

WRITINGS: Silents to Sound: A History of Motion Pictures, Four Winds Press, 1976.

WORK IN PROGRESS: A book on football.

SIDELIGHTS: Juliet Schoen writes that she has had a long-time interest in sports, both as a participant and as a spectator. She considers the changes that have taken place since she first began going to ball games in 1938 to be both depressing and exciting: "Too much money, too little heart."

*   *   *

SCHRAM, Martin 1942-

PERSONAL: Born September 15, 1942, in Chicago, Ill.; son of Marlo J. (a consultant) and Charlene (an artist; maiden name, Fidler) Schram; married Patricia Morgan, May 23, 1964; children: Kenneth Marlo, David Morgan. Education: University of Florida, B.A., 1964. Home: 6309 East Halbert Rd., Bethesda, Md. 20034. Office: Newsday, 1750 Pennsylvania Ave. #304, Washington, D.C. 20006.

CAREER: Miami News, Miami, Fla., reporter, 1963-65; Newsday, Garden City, N.Y., reporter, 1965-67, correspondent in Washington, D.C., 1967-72, Washington bureau chief, 1973—. Author of column, "1600 Pennsylvania Avenue," appearing in Newsday. Notable assignments include presidential summit conferences in Moscow, Vladivostok, Peking, Europe, and the Middle East; special reports from Vietnam, Cuba, Siberia, and the Sino-Soviet border; coverage of the U.S. presidential campaigns of 1968, 1972, and 1976; investigations of Richard Nixon's finances in 1971, and of the Watergate scandal. Awards, honors: James Wright Brown Award, 1965, from Sigma Delta Chi, for public service journalism.

WRITINGS: *Running for President: A Journal of the Carter Campaign*, Pocket Books, 1976; *Running for President, 1976: The Carter Campaign*, Stein & Day, 1977.

*   *   *

SCHREIBER, Elizabeth Anne (Ferguson)   1947-

PERSONAL: Born June 24, 1947, in Indianapolis, Ind.; daughter of Robert Watt (a professor) and Elizabeth Anne (a professor; maiden name, Plummer) Ferguson; married Ralph Walter Schreiber (an ornithologist and writer), April 9, 1972. *Education*: Hollins College, B.A., 1969; University of South Florida, graduate study, 1970-72. *Office*: Natural History Museum of Los Angeles County, 900 Exposition Blvd., Los Angeles, Calif. 90007.

CAREER: High school biology teacher in Tampa, Fla., 1969-70, junior high school biology and math teacher in Tampa, 1971-73; Seabird Research, Inc., Tampa, researcher, 1970-77; Natural History Museum of Los Angeles County, Los Angeles, Calif., research associate, 1976—. *Member*: National Audubon Society, American Ornithologists Union, San Diego Zoo Society. *Awards, honors*: Outstanding science book award from Children's Book Council and National Science Teachers Association, 1975, for *Wonders of Sea Gulls*.

WRITINGS: (With husband, Ralph W. Schreiber) *Wonders of Sea Gulls* (juvenile; with own photographs), Dodd, 1975. Contributor to scientific journals and to Florida nature study magazines.

WORK IN PROGRESS: *Wonders of Terns*, a self-illustrated juvenile book, for Dodd; research on the breeding biology of laughing gulls in Tampa Bay, Fla.

SIDELIGHTS: Elizabeth Schreiber writes briefly: "I feel that scientific knowledge is only useful if it is communicated to others—colleagues and laymen, and used as a tool to help preserve our environment."

*   *   *

SCHREIBER, Ralph W(alter)   1942-

PERSONAL: Born July 6, 1942, in Wooster, Ohio; son of William I. (a college professor) and Clare Adel (a teacher; maiden name, Mentz) Schreiber; married Elizabeth Anne Ferguson (a writer), April 9, 1972. *Education*: College of Wooster, B.A., 1964; University of Maine, M.S., 1966; University of South Florida, Ph.D., 1974. *Office*: Natural History Museum of Los Angeles County, 900 Exposition Blvd., Los Angeles, Calif. 90007.

CAREER: Smithsonian Institution, Washington, D.C., research biologist, 1966-69; Seabird Research, Inc., Tampa, Fla., president, 1972-76; Natural History Museum of Los Angeles County, Los Angeles, Calif., curator of ornithology, 1976—. *Member*: American Ornithologists Union, Wilson Ornithological Society, Cooper Ornithological Society, British Ornithologists Union, Florida Ornithological Society (vice-president, 1975-77), Sigma Xi. *Awards, honors*: Outstanding science book award from Children's Book Council and National Science Teachers Association, 1975, for *Wonders of Sea Gulls*.

WRITINGS: (With J. J. Cook) *Wonders of the Pelican World* (juvenile), Dodd, 1974; (with wife, Elizabeth Anne Schreiber) *Wonders of Sea Gulls* (juvenile; with own photographs), Dodd, 1975. Contributor of more than thirty-five articles to ornithology journals and to *National Geographic* and *Animal Kingdom*.

WORK IN PROGRESS: Research on the biology of marine birds, especially the brown pelican in Florida and tropical sea birds in the Pacific Ocean.

SIDELIGHTS: Schreiber writes that he is primarily interested in scientific research on marine birds but believes that "publishing valid scientific data in a popular manner for 'non-scientist' and children is as important as publishing in the scientific journals."

*   *   *

SCHUKER, Stephen Alan   1939-

PERSONAL: Born February 16, 1939, in New York, N.Y.; son of Louis A. (a high school principal) and Millicent (an educator; maiden name, Milchman) Schuker. *Education*: Cornell University, B.A., 1959; Harvard University, M.A., 1962, Ph.D., 1969; also attended Institut d'Etudes Politiques, 1964-65. *Home*: 143 Walden St., Cambridge, Mass. 02140.

CAREER: Harvard University, Cambridge, Mass., assistant professor, 1968-74, lecturer in history, 1974-75; Brandeis University, Waltham, Mass., lecturer in history, 1975-76. *Military service*: U.S. Naval Reserve, active duty as assistant head of historical research in Naval History Division of Office of Chief of Naval Operations, 1959-61, with Naval Reserve Intelligence Division, 1961-64; became lieutenant senior grade. *Member*: American Historical Association, Telluride Association. *Awards, honors*: National Endowment for the Humanities fellowship, 1972-73; American Council of Learned Societies fellowship, 1976-77; Gilbert Chinard Prize from Society for French Historical Studies, 1976, for *The End of French Predominance in Europe*.

WRITINGS: *The End of French Predominance in Europe: The Financial Crisis of 1924 and the Adoption of the Dawes Plan*, University of North Carolina Press, 1976. Contributor to *Dictionary of American History, Dictionary of American Biography*, and to history journals.

WORK IN PROGRESS: *The Struggle for the Rhineland, 1918-1924; European Reconstruction after the Great War, 1918-1925.*

SIDELIGHTS: Schuker comments that he is a specialist on diplomatic, economic, and business history of western Europe and the United States, who has pioneered the technique of using business and banking archives to illuminate problems of international relations. He is also an authority on European diplomatic archives who has served as a consultant to the U.S. Public Documents Commission.

*   *   *

SCHULLER, Gunther   1925-

PERSONAL: Born November 22, 1925, in New York, N.Y. *Education*: Private study of composition, flute, and French horn. *Office*: New England Conservatory of Music, 290 Huntington Ave., Boston, Mass. 02115.

CAREER: New York Philharmonic Orchestra, New York, N.Y., played French horn under Arturo Toscanini, 1942; played French horn in Ballet Theatre Orchestra under Antal Dorati, 1943; Cincinnati Symphony, Cincinnati, Ohio, solo French horn player, 1943-44; Metropolitan Opera Orchestra, New York City, solo French horn player, 1944-59; musical composer, 1959-67; New England Conservatory of Music, Boston, Mass., president, 1967—, presented the conservatory's "Ragtime Ensemble," 1972. Teacher at Manhattan School of Music, 1952-64; Berkshire Music Center, acting head of composition department, 1963-65, head of department, 1965-69, artistic co-director of Tanglewood, beginning, 1969; associate professor at Yale University, until 1967. Organized and conducted "Twentieth Century Innovations," a concert series for Carnegie Hall Corp., 1963-65. Host of "Changing Music," a series on WGBH-Television, 1973; broadcast "Contemporary Music in Evolution," a weekly series on WBAI-Radio. Has made guest appearances as conductor of symphony orchestras in the United States and Canada, and in Europe, has conducted British Broadcasting Corp. Symphony, Philharmonic Orchestra of London, French Radio Orchestra, Symphony Orchestra of Bavarian Radio, and Tonhalle Orchestra of Zurich.

MEMBER: National Institute of Arts and Letters, National Council of the Arts. *Awards, honors:* National Institute of Arts and Letters award, 1960; Brandeis creative arts award, 1960; Darius Milhaud Award, 1964, for film score of Polish film "Yesterday in Fact"; D.Mus. from Northwestern University, 1967, University of Illinois, 1968, Colby College, 1969, and Williams College, 1975; Deems Taylor Award from American Society of Composers, Authors, and Publishers, 1970, for *Early Jazz: Its Roots and Musical Development;* Alice M. Ditson Conducting Award from Columbia University, 1970; Rodgers and Hammerstein Award, 1971; Grammy Award for chamber music from National Academy of Recording Arts, 1973, for recording "Scott Joplin: The Red Back Book"; has also been awarded Guggenheim fellowships.

WRITINGS: Horn Technique, Oxford University Press, 1962; *Early Jazz: Its Roots and Musical Development,* Oxford University Press, 1968.

Musical compositions: "Horn Concerto," "Symphony for Brass and Percussion," "Concerto for Orchestra," "Spectra," "Seven Studies on Themes of Paul Klee," "Variants" (ballet), "The Visitation" (opera), "String Quartet #1," "Music for Brass Quintet," "Double Quintet for Woodwinds and Brass," "The Sacred Cantata: Psalm XCVIII," "Triplum," "The Fisherman and His Wife" (children's opera), "Concerto de Camera," "The Power within Us" (oratorio), "Tre Invenzione," "Capriccio Stravagante," "Conversations" (jazz). Also composer of a work for the Washington, D.C. Bicentennial Commission.

WORK IN PROGRESS: Continuing his history of jazz with a sequel to *Early Jazz;* composing a violin concerto for Lucerne Festival, a horn concerto, and a trumpet concerto.

SIDELIGHTS: Schuller, as a composer, has received commissions from major American orchestras, and from Ford Foundation, New York City Ballet, Hamburg State Opera, from private music foundations, the American Guild of Organists, Junior League of Boston, and Music Educators National Conference. He has long been associated with John Lewis and the Modern Jazz Quartet. His "Ragtime Ensemble" at New England Conservatory of Music has been recorded on "Scott Joplin: The Red Back Book," for Angel Records. The conservatory is planning to establish in his honor the Gunther Schuller Fund for Studies in American Music.

*   *   *

SCHURMACHER, Emile C. 1903(?)-1976

1903(?)—December 24, 1976; American newspaperman and author; wrote seventeen nonfiction adventure books and biographies. He died in Mount Kisco, N.Y. Obituaries: *New York Times,* December 27, 1976.

SCHWALBERG, Carol(yn Ernestine Stein) 1930- (Hal Bolling; Phyllis Jenkins; Blanche La Fontaine, Lorelei Levy; Carl Shorter; Charles Stein; Barbara Ullman)

PERSONAL: Born February 11, 1930, in New York, N.Y.; daughter of Arthur (a butcher) and Madeline (a stenographer; maiden name, Schoenberg) Stein; married Robert M. Schwalberg (a photographer), August 24, 1952 (divorced, 1958). *Education:* New York University, B.A., 1950; also attended Fordham University, New School for Social Research, Alliance Francaise, French Institute, Cooper Union, Pierce College, Santa Monica City College, and University of California, Los Angeles. *Home address:* P.O. Box 197, Topanga, Calif. 90290. *Agent:* James Brown Associates, Inc., 22 East 60th St., New York, N.Y. 10022.

CAREER: McCall Corp., New York, N.Y., copy chief of *McCall's Needlework and Crafts,* 1955-56; Street & Smith, New York City, staff writer for *Science World,* 1957; free-lance writer, 1958—; *Scholastic Roto,* New York City, editor, 1963-64; *School Bank News,* New York City, editor-in-chief, 1971-73. *Member:* Authors Guild of Authors League of America, American Society of Journalists and Authors, Society of Children's Book Writers. *Awards, honors:* Grant from Wurlitzer Foundation, summer, 1972.

WRITINGS: (Contributor) Adelaide Hall, editor, *New Modern Reading Skill Text Series,* Book I, C. E. Merrill, 1966; *From Cattle to Credit Cards: The History of Money,* Meredith Corp., 1969; (contributor) *The Print* (photography book), Time, Inc., 1970; *Light and Shadow,* Parents' Magazine Press, 1972; (contributor) *How to Get Things Done in New York,* Dutton, 1973; *Doing It: Or, How to Give the Perfect Orgy,* Dell, 1973. Author of film review column "Far-Out and Foreign" (under pseudonym Barbara Ullman) in *Better Home Movie Making,* 1965-66; author of photographic review column "Camera" in *Village Voice,* 1961-64. Contributor, sometimes under pseudonyms, of more than two hundred articles and photographs to photography journals and popular magazines, including *Holiday, Cosmopolitan, Seventeen, Woman's Day, Penthouse,* and *American Way.*

WORK IN PROGRESS: How They Invented Applesauce, a juvenile fantasy; *Tickles, Itches, and Sneezes,* nonfiction for children; *How the Losers Won the Race,* a novel.

SIDELIGHTS: Carol Schwalberg writes: "My love affair with words began early: I talked before I walked. As a child, nothing delighted me more than hearing my mother tell a story. After I discovered that relating funny anecdotes about my family won me friends, I became a writer.... Reporting about ordinary Americans is my current focus of interest."

*   *   *

SCHWARTZ, Bertie G. 1901(?)-1976

1901(?)—September 22, 1976; American authority on books dealing with Jewish culture and co-author of a book on Judaism; associated with many Jewish philanthropic organizations. She died in New York City. Obituaries: *New York Times,* September 24, 1976.

*   *   *

SCOLNICK, Sylvan 1930(?)-1976

1930(?)—September 2, 1976; American writer and lecturer. He confessed to a series of crimes and gave authorities information that led to the arrests of numerous others; after serving a prison sentence, wrote his autobiography. He died in Cherry Hill, N.J. Obituaries: *New York Times*, September 3, 1976.

* * *

SCOTT, John 1912-1976

March 26, 1912—December 1, 1976; American authority on the Soviet Union, journalist, radio commentator, lecturer, and author of books on the Soviet Union, Europe, and the world food crisis. He died in Chicago, Ill. Obituaries: *New York Times*, December 3, 1976. (See index for previous *CA* sketch)

* * *

SCOTT, Kenneth 1900-

PERSONAL: Born May 4, 1900, in Waterbury, Conn.; son of John Linus (a manufacturer) and Julie (Cooke) Scott; married Aurelia Grether (a professor of English), June 17, 1926; children: Jean Helen, Kenneth John. *Education:* Williams College, A.B., 1921; attended American School of Classical Studies, Athens, Greece, 1921-22; University of Wisconsin, Madison, M.A., 1923, Ph.D., 1925. *Politics:* Republican. *Religion:* Episcopalian. *Home:* 42-05 243 St., Douglaston, N.Y. 11363.

CAREER: University of Wisconsin, Madison, instructor in Latin, 1923-24, assistant professor of classics, 1925-27; Yale University, New Haven, Conn., assistant professor of Latin, 1927-29; Western Reserve University (now Case Western Reserve University), Cleveland, Ohio, professor of classics, 1929-42; master of classics and modern languages at private school in Concord, N.H., 1942-47, and of modern languages at a private school in Simsbury, Conn., 1947-48; Upsala College, East Orange, N.J., professor of classical languages, 1948-49; Wagner College, Staten Island, N.Y., professor of modern languages, 1949-59, chairman of department, 1950-59; Queensborough College of the City University of New York, Bayside, N.Y., assistant professor, 1960-61, associate professor, 1961-62, professor of foreign languages and chairman of department, 1962-65; Queens College of the City University of New York, Flushing, N.Y., professor of history, 1965-70, professor emeritus, 1970—.

MEMBER: American Society of Genealogists (fellow), American Philological Association, National Genealogical Society, New York Historical Society, New York Genealogical and Biographical Society (member of board of trustees). *Awards, honors:* Markham traveling fellowship, University of Berlin, 1926-27; Guggenheim fellowship, 1934; commander of the Order of St. Agatha (San Marino), 1937; knight of the Order of the Crown (Italy), 1938.

WRITINGS: (With Karl P. Harrington) *Selections from Latin Prose and Poetry*, Ginn, 1933; (with R. S. Rogers and Margaret Ward) *Caesaris Augusti Res Gestae et Fragmenta* (title means "Deeds and Fragments of Caesar Augustus"), Heath, 1935; *The Imperial Cult under the Flavians*, W. Kohlhammer Verlag, 1936; *Notes on the Bowman, Harter, and Sauer Families*, Warner Press, 1948.

Counterfeiting in Colonial New York, American Numismatic Society, 1953; *Counterfeiting in Colonial Pennsylvania*, American Numismatic Society, 1955; *Counterfeiting in Colonial America*, Oxford University Press, 1957; *Counterfeiting in Colonial Connecticut*, American Numismatic Society, 1957; *Counterfeiting in Colonial Rhode Island*, Rhode Island Historical Society, 1960; (with Julius Bloch, Leo Hershkowitz, and Constance Sherman) *An Account of Her Majesty's Revenue in the Province of New York, 1701-*

1709, Gregg, 1967; *Genealogical Data from New York Administration Bonds, 1753-1799*, New York Genealogical and Biographical Society, 1969; *Jasper Danckaert's Diary of Our Second Trip from Holland to New Netherlands*, Gregg, 1969.

Genealogical Data from the New York Post-Boy, 1743-1773, National Genealogical Society, 1970; *The Voyages and Travels of Francis Goelet, 1746-1758*, Gregg, 1970; (with James Owre) *Genealogical Data from Inventories of New York Estates, 1666-1825*, New York Genealogical Society, 1970; *Genealogical Data from Further New York Administration Bonds*, New York Genealogical and Biographical Society, 1971; *Genealogical Data from the Pennsylvania Chronicle, 1767-1774*, National Genealogical Society, 1971; *Records of the Chancery Court of New York—Guardianships, 1691-1815*, Holland Society of New York, 1971; *Calendar of New York Colonial Commissions Book, Volume IV: 1770-1776*, National Society of Colonial Dames in the State of New York, 1972; *Genealogical Data from Administration Papers from the New York State Court of Appeals in Albany*, National Society of Colonial Dames in the State of New York, 1972; *The Slave Insurrection in New York in 1712*, Bobbs-Merrill, 1972; *New York Marriage Bonds, 1753-1783*, St. Nicholas Society in the City of New York, 1972; *Rivington's New York Newspaper: Excerpts from a Loyalist Press, 1773-1783*, New York Historical Society, 1973; *Genealogical Abstracts from the American Weekly Mercury, 1719-1746*, Genealogical Publishing, 1974; *Abstracts from Ben Franklin's Pennsylvania Gazette, 1728-1748*, Genealogical Publishing, 1975; *New York: State Census of Albany County Towns in 1790*, Genealogical Publishing, 1975; (with Kenn Stryker-Rodda) *Denizations, Naturalizations and Oaths of Allegiance in Colonial New York*, Genealogical Publishing, 1975; (with Kristin L. Gibbons) *The New York Magazine: Marriages and Deaths, 1790-1797*, Polyanthos, 1975; (with Susan E. Klaffky) *A History of the Joseph Lloyd Manor House*, Society for the Preservation of Long Island Antiquities, 1976; (editor with Stryker-Rodda) E. B. O'Callaghan, *The Minutes of the Orphanmasters of New Amsterdam, 1663-1668*, Genealogical Publishing, 1976; *Abstracts (Mainly Deaths) from the Pennsylvania Gazette, 1775-1783*, Genealogical Publishing, 1976; *Joseph Gavit's American Deaths and Marriages, 1784-1829: An Index to Non-Principal Names*, Polyanthos, 1976; (editor with Stryker-Rodda) O'Callaghan, translator, *The Register of Solomon Lachaire: Notary Public of New Amsterdam, 1661-1662*, Genealogical Publishing, 1977; *Genealogical Data from Colonial New York Newspapers*, Genealogical Publishing, 1977; (with Stryker-Rodda) *Varied Genealogical Data: A Complete List of Addressed Letters Left in the Post Offices of Philadelphia, Lancaster, Chester, Trenton and Wilmington between 1748-1780*, Genealogical Publishing, 1977; (with Janet R. Clarke) *Abstracts from the Pennsylvania Gazette, 1748-1755*, Genealogical Publishing, 1977; (editor with Rosanne K. Conway) *Abstracts from Colonial Connecticut Newspapers: New Haven, 1755-1775*, Polyanthos, 1977. Contributing editor of *National Genealogical Society Quarterly*.

WORK IN PROGRESS: A book about early naturalizations for Genealogical Publishing Co.

SIDELIGHTS: Scott writes that he reads Latin and Greek, and speaks Italian, French, German, Spanish, modern Greek, Danish, and Turkish.

SCRIBNER, Charles, Jr. 1921-

PERSONAL: Born July 13, 1921, in Quogue, N.Y.; son of Charles (a publisher) and Vera Gordon (Bloodgood) Scribner; married Dorothy Joan Sunderland, July 16, 1949; children: Charles III, Blair Sunderland, John. *Education:* Princeton University, A.B. (summa cum laude), 1943. *Politics:* Independent. *Religion:* Episcopalian. *Home:* 211 East 70th St., New York, N.Y. 10021. *Office:* Charles Scribner's Sons, 597 Fifth Ave., New York, N.Y. 10017.

CAREER: Charles Scribner's Sons, New York, N.Y., advertising manager, 1946-48, production manager and vice-president, 1948-50, president, 1952-77, chairman, 1977—. Princeton University Press, president, 1957-68, now trustee; trustee of Princeton University, 1969—; president of American Book Publishers Council, 1966-68; director of Woodrow Wilson Foundation. *Military service:* U.S. Naval Reserve, active duty, 1943-46, 1950-52; became lieutenant senior grade.

MEMBER: History of Science Society, Phi Beta Kappa, Racquet and Tennis Club (New York), University Club (New York), Princeton Club (New York), Church Club (New York), Nassau Club (Princeton). *Awards, honors:* M.A. from Princeton University, 1966; Curtis Benjamin Award for Creative Publishing from Association of American Publishers, 1976.

WRITINGS: (Editor and author of introduction) *The Enduring Hemingway,* Scribner, 1974; (translator) Jacob and Wilhelm Grimm, *Hansel and Gretel* (juvenile), Scribner, 1975. Contributor to academic journals and to *National Wildlife.*

WORK IN PROGRESS: Translating *Doppelfinten,* by Gabriel Laub; *The Devil's Bridge,* for children; writing the introduction for *The Scribner-Bantam Dictionary.*

SIDELIGHTS: Scribner writes: "As a book publisher I do not have as much time as I'd like to *write* books. . . . My first attempt at fiction was the text for a children's book *The Devil's Bridge.* This was a retelling of an ancient French legend, which I remember reading as a schoolboy. I am hoping to try my hand at similar projects in the future.

"I was a classics major at Princeton and have given lectures on the value of Latin as well as on other general topics dealing with poetry, writing, language, and education. For more than twenty-five years I have had a strong interest in history of science and intellectual history, and these have led to our publication of *Dictionary of Scientific Biography* and *Dictionary of the History of Ideas.*" He is the fourth consecutive Charles Scribner to head the family publishing firm, founded in 1846.

*   *   *

SEDLACEK, William E(dward) 1939-

PERSONAL: Born January 4, 1939, in Chicago, Ill.; son of Edward Joseph (a painter) and Valborg (a china painter; maiden name, Jensen) Sedlacek; married Jeannette Gehring (a librarian); children: Joseph Sung. *Education:* Iowa State University, B.S., 1960, M.S., 1961; Kansas State University, Ph.D., 1966. *Politics:* "The elimination of racism is the key to world peace." *Religion:* "We all can learn and determine our own lives, more than most do now." *Home:* 1217 Highland Dr., Silver Spring, Md. 20910. *Office:* Counseling Center, Shoemaker Building, University of Maryland, College Park, Md. 20742.

CAREER: Researcher, instructor, and summer employment director at various universities, and at Greater Kansas City Mental Health Foundation, 1960-64; Association of American Medical Colleges, Washington, D.C., research psychologist, 1964-66, acting assistant director for basic research of the division of education, 1966-67; University of Maryland, College Park, assistant professor, 1967-71, associate professor of measurement and statistics, 1971—, assistant director of counseling center and director of testing, research, and data processing, 1967—. Part-time associate professor of psychology, Roosevelt University, 1966-67. Consultant to Public Health Service, American Society of Allied Health Professionals, Association of American Medical Colleges, and other organizations. Lecturer.

MEMBER: American Educational Research Association, American Personnel and Guidance Association (member of National Commission on Academic Testing and Prediction, 1968—), American Psychological Association, Eastern Psychological Association, Institute for Continuing Professional Education, Interamerican Society of Psychology, Midwestern Psychological Association, National Council on Measurement in Education, Association of American Medical Colleges, Psi Chi.

WRITINGS: (With Glenwood C. Brooks, Jr.) *Racism in American Education: A Model for Change,* Nelson-Hall, 1976. Also author (with Brooks) of *Situational Attitude Scale* (SAS), Natresources. Contributor of articles and reviews to professional journals. Editor, *Counseling and Personnel Services Journal,* 1969; member of editorial board, *College Student Journal,* 1972-75.

WORK IN PROGRESS: A book, *The I Hate to Do Research Handbook;* more than fifty research projects dealing with racism, sexism, nutritional behavior of children, and educational evaluation.

SIDELIGHTS: Sedlacek told *CA:* "My main interest is to demonstrate that social change is possible through the translation of research and systematic thought into simple tasks which most people can accomplish. *Racism in American Education* attempts to do this for what I feel is the central issue in world conflict. My next book will be an attempt to demonstrate how to do the research which will accomplish change in many areas."

*   *   *

SEEGER, Pete(r R.) 1919-

PERSONAL: Born May 3, 1919, in New York, N.Y.; son of Charles (a conductor, musicologist, and educator) and Constance de Clyver (a violinist and teacher; maiden name, Edson) Seeger; married Toshi Aline Ohta, July 20, 1943; children: Daniel Adams, Mike Salter, Virginia. *Education:* Attended Harvard University, 1936-38. *Home:* Dutchess Junction, Beacon, N.Y. 12508. *Agent:* Harold Leventhal, 200 West 57th St., New York, N.Y. 10019.

CAREER: Folksinger, composer, musicologist, writer. Library of Congress, Archive of American Folk Song, Washington, D.C., archive assistant, 1939-40; founding member of the Almanac Singers (touring group), 1940-41; toured the southern and southwestern states and Mexico with folksinger, Woody Guthrie, 1941-42; co-founder and national director of People's Songs, Inc. (songwriters' union), 1945; toured the United States with Progressive Party presidential candidate, Henry Wallace, 1948; founding member of the Weavers (folksinging quartet), 1948-52; solo world concert tour, 1952-55 (including "American Folk Music and Its Origins" concert series at Columbia University's Institute of Arts and Sciences, 1954-55); rejoined and toured with the Weavers, 1955-57; host of "Rainbow Quest" program on

National Educational Television (NET), 1955-56. Has appeared in two motion pictures, "To Hear My Banjo Play," 1946, and "Tell Me that You Love Me, Junie Moon," 1970; on national television and radio programs, and at colleges, nightclubs' and theatres (including Carnegie Hall and Town Hall) around the world; recorded over eighty record albums for various companies, including Folkways, Columbia, Decca, Warner Brothers, and Vanguard; produced, with wife, Toshi, some fifteen educational short subjects for Folklore Research Films; has appeared at the National Folk Festival in St. Louis and was instrumental in organizing the Newport (R.I.) Folk Festivals; chairman of the board, Hudson River Sloop Restoration, Inc., 1967-70. *Military service:* U.S. Army Special Services, entertained troops in the United States and the South Pacific, 1942-45.

WRITINGS: American Favorite Ballads, Oak, 1961; *The Steel Drums of Kim Loy Wong* (instruction manual), Oak, 1962; (with Jerry Silverman), *The Folksinger's Guitar Guide,* Oak, 1962; (author of introduction) Woody Guthrie, *Woody Guthrie Folksongs: A Collection of Songs by America's Foremost Balladeer,* Ludlow, 1963; *Steel Drums and How to Play Them* (instruction manual; based on *The Steel Drums of Kim Loy Wong*), Oak, 1964; (with Julius Lester) *The Twelve-String Guitar as Played by Leadbelly,* Oak, 1965; (author of preface) Don McClean, editor and compiler, *Songs and Sketches of the First Clearwater Crew,* North River Press, 1970; *The Incomplete Folksinger,* edited by Joe Metcalf Schwartz, Simon & Schuster, 1972; *Henscratches and Flyspecks: or, How to Read Melodies from Songbooks in Twelve Confusing Lessons,* Berkeley Press, 1973; (with father, Charles Seeger) *The Foolish Frog,* Macmillan, 1973.

Also author of *The Bells of Rhymney,* 1964; (with John Cohen), *New Lost City Ramblers Songbook,* 1965; *How to Play the Five-String Banjo,* published by Oak; *Pete Seeger on Record,* published by Peer-Southern.

Writer of children's songs, folk ballads, labor songs, and freedom songs, including, "Where Have All the Flowers Gone?," (with Lee Hays) "If I Had a Hammer," and (in collaboration with The Weavers) "Kisses Sweeter Than Wine," and "Turn, Turn, Turn."

Contributor of articles to periodicals, including *Environment* and *Broadside.* Member of editorial staff, *Sing Out!*

SIDELIGHTS: Recalling the beginning of his career in music Seeger wrote: "In 1935 I was sixteen years old, playing tenor banjo in the school jazz band. I was uninterested in the classical music which my parents taught at Julliard. That summer I visited a square dance festival in Asheville, North Carolina, and fell in love with the old fashioned five-string banjo, rippling out a rhythm to one fascinating song after another. I liked the rhythms. I liked the melodies, time tested by generations of singers. Above all, I liked the words.

"Compared to the trivialities of most popular songs, the words of these songs had all the meat of human life in them. They sang of heroes, outlaws, murderers, fools. They weren't afraid of being tragic instead of just sentimental. They weren't afraid of being scandalous instead of giggly or cute. Above all, they seemed frank, straightforward, honest. By comparison, it seemed to me that too many art songs were concerned with being elegant and too many pop songs were concerned with being clever.

"So in 1935 I tried learning some of this music . . . I'm still learning. I've found out that some of the simplest music is some of the most difficult to do. I've also found, of course,

that America has in it as many different kinds of folk music as there are folks. We have not only the strains from Ireland and Scotland, France and Germany, but Africa and Mexico, and a hundred other countries."

Touring with Woody Guthrie in the early 1940's, Seeger sang at migrant camps and union halls. He collaborated on writing labor and anti-fascist songs and helped organize labor unions. But, when communists were purged from the unions in the late 1940's, Seeger was blacklisted by both the entertainment world and the labor movement.

In 1955, Seeger was called before a subcommittee of the House Un-American Activities Committee investigating alleged subversive influences in the entertainment field. Instead of citing the Fifth Amendment (which allows the individual to avoid self-incrimination and would have safeguarded him from prosecution), Seeger refused to answer questions regarding his political beliefs or associations and chose to cite the First Amendment (guaranteeing freedom of speech and association). At the time of the hearing he said, "In my whole life I have never done anything of any conspiritorial nature. I resent very much and very deeply the implication of being called before this committee."

Seeger was indicted on ten counts of contempt of Congress and in March of 1961 he went on trial before the U.S. District Court in New York City. He was found guilty on all counts and sentenced to serve one year in prison. Upon sentencing Seeger stated, "I have never in my life supported or done anything subversive to my country, I am proud that I have never refused to sing for any organization because I disagreed with its beliefs." Then, to reaffirm his position, Seeger offered to sing a song. The court denied him permission to do so.

On May 18, 1962, the U.S. Court of Appeals reversed Seeger's conviction by unanimous decision. Even though the indictment had been dismissed, Seeger was banned from some television networks and his concerts were picketed by various conservative organizations. In 1963, when ABC banned Seeger from appearing in "Hootenanny," its weekly folk music program, Joan Baez and several other performers refused invitations to appear. ABC later issued a statement that it would consider allowing Seeger to appear if he would agree to sign an affidavit concerning his political affiliations. Seeger refused on constitutional grounds. The controversy surrounding Seeger has waned considerably since the 1960's, but it has not disappeared.

With the release of his 1965 record album, "God Bless the Grass," Seeger launched himself into a fight to save the environment. His main effort has focused on the restoration of the Hudson River (which has been called "unswimmable, at times unsmellable, and usually undescribable"). Seeger had witnessed the decay of the river valley from his home, a hand built, two-room log cabin on the river's east side. He conceived that a publically owned, life-sized model of a historic Hudson River sloop could rekindle an interest in the river and perhaps insure its future. He and a few dedicated others formed a public corporation which they called the Hudson River Sloop Restoration, Inc. The profits of a series of "sloop concerts", totaling more than $60,000, were donated by Seeger, and in 1968 the ship, *Clearwater,* was built.

Now one of the best known sailing vessels in the country, *Clearwater* carries the environmental message to waterfront communities for "sloop festivals." Here, civic groups and local branches of national organizations are welcomed to gather and discuss ecological problems. The *Clearwater* crew gives free river rides while offering lectures on environment and water beautification. Often Seeger is in the midst of the activities, talking to people and urging them to become active in saving the environment: "Who's going to clean up this river of ours? No polluter, no politician, is going to lift a finger unless we insist on it. So we have to make ourselves heard. We're all in this environmental thing together. Not even a millionaire can escape it. Every breast-fed baby in the country—from rich and poor families alike—is drinking DDT in its mother's milk. All urban dwellers are breathing bad air. We've got to take action right now. We've got to solve this problem before it solves us."

Writer Jack Hope observed that while listening to Seeger speak one may recognize the influence of various contemporary social thinkers ranging from biologist Paul Erlich to Reverend Martin Luther King, Jr. Hope explained that "perhaps Seeger's world view is simply the predictable philosophical outcome of a lifetime devoted to human welfare . . . And probably the fundamental appeal of Peter Seeger's relatively homespun messages has something to do with the fact that his words are an accurate reflection of his own lifestyle."

It is difficult to predict what the final success of the *Clearwater* project will amount to, but Hope concludes that this much is certain: "the popularity of Seeger, his enthusiasm and sincerity and idealism, all have helped to draw support to the environmental cause and have created some of the optimism and hopefulness that have been traditionally lacking from the voice of the environmental movement."

AVOCATIONAL INTERESTS: Skiing, sailing, rambling through the woods.

BIOGRAPHICAL/CRITICAL SOURCES: Sing Out!, May, 1954; Ray Lawless, *Folksingers and Folk Songs in America,* Longmans, 1960; *Hi Fi,* January, 1963; *Ramparts,* November 30, 1968; *Conservationist,* June, 1969; *Look,* August, 1969; *National Wildlife,* February, 1970; *Popular Science,* August, 1970; *Environment,* March, 1971; *Audubon,* March, 1971; *Saturday Review,* May 13, 1973; *Rolling Stone,* March 10, 1977.

* * *

SEGAL, Abraham 1911(?)-1977

1911(?)—May 24, 1977; American author best known for *The Eternal People* and *Joseph and His Brothers.* He taught English in Philadelphia schools before directing the education department of the Union of American Hebrew Congregations. Segal died in New York City. Obituaries: *New York Times,* May 26, 1977.

* * *

SEGAL, Fred 1924(?)-1976

PERSONAL: Married Jackie Klein; children: Gretchen, Vicki, Nicholas, Harry. *Residence:* Woodland Hills, Calif.

CAREER: Novelist and playwright.

WRITINGS: The Broken Field Runner, New American Library, 1967. Also author of plays, and of screenplay, "A Separate Peace," 1972.

OBITUARIES: New York Times, May 30, 1976.*

(Died May 28, 1976, in Santa Monica, Calif.)

* * *

SEKLER, Eduard F(ranz) 1920-

PERSONAL: Born September 30, 1920, in Vienna, Austria;

came to the United States in 1955; son of Eduard Jakob (an actor) and Elisabeth (Demmel) Sekler; married Mary Patricia May (an art historian), July 21, 1962. *Education:* Vienna Technical University, Dipl. Ing., 1945; School for Planning and Regional Research, London, England, certificate, 1947; Warburg Institute, London, Ph.D., 1948. *Home:* 21 Gibson St., Cambridge, Mass. 02138. *Office:* Carpenter Center for Visual Arts, Harvard University, Cambridge, Mass. 02138.

CAREER: Vienna Technical University, Vienna, Austria, assistant lecturer, 1945-53, lecturer in architecture, 1953-60; Harvard University, Cambridge, Mass., visiting professor, 1955-56, associate professor, 1956-60, professor of architecture, 1960-70, Osgood Hooker Professor of Visual Arts, 1970—, director of Carpenter Center of Visual Arts, 1966-76. Member of board of directors of Architectural Heritage, Inc., 1969-75; member of Cambridge Arts Council. Head of UNESCO international team for "Masterplan for the Conservation of the Cultural Heritage of the Kathmandu Valley," 1975; architectural designer of single-family and multiple-family dwellings in Vienna and of public structures and exhibitions; has had exhibitions at Harvard University and Museum of the Philadelphia Civic Center.

MEMBER: International Council of Monuments and Sites, Society of Architectural Historians (member of board of directors, 1963-66, 1970-73), Royal Town Planning Institute (honorary corresponding member), Architectural Association (London), Society of Registered Architects (Vienna). *Awards, honors:* A.M. from Harvard University, 1960; Guggenheim fellowships, 1961-62, 1962-63; fellow of American Academy of Arts and Sciences, 1968; Cross of Honor for Science and Art (Austria), 1970.

WRITINGS: Annus mirabilis: Zeitgemaesse Gedanken zu einer Wiederaufbauplanung der Vergangenheit (title means "Timely Thoughts on a Reconstruction Plan of the Past"), Dokumentationszentrum fuer Technik und Wirtschaft, 1951; *Das Punkthaus im europaeischen Wohnungsbau* (title means "Pointhouses in European Housing"), Dokumentationszentrum fuer Technik und Wirtschaft, 1952; *Wren and His Place in European Architecture,* Faber, 1956.

(Editor) *Historic Urban Spaces,* four volumes, Carpenter Center for the Visual Arts, Harvard University, 1962-71; *Proportion: A Measure of Order,* Carpenter Center for the Visual Arts, Harvard University, 1965; (contributor) Gyorgy Kepes, editor, *Structure in Art and in Science,* Braziller, 1965; (contributor) *The Fine Arts and the University,* York University, 1965; (editor and contributor) *Bauhaus: A Teaching Idea,* Carpenter Center for the Visual Arts, Harvard University, 1967; (editor and contributor) *Form from Process: The Thonet Chair,* Carpenter Center for the Visual Arts, Harvard University, 1967; (contributor) Douglas Fraser and others, editors, *Essays in the History of Architecture Presented to Rudolf Wittkower,* Phaidon, 1967.

(With Carl Pruscha, Raymond Allchin, and others) *Kathmandu Valley: The Preservation of Physical Environment and Cultural Heritage, Protective Inventory,* two volumes, Schroll, 1975; (contributor) Mary Henle, editor, *Perspectives on Vision,* Springer, 1976; (editor and contributor) *Master Plan for the Conservation of the Cultural Heritage in the Kathmandu Valley,* UNESCO, 1977; (with William Curtis) *Le Corbusier at Work: The Genesis of the Carpenter Center for the Visual Arts,* Harvard University Press, 1977.

Contributor to *Oxford Companion to Art, Encyclopaedia Britannica, American People's Encyclopedia, Collier's Encyclopedia, Encyclopedia of World Art,* and *Neue*

Deutsche Biographie. Contributor to architecture journals and other scholarly periodicals.

WORK IN PROGRESS: A monograph on the architecture of Josef Hoffmann; research on historic urban spaces and their conservation and on architectural theory.

SIDELIGHTS: Sekler writes: "I am concerned with the relation of past and future in our environment, particularly in architecture; with architecture as a humanity; with the right balance between change and continuity; with a framework of values I can pass on to my students." *Avocational interests:* International travel ("usually to places rich in historic monuments"), sketching, photography.

* * *

SELF, Edwin F(orbes) 1920-

PERSONAL: Born June 15, 1920, in Dundee, Scotland; came to the United States in 1921, naturalized citizen, 1941; son of Robert Henry and Agnes Wilson (Dick) Self; married Dorothy McCloskey, November 1, 1942; married second wife, Gloria Winke (an editor), August 18, 1951; children: Joan (Mrs. Harry Merrick), Robert, Winke (Mrs. George Dianasopolis), Carey (Mrs. Tai Gen Jar). *Education:* Dartmouth College, A.B. (magna cum laude), 1942. *Residence:* La Jolla, Calif. *Office: San Diego,* 3254 Rosecrans, San Diego, Calif. 92110.

CAREER/WRITINGS: La Jolla Light, La Jolla, Calif., advertising manager, 1946; *North Shores Sentinel,* San Diego, Calif., editor and publisher, 1946-48; *San Diego,* San Diego, publisher and editor-in-chief, 1948—. Sports reporter for *San Diego Sun,* summers, 1936-37; business manager of *Frontier,* 1949-55. Contributor to magazines and newspapers, including *Town and Country, Los Angeles, Nation,* and *Frontier.* Also co-author of *San Diego: Portrait of a Spectacular City,* 1969. Consultant to *Psychology Today, Washingtonian,* and *San Francisco.* Member of California State Board of Architectural Examiners, 1966-68; member of board of directors of Francis Parker School, 1969-71; member of board of directors of San Diego Convention and Visitors Bureau, 1962-68. *Military service:* U.S. Coast Guard, 1942-46; served in Okinawa; became lieutenant senior grade.

MEMBER: La Jolla Museum of Art, San Diego Chamber of Commerce, Phi Beta Kappa, Delta Tau Delta, Sigma Delta Chi. *Awards, honors:* Telesis Award from local chapter of American Institute of Planners, 1963, for contributions to urban environment planning; John Swett Award from California Teachers Association, 1966; public information award from state council of American Institute of Architects, 1970, for urban environment reporting.

* * *

SELG, Herbert 1935-

PERSONAL: Born June 13, 1935, in Oberhausen, Germany; son of Konrad and Luise (Koch) Selg; married Renate Brandenburg, August 28, 1962; children: Thomas, Olaf. *Education:* University of Bonn, Ph.D., 1960; University of Freiburg, habilitation, 1967. *Home:* Kloster-Langheim, Strasse 44, Bamberg, West Germany. *Office:* Gesamthochschule, Bamberg, West Germany.

CAREER: Padagog Hochschule, Braunschweig, Germany, professor of psychology, 1969-72; Free University of Berlin, Berlin, Germany, professor of psychology, 1972-75; Gesamthochschule, Bamberg, Germany, professor of psychology, 1975—. *Member:* Deutsche Gesellschaft fur Psychologie.

WRITINGS: Einfuhrung in die experimentelle Psychologie, Kohlhammer, 1966; *Diagnostik der Aggressivitat,* Verlag fur Psychologie, 1968; (editor) *Zur Aggression verdammt?,* Kohlhammer, 1971, translation by Arnold Pomerans published as *The Making of Human Aggression,* St. Martin's, 1975; (with Werner Bauer) *Forschungsmethoden der Psychologie,* Kohlhammer, 1971; *Entwicklung und Lernen,* Waisenhaus-Buchdruckerie und Verlag, 1972; (with Ulrich Mees) *Menshhliche Aggressivitat,* Verlag fur Psychologie, 1974; (with Mees) *Verhaltensbeobachtung und padagogische Verhaltens modifikation,* Klett, 1977.

WORK IN PROGRESS: Research on aggression, modeling, and dyslexia.

SIDELIGHTS: Dr. Selg told *CA* he considers B. F. Skinner to be the most influential figure in modern psychology.

* * *

SELIGMAN, Eustace 1889(?)-1976

1889(?)—September 5, 1976; American lawyer, civic leader, and writer on international affairs. In 1917 he co-founded the Voluntary Defenders Committee which later became part of the Legal Aid Society, and he was president of Legal Aid for fifteen years. He died in New York City. Obituaries: *New York Times,* September 7, 1976.

* * *

SELL, Ted 1928-

PERSONAL: Born September 15, 1928, in Iowa; son of Clifford P. (a newspaperman) and Nona M. (Watson) Sell; married wife, Anita, September 1, 1951 (divorced, 1973); children: Kathleen, Blake, Brian. *Education:* Drake University, B.A., 1953. *Politics:* Independent. *Religion:* None. *Home and office:* 2401 Calvert St. N.W., Washington, D.C. 20008. *Agent:* Mitchell P. Hamilburg Agency, 292 South La Cienega Blvd., Suite 212, Beverly Hills, Calif. 90211.

CAREER: Los Angeles Times, Los Angeles, Calif., reporter, foreign correspondent, and Washington correspondent, 1953-73; free-lance writer and consultant in Washington, D.C., 1973-76. *Military service:* U.S. Marine Corps, 1945-48, 1950-51; became sergeant. *Member:* Phi Beta Kappa.

WRITINGS: (Co-author) *Six Days in June,* New American Library, 1967.

* * *

SEVAREID, (Arnold) Eric 1912-

PERSONAL: Born November 26, 1912, in Velva, N.D.; son of Alfred (a banker) and Clare (Hougen) Sevareid; married Lois Finger, May 18, 1935 (divorced, August 16, 1962); married Belen Marshall (a musician), February 28, 1963 (separated, 1973); children: (first marriage) Michael and Peter (twins); (second marriage) Christina. *Education:* University of Minnesota, B.A., 1935; graduate study at London School of Economics and Political Science, 1937, and at Alliance Francaise, 1938. *Politics:* "Liberal on domestic affairs and increasingly conservative on foreign affairs." *Religion:* Lutheran. *Office:* CBS News, 2020 M St. N.W., Washington, D.C. 20036.

CAREER: Minneapolis Journal, Minneapolis, Minn., reporter, 1936-37; *New York Herald Tribune* (Paris edition), reporter, 1938, city editor, 1939; Columbia Broadcasting System (CBS), New York City, war correspondent in

France and London, 1939-40, member of Washington News Bureau, 1940-43, war correspondent in China, 1943, covered World War II Italian campaign, 1944, covered the United Nations conference on international organization in San Francisco, Calif., 1945, chief correspondent at Washington News Bureau, 1946-59; roving European correspondent based in London, 1959-61, moderator for various telecasts in New York City, 1961-64, national correspondent in Washington, D.C., and commentator on "CBS Evening News with Walter Cronkite," 1964-1977. Host and science reporter for "Conquest," 1957-58, interviewer and host of "Conversations with Eric Sevareid," 1975-77, and moderator and/or contributor to television programs, including "Years of Crisis," "The Great Challenge," "Town Meeting of the World," "The College Turmoil," "Justice in America," and "Storm over the Supreme Court," all for CBS. Notable assignments include coverage of presidential conventions and elections since 1948, coverage of South Vietnam in 1966, coverage of the resignations of Vice-President Spiro Agnew and President Richard Nixon, and interviews with President Gerald Ford, Willy Brandt, Adlai Stevenson, George Kennan, Marietta Tree, Leo Rosten, John McCloy, Anne Morrow Lindbergh, and other internationally known figures. Night city editor in Paris, United Press International (UPI), 1939. Columnist. Lecturer.

MEMBER: National Press Club, Overseas Writers, Radio Correspondents Association, Garrick Club, Sigma Delta Chi. *Awards, honors:* George Foster Peabody Award, 1950, 1964, and 1967; Page One Award, 1965, from the New York Newspaper Guild, for a story on Adlai Stevenson; Emmy Award from National Academy of Television Arts and Sciences; Teddy Roosevelt Rough Riders Award from the State of North Dakota; Distinguished Achievement of the Year Award from the University of Southern California; Order of the Crown from Belgium; Freedom Medal from Norway; One World Award; Alfred I. DuPont Award; two Overseas Press Club awards; George Polk Memorial Award; Outstanding Achievement Award of the University of Minnesota; Brotherhood Award of the National Conference of Christians and Jews; Sidney Hillman Foundation Award; National Headliners Award; gold medal award from the National Institute of Social Sciences; has received honorary degrees from Wittenburg College, University of Maryland, Temple University, Cornell College (Mount Vernon, Iowa), Luther College, University of North Dakota, Colgate University, and Boston University.

WRITINGS: Canoeing with the Cree, Macmillan, 1935, reprinted by Minnesota Historical Society, 1968; *Not So Wild a Dream* (autobiography), Knopf, 1946, reissued, 1965, reissued by Atheneum, 1976; *In One Ear: 107 Snapshots of Men and Events which Make a Far-Reaching Panorama of the American Situation at Mid-Century* (essays), Knopf, 1952; *Small Sounds in the Night: A Collection of Capsule Commentaries on the American Scene,* Knopf, 1956; (editor) *Candidates 1960: Behind the Headlines in the Presidential Race,* Basic Books, 1959; *This Is Eric Sevareid* (essays), McGraw, 1964; (with Robert A. Smith) *Washington: Magnificent Capital,* Doubleday, 1965.

Author of syndicated weekly column appearing in more than one hundred newspapers. Contributor of articles to periodicals, including *Look* and *Saturday Review.* Author of phonorecords, "National News, Local Control," produced by Center for the Study of Democratic Institutions, 1973, and "An Ear to the Sounds of Our History," produced by CBS News, 1974.

BIOGRAPHICAL/CRITICAL SOURCES: Akron Beacon

Journal, June 30, 1974; *National Review,* August 15, 1975; *New Republic,* September 20, 1975; *Saturday Review,* October 2, 1976, November 27, 1976.

* * *

SEVELA, Efraim 1928-

PERSONAL: Born March 8, 1928, in Bobruisk, Soviet Union; son of Joel E. (a sportsman) and Rachel (Gelfand) Sevela; married Julia Gendelstein (an actress), September 19, 1958; children: Maria, Danial. *Education:* University of Minsk, student, 1945-48. *Home:* 315 West 57th St., Apt. 15G, New York, N.Y. 10019.

CAREER: Worked as journalist in Vilna, Soviet Union, and as script writer and film director in Moscow, Soviet Union; writer. *Member:* Union of Soviet Filmmakers.

WRITINGS: Legends from Invalid Street, Doubleday, 1974; *Truth Is for Strangers,* Doubleday, 1976. Author of plays and scripts for eight feature films, all in the Soviet Union, in Russian.

WORK IN PROGRESS: Two books, *Last Convulsions; Stop the Plane—I'll Get Off.*

SIDELIGHTS: Sevela writes that he was a member of the group of Soviet Jews who made the first political strike in Moscow that led to the beginning of the immigration to Israel.

* * *

SEYMOUR, Charles, Jr. 1912-1977

February 26, 1912—April 7, 1977; American art historian, educator, founder of Yale University's program for professional conservation of art works, leader of the American committee working to rescue Italian art after the Florentine flood (1966), and author of books on Italian Renaissance art and on medieval art and architecture. He died in New Haven, Conn. Obituaries: *New York Times,* April 9, 1977; *AB Bookman's Weekly,* June 20, 1977. (See index for previous *CA* sketch)

* * *

SHADOWITZ, Albert 1915-

PERSONAL: Born May 5, 1915, in Brooklyn, N.Y.; son of Joseph and Sarah Anna (Luntz) Shadovitz; married Edith Goldstein (a librarian), August 8, 1941; children: Naomi, Sarah (Mrs. Ronald Cohen), Rebecca. *Education:* Polytechnic Institute of Brooklyn, B.E.E., 1935; New York University, Ph.D., 1958. *Politics:* "Anti-Communist." *Religion:* Jewish ("in a very poor way"). *Home:* 63 Mountainview Ave., Nutley, N.J. 07110. *Office:* Department of Physics, Fairleigh Dickinson University, Teaneck, N.J. 07666.

CAREER: Aberdeen Proving Ground, Md., junior engineer, 1941-43; International Telegraph & Telephone Co., Nutley, N.J., electronic development engineer, 1943-51; electronics engineer for small electronic companies, 1951-58; Fairleigh Dickinson University, Teaneck, N.J., professor of physics, 1958—. *Member:* American Physical Society, American Association for the Advancement of Science, American Society for Psychical Research. *Awards, honors:* Fellowship from University of Liverpool, 1967.

WRITINGS: Special Relativity, Saunders, 1968; *The Electromagnetic Field,* McGraw, 1975; (with Peter Walsh) *The Dark Side of Knowledge,* Addison-Wesley, 1976.

WORK IN PROGRESS: A technical problem in physics.

SIDELIGHTS: Shadowitz changed professions rather late

in life because he came to feel that "engineering is not a rewarding field of work for anyone intelligent—unless he is rapacious, or rich—because engineers are only exploited hired hands."

Of his most recent book, he writes: "I helped introduce an elective course, Nature and the Occult, into the physics curriculum at Fairleigh Dickinson University. The course was designed to attract liberal arts students, who usually hate anything connected with physics. I meant to explain to these students my belief, common to almost all scientists, that in this world we needed only insight and patience to explain everything rationally, including the mysterious attractions of the occult. It didn't quite work out that way. In the course of four years of investigating this field I gradually changed my view that everything in the occult was humbug. As I see it now, there is more to the glistening occult than fool's gold, though there is much of that. At any rate the notes for the course, transmuted to a book, are responsible for my transition from a writer of technical books and articles for the specialist to a writer of nonfiction literature for the general public."

*   *   *

SHAHA, Rishikesh   1925-

PERSONAL: Born May 16, 1925, in Tansen, Nepal; son of Tarak Buhadur (in government service) and Madan Divyeshvari (Rana) Shaha; married Siddhanta Rana, July 12, 1946; children: Shri Prakash (son). *Education:* Patna University, B.A., 1943, M.A. (English), 1945; Allahabad University, M.A. (political science), 1954. *Politics:* Democratic socialism. *Religion:* "Non-practising Hindu." *Home and office:* Shri Nivas, Kamal Pokhari, Kathmandu, Nepal.

CAREER: Tri-Chandra College, Kathmandu, Nepal, teacher of English and Nepali, 1945-48; Nepal Democratic Congress, Calcutta, India, later Kathmandu, founding member, 1948-49, leader, 1950-52; Nepal Advisory Assembly, Kathmandu, leader of the opposition, 1950-52; Nepali Congress, Kathmandu, general secretary, 1953-55; United Nations representative from Nepal and first residential ambassador to the United States, both 1956-60; Nepali minister of finance, 1960-62, minister of foreign affairs, 1962; special ambassador at large with cabinet rank, 1962-63; chairman of standing committee of the King's Council, 1963-64; East-West Center, Honolulu, Hawaii, senior fellow, 1965-66; member of Nepal's national legislature (from graduates' constituency), 1967-71; University of California, Berkeley, regents' professor in the department of political science, 1971-72; president of Nepal Council of World Affairs, 1973-75; Smithsonian Institution, Washington, D.C., fellow of Woodrow Wilson International Center for Scholars, 1976—. Chairman of Royal Commission for the Drafting of the 1962 Constitution of Nepal; visiting professor at Jawaharlal Nehru University, 1971. *Member:* Amnesty International (president of Nepal chapter, 1973-75), Nepal Nature Conservation Society (president, 1973-75), All-Nepal College and University Teachers Association (past chairman), Nepali Literary Society (past chairman).

WRITINGS: Nepal and the World, Khoj Parisad, Nepali Congress, 1954; *Heroes and Builders of Nepal,* Oxford University Press, 1965; *Notes on Hunting and Wild Life Conservation in Nepal,* privately printed, 1970; *Nepali Politics: Retrospect and Prospect,* Oxford University Press, 1975; *An Introduction to Nepal,* Ratna Pustak Bhandur, 1976.

In Nepali: *Igbal and Nazrul* (translations of poems), Pakistan Embassy (Kathmandu), 1969; *Sarbajanik Suraksha Kanoon Ra Bandi Pratyakshikaran* (title means "Public Security Act and Habeas Corpus"), privately printed, 1970; *Dalabihin Panchayati Prajatantrayek Adhikarik Prarup* (title means "Partyless Panchayat Democracy: An Authoritative Outline"), privately printed, 1970.

Contributor to international journals, in English and Nepali.

WORK IN PROGRESS: A History of Nepal.

SIDELIGHTS: In the second emergency session of the United Nations General Assembly (October, 1956), Shaha was the first among the Asian non-aligned nations to declare support on behalf of his country for the resolution condemning Russian action in Hungary. Burma and Ceylon followed in agreement.

Shaha was critically stabbed in Central Park on the opening day of the September, 1957, General Assembly. He maintained, however, that hoodlums are hoodlums everywhere in the world and that it could have happened to him even in his own capital.

He won acclaim by telling off Kruschev in the General Assembly of 1960, sometimes called "the session of the shoe and the broken gavel." Shaha said that "new members of the United Nations are not likely to be bullied or blackmailed by a show of force into accepting a super power's line of thought, because they value their freedom of judgement and action."

In 1961, Shaha was elected chairman of the international committee set up by the General Assembly to investigate the circumstances leading to the death of Dag Hammarskjoeld.

He reported that he has been imprisoned several times in connection with his agitation for human rights and the rule of law in Nepal. In May, 1977, his latest period of detention, Shaha was arrested for the publication of his article "Recent Amendments to the Constitution of Nepal," published in the *India Left Review* in August, 1976.

In addition, Shaha has participated in international conferences of lawyers and jurists, and he has traveled widely in Europe, India, China, Japan, and Africa.

AVOCATIONAL INTERESTS: Reading, shooting, swimming.

*   *   *

SHAPCOTT, Thomas William   1935-

PERSONAL: Born March 21, 1935, in Ipswich, Australia; son of Harold (an accountant) and Dorothy (Gillespie) Shapcott; married Margaret Hodge (a teacher), April 18, 1960; children: Katherine, Alison, Richard, Isabel. *Education:* University of Queensland, B.A., 1969. *Home:* 11 Burnett St., Ipswich, Queensland 4305, Australia. *Office:* Shapcott & Shapcott, 6 Ellenborough St., Ipswich, Queensland 4305, Australia.

CAREER: H. S. Shapcott (public accountant), Ipswich, Australia, clerk, 1951-63; Shapcott & Shapcott (accountants), Ipswich, partner, 1963-72, sole principal, 1972—. Secretary, Ipswich Fire Brigade, 1970—. *Member:* Australia Council Literature Board (deputy chairman, 1973-76). *Awards, honors:* Grace Leven Prize for poetry, 1961, for *Time on Fire;* Sir Thomas White Memorial Prize for poetry, 1967, for *A Taste of Salt Water;* Sydney Myer Charity Trust Award, 1967, for *A Taste of Salt Water,* and 1969, for *Inwards to the Sun;* Churchill fellowship to United States and England, 1972.

WRITINGS—Poems: *Time on Fire,* Jacaranda Press, 1961;

Twelve Bagatelles, Australian Letters, 1962; *The Mankind Thing,* Jacaranda Press, 1964; *Sonnets 1960/1963,* B. Donaghey, 1964; *A Taste of Salt Water,* Angus & Robertson, 1967; *Inwards to the Sun,* University of Queensland Press, 1969; *Fingers at Air: Experimental Poems,* privately printed, 1969; *Begin with Walking,* University of Queensland Press, 1972; *Interim Report,* privately printed, 1972; *Shabbytown Calendar,* University of Queensland Press, 1976; *Seventh Avenue Poems,* Angus & Robertson, 1976.

Other: *Focus on Charles Blackman* (art monograph), University of Queensland Press, 1967; (editor with Rodney Hall) *New Impulses in Australian Poetry,* University of Queensland Press, 1968; (editor) *Australian Poetry Now,* Sun Books, 1970; *The Seven Deadly Sins* (opera libretto), privately printed, 1970; (editor) *Poets on Record,* University of Queensland Press, 1970-73; (editor) *Contemporary American and Australian Poetry,* University of Queensland Press, 1976.

WORK IN PROGRESS: Selected Poems 1956/1976, publication by University of Queensland Press expected 1978; a novel.

SIDELIGHTS: Sharcott told *CA:* "I am deeply interested in the development of poetry in Australia and in its wider relevance in English speaking contexts. My own development has been from lyrical celebratory beginnings, through increasing awareness of social process to (most recently) a sense of regional mythology within a world in flux. I do not see myself as a regional poet, though; rather, as one man rediscovering himself through others."

* * *

SHARPE, Grant W(illiam) 1925-

PERSONAL: Born May 15, 1925, in Kentfield, Calif.; son of Frank W. and Lillian (Grant) Sharpe; married Wenonah Finch, April 3, 1948; children: Christopher, Kathryn, Charles, Loretta, Paul, Patrick, Frederick, Rosemary, Eileena. *Education:* University of Washington, Seattle, B.S. and M.F., both 1951, Ph.D., 1956. *Home:* 12724 42nd N.E., Seattle, Wash. 98125. *Office:* College of Forest Resources, University of Washington, Seattle, Wash. 98195.

CAREER: Flathead National Forest, Missoula, Mont., in forest fire protection, 1948; U.S. Plywood Corp., Seattle, Wash., exhibit preparer, 1952-55; University of Michigan, Ann Arbor, assistant professor of forestry, 1956-61, associate professor of outdoor recreation, 1961-66; University of Washington, Seattle, professor of outdoor recreation, 1967—. Visiting scientist lecturer for Society of American Foresters and National Science Foundation, 1965-66. Park naturalist for National Park Service, summers, 1949-63; member of resource development screening committee of National Research Council's Council for International Exchange of Scholars, 1975-77. Member of Michigan Parks and Recreation Commission, 1961; vice-chairman of Michigan Natural Areas Council, 1964-65; member of Michigan Civil Service Oral Appraisal Board, 1965. Member of Seattle Municipal Art Commission, 1968-69. *Military service:* U.S. Navy, 1943-46.

MEMBER: Society of American Foresters, Association of Interpretive Naturalists (founding member; fellow; member of board of directors, 1966-67; regional chairman, 1973-74), American Society of Landscape Architects (honorary member), Western Interpreters Association, Sigma Xi, Phi Sigma, Xi Sigma Phi. *Awards, honors:* Meritorious service award from Association of Interpretive Naturalists, 1972.

WRITINGS: (With wife, Wenonah Sharpe) *101 Wildflowers of Glacier National Park,* Glacier Natural History Association, 1952; (with W. Sharpe) *101 Wildflowers of Olympic National Park,* University of Washington Press, 1954; (with W. Sharpe) *101 Wildflowers of Mount Ranier National Park,* University of Washington Press, 1957; (with W. Sharpe) *101 Wildflowers of Shenandoah National Park,* University of Washington Press, 1958; (with W. Sharpe) *101 Wildflowers of Crater Lake National Park,* University of Washington Press, 1959.

(With Shirley W. Allen) *An Introduction to American Forestry,* 3rd edition (Sharpe was not associated with earlier editions), McGraw, 1960; (with Wenonah Sharpe) *101 Wildflowers of Acadia National Park,* University of Washington Press, 1963; (with Robert Searles) *Directory of Interpretive Materials,* Association of Interpretive Naturalists, 1966; *Acadia National Park and the Nearby Coast of Maine,* Golden Press, 1968; (with Shirley W. Allen and Clare Hendee) *Introduction to Forestry,* 4th edition (Sharpe was not associated with earlier editions), McGraw, 1976; (editor and contributor) *Interpreting the Environment,* Wiley, 1976.

Also contributor to *Working with Environmental Factors,* Institute of Forest Products, College of Forest Resources, University of Washington, 1968. Contributor of articles and reviews to professional journals. Member of editorial board of *Journal of Forestry* (associate editor, 1970-72) and *Journal of Leisure Research* (associate editor, 1971-76).

WORK IN PROGRESS: Outdoor Recreation Management, with Charles H. Odegaard, for Wiley.

SIDELIGHTS: Sharpe told *CA:* "Perhaps because I have worked as a naturalist and educator for many years I do not find myself automatically allied with extreme environmentalists. I have worked with these people when I felt their goals to be realistic and balanced, but I have also worked with governmental and private agencies whose concern must be with the total environment. This must include all elements of the human spectrum, from backpackers to trail bike riders. I cannot help but feel that people living today, as well as future generations, must be considered in the allocation of lands and resources for leisure and utilitarian purposes."

AVOCATIONAL INTERESTS: Power boating, canoeing, fishing, photography, growing tomatoes, and scuba diving.

* * *

SHAW, Carolyn Hagner 1903(?)-1977

1903(?)—April 20, 1977; American author, and publisher of *The Social List of Washington.* A social leader in Washington during the Woodrow Wilson years, she wrote a column called, "Modern Manners" for the *Washington Star* and later published a book by the same name. She died in Washington, D.C. Obituaries: *Washington Post,* April 23, 1977.

* * *

SHAW, Lawrence H(ugh) 1940-

PERSONAL: Born August 3, 1940, in Wallace, Idaho; son of Byron T. (a research administrator) and Jane Elizabeth (a teacher; maiden name, Dunn) Shaw; married Sue Olinger (an economist), September 15, 1962; children: Ada, Byron, Amanda, Jane, Emily. *Education:* Dartmouth College, student, 1957-58; George Washington University, A.B. (with distinction), 1961; Harvard University, A.M., 1963, Ph.D., 1964. *Home address:* Route 6, Box 577, Piedmont, S.C. 29673. *Office:* 15 Boyce Ave., Greenville, S.C. 29601.

CAREER: U.S. Department of Agriculture, Washington, D.C., economist in Washington and in Athens, Greece, 1962-66; Vanderbilt University, Nashville, Tenn., assistant professor of economics, 1966-68; B. F. Goodrich Co., Akron, Ohio, director of economic research, 1968-71; Lawrence H. Shaw, Greenville, S.C., economic analyst, 1971—. Author of "What's Ahead for Southern Business?," a weekly column syndicated by Transworld News Service, 1971—. *Member:* National Association of Business Economists, American Economic Association, American Statistical Association, Econometric Society.

WRITINGS: Postwar Growth in Greek Agricultural Output: A Study in Sectoral Output Change, Center for Planning and Economic Research (Athens, Greece), 1969.

SIDELIGHTS: Shaw comments that his syndicated feature "puts national economic events in perspective for the sixteen-state Southern region of the United States. Today's South remains the country's poor relation with income levels only eighty-five per cent of those in the North and West. But change is underway and tomorrow's South will be strikingly different." He considers such questions as "How will the South share in tomorrow's economic prosperity? Will investment opportunities in the region continue to grow? What about unions? What do Southern consumers buy less of with their lower incomes? What will they buy more of in the future?"

*   *   *

SHEA, James J.   1890(?)-1977

1890(?)—January 3, 1977; American business executive and author; board chairman of Milton Bradley, one of the country's largest manufacturer of games, puzzles, and educational materials. He died in Springfield, Mass. Obituaries: *New York Times,* January 4, 1977.

*   *   *

SHEPARD, Sam   1943-
(Slim Shadow)

PERSONAL: Surname originally Rogers; born November 5, 1943, in Fort Sheridan, Ill.; son of Samuel Shepard (a teacher of Spanish) and Elaine (Schook) Rogers; married O-Lan Johnson (an actress), November 9, 1969; children: Jesse Mojo (son). *Education:* Attended Mount Antonio Junior College, 1960-61. *Home:* 62 Pilgrims Lane, London NW3, England. *Agent:* Toby Cole, 234 West 44th St., New York, N.Y. 10036.

CAREER: Conley Arabian Horse Ranch, Chino, Calif., stable hand, 1958-60; actor with Bishop's Co. (repertory touring group), 1962-63; Village Gate, New York City, busboy, 1963-64; Marie's Crisis Cafe, New York City, waiter, 1965; Hickory House, New York City, busboy, 1965-66; writer, 1966—. Rock musician (drums and guitar) with Holy Modal Bounders, 1968. *Awards, honors:* Obie Award from *Village Voice,* for best plays of the Off-Broadway season for "Red Cross," "Icarus's Mother," "Chicago," 1966, "La Turista," 1967, and "Forensic and the Navigators"; fellowships from Yale University, 1967, and University of Minnesota; grants from Guggenheim foundation, and Rockefeller Foundation.

WRITINGS: Hawk Moon: A Book of Short Stories, Poems, and Monologues (limited edition), Black Sparrow Press, 1973.

Plays: "Cowboys," produced in New York City, 1964; "Rocking Chair," produced in New York City, 1964; "Up to Thursday," produced in New York City, 1964; "Dog," produced in New York City, 1964; *Five Plays,* includes "Icarus's Mother" (one-act; produced in New York City, 1965), "Chicago" (one-act; first produced in New York City at Martinique Theatre, April 11, 1966), "Melodrama Play" (one-act; produced in New York City at Cafe La Mama, 1967), "Red Cross" (one-act; produced in New York City at Provincetown Theatre, April 28, 1968), and "Fourteen Hundred Thousand" (one-act; first broadcast as NET Playhouse program, 1969), Bobbs-Merrill, 1968.

Operation Sidewinder (two-act; first produced in New York City at Vivian Beaumont Theatre, March 12, 1970), Bobbs-Merrill, 1970; *The Unseen Hand, and Other Plays,* includes "4-H Club" (produced in New York City, 1965), "Forensic and the Navigators" (one-act; first produced in New York City at Theatre Genesis, St. Mark Church in-the-Bowery, 1968), "The Unseen Hand" (one-act; first produced in New York City at Cafe La Mama, December 26, 1969), "Shaved Splits," (produced in New York City, 1969), "The Holy Ghostly" (one-act; produced in New York City, 1970), and "Back Dog Beast Bait" (one-act; first produced in New York City at American Place Theatre, April 29, 1971), Bobbs-Merrill, 1971; *Mad Dog Blues, and Other Plays,* includes "The Rock Garden" (first produced in New York City, 1964; excerpt produced in "Oh! Calcutta!" in New York City at Eden Theatre, 1969), "Cowboys #2" (one-act; first produced in Los Angeles, 1967), "Cowboy Mouth" (with rock performer Patti Smith; produced in New York City, 1971), and "Mad Dog Blues" (one-act; first produced in New York City at Theatre Genesis, St. Mark Church in-the-Bowery, March 18, 1971), Winter House, 1972; "Blue Bitch," first production, 1973; (with Jean-Claude Van Itallie and Megan Terry) "Nightwalk," first produced in New York City, at St. Clement Church, September 6, 1973. *The Tooth of Crime* [*and*] *Geography of a Horse Dreamer* (the former is a one-act play with rock music, first produced in Princeton, N.J., at McCarter Theatre, 1972), Grove, 1974; "Killer's Head [and] Action," both were first produced in New York City at American Place Theatre, April 15, 1975; *Angel City* [*and*] *Curse of the Starving Class,* Urizen Books, 1976.

Screenplays: (With Robert Frank) "Me and My Brother," 1967; (with Michelangelo Antonioni, Tonino Guerra, Fred Graham, and Clare Peploe) *Zabriskie Point* (released, 1969), Cappelli (Bologna, Italy), 1970, published with Antonioni's *Red Desert,* Simon & Schuster, 1972; (with Murray Mednick) "Ringaleerio," 1971.

SIDELIGHTS: John Lahr called Sam Shepard "perhaps the most ruthlessly experimental and uncompromising" of today's younger writers. He identified Shepard as "the new theater's answer to Harold Pinter—obsessed, cool, precise in language and the control of stage devices. His plays hold up dramatic moments for microscopic scrutiny." While some reviewers have criticized Shepard's experimentation with stage sets and special effects (Marilyn Stasio said that "Operation Sidewinder" was "over-produced with elaborate devices more cinematic than dramatic"), others have been enchanted. Lahr praised Shepard's "eye for texture and surprise." Describing the set of "Red Cross," Lahr said, "Shepard is talking about the flesh—salmon and ugly in front of an all-white set. The violence of his vision of decay takes place in a studied calm—silent and unassuming like the threatening pigment of primary colours."

Shepard's plays evoke widely varied responses from theatre critics. For example, Albert Bermel called "La Turista" a "dead end of infantile sadism, verging on theatrical fascism," while Elizabeth Hardwick described it as a "work of superlative interest." Ms. Hardwick continued: "Sam Shepard . . . possesses the most impressive literary talent and dramatic inventiveness. He is voluble, in love with long, passionate, intense monologues . . . which almost petrify the audience." She also praised Shepard for his decision not to invite reviewers to submit their evaluations of the play and to risk the loss of advertisement which brings people to the theatre. "Perhaps it is only the young people, free of deforming ambitions," Hardwick conjectured, "who would have the courage to submit to such a test."

Adrian Rendle suggested that part of the reason for this disparity of critical opinion was due to "the misunderstandings of some of the directors who append notes on the productions they have done of Shepard's plays. These notes nearly all read like confessions of failure—the truth of the play having hit them after the first performance has been given and I think some of these confessions will show how the author has been misconceived in the theatre." Rendle feels that Shepard must be taken more seriously as a writer, and said of the collection, *Five Plays,* "Here is a writer with enough fire and precision to shake up the *avant garde* world with whom his work is already proving popular."

Commenting on "Geography of a Horse Dreamer," Harold Clurman said: "Shepard is one of the better of our young free-wheeling playwrights. His writing is vernacularly colorful, at moments even eloquent; he possesses an extravagant imagination. There is in him an old-time American saltiness, a quasi-mysticism mixed with a present-day metropolitan vulgarity that manages to be rather sympathetic."

AVOCATIONAL INTERESTS: Greyhound racing, pool, rock and roll, Little Brother Montgomery, Clyde McPhatter, Wyoming, the Sioux Nation, guns, '57 Chevrolets, sheepdogs, highways, buffalo, knives, horse racing, fast women, and various personalities associated with the American West.

BIOGRAPHICAL/CRITICAL SOURCES: New York Review of Books, April 6, 1967; *New Leader,* April 10, 1967; *London Magazine,* December, 1968; *Drama,* Spring, 1969; *Cue,* July 18, 1970; *Nation,* May 3, 1975, January 10, 1976; *New Yorker,* May 5, 1975, December 22, 1975.*

*   *   *

SHEPPARD, Sally   1917-

PERSONAL: Born August 22, 1917, in Knowlton, Quebec, Canada; daughter of Alan K. (a choreographer and Broadway producer) and Esther (Reid) Foster; married Richard Balmain Hutchison, August 25, 1943 (died, January, 1944); married S. Roger Sheppard (an architect), September 1, 1945; children: Stephanie, Hugh, Deborah (Mrs. Ronald John Guy). *Education:* Attended Case Western Reserve University, 1935-36, and Ohio State University, 1936-38. *Politics:* Liberal. *Religion:* Anglican. *Home address:* R.F.D. 6, Brewster, N.Y. 10509.

CAREER: Journalist. Has worked as a reporter and foreign correspondent for *York Gazette,* York, Pa., *Time* (magazine), New York City, and Columbia Broadcasting System (CBS), New York City.

WRITINGS: First Book of Brazil (juvenile), F. Watts, 1962, 2nd edition, 1972; *Indians of the Eastern Woodlands* (juvenile), F. Watts, 1975; *Indians of the Plains* (juvenile), F. Watts, 1976. Also co-author of *The Truth about Weight Control,* for Stein & Day. Contributor to *Vogue.* Editor of *Patent Trader,* 1956.

SIDELIGHTS: Sally Sheppard writes: "I am basically an investigative reporter but with the demise of newspapers I've been forced to write more than report."

*   *   *

SHEPPARD, Walter Lee, Jr.   1911-

PERSONAL: Born June 23, 1911, in Philadelphia, Pa.; son of Walter Lee and Martha Houston (Evans) Sheppard; married Boudinot Oberge Kendall (a secretary); children: (stepsons) Charles H., Jr., John A. *Education:* Cornell University, B.Ch., 1932; University of Pennsylvania, M.S., 1933. *Politics:* Republican. *Religion:* "Liberal Catholic." *Home and office:* 923 Old Manoa Rd., Havertown, Pa. 19083.

CAREER: Registered professional engineer in Delaware and California. Worked various short-term jobs as a chemist, 1933-35; writer of small space copy, N. W. Ayer & Sons, (advertisers), 1936-38; salesperson and assistant to the editor, E. F. Houghton & Co., 1938-41; salesperson, Atlas Mineral Products Co., 1941-45; Tanks & Linings Ltd., Droitwich, England, consultant, 1949-65; district manager and salesperson, Electro Chemical Engineering and Manufacturing Co., 1965-68; Penwalt Corp., Philadelphia, Pa., field sales manager and national account manager of corrosion engineering division, 1968-76; C.C.R.M., Inc., Havertown, Pa., president and consultant of chemically resistant masonry, 1976—. Salesperson and member of committee on acid resistant cement, Amercoat Corp., 1968-76; Board for Certification of Genealogists, founding trustee and president, 1964—. *Military service:* U.S. Army Reserve, Artillery, 1932-71; active duty, 1941-45; served in China-Burma-India Theatre; became lieutenant colonel.

MEMBER: National Association of Corrosion Engineers (local chairperson, 1959-60), National Society of Professional Engineers, American Society for Testing and Materials, Association of Consulting Chemists and Chemical Engineers, American Society of Genealogists (fellow; president, 1970-73), National Genealogical Society, Society of Genealogists (London), Descendents of Illegitimate Sons and Daughters of Kings and Queens of Britain (founder; president, 1968—), New England Historic Genealogical Society, Genealogical Society of Pennsylvania (fellow), Yorkshire Archaeological Society, Welcome Society of Pennsylvania (president, 1966-76), Colonial Society of Pennsylvania (member of council, 1975—), Gilbert and Sullivan Society (president of Philadelphia branch, 1956-60), Phi Kappa Psi (national president, 1968-70), Alpha Chi Sigma, Flagon and Trencher (founder; president, 1967-73), Mayflower Descendents, Sovereign Order of St. John of Jerusalem, Order of the Three Crusades, Savoy Company.

WRITINGS: Ancestors and Descendents of Thomas Stickney Evans and Sarah Ann Fifield, His Wife, privately printed, 1940; (contributor) *Genealogical Research: Methods and Sources,* American Society of Genealogists, 1960; (contributing editor) *Ships and Passengers (to the Delaware),* Genealogical Publishing, 1970; *Feudal Genealogy* (monograph), National Genealogical Society, 1975; (editor) F. L. Weis, *Ancestral Roots of Sixty American Colonists,* Genealogical Publishing, 5th edition, 1976; *Handbook of Chemically Resistant Masonry,* C.C.R.M., Inc., 1977. Contributor of about seventy-five articles to genealogy and engineering journals. Member of editorial board of *Pennsylvania Genealogical Magazine,* 1961-76; contributing editor of *American Genealogist,* 1940—, and *National Genealogical Society Quarterly,* 1955—.

WORK IN PROGRESS: Ancestry of Edward Carlton of Rowley, Massachusetts and Ellen Newton, His Wife.

AVOCATIONAL INTERESTS: History of medieval times and the Dark Ages, the stage (sings in Gilbert and Sullivan productions), films (especially silent films), classical music, theology, the occult, travel, archaeology, puppets, "living conditions and customs throughout the world."

BIOGRAPHICAL/CRITICAL SOURCES: Ubique, spring, 1975.

* * *

SHERER, Robert G(lenn, Jr.) 1940-

PERSONAL: Born March 13, 1940, in Jasper, Ala.; son of Robert Glenn (a businessman) and Esther Lee (a book-keeper; maiden name, Brakefield) Sherer; married Amelia Ann Brookshire (a Methodist minister), June 2, 1968; children: Robert Glenn III, Ann Marie. *Education:* Auburn University, student, 1958-59; University of North Carolina, B.A. (honors), 1962, Ph.D., 1970; Yale University, graduate study, 1962-63; Brown University, M.A., 1967. *Politics:* Democrat. *Religion:* United Methodist. *Home:* 2900 Tower Dr., Marshall, Tex. 75670. *Office:* Department of History and Political Science, Wiley College, Marshall, Tex. 75670.

CAREER: Stetson University, DeLand, Fla., assistant professor of American studies, 1969-71; Alcorn State University, Lorman, Miss., assistant professor, 1971-73, associate professor of American history, 1973-74; Wiley College, Marshall, Tex., professor of history and chairman of department, 1974—.

MEMBER: Organization of American Historians, American Studies Association, Association for the Study of Afro-American Life and History, Southern Historical Association, Texas Historical Association, Phi Beta Kappa, Phi Eta Sigma. *Awards, honors:* Rockefeller fellow at Yale Divinity School, 1962-63; grants from Consortium on Research Training, 1974, 1975, 1976, United Methodist Board of Higher Education, 1975, and National Endowment for the Humanities, 1977.

WRITINGS: Subordination or Liberation?: The Development and Conflicting Theories of Black Education in Nineteenth-Century Alabama, University of Alabama Press, 1977. Contributor of articles and reviews to history and social science journals.

WORK IN PROGRESS: Black Schools and Churches and Their Leaders in the New South; research on black editors during the Progressive Period.

SIDELIGHTS: Sherer writes: "Until recently most American history was written from the perspective of the ruling class, viewing others in society as 'problems' to be dealt with. I join many modern writers in describing, objectively but sympathetically, the lives, cultures, and institutions of groups (for me, blacks and other Southerners) who have been systematically exploited, discriminated against, and segregated. Perhaps naively, I hope that such writing can alleviate some of the injustice in the world by helping the victims of discrimination realize the historical dimensions of their situation and the ones who discriminate understand their victims as persons.

While I do not believe that all people are equally talented in any given field or that we should strive for equal achievement by all, I strongly believe in government limitations on supercorporations and other businesses to guarantee absolute equality of opportunity and every person's equal right to health, housing, clothing, food, education, employment; i.e. the necessary preconditions to the natural, God-given rights of life, liberty, and the *pursuit* of happiness. While in full

agreement with national and international groups working for these goals, I believe that I, and most other individuals, can most effectively move our society toward these goals by social and political activism at the local and state levels (in addition to my writing and teaching these ideas to convey them to others). While these are essentially humanistic goals, I believe that they can be achieved only through religious communities led by persons guided by a religious vision such as the late Dr. Martin Luther King, Jr." *Avocational interests:* Bridge, tennis, local politics, listening to opera, "building models with my children."

* * *

SHERMAN, Eric 1947-

PERSONAL: Born June 29, 1947, in Santa Monica, Calif.; son of Vincent (a film director) and Hedda (Comorau) Sherman. *Education:* Yale University, B.A. (cum laude), 1968. *Politics:* Democrat. *Religion:* Jewish. *Home address:* P.O. Box 845, Malibu, Calif. 90265.

CAREER: Art Center College of Design, Pasadena, Calif., instructor in film, 1975—. Instructor at California Institute of Technology, 1977—. Member of program selection committee for Los Angeles International Film Exposition, 1975—. *Member:* American Film Institute, Society of Motion Picture and Television Engineers.

WRITINGS: (With Martin L. Rubin) *The Director's Event,* Atheneum, 1970; *Directing the Film,* Little, Brown, 1976. Also author of film strips.

Author of oral histories for American Film Institute. Contributor to film journals and newspapers.

WORK IN PROGRESS: A book on healing; film scripts and film script adaptations; writing chapters for a book on directors for Dutton.

* * *

SHERMAN, Jory (Tecumseh) 1932-
(Frank Anvic, Cort Martin, Charlotte A. Sherman, Wilma Tarrant)

PERSONAL: Born October 20, 1932, in St. Paul, Minn.; son of Keith Edward (a franchise consultant) and Mercedes (a stenographer; maiden name, Sheplee) Sherman; married Remy Montes Roxas, June 10, 1951 (deceased); married wife Felicia, August 15, 1958 (divorced December, 1967); married Charlotte Balcom (a writer), March 2, 1968; children: Francis Antonio, Jory Vittorio, Forrest Redmond, Gina Felice, Misty April, Marcus Tecumseh. *Education:* Attended San Francisco State College (now University) and University of Minnesota. *Politics:* Democrat. *Home:* Route 1, Alpena, Ark. 72611. *Agent:* Eleanor Langdon, 457 Oakdale Ave., Chicago, Ill. 60657.

CAREER: Denver Dry Goods, Denver, Colo., advertising copywriter, 1949-50; American President Lines, San Francisco, Calif., computer programmer, 1953-54; Great Plays Co., Lethbridge, Alberta, actor, 1954-55; *San Francisco Examiner,* San Francisco, editor, 1960-61; American Art Enterprise, North Hollywood, Calif., magazine editor, 1961-65; free-lance editor, 1965-67; newspaper columnist, 1965—. San Bernardino County press chairperson for Gerald Brown; press chairperson for John Tunney and Jesse Unruh. Teacher of creative writing for adults. President, MicroDramas Co., Rialto, Calif., 1969-71. Editor, Academy Press, Chatsworth, Calif., 1971-72. *Military service:* U.S. Navy, 1950-53. *Member:* Writers Guild of America, Authors Guild, Western Writers of America, Twin Counties

Press Club (member of board of directors, 1966-70), Desert-Mountain Press Club, Baja California Writers Association. *Awards, honors:* Best newspaper column award from Twin Counties Press Club, 1970; best radio station public service program award from Twin Counties Press Club, 1970 and 1971.

WRITINGS: So Many Rooms, Galley Sail Publications, 1960; *My Face in Wax,* Windfall Press, 1965; *Lust on Canvas,* Anchor Publications, 1965; *The October Scarf,* Challenge Books, 1966; *The Sculptor,* Private Edition Books, 1966; *The Fires of Autumn,* All Star Books, 1967; *Nightsong,* All Star Books, 1968; *Blood Jungle,* Triumph News, 1968; *The Love Rain,* Tecumseh Press, 1971; *There are Ways of Making Love to You,* Tecumseh Press, 1974; *Gun for Hire,* Major Books, 1975; *Ride Hard, Ride Fast,* Major Books, 1976; *Buzzard Bait,* Major Books, 1977.

Under pseudonym Frank Anvic: *The All Girl Crew,* Barclay, 1973; *The Hard Riders,* Barclay, 1973; *We Have Your Daughter,* Brandon Books, 1974; *Bride of Satan,* Brandon Books, 1974.

Under pseudonym Cort Martin: *The Star,* Dominion, 1968; *Quest,* Powell Publications, 1969; *The Edge of Passion,* Saber Books, 1969.

Under pseudonym Charlotte A. Sherman: *The Shuttered Room,* Major Books, 1975.

Under pseudonym Wilma Tarrant: *Her Strange Needs,* Carlyle Communications, 1976; *Trying Out Tricia,* Carlyle Communications, 1976.

Columns: "View on Living," in *Grand Terrace Living,* 1966-67; "Ensenada at Bay," in *Ensenada Hello,* 1966-67; "The New Notebook," in *San Bernardino Independent,* 1970-71; "Baja Notebook," in *Fiesta,* 1972-75; and "Bear with Me," in *Big Bear News,* 1972-75, and *San Bernardino Mountain Highlander,* 1975-76.

Author of two series of educational tapes for radio, "Youth and Drugs" and "Youth and Alcohol," distributed by Classroom World Productions. Contributor of poetry to literary journals. West Coast editor, *Outsider;* advisory editor, *Black Cat Review.*

WORK IN PROGRESS: Falconhood, a gothic novel; *Gates of Breath,* an experimental novel; *Big Bear Valley: Those Were the Days,* a history of the Gold Rush days in Big Bear Lake, California.

SIDELIGHTS: Jory Sherman writes: "I guess I am a compulsive writer. I get charged up by writing. The only way I can relax and get away from writing is to go out into the wilderness, hunt, fish, and be by myself. But even there I am writing in my head. My happiest times are starting a book and finishing one. Right now, these two things occur once a month, which is more pressure than I like. But I'm happy, and I'm where I want to be—on a secluded old farm tucked back in the hills, with my family, my dogs and cats and my stock around me, where things that we've planted are growing."

AVOCATIONAL INTERESTS: Skeet, trap, black powder guns, motorcycling.

BIOGRAPHICAL/CRITICAL SOURCES: Listen (magazine), April, 1971.

*   *   *

SHERRILL, Dorothy 1901-
(April Martin)

PERSONAL: Born May 5, 1901, in South Weymouth, Mass.; daughter of Clinton Hallett (an efficiency expert) and Alma (a teacher; maiden name, Sharp) Googins; married Arthur Miles Sherrill (a writer and publisher), April 19, 1925 (died, 1963); children: Arthur Miles, Jr., Richard Rodman. *Education:* Radcliffe College, B.A. (cum laude), 1922. *Politics:* Republican. *Religion:* Presbyterian. *Home:* 2 Tudor City Pl., New York, N.Y. 10017.

CAREER: Vogue, New York City, member of editorial department, 1923-25; David C. Cook Publishing Co., Wayne, Ill., editor of juvenile books, 1949-51; *Editor's Notebook,* New York City, editor, 1958-61; writer. *Member:* Radcliffe Club, Harvard Club, Smithsonian Institution, Metropolitan Museum. *Awards, honors:* Citation from President Harry S. Truman, 1949, for work in Germany; medal from Freedoms Foundation, 1950.

WRITINGS: Captain from Nantucket (novel), Western Publishing, 1969.

Self-illustrated children's books: *The Story of a Little White Teddy Bear Who Didn't Want to Go to Bed,* Farrar & Rinehart, 1931, reissued, Holt, 1976; *The Story of a Little Yellow Dog and a Little White Bear,* Farrar & Rinehart, 1932; *The Story of Sleepy Sam,* Greenberg, 1932; *The Story of Sleepy Sally,* Greenberg, 1933; *The Story of a Little Duck,* C. E. Merrill, 1935; (under pseudonym April Martin) *Jackie Rabbit and the Last Carrot,* C. E. Merrill, 1935; *The Story of a Little Gray Mouse,* Greenberg, 1945; *The Santa Claus Bears,* Crowell, 1952.

Work represented in anthologies. Contributor to church school publications and popular magazines, including *Vogue, Liberty, Saturday Evening Post,* and *American,* and to *Editor's Notebook.* Member of book review board of Child Study Association of America, 1956-59.

WORK IN PROGRESS: The Story of the Littlest Lion in the World, juvenile; studying Charles II and other Stuarts in Scotland, and the legend of the Loch Ness monster.

SIDELIGHTS: Dorothy Sherrill writes: "People who write for children should experience children, live with them either as teachers, librarians, or parents. German and French are my two foreign languages, in both of which I find wonderful, direct children's stories written by people who not only like and know children but who are writing for *them.* Not for the grown-ups—well-meaning and extravagant though they may be—who buy gift books because they are impressive with their lavish art work and often too sophisticated humor."

AVOCATIONAL INTERESTS: Sailing and living on her yawl, international travel (Scandinavia, England, the Mediterranean).

*   *   *

SHERWIN, Richard E(lliott) 1933-

PERSONAL: Born August 21, 1933, in Malden, Mass.; son of Morris and Edith (Broidy) Sherwin; married Rachel Domke (a Congress organizer), August, 1958; children: Elisabeth Deborah, Yael Tamar, Reuven Jesse. *Education:* University of California, Los Angeles, B.A. (summa cum laude), 1959; Yale University, M.A., 1960, Ph.D., 1963. *Religion:* Jewish. *Home:* Rehov Shlomo Hamelech 97, Herzliyah, Israel. *Office:* Faculty of Humanities, Bar Ilan University, Ramat Gan, Israel.

CAREER: Carleton College, Northfield, Minn., lecturer in English, 1962-64; Bar Ilan University, Ramat Gan, Israel, senior lecturer in English, 1964—, chairman of department, 1972-76, dean of faculty of humanities, 1976—. Visiting senior lecturer at Tel Aviv University, 1965—; visiting professor at University of California, Los Angeles, 1970-71. Member of High Committee of English Teaching in Israel, 1972-76. *Military service:* U.S. Air Force, 1951-55. Zahal Miluim, 1970—. *Member:* University Teachers of English (Israel), Society for Religion in Higher Education (Israel), Modern Language Association of America, Poetry Society of America, Phi Beta Kappa.

WRITINGS: Welcome Home (poems; bilingual edition), Eked, 1977.

Work anthologized in *The Shakespearean World*, edited by M. Roston, [Tel Aviv], 1968; *My Words Feed Others*, edited by Chayyim Zeldis, [New York City], 1974; and *An Anthology of Israeli Poetry in English*. Contributor of several dozen poems and reviews to journals and newspapers internationally, including *Ragnarok, Reconstructionist, Egret, Beloit Poetry Journal, Encounter, Voices,* and *Jewish Spectator*.

WORK IN PROGRESS: Israeli poetry written in English.

SIDELIGHTS: Sherwin writes: "I enjoy reading Juvenal, Martial, Greek Epigrammatists, Ben Jonson, seventeenth and eighteenth century English metaphysicals and satirists, Chinese and Japanese poetry in translation, the Bible, and some modern poetry. I write satires and metaphysical poems (of sorts) which follow logically from my reading interests. Or vice versa. Some of the poems are even readable."

AVOCATIONAL INTERESTS: Ancient history, theology, social psychology.

* * *

SHEW, E(dward) Spencer   1908-1977(?)

November 9, 1908—1977(?); British journalist and mystery writer. Mystery Writers of America awarded him the Edgar prize for his *Encyclopaedia of Murder* in 1962. He died in Weston-super-Mare, England. Obituaries: *AB Bookman's Weekly,* May 9, 1977. (See index for previous *CA* sketch)

* * *

SHIPTON, Eric Earl   1907-1977

August 1, 1907—March 28, 1977; British explorer, mountaineer, and author. He participated in five expeditions to Mt. Everest and was recognized as the leading Himalayan climber of his time. He died at Ansty Manor, near Salisbury, England. Obituaries: *AB Bookman's Weekly,* May 9, 1977.

* * *

SHURDEN, Walter B(yron)   1937-

PERSONAL: Born February 1, 1937, in Greenwood, Miss.; son of Marshal J. (a welder) and Morelle (White) Shurden; married Kay Wilson (a college professor), December 22, 1957; children: Sherry, Paula, Walt. *Education:* Mississippi College, B.A., 1958; New Orleans Baptist Theological Seminary, M.Div., 1961, Th.D., 1967. *Politics:* Democrat. *Home and office:* Department of Religion, Carson-Newman College, Jefferson City, Tenn. 37760.

CAREER: Ordained minister of Baptist Church; Carson-Newman College, Jefferson City, Tenn., associate professor of church history, 1969—. Visiting professor, South Baptist Theological Seminary, 1973. *Member:* American Academy of Religion, American Society of Church History, American Association of University Professors.

WRITINGS: Not a Silent People: Controversies That Have Shaped Southern Baptists, Broadman, 1972.

WORK IN PROGRESS: Researching American Christianity with emphasis on religion in the South.

* * *

SHURKIN, Joel N.   1938-

PERSONAL: Born June 12, 1938, in Orange, N.J.; son of Bernard and Selma Shurkin; married Lorna Greene (a writer), July 4, 1966; children: Jonathan G., Michael R. *Education:* Emory University, B.A., 1960; Temple University, graduate study, 1960-62. *Religion:* Jewish. *Home:* 418 Oak Lane, Wayne, Pa. 19087. *Agent:* Mitchell J. Hamilburg Agency, 292 South La Cienega Blvd., Suite 212, Beverly Hills, Calif. 90211. *Office: Philadelphia Inquirer,* 400 North Broad St., Philadelphia, Pa. 19101.

CAREER: Newark Star-Ledger, Newark, N.J., reporter, 1962-63; United Press International, reporter, 1963-68; Reuters, New York, N.Y., reporter, 1968-72; *Philadelphia Inquirer,* Philadelphia, Pa., science writer, 1972—. *Member:* National Association of Science Writers, Society of Precision Journalists. *Awards, honors:* Aviation-Space Writers Awards, 1974 and 1976.

WRITINGS: Update, Report on Planet Earth, Westminster, 1976; *Variola: The Birth and Death of Smallpox,* Norton, in press.

WORK IN PROGRESS: "Tierra Nova," a television film for Filmline Productions.

* * *

SHUSTER, George Nauman   1894-1977

August 27, 1894—January 25, 1977; American journalist, educator, and author of books on twentieth century Germany, English literature, and education; former president of Hunter College and assistant to the president of the University of Notre Dame, he has been called an interpreter of Roman Catholicism to the modern world. He died in South Bend, Ind. Obituaries: *New York Times,* January 27, 1977; *Current Biography,* March, 1977; *AB Bookman's Weekly,* May 9, 1977.

* * *

SHYER, Marlene Fanta

PERSONAL: Born in Czechoslovakia; daughter of Eric G. and Gertrude (Fanta) Fanta; married Robert M. Shyer (optical manufacturing executive), June 3, 1954; children: Kirby, Christopher, Alison. *Education:* University of Bridgeport, B.S. *Religion:* Unitarian. *Residence:* Larchmont, N.Y. *Agent:* Phyllis Westberg, Harold Ober Associates, 40 East 49th St., New York, N.Y. 10017.

CAREER: Elementary school teacher in Portchester, N.Y., public schools, 1955-57; author, 1962—. *Member:* Writers Guild, Authors League of America.

WRITINGS: Tino, Random House, 1969; *Local Talent,* Bobbs-Merrill, 1974; *Blood in the Snow,* Houghton, 1975. Also writer of television scripts. Contributor of over sixty short stories to popular magazines, including *Redbook, McCall's, Good Housekeeping,* and *Ladies Home Journal.*

WORK IN PROGRESS: A juvenile novel for Scribner, publication expected in spring, 1978.

* * *

SIDHWA, Keki R(attanshah)   1926-

PERSONAL: Born September 29, 1926, in Bombay, India; son of Rattanshah (a businessman) and Mani Sidhwa; married Muriel Christine Price (a teacher), 1960; children: Yasmin, Zarina, Ruxana. *Education:* University of Bombay, B.Sc., 1948; Edinburgh College of Natural Therapeutics, N.D., 1952; British College of Naturopathy and Osteopathy, D.O., 1953. *Home and office:* Shalimar, First Ave., Frinton-on-Sea, England.

CAREER: Marwari Relief Hospital, Calcutta, India, director of therapeutics, 1959; in private practice, 1952—. Shalimar (health home), Frinton-on-Sea, England, director, 1960—. Registered naturopath, osteopath, and natural hygiene practitioner. Has lectured in the United States, Europe, and Asia. *Member:* Incorporated Society of Registered Naturopaths, British Natural Hygiene Society (president).

WRITINGS: Fit for Anything, Thorsons Ltd., 1964, revised edition, 1974; *Words and Music and All Alone* (poems), British Natural Hygiene Society, 1973; *Medical Drugs on Trial: Verdict Guilty,* American Natural Hygiene Press, 1976. Contributor to *Hygienic Review, Health for All,* and *Rude Health.* Magazine editor of *Hygienist.*

WORK IN PROGRESS: Hygienic First Aid; The Magic of Inspiration.

SIDELIGHTS: Sidhwa described himself as a "vegetarian and humanitarian." He told *CA:* "My own life was saved by fasting and diet at age 14 when I was given up to die by medical doctors after seven relapses of typhoid fever, double pneumonia, and a heart murmur and spending eleven months in bed. At age 20 I fell ill again and decided to take up 'Nature-cure' and 'Natural living" methods as my life work, instead of studying to become a surgeon. Since then I have dedicated my life to teaching humanity about the physiological laws of life on which the science of Natural-Hygiene is based. My main criticism of Medicine is that it teaches next to nothing about how to maintain good health and how to prevent illness. It deals mainly with relief of symptoms, which helps to perpetuate diseases and the so-called 'cure' is worse than the disease as exemplified by iatrogenic diseases."

Sidhwa also discussed his views on poetry and religion: "My love of poetry goes back to childhood. I consider poetry as an expression of an inward journey, an attempt to fuse the world of the individual to the world as he finds it, and last but not least, an expression of that creativity which is within us all.

"Being a philosopher at heart, I have strong views on 'organized religion.' The word religion literally means to gather together, i.e., of life's experiences and learning by it and basing our life pattern on reason and instinct. 'Organized religion' divides humanity, just as our prejudices re race, color, culture and nationality. The churches, in attempting to lead us to divinity, totally disregard the humanity. I have been a keen student of 'comparative religions' and have found grains of truths in all of them. What matters is those grains of truths, not the indoctrination, the dogmas and rituals. All religions and their prophets claim to reveal the word of God, and in their very act commit the sin of bigotry. It is very difficult to pinpoint which religion heads the list in bigotry—but after much deliberation I find that the Christian church heads the list. No doubt our Western culture based on such foundations is undergoing mental, moral, and physical degeneration. In brief, a priest comes between Man and his God, a physician comes between Man and his health, a lawyer comes between Man and justice, a teacher comes between Man and wisdom. For all true consciousness is self-conscious, all health is self-healing, all justice is the justice of

one's own conscience, and all true education is self-education. There is but one life-force, and all life is its manifestation—let us respect it and live by it."

*   *   *

SIEGEL, Marcia B. 1932-

PERSONAL: Born September 17, 1932, in New York, N.Y.; daughter of Abraham (a journalist) and Lillian (Straus) Bernstein. *Education:* Connecticut College, B.A., 1954. *Residence:* Brooklyn, N.Y. *Agent:* Wallace & Sheil, Inc., 118 East 61st St., New York, N.Y. 10021. *Office: Soho Weekly News,* 111 Spring St., New York, N.Y. 10003.

CAREER: Writer. Dance critic/contributing editor for *Hudson Review,* 1973—; dance critic for *Soho Weekly News,* 1974—. Director of West Coast Institute for Dance Criticism at Mills College, 1973-75, and Texas Institute for Dance Criticism, 1976-77. *Member:* Phi Beta Kappa. *Awards, honors:* Guggenheim fellowship, 1974-75.

WRITINGS: At the Vanishing Point, Saturday Review Press, 1972; *Please Run on the Playground,* Connecticut Commission on the Arts, 1975; *Watching the Dance Go By,* Houghton, 1977. Contributor of articles and reviews to a variety of journals, including *Arts in Society, Kenyon Review, American Poetry Review, Dance, Time Out,* and *New York,* and to newspapers. Editor, *Dance Scope,* 1964-66; guest editor, *Dance Perspectives,* summer, 1969, and winter, 1971-72.

WORK IN PROGRESS: A book on American choreography, for Houghton.

*   *   *

SILL, Gertrude Grace

PERSONAL: Born in New York, N.Y.; daughter of Edwin J. (a physician) and Gertrude (Keating) Grace; married Davis A. Sill (a textile converter); children: Andrews Grace, Lucinda Bufford. *Education:* Smith College, B.A., 1948; attended Ecole du Louvre, Paris, France, 1949; graduate study at University of Bridgeport, 1977—. *Residence:* Southport, Conn. *Office:* Department of Fine Arts, Fairfield University, Fairfield, Conn. 06430.

CAREER: Fairfield University, Fairfield, Conn., instructor in art history, 1973—. Lecturer at University of Bridgeport, 1977, and at Metropolitan Museum of Art, Frick Collection, Yale Art Gallery, Museum of Art, Science, and Industry, and Silvermine Guild. Executive vice-president of Pequot Library, Southport, Conn. Architectural adviser to Halcyon Films, 1975. *Member:* International Center for Medieval Art, Les Amis du Louvre, College Art Association, Friends of American Art at Yale, Smith College (board member).

WRITINGS: (Compiler with N. C. Weyeth and others) *The Brandywine Inheritance* (catalog), Museum of Art, Science, and Industry, 1974; *A Handbook of Symbols in Christian Art,* Macmillan, 1975. Author of screenplay and on-camera commentary, and photographic supervisor, researcher, and interviewer of "The Hartford Civic Center," a five-part series broadcast by WFSB-TV, Hartford, Conn., 1975. Author of script and slide program, "Introduction to the Metropolitan," Metropolitan Museum of Art, New York, 1973.

WORK IN PROGRESS: Research on George Cope, an American nineteenth-century trompe l'oeil painter; a catalog and show at Brandywine Museum, Chadds Ford, Pa., for 1978.

SIDELIGHTS: Sill told *CA:* "I firmly believe that art is an essential part of life, and by education and exposure should be incorporated into every existence. I also feel art history should be made lively and generally appealing. Academic work need not be so labyrinthine and dull.''

Such thinking is evidently operant in her *Handbook of Symbols in Christian Art.* Martha B. Scott contends that "Gertrude Sill not only turned out a delightful book on a nearly impossible subject, but she made the subject contemporary, exciting, and approachable. . . . Mrs. Sill may be the first art historian to make it accessible to a popular audience." Scott continued, "Sill has made the most of her two widely separated fields—the art of the Middle Ages . . . and the art of 19th Century America. She is both 'living' her interest in her home and 'mining' her scholastic background in her career as a writer, teacher and lecturer. One can readily see why she is in constant demand as a lecturer. Whatever subject she touches . . . she makes it come alive, as though she were on personal terms with the painter or object."

AVOCATIONAL INTERESTS: Travel ("I enjoy traveling to see originals everywhere, lately Greece, Egypt and Kenya").

BIOGRAPHICAL/CRITICAL SOURCES: Bridgeport Sunday Post, December 14, 1975.

* * *

SILVER, Samuel 1915(?)-1976

1915(?)—November 5, 1976; American editor and professor of engineering science at University of California, Berkeley, where he founded the Space Sciences Laboratory. He died in Walnut Creek, Calif. Obituaries: *Washington Post,* November 7, 1976.

* * *

SILVERMAN, Oscar Ansell 1903-1977

February 13, 1903—March, 1977; American author and educator. Director of library at State University of New York at Buffalo where he helped in the acquisition of one of the world's largest collections of James Joyce material. He died in Buffalo, N.Y. Obituaries: *AB Bookman's Weekly,* June 27, 1977.

* * *

SIMS, Naomi 1949-

PERSONAL: Born March 30, 1949, in Oxford, Miss.; married Michael Findlay (an art dealer), August 4, 1973; children: John. *Education:* Attended New York University. *Religion:* Roman Catholic. *Office:* Naomi Sims Collection, 48 East 21st St., New York, N.Y. 10010.

CAREER: Fashion model, 1967-73; Naomi Sims Collection, New York, N.Y., founder and president, 1972—. Writer and lecturer. Member of board of directors, Northside Center for Child Development. *Member:* National Association for the Advancement of Colored People. *Awards, honors:* Model of the Year award, 1969 and 1970, from International Famous Mannequins; New York City Board of Education award, 1970, for teaching underprivileged children in Bedford Stuyvesant; Woman of Achievement medal, 1970, from *Ladies Home Journal;* Woman of Achievement award, 1972, from American Cancer Society; Top Hat Award, 1974, from *Pittsburgh Courier.*

WRITINGS: All About Health and Beauty for the Black Woman, Doubleday, 1976. Contributor of articles to *Redbook, Essence, Encore,* and other periodicals.

SINOR, John 1930-

PERSONAL: Surname is pronounced *Sigh*-ner; born December 24, 1930, in Elk City, Okla.; son of J. D. (a chef) and Orvia (a sales manager; maiden name, Mitchell) Sinor; married Charlene Hodge, August 23, 1950 (divorced, 1968); married Diane Faulk (a teacher and actress), January 19, 1970; children: Michael, Mark, Matthew, Madeline, Michelle; (stepchildren). *Education:* Attended Modesto Junior College, 1953-59, and San Jose State University. *Politics:* Democrat. *Religion:* "Retired Catholic." *Residence:* San Diego, Calif. *Agent:* Paul Sutherland, 4930 Santa Monica Dr., #3, San Diego, Calif. 92107. *Office: San Diego Evening Tribune,* San Diego, Calif. 92112.

CAREER: Free-lance journalist, 1948—. Copley News Service, San Diego, Calif., author of weekly column, "John Sinor Column," syndicated to six hundred newspapers, and of daily column. Also author of daily column in *San Diego Evening Tribune;* member of staff at San Diego State University Extension. *Military service:* U.S. Air Force.

MEMBER: San Diego Press Club, Sigma Delta Chi. *Awards, honors:* National Headliners Award for best local column; California-Arizona Associated Press award for best feature; annual award for best feature story from Copley News Service, 1964; medal of honor from Freedoms Foundation, 1967.

WRITINGS: Eleven Albatrosses in My Bluebird Tree, Joyce Press, 1976; *Finsterhall of San Pasqual,* Joyce Press, 1976.

SIDELIGHTS: Sinor writes that he is "presently working on screenwriting and a desired growth in craft. I intend to write more books and screenplays and hope to do considerable more travel. Interest in daily newspapering is waning, but I intend to keep writing as long as I can." His second book was made into a film by Walt Disney Studios.

AVOCATIONAL INTERESTS: "I've tried all of them. Archery, fishing, hunting, golf, skin diving, photography. . . . Still do some of them occasionally."

* * *

SITARAM, K(ondavagil) S(urya) 1935-

PERSONAL: Born March 29, 1935, in Arsikere, India; came to the United States in 1964; son of Kondavagil and Ananta (Lakshmi) Sitaram; married, 1960; children: one. *Education:* University of Mysore, B.Sc., 1952; University of Oregon, M.S., 1965, Ph.D., 1969. *Office:* Department of Communication, Utah State University, Logan, Utah 84322.

CAREER: Village Industry Board, Mysore, India, publicity officer, 1957-61; Government of India, exhibition officer, 1961-63; University of Hawaii, Honolulu, assistant professor, 1969-74; Governors State University, Park Forest South, Ill., professor of communication science, 1974-76; Utah State University, Logan, visiting professor of communication and head of department, 1976—. *Member:* International Communication Association (vice-president, 1970-72), American Association for the Advancement of Science, Asian Mass Communication Information Center (Singapore). *Awards, honors:* National Science Foundation grant, India, 1972.

WRITINGS: Mass Media and Rural Modernization: The Hindu, Madna, 1970; *What Is Intercultural Communication?,* Wadsworth, 1972; (contributor) Larry Samovar and Richard Porter, editors, *Readings in Intercultural Communication,* Wadsworth, 1972; *Foundations of Intercultural*

Communication, C. E. Merrill, 1976. Contributor to communication journals and to newspapers.

WORK IN PROGRESS: Research on values and communication, scientific and technical communication, and the social effects of mass media, such as television violence; a book on intercultural communication.

SIDELIGHTS: Sitaram writes that his special interests are "intercultural communication, interpersonal communication, and effects of mass media on social behavior." He adds that his many years of study originated as a result of discrimination he and his colleagues experienced as students and as university professors, and what he has seen during his travels in Asia, North America, and Europe.

*   *   *

SITCHIN, Zecharia 1920-

PERSONAL: Born January 11, 1920, in Baku, Russia; son of Isaac and Genia (Barsky) Sitchin; married Frieda Regenbaum, 1941; children: Edna (Mrs. Isidoro Aizenberg), Ella (Mrs. Arthur Feldman). *Education:* University of London, B.Com., 1941. *Agent:* John Farquharson Ltd., 15 Red Lion Sq., London W.C.1, England.

CAREER: Journalist in Palestine/Israel, 1939-52, in United States, 1952-66; president of foreign trade service corporations in New York and London, 1967—. Executive director of American-Israel Chamber of Commerce and Industry, 1953-64; president of American-Israel Pavilion at New York World's Fair, 1964-65. *Military service:* British Army, 1940-44; served in Jerusalem. Israeli Army, 1948-49. *Member:* British Museum Society, American Oriental Society, American Arbitration Association (member of panel of arbitrators), Israel Exploration Society. *Awards, honors:* New York World's Fair award, 1965; founders award from American-Israel Chamber of Commerce and Industry, 1968.

WRITINGS: The Twelfth Planet (nonfiction), Stein & Day, 1976.

WORK IN PROGRESS: Research on the origins of civilization and religion, the ancient Near East, and pre-Colombian civilizations of America.

SIDELIGHTS: Sitchin has traveled extensively in Europe, the Near East, Africa, and North and South America. He knows several modern and ancient (Near Eastern) languages.

*   *   *

SKAAR, Grace Brown 1903-

PERSONAL: Born November 30, 1903, in El Paso, Tex.; daughter of Frank Wardwell and Grace (Blaney) Brown; married Sven Skaar (a writer), July 1, 1940. *Education:* Attended Couinard Art School and Los Angeles Art Center. *Home and office address:* Blue Tent Rd., Nevada City, Calif.

CAREER: Graphic artist and designer. Art director of Chrysons, Hollywood, Calif.

WRITINGS—All self-illustrated books for children: *Nothing but Cats, Cats, Cats,* Young Scott, 1947; *All About Dogs, Dogs, Dogs,* Young Scott, 1947; (with Louise Woodcock) *The Smart Little Kitty,* Addison-Wesley, 1947; (with Woodcock) *The Very Little Dog,* Young Scott, 1947; *What Do They Say,* Young Scott, 1950, revised edition published as *What Do the Animals Say?,* Addison-Wesley, 1968; *The Little Red House,* Young Scott, 1955; *A Boy and His Horse,* William R. Scott, 1958.*

SKLAREWITZ, Norman 1924-

PERSONAL: Born February 1, 1924, in Chicago, Ill.; son of Max and Anne Rae (Datnow) Sklarewitz; married Esther Louise Bohn, 1948; *Education:* Indiana University, A.B., 1948; University of Southern California, M.L.A., 1975. *Home and office:* 321 South San Vicente Blvd., Suite 504, Los Angeles, Calif. 90048.

CAREER: Industrial slide film scriptwriter, magazine editor, and free-lance magazine writer, 1948-56; *Pacific Stars and Stripes,* Tokyo, Japan, feature editor, 1956-59; free-lance correspondent, radio stringer for CBS News, and contributor to newspapers and magazines on Asian affairs from Japan, 1959-63; *Wall Street Journal,* New York, N.Y., staff reporter in New York City, San Francisco, and Japan, 1963-70; *U.S. News and World Report,* Los Angeles, Calif., Los Angeles bureau chief, 1970-74; free-lance writer and photographer, 1974—. Instructor at Pepperdine University, Urban Campus, 1975-76. *Military service:* U.S. Army, 1943-46. *Member:* Society of American Travel Writers, American Society of Journalists and Authors.

WRITINGS: Bamboo Shoots for Breakfast, Tuttle, 1962. Contributor to popular magazines, including *Saturday Evening Post, New West, Skeptic, Coronet, Popular Mechanics, True, TV Guide, Argosy,* and *New Republic,* and to *Christian Science Monitor, Los Angeles Times, National Observer,* and other newspapers.

WORK IN PROGRESS: History of the Shanghai International Settlement, 1842-1941.

SIDELIGHTS: Sklarewitz writes: "After living and working overseas for ten years, I consider myself still a foreign correspondent by virtue of the fact that I continue to report from abroad regularly. I make foreign reporting trips at least four times a year on which I cover economic and political affairs for a wide variety of publications."

*   *   *

SKOLNIK, Alfred 1920(?)-1977

1920(?)—March 10, 1977; American author, editor, and publisher. He died in Washington, D.C. Obituaries: *Washington Post,* March 12, 1977.

*   *   *

SLADEN, Kathleen 1904-

PERSONAL: Born December 31, 1904, in Toronto, Ontario, Canada; daughter of James Edmond and Rachael Sophia Coe; married Gilbert Sladen (a publisher), September 25, 1928; children: Joseph Gilbert, Kathleen Mavourneen (Mrs. Noble Alexander Gow). *Education:* Attended Teachers College, North Bay, Ontario, 1921-22, and Teachers College, Toronto, Ontario, 1925. *Religion:* Anglican. *Home:* 619 Avenue Rd., Apt. 301, Toronto, Ontario, Canada M4Y 2K6. *Office:* S.K.H.S. Publications, 619 Avenue Rd., Room 301, Toronto, Ontario, Canada M4Y 2K6.

CAREER: Teacher in public schools in Widdifield, Ontario, 1923-24, and Silverthorn, Ontario, 1925-28; St. John's Church, York Mills, Ontario, director of religious education, 1937-55; writer, 1950—. Conducted story hours and told stories for public school children in Dunedin, Ontario, 1959-75; chairman of Canadian Council of Churches' children's work committee; member of National Council of Churches of Christ in the U.S. children's work committee. *Member:* Canadian Authors Association. *Awards, honors: Are You in the Picture?* was chosen as a preferred resource book by United Methodist Publishing House, 1973.

WRITINGS—For children: *Billy Goes to Hospital,* Hospital for Sick Children (Toronto, Ontario), 1954; *Growing Up in Worship,* Anglican Church of Canada, 1956; *While You're Sick,* John Knox, 1965; *Are You in the Picture?,* Abingdon, 1973; *Let Them Worship: A Cross-Denomination Book of Worship Resources for Ages Four to Eighteen,* S.K.H.S. Publications, 1976. Author of church school curricula. Contributor of more than five hundred articles to religious publications.

WORK IN PROGRESS: Two children's books; a book of devotions for all ages.

BIOGRAPHICAL/CRITICAL SOURCES: Onward, 1965-68; *Toronto Telegram,* March 18, 1961; *Toronto Star,* February 12, 1977.

* * *

SLOSBERG, Mike 1934-

PERSONAL: Birth-given name is Myron; born August 29, 1934, in Philadelphia, Pa.; son of Sam M. (a real estate agent) and Florence (Frank) Slosberg; married Joan Shidler (a guitar instructor), August 29, 1957; children: Sydney Ellen, Robert Morton. *Education:* Attended Pennsylvania State University, 1952-53, and University of South Carolina, 1954-55; University of Denver, B.S.B.A., 1960. *Home:* 31 Sturges Highway, Westport, Conn. 06880. *Agent:* Eugene Winick, Ernst, Cane, Berner & Gitlin, 7 West 51st St., New York, N.Y. 10019. *Office:* Young & Rubicam, 285 Madison Ave., New York, N.Y. 10017.

CAREER: Young & Rubicam (advertising agency), New York, N.Y., copy writer, 1960-63, copy supervisor, 1963-66, vice-president and creative supervisor, 1966-69, vice-president and creative director, 1969-71, senior vice-president and associate creative director, 1971—. Part-time instructor at Fairfield University. Consultant to Cambridge Research and Development. *Military service:* U.S. Air Force, 1953-57; served as flight engineer; became sergeant. *Member:* Overseas Press Club, Players Club. *Awards, honors:* Copywriter of the Year award from San Francisco Advertising Club, 1962; Cleo awards, 1963-68; American Film Festival awards, 1963-66, 1968; Cannes Film Festival award, 1965.

WRITINGS: Klan-Destined (self-illustrated cartoon book on Ku Klux Klan), Pisani Press (San Francisco, Calif.), 1965; *The August Strangers* (novel), Dial, 1977. Contributor of fiction to *Society for Humanistic Judaism Quarterly Magazine* and to *Broadcasting* magazine.

WORK IN PROGRESS: The Rumplestiltskin Factor, a novel.

SIDELIGHTS: Slosberg told *CA:* "I write for two reasons: I love it, but also feel that business people tend to be one-dimensional. The development of other consuming interests should become an important measurement of a person's success. It helps neutralize the numbing effects of a society of specialists.

"Each of us is our own spinning planet with an outer space to explore. We must, as individuals, experience our Kitty Hawks and our Trans-Atlantic flights; we must develop jets and finally, break the gravitational pull that comes from our own fears or insecurity, lethargy and ennui. It really doesn't make a hell of a lot of difference how far we go. It is the development and direction that counts. Whether I myself am on a moon shot or, like Icarus, heading for disaster near the sun, doesn't matter. I have chosen to think of other things besides fiscal responsibility (whatever that means) and costs per thousand and how to sell. In that way, when I do think of

these things, the subjects for which I am paid to think, it will be with more humanism and perspective.

"The most liberated and effective business people I know are generalists. Because they carry within them the seeds to grow many plants. And so they are free, never to be imprisoned by a lack of alternatives."

AVOCATIONAL INTERESTS: Jogging, tennis, reading.

* * *

SLUSSER, George Edgar 1939-
(Edgar Anstey)

PERSONAL: Born July 14, 1939, in San Francisco, Calif.; son of Raymond Leroy (a teacher and salesman) and Eldo (a commercial artist; maiden name, Kaerth) Slusser; married Daniele Chatelain, July 2, 1965. *Education:* University of California, Berkeley, A.B., 1961; graduate study, University of Tuebingen, 1968-69; Harvard University, Ph.D., 1975. *Home:* 3439 North E St., San Bernardino, Calif. 92405.

CAREER: California State College, San Bernardino, assistant professor of English literature, 1971-75; University of Paris, Nanterre, France, Fulbright lecturer in English literature, 1975-76; free-lance critic and translator from French and German, 1976—. *Military service:* U.S. Army, in counterintelligence operations, 1963-65; became first lieutenant. *Member:* Modern Language Association of America, Phi Beta Kappa. *Awards, honors:* Woodrow Wilson fellowship, 1966; Fulbright fellowships, 1968-69, 1975-76.

WRITINGS: Robert Heinlein: Stranger in His Own Land, Borgo Press, 1976; *The Farthest Shores of Ursula Leguin,* Borgo Press, 1976; (translator) *Balzac: The Centenarian,* Arno, 1976; *Harlan Ellison: Unrepentant Harlequin,* Borgo Press, in press; *The Bradbury Chronicles,* Borgo Press, in press. Contributor to literary journals.

WORK IN PROGRESS: A History of Science Fiction, five volumes, publication by Borgo Press expected in 1978-80; *Rameau's Nephew and His Progeny: The Artist in Search of His Own Genre in Hoffman and Balzac,* completion expected in 1978; *The Fiction of William Styron,* for Borgo Press, 1979; monographs on Arthur C. Clarke, Samuel Delaney, and Frank Herbert, all for Borgo Press; a science fiction novel, under pseudonym Edgar Anstey; translations of works by J. H. Rosny, *The Xipheuz* and *Death of the Earth,* publication expected in 1978.

SIDELIGHTS: "What set me to writing a history of science fiction," Slusser told *CA,* "is that science fiction is more and more the object of academic study. The linguistic structuralists seek a 'grammar' of story forms; Marxists look for 'homologues' to the structures of modern society. These critics prize sf because it is 'popular,' the mechanisms are still visible, untransformed by the hand of the great artist. Unfortunately, they have all the method, but seem to know (or care) little about the vast body of work that is sf. On the other hand, those who have the sweep, who have read widely, seem to lack the method. Many 'histories' to date are mere compendia of fact.

"I propose a history on two simultaneous axes: vertical and horizontal. At any given point, sf mirrors our social structures. Taken in linear fashion, it casts light on the processes of narration—a specific genre, or mode, shapes itself. The point where these two axes meet, the crux of analysis, is the individual work as mythic act. Here social commentary seeks roots in traditional themes and narrative patterns to sustain it, give it universal resonance. Sf is a product of the

Renaissance. The basic myth of Faust expressed a new relation of man to his universe. This myth is still being transformed, reinterpreted. A history of sf then is a history of modern man's literary reactions to his various myths of science.''

AVOCATIONAL INTERESTS: Brewing beer, professional antique restoration.

* * *

SMEDES, Lewis B. 1921-

PERSONAL: Born August 20, 1921, in Michigan; son of Mele (a smith) and Rena (Benedict) Smedes; married Doris Dekker (a librarian), August 5, 1950; children: Catherine, Charles, John. *Education:* Calvin College, A.B., 1947; Calvin Theological Seminary, M.Div., 1950; Free University of Amsterdam, Ph.D., 1953. *Politics:* Democrat. *Religion:* Christian Reformed. *Home:* 475 Fairview, Sierra Madre, Calif. 91024.

CAREER: Calvin College, Grand Rapids, Mich., associate professor of religion, 1957-60, professor of religion, 1960-68; Fuller Theological Seminary, Pasadena, Calif., professor of theology and ethics, 1968—. Guest professor at Free University of Amsterdam, 1976. President of Urban League of Grand Rapids, 1960-65. *Member:* American Society of Christian Ethics. *Awards, honors:* Award for editorial of the year from Church Press Association, 1976, for "The Case of Karen Quinlan."

WRITINGS: The Incarnation, KOK, 1954; *All Things Made New,* Eerdmans, 1967; *Sex for Christians,* Eerdmans, 1976. Co-editor of and contributor to *Reformed Journal.*

WORK IN PROGRESS: Research on nature and the function of moral law and on the concept of moral obligation; a book on Christian love.

* * *

SMITH, Cecil (Howard III) 1917-
(Cecil Howard)

PERSONAL: Born May 22, 1917, in Marlow, Okla.; son of Cecil Howard, Jr. (an engineer) and Elsie (Foster) Smith; married Cleo Morgan (a television producer), July 14, 1961; children: Marcus, Tina. *Education:* Stanford University, student, 1935-37; University of California at Los Angeles, student, 1938-39. *Residence:* Culver City, Calif. *Office: Los Angeles Times,* Times-Mirror Sq., Los Angeles, Calif. 90053.

CAREER/WRITINGS: Los Angeles Times, Los Angeles, Calif., reporter, 1947-52, drama writer, 1952-58, entertainment editor and television columnist/critic, 1958-64, drama critic, 1964-69, critic and author of "The Cecil Smith TV Column," appearing in over one hundred newspapers, 1969—. Author, usually under pseudonym Cecil Howard, of more than fifty network radio plays and more than twenty plays for television; host of television program, "Cecil Smith on Drama," for KCET-TV, 1964-65. *Military service:* U.S. Army Air Forces, 1942-46; became captain; received Distinguished Flying Cross with two Oak Leaf clusters and Air Medal with seven Oak Leaf clusters. *Member:* Critics Consensus, Los Angeles Drama Critics Circle, TV Critics Circle, Los Angeles Press Club. *Awards, honors:* Award from Monte Carlo television festival, 1964, for critical writings.

* * *

SMITH, David C. 1931-

PERSONAL: Born February 7, 1931, in Mt. Clemens,

Mich.; son of Arthur P. (a journalist) and Harriett (Dickson) Smith; married Isabelle Johnston, April 6, 1957; children: Shannon, Erin, Geoffrey, Timothy. *Education:* Attended Central Michigan University, 1954-56; University of Michigan, A.B., 1958; attended American Press Institute, 1966, and Rutgers University, 1969. *Religion:* Protestant. *Home:* 7355 Chula Vista, Birmingham, Mich. 48010. *Office:* Ward's Communications, Inc., 28 West Adams, Detroit, Mich. 48226.

CAREER/WRITINGS: Detroit Times, Detroit, Mich., reporter and financial writer, 1959-60; *Toledo Blade,* Toledo, Ohio, reporter, 1960-61; *Wall Street Journal,* reporter in Cleveland and Los Angeles, 1961-65; *Detroit Free Press,* Detroit, financial editor, 1965-70; *Ward's Auto World* (magazine), Detroit, editor, 1970—. *Member:* Society of American Business and Economic Writers (president, 1972-73), Detroit Press Club (governor, 1976—), Detroit Automobile Writers Group (president, 1975), Society of Automotive Engineers. *Awards, honors:* University of Missouri award for business writing, 1971; Jesse Neal awards from American Business Press, 1974 and 1976.

SIDELIGHTS: Smith wrote: "I was first motivated by my sports coverage for high school and college newspapers. As a part-time large newspaper correspondent, I became involved in covering all aspects of the news—tornadoes, politics, medical, etc. The move into a business specialty was by accident, but I have found it stimulating. The idea's the same—if there's a good story and you're inquisitive by nature, business news coverage can be as stimulating and rewarding as any other area of coverage. Surprisingly, college Spanish and German have proven helpful in my work. Travel has been a vital part of both my newspaper and magazine careers. It makes for a fascinating life—exciting and challenging."

* * *

SMITH, Doris Buchanan 1934-

PERSONAL: Born June 1, 1934, in Washington, D.C.; daughter of Charles A. (an association executive) and Flora (an executive secretary; maiden name, Robinson) Buchanan; married R. Carroll Smith (a building contractor), December 18, 1954; children: Robb, Willie, Randy, Susan, Matthew. *Education:* Attended South Georgia College. *Politics:* Independent. *Religion:* None. *Home and office address:* P.O. Box 1142, Brunswick, Ga. 31520. *Agent:* Paul R. Reynolds, Inc., 12 East 41st St., New York, N.Y. 10017.

CAREER: Writer, 1971—. *Member:* Audubon Society. *Awards, honors:* Georgia children's book award, and book of the year award from Child Study Association, both 1974, both for *A Taste of Blackberries;* named children's book author of the year and general author of the year by Dixie Council of Authors and Journalists, 1974, for *A Taste of Blackberries,* and children's book author, 1976, for *Kelly's Creek;* Bread Loaf fellowship, 1975.

WRITINGS—For children: *A Taste of Blackberries,* Crowell, 1973; *Kick a Stone Home,* Crowell, 1974; *Tough Chauncey,* Morrow, 1974; *Kelly's Creek,* Crowell, 1975; *Up and Over,* Morrow, 1976; *Drumsticks and Dappled Dreams,* Crowell, in press.

WORK IN PROGRESS: An adult novel; adult nonfiction; four juvenile books, one a historical book.

SIDELIGHTS: Doris Smith writes: "I have been writing since I was eleven though only in the last five years was I really taking my writing seriously as a vocation. Determination and a little insanity is what got me there. Some day I may suffer from a 'writer's block' but currently my ideas come so fast that I wish I had six typing hands.

"I love aloneness and love our big family, too, and don't know why I ever thought I could have both. Four children were born to us and we have one whom we raised from the age of twelve. In addition, we have had numerous foster children.

"I'm a strong environmentalist. I'm an eternal optimist and always think things will turn out right in the end."

AVOCATIONAL INTERESTS: Reading, walking, canoeing, bicycling, the woods (especially in the mountains).

* * *

SMITH, Frank (Arthur) 1917-

PERSONAL: Born October 2, 1917, in Wakefield, England; emigrated to United States, 1953; son of David and Elizabeth (Sutcliffe) Smith; married Mollie Bulmer, June 30, 1940; children: Michael, Robert, Lesley, Peter, Charles, Florian, David. *Education:* Doncaster Technical College, certificate, 1944. *Religion:* Latter-day Saints (Mormon). *Home:* 1187 South 1500 East, Bountiful, Utah 84010. *Office:* Genealogical Dept., L.D.S. Church 50, East North Temple, Salt Lake City, Utah 84103.

CAREER: Worked as a coal mines official in South Yorkshire, England, 1937-44; professional genealogist, 1944—; Brigham Young University, Salt Lake City, Utah, instructor in geneology, 1954—; Church of Jesus Christ of the Latterday Saints, Salt Lake City, manager of research services, 1961—. Associate, Institute of Mining Engineers, 1943—. *Member:* Society of Genealogists.

WRITINGS: (With David Gardner) *Genealogical Research in England and Wales,* three volumes, Bookcraft, 1956-64; *A Basic Course in Genealogy,* Bookcraft, 1958; (with Gardner) *A Genealogical Atlas of England & Wales,* Deseret, 1960; (with C. D. Harland) *A Genealogical Atlas of Scotland,* Bookcraft, 1962; (with Harland) *A Genealogical Atlas of Ireland,* Deseret, 1964; *A Genealogical Gazetteer of England,* Genealogical Publishing, 1968; *The Lives and Times of Our English Ancestors,* Everton, 1969; (with Finn A. Thomsen) *Genealogical Guidebook and Atlas of Denmark,* Bookcraft, 1969; (with Thomsen) *Genealogical Guidebook and Atlas of Norway,* Everton, 1970; *A Genealogical Gazetteer of Scotland,* Everton, 1971; (with George Fudge) *L.D.S. Genealogist's Handbook,* Bookcraft, 1972; (with Gardner) *Lists of Immigrants to North America,* Everton, 1976.

WORK IN PROGRESS: The Lives and Times of Our English Ancestors, volume two; *Genealogical Research in England and Wales,* volume four.

SIDELIGHTS: Smith told *CA* that American genealogy poses problems not found in European genealogical research because of lack of church records and the mobility of the American people.

* * *

SMITH, (David) Fred(erick) 1898(?)-1976

1898(?)—August 14, 1976; American writer and pioneer in radio broadcasting who, with Roy E. Larson, developed *Time* magazine's radio program "The March of Time." The show developed into a newsreel and later received an Academy Award for "revolutionizing the newsreel." He also wrote one of the first plays especially created for radio,

"Capricious Mary." He died in New York City. Obituaries: *New York Times,* August 14, 1976; *Washington Post,* August 16, 1976.

* * *

SMITH, Gary R. 1932-

PERSONAL: Born October 20, 1932, in Pocatello, Idaho; son of Alma Gibson, Sr. (a shoe store owner) and Maud Bodell (Jensen) Smith; married Rita Ann Palmer, November 17, 1972; children: Andrew Gibson, Paula Jean. *Education:* Idaho State University, B.A. (business; honors), 1954, B.A. (business education; honors), 1959; University of Idaho, Ed.D. (highest honors), 1969. *Politics:* Republican. *Religion:* Church of Jesus Christ of Latter-day Saints (Mormons). *Home:* 990 East 2680 N., Provo, Utah 84601. *Office:* Department of Business Education, 359 Jesse Knight Building, Brigham Young University, Provo, Utah 84602.

CAREER: Public school teacher in Pocatello, Idaho, 1959-65; Utah State University, Logan, professor of business education, 1967-69; Brigham Young University, Provo, Utah, professor of business education, 1969—. Vice-president of Dale's Auto Supply, 1959—. *Military service:* U.S. Army, 1956-58.

MEMBER: American Vocational Association, National Business Education Association, Council of Distributive Teacher Educators, Western Business Education Association, Utah Business Education Association, Utah Distributive Education Teachers, Utah Vocational Association, Phi Delta Kappa, Phi Kappa Phi, Delta Pi Epsilon. *Awards, honors:* Named deputy marshal of Dodge City, Kan.; outstanding service award from Utah Vocational Association; special recognition award from Distributive Education Clubs of America.

WRITINGS: (With Barbara Sethney Vorndran and Charles S. Winn) *Exploring Marketing Occupations,* McGraw, 1976. Also co-author of *Display and Promotion,* McGraw, 1970, 2nd edition, in press, and *Profiles of Distinction,* Brigham Young University Press, 1975.

WORK IN PROGRESS: Co-editing *Johnny Ain't No Rose.*

SIDELIGHTS: "I have long felt that we are too much concerned in education with knowledge and the regurgitation of facts. Students need to learn more about attitudes and learning how to enjoy life rather than how to recall facts. The materials in *Exploring Marketing Occupations* were designed to give students a hands-on experience at the junior high school level with actual job-related experiences. In *Johnny Ain't No Rose,* we have tried to express our personal philosophy of what education and teaching should be. We need more teachers who will express love and care for students rather than concern for subject matter. People count, things don't.

"I suspect that this feeling for the individual was taught me most effectively by my parents. They have continually given of themselves in the service of others. We all need to be more that way. School would be much less painful for students if they knew they had teachers who would care and were concerned for them. Only when we become more people-oriented will we be able to achieve what we need to do in our educational system.

"As I have the experience of seeing my children grow, I am continually amazed at how readily they are able to give love to others. Yet as we grow older we seem to become more guarded and tend not to give ourselves to others or go out of our way to help them. We all need to become more childlike in our attitudes. We need to study the lives of little children and become like them. In short we need to follow Christ's admonition to become as little children. What a much better world this would then be.''

*   *   *

SMITH, Jack (Clifford) 1916-

PERSONAL: Born August 27, 1916, in Long Beach, Calif.; son of Charles Franklin (a salesman) and Anna Mary (Hughes) Smith; married Denise Bresson (an executive administrator), June 17, 1939; children: Curtis Bresson, Douglas Franklin. *Education:* Attended Bakersfield College. *Religion:* "No affiliation." *Home:* 4251 Camino Real, Los Angeles, Calif. 90065. *Office: Los Angeles Times,* Times-Mirror Sq., Los Angeles, Calif. 90053.

CAREER: Honolulu Advertiser, Honolulu, Hawaii, copy editor, 1940-42; *Los Angeles Daily News,* Los Angeles, Calif., reporter, 1946-49; *Los Angeles Herald-Express,* Los Angeles, reporter, 1950-53; *Los Angeles Times,* Los Angeles, reporter and rewrite man, 1953-58, author of column "Jack Smith," 1958—. *Military service:* U.S. Marine Corps, combat correspondent, 1944-46. *Awards, honors:* National Headliners Award for best column of regional interest, 1975.

WRITINGS: Three Coins in the Birdbath (collection of newspaper columns), Doubleday, 1965; *Smith on Wry* (collection of columns), Doubleday, 1970; *God and Mrs. Gomez* (autobiographical account), Reader's Digest Press, 1974; *The Big Orange* (collection of articles from *Westways*), Ritchie, 1976. Contributor to *Westways.*

*   *   *

SMITH, John Chabot 1915-

PERSONAL: Middle name rhymes with shadow; born September 1, 1915, in Croyden, England; came to United States, 1921; naturalized U.S. citizen, 1943; son of Cecil (a manufacturer) and Christine (Chabot) Smith; married Betty McCarthy (a writer), October 5, 1940; children: Elizabeth (Mrs. Daniel A. Falk), Michael Chabot Smith. *Education:* Princeton University, B.A. (history), 1936; Trinity College, Cambridge, B.A. (history; first class honors), 1938. *Politics:* Independent. *Religion:* Catholic. *Home and office address:* Castle Meadow Rd., Newtown, Conn. 06470. *Agent:* Carl Brandt, Brandt & Brandt, 101 Park Ave., New York, N.Y. 10017.

CAREER: Washington Post, Washington, D.C., reporter, 1939-40; *New York Herald Tribune,* New York City, reporter, 1940-51, correspondent in Washington, D.C., 1940-41, in Rome, 1944-45, in London, 1945-47, and in New York City, 1947-51; American Red Cross, Washington, D.C., public information director of Far Eastern area in Tokyo, Japan, 1951-53; Worthington Corp., New York City, public relations director, 1953-57; General Electric Co., New York City, public affairs analyst, 1957-65; Famous Writers School, Westport, Conn., instructor, 1965-72; *Newtown Bee,* Newtown, Conn., news editor, 1972-73; free-lance writer, 1973—. *Member:* Phi Beta Kappa.

WRITINGS: Alger Hiss: The True Story, Holt, 1976, updated edition, Penguin, 1977; *The Children of Master O'Rourke,* Holt, 1977. Contributor to *Saturday Evening Post, Colliers, This Week,* and to *Fairfield County.*

WORK IN PROGRESS: A novel.

SIDELIGHTS: The controversy over who was lying in 1948—U.S. State Department aide Alger Hiss, who swore he wasn't a spy, or Whittaker Chambers, an admitted Communist agent who testified that Hiss passed him secret U.S. documents—is raging again, this time centered on the publication of Smith's book, *Alger Hiss: The True Story.*

In a comprehensive review of all the evidence, including much that was not known at the time of Hiss's trials in 1949-50, Smith concluded that Hiss was innocent. The book was immediately attacked by Allen Weinstein, who argued in a variety of magazine and newspaper articles that Hiss must have been guilty, and said he was writing a book to prove it. When this was written, that book had not appeared.

Smith, who covered both Hiss's trials for the *New York Herald Tribune,* recently told a *Publishers Weekly* interviewer that "even after the second trial, I felt I didn't know the truth. The testimony of witnesses was wildly conflicting." He contended that "nothing made sense. However, I had formed the impression that Whittaker Chambers . . . was a pathological liar. And I wasn't convinced that any actual espionage had taken place."

An initial hearing by the House Un-American Activities Committee (HUAC) investigating Chambers's allegations that he had known Hiss to be a member of a Communist apparatus ten years earlier nearly led to dismissal of the allegations as being completely false. Hiss claimed not to have known anyone by the name Whittaker Chambers. As Smith explained at the debate between Weinstein and himself at Princeton University on April 13, 1976, "Hiss never did 'admit he knew Chambers'—he only identified the man who now called himself Whittaker Chambers as a man who had previously called himself George Crosley. And as a matter of fact Whittaker Chambers wasn't the man's real name anyhow—that was just the pseudonym he used as a senior editor of *Time* magazine. His real name was Jay Vivian Chambers, but the public didn't know that until it came out in the trials the following year.

"Thus the first of Chambers's many perjuries took place when he was sworn in by the House Un-American Activities Committee, and stated under oath that his name was 'Whittaker Chambers.' If he had said instead that his name was Jay Vivian Chambers, but that he was currently using the name Whittaker Chambers, and had also been known at various times as Carl, David Breen, Lloyd Cantwell, Bob, Eugene, John Kelly, and various other names—even if he had forgotten to mention George Crosley, Mr. Hiss would have known that he was dealing with a many-named accuser, and the whole history of this case would have been different."

Smith noted that "Chambers, of course, denied that he ever used the name that Mr. Hiss knew him by, and [Congressman Richard M.] Nixon," who at that time had insisted the HUAC investigations continue, "succeeded in getting the press and public so confused by the whole shell game that most people believed Nixon and Chambers, and decided that Mr. Hiss must be a liar, as Nixon said he was." It was Robert Sherrill who observed recently that the troubling aspects of Chambers's "relationship with Hiss is just as much a mystery as it ever was. In his book, *Witness,* Chambers, with his usual hyperbole, says 'Alger Hiss and his wife I had come to regard as friends as close as a man ever makes in life,' but as Smith points out—and as Weinstein also used to point out—Chambers was full of wrong information about his 'close friend'; he erroneously testified that Hiss was deaf in one ear, erroneously testified that the Hisses were teetotalers, erroneously testified about the Hisses' church ties, erroneously described Hiss's stepson Timmy as 'a puny little boy.'"

Smith contended that "Chambers told so many lies, and admitted telling so many lies, that he established a track record for lying that as far as I know has never been equalled, at least in American history. Certainly Chambers must have told the truth sometimes about some things, but it takes a lot of careful checking to determine how much truth was in any particular statement made by that extraordinary man. You can't just take what he said at face value—you have to check every word of it, and sometimes every nuance of expression and context."

If Chambers was lying then, as Smith contends, the question is why? What was he going to benefit from such a charade? And "perhaps the biggest question of all over Chambers," Sherrill offered, "is this: was he a double agent? Did he pretend to be a Communist so that he could set up the right people as patsies in such a way as to establish the frenzied anti-Communist atmosphere . . .?"

Smith himself remarked that "the Hiss case readied the American public for McCarthyism. People thought that if such an important government man as Hiss, a man deeply involved in Roosevelt's New Deal programs, could be convicted as a Communist, who could tell how many others there were?" The case did prove to be extremely divisive, and Sherrill observed that "the left was split, some liberals claiming that Hiss was the victim of a conspiracy and that his martyrdom was the foundation for the McCarthy era, some claiming that he was guilty as hell and deserved punishment for giving substance to the warnings of the right wing." Sherrill pointedly noted, "They were certainly right on that last point; Richard Nixon made his reputation as the one member of the House Un-American Activities Committee most devoted to Chambers."

Sherrill placed Smith's book in direct lineage of Fred Cook's *Unfinished Story of Alger Hiss,* Meyer Zeligs's *Friendship and Fratricide,* and Hiss's own account, *In the Court of Public Opinion.* He observed that Smith drew from these books, as well as from Chambers's autobiography, *Witness,* and that Smith interviewed widely, studied the court records, and revived his own memories of the trials. "There is some new stuff," Sherrill conceded. "None of the book's virtues can overcome, nor its faults equal, however, its one basic shortcoming, which is that *The True Story* was obsolete, through no fault of Smith's, before it got off the press." Sherrill anticipated that materials from the Federal Bureau of Investigation's files on the Hiss case that were being released for the first time as a result of lawsuits under the Freedom of Information Act, would shed new light on the case.

Weinstein also hoped to find new evidence in the FBI papers, and frequently mentioned the fifteen thousand pages that had been released between the time Smith's book went to press and the day it was published. His attack on the book received front-page treatment in the *New York Times* and the *Washington Post,* but as Sherrill pointed out, these new stories "missed the most striking feature of Weinstein's review. . . . Weinstein made very little use of those newly-available 15,000 pages."

By the end of the year the number of FBI pages released had grown to more than twenty thousand, and Smith wrote his own evaluation of them in a supplementary chapter to the Penguin edition of his book. Summing them up in a preface to that edition, he wrote: "As might be expected, the FBI papers add nothing significant to the evidence against Hiss that was brought out in the trials; the prosecution used every scrap it had, especially in the second trial. Nor do the FBI papers add anything significant to the evidence in Hiss's favor brought out by the defense; it would be surprising if they did, for that is not what the FBI was looking for. . . .

"Thus, the FBI papers throw little new light on the facts in the case, though they add more details to what was already known. They do nothing to alter any of the facts presented in this book, and they do not answer any of the questions raised. . . . They are important because of the light they shed on the way the FBI operated in 1948-52, which is another subject altogether." It was a subject that related to the question of whether "the government violated Hiss's constitutional rights in the way they handled the case," and this question Hiss was preparing to test in the courts when all the FBI materials were received and examined.

At the time he wrote the first edition of his book, Smith hadn't seen those pages, but Weinstein didn't consult them either to answer the most important question raised by Smith's book: Was a fake typewriter used to frame Hiss? This question of the typewriter used in copying documents allegedly passed by Hiss to Chambers has not conclusively been resolved, and Sherrill pointed out that "Smith offers a variety of possible conspiracies, and Weinstein . . . receives them with undisguised ridicule. But this is the *new* Weinstein, the Weinstein of 1976. The Weinstein of 1971 . . . allowed for the possibility of conspiracy."

Athan Theoharis noted, too, that "Weinstein faults [Smith] for failing to consult and consider the available evidence. That same charge applied equally as well to Professor Weinstein's conclusions. . . . Not only does the evidence he cites not bear the weight of his conclusions but he has failed to address important questions surrounding this case and to await the complete FBI files bearing on this case." Considering that the FBI observed that its files on Hiss consist of fifty-three thousand pages, and that only fifteen thousand pages were released on January 31, 1976, Theoharis stated he found "it amazing that Weinstein could have concluded 'long before the FBI files were open to me' that Hiss was guilty." To that end, Theoharis allowed that since the questions surrounding the Hiss case remain unanswered, "Weinstein's account is not definitive, and he does his case a disservice by suggesting that only those are truly open-minded and nonpartisan who concur in his judgment that Hiss is guilty."

Smith told *CA:* "It's an old principle of the writer's art that nothing is more difficult than changing people's minds, once their minds are made up. You can't settle an argument just by finding out the truth. Something dramatic has to happen in front of people's eyes, and even then a lot of people won't believe it.

"I was skeptical about the Hiss case from the beginning, and when the trials ended it seemed as much of a mystery as ever. But most people had their minds made up, and the world went on as though the jury's verdict had ended the matter. Only when I read Zeligs's psychiatric study of Hiss and Chambers, published in 1967, did I begin to see that the matter wasn't ended. There were clues by which the mystery might be unraveled.

"Then for the first time I read the famous first chapter of Nixon's *Six Crises,* and compared it with published records and other reminiscences of what had gone on in and around the House Un-American Activities Committee before the trials began—the HUAC transcript, Chambers's *Witness,* Andrews's *A Tragedy of History,* Stripling's *Red Plot,* and my own scrapbook of clippings from the trial days.

"Putting it all together, it was clear that a lot more lies had been told than the ones Hiss was accused of—and the ones Chambers had admitted. I wanted to go over the ground again, examine all the records, cross-question Alger Hiss myself, interview everyone else involved in the case, and see if I could arrive at the truth. Until then I had never even interviewed Hiss, and hardly spoken to him. I had only listened and watched him in the courtroom.

"This was before Watergate, and when I talked to publishers about the idea, they weren't interested. Obviously one of the major liars involved was Richard Nixon, and he was then president of the United States. No reputable publisher wanted a book of this kind that would show the president up as a liar.

"Then came Watergate, the dramatic happening that took place before everybody's eyes, and people began to doubt Nixon's word. I got my contract, started cross-examining Hiss, and had most of the research done by the time Nixon left the White House. Nixon wouldn't see me, of course; he didn't even acknowledge my request for an interview. What had happened at the beginning of his career must have seemed trivial to him as it ended.

"I expected storms of opposition and argument when my book came out, but only Allen Weinstein, a young college professor, took up the cudgels against me. I didn't think he was very effective, because he had no answers for anything I had written in my book. He refuted nothing and disputed nothing in it; except my conclusion. He was content to repeat old lies Chambers had told, and twist things around in the artfully deceptive double-talk Nixon used to use. But he reassured those who believed in Nixon and Chambers by promising to write a book that would prove me wrong, and they were content to wait for it. He hasn't done that yet, and I don't believe he can do it, but as far as I know he's still trying.

"Meanwhile those who always believed Hiss was innocent have loved my book, and those who always believed him guilty have largely ignored it. A few have written to me to say it raised doubts in their minds, but they are very few. It is the younger generation, uninfluenced by the passions of 1948-50, who seem to be the most interested."

Asked whether he would continue to tackle political controversy in other books, Smith told CA: "For my second book, The Children of Master O'Rourke, I chose a subject as far away from the passions of American politics as I could. I had once visited Ireland with my wife, whose family came from there four generations ago, and fallen in love with it. Here was another mystery—a peaceful and beautiful land, a nation of friendly, gentle, and imaginative people, yet a history of ferocious bloodshed, which had flared again in the six northern counties under English rule. How could such contradictions be explained? What were the rights and wrongs of the ancient quarrel?

"This time I made no attempt to find the answers; the questions were too complex and went back too many centuries. Instead I set out to discover what it feels like to live in such a country, and what life in the new Irish nation has been like since independence was achieved barely two generations ago. My wife and I lived more than a year in Ireland gathering material for the book, which is based mainly on tape-recorded interviews.

"The result is the story of fifteen children who grew up in rural Ireland in the first generation of the nation's independence; of their mother and father, the local schoolmaster, who had done his bit in the fight for independence; and of what happened when the children grew up and left home to make their own fortunes, nine of them in Ireland, three in England, two in America, and one in Africa. The politics and the bloodshed form part of the background of the story; the story itself is a personal drama of family life.

"Some of this story had to be fictionalized, to protect the privacy of the family I have called O'Rourke, and dramatize their recollections. It was my first attempt at fiction, and it has emboldened me to undertake a work of pure fiction for my next book. It is a novel, light and entertaining with no political overtones, and as yet untitled."

BIOGRAPHICAL/CRITICAL SOURCES: Baltimore Sun, March 14, 1976; Chicago Tribune, March 18, 1976; Bridgeport Sunday Post, March 21, 1976; San Francisco Examiner, March 24, 1976; Lewiston Evening Journal, March 27, 1976; Newsweek, March 29, 1976; Publishers Weekly, March 29, 1976; Time, March 29, 1976; Harper's, April 1, 1976; New York Review of Books, April 1, 1976, May 27, 1976, November 25, 1976; Monterey Sunday Peninsula Herald, April 4, 1976; New York Times Book Review, April 25, 1976.

*   *   *

SMITH, Marion Jaques 1899-

PERSONAL: Born November 16, 1899, in Haverhill, Mass.; daughter of Frank Waterman (a contractor and carpenter) and Edna Lee (Parks) Jaques; married H. Kenneth Smith (a marine electrician), November 9, 1935; children: Lucy Lee (Mrs. Robert S. Trial, Jr.). Education: University of Maine, B.S., 1932; also attended Gorham Normal School, Clark University, Boston University, and Harvard University. Politics: Conservative Republican. Religion: Episcopal. Home: 893 High St., Bath, Me. 04530.

CAREER: Rural teacher in Maine, 1920-21, helping teacher, 1923; elementary school teacher in West Bath, Me., 1925-26, social studies teacher in Bath, Me., 1926-30, elementary school teacher in Bath, 1931-39; Bath Junior High School, Bath, Me., social studies teacher, 1954-63; writer, 1963—. Member of local citizens' advisory committee. Member: National Federation of Business and Professional Women's Clubs (honorary member), National Teachers Association, Maine Teachers Association, Bath-Brunswick Business and Professional Women's Club (vice-regent), Bath Retired Teachers Association, Brunswick Retired Teachers Association, Daughters of the American Revolution (vice-regent of local chapter), Daughters of American Colonists.

WRITINGS: A History of Maine: From Wilderness to Statehood, Falmouth Publishing House, 1949; On the Way North: A Mother Bear's Troubled Trip (self-illustrated juvenile), Bond Wheelwright Co., 1967; Pokey and Timothy of Stonehouse Farm (self-illustrated juvenile), Bond Wheelwright Co., 1973.

WORK IN PROGRESS: A biography of William King, Maine's first governor.

SIDELIGHTS: Marion Smith grew up in Bath, Maine, and still lives there. She spent her childhood and young adult years living on her parents' farm or at the home of a great aunt and uncle, who refreshed her knowledge of local history. She began writing her own history of Maine when she found that standard elementary texts were "old and dull," and eventually for younger children made several stories, handprinted and illustrated in pen and ink, that taught history through the eyes of a little black bear. These stories have been collected and published as On the Way North.

SMITH, Mary Ellen
(Mike Smith)

PERSONAL: Born in Melbourne, Fla.; daughter of Charles E. (a teacher) and Addie (a teacher; maiden name, Wallace) Shull; married Tom Q. Smith (a news writer; died June 6, 1954). *Education:* Attended Rollins College and Chicago Academy of Fine Arts. *Politics:* Democrat. *Religion:* Christian Scientist. *Home:* 2740 Southwest 31st Pl., Miami, Fla. 33133.

CAREER: Florida Power & Light Co., Miami, author and producer of "Builders of South Florida," a weekly radio program, 1947-70; writer of nonfiction books for children and adults, 1959—. *Member:* Women in Communications, Tropical Audubon Society, National Audubon Society, Historical Association of South Florida. *Awards, honors:* Headliner award from Miami chapter of Theta Sigma Phi, 1960.

WRITINGS: Picture Writing from Ancient Southern Mexico, University of Oklahoma Press, 1973.

Under name Mike Smith: (With husband, Tom Q. Smith) *Forty-Seven Ways to Make Money in Florida,* Coral Gables, 1952; *South Florida Frontiers,* Florida Power & Light Co., 1957; *Florida: A Way of Life* (juvenile), Dutton, 1959; *Better Cricket for Boys,* revised edition, International Publications Service, 1972; (contributor) *Beauty of the Outdoor World,* Country Beautiful, 1973; *Success in Football,* Transatlantic, 1974; (with Virginia Matusek) *Guide to the Everglades,* Trend House, 1975; *Better Cricket* (juvenile), Soccer Associates, 1976.

Author of filmstrip script and photographer of "Everglades: Sunlit Wilderness," Outdoor Pictures, 1975.

WORK IN PROGRESS: A children's book, *The Happy Alligator.*

SIDELIGHTS: Smith writes: "I have always been interested in the outdoors. I am also interested in history, especially early history of Florida. I come of a long line of teachers, but early in life decided to become an artist or writer rather than a teacher. I am now interested in outdoor photography, and find this an excellent medium of communication to both children and adults."

* * *

SMITH, Mildred Nelson 1918-

PERSONAL: Born January 30, 1918, in Guilford, Mo.; daughter of Alma (a farmer) and Tony J. Nelson; married Delbert D. Smith (a clergyman), September 18, 1949; children: Howard Alan, Ronald Kenneth, Steven Lynn, Karen Marie, Douglas Dean. *Education:* Northwest Missouri State University, B.S., 1941; Iowa State University, M.S., 1946. *Religion:* Reorganized Church of Jesus Christ of Latter-day Saints. *Home:* 2501 Broadway Ave., Saskatoon, Saskatchewan, Canada S7J 0Z2.

CAREER: Elementary school teacher in Barnard, Mo., 1936-40; Farm Security Administration, Charleston, Mo., home management supervisor, 1941-42; Office of Labor, War Food Administration, East Prairie, Mo., manager of farm labor supply center, 1942-44; U.S. Department of Agriculture, Iowa State University, Ames, extension nutritionist, 1946-51; writer.

WRITINGS: The Master's Touch, Herald House, 1973; *Word of Wisdom: Principle with Promise,* Herald House, 1977.

WORK IN PROGRESS: Word of Wisdom Helps, a cookbook.

SMITH, Robert A(rthur) 1944-

PERSONAL: Born August 23, 1944, in England; son of Arthur Ryan (an aviation executive) and Dianne (Coss) Smith; married Renee Alice Yvette Quevillon (a translator), August 25, 1973; children: Stephanie. *Education:* University of Calgary, student, 1963-65; Queen's University, Kingston, Ontario, Ph.D., 1972. *Politics:* Conservative. *Religion:* Agnostic. *Residence:* Toronto, Ontario, Canada. *Agent:* Al Zuckerman, 132 West 31st St., New York, N.Y. 10001. *Office: Educational Digest,* Maclean-Hunter, 481 University Ave., Toronto, Ontario, Canada M5W 1A7.

CAREER: Southam Business Publications, Toronto, Ontario, research assistant, 1969; *Canadian Pulp and Paper Industry,* Toronto, Ontario, technical editor, 1973; *Educational Digest,* Toronto, Ontario, editor, 1973—. Has worked as disc jockey for CKXL-Radio and prop man at CHCT-Television.

WRITINGS: The Kramer Project (novel), Doubleday, 1975; *The Prey of the Werewolves,* Fawcett, 1977.

WORK IN PROGRESS: The Fox Trap, a spy novel.

SIDELIGHTS: Smith writes: "*The Kramer Project* grew out of information collected while interviewing scientists and researchers for work at Southam Business and as technical editor of *Canadian Pulp and Paper Industry.* I have traveled extensively throughout Europe, and believe that time is growing short if we are to save industrial democracy and humanity itself." He adds, "I am an intense individualist, and avoid organizations and groups."

* * *

SMITH, Robert Paul 1915-1977

April 16, 1915—January 30, 1977; American writer who argued that children should be allowed to lead unstructured lives, best known for *Where Did You Go? Out. What Did You Do? Nothing.,* a book of childhood recollections, and for co-authoring "The Tender Trap," a Broadway play which was later adapted for the screen. He died in New York City. Obituaries: *New York Times,* January 31, 1977; *Newsweek,* February 14, 1977.

* * *

SMITH, Roger H(askell) 1932-

PERSONAL: Born April 25, 1932, in Detroit, Mich.; son of Demonte Haskell (a chemist) and Catherine (Linn) Smith; married Beverly Chew Bates, February 18, 1956; children: Roger Haskell, Jr. (deceased), William Boulton. *Education:* Yale University, B.A., 1954. *Politics:* Democrat. *Religion:* "Anglo-Catholic." *Home:* 92 Grove St., New York, N.Y. 10014. *Agent:* John Cushman Associates, 25 West 43rd St., New York, N.Y. 10036. *Office: Publishers' Weekly,* 1180 Avenue of the Americas, New York, N.Y. 10036.

CAREER: Publishers' Weekly, New York, N.Y., 1954—, began as assistant editor, served as news editor and executive editor, currently contributing editor. Member of board of directors of American Historical Institute and Council on Interracial Books for Children. *Member:* International P.E.N. (member of executive board of American Center), Association of American Publishers, Players Club, Devon Yacht Club.

WRITINGS: The American Reading Public, Bowker, 1963; *Paperback Parnassus: The Birth, the Development, the Pending Crises of the Modern American Paperbound Book,* Westview Press, 1976. Contributor to magazines, including

Saturday Review and *New Republic*, as well as to newspapers.

WORK IN PROGRESS: Biographies of James Agee and James H. Flye.

* * *

SMITH, Ruth Schluchter   1917-

PERSONAL: Born October 18, 1917, in Detroit, Mich.; daughter of Clayton John and Gertrude (Kastler) Schluchter; married Thomas Guilford Smith (a manufacturers' representative and engineer), September 28, 1946; children: Pemberton III. *Education:* Wayne State University, A.B., 1939; University of Michigan, A.B. in L.S., 1942. *Politics:* Republican. *Religion:* Methodist. *Home:* 5304 Glenwood Rd., Bethesda, Md. 20014. *Office:* Institute for Defense Analyses, 400 Army Navy Dr., Arlington, Va. 22202.

CAREER: Detroit Public Library, Detroit, Mich., junior librarian, 1936-43; University of Pennsylvania, Moore School of Electrical Engineering, Philadelphia, research assistant, 1946-47; Bethesda Methodist Church Library, Bethesda, Md., librarian, 1955-61; Institute for Defense Analyses, Arlington, Va., reference librarian and chief of reader services, 1961-65, chief of unclassified library section, 1965-67, head librarian, 1967-75, manager of technical information services, 1975—. *Military service:* U.S. Naval Reserve, Women Accepted for Volunteer Emergency Service (WAVES), 1943-46; became lieutenant, junior grade. *Member:* Church and Synagogue Library Association (founding member and president, 1967-68, member of executive board, 1967-77), Special Libraries Association (chairperson of aerospace division, 1975-76), American Society for Information Science.

WRITINGS: Outline for Building Vitality in Your Church Library, Church Library Council, 1961; (with Robert Collins) *Lasers* (bibliography) Institute for Defense Analyses, 1963; (with Jay Schwartz, J. Kaiser and Joseph Aein) *Multiple Access to a Common Radio Repeater* (bibliography), Institute for Defense Analyses, 1964; *Publicity for a Church Library,* Zondervan, 1966; (contributor) Allen Kent and Harold Lancour, editors, *Encyclopedia of Library and Information Science,* Volume 4, Dekker, 1970; *Workshop Planning,* Church and Synagogue Library Association, 1972; *Getting the Books Off the Shelves,* Hawthorn, 1975; (with Claudia Hannaford) *Promotion Planning,* Church and Synagogue Library Association, 1975, *Cataloging Books Step-by-Step,* Church and Synagogue Library Association, 1977.

Author of scripts for video presentations. Contributor to *Special Libraries, Library Journal, New Christian Advocate,* and other periodicals.

SIDELIGHTS: Smith told *CA:* "A life long enthusiasm for libraries, seasoned by an early interest in journalism, just naturally gave birth to writing—most of it interpretive reporting based on experience in the library field. As an administrator of a scientific research library, I have dealt with the problems of coping with federal government information sources and services, organizing user feedback groups and participating in cooperative library networks. As the chairman of a church library committee and formerly a church librarian, I have described the challenges of organizing and administering a church library ministry, promoting and publicizing its services, and inspiring or training volunteer workers through workshops and interfaith library fellowship activities."

SMOLICH, Yurik K.   1899(?)-1976

1899(?)—August 16, 1976; Ukrainian-born journalist and author whose works included crime stories, satires, and science fiction novels. Obituaries: *New York Times,* August 31, 1976.

* * *

SMYTHE, Hugh H(eyne)   1913-1977

August 19, 1913—June 22, 1977; American sociologist, diplomat, and author. An expert on the sociological status of blacks, he collaborated with W.E.B. Dubois, Jr., on one of the first detailed studies in this field. He later assisted Gunnar Myrdal in the writing of a book regarded as a classic work on race relations. He served as U.S. ambassador to Syria and Malta. He died in New York City. Obituaries: *New York Times,* June 26, 1977. (See index for previous *CA* sketch)

* * *

SODERLIND, Arthur E(dwin)   1920-

PERSONAL: Born August 15, 1920, in Brooklyn, N.Y.; son of Arthur J. and Beda I. (Seaholm) Soderlind; married Dorothy A. Neumann (a registered nurse), August 7, 1948; children: Sheryl Soderlind-Jervis, Linda Turner, Deborah. *Education:* New York College for Teachers (now State University of New York at Albany), B.A., 1947, M.A., 1948; State University of Iowa, Ph.D., 1961. *Religion:* Lutheran. *Home:* 18 Simsbury Manor Dr., Weatogue, Conn. 06089. *Office:* Bureau of Elementary and Secondary Education, State Department of Education, 165 Capitol Ave., Hartford, Conn. 06115.

CAREER: High school teacher in Pawling, N.Y., 1948-49; Minot State Teachers College, Minot, N.D., supervisor of student teachers, 1950-52; State University of Iowa, Iowa City, supervisor of social studies student teachers, 1952-53; State University of New York at Albany, social studies supervisor of student teachers, 1953-61; Connecticut State Department of Education, Hartford, social studies consultant in bureau of elementary and secondary education, 1961—. Adjunct professor of history at University of Hartford. Member of board of directors, Lutheran Theological Seminary, Philadelphia, Pa., 1962-74. *Member:* National Council for the Social Studies (served variously as secretary, program chairperson, and president of Capital District council; secretary-treasurer of Iowa council; treasurer of New York state council; and member of board of directors of Connecticut council), Pi Gamma Mu, Phi Alpha Theta.

WRITINGS: Colonial Histories: Connecticut, Thomas Nelson, 1976. Author of curriculum bulletins and National Council for the Social Studies bulletins; contributor to *Biographical Dictionary of American Educators.* Member of editorial board, "Connecticut History" series, Pequot Press, 1975.

WORK IN PROGRESS: A book on Roger Sherman of Connecticut.

SIDELIGHTS: Soderlind told *CA:* "In the elementary and secondary schools of this state there is a renewed interest in local and state history as a result of the Bicentennial. This and the interest in ethnic studies has brought about an increased awareness of our heritage."

* * *

SOELLE, Dorothee   1929-

PERSONAL: Born September 30, 1929, in Cologne, Germany; daughter of Hans C. Nipperdey (a professor); married Dietrich Soelle, June 3, 1954 (divorced, 1963); married Fulbert Steffensky (a professor), October 24, 1969; children: Martin, Michaela, Caroline, Mirjim. *Education:* Attended University of Cologne and University of Freiburg; University of Goettingen, degree of philosophy, 1954. *Religion:* Evangelical Church of Germany. *Home:* 99 Claremont Ave., New York, N.Y. 10027; and 5 Koln 41, Pauliplatz 7, Federal Republic of Germany.

CAREER: Instructor in German and religion in West German high schools, 1954-60; Technical University of Aachen, Philosophical Institute, Aachen, Germany, research assistant, 1962-64; University of Cologne, Institute for Germanistick, Cologne, Germany, teacher, 1964-67, lecturer in German literature, 1971-75; Union Theological Seminary, New York, N.Y., visiting lecturer in systematic theology, 1975-77, Harry Emerson Fosdick Visiting Professor, 1977—. Lecturer, University of Maine, 1972-75. *Member:* Royal Scientific Academy of Utrecht, P.E.N. *Awards, honors:* Grant from the German Society for Research, 1967; Theodore Heuss Medal, 1974; honorary doctorate from Protestant Faculty, Paris, France.

WRITINGS: Stellvertretung: Ein Kapitel Theologie nach dem Tode Gottes, [Stuttgart], 1965, translation published as *Christ the Representative,* Fortress, 1967; *Die Wahrheit ist konkret,* [Olten], 1967, translation published as *The Truth is Concrete,* Herder, 1969; *Atheistisch an Gott glauben* (title means "Atheistically Believing in God"), [Olten], 1968; *Phantasie und Gehorsam: Ueberlegungen zu einer kuenftigen christlichen Ethick,* [Stuttgart], translation by Lawrence W. Denef published as *Beyond Mere Obedience,* Augsburg, 1970; *Meditationen und Gebrauchstexte* (title means "Meditations and Usable Texts"), Wolfgang-Fietkau Verlag, 1969; (editor with husband, Fulbert Steffensky) *Politisches Nachtgebet in Koeln* (title means "Political Evening Prayer"), [Stuttgart], Volume I, 1969, Volume II, 1970; *Das Recht, ein anderer zu werden: Theologische Texte* (title means "The Right to Become Another"), [Neuwied], 1971; *Politische Theologie: Auseinandersetzung mit Rudolph Bultmann,* [Stuttgart], 1971, translation by John Shelley published as *Political Theology,* Fortress, 1974; *Realisation: Studien zum Verhaeltnis von Theologie und Dichtung nach der Aufklaerung* (title means "Realization: Studies Toward the Relation of Theology and Literature After the Enlightenment"), [Neuwied], 1973; *Leiden: Thesen der Theologie,* [Stuttgart], 1973, translation by Everett Kalin published as *Suffering,* Fortress, 1975; *Die revolutionaere Geduld: Gedichte,* Wolfgang-Fietkau Verlag, 1974, translation by Bob and Rita Kimber published as *Revolutionary Patience,* Orbis, 1977; *Die Hinreise: Zur Religioesen Erfahrung—Teste and Ueberlegvngen,* [Stuttgart], 1976, translation published as *Death by Bread Alone,* Fortress, 1976. Free-lance writer for German radio and television networks.

WORK IN PROGRESS: Cross and Class Struggle, for Beacon Press.

SIDELIGHTS: Dorothee Soelle and her husband Fulbert Steffensky founded the ecumenical group "Political Evening Prayer." She described it as a movement of "theological-political reflection and action, with aims at an understanding of and feeling for the crucified Christ today, and how Christians need to respond."

* * *

SOLOMON, Stephen D(avid) 1950-

PERSONAL: Born January 5, 1950, in Philadelphia, Pa.; son of Philip Goldman (a salesman) and Dolores (in personnel; maiden name, Pomerantz) Solomon. *Education:* Pennsylvania State University, B.A., 1971; Georgetown University, J.D., 1975. *Home:* 4020 Westaway Dr., Lafayette Hill, Pa. 19444. *Agent:* Ray Lincoln, 4 Surrey Rd., Melrose Park, Pa. 19126.

CAREER: Center for the Study of Responsive Law, Washington, D.C., member of staff, 1971; *Today's Post,* Fort Washington, Pa., reporter, 1973; "Washington Merry-Go-Round" (Jack Anderson's syndicated column), Washington, D.C., reporter, 1973-74; free-lance writer, 1974—. Admitted to Bar of Supreme Court of Pennsylvania.

MEMBER: Pennsylvania Bar Association, Phi Beta Kappa, Sigma Delta Chi, Phi Kappa Phi. *Awards, honors:* Gerald Loeb Award from University of California, Los Angeles, John Hancock Award for Excellence from John Hancock Mutual Life Insurance Co., Sidney Hillman Prize from Sidney Hillman Foundation, and story of the year award from Conference of Locally Edited Sunday Magazines, all 1976, all for newspaper article "Fifty-Four Who Died."

WRITINGS: (With Philip Boffey and others) *The Brain Bank of America,* McGraw, 1975; (with Willard S. Randall) *Building 6: The Tragedy at Bridesburg,* Little, Brown, 1977. Contributor to magazines, including *Nation, New Republic,* and *Popular Science.*

WORK IN PROGRESS: A political novel; research on "the often disastrous effects of uncontrolled technology and industrialization on the public health; this encompasses vital issues of ecology, health, and corporate responsibility," with publication expected to result.

SIDELIGHTS: Solomon writes: "One of the important motivating circumstances of my career was the political activism and social upheaval of the late sixties and early seventies, which helped stimulate my interest in politics, law, and the environment. I pursue these subjects today with my writing.

"In 1975, I teamed with another free-lance writer to investigate cancer deaths among workers at a chemical company in Philadelphia. *Building 6* is an expansion of the magazine article that resulted from that investigation, and my work gave me a rare glimpse at the human tragedy that can result from uncontrolled technology. In this book and other writings, I hope to show that control of dangerous industrial chemicals and manufacturing processes can greatly improve public health and the quality of life while still permitting most of the conveniences we have come to enjoy."

AVOCATIONAL INTERESTS: Reading, theater, vegetable gardening, outdoor sports.

* * *

SOLZHENITSYN, Aleksandr I(sayevich) 1918-

PERSONAL: Surname pronounced Sohl-zhe-*neet*-sin; born December 11, 1918, in Kislovodsk, Russia, grew up in Rostov-on-Don, U.S.S.R.; father was a student at Moscow University, then an army volunteer, 1914, served as an artillery officer in World War I, and died, 1918, six months before Aleksandr's birth; mother was a typist and stenographer; married Natalya Reshetovskaya (a professor and research chemist), April 27, 1940 (divorced at his request because of his imprisonment); remarried Natalya Reshetovskaya, 1956 (divorced, 1972); married Natalya Svetlova (a mathematics teacher), April, 1973; children (from marriage to Svetlova): Yermoli, Ignat, Stepan (sons); stepchildren: one son. *Education:* Moscow Institute of History, Philosophy, and Literature, correspondence course in philology, 1939-41; University of Rostov, degree in mathematics and physics, 1941. *Residence:* Cavendish, Vermont.

CAREER: First Secondary School, Morozovka, Rostov, U.S.S.R., physics teacher, 1941; arrested February 9, 1945, while serving as the commander of a Soviet Army artillery battery after certain of his letters containing oblique derogatory references to Stalin were discovered by counter-intelligence agents; sent to Greater Lubyanka Prison, Moscow; convicted without a hearing by a three-man tribunal and sentenced to eight years in prison for anti-Soviet agitation and for attempting to organize an anti-Soviet group; sent to Butyrki Prison, Moscow, and worked on a construction project near Moscow during 1946; transferred to Marfino Prison (a research institute in Moscow, later to become "Mavrina" prison in *The First Circle*) where he worked as a mathematician in radio and telephone communications research, 1947-50; sent to Ekibastuz labor camp in Kazakhstan in Asian U.S.S.R. where he worked as a bricklayer and carpenter on the construction of a powerplant, 1950-53; developed cancer while at Ekibastuz, and underwent surgery, February 12, 1952; released from prison, March 5, 1953, the day of Stalin's death; exiled to Kok-Terek in Kazakhstan where he taught mathematics and began writing; allowed to travel to Tashkent where he spent several months undergoing radiation therapy for treatment of cancer, 1954; pronounced cured and sent back to Kok-Terek to continue teaching; released from exile in June, 1956, and his convictions were removed from official records; settled in Riazan, 120 miles southeast of Moscow, where he taught mathematics and physics in a secondary school; enjoyed his first success as a writer with the publication of *One Day in the Life of Ivan Denisovich,* 1962; began teaching part time and eventually resigned his teaching position to become a full-time writer; *One Day in the Life of Ivan Denisovich* (which originally brought Solzhenitsyn praise at the height of Krushchev's de-Stalinization program, 1962-63) became the basis for the government's unfavorable policy regarding the writer beginning in 1963; Solzhenitsyn was banned from the teaching profession and forbidden to live in Moscow; despite his attempts to regain official sanction, Solzhenitsyn was unable to publish his work in the Soviet Union after 1963; he became an outspoken critic of the Soviet political system, writing articles and letters describing the "stupidity and shortsightedness" of those in power; such actions gained him a large following in his country, and his manuscripts were circulated in *samizdat* (hand-copied or typed) form; KGB (secret police) confiscated his manuscripts, searched his friends' houses, and eventually banished his second wife, Natalya Svetlova, from her teaching position; in 1973 the KGB found a hidden manuscript of *The Gulag Archipelago* (Solzhenitsyn's most explicit work condemning the Soviet prison system); he subsequently authorized a French publication of the book (the only authorized non-Soviet publication of his work at that time) in 1973; publication of *The Gulag Archipelago* and world reaction to it led to Solzhenitsyn's arrest, February 12, 1974; he was taken to Lefortovo Prison and charged with treason; during his interrogation he read a prepared statement proclaiming that any court appointed to try him was incompetent, that he would refuse to answer any questions, and that he would not perform any work if imprisoned; on February 13, 1974, he was flown to exile in West Germany; he subsequently took up residence in Zurich, Switzerland, where he was joined by his wife and children in March, 1974; Solzhenitsyn spent the next two years living in Zurich, writing, and travelling around Eu-

rope; in August, 1976, he moved to the United States and presently lives in Vermont with his family; he continues to write and is in the process of starting a non-profit publishing company to distribute his own works as well as those on Russian culture, religion, and history. *Military service:* Soviet Army, 1941-45; became captain of artillery unit; decorated twice; stripped of rank and decorations when arrested (see above).

MEMBER: Union of Soviet Writers (expelled, 1969), American Academy of Arts and Sciences. *Awards, honors:* Nominated for Lenin Prize, 1964; Prix du Meilleur Livre Etranger (France), 1969, for *The First Circle* and *Cancer Ward;* Nobel Prize for Literature, 1970.

WRITINGS: Odin den'Ivana Denisovicha (short novel), published in *Novy Mir,* November 20, 1962, published in book form by Flegon Press (London), 1962, [Moscow], 1963, English translation by Ralph Parker published as *One Day in the Life of Ivan Denisovich,* Dutton, 1963, English translation by Max Hayward and Ronald Hingley published under same title, Praeger, 1963, English translation by Gillon Aitken published under same title, Farrar, Straus, 1971; *Dlya polzy'dela* (short novel), published in *Novy Mir,* July, 1963, published in book form by Russian Language Specialties (Chicago), 1963, English translation by David Floyd and Hayward published as *For the Good of the Cause,* Praeger, 1964; *Sluchay na stantsii Krechetovka* Matrenin dvor (two short novels; titles mean "An Incident at Krechetovka Station" and "Matryona's House"), published in *Novy Mir,* January, 1963, published in book form by Flegon Press, 1963, English translation by Paul W. Blackstock published as *We Never Make Mistakes,* University of South Carolina Press, 1963; "Ztiudy i Krokhotnye Rasskazy" (short story), published in *Grani* (Frankfurt), Number 56, 1964, published in *Den Oka-Fluss Entlang,* Possev-Verlag, 1965, published in book form as *Krokhotnye Rasskazy,* Librarie des Cinq Continents (Paris), 1970.

Sochininiia (selected works), [Frankfurt], 1966; *V kruge pervom* (novel), manuscript confiscated in U.S.S.R., 1965, scheduled for publication in *Novy Mir,* December, 1967, and suddenly withdrawn, published by Harper, 1968, English translation by Thomas P. Whitney published as *The First Circle,* Harper, 1968, English translation by Michael Guybon published under same title, Harvill, 1968; *Rakovyl korpus* (novel), accepted for publication by *Novy Mir,* January, 1968, then cancelled, first part published by Mondadori (Switzerland), 1968, entire book (100 copies) published by Bodley Head (London), 1968, published by YMCA Press (Paris), 1970, English translation by Nicholas Bethell and David Burg published as *Cancer Ward,* Bodley Head, first part, 1968, second part, 1969, English translation of entire book by Bethell and Burg published as *The Cancer Ward,* Farrar, Straus, 1969, English translation of entire book by Rebecca Frank published under same title, Dial, 1968; *Olen'i shalashovka* (play), Flegon Press (London), 1968, English translation by Bethell and Burg published as *The Love Girl and the Innocent* (adaptation by Paul Avila Mayer produced as "A Play by Aleksandr Solzhenitsyn" in Minneapolis at Tyrone Guthrie Theatre, October 13, 1970), Farrar, Straus, 1969; *Svecha na vetru* (play), Flegon Press, 1968, published in *Grani* (Frankfurt), March, 1969, English translation by Keith Armes and Arthur Hudgins published as *Candle in the Wind,* University of Minnesota Press, 1973; *Les Droits de l'ecrivain* (title means "The Rights of the Writer"), Editions du Seuil, 1969.

Avgust chetyrnadtsatogo (historical novel), Flegon Press (London), 1971, English translation by Michael Glenny published as *August 1914*, Farrar, Straus, 1972; *Stories and Prose Poems by Aleksandr Solzhenitsyn*, English translation by Glenny, Farrar, Straus, 1971; *Six Etudes by Aleksandr Solzhenitsyn*, English translation by James G. Walker, College City Press, 1971; *Nobelevskara lektsira po literature*, YMCA Press (Paris), 1972, English translation by F. D. Reeve published as *Nobel Lecture by Aleksandr Solzhenitsyn*, Farrar, Straus, 1972; *A Lenten Letter to Pimen, Patriarch of All Russia*, English translation by Theofanis G. Staurou, Burgess, 1972; *Arkhipelag GULag, 1918-1956: Op'bit khudozhestvennopo issledovanija*, YMCA Press, 1973, English translation of Volume I by Thomas P. Whitney published as *The Gulag Archipelago, 1918-1956: An Experiment in Literary Investigation*, Volume I, Parts 1 and 2, Harper, 1974, English translation of Volume II by Whitney published as *The Gulag Archipelago*, Volume II, Parts 3 and 4, Harper, 1976; *Mir i nasilie* (title means "Peace and Violence"), [Frankfurt], 1974; *Prusskie nochi: pozma napisappaja v lagere v 1950* (title means "Prussian Nights: Epic Poems Written at the Forced Labor Camp, 1950"), YMCA Press, 1974; *Pis'mo vozhdram Sovetskogo Soruza*, YMCA Press, 1974, English translation by Hilary Sternberg published as *Letter to the Soviet Leaders*, Harper, 1974; *Solzhenitsyn: A Pictorial Autobiography* (photographs by Solzhenitsyn and family members; includes short autobiography written for the Nobel Foundation, 1972), Farrar, Straus, 1974.

Bodalsra telenok s dubom, YMCA Press (Paris), 1975, English translation published as *The Calf and the Oak*, Association Press, 1975; *Lenin v Tsiurikhe*, YMCA Press, 1975, English translation by H. T. Willetts published as *Lenin in Zurich*, Farrar, Straus, 1976; *Amerikanskie rechi* (title means "American Speeches"), YMCA Press, 1975; (with others) *From under the Rubble*, English translation by Michael Scammell, Little, Brown, 1975, published as *From under the Ruins*, Association Press, 1975; (with others) *Detente: Prospects for Democracy and Dictatorship*, Transaction Books, 1975; *Warning to the West*, Farrar, Straus, 1976; *Great Works of Aleksandr Solzhenitsyn*, Bantam, in press.

Unpublished writings and unproduced plays, some confiscated by the Soviet Government: "The Right Hand" (stories); "The Light That Is in You" (play); "The Tanks Know the Truth" (screenplay); "Feast of the Victors" (play; later renounced by Solzhenitsyn), written in prison, 1949, excerpts published in *Die Zeit* (Germany), December, 1969. Contributor of poems to *New Leader*.

WORK IN PROGRESS: Additional parts of *The Gulag Archipelago;* additional volumes of *August 1914;* novels.

SIDELIGHTS: Although the West generally considers Solzhenitsyn to be Russia's greatest living novelist, and although a sympathetic Russian writer, Yevgeny Yevtushenko, regarded him as "our only living classic," most of Solzhenitsyn's compatriots have had the opportunity to read only three of his stories and his first novel, which was published on Khrushchev's order during his era of de-Stalinization. Solzhenitsyn came to be regarded as dangerous to the regime—as was Boris Pasternak—only more so, because, as one writer sympathetic to the Kremlin noted, "Pasternak was a man detached from life, while Solzhenitsyn is combative, determined." Propagandists have called him psychologically unbalanced, a willing tool of the West, even a defector to Egypt. While still residing in the Soviet Union, he was accused of sending his manuscripts to the West, even though he publicly protested against all publication abroad. Since Solzhenitsyn maintains that the secret police raided his

apartment and seized many of his manuscripts, certain observers believe that the Soviet Government may have sent the manuscripts out of the country as a pretext for bringing him to a trial reminiscent of the Sinyavsky-Daniel case. (Harrison E. Salisbury believes, however, that the manuscripts reached the West through Czech sources.) Repeatedly Solzhenitsyn was asked by the secretariat of the Union of Soviet Writers to repudiate his position, but he always refused.

Solzhenitsyn first attracted worldwide attention when, in May of 1967, he sent a letter to a congress of the Union of Soviet Writers, a meeting he was not permitted to attend, stating that his country's literature has been enduring censorship for decades and calling for "the abolition of all censorship, overt or hidden, of all fictional writing." He further charged the government with cancelling his public readings, adding, "My work has thus been finally smothered, gagged, and slandered." Eighty-two of the 6,500 members of the Union petitioned in his behalf, with no success. On June 26, 1968, he was officially denounced in an editorial in *Literaturnaya Gazeta*. After this denunciation Christopher Russell wrote, "Not only are the works banned, no one is allowed to mention his name in print, or even to quote from his writings except to condemn him." The *Times Literary Supplement* reported that Solzhenitsyn was quoted as saying that he was less afraid of dying of cancer than of being "accidentally" killed by the secret police. This fear may have accounted, at least in part, for his opposition to the publication of his works abroad, even though he maintains, as others often do, that many of his English translations are poor since they were rushed into print. "It seems to me," says Victor Erlich, "that the publishers [were] playing fast and loose with Solzhenitsyn's personal safety, showing a callous disregard for his expressed wishes." (Bodley Head, Harper, and Praeger, however, reportedly held sizable sums of money for him.) Furthermore, Solzhenitsyn never authorized or aided the underground "publication" of his work in the U.S.S.R., but, as Jeri Laber said, "dedicated anonymous readers have painstakingly typed out entire manuscripts of his unpublished works, and as many as 5,000 copies of his novels are circulating privately throughout the Soviet Union."

"Solzhenitsyn's world is one of almost private Russian concern and grief," writes a *Time* magazine reporter, a place "which no Westerner may lightly enter or vulgarize in glib anti-Communist terms. Those who have not been through the agonies of the camps, the shocks of alternating liberalization and repression, can scarcely pass judgment.... But Solzhenitsyn brings the reader, any reader, closer to the truth. Essentially, his books are about freedom—including the freedom that sometimes can be found only when a man has been stripped of everything." Through his autobiographical novels (he can be readily likened to Ivan Denisovich, Gleb Nerzhin in *The First Circle*, and Kostoglotov in *The Cancer Ward*) Solzhenitsyn has become, writes Laber, "the symbol and the embodiment of an undaunted creative spirit. In prison, where he lacked even the rudiments of his trade, a pencil and paper, he learned to compose whole stories in his head, committing them to memory, editing them and memorizing them again. Then he recited them to his fellow prisoners who, in turn, memorized them and repeated them to others, thus creating a whole new genre of oral literature." Solzhenitsyn has said that "perhaps more great thoughts have been burned than published," and has concluded that, if necessary, he "could probably do it all over again from memory."

As a novelist, "the most appealing thing about Aleksandr

Solzhenitsyn," writes Alexander Shoumatoff, "is his whole-hearted revision to the methods of 19th-century realism. There is something instantly familiar in the sound of his novels. It is the voice of his master, Tolstoy, the voice of Russian realism with its shrewd physical apprehension of human conflict. One never imagined writing like this would happen again." Salisbury adds: "When comparisons of Solzhenitsyn are made with Tolstoy, Dostoevsky and Turgenev this is not hyperbole. He is, curiously, a major 19th-century novelist suddenly appearing in the last half of the 20th century. No *nouvelle vague* tendencies here; no sign of blurred technique, soft focus, existentialist philosophy. Just hard-edged prose, honed Toledo-sharp, sureness of colloquial language and an implicit accuracy of scene which has its links with Hugo, Dickens, Thackeray, Balzac, Zola. . . . Solzhenitsyn is no fantasist. He tells it like it is. The penal society of which he writes *is* Russia, not some Orwellian concept. It is Russia, here and now; as it was yesterday and last month and for a hundred years before that."

One Day in the Life of Ivan Denisovich, based on Solzhenitsyn's own experiences in a labor camp, was the first book ever to describe such a camp in detail. Ernst Pawel calls the book a masterpiece, "a work squarely in the mainstream of Russia's literary tradition and comparable to some of its greatest examples. . . . Solzhenitsyn speaks very much for himself, and in a voice of his own." Although Irving Howe disallows the word "masterpiece," he considers the book nevertheless remarkable: "*One Day* yields, more than anything else, a beautiful sense of its author as a Chekhovian figure: simple, free of literary affectation, wholly serious." As a novel, he adds, the work "is modest in scope, pure in tone, utterly authentic in treatment, but with a number of severe limitations. . . . In *One Day* tautness of realistic notation becomes a means of limiting imaginative power, and the need for faithful recollection [becomes] a cause for repressing the dangers of meaning. The book is emotionally parched."

With *The First Circle,* writes Timothy Foote, "Solzhenitsyn confirms his earlier promise as the one Russian novelist likely to become not merely a partisan chronicler of Soviet agonies but the enduring Dante of Stalin's latter-day political Inferno." As Guy Davenport maintains, "Only the mice in the wainscoting know more about Stalin when he was alone; no one reading these pages will ever again disparage the imagination of an artist. . . . If Solzhenitsyn's only novel to be published in Russia, *One Day in the Life of Ivan Denisovich,* was useful to Khrushchev as an anti-Stalinist document, *The First Circle* is directed at the entire Soviet experiment and system, condemning, with dignity and a philosophically controlled passion, its poisonous hypocrisy and leaden tyranny. For us it is one of the century's bitterest novels." The *Virginia Quarterly Review* writer says that this is "very clearly a great book, perhaps the finest novel to come out of Europe and America since the 1930's. Solzhenitsyn may not yet be Tolstoy's equal, but in one sense Tolstoy was not Solzhenitsyn's. Tolstoy did not spend eleven years in . . . Stalinist prison [and exile]. Aleksandr Solzhenitsyn came out of the camp with his health ruined, but his genius was unimpaired; prison indeed sharpened his talents, as it frequently has for the great Russian writers. . . . The point of his novels is that twentieth-century existence involves only jailer and prisoner."

The First Circle describes four days in the life of a special prison camp outside Moscow in 1949. (As Davenport notes, at this time there were "more political prisoners in Russia than there were people in France.") The prisoners in this camp were not criminals but rather intelligent people whose minds were a potential danger to the regime. In the camp, according to the *Virginia Quarterly Review,* the prisoners "were building tools which would help increase the prison population. It was, like all prisons, a kind of hell; but compared with the mines of the Arctic or the Siberian lumber camps, it was like the 'first circle' of hell." The prisoners "rotted physically and spiritually—yet a few, but an important few, were in the end purified and even exalted. . . . The prisoner became the moral superior of the jailer, and the tyrant knew it." The horrors, Salisbury correctly asserts, have been stated and restated in many books, "almost to ennui. Now, however, the towering figure of Solzhenitsyn appears. He, like Dostoevsky, is a survivor. . . . And when he writes of that society-within-a-society it is as though we had never before experienced it. In his work, terror is so workaday, brutality so banal, that we know every line he writes is true." Comparing the work, as many have done, to earlier Russian novels, Laber notes that Nerzhin, the protagonist, "hoped at first to find simplicity and truth among the People, believing that true wisdom is the monopoly of those who work with their own hands. Unlike his Tolstoyan counterparts, however, he did not condescend to 'go to the People.' Thrown among them as an equal in the labor camps, he understands finally that they 'had no homespun superiority to him' and lacked 'that personal point of view which becomes more precious than life itself.'" Nerzhin believed, however, that "a person shouldn't regard prison solely as a curse but also as a blessing," a place where, after having lost his possessions, his relations and friends, and his opportunity to speak as he believes, a man may become entirely free.

F. D. Reeve fears that many Americans will read *The First Circle* merely as "an indictment of the political and social structure of the Soviet Union, encouraged in their belief by Solzhenitsyn's repudiation of his mansucript and his disavowal . . . of any involvement in Western publication. . . . [But] *The First Circle* is not simply another expose of prison life, continuing Dostoevsky, Tolstoy, and Chekhov" in their damnation "of a corrupt, illegal society. . . . Solzhenitsyn's novel is one of the steps in the completion of the literature of the Twenties and Thirties. . . . In spite of the perversions of modern man, some men see the good and live by their vision, even if it perverts their lives. . . . This book is a more nearly exact and more stimulating documentary than any we have yet had of the terms under which men have been and still are imprisoned for political deviation in the Soviet Union. [But] it is a sociological document relevant for us all—for us in the United States, too. Solzhenitsyn's analysis of the butcher-like amorality of contemporary men absorbed in the niceties of trimming a carcass whose former life they thought they did not need and therefore undervalued is couched in a superbly artful fiction. Like Tolstoy, he is a man of great talent and of stupendous moral dignity. This tale is not fantasy; nor is it titillation—though there are some comic caricatures of guards and some slapstick. It cuts in our inherited system of value like a scalpel, then presses the heaviest, hardest question on us. . . . It establishes [Solzhenitsyn] as one of the classic writers of contemporary European literature."

One of the few critics who finds some fault, at least with the English versions, is Maurice Friedberg, who writes: "Belonging to the humanitarian tradition of great Russian novels, *The First Circle* has most of their strengths and weaknesses. A major historical document, it discusses some of the basic human predicaments, and contributes to our knowledge of Russia, as well as of ourselves. On the other hand, its construction is somewhat loose; the principal characters are occasionally verbose, and some of the discussions are mere intellectual gymnastics. Nevertheless, *The First Circle* is a splendid book.'' Laber, who considers the book ''a more compelling and devastating indictment of Soviet terror than anything else in print,'' adds: ''But [Solzhenitsyn] is not a polemicist. A thoughtful and serious writer, totally immersed in the style and traditions of Tolstoy and Turgenev, he has chosen prison as a setting to reveal man's search for inner freedom and spiritual peace. His prisoner-scientists are the Prince Andreys and Pierres of the 20th century.'' Foote suspects that *The First Circle* ''will be read and reread long after the East-West propaganda war has been forgotten. For its real concern is the brotherhood of prisoners, the small contrivances of men to endure in adversity, not as heroes but as human beings.'' And, Lask concludes: ''In its humanity and knowledge of human suffering, *The First Circle* does not admit to criticism. Anything one could say would be paltry. It is the fate of Russian novels to be political. And *The First Circle* is overwhelmingly so. But it is also a compassionate commentary on the human condition. It is at once classic and contemporary. Reading it, we know that it has been with us for years, just as we know that future generations will read it with wonder and with awe.''

The Cancer Ward was similarly received by the critics, praised for its honesty and its mastery of traditional storytelling, criticized for its loose, episodic structure. The *Times Literary Supplement* reviewer states that the novel is ''overwhelmingly—to the minutest clinical detail—a novel about cancer. Cancer dominates the life of every character—the patients, the patients' relatives, the doctors and nurses. Every character therefore is involved with the threat or presence of death, in impudent contradiction of the wide-eyed, immortal optimism of official Soviet ideology.... Up to a point ... cancer in *Cancer Ward* has a function similar to that of Death in a medieval mystery play. In its own good time it strikes down the brazen optimists and the rotten bullies of Soviet society. But it strikes down the innocent too.... The only consolation for the carefree and innocent who are struck down ... is one which is firmly rooted in Russian literature: that suffering (whether through illness or through injustice) makes a better man of you.'' The same reviewer adds that, ''in some ways, *Cancer Ward* is an example of what socialist realism might have become if it had been allowed to develop naturally from its roots in the nineteenth century, in Tolstoy in particular. In spite of the pervading gloom, a large proportion of its characters are in fact monumentally disinterested exponents of Soviet heroism.'' As *Time* magazine notes, there is the danger here, as in all of Solzhenitsyn's novels, for Americans to view the author ''merely as a champion of democratic values in the Communist world, a courageous attacker of evils peculiar to Stalinism. But he is much more. Stripped of all illusions by years of war, prison, exile, poverty and sickness, the Solzhenitsyn figure uncompromisingly asserts that modern man can arm himself against the fear of death only with life itself. He must do so by reducing life to complete simplicity, seeing it with unblinking honesty but loving and prizing it nevertheless. If Solzhenitsyn is against cruelty, hypocrisy and loss of freedom, he is also against the distracting things that freedom—with its consequent financial inequality—engenders. Snobbery, status seeking, self-importance, the acquisition of consumer goods, materialism—everything, in short, that tends to repress the natural piety of men.... Solzhenitsyn's heroes have spent a lifetime learning the absolute value of simplicity.''

In contrast to the outstanding critical acclaim received by his

novels, two of Solzhenitsyn's plays, published in 1968 and 1969, met with mixed reactions from reviewers. *The Love Girl and the Innocent* ''often suffers from a sentimentality and a lack of restraint that occasionally mar even [Solzhenitsyn's] mature work,'' notes Maurice Friedberg; however, Helen Michnic feels that ''Solzhenitsyn writes of what he himself had endured. He is both martyr and witness to martyrdom. And he has found a way of involving the audience relentlessly in the horror he has known by transforming the theater itself into his prison camp.... [*The Love Girl and the Innocent*] is a stoic's passionate work, harrowing, realistic, and satirical.'' Reviewing *Candle in the Wind*, Daniel Coogan says: ''Unfortunately, the author has chosen the wrong vehicle to convey the moral indignation which fills him. He would have done better to write a novel on this subject. This parable, for parable it is, is not well-suited to the stage.... Solzhenitsyn himself ... does not consider this work to be a good play. The philosophical dialogue about the pros and cons of scientific control of the spirit of man is heavy, static and largely undramatic. Not one flash of humor lightens the intense seriousness of the mood.'' ''The importance of *Candle in the Wind* in Solzhenitsyn's oeuvre,'' H. E. Salisbury feels, ''is that it is one of two plays he is known to have completed—and it is his only work that, ostensibly, does not possess Russia as its locale.... The literalness of the rendition is in keeping with Solzhenitsyn's preference for a precise version even at the cost of smoothness and readability.''

On October 8, 1970, it was announced that Aleksandr Solzhenitsyn had been awarded the Nobel Prize for Literature. Christopher Moody writes: ''Mindful, no doubt, of the pressure brought to bear upon Pasternak to oblige him to reject his Nobel Prize, [Solzhenitsyn] immediately made public his acceptance and said that 'as far as it depends on me, I intend to receive the Prize in person on the traditional day.' Unfortunately for Solzhenitsyn, it did not depend on him. The Soviet press responded to the award with unaccustomed speed.... *Izvestia* printed a statement by the Union of [Soviet] Writers which deplored the award and described it as a politically hostile act.'' As a result of pressure by the Soviet press, and because of his feeling that he would be denied re-entry to his country if he travelled to Sweden to claim the award, Solzhenitsyn wrote a letter to the Nobel Foundation stating that he could not attend the presentation ceremony. Enclosed with this letter was the lecture which the author was to have given in Sweden; the lecture was later published as *Nobel Lecture by Aleksandr Solzhenitsyn* and came to be accepted as a statement of Solzhenitsyn's philosophy. Edward Weeks calls the lecture ''the most eloquent response in the long history of the [Nobel] Prizes.... One must read Solzhenitsyn's lecture to feel the full force of his argument and the fortitude which prompted it.'' Describing the lecture as ''lyrical, prophetic, bitingly satiric,'' J. F. Smith sees it as ''a magnificent and moving statement of the artist's role as the conscience of mankind.'' M. S. Cosgrave believes that Solzhenitsyn ''has written an extraordinarily moving testament to the power of art and literature as a uniting force in the modern world.''

With the publication of *August 1914* in 1971, Solzhenitsyn broke his long-standing tradition of refusing to authorize publication of his banned books outside of the Soviet Union. The reason for this unexpected move, according to Patricia Blake, was that the author was ''unable to stoop to the 'indignity' of observing the Soviet censors' dictate that the G in God be written in lower case, while K.G.B. (the initials of the State Security Committee, the secret police) must be capitalized.'' Moody says that ''Solzhenitsyn wrote that the idea of writing it first came to him in 1936 and that he had never ceased to regard it as the principal literary task of his life. . . . *August 1914* is conceived as only the first part of a multivolume work which [Solzhenitsyn] expects will take him as long as twenty years to complete and the plan of which is already quite clear in his mind.'' Even though *August 1914* deals with a period of Russian history which preceded the 1917 revolution, it is still considered dangerous to the Soviet system of government; an *Economist* reviewer explains: ''The view of history this book expresses runs completely counter to the official marxist view that the revolution was the culmination of a long and inevitable historical process. It could not be construed as anti-Soviet, nor, even, anti-Russian. Solzhenitsyn's love for his country is deep and sincere. But it could be called un-Soviet in its utter disregard for the official version of life and history, its passionate search for the truth and, indeed in its pity for Russia. The book's leitmotif is the sentence: 'I am sorry for Russia.' These, in the eyes of his critics and detractors in Russia, are sins. They are, of course, Solzhenitsyn's greatest strengths as a writer.'' Simon Karlinsky feels that ''thematically and stylistically the book constitutes an entirely new departure for Solzhenitsyn; and it is, if anything, even more remarkable than his other work. . . . The precision of his battle scenes should delight the military history buff. But readers usually given to skipping military passages will also be gripped by the vivid portrayals of the participants and observers of these battles.'' The comparison to Tolstoy is inevitable since *August 1914* and *War and Peace* share a common theme; Blake writes that both writers ''turned to one of fiction's most compelling themes, war, with its incomparable range of grandeur and grief. Tolstoy was mesmerized by the Napoleonic war, Solzhenitsyn by World War I. Solzhenitsyn evidently views the events of August, 1914, as the turning point in modern Russian history that led to the October revolution, civil war, and the consolidation of the Bolshevik regime. Like Tolstoy, Solzhenitsyn has achieved a superb balance in considering the impact of war on the lives of individuals and on the life of the nation.''

The Gulag Archipelago, written between 1958 and 1968, was authorized for publication in 1973. Like *August 1914,* this work is to be divided into many parts, the number of which is, as yet, unknown. Unlike any of Solzhenitsyn's previous works, however, it is not fiction; as the subtitle indicates, the author defines it as ''An Experiment in Literary Investigation.'' According to Christopher Moody, this genre expresses Solzhenitsyn's duty toward those who did not live to tell the story of the labor camps: ''Justice demanded that they be given a memorial. [The author] was determined to provide that memorial. He was determined, too, that the record of the Soviet terror should not be lost, even if all the documents were destroyed. Unable to consult the archives [because he had been banned from Moscow and the official sources of information], he augmented his own recollections with the testimony of 227 survivors whose reports, memoirs, and letters he collected to produce a veritable encyclopaedia of Soviet forced labour and the injustices which condemned millions to endure it. . . . *The Gulag Archipelago* is Solzhenitsyn's personal statement, an act of contrition for himself and his generation. They all submitted weakly to evil or stood idly by. And hundreds of thousands actually participated in it. Solzhenitsyn looks back with shame on his behaviour as an officer and wonders how easily he too might have ended up on the other side. As in *August 1914,* Solzhenitsyn acknowledges collective responsibility. Those

who did not resist are the guilty, including himself.'' G. F. Kennan feels that the work contains some historical inaccuracies which may be inevitable considering its nature. Kennan writes: ''Solzhenitsyn, incomparable in his treatment of the ordinary victims of the system, shows himself curiously helpless when it comes to picturing the senior figures of the regime: they emerge as caricatures, not as real human beings. . . . [But the work] achieves, in its massiveness, its fierce frankness, and its compelling detail, an authority no amount of counterpropaganda will ever be able to shake. . . . [*The Gulag Archipelago* emerges] as the greatest and most powerful single indictment of a political regime ever to be leveled in modern times. . . . It is impossible to believe that this book can have anything less than a major effect on the Soviet regime.'' The value of the work as a strictly historical account is also questioned by S. F. Cohen; he believes that ''as a chronicle of . . . holocaust, [the book] is an extraordinary achievement. As historical explanation, it is less successful. . . . Solzhenitsyn's reconstruction of this secret 'country' within the country is itself a heroic accomplishment under Soviet conditions.''

More important than the historical value of *The Gulag Archipelago,* perhaps even more important than its descriptions of the Soviet labor camps, is Solzhenitsyn's challenge to certain basic beliefs concerning the beginnings of the camps and Lenin's involvement with them. P. S. Prescott writes: ''More important than the recitation of atrocities is the author's carefully buttressed argument that . . . indiscriminate political persecution resulting in show trials and wholesale extermination of regional groups, was not a pathological Stalinist deviation, but a result of Lenin's belief in the necessity of terror, a program that began in 1918 and continues even now. . . . [The] case made by Solzhenitsyn in these pages is nothing short of staggering.'' Robert Conquest agrees that the real significance of the work lies in its condemnation of Lenin, a figure of glory and adoration in the Soviet Union. ''What is there about *Gulag Archipelago* that made it a kind of last straw and that drove the politburo to its reckless and arbitrary arrest and expulsion of its author?'' Conquest asks. ''First of all, Solzhenitsyn does not put the blame solely on Stalin and the 'personality cult.' He traces the long evolution of terror . . . back to early Soviet times. . . . [He] breaks totally with the myth . . . of a constructive and humane Lenin. Solzhenitsyn compounds this 'blasphemy' by a comparison between Soviet standards of terror and those of czardom.''

Even though the conflict between Aleksandr Solzhenitsyn and the Soviet Government can be traced back to 1945, it was not until the 1974 publication of *The Gulag Archipelago* that the authorities decided to take the final step. For many years the Soviet press had mentioned the author only in a negative context, his books could not be published, and the homes of his family and friends were subjected to searches. As this harrassment continued, Solzhenitsyn became more belligerent, refusing to talk to the Soviet press, but granting occasional interviews to Western journalists. Rumors circulated about the existence of a manuscript in which the dissident author offered eyewitness acounts of the labor camps; the manuscript was said to place the blame for the death of millions of people, not on Stalin, but on Lenin. These rumors became widely spread not only in the Soviet Union but also in the West, where publication of the work was eagerly awaited.

In August, 1973, the KGB interrogated Elizaveta Voronianskaia, Solzhenitsyn's typist, and forced her to disclose the location of the hidden manuscript. Voronianskaia hanged herself after revealing this information. Although Solzhenitsyn never intended to publish *The Gulag Archipelago* until after the deaths of several of his informants, he authorized his representatives in Paris to proceed with the publication after he heard the news of Voronianskaia's suicide. On September 6, 1973, Solzhenitsyn released a short statement to Western correspondents detailing these events. After this statement was publicized, a representative of the KGB reportedly proposed a deal to the author; the government would authorize publication of *Cancer Ward* in the Soviet Union if Solzhenitsyn would stop *The Gulag Archipelago* from going to press and postpone publication of the work for at least twenty years. To gain valuable time while the book was actually being printed, he implied that he was interested in the KGB's proposal.

On December 28, 1973, *The Gulag Archipelago* was released by YMCA Press in Paris. The response of the Soviet press was immediate; a campaign began in early January and continued through February in which Solzhenitsyn was accused of being a pathological liar who had fabricated the entire book. He was called anti-Soviet, anti-socialist, and even pro-Nazi. In an interview with Western journalists, Solzhenitsyn encouraged his countrymen to show their support "not by any physical acts, but by rejecting the lie and by refusing to participate personally in the lie." On February 8, 1974, Solzhenitsyn received a summons demanding that he report to the state prosecutor's office; he did not comply. On February 11, 1974, he received a second summons, which he also ignored. On February 12, 1974, he was arrested at the home of his second wife, Natalya Svetlova, and taken to Lefortovo Prison in Moscow. He spent the night under the assumption that he was to be executed the next day. At 1:00 PM, February 13, 1974, he was put on an airplane; only after landing in West Germany did he realize that he had been stripped of his Soviet citizenship and deported. Aleksandr Solzhenitsyn thus became only the second citizen in the history of the Soviet Union to be forcibly exiled abroad (Leon Trotsky was the first).

Solzhenitsyn's first place of sanctuary was the home of his friend, Heinrich Boell, in Frankfurt. Assured by the Soviet Government that his family would be permitted to join him as soon as possible, Solzhenitsyn began to seek a permanent place of residence. According to *Newsweek:* "Sweden's Prime Minister, Olof Palme and Britain's Prime Minister, Edward Heath joined West Germany's Willy Brandt in offering to take the writer in. In Washington, [Secretary of State, Henry] Kissinger said that Solzhenitsyn 'would certainly be welcome to reside in the United States if he desires.'" Despite such offers, the writer chose to go no farther than Switzerland, the home of his friend, lawyer, and representative, Dr. Fritz Heeb. Later in 1974 Solzhenitsyn was joined in Zurich by his wife, their three sons, and his stepson. For two years, the writer travelled around Europe, sightseeing and lecturing in Madrid, Oslo, Paris, and London; he also went to Stockholm to accept the Nobel Prize four years after he had won it. In August, 1976, he moved to the United States, reportedly to avoid harassment by the KGB. Solzhenitsyn is now living in the small town of Cavendish, Vermont.

With the publication of *The Gulag Archipelago*, Parts 3 and 4, in 1975, Solzhenitsyn continued his assault on the Soviet prison system from his exile. Patricia Blake writes: "Here the extended metaphor of the archipelago is joined by an image that informed Solzhenitsyn's novel *The Cancer Ward*. Evoking his experience of cancer, he perceives the camps as a tumor that, in metastasizing, infected the whole nation with its poison. . . . The number and force of the examples Solzhenitsyn offers to illustrate this 'cancer of the soul' are overwhelming. . . . He repeatedly suggests that it would have been impossible to institutionalize police terror if the majority of Soviet citizens had not behaved like 'rabbits.' . . . Some of this may be hyperbolic. Nonetheless, it is once again clear that Solzhenitsyn and Right alone can move tyrants, subvert power, and alter the course of history." Since his eviction from his country, the author has become no less pointed in his criticism of Lenin and, in particular, Stalin, the "Great Evildoer." Reviewing *The Gulag Archipelago*, Parts 3 and 4, Arthur Cooper explains: "Stalin is accused of expanding the system of camps and filling them with innocent citizens in order to force modernization of the country through his Five Year Plans. . . . The precise number of deaths will never be known, but Solzhenitsyn estimates that from the revolution to 1959, a total of 66 million prisoners died. . . . Everyone must acknowledge [Solzhenitsyn's] determination to seek and tell the truth."

Solzhenitsyn told Pavel Licko that the writer's principal task is to be aware of every mistake in the social development of his country: "The writer," he says, "must be all nerves. . . . Good literature arises out of pain. That is why I pin my literary hopes on Eastern Europe." And the pain out of which he himself writes has allowed him to achieve, as Patricia Blake maintains, "what Camus deemed impossible: [his books] compel the human imagination to participate in the agony and murder of millions that have been the distinguishing feature of our age. Such a task could only have been accomplished by literature, performing here what may be, after the historical cataclysm of Stalinism and Nazism, its highest cathartic function."

Solzhenitsyn continues to assert the indomitableness of the human spirit and the responsibility of the writer. He once said: "One can build the Empire State Building, discipline the Prussian army, raise the official hierarchy above the throne of the Almighty, yet fail to overcome the unaccountable spiritual superiority of certain human beings." The task of the writer, he believes, is "to treat universal and eternal themes: the mysteries of the heart and conscience, the collision between life and death, [and] the triumph over spiritual anguish."

One Day in the Life of Ivan Denisovich was filmed in Norway in 1971; Ronald Harwood's screenplay adaptation, under the same title, was directed by Casper Wrede and starred Tom Courtenay in the title role. Most of Solzhenitsyn's books have been published in Russian, English, German, French, and Spanish, and many in Italian, Polish, Portugese, and Japanese. *One Day in the Life of Ivan Denisovich* was also published in Cuba. Aleksandr Solzhenitsyn speaks German fluently, and his English is said to be improving greatly since his move to the United States.

AVOCATIONAL INTERESTS: Photography, bicycling, hiking, gardening.

BIOGRAPHICAL/CRITICAL SOURCES—Periodicals: *Christian Science Monitor*, January 24, 1963; *Nation*, February 2, 1963, March 2, 1974, October 19, 1974; *New Republic*, May 11, 1963, October 19, 1968, March 2, 1974, August 16, 1975; *New York Times*, June 5, 1967, June 11, 1968, June 27, 1968, September 11, 1968, April 12, 1970, June 19, 1971, July 11, 1971, December 24, 1971, January 23, 1977; *Washington Post*, August 15, 1968, September 17, 1968, November 16, 1968, December 16, 1968, October 3, 1971, April 3, 1972, March 24, 1973; *Life*, September 9, 1968; *Saturday Review*, September 14, 1968, November 9, 1968, February

21, 1970, August 23, 1975; *New York Times Book Review,* September 15, 1968, October 27, 1968, September 10, 1972, September 9, 1973, June 16, 1974, October 26, 1975; *Listener,* September 19, 1968; *Times Literary Supplement,* September 19, 1968, July 2, 1971; *Time,* September 27, 1968, November 8, 1968, May 14, 1973, May 28, 1973, September 10, 1973, January 7, 1974, January 14, 1974, January 28, 1974, February 11, 1974, February 18, 1974, February 25, 1974, March 4, 1974, April 22, 1974; *Book World,* October 6, 1968, June 6, 1969; *National Review,* November 19, 1968, January 18, 1974, February 15, 1974, March 1, 1974, March 15, 1974, March 29, 1974, May 10, 1974, August 15, 1975, October 15, 1976; *Variety,* August 20, 1969, December 17, 1969; *Virginia Quarterly Review,* winter, 1969.

New York Review of Books, March 26, 1970, March 21, 1974, June 13, 1974; *Economist,* September 23, 1972, December 1, 1973; *Detroit Free Press,* October 3, 1972, December 26, 1976; *Newsweek,* January 22, 1973, September 3, 1973, January 7, 1974, January 14, 1974, February 25, 1974, March 4, 1974, March 18, 1974, July 1, 1974, July 28, 1975, November 3, 1975, November 10, 1975; *Atlantic,* April, 1973, April, 1974; *Commonweal,* May 23, 1973, August 9, 1974, August 1, 1975; *U.S. News and World Report,* September 10, 1973, January 14, 1974; *America,* September 22, 1973; *Saturday Review/World,* April 20, 1974; *Ramparts,* June, 1974; *Harper's,* July, 1974; *Reader's Digest,* September, 1974, October, 1975, December, 1975; *Yale Review,* October, 1975.

Books: Leopold Labedz, editor, *Solzhenitsyn: A Documentary Record,* Harper, 1971; Abraham Rothberg, *Aleksandr Solzhenitsyn: The Major Novels,* Cornell University Press, 1971; David Burg and George Feifer, *Solzhenitsyn,* Stein & Day, 1973; John B. Dunlop, Richard Haugh, and Alexis Klimoff, editors, *Aleksandr Solzhenitsyn: Critical Essays and Documentary Materials,* Nordland, 1973, revised edition, 1975; Blythe F. Finke, *Aleksandr Solzhenitsyn: Beleaguered Literary Giant of the U.S.S.R.,* Har. Sam. Press, 1973; *Comtemporary Literary Criticism,* Gale, Volume I, 1973, Volume II, 1974, Volume IV, 1975, Volume VII, 1977; Eneberg Kaa, *Aleksandr Solzhenitsyn: A Biography,* Third Press, 1973; Zhores Medvedov, *Ten Years After Ivan Denisovich,* Knopf, 1973; Allen Myers, *Solzhenitsyn in Exile,* Path Press, 1974; Aleksandr I. Solzhenitsyn, *Solzhenitsyn: A Pictorial Autobiography,* Farrar, Straus, 1974; Natalya A. Reshetovskaya, *Sanya: My Life With Aleksandr Solzhenitsyn,* Bobbs-Merrill, 1975; Solzhenitsyn, *The Calf and the Oak,* Association Press, 1975; Vera V. Carpovich, *Solzhenitsyn's Peculiar Vocabulary,* Technical Dictionaries Co., 1976; Stephen Carter, *The Politics of Solzhenitsyn,* Holmes & Meier, 1976; Kathryn B. Feuer, editor, *Solzhenitsyn,* Spectrum, 1976; Christopher Moody, *Solzhenitsyn,* Harper, 1976; Niels C. Nielson, Jr., *Solzhenitsyn's Religion,* Pillar Books, 1976.†

* * *

SOMERVILLE, (Henry) Lee 1915-

PERSONAL: Born June 4, 1915, in Texas; son of Henry Chambers (a teacher) and Rosa Lee (a teacher; maiden name, Hart) Somerville; married Margaret Alsip, December 20, 1940 (divorced, 1960); married Emily Catherine Moore (a teacher), July 10, 1961; children: (first marriage) George, Richard, Mary (Mrs. Edward Bean); (second marriage) Kathleen, Jeanie. *Education:* Sam Houston University, B.A., 1946; Texas A & M University, M.Ed., 1957; further graduate study at University of Oklahoma, 1965-66, and East Texas State University, 1975. *Politics:* Conservative.

Religion: Protestant. *Home:* 3345 Pine Bluff, Paris, Tex. 75460.

CAREER: U.S. Army Air Forces, career officer, 1941-45; principal of high school in Detroit, Tex., 1946-47; Lamar Business College, Paris, Tex., vocational director, 1948-51; U.S. Air Force, career officer, 1951-64, retiring as lieutenant colonel; rancher, forester, and writer. *Member:* Mystery Writers of America, Mensa, American Legion (local commander, 1975-76), Shriners, Scottish Rite (local president, 1975), Masons. *Awards, honors:* Named Red River County Forest Conservationist of the Year, 1975.

WRITINGS: The Charge of the Model T's (historical comedy; novel), Naylor, 1972. Contributor of about ninety articles and stories to magazines, including *Today's Health, Air Force, Columbia* and mystery magazines.

WORK IN PROGRESS: Blood of Bulls, a historical novel, set on the Texas border in 1819; *The Hunting Season,* a contemporary mystery novel, set in Northeast Texas.

SIDELIGHTS: Somerville writes: "I like to get paid for telling stories. As a veteran of two wars, I want to show what it was really like to be in battle. Part of this motivation is rebellion against lies in textbooks and history books; part of it is the desire to make people understand what combat is really like. Even in comedy, such as the novel *Charge of the Model T's,* I get to write about little-known happenings. My current book, *The Blood of the Bulls,* is based on an almost unknown skirmish in 1819—a shooting scrape wherein a U.S. army captain rode to the rescue of Indians and took the Indian side against white settlers."

As an Air Force officer, Somerville taught at Texas A & M University, served as chief of internal information for Air Research and Development Command, as a missile commander and squadron commander abroad. Assignments included Saudi Arabia, Japan, Philippines, and Puerto Rico. Now he owns about five hundred acres in Texas, much of it in pine trees.

* * *

SOPER, Fred L. 1894(?)-1977

1894(?)—February 9, 1977; American author and international public health specialist; spent twenty-two years in Latin America for the Rockefeller Foundation where he developed new techniques for control and eradication of malaria, yellow fever, and other diseases. In 1946 he received the first annual Lasker Awards of the American Public Health Association for research in improving the health and life expectancy of millions. He died in Chevy Chase, Md. Obituaries: *New York Times,* February 11, 1977.

* * *

SOUZA, Raymond D(ale) 1936-

PERSONAL: Born March 11, 1936, in Attleboro, Mass.; son of Joseph B. (a worker in a jewelry factory) and Linda (Pimental) Souza; married Martha Heckmaster (a teacher of Spanish), December 23, 1966; children: Richard, Robert. *Education:* Attended University of Massachusetts, 1954-56; Drury College, B.A. (magna cum laude), 1958; University of Missouri, M.A., 1960, Ph.D., 1964. *Home:* 1732 West 21st Street Ter., Lawrence, Kan. 66044. *Office:* Department of Spanish and Portuguese, University of Kansas, Lawrence, Kan. 66044.

CAREER: High school teacher of Spanish in Salem, Mo., 1958-59; Kent State University, Kent, Ohio, instructor in

Spanish, 1961-62; University of Kansas, Lawrence, assistant professor, 1963-68, associate professor, 1968-73, professor of Spanish, 1973—, chairman of department, 1968-74, director of summer school in Guadalajara, Mexico, 1969-71. *Member:* Instituto Internacional de Literatura Iberoamericana, Modern Language Association of America, American Association of Teachers of Spanish and Portuguese, American Numismatic Association, Kansas Foreign Language Association. *Awards, honors:* Ford Foundation research grants, 1966 and 1968; American Philosophical Society grant, 1968.

WRITINGS: (Contributor) Philip B. Taylor, Jr., editor, *Contemporary Latin America,* Center of International Studies, University of Houston, 1970; *Major Cuban Novelists: Innovation and Tradition,* University of Missouri Press, 1976. Contributor of about twenty-five articles and reviews to language and Spanish studies journals.

WORK IN PROGRESS: Lino Novas Calvo, for Twayne, completion expected in 1978.

SIDELIGHTS: Souza writes: "My research and publications deal with Spanish American literature of the nineteenth and twentieth centuries, and I am particularly interested in prose fiction and poetry. I have never been able to separate teaching from research because I find that a dynamic relationship exists between these two activities. Discoveries and knowledge gained in research inevitably find expression in class, and new ideas uncovered while teaching have resulted in exciting research."

AVOCATIONAL INTERESTS: Numismatics, sailing.

* * *

SPALDING, Jack 1913-

PERSONAL: Born February 7, 1913, in Atlanta, Ga.; son of Hughes (an attorney) and Bolling (Phinizy) Spalding; married Anne Gowen, June 25, 1955; children: Charles, Elizabeth, John, James, Mary Anne. *Education:* Attended Georgetown University, 1933-34; University of Georgia, A.B., 1936. *Politics:* Independent Democrat. *Religion:* Roman Catholic. *Home:* 6905 Riverside Dr. N.W., Atlanta, Ga. 30328. *Office: Atlanta Journal,* Box 4689, Atlanta, Ga. 30302.

CAREER/WRITINGS: United Fruit Co., timekeeper in Puerto Barrios, Guatemala, and in California, 1936-37; *Atlanta Constitution,* Atlanta, Ga., 1938-39; United Press, reporter in Atlanta and New York City, 1940-41; stockbroker in Atlanta, 1946-50; *Atlanta Journal,* Atlanta, reporter, 1951-56, editor, 1956—. *Military service:* U.S. Naval Reserve, 1942-46. *Member:* Georgia Historical Society, Atlanta Press Club, High Museum of Art (president and member of board of sponsors), Atlanta Arts Alliance (vice-chairman of board of trustees), Atlanta Historical Society (first vice-president), Travelers Aid Society of Atlanta (former president), Sigma Delta Chi, Chi Phi, Piedmont Driving Club, Nine O'Clocks Club, American Legion.

* * *

SPEISER, Jean

PERSONAL: Daughter of George (a physician) and Eloise (Perison) Speiser. *Education:* University of Nebraska, A.B. *Home:* 17 East 70th St., New York, N.Y. 10021. *Office:* United Nations Children's Fund, United Nations, New York, N.Y.

CAREER: Worked as editor for *Life* magazine, photographer for U.S. Information Agency and National Park Service, associate producer for National Broadcasting Corp. (NBC), reporter for *Omaha World Herald,* and as picture editor for United Nations Children's Fund. *Member:* Women's National Press Club.

WRITINGS: River in the Dark, John Day, 1958; *UNICEF and the World,* John Day, 1965; *Schools Are Where You Find Them* (juvenile), John Day, 1971. Contributor of articles on children and travel to popular magazines.

* * *

SPENCER, Metta Wells 1931-

PERSONAL: Born August 29, 1931, in Calera, Okla.; daughter of H. C. and Gladys (Turner) Wells; married Robert Spencer (divorced); children: Jonathan. *Education:* University of California, Berkeley, A.B., 1963, M.A., 1966, Ph.D., 1969. *Religion:* Anglican. *Home:* 155 Marlee Ave., Apt. 201, Toronto, Ontario, Canada. *Office:* Erindale College, University of Toronto, Mississauga, Ontario, Canada.

CAREER: College of the Holy Names, Oakland, Calif., lecturer in sociology, 1964-66; Harvard University, Cambridge, Mass., senior research assistant at Center for International Affairs, 1967, research sociologist, 1968-69; Survey Research Center, Berkeley, Calif., research sociologist, 1969-71; University of Toronto, Erindale College, Mississauga, Ontario, assistant professor, 1971-76, associate professor of sociology, 1976—. Assistant professor at University of Massachusetts, Boston, 1968-69; acting assistant professor at California State College, Hayward, 1970; lecturer at Mills College, 1971, and Ontario Institute for Studies in Education, 1972.

WRITINGS: (Contributor) S. M. Lipset, editor, *Student Politics,* Basic Books, 1967; (contributor) Philip G. Altbach, editor, *The Student Revolution,* Lalvani, 1970; (with Robert Wuthnow, Charles Y. Glock, and Jane Piliavin) *Adolescent Prejudice,* Harper, 1975; *The Foundations of Modern Sociology,* Prentice-Hall, 1976. Contributor to sociological journals.

WORK IN PROGRESS: A study of the philosophical assumptions underlying the various "subcultures" of psychotherapy.

* * *

SPERRY, Byrne Hope 1902-
(Byrne Hope Sanders)

PERSONAL: Born May 2, 1902, in Port Elizabeth, South Africa; emigrated to Canada in 1910; daughter of Harry (a lawyer) and Lucy E. (Bing) Sanders; married Frank M. Sperry (an artist), August 17, 1934; children: Dodie (Mrs. W. J. Finlayson), David. *Education:* Attended high school in Norwich, Ontario. *Religion:* Anglican. *Home:* 364 Bessborough Dr., Toronto, Ontario, Canada M4G 3L2.

CAREER: Sentinel-Review, Woodstock, Ontario, women's editor, author of daily column "Splashes from the Ink Pot," and assistant editor of its publication *Rod and Gun in Canada,* 1919-22; T. Eaton & Co. (department store chain), Toronto, Ontario, member of advertising staff, 1923-26; *Business Woman,* Toronto, editor, 1926-29; *Chatelaine,* Toronto, editor, 1929-51; Canadian Institute of Public Opinion (Gallup Poll), Toronto, director, 1951-71; writer, 1971—. Head of consumers' branch of Wartime Prices and Trade Board, 1942-46; member of Dollar-Sterling Trade Board. *Awards, honors:* Commander of Order of the British Empire, 1947.

WRITINGS—All under name Byrne Hope Sanders: *Emily*

Murphy, Crusader (biography of Canada's first woman magistrate), Macmillan (Canada), 1945; (with Margaret Aitken) *Hey Ma: I Did It,* Clarke-Irwin, 1953; *Famous Women: Carr, Hind, Cullen, Murphy,* Clarke-Irwin, 1958. Contributor to magazines for children.

SIDELIGHTS: Byrne Sperry writes: "In developing what I have always felt my natural avocation, that of author, I have been a refugee from a career in newspaper writing and magazine editing, plus administration, and Heaven help me, even statistics.

"Born in South Africa, my forebears were mainly English, Irish, German and Italian. . . . Various calamities forced my lawyer father to leave South Africa with his wife and four children, all born in that beautiful but tragic country; [we] came to Canada in 1910. Three of us children entered journalistic life. In my case, sketches and brief articles appeared in several big week-end newspapers from the time I was twelve."

BIOGRAPHICAL/CRITICAL SOURCES: Carolyn Cox, *Canadian Strength,* Ryerson, 1946.

*   *   *

SPINA, Tony 1914-

PERSONAL: Born September 10, 1914, in Detroit, Mich.; son of Costan (a designer) and Julia (Perry) Spina; married Frances Leto, March 2, 1946; children: Costan II, Julia, Kathryn. *Education:* Detroit Institute of Technology, B.A., 1939. *Religion:* Roman Catholic. *Home:* 3525 Squirrel Rd., Bloomfield Hills, Mich. 48013. *Office: Detroit Free Press,* 321 West Lafayette, Detroit, Mich. 48231.

CAREER: Detroit Free Press, Detroit, Mich., staff photographer, 1946-52, chief photographer, 1952—, author of "Tony Spina's Questions and Answers," 1972—. Author of "Tony Spina: Photography," a column syndicated by Knight Newspapers Wire Service, 1972—. Photojournalism instructor at Wayne State University and Oakland University. *Military service:* U.S. Navy, chief photographer, 1941-46; served in European and Asiatic-Pacific theaters; received three battle stars.

MEMBER: National Press Photographers Association, Michigan Press Photographers Association, Detroit Press Club, Rome Press Club. *Awards, honors:* Nearly five hundred national and international photography awards; named Knight of St. Gregory by Pope Paul VI, 1965; member of Pulitzer Prize team from *Detroit Free Press,* 1968, for coverage of the 1967 riot in Detroit.

WRITINGS: The Making of the Pope (on Pope John XXIII), A. S. Barnes, 1960; *The Pope and the Council,* A. S. Barnes, 1963; *This Was the President: John F. Kennedy,* A. S. Barnes, 1964; *Press Photographer,* A. S. Barnes, 1968.

SIDELIGHTS: Spina was the first newspaperman to interview and photograph Pope John XXIII at the Vatican after his election. In the United States, he has covered presidential inaugurations and conventions since 1952.

*   *   *

SPRINGER, L(ois) Elsinore 1911-

PERSONAL: Born September 15, 1911, in Elgin, Ill.; daughter of Edward Bowen and Catherine (Wightman) Springer. *Education:* University of Colorado, student, 1927; Mt. Holyoke College, B.A., 1931; University of Chicago, graduate study, 1931-32; Wheaton College, Wheaton, Ill.,

M.A., 1939. *Religion:* Presbyterian. *Home address:* Rt. 2, Box 202, Arden, N.C. 28704.

CAREER: High school English teacher in Geneva, Ill., 1936-64; County Audio-Visual Center, Asheville, N.C., library cataloger, 1964-69; writer, 1969—. Director of local community theater, 1933-36. *Member:* National League of American Pen Women, Daughters of the American Revolution, Aurora Historical Society (life member). *Awards, honors:* First prize from Chicago Suburban Poetry Contest, 1940, for "Fog"; second prize from American Garden Guild, 1951, for magazine article on growing exotic lilies; biennial award from National League of American Pen Women, 1974, for *Collectors' Book of Bells;* Copley Newspaper Award, 1976, for bicentennial feature "My Most Memorable Ancestor."

WRITINGS: Primitive Life (juvenile), Row, Peterson, 1941; *Fishing Banks* (juvenile), Row, Peterson, 1942; *Chimes: An Anthology,* Cuneo, 1949; *Collectors' Book of Bells,* Crown, 1972; *That Vanishing Sound,* Crown, 1976. Contributing editor of *Hobbies.*

WORK IN PROGRESS: Research for a third book on bells, tracing world cultures as revealed by their use of bells; historical sketches based on original unpublished diaries and letters from eighteenth-century New England.

SIDELIGHTS: Elsinore Springer writes: "After a rather eclectic lot of writing at intervals over the years, the main thrust of my writing in the 1970's relates to cultural history as reflected through a single man-made object—bells, in all their many variations both functional and decorative. The challenge is to keep such 'meaty' books on the popular level, for they embrace not only historical fact but also folklore, technical information, anecdote, and how-to collect, document, preserve, etc.

"As an illustration, *That Vanishing Sound* looks at American history through the sound of bells from colonial times on, during those days when that sound was common over the land and bell-founding was a major industry, to the present decline and virtual disappearance of such sounds. It touches on great names in the annals of bell-making, on the appeal sounding bells have had for writers and composers, and on the recent revival of interest in bells as performing instruments in the world of music."

AVOCATIONAL INTERESTS: Amateur naturalist and photographer, supporter of Humane Education Movement.

*   *   *

STAFFORD, Kim R(obert) 1949-

PERSONAL: Born October 15, 1949, in Portland, Ore.; son of William E. (a poet and teacher) and Dorothy (a teacher; maiden name, Frantz) Stafford; married Beverly Beech (a librarian), 1970. *Education:* University of Oregon, B.A., 1971, M.A., 1973. *Religion:* Church of the Brethren. *Home:* 9331 Southwest 20th Pl., Portland, Ore. 97219.

CAREER: Oral historian in Florence, Ore., 1975-76; apprentice printer in Port Townsend, Wash., 1976; writer, 1976—. *Member:* Modern Language Association of America, American Folklore Society, Early English Text Society. *Awards, honors:* National Endowment for the Arts creative writing fellowship, 1976.

WRITINGS: (With father, William E. Stafford) *Braided Apart* (poems), Confluence Press, 1976; *A Gypsy's History of the World* (poems), Copper Canyon Press, 1976.

WORK IN PROGRESS: Editing *Echoes of the Wind,* an

anthology of poems written by children; research on medieval literature.

SIDELIGHTS: Stafford writes: "While working in the Idaho Poet in the Schools Program, I read the following poem by a third-grader: 'Swans sing before they die./Should people?' Later, I dreamed about the 'Shakespearean bullet'—a tiny sphere of wood containing a coil of steel that expands after penetrating the heart, causing exhilaration and laughter. Having planted twenty-two fruit trees in my yard, I find myself homesick for the road. I've always had the gypsy-foot, ready to jump into the daylight."

* * *

STANDRING, Gillian 1935-

PERSONAL: Born August 2, 1935, in Kew, Surrey, England; daughter of Ian W. (an engineer) and Beryl (Smith) Standring. *Education:* Attended Girton College, Cambridge, 1953-56, and University of London, 1957-58. *Home:* 113 Fortess Rd., Tufnell Park, London N.W.5, England. *Office:* Zoological Society of London, Regent's Park, London N.W.1, England.

CAREER: Biology teacher in a girls' school in London, England, 1958-63; Children's Museum, Boston, Mass., museum assistant, 1963-66; biology teacher and head of department at girls' school in London, England, 1967-72; London Zoo, London, England, assistant education officer, 1972—. *Member:* Institute of Biology, Association for Science Education, Fauna Preservation Society.

WRITINGS: (With Peter Credland) *The Living Waters,* Aldus-Jupiter, 1975; *Seas and Oceans,* Danbury Press, 1975; *Zoo Quiz Book,* Collins, in press. Contributor to animal and zoo magazines, and *Nursing Times.*

WORK IN PROGRESS: Research for a book on the natural history of hoofed mammals.

* * *

STANLEY, Leo Leonidas 1886-

PERSONAL: Born March 8, 1886, in Buena Vista, Ore.; son of Hartwell (a physician) and Emma (Irish) Stanley; married Romaine Woods, 1912 (died December, 1926); married Bernice Holthouse Campbell, October 15, 1938. *Education:* Stanford University, B.S., 1907; Cooper Medical College, M.D., 1912. *Politics:* Republican. *Home:* Crest Farm, Fairfax, Calif. 94930.

CAREER: California State Prison, San Quentin, Calif., chief surgeon, 1913-41, 1945-51; Marin Municipal Water District, Marin County, Calif., director, 1946-71; relief surgeon on Pacific liners including the Lurline, the Wilson and the Roosevelt, 1964—; *San Miguel Banner,* San Miguel, Calif., columnist. Writer. *Military service:* U.S. Naval Reserves, 1935-51; active duty as surgeon, 1941-45; retired as captain. *Member:* American Medical Association, American College of Surgeons (fellow), Western Association of Railroad Surgeons.

WRITINGS: Men at Their Worst, Doubleday, 1938; *Marin People,* Marin Historical Society, 1970; *My Most Unforgettable Convicts,* Greywood (Canada), 1971; *San Miguel at the Turn of the Century,* Valley Publishing, 1976. Contributor to *San-Rafael Independent-Journal, San Miguel Banner,* and other periodicals.

WORK IN PROGRESS: Dolores Martinez, a history of one of the first women prisoners at San Quentin; *Men at Their Best,* an account of four years of war; *Now Hear This,* stories and anecdotes of the sea.

SIDELIGHTS: All of the proceeds from the sale of *San Miguel at the Turn of the Century* are being donated by Stanley to Friends of Adobe, an organization whose purpose is to restore old buildings and reacquaint the area with its past.

* * *

STAPLES, Reginald Thomas 1911-
(Howard Bridges, James Sinclair, Robert Tyler Stevens)

PERSONAL: Born November 26, 1911, in London, England; son of William George (a naval officer) and Mary Jane (Brady) Staples; married Florence Anne Hume (a company director), June 12, 1937; children: Jeffery Charles. *Education:* Attended secondary school in London, England. *Politics:* "Distrust modern politics. Distrust all politicians even more." *Religion:* Anglican. *Home:* Wenvoe, Peter Ave., Oxted, Surrey, England. *Agent:* Patsy Brougham, King's Reach Tower, London S.E.1, England. *Office:* Vista Sports Ltd., Sydenham Rd., Croydon, Surrey, England.

CAREER: Winemaker's apprentice at Pedro Domecq (winemaking firm), 1928-30; worked in office for Blue Star Shipping Co., 1930-40, 1946-50; assistant editor for Home Publishing Co., 1950-53; Staples & Hancock Ltd., founder, 1953, director, 1953-66; managing director of Town & Country Studios Ltd. (commercial photographers), 1966—. Chairman of board of directors of Fullerton & Lloyd Ltd. (magazine publishers), 1953—, and of Vista Sports Ltd., 1970—. *Military service:* British Army, Royal Artillery, 1940-46; served in the Middle East; became sergeant. *Member:* Brevet Flying Club.

WRITINGS—All historical novels; under pseudonym James Sinclair: *Warrior Queen* (the story of Boadicea), Souvenir Press, in press.

Under pseudonym Robert Tyler Stevens: *The Summer Day Is Done,* Doubleday, 1976; *Flight from Bucharest,* Souvenir Press, 1977; *Appointment in Sarajevo,* Souvenir Press, in press.

WORK IN PROGRESS: The Night Earth Femina Broke Out; Search for the Romanovs, a sequel to *The Summer Day Is Done,* under pseudonym Robert Tyler Stevens; *Canis the Briton,* a sequel to *Warrior Queen,* under pseudonym James Sinclair; *Curtains for Felicity and Co.,* a modern thriller, under pseudonym Howard Bridges.

SIDELIGHTS: Staples told *CA:* "My spare time pleasure—writing. Wrote millions of words of rubbish over a period of many years. Came down from the mountain of garbage five years ago to apply myself more seriously. Still wrote rubbish but it read better. *Woman* magazine had a rush of blood and accepted *The Summer Day Is Done* for serialisation, giving it press and television coverage. Same magazine has just asked to serialise *Appointment in Sarajevo,* story based on the assassination of Franz Ferdinand in 1914.

"Currently working on *The Night Earth Femina Broke Out*—inspired by the magnetic American feminist, Constance Goodheart. The women of the world see the men off, and Constance becomes first President of Earth Femina, the world of women and purism and who mounts whom."

AVOCATIONAL INTERESTS: "Spare time pursuits—squash, tennis, badminton, hockey, soccer, cricket, golf. Gave them all up in turn, except golf, to save myself dropping dead while life was still beautiful."

STAPLETON, Jean 1942-

PERSONAL: Born June 24, 1942, in Albuquerque, N.M.; daughter of James L. and Mary (a teacher and librarian; maiden name, Behrman) Stapleton; married John F. Clegg, April 15, 1965 (died September 15, 1972); married Richard Bright (a marriage and family counselor), January 13, 1973; children: (stepchildren) Lynn, Paul. *Education:* University of New Mexico, B.A., 1964; Northwestern University, M.S., 1968. *Politics:* Democrat. *Religion:* Methodist. *Home:* 3232 Philo St., Los Angeles, Calif. 90064. *Office:* Department of Journalism, East Los Angeles College, 1301 Brooklyn Ave., Monterey Park, Calif. 91754.

CAREER: Elementary school teacher in Carrizozo, N.M., 1964-65; junior high school English teacher in Albuquerque, N.M., 1965-66; *Glenview Announcements,* Glenview, Ill., reporter, 1967-68; *Angeles Mesa News Advertiser,* Los Angeles, Calif., reporter, 1968-69; City News Service/Radio News West Wire Service, Los Angeles, Calif., reporter, 1969-71; press secretary for "Supervisor Dorn Campaign" in Los Angeles, Calif., 1972; East Los Angeles College, Monterey Park, Calif., assistant professor, 1973-76, associate professor of journalism, 1976—, head of department, 1975—.

MEMBER: Women in Communications, National Organization for Women (vice-president of local chapter, 1971-72; president, 1973-74; secretary, 1976-77), National Women's Political Caucus, Society of Professional Journalists, Journalism Association of Community Colleges (southern California vice-president, 1975-76), Journalism Professors Association of Los Angeles (president, 1976-77), Sigma Delta Chi.

WRITINGS: (Contributor) Joyce Slayton Mitchell, editor, *Other Choices for Becoming a Woman,* Dell, 1975; (with husband, Richard Bright) *Equal Marriage,* Abingdon, 1976. Contributor to magazines, including *Eighteen Almanac* and *Christian Home,* and to newspapers.

WORK IN PROGRESS: Book on dating for teenagers, including non-sexist dating, with Richard Bright.

SIDELIGHTS: Stapleton told *CA:* "I have been active in the feminist movement since 1969. Feminism is commonly thought to be incompatible with marriage, raising children, dating, religion, and many other aspects of life, so much of what I write is aimed at dispelling that myth. *Equal Marriage* not only shows that marriage and equality are compatible, but it also tells how to have an equal marriage, both for those just marrying and for those who have been married for some time. Now I am interested in helping teenagers learn that dating does not have to be a stereotyped relationship."

* * *

STARKIE, Walter 1894-1976

August 9, 1894—November 2, 1976; British-born educator and author best known for his delightful tales of gypsy life; four of his seventeen books dealt with his experiences living with the gypsies of Europe. He was a former directorial board member of Ireland's Abbey Theatre, and he taught romance languages at Trinity College for more than twenty years. He died in Madrid, Spain, where he had made his home since 1942. Obituaries: *New York Times,* November 9, 1976; *Current Biography,* February, 1977.

* * *

STAROBIN, Joseph R(obert) 1913-1976

December 19, 1913—November 6, 1976; American editor, educator, and author; former foreign editor and member of the editorial board of the *Daily Worker.* After leaving the Communist Party in 1954, he wrote many articles and books to explain what he believed was wrong with Communist dogma. He died in New York City. Obituaries: *New York Times,* November 8, 1976. (See index for previous *CA* sketch)

* * *

STARR, Frank 1938-

PERSONAL: Born March 16, 1938, in Frankfort, Ind.; son of Robert (a journalist) and Mary (a journalist; maiden name, Shay) Starr; married Hannelore Tauss (an administrative assistant), August 4, 1962. *Education:* Indiana University, A.B. *Home:* 4541 N. 25th Rd., Arlington, Va. 22207. *Office:* 1707 H St., Washington, D.C. 20006.

CAREER/WRITINGS: City News Bureau of Chicago, Chicago, Ill., reporter, 1963; *Chicago Tribune,* Chicago, reporter, 1963-67, Moscow bureau chief, 1967-70, Washington bureau chief, 1971-74, columnist, 1974—. Notable assignments include the development of domestic political dissent in the Soviet Union, 1967-70, Soviet invasion of Czechoslovakia, 1968, and the Soviet Union-China border disputes, 1969. *Military service:* U.S. Army, 1959-63; became first lieutenant.

SIDELIGHTS: Starr told *CA:* "My major interest is in foreign policy, with professional experience in Asia, Middle East, Europe, and the Soviet Union." *Avocational interests:* Sailing, music and theatre.

* * *

STEELMAN, Robert J(ames) 1914-

PERSONAL: Born March 7, 1914, in Columbus, Ohio; son of Charles William and Nell (Blair) Steelman; married Janet Eyler, August 23, 1941; children: Karen (Mrs. Gene Berson), Michael. *Education:* Ohio State University, B.S., 1938. *Politics:* "Unaffiliated." *Religion:* Presbyterian. *Home and office:* 875 Amiford Dr., San Diego, Calif. 92107. *Agent:* Robert P. Mills Ltd., 156 East 52nd St., New York, N.Y. 10022.

CAREER: U.S. Army, Signal Corps, civilian electronics engineer, 1939-46; U.S. Navy, civilian electronics engineer, 1946-69.

WRITINGS: Stages South, Ace Books, 1956; *Apache Wells,* Ballantine, 1959; *Winter of the Sioux,* Ballantine, 1959; *Call of the Arctic* (Arctic adventure novel), Coward, 1960; *Ambush at Three Rivers,* Ballantine, 1964; *Cheyenne Vengeance,* Doubleday, 1974; *Dakota Territory,* Ballantine, 1974; *The Fox Dancer,* Doubleday, 1975; *Sun Boy,* Doubleday, 1975; *Portrait of a Sioux,* Doubleday, 1976; *Lord Apache,* Doubleday, 1977; *The Galvanized Reb,* Doubleday, 1977. Contributor to Western magazines, including *Ranch Romances,* and to men's adventure magazines.

WORK IN PROGRESS: Continuing research on the frontier West.

SIDELIGHTS: Steelman comments: "My writing is largely of the Old West. I try hard to make my books authoritative and true to the times. Perhaps my principal aim is to do what I can to elevate the 'western' to some literary significance, rather than see it condemned to a second-rate genre status."

BIOGRAPHICAL/CRITICAL SOURCES: Roundup, July, 1957.

STEINMAN, Lisa Malinowski 1950-

PERSONAL: Born April 8, 1950, in Willimantic, Conn.; daughter of Zenon S. (a professor) and Shirley (a college administrator; maiden name, Nathanson) Malinowski; married James A. Steinman (a medical technician), April 13, 1968. *Education:* Cornell University, B.A. (with distinction), 1971, M.F.A., 1973, Ph.D., 1976. *Politics:* "Yes." *Home:* 4995 Southeast 30th Ave., Apt. 87, Portland, Ore. 97202. *Office:* Department of English, Reed College, Portland, Ore. 97202.

CAREER: Reed College, Portland, Ore., visiting assistant professor of English, 1976-77. Member of board of directors of Ithaca Poetry Center. Staff member of Connecticut Union for the Revitalization of Education, 1968; resource person for Aspen Institute of Humanistic Studies, 1972. *Member:* Modern Language Association of America, Society for Values in Higher Education, Poets and Writers, Phi Beta Kappa, Phi Kappa Phi. *Awards, honors:* Honorable mention from Academy of American Poets, 1975.

WRITINGS: Lost Poems, Ithaca House, 1976.

Anthologized in *National Poetry Anthology,* edited by Mel McKee, DeKalb College, 1974; *The Anthology,* edited by A. R. Ammons, Society for the Humanities, Cornell University, 1974; *Anthology of New American Poetry,* edited by Mark Lang Horne, American Poetry Press, 1974. Author of "View from the Yurt," column in *Newfield News,* 1974-76. Contributor to literary journals, including *Jeopardy, Alkahest, Tennessee Poetry Journal, Stone, Foxfire, Epoch,* and *Dekalb Literary Journal.* Editor of *Epoch,* 1972-75.

WORK IN PROGRESS: After the Fire, a book of poems; a critical study of Wallace Stevens.

SIDELIGHTS: Lisa Steinman writes: "For seven years, I lived on a small communal farm in upstate New York, which I helped to found. The feeling of community, of family, is important to me, and seems to me to be what is missing from much of American life. For a while, I enjoyed mixing the best of the academic life with the best of the life in rural, upstate New York. Unfortunately, both the academics and the non-academics look with suspicion on each other, making anyone attempting to live in the two worlds a stranger in both."

* * *

STEITZ, Edward S. 1920-

PERSONAL: Born November 7, 1920, in Brooklyn, N.Y.; son of Charles (in insurance) and Magdaline (Esch) Steitz; married June Harrison (a librarian), January 18, 1946; children: Steve, Nancy, Robert. *Education:* Cornell University, B.S., 1943; Springfield College, M.Ed., 1948, D.P.E., 1963. *Home:* 141 Elm St., East Longmeadow, Mass. 01028. *Office:* School of Physical Education, Springfield College, Springfield, Mass. 01109.

CAREER: Springfield College, Springfield, Mass., professor of physical education, 1948—, assistant director of athletics, 1954-56, director of athletics and head varsity basketball coach, 1956—. Charter member of board of trustees and executive committee of Naismith Memorial Basketball Hall of Fame; member of James Lynah Memorial Committee. Former member of executive committee and member of board of directors of U.S. Olympic Committee (also member of executive committee of administration and drug abuse committee and chairman of officials selection committee); member of executive committee of Special Olympics (for the mentally retarded); vice-chairman of U.S.

Olympic Basketball Committee (member of selection committee for Tokyo and Mexico City Olympic Games). Member of U.S. State Department panel of experts on international sports; member of U.S. People-to-People Sports Committee. Member of executive committee of National Basketball Rules Committee of the United States and Canada; member of selection committee of National Invitational Basketball Tournament; member of executive committee of National Summer Youth Sports Program (of the President's Council on Fitness); member of national rules committee for Little League Baseball; U.S. representative to World Congress of the International Federation of Basketball, World Congress of Basketball at the Olympic Games, and International Basketball Federation's basketball rules committee. President of Eastern Intercollegiate Gymnastics League; president of New England Conference on Athletics (also chairman of basketball committee); member of executive council of Eastern College Athletic Conference (also chairman of principles and policies committee); national chairman of Young Men's Christian Association Basketball Championship Committee. Has conducted clinics in Greenland, Iceland, France, Germany, Italy, Guadalupe, Trinidad and Tobago, Japan, Ceylon, India, Pakistan, Thailand, Hong Kong, Uruguay, Brazil, Mexico, Yugoslavia, Colombia, Panama, Bermuda, Greece, the Soviet Union, and Sweden; basketball consultant for ten films. *Military service:* U.S. Army, 1942-46; served in Africa, Italy, and France; received six battle stars.

MEMBER: International Association of Approved Basketball Officials (honorary life member), National Collegiate Athletic Association (member of executive committee; president of College Division Basketball Tournament Committee; chairman of National Volleyball Committee), Basketball Federation of the United States (president), American Association for Health, Physical Education and Recreation (member of executive council of Division of Men's Athletics), National Association of College Athletic Directors of America (member of Basketball Hall of Fame committee), National Basketball Coaches Association (chairman of research committee), Amateur Basketball Association of the United States of America (member of council), Collegiate Basketball Officials Association (honorary life member), Eastern College Athletic Basketball Association (president), New England Basketball Coaches Association, New England Track and Field Association (member of executive committee), New England Football Officials Association (chairman of executive committee), New England Wrestling Association (member of executive committee), Massachusetts Association for Health, Physical Education and Recreation. *Awards, honors:* Metropolitan award from National Basketball Coaches Association; medallion and citation from U.S. State Department; India's National Tournament for Youth and its trophy have been named in his honor; highest award of merit from International Association of Approved Basketball Officials, 1974; Walter Brown Award; elected to Basketball Hall of Fame, 1976.

WRITINGS: Illustrated Basketball Rules, Doubleday, 1976; *The Art of Officiating,* Prentice-Hall, 1977. Also editor of *Athletic Administration in Colleges and Universities,* National Association of Collegiate Directors of Athletics and American Association for Health, Physical Education and Recreation. Contributor of more than two hundred articles to magazines. Co-editor of *Basketball Case Book,* 1967—; editor of *Basketball Rules of the United States and Canada.*

SIDELIGHTS: In 1965, Steitz directed his basketball team

from Springfield College on a world tour for the U.S. State Department.

* * *

STENSBOEL, Ottar 1930-

PERSONAL: Born June 10, 1930, in Norway; son of Otto and Bergljot (Eikebraaten) Stensboel; married Bjoerg Berge, August 7, 1953; children: Hilde, Mette, Bjoern-ove, Trond. *Education:* Attended Norwegian Air Force Academy, 1950, and Air Force Staff College, 1967. *Politics:* Conservative. *Home:* Kvaernstuv 15A, 1482 Nittedal, Norway.

CAREER: Norwegian Air Force, career officer, 1950—, including NATO service; present rank, lieutenant colonel. Consultant on strategic studies to Norwegian Institute for International Affairs. *Member:* Norwegian Aero Club. *Awards, honors:* Norwegian and Scandinavian championships in radio control soaring.

WRITINGS: RC Glidere (title means "Radio Control Gliders"), Norwegian Aero Club, 1967; *Modellflyhaandboken,* Schibstedt, 1972, translation by author published as *Model Flying Handbook,* Sterling, 1976. Author of columns in *Flynytt, RC Modellar,* and *Radio Control Modeller.*

WORK IN PROGRESS: A book on airfoils for radio control sailplanes.

AVOCATIONAL INTERESTS: Sports (running and cross-country skiing), travel.

* * *

STEPHENS, Joyce 1941-

PERSONAL: Born December 24, 1941, in Kansas City, Kan.; daughter of Clarence A. (a post office employee) and Nellie R. (a post office employee; maiden name, Whitworth) Owens; married Robert L. Stephens (an artist), June 8, 1963. *Education:* St. Louis University, B.S., 1963; University of Hawaii, M.A., 1966; Wayne State University, Ph.D., 1973. *Politics:* "Left of Abbie Hoffman." *Religion:* "Never touch it." *Home address:* P.O. Box 401, Shawnee Mission, Kan. 66201.

CAREER: University of Detroit, Detroit, Mich., instructor in sociology, 1971-73; Luther College, Decorah, Iowa, assistant professor of sociology, 1973-74; University of Queensland, Brisbane, Australia, lecturer in sociology, 1974-76; writer, 1976—. Chairperson of 139 Club's Drop-In Centre for Homeless People. *Member:* American Sociological Association, Sociological Association of Australia and New Zealand.

WRITINGS: Loners, Losers, and Lovers, University of Washington Press, 1976. Contributor to sociology journals.

WORK IN PROGRESS: A book on women academics; a book on deviant occupations.

SIDELIGHTS: Joyce Stephens writes: "I've got sixty years to kill, might as well do something interesting." *Avocational interests:* Cats, sex, dangerous drugs, travel ("not necessarily in that order").

* * *

STERN, Frederick M. 1890(?)-1977

1890(?)—May 6, 1977; German-born author, best known for *The Junker Menace,* an expose of the roots of Nazism. He died at his home in New York City. Obituaries: *New York Times,* May 9, 1977.

STERN, Gerald M(ann) 1937-

PERSONAL: Born April 5, 1937, in Chicago, Ill.; son of Lloyd (an author and businessman) and Fan (a business-woman; maiden name, Wener) Stern; married Linda Stone (a child therapist), December 20, 1969; children: Eric, Jesse. *Education:* University of Pennsylvania, B.S., 1958; Harvard University, L.L.B., 1961. *Agent:* Robert Lescher, 155 East 71st St., New York, N.Y. 10021. *Office:* Rogovin, Stern & Huge, 1730 Rhode Island Ave. N.W., Washington, D.C. 20036.

CAREER: United States Department of Justice, Department of Civil Rights, Washington, D.C., attorney, 1961-64; Arnold & Porter (law firm), Washington, D.C., partner, 1964-76; Rogovin, Stern & Huge, Washington, D.C., partner, 1976—. *Member:* American Trial Lawyers Association, American Bar Association.

WRITINGS: (Contributor) Leon Friedman, editor, *Southern Justice,* Panthcon, 1965; *The Buffalo Creek Disaster,* Random House, 1976.

* * *

STERN, Harold P. 1922-1977

May 3, 1922—April 3, 1977; American author, expert on Japanese art, and director of Freer Gallery of Art in Washington, D.C. During World War II, he was assigned to Japanese language study by U.S. Army Intelligence and turned to the study of Far Eastern art history after the war. He died in Washington, D.C. Obituaries: *New York Times,* April 4, 1977; *Washington Post,* April 4, 1977; *AB Bookman's Weekly,* July 25, 1977.

* * *

STERN, Harry Joshua 1897-

PERSONAL: Born April 24, 1897, in Lithuania; immigrated to the United States in 1903; immigrated to Canada, 1927; son of Morris and Hinda (Markson) Stern; married Sylvia Goldstein, July 4, 1937; children: Stephanie Glaymon, Justine Bloomfield. *Education:* Hebrew Union College, B.H.L., 1919, rabbi, 1922; University of Cincinnati, B.A., 1920; University of Chicago, graduate study, 1926. *Home:* 3238 Boulevard, Westmount, Quebec, Canada. *Office:* 4100 Sherbrooke St. W., Westmount, Quebec, Canada.

CAREER: Rabbi of Jewish congregations in Uniontown, Pa., 1922-27; Temple Emanu-El, Montreal, Quebec, rabbi, 1927-72, rabbi emeritus, 1972—. Overseer of Hebrew Union College's Jewish Institute of Religion; secretary of the first World Jewish Congress (Geneva), 1936; first chairman of Canadian Conference of Reform Rabbis; co-founder of Board of Jewish Ministers of Greater Montreal and of Synagogue Council of Greater Montreal; member of Federated Zionist Organization of Canada and Canadian Jewish Congress; member of board of directors of Canadian Foundation for Jewish Culture and of Zionist Revisionists; founder of Institute on Judaism for Christian Clergy and Educators, College of Jewish Studies, Book Lovers' Forum, and Aron Museum.

MEMBER: Canadian Penal Association, Biblical Society of Canada, Royal Empire Society (past vice-president), Central Conference of American Rabbis (honorary life member), Union of American Hebrew Congregations, Jewish Chautauqua Society of America (life member), American Academy of Political and Social Science, B'nai B'rith, Masons, Pi Lambda Phi, Kiwanis International, Canadian Club. *Awards, honors:* King George VI Coronation Medal from Government of Great Britain, 1937; B'nai B'rith humanitarian award, 1967; Legion of Honor from Kiwanis International. Honorary degrees include LL.D. from McGill University, 1938, D.D. from Hebrew Union College's Jewish Institute of Religion, 1947, and Litt.D. from College of Steubenville.

WRITINGS: Judaism in the War of Ideas: A Collection of Addresses, Bloch Publishing, 1937; *The Jewish Spirit Triumphant: A Collection of Addresses,* Bloch Publishing, 1943; *Martyrdom and Miracle: A Collection of Addresses,* Bloch Publishing, 1950; *Entrusted with Spiritual Leadership,* Hebrew Union College, Jewish Institute of Religion, 1958; *One World or No World,* Bloch Publishing, 1973. Also author of *Jew and Christian,* 1927, *My Pilgrimage to Israel,* 1951, *Europe and Israel Revisited,* and *Israel Revisited,* 1970. Author of pamphlets. Contributing editor to *Canadian Jewish Chronicle* and *Canadian Jewish Review.*

*　　*　　*

STEVENS, Carla M(cBride)　1928-

PERSONAL: Born March 26, 1928, in New York, N.Y.; daughter of Charles James (an engineer) and Marie (an opera singer; maiden name, Minon) McBride; married Leonard A. Stevens (a writer), December 18, 1954; children: Timothy, Brooke, Sara, April. *Education:* New York University, B.A., 1946, M.A., 1949. *Residence:* Bridgewater, Conn.

CAREER: Chairman of primary school in New York, N.Y., 1946-55; Addison-Wesley Publishing Co., Inc., New York City, juvenile editor of "Young Scott Books," 1955-69; New School for Social Research, New York City, instructor, 1969—. Member of board of directors of Regional Educational Services Center, 1967-70, and Pratt Education Center, 1969-74.

WRITINGS—All for children: Rabbit and Skunk and the Scary Rock, Scholastic Book Services, 1962; *Catch a Cricket,* Addison-Wesley, 1964; *Rabbit and Skunk and the Big Fight,* Scholastic Book Services, 1966; *The Birth of Sunset's Kittens* (illustrated with photographs by husband, Leonard A. Stevens), Addison-Wesley, 1969; *Your First Pet and How to Take Care of It,* Macmillan, 1974; *Hooray for Pig!,* Seabury, 1975; *How to Make Possum's Honey Bread,* Seabury, 1976; *Stories from a Snowy Meadow,* Seabury, 1976; *Bear's Magic and Other Stories,* Scholastic Book Services, 1976; *Insect Pets,* Greenwillow Books, 1978; *Pigs and Blue Flag,* Seabury, in press. Also author of *Spooks,* 1968.

WORK IN PROGRESS: Walk Down My Garden Path, for children.

AVOCATIONAL INTERESTS: Weaving, botany, early American history (especially the westward movement).

*　　*　　*

STEWARD, Hal D(avid)　1922-

PERSONAL: Born December 2, 1922, in Chatham County, Ga.; son of Owen B. (in the military) and Margaret A. (Martin) Steward; married Dawn J. Bentata, August 18, 1945 (died April 9, 1967); married Marshall Rose Heinz, November, 1967 (divorced, 1969); married Peggy Jo Ann Morgan, November, 1973 (divorced, 1974). *Education:* Boston University, B.S., 1961; La Salle Extension University, LL.B., 1949. *Politics:* Republican. *Home:* 211 West Hanson St., Apt. 7, Centralia, Wash. 98531. *Office: Daily Chronicle,* P.O. Box 580, Centralia, Wash. 98531.

CAREER: Fort Collins Coloradoan, Fort Collins, Colo., sports writer, 1939; U.S. Army, career officer, 1941-61, re-

tiring as lieutenant colonel; *Fairbanks News-Miner,* Fairbanks, Alaska, Washington correspondent, 1947-48; *Los Angeles Examiner,* Los Angeles, Calif., staff reporter, 1961-62; *San Diego Union,* San Diego, Calif., staff reporter, 1962-64; North American Newspaper Alliance, New York, N.Y., national correspondent, 1965-70; Copley News Service, San Diego, foreign correspondent, 1965-66; Gemini News Service, London, England, U.S. correspondent, 1972-74; *Business Opportunities Journal,* San Diego, editor and co-publisher, 1973-74; *Milliyet,* Istanbul, Turkey, U.S. correspondent, 1974-75; *Daily Chronicle,* Centralia-Chehalis, Wash., associate editor, 1975, executive editor, 1976—, author of column (also appearing in nearby suburban weekly newspapers), 1975—. Author of "Secrets of Success," a column syndicated by Trans-World News Service, 1975—. Part-time instructor at Centralia College; instructor at University of California, San Diego; professor of English and chairman of Division of Humanities at Rust College, 1968; lecturer at colleges and universities. Special executive assistant to lieutenant-governor of California; assistant director of California Department of Human Resources Development.

MEMBER: Authors Guild of Authors League of America, American Society of Newspaper Editors, National Conference of Editorial Writers, Army and Navy Club, National Pilots Association, Aircraft Owners and Pilots Association, Association of Retired Intelligence Officers, Canadian Owners and Pilots Association, San Diego Press Club, Sacramento Press Club, Signia Delta Chi. *Awards, honors:* Copley Journalism Award from *San Diego Union,* 1963, for outstanding initiative and originality in reporting.

WRITINGS: Thunderbolt, Armored Cavalry Journal Press, 1949; *The Spy and the Pirate Queen* (novel), Publishers Export, 1967; *Assassin's Hideaway* (novel), Publishers Export, 1967; (contributor) *The Creative Writer,* Writer's Digest, 1969; (contributor) *Writer's Handbook,* The Writer, 1969; *The Successful Writer's Guide,* Parker Publications, 1970; *Money-Making Secrets of the Millionaires,* Parker Publications, 1972.

Contributor of several hundred articles to magazines.

AVOCATIONAL INTERESTS: International travel (more than sixty countries), flying (licensed commercial pilot).

BIOGRAPHICAL/CRITICAL SOURCES: (Centralia) *Daily Chronicle,* August 7, 1975; *WDS Forum,* autumn, 1975.

*　　*　　*

STEWART, Harold C.　1891(?)-1976

1891(?)—December 21, 1976; American educator and writer in the field of child care and public health; internationally known for his twenty-five year study of the growth and development of 134 individuals from birth to maturity. He taught at Harvard University for thirty-seven years. While spending eighteen months in a German prison camp during World War II, he persuaded the Germans to allow him to serve as physician to his fellow prisoners. He died in Brookline, Mass. Obituaries: *New York Times,* December 24, 1976.

*　　*　　*

STEWART, Harold Frederick　1916-

PERSONAL: Born December 14, 1916, in Sydney, Australia. *Education:* Attended University of Sydney. *Home:* Hotel Shirakuse, Higashisenouchichi 29, Kitashirakawa, Sakyo-ku, Kyoto, Japan 606.

CAREER: Lecturer for Victorian Council of Adult Education, Victoria, Australia, during the 1940's; broadcaster for Australian Broadcasting Commission in Australia, during the 1950's. Poet, essayist and translator. *Military service:* Australian Army, 1942-46. *Member:* Australian Society of Authors. *Awards, honors:* Awarded *Sydney Morning Herald* prize for poetry.

WRITINGS: (With James McAuley) *The Darkening Ecliptic,* Reed & Harris (Melbourne), 1944, published as *Poems,* Lansdowne Press, 1961; *Phoenix Wings* (poems), Angus & Robertson, 1948; *Orpheus and Other Poems,* Angus & Robertson, 1956; *A Net of Fireflies* (haiku translations and essay), Tuttle, 1960; *A Chime of Windbells* (haiku translations and essay), Tuttle, 1969.

WORK IN PROGRESS: New Phoenix Wings (collected poems); a collection of twelve long poems, twelve essays and twelve color woodblock prints, tentatively entitled *By the Old Walls of Kyoto;* a translation of the medieval Japanese Buddhist text *Tannisho,* in collaboration with a Shin Buddhist scholar-priest.

* * *

STIMMEL, Barry 1939-

PERSONAL: Born October 8, 1939, in Brooklyn, N.Y.; son of Abraham and Mabel (Bovit) Stimmel; married Barbara Barovick (an analyst); children: Alexander. *Education:* Brooklyn College (now of the City University of New York), B.S., 1960; State University of New York Downstate Medical Center, M.D., 1964. *Residence:* New York, N.Y. *Office:* Mt. Sinai School of Medicine, City University of New York, 100th St. and 5th Ave., New York, N.Y. 10029.

CAREER: Internist, 1969—; cardiologist, 1970—. Mt. Sinai School of Medicine of City University of New York, associate dean of admissions and academic and student affairs, 1971—, associate professor of medicine, 1975—. Executive director of Methadone Maintenance and Aftercare Treatment Program (MMATP), 1975—. Member of advisory committee of National Center for Urban Problems at City University of New York, 1970-71, and of New York State Office of Drug Abuse Services, 1976—; member of scientific advisory board of National Council on Drug Abuse, 1976—; member of committee on planning, priorities, and evaluations of New York Metropolitan Regional Medical Program, 1971-73. *Military service:* U.S. Navy, physician, 1965-67; became lieutenant senior grade.

MEMBER: American Heart Association, National Association for the Prevention of Addiction to Narcotics, American Association for Higher Education, Society for the Study of Addiction to Alcohol, American Society of Internal Medicine, American Association of University Professors, American College of Cardiology, American Board of Internal Medicine, National Board of Medical Examiners, American Association of Physician Assistants (member of advisory board, 1972-73), New York Heart Association.

WRITINGS: Heroin Dependency: Medical, Social, and Economic Aspects, Stratton Intercontinental Medical Book Corp., 1975.

Contributor: E. Donoso, editor, *Drugs in Cardiology,* Stratton Intercontinental Medical Book Corp., 1975; S. Rahimtolla, editor, *Infective Endocarditis,* Grune, in press; A. Schecter and S. Mule, editors, *Rehabilitation and Treatment Aspects of Drug Dependence,* CRC Press, in press. Contributor of about forty-five articles to professional journals. Member of editorial board of *American Journal of Drug and Alcohol Abuse.*

WORK IN PROGRESS: Research on medical education, drug dependency, and cardiology.

SIDELIGHTS: Stimmel writes: "Dissemination of knowledge to all interested in learning has been a prime motivating factor in my writing. All too often one's thoughts developed from completely erroneous concepts become prejudices which are extremely difficult to overcome. My book on heroin dependency attempts to objectively assess the various aspects of heroin addiction from a social and psychological as well as medical standpoint to provide any interested reader with the opportunity to learn more about this disabling illness."

* * *

STITT, Milan 1941-

PERSONAL: Born February 9, 1941, in Detroit, Mich.; son of Howard (a truant officer) and Audrien (Prindle) Stitt; married Lenore Richars, 1962 (marriage dissolved, 1965). *Education:* University of Michigan, B.A., 1963; Yale University, M.F.A., 1966. *Agent:* Helen Merrill, 337 West 22nd St., New York, N.Y. 10011.

CAREER: Detroit Free Press, Detroit, Mich., drama critic, 1961-63; American Shakespeare Festival, Stratford, Conn., assistant press representative, 1965; Long Warf Theatre, New Haven, Conn., projects director, 1965-66; American Shakespeare Festival, special projects director, 1967-68; American Place Theatre, New York, N.Y., development coordinator, 1968-70; New York Public Library, New York City, public relations representative, 1971-72, associate chief of public relations, 1972—; Triad Playwrights Co., New York City, executive director, 1974—; actor, playwright, and producer. Host and moderator of WNYC-TV talk show, "Between the Lions," 1973-74. *Member:* Dramatists Guild, Authors League of America, P.E.N. *Awards, honors:* Avery Hopwood Playwriting Award, 1961, for "Towers of Achievement," and 1963, for "The First R" and "Take a Little Chance".

WRITINGS—All plays: "Towers of Achievement" (one-act), first produced in Ann Arbor, Mich., 1961; "The First R" (one-act), first produced in Wallingford, Conn., at Moran Junior High School, 1963; "Take a Little Chance," first produced in Ann Arbor, 1963; (with Victor Miller) "In the Pursuit," first produced in New Haven, Conn., at Hofbrau Haus, 1967; "Edie's Home," first produced in New York City at Stage One, August, 1974; *The Runner Stumbles* (first produced in New York City at Manhattan Theatre Club, December, 1974; revised version first produced in Stamford, Conn., at Hartman Theatre, December 30, 1975, and on Broadway at Little Theatre, May 18, 1976), James T. White, 1976.

Play anthologized in *Best Plays of 1975-76,* edited by Otis L. Guernsey, Jr., Dodd, 1976.

WORK IN PROGRESS: "I, Hitler," a play.

SIDELIGHTS: Stitt's well-received play "The Runner Stumbles" was twelve years in the making.

* * *

STIVENS, Dal(las George) 1911-

PERSONAL: Born December 31, 1911, in Blayney, Australia; son of Francis and Jane (Abbott) Stivens; married Mary Burke, 1939 (died 1941); married Winifred Wright,

September 22, 1945; children: Katrin, Christopher. *Home:* 5 Middle Harbor Rd., Lindfield, New South Wales, Australia. 2070.

CAREER: Served in Australian Department of Information, 1944-50; Australia House, London, England, press officer, 1949-50; Australian Society of Authors, Sydney, foundation president, 1963-64, vice president, 1964 and 1966, president, 1967-73; writer and painter. Commonwealth Literature Fund lecturer at University of Adelaide, 1963. Chairman of literary committee of Captain Cook Bicentenary Celebrations, 1969-70; member of New South Wales advisory committee of Australian Broadcasting Commission, 1970-73. One-man show of paintings held in Sydney, 1974. *Military service:* Australian Army, 1943-44; served in Education Service. *Awards, honors:* Commonwealth Literary Fund fellowship, 1951, 1962, 1970; Miles Franklin Award for best Australian novel, 1970, for *A Horse of Air.*

WRITINGS—Novels: *Jimmy Brockett,* Britannicus Liber, 1951; *The Wide Arch,* Angus & Robertson, 1958; *Three Persons Make a Tiger,* Cheshire, 1968; *A Horse of Air,* Angus & Robertson, 1970.

Short stories: *The Tramp and Other Stories,* macmillan, 1936; *The Courtship of Uncle Henry,* Reed & Harris, 1946; *The Gambling Ghost and Other Stories,* Angus & Robertson, 1953; *Ironbark Bill,* Angus & Robertson, 1955; *The Scholarly Mouse and Other Tales,* Angus & Robertson, 1957; *Selected Stories, 1936-1968,* Angus & Robertson, 1970; *The Unicorn and Other Tales,* Wild & Woolley, 1976.

Other: (With Barbara Jeffries) *A Guide to Book Contracts,* Australian Society of Authors, 1957; (editor) *Coast to Coast: Australian Stories, 1957-58,* Angus & Robertson, 1959; *The Incredible Egg* (natural history), Weybright & Talley, 1974.

Contributor to natural history periodicals, including *Wildlife, Pacific Discovery, Animal Kingdom,* and *Natural History.*

WORK IN PROGRESS: Book of drawings with text; a novel, short stories, paintings, and drawings.

SIDELIGHTS: Asked if he would describe himself as a regional writer, Stivens told *CA:* "Not really. Some works are regional in that the setting is Australian. But much of my writing—particularly the fables—have no regional setting. In the past prominent Australian writers called me cosmopolitan." *Avocational interests:* Theater, natural history, travel, art, music.

*   *   *

STIVERS, Robert L(loyd)   1940-

PERSONAL: Born April 25, 1940, in Cincinnati, Ohio; son of Lloyd Edward (a salesman) and Margaret (Schiele) Stivers; married Sylvia Knott (a nurse), January 11, 1964; children: Laura, Mark. *Education:* Yale University, A.B., 1962; Union Theological Seminary, New York, N.Y., M.Div., 1969; Columbia University, M.Phil., 1971, Ph.D., 1973. *Religion:* Presbyterian. *Home:* 9524 47th St. W., Tacoma, Wash. 98466. *Office:* Department of Religion, Pacific Lutheran University, Tacoma, Wash. 98447.

CAREER: Columbia University, New York, N.Y., instructor in contemporary civilization, 1972-73; Union Theological Seminary, New York, N.Y., administrative officer and teaching assistant in Christian ethics, 1972-73; Pacific Lutheran University, Tacoma, Wash., instructor in theology, Christian ethics, and sociology of religion, 1974—. Ordained clergyman in United Presbyterian Church, 1974.

Military service: U.S. Navy, weapons officer, 1962-66; served in Vietnam; became lieutenant. *Member:* American Academy of Religion, American Society of Christian Ethics.

WRITINGS: The Sustainable Society, Westminster, 1976.

WORK IN PROGRESS: Outlines for "a sustainable ethic."

SIDELIGHTS: Stivers writes: "Underlying my work is the perspective of Christian Realism. This perspective was worked out by the American theologian Reinhold Niebuhr. My main effort is to relate the insights of Christianity to current social problems using Christian Realism as a basic perspective. I believe that currently we suffer socially from a lack of any current vision of the future. I hope that my work in conjunction with work of others will help to overcome this lack."

*   *   *

STOKELY, James R(orex), Jr.   1913-1977

October 8, 1913—June 20, 1977; American poet, author, and conservationist; author, often with his wife Bonnie Wilma Dykeman, of books and articles primarily about the South. He died in Newport, Tenn. Obituaries: *New York Times,* June 22, 1977; *Washington Post,* June 23, 1977. (See index for previous *CA* sketch)

*   *   *

STOKES, Carl B(urton)   1927-

PERSONAL: Born June 21, 1927, in Cleveland, Ohio; son of Charles (a laborer) and Louise (Wiggins) Stokes; married Shirley Edwards, January 30, 1958 (divorced, 1973); children: Carl, Cordi, Cordell. *Education:* University of Minnesota, B.S., 1954; Cleveland Marshall School of Law, J.D., 1957. *Religion:* Protestant. *Home:* 1175 York Ave., New York, N.Y. 10021. *Office:* NBC TV News, 30 Rockefeller Plaza, New York, N.Y. 10021.

CAREER: Cleveland Municipal Court, Cleveland, Ohio, probation officer, 1954-58; City of Cleveland, assistant prosecutor, 1958-62; Democratic representative to Ohio State Legislature, 1962-67; Mayor of Cleveland, 1967-71; WNBC-TV, New York, N.Y., commentator, 1972—. Admitted to Ohio bar, 1957, and New York state bar, 1974; partner in firm of Stokes & Stokes, 1962-67; member of executive committee, National League of Cities, 1968-71, president-elect, 1970-71; member of advisory board, U.S. Conference of Mayors, 1968-71; member of steering committee, National Urban Coalition, 1968—; member of advisory committee, Urban America, 1969-71; member of policy committee, National Democratic Committee, 1969-71; honorary chairman, 21st Congressional District caucus, 1970-72. *Military service:* U.S. Army, 1945-46. *Member:* National Association for the Advancement of Colored People (NAACP), Elk, Gamma Eta Gamma, Kappa Alpha Psi. *Awards, honors:* Community of Philadelphia fellow, 1968; Chubb Fellow at Yale University, 1969; Massachusetts Commonwealth Protestants, Catholics and Jews Award, 1969; Equal Opportunity Award, 1970, from National Urban League; Horatio Alger Award, 1970; Pacesetter Award, 1971, from Young People Division of Jewish Community of Federation of Chicago; Outstanding Achievement Award, 1971, from University of Minnesota Law School; ten honorary degrees from universities and colleges in United States, including Tufts University, University of Cincinnati, St. Francis College, Boston University, and Oberlin College.

WRITINGS: The Quality of the Environment, University

of Oregon Press, 1968; *Promises of Power*, Simon & Schuster, 1973. Contributor to *Heights, Highlights, Playboy, Tuesday, Washington Law Review*, and other periodicals.

WORK IN PROGRESS: A story of a black man who won election as President of the United States.

SIDELIGHTS: Stokes told *CA:* "I've relied heavily on my political and government experiments to bring analysis and insight to the reporting of urban affairs. Much of my reporting involves current stories on office holders and their failure to perform in the public interest. My commentaries on urban problems try to define solutions and exhort action."

CA asked Stokes if he intends to return to politics. He responded: "I have found being a journalist gives me all the satisfactions I enjoyed as a professional politician plus the freedom to comment without narrow, partisan restrictions. This makes it highly unlikely that I'd ever return to elective politics. Many of the same needs are served in being a news commentator that are enjoyed by an influential politician: ability to affect changes, ego and status."

* * *

STOKES, Geoffrey 1940-

PERSONAL: Born May 3, 1940, in Newton, Mass.; son of William J. (in advertising) and Ruth (a librarian; maiden name, Corkery) Stokes; married wife, Judith, September, 1961 (divorced, 1967); children: Liam, Timothy. *Education:* Fairfield University, A.B., 1961; Ohio University, M.A., 1963; New York University, M.P.A., 1972. *Politics:* "Left." *Religion:* None. *Home:* 317 East 10th St., New York, N.Y. 10009. *Agent:* Helen Brann Agency, 14 Sutton Pl. S., New York, N.Y. 10022. *Office: Village Voice*, 80 University Pl., New York, N.Y. 10003.

CAREER: Fordham University, Bronx, N.Y., instructor in English, 1965-66; employed by the City of New York, eventually as assistant administrator, 1966-73; now a staff writer for *Village Voice*, New York City. Assistant professor at State University of New York at Stony Brook, 1971-72. *Awards, honors:* Deems Taylor Award from American Society of Composers, Authors and Publishers, 1976, for *Star-Making Machinery;* media award from New York State Bar Association, 1976, for outstanding legal journalism.

WRITINGS: Star-Making Machinery, Bobbs-Merrill, 1976. Contributor to popular magazines, including *Harper's, Ms., Oui*, and *New York Times Magazine*.

* * *

STOKESBURY, Leon 1945-

PERSONAL: Born December 5, 1945, in Oklahoma City, Okla.; son of Leon B. and Jennie (Smith) Stokesbury. *Education:* Lamar University, B.A., 1968; University of Arkansas, M.A., 1972, M.F.A., 1972, further graduate study, 1972—. *Office:* Department of English, University of Arkansas, Fayetteville, Ark. 72701.

CAREER: Lamar University, Beaumont, Tex., instructor in English, 1972-75. *Awards, honors:* First prize in *Southern Poetry Review*'s Collegiate Poetry Contest, 1971, for "To Laura Phelan."

WRITINGS: Often in Different Landscapes (poems), University of Texas Press, 1976.

Work anthologized in *Best Poems of 1971: Borestone Mountain Poetry Awards, 1972*, edited by Lionel Stevenson, Pacific Books, 1972.

WORK IN PROGRESS: Poor Driving in Uganda, poems.

SIDELIGHTS: "Mostly I just hang around and go to the movies a lot," Stokesbury told *CA*. "I really like the movies. I eat a lot and drink a lot. I went to Austin, Texas once. It was closed."

* * *

STONBERG, Selma F(ranks)

PERSONAL: Born in Lawrence, Mass.; daughter of Samuel (a merchant) and Frances (Fishman) Franks; married Abraham Stonberg, August 13, 1935; children: Jane Rakatansky, Barbara (Mrs. Robert W. Morrison), Margery (Mrs. Alberto Berti). *Education:* Attended Radcliffe College, 1933-34; Smith College, A.B., 1935; graduate study at Boston University, 1951-52. *Home:* 280 Boylston St., Chestnut Hill, Mass. 02167. *Office:* Park Pl., Newtonville, Mass. 02160.

CAREER: Newton Junior College, Newtonville, Mass., associate professor of English, 1956—. Research assistant at Harvard University, 1963-68; visiting professor at Honolulu Community College, 1967. *Member:* College English Association (national director, 1968-69), National Council of Teachers of English (member of executive committee, 1966-67; director, 1969-72), College Conference on Composition and Communication (member of executive committee of New England region, 1966-67), Association of English Teachers in Two-Year Colleges (executive secretary, 1964-67), American Association of University Professors, American Association of Junior Colleges, Association of New England Public Junior Colleges.

WRITINGS: From Start to Finish, Houghton, 1970. Editor of newsletter of Association of New England Public Junior Colleges, 1962-63; editor for Association of English Teachers in Two-Year Colleges, 1964-67.

* * *

STONE, Marvin Lawrence 1924-

PERSONAL: Born February 26, 1924, in Burlington Vt.; son of Samuel and Anita (Abrams) Stone; married Sydell Magelaner, November 20, 1949; children: Jamie, Stacey, Torren. *Education:* Marshall College, B.A., 1947; Columbia University, M.S., 1949; Marshall University, Litt.D., 1968. *Home:* 6368 Waterway Dr., Lake Barcroft, Falls Church, Va. 22044. *Office:* 2300 N St. N.W., Washington, D.C. 20037.

CAREER: Herald-Dispatch, Huntington, W.Va., assignment reporter, 1941-43, 1946-48; International News Service, New York, N.Y., European correspondent, 1949-52, Far Eastern director, 1952-58; *U.S. News and World Report*, Washington, D.C., associate editor, 1960-66, general editor, 1966-68, associate executive editor, 1969-70, senior associate executive editor, 1971-72, executive editor, 1973-76, editor-in-chief, 1976—. Sloan Foundation fellow in science, Columbia University, 1958-59. *Military service:* U.S. Navy Reserve, 1943-46; became lieutenant, junior grade. *Member:* Overseas Writers, White House Correspondents Association, American Academy of Political and Social Scientists, Overseas Press Club, Correspondents of Japan (president, 1956-57), International of Washington, Sigma Delta·Chi. *Awards, honors:* Pulitzer traveling fellow, 1950; Columbia Journalism 50th Anniversary Honor Award, 1963; Marshall University Distinguished Alumnus Award, 1973.

WRITINGS: Man in Space, Doubleday, 1960.

STOVER, Allan C. 1938-

PERSONAL: Born June 28, 1938, in Cleveland, Ohio; son of Paul James (a railway clerk) and Blanche (Scramlin) Stover; married Elizabeth Bagaporo, September 6, 1971; children: Grace, Natalie. *Education:* Pacific State University, B.S.E.E. (with highest honors), 1962; Florida Institute of Technology, graduate study, 1964; Vanderbilt University, further graduate study, 1974—. *Residence:* South America. *Office:* Westinghouse Electric, MS 7600-FAV, P.O. Box 1624, Baltimore, Md.

CAREER: Westinghouse Electric, Baltimore, Md., senior engineer, 1975—. Registered professional engineer in California; licensed able seaman (unlimited). *Military service:* U.S. Coast Guard, 1953-56.

MEMBER: Precision Instruments Association (senior member), Instrument of America (senior member), Institute of Electrical and Electronic Engineers, Precision Measurements Association of the Philippines (founder and first president). *Awards, honors:* Outstanding science book of the year award from National Science Teachers Association and Children's Book Council, 1974, for *You and the Metric System.*

WRITINGS: You and the Metric System (juvenile), Dodd, 1974. Contributor to technical journals.

WORK IN PROGRESS: A book on disasters; a science book on computers.

SIDELIGHTS: Stover writes: "I began to write late in life, at the age of thirty-two. . . . I write at night and on the weekends. I enjoy writing more than I would a hobby. I enjoy taking a complex subject and breaking it down so the casual reader will understand it. I want to write more books that people understand and enjoy.

"I helped the Philippine Government in their changeover to the metric system. This gave me the idea to write a book on the subject, since it was obvious the United States would soon change to metric. I also knew that many books on the subject would be difficult for the student and casual reader alike to understand. I wanted my book to be one that would be easy to understand . . . but still contain everything everyone should know about the metric system. I have visited many countries where metric units were used, so I had a feel for the system. I lived for nine years in the Philippines, almost two years in South America, and was assigned for two years to islands in the Pacific. I have visited Mexico, Okinawa, Taiwan, Japan, West and East Germany, Hong Kong, Nicaragua, Belize, Panama, Colombia, Ecuador, Zaire, South Africa, Antigua, Bahamas, Trinidad, Cuba, Jamaica, Haiti, Puerto Rico, Virgin Islands, Netherlands Antilles. . . ."

*   *   *

STRAIN, Lucille Brewton

PERSONAL: Born in Pamplico, S.C.; daughter of William O. (a clergyman and school principal) and Jurheutha (a teacher; maiden name, Gibbs) Brewton; married Winston M. Strain, November 20, 1957; children: Rada Ruth Higgins. *Education:* Benedict College, B.A., 1943; Ohio State University, M.Ed., 1952, Ph.D., 1965. *Politics:* Independent. *Religion:* Presbyterian. *Home:* 4701 Willard Ave., Apt. 1514, Chevy Chase, Md. 20015. *Office:* Department of Graduate Studies, Bowie State College, Bowie, Md. 20715.

CAREER: Sacramento State University, Sacramento, Calif., assistant professor of education, 1965-67; University of Miami, Coral Gables, Fla., associate professor of educa-

tion, 1967-69; Kent State University, Kent, Ohio, associate professor of education, 1970-72; American University, Washington, D.C., associate professor of education, 1972-74; Howard University, Washington, D.C., professor of education and director of elementary education, 1974-75; Bowie State College, Bowie, Md., professor of education, 1975—. *Member:* International Reading Association, National Council of Teachers of English, Association for Supervision and Curriculum Development, Phi Delta Kappa.

WRITINGS: Accountability in Reading Instruction, C. E. Merrill, 1976.

WORK IN PROGRESS: Basics in Reading for All Learners; co-authoring *School-Community Relations.*

SIDELIGHTS: Strain writes: "In no other area of the curriculum is the demand for accountability so compelling and so relevant as in reading. As is widely recognized, an individual's ability to read is essential for progress in all academic endeavors and for success in living in a democratic society. At both undergraduate and graduate levels of education, preparation of teachers for service in the schools should provide for priority attention to their competencies for changing learners' behaviors to those behaviors required for effective reading. Teachers of reading should be assisted in developing a perspective that includes seeing reading achievement in its relationship to all aspects of living. A vital part of this perspective is that effective reading instruction requires more of the teacher than mere knowledge of skills and concepts in the content of reading. Teachers' attitudes toward, and interests in, reading should be positive in nature for these affect attitudes and interests of learners. Teachers who are effective in reading instruction must be skilled, also, in applying techniques of need assessment of learners, determining appropriate objectives of instruction, individualizing instruction, and evaluating instruction and its results. All of these procedures must be performed in such a way that the best of humanistic education is a constant and continuous goal."

*   *   *

STRAUSS, Hans 1898(?)-1977

1898(?)—May 6, 1977; German-born neurologist, electroencephalography expert, and author of books in his field. He died in New York City. Obituaries: *New York Times,* May 10, 1977.

*   *   *

STRODE, Hudson 1892-1976

October 31, 1892—September 22, 1976; American author and educator; author of travel books and articles (most notably on Scandinavia), and a three volume biography of Jefferson Davis. His fiction writing classes at the University of Alabama were known for fostering writers. He died in Tuscaloosa, Ala. Obituaries: *New York Times,* September 23, 1976; *Washington Post,* September 24, 1976. (See index for previous *CA* sketch)

*   *   *

STROUT, Richard L(ee) 1898-
(T.R.B.)

PERSONAL: Born March 14, 1898, in Cohoes, N.Y.; son of George Morris (a teacher) and Mary Susan (Lang) Strout; married Edith R. Mayne, January 15, 1924 (died, January, 1932); married Ernestine Wilke, September 4, 1939; children: Alan Mayne, Phyllis Mayne Strout Morris, Nancy

Ewing, Elizabeth Wilke Strout Zimmermann, Mary Newman Strout Rubeiz. *Education:* Harvard University, A.B., 1919, M.A., 1923. *Home:* 4517 Garfield St. N.W., Washington, D.C. 20007. *Office: Christian Science Monitor,* 910 16th St. N.W., Washington, D.C. 20006.

CAREER: Sheffield Independent, Sheffield, England, staff member, 1919; *Boston Post,* Boston, Mass., reporter, 1921; *Christian Science Monitor,* Boston, reporter, 1921-25, reporter with Washington Bureau, 1925—. Most recent assignments in the areas of politics and economics have included political conventions; also worked as war correspondent during World War II (covered "D-Day" landing in Normandy). *Military service:* U.S. Army, Infantry, during World War I; became second lieutenant.

MEMBER: National Press Club, Overseas Writers Club, Cosmos Club, Sigma Delta Chi (fellow). *Awards, honors:* George Polk Memorial Award for National Reporting from Long Island University, 1958; Fourth Estate Award from National Press Club, 1975.

WRITINGS: (With E. B. White) *Farewell to the Model T,* Putnam, 1936; (editor) *Isabella Maud Rittenhouse, Maud,* Macmillan, 1939. Author of a column in *New Republic,* under pseudonym T.R.B., 1943—. Contributor to magazines, including *Harper's* and *New York Times Magazine,* and newspapers.

*   *   *

STUART, Forbes 1924-

PERSONAL: Born August 14, 1924, in Cape Town, South Africa; son of Charles Edward (a businessman and electrical engineer) and Beatrice (Darvall) Stuart; married, 1953 (divorced, 1971); children: Lara. *Education:* University of Cape Town, B.A., 1947. *Politics:* Socialist. *Religion:* Agnostic ("baptised Weslyan Methodist"). *Home and office:* Lynwood, Lyndale, London N.W.2, England. *Agent:* Bolt & Watson, 8 Storey's Gate, Westminster, London S.W.1, England.

CAREER: Writer of documentary and educational films in Pretoria, South Africa, 1948-51; language teacher and telephonist in London, Paris, and Cologne, 1951-54; Shell South Africa Pty. Ltd., film producer and promoter, 1955-62; Smith, Kline & French, Welwyn Garden City, England, public relations executive and editor of journals, 1962-65; E. S. & A. Robinson Ltd. (packaging firm), London, England, public relations executive and editor of journals, 1965-69; free-lance writer in London, 1970—. Guide, lecturer, and director of summer tours in England, 1971—. Occasional college lecturer. *Military service:* South African Air Force, 1943-46. *Member:* Guild of Guide Lecturers. *Awards, honors:* Runner-up award for best older children's nonfiction book from *Times Educational Supplement,* 1972, for *A Medley of Folk Songs; The Magic Horns* named one of the children's books of the year by National Book League (England), 1974.

WRITINGS: South African Towns Tell Tales, Afrikaanse Pers Beperk (Johannesburg), 1954; *Horned Animals Only,* Thomas Nelson Educational (Edinburgh), 1966; *The Boy on the Ox's Back,* Hamish Hamilton, 1971; *A Medley of Folk Songs,* Kestrel Books, 1971; *Stories of Britain in Song,* Kestrel Books, 1972; *The Magic Bridle,* Muller, 1974, published as *The Witch's Bridle and Other Occult Tales,* Dutton, 1975; *The Magic Horns,* Abelard-Schuman, 1974, Addison-Wesley, 1976; *The Dancer of Burton Fair,* Abelard-Schuman, 1977. Also author of the as yet unpublished manuscripts, *A Week in London* (guide book), *King of the Wild*

Cats (book of African tales), *The Mermaid's Revenge* (book of British tales), and *Great Gulp* (a short novel for children). Writer of about 150 radio plays for South African Broadcasting Corp., 1947-62.

WORK IN PROGRESS: My Friend Turpin, a novel for twelve-year-olds; *Wild Edric, 1066,* a short novel for children.

SIDELIGHTS: Forbes Stuart told *CA:* "I have been writing all my life—journalism, documentary films, public relations handouts, and dramatized radio features. But I didn't begin to write seriously until I was 36 years old. I finally quit public relations at the age of 46, and borrowed some money on my insurance policy to buy one year of writing. I knew that my gift, which is a very small one, had somehow survived the ravages of the public relations market place and was viable, if I applied energy to it.

"Within three months, two books had been commissioned and another was accepted for publication. I was conscious now of how public relations differed from reality, and this has become something of an obsession with me. I write specifically for young people, and I want them to find out what really happened in the past, to take my books and say, 'Well, that's different from what they told us at school. I'll go to the library and do some research and see what really happened.'"

During the past seven years, Stuart has done a great deal of research at the British Museum reading room. "I worked first on African folklore (which I had started before I left South Africa in 1962, because I could no longer shoulder the responsibility of what was being done there in my name as a white voter), went into British history for my folksong books, and kept being referred to books on British folklore. This was to become a very exciting and fruitful field for me."

Although his folktale and folksong collections are suitable for young people and adults, Stuart now proposes to move into the adult market with books that will "take the public relations out of English history. Here is a world where, for example, the Tudors turned Richard III, the last of the Plantagenets, into a hunchback so effectively that to millions of people today—five hundred years afterward—he is still a hunchback, although one of his shoulders was a trifle lower than the other. Nothing can be done about the future until one understands the present and the past, and that is one of my motivations in writing."

Stuart told *CA* his great ambition is to write a novel about his marriage and how it broke up. "This will not be a bitter tragedy, but a picaresque comedy, broad as a folksong, hilarious, but with the undertones of drama and tragedy. Again, there is a didactic side to this work. Perhaps it will prevent others from making my mistake, which was to turn a flesh-and-blood woman into my own romantic projection.

"But I believe I began writing stories and novels for children and young people after being inspired by all the tales I read to my daughter Lara every night of her young life. The late Alison Uttley's *Magic in My Pocket* made a profound impression on me at that time; I am now re-reading it in paperback for my own pleasure.

"Because my books haven't started making enough money to keep body and soul together," Stuart says, "I spend my summers as a tour director and guide-lecturer, taking visitors—particularly Americans—on extended tours of the British Isles, during which I relate history, sing folksongs (Bernard Shaw said that the way to hell is paved with amateur musicians), and read tales from my British folklore collections. I teach and I learn, which makes it lively.

"I have come to love the cathedrals that I take visitors to, and I find joy in art galleries and great paintings. Not only joy, but knowledge. Cezanne, for example, has taught me how to write my marriage-break-up novel. Close to one of his paintings, all you see is squares. Step back, and they jell into a scene. That is what my book will have to do. The reader will put the squares together and find out himself what it's all about."

Forbes Stuart concludes: "I have enough material to keep me writing until I die. And I hope to live for a long time yet. I should mention at the end of this self-indulgent autobiography that I owe a great debt to my father, a Scotsman who recited thousands of lines of Robert Burns to me, by heart, and much of Robert Service, and Shakespeare, and told me stories of his own making as well. He also tried to tell history truthfully. When he died at 71, the magazines on his bedside table were *New Statesman, Economist,* and *Saturday Review of Literature.*"

AVOCATIONAL INTERESTS: Reading poetry aloud, and listening to music (classical, folk, popular, and jazz).

* * *

STURGES, Patricia P(atterson) 1930-

PERSONAL: Born May 4, 1930, in Glendale, Calif.; daughter of Myrl Alonzo (a banker) and Adelya (a secretary; maiden name, Hajny) Patterson; married Franklin W. Sturges (a professor of science), June 15, 1952; children: Sheryl Dee, Karen Meryl. *Education:* Santa Monica City College, A.A., 1950; San Jose State College, B.A. (with great distinction), 1952; Temple University, M.S.Ed., 1969; also attended Cornell University, Southern Oregon College, and Oregon State University. *Residence:* Shepherdstown, W.Va. 25443.

CAREER: Elementary school teacher in Corvallis, Ore., 1952-57; substitute teacher in Abingdon, Pa., 1969-71; elementary school teacher in Harper's Ferry, W.Va., 1972-76, head teacher, 1975-76; Shepherdstown Elementary School, Shepherdstown, W.Va., teacher, 1976—. *Member:* National Education Association, Audubon Society, Wilderness Society, West Virginia Education Association, Zero Population Growth.

WRITINGS: The Endless Chain of Nature: Experiment at Hubbard Brook (juvenile), Westminster, 1976. Contributor to *Living Wilderness* and *Nature and Science,* Teacher's Edition.

WORK IN PROGRESS: Research on population; women's changing roles, goals, and activities; community interrelationships in nature; the environment; pollution; energy; education.

SIDELIGHTS: Patricia Sturges writes: "My family has traveled widely in the United States including Alaska. We have camped in many places and backpacked as a family. As we travel I ask questions and my husband, an ecologist, is quick to point out the ecological interrelationships that make travel so interesting for him. I would like to capture these enriching views of the landscape to share with others.

"I feel that it is important that all nations and individuals face environmental problems and seek solutions. I feel it is more humane to limit our world populations by self control and self determination than to limit our numbers by famine, starvation, and wars caused by nations seeking economic resources and space for their burgeoning populations.

"Through *The Endless Chain* I sought to share my observations of researchers and some environmental problems. At the same time I tried to picture for future ecologists what their professions may entail."

* * *

STURTEVANT, Peter M(ann), Jr. 1943-

PERSONAL: Born February 27, 1943, in Northampton, Mass.; son of Peter (a minister) and Katherine (Hobson) Sturtevant; married Anne Fitzpatrick (a psychologist), July 12, 1969; children: Amanda. *Education:* Wilmington College, B.A., 1965; University of Iowa, M.A., 1967. *Religion:* Episcopal. *Home:* 90 Riverside Dr., New York, N.Y. 10024. *Office:* CBS News, 524 West 57th St., New York, N.Y. 10019.

CAREER/WRITINGS: Columbia Broadcasting System (CBS) News, New York, N.Y., editor and producer, Washington bureau, 1967-70, Saigon bureau chief, 1971-72, Northeast bureau chief, 1973, national editor, 1973—. Notable assignments include the Vietnam War, anti-war demonstrations in Washington, D.C., the Robert Kennedy and Martin Luther King assassinations, the first lunar landing, 1971 Indo-Pakistan War, and the 1976 Bicentennial Day. *Member:* Sigma Delta Chi.

SIDELIGHTS: CA asked Sturtevant his opinion of the reinvestigations of the King and Kennedy assassinations. "My personal opinion," he responded, "is that the House committee investigations may be useful in that it now seems likely that they will shed some new light on the motives of the accused and convicted, and may indicate there were others involved in the plotting. Any investigation which seeks to illuminate the shadows of past events is useful if carried out thoughtfully and honestly. The citizens of this country have every right to know more about events which have shaped our recent history, as well as to understand current events."

Sturtevant has travelled in over thirty-six countries, and speaks French and Vietnamese.

* * *

SUCHOFF, Benjamin 1918-

PERSONAL: Born January 19, 1918, in New York, N.Y.; son of Aaron (a manufacturer) and Sadie (Leishin) Suchoff; married Eleanor Rosen; children: Michael Alan, Susan Carol, Deborah Ann. *Education:* Cornell University, B.S., 1940; New York University, M.A., 1949, Ed.D., 1956. *Home:* 2 Tulip St., Cedarhurst, N.Y. 11516. *Office:* New York Bartok Archive, P.O. Box 717, Lynbrook, N.Y. 11563.

CAREER: Hewlett-Woodmere Public Schools, Hewlett, N.Y., district director of music, 1950—. Curator of New York Bartok Archive, 1953-67, director, 1968—, trustee of estate of Bela Bartok, 1968—. Adjunct professor at Center for Contemporary Arts and Letters, at State University of New York at Stony Brook, 1973—. *Military service:* U.S. Army, 1941-45.

MEMBER: International Folk Music Council, International Musicological Society, American Society of Composers, Authors and Publishers, American Musicological Society, Society for Ethnomusicology, College Music Society, Association for Computing Machinery, National Education Association, Music Educators National Conference, New York State School Music Association, New York State Council of Administrators of Music Education, Nassau

Music Educators Association, Composer's Laboratory of New York (fellow, 1940). *Awards, honors:* New York University Founders Day Award, 1957; American Council of Learned Societies grant, 1966.

WRITINGS: (Editor) *Bartok: Rumanian Folk Music,* five volumes, Nijhoff, 1967-75; *Guide to Bartok's Mikrokosmos,* Boosey & Hawkes, 1970; *Electronic Music Techniques,* Multivox Corp., 1975; (editor) *Bartok: Turkish Folk Music from Asia Minor,* Princeton University Press, 1976; (editor) *Bela Bartok Essays,* St. Martin's, 1976.

Composer of more than 200 musical works and arrangements for chorus, piano, band, and instrumental ensemble.

WORK IN PROGRESS: Editing *Bartok: Yugoslav Folk Music,* three volumes, for State University of New York Press; writing an electronic music curriculum satellite for use with basic classroom music texts.

SIDELIGHTS: Suchoff writes: "My interests in music include composition, the literary aspect, pedagogy, and the scientific area, as well as performing (piano). I count myself fortunate, indeed, to have the opportunity to serve as a pioneer in the area of computerized music research and that of electronic music curriculum development in music education."

* * *

SUMMERS, Anthony (Bruce) 1942-

PERSONAL: Born December 21, 1942, in Bournemouth, England; son of Frederick Ernest (a hotelier) and Enid Elizabeth (a hotelier; maiden name, Shaw) Summers. *Education:* New College, Oxford, B.A. (honors), 1964. *Residence:* County Waterford, Republic of Ireland. *Agent:* Deborah Rogers Agency, 29 Goodge St., London W.1, England.

CAREER: Swiss Broadcasting Corp., Berne, Switzerland, newsreader and writer, 1964; British Broadcasting Corp., London, England, researcher and senior producer of "Panorama," and "24-Hours"; writer, 1974—. *Member:* National Union of Journalists, Association of Broadcasting Staff, Association of Cinema Technicians.

WRITINGS: (With Tom Mangold) *The File on the Tsar: The Fate of the Romanovs ... Dramatic New Evidence,* Harper, 1976. Producer of documentary presentations on foreign affairs and politics for British Broadcasting Corp.

WORK IN PROGRESS: A book on espionage.

SIDELIGHTS: Summers writes: "I am now retained by the BBC for only a part of the year. The main part of my time will now be taken up with not only writing but working a small farm in Ireland, which I am reclaiming from wilderness." His journalistic work has taken him all over the world.

* * *

SUMMERS, Robert S(amuel) 1933-

PERSONAL: Born September 19, 1933, in Halfway, Ore.; son of Orson (a farmer) and Estella (a farmer; maiden name, Robertson) Summers; married Dorothy Kopp, 1955; children: Brent, William, Thomas, Elizabeth Anne, Robert. *Education:* University of Oregon, B.S., 1955; Harvard University, LL.B., 1959; further graduate study at Oxford University, 1964-65, 1974-75. *Office:* School of Law, Cornell University, Ithaca, N.Y. 14850.

CAREER: King, Miller, Anderson, Nash & Yerke, Portland, Ore., associate, 1959-60; University of Oregon, Eugene, assistant professor of law, 1960-63; Stanford University, Stanford, Calif., visiting associate professor of law, 1963-64; University of Oregon, associate professor, 1964-68, professor of law, 1968-69; Cornell University, Ithaca, N.Y., professor of law, 1969-76, McRoberts Professor of Law, 1976. Visiting professor (summers) at Indiana University, 1969, University of Michigan, 1974, University of Warwick, 1975, and University of Miami, Coral Gables, Fla., 1976. Member of board of visitors at University of Oregon; member of the Bar in Oregon and the State of New York.

MEMBER: International Association of Philosophers of Law, American Society for Political and Legal Philosophy, Association of American Law Schools, Phi Beta Kappa. *Awards, honors:* Fulbright fellowship, University of Southampton, 1954-55; Social Science Research Council fellowship, Oxford University, 1964-65.

WRITINGS: (Contributor) Dennis Lloyd, editor, *Introduction to Jurisprudence,* Praeger, 1959, 3rd edition, 1972; (with Charles Howard) *Law, Its Nature, Functions, and Limits,* Prentice-Hall, 1965, 2nd edition, 1972; (editor and author of introduction) *Essays in Legal Philosophy,* University of California Press, 1968; (contributor) Graham Hughes, editor, *Law, Reason and Justice,* New York University Press, 1969; (with Richard Speidel and James White) *Teaching Materials on Commercial Transactions,* West Publishing, 1969; (with Speidel and White) *Teaching Materials on Commercial and Consumer Law,* West Publishing, 1969, 2nd edition, 1974.

(Editor and author of introduction) *More Essays in Legal Philosophy,* University of California Press, 1971; (with White) *The Uniform Commercial Code,* West Publishing, 1972; (with Gail Hubbard and A. Bruce Campbell) *Justice and Order Through Law* (high school text), Ginn, 1973; (with Campbell and John Bozzone) *The American Legal System* (junior high school text), Ginn, 1973; (contributor) Joseph Raz and Peter Hacker, editors, *Festschrift for H.L.A. Hart,* Oxford University Press, 1977. Contributor of about thirty-five articles and reviews to law and philosophy journals. Editor of *Cornell Law Forum.*

WORK IN PROGRESS: Teaching materials on jurisprudence and the legal process; a study of two kinds of reasoning in the common law.

* * *

SUMNER, Richard (William) 1949-

PERSONAL: Born May 20, 1949, in Leamington Spa, England; son of Samuel Tomlinson (a chief ambulance officer) and Ethel Miriam (a teacher) Sumner. *Education:* University of Kent at Canterbury, B.A. (honors), 1970; University of London, certificate in education, 1971, M.A., 1974. *Politics:* "Royalist with Jacobite leanings." *Religion:* Christian. *Home:* Cerdic House, 17 Tower Rd. W., St. Leonards-on-Sea, Sussex, England. *Agent:* John Cushman Associates, 25 West 43rd St., New York, N.Y. 10017.

CAREER: Wandsworth Technical College, London, England, lecturer in history, 1971-73; writer, 1973—. *Member:* Society of Authors, Royal Stuart Society and Royalist League.

WRITINGS: Mistress of the Streets (historical novel), Milton House Books, 1974; *Mistress of the Boards* (historical novel), Random House, 1976.

WORK IN PROGRESS: Royal Throne of Kings, a historical biography, publication expected in 1978; *Mistress of the King,* a historical novel.

SIDELIGHTS: Sumner comments: "It is my aim to produce historical novels which really succeed in evoking the atmosphere of times past and to combine readable dialogue and description with dependable historical accuracy and academic research. It is also my aim both now and in the future to centre my books around the history and reigns of the Royal House of Stuart in which I have an especial interest."

AVOCATIONAL INTERESTS: French cooking, riding, early Renaissance art, antique furniture, heraldry, Scottish folk music.

* * *

SUMWALT, Martha Murray 1924-

PERSONAL: Born September 8, 1924, in Cameron, S.C.; daughter of Ben M. (a farmer) and Edna (Jennings) Keller; married Robert Sumwalt (an international business consultant), September 5, 1948. *Education:* University of South Carolina, A.B., 1944; University of Miami, Coral Gables, Fla., M.A., 1967. *Home address:* Orangeburg, S.C. 29115.

CAREER: Burdine's Department Store, Miami, Fla., magazine editor and photographer, 1955-58; *Miamian* (magazine), Miami, Fla., magazine editor and photographer, 1958-61; writer. *Member:* American Association of University Women, Industrial Editors of South Florida, South Florida Historical Society, Friends of the Library (Miami).

WRITINGS: Colombia in Pictures, Sterling, 1968; *Ecuador in Pictures,* Sterling, 1969, revised edition, 1971; *Surinam in Pictures,* Sterling, 1971. Contributor to *Encyclopedia Americana.*

SIDELIGHTS: Martha Sumwalt has spent prolonged periods of time in South America, Europe, the Middle East, the Orient, and Africa, and writes that she is particularly intrigued by the similarities between artifacts found in South America and the Middle East.

* * *

SUPRANER, Robyn 1930-
(Erica Frost, Elizabeth Warren)

PERSONAL: Surname is pronounced Soo-*pray*-ner; born September 14, 1930, in New York, N.Y.; daughter of Mortimer (an insurance broker) and Dorothy (Kalmanowitz) Rubenstein; married Leon Supraner (a photographer), December 16, 1950; children: Keith, Scott, Dennis, Lauren. *Education:* Attended Pratt Institute and Parson's School of Design, 1944-48, and Adelphi University, 1948-51. *Politics:* "Feminist." *Residence:* Roslyn Harbor, N.Y. *Agent:* McIntosh & Otis, Inc., 475 Fifth Ave., New York, N.Y. 10017.

CAREER: Free-lance song writer, 1962-72 (songs have been recorded by popular recording artists, including Chubby Checker, Mel Torme, and Johnny Winter); writer, 1970—. Taught creative dramatics at Roslyn Creative Arts Workshop, 1973-74.

WRITINGS—For children: Draw Me a Circle, Simon & Schuster, 1970; *Draw Me a Square,* Simon & Schuster, 1970; *Draw Me a Triangle,* Simon & Schuster, 1970; *Would You Rather Be a Tiger?,* Houghton, 1973; *Think About It, You Might Learn Something,* Houghton, 1973; *It's Not Fair!* (Junior Literary Guild selection), Warne, 1976; *Giggly, Wiggly, Snickety-Snick,* Parents' Magazine Press, 1977.

Author of twelve single-concept learning books for Columbia Broadcasting System (CBS), published by Shelley Graphics, 1971; author of other learning books published by Shelley Graphics, 1972, and of a sixteen-volume dictionary for children and other learning books, published by Educational Reading Service, 1972—; also author of books with cassette tapes, under pseudonyms Erica Frost and Elizabeth Warren, for Educational Reading Service, 1975.

WORK IN PROGRESS: A series of eleven mystery books for beginning readers, and another sixteen-volume dictionary, all for Educational Reading Service.

SIDELIGHTS: Robyn Supraner writes: "Since I was little, I have tried to understand my life by writing things down. Many of my books spring from the bewilderments of my childhood. I was a bewildered child, and now, as a parent, I am a bewildered adult.

"I was almost six when my sister was born. I had wanted a brother. When, in spite of my injunctions, my sister was born, I wept for my lost place and my parents' cruel disregard. It wasn't fair. Some thirty odd years later, still smarting, I started and completed *It's Not Fair!*

"Now, I live on a wooded hillside in Roslyn Harbor. My house is large and rambling and slowly emptying itself of children who are growing up."

AVOCATIONAL INTERESTS: Indoor gardening, nature in general.

* * *

SURGE, Frank 1931-

PERSONAL: Born September 27, 1931, in Buhl, Minn.; son of Paul (an iron miner) and Florence Surge. *Education:* University of Minnesota, M.A., 1954. *Home:* 947 Pleasant St., #4-A, Oak Park, Ill. 60302.

CAREER: Glenbard East High School, Lombard, Ill., English teacher, 1970—.

WRITINGS—For children: Western Outlaws, Lerner, 1968; *Western Lawmen,* Lerner, 1968; *Famous Spies,* Lerner, 1969; *Singers of the Blues,* Lerner, 1969.

* * *

SVIRSKY, Grigori 1921-

PERSONAL: Born September 29, 1921, in Ufa, U.S.S.R.; immigrated to Israel, 1972; son of Cezar Rozenbert (a fitter) and Goda Svirsky (a bookkeeper); married Polina Zabejenskaia (a chemist), January 25, 1949; children: Efim. *Education:* Attended Moscow Law School, 1939; State University of Moscow, M.A., 1951. *Politics:* Democrat. *Address:* 27 Thorncliffe Park Dr., Apt. 404, Toronto, Ontario M4H 1J2, Canada; and Etzel St. 12/27, French Hill, Jerusalem, Israel.

CAREER: Author of novels, short stories, and film scenarios in Russia, 1947-64; work removed from publication, 1964, because of outspoken criticism of Soviet censorship; expelled from Communist party, 1968; editorial assistant for Russian journal *Novyi mir,* 1956-70; received grant from Union of Soviet Writers to gather materials for never-published novel about Russian artic, 1970; immigrated to Israel, 1972. Lecturer at higher education institutions in Soviet Union and occasional teacher of creative writing at State University of Moscow, 1948-56; visiting professor of modern Russian literature, University of Toronto, 1975. *Military service:* Soviet Air Force, 1938-46; received nine decorations. *Member:* Authors League of America, Authors Guild, P.E.N. Club.

WRITINGS—Fiction: Zapoved' druzhby (novel; title means "The Command of Friendship"), Voengis (Moscow), 1947; *Zdravstvuy, universitet!,* Volume I (novel; title means "Greetings, University!"), [Moscow], 1952; *Leninsky prospekt* (novel; title means "Lenin Prospect"), [Moscow], 1962, 2nd edition, 1964; *Polyarnaya tragediya* (collection of short stories; title means "The Polar Tragedy"), Possev-Verlag (Frankfort, West Germany), 1976. Also author of as yet unpublished novel, *Gosudarstvennyi ekzamen*, 1964, and of two novels, *Tikhiye mesta*, 1967, and *Zdravstvui, universitet!*, Volume II' 1968, both printed in the U.S.S.R. and destroyed.

Nonfiction: *Zslozhniki* (autobiography), YMCA Press (Paris, France), 1974, translation by Gordon Clough published as *Hostages: The Personal Testimony of a Soviet Jew*, Knopf, 1976. Also author of critical study, *Zhanr, Stil e Kompositsia "Dela Artamonovikh" M. Gorkogo*, forbidden publication in U.S.S.R., 1952.

Filmscripts: "Tichiye mesta" (title means "The Quiet Place"), produced in Moscow, 1966; "Korol pamira" (adapted from author's short story; title means "King of the Pamirs"), Moscow, 1967; "Evrei nalevo" (title means "Jews To the Left!"), Jerusalem, 1972.

Contributor of short stories, essays, critical articles, and sociological studies to journals.

WORK IN PROGRESS: Literature of Spiritual Resistance, 1946-1976, a book on contemporary Russian literature.

SIDELIGHTS: Svirsky forfeited his position as a successful Russian novelist because of his public statements "attacking the role of censorship in Soviet literature and the 'Great-Russian' nationalist chauvinism of such figures as Vasilii Smirnov, chief editor of *Druzhba norodov*." These speeches and statements led to his expulsion from the Party and to a ban on the publication of his writings. With the loss of his income from royalty fees, he took a job offered by his friends on the journal *Novyi mir*. In 1970 he was offered a chance to "reinstate himself." The Union of Soviet Writers, through the influence of his friends, gave Svirsky a grant to write an "optimistic and 'life-asserting' novel" of the Russian far north. He told *CA:* "However, the novel was not, and could not be, written."

In the north Svirsky found that "the setting and background hardly correspond to the official picture of the Soviet north as a flourishing region, tamed and civilized by human effort despite its remoteness and arctic climate." Svirsky told *CA* he saw "a land whose terrain and population were permanently scarred by the marks and memories of the Stalinist labor camps." He found "former prisoners still continue to settle scores with former camp guards, state law still contrives to make criminals of the innocent, protest is suppressed, and there is a general sense of misrule by authority and grievance and demoralization among the ordinary citizens." He returned to Moscow, and unable to write the book he decided to emigrate to Israel.

A reviewer for the *Economist* said of his book *Hostages:* "It is at once the *Bildungsroman* of a young couple painfully learning what it means to be Jewish in the Soviet Union, a history of anti-semitism in the Russian empire, a cry of agony and a tale of defiance. . . . This story movingly illustrates how persecution makes nationalists and why would-be emigrants to Israel increased from a trickle to a flood. It is sometimes asked: 'Why make so much fuss about Soviet persecution of the Jews, when so many others are oppressed in that "prison of nations"?' This book gives the answer."

When asked about the difficulty of getting his manuscripts published in the original Russian, Svirsky replied: "I

thought I was going to write all my life in Russian. I knew contemporary colloquial Russian; its nuances and its dialects as well as its professional jargon. I believe I will never know English as well as Russian."

* * *

SWAIM, Lawrence 1942-

PERSONAL: Born March 19, 1942, in Kinsley, Kan.; son of Roland Quinn (a teacher) and Eugenia Francis (a music teacher; maiden name, Nipps) Swaim; married Linn Wreszin (an employment counselor), February 6, 1962; children: Abigail Ann, Matthew Edward. *Education:* Attended junior colleges. *Politics:* "Democratic Socialist." *Religion:* "Liberal Christian." *Home:* 1224 DeHaro St., San Francisco, Calif. 94107.

CAREER: U.S. Postal Service, vice-president of United Federation of Postal Clerks, Local 2, 1966-74; writer, 1974—. Active in union politics. Member of Democratic Socialist Organizing Committee. *Member:* Authors Guild.

WRITINGS: Waiting for the Earthquake (novel), Little, Brown, 1977. Author of "Labor Scene," a column in *Forecast*, 1966-74. Contributor of articles and poems to magazines, including *North American Review, Nation*, and *In These Times*.

WORK IN PROGRESS: Another novel; a long essay on the future of America; a short history of the Swaim family in America.

SIDELIGHTS: Swaim writes: "I ran away from home when fourteen. I am self-educated essentially, which I consider a definite asset.

"I am deeply interested in value systems, what causes them and what happens when they fall apart. I believe the job of a novelist is to look closely at the manners and morals of a given time and place, as well as describing in an engrossing way its look and feel.

"I would like to write novels, political journalism, essays, plays, screenplays, and make films of all varieties, including documentaries.

"I have been most deeply influenced by the work of George Orwell."

* * *

SWARTZ, Jon D(avid) 1934-

PERSONAL: Born December 28, 1934, in Houston, Tex.; son of Orville E. (a merchant) and Nina June (Baker) Swartz; married Carol Ann Joseph Hampton (an artist), October 20, 1966; children: Eric Jason McFarland, Sally Katherine Baker, Edward Joseph Bryson. *Education:* University of Texas, B.A., 1956, M.A., 1961, Ph.D., 1969. *Politics:* Democrat. *Religion:* Unitarian-Universalist. *Home:* 2102 Redbud Ave., Odessa, Tex. 79761. *Office:* Department of Psychology, Lab 411, University of Texas of the Permian Basin, University & Parkway, Odessa, Tex. 79762.

CAREER: University of Texas, Austin, assistant professor of educational psychology, 1969-72, research scientist at Hogg Foundation for Mental Health, 1972-74; University of Texas of the Permian Basin, Odessa, associate professor of psychology, 1974—, chairman of department of psychology, 1974—, chairman of department of anthropology and sociology, 1975—, co-chairman of advisory board of Human Potentials Center, 1975—. Member of Odessa mayor's Drug Abuse Authority, 1975—; member of executive committee of Western Research Conference on Mental Retardation,

1976—; member of citizens advisory board of Permian Basin Community Centers for Mental Health and Mental Retardation, 1977—.

MEMBER: International Society for the Study of Behavioral Development, International Association of Applied Psychology, International Council on Education for Teaching, Interamerican Society of Psychology, American Psychological Association (fellow), American Anthropological Association (fellow), American Association for the Advancement of Science (fellow), American Association on Mental Deficiency (fellow), Society for Personality Assessment (fellow), American Sociological Association, American Association of University Professors, American Academy on Mental Retardation, Royal Anthropological Institute of Great Britain and Ireland (fellow), Southwestern Psychological Association, Southwest Sociological Association, Texas Psychological Association, Texas Association on Mental Deficiency, Sigma Xi, Psi Chi, Phi Kappa Phi, Mu Alpha Nu, Delta Tau Kappa. *Awards, honors:* U.S. Office of Education fellowship, 1964-66; Spencer fellowship from National Academy of Education, 1972; senior postdoctoral fellowship in community psychology and community mental health, 1973-74.

WRITINGS: (With W. H. Holtzman) *Inkblot Perception and Personality,* University of Texas Press, 1961; (with C. C. Cleland) *Mental Retardation: Approaches to Institutional Change,* Grune, 1969; (with Cleland) *Administrative Issues in Institutions for the Mentally Retarded: Prescriptive Practices and Emergent Topics,* Hogg Foundation for Mental Health, 1972; *Holtzman Inkblot Technique Annotated Bibliography,* Printing Division, University of Texas, 1973; *Multihandicapped Mentally Retarded: Training and Enrichment Strategies,* Hogg Foundation for Mental Health, 1973; (with Holtzman and Rogelio Diaz-Guerrero) *Personality Development in Two Cultures: A Longitudinal Study of School Children in Mexico and the United States,* University of Texas Press, 1975; (editor with Cleland and Larry W. Talkington) *The Profoundly Mentally Retarded: Second Annual Conference Proceedings,* Western Research Conference, 1976.

Co-author of "Holtzman Inkblot Technique" tests, Psychological Corp., 1961, and "Swartz-Holtzman Group Form of the Holtzman Inkblot Technique," Psychological Corp., 1963. Author of "Re Reviewers and Reviewed" column in *Journal of Biological Psychology.* Contributor of more than two hundred articles and reviews to scientific and professional journals. Associate editor of *American Corrective Therapy Journal,* 1971—; editorial associate of *Current Anthropology,* 1971—; book review editor of *Journal of Biological Psychology,* 1972—; member of editorial advisory board of *Phi Kappa Phi Journal,* 1976—. Special manuscript consultant of *Journal of Educational Psychology,* 1971-72; member of manuscript review board of *Human Organization,* 1976—; manuscript consultant of University of Texas Press, Springer Publishing, Nelson-Hall, Allyn & Bacon, and Prentice-Hall.

WORK IN PROGRESS: Power to Parents: Parents as Teachers, with Robert N. Rothstein and Joel Greenspoon; continuing research on perceptional-cognitive development of individuals throughout their lifespan, especially Mexican-Americans; continuing research on the mentally retarded, especially the profoundly retarded.

SIDELIGHTS: Swartz writes: "For as long as I can remember, I have wanted to be both a writer and a scientist. Even while an undergraduate majoring in English and taking every creative writing course available, I still had dreams of being a scientist. When I took my first course in psychology, I knew that this was it—a science that allowed (even required) one to write for publication! In my first semester in graduate school, I discovered that over half of the first year students in the clinical psychology program had undergraduate degrees in English literature. I now spend almost as much time writing as I do teaching—a happy circumstance for one who has always wanted both to write and do research."

AVOCATIONAL INTERESTS: Chess, model ships, book collecting.

BIOGRAPHICAL/CRITICAL SOURCES: American Corrective Therapy Journal, July, 1971, January, 1976; *Contemporary Psychology,* June, 1976.

* * *

SWIFT, Hildegarde Hoyt 1890(?)-1977

1890(?)—January 10, 1977; American biographer and author of books for children, best known for *The Railroad to Freedom,* an illustrated biography of Harriet Tubman. She died in Redland, Calif. Obituaries: *New York Times,* January 11, 1977; *AB Bookman's Weekly,* March 14, 1977.

* * *

SWIFT, Kate 1923-

PERSONAL: Born December 9, 1923, in Yonkers, N.Y.; daughter of Otis Peabody (a journalist) and E. Longworth (a journalist) Swift. *Education:* Connecticut College, student, 1941-43; University of North Carolina, A.B., 1944; New York University, graduate study. *Politics:* Democrat. *Home and office address:* P.O. Box 94, East Haddam, Conn. 06423. *Agent:* Virginia Barber, 44 Greenwich Ave., New York, N.Y. 10011.

CAREER: National Broadcasting Co. (NBC), New York, N.Y., newsroom copy runner, 1944; Port of New Orleans Authority, New Orleans, La., editorial assistant, 1946-47; *Time,* New York, N.Y., editorial assistant, 1947-48; Girl Scouts of the U.S.A., New York City, public relations news writer, 1948-53; American Museum of Natural History, New York City, science writer, 1954-65; Yale University, New Haven, Conn., director of news bureau at School of Medicine, 1965-70; free-lance writer and editor, 1970—. Member of East Haddam Democratic Town Committee and East Haddam Charter Commission. *Military service:* U.S. Army, Women's Army Corps, 1945-46. *Member:* National Association of Science Writers, Womens Institute for Freedom of the Press.

WRITINGS: (With Casey Miller) *Words and Women,* Doubleday, 1976. Contributor to magazines, including *New York, Ms.,* and *New York Times Magazine.*

SIDELIGHTS: Kate Swift, with her co-author Casey Miller, wrote: "We have an editorial partnership known as Miller/Swift, and it was out of our work as free-lance editors that we became interested in the effect of language on women. After writing two articles on the subject ('Desexing the English Language' and 'One Small Step for Genkind') we found we had barely scratched the surface of this topic, which until recently was ignored. *Words and Women* is an expansion of the evidence presented in the articles and is primarily drawn from contemporary sources with historical material as backup. We document many changes occurring in English today as a result of women's changing perceptions of themselves."

SWIGART, Rob 1941-

PERSONAL: Surname is pronounced with a long "i"; born January 7, 1941, in Chicago, Ill.; son of Eugene (a businessman) and Ruth (an actress and theatrical producer; maiden name, Robison) Swigart; married Jane Bugas (a psychotherapist), March 26, 1969; children: Saramanda Nell. *Education:* Princeton University, B.A., 1962; State University of New York at Buffalo, Ph.D., 1972. *Politics:* "Buddhist." *Religion:* Zen. *Home:* 255 Cerrito Ave., Redwood City, Calif. 94061. *Agent:* Ellen Levine, Curtis Brown Ltd., 575 Madison Ave., New York, N.Y. 10022. *Office:* Department of English, San Jose State University, San Jose, Calif. 95114.

CAREER: Cincinnati Enquirer, Cincinnati, Ohio, reporter, 1963; Harper & Row Publishers, Inc., New York City, salesman, 1965-69; San Jose State University, San Jose, Calif., assistant professor of English, 1972—. Owner, producer, cameraman, editor, and sound recordist for Marley & Swigart Films, 1973—. *Military service:* U.S. Army, 1964-65. U.S. Army Reserve, 1965-70. *Member:* Modern Language Association of America.

WRITINGS: Still Lives (poems), No Dead Lines, 1976; *Little America* (novel), Houghton, 1977; *A.K.A.* (novel), Houghton, in press.

Documentary film scripts: "Inishmaan: Beyond the Pale" and "Firstborn." Contributor of an article and poems to literary journals, including *Poetry, Atlantic Monthly, New York Quarterly, Choice, Poetry Northwest,* and *Antaeus.*

WORK IN PROGRESS: Construction Zone, poems; *Yesterday, Today and Tomorrow* (tentative title), a novel; translating and writing about *Ono no Komachi;* a film script from *Little America.*

SIDELIGHTS: Swigart writes: "I'm concerned in poetry with the individual's place in his history and worldview, especially as defined by science—physics, biology, etc. In novels, the comic (black humor?) form: birth, conflict, death, and resurrection. Essentially I am a WASP optimist." *Avocational interests:* Flying (pilot).

*   *   *

SZANTON, Peter L(oeb) 1930-

PERSONAL: Born November 7, 1930, in New York, N.Y.; son of Jules G. (a businessman) and Carolyn (a teacher; maiden name, Loeb) Szanton; married Eleanor Stokes (a consultant), June 22, 1957; children: Nathan Stokes, Andrew Emlew, Sarah Loeb. *Education:* Harvard University, A.B., 1952, A.M., 1955, LL.B., 1958. *Home:* 3458 Macomb St. N.W., Washington, D.C. 20016. *Office:* 11 Dupont Circle N.W., Suite 807, Washington, D.C. 20036.

CAREER: U.S. District Court, San Francisco, Calif., law clerk, 1958-59; attorney in New York, N.Y., 1959-62; member of policy planning staff of Assistant Secretary of Defense for International Security Affairs in Washington, D.C. (responsible for North Atlantic Treatory Organization planning), 1962-65; Bureau of the Budget, Washington, D.C., deputy director of program evaluation staff, 1965-67; Rand Corp., New York, N.Y., president of New York City-Rand Institute, 1967-71; Harvard University, Cambridge, Mass., fellow of Institute of Politics, 1971-72; Rand Corp., senior staff member, 1972-73; Commission on Organization of the Government for the Conduct of Foreign Policy (Murphy Commission), Washington, D.C., research director, 1973-75; independent researcher and writer, 1975—. Instructor at Harvard University, 1957-58. Consultant to National Science Foundation, Organization for Economic Cooperation and Development, Ford Foundation, Clark Foundation, Whitney Foundation, and Civil Service Institute of Israel. *Military service:* U.S. Army, 1952-54; served in Korea.

WRITINGS: (Contributor) *The Engineer and the City,* National Academy of Engineering, 1969; (contributor) A. W. Drake and other editors, *Analysis of Public Systems,* M.T.T. Press, 1972; (contributor) Henry Owen and Charles Schultze, editors, *Setting National Priorities,* Brookings Institution, 1976; *Remaking Foreign Policy: The Organizational Connection,* Basic Books, 1976. Contributor to law journals and to *Operations Research* and *Foreign Policy.*

WORK IN PROGRESS: A study of the attempts of U.S. city governments, since 1960, to use external advice and expertise, especially from universities.

SIDELIGHTS: Szanton writes: "Interest in public affairs took me from law practice to government. Experience in government made me interested in why government works so poorly, and what might realistically be done about it. Anyone concerned with these questions had better have consoling avocations and a happy family. Fortunately, I do."

BIOGRAPHICAL/CRITICAL SOURCES: Paul Dickson, *Think Tanks,* Atheneum, 1971; Martin Greenberger and others, editors, *Models in the Policy Process,* Russell Sage, 1976.

*   *   *

TAFT, Philip 1902-1976

March 22, 1902—November 17, 1976; American author, professor emeritus of economics at Brown University, and a leading historian of the American labor movement. He died in East Providence, R.I. Obituaries: *New York Times,* November 19, 1976; *Washington Post,* November 20, 1976.

*   *   *

TAFURI, Manfredo 1935-

PERSONAL: Born November 4, 1935, in Rome, Italy; son of Simmaco (an engineer) and Elena (Trevi) Tafuri; married Giuseppina Rapisarda (a professor), June 15, 1966; children: Dafne. *Education:* University of Rome, M. Arch., 1960. *Politics:* Partito Comunista Italiano. *Home:* 86, Piazza di Trevi, Rome, Italy. *Office:* 70, Piazza dei Caprettari, Rome, Italy.

CAREER: Instituto Universitario di Architettura di Venezia, Tolentini, Italy, professor of history of architecture, 1968—. Director, Institute of History, Instituto Universitario di Architettura, Venice, 1968—; member of board of directors, Centro Internazionale di Studi di Architettura "Andrea Palladio," 1974—; member of board of directors of architectural magazine, *Casabella,* 1977—. Lecturer.

WRITINGS: L'Architettura moderna in Giappone, Cappelli (Bologna), 1964; *Ludovico Quaroni e lo sviluppo dell'archtettura moderna in Italia,* Edizioni di Comunita, 1964; *Teorie e Storia dell'architettura,* Laterza, 1968; *Jacopo Sansovino e l'architettura dell '500 a Venezia,* Marsilio, 1969; *L'Architettura dell'umanesimo,* Laterza, 1969; (with Luigi Salerno and Luigi Spezzaferro) *Via Giulia: Un'Utopia urbana del '500,* Staderini, 1973; *Progetto e utopia,* Laterza, 1973, translation by Barbara Luigi La Penta published as *Architecture and Utopia,* M.I.T. Press, 1976; (with Giorgio Ciucci, Francesco Dal Co, and Mario Manieri-Elia) *La Citta Americana,* Laterza, 1973; (with Dal Co) *Architettura Contemporanea,* Electa, 1976.

Contributor of articles on architecture to *Casabella, Contropiano, Oppositions, Lotus, Archithese,* and other periodicals.

WORK IN PROGRESS: Research on architecture and planning in the New Deal age in the U.S.

SIDELIGHTS: Tafuri told *CA:* "My historical research is based on a Marxist methodology, for the criticism of the modern and contemporaries ideologies. In this sense the history of art, of the architecture, of the urban planning, is, for me, an approach to the discovery of the most advanced Capitalist strategies, in relationship to the utopias of the intellectual work. The crisis of the avant-gardes and of the contemporary architecture are at the center of my interests. I am convinced that the history cannot change, alone, the present social and economical establishment: but it may aid the architects to understand the real situation of their work, in the perspective of a general and radical development."

* * *

TAHIR, Abe M(ahmoud), Jr. 1931-

PERSONAL: Born February 18, 1931, in Greenwood, Miss.; son of Mahmoud and Mary (Ollie) Tahir. *Education:* University of Mississippi, B.B.A., 1953; George Washington University, M.B.A., 1960. *Religion:* Roman Catholic.

CAREER: Tahir Gallery, New Orleans, La., co-owner, 1966—.

WRITINGS: Hnizdovsky Woodcuts: 1944-1975, Pelican, 1976.

* * *

TALBOT, Gordon (Gray) 1928-

PERSONAL: Born June 17, 1928, in Utica, N.Y.; son of Clio Earl and Jane (Arnold) Talbot; married Janet Tuttle, August 20, 1949; children: David, Carol. *Education:* Houghton College, B.A., 1949; Nyack College, Th.B., 1951; Wheaton College, Wheaton, Ill., M.A., 1956; New York University, Ph.D., 1968. *Politics:* Republican. *Office:* Christian Schools, Inc., Glen Cove, Maine 04846.

CAREER: Pastor of Christian and Missionary Alliance church in Batavia, N.Y., 1952-54; Bryan College, Dayton, Tenn., instructor in Christian education, 1955-57; Houghton College, Houghton, N.Y., instructor in Christian education, 1957-60; director of Christian education for a Baptist church in Des Moines, Iowa, 1960-63; Detroit Bible College, Detroit, Mich., professor of Christian education, 1963-70, chairman of department, 1964-70; Canadian Bible College, Regina, Saskatchewan, professor of Christian education, 1970-71; free-lance curriculum writer in Houghton, 1971-75; Winnipeg Bible College, Otterburne, Manitoba, professor of Christian education, 1975-76; Christian Schools, Inc., Glen Cove, Maine, president, 1976—.

WRITINGS: The Breakdown of Authority, Revell, 1976; *How to Study Your Bible,* Back to the Bible Broadcast Correspondence School, 1976; *Overcoming Materialism,* Herald Press, 1977. Contributor of about two hundred articles to religious periodicals.

SIDELIGHTS: Talbot describes himself as "a declared conservative in religion, politics, and life-style." His Christian Schools, Inc. operates a Bible college and a Christian academy in Glen Cove.

TANNER, Edward Everett III 1921-1976
(Patrick Dennis, Virginia Rowans)

May 16, 1921—November 6, 1976; American novelist under pseudonyms Patrick Dennis and Virginia Rowans, best known for his *Auntie Mame* written under the Dennis pseudonym; holds record as the only author to have three novels on the *New York Times* best-sellers list at once (eight weeks in 1956). His novels have been adapted for stage, films, and television, including the stage play "Auntie Mame" which was later filmed and was most recently re-adapted as the Broadway musical "Mame." He served as an ambulance driver during World War II and later worked as a publishing executive under name Pat Tanner. He died in New York City. Obituaries: *New York Times,* November 7, 1976; *Washington Post,* November 7, 1976; *Publishers Weekly,* November 15, 1976; *Newsweek,* November 22, 1976; *Time,* November 22, 1976; *Current Biography,* February, 1977.

* * *

TANNER, Louise S(tickney) 1922-

PERSONAL: Born February 16, 1922, in New York, N.Y.; daughter of Henry Austin (a lawyer) and Helen (a poet; maiden name, Frith) Stickney; married Edward E. Tanner (an author under pseudonym Patrick Dennis), December 17, 1948 (died, 1976); children: Michael, Elizabeth. *Education:* Vassar College, B.A., 1944. *Politics:* Democrat. *Religion:* Roman Catholic. *Agent:* McIntosh & Otis, Inc., 475 Fifth Ave., New York, N.Y. 10017.

CAREER: Conde Nast Publications, New York City, editorial copywriter, 1944-46; *Good Housekeeping,* New York City, editorial copywriter, 1946-47; Franklin Spier, Inc., New York City, advertising copywriter, 1947-57; writer, 1957—. *Member:* Authors League, P.E.N., New York Civil Liberties Union. *Awards, honors:* First prize in older reader juvenile division from *Chicago Tribune* Children's Spring Book Festival, 1972, for *Reggie and Nilma.*

WRITINGS—Adult books, except as noted: *Here Today,* Crowell, 1959; *Miss Bannister's Girls,* Farrar, Straus, 1963; *All the Things We Were,* Doubleday, 1968; *Reggie and Nilma: A New York City Story* (juvenile), Farrar, Straus, 1971; *Dr. I.R.T.,* Coward, 1976.

WORK IN PROGRESS: Put Me in the Picture, a collection of plays, classroom activities, and slide shows which have successfully encouraged participation in an East Harlem classroom.

SIDELIGHTS: Tanner told *CA:* "I used to write advertising copy for a firm whose biggest bread-and-butter author produced, with the rhythm of the seasons, an annual historical novel, a biblical novel, and a novel featuring a masterful surgeon and an adoring nurse. I have always envied this man, for this is the way to build an audience. My books cause my favorite bookseller to remark 'now which section do we put *this* one in?' This, alas, doesn't make me anyone's bread-and-butter author.

"My motley works do, however, have an underlying theme: the extent to which we are all formed by the peer pressures of our youth. My first book *Here Today* described several young people who crashed into print when the public held one set of assumptions, and who found themselves in bitter obscurity when these assumptions went down the drain. My own attitudes were formed by the 1930's and by a girl's school in which I rejected all that was taught. *All the Things We Were* and *Miss Bannister's Girls* describe the art-deco millieu of my salad days. *Reggie and Nilma* and *Dr. I.R.T.*

deal with contemporary kids caught in the racial tensions of New York City. My bookstore dealer scratched his head in the usual dilemma. (One publisher opted for the adult shelf, while the other hoped for spillover sales due to proximity to *Peter Rabbit*.)

"Presently I'm at work on another complete departure, a true tale set in a New England town where I was dragged kicking and screaming as a child. My parents had an enthusiasm, unshared by me, for collapsed barns, country graveyards, and tombstone rubbings. Today the polarization between black and white, which was the subject of *Reggie and Nilma,* has moved northward to this leafy paradise, which was once a cradle of Abolitionism. A vision of big money has dazzled the churchgoing children of farmers as the plans for a new shopping plaza are unveiled. A rural Arcadia has been quietly transformed, in my opinion, by the subtlest of gentleman's agreements.

"Caught in this drama of changing values is an indomitable old lady, clinging to the rocky hillside farm she calls her homestead. The pop culture of *her* childhood goes back to the slave songs, the 'soldier pieces' of the Civil War. Fact and fiction are strangely intermingled in her memories of nine decades. Let the bookseller do with them what he will."

* * *

TANOBE, Miyuki 1937-

PERSONAL: Born December 20, 1937, in Japan; came to Canada, 1971; naturalized Canadian citizen, 1976; daughter of Tomizo (an opthamologist and violinist) and Yuki (a singer and koto player; maiden name, Hayase) Tanobe; married Maurice Savignac (a researcher), December 10, 1971. *Education:* University of Tokyo, diploma in arts and license for teaching, 1960; also attended Ecole superieure nationale des Beaux Arts, Paris, 1963-65. *Home:* Saint-Antoine-sur-Richelieu, Vercheres County, Quebec, Canada YOL 1RO.

CAREER: Painter. Has had solo exhibitions at Galerie L'Art Francais, Montreal, Quebec, 1972 and 1974, Japanese Pavillon, Montreal, 1973, and Marlborough-Godard, Montreal, and Toronto, Ontario, 1976. *Awards, honors:* Children's Book Showcase Award, 1976, for *I Love You, Quebec: Je T'aime.*

WRITINGS—Self-illustrated; juveniles: *Miyuke in Quebec,* Scribner, 1976; *I Love You, Quebec: Je T'aime,* Tundra Books, 1976.

WORK IN PROGRESS: "A synthesis on Quebec life, in cities and country."

SIDELIGHTS: Tanobe told *CA:* "After studying in Paris and sketching in Greece and Africa, I arrived in Montreal where I caught the French Canadian soul and, by painting the lanes and streets of popular districts in Montreal and Quebec cities, I discovered the warmth of the working classes."

* * *

TARLOV, I. M. 1905(?)-1977

1905(?)—June 4, 1977; American author and professor of neurology and neurosurgery at New York Medical College. He died in Nantucket, Mass. Obituaries: *New York Times,* June 7, 1977.

* * *

TAUBE, Lester S. 1920-

PERSONAL: Born June 5, 1920, in Trenton, N.J.; son of John and Dora Taube; married Ursula Poehlmann (a translator and interpreter); children: Mark, Cheryl, John, Erica. *Education:* Attended Rutgers University and U.S. Army Command and Staff College. *Politics:* "Right of center." *Residence:* Willingboro, N.J. *Agent:* Maximilian Becker, 115 East 82nd St., New York, N.Y. 10028.

CAREER: U.S. Army, career officer, entered service, 1936, served in Bismarck Archipelago and in Iwo Jima, served as adviser to Turkish Army and as general staff officer in Europe, retiring as colonel. Also worked as archives assistant in Washington, D.C., home improvement salesman in Florida, manager of electronics manufacturing plant in California, general manager of paper stock company in Pennsylvania, owner of log and pulpwood cutting company in Canada, owner of automobile repair garages in New Jersey, insurance consultant in New Jersey, president of laundry chain in France, and coordinator of U.S. Army laundries in Germany.

WRITINGS—Novels: *Myer for Hire,* W. H. Allen, 1970; *The Cossack Cowboy,* W. H. Allen, 1971. Also author of *The Grabbers,* 1969, published in the United States as *The Diamond Boomerang,* and *Peter Krimsov,* 1970.

WORK IN PROGRESS—Novels: *The Family; A Land of Thunder; Atonement for Iwo;* a sequel for *Peter Krimsov.*

SIDELIGHTS: Taube has fought on or visited the Pacific Islands, Japan, Korea, and most of the countries in Europe. He writes that researching his books has led him "from the back streets of crime to plush yachting circles." His novels reflect his "love of travel, brushes with danger, and the pitting of man, with all his fears, weaknesses, and yearnings, against sudden, seemingly insurmountable odds." For five years he and his family spent summers on their yacht *Ulrica* on the Cote d'Azur of France and winters in the Tyrolean mountains of Austria. He returned to the United States in 1975, and wrote: "It was time to come home. There are roots which one overlooks in the excitement of new faces and places."

His books have been published in Germany, Italy, the Netherlands, Denmark, Portugal, and Japan.

AVOCATIONAL INTERESTS: Horseback riding, watching bullfights, reading historical novels.

* * *

TAUBER, Abraham 1915(?)-1977

1915(?)—March 6, 1977; American author, founding dean of Bronx Community College, and chairman of speech and drama department at Yeshiva University. He died in New York City. Obituaries: *New York Times,* March 8, 1977.

* * *

TAYLOR, Andrew (McDonald) 1940-

PERSONAL: Born March 19, 1940, in Warrnambool, Victoria, Australia; son of John McDonald (a lawyer) and Margaret (Fraser) Taylor; married Jill Burriss, January 31, 1965 (separated, 1975); children: Travis. *Education:* University of Melbourne, B.A. (first class honors), 1961, M.A. (first class honors), 1970; State University of New York at Buffalo, further graduate study, 1970-71. *Politics:* "Unattached Left." *Home:* 334 Halifax St., Adelaide, South Australia 5000, Australia. *Office:* Department of English, University of Adelaide, Adelaide, South Australia 5001, Australia.

CAREER: British Institute, Rome, Italy, English teacher, 1964-65; University of Melbourne, Melbourne, Australia,

Lockie Fellow in Australia Literature, 1965-69; University of Adelaide, Adelaide, Australia, lecturer, 1971-74, senior lecturer in English, 1974—. Helped to organize Adelaide's "Friendly Street" poetry readings; member of writers' week committee of Adelaide Festival of Arts. Consultant to Australian Broadcasting Commission. *Member:* Australian and New Zealand American Studies Association, English Teachers Association of South Australia. *Awards, honors:* American Council of Learned Societies fellowship, 1970-71.

WRITINGS: (Editor) *Byron, Selected Poems,* Cassell, 1971; *The Cool Change* (poems), University of Queensland Press, 1971; *Ice Fishing* (poems), University of Queensland Press, 1973; *The Invention of Fire* (poems), University of Queensland Press, 1976; *The Cat's Chin and Ears: A Bestiary,* Angus & Robertson, 1976; *Parabolas: Prose Poems,* Makar Press, 1976. Author of radio scripts on poetry for Australian Broadcasting Commission. Contributor to magazines and newspapers.

WORK IN PROGRESS: A book of poems; a novel (or very long story); prose poems and "experiments in prose."

SIDELIGHTS: Taylor writes: "Several years living in Europe and several in the U.S.A., Canada, and Mexico have counteracted Australia's isolation (my involvement with Adelaide Festival of Arts is another attempt at this). But I also like watching plants grow slowly and resolutely in one place. . . ." He adds that his interests are in "modern psychology and phenomenology, in origins (my own rather than my country's)."

AVOCATIONAL INTERESTS: Travel, gardening, animals, children.

* * *

TAYLOR, Bernard 1937-

PERSONAL: Born October 2, 1937, in Wiltshire, England; son of Albert Ernest (a cooper) and Edna (Tanner) Taylor. *Education:* Attended Swindon College of Art, 1956-58, and Chelsea College of Art, 1958-60; University of Birmingham, B.A. (honors), 1961. *Residence:* London, England. *Agent:* Harvey Unna and Stephen Durbridge, 14 Beaumont Mews, London W.1, England.

CAREER: Lived in the United States in the 1960's for six years, working as a teacher, a painter, a book illustrator, and then as an actor; since returning to England in 1969, has continued with his acting career; writer, 1969—. Playwright-in-residence at Queen's Theatre, Hornchurch, England, 1975-76. *Military service:* Royal Air Force, 1952-54. *Awards, honors:* Most promising new playwright award, 1975, for "Mice on the First Floor."

WRITINGS: The Godsend (novel), St. Martin's, 1976; *Sweetheart, Sweetheart* (novel), Souvenir Press, 1977, St. Martin's, in press.

Plays: "Daughter of the Apaches" (two-act), produced in Hornchurch, England, at Queen's Theatre, 1974; "Mice on the First Floor" (three-act), produced in Hornchurch at Queen's Theatre, 1975.

Author of scripts for comedy series, "Maggie—It's Me!," for British Broadcasting Corp. (BBC)-TV.

Work represented in anthologies, *Eighth Fontana Book of Horror,* edited by Mary Danby, Fontana, 1973; *Frighteners,* edited by Danby, Fontana, 1974; *Year's Best Horror Stories III,* edited by Richard Davis, Daw Books, 1975; and *Frighteners II,* edited by Danby, Fontana, 1976.

Contributor of illustrations for children's books and wom-en's magazines, and to *Harper's;* designer of cover for Dutch edition of own novel, *The Godsend,* and British edition of own novel, *Sweetheart, Sweetheart.*

WORK IN PROGRESS: Plays for the theatre and for television.

* * *

TAYLOR, Carl 1937-

PERSONAL: Born January 3, 1937, in New York, N.Y.; son of Carl (a lawyer) and Pauline (Billings) Taylor; married Ching-Wen Pu (a teacher), March 20, 1970; children: May Tran. *Education:* Harvard University, B.A., 1959; Johns Hopkins School of Advanced International Studies, M.A., 1962. *Home address:* River Rd., Woodstock, Vt. 05091.

CAREER: U.S. Department of State, Washington, D.C., foreign service officer, 1962—. Special lecturer at University of Indonesia, 1963-64. *Military service:* U.S. Army Reserve, 1956-62. *Member:* American Foreign Service Association, Indonesia-America Friendship Association.

WRITINGS: Getting to Know Indonesia, Coward, 1961; *Getting to Know Burma,* Coward, 1962. Contributor to economics, history, and Asian studies journals.

SIDELIGHTS: Taylor speaks Indonesian, Burmese, and German. *Avocational interests:* Fishing, hiking, woodchopping.

BIOGRAPHICAL/CRITICAL SOURCES: Robert O. Tilman, *Asian Specialists,* Interuniversity Southeast Asian Committee, Association for Asian Studies, 1969.

* * *

TAYLOR, Ray J. 1918(?)-1977

1918(?)—April 21, 1977; American editor, writer, and executive of trade newspapers and magazines. He died in Washington, D.C. Obituaries: *Washington Post,* April 23, 1977.

* * *

TAYLOR, Ross McLaury 1909(?)-1977

1909(?)—March 16, 1977; American author and authority on the American Southwest; former chairman of department of American studies at Wichita State University. Obituaries: *AB Bookman's Weekly,* May 9, 1977.

* * *

TEICHER, Morton I(rving) 1920-

PERSONAL: Born March 10, 1920, in New York, N.Y.; son of Sam and Celia (Roth) Teicher; married Mildred Adler, October 4, 1941; children: Phyllis Goldman, Oren. *Education:* City College of New York (now City College of the City University of New York), B.S.S., 1940; University of Pennsylvania, M.S.W., 1942; University of Toronto, Ph.D., 1956. *Politics:* Democrat. *Religion:* Jewish. *Home:* 905 East Franklin St., Chapel Hill, N.C. 27514. *Office:* School of Social Work, University of North Carolina, Chapel Hill, N.C. 27514.

CAREER: U.S. Veterans Administration, Boston, Mass., chief social worker, 1946-48; University of Toronto, Toronto, Ontario, assistant professor of social work, 1948-56; Yeshiva University, New York, N.Y., professor of social work, 1956-72; University of North Carolina, Chapel Hill, professor of social work and dean, 1972—. *Military service:* U.S. Army, 1942-46, became first lieutenant; served in China, Burma, and India. *Member:* American Anthropological Association, Society for Applied Anthropology, National Association of Social Workers, American Association for the Advancement of Science, American Association of University Professors, Council on Social Work Education, Gerontological Society, Otto Rank Society. *Awards, honors:* Certificate of Appreciation from Westchester County, N.Y., 1967.

WRITINGS: Windigo Psychosis, University of Washington Press, 1960; (contributor) Myron A. Coler, editor, *Essays on Creativity in the Sciences,* New York University Press, 1963; (editor and contributor) *Values in Social Work,* National Association of Social Workers, 1967. Contributor of articles to professional journals.

* * *

TEICHMANN, Howard Miles   1916-

PERSONAL: Born January 22, 1916, in Chicago, Ill.; son of Jack (a businessman) and Rose (Berliner) Teichmann; married Evelyn Goldstein (a writer), April 2, 1939; children: Judith. *Education:* University of Wisconsin, B.A., 1938. *Home:* 863 Park Ave., New York, N.Y. 10021. *Office:* Department of English, Barnard College, Columbia University, 606 West 120th St., New York, N.Y. 10027.

CAREER: "Orson Welles's Mercury Theatre of the Air," New York, N.Y., stage manager, 1938-40, writer of scripts, 1939-40, producer, 1940-41; Office of War Information, New York City, senior editor, overseas branch, 1942-43; expert consultant in radio to General Brehon Somervell, Washington, D.C., 1943-45; Columbia University, New York City, lecturer, 1946, professor of English, 1947—. Cultural consultant and vice president, Shubert Theatrical Enterprises, 1962-72. *Member:* Dramatists Guild, Sigma Delta Chi, Zeta Beta Tau. *Awards, honors:* University of Wisconsin Distinguished Service Award, 1959.

WRITINGS—Plays: (With George S. Kaufman) *The Solid Gold Cadillac* (two-act), Random House, 1954; *Miss Lonelyhearts* (two-act), Dramatists Play Service, 1959; *The Girls in 509* (two-act), Samuel French, 1959; *Julia, Jake and Uncle Joe* (two-act), Samuel French, 1961; *A Rainy Day in Newark* (two-act), Samuel French, 1964.

Nonfiction: *George S. Kaufman,* Atheneum, 1972; *Smart Aleck—The Wit, World and Life of Alexander Woollcott,* Morrow, 1976.

Also author of radio dramas produced on "Mercury Theatre of the Air," "Campbell Playhouse," "Helen Hayes Theatre," "Texaco Star Theatre," "CBS Workshop," "Cavalcade of America," "Gertrude Lawrence Review," "They Live Forever," "Ford Theatre of the Air," and others.

Author of television dramas for "Theatre USA," "Showtime USA," "USA Canteen," and others.

WORK IN PROGRESS: A color portrait of Alice Roosevelt Longworth.

* * *

THACHER, Alida McKay   1951-

PERSONAL: Born January 7, 1951, in Bloomington, Ind.; daughter of Henry C., Jr. (a professor of computer science) and Ann (a writer; maiden name, Peters) Thacher. *Education:* University of Wisconsin, Madison, B.A., 1972, graduate study, 1975—. *Home:* 600 South Brearly, Madison, Wis. 53703.

CAREER: Western Publishing Co., Inc., Racine, Wis., editorial assistant, 1972-74; writer and designer of audio-visual instructional materials, 1974—.

WRITINGS—For children: *Golden Shoe Book,* Western Publishing, 1974; *Elephant on Wheels,* Western Publishing, 1974; *Raising a Racket: Rosie Casals,* Raintree, 1976; *In the Center: Kareem Abdul-Jabbar,* Raintree, 1976.

WORK IN PROGRESS: "A Timely Disaster," a play for children.

SIDELIGHTS: Alida Thacher writes: "Perhaps the most vital conscious theme to me while writing juvenile literature is that of the importance and beauty of individuality. Too many of us unconsciously feed stereotyped, expected roles to children; we don't encourage and nurture the unexpected in the individual. I expect to continue expanding on this theme as I begin to explore children's film and children's video."

* * *

THARAUD, Lucien Rostaing, Jr.   1953-
(Ross Tharaud)

PERSONAL: Surname is pronounced like "thorough"; born September 8, 1953, in New York, N.Y.; son of Lucien Rostaing (a lawyer) and Cynthia (a university administrator; maiden name, James) Tharaud. *Education:* Cornell University, B.A. (summa cum laude), 1975. *Home:* 521 High St., Marquette, Mich. 49855. *Office:* AMCAB, 600 Altamont, Marquette, Mich. 49855.

CAREER: AMCAB, Marquette, Mich., social worker with delinquent youth. Member of local Planned Parenthood group. *Awards, honors:* Carson-Bishop Prize from Cornell University, 1975; George Harmon Cote Award in American Literature and Creative Writing, 1975.

WRITINGS—Under name Ross Tharaud: (Editor with others) *The First Anthology,* Society of Humanities, Cornell University, 1974; *Openings* (poems), Ithaca House, 1976. Contributor of poems to magazines.

WORK IN PROGRESS: Poems and short stories; essays.

SIDELIGHTS: Tharaud writes: "Specifically, the scope of my endeavor in life is so large as to be positively vague or thereabouts, almost certain to exceed my grasp. But grasping's what matters. Or rather grasping without *grasping,* otherwise termed living. I would explore, insofar as time and ability and circumstance permit, every area of the human tragicomedy. And enjoy while doing it. Education is not a noun but a way of being.

>   "Beginnings with
>   and through
>   which I
>   discerned: keyholes,
>   cracks, chinks; also
>   swallowing ground maws
>   that would have
>   sucked my steps
>   in; lenses, sometimes dim;
>   gaps between teeth
>   of traps I set
>   for an animal named
>   meaning; the slot of a tilted
>   transom or whistle
>   hidden under a bottle-cap;
>   —find and widen them, I said,
>   preserve initial conditions in
>   a box.

>   "Outside, all the time,

revolved particles
of dust and quick
dance steps; mica jewels.
There were inklings on the run.
But only a coil of loose wind
would spring me."

AVOCATIONAL INTERESTS: Tae kwon do (blue belt).

* * *

THEKAEKARA, Matthew P(othen) 1914-1976

March 21, 1914—November 25, 1976; Indian-born Jesuit Roman Catholic priest, physicist, inventor, and author. He invented the mercury pool as a precision tool of the alignment of instruments for orbiting observations, and the cone radiometer. A research physicist at Goddard Space Flight Center of the National Aeronautics and Space Administration in Maryland, his most important contribution to space exploration is considered to be his recalculation of the solar constant. He died in Prince George County, Md. Obituaries: *Washington Post,* November 27, 1976.

* * *

THELIN, John R(obert) 1947-

PERSONAL: Born October 15, 1947, in Newton, Mass.; son of George Willard (an engineer and designer) and Rozalija (Komarec) Thelin. *Education:* Brown University, A.B. (cum laude), 1969; University of California, Berkeley, M.A., 1972, Ph.D., 1973. *Home:* 13342 Del Monte, 5-K, Seal Beach, Calif. 90740.

CAREER: University of California, Berkeley, editor and lecturer in sociology of education and history, 1973-74; University of Kentucky, Lexington, assistant professor of history of education, 1974-77; Marquandia Society, Los Angeles, Calif., curator, 1977—. *Member:* History of Education Society, American Educational Studies Association, Marquandia Society, California Historical Society, Amherst Historical Society, Phi Beta Kappa.

WRITINGS: The Cultivation of Ivy: A Saga of the College in America, Schenkman, 1976. Contributor to history and education journals, and to *Down River, Berkshire Review,* and *Runner's World.*

WORK IN PROGRESS: Research on legal and regional history, especially on the social history of California, 1890-1970; analyzing social and educational policies, especially in higher education; studying Raymond Chandler's Los Angeles, about 1920-1950.

SIDELIGHTS: Thelin comments that his aim is to write history for non-historians. His main interest "is in the use of historical methods for understanding the recent past"; he uses unorthodox sources, artifacts, documents, and icons; he studies mass culture and institutions, commercial art, and architectural forms. *Avocational interests:* Long-distance running, European travel (especially Yugoslavia).

* * *

THIEDA, Shirley Ann 1943-

PERSONAL: Born May 31, 1943, in Illinois; daughter of Edward Simon (a leadman for an electrical appliance company) and Bessie Anne (Milota) Thieda. *Education:* Morton Junior College, A.A., 1963; University of Illinois, student, 1963-66; Southern Illinois University, B.A., 1967; New Mexico Institute of Technology and Mining, M.S., 1971. *Politics:* Independent. *Religion:* Roman Catholic. *Home:*

1200 Madeira Dr. S.E., #125, Albuquerque, N.M. 87108. *Office:* Pioneer Nuclear, Inc., 2532 Vermont N.E., Albuquerque, N.M. 87110.

CAREER: Illinois Geological Survey, Urbana, technical assistant, 1965-66; substitute teacher in West Berwyn, Ill., 1968; high school science teacher in Ruidoso, N.M., 1968-71, and Socorro, N.M., 1971-72; mid-school science teacher in Santa Rosa, N.M., 1972-74; Pioneer Nuclear, Inc., Albuquerque, N.M., office geologist, 1974—. *Member:* National Teachers Association, Amateur Hockey Association, New Mexico Teachers Association, New Mexico Hockey Booster Club, Ruidoso Teachers Association, Thirty/Thirty Club (hockey club; novice member), Kappa Kappa Iota.

WRITINGS: Fast Ice (juvenile), Franklin Publishing, 1975.

WORK IN PROGRESS: Gentleman's Dilemma, a western romance; *Volcanism of New Mexico; The Creeping Killer,* science fiction; *My Grandmother Was a Bootlegger,* a comedy; *Super-G,* about geologists.

SIDELIGHTS: Shirley Thieda writes that she has recently renewed her active interest in hockey, by playing and coaching, but her book on hockey was begun while she was still a high school student. She comments: "I would never want to write for my livelihood because it's too hard, but I do enjoy it when I have time and as a hobby. If I had to do it over again, however, I would because it was an invaluable experience and it provided many opportunities for me."

AVOCATIONAL INTERESTS: Collecting fossils, rocks, and minerals, photography, travel (Mexico and Canada).

* * *

THIELICKE, Helmut 1908-

PERSONAL: Born December 4, 1908, in Wueppertal-Barmen, Germany; son of Reinhard and Laura (Koehler) Thielicke; married Marie-Luise Herrmann, September 28, 1937; children: Wolfram, Berthold, Elisabeth, Rainer. *Education:* Attended University of Greifswald, University of Marburg, and University of Bonn; University of Erlangen, Dr.Phil., 1932, Dr.Theol., 1934. *Religion:* Lutheran. *Home:* Barkenkoppel 2, 2000 Hamburg 65, West Germany. *Office:* Sedanstrasse 19, 2000 Hamburg 13, West Germany.

CAREER: University of Heidelberg, Heidelberg, Germany, professor, 1936-40, ordained priest in Lutheran Church, 1941; parish priest in Ravensburg, Germany, 1941-42; head of Theological Office of Wuerttemberg Church, 1943-45; University of Tuebingen, Tuebingen, Germany, professor of systematic theology, 1945-54, rector of the university, 1951; University of Hamburg, Hamburg, Germany, professor of systematic theology, 1954—, rector of the university, 1960. President of Conference of University Rectors of West Germany, 1951. *Awards, honors:* Great cross of order of merit (West Germany); Dr.Theol., University of Heidelberg, 1946; D.D., University of Glasgow, 1956; LL.D., University of Waterloo (Canada), 1974; Litt.D., Lenoir Rhyne College, 1975.

WRITINGS—Books appearing only in English translation: *Christ and the Meaning of Life: A Book of Sermons and Meditations,* translation by John W. Doberstein, Harper, 1962; *The Silence of God,* translation by Geoffrey Bromiley, Eerdmans, 1962; *The Freedom of the Christian Man: A Christian Confrontation with the Secular Gods,* Harper, 1963.

German books in English translation: (First published anonymously) *Fragen des Christentums an die moderne Welt: Eine christliche Kulturkritik,* Editions Oekumene (Geneva),

1944, published under name as *Fragen des Christentums an die moderne Welt: Untersuchungen zur geistigen und religioesen Driese des Abendlandes*, Mohr (Tuebingen), 1947, translation of chapter 12 by Doberstein published in *Man in God's World*, Harper, 1963; *Tod und Leben: Studien zur christlichen Anthropologie*, Editions Oekumene, c. 1944, translation by Edward Schroeder published as *Death and Life*, Fortress Press, 1970; *Jesus Christus am Scheidewege*, Furche-Verlag (Berlin), 1938, published as *Zwischen Gott und Satan, eine biblische Besinnung*, Furche-Verlag (Tuebingen), 1946, translation by C. C. Barber published as *Between God and Satan*, Eerdmans, 1958.

Der Nihilismus, Reichel (Tuebingen), 1950, translation by Doberstein published as *Nihilism, Its Origin and Nature, With a Christian Answer*, Harper, 1961; *Theologische Ethik*, Volume I: *Prinzipienlehre: Dogmatische, philosophische und kontroverstheologische Grundlegung*, Volume II: *Ethik des Politischen*, Volume III: *Ethik des Besellschaft, des Rechtes, der Sexualitaet, und der Kunst*, Mohr, 1951—, 2nd edition, 1958, translation of abridgment of Volumes I and II by William Lazareth published as *Theological Ethics*, Volume I: *Foundations*, Volume II: *Politics*, Fortress Press, 1966, translation of chapter of Volume III by Doberstein published as *The Ethics of Sex*, Harper, 1964; *Das Gebet, das die Welt umspannt*, Quell-Verlag (Stuttgart), 1953, 13th edition, 1973, translation by Doberstein published as *Our Heavenly Father: Sermons on the Lord's Prayer*, Harper, 1960; *Die Lebensangst und ihre Ueberwindung*, Bertelsmann (Guetersloh), 1954, translation by Geoffrey Bromiley published as *Out of the Depths*, Eerdmans, 1962.

Das Leben kann noch einmal beginnen: Ein Gang durch die Bergpredigt, Quell-Verlag, 1956, 8th edition, 1965, translation by Doberstein published as *Life Can Begin Again: Sermons on the Sermon on the Mount*, Fortress Press, 1963; *Das Bilderbuch Gottes: Reden ueber die Gleichnisse Jesu*, Quell-Verlag, 1957, 3rd edition, 1962, translation by Doberstein published as *The Waiting Father: Sermons on the Parables of Jesus*, Harper, 1959, excerpt from translation published as *The Five Brothers of the Rich Man*, Church Pastoral-Aid Society (London), 1962; *Der Glaube der Christenheit: Unser Welt vor Jesus Christus*, Vendenhoeck & Ruprecht (Goettingen), 1958, 5th edition, 1965, translation of chapters 18-32 by Doberstein published in *Man in God's World*, Harper, 1963; *Kleines geistliches Exerzitium fuer Theologenstudenten*, Agentur des Rauhen Huases (Hamburg), 1959, new edition published as *Kleines Exercitium fuer Theologen*, Furche-Verlag, 1965, translation by Charles Taylor published as *A Little Exercise for Young Theologians*, Eerdmans, 1962; *Vom Schiff ans gesehen: Tagebuch einer Ostasienreise*, Guetersloher Verlagshaus, 1959, translation by Doberstein published as *Voyage to the Far East*, Muhlenberg Press, 1962.

Wie die Welt begann: Der Mensch in der Urgeschichte der Bibel, Quell-Verlag, 1960, translation by Doberstein published as *How the World Began: Man in the First Chapters of the Bible*, Fortress Press, 1961; *Vom geistlichen Reden: Begegnung mit Spurgeon*, Quell-Verlag, 1961, translation by Doberstein published as *Encounter with Spurgeon*, Fortress Press, 1963; *Gespraeche ueber Himmel und Erde: Begegnungen in Amerika*, Quell-Verlag, 1964, 2nd edition, 1965, translation by Doberstein published as *Between Heaven and Earth: Conversations with American Christians*, Harper, 1965.

Leiden an der Kirche: Ein persoenliches Wort, Furche-Verlag, 1965, translation by Doberstein published as *The

Trouble with the Church: A Call for Renewal, Harper, 1965; *Ich glaube: Das Bekanntnis der Christen*, Quell-Verlag, 1965, translation by H. George Anderson and Doberstein published as *I Believe: The Christian's Creed*, Fortress Press, 1968; *Wie modern darf die Theologie sein?*, Quell-Verlag, 1967, published as *Theologisches Denken und verunsicherter Glaube: Eine Hinfuehrung zur "modernen" Theologie*, Herder (Freiburg), 1974, translation by Anderson published as *How Modern Should Theology Be?*, Fortress Press, 1969; *Der evangelische Glaube: Grundzuege der Dogmatik*, Volume I: *Prolegomena: Die Beziehung der Theologie zu den Denkformen der Neuzeit*, Volume II: *Gotteslehre und Christologie*, Mohr, 1968—, translation by Geoffrey Bromiley published as *The Evangelical Faith*, Volume I: *Prolegomena: The Relation of Theology to Modern Thought Forms*, Volume II: *Theology and Christology*, Eerdmans, 1977.

Und wenn Gott waere: Reden ueber die Frage nach Gott, Quell-Verlag, 1970, translation by Anderson published as *How to Believe Again*, Fortress Press, 1972; *Wer darf leben? Ethische Probleme den modernen Medizin*, Goldmann (Munich), 1970, translation published as *The Doctor as Judge of Who Shall Live and Who Shall Die*, Fortress Press, 1976; *So sah ich Afrika; Tagebuch einer Schiffsreise*, Mohr, 1971, translation published as *African Diary: My Search for Understanding*, Word Books (Waco, Tex.), 1974.

Other work: *Das verhaeltnis zwischen dem Ethischen und dem Aesthelischen, eine systematische Untersuchung*, Meiner (Leipzig), 1932; *Geschichte und Existenz: Grundlegung einer evangelichen Geschichtstheologie*, Berteismann, 1935, 2nd edition, Mohn, 1964; *Vernunft und Offenbarung: Eine Studie euber die Religionsphilosophie Lessings*, Bertelsmann, 1936, 3rd edition published as *Offenbarung, Vernunft und Existenz: Studien zur Religionsphilosophie Lessings*, 1957, 5th edition, Mohr, 1957.

Wo ist Gott? Aus einem Briefwechsel, Vandenhoeck & Ruprecht, 1940; *Gottes Wort*, Oekumenische Kommission fuer die Pastoration der Kriegsgefangenen, 1944; *Die Grundgedanken des christlichen Glaubens*, Oekumenische Kommission fuer die Pastoration der Kreigsgefagenen, c. 1944; *Weltanschauung und Glaube*, Deutsche Verlag-Anstalt (Stuttgart), 1946.

Die erzieherische Verantwortung der Universitaet: Grundgragen der Hochschulreform, Mohr, 1952; *Die evangelische Kirche und die Politik: Ethisch-politischer Traktat ueber einige Zietfragen*, Evangelisches Verlagswerk (Stuttgart), 1953; *Mensch und Arbeit im technischen Zeitalter*, Mohr, 1954; *In Amerika ist alles anders: Begegnungen und Beobachtungen*, Furche-Verlag, 1956, revised and enlarged edition published in *Auf Kanzel und Katheder: Aufzeichnungen aus Arbeit und Leben*, 1965; *Mensch zwischen Konstruktionen* (excerpts from *Theologische Ethik*), Cranach (Munich), 1956; *Christliche Verantwortung im Atomzeitalter: Ethisch-politischer Traktat ueuer einige Zeitfragen*, Evangelisches Verlagswerk, 1957; *Begegnungen*, Furche-Verlag, 1957, revised and enlarged edition published in *Auf Kanzel und Katheder: Aufzeichnungen aus Arbeit und Leben*, 1965; *Die Atomquaffe als Frage an die christliche Ethik*, Mohr, 1958; *Die Angst vor der Welt: Zur Begegnung mit dem Nihilismus*, Jugenddienst-Verlag (Wuppertal-Barmen), 1956; *Ethik des Politischen* (excerpt from *Theologische Ethik*), Mohr, 1958.

Brauchen wir Leitbilder? Ein Wort an die Jugend ueber Grosse und Elend der Ideale, Furche-Verlag, 1961; *Das Amt des Beters: Eine Besinnung auf das Wesen des Ge-

betes, Schriftenmissions-Verlag (Gladbeck), 1961; *Das Schweigen Gottes: Fragen von heute an des Evangelium,* Furche-Verlag, 1962; *Unser Leben mit Gott,* Diefel (Wuppertal-Barmen), 1962; *Die Chance, der Freiheit nuetzen,* Bundesdruckerei (Bonn), 1962; *Einfuehrung in die christliche Ethik,* Piper (Munich), 1963; *Der Einzelne und der Apparat: Von der Freiheit des Menschen im technischen Zeitalter,* Furche-Verlag, 1964; (with Ekkehard Othmer) *Deutschland: Demokratie order Vaterland,* Wunderlich (Tuebingen), 1964.

Was ist Wahrheit?, edited by Hans Mueller-Schwefe, Vandenhoeck & Ruprecht, 1965; *Das Schweigen Gottes: Fragen von heute an das Evangelium,* Furche-Verlag, 1965; *Theologie und Zeitgenossenschaft: Gesammelte Aufsaetze,* Wunderlich (Tuebingen), 1967; *Ueber die Angst des heutigen Theologiestudenten vor dem geistlichen Amt,* Mohr, 1967; *Wer darf leben? Der Arzt als Richter,* Wunderlich, 1968; *Kulturkritik der studentischen Rebellion,* Mohr, 1969.

Thielicke-Brevier: Meditationen fuer jeden Tag, compiled and edited by Wolfgang Erk and Heinrich Kuhfuss, Steinkopf (Stuttgart), 1972; *Die geheime Frage nach Gott: Hintergruende unserer geistigen Situation,* Herder, 1972; *Notwendigkeit und Begrenzung des politischen Auftrags der Kirche,* Mohr, 1974; *Das Lachen der Heiligen und Narren: Nachdenklichen ueber Witz und Humor,* Herder, 1974; *Mensch sein, Mensch werden: Entwurf einer christlichen Anthropologie,* Piper, 1976.

Also author of published sermons.

AVOCATIONAL INTERESTS: Photography.

*   *   *

THIRLWALL, John C(onnop, Jr.) 1904-

PERSONAL: Born June 7, 1904, in Brooklyn, N.Y.; son of John Connop and Esther (Weitzel) Thirlwall; married Fuji Yanase, December 17, 1945; children: Thomas Connop, D'arcy Katherine. *Education:* Columbia University, B.A., 1926, Ph.D., 1936. *Home:* 4414 Tibbett Ave., New York, N.Y.

CAREER: Long Island University, Brooklyn, N.Y., instructor in English, 1929-33; College of the City of New York (now City College of the City University of New York), New York, N.Y., began as tutor, 1933, became professor of English, 1956. Instructor at Biarritz American University, 1945; became staff member of Encampment for Citizenship, 1948, and chairman of its education committee, 1954. *Military service:* U.S. Army Air Forces, intelligence officer with Night Photography Reconnaisance Squadron, 1942-46; served in European theater; became captain. *Member:* Modern Language Association of America, American Association of University Professors, American Civil Liberties Union.

WRITINGS: Connop Thirlwall, Historian and Theologian, Macmillan, 1936; (editor with others) *A Bible for the Humanities,* Harper, 1954; *In Another Language: A Record of the Thirty-Year Relationship Between Thomas Mann and His English Translator, Helen T. Lowe-Porter,* Knopf, 1966. Also editor of *Selected Letters of William Carlos Williams,* 1957, *Lost Poems of William Carlos Williams,* 1957, and *Genesis of "Paterson" by William Carlos Williams,* 1962.*

*   *   *

THOMAS, Dorothy Swaine 1899-1977

October 24, 1899—May 1, 1977; American demographer, educator, and author of books in her field; professor emeritus of sociology and co-director of the Center for Population Studies at the University of Pennsylvania. She died in Washington, D.C. Obituaries: *Washington Post,* May 3, 1977. (*CAP*-2; earlier sketch in *CA*-17/18)

*   *   *

THOMAS, William F. 1924-

PERSONAL: Born June 11, 1924, in Bay City, Mich.; son of William and Irene (Billette) Thomas; married Patricia Wendland, December 20, 1948; children: Michael, Peter, Scott. *Education:* Bay City Junior College, A.A., 1948; Northwestern University, B.S., 1950, M.S., 1951. *Home:* 6666 Vickiview Dr., West Hills, Calif. 91304. *Office:* Times Mirror Sq., Los Angeles, Calif. 90053.

CAREER/WRITINGS: Buffalo Evening News, Buffalo, N.Y., assistant chief copy editor, 1950-55; *Sierra Madre News,* Sierra Madre, Calif., editor, 1955-56; *Los Angeles Mirror,* Los Angeles, Calif., editor, 1957-62; *Los Angeles Times,* Los Angeles, metropolitan editor and assistant city editor, 1964-71, executive editor, 1971, executive vice-president and editor, 1972—.

*   *   *

THOMPSON, Fred Dalton 1942-

PERSONAL: Born August 19, 1942, in Tennessee; son of Fletcher (an automobile salesman) and Ruth (Bradley) Thompson; married Sarah Lindsey (a teacher); children: Tony, Daniel, Betsy. *Education:* Florence State College, student, 1960-62; Memphis State University, B.S., 1964; Vanderbilt University, LL.D., 1967. *Politics:* Republican. *Religion:* Christian. *Home:* 808 Sunny Hill Rd., Brentwood, Tenn. 37027. *Office:* Thompson, Liebengood & Crawford, First American Center, Nashville, Tenn. 37238.

CAREER: Thompson, Liebengood & Crawford, Nashville, Tenn., partner in law firm, 1974—. Minority counsel for U.S. Senate Watergate Committee; manager of Middle Tennessee campaign for U.S. Senator Howard Baker, 1972. *Member:* American Bar Association, Tennessee Trial Lawyers Association, Tennessee Bar Association, Nashville Bar Association, Nashville Area Chamber of Commerce.

WRITINGS: At That Point in Time, Quadrangle, 1975. Contributor to law journals.

*   *   *

THOMSON, Roy Herbert 1894-1976

June 5, 1894—August 4, 1976; Canadian publisher who built an empire of 148 newspapers (including *London Times*) and 138 magazines; he owned more newspapers than anyone else in the world. He died in London, England. Obituaries: *New York Times,* August 5, 1976; *Washington Post,* August 5, 1976.

*   *   *

THOMY, Al(fred Marshall)

PERSONAL: Born in Lake City, S.C.; son of Salim Abraham (a merchant) and Blanche (Mauoud) Thomy. *Education:* Attended Guilford College and University of North Carolina. *Religion:* Roman Catholic. *Home:* 2479 Peachtree St. N.E., Atlanta, Ga. 30305. *Office: Atlanta Constitution,* 72 Marietta St., Atlanta, Ga. 30302.

CAREER: Greensboro Daily News, Greensboro, N.C., sports reporter, 1944-49; *Atlanta Constitution,* Atlanta, Ga., sports reporter, 1953-62; *Houston Press,* Houston, Tex., sports reporter and author of column "Diamond Diary," 1963; *Atlanta Times,* Atlanta, Ga., author of column "Al Thomy," 1964-65; *Atlanta Constitution,* professional football writer and author of column "Al Thomy," 1966—. President of Al Thomy Associates (public relations firm), 1964. Member of board of selectors for Pro Football Hall of Fame. *Military service:* U.S. Army, 1953-55; became sergeant.

MEMBER: Pro Football Writers of America. *Awards, honors:* Writing awards from Basketball Writers Association, American Association of Baseball Coaches, and Southern Motorsport Writers; named United Press International sports writer of the year in Georgia, 1975.

WRITINGS: The Ramblin' Wreck, Strode, 1973, revised edition, 1974; *Pepper: An Autobiography of an Unconventional Coach,* Doubleday, 1976. Contributor to *Collegiate Baseball Guide.* Contributor to sports magazines and popular journals, including *Time, Newsweek,* and *Atlanta.*

SIDELIGHTS: Thomy writes: "I think writers are born and not made; there's an inner fire to express yourself and not just witness. I deplore the commercialism of throwing newspaper clippings together and calling it a book. Writers should entertain or have something to say. I admire the simplistic style of Hemingway, who seldom wasted a word."

BIOGRAPHICAL/CRITICAL SOURCES: Greenville News, August 5, 1974.

* * *

THOREN, Arne 1927-

PERSONAL: Born March 24, 1927, in Goteborg, Sweden; son of Jerker (an editor-in-chief) and Helen (Setterberg) Thoren; married Elise Wickes Merritt, April 4, 1951 (divorced, 1964); married Eva Berch, December 28, 1966; children: Stephen, Michele, Peter, Cecilia. *Education:* Attended University of Gothenburg, 1946-48, and University of South Dakota, 1948. *Home:* Otterbaecksvaegen, Hovaas, Sweden. *Office:* Polhemsplatsen 5, Gothenburg, Sweden.

CAREER: Expressen, Stockholm, Sweden, reporter, 1949-51, New York correspondent, 1952-64; Swedish Broadcasting Corp., Stockholm, New York correspondent, 1956-77; *Goeteborgs-Posten,* Gothenburg, Sweden, managing editor, 1977—. Notable assignments include American presidential campaigns, 1948—, all manned space flights in U.S., 1957-76, deaths of John F. Kennedy, Robert Kennedy, Martin Luther King, and Dag Hammarskjold. Chairman of United Nations' Dag Hammarskjold Memorial Scholarship Fund, 1971-74 and 1976. *Member:* United Nations Correspondents Association (president, 1975), Publicistlubben. *Awards, honors:* Stora Journalistpriset, 1969, for coverage of space program.

WRITINGS: (With Ulf Thoren) *Fran Min Sida Sett,* Bonniers (Stockholm), 1968. Contributor of articles to Swedish magazines, including *Vecko-Journalen, Aaret Runt, Roester i Radio/TV,* and *SE.*

WORK IN PROGRESS: A Swedish Travel Guide of New York; Memoirs of My U.S. Years.

SIDELIGHTS: Thoren told *CA:* "I have the greatest respect for American journalism as well as for the work done by my countrymen in the same profession. After 26 years as a correspondent in the United States it is pleasing to note that Swedish journalists and newspapers, as well as the news departments of radio and television, 'borrow' the best of what the U.S. has to offer. There is a great interest for American journalism in Sweden and I myself, as a score of

colleagues in large and small papers, follow the U.S. through magazines as well as newspapers and the correspondents now active in America."

* * *

THURKETTLE, James 1929-

PERSONAL: Born January 10, 1929, in Durham, England; son of Arthur (a butcher) and Mary (Hutchinson) Thurkettle; married Dorothy Joan Ritchie (a teacher); children: Helen, Ian. *Education:* University of Bristol, B.A., 1950; University of Durham, diploma in education, 1951. *Religion:* Church of England. *Home:* 28 Woodvale Rd., Darlington, England.

CAREER: History master in school in Durham County, England, 1951-55; Ankara College, Ankara, Turkey, English master, 1955-59; history master in girls' school in South Shields, Durham, England, 1959-61; Sunnydale Secondary School, Shildon, England, headmaster, 1966—.

WRITINGS: An outline of the Social and Economic History of Britain, 1066-1956, Oxford University Press, 1967, Pergamon, 1968.

* * *

TILLMAN, Stephen Frederick 1900(?)-1977

1900(?)—May 21, 1977; American journalist and veteran of World Wars I and II. He died in Washington, D.C. Obituaries: *Washington Post,* May 22, 1977.

* * *

TILTMAN, Hessell 1897(?)-1976

1897(?)—August 10, 1976; British journalist (a war correspondent in both the Sino-Japanese and Spanish Civil Wars) and author. He died aboard the Polish liner *Jurista* on his way back to Tokyo from Britain. Obituaries: *New York Times,* August 12, 1976.

* * *

TODD, Ian Menzies 1923-

PERSONAL: Born May 27, 1923, in Salonika, Greece; son of Thomas Menzies and Allilat (Dimitroussi) Todd. *Education:* Attended American College of Anatolia, Abbetiuz College, University of London, and London School of Journalism. *Home:* Apt. 54, Guadalupe, San Jose, Costa Rica.

CAREER: Foreign news writer for British Broadcasting Corp. (BBC), London, England; sub-editor of South African Press Association, Johannesburg; deskman of *Canadian Press,* Montreal, Quebec; feature writer for *Ottawa Citizen,* Ottawa, Ontario; police reporter for *Vancouver Daily Province,* Vancouver, British Columbia; magazine editor of Thompson Newspapers, Cape Town, South Africa; supplements editor of *Sydney Daily Telegraph,* Sydney, Australia; managing editor of *Samoa Times;* director of public relations for premier's department in Queensland, Australia; now editor of *Excelsior,* San Jose, Costa Rica. *Military service:* British Army, Black Watch, special operations executive and parachutist; became lieutenant.

WRITINGS: Papua New Guinea: The Moment of Truth, Angus & Robertson, 1974; *Island Realm: A Pacific Panorama,* Angus & Robertson, 1974. Also author of a novel, *Flower of the Goddess;* a detective novel, *Shadow of Her Past;* a biography, *Behind the Japanese Lines;* a historical romance, *Black Bandanna;* and a spy novel, *Ghost of the Assassins.*

WORK IN PROGRESS: A book on Costa Rica's political and historical development; a spy thriller, a sequel to *Ghosts of the Assassins*.

SIDELIGHTS: Todd speaks French, Greek, Spanish, Italian, and Arabic. *Avocational interests:* Chess (championship winner), kung-fu (black belt, 1967).

* * *

TOLMIE, Kenneth Donald 1941-

PERSONAL: Born September 18, 1941, in Halifax, Nova Scotia, Canada; son of Archibald (a factory manager) and Evelyn (Murray) Tolmie; married Ruth MacKenzie (a librarian), August 8, 1962; children: Sarah Katherine, Jane Marianna. *Education:* Mount Allison University, B.F.A. (honors), 1962. *Home:* 649 River Rd. S., Peterborough, Ontario, Canada.

CAREER: Artist, illustrator, and writer. Member of board of directors of INAX Instruments; chairman of Visual Arts Ottawa. Has had one-man shows in Ottawa, Toronto, and Halifax, and group shows and exhibitions in England and New York; his work is represented in collections at National Gallery of Canada, Montreal Museum of Fine Arts, and private collections in the United States, Canada, and Europe. *Member:* Canadian Artists Representation.

WRITINGS: *A Tale of an Egg* (self-illustrated juvenile), Oberon, 1975.

Illustrator: Stuart MacKinnon, *The Welder's Arc*, Oberon, 1969.

SIDELIGHTS: Tolmie has lived and worked in England and Spain.

* * *

TOLSTOY, Mary Koutouzov 1884(?)-1976

1884(?)—November 21, 1976; American-born author, artist, and director of couture houses in Paris; worked as a nurse in French hospitals during borth world wars and worked with the French Resistance during World War II. Her late husband was a nephew of Leo Tolstoy. She died in Paris. *Obituaries: New York Times*, November 25, 1976.

* * *

TOMPERT, Ann 1918-

PERSONAL: Born January 11, 1918, in Detroit, Mich.; daughter of Joseph (a farmer) and Florence (Pollitt) Bakeman; married Robert S. Tompert (in social service), March 31, 1951. *Education:* Siena Heights College, B.A. (summa cum laude); Wayne State University, graduate study. *Politics:* "Independent with Republican leanings." *Religion:* Christian. *Residence:* Marine City, Mich.

CAREER: Teacher in elementary and junior and senior high schools of St. Clair Shores, East Detroit, Grosse Pointe, Marine City, and other cities in Michigan, 1939-59; writer, 1959—. *Member:* Society of Children's Book Writers, River District Hospital Auxiliary (life member; St. Clair, Mich.). *Awards, honors: Little Fox Goes to the End of the World* was named notable children's book by American Library Association, 1976.

WRITINGS—Children's books, except as indicated: *What Makes My Cat Purr?*, Whitman Publishing, 1965; *The Big Whistle*, Whitman Publishing, 1968; *When Rooster Crowed*, Whitman Publishing, 1968; *Maybe a Dog Will Come*, Follett, 1968; *A Horse for Charlie*, Whitman Publishing, 1969; *The Crow, the Kite, and the Golden Umbrella*, Abelard,

1971; *Fun for Ozzie*, Steck, 1971; *Hyacinth, the Reluctant Duck*, Steck, 1972; *It May Come in Handy Someday*, McGraw, 1975; *Little Fox Goes to the End of the World* (Junior Literary Guild selection), Crown, 1976; (editor) *The Way Things Were* (adult autobiography of Marine City, Mich., pioneer, Emily Ward), privately printed, 1976; *Little Otter Remembers*, Crown, 1977. Contributor to children's magazines, including *Jack and Jill*.

WORK IN PROGRESS: A children's book, *The Clever Princess*, for Lollipop Power, Inc.

SIDELIGHTS: The schools Ann Tompert has taught in range from a two-room country schoolhouse in the thumb area of Michigan to the large metropolitan schools of suburban Detroit. In addition, she worked part time in an antique shop and in a local vegetable and flower nursery.

She told *CA:* "I was reared on a small farm on the outskirts of Detroit where my father raised vegetables which were sold at a roadside stand in front of our house; and I have never forgotten my 'roots.' I suppose we were what today would be called 'underprivileged,' but we weren't aware of it. We had few toys so we made our fun. . . . But books were the most important things in my life.

"Because my life has been so influenced by what I read as a child (for example: I knew I wanted to be a writer like Jo Marsh when I read *Little Women*), I am very committed to the idea of fostering positive values in my books for children.

"We as a nation are so dedicated to preserving our physical environment and our quality of life (making ourselves safe from all harm—auto safety, cancer research, pure food laws, etc.); yet, when it comes to dealing with our minds, anything and everything is permissible. I find this very disturbing, to say the least."

AVOCATIONAL INTERESTS: Reading new writers, collecting paperweights and milkglass, working in her wildflower garden, caning chairs, refinishing furniture, sewing, and needlework.

* * *

TORBET, Laura 1942-

PERSONAL: Born August 23, 1942, in Paterson, N.J.; daughter of Earl B. (owner and president of Metalcraft, Inc.) and Ruth (Ehlers) Robbins; married Bruce J. Torbet, September 9, 1967 (divorced, 1971). *Education:* Ohio Wesleyan University, B.A. and B.F.A., 1964. *Home and office:* Laura Torbet Studio, 45 East 22nd St., New York, N.Y. 10010. *Agent:* Sanford J. Greenburger Associates, Inc., 825 Third Ave., New York, N.Y. 10017.

CAREER: *New Jersey Life*, Orange, N.J., managing editor, 1964-65; United Funds of Essex and West Hudson, Newark, N.J., assistant director of public relations, 1965-66; Alitalia Airlines, New York, N.Y., art director, 1966-68; Laura Torbet Studio (graphic design), New York City, owner, 1968—. *Awards, honors:* Graphics and fine arts awards from art directors' clubs, art societies, and art publications.

WRITINGS: *Macrame You Can Wear*, Ballantine, 1972; *Clothing Liberation*, Ballantine, 1972; (with John Thamm) *Leathercraft You Can Wear*, Ballantine, 1974; (with Mario Pei and Salvatore Ramondino) *Dictionary of Foreign Terms*, Delacorte, 1974; *The T-Shirt Book*, Bobbs-Merrill, 1976; *The Complete Book of Skateboarding*, Funk, 1976; *How to Do Everything with Markers*, Bobbs-Merrill, 1976; (with Peter L. Skolnik and Nikki Smith) *Fads: America's Crazes, Fevers, and Fancies*, Crowell, 1977; (with Doug McLaggan) *Squash: How to Play, How to Win*, Dolphin

Books, 1978; *Superflier: The Air Travelers Handbook,* Playboy Press, 1978; (editor) *The Encyclopedia of Crafts,* Avon, in press; *Laura Torbet's Craft Book,* Bobbs-Merrill, in press.

SIDELIGHTS: Torbet told *CA:* "I found my new career in writing after having been an artist and graphic designer for years. An editor at Ballanine Books who had seen craft work of mine written up in several magazines called to ask if I'd write a book on the subject (macrame). When I declined—on the grounds that I knew nothing about writing books and was bored silly with macrame—she charmed and persuaded me over the proverbial publishing lunch.

"I soon found that there was no mystery to writing a book—just a lot of work. I also found that writing non-fiction books is in many ways an ideal situation for me. It gives me an excuse to dabble in just about anything that takes my fancy—from crafts to sports and current fads—and to make a living at the same time. Too, it combines very well with my graphics work: I can 'assemble' the books using the same skills, and the same staff and freelancers as are involved in the graphic studios.

"Truth be told, I'm not crazy about writing, but I like all the other stuff—concept, design, illustration, photography, interviewing, etc. It's also a way of getting a fair return on my art and craftwork which is difficult through the usual gallery and show channels. And I like the 'book business.'"

* * *

TORNABENE, Lyn 1930-

PERSONAL: Born October 13, 1930, in Williamsport, Pa.; daughter of William Lawrence and Frances (Herman) Levitt; married Frank Tornabene (an art publisher), October 30, 1954; children: Wendy-Lyn. *Education:* Pennsylvania State College, B.A., 1952. *Politics:* Liberal. *Religion:* Jewish. *Residence:* Greenwich, Conn. *Agent:* Owen Laster, William Morris Agency, 1350 Avenue of the Americas, New York, N.Y. 10019.

CAREER: Good Housekeeping, New York, N.Y., associate editor, 1954-60; *Cosmopolitan,* New York City, features editor, 1960-64; *Ladies Home Journal,* New York City, articles editor, 1965-67; free-lance writer, 1967—. Consulting editor for Popular Library.

WRITINGS: What's a Jewish Girl, Simon & Schuster, 1966; *I Passed as a Teenager,* Simon & Schuster, 1967; *Long Live the King* (biography of Clark Gable), Putnam, 1977. Author of columns "Lunch Date" in *Cosmopolitan,* 1960-63, and "Walking With" in *McCalls,* 1969. Contributor to popular magazines, including *Family Circle, Saturday Review,* and *Esquire.*

WORK IN PROGRESS: A novel on women, completion expected in 1979; a musical comedy.

SIDELIGHTS: Lyn Tornabene writes: "I am interested in human survival, celebrity, the commonplace. Everyone has a story. . . . I am dedicated to the dignity of women as a cause. I loathe assumptions, cliches, filing cabinets. I wish to declare my subjectivity as a journalist. . . . I don't like to talk. I like anonymity. I hate to be lonely and always am as I write."

AVOCATIONAL INTERESTS: Tennis, reading, cooking, dogs.

* * *

TORREY, Volta (Wray) 1905-

PERSONAL: Born January 31, 1905, in Eddyville, Iowa; son of Wray A. (an engineer) and Bertha (Rowe) Torrey; married Geneva De Fries (a teacher), 1929; children: Thomas Wray. *Education:* University of Nebraska, A.B., 1926; Harvard University, graduate study, 1940. *Politics:* Democrat. *Religion:* Protestant. *Home and office:* 616 G St. S.W., Washington, D.C. 20024.

CAREER: Reporter and editor for newspapers in Omaha, Neb., Chicago, Ill., and New York, N.Y., 1926-43; *Popular Science Monthly,* New York, N.Y., writer and editor, 1944-56; WGBH-Television, Boston, Mass., science reporter, 1956-59; Massachusetts Institute of Technology, Cambridge, editor and publisher, 1959-66; National Aeronautics and Space Administration, Washington, D.C., publications specialist, 1966-76; writer, 1976—. *Member:* National Association of Science Writers (president, 1945), National Press Club, Aviation/Space Writers Association. *Awards, honors:* Charles L. Lawrence Award from Aviation/Space Writers Association, 1969.

WRITINGS: You and Your Congress, Morrow, 1945; *Wind-Catchers: American Windmills of Yesterday and Tomorrow,* Stephen Greene Press, 1976. Contributor to technical and popular journals, including *Atlantic Monthly, Saturday Review, Physics Today,* and *Science Digest.*

WORK IN PROGRESS: Articles about energy and the environment.

* * *

TOTH, Stephen, Jr. 1950-

PERSONAL: Surname rhymes with "both"; born April 11, 1950, in Bemidji, Minn.; son of Stephen (a mechanical engineer) and Elizabeth (Kreydich) Toth; married Sheila Heldenbrand (a writer), May 26, 1972. *Education:* University of Iowa, B.A., 1972. *Politics:* "Love." *Religion:* "Universal." *Home:* 15019 Larch, Lawndale, Calif. 90260.

CAREER: Writer, 1966—. *Member:* Rosicrucian Order, Traditional Martinist Order.

WRITINGS—All poetry: *Gold Rush,* Toothpaste Press, 1972; (with wife, Sheila Heldenbrand) *Morning Glories,* Oyster Press, 1973; *Rota Rooter,* Frontward Books, 1976; *Traveling Light,* Blue Wind Press, 1977. Co-editor of *P. F. Flyer,* 1972-73.

WORK IN PROGRESS: Lost Angels, poems centering on urban life and the history of language; *I Love Lucy,* with wife, Sheila Heldenbrand, for In the Light Books.

SIDELIGHTS: Toth writes that he has been influenced by thirteenth century Persian writers, like Rumi, Attar, Khayyam, and modern influences, including Ted Berrigan, Anselm Hollo, Jack Marshall, and Darrell Gray. He is associated with the poetry movement known as Actualism. Other interests include study of Hebrew, Tarot, Hasidic tales, ancient religious texts and pre-industrial writings.

* * *

TOWNSEND, Charles R(ay) 1929-

PERSONAL: Born November 5, 1929, in Nocona, Tex.; son of Claude Webster (an oil drilling contractor) and Dot (Keck) Townsend; married Mary Louise Smith (an elementary school teacher), April 9, 1950; children: William Donald, Mary Jane, Charles. *Education:* Midwestern State University, B.A., 1960; Baylor University, M.A., 1961; University of Wisconsin, Ph.D., 1968. *Politics:* Democrat. *Religion:* Baptist. *Home:* 507 25th St., Canyon, Tex. 79015. *Office:* Department of History, West Texas State University, Canyon, Tex. 79016.

CAREER: Olsen Steltzer Boot and Saddlery, Henrietta, Tex., sales manager, 1949-54; Nocona Boot Manufacturing Co., Nocona, Tex., sales manager, 1954-55; Olsen Steltzer Boot and Saddlery, sales manager, 1957-60; Hardin-Simmons University, Abilene, Tex., associate professor of history, 1965-67; West Texas State University, Canyon, associate professor, 1967-75, professor of history, 1975—. Member: American Historical Association, Organization of American Historians, American Association of University Professors. Awards, honors: Grammy Award from National Academy of Recording Arts and Sciences and Western Heritage Award from National Cowboy Hall of Fame, both 1975, for Homecoming.

WRITINGS: Homecoming: Reflections on Bob Wills and His Texas Playboys, 1915-1973, United Artists, 1974; Bob Wills and American Music, Capitol, 1976; San Antonio Rose: The Life and Music of Bob Wills, University of Illinois Press, 1976.

WORK IN PROGRESS: Musical Contributions of the American South.

SIDELIGHT: "I am of the opinion," Townsend told CA, "that popular American culture, especially popular music, has been sadly neglected in American history. I hope to encourage young students to help right this wrong by researching and publishing in these neglected areas."

* * *

TRAGER, Helen G. 1910-

PERSONAL: Born October 22, 1910, in New York, N.Y.; daughter of Leon (a businessman) and Anna (Schutte) Gilbson; married Carl Fichandler (divorced, 1936); married Frank N. Trager (a professor of international affairs), October 9, 1936. Education: New York University, B.S., 1941, M.A., 1948, Ph.D., 1958. Politics: "Was a Norman Thomas Socialist until World War II. Unaffiliated since." Home: Hunt Lane, North Salem, N.Y. 10560.

CAREER: Substitute teacher in New York City public schools, 1930-39; Bureau for Intercultural Education, New York City, director of age-level studies, 1943-45 and 1948-50, director of Philadelphia early childhood project, 1945-48; University of Rangoon, Rangoon, Burma, honorary visiting professor of education, 1951-53; Brooklyn College, New York City, lecturer in early childhood, 1954-55; Barnard College, New York City, director of education program, 1955-58; U.S. education consultant to Afghanistan, 1959; Bank Street College of Education, New York City, director of field action research, 1960-61; Peace Corps, Washington, D.C., associate director of college and university division, 1961-63; Trustee, North Salem (N.Y.) Free Library, 1964-73; elected trustee, North Salem District School Board, 1971-74.

MEMBER: Association of American Indians, Burma Research Society, Asia Society, Wilderness Society, Association for Asian Studies, Hammond Museum, Kitchiwan Field Service of Brooklyn Botanical Garden, North Salem Historical Society. Awards, honors: William C. Whitney Foundation fellowship in experimental education, 1940-41.

WRITINGS: (Contributor) W. Kilpatrick and W. Ventil, editors, Intercultural Attitudes in the Making, Harper, 1947; (with Marion Radke) They Learn What They Live: Prejudice in Young Children, Harper, 1952; Burma Through Alien Eyes: Missionary Views of the Burmese in the Nineteenth Century, Praeger, 1966; (with Htin Aung) A Kingdom Lost for a Drop of Honey, Parents' Magazine Press, 1968;

(editor) We the Burmese: Voices of Burma, Praeger, 1969; The Schoolhouse at Pinetree Corner, North Salem, New York, 1784-1916, Harbor Hill Press for the North Salem Historical Society, 1976.

Author of reports for vaious organizations, including Asia Society, Foreign Policy Association and U.S. Aid Mission to Afghanistan. Author of curriculum guides, pamphlets, and monographs. Contributor of articles to journals, including Comparative Education, Journal of Psychology, and Childhood Education.

SIDELIGHTS: Trager writes: "The primary emphases in my research, writing, and teaching have been intercultural and international. Since 1951, when my husband and I first went to Asia, we have revisited that part of the world at least seventeen times."

Trager served as an expert witness in the 1951 Clarendon County, N.C., school case. Her testimony concerned the effects of segregation on the personalities of children.

* * *

TRASK, John Jacquelin 1904(?)-1977

1904(?)—June 5, 1977; American business executive and author. He died in Stonington, Conn. Obituaries: New York Times, June 5, 1977.

* * *

TREE, Ronald 1897-1976

PERSONAL: Full name Arthur Ronald Lambert Field Tree; born in Eastbourne, England; son of Arthur Tree; married Nancy Perkin Field, 1920 (divorced); married Mary Endicott Peabody FitzGerald (a partner in urban planning firm), 1947; children: Jeremy, Michael, Penelope; (stepchildren) Frances FitzGerald. Education: Attended Columbia University. Home: 123 E, 79th St., New York, N.Y. and Heron Bay, Barbados.

CAREER: Forum, New York City, managing editor, 1922-26; joint master of the Pytchley Hounds, 1927-33; Conservative member of British Parliament, representing the Harborough division of Leichestershire, 1933-45; parliamentary private secretary to R. S. Hudson (minister of pensions and later secretary to Overseas Trade Department), 1936-38, Sir John Reith, Minister of Information, Right Honorable Alfred Dugg-Cooper and Right Honorable Brendan Bracken (both Parliament ministers), 1940-43, and to Ministry of Town and Country Planning, 1945. Trustee of Wallace Collection. Member of council, University of West Indies. President, Barbados National Trust. Military service: U.S. Navy, aviator, 1914-18. Member: Turf Club, White's Club, Century Club (New York).

WRITINGS: A History of Barbados, Random, 1972; When the Moon Was High: Memoirs of Peace and War (autobiography), Macmillan, 1975.

SIDELIGHTS: Tree counted among his intimate friends some of the most powerful and famous men and women of his time, including historical and political figures as well as filmstars and social celebrities. Winston Churchill was a frequent visitor at Tree's Ditchley Park Estate, especially during the war years when it was feared that the prime minister's country residence might be too vulnerable to Luftwaffe bombings. Churchill first met Henry Hopkins at Ditchley Park, and it was there that many of the details of Lend-Lease were worked out.

The Ditchley Park Estate consisted of a mansion (housing

twenty-four bedrooms, ten bathrooms, and seven reception rooms), along with its numerous outbuildings, thirty tenant farm cottages, and gardens, woods, and lawns covering thirty-three hundred acres. Tree began to feel a tax pinch after he lost his seat in Parliament in a post-war Labor Party sweep. In 1949, he decided to sell Ditchley Park in favor of a Barbados Estate called Heron Bay.

In recent years the Trees divided their time between Heron Bay and a Manhattan apartment friends called "Little Ditchley".

AVOCATIONAL INTERESTS: Yachting, swimming, golf.

OBITUARIES: New York Times, July 15, 1976; *Washington Post,* July 15, 1976; *Time,* July 26, 1976.*

(Died July 14, 1976, in London, England)

*   *   *

TREFETHEN, James B(yron, Jr.)   1916-1976

June 3, 1916—December 30, 1976; American editor and writer; served as director of publications for Wildlife Management Institute, and wrote books and articles on wildlife and conservation. He died in Washington, D.C. Obituaries: *Washington Post,* January 1, 1977. (See index for previous *CA* sketch)

*   *   *

TRETTEL, (Mario) Efrem   1921-

PERSONAL: Born May 17, 1921, in Predazzo, Italy; son of Andrea (a teacher) and Maria (a teacher; maiden name, Dellagiacoma) Trettel. *Education:* Attended Franciscan seminary, 1938-45. *Home:* 3106 Folsom St., San Francisco, Calif. 94110. *Office:* Apostolato Radio Cristiana, 3106 Folsom St., San Francisco, Calif. 94110.

CAREER: Entered Order of the Friars Minor (O.F.M.; Franciscans), 1933, ordained Roman Catholic priest, 1944; priest in Roman Catholic churches in Trento, Italy, 1944-45, and Calabria, Italy, 1945-46; teacher of Franciscan theology in seminary school in Tropea, Italy, 1946-47; missionary in China, 1947-51; lecturer and preacher throughout the Dioceses of Trent, 1951-53; associate pastor in Roman Catholic church in San Francisco, Calif., 1953-67, pastor, 1967-70; Apostolato Radio Cristiana, San Francisco, Calif., director, 1969—. Engaged in religious radio communications, 1954—; chaplain of Italian Catholic Federation, 1954-69; music teacher in Roman Catholic schools in San Francisco, Calif., 1960-64; member of Franciscan Communication Center (Los Angeles, Calif.), 1964-66.

WRITINGS—In English translation: *Fiumi, Risaie, Anime, Nigrizia* (Bologna), 1960, translation by Elsa Micallef published as *Rivers, Rice Fields, Souls: Memoirs of My Mission in China,* Franciscan Herald, 1965; *"Poems" Liriche* (in English and Italian; translation by Micallef and Joseph Maltaman), La Nuova Italia Letteraria (Bergamo), 1961; *Francesco d'Assisi,* Nigrizia, 1972, translation by Lorenzo Perotti published as *Francis,* Franciscan Herald, 1975.

Other work: *Fogli Sparsi* (poems; title means "Scattered Sheets"), Pro Manuscript (Trento), 1950; *Poesie,* Tipografia AOR (Trento), 1952; *Dieci Anni di Esperienze* (articles; title means "Ten Years of Experiences"), Adige, 1976; (editor) *Testimonianza Cristiana* (title means "Christian Witness"), Adige, 1976. Author of column "Program di Istruzione Religiosa" (title means "Program of Religious Instruction") in *I.C.F. Bulletin,* 1954—.

Contributor of poems to literary magazines in Italy.

WORK IN PROGRESS: A collection of poems, 1964-74; composing and writing sacred songs; an autobiography; developing distribution of audio-cassettes for hospitals and convalescent homes.

SIDELIGHTS: Father Trettel studied piano, organ, violin, and composition in Italy; directed choirs, written solo and choir music; and improvised music for radio and television production. He has painted in oils and acrylics, and his photography is now a regular part of his television presentations. Broadcasting since 1954, he began with a weekly in-depth radio program covering a wide variety of topics, but now his work, much of it is for Italian-speaking people, involves radio and television production and the production of audio cassettes.

Trettel writes: "A 'mike' is my pulpit. Not just to preach, but to break the loneliness of many, to awake the interest in life of those who have lost the sense of happy living. To preach goodness, to make someone feel good, is in itself the best sermon one can give. Religion, culture, folklore, traditions, and the very voice of the people you try to reach, constitute necessary elements for a wholesome spiritual-cultural meal."

*   *   *

TREUER, Robert   1926-

PERSONAL: Surname is pronounced *Troy*-er; born January 31, 1926, in Vienna, Austria; came to the United States in 1939, naturalized, 1944; son of Fritz and Mia (Weil) Treuer; married Nancy Nelson, January 31, 1944 (divorced, September, 1967); married Margaret Seelye (an attorney), April 13, 1968; children: Robert Smith, Paul, Derek John, Anton Steven, David Robert. *Education:* Yale University, student, 1944-45; Antioch College, B.A., 1949; Bemidji State College, B.S., 1960. *Home:* 1730 Crestwood Dr. N.W., Washington, D.C. 20011. *Agent:* Elaine Markson, Elaine Markson Literary Agency, Inc., 44 Greenwich Ave., New York, N.Y. 10011. *Office address:* Route 4, Bemidji, Minn. 56601.

CAREER: Union organizer and editor in Wisconsin, 1949-58; free-lance writer and tree farmer in Bemidji, Minn., 1958-60; high school teacher of English in Cass Lake, Minn., 1961-63; Indian tribal manager and organizer in Minnesota, 1963-68; Office of Economic Opportunity, Washington, D.C., grant and personnel manager, 1968-73; U.S. Department of Health, Education and Welfare, Washington, D.C., grant and contract manager, 1973—; writer, 1977—. *Military service:* U.S. Army, 1944-46.

WRITINGS: The Tree Farm (non-fiction), Little, Brown, 1977.

WORK IN PROGRESS: Voyageur Park, non fiction, publication by University of Minnesota Press expected in 1978; *Reservations,* for Little, Brown, in 1979.

SIDELIGHTS: Treuer told *CA:* "It is important to me to live as a socially useful human being, and in most of my adult pursuits I have found satisfaction in that regard, including my writing. It is ironic that as the product of the humanitarian idealism and romanticism of Europe I should find what spiritual peace I have through my contact with the Ojibwe Indian culture, but that is what happened. To some degree my writing reflects this." *Avocational interests:* Classical piano, canoeing, philately, and hiking.

*   *   *

TREWIN, Ion (Courtenay Gill)   1943-

PERSONAL: Surname is pronounced *Trey*-win; born July

13, 1943, in London, England; son of John Courtenay (a writer) and Wendy (a writer; maiden name, Monk) Trewin; married Sue Merry, August 7, 1966; children: Simon Courtenay, Maria Jane Merry. *Education:* Attended secondary school in London, England. *Home:* 48 Cholmeley Cres., Highgate, London N.6, England. *Office: Times,* Gray's Inn Rd., London W.C.1, England.

CAREER: Independent, Plymouth, England, reporter, 1960-63; *Sunday Telegraph,* London, England, feature writer, 1963-67; *Times,* London, England, "Times Diary" column editor, 1967-72, literary editor, 1972—. Member of management committee of Highgate Literary and Scientific Institution. Chairman of judges for Booker Prize for Fiction, of Booker Brothers, 1974; judge for Somerset Maugham Prize, of the Society of Authors, 1976—. *Member:* New Fiction Society (member of board of directors). *Awards, honors:* Ronald Politzer Prize from Publishers Publicity Circle, 1976, for editing *Times* Christmas book supplement and launching paperback pages.

WRITINGS: (Contributor) Sheridan Morley, editor, *Theatre 74,* Hutchinson, 1974; *Journalism,* David & Charles, 1975; *Norfolk Cottage* (memoirs), M. Joseph, 1977. Contributor to literary and publishing journals.

WORK IN PROGRESS: The Life and Career of "Sapper", on H. C. McNeile, creator of "Bulldog Drummond"; *Art and the Railway.*

SIDELIGHTS: Trewin writes that he was "brought up in a book and theatre oriented family. As a journalist I believe that a book must communicate its message to as large a public as possible." *Avocational interests:* Gardening, reading, cricket, Norfolk and Cornwall.

* * *

TRINIDAD, Francisco D., Jr. 1939-
(Corky Trinidad)

PERSONAL: Born May 26, 1939, in Manila, the Philippines; son of Francisco D. and Carolina (Flores) Trinidad; married Hana Gomez, June 10, 1967; children: Emmanuel, Pia Katrina, Lara Maria, Lorenzo. *Education:* University of Ateneo de Manila, B.A., 1960. *Religion:* Roman Catholic. *Residence:* Honolulu, Hawaii. *Office: Honolulu Star-Bulletin,* P.O. Box 3080, Honolulu, Hawaii 96802.

CAREER: Advertising account executive for Nation-Ad, 1960; political cartoonist for *Philippines Herald,* 1960-69; *Honolulu Star-Bulletin,* Honolulu, Hawaii, political cartoonist, 1969—, author of daily comic strip "Aloha Eden" and weekly cartoon "The Gullivers." Professor at Philippine Women's University, 1960-67; presently associate professor at University of Hawaii. *Awards, honors:* Foreign journalism award from University of California, Los Angeles, 1967; cartooning awards from International Salon des Humour, Montreal, Quebec, 1967, 1971.

WRITINGS—Under name Corky Trinidad: *Nguyen Charlie,* Stars & Stripes, 1969; *Sorry 'Bout That, Sarge,* Stars & Stripes, 1969; *Not in This War, Charlie,* Stars & Stripes, 1970; *Aloha Eden* (cartoons), Rainbow Publishing, 1975; (with Thomas Hernandez) *Under the Coconut Tree,* University of Hawaii, 1976. Cartoonist for *Pacific Stars & Stripes,* 1966-70; author of daily syndicated editorial cartoons.

BIOGRAPHICAL/CRITICAL SOURCES: Syd Hoff, *Editorial and Political Cartooning,* Stravon, 1976.

TROUTMAN, Charles (Henry) 1914-

PERSONAL: Born April 3, 1914, in Butler, Pa.; son of Charles Henry (a merchant) and Lena (Dunn) Troutman; married Lois Dickason, February 7, 1942; children: Charles, David, Miriam Troutman de Paredes. *Education:* Wheaton College, Wheaton, Ill., B.S., 1936; graduate study at Michigan State University and University of Michigan, 1939-40. *Religion:* Episcopalian. *Office:* Apartado 10-250, San Jose, Costa Rica.

CAREER: Inter-Varsity Christian Fellowship, member of staff in Canada and the United States, 1936-42, assistant general secretary in the United States, 1946-53, general secretary in Australia, 1956-61, general director in the United States, 1961-65; Community of Latin American Evangelical Ministries, San Jose, Costa Rica, member of personnel staff, 1965—; Spanish Language Institute, San Jose, Calif., president of board of directors, 1969—. Vice-president of Episcopal Diocese of Costa Rica; affiliate of Latin American Mission. *Military service:* U.S. Army, Corps of Engineers, 1942-46; served in the Far East; became first lieutenant. *Member:* American Scientific Affiliation.

WRITINGS: Everything You Want to Know About the Mission Field, But Are Afraid..., Inter-Varsity Press, 1976. Editor of *Penetracion,* 1969-74.

WORK IN PROGRESS: Preparing Christian missionary structures, policies, practices, and personnel for the next generation.

SIDELIGHTS: Troutman told *CA:* "The recent book was an attempt to prepare new missionaries for the differences of living abroad without extra financial subsidies and the problems of living in another culture with a religious/Christian assignment which nevertheless respects the integrity of the individual and his culture."

* * *

TRUMBO, Dalton 1905-1976
(Sam Jackson, Robert Rich)

December 9, 1905—September 10, 1976; American screen writer and novelist. Perhaps the best known of the "Hollywood Ten," the group of film industry authors who were blacklisted for thirteen years, he spent a year in federal prison for refusing to tell the House Un-American Activities Committee if he was a Communist. He was the author of more than sixty screenplays, including the Academy Award winning "The Brave One," written under a pseudonym while he was blacklisted. Trumbo also wrote the novel *Johnny Got His Gun,* which he later filmed. He died in Hollywood, Calif. Obituaries: *New York Times,* September 11, 1976; *Washington Post,* September 11, 1976. (See index for previous *CA* sketch)

* * *

TUCKER, Glenn (Irving) 1892-1976

November 30, 1892—October 27, 1976; American author and Civil War historian; former newspaper reporter and advertising executive. He died in Asheville, N.C. Obituaries: *New York Times,* October 28, 1976; *Washington Post,* October 29, 1976; *AB Bookman's Weekly,* December 20-27, 1976. (See index for previous *CA* sketch)

* * *

TULLY, John (Kimberley) 1923-

PERSONAL: Born July 7, 1923, in Wolverhampton, England; son of John (an actor) and Ruby (an actress; maiden name, Kimberley) Tully; married Margaret Else; children: Richard, David, Katharine, Diana. *Education:* Attended school in North Wales. *Home:* 209 Jersey Rd., Isleworth, Middlesex TW7 4RE, England.

CAREER: Writer for newspapers and for television. *Military service:* Royal Air Force, 1940-45; became sergeant. *Member:* Writers Guild of Great Britain (vice-chairman, 1976-77).

WRITINGS—Juvenile: *The Crocodile*, BBC Publications, 1972; *The Raven and the Cross*, BBC Publications, 1974; *The Glass Knife*, Methuen, 1974; *The White Cat*, Methuen, 1975; *Johnny Goodlooks*, Methuen, 1977.

Film scripts: "The Man from Nowhere," Children's Film Foundation, 1976; "One Hour to Zero," Children's Film Foundation, 1976. Also documentary films for firms including Shell Oil Co., British Gas Council, and Midland Bank.

Also writer of television scripts, including "The Viaduct," 1972, "Thursday's Child," 1973, "Tom's Midnight Garden," 1974, "Kizzy," 1976, and "The Phoenix and the Carpet," 1977; of plays, including "The Crocodile," "The Raven and the Cross," "A King of Argos," "A Choice of Friends," and "The Jo-Jo Tree," and of documentary programs, including material for "Going to Work," "Exploring Science," "Merry-Go-Round," and "Countdown."

WORK IN PROGRESS: Johnny and the Yank, a sequel to *Johnny Goodlooks*.

SIDELIGHTS: Tully writes: "The BBC commissioned me to dramatise a children's novel. Broadcasting dates were fixed. The studio facilities were lined up. All that was lacking was a suitable book to dramatise.

"There are many good novels written for children but few fit the precise demands of time, budget, scope, and aims of a particular TV series. Everyone in the department was reading books furiously, to no avail. At last the producer, in desperation, suggested to me, 'Why don't you write an original television play, and then write the novel to go with it?'

"I snapped up the idea and wrote *The Crocodile*. While the play was in production I started writing the book, with a traumatic realisation that if children were being advised to read it, this had better be good! Not just a 'book of the film' but something worth reading in its own right. I hope I succeeded.

"By the time I had completed a second, similar exercise, *The Raven and the Cross* I had caught the book-writing bug. What tales I could tell if I were not restricted by the mechanics of television! So why not write a book for its own sake, with no holds barred? The result was *The Glass Knife*.

"Drama was and is, I suppose, my first love because I was brought up in the theatre, both sides of my family being up to their hairlines in greasepaint. My grandmother was writing popular melodramas and touring them round England before I was born. My childhood memories are of plays, revues, variety bills, and backstreet digs.

"I have written for a number of adult TV series as well as many children's programmes and I have learned a curious fact, that popular 'adult' material is often the most 'childish.' It's the kids who want to know the truth about the world in terms more thoughtful and sincere." Tully's books have been published in Germany, Sweden, Denmark, and South Africa.

TURNER, Ann W(arren) 1945-

PERSONAL: Born December 10, 1945, in Northampton, Mass.; daughter of Richard Bigelow (a printer) and Marian (an artist; maiden name, Gray) Warren; married Richard E. Turner (a teacher), June 3, 1967. *Education:* Attended University of Manchester, 1965-66; Bates College, B.A., 1967; University of Massachusetts, M.A.T., 1968. *Politics:* Liberal Democrat. *Religion:* Protestant. *Home and office:* 19 High St., Haydenville, Mass. 01039. *Agent:* Craig Virden, Curtis Brown Ltd., 575 Madison Ave., New York, N.Y. 10022.

CAREER: High school English teacher in Great Barrington, Mass., 1968-69; writer, 1969—. Assistant house manager at a home for young women with drug problems; telephone operator for Northampton Hotline (crisis intervention center), 1973-75. *Awards, honors:* First prize from *Atlantic Monthly* college creative writing contest, 1967, for "Athinai."

WRITINGS: Vultures (nonfiction for children), McKay, 1973; *Houses for the Dead* (study of death in several cultures), McKay, 1976.

WORK IN PROGRESS: Rituals of Birth (tentative title), a book on birth rites in different cultures and times, for older children.

SIDELIGHTS: Ann Turner writes: "My upbringing influenced my writing. Possibly because my liberal family was somewhat 'different' from the New Englanders of our town, I grew up being interested in different peoples and cultures. Living in the country and having an artist for a mother gave me a certain way of seeing, an eye for beauty and interest in what others might think ugly or dull; dead weeds, old men and women, fat ladies at the beach, ancient and venerable crows, and vultures. I still live in the country, draw nourishment from it, and write about the seasons in my journal.

"I am concerned with the things that make each culture individual, and the traits that hold us together. To understand ourselves now, I feel we must know the Eskimos, the Aborigines, the ancient Chinese, and Paleolithic man. We are that strange tribe in the jungle; we are the people so old that only their bones and amulets are left. In strange and beautiful ways we are the same, yet different. That is what I write of, and will probably continue writing of for a long, long time."

BIOGRAPHICAL/CRITICAL SOURCES: Daily Hampshire Gazette, October 21, 1976.

*   *   *

TURNER, Francis Joseph 1929-

PERSONAL: Born January 3, 1929, in Windsor, Ontario, Canada; son of Frank Michael (a tailor) and Germaine (Gendron) Turner; married Joanne Catherine Housley (a social worker), July 26, 1958; children: Francis John, Sarah Elizabeth, Anne-Marie. *Education:* University of Western Ontario, B.A. (honors), 1949; University of Ottawa, B.S.W., 1953, M.S.W., 1955; University of Toronto, further graduate study, 1956-58; Columbia University, D.S.W., 1963. *Religion:* Roman Catholic. *Home:* 186 Claremont Ave., Kitchener, Ontario, Canada. *Office:* Faculty of Social Work, Wilfrid Laurier University, Waterloo, Ontario, Canada.

CAREER: Catholic Children's Aid Society, Windsor, Ontario, social worker, 1952-53, 1955-56; Catholic Children's Aid Society, Toronto, Ontario, social worker, 1956-57; Catholic Social Service Bureau, Peterborough, Ontario, assistant director, 1957-59; Catholic Charities, White Plains, N.Y., social worker, summer, 1960; Ontario Hospital, New Toronto, unit supervisor, 1960-62, chief social worker, 1962-63; University of Ottawa, Ottawa, Ontario, assistant professor of social welfare, 1963-66; Waterloo Lutheran University, Waterloo, Ontario, associate professor, 1966-68, professor of social work, 1968-73, dean of Graduate School of Social Work, 1969-73; Wilfrid Laurier University, Waterloo, Ontario, acting academic vice-president, 1974-75, dean of Faculty of Social Work, 1975—. Private practice in social work, 1961—; social worker at Family Service Centre, 1964-68. Kitchener-Waterloo Counselling Service, family social worker, 1972, 1973-75, member of board of directors, 1976. Field instructor at University of Toronto, 1960-63; research associate at Columbia University, 1964-65; professor and head of department of social work at Memorial University of Newfoundland, 1968-69; visiting professor at Oxford University, 1974. Member of board of directors of Ottawa Welfare Council, 1964-66; member of general advisory board of Ryerson Polytechnical Institute, 1967; St. Agatha's Children's Village, chairman of ethical issues committee, 1971, member of board of directors, 1973-76.

MEMBER: International Council on Social Welfare (member of Canadian committee), Canadian Conference on Social Development, National Accreditation Council for the Blind, Catholic Charities Council of Canada, Council on Social Work Education, Ontario Welfare Council, Kitchener-Waterloo Planning Council (president). *Awards, honors:* Research grants from National Department of Health and Welfare, 1964-66, 1966-68, 1969-73, 1972-73, 1974, Social Planning Council of Ottawa, 1966-68, Memorial University of Newfoundland, 1969, Lutheran Church of America, 1970, Family Service Agency of Hamilton, 1971-73, and Atkinson Charitable Foundation, 1972.

WRITINGS: (Editor with P. C. McCabe) *Catholic Social Work: A Contemporary Overview,* Catholic Charities Council of Canada, 1965; *Differential Diagnosis and Treatment in Social Work,* Free Press, 1968, 2nd edition, 1976; *Social Work Treatment: Interlocking Theoretical Approaches,* Free Press, 1973. Contributor of more than thirty articles and reviews to professional journals. Editor of *Social Worker,* 1966-68.

WORK IN PROGRESS: A series on practice in the helping professions for Free Press.

AVOCATIONAL INTERESTS: Sailing, flying (private pilot).

* * *

TURNER, Kay 1932-

PERSONAL: Born December 10, 1932, in India; daughter of John Hayward (an accountant) and Enid (a secretary; maiden name, Jennings) Tubb; married Myles Turner (a game warden), March 10, 1956; children: Lynda Jane, Michael Alan. *Education:* Educated in secondary school in India. *Politics:* British Conservative. *Religion:* Church of England. *Home:* Nyika National Park, Private Bag Chelinda, P.O. Rumphi, Malawi. *Agent:* John Cushman Associates, Inc., 25 West 43rd St., New York, N.Y. 10036.

CAREER: Secretary in Tanzania, 1947-51, Kenya, 1952-53, South Africa, 1953, England, 1954, and Tanzania, 1955; secretary to park wardens and scientists, 1956—.

WRITINGS: Serengeti Home, Dial, 1977. Contributor to *Africana.*

SIDELIGHTS: Kay Turner writes: "I consider conserva-

tion vital, and wrote this book after living for sixteen years in the Serengeti. In its way, it is a plea for conservation. I am unlikely to write another." *Avocational interests:* Painting landscapes, music, travel (Asia, Australia, New Zealand, the United States, Europe, the Middle East), flying (private pilot's license), animals, walking, mountain climbing (climbed Mt. Kilimanjaro), reading, cooking, entertaining, sewing, sailing, tennis.

* * *

TUTKO, Thomas A(rthur) 1931-

PERSONAL: Born September 8, 1931, in Gallitzin, Pa.; son of George Edward (a construction worker) and Alma Theresa (a chambermaid) Tutko; married Carolyn Mae Goodfellow (a nightclub singer), March 31, 1961 (divorced); married Joan Virginia Thompson (a librarian), October 31, 1971 (divorced, 1975); children: Ann Lorraine, Mark Louis, Jane, Sharon. *Education:* Pennsylvania State University, B.S., 1958; Northwestern University, M.A., 1960, Ph.D., 1962. *Office:* Department of Psychology, San Jose State University, San Jose, Calif. 95192.

CAREER: Pipefitter in Detroit, Mich., 1952-54; San Jose State University, San Jose, Calif., assistant professor, 1962-64, associate professor, 1964-66, professor of psychology, 1966—. Research director of Rehabilitation Mental Health Service, 1965-69. *Military service:* U.S. Marine Corps, in supply, 1949-52; served in Panama Canal Zone; became staff sergeant. *Member:* American Psychological Association, California State Psychological Association, California State Marriage and Family Counseling. *Awards, honors:* U.S. Public Health Service grant, 1965-69.

WRITINGS: (With Bruce Ogilvie) *Problem Athletes and How to Handle Them,* Pelham Press; *Motivation in Play, Game, and Sports,* C. C Thomas, 1970; *Clinical Aspects of Sport Psychology,* Quest, 1970; (with Jack Richards) *Psychology of Coaching,* Allyn & Bacon, 1971; (with Richards) *The Coach's Practical Guide to Athletic Motivation,* Allyn & Bacon, 1972; (with Patsy Neal) *Coaching Girls and Women: Psychological Perspectives,* Allyn & Bacon, 1975; (with Nino Tos) *Sports Psyching; Playing Your Best Game All the Time,* Tarcher-Hawthorne, 1976; (with Bill Bruns) *Winning Is Everything and Other American Myths,* Macmillan, 1976. Contributor to *Encyclopedia of Sports Medicine.* Contributor of about thirty articles to professional journals.

WORK IN PROGRESS: Two books on athletics, one dealing with parents and the other with adolescents.

SIDELIGHTS: Tutko writes: "I feel fortunate in being able to combine my profession of psychology and my avocational interest in athletics. For the most part my philosophy is a humanistic one and I hope by my writings to introduce and have developed an individualistic humanistic approach to athletics since I consider it one of the greatest areas of potential growth in our everyday lives."

BIOGRAPHICAL/CRITICAL SOURCES: People, May 13, 1974.

* * *

TWOMBLY, Wells A. 1935-1977

October 24, 1935—May 30, 1977; American sports writer; most recently sports columnist for the *San Francisco Examiner;* also author of books, including *200 Years of Sports in America.* He died in Redwood City, Calif. Obituaries: *New York Times,* May 31, 1977. (See index for previous *CA* sketch)

TYSON, Richard 1944-

PERSONAL: Born December 9, 1944, in Pittsburgh, Pa.; son of Nathan N. (in the steel business) and Geraldine A. Tyson; married Sandy Rudd (a teacher), May 26, 1975; children: Jonathan Simon. *Education:* Columbia University, student, 1962-64; University of Miami, Coral Gables, Fla., B.A., 1967, M.D., 1971. *Agent:* Jeff Feinman, 40 East 49th St., New York, N.Y. 10017. *Office:* 9150 Galloway Rd., Miami, Fla. 33176.

CAREER: Intern and resident at Jackson Memorial Hospital, 1971-73; family physician in private practice, Miami, Fla., 1973—; medical adviser, Miami-Dade Community College, 1971-73. President, CineMed, Inc., 1971-73, Medical One Communications, Inc., 1973-75, Medical One International, Inc., 1975-76, Energenics, Inc., 1976—; director, Bionutritition Institute, 1977—. Professional entertainer and musician, 1961-67; film producer, director, and writer, 1970-75; author, 1975—. *Member:* American Society of Composers, Authors, and Publishers, Dade County Medical Association, Florida Medical Association. *Awards, honors:* Golden Eagle from Council on International Nontheatrical Events, 1971, for motion picture "Sexuality: An Introduction for Medical Students"; Clio Award finalist, 1973, for television spot "Trees Growing Up."

WRITINGS—Books: The Meditation Diet, Playboy Press, 1976; *How to Stop Smoking Through Meditation,* Playboy Press, 1976; (with Leonard Haimes) *How to Triple Your Energy,* Playboy Press, 1977.

Filmscripts: "Emergency," 1973; "Asipsis," 1974. Also writer of twelve other short medical films and three multimedia presentations for physicians.

*   *   *

UDALL, Stewart L(ee) 1920-

PERSONAL: Born January 31, 1920, in St. Johns, Ariz.; son of Levi Stewart (a lawyer and state justice) and Louise (Lee) Udall; married Ermalee Webb, August 1, 1947; children: Thomas, Scott, Lynn, Lori, Denis, James. *Education:* Attended Eastern Arizona Junior College; University of Arizona, LL.B., 1948. *Politics:* Democrat. *Religion:* Church of Jesus Christ of Latter-day Saints. *Office:* 1700 Pennsylvania Ave., Washington, D.C. 20006.

CAREER: Admitted to Arizona State Bar, 1948; Udall & Udall, Tucson, Ariz., partner, 1948-54; U.S. representative from 2nd Arizona district, 1955-60, served on Committee on Interior and Insular Affairs, Committee on Education and Labor, and Joint Committee on Navajo-Hopi Indian Administration; U.S. secretary of interior, 1961-69; Overview Corp., Washington, D.C., chairman of board, 1969—. Adjunct professor of environmental humanism, Yale University, 1969. *Military service:* U.S. Army Air Force, 1944; served in European theatre of operations. *Member:* American Bar Association. *Awards, honors:* Received honorary degrees from institutions, including Syracuse University, 1961, Dickinson College, 1963, and Colby College, 1963.

WRITINGS: The Quiet Crisis, Harper, 1963; (with others) *National Parks of America,* Putnam, 1966, 2nd edition, Country Beautiful, 1972; *1976: Agenda for Tomorrow,* Harcourt, 1968; (author of commentaries with others) James M. Burns, editor, *To Heal and To Build: The Programs of President Lyndon B. Johnson,* McGraw, 1968; *Natural Wonders of America,* Country Beautiful, 1971; *America's Natural Treasures,* Rand McNally, 1971; (with others) *The Energy Balloon,* McGraw, 1974; *The National Parks,*

Grossman, 1974. Writer of "Udall on the Environment," syndicated column, 1970—.

AVOCATIONAL INTERESTS: Hunting, fishing, hiking, tennis, and touch football.

*   *   *

UHL, Alexander H. 1899(?)-1976

1899(?)—August 24, 1976; American-born author, editor, and co-founder of Press Associates, Inc., an independent labor news service in Washington, D.C. He served as Madrid bureau chief of the Associated Press during the Spanish Civil War. He died in Madrid. Obituaries: *Washington Post,* August 26, 1976.

*   *   *

ULICH, Robert 1890(?)-1977

1890(?)—June 17, 1977; German-born philosopher, author. and member of faculty at Harvard University for more than twenty-five years. He died in Germany. Obituaries: *New York Times,* June 18, 1977.

*   *   *

UNGER, Leonard 1934-
   (Len Unger)

PERSONAL: Born June 24, 1934, in Philadelphia, Pa.; son of Bernard (a printer) and Molly Unger; married wife Toby; children: David Eric, Bren Ivan. *Education:* University of California, Los Angeles, B.A.; Goddard College, M.A. *Home:* 1575 El Dorado Dr., Thousand Oaks, Calif. 91360.

CAREER: United Way, Los Angeles, Calif., projects director, 1965-73; Conejo Recreation and Park District, Thousand Oaks, Calif., recreation supervisor, 1973—. Social worker and recreation supervisor. *Military service:* U.S. Army, 1951-53. *Member:* National Association of Social Workers, California Recreation and Park Society.

*WRITINGS—*Under name Len Unger: *Walking: The Perfect Exercise,* Impact Publishers, 1976. Author of film scripts for U.S. Information Agency. Contributor of stories to *Equalizer* and *Westwind.*

WORK IN PROGRESS: Research on stress and the midlife crisis.

*   *   *

UTLEY, (Clifton) Garrick 1939-

PERSONAL: Born November 19, 1939, in Chicago, Ill.; son of Clifton Maxwell (a journalist) and Frayn (a journalist; maiden name, Garrick) Utley; married wife, Gertje, May 25, 1973. *Education:* Carleton College, B.A., 1961; Free University in Berlin, graduate study, 1962-63. *Office:* NBC News, 25 St. James St., London S.W.1, England.

CAREER/WRITINGS: National Broadcasting Corp. (NBC News), television correspondent in Brussels, Belgium, 1963-64, Vietnam, 1964-65, Chicago, Ill., and New York City, 1966, Berlin, Germany, 1966-68, chief of bureau in Paris, France, 1968-71, British correspondent, 1973—. *Military service:* U.S. Army, 1961-62.

*   *   *

VAN DUYN, Janet 1910-

PERSONAL: Born September 23, 1910, in Auburn, N.Y.; daughter of David Montgomery and Ruth (Bartlett) Dunning; married John Van Duyn (a surgeon), December, 1935 (divorced, 1949); children: Ruth Minnich, Barbara (Mrs. Richard H. Bickerstaff, Jr.). *Education:* Vassar College, A.B., 1932. *Politics:* "Registered independent." *Religion:* "Also independent." *Home:* 135 Lyons Plain Rd., Weston, Conn. 06883.

CAREER: Writer, 1968—. Janet Van Duyn told *CA:* "I have done some teaching of English and writing. I have done library work (research), storytelling in the New York Public Library (my first job). I stayed cooped up in many types of worthy offices until the children grew up, but I confess I never really enjoyed *any* job until I was able to pursue my interests in research and writing. That has all happened recently." *Member:* British Museum, Egypt Exploration Society (London, England), Browning Institute (Florence, Italy).

WRITINGS: I Married Them (humorous novel), Howell, Soskin, 1945; *The Egyptians* (for young people), McGraw, 1970; *The Greeks* (for young people), McGraw, 1972; *Builders on the Desert* (children's history), Messner, 1973. Editor-in-chief and chief writer of Bicentennial issue of *Fairfield County* magazine (Westport, Conn.), 1975. Contributor of articles to periodicals.

WORK IN PROGRESS: A book on the first great woman in history, Queen Hatshepsut of Egypt (c. 1500 B.C.); *The Condemned Tower,* pure fiction, "I do not know where it will go at the moment. It keeps after me"; a book on ancient carrier civilizations.

SIDELIGHTS: Ms. Van Duyn wrote: "I am a frustrated traveller, but lucky in that I've been able to visit some of the spots I've been writing about. My greatest love is the ancient past: looking at it, listening to it, visualizing it, and bringing it back to life. I've been to Egypt, Greece, Italy, France. I've spent a lot of time in England. I've written articles on these places. I love cathedrals, organ music, medieval legends. I love languages. I speak French; half-speak Italian; know sixty words of ancient Greek; and I can occasionally read hieroglyphics if they are short."

When asked how she goes about researching a book, Ms. Van Duyn replied: "Research? It's homework pure and simple. It's private; the more help you get the more discouraged you become. It's lonely, but after you get into it your world is suddenly full of people. I cannot use other people's outlines, nor indeed follow one of my own, until I have flopped about in a congenial chaos of unrelated facts. When these cut-and-dried editors ask for outlines I try to give them what they want, but I never follow them.

"For Egypt I began [research] with simple books, worked my way up through the archaeologists like William Mathew Flanders Petrie to the scholars who wrote the Cambridge Ancient History, and that's pretty heady stuff. I didn't despise fiction, Lawrence Durrell, Mika Waltari. I persuaded the curator of Egyptian art in the Metropolitan Museum of Art to check my first draft. He was great, not at all shy about writing "utter nonsense!" in the margins. In this kind of writing one's value judgments are at stake.

"Travel, of course. Go where you can, but not for fun. I never got to Egypt until after my two books were published. But I did go to Greece and I'm glad I waited until the book was three-fourths done. Travel too soon can affect you in an exact opposite manner from a rigid outline. It overstimulates, then confuses with its wealth of material. So the point is, don't fool around; write that book!"

VAN HOESEN, Walter H.   1898(?)-1977

1898(?)—March 17, 1977; American journalist, author, and business executive. He died in Scotch Plains, N.J. Obituaries: *New York Times,* March 19, 1977.

*   *   *

VAN RHEENEN, Gailyn   1946-

PERSONAL: Born January 4, 1946, in Runnells, Iowa; son of Chalmer David (a farmer) and Lorna (Gossilink) Van Rheenen; married Rebecca Jo Lenderman, June 8, 1969; children: Jonathan Lyle, Rebecca Gail. *Education:* Harding College, B.S., 1968; Abilene Christian College, M.S., 1974. *Home and office address:* P.O. Box 194, Sotik, Kenya.

CAREER: Campus minister of the Church of Christ in Tahlequah, Okla, 1969-71; Church of Christ, Sotik, Kenya, rural evangelist, 1972—. Visiting professor at Harding College, 1977-78.

WRITINGS: Church Planting in Uganda: A Comparative Study, William Carey Library, 1976.

WORK IN PROGRESS: A general Bible study book in the Kipsigis language; a study of church growth principles oriented toward the mission movement of the Church of Christ.

SIDELIGHTS: Van Rheenen is fluent in Kiswahili and Kipsigis. He writes that his goals are to "establish self-supporting, self-governing, and self-propagating congregations which are true to the Scriptures and fit the local cultural context. This means we do not finance the church in Kenya but serve as teachers and advisers; and to function with the intention of working ourselves out of a job. Nothing is built which cannot be overseen by Kenyan Christians for the church in Kenya."

*   *   *

VAN RIPER, Frank A(lbert)   1946-

PERSONAL: Given name Francis; born September 4, 1946, in New York, N.Y.; son of Albert (a note teller) and Mildred (a bookkeeper; maiden name, Casullo) Van Riper; married Christine Rossi (a management consultant), October 18, 1970. *Education:* City College of New York, B.A., 1967. *Religion:* Roman Catholic. *Home:* 7501 Democracy Blvd., Bethesda, Md. 20034. *Office: New York Daily News,* 2101 L St. N.W., Suite 407, Washington, D.C. 20037.

CAREER/WRITINGS: New York Herald Tribune, New York, N.Y., stringer and news clerk, 1967; *New York Post,* New York City, assistant to night city editor, 1965-67; *New York Daily News,* New York City, Washington correspondent, 1967—. Notable assignments include U.S. presidential campaigns since 1968, Vietnam antiwar movement, Senate Watergate hearings, House Judiciary Committee Impeachment proceedings, and the Nixon resignation. Author, with William Sherman, of "Pain and Profit, Inc.," a five-part national survey of nursing homes, for New York News Series, 1975. Lecturer. *Member:* White House Correspondents Association, National Press Club, Holland Society of New York, Sigma Delta Chi.

WORK IN PROGRESS: Articles on contemporary politics and government.

SIDELIGHTS: Van Riper told *CA* he "broke many of the major Watergate exclusives, along with James Wieghart: prospective John N. Mitchell coverup indictment, contents of sealed grand jury report on Nixon's Watergate involvement, running exclusives on grand jury and special prosecutor investigations, major series of exclusives on secret evidence presented to House impeachment hearings." Van Riper also "broke copyrighted series of stories on the F.B.I. and National Security Agency interception of international cable traffic, prompting hearings and investigations by Senate Intelligence Committee and House Individual Liberties Subcommittee."

CA asked Van Riper his opinion of the 1977 David Frost/Richard Nixon interviews. "The Nixon/Frost interviews were useful," he responded, "if only as a vehicle for Frost to express indignation for all of us over the things Nixon did, or condoned. They produced hardly anything new.

"Much as I wanted to denigrate Frost, he did an overall excellent job. He did his homework and knew enough to let Nixon do himself in with his own words, particularly as they related to his perverted perception of a President's right to violate the law.

"With Nixon's bathetic apology for 'letting the country down,' I was moved as I thought I would not be. Perhaps it is merely the passage of time, but I feel, with the apology—and of course, the pardon that puts him out of the law's reach—that Watergate, thank God, finally was finished.

"For this reason, I doubt seriously whether there would be any public interest in having other Watergate figures kiss 'n tell for the tube."

AVOCATIONAL INTERESTS: Photography, travel, cooking, wine, tennis.

*   *   *

VARLEY, John 1947-
(Herb Boehm)

PERSONAL: Born in 1947, in Austin, Tex.; son of John E. Varley (an oil worker) and Joan Boehm Varley Litel; married Anet Mconel (a consumer advocate); children: Maurice, Roger, Stefan. *Education:* Attended Michigan State University, 1966. *Politics:* "Rational anarchist." *Religion:* "Lapsed Lutheran." *Home and office:* 595 Louis St., Eugene, Ore. 97402. *Agent:* Kirby McCauley, 220 East 26th St., New York, N.Y. 10010.

CAREER: Writer, 1973—. *Member:* Science Fiction Writers of America.

WRITINGS—Science fiction: *The Opihiuchi Hotline,* Dial, 1977; *Overdrawn at the Memory Bank* (stories), Dial, in press.

Work anthologized in *Best Science Fiction of the Year #5,* edited by Terry Carr, Ballantine, 1976. Contributor to science fiction magazines, including *Magazine of Fantasy and Science Fiction, Galaxy, Amazing, Vertex,* and, under pseudonym Herb Boehm, to *Isaac Asimov's Science Fiction Magazine.*

WORK IN PROGRESS: Titan (tentative title), a science fiction novel; *Song of the Rings,* a series of connected science fiction novellas.

SIDELIGHTS: Varley writes: "I started writing because I needed the money and foolishly thought I could make a living at it; I wrote science fiction because it's what I knew the most about, and because there was not enough science fiction being written of the sort I preferred. I wrote, and continue to write, stories that I like. Enough other people have liked them that I now think of myself as a professional, and hope I never have to look for another line of work."

VAUGHAN, William E(dward) 1915-1977
(Bill Vaughan)

October 8, 1915—February 26, 1977; American editor and writer; associate editor of the *Kansas City Star* and author of the nationally syndicated humorous column "Starbeams." He died in Kansas City, Mo. Obituaries: *New York Times,* February 27, 1977; *Time,* March 14, 1977. (See index for previous *CA* sketch)

*   *   *

VEATCH, Robert M(arlin) 1939-

PERSONAL: Born January 22, 1939, in Utica, N.Y.; son of Cecil R. (a pharmacist) and Regina (Braddock) Veatch; married Laurelyn Lovett (a sociologist), June 17, 1961; children: Paul Martin, Carlton Elliot. *Education:* Purdue University, B.S. (summa cum laude), 1961; University of California, San Francisco, M.S., 1962; Harvard University, B.D. (magna cum laude), 1964, M.A., 1970, Ph.D., 1971. *Home address:* Old Farm Rd., Chappaqua, N.Y. 10514. *Office:* Hastings Center, 360 Broadway, Hastings-on-Hudson, N.Y. 10706.

CAREER: University of Ife, Ibadan, Nigeria, assistant lecturer in pharmacology, 1963; high school teacher of biology in Ogbomosho, Nigeria, 1963-64; Hastings Center, Institute of Society, Ethics and the Life Sciences, Hastings-on-Hudson, N.Y., senior associate and staff director of research group on death and dying, 1970—. Visiting faculty member at Brown University, Vassar College, Manhattanville College, and Dartmouth College. Research associate at Columbia University, 1971-72. *Member:* American Association for the Advancement of Science, American Population Association, American Society of Christian Ethics, American Sociological Association, Society for the Scientific Study of Religion.

WRITINGS: Death, Dying, and the Biological Revolution, Yale University Press, 1976; *Value-Freedom in Science and Technology,* Scholars' Press, 1976.

Editor: (With Sharmon Sollitto) *Bibliography of Society, Ethics, and the Life Sciences,* Hastings Center, 1973, 4th edition, 1976; (with Willard Gaylin and Councilman Morgan) *The Teaching of Medical Ethics,* Hastings Center, 1973; (with Peter Steinfels) *Death Inside Out,* Harper, 1975; (with Roy Branson) *Ethics and Health Policy,* Ballinger, 1976; *Population Policy and Ethics: The American Experience,* Irvington Books, 1976; *Teaching of Bioethics: Report of the Commission on the Teaching of Bioethics,* Hastings Center, 1976; *Case Studies in Medical Ethics,* Harvard University Press, in press.

Contributor of about forty articles to learned journals. Associate editor of *Encyclopedia of Bioethics;* contributing editor of *Hospital Physician;* member of editorial board of *Journal of the American Medical Association.*

WORK IN PROGRESS: Research on medical ethics, the relation of science to public policy, death and dying, and experimentation on human subjects.

*   *   *

VELIKOVSKY, Immanuel 1895-

PERSONAL: Born June 10, 1895, in Vitebsk, Russia, came to the United States in 1939; son of Simon-Yehiel (a Hebrew scholar and publisher) and Belia Rachel (Grodensky) Velikovsky; married Elisheva Kramer (a violinist), April 15, 1923; children: Shulamith (Mrs. Abraham Kogan), Ruth Ruhama (Mrs. Sidney Sicherman). *Education:* Attended University of Edinburgh, Moscow Economic Institute, and

Kharkov University; Moscow Imperial University, M.D., 1921; postdoctoral study at Charite and Kaiser Wilhelm Academy (Berlin) and Monakow Brain Institute; studied psychoanalysis with Wilhelm Stekel, 1933. *Home:* 78 Hartley Ave., Princeton, N.J. 08540.

CAREER: Physician in Palestine, 1923-28, psychotherapist and psychoanalyst in Europe, 1928-39; writer and researcher, 1939—. Organizer and publisher of *Universitatis atque Bibliothecae Hierosolymitanarum,* 1921-24. *Awards, honors:* Dr. Arts and Sciences from University of Lethbridge, 1974.

WRITINGS: Worlds in Collision, Macmillan, 1950; *Ages in Chaos,* Volume I, Doubleday, 1952; *Oedipus and Akhnaton: Myth and History,* Doubleday, 1960; *Peoples of the Sea,* Doubleday, 1977. Also author of *Thirty Days and Nights of Diego Pires on the Bridge of St. Angelo,* 1935, *Time of Isaiah and Homer,* and *Ramses II and His Time.* Contributor to science and psychology journals and to *New York Post.*

SIDELIGHTS: After twenty-seven years, Velikovsky's controversial theories still incense certain members of the scientific community. Yet he has as many supporters as detractors, and even those who can't agree with the theory, stated in *Worlds in Collision,* of cataclysmic upheavals on Earth caused by a comet originating near Jupiter, or the views, stated in *Ages in Chaos,* that re-date much of the history of Egypt, or the theory, stated in *Earth in Upheaval,* that the entire earth was altered by a global catastrophe about thirty-five hundred years ago, must admit that Velikovsky has had a major influence on astronomy and the world of scientists. He has stimulated heated professional discussion, and done much to popularize a scientific field that most laymen had not previously considered.

His work is characterized by careful annotation, which in no way distracts even the non-scientific reader, and, indeed, many of his original claims have since been verified by independent experiment or by recent U.S. space efforts. His views are still being discussed at major university symposia and at meetings of learned societies.

* * *

VERHALEN, Philip A(ndrew) 1934-

PERSONAL: Born April 2, 1934, in Milwaukee, Wis.; son of Andrew Nicolas (an ice cream manufacturer) and Amanda E. (Rose) Verhalen. *Education:* St. Francis de Sales College, Milwaukee, Wis., B.A., 1956; Gregorian University, Rome, S.T.B., 1958, S.T.L., 1960, S.T.D., 1969; additional study at Notre Dame University, 1963, and Loyola University of Chicago, 1964. *Office:* 318 Boylston E., Seattle, Wash. 98102.

CAREER: Entered St. Francis Seminary, Milwaukee, Wis., 1952; ordained Roman Catholic priest in diocese of Spokane, Wash., 1959-76, laicized, 1976; associate pastor in parishes in Spokane, 1960-63; Marycliff High School for Girls, Spokane, administrator, instructor, and chairperson of religious studies department, 1963-66; Seattle University, Seattle, Wash., assistant professor of theology, 1969-71; St. Patrick's College, Menlo Park, Calif., associate professor of theology, 1971-73; College of Great Falls, Great Falls, Mont., assistant professor of theology, 1973-75, chairperson of Danforth Foundation Institute for College Development, 1974; Claremont Graduate School, Claremont, Calif., visiting professor of theology, 1975-76; St. Mary's Parish, Spokane, resource counselor for education program, 1976-77. Bishop White Seminary, Spokane, instructor in Latin and

history, 1960-62, dean of studies, 1968-69; visiting professor of theology at St. Thomas Seminary, Kenmore, Wash., winter, 1970-71, and Seattle University, summers, 1972, 1973, 1975; instructor in adult religious education programs. Resident priest at parish in Seattle, 1969-71. *Member:* American Academy of Religion, Catholic Theological Society of America, Catholic Biblical Association.

WRITINGS: Faith in a Secularized World, Paulist/Newman, 1976. Contributor to *Priest* and *Secular Life.*

WORK IN PROGRESS: A book, *Introduction to Religion.*

AVOCATIONAL INTERESTS: Swimming, tennis, hiking.

* * *

VIDLER, Virginia 1928-

PERSONAL: Born August 24, 1928, in Buffalo, N.Y.; daughter of Clifford M. and Florence (Hescock) Dawson; married Edward White Vidler (a merchant), June 30, 1951; children: Beverly, Donald. *Education:* Attended Rochester Institute of Technology, 1947-49, and Bryant & Stratton Business Institute, 1950-51. *Home and office:* 309 Parkdale Ave., East Aurora, N.Y. 14052.

CAREER: New York Telephone Co., Buffalo, administrative clerk, 1951-52; Moog Valve Aerospace Co., Elma, N.Y., secretary, 1952-53; Vidler's, Inc., East Aurora, N.Y., bookkeeper and vice-president, 1967—. Free-lance photographer and writer. Historian for East Aurora, N.Y. *Member:* Zonta International, National League of American Pen Women (past officer in western New York), Erie County Federation of Historical Societies (member of board of directors), Aurora Historical Society (honorary life member; member of board of directors). *Awards, honors:* Adopted into Wolf Clan of the Seneca Indians in Chattaraugus, N.Y.

WRITINGS: American Indians, Antiques, Arts and Artifacts of the Northeast, 1760-1900, A. S. Barnes, 1975; *Sugarbush Antiques,* A. S. Barnes, in press. Contributor to magazines and newspapers, including *Child Life, Instructor, Antiques Journal,* and *Antique Trader Weekly.*

SIDELIGHTS: Virginia Vidler comments: "Nonfiction history is my specialty with accompanying photography done by my husband]? We do our own darkroom work. I have been selling my work . . . for the past eight years and have given much more away. Moved on to [books] because I enjoy concentrating all of my efforts on one in-depth topic."

AVOCATIONAL INTERESTS: Travel in the northeastern and northwestern United States.

* * *

VILLERE, Sidney Louis 1900-

PERSONAL: Surname is pronounced Vill-e-*ray;* born October 25, 1900, in New Orleans, La.; son of Fernand Louis (a banker) and Marie (Marin y Argote) Villere; married Audrey Mary Catherine Cobb (a genealogist), November, 1926. *Education:* Attended St. Aloysius College. *Politics:* "Grass root conservative." *Religion:* Roman Catholic. *Home and office:* 1668 Dufossat St., New Orleans, La. 70115. *Agent:* Historic New Orleans Collection, 583 Royal St., New Orleans, La.

CAREER: Armstrong & Kock, New Orleans, La., architectural draftsman, 1921-23; Chambers Advertising Agency, New Orleans, artist, 1924-34; Griffin Manufacturing Co.,

New Orleans, district sales manager, 1936-58; genealogist, historian, and translator (specializing in Louisiana Spanish and French colonial families), 1956—. Appraiser of historical collections; public lecturer. Member of Orleans Parish Landmarks Commission, 1958—. *Member:* Society of 1812 (past president; genealogist and historian).

WRITINGS: Canary Islands Migration in Louisiana, 1778-1783, Genealogical Research Society, 1971; *Jacques Philippe Villere: First Native-Born Governor of Louisiana,* Louisiana State University Press, in press. Contributor to genealogy magazines.

WORK IN PROGRESS: The Military Career of Juchereau de St. Denis (founder of Natchitoches in 1714); *History of Bayou Saint John; The Old Faubourg of New Orleans.*

SIDELIGHTS: Villere told *CA:* "I specialize in 18th and 19th century history of the Mississippi Valley. As I stem from pioneer French and Spanish colonial lineage, with ancestors who were the leading officials, I gradually became a leading authority on Latin families, their backgrounds, migrations, etc."

* * *

VISHNIAK, Mark 1883-1976

January 15, 1883—August 31, 1976; Russian author and pre-Bolshevik politician who, in 1918, was secretary of the only freely elected Constituent Assembly in his country's history. He held the post only seventeen hours, until Lenin disbanded the Parliament. He later became *Time* magazine's senior specialist on Soviet affairs. He died in New York City. Vesson died in New York City. Obituaries: *New York Times,* September 3, 1976.

* * *

VISHNY, Michele 1932-

PERSONAL: Born May 27, 1932, in Chicago, Ill.; daughter of Max Alexander (an attorney) and Esther (Silber) Kopstein; married Paul H. Vishny (an attorney), June 22, 1952; children: Deborah, Renana, Miriam. *Education:* Northwestern University, B.S., 1954, M.A., 1965, Ph.D., 1971. *Religion:* Jewish. *Residence:* Skokie, Ill. *Office:* Department of Art History, Northwestern University, 208 Kresge Hall, Evanston, Ill. 60201.

CAREER: University of Illinois at Chicago Circle, Chicago, assistant professor of art history, 1970-72; Northwestern University, Evanston, Ill., assistant professor of art history, 1973—. Assistant professor at Art Institute of Chicago, 1976—. International Survey of Jewish Monuments (treasurer). Consultant to *Encyclopaedia Britannica. Member:* College Art Association of America, Midwest Art History Society, Women's Caucus for Art, Print and Drawing Club (Art Institute of Chicago), Friends of Art (Northwestern University).

WRITINGS: Mordecai Ardon, Abrams, 1975. Contributor to *Encyclopaedia Britannica* and *Art International.*

WORK IN PROGRESS: A critical biographical and iconographic study of Paul Klee.

AVOCATIONAL INTERESTS: Travel (France, Switzerland, Israel, Germany).

* * *

VISSON, Vladimir 1905(?)-1976

1905(?)—October 13, 1976; Russian-born writer and director of exhibitions for Wildenstein Galleries in New York City.

He was in charge of organizing the big loan shows of French masters that for many years have been a regular feature of the spring and fall art seasons in New York. Visson died in New York City. Obituaries: *New York Times,* October 15, 1976.

* * *

VIZEDOM, Monika B(asch) 1929-

PERSONAL: Surname is pronounced *Wise*-dom; born February 5, 1929, in Prague, Czechoslovakia; came to United States in 1940; naturalized citizen, 1950; daughter of Antonin (an economist) and Eleanor (Fuchs) Basch; married Calvin John Vizedom (an antiques dealer and psychiatric social worker), October 5, 1957; children: Malinda Katherine, Amanda Jennifer. *Education:* Cornell University, B.A. (honors), 1950; graduate study at Sorbonne, University of Paris, 1950-51; Columbia University, Ph.D., 1963. *Politics:* Democrat. *Religion:* Agnostic. *Home:* 70 North Main St., Mansfield, Mass. 02048.

CAREER: Hobart and William Smith Colleges, Geneva, N.Y., substitute teacher, 1956-57; Brooklyn College (now of the City University of New York), Brooklyn, N.Y., substitute teacher, 1957-58; Human Relations Area Files, New Haven, Conn., translator from French to English, 1958-60; National Council on Alcoholism, New York City, interviewer, summer, 1960; Rutgers University, New Brunswick, N.J., instructor in anthropology, 1961-62; Columbia University, New York City, staff ethnologist, 1963-64, part-time consultant, 1965-66; Hunter College of the City University of New York, New York City, part-time lecturer in anthropology, 1966-67; University of Minnesota, Minneapolis, assistant professor of anthropology, 1974—.

WRITINGS: (Translator) Arnold Van Gennep, *The Rites of Passage,* University of Chicago Press, 1960; *Rites and Relationships: Rites of Passage and Modern Anthropology,* Sage Publications, 1976. Contributor to *American Oxford Encyclopedia.*

WORK IN PROGRESS: Research on ethnic studies.

SIDELIGHTS: Monika Vizedom writes: "Like many others I have become interested in the links between our society and history and that of other cultures; I believe this trend reflects the realization that the United States is one nation among many rather than a unique archetype with no past and no relatives." She adds: "Although I love writing and talking *per se* I think both activities have been motivated by a philosophical quest, to understand human life and human nature. Having grown up knowing cultural differences, I came to anthropology to try and understand them, rather than to discover them. Having grown up as an intellectual I take delight in late discovered simple pleasures: cooking, sewing, watching my children grow, bicycling on a spring day. I believe that our concept of life has not taken sufficiently into account that people continue to change throughout their lives, rather than stopping when physical growth stops."

* * *

VOGT, Evon Zartman, Jr. 1918-

PERSONAL: Born August 20, 1918, in Gallup, N.M.; son of Evon and Shirley (Bergman) Vogt; married Catherine Christine Hiller, September 4, 1941; children: Shirley Naneen (Mrs. Geza Teleki), Evon Zartman III, Eric Edwards, Charles Anthony. *Education:* University of Chicago, A.B., 1941, M.A., 1946, Ph.D., 1948. *Home:* 221 Mount Auburn

St., Cambridge, Mass. 02139. *Office:* Peabody Museum of American Archaeology and Ethnology, Harvard University, Cambridge, Mass. 02138.

CAREER: Harvard University, Cambridge, Mass., instructor, 1948-50, assistant professor, 1950-55, associate professor, 1955-59, professor of anthropology, 1959—, chairperson of department, 1969—, director of Chiapas project, 1957—, assistant curator of American ethnology at Peabody Museum of American Archaeology and Ethnology, 1950-59, curator of Middle American ethnology, 1960—, member of expeditions to New Mexico, 1947-53, and Mexico, 1954—. Fellow of Center for Advanced Study in the Behavioral Sciences, 1956-57. Member of Division of Anthropology and Psychology for National Research Council, 1955-57; member of advisory panel in anthropology for National Science Foundation, 1964-66. *Military service:* U.S. Naval Reserve, active duty, 1942-46; became lieutenant.

MEMBER: American Academy of Arts and Sciences (fellow), American Anthropological Association (fellow; member of executive board, 1958-60), Society of American Archaeology, American Folklore Society, Royal Anthropological Society of Great Britain and Ireland, Harvard Club (New York City). *Awards, honors:* Bernard de Sahagun Prize from Republic of Mexico, 1969, for *Zinacantan: A Maya Community in the Highlands of the Chiapas.*

WRITINGS: (With Clyde Kluckhohn) *Navaho Means People,* Harvard University Press, 1951; *Navaho Veterans: A Study of Changing Values,* Peabody Museum of American Archaeology and Ethnology, Harvard University, 1951; *Modern Homesteaders: The Life of a Twentieth-Century Frontier Community,* Belknap Press, 1955; (editor with William Armand Lessa) *Reader in Comparative Religion: An Anthropological Approach,* Row, Peterson, 1958, 3rd edition, Harper, 1972; (with Ray Hyman) *Water Witching, U.S.A.,* University of Chicago Press, 1959.

(Editor with Alberto Ruz L.) *Conference on "The Cultural Development of the Maya," Burg Wartenstein, Austria, 1962,* Department of Philosophy and Letters, Universidad Nacional Autonoma de Mexico, 1964; (with Gordon R. Wiley) *Seminar on the Maya,* Department of Anthropology, Harvard University, Volume I: *1964-1965,* 1965, Volume III (Vogt was not associated with Volume II): *1969-1970,* 1969; (editor) *Los Zinacantecos,* 1966; (editor with Ethel M. Albert) *People of Rimrock: A Study of Values in Five Cultures,* Harvard University Press, 1966; (editor) *Handbook of Middle American Indians,* Volumes VII and VIII, University of Texas Press, 1969; *Zinacantan: A Maya Community in the Highlands of Chiapas,* Belknap Press, 1969.

The Zinacantecos of Mexico: A Modern Maya Way of Life, Holt, 1970; (editor) *Harvard Chiapas Project, 1957-1971,* Harvard University, 1971; (editor with Walter W. Taylor and John L. Fischer, and contributor) *Culture and Life: Essays in Memory of Clyde Kluckhohn,* Southern Illinois University Press, 1973. Contributor to professional journals.*

* * *

VOIGT, Ellen Bryant 1943-

PERSONAL: Born May 9, 1943, in Danville, Va.; daughter of Lloyd (a farmer) and Zue (an elementary school teacher; maiden name, Yeatts) Bryant; married Francis George Wilhelm Voigt (a college dean), September 5, 1965; children: Jula Dudley, William Bryant. *Education:* Converse College, B.A., 1964; University of Iowa, M.F.A., 1966. *Home address:* P.O. Box 16, Marshfield, Vt. 05658. *Office:* M.F.A. Writing Program, Goddard College, Plainfield, Vt. 05667.

CAREER: Iowa Wesleyan College, Mount Pleasant, instructor in English, 1966-69; Goddard College, Plainfield, Vt., teacher of literature and writing, 1970—, director of writing program, 1975—. Professional pianist. Member of board of directors of Associated Writing Programs; has given poetry readings at schools and colleges, and served as judge of poetry contests. *Awards, honors:* Grants from Vermont Council on the Arts, 1974-75, and National Endowment for the Arts, 1976-77.

WRITINGS: Claiming Kin (poems), Wesleyan University Press, 1976.

Anthologized in *Poetry in Public Places,* American International Sculpters Symposium, 1977, and *Ardis Anthology of New American Poetry,* edited by David Rigsby, Ardis, 1977.

Contributor to *Nation* and *New Yorker,* and to literary journals, including *Shenandoah, Sewanee Review, American Poetry Review,* and *Southern Review.* Advisory editor of *Arion's Dolphin,* 1971-75.

WORK IN PROGRESS: Poetry.

* * *

von BRAUN, Wernher 1912-1977

March 23, 1912—June 16, 1977; German-born American engineer, author, and pioneer in field of space exploration best known for the development of the German V-2 rocket and American Saturn 5 moon rocket. By the age of twenty von Braun was Germany's top civilian specialist in rocketry. Brought to the United States after World War II, he headed the teams of rocket scientists who succeeded in launching the Explorer I satellite in 1958, Redstone in 1961, and the huge Saturn 5 which carried *Apollo 11* astronauts to the surface of the moon. In 1960 he was named director of NASA's Marshall Space Flight Center. Von Braun died in Alexandria, Va. Obituaries: *New York Times,* June 18, 1977; *Washington Post,* June 18, 1977; *Time,* June 27, 1977; *Newsweek,* June 27, 1977; *Current Biography,* August, 1977. (See index for previous *CA* sketch)

* * *

VON HILDEBRAND, Dietrich 1889-1977 (Peter Ott)

October 12, 1889—January 26, 1977; German-born professor of philosophy and author of more than thirty books on philosophy and morality. He taught in Germany, Austria, France, and the United States. An exponent of traditional Roman Catholic discipline, Von Hildebrand is best known for *In Defense of Purity* and *Trojan Horse in the City of God.* He died in New Rochelle, N.Y. Obituaries: *New York Times,* January 30, 1977; *AB Bookman's Weekly,* March 14, 1977. (See index for previous *CA* sketch)

* * *

VORHEES, Melvin B. 1904(?)-1977

1904(?)—February 6, 1977; American author and editor. He died in Walla Walla, Wash. Obituaries: *New York Times,* February 9, 1977.

* * *

VUONG g(ia) Thuy 1938-

PERSONAL: Born June 6, 1938, in Vietnam; came to the United States in 1967, naturalized citizen, 1977; son of Van Tich and Nguyen Thi Chat. *Education:* University of Saigon, first certificate of law, 1959, licence degree, 1961; College of Advanced Technology, Cardiff, England, postgraduate diploma, 1965; University of York, certificate of linguistic studies, 1966; Sorbonne, University of Paris, Ph.D., 1972. *Residence:* New York, N.Y. *Office:* Regional Cross-Cultural Training and Resource Center, New York City Board of Education, 110 Livingston St., Brooklyn, N.Y. 11201.

CAREER: National Broadcasting Service of Vietnam, Radio Saigon, Saigon, part-time news editor and writer of commentary, 1955-61; teacher of English and French in public elementary schools in Saigon, Vietnam, 1961-64; Cornell University, Ithaca, N.Y., lecturer in Vietnamese, 1967-70; Berlitz School of languages, New York, N.Y., part-time teacher of Vietnamese, 1971-74; New York City Board of Education, New York, N.Y., coordinator of Indochinese program at Regional Cross-Cultural Training and Resource Center, 1975—. Part-time news editor at Vietnam Press (news agency), summer, 1961; program assistant at Vietnamese section of British Broadcasting Corp.—Bush House, summers, 1965-66; director of summer language school of Touring Club de France, summer, 1967; founder and first president of Vietnam House, 1975-76.

WRITINGS: Vietnamese in a Nutshell, with sound recordings, Institute for Language Study, 1975; *American English Exercises,* Books I and II, Cortina, 1973; *Your New Country* (bilingual guide), Macmillan, 1975; *Getting to Know the Vietnamese and Their Culture,* Ungar, 1976; (with David Ashworth) *Basic American English,* with sound recordings, Cortina, in press.

WORK IN PROGRESS: English Grammar for Vietnamese; bilingual educational books.

SIDELIGHTS: Vuong writes: "At this point, my writing has a two-fold purpose: one, to familiarize the non-Vietnamese readers with the culture, language, and customs of the Vietnamese people. This obviously became a necessity in the light of the recent influx of the Vietnamese refugees in the United States. Very few publications and research works on the above areas are available in English. Two, to familiarize the new immigrants with the culture, language, and customs of the American people. This two-pronged approach is an efficient vehicle and a must to help the Vietnamese adjust smoothly to their new and totally alien world and to contribute to this 'melting pot.'"

* * *

WADDY, Charis 1909-

PERSONAL: Born September 24, 1909, in New South Wales, Australia; daughter of Percival Stacy (a clergyman) and Etheldred (a journalist; maiden name, Spittal) Waddy. *Education:* Lady Margaret Hall, Oxford, B.A. (first class honors), 1931; School of Oriental and African Studies, London, Ph.D., 1934. *Religion:* Church of England. *Home:* 12A Norham Rd., Oxford OX2 6SF, England.

CAREER: Writer. Has taught in Middle East and Africa. *Member:* British Society for Middle-East Studies, Council for Arab-British Understanding, Committee for British-Arab University Visits.

WRITINGS: Baalbek Caravans, Librairie du Liban, 1967; *The Muslim Mind,* Longman, 1976. Contributor to Middle East studies journals and to *Times Educational Supplement.*

WORK IN PROGRESS: Women in the Muslim World; The People of the Book, on cooperation in history between monotheistic faiths.

SIDELIGHTS: Although Charis Waddy was born in Australia, she grew up in Jerusalem, in the years that followed World War I. She told *CA:* "The tensions of that formative period, and the common background shared by all three great monotheistic faiths, were part of my thinking even before I began a life-long study of Islam." She was the first woman to study Arabic at Oxford University, specializing in the Arab side of the Crusades.

A Christian herself, Waddy believes that the West may have much to learn from Islam, and that many will find enrichment in the effort to understand it. Her writing "aims at building bridges of understanding, and breaking the stereotypes that block a perceptive insight."

* * *

WAGNER, (Griegg) Marsden 1930-

PERSONAL: Born February 23, 1930, in San Francisco, Calif.; son of Clarence Reuben (a clergyman) and Kavie (a teacher; maiden name, Griegg) Wagner; married Mary Miles, June 20, 1951 (divorced, 1976); children: Dana, Peter, Karen, Karl. *Education:* University of California, Los Angeles, B.S., 1951, M.D., 1955, M.S.P.H. and certification as pediatrician, 1962. *Home:* Nordkrog 18, 2900 Hellerup, Denmark. *Office:* Joint Center for Studies of Health Problems, Juliane Mariesvej 32, 2100 Copenhagen, Denmark.

CAREER: University of California, Los Angeles, assistant professor of pediatrics and public health, 1962-71; University of Copenhagen, Copenhagen, Denmark, visiting professor of pediatrics, 1971—. Pediatrician and researcher at Joint Center for Studies of Health Problems. Director of child health for the State of California, 1970-71. *Military service:* U.S. Air Force, pediatrician, 1957-59; became captain. *Member:* American Academy of Pediatrics, American Public Health Association.

WRITINGS: Sweden's Health-Screening Program for Four-Year-Old Children, National Institute of Mental Health, 1975; *Problems of School Age Children,* World Health Organization, 1976; (with wife, Mary Wagner) *The Danish National Child-Care System: A Successful System as Model for the Reconstruction of American Child Care,* Westview Press, 1976. Contributor of more than thirty articles to scientific journals.

WORK IN PROGRESS: Directing an extensive research project to study fertility behavior (including sexual behavior, contraceptive practices, and abortion practices) in Denmark, with a book expected to result.

SIDELIGHTS: Wagner writes: "I am interested, first, in studying the health systems and the health behaviors in other countries in order that it might be applied to the future development of health care in the United States. Secondly I am interested in bringing information about health care and health behavior to the general public. My book, which was published by the Westview Press in 1976, was written for the general public and is an illustration of both these interests which I intend to continue to pursue in the future."

* * *

WAGNER, Walter F(rederick), Jr. 1926-

PERSONAL: Born October 28, 1926, in Yonkers, N.Y.; son of Walter Frederick (a designer) and Georgia (Lamoreaux) Wagner; married Barbara Jane Alden (a town selectman), March 2, 1952; children: Jonathan, Jennifer Ann, Daniel, Margaret. *Education:* Massachusetts Institute of Technology, S.B., 1949, S.M., 1950. *Home:* 131 Goodhill

Rd., Weston, Conn. 06880. *Office: Architectural Record,* McGraw-Hill Publishing Co., 1220 Avenue of the Americas, New York, N.Y. 10020.

CAREER: Factory Management and Maintenance, New York City, 1950-57, began as assistant editor, became assistant managing editor; *House and Home,* New York City, assistant managing editor, 1957-65; *Popular Boating,* New York City, editor, 1963-65; *Architectural Record,* New York City, executive editor, 1965-68, editor, 1969—. Member of local planning, zoning, and conservation commissions; past president of Weston-Westport Community Theater; consultant to National Endowment for the Arts and American Institute of Architects. *Military service:* U.S. Naval Reserve, active duty, 1945-46. *Member:* American Institute of Architects, Cedar Point Yacht Club. *Awards, honors:* National Magazine Award from American Society of Magazine Editors and Magazine Publishers Association, 1971, for "New Life for Old Buildings."

WRITINGS: (Editor) *Great Houses for View Sites, Beach Sites, Sites in the Woods, Meadow Sites, Sloping Sites, Steep Sites, and Flat Sites,* McGraw, 1976. Also author of *Houses Architects Design for Themselves,* Architectural Record Books.

* * *

WAGONER, John L.   1927-

PERSONAL: Born July 16, 1927, in Claremore, Okla.; son of Sylvanus and Vivian (Nicholson) Wagoner. *Education:* University of Oklahoma, B.A., 1951. *Home:* 6166 Sheridan Rd., Chicago, Ill. 60660. *Office: Chicago Tribune,* 435 N. Michigan Ave., Chicago, Ill. 60611.

CAREER/WRITINGS: Kansas City Star, Kansas City, Mo., writer, 1952-56, editor, 1956-6; *Chicago Tribune,* Chicago, Ill., editor, 1961-70, news editor, 1970—. *Military service:* U.S. Navy. *Member:* Society of Journalists, Chicago Headline Club, Phi Beta Kappa, Sigma Delta Chi.

* * *

WALDMAN, Milton   1895-1976

PERSONAL: Born October 4, 1895, in Cleveland, Ohio; son of Benjamin and Ida (Spire) Waldman; married Marguerite David, July 20, 1934 (died, 1969); children: Guido, Jehanne Marchesi, Giselle. *Education:* Yale University, A.B., 1917; graduate study, Sorbonne, University of Paris, 1922-23. *Home:* 79 Dorset House, Gloucester Place, London NW1, England.

CAREER: Worked as a newspaperman in United States, 1917-22; *London Mercury,* London, England, assistant editor, 1924-27; Longmans Green & Co., London, literary adviser, 1919-24; William Collins Sons & Co., London, literary adviser, 1939-53; Rupert Hart-Davis, Ltd., London, joint managing director, 1952-55; William Collins Sons & Co., literary adviser, 1955-68. Writer. *Military service:* U.S. Army, 1917-18; became first lieutenant. *Member:* Savile Club.

WRITINGS: Americana, Holt, 1925; *Sir Walter Raleigh,* Harper, 1928; *America Conquers Death,* Rudge, 1928; *The Disinherited* (novel), Longmans, 1929; *King, Queen, Jack,* Longmans, 1931; (editor) *The Omnibus Book of Traveller's Tales,* Stein, 1931; *Elizabeth, Queen of England,* Longmans, 1933, published as *England's Elizabeth,* Houghton, 1933; *Joan of Arc,* Little, Brown, 1935; *Biography of a Family,* Houghton, 1936; *Some English Dictators,* Blackie, 1940, Kennikat, 1970; *Rod of Iron,* Houghton, 1941; *Elizabeth and Leicester,* Collins, 1944, Houghton, 1945; *Queen Elizabeth,*

Collins, 1952; *The Lady Mary: A Biography of Mary Tudor,* Scribner, 1972. Editor of The Golden Hind Series.

SIDELIGHTS: In his long career in the London literary world, Waldman knew Thomas Hardy, James Joyce, T. S. Eliot, and H. L. Mencken.

OBITUARIES: New York Times, March 13, 1976; *Publishers Weekly,* March 29, 1976.*

(Died March 6, 1976, in London, England)

* * *

WALKENSTEIN, Eileen   1923-

PERSONAL: Born November 2, 1923, in Philadelphia, Pa.; daughter of Ben (a musician and paperhanger) and Ethel (Teplitsky) Walkenstein; married David Biser, August, 1957 (deceased); children: Daniel, Tara, Seth, Merissa. *Education:* University of Pennsylvania, B.A., 1946; Woman's Medical College, M.D., 1950. *Home:* 323 Washington Ave., Miami Beach, Fla. 33139.

CAREER: Kingsbridge Veterans Administration Hospital, Bronx, N.Y., resident in psychiatry, 1951-54; private practice in psychiatry in New York, N.Y., 1954-64, Los Angeles, Calif., 1964-68, and Miami Beach, Fla., 1968-74; conducted workshops at growth centers in London, Paris, Rome, Florence, and Naples, 1974-76; writer, 1976—.

WRITINGS: Beyond the Couch, Crown, 1973; *Shrunk to Fit,* Coventure Ltd., 1976; *Don't Shrink to Fit!,* Grove, 1976.

Author, producer, and director of video film "Beyond the Couch." Contributor to *American Journal of Psychiatry.* Contributing editor of *Voices: Art and Science of Psychotherapy.*

WORK IN PROGRESS: Nucleus Therapy: Pursuit of the Unicorn; Body Electric (tentative title).

SIDELIGHTS: David Boadella described Eileen Walkenstein "a pedestal-breaker, a shatterer of idols, a human voice crying against the wilderness of expertise in which she was trained, and against which in order to stay alive and in order to help people who came to her for help to become alive, she had to rebel."

What she produced in her book *Beyond the Couch* Boadella described as "immense energy which will infuriate authoritarians everywhere." Walkenstein admitted, "I am tactless, straightforward, and non-dainty in my language. The book is a vernacular, non-technical expression of my feelings in relation to the dehumanization of the human animal and the processes in America, especially American medicine, and more particularly in American psychiatry and psychoanalysis, which help create the human vegetable and uncreate the man.

"In our culture we are fast becoming robots or vegetables, losing touch even with our own tears, losing contact with our innards, leaving our marionette heads to bob and bow to someone else's strings (purse strings? . . . power strings?). My book is my small attempt to put a finger in the dike of this technological-head-robotizing current that threatens to flood us all. I am not only a monomaniac but a multiple one at that! It is my own passion play!"

"Although the book is a great shout for life, there is also deep wisdom in it," Boadella wrote. "At a time when, with the advent of primal therapy, there is great emphasis on the need to yell out one's pain, she offers a simple reminder to those who scream easily: 'if you're a screamer, things are going out of you all the time and you're not allowing anything to come in—spend some time letting things come in—let your breath come in; keep your mouth shut and let others' words come in; look with your eyes and let the others' eyes come in—this trip will take you toward greater contact than is possible in any of your yells. Listen to silence instead of the sound of your own probably blaming, accusatory voice. If you listen intently enough, you'll hear your body singing to its animal rhythm, which your yells have been blotting out.'''

BIOGRAPHICAL/CRITICAL SOURCES: Energy and Character: The Journal of Bioenergetic Research, May, 1973.

* * *

WALKER, (James) Braz(elton) 1934-

PERSONAL: Born May 29, 1934, in Waco, Tex.; son of Virgil Harris and Marie (Brazelton) Walker. *Education:* University of Texas, student, 1952. *Religion:* Episcopalian. *Home:* 315 Crescent Rd., Waco, Tex. 76710.

CAREER: Writer and photographer, specializing in fish, 1955—. *Member:* International Oceanographic Foundation, Cousteau Society, North American Native Fishes Association, Central Texas Professional Photographers Association (honorary life member). *Awards, honors:* Regional self-rehabilitation award from American Corrective Therapy Association, 1968, national achievement award, 1972; Anchor Award from San Francisco Aquarium Society, 1968; distinguished service award, 1968, from Waco Junior Chamber of Commerce; Outstanding Young Men of America award, 1969, from Outstanding Americans Foundation.

WRITINGS: Enjoy Native Fish, Pet Library, 1970; *Bouillabaisse: Aquatic Oddballs*, San Francisco Aquarium Society, 1971; *Tropical Fish Identifier*, Sterling, 1973; *Angelfish*, T.F.H. Publications, 1974; *Sharks and Loaches*, T.F.H. Publications, 1974; *Oddball Fishes and Other Strange Creatures of the Deep*, Sterling, 1975; (editor) *Marine Fish Identifier*, Sterling, 1975; *Keeping and Breeding Cichlids*, T.F.H. Publications, 1977; *Fishes in Fact and Fantasy*, Sterling, in press.

Author of columns "In the Fish Bowl" in *Waco Tribune-Herald*, "About Fish" in *Pets/Supplies/Marketing*, and "Aqua Life" in *Waco Tribune-Herald*. Contributor of articles and photographs to fish and wildlife magazines and to *Medical Research Engineering*. Former senior associate editor of *Aquarium Illustrated*, senior contributing editor of *Aquarium*, and associate editor of *Aquarist's Gazette*.

SIDELIGHTS: Paralyzed by polio in 1952, and dependent upon breathing equipment, Walker has made himself a successful career, with the aid of specially-designed photographic equipment, dictating machine, tape recorder, and typewriter. Once an avid sportsman—active in hunting, fishing, and athletics—he has specialized in photographing and writing about these subjects, a successful and enthusiastic adaptation.

* * *

WALKER, David Clifton 1942-

PERSONAL: Born October 13, 1942, in Maine; son of Clifton N. (a farmer) and Nellie C. Walker; married Mary F. McCarthy, June, 1964 (divorced, 1977); children: Emma Shea Jewett. *Education:* Bowdoin College, A.B., 1964; New College, Oxford, B.Litt., 1967. *Politics:* Democrat. *Home address:* P.O. Box 82, Freedom, Me. 04941. *Office:* Department of English, Colby College, Waterville, Me. 04901.

CAREER: Brattle Book Shop, Boston, Mass., manager, 1966-67; University of Maine, Presque Isle, instructor in English and American literature, 1967-68; University of Canterbury, Christchurch, New Zealand, lecturer in English and American literature, 1968-71; University of Maine, Augusta, part-time assistant professor of English and American literature, 1971-75; Colby College, Waterville, Me., assistant professor of English and American literature, 1975—. Member of advisory panel of Maine State Arts Commission, 1975—; has given poetry readings on radio and at colleges. *Awards, honors:* Fulbright scholarship, 1964-66; won Associated Writing Program Award from Virginia Commonwealth University Series of Contemporary Poets, 1975, for *Moving Out*.

WRITINGS: Fathers (poems), Pumpkin Press, 1975; *Moving Out* (poems), University Press of Virginia, 1976. Author of radio broadcast material for New Zealand Broadcasting Co., 1969. Contributor of articles and reviews to journals. Co-editor of *Edge*, 1970-73.

WORK IN PROGRESS: Tentative Prayers (tentative title), poems.

SIDELIGHTS: Walker writes: "The crucial fact of my life was to grow up on a dirt farm in an era when small farming had begun to die. I am the first in my family to 'break away'—to live differently, read voraciously, and reflect on the pattern of my heritage. Though I feel a debt to a hundred (or a thousand) writers, people, and factors, probably certain poets who have written in and of New England are closest. I was born in the same town as Edwin Arlington Robinson; and he, Frost, Robert Lowell, Louis Coxe, and Emily Dickinson are among those whose work I honor."

AVOCATIONAL INTERESTS: Travel in Europe and the Pacific, football, music, gourmet cooking.

BIOGRAPHICAL/CRITICAL SOURCES: Maine Review, January, 1977.

* * *

WALKER, Frank 1930-

PERSONAL: Born May 31, 1930, in Leeds, England; son of Thomas (a tinsmith) and Ida (Myers) Walker; divorced, 1975; children: David, Elizabeth, Trudie, Beverley. *Education:* Attended elementary school in Leeds, England. *Politics:* "Uncertain, anything but Communist or Fascist." *Religion:* Atheist. *Home:* 31 Berkeley Ave., Leeds 8, West Yorkshire, England. *Agent:* David Higham Associates Ltd., 5-8 Lower John St., Golden Sq., London W1R 11HA, England.

CAREER: Writer, 1969—. *Military service:* Royal Navy, 1948-55. *Member:* Leeds Writers Circle (joint chairman).

WRITINGS: Jack: The Story of a Belgian Sheepdog (novel), M. Joseph, 1976; *The Navvies Are Coming* (novel), M. Joseph, 1976; *Banjo* (novel), M. Joseph, 1977; *Piledriver; or, The Trawl* (historical adventure stories; "Piledriver" is the sequel to *The Navvies Are Coming*), M. Joseph, 1977. Contributor to magazines, including *Writer's Review*.

WORK IN PROGRESS: The Sharks Don't Leave Much; Down the Fever Road, nonfiction; "All the Answers," a one-act play; "Rain on My Face," a television play; two radio plays, "The Best in the Business" and "Puddin'."

SIDELIGHTS: Walker conducted his research for "The Trawl" in the Arctic aboard the trawler "Arctic Cavalier." He writes: "Writing to me is a necessity, sometimes almost a curse, I can't stop and don't think I could if I never had another word published. People are starting to call me an author but I don't feel like one; I don't think I'll ever feel like a real professional but always like a house painter who writes a bit. My hopes for the future are to make a living by writing only just to prove to myself I can do it, and to write something that means something. I haven't a clue what." He adds that one of his ongoing interests is the establishment of a fully phonetic alphabet.

Walker started work at fourteen as a tailor's cutter apprentice; he since has been a hod carrier, window cleaner, salesman, market trader, waiter, building site navvy, steel erector, barman, and house painter. His first novel was rejected by thirteen publishers.

* * *

WALKER, Pamela 1948-

PERSONAL: Born April 28, 1948, in Burlington, Iowa; daughter of Ronald Russell (a vice-president of a direct-mail corporation) and Helen (a secretary; maiden name, Andersen) Walker; married Edgar M. Denniston, November 23, 1968 (divorced, December, 1972). Education: Iowa State University, B.A., 1970; University of Iowa, M.F.A., 1973; also attended Monterrey Technological Institute, 1968, and University of Valencia, 1970. Home: 771 West End Ave., Apt. 4A, New York, N.Y. 10025. Agent: Susan Protter, 156 East 52nd St., New York, N.Y. 10022.

CAREER: Creativity director at a school in Washington, Conn., 1973-74; Saturday Review Book Club, New York City, managing editor, 1974-75; Riverdale Country School, Bronx, N.Y., private tutor (for middle and high school students with learning disabilities), 1976—.

WRITINGS: Twyla, Prentice-Hall, 1973. Contributor to Highlights for Children.

WORK IN PROGRESS: Valentine, a novel; "Avenue C: A Poem by Galway Kinnell," a film.

AVOCATIONAL INTERESTS: Travel (Greece, North Africa), dance, swimming, jogging, bicycling, skiing, music (playing the piano).

* * *

WALLACE, Ed(ward Tatum) 1906-1976

August 9, 1906—October 10, 1976; American author and feature writer for New York Daily News, specializing in human interest stories. He died in New York City. Obituaries: New York Times, October 12, 1976.

* * *

WALLACE, Robert Kimball 1944-

PERSONAL: Born August 2, 1944, in Seattle, Wash.; son of Walter D. (a businessman) and Barbara (Woolley) Wallace; married Gladys Astor Philibert (a piano teacher), June 15, 1968. Education: Whitman College, B.A., 1966; Columbia University, M.A., 1967, Ph.D., 1972. Politics: Democrat. Home: 956 Hatch St., Cincinnati, Ohio 45202. Office: Department of Humanities, Northern Kentucky University, Highland Heights, Ky. 41076.

CAREER: Northern Kentucky University, Highland Heights, assistant professor of American literature, 1972—. Fulbright lecturer at University of Deusto, 1976-77. Member: Modern Language Association of America, American Comparative Literature Association, Kentucky Philological Association. Awards, honors: Woodrow Wilson fellowship, 1966; National Endowment for the Humanities grant, 1974.

WRITINGS: A Century of Music Making: The Lives of Josef and Rosina Lhevinne, Indiana University Press, 1976. Contributor to music, literature, and aesthetics journals, and to American Scholar.

WORK IN PROGRESS: Fiction; research on the relationship between music and literature.

SIDELIGHTS: Wallace writes: "I'm currently spending a year in Spain to live in a culture and language other than my own; also to be able to travel to other European countries to do research on Jane Austen, Emily Bronte, Chopin, Mozart, Mahler, Thomas Mann."

* * *

WALLACH, Mark I(rwin) 1949-

PERSONAL: Born May 19, 1949, in Cleveland, Ohio; son of Ivan A. (a business executive) and Janice (Grossman) Wallach; married Harriet Kinney (a Montessori teacher), August 11, 1974. Education: Wesleyan University, B.A. (magna cum laude), 1971; Harvard University, J.D. (cum laude), 1974. Religion: Jewish. Home: 23538 Duffield Rd., Shaker Heights, Ohio 44122. Office: Baker, Hostetler & Patterson, 1956 Union Commerce Building, Cleveland, Ohio 44115.

CAREER: Law clerk to chief judge of U.S. District Court in Cleveland, Ohio, 1974-75; Baker, Hostetler & Patterson, Cleveland, associate, 1975—. Member of Bar of State of Ohio; member of state legislation committee of Greater Cleveland Citizens League. Member: American Bar Association, Ohio Bar Association, Greater Cleveland Bar Association, Phi Beta Kappa.

WRITINGS: (With Jon Bracker) Christopher Morley, Twayne, 1976. Contributor to law journals and Markham Review.

WORK IN PROGRESS: Research on the new Toxic Substances Control Act; work on profiles of several British and American authors, including Morley.

SIDELIGHTS: Wallach writes: "I am essentially a lawyer who likes to write, and only incidentally (so far) an author. My interest in Morley developed while I was an undergraduate, and eventually led to the Twayne volume. I hope to do further writing for publication, both legal and non-legal, whenever a subject intrigues me sufficiently to compel me to find time for it."

AVOCATIONAL INTERESTS: Listening to classical music, reading, playing racquetball and softball.

* * *

WALTERS, Robert Mark 1938-

PERSONAL: Born August 24, 1938, in New York, N.Y.; son of Edward J. (a builder) and Janet (an interior designer; maiden name, Stoloff) Walters; married Martha Angle (a journalist), September 28, 1969; children: Erica Lee. Education: Lehigh University, B.S., 1960. Home: 3550 Chesapeake St. N.W., Washington, D.C. 20008. Office: Room 1200, 777 14th St. N.W., Washington, D.C. 20005.

CAREER/WRITINGS: United Press International, reporter in Harrisburg, Pa., 1962, bureau manager in Cincinnati, Ohio, 1963; Washington Star, Washington, D.C., reporter, 1964-74; National Journal Reports, Washington, D.C., contributing editor, 1974-76; Parade (magazine), New York City, associate editor, 1974-76; Newspaper Enterprise Association, syndicated columnist, 1977—. Awards, honors: Woodrow Wilson senior fellow, 1973—.

WALTON, W. Robert 1902-

PERSONAL: Born December 4, 1902, in Indiana; son of Vwoefw (a salesman) and Sarah Jeanette (a teacher; maiden name, Collins) Walton; married Hilda Howat, October 5, 1935; children: Sarah Ann (Mrs. Robert G. Schwartz, Jr.), William R. *Education:* Earned B.A. from University of Michigan. *Politics:* Republican. *Religion:* Roman Catholic. *Residence:* Laguna Niguel, Calif. *Office:* Universal Press Syndicate, 6700 Squibb Rd., Mission, Kan. 66202.

CAREER: South Bend Tribune, South Bend, Ind., city editor, 1925-32; Associated Press, reporter in Chicago, Ill., beginning 1932, and Washington, D.C., until 1942; *South Bend Tribune,* managing editor, 1942-52; Studebaker Corp., South Bend, public relations director, 1952-55; Hall Syndicate, New York, N.Y., editor and vice-president, 1955-68; Universal Press Syndicate, Mission, Kan., author of weekly column "A Time to Live," syndicated to forty-one newspapers, 1968—. As a reporter, covered World War II, including the signing of the Japanese surrender. *Member:* Sigma Delta Chi, Dutch Treat Club of New York.

WRITINGS: A Time to Live, Sheed, 1976.

SIDELIGHTS: Walton comments that his syndicated column is directed at the "retired generation" of which he is a member.

* * *

WARD, Chester 1907-1977

October 7, 1907—June 29, 1977; American Navy rear admiral and author. He was an outspoken conservative who frequently warned of growing Soviet might in the 1960's. He served as a judge advocate while in the Navy. Ward died in Honolulu, Hawaii. Obituaries: *New York Times,* July 2, 1977.

* * *

WARD, Maisie 1889-1975

PERSONAL: Birth-given name, Mary Josephine; born January 4, 1889, in Shanklin, Isle of Wight; came to United States, 1940; daughter of Wilfrid (a writer and editor) and Josephine Mary (a novelist; maiden name, Hope) Ward; married Frank Sheed (the publisher and author), April, 1926; children: Rosemary, Wilfrid. *Education:* Educated privately and at school in Cambridge, England. *Religion:* Roman Catholic. *Home:* 7 Tonnele Ave., Jersey City, N.J. 07306.

CAREER: Publisher, biographer, and Catholic activist. Book Reviewer for *Dublin Review,* in the early 1910's; during World War I, worked as a nurse's aide at military hospitals; became charter member of Catholic Evidence Guild (a Roman Catholic street-corner lecturing organization), 1919; with husband, Frank Sheed, co-founded Sheed & Ward (Roman Catholic publishing house) in London, England, 1926, vice-president, 1926-73, opened New York City branch, 1933, sold firm to Universal Press Syndicate, 1973. During residence in United States, 1940-46, became interested in Dorothy Day's *Catholic Worker* and Catherine de Hueck's interracial Friendship House; in England, co-founded Catholic Housing Aid Society with Molly Walsh, 1955, to subsidize families in the purchase of their own homes. Lecturer for Catholic Evidence Guild and other organizations primarily in England and the United States.

WRITINGS—All published by Sheed, except as noted: *St. Bernadino, the People's Preacher,* Herder, 1914; *Father Maturin, a Memoir, with Selected Letters,* Longmans, Green, 1920; (compiler) *Catholic Evidence Training Out-*

lines, 1925, 4th revised edition (with husband, F. J. Sheed), 1939; (translator) Marie Joseph Lagrange, *Christ and Renan: A Commentary on Ernest Renan's "The Life of Jesus,"* Benziger, 1928; (editor) *The English Way: Studies in English Sanctity from St. Bede to Newman,* 1933, reprinted, Books for Libraries, 1968; *The Oxford Groups* (a comparison of the Oxford group with Catholicism), 1937; *The Wilfrid Wards and the Transition,* Volume I: *The Nineteenth Century,* 1934, Volume II: *Insurrection Versus Resurrection,* 1937; (editor) *This Burning Heat* (collection of letters written during World War II), 1941; *Gilbert Keith Chesterton,* 1943; *The Splendor of the Rosary,* 1945, abridged edition published as *The Rosary,* 1957; *Young Mr. Newman,* 1948; *France Pagan?: The Mission of Abbe Godin,* includes Ward's translation and adaptation of *France a Missionary Land?* by Henri Godin and Yves Daniel, 1949.

The Saints in Pictures, 1950; *The Return to Chesterton,* 1952; *Be Not Solicitous: Sidelights on the Providence of God and the Catholic Family,* 1953; (translator) Etienne Gilson, *Choir of Muses,* 1953; *The Authenticity of the Gospels,* 1956; *They Saw His Glory: An Introduction to the Gospels and Acts,* 1956; *Saints Who Made History: The First Five Centuries,* 1959 (published in England as *Early Church Portrait Gallery,* 1959); *Caryll Houselander, That Divine Eccentric,* 1962; *Unfinished Business* (autobiography), 1964; (editor) *The Letters of Caryll Houselander,* 1965; *Robert Browning and His World,* Holt, Volume I: *The Private Face, 1812-1861,* 1967, Volume II: *Two Robert Brownings?, 1861-1889,* 1969; *The Tragi-Comedy of Pen Browning (1849-1912),* introduction by Robert Coles, 1972; *To and Fro on the Earth: The Sequel to an Autobiography,* 1973.

Contributor to *Saturday Review, Commonweal, Tablet, Dublin Review,* and *New York Times.*

SIDELIGHTS: In answer to Maisie Ward's mother's suggestions that there was a genuine need for a Roman Catholic publishing house as concerned with literary and intellectual quality as with piety, the newly married couple founded Sheed & Ward with only £2000 capital and advice from author Hilaire Belloc. Despite the difficulties and setbacks that faced the small publishing house, however, their son Wilfrid later recalled, "I cannot honestly remember any heavy anxiety reaching the house, even when a vintage psychopath posing as manager made off with the lot in 1943 and they had to start from scratch. Instead, there was usually a vague sense of elation—my mother had just discovered the *Catholic Worker,* or the cooperatives in Nova Scotia, or the worker priests in France, and maybe there was a book in it."

Indeed, Maisie's activism was continuously peaking, as Wilfrid noted: "Something was always catching the corner of her eye and she was off like a retriever. She did her own leg work, in the slums of Marseilles or wherever, and came back snorting fire—'Do you realize what's going on there?'"

Maisie's interest in books, too, was ardent, yet Wilfrid described her as not a bookish person. Rather, "books were to wrestle with. They were life itself, as real as their subject matter. . . ." Maisie managed to make one interest work for the other, though. "Her life of Chesterton finally got finished and became a best-seller," Wilfrid wrote, "and she used that and other earnings to help support two communes and God knows what else. Social activism comes and goes with the tides, and most of those Catholic groups were down to a twitch by the late fifties, but hers goes on forever." Her Catholic Housing Aid Society in England, which buys old houses and turns them into low-rent flats, has grown into a national organization. Her interdenominational money-raising activities for a village in India received the recognition and gratitude of the village itself when it threw a three-day festival for Maisie with huge banners saying 'Welcome Mrs. Sheed,' and much dancing and other activity. Wilfrid noted that "she has become more radicalized in later life and has lately been interviewing draft resisters in prison."

Where not herself personally involved in the mainline of some revolutionary activity, Maisie took pride in having published such Catholic revolutionaries as Hans Kung and Charles Davis, philosophers like Jacques Maritain and Paul Claudel, as well as the works of Dorothy Day, Catherine de Hueck, Gertrud von le Fort, Caryll Houselander, and classics such as the letters of St. Therese de Lisieux and *The Confessions of St. Augustine*.

AVOCATIONAL INTERESTS: Reading, walking.

BIOGRAPHICAL/CRITICAL SOURCES: Maisie Ward, *Unfinished Business*, Sheed, 1964; *New York Times*, April 2, 1972; Ward, *To and Fro on the Earth: The Sequel to an Autobiography*, Sheed, 1973.

OBITUARIES: New York Times, January 29, 1975; *AB Bookman's Weekly*, February 17, 1975; *Publishers' Weekly*, February 17, 1975.

(Died January 28, 1975, in New York, N.Y.)

[Sketch verified by husband, Frank Sheed]

* * *

WARD, Paul W. 1905-1976

October 9, 1905—November 24, 1976; American journalist who won the Pulitzer Prize in 1948 for a series of articles on life in the Soviet Union. He was named a chevalier of the French Legion of Honor for reporting on the war for the Free French news agency in World War II. He died in Washington, D.C. Obituaries: *New York Times*, November 25, 1976; *Washington Post*, November 25, 1976.

* * *

WARDLE, David 1930-

PERSONAL: Born March 25, 1930, in Hull, England; son of John Royston (a bank official) and Marjorie (Chamberlain) Wardle; married Pauline Mary Hardy (a teacher), August 7, 1954; children: Susan (Mrs. Keith Longman), Belinda, Jonathan Richard. *Education:* University of Nottingham, B.A., 1951, M.Ed., 1961, Ph.D., 1965. *Home:* 151 Hassall Rd., Alsager, Stoke-on-Trent, England. *Office:* Padgate College, Fearnhead, Warrington, Cheshire, England.

CAREER: Teacher in secondary schools in Nottingham, England, 1955-61, and technical colleges in Loughborough, England, 1964-67; Alsager College of Education, Alsager, England, principal lecturer in education, 1967-71; Padgate College, Fearnhead, Warrington, England, dean of teacher education, 1971—. *Military service:* Royal Air Force, 1952-55; became flying officer.

WRITINGS: English Popular Education, 1780-1970, Cambridge University Press, 1970, revised edition published as *English Popular Education, 1780-1975*, 1976; *Education and Society in Nineteenth Century Nottingham*, Cambridge University Press, 1971; *The Rise of the Schooled Society*, Routledge & Kegan Paul, 1974. Contributor to scholarly journals.

WORK IN PROGRESS: Writing a section on education for *Victoria History of Cheshire*, Volume III, edited by B. E. Harris, publication by Institute of Historical Research expected in 1979.

SIDELIGHTS: Wardle comments: "My particular academic interest is in a study of the pressures—political, economic, social, intellectual—that cause educational change, especially change in the school curriculum."

* * *

WARE, Leonard 1900(?)-1976

1900(?)-September 19, 1976; American journalist, government official, educator, and author. He served with the State Department and as program director of the Department of Interior's Bureau of Indian Affairs. He died in Hanover, N.H. Obituaries: *Washington Post*, September 23, 1976.

* * *

WARNER, Lucille Schulberg

PERSONAL: Born in Mount Vernon, N.Y.; daughter of Sol and Emma (Zeeman) Schulberg; married Henry Goldsmith Warner (a certified public accountant), January 12, 1971; children: (stepchildren) Alison, Marc. *Education:* Attended Carnegie Institute of Technology (now Carnegie-Mellon University). *Home:* 46 Wensley Dr., Great Neck, N.Y. 11021. *Agent:* Charlotte Sheedy, Hoffman-Sheedy Literary Agency, 145 West 86th St., New York, N.Y. 10024.

CAREER: American National Red Cross, public relations correspondent in France and Germany, 1945-47; Young & Rubicam, New York City, advertising copywriter, 1952-59; Compton Advertising Agencies, New York City, advertising copywriter, 1959-62; Time-Life Books, New York City, staff writer, 1962-69; free-lance writer, 1969—. While employed by the Red Cross, worked in a club in Paris; as correspondent toured the American zone of occupied Germany, and broadcast over American Forces Network.

WRITINGS: Historic India, Time-Life, 1968; *From Slave to Abolitionist: The Life of William Wells Brown* (juvenile), Dial, 1976; (with Ann Reit) *Your A to Z Super Personality Quiz* (juvenile), Scholastic Book Services, 1977. Author of film strip series "What Is Poetry" for Caedmon Records.

WORK IN PROGRESS: A young adult novel; another "A to Z" book for teenagers, for Scholastic Book Services; a juvenile book on India; another novel.

SIDELIGHTS: Lucille Warner writes briefly: "After many years of earning my bread by writing, I feel I am now at the start of my career as a writer."

* * *

WARNER, Oliver 1903-1976

February 28, 1903—August 14, 1976; British-born author of naval histories best known for *Warfare Under Sail, Great Sea Battles*, and biographies of Lord Nelson and Joseph Conrad. He died in England. Obituaries: *AB Bookman's Weekly*, October 4, 1976. (See index for previous *CA* sketch)

* * *

WASSERMAN, Gary 1944-

PERSONAL: Born December 1, 1944, in Washington, D.C.; son of Samuel (an engineer) and Helen (a bookkeeper; maiden name, Disman) Wasserman. *Education:* Georgetown University, B.S., 1966; graduate study at Nairobi University, 1970-71, and St. Antony's College, Oxford, 1971-72; Columbia University, M.A., 1967, Ph.D. (with distinction),

1973. *Politics:* "Jewish populist." *Religion:* "Populist Jew." *Home:* 1673 Columbia Rd. N.W., Apt. 600, Washington, D.C. 20009.

CAREER: Medgar Evers College of the City University of New York, Brooklyn, N.Y., assistant professor of political science, 1973-75; issues coordinator for Presidential campaign of Senator Fred Harris, in Washington, D.C., 1975-76; U.S. House of Representatives, Washington, D.C., legislative assistant to Congressman Dave Obey, 1976—. Summer intern for U.S. State Department's Bureau of African Affairs, 1963-66; assistant professor at Columbia University, summers, 1973-74. *Member:* Alpha Sigma Nu, Pi Sigma Alpha. *Awards, honors:* Fulbright-Hays fellowship, 1969-70.

WRITINGS: Politics of Decolonization, Cambridge University Press, 1976; *The Basics of American Politics,* Little, Brown, 1976. Contributor of articles and reviews to academic journals. Assistant editor of *Columbia Journal of World Business,* 1966-67.

SIDELIGHTS: Wasserman told *CA:* "I have studied politics because it asks the most important questions. I have written about politics because there is more to write than there is to do, unfortunately." He speaks French, Spanish, and Swahili.

*   *   *

WASSON, Donald   1914(?)-1976

1914(?)—November 9, 1976; American author and librarian. He died in New York City. Obituaries: *New York Times,* November 12, 1976.

*   *   *

WATERSTON, (Margaret) Elizabeth (Hillman) 1922-

PERSONAL: Born April 18, 1922, in Montreal Quebec, Canada; daughter of Daniel (an engineer) and Bertha (Smith) Hillman; married Douglas Waterston (an administrator), 1949; children: Dan, Jane, Christina, Charlotte, Rosemary. *Education:* Attended McGill University, 1939-42; University of Toronto, B.A., 1944, Ph.D., 1949; Bryn Mawr College, M.A., 1945. *Home:* R.R. 6, Guelph, Ontario, Canada. *Office:* Department of English, University of Guelph, Guelph, Ontario, Canada.

CAREER: Sir George Williams University, Montreal, Quebec, lecturer, 1945-48, assistant professor, 1950-56, acting chairman of department, 1956-58; University of Western Ontario, London, assistant professor, 1958-66; University of Guelph, Guelph, Ontario, associate professor, 1966-71, professor of English and Canadian literature, 1971—, chairman of department, 1974—. *Member:* Humanities Association of Canada (vice-president, 1974—), Canadian Association of Chairmen of English (president, 1975—), Association of Canadian University Teachers of English, Canadian Association of American Studies, Canadian Association of Commonwealth Language and Literature Studies, Association for the Studies of Canadian and Quebec Literature, Association of Canadian Studies (United States). *Awards, honors:* Canada Council grants, 1964, 1970, 1972.

WRITINGS: Pioneers in Agriculture: Massey, McIntosh, Saunders, Clarke, Irwin (Toronto), 1957; (with Munro Beattie) *Composition for Canadian Universities,* Macmillan, 1964; (contributor) C. F. Klinck, editor, *Literary History of Canada,* University of Toronto Press, 1965; *Survey: A Short History of Canadian Literature,* Methuen, 1973;

(editor with D. W. Hoffman) *On Middle Ground,* University of Guelph, 1974.

Contributor to *Dictionary of Canadian Biography.* Contributor of articles to journals in her field, including *Canadian Literature* and *Journal of Canadian Fiction.* Editor of *Canadian Children's Literature;* member of editorial boards of *Canadian Studies in English* and *Scottish Tradition.*

WORK IN PROGRESS: Two children's books, *Bakers's Dozen* and *Once Around the Block;* scholarly work on Canadian and Scottish fiction.

*   *   *

WATSON, Bernard B(ennett)   1911-1977

May 17, 1911—June 8, 1977; American physicist, educator, and author of texts in his field. He was a physics specialist for the U.S. Office of Education and the Labor Department. He died in Bethesda, Md. Obituaries: *Washington Post,* June 10, 1977.

*   *   *

WATSON, Clarissa

PERSONAL: Born in Ashland, Wis.; daughter of Arthur John (a business executive) and Berenice (a composer; maiden name, Miars) Hanson; married Edward Louis Watson; children: Robin, Alden Wentworth. *Education:* Milwaukee Downer College, B.A. (magna cum laude); also attended Layton Art School. *Religion:* Episcopal. *Home address:* Wolver Hollow Rd., Oyster Bay, N.Y. 11771. *Agent:* Barbara Baccus, 304 East 78th St., New York, N.Y. 10021. *Office:* Country Art Gallery, Forest Ave., Locust Valley, N.Y. 11560.

CAREER: Country Art Gallery, Locust Valley, N.Y., co-founder and director, 1953—; portrait painter. Co-founder and director of Country Art Galleries in Westbury and Southampton, N.Y., 1953—. Founder and director of Country Art School, 1953-68. Director of film festivals for Seven Village Arts Council, 1969-71. Art consultant to Adelphi University, 1966-68.

WRITINGS: (Editor) *The Sensuous Carrot,* Stevenson, 1972; *The Fourth Stage of Gainsborough Brown* (suspense story about art world), McKay, 1977. Contributor to *This Week* and to local newspapers.

WORK IN PROGRESS: The Quick Connoisseur, a guide to knowing art; *The Man in the Back Seat,* another suspense about the art world; editing *Long Island Artists,* an anthology.

AVOCATIONAL INTERESTS: France, gourmet cooking, wine, horses, "and art—always and forever art."

*   *   *

WATSON, Goodwin   1899(?)-1976

1899(?)—December 30, 1976; American educator and author. Watson was an early critic of the validity of standard intelligence tests. He died in Longboat Key, Fla. Obituaries: *AB Bookman's Weekly,* February 14, 1977.

*   *   *

WATSON, Pauline   1925- (POLA)

PERSONAL: Born July 24, 1925, in New Iberia, La.; daughter of Luke and Rosalie (Catalano) Bennett; married Jimmy T. Watson, October 19, 1947; children: Cindy (Mrs.

Scott Walling), Jim, Duke, Vicki, Mike. *Education:* Palmer Institute of Authorship, graduate, 1951. *Home:* 24420 Stuebner Airline, Tumball, Tex. 77375.

CAREER: Accountant and office manager for an automobile dealership in New Iberia, La., 1942-47; writer, 1950—. *Member:* Houston Writer's Workshop (president, 1970—), Associated Authors of Children's Literature, Houston (president, 1975—), International Toastmistress Club (secretary and publicity chairman of Houston's Noonday branch, 1968—), Federated Woman's Club (Beaumont, Tex.).

WRITINGS—Children's books: *A Surprise for Mother,* Prentice-Hall, 1976; *Cricket's Cookery,* Open Court, in press; *A Day with Daddy,* Prentice-Hall, in press; *Curley Cat Babysits,* Harcourt, in press.

Writer of weekly column, "Post Oak Patter," in *Bellaire Texan,* 1969—, and of monthly columns, "Kitchen Klatter," 1972—, and "Washboard Wisdom" (under pseudonym POLA), 1974—, both syndicated by Features Unlimited. Work anthologized in *Cricket's Choice,* edited by Clifton Fadiman and Marianne Carus, 1975. Contributor of children's stories and poems to children's magazines, including *My Weekly Reader* and *Cricket,* and of adult stories and articles to popular magazines, including *Woman's Day, Southern Living, Reader's Digest,* and *Parents' Magazine.*

WORK IN PROGRESS: Short, short witch and ghost stories with fun endings for the very young.

SIDELIGHTS: Pauline Watson wrote: "I try to learn something new everyday and to have a long range plan of study toward goals that I have privately set for myself. I have just completed a course on gagwriting which I thoroughly enjoyed."

* * *

WATT, Douglas (Benjamin) 1914-

PERSONAL: Born January 20, 1914, in New York, N.Y.; son of Benjamin (an engineer) and Agnes (Neimann) Watt; married Ray Mantel, November 5, 1937 (deceased); married Ethel Madsen (a theatre producer), August 13, 1951; children: Richard, James, Patricia, Katherine. *Education:* Cornell University, A.B., 1934. *Home:* 27 W. 86th St., New York, N.Y. 10024. *Office:* 220 E. 42nd St., New York, N.Y. 10017.

CAREER/WRITINGS: New York News, New York City, copy boy, 1936-37, radio columnist, 1937-40, drama critic, 1940—; *New Yorker,* New York City, music editor and staff writer, 1946—. Songwriter. *Military service:* U.S. Air Force, 1943-46. *Member:* American Society of Composers, Authors, and Publishers (ASCAP), American Guild of Authors and Composers, New York Drama Critics Circle (vice president, 1975—), Dutch Treat Club.

* * *

WATTS, Peter Christopher 1919-
(Matt Chisholm, Cy James, Duncan Mackinlock, Tom Owen)

PERSONAL: Born December 25, 1919, in London, England; son of Frank (a telegraphist) and Lillian (a musician; maiden name, Thayers) Watts; married Sonia Chism, August 5, 1925; children: Matthew, Jeremy. *Education:* Educated in England. *Home:* 41 Wellington Road, Hatch End, Pinner, Middlesex HA5 4NF, England. *Agent:* A. D. Peters, 10 Buckingham St., London WC2N 6BU, England; and Peter Matson, Marold Matson Co., 22 East 40th St., New York, N.Y. 10016.

CAREER: Writer. *Military service:* British Army, 1940-46; served in North Africa, Syria, and Burma. *Member:* Western Writers of America.

WRITINGS: Out of Yesterday (novel), Hodder & Stoughton, 1950; *Scream and Shout* (novel), Transworld Publications, 1965; *A Dictionary of the Old West,* Knopf, 1977.

All western novels under pseudonym Matt Chisholm; all published by Panther Books, except as indicated: *Halfbreed,* 1958; *Hodge,* 1958; *Riders at the Ford,* 1958; *Hang a Man High,* 1959; *Sutter's Strike,* 1959; *The Saga of Trench Godden,* 1959; *Blood on the Land,* 1959; *Joe Blade,* 1959; *Never Give Ground,* 1959; *Wild Mustanger,* 1959; *The Law of Ben Hodge,* 1959; *A Posse of Violent Men,* 1960; *Fury at Tombstone,* 1960; *Pursuit in the Sun,* 1960; *Prayer for a Gunman,* 1960; *Hangrope for a Gunman,* 1960; *Advance to Death,* 1961; *A Rage of Guns,* 1961; *Bitter Range,* 1962; *Three for Vengeance,* Mayflower Books, 1963; *The Proud Horseman,* Mayflower Books, 1963; *The Last Gun,* 1966; *Cash McCord,* 1966; *Spur to Death,* 1966; *Hunted,* 1966; *Gun Marshall,* 1967; *Range War,* 1967; *Indian Scout,* 1967; *A Gun for Bragg's Woman,* 1967; *Apache Kill,* 1967; *Gun Lust,* 1968; *A Bullet for Brody,* 1968; *High Peak,* 1968; *Spur,* 1968; *Three Canyons to Death,* Mayflower Books, 1968; *The Trail of Fear,* 1968; *Never Give Ground,* 1969.

"The McAllister Series," all under pseudonym Matt Chisholm: *The Hard Men,* Mayflower Books, 1963; *Death at Noon,* Mayflower Books, 1963; *The Hangman Rides Tall,* Mayflower Books, 1963; *McAllister,* Mayflower Books, 1963, Beagle Books, 1971; *Kiowa,* Panther Books, 1967; *Death Trail,* Panther Books, 1967; *Tough to Kill,* Panther Books, 1968; *McAllister Justice,* Panther Books, 1969, Beagle Books, 1971; *Rage of McAllister,* Panther Books, 1969, Beagle Books, 1971; *Hell for McAllister,* Panther Books, 1969, Beagle Books, 1970; *McAllister Strikes,* Panther Books, 1969, Beagle Books, 1971; *Kill McAllister,* Panther Books, 1969, Beagle Books, 1972; *McAllister Rides,* Panther Books, 1969, Beagle Books, 1971; *McAllister Makes War,* Panther Books, 1969, Beagle Books, 1971; *McAllister's Fury,* Panther Books, 1969, Beagle Books, 1971; *McAllister Fights,* Panther Books, 1969, Beagle Books, 1971; *Gunsmoke for McAllister,* Panther Books, 1969, Beagle Books, 1970; *Blood on McAllister,* Panther Books, 1969, Beagle Books, 1970; *McAllister Says No,* Panther Books, 1970, Beagle Books, 1971; *Danger for McAllister,* Panther Books, 1970; *McAllister Gambles,* Panther Books, 1970, Beagle Books, 1971; *Hang McAllister,* Beagle Books, 1970; *Shoot McAllister,* Panther Books, 1970, Beagle Books, 1971; *Trail of McAllister,* Panther Books, 1970, Beagle Books, 1971; *McAllister Runs Wild,* Mayflower Books, 1972; *Brand McAllister,* Mayflower Books, 1972; *Battle of McAllister,* Mayflower Books, 1972; *McAllister Trapped,* Mayflower Books, 1973; *McAllister Must Die,* Mayflower Books, 1974; *Vengeance of McAllister,* Mayflower Books, 1974; *The McAllister Legend,* Mayflower Books, 1974.

"The Storm Series," all under pseudonym Matt Chisholm; all published by Mayflower Books, except as indicated: *Stampede,* Panther Books, 1971; *Hard Texas Trail,* Panther Books, 1971; *Riders West,* 1971; *One Notch to Death,* 1972; *One Man—One Gun,* 1972; *A Breed of Men,* 1973; *Thunder in the West,* 1973; *Battle Fury,* 1973; *Blood on the Hills,* 1973.

Under pseudonym Matt Chisholm, *Indians!* (juvenile), Odhams, 1965.

Under pseudonym Tom Owen: *The Dread and the Glory*

(novel), Panther Books, 1959; *Circus of Horror* (novel), Panther Books, 1960; *The Corgi Sports Almanac,* Corgi, 1965.

Under pseudonym Duncan Mackinlock: *Island of Hell,* Panther Books, 1961.

All western novels under pseudonym Cy James; all published by Panther Books: *The Brasada Guns,* 1961; *The Gun Is my Brother,* 1961; *The Violent Hills,* 1961; *Death Rides Fast,* 1964; *The Battle of Red Rock,* 1964; *Ride the Far Country,* 1964; *Hellion,* 1964; *Hangrope Posse,* 1965; *Gun-Rage,* 1965; *Blood Creek,* 1965; *Gun Hand,* 1965; *Savage Horseman,* 1966; *Man in the Saddle,* 1966; *The Running Gun,* 1966; *My Gun Is Justice,* 1966.

"The Spur Series," under pseudonym Cy James; all published by Mayflower Books: *The Cimmaron Kid,* 1969; *Longhorn,* 1970; *Gun,* 1971; *The Brave Ride Tall,* 1971; *Blood at Sunset,* 1972.

Also author of over forty short stories and novelettes under pseudonyms Matt Chisholm and Cyrus James, including the "McCool Series" and the "Robin Hood Series."

SIDELIGHTS: Watts believes that writing is a craft which, at every level, must be continually practised. He told *CA:* "a working writer should be capable of picking a character out of the air with ease, of weaving a plot at the drop of a hat, able to write under any circumstances and in any surroundings. Writing must not be so much a dedication as a habit."

After publishing his first novel at twenty-six, there followed a ten year period in the "literary wilderness," during which time Watts received "enough rejection slips to paper his walls." After the success of his first Western, Watts produced two full length novels a month. He has since slowed his output of novels and concentrates on "serious work." The acceptance of *Dictionary of the Old West,* Watts told *CA,* "was the culmination of years of fascination with the words and dialects of the American West."

*   *   *

WEAD, R(oy) Douglas   1946-

PERSONAL: Born May 17, 1946, in Muncie, Ind.; son of Roy H. (a college president) and Rosa Mae (Short) Wead; married Gloria Jean Crain, May 29, 1965; children: Shannon Douglas, Scott Douglas. *Education:* Attended Central Bible College. *Religion:* Christian. *Home and office:* 1428 South Forrest Heights, Springfield, Mo. 65804.

CAREER: Restoration, Springfield, Mo., editor, 1973—. Lecturer, nationally and internationally.

WRITINGS—All nonfiction, except as noted: *Father McCarthy Smokes a Pipe and Speaks in Tongues,* Wisdom House, 1972; *Catholic Charismatics,* Creation House, 1973; *Tonight They'll Kill a Catholic,* Creation House, 1974; *The Great Multimillion Dollar Miracle,* Whitaker House, 1975; *Hear His Voice,* Creation House, 1976; *The C. M. Ward Story* (biography), New Leaf, 1976; *The Compassionate Touch,* Creation House, 1977; (with C. M. Ward) *Inspirational Sports Stories,* Creation House, in press. Contributor to religious periodicals, including *Christian Life* and *Logos Journal.*

WORK IN PROGRESS: Head Wound, a novel about an attempt to assassinate the anti-christ; commuting back and forth to India to gather research for another book on world hunger.

SIDELIGHTS: In the early 1970's Wead visited Ireland to gather material for *Tonight They'll Kill a Catholic;* he ac-

companied the Catholic Irish Republican Army (I.R.A.), interviewed Protestant Tommy Herron only days before he was murdered, and was himself ambushed while on patrols with the British Army. The book has been published in eight languages.

BIOGRAPHICAL/CRITICAL SOURCES: Bookseller, June, 1977.

*   *   *

WEART, Edith L.   1898(?)-1977

1898(?)-1977; American author of a series of educational books on medical subjects, for children. She was a leading women's chess player in the 1930's. Weart died in Mamaroneck, N.Y. Obituaries: *New York Times,* January 26, 1977.

*   *   *

WEAVER, Jerry L(ee)   1939-

PERSONAL: Born March 9, 1939, in Columbus, Ohio; son of Lee J. and Martha (Lockheart) Weaver. *Education:* Ohio University, A.B. (honors), 1962, M.A., 1963; University of Pittsburgh, Ph.D., 1969. *Home:* 2909 South Buchanan St., Arlington, Va. 22206. *Office:* Agency for International Development, U.S. Department of State, Washington, D.C. 20523.

CAREER: California State University, Long Beach, assistant professor of political science, 1966-71; University of Texas, Austin, visiting associate professor of government, 1971-72; California State University, Long Beach, associate professor of political science, 1972-76; U.S. Department of State, Washington, D.C., social science analyst for Agency for International Development, 1977—. Visiting associate professor at University of California, Los Angeles, 1975-76, visiting professor, 1976-77; visiting scholar at University of Michigan, 1970; member of board of directors of International Social Science Institute, 1970-71. *Member:* American Society for Public Administration (member of executive committee of section on international and comparative administration, 1975-78). *Awards, honors:* Henry and Grace Doherty fellowship, 1965-66; American Philosophical Society grant, 1971-72.

WRITINGS: Political Dimensions of Rural Development in Latin America, 1950-1967: A Selected Bibliography, California State University, Long Beach, 1968; *Latin American Development: A Selected Bibliography,* Clio Press, 1969; *Health Care Services Use in Orange County, California: A Socio-Economic Analysis,* Center for Political Research, California State University, Long Beach, 1969; *Bureaucracy During a Period of Social Change: The Guatemalan Case,* Institute of Latin American Studies, University of Texas, 1971; *Role Expectations of Latin American Bureaucrats: Hypotheses and Data,* Institute of Latin American Studies, University of Texas, 1971; (contributor) Clarence E. Thurber and Lawrence S. Graham, editors, *Development Administration in Latin America,* Duke University Press, 1973; (contributor) Phillippe C. Schmitter, editor, *Military Rule in Latin America: Functions, Consequences, and Perspectives,* Sage Publications, 1973; (editor) *Latin American Development Administration: Accomplishments of the 1960's, Research Priorities for the 1970's,* Institute of Latin American Studies, University of Texas, 1973; *Conflict and Control in Health Care Administration,* Sage Publications, 1975; (contributor) Kenneth Fidel, editor, *The Military in Developing Countries,* TransAction Books, 1975; *National Health Policy and the Underserved: Ethnic Minorities, Women, and the Elderly,* Mosby, 1976; (contributor) Frank

Baird, editor, *Mexican American: Political Power, Influence, or Resource,* Texas Technological University Press, 1977.

Contributor of about forty articles and reviews to scholarly journals. Index editor of *Advanced Bibliography of Contents: Political Science,* 1969-71, member of executive committee of advisory board, 1969-77; book review editor of *Journal of Comparative Administration,* 1970-74; member of editorial board of *Journal of Health Politics, Policy and Law,* 1975—; member of editorial advisory board of *Administration and Society,* 1975-76; referee for *Journal of Developing Areas, Social Science Quarterly, Journal of Politics, Inquiry,* and Arizona State University Press.

WORK IN PROGRESS: The Politics of Food; The Politics of Population Policies in the Third World.

* * *

WEBB, Samuel C(lement) 1934-

PERSONAL: Born August 14, 1934, in Oak Grove, Mo.; son of Clement Holly and Minnie Vivian (Everman) Webb; married Jane R. Kirk, June 6, 1959; children: Bronson, Jennifer, Mark, Holly. *Education:* University of Missouri, B.S. (civil engineering), 1957, M.S. (business administration), 1959; University of Kansas, Ph.D. (economics), 1968. *Home:* 537 Circle Dr., Wichita, Kan. 67218. *Office:* College of Business Administration, Wichita State University, Wichita, Kan. 67208.

CAREER: Southwestern Bell Telephone Co., St. Louis, Mo., in management, 1959-63; Wichita State University, Wichita, Kan., assistant professor, 1966-70, associate professor, 1970-77, professor of economics, 1977—. Registered professional engineer in Missouri, 1962—; engineer for Black & Veatch, summers, 1954-56. *Military service:* U.S. Army Reserve, 1957-65, active duty, 1957; became captain. *Member:* American Economic Association.

WRITINGS: The Role of Bank Reserves in the Economy, Pitkin, 1971; (contributor) Glenn W. Miller and Jimmy Skaggs, editors, *Metropolitan Wichita,* University Press of Kansas, 1977; *Managerial Economics,* with instructor's manual, Houghton, 1977. Contributor of about a dozen articles and reviews to business, economics, and education journals. Editor of *Business Journal* (at Wichita State University), 1969-71.

WORK IN PROGRESS: Research in the field of monetary economics.

* * *

WEBBER, Irma E(leanor Schmidt) 1904-

PERSONAL: Born August 16, 1904, in San Diego, Calif.; daughter of Eugene Arthur (a civil engineer) and Edna (Allen) Schmidt; married John Milton Webber (a botanist), May 13, 1927; children: Herbert Milton, Irma Jean (Mrs. M. Michael Appleman). *Education:* University of California, Berkeley, A.B. (honors), 1926, M.A., 1927, Ph.D., 1929. *Home:* 500 Arlington Ave., Berkeley, Calif. 94707.

CAREER: Carnegie Institute (now Carnegie-Mellon University), Pittsburgh, Pa., research assistant in paleobotany, 1927-29; U.S. Department of Agriculture, Washington, D.C., agent with Division of Blister Rust Control, 1929-31; Citrus Experiment Station, Riverside, Calif., research assistant, 1932-33; U.S. Department of Agriculture, collaborator with Division of Western Irrigation Agriculture, Bureau of Plant Industry, 1934, Division of Cotton and Other Fiber Crops, 1936-43, Bureau of Plant Industry, Soils, and Agri-

cultural Engineering, 1943-50, botanist, 1950-51, collaborator, 1951-53, in Agricultural Research Service, 1953—. Collaborator with Revista Lilloa (Argentina), 1937—. Botanical art is included in the Kerlan Collection, Hunt Institute, and Carnegie-Mellon University.

MEMBER: California Botanical Society, University of California Alumni Association, Phi Beta Kappa, Sigma Xi, Phi Sigma.

WRITINGS—Self-illustrated children's books: *Up Above and Down Below,* William R. Scott, 1943; *Anywhere in the World,* William R. Scott, 1947; *Bits That Grow Big,* William R. Scott, 1949; *It Looks Like This,* William R. Scott, 1949, revised edition, 1958, reissued as *What Does It Look Like?,* Scholastic Book Services, 1969; *Thanks to Trees,* William R. Scott, 1952. Contributor to scientific journals and children's magazines, including *Jack and Jill* and *Horn Book.*

WORK IN PROGRESS: Work on plants.

SIDELIGHTS: Irma Webber writes: "Many of my friends were botanists and I married a botanical classmate who was the son of a distinguished botanist. Such ties tended to reinforce my interest in botanical research until my young children taught me how eager they were to learn about their environment. Then I began a search for children's books that presented simple, non-technical but factual information about plants and other facets of the environment in attractive form. The paucity of such material about plants prompted me to draw on my botanical background and parental experience to produce *Up Above and Down Below* and subsequent volumes." Her books have been published in Pakistan, Iran, Japan, Italy, and France.

AVOCATIONAL INTERESTS: Gardening, travel.

* * *

WEBER, William John 1927-

PERSONAL: Born September 8, 1927, in Cleveland, Ohio; son of Clarence J. and Edith (James) Weber; married Barbara Ann Haigh, December 23, 1951; children: William James, John Hunt. *Education:* Ohio State University, D.V.M., 1953, M.Sc., 1954. *Home address:* Route 1, Box 368A, Leesburg, Fla. 32748. *Office:* Leesburg Veterinary Hospital, 3600 West Main St., Leesburg, Fla. 32748.

CAREER: Leesburg Veterinary Hospital, Leesburg, Fla., owner and partner, 1954—. Member of advisory council to Florida State Board of Health, 1970. *Military service:* U.S. Air Force, 1945-47. *Member:* American Veterinary Medical Society, Wildlife Society (member of Florida executive board), Florida Veterinary Medical Association (president, 1964-65), Sigma Xi, Phi Zeta. *Awards, honors:* Gold star award from Florida Veterinary Medical Association, 1968, 1970, 1976, veterinarian of the year award, 1969.

WRITINGS—Juvenile: *Wild Orphan Babies, Mammals and Birds: Caring for Them, Setting Them Free* (with own photographs), Holt, 1975; *Wild Orphan Friends,* Holt, 1976. Photography has appeared on greeting cards and other material from Hallmark Cards and American Greetings, and on covers of magazines, including *National Wildlife, Ranger Rick's Nature Magazine, Florida Wildlife, Archery World, Four Seasons Trails, Veterinary Medicine,* and *Florida Veterinary Journal.* Contributor to nature studies, outdoor recreation, and children's magazines, and to veterinary journals.

* * *

WEBSTER, Edna Robb 1896-

PERSONAL: Born June 29, 1896, in Marshalltown, Iowa;

daughter of James Orville (a hotel owner) and Ellen (Lutes) Robb; married William Holcomb Webster (a purchasing agent), July 25, 1918; children: Marjorie Ellen Webster Stacy-Judd, William Robb Webster. *Education:* Attended Iowa State Teacher's College, 1915-16. *Politics:* Republican. *Religion:* Baptist. *Home:* 12848 Milbank St., Studio City, Calif. 91604.

CAREER: Elementary school teacher in Marshalltown, Iowa, and Cleveland, Ohio, 1916-19; Consolidated Aircraft Corp., San Diego, Calif., executive secretary, 1942-45; City of Los Angeles, Los Angeles, Calif., auditor, 1959-66. Writer, 1930—. Explorer. Lecturer. Has appeared on radio and television programs. *Awards, honors:* National poetry award, 1944.

WRITINGS—Novels, except as noted: *Love Preferred: The Romance of a Business Girl*, Grosset, 1932; *Joretta: A Love Story*, Grosset, 1932; *New Faces*, Grosset, 1933; *Lipstick Girl: A Romance of a Little Beauty*, Grosset, 1932; *Dad's Girl: The Story of a Girl Who Deserved to Win*, Grosset, 1933; *Five O'Clock Girl*, A. L. Burt, 1933; *Show Windows*, A. L. Burt, 1934; *The Love Wager*, A. L. Burt, 1934; (with daughter, Marjorie Ellen Webster) *Double Reflections* (poems), Exposition Press, 1947; *Dark Rhapsody*, Wilmar Publishers, 1968; *Price above Rubies*, Wilmar Publishers, 1969; *Rain of Terror*, Wilmar Publishers, 1971; *Grim Holiday*, Wilmar Publishers, 1972; *Early Exploring in Lands of the Maya* (nonfiction), Wilmar Publishers, 1973; *T. A. Willard: Wizard of the Storage Battery* (biography), Wilmar Publishers, 1976. Also ghostwriter of five books.

Contributor of novels serialized in national periodicals, syndicated by Central Press Syndicate and King Features Syndicate, 1930-41; contributor of stories and features to periodicals, including *Ladies' Home Journal, Literary Digest, Forbes, Independent Woman, Music of the West* magazine, and *American* magazine.

WORK IN PROGRESS: Secret of Youth; a novel exposing state marriage and divorce laws; a novel about city government; a murder mystery; a novel about Iowa family life; a historical novel set in South Carolina; collecting published and unpublished features and stories for anthologies.

SIDELIGHTS: Edna Robb Webster made four trips to areas of Mayan civilization in Central America from 1928-36, "before tourists and any modern accommodations," she emphasized. She lived with natives in thatched jungle huts, ate their foods, and carried her own hammock for sleeping. Sometimes she was housed in ancient ruined palaces with archaeological expeditions.

Mrs. Webster has also traveled extensively throughout the United States, Mexico, Europe, Hawaii, and the West Indies. She is proficient in Spanish, German, and Maya, and is able to decipher Mayan hieroglyphs.

* * *

WEEKS, Lewis G(eorge) 1893-1977

May 22, 1893—March 5, 1977; American writer and geologist specializing in oil and natural gas exploration and founder of Weeks Petroleum Corp. Long before the world became aware that there was a shortage of oil and gas he preached the need for conservation and policies that encouraged the search for new reserves and for extending the boundries of oil exploration. He died in Westport, Conn. Obituaries: *New York Times,* March 7, 1977.

WEIGLE, Luther Allan 1880-1976

September 11, 1880—September 2, 1976; American Protestant clergyman, author, and dean emeritus of Yale Divinity School. Considered to be one of the foremost religious educators in the nation, he directed the writing of *The Revised Standard Version of the Bible,* a project that occupied more than forty years. He died in New Haven, Conn. Obituaries: *New York Times,* August 3, 1976; *Washington Post,* August 4, 1976.

* * *

WEIGLE, Marta 1944-

PERSONAL: Birth-given name, Mary Martha; born July 3, 1944, in Janesville, Wis.; daughter of Richard Daniel (a college president) and Mary (Day) Weigle. *Education:* St. John's College, Annapolis, Md., student, 1961-62; Radcliffe College, A.B., 1965; University of Pennsylvania, M.A., 1968, Ph.D., 1971. *Agent:* Alfonso Tafoya, 655 Sixth Ave., Loft 212, New York, N.Y. 10010. *Office:* Department of Anthropology, University of New Mexico, Albuquerque, N.M. 78131.

CAREER: University of New Mexico, Albuquerque, assistant professor, 1972-77, associate professor of folklore, 1977—. Co-owner and manager of Abacus Books, 1973-74. *Member:* American Folklore Society, American Anthropological Association, New Mexico Folklore Society, Texas Folklore Society. *Awards, honors:* Award of honor from New Mexico Cultural Properties Review Committee, 1976; Zia Award from New Mexico Press Women, 1977.

WRITINGS: Follow My Fancy: The Book of Jacks and Jack Games, Dover, 1970; *The Penitentes of the Southwest,* Ancient City Press, 1970; *Brothers of Light, Brothers of Blood: The Penitentes of the Southwest,* University of New Mexico Press, 1976; (author of introduction to reprinted edition) Raymond Otis, *Miguel of the Bright Mountain,* University of New Mexico Press, 1977.

Editor: Lorenzo de Cordova, *Echoes of the Flute,* Ancient City Press, 1972; *Hispanic Villages of Northern New Mexico,* Lightning Tree, 1975; *The Lightning Tree Bicentennial Southwestern Reader for 1976: An Anthology of Folklore with Weekly Calendar,* Lightning Tree, 1975; *The Annual Lightning Tree Southwestern Reader with Weekly Calendar for 1977,* Lightning Tree, 1976; *A Penitente Bibliography,* University of New Mexico Press, 1976.

Author of "Lightning Tree Southwestern Calendar," 1974-75. Contributor to history, anthropology, and folklore journals.

WORK IN PROGRESS: Because the Magic Dreaming, a novel; editing, *Embers,* a book on folklore from Hispanic New Mexico; a photo-essay on the Penitente Brotherhood.

SIDELIGHTS: Marta Weigle writes: "I am a trained folklorist with research-training interests in narrative-narration analysis, mythology, the Hispanic Southwest, women and folklore, folk religion, and verbal art (the ethnography of communication). I am interested in writing fiction, basically novels and contemporary magic tales (Maerchen). I spent an important year in Athens, 1965-66."

* * *

WEINREB, Lloyd L(obell) 1936-

PERSONAL: Born October 9, 1936, in New York, N.Y.; son of Victor (a businessman) and Ernestine (Lobell) Weinreb; married Ruth Plaut (a teacher), May 5, 1963; children: Jennifer, Elizabeth, Nicholas. *Education:* Dartmouth College, B.A., 1957; Oxford University, B.A., 1959; Harvard University, LL.B., 1962. *Home:* 119 Russell Ave., Watertown, Mass. 02172. *Office:* School of Law, Harvard University, Cambridge, Mass. 02138.

CAREER: Harvard University, Cambridge, Mass., assistant professor, 1965-68, professor of law, 1968—. Chairman of board of trustees of Buckingham, Browne & Nichols School.

WRITINGS: Criminal Law: Cases, Comment, Questions, Foundation Press, 1969, 2nd edition, 1975; *Criminal Process: Cases, Comment, Questions,* Foundation Press, 1969, 2nd edition, 1974; (editor) *Leading Constitutional Cases on Criminal Justice,* Foundation Press, 1973, 5th edition, 1977; *Denial of Justice,* Free Press, 1977.

WORK IN PROGRESS: Law As Order (tentative title); research on the connections between legal and political philosophy and history.

BIOGRAPHICAL/CRITICAL SOURCES: Joseph V. Theis and William F. Andrews, Jr., editors, *Points of Law: Criminal Procedure,* Lakeview Publishers, 1970.

*   *   *

WEISBORD, Albert   1900(?)-1977

1900(?)—April 22, 1977; American Marxist scholar, historian, labor organizer, and writer on politics and economics. In 1926 he led thirteen thousand New Jersey textile workers in a strike that lasted one year. He died in Chicago, Ill. Obituaries: *New York Times,* April 28, 1977.

*   *   *

WEST, Anthony C.   1910-

PERSONAL: Born July 1, 1910, in County Down, Northern Ireland; married Olive Mary Burr, 1940; children: Seven daughters, four sons. *Education:* "The 4 'Rs." *Religion:* Christian. *Residence:* Caernarvonshire, Wales. *Agent:* Max Gartenberg, 331 Madison Ave., New York, N.Y. 10017.

CAREER: Novelist; has worked as a jack-of-all-trades. *Military service:* Royal Air Force, 1939-45; served as an air observer and navigator bomber in the Pathfinder Force. *Awards, honors:* Atlantic award, 1946.

WRITINGS: River's End and Other Stories (short stories), McDowell Obolensky, 1957; *The Native Moment,* McDowell Obolensky, 1959; *Rebel to Judgement,* McDowell Obolensky, 1962; *The Ferret Fancier,* MacGibbon & Kee, 1962, Simon & Schuster, 1963; *As Towns with Fire,* MacGibbon and Kee, 1968, Knopf, 1970.

WORK IN PROGRESS: A novel on troubles in Ireland during the 1920's; a novel on the Depression in America.

AVOCATIONAL INTERESTS: Philosophy, Christology.

*   *   *

WESTALL, Robert (Atkinson)   1929-

PERSONAL: Born October 7, 1929, in Tynemouth, England; son of Robert and Maggie Alexandra (Leggett) Westall; married Jean Underhill (an administrator), July 26, 1958; children: (Robert) Christopher. *Education:* University of Durham, B.A. (first class honors), 1953; University of London, D.F.A., 1957. *Politics:* "Right-wing socialist." *Religion:* Society of Friends (Quakers). *Residence:* Northwich, England.

CAREER: Sir John Deane's School, Northwich, England,

art teacher and head of department, 1960—, head of careers guidance, 1970—. Director of Telephone Samaritans of Mid-Cheshire, 1965-75. *Military service:* British Army, Royal Signals, 1953-55. *Awards, honors:* Carnegie Medal from Library Association of Great Britain, 1976, for *The Machine-Gunners.*

WRITINGS: The Machine-Gunners (novel), Macmillan, 1975; *The Wind Eye* (novel), Macmillan, 1976; *The Watch House* (novel), Macmillan, 1977. Staff writer for *Cheshire Life,* 1968-71. Art and architecture critic for *Cheshire Chronicle,* 1962—; art critic for *Guardian,* 1970.

WORK IN PROGRESS: Full Fathom Five, a novel; *The Scarecrows,* a novel; *Mablette,* a novel about witchcraft.

SIDELIGHTS: Westall writes: "I'm a Protestant writer, I suppose. My heroes are always alone with their consciences. Only they aren't battling with Sin; they're battling with fear. Fear of Chaos; which is only another word for things that are too big and complicated to understand—*at present.* Sin is only a by-product—take away the fear, and the Sin drops off of its own accord.

"The main thing to avoid is belonging to any big organisation whether the Roman Catholic Church or the Communist Party—it's paying someone to do your thinking for you.

"Any man is worth listening to, when he's telling you something he's worked out for himself, something he's noticed himself.

"I like little groups of people who meet because they like each other. I like Hippies—the sort you've got to search for, because they've found something good, and gone off to quietly enjoy it. People who try to ram things down your throat don't really believe what they're ramming. They think if they can convince you, maybe they can convince themselves. If I see a herd on the move, I run the other way, instinctively.

"Big beliefs, big organisations are like junk-car yards. Worth looking at, to see if you can find something useful to pull off, buy and use. I like weird customized cars.

"I hate doing public speaking. It wears the surface of an author's mind away. A half-hour speech can use up a month of writing creativity.

"I like cats, because you have to *earn* their friendship; old wall-clocks; Buddhist statues; birdwatching and people-watching; other people's gardens; ruins and the sea. My main avocational interest is designing, building, and sailing model yachts."

*   *   *

WESTERGAARD, John (Harald)   1927-

PERSONAL: Born October 13, 1927, in London, England; son of Otto (a civil engineer) and Inger (a textile buyer; maiden name, Nyrop) Westergaard; married Inge Soerensen, August, 1950 (divorced); married Hanne Larsen (a potter), January, 1975; children: (first marriage) Susan, Michael; (second marriage) Camilla. *Education:* London School of Economics and Political Science, B.Sc., 1951. *Politics:* "Left-wing socialist." *Religion:* None. *Home:* 39 Rutland Park, Sheffield S.10, England. *Office:* Department of Sociological Studies, University of Sheffield, Sheffield S. 10, England.

CAREER: University of London, London School of Economics and Political Science, London, England, assistant lecturer, 1956-59, lecturer, 1959-66, senior lecturer, 1966-70, reader in sociology, 1970-75, research associate and deputy director of Centre for Urban Studies, 1960-75; University of Sheffield, Sheffield, England, professor of sociology and head of department, 1975—. Visiting lecturer at Brown University, 1963-64. Committee member of England's Social Science Research Council, Council for National Academic Awards, and Council for Academic Freedom and Democracy.

WRITINGS: (With Ruth Glass) *London's Housing Needs,* Centre for Urban Studies, University of London, 1965; *Scandinavian Urbanism,* Institute for Organization and Industrial Sociology (Copenhagen), 1968; (with Glass) *Housing in Camden,* London Borough of Camden, 1969; (with Henrietta Resler) *Class in a Capitalist Society: A Study of Contemporary Britain,* Basic Books, 1975.

Contributor: *London: Aspects of Change,* MacGibbon & Kee, 1964; *Social Objectives in Educational Planning,* Organisation for Economic Cooperation and Development, 1967; R. Miliband and J. Saville, editors, *The Socialist Register 1970,* Merlin Press (London), 1970; R. Blackburn, editor, *Ideology in Social Science,* Fontana, 1973; J. Rex, editor, *Approaches to Sociology,* Routledge & Kegan Paul, 1974. Contributor to professional journals.

WORK IN PROGRESS: Continuing research on various aspects of contemporary class structure.

* * *

WHEATON, Anne (Williams) 1892-1977

September 11, 1892—March 23, 1977; American journalist and public relations expert. She served as associate press secretary to President Eisenhower. Wheaton died in Dallas, Tex. Obituaries: *New York Times,* March 26, 1977; *Current Biography,* May, 1977.

* * *

WHEELER, R(obert) E(ric) Mortimer 1890-1976

September 10, 1890—July 22, 1976; British archaeologist, pioneer of modern scientific archaeology, expert on the Roman colonization of England and the ancient civilizations of India, and author. He died in Leatherhead, England. Obituaries: *New York Times,* July 23, 1976; *AB Bookman's Weekly,* August 23-30, 1976.

* * *

WHELTON, Clark 1937-

PERSONAL: Born June 7, 1937, in Mineola, N.Y.; son of Daniel E. (an attorney) and Mary (a nurse; maiden name, Clark) Whelton; married Diane Kellogg (a writer), September, 1961; children: two daughters. *Education:* Bates College, B.A., 1959. *Agent:* Knox Burger, 39½ Washington Sq. S., New York, N.Y. 10012. *Office: Village Voice,* 80 University Pl., New York, N.Y. 10003.

CAREER: Village Voice, New York, N.Y., free-lance writer, 1968-71, staff writer, 1971—. *Military service:* U.S. Army, 1960-61.

WRITINGS: Skyjack (history), Tower, 1970; *CB Baby* (novel), Avon, 1976. Contributor to magazines, including *Esquire* and *Argosy,* and to newspapers.

WORK IN PROGRESS: A novel and a nonfiction book.

* * *

WHISENAND, Paul M. 1935-

PERSONAL: Born July 3, 1935, in Seattle, Wash.; married; children: three. *Education:* University of Southern California, B.S., 1957, M.S., 1963, M.P.A., 1966, Ph.D., 1968. *Home:* 2061 Mandarin Dr., Costa Mesa, Calif. 92626. *Office:* Department of Criminology, California State College, Long Beach, Calif. 90840.

CAREER: Los Angeles Police Department, Los Angeles, Calif., police officer, 1958-59; University of Southern California, Los Angeles, instructor in public administration and interim coordinator of Delinquency Control Institute, 1964-65; California State College, Long Beach, assistant professor, 1965-68, associate professor of criminology, 1968—, chairman of department, 1971—, director of Institute for Police Studies, 1968-71. Acting chief of Covina Police Department, 1969; project manager at Riverside Police Department, 1971-72. Member of California Crime Technological Research Foundation, 1969—; member of Research and Development Task Force of California Council on Criminal Justice, 1969—; member of Center for Minority Group Employment in Criminal Justice and Center for Criminal Justice Agency Organization and Minority Employment Opportunities, both of Marquette University, 1971—. *Military service:* U.S. Army, 1957-58.

MEMBER: International Association of Chiefs of Police, International City Managers' Association, American Society for Public Administration, Criminal Justice Society, National Council on Crime and Delinquency, Public Personnel Association, Urban-Regional Information Systems Association, California Peace Officers Association.

WRITINGS: (With Harold K. Becker and George T. Felkenes) *New Dimensions in Criminal Justice,* Scarecrow, 1968; (with Tug Tamaru) *Automated Police Information Systems,* Wiley, 1970; (with James L. Cline) *Police Patrol,* Prentice-Hall, 1970; *Police Supervision: Theory and Practice,* Prentice-Hall, 1971; (with Felkenes) *Police Patrol Operations,* McCutchan, 1972; (with Cline and Felkenes) *The Police and Their Community,* Goodyear Publishing, in press; (with Fred Ferguson) *The Managing of Police Organizations,* Prentice-Hall, in press. Contributor to management and criminology journals.

* * *

WHISTON, Lionel (Abney) 1895-

PERSONAL: Born January 20, 1895, in Llandudno, Wales; emigrated to U.S., 1910; son of William (a minister) and Ellen (Amies) Whiston; married Irma Hard, June 30, 1917; children: Lionel, William, Ruth. *Education:* Lawrence University, A.B., 1915; Boston University, S.T.B., 1918. *Politics:* Independent. *Religion:* United Church of Christ. *Home:* 22 Dedham St., Wrentham, Mass. 02093.

CAREER: Pastor of Methodist churches in Ormsby, Wis., 1912-15; pastor of Congregational churches in Lunenburg, Mass., 1915-18; pastor of Methodist churches in Verona, N.Y., 1918-20, and Hamilton, N.Y., 1920-28; Calvinistic Congregational Church, Fitchburg, Mass., pastor, 1928-46; Wrentham Congregational Church, Wrentham, Mass., pastor, 1947-62. Writer and retreat master. *Member:* Phi Beta Kappa.

WRITINGS—All published by Word Inc.: *Are You Fun to Live With?,* 1968; *Enjoy the Journey,* 1972; *New Beginnings,* 1976; *Power of a New Life,* 1976; *Through Suffering to Victory,* 1976. Contributor of articles to *Faith at Work,* and other periodicals.

WORK IN PROGRESS: A relational study of the Gospel of John, publication by expected in 1978.

SIDELIGHTS: Rev. Whiston told *CA:* "The most important aspect of the retreats I conduct is depth sharing, the willingness to be known, personal interaction, group support. I make use of silent time during which people are in touch with themselves and with God, following this they share their thoughts, insights, hunches and leadings. Audible and silent prayer is also part of the Retreat.

"I conduct them by first of all opening my own life to the retreatants in depth. This immediately quickens them so that they respond in their groups, speaking to one another in depth. There is a willingness to 'lead from weakness,' to remove the masks and to stop playing games and to become real with each other as they are known with a new quality of transparency.

"There is much more eagerness to attend retreats than thirty years ago, or even fifteen years ago. Moreover, people are more willing now to come to retreats that are not merely planning sessions but are sessions in which we deal with the dynamics of personal interaction—an interaction that is three-fold—one's interaction with God, with others, and with one's self."

* * *

WHITACRE, Donald (DuMont) 1920-

PERSONAL: Born June 29, 1920, in Harveysburg, Ohio; son of Frank (a carpenter) and Helen (Runyan) Whitacre; married Charlene Sherman (a secretary), October 2, 1938; children: Roger Lynn, Gordon Dennis. *Education:* Pacific Oxford College, B.A., 1952, M.A., 1954; Commonwealth University, Ph.D., 1956. *Religion:* Methodist. *Home:* 449 Glenview Dr., Lebanon, Ohio 45036. *Office:* Curious Facts Features, *Western Star,* Lebanon, Ohio 45036.

CAREER: Worked as liaison supervisor for National Cash Register Co., Dayton, Ohio; Ohio Historical Society, worked as district superintendent of Fort Ancient, and superintendent of Fort St. Clair and Fort Ancient; writer of syndicated columns, "Curious Facts About Animal Life" and "Curious Facts About Ohio," for Curious Fact Features, Lebanon, Ohio. Notable assignments include interviews of Louis Bromfield, Earl Wilson, and Lowell Thomas. Lecturer in massotherapy. Consultant in areas of psychology, parapsychology, and physical therapy. *Member:* Masons, Shriners. *Awards, honors:* Awarded D.Litt. from Eastern Nebraska Christian College.

WRITINGS: The Hourglass of Curious Facts, Curious Fact Features, 1943; *Little Known Facts About Ohio,* Richardson Publishing, 1947. Contributor to *Ohio* and *Ohio Conservation.*

* * *

WHITE, Elijah (Brockenborough III) 1938-

PERSONAL: Born May 2, 1938, in Washington, D.C.; son of Elijah Brockenborough, Jr. (a lawyer) and Margaret Elizabeth (a painter; maiden name, Hoyt) White; married Anne Camden Smith, August 31, 1963; children: Anne Camden Spilman White, Rebekah Barrett White. *Education:* Haverford College, A.B. (high honors), 1959; graduate study at University of London, 1960-61; University of California, Berkeley, M.A., 1962; Virginia Theological Seminary, B.D., 1968. *Politics:* "Person/people-oriented." *Home address:* P.O. Box 970, Financial Station, Leesburg, Va. 22075. *Office:* Our Saviour Church, Oatlands, Box 1558, Leesburg, Va. 22075.

CAREER: Our Saviour Church, Oatlands, Leesburg, Va., Episcopalian worker-priest, 1977—. Editor for Rockville

Consulting Group, 1976—. Member of executive board of Diocese of Virginia, 1975-76, and of its Commission to Barbados, 1973-76. A varied career includes jobs as reporter for *Atlantic Monthly,* newspaper editor, post office clerk, Japanese beetle exterminator, missionary in Fiji, dean of a theological college, lifeguard, and sports editor. *Awards, honors:* Woodrow Wilson fellowship, 1959-60; Rotary International fellowship, 1960-61; first prizes for news photography and for editorial writing from Virginia Press Association, 1964.

WRITINGS: Exorcism as a Christian Ministry, Morehouse, 1975. Contributor of articles and reviews to *Living Church* and *Virginia Seminary Journal.*

WORK IN PROGRESS: The Redundant Dragon, for children; *Fiji Fever,* the first volume of an action-mystery series set in Fiji Islands; a play, a comedy "about the rather-recently-rich in northern Virginia's hunt country."

SIDELIGHTS: White writes: "Writing can be fun, but if it's not fun for the writer it'll never be fun for the reader. I've waded through enough of the heavy stuff to realize that, and I've gotten my one mandatory serious book out of my system early. From now on I'm going to write yards of stuff people will enjoy reading because I'll enjoy writing it. And I get up before Trollope did."

* * *

WHITE, G(eorge) Edward 1941-

PERSONAL: Born March 19, 1941, in Northampton, Mass.; son of George L. (a book publisher) and Frances D. (a teacher; maiden name, McCafferty) White; married Susan Valre Davis (a lawyer), December 31, 1966; children: Alexandra Valre, Elisabeth McCafferty Davis. *Education:* Amherst College, B.A., 1963; Yale University, M.A., 1964, Ph.D., 1967; Harvard University, J.D., 1970. *Residence:* Charlottesville, Va. *Office:* School of Law, University of Virginia, Charlottesville, Va. 22903.

CAREER: American Bar Foundation, Chicago, Ill., visiting scholar, 1970-71; U.S. Supreme Court, Washington, D.C., law clerk to Chief Justice Earl Warren, 1971-72; University of Virginia, Charlottesville, assistant professor, 1972-74, associate professor, 1974-76, professor of law, 1977—. *Member:* American Society for Legal History, Phi Beta Kappa.

WRITINGS: The Eastern Establishment and the Western Experience, Yale University Press, 1968; *The American Judicial Tradition,* Oxford University Press, 1976. Contributor to law journals.

WORK IN PROGRESS: The Intellectual Foundations of Tort Law, publication expected in 1978.

* * *

WHITE, James P(atrick) 1940-

PERSONAL: Born September 28, 1940, in Wichita Falls, Tex.; son of Joseph and Minnie (Mann) White; married Janice Lou Turner, September 11, 1961. *Education:* University of Texas, B.A. (with honors), 1961; Vanderbilt University, M.A. (history), 1967; graduate study at Texas Christian University, 1969-71; Brown University, M.A. (creative writing), 1973. *Home:* 3525 Turtle Creek, 5C, Dallas, Tex. 75219. *Agent:* Julie Fallowfield, McIntosh & Otis, Inc., 475 Fifth Ave., New York, N.Y. 10017. *Office:* Department of Creative Writing, University of Texas of the Permian Basin, Odessa, Tex. 79762.

CAREER: Blue Mountain College, Blue Mountain, Miss.,

associate professor of history, 1964-66; free-lance writer in Europe and the U.S., 1967-70; University of Texas of the Permian Basin, Odessa, assistant professor, 1973-74, associate professor of creative writing, 1974—, chairman of creative writing, 1974—; Texas Center for Writers, Dallas, Tex., founder, 1976—. Member of state executive committee, Texas Joint English Committee for Schools and Colleges, 1973-74; state chairman, Conference of College Teachers of English, creative writing section, 1975-76; visiting professor, University of Texas, Dallas, 1977-78. *Member:* Texas Association of Creative Writers (founding president, 1973-74), Association of Writing Programs (member national editorial board, 1973—), Theta Xi, Phi Delta Phi, Phi Alpha Theta, Phi Eta Sigma. *Awards, honors:* Marston fellowship, 1971.

WRITINGS: (Editor) *Bicentennial Collection of Texas Short Stories,* Texas Center for Writers Press, 1974; (editor) *New and Experimental Literature,* Texas Center for Writers Press, 1975; *Birdsong* (novel), Copper Beech Press, 1977.

Plays: "Broadside" (three-act), first produced in Cleveland, Ohio, at Muse Theatre, 1969; "Family Circle" (Three-act), first produced in Providence, R.I., at Brown University, 1973.

Author of series of articles for *Croft Educational Systems,* 1972-76. Contributor of short stories and poetry to over twenty periodicals, including *Kansas Quarterly, Quartet, Arizona Quarterly, Arts and Letters, Mundus Artium,* and *Texas Quarterly;* contributor of articles to *Contemporary Literary Scene, Journal of African History, Markham Review, New Writers,* and other periodicals.

Editor, *Texas Writer's Newsletter,* 1973-76, *Sand,* 1976—; co-editor, *Texas Books in Review,* 1977—.

WORK IN PROGRESS: Co-editing *Stories and Poems #1.*

SIDELIGHTS: White told *CA:* "Writing becomes, I think, a thoughtful matter of searching for the reality of both the actual and the imagined, searching through the careful use of words. Writing classes perhaps are the best courses in the university whereby a student learns discipline with language and concurrently knows how to better appreciate the structure of fine works. I think that ultimately the value of literature is, for the writer, the actual artistic experience and demand of structuring narration; and, for the reader, gaining rewarding insight into what writing is about.

"Obviously, writing is tightly linked with publishing and I think that the best situation for all writers is for society to have a diversified, decentralized system of publishing. The growth of the well-known, profitable regional press is something we can hope for, so that more variety can be published and more writers can find a market for their work."

*   *   *

WHITE, John   1924-

PERSONAL: Born March 5, 1924, in Liverpool, England; son of Harold and Mary (Wilson) White; married Loretta Mae O'Hara, June 25, 1955; children: Scott Wilson, Kevin John, Liana Maria, Leith Harold, Miles Sherman. *Education:* University of Manchester, M.B., Ch.B., 1952. *Religion:* Evangelical. *Residence:* Winnipeg, Manitoba, Canada. *Office:* Health Sciences Centre, 700 William, Winnipeg, Manitoba, Canada R3E 0Z3.

CAREER: Minister of Church of the Way in Winnipeg, Manitoba; associate general secretary of International Fellowship of Evangelical Students, 1955-64; psychiatric resident, 1964-69; psychiatrist, 1969—. Associate professor at University of Manitoba, 1973—. *Member:* Canadian Psychi-

atric Association, Canadian Medical Association, Manitoba Psychiatric Association.

WRITINGS: The Cost of Commitment, Inter-Varsity Press, 1976; *The Fight,* Inter-Varsity Press, 1976; *Eros Defiled,* Inter-Varsity Press, 1977; *Daring to Draw Near,* Inter-Varsity Press, 1977.

WORK IN PROGRESS: A critique of evangelicalism in North America; research on psychological and sociological implications of espionage during the Cold War and period of "detente."

*   *   *

WHITE, K(enneth) D(ouglas)   1908-

PERSONAL: Born November 22, 1908, in Liverpool, England; son of James (a veterinary surgeon) and Gladys (Eveline) White; married Isobel Helen MacKay (an occupational psychologist), June 6, 1936; children: James, Caroline, Catherine. *Education:* University of Liverpool (with honors in classics), B.A., 1929; University of Cambridge, B.A., 1931, M.A., 1936. *Politics:* Liberal. *Religion:* Anglican. *Home:* Garden Flat, 6 Alexander St., London W2, England. *Office:* Department of Humanities, University of Jos, Jos, Nigeria.

CAREER: University of Edinburgh, Edinburgh, Scotland, assistant in Greek, 1931-33; University of Leeds, Leeds, England, assistant lecturer in classics, 1933-38; Rhodes University, Grahamstown, South Africa, professor of classics and head of department, 1938-58; University of Natal, Pietermaritzburg, professor of classics, 1958-62; University of Ibadan, Ibadan, Nigeria, professor of ancient history, 1962-65; University of Reading, Reading, England, professor of classics, 1965-74; University of Jos, Jos, Nigeria, visiting professor in humanities, 1975—. City of Grahamstown, South Africa, city councillor, 1954-58, and deputy mayor, 1956-58; Commonwealth fellow, St. John's College, Cambridge University, 1960-61; visiting professor of classics, University of Toronto, 1971-72; senior research fellow, Leverhulme Trust, 1975-77. *Member:* South African Association of University Teachers (president, 1955-56), Society for Roman Studies (member of council, 1970-71), Classical Association of Nigeria (president, 1964-65).

WRITINGS: Agricultural Implements of the Roman World, Cambridge University Press, 1967; *Roman Farming,* Cornell University Press, 1970; *A Bibliography of Roman Agriculture,* Reading University Press, 1970; *Farm Equipment of the Roman World,* Cambridge University Press, 1975; *Country Life in Classical Times,* Cornell University Press, 1977. Contributor of articles to *Journal of Roman Studies, Antiquity, Classical Review, Latomus,* and other periodicals.

WORK IN PROGRESS: Studies in Roman Agrarian History for Cambridge University Press, publication expected in 1979; *Social and Economic History of the Roman Empire; Greek and Roman Technology; Resources, Technology and Power in the Roman World.*

SIDELIGHTS: "My research interests," White told *CA,* "have been concentrated in recent years on the infrastructure of the Roman Empire, more particularly on the environmental factors and constraints, the sources of power, the raw materials (sources of supply and methods of extraction, etc.), and the technological achievements and limitations. I have travelled extensively in the Mediterranean area in search of material in libraries and museums, as well as on the ground, with the aim of finding correlations between field archaeology, air photography and written sources, in the hope that I might discover the patterns of land settlement and their vicissitudes in the passage of time.

I have, during a teaching career of 45 years, and in seven different universities, had the opportunity of teaching traditional classics in its literary and linguistical aspects as well as in the historical areas of study where I am specially qualified, and at all levels from pass degree to doctorate. I am now working in a new university, where "humanities" represent a broader approach, and where it is my task to justify the study of ancient history as providing a much-needed perspective for men and women destined for leadership in a rapidly developing society, in an age of swift transition from traditional cultures and values into those of the late twentieth century."

*   *   *

WHITEBIRD, J(oanie) 1951-

PERSONAL: Original name, Joan Elizabeth Green, name legally changed in 1974; born July 1, 1951, in Houston, Tex.; daughter of John Henry (an astrologer) and Betty Sue (an astrologer; maiden name, Bledsoe) Green. Education: Educated in Houston, Tex. Politics: "Hard to say. Southern Democrat, if anything at all." Religion: Zen. Home: 305 Fargo, Houston, Tex. 77006. Office: P.O. Box 66285, Houston, Tex. 77006.

CAREER: Varsity Tattler (magazine), Houston, Tex., assistant editor, 1966-67; free-lance journalist in Houston, 1967-68; Houston blaboratory Theatre, Houston, poet-in-residence, 1973; Southern Voice Inc., Houston, staff member and lay-out artist, 1973-74, special features editor, 1974; Contemporary Arts Museum, Houston, curator of poetry and performing arts, 1975-76; Wings Press, Houston, managing editor, 1976—. Instructor in poetry, University of Houston Sundry School, 1975; poet-in-residence for poetry-in-the-schools program, 1975-76. Director of arts workshops; panelist at arts conferences. Poetry reader at coffee houses, fairs, galleries, and theatres. Initiator and president, Southern Seeds Poetry Guild, 1974-75. Awards, honors: Two grants from Texas Commission on the Arts and Humanities, 1975 and 1976.

WRITINGS: The Family Hand Anthology and Collected Letters, Alpha Publishing, 1971; Bootstrap Chronicles (chapbook), Contemporary Arts Museum of Houston, 1975; Naked (chapbook), Thorp Springs Press, 1976; Spare Poems, Texas Portfolio, 1976; (editor with Paul Foreman) Travois: An Anthology of Texas Poetry, Thorp Springs Press, 1976; Birthmark, Second Coming Press, 1977; "The Beautiful Cage" (three-act play; first produced in Houston at Equinox Theatre, fall, 1977). Contributor of poetry and short stories to journals, including Abraxas, Southern Voice, and Southwestern Art Review.

WORK IN PROGRESS: 24, a book of collected poems; And Then There Was . . ., a book of short stories.

SIDELIGHTS: Joanie Whitebird writes: "The summer I turned seventeen I left home by crawling out my front window with a suitcase, a guitar I could not then (nor to this day) play, a one-way plane ticket to Los Angeles and forty dollars in my pocket from working at Howard Johnsons. When I returned to school at the end of the summer, the school system and I, by mutual agreement, parted ways. I concentrated on writing poetry and spent the next several years hitchhiking around the country.

"At eighteen, I took the name Whitebird because the name I had didn't suit me—wasn't mine. Six years later I discov-ered that I am related to John Ross the Cherokee statesman, whose tribal name, roughly translated, means 'white bird.'"

After her first book was published, Whitebird moved to San Francisco and began reading in coffee houses. When she returned to Houston, she was struck by the lack of poetry activity in the city and decided that she wanted to change that. She says, "I saw the potential in Houston, and no one was trying to tap it. I could go back to California permanently or stay in Houston, and I had to ask myself if I believed in the artistic potential of this region enough that I was willing to devote thirty or forty years of my life to it.

"It was at this point in my life that I began working seriously, both in my career and for Texas literature. After a number of attempts to bring together poets in Texas, I arrived at the Contemporary Arts Museum of Houston. The director was interested enough in my ideas to give me permission to direct a couple of performances and to arrange a reading for Robert Creeley. My efforts proved very successful and I was hired as the curator of poetry and performing arts, the only position of its kind that the museum knew of. My tenure there lasted until the museum was destroyed by flood in 1976."

Since then Whitebird has concentrated on writing and on managing Wings Press, which is mainly, but not exclusively, regional. The first publication of Wings Press was a chapbook Small Change, by the Texas poet Vassar Miller in June, 1976.

Whitebird's interests include the study of Cherokee medicine, letter press printing, and scuba diving. She says, "I also paint and do calligrams and visual collages that I call 'poem pieces,' some of which have been exhibited and sold in gallery shows. Although I neither know or study astrology as my parents did, I have a scientific interest in the structure of the Tarot cards, as I believe they relate to other structures such as poetry or language."

BIOGRAPHICAL/CRITICAL SOURCES: Houston Chronical, September 29, 1975, June 20, 1976; Houston Post, November 9, 1975; Austin American-Statesman, August 22, 1975; Texas Portfolio #III, spring, 1977.

*   *   *

WHITFORD, Bessie 1885(?)-1977

1885(?)—April 20, 1977; American author and high school teacher for more than forty years. She died in Washington, D.C. Obituaries: Washington Post, April 25, 1977.

*   *   *

WHITTEMORE, Don
(Louis Norman)

PERSONAL: Born in Geneva, Ill.; son of Kelsey Pickrell (an accountant) and Celia May (a teacher; maiden name, Swaby) Whittemore. Education: University of Iowa, B.A., 1966, M.A., 1968; Sorbonne, University of Paris, further graduate study; University of California, Berkeley, Ph.D., 1973. Home: 719 Jackson St., Albany, Calif. 94706.

CAREER: Teacher at private boys' school in San Francisco, Calif., 1974-75; University of California, Davis, senior writer, 1975—.

WRITINGS: (Editor) Passport to Hollywood, with study guide, McGraw, 1976; (with Theodore Brachfeld) Art America (study guide), McGraw, 1977; Career Planning Resource Manual, McGraw, 1977. Author of film criticism under pseudonym Louis Norman.

WORK IN PROGRESS: Research on Eric Rohmer's *Six Moral Tales.*

SIDELIGHTS: Whittemore writes: "I speak and write French and Italian, having lived in France and Italy for three years. I can read Spanish, Latin and Greek, although I avoid situations where I might have the opportunity to do so. I have acted in over thirty plays and had small, non-speaking parts in two films."

*   *   *

WICKER, Ireene 1905-

PERSONAL: Born November 24, 1905, in Quincy, Ill.; daughter of Kenner (a railroad company employee) and Margaret (a school teacher; maiden name, Hunsaker) Seaton; married Walter Charles Wicker (marriage ended); married Victor Hammer (an art dealer), January 11, 1941; children: (first marriage) Walter Charles, Jr. (deceased); Nancy (adopted daughter). *Education:* Attended University of Illinois, Goodman Theatre School, and Art Institute of Chicago, 1927-30. *Religion:* Presbyterian. *Residence:* New York, N.Y. *Office:* 667 Madison Ave., New York, N.Y. 10021.

CAREER: Actress in stock company, 1917; Goodman Theatre, Chicago, Ill., actress, 1929-30; Columbia Broadcasting System (CBS), Chicago, member of dramatic staff, 1930-36; presented "The Singing Story Lady" on radio in Chicago; National Broadcasting Co. (NBC), New York City, presented "The Singing Story Lady" on the Blue Network, presented children's quiz program, 1942; American Broadcasting Co. (ABC)-Television, co-director of "Merry-Go-Round Children's Theatre," 1951-54; worked in the Shakespearean group of American Theatre Wing, and with Stella Adler and Joseph Kramm, 1955-56; worked for WNYC and WNYC-FM Radio, New York City, 1959-74; now works on syndicated program for Broadcasting Foundation of America, 1974—. Radio actress for NBC, beginning 1931; presented "Ireene Wicker's Music Plays," broadcast by Mutual Broadcasting Co.; coordinated Radio for Children, of Civilian Defense Volunteers Office, 1942; teacher at Stuyvesant Neighborhood House. *Member:* International Radio and Television Society, International Platform Association, National Academy of Television Arts and Sciences, Authors Guild of Authors League of America, American Women in Radio and Television, National League of American Pen Women, Broadcast Pioneers. *Awards, honors:* Awards for children's programs include George Foster Peabody Award from University of Georgia, 1961, and Emmy Award from Academy of Television Arts and Sciences.

*WRITINGS—*For children: *The Singing Lady's Favorite Stories,* Whitman Publishing, 1934; *The Legend of the Christmas Rose* (plays), Samuel French, 1939; *Sing a Song of History* (songs), Irving Berlin, Inc., 1941; (with Beatrice Faber) *Remember the Brave: The Story of Memorial Day* (two-act musical play), ABC Music Corp., 1941; *Sleeping Beauty* (story with music), ABC Music Corp., 1941; (with Faber) *Under the Christmas Tree* (one-act musical play), ABC Music Corp., 1942.

Young Master Artists: Boyhoods of Famous Artists, Bobbs-Merrill, 1965; *Young Music Makers: Boyhoods of Famous Composers,* Bobbs-Merrill, 1965; *How the Ocelots Got Their Spots,* Lyle Stuart, 1976. Also author of *The Little Hunchback Horse* (from a Russian fairy tale), 1942, and *Children's Stories of Famous Composers and Artists.*

*WORK IN PROGRESS—*For children: American Indian Legends; Christmas and Channukah stories; patriotic stories; famous people of America; *Singing Lady's Fairy Tales.*

SIDELIGHTS: Ireene Wicker has made several sound recordings and tape cassettes, including "Kipling's Just So Stories," "Grimm's Fairy Tales," "The Owl and the Pussycat and Other Stories," "Anderson's Fairy Tales," all for Record Guild of America. *Avocational interests:* Collecting music and children's books, music, theater.

*   *   *

WICKHAM, Jean 1903-
(Jean Gordon)

PERSONAL: Born August 27, 1903, in Kingston, N.Y.; daughter of John (a tax accountant) and Elizabeth (Gordon) Koch; married John Wickham (divorced); married Thomas Riley; children: Joan, John, Nancy, Joyce. *Education:* Attended Columbia University, Henderson's School of Oratory, and Damrachs School of Music. *Home:* 123 Washington St., St. Augustine, Fla. 32084.

CAREER: Writer, 1933—. Clothing designer in Boston, Mass., 1934. Restaurant operator in New York, N.Y., 1935.

*WRITINGS—*Under name Jean Gordon: *Pageant of the Rose,* Studio Publications, 1953, 2nd edition, Red Rose Publications, 1961; *Rose Recipes: Customs, Facts, Fancies,* Red Rose Publications, 1958; *Immortal Roses: One Hundred Rose Stories and Vignettes of Famous People and Events,* Red Rose Publications, 1959; *Orange Recipes: Customs, Facts, Fancies,* Red Rose Publications, 1962; *Coffee Recipes: Customs, Facts, Fancies,* Red Rose Publications, 1963; *The Art of Cooking with Roses,* Walker & Co., 1968, new edition, Farrar, Straus, 1974. Contributor to *Roses Incorporated.*

*WORK IN PROGRESS—*Under name Jean Gordon: *Rose Designs,* for use by manufacturers, in advertising, and in libraries.

SIDELIGHTS: Jean Gordon comments: "My desire is to bring beauty to the attention of the public to offset the all-too-constant repetition of doom, disaster, and disease that is being brought to its attention."

*   *   *

WIDGERY, David 1947-

PERSONAL: Born April 27, 1947, in London, England; son of John Howard (a designer) and Margaret (a teacher; maiden name, Finch) Widgery. *Education:* Royal Free Hospital School of Medicine, M.B.B.S., 1972. *Politics:* "International Socialist." *Home:* 2, Chapel Market, Islington, London N.1, England.

CAREER: House physician and surgeon at Bettnal Green Hospital, London, England; senior house officer, St. Marys, Paddington, England, 1973-74, and St. Leonards, Shoredilch, 1974-76; general medical practitioner in East London, England, 1976—.

WRITINGS: The Left in Britain, 1956-1968, Penguin, 1976. Contributor to magazines, including *Oz, Socialist Worker, Time Out, Spare Rib,* and *Heathworker.* Reviews editor for *Socialist Worker,* 1974-75.

WORK IN PROGRESS: Sex and Socialism; British Labour in the Seventies; What's Wrong with Our National Health Service; a Marxist analysis of London.

SIDELIGHTS: Widgery writes that he is active in rank and file trade union politics. His interests are "British and American labour history and sexual radicalism."

WIGFORSS, Ernst   1882(?)-1977

1882(?)—January 3, 1977; Swedish socialist theoritician, finance minister, and author. Two former Swedish prime ministers paid tribute to him as "the most important Social Democrat of his time". He died in Angelholm, Sweden. Obituaries: *New York Times,* January 4, 1977; *Washington Post,* January 5, 1977.

* * *

WILCOX, Desmond   1931-

PERSONAL: Born May 21, 1931, in England. *Education:* Attended grammar school in Cheltenham, England. *Agent:* Jonathan Clowes, 19 Jeffreys Pl., London N.W.1, England. *Office:* British Broadcasting Corp.—Television, Kensington House, Richmond Way, London W14 OAX, England.

CAREER: Went to sea at 15, later worked as reporter for weekly newspaper; *Daily Mirror,* London, England, reporter and foreign correspondent, 1952-60; ITV Rediffusion, London, England, reporter on "This Week," 1960-65; British Broadcasting Corp., London, England, presented and co-edited "Man Alive" television program, 1965-72, head of general features department, 1972—. *Military service:* British Army, 1949-51; became captain. *Member:* Arts Club (London). *Awards, honors:* Richard Dimbleby Award from British Academy of Film and Television Arts, 1971.

WRITINGS: Explorers, BBC Publications, 1975, published as *Ten Who Dared,* Little, Brown, 1977.

WORK IN PROGRESS: Americans, publication by Delacorte expected in 1978.

* * *

WILCOX, Paul L(orentus)   1899-

PERSONAL: Born May 28, 1899, in Kansas; son of Rex V. (an attorney) and Viola (Maulsby) Wilcox; married Ruth Bolton (divorced); married Ila Anderson (divorced); married I. Teddy Klepinger (a secretary), August 12, 1948; children: Robert B., Paul Loren, Rex Vernon. *Education:* Attended College of Idaho, 1916-17. *Religion:* Baptist. *Home:* 2440 Marshall Way, Sacramento, Calif. 95818.

CAREER: Worked in supervision in construction jobs for California State Highway Department, 1918-29, and for Basich Brothers Construction Co., 1929-34; owner of Hanrahan-Wilcox Construction Co., 1934-37; superintendent for various construction companies in California, Idaho, and Alaska, 1937-72; writer, 1972—. Consultant to construction firms, 1970-72. *Military service:* U.S. Navy, 1917-18.

WRITINGS: Alaska and the Job, Branden Press, 1976.

WORK IN PROGRESS: The Prison Camp on the Kern River; The Doers, "personalized biographical sketches of giants and unusual workers in the construction field."

SIDELIGHTS: Wilcox comments: "I like to write about people who get the world's work done. I am one of them." *Avocational interests:* Travel (extensive national and international travel includes two round-the-world experiences).

* * *

WILDE, W(illiam) H(enry)   1923-

PERSONAL: Born November 19, 1923, in Tamworth, New South Wales, Australia; son of William Henry and Ivy May (Corbett) Wilde; married Ena Fay McKeough, December 20, 1948; children: William Ross, Margaret Ruth (Mrs. Terrence William Conn). *Education:* University of Sydney, B.A., 1946, diploma in education, 1947, M.A., 1964. *Home:* 12 Verco St., Hackett, Canberra, Australian Capital Territory 2602, Australia. *Office:* Department of Language and Literature, Faculty of Military Studies, University of New South Wales, Duntroon, Canberra, Australian Capital Territory, Australia.

CAREER: Royal Australian Naval College, Jervis Bay, Australia, master on civil professional staff, 1953-58, senior master, 1958-63; Royal Military College, Canberra, Australia, senior lecturer, 1965-68; University of New South Wales, Canberra, senior lecturer, 1968-76, associate professor of language and literature, 1977—. *Member:* Australian College of Education.

WRITINGS: Three Radicals, Oxford University Press, 1969; *Adam Lindsay Gordon,* Oxford University Press, 1973; *Henry Kendall,* Twayne, 1976. Contributor to *Meanjin* and *National Times.*

WORK IN PROGRESS: Australian Literature to 1900, with B. G. Andrews, for Gale; *The Selected Letters of Dame Mary Gilmore,* with T. Ingles Moore; *The Biography of Dame Mary Gilmore.*

* * *

WILK, Gerard H(ermann)   1902-

PERSONAL: Born September 1, 1902, in Berlin, Germany; came to United States in 1946; naturalized U.S. citizen, 1951; son of Hugo and Doris (Lewitt) Wilk; married Susan Frankl (a music teacher), February 16, 1949; children: Jane. *Education:* University of Goettingen, Doctor of Laws, 1928. *Office:* 74-02 Kessel St., Forest Hills, N.Y. 11375.

CAREER: Attorney-at-law in Berlin, Germany, 1929-33; emigrated to Yugoslavia, 1933; placed in internment camp in Yugoslavia, 1941-43; attached to U.S. Army Psychological Warfare Branch in Bari and Rome, Italy, and Salzburg, Austria, 1944-46; U.S. Information Agency, New York and Washington D.C., writer and broadcaster, 1946-69; freelance writer and correspondent, 1969—. Writer, *American German Review* and *West German Media,* 1975—. *Member:* American Theatre Critics Association, American Council on Germany, Overseas Press Club, Drama Desk.

WRITINGS: Americans from Germany, German Information Center, 1976. Author of over 100 radio plays for "Voice of America" and other programs, 1946-69. Contributor of articles to *American German Review, Deutsche Buehne, Der Tagesspiegel, Commentary, West German Media,* and other periodicals.

WORK IN PROGRESS: Three Centuries of American-German Theatrical Relations; The American Dream—Seen Through German Eyes, for German Information Center.

SIDELIGHTS: Wilk told *CA:* "I have always been aware that during her long history Germany was divided between her rulers and her powerless people. Since the days of the Reformation there were great Germans fighting and dying for freedom. This we call 'the Other Germany.' It is beautiful to live in a country like America, where an immigrant like me can feel himself a devoted American without having been forced to forget or forgo his heritage."

* * *

WILKINSON, Brenda   1946-

PERSONAL: Born January 1, 1946, in Moultrie, Ga.; daughter of Malcolm (in construction) and Ethel (a nurse;

maiden name, Anderson) Scott; separated; children: Kim, Lori. *Education:* Attended Hunter College of the City University of New York. *Home:* 210 West 230th St., Bronx, N.Y. 10463. *Office:* Board of Global Ministries, 475 Riverside Dr., New York, N.Y.

CAREER: Writer. *Member:* Authors Guild of Authors League of America. *Awards, honors:* National Book Award nominee, 1976.

WRITINGS—For children: *Ludell,* Harper, 1975; *Ludell and Willie,* Harper, 1976.

* * *

WILKINSON, Charlotte Jefferson

PERSONAL: Born in Kenton, Ohio; daughter of John Nelson and Olive (Write) Wilkinson. *Education:* Attended Cincinnati Art Academy, Columbia University, and New York University. *Home:* Hotel Dorset, 30 West 54th St., New York, N.Y. 10019.

CAREER: National Broadcasting Network, New York City, creator of weekly show "Fashion and Modern Manners," 1934-35; *Pictorial Review,* New York City, fashion editor, 1935-36; *Patternettes* (magazine), New York City, director, 1936-40; R. H. Macy, New York City, fashion consultant, 1939-46; Budd Co., Philadelphia, Pa., assistant publicity director, 1948-50; *Ready-to-Wear* (trade publication), New York City, fashion editor, 1950-52; Swiss Fabric Group, New York City, fashion co-ordinator, 1952-67; author of syndicated feature "Your Fashion Image," 1968—. Director of merchandizing at Ridgewood Park Junior College, 1938-40. Presented fashion lecture series to colleges and women's clubs; gave lectures and fashion shows at New York World's Fair, 1943. Has also worked as a comparison shopper for New York City department stores, and publicity director for British Colonial Hotel in Nassau. *Member:* American Association of University Women, Fashion Press Weeks, New York Fashion Group, Metropolitan Opera Guild. *Awards, honors:* Commendation award from U.S. Navy, 1946.

WRITINGS: Modern Manners, Whitman Publishing, 1938; *Noah's Ark* (juvenile), Whitman Publishing, 1940; *ABC's of Fashion,* Whitman Publishing, 1948. Author of special features for United Press International and *Tribune* (Nassau).

WORK IN PROGRESS: Short stories; working on a new television show.

* * *

WILKS, Brian 1933-
(Sam Hughes)

PERSONAL: Born November 1, 1933, in Bedford, England; son of John Percival (an engineer) and Gertrude Ivy (Burnage) Wilks; married Marie Hughes, August 22, 1959; children: Jonathan Paul, Jessica Sally. *Education:* University College of North Wales, B.A. (first class honors), 1959, M.A., 1964. *Religion:* Christian. *Home:* 13 Thae Ave., Roundhay, Leeds LS8 1JG, England. *Office:* Department of Education, University of Leeds, Leeds L52 9JT, England.

CAREER: Schoolmaster in Liverpool, England, 1959-62; University of Liverpool, Liverpool, lecturer in English and drama, 1962-68, lecturer in adult education, 1968—, associate lecturer in English, 1974—. Representative for Yorkshire Women's Institute's drama and education committee, 1970-72, and Yorkshire Rural Community Drama Committee, 1972—. Prepared and broadcast an experimental poetry program for schools, for British Broadcasting Corp. (BBC)-

Radio in Nottingham, 1972, and an adult education series for BBC-Radio in Leeds. *Military service:* Royal Air Force, member of air crew, active duty, 1953-55.

WRITINGS: (Contributor) *Drama in Education,* Volumes I-III, Pitman, 1972-75; (editor with Roger Chapman, and author of introduction) *Snap Out of It* (theatre-in-education program), Methuen, 1973; *The Brontes* (biography), Hamlyn, 1975, 2nd edition, 1976.

Plays: (Under pseudonym Sam Hughes) "Wilfred of Ossett" (juvenile), first performed in Leeds, England, at Leeds Playhouse, 1972; (with Alfred Burke) "The Cassocked Savage" (one-man play), first produced in Leeds at Leeds Playhouse, 1976.

Contributor to *Sunday Times.*

WORK IN PROGRESS: Continued research on the Bronte family.

* * *

WILLIAMS, Gurney III 1941-

PERSONAL: Born June 12, 1941, in New York, N.Y.; son of Gurney, Jr. (an editor) and Lois (Jones) Williams; married Linda Payne (a public relations consultant), June 24, 1967; children: Kimberly Payne, Jay. *Education:* Yale University, B.A., 1963; Columbia University, M.S., 1967. *Religion:* Episcopalian. *Residence:* Bronxville, N.Y. *Office:* 17 Sagamore Rd., Bronxville, N.Y. 10708.

CAREER: Newsday, Garden City, N.Y., reporter and editor, 1967-70; free-lance writer, 1970—. *Member:* American Society of Journalists and Authors. *Awards, honors:* Member of *Newsday* team awarded Pulitzer Prize, 1970, for a series of articles on the land dealings of public officials.

WRITINGS: The Zero People (juvenile), Scholastic Book Services, 1974; *Movie Man* (juvenile), Scholastic Book Services, 1975; *Calling Station E–A–R–T–H* (juvenile), Scholastic Book Services, 1975; *Writing Careers* (juvenile), F. Watts, 1976; (editor) *Yachtsman's Choice: The Best of Rudder,* McKay, 1977; *True Escape and Survival Stores,* F. Watts, 1977; (with Joan Glazer) *Introduction to Children's Literature,* McGraw, 1978. Contributor to magazines, including *Family Health, TV Guide,* and *Reader's Digest.*

SIDELIGHTS: Williams told *CA:* "My father was humor editor of *Collier's* and later *Look* magazine; early exposure to writers and artists he knew sparked my interest. Now, working with my own children, I've become fascinated with children's literature at a time when the literature itself has become more vital and lively than ever before. Writing for children today isn't much different from writing for adults. Children are more resilient than many adults know; they like a good story, and reject sham. I'm trying to meet their need for good writing, avoiding cuteness and condescension."

* * *

WILLIAMS, Philip W(alter) 1941-

PERSONAL: Born January 19, 1941, in Niagara Falls, N.Y.; son of Walter E. (a clergyman) and Ruth (Schultz) Williams; married Nancy Arlene Mellish (a teacher), June 13, 1965; children: Jason Philip, Jenna Jill. *Education:* Capital University, B.A., 1963; Lutheran Theological Seminary, B.D., 1967; Andover Newton Theological Seminary, S.T.M., 1970. *Residence:* Wausau, Wis. *Office:* Wausau Hospitals, Maple Hill, Wausau, Wis. 54401.

CAREER: Ordained American Lutheran minister, 1967; assistant pastor of Lutheran church in Baltimore, Md., 1967-

69; Wausau Hospitals, Wausau, Wis., director of pastoral care, 1971—. *Member:* Association for Clinical Pastoral Education, American Protestant Hospital Association (College of Chaplains), Association of Mental Health Clergy.

WRITINGS: When a Loved One Dies, Augsburg, 1976.

WORK IN PROGRESS: "A meditational book on dying."

SIDELIGHTS: Williams comments: "Writing is a creative avocation; my object is to write about areas of living in nontechnical language for 'common consumption.' My publisher believes I have a basic, simple style of writing which can communicate to the so-called 'average person' who wants and needs education, but is put off by technical works." *Avocational interests:* Athletics, gardening, camping.

* * *

WILLIAMS, Robert P. 1906(?)-1977

1906(?)—January 5, 1977; American author, editor, and publisher. He died in Fort Lauderdale, Fla. Obituaries: *Washington Post,* January 6, 1977.

* * *

WILLIAMS, Theodore C(urtis) 1930-

PERSONAL: Born April 6, 1930, in Tuscarora Reservation, N.Y.; son of Eleazer (a medicine man and Sachem chief) and Amelia (a clan mother; maiden name Chew) Williams; married Carol Loomis, January 2, 1954 (divorced, 1971); married E. Lorraine Frost, November 11, 1973; children: Clinton, Thomas, Donna, Robert, Lisa (deceased), Michael, Joseph. *Education:* Attended State University of New York College at Brockport, 1970. *Home:* 458 Hillside Avenue, Rochester, N.Y. 14610.

CAREER: Professional Archers Association, St. Paul, Minn., competitive archer, 1965-67; Eastman Kodak Co., Rochester, N.Y., mobile crane operator, 1966—. *Military service:* U.S. Army Paratroopers, 1948-52. *Awards, honors:* National Indian Literature award for *The Reservation,* 1976.

WRITINGS: The Reservation, Syracuse University Press, 1976. Author of "How To" column in *Eastern Bowhunter,* 1958.

WORK IN PROGRESS: A book on extrasensory perception among the Iroquois.

SIDELIGHTS: "In the first book, *The Reservation,*" Williams told *CA,* "I omitted a chapter on ghost stories because it grew to be book size. Then Carlos Casteneda's writings spurred an interest in Iroquois similarity. My interest in Indian medicines perked up and I began having some E.S.P. experiences. I then began interviewing older Iroquois tribal members to add to the forthcoming book."

* * *

WILLIAMS, William H(enry) 1936-

PERSONAL: Born June 9, 1936, in Port Jervis, N.Y.; son of Henry (an educator) and Esther (Crocker) Williams; married Helen Garrett (a teacher), June 28, 1959; children: David, Mark, Dawn. *Education:* Drew University, A.B., 1958; Yeshiva University, M.S.Ed., 1959; University of Delaware, Ph.D., 1971. *Politics:* "Undeclared." *Religion:* Methodist. *Home:* 238 West Pine, Georgetown, Del. 19947. *Office:* Deleware Technical and Community College, University of Delaware, Georgetown, Del. 19947.

CAREER: High school social studies teacher in Pawling, N.Y., 1959-63; University of Delaware, Georgetown, instructor, 1967-71, assistant professor of history, 1971—. Chairperson of Delaware Humanities Council; director of Sussex County oral history project, 1975—. *Member:* Organization of American Historians, American Association for the History of Medicine, Social Welfare History Group.

WRITINGS: (Editor with Robert Robinson and Ronald Dodd) *Sixteen Miles from Anywhere: A History of Georgetown, Delaware,* Countian Press, 1975; *America's First Hospital: The Pennsylvania Hospital, 1751-1841,* Haverford House, 1976.

WORK IN PROGRESS: Research on the treatment of the poor by American hospitals, 1731-1976.

SIDELIGHTS: Williams writes: "I am particularly interested in the history of medicine because I see physicians as the new priesthood of western society."

* * *

WILLIS, (George) Anthony Armstrong 1897-1976 (A. A., Anthony Armstrong)

PERSONAL: Born January 2, 1897, in Esquimalt, British Columbia; son of Geroge H. A. (in Royal Navy) and Adela Emma Temple (Frere) Willis; married Frances Monica Sealy, 1926; children: one son, two daughters. *Education:* Attended Trinity College, Cambridge. *Home:* The Knapp, Grayswood Rd., Haslemere, Surrey, England.

CAREER: Author, playwright. Began writing for *Punch,* 1924, contributing weekly articles under pseudonym "A.A.," 1925-33; writer of articles and short stories for periodicals, including *New Yorker, County Fair, Strand, Daily Mail, Evening News,* and *Sunday Chronicle;* writer for British Broadcasting Corp. *Military service:* British Army, Royal Engineers, 1915-25; mentioned in dispatches, received Military Cross. Retired to Royal Engineers Reserve of Officers, 1925; invalided out of reserve, 1939. Royal Air Force Volunteer Reserve, squadron leader, 1940-46; founded and edited *Tee Emm* (training magazine); became captain. *Member:* Savage Club. *Awards, honors:* Order of the British Empire, 1944.

WRITINGS—All under pseudonym Anthony Armstrong; historical novels: *Lure of the Past,* Stanley Paul, 1920; *The Love of Prince Rameses,* Stanley Paul, 1921; *The Heart of a Slave-Girl: A Tale of the Underworld of Ancient Rome,* Stanley Paul, 1922; *When Nile Was Young: A Romance of the Eighteenth Egyptian Dynasty,* Hutchinson, 1923; *Wine of Death,* Stanley Paul, 1925.

Humorous novels: *Patrick, Undergraduate,* Stanley Paul, 1926; *Patrick Engaged,* Stanley Paul, 1927; *No Dragon, No Damsel,* Stanley Paul, 1928; *Patrick Helps,* Stanley Paul, 1928.

Cime novels: *The Trail of Fear,* Macrae Smith, 1927 (published in England as *Jimmie Rezaire,* Stanley Paul, 1927); *The Secret Trail,* Methuen, 1928, Macrae Smith, 1929; *The Trail of the Lotto,* Methuen, 1929, Macrae Smith, 1930; *The Trail of the Black King,* Macrae Smith, 1931; *The Poison Trail,* Benn, 1932; (with Herbert Shaw) *Ten Minute Alibi* (based on Armstrong's play of the same name), Methuen, 1934, Penguin, 1938; *No Higher Mountain,* Methuen, 1951; *He Was Found in the Road,* Methuen, 1952; *A Room at the Hotel Ambre,* Doubleday, for the Crime Club, 1956 (published in England as *Spies in Amber,* Methuen, 1956); *The Strange Case of Mr. Pelham,* Doubleday, for the Crime Club, 1957; *One Jump Ahead,* Methuen, 1972.

Country books: *Cottage into House,* Collins, 1936; *We Like the Country,* Collins, 1940; *Village at War,* Collins, 1941;

We Keep Going, Collins, 1946; *The Year at Margarets* (autobiographical), Harrap, 1953.

Humorous works; all published by Methuen, except as indicated: *Warriors at Ease,* 1926; *Percival and I,* 1927; *Warriors Still at Ease,* 1928; *How to Do It,* 1928; *Percival at Play,* 1929; *Livestock in Barracks,* 1929; *Me and Frances,* 1930; *Taxi! Being a Not Too Serious Book about London Taxicabs and Drivers, with a Few Remarks on Their Foreign Cousins,* Hodder & Stoughton, 1930; *Two Legs and Four,* 1930; (compiler) *Yesterdailies: Being Some Extracts from the Press of the Past,* 1931; *Apple and Percival,* 1931; *Selected Warriors* (contains portions of *Warriors at Ease* and *Warriors Still at Ease*), 1932; *Easy Warriors,* 1932; *Britisher on Broadway,* 1932; *The Prince Who Hiccupped and Other Tales,* Benn, 1932; *While You Wait,* 1933; *Anthony Armstrong: An Anthology of His Humorous Work,* 1934; *Thoughts on Things,* 1935; (compiler) *The Laughter Omnibus,* Faber, 1937; *Captain Bayonet and Others,* 1937; *Warriors Paraded* (contains selections from previous *Warriors* volumes, and from *Livestock in Barracks* and *Captain Bayonet and Others*), 1938; *Nothing to Do with the War,* 1940; (editor) *Laughter Parade* (anthology), Faber, 1940; *Warriors at War,* 1941; *The Pack of Pieces: A Fairy Tale for Adults,* M. Joseph, 1942, 2nd edition published as *The Naughty Princess,* M. Joseph, 1945; *Plonk's Party of A.T.C.,* 1942; *Prune's Progress: The Genealogical Tree of Pilot-Officer Percy Prune,* Jenkins, 1942; *Nice Types,* 1943; *More Nice Types,* 1944; *Good Egg! Flights of Fancy,* R. Lesley, 1944; *Prangmere Mess, and Other Tales,* 1945; *Whiskers Will Not Be Worn,* Rockliff, 1945; *Goodbye, Nice Types!,* 1946; *My Friend Serafin,* 1949; *Sappers at War,* Gale & Polden, 1949.

Plays: *In the Dentist's Chair: A One-Act Thriller,* Samuel French, 1931; *At "The Coach and Horses"* (one-act), Year Book Press, 1931; *Well Caught: A Criminal Comedy in Three Acts,* London Play Co., 1932; *Ten-Minute Alibi* (three-act mystery play), Gollancz, 1933, Samuel French, 1934; (with Ian Hay) *Orders Are Orders* (three-act), Samuel French, 1933; *Eleventh Hour* (one-act drama), London Play Co., 1933; (with Harold Simpson) *Without Witness* (thriller), Gollancz, 1934; *Mile-Away Murder* (three-act detective play), London Play Co., 1937; (with Philip King) *Here We Come Gathering* (comedy), Samuel French, 1952; (with Arnold Ridley) *Bellamy* (three-act comedy-farce), Samuel French, 1960. Also author of additional plays, including: "Full House," 1930; "Business with Royalty" (adapted from the German), 1934; "Postal Service," 1937; (with Ronald Crossley) "The Three Pigeons," 1938; "Brains and Brass," 1932, produced as "Sitting on a Fence," 1939; (with Ridley) "The Running Man," 1949; "Horatius" (three plays), for British War Office, 1950; "Jumble Warfare," 1952; "Knight of Night" (farce); "Spies in Amber" (thriller); "No Higher Mountain" (murder mystery); "Happy Ever After."

Nonfiction: *England Our England: A Vague and Unauthenticated Guide to Some English Towns,* A. Dakers, 1948; *Saying Your Prayers: An Approach to Christian Prayer,* G. Bles, 1957; *A Demonstrator on Trial,* Belton Books, 1968; *The Church of England, the Methodists and Society, 1700-1850,* Rowman & Littlefield, 1973.

Author of short works published by Todd, 1943: *The End of the Road; The Garden; Summer Afternoon and the Spad-Gas;* and of booklet, *Science in the Army: A Brief Account of the Scientific Training and Technical Work of the Soldier Today,* H.M.S.O., 1938. Also author of *The After-Breakfast Book,* W. Hodge, 1937; (with Bruce Graeme [pseud-

onym of Graham Montague Jeffries]) *When the Bells Rang: A Tale,* Harrap, 1943.

Writer of treatment for films, "OHMS," 1936, and "Young and Innocent," 1948; author of scripts for weekly program, "Armstrong's Garden," Southern TV, 1958, and for radio series, with others, "Over to You," BBC, 1951; also author of radio plays, "For Love of a Lady," 1948; "The Black King," 1951; "These Radio Times," 1951; "Return," 1953; "At Squinty Abbott's," 1953; "Death Set to Music," 1953; "The Case of Mr. Pelham," 1954; and others. Work is represented in anthologies, including *Modern Masters of Wit and Laughter,* Methuen, 1938, and *Double Death,* compiled by John Chancellor, Gollancz, 1939.

SIDELIGHTS: Ten Minute Alibi was filmed in 1935, *He Was Found in the Road* was released as "Man in the Road," 1955, and *The Strange Case of Mr. Pelham* was filmed as "The Man Who Haunted Himself," 1970. Radio adaptations based on Armstrong's works include "Ten Minute Alibi," 1947, "Without Witness," 1948, and "Mile Away Murder," 1949. *Avocational interests:* Gardening, walking, reading.

OBITUARIES: AB Bookman's Weekly, March 1, 1976.*

(Died February 10, 1976, in England)

*   *   *

WILLS, Jonathan 1947-

PERSONAL: Born June 17, 1947, in Oxford, England; son of John W. E. and Catherine (Smith) Wills; married Ruth D. Liddington, June 24, 1972 (separated); children: Magnus John, Andrew Laurence. *Education:* University of Edinburgh, M.A. (honors), 1969, Ph.D., 1975. *Politics:* "Freelance ecological socialist." *Religion:* "Freelance ecological socialist." *Home:* 10 Nederdale, Lerwick, Shetland Islands, Scotland.

CAREER: Shetland Times, Lerwick, Shetland Islands, Scotland, reporter, 1969; Lighthouse Service, Unst, Shetland Islands, Scotland, supply boat skipper and crew, 1973-76; *Shetland Times,* writer, 1976. Senior producer for Radio Shetland, 1976. Labour candidate for Parliament from Orkney Island, 1973; rector of University of Edinburgh, 1971-72. *Member:* National Union of Journalists, Shetland Motorcycle Club, Shetland Folk Society.

WRITINGS—All for children: *The Travels of Magnus Pole,* Houghton, 1975; *The Gaston Cartoon Annuals, 1968-1970,* University of Edinburgh Press, 1976; *Linda and the Lighthouse,* Canongate, 1976.

Work anthologized in *The Shetland Way of Oil,* edited by John Button, Thuleprint, 1976. Contributor to Scottish magazines and newspapers. Member of editorial committee of *New Shetlander.*

WORK IN PROGRESS—All for children; completion expected in 1978: *Magnus Pole Sails West; The Trow of the Veng; Brusi and the Wreckwood;* and *Magnus Pole and the Holey Holm.* Also doing historical research.

SIDELIGHTS: Wills writes: "I write for kids in the hope that I can get them interested in history. If you're interested in history it's hard to be bored. I write about oil terminals and their dangers because I want to influence adults and children to defend their environment. I also draw and write for money and don't feel embarrassed about it any more. I prefer painting to writing and it shows. I also prefer landscapes to figures. I hope to live to a ripe old age in a world where nuclear power and nuclear weapons are a part of history—to write kids' horror stories about."

BIOGRAPHICAL/CRITICAL SOURCES: *The Sunday Times*, October 18, 1975.

*　　*　　*

WILSON, Charles McMoran   1882-1977
(Charles McMoran Wilson Moran)

November 10, 1882—April 12, 1977; British physician and author best known for *The Anatomy of Courage* and the controversial *Winston Churchill: The Struggle for Survival, 1940-1965*, based on his twenty-five years as Churchill's physician and comrade. During World War I he served as a physician on the battle front for two and one-half years. Wilson died in Hampshire, England. Obituaries: *New York Times*, April 13, 1977; *Washington Post*, April 13, 1977; *Time*, April 25, 1977; *Newsweek*, April 15, 1977; *AB Bookman's Weekly*, June 27, 1977. (*CAP*-2; earlier sketch in *CA*-21/22)

*　　*　　*

WILSON, Earl   1907-

PERSONAL: Born May 3, 1907, in Rockford, Ohio; son of Arthur Earl (a farmer) and Cloe (Huffman) Wilson; married Rosemary Lyons, January 10, 1936; children: Earl Lyons, Jr. *Education:* Attended Heidelberg College; Ohio State University, B.S., 1931. *Religion:* Methodist. *Home:* 340 West 57th St., New York, N.Y. 10019. *Agent:* Arthur Pine, 1780 Broadway, New York, N.Y. 10019. *Office:* 1681 Broadway, New York, N.Y. 10019.

CAREER: Writer and reporter for various newspapers, including *Piqua Daily Call, Columbus Dispatch, International News Service, Akron Beach Journal*, and *Washington Post*, 1923-35; *New York Post*, New York City, writer, 1935, drama, amusement, and nightclub editor and columnist, 1942—. Guest speaker. Radio commentator for WOR-Mutual, 1945. *Member:* Sigma Delta Chi, Alpha Tau Omega, Lambs Club.

WRITINGS: *I Am Gazing Into My Eight-Ball*, Doubleday, 1945; *Pike's Peak or Bust*, Doubleday, 1946; *Let 'Em Eat Cheesecake*, Doubleday, 1949; *Look Who's Abroad Now*, Doubleday, 1953; *NBC Book of Stars*, Pocket Books, 1957; *Earl Wilson's New York*, Simon & Schuster, 1964; *The Show Business Nobody Knows*, Bantam, 1971; *Show Business Laid Bare*, Putnam, 1974; *Sinatra*, Macmillan, 1976. Also author of *Jungle Performers*, 1941. Writer of a syndicated show business column, "It Happened Last Night," appearing in daily newspapers, including *New York Post* and *Detroit Free Press*. Contributor to magazines, including *Saturday Evening Post, Esquire*, and *Liberty*.

SIDELIGHTS: Wilson's career as a newsman began while he was still in high school, writing sports copy for a local weekly. Always a persistent and probing reporter, he has been responsible for many front-page news stories. In 1935 he scooped the world with news that an anti-polio vaccine was in the works. Currently, his entertainment column, full of amusing human interest stories and show business anecdotes, is syndicated in daily newspapers throughout the country. Gathering material for the column, Wilson often stays up all night attending movie premiers, Broadway first nights, and cafe openings. He travels the equivalent of four times around the world annually. "I always take my wife along," he jokes, "because I'm afraid if I don't people will talk—especially my wife."

WILSON, (Leslie) Granville   1912-

PERSONAL: Born February 10, 1912, in Castleford, West Yorkshire, England; son of Smith (a carpenter) and Mary Ann (Shackleton) Wilson; married Irene Dunn, July 27, 1935; children: Joan (Mrs. Maurice Gray), Arnold Ley. *Education:* Educated in Castleford, England. *Home:* 6 Rosemoor Close, Hunmanby, Filey, North Yorkshire YO14 0NB, England.

CAREER: Journalist. *Member:* Society of Authors, Crime Writers Association.

WRITINGS—For children: *The Gateway to Journalism*, Alliance Press, 1946; *Jonathan Enters Journalism*, Chatto & Windus, 1956; *Formula for Murder*, Brown Watson, 1960; *A First Look at Newspapers*, F. Watts, 1974; *A First Look at the Police*, F. Watts, 1976.

Author of television play "Death of an Editor." Work also represented in anthologies.

WORK IN PROGRESS: A play set in the Yorkshire coal field where he was born; research on novelists as psychologists.

SIDELIGHTS: Wilson comments that he is "a compulsive reader. Could read before I was aged five. Began collecting books when I was nine; still at it." He considers reading the most durable of pleasures, and feels that borrowing books is not enough; one should own them.

*　　*　　*

WILSON, Jeanne (Patricia Pauline)   1920-

PERSONAL: Given name is pronounced Zhan; born May 31, 1920, in London, England; daughter of Francis Arthur and Emily Grace (Williams) Staples; married Wilbert Jeffrey-Smith Wilson (a physician; chief medical officer of Jamaica), July 12, 1943; children: Roger Francis Jeffrey-Smith. *Education:* Educated in private schools and drama school in London, England. *Home and office:* 19 Waterloo Rd., #19K, Kingston 10, Jamaica, West Indies.

CAREER: Westminster Hospital, London, England, nurse, 1940-42; Wolmer's Girls School, Kingston, Jamaica, teacher of speech and drama, 1960-67; writer, 1968—. Has performed in more than one hundred radio and stage plays; producer of plays for adults. *Member:* International P.E.N. (Jamaica center), Authors Guild, Society of Authors. *Awards, honors:* Awards of high commendation from Jamaica Independence Festival, 1965, for radio plays "No Medicine for Murder" and "Reality Is Relevant," and 1966, for radio play "No Truth at All."

WRITINGS: *No Medicine for Murder* (mystery novel), Ward, Lock, 1967; *Model for Murder* (mystery novel), Ward, Lock, 1968; *Weep in the Sun* (historical novel), M. Evans, 1976; *Troubled Heritage* (historical novel), M. Evans, 1977; *Holiday with Guns* (juvenile), Macmillan, 1977; *Flight from the Islands* (juvenile stories), Macmillan, in press; *The House that Liked to Travel* (juvenile stories), Macmillan, in press; *Mulatto* (historical novel), M. Evans, in press; (editor) *West Indian Plays for Schools* (seven West Indian plays), Jamaican Publishing House, in press.

Plays: *No Justice in October* (one-act; first produced in Kingston, Jamaica, March, 1961), Evans Brothers, 1967; *A Legacy for Isabel* (one-act; first produced in Kingston at Little Theatre, March, 1962), Evans Brothers, 1967.

Contributor to *Daily Gleaner*.

WORK IN PROGRESS: *The Golden Harlot* (tentative title), a historical novel; research on Hogarth's London, for a historical novel.

SIDELIGHTS: Wilson writes: "The motivation for writing historical fiction is that I have always been extremely interested in history. The history of the West Indies has been written—by West Indians—quite recently—in the last fifteen to twenty years, and there is very little historical fiction written about Jamaica, or the West Indies as a whole. I feel that accuracy is very important in writing historical fiction, and that comprehensive research must be done. I took three years before I began *Weep in the Sun,* and my research covered West Indian history, European history, the histories of law, architecture, money, the Navy, the cost of living, costumes, and social histories. I am well aware that some writers feel that absolute accuracy is not important. I disagree, and I am also well aware that I will be pounced upon if I am caught out in an historical error!"

AVOCATIONAL INTERESTS: Old buildings, reading dictionaries, reference books, and novels, cooking, swimming, travel (Scotland, Wales, Norway, Sweden, the United States, Surinam, Trinidad), cats, the theatre.

*   *   *

WILSON, John A.   1900(?)-1976

1900(?)—August 30, 1976; American author and professor emeritus at University of Chicago where, upon his retirement, a professorship was named in his honor. He spent five years in Luxor, Egypt, as an epigrapher with the University of Chicago Oriental Institute's expedition, and later became director of the institute. He died in Highstown, N.J. Obituaries: *New York Times,* August 31, 1976.

*   *   *

WILSON, John R. M.   1944-

PERSONAL: Born February 16, 1944, in Vancouver, B.C.; became U.S. citizen, 1958; son of John A. R. (a college professor) and Nora M. (a teacher; maiden name, Mains) Wilson; married Mary Ann Ahlberg (a teacher), August 5, 1967; children: Amy Annee Ahlberg, Christine Allison Ahlberg. *Education:* University of California, Santa Barbara, B.A., 1964; Northwestern University, Ph.D., 1971. *Politics:* Democrat. *Religion:* Lutheran Bretheren. *Home:* 1432 East Sheridan, Olathe, Kan. 66061. *Office:* Department of History, Mid-America Nazarene College, Olathe, Kan. 66061.

CAREER: Minot State College, Minot, N.D., instructor, 1966-70, assistant professor of history, 1970-74; Federal Aviation Administration, Washington, D.C., contract historian, 1974-76; Mid-America Nazarene College, Olathe, Kan., associate professor of history, 1976—. Consultant to Dushkin Publishing Group, 1972-76. Democratic candidate for North Dakota state legislature, 1972. *Member:* Organization of American Historians, American Historical Association, Conference on Faith and History.

WRITINGS: Research Guide in History, General Learning Press, 1974; *Turbulence Aloft: The Civil Aeronautics Administration Amid Wars and Rumors of Wars, 1938-1953,* U.S. Government Printing Office, 1977. Contributor to *Proceedings* of the Northern Great Plains History Conference, *Fides et Historia* (journal of the Conference on Faith and History), *Military Affairs,* and other periodicals.

WORK IN PROGRESS: A multi-volume historical directory of Congress.

AVOCATIONAL INTERESTS: Travel, family camping, baseball, other sports, reading.

WILSON, Phyllis Starr   1928-

PERSONAL: Born February 11, 1928, in New Orleans, La.; daughter of Daniel Davis (an accountant) and Anita (Garripy) Starr; married Hugh Hamilton Wilson (a professor of English), December 24, 1958. *Education:* Tulane University, B.A., 1949. *Politics:* Democrat. *Home:* 242 West 12th St., New York, N.Y. 10014. *Office: Glamour,* 350 Madison Ave., New York, N.Y. 10017.

CAREER: Weird Tales, New York, N.Y., secretary and editor, 1950; Conde Nast Publications, New York City, secretary, 1951-55, researcher and staff writer for *Vogue,* 1955-62; *Glamour,* New York City, staff writer, 1962-67, senior editor of copy and features, 1967-71, managing editor, 1971—. Lecturer at colleges. *Member:* American Society of Magazine Writers, English Speaking Union, American Horticultural Society, Cooper Hewit Museum. *Awards, honors:* J. C. Penney Award from University of Missouri, 1969, for medical article.

WRITINGS: (Editor) *Glamour's Beauty and Health Book,* Simon & Schuster, 1972.

SIDELIGHTS: Phyllis Starr Wilson writes that although she had no interest in science fiction, "I worked for *Weird Tales* because it was the only starting job I could get in the magazine field. It provided me with the first year out-of-college experience in the business world. Then I was able to move on to women's magazines which was always my goal."

*   *   *

WILSON, Snoo   1948-

PERSONAL: Born August 2, 1948, in Reading, England; son of Leslie (a teacher) and Pamela (a teacher; maiden name, Boyle) Wilson. *Education:* University of East Anglia, B.A., 1969. *Home:* 41 The Chase, London SW4, England. *Agent:* Clive Goodwin, 79 Cromwell Rd., London SW7, England.

CAREER: Portable Theatre, London, England, associate director, 1969-72; British Broadcasting Co. (BBC), London, script editor of "Play for Today," 1972; Royal Shakespeare Co., London, dramaturge, 1975-76; playwright, actor and director. Director, Scarab Theatre Co., 1977—. *Member:* London Library.

WRITINGS—All plays: "Girl Mas as Pigs" (one-act), first produced in Norwich, England, at University of East Anglia, June, 1967; "Ella Daybellfesse's Machine" (two-act), first produced in Norwich at University of East Anglia, November, 1967; "Between the Acts" (one-act), first produced in Canterbury, England at Kent University, June, 1969; "Charles the Martyr" (one-act), first produced in Southampton, England, 1970; "Device of Angels" (one-act), first produced in Edinburgh, Scotland, at Traverse Theatre, 1970; "Pericles, The Mean Knight" (one-act), first produced in London at Oval House, January, 1970; *Pignight* [and] *Blow Job* (two-acts; the former first produced in Leeds, England, at Civic Hall, January, 1971, the latter first produced in Edinburgh, Scotland, at The Other Pool Theatre, August, 1971), Calder & Boyers, 1972; (with others) *Lay By* (one-act; first produced in Edinburgh at Traverse Theatre, August, 1971), Calder & Boyers, 1972; "Reason" (one-act), first produced in Edinburgh at Traverse Theatre, June, 1972, produced as "Reason: Boswell and Johnson on the Shores of the Eternal Sea" (one-act), in London at Oval House, March, 1972; (with others) "England's Ireland" (two-act), first produced in Amsterdam at

Mickeri, April, 1972; *The Pleasure Principle* (three-act; first produced in London at Royal Court Theatre upstairs, 1973), Methuen, 1974; "Vampire" (three-act), first produced in London at Oval House, February, 1973; "The Beast" (two-act), first produced in London at The Other Place, October, 1974; "The Soul of the White Ant" (one-act), first produced in London, March, 1976; "The Everest Hotel" (two-act), first produced in London at Bush Theatre, January, 1976; "England—England" (two-act), first produced in London at Jeannetta Cochrane Theatre, August, 1977; "The Glad Hand," first produced in London at Royal Court Theatre, October, 1977.

Also author of "Sunday for Seven Days" screenplay, 1971, and numerous teleplays, including "The Good Life," 1971, "Swamp Music," 1972, "More About the Universe," 1972, "The Barium Meal," 1974, "The Trip to Jerusalem," 1974; "Don't Make Waves," 1975, and "A Greenish Man," 1975.

WORK IN PROGRESS: "The Glad Hand," a cowboy play; "Magic Rose," a teleplay trilogy.

SIDELIGHTS: Wilson told *CA:* "I prefer to write for theatre because it can create the oldest magic. The question of its relevance is only asked by passive incredulous individuals who cannot swallow the idea that perception is an act."

* * *

WILSON, Walt(er N.) 1939-

PERSONAL: Born March 26, 1939, in Texas; son of John A. (a brickmason) and Mildred Wilson; married wife Linda D., September 3, 1960 (divorced, July, 1975); married wife Suzanne L. (a probation officer), June 12, 1976; children: Melanie, Walter N., Jr., Michele. *Education:* Howard Payne College, B.A., 1962; Chapman College, M.A., 1975. *Home:* 11 Amber Way, Chico, Calif. 95926. *Office:* Table Mountain School, 51 County Center, Oroville, Calif. 95965.

CAREER: Ordained Southern Baptist minister; minister of Southern Baptist churches in Texas and California, 1958-72; Table Mountain School, Oroville, Calif., teacher and principal, 1973—. Teacher and principal of school in Marysville, Calif., 1966-73; member of governing board of Youth Service Bureau of Yuba-Sutter Counties, 1969-71; member of Juvenile Court School Administrators Council (California), 1970—. *Member:* Correctional Education Association, Court School Educators of Northern California (president, 1974-75), Phi Delta Kappa.

WRITINGS: T.A. for Teens, privately printed, 1974; *Say Hello to Yourself* (transactional analysis for adolescents), Broadman, 1975. Contributor to religious magazines and *Scholastic.*

WORK IN PROGRESS: Editing *Love and Graffite,* an anthology of poems by juvenile delinquents.

SIDELIGHTS: Wilson writes: "As an adolescent, someone reached out to me, he offered to trust me and gave his love unconditionally. That changed the course of my life. That person was an educator in my high school. Mr. Mac believed in me as a person and gave to me the most valuable thing he could give—himself and his time.

"I decided that I wanted to help other juvenile delinquents. As a minister of churches in Texas and California, I worked with adolescents in camps, revivals, and youth programs. My work with juvenile delinquents has been very rewarding. I have listened to their hearts; watched them grow; cried and laughed with them; hurt with them. I hope to publish some of their poems soon which I've been collecting for the last ten years."

WILTON, Elizabeth 1937-

PERSONAL: Born July 27, 1937, in Adelaide, Australia; daughter of J. Raymond (a professor of mathematics) and Winifred (a Young Women's Christian Association worker; maiden name, Welbourn) Wilton; married Charles F. Stevenson (a teacher), December 26, 1970; children: Daniel Charles, Richard Wilton, Catherine Elizabeth. *Education:* Attended Adelaide Teachers College. *Politics:* Australian Labor Party. *Religion:* Society of Friends (Quakers). *Home:* 4 Tindara Ave., Windsor Gardens, South Australia 5087.

CAREER: Education Department, Adelaide, Australia, senior assistant, 1956-64; Crippled Children's Association, Adelaide, teacher of children with cerebral palsy, 1965-67; Education Department, Adelaide, head teacher in special education and guidance, 1968-70. Teacher with local adult illiteracy program. *Member:* Australian Society of Authors.

*WRITINGS—*For children: *A Ridiculous Idea,* Angus & Robertson, 1967; *Riverboat Family* (Junior Literary Guild selection), Angus & Robertson, 1967, Farrar, Straus, 1969; *Red Ribbons and Mr. Anders,* Angus & Robertson, 1970; *Riverview Kids,* Angus & Robertson, 1971.

WORK IN PROGRESS: Face to the Wind; a history of western Victoria, Australia; a biography of Captain William Randall; studying Australian gold rushes.

SIDELIGHTS: "I write because I have to—I cannot help it; it is a sort of disease. I feel it important to collect the stories that old people have to tell of their early days in this country—before those stories are lost forever. I try to emphasise attitudes toward peace, conservation. I am interested in history, children, and educational methods (particularly with reference to reading)." *Avocational interests:* Listening to music, watching ballet, stamp collecting, gardening, Esperanto.

* * *

WINDHAM, Kathryn T(ucker) 1918-

PERSONAL: Born June 2, 1918, in Selma, Ala.; daughter of James Wilson (a banker) and Helen (an insurance agent; maiden name, Tabb) Tucker; married Amasa Benjamin Windham, February 10, 1946 (deceased); children: Kathryn Tabb, Amasa Benjamin, Jr., Helen Ann. *Education:* Huntingdon College, A.B., 1939. *Politics:* Democrat. *Religion:* United Methodist. *Home:* 2004 Royal St., Selma, Ala. 36701.

CAREER: Alabama Journal, Montgomery, police reporter, 1940-42; U.S. Treasury Department, Birmingham, Ala., statewide promoter of war bonds, 1942-44; *Birmingham News,* Birmingham, Ala., state editor, general reporter, and photographer, 1944-46; *Selma Times-Journal,* Selma, Ala., has worked as reporter, city editor, state editor, associate editor, 1960-73; Area Agency on Aging, Camden, Ala., community services planner, 1973—. Member of board of advisers of Alabama State Historical Commission; member of Selma city school board, 1960-72. *Member:* National Association for the Preservation and Perpetuation of Storytelling (member of board of directors). *Awards, honors:* Best nonfiction award from American Library Association, 1975, for *Alabama: One Big Front Porch;* journalism awards from Associated Press and Alabama Press Association, for photography, features, and spot news.

*WRITINGS—*All published by Strode: *Treasured Alabama Recipes,* 1964; (with Margaret Gillis Figh) *Thirteen Alabama Ghosts and Jeffrey,* 1969; *Exploring Alabama,* 1969;

Jeffrey Introduces Thirteen More Southern Ghosts, 1971; *Treasured Tennessee Recipes,* 1972; *Thirteen Georgia Ghosts and Jeffrey,* 1973; *Treasured Georgia Recipes,* 1973; *Thirteen Mississippi Ghosts and Jeffrey,* 1974; *Alabama: One Big Front Porch,* 1975; *Thirteen Tennessee Ghosts and Jeffrey,* 1976.

WORK IN PROGRESS: Collecting Southern ghost tales, games, folklore, and songs; photographing the changing South.

SIDELIGHTS: Kathryn Windham writes: "My desire is to preserve our Southern ghost tales—the true ones—before they are lost. I use a newspaper reporter's training to check the stories, verify dates, names, places, etc. The sites of all the stories can be visited—but I make no promise that the ghosts can be seen! Jeffrey is the 'something' that lives in our house."

* * *

WINFREY, Lee 1932-

PERSONAL: Born July 7, 1932, in Knoxville, Tenn.; son of Charles Houston (a stonemason) and Norma (Wesenberg) Winfrey; married Mary Anne Hight (a secretary), September 10, 1958; children: David Dylan. *Education:* University of Tennessee, B.S., 1966; University of Iowa, M.A., 1968; Harvard University, further graduate study, 1971-72. *Religion:* Baptist. *Home:* 428 Lombard St., Philadelphia, Pa. 19147. *Office: Philadelphia Inquirer,* 400 North Broad St., Philadelphia, Pa. 19101.

CAREER/WRITINGS: Nashville Tennessean, Nashville, Tenn., reporter, 1957-59; *Knoxville News-Sentinel,* Knoxville, Tenn., reporter, 1959-60; United Press International, Miami, Fla., reporter, 1960-62; *Miami Herald,* Miami, Fla., reporter, 1962-63; Knight Newspapers, Washington Bureau, Washington, D.C., correspondent, 1963-66; University of Iowa, Iowa City, instructor in journalism, 1966-68; *Detroit Free Press,* Detroit, Mich., reporter, 1968-71; *Philadelphia Inquirer,* Philadelphia, Pa., author of column "On Television" (also syndicated by Knight newspapers to about sixty other newspapers), 1972—. Covered the occupation of Wounded Knee, the trial of the "Chicago Seven," the shootings at Kent State University, and the revolution in the Dominican Republic in 1965. Contributor to *Nation, Nieman Reports,* and *Photoplay.* Lecturer at colleges and universities, including University of Michigan, University of Pennsylvania, and Temple University. *Military service:* U.S. Army, 1954-56.

MEMBER: National Press Club, Sigma Delta Chi, Pen and Pencil Club. *Awards, honors:* Shared in team award to Knight Newspapers of George Polk Memorial Award from Long Island University, 1971, for covering the shootings at Kent State University; Nieman fellow at Harvard University, 1971-72.

* * *

WINN, Charles S. 1932-

PERSONAL: Born April 15, 1932, in Utah; son of David G. (an educator) and Edith (Hughes) Winn; married Ann Crandall, August 7, 1953; children: Steven, Julie, Sally, Kathy. *Education:* University of Utah, B.S., M.S., Ed.D. *Home:* 720 South 850th E., Bountiful, Utah 84010. *Office:* Utah State Board of Education, 250 East 500th S., Salt Lake City, Utah 84111.

CAREER: Federal Reserve Bank, Salt Lake City, Utah, management trainee, 1957-59; Utah Technical College, Salt Lake City, member of staff, 1959-61; Hercules Powder Co., Salt Lake City, Utah, training coordinator, 1961-63; Utah State Board of Education, Salt Lake City, educational supervisor, 1963—. *Military service:* U.S. Air Force, 1954-57. Utah Air National Guard; became lieutenant colonel. *Member:* Sales and Marketing Executives International, American Vocational Association, National Business Education Association, National Association of State Supervisors of Distributive Education.

WRITINGS—For young people: *Careers in Focus,* McGraw, 1976; *Careers in Marketing,* McGraw, 1976; *Careers in Transportation,* McGraw, 1976; *Careers in Construction,* McGraw, 1976; *Careers in Manufacturing,* McGraw, 1976; *Careers in Science, Fine Arts, and Humanities,* McGraw, 1976.

WORK IN PROGRESS: Careers in Manufacturing and Repair; Careers in Construction, new edition.

* * *

WINSOR, Mary P(ickard) 1943-

PERSONAL: Born August 25, 1943, in New York, N.Y.; daughter of Paul, Jr. (an engineer) and Marion Joyce Winsor; married Bruce Sinclair (a professor), February 15, 1975. *Education:* Radcliffe College, A.B., 1965; Yale University, Ph.D., 1971. *Home:* 550 Spadina Cres., Toronto, Ontario, Canada M5S 2J9. *Office:* Institute for the History and Philosophy of Science and Technology, University of Toronto, Toronto, Ontario, Canada M5S 1A1.

CAREER: University of Toronto, Toronto, Ontario, lecturer, 1969-71, assistant professor, 1971-74, associate professor of the history of science, 1974—. *Member:* History of Science Society (member of council, 1974-76).

WRITINGS: Starfish, Jellyfish, and the Order of Life: Issues in Nineteenth-Century Science, Yale University Press, 1976.

WORK IN PROGRESS: Research for a book covering the history of the Museum of Comparative Zoology, founded by Louis Agassiz.

AVOCATIONAL INTERESTS: Horseback riding.

* * *

WITKE, Roxane 1938-

PERSONAL: Born March 16, 1938, in Oakland, Calif.; daughter of William Earl and Edith (Armann) Heater; divorced; children: Alexandra. *Education:* Stanford University, B.A. (cum laude), 1959; University of Chicago, M.A., 1962; University of California, Berkeley, Ph.D., 1970. *Office:* History Department, State University of New York at Binghamton, Binghamton, N.Y. 13901.

CAREER: San Francisco State College (now University), San Francisco, Calif., visiting lecturer in history, 1968; Mills College, Oakland, Calif., visiting assistant professor of history, 1969-70; State University of New York, Binghamton, assistant professor, 1971-72, associate professor of history, 1972—. Visiting associate professor of history, Stanford University, 1972-73; guest lecturer, Mills College, 1973, and Harvard University, 1974 and 1975. Modern China seminar chairperson of Columbia University seminar series, 1976-77. Host of "White Haired Girl," a Chinese revolutionary ballet, first broadcast by Public Broadcasting Service (PBS), 1974; has taped educational radio programs for Johnson Foundation, 1974, and National Committee on U.S.-China Relations, 1975. Consultant to U.S. Department of State,

1973, and to White House Press Corps, 1975. *Member:* American Historical Association, National Committee on U.S.-China Relations, American Civil Liberties Union, Association for Asian Studies, Asia Society (associate member of China council). *Awards, honors:* American Council of Learned Societies and Social Science Research Council post-doctoral fellowship, 1970-71, and grant, 1973-74; Johnson Foundation grant, 1972-73; National Endowment for the Humanities research grant, 1973-76.

WRITINGS: (With Robert Rinden) *The Red Flag Waves: A Guide to the 'Hung-ch'i p'iao-p'iao' Collection* (monograph), Center for Chinese Studies, University of California, Berkeley, 1968; (contributor) Marilyn B. Young, editor, *Women in China: Studies in Social Change and Feminism,* Center for Chinese Studies, University of Michigan, 1973; (contributor) Peter J. Opitz, editor, *Die Soehne des Drachen: Chinas Weg vom Konfuzianismus zum Kommunismus* (title means "Seeds of the Dragon: The Chinese Way from Confucianism to Communism"), List Verlag, 1974; (editor with Margery Wolf, and contributor) *Women in Chinese Society,* Stanford University Press, 1975; *Comrade Chiang Ch'ing* (Book-of-the-Month Club alternate selection), Little, Brown, 1977.

Contributor to proceedings of International Congress of Chinese Studies; contributor of articles and reviews to *China Quarterly, Science and Society, American Historical Review,* and to *Journal of Asian Studies.* Assistant editor for China, *Journal of Asian Studies,* 1976—.

WORK IN PROGRESS: A study of politics, society, and culture, *Shanghai in the Thirties;* a generational study combining extensive research and interviews with Chinese leaders, tentatively titled *Revolutionary Women Leaders in China.*

SIDELIGHTS: Roxane Witke was invited to China in summer, 1972, to do research on the status of Chinese women. Her research included a lengthy series of interviews with the wife of Chairman Mao Tse-tung, Chiang Ch'ing, then at the height of her power. The interviews had apparently been sanctioned by Premier Chou En-lai who described Witke to Chiang Ch'ing as "young and enthusiastic for China," but for obscure reasons, perhaps because the interviews made Chiang Ch'ing "look too nakedly ambitious," they were soon deemed a mistake, as Time reported.

Witke was promised that official transcripts of the interviews would be sent to her, but instead she received word months later that the interviews were "too long and complicated" to be issued as a Peking-authorized document. She was offered a generous financial incentive to dissuade her from writing her book. The result, however, a book titled *Comrade Chiang Ch'ing,* compiled from the copious notes she had taken during the interviews, is, according to a *Time* magazine reviewer, "the most intimate, detailed and complete English-language biography ever written about anyone in Peking's secretive, secluded leadership, except perhaps Mao himself."

"Witke's book is not merely a remorseless account," wrote Harrison E. Salisbury, "of the manners and mores of Chiang Ch'ing and the 'proletarian imperial style,' although her quick eye catches almost every nuance. But the book is also Chiang Ch'ing's own selective account of her life, her revolutionary career, her years at Mao's side and her role in what remains one of the most complex and bewildering political events of the century—the Great Proletarian Cultural Revolution."

"There are gaps and omission," noted *Time;* "often, Chiang

Ch'ing's story is extremely self-serving. At the same time, her account of turmoil and conflict gives a whole new view to the nature of life at the top in China—ruthless, unpredictable and dangerous.... Without intending to, she makes today's Forbidden City, where the Peking leaders still live and work, seem almost the same as the old intrigue-ridden imperial court that the Communists claim to have eradicated forever."

Time noted that "in trying to move ... to the power that 'sustains interest in the long run,' [Chiang Ch'ing] never won enough power to survive on her own." The fact that she even gave her interviews to Witke "is being used in the current campaign to vilify her past behavior. By talking to an outsider, and showing that outsider intimate details of her private life, Chiang Ch'ing put on the record all the ammunition her enemies would ever need to destroy her." In an earlier report in the *New York Times,* Witke told reporters that Chiang Ch'ing was vulnerable to criticism as a woman in a man's role and because the interviews were an unconventional and irregular act.

Witke told *CA* that she has been interviewed by Morley Safer for a segment of the CBS "Sixty Minutes" television series. Her book *Comrade Chiang Ch'ing* is being translated for publication in several European and Asian editions.

BIOGRAPHICAL/CRITICAL SOURCES: New York Times, February 19, 1973, March 9, 1973, November 28, 1975; *Time,* March 21, 1977; *Los Angeles Times,* April 3, 1977; *Detroit News,* April 17, 1977; *San Francisco Chronicle,* April 17, 1977; *Washington Post,* April 17, 1977.

* * *

WITTENBERG, Rudolph M. 1906-

PERSONAL: Born March 24, 1906, in Berlin, Germany; came to the United States in 1934, naturalized citizen, 1937; son of Hugo and Paula (Katzenstein) Wittenberg; married Diana Polturak, July 18, 1934; children: Helen (Mrs. David Freedman), Sandra (Mrs. Karl Bemesderfer). *Education:* Columbia University, M.S., 1943. *Home:* 845 West End Ave., New York, N.Y. 10025.

CAREER: Psychoanalyst and writer. Free-lance writer in Berlin, Germany, 1929-33; employed by *Prager Tagblatt,* Prague, Czechoslovakia, 1933, and *Norodni Osvoboseni,* Prague, 1934; Western Reserve University (now Case Western Reserve University), Cleveland, Ohio, lecturer in social sciences, 1934; educational director at school of Jewish Board of Guardians, Hawthorne, N.Y., 1937-39; Board of Education, New York City, member of Bureau of Child Guidance project, 1940-52; lecturer at New School for Social Research, New York City, 1945—. Employed in play therapy by Jewish Child Guidance Bureau, Newark, N.J., and Community Service Society, New York City, both 1945. Member of National Committee for Mental Hygiene; supervisor of local Mental Hygiene Institute; member of committee on counseling for Young Men's Christian Association. *Member:* American Orthopsychiatric Association (fellow), Council of Psychoanalytic Therapists (member of board of directors), New York State Psychological Association.

WRITINGS: So You Want to Help People: A Mental Hygiene Primer for Group Leaders, Association Press, 1947; *The Art of Group Discipline: A Mental Hygiene Approach to Leadership,* Association Press, 1951; *On Call For Youth: How to Understand and Help Young People,* Association Press, 1955; *Common Sense About Psychoanalysis,* Doubleday, 1961; *Discipline in the Teens,* Association Press,

1963; *The Troubled Generation: Toward Understanding and Helping the Young Adult,* Association Press, 1967; *Postadolescence: Theoretical and Clinical Aspects of Psychotherapy,* Grune, 1968.

*   *   *

WOLF, Thomas H(oward)   1916-

PERSONAL: Born April 22, 1916, in New York, N.Y.; son of James and Madeleine (Fleisher) Wolf. *Education:* Princeton University, B.A. (magna cum laude), 1937. *Office:* ABC News, 1330 Avenue of the Americas, New York, N.Y. 10019.

CAREER/WRITINGS: Newspaper Enterprise Association (NEA), New York, N.Y., European manager and war correspondent, 1940-46; National Broadcasting Co. (NBC) Radio, New York City, London and Paris correspondent, 1944-45; Pathe News, New York City, script editor, 1947-50; Information Productions, New York City, president, 1951-59; Columbia Broadcasting System (CBS) News, New York City, executive producer, 1960-62; American Broadcasting Co. (ABC) News, New York City, news executive, 1963—. Contributor to *Collier's, Holiday, New Republic,* and other periodicals.

*   *   *

WOLFE, Bertram D(avid)   1896-1977

January 19, 1896—February 21, 1977; American author, professor, and expert on the Soviet Union best known for *Three Who Made a Revolution.* A founding member of the Communist Party in the United States in 1919, Wolfe was acquainted with Stalin, Trotsky, Bukharin, Molotov, and other revolutionary leaders. He was one of the first members of his party to become a resolute foe of Stalin. He had been a senior fellow at the Hoover Institution on War, Revolution and Peace since 1966. Wolfe died in San Jose, Calif. Obituaries: *New York Times,* February 22, 1977. (See index for previous *CA* sketch)

*   *   *

WOLFE, Gerard R(aymond)   1926-

PERSONAL: Born April 2, 1926, in New York, N.Y.; son of Samuel (a controller) and Anna Wolfe. *Education:* City College (now of the City University of New York), B.B.A., 1948; New York University, A.M., 1949; Sorbonne, University of Paris, certificat, 1954; also attended Middlebury College and University of Mexico. *Home:* 7-13 Washington Sq. N., New York, N.Y. 10003. *Office:* Foreign Language Program, New York University, 3 Washington Sq. N., New York, N.Y. 10003.

CAREER: High school French and Spanish teacher in New York, N.Y., 1949-51, and Floral Park, N.Y., 1951-58; New York University, New York, N.Y., lecturer in Spanish and French, 1958-66, associate professor of continuing education, 1966—, director of Peace Corps training program for Turkey, 1966, chairman of university senate educational policies committee, 1974-76, currently director of foreign language program. Lecturer at Hofstra University, 1973—; guest lecturer at Jewish Museum, 1969—. Researcher for American Museum of Natural History, 1959-64; consultant, New York City Landmarks Preservation Committee, 1969—. Guest on radio and television programs. *Military service:* U.S. Army, 1944-46; served in Germany; became technical sergeant; received one combat star.

MEMBER: Modern Language Association of America,

National University Extension Association, National Trust for Historic Preservation, American Council of Teachers of Foreign Languages, American Jewish Historical Society, American Scandinavian Foundation, New York Historical Society, Long Island Historical Society. *Awards, honors:* Winifred Fisher Award for Creative Programming from Adult Education Council of New York, 1976.

WRITINGS: How to Pass Spanish, Yes Books, 1959; *How to Study,* Yes Books, 1960; (editor) W. H. Starr and A. G. Pellegrino, *New Functional French,* American Book Co., 1960; (editor) M. T. Brunetti, *Read, Write, Speak French,* Bantam, 1960; (editor) *Les du Pont* (title means "The Du Ponts"), American Book Co., 1966; *The Peace Corps in Turkey* (training manual), New York University, School of Continuing Education, 1966; *New York: A Guide to the Metropolis,* New York University Press, 1975; (with Jo Renee Fine) *The Synagogues of New York's Lower East Side,* New York University Press, 1977; (editor) Brunetti, *Read, Write, Speak Spanish,* Bantam, 1977. Contributor to travel section of *New York Times.*

WORK IN PROGRESS: Research on New York City's architectural history, on book publishing in America and its influence on New York politics, and on the decline of New York's Lower East Side.

SIDELIGHTS: Wolfe presently teaches, among other things, courses on the architecture and history of New York City. His work for the American Museum of Natural History included twelve summers in Mexico and Latin America conducting photographic research, and additional time photographing the interior regions of Iceland and Greenland. He has also conducted study tours of Mexico and Guatemala. He speaks Spanish, French, Dutch, Portuguese, and German.

AVOCATIONAL INTERESTS: Playing piano and flute.

*   *   *

WOLFE, Henry C.   1898(?)-1976

1898(?)—November 20, 1976; American writer on foreign affairs and lecturer who predicted the alliance between Nazi Germany and the Soviet Union before the outbreak of World War II. He was named to a post with the American Relief Administration by Herbert Hoover, and lived for a time in the Soviet Union. During World War I he served with the French Army and later with an American ambulance unit and the American Red Cross in Italy. He was decorated for his work in international affairs by eleven foreign governments. He died in New York City. Obituaries: *New York Times,* November 23, 1976.

*   *   *

WOLFENSTEIN, Martha   1911(?)-1976

1911(?)—November 30, 1976; American specialist in child psychology, professor of psychiatry, and author of psychological studies. In collaboration with Margaret Meade she wrote *Childhood in Contemporary Cultures,* and was engaged in psychological studies of painters, including Goya and Magritte. She died in New York City. Obituaries: *New York Times,* December 1, 1976.

*   *   *

WOLTERSTORFF, Nicholas Paul   1932-

PERSONAL: Born January 21, 1932, in Minnesota; son of Matthew (a woodworker) and Agnes (Feenstra) Wolterstorff; married Claire Kingma (a writer and speaker), June

25, 1955; children: Amy, Eric, Robert, Nicholas, Christopher. *Education:* Calvin College, A.B., 1953; Harvard University, M.A., 1954, Ph.D., 1957. *Religion:* Reformed Church. *Home:* 58 Sunnybrook S.E., Grand Rapids, Mich. 49506. *Office:* Department of Philosophy, Calvin College, Grand Rapids, Mich. 49506.

CAREER: Yale University, New Haven, Conn., instructor in philosophy, 1957-59; Calvin College, Grand Rapids, Mich., assistant professor, 1959-61, associate professor, 1961-65, professor of philosophy, 1965—. Visiting lecturer at University of Chicago, 1965; visiting professor at University of Texas, University of Notre Dame, University of Michigan, Haverford College, and Temple University. Consultant to National Endowment for the Humanities. *Member:* American Philosophical Association, American Society for Aesthetics. *Awards, honors:* Woodrow Wilson fellowship, 1953; Harbison Award from Danforth Foundation, 1970; National Endowment for the Humanities junior fellowship, 1970-71.

WRITINGS: Religion and the Schools, Eerdmans, 1967; *On Universals,* University of Chicago Press, 1970; *Reason Within the Bounds of Religion,* Eerdmans, 1976.

Contributor: Alvin Plantinga, editor, *Faith and Philosophy,* Eerdmans, 1964; Theodore R. Sizer, editor, *Religion and Public Education,* Houghton, 1967; Michael Loux, editor, *Universals and Particulars,* Doubleday, 1970; Charles Landesman, editor, *The Problem of Universals,* Basic Books, 1971; Clifton J. Orlebeke and Lewis B. Smedes, editors, *God and the Good,* Eerdmans, 1975. Contributor to philosophy and aesthetics journals. Senior editor of *Reformed Journal.*

WORK IN PROGRESS: Works and Worlds of Art, for philosophers; *Art in Action,* "a more informal book."

SIDELIGHTS: Wolterstorff writes: "In aesthetics, I have been trying to break out of the Cartesian tradition of approaching art from the side of consciousness, and trying instead to set art within the context of action. More generally, a perennial concern of mine has been to see how in my own case, and in general, religious commitment is related to theoretical activity."

*   *   *

WOOD, Kenneth 1922-

PERSONAL: Born September 13, 1922, in Sheffield, England; son of Thomas Pashley and Mary Winifred (Horsfield) Wood; married Patricia O'Donnell, April 29, 1962; children: John Michael, Julia. *Education:* University of Sheffield, B.A., 1948, diploma in education, 1949, M.A., 1950. *Politics:* "Inconsistent." *Residence:* Marske-by-the-Sea, Redcar, Cleveland, England. *Agent:* David Higham Associates, 5-8 Lower John St., London W1R 4HA, England.

CAREER: Teacher in Blackpool, England, 1951-52, Briancon, France, 1952-53, Manchester, England, 1953-55, and Middlesbrough, England, 1955—.

WRITINGS: The Gulls (juvenile), Dobson, 1974.

Author of "The Wheel" (radio play), British Broadcasting Corp., 1971.

WORK IN PROGRESS: A Period of Violence, fiction for teenagers.

SIDELIGHTS: Wood writes: "I spent the first ten years of my life in a small village near Sheffield, England, and I think this fact has coloured my outlook: I am by nature inclined to

be introverted, disliking large social gatherings and preferring to have a few close friends. I did a great deal of reading as a child, but I have no recollection of attempting to write fiction. I was middle-aged when I began to write. I regret this: I have many things I would like to say which will probably never be said. As a writer, I try to express something real and meaningful in language that would really be used by the people involved. I am concerned about the plight of individuals trapped in systems—teenagers in large, impersonal schools, for example. I think education offered in schools often fails to meet the needs of today's young people.... My writing is always hard work, as I seek precision of expression.... I fuss interminably over details of dialogue. The characters about which I write appear very real to me. I once did a radio interview about my writing, and found that I could remember the names of the fictional characters but forgot that of the man to whom I was speaking!"

AVOCATIONAL INTERESTS: Ornithology, games, walks by the sea and in the countryside.

*   *   *

WOOD, Lorna 1913-

PERSONAL: Born June 16, 1913, in Pex Hill, Lancashire, England; daughter of Harry (a transport manager) and Amelia (Haney) Wood; married Joseph Swire, August 31, 1938 (divorced); children: Kyrchian (Mrs. William Sweeney), Roger. *Education:* Attended Manchester School of Music. *Politics:* "Haven't any." *Religion:* Roman Catholic. *Address:* c/o Williams & Glyn's Bank, Market Sq., Reading, England.

CAREER: Concert pianist, 1935-38; British Broadcasting Corp., Monitoring Service, London, England, head of Central African Service, 1971-72; writer, 1972—. *Member:* Society of Authors, Writers Guild of Great Britain.

WRITINGS—For children, except as indicated: *The Crumb-Snatchers,* J. Cape, 1933; *Gilded Sprays,* John Long, 1935; *The Hopeful Travellers,* John Long, 1936; *The Smiling Rabbit and Other Stories,* Harrap, 1939; *The Travelling Tree and Other Stories,* Harrap, 1943; *The Finicky Mouse and Other Stories,* E. J. Arnold, 1949.

The Handkerchief Man, E. J. Arnold, 1951; (editor) *Here I Was a Child,* E. J. Arnold, 1952; *Ameliaranne Goes Digging,* Harrap, 1952; *The People in the Garden,* Dent, 1954; *Rescue by Broomstick,* Dent, 1956; *The Hag Calls for Help,* Dent, 1957; *Holiday on Hot Bricks,* Dent, 1958; *Climb by Candlelight,* Dent, 1959; *Seven-League Ballet Shoes,* Dent, 1959; *Hags on Holiday,* Dent, 1960; *The Golden-Haired Family,* Dent, 1961; *Hag in the Castle,* Dent, 1962.

Hags by Starlight, Dent, 1970; *The Brave Adventures of a Shoemaker's Boy,* Dent, 1971; *Panger's Pup,* Dent, 1972. Also author of *Nothing But Danger* (experiences in Spain), and *The Dogs of Pangers.* Contributor to magazines and newspapers in England, including *National Review, Lady,* and *Homes and Gardens.*

SIDELIGHTS: Lorna Wood writes: "I suppose I started to write because there was nothing else I could do! I was brought up in a large, shabby house in the North of England, about four hundred years old and, in those days, very isolated. I was an only child and there was only one neighbour with a daughter my age: *she* was sent to boarding-school at the age of seven so, as I was not sent to school at all, the only juvenile society I had was composed of occasionally visiting cousins. My father was a typical 'English eccentric' and wouldn't hear of school or any education at all. He did, however, consent to music lessons. It was then discovered I was a 'prodigy,' absolute pitch and all: I played at my first concert at seven, enrolled at the Manchester School of Music and announced that I would write a novel to pay my fees! This incredible gamble paid off and that is why my first book was published in 1931. All written in longhand, by candlelight . . . I forgot to say I was brought up without benefit of gas or electricity. Before my marriage, I led a dual existence, playing at concerts and writing. I then went to Spain, during the Spanish War, with my husband. I described my experiences in *Nothing But Danger*. I have travelled in the U.S.S.R., most of the Iron Curtain countries except Albania and Rumania, Turkey, etc. I visit Canada about once a year.''

*   *   *

WOODHAM-SMITH, Cecil (Blanche Fitzgerald) 1896-1977

1896—March 16, 1977; British author and historian who began writing biographies in her late forties. Producing just four major works, including a biography of Florence Nightingale which won the James Tait Black memorial award in 1950, she achieved her reputation as one of the top authorities of nineteenth century British history. She died in London, England. Obituaries: *New York Times*, March 17, 1977; *Washington Post*, March 19, 1977; *Time*, March 28, 1977; *Newsweek*, March 28, 1977; *AB Bookman's Weekly*, May 9, 1977; *Current Biography*, May, 1977.

*   *   *

WOODSTONE, Arthur

PERSONAL: Born in New York, N.Y.; son of Albert Z. (a businessman) and B. F. Woodstone. *Education:* Wagner College, B.A., 1950; graduate study at Columbia University. *Politics:* ''Angry.'' *Residence:* New York, N.Y. *Agent:* Mel Gold, William Morris Agency, 1350 Avenue of the Americas, New York, N.Y. 10019.

CAREER: Editor and writer. *Variety*, New York City, reporter and critic, 1953-63; *Brooklyn Today*, Brooklyn, N.Y., city editor, 1972; Larry Flynt Publications, New York City, editor, 1977—. Public relations expert and communications executive for politicians, including Bella Abzug, George McGovern, John Lindsay, Mary Ann Krupsak, and Judge Jack Weinstein.

WRITINGS: (With Norma Woodstone) *Fortnight in New York*, Percival Marshall, 1965; *Nixon's Head*, St. Martin's, 1972, revised edition, Popular Library, 1976. Contributor to popular magazines, including *New York, Daily News Magazine, Cosmopolitan*, and *This Week*. Former critic for *True*, entertainment editor and critic for *Quest*, and film critic for *Ingenue*.

SIDELIGHTS: Woodstone writes: ''I'm inclined to march to a different drummer, as my present post might indicate, and as might my biography of Nixon, which suggested at the height of his power that a sitting President seemed (to me) to be hell-bent on his own destruction. My work generally takes the dissident, iconoclastic view, although, paradoxically, I have worked for many mainstream publications. I love a fight.''

*   *   *

WOODWARD, Robert Upshur 1943- (Bob Woodward)

PERSONAL: Born March 26, 1943, in Geneva, Ill.; son of

Alfred E. Woodward (a judge) and Jane (Upshur) Woodward Barnes; married Frances R. Barnard, November 29, 1974; children: Mary Taliesin. *Education:* Yale University, B.A., 1965. *Home:* 3027 Q St. N.W., Washington, D.C. 20007. *Agent:* David Obst, Room 1614, 525 Madison Ave., New York, N.Y. 10022. *Office:* Washington Post, 1150 15th St. N.W., Washington, D.C. 20005.

CAREER: Montgomery County Sentinel, Rockville, Md., reporter, 1970-71; *Washington Post*, Washington, D.C., reporter, 1971—. *Military service:* U.S. Naval Reserve, active duty, 1965-70; became lieutenant. *Awards, honors:* Pulitzer Prize in journalism, Drew Pearson Foundation award, Heywood Brun award, George Polk memorial award, Sidney Hillman Foundation award, Worth Bingham prize, and Sigma Delta Chi award, all 1973, all for investigative reporting of Watergate scandal.

WRITINGS—Under name Bob Woodward: (With Carl Bernstein) *All the President's Men*, Simon & Schuster, 1974; (with Bernstein) *The Final Days*, Simon & Schuster, 1976.

WORK IN PROGRESS: Newspaper work.

SIDELIGHTS: Bob Woodward had been with the *Washington Post* eight months on the night police beat when he was called upon to cover the arraignment of five men who had been arrested for breaking into the Democratic National Committee's offices in the Watergate complex. The astonished young reporter learned the burglers had CIA connections and that one of them, James McCord, was an employee of the Committee to Reelect the President. Woodward, teamed with Carl Bernstein, followed the story from a Washington courtroom through a complicated tangle of clandestine political activity into the highest offices of the White House. The affair eventually led, in part due to Woodward and Bernstein's persistant efforts, to the resignation of numerous government officials in the executive branch, including that of President Richard Nixon.

The reporters' first book, *All the President's Men*, was originally planned to be the culmination of their investigative work for their *Washington Post* stories. At the time—October, 1972—Woodward and Bernstein were the only two reporters pursuing the story. The result of the scant attention from the rest of the press was an exclusive pile of information. Information which they intended to use in a book about the secret activities of White House aides, appropriately titled *All the President's Men*. Four chapters of this never finished book were already written when Judge Sirica released to the press a letter he had received from James McCord. In the letter, McCord revealed the involvement of higher-ups in the burglery and the perjury and political pressure that had occurred during his trial. These disclosures sent everyone scrambling on investigations of their own. Woodword and Bernstein watched their lead in evidence dissolve in the ensuing fierce competition for front page scoops. Realizing that by the time their book could be finished it would appear merely to be rehashing well-reported events, they abandoned the idea. Woodward then suggested that instead of writing a book filled with information everybody already knew, the pair should write the story of how they reported the Watergate cover-up.

Bob Woodward wrote the first draft of the new book, leaving blanks for Bernstein's separate accounts. Although admittedly not a good writer, ''he's very fast and he gets it all in,'' explained Bernstein. When the time came for the authors to decide what the new book was to be called they kept the original title.

The story was told in a third person narrative style. The authors worried that a different style or more personal point of view might appear to be an "ego trip" when dealing with their successes, or worse, might become a defense or justification when dealing with their failures. The reporters openly acknowledged their mistakes: They approached grand jury members for information; they revealed a confidential source; and they overstepped all guidelines in certain rights to privacy. As reporters and authors, they wanted to be objective and honest. The third person narrative with its advantage of impartiality, it was decided, allowed them the best opportunity to do this. In addition, said Doris Kearns, "it turns Watergate into a fast moving mystery, a whodunit written with ease if not elegance."

Critics praised the book wholeheartedly for its ability to sustain reader interest, for its behind-the-scenes explanation of the workings of a large metropolitan newspaper, and for its indispensable historical value. The co-authors were commended for their frankness and their fascinating, personal portraits of the men surrounding the president.

Nevertheless a few critical questions were raised. J. A. O'Hare implied that Woodward and Bernstein may have overreacted in their effort not to rehash over-reported events. "Their journalistic preoccupations," he said, "in fact, so dominate the story that the larger chronology often becomes dim." Doris Kearns wished the reporters had taken a more judicial attitude in relating their ethical decisions. "How did they weight the competing values in those decisions?," she asked. "The book does not say. The same dispassionate language which keeps the story moving keeps the reader at the threshold of moral choice; rarely does it permit looking at the decision-making process. Even in incidents which might be revealing—Bernstein's sleepless night after their story implicating Haldeman in the operation of the illegal fund, or Woodward's distress as Judge Sirica jailed a fellow reporter while letting the two *Post* reporters go free for unprofessional behavior—personal struggles of these heroes are merely mentioned. . . . Woodward and Bernstein struck a right balance [between right and wrong], but I think they failed to openly address the moral choices they made. Could the larger questions have been asked in the fast moving narrative? Probably not. Does the need for a fast moving narrative justify leaving them out? Well, I would have preferred a slower, more introspective tale." It should be noted that in spite of such reservations both these critics recommended *All the President's Men*.

The most popular and intriguing aspect by far of *All the President's Men* was the identity of Woodward's highest source. Nicknamed "Deep Throat" by *Post* managing editor Howard Simons, this source steered the reporters through their investigation by corrolating and verifying their information in the best of cloak and dagger fashion. Woodward never revealed Deep Throat's identity because he said the source held a sensitive, high-level government job. Such a mysterious background fired the public's curiosity. Everyone wondered who he could be. Magazines ran articles debating several possibilities. Some fellow journalists scoffed that Woodward was just using an old journalist's trick—inventing Deep Throat, possibly from a composite of various sources—to create interest and to give his information more credibility. All the while, Woodward remained consistent in his defense of Deep Throat's existence. When the subject came up in an interview, and it always did, Woodward ignored the question and reprimanded the interviewer for trying to uncover another journalist's source. His total comment on Deep Throat was limited to: "Some day he'll come forth. If he were to die, I would feel obliged to

reveal his identity. Some day he'll write a really fascinating book. Carl and I would like to work on it with him."

After the completion of *All the President's Men*, the reporters turned their attention back to the final ranklings of Watergate. They began following six senators around for background for a book about the apparent upcoming impeachment trial of Richard Nixon. Work on that book was stopped short when it became obvious that the president was going to resign.

Woodward and Bernstein immediately began another book. This one was to be about the end of the Nixon administration. This subject was picked because the press, while covering the trials of former presidential aides and the ongoing congressional investigations, had done little reporting on the day-to-day operation of the White House. Woodward and Bernstein felt there was a lot of significant news there, overlooked by much of the rest of the press. The authors explained in the foreword to *The Final Days*: "Some of our most reliable sources said that the real story of those final days of the Nixon presidency had not been adequately told; to report that story and sort through the contradictions would require a concentrated effort of perhaps a year or more."

The authors, taking a leave of absence from the *Post*, hired an assistant and quickly fanned out a few days after Nixon's resignation to interview everyone associated with the White House who agreed to talk with them. It was decided beforehand that anyone who gave them information would remain anonymous, and that statements in the book would not be attributed to any of the sources. "We were convinced from covering the Watergate story," said Woodward, "that a guarantee of anonymity made the best opportunity to get the truth." Many sources demanded they not be identified before they consented to be interviewed, and many added that they would publically deny any cooperation after the book appeared. Three hundred and ninety-four people were interviewed in six months. Many of them gave the authors access to their notes, memos, diaries, and logs.

In allowing the sources complete anonymity, Woodward and Bernstein knew they would have to accept responsibility for the accuracy of every statement made in *The Final Days*. To protect their credibility they decided that at least two sources would have to confirm each incident before they would include it in the book. In the foreword, the authors explained, "[when we confronted people we felt] were slanted, self-serving, or otherwise untrustworthy; we used information from them only when we were convinced by more reliable sources of its accuracy." They also said: "If we obtained two versions, we resolved disagreements through re-interviewing. If this proved impossible, we left out any material we could not confirm." Woodward added: "Anything in the book has been checked and rechecked. The more sensitive the material, the higher the standard we applied. There are several things being disputed now that we have as many as six sources for." The cross-checking and confirming of all statements in the book was an enormous task of which the authors were quite proud.

A filing system was set up in an unused *Post* office to organize the mountains of interview material. Files were chronologically arranged anticipating the form the book was to take. Maps and charts were plotted to keep track of the participants. The book rapidly became, especially in the final two weeks of the Nixon presidency, an incredibly detailed, hour-by-hour account. The book's scope was extended from the final one hundred days of the Nixon administration to the last nine months. The authors realized they would have to go as far back as April 30, 1973—the day H. R. Haldeman and John Ehrlichman left the White House—to adequately explain the events. When all the information was in hand, confirmed, and filed, the writing began. That was in March, 1975. Bob Woodward wrote the first half of *The Final Days*, covering the period from April 30, 1973 to late July, 1974.

The publication of *The Final Days* developed into a media event. Highlights of the book had been syndicated by *Time, Newsweek,* and the *New York Daily News. Newsweek* did a two-part, thirty thousand-word excerpt containing many of the most controversial passages. The issue that included the second part was the fastest selling issue in *Newsweek*'s history. Like *All the President's Men, The Final Days* was a sure bet for commercial success. Upon release in 1976, it sold over one-half million copies in the first month. Another record was set in the book industry when paperback rights were sold at one and one half million dollars.

The initial critical response was a furious rage at the disclosure of so much personal information about the First Family. Some critics were aghast at the inclusion of what they called "backstairs gossip." John Osborne felt the relationships between the closest men around the president were reduced to "a barroom brawl." William Safire, the *New York Times* columnist, accused Woodward and Bernstein of ridiculing the President. Others lambasted both the book and the magazine excerpts as an unsavory attempt at profiteering. A reviewer for *Time* pointed out that this is a "troubling problem for journalists: where to draw the line of discretion or taste." "There are lines to be drawn," returned Woodward, "and we drew many of them. But it is impossible to keep out of the narrative the emotional realities that effected the decision-making procedure in the White House.... This is no laundered version of history. It includes material that is normally locked up for 50 years before being made public. It is an accurate account and will stand the test of time."

Questions of propriety aside, the critical response to *The Final Days* was lengthy and conflicting. Everyone seemed to dislike something, many critics taking special offense to the fanfare surrounding the book. However, each reviewer weighed his or her dislikes differently. Some damned the entire book; some left the overall judgements up to the reader; some praised the book, with reservations; the rest remained divided, praising parts, thoroughly unsatisfied with other parts.

The expected criticism about the procedures behind the book was quick in following the initial outbursts. In his discussion of the book, Max Lerner voiced the historian's opinion of anonymous sources: "I am ready to believe that in the vast majority of interviews [the authors] succeeded in checking and double-checking the information. But the self-interest of many of their sources—their public face, their desire to rid themselves of the Watergate taint and get a better role in the drama of history—seems to me an insurmountable obstacle, unless the reader knows who the sources are and can make his own assessment of them.... Which means they are asking us for blind trust. Not only must they have 'relations of trust' (as they put it) with their sources, but also they expect the reader to trust their assessment of the trustworthiness of the sources. It may have been the only way this particular kind of book could have been written, but the leap of faith it asks us for is more of a jump than most of us can make." Entrenched in the historian's sense of fairness, Learner asks, "how we would feel if Richard Nixon, in his . . . memoirs, were to make the same

claim to our leap of faith in trusting his anonymous sources?" Another critic lamented that *The Final Days* has given us 394 Deep Throats to contend with. Woodward disagreed. "The ultimate test," he said, "ought to be: Were our stories credible? Was our book credible? Have they held up?"

The people written about in *The Final Days* were reported to believe the account to be "basically accurate" and without "factual error"; yet most complained the book's total effect was an exaggeration, an overdramatization, and a distortion. These people and a few critics blamed the book's style. *The Final Days* was a narrative written from the omniscent point of view. John Hughes commented: "Woodward and Bernstein were not inside the heads of the participants at the moment crucial events took place, and yet the book unceasingly gives that impression." David Eisenhower said: "Distortion creeps in when they are attributing chains of thought to participants." J. Fred Buzhardt affirmed: "They write about my thought processes. I don't know how they can derive that, for honestly I can't myself." Illustrating the wide dissention among reviewers, Nicholas von Hoffman defended the point of view. "Assuming they have a good base for believing that so-and-so did say or think something close to that at the time, there's no reason to object. Using such devices as 'he thought,' 'it seemed to her,' etc., may make the narrative flow more easily and there's no need to think history has to be dull to be good."

Von Hoffman was far more concerned with the book's procedures. He, in turn, criticized the requirement that two sources confirm each incident. "This two-source principle must be a hold over from daily journalism. You can't be successfully sued for libel if you show that you took the pains to get information from two different sources. That's good in the courtroom but not in the history books. Are you really going to say something didn't happen because there's only one witness?" John Osborne, who called *The Final Days* "the worst job of nationally noted reporting that I've observed during 49 years in the business," complained: "In this book, they profess to report only what they've been told by 'at least two people.' That is crap. What second source could confirm that Henry Kissinger, Fred Buzhardt, David Gergen, Pat Buchanan, Leonard Garment, Ronald Ziegler—naming a few of the many who are thus depicted—'thought' this or that in an elevator, during a dinner or during an office conversation? Some of the best stories I've ever gotten were known to one person only, the person who told me. Woodstein [an often used compound of the co-authors names] must know it's crap. The fact that they persist in the fiction in this book is a sign of insecurity. It supports the perhaps patronizing but in my opinion fair judgment that they comprehended the evil of Watergate and not the totality of the situations, relationships, and motivations of the many of the people who figure in the book."

Von Hoffman also disagreed with the decision to leave out material from untrustworthy sources and material which couldn't be confirmed. "That solves the problem. You eliminate all conflict, uncertainty and ambiguity. Can you imagine how different, how much better, a book they could have written if they had included some of this material?"

The Final Days was called a "nonfiction novel" by one critic, symptomatic of the difficulty critics had trying to categorize the book. It was also described as "investigative journalism," "instant history," "political reporting," "accusatory journalism," and "hot history." Criticism came from two camps—that of history and that of journalism—and both camps found shortcomings judging by their standards and their requirements. Von Hoffman said: "To this Woodward and Bernstein are entitled to complain they're being critized for not writing a book they never intended to write. Nevertheless if all they wanted to do was write the simple, human, and moving story of one man's family they should have written a novel, because by giving us a depoliticised version of these momentously political events they're making a statement whether they're aware of it or not." "But," disagreed Michael Janeway, "that's not Woodward and Bernstein's story. They're not moralists. If the complete story of the Nixon Administration has any morals (in the Aesopian sense), I doubt that more than a handful of indicted or unindicted co-conspirators or sources close to them know right down to the bottom line what they are. Woodward and Bernstein have no pretensions to being anything but reporters. . . . It has been their strength to report what they could get their hands on, ex-police reporters that they are; to find sources to back it up, and to persuade their editors to publish it."

BIOGRAPHICAL/CRITICAL SOURCES: Time, April 22, 1974, December 30, 1974, April 12, 1976, May 3, 1976; *New York Times Book Review,* June 9, 1974; *Philadelphia Bulletin,* July 10, 1974; *Miami Herald,* July 17, 1974; *Newsweek,* April 12, 1976; *New Republic,* April 24, 1976; *Publisher's Weekly,* April 26, 1976; *Christian Science Monitor,* May 19, 1976; *Saturday Review,* May 29, 1976; *Atlantic,* June, 1976; *New York Review of Books,* June 10, 1976; *The Final Days,* Simon & Schuster, 1976.

*   *   *

WORLINE, Bonnie Bess 1914-

PERSONAL: Born August 3, 1914, in El Dorado, Kan.; daughter of Robert H. (an attorney) and Grace (a teacher and social worker; maiden name, Miller) Worline; married Irvill Courtner King (a clergyman and teacher), March 27, 1937; children: Courtner Worline, April Marian (Mrs. Donald Schirmer), Waveland Irvill Robert. *Education:* University of Chicago, A.B., 1935; University of Pittsburgh, M.A., 1945; University of Kansas, further graduate study, 1951-60. *Politics:* Liberal. *Religion:* Protestant. *Home:* 279 J St., Brawley, Calif. 92227. *Office:* Department of English, San Diego State University, 720 Heber, Calexico, Calif. 92213.

CAREER: Hammond Christian Center, Hammond, Ind., resident teacher, 1937; Rankin Christian Center, Rankin, Pa., resident teacher, 1938-40; KCKN-Radio, Kansas City, Kan., continuity editor, 1942-44; Gorham State College, Gorham, Maine, instructor in English, 1946-51, head of department; University of Kansas, Lawrence, instructor in English, 1951-61; San Diego State University, Calexico, Calif., assistant professor of English, 1964—. Director of special education for a high school in Brawley, Calif., 1961-70; director of Hipass Camp for the Retarded; member of local Area Health Planning Commission and Mental Health Association. *Member:* National Council of Teachers of English, California Teachers Association (president, 1965-67), California College and University Faculty Association, Writers Group (Imperial Valley), Imperial Valley Association for the Retarded (organizer).

WRITINGS: Sod House Adventure (juvenile), Longmans, 1956, reissued as *The Children Who Stayed Alone,* Scholastic Book Services, 1965. Author of novelettes, published serially in *Chicago Daily News.* Contributor to magazines and newspapers. Editor of *IMP* (at San Diego State University), 1974-76.

WORK IN PROGRESS: Sod Schoolhouse, a sequel to *The Children Who Stayed Alone; Mythology of the Western World,* for high school students; *Grease the Inside of the Pan!,* a manual for people who work with older retarded children; *What Color Is God's Skin?,* fiction; *Meredith,* novel; *Manzanita Chronicles,* novel; *Defender of Her People: A Biography; Primer of English Composition for Confused Adults.*

SIDELIGHTS: Bonnie Worline writes: "I was born of educated, pioneer-stock parents with a large, close-knit family clan in the background. Winters were spent in Kansas City, summers in the country at family homesteads sharing life with cousins, and at our own summer home in Missouri on the edge of the Ozark region, where I made friends with an entirely different group of people. Sharing daily activities with a large variety of friends, both adults and children, stimulated my interest in learning all sorts of facts and skills, and in telling about them.

"My long-anticipated period of more freedom for writing approaches, although I still accumulate new experiences. The small branch campus of San Diego State University, where I am in charge of English, is four blocks from the Mexican border, in a reclaimed desert area of lush farming lands as flat as the Kansas prairies. Our school has a high percentage of Mexican-Americans, some Mexicans who walk across the border, many valley descendants of immigrants from Japan, China, India, and dust-bowl Oklahoma. We have many older people finishing degrees, professionals of various sorts upgrading their preparation, and bored people seeking enrichment. Every student tends to be a fascinating story.

"Always I have been interested and involved in all the household arts and skills. With my family I have remodeled and decorated old houses, upholstered salvaged furniture, gardened for food, fun, and exercise, continued my work with the education of pre-schoolers. I have been concerned with Special Education, especially of the retarded and of the gifted. I have been active in camping, from family camping . . . to institutional camping. . . . In 1975 I was resident at a camp for children of the very wealthy. Every one of these activities reveals stories which urge recording.

"Pervading all my interests, however, is the lifetime yearning to help children share the delights of reading. All children—the ordinary and extraordinary, the seeing and the blind, the retarded, and especially the gifted (who are often the most educationally deprived of all students). I am saddened by the many children who have meager access to books, whose mass-production oriented schools deprive them of adequate teaching so that they never learn to enjoy reading."

*   *   *

WORTIS, Avi
(Avi)

PERSONAL: Given name is pronounced Ah-vee; son of Joseph (a physician) and Helen (Zunser) Wortis; married wife, Joan (a weaver), November 1, 1963; children: Shaun, Kevin. *Education:* University of Wisconsin, Madison, B.A., 1959, M.A., 1962; Columbia University, M.S.L.S., 1964. *Home:* 89 West Bridge St., New Hope, Pa. 18938. *Agent:* Dorothy Markinko, McIntosh & Otis, Inc., 475 Fifth Ave., New York, N.Y. 10017. *Office:* Roscoe L. West Library, Trenton State College, Trenton, N.J. 08625.

CAREER: New York Public Library, New York, N.Y., librarian for Theatre Collection, 1962-70; Trenton State College, Trenton, N.J., librarian, 1970—. *Member:* Authors Guild, Mystery Writers of America. *Awards, honors: Snail Tale* was named one of the best books of the year by British Book Council, 1973.

WRITINGS: (Contributor) *Performing Arts Resources,* Drama Books, 1974.

All for children; all under name Avi: *Things That Sometimes Happened,* Doubleday, 1970; *Snail Tale: The Adventures of a Rather Snail,* Pantheon, 1972; *No More Magic* (novel), Pantheon, 1975; *Captain Grey* (novel), Pantheon, 1977; *Emily Upham's Revenge* (novel), Pantheon, in press.

Contributor to library journals.

WORK IN PROGRESS: Henry Decides!, for children, under name Avi; a history of American children's literature.

SIDELIGHTS: Wortis writes: "I was born into a family with a writing tradition. Two great-grandfathers had been writers. My grandmother wrote. My parents aspired to become writers too. With a house full of books, being read to every night, a near-by library, the idea that writing was a splendid thing to do could hardly fail to make its mark on me.

"Not surprisingly I was a big reader, reading all sorts of things, children's books, adult books, and not the least, comic books. Beyond reading, my grandparents were excellent story tellers, and my mother read to me and my twin sister (the poet, Emily Ledier) nightly. I can even recall telling my own tales of adventure to a slightly younger cousin when quite young. I do believe that if you want to be a writer you have to read a lot.

"Despite this background my first desire was to become an airplane designer, then a biologist. After my junior year in high-school my parents were informed that I was in desperate need of a tutor for somehow I had never taken the time to learn to write or to spell.

"That summer I met every day with a wonderful teacher who not only taught me writing basics, but also instilled in me the conviction that I wanted to be a writer myself. Perhaps it was stubbornness! It was generally agreed that was one thing I could not possible do!

"My journey to children's literature was not direct. First it was the theatre, playwriting. Then it was writing novels for adult readers. In the meantime I had all kinds of jobs: sign printer (sometimes with spelling mistakes), carpenter, theatre coach, a whole host of jobs I never did with much satisfaction or success.

"At last I found an opportunity to work in a library. I was home at last! There I found no conflict between my desire to write and the demands of good librarianship. Quickly, I enrolled in library school, attending night classes. I still work as a librarian as well as write, so I am surrounded by books, morning, noon, and night.

"Even then it was only when I had children of my own and had begun to invent stories for them that I thought of writing children's books. Once begun I soon left other writing interests and concentrated on books for young people.

"While I am a fast writer, and never at a loss for ideas, I do a very great deal of re-writing, over and over again. I'm never convinced I can't improve a book, be it only a word or two.

"After writing my books a number of times I try them out on my children. Their reactions are always useful. More re-writing and my wife is asked to criticize. More re-writing and then visits to local school rooms. More re-writing! Then to my agent. More re-writing. Then to the publisher. Actually, I do my least re-writing then.

"The history of children's literature fascinates me, and from time to time I teach college courses or speak to groups about it. When I have the time I visit flea markets and used book stores for I am building up a collection of children's books. It makes me proud to put my own books in the midst of them all!"

* * *

WOUDENBERG, Paul Richard   1927-

PERSONAL: Born September 1, 1927, in Highland Park, Ill.; son of John A. and Rosina (Maechtle) Woudenberg; married Emily Wiltse (a reference librarian), May 5, 1967; children: Mary C., Elizabeth L. *Education:* Occidental College, A.B., 1949; Boston University, S.T.B., 1954, Ph.D., 1959. *Home address:* P.O. Box 1334, Pebble Beach, Calif. 93953. *Office address:* P.O. Box 2205, Carmel, Calif. 93921.

CAREER: Ordained Methodist minister, 1949; pastor of Methodist church in Los Angeles, Calif., 1954-61, in Long Beach, Calif., 1961-68, and in Santa Monica, Calif., 1969-74; Church of the Wayfarer, Carmel, Calif., pastor, 1975—. Lecturer at University of California, Los Angeles, 1974—, and University of California, Santa Cruz, 1977. Chief class judge at Pebbles Beach Concourse.

WRITINGS: Ford in the Thirties, Petersen, 1976.

WORK IN PROGRESS: Ford in the Forties; Ford in the Twenties; The Lincoln Motor Car.

* * *

WRIGHT, Arthur Frederick   1913-1977

December 3, 1913—August 11, 1976; American author, history professor at Yale University, and leading scholar in Chinese studies specializing in social and intellectual history of the pre-modern era. During World War II, he spent two and one-half years in a Japanese prison camp. He died in New London, Conn. Obituaries: *New York Times,* August 14, 1976.

* * *

WRIGHT, Benjamin Fletcher   1900-1976

February 8, 1900—November 28, 1976; American educator, author, and authority on constitutional law. He died in Austin, Tex. Obituaries: *New York Times,* November 30, 1976; *Current Biography,* March, 1977.

* * *

WRIGHT, Linda Raney   1945-

PERSONAL: Born April 10, 1945, in San Diego, Calif.; daughter of Ralph D. (in U.S. Air Force) and Laura (a nurse; maiden name, Powell) Raney; married Russell Sims Wright (a college lecturer), May 24, 1975. *Education:* University of California, Berkeley, A.B., 1976. *Residence:* Crestline, Calif.

CAREER: Writer and public speaker, 1972—.

WRITINGS: Raising Children, Tyndale House, 1975. Contributor to popular magazines, including *Ladies' Home Journal* and *Decision,* and to religious magazines.

WORK IN PROGRESS: A book aimed at affecting social issues in the United States.

SIDELIGHTS: Linda Wright comments: "I believe the general public needs to see God's viewpoint on subjects from the Scriptures."

WRIGHT, Russel 1904-1976

April 3, 1904—December 21, 1976; American industrial designer, author, and originator of Washington, D.C.'s Summer-in-the-Parks program (to encourage citizens to make use of the parks). His early career centered around stage and furniture design; many Wright designs are part of permanent collections in the Museum of Modern Art, the Cooper-Hewitt Museum, the Smithsonian Institution, and the Metropolitan Museum. He died in New York City. Obituaries: *Washington Post,* December 25, 1976.

* * *

WYLIE, Craig 1908-1976

March 11, 1908—December 6, 1976; American editor with Houghton Mifflin publishing house. He died in Cambridge, Mass. Obituaries: *New York Times,* December 8, 1976.

* * *

WYNN-JONES, Michael 1941-

PERSONAL: Born September 17, 1941, in Pentre, Wales; son of Edward (a priest) and Dilys (a teacher; maiden name, Spenser) Wynn-Jones; married Delia Smith (a culinary journalist and television broadcaster), September, 1971. *Education:* Worcester College, Oxford, B.A. (honors), 1964. *Home address:* Stowmarket, Suffolk, England.

CAREER: Nova, London, England, assistant editor, 1965-68; *Daily Mirror,* London, England, deputy editor, 1969-70; *Spectator,* London, England, associate editor, 1970-71; editorial consultant and writer, 1971—. *Awards, honors:* Frank Luther Mott Award, 1976, for *The Cartoon History of the American Revolution.*

WRITINGS: The Cartoon History of Britain, Macmillan, 1971; *Lloyds of London,* Hastings House, 1973; *A Newspaper History of the World,* Morrow, 1974; *The Cartoon History of the American Revolution,* Putnam, 1976; *The World One Hundred Years Ago,* Mackay, 1976; *Deadline Disaster,* Regnery, 1976; *The Cartoon History of the Monarchy,* Macmillan, 1977. Contributor to British publications, including *Radio Times* and *Observer.* Editor of *Twentieth Century,* 1966-71.

WORK IN PROGRESS: A biography of George Cruikshank, for Macmillan, completion expected in 1978; a history of British magazines, London Editions, 1979.

SIDELIGHTS: Wynn-Jones comments: "Basically my interest is in *visual* history; e.g., political cartoons, newspapers, photographs, etc., which I try to use as primary historical sources." *Avocational interests:* Cricket, travel, food and wine.

* * *

WYNTER, Edward (John) 1914-

PERSONAL: Born January 24, 1914, in England; son of Edward (a physiotherapist) and Ida (an actress; maiden name, Thomson) Wynter; married Norah Marsh, December 1, 1945; children: John Howard. *Education:* Attended Marine School of South Shields, 1930-35; College of Craft Education, M.C.C.Ed. *Politics:* "Moderate." *Religion:* Church of England. *Home:* 24 West End Ave., Three Bridges, Crawley, Sussex RH10 1SJ, England.

CAREER: Has worked as a marine engineering apprentice, assistant planning engineer for DeHavilland Aricraft Factory, and teacher of crafts, all in England; has worked at a school in Crawley, England, as a metalwork teacher, teacher of geometry and drawing, 1968-76, part-time teacher, 1976—, and head of technical department. *Military service:* Royal Navy, engine room artificer; served in Norway, West Indies, and North and South America. *Member:* Assistant Masters Association.

WRITINGS—For young people: *Metalcraft,* Longman Group, 1966; (editor) Foong Kee Yoong, *Woodwork, Metalwork, and Related Drafting,* Longman Group, 1968; *Woodwork,* Longman Group, 1970; *Using Woodwork Tools,* A. & C. Black, 1974.

WORK IN PROGRESS: Reference Book of Tools, completion expected in 1978; *Technical Drawing,* 1979.

SIDELIGHTS: Wynter writes: "During my early years in teaching, woodwork was the traditional, well established major craft taught in schools. There was a little elementary metalwork being taught in some schools but on the whole this was limited to simple work usually done in a corner of the woodwork room, and more of a sideline. The school courses I planned were as broad as possible, bearing in mind the educational needs of the pupils. Wrought iron work, foundry work, tool making, art metalwork and jewellry were taken to various stages but the accent was on model engineering, and many simple working model steam engines and electric motors were made.

"I consider myself most fortunate to have enjoyed my work so much. The vocational interests of pupils have often been awakened and quite a lot of boys and a few girls have gone into industry to follow courses of training both at the bench and the drawing board.

"Man is a tool-using animal and most people enjoy using their hands and making things. Practical activity balances book learning and makes for a complete person. Increased leisure and mass production are two good reasons why people need to learn how to design and make things for themselves. It is a most satisfying and enjoyable experience to create beautiful objects, and a rewarding experience to arouse and guide this interest in others."

AVOCATIONAL INTERESTS: Gardening, photography, drawing and painting (water colors and oils), "tinkering about at the workbench," "country walks with my wife and our Yorkshire terrier."

* * *

YAFFE, Richard 1903-
(Ben Chanan)

PERSONAL: Born June 10, 1903, in Reading, Pa.; son of Hyman (a glazer) and Ella (Pearlman) Yaffe; married Sara Mishler (an art dealer), June 10, 1928; children: Marc. *Education:* Boston University, A.B., Harvard University, M.A., 1925. *Religion:* Jewish. *Home:* 301 West 108th St., New York, N.Y. 10025. *Office:* United Nations, Room 306, Press Section, New York, N.Y. 10017.

CAREER: Atlantic City Times, Atlantic City, N.J., staff member, 1926; editor and publisher of *Bucks County Independent,* 1927-29; *Philadelphia Inquirer,* Philadelphia, Pa., staff member, 1929-35; *New York Post,* New York City, worked on financial desk, 1935-37; *New York Journal-American,* New York City, copy chief, 1937-40; *PM* (newspaper), New York City, foreign editor, 1940-48; *New York Star,* New York City, news editor, 1948-49; Columbia Broadcasting System (CBS), New York City, special East European correspondent, 1949; *Al Hamishmar* (newspaper), Israel, American correspondent, 1949—; *London Jewish Chronicle,* London, England, New York and United Nations correspondent, 1955—. Notable assignments include coverage of the Greek civil war, Paris Peace Conference, and various national political conventions. Lecturer on journalism and foreign affairs. *Member:* World Union of Jewish Journalists, Foreign Press Association (past president), United Nations Correspondents Association, Overseas Press Club, American Zionist Federation (member of executive committee), Jewish National Fund (member of board), Americans for Progressive Israel (national council chairman), Society of the Silurians, Deadline Club, Sigma Delta Chi.

WRITINGS: (Editor) Raphael Mahler, David Flasker, and Daniel Ben-Naham, *Borochov for Our Day: The Socialist-Zionist View of the Jewish People,* Progressive Zionist League, 1958. Contributor to *National Jewish Monthly, Hadassah, Moment, Nation,* sometimes under pseudonym. Editor of *Israel Horizons;* associate editor of *The Jewish Week* and *Aufbau* (New York).

WORK IN PROGRESS: A Short History of American Jewry, for Shengold.

* * *

YALDEN, Derek William 1940-

PERSONAL: Born November 4, 1940, in Walton-on-Thames, Surrey, England; son of William Henry and Lilian (Oliver) Yalden; married Patricia Elizabeth Brayley (a technician), July 14, 1972. *Education:* University of London, B.Sc., 1962, Ph.D., 1966. *Politics:* Conservative. *Religion:* Atheist. *Office:* Department of Zoology, University of Manchester, Manchester MI3 9PL, England.

CAREER: University of Manchester, Manchester, England, lecturer in vertebrate zoology, 1965—. Has appeared on local and national radio programs. *Member:* British Herpetological Society, Mammal Society, Fauna Preservation Society, American Society of Mammalogists, Derbyshire Naturalists Trust, Surrey Naturalists Trust, Peakland Archaeological Society, Derbyshire Ornithological Society, London Natural History Society, Lancashire and Cheshire Fauna Society, Northwest Staffordshire Field Club.

WRITINGS: (With P. A. Morris) *The Lives of Bats,* David & Charles, 1975. Contributor of about thirty articles to scientific journals and to *Naturalist.*

WORK IN PROGRESS: Mammals of Ethiopia, with a checklist; *Natural History of the Peak District.*

SIDELIGHTS: Yalden has made four trips to Ethiopia to collect specimens, including the Great Abbai Expedition in 1968. He believes that the "ecological approach to conservation" is of paramount importance.

* * *

YOCHELSON, Samuel 1906(?)-1976

1906(?)—November 12, 1976; American psychiatrist, author, and internationally recognized authority on the criminal mind. Yochelson's multi-volume work on the criminal personality illustrates that individual personalities and value systems, and not merely social environment and other outside elements, are important keys to understanding the criminal. He died in St. Louis, Mo. Obituaries: *Washington Post,* November 13, 1976.

* * *

YOUNG, Donald Ramsey 1898-1977

July 5, 1898—March 28, 1977; American sociologist and author of books in his field. He died in Allentown, Pa. Obituaries: *New York Times,* April 22, 1977.

* * *

YOUNG, James V(an) 1936-

PERSONAL: Born June 12, 1936, in Waterloo, Iowa; son of Robert A. (a retail fuel dealer) and Edith (Van Houten) Young; married Virginia Hudson, June 11, 1959; children: Ann Elizabeth, James Hudson. *Education:* University of Iowa, B.A., 1958, J.D., 1960, Ph.D., 1964. *Home:* 320 Goodrich Dr., Warrensburg, Mo. 64093. *Office:* Department of Political Science, Central Missouri State University, Warrensburg, Mo. 64093.

CAREER: University of Iowa, Iowa City, instructor in political science, spring, 1964; St. Olaf College, Northfield, Minn., assistant professor of political science, 1964-68; Central Missouri State University, Warrensburg, assistant professor, 1968-71, associate professor, 1971-75, professor of political science, 1975—, head of department, 1971—.

MEMBER: North American Society for Sport History, Amateur Athletic Union (Missouri Valley), Missouri Political Science Association, Iowa Lettermen's Club, Central Missouri State University Century Club, Central Missouri State University Booster Club, Warrensburg Tiger Booster Club. *Awards, honors:* Physical fitness leadership award from town of Warrensburg, Mo., 1974.

WRITINGS: (With Arthur F. McClure) *Remembering Their Glory: Sports Heroes of the 1940's,* A. S. Barnes, 1977.

WORK IN PROGRESS: Research on censorship of literature in elementary and secondary schools, and on its relationship to constitutional law.

* * *

YOUNG, (Rodney Lee) Patrick (Jr.) 1937-

PERSONAL: Born October 19, 1937, in Ladysmith, Wis.; son of Rodney Lee (a lawyer) and Janice (a medical technologist; maiden name, Wolf) Young; married Leah Ruth Figelman (a reporter), October 8, 1966; children: Justine Rebecca. *Education:* University of Colorado, B.A. (cum laude), 1960. *Home:* 7711 Hyacinth Court, Laurel, Md. 20810. *Office: National Observer,* 11501 Columbia Pike, Silver Spring, Md. 20910.

CAREER: United Press International (UPI), Washington, D.C., reporter, 1960-63; *National Observer,* Silver Spring, Md., staff science writer, 1965—. *Military service:* U.S. Navy, 1963-65. *Member:* Nashville Songwriters Association International, National Association of Science Writers. *Awards, honors:* Journalism award from Society of Abdominal Surgeons, 1972; Howard W. Blakeslee Award from American Heart Association, 1970; award in physics and astronomy from American Institute of Physics and U.S. Steel Foundation, 1974; Russell Cecil Award from Arthritis Foundation, 1976; James T. Grady Award from American Chemical Society, 1977.

WRITINGS: Old Abe: The Eagle Hero (juvenile), Prentice-Hall, 1965; *Drifting Continents, Shifting Seas: An Introduction to Plate Tectonics* (young adult), F. Watts, 1976. Contributor to popular magazines, including *Harper's, Saturday Review,* and *Family Circle.*

* * *

YOURCENAR, Marguerite 1913-

PERSONAL: Born June 8, 1913, in Brussels, Belgium; originally French citizen; naturalized U.S. citizen, 1947; name legally changed in 1947; daughter of Michel and Fernande (de Cartier de Marchienne) de Crayencour. *Education:* Educated privately. *Residence:* Northeast Harbor, Maine.

CAREER: Writer. *Member:* Academie Royale de langue et de litterature francaises de Belgique, American Civil Rights Association. *Awards, honors:* Prix Femina-Vacaresco, 1951, for *Memoires d'Hadrien;* Page One Award from Newspaper Guild of New York, 1955; L.T.D. from Smith College, 1961; Prix Combat, 1963, for ensemble of work; Prix Femina, 1968, for *L'oeuvre au noir;* L.T.D. from Bowdoin College, 1968; L.T.D. from Colby College, 1972; Prix Monaco, 1973, for ensemble of work; Grand Prix National des Lettres from French Ministry of Culture, 1975.

WRITINGS—In English: *Le coup de grace* (novel), Gallimard, 1939, translation by author and Grace Frick published as *Coup de Grace,* Farrar, 1957; *Memoires d'Hadrien* (novel), Plon, 1951, translation by author and Frick published as *Memoirs of Hadrian,* Farrar, 1954; *L'oeuvre au noir* (novel), Gallimard, 1968, translation by the author and Frick published as *The Abyss,* Farrar, 1976.

Other: *La nouvelle Eurydice* (novel), Grasset, 1931; *Pindare,* Grasset, 1932; *Denier du reve* (novel), Grasset, 1934; *Nouvelles Orientales* (novel), Gallimard, 1938; *Les songes et les sorts,* Grasset, 1938; *Electra; ou, La Chute des masques,* Plon, 1954; (author of critique and translator from the Greek with Constantin Dimaras) *Presentation critique de Constantin Cavafy, 1863-1933,* Gallimard, 1958; *Sous benefice d'inventaire,* Gallimard, 1962; *Le mystere d'-Alceste, suivi de qui n'a pas son minotaure?,* Plon, 1963; (translator from the English) *Fleuve profond, somber riviere: Le Negro spirituals,* Gallimard, 1964; *Alexis; ou, Le Traite du vain combat* (novel), revised edition, Plon, 1965; (author of critique, and translator from the English) *Presentation critique d'Hortense Flexner,* Gallimard, 1969; *Theatre* (plays), two volumes, Gallimard, 1971; *Souvenirs pieux,* Gallimard, 1974; *Feux* (poems), new edition, Gallimard, 1974.

Also author of *Les charities d'Alcippe* (poems), 1959. Translator of works by Henry James, Virginia Woolf, and ancient Greek poets. Contributor to French journals and periodicals, including *Le Monde, Le Figaro,* and *Nouvelle Revue Francaise.*

WORK IN PROGRESS: Archives du nord; the third volume of the trilogy *Le Labyrinthe du monde;* an anthology of Greek poetry in French translation.

SIDELIGHTS: Marguerite Yourcenar has been called the foremost practioner of the formidable genre of historical fiction. According to Joseph Epstein, "historical fiction dependably degenerates into a costume ball, at which feeble invention waltzes with false fact." But Yourcenar, he continues, "brings to the genre scholarship and imagination such as to raise it to a position of art."

Although Yourcenar's *Memoirs of Hadrian* is widely recognized as a classic in the genre, her latest historical novel, *The Abyss,* fares somewhat less well with critics. Arthur A. Cohen has noticed the protagonist Zeno, who is a physician and alchemist in 16th century Europe, is not firmly rooted in time or place. Cohen says that Yourcenar is not as interested in Zeno as much as in "the argument of an intelligence able to parse the body in its turmoil, explore the heart in its surging, explicate the mind in the midst of its anxiety and suffering. It is argument, not imagination that marks *The Abyss* in a totally apposite and surprising way to her earlier *Memoirs of Hadrian.* Hadrian is in the round, whereas Zeno is a tapestry figure fabricated of millions of colored threads and miniscule knots each accurately toned and tied, which despite its complexity, is still flat, without perspective and depth of field."

Frank Kermode describes Zeno as "the second deity in this author's cult of the full man, endlessly inquiring, every skeptical, considerate of the body as of the spirit, of the future as well as the present. Does he represent as well as Hadrian this ideal maturity? The answer must be, I think, that this book works less well than its predecessor. Its best chapters are static, speculative; but they are few in relation to the rest, which have to report action and conversation. Perhaps, Zeno is himself inescapably inferior to Hadrian; he is a composite, whom history has not stamped on coins, portraits, and cities."

Still, *The Abyss* is viewed by critics as a substantial achievement. Epstein comments, "Poetry, thought, and learning are the ingredients out of which *The Abyss* has been made. Literary ambition has been added, for there is very little that Mme. Yourcenar does not attempt in this novel, and almost all of what she does attempt, she brings off handsomely."

Kermode concludes, in appreciation of Yourcenar's accomplishment: "Years of passionate scholarship and long dedication to an ideal of humanity as limited, yet in the end, expressed by history, went to its making. The author deserves her special place in the story."

BIOGRAPHICAL/CRITICAL SOURCES: New York Times Book Review, July 11, 1976; *Book World,* July 11, 1976; *New York Review of Books,* October 14, 1976; *Hudson Review,* winter, 1976-77.

*   *   *

ZEITLIN, Solomon   1888(?)-1976

1888(?)—December 28, 1976; Russian-born professor of rabbinics and history, and author of more than four hundred articles and books in his field. He was known for disputing majority opinion and often drew on original sources in Hebrew, Aramaic, Latin, Greek, Slavonic, Russian, Yiddish, German, French, Arabic, and English to support his views. He died in Philadelphia. Obituaries: *New York Times,* December 30, 1976.

*   *   *

ZEMAN, Zbynek Anthony Bohuslav   1928-

PERSONAL: Born October 18, 1928, in Prague, Czechoslovakia; son of Jaroslav and Ruzena (Petnikova) Zeman; married Anthea Sarah Collins, June, 1956; children: Adam, Alexander, Sarah-Sophia. *Education:* University of Prague, student, 1947-48; University of London, B.A. (honors), 1953; Oxford University, D.Phil., 1956. *Home:* 43 Flask Walk, London N.W.3, England. *Office:* University of Lancaster, Bailrigg, Lancaster, England.

CAREER: Oxford University, Oxford, England, research fellow in St. Antony's College, 1959-62; University of St. Andrews, Scotland, lecturer in modern history, 1963-70; Amnesty International, director of research, 1970-73; University of Lancaster, Bailrigg, England, professor of central and southeastern European studies and head of department, 1976—. Director of European Cooperation Research Group, 1973—. Senior consultant to Canadean Ltd. *Member:* Writers and Scholars International (member of council).

WRITINGS: (Editor) *Germany and the Revolution in Russia, 1915-1918: Documents from the Archives of the German Foreign Ministry,* Oxford University Press, 1958; *The*

Break-Up of the Habsburg Empire, 1914-1918: A Study in National and Social Revolution, Oxford University Press, 1961; *Nazi Propaganda,* Oxford University Press, 1964, 2nd edition, 1973; (with Winifred B. Scharlau) *Freibeuter der Revolution: Parvus-Helphand, eine politische Biographie,* Verlag Wissenschaft und Politik, 1964, English translation published as *The Merchant of Revolution: The Life of Alexander Israel Helphand (Parvus), 1867-1924,* Oxford University Press, 1965; (editor and author of introduction) Maxim Gorky, *Lenin: A Biographical Essay,* Oxford University Press, 1967; *Prague Spring: A Report on Czechoslovakia, 1968,* Hill & Wang, 1969.

A Diplomatic History of the First World War, Weidenfeld & Nicolson, 1971, published in the United States as *The Gentlemen Negotiators: A Diplomatic History of the First World War,* Macmillan, 1971; *Twilight of the Habsburgs: The Collapse of the Austro-Hungarian Empire,* American Heritage Press, 1971; *The Masaryks: The Making of Czechoslovakia,* Barnes & Noble, 1976; (with Jan Zoubek) *Comecon Oil and Gas,* Financial Times, 1977.

Member of foreign editorial staff of *The Economist,* 1959-62.

WORK IN PROGRESS: Research on East European agriculture and on East-West relations.

SIDELIGHTS: Zeman writes: "I have been trained as an historian, though my interests moved more and more to international affairs and economics. Currently, practical manifestations of East-West relations are my chief concern, and, doubtless, one day I shall write about this subject, so rich in tension and in past and present misunderstanding."

*   *   *

ZEPKE, Brent Eric   1943-

PERSONAL: Born March 28, 1943, in Camden, N.J.; son of George W. (a businessman) and June (Stackhouse) Zepke; married Anne Whitaker, August 26, 1966; children: Chad Eric, Hollie Anne, Grant Austin. *Education:* University of North Carolina, B.S., 1967; Clemson University, M.S., 1969; University of Tennessee, J.D., 1973; Temple University, LL.M., 1977. *Residence:* Mount Laurel, N.J. *Office:* Gulf Oil Corp., 1 Presidential Blvd., Bala Cynwyd, Pa. 19004.

CAREER: Greenville Technical Institute, Greenville, S.C., instructor in industrial engineering, 1968-69; University of Tennessee, Knoxville, Tenn., instructor in statistics, 1969-71, instructor in business law, 1972-73, instructor in industrial and personnel management, 1971-74; Gulf Oil Corp., Bala Cynwyd, Pa., attorney, 1974—. Principal officer of Consulting Associates, Inc., 1973-74; corporate counsel and research director for Vicon, Inc. (real estate development firm), 1973-74; lecturer at Temple University, 1975-76.

MEMBER: American Bar Association (Labor Law Group), American Trial Lawyers Association, American Institute of Industrial Engineers, New Jersey Bar Association, Pennsylvania Bar Association, Tennessee Bar Association, District of Columbia Bar Association, Phi Alpha Delta. *Awards, honors:* American Jurisprudence Award from Lawyers Cooperative Publishing Co., 1973, for outstanding achievement in estate planning.

WRITINGS: Mathematical Models for Managers, Mulberry Grove, 1972, revised edition, 1973; *Industrial Management: A Numerical Approach,* Mulberry Grove, 1974; *Products and the Consumer,* American Legal Publications, 1975; *Labor Law,* Littlefield, 1976. Author of "Legal-

Ease," a column in *Knoxville,* 1973-74. Contributor to professional journals. Features editor of *General Issue,* 1971-72.

WORK IN PROGRESS: Business Statistics.

SIDELIGHTS: Zepke writes: "All my efforts . . . have been and are towards trying to assist people to maximize their potential, for their benefit as well as for the benefit of society. This maximization must include learning to work with all resources and, most importantly, with other people. The ideal situation would be where everyone has the freedom to succeed or fail on his own abilities and tastes and without inhibiting someone else'e right to do the same."

*   *   *

ZIMMERMAN, Bill   1940-

PERSONAL: Born December 26, 1940, in Chicago, Ill.; son of Sid and Jean (Weissman) Zimmerman. *Education:* University of Chicago, B.S., 1963, Ph.D., 1967. *Address:* c/o Swallow Press, 811 West Junior Ter., Chicago, Ill. 60613.

CAREER: Brooklyn College of the City University of New York, Brooklyn, N.Y., assistant professor of psychology, 1967-69; University of Chicago, Chicago, Ill., assistant professor of social sciences, 1970-71; Medical Aid for Indochina, Cambridge, Mass., national coordinator, 1972-73; national staff member of Indochina Peace Campaign, 1974-75; campaign manager for Tom Hayden's campaign for U.S. Senator from California, 1975-76; writer, 1976—.

WRITINGS: Airlift to Wounded Knee, Swallow Press, 1976.

*   *   *

ZIMMERMAN, William   1940-
(Bill Zimmerman)

PERSONAL: Born April 5, 1940, in Washington, D.C.; son of Clarence M. and Rachel (Dudley) Zimmerman; married Patricia Joan Moore, September 14, 1963; children: Heather Lynn, William Eric, Brad Moore, Christopher Mason. *Education:* Attended Oklahoma University, 1958-59, and George Washington University, 1959-60. *Politics:* Independent. *Home:* Via Cassia 929, Rome, Italy 00189. *Office:* Via Abruzzi 25, Rome, Italy 00187.

CAREER/WRITINGS: WTVR, Richmond, Va., reporter, 1961-63; WKBN-TV, Youngstown, Ohio, reporter, 1963-64; WTOP-TV, Washington, D.C., reporter, 1964-69; WHDH-TV, Boston, Mass., reporter, 1969-71; American Broadcasting Corp. (ABC News), correspondent in Washington, D.C., 1971-75; bureau chief and correspondent in Beirut, Lebanon, 1975-76, bureau chief and correspondent in Rome, Italy, 1976—. Notable assignments include coverage of Black Lung disease controversy in West Virginia, 1967, the national conventions of 1968, Chappaquiddick, 1969, Eagleton's and later Shriver's vice-presidential campaigns, the Watergate scandal, 1973-74, and Vice-President Ford during 1974. *Military service:* U.S. Army, 1960-61, became 2nd lieutenant.

*   *   *

ZMIJEWSKY, Boris   1946-

PERSONAL: Born December 14, 1946, in Regensburg, Germany; came to the United States in 1951, naturalized citizen, 1965; son of Pawlo and Anna (Butanko) Zmijewsky; married Debra Zuckerman, March 7, 1970; children: Peter. *Education:* Educated in secondary schools in New York, N.Y. *Home:* 1225 15th St., Fort Lee, N.J. 07024.

CAREER: Writer, 1969—. *Military service:* U.S. Army, 1966-68.

WRITINGS: (With brother, Steve Zmijewsky, and Mark Ricci) *The Films of John Wayne,* Citadel, 1970; (with S. Zmijewsky) *Elvis: The Films and Career of Elvis Presley,* Citadel, 1976. Author of film script, "KG's," 1974.

WORK IN PROGRESS: A film script, "Rituals."

AVOCATIONAL INTERESTS: Karate, mountain climbing.

* * *

ZUCKMAYER, Carl 1896-1977

December 27, 1896—January 18, 1977; German playwright, satirist, and author best known for his screenplay, "The Blue Angel," which launched Marlene Dietrich's acting career, and for his immensely popular comedy, "The Captain of Koepenick". His works were produced by theatres throughout Europe until Hitler banned his work from the German-speaking stage. He died in Visp, Switzerland. Obituaries: *New York Times,* January 19, 1977; *Time,* January 31, 1977.

* * *

ZUG, Margaret Philbrook 1945(?)-1976

1945(?)—September 8, 1976; American editor, employed by Grosset & Dunlap as managing editor. She died in Hanover, N.H. Obituaries: *New York Times,* August 9, 1976; *Publishers Weekly,* August 27, 1976.

CONTEMPORARY AUTHORS

INDEX (Volumes 1-72)

Including references to all entries in
Contemporary Authors Revised Volumes and Permanent Series†
Contemporary Literary Criticism, Volumes 1-7
Something About the Author, Volumes 1-12

A

A. A.
See Willis, (George) Anthony Armstrong
Aaker, David A(llen) 1938- ... 49-52
Aalto, (Hugo) Alvar (Henrik) 1898-1976 Obituary ... 65-68
Aardema, Verna (Norbera) 1911- ... 7-8R
See also SATA 4
Aaron, Benjamin 1915- ... 23-24R
Aaron, Chester 1923- ... 21-22R
See also SATA 9
Aaron, Daniel 1912- ... 13-14R
Aaron, James Ethridge 1927- . 23-24R
Aaronovitch, Sam 1919- ... 13-14R
Aarons, Edward S(idney) 1916-1975 Obituary ... 57-60
Aaronson, Bernard S(eymour) 1924- ... 29-32R
Aarsleff, Hans 1925- ... 21-22R
Aaseng, Rolf E(dward) 1923- ... 49-52
Abajian, James De Tar 1914- ... 65-68
Abarbanel, Karin 1950- ... 65-68
Abbaanano, Nicola 1901- ... 33-36R
Abbas, Khwaja Ahmad 1914- ... 57-60
Abbazia, Patrick 1937- ... 57-60
Abbe, Elfriede (Martha) 1919- 15-16R
Abbe, George (Bancroft) 1911- 25-28R
Abbey, Edward 1927- ... 45-48
Abbey, Merrill R. 1905- ... 1R
Abbot, Charles G(reeley) 1872-1973 Obituary ... 45-48
Abbott, Alice
See Borland, Kathryn Kilby and Speicher, Helen Ross S(mith)
Abbott, Anthony S. 1935- ... 17-18R
Abbott, Carl (John) 1944- ... 65-68
Abbott, Claude Colleer 1889- ... 7-8R
Abbott, Freeland K(night) 1919-1971 ... CAP-2
Earlier sketch in CA 25-28
Abbott, H(orace) Porter 1940- .. 45-48
Abbott, Jerry (Lynn) 1938- ... 45-48
Abbott, John J(amison) 1930- 17-18R
Abbott, John Janisen ... 17-18R
Abbott, Manager Henry
See Stratemeyer, Edward L.
Abbott, Martin 1922- ... 33-36R
Abbott, May L(aura) 1916- ... 9-10R
Abbott, R(obert) Tucker 1919- . 9-10R
Abbott, Raymond H(erbert) 1942- ... 57-60
Abbott, Richard H(enry) 1936- 33-36R
Abbott, Rowland A(ubrey) S(amuel) 1909- ... 53-56
Abbott, Sidney 1937- ... 41-44
Abbott, Walter M(atthew) 1923- ... 11-12R
Abboushi, W(asif) F(ahmi) 1931- ... 29-32R
Abcarian, Richard 1929- ... 33-36R
Abdallah, Omar
See Humbaraci, D(emir) Arslan
Abdel-Malek, Anouar 1924- .. 29-32R
Abdelsamad, Moustafa H(assan) 1941- ... 53-56
Abdul, Raoul 1929- ... 29-32R
See also SATA 12
Abe, Kobo 1924- ... 65-68
Abel, Alan (Irwin) 1928- ... 19-20R
Abel, Bob 1931- ... 65-68
Abel, Elie 1920- ... 61-64
Abel, Ernest L(awrence) 1943- .. 41-44
Abel, Jeanne 1937- ... 19-20R
Abel, Lionel 1910- ... 61-64
Abel, Raymond 1911- ... SATA-12
Abel, Reuben 1911- ... 37-40
Abel, Theodora M(ead) 1899- ... 57-60
Abel, Theodore 1896- ... 23-24R
Abell, George O(gden) 1927- .. 9-10R
Abell, Kathleen 1938- ... 49-52
See also SATA 9
Abella, Irving Martin 1940- ... 49-52
Abels, Jules 1913- ... 61-64
Abel-Smith, Brian 1926- ... 21-22R
Abelson, Raziel A. 1921- ... 11-12R
Abelson, Robert P(aul) 1928- ... 41-44
Abend, Norman A(nchel) 1931- 33-36R
Aber, William M(cKee) 1929- ... 57-60
Aberbach, Joel D(avid) 1940- ... 45-48
Aberg, Sherrill E. 1924- ... 21-22R
Aberle, David F(riend) 1918- . 21-22R
Aberle, John Wayne 1919- ... 1R
Aberle, Kathleen Gough 1925- 13-14R
Abernathy, David M(yles) 1933- ... 53-56
Abernathy, (M.) Elton 1913- .. 17-18R
Abernathy, M(abra) Glenn 1921- ... 13-14R
Abernethy, Francis Edward 1925- ... 21-22R
Abernethy, George Lawrence 1910- ... 2R
Abernethy, Peter L(ink) 1935- .. 69-72
Abernethy, Robert G(ordon) 1927- ... 21-22R
See also SATA 5
Abernethy, Thomas Perkins 1890- ... CAP-1
Earlier sketch in CA 19-20
Abisch, Roslyn Kroop 1927- .. 21-22R
See also SATA 9
Abisch, Roz
See Abisch, Roslyn Kroop
Ableman, Paul 1927- ... 61-64
Abler, Ronald 1939- ... 53-56
Abodaher, David J. (Naiph) 1919- ... 17-18R
Abrahall, Clare Hoskyns
See Hoskyns-Abrahall, Clare (Constance Drury)
Abraham, Claude K(urt) 1931- 23-24R
Abraham, Henry Julian 1921- ... 5-6R
Abraham, Willard 1916- ... 13-14R
Abraham, William E. 1934- .. 13-14R
Abraham, William I(srael) 1919- ... 25-28R
Abrahams, Howard Phineas 1904- ... 57-60
Abrahams, Peter (Henry) 1919- . 57-60
See also CLC 4
Abrahams, R(aphael) G(arvin) 1934- ... 25-28R
Abrahams, Robert David 1905- CAP-2
Earlier sketch in CA 33-36
Abrahams, Roger D. 1933- .. 11-12R
See also SATA 4
Abrahams, William Miller 1919- ... 61-64
Abrahamsen, David 1903- ... 65-68
Abram, H(arry) S(hore) 1931-1977 ... 29-32
Abramowitz, Jack 1918- ... 7-8R
Abrams, Charles 1901-1970 ... CAP-2
Earlier sketch in CA 23-24
Abrams, George J(oseph) 1918- ... 61-64
Abrams, M(eyer) H(oward) 1912- ... 57-60
Abrams, Peter D(avid) 1936- . 33-36R
Abrams, Richard M. 1932- ... 13-14R
Abrams, Sam(uel) 1935- ... 21-22R
Abramson, Doris E. 1925- ... 25-28R
Abramson, Harold J(ulian) 1934- ... 45-48
Abramson, Joan 1932- ... 25-28R
Abramson, Martin 1921- ... 49-52
Abramson, Michael 1944- ... 69-72
Abramson, Paul R(obert) 1937- ... 61-64
Abrash, Merritt 1930- ... 23-24R
Abrecht, Mary Ellen (Benson) 1945- ... 69-72
Abreu, Maria Isabel 1919- ... 45-48
Abse, Dannie 1923- ... 53-56
See also CLC 7
Abse, David Wilfred 1915- ... 49-52
Abshire, David M. 1926- ... 23-24R
Abt, Clark C(laus) 1929- ... 69-72
Abt, Lawrence Edwin 1915- .. 33-36R
Abu Jaber, Kamel S. 1932- ... 21-22R
Abu-Lughod, Ibrahim Ali 1929- . 5-6R
Abu-Lughod, Janet L(ouise) 1928- ... 65-68
Abun-Nasr, Jamil Miri 1932- ... 69-72
Academic Investor
See Reddaway, W(illiam) Brian
Accola, Louis W(ayne) 1937- . 29-32R
Ace, Goodman 1899- ... 61-64
Achard, George
See Torress, Tereska (Szwarc)
Achard, Marcel
See Ferreol, Marcel Auguste
Achebe, Chinua 1930- ... 4R
See also CLC 1, 3, 5, 7
Acheson, Dean (Gooderham) 1893-1971 ... CAP-2
Obituary ... 33-36R
Earlier sketch in CA 25-28
Acheson, Patricia Castles 1924- ... 3R
Achtemeier, Elizabeth (Rice) 1926- ... 17-18R
Achtemeier, Paul J(ohn) 1927- 17-18R
Achyut
See Birla, Lakshminiwas
Acker, Duane Calvin 1931- ... 33-36R
Acker, William R. B. 1910(?)-1974 Obituary ... 49-52
Ackerman, Bruce A. 1943- ... 53-56
Ackerman, Carl W. 1890-1970 Obituary ... 29-32R
Ackerman, Diane 1948- ... 57-60
Ackerman, Edward A. 1911-1973 Obituary ... 41-44
Ackerman, Eugene (Francis) 1888-1974 ... SATA-10
Ackerman, Gerald M(artin) 1928- ... 45-48
Ackerman, J. Mark 1939- ... 53-56
Ackerman, James S(loss) 1919- ... 9-10R
Ackerman, Nathan W(ard) 1908-1971 ... CAP-2
Earlier sketch in CA 29-32
Ackerman, Robert E(dwin) 1928- ... 45-48
Ackerson, Duane (Wright, Jr.) 1942- ... 33-36R
Ackland, Rodney 1908- ... 57-60
Ackley, Charles Walton 1913- ... 41-44
Ackley, Hugh Gardner 1915- ... 61-64
Ackley, Randall William 1931- ... 53-56
Ackoff, Russell L(incoln) 1919- . 41-44
Ackroyd, Peter R(unham) 1917- ... 25-28R
Ackworth, Robert Charles 1923- ... 5-6R
Acland, James H. 1917- ... 41-44
Acquaye, Alfred Allotey 1939- 25-28R
Acre, Stephen
See Gruber, Frank
Acred, Arthur 1926- ... 25-28R
Acton, Harold Mario Mitchell 1904- ... 4R
Acton, Jay 1949- ... 45-48
Acton, Thomas (Alan) 1948- ... 57-60
Aczel, Tamas 1921- ... 49-52
Adachi, Barbara (Curtis) 1924- .. 49-52
Adair, Ian 1942- ... 69-72
Adair, James R. 1923- ... 19-20R
Adair, John G(lenn) 1933- ... 49-52
Adair, Margaret Weeks ?-1971 . CAP-1
Earlier sketch in CA 13-14
See also SATA 10
Adam, Ben
See Drachman, Julian M(oses)
Adam, Cornel
See Lengyel, Cornel Adam
Adam, Helen 1909- ... 19-20R
Adam, Michael 1919- ... 53-56
Adam, Ruth (Augusta) 1907- . 23-24R
Adam, Thomas R(itchie) 1900- CAP-1
Earlier sketch in CA 19-20
Adamczewski, Zygmunt 1921- 15-16R
Adamec, Ludwig W(arren) 1924- ... 23-24R
Adamov, Arthur 1908-1970 ... CAP-2
Obituary ... 25-28R
Earlier sketch in CA 17-18
See also CLC 4
Adams, A. Don
See Cleveland, Philip Jerome
Adams, A. John 1931- ... 33-36R
Adams, Adrienne 1906- ... 49-52
See also SATA 8
Adams, Alice 1926- ... CLC-6
Adams, Anne H(utchinson) 1935- ... 41-44
Adams, Annette
See Rowland, D(onald) S(ydney)
Adams, Ansel (Easton) 1902- . 21-22R
Adams, Arthur E(ugene) 1917- .. 7-8R
Adams, Arthur Merrihew 1908- . 53-56
Adams, Betsy
See Pitcher, Gladys
Adams, Charles J(oseph) 1924- ... 17-18R
Adams, Christopher
See Hopkins, Kenneth
Adams, Cindy ... 23-24R
Adams, Clifton 1919- ... 13-14R
Adams, Clinton 1918- ... 33-36R
Adams, Don(ald Kendrick) 1925- ... 33-36R
Adams, E(lie) M(aynard) 1919- ... 3R
Adams, Elsie B(onita) 1932- ... 69-72
Adams, F(rank) Ramsay 1883-1963 ... 7-8R
Adams, Florence 1932- ... 49-52
Adams, Francis A(lexandre) 1874-1975 Obituary ... 61-64
Adams, Frank C(lyde) 1916- ... 69-72
Adams, George Worthington 1905- ... 41-44
Adams, Georgia Sachs 1913- ... 37-40
Adams, Graham, Jr. 1928- ... 17-18R
Adams, Harlen M(artin) 1904- . CAP-1
Earlier sketch in CA 13-14
Adams, Harriet S(tratemeyer) .. 19-20R
See also SATA 1
Adams, Harrison
See Stratemeyer, Edward L.
Adams, Hazard 1926- ... 9-10R
See also SATA 6
Adams, Henry H(itch) 1917- .. 21-22R
Adams, Henry Mason 1907- ... CAP-1
Earlier sketch in CA 17-18
Adams, Henry T.
See Ransom, Jay Ellis
Adams, Herbert Mayow 1893- . CAP-2
Earlier sketch in CA 25-28
Adams, J(ames) Donald 1891- ... 2R
Adams, James F(rederick) 1927- ... 19-20R
Adams, James Luther 1901- ... 41-44
Adams, James R(owe) 1934- ... 41-44
Adams, Joey 1911- ... 49-52
Adams, John Clarke 1910- ... 3R
Adams, John F(estus) 1930- . 33-36R
Adams, John Paul
See Kinnaird, Clark
Adams, John R. 1900- ... 25-28R
Adams, Julian 1919- ... 25-28R
Adams, Kramer A. 1920- ... 11-12R
Adams, L(ouis) Jerold 1939- ... 49-52
Adams, Laura 1943- ... 53-56
Adams, Laurie 1941- ... 53-56
Adams, Leon D(avid) 1905- ... 45-48
Adams, Leonie (Fuller) 1899- .. CAP-1
Earlier sketch in CA 9-10
Adams, Lowell
See Joseph, James Herz
Adams, Marion 1932- ... 41-44
Adams, Michael (Evelyn) 1920- 33-36R
Adams, Nathan Miller 1934- ... 45-48
Adams, Paul L(ieber) 1924- ... 61-64
Adams, Percy G(uy) 1914- ... 4R
Adams, Ramon Frederick 1889-1976 Obituary ... 65-68
Adams, Richard 1920- ... 49-52
See also CLC 4, 5
See also SATA 7
Adams, Richard N(ewbold) 1924- ... 29-32R
Adams, Richard P(errill) 1917-1977 ... CAP-2
Obituary ... 69-72
Earlier sketch in CA 33-36
Adams, Robert (Franklin) 1932- ... 69-72
Adams, Robert Martin 1915- ... 5-6R
Adams, Robert McCormick 1926- ... 61-64
Adams, Robert P. 1910- ... 13-14R
Adams, Russell B(aird), Jr. 1937- ... 69-72
Adams, Russell L. 1930- ... 53-56
Adams, Sally Pepper ... 41-44
Adams, Sam 1934- ... 57-60
Adams, Sexton 1936- ... 25-28R
Adams, T(homas) W(illiam) 1933- ... 25-28R
Adams, Terrence Dean 1935- . 33-36R
Adams, Theodore Floyd 1898- . CAP-1
Earlier sketch in CA 11-12
Adams, Thomas F. 1927- ... 15-16R
Adams, Walter 1922- ... 2R
Adamson, David Grant 1927- . 15-16R
Adamson, Donald 1939- ... 53-56
Adamson, Ed(ward Joseph) 1915(?)-1972 Obituary ... 37-40
Adamson, Frank
See Adams, Robert (Franklin)
Adamson, Gareth 1925- ... 13-14R
Adamson, Graham
See Groom, Arthur William
Adamson, Hans Christian 1890-1968 ... 5-6R
Adamson, Joe
See Adamson, Joseph III
Adamson, Joseph III 1945- ... 45-48
Adamson, Joy (-Friederike Victoria) 1910- ... 69-72
See also SATA 11
Adamson, Wendy Writson 1942- ... 53-56
Adamson, William Robert 1927- ... 23-24R
Adas, Michael 1943- ... 53-56
Adburgham, Alison Haig 1912- CAP-1
Earlier sketch in CA 9-10
Adcock, Almey St. John 1894- .. 65-68

† R refers to *Contemporary Authors* Revised Volumes.
CAP refers to volumes in the *Contemporary Authors—Permanent Series.*

Roy, Katherine (Morris) 1907- 3R
Roy, Liam
See Scarry, Patricia (Murphy)
Roy, Michael 1913-1976 61-64
Obituary 65-68
Roy, Mike
See Roy, Michael
Roy, Reginald H(erbert) 1922- .. 49-52
Royal, Claudia Smith 1904- 7-8R
Royal, Denise 1935- 25-28R
Royce, James E(mmet) 1914- 3R
Royce, Kenneth 1920- 13-14R
Royce, Patrick M(ilan) 1922- . 15-16R
Royce, R(ussell) Joseph 1921- 23-24R
Royer, Fanchon 1902- 7-8R
Roylance, William H(erbert)
1927- 61-64
Royle, Edward 1944- 61-64
Royster, Philip M. 1943- 65-68
Royster, Salibelle 1895-1975 .. CAP-2
Earlier sketch in CA 25-28
Royster, Vermont (Connecticut)
1914- 21-22R
Rozeboom, William W(arren)
1928- 17-18R
Rozek, Evalyn Robillard 1941- .. 61-64
Rozental, Alek A(ron) 1920- .. 33-36R
Rozwenc, Edwin C(harles)
1915-1974 ...... CAP-1
Earlier sketch in CA 13-14
Ruane, Gerald P(atrick) 1934- .. 69-72
Ruano, Araimiro 1924- 33-36R
Ruark, Gibbons 1941- 33-36R
See also CLC 3
Ruark, Robert (Chester)
1915-1965 ...... CAP-2
Obituary 25-28R
Earlier sketch in CA 19-20
Rubadeau, Duane O. 1927- .. 29-32R
Rubashov, Schneor Zalman
See Shazar, (Schneor) Zalman
Rubel, Arthur J. 1924- 41-44
Rubel, Maximilien 1905- CAP-1
Earlier sketch in CA 11-12
Ruben, Brent David 1944- 41-44
Rubens, Bernice 1923- 25-28R
Rubens, Jeff 1941- 25-28R
Rubenstein, Boris B.
1907(?)-1974 Obituary 53-56
Rubenstein, Richard E(dward)
1938- 29-32R
Rubenstein, Richard L(owell)
1924- 21-22R
Rubenstein, (Clarence) Robert
1926- 21-22R
Rubenstone, Jessie 1912- 69-72
Rubicam, Harry Cogswell, Jr.
1902- CAP-2
Earlier sketch in CA 17-18
Rubin, Arnold P(erry) 1946- 69-72
Rubin, David Lee 1939- 41-44
Rubin, Duane R(oger) 1931- ... 57-60
Rubin, Eli Z(under) 1922- 17-18R
Rubin, Frederick 1926- 33-36R
Rubin, Isadore 1912-1970 .... CAP-1
Obituary 29-32R
Earlier sketch in CA 15-16
Rubin, Israel 1923- 37-40
Rubin, Jacob A. 1910-1972 ... CAP-1
Obituary 37-40
Earlier sketch in CA 11-12
Rubin, Jerry 1938- 69-72
Rubin, Larry (Jerome) 1930- ... 5-6R
Rubin, Leona G(reenstone)
1920- 49-52
Rubin, Lillian Breslow 1924- ... 65-68
Rubin, Louis D(ecimus), Jr.
1923- 3R
Rubin, Mark 1946- 53-56
Rubin, Michael 1935- 1R
Rubin, Morton 1923- 41-44
Rubin, Vitalii 1923- 69-72
Rubin, Zick 1944- 49-52
Rubinoff, (M.) Lionel 1930- .. 25-28R
Rubinstein, Alvin Zachary
1927- 9-10R
Rubinstein, Amnon 1931- ... 15-16R
Rubinstein, E(lliott) 1936- 41-44
Rubinstein, Hilary 1926- 57-60
Rubinstein, Moshe F(ajwel)
1930- 57-60
Rubinstein, Paul (Arthur) 61-64
Rubinstein, S(amuel) Leonard
1922- 45-48
Rubinstein, Stanley (Jack)
1890-1975 ...... CAP-2
Earlier sketch in CA 29-32
Rublowsky, John M(artin)
1928- 17-18R
Rubsamen, Walter H. 1911- .. 13-14R
Rubulis, Aleksis 1922- 37-40
Ruby, Kathryn 1947- 65-68
Ruby, Robert Holmes 1921- .. 19-20R
Ruchames, Louis 1917-1976 ..... 2R
Obituary 65-68
Ruchelman, Leonard I. 1933- . 29-32R
Ruchlis, Hy(man) 1913- 4R
See also SATA 3
Ruck, Amy Roberta 1878- 7-8R
Ruck, Berta
See Ruck, Amy Roberta
Ruck, Carl A(nton) P(aul)
1935- 25-28R
Rucker, Bryce W(ilson) 1921- 11-12R
Rucker, (Egbert) Darnell 1921- .. 41-44
Rucker, Frank Warren 1886- 4R
Rucker, Helen (Bornstein) 1R
Rucker, W(infred) Ray 1920- . 13-14R
Rudd, Margaret
See Newlin, Margaret Rudd
Rudd, Margaret T(homas)
1907- 19-20R
Rudder, Robert S(ween) 1937- . 53-56
Rudder, Virginia L. 1941- 65-68
Ruddock, Ralph 1913- 53-56
Rude, George F. E(lliot) 1910- . 7-8R
Rudelius, William 1931- 45-48
Ruder, William 1921- 19-20R
Rudhart, Alexander 1930- 61-64
Rudhyar, Dane 1895- 29-32R
Rudinsky, Joseph F(rancis)
1891- 5-6R
Rudisill, D(orus) P(aul) 1902- .. 45-48
Rudnick, Hans H(einrich)
1935- 41-44
Rudnick, Milton Leroy 1927- 2R
Rudnik, Raphael 1933- 29-32R
See also CLC 7
Rudofsky, Bernard 1905- 17-18R
Rudolf, Anthony 1942- 61-64
Rudolph, Donna Keyse 1934- . 33-36R
Rudolph, Erwin Paul 1916- ... 33-36R
Rudolph, Frederick 1920- ... 11-12R
Rudolph, L(avere) C(hristian)
1921- 7-8R
Rudolph, Lee (Norman) 1948- .. 57-60
Rudolph, Lloyd I(rving) 1927- .. 57-60
Rudolph, Marguerita 1908- .. 33-36R
Rudolph, Nancy 1923- 57-60
Rudolph, Robert S. 1937- 41-44
Rudolph, Susanne Hoeber
1930- 25-28R
Rudomin, Esther
See Hautzig, Esther Rudomin
Rudrum, Alan (William) 1932- 25-28R
Rudy, Peter 1922- 53-56
Rudy, Willis 1920- 37-40
Rue, John E. 1924- 21-22R
Rue, Leonard Lee III 1926- 4R
Ruebsaat, Helmut J(ohannes)
1920- 61-64
Ruechelle, Randall C(ummings)
1920- 41-44
Rueckert, William H(owe)
1926- 23-24R
Ruedi, Norma Paul
See Ainsworth, Norma
Ruef, John S. 1927- 37-40
Rueff, Jacques (Leon) 1896- ... 65-68
Ruege, Klaus 1934- 65-68
Ruehle, Juergen 1924- 25-28R
Ruehn, Olaf 1911- 4R
Ruesch, Hans 1913- 15-16R
Rueschhoff, Phil H. 1924- ... 29-32R
Ruffini, (Jacopo) Remo 1942- .. 57-60
Ruffle, The
See Tegner, Henry (Stuart)
Ruffo, Vinnie 25-28R
Ruffridge, Frank(lin James)
1931- 25-28R
Rugg, Dean S(prague) 1923- ... 41-44
Ruggiers, Paul G(eorge) 1918- 25-28R
Ruggles, Eleanor 1916- 7-8R
Rugh, Belle Dorman 1908- CAP-1
Earlier sketch in CA 15-16
Rugoff, Milton 1913- 21-22R
Ruitenbeek, Hendrik M(arinus)
1928- 7-8R
Ruiz, Jose Martinez
1873-1967 Obituary 25-28R
Ruiz, Ramon Eduardo 1921- . 25-28R
Ruiz, Roberto 1925- 41-44
Ruiz-Fornells, Enrique 1925- . 33-36R
Ruja, Harry 1912- 41-44
Rukeyser, Louis 1933- 65-68
Rukeyser, Merryle Stanley
1897-1974 ...... CAP-2
Earlier sketch in CA 23-24
Rukeyser, Muriel 1913- 7-8R
See also CLC 6
Rukeyser, William Simon
1939- 69-72
Ruksenas, Algis 1942- 49-52
Ruland, Richard (Eugene)
1932- 21-22R
Ruland, Vernon Joseph 1931- 19-20R
Rule, Jane (Vance) 1931- ... 25-28R
Rulon, Philip Reed 1934- 37-40
Rumaker, Michael 1932- 3R
Rumanes, George N(icholas)
1925- 45-48
Rumbelow, Donald 1940- 49-52
Rumble, Thomas C(lark) 1919- 15-16R
Rumble, Wilfrid E., Jr. 1931- . 25-28R
Rumbold-Gibbs, Henry
See Gibbs, Henry St. John
Clair
Rummel, J(osiah) Francis
1911- 19-20R
Rummel, R(udolph) J(oseph)
1932- 65-68
Rumscheidt, H(ans) Martin
1935- 57-60
Rumsey, Marian (Barritt) 1928- 21-22R
Runciman, (James Cochran)
Steven(son) 1903- 3R
Rundell, Walter, Jr. 1928- ... 11-12R
Rundle, Anne 57-60
Runes, Dagobert D(avid) 1902- 25-28R
Runge, William H(arry) 1927- 2R
Runia, Klaas 1926- 7-8R
Runkel, Philip J(ulian) 1917- . 29-32R
Runkle, Gerald 1924- 37-40
Runyan, Harry (John) 1913-(?) CAP-2
Earlier sketch in CA 23-24
Runyan, John
See Palmer, Bernard
Runyan, Thora J. 1931- 69-72
Runyon, Catherine 1947- 61-64
Runyon, Charles W. 1928- ... 17-18R
Runyon, John H. 1945- 33-36R
Runyon, Richard P. 1925- 45-48
Ruoff, James E. 1925- 41-44
Ruotolo, Lucio P(eter) 1927- ... 41-44
Rupert, Hoover 1917- 2R
Rupert, Raphael Rudolph
1910- CAP-2
Earlier sketch in CA 19-20
Ruple, Wayne Douglas 1950- ... 53-56
Rupp, Richard H(enry) 1934- . 29-32R
Ruppenthal, Karl M. 1917- ... 19-20R
Rus, Vladimir 1931- 17-18R
Rusalem, Herbert 1918- 41-44
Rusch, Hermann G. 1907- 61-64
Rusco, Elmer R(itter) 1928- 65-68
Ruse, Gary Alan 1946- 61-64
Rush, Anne Kent 1945- 61-64
Rush, Joseph H(arold) 1911- ... 5-6R
Rush, Joshua
See Pearlstein, Howard J.
Rush, Michael (David) 1937- ... 61-64
Rush, Myron 1922- 45-48
Rush, N(ixon) Orwin 1907- 45-48
Rush, Ralph E(ugene)
1903-1965 ...... 7-8R
Rush, Richard Henry 1915- 5-6R
Rushing, Jane Gilmore 1925- ... 49-52
Rushmore, Helen 1898- 25-28R
See also SATA 3
Rushmore, Robert (William)
1926- 25-28R
See also SATA 8
Rusinek, Alla 1949- 45-48
Rusk, Ralph Leslie 1888-1962 .. 5-6R
Ruskay, Joseph A. 1910- CAP-2
Earlier sketch in CA 29-32
Ruskay, Sophie 1887- 69-72
Ruskin, Ariane 1935- 15-16R
See also SATA 7
Russ, Joanna 1937- 25-28R
Russ, Lavinia 1904- 25-28R
Russ, William Adam, Jr. 1903- ... 3R
Russel, Robert R(oyal) 1890- . 15-16R
Russell, Albert
See Bixby, Jerome Lewis
Russell, Andy 1915- 21-22R
Russell, Annie V(est)
1880(?)-1974 Obituary 49-52
Russell, Arthur (Wolseley)
1908- CAP-1
Earlier sketch in CA 13-14
Russell, Bertrand (Arthur
William) 1872-1970 .... CAP-1
Obituary 25-28R
Earlier sketch in CA 15-16
Russell, C(harles) Allyn 1920- .. 65-68
Russell, Claude Vivian 1919- . 17-18R
Russell, Colin Archibald 1928- .. 45-48
Russell, Conrad 1937- 33-36R
Russell, D(iana) E(lizabeth)
H(amilton) 1938- 61-64
Russell, D(avid) S(yme) 1916- 15-16R
Russell, Daniel 1937- 41-44
Russell, Diarmuid
1902(?)-1973 Obituary 45-48
Russell, Don(ald Bert) 1899- 2R
Russell, Douglas A(ndrew)
1927- 41-44
Russell, Francis 1910- 25-28R
Russell, Franklin 1926- 19-20R
See also SATA 11
Russell, (Sydney) Gordon
1892- CAP-2
Earlier sketch in CA 29-32
Russell, Helen Ross 1915- ... 33-36R
See also SATA 8
Russell, Ivy E(thel Southern)
1909- 7-8R
Russell, J.
See Bixby, Jerome Lewis
Russell, James
See Harknett, Terry
Russell, James E.
1916-1975 Obituary 57-60
Russell, Jeffrey Burton 1934- . 25-28R
Russell, John 1919- 13-14R
Russell, John David 1928- ... 11-12R
Russell, John L(eonard) 1906- 13-14R
Russell, John L(owry), Jr.
1921- 11-12R
Russell, Josiah Cox 1900- 41-44
Russell, Ken(neth Victor)
1929- 25-28R
Russell, Letty M(andeville)
1929- 57-60
Russell, Maurin
See Russell, Maurine
(Fletcher)
Russell, Maurine (Fletcher)
1899- CAP-1
Earlier sketch in CA 9-10
Russell, Norma Hull Lewis
1902- 7-8R
Russell, Norman H(udson), Jr.
1921- 49-52
Russell, O(liver) Ruth 1897- 57-60
Russell, Patrick
See Sammis, John
Russell, Ray 1924- 3R
Russell, Robert (William)
1924- 2R
Russell, Ronald (Stanley)
1904-1974 ...... CAP-1
Earlier sketch in CA 11-12
Russell, Ross 1909- 2R
Russell, Shane
See Norwood, Victor G(eorge)
C(harles)
Russell, Solveig Paulson 1904- ... 3R
See also SATA 3
Russell, William H. 1911- 61-64
Russell-Wood, A(nthony) J(ohn)
R(ussell) 1939- 57-60
Russett, Bruce M(artin) 1935- .. 7-8R
Russett, Cynthia Eagle 1937- . 21-22R
Russo, Anthony 1933- 61-64
Russo, Giuseppe Luigi 1884- .. CAP-1
Earlier sketch in CA 9-10
Russo, John Paul 1944- 41-44
Russo, Joseph Louis
See Russo, Giuseppe Luigi
Russo, Sarett Rude
1918(?)-1976 Obituary 65-68
Russon, L(eslie) J(ohn) 1907- 19-20R
Rust, Brian Arthur Lovell 1922- . 45-48
Rust, Doris (Dibblin) 13-14R
Rust, Eric C(harles) 1910- ... 15-16R
Rust, Richard Dilworth 1937- . 29-32R
Rustin, Bayard 1910- 53-56
Rustow, Dankwart A(lexander)
1924- 3R
Rutberg, Sidney 1924- 69-72
Rutenber, Culbert G(erow)
1909- CAP-2
Earlier sketch in CA 17-18
Rutgers van der Loeff-Basenau,
An(na) 1910- 9-10R
Ruth, Claire (Merritt)
1900-1976 Obituary 69-72
Ruth, Kent Ringelman 1916- ... 5-6R
Ruth, Rod 1912- SATA-9
Rutherford, Andrew 1929- 5-6R
Rutherford, Douglas
See McConnell, James
Douglas Rutherford
Rutherford, Margaret
1882-1972 Obituary 33-36R
Rutherford, Meg 1932- 29-32R
Rutherford, Michael (Andrew) 45-48
Rutherford, Phillip Roland
1939- 37-40
Ruthin, Margaret SATA-4
Ruthven, K(enneth) K(nowles)
1936- 25-28R
Rutkowski, Edwin H(enry)
1923- 37-40
Rutland, Dodge
See Singleton, Betty
Rutland, Robert A(llen) 1922- .. 45-48
Rutledge, Aaron L(eslie) 1919- .. 45-48
Rutledge, Albert J(ohn) 1934- 33-36R
Rutledge, Archibald (Hamilton)
1883-1973 ...... 5-6R
Obituary 45-48
Rutledge, Dom Denys
See Rutledge, Edward William
Rutledge, Edward William
1906- 7-8R
Rutman, Darrett B(ruce) 1929- 15-16R
Rutman, Gilbert L(ionel) 1935- 25-28R
Rutman, Leo 1935- 45-48
Rutsala, Vern 1934- 11-12R
Rutstein, David D(avis) 1909- 33-36R
Rutstein, Nat(han) 1930- 53-56
Rutstrum, Calvin 1895- 3R
Rutt, M. E.
See Shah, Amina
Rutt, Richard 1925- 11-12R
Ruttan, Vernon W(esley) 1924- . 41-44
Ruttenberg, Stanley H(arvey)
1917- 33-36R
Ruttkowski, Wolgang Victor
1935- 41-44
Rutz, Viola Larkin 1932- 23-24R
See also SATA 12
Rutzebeck, Hjalmar 1889- ... 11-12R
Ruuth, Marianne 1933- 57-60
Ruyerson, James Paul
See Rothweiler, Paul R(oger)
Ruzic, Neil P. 1930- 17-18R
Ryall, Edward W(illiam) 1902- .. 61-64
Ryals, Clyde de L(oache) 1928- 23-24R
Ryan, Alan 1940- 29-32R
Ryan, Alvan Sherman 1912- .. 19-20R
Ryan, Bernard, Jr. 1923- 7-8R
Ryan, Betsy
See Ryan, Elizabeth (Anne)
Ryan, Bob 1946- 49-52
Ryan, Charles W(illiam) 1929- .. 57-60
Ryan, Cornelius John
1920-1974 69-72
Obituary 53-56
See also CLC 7
Ryan, Edwin 1916- 5-6R
Ryan, Elizabeth (Anne) 1943- ... 61-64
Ryan, Herbert J(oseph) 1931- .. 41-44
Ryan, James H(erbert) 1928- ... 53-56
Ryan, Jessica Cadwalader
1915(?)-1972 Obituary 33-36R
Ryan, John (Gerald Christopher)
1921- 49-52
Ryan, John Barry 1933- 57-60
Ryan, John J.
1922(?)-1977 Obituary 69-72
Ryan, John K. 1897- 13-14R
Ryan, Sister Joseph Eleanor 61-64
Ryan, Joseph J.
1910(?)-1976 Obituary 69-72
Ryan, Kevin 1932- 29-32R
Ryan, Lawrence Vincent 1923- .. 5-6R
Ryan, Leonard Eames 1930- . 11-12R
Ryan, Marleigh Grayer 1930- . 19-20R
Ryan, Michael 1946- 49-52
Ryan, Milo 1907- 5-6R
Ryan, Neil Joseph 1930- 13-14R
Ryan, Pat M(artin) 1928- ... 33-36R
Ryan, Patrick J. 1902- CAP-1
Earlier sketch in CA 11-12
Ryan, Peter (Charles) 1939- 61-64
Ryan, Robert Michael 1934- .. 29-32R
Ryan, T. Antoinette 1924- 41-44
Ryan, Thomas Arthur 1911- 41-44
Ryan, Thomas Richard 1897- . 29-32R
Ryan, Tom 1938- 57-60
Ryan, William M(artin) 1918- . 33-36R
Ryans, David Garriott 1909- 7-8R
Ryans, John K(elley), Jr. 1932- . 61-64
Ryback, Eric 1952- 37-40
Rybalka, Michel 1933- 41-44
Rybka, Edward F(rank) 1928- . 33-36R
Rybot, Doris
See Ponsonby, D(oris)
A(lmon)
Rychlak, Joseph F(rank) 1928- .. 37-40
Rycroft, Charles (Frederick)
1914- 21-22R
Rydberg, Ernest E(mil) 1901- . 15-16R
Rydberg, Lou(isa Hampton)
1908- 69-72
Rydell, Forbes
See Forbes, DeLoris Stanton
Rydell, Wendell
See Rydell, Wendy
Rydell, Wendy 33-36R
See also SATA 4
Ryden, Hope 33-36R
See also SATA 8
Ryder, A(rthur) J(ohn) 1913- . 21-22R
Ryder, Ellen 1913- 29-32R
Ryder, Frank G(lessner) 1916- .. 7-8R
Ryder, John 1917- 7-8R
Ryder, Jonathan
See Ludlum, Robert
Ryder, Meyer S. 1909- 21-22R
Ryder, Norman B(urston)
1923- 37-40
Ryder, Ron 1904- 61-64
Ryder, T(homas) A(rthur)
1902- 7-8R
Rye, Bjoern Robinson 1942- ... 61-64
Ryerson, Lowell
See Van Atta, Winfred Lowell
Ryerson, Martin 1907- 15-16R
Ryf, Robert S. 1918- 17-18R
Ryken, Leland 1942- 29-32R
Rykwert, Joseph 1926- 69-72
Ryland, Lee
See Arlandson, Leone
Ryle, Gilbert
1900-1976 Obituary 69-72
Rymer, Alta (May) 1925- 49-52
Rymes, Thomas Kenneth
1932- 37-40
Rynew, Arden N. 1943- 37-40
Ryrie, Charles C(aldwell) 1925- 11-12R
Rywell, Martin 1905-1971 .... CAP-2
Earlier sketch in CA 19-20
Rywkin, Michael 1925- 13-14R
Ryzl, Milan 1928- 29-32R
Rzhevsky, Leonid 1905- 41-44

S

Saab, Edouard
1929-1976 Obituary 65-68
Saalman, Howard 1928- 1R